Jessie Williams

Twenty-Three Plays of

WILLIAM SHAKESPEARE

A NEW TEXT EDITED WITH
INTRODUCTION AND NOTES

BY

WILLIAM ALLAN NEILSON
PRESIDENT EMERITUS OF SMITH COLLEGE

AND CHARLES JARVIS HILL
ASSOCIATE PROFESSOR OF ENGLISH
SMITH COLLEGE

HOUGHTON MIFFLIN COMPANY
BOSTON · NEW YORK · CHICAGO · DALLAS · ATLANTA · SAN FRANCISCO
The Riverside Press Cambridge

The Riverside Press
CAMBRIDGE · MASSACHUSETTS
PRINTED IN THE U.S.A.

PREFACE

THE TEXT, introductions, and notes in the present volume are reprinted from the New Cambridge Edition of *The Complete Plays and Poems of William Shakespeare*. The principles followed in the preparation of that edition are described in the Preface and may be repeated here. The contents of the New Cambridge Edition were based on those of *The Complete Works of William Shakespeare* originally published in the series known as "The Cambridge Poets" in 1906. But both text and apparatus underwent so thorough a revision as to constitute what is virtually a new book. The text has been collated anew with the early Quartos and the First Folio, the punctuation has been revised, notes both textual and explanatory have been placed at the foot of the page instead of being printed at the end of the volume in an appendix and glossary, and the Introductions, besides being brought into accord with the results of recent scholarship, have been considerably expanded by fuller critical discussion.

The fundamental principles and methods governing the treatment of the text have remained the same but have been applied more consistently, and many inadvertent lapses have been corrected. As before, the choice of the old text used as a basis has been dictated by the considerations relevant to each play, and in the special Introductions the grounds for the choice between the Folio and a Quarto are set forth. Stage directions, if modern, are enclosed in [brackets]; when they are substantially those of editions not later than 1623, they are unbracketed, or are set aside by a single bracket only, or, when occurring within a line, are enclosed in (parentheses). In the dialogue, when the text of a play is based on, say, that of the First Folio, and passages absent from the Folio are supplied from a Quarto, such passages are also bracketed. Readings which are due to modern conjecture are similarly marked, and the displaced reading is recorded in the Notes.

Since the publication of the edition of 1906 certain scholars have argued that there can be found in the old editions evidences of a so-called "dramatic punctuation." This punctuation, if it exists, is subject to so many exceptions that the rule is hard to discern, and its reproduction in a modern edition would be hopelessly misleading. A study of the original editions makes it manifest that their punctuation is chiefly the work of the compositors of whom there were many, and these were consistent neither with themselves nor with one another. We have, therefore, repunctuated frankly throughout according to modern usage, gaining, it is hoped, a considerable advantage in clearness without any sacrifice of authority.   The use of the apostrophe has raised some difficult and interesting points, the consideration of which has resulted in a decision of some importance.   In spite of the comparative carelessness of the printing of the First Folio, it has been found that there is clearly discernible a somewhat remarkable consistency in the insertion or omission of the *e* of *ed* endings.   To the practice of the early editions in this regard, therefore, the same respect has been shown as in the case of the text in general; i.e., the original has been departed from only when it seemed fair to believe that there was a mistake of the copyist or printer.   The result is that the *ed* is printed, and was apparently sounded, much more frequently than we are accustomed to see and hear it.   In many cases where no new syllable is added to the line, this preservation of the full ending points to a different elision from that usually made, *threat'ned*, for example, instead of *threaten'd*.   This often leads to a distinct gain in sonority, and sometimes to a marked change in rhythm.   The practice of the early editions is exceptional in the case of monosyllables in *ied*, being on the whole against the use of the apostrophe; so in such cases we have preserved the *e* even when not syllabic, representing, for example, the Folio *dyde* by *died* rather than by the somewhat misleading *di'd*.   Attention has also been paid to the frequent elisions and contractions of the old texts, such as *th'* for *the*, *o'* for *on* or *of*, *t'* for *to*, and *i'* for *in*, since these have often no inconsiderable effect on the rhythm.

In order to make easy the use of the present volume in connection with such standard works of reference as Bartlett's *Concordance*, the line-numbering of the *Globe* edition has been adhered to, with these differences, that the lines are numbered in fives instead of in tens, and the numbering is carried through the prose as well as the verse.

Scholarly opinion on the dates of the dramas has now reached such a degree of harmony as to suggest the arranging of the plays in chronological order, according to the approximate date of composition.   The Folio division into Comedies, Histories, and Tragedies has, however, been preserved; the chronological order being adopted in the case of the Comedies and Tragedies, while for obvious reasons the Histories have been retained in their historical sequence.

The tasks of collation, annotation, and interpretation have been shared by the two editors of the present revision, and for whatever merits or shortcomings it may possess they are jointly responsible.

William A. Neilson

Charles J. Hill

Northampton, Massachusetts

CONTENTS

INTRODUCTION

I. LIFE OF SHAKESPEARE

THE NAME OF SHAKESPEARE was of wide and frequent occurrence in the midlands of England in the sixteenth and preceding centuries; and this fact, along with the scarcity of exact documentary evidence, makes even the immediate ancestry of the dramatist a matter of less than absolute certainty. But there is no reason to doubt that he was the son of one John Shakespeare, a glover and dealer in agricultural produce, who at the time of William's birth was a person of increasing importance in the town of Stratford-on-Avon in Warwickshire. John Shakespeare's wife was Mary Arden, the youngest daughter of Robert Arden, a substantial farmer and landowner of Wilmcote, near Stratford. Their first son and third child, William, was baptized on April 26, 1564, the exact date of his birth being unrecorded. The history of his childhood is purely a matter of inference. He would naturally enter, as Rowe says he did, the grammar school of his native town, since he was entitled to free education there; and from what is known of the usual curricula of such schools at that period it is to be supposed that his studies were chiefly in Latin grammar and literature. Four years after the poet's birth, John Shakespeare had reached the most honorable municipal office, that of High Bailiff; but after 1572 there are signs that his fortunes had begun to decline. He absented himself from the meetings of the town council, and was deprived of office; and the nature of his financial transactions indicates that he was sinking deeply into debt. He may have withdrawn his son from school to aid him in business; for Aubrey, who died in 1697, says of the poet, "I have been told heretofore by some of the neighbours that when he was a boy he exercised his father's trade," which, according to this antiquary, was that of a butcher. Aubrey adds the two often-quoted statements: "When he kill'd a calf, he would doe it in a high style and make a speech. There was at that time another butcher's son in this towne, that was held not at all inferior to him for a naturall witt, his acquaintance, and coetanean, but dyed young."

The only additional information we have regarding Shakespeare's early years in Stratford pertains to his marriage, which took place when he was in his nineteenth year. No record of the actual ceremony has been found, but the date is approximately fixed by a document in the registry of the diocese of Worcester, dated November 28, 1582, in which two Stratford farmers gave bonds to free the bishop of responsibility in case of the subsequent discovery of any impediment rendering invalid the prospective marriage of William Shakespeare to Anne Hathaway. This Anne Hathaway is usually identified with Agnes, daughter of Richard Hathaway, a farmer of Shottery, in the parish of Stratford; and from the inscription on her tombstone it appears that she was eight years older than her husband. On May 26, 1583, the Stratford Registers record the baptism of "Susanna, daughter to William Shakspere;" and in February, 1584, the baptism of "Hamnet and Judeth sonne and daughter to William Shakspere." These few facts comprise all that is certainly known about Shakespeare's life before his removal to London; but mention may be made of two interesting traditions. Aubrey reports, "Though as Ben Johnson says of him, that he had but little Latine and lesse Greek; He understood Latine pretty well: for he had been in his younger yeares a Schoolmaster in the Countrey." The other tradition is thus recorded by Rowe in 1709: "He had, by a misfortune common enough to young fellows, fallen into ill company; and amongst them, some that made a frequent practice of Deer-stealing engag'd him with them more than once in robbing a Park that belong'd to Sir *Thomas Lucy* of *Cherlecot*, near *Stratford*. For this he was prosecuted by that gentleman, as he thought, somewhat too severely; and in order to revenge that ill usage, he made a ballad upon him. And tho' this, probably the first essay of his Poetry, be lost, yet it is said to have been so very bitter, that it redoubled the prosecution against him to that degree, that he was oblig'd to leave his business and family in *Warwickshire*, for some time, and shelter himself in *London*." This exploit is recorded also by Archdeacon Davies of Saperton in Gloucestershire in the latter part of the seventeenth century, and corroboration of a different kind is found in the supposed allusion to Lucy and his coat of arms in the "dozen white luces" on Shallow's "old coat" in *The Merry*

Wives of Windsor, I.i.1–23. Unfortunately for the credibility of the legend, it now appears that Sir Thomas Lucy did not own a deer park, and that, if he had, the poaching of deer was an offence against the Crown, not the local landowner. Belief in a germ of truth in the tradition, moreover, does not carry with it the necessity of supposing that Shakespeare's migration to London was due to Lucy's persecution. Interest in the stage, with which he seems to have become connected soon after his arrival in the metropolis, may have begun before he left home. While he was still a small boy, the actors of the Queen's Company and of the Earl of Worcester's Company were officially received in Stratford by his father as High Bailiff; and four companies visited the town in 1587. Those who place his removal as late as 1587 do so chiefly in order to find in the visit of the theatrical companies in that year a possible motive and occasion for the change.

The circumstances and occupation of Shakespeare on his first arrival in London are as uncertain as the date and cause of his leaving Stratford. Various late traditions unite in assigning to him some humble office in connection with the theatre, that of his holding horses outside the door being first printed in 1753. It is known, however, that by 1592 he had achieved considerable reputation as an actor and had begun to write. The company of which he was early a member, and to which he belonged during the greater part, if not the whole, of his career, was that known successively as the Earl of Leicester's (–1588), Lord Strange's (1588–92), Lord Derby's (1592–94), the Lord Chamberlain's (1594–July, 1596), Lord Hunsdon's (July, 1596–March, 1597), the Lord Chamberlain's (1597–1603), and finally, His Majesty's (1603–). Of the two playhouses in London at the beginning of his career, The Theatre is the one in which his later associations make it probable that he first acted. Others in which this company performed were The Rose, Newington Butts, The Curtain, and, after 1599, The Globe. It is doubtful whether Shakespeare was often on the stage after his company began to occupy The Blackfriars about Christmas, 1609. To these must be added the scenes of the performances given in many provincial towns while the company was touring, from Dover to Bristol and from Richmond to Coventry. There is no satisfactory evidence that Shakespeare ever accompanied any of the English actors who performed in Scotland or on the Continent, or, indeed, that he was ever out of England at all. As to his skill as an actor, Chettle stated in 1592 that he was "exelent in the qualitie he professes," and a later report, recorded by Aubrey, says that he acted "exceedingly well." His name ranks high in the actors' lists of his time; he played in Jonson's *Every Man in his Humour* and *Sejanus*; and tradition associates his name with the parts of the Ghost in *Hamlet* and of Adam in *As You Like It*, neither character, it must be allowed, being one likely to be assigned to the leading performer. That he had thought deeply and wisely on the purpose and methods of theatrical art is proved by the speech of Hamlet to the players.

As early as 1592, Shakespeare's success in theatrical matters was sufficiently marked to call forth an envious attack from Robert Greene, who died in September of that year. Addressing his fellow playwrights, Greene speaks of the actors as "those Puppets ... that spake from our mouths; those Anticks garnisht in our colours. Is it not strange that I, to whom they all haue beene beholding: is it not like that you, to whome they all haue beene beholding, shall (were yee in that case as I am now) bee both at once of them forsaken? Yes trust them not: for there is an vpstart Crow, beautified with our feathers, that with his *Tygers hart wrapt in a Players hyde*, supposes he is as well able to bombast out a blanke verse as the best of you: and beeing an absolute *Iohannes fac totum*, is in his owne conceit the onely Shake-scene in a countrey.... Let those apes imitate your past excellence, and neuer more acquaint them with your admired inuentions; ... for it is pittie men of such rare wits should be subiect to the pleasures of such rude groomes." The words italicized are a parody on the line, "O tiger's heart wrapt in a woman's hide!" which occurs in both *The True Tragedie of Richard Duke of Yorke* and *3 Henry VI*, I.iv.137; and the wordplay in "Shake-scene" confirms the interpretation which finds in the passage a denunciation of Shakespeare, who had incurred Greene's special ill-will as a dramatist as well as an actor. *A Groats-worth of Witte bought with a Million of Repentance*, in which the passage occurs, was published after Greene's death by Henry Chettle, who in December of the same year issued an apology in the prefatory address to his own *Kind-Harts Dreame*. "I am as sory," he says, and he is understood to be speaking of Shakespeare, "as if the originall fault had beene my fault, because myselfe haue seene his demeanor no lesse ciuill than he excelent in the qualitie he professes: Besides, diuers of worship haue reported his vprightnes of dealing, which argues his honesty, and his facetious grace in writting, that aproues his Art."

We thus find Shakespeare at the age of twenty-eight a person of some importance in theatrical circles, and recognized as a man to be reckoned with both as actor and as writer. In the two following years his versatility showed itself still farther in the publication of the highly popular *Venus and Adonis* and *Lucrece*; and the suggestion of good relations with men of rank contained in Chettle's phrase, "divers of worship," is made more definite by the terms of the dedications of these poems to the Earl of Southampton. The history of his next few years is mainly contained in the list of the dramas he produced; but there are other evidences of steady progress in fortune and repute. Already in 1594 he had been summoned to play before the Queen along with the most distinguished actors of the day; and from 1595 till long after his death, appeared a series of publications, poems as well as plays, with which he had nothing to do, but to which unscrupulous publishers attached his name or initials, thus testifying to the market-value of his reputation.

Meantime, in Stratford, his father's affairs were going from bad to worse, until in 1596 the stopping of all actions for debt suggests that the dramatist had returned and restored the family fortunes. In August of that year his only son Hamnet died. In that year, too, an attempt to increase the family prestige was made in the name of John Shakespeare, though probably on the initiative of the poet, by applying to the College of Heralds for the grant of a coat of arms. Two drafts of such a grant are extant dated 1596, assigning to John Shakespeare a shield described thus: "Gould on a Bend Sable a Speare of the first, steeled, argent; and for his creast or cognizaunce a falcon, his winges displayed Argent, standing on a wrethe of his coullors, supporting a Speare Gould steeled as aforesaid, sett vppon a healmett with mantelles and tassclles as hath ben accustomed." The grant does not seem to have been issued at this time; but three years later an application was made for an "exemplification" of the coat, the previous right to wear it being taken for granted. This application was successful, and the Shakespeares were henceforth regarded as entitled to the style of "gentlemen." A more substantial evidence of the improved status of the family was afforded in 1597, when the dramatist bought and repaired New Place, then the largest house in Stratford. He did not, however, take up his permanent residence there till several years later. Various other legal and financial transactions indicate that he had come to be regarded as a man of substance; and his profession was sufficiently remunerative easily to account for this. It has been reckoned that his income as an actor must have averaged before the end of the century about £130 a year, and to this must be added about £20 annually from his plays. After The Globe was built in 1599 he became a shareholder, and the profits from this source are likely to have more than doubled his income. Gifts from patrons were not uncommon, and there may be some ground for the tradition handed down by Rowe from D'Avenant,

that Shakespeare received from Southampton the gift of £1000, though the amount stated seems incredibly large. Money is usually reckoned to have had at that period from five to eight times its present purchasing power; but the difficulty of determining this with certainty, and the fragmentary and inconclusive nature of the bases of our information as to the financial side of the Elizabethan theatre, make it necessary to receive with caution the results of the calculations that have been made of Shakespeare's gains. There is no doubt, however, that he was an extremely successful man, that his affairs were conducted with much practical sense and shrewdness, and that he died rich. In his will he left £350 in money, with a considerable amount of real estate and other property. There is in his life, certainly, no evidence that he shared the alleged incapacity of men of imaginative genius for practical affairs.

Along with this material prosperity, Shakespeare gained steadily in literary reputation. As early as 1598, Francis Meres, in his *Palladis Tamia or Wit's Treasury*, wrote "A Comparative Discourse of our English Poets with Greek, Latin, and Italian Poets;" and here he awards the highest praise to Shakespeare as both poet and playwright. "As the soule of *Euphorbus* was thought to liue in *Pythagoras*: so the sweete wittie soule of *Ouid* liues in mellifluous and hony-tongued *Shakespeare*, witnes his *Venus and Adonis*, his *Lucrece*, his sugred Sonnets among his priuate friends, etc. As *Plautus* and *Seneca* are accounted the best for Comedy and Tragedy among the Latines: so *Shakespeare* among ye English is the most excellent in both kinds for the stage; for Comedy, witnes his *Gentlemen of Verona*, his *Errors*, his *Loue labors lost*, his *Loue labours wonne*, his *Midsummers night dreame*, and his *Merchant of Venice*; for tragedy, his *Richard the 2.*, *Richard the 3.*, *Henry the 4.*, *King Iohn*, *Titus Andronicus*, and his *Romeo and Iuliet*. As *Epius Stolo* said that the Muses would speake with *Plautus* tongue, if they would speak Latin, so I say that the Muses would speak with *Shakespeares* fine filed phrase, if they would speake English."

References by his literary contemporaries are fairly numerous, and are in general in this enthusiastic vein. Allusions to his personality reflect a kindly feeling in the speakers, and indicate a genial disposition in the poet, with a love of wit and good fellowship. Legendary gossip suggesting occasional extreme conviviality need not be taken too seriously, and probably implies nothing more than a fondness for making merry with his friends.

The documentary records of the later years of Shakespeare's life are concerned chiefly with lawsuits and the investment of money. They are of interest chiefly as showing in Shakespeare some of his father's tendency to litigiousness, and that carefulness of his pecuniary interests already referred to. His father died in 1601; his mother in 1608. He was not a shareholder in any of the London theatres at his death, and it is not known when he sold out; but it is conjectured that about 1611 he disposed of these interests and retired to Stratford to enjoy his means in leisure. On April 23, 1616, he died, and two days later was buried beneath the chancel of Stratford Church according to a right acquired as part-owner of the tithes. Within seven years of his death an elaborate monument to his memory was placed in the wall of the church, and in it a colored portrait bust, which has been more than once repainted. The only well-authenticated portrait is the engraving by Martin Droeshout prefixed to the Folio editions of the plays, and this is far from lifelike. It is supposed that Droeshout worked from a painting, but there is yet no general agreement as to which, if any, of the existing claimants was his original. Two seem to have stronger support than the others, that sometimes known as the "Flower Portrait," now hanging in the Memorial Picture Gallery at Stratford; and the "Ely Palace Portrait," now in the possession of the Birthplace Trustees. The former of these is reproduced as the frontispiece to the present volume. Pretended portraits have been fabricated without number, and even those to which no suspicion of fraud attaches, with the one exception of the Droeshout engraving, lack a sufficient pedigree.

Of Shakespeare's immediate family there survived him his wife, his two daughters, and one brother. Mrs. Shakespeare lived till August 6, 1623, dying three months before the publication of the great collected edition of her husband's works known as the First Folio. The elder daughter, Susanna, married Dr. John Hall, and died in 1649, leaving one child, Elizabeth. This Elizabeth Hall, later Mrs. Thomas Nash, and still later Lady Barnard, died in 1670 without issue. The younger daughter, who married Thomas Quiney of Stratford, died in 1662, having outlived her three sons. Lady Barnard was thus the last surviving descendant of the poet. Descendants of his sister Joan, who married William Hart, are still living in England, Australia, and the United States.

II. CHRONOLOGY

The chronology of the works of Shakespeare is, except in the case of the two long poems and a few plays, the result of inferences of varying degrees of certitude. Four main divisions are generally recognized, and each of them has a fairly distinctive content. The first stretches from the undated beginnings of his work as a dramatist till about 1594,

and it contains probably a greater variety of kinds of production than any other. It is no mere guess work to call this a period of experiment. Besides the poems, we find in it representatives of all three kinds of drama then in vogue, Comedy, History, and Tragedy. For whatever reason, he seems after these experiments to have laid aside Tragedy for a time except, perhaps, for the uncertainly dated *Romeo and Juliet*, to take it up again after he had mastered the more technical elements of his art, and had a larger experience of life on which to draw.

In History he may have begun with the revision of the work of others; and when he constructed plays for himself he was clearly under the influence of Marlowe. In *Richard III*, conception of theme and manipulation of character are alike Marlowesque; and both in that play and in *King John* the echo of the "mighty line" of Marlowe is clearly discernible in the versification.

In Comedy the lines of experiment are drawn with singular clearness. In *The Two Gentlemen of Verona* he shows already his interest in the problem of characterization, and in the contrasts of Proteus with Valentine and Julia with Silvia he employs a method of which he was to avail himself again and again. In *The Comedy of Errors* he is concerned mainly with the manipulation of plot and situation, finding his model in the Latin Comedy and contenting himself, as Plautus did, with a treatment of character typical rather than individual. *Love's Labour's Lost* is a playful burlesque upon current fashions, and it derives its interest mainly from its clever dialogue and ingenious playing with language, characterization and plot being alike slight. Of the plays of this period, *The Two Gentlemen* most clearly lays down the lines on which he was first to create masterpieces.

The period from 1595 to 1601 is mainly occupied with Comedy, and the Histories written in this period are more than leavened with Comedy. *Henry IV*, though its serious plot is filled with war and rebellion, owed its popularity to the comic elements centering in Falstaff, and constituting about half of the scenes. *Henry V* is free from any note of tragedy. From *A Midsummer-Night's Dream* to *Twelfth Night* we have a succession of plays of unexampled brilliance, surpassing in structure and dialogue anything that had hitherto been produced on the English stage, and in the creation of character still unrivalled. Touches of seriousness undoubtedly occur in these plays. Again and again, in the midst of the love-in-idleness with which they are chiefly occupied, we are reminded of the real business of life presently to be taken up; not infrequently the humor is mingled with pathos or grave reflection; sometimes the folly of Claudio or the fate of Shylock brings us perilously near the brink of tragedy. Yet all this does not invalidate the statement that the temper of the plays written in the last six years of the century is prevailingly that of Comedy.

Equally undeniable are the change of temper and change of theme after 1601. The intrusion of *Troilus and Cressida, Measure for Measure,* and *All's Well that Ends Well* among the great Tragedies cannot be regarded as an objection to the calling of this the tragic period, since their presence serves in no degree to lighten the gloom. It is clear that for eight or nine years Shakespeare's dominant artistic interest was tragic; that is, he was immersed in the problem of presenting dramatically the results of certain elements of weakness and vice in human character.

About 1610 the tone changes once more. In the so-called Dramatic Romances we continue to see pictured the suffering brought about by sin and weakness; but the colors used are less sombre, and in the end the evil men turn from their ways and live. The dominant characters are men of good will, and the motto of the group is Prospero's saying, "The rarer action is in virtue than in vengeance."

All this has often been summed up before; and it is done here once more partly to gather and make more significant the chronological details scattered through the special introductions, partly to make intelligible the standing discussion as to whether from this arrangement of Shakespeare's literary activity there can be drawn evidence as to his emotional and spiritual history. The meaning of the experimental period will hardly be disputed. The collaborated and revised plays show that Shakespeare at the beginning of his career was glad to take what work was given him to do; and the original plays show him trying his hand upon all the chief dramatic types in vogue. His *Venus and Adonis* and *Lucrece* are only further instances of this versatility and curiosity. Prevailing emotional mood of any distinctive kind in this first period there is none.

With the three later divisions the case is very different. Here the temptation is obvious to interpret them respectively as periods of sunshine, gloom, and placidity in the dramatist's life. Up to a certain point this interpretation need not be quarrelled with. There is an appropriateness to the prime of life in the creation of the buoyant personalities of the Comedies and in the triumphant extrication of them from all the tangle of opposing forces invented only to be foiled. The profundity of reflection and the brooding on the mystery of life, of which the Tragedies give abundant evidence, were only possible, in the degree in which we find them, to a man who had already lived and seen

much. It is hardly possible to refrain from associating the victories of good over evil in the Dramatic Romances with a mood natural to a sane spirit contemplating near the close of his career a world which had brought to him in large measure the things for which he had mainly striven. But it is easy to press this method too far. The succession of the various kinds of drama in Shakespeare's production bears a suggestive relation to what appears to have been the popular demand of the time; and if Tragedy was in vogue at a period when Shakespeare was ripe for writing it, then the world was fortunate in the coincidence. Yet the fact of this and similar coincidences should serve to guard us against supposing that the tone of the Tragedies is necessarily a reflection of gloom or pessimism in Shakespeare's soul. Great imaginative creation is, indeed, but rarely the outcome of experience immediately contemporary. Wordsworth's description of poetry as "emotion recollected in tranquillity," though not a universal formula, is most frequently a true account, and ought in itself to caution us against the dogmatism that is based on the assumption that in drama and sonnet alike "Shakespeare unlocked his heart" and left the door ajar for all the world to see. If we are to find in the poet's work a record, not perhaps of his experience, but of his attitude toward human life and human nature, it must be by methods more subtle and cautious than are implied in the kind of inference we are discussing.

III. SHAKESPEARE'S OPPORTUNITY

The height of Shakespeare's preëminence has frequently led to a manner of speaking which sets him apart from his kind as something abnormal and unaccountable. Without entering into a discussion of the natural history of genius, it is desirable to recount those factors in his age and environment which explain many of his characteristics, even if they do not account for the magnitude of his achievement. For that achievement is of a range and quality so stupendous that it required for its accomplishment the highest degree of coincidence between the hour and the man.

The hour was, indeed, the most propitious that had occurred in the history of England. After the long controversies of the Reformation the country was for the time enjoying a comparative truce among warring sects. This truce was partly induced by the necessity of the nation's presenting a united front against the hostility of Spain; and the period of peril had been succeeded by a mood of exhilaration that resulted naturally from the escape from a formidable danger, and the opening up of a national future of untold possibilities of expansion

Approximate Dates of Composition of Shakespeare's Plays

	Comedies	Histories	Tragedies
I	Comedy of Errors 1591–92 Two Gentlemen 1592 Love's Labour's Lost 1594	1 Henry VI ⎫ 2 Henry VI ⎬ 1590–92 3 Henry VI ⎭ Richard III 1593 King John 1594	Titus Andronicus 1591–92
II	Midsummer-Night's Dream 1595 Merchant of Venice 1596 Taming of the Shrew 1596 Much Ado 1598–99 As You Like It 1599–1600 Merry Wives 1599–1600 Twelfth Night 1600–01	Richard II 1595 1 Henry IV 1597 2 Henry IV 1598 Henry V 1599	Romeo and Juliet 1595 Julius Cæsar 1599
III	Troilus and Cressida 1602 All's Well 1602 Measure for Measure 1604 Pericles 1607–08		Hamlet 1601–02 Othello 1604 King Lear 1605–06 Macbeth 1606 Timon of Athens 1607 Antony and Cleopatra 1607 Coriolanus 1608–09
IV	Cymbeline 1610 Winter's Tale 1611 Tempest 1611	Henry VIII 1613	

and conquest. The compiling of chronicles and of endless narratives of travel and exploration in the Western Ocean expressed and symbolized the rising pride in England's past and England's future; and it supplied the basis for the most distinctively national part of the drama, that flourishing of Chronicle History which found its culmination in the martial rhetoric of *Henry V.*

No small part of the credit for all this belongs to the great Queen. Elizabeth was no lofty idealist, but she served England well. After the extremes in religion which had torn the country apart during the reigns of her two predecessors, Edward VI and Mary Tudor, she imposed on the country a church which was in important respects a compromise, but which was broad enough and tolerant enough to embrace the main body of her subjects. Though she dealt severely with extremists to both the right and left, she achieved a substantial degree of unity and peace.

Her foreign policy also was one of peace, and though the threat of the Great Armada called for a mustering of all the nation's forces, this was a defensive effort, and in general she sought to extend the power of England without impoverishing her by foreign wars. Under these circumstances the country enjoyed a long period of prosperity which made possible, among much merely material luxury and ostentation, a notable flourishing of the arts.

From abroad there reached England at last the full impulse of the Renaissance. The more purely intellectual side of this movement had been delayed by the religious turmoil; but now that this was for the time assuaged, the stimulus to intellectual curiosity and the desire for imaginative entertainment had full scope. Men and books representing all the arts of the Continent poured into England, and hundreds of translations opened to those who could read no language but English the intellectual treasures of antiquity and of modern Italy, France, and Spain. A still less literate public were enabled to share the narrative element in this stream by the presentation of stories on the stage; and the plays based on Plutarch's *Lives* and French and Italian *novelle* represent respectively the classical and the contemporary elements in this contribution.

The drama in England had always largely represented what would have been the common reading matter of the people if the people had been able to read. Miracle plays, Moralities, and Interludes were each merely the translation into action and dialogue of the stories from Scripture and the Saints' Lives, of the characteristic medieval mode of allegory, of the bourgeois humorous and satirical anecdote, which the illiterate populace could receive only by the ear. With the Revival of Learning came a vast expansion in the amount and variety of reading matter, especially on the side of secular literature and, more specifically, of the literature of entertainment; and in the reign of Elizabeth the drama showed a responsive development. In the work of Shakespeare's immediate predecessors, Lyly, Marlowe, Peele, Greene, and Kyd, the three forms of Comedy, History, and Tragedy had, partly under the influence of foreign and classical models, taken fairly definite shape. But they were still primarily dramatic arrangements of narrative rather than drama; and to Shakespeare was offered the opportunity, of which he availed himself magnificently yet gradually, of framing and applying the conception of pure drama as a distinct form of art.

In considering his equipment for this momentous task two elements must be constantly kept in mind: that which he received as an actor and manager, and that which he had as a man well-read in the literature of his time. To the former must be credited a large part of his skill as a practical playwright, a factor that is at last receiving its due in the interpretation of his dramas, and which accounts for this among other facts, that so large a number of his plays are still capable of effective presentation upon the modern stage. As a student of literature, Shakespeare's range was large, but not extraordinary. Latin he had presumably learned at school, and with the works of some half-dozen Latin writers he had begun an acquaintance while a boy. But, in addition to the learned Jonson's ascription to him of "small Latine and lesse Greeke," we have the evidence of the plays themselves that he used translations when he could get them. French he seems to have known fairly well; Italian he may have mastered to the extent of being able to extract the plot of a novel, but this is less certain. There is no evidence that he knew Spanish or Greek. The wide and detailed knowledge of history and fiction and of many arts and trades, the evidences of which lie open on every page, is no greater and no more accurate than would be expected of a mind of the quality of his, of an observation so keen, of sympathies so catholic and so intense.

Some ten years before Shakespeare came to London an important event occurred in the building of The Theatre (1576), the first structure erected primarily for the purpose of acting in England. Up to this time, and for at least a quarter of a century longer, it was customary to use inn-yards for theatrical purposes. This was an improvement on the earlier practice of performing on an improvised platform in an open space; and as time went on some five inns in London had made more or less permanent arrangements for actors and audience. But the erection of The Theatre marks not only the provision of much more convenient facilities for performances and for the collecting of admission fees, but a growing recognition of acting as a profession. Later many more play-houses were erected — The Curtain (1577), The Rose (1587), The Swan (1595), The Globe (1599), The Fortune (1600), and others — and, as we have seen, Shakespeare himself found profit in part ownership.

Before the time of Elizabeth, professional actors were legally classed with vagabonds and had no recognized social status. The performance of stage plays was strongly disapproved by the growing Puritan element in the population on grounds of religion and morality, and the civic authorities were also opposed because of the disorderly crowds which gathered to see them, and because of the risks of spreading the plague. The hostility of the city government led to the building of the theaters in the suburbs, beyond its jurisdiction. Important for the improvement of the status of the players was the practice of enrolling their companies under the protection of powerful noblemen, and this culminated in the patronage of the Court. Indeed, it was the fact that the actors were employed to give plays before the Queen which more than any other prevented the opposition from suppressing them altogether. When James succeeded Elizabeth, he continued and extended the support and encouragement given by court performances, and the dramatic companies passed to the patronage of the different members of the royal family, the actors themselves receiving the status of "grooms of the chamber."

Of an importance only less than the intellectual temper of the time and the moment in the development of the drama was the state of the language and of versification. Along with the enthusiasm for the classics and the cultivation of pure Latinity which characterized the Renaissance there appeared a patriotic desire to refine and dignify the vernaculars of the various countries and, among them, of England. The pedantry of the group of men of letters known as the Areopagus, the Euphuism of Lyly, and the Arcadianism of Sidney were only exaggerated instances of the widespread interest in what could be done with the native speech; and, in spite of grotesque eccentricities, these fashions had served to expand the resources and supple the sinews of English. Writers went back to Chaucer and other older authors to recover words which had dropped out of use, and numbers of Romance words were introduced from French, Italian, and Spanish as well as direct from Latin. Traces of this interest in feats in the manipulation of words are apparent in Shakespeare in *Love's Labour's Lost* and elsewhere; but the more important consideration is that when he came to write his plays he had at hand a linguistic medium whose capacities both in vocabulary and structure had not yet become hardened under the dogmatism of the schools, and whose plasticity proved of inestimable value when wielded by a master. A century earlier the language was too poor in resources for such supreme literary achievement; a century later the settling down of convention had made such daring as Shakespeare showed in subduing it to his use all but impossible. Equal good fortune appears in the matter of prosody. Before Shakespeare began to write, drama in England had thrown off the shackles of stanza and rime which had hampered it for centuries, and had found in blank verse its appointed metre. With unerring instinct Shakespeare seized on this and played on it a variety of melodies such as had not hitherto been dreamed of.

Such are the more obvious factors in time and place which gave Shakespeare his opportunity. Peace and prosperity in the country at large; a rising national spirit, inspired and symbolized by a great Queen; the stimulus of Renaissance thought and imagination; a form of art developed to the precise point at which a great genius might carry it to heights never before reached; a language newly enriched and supplied by ingenious experiment, still plastic and fluent; a metre with possibilities proved by at least one great poet but really only tapped; a stage and a profession just emancipated from medieval crudity and waiting to be developed; a mass of material for plots — histories, romances, stories of the falls of princes — ready to the playwright's hand; these were all at Shakespeare's disposal. But they were also at the disposal of his colleagues of the theatre, and though some of these achieved high distinction, none reached and maintained Shakespeare's level. To understand his accomplishment we must turn to more personal matters.

IV. ACCOMPLISHMENT

In attempting to see what are some of the more important qualities that made it possible for Shakespeare to rise to his opportunity, it will be well to note first some of the negative elements in the case. It was not for sheer invention that Shakespeare was unique or even preëminent in his profession. Every form of drama that he touched he carried to a lofty pitch of perfection, but none of them did he create. In two or three cases he seems to have constructed the plot of a play, but such plots are slight and not distinguished by any striking originality. Whenever possible, he borrowed his stories; and the transformation he worked on them is due to a kind of imagination quite other, if much rarer, than is implied in inventive contrivance. Further, in the mechanics of his plays, he repeated himself freely.

When a device, a situation, a contrast of character, proved successful on the stage, he did not scruple to use it again and again, displaying in the variations he worked on it abundant cleverness, but at the same time an economy of invention, in striking contrast to his lavish prodigality in thought and imagery.

The element in his plays which, one is apt to think, must have struck the more thoughtful among his contemporaries as giving them marked distinction among the works of his predecessors and rivals, is his creation of character. In range, in individuality, above all in the illusion of life, there had been nothing in dramatic literature comparable to this endless procession of actual human beings. Here were no puppets labelled with a quality or a title, no mere walking gentlemen capable of being arranged in amusing situations. The persons of the Shakespearean drama, whenever drawn in detail and set in the foreground, are marked by idiosyncrasy that stops short of caricature, are humorous, pathetic, tender, cruel, profound, shallow, or any mixture of these, just as are the people one knows. In no respect does his genius more closely approach the supernatural than in this of the creation of men and women of a truly human complexity. Other qualities already referred to must also have appealed to the contemporary audience: the brilliance of phrase and sparkle of repartee; the consummate mastery of verse — now sweet and lyrical, now throbbing with passion, now echoing the tread of armies, now heavy with thought; — the ingenuity of the stage-craft; the variety of scene and atmosphere. But to the modern student there are deeper things to be found, which may or may not have been evident to his contemporaries, of some of which the poet himself may not have been explicitly conscious.

It has been frequently charged against Shakespeare that in contrast with poets like Dante and Goethe his work embodies no religion, no philosophy. Whatever of truth there may be in this, it is surely inaccurately phrased. Certain it is he was no fanatic, the propagandist of no sect; what philosophy he had is presented in no systematic scheme. If he had been or done these things, he could not have been the supreme dramatist. But the profoundest thought is not necessarily framed into a scheme; the most philosophical artist need not speak through allegory or abstractions. Philosophical ideas find abundant expression in both the dramas and the sonnets of Shakespeare; *obiter dicta* occur of immense suggestiveness and power; and it is hardly possible to read the plays as a whole without becoming conscious of a characteristic attitude toward human nature and the problems of human life. The expression of this attitude naturally varies with the period and the theme. In the Histories the dominant idea is that which one finds elsewhere in the early narratives of these sad stories of the death of kings. Among the strange paradoxes of the Middle Ages none is more remarkable than the persistence, among the Christian conceptions of the Catholic Church, of the pagan goddess of Fortune. So continually is she referred to as the determining force in the destinies of the great, so awed and reverential is the tone in which her caprices are alluded to, that one is forced to the conclusion that she was to the men of that age no mere figure of speech, but a deity who was always feared and often worshipped. The narratives on which Shakespeare based his Histories were pervaded by this conception, and it survives with impressive effect in the speeches of his characters. How far he personally shared it, it is hard to say; but he availed himself of it in a hundred instances of dramatic irony, and it underlies his melancholy insistence on the merely human limitations that assert themselves in the career of every king. With no lack of appreciation of the pomp of monarchy, he yet asserts in play after play that, whether coupled with the futile piety of Henry VI, the unscrupulous tenacity of Richard III, the policy of Henry IV, or the triumphant effectiveness of Henry V,

'Tis not the balm, the sceptre, and the ball,
The sword, the mace, the crown imperial,
The intertissued robe of gold and pearl,
The farced title running 'fore the King,
The throne he sits on, nor the tide of pomp
That beats upon the high shore of this world,

that can separate the king from the pathos of common humanity.

In the Comedies there is no such unity of idea; but generalized reflection is abundantly evident in the dwelling in successive plays on certain tendencies of human nature and their results in action and character; such tendencies as sentimentalism, cynicism, selfishness, and self-deception. The philosophical significance of these plays stops short, as a rule, of the fifth act. The marrying off, at the close, of all eligible youths and maidens is more a concession to the convention of the happy ending demanded by the particular type of drama than the logical outcome of the characters or their deeds. One is not convinced that Shakespeare believed that this was the way things happened in life; but a comedy must end so, and he provided accordingly a conventional dénouement, too often showing traces of the perfunctoriness of his interest in such an artificial adjustment.

Very different is his treatment of the conclusion of Tragedy. Here the crime or weakness which marks the tragic hero is shown bearing its inevitable fruit in suffering and disaster; and the great Tragedies form the crown of his achievement not only because they deal with the more serious problems of life, but because here are found all the elements of poetry, characterization, and construction, in each of which he had attained mastery in earlier plays, but which now are brought to their loftiest pitch and combined. Nowhere else are the two great dramatic elements of character and plot found in such perfect balance, in such complete interaction; nowhere else are they clothed in language so weighty with thought or so glorified by imagination. But it is in the determination of the catastrophes that the philosophical supremacy of the Tragedies most appears, as it is from these that critics who find evidence of pessimism in Shakespeare produce their proof. "Here," they say, pointing to the fifth act of *King Lear*, "here, at least, Shakespeare loses faith; here good and bad go down together in indiscriminate disaster." But so to observe is, surely, to lose sight of the most profound distinction running through these plays, the distinction between the spiritual and the physical. From *Romeo and Juliet* to *Coriolanus* it is clear that Shakespeare hands over to natural and social law the bodies and temporal fortunes of good and bad alike, and such law is permitted its unrelenting sway. But it is equally clear that he regards the spiritual life of his creations as by no means submerged in this welter of suffering and death. Occasionally, as in *Macbeth*, the hero's spiritual career runs at the end parallel to his worldly fortune; more often, as in *Othello* or *Lear*, the moment of physical disaster witnesses a moral purgation, a spiritual triumph; always it is possible to discern two lines of interest, two kinds of value, two clearly distinguished spheres of existence.

For the lack of correspondence between these two lines of action, the absence in Tragedy of any control of worldly happiness in the interest of the good, he attempts no explanation. For he is not concerned to construct a philosophical system, to preach a gospel. Even the all-pervading distinction just set forth is not preached or argued. It is merely implied because no treatment of the greater issues of human life could be at once true and profound without this implication. Thus this limitation, as it has been regarded by those who would have the poet an explicit philosopher, is no limitation at all, but the mark of his allegiance to the true artistic ideal, the proof that he played his own game according to its own rules, and devoted himself with unparalleled disinterestedness, unparalleled range and profundity of insight, to the picturing of things as they are.

W. A. N.

The Comedy of Errors

THERE HAS BEEN very general agreement in regarding *The Comedy of Errors* as one of the earliest of Shakespeare's productions. A play called *A Comedy of Errors* ("like to Plautus his Menaechmus") is stated in the *Gesta Grayorum* to have been acted by players at Gray's Inn as part of the Christmas revels on December 28, 1594, and there is no reason to doubt that this was the present play. Of internal evidences as to date the most pointed is the reference in III.ii.125–127 to France as "armed and reverted, making war against her heir," which is taken as an allusion to the contest between Henry of Navarre and the Catholic League (1589–1593). But Henry of Navarre was heir to the French throne before the death of Henry III in 1589, and had been at war with France as early as 1585. Thus there is nothing in the passage to prevent the dating of this comedy at the very beginning of Shakespeare's career. In *Four Letters Confuted* by Thomas Nashe, registered on January 12, 1593, there occur the words, "heart and good will, but never a ragge of money." The similarity to the lines of Dromio of Ephesus in IV.iv.88–89,

> Money by me? Heart and good will you might,
> But surely, master, not a rag of money,

suggests a borrowing which might have been either way, or from a common proverbial source. The reference in III.ii.141 to Spain's "whole armadoes of caracks" would have roused a quick response from English audiences for years after 1588; hence it offers little help towards a precise date. The large amount of verbal quibbling in the style of the play; the versification, which is marked by much rime both in couplets and alternates; the considerable amount of doggerel; the rarity of mid-line pauses, run-on lines, and weak or light endings; and the comparative scarcity of prose all point to an early date. The riming fourteen-syllabled lines in which the Dromios often speak belong to the tradition of the early drama, but are happily employed for their purpose. From all this it is a fair conjecture that the play was written about 1591 or 1592, but it may have been some years earlier or two years later.

It was first printed in the First Folio of 1623, and on this the present text is based. It is the shortest of Shakespeare's plays.

The main plot follows closely that of the *Menaechmi* of Plautus. The characters common to Plautus and Shakespeare are the two Antipholuses (Menaechmi), Dromio of Syracuse (Messenio), Adriana (Mulier), the Courtezan (Erotium), and Pinch (Medicus). Shakespeare preserves in the Dromio of Syracuse, whom he borrows, and bestows upon the Dromio of Ephesus, whom he invents, the stock characteristics of the witty slave of Plautus. The part of the Courtezan he conspicuously reduces. In Pinch's attempt to diagnose the madness of Antipholus, there is a strong reminiscence of the Medicus of Plautus. The character of Adriana Shakespeare has changed from the conventional shrew of Plautus into a jealous wife, jealous because devoted to her husband. Luciana, her appealing sister, is Shakespeare's happy invention. The Parasite who plays a large part in the Latin comedy, the cook and maid-servant of the Courtezan, and Senex, the father of Mulier, are all discarded by Shakespeare. Little of the detail is drawn from the Latin play, the most notable borrowings being the humorous treatment of the conjurer, the frequent thrashings of Dromio, and the reproof administered by the Abbess to Adriana, which resembles the remarks addressed to Mulier by Senex.

From the *Amphitruo*, another play by Plautus, are taken the scene (III.i.) in which Antipholus of Ephesus and his Dromio are shut out of their own home, and the notion of "doubling" the slaves as well as their masters. There is no reason for doubting that Shakespeare knew both the plays of Plautus in the original. The parallel passages which have been cited to show that he was indebted to the first English translation of the *Menaechmi*, that of W[illiam] W[arner] published in 1595, are not convincing. Furthermore, if he used this translation at all he must have had access to it in manuscript — a possibility but not a probability. Of the *Amphitruo* there was no English translation before the end of the seventeenth century.

The contention that *The Comedy of Errors* was a reworking of a lost play, *The History of Errors*, performed by the boys of St. Paul's at Hampton Court on January 1, 1577, is not acceptable. We know nothing about that play beyond what the title suggests, and the word "Error" need not have been used in the sense of mistaken identity as in the present play. There are, however, some indications that the text of the play as it has survived represents an abridgment of an earlier version which Shakespeare revised. Some broken lines and obscure passages may be due to cuts, but it is unlikely that the revision was drastic. The occasion for it may well enough have been that performance at Gray's Inn in 1594.

The most reluctant commentator cannot fail to give Shakespeare credit for originality in adding to his central plot the frame story of the separation and ultimate reunion of Ægeon and Æmilia, the parents of the twins. For this enveloping action Shakespeare found his inspiration in the long popular tale of Apollonius of Tyre, accessible to him both in the medieval version in Gower's *Confessio Amantis* and the one in Elizabethan prose by Laurence Twine (1576), and subsequently to be developed by him in his own *Pericles*. The tragic experience of this pair, with its happy ending, and the love of Antipholus of Syracuse for Luciana contribute a warmth and dignity to the play which stand athwart and relieve the artificiality and harshness of the dominant "errors." In the conversations of Luciana and the wandering Antipholus the poetry rises to its highest level, and in the personality of Æmilia is suggested a serene knowledge of the world.

Though one can hardly point out in *The Comedy of Errors* signal foreshadowings of the lyric and emotional richness of Shakespeare's mature comedies, one must recognize the theatrical competence and vitality which the play evinces. Though characterization is meager, a complicated plot is skillfully controlled and made to move swiftly. And the grave tone which the story of Ægeon and Æmilia introduces into the comedy would seem to anticipate the blending of the comic and the serious which was to become a distinctive feature of Shakespeare's later plays.

THE COMEDY OF ERRORS

<hr>

[DRAMATIS PERSONÆ

SOLINUS, *duke of Ephesus.*
ÆGEON, *a merchant of Syracuse.*
ANTIPHOLUS of Ephesus, ⎫ *twin brothers, and*
ANTIPHOLUS of Syracuse, ⎬ *sons to Ægeon and*
⎭ *Æmilia.*
DROMIO of Ephesus, ⎫ *twin brothers, and attend-*
DROMIO of Syracuse, ⎬ *ants on the two Anti-*
⎭ *pholuses.*
BALTHAZAR, *a merchant.*
ANGELO, *a goldsmith.*

First Merchant, *friend to Antipholus of Syra-*
cuse.
Second Merchant, *to whom Angelo is a debtor.*
PINCH, *a schoolmaster.*

ÆMILIA, *wife to Ægeon, an abbess at Ephesus.*
ADRIANA, *wife to Antipholus of Ephesus.*
LUCIANA, *her sister.*
LUCE, *servant to Adriana.*
A Courtezan.

Gaoler, Officers, and other Attendants.

SCENE: *Ephesus.*]

ACT I

SCENE I. [*A hall in the Duke's palace.*]

Enter DUKE, ÆGEON, GAOLER, [Officers,]
and other Attendants.

Æge. Proceed, Solinus, to procure my fall,
And by the doom of death end woes and all.
Duke. Merchant of Syracusa, plead no more;
I am not partial to infringe our laws.
The enmity and discord which of late   5
Sprung from the rancorous outrage of your duke
To merchants, our well-dealing countrymen,
Who, wanting guilders to redeem their lives,
Have seal'd his rigorous statutes with their bloods,
Excludes all pity from our threat'ning looks.   10
For, since the mortal and intestine jars
'Twixt thy seditious countrymen and us,
It hath in solemn synods been decreed,
Both by the Syracusians and ourselves,
To admit no traffic to our adverse towns.   15
Nay, more: if any born at Ephesus
Be seen at any Syracusian marts and fairs;
Again, if any Syracusian born

Come to the bay of Ephesus, he dies,   20
His goods confiscate to the Duke's dispose,
Unless a thousand marks be levied,
To quit the penalty and to ransom him.
Thy substance, valu'd at the highest rate,
Cannot amount unto a hundred marks;   25
Therefore by law thou art condemn'd to die.
Æge. Yet this my comfort: when your words are
done,
My woes end likewise with the evening sun.
Duke. Well, Syracusian, say in brief the cause
Why thou departed'st from thy native home,   30
And for what cause thou cam'st to Ephesus.
Æge. A heavier task could not have been impos'd
Than I to speak my griefs unspeakable;
Yet, that the world may witness that my end
Was wrought by nature, not by vile offence,   35
I'll utter what my sorrow gives me leave.
In Syracusa was I born, and wed
Unto a woman, happy but for me,
And by me [too], had not our hap been bad.
With her I liv'd in joy; our wealth increas'd   40
By prosperous voyages I often made

Act I, sc. i, 4. **partial:** inclined. 8. **guilders:** Dutch silver coins worth about 1s.8d. English. 11. **intestine.** Properly "civil"; here between Greeks. 22. **marks.** A mark was worth 13s.4d. 35. **nature:** natural affection. 39. [too] F2. Om. F1.

To Epidamnum, till my factor's death
And the great care of goods at random left
Drew me from kind embracements of my spouse;
From whom my absence was not six months old 45
Before herself, almost at fainting under
The pleasing punishment that women bear,
Had made provision for her following me,
And soon and safe arrived where I was.
There had she not been long but she became 50
A joyful mother of two goodly sons;
And, which was strange, the one so like the other
As could not be distinguish'd but by names.
That very hour, and in the self-same inn,
A [meaner] woman was delivered 55
Of such a burden, male twins, both alike.
Those, for their parents were exceeding poor,
I bought and brought up to attend my sons.
My wife, not meanly proud of two such boys,
Made daily motions for our home return. 60
Unwilling I agreed. Alas! too soon
We came aboard.
A league from Epidamnum had we sail'd
Before the always wind-obeying deep
Gave any tragic instance of our harm. 65
But longer did we not retain much hope;
For what obscured light the heavens did grant
Did but convey unto our fearful minds
A doubtful warrant of immediate death;
Which though myself would gladly have embrac'd,
Yet the incessant weepings of my wife, 71
Weeping before for what she saw must come,
And piteous plainings of the pretty babes,
That mourn'd for fashion, ignorant what to fear,
Forc'd me to seek delays for them and me. 75
And this it was, for other means was none:
The sailors sought for safety by our boat,
And left the ship, then sinking-ripe, to us.
My wife, more careful for the latter born,
Had fast'ned him unto a small spare mast, 80
Such as seafaring men provide for storms;
To him one of the other twins was bound,
Whilst I had been like heedful of the other.
The children thus dispos'd, my wife and I,
Fixing our eyes on whom our care was fix'd, 85
Fast'ned ourselves at either end the mast;
And floating straight, obedient to the stream,
Was carried towards Corinth, as we thought.
At length the sun, gazing upon the earth,
Dispers'd those vapours that offended us; 90
And, by the benefit of his wished light,
The seas wax'd calm, and we discovered
Two ships from far making amain to us,
Of Corinth that, of Epidaurus this.

But ere they came, — O, let me say no more! 95
Gather the sequel by that went before.
  Duke. Nay, forward, old man; do not break off so;
For we may pity, though not pardon thee.
  Æge. O, had the gods done so, I had not now
Worthily term'd them merciless to us! 100
For, ere the ships could meet by twice five leagues,
We were encount'red by a mighty rock,
Which being violently borne [upon],
Our helpful ship was splitted in the midst;
So that, in this unjust divorce of us, 105
Fortune had left to both of us alike
What to delight in, what to sorrow for.
Her part, poor soul! seeming as burdened
With lesser weight but not with lesser woe,
Was carried with more speed before the wind; 110
And in our sight they three were taken up
By fishermen of Corinth, as we thought.
At length, another ship had seiz'd on us;
And, knowing whom it was their hap to save,
Gave healthful welcome to their shipwreck'd guests;
And would have reft the fishers of their prey, 116
Had not their [bark] been very slow of sail;
And therefore homeward did they bend their course.
Thus have you heard me sever'd from my bliss,
That by misfortunes was my life prolong'd 120
To tell sad stories of my own mishaps.
  Duke. And, for the sake of them thou sorrowest
    for,
Do me the favour to dilate at full
What [hath] befallen of them and [thee] till now.
  Æge. My youngest boy, and yet my eldest care,
At eighteen years became inquisitive 126
After his brother, and importun'd me
That his attendant — so his case was like,
Reft of his brother, but retain'd his name —
Might bear him company in the quest of him; 130
Whom whilst I labour'd of a love to see,
I hazarded the loss of whom I lov'd.
Five summers have I spent in farthest Greece,
Roaming clean through the bounds of Asia,
And, coasting homeward, came to Ephesus; 135
Hopeless to find, yet loath to leave unsought
Or that or any place that harbours men.
But here must end the story of my life;
And happy were I in my timely death,
Could all my travels warrant me they live. 140
  Duke. Hapless Ægeon, whom the fates have
    mark'd
To bear the extremity of dire mishap!
Now, trust me, were it not against our laws,
Against my crown, my oath, my dignity,
Which princes, would they, may not disannul, 145

---

42. **factor's**: agent's. 55. **[meaner]** (S. Walker) *meene* F₁; *poor meane* F₂. 60. **motions**: proposals. 62. Cunningham completes the line "and put to sea, but scarce." 65. **instance**: sign. 69. **doubtful**: uncertain but likely. 74. **for fashion**: in imitation. 103. **[upon]** (Pope). *up* F. 115. **healthful**: saving. 117. **[bark]** F₂. *backe* F₁. 123. **dilate**: relate. 124. **[hath]** ... **[thee]** F₂. *have ... they* F₁. 131. **of**: out of, from. 139. **timely**: speedy. 145. **disannul**: annul.

My soul should sue as advocate for thee.
But, though thou art adjudged to the death,
And passed sentence may not be recall'd
But to our honour's great disparagement,
Yet I will favour thee in what I can.   150
Therefore, merchant, I'll limit thee this day
To seek thy [life] by beneficial help.
Try all the friends thou hast in Ephesus;
Beg thou, or borrow, to make up the sum,
And live; if no, then thou art doom'd to die.   155
Gaoler, take him to thy custody.
    Gaol. I will, my lord.
    Æge. Hopeless and helpless doth Ægeon wend,
But to procrastinate his lifeless end.   [*Exeunt.*

[SCENE II. *The mart.*]

Enter ANTIPHOLUS of Syracuse, DROMIO of Syracuse,
        and [FIRST] MERCHANT.

    1. Mer. Therefore give out you are of Epidam-
        num,
Lest that your goods too soon be confiscate.
This very day a Syracusian merchant
Is apprehended for arrival here;
And, not being able to buy out his life   5
According to the statute of the town,
Dies ere the weary sun set in the west.
There is your money that I had to keep.
    Ant. S. Go bear it to the Centaur, where we host,
And stay there, Dromio, till I come to thee.   10
Within this hour it will be dinner-time;
Till that, I'll view the manners of the town,
Peruse the traders, gaze upon the buildings,
And then return and sleep within mine inn,
For with long travel I am stiff and weary.   15
Get thee away.
    Dro. S. Many a man would take you at your
        word,
And go, indeed, having so good a mean.   [*Exit.*
    Ant. S. A trusty villain, sir, that very oft,
When I am dull with care and melancholy,   20
Lightens my humour with his merry jests.
What, will you walk with me about the town,
And then go to my inn and dine with me?
    1. Mer. I am invited, sir, to certain merchants,
Of whom I hope to make much benefit;   25
I crave your pardon. Soon at five o'clock,
Please you, I'll meet with you upon the mart
And afterward consort you till bed-time.
My present business calls me from you now.

    Ant. S. Farewell till then. I will go lose myself,
And wander up and down to view the city.   31
    1. Mer. Sir, I commend you to your own content.
                                                [*Exit.*
    Ant. S. He that commends me to mine own
        content
Commends me to the thing I cannot get.
I to the world am like a drop of water   35
That in the ocean seeks another drop,
Who, falling there to find his fellow forth,
Unseen, inquisitive, confounds himself.
So I, to find a mother and a brother,
In quest of them, unhappy, lose myself.   40

Enter DROMIO of Ephesus.

Here comes the almanac of my true date.
What now? How chance thou art return'd so soon?
    Dro. E. Return'd so soon! rather approach'd
        too late.
The capon burns, the pig falls from the spit,
The clock hath strucken twelve upon the bell;   45
My mistress made it one upon my cheek,
She is so hot because the meat is cold;
The meat is cold because you come not home;
You come not home because you have no stomach;
You have no stomach having broke your fast;   50
But we that know what 'tis to fast and pray
Are penitent for your default to-day.
    Ant. S. Stop in your wind, sir; tell me this, I pray:
Where have you left the money that I gave you?
    Dro. E. O, — sixpence, that I had o'Wednesday
        last   55
To pay the saddler for my mistress' crupper?
The saddler had it, sir; I kept it not.
    Ant. S. I am not in a sportive humour now.
Tell me, and dally not, where is the money?
We being strangers here, how dar'st thou trust   60
So great a charge from thine own custody?
    Dro. E. I pray you, jest, sir, as you sit at dinner.
I from my mistress come to you in post;
If I return, I shall be post indeed,
For she will [score] your fault upon my pate.   65
Methinks your maw, like mine, should be your [clock]
And strike you home without a messenger.
    Ant. S. Come, Dromio, come, these jests are
        out of season;
Reserve them till a merrier hour than this.
Where is the gold I gave in charge to thee?   70
    Dro. E. To me, sir? Why, you gave no gold to me.
    Ant. S. Come on, sir knave, have done your
        foolishness

152. [life] (Rowe).   *helpe* F. Other conjectures are *store, sum, health.*
    Sc. ii, S.D. ANTIPHOLUS of Syracuse. *Antipholis Erotes* Ff.   9. **host:** lodge.   18. **mean:** means, sum of money.
19. **villain.** Used good-naturedly as "fellow"; also bondman.   21. **humour:** a physiological term in Shakespeare's time,
here meaning "mood" or "disposition." 26. **Soon at:** about.   37. **forth:** out.   41. **almanac...date.** Because they were
born in the same hour, Antipholus can see his age in Dromio.   45. **twelve.** The Elizabethan dinner hour was 11:30.
49. **stomach:** appetite. 52. **penitent:** i.e., doing penance. 53. **wind:** talk. 63. **post:** haste. 64. **post:** post in a tavern
or shop on which reckonings were scored. 65. [score] (Rowe). *scoure* F. 66. [clock] (Pope). *cooke* F.

And tell me how thou hast dispos'd thy charge.

Dro. E. My charge was but to fetch you from
    the mart
Home to your house, the Phœnix, sir, to dinner. 75
My mistress and her sister stays for you.

Ant. S. Now, as I am a Christian, answer me
In what safe place you have bestow'd my money,
Or I shall break that merry sconce of yours
That stands on tricks when I am undispos'd. 80
Where is the thousand marks thou hadst of me?

Dro. E. I have some marks of yours upon my pate,
Some of my mistress' marks upon my shoulders,
But not a thousand marks between you both.
If I should pay your worship those again, 85
Perchance you will not bear them patiently.

Ant. S. Thy mistress' marks? What mistress,
    slave, hast thou?

Dro. E. Your worship's wife, my mistress at
    the Phœnix;
She that doth fast till you come home to dinner,
And prays that you will hie you home to dinner. 90

Ant. S. What, wilt thou flout me thus unto my face,
Being forbid? There, take you that, sir knave.

Dro. E. What mean you, sir? For [God's] sake,
    hold your hands!
Nay, an you will not, sir, I'll take my heels. [*Exit.*

Ant. S. Upon my life, by some device or other 95
The villain is [o'erraught] of all my money.
They say this town is full of cozenage,
As, nimble jugglers that deceive the eye,
Dark-working sorcerers that change the mind,
Soul-killing witches that deform the body, 100
Disguised cheaters, prating mountebanks,
And many such-like liberties of sin.
If it prove so, I will be gone the sooner.
I'll to the Centaur to go seek this slave;
I greatly fear my money is not safe. [*Exit.*] 105

ACT II

[SCENE I. *The house of Antipholus of Ephesus.*]

Enter ADRIANA *and* LUCIANA.

Adr. Neither my husband nor the slave return'd,
That in such haste I sent to seek his master!
Sure, Luciana, it is two o'clock.

Luc. Perhaps some merchant hath invited him
And from the mart he's somewhere gone to dinner. 5
Good sister, let us dine and never fret.
A man is master of his liberty.
Time is their master, and when they see time
They'll go or come; if so, be patient, sister. 9

Adr. Why should their liberty than ours be more?

Luc. Because their business still lies out [o' door].

Adr. Look, when I serve him so, he takes it [ill].

Luc. O, know he is the bridle of your will.

Adr. There's none but asses will be bridled so.

Luc. Why, headstrong liberty is lash'd with woe.
There's nothing situate under heaven's eye 16
But hath his bound; in earth, in sea, in sky,
The beasts, the fishes, and the winged fowls
Are their males' subjects and at their controls;
Man, more divine, the master of all these, 20
Lord of the wide world and wild watery seas,
Indu'd with intellectual sense and souls,
Of more preëminence than fish and fowls,
Are masters to their females, and their lords:
Then let your will attend on their accords. 25

Adr. This servitude makes you to keep unwed.

Luc. Not this, but troubles of the marriage-bed.

Adr. But, were you wedded, you would bear
    some sway.

Luc. Ere I learn love, I'll practise to obey.

Adr. How if your husband start some other-
    where? 30

Luc. Till he came home again, I would forbear.

Adr. Patience unmov'd! no marvel though she
    pause.
They can be meek that have no other cause.
A wretched soul, bruis'd with adversity,
We bid be quiet when we hear it cry; 35
But were we burd'ned with like weight of pain,
As much or more we should ourselves complain;
So thou, that hast no unkind mate to grieve thee,
With urging helpless patience would relieve me;
But, if thou live to see like right bereft, 40
This fool-begg'd patience in thee will be left.

Luc. Well, I will marry one day, but to try.
Here comes your man; now is your husband nigh.

Enter DROMIO *of Ephesus.*

Adr. Say, is your tardy master now at hand?

Dro. E. Nay, he's at two hands with me, and
that my two ears can witness. 46

Adr. Say, didst thou speak with him? Know'st
thou his mind?

Dro. E. Ay, ay, he told his mind upon mine ear.
Beshrew his hand, I scarce could understand it.

Luc. Spake he so doubtfully, thou couldst not
feel his meaning? 51

Dro. E. Nay, he struck so plainly, I could too
well feel his blows; and withal so doubtfully that
I could scarce understand them.

Adr. But say, I prithee, is he coming home? 55
It seems he hath great care to please his wife.

Dro. E. Why, mistress, sure my master is horn-
mad.

---

80. **stands on:** persists in. 93. **[God's]** (Hanmer). *God* F. 96. **[o'erraught]** (Hanmer). *ore-wrought* F. 97. **cozenage:**
cheating. 102. **liberties:** licenses.

Act II, sc. i, 11. **[o' door]** (Capell). *adore* F. 12. **[ill]** F₂. *thus* F₁. 30. **start:** swerve aside. 39. **helpless:** unavailing.
41. **fool-begg'd:** idiotic. 49. **beshrew:** curse. **understand:** with a pun on "stand under." 57. **horn-mad:** mad as a beast.

Adr. Horn-mad, thou villain!

Dro. E.   I mean not cuckold-mad;
But, sure, he is stark mad.

When I desir'd him to come home to dinner,   60
He ask'd me for a [thousand] marks in gold.
"'Tis dinner-time," quoth I; "My gold," quoth he.
"Your meat doth burn," quoth I; "My gold!"
    quoth he.
"Will you come [home]?" quoth I; "My gold!"
    quoth he,
"Where is the thousand marks I gave thee, vil-
    lain?"   65
"The pig," quoth I, "is burn'd"; "My gold!"
    quoth he.
"My mistress, sir," quoth I; "Hang up thy mistress!
I know not thy mistress.   Out on thy mistress!"

Luc. Quoth who?

Dro. E. Quoth my master.   70
"I know," quoth he, "no house, no wife, no mis-
    tress."
So that my [errand] due unto my tongue,
I thank him, I bare home upon my shoulders;
For, in conclusion, he did beat me there.

Adr. Go back again, thou slave, and fetch him
    home.   75

Dro. E. Go back again, and be new beaten home?
For God's sake, send some other messenger.

Adr. Back, slave, or I will break thy pate across.

Dro. E. And he will bless that cross with other
    beating.
Between you I shall have a holy head.   80

Adr. Hence, prating peasant!   Fetch thy master
    home.

Dro. E. Am I so round with you as you with
    me,
That like a football you do spurn me thus?   83
You spurn me hence, and he will spurn me hither.
If I last in this service, you must case me in leather.
    [*Exit.*]

Luc. Fie, how impatience loureth in your face!

Adr. His company must do his minions grace,
Whilst I at home starve for a merry look.
Hath homely age the alluring beauty took
From my poor cheek?   Then he hath wasted it.   90
Are my discourses dull?   Barren my wit?
If voluble and sharp discourse be marr'd,
Unkindness blunts it more than marble hard.
Do their gay vestments his affections bait?
That's not my fault; he's master of my state.   95
What ruins are in me that can be found

By him not ruin'd?   Then is he the ground
Of my defeatures.   My decayed fair
A sunny look of his would soon repair.
But, too unruly deer, he breaks the pale   100
And feeds from home; poor I am but his stale.

Luc. Self-harming jealousy! fie, beat it hence!

Adr. Unfeeling fools can with such wrongs dis-
    pense.
I know his eye doth homage other-where,
Or else what lets it but he would be here?   105
Sister, you know he promis'd me a chain;
Would that [alone, alone] he would detain,
So he would keep fair quarter with his bed!
I see the jewel best enamelled
Will lose his beauty; [and tho'] gold bides still   110
That others touch, [yet] often touching will
[Wear] gold; and no man that hath a name
By falsehood and corruption doth it shame.
Since that my beauty cannot please his eye,
I'll weep what's left away, and weeping die.   115

Luc. How many fond fools serve mad jealousy?
    [*Exeunt.*]

[SCENE II.   *A public place.*]

Enter ANTIPHOLUS *of Syracuse.*

Ant. S. The gold I gave to Dromio is laid up
Safe at the Centaur; and the heedful slave
Is wand'red forth, in care to seek me out.
By computation and mine host's report,
I could not speak with Dromio since at first   5
I sent him from the mart.   See, here he comes.

Enter DROMIO *of Syracuse.*

How now, sir! is your merry humour alter'd?
As you love strokes, so jest with me again.
You know no Centaur?   You receiv'd no gold?
Your mistress sent to have me home to dinner?   10
My house was at the Phœnix?   Wast thou mad
That thus so madly thou didst answer me?

Dro. S. What answer, sir?   When spake I such
    a word?

Ant. S. Even now, even here, not half an hour
    since.   14

Dro. S. I did not see you since you sent me hence,
Home to the Centaur, with the gold you gave me.

Ant. S. Villain, thou didst deny the gold's receipt
And told'st me of a mistress and a dinner;
For which, I hope, thou felt'st I was displeas'd.

61. [thousand] F₄. *hundred* F₁. *1000* F₂,₃. 64. [home] (Hanmer). Om. F. 72. [errand] F₄. *arrant* F₁₋₃. due...
tongue: which should have been given me to deliver in words. 80. holy: i.e., with pun on "full of holes." 82. round: (1)
spherical, (2) plain-spoken. 87. minions: favorites. 94. bait: lure. 98. defeatures: disfigurements. fair: beauty.
101. stale: laughing-stock, possibly stalking horse. 103. dispense: put up. 105. lets: prevents. 107. [alone, alone] F₂.
alone, a love F₁. detain: withhold. 108. keep...with: be true to. 110-111. [and tho']...[yet] (Hanmer conj.) *yet*...
and F. 112. [Wear] (Theobald). *Where* F. The passage (109-113) is confused and very likely corrupt. The following paraphrase may give the meaning: "The best enamelled jewel tarnishes, but though handling does not destroy gold,
nevertheless it will impair it; and no man with a reputation risks shaming it by infidelity and debasement."

Dro. S. I am glad to see you in this merry vein. 20
What means this jest? I pray you, master, tell me.
   Ant. S. Yea, dost thou jeer and flout me in the
      teeth?
Think'st thou I jest? Hold, take thou that, and
   that.   [*Beats Dro.*
   Dro. S. Hold, sir, for God's sake! Now your
      jest is earnest.
Upon what bargain do you give it me?   25
   Ant. S. Because that I familiarly sometimes
Do use you for my fool and chat with you,
Your sauciness will jest upon my love
And make a common of my serious hours.
When the sun shines let foolish gnats make sport, 30
But creep in crannies when he hides his beams.
If you will jest with me, know my aspect
And fashion your demeanour to my looks,
Or I will beat this method in your sconce.   34
   Dro. S. Sconce call you it? So you would
leave battering, I had rather have it a head. An
you use these blows long, I must get a sconce for
my head and insconce it too, or else I shall seek my
wit in my shoulders. But, I pray, sir, why am
I beaten?   40
   Ant. S. Dost thou not know?
   Dro. S. Nothing, sir, but that I am beaten.
   Ant. S. Shall I tell you why?
   Dro. S. Ay, sir, and wherefore; for they say
every why hath a wherefore.   45
   Ant. S. Why, first, — for flouting me; and then,
      wherefore, —
For urging it the second time to me.
   Dro. S. Was there ever any man thus beaten
      out of season,
When in the why and the wherefore is neither
      rhyme nor reason?
Well, sir, I thank you.   50
   Ant. S. Thank me, sir! For what?
   Dro. S. Marry, sir, for this something that you
gave me for nothing.
   Ant. S. I'll make you amends next, to give you
nothing for something. But say, sir, is it dinnertime?
   Dro. S. No, sir. I think the meat wants that
   I have.   57
   Ant. S. In good time, sir; what's that?
   Dro. S. Basting.
   Ant. S. Well, sir, then 't will be dry.   60
   Dro. S. If it be, sir, I pray you, eat none of it.

   Ant. S. Your reason?
   Dro. S. Lest it make you choleric and purchase
me another dry basting.
   Ant. S. Well, sir, learn to jest in good time.
There's a time for all things.   66
   Dro. S. I durst have denied that, before you
were so choleric.
   Ant. S. By what rule, sir?
   Dro. S. Marry, sir, by a rule as plain as the plain
bald pate of father Time himself.   71
   Ant. S. Let's hear it.
   Dro. S. There's no time for a man to recover his
hair that grows bald by nature.
   Ant. S. May he not do it by fine and recovery? 75
   Dro. S. Yes, to pay a fine for a periwig and re-
cover the lost hair of another man.
   Ant. S. Why is Time such a niggard of hair,
being, as it is, so plentiful an excrement?   79
   Dro. S. Because it is a blessing that he bestows
on beasts; and what he hath scanted [men] in hair
he hath given them in wit.
   Ant. S. Why, but there's many a man hath
more hair than wit.
   Dro. S. Not a man of those but he hath the wit
to lose his hair.   86
   Ant. S. Why, thou didst conclude hairy men
plain dealers without wit.
   Dro. S. The plainer dealer, the sooner lost; yet
he loseth it in a kind of jollity.   90
   Ant. S. For what reason?
   Dro. S. For two; and sound [ones] too.
   Ant. S. Nay, not sound, I pray you.
   Dro. S. Sure ones, then.
   Ant. S. Nay, not sure, in a thing falsing.   95
   Dro. S. Certain ones, then.
   Ant. S. Name them.
   Dro. S. The one, to save the money that he
spends in [tiring]; the other, that at dinner they
should not drop in his porridge.   100
   Ant. S. You would all this time have prov'd
there is no time for all things.
   Dro. S. Marry, and did, sir; namely, no time
to recover hair lost by nature.
   Ant. S. But your reason was not substantial,
why there is no time to recover.   106
   Dro. S. Thus I mend it: Time himself is bald
and therefore to the world's end will have bald
followers.

Sc. ii, 22. in the teeth: to my face. **24. earnest:** i.e., with a pun on "earnest-money," a sum laid down to bind a
bargain. **29. common:** public playground. **32. aspect:** (1) expression, (2) disposition (malignant or benign) of planets,
in the old astrology. **34. sconce:** head (but *sort* in l. 35 and *helmet* in l. 37). **38. insconce:** protect. **39. seek ...
shoulders:** i.e., my head will be beaten into my shoulders. **58. In good time:** forsooth. **63. choleric.** Overdone
meat was believed to make one irascible. **64. dry basting:** severe beating. **75. fine and recovery:** a legal pro-
cedure by which entailed estates could be transferred without entail from one owner to another. Antipholus
seems to be punning on *heir* and *hair* (see l. 74). **79. excrement:** outgrowth (of hair). **81. [men]** (Theobald). *them,*F.
86. he ... hair. Reference to the diseases which produce loss of hair. **90. jollity.** This word and *sound* (l. 93) and
falsing (i.e., deceptive, l. 95) play upon the implications of l. 86 (see note). **92. [ones]** F$_2$. Om. F$_1$. **99. [tiring]**
(Pope): dressing the hair. *trying* F. **103. no time** F$_2$. *in no time* F$_1$.

Ant. S. I knew 't would be a bald conclusion. —
But, soft! who wafts us yonder?   111

Enter ADRIANA *and* LUCIANA.

Adr. Ay, ay, Antipholus, look strange and frown,
Some other mistress hath thy sweet aspects;
I am not Adriana, nor thy wife.
The time was once when thou unurg'd wouldst vow
That never words were music to thine ear,   116
That never object pleasing in thine eye,
That never touch well welcome to thy hand,
That never meat sweet-savour'd in thy taste,
Unless I spake, or look'd, or touch'd, or carv'd to
    thee.   120
How comes it now, my husband, O, how comes it,
That thou art then estranged from thyself?
Thyself I call it, being strange to me,
That, undividable, incorporate,
Am better than thy dear self's better part.   125
Ah, do not tear away thyself from me!
For know, my love, as easy mayst thou fall
A drop of water in the breaking gulf
And take unmingled thence that drop again,
Without addition or diminishing,   130
As take from me thyself and not me too.
How dearly would it touch thee to the quick
Shouldst thou but hear I were licentious,
And that this body, consecrate to thee,
By ruffian lust should be contaminate!   135
Wouldst thou not spit at me, and spurn at me,
And hurl the name of husband in my face,
And tear the stain'd skin off my harlot-brow,
And from my false hand cut the wedding-ring
And break it with a deep-divorcing vow?   140
I know thou canst; and therefore see thou do it.
I am possess'd with an adulterate blot;
My blood is mingled with the crime of lust;
For if we two be one and thou play false,
I do digest the poison of thy flesh,   145
Being strumpeted by thy contagion.
Keep then fair league and truce with thy true bed;
I live distain'd, thou undishonoured.

Ant. S. Plead you to me, fair dame? I know
    you not.
In Ephesus I am but two hours old,   150
As strange unto your town as to your talk;
Who, every word by all my wit being scann'd,
Wants wit in all one word to understand.

Luc. Fie, brother! how the world is chang'd
    with you!
When were you wont to use my sister thus?   155
She sent for you by Dromio home to dinner.

Ant. S. By Dromio?
Dro. S. By me?
Adr. By thee; and this thou didst return from
    him,
That he did buffet thee, and in his blows   160
Denied my house for his, me for his wife.

Ant. S. Did you converse, sir, with this gentle-
    woman?
What is the course and drift of your compact?

Dro. S. I, sir? I never saw her till this time.

Ant. S. Villain, thou liest; for even her very words
Didst thou deliver to me on the mart.   166

Dro. S. I never spake with her in all my life.

Ant. S. How can she thus then call us by our
    names,
Unless it be by inspiration?

Adr. How ill agrees it with your gravity   170
To counterfeit thus grossly with your slave,
Abetting him to thwart me in my mood!
Be it my wrong you are from me exempt,
But wrong not that wrong with a more contempt.
Come, I will fasten on this sleeve of thine.   175
Thou art an elm, my husband, I a vine,
Whose weakness married to thy [stronger] state
Makes me with thy strength to communicate.
If aught possess thee from me, it is dross,
Usurping ivy, brier, or idle moss;   180
Who, all for want of pruning, with intrusion
Infect thy sap and live on thy confusion.

Ant. S. To me she speaks; she moves me for her
    theme.
What, was I married to her in my dream?
Or sleep I now and think I hear all this?   185
What error drives our eyes and ears amiss?
Until I know this sure uncertainty,
I'll entertain the [offer'd] fallacy.

Luc. Dromio, go bid the servants spread for
    dinner.

Dro. S. O, for my beads! I cross me for a
    sinner.   190
This is the fairy land. O spite of spites!
We talk with goblins, owls, and sprites.
If we obey them not, this will ensue:
They'll suck our breath or pinch us black and blue.

Luc. Why prat'st thou to thyself and answer'st
    not?   195
Dromio, thou Dromio, thou snail, thou slug, thou
    sot!

Dro. S. I am transformed, master, am [not I]?

Ant. S. I think thou art in mind, and so am I.

Dro. S. Nay, master, both in mind and in my
    shape.   199

---

110. **bald:** senseless. 111. **wafts:** waves to, beckons. 113. **aspects:** glances. 125. **better part:** i.e., soul, spirit. 127. **fall:** let fall. 132. **dearly:** intimately, keenly. 148. **distain'd:** unstained. Many editors read "unstained." 163. **compact:** plot. 172. **mood:** displeasure. 173. **exempt:** separated. 177. **[stronger]** F$_4$. *stranger* F$_{1-3}$. 179. **possess:** take. 180. **idle:** barren, useless. 182. **confusion:** ruin. 183. **moves:** takes. 187. **know:** comprehend. 188. **[offer'd]** (Capell conj.) *free'd* F. 190. **beads:** rosary. 196. **sot:** fool. 197. **[not I]** (Theobald). *I not* F.

Ant. S. Thou hast thine own form.

Dro. S.   No, I am an ape.

Luc. If thou art chang'd to aught, 'tis to an ass.

Dro. S. 'Tis true; she rides me and I long for grass.

'Tis so, I am an ass; else it could never be

But I should know her as well as she knows me.

Adr. Come, come; no longer will I be a fool,   205

To put the finger in the eye and weep

Whilst man and master laughs my woes to scorn.

Come, sir, to dinner. Dromio, keep the gate.

Husband, I'll dine above with you to-day

And shrive you of a thousand idle pranks.   210

Sirrah, if any ask you for your master,

Say he dines forth and let no creature enter.

Come, sister. Dromio, play the porter well.

Ant. S. Am I in earth, in heaven, or in hell?

Sleeping or waking? Mad or well-advis'd?   215

Known unto these, and to myself disguis'd!

I'll say as they say and persever so,

And in this mist at all adventures go.

Dro. S. Master, shall I be porter at the gate?

Adr. Ay; and let none enter, lest I break your pate.   220

Luc. Come, come, Antipholus, we dine too late.

                         [*Exeunt.*

ACT III

SCENE I. [*Before the house of Antipholus of Ephesus.*]

Enter ANTIPHOLUS *of Ephesus,* DROMIO *of Ephesus,* ANGELO, *the goldsmith, and* BALTHAZAR, *the merchant.*

Ant. E. Good Signior Angelo, you must excuse us all;

My wife is shrewish when I keep not hours.

Say that I linger'd with you at your shop

To see the making of her carcanet,

And that to-morrow you will bring it home.   5

But here's a villain that would face me down

He met me on the mart, and that I beat him

And charg'd him with a thousand marks in gold,

And that I did deny my wife and house.   9

Thou drunkard, thou, what didst thou mean by this?

Dro. E. Say what you will, sir, but I know what I know.

That you beat me at the mart, I have your hand to show.

If the skin were parchment and the blows you gave were ink,

Your own handwriting would tell you what I think.

Ant. E. I think thou art an ass.

Dro. E.   Marry, so it doth appear

By the wrongs I suffer and the blows I bear.   16

I should kick, being kick'd; and, being at that pass,

You would keep from my heels and beware of an ass.

Ant. E. You're sad, Signior Balthazar; pray God our cheer

May answer my good will and your good welcome here.   20

Bal. I hold your dainties cheap, sir, and your welcome dear.

Ant. E. O, Signior Balthazar, either at flesh or fish,

A table-full of welcome makes scarce one dainty dish.

Bal. Good meat, sir, is common; that every churl affords.

Ant. E. And welcome more common; for that's nothing but words.   25

Bal. Small cheer and great welcome makes a merry feast.

Ant. E. Ay, to a niggardly host and more sparing guest;

But though my cates be mean, take them in good part;

Better cheer may you have, but not with better heart.

But, soft! my door is lock'd. Go bid them let us in.   30

Dro. E. Maud, Bridget, Marian, Cicely, Gillian, Ginn!

Dro. S. [*Within.*] Mome, malt-horse, capon, coxcomb, idiot, patch!

Either get thee from the door or sit down at the hatch.

Dost thou conjure for wenches, that thou call'st for such store

When one is one too many? Go get thee from the door.   35

Dro. E. What patch is made our porter? My master stays in the street.

Dro. S. [*Within.*] Let him walk from whence he came, lest he catch cold on 's feet.

Ant. E. Who talks within there? Ho, open the door!

Dro. S. [*Within.*] Right, sir; I'll tell you when, an you'll tell me wherefore.

Ant. E. Wherefore? For my dinner. I have not din'd to-day.   40

Dro. S. [*Within.*] Nor to-day here you must not, come again when you may.

Ant. E. What art thou that keep'st me out from the house I owe?

---

210. **shrive:** to hear confession and give absolution.   212. **forth:** out.   215. **well-advis'd:** sane.   218. **at all adventures:** come what may.

Act III, sc. i, 4. **carcanet:** jeweled necklace.   8. **with:** i.e., with the possession of.   28. **cates:** refreshments, provisions.   32. **Mome:** blockhead. **malt-horse:** brewer's horse, hence a dullard. **patch:** fool.   33. **hatch:** a wicket or half-door. 42. **owe:** own.

Dro. S. [*Within.*] The porter for this time, sir, and my name is Dromio.

Dro. E. O villain! thou hast stolen both mine office and my name.
The one ne'er got me credit, the other mickle blame.   45
If thou hadst been Dromio to-day in my place,
Thou wouldst have chang'd thy face for a name, or thy name for an ass.

Enter LUCE [*within*].

Luce. [*Within.*] What a coil is there, Dromio? Who are those at the gate?

Dro. E. Let my master in, Luce.

Luce. [*Within.*] Faith, no; he comes too late;
And so tell your master.

Dro. E.   O Lord, I must laugh!
Have at you with a proverb — Shall I set in my staff?   51

Luce. [*Within.*] Have at you with another; that's — When? Can you tell?

Dro. S. [*Within.*] If thy name be called Luce, — Luce, thou hast answer'd him well.

Ant. E. Do you hear, you minion? You'll let us in, I hope?

Luce. [*Within.*] I thought to have ask'd you.

Dro. S.   [*Within.*] And you said no.

Dro. E. So, come, help: well struck! there was blow for blow.   56

Ant. E. Thou baggage, let me in.

Luce. [*Within.*] Can you tell for whose sake?

Dro. E. Master, knock the door hard.

Luce. [*Within.*] Let him knock till it ache.

Ant. E. You'll cry for this, minion, if I beat the door down.

Luce. [*Within.*] What needs all that, and a pair of stocks in the town?   60

Enter ADRIANA [*within*].

Adr. [*Within.*] Who is that at the door that keeps all this noise?

Dro. S. [*Within.*] By my troth, your town is troubled with unruly boys.

Ant. E. Are you there, wife? You might have come before.

Adr. [*Within.*] Your wife, sir knave! Go, get you from the door.

Dro. E. If you went in pain, master, this knave would go sore.   65

Ang. Here is neither cheer, sir, nor welcome; we would fain have either.

Bal. In debating which was best, we shall part with neither.

Dro. E. They stand at the door, master; bid them welcome hither.

Ant. E. There is something in the wind, that we cannot get in.

Dro. E. You would say so, master, if your garments were thin.   70
Your cake here is warm within; you stand here in the cold.
It would make a man mad as a buck, to be so bought and sold.

Ant. E. Go fetch me something; I'll break ope the gate.

Dro. S. [*Within.*] Break any breaking here, and I'll break your knave's pate.

Dro. E. A man may break a word with [you], sir, and words are but wind —   75
Ay, and break it in your face, so he break it not behind.

Dro. S. [*Within.*] It seems thou want'st breaking. Out upon thee, hind!

Dro. E. Here's too much "out upon thee!" I pray thee, let me in.

Dro. S. [*Within.*] Ay, when fowls have no feathers, and fish have no fin.   79

Ant. E. Well, I'll break in; go borrow me a crow.

Dro. E. A crow without feather? Master, mean you so?
For a fish without a fin, there's a fowl without a feather.
If a crow help us in, sirrah, we'll pluck a crow together.

Ant. E. Go, get thee gone; fetch me an iron crow.

Bal. Have patience, sir; O, let it not be so!   85
Herein you war against your reputation
And draw within the compass of suspect
The unviolated honour of your wife.
Once this, — your long experience of [her] wisdom,
Her sober virtue, years, and modesty,   90
Plead on her part some cause to you unknown;
And doubt not, sir, but she will well excuse
Why at this time the doors are made against you.
Be rul'd by me; depart in patience,
And let us to the Tiger all to dinner;   95
And about evening come yourself alone
To know the reason of this strange restraint.
If by strong hand you offer to break in
Now in the stirring passage of the day,
A vulgar comment will be made of it,   100
And that supposed by the common rout
Against your yet ungalled estimation

---

45. **mickle:** much.   47. **face...ass.** Not satisfactorily explained.   48. **coil:** fuss.   51. **set...staff:** take up my abode.   52. **When...tell?** An expression used to evade a question.   54. **minion:** hussy.   55–56. **I...blow.** These lines seem pointless. Perhaps a line has dropped out, rhyming with *hope.*   65. **If...sore.** Probably corrupt. 67. **part:** depart.   72. **bought and sold:** imposed upon.   75. **[you]** F₂. *your* F₁.   77. **hind:** slave.   80. **crow:** crowbar. 83. **pluck a crow:** pick a bone, settle accounts.   87. **suspect:** suspicion.   89. **Once this:** in short, briefly. **[her]** (Rowe). *your* F.   93. **made:** fastened.   99. **stirring passage:** busy traffic.   100. **vulgar:** public.   102. **ungalled:** unblemished.

That may with foul intrusion enter in
And dwell upon your grave when you are dead;
For slander lives upon succession,   105
For ever hous'd where 't gets possession.

Ant. E. You have prevail'd. I will depart in quiet,
And, in despite of mirth, mean to be merry.
I know a wench of excellent discourse,
Pretty and witty, wild, and yet, too, gentle.   110
There will we dine. This woman that I mean,
My wife — but, I protest, without desert —
Hath oftentimes upbraided me withal.
To her will we to dinner. [*To Ang.*] Get you home
And fetch the chain; by this I know 'tis made.   115
Bring it, I pray you, to the Porpentine;
For there's the house. That chain will I bestow —
Be it for nothing but to spite my wife —
Upon mine hostess there. Good sir, make haste.
Since mine own doors refuse to entertain me,   120
I'll knock elsewhere, to see if they'll disdain me.

Ang. I'll meet you at that place some hour hence.
Ant. E. Do so. This jest shall cost me some
    expense.   [*Exeunt.*

[Scene II. *The same.*]

Enter [Luciana] *and* Antipholus *of Syracuse.*

[*Luc.*] And may it be that you have quite forgot
A husband's office? Shall, Antipholus,
Even in the spring of love, thy love-springs rot?
Shall love, in building, grow so [ruinous]?
If you did wed my sister for her wealth,   5
Then for her wealth's sake use her with more
    kindness;
Or if you like elsewhere, do it by stealth;
Muffle your false love with some show of blind-
    ness;
Let not my sister read it in your eye;
Be not thy tongue thy own shame's orator;   10
Look sweet, speak fair, become disloyalty;
Apparel vice like virtue's harbinger;
Bear a fair presence, though your heart be tainted;
Teach sin the carriage of a holy saint;
Be secret-false. What need she be acquainted?   15
What simple thief brags of his own [attaint]?
'Tis double wrong, to truant with your bed
And let her read it in thy looks at board.
Shame hath a bastard fame, well managed;
Ill deeds is doubled with an evil word.   20

Alas, poor women! make us [but] believe,
Being compact of credit, that you love us;
Though others have the arm, show us the sleeve;
We in your motion turn and you may move us.
Then, gentle brother, get you in again;   25
Comfort my sister, cheer her, call her [wife].
'Tis holy sport to be a little vain,
When the sweet breath of flattery conquers strife.

Ant. S. Sweet mistress, — what your name is else,
    I know not,
Nor by what wonder you do hit of mine, —   30
Less in your knowledge and your grace you show not
Than our earth's wonder, more than earth divine.
Teach me, dear creature, how to think and speak;
Lay open to my earthy, gross conceit,
Smoth'red in errors, feeble, shallow, weak,   35
The folded meaning of your words' deceit.
Against my soul's pure truth why labour you
To make it wander in an unknown field?
Are you a god? Would you create me new?
Transform me then, and to your power I'll yield.
But if that I am I, then well I know   41
Your weeping sister is no wife of mine,
Nor to her bed no homage do I owe.
Far more, far more to you do I decline.
O, train me not, sweet mermaid, with thy note, 45
To drown me in thy sister's flood of tears.
Sing, siren, for thyself, and I will dote;
Spread o'er the silver waves thy golden hairs,
And as a [bed] I'll take [them] and there lie,
And in that glorious supposition think   50
He gains by death that hath such means to die.
Let Love, being light, be drowned if she sink!

Luc. What, are you mad, that you do reason so?
Ant. S. Not mad, but mated; how, I do not know.
Luc. It is a fault that springeth from your eye.   55
Ant. S. For gazing on your beams, fair sun, being
    by.
Luc. Gaze when you should, and that will clear
    your sight.
Ant. S. As good to wink, sweet love, as look on
    night.
Luc. Why call you me love? Call my sister so.
Ant. S. Thy sister's sister.
Luc.   That's my sister.
Ant. S.   No;
It is thyself, mine own self's better part,   61
Mine eye's clear eye, my dear heart's dearer heart,

105. **slander...succession:** slander lives on after its victim is dead. 108. **in...mirth:** though I don't feel merry.
112. **desert:** my deserving it. 116. **Porpentine:** Porcupine (house-sign).
Sc. ii, s.d. [Luciana] F₂. *Iuliana* F₁. 1. [**Luc.**] (Rowe). *Iulia* F. 3. **love-springs:** tender shoots of love.
4. [**ruinous**] (Capell). *ruinate* F. 11. **become disloyalty:** carry infidelity gracefully. 14. **carriage:** demeanor. 15. **What:**
why. 16. [**attaint**] (Rowe): dishonor, possibly conviction of crime. *attaine* F. 21. [**but**] (Theobald). Om. F. 22. **compact
of credit:** wholly credulous. 26. [**wife**] F₂. **wise** F₁. 27. **vain:** insincere. 30. **wonder:** miracle. **hit of:** guess. 32. **our
earth's wonder.** Probably a compliment to Queen Elizabeth. 34. **conceit:** understanding. 36. **folded:** concealed.
44. **decline:** incline. 45. **train:** lure. **note:** voice, music. 49. [**bed**] F₂. **bud** F₁. [**them**] (Edwards conj.) *thee* F. 52.
light: buoyant, aspiring. Cf. *V. A.* 149–150. 54. **mated:** amazed, with quibble on "matched with a wife." 56. **by:**
near you. 58. **wink:** close the eyes.

My food, my fortune, and my sweet hope's aim,
My sole earth's heaven, and my heaven's claim.

Luc. All this my sister is, or else should be.   65

Ant. S. Call thyself sister, sweet, for I am thee.
Thee will I love and with thee lead my life;
Thou hast no husband yet nor I no wife.
Give me thy hand.

Luc.   O, soft, sir! hold you still.
I'll fetch my sister, to get her good will. [*Exit.*   70

Enter DROMIO of Syracuse.

Ant. S. Why, how now, Dromio! Where runn'st
thou so fast?

Dro. S. Do you know me, sir? Am I Dromio?
Am I your man? Am I myself?   74

Ant. S. Thou art Dromio, thou art my man,
thou art thyself.

Dro. S. I am an ass, I am a woman's man, and
besides myself.

Ant. S. What woman's man, and how besides
thyself?   80

Dro. S. Marry, sir, besides myself, I am due to
a woman; one that claims me, one that haunts me,
one that will have me.

Ant. S. What claim lays she to thee?   84

Dro. S. Marry, sir, such claim as you would
lay to your horse; and she would have me as a
beast: not that, I being a beast, she would have me;
but that she, being a very beastly creature, lays
claim to me.

Ant. S. What is she?   90

Dro. S. A very reverend body; ay, such a one
as a man may not speak of without he say "Sir-
reverence." I have but lean luck in the match,
and yet is she a wondrous fat marriage.

Ant. S. How dost thou mean a fat marriage?   95

Dro. S. Marry, sir, she's the kitchen wench and
all grease; and I know not what use to put her to
but to make a lamp of her and run from her by her
own light. I warrant, her rags and the tallow in
them will burn a Poland winter. If she lives   100
till doomsday, she'll burn a week longer than the
whole world.

Ant. S. What complexion is she of?

Dro. S. Swart, like my shoe, but her face nothing
like so clean kept: for why, she sweats; a man   105
may go over shoes in the grime of it.

Ant. S. That's a fault that water will mend.

Dro. S. No, sir, 'tis in grain; Noah's flood could
not do it.

Ant. S. What's her name?   110

Dro. S. Nell, sir; but her name [and] three
quarters, that's an ell and three quarters, will not
measure her from hip to hip.

Ant. S. Then she bears some breadth?

Dro. S. No longer from head to foot than   115
from hip to hip. She is spherical, like a globe; I
could find out countries in her.

Ant. S. In what part of her body stands Ireland?

Dro. S. Marry, sir, in her buttocks; I found it
out by the bogs.   121

Ant. S. Where Scotland?

Dro. S. I found it by the barrenness; hard in the
palm of the hand.

Ant. S. Where France?   125

Dro. S. In her forehead; armed and reverted,
making war against her heir.

Ant. S. Where England?

Dro. S. I looked for the chalky cliffs, but I could
find no whiteness in them; but I guess it   130
stood in her chin, by the salt rheum that ran between France and it.

Ant. S. Where Spain?

Dro. S. Faith, I saw it not; but I felt it hot in
her breath.   135

Ant. S. Where America, the Indies?

Dro. S. Oh, sir, upon her nose, all o'er embel-
lished with rubies, carbuncles, sapphires, declining
their rich aspect to the hot breath of Spain; who
sent whole armadoes of caracks to be ballast at her
nose.   141

Ant. S. Where stood Belgia, the Netherlands?

Dro. S. Oh, sir, I did not look so low. To conclude, this drudge, or diviner, laid claim to me;
called me Dromio; swore I was assur'd to her;   145
told me what privy marks I had about me, as,
the mark of my shoulder, the mole in my neck,
the great wart on my left arm, that I, amaz'd,
ran from her as a witch.
And, I think, if my breast had not been made of
    faith and my heart of steel,   150
She had transform'd me to a curtal dog and made
    me turn i' the wheel.

Ant. S. Go, hie thee presently post to the road;
An if the wind blow any way from shore,
I will not harbour in this town to-night.
If any bark put forth, come to the mart,   155
Where I will walk till thou return to me.
If every one knows us and we know none,
'Tis time, I think, to trudge, pack, and be gone.

Dro. S. As from a bear a man would run for
    life,   159

64. **My ... claim:** My heaven on earth and my claim on heaven hereafter.   93. **Sir-reverence:** i.e., "save your reverence," an expression used as apology for a remark that might offend.   104. **Swart:** dark.   108. **in grain:** ineradicable.
111. **[and]** (Theobald). *is* F.   126. **armed ... heir.** See Introduction for reference to French civil wars. **armed:** also with
"eruptions" of the skin. **reverted:** (1) revolted, (2) receding. **heir:** with a pun on *hair*.   130. **them:** the cliffs, presumably her teeth.   139. **declining:** bending.   140. **armadoes ... caracks:** fleets of galleons. See Introduction.   140. **ballast:**
loaded.   144. **diviner:** sorceress.   145. **assur'd:** betrothed.   151. **curtal dog:** a dog with a docked tail.   **turn ... wheel:** i.e.,
turn the spit by running in a wheel.   152. **presently:** immediately.   **road:** harbor, roadstead.

So fly I from her that would be my wife.   [*Exit.*
Ant. S. There's none but witches do inhabit here;
And therefore 'tis high time that I were hence.
She that doth call me husband, even my soul
Doth for a wife abhor.   But her fair sister,
Possess'd with such a gentle sovereign grace,   165
Of such enchanting presence and discourse,
Hath almost made me traitor to myself.
But, lest myself be guilty to self-wrong,
I'll stop mine ears against the mermaid's song.

Enter ANGELO *with the chain.*

Ang. Master Antipholus —
Ant. S.   Ay, that's my name.
Ang. I know it well, sir; lo, here is the chain.   171
I thought to have ta'en you at the Porpentine;
The chain unfinish'd made me stay thus long.
Ant. S. What is your will that I shall do with
    this?
Ang. What please yourself, sir; I have made it
    for you.   175
Ant. S. Made it for me, sir! I bespoke it not.
Ang. Not once, nor twice, but twenty times you
    have.
Go home with it and please your wife withal;
And soon at supper-time I'll visit you
And then receive my money for the chain.   180
Ant. S. I pray you, sir, receive the money now,
For fear you ne'er see chain nor money more.
Ang. You are a merry man, sir; fare you well.
                                    [*Exit.*
Ant. S. What I should think of this, I cannot tell;
But this I think, there's no man is so vain   185
That would refuse so fair an offer'd chain.
I see a man here needs not live by shifts
When in the streets he meets such golden gifts.
I'll to the mart and there for Dromio stay.   189
If any ship put out, then straight away.   [*Exit.*

ACT IV

SCENE I. [*A public place.*]

Enter SECOND MERCHANT, ANGELO, *and an* OFFICER

2. Mer. You know since Pentecost the sum is due,
And since I have not much importun'd you;
Nor now I had not, but that I am bound
To Persia and want guilders for my voyage.
Therefore make present satisfaction,   5
Or I'll attach you by this officer.
Ang. Even just the sum that I do owe to you
Is growing to me by Antipholus,
And in the instant that I met with you

He had of me a chain.   At five o'clock   10
I shall receive the money for the same.
Pleaseth you walk with me down to his house,
I will discharge my bond and thank you too.

Enter ANTIPHOLUS *of Ephesus and* DROMIO *of*
Ephesus *from the courtezan's.*

Off. That labour may you save; see where he
    comes.
Ant. E. While I go to the goldsmith's house, go
    thou   15
And buy a rope's end; that will I bestow
Among my wife and [her] confederates,
For locking me out of my doors by day.
But, soft! I see the goldsmith.   Get thee gone,
Buy thou a rope and bring it home to me.   20
Dro. E. I buy a thousand pound a year! I buy a
    rope!   [*Exit.*
Ant. E. A man is well holp up that trusts to you.
I promised your presence and the chain,
But neither chain nor goldsmith came to me.
Belike you thought our love would last too long   25
If it were chain'd together, and therefore came not.
Ang. Saving your merry humour, here's the note
How much your chain weighs to the utmost [carat],
The fineness of the gold, and chargeful fashion,
Which doth amount to three odd ducats more   30
Than I stand debted to this gentleman.
I pray you, see him presently discharg'd,
For he is bound to sea and stays but for it.
Ant. E. I am not furnish'd with the present
    money;
Besides, I have some business in the town.   35
Good signior, take the stranger to my house;
And with you take the chain, and bid my wife
Disburse the sum on the receipt thereof.
Perchance I will be there as soon as you.
Ang. Then you will bring the chain to her your-
    self?   40
Ant. E. No; bear it with you, lest I come not
    time enough.
Ang. Well, sir, I will.   Have you the chain about
    you?
Ant. E. An if I have not, sir, I hope you have,
Or else you may return without your money.
Ang. Nay, come, I pray you, sir, give me the
    chain.   45
Both wind and tide stays for this gentleman,
And I, to blame, have held him here too long.
Ant. E. Good Lord! you use this dalliance to
    excuse
Your breach of promise to the Porpentine.
I should have chid you for not bringing it,   50

168. to: of.   185. vain: foolish.
Act IV, sc. i, 6. attach: arrest.   8. growing: due, accruing.   16. bestow: employ.   17. [her] (Rowe).   their F.   21. I...
year.   An obscure remark, but Dromio probably means, "What an idea, that *I* should be sent to buy that by which I shall
get a thousand pounds (thumps) a year!"   22. holp: helped.   28. [carat] (Pope).   *charect* F.

But, like a shrew, you first begin to brawl.

2. *Mer.* The hour steals on; I pray you, sir, dispatch.

Ang. You hear how he importunes me; — the chain!

Ant. E. Why, give it to my wife, and fetch your money.

Ang. Come, come, you know I gave it you even now.   55
Either send the chain or send by me some token.

Ant. E. Fie, now you run this humour out of breath.
Come, where's the chain? I pray you, let me see it.

2. *Mer.* My business cannot brook this dalliance.
Good sir, say whe'r you'll answer me or no;   60
If not, I'll leave him to the officer.

Ant. E. I answer you! What should I answer you?

Ang. The money that you owe me for the chain.

Ant. E. I owe you none till I receive the chain.

Ang. You know I gave it you half an hour since.

Ant. E. You gave me none; you wrong me much to say so.   66

Ang. You wrong me more, sir, in denying it.
Consider how it stands upon my credit.

2. *Mer.* Well, officer, arrest him at my suit.

Off. I do; and charge you in the Duke's name to obey me.   70

Ang. This touches me in reputation.
Either consent to pay this sum for me
Or I attach you by this officer.

Ant. E. Consent to pay thee that I never had!
Arrest me, foolish fellow, if thou dar'st.   75

Ang. Here is thy fee; arrest him, officer.
I would not spare my brother in this case,
If he should scorn me so apparently.

Off. I do arrest you, sir: you hear the suit.

Ant. E. I do obey thee till I give thee bail.   80
But, sirrah, you shall buy this sport as dear
As all the metal in your shop will answer.

Ang. Sir, sir, I shall have law in Ephesus,
To your notorious shame; I doubt it not.

Enter DROMIO *of Syracuse, from the bay.*

Dro. S. Master, there is a bark of Epidamnum
That stays but till her owner comes aboard,   86
And then, sir, she bears away. Our fraughtage, sir,
I have convey'd aboard, and I have bought
The oil, the balsamum, and aqua-vitæ.
The ship is in her trim; the merry wind   90
Blows fair from land; they stay for nought at all
But for their owner, master, and yourself.

Ant. E. How now! a madman! Why, thou peevish sheep,
What ship of Epidamnum stays for me?

Dro. S. A ship you sent me to, to hire waftage.

Ant. E. Thou drunken slave, I sent thee for a rope,   96
And told thee to what purpose and what end.

Dro. S. You sent me for a rope's end as soon.
You sent me to the bay, sir, for a bark.

Ant. E. I will debate this matter at more leisure,   100
And teach your ears to list me with more heed.
To Adriana, villain, hie thee straight;
Give her this key, and tell her, in the desk
That's cover'd o'er with Turkish tapestry
There is a purse of ducats; let her send it.   105
Tell her I am arrested in the street
And that shall bail me. Hie thee, slave, be gone!
On, officer, to prison till it come.

[*Exeunt* [2. *Merchant, Angelo, Officer, and Ant. E.*].

Dro. S. To Adriana! That is where we din'd,
Where Dowsabel did claim me for her husband.
She is too big, I hope, for me to compass.   111
Thither I must, although against my will,
For servants must their masters' minds fulfil.

[*Exit.*

[SCENE II. *The house of Antipholus of Ephesus.*]

Enter ADRIANA *and* LUCIANA.

Adr. Ah, Luciana, did he tempt thee so?
Mightst thou perceive austerely in his eye
That he did plead in earnest? Yea or no?
Look'd he or red or pale, or sad or merrily?
What observation mad'st thou in this case   5
Of his heart's meteors tilting in his face?

Luc. First he deni'd you had in him no right.

Adr. He meant he did me none; the more my spite.

Luc. Then swore he that he was a stranger here.

Adr. And true he swore, though yet forsworn he were.   10

Luc. Then pleaded I for you.

Adr.   And what said he?

Luc. That love I begg'd for you he begg'd of me.

Adr. With what persuasion did he tempt thy love?

Luc. With words that in an honest suit might move.
First he did praise my beauty, then my speech.   15

Adr. Didst speak him fair?

---

60. **answer:** pay.   68. **stands upon:** concerns.   78. **apparently:** openly.   87. **fraughtage:** baggage.   89. **balsamum:** balm.   **aqua-vitæ:** spirits.   90. **in...trim:** rigged and ready to sail.   93. **peevish:** senseless.   95. **waftage:** passage.
98. **rope's end:** hangman's noose.   110. **Dowsabel:** derived from *douce et belle* and here applied ironically to Nell (see III. ii.111).

Sc. ii, 2. **austerely:** soberly.   6. **meteors:** changes of color and expression.   **tilting:** clashing (like the aurora borealis).
8. **spite:** grief.

Luc.   Have patience, I beseech.
Adr. I cannot, nor I will not, hold me still;
My tongue, though not my heart, shall have his will.
He is deformed, crooked, old, and sere,
Ill-fac'd, worse bodied, shapeless everywhere: 20
Vicious, ungentle, foolish, blunt, unkind,
Stigmatical in making, worse in mind.
Luc. Who would be jealous then of such a one?
No evil lost is wail'd when it is gone.
Adr. Ah, but I think him better than I say,   25
And yet would herein others' eyes were worse.
Far from her nest the lapwing cries away.
My heart prays for him, though my tongue do
   curse.

        Enter Dromio *of Syracuse.*

Dro. S. Here! go; the desk, the purse! Sweet,
   now, make haste.   29
Luc. How hast thou lost thy breath?
Dro. S.   By running fast.
Adr. Where is thy master, Dromio? Is he well?
Dro. S. No, he's in Tartar limbo, worse than
   hell.
A devil in an everlasting garment hath him;
One whose hard heart is button'd up with steel;
A fiend, a fairy, pitiless and rough;   35
A wolf, nay, worse, a fellow all in buff;
A back-friend, a shoulder-clapper, one that counter-
   mands
The passages of alleys, creeks, and narrow lands;
A hound that runs counter and yet draws dry-foot
   well;
One that before the judgement carries poor souls to
   hell.   40
Adr. Why, man, what is the matter?
Dro. S. I do not know the matter; he is 'rested on
   the case.
Adr. What, is he arrested? Tell me at whose
   suit.
Dro. S. I know not at whose suit he is arrested
   well;
But he's in a suit of buff which 'rested him, that can
   I tell.   45
Will you send him, mistress, redemption, the money
   in his desk?
Adr. Go fetch it, sister. This I wonder at,
                     [*Exit Luciana.*
[That] he, unknown to me, should be in debt.

Tell me, was he arrested on a band?
Dro. S. Not on a band but on a stronger thing,
A chain, a chain! Do you not hear it ring?   51
Adr. What, the chain?
Dro. S. No, no, the bell; 'tis time that I were
   gone.
It was two ere I left him, and now the clock strikes
   one.
Adr. The hours come back! That did I never
   [hear].   55
Dro. S. O, yes; if any hour meet a sergeant, 'a
   turns back for very fear.
Adr. As if Time were in debt! How fondly dost
   thou reason!
Dro. S. Time is a very bankrupt and owes more
   than he's worth to season.
Nay, he's a thief too; have you not heard men say,
That Time comes stealing on by night and day?
If ['a] be in debt and theft, and a sergeant in the
   way,   61
Hath he not reason to turn back an hour in a day?

        Re-enter Luciana.

Adr. Go, Dromio; there's the money, bear it
   straight,
And bring thy master home immediately.
Come, sister; I am press'd down with conceit —   65
   Conceit, my comfort and my injury.   [*Exeunt.*

      [Scene III. *A public place.*]

      Enter Antipholus *of Syracuse.*

Ant. S. There's not a man I meet but doth salute
   me
As if I were their well-acquainted friend;
And every one doth call me by my name.
Some tender money to me; some invite me;
Some other give me thanks for kindnesses;   5
Some offer me commodities to buy.
Even now a tailor call'd me in his shop
And show'd me silks that he had bought for me
And therewithal took measure of my body.
Sure, these are but imaginary wiles,   10
And Lapland sorcerers inhabit here.

      Enter Dromio *of Syracuse.*

Dro. S. Master, here's the gold you sent me for.
What, have you got the picture of old Adam new-
   apparell'd?

---

18. **his:** its. 22. **Stigmatical:** crooked. **making:** form. 32. **Tartar limbo:** prison. *Limbo,* a region on the outskirts of hell, is qualified by *Tartar,* by which Dromio may have meant the classical Tartarus or the Asiatic people (or both). 33. **everlasting:** durable, i.e., made of *buff* (l. 36), a stout leather worn by police officers. 35. **fairy:** i.e., a *malevolent* sprite. 37. **back-friend:** a false friend; here the police officer who arrests by clapping on the back. **countermands:** forbids entrance into. 38. **creeks:** narrow, winding passages. 39. **counter:** in a direction opposite to that which the game has taken; with a pun on *counter,* a prison. **draws dry-foot:** tracks game by mere scent of the foot. 40. **judgement:** (1) a legal judgement, (2) the Day of Judgement. 42. **case:** legal term. 48. [that] F₂ *thus* F₁. 49. **band:** bond. 55. [hear] F₂ *here* F₁. 56. **'a:** he. 57. **fondly:** foolishly. 58. **season:** opportunity. 61. ['a] (Staunton). *I* F. 65. **conceit:** imagination.

Sc. iii, 11. **Lapland.** Lapland was traditionally famous for witchcraft and sorcery. 13–14. **picture . . . new-apparell'd:** the sergeant. There seems to be a lost allusion here. Theobald inserted *rid of* after *got.*

Ant. S. What gold is this? What Adam dost
thou mean? 15
Dro. S. Not that Adam that kept the Paradise,
but that Adam that keeps the prison; he that goes
in the calf's skin that was kill'd for the Prodigal; he
that came behind you, sir, like an evil angel, and bid
you forsake your liberty. 20
Ant. S. I understand thee not.
Dro. S. No? Why, 'tis a plain case; he that went,
like a bass-viol, in a case of leather; the man, sir,
that, when gentlemen are tired, gives them a sob
and 'rests them; he, sir, that takes pity on de- 25
cayed men and gives them suits of durance; he that
sets up his rest to do more exploits with his mace
than a morris-pike.
Ant. S. What, thou mean'st an officer?
Dro. S. Ay, sir, the sergeant of the band; he 30
that brings any man to answer it that breaks his
band; one that thinks a man always going to bed
and says, "God give you good rest!"
Ant. S. Well, sir, there rest in your foolery. Is
there any [ship] puts forth to-night? May we be
gone? 36
Dro. S. Why, sir, I brought you word an hour
since that the bark Expedition put forth to-night;
and then were you hind'red by the sergeant, to
tarry for the hoy Delay. Here are the angels 40
that you sent for to deliver you.
Ant. S. The fellow is distract, and so am I;
And here we wander in illusions.
Some blessed power deliver us from hence!

Enter a COURTEZAN.

Cour. Well met, well met, Master Antipholus.
I see, sir, you have found the goldsmith now. 46
Is that the chain you promis'd me to-day?
Ant. S. Satan, avoid! I charge thee, tempt me
not.
Dro. S. Master, is this Mistress Satan?
Ant. S. It is the devil. 50
Dro. S. Nay, she is worse, she is the devil's
dam, and here she comes in the habit of a light
wench; and thereof comes that the wenches say,
"God damn me"; that's as much to say, God make
me a light wench. It is written, they appear to 55
men like angels of light; light is an effect of fire, and
fire will burn; *ergo*, light wenches will burn. Come
not near her.
Cour. Your man and you are marvellous merry,
sir. 59

Will you go with me? We'll mend our dinner here?
Dro. S. Master, if [you] do, expect spoon-meat;
or bespeak a long spoon.
Ant. S. Why, Dromio?
Dro. S. Marry, he must have a long spoon that
must eat with the devil. 65
Ant. S. Avoid [then], fiend! What tell'st thou
me of supping?
Thou art, as you are all, a sorceress.
I conjure thee to leave me and be gone.
Cour. Give me the ring of mine you had at
dinner,
Or, for my diamond, the chain you promis'd, 70
And I'll be gone, sir, and not trouble you.
Dro. S. Some devils ask but the parings of one's
nail,
A rush, a hair, a drop of blood, a pin,
A nut, a cherry-stone;
But she, more covetous, would have a chain. 75
Master, be wise; an if you give it her,
The devil will shake her chain and fright us with it.
Cour. I pray you, sir, my ring, or else the chain.
I hope you do not mean to cheat me so?
Ant. S. Avaunt, thou witch! Come, Dromio,
let us go. 80
Dro. S. Fly pride, says the peacock: mistress,
that you know.
[*Exeunt* [*Ant. S. and Dro. S.*].]
Cour. Now, out of doubt Antipholus is mad,
Else would he never so demean himself.
A ring he hath of mine worth forty ducats,
And for the same he promis'd me a chain. 85
Both one and other he denies me now.
The reason that I gather he is mad,
Besides this present instance of his rage,
Is a mad tale he told to-day at dinner,
Of his own doors being shut against his entrance. 90
Belike his wife, acquainted with his fits,
On purpose shut the doors against his way.
My way is now to hie home to his house,
And tell his wife that, being lunatic,
He rush'd into my house and took perforce 95
My ring away. This course I fittest choose;
For forty ducats is too much to lose. [*Exit.*]

[SCENE IV. *A street.*]

Enter ANTIPHOLUS *of Ephesus and* [*the* OFFICER].

Ant. E. Fear me not, man; I will not break away.
I'll give thee, ere I leave thee, so much money,

24. **sob:** "a rest given to a horse to recover its wind" (N.E.D.). 26. **durance:** durable cloth, as well as "prison."
27. **sets ... rest:** stakes his all, with quibble upon "setting" a soldier's pike in "rest" for a charge. **mace:** club carried by
a constable. 28. **morris-pike:** Moorish pike. 35. [ship] F₂. ships F₁. 40. **hoy:** small vessel. **angels:** gold coins worth
about 10s. apiece. 48. **avoid:** away, avaunt. 57. **will burn:** i.e., are diseased. 60. **mend:** amend, supplement.
61. [you] F₂. Om. F₁. **spoon-meat:** food for infants. 65. Proverbial. 66. [then] F₄. thou F₁₋₃. 81. **Fly ... peacock.**
An accusation of dishonesty coming from a dishonest person is as out of place as a warning against pride would be from
the peacock.
Sc. iv, S.D. [*the* OFFICER] (Capell). a *Jailor* F.

To warrant thee, as I am 'rested for.
My wife is in a wayward mood to-day,
And will not lightly trust the messenger.   5
That I should be attach'd in Ephesus,
I tell you, 'twill sound harshly in her ears.

Enter DROMIO *of Ephesus with a rope's-end.*

Here comes my man; I think he brings the money.
How now, sir! have you that I sent you for?

Dro. E. Here's that, I warrant you, will pay
    them all.   10

Ant. E. But where's the money?

Dro. E. Why, sir, I gave the money for the rope.

Ant. E. Five hundred ducats, villain, for a rope?

Dro. E. I'll serve you, sir, five hundred at the
    rate.

Ant. E. To what end did I bid thee hie thee
    home?   15

Dro. E. To a rope's end, sir; and to that end am
I return'd.

Ant. E. And to that end, sir, I will welcome you.
                                    [*Beating him.*]

Off. Good sir, be patient.

Dro. E. Nay, 'tis for me to be patient; I am in
adversity.   21

Off. Good now, hold thy tongue.

Dro. E. Nay, rather persuade him to hold his
hands.

Ant. E. Thou whoreson, senseless villain!   25

Dro. E. I would I were senseless, sir, that I might
not feel your blows.

Ant. E. Thou art sensible in nothing but blows,
and so is an ass.

Dro. E. I am an ass, indeed; you may prove   30
it by my long 'ears. I have served him from the
hour of my nativity to this instant, and have nothing at his hands for my service but blows. When I
am cold, he heats me with beating; when I am
warm, he cools me with beating. I am wak'd   35
with it when I sleep; rais'd with it when I sit; driven
out of doors with it when I go from home; welcom'd
home with it when I return; nay, I bear it on my
shoulders, as a beggar wont her brat; and, I think,
when he hath lam'd me, I shall beg with it from   40
door to door.

Enter ADRIANA, LUCIANA, *the* COURTEZAN, *and a*
    Schoolmaster call'd PINCH.

Ant. E. Come, go along; my wife is coming
    yonder.

Dro. E. Mistress, *respice finem*, respect your end;
or rather, [to] prophesy like the parrot, "beware
the rope's-end."   46

Ant. E. Wilt thou still talk?   [*Beating him.*]

Cour. How say you now? Is not your husband mad?

Adr. His incivility confirms no less.

Good Doctor Pinch, you are a conjurer;   50
Establish him in his true sense again,
And I will please you what you will demand.

Luc. Alas, how fiery and how sharp he looks!

Cour. Mark how he trembles in his ecstasy!

Pinch. Give me your hand and let me feel your
    pulse.   55

Ant. E. There is my hand, and let it feel your
    ear.   [*Striking him.*]

Pinch. I charge thee, Satan, hous'd within this
    man,
To yield possession to my holy prayers
And to thy state of darkness hie thee straight.
I conjure thee by all the saints in heaven!   60

Ant. E. Peace, doting wizard, peace! I am not
    mad.

Adr. O, that thou wert not, poor distressed soul!

Ant. E. You minion, you, are these your cus-
    tomers?
Did this companion with the saffron face
Revel and feast it at my house to-day,   65
Whilst upon me the guilty doors were shut
And I denied to enter in my house?

Adr. O husband, God doth know you din'd at
    home;
Where would you had remain'd until this time,
Free from these slanders and this open shame!   70

Ant. E. Din'd at home! Thou villain, what
    sayest thou?

Dro. E. Sir, sooth to say, you did not dine at
    home.

Ant. E. Were not my doors lock'd up and I shut
    out?

Dro. E. Perdie, your doors were lock'd and you
    shut out.   74

Ant. E. And did not she herself revile me there?

Dro. E. Sans fable, she herself revil'd you there.

Ant. E. Did not her kitchen-maid rail, taunt,
    and scorn me?

Dro. E. Certes, she did; the kitchen-vestal scorn'd
    you.

Ant. E. And did not I in rage depart from thence?

Dro. E. In verity you did; my bones bear witness,
That since have felt the vigour of his rage.   81

Adr. Is't good to soothe him in these contraries?

Pinch. It is no shame. The fellow finds his vein,
And, yielding to him, humours well his frenzy.

Ant. E. Thou hast suborn'd the goldsmith to
    arrest me.   85

Adr. Alas, I sent you money to redeem you.

22. **Good now:** pray you.   28. **sensible:** sensitive.   40. **wont:** is accustomed to.   44. *respice finem.* *Respice funem,* "heed the hangman's rope," was a popular quibble on this phrase.   45. **[to]** (Dyce).   *the* F.   46. **"beware the rope's end":** i.e., beware the hangman's noose; apparently a phrase taught to parrots.   50. **conjurer.** Being able to use Latin, Pinch could exorcise evil spirits.   52. **please:** pay.   54. **ecstasy:** madness.   63. **minion:** darling.   **customers:** guests (both terms used contemptuously).   64. **companion:** fellow.   **saffron:** yellow.   74. *Perdie:* certainly (corruption of *par Dieu*).   76. *Sans:* without.   78. **kitchen-vestal:** i.e., Luce.

By Dromio here, who came in haste for it.
  Dro. E. Money by me! Heart and good-will
    you might,
But surely, master, not a rag of money.
  Ant. E. Went'st not thou to her for a purse of
    ducats?   90
  Adr. He came to me and I deliver'd it.
  Luc. And I am witness with her that she did.
  Dro. E. God and the rope-maker bear me witness
That I was sent for nothing but a rope!
  Pinch. Mistress, both man and master is pos-
    sess'd;   95
I know it by their pale and deadly looks.
They must be bound and laid in some dark room.
  Ant. E. Say, wherefore didst thou lock me forth
    to-day?
And why dost thou deny the bag of gold?   99
  Adr. I did not, gentle husband, lock thee forth.
  Dro. E. And, gentle master, I receiv'd no gold;
But I confess, sir, that we were lock'd out.
  Adr. Dissembling villain, thou speak'st false in
    both.
  Ant. E. Dissembling harlot, thou art false in all
And art confederate with a damned pack   105
To make a loathsome abject scorn of me;
But with these nails I'll pluck out these false eyes
That would behold in me this shameful sport.

Enter three or four, and offer to bind him. He strives.

  Adr. O, bind him, bind him! Let him not come
    near me.
  Pinch. More company! The fiend is strong
    within him.   110
  Luc. Ay me, poor man, how pale and wan he looks!
  Ant. E. What, will you murder me? Thou
    gaoler, thou,
I am thy prisoner. Wilt thou suffer them
To make a rescue?
  Off.   Masters, let him go.
He is my prisoner, and you shall not have him.   115
  Pinch. Go bind this man, for he is frantic too.
        [They offer to bind Dro. E.]
  Adr. What wilt thou do, thou peevish officer?
Hast thou delight to see a wretched man
Do outrage and displeasure to himself?
  Off. He is my prisoner; if I let him go,   120
The debt he owes will be requir'd of me.
  Adr. I will discharge thee e'er I go from thee.
Bear me forth unto his creditor
And, knowing how the debt grows, I will pay it.
Good master doctor, see him safe convey'd   125
Home to my house. O most unhappy day!
  Ant. E. O most unhappy strumpet!
  Dro. E. Master, I am here ent'red in bond for
    you.

  Ant. E. Out on thee, villain! wherefore dost thou
    mad me?
  Dro. E. Will you be bound for nothing? Be
mad, good master; cry "The devil!"   131
  Luc. God help, poor souls, how idly do they talk!
  Adr. Go bear him hence. Sister, go you with me.
Say now, whose suit is he arrested at?
    [Exeunt all but Adriana, Luciana, Officer,
    and Courtezan.
  Off. One Angelo, a goldsmith. Do you know
    him?   135
  Adr. I know the man. What is the sum he owes?
  Off. Two hundred ducats.
  Adr.   Say, how grows it due?
  Off. Due for a chain your husband had of him.
  Adr. He did bespeak a chain for me, but had it
    not.
  Cour. When as your husband all in rage to-day
Came to my house and took away my ring —   141
The ring I saw upon his finger now —
Straight after did I meet him with a chain.
  Adr. It may be so, but I did never see it.
Come, gaoler, bring me where the goldsmith is.
I long to know the truth hereof at large.   146

Enter ANTIPHOLUS *of Syracuse* with his rapier
    drawn, *and* DROMIO *of Syracuse.*

  Luc. God, for thy mercy! they are loose again.
  Adr. And come with naked swords.
Let's call more help to have them bound again.
  Off. Away! they'll kill us.   150
    [Exeunt all [but Ant. S. and Dro. S.]
    as fast as may be, frighted.
  Ant. S. I see these witches are afraid of swords.
  Dro. S. She that would be your wife now ran
    from you.
  Ant. S. Come to the Centaur; fetch our stuff
    from thence;
I long that we were safe and sound aboard.   154
  Dro. S. Faith, stay here this night; they will
surely do us no harm. You saw they speak us fair,
give us gold; methinks they are such a gentle
nation that, but for the mountain of mad flesh that
claims marriage of me, I could find in my heart to
stay here still and turn witch.   160
  Ant. S. I will not stay to-night for all the town;
Therefore away, to get our stuff aboard. *[Exeunt.*

ACT V

SCENE I. *[A street before a Priory.]*

Enter SECOND MERCHANT *and* ANGELO.

  Ang. I am sorry, sir, that I have hind'red you;
But, I protest, he had the chain of me,

---

96. **deadly:** deathlike.   97. **bound . . . room.** This was the regular treatment for lunatics in Shakespeare's day.
117. **peevish:** foolish.   147. **again.** Here F reads *Runne all out.*

Though most dishonestly he doth deny it.

2. Mer. How is the man esteem'd here in the
city?

Ang. Of very reverend reputation, sir,   5
Of credit infinite, highly belov'd,
Second to none that lives here in the city.
His word might bear my wealth at any time.

2. Mer. Speak softly; yonder, as I think, he
walks.

Enter ANTIPHOLUS *of Syracuse and* DROMIO *of*
Syracuse.

Ang. 'Tis so; and that self chain about his neck
Which he forswore most monstrously to have.   11
Good sir, draw near to me, I'll speak to him.
Signior Antipholus, I wonder much
That you would put me to this shame and trouble;
And, not without some scandal to yourself,   15
With circumstance and oaths so to deny
This chain which now you wear so openly.
Beside the charge, the shame, imprisonment,
You have done wrong to this my honest friend,
Who, but for staying on our controversy,   20
Had hoisted sail and put to sea to-day.
This chain you had of me; can you deny it?

Ant. S. I think I had; I never did deny it.

2. Mer. Yes, that you did, sir, and forswore it too.

Ant. S. Who heard me to deny it or forswear it?

2. Mer. These ears of mine, thou know'st, did
hear thee.   26
Fie on thee, wretch! 'Tis pity that thou liv'st
To walk where any honest men resort.

Ant. S. Thou art a villain to impeach me thus.
I'll prove mine honour and mine honesty   30
Against thee presently, if thou dar'st stand.

2. Mer. I dare, and do defy thee for a villain.
                              [*They draw.*

Enter ADRIANA, LUCIANA, *the* COURTEZAN *and*
others.

Adr. Hold, hurt him not, for [God's] sake!
He is mad.
Some get within him; take his sword away.
Bind Dromio too, and bear them to my house.   35

Dro. S. Run, master, run; for God's sake, take
a house!
This is some priory. In, or we are spoil'd!
                    [*Exeunt Ant. S. and Dro. S. to the*
Priory.

Enter the LADY ABBESS.

Abb. Be quiet, people. Wherefore throng you
hither?

Adr. To fetch my poor distracted husband hence.

Let us come in, that we may bind him fast   40
And bear him home for his recovery.

Ang. I knew he was not in his perfect wits.

2. Mer. I am sorry now that I did draw on him.

Abb. How long hath this possession held the
man?

Adr. This week he hath been heavy, sour, sad,
And much different from the man he was;   46
But till this afternoon his passion
Ne'er brake into extremity of rage.

Abb. Hath he not lost much wealth by wreck
of sea?
Buried some dear friend? Hath not else his eye
Stray'd his affection in unlawful love?   51
A sin prevailing much in youthful men,
Who give their eyes the liberty of gazing.
Which of these sorrows is he subject to?   54

Adr. To none of these, except it be the last;
Namely, some love that drew him oft from home.

Abb. You should for that have reprehended him.

Adr. Why, so I did.

Abb.   Ay, but not rough enough.

Adr. As roughly as my modesty would let me.

Abb. Haply, in private.

Adr.   And in assemblies too.

Abb. Ay, but not enough.   61

Adr. It was the copy of our conference.
In bed he slept not for my urging it;
At board he fed not for my urging it;
Alone, it was the subject of my theme;   65
In company I often glanced it;
Still did I tell him it was vile and bad.

Abb. And thereof came it that the man was mad.
The venom clamours of a jealous woman
Poisons more deadly than a mad dog's tooth.   70
It seems his sleeps were hind'red by thy railing,
And thereof comes it that his head is light.
Thou say'st his meat was sauc'd with thy upbraid-
ings;
Unquiet meals make ill digestions,
Thereof the raging fire of fever bred;   75
And what's a fever but a fit of madness?
Thou say'st his sports were hind'red by thy brawls:
Sweet recreation barr'd, what doth ensue
But moody and dull melancholy,
Kinsman to grim and comfortless despair,   80
And at her heels a huge infectious troop
Of pale distemperatures and foes to life?
In food, in sport, and life-preserving rest
To be disturb'd, would mad or man or beast.
The consequence is, then, thy jealous fits   85
Hath scar'd thy husband from the use of wits.

Luc. She never reprehended him but mildly,
When he demean'd himself rough, rude, and wildly.

Act V, sc. i, 8. **bear:** claim.   10. **self:** self-same.   11. **forswore:** vehemently denied.   16. **circumstance:** details.
33. **[God's]** F₃. *God* F₁.   34. **within him:** under his guard.   36. **take:** take to.   49. **of:** at.   51. **stray'd:** led astray.
62. **copy:** topic.   **conference:** conversation.   66. **glanced:** hinted at.   82. **distemperatures:** physical disorders.

Why bear you these rebukes and answer not?

Adr. She did betray me to my own reproof.   90
Good people, enter and lay hold on him.

Abb. No, not a creature enters in my house.

Adr. Then let your servants bring my husband forth.

Abb. Neither. He took this place for sanctuary,
And it shall privilege him from your hands   95
Till I have brought him to his wits again,
Or lose my labour in assaying it.

Adr. I will attend my husband, be his nurse,
Diet his sickness, for it is my office,
And will have no attorney but myself;   100
And therefore let me have him home with me.

Abb. Be patient; for I will not let him stir
Till I have us'd the approved means I have,
With wholesome syrups, drugs, and holy prayers,
To make of him a formal man again.   105
It is a branch and parcel of mine oath,
A charitable duty of my order.
Therefore depart and leave him here with me.

Adr. I will not hence and leave my husband here;
And ill it doth beseem your holiness   110
To separate the husband and the wife.

Abb. Be quiet and depart; thou shalt not have
him.   [*Exit.*]

Luc. Complain unto the Duke of this indignity.

Adr. Come, go. I will fall prostrate at his feet
And never rise until my tears and prayers   115
Have won his Grace to come in person hither
And take perforce my husband from the abbess.

2. Mer. By this, I think, the dial points at five.
Anon, I'm sure, the Duke himself in person
Comes this way to the melancholy vale,   120
The place of [death] and sorry execution,
Behind the ditches of the abbey here.

Ang. Upon what cause?

2. Mer. To see a [reverend] Syracusian merchant
Who put unluckily into this bay   125
Against the laws and statutes of this town,
Beheaded publicly for his offence.

Ang. See where they come; we will behold his
death.

Luc. Kneel to the Duke before he pass the abbey.

Enter DUKE [*attended*], *and* ÆGEON *bareheaded*,
    with the Headsman *and other* Officers.

Duke. Yet once again proclaim it publicly,   130
If any friend will pay the sum for him,
He shall not die; so much we tender him.

Adr. Justice, most sacred Duke, against the
abbess!

Duke. She is a virtuous and a reverend lady;

It cannot be that she hath done thee wrong.   135

Adr. May it please your Grace, Antipholus, my
husband,
Who I made lord of me and all I had
At your important letters, — this ill day
A most outrageous fit of madness took him;
That desperately he hurried through the street, —
With him his bondman, all as mad as he, —   141
Doing displeasure to the citizens
By rushing in their houses, bearing thence
Rings, jewels, any thing his rage did like.
Once did I get him bound and sent him home,   145
Whilst to take order for the wrongs I went
That here and there his fury had committed.
Anon, I wot not by what strong escape,
He broke from those that had the guard of him;
And with his mad attendant and himself,   150
Each one with ireful passion, with drawn swords,
Met us again and, madly bent on us,
Chas'd us away, till, raising of more aid,
We came again to bind them.   Then they fled
Into this abbey, whither we pursu'd them;   155
And here the abbess shuts the gates on us,
And will not suffer us to fetch him out,
Nor send him forth that we may bear him hence.
Therefore, most gracious Duke, with thy command
Let him be brought forth and borne hence for help.

Duke. Long since thy husband serv'd me in
my wars,   161
And I to thee engag'd a prince's word,
When thou didst make him master of thy bed,
To do him all the grace and good I could.
Go, some of you, knock at the abbey-gate   165
And bid the lady abbess come to me.
I will determine this before I stir.

Enter a MESSENGER.

Mess. O mistress, mistress, shift and save
yourself!
My master and his man are both broke loose,
Beaten the maids a-row and bound the doctor,   170
Whose beard they have sing'd off with brands
of fire;
And ever, as it blaz'd, they threw on him
Great pails of puddled mire to quench the hair.
My master preaches patience to him and the while
His man with scissors nicks him like a fool,   175
And sure, unless you send some present help,
Between them they will kill the conjurer.

Adr. Peace, fool! thy master and his man are
here,
And that is false thou dost report to us.

Mess. Mistress, upon my life, I tell you true;

---

100. **attorney:** agent.   105. **formal:** normal.   106. **parcel:** portion.   121. [death] F3.   *depth* F1,2.   **sorry:** sad.   124.
[reverend] F3.   *reverent* F1,2.   132. **so much:** i.e., so much leniency.   138. **important:** urgent. **letters.**   Apparently
Adriana had been a ward of the Duke.   146. **take order:** make reparation.   148. **strong:** violent.   175. **nicks...**
fool: cuts his hair fantastically like a professional jester's.

I have not breath'd almost since I did see it.   181
He cries for you, and vows, if he can take you,
To scorch your face and to disfigure you.
                              [*Cry within.*
Hark, hark! I hear him, mistress. Fly, be gone!
  Duke. Come, stand by me; fear nothing. Guard
     with halberds!   185
  Adr. Ay me, it is my husband! Witness you,
That he is borne about invisible.
Even now we hous'd him in the abbey here;
And now he's there, past thought of human reason.

Enter ANTIPHOLUS *of* Ephesus *and* DROMIO *of*
     Ephesus.

  Ant. E. Justice, most gracious Duke, O, grant
     me justice!   190
Even for the service that long since I did thee,
When I bestrid thee in the wars, and took
Deep scars to save thy life; even for the blood
That then I lost for thee, now grant me justice.
  [*Æge.*] Unless the fear of death doth make me
     dote,   195
I see my son Antipholus and Dromio.
  Ant. E. Justice, sweet prince, against that
     woman there!
She whom thou gav'st to me to be my wife,
That hath abused and dishonoured me
Even in the strength and height of injury!   200
Beyond imagination is the wrong
That she this day hath shameless thrown on me.
  Duke. Discover how, and thou shalt find me just.
  Ant. E. This day, great Duke, she shut the doors
     upon me,
While she with harlots feasted in my house.   205
  Duke. A grievous fault! Say, woman, didst
     thou so?
  Adr. No, my good lord. Myself, he, and my
     sister
To-day did dine together. So befall my soul
As this is false he burdens me withal!
  Luc. Ne'er may I look on day, nor sleep on night,
But she tells to your highness simple truth!   211
  Ang. O perjur'd woman! They are both for-
     sworn.
In this the madman justly chargeth them.
  Ant. E. My liege, I am advised what I say,
Neither disturbed with the effect of wine,   215
Nor heady-rash, provok'd with raging ire,
Albeit my wrongs might make one wiser mad.
This woman lock'd me out this day from dinner.
That goldsmith there, were he not pack'd with her,
Could witness it, for he was with me then;   220
Who parted with me to go fetch a chain,

Promising to bring it to the Porpentine,
Where Balthazar and I did dine together.
Our dinner done, and he not coming thither,
I went to seek him. In the street I met him   225
And in his company that gentleman.
There did this perjur'd goldsmith swear me down
That I this day of him receiv'd the chain,
Which, God he knows, I saw not; for the which
He did arrest me with an officer.   230
I did obey, and sent my peasant home
For certain ducats; he with none return'd.
Then fairly I bespoke the officer
To go in person with me to my house.
By the way we met   235
My wife, her sister, and a rabble more
Of vile confederates. Along with them
They brought one Pinch, a hungry lean-fac'd villain,
A mere anatomy, a mountebank,
A threadbare juggler and a fortune-teller,
A needy, hollow-ey'd, sharp-looking wretch,   240
A living dead man. This pernicious slave,
Forsooth, took on him as a conjurer,
And, gazing in mine eyes, feeling my pulse,
And with no face, as 't were, outfacing me,
Cries out, I was possess'd. Then all together   245
They fell upon me, bound me, bore me thence,
And in a dark and dankish vault at home
There left me and my man, both bound together;
Till, gnawing with my teeth my bonds in sunder,
I gain'd my freedom, and immediately   250
Ran hither to your Grace; whom I beseech
To give me ample satisfaction
For these deep shames and great indignities.
  Ang. My lord, in truth, thus far I witness with
     him,   254
That he din'd not at home, but was lock'd out.
  Duke. But had he such a chain of thee or no?
  Ang. He had, my lord; and when he ran in here,
These people saw the chain about his neck.
  2. Mer. Besides, I will be sworn these ears of
     mine
Heard you confess you had the chain of him   260
After you first forswore it on the mart;
And thereupon I drew my sword on you;
And then you fled into this abbey here,
From whence, I think, you are come by miracle.
  Ant. E. I never came within these abbey-walls,
Nor ever didst thou draw thy sword on me.   266
I never saw the chain, so help me heaven!
And this is false you burden me withal.
  Duke. Why, what an intricate impeach is this!
I think you all have drunk of Circe's cup.   270
If here you hous'd him, here he would have been.

---

183. **scorch:** score, slash.   195. [*Æge.*] *Mar. Fat.* F (i.e., Merchant Father).   203. **Discover:** relate.   205. **harlots:**
lewd fellows, rascals.   209. **burdens:** charges.   214. **am advised:** know very well.   219. **pack'd:** conspiring.   231.
peasant: servant.   238. **anatomy:** skeleton.   242. **took ... as:** pretended to be.   269. **impeach:** accusation.   270.
Circe's cup: the cup of poison which changed men into beasts.

If he were mad, he would not plead so coldly.
You say he din'd at home; the goldsmith here
Denies that saying. Sirrah, what say you?
  Dro. E. Sir, he din'd with her there, at the Por-
pentine.   275
  Cour. He did, and from my finger snatch'd that
ring.
  Ant. E. 'Tis true, my liege, this ring I had of her.
  Duke. Saw'st thou him enter at the abbey here?
  Cour. As sure, my liege, as I do see your grace.
  Duke. Why, this is strange. Go call the abbess
hither.   280
I think you are all mated or stark mad.
                              [*Exit one to the Abbess.*
  Æge. Most mighty Duke, vouchsafe me speak a
word.
Haply I see a friend will save my life
And pay the sum that may deliver me.   284
  Duke. Speak freely, Syracusian, what thou wilt.
  Æge. Is not your name, sir, call'd Antipholus?
And is not that your bondman, Dromio?
  Dro. E. Within this hour I was his bondman, sir,
But he, I thank him, gnaw'd in two my cords.
Now am I Dromio and his man unbound.   290
  Æge. I am sure you both of you remember me.
  Dro. E. Ourselves we do remember, sir, by you;
For lately we were bound, as you are now.
You are not Pinch's patient, are you, sir?
  Æge. Why look you strange on me? You know
me well.   295
  Ant. E. I never saw you in my life till now.
  Æge. O, grief hath chang'd me since you saw me
last,
And careful hours with time's deformed hand
Have written strange defeatures in my face.
But tell me yet, dost thou not know my voice? 300
  Ant. E. Neither.
  Æge. Dromio, nor thou?
  Dro. E.   No, trust me, sir, nor I.
  Æge. I am sure thou dost.
  Dro. E. Ay, sir, but I am sure I do not; and
whatsoever a man denies, you are now bound to
believe him.   306
  Æge. Not know my voice! O time's extremity,
Hast thou so crack'd and splitted my poor tongue
In seven short years, that here my only son
Knows not my feeble key of untun'd cares?   310
Though now this grained face of mine be hid
In sap-consuming winter's drizzled snow,
And all the conduits of my blood froze up,
Yet hath my night of life some memory,
My wasting lamps some fading glimmer left,   315

My dull deaf ears a little use to hear.
All these old witnesses — I cannot err —
Tell me thou art my son Antipholus.
  Ant. E. I never saw my father in my life.   319
  Æge. But seven years since, in Syracusa, boy,
Thou know'st we parted; but perhaps, my son,
Thou sham'st to acknowledge me in misery.
  Ant. E. The Duke and all that know me in the city
Can witness with me that it is not so.
I ne'er saw Syracusa in my life.   325
  Duke. I tell thee, Syracusian, twenty years
Have I been patron to Antipholus,
During which time he ne'er saw Syracusa.
I see thy age and dangers make thee dote.

Re-enter ABBESS, *with* ANTIPHOLUS *of* Syracuse
               and DROMIO *of* Syracuse.

  Abb. Most mighty Duke, behold a man much
wrong'd.   [*All gather to see them.*   330
  Adr. I see two husbands, or mine eyes deceive me.
  Duke. One of these men is Genius to the other;
And so of these. Which is the natural man,
And which the spirit? Who deciphers them?
  Dro. S. I, sir, am Dromio; command him away.
  Dro. E. I, sir, am Dromio; pray, let me stay. 336
  Ant. S. Ægeon art thou not? or else his ghost?
  Dro. S. O, my old master! Who hath bound
him here?
  Abb. Whoever bound him, I will loose his bonds
And gain a husband by his liberty.   340
Speak, old Ægeon, if thou be'st the man
That hadst a wife once call'd Æmilia
That bore thee at a burden two fair sons.
O, if thou be'st the same Ægeon, speak,
And speak unto the same Æmilia!   345
  Æge. If I dream not, thou art Æmilia.
If thou art she, tell me, where is that son
That floated with thee on the fatal raft?
  Abb. By men of Epidamnum he and I
And the twin Dromio all were taken up;   350
But by and by rude fishermen of Corinth
By force took Dromio and my son from them,
And me they left with those of Epidamnum.
What then became of them I cannot tell;
I to this fortune that you see me in.   355
  Duke. [Why, here begins his morning story right.
These two Antipholuses, these two so like,
And these two Dromios, one in semblance, —
Besides her urging of her wreck at sea, —
These are the parents to these children,   360
Which accidentally are met together.]
Antipholus, thou cam'st from Corinth first?

---

272. **coldly:** rationally, coolly.   281. **mated:** confused.   298. **careful:** full of care.   **deformed:** deforming.   299. **de-features:** disfigurations.   310. **my ... cares:** my weak, discordant voice, that has been changed by sorrows.   311. **grained:** furrowed.   315. **lamps:** eyes.   332. **Genius:** attendant spirit.   334. **deciphers:** distinguishes.   343. **burden:** birth. 356-61. In F these lines follow l. 345.   The rearrangement seems clearly necessary.   Perhaps a line has dropped out following 359.

Ant. S. No, sir, not I; I came from Syracuse.

Duke. Stay, stand apart; I know not which is which.

Ant. E. I came from Corinth, my most gracious lord, — 365

Dro. E. And I with him.

Ant. E. Brought to this town by that most famous warrior,

Duke Menaphon, your most renowned uncle.

Adr. Which of you two did dine with me to-day?

Ant. S. I, gentle mistress.

Adr.   And are not you my husband?

Ant. E. No; I say nay to that.   371

Ant. S. And so do I, yet did she call me so;

And this fair gentlewoman, her sister here,

Did call me brother. [*To Luc.*] What I told you then

I hope I shall have leisure to make good;   375

If this be not a dream I see and hear.

Ang. That is the chain, sir, which you had of me.

Ant. S. I think it be, sir; I deny it not.

Ant. E. And you, sir, for this chain arrested me.

Ang. I think I did, sir; I deny it not.   380

Adr. I sent you money, sir, to be your bail,

By Dromio; but I think he brought it not.

Dro. E. No, none by me.

Ant. S. This purse of ducats I receiv'd from you

And Dromio my man did bring them me.   385

I see we still did meet each other's man,

And I was ta'en for him, and he for me,

And thereupon these errors are arose.   388

Ant. E. These ducats pawn I for my father here.

Duke. It shall not need; thy father hath his life.

Cour. Sir, I must have that diamond from you.

Ant. E. There, take it; and much thanks for my good cheer.

Abb. Renowned Duke, vouchsafe to take the pains

To go with us into the abbey here

And hear at large discoursed all our fortunes;   395

And all that are assembled in this place

That by this sympathized one day's error

Have suffer'd wrong, go, keep us company,

And we shall make full satisfaction.

Thirty-three years have I but gone in travail   400

Of you, my sons; and till this present hour

My heavy burden [ne'er] delivered.

The Duke, my husband, and my children both,

And you the calendars of their nativity,

Go to a gossips' feast, and go with me;   405

After so long grief, such nativity!

Duke. With all my heart, I'll gossip at this feast.

[*Exeunt all but Ant. S., Ant. E., Dro. S., and Dro. E.*]

Dro. S. Master, shall I go fetch your stuff from shipboard?

Ant. E. Dromio, what stuff of mine hast thou embark'd?

Dro. S. Your goods that lay at host, sir, in the Centaur.   410

Ant. S. He speaks to me. I am your master, Dromio.

Come, go with us; we'll look to that anon.

Embrace thy brother there; rejoice with him.

[*Exeunt [Ant. S. and Ant. E.].*]

Dro. S. There is a fat friend at your master's house,

That kitchen'd me for you to-day at dinner;   415

She now shall be my sister, not my wife.

Dro. E. Methinks you are my glass, and not my brother.

I see by you I am a sweet-fac'd youth.

Will you walk in to see their gossiping?

Dro. S. Not I, sir; you are my elder.   420

Dro. E. That's a question: how shall we try it?

Dro. S. We'll draw cuts for the senior; till then lead thou first.

Dro. E. Nay, then, thus:

We came into the world like brother and brother;

And now let's go hand in hand, not one before another.   [*Exeunt.* 425

---

386. **still**: continually.   397. **sympathized**: suffered by all.   402. **[ne'er]** (Dyce).   *are* F.   404. **calendars . . . na-tivity**: the Dromios.   Cf. I.ii.41, note.   405. **gossips'.** A gossip is the sponsor in baptism to a child.   406. **grief**: labor.   407. **gossip**: make merry.   410. **lay at host**: were put up.   415. **kitchen'd**: entertained in the kitchen.

The Tragedy of Richard the Third

THE ONLY EXTERNAL evidence for the date of *Richard III* is the publication of the First Quarto in 1597. The marks of Shakespeare's early style, and especially of the influence of Marlowe, are, however, so pronounced as to have led to a general agreement that the play was composed some years before that date, probably about 1593.

The Quarto of 1597 was reprinted in 1598, with the name of Shakespeare on the title page, but without further change. Other Quartos appeared in 1602, 1605, 1612, 1622, 1629, and 1634, but all derive ultimately from the text of 1597. The version in the First Folio is independent, and differs widely in detail from the text of the Quartos. The question of the comparative authority of these texts is exceedingly complicated. Each contains passages essential to the context but lacking in the other. The Folio has besides many additions quite apposite and in the manner of Shakespeare, though the corresponding place in the Quarto shows no lacuna. The difficulty is thus to determine which goes back to the earlier original, and whether Shakespeare himself is responsible for the variations. Opinions still differ widely on these points, but are for the most part agreed that the Folio is to be regarded as the more authentic version; and it is, accordingly, made the basis of the present text. A striking peculiarity of the case is that the variations are too numerous to be plausibly accounted for as mistakes of copyist or printer, and are often so slight in their effect on meaning or rhythm that it is hard to believe them the result of conscious revision. They are very frequently such differences as might be explained by lapse of memory; and it is probable that in the First Quarto we have an exceptionally correct short-hand writer's report of the play, the variations being largely due to the slips of the actors; though some hold that the Quarto is from a transcript of the acting copy, perhaps made by a prompter who often followed his recollection of what he had heard the actors say rather than the manuscript before him.

The chief basis of the action is, as usual, Holin-shed, who, in dealing with the events of Acts I, II, III, and part of IV, follows the history of the reigns of Edward V and Richard III ascribed to Sir Thomas More, and the *Historia Anglica* of Polydore Vergil, as transmitted in the Chronicle of Halle; and who in the story corresponding to the rest of Act IV and to Act V, follows Halle. But before Shakespeare's there had been two, if not more, dramatic treatments of the theme. The *Richardus Tertius* of Dr. Legge is a Latin chronicle play written, perhaps as early as 1573, for performance at the University of Cambridge. *The True Tragedie of Richard III* is anonymous and of uncertain date, but was apparently a sequel to *3 Henry VI*. Both of these contributed to the dramatic tradition of Richard, but that they affected Shakespeare directly or at all remains to be proved. Some details seem to have been gathered from such narratives as those in *The Mirror for Magistrates*.

But it was the Chronicles of Holinshed or Halle which supplied almost all the episodes and the outlines of most of the characters, especially the men. These outlines, however, are in every case filled in by Shakespeare, whose imagination caught up and vitalized the merest hints of character. Most of the famous speeches are purely the invention of the dramatist. The opening soliloquy, the wooing of Anne, the two great cursing scenes in which Margaret of Anjou plays the chief part, the dream and the murder scene of Clarence, and the exchange of repartee between Gloucester and the little Duke of York, are all without foundation in Holinshed. Gloucester's hypocritical pre-occupation with holy exercises on the occasion of the visit of the Mayor and Buckingham with the offer of the crown, is based on the parenthetical phrase, "with a bishop on every hand of him." The substance and tone of the addresses of the rival leaders to their armies in V.iii. are suggested by the Chronicle.

The historical accuracy, in its main lines, of the portrait of Richard is still a matter of dispute among historians. But the falsification, if such there be, is only in a small degree due to Shakespeare; it had already occurred in the authorities from whom he drew the facts for which he supplied a plausible psychological explanation. It is important to remember that Henry Richmond, Richard's final rival, was the grandfather of Queen Elizabeth, and that the stamp of the Machiavellian villain had already been placed on Richard by Tudor historians like More and Polydore Vergil.

It is mainly through the tremendous emphasis on the central figure that Shakespeare passes from the loose structure that had characterized the earlier chronicle plays to the unity that was recognized in calling this drama *The Tragedy of Richard III.* The merely episodic scenes which made up the epic structure of a *Tamburlaine* give place to a series ascending to a climax. For a time it was common to ascribe to Marlowe at least a part in the authorship of *Richard III*, and the fact of his influence is

still generally recognized. But Shakespeare had learned from Seneca and Kyd as well as from Marlowe, and in the present play he achieved a theatrical success beyond that of any predecessor.

The play was very popular in his time, as is shown by the large number of quartos, and it has held the stage down to the present day. The tremendous energy embodied in the main character, the biting quality of his speeches, and the opportunity for full-throated elocution have made the rôle a favorite one with actors; while the lack of subtlety and shading have made Richard vivid to every level of audience. In the histories which followed from *Richard II* to *Henry V*, Shakespeare maintained the structural advances shown in the present play, but abated the melodramatic intensity in the interest of a greater realism.

THE WOODVILLE FAMILY

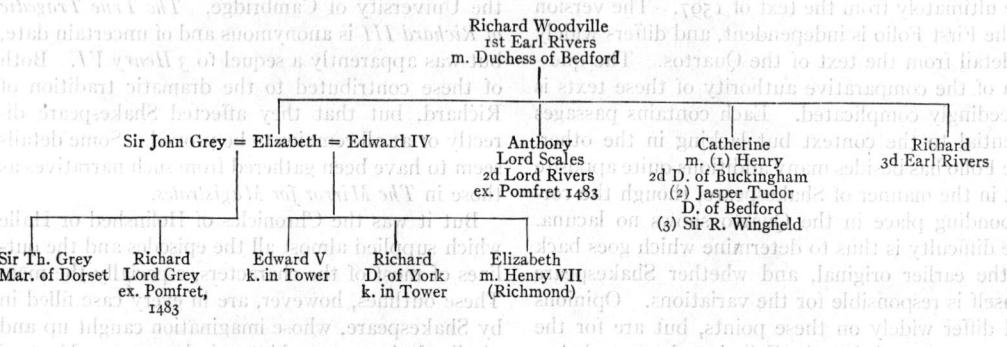

Richard Woodville
1st Earl Rivers
m. Duchess of Bedford

Sir John Grey = Elizabeth = Edward IV   Anthony   Catherine   Richard
                                          Lord Scales   m. (1) Henry   3d Earl Rivers
                                          2d Lord Rivers   2d D. of Buckingham
                                          ex. Pomfret 1483   (2) Jasper Tudor
                                                              D. of Bedford
                                                              (3) Sir R. Wingfield

Sir Th. Grey   Richard   Edward V   Richard   Elizabeth
Mar. of Dorset   Lord Grey   k. in Tower   D. of York   m. Henry VII
                  ex. Pomfret,   k. in Tower   (Richmond)
                  1483

THE TRAGEDY OF
RICHARD THE THIRD

[DRAMATIS PERSONÆ

KING EDWARD IV.
EDWARD, PRINCE OF WALES,
   afterwards KING EDWARD V, } sons to the King.
RICHARD, duke of York,
GEORGE, duke of Clarence,
RICHARD, duke of Gloucester, } brothers to the King.
   afterwards KING RICHARD III,
A young son of Clarence (Edward, E. of War-
   wick).
HENRY, earl of Richmond, afterwards KING
   HENRY VII.
CARDINAL BOURCHIER, archbishop of Canter-
   bury
THOMAS ROTHERHAM, archbishop of York.
JOHN MORTON, bishop of Ely.
DUKE OF BUCKINGHAM.
DUKE OF NORFOLK.
EARL OF SURREY, his son.
EARL RIVERS, brother to Elizabeth.
MARQUIS OF DORSET, } sons to
LORD GREY, } Elizabeth.
EARL OF OXFORD,
LORD HASTINGS, Lord Chamberlain.
LORD STANLEY, called also EARL OF DERBY.
LORD LOVEL.

SIR THOMAS VAUGHAN.
SIR RICHARD RATCLIFF.
SIR WILLIAM CATESBY.
SIR JAMES TYRREL.
SIR JAMES BLUNT.
SIR WALTER HERBERT.
SIR ROBERT BRAKENBURY, lieutenant of the
   Tower.
SIR WILLIAM BRANDON, Keeper in the Tower.
CHRISTOPHER URSWICK, a priest.
Another Priest.
TRESSEL and BERKELEY, gentlemen attending on
   the Lady Anne.
Lord Mayor of London.
Sheriff of Wiltshire.

ELIZABETH, queen to King Edward IV.
MARGARET, widow of King Henry VI.
DUCHESS OF YORK, mother to King Edward IV
   and King Richard III.
LADY ANNE, widow of Edward Prince of Wales,
   son to King Henry VI; afterwards married to
   Richard.
A young Daughter of Clarence (MARGARET
   PLANTAGENET, Countess of Salisbury).

Ghosts of those murdered by Richard III; Lords and other Attendants, a Pursuivant, a Page,
   Scrivener, Citizens, Bishops, Aldermen, Murderers, Messengers, Soldiers, etc.

SCENE: England.]

ACT I

SCENE I. [London. A street.]

Enter RICHARD, DUKE OF GLOUCESTER, solus.

Glou. Now is the winter of our discontent
Made glorious summer by this sun of York;
And all the clouds that lour'd upon our house
In the deep bosom of the ocean buried.

Now are our brows bound with victorious wreaths;
Our bruised arms hung up for monuments; 6
Our stern alarums chang'd to merry meetings,
Our dreadful marches to delightful measures.
Grim-visag'd War hath smooth'd his wrinkled front;
And now, instead of mounting barbed steeds 10
To fright the souls of fearful adversaries,
He capers nimbly in a lady's chamber
To the lascivious pleasing of a lute.

Act I, sc. i, 2. sun: a pun on *son* and *sun*.   King Edward's badge was a sun.   Cf. *3 Henry VI*, II.i.25-40, V.iii.5.   8. measures: dances.   10. barbed: armoured.

But I, that am not shap'd for sportive tricks,
Nor made to court an amorous looking-glass;   15
I, that am rudely stamp'd, and want love's majesty
To strut before a wanton ambling nymph;
I, that am curtail'd of this fair proportion,
Cheated of feature by dissembling nature,
Deform'd, unfinish'd, sent before my time   20
Into this breathing world, scarce half made up,
And that so lamely and unfashionable
That dogs bark at me as I halt by them;
Why, I, in this weak piping time of peace,
Have no delight to pass away the time,   25
Unless to see my shadow in the sun
And descant on mine own deformity.
And therefore, since I cannot prove a lover
To entertain these fair well-spoken days,
I am determined to prove a villain   30
And hate the idle pleasures of these days.
Plots have I laid, inductions dangerous,
By drunken prophecies, libels, and dreams,
To set my brother Clarence and the King
In deadly hate the one against the other;   35
And if King Edward be as true and just
As I am subtle, false, and treacherous,
This day should Clarence closely be mew'd up
About a prophecy, which says that G
Of Edward's heirs the murderer shall be.   40
Dive, thoughts, down to my soul! Here Clarence
     comes.

Enter CLARENCE, *guarded, and* BRAKENBURY.

Brother, good day. What means this armed guard
That waits upon your Grace?
   Clar.   His Majesty,
Tend'ring my person's safety, hath appointed
This conduct to convey me to the Tower.   45
   Glou. Upon what cause?
   Clar.   Because my name is George.
   Glou. Alack, my lord, that fault is none of yours;
He should, for that, commit your godfathers.
O, belike his Majesty hath some intent
That you should be new christ'ned in the Tower.   50
But what's the matter, Clarence? May I know?
   Clar. Yea, Richard, when I know, [for] I protest
As yet I do not; but, as I can learn,
He hearkens after prophecies and dreams,
And from the cross-row plucks the letter G,   55
And says a wizard told him that by G
His issue disinherited should be;
And, for my name of George begins with G,
It follows in his thought that I am he.
These, as I learn, and such like toys as these   60

Have mov'd his Highness to commit me now.
   Glou. Why, this it is, when men are rul'd by
     women.
'Tis not the King that sends you to the Tower;
My Lady Grey his wife, Clarence, 'tis she
That tempts him to this harsh extremity.   65
Was it not she and that good man of worship,
Anthony Woodville, her brother there,
That made him send Lord Hastings to the Tower,
From whence this present day he is delivered?
We are not safe, Clarence; we are not safe.   70
   Clar. By heaven, I think there is no man secure
But the Queen's kindred, and night-walking heralds
That trudge betwixt the King and Mistress Shore.
Heard you not what an humble suppliant
Lord Hastings was [to her for his] delivery?   75
   Glou. Humbly complaining to her deity
Got my Lord Chamberlain his liberty.
I'll tell you what; I think it is our way,
If we will keep in favour with the King,
To be her men and wear her livery.   80
The jealous o'erworn widow and herself,
Since that our brother dubb'd them gentlewomen,
Are mighty gossips in our monarchy.
   Brak. I beseech your Graces both to pardon me;
His Majesty hath straitly given in charge   85
That no man shall have private conference,
Of what degree soever, with your brother.
   Glou. Even so? An't please your worship,
     Brakenbury,
You may partake of anything we say.
We speak no treason, man. We say the King   90
Is wise and virtuous, and his noble queen
Well struck in years, fair, and not jealous;
We say that Shore's wife hath a pretty foot,
A cherry lip, a bonny eye, a passing pleasing tongue;
And that the Queen's kindred are made gentlefolks.
How say you, sir? Can you deny all this?   96
   Brak. With this, my lord, myself have nought
     to do.
   Glou. Naught to do with Mistress Shore! I tell
     thee, fellow,
He that doth naught with her, excepting one,
Were best to do it secretly, alone.   100
   Brak. What one, my lord?
   Glou. Her husband, knave. Wouldst thou
     betray me?
   Brak. I do beseech your Grace to pardon me,
     and withal
Forbear your conference with the noble Duke.
   Clar. We know thy charge, Brakenbury, and
     will obey.   105

---

19. **feature**: general appearance. **dissembling**: cheating.   22. **unfashionable**: badly made.   25. **to pass**: in passing.
27. **descant**: comment variously.   32. **inductions**: preparations.   38. **mew'd up**: caged (like a hawk).   44. **Tend'ring**:
caring for.   52. **[for]** Q.   *but* F.   55. **cross-row**: alphabet.   60. **toys**: trifles.   73. **Mistress Shore**: Jane Shore, wife of a
London goldsmith and mistress of Edward.   75. **[to her for his]** Q.   *for her* F.   78. **way**: best policy.   81. **widow**: Queen
Elizabeth.   83. **mighty gossips**: powerful busybodies.   92. **Well struck**: advanced.

Glou. We are the Queen's abjects and must
　　obey.
Brother, farewell! I will unto the King;
And whatsoe'er you will employ me in,
Were it to call King Edward's widow sister,
I will perform it to enfranchise you.　　110
Meantime, this deep disgrace in brotherhood
Touches me deeper than you can imagine.

Clar. I know it pleaseth neither of us well.

Glou. Well, your imprisonment shall not be long;
I will deliver you, or else lie for you.　　115
Meantime, have patience.

Clar.　　　　I must perforce. Farewell.

[Exeunt Clarence [Brackenbury, and Guard].

Glou. Go, tread the path that thou shalt ne'er
　　return,
Simple, plain Clarence! I do love thee so
That I will shortly send thy soul to heaven,
If heaven will take the present at our hands.　　120
But who comes here? The new-delivered Hastings?

Enter LORD HASTINGS.

Hast. Good time of day unto my gracious lord!

Glou. As much unto my good Lord Chamberlain!
Well are you welcome to the open air.
How hath your lordship brook'd imprisonment?

Hast. With patience, noble lord, as prisoners
　　must;　　126
But I shall live, my lord, to give them thanks
That were the cause of my imprisonment.

Glou. No doubt, no doubt; and so shall Clarence
　　too;
For they that were your enemies are his　　130
And have prevail'd as much on him as you.

Hast. More pity that the eagles should be mew'd
Whiles kites and buzzards play at liberty.

Glou. What news abroad?

Hast. No news so bad abroad as this at home:　　135
The King is sickly, weak, and melancholy,
And his physicians fear him mightily.

Glou. Now, by Saint John, that news is bad
　　indeed.
O, he hath kept an evil diet long,
And overmuch consum'd his royal person.　　140
'Tis very grievous to be thought upon.
Where is he? In his bed?

Hast. He is.

Glou. Go you before, and I will follow you.

[Exit Hastings.

He cannot live, I hope; and must not die　　145
Till George be pack'd with post-horse up to heaven.
I'll in, to urge his hatred more to Clarence
With lies well steel'd with weighty arguments;
And, if I fail not in my deep intent,

Clarence hath not another day to live;　　150
Which done, God take King Edward to his mercy,
And leave the world for me to bustle in!
For then I'll marry Warwick's youngest daughter.
What though I kill'd her husband and her father?
The readiest way to make the wench amends　　155
Is to become her husband and her father,
The which will I; not all so much for love
As for another secret close intent
By marrying her which I must reach unto.
But yet I run before my horse to market:　　160
Clarence still breathes; Edward still lives and
　　reigns;
When they are gone, then must I count my gains.

[Exit.

SCENE II. *[The same. Another street.]*

Enter the corpse of KING HENRY VI, *[*GENTLEMEN*]
with halberds to guard it, [among them* TRESSEL
and BERKELEY;*]* LADY ANNE *being the mourner.*

Anne. Set down, set down your honourable load,
If honour may be shrouded in a hearse,
Whilst I a while obsequiously lament
Th' untimely fall of virtuous Lancaster.

[The coffin is set down.]

Poor key-cold figure of a holy king!　　5
Pale ashes of the house of Lancaster!
Thou bloodless remnant of that royal blood!
Be it lawful that I invocate thy ghost
To hear the lamentations of poor Anne,
Wife to thy Edward, to thy slaught'red son,　　10
Stabb'd by the self-same hand that made these
　　wounds!
Lo, in these windows that let forth thy life
I pour the helpless balm of my poor eyes.
O cursed be the hand that made these holes!
Cursed the heart that had the heart to do it!　　15
Cursed the blood that let this blood from hence!
More direful hap betide that hated wretch
That makes us wretched by the death of thee
Than I can wish to wolves, to spiders, toads,
Or any creeping venom'd thing that lives!　　20
If ever he have child, abortive be it,
Prodigious, and untimely brought to light,
Whose ugly and unnatural aspect
May fright the hopeful mother at the view;
And that be heir to his unhappiness!　　25
If ever he have wife, let her be made
More miserable by the death of him
Than I am made by my young lord and thee!
Come, now towards Chertsey with your holy load,
Taken from Paul's to be interred there;　　30

106. **abjects:** servile subjects.　115. **lie:** i.e., in prison, with a play on the sense of prevaricate.　137. **fear:** fear for.
148. **steel'd:** hardened.
Sc. ii, 3. **obsequiously:** mournfully.

And still, as you are weary of this weight,
Rest you, whiles I lament King Henry's corse.

[The bearers take up the coffin.]

Enter GLOUCESTER

Glou. Stay, you that bear the corse, and set it
   down.
Anne. What black magician conjures up this
   fiend
To stop devoted charitable deeds?   35
Glou. Villains, set down the corse; or, by Saint
   Paul,
I'll make a corse of him that disobeys.
Gent. My lord, stand back, and let the coffin
   pass.
Glou. Unmanner'd dog! stand thou, when I
   command.
Advance thy halberd higher than my breast 40
Or, by Saint Paul, I'll strike thee to my foot
And spurn upon thee, beggar, for thy boldness.

[The coffin is set down again.]

Anne. What, do you tremble? Are you all
   afraid?
Alas, I blame you not, for you are mortal
And mortal eyes cannot endure the devil. 45
Avaunt, thou dreadful minister of hell!
Thou hadst but power over his mortal body,
His soul thou canst not have; therefore, be gone.
Glou. Sweet saint, for charity, be not so curst.
Anne. Foul devil, for God's sake, hence, and
   trouble us not;   50
For thou hast made the happy earth thy hell,
Fill'd it with cursing cries and deep exclaims.
If thou delight to view thy heinous deeds,
Behold this pattern of thy butcheries.
O, gentlemen, see, see! dead Henry's wounds 55
Open their congeal'd mouths and bleed afresh!
Blush, blush, thou lump of foul deformity;
For 'tis thy presence that exhales this blood
From cold and empty veins, where no blood dwells.
Thy deed, inhuman and unnatural, 60
Provokes this deluge most unnatural.
O God, which this blood mad'st, revenge his death!
O earth, which this blood drink'st, revenge his
   death!
Either heaven with lightning strike the murd'rer
   dead,
Or earth gape open wide and eat him quick, 65
As thou dost swallow up this good king's blood
Which his hell-govern'd arm hath butchered!
Glou. Lady, you know no rules of charity,
Which renders good for bad, blessings for curses.
Anne. Villain, thou know'st nor law of God nor
   man.   70
No beast so fierce but knows some touch of pity.

Glou. But I know none, and therefore am no beast.
Anne. O wonderful, when devils tell the truth!
Glou. More wonderful, when angels are so angry.
Vouchsafe, divine perfection of a woman, 75
Of these supposed crimes to give me leave
By circumstance but to acquit myself.
Anne. Vouchsafe, defus'd infection of [a] man,
[For] these known evils but to give me leave
By circumstance to curse thy cursed self. 80
Glou. Fairer than tongue can name thee, let me
   have
Some patient leisure to excuse myself.
Anne. Fouler than heart can think thee, thou
   canst make
No excuse current but to hang thyself.
Glou. By such despair I should accuse myself. 85
Anne. And by despairing shalt thou stand excus'd
For doing worthy vengeance on thyself,
That didst unworthy slaughter upon others.
Glou. Say that I slew them not?
Anne.   Then say they were not slain.
But dead they are, and, devilish slave, by thee. 90
Glou. I did not kill your husband.
Anne.   Why, then he is alive.
Glou. Nay, he is dead; and slain by Edward's
   hands.
Anne. In thy foul throat thou liest! Queen
   Margaret saw
Thy murd'rous falchion smoking in his blood;
The which thou once didst bend against her breast,
But that thy brothers beat aside the point. 96
Glou. I was provoked by her sland'rous tongue
That laid their guilt upon my guiltless shoulders.
Anne. Thou wast provoked by thy bloody mind
That never dreamst on aught but butcheries. 100
Didst thou not kill this king?
Glou.   I grant ye.
Anne. Dost grant me, hedgehog? Then, God
   grant me too
Thou mayst be damned for that wicked deed!
O, he was gentle, mild, and virtuous!
Glou. The better for the King of heaven, that
   hath him. 105
Anne. He is in heaven, where thou shalt never
   come.
Glou. Let him thank me, that holp to send him
   thither,
For he was fitter for that place than earth.
Anne. And thou unfit for any place but hell.
Glou. Yes, one place else, if you will hear me
   name it. 110
Anne. Some dungeon.
Glou.   Your bed-chamber.
Anne. Ill rest betide the chamber where thou
   liest!

54. **pattern:** example. 56. **bleed afresh**—as the bodies of murdered persons were believed to do in the presence of the murderer. 58. **exhales:** draws out. 78. **defus'd:** misshapen. **[a]** Q. Om. F. 79. **[For]** Q. Of F. 84. **current:** that will pass.

Glou. So will it, madam, till I lie with you.

Anne. I hope so.

Glou.   I know so. But, gentle Lady Anne,
To leave this keen encounter of our wits   115
And fall something into a slower method,
Is not the causer of the timeless deaths
Of these Plantagenets, Henry and Edward,
As blameful as the executioner?

Anne. Thou wast the cause, and most accurs'd
effect.   120

Glou. Your beauty was the cause of that effect;
Your beauty, that did haunt me in my sleep
To undertake the death of all the world
So I might live one hour in your sweet bosom.

Anne. If I thought that, I tell thee, homicide,   125
These nails should rend that beauty from my
cheeks.

Glou. These eyes could not endure that beauty's
wreck;
You should not blemish it if I stood by.
As all the world is cheered by the sun,
So I by that; it is my day, my life.   130

Anne. Black night o'ershade thy day, and death
thy life!

Glou. Curse not thyself, fair creature; thou art
both.

Anne. I would I were, to be reveng'd on thee.

Glou. It is a quarrel most unnatural,
To be reveng'd on him that loveth thee.   135

Anne. It is a quarrel just and reasonable,
To be reveng'd on him that kill'd my husband.

Glou. He that bereft thee, lady, of thy husband
Did it to help thee to a better husband.

Anne. His better doth not breathe upon the
earth.   140

Glou. He lives that loves thee better than he
could.

Anne. Name him.

Glou.   Plantagenet.

Anne.   Why, that was he.

Glou. The self-same name, but one of better
nature.

Anne. Where is he?

Glou.   Here. (*She spits at him.*) Why
dost thou spit at me?   145

Anne. Would it were mortal poison for thy sake!

Glou. Never came poison from so sweet a place.

Anne. Never hung poison on a fouler toad.
Out of my sight! Thou dost infect mine eyes.

Glou. Thine eyes, sweet lady, have infected mine.

Anne. Would they were basilisks, to strike thee
dead!   151

Glou. I would they were, that I might die at once,
For now they kill me with a living death.
Those eyes of thine from mine have drawn salt tears,
Sham'd their aspects with store of childish drops.

These eyes, which never shed remorseful tear,   156
No, when my father York and Edward wept
To hear the piteous moan that Rutland made
When black-fac'd Clifford shook his sword at
him;
Nor when thy warlike father, like a child,   160
Told the sad story of my father's death,
And twenty times made pause to sob and weep
That all the standers-by had wet their cheeks
Like trees bedash'd with rain, — in that sad time
My manly eyes did scorn an humble tear;   165
And what these sorrows could not thence exhale
Thy beauty hath, and made them blind with
weeping.
I never sued to friend nor enemy;
My tongue could never learn sweet smoothing
words;
But, now thy beauty is propos'd my fee,   170
My proud heart sues and prompts my tongue to
speak.   [*She looks scornfully at him.*
Teach not thy lip such scorn, for it was made
For kissing, lady, not for such contempt.
If thy revengeful heart cannot forgive,
Lo, here I lend thee this sharp-pointed sword,   175
Which if thou please to hide in this true breast
And let the soul forth that adoreth thee,
I lay it naked to the deadly stroke
And humbly beg the death upon my knee.

     [*He lays his breast open: she offers at it with
     his sword.*

Nay, do not pause; for I did kill King Henry,   180
But 'twas thy beauty that provoked me.
Nay, now dispatch; 'twas I that stabb'd young
Edward,
But 'twas thy heavenly face that set me on.

     [*She falls the sword.*

Take up the sword again, or take up me.

Anne. Arise, dissembler! Though I wish thy
death   185
I will not be thy executioner.

Glou. Then bid me kill myself and I will do it.

Anne. I have already.

Glou.   That was in thy rage.
Speak it again, and even with the word
This hand, which for thy love did kill thy love,
Shall for thy love kill a far truer love;   191
To both their deaths shalt thou be accessary.

Anne. I would I knew thy heart.

Glou. 'Tis figur'd in my tongue.

Anne. I fear me both are false.   195

Glou. Then never man was true.

Anne. Well, well, put up your sword.

Glou. Say, then, my peace is made.

Anne. That shalt thou know hereafter.

Glou. But shall I live in hope?   200

Anne. All men, I hope, live so.

---

117. **timeless:** untimely.   151. **basilisks:** fabulous serpents which killed by a glance.   194. **figur'd:** expressed.

[*Glou.*] Vouchsafe to wear this ring.
[*Anne.* To take is not to give.]

[*Puts on the ring.*]

Glou. Look, how my ring encompasseth thy
     finger,
Even so thy breast encloseth my poor heart.   205
Wear both of them, for both of them are thine.
And if thy poor devoted servant may
But beg one favour at thy gracious hand,
Thou dost confirm his happiness for ever.
     Anne. What is it?   210
     Glou. That it may please you leave these sad
          designs
To him that hath most cause to be a mourner,
And presently repair to Crosby House;
Where, after I have solemnly interr'd
At Chertsey monastery this noble king,   215
And wet his grave with my repentant tears,
I will with all expedient duty see you.
For divers unknown reasons, I beseech you,
Grant me this boon.
     Anne. With all my heart; and much it joys me
          too,   220
To see you are become so penitent.
Tressel and Berkeley, go along with me.
     Glou. Bid me farewell.
     Anne.   'Tis more than you deserve;
But since you teach me how to flatter you,
Imagine I have said farewell already.   225
     [*Exeunt Lady Anne, Tressel, and Berkeley.*
     [*Glou.* Sirs, take up the corse.]
     Gent.   Towards Chertsey, noble lord?
     Glou. No, to White-Friars; there attend my
          coming.   [*Exeunt all but Gloucester.*
Was ever woman in this humour woo'd?
Was ever woman in this humour won?
I'll have her, but I will not keep her long. 230
What! I, that kill'd her husband and his father,
To take her in her heart's extremest hate,
With curses in her mouth, tears in her eyes,
The bleeding witness of my hatred by;
Having God, her conscience, and these bars against
     me,   235
And I no friends to back my suit withal
But the plain devil and dissembling looks,
And yet to win her, all the world to nothing!
Ha!
Hath she forgot already that brave prince,   240
Edward, her lord, whom I some three months since
Stabb'd in my angry mood at Tewksbury?
A sweeter and a lovelier gentleman,
Fram'd in the prodigality of nature,

Young, valiant, wise, and, no doubt, right royal,
The spacious world cannot again afford.   246
And will she yet abase her eyes on me,
That cropp'd the golden prime of this sweet prince
And made her widow to a woeful bed?
On me, whose all not equals Edward's moiety? 250
On me, that halts and am misshapen thus?
My dukedom to a beggarly denier,
I do mistake my person all this while.
Upon my life, she finds, although I cannot,
Myself to be a marvellous proper man.   255
I'll be at charges for a looking-glass,
And entertain a score or two of tailors
To study fashions to adorn my body.
Since I am crept in favour with myself,
I will maintain it with some little cost.   260
But first I'll turn yon fellow in his grave;
And then return lamenting to my love.
Shine out, fair sun, till I have bought a glass,
That I may see my shadow as I pass.   [*Exit.*

SCENE III. [*The palace.*]

Enter QUEEN ELIZABETH, LORD RIVERS, *and*
          LORD GREY.

     Riv. Have patience, madam; there's no doubt
          his Majesty
Will soon recover his accustom'd health.
     Grey. In that you brook it ill, it makes him worse;
Therefore, for God's sake, entertain good comfort,
And cheer his Grace with quick and merry eyes. 5
     Q. Eliz. If he were dead, what would betide on me?
     Grey. No other harm but loss of such a lord.
     Q. Eliz. The loss of such a lord includes all harms.
     Grey. The heavens have bless'd you with a goodly
          son
To be your comforter when he is gone.   10
     Q. Eliz. Ah, he is young, and his minority
Is put unto the trust of Richard Gloucester,
A man that loves not me, nor none of you.
     Riv. Is it concluded he shall be Protector?
     Q. Eliz. It is determin'd, not concluded yet;   15
But so it must be, if the King miscarry.

Enter BUCKINGHAM *and* DERBY.

     Grey. Here comes the lords of Buckingham and
          Derby.
     Buck. Good time of day unto your royal Grace!
     Der. God make your Majesty joyful as you have
          been!
     Q. Eliz. The Countess Richmond, good my Lord
          of Derby,   20

---

202. [*Glou.*] Q. Om. F. 203. [*Anne ... ring*] Q. Om. F. 213. **presently:** at once. 217. **expedient:** speedy. 226.
[*Glou. ... corse.*] Q. Om. F. 250. **Edward's moiety:** half of Edward. 252. **denier:** a small copper coin.
     Sc. iii, 5. quick: lively. 15. **concluded:** put in operation. 20. **Countess Richmond:** Margaret Beaufort, great-grand-
daughter of John of Gaunt, widow of Edmund Tudor, Earl of Richmond, and mother of the future Henry VII, had married
the Earl of Derby.

To your good prayer will scarcely say amen.
Yet, Derby, notwithstanding she's your wife
And loves not me, be you, good lord, assur'd
I hate not you for her proud arrogance.

Der. I do beseech you, either not believe   25
The envious slanders of her false accusers;
Or, if she be accus'd on true report,
Bear with her weakness, which, I think, proceeds
From wayward sickness and no grounded malice.

Q. Eliz. Saw you the King to-day, my Lord of
Derby?   30

Der. But now the Duke of Buckingham and I
Are come from visiting his Majesty.

Q. Eliz. What likelihood of his amendment, lords?

Buck. Madam, good hope; his Grace speaks
cheerfully.

Q. Eliz. God grant him health! Did you confer
with him?   35

Buck. Ay, madam. He desires to make atonement
Between the Duke of Gloucester and your brothers,
And between them and my Lord Chamberlain;
And sent to warn them to his royal presence.

Q. Eliz. Would all were well! but that will never
be.   40
I fear our happiness is at the height.

Enter GLOUCESTER [HASTINGS, *and* DORSET].

Glou. They do me wrong and I will not endure it.
Who is it that complains unto the King
That I, forsooth, am stern and love them not?
By holy Paul, they love his Grace but lightly   45
That fill his ears with such dissentious rumours.
Because I cannot flatter and look fair,
Smile in men's faces, smooth, deceive, and cog,
Duck with French nods and apish courtesy,
I must be held a rancorous enemy.   50
Cannot a plain man live and think no harm
But thus his simple truth must be abus'd
With silken, sly, insinuating Jacks?

Grey. To who in all this presence speaks your
Grace?   54

Glou. To thee, that hast nor honesty nor grace.
When have I injur'd thee? When done thee wrong?
Or thee? or thee? or any of your faction?
A plague upon you all! His royal Grace —
Whom God preserve better than you would wish! —
Cannot be quiet scarce a breathing-while   60
But you must trouble him with lewd complaints.

Q. Eliz. Brother of Gloucester, you mistake the
matter.
The King on his own royal disposition,
And not provok'd by any suitor else,
Aiming, belike, at your interior hatred,   65
That in your outward action shows itself

Against my children, brothers, and myself,
Makes him to send that he may learn the ground.

Glou. I cannot tell. The world is grown so bad   70
That wrens make prey where eagles dare not perch.
Since every Jack became a gentleman,
There's many a gentle person made a Jack.

Q. Eliz. Come, come, we know your meaning,
brother Gloucester;
You envy my advancement and my friends'.   75
God grant we never may have need of you!

Glou. Meantime, God grants that I have need
of you.
Our brother is imprison'd by your means,
Myself disgrac'd, and the nobility
Held in contempt; while great promotions   80
Are daily given to ennoble those
That scarce, some two days since, were worth a
noble.

Q. Eliz. By Him that rais'd me to this careful
height
From that contented hap which I enjoy'd,
I never did incense his Majesty   85
Against the Duke of Clarence, but have been
An earnest advocate to plead for him.
My lord, you do me shameful injury
Falsely to draw me in these vile suspects.

Glou. You may deny that you were not the mean
Of my Lord Hastings' late imprisonment.   91

Riv. She may, my lord, for —

Glou. She may, Lord Rivers! Why, who knows
not so?
She may do more, sir, than denying that.
She may help you to many fair preferments   95
And then deny her aiding hand therein,
And lay those honours on your high desert.
What may she not? She may, ay, marry, may
she, —

Riv. What, marry, may she?

Glou. What, marry may she! Marry with a king,
A bachelor, and a handsome stripling too.   101
I wis your grandam had a worser match.

Q. Eliz. My Lord of Gloucester, I have too long
borne
Your blunt upbraidings and your bitter scoffs.
By heaven, I will acquaint his Majesty   105
Of those gross taunts that oft I have endur'd.
I had rather be a country servant-maid
Than a great queen with this condition,
To be thus baited, scorn'd, and stormed at.
Small joy have I in being England's Queen.   110

Enter old QUEEN MARGARET.

Q. Mar. And less'ned be that small, God I
beseech Him!

29. **wayward:** whimsical.   36. **atonement:** reconciliation.   39. **warn:** summon.   48. **cog:** cheat.   53. **Jacks:** fellows.   61.
lewd: base.   77. **of you:** because of you.   82. **noble:** 6s.8d.   83. **careful:** full of care.   89. **suspects:** suspicions.   102. **I
wis:** assuredly.

Thy honour, state, and seat is due to me.

Glou. What! threat you me with telling of the
King?

[Tell him, and spare not. Look, what I have said]
I will avouch't in presence of the King.   115
I dare adventure to be sent to th' Tower.
'Tis time to speak; my pains are quite forgot.

Q. Mar. Out, devil! I do remember them too
well:
Thou kill'dst my husband Henry in the Tower,
And Edward, my poor son, at Tewksbury.   120

Glou. Ere you were queen, ay, or your husband
king,
I was a pack-horse in his great affairs,
A weeder-out of his proud adversaries,
A liberal rewarder of his friends.
To royalize his blood I spent mine own.   125

Q. Mar. Ay, and much better blood than his or
thine.

Glou. In all which time you and your husband
Grey
Were factious for the house of Lancaster;
And, Rivers, so were you. Was not your husband
In Margaret's battle at Saint Alban's slain?   130
Let me put in your minds, if you forget,
What you have been ere this and what you are;
Withal, what I have been and what I am.

Q. Mar. A murd'rous villain, and so still thou art.

Glou. Poor Clarence did forsake his father,
Warwick,   135
Ay, and forswore himself — which Jesu pardon! —

Q. Mar. Which God revenge!

Glou. To fight on Edward's party for the crown;
And for his meed, poor lord, he is mew'd up.
I would to God my heart were flint, like Edward's;
Or Edward's soft and pitiful, like mine.   141
I am too childish-foolish for this world.

Q. Mar. Hie thee to hell for shame, and leave
this world,
Thou cacodemon! there thy kingdom is.

Riv. My Lord of Gloucester, in those busy days
Which here you urge to prove us enemies,   146
We follow'd then our lord, our sovereign king.
So should we you if you should be our king.

Glou. If I should be! I had rather be a pedlar.
Far be it from my heart, the thought thereof!   150

Q. Eliz. As little joy, my lord, as you suppose
You should enjoy, were you this country's king,
As little joy you may suppose in me
That I enjoy, being the queen thereof.

Q. Mar. A little joy enjoys the queen thereof;
For I am she, and altogether joyless.   156
I can no longer hold me patient.   [*Advancing.*]
Hear me, you wrangling pirates, that fall out
In sharing that which you have pill'd from me!
Which of you trembles not that looks on me?   160

If not that I am queen, you bow like subjects,
Yet that by you depos'd, you quake like rebels?
Ah, gentle villain, do not turn away!

Glou. Foul wrinkled witch, what mak'st thou in
my sight?

Q. Mar. But repetition of what thou hast marr'd;
That will I make before I let thee go.   166

Glou. Wert thou not banished on pain of death?

Q. Mar. I was; but I do find more pain in ban-
ishment
Than death can yield me here by my abode.
A husband and a son thou ow'st to me;   170
And thou a kingdom; all of you allegiance.
This sorrow that I have by right is yours,
And all the pleasures you usurp are mine.

Glou. The curse my noble father laid on thee
When thou didst crown his warlike brows with
paper   175
And with thy scorns drew'st rivers from his eyes
And then, to dry them, gav'st the Duke a clout
Steep'd in the faultless blood of pretty Rutland, —
His curses, then from bitterness of soul
Denounc'd against thee, are all fall'n upon thee;   180
And God, not we, hath plagu'd thy bloody deed.

Q. Eliz. So just is God, to right the innocent.

Hast. O, 'twas the foulest deed to slay that babe,
And the most merciless that e'er was heard of!

Riv. Tyrants themselves wept when it was reported.   185

Dor. No man but prophesied revenge for it.

Buck. Northumberland, then present, wept to
see it.

Q. Mar. What! were you snarling all before I
came,
Ready to catch each other by the throat,
And turn you all your hatred now on me?   190
Did York's dread curse prevail so much with heaven
That Henry's death, my lovely Edward's death,
Their kingdom's loss, my woeful banishment,
Should all but answer for that peevish brat?
Can curses pierce the clouds and enter heaven?   195
Why, then, give way, dull clouds, to my quick
curses!
Though not by war, by surfeit die your king,
As ours by murder to make him a king!
Edward thy son, that now is Prince of Wales,
For Edward our son, that was Prince of Wales,   200
Die in his youth by like untimely violence!
Thyself a queen, for me that was a queen,
Outlive thy glory like my wretched self!
Long mayst thou live to wail thy children's death
And see another, as I see thee now,   205
Deck'd in thy rights as thou art stall'd in mine!
Long die thy happy days before thy death
And, after many length'ned hours of grief,
Die neither mother, wife, nor England's Queen!

Rivers and Dorset, you were standers by   210
And so wast thou, Lord Hastings, when my son
Was stabb'd with bloody daggers: God I pray him,
That none of you may live his natural age,
But by some unlook'd accident cut off!

Glou. Have done thy charm, thou hateful wither'd
    hag!   215

Q. Mar. And leave out thee? Stay, dog, for
thou shalt hear me.
If heaven have any grievous plague in store
Exceeding those that I can wish upon thee,
O, let them keep it till thy sins be ripe,
And then hurl down their indignation   220
On thee, the troubler of the poor world's peace!
The worm of conscience still begnaw thy soul!
Thy friends suspect for traitors while thou liv'st
And take deep traitors for thy dearest friends!
No sleep close up that deadly eye of thine   225
Unless it be while some tormenting dream
Affrights thee with a hell of ugly devils!
Thou elvish-mark'd, abortive, rooting hog!
Thou that wast seal'd in thy nativity
The slave of nature and the son of hell!   230
Thou slander of thy heavy mother's womb!
Thou loathed issue of thy father's loins!
Thou rag of honour! thou detested —

Glou.   Margaret.
Q. Mar.   Richard!
Glou.   Ha!
Q. Mar.   I call thee not.
Glou. I cry thee mercy then, for I did think   235
That thou hadst call'd me all these bitter names.

Q. Mar. Why, so I did; but look'd for no reply.
O, let me make the period to my curse!

Glou. 'Tis done by me, and ends in "Margaret."

Q. Eliz. Thus have you breath'd your curse
    against yourself.   240

Q. Mar. Poor painted queen, vain flourish of my
    fortune!
Why strew'st thou sugar on that bottl'd spider
Whose deadly web ensnareth thee about?
Fool, fool! thou whet'st a knife to kill thyself.
The day will come that thou shalt wish for me   245
To help thee curse this poisonous bunch-back'd
    toad.

Hast. False-boding woman, end thy frantic curse,
Lest to thy harm thou move our patience.

Q. Mar. Foul shame upon you! you have all
    mov'd mine.

Riv. Were you well serv'd you would be taught
    your duty.   250

Q. Mar. To serve me well you all should do me
    duty,
Teach me to be your queen and you my subjects.

O, serve me well and teach yourselves that duty!

Dor. Dispute not with her; she is lunatic.

Q. Mar. Peace, master marquess, you are mala-
    pert;   255
Your fire-new stamp of honour is scarce current.
O, that your young nobility could judge
What 'twere to lose it and be miserable!
They that stand high have many blasts to shake
    them;
And if they fall, they dash themselves to pieces.   260

Glou. Good counsel, marry; learn it, learn it,
    marquess.

Dor. It touches you, my lord, as much as me.

Glou. Ay, and much more; but I was born so high,
Our aery buildeth in the cedar's top
And dallies with the wind and scorns the sun.   265

Q. Mar. And turns the sun to shade; alas! alas!
Witness my son, now in the shade of death,
Whose bright out-shining beams thy cloudy wrath
Hath in eternal darkness folded up.
Your aery buildeth in our aery's nest.   270
O God that seest it, do not suffer it!
As it is won with blood, lost be it so!

Buck. Peace, peace! for shame, if not for charity.

Q. Mar. Urge neither charity nor shame to me.
Uncharitably with me have you dealt,   275
And shamefully my hopes by you are butcher'd.
My charity is outrage, life my shame;
And in that shame still live my sorrow's rage!

Buck. Have done, have done.

Q. Mar. O princely Buckingham, I'll kiss thy
    hand   280
In sign of league and amity with thee.
Now fair befall thee and thy noble house!
Thy garments are not spotted with our blood
Nor thou within the compass of my curse.

Buck. Nor no one here; for curses never pass   285
The lips of those that breathe them in the air.

Q. Mar. I will not think but they ascend the sky
And there awake God's gentle-sleeping peace.
[*Aside to Buck.*] O Buckingham, take heed of
    yonder dog!
Look, when he fawns he bites, and when he bites
His venom tooth will rankle to the death.   291
Have not to do with him, beware of him;
Sin, death, and hell have set their marks on him,
And all their ministers attend on him.

Glou. What doth she say, my Lord of Bucking-
    ham?   295

Buck. Nothing that I respect, my gracious lord.

Q. Mar. What, dost thou scorn me for my gentle
    counsel
And soothe the devil that I warn thee from?
O, but remember this another day,

---

214. **unlook'd:** unexpected.   228. **elvish-mark'd:** deformed by elves.   230. **slave of nature:** born wretch.   241. **vain ...
fortune:** empty ornament of the position which belongs to me.   242. **bottl'd:** big-bellied.   256. **fire-new:** brand new.
264. **aery:** eagle's brood.

When he shall split thy very heart with sorrow, 300
And say poor Margaret was a prophetess!
Live each of you the subjects to his hate,
And he to yours, and all of you to God's!   [*Exit.*
  Buck. My hair doth stand on end to hear her
       curses.
  Riv. And so doth mine. I muse why she's at
       liberty.   305
  Glou. I cannot blame her. By God's holy
       mother,
She hath had too much wrong, and I repent
My part thereof that I have done to her.
  Q. Eliz. I never did her any to my knowledge.
  Glou. Yet you have all the vantage of her wrong.
I was too hot to do somebody good   311
That is too cold in thinking of it now.
Marry, as for Clarence, he is well repaid;
He is frank'd up to fatting for his pains.
God pardon them that are the cause thereof!   315
  Riv. A virtuous and a Christian-like conclusion,
To pray for them that have done scathe to us.
  Glou. So do I ever, being well advis'd.
                            [*Speaks to himself.*
For had I curs'd now, I had curs'd myself.

Enter CATESBY.

  Cates. Madam, his Majesty doth call for you;
And for your Grace; and yours, my noble lord. 321
  Q. Eliz. Catesby, I come. Lords, will you go
       with me?
  Riv. We wait upon your Grace.
                    [*Exeunt all but Gloucester.*
  Glou. I do the wrong, and first begin to brawl.
The secret mischiefs that I set abroach   325
I lay unto the grievous charge of others.
Clarence, who I, indeed, have cast in darkness,
I do beweep to many simple gulls,
Namely, to Derby, Hastings, Buckingham;
And tell them 'tis the Queen and her allies   330
That stir the King against the Duke my brother.
Now, they believe it; and withal whet me
To be reveng'd on Rivers, Dorset, Grey.
But then I sigh, and, with a piece of scripture,
Tell them that God bids us do good for evil;   335
And thus I clothe my naked villainy
With odd old ends stol'n forth of holy writ,
And seem a saint when most I play the devil.

Enter two MURDERERS.

But, soft! here come my executioners.
How now, my hardy, stout, resolved mates!   340
Are you now going to dispatch this thing?
  [*1. Murd.*] We are, my lord; and come to have
       the warrant

That we may be admitted where he is.
  Glou. Well thought upon; I have it here about me.
                            [*Gives the warrant.*
When you have done, repair to Crosby Place.   345
But, sirs, be sudden in the execution;
Withal obdurate, do not hear him plead;
For Clarence is well-spoken and perhaps
May move your hearts to pity if you mark him.
  [*1. Murd.*] Tut, tut, my lord, we will not stand to
       prate.   351
Talkers are no good doers; be assur'd
We go to use our hands and not our tongues.
  Glou. Your eyes drop millstones, when fools' eyes
       fall tears.
I like you, lads; about your business straight. 355
Go, go, dispatch.
  [*1. Murd.*]   We will, my noble lord. [*Exeunt.*]

SCENE IV. [*London.   The Tower.*]

Enter CLARENCE and KEEPER.

  Keep. Why looks your Grace so heavily today?
  Clar. O, I have pass'd a miserable night,
So full of fearful dreams, of ugly sights,
That, as I am a Christian faithful man,
I would not spend another such a night   5
Though 'twere to buy a world of happy days,
So full of dismal terror was the time.
  Keep. What was your dream, my lord? I pray
       you, tell me.
  Clar. Methoughts that I had broken from the
       Tower
And was embark'd to cross to Burgundy;   10
And in my company my brother Gloucester,
Who from my cabin tempted me to walk
Upon the hatches.   There we look'd toward Eng-
       land,
And cited up a thousand heavy times
During the wars of York and Lancaster   15
That had befall'n us.   As we pac'd along
Upon the giddy footing of the hatches,
Methought that Gloucester stumbled, and in falling
Struck me, that thought to stay him, overboard
Into the tumbling billows of the main.   20
O Lord! methought what pain it was to drown!
What dreadful noise of water in mine ears!
What sights of ugly death within mine eyes!
Methoughts I saw a thousand fearful wrecks,
A thousand men that fishes gnaw'd upon,   25
Wedges of gold, great anchors, heaps of pearl,
Inestimable stones, unvalued jewels,
All scatt'red in the bottom of the sea.
Some lay in dead men's skulls; and, in the holes
Where eyes did once inhabit, there were crept, 30

---

305. **muse**: wonder. 314. **frank'd up**: shut up as in a sty. 317. **scathe**: harm. 325. **abroach**: a-going. 328. **gulls**: dupes.
342, 351, 356. **[*1. Murd.*]** (Capell). *Vil.* F.
Sc. iv, 27. **unvalued**: invaluable.

As 'twere in scorn of eyes, reflecting gems,
That woo'd the slimy bottom of the deep
And mock'd the dead bones that lay scatt'red by.
   Keep. Had you such leisure in the time of death
To gaze upon these secrets of the deep?   35
   Clar. Methought I had. And often did I strive
To yield the ghost; but still the envious flood
Stopp'd in my soul and would not let it forth
To find the empty, vast, and wand'ring air,
But smother'd it within my panting bulk,   40
Who almost burst to belch it in the sea.
   Keep. Awak'd you not in this sore agony?
   Clar. No, no, my dream was lengthen'd after
     life.
O, then began the tempest to my soul.
I pass'd, methought, the melancholy flood   45
With that sour ferryman which poets write of,
Unto the kingdom of perpetual night.
The first that there did greet my stranger soul
Was my great father-in-law, renowned Warwick,
Who spake aloud, "What scourge for perjury   50
Can this dark monarchy afford false Clarence?"
And so he vanish'd. Then came wand'ring by
A shadow like an angel, with bright hair
Dabbl'd in blood; and he shriek'd out aloud,
"Clarence is come; false, fleeting, perjur'd Clarence,
That stabb'd me in the field by Tewksbury.   56
Seize on him, Furies, take him unto torment!"
With that, methought, a legion of foul fiends
Environ'd me, and howled in mine ears
Such hideous cries that with the very noise   60
I trembling wak'd, and for a season after
Could not believe but that I was in hell,
Such terrible impression made my dream.
   Keep. No marvel, lord, though it affrighted you;
I am afraid, methinks, to hear you tell it.   65
   Clar. Ah! Keeper, Keeper, I have done these
     things
That now give evidence against my soul
For Edward's sake; and see how he requites me!
O God! if my deep prayers cannot appease thee,
But thou wilt be aveng'd on my misdeeds,   70
Yet execute thy wrath in me alone!
O, spare my guiltless wife and my poor children!
Keeper, I prithee, sit by me a while.
My soul is heavy, and I fain would sleep.
   Keep. I will, my lord. God give your Grace
     good rest!   [*Clarence sleeps.*]   75

Enter BRAKENBURY, *the Lieutenant.*

   Brak. Sorrow breaks seasons and reposing hours,
Makes the night morning and the noon-tide night.
Princes have but their titles for their glories,
An outward honour for an inward toil;
And for unfelt imaginations   80

They often feel a world of restless cares,
So that between their titles and low name
There's nothing differs but the outward fame.

Enter the two MURDERERS.

   1. Murd. Ho! who's here?
   Brak. What wouldst thou, fellow, and how cam'st
     thou hither?   85
   2. Murd. I would speak with Clarence, and I
came hither on my legs.
   Brak. What, so brief?
   1. Murd. 'Tis better, sir, than to be tedious.
Let him see our commission, and talk no more.   91
          [*Brakenbury reads it.*
   Brak. I am in this commanded to deliver
The noble Duke of Clarence to your hands.
I will not reason what is meant hereby,
Because I will be guiltless from the meaning.   95
There lies the Duke asleep, and there the keys.
I'll to the King and signify to him
That thus I have resign'd to you my charge.
          [*Exit* [*with Keeper*].
   1. Murd. You may, sir; 'tis a point of wisdom.
Fare you well.   100
   2. Murd. What, shall we stab him as he sleeps?
   1. Murd. No; he'll say 'twas done cowardly when
he wakes.
   2. Murd. Why, he shall never wake until the
great judgement-day.   106
   1. Murd. Why, then he'll say we stabb'd him
sleeping.
   2. Murd. The urging of that word "judgement"
hath bred a kind of remorse in me.   110
   1. Murd. What, art thou afraid?
   2. Murd. Not to kill him, having a warrant; but
to be damn'd for killing him, from the which no
warrant can defend me.
   1. Murd. I thought thou hadst been resolute.   116
   2. Murd. So I am, to let him live.
   1. Murd. I'll back to the Duke of Gloucester and
tell him so.
   2. Murd. Nay, I prithee, stay a little. I hope
this passionate humour of mine will change. It
was wont to hold me but while one tells twenty.   122
   1. Murd. How dost thou feel thyself now?
   2. Murd. Some certain dregs of conscience are
yet within me.
   1. Murd. Remember our reward when the deed's
done.
   2. Murd. ['Zounds], he dies! I had forgot the
reward.
   1. Murd. Where's thy conscience now?   130
   2. Murd. O, in the Duke of Gloucester's purse.
   1. Murd. When he opens his purse to give us
our reward, thy conscience flies out.

37. **envious**: malicious. 45. **flood**: the river Styx. 46. **ferryman**: Charon. 55. **fleeting**: inconstant. 80. **for unfelt imaginations**: in place of glories imagined but not experienced. 121. **passionate**: compassionate. 128. ['Zounds] Q. *Come* F.

2. *Murd.* 'Tis no matter; let it go.   There's few
or none will entertain it.   135
  1. *Murd.* What if it come to thee again?
  2. *Murd.* I'll not meddle with it; [it is a dangerous thing;] it makes a man a coward.   A man
cannot steal but it accuseth him; a man cannot
swear but it checks him; a man cannot lie with
his neighbour's wife but it detects him. 'Tis a 140
blushing shamefac'd spirit that mutinies in a man's
bosom.   It fills a man full of obstacles.   It made
me once restore a purse of gold that by chance I
found.   It beggars any man that keeps it.   It is
turn'd out of towns and cities for a dangerous 145
thing; and every man that means to live well endeavours to trust to himself and live without it.
['Zounds,] 'tis even now at my elbow, persuading
me not to kill the Duke.   150
  [1.] *Murd.* Take the devil in thy mind, and
believe him not; he would insinuate with thee but
to make thee sigh.
  [2.] *Murd.* I am strong-fram'd, he cannot prevail
with me.   155
  [1.] *Murd.* Spoke like a tall man that respects
thy reputation.   Come, shall we fall to work?
  [2.] *Murd.* Take him on the costard with the
hilts of thy sword, and then throw him into the
malmsey-butt in the next room.   161
  [1.] *Murd.* O excellent device! and make a sop
of him.
  [2.] *Murd.* Soft! He wakes.
  [1.] *Murd.* Strike!
  [2.] *Murd.* No, we'll reason with him.   165
  Clar. Where art thou, Keeper?   Give me a cup
    of wine.
  [1.] *Murd.* You shall have wine enough, my lord,
    anon.
  Clar. In God's name, what art thou?
  [2.] *Murd.* A man, as you are.   170
  Clar. But not, as I am, royal.
  [2.] *Murd.* Nor you, as we are, loyal.
  Clar. Thy voice is thunder but thy looks are
    humble.
  [2.] *Murd.* My voice is now the King's, my looks
    mine own.
  Clar. How darkly and how deadly dost thou
    speak!   175
Your eyes do menace me.   Why look you pale?
Who sent you hither?   Wherefore do you come?
  2. *Murd.* To, to, to —
  Clar. To murder me?
  Both. Ay, ay.

  Clar. You scarcely have the hearts to tell me so,
And therefore cannot have the hearts to do it. 181
Wherein, my friends, have I offended you?
  1. *Murd.* Offended us you have not, but the
    King.
  Clar. I shall be reconcil'd to him again.
  2. *Murd.* Never, my lord; therefore prepare to
    die.   185
  Clar. Are you drawn forth among a world of men
To slay the innocent?   What is my offence?
Where is the evidence that doth accuse me?
What lawful quest have given their verdict up
Unto the frowning judge? or who pronounc'd 190
The bitter sentence of poor Clarence' death?
Before I be convict by course of law,
To threaten me with death is most unlawful.
I charge you, as you hope [to have redemption
By Christ's dear blood shed for our grievous sins,]
That you depart and lay no hands on me.   196
The deed you undertake is damnable.
  1. *Murd.* What we will do, we do upon command.
  2. *Murd.* And he that hath commanded is our
    King.
  Clar. Erroneous vassals! the great King of kings
Hath in the table of his law commanded 201
That thou shalt do no murder.   Will you, then,
Spurn at His edict and fulfil a man's?
Take heed; for He holds vengeance in His hand,
To hurl upon their heads that break His law. 205
  2. *Murd.* And that same vengeance doth He
    hurl on thee
For false forswearing and for murder too.
Thou didst receive the sacrament to fight
In quarrel of the house of Lancaster.
  1. *Murd.* And like a traitor to the name of God
Didst break that vow; and with thy treacherous
    blade   211
Unripp'd'st the bowels of thy sovereign's son.
  2. *Murd.* Whom thou wast sworn to cherish and
    defend.
  1. *Murd.* How canst thou urge God's dreadful
    law to us,
When thou hast broke it in such dear degree? 215
  Clar. Alas! for whose sake did I that ill deed?
For Edward, for my brother, for his sake.
He sends you not to murder me for this,
For in that sin he is as deep as I.   220
If God will be avenged for the deed,
O, know you yet, He doth it publicly.
Take not the quarrel from His powerful arm;
He needs no indirect or lawless course

137. [it ... thing] Q.   Om. F.   148. ['Zounds] Q.   Om. F.   QF give this sentence to *1. Murd.*   151. the devil: i.e., your conscience.   Or, if devil means Satan, taking him into your mind will enable you not to believe your conscience.   151, 156, 162, 167. [1.] 2. QF.   152. insinuate: ingratiate himself.   154, 158. [2.] *1.* QF.   158. costard: head.   161. malmsey-butt: wine cask.   162. sop: cake soaked in wine.   163. [2.] *1.* F.   165, 170, 172, 174. [2.] Q. *1.* F.   In these speeches the ascriptions of F have been departed from to maintain the consistency of the characters.   189. quest: inquest.   192. convict: convicted.   194–95. [to ... sins] Q.   *for any goodnesse* F.   215. dear: grievous.

To cut off those that have offended Him.   225
  1. Murd. Who made thee then a bloody minister,
When gallant-springing brave Plantagenet,
That princely novice, was struck dead by thee?
  Clar. My brother's love, the devil, and my rage.
  1. Murd. Thy brother's love, our duty, and thy
    faults   230
Provoke us hither now to slaughter thee.
  Clar. If you do love my brother, hate not me!
I am his brother and I love him well.
If you are hir'd for meed, go back again,
And I will send you to my brother Gloucester,   235
Who shall reward you better for my life
Than Edward will for tidings of my death.
  2. Murd. You are deceiv'd.   Your brother
    Gloucester hates you.
  Clar. O, no, he loves me and he holds me dear.
Go you to him from me.
  1. Murd.   Ay, so we will.   240
  Clar. Tell him, when that our princely father
    York
Bless'd his three sons with his victorious arm
[And charg'd us from his soul to love each other]
He little thought of this divided friendship.
Bid Gloucester think on this, and he will weep. 245
  1. Murd. Ay, millstones; as he lesson'd us to weep.
  Clar. O, do not slander him, for he is kind.
  1. Murd. Right; as snow in harvest.
Come, you deceive yourself;
'Tis he that sends us to destroy you here.   250
  Clar. It cannot be; for he bewept my fortune
And hugg'd me in his arms and swore with sobs
That he would labour my delivery.
  1. Murd. Why, so he doth, when he delivers you
From this earth's thraldom to the joys of heaven.
  2. Murd. Make peace with God, for you must
    die, my lord.   256
  Clar. Have you that holy feeling in your souls
To counsel me to make my peace with God
And are you yet to your own souls so blind
That you will war with God by murd'ring me? 260
O, sirs, consider, they that set you on
To do this deed will hate you for the deed.
  2. Murd. What shall we do?
  Clar.   Relent, and save your souls.
  1. Murd. Relent! No! 'tis cowardly and womanish.
  Clar. Not to relent is beastly, savage, devilish.
Which of you, if you were a prince's son,   266
Being pent from liberty as I am now,
If two such murderers as yourselves came to you,
Would not entreat for life?
My friend, I spy some pity in thy looks.   270
O, if thine eye be not a flatterer,
Come thou on my side and entreat for me,

As you would beg, were you in my distress.
A begging prince what beggar pities not?
  2. Murd. Look behind you, my lord.   275
  1. Murd. Take that, and that. If all this will
    not do.   [*Stabs him.*
I'll drown you in the malmsey-butt within.
             [*Exit* [*with the body*].
  2. Murd. A bloody deed, and desperately dis-
    patch'd!
How fain, like Pilate, would I wash my hands
Of this most grievous murder!   280

Re-enter First Murderer.

  1. Murd. How now! what mean'st thou, that
    thou help'st me not?
By heaven, the Duke shall know how slack you
    have been!
  2. Murd. I would he knew that I had sav'd his
    brother!
Take thou the fee and tell him what I say,
For I repent me that the Duke is slain.   285
                 [*Exit.*
  1. Murd. So do not I. Go, coward as thou art.
Well, I'll go hide the body in some hole
Till that the Duke give order for his burial;
And when I have my meed I will away;
For this will out, and then I must not stay.   290
                 [*Exit.*

ACT II

Scene I. [*London.   The palace.*]

Flourish.   Enter King Edward *sick,* Queen Eliza-
beth, Dorset, Rivers, Hastings, Buckingham
[Grey, *and others*].
  K. Edw. Why, so: now have I done a good day's
    work.
You peers, continue this united league.
I every day expect an embassage
From my Redeemer to redeem me hence;   4
And more [in] peace my soul shall part to heaven
Since I have made my friends at peace on earth.
[Hastings] and Rivers, take each other's hand;
Dissemble not your hatred, swear your love.
  Riv. By heaven, my soul is purg'd from grudging
    hate;
And with my hand I seal my true heart's love.   10
  Hast. So thrive I as I truly swear the like!
  K. Edw. Take heed you dally not before your
    king
Lest He that is the supreme King of kings
Confound your hidden falsehood and award
Either of you to be the other's end.   15
  Hast. So prosper I as I swear perfect love!

---

243. [And ... other] Q. Om. F.   253. labour: work for. 264-65. *1. Murd. ... devilish.* So Q. After 273 in F.   267.
pent: shut up. 270-72. Before 274 in F.
  Act II, sc. i, 5. [in] Q. *to* F.   7. [Hastings] Q. *Dorset* F.

Riv. And I, as I love Hastings with my heart!

K. Edw. Madam, your self is not exempt from this,
Nor you, son Dorset, Buckingham, nor you;
You have been factious one against the other.   20
Wife, love Lord Hastings, let him kiss your hand;
And what you do, do it unfeignedly.

Q. Eliz. There, Hastings; I will never more remember
Our former hatred, so thrive I and mine!

K. Edw. Dorset, embrace him; Hastings, love
lord marquess.   25

Dor. This interchange of love, I here protest,
Upon my part shall be inviolable.

Hast. And so swear I.   [*They embrace.*]

K. Edw. Now, princely Buckingham, seal thou
this league
With thy embracements to my wife's allies,   30
And make me happy in your unity.

Buck. Whenever Buckingham doth turn his hate
Upon your Grace [*to the Queen*], but with all duteous
love
Doth cherish you and yours, God punish me
With hate in those where I expect most love!   35
When I have most need to employ a friend,
And most assured that he is a friend,
Deep, hollow, treacherous, and full of guile
Be he unto me! This do I beg of Heaven,
When I am cold in love to you or yours.   40
                         [*They embrace.*

K. Edw. A pleasing cordial, princely Buckingham,
Is this thy vow unto my sickly heart.
There wanteth now our brother Gloucester here
To make the blessed period of this peace.

Buck. And, in good time,   45
Here comes Sir Richard Ratcliff and the Duke.

Enter GLOUCESTER *and* RATCLIFF.

Glou. Good morrow to my sovereign king and
queen;   46
And, princely peers, a happy time of day!

K. Edw. Happy, indeed, as we have spent the day.
Gloucester, we have done deeds of charity,
Made peace of enmity, fair love of hate,   50
Between these swelling wrong-incensed peers.

Glou. A blessed labour, my most sovereign lord.
Among this princely heap, if any here
By false intelligence or wrong surmise
Hold me a foe;   55
If I [unwittingly], or in my rage,
Have aught committed that is hardly borne
By any in this presence, I desire
To reconcile me to his friendly peace.

'Tis death to me to be at enmity;   60
I hate it, and desire all good men's love.
First, madam, I entreat true peace of you,
Which I will purchase with my duteous service;
Of you, my noble cousin Buckingham,
If ever any grudge were lodg'd between us;   65
Of you and you, Lord Rivers and of Dorset;
That all without desert have frown'd on me;
Dukes, earls, lords, gentlemen — indeed, of all.
I do not know that Englishman alive
With whom my soul is any jot at odds   70
More than the infant that is born to-night.
I thank my God for my humility.

Q. Eliz. A holy day shall this be kept hereafter.
I would to God all strifes were well compounded.
My sovereign lord, I do beseech your Highness   75
To take our brother Clarence to your grace.

Glou. Why, madam, have I off'red love for this,
To be so flouted in this royal presence?
Who knows not that the gentle Duke is dead?
                         [*They all start.*
You do him injury to scorn his corse.   80

K. Edw. Who knows not he is dead! Who knows
he is?

Q. Eliz. All-seeing Heaven, what a world is this!

Buck. Look I so pale, Lord Dorset, as the rest?

Dor. Ay, my good lord; and no man in the presence
But his red colour hath forsook his cheeks.   85

K. Edw. Is Clarence dead? The order was
revers'd.

Glou. But he, poor man, by your first order died,
And that a winged Mercury did bear;
Some tardy cripple bare the countermand,
That came too lag to see him buried.   90
God grant that some, less noble and less loyal,
Nearer in bloody thoughts, but not in blood,
Deserve not worse than wretched Clarence did,
And yet go current from suspicion!   94

Enter DERBY.

Der. A boon, my sovereign, for my service done!
                         [*Kneels.*]

K. Edw. I prithee, peace; my soul is full of sorrow.

Der. I will not rise, unless your Highness hear me.

K. Edw. Then say at once what is it thou requests.

Der. The forfeit, sovereign, of my servant's life,
Who slew to-day a riotous gentleman   100
Lately attendant on the Duke of Norfolk.

K. Edw. Have I a tongue to doom my brother's
death
And shall that tongue give pardon to a slave?
My brother kill'd no man; his fault was thought,

And yet his punishment was bitter death.   105
Who sued to me for him? Who, in my wrath,
Kneel'd at my feet and bid me be advis'd?
Who spoke of brotherhood? Who spoke of love?
Who told me how the poor soul did forsake
The mighty Warwick and did fight for me?   110
Who told me, in the field at Tewksbury,
When Oxford had me down, he rescued me
And said, "Dear brother, live, and be a king"?
Who told me, when we both lay in the field
Frozen almost to death, how he did lap me   115
Even in his garments, and did give himself,
All thin and naked, to the numb cold night?
All this from my remembrance brutish wrath
Sinfully pluck'd, and not a man of you
Had so much grace to put it in my mind.   120
But when your carters or your waiting-vassals
Have done a drunken slaughter, and defac'd
The precious image of our deaf Redeemer,
You straight are on your knees for pardon, pardon;
And I, unjustly too, must grant it you.   125
    [*Derby rises.*]
But for my brother not a man would speak,
Nor I, ungracious, speak unto myself
For him, poor soul.   The proudest of you all
Have been beholding to him in his life;
Yet none of you would once beg for his life.   130
O God, I fear thy justice will take hold
On me and you, and mine and yours for this!
Come, Hastings, help me to my closet.   Ah, poor
    Clarence! [*Exeunt some with King and Queen.*
    Glou. This is the fruit of rashness! Mark'd you
    not
How that the guilty kindred of the Queen   135
Look'd pale when they did hear of Clarence' death?
O, they did urge it still unto the King!
God will revenge it.   Come, lords, will you go
To comfort Edward with our company.
    Buck. We wait upon your Grace. [*Exeunt.*   140

SCENE II.   [*The palace.*]

Enter the old DUCHESS OF YORK, *with the two*
    CHILDREN *of Clarence.*

Boy. Good grandam, tell us, is our father dead?
Duch. No, boy.
Girl. Why do you weep so oft, and beat your
    breast,
And cry, "O Clarence, my unhappy son!"
    Boy. Why do you look on us, and shake your
    head,   5
And call us orphans, wretches, castaways,
If that our noble father were alive?

Duch. My pretty cousins, you mistake me both.
I do lament the sickness of the King,
As loath to lose him, not your father's death;   10
It were lost sorrow to wail one that's lost.
    Boy. Then you conclude, my grandam, he is dead.
The King mine uncle is to blame for it.
God will revenge it, whom I will importune
With earnest prayers all to that effect.   15
    Girl. And so will I.
    Duch. Peace, children, peace! the King doth love
    you well.
Incapable and shallow innocents,
You cannot guess who caus'd your father's death.
    Boy. Grandam, we can; for my good uncle
        Gloucester   20
Told me the King, provok'd to it by the Queen,
Devis'd impeachments to imprison him.
And when my uncle told me so he wept,
And pitied me and kindly kiss'd my cheek;
Bade me rely on him as on my father,   25
And he would love me dearly as a child.
    Duch. Ah, that deceit should steal such gentle
        shape
And with a virtuous vizor hide deep vice!
He is my son, ay, and therein my shame;
Yet from my dugs he drew not this deceit.   30
    Boy. Think you my uncle did dissemble, gran-
        dam?
    Duch. Ay, boy.
    Boy. I cannot think it.   Hark! what noise is this?

Enter QUEEN ELIZABETH, *with her hair about her*
    ears; RIVERS *and* DORSET *after her.*

    Q. Eliz. Ah, who shall hinder me to wail and weep,
To chide my fortune, and torment myself?   35
I'll join with black despair against my soul
And to myself become an enemy.
    Duch. What means this scene of rude impatience?
    Q. Eliz. To make an act of tragic violence.
Edward, my lord, thy son, our king, is dead.   40
Why grow the branches when the root is gone?
Why wither not the leaves that want their sap?
If you will live, lament; if die, be brief,
That our swift-winged souls may catch the King's,
Or, like obedient subjects, follow him   45
To his new kingdom of ne'er-changing night.
    Duch. Ah, so much interest have I in thy sorrow
As I had title in thy noble husband!
I have bewept a worthy husband's death,
And liv'd with looking on his images;   50
But now two mirrors of his princely semblance
Are crack'd in pieces by malignant death,
And I for comfort have but one false glass,
That grieves me when I see my shame in him.

107. **advis'd:** cautious.   137. **still:** continually.
Sc. ii, 8. **cousins.** Used of any relatives outside the immediate family.   18. **Incapable:** not able to understand.   50. **images:**
sons.

Thou art a widow; yet thou art a mother,   55
And hast the comfort of thy children left:
But death hath snatch'd my husband from mine
    arms
And pluck'd two crutches from my feeble hands,
Clarence and Edward. O, what cause have I,
Thine being but a moiety of my moan,   60
To overgo thy woes and drown thy cries!
  Boy. Ah! aunt, you wept not for our father's
    death;
How can we aid you with our kindred tears?
  Girl. Our fatherless distress was left unmoan'd;
Your widow-dolour likewise be unwept!   65
  Q. Eliz. Give me no help in lamentation,
I am not barren to bring forth complaints.
All springs reduce their currents to mine eyes,
That I, being govern'd by the watery moon,
May send forth plenteous tears to drown the world!
Ah for my husband, for my dear lord Edward!   71
  Chil. Ah for our father, for our dear lord Clarence!
  Duch. Alas for both, both mine, Edward and
    Clarence!
  Q. Eliz. What stay had I but Edward? and he's
    gone.
  Chil. What stay had we but Clarence? and he's
    gone.   75
  Duch. What stays had I but they? and they are
    gone.
  Q. Eliz. Was never widow had so dear a loss!
  Chil. Were never orphans had so dear a loss!
  Duch. Was never mother had so dear a loss!
Alas, I am the mother of these griefs!   80
Their woes are parcell'd, mine is general.
She for an Edward weeps, and so do I;
I for a Clarence weep, so doth not she;
These babes for Clarence weep, [and so do I;
I for an Edward weep,] so do not they.   85
Alas, you three, on me, threefold distress'd,
Pour all your tears! I am your sorrow's nurse,
And I will pamper it with lamentation.
  Dor. Comfort, dear mother. God is much dis-
    pleas'd
That you take with unthankfulness His doing.   90
In common worldly things 'tis call'd ungrateful
With dull unwillingness to repay a debt
Which with a bounteous hand was kindly lent;
Much more to be thus opposite with heaven,
For it requires the royal debt it lent you.   95
  Riv. Madam, bethink you, like a careful mother,
Of the young prince your son. Send straight for
    him;
Let him be crown'd; in him your comfort lives.
Drown desperate sorrow in dead Edward's grave,
And plant your joys in living Edward's throne.   100

  Enter GLOUCESTER, BUCKINGHAM, DERBY,
    HASTINGS, *and* RATCLIFF.

  Glou. Sister, have comfort. All of us have cause
To wail the dimming of our shining star,
But none can help our harms by wailing them.
Madam, my mother, I do cry you mercy;
I did not see your Grace. Humbly on my knee   105
I crave your blessing.
  Duch. God bless thee, and put meekness in thy
    breast,
Love, charity, obedience, and true duty!
  Glou. [*Aside.*] Amen; and make me die a good
    old man!
That is the butt-end of a mother's blessing.   110
I marvel that her Grace did leave it out.
  Buck. You cloudy princes and heart-sorrowing
    peers
That bear this heavy mutual load of moan,
Now cheer each other in each other's love.
Though we have spent our harvest of this king,   115
We are to reap the harvest of his son.
The broken rancour of your high-swoln hates,
But lately splinter'd, knit, and join'd together,
Must gently be preserv'd, cherish'd, and kept.
Me seemeth good, that, with some little train,   120
Forthwith from Ludlow the young prince be fet
Hither to London, to be crown'd our king.
  Riv. Why with some little train, my Lord of
    Buckingham?
  Buck. Marry, my lord, lest, by a multitude,
The new-heal'd wound of malice should break out,
Which would be so much the more dangerous,   126
By how much the estate is green and yet ungovern'd.
Where every horse bears his commanding rein
And may direct his course as please himself,
As well the fear of harm, as harm apparent,   130
In my opinion, ought to be prevented.
  Glou. I hope the King made peace with all of us;
And the compact is firm and true in me.
  Riv. And so in me; and so, I think, in all.
Yet, since it is but green, it should be put   135
To no apparent likelihood of breach,
Which haply by much company might be urg'd;
Therefore I say with noble Buckingham,
That it is meet so few should fetch the Prince.
  Hast. And so say I.   140
  Glou. Then be it so; and go we to determine
Who they shall be that straight shall post to [Lud-
    low].
Madam, and you, my sister, will you go
To give your censures in this business?
  [*Q. Eliz.*}
  [*Duch.* } With all our hearts.]   145
    [*Exeunt all but Buckingham and Gloucester.*

---

68. **All springs reduce:** let all springs lead.   84–85. [**and ... weep**] Q. Om. F.   104. **do ... mercy:** beg your pardon.
112. **cloudy:** gloomy.   118. **splinter'd:** bound in splints.   121. **fet:** fetched.   127. **estate is green:** government is newly
established.   128. **bears:** controls.   142, 154. [**Ludlow**] Q.   *London* F.   144. **censures:** judgments.   145. Q. Om. F.

Buck. My lord, whoever journeys to the Prince,
For God's sake, let not us two stay at home;
For, by the way, I'll sort occasion,
As index to the story we late talk'd of,
To part the Queen's proud kindred from the Prince.
Glou. My other self, my counsel's consistory, 151
My oracle, my prophet, my dear cousin,
I, as a child, will go by thy direction.
Toward [Ludlow] then, for we'll not stay behind.
[Exeunt.

SCENE III. [*London. A street.*]

Enter one CITIZEN *at one door, and* another *at the other.*

1. Cit. Good morrow, neighbour; whither away
so fast?
2. Cit. I promise you, I scarcely know myself.
Hear you the news abroad?
1. Cit.   Yes, that the King is dead.
2. Cit. Ill news, by 'r lady; seldom comes the
better.
I fear, I fear 'twill prove a giddy world.   5

Enter another CITIZEN.

3. Cit. Neighbours, God speed!
1. Cit.   Give you good morrow, sir.
3. Cit. Doth the news hold of good King Edward's
death?
2. Cit. Ay, sir, it is too true; God help the while!
3. Cit. Then, masters, look to see a troublous
world.
1. Cit. No, no; by God's good grace his son shall
reign.   10
3. Cit. Woe to that land that's govern'd by a
child!
2. Cit. In him there is a hope of government,
That in his nonage, council under him,
And in his full and ripened years himself,
No doubt, shall then and till then govern well.   15
1. Cit. So stood the state when Henry the Sixth
Was crown'd in Paris but at nine months old.
3. Cit. Stood the state so? No, no, good friends,
God wot;
For then this land was famously enrich'd
With politic grave counsel; then the King   20
Had virtuous uncles to protect his Grace.
1. Cit. Why, so hath this, both by his father and
mother.
2. Cit. Better it were they all came by his father,
Or by his father there were none at all;
For emulation who shall now be nearest   25
Will touch us all too near, if God prevent not.
O, full of danger is the Duke of Gloucester,

And the Queen's sons and brothers haught and
proud!
And were they to be rul'd, and not to rule,
This sickly land might solace as before.   30
1. Cit. Come, come, we fear the worst; all will be
well.
3. Cit. When clouds are seen, wise men put on
their cloaks;
When great leaves fall, then winter is at hand;
When the sun sets, who doth not look for night?
Untimely storms makes men expect a dearth.   35
All may be well; but, if God sort it so,
'Tis more than we deserve or I expect.
2. Cit. Truly, the hearts of men are full of fear.
You cannot reason almost with a man
That looks not heavily and full of dread.   40
3. Cit. Before the days of change still is it so.
By a divine instinct men's minds mistrust
Ensuing danger; as by proof we see
The water swell before a boist'rous storm.
But leave it all to God. Whither away?   45
2. Cit. Marry, we were sent for to the justices.
3. Cit. And so was I. I'll bear you company.
[Exeunt.

SCENE IV. [*London. The palace.*]

Enter the ARCHBISHOP OF YORK, *the young* DUKE
OF YORK, QUEEN ELIZABETH, *and the* DUCHESS
OF YORK.

Arch. Last night, I heard, they lay at [North-
ampton;
At Stony-Stratford] they do rest to-night.
To-morrow, or next day, they will be here.
Duch. I long with all my heart to see the Prince.
I hope he is much grown since last I saw him.   5
Q. Eliz. But I hear, no; they say my son of York
Has almost overta'en him in his growth.
York. Ay, mother; but I would not have it so.
Duch. Why, my good cousin, it is good to grow.
York. Grandam, one night, as we did sit at sup-
per,   10
My uncle Rivers talk'd how I did grow
More than my brother. "Ay," quoth my uncle
Gloucester,
"Small herbs have grace, great weeds do grow
apace;"
And since, methinks I would not grow so fast,
Because sweet flowers are slow and weeds make
haste.   15
Duch. Good faith, good faith, the saying did not
hold
In him that did object the same to thee.

---

148. **sort occasion:** make opportunity. 149. **index:** introduction. 151. **consistory:** high court.
Sc. iii, 8. **the while:** the times. 13. **nonage:** minority. 30. **solace:** be happy. 36. **sort:** arrange. 39. **reason:** talk.
42. **mistrust:** suspect. 43. **Ensuing.** So in Q and in catchword at foot of page in F. *Pursuing* in text.
Sc. iv, 1, 2. **[Northampton . . . Stony-Stratford]** Q. *Stony Stratford, and at Northampton* F.

He was the wretched'st thing when he was young,
So long a-growing and so leisurely
That, if his rule were true, he should be gracious. 20
　　[*Arch.*] And so, no doubt, he is, my gracious
　　madam.
　　Duch. I hope he is; but yet let mothers doubt.
　　York. Now, by my troth, if I had been remem-
　　b'red
I could have given my uncle's Grace a flout,
To touch his growth nearer than he touch'd mine. 25
　　Duch. How, my young York? I prithee, let me
　　hear it.
　　York. Marry, they say my uncle grew so fast
That he could gnaw a crust at two hours old;
'Twas full two years ere I could get a tooth.
Grandam, this would have been a biting jest.   30
　　Duch. I prithee, pretty York, who told thee this?
　　York. Grandam, his nurse.
　　Duch. His nurse! why, she was dead ere thou
　　wast born.
　　York. If 'twere not she, I cannot tell who told me.
　　Q. Eliz. A parlous boy! Go to, you are too
　　shrewd. 35
　　Duch. Good madam, be not angry with the child.
　　Q. Eliz. Pitchers have ears.

Enter a MESSENGER.

　　Arch. Here comes a messenger. What news?
　　Mess. Such news, my lord, as grieves me to re-
　　port.
　　Q. Eliz. How doth the Prince?
　　Mess.   Well, madam, and in health.
　　Duch. What is thy news?   41
　　Mess. Lord Rivers and Lord Grey are sent to
　　Pomfret,
With them Sir Thomas Vaughan, prisoners.
　　Duch. Who hath committed them?
　　Mess.   The mighty dukes
Gloucester and Buckingham.
　　Arch.   For what offence? 45
　　Mess. The sum of all I can I have disclos'd.
Why or for what the nobles were committed
Is all unknown to me, my gracious lord.
　　Q. Eliz. Ay me, I see the ruin of my house!
The tiger now hath seiz'd the gentle hind; 50
Insulting tyranny begins to jut
Upon the innocent and aweless throne.
Welcome, destruction, blood, and massacre!
I see, as in a map, the end of all.
　　Duch. Accursed and unquiet wrangling days, 55
How many of you have mine eyes beheld!
My husband lost his life to get the crown,
And often up and down my sons were toss'd

For me to joy and weep their gain and loss;
And being seated and domestic broils 60
Clean over-blown, themselves, the conquerors,
Make war upon themselves, brother to brother,
Blood to blood, self against self. O, preposterous
And frantic outrage, end thy damned spleen;
Or let me die, to look on earth no more! 65
　　Q. Eliz. Come, come, my boy; we will to sanc-
　　tuary.
Madam, farewell.
　　Duch.   Stay, I will go with you.
　　Q. Eliz. You have no cause.
　　Arch. [*To the Queen.*] My gracious lady, go;
And thither bear your treasure and your goods.
For my part, I'll resign unto your Grace 70
The seal I keep; and so betide to me
As well I tender you and all of yours!
Go, I'll conduct you to the sanctuary. [*Exeunt.*

ACT III

SCENE I. [*London. A street.*]

The trumpets sound. Enter the young PRINCE, *the*
DUKES OF GLOUCESTER *and* BUCKINGHAM,
CARDINAL [BOURCHIER, CATESBY,] *and others.*

　　Buck. Welcome, sweet prince, to London, to your
　　chamber,
　　Glou. Welcome, dear cousin, my thoughts'
　　sovereign.
The weary way hath made you melancholy.
　　Prince. No, uncle; but our crosses on the way
Have made it tedious, wearisome, and heavy. 5
I want more uncles here to welcome me.
　　Glou. Sweet prince, the untainted virtue of your
　　years
Hath not yet div'd into the world's deceit.
No more can you distinguish of a man
Than of his outward show, which, God he knows, 10
Seldom or never jumpeth with the heart.
Those uncles which you want were dangerous;
Your Grace attended to their sug'red words
But look'd not on the poison of their hearts.
God keep you from them, and from such false
　　friends! 15
　　Prince. God keep me from false friends! but they
　　were none.
　　Glou. My lord, the Mayor of London comes to
　　greet you.

Enter the LORD MAYOR [*and his train*].

　　May. God bless your Grace with health and
　　happy days!

21. [*Arch.*] (Capell). *Car.* Q. *Yor.* F. 25. **touch:** twit on. 35. **parlous:** mischievous. **shrewd:** keen. 46. **can:** know. 51.
Insulting: arrogant. 51-52. **jut Upon:** threaten. 52. **aweless:** not feared. 64. **spleen:** malevolence. 72. **tender:** cherish.
　　Act III, sc. i, 1. **chamber.** London was called "The King's Chamber." 4. **crosses:** unfortunate happenings, i.e., the
arrests. 11. **jumpeth:** agreeth.

Prince. I thank you, good my lord, and thank
you all.   [*Mayor and train retire.*]
I thought my mother and my brother York   20
Would long ere this have met us on the way.
Fie, what a slug is Hastings, that he comes not
To tell us whether they will come or no!

    Enter LORD HASTINGS.

  Buck. And, in good time, here comes the sweating
lord.
  Prince. Welcome, my lord. What, will our
mother come?   25
  Hast. On what occasion, God he knows, not I,
The Queen your mother and your brother York
Have taken sanctuary. The tender prince
Would fain have come with me to meet your Grace,
But by his mother was perforce withheld.   30
  Buck. Fie, what an indirect and peevish course
Is this of hers! Lord Cardinal, will your Grace
Persuade the Queen to send the Duke of York
Unto his princely brother presently?
If she deny, Lord Hastings, go with him   35
And from her jealous arms pluck him perforce.
  Card. My Lord of Buckingham, if my weak
oratory
Can from his mother win the Duke of York,
Anon expect him here; but if she be obdurate
To mild entreaties, God [in heaven] forbid   40
We should infringe the holy privilege
Of blessed sanctuary! Not for all this land
Would I be guilty of so great a sin.
  Buck. You are too senseless-obstinate, my lord,
Too ceremonious and traditional.   45
Weigh it but with the grossness of this age,
You break not sanctuary in seizing him.
The benefit thereof is always granted
To those whose dealings have deserv'd the place
And those who have the wit to claim the place.   50
This prince hath neither claim'd it nor deserv'd it,
And therefore, in mine opinion, cannot have it.
Then, taking him from thence that is not there,
You break no privilege nor charter there.
Oft have I heard of sanctuary men,   55
But sanctuary children ne'er till now.
  Card. My lord, you shall o'er-rule my mind for
once.
Come on, Lord Hastings, will you go with me?
  Hast. I go, my lord.
  Prince. Good lords, make all the speedy haste
you may.   [*Exeunt Cardinal and Hastings.*
Say, uncle Gloucester, if our brother come,   61
Where shall we sojourn till our coronation?
  Glou. Where it think'st best unto your royal self.

If I may counsel you, some day or two
Your Highness shall repose you at the Tower;   65
Then where you please, and shall be thought most
fit
For your best health and recreation.
  Prince. I do not like the Tower, of any place.
Did Julius Cæsar build that place, my lord?
  Buck. He did, my gracious lord, begin that place;
Which, since, succeeding ages have re-edifi'd.   71
  Prince. Is it upon record, or else reported
Successively from age to age, he built it?
  Buck. Upon record, my gracious lord.   74
  Prince. But say, my lord, it were not regist'red,
Methinks the truth should live from age to age,
As 'twere retail'd to all posterity
Even to the general all-ending day.
  Glou. [*Aside.*] So wise so young, they say, do
never live long.
  Prince. What say you, uncle?   80
  Glou. I say, without characters, fame lives long.
[*Aside.*] Thus, like the formal Vice, Iniquity,
I moralize two meanings in one word.
  Prince. That Julius Cæsar was a famous man;
With what his valour did enrich his wit   85
His wit set down to make his valour live.
Death makes no conquest of [this] conqueror,
For now he lives in fame, though not in life.
I'll tell you what, my cousin Buckingham, —
  Buck. What, my gracious lord?   90
  Prince. An if I live until I be a man,
I'll win our ancient right in France again
Or die a soldier as I liv'd a king.
  Glou. [*Aside.*] Short summers lightly have a for-
ward spring.

    Enter young YORK, HASTINGS, *and the* CARDINAL.

  Buck. Now, in good time, here comes the Duke of
York.   95
  Prince. Richard of York! how fares our noble
brother?
  York. Well, my [dread] lord; so must I call you
now.
  Prince. Ay, brother, to our grief, as it is yours.
Too late he died that might have kept that title,
Which by his death hath lost much majesty.   100
  Glou. How fares our cousin, noble Lord of York?
  York. I thank you gentle uncle. O, my lord,
You said that idle weeds are fast in growth:
The Prince my brother hath outgrown me far.
  Glou. He hath, my lord.
  York.   And therefore is he idle?   105
  Glou. O, my fair cousin, I must not say so.
  York. Then is he more beholding to you than I.

---

22. **slug:** snail.   31. **indirect and peevish:** irregular and silly.   40. **[in heaven]** Q. Om. F.   46. **grossness:** laxness,
unscrupulousness.   63. **think'st:** seems.   75. **regist'red:** written down.   81. **characters:** (1) writing, (2) moral qualities.
82. **formal Vice:** regular Vice (of the Moralities).   87. **[this]** Q. *his* F.   94. **lightly:** easily, i.e., are likely to.   97. **[dread]** Q.
deare F.   99. **late:** recently.

Glou. He may command me as my sovereign;
But you have power in me as in a kinsman.
   York. I pray you, uncle, give me this dagger.
   Glou. My dagger, little cousin? With all my
     heart.   111
   Prince. A beggar, brother?
   York. Of my kind uncle, that I know will give,
And being but a toy which is no grief to give. 114
   Glou. A greater gift than that I'll give my cousin.
   York. A greater gift! O, that's the sword to it.
   Glou. Ay, gentle cousin, were it light enough.
   York. O, then, I see, you will part but with light
     gifts;
In weigh'tier things you'll say a beggar nay.
   Glou. It is too weighty for your Grace to wear.
   York. I weigh it lightly, were it heavier.   121
   Glou. What, would you have my weapon, little
     lord?
   York. I would, that I might thank you as you call
     me.
   Glou. How?
   York. Little.   125
   Prince. My Lord of York will still be cross in talk.
Uncle, your Grace knows how to bear with him.
   York. You mean, to bear me, not to bear with me.
Uncle, my brother mocks both you and me.
Because that I am little, like an ape,   130
He thinks that you should bear me on your shoulders.
   Buck. [*Aside to Hastings.*] With what a sharp-
     provided wit he reasons!
To migitate the scorn he gives his uncle,
He prettily and aptly taunts himself.
So cunning and so young is wonderful.   135
   Glou. My lord, will't please you pass along?
Myself and my good cousin Buckingham
Will to your mother, to entreat of her
To meet you at the Tower and welcome you.
   York. What, will you go unto the Tower, my
     lord?   140
   Prince. My Lord Protector [needs] will have it so.
   York. I shall not sleep in quiet at the Tower.
   Glou. Why, what should you fear?
   York. Marry, my uncle Clarence' angry ghost.
My grandam told me he was murder'd there. 145
   Prince. I fear no uncles dead.
   Glou. Nor none that live, I hope.
   Prince. An if they live, I hope I need not fear.
But come, my lord; and with a heavy heart,
Thinking on them, go I unto the Tower.   150
     [*A Sennet. Exeunt all but Gloucester,
      Buckingham, and Catesby.*
   Buck. Think you, my lord, this little prating
     York

Was not incensed by his subtle mother
To taunt and scorn you thus opprobriously?
   Glou. No doubt, no doubt. O, 'tis a perilous boy,
Bold, quick, ingenious, forward, capable.   155
He is all the mother's, from the top to toe.
   Buck. Well, let them rest. Come hither,
     Catesby.
Thou art sworn as deeply to effect what we intend
As closely to conceal what we impart.
Thou know'st our reasons urg'd upon the way; 160
What think'st thou? Is it not an easy matter
To make William Lord Hastings of our mind
For the instalment of this noble duke
In the seat royal of this famous isle?
   Cate. He for his father's sake so loves the Prince
That he will not be won to aught against him. 166
   Buck. What think'st thou, then, of Stanley?
     Will not he?
   Cate. He will do all in all as Hastings doth.
   Buck. Well, then, no more but this: go, gentle
     Catesby,
And, as it were far off, sound thou Lord Hastings
How he doth stand affected to our purpose;   171
And summon him to-morrow to the Tower
To sit about the coronation.
If thou dost find him tractable to us,
Encourage him and tell him all our reasons.   175
If he be leaden, icy, cold, unwilling,
Be thou so too; and so break off the talk,
And give us notice of his inclination;
For we to-morrow hold divided councils,
Wherein thyself shalt highly be employ'd.   180
   Glou. Commend me to Lord William. Tell him,
     Catesby,
His ancient knot of dangerous adversaries
To-morrow are let blood at Pomfret Castle;
And bid my lord, for joy of this good news,
Give Mistress Shore one gentle kiss the more. 185
   Buck. Good Catesby, go, effect this business
     soundly.
   Cate. My good lords both, with all the heed I
     can.
   Glou. Shall we hear from you, Catesby, ere we
     sleep?
   Cate. You shall, my lord.
   Glou. At Crosby House, there shall you find us
     both.   [*Exit Catesby.* 190
   Buck. Now, my lord, what shall we do if we per-
     ceive
Lord Hastings will not yield to our complots?
   Glou. Chop off his head; something we will de-
     termine.
And, look, when I am king, claim thou of me

---

114. **toy:** trifle. 121. **lightly:** as a trifle. 131. **bear.** It was common to have a bear carry an ape on his back. A slur on Richard's shape. 141. **[needs]** Q. Om. F. 150. s.d. **Sennet:** a set of notes on a trumpet. 152. **incensed:** incited.
173. **sit about:** discuss. 179. **divided councils.** Richard and Buckingham consulted separately. 182. **knot:** group. 185.
Mistress Shore, who became Hastings' mistress after Edward IV's death. 192. **complots:** conspiracies.

The earldom of Hereford, and all the movables
Whereof the King my brother was possess'd.   196
  Buck. I'll claim that promise at your Grace's
    hand.
  Glou. And look to have it yielded with all kind-
    ness.
Come, let us sup betimes, that afterwards
We may digest our complots in some form.   200
                          [*Exeunt.*

SCENE II.   *Before Lord Hastings' house.*

Enter a MESSENGER.

  Mess. My lord! my lord!
  Hast. [*Within.*] Who knocks?
  Mess. One from the Lord Stanley.
  Hast. [*Within.*] What is 't o'clock?
  Mess. Upon the stroke of four.   5

Enter LORD HASTINGS.

  Hast. Can't my lord Stanley sleep these tedious
    nights?
  Mess. So it appears by that I have to say.
First, he commends him to your noble self.
  Hast. What then?
  Mess. Then certifies your lordship that this
    night   10
He dreamt the boar had razed off his helm.
Besides, he says there are two councils kept;
And that may be determin'd at the one
Which may make you and him to rue at th' other.
Therefore he sends to know your lordship's pleas-
    ure,   15
If you will presently take horse with him,
And with all speed post with him toward the north
To shun the danger that his soul divines.
  Hast. Go, fellow, go, return unto thy lord;
Bid him not fear the separated councils.   20
His honour and myself are at the one,
And at the other is my good friend Catesby,
Where nothing can proceed that toucheth us
Whereof I shall not have intelligence.
Tell him his fears are shallow, without instance;   25
And for his dreams, I wonder he's so simple
To trust the mock'ry of unquiet slumbers.
To fly the boar before the boar pursues
Were to incense the boar to follow us
And make pursuit where he did mean no chase.
Go, bid thy master rise and come to me;   31
And we will both together to the Tower,
Where, he shall see, the boar will use us kindly.
  Mess. I'll go, my lord, and tell him what you say.
                            [*Exit.*

Enter CATESBY.

  Cate. Many good morrows to my noble lord!   35
  Hast. Good morrow, Catesby; you are early stir-
    ring.
What news, what news, in this our tott'ring state?
  Cate. It is a reeling world, indeed, my lord,
And, I believe, will never stand upright
Till Richard wear the garland of the realm.   40
  Hast. How! wear the garland! Dost thou mean
    the crown?
  Cate. Ay, my good lord.
  Hast. I'll have this crown of mine cut from my
    shoulders
Before I'll see the crown so foul misplac'd.
But canst thou guess that he doth aim at it?   45
  Cate. Ay, on my life; and hopes to find you for-
    ward
Upon his party for the gain thereof;
And thereupon he sends you this good news,
That this same very day your enemies,
The kindred of the Queen, must die at Pomfret.   50
  Hast. Indeed, I am no mourner for that news
Because they have been still my adversaries;
But, that I'll give my voice on Richard's side,
To bar my master's heirs in true descent,
God knows I will not do it, to the death.   55
  Cate. God keep your lordship in that gracious
    mind!
  Hast. But I shall laugh at this a twelve-month
    hence,
That they which brought me in my master's hate,
I live to look upon their tragedy.
Well, Catesby, ere a fortnight make me older,   60
I'll send some packing that yet think not on 't.
  Cate. 'Tis a vile thing to die, my gracious lord,
When men are unprepar'd and look not for it.   65
  Hast. O monstrous, monstrous! and so falls it out
With Rivers, Vaughan, Grey; and so 'twill do
With some men else, that think themselves as safe
As thou and I; who, as thou know'st, are dear
To princely Richard and to Buckingham.   70
  Cate. The Princes both make high account of you,
  [*Aside.*] For they account his head upon the bridge.
  Hast. I know they do, and I have well deserv'd it.

Enter LORD STANLEY.

— Come on, come on [*to Stanley*]; where is your
    boar-spear, man?
Fear you the boar, and go so unprovided?   75
  Stan. My lord, good morrow; good morrow,
    Catesby.
You may jest on, but, by the holy rood,
I do not like these several councils, I.

---

200. **digest:** work out.
Sc. ii, 11. **boar:** Richard. 25. **instance:** grounds. 72. **bridge:** London Bridge, where the heads of traitors were exhibited.

Hast. My lord, I hold my life as dear as yours;
And never in my days, I do protest,   81
Was it so precious to me as 'tis now.
Think you, but that I know our state secure,
I would be so triumphant as I am?
     Stan. The lords at Pomfret, when they rode from
         London,   85
Were jocund, and suppos'd their states were sure,
And they indeed had no cause to mistrust;
But yet, you see, how soon the day o'ercast.
This sudden stab of rancour I misdoubt.
Pray God, I say, I prove a needless coward!   90
What, shall we toward the Tower? The day is
     spent.
     Hast. Come, come, have with you. Wot you
         what, my lord?
To-day the lords you talk of are beheaded.
     Stan. They, for their truth, might better wear
         their heads
Than some that have accus'd them wear their hats.
But come, my lord, let us away.   96

           Enter a PURSUIVANT.

     Hast. Go on before; I'll talk with this good fel-
         low.   [*Exeunt Stanley and Catesby.*
How now, sirrah! how goes the world with thee?
     Purs. The better that your lordship please to
         ask.   99
     Hast. I tell thee, man, 'tis better with me now
Than when thou met'st me last where now we meet.
Then was I going prisoner to the Tower
By the suggestion of the Queen's allies;
But now, I tell thee — keep it to thyself —
This day those enemies are put to death,   105
And I in better state than e'er I was.
     Purs. God hold it, to your honour's good con-
         tent!
     Hast. Gramercy, fellow. There, drink that for
         me.   [*Throws him his purse.*
     Purs. I thank your honour.   [*Exit.*

           Enter a PRIEST.

     Priest. Well met, my lord; I am glad to see your
         honour.   110
     Hast. I thank thee, good Sir John, with all my
         heart.
I am in your debt for your last exercise;
Come the next Sabbath, and I will content you.
     Priest. I'll wait upon your lordship.

           Enter BUCKINGHAM.

     Buck. What, talking with a priest, Lord Cham-
         berlain?
Your friends at Pomfret, they do need the priest;

Your honour hath no shriving work in hand.   116
     Hast. Good faith, and when I met this holy man
The men you talk of came into my mind.
What, go you toward the Tower?
     Buck. I do, my lord; but long I cannot stay there.
I shall return before your lordship thence.   121
     Hast. Nay, like enough, for I stay dinner there.
     Buck. [*Aside.*] And supper too, although thou
         know'st it not.
Come, will you go?
     Hast. I'll wait upon your lordship.   125
                               [*Exeunt.*

         SCENE III.   *Pomfret* [*Castle*].

Enter SIR RICHARD RATCLIFF, *with halberds, carry-
     ing* RIVERS, GREY, *and* VAUGHAN *to death.*

     [*Rat.* Come, bring forth the prisoners.]
     Riv. Sir Richard Ratcliff, let me tell thee this:
To-day shalt thou behold a subject die
For truth, for duty, and for loyalty.
     Grey. God bless the Prince from all the pack of
         you!   5
A knot you are of damned blood-suckers.
     Vaug. You live that shall cry woe for this here-
         after.
     Rat. Dispatch; the limit of your lives is out.
     Riv. O Pomfret, Pomfret! O thou bloody prison,
Fatal and ominous to noble peers!   10
Within the guilty closure of thy walls
Richard the Second here was hack'd to death;
And, for more slander to thy dismal seat,
We give to thee our guiltless blood to drink.
     Grey. Now Margaret's curse is fall'n upon our
         heads,   15
When she exclaim'd on Hastings, you, and I
For standing by when Richard stabb'd her son.
     Riv. Then curs'd she Richard, then curs'd she
         Buckingham,
Then curs'd she Hastings. O, remember, God,
To hear her prayer for them, as now for us!
And for my sister and her princely sons,   20
Be satisfi'd, dear God, with our true blood,
Which, as thou know'st, unjustly must be spilt.
     Rat. Make haste; the hour of death is expiate.
     Riv. Come, Grey, come, Vaughan, let us here
         embrace.
Farewell, until we meet again in heaven.   25
                               [*Exeunt.*

         SCENE IV.   [*The Tower of London.*]

Enter BUCKINGHAM, DERBY, HASTINGS, *the* BISHOP
     OF ELY, RATCLIFF, LOVEL, *with others,* [*and take
     their seats*] *at a table.*

     80. **as yours.** Q reading *as you do yours* is more explicit.   92. **have with you:** come along.   96. S.D. PURSUIVANT: at-
tendant on a herald.   111. **Sir John.** Priests were habitually called Sir.   112. **exercise:** sermon.   116. **shriving work:** confession and absolution.
     Sc. iii, 1. [*Rat....prisoners*] Q. Om. F.   13. **slander:** evil reputation.   23. **expiate:** fully come.

Hast. Now, noble peers, the cause why we are
　　met
Is to determine of the coronation.
In God's name speak, when is the royal day?
　Buck. Is all things ready for the royal time?
　Der. It is, and wants but nomination.　　　5
　Ely. To-morrow, then, I judge a happy day.
　Buck. Who knows the Lord Protector's mind
　　herein?
Who is most inward with the royal Duke?
　Ely. Your Grace, we think, should soonest know
　　his mind.
　Buck. [Who, I, my lord?]　　　　　　　10
We know each other's faces; for our hearts,
He knows no more of mine than I of yours,
Or I of his, my lord, than you of mine.
Lord Hastings, you and he are near in love.
　Hast. I thank his Grace, I know he loves me well;
But for his purpose in the coronation　　　16
I have not sounded him, nor he deliver'd
His gracious pleasure any way therein:
But you, my honourable lords, may name the time;
And in the Duke's behalf I'll give my voice,　20
Which, I presume, he'll take in gentle part.

　　　　　Enter GLOUCESTER.

　Ely. In happy time, here comes the Duke him-
　　self.
　Glou. My noble lords and cousins all, good mor-
　　row.
I have been long a sleeper; but, I trust,
My absence doth neglect no great design　　25
Which by my presence might have been concluded.
　Buck. Had not you come upon your cue, my
　　lord,
William Lord Hastings had pronounc'd your part,—
I mean, your voice, — for crowning of the King.
　Glou. Than my Lord Hastings no man might be
　　bolder;　　　　　　　　　　　30
His lordship knows me well and loves me well.
　[*Hast.* I thank your Grace.]
　Glou.　　　　　　　My lord of Ely!
　[*Ely.*　　　　　　　　My lord?]
　Glou. When I was last in Holborn,
I saw good strawberries in your garden there.
I do beseech you send for some of them.　　35
　Ely. Marry, and will, my lord, with all my heart.
　　　　　　　　　　　　　　　[*Exit.*
　Glou. Cousin of Buckingham, a word with you.
　　　　　　　　　　[*Drawing him aside.*]
Catesby hath sounded Hastings in our business
And finds the testy gentleman so hot
That he will lose his head ere give consent　40
His master's child, as worshipfully he terms it,

Shall lose the royalty of England's throne.
　Buck. Withdraw yourself a while; I'll go with
　　you.　[*Exeunt* [*Gloucester and Buckingham*].
　Der. We have not yet set down this day of tri-
　　umph.
To-morrow, in my judgement, is too sudden;　45
For I myself am not so well provided
As else I would be were the day prolong'd.

　　　　Re-enter BISHOP OF ELY.

　Ely. Where is my Lord, the Duke of Gloucester?
I have sent for these strawberries.
　Hast. His Grace looks cheerfully and smooth this
　　morning.　　　　　　　　　　50
There's some conceit or other likes him well
When that he bids good morrow with such spirit.
I think there's never a man in Christendom
Can lesser hide his love or hate than he;　54
For by his face straight shall you know his heart.
　Der. What of his heart perceive you in his face
By any [likelihood] he show'd to-day?
　Hast. Marry, that with no man here he is of-
　　fended;
For, were he, he had shown it in his looks.
　[*Der.* I pray God he be not, I say.]　　60

　Re-enter GLOUCESTER *and* BUCKINGHAM.

　Glou. I pray you all, tell me what they deserve
That do conspire my death with devilish plots
Of damned witchcraft, and that have prevail'd
Upon my body with their hellish charms?
　Hast. The tender love I bear your Grace, my
　　lord,　　　　　　　　　　　65
Makes me most forward in this princely presence
To doom th' offenders, whosoe'er they be.
I say, my lord, they have deserved death.
　Glou. Then be your eyes the witness of their evil.
Look how I am bewitch'd; behold mine arm　70
Is, like a blasted sapling, wither'd up.
And this is Edward's wife, that monstrous witch,
Consorted with that harlot strumpet Shore,
That by their witchcraft thus have marked me.
　Hast. If they have done this deed, my noble
　　lord, —　　　　　　　　　　75
　Glou. If! Thou protector of this damned
　　strumpet,
Talk'st thou to me of "ifs"? Thou art a traitor!
Off with his head! Now, by Saint Paul I swear,
I will not dine until I see the same.
Lovel and Ratcliff, look that it be done.　　80
The rest, that love me, rise and follow me.
　　　　[*Exeunt all but Hastings, Ratcliff, and
　　　　Lovel.*

Sc. iv, 5. nomination: fixing. 8. inward: intimate. 10. [Who…lord?] Q. Om. F. 20. voice: vote. 32. [Hast.… Grace] [Ely…lord?] Q. Om. F. 47. prolong'd: postponed. 51. conceit: fancy. likes: pleases. 57. [likelihood] Q. livelihood F. 60. [Der.…say] Q. Om. F.

Hast. Woe, woe for England! not a whit for me;
For I, too fond, might have prevented this.
Stanley did dream the boar did raze our helms,
And I did scorn it and disdain to fly.   85
Three times to-day my foot-cloth horse did stum-
    ble,
And started when he look'd upon the Tower,
As loath to bear me to the slaughter-house.
O, now I need the priest that spake to me!
I now repent I told the pursuivant,   90
As too triumphing, how mine enemies
To-day at Pomfret bloodily were butcher'd,
And I myself secure in grace and favour.
O Margaret, Margaret, now thy heavy curse
Is lighted on poor Hastings' wretched head!   95
    Rat. Come, come, dispatch; the Duke would be
        at dinner.
Make a short shrift; he longs to see your head.
    Hast. O momentary grace of mortal men,
Which we more hunt for than the grace of God!
Who builds his hope in air of your good looks
Lives like a drunken sailor on a mast,   101
Ready, with every nod, to tumble down
Into the fatal bowels of the deep.
    Lov. Come, come, dispatch; 'tis bootless to ex-
        claim.
    Hast. O bloody Richard! miserable England!
I prophesy the fearfull'st time to thee   106
That ever wretched age hath look'd upon.
Come, lead me to the block; bear him my head.
They smile at me who shortly shall be dead.
                                        [*Exeunt.*

[SCENE V. *The Tower-walls.*]

Enter GLOUCESTER *and* BUCKINGHAM, *in rotten
    armour, marvellous ill-favoured.*

    Glou. Come, cousin, canst thou quake and change
        thy colour,
Murder thy breath in middle of a word,
And then again begin, and stop again,
As if thou were distraught and mad with terror?
    Buck. Tut, I can counterfeit the deep tragedian,
Speak and look back, and pry on every side,   6
Tremble and start at wagging of a straw,
Intending deep suspicion. Ghastly looks
Are at my service, like enforced smiles;
And both are ready in their offices   10
At any time to grace my stratagems.
But what, is Catesby gone?
    Glou. He is; and, see, he brings the Mayor along.

Enter the MAYOR *and* CATESBY.

    Buck. Lord Mayor, —

    Glou. Look to the drawbridge there!   15
    Buck. Hark! a drum.
    Glou. Catesby, o'erlook the walls.
    Buck. Lord Mayor, the reason we have sent —
    Glou. Look back, defend thee, here are enemies.
    Buck. God and our innocency defend and guard
        us!   20

Enter LOVEL *and* RATCLIFF, *with Hastings' head.*

    Glou. Be patient, they are friends, Ratcliff and
        Lovel.
    Lov. Here is the head of that ignoble traitor,
The dangerous and unsuspected Hastings.
    Glou. So dear I lov'd the man that I must weep.
I took him for the plainest harmless creature   25
That breath'd upon the earth a Christian,
Made him my book wherein my soul recorded
The history of all her secret thoughts.
So smooth he daub'd his vice with show of virtue
That, his apparent open guilt omitted,   30
I mean his conversation with Shore's wife,
He liv'd from all attainder of suspects.
    Buck. Well, well, he was the covert'st shelt'red
        traitor
That ever liv'd.
Would you imagine, or almost believe,   35
Were 't not that by great preservation
We live to tell it, that the subtle traitor
This day had plotted, in the council-house
To murder me and my good lord of Gloucester?
    May. Had he done so?   40
    Glou. What, think you we are Turks or infidels?
Or that we would, against the form of law,
Proceed thus rashly in the villain's death,
But that the extreme peril of the case,
The peace of England, and our persons' safety   45
Enforc'd us to this execution?
    May. Now, fair befall you! he deserv'd his death;
And your good Graces both have well proceeded
To warn false traitors from the like attempts.
I never look'd for better at his hands   50
After he once fell in with Mistress Shore.
    Buck. Yet had we not determin'd he should die
Until your lordship came to see his end;
Which now the loving haste of these our friends,
Something against our meanings, have prevented;
Because, my lord, I would have had you heard   56
The traitor speak, and timorously confess
The manner and the purpose of his treasons;
That you might well have signifi'd the same
Unto the citizens, who haply may   60
Misconstrue us in him and wail his death.
    May. But, my good lord, your Grace's words
        shall serve

---

83. **fond:** foolish. 86. **foot-cloth:** wearing housings or trappings. 100. **in . . . looks:** on your favorable external seeming.
Sc. v, S.D. *rotten:* rusty. 8. **Intending:** pretending. 31. **conversation:** intercourse. 32. **from . . . suspects:** free from all
taint of suspicion. 50, 51. **I . . . Shore.** As in Q. F gives to *Buck.* 55. **prevented:** anticipated.

As well as I had seen and heard him speak;
And do not doubt, right noble princes both,
That I'll acquaint our duteous citizens   65
With all your just proceedings in this case.
    Glou. And to that end we wish'd your lordship here,
T' avoid the censures of the carping world.
    Buck. [But] since you come too late of our intent,
Yet witness what you hear we did intend.   70
And so, my good Lord Mayor, we bid farewell.
                             [Exit Mayor.
    Glou. Go, after, after, cousin Buckingham.
The mayor towards Guildhall hies him in all post.
There, at your meetest vantage of the time,
Infer the bastardy of Edward's children.   75
Tell them how Edward put to death a citizen
Only for saying he would make his son
Heir to the Crown; meaning indeed his house,
Which, by the sign thereof, was termed so.
Moreover, urge his hateful luxury   80
And bestial appetite in change of lust,
Which stretch'd unto their servants, daughters, wives,
Even where his raging eye or savage heart,
Without control, lusted to make a prey.
Nay, for a need, thus far come near my person: 85
Tell them, when that my mother went with child
Of that insatiate Edward, noble York
My princely father then had wars in France;
And, by true computation of the time,
Found that the issue was not his begot;   90
Which well appeared in his lineaments,
Being nothing like the noble Duke my father.
Yet touch this sparingly, as 'twere far off;
Because, my lord, you know my mother lives.
    Buck. Doubt not, my lord, I'll play the orator   95
As if the golden fee for which I plead
Were for myself; and so, my lord, adieu.
    Glou. If you thrive well, bring them to Baynard's Castle,
Where you shall find me well accompanied
With reverend fathers and well-learned bishops.
    Buck. I go; and towards three or four o'clock   101
Look for the news that the Guildhall affords. *[Exit.*
    Glou. Go, Lovel, with all speed to Doctor Shaw;
[To Cate.] Go thou to Friar Penker; bid them both
Meet me within this hour at Baynard's Castle.
                 [Exeunt [all but Gloucester].
Now will I go to take some privy order   106
To draw the brats of Clarence out of sight;
And to give [notice] that no manner person
Have any time recourse unto the princes.   *[Exit.*

[SCENE VI. *The same. A street.*]

Enter a SCRIVENER *with a paper in his hand.*

    Scriv. Here is the indictment of the good Lord Hastings,
Which in a set hand fairly is engross'd
That it may be to-day read o'er in Paul's.
And mark how well the sequel hangs together:
Eleven hours I've spent to write it over,   5
For yesternight by Catesby was it sent me;
The precedent was full as long a-doing;
And yet within these five hours Hastings liv'd,
Untainted, unexamin'd, free, at liberty.
Here's a good world the while! Who is so gross   10
That cannot see this palpable device?
Yet who so bold but says he sees it not?
Bad is the world; and all will come to nought
When such ill dealing must be seen in thought.
                            [Exit.

[SCENE VII. *Baynard's Castle.*]

Enter GLOUCESTER *and* BUCKINGHAM, *at several doors.*

    Glou. How now, how now, what say the citizens?
    Buck. Now, by the holy mother of our Lord,
The citizens are mum, say not a word.
    Glou. Touch'd you the bastardy of Edward's children?
    Buck. I did; with his contract with Lady Lucy,
And his contract by deputy in France;   6
Th' unsatiate greediness of his desire,
And his enforcement of the city wives;
His tyranny for trifles; his own bastardy,
As being got, your father then in France,   10
And his resemblance, being not like the Duke.
Withal I did infer your lineaments,
Being the right idea of your father,
Both in your form and nobleness of mind;
Laid open all your victories in Scotland,   15
Your discipline in war, wisdom in peace,
Your bounty, virtue, fair humility;
Indeed, left nothing fitting for your purpose
Untouch'd or slightly handled in discourse.
And when my oratory drew toward end,   20
I bid them that did love their country's good
Cry, "God save Richard, England's royal king!"
    Glou. And did they so?
    Buck. No, so God help me, they spake not a word;
But, like dumb statuës or breathing stones,   25
Star'd each on other and look'd deadly pale;
Which when I saw, I reprehended them,
And ask'd the Mayor what meant this wilful silence.

69. [But] Q. *Which* F. 74. meetest…time: fittest opportunity. 75. Infer: assert. 80. luxury: sensuality. 85. for a need: if necessary. 108. [notice] Q. *order* F.
Sc. vi, 7. precedent: first draft. 10. gross: stupid.
Sc. vii, 12. infer: adduce.

His answer was, the people were not used
To be spoke to but by the Recorder.   30
Then he was urg'd to tell my tale again,
"Thus saith the Duke, thus hath the Duke inferr'd;"
But nothing spoke in warrant from himself.
When he had done, some followers of mine own,
At lower end of th' hall, hurl'd up their caps,   35
And some ten voices cried, "God save King Rich-
          ard!"
And thus I took the vantage of those few,
"Thanks, gentle citizens and friends," quoth I;
"This general applause and cheerful shout
Argues your wisdom and your love to Richard:"   40
And even here brake off, and came away.
          Glou. What tongueless blocks were they! Would
          they not speak?
[*Buck.* No, by my troth, my lord.]
          Glou. Will not the Mayor then and his brethren
          come?
          Buck. The Mayor is here at hand.   Intend some
          fear;   45
Be not you spoke with but by mighty suit;
And look you get a prayer-book in your hand
And stand between two churchmen, good my lord,—
For on that ground I'll make a holy descant —
And be not easily won to our requests.   50
Play the maid's part, still answer nay and take it.
          Glou. I go; and if you plead as well for them
As I can say nay to thee for myself,
No doubt we'll bring it to a happy issue.
          Buck. Go, go up to the leads; the Lord Mayor
          knocks.   [*Exit* [*Gloucester*].   55

Enter the MAYOR *and* Citizens.

Welcome, my lord!   I dance attendance here;
I think the Duke will not be spoke withal.

Enter CATESBY [*from the castle*].

[Here comes his servant.]
Now, Catesby, what says your lord to my request?
          Cate. He doth entreat your Grace, my noble lord,
To visit him to-morrow or next day.   60
He is within, with two right reverend fathers,
Divinely bent to meditation;
And in no worldly suits would he be mov'd
To draw him from his holy exercise.
          Buck. Return, good Catesby, to the gracious
          Duke;   65
Tell him, myself, the Mayor and Aldermen,
In deep designs, in matter of great moment,
No less importing than our general good,
Are come to have some conference with his Grace.
          Cate. I'll signify so much unto him straight.   70
                                        [*Exit.*

          Buck. Ah, ha, my lord, this prince is not an
          Edward!
He is not lolling on a lewd love-bed,
But on his knees at meditation;
Not dallying with a brace of courtezans,
But meditating with two deep divines;   75
Not sleeping, to engross his idle body,
But praying, to enrich his watchful soul.
Happy were England would this virtuous prince
Take on his Grace the sovereignty thereof;
But, sure, I fear, we shall not win him to it.   80
          May. Marry, God defend his Grace should say us
          nay!
          Buck. I fear he will.   Here Catesby comes again.

Re-enter CATESBY.

Now, Catesby, what says his Grace?
          Cate.   [My lord,]
He wonders to what end you have assembled
Such troops of citizens to come to him,   85
His Grace not being warn'd thereof before.
He fears, my lord, you mean no good to him.
          Buck. Sorry I am my noble cousin should
Suspect me that I mean no good to him.
By heaven, we come to him in perfect love;   90
And so once more return and tell his Grace.
                                   [*Exit Catesby.*
When holy and devout religious men
Are at their beads, 'tis much to draw them thence,
So sweet is zealous contemplation.

Enter GLOUCESTER *aloft, between two* Bishops.
          [CATESBY *returns*.]

          May. See, where his Grace stands 'tween two
          clergymen!   95
          Buck. Two props of virtue for a Christian prince,
To stay him from the fall of vanity;
And, see, a book of prayer in his hand,
True ornaments to know a holy man.
Famous Plantagenet, most gracious prince,   100
Lend favourable ear to our requests,
And pardon us the interruption
Of thy devotion and right Christian zeal.
          Glou. My lord, there needs no such apology.
I do beseech your Grace to pardon me,   105
Who, earnest in the service of my God,
Deferr'd the visitation of my friends.
But, leaving this, what is your Grace's pleasure?
          Buck. Even that, I hope, which pleaseth God above
And all good men of this ungovern'd isle.   110
          Glou. I do suspect I have done some offence
That seems disgracious in the city's eye,
And that you come to reprehend my ignorance.
          Buck. You have, my lord.   Would it might
          please your Grace,

43. [*Buck....* lord] Q. Om. F.   49. make...descant: play a tune with variations.   55. leads: roof.   57. [Here...
servant] Q. Om. F.   76. engross: fatten.   81. defend: forbid.   83. [My lord,] Q. Om. F.   97. fall of: falling into.

On our entreaties, to amend your fault!   115
   Glou. Else wherefore breathe I in a Christian
    land?
   Buck. Know then, it is your fault that you resign
The supreme seat, the throne majestical,
The scep'tred office of your ancestors,
Your state of fortune, and your due of birth,   120
The lineal glory of your royal house,
To the corruption of a blemish'd stock;
Whiles, in the mildness of your sleepy thoughts,
Which here we waken to our country's good,
The noble isle doth want his proper limbs;   125
His face defac'd with scars of infamy,
His royal stock graft with ignoble plants,
And almost should'red in the swallowing gulf
Of dark forgetfulness and deep oblivion.
Which to recure, we heartily solicit   130
Your gracious self to take on you the charge
And kingly government of this your land,
Not as protector, steward, substitute,
Or lowly factor for another's gain;
But as successively, from blood to blood,   135
Your right of birth, your empery, your own.
For this, consorted with the citizens,
Your very worshipful and loving friends,
And by their vehement instigation,
In this just cause come I to move your Grace.   140
   Glou. I cannot tell if to depart in silence
Or bitterly to speak in your reproof
Best fitteth my degree or your condition.
If not to answer, you might haply think
Tongue-ti'd ambition, not replying, yielded   145
To bear the golden yoke of sovereignty
Which fondly you would here impose on me.
If to reprove you for this suit of yours,
So season'd with your faithful love to me,
Then, on the other side, I check'd my friends.   150
Therefore, to speak, and to avoid the first,
And then, in speaking, not to incur the last,
Definitively thus I answer you:
Your love deserves my thanks; but my desert
Unmeritable shuns your high request.   155
First, if all obstacles were cut away,
And that my path were even to the crown
As [my right] revenue and due of birth,
Yet so much is my poverty of spirit,
So mighty and so many my defects,   160
That I would rather hide me from my greatness,
Being a bark to brook no mighty sea,
Than in my greatness covet to be hid
And in the vapour of my glory smother'd.
But, God be thank'd, there is no need of me,   165
And much I need to help you, were there need.
The royal tree hath left us royal fruit

Which, mellow'd by the stealing hours of time,
Will well become the seat of majesty,
And make, no doubt, us happy by his reign.   170
On him I lay that you would lay on me,
The right and fortune of his happy stars,
Which God defend that I should wring from him!
   Buck. My lord, this argues conscience in your
    Grace;
But the respects thereof are nice and trivial,   175
All circumstances well considered.
You say that Edward is your brother's son:
So say we too, but not by Edward's wife;
For first was he contract to Lady Lucy —
Your mother lives a witness to his vow —   180
And afterward by substitute betroth'd
To Bona, sister to the King of France.
These both put off, a poor petitioner,
A care-craz'd mother to a many sons,
A beauty-waning and distressed widow,   185
Even in the afternoon of her best days,
Made prize and purchase of his wanton eye,
Seduc'd the pitch and height of his degree
To base declension and loath'd bigamy.
By her, in his unlawful bed, he got   190
This Edward, whom our manners call the Prince.
More bitterly could I expostulate
Save that, for reverence to some alive,
I give a sparing limit to my tongue.
Then, good my lord, take to your royal self   195
This proffer'd benefit of dignity;
If not to bless us and the land withal,
Yet to draw forth your noble ancestry
From the corruption of abusing times
Unto a lineal true-derived course.   200
   May. Do, good my lord, your citizens entreat
    you.
   Buck. Refuse not, mighty lord, this proffer'd love.
   Cate. O, make them joyful, grant their lawful
    suit!
   Glou. Alas, why would you heap this care on me?
I am unfit for state and majesty.   205
I do beseech you, take it not amiss;
I cannot nor I will not yield to you.
   Buck. If you refuse it, — as, in love and zeal,
Loath to depose the child, your brother's son;
As well we know your tenderness of heart   210
And gentle, kind, effeminate remorse,
Which we have noted in you to your kindred
And equally indeed to all estates, —
Yet know, whe'er you accept our suit or no,
Your brother's son shall never reign our king;   215
But we will plant some other in the throne
To the disgrace and downfall of your house;
And in this resolution here we leave you. —

---

128. **should'red in:** plunged into.   130. **recure:** remedy.   158. **[my right]** Q₂.   *the ripe* F.   *my ripe* Q₁.   166. **much I
need:** I am greatly lacking in ability.   175. **nice:** over-scrupulous.   187. **purchase:** booty.   189. **declension:** decline.
192. **expostulate:** discuss.   199. **of abusing times:** caused by the abuses of the times.   211. **remorse:** pity.   213. **estates:** ranks.

Come, citizens! ['Zounds!] we'll entreat no more.
  [*Glou.* O, do not swear, my Lord of Buckingham.]
            [*Exit Buckingham [with the Citizens].*
  Cate. Call them again, sweet prince, accept their
    suit.   221
If you deny them all the land will rue it.
  Glou. Will you enforce me to a world of cares?
Call them again. [*Catesby goes to the Mayor, and
    exit.*] I am not made of stones,
But penetrable to your kind entreaties,   225
Albeit against my conscience and my soul.

    Re-enter BUCKINGHAM, [CATESBY] *and the rest.*

Cousin of Buckingham, and sage, grave men,
Since you will buckle Fortune on my back
To bear her burden whe'er I will or no,
I must have patience to endure the load.   230
But if black scandal or foul-fac'd reproach
Attend the sequel of your imposition,
Your mere enforcement shall acquittance me
From all the impure blots and stains thereof;
For God doth know, and you may partly see,   235
How far I am from the desire of this.
  May. God bless your Grace! we see it and will say
    it.
  Glou. In saying so you shall but say the truth.
  Buck. Then I salute you with this royal title:
Long live King Richard, England's worthy king!
  All. Amen.   241
  Buck. To-morrow may it please you to be
    crown'd?
  Glou. Even when you please, for you will have it
    so.
  Buck. To-morrow, then, we will attend your
    Grace;
And so most joyfully we take our leave.   245
  Glou. [*To the Bishops.*] Come, let us to our holy
    work again.
Farewell, my cousins; farewell, gentle friends.
                                        [*Exeunt.*

ACT IV

SCENE I. [*Before the Tower.*]

Enter QUEEN ELIZABETH, *the* DUCHESS OF YORK,
  and MARQUESS OF DORSET *at one door;* ANNE,
  DUCHESS OF GLOUCESTER, [*leading* LADY MAR-
  GARET PLANTAGENET, *Clarence's young Daughter*]
  at another door.

  Duch. Who meets us here? My niece Plantage-
    net
Led in the hand of her kind aunt of Gloucester?
Now, for my life, she's wandering to the Tower
On pure heart's love to greet the tender prince.

Daughter, well met.
  Anne.   God give your Graces both   5
A happy and a joyful time of day!
  Q. Eliz. As much to you, good sister! Whither
    away?
  Anne. No farther than the Tower; and, as I
    guess,
Upon the like devotion as yourselves,
To gratulate the gentle princes there.   10
  Q. Eliz. Kind sister, thanks; we'll enter all to-
    gether.

    Enter the lieutenant [BRAKENBURY].

And, in good time, here the lieutenant comes.
Master lieutenant, pray you, by your leave,
How doth the Prince and my young son of York?
  Brak. Right well, dear madam. By your pa-
    tience,   15
I may not suffer you to visit them;
The King hath strictly charg'd the contrary.
  Q. Eliz. The King! Who's that?
  Brak. [I cry you mercy!] I mean the Lord Pro-
    tector.
  Q. Eliz. The Lord protect him from that kingly
    title!   20
Hath he set bounds between their love and me?
I am their mother; who shall bar me from them?
  Duch. I am their father's mother; I will see them.
  Anne. Their aunt I am in law, in love their
    mother;
Then bring me to their sights. I'll bear thy blame
And take thy office from thee, on my peril.   26
  Brak. No, madam, no; I may not leave it so.
I am bound by oath, and therefore pardon me.
                                        [*Exit.*

    Enter LORD STANLEY

  Stan. Let me but meet you, ladies, one hour
    hence,
And I'll salute your Grace of York as mother   30
And reverend looker on of two fair queens.
  [*To Anne.*] Come, madam, you must straight to
    Westminster.
There to be crowned Richard's royal queen.
  Q. Eliz. O, cut my lace asunder that my pent
    heart
May have some scope to beat, or else I swoon   35
With this dead-killing news!
  Anne. Despiteful tidings! O unpleasing news!
  Dor. Be of good cheer. Mother, how fares your
    Grace?
  Q. Eliz. O Dorset, speak not to me, get thee gone!
Death and destruction dogs thee at thy heels;   40
Thy mother's name is ominous to children.
If thou wilt outstrip death, go cross the seas,

And live with Richmond, from the reach of hell.
Go, hie thee, hie thee from this slaughter-house,
Lest thou increase the number of the dead,   45
And make me die the thrall of Margaret's curse,
Nor mother, wife, nor England's counted queen.
    Stan. Full of wise care is this your counsel,
        madam.
Take all the swift advantage of the hours;
You shall have letters from me to my son   50
In your behalf, to meet you on the way.
Be not ta'en tardy by unwise delay.
    Duch. O ill-dispersing wind of misery!
O my accursed womb, the bed of death!
A cockatrice hast thou hatch'd to the world,   55
Whose unavoided eye is murderous.
    Stan. Come, madam, come; I in all haste was
        sent.
    Anne. And I with all unwillingness will go.
O, would to God that the inclusive verge
Of golden metal that must round my brow   60
Were red-hot steel, to sear me to the brains!
Anointed let me be with deadly venom,
And die ere men can say, "God save the Queen!"
    Q. Eliz. Go, go, poor soul, I envy not thy glory;
To feed my humour wish thyself no harm.   65
    Anne. No! why? When he that is my husband
        now
Came to me as I follow'd Henry's corse,
When scarce the blood was well wash'd from his
        hands
Which issued from my other angel husband
And that dear saint which then I weeping follow'd;
O, when, I say, I look'd on Richard's face,   71
This was my wish: "Be thou," quoth I, "accurs'd
For making me, so young, so old a widow!
And, when thou wed'st, let sorrow haunt thy bed;
And be thy wife — if any be so mad —   75
More miserable by the life of thee
Than thou hast made me by my dear lord's death!"
Lo, ere I can repeat this curse again,
Within so small a time, my woman's heart
Grossly grew captive to his honey words   80
And prov'd the subject of mine own soul's curse,
Which hitherto hath held mine eyes from rest;
For never yet one hour in his bed
Did I enjoy the golden dew of sleep,
But with his timorous dreams was still awak'd.   85
Besides, he hates me for my father Warwick,
And will, no doubt, shortly be rid of me.
    Q. Eliz. Poor heart, adieu! I pity thy complain-
        ing.
    Anne. No more than with my soul I mourn for
        yours.

    Dor. Farewell, thou woeful welcomer of glory! 90
    Anne. Adieu, poor soul, that tak'st thy leave of it!
    Duch. [*To Dorset.*] Go thou to Richmond, and
        good fortune guide thee!
    [*To Anne.*] Go thou to Richard, and good angels
        tend thee!
    [*To Queen Eliz.*] Go thou to sanctuary, and good
        thoughts possess thee!
I to my grave, where peace and rest lie with me! 95
Eighty odd years of sorrow have I seen.
And each hour's joy wreck'd with a week of teen.
    Q. Eliz. Stay, yet look back with me unto the
        Tower.
Pity, you ancient stones, those tender babes
Whom envy hath immur'd within your walls,   100
Rough cradle for such little pretty ones!
Rude ragged nurse, old sullen playfellow
For tender princes, use my babies well!
So foolish sorrow bids your stones farewell. [*Exeunt.*

SCENE II. [*London. The palace.*]

Sennet. Enter RICHARD, *in pomp, crowned;* BUCK-
        INGHAM, CATESBY [*a* PAGE, *and others*].

    K. Rich. Stand all apart. Cousin of Bucking-
        ham!
    Buck. My gracious sovereign?
    K. Rich. Give me thy hand. (*Here he ascendeth
        the throne. Sound.*) Thus high, by thy
        advice
And thy assistance, is King Richard seated;
But shall we wear these glories for a day;   5
Or shall they last, and we rejoice in them?
    Buck. Still live they, and for ever let them last!
    K. Rich. Ah, Buckingham, now do I play the
        touch
To try if thou be current gold indeed.
Young Edward lives: think now what I would speak.
    Buck. Say on, my loving lord.   11
    K. Rich. Why, Buckingham, I say, I would be
        king.
    Buck. Why, so you are, my thrice renowned lord.
    K. Rich. Ha! am I king? 'Tis so: but Edward
        lives.
    Buck. True, noble prince.
    K. Rich.   O bitter consequence,
That Edward still should live! "True, noble
        prince!"   16
Cousin, thou wast not wont to be so dull.
Shall I be plain? I wish the bastards dead;
And I would have it suddenly perform'd.
What say'st thou now? Speak suddenly; be brief.
    Buck. Your Grace may do your pleasure.   21

43. **Richmond:** Henry Tudor, son of Margaret Beaufort, later Henry VII. 50. **son:** step-son. Stanley married Henry
Tudor's mother. 55. **cockatrice:** a fabulous monster. 59. **verge:** rim. 80. **Grossly:** stupidly. 97. **teen:** sorrow.
Sc. ii, 8. **touch:** touchstone. 15. **consequence:** (1) answer, (2) fact.

K. Rich. Tut, tut, thou art all ice, thy kindness freezes.
Say, have I thy consent that they shall die?
  Buck. Give me some little breath, some pause, dear lord,
Before I positively speak in this.   25
I will resolve you herein presently.   [*Exit.*
  Cate. [*Aside to a stander by.*] The King is angry;
  see, he gnaws his lip.
  K. Rich. I will converse with iron-witted fools
And unrespective boys; none are for me
That look into me with considerate eyes.   30
High-reaching Buckingham grows circumspect.
Boy!
  Page. My lord?
  K. Rich. Know'st thou not any whom corrupting gold
Will tempt unto a close exploit of death?   35
  Page. I know a discontented gentleman
Whose humble means match not his haughty spirit.
Gold were as good as twenty orators,
And will, no doubt, tempt him to anything.   39
  K. Rich. What is his name?
  Page.   His name, my lord, is Tyrrel.
  K. Rich. I partly know the man; go, call him hither.   [*Exit Page.*
The deep-revolving witty Buckingham
No more shall be the neighbour to my counsels.
Hath he so long held out with me untir'd
And stops he now for breath? Well, be it so.   45

Enter STANLEY.

How now, Lord Stanley, what's the news?
  Stan. Know, my loving lord,
The Marquis Dorset, as I hear, is fled
To Richmond, in the parts where he abides.
     [*Stands apart.*]
  K. Rich. Come hither, Catesby. Rumour it abroad   51
That Anne, my wife, is very grievous sick;
I will take order for her keeping close.
Inquire me out some mean poor gentleman
Whom I will marry straight to Clarence' daughter;
The boy is foolish and I fear not him.   56
Look, how thou dream'st! I say again, give out
That Anne my queen is sick and like to die.
About it; for it stands me much upon
To stop all hopes whose growth may damage me.
     [*Exit Catesby.*]
I must be married to my brother's daughter,   61
Or else my kingdom stands on brittle glass.
Murder her brothers and then marry her!
Uncertain way of gain! But I am in

So far in blood that sin will pluck on sin!   65
Tear-falling pity dwells not in this eye.

     Re-enter [Page, *with* SIR JAMES] TYRREL.

Is thy name Tyrrel?
  Tyr. James Tyrrel, and your most obedient subject.
  K. Rich. Art thou, indeed?
  Tyr.   Prove me, my gracious lord.
  K. Rich. Dar'st thou resolve to kill a friend of mine?   70
  Tyr. Please you;
But I had rather kill two enemies.
  K. Rich. Why, there thou hast it; two deep enemies,
Foes to my rest and my sweet sleep's disturbers
Are they that I would have thee deal upon.   75
Tyrrel, I mean those bastards in the Tower.
  Tyr. Let me have open means to come to them,
And soon I'll rid you from the fear of them.
  K. Rich. Thou sing'st sweet music. Hark, come hither, Tyrrel.
Go, by this token. Rise and lend thine ear.   80
     [*Whispers.*
There is no more but so; say it is done,
And I will love thee and prefer thee for it.
  Tyr. I will despatch it straight.
  [*K. Rich.* Shall we hear from thee, Tyrrel, ere we sleep?
  Tyr. Ye shall, my lord.]   [*Exit.* 85

     Re-enter BUCKINGHAM.

  Buck. My lord, I have consider'd in my mind
The late request that you did sound me in.
  K. Rich. Well, let that rest. Dorset is fled to Richmond.
  Buck. I hear the news, my lord.
  K. Rich. Stanley, he is your wife's son: well, look unto it.   90
  Buck. My lord, I claim the gift, my due by promise.
For which your honour and your faith is pawn'd;
The earldom of Hereford and the movables
Which you have promised I shall possess.
  K. Rich. Stanley, look to your wife. If she convey   95
Letters to Richmond, you shall answer it.
  Buck. What says your Highness to my just request?
  K. Rich. I do remember me, Henry the Sixth
Did prophesy that Richmond should be king,
When Richmond was a little peevish boy.   100
A king, perhaps, [perhaps, —

---

26. **resolve**: inform. 29. **unrespective**: thoughtless. 30. **considerate**: thoughtful. 35. **close exploit**: secret undertaking. 42. **witty**: cunning. 53. **close**: confined. 59. **stands ... upon**: is of great concern to me. 61. **my brother's daughter**: Edward IV's daughter Elizabeth. 84-85. [*K. Rich.* .... lord.] Q. Om. F. 101-121. [**perhaps**, — ... tut] Q. *Buck. May it please you to resolve me in my suit. Rich.* F.

Buck. My lord!

K. Rich. How chance the prophet could not at
    that time
Have told me, I being by, that I should kill him?

Buck. My lord, your promise for the earldom, —

K. Rich. Richmond! When last I was at Exeter,
The mayor in courtesy show'd me the castle   107
And call'd it Rougemont; at which name I started,
Because a bard of Ireland told me once
I should not live long after I saw Richmond.   110

Buck. My lord!

K. Rich. Ay, what's o'clock?

Buck. I am thus bold to put your Grace in mind
Of what you promis'd me.

K. Rich.   Well, but what 's o'clock?

Buck. Upon the stroke of ten.

K. Rich.   Well, let it strike.

Buck. Why let it strike?   116

K. Rich. Because that, like a Jack, thou keep'st
    the stroke
Betwixt thy begging and my meditation.
I am not in the giving vein to-day.

Buck. Why, then resolve me whether you will or
    no.   120

K. Rich. Tut, tut,]
Thou troublest me; I am not in the vein.
                        [*Exeunt all but Buckingham.*

Buck. And is it thus? Repays he my deep service
With such contempt? Made I him king for this?
O, let me think on Hastings, and be gone   125
To Brecknock while my fearful head is on!   [*Exit.*

[SCENE III.   *The same.*]

Enter TYRREL.

Tyr. The tyrannous and bloody act is done,
The most arch deed of piteous massacre
That ever yet this land was guilty of.
Dighton and Forrest, who I did suborn
To do this piece of ruthless butchery,   5
Albeit they were flesh'd villains, bloody dogs,
Melted with tenderness and mild compassion,
Wept like two children in their death's sad story.
"O, thus," quoth Dighton, "lay the gentle babes;"
"Thus, thus," quoth Forrest, "girdling one another
Within their alabaster innocent arms.   11
Their lips were four red roses on a stalk,
Which in their summer beauty kiss'd each other.
A book of prayers on their pillow lay,
Which once," quoth Forrest, "almost chang'd my
    mind;   15
But O! the devil" — there the villain stopp'd;
When Dighton thus told on: "We smothered

The most replenished sweet work of Nature
That from the prime creation e'er she fram'd."
Hence both are gone with conscience and remorse   2c
They could not speak; and so I left them both,
To bear this tidings to the bloody King.

Enter KING RICHARD.

And here he comes. All health, my sovereign lord!

K. Rich. Kind Tyrrel, am I happy in thy news?

Tyr. If to have done the thing you gave in charge
Beget your happiness, be happy then,   2c
For it is done.

K. Rich.   But didst thou see them dead?

Tyr. I did, my lord.

K. Rich.   And buried, gentle Tyrrel?

Tyr. The chaplain of the Tower hath buried
    them;
But where, to say the truth, I do not know.   3c

K. Rich. Come to me, Tyrrel, soon, [at] after-
    supper,
When thou shalt tell the process of their death.
Meantime, but think how I may do thee good
And be inheritor of thy desire.
Farewell till then.   35

Tyr. I humbly take my leave.   [*Exit.*

K. Rich. The son of Clarence have I pent up close;
His daughter meanly have I match'd in marriage;
The sons of Edward sleep in Abraham's bosom,
And Anne my wife hath bid this world good-night.
Now, for I know the Breton Richmond aims   40
At young Elizabeth, my brother's daughter,
And by that knot looks proudly on the crown,
To her go I, a jolly thriving wooer.

Enter RATCLIFF.

Rat. My lord!

K. Rich. Good or bad news, that thou com'st in
    so bluntly?   45

Rat. Bad news, my lord. Morton is fled to Rich-
    mond;
And Buckingham, back'd with the hardy Welshmen,
Is in the field, and still his power increaseth.

K. Rich. Ely with Richmond troubles me more
    near
Than Buckingham and his rash-levied strength.   50
Come, I have learn'd that fearful commenting
Is leaden servitor to dull delay;
Delay leads impotent and snail-pac'd beggary.
Then fiery expedition be my wing,
Jove's Mercury, and herald for a king!   55
Go, muster men! My counsel is my shield;
We must be brief when traitors brave the field.
                        [*Exeunt.*

117. **Jack:** a figure in old clocks that strikes the bell. The general sense is, make an end of begging and leave me to my
meditation.

Sc. iii, 2. arch: extreme. 6. **flesh'd:** accustomed to slaughter. 18. **replenished:** complete. 31. **[at]** Q. *and* F. **after-
supper:** dessert. 34. **inheritor:** possessor. 42. **knot:** alliance. 50. **rash-levied:** hastily raised. 53. **leads:** leads to.

SCENE [IV. *Before the palace.*]

Enter old QUEEN MARGARET.

Q. Mar. So, now prosperity begins to mellow
And drop into the rotten mouth of death.
Here in these confines slily have I lurk'd
To watch the waning of mine enemies.
A dire induction am I witness to,   5
And will to France, hoping the consequence
Will prove as bitter, black, and tragical.
Withdraw thee, wretched Margaret; who comes
    here?   [*Retires.*]

Enter QUEEN ELIZABETH *and the* DUCHESS OF YORK.

Q. Eliz. Ah, my poor princes! ah, my tender
    babes!
My [unblown] flowers, new-appearing sweets!   10
If yet your gentle souls fly in the air
And be not fix'd in doom perpetual,
Hover about me with your airy wings
And hear your mother's lamentation!
Q. Mar. Hover about her; say that right for
    right   15
Hath dimm'd your infant morn to aged night.
Duch. So many miseries have craz'd my voic
That my woe-wearied tongue is still and mute.
Edward Plantagenet, why art thou dead?
Q. Mar. Plantagenet doth quit Plantagenet. 20
Edward for Edward pays a dying debt.
Q. Eliz. Wilt thou, O God, fly from such gentle
    lambs
And throw them in the entrails of the wolf?
When didst thou sleep when such a deed was done?
Q. Mar. When holy Harry died, and my sweet
    son.   25
Duch. Dead life, blind sight, poor mortal living
    ghost,
Woe's scene, world's shame, grave's due by life
    usurp'd,
Brief abstract and record of tedious days,
Rest thy unrest on England's lawful earth,
                          [*Sitting down.*]
Unlawfully made drunk with innocent blood!   30
Q. Eliz. Ah, that thou wouldst as soon afford a
    grave
As thou canst yield a melancholy seat!
Then would I hide my bones, not rest them here.
Ah, who hath any cause to mourn but we?
                      [*Sitting down by her.*]
Q. Mar. [*Coming forward.*] If ancient sorrow be
    most reverend,   35
Give mine the benefit of seniory,
And let my griefs frown on the upper hand.

If sorrow can admit society,
                  [*Sitting down with them.*]
[Tell o'er your woes again by viewing mine.]
I had an Edward, till a Richard kill'd him;   40
I had a [Harry], till a Richard kill'd him:
Thou hadst an Edward, till a Richard kill'd him;
Thou hadst a Richard, till a Richard kill'd him.
Duch. I had a Richard too, and thou didst kill
    him;
I had a Rutland too, thou holp'st to kill him. 45
Q. Mar. Thou hadst a Clarence too, and Richard
    kill'd him.
From forth the kennel of thy womb hath crept
A hell-hound that doth hunt us all to death.
That dog, that had his teeth before his eyes
To worry lambs and lap their gentle blood,   50
That foul defacer of God's handiwork,
That excellent grand tyrant of the earth
That reigns in galled eyes of weeping souls,
Thy womb let loose, to chase us to our graves.
O upright, just, and true-disposing God,   55
How do I thank thee that this carnal cur
Preys on the issue of his mother's body
And makes her pew-fellow with others' moan!
Duch. O Harry's wife, triumph not in my woes!
God witness with me, I have wept for thine.   60
Q. Mar. Bear with me; I am hungry for revenge,
And now I cloy me with beholding it.
Thy Edward he is dead, that kill'd my Edward;
The other Edward dead, to quit my Edward;
Young York he is but boot, because both they   65
Match not the high perfection of my loss.
Thy Clarence he is dead that stabb'd my Edward;
And the beholders of this frantic play,
The adulterate Hastings, Rivers, Vaughan, Grey,
Untimely smother'd in their dusky graves.   70
Richard yet lives, hell's black intelligencer,
Only reserv'd their factor to buy souls
And send them thither; but at hand, at hand,
Ensues his piteous and unpitied end.
Earth gapes, hell burns, fiends roar, saints pray, 75
To have him suddenly convey'd from hence.
Cancel his bond of life, dear God, I pray,
That I may live to say, "The dog is dead!"
Q. Eliz. O, thou didst prophesy the time would
    come
That I should wish for thee to help me curse   80
That bottl'd spider, that foul bunch-back'd toad!
Q. Mar. I call'd thee then vain flourish of my
    fortune;
I call'd thee then poor shadow, painted queen;
The presentation of but what I was;
The flattering index of a direful pageant;   85

Sc. iv, 5. **induction**: beginning. 6. **consequence**: sequel. 10. **[unblown]** Q. *unblowed* F. 15. **right for right**: avenging justice. 17. **craz'd**: cracked. 39. **[Tell...mine]** Q. Om. F. 41. **[Harry]** (Camb. edd.). *Husband* F. *Richard* Q. 52, 53. **That...souls**. So Capell. Transposed in F. 56. **carnal**: carnivorous. 58. **pew-fellow**: companion. 65. **boot**: something added to equalize a bargain. 69. **adulterate**: adulterous, with perhaps the added idea of base metal. 71. **intelligencer**: agent. 85. **index**: beginning.

One heav'd a-high, to be hurl'd down below;
A mother only mock'd with two fair babes;
A dream of what thou wast; a garish flag
To be the aim of every dangerous shot;
A sign of dignity, a breath, a bubble;   90
A queen in jest, only to fill the scene.
Where is thy husband now? Where be thy brothers?
Where be thy two sons? Wherein dost thou joy?
Who sues, and kneels, and says, "God save the
    Queen"?
Where be the bending peers that flattered thee?   95
Where be the thronging troops that followed thee?
Decline all this, and see what now thou art:
For happy wife, a most distressed widow;
For joyful mother, one that wails the name;
For queen, a very caitiff crown'd with care;   100
For one being sued to, one that humbly sues;
For she that scorn'd at me, now scorn'd of me;
For she being fear'd of all, now fearing one;
For she commanding all, obey'd of none.
Thus hath the course of justice whirl'd about   105
And left thee but a very prey to time,
Having no more but thought of what thou wast,
To torture thee the more, being what thou art.
Thou didst usurp my place, and dost thou not
Usurp the just proportion of my sorrow?   110
Now thy proud neck bears half my burden'd yoke
From which even here I slip my wearied head
And leave the burden of it all on thee.
Farewell, York's wife, and queen of sad mischance;
These English woes shall make me smile in France.
  Q. Eliz. O thou well skill'd in curses, stay a while
And teach me how to curse mine enemies!   117
  Q. Mar. Forbear to sleep the night, and fast the
    day;
Compare dead happiness with living woe;
Think that thy babes were sweeter than they were
And he that slew them fouler than he is.   121
Bett'ring thy loss makes the bad causer worse;
Revolving this will teach thee how to curse.
  Q. Eliz. My words are dull; O, quicken them with
    thine!
  Q. Mar. Thy woes will make them sharp and
    pierce like mine.   [*Exit.*   125
  Duch. Why should calamity be full of words?
  Q. Eliz. Windy attorneys to their [client] woes,
Airy succeeders of [intestate] joys,
Poor breathing orators of miseries,
Let them have scope! though what they will impart
Help nothing else, yet do they ease the heart.   131
  Duch. If so, then be not tongue-ti'd; go with me
And in the breath of bitter words let's smother

My damned son that thy two sweet sons smother'd.
The trumpet sounds; be copious in exclaims.   135

  Enter KING RICHARD *and his train, marching,
    with drums and trumpets.*

  K. Rich. Who intercepts me in my expedition?
  Duch. O, she that might have intercepted thee,
By strangling thee in her accursed womb,
From all the slaughters, wretch, that thou hast done!
  Q. Eliz. Hid'st thou that forehead with a golden
    crown   140
Where should be branded, if that right were right,
The slaughter of the prince that ow'd that crown,
And the dire death of my poor sons and brothers?
Tell me, thou villain slave, where are my children?
  Duch. Thou toad, thou toad, where is thy brother
    Clarence?   145
And little Ned Plantagenet, his son?
  Q. Eliz. Where is the gentle Rivers, Vaughan,
    Grey?
  Duch. Where is kind Hastings?
  K. Rich. A flourish, trumpets! strike alarum,
    drums!
Let not the heavens hear these tell-tale women
Rail on the Lord's anointed. Strike, I say!   150
                    [*Flourish. Alarums.*
Either be patient and entreat me fair,
Or with the clamorous report of war
Thus will I drown your exclamations.
  Duch. Art thou my son?
  K. Rich. Ay, I thank God, my father, and your-
    self.   155
  Duch. Then patiently hear my impatience.
  K. Rich. Madam, I have a touch of your condi-
    tion,
That cannot brook the accent of reproof.
  Duch. O, let me speak!
  K. Rich.   Do then; but I'll not hear.
  Duch. I will be mild and gentle in my words.
  K. Rich. And brief, good mother, for I am in
    haste.   161
  Duch. Art thou so hasty? I have stay'd for thee,
God knows, in torment and in agony.
  K. Rich. And came I not at last to comfort you?
  Duch. No, by the holy rood, thou know'st it well,
Thou cam'st on earth to make the earth my hell.   166
A grievous burden was thy birth to me;
Tetchy and wayward was thy infancy;
Thy school-days frightful, desp'rate, wild, and
    furious,   169
Thy prime of manhood daring, bold, and venturous,
Thy age confirm'd proud, subtle, sly, and bloody,

---

90. **sign:** symbol, not the thing itself. 97. **Decline:** recite in order. 100, 101. **For . . . me.** So Q. Transposed in F.
111. **burden'd:** burdensome. 127. **[client]** (Hanmer). *clients* F. 128. **[intestate]** Q: dead without bequeathing anything.
intestine F. 136. **expedition:** haste. 142. **ow'd:** owned. 146. **Ned Plantagenet:** Edward, Earl of Warwick, referred to in
IV.ii.56, but not as a victim of Richard's. 157. **condition:** disposition. 168. **Tetchy:** fretful. 171. **age confirm'd:** settled
middle age.

More mild, but yet more harmful, kind in hatred.
What comfortable hour canst thou name
That ever grac'd me with thy company?
   K. Rich. Faith, none, but Humphrey Hour, that
     call'd your Grace   175
To breakfast once forth of my company.
If I be so disgracious in your eye
Let me march on and not offend you, madam.
Strike up the drum.
   Duch.   I prithee, hear me speak.
   K. Rich. You speak too bitterly.
   Duch.   Hear me a word,
For I shall never speak to thee again.   181
   K. Rich. So.
   Duch. Either thou wilt die by God's just ordinance
Ere from this war thou turn a conqueror,
Or I with grief and extreme age shall perish   185
And never more behold thy face again.
Therefore take with thee my most grievous curse,
Which in the day of battle tire thee more
Than all the complete armour that thou wear'st!
My prayers on the adverse party fight;   190
And there the little souls of Edward's children
Whisper the spirits of thine enemies
And promise them success and victory.
Bloody thou art, bloody will be thy end;
Shame serves thy life and doth thy death attend.
                            [Exit.
   Q. Eliz. Though far more cause, yet much less
     spirit to curse   196
Abides in me; I say amen to her.
   K. Rich. Stay, madam; I must talk a word with
     you.
   Q. Eliz. I have no more sons of the royal blood
For thee to slaughter; for my daughters, Richard,
They shall be praying nuns, not weeping queens; 201
And therefore level not to hit their lives.
   K. Rich. You have a daughter call'd Elizabeth,
Virtuous and fair, royal and gracious.
   Q. Eliz. And must she die for this? O, let her
     live   205
And I'll corrupt her manners, stain her beauty,
Slander myself as false to Edward's bed,
Throw over her the veil of infamy.
So she may live unscarr'd of bleeding slaughter,
I will confess she was not Edward's daughter. 210
   K. Rich. Wrong not her birth, she is a royal
     princess.
   Q. Eliz. To save her life, I'll say she is not so.
   K. Rich. Her life is safest only in her birth.
   Q. Eliz. And only in that safety died her brothers.
   K. Rich. Lo, at their birth good stars were op-
     posite.   215

   Q. Eliz. No, to their lives ill friends were con-
     trary.
   K. Rich. All unavoided is the doom of destiny.
   Q. Eliz. True, when avoided grace makes destiny.
My babes were destin'd to a fairer death
If grace had bless'd thee with a fairer life.   220
   K. Rich. You speak as if that I had slain my
     cousins.
   Q. Eliz. Cousins, indeed; and by their uncle
     cozen'd
Of comfort, kingdom, kindred, freedom, life.
Whose hand soever lanc'd their tender hearts,
Thy head, all indirectly, gave direction.   225
No doubt the murd'rous knife was dull and blunt
Till it was whetted on thy stone-hard heart
To revel in the entrails of my lambs.
But that still use of grief makes wild grief tame,
My tongue should to thy ears not name my boys
Till that my nails were anchor'd in thine eyes; 230
And I, in such a desp'rate bay of death,
Like a poor bark of sails and tackling reft,
Rush all to pieces on thy rocky bosom.
   K. Rich. Madam, so thrive I in my enterprise 235
And dangerous success of bloody wars,
As I intend more good to you and yours
Than ever you or yours by me were harm'd!
   Q. Eliz. What good is cover'd with the face of
     heaven.
To be discover'd, that can do me good?   240
   K. Rich. Th' advancement of your children,
     gentle lady.
   Q. Eliz. Up to some scaffold, there to lose their
     heads?
   K. Rich. Unto the dignity and height of fortune,
The high imperial type of this earth's glory.
   Q. Eliz. Flatter my sorrow with report of it; 245
Tell me what state, what dignity, what honour,
Canst thou demise to any child of mine?
   K. Rich. Even all I have; ay, and myself and all
Will I withal endow a child of thine;
So in the Lethe of thy angry soul   250
Thou drown the sad remembrance of those wrongs
Which thou supposest I have done to thee.
   Q. Eliz. Be brief, lest that the process of thy
     kindness
Last longer telling than thy kindness' date.
   K. Rich. Then know, that from my soul I love
     thy daughter.   255
   Q. Eliz. My daughter's mother thinks it with her
     soul.
   K. Rich. What do you think?
   Q. Eliz. That thou dost love my daughter from
     thy soul.

So from thy soul's love didst thou love her brothers,
And from my heart's love I do thank thee for it.   260
　　K. Rich. Be not so hasty to confound my meaning.
I mean, that with my soul I love thy daughter,
And do intend to make her Queen of England.
　　Q. Eliz. Well then, who dost thou mean shall be
　　her king?
　　K. Rich. Even he that makes her queen.   Who
　　else should be?   265
　　Q. Eliz. What, thou?
　　K. Rich. Even so.   How think you of it?
　　Q. Eliz. How canst thou woo her?
　　K. Rich.   That I would learn of you,
As one being best acquainted with her humour.
　　Q. Eliz. And wilt thou learn of me?
　　K. Rich.   Madam, with all my heart.
　　Q. Eliz. Send to her by the man that slew her
　　brothers   271
A pair of bleeding hearts; thereon engrave
Edward and York; then haply will she weep.
Therefore present to her, — as sometime Margaret
Did to thy father, steep'd in Rutland's blood, —   275
A handkerchief; which, say to her, did drain
The purple sap from her sweet brother's body;
And bid her wipe her weeping eyes withal.
If this inducement move her not to love,
Send her a letter of thy noble deeds.   280
Tell her thou mad'st away her uncle Clarence,
Her uncle Rivers; ay, and, for her sake,
Mad'st quick conveyance with her good aunt Anne.
　　K. Rich. You mock me, madam; this is not the
　　way   284
To win your daughter.
　　Q. Eliz.   There is no other way,
Unless thou couldst put on some other shape
And not be Richard that hath done all this.
　　K. Rich. Say that I did all this for love of her.
　　Q. Eliz. Nay, then indeed she cannot choose but
　　hate thee,
Having bought love with such a bloody spoil.   290
　　K. Rich. Look, what is done cannot be now
　　amended.
Men shall deal unadvisedly sometimes,
Which after hours gives leisure to repent.
If I did take the kingdom from your sons,
To make amends I'll give it to your daughter.   295
If I have kill'd the issue of your womb,
To quicken your increase, I will beget
Mine issue of your blood upon your daughter.
A grandam's name is little less in love
Than is the doting title of a mother;   300
They are as children but one step below,
Even of your mettle, of your very blood;
Of all one pain, save for a night of groans
Endur'd of her, for whom you bid like sorrow.

Your children were vexation to your youth,   305
But mine shall be a comfort to your age.
The loss you have is but a son being king,
And by that loss your daughter is made queen.
I cannot make you what amends I would,
Therefore accept such kindness as I can.   310
Dorset your son, that with a fearful soul
Leads discontented steps in foreign soil,
This fair alliance quickly shall call home
To high promotions and great dignity.
The King, that calls your beauteous daughter wife,
Familiarly shall call thy Dorset brother;   316
Again shall you be mother to a king,
And all the ruins of distressful times
Repair'd with double riches of content.
What! we have many goodly days to see.   320
The liquid drops of tears that you have shed
Shall come again, transform'd to orient pearl,
Advantaging their [loan] with interest
Of ten times double gain of happiness.
Go, then, my mother, to thy daughter go;   325
Make bold her bashful years with your experience;
Prepare her ears to hear a wooer's tale;
Put in her tender heart th' aspiring flame
Of golden sovereignty; acquaint the princess
With the sweet silent hours of marriage joys;   330
And when this arm of mine hath chastised
The petty rebel, dull-brain'd Buckingham,
Bound with triumphant garlands will I come
And lead thy daughter to a conqueror's bed;
To whom I will retail my conquest won.   335
And she shall be sole victress, Cæsar's Cæsar.
　　Q. Eliz. What were I best to say?   Her father's
　　brother
Would be her lord?   Or shall I say, her uncle?
Or, he that slew her brothers and her uncles?
Under what title shall I woo for thee,   340
That God, the law, my honour, and her love
Can make seem pleasing to her tender years?
　　K. Rich. Infer fair England's peace by this alliance.
　　Q. Eliz. Which she shall purchase with still lasting
　　war.
　　K. Rich. Tell her the King, that may command,
　　entreats.   345
　　Q. Eliz. That at her hands which the King's king
　　forbids.
　　K. Rich. Say she shall be a high and mighty
　　queen.
　　Q. Eliz. To wail the title, as her mother doth.
　　K. Rich. Say, I will love her everlastingly.
　　Q. Eliz. But how long shall that title "ever"
　　last?   350
　　K. Rich. Sweetly in force unto her fair life's end.
　　Q. Eliz. But how long fairly shall her sweet life
　　last?

---

283. **conveyance:** riddance.   290. **spoil:** booty.   304. **bid:** did bide, suffered.   323. **[loan]** (Theobald).   *loue* F.   335. **retail:** relate.   343. **Infer:** allege.

K. Rich. As long as heaven and nature lengthens it.

Q. Eliz. As long as hell and Richard likes of it.

K. Rich. Say, I, her sovereign, am her subject low.

Q. Eliz. But she, your subject, loathes such sovereignty.   356

K. Rich. Be eloquent in my behalf to her.

Q. Eliz. An honest tale speeds best being plainly told.

K. Rich. Then plainly to her tell my loving tale.

Q. Eliz. Plain and not honest is too harsh a style.

K. Rich. Your reasons are too shallow and too quick.   361

Q. Eliz. O no, my reasons are too deep and dead;
Too deep and dead, poor infants, in their graves.

K. Rich. Harp not on that string, madam; that is past.

Q. Eliz. Harp on it still shall I till heartstrings break.   365

K. Rich. Now, by my George, my Garter, and my crown, —

Q. Eliz. Profan'd, dishonour'd, and the third usurp'd.

K. Rich. I swear —

Q. Eliz.   By nothing; for this is no oath.
Thy George, profan'd, hath lost his lordly honour;
Thy Garter, blemish'd, pawn'd his knightly virtue;
Thy crown, usurp'd, disgrac'd his kingly glory.   371
If something thou wouldst swear to be believ'd,
Swear then by something that thou hast not wrong'd.

K. Rich. Now, by the world —

Q. Eliz.   'Tis full of thy foul wrongs.

K. Rich. My father's death —

Q. Eliz.   Thy life hath it dishonour'd.   375

K. Rich. Then, by myself —

Q. Eliz.   Thyself [thyself misusest].

K. Rich. Why then, by [God] —

Q. Eliz.   [God's] wrong is most of all.
If thou did'st fear to break an oath with Him,
The unity the King my husband made
Thou hadst not broken, nor my brothers died.   380
If thou hadst fear'd to break an oath by Him,
Th' imperial metal, circling now thy head,
Had grac'd the tender temples of my child,
And both the Princes had been breathing here,
Which now, two tender bedfellows for dust,   385
Thy broken faith hath made the prey for worms.
What canst thou swear by now?

K. Rich.   The time to come.

Q. Eliz. That thou hast wronged in the time o'erpast;
For I myself have many tears to wash

Hereafter time, for time past wrong'd by thee.   390
The children live whose fathers thou hast slaughter'd,
Ungovern'd youth, to wail it with their age;
The parents live whose children thou hast butcher'd,
Old barren plants, to wail it with their age.
Swear not by time to come; for that thou hast
Misus'd ere us'd, by times ill-us'd [o'erpast].   396

K. Rich. As I intend to prosper and repent,
So thrive I in my dangerous affairs
Of hostile arms! Myself myself confound!
Heaven and fortune bar me happy hours!   400
Day, yield me not thy light, nor, night, thy rest!
Be opposite all planets of good luck
To my proceeding, if, with dear heart's love,
Immaculate devotion, holy thoughts,
I tender not thy beauteous princely daughter!   405
In her consists my happiness and thine;
Without her, follows to myself and thee,
Herself, the land, and many a Christian soul,
Death, desolation, ruin, and decay.
It cannot be avoided but by this;   410
It will not be avoided but by this.
Therefore, dear mother, — I must call you so —
Be the attorney of my love to her.
Plead what I will be, not what I have been;
Not my deserts, but what I will deserve.   415
Urge the necessity and state of times,
And be not [peevish-fond] in great designs.

Q. Eliz. Shall I be tempted of the devil thus?

K. Rich. Ay, if the devil tempt you to do good.

Q. Eliz. Shall I forget myself to be myself?   420

K. Rich. Ay, if yourself's remembrance wrong yourself.

Q. Eliz. Yet thou didst kill my children.

K. Rich. But in your daughter's womb I bury them;
Where in that nest of spicery they will breed
Selves of themselves to your recomforture.   425

Q. Eliz. Shall I go win my daughter to thy will?

K. Rich. And be a happy mother by the deed.

Q. Eliz. I go. Write to me very shortly,
And you shall understand from me her mind.

K. Rich. Bear me her true love's kiss; and so, farewell.   [*Exit Queen Elizabeth.* 430
Relenting fool, and shallow changing woman!

Enter RATCLIFF [CATESBY *following*].

How now! what news?

Rat. Most mighty sovereign, on the western coast
Rideth a puissant navy; to our shores
Throng many doubtful hollow-hearted friends,   435
Unarm'd, and unresolv'd to beat them back.

---

361. **quick:** hasty, but in l. 362 it is taken as *living*. 366. **George:** the pendant of St. George and the Dragon which hung from the collar of the Order of the Garter. 376. *K. Rich. . . . misusest*]. So Q. After 373 in F. [thyself misusest] Q. *is self misus'd* F. 377. [God] — [God's], Q. *Heaven. Heavens* F. 396. [o'erpast] Q. *repast* F. 405. **tender:** cherish. 417. [peevish-fond] (Staunton). *pievish, fond* Q. *peevish found* F. 424. **nest of spicery:** a reference to the nest of the Phœnix.

'Tis thought that Richmond is their admiral;
And there they hull, expecting but the aid
Of Buckingham to welcome them ashore.

 K. Rich. Some light-foot friend post to the Duke
  of Norfolk;   440
Ratcliff, thyself, or Catesby; where is he?

 Cate. Here, my good lord.

 K. Rich.   Catesby, fly to the Duke. 442a

 Cate. I will, my lord, with all convenient
  haste.   442b

 K. Rich. [Ratcliff], come hither. Post to Salisbury.
When thou com'st thither, — [*To Catesby.*] Dull
  unmindful villain,
Why stay'st thou here, and go'st not to the Duke?

 Cate. First, mighty liege, tell me your Highness'
  pleasure,   446
What from your Grace I shall deliver to him.

 K. Rich. O, true, good Catesby. Bid him levy
  straight
The greatest strength and power that he can make,
And meet me suddenly at Salisbury.   450

 Cate. I go.   [*Exit.*

 Rat. What, may it please you, shall I do at
  Salisbury?

 K. Rich. Why, what wouldst thou do there before
  I go?

 Rat. Your Highness told me I should post before.

 K. Rich. My mind is chang'd.   456

    Enter LORD STANLEY.

     Stanley, what news with you?

 Stan. None good, my liege, to please you with
  the hearing;
Nor none so bad but may well be reported.

 K. Rich. Hoyday, a riddle! neither good nor bad!
What need'st thou run so many miles about 461
When thou mayst tell thy tale the nearest way?
Once more, what news?

 Stan.   Richmond is on the seas.

 K. Rich. There let him sink, and be the seas on
  him!
White-liver'd runagate, what doth he there? 465

 Stan. I know not, mighty sovereign, but by guess.

 K. Rich. Well, as you guess?

 Stan. Stirr'd up by Dorset, Buckingham, and
  Morton,
He makes for England, here to claim the crown.

 K. Rich. Is the chair empty? Is the sword un-
  sway'd?   470
Is the King dead? the empire unpossess'd?
What heir of York is there alive but we?
And who is England's king but great York's heir?
Then, tell me, what makes he upon the seas? 474

 Stan. Unless for that, my liege, I cannot guess.

 K. Rich. Unless for that he comes to be your liege
You cannot guess wherefore the Welshman comes?
Thou wilt revolt, and fly to him, I fear.

 Stan. No, my good lord, therefore mistrust me
  not.

 K. Rich. Where is thy power, then, to beat him
  back?   480
Where be thy tenants and thy followers?
Are they not now upon the western shore,
Safe-conducting the rebels from their ships?

 Stan. No, my good lord, my friends are in the
  north.

 K. Rich. Cold friends to me! What do they in
  the north   485
When they should serve their sovereign in the west?

 Stan. They have not been commanded, mighty
  King.
Pleaseth your Majesty to give me leave,
I'll muster up my friends and meet your Grace
Where and what time your Majesty shall please.

 K. Rich. Ay, ay, thou wouldst be gone to join
  with Richmond;   491
But I'll not trust thee.

 Stan.   Most mighty sovereign,
You have no cause to hold my friendship doubtful.
I never was nor never will be false.

 K. Rich. Go, then, and muster men; but leave
  behind   496
Your son, George Stanley. Look your heart be
  firm,
Or else his head's assurance is but frail.

 Stan. So deal with him as I prove true to you.
         [*Exit.*

    Enter a Messenger.

 1. Mess. My gracious sovereign, now in Devon-
  shire,   500
As I by friends am well advertised,
Sir Edward Courtney, and the haughty prelate,
Bishop of Exeter, his elder brother,
With many moe confederates, are in arms.

    Enter another MESSENGER.

 2. Mess. In Kent, my liege, the Guildfords are in
  arms;   505
And every hour more competitors
Flock to the rebels, and their power grows strong.

    Enter another MESSENGER.

 3. Mess. My lord, the army of great Buckingham —

 K. Rich. Out on ye, owls! nothing but songs of
  death?   [*He striketh him.* 509
There, take thou that till thou bring better news.

 3. Mess. The news I have to tell your Majesty

---

438. **hull**: drift. 443. **[Ratcliff]** (Rowe). *Catesby* F. 465. **runagate**: renegade. 477. **Welshman**: the Tudors were Welsh.
501. **advertised**: informed. 506. **competitors**: associates.

Is that by sudden floods and fall of waters
Buckingham's army is dispers'd and scatter'd;
And he himself wand'red away alone,
No man knows whither.

 K. Rich.   I cry thee mercy; 515
There is my purse to cure that blow of thine.
Hath any well-advised friend proclaim'd
Reward to him that brings the traitor in?

 3. Mess. Such proclamation hath been made, my
  lord.

    Enter another MESSENGER.

 4. Mess. Sir Thomas Lovel and Lord Marquis
  Dorset, 520
'Tis said, my liege, in Yorkshire are in arms.
But this good comfort bring I to your Highness,
The Breton navy is dispers'd by tempest.
Richmond in Dorsetshire sent out a boat
Unto the shore, to ask those on the banks 525
If they were his assistants, yea or no;
Who answer'd him, they came from Buckingham
Upon his party. He, mistrusting them,
Hois'd sail and made his course again for Brittany.

 K. Rich. March on, march on, since we are up in
  arms; 530
If not to fight with foreign enemies,
Yet to beat down these rebels here at home.

    Re-enter CATESBY.

 Cate. My liege, the Duke of Buckingham is
  taken;
That is the best news. That the Earl of Richmond
Is with a mighty power landed at Milford, 535
Is colder news, but yet they must be told.

 K. Rich. Away towards Salisbury! While we
  reason here
A royal battle might be won and lost.
Some one take order Buckingham be brought
To Salisbury; the rest march on with me. 540
        [Flourish. Exeunt.

    SCENE [V. *Lord Derby's house.*]

Enter DERBY *and* SIR CHRISTOPHER [URSWICK].

 Der. Sir Christopher, tell Richmond this from
  me,
That in the sty of the most deadly boar
My son George Stanley is frank'd up in hold;
If I revolt, off goes young George's head.
The fear of that holds off my present aid. 5
So get thee gone; commend me to thy lord.
Withal say that the Queen hath heartily consented
He should espouse Elizabeth her daughter.
But, tell me, where is princely Richmond now?

 Chris. At Pembroke or at Ha'rford-west in
  Wales. 10
 Der. What men of name resort to him?
 Chris. Sir Walter Herbert, a renowned soldier;
Sir Gilbert Talbot, Sir William Stanley,
Oxford, redoubted Pembroke, Sir James Blunt,
And Rice ap Thomas, with a valiant crew, 15
And many other of great name and worth;
And towards London do they bend their power
If by the way they be not fought withal.

 Der. Well, hie thee to thy lord; I kiss his hand.
My letter will resolve him of my mind. 20
Farewell.   *[Gives letter, and] exeunt.*

      ACT V

  SCENE I. [*Salisbury. An open place.*]

Enter [*the* SHERIFF, *and*] BUCKINGHAM, *with halberds,*
    led to execution.

 Buck. Will not King Richard let me speak with
  him?
 Sher. No, my good lord; therefore be patient.
 Buck. Hastings, and Edward's children, Grey
  and Rivers,
Holy King Henry and thy fair son Edward,
Vaughan, and all that have miscarried 5
By underhand corrupted foul injustice,
If that your moody discontented souls
Do through the clouds behold this present hour,
Even for revenge mock my destruction!
This is All-Souls' day, fellow, is it not? 10
 Sher. It is [my lord].
 Buck. Why, then All-Souls' day is my body's
  doomsday.
This is the day which, in King Edward's time,
I wish'd might fall on me when I was found
False to his children and his wife's allies; 15
This is the day wherein I wish'd to fall
By the false faith of him whom most I trusted;
This, this All-Souls' day to my fearful soul
Is the determin'd respite of my wrongs.
That high All-Seer, which I dallied with, 20
Hath turn'd my feigned prayer on my head
And given in earnest what I begg'd in jest;
Thus doth He force the swords of wicked men
To turn their own points in their masters' bosoms.
Now Margaret's curse falls heavy on my neck: 25
"When he," quoth she, "shall split thy heart with
  sorrow,
Remember Margaret was a prophetess."
Come, lead me, officers, to the block of shame;
Wrong hath but wrong, and blame the due of
  blame.
         [Exeunt.

Sc. v, 3. frank'd: penned. hold: prison.
Act V, sc. i, 7. moody: angry. 11. [my lord] Q. Om. F. 19. determin'd ... wrongs: date fixed to end my wrong-doing.

SCENE II. [*The camp near Tamworth.*]

Enter RICHMOND, OXFORD, BLUNT, HERBERT, *and
others, with drum and colours.*

Richm. Fellows in arms, and my most loving
   friends,
Bruis'd underneath the yoke of tyranny,
Thus far into the bowels of the land
Have we march'd on without impediment;
And here receive we from our father Stanley   5
Lines of fair comfort and encouragement.
The wretched, bloody, and usurping boar,
That spoil'd your summer fields and fruitful vines,
Swills your warm blood like wash and makes his
   trough
In your embowell'd bosoms, this foul swine   10
Is now even in the centre of this isle,
Near to the town of Leicester as we learn.
From Tamworth thither is but one day's march.
In God's name, cheerly on, courageous friends,
To reap the harvest of perpetual peace   15
By this one bloody trial of sharp war.
  Oxf. Every man's conscience is a thousand men
To fight against this guilty homicide.
  Herb. I doubt not but his friends will turn to us.
  Blunt. He hath no friends but what are friends for
   fear,   20
Which in his dearest need will fly from him.
  Richm. All for our vantage. Then, in God's name,
  march!
True hope is swift and flies with swallow's wings,
Kings it makes gods and meaner creatures kings.
                        [*Exeunt.*

[SCENE III.   *Bosworth Field.*]

Enter KING RICHARD, *in arms, with* NORFOLK, *the*
EARL OF SURREY, RATCLIFF [*and others*].

  K. Rich. Here pitch our tent, even here in Bos-
  worth field.
My Lord of Surrey, why look you so sad?
  Sur. My heart is ten times lighter than my looks.
  K. Rich. My Lord of Norfolk, —
  Nor.   Here, most gracious liege.
  K. Rich. Norfolk, we must have knocks; ha!
  must we not?   5
  Nor. We must both give and take, my loving
  lord.
  K. Rich. Up with my tent! Here will I lie to-
  night —
But where to-morrow? Well, all's one for that.
Who hath descried the number of the traitors?
  Nor. Six or seven thousand is their utmost
  power.   10

  K. Rich. Why, our battalia treble that account;
Besides, the King's name is a tower of strength
Which they upon the adverse faction want.
Up with the tent! Come, noble gentlemen,
Let us survey the vantage of the ground.   15
Call for some men of sound direction;
Let's lack no discipline, make no delay;
For, lords, to-morrow is a busy day.   [*Exeunt.*

E.iter [*on the other side of the field*] RICHMOND, SIR
  WILLIAM BRANDON, OXFORD, DORSET [BLUNT,
  and others. Some of the Soldiers *pitch Richmond's
  tent*].

  Richm. The weary sun hath made a golden set
And by the bright [track] of his fiery car   20
Gives token of a goodly day to-morrow.
Sir William Brandon, you shall bear my standard.
Give me some ink and paper in my tent;
I'll draw the form and model of our battle,
Limit each leader to his several charge,   25
And part in just proportion our small power.
My Lord of Oxford, you, Sir William Brandon,
And you, Sir Walter Herbert, stay with me.
The Earl of Pembroke keeps his regiment;
Good Captain Blunt, bear my good-night to him   30
And by the second hour in the morning
Desire the Earl to see me in my tent.
Yet one thing more, good captain, do for me:
Where is Lord Stanley quarter'd, do you know?
  Blunt. Unless I have mista'en his colours much,
Which well I am assur'd I have not done,   36
His regiment lies half a mile at least
South from the mighty power of the King.
  Richm. If without peril it be possible,
Sweet Blunt, make some good means to speak with
  him.   40
And give him from me this most needful note.
  Blunt. Upon my life, my lord, I'll undertake it;
And so, God give you quiet rest to-night!
  Richm. Good-night, good Captain Blunt. Come,
    gentlemen,   [*Exit Blunt.*]
Let us consult upon to-morrow's business.   45
Into my tent; the dew is raw and cold.
               [*They withdraw into the tent.*

Enter [*to his tent*] KING RICHARD, NORFOLK, RAT-
  CLIFF, CATESBY [*and others*].

  K. Rich. What is't o'clock?
  Cate.   It's supper-time, my lord;
It's nine o'clock.
  K. Rich.   I will not sup to-night.
Give me some ink and paper.
What, is my beaver easier than it was,   50
And all my armour laid into my tent?

Sc. ii, 5. father: stepfather. 9. wash: swill. 10. embowell'd: disembowelled.
Sc. iii, 11. battalia: army. 16. direction: military judgment. 20. [track] Q. tract F. 25. Limit: appoint. 29. keeps:
stays with. 50. beaver: face part of the helmet.

Cate. It is, my liege; and all things are in readiness.

K. Rich. Good Norfolk, hie thee to thy charge;
Use careful watch, choose trusty sentinels.

Nor. I go, my lord.   55

K. Rich. Stir with the lark to-morrow, gentle Norfolk.

Nor. I warrant you, my lord.   [*Exit.*

K. Rich. [Catesby!

Cate.] My lord?

K. Rich.   Send out a pursuivant at arms
To Stanley's regiment; bid him bring his power
Before sunrising, lest his son George fall   61
Into the blind cave of eternal night.

                                        [*Exit Catesby.*]

Fill me a bowl of wine. Give me a watch.
Saddle white Surrey for the field to-morrow.
Look that my staves be sound, and not too heavy.
Ratcliff!   66

Rat. My lord?

K. Rich. Saw'st the melancholy Lord Northumberland?

Rat. Thomas the Earl of Surrey, and himself,
Much about cock-shut time, from troop to troop   70
Went through the army, cheering up the soldiers.

K. Rich. So, I am satisfied. Give me a bowl of wine.
I have not that alacrity of spirit
Nor cheer of mind that I was wont to have.
Set it down. Is ink and paper ready?   75

Rat. It is, my lord.

K. Rich.   Bid my guard watch; leave me.
Ratcliff, about the mid of night come to my tent
And help to arm me. Leave me, I say.

          [*Exeunt Ratcliff [and the other Attendants.
          Richard sleeps*].

Enter DERBY *to* RICHMOND *in his tent.* [*Lords and
                    others attending.*]

Der. Fortune and victory sit on thy helm!

Richm. All comfort that the dark night can afford
Be to thy person, noble father-in-law!   81
Tell me, how fares our [loving] mother?

Der. I, by attorney, bless thee from thy mother,
Who prays continually for Richmond's good.
So much for that. The silent hours steal on   85
And flaky darkness breaks within the east.
In brief, — for so, the season bids us be, —
Prepare thy battle early in the morning,
And put thy fortune to th' arbitrement
Of bloody strokes and mortal-staring war.   90
I, as I may — that which I would I cannot, —
With best advantage will deceive the time

And aid thee in this doubtful shock of arms;
But on thy side I may not be too forward
Lest, being seen, thy brother, tender George,   95
Be executed in his father's sight.
Farewell! The leisure and the fearful time
Cuts off the ceremonious vows of love
And ample interchange of sweet discourse
Which so long sund'red friends should dwell upon.
God give us leisure for these rites of love!   101
Once more, adieu! Be valiant, and speed well!

Richm. Good lords, conduct him to his regiment.
I'll strive with troubled noise to take a nap
Lest leaden slumber peise me down to-morrow 105
When I should mount with wings of victory.
Once more, good-night, kind lords and gentlemen.

                    [*Exeunt all but Richmond.*

O Thou whose captain I account myself,
Look on my forces with a gracious eye!
Put in their hands thy bruising irons of wrath   110
That they may crush down with a heavy fall
The usurping helmets of our adversaries!
Make us thy ministers of chastisement
That we may praise Thee in the victory!
To Thee I do commend my watchful soul   115
Ere I let fall the windows of mine eyes.
Sleeping and waking, O, defend me still!   [*Sleeps.*

Enter the Ghost of PRINCE EDWARD, *son to
            Henry the Sixth.*

Ghost. (*To Richard.*) Let me sit heavy on thy
          soul to-morrow!
Think, how thou stabb'dst me in my prime of youth
At Tewksbury. Despair, therefore, and die!   120
(*To Richmond.*) Be cheerful, Richmond; for the
          wronged souls
Of butcher'd princes fight in thy behalf.
King Henry's issue, Richmond, comforts thee.

Enter the Ghost of HENRY THE SIXTH.

Ghost. (*To Richard.*) When I was mortal, my
          anointed body
By thee was punched full of [deadly] holes.   125
Think on the Tower and me. Despair, and die!
Harry the Sixth bids thee despair and die.
(*To Richmond.*) Virtuous and holy, be thou conqueror!
Harry, that prophesied thou shouldst be king,
Doth comfort thee in sleep. Live, and flourish!

Enter the Ghost of CLARENCE.

Ghost. [*To Richard.*] Let me sit heavy in thy soul
          to-morrow!   131
I, that was wash'd to death with fulsome wine,

---

58. [Catesby! *Cate.*] Q. *Ratcliffe. Rat.* F.   63. **watch:** watch-light, candle.   65. **staves:** shafts of my lances.   70. **cock-shut:** sunset.   81. **father-in-law:** stepfather.   82. [loving] Q. *noble* F.   89. **arbitrement:** decision.   92. **With . . . time:** cheat Richard at the best opportunity.   97. **leisure:** lack of leisure.   105. **peise:** weigh.   125. [deadly] Q. Om. F.   132. **fulsome:** cloying.

Poor Clarence, by thy guile betray'd to death!
To-morrow in the battle think on me
And fall thy edgeless sword. Despair, and die!
(*To Richmond.*) Thou offspring of the house of
 Lancaster,   136
The wronged heirs of York do pray for thee.
Good angels guard thy battle! Live, and flourish!

Enter the Ghosts of RIVERS, GREY, *and* VAUGHAN.

 Ghost of R. [*To Richard.*] Let me sit heavy in thy
  soul to-morrow,
Rivers, that died at Pomfret! Despair, and die! 140
 Ghost of G. [*To Richard.*] Think upon Grey, and
  let thy soul despair!
 Ghost of V. [*To Richard.*] Think upon Vaughan,
  and with guilty fear
Let fall thy lance. Despair, and die!
 All. (*To Richmond.*) Awake, and think our
  wrongs in Richard's bosom
Will conquer him! Awake, and win the day! 145

Enter the Ghost of HASTINGS.

 Ghost. [*To Richard.*] Bloody and guilty, guiltily
  awake,
And in a bloody battle end thy days!
Think on Lord Hastings. Despair, and die!
(*To Richmond.*) Quiet untroubled soul, awake,
 awake!
Arm, fight, and conquer, for fair England's sake! 150

Enter the Ghosts of the two young Princes.

 Ghosts. (*To Richard.*) Dream on thy cousins
  smothered in the Tower.
Let us be lead within thy bosom, Richard,
And weigh thee down to ruin, shame, and death!
Thy nephews' souls bid thee despair and die!
(*To Richmond.*) Sleep, Richmond, sleep in peace
 and wake in joy.   155
Good angels guard thee from the boar's annoy!
Live, and beget a happy race of kings!
Edward's unhappy sons do bid thee flourish.

Enter the Ghost of LADY ANNE.

 Ghost. (*To Richard.*) Richard, thy wife, that
  wretched Anne thy wife,
That never slept a quiet hour with thee, 160
Now fills thy sleep with perturbations.
To-morrow in the battle think on me
And fall thy edgeless sword. Despair, and die!
(*To Richmond.*) Thou quiet soul, sleep thou a quiet
 sleep;
Dream of success and happy victory! 165
Thy adversary's wife doth pray for thee.

Enter the Ghost of BUCKINGHAM.

 Ghost. (*To Richard.*) The first was I that help'd
  thee to the crown;
The last was I that felt thy tyranny.
O, in the battle think on Buckingham,
And die in terror of thy guiltiness! 170
Dream on, dream on, of bloody deeds and death;
Fainting, despair; despairing, yield thy breath!
(*To Richmond.*) I died for hope ere I could lend thee
 aid;
But cheer thy heart, and be thou not dismay'd.
God and good angels fight on Richmond's side,
And Richard fall in height of all his pride! 176
  [*The Ghosts vanish. King*] *Richard starts
  out of his dream.*
 K. Rich. Give me another horse! Bind up my
  wounds!
Have mercy, Jesu! — Soft! I did but dream.
O coward conscience, how dost thou afflict me!
The lights burn blue. It is now dead midnight. 180
Cold fearful drops stand on my trembling flesh.
What! do I fear myself? There's none else by.
Richard loves Richard; that is, I am I.
Is there a murderer here? No. Yes, I am.
Then fly. What, from myself? Great reason
 why,   185
Lest I revenge. What, myself upon myself?
Alack, I love myself. Wherefore? For any good
That I myself have done unto myself?
O, no! alas, I rather hate myself
For hateful deeds committed by myself! 190
I am a villain: yet I lie, I am not.
Fool, of thyself speak well; fool, do not flatter.
My conscience hath a thousand several tongues,
And every tongue brings in a several tale,
And every tale condemns me for a villain. 195
Perjury, [perjury,] in the high'st degree;
Murder, stern murder, in the dir'st degree;
All several sins, all us'd in each degree,
Throng to the bar, crying all, Guilty! guilty!
I shall despair. There is no creature loves me,
And if I die no soul shall pity me. 201
Nay, wherefore should they, since that I myself
Find in myself no pity to myself?
Methought the souls of all that I had murder'd
Came to my tent; and every one did threat 205
To-morrow's vengeance on the head of Richard.

Enter RATCLIFF.

 Rat. My lord!
 K. Rich. ['Zounds!] who's there?
 Rat. Ratcliff, my lord; 'tis I. The early village-
 cock
Hath twice done salutation to the morn; 210
Your friends are up and buckle on their armour.

156. **boar's annoy:** harm from Richard.   173. **for hope:** hoping to give aid.   180. **burn blue:** sign of a ghost's presence.
196. [perjury] Q. Om. F.   198. **us'd:** committed.   208. ['Zounds] Q. Om. F.

K. Rich. [O Ratcliff, I have dream'd a fearful dream!
What thinkest thou, will our friends prove all true?
Rat. No doubt, my lord.]
K. Rich. O Ratcliff, I fear, I fear, —
Rat. Nay, good my lord, be not afraid of shadows.
K. Rich. By the apostle Paul, shadows to-night 216
Have struck more terror to the soul of Richard
Than can the substance of ten thousand soldiers
Armed in proof and led by shallow Richmond.
It is not yet near day. Come, go with me; 220
Under our tents I'll play the eaves-dropper,
To hear if any mean to shrink from me. [*Exeunt.*

Enter the LORDS *to* RICHMOND, *sitting in his tent.*
Lords. Good morrow, Richmond!
Richm. Cry mercy, lords and watchful gentlemen,
That you have ta'en a tardy sluggard here. 225
Lords. How have you slept, my lord?
Richm. The sweetest sleep and fairest-boding dreams
That ever ent'red in a drowsy head
Have I since your departure had, my lords.
Methought their souls whose bodies Richard murder'd 230
Came to my tent and cried on victory.
I promise you, my heart is very jocund
In the remembrance of so fair a dream.
How far into the morning is it, lords?
Lords. Upon the stroke of four. 235
Richm. Why, then 'tis time to arm and give direction.

His oration to his soldiers.
More than I have said, loving countrymen,
The leisure and enforcement of the time
Forbids to dwell upon; yet remember this,
God and our good cause fight upon our side; 240
The prayers of holy saints and wronged souls,
Like high-rear'd bulwarks, stand before our faces.
Richard except, those whom we fight against
Had rather have us win than him they follow.
For what is he they follow? Truly, gentlemen,
A bloody tyrant and a homicide; 246
One rais'd in blood, and one in blood establish'd;
One that made means to come by what he hath
And slaughter'd those that were the means to help him;
A base foul stone, made precious by the foil 250
Of England's chair, where he is falsely set;
One that hath ever been God's enemy.
Then, if you fight against God's enemy,
God will in justice ward you as his soldiers;

If you do [sweat] to put a tyrant down, 255
You sleep in peace, the tyrant being slain;
If you do fight against your country's foes,
Your country's fat shall pay your pains the hire;
If you do fight in safeguard of your wives,
Your wives shall welcome home the conquerors; 260
If you do free your children from the sword,
Your children's children quits it in your age.
Then, in the name of God and all these rights,
Advance your standards, draw your willing swords.
For me, the ransom of my bold attempt 265
Shall be this cold corpse on the earth's cold face;
But if I thrive, the gain of my attempt
The least of you shall share his part thereof.
Sound drums and trumpets boldly and cheerfully; 269
God and Saint George! Richmond and victory!
[*Exeunt.*

Re-enter KING RICHARD, RATCLIFF, CATESBY
[*Attendants and Forces*].
K. Rich. What said Northumberland as touching Richmond?
Rat. That he was never trained up in arms.
K. Rich. He said the truth; and what said Surrey then?
Rat. He smil'd and said, "The better for our purpose."
K. Rich. He was in the right; and so indeed it is. [*Clock strikes.* 275
Tell the clock there. Give me a calendar.
Who saw the sun to-day?
Rat. Not I, my lord.
K. Rich. Then he disdains to shine, for by the book
He should have brav'd the east an hour ago.
A black day will it be to somebody. 280
Ratcliff!
Rat. My lord?
K. Rich. The sun will not be seen to-day;
The sky doth frown and lour upon our army.
I would these dewy tears were from the ground.
Not shine to-day! Why, what is that to me 285
More than to Richmond? for the self-same heaven
That frowns on me looks sadly upon him.

Enter NORFOLK.
Nor. Arm, arm, my lord; the foe vaunts in the field.
K. Rich. Come, bustle, bustle; caparison my horse.
Call up Lord Stanley, bid him bring his power. 290
I will lead forth my soldiers to the plain,
And thus my battle shall be ordered:
My foreward shall be drawn [out all] in length,

212–214. [O . . . lord] Q. Om. F. 219. **proof:** tested armor. 250. **foil:** leaf of metal placed under a precious stone to increase its brilliance. 255. [sweat] Q and Holinshed. *sweare* F. 265. **ransom:** price. 276. **Tell:** count (the strokes). 279. **brav'd:** made splendid. 288. **vaunts:** swaggers. 293. **foreward:** vanguard. [out all] Q. Om. F.

Consisting equally of horse and foot;
Our archers shall be placed in the midst;   295
John Duke of Norfolk, Thomas Earl of Surrey,
Shall have the leading of the foot and horse.
They thus directed, we will follow
In the main battle, whose puissance on either side
Shall be well winged with our chiefest horse.   300
This, and Saint George to boot! What think'st
          thou, Norfolk?
          Nor. A good direction, warlike sovereign.
This found I on my tent this morning.
                              [*He sheweth him a paper.*
     [*K. Rich. Reads.*] "Jockey of Norfolk, be not so
          bold,
For Dickon thy master is bought and sold."   305
A thing devised by the enemy.
Go, gentlemen, every man to his charge.
Let not our babbling dreams affright our souls,
For conscience is a word that cowards use,
Devis'd at first to keep the strong in awe.   310
Our strong arms be our conscience, swords our law!
March on, join bravely, let us to't pell-mell;
If not to heaven, then hand in hand to hell.

               His oration to his Army.

What shall I say more than I have inferr'd?
Remember whom you are to cope withal;   315
A sort of vagabonds, rascals, and runaways,
A scum of Bretons and base lackey peasants,
Whom their o'er-cloyed country vomits forth
To desperate [ventures] and assur'd destruction.
You sleeping safe, they bring you to unrest;   320
You having lands, and blest with beauteous wives,
They would restrain the one, distain the other.
And who doth lead them but a paltry fellow,
Long kept in Bretagne at our mother's cost?
A milk-sop, one that never in his life   325
Felt so much cold as over shoes in snow?
Let's whip these stragglers o'er the seas again;
Lash hence these overweening rags of France,
These famish'd beggars, weary of their lives,
Who, but for dreaming on this fond exploit,   330
For want of means, poor rats, had hang'd them-
          selves.
If we be conquered, let men conquer us
And not these bastard Bretons whom our fathers
Have in their own land beaten, bobb'd, and
          thump'd,
And on record, left them the heirs of shame.   335
Shall these enjoy our lands? lie with our wives?
Ravish our daughters? (*Drum afar off.*) Hark!
          I hear their drum.
[Fight], gentlemen of England! fight, [bold] yeomen!

Draw, archers, draw your arrows to the head!
Spur your proud horses hard and ride in blood;   340
Amaze the welkin with your broken staves!

               Enter a MESSENGER.

What says Lord Stanley? Will he bring his power?
     Mess. My lord, he doth deny to come.
     K. Rich. Off with his son George's head!
     Nor. My lord, the enemy is past the marsh;   345
After the battle let George Stanley die.
     K. Rich. A thousand hearts are great within my
          bosom.
Advance our standards, set upon our foes;
Our ancient word of courage, fair Saint George,
Inspire us with the spleen of fiery dragons!   350
Upon them! Victory sits on our [helms].
                              [*Exeunt.*]

          [SCENE IV. *Another part of the field.*]

Alarum. Excursions. Enter [NORFOLK *and forces
          fighting; to him*] CATESBY.

     Cate. Rescue, my Lord of Norfolk, rescue, rescue!
The King enacts more wonders than a man,
Daring an opposite to every danger.
His horse is slain, and all on foot he fights,
Seeking for Richmond in the throat of death.   5
Rescue, fair lord, or else the day is lost!

          Alarums. Enter KING RICHARD.

     K. Rich. A horse! a horse! my kingdom for a
          horse!
     Cate. Withdraw, my lord; I'll help you to a horse.
     K. Rich. Slave, I have set my life upon a cast
And I will stand the hazard of the die.   10
I think there be six Richmonds in the field;
Five have I slain to-day instead of him.
A horse! a horse! my kingdom for a horse!
                              [*Exeunt.*]

          [SCENE V. *Another part of the field.*]

*Alarum. Enter Richard and Richmond; they fight;
     Richard is slain. Retreat and flourish. Re-enter*
     RICHMOND, DERBY, *bearing the crown, with divers
     other Lords.*

     Richm. God and your arms be prais'd, victorious
          friends;
The day is ours, the bloody dog is dead.
     Der. Courageous Richmond, well hast thou
          acquit thee.
Lo, here, these long-usurped royalties
From the dead temples of this bloody wretch   5

---

302. **direction:** plan of battle. 304. [**K. Rich. Reads**] (Capell). Om. F. 314. **inferr'd:** stated. 316. **sort:** gang.
319. [**ventures**] (Capell). *adventures* Q F. 322. **restrain:** deprive you of. **distain:** outrage. 334. **bobb'd:** thrashed. 338.
[**Fight**] Q. *Right* F. [**bold**] Q. *boldly* F. 350. **spleen:** anger. 351. [**helms**] Q. *helpes* F.
     Sc. iv, 3. **opposite:** enemy. 9. **cast:** throw of the dice.

Have I pluck'd off to grace thy brows withal.
Wear it, [enjoy it,] and make much of it.
  Richm. Great God of heaven, say amen to all!
But, tell me, is young George Stanley living?
  Der. He is, my lord, and safe in Leicester town;
Whither, if [it please you], we may [now] with-
    draws us.   11
  Richm. What men of name are slain on either
    side?
  Der. John Duke of Norfolk, Walter Lord
    Ferrers,
Sir Robert Brakenbury, and Sir William Bran-
    don.
  Richm. Inter their bodies as become their births.
Proclaim a pardon to the soldiers fled   16
That in submission will return to us;
And then, as we have ta'en the sacrament,
We will unite the white rose and the red.
Smile heaven upon this fair conjunction,   20
That long have frown'd upon their enmity!
What traitor hears me, and says not amen?

England hath long been mad and scarr'd herself;
The brother blindly shed the brother's blood,
The father rashly slaughtered his own son,   25
The son, compell'd, been butcher to the sire.
All this divided York and Lancaster,
Divided in their dire division,
O, now, let Richmond and Elizabeth,
The true succeeders of each royal house,   30
By God's fair ordinance conjoin together!
And let [their] heirs, God, if thy will be so,
Enrich the time to come with smooth-fac'd Peace,
With smiling Plenty and fair prosperous days!
Abate the edge of traitors, gracious Lord,   35
That would reduce these bloody days again
And make poor England weep in streams of blood!
Let them not live to taste this land's increase
That would with treason wound this fair land's
    peace!
Now civil wounds are stopp'd, Peace lives again;
That she may long live here, God say amen!   41
                           [*Exeunt.*

Sc. v, 7. [enjoy it] Q. Om. F.   **11.** [it please you] Q₂. *you please* F.   [now] Q. Om. F.   **32.** [their] Q. *thy* F.   **35.**
Abate: blunt.   **36. reduce:** bring back.

A Midsummer-Night's Dream

THE FIRST QUARTO of this play appeared in 1600, printed by Thomas Fisher from what certain stage-directions would indicate was a prompter's play-house manuscript. A second Quarto, set up from Q_1 was printed by James Roberts in 1619, but dishonestly dated 1600. The text of the First Folio followed a copy of Roberts's Quarto which apparently had been collated anew with a theatrical prompt-book or had itself served in the play-house, for the Folio text carries more numerous stage-directions as well as divisions into acts and scenes. The present text is based on Q_1.

The date of the play, though not to be ascertained exactly, can at least be discussed in connection with certain definite things. That the play was first devised in celebration of some nobleman's wedding is suggested by the prominence of the marriage of Theseus in the setting, the general masque-like character of the whole, with its abundance of song and dance, and the virtual epithalamium with which it closes. The oblique flattery of Elizabeth in the praise of chastity (I.i.74-75), in the image of the "imperial votaress" in Oberon's vision (II.i.155-165), and in the sovereign courtesy of Theseus toward the faltering tributes of his well-meaning subjects (V.i.89-105) would point further to the actual presence of the Queen. A variety of occasions has been suggested, the most plausible of which is the marriage of the Earl of Derby to Elizabeth Vere at the Court in Greenwich on January 26, 1595. Elizabeth was in fact present at this wedding. Titania's description (II.i.88-114) of the abnormal weather caused by Oberon's brawls reflects in all probability the cold and stormy summer of 1594. Tenable but not wholly convincing is the notion that the fear of the "rude mechanicals" lest the lion affright the ladies (I.ii.76-80) refers to an actual occurrence at the Scottish Court on August 30, 1594, when at a banquet celebrating the baptism of Prince Henry a blackamoor was substituted for the lion which was to have drawn in a triumphal car. To seek an allusion to the death of a particular person in the mourning of the Muses for "the death

of Learning, late deceas'd in beggary" (V.i.52-55) is misguided. Shakespeare may have meant to imply no more than the decline of Learning in general. The matters already noted point to late 1594 or early 1595, and the impression one gains from the style, characterization, and construction of the play and the evidence from the meter fit this date. The lyric beauty and versatility, the crowning grace of this play, may well be the fine flowering of the poetic impulse which was released in Shakespeare by the success of his two poems dedicated to Southampton and the composition of his presumably early sonnets, and which imparted the lyric élan to *Richard II* and *Romeo and Juliet*, plays certainly close to *A Midsummer-Night's Dream* in date.

The text as it has survived carries three possible endings, any of which could be used without raising a question of completeness. The epithalamium and dance of the fairies would make a comely close for a private performance but would be less appropriate upon the public stage. Robin's epilogue, on the other hand, with its petition for applause, seems clearly composed for the general public. Theseus waived the epilogue of the "hempen homespuns," and the play could stop there, but Robin thrust one upon the audience in the theatre! This provision of alternative endings is a proof of adaptation. There is also evidence of revision. In the Quarto printing of V.i.1-84 there is some mislineation which suggests that Shakespeare had added material in the margin of his manuscript without dividing it into pentameter lines and that the compositor incorporated it as he found it. But the argument for extensive revision which has been advanced on the basis of inconsistency in speech-headings is not convincing. Throughout the Quarto some of Robin's speeches are headed *Puck*; some of Oberon's are headed *King*; some of Titania's, *Queen*; some of Bottom's, *Clown*; and in Act V the names of Theseus and Hippolyta give way to *Duke* and *Duch*. The most natural inference from this state of affairs is that Shakespeare, writing rapidly or at intervals and not concerned for consistency in his manuscript, set down in speech-headings whatever designation flashed to mind. But even if one postulates revision from this evidence, it seems odd to do so in the case of some of the alternative headings but not all; yet this is what has been done. Moreover, the texture of the verse assigned to the several characters seems perfectly uniform.

For his plot, which was original, Shakespeare drew upon a variety of sources. For the story of Theseus he had available Chaucer's *Knight's Tale* and Plutarch's *Life of Theseus* in North's translation (1579). From the former he might have got the idea of the marriage festivities of Theseus, the May-day observances, the hunting scene, the name of Philostrate, and some minor details. From the latter he might have taken a few proper names and allusions to the previous adventures of Theseus in love and war. The idea for the love charms he may have found in the *Diana* of Montemayor, whence he took details for the plot of *The Two Gentlemen of Verona*. The story of Pyramus and Thisbe was accessible in Ovid's *Metamorphoses* or in Golding's translation of the same, in Chaucer's *Legend of Good Women*, and in various later forms. The fairy-lore is based mainly on popular tradition, though Ovid applies the name Titania to both Diana and Circe. Oberon had appeared in the romance of *Huon of Bordeaux*, familiar in Shakespeare's time in Berners's translation, and he had already figured on the stage in Robert Greene's *James IV*. Robin Goodfellow, a beneficent goblin who assisted maids and farm hands but who loved mischief and making things "befall preposterously," was widely familiar in English folklore, and though Shakespeare could have read about him in books, he had his mind stored with fairy story in his Warwickshire boyhood.

Like Robin, Bottom and his company of "hempen homespuns" are pure English, even in their names, which derive from the common trades they ply. For example, Bottom the Weaver takes his name from the core or "bottom" of a skein of yarn; Quince is a spelling of "quines" or "quoins," wedges of wood, and thus applicable to a carpenter; Snout is the spout of a kettle, an article familiar enough to tinkers; Snug is a palpably fitting name for a joiner; Flute, the bellows-mender, would also be able to repair the "flutes" or pipes of an

organ. The "tedious brief scene" which these "mechanicals" enact is such a one as a group of Elizabethan villagers might contribute to an entertainment in honor of their queen on one of her royal progresses. The awkwardness of their performance would undoubtedly have been in fact as natural, as expected, and as well tolerated as it is made to be in this play. In the play of the Nine Worthies performed by the clowns in *Love's Labour's Lost* Shakespeare had already had his fling at such "theatricals." It is possible that in "the most lamentable comedy" Shakespeare was burlesquing the exaggerated title-pages of the period, such as that of Thomas Preston's play, "A Lamentable Tragedie Mixed Full Of Pleasant Mirth, Containing The Life Of Cambises, King Of Percia," or that of one of his own Quartos, "The Most Excellent and lamentable Tragedie of Romeo and Juliet." That he intended Quince's play for a burlesque of *Romeo and Juliet* has been suggested.

The advance which *A Midsummer-Night's Dream* registers in Shakespeare's development as a dramatist is notable. The mastery of construction is consummate. The several plots are deftly interwoven; the result is organic unity, not merely geometric design. The handling of character shows Shakespeare's growth equally well. The Athenian aristocrats, the fairies, and Quince's crew all live and have their beings convincingly upon their several planes. To be sure, the four distracted lovers are not highly individual, but it must be clear that Shakespeare had no reason for making them so; it was situation, not personality, which concerned him in their case. Theseus, however, is eminently real; a ruler intelligent, energetic, benevolent, fond of sport, with the saving grace of humor, and withal in love. The supreme creation is, of course, Bottom. More real than any of the eccentrics in *Love's Labour's Lost*, he looks forward to Dogberry and Verges whose malapropisms he anticipates. Upon the fairy world Shakespeare worked a transformation into something all his own, and in so doing permanently modified this field of popular fancy. There is perhaps no one achievement of his genius which has had so pervasive an effect as his treatment of fairies in the present play and in Mercutio's speech on Queen Mab, in *Romeo and Juliet*.

A MIDSUMMER-NIGHT'S DREAM

[DRAMATIS PERSONÆ

THESEUS, *duke of Athens.*
EGEUS, *father to Hermia.*
LYSANDER, *betrothed to Hermia.*
DEMETRIUS, *in love with Hermia.*
PHILOSTRATE, *master of the revels to Theseus.*

QUINCE, *a carpenter,*
BOTTOM, *a weaver,*
FLUTE, *a bellows-
  mender,*   *presenting*
SNOUT, *a tinker,*
SNUG, *a joiner,*
STARVELING, *a tailor,*

PROLOGUE.
PYRAMUS.
THISBE.
WALL.
LION.
MOONSHINE.

HIPPOLYTA, *queen of the Amazons, betrothed to
  Theseus.*
HERMIA, *daughter to Egeus, betrothed to Lysander.*
HELENA, *in love with Demetrius.*

OBERON, *king of the fairies.*
TITANIA, *queen of the fairies.*
ROBIN GOODFELLOW, *a Puck.*
PEASEBLOSSOM,
COBWEB,
MOTH,   *fairies.*
MUSTARDSEED,

Other fairies attending their King and Queen.
Attendants on Theseus and Hippolyta.

SCENE: *Athens, and a wood near it.*]

ACT

[SCENE I. *Athens. The palace of Theseus.*]

Enter THESEUS, HIPPOLYTA, [PHILOSTRATE,]
with others.

The. Now, fair Hippolyta, our nuptial hour
Draws on apace. Four happy days bring in
Another moon; but, O, methinks, how slow
This old moon wanes! She lingers my desires,
Like to a step-dame or a dowager   5
Long withering out a young man's revenue.
  Hip. Four days will quickly steep themselves
    in night;
Four nights will quickly dream away the time;
And then the moon, like to a silver bow
New-bent in heaven, shall behold the night   10
Of our solemnities.
  The.   Go, Philostrate,
Stir up the Athenian youth to merriments;
Awake the pert and nimble spirit of mirth;
Turn melancholy forth to funerals;
The pale companion is not for our pomp.   15
                                    [*Exit Philostrate.*]
Hippolyta, I woo'd thee with my sword,
And won thy love doing thee injuries;
But I will wed thee in another key,
With pomp, with triumph, and with revelling.

Enter EGEUS, HERMIA, LYSANDER, *and* DEME-
TRIUS.

  Ege. Happy be Theseus, our renowned Duke!
  The. Thanks, good Egeus; what's the news with
    thee?   21
  Ege. Full of vexation come I, with complaint
Against my child, my daughter Hermia.
Stand forth, Demetrius. My noble lord,
This man hath my consent to marry her.   25
Stand forth, Lysander: and, my gracious Duke,
This man hath bewitch'd the bosom of my child.

Act I, sc. i, 5. **dowager:** widow with a dowry from an estate. 10. **New-bent** Qq. *Now bent* Ff. 13. **pert:** lively. 15.
companion: fellow, referring to melancholy. 19. **triumph:** public festivity.

Thou, thou, Lysander, thou hast given her rhymes
And interchang'd love-tokens with my child.
Thou hast by moonlight at her window sung 30
With faining voice verses of faining love,
And stol'n the impression of her fantasy
With bracelets of thy hair, rings, gawds, conceits,
Knacks, trifles, nosegays, sweetmeats, — messengers
Of strong prevailment in unhard'ned youth. 35
With cunning hast thou filch'd my daughter's heart,
Turn'd her obedience, which is due to me,
To stubborn harshness; and, my gracious Duke,
Be it so she will not here before your Grace
Consent to marry with Demetrius, 40
I beg the ancient privilege of Athens,
As she is mine, I may dispose of her;
Which shall be either to this gentleman
Or to her death, according to our law
Immediately provided in that case. 45
    The. What say you, Hermia? Be advis'd, fair maid.
To you your father should be as a god,
One that compos'd your beauties, yea, and one
To whom you are but as a form in wax
By him imprinted, and within his power 50
To leave the figure or disfigure it.
Demetrius is a worthy gentleman.
    Her. So is Lysander.
    The.   In himself he is;
But in this kind, wanting your father's voice,
The other must be held the worthier. 55
    Her. I would my father look'd but with my eyes.
    The. Rather your eyes must with his judgement look.
    Her. I do entreat your Grace to pardon me.
I know not by what power I am made bold,
Nor how it may concern my modesty, 60
In such a presence here to plead my thoughts;
But I beseech your Grace that I may know
The worst that may befall me in this case,
If I refuse to wed Demetrius.
    The. Either to die the death or to abjure 65
For ever the society of men.
Therefore, fair Hermia, question your desires,
Know of your youth, examine well your blood,
Whether, if you yield not to your father's choice,
You can endure the livery of a nun, 70
For aye to be in shady cloister mew'd,
To live a barren sister all your life,
Chanting faint hymns to the cold fruitless moon.
Thrice-blessed they that master so their blood

To undergo such maiden pilgrimage; 75
But earthlier happy is the rose distill'd
Than that which withering on the virgin thorn
Grows, lives, and dies in single blessedness.
    Her. So will I grow, so live, so die, my lord,
Ere I will yield my virgin patent up 80
Unto his lordship, whose unwished yoke
My soul consents not to give sovereignty.
    The. Take time to pause; and, by the next new moon —
The sealing-day betwixt my love and me
For everlasting bond of fellowship — 85
Upon that day either prepare to die
For disobedience to your father's will,
Or else to wed Demetrius, as he would,
Or on Diana's altar to protest
For aye austerity and single life. 90
    Dem. Relent, sweet Hermia; and, Lysander, yield
Thy crazed title to my certain right.
    Lys. You have her father's love, Demetrius,
Let me have Hermia's; do you marry him.
    Ege. Scornful Lysander! true, he hath my love,
And what is mine my love shall render him. 96
And she is mine, and all my right of her
I do estate unto Demetrius.
    Lys. I am, my lord, as well deriv'd as he,
As well possess'd; my love is more than his; 100
My fortunes every way as fairly rank'd,
If not with vantage, as Demetrius';
And, which is more than all these boasts can be,
I am belov'd of beauteous Hermia.
Why should not I then prosecute my right? 105
Demetrius, I'll avouch it to his head,
Made love to Nedar's daughter, Helena,
And won her soul; and she, sweet lady, dotes,
Devoutly dotes, dotes in idolatry,
Upon this spotted and inconstant man. 110
    The. I must confess that I have heard so much,
And with Demetrius thought to have spoke thereof;
But, being over-full of self-affairs,
My mind did lose it. But, Demetrius, come;
And come, Egeus; you shall go with me; 115
I have some private schooling for you both.
For you, fair Hermia, look you arm yourself
To fit your fancies to your father's will;
Or else the law of Athens yields you up —
Which by no means we may extenuate — 120
To death, or to a vow of single life.
Come, my Hippolyta; what cheer, my love?
Demetrius and Egeus, go along.
I must employ you in some business

---

31. **faining:** longing.   32. **stol'n ... fantasy:** captured her fancy (by impressing it with gifts).   33. **gawds:** trinkets. **conceits:** devices.   34. **knacks:** knickknacks.   39. **Be it so:** if.   45. **Immediately:** expressly.   51. **disfigure:** obliterate. 54. **in ... kind:** i.e., as a husband.   **voice:** approval.   60. **concern:** beseem.   68. **blood:** passion.   69. **Whether.** One syllable in pronunciation.   71. **mew'd:** shut up (a term from falconry).   80. **patent:** privilege, liberty.   89. **protest:** vow. 92. **crazed:** unsound.   98. **estate unto:** settle upon.   106. **head:** face.   120. **extenuate:** weaken.

Against our nuptial, and confer with you   125
Of something nearly that concerns yourselves.
    Ege. With duty and desire we follow you.
        [*Exeunt all but Lysander and Hermia.*
    Lys. How now, my love! why is your cheek so
    pale?
How chance the roses there do fade so fast?
    Her. Belike for want of rain, which I could well
Beteem them from the tempest of my eyes.   131
    Lys. Ay me! for aught that I could ever read,
Could ever hear by tale or history,
The course of true love never did run smooth;
But, either it was different in blood, —   135
    Her. O cross! too high to be enthrall'd to [low].
    Lys. Or else misgraffed in respect of years, —
    Her. O spite! too old to be engag'd to young.
    Lys. Or else it stood upon the choice of friends, —
    Her. O hell! to choose love by another's eyes.   140
    Lys. Or, if there were a sympathy in choice,
War, death, or sickness did lay siege to it,
Making it momentany as a sound,
Swift as a shadow, short as any dream,
Brief as the lightning in the collied night,   145
That, in a spleen, unfolds both heaven and earth,
And ere a man hath power to say "Behold!"
The jaws of darkness do devour it up:
So quick bright things come to confusion.
    Her. If then true lovers have been ever cross'd,
It stands as an edict in destiny.   151
Then let us teach our trial patience,
Because it is a customary cross,
As due to love as thoughts and dreams and sighs,
Wishes and tears, poor Fancy's followers.   155
    Lys. A good persuasion; therefore, hear me, Her-
    mia.
I have a widow aunt, a dowager
Of great revenue, and she hath no child.
From Athens is her house remote seven leagues;
And she respects me as her only son.   160
There, gentle Hermia, may I marry thee;
And to that place the sharp Athenian law
Cannot pursue us. If thou lov'st me then,
Steal forth thy father's house to-morrow night;
And in the wood, a league without the town,   165
Where I did meet thee once with Helena
To do observance to a morn of May,
There will I stay for thee.
    Her.   My good Lysander!
I swear to thee, by Cupid's strongest bow,
By his best arrow with the golden head,   170
By the simplicity of Venus' doves,
By that which knitteth souls and prospers loves,

And by that fire which burn'd the Carthage queen
When the false Troyan under sail was seen,
By all the vows that ever men have broke,   175
In number more than ever women spoke,
In that same place thou hast appointed me
To-morrow truly will I meet with thee.
    Lys. Keep promise, love. Look, here comes
    Helena.

        Enter HELENA.

    Her. God speed fair Helena! Whither away? 180
    Hel. Call you me fair? That fair again unsay.
Demetrius loves your fair, O happy fair!
Your eyes are lode-stars, and your tongue's sweet
    air
More tuneable than lark to shepherd's ear
When wheat is green, when hawthorn buds appear.
Sickness is catching; O, were favour so,   186
[Yours would] I catch, fair Hermia, ere I go;
My ear should catch your voice, my eye your eye,
My tongue should catch your tongue's sweet mel-
    ody.
Were the world mine, Demetrius being bated,   190
The rest I'll give to be to you translated.
O, teach me how you look, and with what art
You sway the motion of Demetrius' heart.
    Her. I frown upon him, yet he loves me still.
    Hel. O that your frowns would teach my smiles
    such skill!   195
    Her. I give him curses, yet he gives me love.
    Hel. O that my prayers could such affection
    move!
    Her. The more I hate, the more he follows me.
    Hel. The more I love, the more he hateth me.
    Her. His folly, Helena, is no fault of mine.
    Hel. None, but your beauty. Would that fault
    were mine!   201
    Her. Take comfort; he no more shall see my
    face;
Lysander and myself will fly this place.
Before the time I did Lysander see,
Seem'd Athens as a paradise to me;   205
O, then, what graces in my love do dwell,
That he hath turn'd a heaven unto a hell!
    Lys. Helen, to you our minds we will unfold.
To-morrow night, when Phœbe doth behold
Her silver visage in the wat'ry glass,   210
Decking with liquid pearl the bladed grass,
A time that lovers' flights doth still conceal,
Through Athens' gates have we devis'd to steal.
    Her. And in the wood, where often you and I
Upon faint primrose-beds were wont to lie,   215

---

125. **against:** in anticipation of.   131. **Beteem:** allow.   136. **[low]** (Theobald). *love* Q.   137. **misgraffed:** mismatched. 143. **momentany:** momentary.   145. **collied:** blackened.   146. **spleen:** burst of passion.   150. **ever:** always.   155. **Fancy's:** love's.   160. **respects:** regards.   171. **simplicity:** innocence.   173. **Carthage queen:** Dido, who killed herself after the Trojan Aeneas had deserted her.   182. **fair:** beauty.   186. **favour:** beauty.   187. **[Yours would]** (Hanmer). *Your words* Q.   190. **bated:** excepted.   191. **translated:** transformed.   209. **Phœbe:** Diana, the moon.   215. **faint:** pale.

Emptying our bosoms of their counsel [sweet].
There my Lysander and myself shall meet;
And thence from Athens turn away our eyes,
To seek new friends and [stranger companies].
Farewell, sweet playfellow! Pray thou for us;
And good luck grant thee thy Demetrius!   221
Keep word, Lysander; we must starve our sight
From lovers' food till morrow deep midnight.
   Lys. I will, my Hermia.   [*Exit Herm.*
             Helena, adieu:
As you on him, Demetrius dote on you!   225
                        [*Exit.*
   Hel. How happy some o'er other some can be!
Through Athens I am thought as fair as she.
But what of that? Demetrius thinks not so;
He will not know what all but he do know;
And as he errs, doting on Hermia's eyes,   230
So I, admiring of his qualities.
Things base and vile, holding no quantity,
Love can transpose to form and dignity.
Love looks not with the eyes but with the mind,
And therefore is wing'd Cupid painted blind.   235
Nor hath Love's mind of any judgement taste;
Wings and no eyes figure unheedy haste;
And therefore is Love said to be a child,
Because in choice he is so oft beguil'd.
As waggish boys in game themselves forswear,   240
So the boy Love is perjur'd every where:
For ere Demetrius look'd on Hermia's eyne,
He hail'd down oaths that he was only mine;
And when this hail some heat from Hermia felt,
So he dissolv'd, and show'rs of oaths did melt.   245
I will go tell him of fair Hermia's flight;
Then to the wood will he to-morrow night
Pursue her; and for this intelligence
If I have thanks, it is a dear expense.
But herein mean I to enrich my pain,   250
To have his sight thither and back again.
                        [*Exit.*

[SCENE II. *Athens. Quince's house.*]

Enter QUINCE, SNUG, BOTTOM, FLUTE, SNOUT, *and*
             STARVELING.

   Quin. Is all our company here?
   Bot. You were best to call them generally, man
by man, according to the scrip.
   Quin. Here is the scroll of every man's name,
which is thought fit, through all Athens, to play
in our interlude before the Duke and the Duchess, on his wedding-day at night.   7
   Bot. First, good Peter Quince, say what the play

treats on, then read the names of the actors, and so
grow to a point.   10
   Quin. Marry, our play is *The most lamentable
comedy, and most cruel death of Pyramus and
Thisby.*
   Bot. A very good piece of work, I assure you, and
a merry. Now, good Peter Quince, call forth   15
your actors by the scroll. Masters, spread yourselves.
   Quin. Answer as I call you. Nick Bottom, the
weaver.
   Bot. Ready. Name what part I am for, and
proceed.   21
   Quin. You, Nick Bottom, are set down for Pyramus.
   Bot. What is Pyramus? A lover, or a tyrant?
   Quin. A lover, that kills himself most gallant
for love.   26
   Bot. That will ask some tears in the true performing of it. If I do it, let the audience look to
their eyes. I will move storms, I will condole in
some measure. To the rest. Yet my chief humour
is for a tyrant. I could play Ercles rarely, or a   31
part to tear a cat in, to make all split.
       "The raging rocks
         And shivering shocks
         Shall break the locks   35
           Of prison gates;
         And Phibbus' car
         Shall shine from far
         And make and mar
           The foolish Fates."   40
This was lofty! Now name the rest of the players.
This is Ercles' vein, a tyrant's vein; a lover is more
condoling.
   Quin. Francis Flute, the bellows-mender.
   Flu. Here, Peter Quince.   45
   Quin. Flute, you must take Thisby on you.
   Flu. What is Thisby? A wand'ring knight?
   Quin. It is the lady that Pyramus must love.
   Flu. Nay, faith, let not me play a woman; I have
a beard coming.   50
   Quin. That's all one; you shall play it in a mask,
and you may speak as small as you will.
   Bot. An I may hide my face, let me play Thisby
too. I'll speak in a monstrous little voice, "Thisne!
Thisne! Ah Pyramus, my lover dear! thy Thisby
dear, and lady dear!"   56
   Quin. No, no; you must play Pyramus; and,
Flute, you Thisby.
   Bot. Well, proceed.
   Quin. Robin Starveling, the tailor.   60
   Star. Here, Peter Quince.

---

216. **[sweet]** (Theobald). *sweld* Q. 219. **[stranger companies]** (Theobald). *strange companions* Q. 237. **figure:** symbolize.
242. **eyne:** eyes. 248. **intelligence:** news. 249. **dear expense:** costly gain. 251. **his sight:** sight of him.
   Sc. ii, 2. generally: Bottom's error for *severally.* 3. **scrip:** written list. 10. **grow...point:** come to the point. 29.
condole: grieve. 31. **Ercles:** Hercules, a common ranting part in early drama. 31. **make all split,** i.e., with passion. 37.
Phibbus': Phoebus'. 53. **An:** if.

Quin. Robin Starveling, you must play Thisby's mother. Tom Snout, the tinker.

Snout. Here, Peter Quince.

Quin. You, Pyramus' father; myself, Thisby's father; Snug, the joiner, you, the lion's part; 66 and, I hope, here is a play fitted.

Snug. Have you the lion's part written? Pray you, if it be, give it me, for I am slow of study.

Quin. You may do it extempore, for it is no- 70 thing but roaring.

Bot. Let me play the lion too. I will roar, that I will do any man's heart good to hear me. I will roar, that I will make the Duke say, "Let him roar again, let him roar again." 75

Quin. An you should do it too terribly, you would fright the Duchess and the ladies, that they would shriek; and that were enough to hang us all.

All. That would hang us, every mother's son. 80

Bot. I grant you, friends, if you should fright the ladies out of their wits, they would have no more discretion but to hang us; but I will aggravate my voice so that I will roar you as gently as any suck- 85 ing dove; I will roar you an 'twere any night-ingale.

Quin. You can play no part but Pyramus; for Pyramus is a sweet-fac'd man; a proper man, as one shall see in a summer's day; a most lovely gentle- 90 man-like man: therefore you must needs play Pyramus.

Bot. Well, I will undertake it. What beard were I best to play it in?

Quin. Why, what you will.

Bot. I will discharge it in either your straw- 95 colour beard, your orange-tawny beard, your pur-ple-in-grain beard, or your French-crown-colour beard, your perfect yellow.

Quin. Some of your French crowns have no hair at all, and then you will play barefac'd. But, 100 masters, here are your parts; and I am to entreat you, request you, and desire you, to con them by to-morrow night; and meet me in the palace wood, a mile without the town, by moonlight. There will we rehearse, for if we meet in the city, we shall be 105 dogg'd with company, and our devices known. 106 In the meantime I will draw a bill of properties, such as our play wants. I pray you, fail me not.

Bot. We will meet; and there we may rehearse 110 most obscenely and courageously. Take pains; be perfect; adieu.

Quin. At the Duke's oak we meet.

Bot. Enough; hold or cut bow-strings.

[*Exeunt.*

ACT II

[SCENE I. *A wood near Athens.*]

Enter a FAIRY *at one door and* ROBIN GOODFELLOW *at another.*

Robin. How now, spirit! whither wander you?

Fai. Over hill, over dale,
   Thorough bush, thorough brier,
Over park, over pale,
   Thorough flood, thorough fire, 5
I do wander every where,
Swifter than the moon's sphere;
And I serve the fairy Queen,
To dew her orbs upon the green.
The cowslips tall her pensioners be; 10
In their gold coats spots you see;
Those be rubies, fairy favours,
In those freckles live their savours.
I must go seek some dewdrops here
And hang a pearl in every cowslip's ear. 15
Farewell, thou lob of spirits; I'll be gone.
Our Queen and all her elves come here anon.

Robin. The King doth keep his revels here to-night;
Take heed the Queen come not within his sight;
For Oberon is passing fell and wrath, 20
Because that she as her attendant hath
A lovely boy stolen from an Indian king.
She never had so sweet a changeling;
And jealous Oberon would have the child
Knight of his train, to trace the forests wild; 25
But she perforce withholds the loved boy,
Crowns him with flowers, and makes him all her joy;
And now they never meet in grove or green,
By fountain clear, or spangled starlight sheen,
But they do square, that all their elves for fear 30
Creep into acorn-cups and hide them there.

Fai. Either I mistake your shape and making quite,
Or else you are that shrewd and knavish sprite
Call'd Robin Goodfellow. Are not you he
That frights the maidens of the villagery, 35
Skim milk, and sometimes labour in the quern,
And bootless make the breathless housewife churn,
And sometime make the drink to bear no barm,
Mislead night-wanderers, laughing at their harm?
Those that Hobgoblin call you, and sweet Puck, 40

---

83. **aggravate:** Bottom's mistake for *moderate*. 88. **proper:** handsome. 95-98. Bottom, the Weaver, refers glibly to several familiar dyes. 111. **obscenely:** Bottom's mistake for *obscurely*. 114. **hold ... bow-strings.** Apparently an archer's expression. Bottom probably means, "Keep your appointments or everything is off."

Act II, Sc. i, s.d. ROBIN GOODFELLOW. This character is described as a Puck, a name previously applied in English folklore to a minor order of evil spirits. Shakespeare recreates him as he does the fairies. 9. **orbs:** fairy rings. 10. **pensioners.** Elizabeth's bodyguards were called gentlemen pensioners. 13. **savours:** perfumes. 16. **lob:** lout. 20. **passing ... wrath:** exceedingly angry and wrathful. 23. **changeling:** a child exchanged by fairies. 30. **square:** quarrel. **that:** so that. 33. **shrewd:** mischievous. 36. **quern:** handmill. 38. **barm:** yeast.

You do their work, and they shall have good luck.
Are not you he?
    Robin.   Thou speakest aright;
I am that merry wanderer of the night.
I jest to Oberon and make him smile
When I a fat and bean-fed horse beguile,   45
Neighing in likeness of a filly foal;
And sometime lurk I in a gossip's bowl,
In very likeness of a roasted crab,
And when she drinks, against her lips I bob
And on her withered dewlap pour the ale.   50
The wisest aunt, telling the saddest tale,
Sometime for three-foot stool mistaketh me.
Then slip I from her bum, down topples she,
And "tailor" cries, and falls into a cough;
And then the whole quire hold their hips and laugh,
And waxen in their mirth, and neeze, and swear 56
A merrier hour was never wasted there.
But, room, fairy! here comes Oberon.
    Fai. And here my mistress. Would that he were
        gone!

Enter the King of Fairies [OBERON] *at one door with
his train; and the Queen* [TITANIA] *at another with
hers.*

    Obe. Ill met by moonlight, proud Titania.   60
    Tita. What, jealous Oberon! Fairies, skip hence:
I have forsworn his bed and company.
    Obe. Tarry, rash wanton! Am not I thy lord?
    Tita. Then I must be thy lady; but I know
When thou hast stolen away from fairy land,   65
And in the shape of Corin sat all day,
Playing on pipes of corn and versing love
To amorous Phillida. Why art thou here,
Come from the farthest steep of India?
But that, forsooth, the bouncing Amazon,   70
Your buskin'd mistress and your warrior love,
To Theseus must be wedded, and you come
To give their bed joy and prosperity.
    Obe. How canst thou thus for shame, Titania,
Glance at my credit with Hippolyta,   75
Knowing I know thy love to Theseus?
Didst thou not lead him through the glimmering
    night
From Perigenia, whom he ravished?
And make him with fair Ægle break his faith,
With Ariadne, and Antiopa?   80

    Tita. These are the forgeries of jealousy;
And never, since the middle summer's spring,
Met we on hill, in dale, forest or mead,
By paved fountain or by rushy brook,
Or in the beached margent of the sea,   85
To dance our ringlets to the whistling wind,
But with thy brawls thou hast disturb'd our sport.
Therefore the winds, piping to us in vain,
As in revenge, have suck'd up from the sea
Contagious fogs; which, falling in the land,   90
Hath every pelting river made so proud
That they have overborne their continents.
The ox hath therefore stretch'd his yoke in vain,
The ploughman lost his sweat, and the green corn
Hath rotted ere his youth attain'd a beard.   95
The fold stands empty in the drowned field,
And crows are fatted with the murrain flock,
The nine men's morris is fill'd up with mud,
And the quaint mazes in the wanton green
For lack of tread are undistinguishable.   100
The human mortals want their winter [cheer];
No night is now with hymn or carol blest.
Therefore the moon, the governess of floods,
Pale in her anger, washes all the air,
That rheumatic diseases do abound.   105
And thorough this distemperature we see
The seasons alter: hoary-headed frosts
Fall in the fresh lap of the crimson rose,
And on old Hiems' thin and icy crown
An odorous chaplet of sweet summer buds   110
Is, as in mockery, set; the spring, the summer,
The childing autumn, angry winter, change
Their wonted liveries; and the mazed world,
By their increase, now knows not which is which.
And this same progeny of evils comes   115
From our debate, from our dissension;
We are their parents and original.
    Obe. Do you amend it then; it lies in you.
Why should Titania cross her Oberon?
I do but beg a little changeling boy   120
To be my henchman.
    Tita.   Set your heart at rest;
The fairy land buys not the child of me.
His mother was a vot'ress of my order,
And, in the spiced Indian air, by night,
Full often hath she gossip'd by my side,   125
And sat with me on Neptune's yellow sands,

47. **gossip's bowl:** christening-cup. Gossip is used here in the original sense of godmother. 48. **crab:** crab apple. 50. **dewlap:** loose skin on the neck. 51. **aunt:** old woman. **saddest:** soberest. 54. "tailor" cries. Meaning obscure. 56. **waxen:** increase. **neeze:** sneeze. 66–68. **Corin ... Phillida:** names traditional in pastoral poetry. 71. **buskin'd:** wearing high boots. 75. **glance at:** cast reflections on. 79–80. **Ægle ... Ariadne ... Antiopa.** These names of women whom Theseus had loved Shakespeare found in North's *Plutarch.* Antiope is sometimes identified with Hippolyta, but in this speech they are treated as two. 82. **middle summer's spring:** beginning of midsummer. 85. **in:** on. **margent:** margin. 86. **ringlets:** circular dances. 87. **thy brawls.** See Introduction. 91. **pelting:** paltry. Ff read *petty.* 92. **continents:** banks. 97. **murrain:** diseased. 98. **nine men's morris:** a game played in squares marked out on the turf of the village green; something like hopscotch. 99. **mazes:** figures. **wanton:** luxuriant. 101. [cheer] (Theobald conj.). *heere* Q. 106. **distemperature:** disturbance. 109. **Hiems:** the god of winter. 112. **childing:** fruitful. 113. **mazed:** amazed. 117. **original:** origin. 121. **henchman:** page.

Marking th' embarked traders on the flood,
When we have laugh'd to see the sails conceive
And grow big-bellied with the wanton wind;
Which she with pretty and with swimming gait
Following, her womb then rich with my young
    squire,   131
Would imitate, and sail upon the land
To fetch me trifles, and return again,
As from a voyage, rich with merchandise.
But she, being mortal, of that boy did die;   135
And for her sake do I rear up her boy,
And for her sake I will not part with him.

Obe. How long within this wood intend you stay?

Tita. Perchance till after Theseus' wedding-day.
If you will patiently dance in our round   140
And see our moonlight revels, go with us;
If not, shun me, and I will spare your haunts.

Obe. Give me that boy, and I will go with
thee.

Tita. Not for thy fairy kingdom. Fairies, away!
We shall chide downright, if I longer stay.   145
        [Exit [Titania with her train].

Obe. Well, go thy way; thou shalt not from this
    grove
Till I torment thee for this injury.
My gentle Puck, come hither. Thou rememb'rest
Since once I sat upon a promontory,
And heard a mermaid on a dolphin's back   150
Uttering such dulcet and harmonious breath
That the rude sea grew civil at her song,
And certain stars shot madly from their spheres,
To hear the sea-maid's music?

Robin.   I remember.

Obe. That very time I saw, but thou couldst not,
Flying between the cold moon and the earth,   156
Cupid all arm'd. A certain aim he took
At a fair vestal throned by the west,
And loos'd his love-shaft smartly from his bow,
As it should pierce a hundred thousand hearts;
But I might see young Cupid's fiery shaft   161
Quench'd in the chaste beams of the wat'ry moon,
And the imperial vot'ress passed on,
In maiden meditation, fancy-free.
Yet mark'd I where the bolt of Cupid fell.   165
It fell upon a little western flower,
Before milk-white, now purple with love's wound,
And maidens call it love-in-idleness.
Fetch me that flower, the herb I shew'd thee once.
The juice of it on sleeping eye-lids laid   170
Will make or man or woman madly dote
Upon the next live creature that it sees.
Fetch me this herb; and be thou here again
Ere the leviathan can swim a league.

Robin. I'll put a girdle round about the earth   175
In forty minutes.   *[Exit.]*

Obe.   Having once this juice,
I'll watch Titania when she is asleep,
And drop the liquor of it in her eyes.
The next thing then she waking looks upon,
Be it on lion, bear, or wolf, or bull,   180
On meddling monkey, or on busy ape,
She shall pursue it with the soul of love;
And ere I take this charm from off her sight,
As I can take it with another herb,
I'll make her render up her page to me.   185
But who comes here? I am invisible;
And I will overhear their conference.

Enter DEMETRIUS, HELENA *following him.*

Dem. I love thee not, therefore pursue me not.
Where is Lysander and fair Hermia?
The one I'll stay, the other stayeth me.   190
Thou told'st me they were stol'n unto this wood;
And here am I, and wood within this wood
Because I cannot meet my Hermia.
Hence, get thee gone, and follow me no more.

Hel. You draw me, you hard-hearted adamant;
But yet you draw not iron, for my heart   196
Is true as steel. Leave you your power to draw,
And I shall have no power to follow you.

Dem. Do I entice you? Do I speak you fair?
Or, rather, do I not in plainest truth   200
Tell you, I do not nor I cannot love you?

Hel. And even for that do I love you the more.
I am your spaniel, and, Demetrius,
The more you beat me, I will fawn on you.
Use me but as your spaniel, spurn me, strike me,   205
Neglect me, lose me; only give me leave,
Unworthy as I am, to follow you.
What worser place can I beg in your love,—
And yet a place of high respect with me,—
Than to be used as you use your dog?   210

Dem. Tempt not too much the hatred of my
    spirit,
For I am sick when I do look on thee.

Hel. And I am sick when I look not on you.

Dem. You do impeach your modesty too much,
To leave the city and commit yourself   215
Into the hands of one that loves you not;
To trust the opportunity of night
And the ill counsel of a desert place
With the rich worth of your virginity.

Hel. Your virtue is my privilege. For that   220
It is not night when I do see your face,
Therefore I think I am not in the night;
Nor doth this wood lack worlds of company,

148–168. See Introduction. 149. **Since**: when. 158. **vestal**: virgin. 168. **love-in-idleness**: pansy. 190. **stay...stayeth**. Thirlby's conjecture "slay...slayeth" has been followed by many editors. 192. **wood**: mad. 195. **adamant**: probably with both senses of "lode-stone" (magnet) and "hardest metal." 197. **Leave**: give up. 220. **privilege**: safeguard. **For that**: because.

For you in my respect are all the world.
Then how can it be said I am alone,   225
When all the world is here to look on me?

   Dem. I'll run from thee and hide me in the
     brakes,
And leave thee to the mercy of wild beasts.

   Hel. The wildest hath not such a heart as you.
Run when you will, the story shall be chang'd:
Apollo flies, and Daphne holds the chase;   231
The dove pursues the griffin; the mild hind
Makes speed to catch the tiger: bootless speed,
When cowardice pursues and valour flies.

   Dem. I will not stay thy questions; let me go;   235
Or, if thou follow me, do not believe
But I shall do thee mischief in the wood.

   Hel. Ay, in the temple, in the town, the field,
You do me mischief. Fie, Demetrius!
Your wrongs do set a scandal on my sex.   240
We cannot fight for love, as men may do.
We should be woo'd and were not made to woo.
                     [*Exit Dem.*]
I'll follow thee and make a heaven of hell,
To die upon the hand I love so well.   [*Exit.*

   Obe. Fare thee well, nymph. Ere he do leave
     this grove,   245
Thou shalt fly him and he shall seek thy love.

    Re-enter [ROBIN GOODFELLOW].

Hast thou the flower there? Welcome, wanderer.
   Robin. Ay, there it is.
   Obe.   I pray thee, give it me.
I know a bank where the wild thyme blows,
Where oxlips and the nodding violet grows,   250
Quite over-canopi'd with luscious woodbine,
With sweet musk-roses and with eglantine.
There sleeps Titania sometime of the night,
Lull'd in these flowers with dances and delight;
And there the snake throws her enamell'd skin,   255
Weed wide enough to wrap a fairy in;
And with the juice of this I'll streak her eyes,
And make her full of hateful fantasies.
Take thou some of it, and seek through this grove.
A sweet Athenian lady is in love   260
With a disdainful youth. Anoint his eyes,
But do it when the next thing he espies
May be the lady. Thou shalt know the man
By the Athenian garments he hath on.
Effect it with some care, that he may prove   265
More fond on her than she upon her love;
And look thou meet me ere the first cock crow.
   Robin. Fear not, my lord, your servant shall do
so.   [*Exeunt.*

   [SCENE II. *Another part of the wood.*]

    Enter TITANIA, *with her train.*

   Tita. Come, now a roundel and a fairy song;
Then, for the third part of a minute, hence,
Some to kill cankers in the musk-rose buds,
Some war with rere-mice for their leathern wings   4
To make my small elves coats, and some keep back
The clamorous owl that nightly hoots and wonders
At our quaint spirits. Sing me now asleep;
Then to your offices and let me rest.

    THE FAIRIES *sing.*

[1. *Fairy.*] "You spotted snakes with double
    tongue,
   Thorny hedgehogs, be not seen;   10
Newts and blind-worms, do no wrong,
   Come not near our fairy queen."

[*Cho.*] "Philomel, with melody
   Sing in our sweet lullaby;
Lulla, lulla, lullaby; lulla, lulla, lullaby.   15
    Never harm
    Nor spell nor charm
Come our lovely lady nigh.
   So, good night, with lullaby."

1. Fairy. "Weaving spiders, come not here;   20
   Hence, you long-legg'd spinners, hence!
Beetles black, approach not near;
   Worm nor snail, do no offence."

[*Cho.*] "Philomel, with melody," etc.

2. Fairy. Hence, away! now all is well.
   One aloof stand sentinel.   25
        [*Exeunt Fairies.*] *Titania sleeps.*

Enter OBERON [*and squeezes the flower on Titania's*
    eyelids].

   Obe. What thou seest when thou dost wake,
    Do it for thy true-love take,
    Love and languish for his sake.
    Be it ounce, or cat, or bear,   30
    Pard, or boar with bristled hair,
    In thy eye that shall appear
    When thou wak'st, it is thy dear.
    Wake when some vile thing is near.
                     [*Exit.*]

    Enter LYSANDER *and* HERMIA.

   Lys. Fair love, you faint with wand'ring in the
    wood;   35
And to speak troth, I have forgot our way.

---

224. in my respect: to me. 231. Apollo ... chase. According to the myth, Apollo pursued Daphne, but here the situation
is reversed. 232. griffin: a monster having a lion's body and an eagle's head. hind: female of the red deer. 235. questions:
arguments. 244. upon: by. 254. dances and delight: delightful dances. 256. Weed: garment. 257. streak: stroke.
Sc. ii, 1. roundel: circular dance. 3. cankers: cankerworms. 4. rere-mice: bats. 7. quaint: dainty. 11. Newts:
water lizards. 13. Philomel: the nightingale. 30. ounce: lynx. cat: wildcat. 31. Pard: leopard.

We'll rest us, Hermia, if you think it good,
And tarry for the comfort of the day.
Her. Be it so, Lysander. Find you out a bed;
For I upon this bank will rest my head.   40
Lys. One turf shall serve as pillow for us both;
One heart, one bed, two bosoms and one troth.
Her. Nay, good Lysander; for my sake, my dear,
Lie further off yet; do not lie so near.
Lys. O, take the sense, sweet, of my innocence!
Love takes the meaning in love's conference.   46
I mean, that my heart unto yours is knit
So that but one heart we can make of it;
Two bosoms interchained with an oath,
So then two bosoms and a single troth.   50
Then by your side no bed-room me deny;
For lying so, Hermia, I do not lie.
Her. Lysander riddles very prettily.
Now much beshrew my manners and my pride,
If Hermia meant to say Lysander lied.   55
But, gentle friend, for love and courtesy
Lie further off; in humane modesty,
Such separation as may well be said
Becomes a virtuous bachelor and a maid,
So far be distant; and, good night, sweet friend.   60
Thy love ne'er alter till thy sweet life end!
Lys. Amen, amen, to that fair prayer, say I;
And then end life when I end loyalty!
Here is my bed; sleep give thee all his rest!
Her. With half that wish the wisher's eyes be
press'd!   [*They sleep.*   65

Enter [ROBIN GOODFELLOW].

Robin. Through the forest have I gone,
But Athenian found I none,
On whose eyes I might approve
This flower's force in stirring love.
Night and silence — Who is here?   70
Weeds of Athens he doth wear!
This is he, my master said,
Despised the Athenian maid;
And here the maiden, sleeping sound,
On the dank and dirty ground.   75
Pretty soul! she durst not lie
Near this lack-love, this kill-courtesy.
Churl, upon thy eyes I throw
All the power this charm doth owe.
When thou wak'st, let love forbid   80
Sleep his seat on thy eyelid;
So awake when I am gone,
For I must now to Oberon.   [*Exit.*

Enter DEMETRIUS *and* HELENA, *running.*

Hel. Stay, though thou kill me, sweet Demetrius.
Dem. I charge thee, hence, and do not haunt me
thus.   85

Hel. O, wilt thou darkling leave me? Do not so.
Dem. Stay, on thy peril; I alone will go.
[*Exit.*
Hel. O, I am out of breath in this fond chase!
The more my prayer, the lesser is my grace.
Happy is Hermia, wheresoe'er she lies,   90
For she hath blessed and attractive eyes.
How came her eyes so bright? Not with salt tears;
If so, my eyes are oft'ner wash'd than hers.
No, no, I am as ugly as a bear,
For beasts that meet me run away for fear;   95
Therefore no marvel though Demetrius
Do, as a monster, fly my presence thus.
What wicked and dissembling glass of mine
Made me compare with Hermia's sphery eyne?
But who is here? Lysander! on the ground!   100
Dead? or asleep? I see no blood, no wound.
Lysander, if you live, good sir, awake.
Lys. [*Awaking.*] And run through fire I will for
thy sweet sake.
Transparent Helena! Nature shows art,
That through thy bosom makes me see thy heart.
Where is Demetrius? O, how fit a word   106
Is that vile name to perish on my sword!
Hel. Do not say so, Lysander; say not so.
What though he love your Hermia? Lord, what
though?
Yet Hermia still loves you; then be content.   110
Lys. Content with Hermia! No; I do repent
The tedious minutes I with her have spent.
Not Hermia but Helena I love.
Who will not change a raven for a dove?
The will of man is by his reason sway'd;   115
And reason says you are the worthier maid.
Things growing are not ripe until their season,
So I, being young, till now ripe not to reason;
And touching now the point of human skill,
Reason becomes the marshal to my will   120
And leads me to your eyes, where I o'erlook
Love's stories written in Love's richest book.
Hel. Wherefore was I to this keen mockery born?
When at your hands did I deserve this scorn?
Is't not enough, is't not enough, young man,   125
That I did never, no, nor never can,
Deserve a sweet look from Demetrius' eye,
But you must flout my insufficiency?
Good troth, you do me wrong, good sooth you do,
In such disdainful manner me to woo.   130
But fare you well; perforce I must confess
I thought you lord of more true gentleness.
O, that a lady, of one man refus'd,
Should of another therefore be abus'd!   [*Exit.*
Lys. She sees not Hermia. Hermia, sleep thou
there;   135
And never mayst thou come Lysander near!

46. **Love . . . conference:** Love gives lovers true understanding. 68. **approve:** test. 79. **owe:** own. 86. **darkling:** in the dark. 88. **fond:** foolish. 89. **my grace:** the favor I receive. 99. **sphery eyne:** starry eyes. 119. **point . . . skill:** summit of human discernment.

For as a surfeit of the sweetest things
The deepest loathing to the stomach brings,
Or as the heresies that men do leave
Are hated most of those they did deceive,   140
So thou, my surfeit and my heresy,
Of all be hated, but the most of me!
And, all my powers, address your love and might
To honour Helen and to be her knight.   [*Exit.*
Her. [*Awaking.*] Help me, Lysander, help me! do
        thy best   145
To pluck this crawling serpent from my breast!
Ay me, for pity! what a dream was here!
Lysander, look how I do quake with fear.
Methought a serpent eat my heart away,
And you sat smiling at his cruel prey.   150
Lysander! what, remov'd? Lysander! lord!
What, out of hearing? Gone? No sound, no word?
Alack, where are you? Speak, an if you hear;
Speak, of all loves! I swoon almost with fear.
No? then I well perceive you are not nigh.   155
Either death or you I'll find immediately.   [*Exit.*

ACT III

[SCENE I. *The wood. Titania lying asleep.*]

Enter the Clowns [QUINCE, SNUG, BOTTOM, FLUTE,
        SNOUT, *and* STARVELING].

Bot. Are we all met?
Quin. Pat, pat; and here's a marvellous convenient place for our rehearsal. This green plot
shall be our stage, this hawthorn-brake our tiring-
house; and we will do it in action as we will do it before the Duke.   6
Bot. Peter Quince!
Quin. What say'st thou, bully Bottom?
Bot. There are things in this comedy of Pyramus
and Thisby that will never please. First, Pyra-   10
mus must draw a sword to kill himself, which the
ladies cannot abide. How answer you that?
Snout. By'r lakin, a parlous fear.
Star. I believe we must leave the killing out,
when all is done.   16
Bot. Not a whit! I have a device to make all
well. Write me a prologue; and let the prologue
seem to say, we will do no harm with our swords and
that Pyramus is not kill'd indeed; and, for the   20
more better assurance, tell them that I Pyramus am
not Pyramus, but Bottom the weaver. This will
put them out of fear.
Quin. Well, we will have such a prologue; and it
shall be written in eight and six.   25

Bot. No, make it two more; let it be written in
eight and eight.
Snout. Will not the ladies be afeard of the lion?
Star. I fear it, I promise you.
Bot. Masters, you ought to consider with   30
yourselves. To bring in — God shield us! — a lion
among ladies, is a most dreadful thing; for there is
not a more fearful wild-fowl than your lion living;
and we ought to look to't.
Snout. Therefore another prologue must tell he
is not a lion.   36
Bot. Nay, you must name his name, and half his
face must be seen through the lion's neck; and he
himself must speak through, saying thus, or to the
same defect, "Ladies," or "Fair ladies, I would   40
wish you," or "I would request you," or "I would
entreat you, not to fear, not to tremble: my life for
yours. If you think I come hither as a lion, it were
pity of my life. No, I am no such thing; I am a man
as other men are;" and there indeed let him   45
name his name, and tell them plainly he is Snug the
joiner.
Quin. Well, it shall be so. But there is two hard
things; that is, to bring the moonlight into a chamber; for, you know, Pyramus and Thisby meet by
moonlight.   51
Snout. Doth the moon shine that night we play
our play?
Bot. A calendar, a calendar! Look in the almanac! Find out moonshine, find out moonshine.
Quin. Yes, it doth shine that night.   56
Bot. Why, then may you leave a casement of the
great chamber window, where we play, open, and
the moon may shine in at the casement.
Quin. Ay; or else one must come in with a   60
bush of thorns and a lantern, and say he comes to
disfigure, or to present, the person of Moonshine.
Then, there is another thing: we must have a wall
in the great chamber; for Pyramus and Thisby, says
the story, did talk through the chink of a wall.   66
Snout. You can never bring in a wall. What say
you, Bottom?
Bot. Some man or other must present Wall; and
let him have some plaster, or some loam, or some
rough-cast about him, to signify wall; or let him   71
hold his fingers thus, and through that cranny shall
Pyramus and Thisby whisper.
Quin. If that may be, then all is well. Come, sit
down, every mother's son, and rehearse your parts.
Pyramus, you begin. When you have spoken   76
your speech, enter into that brake. And so every
one according to his cue.

150. **prey:** preying.   154. **of all loves:** for love's sake.
Act III, sc. i, 5. **tiring-house:** dressing room.   8. **bully:** "good old"; a term of friendship.   13. **By'r lakin:** by our ladykin,
i.e., the Virgin Mary.   **parlous:** perilous.   25. **eight and six:** alternate lines of eight and six syllables, ballad meter.   32.
lion among ladies. See Introduction.   40. **defect:** error for *effect*.   62. **disfigure:** blunder for *prefigure*.   71. **rough-cast:**
plaster mixed with pebbles.

Enter ROBIN GOODFELLOW [*behind*].

Robin. What hempen home-spuns have we swag-
    g'ring here,
So near the cradle of the fairy queen?   80
What, a play toward! I'll be an auditor;
An actor too perhaps, if I see cause.

Quin. Speak, Pyramus. Thisby, stand forth.

Bot. "Thisby, the flowers of odious savours
    sweet," —

Quin. Odorous, odorous.   85

Bot. —— "odours savours sweet;
So hath thy breath, my dearest Thisby dear.
But hark, a voice! Stay thou but here awhile,
    And by and by I will to thee appear." [*Exit.*

Robin. A stranger Pyramus than e'er play'd here.
                        [*Exit.*]

Flu. Must I speak now?   91

Quin. Ay, marry, must you; for you must understand he goes but to see a noise that he heard, and is
to come again.

Flu. "Most radiant Pyramus, most lily-white
    of hue,   95
Of colour like the red rose on triumphant brier,
Most brisky juvenal and eke most lovely Jew,
    As true as truest horse that yet would never tire,
I'll meet thee, Pyramus, at Ninny's tomb."   99

Quin. "Ninus' tomb," man. Why, you must
not speak that yet; that you answer to Pyramus. You speak all your part at once, cues and all.
Pyramus enter. Your cue is past; it is, "never tire."

Flu. O,—"As true as truest horse, that yet would
never tire."   105

[*Re-enter* ROBIN GOODFELLOW, *and* BOTTOM *with an
ass's head*.]

Bot. "If I were fair, Thisby, I were only thine."

Quin. O monstrous! O strange! we are haunted.
Pray, masters, fly, masters! Help!
        [*Exeunt* [*Quince, Snug, Flute, Snout, and
           Starveling*].

Robin. I'll follow you, I'll lead you about, a-
    round,
Through bog, through bush, through brake,
    through brier,   110
Sometime a horse I'll be, sometime a hound,
    A hog, a headless bear, sometime a fire;
And neigh, and bark, and grunt, and roar, and burn,
Like horse, hound, hog, bear, fire, at every turn.
                        [*Exit.*

Bot. Why do they run away? This is a knavery
of them to make me afeard.   116

Re-enter SNOUT.

Snout. O Bottom, thou art chang'd! What do I
see on thee?

Bot. What do you see? You see an ass-head of
your own, do you?   [*Exit Snout.*]   120

Re-enter QUINCE.

Quin. Bless thee, Bottom! bless thee! thou art
translated.   [*Exit.*

Bot. I see their knavery; this is to make an ass of
me, to fright me, if they could. But I will not stir
from this place, do what they can. I will   125
walk up and down here, and I will sing, that they
shall hear I am not afraid.   [*Sings.*]
  "The ousel cock so black of hue,
    With orange-tawny bill,
  The throstle with his note so true,   130
    The wren with little quill," —

Tita. [*Awaking.*] What angel wakes me from my
    flowery bed?

Bot. [*Sings.*]
  "The finch, the sparrow, and the lark,
    The plain-song cuckoo gray,
  Whose note full many a man doth mark,   135
    And dares not answer nay;" —
for, indeed, who would set his wit to so foolish a
bird? Who would give a bird the lie, though he
cry "cuckoo" never so?

Tita. I pray thee, gentle mortal, sing again.   140
Mine ear is much enamour'd of thy note;
So is mine eye enthralled to thy shape;
And thy fair virtue's force perforce doth move me
On the first view to say, to swear, I love thee.

Bot. Methinks, mistress, you should have   145
little reason for that; and yet, to say the truth,
reason and love keep little company together now-
a-days; the more the pity that some honest neighbours will not make them friends. Nay, I can
gleek upon occasion.   150

Tita. Thou art as wise as thou art beautiful.

Bot. Not so, neither; but if I had wit enough to
get out of this wood, I have enough to serve mine
own turn.

Tita. Out of this wood do not desire to go;   155
Thou shalt remain here, whether thou wilt or no.
I am a spirit of no common rate;
The summer still doth tend upon my state;
And I do love thee; therefore, go with me.
I'll give thee fairies to attend on thee,   160
And they shall fetch thee jewels from the deep,
And sing while thou on pressed flowers dost sleep.
And I will purge thy mortal grossness so

<hr>

81. **toward:** afoot. 97. **brisky juvenal:** lively youth. **Jew:** Probably a nonsensical repetition of the first syllable of *juvenal*. 100. **Ninus:** mythical founder of Babylon, the setting of the tale of Pyramus and Thisbe. 122. **translated:** transformed. 128. **ousel:** blackbird. Q₁ reads *woosel*. 131. **quill:** pipe. 134. **plain-song:** melody without variations. 135-136.
Whose ... nay. The note of the cuckoo sounded not unlike "cuckold," an unwelcome word to husbands. 150. **gleek:** jest
satirically. 158. **still:** always.

That thou shalt like an airy spirit go.
Peaseblossom! Cobweb! Moth! and Mustard-
seed!   165

Enter four Fairies [PEASEBLOSSOM, COBWEB, MOTH,
and MUSTARDSEED].

Peas. Ready.
Cob.   And I.
Moth.   And I.
Mus.   And I.
All.   Where shall we go?
Tita. Be kind and courteous to this gentleman.
Hop in his walks and gambol in his eyes;
Feed him with apricocks and dewberries,
With purple grapes, green figs, and mulberries; 170
The honey-bags steal from the humble-bees,
And for night-tapers crop their waxen thighs
And light them at the fiery glow-worm's eyes,
To have my love to bed and to arise;
And pluck the wings from painted butterflies 175
To fan the moonbeams from his sleeping eyes.
Nod to him, elves, and do him courtesies.
Peas. Hail, mortal!
Cob. Hail!
Moth. Hail!   180
Mus. Hail!
Bot. I cry your worships mercy, heartily. I be-
seech your worship's name.
Cob. Cobweb.
Bot. I shall desire you of more acquaintance, 185
good Master Cobweb. If I cut my finger, I shall
make bold with you. Your name, honest gentle-
man?
Peas. Peaseblossom.
Bot. I pray you commend me to Mistress 190
Squash, your mother, and to Master Peascod, your
father. Good Master Peaseblossom, I shall desire
you of more acquaintance too. Your name, I beseech you, sir?
Mus. Mustardseed.   195
Bot. Good Master Mustardseed, I know your
patience well. That same cowardly, giant-like ox-
beef hath devoured many a gentleman of your
house. I promise you your kindred hath made my
eyes water ere now. I desire you more acquaintance, good Master Mustardseed.   201
Tita. Come, wait upon him; lead him to my
bower.
The moon methinks looks with a wat'ry eye;
And when she weeps, weeps every little flower,
Lamenting some enforced chastity.   205
Tie up my [love's] tongue, bring him silently.
                                          [*Exeunt.*

[SCENE II. *Another part of the wood.*]

Enter OBERON.

Obe. I wonder if Titania be awak'd;
Then, what it was that next came in her eye,
Which she must dote on in extremity.

Enter ROBIN GOODFELLOW.

Here comes my messenger.
                          How now, mad spirit!
What night-rule now about this haunted grove? 5
Robin. My mistress with a monster is in love.
Near to her close and consecrated bower,
While she was in her dull and sleeping hour,
A crew of patches, rude mechanicals,
That work for bread upon Athenian stalls,   10
Were met together to rehearse a play
Intended for great Theseus' nuptial-day.
The shallowest thickskin of that barren sort,
Who Pyramus presented in their sport,
Forsook his scene and ent'red in a brake.   15
When I did him at this advantage take,
An ass's nole I fixed on his head.
Anon his Thisby must be answered,
And forth my mimic comes. When they him spy,
As wild geese that the creeping fowler eye,   20
Or russet-pated choughs, many in sort,
Rising and cawing at the gun's report,
Sever themselves and madly sweep the sky,
So, at his sight, away his fellows fly;
And, at our stamp, here o'er and o'er one falls; 25
He murder cries, and help from Athens calls.
Their sense thus weak, lost with their fears thus
    strong,
Made senseless things begin to do them wrong;
For briers and thorns at their apparel snatch;
Some sleeves, some hats, from yielders all things
    catch.   30
I led them on in this distracted fear,
And left sweet Pyramus translated there;
When in that moment, so it came to pass,
Titania wak'd and straightway lov'd an ass.
Obe. This falls out better than I could devise.
But hast thou yet latch'd the Athenian's eyes   36
With the love-juice, as I did bid thee do?
Robin. I took him sleeping, — that is finish'd
    too, —
And the Athenian woman by his side;
That, when he wak'd, of force she must be ey'd. 40

Enter DEMETRIUS *and* HERMIA.

Obe. Stand close; this is the same Athenian.
Robin. This is the woman, but not this the man.

191. **Squash:** unripe pea pod. 197. **patience:** suffering. 205. **enforced:** violated. 206. **[love's]** (Pope). *lovers* Q.
Sc. ii, 2. **next:** first. 3. **in extremity:** extremely. 5. **night-rule:** diversion planned for the night. 9. **patches:**
yokels. **mechanicals:** artisans. 13. **barren sort:** dull crew. 17. **nole:** head. 19. **mimic:** buffoon, burlesque actor. 21.
choughs: jackdaws. **in sort:** together. 24. **his sight:** sight of him. 36. **latch'd:** anointed. 40. **of force:** perforce.

Dem. O, why rebuke you him that loves you so?
Lay breath so bitter on your bitter foe.

Her. Now I but chide; but I should use thee
    worse,   45
For thou, I fear, hast given me cause to curse.
If thou hast slain Lysander in his sleep,
Being o'er shoes in blood, plunge in knee-deep,
And kill me too.
The sun was not so true unto the day   50
As he to me: would he have stolen away
From sleeping Hermia? I'll believe as soon
This whole earth may be bor'd and that the moon
May through the centre creep and so displease
Her brother's noontide with the Antipodes. 55
It cannot be but thou hast murd'red him;
So should a murderer look, so dread, so grim.

Dem. So should the murd'red look, and so
    should I,
Pierc'd through the heart with your stern cruelty;
Yet you, the murderer, look as bright, as clear, 60
As yonder Venus in her glimmering sphere.

Her. What's this to my Lysander? Where is he?
Ah, good Demetrius, wilt thou give him me?

Dem. I had rather give his carcass to my hounds.

Her. Out, dog! out, cur! thou driv'st me past the
    bounds   65
Of maiden's patience. Hast thou slain him, then?
Henceforth be never numb'red among men!
O, once tell true, tell true, even for my sake!
Durst thou have look'd upon him being awake,
And hast thou kill'd him sleeping? O brave touch!
Could not a worm, an adder, do so much? 71
An adder did it; for with doubler tongue
Than thine, thou serpent, never adder stung.

Dem. You spend your passion on a mispris'd
    mood.
I am not guilty of Lysander's blood; 75
Nor is he dead, for aught that I can tell.

Her. I pray thee, tell me then that he is well.

Dem. An if I could, what should I get therefore?

Her. A privilege never to see me more.
And from thy hated presence part I so: 80
See me no more, whether he be dead or no. [*Exit.*

Dem. There is no following her in this fierce
    vein;
Here therefore for a while I will remain.
So sorrow's heaviness doth heavier grow 84
For debt that bankrupt sleep doth sorrow owe;
Which now in some slight measure it will pay,
If for his tender here I make some stay.
    [*Lies down [and sleeps].*

Obe. What hast thou done? Thou hast mistaken
    quite

And laid the love-juice on some true-love's sight.
Of thy misprision must perforce ensue 90
Some true love turn'd and not a false turn'd true.

Robin. Then fate o'er-rules, that, one man hold-
    ing troth,
A million fail, confounding oath on oath.

Obe. About the wood go swifter than the wind,
And Helena of Athens look thou find. 95
All fancy-sick she is and pale of cheer
With sighs of love, that costs the fresh blood dear.
By some illusion see thou bring her here.
I'll charm his eyes against she do appear.

Robin. I go, I go; look how I go, 100
Swifter than arrow from the Tartar's bow. [*Exit.*

Obe.   Flower of this purple dye,
    Hit with Cupid's archery,
    Sink in apple of his eye.
    When his love he doth espy, 105
    Let her shine as gloriously
    As the Venus of the sky.
    When thou wak'st, if she be by,
    Beg of her for remedy.

    Re-enter ROBIN GOODFELLOW.

Robin. Captain of our fairy band, 110
    Helena is here at hand;
    And the youth, mistook by me,
    Pleading for a lover's fee.
    Shall we their fond pageant see?
    Lord, what fools these mortals be! 115

Obe.   Stand aside. The noise they make
    Will cause Demetrius to awake.

Robin. Then will two at once woo one;
    That must needs be sport alone.
    And those things do best please me 120
    That befall preposterously.

    Enter LYSANDER *and* HELENA.

Lys. Why should you think that I should woo
    in scorn?
Scorn and derision never come in tears.
Look, when I vow, I weep; and vows so born,
    In their nativity all truth appears. 125
How can these things in me seem scorn to you,
Bearing the badge of faith, to prove them true?

Hel. You do advance your cunning more and
    more.
When truth kills truth, O devilish-holy fray!
These vows are Hermia's; will you give her o'er? 130
Weigh oath with oath, and you will nothing
    weigh.
Your vows to her and me, put in two scales,
Will even weigh, and both as light as tales.

70. **touch:** exploit. 71. **worm:** serpent. 74. **on ... mood:** in mistaken anger. 87. **for his tender:** i.e., until sleep tenders itself. 90. **misprision:** mistake. 96. **fancy-sick:** love-sick. **cheer:** face. 97. **sighs ... blood.** It was commonly thought that each sigh took a drop of blood from the heart. 99. **against ... appear:** in anticipation of her appearance. 114. **fond pageant:** foolish exhibition. 119. **alone:** unique. 124–125. **vows ... appears:** vows so born show wholly true.

Lys. I had no judgement when to her I swore.
Hel. Nor none, in my mind, now you give her
    o'er.   135
Lys. Demetrius loves her, and he loves not you.
Dem. [*Awaking.*] O Helen, goddess, nymph,
    perfect, divine!
To what, my love, shall I compare thine eyne?
Crystal is muddy. O, how ripe in show   139
Thy lips, those kissing cherries, tempting grow!
That pure congealed white, high Taurus' snow,
Fann'd with the eastern wind, turns to a crow
When thou hold'st up thy hand. O, let me kiss
This princess of pure white, this seal of bliss!
Hel. O spite! O hell! I see you all are bent
To set against me for your merriment.   146
If you were civil and knew courtesy,
You would not do me thus much injury.
Can you not hate me, as I know you do,
But you must join in souls to mock me too?   150
If you were men, as men you are in show,
You would not use a gentle lady so;
To vow, and swear, and superpraise my parts,
When I am sure you hate me with your hearts.
You both are rivals, and love Hermia;   155
And now both rivals, to mock Helena.
A trim exploit, a manly enterprise,
To conjure tears up in a poor maid's eyes
With your derision! None of noble sort
Would so offend a virgin and extort   160
A poor soul's patience, all to make you sport.
Lys. You are unkind, Demetrius; be not so;
For you love Hermia; this you know I know.
And here, with all good will, with all my heart,
In Hermia's love I yield you up my part;   165
And yours of Helena to me bequeath,
Whom I do love and will do till my death.
Hel. Never did mockers waste more idle breath.
Dem. Lysander, keep thy Hermia; I will none.
If e'er I lov'd her, all that love is gone.   170
My heart to her but as guest-wise sojourn'd,
And now to Helen is it home return'd,
There to remain.
Lys.   Helen, it is not so.
Dem. Disparage not the faith thou dost not
    know,
Lest, to thy peril, thou aby it dear.   175
Look, where thy love comes, yonder is thy dear.

Re-enter HERMIA.

Her. Dark night, that from the eye his function
    takes,
The ear more quick of apprehension makes;

Wherein it doth impair the seeing sense,
It pays the hearing double recompense.   180
Thou art not by mine eye, Lysander, found;
Mine ear, I thank it, brought me to thy sound.
But why unkindly didst thou leave me so?
    Lys. Why should he stay, whom love doth press
    to go?
    Her. What love could press Lysander from my
    side?   185
    Lys. Lysander's love, that would not let him bide,
Fair Helena, who more engilds the night
Than all yon fiery oes and eyes of light.
Why seek'st thou me? Could not this make thee
    know,
The hate I bare thee made me leave thee so?   190
    Her. You speak not as you think. It cannot be.
    Hel. Lo, she is one of this confederacy!
Now I perceive they have conjoin'd all three
To fashion this false sport, in spite of me.
Injurious Hermia! most ungrateful maid!   195
Have you conspir'd, have you with these contriv'd
To bait me with this foul derision?
Is all the counsel that we two have shar'd,
The sisters' vows, the hours that we have spent,
When we have chid the hasty-footed time   200
For parting us, — O, is all forgot?
All school-days' friendship, childhood innocence?
We, Hermia, like two artificial gods,
Have with our needles created both one flower,
Both on one sampler, sitting on one cushion,   205
Both warbling of one song, both in one key,
As if our hands, our sides, voices and minds
Had been incorporate. So we grew together,
Like to a double cherry, seeming parted,
But yet an union in partition;   210
Two lovely berries moulded on one stem;
So, with two seeming bodies but one heart;
Two of the first, [like] coats in heraldry,
Due but to one and crowned with one crest.
And will you rend our ancient love asunder,   215
To join with men in scorning your poor friend?
It is not friendly, 'tis not maidenly.
Our sex, as well as I, may chide you for it,
Though I alone do feel the injury.
    Her. I am amazed at your passionate words.
I scorn you not; it seems that you scorn me.   221
    Hel. Have you not set Lysander, as in scorn,
To follow me and praise my eyes and face?
And made your other love, Demetrius,
Who even but now did spurn me with his foot,
To call me goddess, nymph, divine and rare,   226
Precious, celestial? Wherefore speaks he this

141. **Taurus:** a mountain range in Asia Minor.   144. **seal:** pledge.   153. **parts:** qualities.   160. **extort:** wrest, torture.   169. **will none:** i.e., of her.   175. **aby:** pay for.   177. **his:** its.   188. **oes:** orbs, circles.   195. **Injurious:** insulting.   203. **artificial:** skilled in art.   208. **incorporate:** joined in one body.   213. **Two of the first.** Apparently a heraldic phrase used of two coats of arms (such as those of husband and wife) arranged on either side of a vertical division of the shield, such division being known as "the first" of several possible divisions.   **[like]** (Folks conj.).   *life* Q.

To her he hates?   And wherefore doth Lysander
Deny your love, so rich within his soul,
And tender me, forsooth, affection,   230
But by your setting on, by your consent?
What though I be not so in grace as you,
So hung upon with love, so fortunate,
But miserable most, to love unlov'd?
This you should pity rather than despise.   235
   Her. I understand not what you mean by this.
   Hel. Ay, do, persever, counterfeit sad looks,
Make mouths upon me when I turn my back,
Wink each at other, hold the sweet jest up;
This sport, well carried, shall be chronicled.   240
If you have any pity, grace, or manners,
You would not make me such an argument.
But fare ye well; 'tis partly my own fault,
Which death or absence soon shall remedy.
   Lys. Stay, gentle Helena; hear my excuse,   245
My love, my life, my soul, fair Helena!
   Hel. O excellent!
   Her.   Sweet, do not scorn her so.
   Dem. If she cannot entreat, I can compel.
   Lys. Thou canst compel no more than she entreat.
Thy threats have no more strength than her weak
   [prayers].   250
Helen, I love thee; by my life, I do!
I swear by that which I will lose for thee,
To prove him false that says I love thee not.
   Dem. I say I love thee more than he can do.   254
   Lys. If thou say so, withdraw, and prove it too.
   Dem. Quick, come!
   Her.   Lysander, whereto tends all this?
   Lys. Away, you Ethiope!
   Dem.   No, no; he'll [but]
Seem to break loose.   Take on as you would follow,
But yet come not.   You are a tame man, go!
   Lys. Hang off, thou cat, thou burr!   Vile thing,
   let loose,   260
Or I will shake thee from me like a serpent!
   Her. Why are you grown so rude?   What change
   is this?
Sweet love, —
   Lys.   Thy love!   Out, tawny Tartar, out!
Out, loathed medicine!   O hated potion, hence!
   Her. Do you not jest?
   Hel.   Yes, sooth; and so do you.   265
   Lys. Demetrius, I will keep my word with thee.
   Dem. I would I had your bond, for I perceive
A weak bond holds you. I'll not trust your word.
   Lys. What, should I hurt her, strike her, kill her
   dead?
Although I hate her, I'll not harm her so.   270
   Her. What, can you do me greater harm than
   hate?

Hate me! wherefore?   O me! what news, my love!
Am not I Hermia?   Are not you Lysander?
I am as fair now as I was erewhile.
Since night you lov'd me; yet since night you left
   me: 275
Why, then you left me — O, the gods forbid! —
In earnest, shall I say?
   Lys.   Ay, by my life;
And never did desire to see thee more.
Therefore be out of hope, of question, doubt;
Be certain, nothing truer; 'tis no jest   280
That I do hate thee and love Helena.
   Her. O me! you juggler! you canker-blossom!
You thief of love!   What, have you come by night
And stolen my love's heart from him?
   Hel.   Fine, i' faith!
Have you no modesty, no maiden shame,   285
No touch of bashfulness?   What, will you tear
Impatient answers from my gentle tongue?
Fie, fie! you counterfeit, you puppet, you!
   Her. "Puppet?"   Why so?   Ay, that way goes
   the game.
Now I perceive that she hath made compare   290
Between our statures; she hath urg'd her height;
And with her personage, her tall personage,
Her height, forsooth, she hath prevail'd with him.
And are you grown so high in his esteem,
Because I am so dwarfish and so low?   295
How low am I, thou painted maypole?   Speak,
How low am I?   I am not yet so low
But that my nails can reach unto thine eyes.
   Hel. I pray you, though you mock me, gentlemen,
Let her not hurt me.   I was never curst;   300
I have no gift at all in shrewishness;
I am a right maid for my cowardice.
Let her not strike me.   You perhaps may think,
Because she is something lower than myself,
That I can match her.
   Her.   "Lower!" hark, again. 305
   Hel. Good Hermia, do not be so bitter with me.
I evermore did love you, Hermia,
Did ever keep your counsels, never wrong'd you;
Save that, in love unto Demetrius,
I told him of your stealth unto this wood.   310
He followed you; for love I followed him;
But he hath chid me hence and threat'ned me
To strike me, spurn me, nay, to kill me too.
And now, so you will let me quiet go,
To Athens will I bear my folly back   315
And follow you no further.   Let me go.
You see how simple and how fond I am.
   Her. Why, get you gone; who is't that hinders
   you?
   Hel. A foolish heart, that I leave here behind.

---

237. **sad**: grave.   242. **argument**: subject for scorn.   250. **[prayers]** (Theobald).   *praise* Q.   257. **he'll [but]**. Nicolson conj. for the obviously corrupt *heele* of Q.   272. **what news?** what is the matter?   282. **canker-blossom**: worm that destroys a blossom.   300. **curst**: shrewish.   302. **right**: true.   310. **stealth**: stealing away.

Her. What, with Lysander?

Hel.   With Demetrius.   320

Lys. Be not afraid; she shall not harm thee, Helena.

Dem. No, sir, she shall not, though you take her part.

Hel. O, when she's angry, she is keen and shrewd! She was a vixen when she went to school; And though she be but little, she is fierce.   325

Her. "Little" again! Nothing but "low" and "little"! Why will you suffer her to flout me thus? Let me come to her.

Lys.   Get you gone, you dwarf, You minimus, of hind'ring knot-grass made; You bead, you acorn.

Dem.   You are too officious   330 In her behalf that scorns your services. Let her alone; speak not of Helena; Take not her part; for, if thou dost intend Never so little show of love to her, Thou shalt aby it.

Lys.   Now she holds me not.   335 Now follow, if thou dar'st, to try whose right, Of thine or mine, is most in Helena.

Dem. Follow! Nay, I'll go with thee, cheek by jowl.

                    [*Exeunt Lysander and Demetrius.*

Her. You, mistress, all this coil is 'long of you. Nay, go not back.

Hel.   I will not trust you, I,   340 Nor longer stay in your curst company. Your hands than mine are quicker for a fray; My legs are longer though, to run away.   [*Exit.*

Her. I am amaz'd, and know not what to say.
                                        [*Exit.*

Obe. This is thy negligence. Still thou mistak'st, Or else committ'st thy knaveries wilfully.   346

Robin. Believe me, king of shadows, I mistook. Did not you tell me I should know the man By the Athenian garments he had on? And so far blameless proves my enterprise,   350 That I have 'nointed an Athenian's eyes; And so far am I glad it so did sort, As this their jangling I esteem a sport.

Obe. Thou see'st these lovers seek a place to fight; Hie therefore, Robin, overcast the night.   355 The starry welkin cover thou anon With drooping fog as black as Acheron, And lead these testy rivals so astray As one come not within another's way. Like to Lysander sometime frame thy tongue,   360

Then stir Demetrius up with bitter wrong; And sometime rail thou like Demetrius; And from each other look thou lead them thus, Till o'er their brows death-counterfeiting sleep With leaden legs and batty wings doth creep.   365 Then crush this herb into Lysander's eye; Whose liquor hath this virtuous property, To take from thence all error with his might, And make his eyeballs roll with wonted sight. When they next wake, all this derision   370 Shall seem a dream and fruitless vision; And back to Athens shall the lovers wend With league whose date till death shall never end. Whiles I in this affair do thee employ, I'll to my queen and beg her Indian boy;   375 And then I will her charmed eye release From monster's view, and all things shall be peace.

Robin. My fairy lord, this must be done with haste, For Night's swift dragons cut the clouds full fast, And yonder shines Aurora's harbinger,   380 At whose approach, ghosts, wand'ring here and there, Troop home to churchyards. Damned spirits all, That in crossways and floods have burial, Already to their wormy beds are gone. For fear lest day should look their shames upon, They wilfully themselves exile from light   386 And must for aye consort with black-brow'd night.

Obe. But we are spirits of another sort. I with the Morning's love have oft made sport, And, like a forester, the groves may tread,   390 Even till the eastern gate, all fiery-red, Opening on Neptune with fair blessed beams Turns into yellow gold his salt green streams; But, notwithstanding, haste, make no delay; We may effect this business yet ere day.   [*Exit.*

Robin. Up and down, up and down,   396 I will lead them up and down. I am fear'd in field and town. Goblin, lead them up and down. Here comes one.   400

Re-enter LYSANDER.

Lys. Where art thou, proud Demetrius? Speak thou now.

Robin. Here, villain; drawn and ready. Where art thou?

Lys. I will be with thee straight.

Robin.   Follow me, then, To plainer ground.

                    [*Exit Lysander, as following the voice.*

323. **shrewd:** sharp-tongued.   329. **minimus:** dwarf. **knot-grass:** a weed supposed capable of stunting the growth.   333. **intend:** proffer.   339. **coil:** turmoil. **'long:** because.   352. **sort:** turn out.   357. **Acheron:** river of Hades.   361. **wrong:** taunts.   367. **virtuous:** powerful.   368. **his might:** its power.   379. **night's . . . dragons:** the dragons drawing the car of Night.   380. **Aurora's harbinger:** star announcing the dawn.   383. **crossways . . . burial.** Suicides were buried at crossroads, and like the ghosts of those who had drowned, having thus no proper burial, were believed condemned to cheerless wandering.   389. **Morning's love:** Cephalus, the youth loved by Aurora, or possibly Aurora herself.

Re-enter DEMETRIUS.

Dem.   Lysander, speak again!
Thou runaway, thou coward, art thou fled?   405
Speak! In some bush? Where dost thou hide thy
    head?
Robin. Thou coward, art thou bragging to the
    stars,
Telling the bushes that thou look'st for wars,
And wilt not come? Come, recreant; come, thou
    ˙child,
I'll whip thee with a rod. He is defil'd   410
That draws a sword on thee.
    Dem.   Yea, art thou there?
Robin. Follow my voice. We'll try no manhood
    here.   [*Exeunt.*

[*Re-enter* LYSANDER.]

Lys. He goes before me and still dares me on.
When I come where he calls, then he is gone.
The villain is much lighter-heel'd than I;   415
I followed fast, but faster he did fly,
That fallen am I in dark uneven way,
And here will rest me. Come, thou gentle day!
                        [*Lies down.*
For if but once thou show me thy grey light,
I'll find Demetrius and revenge this spite.   420
                        [*Sleeps.*

Re-enter ROBIN GOODFELLOW *and* DEMETRIUS.

Robin. Ho, ho, ho! Coward, why com'st thou not?
Dem. Abide me, if thou dar'st; for well I wot
Thou runn'st before me, shifting every place,
And dar'st not stand, nor look me in the face.
Where art thou now?
    Robin.   Come hither; I am here.
Dem. Nay, then, thou mock'st me. Thou shalt
    buy this dear,   426
If ever I thy face by daylight see.
Now, go thy way. Faintness constraineth me
To measure out my length on this cold bed.
By day's approach look to be visited.   430
                    [*Lies down and sleeps.*

Re-enter HELENA.

Hel. O weary night, O long and tedious night,
Abate thy hours! Shine, comforts, from the east,
That I may back to Athens by daylight,
From these that my poor company detest.
And sleep, that sometimes shuts up sorrow's eye,
Steal me awhile from mine own company.   436
                    [*Lies down and*] *sleeps.*
Robin. Yet but three? Come one more;
    Two of both kinds makes up four.

Re-enter HERMIA.

Here she comes, curst and sad.

Cupid is a knavish lad,   440
    Thus to make poor females mad.
Her. Never so weary, never so in woe,
    Bedabbled with the dew and torn with briers,
I can no further crawl, no further go;
    My legs can keep no pace with my desires.   445
Here will I rest me till the break of day.
Heavens shield Lysander, if they mean a fray!
                    [*Lies down and sleeps.*
Robin.   On the ground
            Sleep sound.
            I'll apply   450
            To your eye,
    Gentle lover, remedy.
            [*Squeezing the juice on Lysander's eyes.*
            When thou wak'st,
            Thou tak'st
            True delight   455
            In the sight
    Of thy former lady's eye;
    And the country proverb known,
    That every man should take his own,
    In your waking shall be shown.   460
            Jack shall have Jill;
            Nought shall go ill;
The man shall have his mare again, and all shall be
    well.   [*Exit.*

ACT IV

[SCENE I. *The same.*]

[LYSANDER, DEMETRIUS, HELENA, *and* HERMIA,
        lying asleep.]

Enter TITANIA *and Clown* [BOTTOM; PEASEBLOSSOM,
COBWEB, MOTH, MUSTARDSEED,] *and* [*other*]
Fairies [*attending*]; OBERON *behind* [*unseen*].

Tita. Come, sit thee down upon this flow'ry bed,
    While I thy amiable cheeks do coy;
And stick musk-roses in thy sleek smooth head,
    And kiss thy fair large ears, my gentle joy.
Bot. Where's Peaseblossom?   5
Peas. Ready.
Bot. Scratch my head, Peaseblossom. Where's
Mounsieur Cobweb?
Cob. Ready.
Bot. Mounsieur Cobweb, good mounsieur, get
you your weapons in your hand, and kill me a   11
red-hipp'd humble-bee on the top of a thistle; and,
good mounsieur, bring me the honey-bag. Do not
fret yourself too much in the action, mounsieur,
and, good mounsieur, have a care the honey-bag
break not; I would be loath to have you over-   16
flown with a honey-bag, signior. Where's Mounsieur Mustardseed?
Mus. Ready.   19

    Act IV, sc. i, 2. **coy:** caress.

Bot. Give me your neaf, Mounsieur Mustardseed.   Pray you, leave your courtesy, good mounsieur.

Mus. What's your will?

Bot. Nothing, good mounsieur, but to help
Cavalery Cobweb to scratch.   I must to the barber's, mounsieur; for methinks I am marvellous   25
hairy about the face; and I am such a tender ass, if
my hair do but tickle me, I must scratch.

Tita. What, wilt thou hear some music, my
sweet love?

Bot. I have a reasonable good ear in music.   30
Let's have the tongs and the bones.

[Music. Tongs. Rural music.

Tita. Or say, sweet love, what thou desir'st to
eat.

Bot. Truly, a peck of provender; I could munch
your good dry oats.   Methinks I have a great desire to a bottle of hay.   Good hay, sweet hay,
hath no fellow.   36

Tita. I have a venturous fairy that shall seek
The squirrel's hoard, and fetch [for] thee new nuts.

Bot. I had rather have a handful or two of dried
peas.   But, I pray you, let none of your people   40
stir me; I have an exposition of sleep come upon me.

Tita. Sleep thou, and I will wind thee in my arms.
Fairies, be gone, and be always away.

[Exeunt fairies.]

So doth the woodbine the sweet honeysuckle   45
Gently entwist; the female ivy so
Enrings the barky fingers of the elm.
O, how I love thee! how I dote on thee!

[They sleep.]

Enter ROBIN GOODFELLOW.

Obe. [*Advancing.*] Welcome, good Robin.   See'st
thou this sweet sight?
Her dotage now I do begin to pity;   50
For, meeting her of late behind the wood,
Seeking sweet favours for this hateful fool,
I did upbraid her and fall out with her.
For she his hairy temples then had rounded
With coronet of fresh and fragrant flowers;   55
And that same dew, which sometime on the buds
Was wont to swell like round and orient pearls,
Stood now within the pretty flowerets' eyes
Like tears that did their own disgrace bewail.
When I had at my pleasure taunted her   60
And she in mild terms begg'd my patience,
I then did ask of her her changeling child;
Which straight she gave me, and her fairy sent
To bear him to my bower in fairy land.

And, now I have the boy, I will undo   65
This hateful imperfection of her eyes;
And, gentle Puck, take this transformed scalp
From off the head of this Athenian swain,
That, he awaking when the other do,
May all to Athens back again repair,   70
And think no more of this night's accidents
But as the fierce vexation of a dream.
But first I will release the fairy queen.

[Touching her eyes.]

Be as thou wast wont to be;
See as thou wast wont to see: 75
Dian's bud o'er Cupid's flower
Hath such force and blessed power.
Now, my Titania; wake you, my sweet queen.

Tita. My Oberon! what visions have I seen!
Methought I was enamour'd of an ass.   80

Obe. There lies your love.

Tita.   How came these things to pass?
O, how mine eyes do loathe his visage now!

Obe. Silence awhile.   Robin, take off this head.
Titania, music call; and strike more dead
Than common sleep of all these five the sense.   85

Tita. Music, ho! music, such as charmeth sleep!

[Music, still.

Robin. Now, when thou wak'st, with thine own
fool's eyes peep.

Obe. Sound, music!   Come, my queen, take
hands with me,   89
And rock the ground whereon these sleepers be.
Now thou and I are new in amity
And will to-morrow midnight solemnly
Dance in Duke Theseus' house triumphantly
And bless it to all fair prosperity.
There shall the pairs of faithful lovers be   95
Wedded, with Theseus, all in jollity.

Robin. Fairy king, attend and mark;
I do hear the morning lark.

Obe. Then, my queen, in silence sad
Trip we after the night's shade.   100
We the globe can compass soon,
Swifter than the wand'ring moon.

Tita. Come, my lord, and in our flight
Tell me how it came this night
That I sleeping here was found   105
With these mortals on the ground.

[Exeunt. Horns winded [within].

Enter THESEUS, HIPPOLYTA, EGEUS, *and all his
train.*

The. Go, one of you, find out the forester,
For now our observation is perform'd,

---

20. **neaf:** fist.   21. **leave your courtesy:** put on your hat.   24. **Cavalery:** cavaliero, gentleman.   **Cobweb.** We should
expect *Peaseblossom* (cf. l. 7).   31. **tongs...bones:** rustic instruments of music.   35. **bottle:** bundle.   36. **fellow:** equal.
38. **[for]** (Collier conj.). Om. Qq.   41. **exposition of.** He means *disposition to.*   52. **favours:** i.e., flowers for love-tokens.
57. **orient:** eastern.   69. **other:** others.   76. **Dian's bud.** The flower of the *agnus castus* or chaste tree was believed to
preserve chastity.   108. **observation:** observance, May-day rites (cf. I.i.167).

And since we have the vaward of the day,
My love shall hear the music of my hounds.   110
Uncouple in the western valley, let them go.
Despatch, I say, and find the forester.

[Exit an attendant.]

We will, fair queen, up to the mountain's top
And mark the musical confusion
Of hounds and echo in conjunction.   115
  Hip. I was with Hercules and Cadmus once,
When in a wood of Crete they bay'd the bear
With hounds of Sparta.   Never did I hear
Such gallant chiding; for, besides the groves,
The skies, the fountains, every region near   120
Seem'd all one mutual cry.   I never heard
So musical a discord, such sweet thunder.
  The. My hounds are bred out of the Spartan kind,
So flew'd, so sanded, and their heads are hung
With ears that sweep away the morning dew;   125
Crook-knee'd, and dew-lapp'd like Thessalian bulls;
Slow in pursuit, but match'd in mouth like bells,
Each under each.   A cry more tuneable
Was never holla'd to, nor cheer'd with horn,
In Crete, in Sparta, nor in Thessaly.   130
Judge when you hear.   But, soft! what nymphs are
    these?
  Ege. My lord, this is my daughter here asleep;
And this, Lysander; this Demetrius is;
This Helena, old Nedar's Helena.
I wonder of their being here together.   135
  The. No doubt they rose up early to observe
The rite of May, and, hearing our intent,
Came here in grace of our solemnity.
But speak, Egeus; is not this the day
That Hermia should give answer of her choice?
  Ege. It is, my lord.   141
  The. Go, bid the huntsmen wake them with their
    horns.

*[Horns and shout within.   Lys., Dem., Hel.,
    and Her. wake and start up.*

Good morrow, friends.   Saint Valentine is past;
Begin these wood-birds but to couple now?
  Lys. Pardon, my lord.
  The.   I pray you all, stand up.
I know you two are rival enemies;   146
How comes this gentle concord in the world,
That hatred is so far from jealousy
To sleep by hate and fear no enmity?
  Lys. My lord, I shall reply amazedly,   150
Half sleep, half waking; but as yet, I swear,
I cannot truly say how I came here.
But, as I think, — for truly would I speak,
And now I do bethink me, so it is, —

I came with Hermia hither.   Our intent   155
Was to be gone from Athens, where we might,
Without the peril of the Athenian law —
  Ege. Enough, enough, my lord; you have enough.
I beg the law, the law, upon his head.
They would have stol'n away; they would, De-   160
    metrius,
Thereby to have defeated you and me,
You of your wife, and me of my consent,
Of my consent that she should be your wife.
  Dem. My lord, fair Helen told me of their stealth,
Of this their purpose hither to this wood;   165
And I in fury hither follow'd them,
Fair Helena in fancy following me.
But, my good lord, I wot not by what power, —
But by some power it is, — my love to Hermia,
Melted as [is] the snow, seems to me now   170
As the remembrance of an idle gaud
Which in my childhood I did dote upon;
And all the faith, the virtue of my heart,
The object and the pleasure of mine eye,
Is only Helena.   To her, my lord,   175
Was I betroth'd ere I saw Hermia;
But like a sickness did I loathe this food;
But, as in health, come to my natural taste,
Now I do wish it, love it, long for it,
And will for evermore be true to it.   180
  The. Fair lovers, you are fortunately met;
Of this discourse we more will hear anon.
Egeus, I will overbear your will;
For in the temple, by and by, with us
These couples shall eternally be knit.   185
And, for the morning now is something worn,
Our purpos'd hunting shall be set aside.
Away with us to Athens; three and three,
We'll hold a feast in great solemnity.
Come, Hippolyta.   190

[Exeunt The., Hip., Ege., and train.

  Dem. These things seem small and undistin-
    guishable,
Like far-off mountains turned into clouds.
  Her. Methinks I see these things with parted eye,
When every thing seems double.
  Hel.   So methinks;
And I have found Demetrius like a jewel,   195
Mine own, and not mine own.
  Dem.   [But] are you sure
That we are [now] awake?   It seems to me
That yet we sleep, we dream.   Do not you think
The Duke was here, and bid us follow him?
  Her. Yea; and my father.
  Hel.   And Hippolyta.   200

---

109. vaward: vanguard.   119. chiding: baying.   124. flew'd: with large chaps.   sanded: of sandy color.   128. **Each
...each:** with varied pitch.   Elizabethan huntsmen coveted packs of hounds whose cries would blend.   cry: pack.   138.
solemnity: marriage ceremony.   143. **Saint Valentine.**   Birds were popularly supposed to choose their mates on Valentine's day.   156. where: to a place where.   157. Without: beyond.   170. [is] (Steevens).   Om. Qq. Ff.   193. parted: out of focus.
196–97. [But] ... awake?   (Steevens conj.).   *Are you sure that we are awake?*   Qq. Om. Ff.

Lys. And he did bid us follow to the temple.

Dem. Why, then, we are awake. Let's follow him;
And by the way let us recount our dreams.

[*Exeunt lovers.*

Bot. (*Awaking.*) When my cue comes, call me, and I will answer. My next is, "Most fair Pyramus." Heigh-ho! Peter Quince! Flute, the bellows-mender! Snout, the tinker! Starveling! 207 God's my life, stolen hence, and left me asleep! I have had a most rare vision. I have had a dream, past the wit of man to say what dream it 210 was. Man is but an ass, if he go about to expound this dream. Methought I was — there is no man can tell what. Methought I was, — and methought I had, — but man is but a patch'd fool, if he will offer to say what methought I had. The eye of 215 man hath not heard, the ear of man hath not seen, man's hand is not able to taste, his tongue to conceive, nor his heart to report, what my dream was. I will get Peter Quince to write a ballad of this dream. It shall be called "Bottom's Dream," 220 because it hath no bottom; and I will sing it in the latter end of a play, before the Duke; peradventure, to make it the more gracious, I shall sing it at her death. [*Exit.*

[SCENE II. *Athens. Quince's house.*]

Enter QUINCE, FLUTE, SNOUT, *and* STARVELING.

Quin. Have you sent to Bottom's house? Is he come home yet?

Star. He cannot be heard of. Out of doubt he is transported.

Flu. If he come not, then the play is marr'd. It goes not forward, doth it? 6

Quin. It is not possible. You have not a man in all Athens able to discharge Pyramus but he.

Flu. No, he hath simply the best wit of any handicraft man in Athens. 10

Snout. Yea, and the best person too; and he is a very paramour for a sweet voice.

Flu. You must say "paragon"; a paramour is, God bless us, a thing of naught.

Enter SNUG.

Snug. Masters, the Duke is coming from the 15 temple, and there is two or three lords and ladies more married. If our sport had gone forward, we had all been made men.

Flu. O sweet bully Bottom! Thus hath he lost sixpence a day during his life; he could not 20 have 'scaped sixpence a day. An the Duke had not given him sixpence a day for playing Pyramus, I'll

be hang'd. He would have deserved it. Sixpence a day in Pyramus, or nothing.

Enter BOTTOM.

Bot. Where are these lads? Where are these hearts? 26

Quin. Bottom! O most courageous day! O most happy hour!

Bot. Masters, I am to discourse wonders, but ask me not what; for if I tell you, I am no true 30 Athenian. I will tell you everything, right as it fell out.

Quin. Let us hear, sweet Bottom.

Bot. Not a word of me. All that I will tell you is, that the Duke hath dined. Get your apparel 35 together, good strings to your beards, new ribbons to your pumps; meet presently at the palace; every man look o'er his part; for the short and the long is, our play is preferr'd. In any case, let Thisby have clean linen; and let not him that plays the 40 lion pare his nails, for they shall hang out for the lion's claws. And, most dear actors, eat no onions nor garlic, for we are to utter sweet breath; and I do not doubt but to hear them say, it is a sweet comedy. No more words; away! go, away! 46

[*Exeunt.*

ACT V

[SCENE I. *Athens. The palace of Theseus.*]

Enter THESEUS, HIPPOLYTA, PHILOSTRATE, Lords
[*and* Attendants].

Hip. 'Tis strange, my Theseus, that these lovers
    speak of.

The. More strange than true; I never may believe
These antique fables, nor these fairy toys.
Lovers and madmen have such seething brains,
Such shaping fantasies, that apprehend 5
More than cool reason ever comprehends.
The lunatic, the lover, and the poet
Are of imagination all compact.
One sees more devils than vast hell can hold;
That is, the madman. The lover, all as frantic, 10
Sees Helen's beauty in a brow of Egypt.
The poet's eye, in a fine frenzy rolling,
Doth glance from heaven to earth, from earth to
    heaven;
And as imagination bodies forth
The forms of things unknown, the poet's pen 15
Turns them to shapes and gives to airy nothing
A local habitation and a name.
Such tricks hath strong imagination,

211. go about: attempt. 214. patch'd: wearing motley. 224. at her death, i.e., Thisbe's.
Sc. ii, 14. thing of naught: naughty thing. 20. sixpence a day, i.e., as royal pension. 39. preferr'd: chosen.
Act V, sc. i, 4–22. See Introduction. 8. compact: composed. 11. Helen: Helen of Troy. brow of Egypt: gypsy's face.

That, if it would but apprehend some joy,
It comprehends some bringer of that joy;   20
Or in the night, imagining some fear,
How easy is a bush suppos'd a bear!
  Hip. But all the story of the night told over,
And all their minds transfigur'd so together,
More witnesseth than fancy's images,   25
And grows to something of great constancy;
But, howsoever, strange and admirable.

Enter lovers, LYSANDER, DEMETRIUS, HERMIA, *and*
                HELENA.

  The. Here come the lovers, full of joy and mirth.
Joy, gentle friends! joy and fresh days of love
Accompany your hearts!
  Lys.   More than to us   30
Wait in your royal walks, your board, your bed!
  The. Come now; what masques, what dances
    shall we have,
To wear away this long age of three hours
Between our after-supper and bed-time?
Where is our usual manager of mirth?   35
What revels are in hand? Is there no play
To ease the anguish of a torturing hour?
Call Philostrate.
  Phil.   Here, mighty Theseus.
  The. Say, what abridgement have you for this
    evening?
What masque? what music? How shall we be-
    guile   40
The lazy time, if not with some delight?
  Phil. There is a brief how many sports are ripe.
Make choice of which your Highness will see first.
                      [*Giving a paper.*]
  The. [*Reads.*] "The battle with the Centaurs,
    to be sung
By an Athenian eunuch to the harp."   45
We'll none of that: that have I told my love,
In glory of my kinsman Hercules.
"The riot of the tipsy Bacchanals,
Tearing the Thracian singer in their rage."
That is an old device; and it was play'd   50
When I from Thebes came last a conqueror.
"The thrice three Muses mourning for the death
Of Learning, late deceas'd in beggary."
That is some satire, keen and critical,
Not sorting with a nuptial ceremony.   55
"A tedious brief scene of young Pyramus
And his love Thisbe; very tragical mirth."
Merry and tragical! Tedious and brief!
That is, hot ice and wondrous strange snow.

How shall we find the concord of this discord?   60
  Phil. A play there is, my lord, some ten words
    long,
Which is as brief as I have known a play;
But by ten words, my lord, it is too long,
Which makes it tedious; for in all the play
There is not one word apt, one player fitted.   65
And tragical, my noble lord, it is;
For Pyramus therein doth kill himself.
Which, when I saw rehears'd, I must confess,
Made mine eyes water; but more merry tears
The passion of loud laughter never shed.   70
  The. What are they that do play it?
  Phil. Hard-handed men that work in Athens
    here,
Which never labour'd in their minds till now,
And now have toil'd their unbreath'd memories
With this same play, against your nuptial.   75
  The. And we will hear it.
  Phil.   No, my noble lord;
It is not for you. I have heard it over,
And it is nothing, nothing in the world;
Unless you can find sport in their intents,
Extremely stretch'd and conn'd with cruel pain,   80
To do you service.
  The.   I will hear that play;
For never anything can be amiss,
When simpleness and duty tender it.
Go, bring them in; and take your places, ladies.
                      [*Exit Philostrate.*]
  Hip. I love not to see wretchedness o'er-charged,
And duty in his service perishing.   86
  The. Why, gentle sweet, you shall see no such
    thing.
  Hip. He says they can do nothing in this kind.
  The. The kinder we, to give them thanks for
    nothing.
Our sport shall be to take what they mistake;   90
And what poor duty cannot do, noble respect
Takes it in might, not merit.
Where I have come, great clerks have purposed
To greet me with premeditated welcomes;
Where I have seen them shiver and look pale,   95
Make periods in the midst of sentences,
Throttle their practis'd accent in their fears,
And in conclusion dumbly have broke off,
Not paying me a welcome. Trust me, sweet,
Out of this silence yet I pick'd a welcome;   100
And in the modesty of fearful duty
I read as much as from the rattling tongue
Of saucy and audacious eloquence.

---

26. **constancy:** certainty. 39. **abridgement:** pastime. 42. **brief:** list, schedule. 44. **Centaurs.** The Centaurs and the Lapithae fought at a wedding which Theseus would remember, since he had taken part on the side of the latter. 48–49. **The riot . . . rage.** Orpheus, the poet-musician, was killed by the frenzied women followers of Bacchus. 52. **The thrice three Muses.** A topical reference has been seen in these lines, but no explanation is satisfactory. 55. **sorting with:** befitting. 74. **unbreath'd:** unpractised. 80. **stretch'd:** strained. 85. **wretchedness o'ercharged:** weakness overburdened. 92. **takes . . . merit:** takes the will for the deed. 93. **clerks:** scholars.

Love, therefore, and tongue-ti'd simplicity
In least speak most, to my capacity.   105

[Re-enter PHILOSTRATE.*]*

Phil. So please your Grace, the Prologue is address'd.
The. Let him approach.   *[Flourish of trumpets.*

Enter [QUINCE *for*] *the* Prologue.

Pro. If we offend, it is with our good will.
That you should think, we come not to offend,
But with good will.   To show our simple skill,   110
That is the true beginning of our end.
Consider then we come but in despite.
We do not come as minding to content you,
Our true intent is.   All for your delight
We are not here.   That you should here repent
        you,   115
The actors are at hand, and by their show
You shall know all that you are like to know.
The. This fellow doth not stand upon points.
Lys. He hath rid his prologue like a rough colt;
he knows not the stop.   A good moral, my lord: it is
not enough to speak, but to speak true.   121
Hip. Indeed he hath play'd on this prologue like
a child on a recorder; a sound, but not in govern-
ment.
The. His speech was like a tangled chain;   125
nothing impaired, but all disordered.   Who is next?

Enter with a trumpet before them, PYRAMUS *and*
THISBE, WALL, MOONSHINE, *and* LION.

Pro. Gentles, perchance you wonder at this show;
But wonder on till truth make all things plain.
This man is Pyramus, if you would know;   130
This beauteous lady Thisby is certain.
This man, with lime and rough-cast, doth present
Wall, that vile Wall which did these lovers sunder;
And through Wall's chink, poor souls, they are con-
        tent
To whisper.   At the which let no man wonder.   135
This man, with lantern, dog, and bush of thorn,
Presenteth Moonshine; for, if you will know,
By moonshine did these lovers think no scorn
To meet at Ninus' tomb, there, there to woo.
This grisly beast, which Lion hight by name,   140
The trusty Thisby, coming first by night,
Did scare away, or rather did affright;
And, as she fled, her mantle she did fall,
Which Lion vile with bloody mouth did stain.
Anon comes Pyramus, sweet youth and tall,   145

And finds his trusty Thisby's mantle slain;
Whereat, with blade, with bloody blameful blade,
He bravely broach'd his boiling bloody breast;
And Thisby, tarrying in mulberry shade,
His dagger drew, and died.   For all the rest,   150
Let Lion, Moonshine, Wall, and lovers twain
At large discourse, while here they do remain.
        *[Exeunt Prologue, Thisbe, Lion, and Moon-
            shine.*
The. I wonder if the lion be to speak.
Dem. No wonder, my lord; one lion may, when
many asses do.   155
Wall. In this same interlude it doth befall
That I, one Snout by name, present a wall;
And such a wall, as I would have you think,
That had in it a crannied hole or chink,
Through which the lovers, Pyramus and Thisby,   160
Did whisper often very secretly.
This loam, this rough-cast, and this stone doth show
That I am that same wall; the truth is so;
And this the cranny is, right and sinister,
Through which the fearful lovers are to whisper.   165
The. Would you desire lime and hair to speak
better?
Dem. It is the wittiest partition that ever I heard
discourse, my lord.   169

Enter PYRAMUS.

The. Pyramus draws near the wall.   Silence!
Pyr. O grim-look'd night!   O night with hue so
        black!
O night, which ever art when day is not!
O night, O night! alack, alack, alack,
I fear my Thisby's promise is forgot!
And thou, O wall, O sweet, O lovely wall,   175
That stand'st between her father's ground and
        mine!
Thou wall, O wall, O sweet and lovely wall,
Show me thy chink, to blink through with mine
        eyne!   *[Wall holds up his fingers.]*
Thanks, courteous wall; Jove shield thee well for
        this!
But what see I?   No Thisby do I see.   180
O wicked wall, through whom I see no bliss!
Curs'd be thy stones for thus deceiving me!
The. The wall, methinks, being sensible, should
curse again.
Pyr. No, in truth, sir, he should not.   "De-   185
ceiving me" is Thisby's cue.   She is to enter now,
and I am to spy her through the wall.   You shall
see it will fall pat as I told you.   Yonder she
comes.

---

105. **to my capacity:** in my opinion.   In the sympathetic speech of Theseus a tribute was very likely intended to the
graciousness of Queen Elizabeth, who may on some occasion have witnessed this play.   106. **address'd:** ready.   108 ff.
The comic device of misconstruing punctuation had been used some sixty years before in *Ralph Roister Doister.*   118. **stand
...points.**   A quibble upon (1) "to be scrupulous" and (2) "heed punctuation."   123. **recorder:** an instrument like a
flageolet.   124. **government:** control.   140. **hight:** is called.   148. **broach'd:** stabbed.   183. **sensible:** capable of feeling.

Enter THISBE.

This. O wall, full often hast thou heard my moans,

For parting my fair Pyramus and me!   191

My cherry lips have often kiss'd thy stones,

Thy stones with lime and hair knit up in thee.

Pyr. I see a voice! Now will I to the chink,

To spy an I can hear my Thisby's face.   195

Thisby!

This. My love, thou art my love, I think.

Pyr. Think what thou wilt, I am thy lover's grace;

And, like Limander, am I trusty still.

This. And I like Helen, till the Fates me kill.   200

Pyr. Not Shafalus to Procrus was so true.

This. As Shafalus to Procrus, I to you.

Pyr. O, kiss me through the hole of this vile wall!

This. I kiss the wall's hole, not your lips at all.

Pyr. Wilt thou at Ninny's tomb meet me straightway?   205

This. 'Tide life, 'tide death, I come without delay.   [*Exeunt Pyramus and Thisbe.*]

Wall. Thus have I, Wall, my part discharged so;

And, being done, thus Wall away doth go.   [*Exit.*

The. Now is the moon used between the two neighbours.

Dem. No remedy, my lord, when walls are so wilful to hear without warning.   211

Hip. This is the silliest stuff that ever I heard.

The. The best in this kind are but shadows; and the worst are no worse, if imagination amend them.

Hip. It must be your imagination then, and   216 not theirs.

The. If we imagine no worse of them than they of themselves, they may pass for excellent men. Here come two noble beasts in, a man and a lion.   221

Enter LION *and* MOONSHINE.

Lion. You, ladies, you, whose gentle hearts do fear

The smallest monstrous mouse that creeps on floor,

May now perchance both quake and tremble here,

When lion rough in wildest rage doth roar.   225

Then know that I, as Snug the joiner, am

A lion fell, nor else no lion's dam;

For, if I should as lion come in strife

Into this place, 'twere pity on my life.

The. A very gentle beast, and of a good   230 conscience.

Dem. The very best at a beast, my lord, that e'er I saw.

Lys. This lion is a very fox for his valour.

The. True; and a goose for his discretion.   235

Dem. Not so, my lord; for his valour cannot carry his discretion, and the fox carries the goose.

The. His discretion, I am sure, cannot carry his valour; for the goose carries not the fox. It is   240 well; leave it to his discretion, and let us hearken to the moon.

Moon. This lantern doth the horned moon present; —

Dem. He should have worn the horns on his head.   245

The. He is no crescent, and his horns are invisible within the circumference.

Moon. This lantern doth the horned moon present;

Myself the man i' th' moon do seem to be.

The. This is the greatest error of all the rest. The man should be put into the lantern.   251 How is it else the man i' th' moon?

Dem. He dares not come there for the candle; for, you see, it is already in snuff.

Hip. I am aweary of this moon. Would he would change!   256

The. It appears, by his small light of discretion, that he is in the wane; but yet, in courtesy, in all reason, we must stay the time.

Lys. Proceed, Moon.   260

Moon. All that I have to say, is, to tell you that the lantern is the moon; I, the man i' th' moon; this thorn-bush, my thorn-bush; and this dog, my dog.

Dem. Why, all these should be in the lantern;   265 for all these are in the moon. But, silence! here comes Thisbe.

Re-enter THISBE.

This. This is old Ninny's tomb. Where is my love?

Lion. (*Roaring.*) Oh —— [*Thisbe runs off.*

Dem. Well roar'd, Lion.   270

The. Well run, Thisbe.

Hip. Well shone, Moon. Truly, the moon shines with a good grace.

[*The Lion shakes Thisbe's mantle and exit.*]

The. Well mous'd, Lion.

Re-enter PYRAMUS.

Dem. And then came Pyramus.

Lys. And so the lion vanish'd.   275

Pyr. Sweet Moon, I thank thee for thy sunny beams;

199–200. **Limander . . . Helen**: blunders for *Hero* and *Leander*.   201. **Shafalus to Procrus**: blunder for *Cephalus to Procris*, also famous lovers.   206. **'Tide**: betide.   209. **moon used**. Qq. *morall downe* Ff. Pope's conj. *mural down* has been generally followed. All are unsatisfactory.   221. **man**. Many edd. emend to *moon*.   226. **as**. Qq. *one* Ff.   244. **horns . . . head**. The inescapable jest about the "horns" of the "cuckold."   254. **in snuff**: quibble on (1) "offended" and (2) "in need of snuffing."

I thank thee, Moon, for shining now so bright;
For, by thy gracious, golden, glittering [gleams],
  I trust to take of truest Thisby sight.   280
    But stay, O spite!
    But mark, poor knight,
  What dreadful dole is here!
    Eyes, do you see?
    How can it be?   285
  O dainty duck! O dear!
    Thy mantle good,
    What, stain'd with blood!
  Approach, ye Furies fell!
    O Fates, come, come,   290
    Cut thread and thrum;
  Quail, crush, conclude, and quell!
The. This passion, and the death of a dear friend,
would go near to make a man look sad.
Hip. Beshrew my heart, but I pity the man. 295
Pyr. O wherefore, Nature, didst thou lions frame?
Since lion vile hath here deflow'r'd my dear;
Which is — no, no — which was the fairest dame
That liv'd, that lov'd, that lik'd, that look'd with
    cheer.
    Come, tears, confound;   300
    Out, sword, and wound
  The pap of Pyramus;
    Ay, that left pap,
    Where heart doth hop.   [*Stabs himself.*]
  Thus die I, thus, thus, thus.   305
    Now am I dead,
    Now am I fled;
  My soul is in the sky.
    Tongue, lose thy light;   309
    Moon, take thy flight.   [*Exit Moonshine.*]
  Now die, die, die, die, die.   [*Dies.*]
Dem. No die, but an ace, for him; for he is but one.
Lys. Less than an ace, man, for he is dead; he is
nothing.   315
The. With the help of a surgeon he might yet re-
cover, and yet prove an ass.
Hip. How chance Moonshine is gone before
Thisbe comes back and finds her lover?

Re-enter THISBE.

The. She will find him by starlight. Here 320
she comes; and her passion ends the play.
Hip. Methinks she should not use a long one for
such a Pyramus. I hope she will be brief.
Dem. A mote will turn the balance, which Pyramus, which Thisbe, is the better; he for a man, 325
God warrant us; she for a woman, God bless us.
Lys. She hath spied him already with those sweet
eyes.

Dem. And thus she moans, *videlicet:* —   330
This. Asleep, my love?
    What, dead, my dove?
  O Pyramus, arise!
    Speak, speak! Quite dumb?
    Dead, dead? A tomb   335
  Must cover thy sweet eyes.
    These lily lips,
    This cherry nose,
  These yellow cowslip cheeks,
    Are gone, are gone!   340
    Lovers, make moan.
  His eyes were green as leeks.
    O Sisters Three,
    Come, come to me,
  With hands as pale as milk;   345
    Lay them in gore,
    Since you have shore
  With shears his thread of silk.
    Tongue, not a word!
    Come, trusty sword;   350
  Come, blade, my breast imbrue!
           [*Stabs herself.*]
    And, farewell, friends;
    Thus, Thisby ends.
  Adieu, adieu, adieu.   [*Dies.*]
The. Moonshine and Lion are left to bury 355
the dead.
Dem. Ay, and Wall too.
Bot. [*Starting up.*] No, I assure you; the wall is
down that parted their fathers. Will it please you
to see the epilogue, or to hear a Bergomask dance
between two of our company?   361
The. No epilogue, I pray you; for your play needs
no excuse. Never excuse; for when the players are
all dead, there need none to be blamed. Marry, if
he that writ it had played Pyramus and hang'd 365
himself in Thisbe's garter, it would have been a fine
tragedy; and so it is, truly; and very notably discharg'd. But, come, your Bergomask; let your
epilogue alone.   [*A dance.*]
The iron tongue of midnight hath told twelve. 370
Lovers, to bed; 'tis almost fairy time.
I fear we shall out-sleep the coming morn
As much as we this night have overwatch'd.
This palpable-gross play hath well beguil'd
The heavy gait of night. Sweet friends, to bed.
A fortnight hold we this solemnity   376
In nightly revels and new jollity.   [*Exeunt.*

Enter ROBIN GOODFELLOW.

Robin. Now the hungry lion roars,
    And the wolf [behowls] the moon;

---

279. **[gleams]** (Knight). *beames* Q. 283. **dole:** grief. 291. **thrum:** the loose threads at the end of the web. 292. **quail:** overpower. **quell:** kill. 312. **ace:** the lowest cast of the dice. 330. **moans.** Qq. Ff. *means:* laments. **videlicet:** as follows. 343. **Sisters three:** the Fates. 351. **imbrue:** stain with blood. 360. **Bergomask dance:** a rustic dance named from Bergamo in Italy. 374. **palpable-gross:** palpably crude. 379. **[behowls]** (Warburton). *beholds* Q.

Whilst the heavy ploughman snores,   380
  All with weary task fordone.
Now the wasted brands do glow,
  Whilst the screech-owl, screeching loud,
Puts the wretch that lies in woe
  In remembrance of a shroud.   385
Now it is the time of night
  That the graves, all gaping wide,
Every one lets forth his sprite,
  In the church-way paths to glide.
And we fairies, that do run   390
  By the triple Hecate's team
From the presence of the sun,
  Following darkness like a dream,
Now are frolic.   Not a mouse
Shall disturb this hallowed house.   395
I am sent with broom before,
To sweep the dust behind the door.

Enter OBERON *and* TITANIA *with their train.*

Obe. Through the house give glimmering light
  By the dead and drowsy fire,
Every elf and fairy sprite   400
  Hop as light as bird from brier;
And this ditty, after me,
Sing, and dance it trippingly.
Tita. First, rehearse your song by rote,
  To each word a warbling note.   405
Hand in hand, with fairy grace,
Will we sing, and bless this place.
           [Song [and dance].
Obe. Now, until the break of day,
Through this house each fairy stray.
To the best bride-bed will we,   410
Which by us shall blessed be;

And the issue there create
Ever shall be fortunate.
So shall all the couples three
Ever true in loving be;   415
And the blots of Nature's hand
Shall not in their issue stand;
Never mole, harelip, nor scar,
Nor mark prodigious, such as are
Despised in nativity,   420
Shall upon their children be.
With this field-dew consecrate,
Every fairy take his gait,
And each several chamber bless,
Through this palace, with sweet peace;   425
And the owner of it blest
Ever shall in safety rest.
Trip away; make no stay;
Meet me all by break of day.
      [Exeunt [Oberon, Titania, and train].
Robin. If we shadows have offended,   430
  Think but this, and all is mended,
That you have but slumb'red here
  While these visions did appear.
And this weak and idle theme,
  No more yielding but a dream,   435
Gentles, do not reprehend.
  If you pardon, we will mend.
And, as I am an honest Puck,
  If we have unearned luck
Now to 'scape the serpent's tongue,   440
  We will make amends ere long;
Else the Puck a liar call.
  So, good night unto you all.
Give me your hands, if we be friends,
  And Robin shall restore amends.   445
                     [Exit.]

---

381. **fordone:** worn out.   391. **triple Hecate's.**   Hecate ruled in three capacities: as Diana on earth, as Cynthia in heaven, and as Proserpine in hell.   394. **frolic:** merry.   397. **behind:** from behind.   419. **prodigious:** unnatural.   440. **serpent's tongue:** hissing.   444. **Give . . . hands:** applaud.

The Tragedy of Richard the Second

RICHARD II WAS entered in the Stationers' Register on August 29, 1597, and the First Quarto was published anonymously the same year. Two other quartos appeared in 1598 (with Shakespeare's name on the title page), a fourth, containing the abdication scene for the first time (IV.i.154–318), in 1608, and a fifth in 1615. The present text is based upon that of the First Quarto, which was probably printed from the author's manuscript. For the abdication scene the First Folio has been used as a basis, since it seems to follow a corrected copy of the Fifth Quarto.

The date of composition of Richard II is tied up with the question of the relation of the play to Daniel's Civil Wars between Lancaster and York, which was registered on October 11, 1594, and published in 1595. There is, however, as yet no agreement among scholars as to whether there is any indebtedness between the poem and the play, and, if there is, on which side. A supposed allusion to Richard II has been found in an invitation sent to Sir Robert Cecil by Sir Edward Hoby to visit him at his house in Canon Row on December 9, 1595, where "a gate for your supper shal be open, and K. Richard present him selfe to your vewe." But it is by no means certain that the reference is to a play at all, or that, if it is, that it was to Shakespeare's, or that the Richard was Richard the second. On grounds of style and versification it is generally held that the date is close to that of A Midsummer-Night's Dream and of King John, and a reasonable conjecture is 1595.

The main source of the action is Holinshed's Chronicles of England, Scotland, and Ireland. Subsidiary sources are Froissart's Chronicle, which he knew in Lord Berners's translation; possibly one or two other French chronicles; and an earlier play on the Duke of Gloucester, known as Thomas of Woodstock. But the chief interest lies in those elements that are due to the dramatist's imagination. The parts played and the speeches uttered by the female characters are entirely Shakespeare's. Historically, the Queen was only eleven years old

at the date of her husband's deposition; and the Duchess of York was only the stepmother of Aumerle. The treatment of the character of John of Gaunt follows Froissart rather than Holinshed, but of the great speech on the glory of England there is no hint in the sources. This speech, with others such as the closing lines of King John, points to the inference that the dramatist deliberately used the opportunities given in the historical plays to appeal to the patriotic enthusiasm of the Elizabethan Englishman.

The greatest achievement in the play is in the creation, or interpretation, of the character of Richard himself, and in the poetry of his speeches. The chronicles supplied the outline of his action, but little characterization beyond charges of self-indulgence and subjection to unworthy favorites. Richard's love of the spectacular and his enjoyment of his own emotions even of misery and despair, along with his tendency to substitute fluent and poetical utterance for deeds, are all the conception of the dramatist. The resignation of the crown actually took place in the presence of a few lords in Richard's chamber in the Tower, so that the amazing exhibition of sentimental vanity in the abdication scene is purely Shakespearean. The hints of the character of Bolingbroke are also mainly invented, and prepare the ground for the more elaborate treatment in 1 and 2 Henry IV. Holinshed speaks of his popularity, but gives nothing of such causes of it as are indicated in the description of his courtship of the common people in I.iv. 23–36. Throughout, even when the details of the episode are borrowed from the chronicle, as in the conspiracy in which Aumerle is involved, the speeches are purely imaginary, hardly a hint of the diction being derived from the sources.

The tragedy was highly successful when first produced, Queen Elizabeth herself being the authority for the statement that "this tragedy was played forty times in open streets and houses." It was in the same conversation with the keeper of the Tower records that she is reported as saying, "I am

Richard II, know ye not that?" The uncertainty of the succession to the throne, and the existence of factions favoring the various candidates, seem to have made the Queen sensitive about treatments of the deposition of kings. Grounds for her uneasiness may be found in the performance of the play at the Globe Theatre on February 7, 1601, the afternoon before the outbreak of Essex's rebellion. This was arranged for by partisans of Essex, who induced the Chamberlain's Men to give it (though they felt it was too old to draw an audience) by paying them a special honorarium of forty shillings. At the trial of Essex, this performance was adduced in evidence against him. The absence of the abdication scene in all the editions published during Elizabeth's lifetime is further evidence that the subject was felt to be a delicate one.

Shakespeare was, of course, fully aware that in the deposition and murder of Richard and the usurpation of Bolingbroke lay the seeds of the civil dissensions he had already presented in the three parts of *Henry VI* and *Richard III*. But it seems clear that his interest lay less in presenting a case for either side in the quarrels of York and Lancaster than in the human beings who were the agents or the victims in the long drawn out struggle. Richard's weaknesses and selfishness are not disguised, yet neither are they so emphasized as to lead us to deny him sympathy or to obscure his tragedy. Bolingbroke's grievances are palpable enough, yet we are shown clearly the steps by which he proceeds from seeking to vindicate his just claims to seizing the opportunities Fortune offers him till he becomes guilty of usurpation.

The spellings "Bullingbroke," "Herford," "Barkly," "Callice" (Calais), and "Cotshall" or "Coltshold" (Cotswold) in the old copies, indicate the Elizabethan pronunciation of these names.

SONS OF EDWARD III

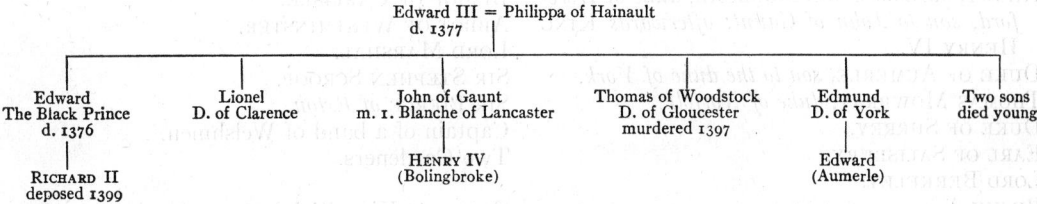

Edward III = Philippa of Hainault
d. 1377

Edward
The Black Prince
d. 1376

Richard II
deposed 1399

Lionel
D. of Clarence

John of Gaunt
m. 1. Blanche of Lancaster

Henry IV
(Bolingbroke)

Thomas of Woodstock
D. of Gloucester
murdered 1397

Edmund
D. of York

Edward
(Aumerle)

Two sons
died young

THE TRAGEDY OF
RICHARD THE SECOND

KING RICHARD II

JOHN OF GAUNT, *duke of Lancaster*, } *uncles*
EDMUND OF LANGLEY, *duke of York*, } *to the King.*

HENRY, *surnamed* BOLINGBROKE, *duke of Hereford, son to John of Gaunt; afterwards* KING HENRY IV.

DUKE OF AUMERLE, *son to the duke of York.*
THOMAS MOWBRAY, *duke of Norfolk.*
DUKE OF SURREY.
EARL OF SALISBURY.
LORD BERKELEY.
BUSHY, }
BAGOT, } *servants to King Richard.*
GREEN, }
EARL OF NORTHUMBERLAND.

HENRY PERCY, *surnamed* HOTSPUR, *his son.*
LORD ROSS.
LORD WILLOUGHBY.
LORD FITZWATER.
BISHOP OF CARLISLE.
ABBOT OF WESTMINSTER.
LORD MARSHAL.
SIR STEPHEN SCROOP.
SIR PIERCE *of Exton.*
Captain of a band of Welshmen.
Two Gardeners.

QUEEN *to King Richard.*
DUCHESS OF YORK.
DUCHESS OF GLOUCESTER.
Lady attending on the Queen.

Lords, Heralds, Officers, Soldiers, Keeper, Messenger, Groom, and other Attendants.

SCENE: *England and Wales.*]

ACT I

SCENE I. [*London. King Richard's palace.*]

Enter KING RICHARD, JOHN OF GAUNT, *with other* Nobles *and* Attendants.

K. Rich. Old John of Gaunt, time-honoured
Lancaster,
Hast thou, according to thy oath and band,
Brought hither Henry Hereford thy bold son,
Here to make good the boist'rous late appeal,
Which then our leisure would not let us hear, 5
Against the Duke of Norfolk, Thomas Mowbray?
Gaunt. I have, my liege.
K. Rich. Tell me, moreover, hast thou sounded
him
If he appeal the Duke on ancient malice,
Or worthily, as a good subject should, 10

On some known ground of treachery in him?
Gaunt. As near as I could sift him on that argument,
On some apparent danger seen in him
Aim'd at your Highness, no inveterate malice.
K. Rich. Then call them to our presence.
[*Exeunt some Attendants.*] Face to face, 15
And frowning brow to brow, ourselves will hear
The accuser and the accused freely speak.
High-stomach'd are they both and full of ire,
In rage deaf as the sea, hasty as fire.

Enter BOLINGBROKE *and* MOWBRAY [*with Attendants*].

Boling. Many years of happy days befall 20
My gracious sovereign, my most loving liege!
Mow. Each day still better other's happiness

Act I, sc. i, 2. **band**: bond. 4. **appeal**: accusation. 18. **High-stomach'd**: haughty and wrathful.

Until the heavens, envying earth's good hap,
Add an immortal title to your crown!
   K. Rich. We thank you both; yet one but flatters
      us,   25
As well appeareth by the cause you come,
Namely, to appeal each other of high treason.
Cousin of Hereford, what dost thou object
Against the Duke of Norfolk, Thomas Mowbray?
   Boling. First, heaven be the record to my speech!
In the devotion of a subject's love,   31
Tend'ring the precious safety of my prince,
And free from other misbegotten hate,
Come I appellant to this princely presence.
Now, Thomas Mowbray, do I turn to thee,   35
And mark my greeting well; for what I speak
My body shall make good upon this earth,
Or my divine soul answer it in heaven.
Thou art a traitor and a miscreant,
Too good to be so, and too bad to live,   40
Since the more fair and crystal is the sky,
The uglier seem the clouds that in it fly.
Once more, the more to aggravate the note,
With a foul traitor's name stuff I thy throat
And wish, so please my sovereign, ere I move, 45
What my tongue speaks my right drawn sword may
      prove.
   Mow. Let not my cold words here accuse my zeal.
'Tis not the trial of a woman's war,
The bitter clamour of two eager tongues,
Can arbitrate this cause betwixt us twain;   50
The blood is hot that must be cool'd for this.
Yet can I not of such tame patience boast
As to be hush'd and nought at all to say.
First, the fair reverence of your Highness curbs me
From giving reins and spurs to my free speech, 55
Which else would post until it had return'd
These terms of treason doubled down his throat.
Setting aside his high blood's royalty,
And let him be no kinsman to my liege,
I do defy him and I spit at him,   60
Call him a slanderous coward and a villain;
Which to maintain I would allow him odds
And meet him, were I tied to run afoot
Even to the frozen ridges of the Alps,
Or any other ground inhabitable   65
Where ever Englishman durst set his foot.
Meantime let this defend my loyalty:
By all my hopes, most falsely doth he lie.
   Boling. Pale trembling coward, there I throw
      my gage,
Disclaiming here the kindred of the King,   70
And lay aside my high blood's royalty,

Which fear, not reverence, makes thee to except.
If guilty dread have left thee so much strength
As to take up mine honour's pawn, then stoop.
By that and all the rites of knighthood else,   75
Will I make good against thee, arm to arm,
What I have spoke or thou canst worse devise.
   Mow. I take it up; and by that sword I swear
Which gently laid my knighthood on my shoulder,
I'll answer thee in any fair degree   80
Or chivalrous design of knightly trial;
And when I mount, alive may I not light
If I be traitor or unjustly fight!
   K. Rich. What doth our cousin lay to Mowbray's
      charge?
It must be great that can inherit us   85
So much as of a thought of ill in him.
   Boling. Look, what I speak, my life shall prove
      it true:
That Mowbray hath receiv'd eight thousand nobles
In name of lendings for your Highness' soldiers,
The which he hath detain'd for lewd employments,
Like a false traitor and injurious villain.   91
Besides I say, and will in battle prove,
Or here or elsewhere to the furthest verge
That ever was survey'd by English eye,
That all the treasons for these eighteen years   95
Complotted and contrived in this land
Fetch from false Mowbray their first head and
      spring.
Further I say, and further will maintain
Upon his bad life to make all this good,
That he did plot the Duke of Gloucester's death,
Suggest his soon-believing adversaries,   101
And consequently, like a traitor coward,
Sluic'd out his innocent soul through streams of
      blood;
Which blood, like sacrificing Abel's, cries,
Even from the tongueless caverns of the earth, 105
To me for justice and rough chastisement;
And, by the glorious worth of my descent,
This arm shall do it, or this life be spent.
   K. Rich. How high a pitch his resolution soars!
Thomas of Norfolk, what say'st thou to this?   110
   Mow. O, let my sovereign turn away his face
And bid his ears a little while be deaf,
Till I have told this slander of his blood
How God and good men hate so foul a liar.
   K. Rich. Mowbray, impartial are our eyes and
      ears.   115
Were he my brother, nay, my kingdom's heir,
As he is but my father's brother's son,
Now, by [my] sceptre's awe, I make a vow,

---

32. **Tend'ring**: holding dear.   34. **appellant**: accuser.   43. **note**: stigma.   47. **accuse my zeal**: accuse me for lacking zeal.   49. **eager**: biting.   63. **tied**: obliged.   65. **inhabitable**: uninhabitable.   74. **pawn**: pledge (his glove).   85. **inherit us**: make us have.   88. **nobles**: coins worth 6s.8d.   90. **lewd**: base.   100. **Gloucester's**. Thomas of Woodstock, uncle of Richard and Bolingbroke, murdered at Calais, 1397.   101. **Suggest**: incite.   102. **consequently**: afterwards. 118. **[my]** F. Om. Q.

Such neighbour nearness to our sacred blood
Should nothing privilege him, nor partialize   120
The unstooping firmness of my upright soul. .
He is our subject, Mowbray; so art thou.
Free speech and fearless I to thee allow.

Mow. Then, Bolingbroke, as low as to thy heart,
Through the false passage of thy throat, thou liest.
Three parts of that receipt I had for Calais   126
Disburs'd I duly to his Highness' soldiers;
The other part reserv'd I by consent,
For that my sovereign liege was in my debt
Upon remainder of a dear account,   130
Since last I went to France to fetch his queen.
Now swallow down that lie.   For Gloucester's
      death,
I slew him not; but to my own disgrace
Neglected my sworn duty in that case.
For you, my noble Lord of Lancaster,   135
The honourable father to my foe,
Once did I lay an ambush for your life,
A trespass that doth vex my grieved soul;
But ere I last receiv'd the sacrament
I did confess it, and exactly begg'd   140
Your Grace's pardon; and I hope I had it.
This is my fault.   As for the rest appeal'd,
It issues from the rancour of a villain,
A recreant and most degenerate traitor;
Which in myself I boldly will defend;   145
And interchangeably hurl down my gage
Upon this overweening traitor's foot
To prove myself a loyal gentleman
Even in the best blood chamber'd in his bosom.
In haste whereof, most heartily I pray   150
Your Highness to assign our trial day.

K. Rich. Wrath-kindled gentlemen, be rul'd by
      me;
Let's purge this choler without letting blood.
This we prescribe, though no physician;
Deep malice makes too deep incision.   155
Forget, forgive; conclude and be agreed;
Our doctors say this is no month to bleed.
Good uncle, let this end where it begun;
We'll calm the Duke of Norfolk, you your son.   159

Gaunt. To be a make-peace shall become my age.
Throw down, my son, the Duke of Norfolk's gage.

K. Rich. And, Norfolk, throw down his.

Gaunt.   When, Harry, when!
Obedience bids I should not bid again.

K. Rich. Norfolk, throw down, we bid; there is
      no boot.

Mow. Myself I throw, dread sovereign, at thy
      foot;   165
My life thou shalt command, but not my shame.

The one my duty owes; but my fair name,
Despite of death that lives upon my grave,
To dark dishonour's use thou shalt not have.
I am disgrac'd, impeach'd, and baffl'd here,   170
Pierc'd to the soul with slander's venom'd spear,
The which no balm can cure but his heart-blood
Which breath'd this poison.

K. Rich.   Rage must be withstood;
Give me his gage.   Lions make leopards tame.

Mow. Yea, but not change his spots.   Take but
      my shame,   175
And I resign my gage.   My dear dear lord,
The purest treasure mortal times afford
Is spotless reputation; that away,
Men are but gilded loam or painted clay.
A jewel in a ten-times-barr'd-up chest   180
Is a bold spirit in a loyal breast.
Mine honour is my life; both grow in one;
Take honour from me, and my life is done.
Then, dear my liege, mine honour let me try;
In that I live, and for that will I die.   185

K. Rich. Cousin, throw up your gage.   Do you
      begin.

Boling. O, God defend my soul from such deep
      sin!
Shall I seem crest-fallen in my father's sight,
Or with pale beggar-fear impeach my height
Before this out-dar'd dastard?   Ere my tongue   190
Shall wound my honour with such feeble wrong
Or sound so base a parle, my teeth shall tear
The slavish motive of recanting fear,
And spit it bleeding in his high disgrace,
Where shame doth harbour, even in Mowbray's
      face.   [*Exit Gaunt.* 195

K. Rich. We were not born to sue, but to com-
      mand;
Which since we cannot do to make you friends,
Be ready, as your lives shall answer it,
At Coventry, upon Saint Lambert's day.
There shall your swords and lances arbitrate   200
The swelling difference of your settled hate.
Since we cannot atone you, we shall see
Justice design the victor's chivalry.
Lord Marshal, command our officers at arms
Be ready to direct these home alarms. [*Exeunt.* 205

SCENE II. [*London.   The Duke of Lancaster's
palace.*]

Enter JOHN OF GAUNT *with the* DUCHESS OF
GLOUCESTER.

Gaunt. Alas, the part I had in Woodstock's blood
Doth more solicit me than your exclaims

---

126. **receipt:** money received.   130. **dear:** large.   150. **In haste whereof:** to hasten which.   156. **conclude:** come to terms.
164. **boot:** remedy, alternative.   170. **baffl'd:** put to shame.   174. **gage:** glove given as a challenge.   177. **mortal times:** a
man's life.   189. **impeach my height:** disgrace my rank.   193. **motive:** i.e., his tongue.   199. **Saint Lambert's day:** Sept. 17.
202. **atone:** reconcile.   203. **design:** designate.

To stir against the butchers of his life!
But since correction lieth in those hands
Which made the fault that we cannot correct,   5
Put we our quarrel to the will of Heaven;
Who, when they see the hours ripe on earth,
Will rain hot vengeance on offenders' heads.
   Duch. Finds brotherhood in thee no sharper spur?
Hath love in thy old blood no living fire?   10
Edward's seven sons, whereof thyself art one,
Were as seven vials of his sacred blood,
Or seven fair branches springing from one root.
Some of those seven are dried by nature's course,
Some of those branches by the Destinies cut;   15
But Thomas, my dear lord, my life, my Gloucester,
One vial full of Edward's sacred blood,
One flourishing branch of his most royal root,
Is crack'd, and all the precious liquor spilt,
Is hack'd down, and his summer leaves all faded,   20
By Envy's hand and Murder's bloody axe.
Ah, Gaunt, his blood was thine! That bed, that womb,
That mettle, that self-mould, that fashion'd thee
Made him a man; and though thou liv'st and breath'st,
Yet art thou slain in him. Thou dost consent   25
In some large measure to thy father's death,
In that thou seest thy wretched brother die,
Who was the model of thy father's life.
Call it not patience, Gaunt; it is despair.
In suff'ring thus thy brother to be slaught'red,
Thou show'st the naked pathway to thy life,   31
Teaching stern Murder how to butcher thee.
That which in mean men we entitle patience
Is pale cold cowardice in noble breasts.
What shall I say? To safeguard thine own life   35
The best way is to venge my Gloucester's death.
   Gaunt. God's is the quarrel; for God's substitute,
His deputy anointed in His sight,
Hath caus'd his death; the which if wrongfully,
Let Heaven revenge; for I may never lift   40
An angry arm against His minister.
   Duch. Where then, alas, may I complain myself?
   Gaunt. To God, the widow's champion and defence.
   Duch. Why, then, I will. Farewell, old Gaunt!
Thou go'st to Coventry, there to behold   45
Our cousin Hereford and fell Mowbray fight.
O, [sit] my husband's wrongs on Hereford's spear,
That it may enter butcher Mowbray's breast!
Or, if misfortune miss the first career,
Be Mowbray's sins so heavy in his bosom   50
That they may break his foaming courser's back,
And throw the rider headlong in the lists,
A caitiff recreant to my cousin Hereford!
Farewell, old Gaunt! Thy sometimes brother's wife

With her companion grief must end her life.   55
   Gaunt. Sister, farewell; I must to Coventry.
As much good stay with thee as go with me!
   Duch. Yet one word more! Grief boundeth where [it falls],
Not with the empty hollowness, but weight.
I take my leave before I have begun,   60
For sorrow ends not when it seemeth done.
Commend me to thy brother, Edmund York.
Lo, this is all: — nay, yet depart not so;
Though this be all, do not so quickly go;
I shall remember more. Bid him — ah, what? —
With all good speed at Plashy visit me.   66
Alack, and what shall good old York there see
But empty lodgings and unfurnish'd walls,
Unpeopled offices, untrodden stones?   69
And what hear there for welcome but my groans?
Therefore commend me; let him not come there
To seek out sorrow that dwells everywhere.
Desolate, desolate, will I hence and die.
The last leave of thee takes my weeping eye.
                     [Exeunt.

SCENE III. *[The lists at Coventry.]*

Enter the LORD MARSHAL *and the* DUKE OF AUMERLE.

   Mar. My Lord Aumerle, is Harry Hereford arm'd?
   Aum. Yea, at all points; and longs to enter in.
   Mar. The Duke of Norfolk, sprightfully and bold,
Stays but the summons of the appellant's trumpet.
   Aum. Why, then, the champions are prepar'd, and stay   5
For nothing but his Majesty's approach.

The trumpets sound, and the KING *enters with his nobles,* GAUNT, BUSHY, BAGOT, GREEN, *and others. When they are set, enter* MOWBRAY *in arms, defendant, with a* HERALD.

   K. Rich. Marshal, demand of yonder champion
The cause of his arrival here in arms.
Ask him his name, and orderly proceed
To swear him in the justice of his cause.   10
   Mar. In God's name and the King's, say who thou art
And why thou com'st thus knightly clad in arms,
Against what man thou com'st, and what thy quarrel.
Speak truly, on thy knighthood and thy oath;
And so defend thee Heaven and thy valour!   15
   Mow. My name is Thomas Mowbray, Duke of Norfolk;
Who hither come engaged by my oath —

Sc. ii, 4. **those hands:** Richard's. 21. **Envy's:** Malice's. 28. **model:** copy. 46. **cousin:** kinsman; here, nephew. 47. **[sit]** F. *set* Q. 49. **career:** charge. 58. **[it falls]** F. *is fals* Q. 69. **offices:** service quarters.

Which God defend a knight should violate! —
Both to defend my loyalty and truth
To God, my King, and my succeeding issue,   20
Against the Duke of Hereford that appeals me;
And, by the grace of God and this mine arm,
To prove him, in defending of myself,
A traitor to my God, my King, and me:
And as I truly fight, defend me Heaven!   25

The trumpets sound. Enter BOLINGBROKE,
appellant, in armour, with a HERALD.

  K. Rich. Marshal, ask yonder knight in arms,
Both who he is and why he cometh hither
Thus plated in habiliments of war,
And formally, according to our law,
Depose him in the justice of his cause.   30
  Mar. What is thy name? and wherefore com'st
     thou hither
Before King Richard in his royal lists?
Against whom comest thou? and what's thy quarrel?
Speak like a true knight, so defend thee Heaven!
  Boling. Harry of Hereford, Lancaster, and Derby
Am I; who ready here do stand in arms   36
To prove, by God's grace and my body's valour
In lists on Thomas Mowbray, Duke of Norfolk,
That he's a traitor, foul and dangerous,
To God of heaven, King Richard, and to me;   40
And as I truly fight, defend me Heaven!
  Mar. On pain of death, no person be so bold
Or daring-hardy as to touch the lists,
Except the Marshal and such officers
Appointed to direct these fair designs.   45
  Boling. Lord Marshal, let me kiss my sovereign's
     hand
And bow my knee before his Majesty;
For Mowbray and myself are like two men
That vow a long and weary pilgrimage.
Then let us take a ceremonious leave   50
And loving farewell of our several friends.
  Mar. The appellant in all duty greets your
     Highness,
And craves to kiss your hand and take his leave.
  K. Rich. We will descend and fold him in our arms.
Cousin of Hereford, as thy cause is right   55
So be thy fortune in this royal fight!
Farewell, my blood; which if to-day thou shed,
Lament we may, but not revenge thee dead.
  Boling. O, let no noble eye profane a tear
For me, if I be gor'd with Mowbray's spear.   60
As confident as is the falcon's flight
Against a bird, do I with Mowbray fight.
My loving lord, I take my leave of you;
Of you, my noble cousin, Lord Aumerle;
Not sick, although I have to do with death,   65
But lusty, young, and cheerly drawing breath.

Lo, as at English feasts, so I regreet
The daintiest last, to make the end most sweet:
O thou, the earthly author of my blood,
Whose youthful spirit, in me regenerate,   70
Doth with a twofold vigour lift me up
To reach at victory above my head,
Add proof unto mine armour with thy prayers,
And with thy blessings steel my lance's point
That it may enter Mowbray's waxen coat,   75
And furbish new the name of John o' Gaunt,
Even in the lusty haviour of his son.
  Gaunt. God in thy good cause make thee pros-
     perous!
Be swift like lightning in the execution;
And let thy blows, doubly redoubled,   80
Fall like amazing thunder on the casque
Of thy adverse pernicious enemy.
Rouse up thy youthful blood, be valiant, and
     live.
  Boling. Mine innocency and Saint George to
     thrive!
  Mow. However God or Fortune cast my lot,   85
There lives or dies, true to King Richard's throne,
A loyal, just, and upright gentleman.
Never did captive with a freer heart
Cast off his chains of bondage and embrace
His golden uncontroll'd enfranchisement,   90
More than my dancing soul doth celebrate
This feast of battle with mine adversary.
Most mighty liege and my companion peers,
Take from my mouth the wish of happy years.
As gentle and as jocund as to jest   95
Go I to fight; truth hath a quiet breast.
  K. Rich. Farewell, my lord; securely I espy
Virtue with valour couched in thine eye.
Order the trial, Marshal, and begin.
  Mar. Harry of Hereford, Lancaster, and Derby,
Receive thy lance; and God defend the right!   101
  Boling. Strong as a tower in hope, I cry amen.
  Mar. [*To an officer.*] Go bear this lance to Thomas,
     Duke of Norfolk.
  1. Her. Harry of Hereford, Lancaster, and Derby,
Stands here for God, his sovereign, and himself,   105
On pain to be found false and recreant,
To prove the Duke of Norfolk, Thomas Mowbray,
A traitor to his God, his king, and him;
And dares him to set forward to the fight.
  2. Her. Here standeth Thomas Mowbray, Duke
     of Norfolk,   110
On pain to be found false and recreant,
Both to defend himself and to approve
Henry of Hereford, Lancaster, and Derby,
To God, his sovereign, and to him disloyal;
Courageously and with a free desire   115
Attending but the signal to begin.

Sc. iii, 18. **defend:** forbid.   30. **Depose:** swear.   67. **regreet:** salute.   73. **proof:** power of resistance.   81. **amazing:** be-
wildering.   112. **approve:** prove.

Mar. Sound, trumpets; and set forward, com-
    batants.   [*A charge sounded.*
Stay! The King hath thrown his warder down.
    K. Rich. Let them lay by their helmets and their
        spears,
And both return back to their chairs again.   120
Withdraw with us; and let the trumpets sound
While we return these dukes what we decree.
                                    [*A long flourish.*
Draw near
And list what with our council we have done.
For that our kingdom's earth should not be soil'd
With that dear blood which it hath fostered;   126
And for our eyes do hate the dire aspect
Of civil wounds plough'd up with neighbours' sword;
And for we think the eagle-winged pride
Of sky-aspiring and ambitious thoughts,   130
With rival-hating envy, set on you
To wake our peace, which in our country's cradle
Draws the sweet infant breath of gentle sleep;
Which, so rous'd up with boist'rous untun'd drums,
With harsh-resounding trumpets' dreadful bray,
And grating shock of wrathful iron arms,   136
Might from our quiet confines fright fair Peace
And make us wade even in our kindred's blood;
Therefore, we banish you our territories.
You, cousin Hereford, upon pain of life,   140
Till twice five summers have enrich'd our fields
Shall not regreet our fair dominions,
But tread the stranger paths of banishment.
    Boling. Your will be done. This must my com-
        fort be,
That sun that warms you here shall shine on me;   145
And those his golden beams to you here lent
Shall point on me and gild my banishment.
    K. Rich. Norfolk, for thee remains a heavier doom,
Which I with some unwillingness pronounce.
The sly, slow hours shall not determinate   150
The dateless limit of thy dear exile;
The hopeless word of "never to return"
Breathe I against thee, upon pain of life.
    Mow. A heavy sentence, my most sovereign liege,
And all unlook'd for from your Highness' mouth.
A dearer merit, not so deep a maim   156
As to be cast forth in the common air,
Have I deserved at your Highness' hands.
The language I have learn'd these forty years,
My native English, now I must forgo;   160
And now my tongue's use is to me no more
Than an unstringed viol or a harp,
Or like a cunning instrument cas'd up,
Or, being open, put into his hands
That knows no touch to tune the harmony.   165
Within my mouth you have engaol'd my tongue,
Doubly portcullis'd with my teeth and lips;

And dull unfeeling barren ignorance
Is made my gaoler to attend on me.
I am too old to fawn upon a nurse,   170
Too far in years to be a pupil now.
What is thy sentence [then] but speechless death,
Which robs my tongue from breathing native
    breath?
    K. Rich. It boots thee not to be compassionate.
After our sentence plaining comes too late.   175
    Mow. Then thus I turn me from my country's
        light,
To dwell in solemn shades of endless night.
    K. Rich. Return again, and take an oath with thee.
Lay on our royal sword your banish'd hands;
Swear by the duty that you owe to God —   180
Our part therein we banish with yourselves —
To keep the oath that we administer:
You never shall, so help you truth and God!
Embrace each other's love in banishment;
Nor never look upon each other's face;   185
Nor never write, regreet, nor reconcile
This louring tempest of your home-bred hate;
Nor never by advised purpose meet
To plot, contrive, or complot any ill
'Gainst us, our state, our subjects, or our land.   190
    Boling. I swear.
    Mow. And I, to keep all this.
    Boling. Norfolk, so far as to mine enemy: —
By this time, had the King permitted us,
One of our souls had wand'red in the air,   195
Banish'd this frail sepulchre of our flesh
As now our flesh is banish'd from this land;
Confess thy treasons ere thou fly the realm;
Since thou hast far to go, bear not along
The clogging burden of a guilty soul.   200
    Mow. No, Bolingbroke; if ever I were traitor,
My name be blotted from the book of life,
And I from heaven banish'd as from hence!
But what thou art, God, thou, and I do know;
And all too soon, I fear, the King shall rue.   205
Farewell, my liege. Now no way can I stray;
Save back to England, all the world's my way.
                                    [*Exit.*
    K. Rich. Uncle, even in the glasses of thine eyes
I see thy grieved heart. Thy sad aspect
Hath from the number of his banish'd years   210
Pluck'd four away. [*To Boling.*] Six frozen winters
        spent,
Return with welcome home from banishment.
    Boling. How long a time lies in one little word!
Four lagging winters and four wanton springs
End in a word: such is the breath of kings.   215
    Gaunt. I thank my liege that in regard of me
He shortens four years of my son's exile;
But little vantage shall I reap thereby,

118. **warder:** baton. 122. **return:** inform. 150. **determinate:** end. 151. **dear:** keenly felt. 156. **maim:** penalty.
172. **[then]** F. Om. Q. 174. **compassionate:** self-pitying. 175. **plaining:** complaining.

For, ere the six years that he hath to spend
Can change their moons and bring their times about,
My oil-dri'd lamp and time-bewasted light   221
Shall be extinct with age and endless night;
My inch of taper will be burnt and done,
And blindfold Death not let me see my son.
    K. Rich. Why, uncle, thou hast many years to
live.   225
    Gaunt. But not a minute, King, that thou canst
give.
Shorten my days thou canst with sullen sorrow,
And pluck nights from me, but not lend a morrow.
Thou canst help Time to furrow me with age,
But stop no wrinkle in his pilgrimage.   230
Thy word is current with him for my death,
But dead, thy kingdom cannot buy my breath.
    K. Rich. Thy son is banish'd upon good advice,
Whereto thy tongue a party-verdict gave.
Why at our justice seem'st thou then to lour?   235
    Gaunt. Things sweet to taste prove in digestion
sour.
You urg'd me as a judge; but I had rather
You would have bid me argue like a father.
O, had it been a stranger, not my child,
To smooth his fault I should have been more mild.
A partial slander sought I to avoid,   241
And in the sentence my own life destroy'd.
Alas, I look'd when some of you should say
I was too strict to make mine own away;
But you gave leave to my unwilling tongue   245
Against my will to do myself this wrong.
    K. Rich. Cousin, farewell; and, uncle, bid him so.
Six years we banish him, and he shall go.
          [Flourish. Exeunt [King Richard and train].
    Aum. Cousin, farewell! What presence must not
know,
From where you do remain let paper show.   250
    Mar. My lord, no leave take I; for I will ride,
As far as land will let me, by your side.
    Gaunt. O, to what purpose dost thou hoard thy
words,
That thou return'st no greeting to thy friends?
    Boling. I have too few to take my leave of you,
When the tongue's office should be prodigal   256
To breathe the abundant dolour of the heart.
    Gaunt. Thy grief is but thy absence for a time.
    Boling. Joy absent, grief is present for that time.
    Gaunt. What is six winters? They are quickly
gone.   260
    Boling. To men in joy; but grief makes one hour
ten.
    Gaunt. Call it a travel that thou tak'st for
pleasure.
    Boling. My heart will sigh when I miscall it so,

Which finds it an enforced pilgrimage.
    Gaunt. The sullen passage of thy weary steps
Esteem as foil wherein thou art to set   266
The precious jewel of thy home return.
    Boling. Nay, rather, every tedious stride I make
Will but remember me what a deal of world
I wander from the jewels that I love.   270
Must I not serve a long apprenticehood
To foreign passages, and in the end,
Having my freedom, boast of nothing else
But that I was a journeyman to grief?
    Gaunt. All places that the eye of heaven visits
Are to a wise man ports and happy havens.   276
Teach thy necessity to reason thus:
There is no virtue like necessity.
Think not the King did banish thee,
But thou the King. Woe doth the heavier sit   280
Where it perceives it is but faintly borne.
Go, say I sent thee forth to purchase honour
And not the King exil'd thee; or suppose
Devouring pestilence hangs in our air
And thou art flying to a fresher clime.   285
Look, what thy soul holds dear, imagine it
To lie that way thou goest, not whence thou com'st.
Suppose the singing birds musicians,
The grass whereon thou tread'st the presence strew'd,
The flowers fair ladies, and thy steps no more   290
Than a delightful measure or a dance;
For gnarling sorrow hath less power to bite
The man that mocks at it and sets it light.
    Boling. O, who can hold a fire in his hand
By thinking on the frosty Caucasus?   295
Or cloy the hungry edge of appetite
By bare imagination of a feast?
Or wallow naked in December snow
By thinking on fantastic summer's heat?
O, no! the apprehension of the good   300
Gives but the greater feeling to the worse.
Fell Sorrow's tooth doth never rankle more
Than when he bites, but lanceth not the sore.
    Gaunt. Come, come, my son, I'll bring thee on
thy way;
Had I thy youth and cause, I would not stay.
    Boling. Then, England's ground, farewell; sweet
soil, adieu;   306
My mother, and my nurse, that bears me yet!
Where'er I wander, boast of this I can,
Though banish'd, yet a trueborn Englishman.
          [Exeunt.

SCENE IV. [The Court.]

Enter the KING, with BAGOT and GREEN at one door;
          and the DUKE OF AUMERLE at another.

    K. Rich. We did observe. Cousin Aumerle,

How far brought you high Hereford on his way?
  Aum. I brought high Hereford, if you call him so,
But to the next highway, and there I left him.
  K. Rich. And say, what store of parting tears
    were shed? 5
  Aum. Faith, none for me; except the northeast
    wind,
Which then blew bitterly against our faces,
Awak'd the sleeping rheum, and so by chance
Did grace our hollow parting with a tear.
  K. Rich. What said our cousin when you parted
    with him? 10
  Aum. "Farewell!"
And, for my heart disdained that my tongue
Should so profane the word, that taught me craft
To counterfeit oppression of such grief
That words seem'd buried in my sorrow's grave. 15
Marry, would the word "farewell" have length'ned
    hours
And added years to his short banishment,
He should have had a volume of farewells;
But since it would not, he had none of me. 19
  K. Rich. He is our [cousin, cousin]; but 'tis doubt,
When time shall call him home from banishment,
Whether our kinsman come to see his friends.
Ourself and Bushy, [Bagot here and Green]
Observ'd his courtship to the common people;
How he did seem to dive into their hearts 25
With humble and familiar courtesy,
What reverence he did throw away on slaves,
Wooing poor craftsmen with the craft of smiles
And patient underbearing of his fortune,
As 'twere to banish their affects with him. 30
Off goes his bonnet to an oyster-wench;
A brace of draymen bid God speed him well
And had the tribute of his supple knee,
With "Thanks, my countrymen, my loving friends,"
As were our England in reversion his, 35
And he our subjects' next degree in hope.
  Green. Well, he is gone; and with him go these
    thoughts.
Now for the rebels which stand out in Ireland,
Expedient manage must be made, my liege,
Ere further leisure yield them further means 40
For their advantage and your Highness' loss.
  K. Rich. We will ourself in person to this war;
And, for our coffers, with too great a court
And liberal largess, are grown somewhat light,
We are enforc'd to farm our royal realm; 45
The revenue whereof shall furnish us
For our affairs in hand. If that come short,
Our substitutes at home shall have blank charters;
Whereto, when they shall know what men are rich,

They shall subscribe them for large sums of gold 50
And send them after to supply our wants,
For we will make for Ireland presently.

          Enter BUSHY.
[Bushy, what news?]
  Bushy. Old John of Gaunt is grievous sick, my
    lord,
Suddenly taken; and hath sent post haste 55
To entreat your Majesty to visit him.
  K. Rich. Where lies he?
  Bushy. At Ely House.
  K. Rich. Now put it, God, in the physician's
    mind
To help him to his grave immediately! 60
The lining of his coffers shall make coats
To deck our soldiers for these Irish wars.
Come, gentlemen, let's all go visit him.
Pray God we may make haste, and come too late!
    [*All.*] Amen.   [*Exeunt.* 65

ACT II

SCENE I. [*London. Ely House.*]

Enter JOHN OF GAUNT, *sick, with the* DUKE OF
YORK, *etc.*

  Gaunt. Will the King come, that I may breathe
    my last
In wholesome counsel to his unstaid youth?
  York. Vex not yourself, nor strive not with your
    breath;
For all in vain comes counsel to his ear.
  Gaunt. O, but they say the tongues of dying men
Enforce attention like deep harmony. 6
Where words are scarce, they are seldom spent in vain,
For they breathe truth that breathe their words in
    pain.
He that no more must say is listened more
    Than they whom youth and ease have taught to
    glose. 10
More are men's ends mark'd than their lives before.
    The setting sun, and music at the close,
As the last taste of sweets, is sweetest last,
Writ in remembrance more than things long past.
Though Richard my life's counsel would not hear,
My death's sad tale may yet undeaf his ear. 16
  York. No; it is stopp'd with other flattering
    sounds,
As praises, of whose taste the wise are found,
Lascivious metres, to whose venom sound
The open ear of youth doth always listen; 20
Report of fashions in proud Italy,

Sc. iv, 20. [cousin, cousin] F. *coosens coosin* Q. 23. [Bagot ... Green] Q₆. Om. Q₁. 29. underbearing: endurance.
30. affects: affections. 39. Expedient manage: swift handling. 45. farm: lease the revenues. 48. blank charters: i.e., to
be filled in at the king's pleasure. 53. [Bushy, what news?] F. *with news* (as part of s.d.) Q. 65. [All.] (Staunton). Om. Q.
Act II, sc. i, 10. glose: flatter. 18. of ... found Q. *of his state: then there are found* Ff. Obviously corrupt. Many edd.
read *fond* for *found.*

Whose manners still our tardy, apish nation
Limps after in base imitation.
Where doth the world thrust forth a vanity —
So it be new, there's no respect how vile —   25
That is not quickly buzz'd into his ears?
Then all too late comes counsel to be heard
Where will doth mutiny with wit's regard.
Direct not him whose way himself will choose;
'Tis breath thou lack'st, and that breath wilt thou
     lose.   30
   Gaunt. Methinks I am a prophet new inspir'd
And thus expiring do foretell of him:
His rash fierce blaze of riot cannot last,
For violent fires soon burn out themselves;
Small showers last long, but sudden storms are
     short;   35
He tires betimes that spurs too fast betimes;
With eager feeding food doth choke the feeder;
Light vanity, insatiate cormorant,
Consuming means, soon preys upon itself.
This royal throne of kings, this sceptred isle,   40
This earth of majesty, this seat of Mars,
This other Eden, demi-paradise,
This fortress built by Nature for herself
Against infection and the hand of war,
This happy breed of men, this little world,   45
This precious stone set in the silver sea,
Which serves it in the office of a wall
Or as a moat defensive to a house
Against the envy of less happier lands,
This blessed plot, this earth, this realm, this
     England,   50
This nurse, this teeming womb of royal kings,
Fear'd by their breed and famous by their birth,
Renowned for their deeds as far from home,
For Christian service and true chivalry,
As is the sepulchre in stubborn Jewry,   55
Of the world's ransom, blessed Mary's Son,
This land of such dear souls, this dear dear land,
Dear for her reputation through the world,
Is now leas'd out, I die pronouncing it,
Like to a tenement or pelting farm.   60
England, bound in with the triumphant sea,
Whose rocky shore beats back the envious siege
Of wat'ry Neptune, is now bound in with shame,
With inky blots and rotten parchment bonds.
That England, that was wont to conquer others,   65
Hath made a shameful conquest of itself.
Ah, would the scandal vanish with my life,
How happy then were my ensuing death!

     Enter KING RICHARD *and* QUEEN, AUMERLE,
   BUSHY, GREEN, BAGOT, ROSS, *and* WILLOUGHBY.

   York. The King is come. Deal mildly with his
     youth;

For young hot colts being rag'd do rage the more.
   Queen. How fares our noble uncle Lancaster?   71
   K. Rich. What comfort, man? How is't with
     aged Gaunt?
   Gaunt. O, how that name befits my composition!
Old Gaunt indeed, and gaunt in being old.
Within me Grief hath kept a tedious fast;   75
And who abstains from meat that is not gaunt?
For sleeping England long time have I watch'd;
Watching breeds leanness, leanness is all gaunt.
The pleasure that some fathers feed upon,
Is my strict fast; I mean, my children's looks;   80
And therein fasting, hast thou made me gaunt.
Gaunt am I for the grave, gaunt as a grave,
Whose hollow womb inherits nought but bones.
   K. Rich. Can sick men play so nicely with their
     names?
   Gaunt. No, misery makes sport to mock itself.   85
Since thou dost seek to kill my name in me,
I mock my name, great King, to flatter thee.
   K. Rich. Should dying men flatter with those
     that live?
   Gaunt. No, no, men living flatter those that die.
   K. Rich. Thou, now a-dying, say'st thou flatterest
     me.   90
   Gaunt. O, no! thou diest, though I the sicker be.
   K. Rich. I am in health, I breathe, and see thee ill.
   Gaunt. Now He that made me knows I see thee ill;
Ill in myself to see, and in thee seeing ill.
Thy death-bed is no lesser than thy land   95
Wherein thou liest in reputation sick;
And thou, too careless patient as thou art,
Commit'st thy anointed body to the cure
Of those physicians that first wounded thee.
A thousand flatterers sit within thy crown,   100
Whose compass is no bigger than thy head;
And yet, [incaged] in so small a verge,
The waste is no whit lesser than thy land.
O, had thy grandsire with a prophet's eye
Seen how his son's son should destroy his sons,   105
From forth thy reach he would have laid thy shame,
Deposing thee before thou wert possess'd,
Which art possess'd now to depose thyself.
Why, cousin, wert thou regent of the world,
It were a shame to let this land by lease;   110
But for thy world enjoying but this land,
Is it not more than shame to shame it so?
Landlord of England art thou now, not king.
Thy state of law is bondslave to the law,
And thou —
   K. Rich. A lunatic lean-witted fool,   115
Presuming on an ague's privilege,
Dar'st with thy frozen admonition
Make pale our cheek, chasing the royal blood
With fury from his native residence.

---

25. **no respect:** no matter. 28. **wit's regard:** respect for reason. 52. **by:** for. 60. **pelting:** paltry. 73. **composition:** condition. 83. **inherits:** holds. 84. **nicely:** delicately, subtly. 102. **[incaged]** F. *inraged* Q. **verge:** circle.

Now, by my seat's right royal majesty, 120
Wert thou not brother to great Edward's son,
This tongue that runs so roundly in thy head
Should run thy head from thy unreverent shoulders.
Gaunt. O, spare me not, my brother Edward's
        son,
For that I was his father Edward's son. 125
That blood already, like the pelican,
Hast thou tapp'd out and drunkenly carous'd.
My brother Gloucester, plain well-meaning soul,
Whom fair befall in heaven 'mongst happy souls!
May be a precedent and witness good 130
That thou respect'st not spilling Edward's blood.
Join with the present sickness that I have,
And thy unkindness be like crooked age,
To crop at once a too long withered flower.
Live in thy shame, but die not shame with thee!
These words hereafter thy tormentors be! 136
Convey me to my bed, then to my grave;
Love they to live that love and honour have.
        [*Exit* [*borne off by his Attendants*].
    K. Rich. And let them die that age and sullens
        have;
For both hast thou, and both become the grave.
    York. I do beseech your Majesty, impute his
        words 141
To wayward sickliness and age in him.
He loves you, on my life, and holds you dear
As Harry Duke of Hereford, were he here.
    K. Rich. Right, you say true.   As Hereford's
        love, so his; 145
As theirs, so mine; and all be as it is.

Enter NORTHUMBERLAND.

    North. My liege, old Gaunt commends him to
        your Majesty.
    K. Rich. What says he?
    North.   Nay, nothing; all is said.
His tongue is now a stringless instrument;
Words, life, and all, old Lancaster hath spent. 150
    York. Be York the next that must be bankrupt so!
Though death be poor, it ends a mortal woe.
    K. Rich. The ripest fruit first falls, and so doth he;
His time is spent, our pilgrimage must be.
So much for that.   Now for our Irish wars. 155
We must supplant those rough rug-headed kerns,
Which live like venom where no venom else
But only they have privilege to live.
And for these great affairs do ask some charge,
Towards our assistance we do seize to us 160
The plate, coin, revenues, and moveables,
Whereof our uncle Gaunt did stand possess'd.

    York. How long shall I be patient?   Ah, how long
Shall tender duty make me suffer wrong? 164
Not Gloucester's death, nor Hereford's banishment
Not Gaunt's rebukes, nor England's private wrongs,
Nor the prevention of poor Bolingbroke
About his marriage, nor my own disgrace,
Have ever made me sour my patient cheek,
Or bend one wrinkle on my sovereign's face. 170
I am the last of noble Edward's sons,
Of whom thy father, Prince of Wales, was first.
In war was never lion rag'd more fierce,
In peace was never gentle lamb more mild,
Than was that young and princely gentleman. 175
His face thou hast, for even so look'd he,
Accomplish'd with the number of thy hours;
But when he frown'd, it was against the French
And not against his friends.   His noble hand
Did win what he did spend and spent not that 180
Which his triumphant father's hand had won.
His hands were guilty of no kindred blood,
But bloody with the enemies of his kin.
O Richard!   York is too far gone with grief,
Or else he never would compare between. 185
    K. Rich. Why, uncle, what's the matter?
    York.   O my liege,
Pardon me, if you please; if not, I, pleas'd
Not to be pardon'd, am content withal.
Seek you to seize and gripe into your hands
The royalties and rights of banish'd Hereford? 190
Is not Gaunt dead, and doth not Hereford live?
Was not Gaunt just, and is not Harry true?
Did not the one deserve to have an heir?
Is not his heir a well-deserving son?
Take Hereford's rights away, and take from Time
His charters and his customary rights; 196
Let not to-morrow then ensue to-day;
Be not thyself; for how art thou a king
But by fair sequence and succession?
Now, afore God — God forbid I say true! — 200
If you do wrongfully seize Hereford's rights,
Call in the letters patents that he hath
By his attorneys general to sue
His livery, and deny his off'red homage,
You pluck a thousand dangers on your head, 205
You lose a thousand well-disposed hearts
And prick my tender patience to those thoughts
Which honour and allegiance cannot think.
    K. Rich. Think what you will, we seize into our
        hands
His plate, his goods, his money, and his lands. 210
    York. I'll not be by the while.   My liege, fare-
        well!

132–34. **Join . . . flower:** Let thy unkindness join with my sickness to end my life.   156. **rug-headed kerns:** shock-headed troops.   157. **venom:** venomous animals, the snakes St. Patrick banished.   159. **charge:** expense.   166. **Gaunt's rebukes:** insults to Gaunt.   167–68. **prevention . . . marriage.**   Richard had intervened to prevent Bolingbroke's marriage to the cousin of the King of France.   177. **Accomplish'd . . . hours:** at thy age.   203–04. **sue His livery:** claim his inheritance.

What will ensue hereof, there's none can tell;
But by bad courses may be understood
That their events can never fall out good.   [*Exit.*
    K. Rich. Go, Bushy, to the Earl of Wiltshire
        straight.   215
Bid him repair to us to Ely House
To see this business. To-morrow next
We will for Ireland; and 'tis time, I trow;
And we create, in absence of ourself,
Our uncle York lord governor of England;   220
For he is just and always lov'd us well.
Come on, our queen; to-morrow must we part.
Be merry, for our time of stay is short.
            [*Flourish. Exeunt King, Queen, Aumerle,
                Bushy, Green, and Bagot.*
    North. Well, lords, the Duke of Lancaster is dead.
    Ross. And living too; for now his son is duke. 225
    Willo. Barely in title, not in revenues.
    North. Richly in both, if Justice had her right.
    Ross. My heart is great; but it must break with
        silence,
Ere 't be disburden'd with a liberal tongue.
    North. Nay, speak thy mind; and let him ne'er
        speak more   230
That speaks thy words again to do thee harm!
    Willo. Tends that thou wouldst speak to the
        Duke of Hereford?
If it be so, out with it boldly, man;
Quick is mine ear to hear of good towards him.
    Ross. No good at all that I can do for him;   235
Unless you call it good to pity him,
Bereft and gelded of his patrimony.
    North. Now, afore God, 'tis shame such wrongs
        are borne
In him, a royal prince, and many moe
Of noble blood in this declining land.   240
The King is not himself, but basely led
By flatterers; and what they will inform,
Merely in hate, 'gainst any of us all,
That will the King severely prosecute
'Gainst us, our lives, our children, and our heirs. 245
    Ross. The commons hath he pill'd with grievous
        taxes,
And quite lost their hearts; the nobles hath he fin'd
For ancient quarrels, and quite lost their hearts.
    Willo. And daily new exactions are devis'd,
As blanks, benevolences, and I wot not what.   250
But what, o' God's name, doth become of this?
    North. Wars hath not wasted it, for warr'd he
        hath not,
But basely yielded upon compromise
That which his noble ancestors achiev'd with blows.
More hath he spent in peace than they in wars.   255
    Ross. The Earl of Wiltshire hath the realm in farm.

    Willo. The King's grown bankrupt, like a broken
        man.
    North. Reproach and dissolution hangeth over
        him.
    Ross. He hath not money for these Irish wars,
His burdenous taxations notwithstanding,   260
But by the robbing of the banish'd Duke.
    North. His noble kinsman: most degenerate king!
But, lords, we hear this fearful tempest sing,
Yet seek no shelter to avoid the storm;
We see the wind sit sore upon our sails,   265
And yet we strike not, but securely perish.
    Ross. We see the very wreck that we must suffer;
And unavoided is the danger now,
For suffering so the causes of our wreck.
    North. Not so; even through the hollow eyes of
        death   270
I spy life peering; but I dare not say
How near the tidings of our comfort is.
    Willo. Nay, let us share thy thoughts, as thou
        dost ours.
    Ross. Be confident to speak, Northumberland.
We three are but thyself; and, speaking so,   275
Thy words are but as thoughts; therefore, be
        bold.
    North. Then thus: I have from Le Port Blanc, a
        bay
In Brittany, receiv'd intelligence
That Harry Duke of Hereford, Rainold Lord
        Cobham,
[The son and heir of th' Earl of Arundel,]   280
That late broke from the Duke of Exeter,
His brother, Archbishop late of Canterbury,
Sir Thomas Erpingham, Sir John Ramston,
Sir John Norbery, Sir Robert Waterton, and
        Francis Coines,
All these, well furnish'd by the Duke of Bretagne 285
With eight tall ships, three thousand men of war,
Are making hither with all due expedience
And shortly mean to touch our northern shore.
Perhaps they had ere this, but that they stay
The first departing of the King for Ireland.   290
If then we shall shake off our slavish yoke,
Imp out our drooping country's broken wing,
Redeem from broking pawn the blemish'd crown,
Wipe off the dust that hides our sceptre's gilt,
And make high majesty look like itself,   295
Away with me in post to Ravenspurgh;
But if you faint, as fearing to do so,
Stay and be secret, and myself will go.
    Ross. To horse, to horse! urge doubts to them
        that fear.   299
    Willo. Hold out my horse, and I will first be there.
                                                [*Exeunt.*

---

228. **great:** swollen, full.   229. **liberal:** free.   246. **pill'd:** robbed.   250. **blanks.** Cf. I.iv.48, note.   **benevolences:** forced loans.   265. **sit sore:** press hard.   266. **securely:** carelessly.   280. This line is substantially from Holinshed. Om. QF.
281. **broke from:** escaped the custody of.   292. **Imp out:** mend by grafting.   293. **broking pawn:** the pawnbroker.

Scene II. [*Windsor Castle.*]

Enter Queen, Bushy, *and* Bagot.

Bushy. Madam, your Majesty is too much sad.
You promis'd, when you parted with the King,
To lay aside life-harming heaviness
And entertain a cheerful disposition.

Queen. To please the King I did; to please myself
I cannot do it; yet I know no cause   6
Why I should welcome such a guest as Grief,
Save bidding farewell to so sweet a guest
As my sweet Richard. Yet again, methinks,
Some unborn sorrow, ripe in fortune's womb,   10
Is coming towards me, and my inward soul
With nothing trembles. At something it grieves,
More than with parting from my lord the King.

Bushy. Each substance of a grief hath twenty
    shadows,
Which shows like grief itself, but is not so;   15
For sorrow's eye, glazed with blinding tears,
Divides one thing entire to many objects,
Like perspectives, which rightly gaz'd upon
Show nothing but confusion, ey'd awry
Distinguish form; so your sweet Majesty,   20
Looking awry upon your lord's departure,
Find shapes of grief, more than himself, to wail;
Which, look'd on as it is, is nought but shadows
Of what it is not. Then, thrice-gracious Queen,
More than your lord's departure weep not. More's
    not seen;   25
Or if it be, 'tis with false sorrow's eye,
Which for things true weeps things imaginary.

Queen. It may be so; but yet my inward soul
Persuades me it is otherwise. Howe'er it be,
I cannot but be sad; so heavy sad   30
As, though on thinking on no thought I think,
Makes me with heavy nothing faint and shrink.

Bushy. 'Tis nothing but conceit, my gracious
    lady.

Queen. 'Tis nothing less: conceit is still deriv'd
From some forefather grief; mine is not so,   35
For nothing hath begot my something grief,
Or something hath the nothing that I grieve.
'Tis in reversion that I do possess;
But what it is, that is not yet known; what,
I cannot name; 'tis nameless woe, I wot.   40

Enter Green.

Green. God save your Majesty! and well met,
    gentlemen.
I hope the King is not yet shipp'd for Ireland.

Queen. Why hop'st thou so? 'Tis better hope he is;
For his designs crave haste, his haste good hope.
Then wherefore dost thou hope he is not shipp'd? 45

Green. That he, our hope, might have retir'd his
    power,

And driven into despair an enemy's hope,
Who strongly hath set footing in this land.
The banish'd Bolingbroke repeals himself,
And with uplifted arms is safe arriv'd   50
At Ravenspurgh.

Queen.   Now God in heaven forbid!

Green. Ah, madam, 'tis too true; and, that is
    worse,
The Lord Northumberland, his son young Henry
    Percy,
The Lords of Ross, Beaumond, and Willoughby,
With all their powerful friends, are fled to him. 55

Bushy. Why have you not proclaim'd Northum-
    berland
And all the rest revolted faction traitors?

Green. We have; whereupon the Earl of Worces-
    ter
Hath broken his staff, resign'd his stewardship,
And all the household servants fled with him   60
To Bolingbroke.

Queen. So, Green, thou art the midwife to my
    woe,
And Bolingbroke my sorrow's dismal heir.
Now hath my soul brought forth her prodigy,
And I, a gasping new-deliver'd mother,   65
Have woe to woe, sorrow to sorrow join'd.

Bushy. Despair not, madam.

Queen.   Who shall hinder me?
I will despair, and be at enmity
With cozening hope. He is a flatterer,
A parasite, a keeper back of death,   70
Who gently would dissolve the bands of life,
Which false hope lingers in extremity.

Enter York.

Green. Here comes the Duke of York.

Queen. With signs of war about his aged neck.
O, full of careful business are his looks!   75
Uncle, for God's sake, speak comfortable words.

York. Should I do so, I should belie my thoughts.
Comfort's in heaven, and we are on the earth,
Where nothing lives but crosses, cares, and grief.
Your husband, he is gone to save far off,   80
Whilst others come to make him lose at home.
Here am I left to underprop his land,
Who, weak with age, cannot support myself.
Now comes the sick hour that his surfeit made;
Now shall he try his friends that flatter'd him. 85

Enter a Servant.

Serv. My lord, your son was gone before I came.

York. He was? Why, so! go all which way it will!
The nobles they are fled; the commons they are
    cold,
And will, I fear, revolt on Hereford's side.   89

Sc. ii, 18. **perspectives:** optical glasses. **rightly:** straight. 33. **conceit:** imagination. 34. **still:** always. 46. **retir'd:**
brought back. 52. **that:** what. 69. **cozening:** cheating. 72. **lingers:** prolongs. 75. **careful:** anxious.

Sirrah, get thee to Plashy, to my sister Gloucester;
Bid her send me presently a thousand pound.
Hold, take my ring.

Serv. My lord, I had forgot to tell your lordship,
To-day, as I came by, I called there, —
But I shall grieve you to report the rest.   95

York. What is't, knave?

Serv. An hour before I came, the Duchess died.

York. God for his mercy! what a tide of woes
Comes rushing on this woeful land at once!
I know not what to do. I would to God,   100
So my untruth had not provok'd him to it,
The King had cut off my head with my brother's.
What, are there no posts dispatch'd for Ireland?
How shall we do for money for these wars?
Come, sister, — cousin, I would say, — pray,
        pardon me.   105
Go, fellow, get thee home, provide some carts
And bring away the armour that is there.
                              [*Exit Servant.*]
Gentlemen, will you go muster men? If I
Know how or which way to order these affairs
Thus thrust disorderly into my hands,   110
Never believe me. Both are my kinsmen:
Th' one is my sovereign, whom both my oath
And duty bids defend; t'other again
Is my kinsman, whom the King hath wrong'd,
Whom conscience and my kindred bids to right. 115
Well, somewhat we must do. Come, cousin, I'll
Dispose of you.
Gentlemen, go, muster up your men,
And meet me presently at Berkeley.
I should to Plashy too,   120
But time will not permit. All is uneven,
And everything is left at six and seven.
                        [*Exeunt York and Queen.*

Bushy. The wind sits fair for news to go for
        Ireland,
But none returns. For us to levy power
Proportionable to the enemy   125
Is all unpossible.

Green. Besides, our nearness to the King in love
Is near the hate of those love not the King.

Bagot. And that's the wavering commons, for
        their love
Lies in their purses; and whoso empties them 130
By so much fills their hearts with deadly hate.

Bushy. Wherein the King stands generally con-
        demn'd.

Bagot. If judgement lie in them, then so do we,
Because we ever have been near the King.

Green. Well, I will for refuge straight to Bristol
        castle: 135
The Earl of Wiltshire is already there.

Bushy. Thither will I with you; for little office
The hateful commons [will] perform for us.

Except like curs to tear us all to pieces.
Will you go along with us?   140

Bagot. No; I will to Ireland to his Majesty.
Farewell! If heart's presages be not vain,
We three here part that ne'er shall meet again.

Bushy. That's as York thrives to beat back
        Bolingbroke.

Green. Alas, poor duke! the task he undertakes
Is numb'ring sands and drinking oceans dry. 146
Where one on his side fights, thousands will fly.
Farewell at once, for once, for all, and ever.

Bushy. Well, we may meet again.

Bagot.   I fear me, never.
                              [*Exeunt.*

SCENE III. [*Wilds in Gloucestershire.*]

Enter BOLINGBROKE *and* NORTHUMBERLAND
        [*with forces*].

Boling. How far is it, my lord, to Berkeley now?

North. Believe me, noble lord,
I am a stranger here in Gloucestershire.
These high wild hills and rough uneven ways   4
Draws out our miles, and makes them wearisome;
And yet your fair discourse hath been as sugar,
Making the hard way sweet and delectable.
But I bethink me what a weary way
From Ravenspurgh to Cotswold will be found
In Ross and Willoughby, wanting your company, 10
Which, I protest, hath very much beguil'd
The tediousness and process of my travel.
But theirs is sweet'ned with the hope to have
The present benefit which I possess;
And hope to joy is little less in joy   15
Than hope enjoy'd. By this the weary lords
Shall make their way seem short, as mine hath done
By sight of what I have, your noble company.

Boling. Of much less value is my company
Than your good words. But who comes here? 20

Enter HENRY PERCY.

North. It is my son, young Harry Percy,
Sent from my brother Worcester, whencesoever.
Harry, how fares your uncle?

Percy. I had thought, my lord, to have learn'd
        his health of you.

North. Why, is he not with the Queen?   25

Percy. No, my good lord; he hath forsook the
        court,
Broken his staff of office, and dispers'd
The household of the King.

North.   What was his reason?
He was not so resolv'd when last we spake together.

Percy. Because your lordship was proclaimed
        traitor.   30
But he, my lord, is gone to Ravenspurgh

To offer service to the Duke of Hereford,
And sent me over by Berkeley, to discover
What power the Duke of York had levied there;
Then with directions to repair to Ravenspurgh. 35
   North. Have you forgot the Duke of Hereford,
     boy?
   Percy. No, my good lord, for that is not forgot
Which ne'er I did remember. To my knowledge,
I never in my life did look on him.
   North. Then learn to know him now; this is the
     Duke. 40
   Percy. My gracious lord, I tender you my
     service,
Such as it is, being tender, raw, and young;
Which elder days shall ripen and confirm
To more approved service and desert.
   Boling. I thank thee, gentle Percy; and be sure
I count myself in nothing else so happy 46
As in a soul rememb'ring my good friends;
And, as my fortune ripens with thy love,
It shall be still thy true love's recompense.
My heart this covenant makes, my hand thus
     seals it. 50
   North. How far is it to Berkeley? and what stir
Keeps good old York there with his men of war?
   Percy. There stands the castle, by yon tuft of
     trees,
Mann'd with three hundred men, as I have heard;
And in it are the Lords of York, Berkeley, and
     Seymour; 55
None else of name and noble estimate.

     Enter Ross *and* WILLOUGHBY.

   North. Here come the Lords of Ross and Wil-
     loughby,
Bloody with spurring, fiery-red with haste.
   Boling. Welcome, my lords. I wot your love
     pursues
A banish'd traitor. All my treasury 60
Is yet but unfelt thanks, which more enrich'd
Shall be your love and labour's recompense.
   Ross. Your presence makes us rich, most noble
     lord.
   Willo. And far surmounts our labour to attain it.
   Boling. Evermore thanks, the exchequer of the
     poor, 65
Which, till my infant fortune comes to years,
Stands for my bounty. But who comes here?

     Enter BERKELEY.

   North. It is my Lord of Berkeley, as I guess.
   Berk. My Lord of Hereford, my message is to you.
   Boling. My lord, my answer is — to Lancaster;
And I am come to seek that name in England; 71

And I must find that title in your tongue,
Before I make reply to aught you say.
   Berk. Mistake me not, my lord; 'tis not my
     meaning
To raze one title of your honour out. 75
To you, my lord, I come, what lord you will,
From the most gracious regent of this land,
The Duke of York, to know what pricks you on
To take advantage of the absent time 79
And fright our native peace with [self-born] arms.

     Enter YORK [*attended*].

   Boling. I shall not need transport my words by
     you;
Here comes his Grace in person. My noble uncle!
                    [*Kneels.*]
   York. Show me thy humble heart, and not thy
     knee,
Whose duty is deceiveable and false.
   Boling. My gracious uncle — 85
   York. Tut, tut!
Grace me no grace, nor uncle me no uncle.
I am no traitor's uncle; and that word "grace"
In an ungracious mouth is but profane.
Why have those banish'd and forbidden legs 90
Dar'd once to touch a dust of England's ground?
But then more "why?" Why have they dar'd to
     march
So many miles upon her peaceful bosom,
Frighting her pale-fac'd villages with war
And ostentation of despised arms? 95
Com'st thou because the anointed King is hence?
Why, foolish boy, the King is left behind,
And in my loyal bosom lies his power.
Were I but now the lord of such hot youth
As when brave Gaunt, thy father, and myself 100
Rescued the Black Prince, that young Mars of men,
From forth the ranks of many thousand French,
O, then how quickly should this arm of mine,
Now prisoner to the palsy, chastise thee
And minister correction to thy fault! 105
   Boling. My gracious uncle, let me know my fault.
On what condition stands it and wherein?
   York. Even in condition of the worst degree,
In gross rebellion and detested treason.
Thou art a banish'd man, and here art come 110
Before the expiration of thy time,
In braving arms against thy sovereign.
   Boling. As I was banish'd, I was banish'd Here-
     ford;
But as I come, I come for Lancaster.
And, noble uncle, I beseech your Grace 115
Look on my wrongs with an indifferent eye.
You are my father, for methinks in you

Sc. iii, 61. **unfelt:** which I cannot make you feel. 79. **absent time:** time of the King's absence. 80. **[self-born]** F₃: domestic. *selfeborne* Q. 84. **deceiveable:** deceptive. 95. **despised:** despicable. 107. **condition:** quality. 112. **braving:** defiant. 116. **indifferent:** impartial.

I see old Gaunt alive. O, then, my father,
Will you permit that I shall stand condemn'd
A wandering vagabond; my rights and royalties 120
Pluck'd from my arms perforce, and given away
To upstart unthrifts? Wherefore was I born?
If that my cousin king be King of England,
It must be granted I am Duke of Lancaster.
You have a son, Aumerle, my noble cousin; 125
Had you first died, and he been thus trod down,
He should have found his uncle Gaunt a father
To rouse his wrongs and chase them to the bay.
I am deni'd to sue my livery here,
And yet my letters patents give me leave. 130
My father's goods are all distrain'd and sold,
And these and all are all amiss employ'd.
What would you have me do? I am a subject
And I challenge law. Attorneys are denied me;
And therefore personally I lay my claim 135
To my inheritance of free descent.
    North. The noble Duke hath been too much
        abus'd.
    Ross. It stands your Grace upon to do him right.
    Willo. Base men by his endowments are made
        great.
    York. My lords of England, let me tell you this:
I have had feeling of my cousin's wrongs 141
And labour'd all I could to do him right;
But in this kind to come, in braving arms,
Be his own carver and cut out his way,
To find out right with wrong — it may not be; 145
And you that do abet him in this kind
Cherish rebellion and are rebels all.
    North. The noble Duke hath sworn his coming is
But for his own; and for the right of that
We all have strongly sworn to give him aid; 150
And let him ne'er see joy that breaks that oath!
    York. Well, well, I see the issue of these arms.
I cannot mend it, I must needs confess,
Because my power is weak and all ill left;
But if I could, by Him that gave me life, 155
I would attach you all and make you stoop
Unto the sovereign mercy of the King;
But since I cannot, be it known to you
I do remain as neuter. So, fare you well;
Unless you please to enter in the castle 160
And there repose you for this night.
    Boling. An offer, uncle, that we will accept.
But we must win your Grace to go with us
To Bristol castle, which they say is held
By Bushy, Bagot, and their complices, 165
The caterpillars of the commonwealth,
Which I have sworn to weed and pluck away.
    York. It may be I will go with you; but yet I'll
        pause,

For I am loath to break our country's laws.
Nor friends nor foes, to me welcome you are. 170
Things past redress are now with me past care.
                                        [*Exeunt.*

SCENE IV. [*A camp in Wales.*]

Enter SALISBURY *and a* Welsh CAPTAIN.

    Cap. My Lord of Salisbury, we have stay'd ten
        days
And hardly kept our countrymen together,
And yet we hear no tidings from the King;
Therefore we will disperse ourselves. Farewell!
    Sal. Stay yet another day, thou trusty Welsh-
        man. 5
The King reposeth all his confidence in thee.
    Cap. 'Tis thought the King is dead; we will not
        stay.
The bay-trees in our country are all wither'd
And meteors fright the fixed stars of heaven;
The pale-fac'd moon looks bloody on the earth 10
And lean-look'd prophets whisper fearful change;
Rich men look sad and ruffians dance and leap,
The one in fear to lose what they enjoy,
The other to enjoy by rage and war.
These signs forerun the death or fall of kings. 15
Farewell! Our countrymen are gone and fled,
As well assur'd Richard their king is dead. [*Exit.*
    Sal. Ah, Richard, with the eyes of heavy mind
I see thy glory like a shooting star
Fall to the base earth from the firmament. 20
Thy sun sets weeping in the lowly west,
Witnessing storms to come, woe, and unrest.
Thy friends are fled to wait upon thy foes,
And crossly to thy good all fortune goes. [*Exit.*

ACT III

SCENE I. [*Bristol. Before the castle.*]

Enter BOLINGBROKE, YORK, NORTHUMBERLAND,
ROSS, PERCY, WILLOUGHBY, *with* BUSHY *and*
GREEN, *prisoners.*

    Boling. Bring forth these men.
Bushy and Green, I will not vex your souls —
Since presently your souls must part your bodies —
With too much urging your pernicious lives,
For 'twere no charity; yet, to wash your blood 5
From off my hands, here in the view of men
I will unfold some causes of your deaths.
You have misled a prince, a royal king,
A happy gentleman in blood and lineaments,
By you unhappied and disfigur'd clean. 10
You have in manner with your sinful hours

Made a divorce betwixt his queen and him,
Broke the possession of a royal bed
And stain'd the beauty of a fair queen's cheeks
With tears drawn from her eyes by your foul wrongs.
Myself, a prince by fortune of my birth,   16
Near to the King in blood, and near in love
Till you did make him misinterpret me,
Have stoop'd my neck under your injuries,
And sigh'd my English breath in foreign clouds,   20
Eating the bitter bread of banishment;
Whilst you have fed upon my signories,
Dispark'd my parks and fell'd my forest woods,
From my own windows torn my household coat,
Raz'd out my imprese, leaving me no sign,   25
Save men's opinions and my living blood,
To show the world I am a gentleman.
This and much more, much more than twice all this,
Condemns you to the death. See them delivered
   over
To execution and the hand of death.   30
  Bushy. More welcome is the stroke of death to me
Than Bolingbroke to England. Lords, farewell!
  Green. My comfort is that heaven will take our
   souls
And plague injustice with the pains of hell.
  Boling. My Lord Northumberland, see them
   dispatch'd.   35
      [*Exeunt Northumberland and others, with
         the prisoners.*]
Uncle, you say the Queen is at your house.
For God's sake, fairly let her be entreated.
Tell her I send to her my kind commends;
Take special care my greetings be delivered.
  York. A gentleman of mine I have dispatch'd   40
With letters of your love to her at large.
  Boling. Thanks, gentle uncle.   Come, lords,
   away,
To fight with Glendower and his complices.
A while to work, and after holiday.   [*Exeunt.*

SCENE II. [*The coast of Wales. A castle in view.*]

Drums: flourish and colours. Enter KING RICHARD,
the BISHOP OF CARLISLE, AUMERLE, *and Soldiers.*

  K. Rich. Barkloughly castle call they this at
   hand?
  Aum. Yea, my lord. How brooks your Grace the
   air,
After your late tossing on the breaking seas?
  K. Rich. Needs must I like it well; I weep for joy
To stand upon my kingdom once again.   5
Dear earth, I do salute thee with my hand,
Though rebels wound thee with their horses' hoofs.
As a long-parted mother with her child

Plays fondly with her tears and smiles in meeting,
So, weeping, smiling, greet I thee, my earth,   10
And do thee favours with my royal hands.
Feed not thy sovereign's foe, my gentle earth,
Nor with thy sweets comfort his ravenous sense;
But let thy spiders, that suck up thy venom,
And heavy-gaited toads lie in their way,   15
Doing annoyance to the treacherous feet
Which with usurping steps do trample thee.
Yield stinging nettles to mine enemies;
And when they from thy bosom pluck a flower,
Guard it, I pray thee, with a lurking adder   20
Whose double tongue may with a mortal touch
Throw death upon thy sovereign's enemies.
Mock not my senseless conjuration, lords.
This earth shall have a feeling, and these stones
Prove armed soldiers, ere her native king   25
Shall falter under foul rebellion's arms.
  Car. Fear not, my lord; that Power that made
   you king
Hath power to keep you king in spite of all.
The means that heavens yield must be embrac'd,
And not neglected; else, [if] heaven would   30
And we will not, heaven's offer we refuse,
The proffer'd means of succour and redress.
  Aum. He means, my lord, that we are too remiss,
Whilst Bolingbroke, through our security,   34
Grows strong and great in substance and in power.
  K. Rich. Discomfortable cousin! know'st thou not
That when the searching eye of heaven is hid
Behind the globe, that lights the lower world,
Then thieves and robbers range abroad unseen
In murders and in outrage boldly here;   40
But when from under this terrestrial ball
He fires the proud tops of the eastern pines
And darts his light through every guilty hole,
Then murders, treasons, and detested sins,
The cloak of night being pluck'd from off their
   backs,   45
Stand bare and naked, trembling at themselves?
So when this thief, this traitor, Bolingbroke,
Who all this while hath revell'd in the night
Whilst we were wand'ring with the antipodes,
Shall see us rising in our throne, the east,   50
His treasons will sit blushing in his face,
Not able to endure the sight of day,
But, self-affrighted, tremble at his sin.
Not all the water in the rough rude sea
Can wash the balm off from an anointed king;   55
The breath of worldly men cannot depose
The deputy elected by the Lord.
For every man that Bolingbroke hath press'd
To lift shrewd steel against our golden crown,
God for his Richard hath in heavenly pay   60

22. **signories:** estates. 23. **Dispark'd:** thrown open. 24. **coat:** coat of arms. 25. **imprese:** device with motto.
Sc. ii, 2. **brooks:** enjoys. 21. **double:** forked. 23. **conjuration:** appeal. 25. **native:** by right of birth. 30. **[if]** (Pope).
Om. Q. 34. **security:** lack of care. 38. **that.** The antecedent is *eye.* 58. **press'd:** impressed, conscripted.

A glorious angel; then, if angels fight,
Weak men must fall, for Heaven still guards the
          right.

Enter SALISBURY.

Welcome, my lord.   How far off lies your power?
  Sal. Nor near nor farther off, my gracious lord,
Than this weak arm.   Discomfort guides my
          tongue   65
And bids me speak of nothing but despair.
One day too late, I fear me, noble lord,
Hath clouded all thy happy days on earth.
O, call back yesterday, bid time return,
And thou shalt have twelve thousand fighting men!
To-day, to-day, unhappy day, too late,   71
O'erthrows thy joys, friends, fortune, and thy state;
For all the Welshmen, hearing thou wert dead,
Are gone to Bolingbroke, dispers'd, and fled.
  Aum. Comfort, my liege; why looks your Grace
          so pale?   75
  K. Rich. But now the blood of twenty thousand
          men
Did triumph in my face, and they are fled;
And, till so much blood thither come again,
Have I not reason to look pale and dead?
All souls that will be safe fly from my side,   80
For time hath set a blot upon my pride.
  Aum. Comfort, my liege; remember who you are.
  K. Rich. I had forgot myself; am I not King?
Awake, thou coward majesty! thou sleepest.
Is not the King's name twenty thousand names?   85
Arm, arm, my name! a puny subject strikes
At thy great glory.   Look not to the ground,
Ye favourites of a king; are we not high?
High be our thoughts.   I know my uncle York
Hath power enough to serve our turn.   But who
          comes here?   90

Enter SCROOP.

  Scroop. More health and happiness betide my
          liege
Than can my care-tun'd tongue deliver him!
  K. Rich. Mine ear is open and my heart prepar'd.
The worst is worldly loss thou canst unfold.
Say, is my kingdom lost?   Why, 'twas my care;   95
And what loss is it to be rid of care?
Strives Bolingbroke to be as great as we?
Greater he shall not be; if he serve God,
We'll serve Him too and be his fellow so.
Revolt our subjects?   That we cannot mend;   100
They break their faith to God as well as us.
Cry woe, destruction, ruin, and decay:
The worst is death, and death will have his day.
  Scroop. Glad am I that your Highness is so arm'd
To bear the tidings of calamity.   105

Like an unseasonable stormy day
Which makes the silver rivers drown their shores
As if the world were all dissolv'd to tears,
So high above his limits swells the rage
Of Bolingbroke, covering your fearful land   110
With hard bright steel and hearts harder than steel.
White-beards have arm'd their thin and hairless
          scalps
Against thy majesty; boys, with women's voices,
Strive to speak big, and clap their female joints
In stiff unwieldy arms against thy crown;   115
Thy very beadsmen learn to bend their bows
Of double-fatal yew against thy state;
Yea, distaff-women manage rusty bills
Against thy seat: both young and old rebel,
And all goes worse than I have power to tell.   120
  K. Rich. Too well, too well thou tell'st a tale so ill.
Where is the Earl of Wiltshire?   Where is Bagot?
What is become of Bushy?   Where is Green?
That they have let the dangerous enemy
Measure our confines with such peaceful steps? 125
If we prevail, their heads shall pay for it.
I warrant they have made peace with Bolingbroke.
  Scroop. Peace have they made with him indeed,
          my lord.
  K. Rich. O villains, vipers, damn'd without re-
          demption!
Dogs, easily won to fawn on any man!   130
Snakes, in my heart-blood warm'd, that sting my
          heart!
Three Judases, each one thrice worse than Judas!
Would they make peace?   Terrible hell make war
Upon their spotted souls for this [offence]!
  Scroop. Sweet love, I see, changing his property,
Turns to the sourest and most deadly hate.   136
Again uncurse their souls; their peace is made
With heads, and not with hands.   Those whom you
          curse
Have felt the worst of death's destroying wound
And lie full low, grav'd in the hollow ground. 140
  Aum. Is Bushy, Green, and the Earl of Wiltshire
          dead?
  Scroop. Ay, all of them at Bristol lost their heads.
  Aum. Where is the Duke my father with his
          power?
  K. Rich. No matter where; of comfort no man
          speak.
Let's talk of graves, of worms, and epitaphs;   145
Make dust our paper and with rainy eyes
Write sorrow on the bosom of the earth.
Let's choose executors and talk of wills;
And yet not so; for what can we bequeath
Save our deposed bodies to the ground?   150
Our lands, our lives, and all are Bolingbroke's,
And nothing can we call our own but death,

---

116. **beadsmen:** almsmen who prayed for the King.   117. **double-fatal:** causing death in two ways.   The wood was used
for bows, and the berries are poisonous.   118. **bills:** two-handed axes.   134. **[offence]** F.   Om. Q (ending line 133 with *hell*).

And that small model of the barren earth
Which serves as paste and cover to our bones.
For God's sake, let us sit upon the ground   155
And tell sad stories of the death of kings:
How some have been depos'd; some slain in war;
Some haunted by the ghosts they have depos'd;
Some poison'd by their wives; some sleeping kill'd;
All murdered: for within the hollow crown   160
That rounds the mortal temples of a king
Keeps Death his court, and there the antic sits,
Scoffing his state and grinning at his pomp,
Allowing him a breath, a little scene,
To monarchize, be fear'd, and kill with looks,   165
Infusing him with self and vain conceit,
As if this flesh which walls about our life
Were brass impregnable; and humour'd thus
Comes at the last and with a little pin
Bores through his castle wall, and — farewell
      king!   170
Cover your heads, and mock not flesh and blood
With solemn reverence. Throw away respect,
Tradition, form, and ceremonious duty;
For you have but mistook me all this while.
I live with bread like you, feel want,   175
Taste grief, need friends: subjected thus,
How can you say to me I am a king?
    Car. My lord, wise men ne'er sit and wail their
      woes,
But presently prevent the ways to wail.
To fear the foe, since fear oppresseth strength,   180
Gives in your weakness strength unto your foe,
And so your follies fight against yourself.
Fear, and be slain; no worse can come to fight;
And fight and die is death destroying death,
Where fearing dying pays death servile breath.   185
    Aum. My father hath a power; inquire of him,
And learn to make a body of a limb.
    K. Rich. Thou chid'st me well. Proud Boling-
      broke, I come
To change blows with thee for our day of doom.
This ague fit of fear is over-blown;   190
An easy task it is to win our own.
Say, Scroop, where lies our uncle with his power?
Speak sweetly, man, although thy looks be sour.
    Scroop. Men judge by the complexion of the sky
The state and inclination of the day;   195
So may you by my dull and heavy eye,
My tongue hath but a heavier tale to say.
I play the torturer by small and small
To lengthen out the worst that must be spoken.
Your uncle York is join'd with Bolingbroke,   200
And all your northern castles yielded up,
And all your southern gentlemen in arms
Upon his party.
    K. Rich.   Thou hast said enough.

[*To Aumerle.*] Beshrew thee, cousin, which didst
      lead me forth
Of that sweet way I was in to despair!   205
What say you now? What comfort have we now?
By heaven, I'll hate him everlastingly
That bids me be of comfort any more.
Go to Flint castle; there I'll pine away;
A king, woe's slave, shall kingly woe obey.   210
That power I have, discharge; and let them go
To ear the land that hath some hope to grow,
For I have none. Let no man speak again
To alter this, for counsel is but vain.
    Aum. My liege, one word.
    K. Rich.   He does me double wrong   215
That wounds me with the flatteries of his tongue.
Discharge my followers; let them hence away,
From Richard's night to Bolingbroke's fair day.
                                          [*Exeunt.*]

SCENE III. [*Wales. Before Flint Castle.*]

Enter, with drum and colours, BOLINGBROKE, YORK,
      NORTHUMBERLAND, *Attendants* [*and forces*].

    Boling. So that by this intelligence we learn
The Welshmen are dispers'd, and Salisbury
Is gone to meet the King, who lately landed
With some few private friends upon this coast.
    North. The news is very fair and good, my lord.
Richard not far from hence hath hid his head.   6
    York. It would beseem the Lord Northumberland
To say King Richard. Alack the heavy day
When such a sacred king should hide his head!
    North. Your Grace mistakes; only to be brief   10
Left I his title out.
    York.   The time hath been,
Would you have been so brief with him, he would
Have been so brief [with you], to shorten you,
For taking so the head, your whole head's length.
    Boling. Mistake not, uncle, further than you
      should.   15
    York. Take not, good cousin, further than you
      should,
Lest you mistake the heavens are o'er our heads.
    Boling. I know it, uncle, and oppose not myself
Against their will. But who comes here?

Enter PERCY.

Welcome, Harry. What, will not this castle yield?
    Percy. The castle royally is mann'd, my lord,   21
Against thy entrance.
    Boling. Royally!
Why, it contains no king?
    Percy.   Yes, my good lord,
It doth contain a king. King Richard lies   25
Within the limits of yon lime and stone;

---

162. **antic:** grotesque figure. 168. **humour'd thus:** having humored him thus. 212. **ear:** plow.
Sc. iii, 13. [**with you**] F. Om. Q. 14. **head:** title.

And with him are the Lord Aumerle, Lord Salisbury,
Sir Stephen Scroop, besides a clergyman
Of holy reverence; who, I cannot learn.
    North. O, belike it is the Bishop of Carlisle. 30
    Boling. Noble lords,
Go to the rude ribs of that ancient castle;
Through brazen trumpet send the breath of parley
Into his ruin'd ears, and thus deliver:
Henry Bolingbroke 35
On both his knees doth kiss King Richard's hand
And sends allegiance and true faith of heart
To his most royal person, hither come
Even at his feet to lay my arms and power,
Provided that my banishment repeal'd 40
And lands restor'd again be freely granted.
If not, I'll use the advantage of my power
And lay the summer's dust with showers of blood
Rain'd from the wounds of slaughtered Englishmen;
The which, how far off from the mind of Bolingbroke
It is, such crimson tempest should bedrench 46
The fresh green lap of fair King Richard's land,
My stooping duty tenderly shall show.
Go, signify as much, while here we march
Upon the grassy carpet of this plain. 50
Let's march without the noise of threat'ning drum,
That from this castle's tattered battlements
Our fair appointments may be well perus'd.
Methinks King Richard and myself should meet
With no less terror than the elements 55
Of fire and water, when their thund'ring shock
At meeting tears the cloudy cheeks of heaven.
Be he the fire, I'll be the yielding water;
The rage be his, whilst on the earth I rain
My waters — on the earth, and not on him. 60
March on, and mark King Richard how he looks.

Parle without, and answer within: then a flourish.
    Enter on the walls, KING RICHARD, *the* BISHOP OF
  CARLISLE, AUMERLE, SCROOP, *and* SALISBURY.

See, see, King Richard doth himself appear,
As doth the blushing discontented sun
From out the fiery portal of the east,
When he perceives the envious clouds are bent 65
To dim his glory and to stain the track
Of his bright passage to the occident.
    York. Yet looks he like a king! Behold, his eye,
As bright as is the eagle's, lightens forth
Controlling majesty. Alack, alack, for woe, 70
That any harm should stain so fair a show!
    K. Rich. We are amaz'd; and thus long have we
      stood   [*To North.*]
To watch the fearful bending of thy knee,
Because we thought ourself thy lawful king;
And if we be, how dare thy joints forget 75
To pay their awful duty to our presence?

If we be not, show us the hand of God
That hath dismiss'd us from our stewardship;
For well we know, no hand of blood and bone
Can gripe the sacred handle of our sceptre, 80
Unless he do profane, steal, or usurp.
And though you think that all, as you have done,
Have torn their souls by turning them from us,
And we are barren and bereft of friends,
Yet know, my master, God omnipotent, 85
Is mustering in his clouds on our behalf
Armies of pestilence; and they shall strike
Your children yet unborn and unbegot,
That lift your vassal hands against my head
And threat the glory of my precious crown. 90
Tell Bolingbroke — for yon methinks he stands —
That every stride he makes upon my land
Is dangerous treason. He is come to open
The purple testament of bleeding war;
But ere the crown he looks for live in peace, 95
Ten thousand bloody crowns of mothers' sons
Shall ill become the flower of England's face,
Change the complexion of her maid-pale peace
To scarlet indignation, and bedew
Her pastures' grass with faithful English blood. 100
    North. The King of heaven forbid our lord the
      King
Should so with civil and uncivil arms
Be rush'd upon! Thy thrice noble cousin
Harry Bolingbroke doth humbly kiss thy hand;
And by the honourable tomb he swears 105
That stands upon your royal grandsire's bones,
And by the royalties of both your bloods,
Currents that spring from one most gracious head,
And by the buried hand of warlike Gaunt,
And by the worth and honour of himself, 110
Comprising all that may be sworn or said,
His coming hither hath no further scope
Than for his lineal royalties, and to beg
Enfranchisement immediate on his knees;
Which on thy royal party granted once, 115
His glittering arms he will commend to rust,
His barbed steeds to stables, and his heart
To faithful service of your Majesty.
This swears he, as he is [a prince, is] just;
And, as I am a gentleman, I credit him. 120
    K. Rich. Northumberland, say thus the King
      returns:
His noble cousin is right welcome hither;
And all the number of his fair demands
Shall be accomplish'd without contradiction.
With all the gracious utterance thou hast 125
Speak to his gentle hearing kind commends.
      [*Northumberland withdraws to Bolingbroke.*]
  [*To Aumerle.*] We do debase ourselves, cousin, do
    we not,

---

73. **watch:** wait for. 102. **civil:** as in civil war. The other sense is played on in *uncivil.* 115. **party:** part. 119. [a
prince, is] F₁. *princesse* Q. 121. **returns:** replies.

To look so poorly and to speak so fair?
Shall we call back Northumberland, and send
Defiance to the traitor, and so die?   130
    Aum. No, good my lord; let's fight with gentle
        words
Till time lend friends, and friends their helpful
        swords.
    K. Rich. O God, O God! that e'er this tongue of
        mine
That laid the sentence of dread banishment
On yon proud man, should take it off again   135
With words of sooth! O that I were as great
As is my grief, or lesser than my name!
Or that I could forget what I have been,
Or not remember what I must be now!
Swell'st thou, proud heart? I'll give thee scope to
        beat,   140
Since foes have scope to beat both thee and me.
    Aum. Northumberland comes back from Boling-
        broke.
    K. Rich. What must the King do now? Must he
        submit?
The King shall do it. Must he be depos'd?
The King shall be contented. Must he lose   145
The name of king? O' God's name, let it go.
I'll give my jewels for a set of beads,
My gorgeous palace for a hermitage,
My gay apparel for an almsman's gown,
My figur'd goblets for a dish of wood,   150
My sceptre for a palmer's walking-staff,
My subjects for a pair of carved saints,
And my large kingdom for a little grave,
A little little grave, an obscure grave;
Or I'll be buried in the King's highway,   155
Some way of common trade, where subjects' feet
May hourly trample on their sovereign's head;
For on my heart they tread now whilst I live,
And buried once, why not upon my head?
Aumerle, thou weep'st, my tender-hearted cousin!   161
We'll make foul weather with despised tears.
Our sighs and they shall lodge the summer corn,
And make a dearth in this revolting land.
Or shall we play the wantons with our woes
And make some pretty match with shedding tears?
As thus, to drop them still upon one place,   166
Till they have fretted us a pair of graves
Within the earth; and, therein laid, — there lies
Two kinsmen digg'd their graves with weeping eyes.
Would not this ill do well? Well, well, I see   170
I talk but idly, and you laugh at me.
Most mighty prince, my Lord Northumberland,
What says King Bolingbroke? Will his Majesty
Give Richard leave to live till Richard die?
You make a leg, and Bolingbroke says ay.   175
    North. My lord, in the base court he doth attend

To speak with you, may it please you to come down.
    K. Rich. Down, down I come; like glist'ring
        Phaethon,
Wanting the manage of unruly jades.
In the base court? Base court, where kings grow
        base,   180
To come at traitors' calls and do them grace.
In the base court? Come down? Down, court!
        down, king!
For night-owls shriek where mounting larks should
        sing.   [*Exeunt from above.*]
    Boling. What says his Majesty?
    North.   Sorrow and grief of heart
Makes him speak fondly, like a frantic man;   185
Yet he is come.

[*Enter* KING RICHARD *and his* Attendants *below.*]

    Boling. Stand all apart,
And show fair duty to his Majesty.   [*He kneels down.*
My gracious lord, —
    K. Rich. Fair cousin, you debase your princely
        knee   190
To make the base earth proud with kissing it.
Me rather had my heart might feel your love
Than my unpleas'd eye my see your courtesy.
Up, cousin, up; your heart is up, I know,
Thus high at least [*touching his own head*], although
        your knee be low.   195
    Boling. My gracious lord, I come but for mine
        own.
    K. Rich. Your own is yours, and I am yours, and
        all.
    Boling. So far be mine, my most redoubted lord,
As my true service shall deserve your love.
    K. Rich. Well you deserve; they well deserve to
        have   200
That know the strong'st and surest way to get.
Uncle, give me your hands: nay, dry your eyes;
Tears show their love, but want their remedies.
Cousin, I am too young to be your father,
Though you are old enough to be my heir.   205
What you will have, I'll give, and willing too;
For do we must what force will have us do.
Set on towards London, cousin, is it so?
    Boling. Yea, my good lord.
    K. Rich.   Then I must not say no.
        [*Flourish. Exeunt.*

SCENE IV. [*Langley. The Duke of York's garden.*]

    Enter the QUEEN *and two* LADIES.

    Queen. What sport shall we devise here in this
        garden
To drive away the heavy thought of care?

---

136. **words of sooth:** smooth words. 162. **lodge:** lay flat. 167. **fretted:** worn. 175. **leg:** obeisance. 176. **base court:** lower (outer) courtyard. 179. **Wanting . . . of:** lacking the ability to control. 185. **fondly:** foolishly.

Lady. Madam, we'll play at bowls.
Queen. 'Twill make me think the world is full of
  rubs,
And that my fortune runs against the bias.   5
Lady. Madam, we'll dance.
Queen. My legs can keep no measure in delight,
When my poor heart no measure keeps in grief;
Therefore, no dancing, girl; some other sport.
Lady. Madam, we'll tell tales.   10
Queen. Of sorrow or of [joy]?
Lady.   Of either, madam.
Queen. Of neither, girl;
For if of joy, being altogether wanting,
It doth remember me the more of sorrow;
Or if of grief, being altogether had,   15
It adds more sorrow to my want of joy;
For what I have I need not to repeat,
And what I want it boots not to complain.
Lady. Madam, I'll sing.
Queen.   'Tis well that thou hast cause;
But thou shouldst please me better wouldst thou
  weep.   20
Lady. I could weep, madam, would it do you
  good.
Queen. And I could sing, would weeping do me
  good,
And never borrow any tear of thee.

Enter a GARDENER *and two* SERVANTS.

But stay, here come the gardeners.
Let's step into the shadow of these trees.   25
My wretchedness unto a row of pins,
They'll talk of state; for every one doth so
Against a change; woe is forerun with woe.
            [*Queen and Ladies retire.*]
Gard. Go, bind thou up yon dangling apricocks,
Which, like unruly children, make their sire   30
Stoop with oppression of their prodigal weight;
Give some supportance to the bending twigs.
Go thou, and like an executioner,
Cut off the heads of too fast growing sprays,
That look too lofty in our commonwealth;   35
All must be even in our government.
You thus employ'd, I will go root away
The noisome weeds, which without profit suck
The soil's fertility from wholesome flowers.
Serv. Why should we in the compass of a pale   40
Keep law and form and due proportion,
Showing, as in a model, our firm estate,
When our sea-walled garden, the whole land,
Is full of weeds, her fairest flowers chok'd up,
Her fruit-trees all unprun'd, her hedges ruin'd,   45
Her knots disorder'd and her wholesome herbs
Swarming with caterpillars?

Gard.   Hold thy peace.
He that hath suffer'd this disordered spring
Hath now himself met with the fall of leaf.
The weeds which his broad-spreading leaves did
  shelter,   50
That seem'd in eating him to hold him up,
Are pluck'd up root and all by Bolingbroke,
I mean the Earl of Wiltshire, Bushy, Green.
Serv. What, are they dead?
Gard.   They are; and Bolingbroke
Hath seiz'd the wasteful King. O, what pity is it
That he had not so trimm'd and dress'd his land   56
As we this garden! [We] at time of year
Do wound the bark, the skin of our fruit-trees,
Lest, being over-proud in sap and blood,
With too much riches it confound itself;   60
Had he done so to great and growing men,
They might have liv'd to bear and he to taste
Their fruits of duty. Superfluous branches
We lop away, that bearing boughs may live;
Had he done so, himself had borne the crown,   65
Which waste of idle hours hath quite thrown down.
Serv. What, think you the King shall be depos'd?
Gard. Depress'd he is already, and depos'd
'Tis doubt he will be. Letters came last night
To a dear friend of the good Duke of York's,   70
That tell black tidings.
Queen. O, I am press'd to death through want
  of speaking!   [*Coming forward.*]
Thou, old Adam's likeness, set to dress this garden,
How dares thy harsh rude tongue sound this un-
  pleasing news?
What Eve, what serpent, hath suggested thee   75
To make a second fall of cursed man?
Why dost thou say King Richard is depos'd?
Dar'st thou, thou little better thing than earth,
Divine his downfall? Say, where, when, and how,
Cam'st thou by this ill tidings? Speak, thou wretch.
Gard. Pardon me, madam; little joy have I   81
To breathe this news; yet what I say is true.
King Richard, he is in the mighty hold
Of Bolingbroke. Their fortunes both are weigh'd.
In your lord's scale is nothing but himself,   85
And some few vanities that make him light;
But in the balance of great Bolingbroke,
Besides himself, are all the English peers,
And with that odds he weighs King Richard down.
Post you to London, and you'll find it so;   90
I speak no more than every one doth know.
Queen. Nimble Mischance, that art so light of
  foot,
Doth not thy embassage belong to me,
And am I last that knows it? O, thou think'st
To serve me last, that I may longest keep   95

Thy sorrow in my breast. Come, ladies, go,
To meet at London London's king in woe.
What, was I born to this, that my sad look
Should grace the triumph of great Bolingbroke?
Gardener, for telling me these news of woe,   100
Pray God the plants thou graft'st may never grow.
                [*Exeunt [Queen and Ladies*].
  Gard. Poor queen! so that thy state might be no
     worse,
I would my skill were subject to thy curse.
Here did she fall a tear; here in this place
I'll set a bank of rue, sour herb of grace.   105
Rue, even for ruth, here shortly shall be seen,
In the remembrance of a weeping queen. [*Exeunt.*

ACT IV

Scene I. [*London. Westminster Hall.*]

Enter as to the Parliament Bolingbroke, Aumerle,
Northumberland, Percy, Fitzwater, Surrey,
the Bishop of Carlisle, *the* Abbot of Westminster [*and another* Lord], Herald, *and* Officers.

  Boling. Call forth Bagot.

            Enter Bagot.

Now, Bagot, freely speak thy mind;
What thou dost know of noble Gloucester's death,
Who wrought it with the King, and who perform'd
The bloody office of his timeless end.   5
  Bagot. Then set before my face the Lord Aumerle.
  Boling. Cousin, stand forth, and look upon that
    man.
  Bagot. My Lord Aumerle, I know your daring
    tongue
Scorns to unsay what once it hath deliver'd.
In that dead time when Gloucester's death was
    plotted,   10
I heard you say, "Is not my arm of length,
That reacheth from the restful English court
As far as Calais, to mine uncle's head?"
Amongst much other talk, that very time,
I heard you say that you had rather refuse   15
The offer of an hundred thousand crowns
Than Bolingbroke's return to England;
Adding withal, how blest this land would be
In this your cousin's death.
  Aum.   Princes and noble lords,
What answer shall I make to this base man?   20
Shall I so much dishonour my fair stars
On equal terms to give [him] chastisement?
Either I must, or have mine honour soil'd
With the attainder of his slanderous lips.
There is my gage, the manual seal of death,   25
That marks thee out for hell. I say, thou liest,

And will maintain what thou hast said is false
In thy heart-blood, though being all too base
To stain the temper of my knightly sword.   29
  Boling. Bagot, forbear; thou shalt not take it up.
  Aum. Excepting one, I would he were the best
In all this presence that hath mov'd me so.
  Fitz. If that thy valour stand on sympathy,
There is my gage, Aumerle, in gage to thine.
By that fair sun which shows me where thou stand'st,
I heard thee say, and vauntingly thou spak'st it,   36
That thou wert cause of noble Gloucester's death.
If thou deny'st it twenty times, thou liest;
And I will turn thy falsehood to thy heart,
Where it was forged, with my rapier's point.   40
  Aum. Thou dar'st not, coward, live to see that
    day.
  Fitz. Now, by my soul, I would it were this hour.
  Aum. Fitzwater, thou art damn'd to hell for this.
  Percy. Aumerle, thou liest; his honour is as true
In this appeal as thou art all unjust;   45
And that thou art so, there I throw my gage,
To prove it on thee to the extremest point
Of mortal breathing. Seize it, if thou dar'st.
  Aum. An if I do not, may my hands rot off
And never brandish more revengeful steel   50
Over the glittering helmet of my foe!
  Another Lord. I task the earth to the like, for-
    sworn Aumerle;
And spur thee on with full as many lies
As may be holloa'd in thy treacherous ear
From sun to sun. There is my honour's pawn;   55
Engage it to the trial, if thou dar'st.
  Aum. Who sets me else? By heaven, I'll throw
    at all!
I have a thousand spirits in one breast,
To answer twenty thousand such as you.
  Surrey. My Lord Fitzwater, I do remember well
The very time Aumerle and you did talk.   61
  Fitz. 'Tis very true; you were in presence then,
And you can witness with me this is true.
  Surrey. As false, by heaven, as heaven itself is
    true.
  Fitz. Surrey, thou liest.
  Surrey.   Dishonourable boy!
That lie shall lie so heavy on my sword,   66
That it shall render vengeance and revenge
Till thou the lie-giver and that lie do lie
In earth as quiet as thy father's skull;
In proof whereof, there is my honour's pawn;
Engage it to the trial, if thou dar'st.   71
  Fitz. How fondly dost thou spur a forward horse!
If I dare eat, or drink, or breathe, or live,
I dare meet Surrey in a wilderness
And spit upon him, whilst I say he lies,   75
And lies, and lies. There is [my] bond of faith,

Act IV, sc. i, 5. **timeless:** untimely. 10. **dead:** fatal. 21. **stars:** destiny. 22. **[him]** F. *them* Q₁, *my* Q₂. 33. **sympathy:**
equality of rank. 57. **sets:** challenges. 76. **[my]** Q₃. Om. Q₁.

To tie thee to my strong correction.
As I intend to thrive in this new world,
Aumerle is guilty of my true appeal;
Besides, I heard the banish'd Norfolk say   80
That thou, Aumerle, didst send two of thy men
To execute the noble Duke at Calais.
   Aum. Some honest Christian trust me with a
      gage
That Norfolk lies. Here do I throw down this,
If he may be repeal'd, to try his honour.   85
   Boling. These differences shall all rest under gage
Till Norfolk be repeal'd. Repeal'd he shall be,
And, though mine enemy, restor'd again
To all his lands and signories. When he's return'd,
Against Aumerle we will enforce his trial.   90
   Car. That honourable day shall ne'er be seen.
Many a time hath banish'd Norfolk fought
For Jesu Christ in glorious Christian field,
Streaming the ensign of the Christian cross
Against black pagans, Turks, and Saracens;   95
And, toil'd with works of war, retir'd himself
To Italy; and there at Venice gave
His body to that pleasant country's earth,
And his pure soul unto his captain Christ,
Under whose colours he had fought so long.   100
   Boling. Why, Bishop, is Norfolk dead?
   Car. As surely as I live, my lord.
   Boling. Sweet Peace conduct his sweet soul to
      the bosom
Of good old Abraham! Lords appellants,
Your differences shall all rest under gage   105
Till we assign you to your days of trial.

Enter YORK [*attended*].

   York. Great Duke of Lancaster, I come to thee
From plume-pluck'd Richard; who with willing soul
Adopts thee heir, and his high sceptre yields
To the possession of thy royal hand.   110
Ascend his throne, descending now from him;
And long live Henry, fourth of that name!
   Boling. In God's name, I'll ascend the regal
      throne.
   Car. Marry, God forbid!
Worst in this royal presence may I speak,   115
Yet best beseeming me to speak the truth.
Would God that any in this noble presence
Were enough noble to be upright judge
Of noble Richard! Then true noblesse would
Learn him forbearance from so foul a wrong.   120
What subject can give sentence on his king?
And who sits here that is not Richard's subject?
Thieves are not judg'd but they are by to hear,
Although apparent guilt be seen in them;
And shall the figure of God's majesty,   125
His captain, steward, deputy elect,

Anointed, crowned, planted many years,
Be judg'd by subject and inferior breath,
And he himself not present? O, forfend it, God,
That in a Christian climate souls refin'd   130
Should show so heinous, black, obscene a deed!
I speak to subjects, and a subject speaks,
Stirr'd up by God, thus boldly for his king.
My Lord of Hereford here, whom you call king,
Is a foul traitor to proud Hereford's king;   135
And if you crown him, let me prophesy,
The blood of English shall manure the ground,
And future ages groan for this foul act.
Peace shall go sleep with Turks and infidels,
And in this seat of peace tumultuous wars   140
Shall kin with kin and kind with kind confound.
Disorder, horror, fear, and mutiny
Shall here inhabit, and this land be call'd
The field of Golgotha and dead men's skulls.
O, if you raise this house against this house,   145
It will the woefullest division prove
That ever fell upon this cursed earth.
Prevent it, resist it, let it not be so,
Lest child, child's children, cry against you "woe!"
   North. Well have you argued, sir; and, for your
      pains   150
Of capital treason we arrest you here.
My Lord of Westminster, be it your charge
To keep him safely till his day of trial.
May it please you, lords, to grant the commons'
      suit?
   Boling. Fetch hither Richard, that in common
      view   155
He may surrender; so we shall proceed
Without suspicion.
   York.   I will be his conduct. [*Exit.*
   Boling. Lords, you that here are under our arrest,
Procure your sureties for your days of answer.
Little are we beholding to your love,   160
And little look'd for at your helping hands.

Re-enter YORK, *with* RICHARD [*and* Officers
      bearing the crown and sceptre].

   K. Rich. Alack, why am I sent for to a king
Before I have shook off the regal thoughts
Wherewith I reign'd? I hardly yet have learn'd
To insinuate, flatter, bow, and bend my knee.   165
Give sorrow leave a while to tutor me
To this submission. Yet I well remember
The favours of these men. Were they not mine?
Did they not sometime cry, "All hail!" to me?
So Judas did to Christ; but He, in twelve,   170
Found truth in all but one; I, in twelve thousand,
      none.
God save the King! — Will no man say amen?
Am I both priest and clerk? Well then, amen.

God save the King! although I be not he;
And yet, amen, if heaven do think him me. — 175
To do what service am I sent for hither?
   York. To do that office of thine own good will
Which tired majesty did make thee offer,
The resignation of thy state and crown
To Henry Bolingbroke.   180
   K. Rich. Give me the crown. Here, cousin,
      seize the crown;
Here, cousin,
On this side my hand, and on that side thine.
Now is this golden crown like a deep well
That owes two buckets, filling one another,   185
The emptier ever dancing in the air,
The other down, unseen, and full of water.
That bucket down and full of tears am I,
Drinking my griefs, whilst you mount up on high.
   Boling. I thought you had been willing to resign.
   K. Rich. My crown I am; but still my griefs are
      mine.   191
You may my glories and my state depose,
But not my griefs; still am I king of those.
   Boling. Part of your cares you give me with your
      crown.
   K. Rich. Your cares set up do not pluck my cares
      down.   195
My care is loss of care, by old care done;
Your care is gain of care, by new care won.
The cares I give I have, though given away;
They 'tend the crown, yet still with me they stay.
   Boling. Are you contented to resign the crown?
   K. Rich. Ay, no; no, ay; for I must nothing be;
Therefore no no, for I resign to thee.   202
Now mark me, how I will undo myself.
I give this heavy weight from off my head
And this unwieldy sceptre from my hand,   205
The pride of kingly sway from out my heart.
With mine own tears I wash away my balm,
With mine own hands I give away my crown,
With mine own tongue deny my sacred state,
With mine own breath release all duteous oaths. 210
All pomp and majesty I do forswear;
My manors, rents, revenues I forgo;
My acts, decrees, and statutes I deny.
God pardon all oaths that are broke to me!
God keep all vows unbroke are made to thee!   215
Make me, that nothing have, with nothing griev'd,
And thou with all pleas'd, that hast all achiev'd!
Long mayst thou live in Richard's seat to sit,
And soon lie Richard in an earthy pit!
God save King Henry, unking'd Richard says,   220
And send him many years of sunshine days!
— What more remains?
   North.   No more, but that you read
                    [Presenting a paper.]

These accusations and these grievous crimes
Committed by your person and your followers
Against the state and profit of this land;   225
That, by confessing them, the souls of men
May deem that you are worthily depos'd.
   K. Rich. Must I do so? and must I ravel out
My weav'd-up follies? Gentle Northumberland,
If thy offences were upon record,   230
Would it not shame thee in so fair a troop
To read a lecture of them? If thou wouldst,
There shouldst thou find one heinous article,
Containing the deposing of a king
And cracking the strong warrant of an oath,   235
Mark'd with a blot, damn'd in the book of heaven.
Nay, all of you that stand and look upon me
Whilst that my wretchedness doth bait myself,
Though some of you with Pilate wash your hands
Showing an outward pity; yet you Pilates   240
Have here deliver'd me to my sour cross,
And water cannot wash away your sin.
   North. My lord, dispatch; read o'er these articles.
   K. Rich. Mine eyes are full of tears, I cannot see;
And yet salt water blinds them not so much   245
But they can see a sort of traitors here.
Nay, if I turn mine eyes upon myself,
I find myself a traitor with the rest;
For I have given here my soul's consent
To undeck the pompous body of a king;   250
Made glory base, a sovereignty a slave,
Proud majesty a subject, state a peasant.
   North. My lord, —
   K. Rich. No lord of thine, thou haught insulting
      man,
Nor no man's lord. I have no name, no title;   255
No, not that name was given me at the font,
But 'tis usurp'd. Alack the heavy day,
That I have worn so many winters out
And know not now what name to call myself!
O that I were a mockery king of snow,   260
Standing before the sun of Bolingbroke,
To melt myself away in water-drops!
Good king, great king, and yet not greatly good,
An if my word be sterling yet in England,
Let it command a mirror hither straight,   265
That it may show me what a face I have
Since it is bankrupt of his majesty.
   Boling. Go some of you and fetch a looking-glass.
                    [Exit an attendant.]
   North. Read o'er this paper while the glass doth
      come.
   K. Rich. Fiend, thou torments me e'er I come to
      hell!   270
   Boling. Urge it no more, my Lord Northumber-
      land.
   North. The commons will not then be satisfi'd.

---

246. **sort:** group. 250. **pompous:** glorious. 252. **state:** kingship. 254. **haught:** haughty, arrogant. 264. **sterling:** current, valid. 269. **while:** till.

K. Rich. They shall be satisfi'd. I'll read enough,
When I do see the very book indeed
Where all my sins are writ, and that's myself. 275

Re-enter Attendant, *with a glass.*

Give me that glass, and therein will I read.
No deeper wrinkles yet? Hath sorrow struck
So many blows upon this face of mine,
And made no deeper wounds? O flatt'ring glass,
Like to my followers in prosperity, 280
Thou dost beguile me! Was this face the face
That every day under his household roof
Did keep ten thousand men? Was this the face
That, like the sun, did make beholders wink?
Is this the face which fac'd so many follies, 285
That was at last out-fac'd by Bolingbroke?
A brittle glory shineth in this face;
As brittle as the glory is the face,
                    [*Dashes the glass against the ground.*]
For there it is, crack'd in an hundred shivers.
Mark, silent king, the moral of this sport, 290
How soon my sorrow hath destroy'd my face.
Boling. The shadow of your sorrow hath de-
    stroy'd
The shadow of your face.
    K. Rich.   Say that again.
The shadow of my sorrow! Ha! let's see.
'Tis very true, my grief lies all within;
And these external manners of laments 295
Are merely shadows to the unseen grief
That swells with silence in the tortur'd soul.
There lies the substance; and I thank thee, King,
For thy great bounty, that not only giv'st 300
Me cause to wail but teachest me the way
How to lament the cause. I'll beg one boon,
And then be gone and trouble you no more.
Shall I obtain it?
    Boling.   Name it, fair cousin.
    K. Rich. "Fair cousin"? I am greater than a
        king; 305
For when I was a king my flatterers
Were then but subjects; being now a subject,
I have a king here to my flatterer.
Being so great, I have no need to beg.
    Boling. Yet ask. 310
    K. Rich. And shall I have?
    Boling. You shall.
    K. Rich. Then give me leave to go.
    Boling. Whither?
    K. Rich. Whither you will, so I were from your
        sights. 315
    Boling. Go, some of you convey him to the
        Tower.

K. Rich. O, good! convey! Conveyers are you all,
That rise thus nimbly by a true king's fall.
            [*Exeunt King Richard, some Lords, and a
                Guard.*]
    Boling. On Wednesday next we solemnly pro-
        claim
Our coronation. Lords, be ready all. 320
        [*Exeunt all but the Bishop of Carlisle, the
            Abbot of Westminster, and Aumerle.*
    Abbot. A woeful pageant have we here beheld.
    Car. The woe's to come; the children yet unborn
Shall feel this day as sharp to them as thorn.
    Aum. You holy clergymen, is there no plot
To rid the realm of this pernicious blot? 325
    Abbot. My lord,
Before I freely speak my mind herein,
You shall not only take the sacrament
To bury mine intents, but also to effect
Whatever I shall happen to devise. 330
I see your brows are full of discontent,
Your hearts of sorrow, and your eyes of tears.
Come home with me to supper; [and] I'll lay
A plot shall show us all a merry day.   [*Exeunt.*

ACT V

Scene I. [*London. A street leading to the Tower.*]

Enter the Queen *with her* Attendants.

Queen. This way the King will come; this is the
    way
To Julius Cæsar's ill-erected tower,
To whose flint bosom my condemned lord
Is doom'd a prisoner by proud Bolingbroke.
Here let us rest, if this rebellious earth 5
Have any resting for her true king's queen.

Enter Richard *and* Guard.

But soft, but see, or rather do not see,
My fair rose wither; yet look up, behold,
That you in pity may dissolve to dew
And wash him fresh again with true-love tears. 10
Ah, thou, the model where old Troy did stand,
Thou map of honour, thou King Richard's tomb,
And not King Richard; thou most beauteous inn,
Why should hard-favour'd Grief be lodg'd in thee,
When Triumph is become an alehouse guest? 15
    K. Rich. Join not with grief, fair woman, do
        not so,
To make my end too sudden. Learn, good soul,
To think our former state a happy dream,
From which awak'd, the truth of what we are
Shows us but this. I am sworn brother, sweet, 20

296. to: compared to. 308. to: as. 317. Conveyers: thieves. 319. On F₁. *Let it be so, and loe on* Q. proclaim Q.
set down F₁. 320. be ready all Q. *prepare yourselves* F₁. 333. [and] (Pope). Om. Qq Ff.
Act V, sc. i, 2. ill-erected: erected for evil ends. The Tower was, in fact, built by William the Conqueror. 11. model:
ground plan. She compares Richard to a mere plan of a ruined city, then to a mere outline of majesty.

To grim Necessity; and he and I
Will keep a league till death. Hie thee to France
And cloister thee in some religious house.
Our holy lives must win a new world's crown,
Which our profane hours here have thrown down.
  Queen. What, is my Richard both in shape and
    mind   26
Transform'd and weak'ned? Hath Bolingbroke
    depos'd
Thine intellect? Hath he been in thy heart?
The lion dying thrusteth forth his paw,
And wounds the earth, if nothing else, with rage 30
To be o'erpower'd; and wilt thou, pupil-like,
Take the correction, mildly kiss the rod,
And fawn on rage with base humility,
Which art a lion and the king of beasts?
  K. Rich. A king of beasts, indeed; if aught but
    beasts,   35
I had been still a happy king of men.
Good sometime queen, prepare thee hence for
    France.
Think I am dead, and that even here thou tak'st,
As from my death-bed, thy last living leave.
In winter's tedious nights sit by the fire   40
With good old folks and let them tell thee tales
Of woeful ages long ago betid;
And ere thou bid good night, to quite their griefs
Tell thou the lamentable tale of me
And send the hearers weeping to their beds.   45
For why, the senseless brands will sympathize
The heavy accent of thy moving tongue,
And in compassion weep the fire out;
And some will mourn in ashes, some coal-black,
For the deposing of a rightful king.   50

Enter NORTHUMBERLAND [*and others*].

  North. My lord, the mind of Bolingbroke is
    chang'd;
You must to Pomfret, not unto the Tower.
And, madam, there is order ta'en for you;
With all swift speed you must away to France.
  K. Rich. Northumberland, thou ladder where-
    withal   55
The mounting Bolingbroke ascends my throne,
The time shall not be many hours of age
More than it is, ere foul sin gathering head
Shall break into corruption. Thou shalt think,
Though he divide the realm and give thee half, 60
It is too little, helping him to all;
[And] he shall think that thou, which know'st the
    way
To plant unrightful kings, wilt know again,
Being ne'er so little urg'd, another way
To pluck him headlong from the usurped throne. 65

The love of wicked men converts to fear,
That fear to hate, and hate turns one or both
To worthy danger and deserved death.
  North. My guilt be on my head, and there an end.
Take leave and part; for you must part forthwith.
  K. Rich. Doubly divorc'd! Bad men, you vio-
    late   71
A twofold marriage, 'twixt my crown and me,
And then betwixt me and my married wife.
Let me unkiss the oath 'twixt thee and me;
And yet not so, for with a kiss 'twas made.   75
Part us, Northumberland; I towards the north,
Where shivering cold and sickness pines the clime;
My wife to France; from whence, set forth in pomp,
She came adorned hither like sweet May,
Sent back like Hallowmas or short'st of day.   80
  Queen. And must we be divided? Must we part?
  K. Rich. Ay, hand from hand, my love, and heart
    from heart.
  Queen. Banish us both, and send the King with
    me.
  [*North.*] That were some love but little policy.
  Queen. Then whither he goes, thither let me go.
  K. Rich. So two, together weeping, make one
    woe.   86
Weep thou for me in France, I for thee here;
Better far off than near, be ne'er the near.
Go, count thy way with sighs; I mine with groans.
  Queen. So longest way shall have the longest
    moans.   90
  K. Rich. Twice for one step I'll groan, the way
    being short,
And piece the way out with a heavy heart.
Come, come, in wooing sorrow let's be brief,
Since, wedding it, there is such length in grief.
One kiss shall stop our mouths, and dumbly part;
Thus give I mine, and thus take I thy heart.   96
  Queen. Give me mine own again; 'twere no good
    part
To take on me to keep and kill thy heart. —
So, now I have mine own again, be gone,
That I may strive to kill it with a groan.   100
  K. Rich. We make woe wanton with this fond
    delay.
Once more, adieu; the rest let sorrow say.
                                  [*Exeunt.*

SCENE II. [*London. The Duke of York's palace.*]

Enter YORK *and his* DUCHESS.

  Duch. My lord, you told me you would tell the
    rest,
When weeping made you break the story off,
Of our two cousins coming into London.

43. **quite ... griefs:** requite their sad tales. 62. **[And]** (Rowe). Om. Qq Ff. 68. **worthy:** well-earned. 77. **pines:** makes painful. 80. **Hallowmas ... day.** Nov. 1 or Dec. 21. 84. **[North.]** Ff. *King* Q. 88. **be ... near:** if we can never meet. *Near* is comparative.

York. Where did I leave?

Duch.   At that sad stop, my lord,
Where rude misgovern'd hands from windows' tops
Threw dust and rubbish on King Richard's head.   6

York. Then, as I said, the Duke, great Boling-
   broke,
Mounted upon a hot and fiery steed
Which his aspiring rider seem'd to know,
With slow but stately pace kept on his course,   10
Whilst all tongues cried, "God save thee, Boling-
   broke!"
You would have thought the very windows spake,
So many greedy looks of young and old
Through casements darted their desiring eyes
Upon his visage, and that all the walls   15
With painted imagery had said at once,
"Jesu preserve thee! Welcome, Bolingbroke!"
Whilst he, from the one side to the other turning,
Bareheaded, lower than his proud steed's neck,
Bespake them thus: "I thank you, countrymen."
And thus still doing, thus he pass'd along.   21

Duch. Alack, poor Richard! where rode he the
   whilst?

York. As in a theatre, the eyes of men,
After a well-grac'd actor leaves the stage,
Are idly bent on him that enters next,   25
Thinking his prattle to be tedious;
Even so, or with much more contempt, men's eyes
Did scowl on gentle Richard. No man cried,
"God save him!"
No joyful tongue gave him his welcome home;
But dust was thrown upon his sacred head,   30
Which with such gentle sorrow he shook off,
His face still combating with tears and smiles,
The badges of his grief and patience,
That had not God, for some strong purpose, steel'd
The hearts of men, they must perforce have melted,
And barbarism itself have pitied him.   36
But Heaven hath a hand in these events,
To whose high will we bow our calm contents.
To Bolingbroke are we sworn subjects now,
Whose state and honour I for aye allow.   40

Enter AUMERLE.

Duch. Here comes my son Aumerle.

York.   Aumerle that was;
But that is lost for being Richard's friend,
And, madam, you must call him Rutland now.
I am in parliament pledge for his truth
And lasting fealty to the new-made king.   45

Duch. Welcome, my son! Who are the violets now
That strew the green lap of the new come spring?

Aum. Madam, I know not, nor I greatly care not.
God knows I had as lief be none as one.

York. Well, bear you well in this new spring of
   time,   50

Lest you be cropp'd before you come to prime.
What news from Oxford? Do these jousts and
   triumphs hold?

Aum. For aught I know, my lord, they do.

York. You will be there, I know.

Aum. If God prevent not, I purpose so.   55

York. What seal is that, that hangs without thy
   bosom?
Yea, look'st thou pale? Let me see the writing.

Aum. My lord, 'tis nothing.

York.   No matter, then, who see it.
I will be satisfied; let me see the writing.

Aum. I do beseech your Grace to pardon me.   60
It is a matter of small consequence,
Which for some reasons I would not have seen.

York. Which for some reasons, sir, I mean to see.
I fear, I fear, —

Duch.   What should you fear?
'Tis nothing but some band that he is ent'red into
For gay apparel 'gainst the triumph day.   66

York. Bound to himself! What doth he with a
   bond
That he is bound to? Wife, thou art a fool.
Boy, let me see the writing.

Aum. I do beseech you, pardon me. I may not
   show it.   70

York. I will be satisfied; let me see it, I say.
   [*He plucks it out of his bosom and reads it.*]
Treason! foul treason! Villain! traitor! slave!

Duch. What is the matter, my lord?

York. Ho! who is within there?

                                 [*Enter a* Servant.]

                                   Saddle my horse.
God for his mercy, what treachery is here!   75

Duch. Why, what is it, my lord?

York. Give me my boots, I say; saddle my horse.
                                     [*Exit Servant.*]
Now, by mine honour, by my life, by my troth,
I will appeach the villain.

Duch.   What is the matter?

York. Peace, foolish woman.   80

Duch. I will not peace. What is the matter,
   Aumerle?

Aum. Good mother, be content; it is no more
Than my poor life must answer.

Duch.   Thy life answer!

York. Bring me my boots; I will unto the King.

Re-enter Servant *with boots.*

Duch. Strike him, Aumerle. Poor boy, thou art
   amaz'd.   85
— Hence, villain! never more come in my sight.

York. Give me my boots, I say.

Duch. Why, York, what wilt thou do?
Wilt thou not hide the trespass of thine own?

Sc. ii, 40. **allow:** acknowledge.   79. **appeach:** impeach, accuse.   85. **amaz'd:** dumbfounded.

Have we more sons? or are we like to have?   90
Is not my teeming date drunk up with time,
And wilt thou pluck my fair son from mine age,
And rob me of a happy mother's name?
Is he not like thee? Is he not thine own?
York. Thou fond mad woman,   95
Wilt thou conceal this dark conspiracy?
A dozen of them here have ta'en the sacrament,
And interchangeably set down their hands,
To kill the King at Oxford.
Duch.   He shall be none;
We'll keep him here; then what is that to him?   100
York. Away, fond woman! were he twenty times
my son,
I would appeach him.
Duch.   Hadst thou groan'd for him
As I have done, thou wouldst be more pitiful.
But now I know thy mind; thou dost suspect
That I have been disloyal to thy bed,   105
And that he is a bastard, not thy son.
Sweet York, sweet husband, be not of that mind.
He is as like thee as a man may be,
Not like to me, or any of my kin,
And yet I love him.
York.   Make way, unruly woman!   110
[*Exit.*
Duch. After, Aumerle! mount thou upon his
horse;
Spur post, and get before him to the King,
And beg thy pardon ere he do accuse thee.
I'll not be long behind; though I be old,
I doubt not but to ride as fast as York.   115
And never will I rise up from the ground
Till Bolingbroke have pardon'd thee. Away, be
gone! [*Exeunt.*

Scene III. [*Windsor Castle.*]

Enter BOLINGBROKE, PERCY, *and other* Lords.

Boling. Can no man tell me of my unthrifty son?
'Tis full three months since I did see him last.
If any plague hang over us, 'tis he.
I would to God, my lords, he might be found.
Inquire at London, 'mongst the taverns there,   5
For there, they say, he daily doth frequent,
With unrestrained loose companions,
Even such, they say, as stand in narrow lanes
And beat our watch and rob our passengers;
Which he, young wanton and effeminate boy,   10
Takes on the point of honour to support
So dissolute a crew.
Percy. My lord, some two days since I saw the
Prince,
And told him of those triumphs held at Oxford.
Boling. And what said the gallant?   15

Percy. His answer was, he would unto the stews,
And from the common'st creature pluck a glove
And wear it as a favour; and with that
He would unhorse the lustiest challenger.
Boling. As dissolute as desperate; yet through
both   20
I see some sparks of better hope, which elder years
May happily bring forth. But who comes here?

Enter AUMERLE, *amazed.*

Aum. Where is the King?
Boling. What means our cousin, that he stares
and looks
So wildly?   25
Aum. God save your Grace! I do beseech your
Majesty,
To have some conference with your Grace alone.
Boling. Withdraw yourselves, and leave us here
alone. [*Exeunt Percy and Lords.*]
What is the matter with our cousin now?   29
Aum. For ever may my knees grow to the earth,
[*Kneeling.*]
My tongue cleave to my roof within my mouth,
Unless a pardon ere I rise or speak.
Boling. Intended or committed was this fault?
If on the first, how heinous e'er it be,
To win thy after-love I pardon thee.   35
Aum. Then give me leave that [I] may turn the
key,
That no man enter till my tale be done.
Boling. Have thy desire.
[*Aumerle locks the door.*] *York knocks at
the door and crieth.*
York. (*Within.*) My liege, beware! Look to
thyself;
Thou hast a traitor in thy presence there.   40
Boling. Villain, I'll make thee safe. [*Drawing.*]
Aum. Stay thy revengeful hand; thou hast no
cause to fear.
York. [*Within.*] Open the door, secure, fool-
hardy King!
Shall I for love speak treason to thy face?
Open the door, or I will break it open.   45

Enter YORK.

Boling. What is the matter, uncle? Speak;
Recover breath; tell us how near is danger
That we may arm us to encounter it.
York. Peruse this writing here, and thou shalt
know
The treason that my haste forbids me show.   50
Aum. Remember, as thou read'st, thy promise
pass'd.
I do repent me; read not my name there.
My heart is not confederate with my hand.

York. It was, villain, ere thy hand did set it
down.
I tore it from the traitor's bosom, King;   55
Fear, and not love, begets his penitence.
Forget to pity him, lest thy pity prove
A serpent that will sting thee to the heart.
Boling. O heinous, strong, and bold conspiracy!
O loyal father of a treacherous son!   60
Thou sheer, immaculate, and silver fountain,
From whence this stream through muddy passages
Hath held his current and defil'd himself!
Thy overflow of good converts to bad,
And thy abundant goodness shall excuse   65
This deadly blot in thy digressing son.
York. So shall my virtue be his vice's bawd;
And he shall spend mine honour with his shame,
As thriftless sons their scraping fathers' gold.
Mine honour lives when his dishonour dies,   70
Or my sham'd life in his dishonour lies.
Thou kill'st me in his life; giving him breath,
The traitor lives, the true man's put to death.
Duch. (*Within.*) What ho, my liege! for God's
sake, let me in.
Boling. What shrill-voiced suppliant makes this
eager cry?   75
Duch. A woman, and thy aunt, great King; 'tis
I.
Speak with me, pity me, open the door!
A beggar begs that never begg'd before.
Boling. Our scene is alt'red from a serious thing,
And now chang'd to "The Beggar and the King."
My dangerous cousin, let your mother in: 81
I know she's come to pray for your foul sin.
York. If thou do pardon, whosoever pray,
More sins for this forgiveness prosper may.
This fest'red joint cut off, the rest rest sound;   85
This let alone will all the rest confound.

Enter DUCHESS.

Duch. O King, believe not this hard-hearted
man!
Love loving not itself none other can.
York. Thou frantic woman, what dost thou make
here?
Shall thy old dugs once more a traitor rear?   90
Duch. Sweet York, be patient. Hear me, gentle
liege.   [*Kneels.*]
Boling. Rise up, good aunt.
Duch.   Not yet, I thee beseech.
For ever will I walk upon my knees,
And never see day that the happy sees,
Till thou give joy; until thou bid me joy   95
By pardoning Rutland, my transgressing boy.
Aum. Unto my mother's prayers I bend my
knee.   [*Kneels.*]

York. Against them both my true joints bended
be.   [*Kneels.*]
Ill mayst thou thrive, if thou grant any grace!   99
Duch. Pleads he in earnest? Look upon his face;
His eyes do drop no tears, his prayers are in jest;
His words come from his mouth, ours from our
breast.
He prays but faintly and would be deni'd;
We pray with heart and soul and all beside.
His weary joints would gladly rise, I know;   105
Our knees [shall] kneel till to the ground they grow.
His prayers are full of false hypocrisy;
Ours of true zeal and deep integrity.
Our prayers do out-pray his; then let them have
That mercy which true prayer ought to have.   110
Boling. Good aunt, stand up.
Duch.   Nay, do not say, "Stand up";
Say "Pardon" first, and afterwards "Stand up."
An if I were thy nurse, thy tongue to teach,
"Pardon" should be the first word of thy speech.
I never long'd to hear a word till now.   115
Say "pardon," King; let pity teach thee how.
The word is short, but not so short as sweet;
No word like "pardon" for kings' mouths so meet.
York. Speak it in French, King; say, "*Pardonne
moi.*"
Duch. Dost thou teach pardon pardon to de-
stroy?   120
Ah, my sour husband, my hard-hearted lord,
That set'st the word itself against the word!
Speak "pardon" as 'tis current in our land;
The chopping French we do not understand.
Thine eye begins to speak; set thy tongue there;
Or in thy piteous heart plant thou thine ear;   126
That, hearing how our plaints and prayers do
pierce,
Pity may move thee "pardon" to rehearse.
Boling. Good aunt, stand up.
Duch.   I do not sue to stand;
Pardon is all the suit I have in hand.   130
Boling. I pardon him, as God shall pardon me.
Duch. O happy vantage of a kneeling knee!
Yet am I sick for fear: speak it again.
Twice saying "pardon" doth not pardon twain,
But makes one pardon strong.
Boling. I pardon him with all my heart.   135
Duch. A god on earth thou art.
Boling. But for our trusty brother-in-law and the
abbot,
With all the rest of that consorted crew,
Destruction straight shall dog them at the heels.
Good uncle, help to order several powers   140
To Oxford, or where'er these traitors are.
They shall not live within this world, I swear,
But I will have them, if I once know where.

Uncle, farewell; and, cousin, adieu!   144
Your mother well hath pray'd, and prove you true.
   Duch. Come, my old son; I pray God make thee
   new.   [*Exeunt.*

[SCENE IV. *Another room in the same.*]

Enter EXTON *and* SERVANT.

   Exton. Didst thou not mark the King, what
   words he spake,
"Have I no friend will rid me of this living fear?"
Was it not so?
   Serv.   These were his very words.
   Exton. "Have I no friend?" quoth he. He spake
   it twice,
And urg'd it twice together, did he not?   5
   Serv. He did.
   Exton. And speaking it, he wishtly look'd on me
As who should say, "I would thou wert the man
That would divorce this terror from my heart;"
Meaning the King at Pomfret. Come, let's go.
I am the King's friend, and will rid his foe.   11
                       [*Exeunt.*

SCENE [V. *Pomfret Castle. A ward room.*]

Enter KING RICHARD.

   K. Rich. I have been studying how I may com-
   pare
This prison where I live unto the world;
And for because the world is populous
And here is not a creature but myself,
I cannot do it; yet I'll hammer it out.   5
My brain I'll prove the female to my soul,
My soul the father; and these two beget
A generation of still-breeding thoughts,
And these same thoughts people this little world,
In humours like the people of this world.   10
For no thought is contented. The better sort,
As thoughts of things divine, are intermix'd
With scruples and do set the word itself
Against the word:
As thus, "Come, little ones," and then again,
"It is as hard to come as for a camel   16
To thread the postern of a small needle's eye."
Thoughts tending to ambition, they do plot
Unlikely wonders: how these vain weak nails
May tear a passage through the flinty ribs   20
Of this hard world, my ragged prison walls,
And, for they cannot, die in their own pride.
Thoughts tending to content flatter themselves
That they are not the first of fortune's slaves,
Nor shall not be the last; like silly beggars 25

Who, sitting in the stocks, refuge their shame,
That many have and others must sit there;
And in this thought they find a kind of ease,
Bearing their own misfortunes on the back
Of such as have before endur'd the like.   30
Thus play I in one person many people,
And none contented. Sometimes am I king;
Then treasons make me wish myself a beggar;
And so I am. Then crushing penury
Persuades me I was better when a king;   35
Then am I king'd again: and by and by
Think that I am unking'd by Bolingbroke,
And straight am nothing. But whate'er I be,
Nor I nor any man that but man is
With nothing shall be pleas'd, till he be eas'd 40
With being nothing. Music do I hear?   [*Music.*
Ha, ha! keep time! How sour sweet music is,
When time is broke and no proportion kept!
So is it in the music of men's lives.
And here have I the daintiness of ear   45
To check time broke in a disordered string;
But for the concord of my state and time
Had not an ear to hear my true time broke.
I wasted time, and now doth Time waste me;   49
For now hath Time made me his numb'ring clock.
My thoughts are minutes; and with sighs they jar
Their watches on unto mine eyes, the outward
   watch,
Whereto my finger, like a dial's point,
Is pointing still, in cleansing them from tears.
Now sir, the sound that tells what hour it is   55
Are clamorous groans, which strike upon my heart,
Which is the bell. So sighs and tears and groans
Show minutes, times, and hours; but my time
Runs posting on in Bolingbroke's proud joy,
While I stand fooling here, his Jack o' th' clock. 60
This music mads me; let it sound no more;
For though it have holp madmen to their wits,
In me it seems it will make wise men mad.
Yet blessing on his heart that gives it me!
For 'tis a sign of love; and love to Richard   65
Is a strange brooch in this all-hating world.

Enter a GROOM *of the Stable.*

   Groom. Hail, royal prince!
   K. Rich.   Thanks, noble peer!
The cheapest of us is ten groats too dear.
What art thou? and how com'st thou hither,
Where no man never comes but that sad dog   70
That brings me food to make misfortune live?
   Groom. I was a poor groom of thy stable, King,
When thou wert king; who, travelling towards York,
With much ado at length have gotten leave

Sc. iv, 7. **wishtly:** wistfully. 11. **rid:** destroy.
Sc. v, 8. **still-breeding:** ever-breeding. 10. **humours:** individual peculiarities. 21. **ragged:** rough. 46. **check:** object to.
51. **jar:** tick. 60. **Jack:** the figure that strikes the hours. 66. **brooch:** ornament. 67–68. **royal ... noble ... ten groats.**
Ten groats made 3*s*.4*d.*, the difference between a royal (10*s.*) and a noble (6*s*.8*d.*).

To look upon my sometimes royal master's face.   75
O, how it yearn'd my heart when I beheld
In London streets, that coronation-day,
When Bolingbroke rode on roan Barbary,
That horse that thou so often hast bestrid,
That horse that I so carefully have dress'd!   80
   K. Rich. Rode he on Barbary? Tell me, gentle
     friend,
How went he under him?
   Groom. So proudly as if he disdain'd the ground.
   K. Rich. So proud that Bolingbroke was on his
     back!
That jade hath eat bread from my royal hand;   85
This hand hath made him proud with clapping him.
Would he not stumble? Would he not fall down,
Since pride must have a fall, and break the neck
Of that proud man that did usurp his back?
Forgiveness, horse! why do I rail on thee,   90
Since thou, created to be aw'd by man,
Wast born to bear? I was not made a horse;
And yet I bear a burden like an ass,
Spurr'd, gall'd, and tir'd by jauncing Bolingbroke.

Enter KEEPER, *with a dish.*

   Keep. Fellow, give place; here is no longer stay.
   K. Rich. If thou love me, 'tis time thou wert
     away.   96
   Groom. What my tongue dares not, that my heart
     shall say.   [*Exit.*
   Keep. My lord, will 't please you to fall to?
   K. Rich. Taste of it first, as thou art wont to do.
   Keep. My lord, I dare not. Sir Pierce of Exton,
who lately came from the King, commands the con-
trary.   102
   K. Rich. The devil take Henry of Lancaster and
     thee!
Patience is stale, and I am weary of it.
   Keep. Help, help, help!   105

Enter EXTON *and* Servants [*armed*].

   K. Rich. How now! what means death in this
     rude assault?
Villain, thy own hand yields thy death's instru-
     ment.
     [*Snatching an axe from a Servant and kill-*
     ing him.]
Go thou, and fill another room in hell.
     [*He kills another.*] *Here Exton strikes him*
     down.
That hand shall burn in never-quenching fire
That staggers thus my person. Exton, thy fierce
     hand   110
Hath with the King's blood stained the King's own
     land.
Mount, mount, my soul! thy seat is up on high;

Whilst my gross flesh sinks downward, here to die.
     [*Dies.*]
   Exton. As full of valour as of royal blood!
Both have I spill'd; O would the deed were good!
For now the devil, that told me I did well,   116
Says that this deed is chronicled in hell.
This dead king to the living king I'll bear:
Take hence the rest, and give them burial here.
     [*Exeunt.*

SCENE [VI. *Windsor Castle.*]

Flourish. *Enter* BOLINGBROKE, YORK, *with*
other Lords, *and* Attendants.

   Boling. Kind uncle York, the latest news we hear
Is that the rebels hath consum'd with fire
Our town of Cicester in Gloucestershire;
But whether they be ta'en or slain we hear not.

Enter NORTHUMBERLAND.

Welcome, my lord, what is the news?   5
   North. First, to thy sacred state wish I all happi-
     ness.
The next news is, I have to London sent
The heads of Oxford, Salisbury, Blunt, and Kent.
The manner of their taking may appear
At large discoursed in this paper here.   10
   Boling. We thank thee, gentle Percy, for thy
     pains;
And to thy worth will add right worthy gains.

Enter FITZWATER.

   Fitz. My lord, I have from Oxford sent to London
The heads of Brocas and Sir Bennet Seely,
Two of the dangerous consorted traitors   15
That sought at Oxford thy dire overthrow.
   Boling. Thy pains, Fitzwater, shall not be forgot;
Right noble is thy merit, well I wot.

Enter PERCY, *and the* BISHOP OF CARLISLE.

   Percy. The grand conspirator, Abbot of West-
     minster,
With clog of conscience and sour melancholy   20
Hath yielded up his body to the grave;
But here is Carlisle living, to abide
Thy kingly doom and sentence of his pride.
   Boling. Carlisle, this is your doom:
Choose out some secret place, some reverend room,
More than thou hast, and with it joy thy life.   26
So as thou liv'st in peace, die free from strife;
For though mine enemy thou hast ever been,
High sparks of honour in thee have I seen.

Enter EXTON, *with* [Attendants *bearing*] *a coffin.*

   Exton. Great King, within this coffin I present

---

76. **yearn'd**: made ache.   94. **jauncing**: prancing.
Sc. vi, 26. **joy**: enjoy.

Thy buried fear.   Herein all breathless lies   31
The mightiest of thy greatest enemies,
Richard of Bordeaux, by me hither brought.
   Boling. Exton, I thank thee not; for thou hast
       wrought
A deed of slander with thy fatal hand   35
Upon my head and all this famous land.
   Exton. From your own mouth, my lord, did I
       this deed.
   Boling. They love not poison that do poison need,
Nor do I thee.   Though I did wish him dead,
I hate the murderer, love him murdered.   40

The guilt of conscience take thou for thy labour,
But neither my good word nor princely favour.
With Cain go wander through [the] shades of night,
And never show thy head by day nor light.
Lords, I protest, my soul is full of woe   45
That blood should sprinkle me to make me grow.
Come, mourn with me for what I do lament,
And put on sullen black incontinent.
I'll make a voyage to the Holy Land,
To wash this blood off from my guilty hand.   50
March sadly after; grace my mournings here
In weeping after this untimely bier.   [*Exeunt.*

43. **[the]** Q$_2$. Om. Q$_1$.   48. **incontinent:** at once.

The Tragedy of Romeo and Juliet

THE FIRST QUARTO of *Romeo and Juliet* was printed in 1597 with a title page stating that "it hath been often (with great applause) plaid publiquely, by the right Honourable the L. of Hunsdon his Seruants." This notice proves it to have been on the stage between July 22, 1596 and March 17, 1597, for only during that interval did Shakespeare's company go by the name of "Lord Hunsdon's servants." Further evidence for date is purely internal. Undue attention has been paid to the Nurse's remark (I.iii.23,35), "'tis since the earthquake now eleven years," which has been held to point to 1591 as the date of composition, because there was an earthquake in London in 1580. But Shakespeare is giving the Nurse a realistic basis for computing Juliet's age, and although he may have been reminded of the actual earthquake, the figure eleven is probably fortuitous. More compelling with reference to date, is the pervasive lyrical impulse. For despite the abundance of quibbling and of "conceited" verse, the play has much lyric beauty of a high order. The affinity of *Romeo and Juliet* with Shakespeare's Sonnets has often been remarked, and, though a tragedy, the play is a kind of hymn to the omnipotence of love. A proper date, therefore, would seem to be 1595, which would associate it with *Love's Labour's Lost*, *A Midsummer Night's Dream* and *Richard II*, in all of which plays lyricism is a marked feature.

The First Quarto prints a mangled text, copy for which was apparently provided by a reporter whose memory was perhaps eked out by some notes. Very likely he was a minor player, though he does not reveal himself by such superior rendering of particular parts as betrays the piratical actors behind the "bad" Quartos of *Hamlet* and *The Merry Wives*. The text is disfigured by mislineation and corrupt metre, by transposition of lines and phrases, and by paraphrase. In 1599 appeared the Second Quarto, "Newly corrected, augmented, and amended," but it was carelessly set up, with the result that it contains some errors which, paradoxically, can be rectified by readings from the First. The Second Quarto

contains 775 more lines than the First. From this discrepancy it has been argued that the First Quarto represents an earlier version of the play. It is more likely, however, that the texts of both Quartos derive ultimately from the same acting version, and that the brevity of the First Quarto is owing to the reporter's sins of omission and, perhaps, to a few cuts made for performances in 1597. Certain typographical likenesses suggest that the Second Quarto may have been set up in part from a corrected copy of the First. A Third Quarto was printed (1609) from the Second, and a Fourth (undated) from the Third, and a Fifth (1637) from the Fourth. The Folio reprints the Third Quarto. The Second Quarto is consequently the authority, and forms the basis of the present edition.

The story of Romeo and Juliet, who stand among the great lovers in the world's literature, has a long and fascinating lineage. The device of escaping from an unwelcome marriage by means of a sleeping potion is found in the *Ephesiaca* of Xenophon of Ephesus about the fourth century. At some time or other this element became merged with a tragic tale of ill-fated lovers, who were the forbears of Romeo and Juliet. Such a tale is the thirty-third in a collection by Masuccio of Salerno (1476), but the earliest version which is a direct ancestor of Shakespeare's plot is the *Historia di due nobili Amanti* by Luigi da Porto (c. 1530). The progress of the story toward its Shakespearean form continues through a version in the *Novelle* of Matteo Bandello (1554), a translation of the same by Boisteau in his *Histoires Tragiques* (1559), an English poem by Arthur Brooke, *The Tragicall Historye of Romeus and Juliet* (1562), and a prose tale in Painter's *Palace of Pleasure* (1567).

The main lines of the action and of the chief characters were thus already laid down before Shakespeare worked on the story. The dramatic essentials are present, indeed, in the version of da Porto, who sets the scene in Verona, introduces the feud of the Montecchi and Cappelletti, and gives the names Romeo and Giulietta, Tebaldo (Tybalt), and

Lorenzo (the Friar). But in this version Romeo goes to the Capulets' feast in pursuit of a cruel mistress (though he falls in love with Juliet there); Romeo is already in possession of poison; Juliet revives in the tomb before Romeo expires, and kills herself, not with her lover's dagger, but by holding her breath until she dies. In Bandello a new stress is given to Romeo's antecedent love affair; Romeo goes to the Capulets', not in pursuit of his cruel lady but in order to see new beauties; the undesired bridegroom is named Paris; and Juliet's Nurse is introduced as the lovers' go-between. The major contribution of Boisteau is the scene with the Apothecary (from a hint in Bandello) and an alteration in the ending whereby Juliet is made to awake after the death of Romeo and to kill herself with his dagger. The poem of Brooke is tedious and pedestrian, but in it the Nurse is developed as a comic character, and the episode of Romeo's distraction at the Friar's cell and a picture of his misery in exile are added. In an address "To the Reader" Brooke states that he "saw the same argument lately set forth on stage," but the play he mentions has not survived. The notion that Shakespeare was indebted to this lost play is superfluous, for Shakespeare's drama is derived directly and, to all appearances, exclusively from the poem of Brooke.

Shakespeare works a notable transformation in his material. He compresses the action, which in Brooke had covered nine months, to five days, and reduces Juliet's age from sixteen to fourteen. The important changes, however, lie in the enrichment of characterization. Tybalt's hatred is underscored by his early introduction at the Capulets' ball, where he recognizes Romeo. Romeo fights Tybalt to avenge the death of Mercutio, whom he had striven to pacify (III.i.87–136), not, as in Brooke, because Tybalt challenges him in one of the common brawls of Montagues and Capulets. Mercutio is Shakespeare's brilliant creation from a mere supernumerary in Brooke. The Nurse is perfected as a comic figure. Shakespeare expands the rôle of Paris, ennobling his character and adding his death at Juliet's tomb, and he develops the characters of Benvolio, Lady Capulet, Montague, and Lady Montague from hints in Brooke. The crowning achievement is the poetry. This tragedy of star-crossed lovers is one of the great love poems in an age rich in amorous poetry. Shakespeare has "loaded every rift with ore." It is not, on the other hand, of uniform quality. There is considerable verbal extravagance and mere rhetoric (e.g., I.i.170–201; III.iii.17–51); there are bravura pieces (e.g., I.iv.53–94; III.ii.1–31; IV.iii.14–58); but the finest passages, though they may lack the deep tonal qualities of Shakespeare's mature verse, are very beautiful indeed.

The lyric vitality of this play is in accord with the youthful passion it celebrates. For there can be no doubt about Shakespeare's attitude toward the lovers. He has written *con amore*, sympathetic with them at every turn. To seek the cause of their "piteous overthrow" in some inherent guilt or tragic flaw, in filial disobedience or sensuality or rashness, is entirely mistaken. To know Shakespeare's feelings one need only consult one's own, which, unless one is an incorrigible moralist or has never been in love, will not be expressed in an ethical judgment. Shakespeare has written it clear in his text that his drama is a tragedy of fate. The Prologue announces the fact unambiguously, and many other passages express the hostility of Fortune and the stars, or are fraught with foreboding (I.iv. 106–11; I.v.119–22; II.ii.116–20; II.vi.6–8; III.i. 124–25, 141; III.v.54–59; V.i.24; V.iii.108–12). Romeo's exultant image of a pilot adventuring for rich merchandise (II.ii.82–84) has its fateful transmutation in the "desperate pilot" shattering upon the rocks his "sea-sick weary bark" (V.iii.117–18). The imminence of Fate is enhanced by the feud; indeed, in the perspective of the victims the feud is Fate, for without it there would have been no obstacle to their happiness. The "ancient grudge" breaks out ominously in the first (and theatrically admirable) scene of the play; Mercutio, dying because of it, cries "a plague o' both your houses"; and Tybalt's death and Romeo's banishment are owing to it. The death of the lovers is in reality, however indirectly, a consequence; for the accident preventing the delivery of the Friar's letter is subservient to a Fate already too well implemented. And after this chastening fulfillment the grieving families are reconciled. In the wickedness of this mortal enmity lies the moral of the play, if Shakespeare intended any at all.

Romeo and Juliet is a genuinely moving rather than a great play. It has emotional intensity rather than spiritual depth. The lives of the protagonists are not wrecked through dangerous propensities within themselves. Shakespeare is not here picturing the moral havoc which is unleashed through base desires or guilty passions, through ruinous self-deception, or through malice poisoning the very springs of virtue in men. Neither experience nor inclination, presumably, yet summoned him to such endeavor. But when, nearly a decade later, Shakespeare came to treat of these things, the time very likely had passed when he could portray so affectingly the simple passion and heartbreak of youth.

THE TRAGEDY OF ROMEO AND JULIET

[DRAMATIS PERSONÆ

ESCALUS, *Prince of Verona.*
PARIS, *a young nobleman, kinsman to the prince.*
MONTAGUE, } *heads of two houses at variance*
CAPULET, } *with each other.*
An old man, of the Capulet family.
ROMEO, *son to Montague.*
MERCUTIO, *kinsman to the prince, and friend to Romeo.*
BENVOLIO, *nephew to Montague, and cousin to Romeo.*
TYBALT, *nephew to Lady Capulet.*
FRIAR LAURENCE, } *Franciscans.*
FRIAR JOHN, }
BALTHASAR, *servant to Romeo.*
ABRAHAM, *servant to Montague.*

SAMPSON, } *servants to Capulet.*
GREGORY, }
PETER, *servant to Juliet's nurse.*
An Apothecary.
Three Musicians.
Page to Paris; *another Page.*
An Officer.

LADY MONTAGUE, *wife to Montague.*
LADY CAPULET, *wife to Capulet.*
JULIET, *daughter to Capulet.*
Nurse to Juliet.

Chorus.

Citizens of Verona; several Men and Women, kinsfolk to both houses; Maskers, Guards, Watchmen, and Attendants.

SCENE: *Verona; Mantua.*]

PROLOGUE

Two households, both alike in dignity,
    In fair Verona, where we lay our scene,
From ancient grudge break to new mutiny,
    Where civil blood makes civil hands unclean.
From forth the fatal loins of these two foes   5
    A pair of star-cross'd lovers take their life;
Whose misadventur'd piteous overthrows
    Doth with their death bury their parents' strife.
The fearful passage of their death-mark'd love,
    And the continuance of their parents' rage,   10
Which, but their children's end, nought could re-
    move,
Is now the two hours' traffic of our stage;
    The which if you with patient ears attend,
What here shall miss, our toil shall strive to
    mend.

ACT I

SCENE I. [*Verona. A public place.*]

Enter SAMPSON *and* GREGORY, *of the house of Capulet, with swords and bucklers.*

Sam. Gregory, on my word, we'll not carry coals.
Gre. No, for then we should be colliers.
Sam. I mean, an we be in choler, we'll draw.   5
Gre. Ay, while you live, draw your neck out of collar.
Sam. I strike quickly, being mov'd.
Gre. But thou art not quickly mov'd to strike.
Sam. A dog of the house of Montague moves me.   10
Gre. To move is to stir, and to be valiant is to stand; therefore, if thou art mov'd, thou run'st away.

Prol., 3. **mutiny:** discord. 6. **star-cross'd:** doomed by the stars.
Act I, sc. i, 1. **carry coals:** submit to insult. 7. **mov'd:** angered.

Sam. A dog of that house shall move me to stand. I will take the wall of any man or maid of Montague's.   16

Gre. That shows thee a weak slave; for the weakest goes to the wall.

Sam. 'Tis true; and therefore women, being the weaker vessels, are ever thrust to the wall; therefore I will push Montague's men from the wall, and thrust his maids to the wall.   22

Gre. The quarrel is between our masters and us their men.

Sam. 'Tis all one, I will show myself a tyrant. When I have fought with the men, I will be [cruel] with the maids; I will cut off their heads.   28

Gre. The heads of the maids?

Sam. Ay, the heads of the maids, or their maidenheads; take it in what sense thou wilt.

Gre. They must take it in sense that feel it.

Sam. Me they shall feel while I am able to stand; and 'tis known I am a pretty piece of flesh.   35

Gre. 'Tis well thou art not fish; if thou hadst, thou hadst been poor John. Draw thy tool; here comes [two] of the house of Montagues.

Enter two other serving-men [ABRAHAM *and* BALTHASAR].

Sam. My naked weapon is out. **Quarrel!** I will back thee.   40

Gre. How! turn thy back and **run**?

Sam. Fear me not.

Gre. No, marry; I fear thee!

Sam. Let us take the law of our sides; let them begin.   45

Gre. I will frown as I pass by, and let them take it as they list.

Sam. Nay, as they dare. I will bite my thumb at them; which is disgrace to them, if they bear it.   50

Abr. Do you bite your thumb at us, sir?

Sam. I do bite my thumb, sir.

Abr. Do you bite your thumb at us, sir?

Sam. [*Aside to Gre.*] Is the law of our side, if I say ay?   55

Gre. No.

Sam. No, sir, I do not bite my **thumb** at you, sir; but I bite my thumb, sir.

Gre. Do you quarrel, sir?

Abr. Quarrel, sir? No, sir.   60

Sam. But if you do, sir, **I am for you.** I serve as good a man as you.

Abr. No better.

Sam. Well, sir.

Enter BENVOLIO.

Gre. Say "better"; here comes one of my master's kinsmen.   66

Sam. Yes, better, sir.

Abr. You lie.

Sam. Draw, if you be men. Gregory, remember thy [swashing] blow.   [*They fight.*   70

Ben. Part, fools!
Put up your swords; you know not what you do.
                          [*Beats down their swords.*]

Enter TYBALT.

Tyb. What, art thou drawn among these heartless hinds?
Turn thee, Benvolio, look upon thy death.

Ben. I do but keep the peace. Put up thy sword,   75
Or manage it to part these men with me.

Tyb. What, drawn, and talk of peace! I hate the word
As I hate hell, all Montagues, and thee.
Have at thee, coward!   [*They fight.*

Enter three or four Citizens [*and* OFFICERS], *with clubs or partisans.*

Off. Clubs, bills, and partisans! Strike! Beat them down!   80
Down with the Capulets! down with the Montagues!

Enter CAPULET *in his gown, and* LADY CAPULET.

Cap. What noise is this? Give me my long sword, ho!

La. Cap. A crutch, a crutch! why call you for a sword?

Cap. My sword, I say! Old Montague is come,
And flourishes his blade in spite of me.   85

Enter MONTAGUE *and* LADY MONTAGUE.

Mon. Thou villain Capulet, — Hold me not, let me go.

La. Mon. Thou shalt not stir one foot to seek a foe.

Enter PRINCE ESCALUS, *with his train.*

Prin. Rebellious subjects, enemies to peace,
Profaners of this neighbour-stained steel, —
Will they not hear? — What, ho! you men, you beasts,   90

---

15. **take the wall.** Keeping to the side of the walk next to the wall was the pedestrian's best protection in the dirty streets of Shakespeare's day. To "take the wall" could be insulting, just as to yield it was courteous.   27. [**cruel**] Q₄. **civil** Q₂.   37. **poor John:** salt hake.   38. [**two**] Q₁.   Om. Q₂.   66. **here ... kinsmen.** Tybalt is sighted.   70. [**swashing**] Q₄: crushing.   **washing** Q₂.   73. **heartless hinds:** cowardly servants.   80. **Clubs:** a cry of the London apprentices, who wielded clubs.   **bills:** battle-axes.   **partisans:** pikes or spears with two-edged knives affixed.   85. **spite:** defiance.   89. **neighbour-stained:** stained with neighbor's blood.

That quench the fire of your pernicious rage
With purple fountains issuing from your veins,
On pain of torture, from those bloody hands
Throw your mistemper'd weapons to the ground,
And hear the sentence of your moved prince.   95
Three civil brawls, bred of an airy word,
By thee, old Capulet, and Montague,
Have thrice disturb'd the quiet of our streets,
And made Verona's ancient citizens
Cast by their grave beseeming ornaments   100
To wield old partisans, in hands as old,
Cank'red with peace, to part your cank'red hate;
If ever you disturb our streets again
Your lives shall pay the forfeit of the peace.
For this time, all the rest depart away.   105
You, Capulet, shall go along with me;
And, Montague, come you this afternoon,
To know our farther pleasure in this case,
To old Free-town, our common judgement-place.
Once more, on pain of death, all men depart.   110
    [Exeunt [all but Montague, Lady Montague,
        and Benvolio].
    Mon. Who set this ancient quarrel new abroach?
Speak, nephew, were you by when it began?
    Ben. Here were the servants of your adversary,
And yours, close fighting ere I did approach.
I drew to part them. In the instant came   115
The fiery Tybalt, with his sword prepar'd,
Which, as he breath'd defiance to my ears,
He swung about his head and cut the winds,
Who, nothing hurt withal, hiss'd him in scorn.
While we were interchanging thrusts and blows,   120
Came more and more and fought on part and part,
Till the Prince came, who parted either part.
    La. Mon. O, where is Romeo? Saw you him
to-day?
Right glad I am he was not at this fray.
    Ben. Madam, an hour before the worshipp'd
        sun   125
Peer'd forth the golden window of the east,
A troubled mind [drave] me to walk abroad;
Where, underneath the grove of sycamore
That westward rooteth from [the city's] side,
So early walking did I see your son.   130
Towards him I made, but he was ware of me
And stole into the covert of the wood.
I, measuring his affections by my own,
Which then most sought where most might not be
        found,
Being one too many by my weary self,
Pursued my humour not pursuing his,   135
And gladly shunn'd who gladly fled from me.
    Mon. Many a morning hath he there been seen,
With tears augmenting the fresh morning's dew,

Adding to clouds more clouds with his deep sighs;
But all so soon as the all-cheering sun   140
Should in the farthest east begin to draw
The shady curtains from Aurora's bed,
Away from light steals home my heavy son,
And private in his chamber pens himself,
Shuts up his windows, locks fair daylight out,   145
And makes himself an artificial night.
Black and portentous must this humour prove
Unless good counsel may the cause remove.
    Ben. My noble uncle, do you know the cause?
    Mon. I neither know it nor can learn of him.   150
    Ben. Have you importun'd him by any means?
    Mon. Both by myself and many other friends;
But he, his own affections' counsellor,
Is to himself — I will not say how true —
But to himself so secret and so close,   155
So far from sounding and discovery,
As is the bud bit with an envious worm
Ere he can spread his sweet leaves to the air
Or dedicate his beauty to the [sun].
Could we but learn from whence his sorrows grow,
We would as willingly give cure as know.   161

Enter ROMEO.

    Ben. See, where he comes! So please you, step
        aside;
I'll know his grievance, or be much deni'd.
    Mon. I would thou wert so happy by thy stay
To hear true shrift. Come, madam, let's away.   165
        [Exeunt [Montague and Lady].
    Ben. Good morrow, cousin.
    Rom.   Is the day so young?
    Ben. But new struck nine.
    Rom.   Ay me! sad hours seem long.
Was that my father that went hence so fast?
    Ben. It was. What sadness lengthens Romeo's
        hours?
    Rom. Not having that which, having, makes
        them short.   170
    Ben. In love?
    Rom. Out —
    Ben. Of love?
    Rom. Out of her favour, where I am in love.
    Ben. Alas, that love, so gentle in his view,   175
Should be so tyrannous and rough in proof!
    Rom. Alas, that love, whose view is muffled still,
Should, without eyes, see pathways to his will!
Where shall we dine? O me! What fray was here?
Yet tell me not, for I have heard it all.   180
Here's much to do with hate, but more with love.
Why, then, O brawling love! O loving hate!
O anything, of nothing first [create]!
O heavy lightness! serious vanity!

---

94. **mistemper'd:** angry. 102. **Cank'red:** (1) rusted, (2) malignant. 111. **set...abroach:** tap and leave running. 127. [drave] F. *drive* Q₂. 129. [the city's] Q₁. *this city* Q₂. 133. **affections:** inclinations. 134. **where...found:** the most unfrequented place. 157. **envious:** malicious. 159. [sun] (Theobald). *same* Q₂. 165. **shrift:** confession. 175. **view:** looks. 176. **proof:** experience. 183. [create] Q₁. *created* Q₂.

Mis-shapen chaos of [well-seeming] forms!   185
Feather of lead, bright smoke, cold fire, sick health!
Still-waking sleep, that is not what it is!
This love feel I, that feel no love in this.
Dost thou not laugh?

   Ben.   No, coz, I rather weep.

   Rom. Good heart, at what?

   Ben.   At thy good heart's oppression.   190

   Rom. Why, such is love's transgression.
Griefs of mine own lie heavy in my breast,
Which thou wilt propagate to have it prest
With more of thine.   This love that thou hast shown
Doth add more grief to too much of mine own.   195
Love is a smoke made with the fume of sighs;
Being purg'd, a fire sparkling in lovers' eyes;
Being vex'd, a sea nourish'd with [lovers'] tears.
What is it else?   A madness most discreet,
A choking gall, and a preserving sweet.   200
Farewell, my coz.

   Ben.   Soft! I will go along.
An if you leave me so, you do me wrong.

   Rom. Tut, I have [left] myself; I am not here.
This is not Romeo; he's some otherwhere.

   Ben. Tell me in sadness, who is that you love? 205

   Rom. What, shall I groan and tell thee?

   Ben.   Groan! why, no;
But sadly tell me who.

   Rom. [Bid a] sick man in sadness [make] his
     will, —
Ah, word ill urg'd to one that is so ill!
In sadness, cousin, I do love a woman.   210

   Ben. I aim'd so near when I suppos'd you lov'd.

   Rom. A right good mark-man! And she's fair I
     love.

   Ben. A right fair mark, fair coz, is soonest hit.

   Rom. Well, in that hit you miss.   She'll not be
     hit
With Cupid's arrow; she hath Dian's wit;   215
And, in strong proof of chastity well arm'd,
From Love's weak childish bow she lives [un-
     harm'd].
She will not stay the siege of loving terms,
Nor bide th' encounter of assailing eyes,
Nor ope her lap to saint-seducing gold.   220
O, she is rich in beauty, only poor
That, when she dies, with beauty dies her store.

   Ben. Then she hath sworn that she will still live
     chaste?

   Rom. She hath, and in that sparing make huge
     waste;
For beauty starv'd with her severity   225
Cuts beauty off from all posterity.

She is too fair, too wise, wisely too fair,
To merit bliss by making me despair.
She hath forsworn to love, and in that vow
Do I live dead that live to tell it now.   230

   Ben. Be rul'd by me, forget to think of her.

   Rom. O, teach me how I should forget to think.

   Ben. By giving liberty unto thine eyes;
Examine other beauties.

   Rom.   'Tis the way
To call hers, exquisite, in question more.   235
These happy masks that kiss fair ladies' brows,
Being black, puts us in mind they hide the fair;
He that is strucken blind cannot forget
The precious treasure of his eyesight lost.
Show me a mistress that is passing fair,   240
What doth her beauty serve, but as a note
Where I may read who pass'd that passing fair?
Farewell! Thou canst not teach me to forget.

   Ben. I'll pay that doctrine, or else die in debt.
                          [*Exeunt.*

[SCENE II.   *A street.*]

Enter CAPULET, PARIS, *and the Clown* [*a* SERVANT].

   Cap. But Montague is bound as well as I,
In penalty alike; and 'tis not hard, I think,
For men so old as we to keep the peace.

   Par. Of honourable reckoning are you both;
And pity 'tis you liv'd at odds so long.   5
But now, my lord, what say you to my suit?

   Cap. But saying o'er what I have said before.
My child is yet a stranger in the world;
She hath not seen the change of fourteen years.
Let two more summers wither in their pride,   10
Ere we may think her ripe to be a bride.

   Par. Younger than she are happy mothers made.

   Cap. And too soon marr'd are those so early made.
[The] earth hath swallow'd all my hopes but she;
She is the hopeful lady of my earth;   15
But woo her, gentle Paris, get her heart,
My will to her consent is but a part;
An she [agree], within her scope of choice
Lies my consent and fair according voice.
This night I hold an old accustom'd feast,   20
Whereto I have invited many a guest,
Such as I love; and you, among the store
One more, most welcome, makes my number more.
At my poor house look to behold this night
Earth-treading stars that make dark heaven light.   25
Such comfort as do lusty young men feel
When well-apparell'd April on the heel
Of limping winter treads, even such delight

185. **[well-seeming]** Q4.   *well-seeing* Q2.   193. **to have:** by having.   198. **[lovers']** (Pope).   *a lovers* Q1.   *loving* Q2. 203. **[left]** (Allen conj.).   *lost* Q2.   205. **sadness:** seriousness.   208. **[Bid a]... [make]** Q1.   *A... makes* Q2.   215. **wit:** mind, purpose.   216. **proof:** armor.   217. **[unharm'd]** Q1.   *uncharm'd* Q2.   218. **stay:** bide.   222. **store:** riches.   235. **in... more:** into greater consideration.   244. **pay... doctrine:** teach that lesson.

    Sc. ii, 4. **reckoning:** repute.   14. **[The]** Q4.   Om. Q2.   15. **earth:** body, or world.   18. **[agree]** F.   *agreed* Q2.

Among fresh [female] buds shall you this night
Inherit at my house. Hear all, all see, 30
And like her most whose merit most shall be;
Which [on] more view of, many, mine being one,
May stand in number, though in reckoning none.
Come, go with me. [*To Servant.*] Go, sirrah, trudge
    about
Through fair Verona; find those persons out 35
Whose names are written there, and to them say
My house and welcome on their pleasure stay.

                  [Exeunt [Capulet and Paris].

Serv. Find them out whose names are written
here! It is written that the shoemaker should
meddle with his yard and the tailor with his last, the
fisher with his pencil and the painter with his nets;
but I am sent to find those persons whose names are
here writ, and can never find what names the writing
person hath here writ. I must to the learned. — In
good time. 45

Enter BENVOLIO *and* ROMEO.

Ben. Tut, man, one fire burns out another's burn-
    ing,
One pain is less'ned by another's anguish;
Turn giddy, and be help by backward turning;
One desperate grief cures with another's languish.
Take thou some new infection to thy eye, 50
And the rank poison of the old will die.
Rom. Your plaintain-leaf is excellent for that.
Ben. For what, I pray thee?
Rom.   For your broken shin.
Ben. Why, Romeo, art thou mad?
Rom. Not mad, but bound more than a madman
    is; 55
Shut up in prison, kept without my food,
Whipp'd and tormented and — God-den, good fellow.
Serv. God gi' god-den. I pray, sir, can you read?
Rom. Ay, mine own fortune in my misery. 60
Serv. Perhaps you have learn'd it without book.
But, I pray, can you read anything you see?
Rom. Ay, if I know the letters and the language.
Serv. Ye say honestly. Rest you merry!
Rom. Stay, fellow; I can read. 66
(*Reads.*) "Signior Martino and his wife and
daughters; County Anselme and his beauteous sisters;
the lady widow of Vitruvio; Signior Placentio and
his lovely nieces; Mercutio and his brother Valen-
tine; mine uncle Capulet, his wife, and daughters;
my fair niece Rosaline; Livia; Signior Valentio and
his cousin Tybalt; Lucio and the lively Helena." 74
A fair assembly: whither should they come?
Serv. Up.

Rom. Whither? To supper?
Serv. To our house.
Rom. Whose house?
Serv. My master's. 80
Rom. Indeed, I should have ask'd you that before.
Serv. Now I'll tell you without asking. My master
is the great rich Capulet; and if you be not of the
house of Montagues, I pray, come and crush a cup of
wine. Rest you merry!   *[Exit.* 86
Ben. At this same ancient feast of Capulet's
Sups the fair Rosaline whom thou so loves,
With all the admired beauties of Verona.
Go thither; and with unattainted eye 90
Compare her face with some that I shall show,
And I will make thee think thy swan a crow.
Rom. When the devout religion of mine eye
Maintains such falsehood, then turn tears to [fires];
And these, who, often drown'd, could never die, 95
Transparent heretics, be burnt for liars!
One fairer than my love! The all-seeing sun
Ne'er saw her match since first the world begun.
Ben. Tut, you saw her fair, none else being by,
Herself pois'd with herself in either eye; 100
But in that crystal scales let there be weigh'd
Your lady's love against some other maid
That I will show you shining at this feast,
And she shall scant show well that now seems best.
Rom. I'll go along no such sight to be shown, 105
But to rejoice in splendour of mine own. *[Exeunt.]*

[SCENE III. *A room in Capulet's house.*]

Enter LADY CAPULET *and* NURSE.

La. Cap. Nurse, where's my daughter? Call
    her forth to me.
Nurse. Now, by my maidenhead at twelve year
    old.
I bade her come. What, lamb! What, ladybird!
God forbid! — Where's this girl? What, Juliet!

Enter JULIET.

Jul. How now! Who calls?
Nurse.   Your mother.
Jul.   Madam, I am here.
What is your will?
La. Cap. This is the matter. — Nurse, give leave a
    while,
We must talk in secret. — Nurse, come back again;
I have rememb'red me, thou 's hear our counsel.
Thou know'st my daughter 's of a pretty age. 10
Nurse. Faith, I can tell her age unto an hour.
La. Cap. She's not fourteen.

---

29. **[female]** Q₁. *fennell* Q₂. 30. **Inherit:** possess. 32. **[on]** Q₄. *one* Q₂. 48. **backward:** in the reverse direction. 57. **God-den:** good evening. 84. **crush:** drink. 87. **ancient:** customary. 90. **unattainted:** unprejudiced. 94. **[fires]** (Pope). *fire* Q₂. 95. **these:** i.e., my eyes. 100. **pois'd:** balanced.

    Sc. iii, 4. **God forbid:** i.e., that anything is wrong. 2–78. Q₂ prints the Nurse's speeches in prose and in italics. 9. **thou's:** thou shalt.

Nurse.   I'll lay fourteen of my teeth, —
And yet, to my teen be it spoken, I have but four, —
She 's not fourteen. How long is it now
To Lammas-tide?

La. Cap.   A fortnight and odd days.   15

Nurse. Even or odd, of all days in the year,
Come Lammas-eve at night shall she be fourteen.
Susan and she — God rest all Christian souls! —
Were of an age. Well, Susan is with God;
She was too good for me. But, as I said,   20
On Lammas-eve at night shall she be fourteen;
That shall she, marry; I remember it well.
'Tis since the earthquake now eleven years,
And she was wean'd, — I never shall forget it —
Of all the days of the year, upon that day;   25
For I had then laid wormwood to my dug,
Sitting in the sun under the dove-house wall;
My lord and you were then at Mantua; —
Nay, I do bear a brain; — but, as I said,
When it did taste the wormwood on the nipple   30
Of my dug and felt it bitter, pretty fool,
To see it tetchy and fall out wi' the dug!
Shake, quoth the dove-house; 'twas no need, I trow,
To bid me trudge.
And since that time it is eleven years;   35
For then she could stand high-lone; nay, by the rood,
She could have run and waddled all about;
For even the day before, she broke her brow;
And then my husband — God be with his soul!
'A was a merry man — took up the child.   40
"Yea," quoth he, "dost thou fall upon thy face?
Thou wilt fall backward when thou hast more wit;
Wilt thou not, Jule?" and, by my holidame,
The pretty wretch left crying and said, "Ay."
To see, now, how a jest shall come about!   45
I warrant, an I should live a thousand years,
I never should forget it. "Wilt thou not, Jule?"
          quoth he;
And, pretty fool, it stinted and said, "Ay."

La. Cap. Enough of this; I pray thee, hold thy
          peace.

Nurse. Yes, madam; yet I cannot choose but
          laugh   50
To think it should leave crying and say, "Ay."
And yet, I warrant, it had upon it brow
A bump as big as a young cock'rel's stone;
A perilous knock; and it cried bitterly.
"Yea," quoth my husband, "fall'st upon thy face?
Thou wilt fall backward when thou comest to age;   56
Wilt thou not, Jule?" It stinted and said, "Ay."

Jul. And stint thou too, I pray thee, nurse, say I.

Nurse. Peace, I have done. God mark thee to his
          grace!

Thou wast the prettiest babe that e'er I nurs'd.   60
An I might live to see thee married once,
I have my wish.

La. Cap. Marry, that "marry" is the very theme
I came to talk of. Tell me, daughter Juliet,
How stands your dispositions to be married?   65

Jul. It is an [honour] that I dream not of.

Nurse. An [honour]! were not I thine only nurse,
I would say thou hadst suck'd wisdom from thy teat.

La. Cap. Well, think of marriage now; younger
          than you,
Here in Verona, ladies of esteem,   70
Are made already mothers. By my count,
I was your mother much upon these years
That you are now a maid. Thus then in brief:
The valiant Paris seeks you for his love.

Nurse. A man, young lady! Lady, such a man   75
As all the world — why, he's a man of wax.

La. Cap. Verona's summer hath not such a flower.

Nurse. Nay, he's a flower; in faith, a very flower.

La. Cap. What say you? Can you love the gentle-
          man?
This night you shall behold him at our feast;   80
Read o'er the volume of young Paris' face
And find delight writ there with beauty's pen;
Examine every married lineament
And see how one another lends content,
And what obscur'd in this fair volume lies   85
Find written in the margent of his eyes.
This precious book of love, this unbound lover,
To beautify him, only lacks a cover.
The fish lives in the sea, and 'tis much pride
For fair without the fair within to hide.   90
That book in many's eyes doth share the glory,
That in gold clasps locks in the golden story;
So shall you share all that he doth possess,
By having him, making yourself no less.   94

Nurse. No less! nay, bigger; women grow by men.

La. Cap. Speak briefly, can you like of Paris' love?

Jul. I'll look to like, if looking liking move;
But no more deep will I endart mine eye
Than your consent gives strength to make [it] fly.   99

Enter SERVANT.

Serv. Madam, the guests are come, supper serv'd
up, you call'd, my young lady ask'd for, the nurse
curs'd in the pantry, and everything in extremity. I
must hence to wait; I beseech you, follow straight.
          [*Exit.*

La. Cap. We follow thee. Juliet, the County
          stays.   105

Nurse. Go, girl, seek happy nights to happy days.
          [*Exeunt.*

---

12. **lay:** wager. 13. **teen:** sorrow. 15. **Lammas-tide:** August 1st. 29. **bear a brain:** i.e., have a great memory. 32. **tetchy:** fretful. 36. **high-lone:** quite alone. 43. **holidame:** i.e., halidom, holiness. 48. **stinted:** ceased. 53. **cock'rel's:** a young cock's. 66, 67. **[honour]** Q1. *houre* Q2. 76. **man of wax:** as handsome as a wax figure. 83. **married:** harmonious. 86. **margent:** margin. 89. **The . . . sea:** i.e., the lover is yet uncaught. 99. **[it]** Q1. Om. Q2. 105. **stays:** waits.

[SCENE IV. *A street.*]

Enter ROMEO, MERCUTIO, BENVOLIO, *with five or six other* Maskers, Torch-bearers.

Rom. What, shall this speech be spoke for our excuse?
Or shall we on without apology?
   Ben. The date is out of such prolixity.
We'll have no Cupid hoodwink'd with a scarf,
Bearing a Tartar's painted bow of lath,   5
Scaring the ladies like a crow-keeper;
[Nor no without-book prologue, faintly spoke
After the prompter, for our entrance;]
But let them measure us by what they will,
We'll measure them a measure and be gone.   10
   Rom. Give me a torch. I am not for this ambling;
Being but heavy, I will bear the light.
   Mer. Nay, gentle Romeo, we must have you dance.
   Rom. Not I, believe me. You have dancing shoes
With nimble soles; I have a soul of lead   15
So stakes me to the ground I cannot move.
   Mer. You are a lover; borrow Cupid's wings,
And soar with them above a common bound.
   Rom. I am too sore enpierced with his shaft
To soar with his light feathers, and so bound   20
I cannot bound a pitch above dull woe.
Under love's heavy burden do I sink.
   [*Mer.*] And, to sink in it, should you burden love;
Too great oppression for a tender thing.
   Rom. Is love a tender thing? It is too rough,   25
Too rude, too boist'rous, and it pricks like thorn.
   Mer. If love be rough with you, be rough with love;
Prick love for pricking, and you beat love down. —
Give me a case to put my visage in,   [*Puts on a mask.*]
A visor for a visor! what care I   30
What curious eye doth quote deformities?
Here are the beetle brows shall blush for me.
   Ben. Come, knock and enter; and no sooner in,
But every man betake him to his legs.
   Rom. A torch for me; let wantons light of heart 35
Tickle the senseless rushes with their heels,
For I am proverb'd with a grandsire phrase:
I'll be a candle-holder, and look on.
The game was ne'er so fair, and I am [done].
   Mer. Tut, dun's the mouse, the constable's own word.   40
If thou art Dun, we'll draw thee from the mire

Or, save your reverence, love, wherein thou stickest
Up to the ears. Come, we burn daylight, ho!
   Rom. Nay, that's not so.
   Mer.   I mean, sir, in delay
We waste our lights in vain, [like] lights by day.   45
Take our good meaning, for our judgement sits
Five times in that ere once in our [five] wits.
   Rom. And we mean well in going to this mask;
But 'tis no wit to go.
   Mer.   Why, may one ask?   49
   Rom. I dream'd a dream to-night.
   Mer.   And so did I.
   Rom. Well, what was yours?
   Mer.   That dreamers often lie.
   Rom. In bed asleep, while they do dream things true.
   Mer. O, then, I see Queen Mab hath been with you.
She is the fairies' midwife, and she comes
In shape no bigger than an agate-stone   55
On the fore-finger of an alderman,
Drawn with a team of little atomies
Over men's noses as they lie asleep;
Her waggon-spokes made of long spinners' legs,
The cover of the wings of grasshoppers,   60
Her traces of the smallest spider web,
Her collars of the moonshine's wat'ry beams,
Her whip of cricket's bone, the lash of film,
Her waggoner a small grey-coated gnat,
Not half so big as a round little worm   65
Prick'd from the lazy finger of a [maid];
Her chariot is an empty hazel-nut
Made by the joiner squirrel, or old grub,
Time out o' mind the fairies' coachmakers.
And in this state she gallops night by night   70
Through lovers' brains, and then they dream of love;
On courtiers' knees, that dream on curtsies straight;
O'er lawyers' fingers, who straight dream on fees;
O'er ladies' lips, who straight on kisses dream,
Which oft the angry Mab with blisters plagues, 75
Because their breath with sweetmeats tainted are.
Sometime she gallops o'er a courtier's nose,
And then dreams he of smelling out a suit;
And sometime comes she with a tithe-pig's tail
Tickling a parson's nose as 'a lies asleep,   80
Then he dreams of another benefice.
Sometime she driveth o'er a soldier's neck,
And then dreams he of cutting foreign throats,

Sc. iv, 1. speech. Maskers used to be preceded by one who made a speech. **4. hoodwink'd:** blindfolded. **6. crow-keeper:** scarecrow. **7–8.** [**Nor . . . entrance**] Q₁. Om. Q₂. **10. measure:** dance. **23.** [*Mer.*] Q₄. *Horatio* Q₂. **29. case:** mask. **30. visor . . . visor:** mask for a mask-like (i.e., ugly) face. **31. quote:** notice. **36. rushes.** Rushes were used as floor covering. **37. grandsire phrase:** old proverb, viz., "A good candle-holder (i.e., onlooker) proves a good gamester" (l. 38). Another seems to be echoed in l. 39: "He is wise who gives over (is done) when the game is fairest." **39.** [**done**] Q₁. *dum* Q₂. *dun* Q₃. **40. dun's the mouse.** A stock phrase apparently meaning "keep still." **41. Dun.** Alluding to an old Christmas game, "Dun is in the mire." A heavy log representing a horse stuck in the mud is hauled out by the players. **42. Or . . . love.** Many edd. read *Of this sir-reverence love,* from Q₁. **45.** [**like**] (Johnson). *lights* Q₂. **47.** [**five**] (Wilbraham conj.). *fine* Q₂. **53–91. O . . . bodes.** So Q₁. Prose Q₂. **66.** [**maid**] Q₁. *man* Q₂. **79. tithe-pig's:** pig paid as part of parish dues.

Of breaches, ambuscadoes, Spanish blades,
Of healths five fathom deep; and then anon   85
Drums in his ear, at which he starts and wakes,
And being thus frighted swears a prayer or two
And sleeps again. This is that very Mab
That plats the manes of horses in the night,
And bakes the elf-locks in foul sluttish hairs,   90
Which, once untangled, much misfortune bodes.
This is the hag, when maids lie on their backs,
That presses them and learns them first to bear,
Making them women of good carriage.
This is she——
    Rom.   Peace, peace, Mercutio, peace!   95
Thou talk'st of nothing.
    Mer.   True, I talk of dreams,
Which are the children of an idle brain,
Begot of nothing but vain fantasy,
Which is as thin of substance as the air
And more inconstant than the wind, who wooes   100
Even now the frozen bosom of the north,
And, being anger'd, puffs away from thence,
Turning his [face] to the dew-dropping south.
    Ben. This wind you talk of blows us from our-
        selves.
Supper is done, and we shall come too late.   105
    Rom. I fear, too early; for my mind misgives
Some consequence yet hanging in the stars
Shall bitterly begin his fearful date
With this night's revels, and expire the term
Of a despised life clos'd in my breast   110
By some vile forfeit of untimely death.
But He that hath the steerage of my course
Direct my [sail]! On, lusty gentlemen!
    Ben. Strike, drum.   [*They march about the stage.
                                        [Exeunt.*]

[SCENE V. *A hall in Capulet's house.*]

[*Musicians waiting.*] *Enter* SERVING-MEN, *with
                napkins.*

[*1.*] *Serv.* Where's Potpan, that he helps not to
take away? He shift a trencher! He scrape a
trencher!

[*2.*] *Serv.* When good manners shall lie all in one
or two men's hands, and they unwash'd too, 'tis a
foul thing.   6

[*1.*] *Serv.* Away with the joint-stools, remove the
court-cupboard, look to the plate. Good thou, save
me a piece of marchpane; and, as thou loves me, let
the porter let in Susan Grindstone and Nell. Antony
and Potpan!   11

2. Serv. Ay, boy, ready.

[*1.*] *Serv.* You are look'd for and call'd for, ask'd
for and sought for, in the great chamber.

3. Serv. We cannot be here and there too. Cheerly,
boys; be brisk a while, and the longer liver take
all.   [*They retire.*] 17

Enter [CAPULET, *with* JULIET, TYBALT, *and others of
    his house, meeting*] *the* Guests, ROMEO, *and other*
    Maskers.

    Cap. Welcome, gentlemen! Ladies that have
        their toes
Unplagu'd with corns will walk [a bout] with you.
Ah, my mistresses, which of you all   20
Will now deny to dance? She that makes dainty,
She, I'll swear, hath corns. Am I come near ye
        now?
Welcome, gentlemen! I have seen the day
That I have worn a visor and could tell
A whispering tale in a fair lady's ear,   25
Such as would please; 'tis gone, 'tis gone, 'tis gone.
You are welcome, gentlemen! Come, musicians,
        play.   [*Music plays, and they dance.*]
A hall, a hall! give room! and foot it, girls.
More light, you knaves; and turn the tables up,
And quench the fire, the room is grown too hot. 30
Ah, sirrah, this unlook'd-for sport comes well.
Nay, sit, nay, sit, good cousin Capulet,
For you and I are past our dancing days.
How long is't now since last yourself and I
Were in a mask?
    2. Cap.   By 'r lady, thirty years.   35
    Cap. What, man! 'tis not so much, 'tis not so much.
'Tis since the nuptial of Lucentio,
Come Pentecost as quickly as it will,
Some five and twenty years; and then we mask'd.
    2. Cap. 'Tis more, 'tis more. His son is elder, sir;
His son is thirty.
    Cap.   Will you tell me that?   41
His son was but a ward two years ago.
    Rom. [*To a Serving-man.*] What lady's that which
        doth enrich the hand
Of yonder knight?
    Serv. I know not, sir.   45
    Rom. O, she doth teach the torches to burn bright!
It seems she hangs upon the cheek of night
As a rich jewel in an Ethiop's ear;
Beauty too rich for use, for earth too dear!
So shows a snowy dove trooping with crows,   50
As yonder lady o'er her fellows shows.
The measure done, I'll watch her place of stand,
And, touching hers, make blessed my rude hand.
Did my heart love till now? Forswear it, sight!
For I ne'er saw true beauty till this night.   55
    Tyb. This, by his voice, should be a Montague.
Fetch me my rapier, boy. What dares the slave
Come hither, cover'd with an antic face,

---

90. **elf-locks:** hair tangled by elves.   103. **[face]** Q₁.   *side* Q₂.   **dew-dropping:** rainy.   113. **[sail]** Q₁.   *sute* Q₂.
Sc. v, 7. **joint-stools:** folding stools.   8. **court-cupboard:** sideboard.   9. **marchpane:** marzipan, cake made of almond
paste.   19. **[a bout]** (Daniel).   *about* Q₂.   To "walk a bout" is to tread a measure.   28. **A hall:** make room.

To fleer and scorn at our solemnity?
Now, by the stock and honour of my kin,　60
To strike him dead I hold it not a sin.
　Cap. Why, how now, kinsman! wherefore storm
　　you so?
　Tyb. Uncle, this is a Montague, our foe,
A villain that is hither come in spite
To scorn at our solemnity this night.　65
　Cap. Young Romeo is it?
　Tyb. 　　　　'Tis he, that villain Romeo.
　Cap. Content thee, gentle coz, let him alone,
'A bears him like a portly gentleman;
And, to say truth, Verona brags of him
To be a virtuous and well-govern'd youth.　70
I would not for the wealth of all this town
Here in my house do him disparagement;
Therefore be patient, take no note of him;
It is my will, the which if thou respect,
Show a fair presence and put off these frowns,　75
An ill-beseeming semblance for a feast.
　Tyb. It fits, when such a villain is a guest.
I'll not endure him.
　Cap. 　　　　He shall be endur'd.
What, goodman boy! I say he shall; go to!
Am I the master here, or you? Go to!　80
You'll not endure him! God shall mend my soul!
You'll make a mutiny among my guests!
You will set cock-a-hoop! You'll be the man!
　Tyb. Why, uncle, 'tis a shame.
　Cap. 　　　　　　Go to, go to;
You are a saucy boy. Is't so, indeed?　85
This trick may chance to scathe you; I know what.
You must contrary me! Marry, 'tis time. —
Well said, my hearts! — You are a princox; go;
Be quiet, or — More light, more light! — for shame!
I'll make you quiet. — What, cheerly, my hearts!　90
　Tyb. Patience perforce with wilful choler meeting
Makes my flesh tremble in their different greeting.
I will withdraw; but this intrusion shall
Now seeming sweet convert to bitt'rest gall. [*Exit.*
　Rom. [*To Juliet.*] If I profane with my unworthiest
　　hand　95
This holy shrine, the gentle [fine] is this:
My lips, two blushing pilgrims, ready stand
To smooth that rough touch with a tender kiss.
　Jul. Good pilgrim, you do wrong your hand too
　　much,
Which mannerly devotion shows in this;　100
For saints have hands that pilgrims' hands do touch,
And palm to palm is holy palmers' kiss.
　Rom. Have not saints lips, and holy palmers too?
　Jul. Ay, pilgrim, lips that they must use in
　　prayer.

　Rom. O, then, dear saint, let lips do what hands
　　do;　105
They pray, grant thou, lest faith turn to despair.
　Jul. Saints do not move, though grant for prayers'
　　sake.
　Rom. Then move not while my prayer's effect I
　　take.
Thus from my lips, by thine, my sin is purg'd.
　　　　　　　　　　　　[*Kissing her.*]
　Jul. Then have my lips the sin that they have
　　took.　110
　Rom. Sin from my lips? O trespass sweetly urg'd!
Give me my sin again. [*Kissing her again.*
　Jul. 　　　　You kiss by the book.
　Nurse. Madam, your mother craves a word with
　　you.
　Rom. What is her mother?
　Nurse. 　　　　Marry, bachelor,
Her mother is the lady of the house,　115
And a good lady, and a wise and virtuous.
I nurs'd her daughter, that you talk'd withal;
I tell you, he that can lay hold of her
Shall have the chinks.
　Rom. 　　　　Is she a Capulet?
O dear account! my life is my foe's debt.　120
　Ben. Away, be gone; the sport is at the best.
　Rom. Ay, so I fear; the more is my unrest.
　Cap. Nay, gentlemen, prepare not to be gone;
We have a trifling foolish banquet towards.
Is it e'en so? Why, then, I thank you all;　125
I thank you, honest gentlemen; good-night.
More torches here! Come on then, let's to bed.
Ah, sirrah, by my fay, it waxes late;
I'll to my rest.
　　　[*All but Juliet and Nurse begin to go out.*]
　Jul. Come hither, nurse. What is yond gentle-
　　man?　130
　Nurse. The son and heir of old Tiberio.
　Jul. What's he that now is going out of door?
　Nurse. Marry, that, I think, be young Petruchio.
　Jul. What's he that follows here, that would not
　　dance?
　Nurse. I know not.　135
　Jul. Go, ask his name. — If he be married,
My grave is like to be my wedding-bed.
　Nurse. His name is Romeo, and a Montague;
The only son of your great enemy.
　Jul. My only love sprung from my only hate!　140
Too early seen unknown, and known too late!
Prodigious birth of love it is to me
That I must love a loathed enemy.
　Nurse. What's this? what's this?
　Jul. 　　　　A rhyme I learn'd even now

---

59. **fleer:** mock. **solemnity:** feast. 68. **portly:** dignified. 83. **set cock-a-hoop:** throw things into disorder. 88. **princox:** saucy boy. 91. **perforce:** enforced. 95–108. These lines make a sonnet in the Shakespearean form. 96. **[fine]** (Theobald). *sin* Q₂. 97. **ready** Q₁. *did readie* Q₂. 112. **by the book:** methodically. 119. **chinks:** money. 120. **my foe's debt:** i.e., in the power of my foe. 124. **towards:** coming. 142. **Prodigious:** ominous.

Of one I danc'd withal.

     [One calls within, "Juliet."
Nurse.   Anon, anon!   145
Come, let's away; the strangers all are gone.

            [Exeunt.

[ACT II]

[PROLOGUE]

[Enter] CHORUS.

[*Chor.*] Now old Desire doth in his death-bed lie,
 And young Affection gapes to be his heir;
That fair for which love groan'd for and would die,
 With tender Juliet [match'd] is now not fair.
Now Romeo is belov'd and loves again,   5
 Alike bewitched by the charm of looks,
But to his foe suppos'd he must complain,
 And she steal love's sweet bait from fearful hooks.
Being held a foe, he may not have access
 To breathe such vows as lovers use to swear;   10
And she as much in love, her means much less
 To meet her new-beloved anywhere.
But passion lends them power, time means, to meet,
Temp'ring extremities with extreme sweet. [*Exit.*]

[SCENE I.   *A lane by the wall of Capulet's orchard.*]

Enter ROMEO, *alone.*

Rom. Can I go forward when my heart is here?
Turn back, dull earth, and find thy centre out.

 [He climbs the wall, and leaps down within it.]

Enter BENVOLIO *with* MERCUTIO.

Ben. Romeo! my cousin Romeo!
Mer.   He is wise;
And, on my life, hath stol'n him home to bed.
Ben. He ran this way, and leap'd this orchard
  wall.   5
Call, good Mercutio.
[*Mer.*]   Nay, I'll conjure too.
Romeo! humours! madman! passion! lover!
Appear thou in the likeness of a sigh!
Speak but one rhyme, and I am satisfied;
Cry but "Ay me!" [pronounce] but "love" and
  ["dove"];   10
Speak to my gossip Venus one fair word,
One nick-name for her purblind son and [heir],
Young [Adam] Cupid, he that shot so [trim],
When King Cophetua lov'd the beggar-maid!
He heareth not, he stirreth not, he moveth not; 15

The ape is dead, and I must conjure him.
I conjure thee by Rosaline's bright eyes,
By her high forehead and her scarlet lip,
By her fine foot, straight leg, and quivering thigh,
And the demesnes that there adjacent lie,   20
That in thy likeness thou appear to us!
 Ben. An if he hear thee, thou wilt anger him.
 Mer. This cannot anger him; 'twould anger him
To raise a spirit in his mistress' circle,
Of some strange nature, letting it there stand   25
Till she had laid it and conjur'd it down.
That were some spite; my invocation
Is fair and honest; in his mistress' name
I conjure only but to raise up him.
 Ben. Come, he hath hid himself among these
  trees   30
To be consorted with the humorous night.
Blind is his love and best befits the dark.
 Mer. If Love be blind, Love cannot hit the mark.
Now will he sit under a medlar tree
And wish his mistress were that kind of fruit   35
As maids call medlars, when they laugh alone.
O, Romeo, that she were, O, that she were
An open [*et cetera*], thou a poperin pear!
Romeo, good-night; I'll to my truckle-bed;
This field-bed is too cold for me to sleep.   40
Come, shall we go?
 Ben.   Go, then; for 'tis in vain
To seek him here that means not to be found.

        [Exeunt [Ben. and Mer.].

[SCENE II.   *Capulet's orchard.*

ROMEO *advances from the wall.*]

 Rom. He jests at scars that never felt a wound.

    [Juliet appears above at her window.]

But, soft! what light through yonder window
  breaks?
It is the east, and Juliet is the sun.
Arise, fair sun, and kill the envious moon,
Who is already sick and pale with grief   5
That thou, her maid, art far more fair than she.
Be not her maid, since she is envious;
Her vestal livery is but sick and green,
And none but fools do wear it; cast it off.
It is my lady, O, it is my love!   10
O, that she knew she were!
She speaks, yet she says nothing; what of that?
Her eye discourses; I will answer it. —
I am too bold, 'tis not to me she speaks.
Two of the fairest stars in all the heaven,   15

 Act II, Prol., 4. [**match'd**] F.   *match* Q₂.
 Sc., i, 2. dull earth. Romeo means himself.   **6.** [**Mer.**] Q₁.   Continued to Benvolio Q₂.   **10.** [**pronounce**] Q₁.   *provaunt* Q₂.
[**"dove"**] Q₁.   *day* Q₂.   **11. gossip:** friend.   **12. purblind:** totally blind.   [**heir**] Q₁.   *her* Q₂.   **13.** [**Adam**] (Upton conj.).   *Abraham* Q₂.   Adam is Adam Bell, famous archer of the old ballads.   [**trim**] Q₁.   *true* Q₂.   Trim is the word used in the ballad of King Cophetua.   **27. spite:** vexation.   **31. humorous:** damp.   **34. medlar:** a fruit like an apple.   **38.** [**et cetera**] Q₁. or Q₂.   **poperin:** a Flemish variety of pear.   **39. truckle-bed:** small bed (made to slip under a larger).

Having some business, [do] entreat her eyes
To twinkle in their spheres till they return.
What if her eyes were there, they in her head?
The brightness of her cheek would shame those
    stars,
As daylight doth a lamp; her eyes in heaven   20
Would through the airy region stream so bright
That birds would sing and think it were not night.
See, how she leans her cheek upon her hand!
O, that I were a glove upon that hand,
That I might touch that cheek!

    Jul.   Ay me!
    Rom.   She speaks!
O, speak again, bright angel! for thou art   26
As glorious to this night, being o'er my head,
As is a winged messenger of heaven
Unto the white-upturned wond'ring eyes
Of mortals that fall back to gaze on him   30
When he bestrides the lazy-[pacing] clouds
And sails upon the bosom of the air.

    Jul. O Romeo, Romeo! wherefore art thou
    Romeo?
Deny thy father and refuse thy name;
Or, if thou wilt not, be but sworn my love,   35
And I'll no longer be a Capulet.

    Rom. [*Aside.*] Shall I hear more, or shall I speak
    at this?
    Jul. 'Tis but thy name that is my enemy;
Thou art thyself, though not a Montague.
What's Montague? It is nor hand, nor foot,   40
Nor arm, nor face, [nor any other part]
Belonging to a man. O, be some other name!
What's in a name? That which we call a rose
By any other word would smell as sweet;
So Romeo would, were he not Romeo call'd,   45
Retain that dear perfection which he owes
Without that title. Romeo, doff thy name,
And for thy name, which is no part of thee,
Take all myself.

    Rom.   I take thee at thy word.
Call me but love, and I'll be new baptiz'd;   50
Henceforth I never will be Romeo.

    Jul. What man art thou that thus bescreen'd in
    night
So stumblest on my counsel?

    Rom.   By a name
I know not how to tell thee who I am.
My name, dear saint, is hateful to myself,   55
Because it is an enemy to thee;
Had I it written, I would tear the word.

    Jul. My ears have yet not drunk a hundred words
Of thy tongue's uttering, yet I know the sound.
Art thou not Romeo, and a Montague?   60

    Rom. Neither, fair maid, if either thee dislike.
    Jul. How cam'st thou hither, tell me, and where-
    fore?
The orchard walls are high and hard to climb,
And the place death, considering who thou art,
If any of my kinsmen find thee here.   65

    Rom. With love's light wings did I o'erperch
    these walls;
For stony limits cannot hold love out,
And what love can do, that dares love attempt;
Therefore thy kinsmen are no stop to me.

    Jul. If they do see thee, they will murder thee.   70
    Rom. Alack, there lies more peril in thine eye
Than twenty of their swords! Look thou but sweet,
And I am proof against their enmity.

    Jul. I would not for the world they saw thee here.
    Rom. I have night's cloak to hide me from their
    eyes;   75
And but thou love me, let them find me here.
My life were better ended by their hate,
Than death prorogued, wanting of thy love.

    Jul. By whose direction found'st thou out this
    place?
    Rom. By Love, that first did prompt me to in-
    quire;   80
He lent me counsel and I lent him eyes.
I am no pilot; yet, wert thou as far
As that vast shore [wash'd] with the farthest sea,
I should adventure for such merchandise.

    Jul. Thou know'st the mask of night is on my
    face,   85
Else would a maiden blush bepaint my cheek
For that which thou hast heard me speak to-night.
Fain would I dwell on form, fain, fain deny
What I have spoke; but farewell compliment!
Dost thou love me? I know thou wilt say "Ay,"
And I will take thy word; yet, if thou swear'st,   91
Thou mayst prove false. At lovers' perjuries,
They say, Jove laughs. O gentle Romeo,
If thou dost love, pronounce it faithfully;
Or if thou think'st I am too quickly won,   95
I'll frown and be perverse and say thee nay, —
So thou wilt woo; but else, not for the world.
In truth, fair Montague, I am too fond,
And therefore thou mayst think my ['haviour] light;
But trust me, gentleman, I'll prove more true   100
Than those that have [more cunning] to be strange.
I should have been more strange, I must confess,
But that thou overheard'st, ere I was ware,
My true love's passion; therefore pardon me,
And not impute this yielding to light love,   105
Which the dark night hath so discovered.

    Rom. Lady, by yonder blessed moon I vow

    Sc. ii, 16. **[do]** F. *to* Q2. 31. **[pacing]** Q1. *puffing* Q2. 41. **[nor . . . part]** Q1. Om. Q2. 42. **O . . . name.** After *face* in l. 41 Q2. Q1 omits 42. 44. **word** Q2. *name* Q1. 46. **owes:** possesses. 61. **dislike:** displease. 78. **prorogued:** postponed. 83. **[wash'd]** Q4. *washeth* Q2. 89. **compliment:** convention. 99. **['haviour]** *haviour* Q1. *behaviour* Q2. 101. **[more cunning]** Q1. *coying* Q2. **strange:** reserved, distant. 107. **vow** Q2. *swear* Q1.

That tips with silver all these fruit-tree tops —
  Jul. O, swear not by the moon, the inconstant moon,
That monthly changes in her circled orb,   110
Lest that thy love prove likewise variable.
  Rom. What shall I swear by?
  Jul.   Do not swear at all;
Or, if thou wilt, swear by thy gracious self,
Which is the god of my idolatry,   114
And I'll believe thee.
  Rom.   If my heart's dear love —
  Jul. Well, do not swear. Although I joy in thee,
I have no joy of this contract to-night;
It is too rash, too unadvis'd, too sudden,
Too like the lightning, which doth cease to be
Ere one can say it lightens. Sweet, good-night!
This bud of love, by summer's ripening breath, 121
May prove a beauteous flower when next we meet.
Good-night, good-night! as sweet repose and rest
Come to thy heart as that within my breast!
  Rom. O, wilt thou leave me so unsatisfied? 125
  Jul. What satisfaction canst thou have to-night?
  Rom. Th' exchange of thy love's faithful vow for mine.
  Jul. I gave thee mine before thou didst request it;
And yet I would it were to give again.
  Rom. Wouldst thou withdraw it? For what purpose, love? 130
  Jul. But to be frank, and give it thee again.
And yet I wish but for the thing I have.
My bounty is as boundless as the sea,
My love as deep; the more I give to thee,
The more I have, for both are infinite. 135
                        [Nurse] calls within.
I hear some noise within; dear love, adieu!
Anon, good nurse! Sweet Montague, be true.
Stay but a little, I will come again.   *[Exit, above.]*
  Rom. O blessed, blessed night! I am afeard,
Being in night, all this is but a dream, 140
Too flattering-sweet to be substantial.

         [Re-enter JULIET, *above.]*

  Jul. Three words, dear Romeo, and good-night indeed.
If that thy bent of love be honourable,
Thy purpose marriage, send me word to-morrow,
By one that I'll procure to come to thee, 145
Where and what time thou wilt perform the rite;
And all my fortunes at thy foot I'll lay
And follow thee my lord throughout the world.
  [Nurse.] (*Within.*) Madam!
  Jul. I come, anon. — But if thou mean'st not well, 150
I do beseech thee —

  [Nurse.] (*Within.*) Madam!
  Jul.   By and by, I come: —
To cease thy suit, and leave me to my grief.
To-morrow will I send.
  Rom.   So thrive my soul —
  Jul. A thousand times good-night! *[Exit [above].*
  Rom. A thousand times the worse, to want thy light. 155
Love goes toward love, as schoolboys from their books,
But love from love, toward school with heavy looks.
                    [Retiring.]

     Re-enter JULIET, *above.*

  Jul. Hist! Romeo, hist! O, for a falconer's voice,
To lure this tassel-gentle back again! 160
Bondage is hoarse, and may not speak aloud;
Else would I tear the cave where Echo lies,
And make her airy tongue more hoarse than [mine],
With repetition of my [Romeo's name.]
Romeo!
  Rom. It is my soul, that calls upon my name.
How silver-sweet sound lovers' tongues by night, 166
Like softest music to attending ears!
  Jul. Romeo!
  Rom.   My [dear]?
  Jul.   What o'clock to-morrow
Shall I send to thee?
  Rom.   By the hour of nine.
  Jul. I will not fail; 'tis twenty year till then. 170
I have forgot why I did call thee back.
  Rom. Let me stand here till thou remember it.
  Jul. I shall forget, to have thee still stand there,
Rememb'ring how I love thy company.
  Rom. And I'll still stay, to have thee still forget,
Forgetting any other home but this. 176
  Jul. 'Tis almost morning, I would have thee gone; —
And yet no farther than a wanton's bird,
That lets it hop a little from [her] hand,
Like a poor prisoner in his twisted gyves, 180
And with a [silk] thread plucks it back again,
So loving-jealous of his liberty.
  Rom. I would I were thy bird.
  Jul.   Sweet, so would I;
Yet I should kill thee with much cherishing.
Good-night, good-night! Parting is such sweet sorrow, 185
That I shall say good-night till it be morrow.
                  [Exit, above.]
  Rom. Sleep dwell upon thine eyes, peace in thy breast!
Would I were sleep and peace, so sweet to rest!

131. **frank**: generous. 143. **bent**: inclination. 149, 151. [*Nurse*] (Capell). Om. Q₂. 151. **By and by**: immediately. 160. **tassel-gentle**: male hawk. 163. [mine] Q₄. Om. Q₂. 164. [Romeo's name] Q₁. Om. Q₂. 168. [dear] Q₄. *Neece* Q₂. 179. [her] Q₁. *his* Q₂. 180. **gyves**: fetters. 181. [silk] Q₁. *silken* Q₂. 188. After *rest* Q₂ inserts iii.1–4.

Hence will I to my ghostly [father's] cell,
His help to crave, and my dear hap to tell.   190

[*Exit.*

[SCENE III.   *Friar Laurence's cell.*]

Enter FRIAR [LAURENCE], *with a basket.*

Fri. L. The grey-ey'd morn smiles on the frown-
    ing night,
Chequ'ring the eastern clouds with streaks of light,
And flecked darkness like a drunkard reels
From forth day's path and Titan's [fiery] wheels.
Now, ere the sun advance his burning eye,   5
The day to cheer and night's dank dew to dry,
I must up-fill this osier cage of ours
With baleful weeds and precious-juiced flowers.
The earth, that's nature's mother, is her tomb;
What is her burying grave, that is her womb;   10
And from her womb children of divers kind
We sucking on her natural bosom find:
Many for many virtues excellent,
None but for some, and yet all different.
O, mickle is the powerful grace that lies   15
In plants, herbs, stones, and their true qualities;
For nought so vile that on the earth doth live
But to the earth some special good doth give,
Nor aught so good but, strain'd from that fair use,
Revolts from true birth, stumbling on abuse.   20
Virtue itself turns vice, being misapplied;
And vice [sometime's] by action dignified.

Enter ROMEO.

Within the infant rind of this weak flower
Poison hath residence and medicine power;
For this, being smelt, with that part cheers each
    part;   25
Being tasted, [slays] all senses with the heart.
Two such opposed kings encamp them still
In man as well as herbs, grace and rude will;
And where the worser is predominant,
Full soon the canker death eats up that plant.   30
Rom. Good morrow, father.
Fri. L.   *Benedicite!*
What early tongue so sweet saluteth me?
Young son, it argues a distempered head
So soon to bid good morrow to thy bed.
Care keeps his watch in every old man's eye,   35
And where care lodges, sleep will never lie;
But where unbruised youth with unstuff'd brain
Doth couch his limbs, there golden sleep doth reign;
Therefore thy earliness doth me assure
Thou art up-rous'd with some distemp'rature;   40
Or if not so, then here I hit it right,

Our Romeo hath not been in bed to-night.
Rom. That last is true; the sweeter rest was mine.
Fri. L. God pardon sin! Wast thou with Rosa-
    line?
Rom. With Rosaline, my ghostly father? No!
I have forgot that name, and that name's woe.   46
Fri. L. That's my good son; but where hast thou
    been, then?
Rom. I'll tell thee ere thou ask it me again.
I have been feasting with mine enemy,
Where on a sudden one hath wounded me   50
That's by me wounded; both our remedies
Within thy help and holy physic lies.
I bear no hatred, blessed man, for, lo,
My intercession likewise steads my foe.
Fri. L. Be plain, good son, and homely in thy
    drift;   55
Riddling confession finds but riddling shrift.
Rom. Then plainly know my heart's dear love is
    set
On the fair daughter of rich Capulet.
As mine on hers, so hers is set on mine;
And all combin'd, save what thou must combine   60
By holy marriage.   When and where and how
We met, we woo'd, and made exchange of vow,
I'll tell thee as we pass; but this I pray,
That thou consent to marry us to-day.
Fri. L. Holy Saint Francis, what a change is
    here!   65
Is Rosaline, that thou didst love so dear,
So soon forsaken?   Young men's love then lies
Not truly in their hearts, but in their eyes.
Jesu Maria, what a deal of brine
Hath wash'd thy sallow cheeks for Rosaline!   70
How much salt water thrown away in waste,
To season love, that of it doth not taste!
The sun not yet thy sighs from heaven clears,
Thy old groans yet [ring] in mine ancient ears;
Lo, here upon thy cheek the stain doth sit   75
Of an old tear that is not wash'd off yet.
If e'er thou wast thyself and these woes thine,
Thou and these woes were all for Rosaline.
And art thou chang'd? Pronounce this sentence
    then:
Women may fall, when there's no strength in men.
Rom. Thou chid'st me oft for loving Rosaline.   81
Fri. L. For doting, not for loving, pupil mine.
Rom. And bad'st me bury love.
Fri. L.   Not in a grave,
To lay one in, another out to have.
Rom. I pray thee, chide me not. Her I love
    now   85
Doth grace for grace and love for love allow;

189. **ghostly:** spiritual. **[father's]** Q₁. *Friers close* Q₂. 190. **dear hap:** good fortune.
    Sc. iii, 4. **[fiery]** Q₁. *burning* Q₂. 7. **osier cage:** willow basket. 22. **[sometime's]** (Capell). *sometimes* Q₁. *sometime* Q₂. 25. **that part:** i.e., the odor. 26. **[slays]** F. *stays* Q₂. 30. **canker:** canker-worm. 33. **distempered:** sick. 56. **shrift:** absolution. 74. **[ring]** Q₄. *ringing* Q₂.

The other did not so.

Fri. L.　　　　O, she knew well
Thy love did read by rote that could not spell.
But come, young waverer, come, go with me,
In one respect I'll thy assistant be;　90
For this alliance may so happy prove
To turn your households' rancour to pure love.

Rom. O, let us hence; I stand on sudden haste.

Fri. L. Wisely and slow; they stumble that run
　fast.　　　　　　　　　　　　　[*Exeunt.*

[SCENE IV.　*A street.*]

Enter BENVOLIO *and* MERCUTIO.

Mer. Where the devil should this Romeo be?
Came he not home to-night?

Ben. Not to his father's; I spoke with his man.

Mer. Why, that same pale hard-hearted wench,
　　that Rosaline,
Torments him so, that he will sure run mad.　5

Ben. Tybalt, the kinsman of old Capulet,
Hath sent a letter to his father's house.

Mer. A challenge, on my life.

Ben. Romeo will answer it.

Mer. Any man that can write may answer a letter.　10

Ben. Nay, he will answer the letter's master,
how he dares, being dared.

Mer. Alas, poor Romeo! he is already dead;
stabb'd with a white wench's black eye; run through
the ear with a love song; the very pin of his heart
cleft with the blind bow-boy's butt-shaft: and is he
a man to encounter Tybalt?　17

Ben. Why, what is Tybalt?

Mer. More than prince of cats. O, he's the
courageous captain of compliments. He fights
as you sing prick-song; keeps time, distance, and
proportion; he rests his minim rests, one, two,　22
and the third in your bosom: the very butcher of a
silk button; a duellist, a duellist; a gentleman of the
very first house, of the first and second cause. Ah,
the immortal *passado!* the *punto reverso!* the *hai!*

Ben. The what?　28

Mer. The pox of such antic, lisping, affecting
[fantasticoes]; these new tuners of accent! "By
Jesu, a very good blade! a very tall man! a very
good whore!" Why, is not this a lamentable thing,
grandsire, that we should be thus afflicted with these

strange flies, these fashion-mongers, these [*perdona-
mi's*], who stand so much on the new form, that
they cannot sit at ease on the old bench? O, their
bones, their bones!　37

Enter ROMEO.

Ben. Here comes Romeo, here comes Romeo.

Mer. Without his roe, like a dried herring: O
flesh, flesh, how art thou fishified! Now is he for the
numbers that Petrarch flowed in. Laura to his lady
was a kitchen-wench (marry, she had a better
love to be-rhyme her); Dido a dowdy; Cleopatra　43
a gipsy; Helen and Hero hildings and harlots;
Thisbe, a grey eye or so, but not to the purpose.
Signior Romeo, *bonjour!* There's a French salutation to your French slop. You gave us the counterfeit fairly last night.

Rom. Good morrow to you both. What counterfeit did I give you?　50

Mer. The slip, sir, the slip; can you not conceive?

Rom. Pardon, good Mercutio, my business was
great; and in such a case as mine a man may strain
courtesy.　55

Mer. That's as much as to say, such a case as
yours constrains a man to bow in the hams.

Rom. Meaning, to curtsy.

Mer. Thou hast most kindly hit it.

Rom. A most courteous exposition.　60

Mer. Nay, I am the very pink of courtesy.

Rom. Pink for flower.

Mer. Right.

Rom. Why, then is my pump well flower'd.　64

Mer. Sure wit! Follow me this jest now till thou
hast worn out thy pump, that, when the single sole
of it is worn, the jest may remain, after the wearing,
solely singular.

Rom. O single-sol'd jest, solely singular for the
singleness!　70

Mer. Come between us, good Benvolio; my wits
faint.

Rom. Switch and spurs, switch and spurs; or I'll
cry a match.　74

Mer. Nay, if our wits run the wild-goose chase,
I am done, for thou hast more of the wild-goose in
one of thy wits than, I am sure, I have in my whole
five. Was I with you there for the goose?　80

Rom. Thou wast never with me for anything
when thou wast not there for the goose.

88. **rote:** memory. 93. **stand on:** insist on.

Sc. iv, 15. **pin:** peg in center of a target. 16. **butt-shaft:** blunt arrow. 19. **prince of cats.** The king of the cats in *Reynard the Fox* was called Tibalt. 21. **prick-song:** music sung from written notes. 25. **first house:** best school (of fencing). 26. **of ... cause:** i.e., very ready to quarrel. A satirical reference to the manuals which codified the reasons for quarreling. 27. **passado:** forward thrust; **punto reverso:** back-handed thrust; **hai:** home thrust. 30. [**fantasticoes**] Q_1; coxcombs. **phantacies** Q_2. 31. **tall:** brave. 34. [**perdona-mi's**] Q_4: pardon me's (Ital.). **pardons mees** Q_2. 36. **form:** (1) fashion, (2) bench. 37. **bones.** Pun on *bons* (Fr.). 41. **numbers:** verses. 44. **hildings:** good-for-nothings. 47. **slop:** loose breeches (French fashion). 50-51. **counterfeit ... slip.** Counterfeit coins were called *slips*. 59. **kindly:** naturally. 70. **singleness:** silliness. 75. **wild-goose chase:** a cross-country riding game, in which the leader could pick whatever course he chose and the others had to follow. The object was to capture the lead.

Mer. I will bite thee by the ear for that jest.

Rom. Nay, good goose, bite not.

Mer. Thy wit is a very bitter sweeting; it is a most sharp sauce.

Rom. And is it not, then, well serv'd in to a sweet goose? 86

Mer. O, here's a wit of cheveril, that stretches from an inch narrow to an ell broad!

Rom. I stretch it out for that word "broad"; which added to the goose, proves thee far and wide a broad goose. 91

Mer. Why, is not this better now than groaning for love? Now art thou sociable, now art thou Romeo, now art thou what thou art, by art as well as by nature; for this drivelling love is like a great natural, that runs lolling up and down to hide his bauble in a hole. 97

Ben. Stop there, stop there.

Mer. Thou desir'st me to stop in my tale against the hair.

Ben. Thou wouldst else have made thy tale large. 102

Mer. O, thou art deceiv'd; I would have made it short; for I was come to the whole depth of my tale, and meant, indeed, to occupy the argument no longer. 106

Rom. Here's goodly gear!

Enter NURSE *and her man* [PETER].

A sail, a sail!

Mer. Two, two; a shirt and a smock.

Nurse. Peter! 110

Peter. Anon!

Nurse. My fan, Peter.

Mer. Good Peter, to hide her face; for her fan's the fairer face.

Nurse. God ye good morrow, gentlemen. 115

Mer. God ye good den, fair gentlewoman.

Nurse. Is it good den?

Mer. 'Tis no less, I tell ye; for the bawdy hand of the dial is now upon the prick of noon.

Nurse. Out upon you! what a man are you! 120

Rom. One, gentlewoman, that God hath made [for] himself to mar.

Nurse. By my troth, it is well said; "for himself to mar," quoth 'a! Gentlemen, can any of you tell me where I may find the young Romeo? 125

Rom. I can tell you; but young Romeo will be older when you have found him than he was when you sought him. I am the youngest of that name, for fault of a worse.

Nurse. You say well. 130

Mer. Yea, is the worst well? Very well took, i' faith; wisely, wisely.

Nurse. If you be he, sir, I desire some confidence with you.

Ben. She will indite him to some supper. 135

Mer. A bawd, a bawd, a bawd! So ho!

Rom. What hast thou found?

Mer. No hare, sir; unless a hare, sir, in a lenten pie, that is something stale and hoar ere it be spent. [*Sings.*] 140

　　"An old hare hoar,
　　　And an old hare hoar,
　　Is very good meat in lent;
　　　But a hare that is hoar
　　　Is too much for a score, 145
　　When it hoars ere it be spent."

Romeo, will you come to your father's? We'll to dinner thither.

Rom. I will follow you.

Mer. Farewell, ancient lady; farewell, [*singing*] "lady, lady, lady." 151

[*Exeunt Mercutio and Benvolio.*

Nurse. I pray you, sir, what saucy merchant was this, that was so full of his ropery?

Rom. A gentleman, nurse, that loves to hear himself talk, and will speak more in a minute than he will stand to in a month. 157

Nurse. An 'a speak anything against me, I'll take him down, an 'a were lustier than he is, and twenty such Jacks; and if I cannot, I'll find those that shall. Scurvy knave! I am none of his flirt-gills; I am none of his skains-mates. — And thou must stand by too, and suffer every knave to use me at his pleasure! 164

Peter. I saw no man use you at his pleasure; if I had, my weapon should quickly have been out. I warrant you, I dare draw as soon as another man, if I see occasion in a good quarrel, and the law on my side. 169

Nurse. Now, afore God, I am so vex'd that every part about me quivers. Scurvy knave! Pray you, sir, a word: and as I told you, my young lady bid me inquire you out; what she bid me say, I will keep to myself. But first let me tell ye, if ye should lead her [into] a fool's paradise, as they say, it [175 were a very gross kind of behaviour, as they say; for the gentlewoman is young, and, therefore, if you should deal double with her, truly it were an ill thing to be off'red to any gentlewoman, and very weak dealing. 181

Rom. Nurse, commend me to thy lady and mistress. I protest unto thee —

---

85. **sweeting:** a variety of apple.　87. **cheveril:** kid leather.　88. **ell:** 45 inches.　96. **natural:** idiot.　100. **hair:** i.e., grain.　102. **large:** i.e., with a pun on sense of *gross, lewd*.　107. **gear:** matter.　122. **[for]** Q₁. Om. Q₂.　134. **confidence:** blunder for *conference*.　135. **indite:** Benvolio's intentional malapropism for *invite*.　136. **So ho:** hunter's cry when sighting a hare.　153. **ropery:** roguery.　160. **Jacks:** saucy fellows.　162. **flirt-gills:** flirting women.　**skains-mates.** A derogatory term not occurring elsewhere.　175. **[into]** Q₁. *in* Q₂.

Nurse. Good heart, and, i' faith, I will tell her as much. Lord, Lord, she will be a joyful woman.   186

Rom. What wilt thou tell her, nurse? Thou dost not mark me.

Nurse. I will tell her, sir, that you do protest; which, as I take it, is a gentlemanlike offer.

Rom. Bid her devise   191
Some means to come to shrift this afternoon;
And there she shall at Friar Laurence' cell
Be shriv'd and married. Here is for thy pains.

Nurse. No, truly, sir; not a penny.   195

Rom. Go to; I say you shall.

Nurse. This afternoon, sir? Well, she shall be there.

Rom. And stay, good nurse; — behind the abbey wall
Within this hour my man shall be with thee,   200
And bring thee cords made like a tackled stair;
Which to the high top-gallant of my joy
Must be my convoy in the secret night.
Farewell; be trusty, and I'll quit thy pains.
Farewell; commend me to thy mistress.   205

Nurse. Now God in heaven bless thee! Hark you, sir.

Rom. What say'st thou, my dear nurse?

Nurse. Is your man secret? Did you ne'er hear say,
"Two may keep counsel, putting one away"?

Rom. [I] warrant thee, my man's as true as steel.   210

Nurse. Well, sir; my mistress is the sweetest lady — Lord, Lord! when 'twas a little prating thing, — O, there is a nobleman in town, one Paris, that would fain lay knife aboard; but she, good soul, had as lief see a toad, a very toad, as see   215
him. I anger her sometimes and tell her that Paris is the properer man; but, I'll warrant you, when I say so, she looks as pale as any clout in the versal world. Doth not rosemary and Romeo begin both with a letter?   220

Rom. Ay, nurse; what of that? Both with an R.

Nurse. Ah, mocker! that's the dog's name. R is for the — No; I know it begins with some other letter — and she hath the prettiest sententious of it, of you and rosemary, that it would do you good to hear it.   227

Rom. Commend me to thy lady.

Nurse. Ay, a thousand times. [*Exit Romeo.*] Peter!

Pet. Anon!

Nurse. Before, and apace.   [*Exeunt.* 232

[SCENE V. *Capulet's orchard.*]

Enter JULIET.

Jul. The clock struck nine when I did send the nurse;
In half an hour she promis'd to return.
Perchance she cannot meet him: that's not so.
O, she is lame! Love's heralds should be thoughts,
Which ten times faster [glide] than the sun's beams   5
Driving back shadows over louring hills;
Therefore do nimble-pinion'd doves draw Love,
And therefore hath the wind-swift Cupid wings.
Now is the sun upon the highmost hill
Of this day's journey, and from nine till twelve 10
Is three long hours, yet she is not come.
Had she affections and warm youthful blood,
She would be as swift in motion as a ball;
My words would bandy her to my sweet love,
And his to me;   15
But old folks, [marry,] feign as they were dead,
Unwieldy, slow, heavy and pale as lead.

Enter NURSE [*and* PETER].

O God, she comes! O honey nurse, what news?
Hast thou met with him? Send thy man away.

Nurse. Peter, stay at the gate.   [*Exit Peter.* 20

Jul. Now, good sweet nurse, — O Lord, why look'st thou sad?
Though news be sad, yet tell them merrily;
If good, thou sham'st the music of sweet news
By playing it to me with so sour a face.

Nurse. I am a-weary, give me leave a while.   25
Fie, how my bones ache! What a jaunce have I [had]!

Jul. I would thou hadst my bones, and I thy news.
Nay, come, I pray thee, speak; good, good nurse, speak.

Nurse. Jesu, what haste! Can you not stay a while?
Do you not see that I am out of breath?   30

Jul. How art thou out of breath, when thou hast breath
To say to me that thou art out of breath?
Th' excuse that thou dost make in this delay
Is longer than the tale thou dost excuse.
Is thy news good, or bad? Answer to that;   35
Say either, and I'll stay the circumstance.
Let me be satisfied, is't good or bad?

Nurse. Well, you have made a simple choice; you know not how to choose a man. Romeo! no, not he. Though his face be better than any man's, 40

---

201. **tackled stair:** rope ladder. 202. **top-gallant:** summit. 203. **convoy:** conveyance. 210. **[I]** F₂. Om. Q₂. 217. **properer:** handsomer. 218. **clout:** rag. **versal:** universal. 225. **sententious:** blunder for *sentences,* i.e., proverbs. **Sc. v,** 5. **[glide]** F₄. *glides* Q₂. 14. **bandy:** toss. 16. **[marry]** (Johnson). *many* Q₂. 26. **jaunce:** jaunt. **[had]** F. Om. Q₂. 36. **stay the circumstance:** wait for details.

yet his leg excels all men's; and for a hand, and a
foot, and a body, though they be not to be talk'd
on, yet they are past compare.　He is not the
flower of courtesy, but, I'll warrant him, as gentle
as a lamb.　Go thy ways, wench; serve God.　What,
have you din'd at home?　　　　　　　　　　　46
　Jul.　No, no!　But all this did I know before.
What says he of our marriage?　What of that?
　Nurse.　Lord, how my head aches!　What a head
　　have I!
It beats as it would fall in twenty pieces.　　50
My back o' t' other side, — O, my back, my back!
Beshrew your heart for sending me about
To catch my death with jauncing up and down!
　Jul.　I' faith, I am sorry that thou art not well.
Sweet, sweet, sweet nurse, tell me, what says my
　　love?　　　　　　　　　　　　　　　　55
　Nurse.　Your love says, like an honest gentle-
man, and a courteous, and a kind, and a handsome,
and, I warrant, a virtuous, — Where is your
mother?
　Jul.　Where is my mother!　why, she is within; 60
Where should she be?　How oddly thou repliest!
"Your love says, like an honest gentleman,
'Where is your mother?'"
　Nurse.　　　　　　　　　O God's lady dear!
Are you so hot?　Marry, come up, I trow;
Is this the poultice for my aching bones?　　65
Henceforward do your messages yourself.
　Jul.　Here's such a coil! — Come, what says
　　Romeo?
　Nurse.　Have you got leave to go to shrift today?
　Jul.　I have.
　Nurse.　Then hie you hence to Friar Laurence'
　　cell;　　　　　　　　　　　　　　　70
There stays a husband to make you a wife.
Now comes the wanton blood up in your cheeks;
They'll be in scarlet straight at any news.
Hie you to church; I must another way,
To fetch a ladder, by the which your love　　75
Must climb a bird's nest soon when it is dark.
I am the drudge and toil in your delight,
But you shall bear the burden soon at night.
Go; I'll to dinner; hie you to the cell.
　Jul.　Hie to high fortune!　Honest nurse, fare-
　　well.　　　　　　　　　　　[*Exeunt.* 80

[SCENE VI.　*Friar Laurence's cell.*]

Enter FRIAR LAURENCE *and* ROMEO.

　Fri. L.　So smile the heavens upon this holy act,
That after-hours with sorrow chide us not!
　Rom.　Amen, amen! but come what sorrow can,
It cannot countervail th' exchange of joy

That one short minute gives me in her sight.　　5
Do thou but close our hands with holy words,
Then love-devouring Death do what he dare;
It is enough I may but call her mine.
　Fri. L.　These violent delights have violent ends,
And in their triumph die, like fire and powder,　10
Which as they kiss consume.　The sweetest honey
Is loathsome in his own deliciousness
And in the taste confounds the appetite:
Therefore love moderately; long love doth so;
Too swift arrives as tardy as too slow.　　15

Enter JULIET.

Here comes the lady.　O, so light a foot
Will ne'er wear out the everlasting flint.
A lover may bestride the gossamer
That idles in the wanton summer air,
And yet not fall; so light is vanity.　　20
　Jul.　Good even to my ghostly confessor.
　Fri. L.　Romeo shall thank thee, daughter, for us
　　both.
　Jul.　As much to him, else is his thanks too much.
　Rom.　Ah, Juliet, if the measure of thy joy
Be heap'd like mine, and that thy skill be more　25
To blazon it, then sweeten with thy breath
This neighbour air, and let rich music's tongue
Unfold the imagin'd happiness that both
Receive in either by this dear encounter.
　Jul.　Conceit, more rich in matter than in words,
Brags of his substance, not of ornament.　　31
They are but beggars that can count their worth;
But my true love is grown to such excess
I cannot sum up sum of half my wealth.
　Fri. L.　Come, come with me, and we will make
　　short work;　　　　　　　　　　35
For, by your leaves, you shall not stay alone
Till Holy Church incorporate two in one. [*Exeunt.*

[ACT III]

[SCENE I.　*A public place.*]

Enter MERCUTIO, BENVOLIO, *and men.*

　Ben.　I pray thee, good Mercutio, let's retire.
The day is hot, the Capulets abroad,
And, if we meet, we shall not scape a brawl,
For now, these hot days, is the mad blood stirring. 4
　Mer.　Thou art like one of these fellows that,
when he enters the confines of a tavern, claps
his sword upon the table and says, "God send me
no need of thee!" and by the operation of the
second cup draws him on the drawer, when indeed
there is no need.　　　　　　　　　　10
　Ben.　Am I like such a fellow?
　Mer.　Come, come, thou art as hot a Jack in thy

67.　coil: fuss.
Sc. vi, 4.　countervail: equal.　13.　confounds: destroys.　26.　blazon: proclaim.　30.　Conceit: imagination.
Act III, sc. i, 9.　drawer: tapster.

mood as any in Italy, and as soon moved to be moody, and as soon moody to be moved.

Ben. And what to? 15

Mer. Nay, an there were two such, we should have none shortly, for one would kill the other. Thou! why, thou wilt quarrel with a man that hath a hair more or a hair less in his beard than thou hast. Thou wilt quarrel with a man for cracking nuts, 20 having no other reason but because thou hast hazel eyes. What eye but such an eye would spy out such a quarrel? Thy head is as full of quarrels as an egg is full of meat, and yet thy head hath been beaten as addle as an egg for quarrelling. Thou hast quarrell'd with a man for coughing in the 26 street, because he hath wakened thy dog that hath lain asleep in the sun. Didst thou not fall out with a tailor for wearing his new doublet before Easter? with another for tying his new shoes with old riband? And yet thou wilt tutor me for quarrelling! 30

Ben. An I were so apt to quarrel as thou art, any man should buy the fee-simple of my life for an hour and a quarter. 36

Mer. The fee-simple! O simple!

Enter TYBALT, Petruchio, *and others.*

Ben. By my head, here comes the Capulets.

Mer. By my heel, I care not.

Tyb. Follow me close, for I will speak to them. Gentlemen, good den; a word with one of you. 41

Mer. And but one word with one of us? Couple it with something; make it a word and a blow.

Tyb. You shall find me apt enough to that, sir, an you will give occasion.

Mer. Could you not take some occasion without giving? 47

Tyb. Mercutio, thou consortest with Romeo,—

Mer. Consort! what, dost thou make us minstrels? An thou make minstrels of us, look to hear nothing but discords. Here's my fiddlestick; here's that shall make you dance. 'Zounds, consort! 52

Ben. We talk here in the public haunt of men. Either withdraw unto some private place, Or reason coldly of your grievances, 55 Or else depart; here all eyes gaze on us.

Mer. Men's eyes were made to look, and let them gaze; I will not budge for no man's pleasure, I.

Enter ROMEO.

Tyb. Well, peace be with you, sir; here comes my man.

Mer. But I'll be hang'd, sir, if he wear your livery. 60 Marry, go before to field, he'll be your follower; Your worship in that sense may call him "man."

Tyb. Romeo, the love I bear thee can afford No better term than this: thou art a villain.

Rom. Tybalt, the reason that I have to love thee 65 Doth much excuse the appertaining rage To such a greeting. Villain am I none; Therefore farewell; I see thou know'st me not.

Tyb. Boy, this shall not excuse the injuries That thou hast done me; therefore turn and draw.

Rom. I do protest I never injur'd thee, 71 But love thee better than thou canst devise Till thou shalt know the reason of my love; And so, good Capulet,—which name I tender As dearly as mine own,—be satisfied. 75

Mer. O calm, dishonourable, vile submission! *Alla stoccata* carries it away. [*Draws.*] Tybalt, you rat-catcher, will you walk?

Tyb. What wouldst thou have with me? 79

Mer. Good king of cats, nothing but one of your nine lives; that I mean to make bold withal, and, as you shall use me hereafter, dry-beat the rest of the eight. Will you pluck your sword out of his pilcher by the ears? Make haste, lest mine be about your ears ere it be out. 85

Tyb. I am for you. [*Drawing.*]

Rom. Gentle Mercutio, put thy rapier up.

Mer. Come, sir, your *passado*. [*They fight.*]

Rom. Draw, Benvolio; beat down their weapons. Gentlemen, for shame, forbear this outrage! 90 Tybalt, Mercutio, the Prince expressly hath Forbid this bandying in Verona streets. Hold, Tybalt! Good Mercutio!

[*Tybalt under Romeo's arm thrusts Mercutio, and flies.*

Mer. I am hurt. A plague o' both [your] houses! I am sped. Is he gone, and hath nothing?

Ben. What, art thou hurt?

Mer. Ay, ay, a scratch, a scratch; marry, 'tis enough. 96 Where is my page? Go, villain, fetch a surgeon.

[*Exit Page.*]

Rom. Courage, man; the hurt cannot be much.

Mer. No, 'tis not so deep as a well, nor so wide as a church-door; but 'tis enough, 'twill serve. Ask for me to-morrow, and you shall find me a grave [101 man. I am pepper'd, I warrant, for this world. A plague o' both your houses! 'Zounds, a dog, a rat, a mouse, a cat, to scratch a man to death! a braggart, a rogue, a villain, that fights by the book of

---

14. **moody:** angry. 35. **fee-simple:** absolute possession. 52. **'Zounds:** by God's wounds. 61. **field:** i.e., for duelling. 77. *Alla stoccata:* "with the thrust" — meaning Tybalt. Cf. II.iv.19–27. **carries it away:** wins. 82. **dry-beat:** thrash without drawing blood. 84. **pilcher:** scabbard. 94. **[your]** (Dyce). Om. Q₂; *the* F. **sped:** done for.

arithmetic! Why the devil came you between us?
I was hurt under your arm.   108
   Rom. I thought all for the best.
   Mer. Help me into some house, Benvolio,
Or I shall faint. A plague o' both your houses!
They have made worms' meat of me. I have it,
And soundly too. Your houses!   113
               [Exeunt [Mercutio and Benvolio].
   Rom. This gentleman, the Prince's near ally,
My very friend, hath got this mortal hurt
In my behalf; my reputation stain'd
With Tybalt's slander, — Tybalt, that an hour
Hath been my cousin! O sweet Juliet,
Thy beauty hath made me effeminate
And in my temper soft'ned valour's steel!   120

Re-enter BENVOLIO.

   Ben. O Romeo, Romeo, brave Mercutio's dead!
That gallant spirit hath aspir'd the clouds,
Which too untimely here did scorn the earth.
   Rom. This day's black fate on moe days doth
     depend;
This but begins the woe others must end.   125
   Ben. Here comes the furious Tybalt back again.

Re-enter TYBALT.

   Rom. [Alive], in triumph! and Mercutio slain!
Away to heaven, respective lenity,
And [fire-eyed] fury be my conduct now!
Now, Tybalt, take the "villain" back again   130
That late thou gav'st me; for Mercutio's soul
Is but a little way above our heads,
Staying for thine to keep him company.
Either thou, or I, or both, must go with him.
   Tyb. Thou, wretched boy, that didst consort him
     here,   135
Shalt with him hence.
   Rom.   This shall determine that.
               [They fight; Tybalt falls.
   Ben. Romeo, away, be gone!
The citizens are up, and Tybalt slain.
Stand not amaz'd; the Prince will doom thee death
If thou art taken. Hence, be gone, away!   140
   Rom. O, I am fortune's fool!
   Ben.   Why dost thou stay?
                    [Exit Romeo.

Enter CITIZENS.

   [A] Cit. Which way ran he that kill'd Mercutio?
Tybalt, that murderer, which way ran he?
   Ben. There lies that Tybalt.
   [A] Cit.   Up, sir, go with me;
I charge thee in the Prince's name, obey.   145

   Enter PRINCE, MONTAGUE, CAPULET, *their*
             WIVES, *and all.*

   Prin. Where are the vile beginners of this fray?
   Ben. O noble Prince, I can discover all
The unlucky manage of this fatal brawl.
There lies the man, slain by young Romeo,
That slew thy kinsman, brave Mercutio.   150
   La. Cap. Tybalt, my cousin! O my brother's
     child!
O Prince! O cousin! husband! O, the blood is
     spilt
Of my dear kinsman! Prince, as thou art true,
For blood of ours, shed blood of Montague.
O cousin, cousin!   155
   Prin. Benvolio, who began this bloody fray?
   Ben. Tybalt, here slain, whom Romeo's hand did
     slay!
Romeo that spoke him fair, bid him bethink
How nice the quarrel was, and urg'd withal
Your high displeasure; all this, uttered   160
With gentle breath, calm look, knees humbly bow'd,
Could not take truce with the unruly spleen
Of Tybalt deaf to peace, but that he tilts
With piercing steel at bold Mercutio's breast,
Who, all as hot, turns deadly point to point,   165
And, with a martial scorn, with one hand beats
Cold death aside, and with the other sends
It back to Tybalt, whose dexterity
Retorts it. Romeo he cries aloud,
"Hold, friends! friends, part!" and, swifter than
     his tongue,   170
His [agile] arm beats down their fatal points,
And 'twixt them rushes; underneath whose arm
An envious thrust from Tybalt hit the life
Of stout Mercutio, and then Tybalt fled;
But by and by comes back to Romeo,   175
Who had but newly entertain'd revenge,
And to't they go like lightning, for, ere I
Could draw to part them, was stout Tybalt slain,
And, as he fell, did Romeo turn and fly.
This is the truth, or let Benvolio die.   180
   La. Cap. He is a kinsman to the Montague;
Affection makes him false; he speaks not true.
Some twenty of them fought in this black strife,
And all those twenty could but kill one life.
I beg for justice, which thou, Prince, must give;
Romeo slew Tybalt, Romeo must not live.   186
   Prin. Romeo slew him, he slew Mercutio;
Who now the price of his dear blood doth owe?
   [Mon.] Not Romeo, Prince, he was Mercutio's
     friend;
His fault concludes but what the law should end,
The life of Tybalt.

---

114. **ally:** kinsman. 122. **aspir'd:** mounted to. 124. **moe:** more. 127. **[Alive]** Q₁. *He gan* Q₂. 128. **respective:** considerate. 129. **[fire-eyed]** Q₁. *fier end* Q₂; *fire and* F. **conduct:** guide. 139. **amaz'd:** stupefied. 147. **discover:** reveal. 148. **manage:** conduct. 159. **nice:** foolish. 171. **[agile]** Q₁. *aged* Q₂. 189. **[Mon.]** Q₄. *Capu* Q₂.

Prin.   And for that offence   191
Immediately we do exile him hence.
I have an interest in your [hate's] proceeding,
My blood for your rude brawls doth lie a-bleeding;
But I'll amerce you with so strong a fine   195
That you shall all repent the loss of mine.
[I] will be deaf to pleading and excuses;
Nor tears nor prayers shall purchase out abuses;
Therefore use none.   Let Romeo hence in haste,
Else, when he's found, that hour is his last.   200
Bear hence this body and attend our will.
Mercy but murders, pardoning those that kill.
                                        [Exeunt.

[SCENE II.   Capulet's orchard.]

Enter JULIET, alone.

Jul. Gallop apace, you fiery-footed steeds,
Towards Phœbus' lodging; such a waggoner
As Phaethon would whip you to the west,
And bring in cloudy night immediately.
Spread thy close curtain, love-performing night,   5
That runaway's eyes may wink, and Romeo
Leap to these arms untalk'd of and unseen!
Lovers can see to do their amorous rites
By their own beauties; or, if love be blind,
It best agrees with night.   Come, civil night,   10
Thou sober-suited matron, all in black,
And learn me how to lose a winning match,
Play'd for a pair of stainless maidenhoods.
Hood my unmann'd blood, bating in my cheeks,
With thy black mantle, till strange love grow bold,
Think true love acted simple modesty.   16
Come, night; come, Romeo; come, thou day in
         night;
For thou wilt lie upon the wings of night,
Whiter than new snow [on] a raven's back.
Come, gentle night, come, loving, black-brow'd
         night,   20
Give me my Romeo; and, when [he] shall die,
Take him and cut him out in little stars,
And he will make the face of heaven so fine
That all the world will be in love with night
And pay no worship to the garish sun.   25
O, I have bought the mansion of a love,
But not possess'd it, and, though I am sold,
Not yet enjoy'd.   So tedious is this day
As is the night before some festival
To an impatient child that hath new robes   30
And may not wear them.   O, here comes my nurse,

Enter NURSE, with cords.

And she brings news; and every tongue that speaks
But Romeo's name speaks heavenly eloquence.
Now, nurse, what news?   What hast thou there?
         The cords
That Romeo bid thee fetch?
   Nurse.   Ay, ay, the cords. 35
                                    [Throws them down.]
   Jul. Ay me! what news?   Why dost thou wring
         thy hands?
   Nurse. Ah, well-a-day! he's dead, he's dead, he's
         dead!
We are undone, lady, we are undone!
Alack the day! he's gone, he's kill'd, he's dead!
   Jul. Can heaven be so envious?
   Nurse.   Romeo can, 40
Though heaven cannot. O Romeo, Romeo!
Who ever would have thought it?   Romeo!
   Jul. What devil art thou, that dost torment me
         thus?
This torture should be roar'd in dismal hell.
Hath Romeo slain himself?   Say thou but ay,   45
And that bare vowel I shall poison more
Than the death-darting eye of cockatrice.
I am not I, if there be such an ay;
Or those eyes shut, that makes thee answer ay.
If he be slain, say ay; or if not, no.   50
Brief sounds determine [of] my weal or woe.
   Nurse. I saw the wound, I saw it with mine
         eyes, —
God save the mark! — here on his manly breast.
A piteous corse, a bloody piteous corse!
Pale, pale as ashes, all bedaub'd in blood,   55
All in gore-blood; I swounded at the sight.
   Jul. O, break, my heart! poor bankrupt, break
         at once!
To prison, eyes, ne'er look on liberty!
Vile earth, to earth resign; end motion here;
And thou and Romeo press [one] heavy bier!   60
   Nurse. O Tybalt, Tybalt, the best friend I
         had!
O courteous Tybalt! honest gentleman!
That ever I should live to see thee dead!
   Jul. What storm is this that blows so contrary?
Is Romeo slaught'red, and is Tybalt dead?   65
My dearest cousin, and my dearer lord?
Then, dreadful trumpet, sound the general doom!
For who is living, if those two are gone?
   Nurse. Tybalt is gone, and Romeo banished;
Romeo that kill'd him, he is banished.   70

193. [hate's] Q₁. hearts Q₂. 195. amerce: punish by fine. 197. [I] Q₁. It Q₂.
Sc. ii, 6. runaway's. Unexplained and probably corrupt. There is no apostrophe in the early texts. The stars, sun,
moon, Phaeton, Cupid, and many others have been suggested as the runaway. wink: close. 9. By Q₄. And by Q₂. 10.
civil: grave. 14. Hood: cover; unmann'd: untamed; bating: fluttering. Terms from falconry. The hawk was blindfolded to
keep it quiet. 19. [on] F₂. upon Q₂. 21. [he] Q₄. I Q₂. 47. cockatrice: fabulous animal which killed by its glance.
49. those eyes: i.e., Romeo's. 51. [of] F. Om. Q₂. 60. [one] Q₄. on Q₂.

Jul. O God! did Romeo's hand shed Tybalt's
    blood?
Nurse. It did, it did; alas the day, it did!
Jul. O serpent heart, hid with a flow'ring face!
Did ever dragon keep so fair a cave?
Beautiful tyrant! fiend angelical!   75
[Dove-feather'd] raven! wolvish ravening lamb!
Despised substance of divinest show!
Just opposite to what thou justly seem'st,
A [damned] saint, an honourable villain!
O nature, what hadst thou to do in hell,   80
When thou didst bower the spirit of a fiend
In mortal paradise of such sweet flesh?
Was ever book containing such vile matter
So fairly bound? O, that deceit should dwell
In such a gorgeous palace!
    Nurse.   There's no trust,   85
No faith, no honesty in men; all perjur'd,
All forsworn, all naught, all dissemblers.
Ah, where's my man? Give me some *aqua vitæ;*
These griefs, these woes, these sorrows make me old.
Shame come to Romeo!
    Jul.   Blister'd be thy tongue
For such a wish! he was not born to shame.   91
Upon his brow shame is asham'd to sit;
For 'tis a throne where honour may be crown'd
Sole monarch of the universal earth.
O, what a beast was I to chide at him!   95
    Nurse. Will you speak well of him that kill'd
        your cousin?
Jul. Shall I speak ill of him that is my husband?
Ah, poor my lord, what tongue shall smooth thy
    name,
When I, thy three-hours wife, have mangled it?
But, wherefore, villain, didst thou kill my cousin?
That villain cousin would have kill'd my hus-
    band.   101
Back, foolish tears, back to your native spring;
Your tributary drops belong to woe,
Which you, mistaking, offer up to joy.
My husband lives that Tybalt would have slain;
And Tybalt's dead that would have slain my hus-
    band.   106
All this is comfort; wherefore weep I then?
Some word there was, worser than Tybalt's death,
That murd'red me; I would forget it fain;
But, O, it presses to my memory   110
Like damned guilty deeds to sinners' minds:
"Tybalt is dead, and Romeo — banished."
That "banished," that one word "banished,"
Hath slain ten thousand Tybalts. Tybalt's death
Was woe enough, if it had ended there;   115
Or, if sour woe delights in fellowship
And needly will be rank'd with other griefs,

Why follow'd not, when she said, "Tybalt's dead,"
Thy father, or thy mother, nay, or both,   119
Which modern lamentation might have mov'd?
But with a rear-ward following Tybalt's death,
"Romeo is banished," to speak that word,
Is father, mother, Tybalt, Romeo, Juliet,
All slain, all dead. "Romeo is banished!"
There is no end, no limit, measure, bound,   125
In that word's death; no words can that woe sound.
Where is my father and my mother, nurse?
    Nurse. Weeping and wailing over Tybalt's corse.
Will you go to them? I will bring you thither.
    Jul. Wash they his wounds with tears? Mine
        shall be spent,   130
When theirs are dry, for Romeo's banishment.
Take up those cords. Poor ropes, you are beguil'd,
Both you and I, for Romeo is exil'd.
He made you for a highway to my bed,
But I, a maid, die maiden-widowed.   135
Come, cords, come, nurse; I'll to my wedding-bed;
And death, not Romeo, take my maidenhead!
    Nurse. Hie to your chamber. I'll find Romeo
To comfort you; I wot well where he is.
Hark ye, your Romeo will be here at night.   140
I'll to him; he is hid at Laurence' cell.
    Jul. O, find him! Give this ring to my true
        knight,
And bid him come to take his last farewell.
                           [*Exeunt.*

    [Scene III. *Friar Laurence's cell.*]

    Enter Friar Laurence, Romeo [*following*].

    Fri. L. Romeo, come forth; come forth, thou
        fearful man:
Affliction is enamour'd of thy parts,
And thou art wedded to calamity.
    Rom. Father, what news? What is the Prince's
        doom?
What sorrow craves acquaintance at my hand,   5
That I yet know not?
    Fri. L.   Too familiar
Is my dear son with such sour company.
I bring thee tidings of the Prince's doom.
    Rom. What less than dooms-day is the Prince's
        doom?
    Fri. L. A gentler judgement vanish'd from his
        lips,   10
Not body's death, but body's banishment.
    Rom. Ha, banishment! Be merciful, say
        "death";
For exile hath more terror in his look,
Much more than death. Do not say "banish-
    ment"!

76. **[Dove-feather'd]** (Theobald). *Ravenous dovefeatherd* Q2.   78. **Just:** exact.   79. **[damned]** Q4. *dimme* Q2.   81.
bower: lodge.   117. **needly:** necessarily.   120. **modern:** ordinary.   126. **sound:** (1) express, (2) fathom.
    Sc. iii, 1. **fearful:** full of fear.   10. **vanish'd:** issued.

Fri. L. Here from Verona art thou banished. 15
Be patient, for the world is broad and wide.
  Rom. There is no world without Verona walls,
But purgatory, torture, hell itself.
Hence "banished" is banish'd from the world,
And world's exile is death; then "banished" 20
Is death mis-term'd. Calling death "banishment,"
Thou cut'st my head off with a golden axe,
And smil'st upon the stroke that murders me.
  Fri. L. O deadly sin! O rude unthankfulness!
Thy fault our law calls death; but the kind prince,
Taking thy part, hath rush'd aside the law, 26
And turn'd that black word "death" to "banish-
    ment."
This is dear mercy, and thou seest it not.
  Rom. 'Tis torture, and not mercy. Heaven is
    here,
Where Juliet lives; and every cat and dog 30
And little mouse, every unworthy thing,
Live here in heaven and may look on her;
But Romeo may not. More validity,
More honourable state, more courtship lives
In carrion-flies than Romeo; they may seize 35
On the white wonder of dear Juliet's hand
And steal immortal blessing from her lips,
Who, even in pure and vestal modesty,
Still blush, as thinking their own kisses sin;
But Romeo may not; he is banished. 40
This may flies do, when I from this must fly;
They are free men, but I am banished:
And say'st thou yet that exile is not death?
Hadst thou no poison mix'd, no sharp-ground knife,
No sudden mean of death, though ne'er so mean,
But "banished" to kill me? — "Banished"? 46
O friar, the damned use that word in hell;
Howling attends it. How hast thou the heart,
Being a divine, a ghostly confessor,
A sin-absolver, and my friend profess'd, 50
To mangle me with that word "banished"?
  Fri. L. [Thou] fond mad man, hear me a little
    speak.
  Rom. O, thou wilt speak again of banishment.
  Fri. L. I'll give thee armour to keep off that
    word;
Adversity's sweet milk, philosophy, 55
To comfort thee, though thou art banished.
  Rom. Yet "banished"? Hang up philosophy!
Unless philosophy can make a Juliet,
Displant a town, reverse a prince's doom,
It helps not, it prevails not. Talk no more. 60
  Fri. L. O, then I see that madmen have no ears.
  Rom. How should they, when that wise men
    have no eyes?
  Fri. L. Let me dispute with thee of thy estate.

  Rom. Thou canst not speak of that thou dost
    not feel.
Wert thou as young as I, Juliet thy love, 65
An hour but married, Tybalt murdered,
Doting like me and like me banished,
Then mightst thou speak, then mightst thou tear
    thy hair,
And fall upon the ground, as I do now,
Taking the measure of an unmade grave. 70
                        [*Knocking within.*
  Fri. L. Arise; one knocks. Good Romeo, hide
    thyself.
  Rom. Not I; unless the breath of heart-sick
    groans,
Mist-like, infold me from the search of eyes.
                                  [*Knocking.*
  Fri. L. Hark, how they knock! Who's there?
    Romeo, arise;
Thou wilt be taken. — Stay a while! — Stand
    up; [*Knocking.* 75
Run to my study. — By and by! — God's will,
What simpleness is this! — I come, I come!
                                  [*Knocking.*
Who knocks so hard? Whence come you? What's
    your will?

Enter NURSE.

  Nurse. Let me come in, and you shall know my
    errand.
I come from Lady Juliet.
  Fri. L.   Welcome, then. 80
  Nurse. O holy friar, O, tell me, holy friar,
Where is my lady's lord, where's Romeo?
  Fri. L. There on the ground, with his own tears
    made drunk.
  Nurse. O, he is even in my mistress' case,
Just in her case! O woeful sympathy! 85
Piteous predicament! Even so lies she,
Blubb'ring and weeping, weeping and blubb'ring.
Stand up, stand up; stand, an you be a man.
For Juliet's sake, for her sake, rise and stand;
Why should you fall into so deep an O? 90
  Rom. Nurse!
  Nurse. Ah sir! ah sir! Death's the end of all.
  Rom. Spak'st thou of Juliet? How is it with
    her?
Doth not she think me an old murderer,
Now I have stain'd the childhood of our joy 95
With blood remov'd but little from her own?
Where is she? and how doth she? and what says
My conceal'd lady to our cancell'd love?
  Nurse. O, she says nothing, sir, but weeps and
    weeps;
And now falls on her bed; and then starts up, 100

---

17. **without:** outside. 33. **validity:** worth. 40–43. **But . . . death.** In Q₂ the order of the lines is 41, 43, 40, (41), 42. (41) reads *Flies may do this*, etc. 45. **mean . . . mean:** means . . . base. 52. **[Thou]** Q₁. *Then* Q₂. **fond:** foolish. 63. **dispute:** discuss. **estate:** situation. 90. **O:** i.e., groan. 98. **conceal'd:** secretly married.

And Tybalt calls; and then on Romeo cries,
And then down falls again.

Rom.   As if that name,
Shot from the deadly level of a gun,
Did murder her, as that name's cursed hand
Murder'd her kinsman.   O, tell me, friar, tell me,
In what vile part of this anatomy   106
Doth my name lodge?   Tell me, that I may sack
The hateful mansion.

                    [*He offers to stab himself, and the Nurse
                    snatches the dagger away.*

Fri. L.   Hold thy desperate hand!
Art thou a man?   Thy form cries out thou art;
Thy tears are womanish; thy wild acts denote   110
The unreasonable fury of a beast.
Unseemly woman in a seeming man,
And ill-beseeming beast in seeming both,
Thou hast amaz'd me!   By my holy order,
I thought thy disposition better temper'd.   115
Hast thou slain Tybalt?   Wilt thou slay thyself,
And slay thy lady that in thy life [lives],
By doing damned hate upon thyself?
Why rail'st thou on thy birth, the heaven, and
     earth?
Since birth, and heaven, and earth, all three do
     meet   120
In thee at once, which thou at once wouldst lose.
Fie, fie, thou sham'st thy shape, thy love, thy wit;
Which, like a usurer, abound'st in all,
And usest none in that true use indeed
Which should bedeck thy shape, thy love, thy wit.
Thy noble shape is but a form of wax,   126
Digressing from the valour of a man;
Thy dear love sworn but hollow perjury,
Killing that love which thou hast vow'd to cherish;
Thy wit, that ornament to shape and love,   130
Mis-shapen in the conduct of them both,
Like powder in a skilless soldier's flask,
Is set a-fire by thine own ignorance,
And thou dismemb'red with thine own defence.
What, rouse thee, man! thy Juliet is alive,   135
For whose dear sake thou wast but lately dead:
There art thou happy.   Tybalt would kill thee,
But thou slewest Tybalt: there art thou happy.
The law that threat'ned death becomes thy friend
And turns it to exile: there art thou happy.   140
A pack of blessings light upon thy back;
Happiness courts thee in her best array;
But, like a misbehav'd and sullen wench,
Thou [pout'st upon] thy fortune and thy love.
Take heed, take heed, for such die miserable.   145
Go, get thee to thy love, as was decreed;
Ascend her chamber; hence, and comfort her.
But look thou stay not till the watch be set,

For then thou canst not pass to Mantua,
Where thou shalt live till we can find a time   150
To blaze your marriage, reconcile your friends,
Beg pardon of the Prince, and call thee back
With twenty hundred thousand times more joy
Than thou went'st forth in lamentation.
Go before, nurse; commend me to thy lady;   155
And bid her hasten all the house to bed,
Which heavy sorrow makes them apt unto.
Romeo is coming.

Nurse.   O Lord, I could have stay'd here all the
     night
To hear good counsel.   O, what learning is!   160
My lord, I'll tell my lady you will come.

Rom.   Do so, and bid my sweet prepare to chide.
                    [*Nurse offers to go in, and turns again.*

Nurse.   Here, sir, a ring she bid me give you, sir.
Hie you, make haste, for it grows very late.

Rom.   How well my comfort is reviv'd by this!
                    [*Exit Nurse.*

Fri. L.   Go hence; good-night; and here stands all
     your state: 166
Either be gone before the watch be set,
Or by the break of day disguis'd from hence.
Sojourn in Mantua; I'll find out your man,
And he shall signify from time to time   170
Every good hap to you that chances here.
Give me thy hand; 'tis late.   Farewell; good-night.

Rom.   But that a joy past joy calls out on me,
It were a grief, so brief to part with thee.
Farewell.   [*Exeunt.*   175

[SCENE IV.   *A room in Capulet's house.*]

Enter CAPULET, LADY CAPULET, *and* PARIS.

Cap.   Things have fallen out, sir, so unluckily
That we have had no time to move our daughter.
Look you, she lov'd her kinsman Tybalt dearly,
And so did I.   Well, we were born to die.
'Tis very late, she'll not come down to-night;   5
I promise you, but for your company,
I would have been a-bed an hour ago.

Par.   These times of woe afford no times to woo.
Madam, good-night; commend me to your daughter.

La. Cap.   I will, and know her mind early to-
     morrow;   10
To-night she's mewed up to her heaviness.

Cap.   Sir Paris, I will make a desperate tender
Of my child's love.   I think she will be rul'd
In all respects by me; nay, more, I doubt it not.
Wife, go you to her ere you go to bed;   15
Acquaint her here of my son Paris' love;
And bid her — mark you me? — on Wednesday
     next —

---

117. **[lives]** F4.   *lies* Q2.   123. **Which:** who.   134. **defence:** weapon.   144. **[pout'st upon]** Q5.   *puts up* Q2.   151. **blaze:** announce.   166. **here ... state:** i.e., this is the situation.   174. **brief:** hastily.
     Sc. iv, 11. mewed: shut.   12. **desperate tender:** bold offer.

But, soft! what day is this?
  Par.   Monday, my lord.
  Cap. Monday! ha, ha! Well, Wednesday is too
    soon,
O' Thursday let it be, — o' Thursday, tell her, 20
She shall be married to this noble earl.
Will you be ready? Do you like this haste?
We'll keep no great ado, — a friend or two;
For, hark you, Tybalt being slain so late,
It may be thought we held him carelessly, 25
Being our kinsman, if we revel much;
Therefore we'll have some half a dozen friends,
And there an end. But what say you to Thursday?
  Par. My lord, I would that Thursday were to-
    morrow.
  Cap. Well, get you gone; o' Thursday be it,
    then. 30
Go you to Juliet ere you go to bed;
Prepare her, wife, against this wedding-day.
Farewell, my lord. Light to my chamber, ho!
Afore me! it is so very late that we
May call it early by and by. Good-night. 35
                           [*Exeunt.*

[SCENE V. *Capulet's orchard.*]

Enter ROMEO *and* JULIET, *aloft.*

  Jul. Wilt thou be gone? it is not yet near day.
It was the nightingale, and not the lark,
That pierc'd the fearful hollow of thine ear;
Nightly she sings on yond pomegranate-tree.
Believe me, love, it was the nightingale. 5
  Rom. It was the lark, the herald of the morn,
No nightingale. Look, love, what envious streaks
Do lace the severing clouds in yonder east.
Night's candles are burnt out, and jocund day
Stands tiptoe on the misty mountain tops. 10
I must be gone and live, or stay and die.
  Jul. Yond light is not day-light, I know it, I;
It is some meteor that the sun exhales
To be to thee this night a torch-bearer
And light thee on thy way to Mantua; 15
Therefore stay yet; thou need'st not to be gone.
  Rom. Let me be ta'en, let me be put to death;
I am content, so thou wilt have it so.
I'll say yon grey is not the morning's eye,
'Tis but the pale reflex of Cynthia's brow; 20
Nor that is not the lark, whose notes do beat
The vaulty heaven so high above our heads.
I have more care to stay than will to go.
Come, death, and welcome! Juliet wills it so.
How is't, my soul? Let's talk; it is not day. 25
  Jul. It is, it is! Hie hence, be gone, away!
It is the lark that sings so out of tune,

Straining harsh discords and unpleasing sharps.
Some say the lark makes sweet division;
This doth not so, for she divideth us. 30
Some say the lark and loathed toad change eyes;
O, now I would they had chang'd voices too,
Since arm from arm that voice doth us affray,
Hunting thee hence with hunt's-up to the day.
O, now be gone; more light and light it grows. 35
  Rom. More light and light; more dark and dark
    our woes!

Enter NURSE [*from the chamber*].

  Nurse. Madam!
  Jul. Nurse?
  Nurse. Your lady mother is coming to your
    chamber.
The day is broke; be wary, look about. [*Exit.* 40
  Jul. Then, window, let day in, and let life out.
  Rom. Farewell, farewell! One kiss, and I'll
    descend.   [*He goeth down.*
  Jul. Art thou gone so? Love, lord, ay, husband,
    friend!
I must hear from thee every day in the hour,
For in a minute there are many days. 45
O, by this count I shall be much in years
Ere I again behold my Romeo!
  Rom. [*From below.*] Farewell!
I will omit no opportunity
That may convey my greetings, love, to thee. 50
  Jul. O, think'st thou we shall ever meet again?
  Rom. I doubt it not; and all these woes shall
    serve
For sweet discourses in our times to come.
  Jul. O God, I have an ill-divining soul!
Methinks I see thee, now thou art [below], 55
As one dead in the bottom of a tomb.
Either my eyesight fails, or thou look'st pale.
  Rom. And trust me, love, in my eye so do you;
Dry sorrow drinks our blood. Adieu, adieu!
  Jul. O Fortune, Fortune! all men call thee
    fickle; 60
If thou art fickle, what dost thou with him
That is renown'd for faith? Be fickle, Fortune;
For then, I hope, thou wilt not keep him long,
But send him back.

Enter LADY CAPULET.

  La. Cap. Ho, daughter! are you up? 65
  Jul. Who is't that calls? It is my lady mother.
Is she not down so late, or up so early?
What unaccustom'd cause procures her hither?
  La. Cap. Why, how now, Juliet?
  Jul.   Madam, I am not well.

Sc. v, 20. **Cynthia's:** the moon's.   23. **care:** desire.   28. **sharps:** high notes.   29. **division:** melody.   34. **hunt's-up:** a song to waken hunters.   54. **ill-divining:** foreboding evil.   55. **[below]** Q₁. *so low* Q₂.   59. **Dry sorrow.** Sorrow was believed to dry up the blood.

La. Cap. Evermore weeping for your cousin's
      death?   70
What, wilt thou wash him from his grave with
      tears?
An if thou couldst, thou couldst not make him live;
Therefore, have done.   Some grief shows much of
      love,
But much of grief shows still some want of wit.
    Jul. Yet let me weep for such a feeling loss.   75
    La. Cap. So shall you feel the loss, but not the
      friend
Which you weep for.
    Jul.   Feeling so the loss,
I cannot choose but ever weep the friend.
    La. Cap. Well, girl, thou weep'st not so much
      for his death,   79
As that the villain lives which slaughter'd him.
    Jul. What villain, madam?
    La. Cap.   That same villain, Romeo.
    Jul. [*Aside.*] Villain and he be many miles
      asunder. —
God pardon [him]!   I do, with all my heart;
And yet no man like he doth grieve my heart.
    La. Cap. That is, because the traitor murderer
      lives.   85
    Jul. Ay, madam, from the reach of these my
      hands.
Would none but I might venge my cousin's death!
    La. Cap. We will have vengeance for it, fear thou
      not;
Then weep no more.   I'll send to one in Mantua,
Where that same banish'd runagate doth live,   90
Shall give him such an unaccustom'd dram
That he shall soon keep Tybalt company;
And then, I hope, thou wilt be satisfied.
    Jul. Indeed, I never shall be satisfied
With Romeo, till I behold him — dead —   95
Is my poor heart, so for a kinsman vex'd.
Madam, if you could find out but a man
To bear a poison, I would temper it
That Romeo should, upon receipt thereof,   99
Soon sleep in quiet.   O, how my heart abhors
To hear him nam'd, and cannot come to him
To wreak the love I bore my cousin [Tybalt]
Upon his body that hath slaughter'd him!
    La. Cap. Find thou the means, and I'll find such
      a man.
But now I'll tell thee joyful tidings, girl.   105
    Jul. And joy comes well in such a needy time.
What are they, [I] beseech your ladyship?
    La. Cap. Well, well, thou hast a careful father,
      child;
One who, to put thee from thy heaviness,

Hath sorted out a sudden day of joy   110
That thou expects not nor I look'd not for.
    Jul. Madam, in happy time, what day is that?
    La. Cap. Marry, my child, early next Thursday
      morn
The gallant, young, and noble gentleman,
The County Paris, at Saint Peter's Church,   115
Shall happily make thee there a joyful bride.
    Jul. Now, by Saint Peter's Church and Peter
      too,
He shall not make me there a joyful bride.
I wonder at this haste that I must wed
Ere he that should be husband comes to woo.   120
I pray you, tell my lord and father, madam,
I will not marry yet; and, when I do, I swear,
It shall be Romeo, whom you know I hate,
Rather than Paris.   These are news indeed!
    La. Cap. Here comes your father; tell him so
      yourself,   125
And see how he will take it at your hands.

              Enter CAPULET *and* NURSE

    Cap. When the sun sets, the [air] doth drizzle
      dew;
But for the sunset of my brother's son
It rains downright.
How now! a conduit, girl?   What, still in tears?
Evermore show'ring?   In one little body   131
Thou counterfeits a bark, a sea, a wind:
For still thy eyes, which I may call the sea,
Do ebb and flow with tears; the bark thy body is,
Sailing in this salt flood; the winds, thy sighs,   135
Who, raging with thy tears, and they with them,
Without a sudden calm, will overset
Thy tempest-tossed body.   How now, wife!
Have you delivered to her our decree?
    La. Cap. Ay, sir; but she will none, she gives you
      thanks.   140
I would the fool were married to her grave!
    Cap. Soft! take me with you, take me with you,
      wife.
How! will she none?   Doth she not give us thanks?
Is she not proud?   Doth she not count her blest,
Unworthy as she is, that we have wrought   145
So worthy a gentleman to be her bride?
    Jul. Not proud you have; but thankful that you
      have.
Proud can I never be of what I hate;
But thankful even for hate that is meant love.
    Cap. How how, how how, chop-logic!   What is
      this?   150
"Proud," and "I thank you," and "I thank you
      not;"

And yet "not proud."   Mistress minion, you,
Thank me no thankings, nor proud me no prouds,
But fettle your fine joints 'gainst Thursday next,
To go with Paris to Saint Peter's Church,   155
Or I will drag thee on a hurdle thither.
Out, you green-sickness carrion!   Out, you bag-
    gage!
You tallow-face!
  La. Cap.   Fie, fie! what, are you mad?
  Jul. Good father, I beseech you on my knees,
Hear me with patience but to speak a word.   160
  Cap. Hang thee, young baggage! disobedient
    wretch!
I tell thee what: get thee to church o' Thursday,
Or never after look me in the face.
Speak not, reply not, do not answer me!
My fingers itch.   Wife, we scarce thought us blest
That God had lent us but this only child;   166
But now I see this one is one too much,
And that we have a curse in having her.
Out on her, hilding!
  Nurse.   God in heaven bless her!
You are to blame, my lord, to rate her so.   170
  Cap. And why, my lady Wisdom?   Hold your
    tongue,
Good prudence; smatter with your gossips, go.
  Nurse. I speak no treason.
  [*Cap.*]   O, God ye god-den.
  [*Nurse.*] May not one speak?
  Cap.   Peace, you mumbling fool!
Utter your gravity o'er a gossip's bowl;   175
For here we need it not.
  La. Cap.   You are too hot.
  Cap. God's bread! it makes me mad.
Day, night, hour, tide, time, work, play,
Alone, in company, still my care hath been
To have her match'd; and having now provided 180
A gentleman of noble parentage,
Of fair demesnes, youthful and nobly [train'd],
Stuff'd, as they say, with honourable parts,
Proportion'd as one's thought would wish a man;
And then to have a wretched puling fool,   185
A whining mammet, in her fortune's tender
To answer, "I'll not wed; I cannot love,
I am too young; I pray you, pardon me."
But, an you will not wed, I'll pardon you.
Graze where you will, you shall not house with me.
Look to't, think on't, I do not use to jest.   191
Thursday is near; lay hand on heart, advise.
An you be mine, I'll give you to my friend;
An you be not, hang, beg, starve, die in the streets,
For, by my soul, I'll ne'er acknowledge thee,   195
Nor what is mine shall never do thee good.

Trust to't, bethink you; I'll not be forsworn.
                                    [*Exit.*
  Jul. Is there no pity sitting in the clouds,
That sees into the bottom of my grief?
O, sweet my mother, cast me not away!   200
Delay this marriage for a month, a week;
Or, if you do not, make the bridal bed
In that dim monument where Tybalt lies.
  La. Cap. Talk not to me, for I'll not speak a word.
Do as thou wilt, for I have done with thee.   205
                                    [*Exit.*
  Jul. O God! — O nurse, how shall this be pre-
    vented?
My husband is on earth, my faith in heaven;
How shall that faith return again to earth,
Unless that husband send it me from heaven
By leaving earth?   Comfort me, counsel me!   210
Alack, alack, that heaven should practise strat-
    agems
Upon so soft a subject as myself!
What say'st thou?   Hast thou not a word of joy?
Some comfort, nurse.
  Nurse.   Faith, here it is.
Romeo is banish'd; and all the world to nothing 215
That he dares ne'er come back to challenge you;
Or, if he do, it needs must be by stealth.
Then, since the case so stands as now it doth,
I think it best you married with the County.
O, he's a lovely gentleman!   220
Romeo's a dishclout to him.   An eagle, madam,
Hath not so green, so quick, so fair an eye
As Paris hath.   Beshrew my very heart,
I think you are happy in this second match,
For it excels your first; or if it did not,   225
Your first is dead; or 'twere as good he were
As living here and you no use of him.
  Jul. Speak'st thou from thy heart?
  Nurse. And from my soul too; else beshrew them
    both.
  Jul. Amen!
  Nurse. What?
  Jul. Well, thou hast comforted me marvellous
    much.   230
Go in; and tell my lady I am gone,
Having displeas'd my father, to Laurence' cell,
To make confession and to be absolv'd.
  Nurse. Marry, I will; and this is wisely done.
                                    [*Exit.*]
  Jul. Ancient damnation!   O most wicked fiend!
Is it more sin to wish me thus forsworn,   236
Or to dispraise my lord with that same tongue
Which she hath prais'd him with above compare
So many thousand times?   Go, counsellor;

152. **minion:** spoiled child.   154. **fettle:** prepare.   156. **hurdle:** conveyance for criminals.   157. **green-sickness:** anemia (suggesting Juliet's paleness).   172. **smatter:** chatter.   173. [*Cap.*] Q₄.   Given to Nurse in Q₂.   182. **demesnes:**
estates.   [**train'd**] Q₁.   *liand* Q₂.   *allied* F.   186. **mammet:** doll.   **in ... tender:** when good fortune is offered her.   192.
advise: consider.   227. **here:** i.e., in this world.

Thou and my bosom henceforth shall be twain.
I'll to the friar, to know his remedy;   241
If all else fail, myself have power to die.   [*Exit.*

[ACT IV]

[SCENE I. *Friar Laurence's cell.*]

Enter FRIAR LAURENCE *and* PARIS.

Fri. L. On Thursday, sir? The time is very
    short.
Par. My father Capulet will have it so,
And I am nothing slow to slack his haste.
Fri. L. You say you do not know the lady's
    mind.
Uneven is the course, I like it not.   5
Par. Immoderately she weeps for Tybalt's
    death,
And therefore have I little [talk'd] of love,
For Venus smiles not in a house of tears.
Now, sir, her father counts it dangerous
That she do give her sorrow so much sway,   10
And in his wisdom hastes our marriage
To stop the inundation of her tears;
Which, too much minded by herself alone,
May be put from her by society.
Now do you know the reason of this haste.   15
Fri. L. [*Aside.*] I would I knew not why it should
    be slow'd.
Look, sir, here comes the lady toward my cell.

Enter JULIET.

Par. Happily met, my lady and my wife!
Jul. That may be, sir, when I may be a wife.
Par. That may be must be, love, on Thursday
    next.   20
Jul. What must be shall be.
Fri. L.   That's a certain text.
Par. Come you to make confession to this
    father?
Jul. To answer that, I should confess to you.
Par. Do not deny to him that you love me.
Jul. I will confess to you that I love him.   25
Par. So will ye, I am sure, that you love me.
Jul. If I do so, it will be of more price,
Being spoke behind your back, than to your face.
Par. Poor soul, thy face is much abus'd with tears.
Jul. The tears have got small victory by that,   30
For it was bad enough before their spite.
Par. Thou wrong'st it, more than tears, with
    that report.
Jul. That is no slander, sir, which is a truth;
And what I spake, I spake it to my face.

Par. Thy face is mine, and thou hast sland'red
    it.   35
Jul. It may be so, for it is not mine own.
Are you at leisure, holy father, now;
Or shall I come to you at evening mass?
Fri. L. My leisure serves me, pensive daughter,
    now.
My lord, we must entreat the time alone.   40
Par. God shield I should disturb devotion!
Juliet, on Thursday early will I rouse ye;
Till then, adieu; and keep this holy kiss.   [*Exit.*
Jul. O, shut the door! and when thou hast done
    so,
Come weep with me, past hope, past care, past
    help!   45
Fri. L. O Juliet, I already know thy grief;
It strains me past the compass of my wits.
I hear thou must, and nothing may prorogue it,
On Thursday next be married to this County.
Jul. Tell me not, friar, that thou hear'st of this,   50
Unless thou tell me how I may prevent it.
If, in thy wisdom, thou canst give no help,
Do thou but call my resolution wise,
And with this knife I'll help it presently.
God join'd my heart and Romeo's, thou our hands;
And ere this hand, by thee to Romeo's seal'd,   56
Shall be the label to another deed,
Or my true heart with treacherous revolt
Turn to another, this shall slay them both.
Therefore, out of thy long-experienc'd time,   60
Give me some present counsel, or, behold,
'Twixt my extremes and me this bloody knife
Shall play the umpire, arbitrating that
Which the commission of thy years and art
Could to no issue of true honour bring.   65
Be not so long to speak; I long to die
If what thou speak'st speak not of remedy.
Fri. L. Hold, daughter! I do spy a kind of hope,
Which craves as desperate an execution
As that is desperate which we would prevent.   70
If, rather than to marry County Paris,
Thou hast the strength of will to [slay] thyself,
Then is it likely thou wilt undertake
A thing like death to chide away this shame,
That cop'st with Death himself to scape from it;   75
And, if thou dar'st, I'll give thee remedy.
Jul. O, bid me leap, rather than marry Paris,
From off the battlements of any tower,
Or walk in thievish ways, or bid me lurk
Where serpents are; chain me with roaring bears,   80
Or hide me nightly in a charnel-house,
O'er-cover'd quite with dead men's rattling bones,
With reeky shanks and yellow chapless skulls;
Or bid me go into a new-made grave

Act IV, sc. i, 5. **Uneven:** irregular.   7. **[talk'd]** Q₅. *talke* Q₂.   41. **shield:** forbid.   45. **care** Q₂. *cure* Q₁.   57. **label:** seal.
62. **extremes:** extremities.   64. **commission:** authority.   72. **[slay]** Q₁. *stay* Q₂.   75. **cop'st with:** wouldest encounter.
79. **thievish:** full of thieves.   81. **hide** Q₂. *shut* Q₁.   83. **reeky:** foul smelling. **chapless:** jawless.

And hide me with a dead man in his [shroud], —
Things that, to hear them told, have made me trem-
ble;   86
And I will do it without fear or doubt,
To live an unstain'd wife to my sweet love.
   Fri. L. Hold, then. Go home, be merry, give
consent
To marry Paris. Wednesday is to-morrow.   90
To-morrow night look that thou lie alone;
Let not the nurse lie with thee in thy chamber.
Take thou this vial, being then in bed,
And this [distilled] liquor drink thou off;
When presently through all thy veins shall run   95
A cold and drowsy humour; for no pulse
Shall keep his native progress, but surcease;
No warmth, no [breath] shall testify thou livest;
The roses in thy lips and cheeks shall fade
To [paly] ashes, thy eyes' windows fall,   100
Like death when he shuts up the day of life;
Each part, depriv'd of supple government,
Shall, stiff and stark and cold, appear like death:
And in this borrowed likeness of shrunk death
Thou shalt continue two and forty hours,   105
And then awake as from a pleasant sleep.
Now, when the bridegroom in the morning comes
To rouse thee from thy bed, there art thou dead.
Then, as the manner of our country is,
[In] thy best robes uncovered on the bier   110
Thou shall be borne to that same ancient vault
Where all the kindred of the Capulets lie.
In the mean time, against thou shalt awake,
Shall Romeo by my letters know our drift,
And hither shall he come; and he and I   115
Will watch thy waking, and that very night
Shall Romeo bear thee hence to Mantua.
And this shall free thee from this present shame;
If no inconstant toy, nor womanish fear,
Abate thy valour in the acting it.   120
   Jul. Give me, give me! O, tell not me of fear!
   Fri. L. Hold; get you gone, be strong and pros-
perous
In this resolve. I'll send a friar with speed
To Mantua, with my letters to thy lord.
   Jul. Love give me strength! and strength shall
help afford.   125
Farewell, dear father!   [*Exeunt.*

[SCENE II. *Hall in Capulet's house.*]

Enter CAPULET, LADY CAPULET, NURSE, *and*
SERVING-MEN, *two or three.*

   Cap. So many guests invite as here are writ.
[*Exit 1. Servant.*]

Sirrah, go hire me twenty cunning cooks.
   [2.] *Serv.* You shall have none ill, sir; for I'll try
if they can lick their fingers.
   Cap. How canst thou try them so?   5
   [2.] *Serv.* Marry, sir, 'tis an ill cook that cannot
lick his own fingers; therefore he that cannot lick his
fingers goes not with me.
   Cap. Go, be gone.   [*Exit 2. Servant.*]
We shall be much unfurnish'd for this time.   10
What, is my daughter gone to Friar Laurence?
   Nurse. Ay, forsooth.
   Cap. Well, he may chance to do some good on
her.
A peevish self-will'd harlotry it is.

Enter JULIET.

   Nurse. See where she comes from shrift with
merry look.   15
   Cap. How now, my headstrong! where have you
been gadding?
   Jul. Where I have learn'd me to repent the sin
Of disobedient opposition
To you and your behests, and am enjoin'd
By holy Laurence to fall prostrate here   20
And beg your pardon. Pardon, I beseech you!
Henceforward I am ever rul'd by you.
   Cap. Send for the County; go tell him of this.
I'll have this knot knit up to-morrow morning.
   Jul. I met the youthful lord at Laurence' cell   25
And gave him what becomed love I might,
Not stepping o'er the bounds of modesty.
   Cap. Why, I am glad on't; this is well; stand
up.
This is as 't should be. Let me see the County;
Ay, marry, go, I say, and fetch him hither.   30
Now, afore God! this reverend holy friar,
All our whole city is much bound to him.
   Jul. Nurse, will you go with me into my closet
To help me sort such needful ornaments
As you think fit to furnish me to-morrow?   35
   La. Cap. No, not till Thursday; there is time
enough.
   Cap. Go, nurse, go with her; we'll to church to-
morrow.   [*Exeunt Juliet and Nurse.*
   La. Cap. We shall be short in our provision;
'Tis now near night.
   Cap.   Tush, I will stir about,
And all things shall be well, I warrant thee, wife;
Go thou to Juliet, help to deck up her.   41
I'll not to bed to-night; let me alone;
I'll play the housewife for this once. What, ho!
They are all forth. Well, I will walk myself
To County Paris, to prepare up him   45

85. [shroud] Q4. Om. Q2. 94. [distilled] Q1. *distilling* Q2. 98. [breath] Q1. *breast* Q2. 100. [paly] Q5. *many* Q2.
110. [In] *Is* Q2. bier. After l. 110 Qq Ff print a line "Be borne to burial in thy kindreds grave," probably an unerased
alternative for l. 111. 113. **against:** in preparation for the time when. 119. **toy:** whim.
Sc. ii, 14. **peevish:** refractory. **harlotry:** wench. 26. **becomed:** fitting.

Against to-morrow.　My heart is wondrous light,
Since this same wayward girl is so reclaim'd.
　　　　　　　　　　　　　　　　　　　[*Exeunt.*

[SCENE III.　*Juliet's chamber.*]
Enter JULIET *and* NURSE.

Jul. Ay, those attires are best; but, gentle nurse,
I pray thee, leave me to myself to-night;
For I have need of many orisons
To move the heavens to smile upon my state,
Which, well thou know'st, is cross and full of sin. 5

Enter LADY CAPULET.

La. Cap. What, are you busy, ho?　Need you my
　　help?
Jul. No, madam; we have cull'd such necessaries
As are behoveful for our state to-morrow.
So please you, let me now be left alone,
And let the nurse this night sit up with you;　10
For, I am sure, you have your hands full all,
In this so sudden business.
La. Cap.　　　　　　　Good-night.
Get thee to bed, and rest; for thou hast need.
　　　　　　[*Exeunt* [*Lady Capulet and Nurse*].
Jul. Farewell!　God knows when we shall meet
　　again.
I have a faint cold fear thrills through my veins, 15
That almost freezes up the heat of life.
I'll call them back again to comfort me.
Nurse! — What should she do here?
My dismal scene I needs must act alone.
Come, vial.　　　　　　　　　　　　20
What if this mixture do not work at all?
Shall I be married then to-morrow morning?
No, no; this shall forbid it.　Lie thou there.
　　　　　　　　　　[*Laying down her dagger.*]
What if it be a poison, which the friar
Subtly hath minist'red to have me dead,　25
Lest in this marriage he should be dishonour'd
Because he married me before to Romeo?
I fear it is; and yet, methinks, it should not,
For he hath still been tried a holy man.
How if, when I am laid into the tomb,　30
I wake before the time that Romeo
Come to redeem me?　There's a fearful point!
Shall I not then be stifled in the vault,
To whose foul mouth no healthsome air breathes in,
And there die strangled ere my Romeo comes?　35
Or, if I live, is it not very like
The horrible conceit of death and night,
Together with the terror of the place, —

As in a vault, an ancient receptacle,
Where, for this many hundred years, the bones　40
Of all my buried ancestors are pack'd;
Where bloody Tybalt, yet but green in earth,
Lies fest'ring in his shroud; where, as they say,
At some hours in the night spirits resort; —
Alack, alack, is it not like that I,　45
So early waking, — what with loathsome smells,
And shrieks like mandrakes' torn out of the earth,
That living mortals, hearing them, run mad; —
O, if I wake, shall I not be distraught,
Environed with all these hideous fears,　50
And madly play with my forefathers' joints,
And pluck the mangled Tybalt from his shroud,
And, in this rage, with some great kinsman's bone
As with a club, dash out my desperate brains?
O, look! methinks I see my cousin's ghost　55
Seeking out Romeo, that did spit his body
Upon a rapier's point.　Stay, Tybalt, stay!
Romeo, [I come!　This do I] drink to thee.
　　　[*She falls upon her bed, within the curtains.*

[SCENE IV.　*Hall in Capulet's house.*]
Enter LADY CAPULET *and* NURSE.

La. Cap. Hold, take these keys and fetch more
　　spices, nurse.
Nurse. They call for dates and quinces in the
　　pastry.

Enter CAPULET.

Cap. Come, stir, stir, stir! the second cock hath
　　crow'd,
The curfew-bell hath rung, 'tis three o'clock.
Look to the bak'd meats, good Angelica;　5
Spare not for cost.
Nurse.　　　　　　Go, you cot-quean, go,
Get you to bed.　Faith, you'll be sick to-morrow
For this night's watching.
Cap. No, not a whit!　What! I have watch'd ere
　　now
All night for lesser cause, and ne'er been sick.　10
La. Cap. Ay, you have been a mouse-hunt in
　　your time;
But I will watch you from such watching now.
　　　　　　[*Exeunt Lady Capulet and Nurse.*
Cap. A jealous-hood, a jealous-hood!

Enter three or four [SERVING-MEN,] *with spits,
logs, and baskets.*
　　　　　　　　　　　　　　Now, fellow,
What's there?

Sc. iii, 5. **cross:** perverse.　8. **behoveful:** needful.　29. **still:** ever.　**tried:** proved.　37. **conceit:** idea.　47. **mandrakes'.**
The root of the mandrake plant was believed to utter a shriek when pulled up.　58. **[I come!　This do I]** Q₁.　*Romeo, Romeo, heeres drinke,* I Q₂.

Sc. iv, 2. **pastry:** pastry-room, pantry.　5. **bak'd meats:** meat pies.　6. **cot-quean:** man who plays housewife.　11. **mouse-hunt:** woman-chaser.　13. **jealous-hood:** jealous person.

[*1. Serv.*] Things for the cook, sir; but I know not
what.

Cap. Make haste, make haste. [*Exit 1. Serv.*]
Sirrah, fetch drier logs: 15
Call Peter, he will show thee where they are.

[*2. Serv.*] I have a head, sir, that will find out logs,
And never trouble Peter for the matter.

Cap. Mass, and well said; a merry whoreson, ha!
Thou shalt be logger-head. [*Exit 2. Serv.*] Good
[faith], 'tis day. 20
The County will be here with music straight,
For so he said he would. I hear him near.
[*Music within.*]
Nurse! Wife! What, ho! What, nurse, I say!

Re-enter NURSE.

Go waken Juliet, go and trim her up;
I'll go and chat with Paris. Hie, make haste, 25
Make haste; the bridegroom he is come already.
Make haste, I say. [*Exeunt.*]

[SCENE V. *Juliet's chamber.*]

[*Enter* NURSE.]

Nurse. Mistress! what, mistress! Juliet! —
Fast, I warrant her, she. —
Why, lamb! why, lady! fie, you slug-a-bed!
Why, love! I say, madam! sweetheart! why, bride!
What, not a word? You take your penny-worths
now;
Sleep for a week; for the next night, I warrant, 5
The County Paris hath set up his rest
That you shall rest but little. God forgive me!
Marry, and amen, how sound is she asleep!
I needs must wake her. Madam, madam, madam!
Ay, let the County take you in your bed; 10
He'll fright you up, i' faith. Will it not be?
[*Draws back the curtains.*]
What, dress'd, and in your clothes! and down again!
I must needs wake you. Lady! lady! lady!
Alas, alas! Help, help! my lady's dead!
O, well-a-day, that ever I was born! 15
Some *aqua vitæ*, ho! My lord! my lady!

Enter LADY CAPULET.

La. Cap. What noise is here?
Nurse. O lamentable day!
La. Cap. What is the matter?
Nurse. Look, look! O heavy day!
La. Cap. O me, O me! My child, my only life,
Revive, look up, or I will die with thee! 20
Help, help! Call help.

Enter CAPULET.

Cap. For shame, bring Juliet forth; her lord is
come.
Nurse. She's dead, deceas'd, she's dead; alack
the day!
La. Cap. Alack the day, she's dead, she's dead,
she's dead!
Cap. Ha! let me see her. Out, alas! she's cold;
Her blood is settled, and her joints are stiff; 26
Life and these lips have long been separated.
Death lies on her like an untimely frost
Upon the sweetest flower of all the field.
Nurse. O lamentable day!
La. Cap. O woeful time! 30
Cap. Death, that hath ta'en her hence to make
me wail,
Ties up my tongue, and will not let me speak.

Enter FRIAR LAURENCE *and* PARIS, *with*
MUSICIANS.

Fri. L. Come, is the bride ready to go to church?
Cap. Ready to go, but never to return. —
O son! the night before thy wedding-day 35
Hath Death lain with thy wife. There she lies,
Flower as she was, deflowered by him.
Death is my son-in-law, Death is my heir;
My daughter he hath wedded. I will die
And leave him all; life, living, all is Death's. 40
Par. Have I thought [long] to see this morning's
face,
And doth it give me such a sight as this?
La. Cap. Accurs'd, unhappy, wretched, hateful
day!
Most miserable hour that e'er Time saw
In lasting labour of his pilgrimage! 45
But one, poor one, one poor and loving child,
But one thing to rejoice and solace in,
And cruel Death hath catch'd it from my sight!
Nurse. O woe! O woeful, woeful, woeful day!
Most lamentable day, most woeful day, 50
That ever, ever, I did yet behold!
O day! O day! O day! O hateful day!
Never was seen so black a day as this.
O woeful day, O woeful day!
Par. Beguil'd, divorced, wronged, spited, slain!
Most detestable Death, by thee beguil'd, 56
By cruel cruel thee quite overthrown!
O love! O life! not life, but love in death!
Cap. Despis'd, distressed, hated, martyr'd,
kill'd!
Uncomfortable time, why cam'st thou now 60
To murder, murder our solemnity?
O child! O child! my soul, and not my child!

14. [*1. Serv.*] (Capell). *Fel.* (i.e., Fellow) Q₂. 17. [*2. Serv.*] (Capell). *Fel.* Q₂. 20. **logger-head:** blockhead. [**faith**]
Q₄. *father* Q₂.
Sc. v, 2. **Fast:** i.e., fast asleep. 6. **set...rest:** resolved. 41. **thought [long]** Q₃: longed. *thought love* Q₂.

Dead art thou! Alack! my child is dead;
And with my child my joys are buried.

  Fri. L. Peace, ho, for shame! Confusion's
[cure] lives not   65
In these confusions. Heaven and yourself
Had part in this fair maid; now heaven hath all,
And all the better is it for the maid.
Your part in her you could not keep from death,
But heaven keeps his part in eternal life.   70
The most you sought was her promotion,
For 'twas your heaven she should be advanc'd;
And weep ye now, seeing she is advanc'd
Above the clouds, as high as heaven itself?
O, in this love, you love your child so ill   75
That you run mad, seeing that she is well.
She's not well married that lives married long;
But she's best married that dies married young.
Dry up your tears, and stick your rosemary
On this fair corse; and, as the custom is,   80
[In all] her best array bear her to church;
For though [fond] nature bids us all lament,
Yet nature's tears are reason's merriment.

  Cap. All things that we ordained festival,
Turn from their office to black funeral;   85
Our instruments to melancholy bells,
Our wedding cheer to a sad burial feast,
Our solemn hymns to sullen dirges change,
Our bridal flowers serve for a buried corse,
And all things change them to the contrary.   90

  Fri. L. Sir, go you in; and, madam, go with him;
And go, Sir Paris; every one prepare
To follow this fair corse unto her grave.
The heavens do lour upon you for some ill;
Move them no more by crossing their high will.   95
    [*Exeunt* [*Capulet, Lady Capulet, Paris, and
      Friar*].

  [*1.*] *Mus.* Faith, we may put up our pipes and be
gone.

  Nurse. Honest good fellows, ah, put up, put up;
For, well you know, this is a pitiful case.   [*Exit.*

  [*1.*] *Mus.* Ay, by my troth, the case may be
amended.   101

Enter [PETER].

  Pet. Musicians, O, musicians, "Heart's ease,
Heart's ease!" O, an you will have me live, play
"Heart's ease."

  [*1.*] *Mus.* Why "Heart's ease"?   105

  Pet. O, musicians, because my heart itself plays
"My heart is full [of woe]." O, play me some merry
dump to comfort me.

  [*1.*] *Mus.* Not a dump we; 'tis no time to play
now.   110

  Pet. You will not, then?

  [*1.*] *Mus.* No.

  Pet. I will then give it you soundly.

  [*1.*] *Mus.* What will you give us?

  Pet. No money, on my faith, but the gleek; I will
give you the minstrel.   116

  [*1.*] *Mus.* Then will I give you the serving-creature.

  Pet. Then will I lay the serving-creature's dagger
on your pate. I will carry no crotchets; I'll *re* you,
I'll *fa* you. Do you note me?   121

  [*1.*] *Mus.* An you *re* us and *fa* us, you note us.

  [*2.*] *Mus.* Pray you, put up your dagger, and put
out your wit.

  Pet. Then have at you with my wit! I will dry-
beat you with an iron wit, and put up my iron dagger. Answer me like men: 127
    "When griping griefs the heart doth wound,
      [And doleful dumps the mind oppress,]
    Then music with her silver sound" —   130
why "silver sound"? Why "music with her silver
sound"? What say you, Simon Catling?

  [*1.*] *Mus.* Marry, sir, because silver hath a sweet
sound.   134

  Pet. [Pretty!] What say you, Hugh Rebeck?

  2. Mus. I say, "silver sound," because musicians sound for silver.

  Pet. [Pretty] too! What say you, James Sound-
post?

  3. Mus. Faith, I know not what to say.   140

  Pet. O, I cry you mercy; you are the singer; I will
say for you. It is "music with her silver sound,"
because musicians have no gold for sounding:
    "Then music with her silver sound   145
    With speedy help doth lend redress."   [*Exit.*

  1. Mus. What a pestilent knave is this same!

  2. Mus. Hang him, Jack! Come, we'll in here,
tarry for the mourners, and stay dinner.   150
    [*Exeunt.*

[ACT V]

[SCENE I. *Mantua. A street.*]

Enter ROMEO.

  Rom. If I may trust the flattering truth of sleep,
My dreams presage some joyful news at hand.
My bosom's lord sits lightly in his throne,
And all this day an unaccustom'd spirit

65. [cure] (Theobald). *care* Q2. 79. **rosemary:** an herb (symbolic of remembrance). 81. **[In all]** Q1. *And in* Q2. 82. [fond] F2. *some* Q2. 102. s.d. [PETER] Q4. *Will Kemp* Q2. Kemp, the low comedian in Shakespeare's company, apparently acted Peter. 107. [of woe] Q4. Om. Q2. 108. **dump:** mournful tune. 115. **gleek:** gibe. 120. **carry:** endure. **crotchets:** (1) whims, (2) quarter notes. 124. **put out:** exert. 125. **Then... wit.** So Q4. Cont. to *2. Mus.* in Q2. 129. **[And ... oppress]** Q1. Om. Q2. 135, 138. **[Pretty]** (Pope). *Prates* Q2. 141. **singer.** Peter's joke is that as a singer the musician can only *sing*, not *say.*
Act V, sc. i, 3. **bosom's lord:** heart.

Lifts me above the ground with cheerful thoughts.
I dreamt my lady came and found me dead — 6
Strange dream, that gives a dead man leave to
    think! —
And breath'd such life with kisses in my lips
That I reviv'd and was an emperor.
Ah me! how sweet is love itself possess'd, 10
When but love's shadows are so rich in joy!

Enter BALTHASAR, *his man, booted.*

News from Verona! — How now, Balthasar!
Dost thou not bring me letters from the friar?
How doth my lady? Is my father well?
How [fares my] Juliet? that I ask again; 15
For nothing can be ill, if she be well.
  Bal. Then she is well, and nothing can be ill.
Her body sleeps in Capel's monument,
And her immortal part with angels lives.
I saw her laid low in her kindred's vault, 20
And presently took post to tell it you.
O, pardon me for bringing these ill news,
Since you did leave it for my office, sir.
  Rom. Is it [even] so? Then I [defy] you,
    stars!
Thou know'st my lodging; get me ink and paper 25
And hire post-horses; I will hence to-night.
  Bal. I do beseech you, sir, have patience.
Your looks are pale and wild, and do import
Some misadventure.
  Rom.   Tush, thou art deceiv'd:
Leave me, and do the thing I bid thee do. 30
Hast thou no letters to me from the friar?
  Bal. No, my good lord.
  Rom.   No matter; get thee gone
And hire those horses; I'll be with thee straight.
                         [*Exit Balthasar.*
Well, Juliet, I will lie with thee to-night.
Let's see for means. O mischief, thou art swift 35
To enter in the thoughts of desperate men!
I do remember an apothecary, —
And hereabouts 'a dwells, — which late I noted
In tatt'red weeds, with overwhelming brows,
Culling of simples; meagre were his looks, 40
Sharp misery had worn him to the bones;
And in his needy shop a tortoise hung,
An alligator stuff'd, and other skins
Of ill-shap'd fishes; and about his shelves
A beggarly account of empty boxes, 45
Green earthen pots, bladders and musty seeds,
Remnants of packthread and old cakes of roses
Were thinly scattered, to make up a show.
Noting this penury, to myself I said,
"An if a man did need a poison now, 50
Whose sale is present death in Mantua,
Here lives a caitiff wretch would sell it him."

O, this same thought did but forerun my need;
And this same needy man must sell it me.
As I remember, this should be the house. 55
Being holiday, the beggar's shop is shut.
What, ho! apothecary!

Enter APOTHECARY.

  Ap.   Who calls so loud?
  Rom. Come hither, man. I see that thou art
    poor.
Hold, there is forty ducats. Let me have
A dram of poison, such soon-speeding gear 60
As will disperse itself through all the veins
That the life-weary taker may fall dead,
And that the trunk may be discharg'd of breath
As violently as hasty powder fir'd
Doth hurry from the fatal cannon's womb. 65
  Ap. Such mortal drugs I have; but Mantua's law
Is death to any he that utters them.
  Rom. Art thou so bare and full of wretchedness,
And fear'st to die? Famine is in thy cheeks,
Need and oppression starveth in thy eyes, 70
Contempt and beggary hangs upon thy back;
The world is not thy friend nor the world's law;
The world affords no law to make thee rich;
Then be not poor, but break it, and take this.
  Ap. My poverty, but not my will, consents. 75
  Rom. I [pay] thy poverty, and not thy will.
  Ap. Put this in any liquid thing you will,
And drink it off; and, if you had the strength
Of twenty men, it would dispatch you straight.
  Rom. There is thy gold, worse poison to men's
    souls, 80
Doing more murder in this loathsome world,
Than these poor compounds that thou mayst not
    sell.
I sell thee poison; thou hast sold me none.
Farewell! Buy food, and get thyself in flesh.
Come, cordial and not poison, go with me 85
To Juliet's grave; for there must I use thee.
                         [*Exeunt.*

[SCENE II. *Verona. Friar Laurence's cell.*]

Enter FRIAR JOHN.

  Fri. J. Holy Franciscan friar! brother, ho!

Enter FRIAR LAURENCE.

  Fri. L. This same should be the voice of Friar
    John.
Welcome from Mantua! What says Romeo?
Or, if his mind be writ, give me his letter.
  Fri. J. Going to find a bare-foot brother out, 5
One of our order, to associate me,
Here in this city visiting the sick,

---

  15. [fares my] Q₁. *doth my Lady* Q₂. 24. [even] F. *in* Q₂. [defy] Q₁. *denie* Q₂. 40. **simples:** medicinal herbs. 63. **trunk:** body. 67. **utters:** sells. 76. [pay] Q₁. *pray* Q₂. 85. **cordial:** restorative.

And finding him, the searchers of the town,
Suspecting that we both were in a house
Where the infectious pestilence did reign,   10
Seal'd up the doors and would not let us forth,
So that my speed to Mantua there was stay'd.
   Fri. L. Who bare my letter, then, to Romeo?
   Fri. J. I could not send it, — here it is again, —
Nor get a messenger to bring it thee,   15
So fearful were they of infection.
   Fri. L. Unhappy fortune! By my brotherhood,
The letter was not nice but full of charge
Of dear import, and the neglecting it
May do much danger. Friar John, go hence;   20
Get me an iron crow, and bring it straight
Unto my cell.
   Fri. J. Brother, I'll go and bring it thee. [*Exit.*
   Fri. L. Now must I to the monument alone;
Within this three hours will fair Juliet wake.   25
She will beshrew me much that Romeo
Hath had no notice of these accidents;
But I will write again to Mantua,
And keep her at my cell till Romeo come;
Poor living corse, clos'd in a dead man's tomb!   30
                         [*Exit.*

[SCENE III. *A churchyard; in it a tomb belonging to the Capulets.*]

Enter PARIS, *and his* PAGE *with flowers and sweet water* [*and a torch*].

   Par. Give me thy torch, boy. Hence, and stand
      aloof.
Yet put it out, for I would not be seen.
Under yond [yew-tree] lay thee all along,
Holding [thine] ear close to the hollow ground;
So shall no foot upon the churchyard tread,   5
Being loose, unfirm, with digging up of graves,
But thou shalt hear it. Whistle then to me,
As signal that thou hear'st something approach.
Give me those flowers. Do as I bid thee, go.
   Page. [*Aside.*] I am almost afraid to stand alone
Here in the churchyard; yet I will adventure.   11
                         [*Retires.*
   Par. Sweet flower, with flowers thy bridal bed I
      strew, —
O woe! thy canopy is dust and stones —
Which with sweet water nightly I will dew,
Or, wanting that, with tears distill'd by moans.
The obsequies that I for thee will keep   16
Nightly shall be to strew thy grave and weep.
                    [*The Page whistles.*
The boy gives warning something doth approach.
What cursed foot wanders this way to-night,
To cross my obsequies and true love's rite?   20

What, with a torch! Muffle me, night, a while.
                         [*Retires.*]

Enter ROMEO *and* [BALTHASAR], *with a torch, a mattock, and a crow of iron.*

   Rom. Give me that mattock and the wrenching
      iron.
Hold, take this letter; early in the morning
See thou deliver it to my lord and father.
Give me the light. Upon thy life I charge thee,   25
Whate'er thou hear'st or seest, stand all aloof,
And do not interrupt me in my course.
Why I descend into this bed of death
Is partly to behold my lady's face,
But chiefly to take thence from her dead finger   30
A precious ring, a ring that I must use
In dear employment; therefore hence, be gone.
But if thou, jealous, dost return to pry
In what I farther shall intend to do,
By heaven, I will tear thee joint by joint   35
And strew this hungry churchyard with thy limbs.
The time and my intents are savage-wild,
More fierce and more inexorable far
Than empty tigers or the roaring sea.
   [*Bal.*] I will be gone, sir, and not trouble ye.   40
   Rom. So shalt thou show me friendship. Take
      thou that;
Live, and be prosperous; and farewell, good fellow.
   [*Bal.*] [*Aside.*] For all this same, I'll hide me
      hereabout.
His looks I fear, and his intents I doubt. [*Retires.*]
   Rom. Thou detestable maw, thou womb of
      death,   45
Gorg'd with the dearest morsel of the earth,
Thus I enforce thy rotten jaws to open,
And, in despite, I'll cram thee with more food!
                    [*Opens the tomb.*]
   Par. This is that banish'd haughty Montague,
That murd'red my love's cousin, with which grief,
It is supposed, the fair creature died;   51
And here is come to do some villanous shame
To the dead bodies. I will apprehend him.
                  [*Comes forward.*]
Stop thy unhallowed toil, vile Montague!
Can vengeance be pursued further than death?   55
Condemned villain, I do apprehend thee.
Obey, and go with me; for thou must die.
   Rom. I must indeed; and therefore came I
      hither.
Good gentle youth, tempt not a desperate man.
Fly hence, and leave me; think upon these gone,   60
Let them affright thee. I beseech thee, youth,
Put not another sin upon my head,
By urging me to fury: O, be gone!

Sc. ii, 8. **searchers**: i.e., health officers. 18. **nice**: trivial. **charge**: importance. 21. **crow**: crowbar. 26. **beshrew**: censure. Sc. iii, 3. **[yew-tree]** Q1. *young trees* Q2. **all along**: prone. 4. **[thine]** Q1. *thy* Q2. 14. **sweet**: perfumed. 22. s.d. **[BALTHASAR]** Q1. *Peter* Q2. 33. **jealous**: suspicious. 40, 43. **[Bal.]** Q4. *Pet.* Q2.

By heaven, I love thee better than myself;
For I come hither arm'd against myself.   65
Stay not, be gone; live, and hereafter say
A madman's mercy bid thee run away.

   Par. I do defy thy [conjurations]
And apprehend thee for a felon here.

   Rom. Wilt thou provoke me? Then have at
     thee, boy!   [*They fight.* 70

   [*Page.*] O Lord, they fight! I will go call the
     watch.   [*Exit.*]

   Par. O, I am slain! [*Falls.*] If thou be merciful,
Open the tomb, lay me with Juliet.   [*Dies.*]

   Rom. In faith, I will. Let me peruse this
     face.
Mercutio's kinsman, noble County Paris!   75
What said my man, when my betossed soul
Did not attend him as we rode? I think
He told me Paris should have married Juliet.
Said he not so? Or did I dream it so?
Or am I mad, hearing him talk of Juliet,   80
To think it was so? O, give me thy hand,
One writ with me in sour misfortune's book!
I'll bury thee in a triumphant grave.
A grave? O, no! a lantern, slaught'red youth,
For here lies Juliet, and her beauty makes   85
This vault a feasting presence full of light.
Death, lie thou there, by a dead man interr'd.
          [*Laying Paris in the tomb.*]
How oft when men are at the point of death
Have they been merry! which their keepers call
A lightning before death. O, how may I   90
Call this a lightning? O my love! my wife!
Death, that hath suck'd the honey of thy breath,
Hath had no power yet upon thy beauty.
Thou art not conquer'd; beauty's ensign yet
Is crimson in thy lips and in thy cheeks,   95
And death's pale flag is not advanced there.
Tybalt, li'st thou there in thy bloody sheet?
O, what more favour can I do to thee,
Than with that hand that cut thy youth in twain
To sunder his that was thine enemy?   100
Forgive me, cousin! Ah, dear Juliet,
Why art thou yet so fair? Shall I believe
That unsubstantial Death is amorous,
And that the lean abhorred monster keeps
Thee here in dark to be his paramour?   105
For fear of that, I still will stay with thee,
And never from this [palace] of dim night
Depart again. Here, here will I remain
With worms that are thy chamber-maids; O, here
Will I set up my everlasting rest,   110
And shake the yoke of inauspicious stars

From this world-wearied flesh. Eyes, look your
     last!
Arms, take your last embrace! and, lips, O you
The doors of breath, seal with a righteous kiss
A dateless bargain to engrossing death!   115
Come, bitter conduct, come, unsavoury guide!
Thou desperate pilot, now at once run on
The dashing rocks thy sea-sick weary bark!
Here's to my love! [*Drinks.*] O true apothe-
     cary!
Thy drugs are quick. Thus with a kiss I die.   120
          [*Dies.*]

  Enter FRIAR LAURENCE, *with lantern, crow,*
         and spade.

   Fri. L. Saint Francis be my speed! how oft to-
     night
Have my old feet stumbled at graves! Who's
     there?

   Bal. Here's one, a friend, and one that knows
     you well.

   Fri. L. Bliss be upon you! Tell me, good my
     friend,
What torch is yond, that vainly lends his light
To grubs and eyeless skulls? As I discern,   126
It burneth in the Capels' monument.

   Bal. It doth so, holy sir; and there's my master,
One that you love.

   Fri. L.   Who is it?

   Bal.   Romeo.   129

   Fri. L. How long hath he been there?

   Bal.   Full half an hour.

   Fri. L. Go with me to the vault.

   Bal.   I dare not, sir.
My master knows not but I am gone hence;
And fearfully did menace me with death
If I did stay to look on his intents.

   Fri. L. Stay, then; I'll go alone. Fear comes
     upon me: 135
O, much I fear some ill unthrifty thing.

   Bal. As I did sleep under this [yew]-tree here,
I dreamt my master and another fought,
And that my master slew him.

   Fri. L.   Romeo!
          [*Advances.*]
Alack, alack, what blood is this, which stains   140
The stony entrance of this sepulchre?
What mean these masterless and gory swords
To lie discolour'd by this place of peace?
          [*Enters the tomb.*]
Romeo! O, pale! Who else? What, Paris too?
And steep'd in blood? Ah, what an unkind hour

---

68. [conjurations] Q1. *commiration* Q2. 71. [*Page.*] Q4. Om. Q2. *Pet.* F. 86. **presence:** presence-chamber. 89. **keepers:** nurses. 107. [**palace**] Q1. *pallat* Q2. After this line, and before l. 108, Q2 and F insert: "Depart againe, come lye thou in my arme,/Heer's to thy health, where ere thou tumblest in./O true Appothecarie!/Thy drugs are quicke. Thus with a kisse I die." 115. **dateless:** eternal. **engrossing:** monopolizing. 136. **unthrifty:** unlucky (which F reads). 137. [**yew**] (Pope). *yong* Q2.

Is guilty of this lamentable chance!   146
The lady stirs.   [*Juliet rises.*
    Jul. O comfortable friar! where is my lord?
I do remember well where I should be,
And there I am.   Where is my Romeo?   150
                              [*Noise within.*]
    Fri. L. I hear some noise. Lady, come from
        that nest
Of death, contagion, and unnatural sleep.
A greater power than we can contradict
Hath thwarted our intents. Come, come away.
Thy husband in thy bosom there lies dead;   155
And Paris too.   Come, I'll dispose of thee
Among a sisterhood of holy nuns.
Stay not to question, for the watch is coming;
Come, go, good Juliet [*Noise again*], I dare no longer
        stay.   [*Exit Fri. Lau.*
    Jul. Go, get thee hence, for I will not away.   160
What's here?   A cup, clos'd in my true love's hand?
Poison, I see, hath been his timeless end.
O churl! drunk all, and left no friendly drop
To help me after?   I will kiss thy lips;
Haply some poison yet doth hang on them,   165
To make me die with a restorative.
Thy lips are warm.

        Enter WATCH, *with the* PAGE *of Paris.*
    [*1.*] *Watch.* Lead, boy; which way?
    Jul. Yea, noise?   Then I'll be brief.   O happy
        dagger!   [*Snatching Romeo's dagger.*]
This is thy sheath (*Stabs herself*); there rust, and
        let me die.   170
        -       [*Falls* [*on Romeo's body, and dies*].
    [*Page.*] This is the place; there, where the torch
        doth burn.
    [*1.*] *Watch.* The ground is bloody; search about
        the churchyard.
Go, some of you, whoe'er you find attach.
                              [*Exeunt some.*]
Pitiful sight! here lies the County slain;
And Juliet bleeding, warm, and newly dead,   175
Who here hath lain this two days buried.
Go, tell the Prince; run to the Capulets;
Raise up the Montagues; some others search.
                              [*Exeunt others.*]
We see the ground whereon these woes do lie;
But the true ground of all these piteous woes   180
We cannot without circumstance descry.

    Re-enter [*some of the* WATCH, *with*] BALTHASAR.
    [*2.*] *Watch.* Here's Romeo's man; we found him
        in the churchyard.
    [*1.*] *Watch.* Hold him in safety till the Prince
        come hither.

    Re-enter another WATCHMAN, *with* FRIAR LAURENCE.
    [*3.*] *Watch.* Here is a friar, that trembles, sighs,
        and weeps.
We took this mattock and this spade from him,   185
As he was coming from this churchyard's side.
    [*1.*] *Watch.* A great suspicion.   Stay the friar too.

        Enter the PRINCE [*and Attendants*].
    Prince. What misadventure is so early up,
That calls our person from our morning rest?

    Enter CAPULET, LADY CAPULET, *and others.*
    Cap. What should it be, that [they] so shriek
        abroad?   190
    La. Cap. Oh! the people in the street cry Romeo,
Some Juliet, and some Paris; and all run,
With open outcry, toward our monument.
    Prince. What fear is this which startles in [our]
        ears?
    [*1.*] *Watch.* Sovereign, here lies the County Paris
        slain;   195
And Romeo dead; and Juliet, dead before,
Warm and new kill'd.
    Prince. Search, seek, and know how this foul
        murder comes.
    [*1.*] *Watch.* Here is a friar, and slaughter'd
        Romeo's man,
With instruments upon them, fit to open   200
These dead men's tombs.
    Cap. O heavens!   O wife, look how our daughter
        bleeds!
This dagger hath mista'en, — for, lo, his house
Is empty on the back of Montague, —
And it mis-sheathed in my daughter's bosom!   205
    La Cap. O me! this sight of death is as a bell,
That warns my old age to a sepulchre.

        Enter MONTAGUE [*and others*].
    Prince. Come, Montague; for thou art early up
To see thy son and heir [more early] down.
    Mon. Alas, my liege, my wife is dead to-night;   210
Grief of my son's exile hath stopp'd her breath.
What further woe conspires against mine age?
    Prince. Look, and thou shalt see.
    Mon. O thou untaught! what manners is in this,
To press before thy father to a grave?   215
    Prince. Seal up the mouth of outrage for a while,
Till we can clear these ambiguities,
And know their spring, their head, their true de-
        scent;
And then will I be general of your woes
And lead you even to death.   Meantime forbear,
And let mischance be slave to patience.   221

---

148. **comfortable:** comforting.   162. **timeless:** untimely.   168. [*1.*] *Watch.* For the speeches of the 1st Watch, the headings of Q2 are *Watch* or *Chief Watch*; for those of the 2d Watch and 3d Watch, *Watch.*   171. [**Page**] (Capell).   *Watch boy* Q2.   **173. attach:** arrest.   190. [**they**] F.   *is* Q2.   194. [**our**] (Johnson conj.).   *your* Q2.   203. **house:** scabbard.   209. [**more early**] Q1.   *now earling* Q2.   216. **outrage:** outcry.

Bring forth the parties of suspicion.

 Fri. L. I am the greatest, able to do least,
Yet most suspected, as the time and place
Doth make against me, of this direful murder; 225
And here I stand, both to impeach and purge
Myself condemned and myself excus'd.

 Prince. Then say at once what thou dost know
  in this.

 Fri. L. I will be brief, for my short date of breath
Is not so long as is a tedious tale. 230
Romeo, there dead, was husband to that Juliet;
And she, there dead, [that] Romeo's faithful wife.
I married them; and their stol'n marriage-day
Was Tybalt's dooms-day, whose untimely death
Banish'd the new-made bridegroom from this city,
For whom, and not for Tybalt, Juliet pin'd. 236
You, to remove that siege of grief from her,
Betroth'd and would have married her perforce
To County Paris. Then comes she to me,
And, with wild looks, bid me devise some mean
To rid her from this second marriage, 241
Or in my cell there would she kill herself.
Then gave I her, so tutor'd by my art,
A sleeping potion; which so took effect
As I intended, for it wrought on her 245
The form of death. Meantime I writ to Romeo,
That he should hither come as this dire night
To help to take her from her borrowed grave,
Being the time the potion's force should cease.
But he which bore my letter, Friar John, 250
Was stay'd by accident, and yesternight
Return'd my letter back. Then all alone
At the prefixed hour of her waking,
Came I to take her from her kindred's vault;
Meaning to keep her closely at my cell, 255
Till I conveniently could send to Romeo;
But when I came, some minutes ere the time
Of her awak'ning, here untimely lay
The noble Paris and true Romeo dead.
She wakes; and I entreated her come forth 260
And bear this work of heaven with patience.
But then a noise did scare me from the tomb;
And she, too desperate, would not go with me,
But, as it seems, did violence on herself.
All this I know; and to the marriage 265
Her nurse is privy; and, if aught in this
Miscarried by my fault, let my old life
Be sacrific'd, some hour before his time,

Unto the rigour of severest law. 269

 Prince. We still have known thee for a holy man.
Where's Romeo's man? What can he say to
  this?

 Bal. I brought my master news of Juliet's death;
And then in post he came from Mantua
To this same place, to this same monument.
This letter he early bid me give his father, 275
And threat'ned me with death, going in the vault,
If I departed not and left him there.

 Prince. Give me the letter; I will look on it.
Where is the County's page, that rais'd the watch?
Sirrah, what made your master in this place? 280

 Page. He came with flowers to strew his lady's
  grave;
And bid me stand aloof, and so I did.
Anon comes one with light to ope the tomb,
And by and by my master drew on him;
And then I ran away to call the watch. 285

 Prince. This letter doth make good the friar's
  words,
Their course of love, the tidings of her death.
And here he writes that he did buy a poison
Of a poor 'pothecary, and therewithal
Came to this vault to die, and lie with Juliet. 290
Where be these enemies? Capulet! Montague!
See, what a scourge is laid upon your hate,
That Heaven finds means to kill your joys with
  love.
And I for winking at your discords too 294
Have lost a brace of kinsmen. All are punish'd.

 Cap. O brother Montague, give me thy hand.
This is my daughter's jointure, for no more
Can I demand.

 Mon.   But I can give thee more;
For I will raise her statue in pure gold;
That whiles Verona by that name is known, 300
There shall no figure at such rate be set
As that of true and faithful Juliet.

 Cap. As rich shall Romeo's by his lady's lie,
Poor sacrifices of our enmity!

 Prince. A glooming peace this morning with it
  brings; 305
The sun, for sorrow, will not show his head.
Go hence, to have more talk of these sad things;
 Some shall be pardon'd, and some punished:
For never was a story of more woe
Than this of Juliet and her Romeo. [*Exeunt.* 310

---

 232. [that] Q4. *thats* Q2. 247. as this: this very. 255. closely: secretly. 297. jointure: marriage portion. 301. rate: value.

The Merchant of Venice

ON JULY 22, 1598, James Roberts entered *The Marchaunt of Venyce or otherwise called the Jewe of Venyce* in the Stationers' Register. The entry was presumably a "staying entry" to prevent piracy, for no Quarto appeared until 1600, when Roberts printed the play for Thomas Heyes, to whom he had, as witnessed by an entry of October 28, 1600, transferred his right. A second Quarto, purporting by its title page to have been printed by Roberts in 1600, has been proved to be one of the spuriously dated Quartos issued by Pavier in 1619. It has also been shown that this Quarto, formerly believed to be the earlier, and the text of the First Folio were each set up independently from the Heyes Quarto. Thus the Heyes Quarto now stands as the proper basis for any modern text.

As to the date of the play, there is not much to go upon. It is mentioned by Meres in his list of 1598, but it is undoubtedly earlier. In 1594 Dr. Roderigo Lopez, a prominent Jewish physician who had gained the distinction of serving the Queen herself, was hanged in London on a charge of treason and conspiracy to murder Elizabeth and the Portuguese pretender, Antonio Perez. It has been suggested that the present play was prepared about this time to take advantage of the popular excitement created by that affair. The notion gains support from the fact that rivals of Shakespeare's company were apparently making capital of it, for during the summer and fall of 1594 the Admiral's Men staged a highly successful revival of Marlowe's sensational *Jew of Malta*. Tenuous corroboration of the theory may be found in the occurrence of the name Antonio as that of the intended victim in both history and the drama, and in the possible though doubtful allusion to Lopez in Gratiano's abuse of Shylock in IV.i.133–38. The maturity exhibited in the workmanship of the play, however, has made scholars reluctant to accept a date earlier than 1596. Nevertheless, though the text probably was not earlier than 1596, the idea for the play may have originated in the events of 1594.

The main plot of the play is unquestionably de-

rived from the story of Giannetto, the first novel of the fourth day in Ser Giovanni Fiorentino's *Il Pecorone* (written about 1378, though not printed until 1558), which combines the stories of the bond and the rings, sets the principal action in Venice, and names Belmont as the lady's residence. Suitors of the lady are to win her, however, not by a choice among caskets but by wooing her throughout a whole night, a consummation which the lady seeks to prevent by sleeping-potions administered in their drink. The one who ultimately gains her is successful only because the lady's maid-in-waiting kindly betrays the secret of the potion. The winning of Portia by the suitor who should choose correctly among caskets of gold, silver, and lead was probably suggested by a story in the *Gesta Romanorum*, a miscellaneous collection of tales dating from the Middle Ages, of which a popular translation had appeared in 1577. In the version in the *Gesta* the test is imposed by the Emperor of Rome upon a foreign princess to determine her worthiness to become his wife. No specific source has been discovered for Jessica's part in the play, but Shakespeare may have found the hint in the rôle of Abigail, the daughter of Marlowe's Jew of Malta, who also had a Christian lover. Mention should be made of a lost play called *The Jew*, of which the sole surviving record is a reference by Stephen Gosson in his *School of Abuse* (1579), describing it as "representing the greediness of worldly chusers, and bloody mindes of Usurers." From this description critics have inferred a play combining the story of the caskets with that of the pound of flesh. It is a likely conjecture, yet so long as the play remains undiscovered it is futile to speculate upon what it may have supplied to Shakespeare; and it is going far beyond the evidence to conjecture that *The Merchant of Venice* as we know it, is in fact *The Jew* adapted (after possible intermediate handlings) by Shakespeare in 1594 and further revised by him some time before 1600.

The two chief elements of the plot belong independently to old and widespread traditions. The story of the pound of flesh occurs in the medieval *Dolopathos* by Joannes de Alta Silva, the *Gesta Romanorum*, the Middle English *Cursor Mundi*, a ballad on the cruelty of "Gernutus the Jew," and *Histoires Tragiques*, a book of declamations by Alexandre Silvayn, of which an English translation, *The Orator*, appeared in 1596. The last named is of particular interest because it may be that the argument of a Jew before his judge supplied hints for some of Shylock's lines in the court scene. If the suggested indebtedness is real, it supports 1596 as the earliest possible date for the play. The story of the caskets appears, with different motivation, in the Greek romance of *Barlaam and Josaphat*, the *Speculum Historiale* (XV, 10) of Vincent of Beauvais, the *Legenda Aurea* (cap. 176), the *Decameron* (X, I) of Boccaccio, and the *Confessio Amantis* (V, 2273–2390) of John Gower.

The Merchant of Venice is unlike Shakespeare's other romantic comedies in not having love as the central interest. There are, to be sure, three pairs of lovers, but their affairs, though they bear upon the main plot significantly, are nevertheless subordinate issues. The protagonists are clearly Antonio and Shylock. Friendship, however, as exalted in the Renaissance conception over the love of man for woman, does constitute an important element in the main plot. Without demur Antonio equips Bassanio, already deep in his debt for like services, in his expedition to Belmont, and weeps, we are told, at his departure thither. Indeed, the melancholy from which Antonio is suffering when first we meet him seems to be owing to an intuition that something is about to deprive him of his friend. That some modern critics have found this devotion misplaced is nothing to the point. Antonio did not, and neither, certainly, did Shakespeare, who in his Sonnets celebrated friendship, making it superior to love. Antonio, however, receives his reward, for in his time of crisis Bassanio returns to him bearing twice the sum he owes the Jew. That the instigation as well as the bounty comes from Portia is perhaps little to Bassanio's credit, but this Antonio does not know, and he ultimately learns that in "losing" one friend he has gained another.

The question of anti-Semitism in this play has been widely discussed. There can be no doubt that Shakespeare intentionally endowed Shylock with traits which have fostered the traditional antipathy to his race. Shylock is an avaricious moneylender; he has a burning racial pride, with a con-comitant scorn for his Gentile oppressors. He is despised by all the members of Antonio's circle, whose enmity would probably be shared by many of Shakespeare's contemporaries. But Shakespeare, with his rare creative gift for understanding and humanizing all sorts and conditions of men, did not find it possible to make of Shylock simply a conventional monster of avaricious cruelty. Rather he has made him at many points affectingly human. He has let him be eloquent upon the sufferings of his race and the common humanity of Jew and Gentile. And he has taken care to afford him comprehensible motivation for the relentlessness which the traditional story of the pound of flesh demanded. A judicious reading of the text shows that it was not primarily Antonio's forfeiture which made Shylock greedy to exact the literal penalty of the bond. Originally Shylock had said that the terms of the bond were named "in merry sport," and there is no real reason to accuse him of diabolical insincerity. The chances of Antonio's failing must have appeared as remote to him as to anyone else. The terms may well enough have been no more than awkward jesting after his offer, out of a protested desire to be friends with Antonio, to forgo his customary "usury." In any event, when Shylock is first informed of Antonio's losses, he hardly leaps to his chances as he should have done if from the beginning he had been thirsting for Antonio's ruin. At that moment his mind is racked by the discovery of his daughter's elopement; she, his own flesh and blood, has deceived and robbed him, running off with a Christian aided and abetted by Antonio's friends. That is what tortures him and goads him, once his opportunity has dawned upon him, into a fanatical desire for revenge. And in the initial frenzy of his grief, sympathy for Shylock cannot be denied. He is a father, terribly wronged.

In the end, however, Shylock is a defeated and a broken man. His lust for inexorable justice was evil, and the play is a comedy wherein the figure obstructing the happiness of those destined to be blest must be thwarted. The penalty that he renounce his religion appears to us today as a wanton cruelty, but to Shakespeare's contemporaries it probably did not seem so. Critics have, indeed, suggested that they would regard it as an act of charity to admit Shylock to the benefits of Christian sacraments. However that may be, it is impossible to accuse Shakespeare, who made of Shylock so intensely human a figure, of anti-Semitism.

THE MERCHANT OF VENICE

ACT I

[SCENE I. Venice. A street.]

Enter ANTONIO, SALARINO, *and* SALANIO.

Ant. In sooth, I know not why I am so sad.
It wearies me; you say it wearies you;
But how I caught it, found it, or came by it,
What stuff 'tis made of, whereof it is born,
I am to learn;   5
And such a want-wit sadness makes of me,
That I have much ado to know myself.
  Salar. Your mind is tossing on the ocean,
There, where your argosies with portly sail,
Like signiors and rich burghers on the flood,   10
Or, as it were, the pageants of the sea,
Do overpeer the petty traffickers
That curtsy to them, do them reverence,
As they fly by them with their woven wings.
  Salan. Believe me, sir, had I such venture forth,
The better part of my affections would   16
Be with my hopes abroad. I should be still
Plucking the grass to know where sits the wind,
Peering in maps for ports and piers and roads;
And every object that might make me fear   20
Misfortune to my ventures, out of doubt
Would make me sad.
  Salar.   My wind cooling my broth
Would blow me to an ague when I thought
What harm a wind too great might do at sea.
I should not see the sandy hour-glass run   25
But I should think of shallows and of flats,
And see my wealthy Andrew dock'd in sand,
Vailing her high-top lower than her ribs
To kiss her burial. Should I go to church
And see the holy edifice of stone,   30
And not bethink me straight of dangerous rocks,
Which, touching but my gentle vessel's side,
Would scatter all her spices on the stream,
Enrobe the roaring waters with my silks,
And, in a word, but even now worth this,   35
And now worth nothing? Shall I have the thought

Act I, sc. i, 5. **am to learn:** have not learned.   9. **argosies:** large merchant ships.   **portly:** billowing.   11. **pageants:** the wheeled stages of the Miracle Plays.   15. **venture forth:** investment at stake.   17. **still:** constantly.   19. **roads:** anchorages.   27. **Andrew:** name of a ship.   28. **Vailing:** lowering.   **high-top:** masthead.

To think on this, and shall I lack the thought
That such a thing bechanc'd would make me sad?
But tell not me; I know Antonio
Is sad to think upon his merchandise.   40
   Ant. Believe me, no.   I thank my fortune for it,
My ventures are not in one bottom trusted,
Nor to one place; nor is my whole estate
Upon the fortune of this present year:
Therefore my merchandise makes me not sad.   45
   Salar. Why, then you are in love.
   Ant.   Fie, fie!
   Salar. Not in love neither?   Then let us say you
      are sad
Because you are not merry; and 'twere as easy
For you to laugh and leap and say you are merry
Because you are not sad.   Now, by two-headed
      Janus,   50
Nature hath fram'd strange fellows in her time;
Some that will evermore peep through their eyes
And laugh like parrots at a bag-piper,
And other of such vinegar aspect
That they'll not show their teeth in way of smile
Though Nestor swear the jest be laughable.   56

   Enter BASSANIO, LORENZO, *and* GRATIANO.

   Salan. Here comes Bassanio, your most noble
      kinsman,
Gratiano, and Lorenzo.   Fare ye well;
We leave you now with better company.
   Salar. I would have stay'd till I had made you
      merry,   60
If worthier friends had not prevented me.
   Ant. Your worth is very dear in my regard.
I take it, your own business calls on you
And you embrace th' occasion to depart.
   Salar. Good morrow, my good lords.   65
   Bass. Good signiors both, when shall we laugh?
      Say, when?
You grow exceeding strange.   Must it be so?
   Salar. We'll make our leisures to attend on yours.
            [*Exeunt Salarino and Salanio.*
   Lor. My Lord Bassanio, since you have found
      Antonio,
We two will leave you; but at dinner-time,   70
I pray you, have in mind where we must meet.
   Bass. I will not fail you.
   Gra. You look not well, Signior Antonio;
You have too much respect upon the world.
They lose it that do buy it with much care.   75
Believe me, you are marvellously chang'd.
   Ant. I hold the world but as the world, Gratiano,
A stage where every man must play a part,

And mine a sad one.
   Gra.   Let me play the fool!
With mirth and laughter let old wrinkles come,   80
And let my liver rather heat with wine
Than my heart cool with mortifying groans.
Why should a man, whose blood is warm within,
Sit like his grandsire cut in alabaster,
Sleep when he wakes, and creep into the jaundice   85
By being peevish?   I tell thee what, Antonio —
I love thee, and it is my love that speaks —
There are a sort of men whose visages
Do cream and mantle like a standing pond,
And do a wilful stillness entertain,   90
With purpose to be dress'd in an opinion
Of wisdom, gravity, profound conceit,
As who should say, "I am Sir Oracle,
And when I ope my lips let no dog bark!"
O my Antonio, I do know of these   95
That therefore only are reputed wise
For saying nothing, when, I am very sure,
If they should speak, would almost damn those ears
Which, hearing them, would call their brothers
      fools.
I'll tell thee more of this another time;   100
But fish not with this melancholy bait
For this fool gudgeon, this opinion.
Come, good Lorenzo.   Fare ye well awhile;
I'll end my exhortation after dinner.
   Lor. Well, we will leave you then till dinner-time.
I must be one of these same dumb wise men,   106
For Gratiano never lets me speak.
   Gra. Well, keep me company but two years moe,
Thou shalt not know the sound of thine own tongue.
   Ant. Farewell!   I'll grow a talker for this gear.
   Gra. Thanks, i' faith, for silence is only com-
      mendable   111
In a neat's tongue dri'd and a maid not vendible.
            [*Exeunt* [*Gratiano and Lorenzo*].
   Ant. Is that any thing now?
   Bass. Gratiano speaks an infinite deal of nothing,
more than any man in all Venice.   His reasons are
as two grains of wheat hid in two bushels of   116
chaff; you shall seek all day ere you find them, and
when you have them, they are not worth the search.
   Ant. Well, tell me now what lady is the same
To whom you swore a secret pilgrimage,   120
That you to-day promis'd to tell me of?
   Bass. 'Tis not unknown to you, Antonio,
How much I have disabled mine estate
By something showing a more swelling port   124
Than my faint means would grant continuance.
Nor do I now make moan to be abridg'd

---

42. **bottom:** ship.   50. **Janus:** a Roman god represented with two faces, one smiling, the other grave.   56. **Nestor:** a character of signal gravity in the *Iliad*.   61. **prevented:** anticipated.   67. **strange:** reserved, cold.   74. **have...upon:** give too much thought to.   82. **mortifying:** killing.   89. **mantle:** become covered with scum.   91. **opinion:** reputation. 92. **conceit:** thought.   98–99. **damn...fools.** An allusion to Matthew v.22: "Whosoever shall say to his brother... 'Thou fool,' shall be in danger of hell fire."   102. **gudgeon:** a small fish.   108. **moe:** more.   110. **for...gear:** because of this harangue.   112. **neat's:** ox's.   **vendible:** marriageable.

From such a noble rate; but my chief care
Is to come fairly off from the great debts
Wherein my time something too prodigal
Hath left me gag'd. To you, Antonio, 130
I owe the most, in money and in love,
And from your love I have a warranty
To unburden all my plots and purposes
How to get clear of all the debts I owe.

Ant. I pray you, good Bassanio, let me know it;
And if it stand, as you yourself still do, 136
Within the eye of honour, be assur'd
My purse, my person, my extremest means,
Lie all unlock'd to your occasions.

Bass. In my school-days, when I had lost one
shaft, 140
I shot his fellow of the self-same flight
The self-same way with more advised watch
To find the other forth, and by adventuring both
I oft found both. I urge this childhood proof,
Because what follows is pure innocence. 145
I owe you much, and, like a wilful youth,
That which I owe is lost; but if you please
To shoot another arrow that self way
Which you did shoot the first, I do not doubt,
As I will watch the aim, or to find both 150
Or bring your latter hazard back again
And thankfully rest debtor for the first.

Ant. You know me well, and herein spend but
time
To wind about my love with circumstance;
And out of doubt you do me now more wrong 155
In making question of my uttermost
Than if you had made waste of all I have.
Then do but say to me what I should do
That in your knowledge may by me be done,
And I am prest unto it; therefore, speak. 160

Bass. In Belmont is a lady richly left;
And she is fair and, fairer than that word,
Of wondrous virtues. Sometimes from her eyes
I did receive fair speechless messages.
Her name is Portia, nothing undervalu'd 165
To Cato's daughter, Brutus' Portia.
Nor is the wide world ignorant of her worth,
For the four winds blow in from every coast
Renowned suitors; and her sunny locks
Hang on her temples like a golden fleece, 170
Which makes her seat of Belmont Colchis' strand,
And many Jasons come in quest of her.
O my Antonio, had I but the means
To hold a rival place with one of them,
I have a mind presages me such thrift, 175
That I should questionless be fortunate!

Ant. Thou know'st that all my fortunes are at sea;

Neither have I money nor commodity
To raise a present sum. Therefore go forth;
Try what my credit can in Venice do. 180
That shall be rack'd, even to the uttermost,
To furnish thee to Belmont, to fair Portia.
Go, presently inquire, and so will I,
Where money is; and I no question make
To have it of my trust or for my sake. 185
[*Exeunt.*

SCENE II. [*Belmont. A room in Portia's house.*]

Enter PORTIA *with her waiting-woman,* NERISSA.

Por. By my troth, Nerissa, my little body is
aweary of this great world.

Ner. You would be, sweet madam, if your miseries were in the same abundance as your good fortunes are; and yet, for aught I see, they are as 5
sick that surfeit with too much as they that starve
with nothing. It is no mean happiness, therefore,
to be seated in the mean. Superfluity comes sooner
by white hairs, but competency lives longer. 10

Por. Good sentences and well pronounc'd.

Ner. They would be better, if well followed.

Por. If to do were as easy as to know what were
good to do, chapels had been churches and poor
men's cottages princes' palaces. It is a good di- 15
vine that follows his own instructions; I can easier
teach twenty what were good to be done, than to be
one of the twenty to follow mine own teaching.
The brain may devise laws for the blood, but a hot
temper leaps o'er a cold decree; such a hare is 20
madness the youth, to skip o'er the meshes of good
counsel the cripple. But this reasoning is not in the
fashion to choose me a husband. O me, the word
choose! I may neither choose who I would nor refuse who I dislike; so is the will of a living 25
daughter curb'd by the will of a dead father. Is
it not hard, Nerissa, that I cannot choose one nor
refuse none? 29

Ner. Your father was ever virtuous, and holy
men at their death have good inspirations; therefore the lott'ry that he hath devised in these three
chests of gold, silver, and lead, whereof who chooses
his meaning chooses you, will, no doubt, never be
chosen by any rightly but one who you shall 35
rightly love. But what warmth is there in your
affection towards any of these princely suitors that
are already come?

Por. I pray thee, over-name them; and as thou
namest them, I will describe them; and, accord- 40
ing to my description, level at my affection.

Ner. First, there is the Neapolitan prince.

127. **rate:** style of living. 129. **time:** way of life. 130. **gag'd:** pledged. 143. **forth:** out. 144. **proof:** experience. 160.
prest: ready. 166. **Brutus' Portia.** See *Julius Caesar.* 172. **Jasons.** Jason obtained the famous golden fleece at Colchis.
175. **thrift:** success. 181. **rack'd:** stretched. 183. **presently:** at once.

Sc. ii, 9. **comes...by:** causes sooner. 11. **sentences:** maxims. 25-26. **will...will:** desire...testament. 41. **level at:**
aim at, judge of.

Por. Ay, that's a colt indeed, for he doth nothing but talk of his horse; and he makes it a great 45 appropriation to his own good parts, that he can shoe him himself. I am much afeard my lady his mother played false with a smith.

Ner. Then is there the County Palatine.

Por. He doth nothing but frown, as who 50 should say, "An you will not have me, choose." He hears merry tales and smiles not. I fear he will prove the weeping philosopher when he grows old, being so full of unmannerly sadness in his youth. I had rather be married to a death's- 55 head with a bone in his mouth than to either of these. God defend me from these two!

Ner. How say you by the French lord, Monsieur Le Bon?   59

Por. God made him, and therefore let him pass for a man. In truth, I know it is a sin to be a mocker; but, he! why, he hath a horse better than the Neapolitan's, a better bad habit of frowning than the Count Palatine. He is every man in no man. If a throstle sing, he falls straight a cap'r- 65 ing. He will fence with his own shadow. If I should marry him, I should marry twenty husbands. If he would despise me, I would forgive him, for if he love me to madness, I shall never requite him. 70

Ner. What say you, then, to Falconbridge, the young baron of England?

Por. You know I say nothing to him, for he understands not me, nor I him. He hath neither Latin, French, nor Italian, and you will come 75 into the court and swear that I have a poor penny-worth in the English. He is a proper man's picture, but, alas, who can converse with a dumb-show? How oddly he is suited! I think he bought his doublet in Italy, his round hose in France, his 80 bonnet in Germany, and his behaviour everywhere.

Ner. What think you of the Scottish lord, his neighbour?

Por. That he hath a neighbourly charity in 85 him, for he borrowed a box of the ear of the English-man and swore he would pay him again when he was able. I think the Frenchman became his surety and seal'd under for another.

Ner. How like you the young German, the Duke of Saxony's nephew?   91

Por. Very vilely in the morning, when he is sober, and most vilely in the afternoon, when he is drunk. When he is best, he is a little worse than a man, and when he is worst, he is little better than a beast. 95 An the worst fall that ever fell, I hope I shall make shift to go without him.

Ner. If he should offer to choose, and choose the right casket, you should refuse to perform your father's will if you should refuse to accept him. 102

Por. Therefore, for fear of the worst, I pray thee, set a deep glass of rhenish wine on the contrary casket, for if the devil be within and that tempta-tion without, I know he will choose it. I will do 106 anything, Nerissa, ere I will be married to a sponge.

Ner. You need not fear, lady, the having any of these lords. They have acquainted me with 110 their determinations; which is, indeed, to return to their home and to trouble you with no more suit, unless you may be won by some other sort than your father's imposition depending on the caskets. 115

Por. If I live to be as old as Sibylla, I will die as chaste as Diana, unless I be obtained by the man-ner of my father's will. I am glad this parcel of wooers are so reasonable, for there is not one among them but I dote on his very absence, and I pray 120 God grant them a fair departure.

Ner. Do you not remember, lady, in your father's time, a Venetian, a scholar and a soldier, that came hither in company of the Marquis of Montferrat?

Por. Yes, yes, it was Bassanio, — as I think, so was he call'd.   128

Ner. True, madam. He, of all the men that ever my foolish eyes look'd upon, was the best deserving a fair lady.   131

Por. I remember him well, and I remember him worthy of thy praise.

Enter a SERVING-MAN.

How now! what news?

Serv. The four strangers seek for you, madam, to take their leave; and there is a forerunner come 136 from a fifth, the Prince of Morocco, who brings word the Prince his master will be here tonight. 139

Por. If I could bid the fifth welcome with so good a heart as I can bid the other four farewell, I should be glad of his approach. If he have the condition of a saint and the complexion of a devil, I had rather he should shrive me than wive me. 145 Come, Nerissa. Sirrah, go before. While we shut the gates upon one wooer, another knocks at the door.   [*Exeunt.*

[SCENE III. *Venice. A public place.*]

Enter BASSANIO *and* SHYLOCK *the Jew.*

Shy. Three thousand ducats; well.

Bass. Ay, sir, for three months.

Shy. For three months; well.

---

51. **choose:** i.e., do what you please.   53. **weeping philosopher:** Heraclitus.   76. **proper:** handsome.   78. **suited:** dressed.   79. **round hose:** breeches.   81. **Scottish** Qq. F reads *other*, probably substituted in deference to King James. 88-89. **Frenchman ... another:** i.e., the Frenchman pledged himself to pay the Englishman with another blow. An allusion to the old alliance between France and Scotland.   96. **fall ... fell:** befall ... befell.   115. **imposition:** conditions. 116. **Sibylla:** the Cumaean Sibyl, to whom Apollo granted as many years as there were grains in her handful of sand. 134. **four.** Nerissa has named six suitors.   143. **condition:** disposition.   145. **shrive me:** hear my confession.

Bass. For the which, as I told you, Antonio shall
be bound.   5

Shy. Antonio shall become bound; well.

Bass. May you stead me? Will you pleasure
me? Shall I know your answer?

Shy. Three thousand ducats for three months,
and Antonio bound.   10

Bass. Your answer to that.

Shy. Antonio is a good man.

Bass. Have you heard any imputation to the
contrary?

Shy. Ho, no, no, no, no! My meaning in   15
saying he is a good man is to have you understand
me that he is sufficient. Yet his means are in supposition: he hath an argosy bound to Tripolis, another to the Indies; I understand, moreover, upon
the Rialto, he hath a third at Mexico, a fourth   20
for England, and other ventures he hath, squand'red
abroad. But ships are but boards, sailors but men;
there be land-rats and water-rats, water-thieves and
land-thieves, I mean pirates, and then there is the
peril of waters, winds, and rocks. The man is,   25
notwithstanding, sufficient. Three thousand ducats:
I think I may take his bond.

Bass. Be assured you may.

Shy. I will be assured I may; and, that I may   30
be assured, I will bethink me. May I speak with
Antonio?

Bass. If it please you to dine with us.

Shy. Yes, to smell pork; to eat of the habitation
which your prophet the Nazarite conjured the   35
devil into. I will buy with you, sell with you, talk
with you, walk with you, and so following; but I
will not eat with you, drink with you, nor pray with
you. What news on the Rialto? Who is he comes
here?   40

Enter ANTONIO.

Bass. This is Signior Antonio.

Shy. [*Aside.*] How like a fawning publican he
    looks!
I hate him for he is a Christian.
But more for that in low simplicity
He lends out money gratis, and brings down   45
The rate of usance here with us in Venice.
If I can catch him once upon the hip,
I will feed fat the ancient grudge I bear him.
He hates our sacred nation, and he rails,
Even there where merchants most do congregate,
On me, my bargains, and my well-won thrift,   51
Which he calls interest. Cursed be my tribe,

If I forgive him!

Bass.   Shylock, do you hear?

Shy. I am debating of my present store,
And, by the near guess of my memory,   55
I cannot instantly raise up the gross
Of full three thousand ducats. What of that?
Tubal, a wealthy Hebrew of my tribe,
Will furnish me. But soft! how many months
Do you desire? [*To Ant.*] Rest you fair, good
    signior;   60
Your worship was the last man in our mouths.

Ant. Shylock, albeit I neither lend nor borrow
By taking nor by giving of excess,
Yet, to supply the ripe wants of my friend,
I'll break a custom. Is he yet possess'd   65
How much ye would?

Shy.   Ay, ay, three thousand ducats.

Ant. And for three months.

Shy. I had forgot; three months; you told me so.
Well then, your bond; and let me see; — but hear
    you;
Methought you said you neither lend nor borrow   70
Upon advantage.

Ant.   I do never use it.

Shy. When Jacob graz'd his uncle Laban's
    sheep —
This Jacob from our holy Abram was,
As his wise mother wrought in his behalf,
The third possessor; ay, he was the third —   75

Ant. And what of him? Did he take interest?

Shy. No, not take int'rest, not, as you would say,
Directly int'rest. Mark what Jacob did.
When Laban and himself were compromis'd   79
That all the eanlings which were streak'd and pied
Should fall as Jacob's hire, the ewes, being rank,
In end of autumn turned to the rams,
And, when the work of generation was
Between these woolly breeders in the act,
The skilful shepherd pill'd me certain wands   85
And, in the doing of the deed of kind,
He stuck them up before the fulsome ewes,
Who then conceiving did in eaning time
Fall parti-colour'd lambs, and those were Jacob's.
This was a way to thrive, and he was blest;   90
And thrift is blessing, if men steal it not.

Ant. This was a venture, sir, that Jacob serv'd
    for;
A thing not in his power to bring to pass,
But sway'd and fashion'd by the hand of Heaven.
Was this inserted to make interest good?   95
Or is your gold and silver ewes and rams?

Sc. iii, 7. **stead:** help. 20. **Rialto:** the mart of Venice. 35. **Nazarite:** Nazarene. The reference is to Christ's driving
out devils from men into swine. (Luke vii.32–33.) 42. **publican:** term of scorn. 46. **usance:** interest. 47. **catch . . .
hip:** a wrestling term. 65–66. **Is . . . would.** Q₁. *Are you resolv'd, How much he would have* Q₂. **possess'd:** informed.
71. **Upon advantage:** for profit. 75. **possessor:** i.e., of God's promise to Abraham. 78–89. **Mark . . . Jacob's.** See Genesis
xxx.35–43. 79. **compromis'd:** agreed. 80. **eanlings:** new-born lambs. **pied:** spotted. 85. **pill'd:** peeled. 86. **kind:**
nature. 89. **Fall:** give birth to.

Shy. I cannot tell; I make it breed as fast.
But note me, signior.
    Ant.   Mark you this, Bassanio,
The devil can cite Scripture for his purpose.
An evil soul producing holy witness   100
Is like a villain with a smiling cheek,
A goodly apple rotten at the heart.
O, what a goodly outside falsehood hath!
    Shy. Three thousand ducats; 'tis a good round
        sum.
Three months from twelve; then, let me see; the
        rate —   105
    Ant. Well, Shylock, shall we be beholding to
        you?
    Shy. Signior Antonio, many a time and oft
In the Rialto you have rated me
About my moneys and my usances.
Still have I borne it with a patient shrug,   110
For suff'rance is the badge of all our tribe.
You call me misbeliever, cut-throat dog,
And spit upon my Jewish gaberdine,
And all for use of that which is mine own.
Well then, it now appears you need my help.   115
Go to, then! You come to me, and you say,
"Shylock, we would have moneys;" you say so —
You, that did void your rheum upon my beard
And foot me as you spurn a stranger cur
Over your threshold; moneys is your suit.   120
What should I say to you? Should I not say,
"Hath a dog money? Is it possible
A cur can lend three thousand ducats?" Or
Shall I bend low and in a bondman's key,
With bated breath and whisp'ring humbleness,   125
Say this:
"Fair sir, you spat on me on Wednesday last;
You spurn'd me such a day; another time
You call'd me dog; and for these courtesies
I'll lend you thus much moneys"?   130
    Ant. I am as like to call thee so again,
To spit on thee again, to spurn thee too.
If thou wilt lend this money, lend it not
As to thy friends; for when did friendship take
A breed for barren metal of his friend?   135
But lend it rather to thine enemy,
Who, if he break, thou mayst with better face
Exact the penalty.
    Shy.   Why, look you, how you storm!
I would be friends with you and have your love,
Forget the shames that you have stain'd me with,
Supply your present wants, and take no doit   141
Of usance for my moneys, and you'll not hear me.
This is kind I offer.
    Bass. This were kindness.
    Shy.   This kindness will I show.

Go with me to a notary, seal me there   145
Your single bond; and, in a merry sport,
If you repay me not on such a day,
In such a place, such sum or sums as are
Express'd in the condition, let the forfeit
Be nominated for an equal pound   150
Of your fair flesh, to be cut off and taken
In what part of your body pleaseth me.
    Ant. Content, i'faith, I'll seal to such a bond,
And say there is much kindness in the Jew.
    Bass. You shall not seal to such a bond for me;
I'll rather dwell in my necessity.   156
    Ant. Why, fear not, man; I will not forfeit it.
Within these two months, that's a month before
This bond expires, I do expect return
Of thrice three times the value of this bond. 160
    Shy. O father Abram, what these Christians are,
Whose own hard dealings teaches them suspect
The thoughts of others! Pray you, tell me this:
If he should break his day, what should I gain
By the exaction of the forfeiture?   165
A pound of man's flesh taken from a man
Is not so estimable, profitable neither,
As flesh of muttons, beefs, or goats. I say,
To buy his favour, I extend this friendship.
If he will take it, so; if not, adieu;   170
And, for my love, I pray you wrong me not.
    Ant. Yes, Shylock, I will seal unto this bond.
    Shy. Then meet me forthwith at the notary's;
Give him direction for this merry bond,
And I will go and purse the ducats straight,   175
See to my house, left in the fearful guard
Of an unthrifty knave, and presently
I will be with you.   [*Exit* [*Shylock*].
    Ant. Hie thee, gentle Jew.
The Hebrew will turn Christian; he grows kind.
    Bass. I like not fair terms and a villain's mind.
    Ant. Come on; in this there can be no dismay; 181
My ships come home a month before the day.
                                        [*Exeunt.*

ACT II

[SCENE I. *Belmont. A room in Portia's house.*]

Enter [*the* PRINCE OF] *Morocco, a tawny Moor, all
in white, and three or four followers accordingly,
with* PORTIA, NERISSA, *and their train. Flourish
of cornets.*

    Mor. Mislike me not for my complexion,
The shadowed livery of the burnish'd sun,
To whom I am a neighbour and near bred.
Bring me the fairest creature northward born,
Where Phœbus' fire scarce thaws the icicles,   5

108. **rated**: reviled. 113. **gaberdine**: cloak. 135. **breed**: increase, interest. 137. **Who**: from whom. **break**: fail. 141. **doit**: a small Dutch coin; cf. a farthing. 146. **single**: without endorsement. 150. **equal**: exact. 176. **fearful**: precarious.
    Act II, sc. i, 2. shadowed livery: black uniform, as if Morocco were the "retainer" of the sun.

And let us make incision for your love,
To prove whose blood is reddest, his or mine.
I tell thee, lady, this aspect of mine
Hath fear'd the valiant. By my love I swear
The best-regarded virgins of our clime   10
Have lov'd it too. I would not change this hue,
Except to steal your thoughts, my gentle queen.

Por. In terms of choice I am not solely led
By nice direction of a maiden's eyes;
Besides, the lott'ry of my destiny   15
Bars me the right of voluntary choosing.
But if my father had not scanted me
And hedg'd me by his wit, to yield myself
His wife who wins me by that means I told you,
Yourself, renowned Prince, then stood as fair   20
As any comer I have look'd on yet
For my affection.

Mor.   Even for that I thank you;
Therefore, I pray you, lead me to the caskets
To try my fortune. By this scimitar
That slew the Sophy and a Persian prince   25
That won three fields of Sultan Solyman,
I would o'erstare the sternest eyes that look,
Outbrave the heart most daring on the earth,
Pluck the young sucking cubs from the she-bear,
Yea, mock the lion when he roars for prey,   30
To win thee, lady. But, alas the while!
If Hercules and Lichas play at dice
Which is the better man, the greater throw
May turn by fortune from the weaker hand.
So is Alcides beaten by his [page];   35
And so may I, blind fortune leading me,
Miss that which one unworthier may attain,
And die with grieving.

Por.   You must take your chance,
And either not attempt to choose at all,
Or swear before you choose, if you choose wrong   40
Never to speak to lady afterward
In way of marriage; therefore be advis'd.

Mor. Nor will not. Come, bring me unto my
chance.

Por. First, forward to the temple. After dinner
Your hazard shall be made.

Mor.   Good fortune then!   45
To make me blest or cursed'st among men.

                    [*Cornets, and exeunt.*

[SCENE II. *Venice. A street.*]

Enter the Clown [LAUNCELOT] *alone.*

Laun. Certainly my conscience will serve me to

run from this Jew my master. The fiend is at mine
elbow and tempts me, saying to me, "Gobbo,
Launcelot Gobbo, good Launcelot," or "good
Gobbo," or "good Launcelot Gobbo, use your   5
legs, take the start, run away." My conscience
says, "No; take heed, honest Launcelot; take heed,
honest Gobbo," or, as aforesaid, "honest Launcelot
Gobbo; do not run; scorn running with thy heels."
Well, the most courageous fiend bids me pack.   10
"Via!" says the fiend; "away!" says the fiend;
"for the heavens, rouse up a brave mind," says the
fiend, "and run." Well, my conscience, hanging
about the neck of my heart, says very wisely to me,
"My honest friend Launcelot, being an honest   15
man's son," or rather an honest woman's son; for,
indeed, my father did something smack, something
grow to, he had a kind of taste, — well, my conscience says, "Launcelot, budge not." "Budge," says
the fiend. "Budge not," says my conscience. "Conscience," say I, "you counsel well;" "Fiend,"   20
say I, "you counsel well." To be rul'd by my
conscience, I should stay with the Jew my master,
who, God bless the mark, is a kind of devil; and, to
run away from the Jew, I should be rul'd by the   26
fiend, who, saving your reverence, is the devil himself. Certainly the Jew is the very devil incarnation; and, in my conscience, my conscience is but a
kind of hard conscience, to offer to counsel me to
stay with the Jew. The fiend gives the more   31
friendly counsel. I will run, fiend; my heels are at
your commandment; I will run.

Enter Old GOBBO, *with a basket.*

Gob. Master young man, you, I pray you, which
is the way to master Jew's?   35

Laun. [*Aside.*] O heavens! this is my true-begot-
ten father, who, being more than sand-blind, high-
gravel blind, knows me not. I will try confusions
with him.

Gob. Master young gentleman, I pray you, which
is the way to master Jew's?   41

Laun. Turn up on your right hand at the next
turning, but at the next turning of all, on your left;
marry at the very next turning, turn of no hand, but
turn down indirectly to the Jew's house.   46

Gob. By God's sonties, 'twill be a hard way to
hit. Can you tell me whether one Launcelot, that
dwells with him, dwell with him or no?

Laun. Talk you of young Master Launcelot?
[*Aside.*] Mark me now; now will I raise the   50
waters. — Talk you of young Master Launcelot?

13. **terms:** matters.   14. **nice:** fastidious.   17. **scanted:** restricted.   18. **wit:** wisdom, ingenuity.   25. **Sophy:** Shah of
Persia.   26. **Solyman:** Turkish Sultan (1520–1566).   32. **Lichas:** servant of Hercules (Alcides).   35. **[page]** (Theobald).
rage Qq.   44. **to the temple:** i.e., to take your oath.
Sc. ii, 10. pack: begone.   17–19. Launcelot means that his father was barely honest.   23. **well. To be** Q₁.   *ill. To*
be Q₂.   25. **God . . . mark:** a phrase of apology.   27. **incarnation** Q₁.   *incarnall* Q₂.   Incarnate.   33. **commandment** Q₁.
command Q₂.   37. **high-gravel blind:** Launcelot's original term for something less than stone-blind and more than sand-blind.
38. **confusions** Q₁.   *conclusions* Q₂.   47. **sonties:** diminutive of *sonts*, i.e., saints.   51. **waters:** tears.

Gob. No master, sir, but a poor man's son. His father, though I say 't, is an honest exceeding poor man and, God be thanked, well to live.   55

Laun. Well, let his father be what 'a will, we talk of young Master Launcelot.

Gob. Your worship's friend and Launcelot, sir.

Laun. But I pray you, ergo, old man, ergo, I beseech you, talk you of young Master Launcelot.   60

Gob. Of Launcelot, an't please your mastership.

Laun. Ergo, Master Launcelot. Talk not of Master Launcelot, father; for the young gentleman, according to Fates and Destinies and such odd   65 sayings, the Sisters Three and such branches of learning, is indeed deceased, or, as you would say in plain terms, gone to heaven.

Gob. Marry, God forbid! The boy was the very staff of my age, my very prop.   70

Laun. [*Aside.*] Do I look like a cudgel or a hovel-post, a staff or a prop? — Do you know me, father?

Gob. Alack the day, I know you not, young gentleman; but I pray you, tell me, is my boy, God rest his soul, alive or dead?   75

Laun. Do you not know me, father?

Gob. Alack, sir, I am sand-blind; I know you not.

Laun. Nay, indeed, if you had your eyes, you might fail of the knowing me; it is a wise fa-   80 ther that knows his own child. Well, old man, I will tell you news of your son. Give me your blessing; truth will come to light; murder cannot be hid long; a man's son may, but in the end truth will out.   85

Gob. Pray you, sir, stand up. I am sure you are not Launcelot, my boy.

Laun. Pray you, let's have no more fooling about it, but give me your blessing. I am Launcelot, your boy that was, your son that is, your child that shall be.   91

Gob. I cannot think you are my son.

Laun. I know not what I shall think of that; but I am Launcelot, the Jew's man, and I am sure Margery your wife is my mother.   95

Gob. Her name is Margery, indeed. I'll be sworn, if thou be Launcelot, thou art mine own flesh and blood. Lord worshipp'd might he be! what a beard hast thou got! Thou has got more hair on thy chin than Dobbin my fill-horse has on his tail.   101

Laun. It should seem, then, that Dobbin's tail grows backward. I am sure he had more hair of his tail than I have of my face when I last saw him.   105

Gob. Lord, how art thou chang'd! How dost thou and thy master agree? I have brought him a present. How 'gree you now?

Laun. Well, well: but, for mine own part, as I

have set up my rest to run away, so I will not   110 rest till I have run some ground. My master's a very Jew. Give him a present! give him a halter. I am famish'd in his service; you may tell every finger I have with my ribs. Father, I am glad you are come; give me your present to one Master   115 Bassanio, who, indeed, gives rare new liveries. If I serve not him, I will run as far as God has any ground. O rare fortune! here comes the man. To him, father; for I am a Jew, if I serve the Jew any longer.   120

Enter BASSANIO, *with* [LEONARDO *and other*] *followers.*

Bass. You may do so; but let it be so hasted that supper be ready at the farthest by five of the clock. See these letters delivered; put the liveries to making, and desire Gratiano to come anon to my lodging.   [*Exit one of his men.* 125

Laun. To him, father.

Gob. God bless your worship!

Bass. Gramercy! wouldst thou aught with me?

Gob. Here's my son, sir, a poor boy, —   129

Laun. Not a poor boy, sir, but the rich Jew's man; that would, sir, as my father shall specify —

Gob. He hath a great infection, sir, as one would say, to serve —   134

Laun. Indeed, the short and the long is, I serve the Jew, and have a desire, as my father shall specify —

Gob. His master and he, saving your worship's reverence, are scarce cater-cousins —   139

Laun. To be brief, the very truth is that the Jew, having done me wrong, doth cause me, as my father, being, I hope, an old man, shall frutify unto you —

Gob. I have here a dish of doves that I would bestow upon your worship, and my suit is —   145

Laun. In very brief, the suit is impertinent to myself, as your worship shall know by this honest old man; and, though I say it, though old man, yet poor man, my father.

Bass. One speak for both. What would you?   150

Laun. Serve you, sir.

Gob. That is the very defect of the matter, sir.

Bass. I know thee well; thou hast obtain'd thy suit.

Shylock thy master spoke with me this day,
And hath preferr'd thee, if it be preferment   155
To leave a rich Jew's service, to become
The follower of so poor a gentleman.

Laun. The old proverb is very well parted between my master Shylock and you, sir: you have the grace of God, sir, and he hath enough.   160

---

55. **well to live:** well to do. 59. **ergo:** therefore (here meaningless). 71. **hovel-post:** support used for a shed. 85. **in the end** Q1. *at the length* Q2. 99. **beard.** Launcelot has kneeled with his back to his father. 101. **fill-horse:** shaft-horse. 110. **set . . . rest:** resolved. 113. **tell:** count. 128. **Gramercy:** many thanks. 133. **infection:** blunder for *affection.* 139. **cater-cousins:** good friends. 143. **frutify:** blunder for *certify.* 152. **defect:** blunder for *effect* (heart). 158. **proverb:** "God's grace is gear enough."

Bass. Thou speak'st it well. Go, father, with thy
     son.
Take leave of thy old master, and inquire
My lodging out.   Give him a livery
More guarded than his fellows'; see it done.   164
     Laun. Father, in.   I cannot get a service, no;
I have ne'er a tongue in my head. [*Looks on his
palm.*]   Well, if any man in Italy have a fairer
table, which doth offer to swear upon a book, I shall
have good fortune.   Go to, here's a simple line of
life!   Here's a small trifle of wives!   Alas, fifteen
wives is nothing!   Eleven widows and nine   170
maids is a simple coming-in for one man.   And then
to 'scape drowning thrice, and to be in peril of my
life with the edge of a feather-bed; here are simple
scapes.   Well, if Fortune be a woman, she's a good
wench for this gear.   Father, come; I'll take my   175
leave of the Jew in the twinkling [of an eye].
          [*Exeunt Launcelot [and old Gobbo].*
     Bass. I pray thee, good Leonardo, think on this:
These things being bought and orderly bestow'd,
Return in haste, for I do feast to-night   180
My best esteem'd acquaintance.   Hie thee, go.
     Leon. My best endeavours shall be done herein.

          Enter GRATIANO.

     Gra. Where is your master?
     Leon.   Yonder, sir, he walks.
          [*Exit.*
     Gra. Signior Bassanio!
     Bass. Gratiano!   185
     Gra. I have a suit to you.
     Bass.   You have obtain'd it.
     Gra. You must not deny me; I must go with you
to Belmont.
     Bass. Why, then you must.   But hear thee,
          Gratiano;
Thou art too wild, too rude and bold of voice;   190
Parts that become thee happily enough
And in such eyes as ours appear not faults;
But where thou art not known, why, there they
          show
Something too liberal.   Pray thee, take pain
To allay with some cold drops of modesty   195
Thy skipping spirit, lest through thy wild behaviour
I be misconst'red in the place I go to,
And lose my hopes.
     Gra.   Signior Bassanio, hear me:
If I do not put on a sober habit,
Talk with respect and swear but now and then,   200
Wear prayer-books in my pocket, look demurely,
Nay more, while grace is saying, hood mine eyes
Thus with my hat, and sigh and say Amen,

Use all the observance of civility,
Like one well studied in a sad ostent   205
To please his grandam, never trust me more.
     Bass. Well, we shall see your bearing.
     Gra. Nay, but I bar to-night; you shall not gauge
          me
By what we do to-night.
     Bass.   No, that were pity.
I would entreat you rather to put on   210
Your boldest suit of mirth, for we have friends
That purpose merriment.   But fare you well!
I have some business.
     Gra. And I must to Lorenzo and the rest;   214
But we will visit you at supper-time.   [*Exeunt.*

          [SCENE III.   *The same.   A room in Shylock's
                    house.*]

     Enter JESSICA *and the Clown* [LAUNCELOT].

     Jes. I am sorry thou wilt leave my father so.
Our house is hell, and thou, a merry devil,
Didst rob it of some taste of tediousness.
But fare thee well, there is a ducat for thee;
And, Launcelot, soon at supper shalt thou see   5
Lorenzo, who is thy new master's guest.
Give him this letter; do it secretly;
And so farewell.   I would not have my father
See me in talk with thee.   9
     Laun. Adieu! tears exhibit my tongue.   Most
beautiful pagan, most sweet Jew! if a Christian do
not play the knave and get thee, I am much de-
ceived.   But, adieu! these foolish drops do some-
thing drown my manly spirit.   Adieu!   [*Exit.*
     Jes. Farewell, good Launcelot.   15
Alack, what heinous sin is it in me
To be asham'd to be my father's child!
But though I am a daughter to his blood,
I am not to his manners.   O Lorenzo,
If thou keep promise, I shall end this strife,   20
Become a Christian and thy loving wife.   [*Exit.*

          [SCENE IV.   *The same.   A street.*]

     Enter GRATIANO, LORENZO, SALARINO, *and*
               SALANIO.

     Lor. Nay, we will slink away in supper-time,
Disguise us at my lodging and return,
All in an hour.
     Gra. We have not made good preparation.
     Salar. We have not spoke us yet of torch-bearers.
     Salan. 'Tis vile, unless it may be quaintly
          order'd,
And better in my mind not undertook.

164. **guarded:** ornamented with braid.   168. **table:** palm.   169. **simple:** poor or small (ironical).   176. **[of an eye]** Q₂.
Om. Q₁.   194. **liberal:** free and easy.   199. **habit:** demeanor.   205. **sad ostent:** grave deportment.
Sc. iii, 10. **exhibit:** blunder for *inhibit.*
Sc. iv, 5. **spoke...of:** yet bespoken.   6. **quaintly:** elegantly.

Lor. 'Tis now but four o'clock; we have two hours
To furnish us.

Enter LAUNCELOT, *with a letter.*

     Friend Launcelot, what's the news?
Laun. An it shall please you to break up this, it
shall seem to signify.   11
Lor. I know the hand; in faith, 'tis a fair hand,
And whiter than the paper it writ on
Is the fair hand that writ.
Gra.   Love-news, in faith.
Laun. By your leave, sir.   15
Lor. Whither goest thou?
Laun. Marry, sir, to bid my old master the Jew,
to sup to-night with my new master the Christian.
Lor. Hold, here, take this. Tell gentle Jessica 20
I will not fail her; speak it privately; go.
         [*Exit Launcelot.*
Gentlemen,
Will you prepare you for this masque to-night?
I am provided of a torch-bearer. 24
Salar. Ay, marry, I'll be gone about it straight.
Salan. And so will I.
Lor.   Meet me and Gratiano
At Gratiano's lodging some hour hence.
Salar. 'Tis good we do so.
     [*Exeunt [Salar. and Salan.].*
Gra. Was not that letter from fair Jessica?
Lor. I must needs tell thee all. She hath directed
How I shall take her from her father's house, 31
What gold and jewels she is furnish'd with,
What page's suit she hath in readiness.
If e'er the Jew her father come to heaven,
It will be for his gentle daughter's sake; 35
And never dare misfortune cross her foot,
Unless she do it under this excuse,
That she is issue to a faithless Jew.
Come, go with me; peruse this as thou goest. 39
Fair Jessica shall be my torch-bearer. [*Exeunt.*

[SCENE V. *The same. Before Shylock's house.*]

Enter the Jew [SHYLOCK] *and* LAUNCELOT.

Shy. Well, thou shalt see, thy eyes shall be thy judge,
The difference of old Shylock and Bassanio. —
What, Jessica! — Thou shalt not gormandise,
As thou hast done with me, — What, Jessica! —
And sleep and snore, and rend apparel out; — 5
Why, Jessica, I say!
Laun.   Why, Jessica!

Shy. Who bids thee call? I do not bid thee call.
Laun. Your worship was wont to tell me I could
do nothing without bidding.

Enter JESSICA.

Jes. Call you? What is your will? 10
Shy. I am bid forth to supper, Jessica.
There are my keys. But wherefore should I go?
I am not bid for love; they flatter me;
But yet I'll go in hate, to feed upon
The prodigal Christian. Jessica, my girl, 15
Look to my house. I am right loath to go.
There is some ill a-brewing towards my rest,
For I did dream of money-bags to-night.
Laun. I beseech you, sir, go. My young master
doth expect your reproach. 20
Shy. So do I his.
Laun. And they have conspired together. I will
not say you shall see a masque; but if you do, then
it was not for nothing that my nose fell a-bleeding
on Black Monday last at six o'clock i' th' morn- 25
ing, falling out that year on Ash Wednesday was four
year, in th' afternoon.
Shy. What, are there masques? Hear you me,
Jessica.
Lock up my doors; and when you hear the drum
And the vile squealing of the wry-neck'd fife, 30
Clamber not you up to the casements then,
Nor thrust your head into the public street
To gaze on Christian fools with varnish'd faces,
But stop my house's ears, I mean my casements.
Let not the sound of shallow fopp'ry enter 35
My sober house. By Jacob's staff I swear
I have no mind of feasting forth to-night;
But I will go. Go you before me, sirrah;
Say I will come.
Laun. I will go before, sir. Mistress, look out at
window, for all this; 41
   There will come a Christian by,
    Will be worth a Jewess' eye. [*Exit.*]
Shy. What says that fool of Hagar's offspring, ha?
Jes. His words were "Farewell, Mistress!"
nothing else. 45
Shy. The patch is kind enough, but a huge feeder;
Snail-slow in profit, and he sleeps by day
More than the wild-cat. Drones hive not with me;
Therefore I part with him, and part with him
To one that I would have him help to waste 50
His borrowed purse. Well, Jessica, go in.
Perhaps I will return immediately.
Do as I bid you, shut doors after you;
Fast bind, fast find;
A proverb never stale in thrifty mind. [*Exit.* 55

---

10. **up:** open. 36. **dare:** i.e., will dare. **foot:** i.e., path. 38. **faithless:** unbelieving.
Sc. v, 18. **to-night:** last night. 20. **reproach:** blunder for *approach.* 30. **wry-neck'd fife:** fife-player holding his head awry. 33. **varnish'd faces:** painted faces or masks. 44. **fool of Hagar's offspring:** Ishmaelite, a term of reproach. 46. **patch:** fool.

Jes. Farewell; and if my fortune be not cross'd,
I have a father, you a daughter, lost.   [*Exit.*

[SCENE VI.   *The same.*]

Enter GRATIANO *and* SALARINO, *masked.*

Gra. This is the pent-house under which Lorenzo
Desir'd us to make stand.
Salar.   His hour is almost past.
Gra. And it is marvel he out-dwells his hour,
For lovers ever run before the clock.
Salar. O, ten times faster Venus' pigeons fly   5
To seal love's bonds new-made than they are wont
To keep obliged faith unforfeited!
Gra. That ever holds.   Who riseth from a feast
With that keen appetite that he sits down?
Where is the horse that doth untread again   10
His tedious measures with the unbated fire
That he did pace them first?   All things that are,
Are with more spirit chased than enjoy'd.
How like a younker or a prodigal
The scarfed bark puts from her native bay,   15
Hugg'd and embraced by the strumpet wind!
How like the prodigal doth she return,
With over-weather'd ribs and ragged sails,
Lean, rent, and beggar'd by the strumpet wind!
Salar. Here comes Lorenzo; more of this here-
after.   20

Enter LORENZO.

Lor. Sweet friends, your patience for my long
abode;
Not I, but my affairs, have made you wait.
When you shall please to play the thieves for wives,
I'll watch as long for you then.   Approach;
Here dwells my father Jew.   Ho! who's within?   25

Enter JESSICA, *above* [*in boy's clothes*].

Jes. Who are you?   Tell me for more certainty,
Albeit I'll swear that I do know your tongue.
Lor. Lorenzo, and thy love.
Jes. Lorenzo, certain, and my love indeed,
For who love I so much?   And now who knows
But you, Lorenzo, whether I am yours?   31
Lor. Heaven and thy thoughts are witness that
thou art.
Jes. Here, catch this casket; it is worth the pains.
I am glad 'tis night, you do not look on me,
For I am much asham'd of my exchange.   35
But love is blind and lovers cannot see
The pretty follies that themselves commit;
For if they could, Cupid himself would blush
To see me thus transformed to a boy.   39

Lor. Descend, for you must be my torchbearer.
Jes. What, must I hold a candle to my shames?
They in themselves, good sooth, are too too light.
Why, 'tis an office of discovery, love;
And I should be obscur'd.
Lor.   So are you, sweet,
Even in the lovely garnish of a boy.   45
But come at once;
For the close night doth play the runaway,
And we are stay'd for at Bassanio's feast.
Jes. I will make fast the doors, and gild myself
With some moe ducats, and be with you straight.
[*Exit above.*
Gra. Now, by my hood, a [Gentile] and no Jew.
Lor. Beshrew me but I love her heartily;   52
For she is wise, if I can judge of her,
And fair she is, if that mine eyes be true,
And true she is, as she hath prov'd herself,   55
And therefore, like herself, wise, fair, and true,
Shall she be placed in my constant soul.

Enter JESSICA [*below*].

What, art thou come?   On, gentlemen; away!
Our masquing mates by this time for us stay.
[*Exit* [*with Jessica and Salarino*].

Enter ANTONIO.

Ant. Who's there?   60
Gra. Signior Antonio!
Ant. Fie, fie, Gratiano! where are all the rest?
'Tis nine o'clock; our friends all stay for you.
No masque to-night; the wind is come about,
Bassanio presently will go aboard.   65
I have sent twenty out to seek for you.
Gra. I am glad on't.   I desire no more delight
Than to be under sail and gone to-night.   [*Exeunt.*

[SCENE VII.   *Belmont.   A room in Portia's house.*]
[*Flourish of cornets.*]   *Enter* PORTIA *with* [*the* PRINCE
OF] MOROCCO, *and their trains.*

Por. Go draw aside the curtains and discover
The several caskets to this noble prince.
Now make your choice.
Mor. The first, of gold, who this inscription bears,
"Who chooseth me shall gain what many men
desire;"   5
The second, silver, which this promise carries,
"Who chooseth me shall get as much as he deserves;"
This third, dull lead, with warning all as blunt,
"Who chooseth me must give and hazard all he
hath."
How shall I know if I do choose the right?   10

<hr>

Sc. vi, 1. **pent-house**: projecting roof.   5. **Venus' pigeons**: the doves that drew Venus's chariot.   7. **obliged**: plighted.
10. **untread**: retrace.   14. **younker**: youngster.   15. **scarfed**: decked with flags.   42. **light**: wanton.   43. **office of dis-**
covery: i.e., the business of torches is to reveal.   45. **garnish**: garb.   47. **close**: dark, secret.   51. [Gentile] Q2.   *gentle* Q1.
In either case, there is a quibble.
Sc. vii, 1. **discover**: disclose.

Por. The one of them contains my picture, Prince:
If you choose that, then I am yours withal.

   Mor. Some god direct my judgement!   Let me
see;
I will survey th' inscriptions back again.
What says this leaden casket?   15
"Who chooseth me must give and hazard all he
    hath."
Must give: for what?   For lead?   Hazard for
lead?
This casket threatens.   Men that hazard all
Do it in hope of fair advantages;
A golden mind stoops not to shows of dross.   20
I'll then nor give nor hazard aught for lead.
What says the silver with her virgin hue?
"Who chooseth me shall get as much as he de-
    serves."
As much as he deserves!   Pause there, Morocco,
And weigh thy value with an even hand.   25
If thou be'st rated by thy estimation,
Thou dost deserve enough; and yet enough
May not extend so far as to the lady;
And yet to be afeard of my deserving
Were but a weak disabling of myself.   30
As much as I deserve!   Why, that's the lady.
I do in birth deserve her, and in fortunes,
In graces, and in qualities of breeding;
But more than these, in love I do deserve.
What if I stray'd no farther, but chose here?   35
Let's see once more this saying grav'd in gold:
"Who chooseth me shall gain what many men de-
    sire."
Why, that's the lady; all the world desires her.
From the four corners of the earth they come
To kiss this shrine, this mortal-breathing saint. 40
The Hyrcanian deserts and the vasty wilds
Of wide Arabia are as throughfares now
For princes to come view fair Portia.
The watery kingdom, whose ambitious head
Spits in the face of heaven, is no bar   45
To stop the foreign spirits, but they come
As o'er a brook to see fair Portia.
One of these three contains her heavenly picture.
Is't like that lead contains her?   'Twere damnation
To think so base a thought.   It were too gross 50
To rib her cerecloth in the obscure grave.
Or shall I think in silver she's immur'd,
Being ten times undervalu'd to tri'd gold?
O sinful thought!   Never so rich a gem
Was set in worse than gold.   They have in England
A coin that bears the figure of an angel   56
Stamped in gold, but that's insculp'd upon;
But here an angel in a golden bed
Lies all within.   Deliver me the key.
Here do I choose, and thrive I as I may!   60

   Por. There, take it, Prince; and if my form lie
there,
Then I am yours.   [*He unlocks the golden casket.*]
   Mor.   O hell! what have we here?
A carrion Death within whose empty eye
There is a written scroll!   I'll read the writing.
[*Reads.*] "All that glisters is not gold;   65
    Often have you heard that told.
    Many a man his life hath sold
    But my outside to behold.
    Gilded [tombs] do worms infold.
    Had you been as wise as bold,   70
    Young in limbs, in judgement old,
    Your answer had not been inscroll'd.
    Fare you well; your suit is cold."
   Cold, indeed; and labour lost:
Then, farewell, heat, and welcome, frost!   75
Portia, adieu.   I have too griev'd a heart
To take a tedious leave; thus losers part.
             [*Exit.   Flourish of cornets.*
   Por. A gentle riddance.   Draw the curtains, go.
Let all of his complexion choose me so.   [*Exeunt.*

[SCENE VIII.   *Venice.   A street.*]

Enter SALARINO *and* SALANIO.

   Salar. Why, man, I saw Bassanio under sail.
With him is Gratiano gone along,
And in their ship I'm sure Lorenzo is not.
   Salan. The villain Jew with outcries rais'd the
    Duke,
Who went with him to search Bassanio's ship.   5
   Salar. He came too late, the ship was under sail;
But there the Duke was given to understand
That in a gondola were seen together
Lorenzo and his amorous Jessica.
Besides, Antonio certified the Duke   10
They were not with Bassanio in his ship.
   Salan. I never heard a passion so confus'd,
So strange, outrageous, and so variable
As the dog Jew did utter in the streets.   14
"My daughter!   O my ducats!   O my daughter!
Fled with a Christian!   O my Christian ducats!
Justice! the law! my ducats, and my daughter!
A sealed bag, two sealed bags of ducats,
Of double ducats, stol'n from me by my daughter!
And jewels, two stones, two rich and precious stones,
Stol'n by my daughter!   Justice! find the girl;   21
She hath the stones upon her, and the ducats."
   Salar. Why, all the boys in Venice follow him,
Crying, his stones, his daughter, and his ducats.
   Salan. Let good Antonio look he keep his day, 25
Or he shall pay for this.
   Salar.   Marry, well remem'bred.

   30. **disabling:** undervaluing.   41. **Hyrcanian.** Hyrcania was a district in Asia.   51. **rib:** wrap, hold.   **cerecloth:** shroud.
63. **carrion Death:** death's head.   69. **[tombs]** (Johnson conj.).   *timber* Qq.

I reason'd with a Frenchman yesterday,
Who told me, in the narrow seas that part
The French and English, there miscarried
A vessel of our country richly fraught.   30
I thought upon Antonio when he told me;
And wish'd in silence that it were not his.
    Salan. You were best to tell Antonio what you
        hear;
Yet do not suddenly, for it may grieve him.
    Salar. A kinder gentleman treads not the earth.
I saw Bassanio and Antonio part;   36
Bassanio told him he would make some speed
Of his return; he answer'd, "Do not so;
Slubber not business for my sake, Bassanio,
But stay the very riping of the time;   40
And for the Jew's bond which he hath of me,
Let it not enter in your mind of love.
Be merry, and employ your chiefest thoughts
To courtship and such fair ostents of love
As shall conveniently become you there."   45
And even there, his eye being big with tears,
Turning his face, he put his hand behind him,
And with affection wondrous sensible
He wrung Bassanio's hand; and so they parted.
    Salan. I think he only loves the world for him. 50
I pray thee, let us go and find him out
And quicken his embraced heaviness
With some delight or other.
    Salar.   Do we so.   [*Exeunt.*

[SCENE IX.   *Belmont.   A room in Portia's house.*]

Enter NERISSA *with a* Servitor.

    Ner. Quick, quick, I pray thee; draw the curtain
        straight.
The Prince of Arragon hath ta'en his oath,
And comes to his election presently.

Flourish of cornets.   Enter the PRINCE OF ARRAGON,
    PORTIA, *and their trains.*

    Por. Behold, there stand the caskets, noble
        Prince.
If you choose that wherein I am contain'd,   5
Straight shall our nuptial rites be solemniz'd;
But if you fail, without more speech, my lord,
You must be gone from hence immediately.
    Ar. I am enjoin'd by oath to observe three things:
First, never to unfold to any one   10
Which casket 'twas I chose; next, if I fail
Of the right casket, never in my life
To woo a maid in way of marriage;
Lastly,
If I do fail in fortune of my choice,   15
Immediately to leave you and be gone.

    Por. To these injunctions every one doth swear
That comes to hazard for my worthless self.
    Ar. And so have I address'd me.   Fortune now
To my heart's hope!   Gold; silver; and base lead. 20
"Who chooseth me must give and hazard all he
        hath."
You shall look fairer, ere I give or hazard.
What says the golden chest?   Ha! let me see:
"Who chooseth me shall gain what many men de-
        sire."
What many men desire!   That many may be
        meant   25
By the fool multitude, that choose by show,
Not learning more than the fond eye doth teach;
Which pries not to th' interior, but, like the martlet,
Builds in the weather on the outward wall,
Even in the force and road of casualty.   30
I will not choose what many men desire,
Because I will not jump with common spirits
And rank me with the barbarous multitudes.
Why, then to thee, thou silver treasure-house;
Tell me once more what title thou dost bear: 35
"Who chooseth me shall get as much as he de-
        serves;"
And well said too; for who shall go about
To cozen fortune and be honourable
Without the stamp of merit?   Let none presume
To wear an undeserved dignity.   40
O, that estates, degrees, and offices
Were not deriv'd corruptly, and that clear honour
Were purchas'd by the merit of the wearer!
How many then should cover that stand bare!
How many be commanded that command!   45
How much low peasantry would then be glean'd
From the true seed of honour! and how much honour
Pick'd from the chaff and ruin of the times
To be new-varnish'd!   Well, but to my choice:
"Who chooseth me shall get as much as he deserves."
I will assume desert.   Give me a key for this,   51
And instantly unlock my fortunes here.
                [*He opens the silver casket.*]
    Por. Too long a pause for that which you find
        there.
    Ar. What's here?   The portrait of a blinking idiot,
Presenting me a schedule!   I will read it.   55
How much unlike art thou to Portia!
How much unlike my hopes and my deservings!
"Who chooseth me shall have as much as he de-
        serves."
Did I deserve no more than a fool's head?
Is that my prize?   Are my deserts no better?   60
    Por. To offend and judge are distinct offices
And of opposed natures.
    Ar.   What is here?

Sc. viii, 27. **reason'd**: talked.   39. **Slubber**: do slovenly.   44. **ostents**: demonstrations.   48. **sensible**: intense.
Sc. ix, 19. **address'd**: prepared.   27. **fond**: foolish.   28. **martlet**: martin.   29. **in**: exposed to.   30. **casualty**: mischance.
32. **jump**: agree.   38. **cozen**: cheat.   44. **cover**: put on their hats.   46. **glean'd**: picked out, i.e., separated.   47. **seed of
honour**: nobility.   61–62. **To . . . natures**: i.e., Having taken your chance, you are not entitled to quarrel with the outcome.

[*Reads.*] "The fire seven times tried this;
Seven times tried that judgement is,
That did never choose amiss.   65
Some there be that shadows kiss,
Such have but a shadow's bliss.
There be fools alive, iwis,
Silver'd o'er; and so was this.
Take what wife you will to bed,   70
I will ever be your head.
So be gone; you are sped."

Still more fool I shall appear
By the time I linger here.
With one fool's head I came to woo,   75
But I go away with two.
Sweet, adieu. I'll keep my oath,
Patiently to bear my wroth.
                [*Exeunt Arragon and train.*]
  Por. Thus hath the candle sing'd the moth.
O, these deliberate fools! When they do choose,   80
They have the wisdom by their wit to lose.
  Ner. The ancient saying is no heresy,
Hanging and wiving goes by destiny.
  Por. Come, draw the curtain, Nerissa.

                Enter a MESSENGER.

  Mess. Where is my lady?
  Por.   Here; what would my lord?   85
  Mess. Madam, there is alighted at your gate
A young Venetian, one that comes before
To signify th' approaching of his lord;
From whom he bringeth sensible regreets,
To wit, besides commends and courteous breath,   90
Gifts of rich value. Yet I have not seen
So likely an ambassador of love.
A day in April never came so sweet,
To show how costly summer was at hand,
As this fore-spurrer comes before his lord.   95
  Por. No more, I pray thee. I am half afeard
Thou wilt say anon he is some kin to thee,
Thou spend'st such high-day wit in praising him.
Come, come, Nerissa, for I long to see
Quick Cupid's post that comes so mannerly.   100
  Ner. Bassanio, lord Love, if thy will it be!
                                [*Exeunt.*

ACT III

[SCENE I. *Venice. A street.*]

Enter SALANIO *and* SALARINO.

  Salan. Now, what news on the Rialto?
  Salar. Why, yet it lives there uncheck'd that Antonio hath a ship of rich lading wrack'd on the narrow seas; the Goodwins, I think they call the place; a very dangerous flat, and fatal, where the   5
carcases of many a tall ship lie buried, as they say, if my gossip Report be an honest woman of her word.
  Salan. I would she were as lying a gossip in that as ever knapp'd ginger or made her neighbours   10
believe she wept for the death of a third husband. But it is true, without any slips of prolixity or crossing the plain highway of talk, that the good Antonio, the honest Antonio, — O that I had a title good enough to keep his name company! —   16
  Salar. Come, the full stop.
  Salan. Ha! what sayest thou? Why, the end is, he hath lost a ship.
  Salar. I would it might prove the end of his losses.   21
  Salan. Let me say Amen betimes, lest the devil cross my prayer, for here he comes in the likeness of a Jew.

                Enter SHYLOCK.

How now, Shylock! what news among the merchants?   26
  Shy. You knew, none so well, none so well as you, of my daughter's flight.
  Salar. That's certain. I, for my part, knew the tailor that made the wings she flew withal.   30
  Salan. And Shylock, for his own part, knew the bird was fledg'd; and then it is the complexion of them all to leave the dam.
  Shy. She is damn'd for it.
  Salar. That's certain, if the devil may be her judge.   36
  Shy. My own flesh and blood to rebel!
  Salan. Out upon it, old carrion! Rebels it at these years?
  Shy. I say, my daughter is my flesh and my blood.   40
  Salar. There is more difference between thy flesh and hers than between jet and ivory; more between your bloods than there is between red wine and rhenish. But tell us, do you hear whether Antonio have had any loss at sea or no?   45
  Shy. There I have another bad match. A bankrupt, a prodigal, who dare scarce show his head on the Rialto; a beggar, that was us'd to come so smug upon the mart; let him look to his bond. He was wont to call me usurer; let him look to his bond.   50
He was wont to lend money for a Christian courtesy; let him look to his bond.
  Salar. Why, I am sure, if he forfeit, thou wilt not take his flesh. What's that good for?

68. iwis: certainly. 78. wroth: chagrin. 89. sensible regreets: moving greetings. 94. costly: lavish. 98. high-day: holiday, high-flown.
  Act III, sc. i, 2. it...uncheck'd: there is an unconfirmed report. 4. Goodwins: Goodwin Sands, off the mouth of the Thames. 10. knapp'd: chewed. 32. complexion: instinct. 46. match: bargain.

Shy. To bait fish withal. If it will feed nothing else, it will feed my revenge. He hath disgrac'd 56 me, and hind'red me half a million; laugh'd at my losses, mock'd at my gains, scorn'd my nation, thwarted my bargains, cool'd my friends, heated mine enemies; and what's his reason? I am a 60 Jew. Hath not a Jew eyes? Hath not a Jew hands, organs, dimensions, senses, affections, passions; fed with the same food, hurt with the same weapons, subject to the same diseases, heal'd by the same means, warm'd and cool'd by the same winter 65 and summer, as a Christian is? If you prick us, do we not bleed? If you tickle us, do we not laugh? If you poison us, do we not die? And if you wrong us, shall we not revenge? If we are like you in the rest, we will resemble you in that. If a Jew 70 wrong a Christian, what is his humility? Revenge. If a Christian wrong a Jew, what should his suffer-ance be by Christian example? Why, revenge. The villainy you teach me, I will execute, and it shall go hard but I will better the instruction. 76

Enter a [SERVANT].

Serv. Gentlemen, my master Antonio is at his house and desires to speak with you both.
Salar. We have been up and down to seek him.

Enter TUBAL.

Salan. Here comes another of the tribe; a 80 third cannot be match'd, unless the devil himself turn Jew. [*Exeunt* [*Salan., Salar., and Servant*].
Shy. How now, Tubal! what news from Genoa? Hast thou found my daughter?
Tub. I often came where I did hear of her, but cannot find her. 86
Shy. Why, there, there, there, there! A dia-mond gone, cost me two thousand ducats in Frank-fort! The curse never fell upon our nation till now. I never felt it till now. Two thousand ducats 90 in that; and other precious, precious jewels. I would my daughter were dead at my foot, and the jewels in her ear! Would she were hears'd at my foot, and the ducats in her coffin! No news of them? Why so? And I know not what's spent 95 in the search. Why, thou loss upon loss! the thief gone with so much, and so much to find the thief; and no satisfaction, no revenge, nor no ill luck stirring but what lights o' my shoulders, no sighs but o' my breathing, no tears but o' my 100 shedding.
Tub. Yes, other men have ill luck too. Antonio, as I heard in Genoa, —
Shy. What, what, what? Ill luck, ill luck?

Tub. Hath an argosy cast away, coming from Tripolis. 106
Shy. I thank God, I thank God. Is it true, is it true?
Tub. I spoke with some of the sailors that es-caped the wreck. 110
Shy. I thank thee, good Tubal; good news, good news! Ha, ha! [Heard] in Genoa?
Tub. Your daughter spent in Genoa, as I heard, in one night fourscore ducats.
Shy. Thou stick'st a dagger in me. I shall 115 never see my gold again. Fourscore ducats at a sitting! Fourscore ducats!
Tub. There came divers of Antonio's creditors in my company to Venice, that swear he cannot choose but break. 120
Shy. I am very glad of it. I'll plague him; I'll torture him. I am glad of it.
Tub. One of them showed me a ring that he had of your daughter for a monkey.
Shy. Out upon her! Thou torturest me, 125 Tubal. It was my turquoise; I had it of Leah when I was a bachelor. I would not have given it for a wilderness of monkeys.
Tub. But Antonio is certainly undone.
Shy. Nay, that's true, that's very true. Go, 130 Tubal, fee me an officer; bespeak him a fortnight before. I will have the heart of him, if he forfeit; for, were he out of Venice, I can make what mer-chandise I will. Go, go, Tubal, and meet me at our synagogue; go, good Tubal; at our synagogue, 135 Tubal. [*Exeunt.*

[SCENE II. *Belmont. A room in Portia's house.*]

Enter BASSANIO, PORTIA, GRATIANO, [NERISSA,] *and all their train.*

Por. I pray you, tarry. Pause a day or two
Before you hazard; for, in choosing wrong,
I lose your company; therefore forbear awhile.
There's something tells me, but it is not love,
I would not lose you; and, you know yourself, 5
Hate counsels not in such a quality.
But lest you should not understand me well, —
And yet a maiden hath no tongue but thought, —
I would detain you here some month or two
Before you venture for me. I could teach you 10
How to choose right, but then I am forsworn.
So will I never be; so may you miss me;
But if you do, you'll make me wish a sin,
That I had been forsworn. Beshrew your eyes,
They have o'erlook'd me and divided me; 15
One half of me is yours, the other half yours,
Mine own, I would say; but if mine, then yours,

And so all yours. O, these naughty times
Puts bars between the owners and their rights.
And so, though yours, not yours. Prove it so, 20
Let fortune go to hell for it, not I.
I speak too long; but 'tis to peize the time,
To eke it and to draw it out in length,
To stay you from election.
   Bass.   Let me choose;
For as I am, I live upon the rack. 25
   Por. Upon the rack, Bassanio! Then confess
What treason there is mingled with your love.
   Bass. None but that ugly treason of mistrust,
Which makes me fear th' enjoying of my love.
There may as well be amity and life 30
'Tween snow and fire, as treason and my love.
   Por. Ay, but I fear you speak upon the rack,
Where men enforced do speak anything.
   Bass. Promise me life, and I'll confess the truth.
   Por. Well then, confess and live.
   Bass.   "Confess and love"
Had been the very sum of my confession. 36
O happy torment, when my torturer
Doth teach me answers for deliverance!
But let me to my fortune and the caskets.
   Por. Away, then! I am lock'd in one of them;
If you do love me, you will find me out. 41
Nerissa and the rest, stand all aloof.
Let music sound while he doth make his choice;
Then, if he lose, he makes a swan-like end,
Fading in music. That the comparison 45
May stand more proper, my eye shall be the stream
And watery death-bed for him. He may win;
And what is music then? Then music is
Even as the flourish when true subjects bow
To a new-crowned monarch; such it is 50
As are those dulcet sounds in break of day
That creep into the dreaming bridegroom's ear
And summon him to marriage. Now he goes,
With no less presence but with much more love,
Than young Alcides, when he did redeem 55
The virgin tribute paid by howling Troy
To the sea-monster. I stand for sacrifice;
The rest aloof are the Dardanian wives,
With bleared visages, come forth to view
The issue of the exploit. Go, Hercules! 60
Live thou, I live. With much, much more dismay
I view the fight than thou that mak'st the fray.

    A song, the whilst BASSANIO *comments on the
      caskets to himself.*

    Tell me where is fancy bred,
      Or in the heart or in the head?
    How begot, how nourished? 65
      Reply, reply.

      It is engend'red in the eyes,
      With gazing fed; and fancy dies
      In the cradle where it lies.
         Let us all ring fancy's knell; 70
         I'll begin it, — Ding, dong, bell.
   All. Ding, dong, bell.

   Bass. So may the outward shows be least them-
selves;
The world is still deceiv'd with ornament.
In law, what plea so tainted and corrupt 75
But, being season'd with a gracious voice,
Obscures the show of evil? In religion,
What damned error but some sober brow
Will bless it and approve it with a text,
Hiding the grossness with fair ornament? 80
There is no vice so simple but assumes
Some mark of virtue on his outward parts.
How many cowards, whose hearts are all as false
As stairs of sand, wear yet upon their chins
The beards of Hercules and frowning Mars, 85
Who, inward search'd, have livers white as milk;
And these assume but valour's excrement
To render them redoubted! Look on beauty,
And you shall see 'tis purchas'd by the weight;
Which therein works a miracle in nature, 90
Making them lightest that wear most of it.
So are those crisped snaky golden locks,
Which make such wanton gambols with the wind
Upon supposed fairness, often known
To be the dowry of a second head, 95
The skull that bred them in the sepulchre.
Thus ornament is but the guiled shore
To a most dangerous sea; the beauteous scarf
Veiling an Indian beauty; in a word,
The seeming truth which cunning times put on
T' entrap the wisest. Therefore, then, thou gaudy
    gold, 101
Hard food for Midas, I will none of thee;
Nor none of thee, thou pale and common drudge
'Tween man and man; but thou, thou meagre lead,
Which rather threat'nest than dost promise aught,
Thy plainness moves me more than eloquence; 106
And here choose I. Joy be the consequence!
   Por. [*Aside.*] How all the other passions fleet
    to air,
As doubtful thoughts, and rash-embrac'd despair,
And shudd'ring fear, and green-ey'd jealousy! 110
O love, be moderate; allay thy ecstasy;
In measure rein thy joy; scant this excess!
I feel too much thy blessing; make it less,
For fear I surfeit.
   Bass.   What find I here? 115
           [*Opening the leaden casket.*]

---

   18. **naughty:** wicked. 22. **peize:** retard (by weighting down). 55. **Alcides:** i.e., Hercules, who rescued the Trojan princess Hesione. 58. **Dardanian:** Trojan. 63. **fancy:** love. 79. **approve:** confirm. 81. **simple:** unmixed. 87. **valour's excrement:** a brave man's beard. 88. **redoubted:** feared. 94. **supposed:** artificial. 97. **guiled:** treacherous. 102. **Midas:** the Phrygian king who turned whatever he touched to gold.

Fair Portia's counterfeit!   What demi-god
Hath come so near creation?   Move these eyes?
Or whether, riding on the balls of mine,
Seem they in motion?   Here are sever'd lips,
Parted with sugar breath; so sweet a bar   120
Should sunder such sweet friends.   Here in her
    hairs
The painter plays the spider, and hath woven
A golden mesh t' entrap the hearts of men
Faster than gnats in cobwebs.   But her eyes, —
How could he see to do them?   Having made one,
Methinks it should have power to steal both his   126
And leave itself unfurnish'd.   Yet look, how far
The substance of my praise doth wrong this shadow
In underprizing it, so far this shadow
Doth limp behind the substance.   Here's the scroll,
The continent and summary of my fortune.   131
[*Reads.*]   "You that choose not by the view,
    Chance as fair and choose as true!
    Since this fortune falls to you,
    Be content and seek no new.   135
    If you be well pleas'd with this
    And hold your fortune for your bliss,
    Turn you where your lady is
    And claim her with a loving kiss."
A gentle scroll.   Fair lady, by your leave;   140
I come by note, to give and to receive.
Like one of two contending in a prize,
That thinks he hath done well in people's eyes,
Hearing applause and universal shout,
Giddy in spirit, still gazing in a doubt   145
Whether those peals of praise be his or no;
So, thrice-fair lady, stand I, even so,
As doubtful whether what I see be true,
Until confirm'd, sign'd, ratified by you.
   Por.   You see me, Lord Bassanio, where I stand,
Such as I am.   Though for myself alone   151
I would not be ambitious in my wish
To wish myself much better; yet, for you
I would be trebled twenty times myself,
A thousand times more fair, ten thousand times   155
More rich; that only to stand high in your account,
I might in virtues, beauties, livings, friends,
Exceed account.   But the full sum of me
Is sum of — something, which, to term in gross,   160
Is an unlesson'd girl, unschool'd, unpractis'd;
Happy in this, she is not yet so old
But she may learn; happier than this,
She is not bred so dull but she can learn;
Happiest of all is that her gentle spirit   165
Commits itself to yours to be directed,
As from her lord, her governor, her king.
Myself and what is mine to you and yours
Is now converted.   But now I was the lord

Of this fair mansion, master of my servants,   170
Queen o'er myself; and even now, but now,
This house, these servants, and this same myself
Are yours, my lord; I give them with this ring;
Which when you part from, lose, or give away,
Let it presage the ruin of your love   175
And be my vantage to exclaim on you.
   Bass.   Madam, you have bereft me of all words,
Only my blood speaks to you in my veins;
And there is such confusion in my powers,
As, after some oration fairly spoke   180
By a beloved prince, there doth appear
Among the buzzing pleased multitude;
Where every something, being blent together,
Turns to a wild of nothing, save of joy   184
Express'd and not express'd.   But when this ring
Parts from this finger, then parts life from hence;
O, then be bold to say Bassanio's dead!
   Ner.   My lord and lady, it is now our time,
That have stood by and seen our wishes prosper,
To cry good joy.   Good joy, my lord and lady!
   Gra.   My Lord Bassanio and my gentle lady,
I wish you all the joy that you can wish,   192
For I am sure you can wish none from me;
And when your honours mean to solemnize
The bargain of your faith, I do beseech you,   195
Even at that time I may be married too.
   Bass.   With all my heart, so thou canst get a wife.
   Gra.   I thank your lordship, you have got me one.
My eyes, my lord, can look as swift as yours.
You saw the mistress, I beheld the maid;   200
You lov'd, I lov'd; for intermission
No more pertains to me, my lord, than you.
Your fortune stood upon the caskets there,
And so did mine too, as the matter falls;
For, wooing here until I sweat again,   205
And swearing till my very roof was dry
With oaths of love, at last, if promise last,
I got a promise of this fair one here
To have her love, provided that your fortune
Achiev'd her mistress.
   Por.   Is this true, Nerissa?   210
   Ner.   Madam, it is, so you stand pleas'd withal.
   Bass.   And do you, Gratiano, mean good faith?
   Gra.   Yes, faith, my lord.
   Bass.   Our feast shall be much honour'd in your
     marriage.   215
   Gra.   We'll play with them the first boy for a
thousand ducats.
   Ner.   What, and stake down?
   Gra.   No; we shall ne'er win at that sport and
stake down.   220
But who comes here?   Lorenzo and his infidel?
What, and my old Venetian friend Salerio?

---

116. **counterfeit**: portrait.   127. **unfurnish'd**: without its mate.   131. **continent**: container.   141. **note**: direction.   142. **prize**: competition.   156. **account**: opinion.   159. **account**: reckoning.   176. **vantage**: opportunity.   **exclaim on**: reproach.   201. **intermission**: inactivity.   The punctuation is Theobald's (Qq read *lov'd for*,).   206. **roof**: i.e., of my mouth.

Enter LORENZO, JESSICA, *and* SALERIO, *a messenger from Venice.*

Bass. Lorenzo and Salerio, welcome hither,
If that the youth of my new interest here
Have power to bid you welcome.   By your leave
I bid my very friends and countrymen,   226
Sweet Portia, welcome.

Por.   So do I, my lord:
They are entirely welcome.

Lor. I thank your honour.   For my part, my lord,
My purpose was not to have seen you here;   230
But meeting with Salerio by the way,
He did intreat me, past all saying nay,
To come with him along.

Saler.   I did, my lord;
And I have reason for it.   Signior Antonio
Commends him to you.   [*Gives Bassanio a letter.*]

Bass.   Ere I ope his letter,   235
I pray you, tell me how my good friend doth.

Saler. Not sick, my lord, unless it be in mind,
Nor well, unless in mind.   His letter there
Will show you his estate.   [*Bass. opens the letter.*

Gra. Nerissa, cheer yond stranger; bid her wel-
come.   240
Your hand, Salerio.   What's the news from Venice?
How doth that royal merchant, good Antonio?
I know he will be glad of our success;
We are the Jasons, we have won the fleece.

Saler. I would you had won the fleece that he
hath lost.   245

Por. There are some shrewd contents in yon
same paper
That steals the colour from Bassanio's cheek.
Some dear friend dead; else nothing in the world
Could turn so much the constitution
Of any constant man.   What, worse and worse!
With leave, Bassanio; I am half yourself,   251
And I must freely have the half of anything
That this same paper brings you.

Bass.   O sweet Portia,
Here are a few of the unpleasant'st words
Than ever blotted paper!   Gentle lady,   255
When I did first impart my love to you,
I freely told you all the wealth I had
Ran in my veins; I was a gentleman.
And then I told you true; and yet, dear lady,
Rating myself at nothing, you shall see   260
How much I was a braggart.   When I told you
My state was nothing, I should then have told you
That I was worse than nothing; for, indeed,
I have engag'd myself to a dear friend,
Engag'd my friend to his mere enemy,   265
To feed my means.   Here is a letter, lady;
The paper as the body of my friend,

And every word in it a gaping wound,
Issuing life-blood.   But is it true, Salerio?
Hath all his ventures fail'd?   What?   Not one hit?
From Tripolis, from Mexico, and England,   271
From Lisbon, Barbary, and India?
And not one vessel scape the dreadful touch
Of merchant-marring rocks?

Saler.   Not one, my lord.
Besides, it should appear, that if he had   275
The present money to discharge the Jew,
He would not take it.   Never did I know
A creature that did bear the shape of man
So keen and greedy to confound a man.
He plies the Duke at morning and at night,   280
And doth impeach the freedom of the state,
If they deny him justice.   Twenty merchants,
The Duke himself, and the magnificoes
Of greatest port, have all persuaded with him;
But none can drive him from the envious plea   285
Of forfeiture, of justice, and his bond.

Jes. When I was with him I have heard him
swear
To Tubal and to Chus, his countrymen,
That he would rather have Antonio's flesh
Than twenty times the value of the sum   290
That he did owe him; and I know, my lord,
If law, authority, and power deny not,
It will go hard with poor Antonio.

Por. Is it your dear friend that is thus in trouble?

Bass. The dearest friend to me, the kindest man,
The best-condition'd and unwearied spirit   296
In doing courtesies, and one in whom
The ancient Roman honour more appears
Than any that draws breath in Italy.

Por. What sum owes he the Jew?   300

Bass. For me, three thousand ducats.

Por.   What, no more?
Pay him six thousand, and deface the bond;
Double six thousand, and then treble that,
Before a friend of this description
Shall lose a hair through Bassanio's fault.   305
First go with me to church and call me wife,
And then away to Venice to your friend;
For never shall you lie by Portia's side
With an unquiet soul.   You shall have gold
To pay the petty debt twenty times over.   310
When it is paid, bring your true friend along.
My maid Nerissa and myself meantime
Will live as maids and widows.   Come, away!
For you shall hence upon your wedding-day.
Bid your friends welcome, show a merry cheer;   315
Since you are dear bought, I will love you dear.
But let me hear the letter of your friend.
    [*Bass.   Reads.*]   "Sweet Bassanio, my ships have

226. **very**: true.   239. **estate**: condition.   246. **shrewd**: evil, bitter.   249. **constitution**: state of mind.   250. **constant**:
steady.   265. **mere**: absolute.   276. **present**: ready.   281. **impeach**: call in question.   283. **magnificoes**: grandees.   284.
port: prestige.   285. **envious**: spiteful.   315. **cheer**: face.

all miscarried, my creditors grow cruel, my estate
is very low, my bond to the Jew is forfeit; and   320
since in paying it, it is impossible I should live, all
debts are cleared between you and I, if I might but
see you at my death. Notwithstanding, use your
pleasure; if your love do not persuade you to come,
let not my letter."   325

Por. O love, dispatch all business, and be gone!
Bass. Since I have your good leave to go away,
    I will make haste; but, till I come again,
No bed shall e'er be guilty of my stay,
    Nor rest be interposer 'twixt us twain.   330

                              [*Exeunt.*

[SCENE III. *Venice. A street.*]

Enter the Jew [SHYLOCK], [SALARINO], ANTONIO,
                and Gaoler.

Shy. Gaoler, look to him; tell not me of mercy.
This is the fool that lent out money gratis!
Gaoler, look to him.
    Ant.   Hear me yet, good Shylock.
    Shy. I'll have my bond; speak not against my
        bond.
I have sworn an oath that I will have my bond.   5
Thou call'dst me dog before thou hadst a cause;
But, since I am a dog, beware my fangs.
The Duke shall grant me justice. I do wonder,
Thou naughty gaoler, that thou art so fond
To come abroad with him at his request.   10
    Ant. I pray thee, hear me speak.
    Shy. I'll have my bond; I will not hear thee speak.
I'll have my bond; and therefore speak no more.
I'll not be made a soft and dull-ey'd fool
To shake the head, relent, and sigh, and yield   15
To Christian intercessors. Follow not;
I'll have no speaking; I will have my bond. [*Exit.*
    Sal[*ar*]. It is the most impenetrable cur
That ever kept with men.
    Ant.   Let him alone;
I'll follow him no more with bootless prayers.   20
He seeks my life; his reason well I know:
I oft deliver'd from his forfeitures
Many that have at times made moan to me;
Therefore he hates me.
    Sal[*ar*].   I am sure the Duke
Will never grant this forfeiture to hold.   25
    Ant. The Duke cannot deny the course of law;
For the commodity that strangers have
With us in Venice, if it be denied,
Will much impeach the justice of the state,
Since that the trade and profit of the city   30
Consisteth of all nations. Therefore, go.
These griefs and losses have so bated me,

That I shall hardly spare a pound of flesh
To-morrow to my bloody creditor.
Well, gaoler, on. Pray God, Bassanio come   35
To see me pay his debt, and then I care not!
                              [*Exeunt.*

[SCENE IV. *Belmont. A room in Portia's house.*]

Enter PORTIA, NERISSA, LORENZO, JESSICA, *and*
        [BALTHASAR,] *a man of Portia's.*

Lor. Madam, although I speak it in your pres-
        ence,
You have a noble and a true conceit
Of god-like amity, which appears most strongly
In bearing thus the absence of your lord.
But if you knew to whom you show this honour,   5
How true a gentleman you send relief,
How dear a lover of my lord your husband,
I know you would be prouder of the work
Than customary bounty can enforce you.
    Por. I never did repent for doing good,   10
Nor shall not now: for in companions
That do converse and waste the time together,
Whose souls do bear an egal yoke of love,
There must be needs a like proportion
Of lineaments, of manners, and of spirit;   15
Which makes me think that this Antonio,
Being the bosom lover of my lord,
Must needs be like my lord. If it be so,
How little is the cost I have bestow'd
In purchasing the semblance of my soul   20
From out the state of hellish cruelty!
This comes too near the praising of myself,
Therefore no more of it. Hear other things.
Lorenzo, I commit into your hands
The husbandry and manage of my house   25
Until my lord's return. For mine own part,
I have toward heaven breath'd a secret vow
To live in prayer and contemplation,
Only attended by Nerissa here,
Until her husband and my lord's return.   30
There is a monastery two miles off;
And there we will abide. I do desire you
Not to deny this imposition,
The which my love and some necessity
Now lays upon you.
    Lor.   Madam, with all my heart   35
I shall obey you in all fair commands.
    Por. My people do already know my mind,
And will acknowledge you and Jessica
In place of Lord Bassanio and myself.
So fare you well till we shall meet again.   40
    Lor. Fair thoughts and happy hours attend on
        you!

Sc. iii. s.d. [SALARINO] Q₂. *Salerio* Q₁. *Solanio* F₁. 19. kept: dwelt. 27. commodity: commercial privileges. 33.
bated: reduced.
    Sc. iv, 2. conceit: conception. 9. enforce you: i.e., make you be. 13. egal: equal. 25. husbandry: economy.

Jes. I wish your ladyship all heart's content.

Por. I thank you for your wish, and am well pleas'd
To wish it back on you.   Fare you well, Jessica.
                    [*Exeunt [Jessica and Lorenzo].*
Now, Balthasar,   45
As I have ever found thee honest-true,
So let me find thee still.   Take this same letter,
And use thou all th' endeavour of a man
In speed to [Padua].   See thou render this
Into my cousin's hands, Doctor Bellario;   50
And, look, what notes and garments he doth give
            thee,
Bring them, I pray thee, with imagin'd speed
Unto the [traject], to the common ferry
Which trades to Venice.   Waste no time in words,
But get thee gone.   I shall be there before thee. 55
Balth. Madam, I go with all convenient speed.
                                    [*Exit.*
Por. Come on, Nerissa; I have work in hand
That you yet know not of.   We'll see our husbands
Before they think of us.

Ner.   Shall they see us?

Por. They shall, Nerissa; but in such a habit 60
That they shall think we are accomplished
With that we lack.   I'll hold thee any wager,
When we are both accoutred like young men,
I'll prove the prettier fellow of the two,
And wear my dagger with the braver grace,   65
And speak between the change of man and boy
With a reed voice, and turn two mincing steps
Into a manly stride, and speak of frays
Like a fine bragging youth, and tell quaint lies,
How honourable ladies sought my love,   70
Which I denying, they fell sick and died.
I could not do withal.   Then I'll repent,
And wish, for all that, that I had not kill'd them;
And twenty of these puny lies I'll tell,
That men shall swear I have discontinued school 75
Above a twelvemonth.   I have within my mind
A thousand raw tricks of these bragging Jacks,
Which I will practise.

Ner.   Why, shall we turn to men?

Por. Fie, what a question's that,
If thou wert near a lewd interpreter!   80
But come, I'll tell thee all my whole device
When I am in my coach, which stays for us
At the park gate; and therefore haste away,
For we must measure twenty miles to-day.
                                    [*Exeunt.*

[SCENE V.   *The same.   A garden.*]

Enter Clown [LAUNCELOT] *and* JESSICA.

Laun. Yes, truly; for, look you, the sins of the

father are to be laid upon the children; therefore, I
promise you, I fear you.   I was always plain with
you, and so now I speak my agitation of the matter;
therefore be o' good cheer, for truly I think you   5
are damn'd.   There is but one hope in it that can
do you any good; and that is but a kind of bastard
hope neither.

Jes. And what hope is that, I pray thee?   10

Laun. Marry, you may partly hope that your
father got you not, that you are not the Jew's
daughter.

Jes. That were a kind of bastard hope, indeed.
So the sins of my mother should be visited upon me.

Laun. Truly then I fear you are damn'd both   17
by father and mother; thus when I shun Scylla, your
father, I fall into Charybdis, your mother.   Well,
you are gone both ways.   20

Jes. I shall be sav'd by my husband.   He hath
made me a Christian.

Laun. Truly, the more to blame he; we were
Christians enow before; e'en as many as could well
live, one by another.   This making of Christians 25
will raise the price of hogs.   If we grow all to be
pork-eaters, we shall not shortly have a rasher on
the coals for money.

Enter LORENZO.

Jes. I'll tell my husband, Launcelot, what you
say.   Here he comes.   30

Lor. I shall grow jealous of you shortly, Launcelot, if you thus get my wife into corners.

Jes. Nay, you need not fear us, Lorenzo; Launcelot and I are out.   He tells me flatly there is no
mercy for me in heaven because I am a Jew's   35
daughter; and he says, you are no good member of
the commonwealth, for in converting Jews to
Christians, you raise the price of pork.   39

Lor. I shall answer that better to the commonwealth than you can the getting up of the negro's
belly.   The Moor is with child by you, Launcelot.

Laun. It is much that the Moor should be
more than reason; but if she be less than an
honest woman, she is indeed more than I took   46
her for.

Lor. How every fool can play upon the word!
I think the best grace of wit will shortly turn into
silence, and discourse grow commendable in   50
none only but parrots.   Go in, sirrah; bid them
prepare for dinner.

Laun. That is done, sir; they have all stomachs.

Lor. Goodly Lord, what a wit-snapper are you!
Then bid them prepare dinner.   56

Laun. That is done too, sir; only cover is the
word.

---

49. **[Padua]** (Theobald conj.).   *Mantua* Qq. (Cf. iv.i.109.) Padua was famous for its law school.   52. **imagin'd speed:**
all imaginable speed.   53. **[traject]** (Rowe): crossing.   *tranect* Qq.   61. **accomplished:** provided.   72. **do withal:** help it.

Sc. v, 3. **fear you:** i.e., fear for you.   4. **agitation:** blunder for *cogitation.*   34. **are out:** have quarreled.   52. **stomachs:**
appetites, with a quibble.

Lor. Will you cover then, sir?

Laun. Not so, sir, neither; I know my duty. 59

Lor. Yet more quarrelling with occasion! Wilt thou show the whole wealth of thy wit in an instant? I pray thee, understand a plain man in his plain meaning: go to thy fellows; bid them cover the table, serve in the meat, and we will come in to dinner. 65

Laun. For the table, sir, it shall be serv'd in; for the meat, sir, it shall be cover'd; for your coming in to dinner, sir, why, let it be as humours and conceits shall govern. [*Exit.*

Lor. O dear discretion, how his words are suited! The fool hath planted in his memory 71
An army of good words; and I do know
A many fools, that stand in better place,
Garnish'd like him, that for a tricksy word
Defy the matter. How cheer'st thou, Jessica? 75
And now, good sweet, say thy opinion,
How dost thou like the Lord Bassanio's wife?

Jes. Past all expressing. It is very meet
The Lord Bassanio live an upright life;
For, having such a blessing in his lady, 80
He finds the joys of heaven here on earth;
And if on earth he do not [merit them],
In reason he should never come to heaven.
Why, if two gods should play some heavenly match
And on the wager lay two earthly women, 85
And Portia one, there must be something else
Pawn'd with the other, for the poor rude world
Hath not her fellow.

Lor.   Even such a husband
Hast thou of me as she is for a wife.

Jes. Nay, but ask my opinion too of that. 90

Lor. I will anon; first, let us go to dinner.

Jes. Nay, let me praise you while I have a stomach.

Lor. No, pray thee, let it serve for table-talk;
Then, howsome'er thou speak'st, 'mong other things
I shall digest it.

Jes.   Well, I'll set you forth. 95
[*Exeunt.*

ACT IV

[SCENE I. *Venice. A court of justice.*]

Enter the DUKE, *the* Magnificoes, ANTONIO, BASSANIO, GRATIANO [SALERIO, *and others*].

Duke. What, is Antonio here?

Ant. Ready, so please your Grace.

Duke. I am sorry for thee. Thou art come to answer
A stony adversary, an inhuman wretch
Uncapable of pity, void and empty 5
From any dram of mercy.

Ant.   I have heard
Your Grace hath ta'en great pains to qualify
His rigorous course; but since he stands obdurate
And that no lawful means can carry me
Out of his envy's reach, I do oppose 10
My patience to his fury, and am arm'd
To suffer, with a quietness of spirit,
The very tyranny and rage of his.

Duke. Go one, and call the Jew into the court.

Saler. He is ready at the door. He comes, my lord. 15

Enter SHYLOCK.

Duke. Make room, and let him stand before our face.
Shylock, the world thinks, and I think so too,
That thou but lead'st this fashion of thy malice
To the last hour of act; and then 'tis thought
Thou'lt show thy mercy and remorse more strange
Than is thy strange apparent cruelty; 21
And where thou now exact'st the penalty,
Which is a pound of this poor merchant's flesh,
Thou wilt not only loose the forfeiture,
But, touch'd with humane gentleness and love, 25
Forgive a moiety of the principal;
Glancing an eye of pity on his losses,
That have of late so huddled on his back,
Enow to press a royal merchant down
And pluck commiseration of his state 30
From brassy bosoms and rough hearts of flint,
From stubborn Turks and Tartars, never train'd
To offices of tender courtesy.
We all expect a gentle answer, Jew.

Shy. I have possess'd your Grace of what I purpose; 35
And by our holy Sabbath have I sworn
To have the due and forfeit of my bond.
If you deny it, let the danger light
Upon your charter and your city's freedom.
You'll ask me why I rather choose to have 40
A weight of carrion flesh than to receive
Three thousand ducats. I'll never answer that;
But say it is my humour. Is it answer'd?
What if my house be troubled with a rat
And I be pleas'd to give ten thousand ducats 45
To have it ban'd? What, are you answer'd yet?

---

58. **cover:** (1) set the table, (2) put on your hat. 60. **quarrelling...occasion:** quibbling. 70. **suited:** dressed up, or adapted. 74. **Garnish'd:** equipped. **tricksy:** fantastic. 75. **matter:** i.e., true sense. 82. **[merit them]** (Clar. conj.). *meane it, it* Q₁. *meane it, then* Q₂. If Q₂ is followed, the sense would seem to be, "intend to live an upright life." 87. **Pawn'd:** staked. 95. **set you forth:** (1) extol, (2) serve up.

Act IV, sc. i, 7. **qualify:** moderate. 18. **fashion:** way of expressing. 20. **remorse:** pity. **strange:** extraordinary. 26. **moiety:** part. 29. **enow:** enough. 43. **humour:** whim. 46. **ban'd:** poisoned.

Some men there are love not a gaping pig;
Some, that are mad if they behold a cat;
And others, when the bagpipe sings i' th' nose,
Cannot contain their urine: for affection,   50
Master of passion, sways it to the mood
Of what it likes or loathes.   Now, for your answer:
As there is no firm reason to be rend'red
Why he cannot abide a gaping pig;
Why he, a harmless necessary cat;   55
Why he, a woollen bagpipe; but of force
Must yield to such inevitable shame
As to offend, himself being offended;
So can I give no reason, nor I will not,
More than a lodg'd hate and a certain loathing   60
I bear Antonio, that I follow thus
A losing suit against him.   Are you answer'd?
    Bass. This is no answer, thou unfeeling man,
To excuse the current of thy cruelty.
    Shy. I am not bound to please thee with my an-
        swers.   65
    Bass. Do all men kill the things they do not love?
    Shy. Hates any man the thing he would not kill?
    Bass. Every offence is not a hate at first.
    Shy. What, wouldst thou have a serpent sting
        thee twice?
    Ant. I pray you, think, you question with the
        Jew.   70
You may as well go stand upon the beach
And bid the main flood bate his usual height;
You may as well use question with the wolf
Why he hath made the ewe bleat for the lamb;
You may as well forbid the mountain pines   75
To wag their high tops and to make no noise
When they are fretten with the gusts of heaven;
You may as well do any thing most hard,
As seek to soften that — than which what's
        harder? —
His Jewish heart.   Therefore, I do beseech you,   80
Make no moe offers, use no farther means,
But with all brief and plain conveniency
Let me have judgement and the Jew his will.
    Bass. For thy three thousand ducats here is six.
    Shy. If every ducat in six thousand ducats   85
Were in six parts, and every part a ducat,
I would not draw them; I would have my bond.
    Duke. How shalt thou hope for mercy, rendering
        none?
    Shy. What judgement shall I dread, doing no
        wrong?
You have among you many a purchas'd slave,   90
Which, like your asses and your dogs and mules,
You use in abject and in slavish parts,
Because you bought them.   Shall I say to you,
"Let them be free!   Marry them to your heirs!
Why sweat they under burdens?   Let their beds   95

Be made as soft as yours and let their palates
Be season'd with such viands"?   You will answer,
"The slaves are ours."   So do I answer you.
The pound of flesh, which I demand of him,
Is dearly bought; 'tis mine and I will have it.   100
If you deny me, fie upon your law!
There is no force in the decrees of Venice.
I stand for judgement!   Answer: shall I have it?
    Duke. Upon my power I may dismiss this court,
Unless Bellario, a learned doctor,   105
Whom I have sent for to determine this,
Come here to-day.
    Saler.   My lord, here stays without
A messenger with letters from the doctor,
New come from Padua.
    Duke. Bring us the letters; call the messenger.   110
    Bass. Good cheer, Antonio!   What, man, courage
        yet!
The Jew shall have my flesh, blood, bones, and all,
Ere thou shalt lose for me one drop of blood.
    Ant. I am a tainted wether of the flock,
Meetest for death.   The weakest kind of fruit   115
Drops earliest to the ground, and so let me.
You cannot better be employ'd, Bassanio,
Than to live still and write mine epitaph.

    Enter NERISSA [*dressed like a lawyer's clerk*].
    Duke. Came you from Padua, from Bellario?
    Ner. From both, my lord.   Bellario greets your
        Grace.   [*Presenting a letter.*]
    Bass. Why dost thou whet thy knife so ear-
        nestly?   121
    Shy. To cut the forfeiture from that bankrupt
        there.
    Gra. Not on thy sole, but on thy soul, harsh Jew,
Thou mak'st thy knife keen; but no metal can,   124
No, not the hangman's axe, bear half the keenness
Of thy sharp envy.   Can no prayers pierce thee?
    Shy. No, none that thou hast wit enough to make.
    Gra. O, be thou damn'd, inexecrable dog!
And for thy life let justice be accus'd.
Thou almost mak'st me waver in my faith   130
To hold opinion with Pythagoras,
That souls of animals infuse themselves
Into the trunks of men.   Thy currish spirit
Govern'd a wolf, who, hang'd for human slaughter,
Even from the gallows did his fell soul fleet,   135
And, whilst thou lay'st in thy unhallowed dam,
Infus'd itself in thee; for thy desires
Are wolvish, bloody, starv'd, and ravenous.
    Shy. Till thou canst rail the seal from off my
        bond,
Thou but offend'st thy lungs to speak so loud.   140
Repair thy wit, good youth, or it will fall
To cureless ruin.   I stand here for law.

---

47. **gaping pig:** a pig roasted whole with its mouth open.   50. **affection:** natural inclination.   70. **question:** argue.
77. **fretten:** fretted.   87. **draw:** take.   92. **parts:** tasks.   140. **offend'st:** injurest.

Duke. This letter from Bellario doth commend
A young and learned doctor to our court.
Where is he?

Ner.   He attendeth here hard by   145
To know your answer, whether you'll admit him.

Duke. With all my heart.   Some three or four of
          you
Go give him courteous conduct to this place.
Meantime the court shall hear Bellario's letter.   149

[*Clerk.   Reads.*]   "Your Grace shall understand
that at the receipt of your letter I am very sick; but
in the instant that your messenger came, in loving
visitation was with me a young doctor of Rome.
His name is Balthazar.   I acquainted him with the
cause in controversy between the Jew and   155
Antonio the merchant.   We turned o'er many
books together.   He is furnished with my opinion;
which, bett'red with his own learning, the greatness
whereof I cannot enough commend, comes with
him, at my importunity, to fill up your Grace's   160
request in my stead.   I beseech you, let his lack of
years be no impediment to let him lack a reverend
estimation; for I never knew so young a body with
so old a head.   I leave him to your gracious acceptance, whose trial shall better publish his commendation."   166

Enter PORTIA *for* BALTHAZAR.

Duke. You hear the learn'd Ballario, what he
          writes;
And here, I take it, is the doctor come.
Give me your hand.   Come you from old Bellario?

Por. I did, my lord.

Duke.   You are welcome; take your place.
Are you acquainted with the difference   171
That holds this present question in the court?

Por. I am informed throughly of the cause.
Which is the merchant here, and which the Jew?

Duke. Antonio and old Shylock, both stand
          forth.   175

Por. Is your name Shylock?

Shy.   Shylock is my name.

Por. Of a strange nature is the suit you follow;
Yet in such rule that the Venetian law
Cannot impugn you as you do proceed.
You stand within his danger, do you not?   180

Ant. Ay, so he says.

Por.   Do you confess the bond?

Ant. I do.

Por.   Then must the Jew be merciful.

Shy. On what compulsion must I?   Tell me that.

Por. The quality of mercy is not strain'd.
It droppeth as the gentle rain from heaven   185
Upon the place beneath.   It is twice blest:
It blesseth him that gives and him that takes.

'Tis mightiest in the mightiest; it becomes
The throned monarch better than his crown.
His sceptre shows the force of temporal power,   190
The attribute to awe and majesty,
Wherein doth sit the dread and fear of kings;
But mercy is above the sceptred sway;
It is enthroned in the hearts of kings;
It is an attribute to God himself;   195
And earthly power doth then show likest God's
When mercy seasons justice.   Therefore, Jew,
Though justice be thy plea, consider this,
That, in the course of justice, none of us
Should see salvation.   We do pray for mercy,   200
And that same prayer doth teach us all to render
The deeds of mercy.   I have spoke thus much
To mitigate the justice of thy plea,
Which if thou follow, this strict court of Venice
Must needs give sentence 'gainst the merchant
          there.   205

Shy. My deeds upon my head!   I crave the law,
The penalty and forfeit of my bond.

Por. Is he not able to discharge the money?

Bass. Yes, here I tender it for him in the court;
Yea, twice the sum.   If that will not suffice,   210
I will be bound to pay it ten times o'er,
On forfeit of my hands, my head, my heart.
If this will not suffice, it must appear
That malice bears down truth.   And I beseech you,
Wrest once the law to your authority;   215
To do a great right, do a little wrong,
And curb this cruel devil of his will.

Por. It must not be; there is no power in Venice
Can alter a decree established.
'Twill be recorded for a precedent,   220
And many an error by the same example
Will rush into the state.   It cannot be.

Shy. A Daniel come to judgement! yea, a Daniel!
O wise young judge, how I do honour thee!

Por. I pray you, let me look upon the bond.   225

Shy. Here 'tis, most reverend doctor, here it is.

Por. Shylock, there's thrice thy money off'red
          thee.

Shy. An oath, an oath, I have an oath in heaven!
Shall I lay perjury upon my soul?
No, not for Venice.

Por.   Why, this bond is forfeit;   230
And lawfully by this the Jew may claim
A pound of flesh, to be by him cut off
Nearest the merchant's heart.   Be merciful;
Take thrice thy money; bid me tear the bond.

Shy. When it is paid according to the tenour.
It doth appear you are a worthy judge;   236
You know the law, your exposition
Hath been most sound.   I charge you by the law,
Whereof you are a well-deserving pillar,

---

171. **difference:** dispute.   184. **strain'd:** constrained, forced.   214. **truth:** honesty.   223. **Daniel.** In the Apocryphal book of *Susannah*, Daniel is a judge.

Proceed to judgement.   By my soul I swear   240
There is no power in the tongue of man
To alter me.   I stay here on my bond.

Ant. Most heartily I do beseech the court
To give the judgement.

Por.   Why then, thus it is: 244
You must prepare your bosom for his knife, —

Shy. O noble judge!   O excellent young man!

Por. For the intent and purpose of the law
Hath full relation to the penalty
Which here appeareth due upon the bond.

Shy. 'Tis very true.   O wise and upright judge!
How much more elder art thou than thy looks!   251

Por. Therefore lay bare your bosom.

Shy.   Ay, his breast;
So says the bond; doth it not, noble judge?
"Nearest his heart;" those are the very words.

Por. It is so.   Are there balance here to weigh
The flesh?

Shy.   I have them ready.   256

Por. Have by some surgeon, Shylock, on your
        charge,
To stop his wounds, lest he do bleed to death.

Shy. Is it so nominated in the bond?

Por. It is not so express'd; but what of that?   260
'Twere good you do so much for charity.

Shy. I cannot find it; 'tis not in the bond.

Por. You, merchant, have you anything to say?

Ant. But little; I am arm'd and well prepar'd.
Give me your hand, Bassanio; fare you well!   265
Grieve not that I am fall'n to this for you;
For herein Fortune shows herself more kind
Than is her custom.   It is still her use
To let the wretched man outlive his wealth,
To view with hollow eye and wrinkled brow   270
An age of poverty; from which ling'ring penance
Of such a misery doth she cut me off.
Commend me to your honourable wife.
Tell her the process of Antonio's end;
Say how I lov'd you, speak me fair in death,   275
And, when the tale is told, bid her be judge
Whether Bassanio had not once a love.
Repent but you that you shall lose your friend,
And he repents not that he pays your debt;
For if the Jew do cut but deep enough,   280
I'll pay it instantly with all my heart.

Bass. Antonio, I am married to a wife
Which is as dear to me as life itself;
But life itself, my wife, and all the world,
Are not with me esteem'd above thy life.   285
I would lose all, ay, sacrifice them all
Here to this devil, to deliver you.

Por. Your wife would give you little thanks for
        that,
If she were by, to hear you make the offer.

Gra. I have a wife, who, I protest, I love;   290
I would she were in heaven, so she could
Entreat some power to change this currish Jew.

Ner. 'Tis well you offer it behind her back.
The wish would make else an unquiet house.

Shy. These be the Christian husbands.   I have a
        daughter;   295
Would any of the stock of Barrabas
Had been her husband rather than a Christian!
                                                [*Aside.*]
We trifle time.   I pray thee, pursue sentence.

Por. A pound of that same merchant's flesh is
        thine.
The court awards it, and the law doth give it.   300

Shy. Most rightful judge!

Por. And you must cut this flesh from off his
        breast.
The law allows it, and the court awards it.

Shy. Most learned judge!   A sentence!   Come,
        prepare!

Por. Tarry a little; there is something else.   305
This bond doth give thee here no jot of blood;
The words expressly are " a pound of flesh."
Take then thy bond, take thou thy pound of
        flesh;
But, in the cutting it, if thou dost shed
One drop of Christian blood, thy lands and goods
Are, by the laws of Venice, confiscate   311
Unto the state of Venice.

Gra. O upright judge!   Mark, Jew: O learned
        judge!

Shy. Is that the law?

Por.   Thyself shall see the act;
For, as thou urgest justice, be assur'd   315
Thou shalt have justice, more than thou desir'st.

Gra. O learned judge!   Mark, Jew: a learned
        judge!

Shy. I take this offer, then; pay the bond thrice
And let the Christian go.

Bass.   Here is the money.

Por. Soft!   320
The Jew shall have all justice.   Soft! no haste.
He shall have nothing but the penalty.

Gra. O Jew! an upright judge, a learned judge!

Por. Therefore prepare thee to cut off the flesh.
Shed thou no blood, nor cut thou less nor more   325
But just a pound of flesh.   If thou tak'st more
Or less than a just pound, be it but so much
As makes it light or heavy in the substance
Or the division of the twentieth part
Of one poor scruple, nay, if the scale do turn   330
But in the estimation of a hair,
Thou diest and all thy goods are confiscate.

Gra. A second Daniel!   A Daniel, Jew!
Now, infidel, I have you on the hip.

248. relation to: bearing upon.   **296. Barrabas:** the thief freed by Pilate.   **328–29. in ... division:** by the whole or the fraction.   **330. scruple:** 20 grains.

Por. Why doth the Jew pause?   Take thy for-
feiture.   335
Shy. Give me my principal, and let me go.
Bass. I have it ready for thee; here it is.
Por. He hath refus'd it in the open court.
He shall have merely justice and his bond.
Gra. A Daniel, still say I, a second Daniel!   340
I thank thee, Jew, for teaching me that word.
Shy. Shall I not have barely my principal?
Por. Thou shalt have nothing but the forfeiture,
To be so taken at thy peril, Jew.
Shy. Why, then the devil give him good of it!
I'll stay no longer question.
Por.   Tarry, Jew: 346
The law hath yet another hold on you.
It is enacted in the laws of Venice,
If it be prov'd against an alien
That by direct or indirect attempts   350
He seek the life of any citizen,
The party 'gainst the which he doth contrive
Shall seize one half his goods; the other half
Comes to the privy coffer of the state;
And the offender's life lies in the mercy   355
Of the Duke only, 'gainst all other voice:
In which predicament, I say, thou stand'st;
For it appears, by manifest proceeding,
That indirectly, and directly too,
Thou hast contriv'd against the very life   360
Of the defendant; and thou hast incurr'd
The danger formerly by me rehears'd.
Down therefore and beg mercy of the Duke.
Gra. Beg that thou mayst have leave to hang
thyself;
And yet, thy wealth being forfeit to the state,   365
Thou hast not left the value of a cord;
Therefore thou must be hang'd at the state's charge.
Duke. That thou shalt see the difference of our
spirit,
I pardon thee thy life before thou ask it.
For half thy wealth, it is Antonio's;   370
The other half comes to the general state,
Which humbleness may drive unto a fine.
Por. Ay, for the state, not for Antonio.
Shy. Nay, take my life and all; pardon not that.
You take my house when you do take the prop   375
That doth sustain my house; you take my life
When you do take the means whereby I live.
Por. What mercy can you render him, Antonio?
Gra. A halter gratis; nothing else, for God's sake.
Ant. So please my lord the Duke and all the court
To quit the fine for one half of his goods,   381
I am content; so he will let me have
The other half in use, to render it,
Upon his death, unto the gentleman
That lately stole his daughter: 385

Two things provided more, that, for this favour,
He presently become a Christian;
The other, that he do record a gift,
Here in the court, of all he dies possess'd,
Unto his son Lorenzo and his daughter.   390
Duke. He shall do this, or else I do recant
The pardon that I late pronounced here.
Por. Art thou contented, Jew?   What dost thou
say?
Shy. I am content.
Por.   Clerk, draw a deed of gift.
Shy. I pray you, give me leave to go from hence.
I am not well.   Send the deed after me,   396
And I will sign it.
Duke.   Get thee gone, but do it.
Gra. In christening shalt thou have two god-
fathers:
Had I been judge, thou shouldst have had ten more,
To bring thee to the gallows, not the font.   400
                                    [*Exit [Shylock*].
Duke. Sir, I entreat you home with me to dinner.
Por. I humbly do desire your Grace of pardon.
I must away this night toward Padua,
And it is meet I presently set forth.
Duke. I am sorry that your leisure serves you not.
Antonio, gratify this gentleman;   406
For, in my mind, you are much bound to him.
                          [*Exeunt Duke and his train.*
Bass. Most worthy gentleman, I and my friend
Have by your wisdom been this day acquitted
Of grievous penalties; in lieu whereof   410
Three thousand ducats, due unto the Jew,
We freely cope your courteous pains withal.
Ant. And stand indebted, over and above,
In love and service to you evermore.
Por. He is well paid that is well satisfied;   415
And I, delivering you, am satisfied
And therein do account myself well paid.
My mind was never yet more mercenary.
I pray you, know me when we meet again.
I wish you well, and so I take my leave.   420
Bass. Dear sir, of force I must attempt you
further.
Take some remembrance of us, as a tribute,
Not as fee.   Grant me two things, I pray you,
Not to deny me, and to pardon me.
Por. You press me far, and therefore I will yield.
[*To Ant.*] Give me your gloves, I'll wear them for
your sake;   426
[*To Bass.*] And, for your love, I'll take this ring
from you.
Do not draw back your hand; I'll take no more;
And you in love shall not deny me this.
Bass. This ring, good sir, alas, it is a trifle!   430
I will not shame myself to give you this.

372. **drive:** reduce.   381. **quit:** remit.   383. **use:** trust.   399. **ten more:** i.e., to make a jury of twelve.   406. **gratify:**
reward.   410. **lieu:** return.   412. **cope:** requite.

Por. I will have nothing else but only this;
And now methinks I have a mind to it.
   Bass. There's more depends on this than on the
    value.
The dearest ring in Venice will I give you,   435
And find it out by proclamation;
Only for this, I pray you, pardon me.
   Por. I see, sir, you are liberal in offers.
You taught me first to beg; and now methinks
You teach me how a beggar should be answer'd. 440
   Bass. Good sir, this ring was given me by my
    wife;
And when she put it on, she made me vow
That I should neither sell nor give nor lose it.
   Por. That 'scuse serves many men to save their
    gifts.
An if your wife be not a mad-woman,   445
And know how well I have deserv'd this ring,
She would not hold out enemy for ever,
For giving it to me. Well, peace be with you!
             [Exeunt [Portia and Nerissa].
   Ant. My Lord Bassanio, let him have the ring.
Let his deservings and my love withal   450
Be valued 'gainst your wife's commandement.
   Bass. Go, Gratiano, run and overtake him;
Give him the ring, and bring him, if thou canst,
Unto Antonio's house. Away! make haste.
                  [Exit Gratiano.
Come, you and I will thither presently;   455
And in the morning early will we both
Fly toward Belmont. Come, Antonio.   *[Exeunt.*

      [SCENE II. *The same. A street.*]

     Enter PORTIA *and* NERISSA.

   Por. Inquire the Jew's house out, give him this
    deed
And let him sign it. We'll away to-night,
And be a day before our husbands home.
This deed will be well welcome to Lorenzo.

        Enter GRATIANO.

   Gra. Fair sir, you are well o'erta'en.   5
My Lord Bassanio upon more advice
Hath sent you here this ring, and doth entreat
Your company at dinner.
   Por.   That cannot be.
His ring I do accept most thankfully,
And so, I pray you, tell him; furthermore,   10
I pray you, show my youth old Shylock's house.
   Gra. That will I do.
   Ner.   Sir, I would speak with you.
[Aside to Por.] I'll see if I can get my husband's ring,

Which I did make him swear to keep for ever.
   Por. [*Aside to Ner.*] Thou mayst, I warrant.
   We shall have old swearing   15
That they did give the rings away to men;
But we'll outface them, and outswear them too.
[*Aloud.*] Away! make haste. Thou know'st where
   I will tarry.
   Ner. Come, good sir, will you show me to this
    house?   *[Exeunt.*

            ACT V

  [SCENE I. *Belmont. Avenue to Portia's house.*]

     Enter LORENZO *and* JESSICA.

   Lor. The moon shines bright. In such a night as
    this,
When the sweet wind did gently kiss the trees
And they did make no noise, in such a night
Troilus methinks mounted the Troyan walls,
And sigh'd his soul toward the Grecian tents,   5
Where Cressid lay that night.
   Jes.   In such a night
Did Thisbe fearfully o'ertrip the dew,
And saw the lion's shadow ere himself
And ran dismay'd away.
   Lor.   In such a night
Stood Dido with a willow in her hand   10
Upon the wild sea banks, and waft her love
To come again to Carthage.
   Jes.   In such a night
Medea gathered the enchanted herbs
That did renew old Æson.
   Lor.   In such a night
Did Jessica steal from the wealthy Jew,   15
And with an unthrift love did run from Venice
As far as Belmont.
   Jes.   In such a night
Did young Lorenzo swear he lov'd her well,
Stealing her soul with many vows of faith
And ne'er a true one.
   Lor.   In such a night   20
Did pretty Jessica, like a little shrew,
Slander her love, and he forgave it her.
   Jes. I would out-night you, did no body come;
But, hark, I hear the footing of a man.

      Enter a MESSENGER.

   Lor. Who comes so fast in silence of the night?   25
   Mess. A friend.
   Lor. A friend! what friend? Your name, I pray
    you, friend?
   Mess. Stephano is my name; and I bring word
My mistress will before the break of day

434. depends...on Q₁. *then this depends upon* Q₂.
Sc. ii, 6. **advice**: consideration. 15. **old**: plentiful.
Act V, sc. i, 4-6. Reminiscent of Chaucer's *Troilus and Criseyde*, V.647-72. 10. **willow**: symbol of forsaken love.
11. **waft**: waved.

Be here at Belmont. She doth stray about   30
By holy crosses, where she kneels and prays
For happy wedlock hours.

Lor.   Who comes with her?

Mess. None but a holy hermit and her maid.
I pray you, is my master yet return'd?

Lor. He is not, nor we have not heard from him.
But go we in, I pray thee, Jessica,   36
And ceremoniously let us prepare
Some welcome for the mistress of the house.

Enter Clown [LAUNCELOT].

Laun. Sola, sola! wo ha, ho! sola, sola!

Lor. Who calls?   40

Laun. Sola! did you see Master Lorenzo and
[Mistress] Lorenzo? Sola, sola!

Lor. Leave holloaing, man; here.

Laun. Sola! where? where?

Lor. Here.   45

Laun. Tell him there's a post come from my master, with his horn full of good news. My master will be here ere morning.   [*Exit.*]

Lor. Sweet soul, let's in, and there expect their
coming.
And yet no matter; why should we go in?   50
My friend Stephano, signify, I pray you,
Within the house, your mistress is at hand;
And bring your music forth into the air.
    [*Exit Mess.*]
How sweet the moonlight sleeps upon this bank!
Here will we sit and let the sounds of music   55
Creep in our ears. Soft stillness and the night
Become the touches of sweet harmony.
Sit, Jessica. Look how the floor of heaven
Is thick inlaid with patines of bright gold.
There's not the smallest orb which thou behold'st   60
But in his motion like an angel sings,
Still quiring to the young-ey'd cherubins.
Such harmony is in immortal souls;
But whilst this muddy vesture of decay
Doth grossly close it in, we cannot hear it.   65

[*Enter* Musicians.]

Come, ho! and wake Diana with a hymn;
With sweetest touches pierce your mistress' ear
And draw her home with music.   [*Play Music.*

Jes. I am never merry when I hear sweet music.

Lor. The reason is, your spirits are attentive;
For do but note a wild and wanton herd,   71
Or race of youthful and unhandled colts,
Fetching mad bounds, bellowing and neighing loud,
Which is the hot condition of their blood,
If they but hear perchance a trumpet sound,   75

Or any air of music touch their ears,
You shall perceive them make a mutual stand,
Their savage eyes turn'd to a modest gaze
By the sweet power of music; therefore the poet
Did feign that Orpheus drew trees, stones, and
        floods;   80
Since nought so stockish, hard, and full of rage,
But music for the time doth change his nature.
The man that hath no music in himself,
Nor is not mov'd with concord of sweet sounds,
Is fit for treasons, stratagems, and spoils.   85
The motions of his spirit are dull as night
And his affections dark as Erebus.
Let no such man be trusted. Mark the music.

Enter PORTIA *and* NERISSA.

Por. That light we see is burning in my hall.
How far that little candle throws his beams!   90
So shines a good deed in a naughty world.

Ner. When the moon shone, we did not see the
candle.

Por. So doth the greater glory dim the less.
A substitute shines brightly as a king
Until a king be by; and then his state   95
Empties itself, as doth an inland brook
Into the main of waters. Music! Hark!

Ner. It is your music, madam, of the house.

Por. Nothing is good, I see, without respect;
Methinks it sounds much sweeter than by day.   100

Ner. Silence bestows that virtue on it, madam.

Por. The crow doth sing as sweetly as the lark
When neither is attended, and I think
The nightingale, if she should sing by day,
When every goose is cackling, would be thought
No better a musician than the wren.   106
How many things by season season'd are
To their right praise and true perfection!
Peace, ho! the Moon sleeps with Endymion
And would not be awak'd.   [*Music ceases.*

Lor.   That is the voice,
Or I am much deceiv'd, of Portia.   111

Por. He knows me as the blind man knows the
cuckoo,
By the bad voice.

Lor.   Dear lady, welcome home!

Por. We have been praying for our husbands'
welfare,
Which speed, we hope, the better for our words.   115
Are they return'd?

Lor.   Madam, they are not yet;
But there is come a messenger before,
To signify their coming.

Por.   Go in, Nerissa;

---

39. **Sola:** perhaps imitation of a postman's horn.   41–42. **Master ... Lorenzo.** Q₁ reads *M. Lorenzo & M. Lorenzo.*
49. **expect:** await.   59. **patines:** disks.   77. **mutual:** simultaneous.   79. **the poet:** Ovid.   81. **stockish:** wooden, unfeeling.
87. **affections:** passions. **Erebus:** the hell of classical mythology.   91. **naughty:** wicked.   99. **respect:** reference to something.   103. **attended:** heeded.   109. **Endymion:** a shepherd loved by Diana.

Give order to my servants that they take
No note at all of our being absent hence;   120
Nor you, Lorenzo; Jessica, nor you.
                                    [A tucket sounds.
  Lor. Your husband is at hand; I hear his trumpet.
We are no tell-tales, madam; fear you not.
  Por. This night methinks is but the daylight sick;
It looks a little paler.   'Tis a day,   125
Such as the day is when the sun is hid.

    Enter BASSANIO, ANTONIO, GRATIANO, and
                their followers.

  Bass. We should hold day with the Antipodes,
If you would walk in absence of the sun.
  Por. Let me give light, but let me not be light;
For a light wife doth make a heavy husband,   130
And never be Bassanio so for me.
But God sort all!   You're welcome home, my lord.
  Bass. I thank you, madam.   Give welcome to my
    friend.
This is the man, this is Antonio,
To whom I am so infinitely bound.   135
  Por. You should in all sense be much bound to
    him,
For, as I hear, he was much bound for you.
  Ant. No more than I am well acquitted of.
  Por. Sir, you are very welcome to our house.
It must appear in other ways than words,   140
Therefore I scant this breathing courtesy.
  Gra. [To Ner.]   By yonder moon I swear you do
    me wrong;
In faith, I gave it to the judge's clerk.
Would he were gelt that had it, for my part,
Since you do take it, love, so much at heart.   145
  Por. A quarrel, ho, already!   What's the matter?
  Gra. About a hoop of gold, a paltry ring
That she did give me, whose posy was
For all the world like cutler's poetry
Upon a knife, "Love me, and leave me not."   150
  Ner. What talk you of the posy or the value?
You swore to me, when I did give it you,
That you would wear it till your hour of death,
And that it should lie with you in your grave.   154
Though not for me, yet for your vehement oaths,
You should have been respective and have kept it.
Gave it a judge's clerk!   No, God's my judge,
The clerk will ne'er wear hair on's face that had it.
  Gra. He will, an if he live to be a man.
  Ner. Ay, if a woman live to be a man.   160
  Gra. Now, by this hand, I gave it to a youth,
A kind of boy, a little scrubbed boy,
No higher than thyself, the judge's clerk,
A prating boy, that begg'd it as a fee.
I could not for my heart deny it him.   165

  Por. You were to blame, I must be plain with
    you,
To part so slightly with your wife's first gift;
A thing stuck on with oaths upon your finger
And so riveted with faith unto your flesh.
I gave my love a ring, and made him swear   170
Never to part with it; and here he stands.
I dare be sworn for him he would not leave it
Nor pluck it from his finger for the wealth
That the world masters.   Now, in faith, Gratiano,
You give your wife too unkind a cause of grief.   175
An 'twere to me, I should be mad at it.
  Bass. [Aside.]   Why, I were best to cut my left
    hand off
And swear I lost the ring defending it.
  Gra. My Lord Bassanio gave his ring away
Unto the judge that begg'd it, and indeed   180
Deserv'd it too; and then the boy, his clerk,
That took some pains in writing, he begg'd mine;
And neither man nor master would take aught
But the two rings.
  Por.   What ring gave you, my lord?
Not that, I hope, which you receiv'd of me.   185
  Bass. If I could add a lie unto a fault,
I would deny it; but you see my finger
Hath not the ring upon it; it is gone.
  Por. Even so void is your false heart of truth.
By heaven, I will ne'er come in your bed   190
Until I see the ring.
  Ner.   Nor I in yours
Till I again see mine.
  Bass.   Sweet Portia,
If you did know to whom I gave the ring,
If you did know for whom I gave the ring,
And would conceive for what I gave the ring,   195
And how unwillingly I left the ring,
When nought would be accepted but the ring,
You would abate the strength of your displeasure.
  Por. If you had known the virtue of the ring,
Or half her worthiness that gave the ring,   200
Or your own honour to contain the ring,
You would not then have parted with the ring.
What man is there so much unreasonable,
If you had pleas'd to have defended it
With any terms of zeal, wanted the modesty   205
To urge the thing held as a ceremony?
Nerissa teaches me what to believe:
I'll die for't but some woman had the ring.
  Bass. No, by my honour, madam, by my soul,
No woman had it, but a civil doctor,   210
Which did refuse three thousand ducats of me
And begg'd the ring; the which I did deny him
And suffer'd him to go displeas'd away;
Even he that had held up the very life

---

121. S.D. tucket: flourish on a trumpet.   132. sort: dispose.   141. breathing courtesy: courteous talk.   148. posy:
motto.   156. respective: careful, mindful.   162. scrubbed: stunted.   201. contain: retain.   206. urge: demand.   ceremony: something sacred.   210. civil doctor: doctor of civil law.

Of my dear friend.   What should I say, sweet lady?
I was enforc'd to send it after him;   216
I was beset with shame and courtesy;
My honour would not let ingratitude
So much besmear it.   Pardon me, good lady;
For, by these blessed candles of the night,   220
Had you been there, I think you would have begg'd
The ring of me to give the worthy doctor.
    Por. Let not that doctor e'er come near my house.
Since he hath got the jewel that I lov'd,
And that which you did swear to keep for me,   225
I will become as liberal as you.
I'll not deny him any thing I have,
No, not my body nor my husband's bed.
Know him I shall, I am well sure of it.
Lie not a night from home.   Watch me like Argus.
If you do not, if I be left alone,   231
Now, by mine honour, which is yet mine own,
I'll have that doctor for my bedfellow.
    Ner. And I his clerk; therefore be well advis'd
How you do leave me to mine own protection.   235
    Gra. Well, do you so; let not me take him then;
For if I do, I'll mar the young clerk's pen.
    Ant. I am th' unhappy subject of these quarrels.
    Por. Sir, grieve not you; you are welcome not-
        withstanding.
    Bass. Portia, forgive me this enforced wrong;   240
And in the hearing of these many friends
I swear to thee, even by thine own fair eyes,
Wherein I see myself —
    Por.   Mark you but that!
In both my eyes he doubly sees himself,
In each eye, one.   Swear by your double self,   245
And there's an oath of credit.
    Bass.   Nay, but hear me.
Pardon this fault, and by my soul I swear
I never more will break an oath with thee.
    Ant. I once did lend my body for his wealth,
Which, but for him that had your husband's ring,
Had quite miscarried.   I dare be bound again,   251
My soul upon the forfeit, that your lord
Will never more break faith advisedly.
    Por. Then you shall be his surety.   Give him this
And bid him keep it better than the other.   255
    Ant. Here, Lord Bassanio; swear to keep this
        ring.
    Bass. By heaven, it is the same I gave the doctor!
    Por. I had it of him.   Pardon me, Bassanio;
For, by this ring, the doctor lay with me.
    Ner. And pardon me, my gentle Gratiano;   260
For that same scrubbed boy, the doctor's clerk,

In lieu of this last night did lie with me.
    Gra. Why, this is like the mending of highways
In summer, where the ways are fair enough.
What, are we cuckolds ere we have deserv'd it?   265
    Por. Speak not so grossly.   You are all amaz'd.
Here is a letter; read it at your leisure.
It comes from Padua, from Bellario.
There you shall find that Portia was the doctor,
Nerissa there her clerk.   Lorenzo here   270
Shall witness I set forth as soon as you
And even but now return'd; I have not yet
Ent'red my house.   Antonio, you are welcome;
And I have better news in store for you
Than you expect.   Unseal this letter soon;   275
There you shall find three of your argosies
Are richly come to harbour suddenly.
You shall not know by what strange accident
I chanced on this letter.
    Ant.   I am dumb.   279
    Bass. Were you the doctor and I knew you not?
    Gra. Were you the clerk that is to make me
        cuckold?
    Ner. Ay, but the clerk that never means to do it,
Unless he live until he be a man.
    Bass. Sweet doctor, you shall be my bedfellow.
When I am absent, then lie with my wife.   285
    Ant. Sweet lady, you have given me life and liv-
        ing;
For here I read for certain that my ships
Are safely come to road.
    Por.   How now, Lorenzo!
My clerk hath some good comforts too for you.
    Ner. Ay, and I'll give them him without a fee.   290
There do I give to you and Jessica,
From the rich Jew, a special deed of gift,
After his death, of all he dies possess'd of.
    Lor. Fair ladies, you drop manna in the way
Of starved people.
    Por.   It is almost morning,   295
And yet I am sure you are not satisfied
Of these events at full.   Let us go in;
And charge us there upon inter'gatories,
And we will answer all things faithfully.
    Gra. Let it be so.   The first inter'gatory   300
That my Nerissa shall be sworn on is,
Whether till the next night she had rather stay,
Or go to bed now, being two hours to day.
But were the day come, I should wish it dark,
Till I were couching with the doctor's clerk.   305
Well, while I live I'll fear no other thing
So sore as keeping safe Nerissa's ring.   [*Exeunt.*

230. **like Argus:** i.e. with a hundred eyes.   245. **double:** deceitful.   249. **wealth:** weal, welfare.   298. **charge ... inter'-**
gatories: question us under oath.   306. **fear:** be anxious about.

The First Part of Henry the Fourth

ON FEBRUARY 25, 1598, there was entered in the Stationers' Register *The historye of Henry the iiiith with his battaile of Shrewsburye against Henry Hottspurre of The Northe with the conceipted mirth of Sir John Ffalstoff.* The First Quarto appeared the same year, and others, each printed from the preceding one, followed in 1599, 1603, 1604, 1608, 1613, and 1622. The First Folio was printed from the Fifth Quarto. The basis for the present text is the First Quarto.

There is no evidence of the date of composition before the entry in the Stationers' Register, but the play was obviously written after *Richard II*, judging from the treatment of the character of Bolingbroke, which is clearly developed on the lines laid down in the earlier play. Meres lists *Henry IV* among the Tragedies, and may be presumed to refer to Part I. The date 1597 is generally accepted. The number of editions as well as the frequency of allusion to Falstaff show it to have been the most successful of the histories.

The political part of the plot is founded on Holinshed's *Chronicles* (2d edition, 1587), the speeches, as usually in the English historical plays, being elaborated from the merest hints. The outstanding creation in the serious plot, apart from the Prince, is the opposing figure of Hotspur, whom Shakespeare clearly conceived for the purpose of psychological contrast. In fact, Hotspur was slightly older than the King, and his age is reduced in order to match that of Hal, who is presented as older than his real age, which at the time of the battle of Shrewsbury was only sixteen. Prince Hal does not appear in *Richard II*, but the King speaks of him as "unthrifty," "young wanton and effeminate boy," "as dissolute as desperate," and the associate of ruffians and robbers, though with "sparks of better hope" (V.iii.1–22). This is a slightly darker picture than we get in the present play, for though some of its features are corroborated, Shakespeare is careful to keep the Prince's wildness within limits, however disreputable his associates. Elaborate preparation for his future greatness is made in the

soliloquy in the end of I.ii, and this priggish and hypocritical speech has been defended or explained away as a kind of exposition by the author, the soliloquy serving the purpose of a chorus. Be this as it may, the fact that it is uttered by Hal himself leaves an unpleasant impression of insincerity on the reader.

For the comic scenes Shakespeare gathered some names and incidents from *The Famous Victories of Henry V*, a very crude history-comedy printed in 1598, but licensed in 1594, and acted certainly as early as 1588. The robbery at Gadshill, the Tavern in Eastcheap, Hal's relation to his boon companions and to the Lord Chief Justice, his reconciliation to his father, the episode of the crown, and the final abandonment of his tavern friends, are all presented in rude form in *The Famous Victories*. But the method of treatment is such as to offer barely more suggestion than the bald narrative of Holinshed. In the sixth scene a Sir John Oldcastle is introduced who speaks some half-dozen lines, including one referring to Henry IV: "He is a good old man, God take him to his mercy the sooner." This seems to be the germ of Falstaff, who was called Oldcastle when *I Henry IV* was first produced. The historical Sir John Oldcastle was a well-known nobleman of the time of Henry V, who was burned as a Lollard. His descendants were influential in the time of Elizabeth, and it is supposed that the change of name was made under pressure from them. The epilogue to the second part of *Henry IV* contains the explicit statement, "for Oldcastle died a martyr, and this is not the man." The name Falstaff seems to be derived from that of Sir John Fastolfe who appears (unhistorically) as a coward in *I Henry VI*.

The historical action presented occupied little more than a year (June, 1402–July, 1403), and in the play is compressed into a few months. Culminating as it does in the battle of Shrewsbury, the play has more unity and compactness than most of the histories. Its importance in the development of the chronicle history as a dramatic form lies in the great expansion of the comic element. In this,

of course, the main element is Falstaff, the greatest
of Shakespeare's comic creations, and in the opinion
of many the greatest comic figure in literature. It
is indeed difficult to find a parallel to the amazing
vitality with which he is endowed, to his great gift
of language, to his readiness of wit, to his imper-
turbable good humor, and to the charm which over-
comes his grossness. Critical attention has been
curiously attracted to the question as to whether he
was a coward. The association of his name with
that of Sir John Fastolfe, the Prince's upbraiding
after the Gadshill affair, and his soliloquy on honor
at the battle of Shrewsbury have led to this charge;
while he has found valiant defenders who have explained all this away. There is evidence enough
that he did not lack courage, but he practiced a discreet economy in its employment. *touché*

DESCENT OF THE MORTIMERS

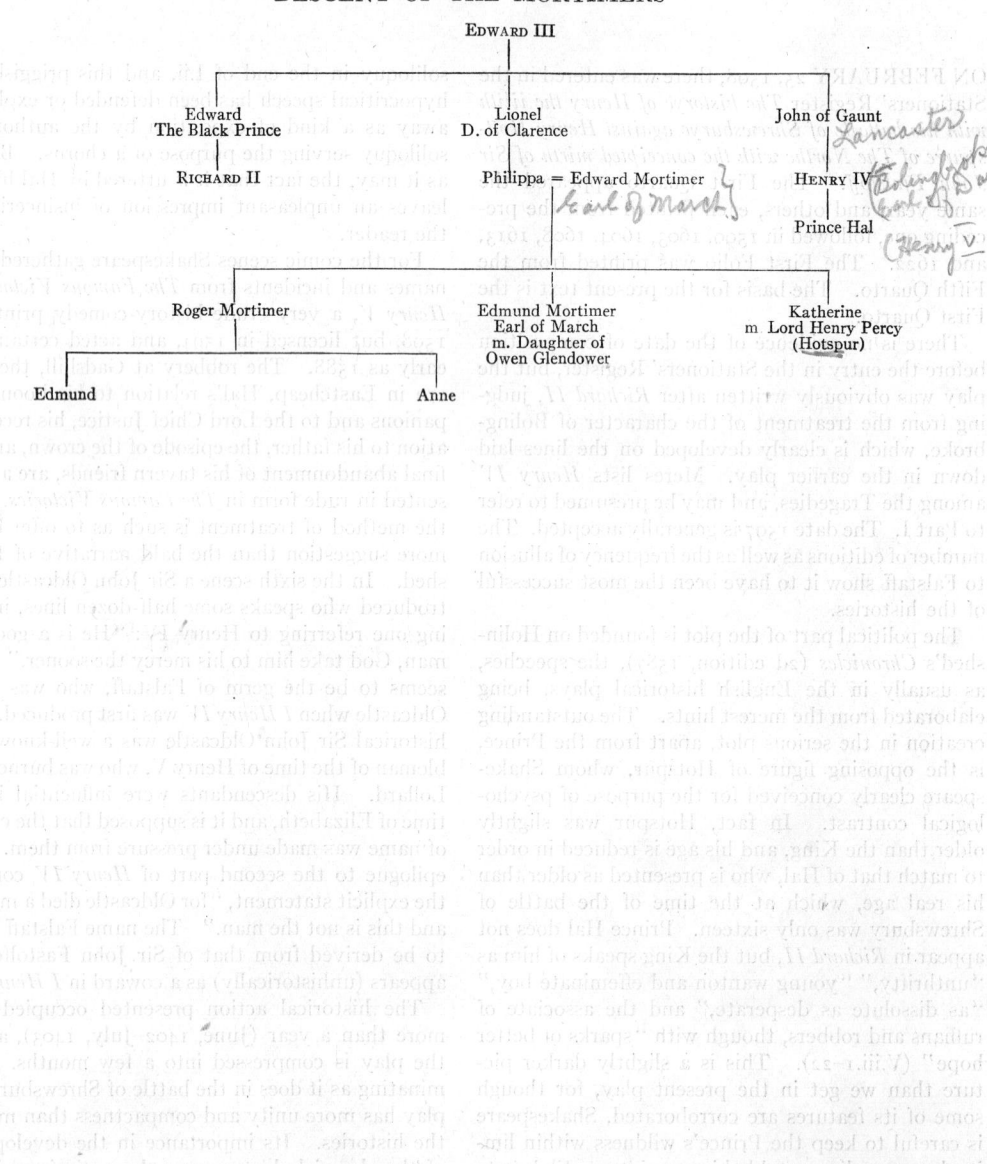

THE FIRST PART OF HENRY THE FOURTH

— Rebel

[DRAMATIS PERSONÆ

KING HENRY IV.
HENRY, PRINCE OF WALES, } sons to the King.
PRINCE JOHN OF LANCASTER, }
EARL OF WESTMORELAND.
SIR WALTER BLUNT.
THOMAS PERCY, *earl of Worcester.*
HENRY PERCY, *earl of Northumberland.*
HENRY PERCY, *surnamed* HOTSPUR, *his son.*
EDMUND MORTIMER, *earl of March.*
RICHARD SCROOP, *archbishop of York.*
ARCHIBALD, *earl of Douglas.*
OWEN GLENDOWER.
SIR RICHARD VERNON.
SIR JOHN FALSTAFF.

SIR MICHAEL, *a friend to the archbishop of York.*
POINS.
GADSHILL.
PETO.
BARDOLPH.

LADY PERCY, *wife to Hotspur, and sister to Mortimer.*
LADY MORTIMER, *daughter to Glendower, and wife to Mortimer.*
MISTRESS QUICKLY, *hostess of a tavern in East-cheap.*

Lords, Officers, Sheriff, Vintner, Chamberlain, Drawers, two Carriers, Travellers, and Attendants.

SCENE: *England and Wales.*]

ACT I

SCENE I. [*London. The palace.*]

Enter KING HENRY, LORD JOHN OF LANCASTER, *the* EARL OF WESTMORELAND, [SIR WALTER BLUNT] *with others.*

King. So shaken as we are, so wan with care,
Find we a time for frighted Peace to pant
And breathe short-winded accents of new broils
To be commenc'd in strands afar remote.
No more the thirsty entrance of this soil   5
Shall daub her lips with her own children's blood;
No more shall trenching war channel her fields,
Nor bruise her flowerets with the armed hoofs
Of hostile paces.   Those opposed eyes,
Which, like the meteors of a troubled heaven,   10
All of one nature, of one substance bred,

Did lately meet in the intestine shock
And furious close of civil butchery,
Shall now, in mutual well-beseeming ranks,
March all one way and be no more oppos'd   15
Against acquaintance, kindred, and allies.
The edge of war, like an ill-sheathed knife,
No more shall cut his master.   Therefore, friends,
As far as to the sepulchre of Christ,
Whose soldier now, under whose blessed cross   20
We are impressed and engag'd to fight,
Forthwith a power of English shall we levy,
Whose arms were moulded in their mother's womb
To chase these pagans in those holy fields
Over whose acres walk'd those blessed feet   25
Which fourteen hundred years ago were nail'd
For our advantage on the bitter cross.
But this our purpose now is twelve month old,
And bootless 'tis to tell you we will go;

Act I, sc. i, 5. **thirsty entrance:** parched mouth.   12. **intestine:** internal.   14. **mutual:** united.   22. **power:** force.

Therefore we meet not now.   Then let me hear 30
Of you, my gentle cousin Westmoreland,
What yesternight our council did decree
In forwarding this dear expedience.

West. My liege, this haste was hot in question
And many limits of the charge set down 35
But yesternight; when all athwart there came
A post from Wales loaden with heavy news;
Whose worst was, that the noble Mortimer,
Leading the men of Herefordshire to fight
Against the irregular and wild Glendower, 40
Was by the rude hands of that Welshman taken,
A thousand of his people butchered;
Upon whose dead corpse there was such misuse,
Such beastly shameless transformation,
By those Welshwomen done as may not be 45
Without much shame retold or spoken of.

King. It seems then that the tidings of this broil
Brake off our business for the Holy Land.

West. This match'd with other did, my gracious
     lord;
For more uneven and unwelcome news 50
Came from the north, and thus it did import:
On Holy-rood day, the gallant Hotspur there,
Young Harry Percy, and brave Archibald,
That ever-valiant and approved Scot,
At Holmedon met, 55
Where they did spend a sad and bloody hour,
As by discharge of their artillery
And shape of likelihood the news was told;
For he that brought them, in the very heat
And pride of their contention did take horse, 60
Uncertain of the issue any way.

King. Here is a dear, a true industrious friend,
Sir Walter Blunt, new lighted from his horse,
Stain'd with the variation of each soil
Betwixt that Holmedon and this seat of ours; 65
And he hath brought us smooth and welcome news.
The Earl of Douglas is discomfited.
Ten thousand bold Scots, two and twenty knights,
Balk'd in their own blood did Sir Walter see
On Holmedon's plains. Of prisoners, Hotspur took
Murdoch Earl of Fife and eldest son 71
To beaten Douglas; and the Earl of Athole,
Of Moray, Angus, and Menteith.
And is not this an honourable spoil?
A gallant prize, ha, cousin, is it not? 75

West. In faith,
It is a conquest for a prince to boast of.

King. Yea, there thou mak'st me sad, and mak'st
     me sin

In envy that my Lord Northumberland
Should be the father to so blest a son; 80
A son who is the theme of Honour's tongue,
Amongst a grove the very straightest plant,
Who is sweet Fortune's minion and her pride;
Whilst I, by looking on the praise of him,
See riot and dishonour stain the brow 85
Of my young Harry.   O that it could be prov'd
That some night-tripping fairy had exchang'd
In cradle-clothes our children where they lay,
And call'd mine Percy, his Plantagenet!
Then would I have his Harry and he mine. 90
But let him from my thoughts.   What think you,
     coz,
Of this young Percy's pride?   The prisoners
Which he in this adventure hath surpris'd
To his own use he keeps; and sends me word,
I shall have none but Murdoch Earl of Fife. 95

West. This is his uncle's teaching; this is
     Worcester,
Malevolent to you in all aspects;
Which makes him prune himself and bristle up
The crest of youth against your dignity.

King. But I have sent for him to answer this;
And for this cause awhile we must neglect 101
Our holy purpose to Jerusalem.
Cousin, on Wednesday next our council we
Will hold at Windsor.   So inform the lords;
But come yourself with speed to us again, 105
For more is to be said and to be done
Than out of anger can be uttered.

West. I will, my liege.   [*Exeunt.*

SCENE II. [*London.   An apartment of the Prince's.*]

Enter the PRINCE OF WALES *and* FALSTAFF.

Fal. Now, Hal, what time of day is it, lad?

Prince. Thou art so fat-witted, with drinking of
old sack and unbuttoning thee after supper and
sleeping upon benches after noon, that thou hast
forgotten to demand that truly which thou wouldest
truly know.   What a devil hast thou to do 6
with the time of the day? Unless hours were cups
of sack, and minutes capons, and clocks the tongues
of bawds, and dials the signs of leaping-houses, and
the blessed sun himself a fair hot wench in flame-
coloured taffeta, I see no reason why thou shouldest
be so superfluous to demand the time of the day. 13

Fal. Indeed, you come near me now, Hal; for
we that take purses go by the moon and the seven
stars, and not by Phœbus, he, "that wand'ring

---

30. **Therefore:** for this.   33. **dear expedience:** expedition close to my heart.   35. **charge:** expense.   36. **athwart:** across
(the plan).   43. **corpse.** A plural. Q spells *corpes.*   44. **transformation:** mutilation.   50. **uneven.** Cf. *smooth,* l. 66.
52. **Holy-rood day:** Sept. 14 (1402).   Mortimer's defeat was on June 22.   69. **Balk'd:** piled up in ridges.   71-72. **eldest...**
Douglas. In fact, Murdoch was son to the Duke of Albany.   76-77. **In faith It is** (Malone). Q gives these words to King.
83. **minion:** darling.   98. **prune:** preen.
   Sc. ii, 3. **sack:** a sweet Spanish wine, sherry.   9. **leaping-houses:** brothels.   15. **seven stars:** Pleiades.

knight so fair." And, I prithee, sweet wag, when thou art a king, as, God save thy Grace, — Majesty I should say, for grace thou wilt have none, — 20

Prince. What, none?

Fal. No, by my troth, not so much as will serve to be prologue to an egg and butter.

Prince. Well, how then? Come, roundly, roundly. 25

Fal. Marry, then, sweet wag, when thou art king, let not us that are squires of the night's body be called thieves of the day's beauty. Let us be Diana's foresters, gentlemen of the shade, minions of the moon; and let men say we be men of good government, being govern'd, as the sea is, by our noble and chaste mistress the moon, under whose countenance we steal. 33

Prince. Thou say'st well, and it holds well too; for the fortune of us that are the moon's men doth ebb and flow like the sea, being governed, as the sea is, by the moon. As, for proof, now: a purse of gold most resolutely snatch'd on 38 Monday night and mostly dissolutely spent on Tuesday morning; got with swearing "Lay by" and spent with crying "Bring in;" now in as low an ebb as the foot of the ladder, and by and by in as high a flow as the ridge of the gallows. 43

Fal. By the Lord, thou say'st true, lad. And is not my hostess of the tavern a most sweet wench?

Prince. As the honey of Hybla, my old lad of the castle. And is not a buff jerkin a most sweet robe of durance? 49

Fal. How now, how now, mad wag! What, in thy quips and thy quiddities, what a plague have I to do with a buff jerkin?

Prince. Why, what a pox have I to do with my hostess of the tavern? 54

Fal. Well, thou hast call'd her to a reckoning many a time and oft.

Prince. Did I ever call for thee to pay thy part?

Fal. No; I'll give thee thy due, thou hast paid all there. 60

Prince. Yea, and elsewhere, so far as my coin would stretch; and where it would not, I have us'd my credit. 63

Fal. Yea, and so us'd it that, were it not here apparent that thou art heir apparent — But, I prithee, sweet wag, shall there be gallows standing in England when thou art king? and resolution thus fobb'd as it is with the rusty curb of old father antic the law? Do not thou, when thou art king, hang a thief. 70

Prince. No; thou shalt.

Fal. Shall I? O rare! By the Lord, I'll be a brave judge.

Prince. Thou judgest false already. I mean, thou shalt have the hanging of the thieves and so become a rare hangman. 76

Fal. Well, Hal, well; and in some sort it jumps with my humour as well as waiting in the court, I can tell you.

Prince. For obtaining of suits? 80

Fal. Yea, for obtaining of suits, whereof the hangman hath no lean wardrobe. 'Sblood, I am as melancholy as a gib cat or a lugg'd bear.

Prince. Or an old lion, or a lover's lute. 84

Fal. Yea, or the drone of a Lincolnshire bagpipe.

Prince. What sayest thou to a hare, or the melancholy of Moor-ditch? 88

Fal. Thou hast the most unsavoury similes and art indeed the most comparative, rascalliest, sweet young prince. But, Hal, I prithee, trouble me no more with vanity. I would to God thou and I knew where a commodity of good names were to be bought. An old lord of the council rated me 94 the other day in the street about you, sir, but I mark'd him not; and yet he talk'd very wisely, but I regarded him not; and yet he talk'd wisely, and in the street too.

Prince. Thou didst well; for wisdom cries out in the streets, and no man regards it. 100

Fal. O, thou hast damnable iteration and art indeed able to corrupt a saint. Thou hast done much harm upon me, Hal; God forgive thee for it! Before I knew thee, Hal, I knew nothing; and now am I, if a man should speak truly, little 105 better than one of the wicked. I must give over this life, and I will give it over. By the Lord, an I do not, I am a villain. I'll be damn'd for never a king's son in Christendom.

Prince. Where shall we take a purse tomorrow, Jack? 111

Fal. 'Zounds, where thou wilt, lad; I'll make one. An I do not, call me villain and baffle me.

Prince. I see a good amendment of life in thee; from praying to purse-taking.

Fal. Why, Hal, 'tis my vocation, Hal. 'Tis no sin for a man to labour in his vocation. 117

Enter POINS.

Poins! Now shall we know if Gadshill have set a match. O, if men were to be saved by merit, what hole in hell were hot enough for him? This

---

25. **roundly:** directly. 47. **Hybla:** a town in Sicily. 49. **durance:** (1) lasting stuff, (2) imprisonment (because worn by sheriff's officers). 51. **quiddities:** hairsplittings. 68. **fobb'd:** cheated. 69. **antic:** clown. 77. **jumps:** agrees. 82. **no . . . wardrobe.** The hangman inherited the clothes of his victims. 83. **gib cat:** tomcat. **lugg'd:** led. 88. **Moor-ditch:** a swamp just outside the walls. 90. **comparative:** comparison-making. 93. **commodity:** supply. 99-100. **wisdom . . . regards it.** *Proverbs* I.20–24. Om. Ff. 101. **damnable iteration:** quoting for an evil end. 113. **baffle:** disgrace. 118. **Gadshill.** This confusing name is taken from *The Famous Victories of Henry V.* **set a match:** arranged a meeting.

is the most omnipotent villain that ever cried "Stand!" to a true man.

Prince. Good morrow, Ned.   123

Poins. Good morrow, sweet Hal. What says Monsieur Remorse? What says Sir John Sack and Sugar? Jack! how agrees the devil and thee about thy soul, that thou soldest him on Good Friday last for a cup of Madeira and a cold capon's leg?   129

Prince. Sir John stands to his word, the devil shall have his bargain; for he was never yet a breaker of proverbs. He will give the devil his due.

Poins. Then art thou damn'd for keeping thy word with the devil.   135

Prince. Else he had been damn'd for cozening the devil.

Poins. But, my lads, my lads, to-morrow morning by four o'clock early, at Gadshill! There are pilgrims going to Canterbury with rich offerings, 140 and traders riding to London with fat purses. I have vizards for you all; you have horses for yourselves. Gadshill lies to-night in Rochester. I have bespoke supper to-morrow night in Eastcheap. We may do it as secure as sleep. If you will go, 145 I will stuff your purses full of crowns; if you will not, tarry at home and be hang'd.

Fal. Hear ye, Yedward; if I tarry at home and go not, I'll hang you for going.   150

Poins. You will, chops?

Fal. Hal, wilt thou make one?

Prince. Who, I rob? I a thief? Not I, by my faith.   154

Fal. There's neither honesty, manhood, nor good fellowship in thee, nor thou cam'st not of the blood royal, if thou dar'st not stand for ten shillings.

Prince. Well, then, once in my days I'll be a madcap.   160

Fal. Why, that's well said.

Prince. Well, come what will, I'll tarry at home.

Fal. By the lord, I'll be a traitor then, when thou art king.   165

Prince. I care not.

Poins. Sir John, I prithee, leave the Prince and me alone. I will lay him down such reasons for this adventure that he shall go.   169

Fal. Well, God give thee the spirit of persuasion and him the ears of profiting, that what thou speakest may move and what he hears may be believed, that the true prince may, for recreation sake, prove a false thief; for the poor abuses of the time want countenance. Farewell; you shall find me in Eastcheap.   176

Prince. Farewell, [thou] latter spring! Farewell, All-hallown summer!   [*Exit Falstaff.*]

Poins. Now, my good sweet honey lord, ride with us to-morrow; I have a jest to execute that 180 I cannot manage alone. Falstaff [Bardolph, Peto,] and Gadshill shall rob those men that we have already waylaid; yourself and I will not be there; and when they have the booty, if you and I do not rob them, cut this head off from my shoulders.

Prince. How shall we part with them in setting forth?   188

Poins. Why, we will set forth before or after them and appoint them a place of meeting, wherein it is at our pleasure to fail, and then will they adventure upon the exploit themselves; which they shall have no sooner achieved, but we'll set upon them.   194

Prince. Yea, but 'tis like that they will know us by our horses, by our habits, and by every other appointment, to be ourselves.   197

Poins. Tut! our horses they shall not see — I'll tie them in the wood; our vizards we will change after we leave them; and, sirrah, I have cases of buckram for the nonce, to immask our noted outward garments.   202

Prince. Yea, but I doubt they will be too hard for us.

Poins. Well, for two of them, I know them to be as true-bred cowards as ever turn'd back; and for the third, if he fight longer than he sees 207 reason, I'll forswear arms. The virtue of this jest will be the incomprehensible lies that this same fat rogue will tell us when we meet at supper; how thirty, at least, he fought with; what wards, what blows, what extremities he endured; and in the reproof of this lies the jest.   213

Prince. Well, I'll go with thee. Provide us all things necessary and meet me to-morrow night in Eastcheap; there I'll sup. Farewell.

Poins. Farewell, my lord.   [*Exit.*

Prince. I know you all, and will a while uphold The unyok'd humour of your idleness.
Yet herein will I imitate the sun,   220
Who doth permit the base contagious clouds
To smother up his beauty from the world,
That when he please again to be himself
Being wanted, he may be more wond'red at
By breaking through the foul and ugly mists   225
Of vapours that did seem to strangle him.
If all the year were playing holidays,
To sport would be as tedious as to work;
But when they seldom come, they wish'd for come,
And nothing pleaseth but rare accidents.   230

---

136. **cozening:** cheating. 151. **chops:** fat-face. 157. **royal:** punning on *royal,* a coin worth 10*s.* 177. **[thou]** (Pope). *the* Qq Ff. 178. **All-hallown summer:** belated summer, youth in age. 181. **[Bardolph, Peto]** (Theobald). *Harvey, Rossill* Qq Ff — names of the actors. 200. **cases of buckram:** suits of linen stiffened with paste. 201. **nonce:** occasion. **noted:** known. 211. **wards:** postures of defense. 213. **reproof:** refutation. 230. **accidents:** incidents.

So, when this loose behaviour I throw off
And pay the debt I never promised,
By how much better than my word I am,
By so much shall I falsify men's hopes;
And like bright metal on a sullen ground, 235
My reformation, glitt'ring o'er my fault,
Shall show more goodly and attract more eyes
Than that which hath no foil to set it off.
I'll so offend, to make offence a skill,
Redeeming time when men think least I will. 240
    [*Exit.*

SCENE III. [*London. The palace.*]

Enter the KING, NORTHUMBERLAND, WORCESTER,
    HOTSPUR, SIR WALTER BLUNT, *with others.*

    King. My blood hath been too cold and tem-
        perate,
Unapt to stir at these indignities,
And you have found me; for accordingly
You tread upon my patience. But be sure
I will from henceforth rather be myself, 5
Mighty and to be fear'd, than my condition;
Which hath been smooth as oil, soft as young down,
And therefore lost that title of respect
Which the proud soul ne'er pays but to the proud.
    Wor. Our house, my sovereign liege, little de-
        serves 10
The scourge of greatness to be us'd on it;
And that same greatness too which our own hands
Have holp to make so portly.
    North. My lord,—
    King. Worcester, get thee gone; for I do see 15
Danger and disobedience in thine eye.
O, sir, your presence is too bold and peremptory,
And majesty might never yet endure
The moody frontier of a servant brow. 19
You have good leave to leave us. When we need
Your use and counsel, we shall send for you.
    [*Exit Worcester.*
You were about to speak.
    North.   Yea, my good lord.
Those prisoners in your Highness' name demanded,
Which Harry Percy here at Holmedon took,
Were, as he says, not with such strength denied 25
As is delivered to your Majesty.
Either envy, therefore, or misprision
Is guilty of this fault, and not my son.
    Hot. My liege, I did deny no prisoners.
But I remember, when the fight was done, 30
When I was dry with rage and extreme toil,

Breathless and faint, leaning upon my sword,
Came there a certain lord, neat, trimly dress'd,
Fresh as a bridegroom; and his chin new reap'd
Show'd like a stubble-land at harvest-home. 35
He was perfumed like a milliner;
And 'twixt his finger and his thumb he held
A pouncet-box, which ever and anon
He gave his nose and took't away again;
Who therewith angry, when it next came there, 40
Took it in snuff; and still he smil'd and talk'd,
And as the soldiers bore dead bodies by,
He call'd them untaught knaves, unmannerly,
To bring a slovenly unhandsome corse
Betwixt the wind and his nobility. 45
With many holiday and lady terms
He question'd me; amongst the rest, demanded
My prisoners in your Majesty's behalf.
I then, all smarting with my wounds being cold,
To be so pest'red with a popinjay, 50
Out of my grief and my impatience
Answer'd neglectingly — I know not what,
He should, or he should not; for he made me mad
To see him shine so brisk and smell so sweet
And talk so like a waiting-gentlewoman 55
Of guns and drums and wounds, — God save the
        mark! —
And telling me the sovereign'st thing on earth
Was parmaceti for an inward bruise;
And that it was great pity, so it was,
This villanous salt-petre should be digg'd 60
Out of the bowels of the harmless earth,
Which many a good tall fellow had destroy'd
So cowardly; and but for these vile guns,
He would himself have been a soldier.
This bald unjointed chat of his, my lord, 65
I answered indirectly, as I said;
And I beseech you, let not his report
Come current for an accusation
Betwixt my love and your high Majesty.
    Blunt. The circumstance considered, good my
        lord, 70
Whate'er Lord Harry Percy then had said
To such a person and in such a place,
At such a time, with all the rest retold,
May reasonably die and never rise
To do him wrong or any way impeach 75
What then he said, so he unsay it now.
    King. Why, yet he doth deny his prisoners
But with proviso and exception
That we at our own charge shall ransom straight
His brother-in-law, the foolish Mortimer; 80

---

235. **sullen:** dark. 238. **foil:** leaf of metal under a gem.
  Sc. iii, 6. **condition:** natural bent. 19. **frontier:** forehead. The word meant also outwork, fortification. 27. **misprision:** misunderstanding. 38. **pouncet-box:** perfume box. 40. **Who:** which (nose). 41. **Took...snuff:** was offended. 50. **popinjay:** parrot. 51. **grief:** pain. 58. **parmaceti:** spermaceti, sperm of the whale. 62. **tall:** brave. 66. **indirectly:** vaguely. 68. **Come current:** be accepted as valid. 75. **impeach:** call in question. 78. **But...exception:** unless on the condition.

Who, on my soul, hath wilfully betray'd
The lives of those that he did lead to fight
Against that great magician, damn'd Glendower,
Whose daughter, as we hear, the Earl of March
Hath lately married. Shall our coffers, then,   85
Be emptied to redeem a traitor home?
Shall we buy treason, and indent with fears,
When they have lost and forfeited themselves?
No, on the barren mountains let him starve;
For I shall never hold that man my friend   90
Whose tongue shall ask me for one penny cost
To ransom home revolted Mortimer.

   Hot. Revolted Mortimer!
He never did fall off, my sovereign liege,
But by the chance of war. To prove that true   95
Needs no more but one tongue for all those wounds,
Those mouthed wounds, which valiantly he took,
When on the gentle Severn's sedgy bank,
In single opposition, hand to hand,
He did confound the best part of an hour   100
In changing hardiment with great Glendower.
Three times they breath'd and three times did they
    drink,
Upon agreement, of swift Severn's flood;
Who then, affrighted with their bloody looks,
Ran fearfully among the trembling reeds,   105
And hid his crisp head in the hollow bank
Bloodstained with these valiant combatants.
Never did [base] and rotten policy
Colour her working with such deadly wounds,
Nor never could the noble Mortimer   110
Receive so many, and all willingly.
Then let not him be slandered with revolt.

   King. Thou dost belie him, Percy, thou dost
    belie him;
He never did encounter with Glendower.
I tell thee,   115
He durst as well have met the devil alone
As Owen Glendower for an enemy.
Art thou not asham'd? But, sirrah, henceforth
Let me not hear you speak of Mortimer.
Send me your prisoners with the speediest means,
Or you shall hear in such a kind from me   121
As will displease you. My Lord Northumberland,
We license your departure with your son.
Send us your prisoners, or you'll hear of it.

    [*Exeunt King Henry* [*Blunt, and train*].

   Hot. An if the devil come and roar for them,   125
I will not send them. I will after straight
And tell him so; for I will ease my heart,
Albeit I make a hazard of my head.

   North. What, drunk with choler? Stay and
    pause a while.
Here comes your uncle.

Re-enter WORCESTER.

   Hot.   Speak of Mortimer!   130
'Zounds, I will speak of him; and let my soul
Want mercy if I do not join with him.
Yea, on his part I'll empty all these veins,
And shed my dear blood drop by drop in the dust,
But I will lift the down-trod Mortimer   135
As high in the air as this unthankful king,
As this ingrate and cank'red Bolingbroke.

   North. Brother, the King hath made your
    nephew mad.

   Wor. Who struck this heat up after I was gone?

   Hot. He will, forsooth, have all my prisoners;   140
And when I urg'd the ransom once again
Of my wife's brother, then his cheek look'd pale,
And on my face he turn'd an eye of death,
Trembling even at the name of Mortimer.

   Wor. I cannot blame him. Was not he pro-
    claim'd   145
By Richard, that dead is, the next of blood?

   North. He was; I heard the proclamation.
And then it was when the unhappy king, —
Whose wrongs in us God pardon! — did set forth
Upon his Irish expedition;   150
From whence he intercepted did return
To be depos'd and shortly murdered.

   Wor. And for whose death we in the world's wide
    mouth
Live scandaliz'd and foully spoken of.

   Hot. But, soft, I pray you; did King Richard then
Proclaim my brother Edmund Mortimer   156
Heir to the crown?

   North.   He did; myself did hear it.

   Hot. Nay, then I cannot blame his cousin king,
That wish'd him on the barren mountains starve.
But shall it be that you, that set the crown   160
Upon the head of this forgetful man
And for his sake wear the detested blot
Of murderous subornation, shall it be,
That you a world of curses undergo,
Being the agents or base second means,   165
The cords, the ladder, or the hangman rather?
O, pardon me that I descend so low
To show the line and the predicament
Wherein you range under this subtle king!
Shall it for shame be spoken in these days,   170
Or fill up chronicles in time to come,
That men of your nobility and power
Did gage them both in an unjust behalf,
As both of you — God pardon it! — have done,
To put down Richard, that sweet lovely rose,   175
And plant this thorn, this canker, Bolingbroke?
And shall it in more shame be further spoken,
That you are fool'd, discarded, and shook off

---

87. **indent:** make a contract. 100. **confound:** spend. 101. **hardiment:** valiant blows. 106. **crisp:** rippled. 108. **[base]** Ff. *bare* Qq. 137. **cank'red:** malignant. 163. **subornation:** persuading to commit a crime. 168. **predicament:** situation. 173. **gage:** engage.

By him for whom these shames ye underwent?
No; yet time serves wherein you may redeem   180
Your banish'd honours and restore yourselves
Into the good thoughts of the world again,
Revenge the jeering and disdain'd contempt
Of this proud king, who studies day and night
To answer all the debt he owes to you   185
Even with the bloody payment of your deaths.
Therefore, I say, —
  Wor.   Peace, cousin, say no more;
And now I will unclasp a secret book,
And to your quick-conceiving discontents
I'll read you matter deep and dangerous,   190
As full of peril and adventurous spirit
As to o'er-walk a current roaring loud
On the unsteadfast footing of a spear.
  Hot. If he fall in, good night! or sink or swim.
Send Danger from the east unto the west,   195
So Honour cross it from the north to south,
And let them grapple.   O, the blood more stirs
To rouse a lion than to start a hare!
  North. Imagination of some great exploit
Drives him beyond the bounds of patience.   200
  [*Hot.*] By heaven, methinks it were an easy leap,
To pluck bright Honour from the pale-fac'd moon,
Or dive into the bottom of the deep,
Where fathom-line could never touch the ground
And pluck up drowned Honour by the locks;   205
So he that doth redeem her thence might wear
Without corrival all her dignities.
But out upon this half-fac'd fellowship!
  Wor. He apprehends a world of figures here,
But not the form of what he should attend.   210
Good cousin, give me audience for a while.
  Hot. I cry you mercy.
  Wor.   Those same noble Scots
That are your prisoners, —
  Hot.   I'll keep them all!
By God, he shall not have a Scot of them;
No, if a Scot would save his soul, he shall not!   215
I'll keep them, by this hand.
  Wor.   You start away
And lend no ear unto my purposes.
Those prisoners you shall keep.
  Hot.   Nay, I will; that's flat.
He said he would not ransom Mortimer;
Forbade my tongue to speak of Mortimer;   220
But I will find him when he lies asleep
And in his ear I'll holla "Mortimer!"
Nay,
I'll have a starling shall be taught to speak
Nothing but "Mortimer," and give it him   225
To keep his anger still in motion.
  Wor. Hear you, cousin; a word.

  Hot. All studies here I solemnly defy,
Save how to gall and pinch this Bolingbroke;
And that same sword-and-buckler Prince of Wales,
But that I think his father loves him not   231
And would be glad he met with some mischance,
I would have him poison'd with a pot of ale.
  Wor. Farewell, kinsman!   I'll talk to you
When you are better temper'd to attend.   235
  North. Why, what a wasp-stung and impatient fool
Art thou to break into this woman's mood,
Tying thine ear to no tongue but thine own!
  Hot. Why, look you, I am whipp'd and scourg'd with rods,
Nettled and stung with pismires, when I hear   240
Of this vile politician, Bolingbroke.
In Richard's time, — what do you call the place? —
A plague upon it, it is in Gloucestershire;
'Twas where the madcap duke his uncle kept,
His uncle York; where I first bow'd my knee   245
Unto this king of smiles, this Bolingbroke, —
'Sblood! —
When you and he came back from Ravenspurgh —
  North. At Berkeley castle.
  Hot. You say true.   250
Why, what a candy deal of courtesy
This fawning greyhound then did proffer me!
Look, "when his infant fortune came to age,"
And "gentle Harry Percy," and "kind cousin;"
O, the devil take such cozeners! — God forgive me!
Good uncle, tell your tale; [for] I have done.   256
  Wor. Nay, if you have not, to't again;
We'll stay your leisure.
  Hot.   I have done, i' faith.
  Wor. Then once more to your Scottish prisoners.
Deliver them up without their ransom straight,   260
And make the Douglas' son your only mean
For powers in Scotland; which, for divers reasons
Which I shall send you written, be assur'd,
Will easily be granted.   You, my lord,
           [*To Northumberland.*
Your son in Scotland being thus employ'd,   265
Shall secretly into the bosom creep
Of that same noble prelate, well belov'd,
The Archbishop.
  Hot. Of York, is it not?
  Wor. True; who bears hard   270
His brother's death at Bristol, the Lord Scroop.
I speak not this in estimation,
As what I think might be, but what I know
Is ruminated, plotted, and set down,
And only stays but to behold the face   275
Of that occasion that shall bring it on.
  Hot. I smell it.   Upon my life, it will do well.

183. disdain'd: full of disdain.   201. [*Hot.*] Q5.   Om. Q1–4.   208. half-fac'd: half-hearted.   228. defy: renounce.   240. pismires: ants.   244. kept: lived.   251. candy: sugary.   256. [for] F. Om. Qq.   261. mean: agent.   272. estimation: inference.

North. Before the game's afoot, thou still let'st
    slip.

Hot. Why, it cannot choose but be a noble plot.
And then the power of Scotland and of York,   280
To join with Mortimer, ha?

Wor.   And so they shall.

Hot. In faith, it is exceedingly well aim'd.

Wor. And 'tis no little reason bids us speed,
To save our heads by raising of a head;
For, bear ourselves as even as we can,   285
The King will always think him in our debt,
And think we think ourselves unsatisfied,
Till he hath found a time to pay us home.
And see already how he doth begin
To make us strangers to his looks of love.   290

Hot. He does, he does. We'll be reveng'd on him.

Wor. Cousin, farewell! No further go in this
Than I by letters shall direct your course.
When time is ripe, which will be suddenly,
I'll steal to Glendower and Lord Mortimer;   295
Where you and Douglas and our powers at once,
As I will fashion it, shall happily meet
To bear our fortunes in our own strong arms,
Which now we hold at much uncertainty.

North. Farewell, good brother! We shall thrive,
    I trust.   300

Hot. Uncle, adieu! O, let the hours be short
Till fields and blows and groans applaud our sport!
                  [*Exeunt.*

ACT II

SCENE I. [*Rochester. An inn yard.*]

Enter a CARRIER *with a lantern in his hand.*

1. Car. Heigh-ho! an it be not four by the day,
I'll be hang'd. Charles' wain is over the new
chimney, and yet our horse not pack'd. What,
ostler!   4

Ost. [*Within.*] Anon, anon.

1. Car. I prithee, Tom, beat Cut's saddle, put a
few flocks in the point. Poor jade, is wrung in
the withers out of all cess.   8

Enter another CARRIER.

2. Car. Peas and beans are as dank here as a
dog, and that is the next way to give poor jades
the bots. This house is turned upside down since
Robin Ostler died.

1. Car. Poor fellow, never joy'd since the price
of oats rose; it was the death of him.   14

2. Car. I think this be the most villanous house
in all London road for fleas. I am stung like a
tench.

1. Car. Like a tench! by the mass, there is ne'er
a king christen could be better bit than I have
been since the first cock.   20

2. Car. Why, they will allow us ne'er a jordan,
and then we leak in your chimney; and your
chamber-lye breeds fleas like a loach.

1. Car. What, ostler! come away and be hang'd!
Come away.   25

2. Car. I have a gammon of bacon and two razes
of ginger, to be delivered as far as Charing-
cross.   28

1. Car. God's body! the turkeys in my pannier
are quite starved. What, ostler! A plague on
thee! hast thou never an eye in thy head? Canst
not hear? An't were not as good deed as drink,
to break the pate on thee, I am a very villain.
Come, and be hang'd! Hast no faith in thee?   35

Enter GADSHILL.

Gads. Good morrow, carriers. What's o'clock?

[1.] Car. I think it be two o'clock.

Gads. I prithee, lend me thy lantern, to see my
gelding in the stable.

1. Car. Nay, by God, soft; I know a trick worth
two of that, i' faith.

Gads. I pray thee, lend me thine.

2. Car. Ay, when? canst tell? Lend me thy
lantern, quoth he? Marry, I'll see thee hang'd first.

Gads. Sirrah carrier, what time do you mean to
come to London?   46

2. Car. Time enough to go to bed with a candle,
I warrant thee. Come, neighbour Mugs, we'll
call up the gentlemen. They will along with
company, for they have great charge.   51
              [*Exeunt Carriers.*

Enter CHAMBERLAIN.

Gads. What, ho! chamberlain!

Cham. At hand, quoth pick-purse.

Gads. That's even as fair as — at hand, quoth
the chamberlain; for thou variest no more from
picking of purses than giving direction doth from
labouring; thou lay'st the plot how.   57

Cham. Good morrow, Master Gadshill. It holds
current that I told you yesternight: there's a
franklin in the Wild of Kent hath brought three
hundred marks with him in gold. I heard him
tell it to one of his company last night at supper;
a kind of auditor; one that hath abundance of
charge too, God knows what. They are up already, and call for eggs and butter. They will
away presently.   66

Gads. Sirrah, if they meet not with Saint
Nicholas' clerks, I'll give thee this neck.

Act II, sc. i, 2. Charles' wain: the Great Bear. **5. Anon:** at once. **7. flocks:** tufts of wool. **8. cess:** measure. **11. bots:** worms. **17. tench:** a spotted fish. **23. chamber-lye:** urine. **loach:** fish. **26. razes:** bundles of roots. **40. soft:** go slow. **51. charge:** valuables. **60. Wild:** Weald, forest. **61. marks:** 13s.4d. **67–68. Saint Nicholas' clerks:** highwaymen.

Cham. No, I'll none of it. I pray thee, keep that for the hangman; for I know thou worshipp'st Saint Nicholas as truly as a man of falsehood may.   72

Gads. What talkest thou to me of the hangman? If I hang, I'll make a fat pair of gallows; for if I hang, old Sir John hangs with me, and thou know'st he is no starveling. Tut! there are other Troians that thou dream'st not of, the which for sport sake are content to do the profession 78 some grace, that would, if matters should be look'd into, for their own credit sake, make all whole. I am joined with no foot land-rakers, no long-staff sixpenny strikers, none of these mad mustachio purple-hued malt-worms; but with nobility and tranquillity, burgomasters and great oneyers; such as can hold in, such as will strike sooner than 85 speak, and speak sooner than drink, and drink sooner than pray; and yet, 'zounds, I lie; for they pray continually to their saint, the commonwealth; or rather, not pray to her, but prey on her, for they ride up and down on her and make her their boots.   91

Cham. What, the commonwealth their boots? Will she hold out water in foul way?

Gads. She will, she will; justice hath liquor'd her. We steal as in a castle, cock-sure; we have the receipt of fern-seed, we walk invisible.   96

Cham. Nay, by my faith, I think you are more beholding to the night than to fern-seed for your walking invisible.

Gads. Give me thy hand. Thou shalt have a share in our purchase, as I am a true man.   101

Cham. Nay, rather let me have it as you are a false thief.

Gads. Go to; *homo* is a common name to all men. Bid the ostler bring my gelding out of the stable. Farewell, you muddy knave.   [*Exeunt.* 106

SCENE II. [*The highway, near Gadshill.*]

Enter PRINCE HENRY *and* POINS.

Poins. Come, shelter, shelter! I have remov'd Falstaff's horse, and he frets like a gumm'd velvet.
                                        [*They step back.*]
Prince. Stand close.

Enter FALSTAFF.

Fal. Poins! Poins, and be hang'd! Poins!   4
Prince. [*Coming forward.*] Peace, ye fat-kidney'd rascal! what a brawling dost thou keep!
Fal. Where's Poins, Hal?

Prince. He is walk'd up to the top of the hill; I'll go seek him.   [*Withdraws.*] 9
Fal. I am accurs'd to rob in that thief's company. The rascal hath removed my horse, and tied him I know not where. If I travel but four foot by the squire further afoot, I shall break my wind. Well, I doubt not but to die a fair death for all this, if I scape hanging for killing that 15 rogue. I have forsworn his company hourly any time this two and twenty years, and yet I am be-witch'd with the rogue's company. If the rascal have not given me medicines to make me love him, I'll be hang'd. It could not be else; I have 20 drunk medicines. Poins! Hal! a plague upon you both! Bardolph! Peto! I'll starve ere I'll rob a foot further. An 'twere not as good a deed as drink, to turn true man and to leave these rogues, I am the veriest varlet that ever chewed 25 with a tooth. Eight yards of uneven ground is threescore and ten miles afoot with me; and the stony-hearted villains know it well enough. A plague upon it when thieves cannot be true one to another! (*They whistle.*) Whew! A 30 plague upon you all! Give me my horse, you rogues; give me my horse, and be hang'd!

Prince. [*Coming forward.*] Peace, ye fat-guts! lie down. Lay thine ear close to the ground and list if thou canst hear the tread of travellers. 35
Fal. Have you any levers to lift me up again, being down? 'Sblood, I'll not bear mine own flesh so far afoot again for all the coin in thy father's exchequer. What a plague mean ye to colt me thus?   40
Prince. Thou liest; thou art not colted, thou art uncolted.
Fal. I prithee, good Prince Hal, help me to my horse, good king's son.
Prince. Out, ye rogue! shall I be your ostler? 45
Fal. Hang thyself in thine own heir-apparent garters! If I be ta'en, I'll peach for this. An I have not ballads made on you all and sung to filthy tunes, let a cup of sack be my poison. When a jest is so forward, and afoot too! I hate it.   50

Enter GADSHILL [BARDOLPH, *and* PETO *with him*].

Gads. Stand.
Fal. So I do, against my will.
Poins. [*Coming forward.*] O, 'tis our setter; I know his voice. Bardolph, what news?   54
Bard. Case ye, case ye; on with your vizards. There's money of the King's coming down the hill; 'tis going to the King's exchequer.

---

77. **Troians:** fellows. 81. **foot land-rakers:** footpads. 82. **long-staff ... strikers:** petty thieves. 83. **mustachio ... malt-worms:** topers with mustaches dyed with ale. 84. **oneyers:** ones. 91. **boots.** With a pun on *booty.* 93. **foul:** muddy. 94. **liquor'd:** waterproofed. 101. **purchase:** booty.

Sc. ii, 2. **gumm'd:** stiffened with gum. 13. **squire:** square, foot-rule. 15. **for:** in spite of. 39. **colt:** fool. 53. **setter:** arranger (Gadshill).

Fal. You lie, ye rogue; 'tis going to the King's tavern.

Gads. There's enough to make us all. 60

Fal. To be hang'd.

Prince. Sirs, you four shall front them in the narrow lane; Ned Poins and I will walk lower. If they scape from your encounter, then they light on us. 65

Peto. How many be there of them?

Gads. Some eight or ten.

Fal. 'Zounds, will they not rob us?

Prince. What, a coward, Sir John Paunch?

Fal. Indeed, I am not John of Gaunt, your grandfather; but yet no coward, Hal. 71

Prince. Well, we leave that to the proof.

Poins. Sirrah Jack, thy horse stands behind the hedge; when thou need'st him, there thou shalt find him. Farewell, and stand fast. 75

Fal. Now cannot I strike him, if I should be hang'd.

Prince. [*Aside.*] Ned, where are our disguises.

Poins. [*Aside.*] Here, hard by. Stand close.

[*Exeunt Prince and Poins.*]

Fal. Now, my masters, happy man be his dole, say I. Every man to his business. 81

Enter the TRAVELLERS.

[*1.*] *Trav.* Come, neighbour; the boy shall lead our horses down the hill. We'll walk afoot a while, and ease our legs.

Thieves. Stand!

Travellers. Jesus bless us! 86

Fal. Strike; down with them! Cut the villains' throats! Ah! whoreson caterpillars! bacon-fed knaves! they hate us youth. Down with them! Fleece them!

Travellers. O, we are undone, both we and ours for ever! 92

Fal. Hang ye, gorbellied knaves, are ye undone? No, ye fat chuffs; I would your store were here! On, bacons, on! What, ye knaves! young men must live. You are grandjurors, are ye? We'll jure ye, faith. 97

[*Here they rob them and bind them. Exeunt.*]

Re-enter PRINCE HENRY *and* POINS [*in buckram*].

Prince. The thieves have bound the true men. Now, could thou and I rob the thieves and go merrily to London, it would be argument for a week, laughter for a month, and a good jest for ever.

Poins. Stand close; I hear them coming. 103

Enter the Thieves again.

Fal. Come, my masters, let us share, and then

to horse before day. An the Prince and Poins be not two arrant cowards, there's no equity stirring. There's no more valour in that Poins than in a wild-duck. 108

Prince. Your money!

Poins. Villains!

[*As they are sharing, the Prince and Poins set upon them; they all run away; and Falstaff, after a blow or two, runs away too, leaving the booty behind them.*]

Prince. Got with much ease. Now merrily to horse.
The thieves are all scatt'red and possess'd with fear
So strongly that they dare not meet each other;
Each takes his fellow for an officer.
Away, good Ned. Falstaff sweats to death, 115
And lards the lean earth as he walks along.
Were't not for laughing, I should pity him.

Poins. How the [fat] rogue roar'd! [*Exeunt.*

SCENE III. [*Warkworth Castle.*]

Enter HOTSPUR, *solus, reading a letter.*

Hot. "But, for mine own part, my lord, I could be well contented to be there, in respect of the love I bear your house." He could be contented: why is he not, then? In respect of the love he bears our house: he shows in this, he loves his 5 own barn better than he loves our house. Let me see some more. "The purpose you undertake is dangerous;" — why, that's certain. 'Tis dangerous to take a cold, to sleep, to drink; but I tell you, my lord fool, out of this nettle, danger, we pluck this flower, safety. "The purpose you 10 undertake is dangerous; the friends you have named uncertain; the time itself unsorted; and your whole plot too light for the counterpoise of so great an opposition." Say you so, say you so? I say unto you again, you are a shallow, cowardly 15 hind, and you lie. What a lack-brain is this! By the Lord, our plot is a good plot as ever was laid; our friends true and constant: a good plot, good friends, and full of expectation; an excellent plot, very good friends. What a frosty- 20 spirited rogue is this! Why, my Lord of York commends the plot and the general course of the action. 'Zounds, an I were now by this rascal, I could brain him with his lady's fan. Is there not my father, my uncle, and myself? Lord 25 Edmund Mortimer, my Lord of York, and Owen Glendower? Is there not besides the Douglas? Have I not all their letters to meet me in arms by the ninth of the next month? and are they

not some of them set forward already? What 30
a pagan rascal is this! an infidel! Ha! you shall
see now in very sincerity of fear and cold heart,
will he to the King and lay open all our proceedings. O, I could divide myself and go to buffets,
for moving such a dish of skim-milk with so 35
honourable an action! Hang him! let him tell
the King; we are prepared. I will set forward
to-night. — *have to start sooner than intended.*

Enter LADY PERCY.

How now, Kate! I must leave you within these
two hours.

Lady. O, my good lord, why are you thus alone?
For what offence have I this fortnight been   41
A banish'd woman from my Harry's bed?
Tell me, sweet lord, what is't that takes from thee
Thy stomach, pleasure, and thy golden sleep?
Why dost thou bend thine eyes upon the earth, 45
And start so often when thou sit'st alone?
Why hast thou lost the fresh blood in thy cheeks,
And given my treasures and my rights of thee
To thick-ey'd musing and curst melancholy?
In thy faint slumbers I by thee have watch'd, 50
And heard thee murmur tales of iron wars;
Speak terms of manage to thy bounding steed;
Cry "Courage! to the field!"   And thou hast
talk'd
Of sallies and retires, of trenches, tents,
Of palisadoes, frontiers, parapets,   55
Of basilisks, of cannon, culverin,
Of prisoners' ransom, and of soldiers slain,
And all the currents of a heady fight.
Thy spirit within thee hath been so at war
And thus hath so bestirr'd thee in thy sleep, 60
That beads of sweat have stood upon thy brow,
Like bubbles in a late-disturbed stream;
And in thy face strange motions have appear'd,
Such as we see when men restrain their breath
On some great sudden hest. O, what portents are
those?   65
Some heavy business hath my lord in hand,
And I must know it, else he loves me not.

Hot. What, ho!

[Enter SERVANT.]

Is Gilliams with the packet gone?

Serv. He is, my lord, an hour ago.

Hot. Hath Butler brought those horses from the
sheriff?   70

Serv. One horse, my lord, he brought even
now.

Hot. What horse? Roan, a crop-ear, is it not?

Serv. It is, my lord.

Hot.   That roan shall be my throne.
Well, I will back him straight. O *Esperance!*
Bid Butler lead him forth into the park.   75
[*Exit Servant.*]

Lady. But hear you, my lord.

Hot. What say'st thou, my lady?

Lady. What is it carries you away?

Hot. Why, my horse, my love, my horse.

Lady. Out, you mad-headed ape!   80
A weasel hath not such a deal of spleen
As you are toss'd with. In faith,
I'll know your business, Harry, that I will.
I fear my brother Mortimer doth stir
About his title, and hath sent for you   85
To line his enterprise; but if you go, —

Hot. So far afoot, I shall be weary, love.

Lady. Come, come, you paraquito, answer me
Directly unto this question that I ask.
In faith, I'll break thy little finger, Harry, 90
An if thou wilt not tell me all things true.

Hot. Away.
Away, you trifler! Love! I love thee not,
I care not for thee, Kate. This is no world
To play with mammets and to tilt with lips.   95
We must have bloody noses and crack'd crowns,
And pass them current too. God's me, my
horse!
What say'st thou, Kate? What would'st thou
have with me?

Lady. Do you not love me? Do you not, indeed?
Well, do not then; for since you love me not, 100
I will not love myself. Do you not love me?
Nay, tell me if you speak in jest or no.

Hot. Come, wilt thou see me ride?
And when I am o' horseback, I will swear
I love thee infinitely. But hark you, Kate; 105
I must not have you henceforth question me
Whither I go, nor reason whereabout.
Whither I must, I must; and, to conclude,
This evening must I leave you, gentle Kate.
I know you wise; but yet no farther wise   110
Than Harry Percy's wife. Constant you are,
But yet a woman; and for secrecy,
No lady closer; for I well believe
Thou wilt not utter what thou dost not know;
And so far will I trust thee, gentle Kate.   115

Lady. How! so far?

Hot. Not an inch further. But hark you, Kate:
Whither I go, thither shall you go too;
To-day will I set forth, to-morrow you.
Will this content you, Kate?

Lady.   It must of force. 120
[*Exeunt.*

44. **stomach:** appetite. 52. **manage:** horse-training. 55. **frontiers:** outworks. 56. **basilisks:** brass cannon. **culverin:**
long cannon. 65. **hest:** demand. 74. *Esperance:* Hope; the Percy motto. 86. **line:** support. 95. **mammets:** dolls.
107. **whereabout:** about what.

SCENE IV. [*The Boar's-Head Tavern, Eastcheap.*]

Enter the PRINCE *and* POINS.

Prince. Ned, prithee, come out of that fat room, and lend me thy hand to laugh a little.

Poins. Where hast been, Hal?

Prince. With three or four loggerheads amongst three or four score hogsheads. I have sounded 5 the very base-string of humility. Sirrah, I am sworn brother to a leash of drawers; and can call them all by their christen names, as Tom, Dick, and Francis. They take it already upon their salvation, that though I be but Prince of Wales, 10 yet I am the king of courtesy; and tell me flatly I am no proud Jack, like Falstaff, but a Corinthian, a lad of mettle, a good boy, (by the Lord, so they call me,) and when I am King of England, I shall command all the good lads in Eastcheap. 15 They call drinking deep, dyeing scarlet; and when you breathe in your watering, they cry "hem!" and bid you play it off. To conclude, I am so good a proficient in one quarter of an hour, that I can drink with any tinker in his own language 20 during my life. I tell thee, Ned, thou hast lost much honour, that thou wert not with me in this action. But, sweet Ned, — to sweeten which name of Ned, I give thee this pennyworth of sugar, clapp'd even now into my hand by an under- 25 skinker, one that never spake other English in his life than "Eight shillings and sixpence," and "You are welcome," with this shrill addition, "Anon, anon, sir! Score a pint of bastard in the Half-moon," or so. But, Ned, to drive away the 30 time till Falstaff come, I prithee, do thou stand in some by-room, while I question my puny drawer to what end he gave me the sugar; and do thou never leave calling "Francis," that his tale to me may be nothing but "Anon." Step aside, 35 and I'll show thee a [precedent].

Poins. Francis!

Prince. Thou art perfect.

Poins. Francis!   [*Exit Poins.*] 40

Enter drawer [FRANCIS].

Fran. Anon, anon, sir. Look down into the Pomgarnet, Ralph.

Prince. Come hither, Francis.

Fran. My lord?

Prince. How long hast thou to serve, Francis? 45

Fran. Forsooth, five years, and as much as to —

Poins. [*Within.*] Francis!

Fran. Anon, anon, sir. 49

Prince. Five year! by 'r lady, a long lease for the clinking of pewter. But, Francis, darest thou be so valiant as to play the coward with thy indenture and show it a fair pair of heels and run from it? 54

Fran. O Lord, sir, I'll be sworn upon all the books in England, I could find in my heart —

Poins. [*Within.*] Francis!

Fran. Anon, sir.

Prince. How old art thou, Francis?

Fran. Let me see — about Michaelmas next I shall be — 61

Poins. [*Within.*] Francis!

Fran. Anon, sir. Pray you, stay a little, my lord.

Prince. Nay, but hark you, Francis: for the sugar thou gavest me, 'twas a pennyworth, was't not? 66

Fran. O Lord, I would it had been two!

Prince. I will give thee for it a thousand pound. Ask me when thou wilt, and thou shalt have it. 70

Poins. [*Within.*] Francis!

Fran. Anon, anon.

Prince. Anon, Francis? No, Francis; but to-morrow, Francis; or Francis, o' Thursday; or indeed, Francis, when thou wilt. But, Francis!

Fran. My lord? 76

Prince. Wilt thou rob this leathern jerkin, crystal-button, not-pated, agate-ring, puke-stocking, caddis-garter, smooth-tongue, Spanish-pouch, — 80

Fran. O Lord, sir, who do you mean?

Prince. Why, then, your brown bastard is your only drink; for look you, Francis, your white canvas doublet will sully. In Barbary, sir, it cannot come to so much. 85

Fran. What, sir?

Poins. [*Within.*] Francis!

Prince. Away, you rogue! dost thou not hear them call? 89

[*Here they both call him; the drawer stands amazed, not knowing which way to go.*]

Enter VINTNER.

Vint. What, stand'st thou still, and hear'st such a calling? Look to the guests within. [*Exit Francis.*] My lord, old Sir John with half-a-dozen more are at the door; shall I let them in? 94

Prince. Let them alone a while, and then open the door. [*Exit Vintner.*] Poins!

Poins. [*Within.*] Anon, anon, sir.

Re-enter POINS.

Prince. Sirrah, Falstaff and the rest of the thieves are at the door; shall we be merry? 99

Sc. iv, 1. fat: vat. 12. Corinthian: a gay blade. 17. watering: drinking. 25. under-skinker: tapster's assistant. 29. bastard: a Spanish wine. Half-moon: name of a room in the inn, like *Pomgarnet* in l. 42. 36. [precedent] (Pope): example. *present* Q, *president* Ff. 42. Pomgarnet: Pomegranate. 53. indenture: apprentice's contract. 77–80. Describing the vintner (l. 90). 78. not-pated: close-cropped. puke: dark gray. 79. caddis: worsted. Spanish: of Spanish leather.

Poins. As merry as crickets, my lad. But hark ye; what cunning match have you made with this jest of the drawer? Come, what's the issue?   103

Prince. I am now of all humours that have showed themselves humours since the old days of goodman Adam to the pupil age of this present twelve o'clock at midnight.

[*Re-enter* FRANCIS.]

What's o'clock, Francis?

Fran. Anon, anon, sir.   [*Exit.*]   109

Prince. That ever this fellow should have fewer words than a parrot, and yet the son of a woman! His industry is upstairs and downstairs; his eloquence the parcel of a reckoning. I am not yet of Percy's mind, the Hotspur of the north; he that kills me some six or seven dozen of Scots at a   115 breakfast, washes his hands, and says to his wife, "Fie upon this quiet life! I want work." "O my sweet Harry," says she, "how many hast thou kill'd to-day?" "Give my roan horse a drench," says he; and answers, "Some fourteen," an   120 hour after; "a trifle, a trifle." I prithee, call in Falstaff. I'll play Percy, and that damn'd brawn shall play Dame Mortimer his wife. "Rivo!" says the drunkard. Call in ribs, call in tallow.   125

Enter FALSTAFF [GADSHILL, BARDOLPH, *and* PETO; FRANCIS *following with wine*].

Poins. Welcome, Jack! Where hast thou been?

Fal. A plague of all cowards, I say, and a vengeance too! marry, and amen! Give me a cup of sack, boy. Ere I lead this life long, I'll sew nether stocks, and mend them and foot them too. A plague of all cowards! Give me a cup of sack, rogue. Is there no virtue extant?   132

[*He drinketh.*

Prince. Didst thou never see Titan kiss a dish of butter, pitiful-hearted Titan, that melted at the sweet tale of the [sun]? If thou didst, then behold that compound.   136

Fal. You rogue, here's lime in this sack too. There is nothing but roguery to be found in villanous man; yet a coward is worse than a cup of sack with lime in it. A villanous coward! Go   140 thy ways, old Jack; die when thou wilt, if manhood, good manhood, be not forgot upon the face of the earth, then am I a shotten herring. There lives not three good men unhang'd in England; and one of them is fat and grows old. God help   145

the while! a bad world, I say. I would I were a weaver; I could sing psalms or anything. A plague of all cowards, I say still.

Prince. How now, wool-sack! what mutter you?   149

Fal. A king's son! If I do not beat thee out of thy kingdom with a dagger of lath, and drive all thy subjects afore thee like a flock of wild-geese, I'll never wear hair on my face more. You Prince of Wales!   154

Prince. Why, you whoreson round man, what's the matter?

Fal. Are not you a coward? Answer me to that; and Poins there?

Poins. 'Zounds, ye fat paunch, an ye call me coward, by the Lord, I'll stab thee.   160

Fal. I call thee coward! I'll see thee damn'd ere I call thee coward; but I would give a thousand pound I could run as fast as thou canst. You are straight enough in the shoulders; you care not who sees your back. Call you that backing of your friends? A plague upon such backing! give me them that will face me. Give me a cup of sack. I am a rogue, if I drunk to-day.   169

Prince. O villain! thy lips are scarce wip'd since thou drunk'st last.

Fal. All's one for that. (*He drinketh.*) A plague of all cowards, still say I.

Prince. What's the matter?   174

Fal. What's the matter! There be four of us here have ta'en a thousand pound this day morning.

Prince. Where is it, Jack? where is it?

Fal. Where is it! Taken from us it is; a hundred upon poor four of us.   180

Prince. What, a hundred, man?

Fal. I am a rogue, if I were not at half-sword with a dozen of them two hours together. I have scaped by miracle. I am eight times thrust through the doublet, four through the hose; my   185 buckler cut through and through; my sword hack'd like a hand-saw — *ecce signum!* I never dealt better since I was a man; all would not do. A plague of all cowards! Let them speak; if they speak more or less than truth, they are villains and the sons of darkness.   191

[*Prince.*] Speak, sirs; how was it?

[*Gads.*] We four set upon some dozen —

Fal. Sixteen at least, my lord.

[*Gads.*] And bound them.   195

Peto. No, no, they were not bound.

102. **match**: game. 106. **pupil age**: youth. 113. **parcel**: item. 119. **drench**: bran and water. 124. "**Rivo!**": a reveller's exclamation. 130. **nether stocks**: stockings. 133. **Titan**: Hyperion, the sun. 134. **that**. The antecedent is *butter*. 135. [sun] Q₃F₁. *sonnes* Q₁. 137. **lime**: used as a preservative. 143. **shotten**: having spawned. 146. **the while**: the times. 182. **at half-sword**: at close quarters. 187. *ecce signum*: behold the proof. 192. [*Prince*] Ff. *Gad*. Qq. 193, 195, 199. [*Gads.*] Ff. *Ross*. Qq. Cf. I.ii.181, note.

Fal. You rogue, they were bound, every man of them, or I am a Jew else, an Ebrew Jew.

[*Gads.*] As we were sharing, some six or seven fresh men set upon us —   200

Fal. And unbound the rest, and then come in the other.

Prince. What, fought you with them all?   203

Fal. All! I know not what you call all; but if I fought not with fifty of them, I am a bunch of radish. If there were not two or three and fifty upon poor old Jack, then am I no two-legg'd creature.

Prince. Pray God you have not murd'red some of them.   210

Fal. Nay, that's past praying for; I have pepper'd two of them. Two I am sure I have paid, two rogues in buckram suits. I tell thee what, Hal, if I tell thee a lie, spit in my face, call me horse. Thou knowest my old ward: here I lay, and thus I bore my point. Four rogues in buckram let drive at me —   217

Prince. What, four? Thou saidst but two even now.

Fal. Four, Hal; I told thee four.

Poins. Ay, ay, he said four.   221

Fal. These four came all a-front, and mainly thrust at me. I made me no more ado but took all their seven points in my target, thus.

Prince. Seven? why, there were but four even now.   226

Fal. In buckram?

Poins. Ay, four, in buckram suits.

Fal. Seven, by these hilts, or I am a villain else.   230

Prince. Prithee, let him alone; we shall have more anon.

Fal. Dost thou hear me, Hal?

Prince. Ay, and mark thee too, Jack.   234

Fal. Do so, for it is worth the listening to. These nine in buckram that I told thee of —

Prince. So, two more already.

Fal. Their points being broken, —

Poins. Down fell their hose.   239

Fal. Began to give me ground; but I followed me close, came in foot and hand, and with a thought seven of the eleven I paid.

Prince. O monstrous! eleven buckram men grown out of two!   244

Fal. But, as the devil would have it, three misbegotten knaves in Kendal green came at my back and let drive at me; for it was so dark, Hal, that thou couldst not see thy hand.   248

Prince. These lies are like their father that begets them; gross as a mountain, open, palpable.

Why thou clay-brain'd guts, thou knotty-pated fool, thou whoreson, obscene, greasy tallow-catch, —   253

Fal. What, art thou mad? art thou mad? Is not the truth the truth?

Prince. Why, how couldst thou know these men in Kendal green, when it was so dark thou couldst not see thy hand? Come, tell us your reason; what say'st thou to this?   259

Poins. Come, your reason, Jack, your reason.

Fal. What, upon compulsion? 'Zounds, an I were at the strappado, or all the racks in the world, I would not tell you on compulsion. Give you a reason on compulsion! If reasons were as plenty as blackberries, I would give no man a reason upon compulsion, I.   266

Prince. I'll be no longer guilty of this sin. This sanguine coward, this bed-presser, this horseback-breaker, this huge hill of flesh, —   269

Fal. 'Sblood, you starveling, you elf-skin, you dried neat's tongue, you bull's pizzle, you stockfish! O for breath to utter what is like thee! you tailor's-yard, you sheath, you bowcase, you vile standing-tuck, —   274

Prince. Well, breathe a while, and then to it again; and when thou hast tired thyself in base comparisons, hear me speak but this: —

Poins. Mark, Jack.   278

Prince. We two saw you four set on four and bound them, and were masters of their wealth. Mark now, how a plain tale shall put you down. Then did we two set on you four; and, with a word, out-fac'd you from your prize, and have it, yea, and can show it you here in the house; and, Falstaff, you carried your guts away as nimbly, with as   285 quick dexterity, and roar'd for mercy, and still run and roar'd, as ever I heard bull-calf. What a slave art thou, to hack thy sword as thou hast done, and then say it was in fight! What trick, what device, what starting-hole, canst thou now find out to hide thee from this open and apparent shame?   292

Poins. Come, let's hear, Jack; what trick hast thou now?

Fal. By the Lord, I knew ye as well as he that made ye. Why, hear you, my masters. Was it for me to kill the heir-apparent? Should I turn upon the true prince? Why, thou knowest I am as valiant as Hercules; but beware instinct; the lion will not touch the true prince. Instinct is a great matter; I was now a coward on in-   300 stinct. I shall think the better of myself and thee during my life; I for a valiant lion, and thou for a true prince. But, by the Lord, lads, I am

---

222. **mainly:** powerfully. 224. **target:** shield. 238. **points:** (1) of swords, (2) tagged laces, holding garments together. 253. **catch:** tub. 262. **strappado:** a torture of Spanish origin. 271. **neat's:** ox's. 271. **stockfish:** dried cod. 274. **tuck:** rapier. 290. **starting-hole:** loophole.

glad you have the money. Hostess, clap to the doors! Watch to-night, pray to-morrow. 305 Gallants, lads, boys, hearts of gold, all the titles of good fellowship come to you! What, shall we be merry? Shall we have a play extempore?

Prince. Content; and the argument shall be thy running away. 311

Fal. Ah, no more of that, Hal, an thou lovest me!

Enter HOSTESS.

Host. O Jesu, my lord the Prince!

Prince. How now, my lady the hostess! what say'st thou to me? 316

Host. Marry, my lord, there is a nobleman of the court at door would speak with you. He says he comes from your father.

Prince. Give him as much as will make him a royal man, and send him back again to my mother.

Fal. What manner of man is he? 323

Host. An old man.

Fal. What doth Gravity out of his bed at midnight? Shall I give him his answer? 326

Prince. Prithee, do, Jack.

Fal. Faith, and I'll send him packing. [*Exit.*

Prince. Now, sirs, by 'r lady, you fought fair; so did you, Peto; so did you, Bardolph. You are lions too, you ran away upon instinct, you will not touch the true prince; no, fie! 332

Bard. Faith, I ran when I saw others run.

Prince. Faith, tell me now in earnest, how came Falstaff's sword so hack'd?

Peto. Why, he hack'd it with his dagger, and said he would swear truth out of England but he would make you believe it was done in fight, and persuaded us to do the like. 339

Bard. Yea, and to tickle our noses with speargrass to make them bleed, and then to beslubber our garments with it and swear it was the blood of true men. I did that I did not this seven year before, I blush'd, to hear his monstrous devices. 344

Prince. O villain, thou stolest a cup of sack eighteen years ago, and wert taken with the manner, and ever since thou hast blush'd extempore. Thou hadst fire and sword on thy side, and yet thou ran'st away; what instinct hadst thou for it? 350

Bard. My lord, do you see these meteors? Do you behold these exhalations?

[*Pointing to his own face.*]

Prince. I do.

Bard. What think you they portend?

Prince. Hot livers and cold purses. 355

Bard. Choler, my lord, if rightly taken.

Re-enter FALSTAFF.

Prince. No, if rightly taken, halter. Here comes lean Jack, here comes bare-bone. How now, my sweet creature of bombast! How long is 't ago, Jack, since thou sawest thine own knee? 361

Fal. My own knee? When I was about thy years, Hal, I was not an eagle's talon in the waist; I could have crept into any alderman's thumb-ring. A plague of sighing and grief! it blows a man up like a bladder. There's villanous news abroad. 366 Here was Sir John Bracy from your father; you must to the court in the morning. That same mad fellow of the north, Percy, and he of Wales that gave Amamon the bastinado and made Lucifer cuckold and swore the devil his true liegeman upon the cross of a Welsh hook — what a plague call you him? 373

Poins. O, Glendower.

Fal. Owen, Owen, the same; and his son-in-law Mortimer, and old Northumberland, and that sprightly Scot of Scots, Douglas, that runs o' horseback up a hill perpendicular, —

Prince. He that rides at high speed and with his pistol kills a sparrow flying. 380

Fal. You have hit it.

Prince. So did he never the sparrow.

Fal. Well, that rascal hath good mettle in him; he will not run. 384

Prince. Why, what a rascal art thou then, to praise him so for running!

Fal. O' horseback, ye cuckoo; but afoot he will not budge a foot.

Prince. Yes, Jack, upon instinct. 389

Fal. I grant ye, upon instinct. Well, he is there too, and one Murdoch, and a thousand blue-caps more. Worcester is stolen away tonight. Thy father's beard is turn'd white with the news. You may buy land now as cheap as stinking mackerel. 395

Prince. Why, then, it is like, if there come a hot June and this civil buffeting hold, we shall buy maidenheads as they buy hob-nails, by the hundreds. 399

Fal. By the mass, lad, thou say'st true; it is like we shall have good trading that way. But tell me, Hal, art not thou horrible afeard? Thou being heir-apparent, could the world pick thee out three such enemies again as that fiend Douglas, that spirit Percy, and that devil Glendower? Art thou not horribly afraid? Doth not thy blood thrill at it? 407

---

305. **Watch:** wake. 321. **royal:** A play on *noble* and *royal* as names of coins worth respectively 6s.8d. and 10s. 346. **with...manner:** in the act. 355. **Hot...purses:** drunkenness and poverty. 357. **halter:** with a pun on *choler, collar.* 360. **bombast:** cotton wadding. 370. **Amamon:** a devil. 372. **Welsh hook:** a bill with a curved blade. 391. **blue-caps:** blue bonnets, Scots.

Prince. Not a whit, i' faith; I lack some of thy instinct.

Fal. Well, thou wilt be horribly chid tomorrow when thou comest to thy father. If thou love me, practise an answer.   412

Prince. Do thou stand for my father, and examine me upon the particulars of my life.

Fal. Shall I? Content. This chair shall be my state, this dagger my sceptre, and this cushion my crown.   417

Prince. Thy state is taken for a join'd-stool, thy golden sceptre for a leaden dagger, and thy precious rich crown for a pitiful bald crown!   420

Fal. Well, an the fire of grace be not quite out of thee, now shalt thou be moved. Give me a cup of sack to make my eyes look red, that it may be thought I have wept; for I must speak in passion, and I will do it in King Cambyses' vein.   426

Prince. Well, here is my leg.

Fal. And here is my speech. Stand aside, nobility.

Host. O Jesu, this is excellent sport, i' faith!

Fal. Weep not, sweet queen; for trickling tears are vain.   431

Host. O, the father, how he holds his countenance!

Fal. For God's sake, lords, convey my [tristful] queen;
For tears do stop the flood-gates of her eyes.   435

Host. O Jesu, he doth it as like one of these harlotry players as ever I see!

Fal. Peace, good pint-pot; peace, good ticklebrain. Harry, I do not only marvel where thou spendest thy time, but also how thou art accompanied; for though the camomile, the more it is trodden on the faster it grows, [yet] youth, the more it is wasted the sooner it wears. That thou art my son, I have partly thy mother's word, partly my own opinion, but chiefly a villanous trick of thine eye and a foolish hanging of thy nether lip, that doth warrant me. If then thou be son to me, here lies the point; why, being son to me, art thou so pointed at? Shall the blessed sun of heaven prove a micher and eat blackberries? a question not to be ask'd. Shall the son of England prove a thief and take purses? a question to be ask'd. There is a thing, Harry, which thou hast often heard of and it is known to many in our land by the name of pitch. This pitch, as ancient writers do report, doth defile; so doth the company thou keepest; for, Harry, now I do not speak to thee in drink but in tears; not in pleasure but in

passion, not in words only, but in woes also; and yet there is a virtuous man whom I have often noted in thy company, but I know not his name.   461

Prince. What manner of man, an it like your Majesty?

Fal. A goodly portly man, i' faith, and a corpulent; of a cheerful look, a pleasing eye, and a most noble carriage; and, as I think, his age some fifty, or, by 'r lady, inclining to threescore; and now I remember me, his name is Falstaff. If that man should be lewdly given, he deceiveth me; for, Harry, I see virtue in his looks. If then the tree may be known by the fruit, as the fruit by the tree, then, peremptorily I speak it, there is virtue in that Falstaff; him keep with, the rest banish. And tell me now, thou naughty varlet, tell me, where hast thou been this month?   475

Prince. Dost thou speak like a king? Do thou stand for me, and I'll play my father.

Fal. Depose me? If thou dost it half so gravely, so majestically, both in word and matter, hang me up by the heels for a rabbit-sucker or a poulter's hare.   481

Prince. Well, here I am set.

Fal. And here I stand. Judge, my masters.

Prince. Now, Harry, whence come you?

Fal. My noble lord, from Eastcheap.   485

Prince. The complaints I hear of thee are grievous.

Fal. 'Sblood, my lord, they are false. — Nay, I'll tickle ye for a young prince, i' faith.   489

Prince. Swearest thou, ungracious boy? Henceforth ne'er look on me. Thou art violently carried away from grace. There is a devil haunts thee in the likeness of an old fat man; a tun of man is thy companion. Why dost thou converse with that trunk of humours, that bolting-hutch of beastliness, that swollen parcel of dropsies, that hugh bombard of sack; that stuff'd cloak-bag of guts, that roasted Manningtree ox with the pudding in his belly, that reverend vice, that grey iniquity, that father ruffian, that vanity in years? Wherein is he good, but to taste sack and drink it? wherein neat and cleanly, but to carve a capon and eat it? wherein cunning, but in craft? wherein crafty, but in villainy? wherein villanous, but in all things? wherein worthy, but in nothing?   505

Fal. I would your Grace would take me with you. Whom means your Grace?

Prince. That villanous abominable misleader of youth, Falstaff, that old white-bearded Satan.

Fal. My lord, the man I know.   510

---

416. **state:** throne. 418. **join'd-stool:** wooden stool. 426. **King Cambyses' vein:** Preston's *Cambyses* (1570) was the type of the bombastic tragedy. Falstaff imitates the style in ll. 431, 434-35. 427. **leg:** obeisance. 434. **[tristful]** (Rowe). *trustful* Q. 438. **tickle-brain:** strong drink. 441-475. In these speeches Falstaff parodies the style of Lyly's *Euphues.* 442. **[yet]** F. *so* Q. 450. **micher:** truant. 480. **rabbit-sucker:** young rabbit. **poulter's:** poulterer's. 495. **bolting-hutch:** miller's chest. 497. **bombard:** a large leather vessel for liquor. 498. **Manningtree:** an agricultural town in Essex.

Prince. I know thou dost.

Fal. But to say I know more harm in him than in myself, were to say more than I know. That he is old, the more the pity, his white hairs do witness it; but that he is, saving your reverence, a 515 whoremaster, that I utterly deny. If sack and sugar be a fault, God help the wicked! If to be old and merry be a sin, then many an old host that I know is damn'd. If to be fat be to be hated, then Pharaoh's lean kine are to be loved. No, my 520 good lord; banish Peto, banish Bardolph, banish Poins; but for sweet Jack Falstaff, kind Jack Falstaff, true Jack Falstaff, valiant Jack Falstaff, and therefore more valiant, being, as he is, old Jack Falstaff, banish not him thy Harry's company, 525 banish not him thy Harry's company. Banish plump Jack, and banish all the world.

Prince. I do, I will.

[*A knocking heard. Exeunt Hostess, Francis, and Bardolph.*]

Re-enter BARDOLPH, *running.*

Bard. O, my lord, my lord! the sheriff with a most monstrous watch is at the door. 530

Fal. Out, ye rogue! Play out the play; I have much to say in the behalf of that Falstaff.

Re-enter the HOSTESS.

Host. O Jesu, my lord, my lord!

Prince. Heigh, heigh! the devil rides upon a fiddlestick. What's the matter? 535

Host. The sheriff and all the watch are at the door; they are come to search the house. Shall I let them in?

Fal. Dost thou hear, Hal? Never call a true piece of gold a counterfeit. Thou art essentially mad, without seeming so. 541

Prince. And thou a natural coward, without instinct.

Fal. I deny your major. If you will deny the sheriff, so; if not, let him enter. If I become not a cart as well as another man, a plague on my bringing up! I hope I shall as soon be strangled with a halter as another. 548

Prince. Go, hide thee behind the arras; the rest walk up above. Now, my masters, for a true face and good conscience.

Fal. Both which I have had; but their date is out, and therefore I'll hide me. [*Exit.* 553

Prince. Call in the sheriff.

[*Exeunt all except the Prince and Peto.*]

Enter SHERIFF *and the* CARRIER.

Now, master sheriff, what is your will with me?

Sher. First, pardon me, my lord. A hue and cry
Hath followed certain men unto this house.

Prince. What men?

Sher. One of them is well known, my gracious lord,
A gross fat man.

Car.   As fat as butter. 560

Prince. The man, I do assure you, is not here,
For I myself at this time have employ'd him.
And, sheriff, I will engage my word to thee
That I will, by to-morrow dinner-time,
Send him to answer thee or any man 565
For anything he shall be charg'd withal.
And so let me entreat you leave the house.

Sher. I will, my lord. There are two gentlemen
Have in this robbery lost three hundred marks.

Prince. It may be so. If he have robb'd these men, 570
He shall be answerable; and so farewell.

Sher. Good night, my noble lord.

Prince. I think it is good morrow, is it not?

Sher. Indeed, my lord, I think it be two o'clock.
[*Exeunt [Sheriff and Carrier].*

Prince. This oily rascal is known as well as Paul's. Go, call him forth. 576

Peto. Falstaff! — Fast asleep behind the arras, and snorting like a horse.

Prince. Hark, how hard he fetches breath. Search his pockets. (*He searcheth his pockets, and findeth certain papers.*) What hast thou found? 582

Peto. Nothing but papers, my lord.

Prince. Let's see what they be. Read them.

Peto. [*Reads.*]

Item, A capon . . . . 2s. 2d.
Item, Sauce . . . . 4d.
Item, Sack, two gallons . . . . 5s. 8d.
Item, Anchovies and sack after supper 2s. 6d.
Item, Bread . . . . ob.

Prince. O monstrous! but one half-penny- 591
worth of bread to this intolerable deal of sack! What there is else, keep close; we'll read it at more advantage. There let him sleep till day. I'll to the court in the morning. We must all to the 595 wars, and thy place shall be honourable. I'll procure this fat rogue a charge of foot; and I know his death will be a march of twelve-score. The money shall be paid back again with advantage. Be with [me] betimes in the morning; and so, good morrow, Peto. 601

Peto. Good morrow, good my lord. [*Exeunt.*

544. **major:** major premise. 546. **cart:** the hangman's cart. 549. **arras:** tapestry hangings. 576. **Paul's:** St. Paul's Cathedral. 590. **ob.:** obolus; here, a halfpenny. 598. **death . . . twelve-score:** a march of 240 yards will kill him. 599. **advantage:** interest. 600. [**me**] F. *the* Q.

ACT III

SCENE I. [*Bangor. The Archdeacon's house.*]

Enter HOTSPUR, WORCESTER, MORTIMER, *and*
GLENDOWER.

Mort. These promises are fair, the parties sure,
And our induction full of prosperous hope.

Hot. Lord Mortimer, and cousin Glendower,
Will you sit down?
And uncle Worcester, — a plague upon it!   5
I have forgot the map.

Glend.   No, here it is.
Sit, cousin Percy; sit, good cousin Hotspur,
For by that name as oft as Lancaster
Doth speak of you, his cheek looks pale and with
A rising sigh he wisheth you in heaven.   10

Hot. And you in hell, as oft as he hears Owen
Glendower spoke of.

Glend. I cannot blame him. At my nativity
The front of heaven was full of fiery shapes,
Of burning cressets; and at my birth   15
The frame and huge foundation of the earth
Shak'd like a coward.

Hot. Why, so it would have done at the same
season, if your mother's cat had but kitten'd,
though yourself had never been born.   20

Glend. I say the earth did shake when I was born.

Hot. And I say the earth was not of my mind,
If you suppose as fearing you it shook.

Glend. The heavens were all on fire, the earth did
tremble.

Hot. O, then the earth shook to see the heavens
on fire,   25
And not in fear of your nativity.
Diseased nature oftentimes breaks forth
In strange eruptions; oft the teeming earth
Is with a kind of colic pinch'd and vex'd
By the imprisoning of unruly wind   30
Within her womb; which, for enlargement striving,
Shakes the old beldam earth, and topples down
Steeples and moss-grown towers. At your birth
Our grandam earth, having this distemperature,
In passion shook.

Glend.   Cousin, of many men   35
I do not bear these crossings. Give me leave
To tell you once again that at my birth
The front of heaven was full of fiery shapes,
The goats ran from the mountains, and the herds
Were strangely clamorous to the frighted fields.
These signs have mark'd me extraordinary;   41
And all the courses of my life do show
I am not in the roll of common men.
Where is he living, clipp'd in with the sea
That chides the banks of England, Scotland, Wales,

Which calls me pupil, or hath read to me?   46
And bring him out that is but woman's son
Can trace me in the tedious ways of art
And hold me pace in deep experiments.

Hot. I think there's no man speaks better Welsh.
I'll to dinner.   51

Mort. Peace, cousin Percy; you will make him
mad.

Glend. I can call spirits from the vasty deep.

Hot. Why, so can I, or so can any man;
But will they come when you do call for them?   55

Glend. Why, I can teach you, cousin, to command
The devil.

Hot. And I can teach thee, coz, to shame the
devil
By telling truth. "Tell truth and shame the devil."
If thou have power to raise him, bring him hither,
And I'll be sworn I have power to shame him
hence.   61
O, while you live, tell truth and shame the devil!

Mort. Come, come, no more of this unprofitable
chat.

Glend. Three times hath Henry Bolingbroke
made head
Against my power; thrice from the banks of Wye
And sandy-bottom'd Severn have I sent him   66
Bootless home and weather-beaten back.

Hot. Home without boots, and in foul weather
too!
How scapes he agues, in the devil's name?

Glend. Come, here's the map. Shall we divide
our right   70
According to our threefold order ta'en?

Mort. The Archdeacon hath divided it
Into three limits very equally.
England, from Trent and Severn hitherto,
By south and east is to my part assign'd;   75
All westward, Wales beyond the Severn shore,
And all the fertile land within that bound,
To Owen Glendower; and, dear coz, to you
The remnant northward, lying off from Trent.
And our indentures tripartite are drawn;   80
Which being sealed interchangeably,
A business that this night may execute,
To-morrow, cousin Percy, you and I
And my good Lord of Worcester will set forth
To meet your father and the Scottish power,   85
As is appointed us, at Shrewsbury.
My father Glendower is not ready yet,
Nor shall we need his help these fourteen days.
Within that space you may have drawn together
Your tenants, friends, and neighbouring gentle-
men.   90

Glend. A shorter time shall send me to you, lords;

Act III, sc. i, 2. **induction:** beginning.   15. **cressets:** fire baskets; here, meteors.   34. **distemperature:** disorder.   46. **read to:** taught.   48. **trace:** follow.   **art:** magic.   67. **Bootless:** without advantage.   74. **hitherto:** to this point.

And in my conduct shall your ladies come,
From whom you now must steal and take no leave,
For there will be a world of water shed
Upon the parting of your wives and you.   95
 Hot. Methinks my moiety, north from Burton here,
In quantity equals not one of yours.
See how this river comes me cranking in,
And cuts me from the best of all my land
A huge half-moon, a monstrous cantle out.   100
I'll have the current in this place damm'd up;
And here the smug and silver Trent shall run
In a new channel, fair and evenly.
It shall not wind with such a deep indent,
To rob me of so rich a bottom here.   105
 Glend. Not wind? It shall, it must; you see it doth.
 Mort. Yea, but
Mark how he bears his course, and runs me up
With like advantage on the other side;
Gelding the opposed continent as much   110
As on the other side it takes from you.
 Wor. Yea, but a little charge will trench him here
And on this north side win this cape of land;
And then he runs straight and even.
 Hot. I'll have it so; a little charge will do it.   115
 Glend. I'll not have it alt'red.
 Hot.   Will not you?
 Glend. No, nor you shall not.
 Hot.   Who shall say me nay?
 Glend. Why, that will I.
 Hot. Let me not understand you, then; speak it in Welsh.   120
 Glend. I can speak English, lord, as well as you;
For I was train'd up in the English court;
Where, being but young, I framed to the harp
Many an English ditty lovely well
And gave the tongue a helpful ornament,   125
A virtue that was never seen in you.
 Hot. Marry,
And I am glad of it with all my heart.
I had rather be a kitten and cry mew
Than one of these same metre ballad-mongers.
I had rather hear a brazen canstick turn'd,   131
Or a dry wheel grate on the axle-tree,
And that would set my teeth nothing on edge,
Nothing so much as mincing poetry.
'Tis like the forc'd gait of a shuffling nag.   135
 Glend. Come, you shall have Trent turn'd.
 Hot. I do not care. I'll give thrice so much land
To any well-deserving friend;
But in the way of bargain, mark ye me,

I'll cavil on the ninth part of a hair.   140
Are the indentures drawn? Shall we be gone?
 Glend. The moon shines fair; you may away by night.
I'll haste the writer, and withal
Break with your wives of your departure hence.
I am afraid my daughter will run mad,   145
So much she doteth on her Mortimer. [*Exit.*
 Mort. Fie, cousin Percy! how you cross my father!
 Hot. I cannot choose. Sometimes he angers me
With telling me of the moldwarp and the ant,
Of the dreamer Merlin and his prophecies,   150
And of a dragon and a finless fish,
A clip-wing'd griffin and a moulten raven,
A couching lion and a ramping cat,
And such a deal of skimble-skamble stuff
As puts me from my faith. I tell you what: 155
He held me last night at least nine hours
In reckoning up the several devils' names
That were his lackeys. I cried "hum," and "well, go to,"
But mark'd him not a word. O, he is as tedious
As a tired horse, a railing wife;   160
Worse than a smoky house. I had rather live
With cheese and garlic in a windmill, far,
Than feed on cates and have him talk to me
In any summer-house in Christendom.
 Mort. In faith, he is a worthy gentleman,   165
Exceedingly well read, and profited
In strange concealments, valiant as a lion
And wondrous affable, and as bountiful
As mines of India. Shall I tell you, cousin?
He holds your temper in a high respect   170
And curbs himself even of his natural scope
When you come 'cross his humour. Faith, he does.
I warrant you, that man is not alive
Might so have tempted him as you have done,
Without the taste of danger and reproof.   175
But do not use it oft, let me entreat you.
 Wor. In faith, my lord, you are too wilful-blame;
And since your coming hither have done enough
To put him quite besides his patience.
You must needs learn, lord, to amend this fault.   180
Though sometimes it show greatness, courage, blood, —
And that's the dearest grace it renders you, —
Yet oftentimes it doth present harsh rage,
Defect of manners, want of government,
Pride, haughtiness, opinion, and disdain;   185
The least of which haunting a nobleman
Loseth men's hearts and leaves behind a stain
Upon the beauty of all parts besides,

96. **moiety:** share. 100. **cantle:** piece, corner. 104. **indent:** indentation. 110. **Gelding:** cutting off from. **continent:** land. 112. **charge:** cost. 131. **canstick:** candlestick. 149. **moldwarp:** mole. This and the following lines refer to a prophecy mentioned by Holinshed. 163. **cates:** delicacies. 166. **profited:** proficient. 167. **concealments:** occult arts. 177. **wilful-blame:** wilfully to blame. 183. **present:** indicate. 184. **government:** self-control.

Beguiling them of commendation.
Hot. Well, I am school'd. Good manners be
  your speed!   190
Here come our wives, and let us take our leave.

Re-enter GLENDOWER *with the ladies.*

Mort. This is the deadly spite that angers me;
My wife can speak no English, I no Welsh.
Glend. My daughter weeps; she will not part
  with you.
She'll be a soldier too, she'll to the wars.   195
Mort. Good father, tell her that she and my aunt
  Percy
Shall follow in your conduct speedily.
  [*Glendower speaks to her in Welsh, and she
    answers him in the same.*
Glend. She is desperate here; a peevish self-
will'd harlotry, one that no persuasion can do good
upon.   [*The lady speaks in Welsh.* 200
Mort. I understand thy looks. That pretty
  Welsh
Which thou pourest down from these swelling
  heavens
I am too perfect in; and, but for shame,
In such a parley should I answer thee.
  [*The lady speaks again in Welsh.*
I understand thy kisses and thou mine,   205
And that's a feeling disputation.
But I will never be a truant, love,
Till I have learn'd thy language; for thy tongue
Makes Welsh as sweet as ditties highly penn'd,
Sung by a fair queen in a summer's bower,   210
With ravishing division, to her lute.
Glend. Nay, if you melt, then will she run mad.
  [*The lady speaks again in Welsh.*
Mort. O, I am ignorance itself in this!
Glend. She bids you on the wanton rushes lay
  you down
And rest your gentle head upon her lap,   215
And she will sing the song that pleaseth you
And on your eyelids crown the god of sleep,
Charming your blood with pleasing heaviness,
Making such difference 'twixt wake and sleep
As is the difference 'twixt day and night   220
The hour before the heavenly-harness'd team
Begins his golden progress in the east.
Mort. With all my heart I'll sit and hear her
  sing.
By that time will our book, I think be drawn.
Glend. Do so;   225
And those musicians that shall play to you
Hang in the air a thousand leagues from hence,
And straight they shall be here. Sit, and attend.
Hot. Come, Kate, thou art perfect in lying down.

Come, quick, quick, that I may lay my head in thy
lap.   231
Lady P. Go, ye giddy goose. [*The music plays.*
Hot. Now I perceive the devil understands
  Welsh;
And 'tis no marvel he is so humorous.
By 'r lady, he is a good musician.   235
Lady P. Then should you be nothing but musical,
for you are altogether governed by humours. Lie
still, ye thief, and hear the lady sing in Welsh.
Hot. I had rather hear Lady, my brach, howl in
Irish.   241
Lady P. Wouldst thou have thy head broken?
Hot. No.
Lady P. Then be still.
Hot. Neither; 'tis a woman's fault.   245
Lady P. Now God help thee!
Hot. To the Welsh lady's bed.
Lady P. What's that?
Hot. Peace! she sings.
  [*Here the lady sings a Welsh song.*
Hot. Come, Kate, I'll have your song too.   250
Lady P. Not mine, in good sooth.
Hot. Not yours, in good sooth! Heart, you
swear like a comfit-maker's wife. "Not you, in
good sooth," and "as true as I live," and "as God
shall mend me," and "as sure as day;"   255
And givest such sarcenet surety for thy oaths
As if thou never walk'st further than Finsbury.
Swear me, Kate, like a lady as thou art,
A good mouth-filling oath, and leave "in sooth,"
And such protest of pepper-gingerbread,   260
To velvet-guards and Sunday-citizens.
Come, sing.
Lady P. I will not sing.
Hot. 'Tis the next way to turn tailor, or be red-
breast teacher. An the indentures be drawn, 265
I'll away within these two hours; and so, come in
when ye will.   [*Exit.*
Glend. Come, come, Lord Mortimer; you are as
  slow
As hot Lord Percy is on fire to go.
By this our book is drawn. We'll but seal,   270
And then to horse immediately.
Mort.   With all my heart.
  [*Exeunt.*

SCENE II. [*London. The palace.*]

Enter the KING, PRINCE OF WALES, *and others.*

King. Lords, give us leave; the Prince of Wales
  and I
Must have some private conference; but be near
  at hand,

---

199. **harlotry:** hussy. 211. **division:** modulation. 224. **book:** the threefold agreement. 240. **brach:** bitch. 253. **comfit-maker's:** confectioner's. 256. **sarcenet:** silky. 257. **Finsbury:** a recreation ground outside London. 261. **velvet-guards:** velvet trimmings such as the citizens' wives wore. 265. **red-breast teacher:** teacher of song birds.

For we shall presently have need of you.
                                    [Exeunt Lords.
I know not whether God will have it so,
For some displeasing service I have done,   5
That, in his secret doom, out of my blood
He'll breed revengement and a scourge for me;
But thou dost in thy passages of life
Make me believe that thou art only mark'd
For the hot vengeance and the rod of heaven   10
To punish my mistreadings.   Tell me else,
Could such inordinate and low desires,
Such poor, such bare, such lewd, such mean
        attempts,
Such barren pleasures, rude society,
As thou art match'd withal and grafted to,   15
Accompany the greatness of thy blood
And hold their level with thy princely heart?
   Prince. So please your Majesty, I would I could
Quit all offences with as clear excuse
As well as I am doubtless I can purge   20
Myself of many I am charg'd withal.
Yet such extenuation let me beg,
As, in reproof of many tales devis'd,
Which oft the ear of greatness needs must hear,
By smiling pick-thanks and base newsmongers,   25
I may, for some things true, wherein my youth
Hath faulty wand'red and irregular,
Find pardon on my true submission.
   King. God pardon thee! yet let me wonder,
     Harry,
At thy affections, which do hold a wing   30
Quite from the flight of all thy ancestors.
Thy place in council thou hast rudely lost,
Which by thy younger brother is suppli'd,
And art almost an alien to the hearts
Of all the court and princes of my blood.   35
The hope and expectation of thy time
Is ruin'd, and the soul of every man
Prophetically do forethink thy fall.
Had I so lavish of my presence been,
So common-hackney'd in the eyes of men,   40
So stale and cheap to vulgar company,
Opinion, that did help me to the crown,
Had still kept loyal to possession
And left me in reputeless banishment,
A fellow of no mark nor likelihood.   45
By being seldom seen, I could not stir
But like a comet I was wond'red at;
That men would tell their children, "This is he;"
Others would say, "Where, which is Bolingbroke?"
And then I stole all courtesy from heaven,   50
And dress'd myself in such humility
That I did pluck allegiance from men's hearts,

Loud shouts and salutations from their mouths,
Even in the presence of the crowned King.
Thus did I keep my person fresh and new,   55
My presence, like a robe pontifical,
Ne'er seen but wond'red at; and so my state,
Seldom but sumptuous, show'd like a feast
And won by rareness such solemnity.
The skipping King, he ambled up and down   60
With shallow jesters and rash bavin wits,
Soon kindled and soon burnt; carded his state,
Mingled his royalty with cap'ring fools,
Had his great name profaned with their scorns,
And gave his countenance, against his name   65
To laugh at gibing boys and stand the push
Of every beardless vain comparative;
Grew a companion to the common streets,
Enfeoff'd himself to popularity;
That, being daily swallowed by men's eyes,   70
They surfeited with honey and began
To loathe the taste of sweetness, whereof a little
More than a little is by much too much.
So when he had occasion to be seen,
He was but as the cuckoo is in June,   75
Heard, not regarded; seen, but with such eyes
As, sick and blunted with community,
Afford no extraordinary gaze
Such as is bent on sun-like majesty
When it shines seldom in admiring eyes;   80
But rather drows'd and hung their eyelids down,
Slept in his face and rend'red such aspect
As cloudy men use to their adversaries,
Being with his presence glutted, gorg'd, and full.
And in that very line, Harry, standest thou;   85
For thou hast lost thy princely privilege
With vile participation. Not an eye
But is a-weary of thy common sight,
Save mine, which hath desir'd to see thee more;
Which now doth that I would not have it do,   90
Make blind itself with foolish tenderness.
   Prince. I shall hereafter, my thrice gracious lord,
Be more myself.
   King.   For all the world
As thou art to this hour was Richard then
When I from France set foot at Ravenspurgh,   95
And even as I was then is Percy now.
Now, by my sceptre and my soul to boot,
He hath more worthy interest to the state
Than thou, the shadow of succession.
For of no right, nor colour like to right,   100
He doth fill fields with harness in the realm,
Turns head against the lion's armed jaws,
And, being no more in debt to years than thou,
Leads ancient lords and reverend bishops on

   Sc. ii, 6. doom: judgment. **19. Quit:** clear myself of. **23. reproof:** refutation. **25. pick-thanks:** busybodies, flatterers.
36. time: reign. **43. possession:** i.e., Richard II. **61. bavin:** brushwood. **62. carded:** diluted. **67. comparative:** would-
be wit. **69. Enfeoff'd:** became a vassal. **77. community:** familiarity. **87. participation:** fellowship. **98. interest:** claim.
101. harness: armor.

To bloody battles and to bruising arms.   105
What never-dying honour hath he got
Against renowned Douglas! whose high deeds,
Whose hot incursions and great name in arms
Holds from all soldiers chief majority
And military title capital   110
Through all the kingdoms that acknowledge Christ.
Thrice hath this Hotspur, Mars in swathling clothes,
This infant warrior, in his enterprises
Discomfited great Douglas, ta'en him once,
Enlarged him and made a friend of him,   115
To fill the mouth of deep defiance up
And shake the peace and safety of our throne.
And what say you to this? Percy, Northumberland,
The Archbishop's grace of York, Douglas, Mortimer,
Capitulate against us and are up.   120
But wherefore do I tell these news to thee?
Why, Harry, do I tell thee of my foes,
Which art my near'st and dearest enemy?
Thou that art like enough, through vassal fear,
Base inclination, and the start of spleen,   125
To fight against me under Percy's pay,
To dog his heels and curtsy at his frowns,
To show how much thou art degenerate.
 Prince. Do not think so; you shall not find it so:
And God forgive them that so much have sway'd
Your Majesty's good thoughts away from me!   131
I will redeem all this on Percy's head,
And in the closing of some glorious day
Be bold to tell you that I am your son;
When I will wear a garment all of blood   135
And stain my favours in a bloody mask,
Which, wash'd away, shall scour my shame with it.
And that shall be the day, whene'er it lights,
That this same child of honour and renown,
This gallant Hotspur, this all-praised knight,   140
And your unthought-of Harry chance to meet.
For every honour sitting on his helm,
Would they were multitudes, and on my head
My shames redoubled! For the time will come
That I shall make this northern youth exchange   145
His glorious deeds for my indignities.
Percy is but my factor, good my lord,
To engross up glorious deeds on my behalf;
And I will call him to so strict account
That he shall render every glory up,   150
Yea, even the slightest worship of his time,
Or I will tear the reckoning from his heart.
This, in the name of God, I promise here;
The which if He be pleas'd I shall perform,
I do beseech your Majesty may salve   155

The long-grown wounds of my intemperance.
If not, the end of life cancels all bands;
And I will die a hundred thousand deaths
Ere break the smallest parcel of this vow.   159
 King. A hundred thousand rebels die in this.
Thou shalt have charge and sovereign trust herein.

Enter BLUNT.

How now, good Blunt? Thy looks are full of speed.
 Blunt. So hath the business that I come to speak of.
Lord Mortimer of Scotland hath sent word
That Douglas and the English rebels met   165
The eleventh of this month at Shrewsbury.
A mighty and a fearful head they are,
If promises be kept on every hand,
As ever off'red foul play in a state.
 King. The Earl of Westmoreland set forth to-day,   170
With him my son, Lord John of Lancaster,
For this advertisement is five days old.
On Wednesday next, Harry, you shall set forward;
On Thursday we ourselves will march. Our meeting
Is Bridgenorth: and, Harry, you shall march   175
Through Gloucestershire; by which account,
Our business valued, some twelve days hence
Our general forces at Bridgenorth shall meet.
Our hands are full of business; let's away.
Advantage feeds him fat, while men delay.   180
                                        [*Exeunt.*

SCENE III. [*Eastcheap. The Boar's-Head Tavern.*]

Enter FALSTAFF *and* BARDOLPH.

 Fal. Bardolph, am I not fallen away vilely since this last action? Do I not bate? Do I not dwindle? Why, my skin hangs about me like an old lady's loose gown; I am withered like an old apple-john. Well, I'll repent, and that suddenly, while I am   5
in some liking. I shall be out of heart shortly, and then I shall have no strength to repent. An I have not forgotten what the inside of a church is made of, I am a peppercorn, a brewer's horse. The inside of a church! Company, villanous company, hath   10
been the spoil of me.
 Bard. Sir John, you are so fretful, you cannot live long.   14
 Fal. Why, there is it. Come sing me a bawdy song; make me merry. I was as virtuously given

109. **majority**: supremacy.   120. **Capitulate**: combine.   **up**: in rebellion.   136. **favours**: features.   147. **factor**: agent.
148. **engross up**: gather.   164. **Lord ... Scotland**: Dunbar, the Scottish Earl of March, confused with the English Mortimer.
167. **head**: force.   172. **advertisement**: information.   177. **Our ... valued**: the time necessary for our business being considered.
 Sc. iii, 4. **apple-john**: an apple that keeps its flavor after it is shriveled.   6. **liking**: bodily condition.

as a gentleman need to be; virtuous enough, swore little, dic'd not above seven times a week, went to a bawdy-house not above once in a quarter — of an hour, paid money that I borrowed — three or 20 four times, lived well and in good compass; and now I live out of all order, out of all compass.

Bard. Why, you are so fat, Sir John, that you must needs be out of all compass, out of all reasonable compass, Sir John. 26

Fal. Do thou amend thy face, and I'll amend my life. Thou art our admiral; thou bearest the lantern in the poop, but 'tis in the nose of thee. Thou art the Knight of the Burning Lamp. 30

Bard. Why, Sir John, my face does you no harm.

Fal. No, I'll be sworn; I make as good use of it as many a man doth of a Death's-head or a *memento mori;* I never see thy face but I think upon hell- 35 fire and Dives that lived in purple; for there he is in his robes, burning, burning. If thou wert any way given to virtue, I would swear by thy face; my oath should be, "By this fire, that's God's angel;" but thou art altogether given over, and wert 40 indeed, but for the light in thy face, the son of utter darkness. When thou ran'st up Gadshill in the night to catch my horse, if I did not think thou hadst been an *ignis fatuus* or a ball of wildfire, there's no purchase in money. O, thou art a 45 perpetual triumph, an everlasting bonfire-light! Thou hast saved me a thousand marks in links and torches, walking with thee in the night betwixt tavern and tavern; but the sack that thou hast drunk me would have bought me lights as good 50 cheap at the dearest chandler's in Europe. I have maintain'd that salamander of yours with fire any time this two and thirty years; God reward me for it! 55

Bard. 'Sblood, I would my face were in your belly!

Fal. God-a-mercy! so should I be sure to be heart-burn'd.

Enter HOSTESS.

How now, Dame Partlet the hen! have you inquir'd yet who pick'd my pocket? 61

Host. Why, Sir John, what do you think, Sir John? Do you think I keep thieves in my house? I have search'd, I have inquired, so has my husband, man by man, boy by boy, servant by 65 servant. The [tithe] of a hair was never lost in my house before.

Fal. Ye lie, hostess. Bardolph was shav'd and lost many a hair; and I'll be sworn my pocket was pick'd. Go to, you are a woman, go. 70

Host. Who? I? No; I defy thee. God's light, I was never call'd so in mine own house before.

Fal. Go to, I know you well enough.

Host. No, Sir John; you do not know me, Sir John. I know you, Sir John; you owe me 75 money, Sir John; and now you pick a quarrel to beguile me of it. I bought you a dozen of shirts to your back.

Fal. Dowlas, filthy dowlas. I have given them away to bakers' wives; they have made bolters of them. 81

Host. Now, as I am a true woman, holland of eight shillings an ell. You owe money here besides, Sir John, for your diet and by-drinkings, and money lent you, four and twenty pound. 86

Fal. He had his part of it; let him pay.

Host. He? Alas, he is poor; he hath nothing.

Fal. How! poor? Look upon his face; what call you rich? Let them coin his nose, let them 90 coin his cheeks. I'll not pay a denier. What, will you make a younker of me? Shall I not take mine ease in mine inn but I shall have my pocket pick'd? I have lost a seal-ring of my grandfather's worth forty mark. 95

Host. O Jesu, I have heard the Prince tell him, I know not how oft, that that ring was copper!

Fal. How! the Prince is a Jack, a sneak-cup. 'Sblood, an he were here, I would cudgel him like a dog, if he would say so. 101

Enter the PRINCE [*and* PETO], *marching, and* FALSTAFF *meets them playing on his truncheon like a fife.*

How now, lad! is the wind in that door, i' faith? Must we all march?

Bard. Yea, two and two, Newgate fashion.

Host. My lord, I pray you, hear me. 105

Prince. What say'st thou, Mistress Quickly? How doth thy husband? I love him well; he is an honest man.

Host. Good my lord, hear me.

Fal. Prithee, let her alone, and list to me. 110

Prince. What say'st thou, Jack?

Fal. The other night I fell asleep here behind the arras and had my pocket pick'd. This house is turn'd bawdy-house; they pick pockets.

Prince. What didst thou lose, Jack? 115

Fal. Wilt thou believe me, Hal? Three or four bonds of forty pound a-piece, and a seal-ring of my grandfather's.

Prince. A trifle, some eight-penny matter.

Host. So I told him, my lord, and I said I 120 heard your Grace say so; and, my lord, he speaks

---

28. **admiral:** flagship. 36. **Dives:** the rich man in *Luke* xvi.19-31. 44. *ignis fatuus:* will o' the wisp. 46. **triumph:** public celebration. 47. **links:** torches. 66. **[tithe]** (Theobald). *tight* Q. 79. **Dowlas:** coarse linen. 80. **bolters:** sieves for flour. 82. **holland:** fine linen. 84. **by-drinkings:** i.e., between meals. 91. **denier:** tenth of a penny. 92. **younker:** novice. 99. **Jack:** knave. **sneak-cup:** a shirker in drinking. 104. **Newgate:** a London prison.

most vilely of you, like a foul-mouth'd man as he is, and said he would cudgel you.

Prince. What! he did not?

Host. There's neither faith, truth, nor woman-hood in me else. 126

Fal. There's no more faith in thee than in a stew'd prune; nor no more truth in thee than in a drawn fox; and for womanhood, Maid Marian may be the deputy's wife of the ward to thee. Go, you thing, go. 131

Host. Say, what thing? what thing?

Fal. What thing? Why, a thing to thank God on.

Host. I am no thing to thank God on, I 135 would thou shouldst know it. I am an honest man's wife; and, setting thy knighthood aside, thou art a knave to call me so.

Fal. Setting thy womanhood aside, thou art a beast to say otherwise. 140

Host. Say, what beast, thou knave, thou?

Fal. What beast? Why, an otter.

Prince. An otter, Sir John! Why an otter?

Fal. Why, she's neither fish nor flesh; a man knows not where to have her. 145

Host. Thou art an unjust man in saying so. Thou or any man knows where to have me, thou knave, thou!

Prince. Thou say'st true, hostess; and he slanders thee most grossly. 150

Host. So he doth you, my lord; and said this other day you ought him a thousand pound.

Prince. Sirrah, do I owe you a thousand pound?

Fal. A thousand pound, Hal! A million. 155 Thy love is worth a million; thou ow'st me thy love.

Host. Nay, my lord, he called you Jack, and said he would cudgel you.

Fal. Did I, Bardolph? 160

Bard. Indeed, Sir John, you said so.

Fal. Yea, if he said my ring was copper.

Prince. I say 'tis copper. Dar'st thou be as good as thy word now? 164

Fal. Why, Hal, thou know'st, as thou art but man, I dare; but as thou art Prince, I fear thee as I fear the roaring of the lion's whelp.

Prince. And why not as the lion?

Fal. The King himself is to be feared as the lion. Dost thou think I'll fear thee as I fear thy 170 father? Nay, an I do, I pray God my girdle break.

Prince. O, if it should, how would thy guts fall about thy knees! But, sirrah, there's no room for faith, truth, nor honesty in this bosom of thine;

it is all filled up with guts and midriff. Charge 175 an honest woman with picking thy pocket! Why, thou whoreson, impudent, emboss'd rascal, if there were anything in thy pocket but tavern-reckonings, memorandums of bawdy-houses, and one poor penny-worth of sugar-candy to make thee long- 180 winded, if thy pocket were enrich'd with any other injuries but these, I am a villain. And yet you will stand to it; you will not pocket up wrong. Art thou not asham'd? 184

Fal. Dost thou hear, Hal? Thou know'st in the state of innocency Adam fell; and what should poor Jack Falstaff do in the days of villany? Thou seest I have more flesh than another man, and therefore more frailty. You confess then, you pick'd my pocket? 190

Prince. It appears so by the story.

Fal. Hostess, I forgive thee. Go, make ready breakfast; love thy husband, look to thy servants, cherish thy guests. Thou shalt find me tractable to any honest reason; thou seest I am pacified 195 still. Nay, prithee, be gone. [*Exit Hostess.*

Now, Hal, to the news at court. For the rob-bery, lad, how is that answered?

Prince. O, my sweet beef, I must still be good angel to thee. The money is paid back again. 200

Fal. O, I do not like that paying back; 'tis a double labour.

Prince. I am good friends with my father and may do anything. 204

Fal. Rob me the exchequer the first thing thou doest, and do it with unwash'd hands too.

Bard. Do, my lord.

Prince. I have procured thee, Jack, a charge of foot. 209

Fal. I would it had been of horse. Where shall I find one that can steal well? O for a fine thief, of the age of two and twenty or thereabouts! I am heinously unprovided. Well, God be thanked for these rebels, they offend none but the virtues. I laud them, I praise them. 215

Prince. Bardolph!

Bard. My lord?

Prince. Go bear this letter to Lord John of Lancaster, to my brother John; this to my Lord of Westmoreland. [*Exit Bardolph.*] Go, Peto, 220 to horse, to horse; for thou and I have thirty miles to ride yet ere dinner time. [*Exit Peto.*] Jack, meet me to-morrow in the Temple hall at two o'clock in the afternoon.

There shalt thou know thy charge, and there 225 receive

Money and order for their furniture.

128. **stew'd prune:** harlot. 129. **drawn:** i.e., out of his hole, and seeking to trick his pursuers. **Maid Marian:** a character in Robin Hood ballads and May-games, not admired by Puritanical burgesses. 145. **have:** find, place. 152. **ought:** owed. 177. **emboss'd:** swollen. 182. **injuries:** incriminating articles. 206. **with unwash'd hands:** hastily. 226. **furniture:** equipment.

The land is burning; Percy stands on high;
And either we or they must lower lie.   [*Exit.*]
  Fal. Rare words! brave world! Hostess, my
    breakfast, come!
O, I could wish this tavern were my drum!   230
                         [*Exit.*]

ACT IV

SCENE I. [*The rebel camp near Shrewsbury.*]
  Enter HOTSPUR, WORCESTER, *and* DOUGLAS.

  Hot. Well said, my noble Scot! If speaking
    truth
In this fine age were not thought flattery,
Such attribution should the Douglas have
As not a soldier of this season's stamp
Should go so general current through the world.   5
By God, I cannot flatter; I do defy
The tongues of soothers; but a braver place
In my heart's love hath no man than yourself.
Nay, task me to my word; approve me, lord.
  Doug. Thou art the king of honour.   10
No man so potent breathes upon the ground
But I will beard him.

    Enter a MESSENGER *with letters.*

  Hot.   Do so, and 'tis well. —
What letters hast thou there? — I can but thank
    you.
  Mess. These letters come from your father.
  Hot. Letters from him! Why comes he not
    himself?   15
  Mess. He cannot come, my lord; he is grievous
    sick.
  Hot. 'Zounds! how has he the leisure to be sick
In such a justling time? Who leads his power?
Under whose government come they along?
  Mess. His letters bears his mind, not I, my
    [lord].   20
  Wor. I prithee, tell me, doth he keep his bed?
  Mess. He did, my lord, four days ere I set forth;
And at the time of my departure thence
He was much fear'd by his physicians.
  Wor. I would the state of time had first been
    whole   25
Ere he by sickness had been visited.
His health was never better worth than now.
  Hot. Sick now! droop now! This sickness doth
    infect
The very life-blood of our enterprise;
'Tis catching hither, even to our camp.   30

He writes me here, that inward sickness —
And that his friends by deputation could not
So soon be drawn, nor did he think it meet
To lay so dangerous and dear a trust
On any soul remov'd but on his own.   35
Yet doth he give us bold advertisement
That with our small conjunction we should on
To see how fortune is dispos'd to us;
For, as he writes, there is no quailing now,
Because the King is certainly possess'd   40
Of all our purposes. What say you to it?
  Wor. Your father's sickness is a maim to us.
  Hot. A perilous gash, a very limb lopp'd off.
And yet, in faith, 'tis not; his present want
Seems more than we shall find it. Were it good   45
To set the exact wealth of all our states
All at one cast? to set so rich a main
On the nice hazard of one doubtful hour?
It were not good; for therein should we read
The very bottom and the soul of hope,   50
The very list, the very utmost bound
Of all our fortunes.
  Doug.   Faith, and so we should;
Where now remains a sweet reversion.
We may boldly spend upon the hope of what
[Is] to come in.   55
A comfort of retirement lives in this.
  Hot. A rendezvous, a home to fly unto,
If that the devil and mischance look big
Upon the maidenhead of our affairs.
  Wor. But yet I would your father had been
    here.   60
The quality and hair of our attempt
Brooks no division. It will be thought
By some that know not why he is away
That wisdom, loyalty, and mere dislike
Of our proceedings kept the earl from hence;   65
And think how such an apprehension
May turn the tide of fearful faction
And breed a kind of question in our cause.
For well you know we of the off'ring side
Must keep aloof from strict arbitrement,   70
And stop all sight-holes, every loop from whence
The eye of reason may pry in upon us.
This absence of your father's draws a curtain,
That shows the ignorant a kind of fear
Before not dreamt of.
  Hot.   You strain too far.   75
I rather of his absence make this use:
It lends a lustre and more great opinion,
A larger dare to our great enterprise,
Than if the earl were here; for men must think,

Act IV, sc. i, 7. **soothers:** flatterers. 9. **approve:** test. 20. [lord] (Capell). *mind* Q. 32. **deputation:** deputy, agent. 35. **remov'd:** other. 36. **advertisement:** advice. 37. **conjunction:** allied force. 44. **want:** absence. 46. **set:** stake. 47. **main:** stake. 48. **nice:** delicate. 51. **list:** limit. 53. **Where:** whereas. **reversion:** something to fall back on. 55. [Is] F. *'tis* Q. 58–59. **look…maidenhead:** frown upon the early stages. 61. **hair:** fiber, quality. 69. **off'ring:** attacking. 70. **arbitrement:** judicial decision.

If we without his help can make a head   80
To push against a kingdom, with his help
We shall o'erturn it topsy-turvy down.
Yet all goes well, yet all our joints are whole.

   Doug. As heart can think. There is not such a
     word
Spoke of in Scotland as this term of fear.   85

Enter Sir Richard Vernon.

   Hot. My cousin Vernon! welcome, by my soul.
   Ver. Pray God my news be worth a welcome,
     lord.
The Earl of Westmoreland, seven thousand strong,
Is marching hitherwards; with him Prince John.
   Hot. No harm. What more?
   Ver.   And further, I have learn'd,
The King himself in person is set forth,   91
Or hitherwards intended speedily,
With strong and mighty preparation.
   Hot. He shall be welcome too. Where is his son,
The nimble-footed madcap Prince of Wales,   95
And his comrades, that daff'd the world aside
And bid it pass?
   Ver.   All furnish'd, all in arms;
All plum'd like estridges that with the wind
Bated, like eagles having lately bath'd;
Glittering in golden coats, like images;   100
As full of spirit as the month of May
And gorgeous as the sun at midsummer;
Wanton as youthful goats, wild as young bulls.
I saw young Harry with his beaver on,
His cuisses on his thighs, gallantly arm'd,   105
Rise from the ground like feathered Mercury,
And vaulted with such ease into his seat
As if an angel dropp'd down from the clouds
To turn and wind a fiery Pegasus
And witch the world with noble horsemanship.   110
   Hot. No more, no more! Worse than the sun
     in March,
This praise doth nourish agues. Let them come!
They come like sacrifices in their trim,
And to the fire-ey'd maid of smoky war
All hot and bleeding will we offer them.   115
The mailed Mars shall on his altar sit
Up to the ears in blood. I am on fire
To hear this rich reprisal is so nigh
And yet not ours. Come, let me taste my horse,
Who is to bear me like a thunderbolt   120
Against the bosom of the Prince of Wales.
Harry to Harry shall, hot horse to horse,
Meet and ne'er part till one drop down a corse.
O that Glendower were come!
   Ver.   There is more news.

I learn'd in Worcester, as I rode along,   125
He [cannot] draw his power this fourteen days.
   Doug. That's the worst tidings that I hear of
     [yet].
   Wor. Ay, by my faith, that bears a frosty
     sound.
   Hot. What may the King's whole battle reach
     unto?
   Ver. To thirty thousand.
   Hot.   Forty let it be!   130
My father and Glendower being both away,
The powers of us may serve so great a day.
Come, let us take a muster speedily.
Doomsday is near; die all, die merrily.
   Doug. Talk not of dying; I am out of fear   135
Of death or death's hand for this one half-year.
                          [Exeunt.

Scene II. [*A public road near Coventry.*]

Enter Falstaff and Bardolph.

   Fal. Bardolph, get thee before to Coventry; fill
me a bottle of sack. Our soldiers shall march
through; we'll to Sutton Cophill to-night.
   Bard. Will you give me money, captain?
   Fal. Lay out, lay out.   5
   Bard. This bottle makes an angel.
   Fal. An if it do, take it for thy labour; and if it
make twenty, take them all; I'll answer the coinage. Bid my lieutenant Peto meet me at town's
end.   10
   Bard. I will, captain; farewell.   *[Exit.*
   Fal. If I be not ashamed of my soldiers, I am a
sous'd gurnet. I have misus'd the King's press
damnably. I have got, in exchange of a hundred
and fifty soldiers, three hundred and odd pounds.   15
I press me none but good householders, yeoman's
sons; inquire me out contracted bachelors, such as
had been ask'd twice on the banns; such a commodity of warm slaves, as had as lieve hear the
devil as a drum; such as fear the report of a   20
caliver worse than a struck fowl or a hurt wild-
duck. I press'd me none but such toasts-and-
butter, with hearts in their bellies no bigger than
pins' heads; and they have bought out their
services; and now my whole charge consists of   25
ancients, corporals, lieutenants, gentlemen of
companies — slaves as ragged as Lazarus in the
painted cloth, where the glutton's dogs licked his
sores; and such as, indeed, were never soldiers, but
discarded unjust serving-men, younger sons   30
to younger brothers, revolted tapsters and ostlers
trade-fallen, the cankers of a calm world and a

---

    96. **daff'd**: thrust. 98. **estridges**: ostriches. 99. **Bated**: beat their wings. 104. **beaver**: (face part of the) helmet.
118. **reprisal**: prize. 126. **[cannot]** Q5. *can* Q1. 127. **[yet]** Q5. *it* Q1.
    Sc. ii, 6. **angel**: 10s. 13. **sous'd gurnet**: pickled fish. **press**: warrant for conscripting. 18. **commodity**: lot. 19.
warm: comfortable. 21. **caliver**: musket. 26. **ancients**: ensigns. 32. **trade-fallen**: out of work.

long peace, ten times more dishonourable ragged than an old feaz'd ancient: and such have I, to fill up the rooms of them as have bought out their 35 services, that you would think that I had a hundred and fifty tatter'd prodigals lately come from swine-keeping, from eating draff and husks. A mad fellow met me on the way and told me I had un-loaded all the gibbets and press'd the dead 40 bodies. No eye hath seen such scarecrows. I'll not march through Coventry with them, that's flat. Nay, and the villains march wide betwixt the legs, as if they had gyves on; for indeed I had the most of them out of prison. There's but a 45 shirt and a half in all my company; and the half shirt is two napkins tack'd together and thrown over the shoulders like an herald's coat without sleeves; and the shirt, to say the truth, stolen from my host at Saint Alban's, or the red-nose inn- 50 keeper of Daventry. But that's all one; they'll find linen enough on every hedge.

Enter the PRINCE *and* WESTMORELAND.

Prince. How now, blown Jack! how now, quilt! 54
Fal. What, Hal! how now, mad wag! What a devil dost thou in Warwickshire? My good Lord of Westmoreland, I cry you mercy! I thought your honour had already been at Shrewsbury. 59
West. Faith, Sir John, 'tis more than time that I were there, and you too; but my powers are there already. The King, I can tell you, looks for us all. We must away all night.
Fal. Tut, never fear me. I am as vigilant as a cat to steal cream. 65
Prince. I think, to steal cream indeed, for thy theft hath already made thee butter. But tell me, Jack, whose fellows are these that come after?
Fal. Mine, Hal, mine.
Prince. I did never see such pitiful rascals. 70
Fal. Tut, tut; good enough to toss; food for powder, food for powder; they'll fill a pit as well as better. Tush, man, mortal men, mortal men.
West. Ay, but, Sir John, methinks they are exceeding poor and bare, too beggarly. 75
Fal. Faith, for their poverty, I know not where they had that; and for their bareness, I am sure they never learn'd that of me.
Prince. No, I'll be sworn; unless you call three fingers on the ribs bare. But, sirrah, make haste. Percy is already in the field. 81
Fal. What, is the King encamp'd?
West. He is, Sir John. I fear we shall stay too long.
Fal. Well,

To the latter end of a fray and the beginning of a feast 85
Fits a dull fighter and a keen guest. [*Exeunt.*

SCENE III. [*The rebel camp near Shrewsbury.*]

Enter HOTSPUR, WORCESTER, DOUGLAS, *and* VERNON.

Hot. We'll fight with him to-night.
Wor.   It may not be.
Doug. You give him then advantage.
Ver.   Not a whit.
Hot. Why say you so? Looks he not for supply?
Ver. So do we.
Hot.   His is certain, ours is doubtful.
Wor. Good cousin, be advis'd; stir not to-night. 5
Ver. Do not, my lord.
Doug.   You do not counsel well.
You speak it out of fear and cold heart.
Ver. Do me no slander, Douglas. By my life,
And I dare well maintain it with my life,
If well-respected honour bid me on 10
I hold as little counsel with weak fear
As you, my lord, or any Scot that this day lives.
Let it be seen to-morrow in the battle
Which of us fears.
Doug.   Yea, or to-night.
Ver.   Content.
Hot. To-night, say I. 15
Ver. Come, come, it may not be. I wonder much,
Being men of such great leading as you are,
That you foresee not what impediments
Drag back our expedition. Certain horse
Of my cousin Vernon's are not yet come up. 20
Your uncle Worcester's horse came but to-day;
And now their pride and mettle is asleep,
Their courage with hard labour tame and dull,
That not a horse is half the half of himself.
Hot. So are the horses of the enemy 25
In general, journey-bated and brought low.
The better part of ours are full of rest.
Wor. The number of the King exceedeth ours.
For God's sake, cousin, stay till all come in.
[*The trumpet sounds a parley.*

Enter SIR WALTER BLUNT.

Blunt. I come with gracious offers from the King,
If you vouchsafe me hearing and respect. 31
Hot. Welcome, Sir Walter Blunt; and would to God
You were of our determination!
Some of us love you well; and even those some

34. **feaz'd ancient:** torn flag. 38. **draff:** swill. 44. **gyves:** fetters. 63. **all night:** marching all night. Ff read *all to night.* Sc. iii, 3. **supply:** reinforcements. 17. **leading:** leadership. 26. **journey-bated:** weary from travel. 33. **determination:** party.

Envy your great deservings and good name,   35
Because you are not of our quality,
But stand against us like an enemy.

   Blunt. And God defend but still I should stand
     so,
So long as out of limit and true rule
You stand against anointed majesty.   40
But to my charge.   The King hath sent to know
The nature of your griefs, and whereupon
You conjure from the breast of civil peace
Such bold hostility, teaching his duteous land
Audacious cruelty.   If that the King   45
Have any way your good deserts forgot,
Which he confesseth to be manifold,
He bids you name your griefs; and with all speed
You shall have your desires with interest
And pardon absolute for yourself and these   50
Herein misled by your suggestion.

   Hot. The King is kind; and well we know the
     King
Knows at what time to promise, when to pay.
My father and my uncle and myself
Did give him that same royalty he wears;   55
And when he was not six and twenty strong,
Sick in the world's regard, wretched and low,
A poor unminded outlaw sneaking home,
My father gave him welcome to the shore;
And when he heard him swear and vow to God   60
He came but to be Duke of Lancaster,
To sue his livery and beg his peace,
With tears of innocence and terms of zeal,
My father, in kind heart and pity mov'd,
Swore him assistance and perform'd it too.   65
Now when the lords and barons of the realm
Perceiv'd Northumberland did lean to him,
The more and less came in with cap and knee;
Met him in boroughs, cities, villages,
Attended him on bridges, stood in lanes,   70
Laid gifts before him, proffer'd him their oaths,
Gave him their heirs as pages, followed him
Even at the heels in golden multitudes.
He presently, as greatness knows itself,
Steps me a little higher than his vow   75
Made to my father, while his blood was poor,
Upon the naked shore at Ravenspurgh;
And now, forsooth, takes on him to reform
Some certain edicts and some strait decrees
That lie too heavy on the commonwealth,   80
Cries out upon abuses, seems to weep
Over his country's wrongs; and by this face,
This seeming brow of justice, did he win
The hearts of all that he did angle for;
Proceeded further; cut me off the heads   85
Of all the favourites that the absent king

In deputation left behind him here,
When he was personal in the Irish war.

   Blunt. Tut, I came not to hear this.

   Hot.   Then to the point.
In short time after, he depos'd the King;   90
Soon after that, depriv'd him of his life;
And in the neck of that, task'd the whole state.
To make that worse, suffer'd his kinsman March,
Who is, if every owner were well plac'd,
Indeed his king, to be engag'd in Wales,   95
There without ransom to lie forfeited;
Disgrac'd me in my happy victories,
Sought to entrap me by intelligence;
Rated mine uncle from the council-board;
In rage dismiss'd my father from the court;   100
Broke oath on oath, committed wrong on wrong,
And in conclusion drove us to seek out
This head of safety; and withal to pry
Into his title, the which we find
Too indirect for long continuance.   105

   Blunt. Shall I return this answer to the King?

   Hot. Not so, Sir Walter; we'll withdraw a while.
Go to the King; and let there be impawn'd
Some surety for a safe return again,
And in the morning early shall mine uncle   110
Bring him our purposes: and so farewell.

   Blunt. I would you would accept of grace and
     love.

   Hot. And may be so we shall.

   Blunt.   Pray God you do.
                           [Exeunt.

SCENE IV. [*York.   The Archbishop's palace.*]

Enter the ARCHBISHOP OF YORK *and* SIR MICHAEL.

   Arch. Hie, good Sir Michael; bear this sealed
     brief
With winged haste to the Lord Marshal,
This to my cousin Scroop, and all the rest
To whom they are directed.   If you knew
How much they do import, you would make haste.

   Sir M. My good lord,   6
I guess their tenour.

   Arch.   Like enough you do.
To-morrow, good Sir Michael, is a day
Wherein the fortune of ten thousand men
Must bide the touch; for, sir, at Shrewsbury,   10
As I am truly given to understand,
The King with mighty and quick-raised power
Meets with Lord Harry; and, I fear, Sir Michael,
What with the sickness of Northumberland,
Whose power was in the first proportion,   15
And what with Owen Glendower's absence thence,
Who with them was a rated sinew too

---

36. **quality:** party.   62. **sue his livery:** claim his inheritance.   79. **strait:** strict.   88. **personal:** in person.   92. **task'd:** taxed.   98. **intelligence:** spies.   99. **Rated:** scolded.   103. **head of safety:** safety by armed force.
   Sc. iv, 15. **proportion:** magnitude.   17. **rated sinew:** force counted on.

And comes not in, o'er-rul'd by prophecies,
I fear the power of Percy is too weak
To wage an instant trial with the King.   20
Sir M. Why, my good lord, you need not fear;
There is Douglas and Lord Mortimer.
Arch. No, Mortimer is not there.
Sir M. But there is Murdoch, Vernon, Lord
     Harry Percy,
And there is my Lord of Worcester, and a head   25
Of gallant warriors, noble gentlemen.
Arch. And so there is; but yet the King hath
     drawn
The special head of all the land together:
The Prince of Wales, Lord John of Lancaster,
The noble Westmoreland, and warlike Blunt;   30
And many moe corrivals and dear men
Of estimation and command in arms.
Sir M. Doubt not, my lord, they shall be well
     oppos'd.
Arch. I hope no less, yet needful 'tis to fear;
And, to prevent the worst, Sir Michael, speed;   35
For if Lord Percy thrive not, ere the King
Dismiss his power he means to visit us,
For he hath heard of our confederacy,
And 'tis but wisdom to make strong against him.
Therefore make haste. I must go write again   40
To other friends; and so farewell, Sir Michael.
                                        [*Exeunt.*

ACT V

SCENE I. [*The King's camp near Shrewsbury.*]

Enter the KING, PRINCE OF WALES, LORD JOHN OF
LANCASTER, SIR WALTER BLUNT, *and* FALSTAFF.

King. How bloodily the sun begins to peer
Above yon [busky] hill! The day looks pale
At his distemperature.
Prince.   The southern wind
Doth play the trumpet to his purposes,
And by his hollow whistling in the leaves   5
Foretells a tempest and a blust'ring day.
King. Then with the losers let it sympathize,
For nothing can seem foul to those that win.
                                   [*The trumpet sounds.*

Enter WORCESTER [*and* VERNON].

How now, my Lord of Worcester! 'tis not well
That you and I should meet upon such terms   10
As now we meet. You have deceiv'd our trust,
And made us doff our easy robes of peace,
To crush our old limbs in ungentle steel.
This is not well, my lord, this is not well.
What say you to it? Will you again unknit   15

This churlish knot of all-abhorred war?
And move in that obedient orb again
Where you did give a fair and natural light,
And be no more an exhal'd meteor,
A prodigy of fear and a portent   20
Of broached mischief to the unborn times?
Wor. Hear me, my liege.
For mine own part, I could be well content]
To entertain the lag-end of my life
With quiet hours; for I [do] protest,   25
I have not sought the day of this dislike.
King. You have not sought it! How comes it,
     then?
Fal. Rebellion lay in his way, and he found it.
Prince. Peace, chewet, peace!
Wor. It pleas'd your Majesty to turn your looks
Of favour from myself and all our house;   31
And yet I must remember you, my lord,
We were the first and dearest of your friends.
For you my staff of office did I break
In Richard's time; and posted day and night   35
To meet you on the way, and kiss your hand,
When yet you were in place and in account
Nothing so strong and fortunate as I.
It was myself, my brother, and his son,
That brought you home and boldly did outdare
The dangers of the time. You swore to us,   41
And you did swear that oath at Doncaster,
That you did nothing purpose 'gainst the state;
Nor claim no further than your new-fall'n right,
The seat of Gaunt, dukedom of Lancaster.   45
To this we swore our aid. But in short space
It rain'd down fortune show'ring on your head;
And such a flood of greatness fell on you,
What with our help, what with the absent King,
What with the injuries of a wanton time,   50
The seeming sufferances that you had borne,
And the contrarious winds that held the King
So long in his unlucky Irish wars
That all in England did repute him dead;
And from this swarm of fair advantages   55
You took occasion to be quickly woo'd
To gripe the general sway into your hand;
Forgot your oath to us at Doncaster;
And being fed by us you us'd us so
As that ungentle gull, the cuckoo's bird,   60
Useth the sparrow; did oppress our nest;
Grew by our feeding to so great a bulk
That even our love durst not come near your sight
For fear of swallowing; but with nimble wing
We were enforc'd, for safety sake, to fly   65
Out of your sight and raise this present head;
Whereby we stand opposed by such means
As you yourself have forg'd against yourself

---

31. **moe**: more. **corrivals**: associates.
  Act V, sc. i, S.D. SIR (Capell). *Earle of Westmorland, Sir* Qq Ff. 2. **[busky]** Ff: wooded. *bulky* Q. 3. **distemperature:**
abnormal appearance. 21. **broached:** set going. 25. **[do]** F. Om. Qq. 29. **chewet:** jackdaw. 60. **gull, bird:** nestling.

Development of character of Prince reaches climax in this act

By unkind usage, dangerous countenance,
And violation of all faith and troth 70
Sworn to us in your younger enterprise.
    King. These things indeed you have articulate,
Proclaim'd at market-crosses, read in churches,
To face the garment of rebellion
With some fine colour that may please the eye 75
Of fickle changelings and poor discontents,
Which gape and rub the elbow at the news
Of hurly-burly innovation.
And never yet did insurrection want
Such water-colours to impaint his cause; 80
Nor moody beggars, starving for a time
Of pell-mell havoc and confusion.
    Prince. In both your armies there is many a soul
Shall pay full dearly for this encounter,
If once they join in trial. Tell your nephew, 85
The Prince of Wales doth join with all the world
In praise of Henry Percy. By my hopes,
This present enterprise set off his head,
I do not think a braver gentleman,
More active-valiant or more valiant-young, 90
More daring or more bold, is now alive
To grace this latter age with noble deeds.
For my part, I may speak it to my shame,
I have a truant been to chivalry;
And so I hear he doth account me too; 95
Yet this before my father's majesty:
I am content that he shall take the odds
Of his great name and estimation,
And will, to save the blood on either side,
Try fortune with him in a single fight. 100
    King. And, Prince of Wales, so dare we venture thee,
Albeit considerations infinite
Do make against it. No, good Worcester, no,
We love our people well; even those we love
That are misled upon your cousin's part; 105
And, will they take the offer of our grace,
Both he and they and you, yea, every man
Shall be my friend again and I'll be his.
So tell your cousin, and bring me word
What he will do. But if he will not yield, 110
Rebuke and dread correction wait on us
And they shall do their office. So, be gone;
We will not now be troubled with reply.
We offer fair; take it advisedly.
         [*Exeunt Worcester* [*and Vernon*].
    Prince. It will not be accepted, on my life. 115
The Douglas and the Hotspur both together
Are confident against the world in arms.
    King. Hence, therefore, every leader to his charge,
For, on their answer, will we set on them;

And God befriend us, as our cause is just! 120
         [*Exeunt all but the Prince of Wales and Falstaff.*
    Fal. Hal, if thou see me down in the battle and bestride me, so; 'tis a point of friendship.
    Prince. Nothing but a colossus can do thee that friendship. Say thy prayers, and farewell.
    Fal. I would 'twere bed-time, Hal, and all well.
    Prince. Why, thou owest God a death. 127
         [*Exit.*]
    Fal. 'Tis not due yet; I would be loath to pay him before his day. What need I be so forward with him that calls not on me? Well, 'tis no 130 matter; honour pricks me on. Yea, but how if honour prick me off when I came on? How then? Can honour set to a leg? No. Or an arm? No. Or take away the grief of a wound? No. Honour hath no skill in surgery, then? No. What is 135 honour? A word. What is in that word honour? What is that honour? Air; a trim reckoning! Who hath it? He that died o' Wednesday. Doth he feel it? No. Doth he hear it? No. 'Tis insensible, then? Yea, to the dead. But will 140 [it] not live with the living? No. Why? Detraction will not suffer it. Therefore I'll none of it. Honour is a mere scutcheon: and so ends my catechism.   [*Exit.*

SCENE II.   [*The rebel camp.*]

Enter WORCESTER *and* VERNON.

    Wor. O, no, my nephew must not know, Sir Richard,
The liberal and kind offer of the King.
    Ver. 'Twere best he did.
    Wor.   Then are we all [undone].
It is not possible, it cannot be,
The King should keep his word in loving us. 5
He will suspect us still, and find a time
To punish this offence in other faults.
Supposition all our lives shall be stuck full of eyes;
For treason is but trusted like the fox,
Who, ne'er so tame, so cherish'd and lock'd up, 10
Will have a wild trick of his ancestors.
Look how we can, or sad or merrily,
Interpretation will misquote our looks,
And we shall feed like oxen at a stall,
The better cherish'd, still the nearer death. 15
My nephew's trespass may be well forgot;
It hath the excuse of youth and heat of blood,
And an adopted name of privilege,
A hare-brain'd Hotspur, govern'd by a spleen.
All his offences live upon my head 20
And on his father's. We did train him on,
And, his corruption being ta'en from us,

---

72. **articulate:** stated in articles.   78. **innovation:** rebellion.   88. **set...head:** apart.   141. **[it]** Q2. Om. Q1.
Sc. ii, 3. **[undone]** Q5.   *under one* Q1.   8. **Supposition:** suspicion.

We, as the spring of all, shall pay for all.
Therefore, good cousin, let not Harry know,
In any case, the offer of the King.   25
    Ver. Deliver what you will; I'll say 'tis so.
Here comes your cousin.

Enter HOTSPUR [*and* DOUGLAS].

    Hot. My uncle is return'd;
Deliver up my Lord of Westmoreland.
Uncle, what news?   30
    Wor. The King will bid you battle presently.
    Doug. Defy him by the Lord of Westmoreland.
    Hot. Lord Douglas, go you and tell him so.
    Doug. Marry, and shall, and very willingly.
                                        [*Exit.*
    Wor. There is no seeming mercy in the King.   35
    Hot. Did you beg any?   God forbid!
    Wor. I told him gently of our grievances,
Of his oath-breaking; which he mended thus,
By now forswearing that he is forsworn.
He calls us rebels, traitors; and will scourge   40
With haughty arms this hateful name in us.

Re-enter DOUGLAS.

    Doug. Arm, gentlemen; to arms! for I have
        thrown
A brave defiance in King Henry's teeth,
And Westmoreland, that was engag'd, did bear it;
Which cannot choose but bring him quickly on.
    Wor. The Prince of Wales stepp'd forth before
        the King,   46
And, nephew, challeng'd you to single fight.
    Hot. O, would the quarrel lay upon our heads,
And that no man might draw short breath to-day
But I and Harry Monmouth!   Tell me, tell me,   50
How show'd his tasking?   Seem'd it in contempt?
    Ver. No, by my soul; I never in my life
Did hear a challenge urg'd more modestly,
Unless a brother should a brother dare
To gentle exercise and proof of arms.   55
He gave you all the duties of a man,
Trimm'd up your praises with a princely tongue,
Spoke your deservings like a chronicle,
Making you ever better than his praise
By still dispraising praise valued with you;   60
And, which became him like a prince indeed.
He made a blushing cital of himself,
And chid his truant youth with such a grace
As if he mast'red there a double spirit
Of teaching and of learning instantly.   65
There did he pause; but let me tell the world,
If he outlive the envy of this day,
England did never owe so sweet a hope,
So much misconstrued in his wantonness.
    Hot. Cousin, I think thou art enamoured   70

On his follies.   Never did I hear
Of any prince so wild a liberty.
But be he as he will, yet once ere night
I will embrace him with a soldier's arm
That he shall shrink under my courtesy.   75
Arm, arm with speed! and, fellows, soldiers, friends,
Better consider what you have to do
Than I, that have not well the gift of tongue,
Can lift your blood up with persuasion.

Enter a MESSENGER.

    Mess. My lord, here are letters for you.   80
    Hot. I cannot read them now.
O gentlemen, the time of life is short!
To spend that shortness basely were too long,
If life did ride upon a dial's point,
Still ending at the arrival of an hour.   85
An if we live, we live to tread on kings;
If die, brave death, when princes die with us!
Now, for our consciences, the arms are fair
When the intent of bearing them is just.

Enter another MESSENGER.

    [2.] *Mess.* My lord, prepare; the King comes on
        apace.   90
    Hot. I thank him that he cuts me from my tale,
For I profess not talking; only this —
Let each man do his best; and here draw I
A sword, whose temper I intend to stain
With the best blood that I can meet withal   95
In the adventure of this perilous day.
Now *Esperance!*   Percy!   and set on.
Sound all the lofty instruments of war,
And by that music let us all embrace;
For, heaven to earth, some of us never shall   100
A second time do such a courtesy.
                    [*They embrace [and exeunt].*

[SCENE III. *Plain between the camps.*]

*The trumpets sound.   The King enters with his power
and passes over.   Alarum to the battle.   Then
enter* DOUGLAS *and* SIR WALTER BLUNT.

    Blunt. What is thy name, that in the battle thus
Thou crossest me?   What honour dost thou seek
Upon my head?
    Doug.   Know then, my name is Douglas;
And I do haunt thee in the battle thus
Because some tell me that thou art a king.   5
    Blunt. They tell thee true.
    Doug. The Lord of Stafford dear to-day hath
        bought
Thy likeness, for instead of thee, King Harry,
This sword hath ended him.   So shall it thee,
Unless thou yield thee as my prisoner.   10

44. **engag'd:** held as hostage.   51. **tasking:** challenge.   56. **duties:** due merits.   60. **valued:** compared.   62. **cital:** mention.   67. **envy:** malice.   68. **owe:** own.

Blunt. I was not born a yielder, thou proud Scot;
And thou shalt find a king that will revenge
Lord Stafford's death.

           [*They fight. Douglas kills Blunt.*

Enter HOTSPUR.

Hot. O Douglas, hadst thou fought at Holmedon
    thus,
I never had triumph'd upon a Scot.   16
    Doug. All's done, all's won; here breathless lies
        the King.
    Hot. Where?
    Doug. Here.
    Hot. This, Douglas? No. I know this face
full well.
A gallant knight he was, his name was Blunt;   20
Semblably furnish'd like the King himself.
    Doug. Ah! "fool" go with thy soul, whither it
       goes!
A borrowed title hast thou bought too dear.
Why didst thou tell me that thou wert a king?   24
    Hot. The King hath many marching in his coats.
    Doug. Now, by my sword, I will kill all his coats;
I'll murder all his wardrobe, piece by piece,
Until I meet the King.
    Hot.   Up, and away!
Our soldiers stand full fairly for the day.   29
           [*Exeunt.*

Alarum. Enter FALSTAFF, *solus.*

Fal. Though I could scape shot-free at London,
I fear the shot here; here's no scoring but upon
the pate. Soft! who are you? Sir Walter Blunt.
There's honour for you! Here's no vanity! I
am as hot as molten lead, and as heavy too. God
keep lead out of me! I need no more weight   35
than mine own bowels. I have led my ragamuffins
where they are pepper'd. There's not three of
my hundred and fifty left alive; and they are for
the town's end, to beg during life. But who
comes here?   40

Enter the PRINCE.

Prince. What, stands thou idle here? Lend me
    thy sword.
Many a nobleman lies stark and stiff
Under the hoofs of vaunting enemies,
Whose deaths are yet unreveng'd. I prithee, lend
    me thy sword.   44
    Fal. O Hal, I prithee, give me leave to breathe
a while. Turk Gregory never did such deeds in
arms as I have done this day. I have paid Percy,
I have made him sure.

Prince. He is, indeed; and living to kill thee. I
prithee, lend me thy sword.   50
    Fal. Nay, before God, Hal, if Percy be alive,
thou gets not my sword; but take my pistol, if thou
wilt.
    Prince. Give it me. What, is it in the case?
    Fal. Ay, Hal; 'tis hot, 'tis hot. There's that
will sack a city.   56
        [*The Prince draws it out, and finds it to
         be a bottle of sack.*
    Prince. What, is it a time to jest and dally now?
        [*He throws the bottle at him. Exit.*
    Fal. Well, if Percy be alive, I'll pierce him. If
he do come in my way, so; if he do not, if I   60
come in his willingly, let him make a carbonado
of me. I like not such grinning honour as Sir
Walter hath. Give me life, which if I can save,
so; if not, honour comes unlook'd for, and there's
an end.   [*Exit.*   65

SCENE [IV. *Another part of the field.*]

Alarum. Excursions. Enter the KING, *the* PRINCE
[*wounded*], LORD JOHN OF LANCASTER, *and* EARL
OF WESTMORELAND.

King. I prithee,
Harry, withdraw thyself; thou bleedest too much.
Lord John of Lancaster, go you with him.
    Lan. Not I, my lord, unless I did bleed too.
    Prince. I beseech your Majesty, make up,   5
Lest your retirement do amaze your friends.
    King. I will do so.
My Lord of Westmoreland, lead him to his tent.
    West. Come, my lord, I'll lead you to your tent.
    Prince. Lead me, my lord? I do not need your
    help: 10
And God forbid a shallow scratch should drive
The Prince of Wales from such a field as this,
Where stain'd nobility lies trodden on,
And rebels' arms triumph in massacres!
    Lan. We breathe too long. Come, cousin
    Westmoreland,   15
Our duty this way lies; for God's sake, come.
        [*Exeunt Prince John and Westmoreland.*]
    Prince. By God, thou hast deceiv'd me, Lan-
    caster;
I did not think thee lord of such a spirit.
Before, I lov'd thee as a brother, John;
But now, I do respect thee as my soul.   20
    King. I saw him hold Lord Percy at the point
With lustier maintenance than I did look for
Of such an ungrown warrior.
    Prince.   O, this boy
Lends mettle to us all!   [*Exit.*

Sc. iii, 21. **Semblably:** similarly.   30. **shot-free:** without paying.   46. **Turk Gregory:** Pope Gregory VII (Hildebrand).
61. **carbonado:** meat slashed for broiling.
    Sc. iv, 5. **make up:** advance.   6. **amaze:** confound.   22. **maintenance:** endurance.

Enter DOUGLAS.

Doug. Another king! they grow like Hydra's
heads.   25
I am the Douglas, fatal to all those
That wear those colours on them.   What art thou,
That counterfeit'st the person of a king?

King. The King himself; who, Douglas, grieves
at heart
So many of his shadows thou hast met   30
And not the very King.   I have two boys
Seek Percy and thyself about the field;
But, seeing thou fall'st on me so luckily,
I will assay thee; [so,] defend thyself.

Doug. I fear thou art another counterfeit;   35
And yet, in faith, thou bear'st thee like a king.
But mine I am sure thou art, whoe'er thou be,
And thus I win thee.

They fight; the King being in danger, re-enter
PRINCE OF WALES.

Prince. Hold up thy head, vile Scot, or thou art
like
Never to hold it up again!   The spirits   40
Of valiant Shirley, Stafford, Blunt, are in my arms.
It is the Prince of Wales that threatens thee,
Who never promiseth but he means to pay.
                                    [*They fight: Douglas flies.*
Cheerly, my lord, how fares your Grace?
Sir Nicholas Gawsey hath for succour sent,   45
And so hath Clifton.   I'll to Clifton straight.

King. Stay, and breathe a while.
Thou hast redeem'd thy lost opinion,
And show'd thou mak'st some tender of my life
In this fair rescue thou hast brought to me.   50

Prince. O God! they did me too much injury
That ever said I heark'ned for your death.
If it were so, I might have let alone
The insulting hand of Douglas over you,
Which would have been as speedy in your end   55
As all the poisonous potions in the world,
And sav'd the treacherous labour of your son.

King. Make up to Clifton.   I'll to Sir Nicholas
Gawsey.   [*Exit.*

Enter HOTSPUR.

Hot. If I mistake not, thou art Harry Monmouth.

Prince. Thou speak'st as if I would deny my
name.   60

Hot. My name is Harry Percy.

Prince.   Why, then I see
A very valiant rebel of the name.
I am the Prince of Wales; and think not, Percy,
To share with me in glory any more.

Two stars keep not their motion in one sphere,   65
Nor can one England brook a double reign
Of Harry Percy and the Prince of Wales.

Hot. Nor shall it, Harry; for the hour is come
To end the one of us; and would to God
Thy name in arms were now as great as mine!   70

Prince. I'll make a greater ere I part from thee,
And all the budding honours on thy crest
I'll crop, to make a garland for my head.

Hot. I can no longer brook thy vanities.
                                            [*They fight.*

Enter FALSTAFF.

Fal. Well said, Hal! to it, Hal!   Nay, you shall
find no boy's play here, I can tell you.   76

*Re-enter Douglas; he fights with Falstaff, who falls
down as if he were dead [and exit Douglas.   Hotspur
is wounded, and falls].*

Hot. O, Harry, thou hast robb'd me of my youth!
I better brook the loss of brittle life
Than those proud titles thou hast won of me.
They wound my thoughts worse than thy sword
my flesh.   80
But thoughts, the slaves of life, and life, time's fool,
And time, that takes survey of all the world,
Must have a stop.   O, I could prophesy,
But that the earthy and cold hand of death
Lies on my tongue.   No, Percy, thou art dust, 85
And food for —   [*Dies.*

Prince. For worms, brave Percy.   Fare thee
well, great heart!
Ill-weav'd ambition, how much art thou shrunk!
When that this body did contain a spirit,
A kingdom for it was too small a bound;   90
But now two paces of the vilest earth
Is room enough.   This earth that bears thee dead
Bears not alive so stout a gentleman.
If thou wert sensible of courtesy,
I should not make so dear a show of zeal.   95
But let my favours hide thy mangled face;
And, even in thy behalf, I'll thank myself
For doing these fair rites of tenderness.
Adieu, and take thy praise with thee to heaven!
Thy ignominy sleep with thee in the grave,   100
But not rememb'red in thy epitaph!
                        [*He spieth Falstaff on the ground.*
What, old acquaintance! could not all this flesh
Keep in a little life?   Poor Jack, farewell!
I could have better spar'd a better man.
O, I should have a heavy miss of thee   105
If I were much in love with vanity!

---

34. **[so]** Ff. *and* Q.   48. **opinion:** reputation.   49. **mak'st . . . of:** hast some regard for.   77. S.D. **[and . . . falls]** (Steevens).
the Prince killeth Percie Qq Ff.   81. **thoughts, the slaves** Q.   F reads *thought's the slave.*   But probably *slaves* is in apposition
with *thoughts, fool* with *life*, and *thoughts, fool*, and *time* are all subjects of *Must.*   96. **favours.**   He covers Hotspur's face
with a scarf, or the like.   100. **ignominy:** pronounced *ignomy* which Ff read.

Death hath not struck so fat a deer to-day,
Though many dearer, in this bloody fray.
Embowell'd will I see thee by and by; 109
Till then in blood by noble Percy lie. [*Exit.*

 Fal. (*Rising up.*) Embowell'd! if thou embowel
me to-day, I'll give you leave to powder me and
eat me too to-morrow. 'Sblood, 'twas time to
counterfeit, or that hot termagant Scot had paid
me scot and lot too. Counterfeit? I lie, I am 115
no counterfeit. To die is to be a counterfeit, for
he is but the counterfeit of a man who hath not
the life of a man; but to counterfeit dying, when a
man thereby liveth, is to be no counterfeit, but the
true and perfect image of life indeed. The 120
better part of valour is discretion; in the which
better part I have saved my life. 'Zounds, I am
afraid of this gunpowder Percy though he be dead.
How, if he should counterfeit too and rise? By
my faith, I am afraid he would prove the better 125
counterfeit. Therefore I'll make him sure; yea,
and I'll swear I kill'd him. Why may not he
rise as well as I? Nothing confutes me but eyes,
and nobody sees me. Therefore, sirrah [*stabbing
him*], with a new wound in your thigh, come 130
you along with me.

    [*Takes up Hotspur on his back.*

Re-enter the PRINCE OF WALES *and* LORD JOHN
    OF LANCASTER.

 Prince. Come, brother John; full bravely hast
  thou flesh'd
Thy maiden sword.
 Lan.   But, soft! whom have we here?
Did you not tell me this fat man was dead? 135
 Prince. I did; I saw him dead,
Breathless and bleeding on the ground. Art thou
  alive?
Or is it fantasy that plays upon our eyesight?
I prithee, speak; we will not trust our eyes 139
Without our ears. Thou art not what thou seem'st.
 Fal. No, that's certain; I am not a double man;
but if I be not Jack Falstaff, then am I a Jack.
There is Percy [*throwing the body down*]. If your
father will do me any honour, so; if not, let him
kill the next Percy himself. I look to be either earl
or duke, I can assure you. 146
 Prince. Why, Percy I kill'd myself, and saw
  thee dead.
 Fal. Didst thou? Lord, Lord, how this world
is given to lying! I grant you I was down and
out of breath, and so was he; but we rose both 150
at an instant and fought a long hour by Shrewsbury clock. If I may be believed, so; if not, let
them that should reward valour bear the sin
upon their own heads. I'll take it upon my death,
I gave him this wound in the thigh. If the man 155

were alive and would deny it, 'zounds, I would
make him eat a piece of my sword.
 Lan. This is the strangest tale that ever I
  heard.
 Prince. This is the strangest fellow, brother John.
Come, bring your luggage nobly on your back. 160
For my part, if a lie may do thee grace,
I'll gild it with the happiest terms I have.

    [*A retreat is sounded.*
The trumpet sounds retreat; the day is ours.
Come, brother, let us to the highest of the field,
To see what friends are living, who are dead. 165

   [*Exeunt* [*Prince of Wales and Lancaster*].

 Fal. I'll follow, as they say, for reward. He
that rewards me, God reward him! If I do grow
great, I'll grow less; for I'll purge, and leave
sack, and live cleanly as a nobleman should do.

    [*Exit.*

SCENE [V. *Another part of the field.*]

The trumpets sound. Enter the KING, PRINCE OF
 WALES, LORD JOHN OF LANCASTER, EARL OF
 WESTMORELAND, *with* WORCESTER *and* VERNON
 prisoners.

 King. Thus ever did rebellion find rebuke.
Ill-spirited Worcester! did not we send grace,
Pardon, and terms of love to all of you?
And wouldst thou turn our offers contrary?
Misuse the tenour of thy kinsman's trust? 5
Three knights upon our party slain to-day,
A noble earl, and many a creature else
Had been alive this hour,
If like a Christian thou hadst truly borne
Betwixt our armies true intelligence. 10
 Wor. What I have done my safety urg'd me to;
And I embrace this fortune patiently,
Since not to be avoided it falls on me.
 King. Bear Worcester to the death and Vernon
  too.
Other offenders we will pause upon. 15

   [*Exeunt Worcester and Vernon* [*guarded*].
How goes the field?
 Prince. The noble Scot, Lord Douglas, when he
  saw
The fortune of the day quite turn'd from him,
The noble Percy slain, and all his men
Upon the foot of fear, fled with the rest; 20
And falling from a hill, he was so bruis'd
That the pursuers took him. At my tent
The Douglas is; and I beseech your Grace
I may dispose of him.
 King.   With all my heart.
 Prince. Then, brother John of Lancaster, to
  you
This honourable bounty shall belong. 26

---

112. **powder:** salt. 115. **scot and lot:** completely. 141. **double:** referring to the body of Hotspur he is carrying.

Go to the Douglas, and deliver him
Up to his pleasure, ransomless and free.
His valours shown upon our crests to-day
Have taught us how to cherish such high deeds   30
Even in the bosom of our adversaries.

   Lan. I thank your Grace for this high courtesy,
Which I shall give away immediately.

   King. Then this remains, that we divide our
     power.
You, son John, and my cousin Westmoreland   35

Towards York shall bend you with your dearest
   speed,
To meet Northumberland and the prelate Scroop,
Who, as we hear, are busily in arms.
Myself and you, son Harry, will towards Wales,
To fight with Glendower and the Earl of March.
Rebellion in this land shall lose his sway,   41
Meeting the check of such another day;
And since this business so fair is done,
Let us not leave till all our own be won.   [*Exeunt.*

The Second Part of Henry the Fourth

ON THE TWENTY-THIRD OF AUGUST, 1600, the Second Part of *Henry IV* was entered in the Stationers' Register, and the first and only Quarto was published in the same year with the title: *The Second part of Henrie the fourth, continuing to his death, and coronation of Henri the fift. With the humours of Sir John Falstaffe, and Swaggering Pistoll.* Though the Quarto lacks about 170 lines which appear in the Folio, recent opinion tends to the conclusion that the earlier publication is nearer to Shakespeare's manuscript, and may have been printed from that manuscript. The Folio text lacks 40 lines given by the Quarto and bears marks of revision that suggest that it was printed from a transcript of a prompt-book. The present text is based upon the Quarto, except for the missing 170 lines for which the Folio is the only source. These are enclosed in brackets in the present text.

The reasons for the omissions in the Quarto have been the subject of much discussion. It is not likely, judging from the awkwardness with which the cuts are made, that they were intended merely to produce an acting version. Some may have been due to inadvertence and difficulty in reading the manuscript; others point to political reasons. Eleven references to Richard II appear in the Folio, all of which have been cut out of the Quarto, and it is impossible not to connect this with the Queen's attitude towards Richard's abdication discussed in the Introduction to *Richard II*. Other omissions, such as references to the right of rebellion, may have been due to the political tension during the trial of Essex.

It is evident that the writing of Part II followed closely on that of Part I, and there is general agreement on 1598 as the date of composition.

As in the case of Part I, the historical material is taken chiefly from Holinshed's *Chronicles*. The story of the attack on the Chief Justice follows the account given in Elyot's *Governour* (1531), which had been reproduced in Stow's *Annals*, in either of which Shakespeare may have read it. Suggestions for the scene of the recruiting in Gloucestershire and of the rejection of Falstaff are to be found in the old play, *The Famous Victories of Henry the Fifth*, from which he borrowed in Part I, but they are only suggestions.

Many critics have found Part II inferior to Part I, and it must be admitted that the serious part of the play provides no such dramatic contrast of character as that between Hotspur and the Prince in the earlier play. Nor does the victory over the rebels obtained by the treachery of Prince John compare in effectiveness with the climax provided by the battle of Shrewsbury. Shakespeare had the disadvantage also of having to make a plot out of the same kind of material as he had just used — the fomenting of conspiracy and the overthrow of rebellion. This difficulty is probably responsible for the increased amount of space given to comic scenes.

The theme of the relation of father and son is, however, developed much more fully and with much more emotional power. There is in the treatment of the King's despair over the Prince's wildness a characteristic strain of Shakespeare's favorite device of dramatic irony. The audience of Elizabeth's time all knew that Hal was to turn out all right, and Shakespeare made sure they would not forget it by making the Prince remind them of it as early as the end of I.ii of Part I. This does not detract from the pathos of Henry's anxiety and depression, but it makes possible a fuller enjoyment of the comedy element.

Whatever may be thought of the comparative merit of the historical scenes, there is no decline in the part of the play carried by Falstaff. The conversations between him and the Chief Justice, the Tavern riots in which Mrs. Quickly is developed from the sketch in Part I and Doll Tearsheet and Pistol are added to the group, and the scenes with Shallow and Silence in Gloucestershire are among the greatest triumphs of Shakespearean comedy. The part played by the Prince in these is a diminishing one, the dramatist clearly preparing him and us for his final withdrawal. When this occurs in the great scene following the coronation and the reconciliation with the Lord Chief Justice, the transformation of the wild prince into the hero-king is complete. This had obviously been contemplated by Shakespeare from the first and was, of course, inevitable. Yet few episodes in these plays have been more bitterly resented than the rejection of Falstaff. Much argument has been waged in attack and defense, all of which goes to show how completely and perhaps uniquely Shakespeare has succeeded in producing in his greatest comic creation the absolute illusion of reality.

THE SECOND PART OF HENRY THE FOURTH

[DRAMATIS PERSONÆ]

RUMOUR, *the Presenter.*
KING HENRY IV.
HENRY, PRINCE [OF WALES], *afterwards crowned* Henry V.
PRINCE JOHN OF LANCASTER, } *sons to Henry*
[PRINCE] HUMPHREY OF } *IV and breth-*
  GLOUCESTER, } *ren to Henry*
THOMAS [DUKE] OF CLARENCE, } *V.*
[EARL OF] NORTHUMBERLAND, }
[SCROOP,] *archbishop of York,* }
[LORD] MOWBRAY, } *opposites*
[LORD] HASTINGS, } *against King*
LORD BARDOLPH, } *Henry IV.*
TRAVERS, } *retainers of North-*
MORTON, } *umberland,*
[SIR JOHN] COLVILLE, }
[EARL OF] WARWICK, }
[EARL OF] WESTMORELAND, }
[EARL OF] SURREY, } *of the King's*
GOWER, } *Party.*
HARCOURT, }
LORD CHIEF JUSTICE, }

[SIR JOHN] FALSTAFF, }
HIS PAGE, }
POINS, }
BARDOLPH, } *irregular Humourists.*
PISTOL, }
PETO, }
SHALLOW, } *both country Justices.*
SILENCE, }
DAVY, *servant to Shallow.*
FANG *and* SNARE, *two Sergeants.*
MOULDY, }
SHADOW, }
WART, } *country soldiers.*
FEEBLE, }
BULLCALF, }

NORTHUMBERLAND'S WIFE.
[LADY PERCY], *Percy's Widow.*
QUICKLY, *hostess [of a tavern in Eastcheap].*
DOLL TEARSHEET.

[Lords and attendants; Porter] Drawers, Beadles, Grooms [Servants, etc. A Dancer as] Epilogue.

[SCENE: *England.*]

INDUCTION

[*Warkworth. Before the castle.*]

Enter RUMOUR, *painted full of tongues.*

Rum. Open your ears; for which of you will stop
The vent of hearing when loud Rumour speaks?
I, from the orient to the drooping west,
Making the wind my post-horse, still unfold
The acts commenced on this ball of earth. 5
Upon my tongues continual slanders ride,
The which in every language I pronounce,
Stuffing the ears of men with false reports.
I speak of peace, while covert enmity
Under the smile of safety wounds the world; 10
And who but Rumour, who but only I,
Make fearful musters and prepar'd defence,
Whiles the big year, swoln with some other grief,
Is thought with child by the stern tyrant war,
And no such matter? Rumour is a pipe 15
Blown by surmises, jealousies, conjectures,
And of so easy and so plain a stop

The list of Dramatis Personæ is substantially as given in F₁.

That the blunt monster with uncounted heads,
The still-discordant wav'ring multitude,
Can play upon it. But what need I thus   20
My well-known body to anatomize
Among my household? Why is Rumour here?
I run before King Harry's victory,
Who in a bloody field by Shrewsbury
Hath beaten down young Hotspur and his troops,
Quenching the flame of bold rebellion   26
Even with the rebel's blood. But what mean I
To speak so true at first? My office is
To noise abroad that Harry Monmouth fell
Under the wrath of noble Hotspur's sword,   30
And that the King before the Douglas' rage
Stoop'd his anointed head as low as death.
This have I rumour'd through the peasant towns
Between that royal field of Shrewsbury
And this worm-eaten [hold] of ragged stone,   35
[Where] Hotspur's father, old Northumberland,
Lies crafty-sick. The posts come tiring on,
And not a man of them brings other news
Than they have learn'd of me. From Rumour's
     tongues
They bring smooth comforts false, worse than true
     wrongs.   [*Exit.*   40

ACT I

SCENE [I. *The same.*]

Enter LORD BARDOLPH *at one door.*

L. Bard. Who keeps the gate here, ho?
     [*The* PORTER *opens the gate.*]
                Where is the Earl?
Port. What shall I say you are?
L. Bard.   Tell thou the Earl
That the Lord Bardolph doth attend him here.
Port. His lordship is walk'd forth into the
     orchard.
Please it your honour, knock but at the gate,   5
And he himself will answer.

Enter NORTHUMBERLAND.

L. Bard.   Here comes the Earl.
                     [*Exit Porter.*]
North. What news, Lord Bardolph? Every
     minute now
Should be the father of some stratagem.
The times are wild; contention, like a horse
Full of high feeding, madly hath broke loose   10
And bears down all before him.
L. Bard.   Noble Earl,
I bring you certain news from Shrewsbury.
North. Good, an God will!
L. Bard.   As good as heart can wish.
The King is almost wounded to the death;

And, in the fortune of my lord your son,   15
Prince Harry slain outright; and both the Blunts
Kill'd by the hand of Douglas; young Prince John
And Westmoreland and Stafford fled the field;
And Harry Monmouth's brawn, the hulk Sir John,
Is prisoner to your son. O, such a day,   20
So fought, so followed, and so fairly won,
Came not till now to dignify the times,
Since Cæsar's fortunes!
North.   How is this deriv'd?
Saw you the field? Came you from Shrewsbury?
L. Bard. I spake, with one, my lord, that came
     from thence,   25
A gentleman well bred and of good name,
That freely rend'red me these news for true.

Enter TRAVERS.

North. Here comes my servant Travers, who I
     sent
On Tuesday last to listen after news.
L. Bard. My lord, I over-rode him on the way;
And he is furnish'd with no certainties   31
More than he haply may retail from me.
North. Now, Travers, what good tidings comes
     with you?
Tra. My lord, Sir John Umfrevile turn'd me back
With joyful tidings; and, being better hors'd,   35
Out-rode me. After him came spurring hard
A gentleman, almost forspent with speed,
That stopp'd by me to breathe his bloodied horse.
He ask'd the way to Chester; and of him
I did demand what news from Shrewsbury.   40
He told me that rebellion had bad luck,
And that young Harry Percy's spur was cold.
With that, he gave his able horse the head,
And bending forward struck his armed heels
Against the panting sides of his poor jade   45
Up to the rowel-head, and starting so
He seem'd in running to devour the way,
Staying no longer question.
North.   Ha! Again.
Said he young Harry Percy's spur was cold?
Of Hotspur Coldspur? That rebellion   50
Had met ill luck?
L. Bard.   My lord, I'll tell you what:
If my young lord your son have not the day,
Upon mine honour, for a silken point
I'll give my barony. Never talk of it.
North. Why should that gentleman that rode
     by Travers   55
Give then such instances of loss?
L. Bard.   Who, he?
He was some hilding fellow that had stolen
The horse he rode on, and, upon my life,
Spoke at a venture. Look, here comes more news.

Ind., 18. **blunt**: stupid. 29. **Harry Monmouth**: Prince Henry. 35. **[hold]** (Theobald). *hole* QF. 36. **[Where]** F. *When* Q.
Act I, sc. i, 19. **brawn**: mass of flesh. 53. **point**: lace, tying doublet to breeches. 57. **hilding**: worthless.

Enter MORTON.

North. Yea, this man's brow, like to a title-leaf,
Foretells the nature of a tragic volume.   61
So looks the strand whereon the imperious flood
Hath left a witness'd usurpation.
Say, Morton, didst thou come from Shrewsbury?
  Mor. I ran from Shrewsbury, my noble lord,   65
Where hateful Death put on his ugliest mask
To fright our party.
  North.   How doth my son and brother?
Thou tremblest; and the whiteness in thy cheek
Is apter than thy tongue to tell thy errand.
Even such a man, so faint, so spiritless,   70
So dull, so dead in look, so woe-begone,
Drew Priam's curtain in the dead of night
And would have told him half his Troy was burnt;
But Priam found the fire ere he his tongue,
And I my Percy's death ere thou report'st it.   75
This thou wouldst say, "Your son did thus and
        thus;
Your brother thus; so fought the noble Douglas;"
Stopping my greedy ear with their bold deeds;
But in the end, to stop my ear indeed,
Thou hast a sigh to blow away this praise,   80
Ending with "Brother, son, and all are dead."
  Mor. Douglas is living, and your brother yet;
But, for my lord your son, —
  North.   Why, he is dead.
See what a ready tongue suspicion hath!
He that but fears the thing he would not know   85
Hath by instinct knowledge from others' eyes
That what he fear'd is chanc'd. Yet speak, Morton;
Tell thou an earl his divination lies,
And I will take it as a sweet disgrace
And make thee rich for doing me such wrong.   90
  Mor. You are too great to be by me gainsaid;
Your spirit is too true, your fears too certain.
  North. Yet, for all this, say not that Percy's dead.
I see a strange confession in thine eye.
Thou shak'st thy head and hold'st it fear or sin   95
To speak a truth. If he be slain, [say so;]
The tongue offends not that reports his death;
And he doth sin that doth belie the dead,
Not he which says the dead is not alive.
Yet the first bringer of unwelcome news   100
Hath but a losing office, and his tongue
Sounds ever after as a sullen bell,
Rememb'red tolling a departing friend.
  L. Bard. I cannot think, my lord, your son is
        dead.
  Mor. I am sorry I should force you to believe   105
That which I would to God I had not seen;
But these mine eyes saw him in bloody state,
Rend'ring faint quittance, wearied and outbreath'd,

To Harry Monmouth; whose swift wrath beat down
The never-daunted Percy to the earth,   110
From whence with life he never more sprung up.
In few, his death, whose spirit lent a fire
Even to the dullest peasant in his camp,
Being bruited once, took fire and heat away
From the best-temper'd courage in his troops;   115
For from his metal was his party steel'd;
Which once in him abated, all the rest
Turn'd on themselves, like dull and heavy lead.
And as the thing that's heavy in itself
Upon enforcement flies with greatest speed,   120
So did our men, heavy in Hotspur's loss,
Lend to this weight such lightness with their fear
That arrows fled not swifter toward their aim
Than did our soldiers, aiming at their safety,
Fly from the field. Then was that noble Worcester
[Too] soon ta'en prisoner; and that furious Scot,   126
The bloody Douglas, whose well-labouring sword
Had three times slain th' appearance of the King,
Gan vail his stomach and did grace the shame
Of those that turn'd their backs, and in his flight,
Stumbling in fear, was took. The sum of all   131
Is that the King hath won, and hath sent out
A speedy power to encounter you, my lord,
Under the conduct of young Lancaster
And Westmoreland. This is the news at full.   135
  North. For this I shall have time enough to
        mourn.
In poison there is physic; and these news,
Having been well, that would have made me sick,
Being sick, have in some measure made me well.
And as the wretch whose fever-weak'ned joints,
Like strengthless hinges, buckle under life,   141
Impatient of his fit, breaks like a fire
Out of his keeper's arms, even so my limbs,
Weak'ned with grief, being now enrag'd with grief,
Are thrice themselves. Hence, therefore, thou nice
        crutch!   145
A scaly gauntlet now with joints of steel
Must glove this hand; and hence, thou sickly quoif!
Thou art a guard too wanton for the head
Which princes, flesh'd with conquest, aim to hit.
Now bind my brows with iron; and approach   150
The ragged'st hour that time and spite dare bring
To frown upon th' enrag'd Northumberland!
Let heaven kiss earth! Now let not Nature's hand
Keep the wild flood confin'd! Let order die!
And let this world no longer be a stage   155
To feed contention in a ling'ring act;
But let one spirit of the first-born Cain
Reign in all bosoms, that, each heart being set
On bloody courses, the rude scene may end,
And darkness be the burier of the dead!   160

---

63. **witness'd:** witness of.   87. **is chanc'd:** has happened.   96. **[say so]** F. Om. Q.   112. **In few:** in short.   126. **[Too]**
F. *So* Q.   129. **Gan ... stomach:** began to lower his courage.   144. **grief:** pain. The second *grief* has its modern sense.
145. **nice:** effeminate.   147. **quoif:** cap.   148. **wanton:** luxurious.   149. **flesh'd:** made fierce.

[Tra.] This strained passion doth you wrong, my
    lord.
L. Bard. Sweet Earl, divorce not wisdom from
    your honour.
Mor. The lives of all your loving complices
[Lean] on your health; the which, if you give o'er
To stormy passion, must perforce decay. 165
[You cast th' event of war, my noble lord,
And summ'd the account of chance before you said,
"Let us make head." It was your presurmise
That in the dole of blows your son might drop.
You knew he walk'd o'er perils, on an edge, 170
More likely to fall in than to get o'er;
You were advis'd his flesh was capable
Of wounds and scars, and that his forward spirit
Would lift him where most trade of danger rang'd;
Yet did you say, "Go forth!" and none of this, 175
Though strongly apprehended, could restrain
The stiff-borne action. What hath then befall'n,
Or what hath this bold enterprise brought forth,
More than that being which was like to be?]
L. Bard. We all that are engaged to this loss 180
Knew that we ventur'd on such dangerous seas
That if we wrought out life 'twas ten to one;
And yet we ventur'd, for the gain propos'd
Chok'd the respect of likely peril fear'd;
And since we are o'erset, venture again. 185
Come, we will all put forth, body and goods.
Mor. 'Tis more than time; and, my most noble
    lord,
I hear for certain and [do] speak the truth,
[The gentle Archbishop of York is up
With well-appointed powers. He is a man 190
Who with a double surety binds his followers.
My lord your son had only but the corpse,
But shadows and the shows of men, to fight;
For that same word, rebellion, did divide
The action of their bodies from their souls; 195
And they did fight with queasiness, constrain'd
As men drink potions, that their weapons only
Seem'd on our side; but, for their spirits and souls,
This word, rebellion, it had froze them up,
As fish are in a pond. But now the Bishop 200
Turns insurrection to religion.
Suppos'd sincere and holy in his thoughts,
He's follow'd both with body and with mind;
And doth enlarge his rising with the blood
Of fair King Richard, scrap'd from Pomfret stones;
Derives from heaven his quarrel and his cause; 206
Tells them he doth bestride a bleeding land,
Gasping for life under great Bolingbroke;

And more and less do flock to follow him.]
North. I knew of this before; but, to speak truth,
This present grief had wip'd it from my mind. 211
Go in with me; and counsel every man
The aptest way for safety and revenge.
Get posts and letters, and make friends with
    speed, —
Never so few, and never yet more need. 215
                       [Exeunt.

SCENE [II. *London. A street.*]
Enter FALSTAFF, *with his* PAGE *bearing his
sword and buckler.*

Fal. Sirrah, you giant, what says the doctor to
my water?
Page. He said, sir, the water itself was a good
healthy water; but, for the party that ow'd it,
he might have moe diseases than he knew for. 6
Fal. Men of all sorts take a pride to gird at me.
The brain of this foolish-compounded clay, man,
is not able to invent anything that intends to
laughter more than I invent or is invented on 10
me. I am not only witty in myself, but the cause
that wit is in other men. I do here walk before
thee like a sow that hath overwhelm'd all her
litter but one. If the Prince put thee into my
service for any other reason than to set me off, 15
why then I have no judgement. Thou whoreson
mandrake, thou art fitter to be worn in my cap
than to wait at my heels. I was never mann'd
with an agate till now; but I will inset you neither
in gold nor silver, but in vile apparel, and 20
send you back again to your master, for a jewel, —
the juvenal, the Prince your master, whose chin
is not yet fledg'd. I will sooner have a beard grow
in the palm of my hand than he shall get one off
his cheek; and yet he will not stick to say his 25
face is a face royal. God may finish it when he
will, 'tis not a hair amiss yet. He may keep it
still at a face royal, for a barber shall never earn
sixpence out of it; and yet he'll be crowing as if
he had writ man ever since his father was a 30
bachelor. He may keep his own grace, but he's
almost out of mine, I can assure him. What said
Master Dommelton about the satin for my short
cloak and my slops? 34
Page. He said, sir, you should procure him
better assurance than Bardolph. He would not
take his band and yours. He lik'd not the security. 38

161. **[Tra.]** (Capell). *Umfr.* Q. 164. **[Lean]** F. *Leave* Q. 166–79. F. Om. Q. 166. **cast th' event:** considered the outcome. 168. **make head:** gather troops. 169. **dole:** dealing. 172. **advis'd:** aware. 172–73. **capable Of:** susceptible to. 180. **engaged to:** involved in. 182. **That ... one:** that it was ten to one against our surviving. 184. **Chok'd the respect:** checked consideration. 186. **put forth:** stake. 188. **[do]** F. *dare* Q. 189–209. F. Om. Q. 192. **corpse:** bodies. 196. **queasiness:** nausea.

Sc. ii, 5. **ow'd:** owned. 17. **mandrake:** plant with a forked root. 19. **agate:** a stone often carved into little figures. 26, 28. **royal:** with a pun on *royal,* a coin bearing the king's head. 34. **slops:** wide breeches. 37. **band:** bond.

Fal. Let him be damn'd like the glutton! Pray God his tongue be hotter! A whoreson Achitophel! a rascally yea-for-sooth knave! to bear a gentleman in hand, and then stand upon security! The whoreson smooth-pates do now wear nothing but high shoes, and bunches of keys at their girdles; and if a man is through with them in honest 45 taking up, then they must stand upon security. I had as lief they would put ratsbane in my mouth as offer to stop it with security. I look'd 'a should have sent me two and twenty yards of satin, as I am a true knight, and he sends me security. 50 Well, he may sleep in security; for he hath the horn of abundance, and yet the lightness of his wife shines through it; and yet cannot he see; though he have his own lanthorn to light him. Where's Bardolph? 55

Page. He's gone [into] Smithfield to buy your worship a horse.

Fal. I bought him in Paul's, and he'll buy me a horse in Smithfield. An I could get me but a wife in the stews, I were mann'd, hors'd, and wiv'd. 61

Enter the Lord Chief Justice *and* Servant.

Page. Sir, here comes the nobleman that committed the Prince for striking him about Bardolph.

Fal. Wait close; I will not see him. 65

Ch. Just. What's he that goes there?

Serv. Falstaff, an 't please your lordship.

Ch. Just. He that was in question for the robbery? 69

Serv. He, my lord; but he hath since done good service at Shrewsbury, and, as I hear, is now going with some charge to the Lord John of Lancaster.

Ch. Just. What, to York? Call him back again.

Serv. Sir John Falstaff! 76

Fal. Boy, tell him I am deaf.

Page. You must speak louder; my master is deaf. 79

Ch. Just. I am sure he is, to the hearing of anything good. Go, pluck him by the elbow; I must speak with him.

Serv. Sir John! 83

Fal. What! a young knave, and begging! Is there not wars? Is there not employment? Doth not the King lack subjects? Do not the rebels need soldiers? Though it be a shame to be on any side but one, it is worse shame to beg than to be on the worst side, were it worse than the name of rebellion can tell how to make it. 90

Serv. You mistake me, sir.

Fal. Why, sir, did I say you were an honest man? Setting my knighthood and my soldiership aside, I had lied in my throat, if I had said so. 94

Serv. I pray you, sir, then set your knighthood and your soldiership aside; and give me leave to tell you you lie in your throat if you say I am any other than an honest man. 98

Fal. I give thee leave to tell me so! I lay aside that which grows to me! If thou get'st any leave of me, hang me; if thou tak'st leave, thou wert better be hang'd. You hunt counter; hence! avaunt! 103

Serv. Sir, my lord would speak with you.

Ch. Just. Sir John Falstaff, a word with you.

Fal. My good lord! God give your lordship good time of day. I am glad to see your lordship abroad. I heard say your lordship was sick; I 108 hope your lordship goes abroad by advice. Your lordship, though not clean past your youth, [hath] yet some smack of [age] in you, some relish of the saltness of time in you; and I most humbly beseech your lordship to have a reverent care of your health. 114

Ch. Just. Sir John, I sent for you before your expedition to Shrewsbury.

Fal. An't please your lordship, I hear his Majesty is return'd with some discomfort from Wales. 119

Ch. Just. I talk not of his Majesty. You would not come when I sent for you.

Fal. And I hear, moreover, his Highness is fallen into this same whoreson apoplexy.

Ch. Just. Well, God mend him! I pray you, let me speak with you. 126

Fal. This apoplexy, as I take it, is a kind of lethargy, an't please your lordship, a kind of sleeping in the blood, a whoreson tingling.

Ch. Just. What tell you me of it? Be it as it is. 130

Fal. It hath it original from much grief, from study, and perturbation of the brain. I have read the cause of his effects in Galen. It is a kind of deafness. 134

Ch. Just. I think you are fallen into the disease; for you hear not what I say to you.

[Fal.] Very well, my lord, very well. Rather, an 't please you, it is the disease of not listening, the malady of not marking, that I am troubled withal. 140

Ch. Just. To punish you by the heels would

---

39. **glutton:** Dives (*Luke* xvi.19). 40. **Achitophel:** Absalom's adviser (II *Samuel*, xv ff.). 41. **yea-for-sooth:** a mild oath. 42. **bear . . . in hand:** lead on. 45. **through:** straightforward. 46. **taking up:** ordering on credit. 52–54. **horn . . . lanthorn:** a play on **horn** (1) cornucopia, (2) the sign of the cuckold, and (3) the window of a lantern. 55. **Where's Bardolph?** Q inserts in l. 53, before *and yet.* 56. **[into]** F. *in* Q. 58. **Paul's.** Men seeking service paraded in St. Paul's. 60. **stews:** houses of ill fame. 72. **charge:** troops. 102. **counter:** in the wrong direction. 110. **[hath]** F. *have* Q. 111. **[age]** F. *an ague* Q. 137. **[Fal.]** F. *Old.* Q. A trace of Oldcastle, the earlier name for Falstaff. See Introduction to Part I.

amend the attention of your ears; and I care not
if I do become your physician.   143

Fal. I am as poor as Job, my lord, but not so
patient. Your lordship may minister the potion
of imprisonment to me in respect of poverty; but
how I should be your patient to follow your pre-
scriptions, the wise may make some dram of a
scruple, or indeed a scruple itself.   149

Ch. Just. I sent for you, when there were matters
against you for your life, to come speak with me.

Fal. As I was then advis'd by my learned counsel
in the laws of this land-service, I did not come.   155

Ch. Just. Well, the truth is, Sir John, you live
in great infamy.

Fal. He that buckles himself in my belt cannot
live in less.

Ch. Just. Your means are very slender, and your
waste is great.   161

Fal. I would it were otherwise; I would my
means were greater, and my waist [slenderer].

Ch. Just. You have misled the youthful prince.

Fal. The young prince hath misled me. I am
the fellow with the great belly, and he my dog.   166

Ch. Just. Well, I am loath to gall a new-heal'd
wound. Your day's service at Shrewsbury hath
a little gilded over your night's exploit on Gadshill.
You may thank th' unquiet time for your quiet
o'er-posting that action.   171

Fal. My lord?

Ch. Just. But since all is well, keep it so. Wake
not a sleeping wolf.

Fal. To wake a wolf is as bad as smell a fox.   176

Ch. Just. What! you are as a candle, the better
part burnt out.

Fal. A wassail candle, my lord, all tallow. If
I did say of wax, my growth would approve the
truth.   181

Ch. Just. There is not a white hair in your face
but should have his effect of gravity.

Fal. His effect of gravy, gravy, gravy.

Ch. Just. You follow the young prince up and
down, like his ill angel.   186

Fal. Not so, my lord. Your ill angel is light;
but I hope he that looks upon me will take me
without weighing; and yet, in some respects, I
grant, I cannot go. I cannot tell. Virtue is of   190
so little regard in these costermongers' times that
true Valour is turned bear-herd; Pregnancy is made
a tapster, and his quick wit wasted in giving reckonings; all the other gifts appertinent to man, as
the malice of [this] age shapes them, are not   195
worth a gooseberry. You that are old consider

not the capacities of us that are young; you do
measure the heat of our livers with the bitterness
of your galls; and we that are in the vaward of our
youth, I must confess, are wags too.   200

Ch. Just. Do you set down your name in the
scroll of youth, that are written down old with
all the characters of age? Have you not a moist
eye, a dry hand, a yellow cheek, a white beard,
a decreasing leg, an increasing belly? Is not   205
your voice broken, your wind short, your chin
double, your wit single, and every part about
you blasted with antiquity? And will you yet
call yourself young? Fie, fie, fie, Sir John!   209

Fal. My lord, I was born about three of the
clock in the afternoon, with a white head and
something a round belly. For my voice, I have
lost it with hallooing and singing of anthems. To
approve my youth further, I will not. The truth is,
I am only old in judgement and understanding;   215
and he that will caper with me for a thousand
marks, let him lend me the money, and have at
him! For the box of the ear that the Prince gave
you, he gave it like a rude prince, and you took
it like a sensible lord. I have check'd him for it,
and the young lion repents; marry, not in ashes
and sackcloth, but in new silk and old sack.   222

Ch. Just. Well, God send the Prince a better
companion!

Fal. God send the companion a better prince!
I cannot rid my hands of him.   226

Ch. Just. Well, the King hath sever'd you [and
Prince Harry]. I hear you are going with Lord
John of Lancaster against the Archbishop and the
Earl of Northumberland.   230

Fal. Yea, I thank your pretty sweet wit for it.
But look you pray, all you that kiss my lady
Peace at home, that our armies join not in a hot
day; for, by the Lord, I take but two shirts out with
me, and I mean not to sweat extraordinarily.   235
If it be a hot day, and I brandish anything but a
bottle, I would I might never spit white again.
There is not a dangerous action can peep out his
head but I am thrust upon it. Well, I cannot last
ever; but it was alway yet the trick of our   240
English nation, if they have a good thing, to make
it too common. If ye will needs say I am an old
man, you should give me rest. I would to God
my name were not so terrible to the enemy as it is.
I were better to be eaten to death with a rust than
to be scoured to nothing with perpetual motion.   247

Ch. Just. Well, be honest, be honest; and God
bless your expedition!

---

148. **dram of a scruple**: trifle of a doubt, punning on *scruple*, a small weight. 163. **[slenderer]** F. *slander* Q. 171. **o'er-**
posting: getting over the results of. 179. **wassail**: festival. 187. **angel**: a pun on *angel*, the coin. **light**: underweight. 190.
go: pass (as genuine). 191. **costermongers'**: i.e., commercial. 192. **Pregnancy**: readiness of wit. 195. **[this]** F. *his* Q.
199. **vaward**: vanguard. 222. **sack**: Spanish wine. 227. **[and Prince Harry]** F. Om. Q. 237. **spit white**. Not satisfactorily
explained. "Be thirsty" is a possible meaning. 240–247. Q. Om. F.

Fal. Will your lordship lend me a thousand pound to furnish me forth?

Ch. Just. Not a penny, not a penny; you are too impatient to bear crosses. Fare you well! Commend me to my cousin Westmoreland.   254

           [*Exeunt Chief Justice and Servant.*]

Fal. If I do, fillip me with a three-man beetle. A man can no more separate age and covetousness than 'a can part young limbs and lechery; but the gout galls the one, and the pox pinches the other, and so both the degrees prevent my curses. Boy!

Page. Sir?   261

Fal. What money is in my purse?

Page. Seven groats and two pence.   263

Fal. I can get no remedy against this consumption of the purse. Borrowing only lingers and lingers it out, but the disease is incurable. Go bear this letter to my Lord of Lancaster; this to the Prince; this to the Earl of Westmoreland; and this to old Mistress Ursula, whom I have weekly sworn to marry since I perceiv'd the first white 270 hair of my chin. About it. You know where to find me. [*Exit Page.*] A pox of this gout! or, a gout of this pox! for the one or the other plays the rogue with my great toe. 'Tis no matter if I do halt; I have the wars for my colour, and my pension shall seem the more reasonable. A good wit will make use of anything. I will turn diseases to commodity.   [*Exit.* 278

SCENE [III. *York. The Archbishop's palace.*]

Enter the ARCHBISHOP, *the* Lords HASTINGS, MOWBRAY (EARL MARSHAL), *and* BARDOLPH.

Arch. Thus have you heard our cause and known
     our means;
And, my most noble friends, I pray you all,
Speak plainly your opinions of our hopes.
And first, Lord Marshal, what say you to it?

Mowb. I well allow the occasion of our arms;   5
But gladly would be better satisfied
How in our means we should advance ourselves
To look with forehead bold and big enough
Upon the power and puissance of the King.

Hast. Our present musters grow upon the file   10
To five and twenty thousand men of choice;
And our supplies live largely in the hope
Of great Northumberland, whose bosom burns
With an incensed fire of injuries.

L. Bard. The question then, Lord Hastings,
     standeth thus: 15

Whether our present five and twenty thousand
May hold up head without Northumberland?

Hast. With him, we may.

L. Bard.   Yea, marry, there's the point!
But if without him we be thought too feeble,
My judgement is, we should not step too far   20
[Till we had his assistance by the hand;
For, in a theme so bloody-fac'd as this,
Conjecture, expectation, and surmise
Of aids incertain should not be admitted].

Arch. 'Tis very true, Lord Bardolph; for indeed
It was young Hotspur's case at Shrewsbury.   26

L. Bard. It was, my lord; who lin'd himself with
     hope,
Eating the air, and promise of supply,
Flatt'ring himself in project of a power
Much smaller than the smallest of his thoughts;   30
And so, with great imagination
Proper to madmen, led his powers to death,
And winking leap'd into destruction.

Hast. But, by your leave, it never yet did hurt
To lay down likelihoods and forms of hope.   35

L. Bard. [Yes, if this present quality of war
Needed the instant action. A cause on foot
Lives so in hope as in an early spring
We see th' appearing buds, which to prove fruit
Hope gives not so much warrant, as despair   40
That frosts will bite them. When we mean to build,
We first survey the plot, then draw the model;
And when we see the figure of the house,
Then must we rate the cost of the erection;
Which if we find outweighs ability,   45
What do we then but draw anew the model
In fewer offices, or at least desist
To build at all? Much more, in this great work,
Which is almost to pluck a kingdom down
And set another up, should we survey   50
The plot of situation and the model,
Consent upon a sure foundation,
Question surveyors, know our own estate,
How able such a work to undergo,
To weigh against his opposite; or else]   55
We fortify in paper and in figures,
Using the names of men instead of men;
Like one that draws the model of a house
Beyond his power to build it; who, half through,
Gives o'er and leaves his part-created cost   60
A naked subject to the weeping clouds
And waste for churlish winter's tyranny.

Hast. Grant that our hopes, yet likely of fair
     birth,

---

253. **crosses:** (1) afflictions, (2) coins.   255. **fillip...beetle:** toss me into the air from the end of a board, the other end being struck by a rammer worked by three men.   260. **degrees:** kinds (of disease). **prevent:** anticipate.   275. **colour:** excuse.   278. **commodity:** advantage.

Sc. iii, 10. **file:** list.   12. **supplies:** reinforcements.   21–24. F. Om. Q.   27. **lin'd:** supported.   29. **project:** idea.   33. **winking:** with eyes shut.   36–55. F. Om. Q.   37. **Needed** (Gould conj.). *Indeed* F.   47. **offices:** rooms for service.   52. **Consent:** agree.   53. **estate:** resources.   55. **weigh...opposite:** balance the expenditure.   60. **part-created cost:** expensive half-built house.

Should be still-born, and that we now possess'd
The utmost man of expectation,   65
I think we are [a] body strong enough,
Even as we are, to equal with the King.

   L. Bard. What, is the King but five and twenty
      thousand?

   Hast. To us no more; nay, not so much, Lord
Bardolph.
For his divisions, as the times do brawl,   70
[Are] in three heads: one power against the French,
And one against Glendower; perforce a third
Must take up us. So is the unfirm King
In three divided; and his coffers sound
With hollow poverty and emptiness.   75

   Arch. That he should draw his several strengths
      together
And come against us in full puissance,
Need not be dreaded.

   Hast.   If he should do so,
[To] French and Welsh he leaves his back unarm'd,
They baying him at the heels. Never fear that.

   L. Bard. Who is it like should lead his forces
      hither?   81

   Hast. The Duke of Lancaster and Westmoreland;
Against the Welsh, himself and Harry Monmouth;
But who is substituted 'gainst the French,
I have no certain notice.

   [*Arch.*   Let us on,   85
And publish the occasion of our arms.
The commonwealth is sick of their own choice;
Their over-greedy love hath surfeited.
An habitation giddy and unsure
Hath he that buildeth on the vulgar heart.   90
O thou fond many, with what loud applause
Didst thou beat heaven with blessing Bolingbroke
Before he was what thou wouldst have him be!
And being now trimm'd in thine own desires,
Thou, beastly feeder, art so full of him,   95
That thou provok'st thyself to cast him up.
So, so, thou common dog, didst thou disgorge
Thy glutton bosom of the royal Richard;
And now thou wouldst eat thy dead vomit up,
And howl'st to find it. What trust is in these
      times?   100
They that, when Richard liv'd, would have him die,
Are now become enamour'd on his grave.
Thou, that threw'st dust upon his goodly head
When through proud London he came sighing on
After th' admired heels of Bolingbroke,   105
Cri'st now, "O earth, yield us that king again,
And take thou this!" O thoughts of men accurs'd!
Past and to come seems best; things present
      worst.]

   Mowb. Shall we go draw our numbers and set on?

   Hast. We are Time's subjects, and Time bids
be gone.   [*Exeunt.*   110

ACT II

SCENE I. [*London. A street.*]

Enter HOSTESS, FANG [*and his Boy with her,*]
    and SNARE *following.*

   Host. Master Fang, have you ent'red the action?

   Fang. It is ent'red.

   Host. Where's your yeoman? Is't a lusty
yeoman? Will 'a stand to't?   5

   Fang. Sirrah, where's Snare?

   Host. O Lord, ay! good Master Snare.

   Snare. Here, here.

   Fang. Snare, we must arrest Sir John Falstaff.

   Host. Yea, good Master Snare; I have ent'red
him and all.   11

   Snare. It may chance cost some of us our lives,
for he will stab.

   Host. Alas the day! take heed of him. He
stabb'd me in mine own house, [and that] most   15
beastly. In good faith, 'a cares not what mischief
he does, if his weapon be out. He will foin like
any devil; he will spare neither man, woman, nor
child.   19

   Fang. If I can close with him, I care not for his
thrust.

   Host. No, nor I neither. I'll be at your elbow.

   Fang. An I but fist him once; an 'a come but
within my vice, —   24

   Host. I am undone by his going; I warrant you,
he's an infinitive thing upon my score. Good
Master Fang, hold him sure. Good Master Snare,
let him not scape. 'A comes continuantly to Pie-
corner — saving your manhoods — to buy a saddle;
and he is indited to dinner to the Lubber's-head   30
in Lumbert street, to Master Smooth's the silk-
man. I pray you, since my exion is ent'red and
my case so openly known to the world, let him be
brought in to his answer. A hundred mark is a
long one for a poor lone woman to bear; and I   35
have borne, and borne, and borne, and have been
fubb'd off, and fubb'd off, and fubb'● off, from this
day to that day, that it is a shame to be thought on.
There is no honesty in such dealing; unless a woman
should be made an ass and a beast, to bear   40
every knave's wrong. Yonder he comes; and that
arrant malmsey-nose knave, Bardolph, with him.
Do your offices, do your offices, Master Fang and
Master Snare; do me, do me, do me your offices.   45

66. [a] F. *so* Q. 70. do brawl: are disturbed. 71. [Are] F. *And* Q. 78. be F. *to be* Q. 79. [To] (Capell). Om. Q.
85–108. F. Om. Q. 91. fond many: foolish multitude.
   Act II, sc. i, 10. ent'red: brought suit against. 15. [and that] F. Om. Q. 17. foin: thrust. 24. vice: grasp. 30. indited: invited. 32. exion: action. 42. malmsey-nose: red nose from drinking wine.

F. loses sympathy of audience because he treats H. badly.

Enter FALSTAFF, BARDOLPH, *and* PAGE.

Fal. How now! whose mare's dead? What's the matter?

Fang. [Sir John,] I arrest you at the suit of Mistress Quickly.

Fal. Away, varlets! Draw, Bardolph; cut me off the villain's head. Throw the quean in the channel. 52

Host. Throw me in the channel! I'll throw thee in the channel. Wilt thou? wilt thou? thou bastardly rogue! Murder, murder! Ah, thou honeysuckle villain! wilt thou kill God's officers and the King's? Ah, thou honey-seed rogue! thou art a honey-seed, a man-queller, and a woman-queller. 59

Fal. Keep them off, Bardolph.

Fang. A rescue! a rescue!

Host. Good people, bring a rescue or two. Thou wo't, wo't thou? thou wo't, wo't ta? Do, do, thou rogue! do, thou hempseed! 64

Page. Away, you scullion! you rampallian! you fustilarian! I'll tickle your catastrophe.

Enter the LORD CHIEF JUSTICE, *and his men.*

Ch. Just. What is the matter? Keep the peace here, ho!

Host. Good my lord, be good to me. I beseech you, stand to me. 70

Ch. Just. How now, Sir John! what, are you brawling here? Doth this become your place, your time and business? You should have been well on your way to York. Stand from him, fellow; wherefore hang'st thou upon him? 74

Host. O my most worshipful lord, an't please your Grace, I am a poor widow of Eastcheap, and he is arrested at my suit.

Ch. Just. For what sum? 78

Host. It is more than for some, my lord; it is for all I have. He hath eaten me out of house and home; he hath put all my substance into that fat belly of his: but I will have some of it out again, or I will ride thee o' nights like the mare. 83

Fal. I think I am as like to ride the mare, if I have any vantage of ground to get up.

Ch. Just. How comes this, Sir John? [Fie!] what man of good temper would endure this tempest of exclamation? Are you not asham'd to enforce a poor widow to so rough a course to come by her own? 90

Fal. What is the gross sum that I owe thee?

Host. Marry, if thou wert an honest man, thyself and the money too. Thou didst swear to me upon a parcel-gilt goblet, sitting in my Dolphin chamber, at the round table, by a sea-coal fire, 95 upon Wednesday in Wheeson week, when the Prince broke thy head for liking his father to a singing-man of Windsor, thou didst swear to me then, as I was washing thy wound, to marry me and make me my lady thy wife. Canst thou 100 deny it? Did not goodwife Keech, the butcher's wife, come in then and call me gossip Quickly? coming in to borrow a mess of vinegar, telling us she had a good dish of prawns; whereby thou didst desire to eat some; whereby I told thee they 105 were ill for a green wound? And didst thou not, when she was gone downstairs, desire me to be no more so familiarity with such poor people, saying that ere long they should call me madam? And didst thou not kiss me and bid me fetch thee thirty shillings? I put thee now to thy book-oath. Deny it, if thou canst. 112

Fal. My lord, this is a poor mad soul; and she says up and down the town that her eldest son is like you. She hath been in good case, and the truth is, poverty hath distracted her. But for these foolish officers, I beseech you I may have redress against them. 118

Ch. Jus. Sir John, Sir John, I am well acquainted with your manner of wrenching the true cause the false way. It is not a confident brow, nor the throng of words that come with such more than impudent sauciness from you, can thrust me 123 from a level consideration. You have, as it appears to me, practis'd upon the easy-yielding spirit of this woman, and made her serve your uses both in purse and in person.

Host. Yea, in truth, my lord. 128

Ch. Just. Pray thee, peace. Pay her the debt you owe her, and unpay the villainy you have done with her. The one you may do with sterling money, and the other with current repentance. 132

Fal. My lord, I will not undergo this sneap without reply. You call honourable boldness impudent sauciness; if a man will make curtsy and say nothing, he is virtuous. No, my lord, my humble duty rememb'red, I will not be your suitor. I say to you, I do desire deliverance from these officers, being upon hasty employment in the King's affairs. 140

Ch. Just. You speak as having power to do wrong; but answer in th' effect of your reputation, and satisfy the poor woman.

Fal. Come hither, hostess. 144

H. details unrelates to her topic

F. getting to familiar with P.

F. tries to slide out of N. charge slander

48. [Sir John] F. Om. Q. 51. quean: hussy. 52. channel: gutter. 55. honey-suckle: i.e., homicidal. 57. honey-seed: i.e., homicide. 66. catastrophe: end, backside. 83. mare: nightmare. 86. [Fie] F. Om. Q. 94. parcel-gilt: gilded on the inside. 96. Wheeson: Whitsun(day). 104. prawns: shrimps. 106. green: new. 115. in good case: prosperous. 124. level: just. 132. current: real. 133. sneap: rebuke. 142. in th' effect of: suitably to.

Enter GOWER.

Ch. Just. Now, Master Gower, what news?

Gow. The King, my lord, and Harry Prince of Wales
Are near at hand. The rest the paper tells.

Fal. As I am a gentleman.

Host. Faith, you said so before. 149

Fal. As I am a gentleman. Come, no more words of it.

Host. By this heavenly ground I tread on, I must be fain to pawn both my plate and the tapestry of my dining-chambers. 154

Fal. Glasses, glasses, is the only drinking; and for thy walls, a pretty slight drollery, or the story of the Prodigal, or the German hunting in water-work, is worth a thousand of these bed-hangers and these fly-bitten tapestries. Let it be ten pound, if thou canst. Come, an't were not 160 for thy humours, there's not a better wench in England. Go, wash thy face, and draw the action. Come, thou must not be in this humour with me; dost not know me? Come, come, I know thou wast set on to this. 165

Host. Pray thee, Sir John, let it be but twenty nobles. I' faith, I am loath to pawn my plate, so God save me, la!

Fal. Let it alone; I'll make other shift. You'll be a fool still. 170

Host. Well, you shall have it, though I pawn my gown. I hope you'll come to supper. You'll pay me altogether?

Fal. Will I live? [*To Bardolph.*] Go, with her, with her; hook on, hook on. 175

Host. Will you have Doll Tearsheet meet you at supper?

Fal. No more words; let's have her.

[*Exeunt Hostess, Bardolph, Officers, and Boy.*]

Ch. Just. I have heard better news.

Fal. What's the news, my lord? 180

Ch. Just. Where lay the King to-night?

Gow. At [Basingstoke], my lord.

Fal. I hope, my lord, all's well. What is the news, my lord?

Ch. Just. Come all his forces back? 185

Gow. No; fifteen hundred foot, five hundred horse,
Are march'd up to my Lord of Lancaster.
Against Northumberland and the Archbishop.

Fal. Comes the King back from Wales, my noble lord?

Ch. Just. You shall have letters of me presently. Come, go along with me, good Master Gower. 191

Fal. My lord!

Ch. Just. What's the matter?

Fal. Master Gower, shall I entreat you with me to dinner? 195

Gow. I must wait upon my good lord here; I thank you, good Sir John.

Ch. Just. Sir John, you loiter here too long, being you are to take soldiers up in counties as you go. 200

Fal. Will you sup with me, Master Gower?

Ch. Just. What foolish master taught you these manners, Sir John?

Fal. Master Gower, if they become me not, he was a fool that taught them me. This is the right fencing grace, my lord; tap for tap, and so part fair. 207

Ch. Just. Now the Lord lighten thee! thou art a great fool. [*Exeunt.*]

SCENE II. [*London. Another street.*]

Enter PRINCE HENRY *and* POINS.

Prince. Before God, I am exceeding weary.

Poins. Is't come to that? I had thought weariness durst not have attach'd one of so high blood. 4

Prince. Faith, it does me, though it discolours the complexion of my greatness to acknowledge it. Doth it not show vilely in me to desire small beer?

Poins. Why, a prince should not be so loosely studied as to remember so weak a composition. 10

Prince. Belike then my appetite was not princely got, for, by my troth, I do now remember the poor creature, small beer. But, indeed, these humble considerations make me out of love with my greatness. What a disgrace is it to me 15 to remember thy name! or to know thy face to-morrow! or to take note how many pair of silk stockings thou hast, [viz.], these, and those that were thy peach-colour'd [ones]! or to bear the inventory of thy shirts, as, one for superfluity, and another for use! But that the tennis- 20 court-keeper knows better than I; for it is a low ebb of linen with thee when thou keepest not racket there; as thou hast not done a great while, because the rest of the low countries have [made a shift to] eat up thy holland. And God knows, 25 whether those that bawl out the ruins of thy linen shall inherit his kingdom: but the midwives say

155. **Glasses:** i.e., in place of silver goblets. 156. **drollery:** a comic scene. 157. **water-work:** water-color. 161. **humours:** whims, moods. 162. **draw:** withdraw. 182. **[Basingstoke]** F. *Billingsgate* Q. 199. **take . . . up:** recruit.
Sc. ii, S.D. POINS. (Rowe). *Poins, sir Iohn Russel, with other* Q. 5–6. **discolours the complexion** Q. makes blush. 10. **studied:** disposed. 18. **[viz.]** F. *with* Q. 19. **[ones]** F. *once* Q. 25. **[made a shift to]** F. Om. Q. **holland:** linen, with pun on *Holland.* 26. **those . . . linen:** his children, who wear his cast-off shirts. 26–30. Q. Om. F.

the children are not in the fault; whereupon the world increases, and kindreds are mightily strengthened.   30

Poins. How ill it follows, after you have laboured so hard, you should talk so idly! Tell me, how many good young princes would do so, their fathers being so sick as yours at this time is?

Prince. Shall I tell thee one thing, Poins?   35

Poins. Yes, faith; and let it be an excellent good thing.

Prince. It shall serve among wits of no higher breeding than thine.

Poins. Go to; I stand the push of your one thing that you will tell.   41

Prince. Marry, I tell thee, it is not meet that I should be sad, now my father is sick; albeit I could tell to thee, as to one it pleases me, for fault of a better, to call my friend, I could be sad, and sad indeed too.

Poins. Very hardly upon such a subject.   47

Prince. By this hand, thou think'st me as far in the devil's book as thou and Falstaff for obduracy and persistency. Let the end try the man. But I tell thee, my heart bleeds inwardly that my father is so sick; and keeping such vile company as thou art hath in reason taken from me all ostentation of sorrow.   54

Poins. The reason?

Prince. What wouldst thou think of me, if I should weep?

Poins. I would think thee a most princely hypocrite.   59

Prince. It would be every man's thought; and thou art a blessed fellow to think as every man thinks. Never a man's thought in the world keeps the road-way better than thine. Every man would think me an hypocrite indeed. And what accites your most worshipful thought to think so?   65

Poins. Why, because you have been so lewd and so much engraffed to Falstaff.

Prince. And to thee.   68

Poins. By this light, I am well spoke on; I can hear it with mine own ears. The worst that they can say of me is that I am a second brother and that I am a proper fellow of my hands; and those two things, I confess, I cannot help. By the mass, here comes Bardolph.   74

Enter BARDOLPH and PAGE.

Prince. And the boy that I gave Falstaff. 'A had him from me Christian; and look, if the fat villain have not transform'd him ape.

Bard. God save your Grace!

Prince. And yours, most noble Bardolph!   79

Poins. Come, you virtuous ass, you bashful fool, must you be blushing? Wherefore blush you now? What a maidenly man-at-arms are you become! Is't such a matter to get a pottle-pot's maidenhead?   84

Page. 'A calls me e'en now, my lord, through a red lattice, and I could discern no part of his face from the window. At last I spied his eyes, and methought he had made two holes in the ale-wife's [new] petticoat and so peep'd through.

Prince. Has not the boy profited?   90

Bard. Away, you whoreson upright rabbit, away!

Page. Away, you rascally Althæa's dream, away!   94

Prince. Instruct us, boy; what dream, boy?

Page. Marry, my lord, Althæa dream'd she was delivered of a fire-brand; and therefore I call him her dream.

Prince. A crown's worth of good interpretation. There 'tis, boy.   100

Poins. O, that this [good] blossom could be kept from cankers! Well, there is sixpence to preserve thee.

Bard. An you do not make him hang'd among you, the gallows shall have wrong.   105

Prince. And how doth thy master, Bardolph?

Bard. Well, my lord. He heard of your Grace's coming to town. There's a letter for you.

Poins. Deliver'd with good respect. And how doth the martlemas, your master?   110

Bard. In bodily health, sir.

Poins. Marry, the immortal part needs a physician; but that moves not him. Though that be sick, it dies not.   114

Prince. I do allow this wen to be as familiar with me as my dog, and he holds his place, for look you how he writes.   117

Poins. [*Reads.*] "John Falstaff, knight," — every man must know that, as oft as he has occasion to name himself; even like those that are kin to the King, for they never prick their finger but they say, "There's some of the King's blood spilt." "How comes that?" says he, that   124 takes upon him not to conceive. The answer is as ready as a [borrower's] cap, "I am the King's poor cousin, sir."

Prince. Nay, they will be kin to us, or they will fetch it from Japhet. But the letter: 128 "Sir John Falstaff, knight, to the son of the King nearest his father, Harry Prince of Wales, greeting."

Poins. Why, this is a certificate.

Prince. Peace!   133

---

64. **accites:** prompts. 83. **pottle-pot:** two-quart pot. 89. **[new]** F. Om. Q. 101. **[good]** F. Om. Q. 102. **cankers:** canker-worms. 110. **martlemas:** fatted ox, killed at Martinmas (Nov. 11). 115. **wen:** tumor. 126. **[borrower's]** (Theobald). *borrowed* QF. 128. **Japhet:** son of Noah.

"I will imitate the honourable Romans in brevity."

Poins. He sure means brevity in breath, short-winded.

[*Prince.*] "I commend me to thee, I commend thee, and I leave thee. Be not too familiar with Poins; for he misuses thy favours so much that he swears thou art to marry his sister Nell. Repent at idle times as thou mayest; and so, farewell. 141

"Thine, by yea and no, which is as much as to say, as thou usest him, JACK FALSTAFF with my [familiars,] JOHN with my brothers and sisters, and SIR JOHN with all Europe." 146

Poins. My lord, I'll steep this letter in sack and make him eat it.

Prince. That's to make him eat twenty of his words. But do you use me thus, Ned? Must I marry your sister? 151

Poins. God send the wench no worse fortune! But I never said so.

Prince. Well, thus we play the fools with the time, and the spirits of the wise sit in the clouds and mock us. Is your master here in London? 157

Bard. Yea, my lord.

Prince. Where sups he? Doth the old boar feed in the old frank? 161

Bard. At the old place, my lord, in Eastcheap.

Prince. What company?

Page. Ephesians, my lord, of the old church.

Prince. Sup any women with him?

Page. None, my lord, but old Mistress Quickly and Mistress Doll Tearsheet. 167

Prince. What pagan may that be?

Page. A proper gentlewoman, sir, and a kins-woman of my master's.

Prince. Even such kin as the parish heifers are to the town bull. Shall we steal upon them, Ned, at supper? 173

Poins. I am your shadow, my lord; I'll follow you.

Prince. Sirrah, you boy, and Bardolph, no word to your master that I am yet come to town. There's for your silence. 178

Bard. I have no tongue, sir.

Page. And for mine, sir, I will govern it.

Prince. Fare you well; go. [*Exeunt Bardolph and Page.*] This Doll Tearsheet should be some road. 183

Poins. I warrant you, as common as the way between Saint Alban's and London.

Prince. How might we see Falstaff bestow him-self to-night in his true colours, and not ourselves be seen? 188

Poins. Put on two leathern jerkins and aprons, and wait upon him at his table as drawers. 191

Prince. From a God to a bull? a heavy descen-sion! It was Jove's case. From a prince to a prentice? a low transformation! That shall be mine; for in everything the purpose must weigh with the folly. Follow me, Ned. [*Exeunt.* 196

SCENE III. [*Warkworth. Before the castle.*]

Enter NORTHUMBERLAND, LADY NORTHUM-BERLAND, *and* LADY PERCY.

North. I pray thee, loving wife, and gentle daughter,
Give even way unto my rough affairs;
Put not you on the visage of the times
And be like them to Percy troublesome.

Lady N. I have given over, I will speak no more.   5
Do what you will; your wisdom be your guide.

North. Alas, sweet wife, my honour is at pawn;
And, but my going, nothing can redeem it.

Lady P. O yet, for God's sake, go not to these wars!
The time was, father, that you broke your word   10
When you were more endear'd to it than now;
When your own Percy, when my heart's dear Harry,
Threw many a northward look to see his father
Bring up his powers; but he did long in vain.
Who then persuaded you to stay at home?   15
There were two honours lost, yours and your son's.
For yours, the God of heaven brighten it!
For his, it stuck upon him as the sun
In the grey vault of heaven, and by his light
Did all the chivalry of England move   20
To do brave acts. He was indeed the glass
Wherein the noble youth did dress themselves.
[He had no legs, that practis'd not his gait;
And speaking thick, which nature made his blemish,
Became the accents of the valiant;   25
For those that could speak low and tardily
Would turn their own perfection to abuse
To seem like him; so that in speech, in gait,
In diet, in affections of delight,
In military rules, humours of blood,   30
He was the mark and glass, copy and book,
That fashion'd others. And him, O wondrous him!
O miracle of men! him did you leave,
Second to none, unseconded by you,

---

138. **[Prince]** (Theobald). Om. Q.   144. **[familiars]** F. *family* Q.   161. **frank:** sty.   164. **Ephesians:** boon companions.
168. **pagan:** harlot.   183. **road:** harlot.   186. **bestow:** behave.   192. **God...bull:** an allusion to the story of Jove and Europa.   196. **weigh with:** equal.

Sc. iii, 11. **endear'd:** bound.   23–45. F. Om. Q.   24. **thick:** hurriedly.   29. **affections of delight:** favorite occupations.
30. **humours of blood:** temperament.

To look upon the hideous god of war   35
In disadvantage; to abide a field
Where nothing but the sound of Hotspur's name
Did seem defensible: so you left him.
Never, O never, do his ghost the wrong
To hold your honour more precise and nice   40
With others than with him! Let them alone.
The Marshal and the Archbishop are strong.
Had my sweet Harry had but half their numbers,
To-day might I, hanging on Hotspur's neck,
Have talk'd of Monmouth's grave.]
   North.   Beshrew your heart,
Fair daughter, you do draw my spirits from me   46
With new lamenting ancient oversights.
But I must go and meet with danger there,
Or it will seek me in another place
And find me worse provided.
   Lady N.   O, fly to Scotland
Till that the nobles and the armed commons   51
Have of their puissance made a little taste.
   Lady P. If they get ground and vantage of the
     King,
Then join you with them, like a rib of steel,
To make strength stronger; but, for all our loves,   55
First let them try themselves. So did your son;
He was so suff'red; so came I a widow;
And never shall have length of life enough
To rain upon remembrance with mine eyes,
That it may grow and sprout as high as heaven,
For recordation to my noble husband.   61
   North. Come, come, go in with me. 'Tis with
     my mind
As with the tide swell'd up unto his height,
That makes a still stand, running neither way.
Fain would I go to meet the Archbishop,   65
But many thousand reasons hold me back.
I will resolve for Scotland. There am I
Till time and vantage crave my company.
                    [Exeunt.

SCENE IV. [*London. The Boar's-Head Tavern
in Eastcheap.*]

Enter two DRAWERS.

[*1. Draw.*] What the devil hast thou brought
there? Apple-johns? Thou know'st Sir John
cannot endure an apple-john.   3
   2. Draw. Mass, thou say'st true. The Prince
once set a dish of apple-johns before him, and told
him there were five more Sir Johns, and, putting
off his hat, said, "I will now take my leave of these
six dry, round, old, wither'd knights." It ang'red

him to the heart; but he hath forgot that.   10
   [*1. Draw.*] Why, then, cover, and set them down;
and see if thou canst find out Sneak's noise. Mistress Tearsheet would fain hear some music. Dispatch! The room where they supped is too hot;
they'll come in straight.   15
   [*2. Draw.*] Sirrah, here will be the Prince and
Master Poins anon; and they will put on two of
our jerkins and aprons; and Sir John must not
know of it. Bardolph hath brought word.   20
   1. Draw. By the mass, here will be old utis; it
will be an excellent stratagem.
   [*2. Draw.*] I'll see if I can find out Sneak. [*Exit.*

Enter HOSTESS *and* DOLL TEARSHEET.

   Host. I' faith, sweetheart, methinks now you
are in an excellent good temperality. Your   25
pulsidge beats as extraordinarily as heart would
desire; and your colour, I warrant you, is as red
as any rose, in good truth, la! But, i' faith, you
have drunk too much canaries; and that's a marvellous searching wine, and it perfumes the blood ere
one can say, "What's this?" How do you now?   32
   Dol. Better than I was. Hem!
   Host. Why, that's well said; a good heart's
worth gold. Lo, here comes Sir John.   35

Enter FALSTAFF.

   Fal. [*Singing.*] "When Arthur first in court"—
Empty the jordan. [*Exit 1. Drawer.*]—[*Singing.*]
"And was a worthy king." How now, Mistress
Doll!
   Host. Sick of a calm; yea, good faith.   40
   Fal. So is all her sect; an they be once in a calm,
they are sick.
   Dol. A pox damn you, you muddy rascal, is that
all the comfort you give me?
   Fal. You make fat rascals, Mistress Doll.   45
   Dol. I make them? Gluttony and diseases make
[them]; I make them not.
   Fal. If the cook help to make the gluttony, you
help to make the diseases, Doll. We catch of you,
Doll, we catch of you. Grant that, my poor virtue,
grant that.   51
   Dol. Yea, joy, our chains and our jewels.
   Fal. Your brooches, pearls, and ouches. For to
serve bravely is to come halting off, you know; to
come off the breach with his pike bent bravely, and
to surgery bravely; to venture upon the charg'd
chambers bravely, —   57
   Dol. Hang yourself, you muddy conger, hang
yourself!

61. **recordation:** memorial.
  Sc. iv, 1, 11. [*1. Draw.*] F. *Francis* Q. 2. **Apple-johns:** wrinkled winter apples. 12. **noise:** band of musicians. 14.
Dispatch (Pope). Dra. *Dispatch* Q. 16, 23. [*2. Draw.*] F. *Francis* Q. 20. **word** F. *word.* *Enter Will* Q. 21. **old utis:**
great sport. 36. **"When Arthur, etc."** Fragment of the ballad *Sir Lancelot du Lake.* 37. **jordan:** chamber-pot.
40. **calm:** qualm. 47. **[them]** F. Om. Q. 53. **ouches:** jewels. 57. **chambers:** small cannon. 58. **conger:** eel.

Host. By my troth, this is the old fashion; you two never meet but you fall to some discord. You are both, i' good truth, as rheumatic as two dry 62 toasts; you cannot one bear with another's confirmities. What the good-year! one must bear, and that must be you; you are the weaker vessel, as they say, the emptier vessel. 66

Dol. Can a weak empty vessel bear such a huge full hogshead? There's a whole merchant's venture of Bourdeaux stuff in him; you have not seen a hulk better stuff'd in the hold. Come, I'll be friends with thee, Jack. Thou art going to the wars; and whether I shall ever see thee again or no, there is nobody cares. 73

Re-enter [FIRST] DRAWER.

[1.] *Draw.* Sir, Ancient Pistol's below, and would speak with you.

Dol. Hang him, swaggering rascal! let him not come hither. It is the foul-mouth'd'st rogue in England. 78

Host. If he swagger, let him not come here; no, by my faith. I must live among my neighbours; I'll no swaggerers. I am in good name and fame with the very best. Shut the door; there comes no swaggerers here. I have not liv'd all this while, to have swaggering now. Shut the door, I pray you.

Fal. Dost thou hear, hostess? 86

Host. Pray ye, pacify yourself, Sir John. There comes no swaggerers here.

Fal. Dost thou hear? It is mine ancient. 89

Host. Tilly-fally, Sir John, ne'er tell me; and your ancient swaggerer comes not in my doors. I was before Master Tisick, the deputy, t'other day; and, as he said to me, 'twas no longer ago than Wednesday last, "I' good faith, neighbour Quickly," says he; Master Dumbe, our minister, 95 was by then; "neighbour Quickly," says he, "receive those that are civil; for," said he, "you are in an ill name." Now 'a said so, I can tell whereupon; "for," says he, "you are an honest woman, and well thought on; therefore take heed what 100 guests you receive. Receive," says he, "no swaggering companions." There comes none here. You would bless you to hear what he said. No, I'll no swaggerers. 104

Fal. He's no swaggerer, hostess; a tame cheater, i' faith; you may stroke him as gently as a puppy greyhound. He'll not swagger with a Barbary hen, if her feathers turn back in any show of resistance. Call him up, drawer. [*Exit* 1. *Drawer.*] 109

Host. Cheater, call you him? I will bar no honest man my house, nor no cheater; but I do

not love swaggering, by my troth. I am the worse, when one says swagger. Feel, masters, how I shake; look you, I warrant you. 114

Dol. So you do, hostess.

Host. Do I? yea, in very truth, do I, an 'twere an aspen leaf. I cannot abide swaggerers.

Enter PISTOL, BARDOLPH, *and* PAGE.

Pist. God save you, Sir John! 119

Fal. Welcome, Ancient Pistol. Here, Pistol, I charge you with a cup of sack; do you discharge upon mine hostess.

Pist. I will discharge upon her, Sir John, with two bullets. 124

Fal. She is pistol-proof, sir; you shall hardly offend her.

Host. Come, I'll drink no proofs nor no bullets. I'll drink no more than will do me good, for no man's pleasure, I. 129

Pist. Then to you, Mistress Dorothy; I will charge you.

Dol. Charge me! I scorn you, scurvy companion. What! you poor, base, rascally, cheating, lacklinen mate! Away, you mouldy rogue, away! I am meat for your master. 135

Pist. I know you, Mistress Dorothy.

Dol. Away, you cut-purse rascal! you filthy bung, away! By this wine, I'll thrust my knife in your mouldy chaps, an you play the saucy cuttle with me. Away, you bottle-ale rascal! you basket-hilt stale juggler, you! Since when, I pray you, sir? God's light, with two points on your shoulder? Much! 143

Pist. God let me not live, but I will murder your ruff for this.

Fal. No more, Pistol; I would not have you go off here. Discharge yourself of our company, Pistol.

Host. No, good Captain Pistol; not here, sweet captain. 150

Dol. Captain! thou abominable damn'd cheater, art thou not ashamed to be call'd captain? An captains were of my mind, they would truncheon you out for taking their names upon you before you have earn'd them. You a captain! you 155 slave, for what? For tearing a poor whore's ruff in a bawdy-house? He a captain! Hang him, rogue! he lives upon mouldy stew'd prunes and dried cakes. A captain! God's light, these villains will make the word as odious as the word 160 "occupy"; which was an excellent good word before it was ill sorted; therefore captains had need look to't.

---

64. **What the good-year!** A common expletive. 74. **Ancient:** ensign. 102. **companions:** fellows. 105. **cheater:** swindler. Some have seen in l. 110, a confusion with *escheator*, a fiscal officer. 107. **Barbary hen:** Guinea hen. 138. **bung:** pickpocket. 139. **cuttle:** cut-purse. 142. **points:** laces. 161. **"occupy":** fornicate. 162. **ill sorted:** fallen into evil company.

F whole atmosphere of inn degenerated.

Bard. Pray thee, go down, good ancient.

Fal. Hark thee hither, Mistress Doll.   165

Pist. Not I. I tell thee what, Corporal Bardolph, I could tear her. I'll be reveng'd of her.

Page. Pray thee, go down.

Pist. I'll see her damn'd first; to Pluto's damn'd lake, by this hand, to the infernal deep, with Erebus and tortures vile also. Hold hook and line, say I. Down, down, dogs! down, faitors! Have we not Hiren here?   173

Host. Good Captain Peesel, be quiet; 'tis very late, i' faith. I beseek you now, aggravate your choler.

Pist. These be good humours, indeed! Shall pack-horses

And hollow pamper'd jades of Asia,

Which cannot go but thirty mile a-day,   179

Compare with Cæsars and with Cannibals

And Troian Greeks? Nay, rather damn them with

King Cerberus, and let the welkin roar.

Shall we fall foul for toys?

Host. By my troth, captain, these are very bitter words.   185

Bard. Be gone, good ancient. This will grow to a brawl anon.

Pist. [Die] men like dogs! Give crowns like pins! Have we not Hiren here?   189

Host. O' my word, captain, there's none such here. What the good-year! do you think I would deny her? For God's sake, be quiet.

Pist. Then feed, and be fat, my fair Calipolis. Come, give 's some sack.   194

"*Si fortune me tormente, sperato me contento.*"

Fear we broadsides? No, let the fiend give fire.

Give me some sack; and, sweetheart, lie thou there.   [*Laying down his sword.*]

Come we to full points here; and are etceteras nothings?

Fal. Pistol, I would be quiet.   199

Pist. Sweet knight, I kiss thy neaf. What! we have seen the seven stars.

Dol. For God's sake, thrust him downstairs. I cannot endure such a fustian rascal.

Pist. Thrust him downstairs! Know we not Galloway nags?   205

Fal. Quoit him down, Bardolph, like a shove-groat shilling. Nay, an 'a do nothing but speak nothing, 'a shall be nothing here.

Bard. Come, get you downstairs.

Pist. What! shall we have incision? Shall we imbrue?   [*Snatching up his sword.*]   210

Then death rock me asleep, abridge my doleful days!

Why, then, let grievous, ghastly, gaping wounds

Untwine the Sisters Three! Come, Atropos, I say!

Host. Here's goodly stuff toward!   214

Fal. Give me my rapier, boy.

Dol. I pray thee, Jack, I pray thee, do not draw.

Fal. Get you downstairs.   218

[*Drawing, and driving Pistol out.*]

Host. Here's a goodly tumult! I'll forswear keeping house, afore I'll be in these tirrits and frights. So; murder, I warrant now. Alas, alas! put up your naked weapons, put up your naked weapons.   [*Exeunt Pistol and Bardolph.*]   223

Dol. I pray thee, Jack, be quiet; the rascal's gone. Ah, you whoreson little valiant villain, you!

Host. Are you not hurt i' the groin? Methought 'a made a shrewd thrust at your belly.   228

[*Re-enter* BARDOLPH.]

Fal. Have you turn'd him out o' doors?

Bard. Yea, sir; the rascal's drunk. You have hurt him, sir, i' the shoulder.

Fal. A rascal! to brave me!   232

Dol. Ah, you sweet little rogue, you! Alas, poor ape, how thou sweat'st! Come, let me wipe thy face. Come on, you whoreson chops. Ah, rogue! i' faith, I love thee. Thou art as valorous as Hector of Troy, worth five of Agamemnon, and ten times better than the Nine Worthies. Ah, villain!   239

Fal. A rascally slave! I will toss the rogue in a blanket.

Dol. Do, an thou dar'st for thy heart. An thou dost, I'll canvass thee between a pair of sheets.   244

Enter Music.

Page. The music is come, sir.

Fal. Let them play. Play, sirs. Sit on my knee, Doll. A rascal bragging slave! The rogue fled from me like quicksilver.   248

Dol. I' faith, and thou follow'dst him like a church. Thou whoreson little tidy Bartholomew boar-pig, when wilt thou leave fighting o' days and foining o' nights, and begin to patch up thine old body for heaven?   253

Enter [*behind,*] PRINCE HENRY *and* POINS, *disguised.*

Fal. Peace, good Doll! do not speak like a death's-head. Do not bid me remember mine end.

Dol. Sirrah, what humour's the Prince of?

Fal. A good shallow young fellow. 'A would

172. **faitors**: swindlers. 173. **Hiren**. Not satisfactorily explained. 175. **aggravate**. As often, Quickly says the opposite of what she means. 188. **[Die]** F. Om. Q. 195. "If fortune torments me, hope contents me." 198. **points**: stops. 200. **neaf**: fist. 207. **shove-groat**: a game where coins were aimed at a mark. 213. **Atropos**: one of the three Fates. 214. **toward**: coming. 235. **chops**: fat face. 250. **Bartholomew boar-pig**: roast pig was the chief dish at the fair on St. Bartholomew's Day. 252. **foining**: thrusting.

have made a good pantler; 'a would ha' chipp'd
bread well.   259

Dol. They say Poins has a good wit.

Fal. He a good wit? Hang him, baboon! His
wit's as thick as Tewksbury mustard; there's no
more conceit in him than is in a mallet.   263

Dol. Why does the Prince love him so, then?

Fal. Because their legs are both of a bigness, and
he plays at quoits well, and eats conger and fennel,
and drinks off candles' ends for flap-dragons, and
rides the wild-mare with the boys, and jumps upon
join'd stools, and swears with a good grace, and
wears his boots very smooth, like unto the sign 270
of The Leg, and breeds no bate with telling of discreet stories; and such other gambol faculties 'a
has, that show a weak mind and an able body, for
the which the Prince admits him. For the Prince
himself is such another; the weight of a hair will
turn the scales between their avoirdupois.   277

Prince. Would not this nave of a wheel have his
ears cut off?

Poins. Let's beat him before his whore.

Prince. Look, whe'er the wither'd elder hath not
his poll claw'd like a parrot.   282

Poins. Is it not strange that desire should so
many years outlive performance?

Fal. Kiss me, Doll.

Prince. Saturn and Venus this year in conjunction! What says the almanac to that?   287

Poins. And, look, whether the fiery Trigon, his
man, be not lisping to his master's old tables, his
note-book, his counsel-keeper.

Fal. Thou dost give me flattering busses.

Dol. By my troth, I kiss thee with a most constant heart.   293

Fal. I am old, I am old.

Dol. I love thee better than I love e'er a scurvy
young boy of them all.   296

Fal. What stuff wilt have a kirtle of? I shall
receive money o' Thursday. Shalt have a cap to-
morrow. A merry song, come! It grows late;
we'll to bed. Thou 'forget me when I am gone.   300

Dol. By my troth, thou't set me a-weeping, an
thou say'st so. Prove that ever I dress myself
handsome till thy return. Well, hearken a' th'
end.

Fal. Some sack, Francis.   305

Prince. } Anon, anon, sir.
Poins. }

[Coming forward.]

Fal. Ha! a bastard son of the King's? And art
not thou Poins his brother?

Prince. Why, thou globe of sinful continents,
what a life dost thou lead!   310

Fal. A better than thou. I am a gentleman; thou
art a drawer.

Prince. Very true, sir; and I come to draw you
out by the ears.   314

Host. O, the Lord preserve thy Grace! By my
troth, welcome to London. Now, the Lord bless
that sweet face of thine! O Jesu, are you come
from Wales?

Fal. Thou whoreson mad compound of majesty,
by this light flesh and corrupt blood, thou art
welcome.   321

Dol. How, you fat fool! I scorn you.

Poins. My lord, he will drive you out of your
revenge and turn all to a merriment, if you take
not the heat.   325

Prince. You whoreson candle-mine, you, how
vilely did you speak of me even now before this
honest, virtuous, civil gentlewoman!

Host. God's blessing of your good heart! and
so she is, by my troth.   330

Fal. Didst thou hear me?

Prince. Yea, and you knew me, as you did when
you ran away by Gadshill. You knew I was at
your back, and spoke it on purpose to try my
patience.   335

Fal. No, no, no; not so; I did not think thou
wast within hearing.

Prince. I shall drive you then to confess the
wilful abuse, and then I know how to handle you.

Fal. No abuse, Hal, o' mine honour; no abuse.

Prince. Not to dispraise me, and call me pantler
and bread-chipper and I know not what?   342

Fal. No abuse, Hal.

Poins. No abuse?   344

Fal. No abuse, Ned, i' the world; honest Ned,
none. I disprais'd him before the wicked, that the
wicked might not fall in love with [him]; in which
doing, I have done the part of a careful friend and
a true subject, and thy father is to give me thanks
for it. No abuse, Hal; none, Ned, none; no, faith,
boys, none.   351

Prince. See now, whether pure fear and entire
cowardice doth not make thee wrong this virtuous
gentlewoman to close with us? Is she of the
wicked? Is thine hostess here of the wicked? Or
is thy boy of the wicked? Or honest Bardolph,
whose zeal burns in his nose, of the wicked?   357

Poins. Answer, thou dead elm, answer.

Fal. The fiend hath prick'd down Bardolph ir-
recoverable; and his face is Lucifer's privy-kitchen,

258. **pantler:** servant in the pantry. 263. **conceit:** wit. 267. **for flap-dragons:** floating on burning brandy. 268. **wild-mare:** see-saw. 271. **bate:** strife. 278. **nave:** hub, with pun on *knave.* 288. **fiery Trigon.** The Zodiac was divided into four "trigons" of three signs, characterized as fiery, airy, watery, and earthy. 289. **tables:** account book, i.e., Quickly. 291. **busses:** kisses. 320. **light...blood:** i.e., Doll. 325. **take...heat:** strike not when the iron is hot. 326. **candle-mine:** mass of tallow. 347. **[him]** F. *thee* Q. 353. **close with:** pacify. 359. **prick'd:** marked.

where he doth nothing but roast malt-worms. For
the boy, there is a good angel about him; but the
devil blinds him too.   363
Prince. For the women?
Fal. For one of them, she is in hell already, and
burns poor souls. For the other, I owe her money;
and whether she be damn'd for that, I know not.
Host. No, I warrant you.   369
Fal. No, I think thou art not; I think thou art
quit for that. Marry, there is another indictment
upon thee, for suffering flesh to be eaten in thy
house, contrary to the law; for the which I think
thou wilt howl.   374
Host. All victuallers do so. What's a joint of
mutton or two in a whole Lent?
Prince. You, gentlewoman,—
Dol. What says your Grace?
Fal. His grace says that which his flesh rebels
against.   [*Peto knocks at door.* 380
Host. Who knocks so loud at door? Look to
th' door there, Francis.

Enter PETO.

Prince. Peto, how now! what news?
Peto. The King your father is at Westminster;
And there are twenty weak and wearied posts 385
Come from the north; and, as I came along,
I met and overtook a dozen captains,
Bare-headed, sweating, knocking at the taverns,
And asking every one for Sir John Falstaff.
Prince. By heaven, Poins, I feel me much to
    blame   390
So idly to profane the precious time,
When tempest of commotion, like the south
Borne with black vapour, doth begin to melt
And drop upon our bare unarmed heads.   394
Give me my sword and cloak. Falstaff, good night.
    [*Exeunt Prince Henry, Poins, [Peto, and
        Bardolph.*]
Fal. Now comes in the sweetest morsel of the
night, and we must hence and leave it unpick'd.
[*Knocking within.*] More knocking at the door!

[*Re-enter* BARDOLPH.]

How now! what's the matter?   400
Bard. You must away to court, sir, presently;
A dozen captains stay at door for you.
Fal. [*To the Page.*] Pay the musicians, sirrah.
Farewell, hostess; farewell, Doll. You see, my
good wenches, how men of merit are sought after.
The undeserver may sleep when the man of action
is call'd on. Farewell, good wenches; if I be not
sent away post, I will see you again ere I go. 408

Dol. I cannot speak. If my heart be not ready
to burst, — well, sweet Jack, have a care of thyself.
Fal. Farewell, farewell.
            [*Exeunt Falstaff [and Bardolph.*]
Host. Well, fare thee well. I have known thee
these twenty-nine years, come peascod-time; but
an honester and truer-hearted man, — well, fare
thee well.   415
Bard. [*Within.*] Mistress Tearsheet!
Host. What's the matter?
Bard. [*Within.*] Bid Mistress Tearsheet come to
my master.
Host. O, run, Doll, run; run, good Doll. Come.
(*She comes blubbered.*) Yea, will you come,
Doll?   [*Exeunt.* 421

ACT III

SCENE I. [*Westminster. The palace.*]

Enter the KING *in his nightgown, with a* Page.

King. Go call the Earls of Surrey and of War-
    wick;
But, ere they come, bid them o'er-read these letters
And well consider of them. Make good speed.
                                            [*Exit Page.*
How many thousand of my poorest subjects
Are at this hour asleep! O Sleep, O gentle Sleep,   5
Nature's soft nurse, how have I frighted thee
That thou no more wilt weigh my eyelids down
And steep my senses in forgetfulness?
Why rather, Sleep, liest thou in smoky cribs,
Upon uneasy pallets stretching thee,   10
And hush'd with buzzing night-flies to thy slumber,
Than in the perfum'd chambers of the great
Under the canopies of costly state,
And lull'd with sound of sweetest melody?
O thou dull god, why liest thou with the vile   15
In loathsome beds, and leav'st the kingly couch
A watch-case or a common 'larum-bell?
Wilt thou upon the high and giddy mast
Seal up the ship-boy's eyes, and rock his brains
In cradle of the rude imperious surge   20
And in the visitation of the winds,
Who take the ruffian billows by the top,
Curling their monstrous heads and hanging them
With deaf'ning clamour in the slippery clouds,
That, with the hurly, death itself awakes?   25
Canst thou, O partial Sleep, give thy repose
To the wet [sea-boy] in an hour so rude,
And in the calmest and most stillest night,
With all appliances and means to boot,
Deny it to a king? Then happy low, lie down!   30
Uneasy lies the head that wears a crown.

361. malt-worms: beer tipplers. 392. south: south wind. 393. Borne: laden.
Act III, sc. i, S.D. nightgown: dressing gown. 9. cribs: cabins. 17. watch-case: sentry-box. 27. [sea-boy] F. season Q.

Enter WARWICK *and* SURREY.

War. Many good morrows to your Majesty!

King. Is it good morrow, lords?

War. 'Tis one o'clock, and past.

King. Why, then, good morrow to you all, my
lords. 35

Have you read o'er the letters that I sent you?

War. We have, my liege.

King. Then you perceive the body of our kingdom

How foul it is; what rank diseases grow,

And with what danger, near the heart of it. 40

War. It is but as a body yet distemper'd;

Which to his former strength may be restor'd

With good advice and little medicine.

My Lord Northumberland will soon be cool'd.

King. O God! that one might read the book of
fate, 45

And see the revolution of the times

Make mountains level, and the continent,

Weary of solid firmness, melt itself

Into the sea! and, other times, to see

The beachy girdle of the ocean 50

Too wide for Neptune's hips; how chances mock,

And changes fill the cup of alteration

With divers liquors! O, if this were seen,

The happiest youth, viewing his progress through,

What perils past, what crosses to ensue, 55

Would shut the book, and sit him down and die.

'Tis not ten years gone

Since Richard and Northumberland, great friends,

Did feast together, and in two years after

Were they at wars. It is but eight years since 60

This Percy was the man nearest my soul,

Who like a brother toil'd in my affairs

And laid his love and life under my foot;

Yea, for my sake, even to the eyes of Richard

Gave him defiance. But which of you was by —

You, cousin Nevil, as I may remember — 66

[*To Warwick.*]

When Richard, with his eye brimful of tears,

Then check'd and rated by Northumberland,

Did speak these words, now prov'd a prophecy?

"Northumberland, thou ladder by the which 70

My cousin Bolingbroke ascends my throne, —"

Though then, God knows, I had no such intent,

But that necessity so bow'd the state

That I and greatness were compell'd to kiss; —

"The time shall come," thus did he follow it, 75

"The time will come, that foul sin, gathering head,

Shall break into corruption:" so went on,

Foretelling this same time's condition

And the division of our amity.

War. There is a history in all men's lives, 80

Figuring the nature of the times deceas'd;

The which observ'd, a man may prophesy,

With a near aim, of the main chance of things

As yet not come to life, [which] in their seeds

And weak beginnings lie intreasured. 85

Such things become the hatch and brood of time;

And by the necessary form of this

King Richard might create a perfect guess

That great Northumberland, then false to him,

Would of that seed grow to a greater falseness, 90

Which should not find a ground to root upon

Unless on you.

King. Are these things then necessities?

Then let us meet them like necessities.

And that same word even now cries out on us.

They say the Bishop and Northumberland 95

Are fifty thousand strong.

War. It cannot be, my lord.

Rumour doth double, like the voice and echo,

The numbers of the fear'd. Please it your Grace

To go to bed. Upon my soul, my lord,

The powers that you already have sent forth 100

Shall bring this prize in very easily.

To comfort you the more, I have receiv'd

A certain instance that Glendower is dead.

Your Majesty hath been this fortnight ill,

And these unseason'd hours perforce must add 105

Unto your sickness.

King. I will take your counsel:

And were these inward wars once out of hand,

We would, dear lords, unto the Holy Land.

[*Exeunt.*

SCENE II. [*Gloucestershire. Before Justice Shallow's house.*]

Enter SHALLOW *and* SILENCE [*meeting*]; MOULDY,
SHADOW, WART, FEEBLE, BULLCALF [*a Servant
or two with them*].

Shal. Come on, come on, come on, sir; give me
your hand, sir, give me your hand, sir. An early
stirrer, by the rood! And how doth my good cousin Silence?

Sil. Good morrow, good cousin Shallow. 5

Shal. And how doth my cousin, your bedfellow?
and your fairest daughter and mine, my god-
daughter Ellen?

Sil. Alas, a black ousel, cousin Shallow! 9

Shal. By yea and no, sir, I dare say my cousin
William is become a good scholar. He is at Oxford
still, is he not?

Sil. Indeed, sir, to my cost. 13

Shal. 'A must, then, to the Inns o' Court shortly.

32. S.D. SURREY. F. *Surrey, and sir Iohn Blunt* Q. 70 ff. See *Rich. II*, V.i.55 ff. 84. [which] F. *who* Q. 103. **instance:**
proof.

Sc. ii, 9. **ousel:** blackbird.

I was once of Clement's Inn, where I think they will talk of mad Shallow yet.   16

Sil. You were call'd lusty Shallow then, cousin.

Shal. By the mass, I was call'd anything; and I would have done anything indeed too, and roundly too. There was I, and little John Doit of Stafford-shire, and black George Barnes, and Francis Pick-bone, and Will Squele, a Cots'ol' man. You had not four such swingebucklers in all the Inns o' Court again; and I may say to you, we knew where   25
the bona robas were and had the best of them all at commandment. Then was Jack Falstaff, now Sir John, a boy, and page to Thomas Mowbray, Duke of Norfolk.

Sil. Cousin, this Sir John that comes hither anon about soldiers?   31

Shal. The same Sir John, the very same. I see him break Skogan's head at the court-gate, when 'a was a crack not thus high; and the very same day did I fight with one Sampson Stockfish, a fruiterer, behind Gray's Inn. Jesu, Jesu, the mad days that I have spent! And to see how many of my old acquaintance are dead!   38

Sil. We shall all follow, cousin.

Shal. Certain, 'tis certain; very sure, very sure. Death, as the Psalmist saith, is certain to all; all shall die. How a good yoke of bullocks at Stamford fair?   43

Sil. By my troth, I was not there.

Shal. Death is certain. Is old Double of your town living yet?

Sil. Dead, sir.   47

Shal. Jesu, Jesu, dead! 'A drew a good bow; and dead! 'A shot a fine shoot. John o' Gaunt loved him well, and betted much money on his head. Dead! 'a would have clapp'd i' th' clout at twelve score; and carried you a forehand shaft at fourteen and fourteen and a half, that it would have done a man's heart good to see. How a score of ewes now?   55

Sil. Thereafter as they be, a score of good ewes may be worth ten pounds.

Shal. And is old Double dead?

Sil. Here come two of Sir John Falstaff's men, as I think.   60

Enter BARDOLPH *and one with him.*

Good morrow, honest gentlemen.

Bard. I beseech you, which is Justice Shallow?

Shal. I am Robert Shallow, sir; a poor esquire of this county, and one of the King's justices of the peace. What is your good pleasure with me?   65

Bard. My captain, sir, commends him to you;

my captain, Sir John Falstaff, a tall gentleman, by heaven, and a most gallant leader.

Shal. He greets me well, sir. I knew him a good backsword man. How doth the good knight? May I ask how my lady his wife doth?   71

Bard. Sir, pardon; a soldier is better accom-modated than with a wife.

Shal. It is well said, in faith, sir; and it is well said indeed too. Better accommodated! it is good; yea, indeed, is it. Good phrases are surely, and ever were, very commendable. Accommodated! it comes of *accommodo*. Very good; a good phrase.

Bard. Pardon, sir; I have heard the word.   80
Phrase call you it? By this day, I know not the phrase; but I will maintain the word with my sword to be a soldier-like word, and a word of exceeding good command, by heaven. Accommodated;   84
that is, when a man is, as they say, accommodated; or when a man is, being, whereby 'a may be thought to be accommodated; which is an excellent thing.

Enter FALSTAFF.

Shal. It is very just. Look, here comes good Sir John. Give me your good hand, give me your   90
worship's good hand. By my troth, you like well and bear your years very well. Welcome, good Sir John.

Fal. I am glad to see you well, good Master Robert Shallow. Master Surecard, as I think?   95

Shal. No, Sir John; it is my cousin Silence, in commission with me.

Fal. Good Master Silence, it well befits you should be of the peace.

Sil. Your good worship is welcome.   100

Fal. Fie! this is hot weather, gentlemen. Have you provided me here half a dozen sufficient men?

Shal. Marry, have we, sir. Will you sit?

Fal. Let me see them, I beseech you.   105

Shal. Where's the roll? where's the roll? where's the roll? Let me see, let me see, let me see. So, so, so, so, so, so, so; yea, marry, sir. Ralph Mouldy! Let them appear as I call; let them do so, let them do so. Let me see; where is Mouldy?   111

Moul. Here, an it please you.

Shal. What think you, Sir John? A good-limb'd fellow; young, strong, and of good friends.

Fal. Is thy name Mouldy?   115

Moul. Yea, an't please you.

Fal. 'Tis the more time thou wert us'd.

Shal. Ha, ha, ha! most excellent, i' faith! Things that are mouldy lack use. Very singular good! In faith, well said, Sir John, very well said.

Fal. Prick him.   [*John pricks him.*   121

Moul. I was prick'd well enough before, an you

---

27. **bona robas:** harlots.   51–52. **clapp'd . . . score:** hit the bull's-eye at 240 yards.   52. **forehand:** for straightforward shooting.   67. **tall:** brave.   70. **backsword man:** single-stick fencer.   72. **accommodated:** furnished. Shallow's remarks show that it was an innovation.   91. **like well:** are in good condition.

could have let me alone. My old dame will be undone now for one to do her husbandry and her
drudgery. You need not to have prick'd me; there
are other men fitter to go out than I. 126

Fal. Go to; peace, Mouldy; you shall go.
Mouldy, it is time you were spent.

Moul. Spent!

Shal. Peace, fellow, peace; stand aside; know
you where you are? For the other, Sir John, let
me see. Simon Shadow! 132

Fal. Yea, marry, let me have him to sit under;
he's like to be a cold soldier.

Shal. Where's Shadow?

Shad. Here, sir.

Fal. Shadow, whose son art thou? 137

Shad. My mother's son, sir.

Fal. Thy mother's son! like enough, and thy
father's shadow. So the son of the female is the
shadow of the male. It is often so, indeed; but
much of the father's substance! 142

Shal. Do you like him, Sir John?

Fal. Shadow will serve for summer. Prick
him, for we have a number of shadows to fill up
the muster-book. 146

Shal. Thomas Wart!

Fal. Where's he?

Wart. Here, sir.

Fal. Is thy name Wart? 150

Wart. Yea, sir.

Fal. Thou art a very ragged wart.

Shal. Shall I prick him, Sir John?

Fal. It were superfluous; for [his] apparel is
built upon his back and the whole frame stands
upon pins. Prick him no more. 156

Shal. Ha, ha, ha! you can do it, sir; you can do
it; I commend you well. Francis Feeble!

Fee. Here, sir.

[*Fal.*] What trade art thou, Feeble? 160

Fee. A woman's tailor, sir.

Shal. Shall I prick him, sir?

Fal. You may; but if he had been a man's
tailor, he'd ha' prick'd you. Wilt thou make as
many holes in an enemy's battle as thou hast done
in a woman's petticoat? 166

Fee. I will do my good will, sir; you can have no
more.

Fal. Well said, good woman's tailor! well said,
courageous Feeble! Thou wilt be as valiant as the
wrathful dove or most magnanimous mouse. Prick
the woman's tailor. Well, Master Shallow; deep,
Master Shallow. 173

Fee. I would Wart might have gone, sir.

Fal. I would thou wert a man's tailor, that thou
mightst mend him and make him fit to go. I cannot put him to a private soldier that is the leader

of so many thousands. Let that suffice, most
forcible Feeble.

Fee. It shall suffice, sir. 180

Fal. I am bound to thee, reverend Feeble. Who
is next?

Shal. Peter Bullcalf o' th' green!

Fal. Yea, marry, let's see Bullcalf.

Bull. Here, sir. 185

Fal. 'Fore God, a likely fellow! Come, prick
me Bullcalf till he roar again.

Bull. O Lord! good my lord captain, —

Fal. What, dost thou roar before thou art
prick'd? 190

Bull. O Lord, sir! I am a diseased man.

Fal. What disease hast thou?

Bull. A whoreson cold, sir, a cough, sir, which I
caught with ringing in the King's affairs upon his
coronation-day, sir. 195

Fal. Come, thou shalt go to the wars in a gown.
We will have away thy cold; and I will take such
order that thy friends shall ring for thee. Is here
all? 199

Shal. Here is two more call'd than your number;
you must have but four here, sir. And so, I pray
you, go in with me to dinner.

Fal. Come, I will go drink with you, but I cannot tarry dinner. I am glad to see you, by my
troth, Master Shallow. 205

Shal. O, Sir John, do you remember since we
lay all night in the windmill in Saint George's field?

Fal. No more of that, [good] Master Shallow
[no more of that].

Shal. Ha! 'twas a merry night. And is Jane
Nightwork alive? 211

Fal. She lives, Master Shallow.

Shal. She never could away with me.

Fal. Never, never; she would always say she
could not abide Master Shallow. 215

Shal. By the mass, I could anger her to the
heart. She was then a bona roba. Doth she hold
her own well?

Fal. Old, old, Master Shallow. 219

Shal. Nay, she must be old; she cannot choose
but be old; certain she's old; and had Robin Nightwork by old Nightwork before I came to Clement's
Inn.

Sil. That's fifty-five year ago. 224

Shal. Ha, cousin Silence, that thou hadst seen
that that this knight and I have seen! Ha, Sir
John, said I well?

Fal. We have heard the chimes at midnight,
Master Shallow. 229

Shal. That we have, that we have, that we have;
in faith, Sir John, we have. Our watchword was
"Hem, boys!" Come, let's to dinner; come, let's

154. [his] F. Om. Q. 160. [*Fal.*] (Theobald). *Shal.* QF. 178. **thousands:** i.e., of lice. 208. [good] F. Om. Q. 209. [no ... that] F. Om. Q.

to dinner. Jesu, the days that we have seen!
Come, come.   234

[*Exeunt* [*Falstaff and the Justices*].

Bull. Good Master Corporate Bardolph, stand
my friend; and here's four Harry ten shillings in
French crowns for you. In very truth, sir, I had
as lief be hang'd, sir, as go; and yet, for mine own
part, sir, I do not care; but rather, because I   239
am unwilling, and, for mine own part, have a desire
to stay with my friends; else, sir, I did not care,
for mine own part, so much.

Bard. Go to; stand aside.   243

Moul. And, good master corporal captain, for
my [old] dame's sake, stand my friend. She has
nobody to do anything about her when I am gone;
and she is old, and cannot help herself. You shall
have forty, sir.

Bard. Go to; stand aside.   249

Fee. By my troth, I care not; a man can die but
once; we owe God a death. I'll ne'er bear a base
mind. An't be my destiny, so; an't be not, so.
No man's too good to serve 's prince; and let it go
which way it will, he that dies this year is quit for
the next.   255

Bard. Well said; th' art a good fellow.

Fee. Faith, I'll bear no base mind.

Re-enter FALSTAFF *and the* JUSTICES.

Fal. Come, sir, which men shall I have?

Shal. Four of which you please.

Bard. [*Aside to Fal.*] Sir, a word with you. I
have three pound to free Mouldy and Bullcalf. 261

Fal. Go to; well.

Shal. Come, Sir John, which four will you have?

Fal. Do you choose for me.

Shal. Marry, then, Mouldy, Bullcalf, Feeble,
and Shadow.   267

Fal. Mouldy and Bullcalf! for you, Mouldy,
stay at home till you are past service; and for your
part, Bullcalf, grow till you come unto it. I will
none of you.

Shal. Sir John, Sir John, do not yourself wrong.
They are your likeliest men, and I would have
you serv'd with the best.   274

Fal. Will you tell me, Master Shallow, how to
choose a man? Care I for the limb, the thews, the
stature, bulk, and big assemblance of a man!
Give me the spirit, Master Shallow. Here's
Wart; you see what a ragged appearance it is. 'A
shall charge you and discharge you with the   280
motion of a pewterer's hammer, come off and on
swifter than he that gibbets on the brewer's bucket.
And this same half-fac'd fellow, Shadow; give me

this man. He presents no mark to the enemy; the
foeman may with as great aim level at the   285
edge of a penknife. And for a retreat; how swiftly
will this Feeble the woman's tailor run off! O, give
me the spare men, and spare me the great ones.
Put me a caliver into Wart's hand, Bardolph. 290

Bard. Hold, Wart, traverse; thus, thus, thus.

Fal. Come, manage me your caliver. So: very
well; go to; very good, exceeding good. O, give
me always a little, lean, old, chapt, bald shot.
Well said, i' faith, Wart; thou'rt a good scab.
Hold, there's a tester for thee.   296

Shal. He is not his craft's master; he doth not
do it right. I remember at Mile-end Green, when
I lay at Clement's Inn, — I was then Sir Dagonet
in Arthur's show, — there was a little quiver fellow, and 'a would manage you his piece thus; 301
and 'a would about and about, and come you in
and come you in. "Rah, tah, tah," would 'a say;
"bounce" would 'a say; and away again would 'a
go, and again would 'a come. I shall ne'er see such
a fellow.   306

Fal. These fellows will do well, Master Shallow.
God keep you, Master Silence; I will not use many
words with you. Fare you well, gentlemen both;
I thank you. I must a dozen mile to-night. Bardolph, give the soldiers coats.   311

Shal. Sir John, the Lord bless you! God
prosper your affairs! God send us peace! At your
return visit our house; let our old acquaintance be re-
newed. Peradventure I will with ye to the court. 316

Fal. 'Fore God, would you would [Master
Shallow].

Shal. Go to; I have spoke at a word. God keep
you!   320

Fal. Fare you well, gentle gentlemen. [*Exeunt
Justices.*] On, Bardolph; lead the men away.
[*Exeunt Bardolph, recruits, etc.*] As I return, I
will fetch off these justices. I do see the bottom
of Justice Shallow. Lord, Lord, how subject we
old men are to this vice of lying! This same   326
starv'd justice hath done nothing but prate to me of
the wildness of his youth, and the feats he hath
done about Turnbull Street; and every third word
a lie, duer paid to the hearer than the Turk's   330
tribute. I do remember him at Clement's Inn
like a man made after supper of a cheese-paring.
When 'a was naked, he was, for all the world,
like a forked radish, with a head fantastically
carv'd upon it with a knife. 'A was so forlorn,   335
that his dimensions to any thick sight were invincible. 'A was the very genius of famine, yet lecherous as a monkey, and the whores called him man-

---

245. [old] F. Om. Q. 277. **assemblance:** appearance. 282. **gibbets:** hangs on the yoke. 290. **caliver:** musket. 291.
traverse: march. 296. **tester:** sixpence. 300. **Arthur's show.** A company of London archers gave an annual exhibition at
Mile-End Green, each taking the name of one of King Arthur's knights. Sir Dagonet was the fool. 300. **quiver:** nimble.
317. [**Master Shallow**] F. Om. Q. 319. **at a word:** in one word. 324. **fetch off:** fleece. 330. **duer:** more duly. 337. **invincible:** not discernible.

drake. 'A came ever in the rearward of the fashion, and sung those tunes to the overscutch'd 340 huswives that he heard the carmen whistle, and sware they were his fancies or his good-nights. And now is this Vice's dagger become a squire, and talks as familiarly of John o' Gaunt as if he had been sworn brother to him; and I'll be sworn 345 'a ne'er saw him but once in the Tilt-yard; and then he burst his head for crowding among the marshal's men. I saw it, and told John o' Gaunt he beat his own name; for you might have thrust him and all his apparel into an eel-skin. The case of a 350 treble hautboy was a mansion for him, a court; and now has he land and beeves. Well, I'll be acquainted with him, if I return; and 't shall go hard but I will make him a philosopher's two stones to me. If the young dace be a bait for the old 355 pike, I see no reason in the law of nature but I may snap at him. Let time shape, and there an end.

[*Exit.*]

ACT IV

Scene I. [*Yorkshire.*] *Within the Forest of Gaultree.*

Enter the Archbishop of York, Mowbray, Hastings [*and others*].

Arch. What is this forest call'd?

Hast. 'Tis Gaultree Forest, an't shall please your Grace.

Arch. Here stand, my lords; and send discoverers forth
To know the numbers of our enemies.

Hast. We have sent forth already.

Arch.   'Tis well done.
My friends and brethren in these great affairs,   6
I must acquaint you that I have receiv'd
New-dated letters from Northumberland;
Their cold intent, tenour, and substance, thus:
Here doth he wish his person, with such powers   10
As might hold sortance with his quality,
The which he could not levy; whereupon
He is retir'd, to ripe his growing fortunes,
To Scotland; and concludes in hearty prayers
That your attempts may overlive the hazard   15
And fearful meeting of their opposite.

Mowb. Thus do the hopes we have in him touch ground
And dash themselves to pieces.

Enter a Messenger.

Hast.   Now, what news?

Mess. West of this forest, scarcely off a mile,

In goodly form comes on the enemy;   20
And, by the ground they hide, I judge their number
Upon or near the rate of thirty thousand.

Mowb. The just proportion that we gave them out.
Let us sway on and face them in the field.

Arch. What well-appointed leader fronts us here?   25

Enter Westmoreland.

Mowb. I think it is my Lord of Westmoreland.

West. Health and fair greeting from our general,
The Prince, Lord John and Duke of Lancaster.

Arch. Say on, my Lord of Westmoreland, in peace,
What doth concern your coming.

West.   [Then, my lord,]
Unto your Grace do I in chief address   31
The substance of my speech. If that rebellion
Came like itself, in base and abject routs,
Led on by bloody youth, guarded with [rags,]
And countenanc'd by boys and beggary, —   35
I say, if damn'd commotion so appear'd
In his true, native, and most proper shape,
You, reverend father, and these noble lords
Had not been here to dress the ugly form
Of base and bloody insurrection   40
With your fair honours. You, Lord Archbishop,
Whose see is by a civil peace maintain'd,
Whose beard the silver hand of peace hath touch'd,
Whose learning and good letters peace hath tutor'd,
Whose white investments figure innocence,   45
The dove, and very blessed spirit of peace,
Wherefore do you so ill translate yourself
Out of the speech of peace that bears such grace,
Into the harsh and boist'rous tongue of war;
Turning your books to graves, your ink to blood,
Your pens to lances and your tongue divine   51
To a loud trumpet and a point of war?

Arch. Wherefore do I this? so the question stands.
Briefly to this end: we are all diseas'd,
[And with our surfeiting and wanton hours   55
Have brought ourselves into a burning fever,
And we must bleed for it; of which disease
Our late king, Richard, being infected, died.
But, my most noble Lord of Westmoreland,
I take not on me here as a physician,   60
Nor do I as an enemy to peace
Troop in the throngs of military men;
But rather show awhile like fearful war
To diet rank minds sick of happiness,
And purge the obstructions which begin to stop   65

339. mandrake: a plant with a forked root. 340. overscutch'd huswives: worn-out strumpets. 342. fancies, goodnights: types of songs. 343. Vice: a character in the morality plays who carried a dagger of lath. 351. hautboy: oboe. 354. philosopher's two stones: as valuable as two philosopher's stones, which were supposed to change base metals to gold.

Act IV, sc. i, 11. sortance: accord. 23. just...out: exact number we estimated. 30. [Then, my lord] F. Om. Q. 34. guarded: dressed. [rags] (Singer). rage QF. 52. point: note of a trumpet. 55–79. F. Om. Q.

Our very veins of life.   Hear me more plainly.
I have in equal balance justly weigh'd
What wrongs our arms may do, what wrongs we
suffer,
And find our griefs heavier than our offences.
We see which way the stream of time doth run,   70
And are enforc'd from our most quiet there
By the rough torrent of occasion;
And have the summary of all our griefs,
When time shall serve, to show in articles;
Which long ere this we offer'd to the King,   75
And might by no suit gain our audience.
When we are wrong'd and would unfold our griefs,
We are deni'd access unto his person
Even by those men that most have done us wrong.]
The dangers of the days but newly gone,   80
Whose memory is written on the earth
With yet appearing blood, and the examples
Of every minute's instance, present now,
Hath put us in these ill-beseeming arms,
Not to break peace or any branch of it,   85
But to establish here a peace indeed,
Concurring both in name and quality.
    West. When ever yet was your appeal denied?
Wherein have you been galled by the King?   89
What peer hath been suborn'd to grate on you
That you should seal this lawless bloody book
Of forg'd rebellion with a seal divine
And consecrate commotion's bitter edge?
    Arch. My brother general, the commonwealth,
To brother born an household cruelty.   95
I make my quarrel in particular.
    West. There is no need of any such redress;
Or if there were, it not belongs to you.
    Mowb. Why not to him in part, and to us all
That feel the bruises of the days before,   100
And suffer the condition of these times
To lay a heavy and unequal hand
Upon our honours?
    West.   [O, my good Lord Mowbray,
Construe the times to their necessities,
And you shall say indeed, it is the time,   105
And not the King, that doth you injuries.
Yet for your part, it not appears to me
Either from the King or in the present time
That you should have an inch of any ground
To build a grief on. Were you not restor'd   110
To all the Duke of Norfolk's signories,
Your noble and right well-rememb'red father's?
    Mowb. What thing, in honour, had my father
lost,
That need to be reviv'd and breath'd in me?   114

The King that lov'd him, as the state stood then,
Was, force perforce, compell'd to banish him;
And then that Henry Bolingbroke and he,
Being mounted and both roused in their seats,
Their neighing coursers daring of the spur,   119
Their armed staves in charge, their beavers down,
Their eyes of fire sparkling through sights of steel,
And the loud trumpet blowing them together,
Then, then, when there was nothing could have stay'd
My father from the breast of Bolingbroke,   124
O, when the King did throw his warder down —
His own life hung upon the staff he threw, —
Then threw he down himself and all their lives
That by indictment and by dint of sword
Have since miscarried under Bolingbroke.
    West. You speak, Lord Mowbray, now you
know not what.   130
The Earl of Hereford was reputed then
In England the most valiant gentleman.
Who knows on whom Fortune would then have
smil'd?
But if your father had been victor there,
He ne'er had borne it out of Coventry;   135
For all the country in a general voice
Cried hate upon him; and all their prayers and love
Were set on Hereford, whom they doted on
And bless'd and grac'd and did, more than the
King, —]
But this is mere digression from my purpose.   140
Here come I from our princely general
To know your griefs; to tell you from his Grace
That he will give you audience; and wherein
It shall appear that your demands are just,
You shall enjoy them, everything set off   145
That might so much as think you enemies.
    Mowb. But he hath forc'd us to compel this offer;
And it proceeds from policy, not love.
    West. Mowbray, you overween to take it so;
This offer comes from mercy, not from fear.   150
For, lo! within a ken our army lies,
Upon mine honour, all too confident
To give admittance to a thought of fear.
Our battle is more full of names than yours,
Our men more perfect in the use of arms,   155
Our armour all as strong, our cause the best;
Then reason will our hearts should be as good.
Say you not then our offer is compell'd.
    Mowb. Well, by my will we shall admit no parley.
    West. That argues but the shame of your offence.
A rotten case abides no handling.   161
    Hast. Hath the Prince John a full commission,
In very ample virtue of his father,

---

69. **griefs:** grievances. 94-96. These lines are obviously defective. F. omits 95. York's brother, Scroop, had been exe-cuted by Henry. 103-139. F. Om. Q. 104. **to:** according to. 114. **breath'd:** have life breathed into it. 115 ff. Cf. *Rich. II,* I.iii.118 ff. 116. **force** (Theobald). *forc'd* F. 120. **armed . . . charge:** lances in rest. **beavers:** visors. 125. **warder:** staff. 129. **miscarried:** perished. 131. **Hereford:** Bolingbroke. 145. **set off:** disregarded. 151. **a ken:** sight. 157. **will:** will show. 163. **virtue:** power.

To hear and absolutely to determine
Of what conditions we shall stand upon?   165
    West. That is intended in the general's name.
I muse you make so slight a question.
    Arch. Then take, my Lord of Westmoreland, this
        schedule,
For this contains our general grievances.
Each several article herein redress'd,   170
All members of our cause, both here and hence,
That are insinew'd to this action,
Acquitted by a true substantial form,
And present execution of our wills
To us and to our purposes confin'd,   175
We come within our awful banks again
And knit our powers to the arm of peace.
    West. This will I show the general. Please you,
        lords,
In sight of both our battles we may meet;
And either end in peace, which God so frame!   180
Or to the place of diff'rence call the swords
Which must decide it.   [*Exit West.*
    Arch.   My lord, we will do so.
    Mowb. There is a thing within my bosom tells
        me
That no conditions of our peace can stand.
    Hast. Fear you not that. If we can make our
        peace   185
Upon such large terms and so absolute
As our conditions shall consist upon,
Our peace shall stand as firm as rocky mountains.
    Mowb. Yea, but our valuation shall be such
That every slight and false-derived cause,   190
Yea, every idle, nice, and wanton reason
Shall to the King taste of this action;
That, were our royal faiths martyrs in love,
We shall be winnow'd with so rough a wind
That even our corn shall seem as light as chaff   195
And good from bad find no partition.
    Arch. No, no, my lord. Note this: the King is
        weary
Of dainty and such picking grievances;
For he hath found to end one doubt by death
Revives two greater in the heirs of life,   200
And therefore will he wipe his tables clean
And keep no tell-tale to his memory
That may repeat and history his loss
To new remembrance; for full well he knows
He cannot so precisely weed this land   205
As his misdoubts present occasion.
His foes are so enrooted with his friends
That, plucking to unfix an enemy,
He doth unfasten so and shake a friend;

So that this land, like an offensive wife   210
That hath enrag'd him on to offer strokes,
As he is striking, holds his infant up
And hangs resolv'd correction in the arm
That was uprear'd to execution.
    Hast. Besides, the King hath wasted all his rods
On late offenders, that he now doth lack   216
The very instruments of chastisement;
So that his power, like to a fangless lion,
May offer, but not hold.
    Arch.   'Tis very true;
And therefore be assur'd, my good Lord Marshal,
If we do now make our atonement well,   221
Our peace will, like a broken limb united,
Grow stronger for the breaking.
    Mowb.   Be it so.
Here is return'd my Lord of Westmoreland.

Re-enter WESTMORELAND.

    West. The Prince is here at hand. Pleaseth
        your lordship   225
To meet his Grace just distance 'tween our armies.
    Mowb. Your Grace of York, in God's name, then,
        set forward.
    Arch. Before, and greet his Grace. My lord,
        we come.   [*Exeunt.*

[SCENE II. *Another part of the forest.*]

Enter [*from one side,* MOWBRAY, *attended; afterwards the* ARCHBISHOP, HASTINGS, *and others:
from the other side,*] PRINCE JOHN OF LANCASTER
[*and* WESTMORELAND; *Officers, and others with
them*].

    Lan. You are well encount'red here, my cousin
        Mowbray.
Good day to you, gentle Lord Archbishop;
And so to you, Lord Hastings, and to all.
My Lord of York, it better show'd with you
When that your flock, assembled by the bell,   5
Encircled you to hear with reverence
Your exposition on the holy text
Than now to see you here an iron man,
Cheering a rout of rebels with your drum,
Turning the Word to sword and life to death.   10
That man that sits within a monarch's heart
And ripens in the sunshine of his favour,
Would he abuse the countenance of the King,
Alack, what mischiefs might he set abroach
In shadow of such greatness! With you, Lord
        Bishop,   15
It is even so. Who hath not heard it spoken

---

166. **intended:** implied.   172. **insinew'd to:** involved in.   174-75. The immediate carrying out of our wishes as regards
ourselves and our plans.   176. **awful banks:** bounds of respect.   187. **upon:** of.   189. **valuation:** i.e., by the king.   193.
were ... love: though our fidelity to the king were as intense as the faith of martyrs.   198. **picking:** trifling.   203. **history:**
record.   213. **hangs resolv'd correction:** checks intended punishment.   219. **offer:** threaten.   226. **just:** precise.
Sc. ii, 8. **man** F.   *man talking* Q.   14. **set abroach:** start.

How deep you were within the books of God?
To us the speaker in His parliament;
To us the imagin'd voice of God himself;
The very opener and intelligencer 20
Between the grace, the sanctities, of Heaven
And our dull workings. O, who shall believe
But you misuse the reverence of your place,
[Employ] the countenance and grace of Heaven,
As a false favourite doth his prince's name, 25
In deeds dishonourable? You have ta'en up,
Under the counterfeited zeal of God,
The subjects of His substitute, my father,
And both against the peace of Heaven and him
Have here upswarm'd them.
    Arch.   Good my Lord of Lancaster,
I am not here against your father's peace; 31
But, as I told my Lord of Westmoreland,
The time misord'red doth, in common sense,
Crowd us and crush us to this monstrous form
To hold our safety up. I sent your Grace 35
The parcels and particulars of our grief,
The which hath been with scorn shov'd from the
    court,
Whereon this Hydra son of war is born;
Whose dangerous eyes may well be charm'd asleep
With grant of our most just and right desires; 40
And true obedience, of this madness cur'd,
Stoop tamely to the foot of majesty.
    Mowb. If not, we ready are to try our fortunes
To the last man.
    Hast.   And though we here fall down,
We have supplies to second our attempt. 45
If they miscarry, theirs shall second them;
And so success of mischief shall be born,
And heir from heir shall hold this quarrel up
Whiles England shall have generation.
    Lan. You are too shallow, Hastings, much too
    shallow, 50
To sound the bottom of the after-times.
    West. Pleaseth your Grace to answer them
    directly
How far forth you do like their articles.
    Lan. I like them all, and do allow them well,
And swear here, by the honour of my blood, 55
My father's purposes have been mistook,
And some about him have too lavishly
Wrested his meaning and authority.
My lord, these griefs shall be with speed redress'd;
Upon my soul, they shall. If this may please
    you, 60
Discharge your powers unto their several counties,
As we will ours; and here between the armies
Let's drink together friendly and embrace,
That all their eyes may bear those tokens home

Of our restored love and amity. 65
    Arch. I take your princely word for these re-
    dresses.
    Lan. I give it you, and will maintain my word;
And thereupon I drink unto your Grace.
    [*Hast.*] Go, captain, and deliver to the army
This news of peace. Let them have pay, and
    part. 70
I know it will well please them. Hie thee, captain.
                       [*Exit* [*Officer*].
    Arch. To you, my noble Lord of Westmoreland.
    West. I pledge your Grace; and, if you knew
    what pains
I have bestow'd to breed this present peace,
You would drink freely. But my love to ye 75
Shall show itself more openly hereafter.
    Arch. I do not doubt you.
    West.   I am glad of it.
Health to my lord and gentle cousin, Mowbray.
    Mowb. You wish me health in very happy
    season;
For I am, on the sudden, something ill. 80
    Arch. Against ill chances men are ever merry;
But heaviness foreruns the good event.
    West. Therefore be merry, coz; since sudden
    sorrow
Serves to say thus, some good thing comes to-
    morrow.
    Arch. Believe me, I am passing light in spirit. 85
    Mowb. So much the worse, if your own rule be
    true.   [*Shouts* [*within*].
    Lan. The word of peace is rend'red. Hark, how
    they shout!
    Mowb. This had been cheerful after victory.
    Arch. A peace is of the nature of a conquest;
For then both parties nobly are subdu'd, 90
And neither party loser.
    Lan.   Go, my lord,
And let our army be discharged too.
And, good my lord, so please you, let your trains
March by us, that we may peruse the men
               [*Exit* [*Westmoreland*].
We should have cop'd withal.
    Arch.   Go, good Lord Hastings,
And, ere they be dismiss'd, let them march by. 96
                  [*Exit* [*Hastings*].

Re-enter WESTMORELAND.

    Lan. I trust, lords, we shall lie to-night together.
Now cousin, wherefore stands our army still?
    West. The leaders, having charge from you to
    stand,
Will not go off until they hear you speak. 100
    Lan. They know their duties.

20. opener: interpreter. intelligencer: intermediary. 24. [Employ] F. *Imply* Q. 26. ta'en up: enlisted. 36. parcels: details. 38. Hydra: many-headed. 47. success: succession. 69. [Hast.] F. *Prince* Q. 81. Against: before. 87. rend'red: given out. 95. cop'd: fought.

Re-enter HASTINGS.

Hast. My lord, our army is dispers'd already.
Like youthful steers unyok'd, they take their
    courses
East, west, north, south; or, like a school broke up,
Each hurries toward his home and sporting-
    place.   105
West. Good tidings, my Lord Hastings; for the
    which
I do arrest thee, traitor, of high treason;
And you, Lord Archbishop, and you, Lord Mow-
    bray,
Of capital treason I attach you both.
Mowb. Is this proceeding just and honourable?
West. Is your assembly so?   111
Arch. Will you thus break your faith?
Lan.   I pawn'd thee none.
I promis'd you redress of these same grievances
Whereof you did complain; which, by mine honour,
I will perform with a most Christian care.   115
But for you, rebels, look to taste the due
Meet for rebellion [and such acts as yours].
Most shallowly did you these arms commence,
Fondly brought here and foolishly sent hence.
Strike up our drums, pursue the scatt'red stray. 120
God, and not we, hath safely fought to-day.
Some guard [these traitors] to the block of death,
Treason's true bed and yielder up of breath.
                                        [*Exeunt.*

[SCENE III.   *Another part of the forest.*]

Alarums. Excursion. Enter FALSTAFF *and*
    COLVILLE [*meeting*].

Fal. What's your name, sir? Of what condition
are you, and of what place, [I pray]?
Col. I am a knight, sir; and my name is Colville
of the Dale.   4
Fal. Well, then, Colville is your name, a knight
is your degree, and your place the Dale. Colville
shall be still your name, a traitor your degree, and
the dungeon your place, a place deep enough; so
shall you be still Colville of the Dale.   10
Col. Are not you Sir John Falstaff?
Fal. As good a man as he, sir, whoe'er I am. Do
ye yield, sir? or shall I sweat for you? If I do
sweat, they are the drops of thy lovers, and they
weep for thy death; therefore rouse up fear and
trembling, and do observance to my mercy.   17
Col. I think you are Sir John Falstaff, and in
that thought yield me.
Fal. I have a whole school of tongues in this belly
of mine, and not a tongue of them all speaks any

other word but my name. An I had but a belly of
any indifferency, I were simply the most active   23
fellow in Europe. My womb, my womb, my
womb, undoes me. Here comes our general.

Enter PRINCE JOHN OF LANCASTER, WEST-
    MORELAND, [BLUNT] *and others.*

Lan. The heat is past; follow no further now. 27
Call in the powers, good cousin Westmoreland.
                            [*Exit Westmoreland.*]
Now, Falstaff, where have you been all this while?
When everything is ended, then you come.
These tardy tricks of yours will, on my life,
One time or other break some gallows' back.   32
Fal. I would be sorry, my lord, but it should be
thus. I never knew yet but rebuke and check was
the reward of valour. Do you think me a swallow,
an arrow, or a bullet? Have I, in my poor and old
motion, the expedition of thought? I have   37
speeded hither with the very extremest inch of
possibility; I have found'red ninescore and odd
posts; and here, travel-tainted as I am, have, in my
pure and immaculate valour, taken Sir John Colville of the Dale, a most furious knight and valor- 42
ous enemy. But what of that? He saw me, and
yielded; that I may justly say, with the hook-
nos'd fellow of Rome, "I came, saw, and overcame."
Lan. It was more of his courtesy than your deserving.   48
Fal. I know not. Here he is, and here I yield
him; and I beseech your Grace, let it be book'd
with the rest of this day's deeds; or, by the Lord, I
will have it in a particular ballad else, with mine
own picture on the top on't, Colville kissing my
foot; to the which course if I be enforc'd, if you do
not all show like gilt twopences to me, and I in   55
the clear sky of fame o'ershine you as much as the
full moon doth the cinders of the element, which
show like pins' heads to her, believe not the word
of the noble. Therefore let me have right, and let
desert mount.   61
Lan. Thine's too heavy to mount.
Fal. Let it shine, then.
Lan. Thine's too thick to shine.
Fal. Let it do something, my good lord, that
may do me good, and call it what you will.   66
Lan. Is thy name Colville?
Col. It is, my lord.
Lan. A famous rebel art thou, Colville.
Fal. And a famous true subject took him.   70
Col. I am, my lord, but as my betters are
That led me hither. Had they been rul'd by me,
You should have won them dearer than you have.
Fal. I know not how they sold themselves; but

117. [and . . . yours] F. Om. Q.   120. stray: stragglers.   122. [these traitors] F. *this traitor* Q.
Sc. iii, 1. condition: rank.   2. [I pray] F. Om. Q.   23. indifferency: moderate bulk.   37. expedition: speed.   40. posts:
horses.   45. Rome F. *Rome, there cosin* Q.   57. cinders of the element: stars.

thou, like a kind fellow, gav'st thyself away gratis;
and I thank thee for thee.   76

Re-enter WESTMORELAND.

Lan. Now, have you left pursuit?

West. Retreat is made and execution stay'd.

Lan. Send Colville with his confederates
To York, to present execution.   80
Blunt, lead him hence; and see you guard him sure.
    [Exeunt [Blunt and others] with Colville.
And now dispatch we toward the court, my lords;
I hear the King my father is sore sick.
Our news shall go before us to his Majesty,
Which, cousin, you shall bear to comfort him,
And we with sober speed will follow you.   86

Fal. My lord, I beseech you, give me leave to go
Through Gloucestershire; and, when you come to
    court,
Stand my good lord, [pray,] in your good report.

Lan. Fare you well, Falstaff. I, in my condition,   90
Shall better speak of you than you deserve.
    [Exeunt [all but Falstaff].

Fal. I would you had [but] the wit; 'twere better
than your dukedom. Good faith, this same young
sober-blooded boy doth not love me, nor a man
cannot make him laugh; but that's no marvel, 95
he drinks no wine. There's never none of these
demure boys come to any proof; for thin drink doth
so over-cool their blood, and making many fish-
meals, that they fall into a kind of male green-
sickness; and then, when they marry, they get 100
wenches. They are generally fools and cowards;
which some of us should be too, but for inflammation. A good sherris-sack hath a two-fold operation in it. It ascends me into the brain; dries me
there all the foolish and dull and crudy vapours 105
which environ it; makes it apprehensive, quick,
forgetive, full of nimble, fiery, and delectable
shapes; which, delivered o'er to the voice, the
tongue, which is the birth, becomes excellent wit.
The second property of your excellent sherris 110
is, the warming of the blood; which, before cold and
settled, left the liver white and pale, which is the
badge of pusillanimity and cowardice; but the
sherris warms it and makes it course from the inwards to the parts extremes. It illumineth the 115
face, which as a beacon gives warning to all the
rest of this little kingdom, man, to arm; and then
the vital commoners and inland petty spirits
muster me all to their captain, the heart, who, 120
great and puff'd up with this retinue, doth any deed
of courage; and this valour comes of sherris. So

that skill in the weapon is nothing without sack,
for that sets it a-work; and learning a mere hoard
of gold kept by a devil, till sack commences it 125
and sets it in act and use. Hereof comes it that
Prince Harry is valiant; for the cold blood he did
naturally inherit of his father, he hath, like lean,
sterile, and bare land, manured, husbanded, and
till'd with excellent endeavour of drinking good 130
and good store of fertile sherris, that he is become
very hot and valiant. If I had a thousand sons,
the first humane principle I would teach them
should be, to forswear thin potations and to addict
themselves to sack.   135

Enter BARDOLPH.

How now, Bardolph?

Bard. The army is discharged all and gone.

Fal. Let them go. I'll through Gloucestershire; and there will I visit Master Robert Shallow,
esquire. I have him already tempering between my
finger and my thumb, and shortly will I seal with
him. Come away.   *[Exeunt.* 142

SCENE [IV. *Westminster. The Jerusalem
Chamber.*]

Enter the KING, *the* PRINCES THOMAS OF CLARENCE
and HUMPHREY OF GLOUCESTER, WARWICK [*and
others*].

King. Now, lords, if God doth give successful
    end
To this debate that bleedeth at our doors,
We will our youth lead on to higher fields,
And draw no swords but what are sanctifi'd.
Our navy is address'd, our power collected,   5
Our substitutes in absence well invested,
And everything lies level to our wish.
Only, we want a little personal strength;
And pause us, till these rebels, now afoot,
Come underneath the yoke of government.   10

War. Both which we doubt not but your Ma-
    jesty
Shall soon enjoy.

King.   Humphrey, my son of Gloucester,
Where is the Prince your brother?

Glou. I think he's gone to hunt, my lord, at
    Windsor.

King. And how accompanied?

Glou.   I do not know, my lord.

King. Is not his brother, Thomas of Clarence,
    with him?   16

Glou. No, my good lord; he is in presence here.

Clar. What would my lord and father?

---

89. [pray] F. Om. Q. 90. condition: official capacity. 92. [but] F. Om. Q. 97. come to any proof: develop
well. 99. green-sickness: anemia. 102. inflammation: i.e., by drink. 103. sherris-sack: sherry. 107. forgetive: inventive. 140. tempering: softening.
Sc. iv, 3. higher fields: Palestine. 5. address'd: ready.

King. Nothing but well to thee, Thomas of
   Clarence.
How chance thou art not with the Prince thy
   brother?   20
He loves thee, and thou dost neglect him, Thomas.
Thou hast a better place in his affection
Than all thy brothers. Cherish it, my boy,
And noble offices thou mayst effect
Of mediation, after I am dead,   25
Between his greatness and thy other brethren.
Therefore omit him not; blunt not his love,
Nor lose the good advantage of his grace
By seeming cold or careless of his will.
For he is gracious, if he be observ'd;   30
He hath a tear for pity, and a hand
Open as day for [melting] charity;
Yet notwithstanding, being incens'd, he's flint,
As humorous as winter, and as sudden
As flaws congealed in the spring of day.   35
His temper, therefore, must be well observ'd.
Chide him for faults, and do it reverently
When you perceive his blood inclin'd to mirth;
But, being moody, give him time and scope,
Till that his passions, like a whale on ground,   40
Confound themselves with working. Learn this,
   Thomas,
And thou shalt prove a shelter to thy friends,
A hoop of gold to bind thy brothers in,
That the united vessel of their blood,
Mingled with venom of suggestion,   45
(As, force perforce, the age will pour it in),
Shall never leak, though it do work as strong
As aconitum or rash gunpowder.
  Clar. I shall observe him with all care and love.
  King. Why art thou not at Windsor with him,
   Thomas?   50
  Clar. He is not there to-day; he dines in London.
  King. And how accompanied? [Canst thou tell
   that?]
  Clar. With Poins, and other his continual fol-
   lowers.
  King. Most subject is the fattest soil to weeds,
And he, the noble image of my youth,   55
Is overspread with them; therefore my grief
Stretches itself beyond the hour of death.
The blood weeps from my heart when I do shape
In forms imaginary the unguided days
And rotten times that you shall look upon   60
When I am sleeping with my ancestors.
For when his headstrong riot hath no curb,
When rage and hot blood are his counsellors,
When means and lavish manners meet together,
O, with what wings shall his affections fly   65

Towards fronting peril and oppos'd decay!
  War. My gracious lord, you look beyond him
   quite.
The Prince but studies his companions
Like a strange tongue, wherein, to gain the lan-
   guage,
'Tis needful that the most immodest word   70
Be look'd upon and learn'd; which once attain'd,
Your Highness knows, comes to no further use
But to be known and hated. So, like gross terms,
The Prince will in the perfectness of time
Cast off his followers; and their memory   75
Shall as a pattern or a measure live,
By which his Grace must mete the lives of others,
Turning past evils to advantages.
  King. 'Tis seldom when the bee doth leave her
   comb
In the dead carrion.

            Enter WESTMORELAND.

            Who's here? Westmoreland?
  West. Health to my sovereign, and new happi-
   ness   81
Added to that that I am to deliver!
Prince John your son doth kiss your Grace's hand.
Mowbray, the Bishop Scroop, Hastings and all
Are brought to the correction of your law.   85
There is not now a rebel's sword unsheath'd,
But Peace puts forth her olive everywhere.
The manner how this action hath been borne
Here at more leisure may your Highness read,
With every course in his particular.   90
  King. O Westmoreland, thou art a summer bird,
Which ever in the haunch of winter sings
The lifting up of day.

           Enter HARCOURT.

            Look, here's more news.
  Har. From enemies heaven keep your Majesty;
And, when they stand against you, may they fall   95
As those that I am come to tell you of!
The Earl Northumberland and the Lord Bardolph,
With a great power of English and of Scots,
Are by the sheriff of Yorkshire overthrown.
The manner and true order of the fight   100
This packet, please it you, contains at large.
  King. And wherefore should these good news
   make me sick?
Will Fortune never come with both hands full,
But [write] her fair words still in foulest [letters]?
She either gives a stomach and no food;   105
Such are the poor, in health; or else a feast
And takes away the stomach; such are the rich,

---

27. **omit:** neglect. 30. **observ'd:** paid respect to. 32. **[melting]** F. *meeting* Q. 34. **humorous:** capricious. 35. **flaws:**
blasts of wind. 45. **suggestion:** gossip. 48. **aconitum:** a poisonous plant. 52. **[Canst . . . that]** F. Om. Q. 66. **oppos'd
decay:** decay facing him. 67. **look beyond:** misinterpret. 92. **haunch:** latter end. 104. **[write] . . . [letters]** F. *wet . . .
termes* Q.

Crown Scene (handwritten)

That have abundance and enjoy it not.
I should rejoice now at this happy news;
And now my sight fails, and my brain is giddy.
O me! come near me; now I am much ill.   111
  Glou. Comfort, your Majesty!
  Clar.   O my royal father!
  West. My sovereign lord, cheer up yourself,
    look up.
  War. Be patient, Princes; you do know, these
    fits
Are with his Highness very ordinary.   115
Stand from him, give him air. He'll straight be
    well.
  Clar. No, no, he cannot long hold out these pangs.
The incessant care and labour of his mind
Hath wrought the mure that should confine it in
So thin that life looks through [and will break
    out].   120
  Glou. The people fear me; for they do observe
Unfather'd heirs and loathly births of nature.
The seasons change their manners, as the year
Had found some months asleep and leap'd them
    over.
  Clar. The river hath thrice flow'd, no ebb be-
    tween;   125
And the old folk, time's doting chronicles,
Say it did so a little time before
That our great-grandsire, Edward, sick'd and
    died.
  War. Speak lower, Princes, for the King re-
    covers.
  Glou. This apoplexy will certain be his end. 130
  King. I pray you, take me up, and bear me hence
Into some other chamber. [Softly, pray.]
            [*Exeunt. The King is borne out.*]

- [SCENE V. *Another chamber.*
The KING *lying on a bed:* CLARENCE, GLOUCESTER,
  WARWICK, *and others in attendance.*]

  King. Let there be no noise made, my gentle
    friends,
Unless some dull and favourable hand
Will whisper music to my weary spirit.
  Wor. Call for the music in the other room.
  King. Set me the crown upon my pillow here. 5
  Clar. His eye is hollow, and he changes much.
  War. Less noise, less noise!

            Enter PRINCE HENRY.

  Prince.   Who saw the Duke of Clarence?
  Clar. I am here, brother, full of heaviness.
  Prince. How now! rain within doors, and none
    abroad!

  Prince.   How doth the King?   10
  Glou. Exceeding ill.
  Prince.   Heard he the good news yet?
Tell it him.
  Glou. He [alt'red] much upon the hearing it.
  Prince. If he be sick with joy, he'll recover with-
out physic.   15
  War. Not so much noise, my lords. Sweet
    Prince, speak low;
The King, your father, is dispos'd to sleep.
  Clar. Let us withdraw into the other room.
  War. Will't please your Grace to go along with
    us?
  Prince. No; I will sit and watch here by the
    King.   [*Exeunt all but the Prince.*] 20
Why doth the crown lie there upon his pillow,
Being so troublesome a bedfellow?
O polish'd perturbation! golden care!
That keep'st the ports of slumber open wide
To many a watchful night! Sleep with it now! 25
Yet not so sound and half so deeply sweet
As he whose brow with homely biggen bound
Snores out the watch of night. O majesty!
When thou dost pinch thy bearer, thou dost sit
Like a rich armour worn in heat of day, 30
That scald'st with safety. By his gates of breath
There lies a downy feather which stirs not.
Did he suspire, that light and weightless down
Perforce must move. My gracious lord! my father!
This sleep is sound indeed; this is a sleep 35
That from this golden rigol hath divorc'd
So many English kings. Thy due from me
Is tears and heavy sorrows of the blood,
Which nature, love, and filial tenderness
Shall, O dear father, pay thee plenteously. 40
My due from thee is this imperial crown,
Which, as immediate from thy place and blood,
Derives itself to me. [*Puts on the crown.*] Lo,
    where it sits,
Which God shall guard; and put the world's whole
    strength
Into one giant arm, it shall not force 45
This lineal honour from me. This from thee
Will I to mine leave, as 'tis left to me.   [*Exit.*
  King. Warwick! Gloucester! Clarence!

  Re-enter WARWICK, GLOUCESTER, CLARENCE
            [*and the rest*].

  Clar. Doth the King call?
  War. What would your Majesty? [How fares
    your Grace?] 50
  King. Why did you leave me here alone, my
    lords?

119. **wrought the mure:** worn away the wall.   120. **[and ... out]** F. Om. Q.   121. **fear:** frighten.   132. **[Softly,
pray]** F. Om. Q.
Sc. v, 2. **dull:** soft.   27. **biggen:** nightcap.   31. **with:** giving.   36. **rigol:** circle.   50. **[How fares your Grace?]** F. Om. Q.

Clar. We left the Prince my brother here, my
   liege,
Who undertook to sit and watch by you.
  King. The Prince of Wales! Where is he? Let
   me see him.
He is not here. 55
  War. This door is open; he is gone this way.
  Glou. He came not through the chamber where
   we stay'd.
  King. Where is the crown? Who took it from
   my pillow?
  War. When we withdrew, my liege, we left it
   here.
  King. The Prince hath ta'en it hence. Go, seek
   him out. 60
Is he so hasty that he doth suppose
My sleep my death?
Find him, my Lord of Warwick; chide him hither.
                    [*Exit Warwick.*]
This part of his conjoins with my disease,
And helps to end me. See, sons, what things you
   are! 65
How quickly nature falls into revolt
When gold becomes her object!
For this the foolish over-careful fathers
Have broke their sleep with thoughts, their brains
   with care,
Their bones with industry; 70
For this they have engrossed and pil'd up
The cank'red heaps of strange-achieved gold;
For this they have been thoughtful to invest
Their sons with arts and martial exercises;
When, like the bee, tolling from every flower 75
[The virtuous sweets],
Our thighs pack'd with wax, our mouths with
   honey,
We bring it to the hive, and, like the bees,
Are murd'red for our pains. This bitter taste
Yields his engrossments to the ending father. 80

           Re-enter WARWICK.

Now, where is he that will not stay so long
Till his friend sickness hath determin'd me?
  War. My lord, I found the Prince in the next
   room,
Washing with kindly tears his gentle cheeks,
With such a deep demeanour in great sorrow 85
That Tyranny, which never quaff'd but blood,
Would, by beholding him, have wash'd his knife
With gentle eye-drops. He is coming hither.
  King. But wherefore did he take away the crown?

          Re-enter PRINCE HENRY.

Lo, where he comes. Come hither to me, Harry. 90

Depart the chamber, leave us here alone.
           [*Exeunt [Warwick and the rest].*
  Prince. I never thought to hear you speak again.
  King. Thy wish was father, Harry, to that
   thought.
I stay too long by thee, I weary thee.
Dost thou so hunger for mine empty chair 95
That thou wilt needs invest thee with mine honours
Before thy hour be ripe? O foolish youth!
Thou seek'st the greatness that will overwhelm
   thee.
Stay but a little; for my cloud of dignity
Is held from falling with so weak a wind 100
That it will quickly drop. My day is dim.
Thou hast stol'n that which after some few hours
Were thine without offence; and at my death
Thou hast seal'd up my expectation.
Thy life did manifest thou lov'dst me not, 105
And thou wilt have me die assur'd of it.
Thou hid'st a thousand daggers in thy thoughts,
Which thou hast whetted on thy stony heart
To stab at half an hour of my life.
What! canst thou not forbear me half an hour? 110
Then get thee gone and dig my grave thyself,
And bid the merry bells ring to thine ear
That thou art crowned, not that I am dead.
Let all the tears that should bedew my hearse
Be drops of balm to sanctify thy head; 115
Only compound me with forgotten dust;
Give that which gave thee life unto the worms.
Pluck down my officers, break my decrees;
For now a time is come to mock at form.
Harry the Fifth is crown'd! Up, vanity! 120
Down, royal state! All you sage counsellors,
   hence!
And to the English court assemble now,
From every region, apes of idleness!
Now, neighbour confines, purge you of your scum!
Have you a ruffian that will swear, drink, dance, 125
Revel the night, rob, murder, and commit
The oldest sins the newest kind of ways?
Be happy, he will trouble you no more.
England shall double gild his treble guilt,
England shall give him office, honour, might; 130
For the fifth Harry from curb'd license plucks
The muzzle of restraint, and the wild dog
Shall flesh his tooth on every innocent.
O my poor kingdom, sick with civil blows!
When that my care could not withhold thy riots,
What wilt thou do when riot is thy care? 136
O, thou wilt be a wilderness again,
Peopled with wolves, thy old inhabitants!
  Prince. O, pardon me, my liege! but for my tears,
The moist impediments unto my speech, 140
I had forestall'd this dear and deep rebuke

---

64. **part:** deed. 69. **thoughts:** worries. 71. **engrossed:** accumulated. 72. **cank'red:** tarnished. 76. **[The ... sweets]**
F. Om. Q. 82. **determin'd:** ended. 84. **kindly:** natural. 104. **seal'd up:** confirmed. 141. **dear:** cutting to the heart.

Ere you with grief had spoke and I had heard
The course of it so far.　There is your crown;
And He that wears the crown immortally
Long guard it yours!　If I affect it more　145
Than as your honour and as your renown,
Let me no more from this obedience rise,　[Kneels.]
Which my most inward, true, and duteous spirit
Teacheth, this prostrate and exterior bending.
God witness with me, when I here came in,　150
And found no course of breath within your Majesty,
How cold it struck my heart!　If I do feign,
O, let me in my present wildness die
And never live to show th' incredulous world
The noble change that I have purposed!　155
Coming to look on you, thinking you dead,
And dead almost, my liege, to think you were,
I spake unto this crown as having sense,
And thus upbraided it: "The care on thee depending
Hath fed upon the body of my father;　160
Therefore, thou best of gold art [worst of] gold.
Other, less fine in carat, [is] more precious,
Preserving life in medicine potable;
But thou, most fine, most honour'd, most renown'd,
Hast eat thy bearer up."　Thus, my most royal liege,　165
Accusing it, I put it on my head,
To try with it, as with an enemy
That had before my face murdered my father,
The quarrel of a true inheritor.
But if it did infect my blood with joy,　170
Or swell my thoughts to any strain of pride;
If any rebel or vain spirit of mine
Did with the least affection of a welcome
Give entertainment to the might of it,
Let God for ever keep it from my head　175
And make me as the poorest vassal is
That doth with awe and terror kneel to it!
　King.　[O my son,]
God put it in thy mind to take it hence,
That thou mightst win the more thy father's love,
Pleading so wisely in excuse of it!　181
Come hither, Harry, sit thou by my bed;
And hear, I think, the very latest counsel
That ever I shall breathe.　God knows, my son,
By what by-paths and indirect crook'd ways　185
I met this crown; and I myself know well
How troublesome it sat upon my head.
To thee it shall descend with better quiet,
Better opinion, better confirmation;
For all the soil of the achievement goes　190

With me into the earth.　It seem'd in me
But as an honour snatch'd with boist'rous hand,
And I had many living to upbraid
My gain of it by their assistances;
Which daily grew to quarrel and to bloodshed,　195
Wounding supposed peace.　All these bold fears
Thou see'st with peril I have answered;
For all my reign hath been but as a scene
Acting that argument; and now my death
Changes the mode; for what in me was purchas'd
Falls upon thee in a more fairer sort;　201
So thou the garland wear'st successively.
Yet, though thou stand'st more sure than I could do,
Thou art not firm enough, since griefs are green;
And all [my] friends, which thou must make thy friends,　205
Have but their stings and teeth newly ta'en out,
By whose fell working I was first advanc'd
And by whose power I well might lodge a fear
To be again displac'd; which to avoid,
I cut them off; and had a purpose now　210
To lead out many to the Holy Land,
Lest rest and lying still might make them look
Too near unto my state.　Therefore, my Harry,
Be it thy course to busy giddy minds
With foreign quarrels, that action, hence borne out,
May waste the memory of the former days.　216
More would I, but my lungs are wasted so
That strength of speech is utterly deni'd me.
How I came by the crown, O God forgive;
And grant it may with thee in true peace live!　220
　Prince.　[My gracious liege,]
You won it, wore it, kept it, gave it me;
Then plain and right must my possession be,
Which I with more than with a common pain
'Gainst all the world will rightfully maintain.　225

Enter LORD JOHN OF LANCASTER and WARWICK.

　King.　Look, look, here comes my John of Lancaster.
　Lan.　Health, peace, and happiness to my royal father!
　King.　Thou bring'st me happiness and peace, son John;
But health, alack, with youthful wings is flown
From this bare wither'd trunk.　Upon thy sight　230
My worldly business makes a period.
Where is my Lord of Warwick?
　Prince.　　　　　　　My Lord of Warwick!
　King.　Doth any name particular belong
Unto the lodging where I first did swoon?
　War.　'Tis call'd Jerusalem, my noble lord.　235

145. affect: love.　161. [worst of] F.　worse than Q.　162. [is] F.　Om. Q.　163. potable: drinkable.　Gold was valued as a medicine.　171. strain: tendency.　178. [O my son] F.　Om. Q.　189. opinion: support of public opinion.　200. purchas'd: acquired (often wrongly).　202. successively: by inheritance.　205. [my] (Tyrwhitt conj.).　thy QF.　207. fell: violent.　215. hence: abroad.　221. [My gracious liege] F.　Om. Q.　224. pain: effort.　230. Upon thy sight: seeing thee.　235. Jerusalem: a chamber in Westminster Abbey.

King. Laud be to God! even there my life must
end.
It hath been prophesi'd to me many years,
I should not die but in Jerusalem;
Which vainly I suppos'd the Holy Land.
But bear me to that chamber; there I'll lie;   240
In that Jerusalem shall Harry die.   [*Exeunt.*

ACT V

SCENE I. [*Gloucestershire. Shallow's house.*]

Enter SHALLOW, FALSTAFF, BARDOLPH, *and* Page.

Shal. By cock and pie, sir, you shall not away
to-night. What, Davy, I say!

Fal. You must excuse me, Master Robert
Shallow.   4

Shal. I will not excuse you; you shall not be
excus'd; excuses shall not be admitted; there is no
excuse shall serve; you shall not be excus'd. Why,
Davy!

[*Enter* DAVY.]

Davy. Here, sir.   9

Shal. Davy, Davy, Davy, Davy, let me see,
Davy; let me see, Davy; let me see. Yea, marry,
William cook, bid him come hither. Sir John, you
shall not be excus'd.

Davy. Marry, sir, thus; those precepts cannot
be serv'd; and, again, sir, shall we sow the headland
with wheat?   16

Shal. With red wheat, Davy. But for William
cook: are there no young pigeons?

Davy. Yes, sir. Here is now the smith's note for
shoeing and plough-irons.   20

Shal. Let it be cast and paid. Sir John, you
shall not be excus'd.

Davy. Now, sir, a new link to the bucket must
needs be had; and, sir, do you mean to stop any of
William's wages, about the sack he lost [the other
day] at Hinckley fair?   26

Shal. 'A shall answer it. Some pigeons, Davy,
a couple of short-legg'd hens, a joint of mutton, and
any pretty little tiny kickshaws, tell William cook.

Davy. Doth the man of war stay all night, sir?   31

Shal. Yea, Davy; I will use him well. A friend
i' th' court is better than a penny in purse. Use his
men well, Davy; for they are arrant knaves, and
will backbite.   36

Davy. No worse than they are backbitten, sir;
for they have marvellous foul linen.

Shal. Well conceited, Davy. About thy business, Davy.   40

Davy. I beseech you, sir, to countenance William
Visor of Woncot against Clement Perkes o' th' hill.

Shal. There is many complaints, Davy, against
that Visor. That Visor is an arrant knave, on my
knowledge.   46

Davy. I grant your worship that he is a knave,
sir; but yet, God forbid, sir, but a knave should
have some countenance at his friend's request. An
honest man, sir, is able to speak for himself, when a
knave is not. I have serv'd your worship truly,   51
sir, this eight years; and if I cannot once or twice in
a quarter bear out a knave against an honest man, I
have [but a very] little credit with your worship.
The knave is mine honest friend, sir; therefore, I
beseech you, let him be countenanc'd.   57

Shal. Go to; I say he shall have no wrong. Look
about, Davy. [*Exit Davy.*] Where are you, Sir
John? Come, come, come, off with your boots.
Give me your hand, Master Bardolph.   62

Bard. I am glad to see your worship.

Shal. I thank thee with [all] my heart, kind
Master Bardolph: and welcome, my tall fellow [*to
the Page*]. Come, Sir John.   66

Fal. I'll follow you, good Master Robert Shallow. [*Exit Shallow.*] Bardolph, look to our
horses. [*Exeunt Bardolph and Page.*] If I were
saw'd into quantities, I should make four dozen   70
of such bearded hermits' staves as Master Shallow.
It is a wonderful thing to see the semblable coherence of his men's spirits and his. They, by
observing him, do bear themselves like foolish
justices; he, by conversing with them, is turn'd   75
into a justice-like serving-man. Their spirits are
so married in conjunction with the participation of
society that they flock together in consent, like so
many wild-geese. If I had a suit to Master Shallow, I would humour his men with the imputa-   80
tion of being near their master; if to his men, I
would curry with Master Shallow that no man
could better command his servants. It is certain
that either wise bearing or ignorant carriage is
caught, as men take diseases, one of another;   85
therefore let men take heed of their company. I
will devise matter enough out of this Shallow to
keep Prince Harry in continual laughter the wearing out of six fashions, which is four terms, or two
actions, and 'a shall laugh without intervallums.   90
O, it is much that a lie with a slight oath and a jest
with a sad brow will do with a fellow that never had
the ache in his shoulders! O, you shall see him
laugh till his face be like a wet cloak ill laid up.   95

Act V, sc. i, 14. **precepts:** summonses. 21. **cast:** reckoned. 25-26. **[the other day]** F. Om. Q. 29. **kickshaws:** fancy
dishes. 39. **Well conceited:** wittily said. 41. **countenance:** favor. 54. **[but a very]** F. Om. Q. 64. **[all]** F. Om. Q.
72. **semblable coherence:** similarity. 78. **consent:** agreement. 89. **terms:** i.e., of court. 90. **actions:** lawsuits. 92. **sad:**
serious.

Shal. [*Within.*] Sir John!

Fal. I come, Master Shallow; I come, Master Shallow.　　　　　　　　　　　　　　　　[*Exit.*

SCENE II. [*Westminster. The palace.*]

Enter WARWICK *and the* LORD CHIEF JUSTICE [*meeting*].

War. How now, my Lord Chief Justice; whither away?

Ch. Just. How doth the King?

War. Exceeding well; his cares are now all ended.

Ch. Just. I hope, not dead.

War.　　　　　　　He's walk'd the way of nature;
And to our purposes he lives no more.　　　　5

Ch. Just. I would his Majesty had call'd me with him.
The service that I truly did his life
Hath left me open to all injuries.

War. Indeed I think the young King loves you not.

Ch. Just. I know he doth not, and do arm myself　　　　　　　　　　　　　　　　　10
To welcome the condition of the time,
Which cannot look more hideously upon me
Than I have drawn it in my fantasy.

Enter LANCASTER, CLARENCE, GLOUCESTER [WESTMORELAND, *and others*].

War. Here come the heavy issue of dead Harry:
O that the living Harry had the temper　　15
Of him, the worst of these three gentlemen!
How many nobles then should hold their places,
That must strike sail to spirits of vile sort!

Ch. Just. O God, I fear all will be overturn'd!

Lan. Good morrow, cousin Warwick, good morrow.　　　　　　　　　　　　　　　20

Glou. }
Clar. } Good morrow, cousin.

Lan. We meet like men that had forgot to speak.

War. We do remember; but our argument
Is all too heavy to admit much talk.

Lan. Well, peace be with him that hath made us heavy!　　　　　　　　　　　　　25

Ch. Just. Peace be with us, lest we be heavier!

Glou. O, good my lord, you have lost a friend indeed;
And I dare swear you borrow not that face
Of seeming sorrow; it is sure your own.

Lan. Though no man be assur'd what grace to find,　　　　　　　　　　　　　　　30
You stand in coldest expectation.
I am the sorrier; would 'twere otherwise!

Clar. Well, you must now speak Sir John Falstaff fair;
Which swims against your stream of quality.

Ch. Just. Sweet princes, what I did, I did in honour,　　　　　　　　　　　　　　　35
Led by th' impartial conduct of my soul;
And never shall you see that I will beg
A ragged and forestall'd remission.
If truth and upright innocency fail me,
I'll to the King my master that is dead,　　40
And tell him who hath sent me after him.

War. Here comes the Prince.

Enter KING HENRY THE FIFTH [*attended*].

Ch. Just. Good morrow; and God save your Majesty!

King. This new and gorgeous garment, majesty,
Sits not so easy on me as you think.　　45
Brothers, you mix your sadness with some fear.
This is the English, not the Turkish court;
Not Amurath an Amurath succeeds,
But Harry Harry. Yet be sad, good brothers,
For, by my faith, it very well becomes you.　50
Sorrow so royally in you appears
That I will deeply put the fashion on
And wear it in my heart. Why then, be sad;
But entertain no more of it, good brothers,
Than a joint burden laid upon us all.　　55
For me, by heaven, I bid you be assur'd,
I'll be your father and your brother too.
Let me but bear your love, I'll bear your cares.
Yet weep that Harry's dead, and so will I;
But Harry lives, that shall convert those tears　60
By number into hours of happiness.

Princes. We hope no other from your Majesty.

King. You all look strangely on me, and you most.
You are, I think, assur'd I love you not.

Ch. Just. I am assur'd, if I be measur'd rightly,
Your Majesty hath no just cause to hate me.　66

King. No?
How might a prince of my great hopes forget
So great indignities you laid upon me?
What! rate, rebuke, and roughly send to prison　70
The immediate heir of England! Was this easy?
May this be wash'd in Lethe, and forgotten?

Ch. Just. I then did use the person of your father;
The image of his power lay then in me;
And, in th' administration of his law,　　75
Whiles I was busy for the commonwealth,
Your Highness pleased to forget my place,
The majesty and power of law and justice,
The image of the King whom I presented,
And struck me in my very seat of judgement;　80

Sc. ii, 23. **argument:** subject. 34. **stream of quality:** tendency of your character. 38. **ragged:** beggarly. **forestall'd:** destined to be refused. 48. **Amurath:** a Turkish emperor who, on his accession, strangled his five brothers. 71. **easy:** a small thing. 73. **use the person of:** represent.

Whereon, as an offender to your father,
I gave bold way to my authority
And did commit you. If the deed were ill,
Be you contented, wearing now the garland,
To have a son set your decrees at nought?   85
To pluck down justice from your awful bench?
To trip the course of law and blunt the sword
That guards the peace and safety of your person?
Nay, more, to spurn at your most royal image
And mock your workings in a second body?   90
Question your royal thoughts, make the case yours:
Be now the father and propose a son,
Hear your own dignity so much profan'd,
See your most dreadful laws so loosely slighted,
Behold yourself so by a son disdained;   95
And then imagine me taking your part
And in your power soft silencing your son.
After this cold considerance, sentence me;
And, as you are a king, speak in your state
What I have done that misbecame my place,   100
My person, or my liege's sovereignty.

  King. You are right, Justice, and you weigh this
      well,
Therefore still bear the balance and the sword,
And I do wish your honours may increase,
Till you do live to see a son of mine   105
Offend you and obey you, as I did.
So shall I live to speak my father's words:
"Happy am I, that have a man so bold,
That dares do justice on my proper son;
And not less happy, having such a son   110
That would deliver up his greatness so
Into the hands of justice." You did commit me;
For which I do commit into your hand
Th' unstained sword that you have us'd to bear,
With this remembrance, that you use the same   115
With the like bold, just, and impartial spirit
As you have done 'gainst me. There is my hand.
You shall be as a father to my youth,
My voice shall sound as you do prompt mine ear,
And I will stoop and humble my intents   120
To your well-practis'd wise directions.
And, princes all, believe me, I beseech you,
My father is gone wild into his grave,
For in his tomb lie my affections;
And with his spirit sadly I survive,   125
To mock the expectation of the world,
To frustrate prophecies, and to raze out
Rotten opinion, who hath writ me down
After my seeming. The tide of blood in me
Hath proudly flow'd in vanity till now: 130
Now doth it turn and ebb back to the sea,
Where it shall mingle with the state of floods

And flow henceforth in formal majesty.
Now call we our high court of parliament;
And let us choose such limbs of noble counsel   135
That the great body of our state may go
In equal rank with the best govern'd nation;
That war, or peace, or both at once, may be
As things acquainted and familiar to us;
In which you, father, shall have foremost hand.   140
Our coronation done, we will accite,
As I before rememb'red, all our state;
And, God consigning to my good intents,
No prince nor peer shall have just cause to say,
God shorten Harry's happy life one day!   145
                              [*Exeunt.*

SCENE III. [*Gloucestershire.   Shallow's orchard.*]

          Enter FALSTAFF, SHALLOW, SILENCE, DAVY,
              BARDOLPH, *and the* Page.

  Shal. Nay, you shall see my orchard, where,
in an arbour, we will eat a last year's pippin of
mine own graffing, with a dish of caraways, and
so forth, — come, cousin Silence, — and then to
bed.   5
  Fal. 'Fore God, you have here a goodly dwelling
and [a] rich.
  Shal. Barren, barren, barren; beggars all, beggars all, Sir John: marry, good air.   Spread,
Davy; spread, Davy.   Well said, Davy.   10
  Fal. This Davy serves you for good uses; he is
your serving-man and your husband.
  Shal. A good varlet, a good varlet, a very good
varlet, Sir John.   By the mass, I have drunk
too much sack at supper.   A good varlet.   Now
sit down, now sit down.   Come, cousin.   16
  Sil. Ah, sirrah! quoth-a, we shall
[*Singing.*]
"Do nothing but eat, and make good cheer,
    And praise God for the merry year,
    When flesh is cheap and females dear,   20
    And lusty lads roam here and there
            So merrily,
    And ever among so merrily."
  Fal. There's a merry heart!   Good Master
Silence, I'll give you a health for that anon.   25
  Shal. Give Master Bardolph some wine, Davy.
  Davy. Sweet sir, sit; I'll be with you anon;
most sweet sir, sit.   Master page, good master
page, sit.   Proface!   What you want in meat, we'll
have in drink; but you must bear.   The heart's
all.   [*Exit.*] 32
  Shal. Be merry, Master Bardolph; and, my little
soldier there, be merry.

---

  90. second body: deputy.   92. propose: imagine.   98. considerance: consideration.   99. state: royal capacity.   109.
proper: own.   123. wild: carrying my wildness.   124. affections: previous inclinations.   125. sadly: soberly.   132. state
of floods: ocean's majesty.   141. accite: summon.   142. rememb'red: mentioned.   143. consigning: assenting.
    Sc. iii, 3. graffing: grafting.   10. said: done.   12. husband: manager.   29. Proface: your health!

Sil. [*Singing.*] "Be merry, be merry, my wife
    has all;
    For women are shrews, both short and
      tall.
    'Tis merry in hall when beards wag all,
      And welcome merry Shrove-tide.
    Be merry, be merry."   39
Fal. I did not think Master Silence had been a
man of this mettle.
Sil. Who? I? I have been merry twice and
once ere now.

Re-enter DAVY.

Davy. There's a dish of leather-coats for you.
                          [*To Bardolph.*]
Shal. Davy!   45
Davy. Your worship! I'll be with you straight.
A cup of wine, sir?
Sil. [*Singing.*] "A cup of wine that's brisk and
      fine,
    And drink unto the leman mine;
      And a merry heart lives long-a."   50
Fal. Well said, Master Silence.
Sil. An we shall be merry, now comes in the
sweet o' th' night.
Fal. Health and long life to you, Master
Silence.   55
Sil. [*Singing.*] "Fill the cup, and let it come;
    I'll pledge you a mile to the bottom."
Shal. Honest Bardolph, welcome. If thou
want'st anything, and wilt not call, beshrew thy
heart. Welcome, my little tiny thief [*to the Page*],
and welcome indeed too. I'll drink to Master Bar-
dolph, and to all the cabileros about London.   63
Davy. I hope to see London once ere I die.
Bard. An I might see you there, Davy, —
Shal. By the mass, you'll crack a quart together,
ha! will you not, Master Bardolph?
Bard. Yea, sir, in a pottle-pot.   68
Shal. By God's liggens, I thank thee. The
knave will stick by thee, I can assure thee that.
'A will not out; [he is] true bred.
Bard. And I'll stick by him, sir.   72
                        [*One knocks at door.*
Shal. Why, there spoke a king. Lack nothing;
be merry! Look who's at door there. Ho! who
knocks?   [*Exit Davy.*]
Fal. Why, now you have done me right.   76
    [*To Silence, seeing him take off a bumper.*]
Sil. [*Singing.*] "Do me right,
      And dub me knight:
        S'amingo."
Is't not so?   80

Fal. 'Tis so.
Sil. Is't so? Why then, say an old man can
do somewhat.

[Re-enter DAVY.]

Davy. An't please your worship, there's one
Pistol come from the court with news.   85
Fal. From the court! Let him come in.

Enter PISTOL.

How now, Pistol!
Pist. Sir John, God save you!
Fal. What wind blew you hither, Pistol?   89
Pist. Not the ill wind which blows no man to
good. Sweet knight, thou art now one of the
greatest men in this realm.
Sil. By 'r lady, I think 'a be, but goodman Puff
of Barson.
Pist. Puff!   95
Puff i' thy teeth, most recreant coward base!
Sir John, I am thy Pistol and thy friend,
And helter-skelter have I rode to thee,
And tidings do I bring, and lucky joys
And golden times and happy news of price.   100
Fal. I pray thee now, deliver them like a man
of this world.
Pist. A foutra for the world and worldlings base!
I speak of Africa and golden joys.
Fal. O base Assyrian knight, what is thy news?
Let King Cophetua know the truth thereof.   106
Sil. [*Singing.*] "And Robin Hood, Scarlet, and
    John."
Pist. Shall dunghill curs confront the Helicons?
And shall good news be baffled?
Then, Pistol, lay thy head in Furies' lap.   110
Sil. Honest gentleman, I know not your breeding.
Pist. Why then, lament therefore.
Shal. Give me pardon, sir. If, sir, you come
with news from the court, I take it there's but
two ways, either to utter them, or to conceal them.
I am, sir, under the King, in some authority.   118
Pist. Under which king, Besonian? Speak, or
    die.
Shal. Under King Harry.
Pist.   Harry the Fourth or Fifth?
Shal. Harry the Fourth.
Pist.   A foutra for thine office!
Sir John, thy tender lambkin now is king;   122
Harry the Fifth's the man. I speak the truth.
When Pistol lies, do this, and fig me like
The bragging Spaniard.
Fal. What, is the old king dead?   126

---

44. **leather-coats:** russet apples.   49. **leman:** sweetheart.   63. **cabileros:** gallants.   68. **pottle-pot:** two-quart tankard.
69. **liggens:** lifekins (?).   71. **[he is]** F.   *a tis* Q.   76. **done me right:** matched me (in drinking).   79. **S'amingo:** San
Domingo.   93. **but:** except.   103. **foutra:** a coarse term of contempt.   119. **Besonian:** base fellow.   124. **fig:** insult by
thrusting the thumb between the fingers.

Pist. As nail in door.   The things I speak are just.

Fal. Away, Bardolph! saddle my horse.   Master Robert Shallow, choose what office thou wilt in the land, 'tis thine.   Pistol, I will double-charge thee with dignities.   131

Bard. O joyful day!
I would not take a [knighthood] for my fortune.

Pist. What! I do bring good news.   134

Fal. Carry Master Silence to bed.   Master Shallow, my Lord Shallow, — be what thou wilt; I am Fortune's steward — get on thy boots. We'll ride all night.   O sweet Pistol!   Away, Bardolph! [*Exit Bard.*]   Come, Pistol, utter more to me; and withal devise something to do thyself good.   Boot, boot, Master Shallow!   140 I know the young king is sick for me.   Let us take any man's horses; the laws of England are at my commandment.   Blessed are they that have been my friends; and woe to my Lord Chief Justice!   145

Pist. Let vultures vile seize on his lungs also! "Where is the life that late I led?" say they. Why here it is; welcome these pleasant days! [*Exeunt.*

SCENE IV. [*London.   A street.*]

Enter BEADLES, [*dragging in*] HOSTESS QUICKLY *and* DOLL TEARSHEET.

Host. No, thou arrant knave; I would to God that I might die, that I might have thee hang'd. Thou hast drawn my shoulder out of joint.

[*1. Bead.*] The constables have delivered her over to me; and she shall have whipping cheer enough, I warrant her.   There hath been a man or two lately kill'd about her.   7

Dol. Nut-hook, nut-hook, you lie.   Come on! I'll tell thee what, thou damn'd tripe-visag'd rascal, an the child I now go with do miscarry, thou wert better thou hadst struck thy mother, thou paper-fac'd villain!   12

Host. O the Lord, that Sir John were come! He would make this a bloody day to somebody.   But I pray God the fruit of her womb miscarry.

[*1. Bead.*] If it do, you shall have a dozen of cushions again; you have but eleven now.   Come, I charge you both go with me; for the man is dead that you and Pistol beat amongst you.   19

Dol. I'll tell you what, you thin man in a censer, I will have you as soundly swinged for this, — you

blue-bottle rogue, you filthy famish'd correctioner, if you be not swinged, I'll forswear half-kirtles.   24

[*1. Bead.*] Come, come, you she knight-errant, come.

Host. O God, that right should thus overcome might!   Well, of sufferance comes ease.

Dol. Come, you rogue, come; bring me to a justice.   30

Host. Ay, come, you starv'd blood-hound.

Dol. Goodman death, goodman bones!

Host. Thou atomy, thou!

Dol. Come, you thin thing; come, you rascal.

[*1. Bead.*] Very well.   [*Exeunt.* 35

SCENE V. [*A public place near Westminster Abbey.*]

Enter two GROOMS, *strewing rushes.*

1. Groom. More rushes, more rushes.

2. Groom. The trumpets have sounded twice.

1. Groom. 'Twill be two o'clock ere they come from the coronation.   Dispatch, dispatch.   4 [*Exeunt.*

Trumpets sound, and the King and his train pass over the stage.   After them enter FALSTAFF, SHALLOW, PISTOL, BARDOLPH, *and* PAGE.

Fal. Stand here by me, Master Robert Shallow; I will make the King do you grace.   I will leer upon him as 'a comes by; and do but mark the countenance that he will give me.

Pist. God bless thy lungs, good knight.   9

Fal. Come here, Pistol; stand behind me.   O, if I had time to have made new liveries, I would have bestowed the thousand pound I borrowed of you.   But 'tis no matter; this poor show doth better; this doth infer the zeal I had to see him.

[*Shal.*] It doth so.   16

Fal. It shows my earnestness of affection, —

Shal. It doth so.

Fal. My devotion, —

Shal. It doth, it doth, it doth.   20

Fal. As it were, to ride day and night; and not to deliberate, not to remember, not to have patience to shift me, —

Shal. It is best, certain.   24

[*Fal.*] But to stand stained with travel and sweating with desire to see him; thinking of nothing else, putting all affairs else in oblivion, as if there were nothing else to be done but to see him.   29

133. [knighthood] F.   *knight* Q.
Sc. iv, s.d. BEADLES F.   Q reads *Sincklo*, the name of the actor.   4, 16, 25, 35.   [*1. Bead.*] (Malone).   *Sincklo* Q.   *Off.* F. 8. nut-hook: catchpole.   8, 20, etc. *Dol.* F.   *Whoore* Q.   17. cushions: i.e., to simulate pregnancy.   20. thin...censer: a figure in low relief embossed on the bottom of a censer.   22. blue-bottle: Beadles wore blue coats.   24. half-kirtles: short skirts.   28. sufferance: suffering.   33. atomy: confusion of *atom* and *anatomy*, skeleton.
Sc. v, 12. bestowed: used.   16. [*Shal.*] F.   *Pist.* Q.   23. shift me: change my clothes.   25. [*Fal.*] F.   Om. Q.

Pist. 'Tis "*semper idem*," for "*obsque hoc nihil est.*" 'Tis all in every part.

Shal. 'Tis so, indeed.

Pist. My knight, I will inflame thy noble liver,
And make thee rage.
Thy Doll, and Helen of thy noble thoughts, 35
Is in base durance and contagious prison;
Hal'd thither
By most mechanical and dirty hand.
Rouse up revenge from ebon den with fell Alecto's snake,
For Doll is in.   Pistol speaks nought but truth. 40

Fal. I will deliver her.

Pist. There roar'd the sea, and trumpet-clangor sounds.

The trumpets sound. Enter the KING *and his train, the* LORD CHIEF JUSTICE [*among them*].

Fal. God save thy Grace, King Hal! my royal Hal! 44

Pist. The heavens thee guard and keep, most royal imp of fame!

Fal. God save thee, my sweet boy!

King. My Lord Chief Justice, speak to that vain man.

Ch. Just. Have you your wits? Know you what 'tis you speak?

Fal. My king! my Jove! I speak to thee, my heart! 50

King. I know thee not, old man; fall to thy prayers.
How ill white hairs become a fool and jester!
I have long dreamt of such a kind of man,
So surfeit-swell'd, so old, and so profane;
But, being awak'd, I do despise my dream. 55
Make less thy body hence, and more thy grace;
Leave gormandizing; know the grave doth gape
For thee thrice wider than for other men.
Reply not to me with a fool-born jest.
Presume not that I am the thing I was; 60
For God doth know, so shall the world perceive,
That I have turn'd away my former self;
So will I those that kept me company.
When thou dost hear I am as I have been,
Approach me, and thou shalt be as thou wast, 65
The tutor and the feeder of my riots.
Till then, I banish thee, on pain of death,
As I have done the rest of my misleaders,
Not to come near our person by ten mile.
For competence of life I will allow you, 70
That lack of means enforce you not to evils;
And, as we hear you do reform yourselves,
We will, according to your strengths and qualities,
Give you advancement. Be it your charge, my lord,
To see perform'd the tenour of my word. 75
Set on.   [*Exeunt King* [*etc.*].

Fal. Master Shallow, I owe you a thousand pound.

Shal. Yea, marry, Sir John; which I beseech you to let me have home with me. 80

Fal. That can hardly be, Master Shallow. Do not you grieve at this; I shall be sent for in private to him. Look you, he must seem thus to the world. Fear not your advancements; I will be the man yet that shall make you great. 85

Shal. I cannot well perceive how, unless you should give me your doublet and stuff me out with straw. I beseech you, good Sir John, let me have five hundred of my thousand.

Fal. Sir, I will be as good as my word. This that you heard was but a colour. 91

Shal. A colour that I fear you will die in, Sir John.

Fal. Fear no colours; go with me to dinner. Come, Lieutenant Pistol; come, Bardolph. I shall be sent for soon at night. 96

Re-enter PRINCE JOHN, *the* LORD CHIEF JUSTICE [*Officers with them*].

Ch. Just. Go, carry Sir John Falstaff to the Fleet. Take all his company along with him.

Fal. My lord, my lord, —

Ch. Just. I cannot now speak; I will hear you soon. 100
Take them away.

Pist. Si fortuna me tormenta, spera contenta.
    [*Exeunt all but Prince John and the Chief Justice.*

Lan. I like this fair proceeding of the King's.
He hath intent his wonted followers
Shall all be very well provided for; 105
But all are banish'd till their conversations
Appear more wise and modest to the world.

Ch. Just. And so they are.

Lan. The King hath call'd his parliament, my lord.

Ch. Just. He hath. 110

Lan. I will lay odds that, ere this year expire,
We bear our civil swords and native fire
As far as France. I heard a bird so sing,
Whose music, to my thinking, pleas'd the King.
Come, will you hence?   [*Exeunt.* 115

EPILOGUE

[Spoken by a DANCER.*]*

First my fear; then my curtsy; last my speech.
My fear is, your displeasure; my curtsy, my duty;
and my speech, to beg your pardons. If you

30–31. **semper ... est:** "always the same" for "without this there is nothing." 38. **mechanical:** low-class. 39. **Alecto:** a Fury. 91–94. **colour ... colours:** pun on (1) pretext, (2) collar, (3) flags. 97. **Fleet:** a prison. 106. **conversations:** behavior.

look for a good speech now, you undo me; for what I have to say is of mine own making; and 5 what indeed I should say will, I doubt, prove mine own marring. But to the purpose, and so to the venture. Be it known to you, as it is very well, I was lately here in the end of a displeasing play, to pray your patience for it and to promise you 10 a better. I meant indeed to pay you with this; which, if like an ill venture it come unluckily home, I break, and you, my gentle creditors, lose. Here I promis'd you I would be, and here I commit my body to your mercies. Bate me some and I 15 will pay you some and, as most debtors do, promise you infinitely.

If my tongue cannot entreat you to acquit me, will you command me to use my legs? And yet that were but light payment, to dance out of your debt. But a good conscience will make 20 any possible satisfaction, and so would I. All the gentlewomen here have forgiven me; if the gentlemen will not, then the gentlemen do not agree with the gentlewomen, which was never seen [before] in such an assembly. 26

One word more, I beseech you. If you be not too much cloy'd with fat meat, our humble author will continue the story, with Sir John in it, and make you merry with fair Katharine of France; 30 where, for anything I know, Falstaff shall die of a sweat, unless already 'a be kill'd with your hard opinions; for Oldcastle died a martyr, and this is not the man. My tongue is weary; when my legs are too, I will bid you good night; and so I kneel 35 down before you; but, indeed, to pray for the Queen.

Epi., 9. **displeasing play.** Not identified. 13. **break:** go bankrupt. 15. **Bate:** abate, remit. 26. **[before]** F. Om. Q. 33. **Oldcastle.** See Introduction to Part I. 35–36. **and ... Queen** F (omitting *I*). Q inserts at l. 17.

[handwritten notes]

The Life of Henry the Fifth

OF FEW OF SHAKESPEARE'S PLAYS can the date of composition be fixed with such accuracy and precision as that of *Henry the Fifth*. The Prologue to Act V contains the following lines:

> As, by a lower but loving likelihood,
> Were now the general of our gracious Empress,
> As in good time he may, from Ireland coming,
> Bringing rebellion broached on his sword,

The allusion is clear to the expedition led by the Earl of Essex, who left for Ireland on March 27, 1599, and returned unannounced to London on September 28th of the same year. As Essex's failure had been foreseen for some time before his return, the passage must have been written by midsummer, 1599. The play is not listed by Meres.

Following the entry in the Stationers' Register of August 4, 1600, a Quarto edition appeared in that year and was reprinted in 1602 and 1619. It differs, however, in the source of the text from the First Folio, on which the present edition is based. The Quarto text is less than half the length of the version in the Folio, and is so badly mangled and corrupted that it is now generally agreed that it is a pirated edition printed from notes taken at a performance, and perhaps from other sources surreptitiously obtained. The theory that it represents an early draft of the play is not supported by a close comparison of the texts.

The source of the serious plot is, as usual in the Histories, the *Chronicles* of Holinshed. Shakespeare follows the main trend of actual events, altering the order only slightly, but condensing the action from six years. The long speeches throughout are, but for a few hints, altogether his, with the exception of the genealogical argument of the Archbishop of Canterbury, I.ii, which follows Holinshed with remarkable closeness. The following passage shows how little change was necessary to transform Holinshed's prose into blank verse:

"Hugh Capet also, (who usurped the crowne upon

Charles duke of Loraine, the sole heire male of the line and stocke of Charles the great,) to make his title seeme true, and appeare good, (though in deed it was starke naught,) conveied himselfe as heire to the ladie Lingard, daughter to King Charlemaine, sonne to Lewes the emperour, that was son to Charles the great." (Holinshed, iii.545)

> Hugh Capet also, who usurp'd the crown
> Of Charles the Duke of Lorraine, sole heir male
> Of the true line and stock of Charles the Great,
> To find his title with some shows of truth,
> Though, in pure truth, it was corrupt and naught,
> Convey'd himself as th' heir to th' Lady Lingare,
> Daughter to Charlemain, who was the son
> To Lewis the Emperor, and Lewis the son
> Of Charles the Great. (I.ii.69–77.)

On the other hand the spirited retort to the Dauphin on the tennis balls in I.ii.259–296, is elaborated from a single sentence. "Wherfore the K. wrote to him, that yer ought long, he would tosse him some London balles that perchance should shake the walles of the best court in France." (Holinshed, iii.545.) The scenes in which Pistol and his fellows appear have, of course, no original; and the group of subordinate officers, Fluellen, Macmorris, and Captain Jamy, with Bates and Williams and the glove episode, are all purely Shakespearean. The pardoning of the man who had railed against the king is a skillful invention to lead up to the unmasking and self-condemnation of the conspirators. The happy personal relations existing among the English are brought out in Henry's speeches to old Erpingham, in the description of the deaths of Suffolk and York, in the conversation between the king and the common soldiers, in the splendid eloquence of such speeches as those of Henry before Harfleur and on St. Crispin's Day, all of which are absent from the chronicles; and, conversely, the vain boasting of the French lords before the battle is created out of a mere hint that they passed the night in merriment and were contemptuous of their opponents. Again, additional stress is laid by Shakespeare on Henry's piety, his soliloquy and prayer before Agincourt being without historical basis. Yet the main lines of his character are those laid down by Holinshed and earlier writers.

The French lesson of the Princess is original; but the wooing is foreshadowed in the crude play of *The Famous Victories of Henry the Fifth,* which had already supplied hints for *Henry IV.* This play also uses the Dauphin's gift of tennis balls, and contains dialect parts which may have suggested the Welsh, Scottish, and Irish parts here; and a scene in which a Frenchman tries to hold an Englishman for ransom bears a certain resemblance to Pistol's treatment of his French captive. The stealing of the pyx and the fate, though not the character, of Bardolph are historical. The Dauphin was not in fact present at the battle of Agincourt, nor were Bedford, Westmoreland, or Warwick. The simile of the bees in Canterbury's speech (I.ii.187–204) may have been suggested by a passage in Lyly's *Euphues and his England,* which in turn is based on Pliny.

As has been pointed out in previous introductions, Shakespeare had planned, while writing the immediately preceding histories, the ultimate development of Henry into the heroic figure of the ideal English king. The completion of his regeneration is explicitly announced by the Archbishop of Canterbury in the first scene of the present play. Henry is no longer exhibited as a master of spar-

kling repartee, but stress is laid on his judgment and his piety. He retains, however, his power over words, as is shown in the great heroic speeches, in the soliloquy on ceremony, and in the wooing of Katharine. His capacity for dealing with the common people is exhibited in the moving prose of the scene with Bates and Williams (IV.1), in which "mean and gentle all behold ... a little touch of Harry in the night."

The Epilogue to the second part of *Henry the Fourth* had promised to continue "the story with Sir John in it," but it is obvious enough that the association of the king with Falstaff would have been impossible in a play with the temper of *Henry the Fifth.* In place of it we have the hostess's incomparable account of his death — a passage which owes much to the most celebrated of all textual emendations: the change by Theobald of "and a Table of greene fields" into "and 'a babbled of green fields."

With the exception of the collaborated *Henry VIII,* this play was the last to be written of Shakespeare's histories. The crises in English history before the Tudor period which gave good dramatic opportunity were well-nigh exhausted, and the limitations of the form of the chronicle play must have been increasingly irksome to Shakespeare's developed artistic sense. *Henry the Fifth* forms an appropriate close to the series, bringing, as it does, the patriotic fervor underlying them all to its highest expression.

THE CLAIM OF HENRY V TO THE FRENCH THRONE

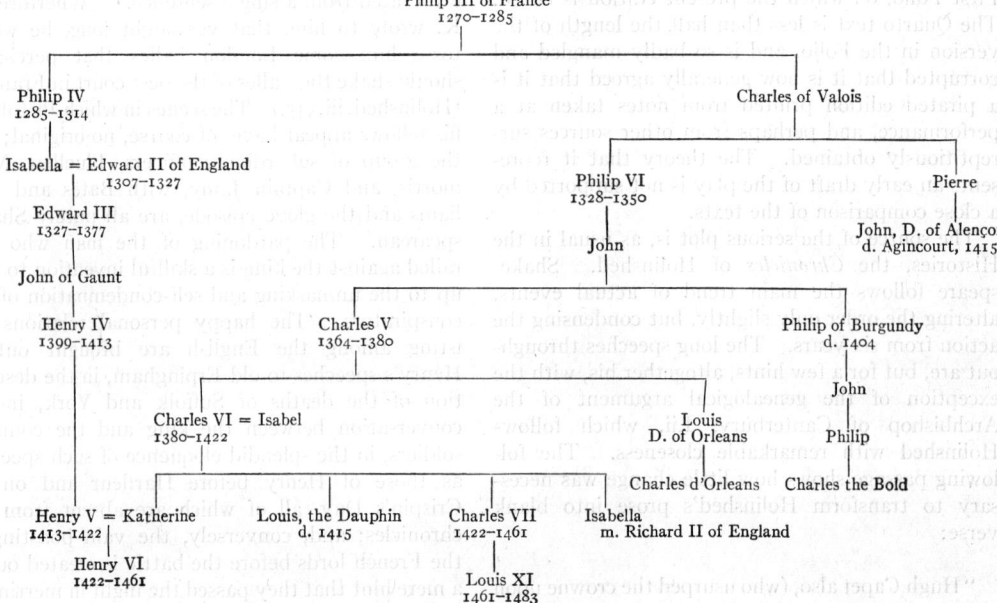

Philip III of France
1270–1285

Philip IV
1285–1314

Isabella = Edward II of England
1307–1327

Edward III
1327–1377

John of Gaunt

Henry IV
1399–1413

Charles V
1364–1380

Charles VI = Isabel
1380–1422

Henry V = Katherine   Louis, the Dauphin   Charles VII   Isabella
1413–1422   d. 1415   1422–1461   m. Richard II of England

Henry VI
1422–1461

Louis XI
1461–1483

Charles of Valois

Philip VI
1328–1350

John

John, D. of Alençon
d. Agincourt, 1415

Pierre

Philip of Burgundy
d. 1404

John

Louis
D. of Orleans

Philip

Charles d'Orleans   Charles the Bold

THE LIFE OF HENRY THE FIFTH

[DRAMATIS PERSONÆ

KING HENRY V.
DUKE OF GLOUCESTER,⎫ brothers to the King.
DUKE OF BEDFORD,   ⎭
DUKE OF EXETER, uncle to the King.
DUKE OF YORK, cousin to the King.
EARLS OF SALISBURY, WESTMORELAND, and
   WARWICK.
ARCHBISHOP OF CANTERBURY.
BISHOP OF ELY.
EARL OF CAMBRIDGE.
LORD SCROOP.
SIR THOMAS GREY.
SIR THOMAS ERPINGHAM,⎫
GOWER,   ⎪
FLUELLEN,   ⎬ officers in King
MACMORRIS,   ⎪ Henry's army.
JAMY,   ⎭
BATES, ⎫
COURT, ⎬ soldiers in the same.
WILLIAMS,⎭
PISTOL.
NYM.

BARDOLPH.
BOY.
A Herald.

CHARLES VI, king of France.
LEWIS, the Dauphin.
DUKES OF BURGUNDY, ORLEANS, and BOURBON.
The Constable of France.
RAMBURES, ⎫ French Lords.
GRANDPRÉ,⎭
Governor of Harfleur.
MONTJOY, a French Herald.
Ambassadors to the King of England.

ISABEL, queen of France.
KATHARINE, daughter to Charles and Isabel.
ALICE, a lady attending on her.
HOSTESS of a tavern in Eastcheap, formerly Mistress Quickly, and now married to Pistol.

CHORUS.

Lords, Ladies, Officers, Soldiers, Citizens, Messengers, and Attendants.

SCENE: England; afterwards France.]

PROLOGUE

Enter [CHORUS].

[*Chor.*] O for a Muse of fire, that would ascend
The brightest heaven of invention,
A kingdom for a stage, princes to act,
And monarchs to behold the swelling scene!
Then should the warlike Harry, like himself,   5
Assume the port of Mars; and at his heels,
Leash'd in like hounds, should famine, sword, and
   fire
Crouch for employment. But pardon, gentles all,

The flat unraised spirits that hath dar'd
On this unworthy scaffold to bring forth   10
So great an object. Can this cockpit hold
The vasty fields of France? Or may we cram
Within this wooden O the very casques
That did affright the air at Agincourt?
O, pardon! since a crooked figure may   15
Attest in little place a million;
And let us, ciphers to this great accompt,
On your imaginary forces work.
Suppose within the girdle of these walls
Are now confin'd two mighty monarchies,   20

Prol., 13. **wooden O**: circular theater, probably the newly built Globe. 16. **Attest**: represent. 18. **imaginary**: imaginative.

Whose high upreared and abutting fronts
The perilous narrow ocean parts asunder;
Piece out our imperfections with your thoughts;
Into a thousand parts divide one man,
And make imaginary puissance;   25
Think, when we talk of horses, that you see them
Printing their proud hoofs i' th' receiving earth.
For 'tis your thoughts that now must deck our
    kings,
Carry them here and there, jumping o'er times,
Turning the accomplishment of many years   30
Into an hour-glass: for the which supply,
Admit me Chorus to this history;
Who, prologue-like, your humble patience pray
Gently to hear, kindly to judge, our play.   [Exit.

ACT I

SCENE I. [London.   An ante-chamber in the
      King's palace.]

Enter the ARCHBISHOP OF CANTERBURY and the
     BISHOP OF ELY.

Cant. My lord, I'll tell you: that self bill is urg'd
Which in th' eleventh year of the last king's reign
Was like, and had indeed against us pass'd,
But that the scambling and unquiet time
Did push it out of farther question.   5
   Ely. But how, my lord, shall we resist it now?
   Cant. It must be thought on. If it pass against
     us,
We lose the better half of our possession;
For all the temporal lands which men devout
By testament have given to the Church   10
Would they strip from us; being valu'd thus:
As much as would maintain, to the King's honour,
Full fifteen earls and fifteen hundred knights,
Six thousand and two hundred good esquires;
And, to relief of lazars and weak age,   15
Of indigent faint souls past corporal toil,
A hundred almshouses right well suppli'd;
And to the coffers of the King beside,
A thousand pounds by th' year. Thus runs the
    bill.
   Ely. This would drink deep.
   Cant.   'Twould drink the cup and all.   20
   Ely. But what prevention?
   Cant. The King is full of grace and fair regard.
   Ely. And a true lover of the holy Church.
   Cant. The courses of his youth promis'd it not.
The breath no sooner left his father's body,   25
But that his wildness, mortifi'd in him,

Seem'd to die too; yea, at that very moment
Consideration like an angel came
And whipp'd th' offending Adam out of him,
Leaving his body as a paradise   30
T' envelop and contain celestial spirits.
Never was such a sudden scholar made;
Never came reformation in a flood
With such a heady currance, scouring faults;
Nor never Hydra-headed wilfulness   35
So soon did lose his seat, and all at once,
As in this king.
   Ely.   We are blessed in the change.
   Cant. Hear him but reason in divinity,
And, all-admiring, with an inward wish
You would desire the King were made a prelate;   40
Hear him debate of commonwealth affairs,
You would say it hath been all in all his study;
List his discourse of war, and you shall hear
A fearful battle rend'red you in music;
Turn him to any cause of policy,   45
The Gordian knot of it he will unloose,
Familiar as his garter; that, when he speaks,
The air, a charter'd libertine, is still,
And the mute wonder lurketh in men's ears
To steal his sweet and honey'd sentences;   50
So that the art and practic part of life
Must be the mistress to this theoric:
Which is a wonder how his Grace should glean it,
Since his addiction was to courses vain,
His companies unletter'd, rude, and shallow,   55
His hours fill'd up with riots, banquets, sports,
And never noted in him any study,
Any retirement, any sequestration
From open haunts and popularity.
   Ely. The strawberry grows underneath the
     nettle,   60
And wholesome berries thrive and ripen best
Neighbour'd by fruit of baser quality;
And so the Prince obscur'd his contemplation
Under the veil of wildness; which, no doubt,
Grew like the summer grass, fastest by night,   65
Unseen, yet crescive in his faculty.
   Cant. It must be so; for miracles are ceas'd,
And therefore we must needs admit the means
How things are perfected.
   Ely.   But, my good lord,
How now for mitigation of this bill   70
Urg'd by the commons? Doth his Majesty
Incline to it, or no?
   Cant.   He seems indifferent,
Or rather swaying more upon our part
Than cherishing th' exhibiters against us;
For I have made an offer to his Majesty,   75

31. the which supply: filling the gaps.
Act I, sc. i, 1. self: same. 4. scambling: disorderly. 15. lazars: lepers. 28. Consideration: reflection. 34. heady currance: violent current. 45. cause: question. 48. charter'd: licensed. 59. popularity: association with common people. 66. crescive ... faculty: growing in its natural power. 74. exhibiters: promoters.

Upon our spiritual convocation
And in regard of causes now in hand,
Which I have open'd to his Grace at large,
As touching France, to give a greater sum
Than ever at one time the clergy yet   80
Did to his predecessors part withal.
    Ely. How did this offer seem receiv'd, my lord?
    Cant. With good acceptance of his Majesty;
Save that there was not time enough to hear,
As I perceiv'd his Grace would fain have done,   85
The severals and unhidden passages
Of his true titles to some certain dukedoms,
And generally to the crown and seat of France
Deriv'd from Edward, his great-grandfather.
    Ely. What was th' impediment that broke this
      off?   90
    Cant. The French ambassador upon that instant
Crav'd audience; and the hour, I think, is come
To give him hearing.   Is it four o'clock?
    Ely. It is.
    Cant. Then go we in, to know his embassy;   95
Which I could with a ready guess declare
Before the Frenchman speak a word of it.
    Ely. I'll wait upon you, and I long to hear it.
                                     [Exeunt.

[SCENE II.   *The same.   The presence chamber.*]

Enter KING HENRY, GLOUCESTER, BEDFORD,
    EXETER, WARWICK, WESTMORELAND [*and*
    Attendants].

    K. Hen. Where is my gracious Lord of Canter-
    bury?
    Exe. Not here in presence.
    K. Hen.   Send for him, good uncle.
    West. Shall we call in th' ambassador, my liege?
    K. Hen. Not yet, my cousin.   We would be
    resolv'd,
Before we hear him, of some things of weight   5
That task our thoughts, concerning us and France.

Enter the ARCHBISHOP OF CANTERBURY *and the*
    BISHOP OF ELY

    Cant. God and his angels guard your sacred
    throne
And make you long become it!
    K. Hen.   Sure we thank you.
My learned lord, we pray you to proceed
And justly and religiously unfold   10
Why the law Salique that they have in France
Or should, or should not, bar us in our claim;

And God forbid, my dear and faithful lord,
That you should fashion, wrest, or bow your
    reading,
Or nicely charge your understanding soul   15
With opening titles miscreate, whose right
Suits not in native colours with the truth;
For God doth know how many now in health
Shall drop their blood in approbation
Of what your reverence shall incite us to.   20
Therefore take heed how you impawn our person,
How you awake our sleeping sword of war.
We charge you, in the name of God, take heed;
For never two such kingdoms did contend
Without much fall of blood, whose guiltless drops
Are every one a woe, a sore complaint   26
'Gainst him whose wrong gives edge unto the
    swords
That makes such waste in brief mortality.
Under this conjuration speak, my lord;
For we will hear, note, and believe in heart   30
That what you speak is in your conscience wash'd
As pure as sin with baptism.
    Cant. Then hear me, gracious sovereign, and you
    peers,
That owe yourselves, your lives, and services
To this imperial throne.   There is no bar   35
To make against your Highness' claim to France
But this, which they produce from Pharamond:
"*In terram Salicam mulieres ne succedant,*"
"No woman shall succeed in Salique land;"
Which Salique land the French unjustly gloze   40
To be the realm of France, and Pharamond
The founder of this law and female bar.
Yet their own authors faithfully affirm
That the land Salique is in Germany,
Between the floods of Sala and of Elbe;   45
Where Charles the Great, having subdu'd the
    Saxons,
There left behind and settled certain French;
Who, holding in disdain the German women
For some dishonest manners of their life,
Establish'd then this law, to wit, no female   50
Should be inheritrix in Salique land;
Which Salique, as I said, 'twixt Elbe and Sala,
Is at this day in Germany call'd Meisen.
Then doth it well appear the Salique law
Was not devised for the realm of France;   55
Nor did the French possess the Salique land
Until four hundred one and twenty years
After defunction of King Pharamond,
Idly suppos'd the founder of this law,
Who died within the year of our redemption   60

    76. **Upon ... convocation:** on behalf of the assembly of clergy.   86. **severals:** details.   **unhidden passages:** clear de-
rivation.
    Sc. ii, 4. **resolv'd:** clear in our minds.   11. **law Salique.** Henry's claim to the French throne was through Isabella, daugh-
ter of Philip IV of France and wife of Edward II, Henry's great-great-grandfather.   15. **nicely:** sophistically.   19–20. **approbation Of:** making good.   21. **impawn:** commit.   40. **gloze:** interpret.   49. **dishonest:** unchaste.   58. **defunction:** death.

Four hundred twenty-six; and Charles the Great
Subdu'd the Saxons, and did seat the French
Beyond the river Sala, in the year
Eight hundred five. Besides, their writers say,
King Pepin, which deposed Childeric,   65
Did, as heir general, being descended
Of Blithild, which was daughter to King Clothair,
Make claim and title to the crown of France.
Hugh Capet also, who usurp'd the crown
Of Charles the Duke of Lorraine, sole heir male   70
Of the true line and stock of Charles the Great,
To find his title with some shows of truth,
Though, in pure truth, it was corrupt and naught,
Convey'd himself as th' heir to th' Lady Lingare,
Daughter to Charlemain, who was the son   75
To Lewis the Emperor, and Lewis the son
Of Charles the Great. Also, King Lewis the Tenth,
Who was sole heir to the usurper Capet,
Could not keep quiet in his conscience,
Wearing the crown of France, till satisfied   80
That fair Queen Isabel, his grandmother,
Was lineal of the Lady Ermengare,
Daughter to Charles, the foresaid Duke of Lorraine;
By the which marriage the line of Charles the
    Great
Was re-united to the crown of France.   85
So that, as clear as is the summer's sun,
King Pepin's title and Hugh Capet's claim,
King Lewis his satisfaction, all appear
To hold in right and title of the female.
So do the kings of France unto this day,   90
Howbeit they would hold up this Salique law
To bar your Highness claiming from the female,
And rather choose to hide them in a net
Than amply to imbar their crooked titles
Usurp'd from you and your progenitors.   95
  K. Hen. May I with right and conscience make
    this claim?
  Cant. The sin upon my head, dread sovereign!
For in the book of Numbers is it writ,
When the man dies, let the inheritance
Descend unto the daughter. Gracious lord,   100
Stand for your own! Unwind your bloody flag!
Look back into your mighty ancestors!
Go, my dread lord, to your great-grandsire's tomb,
From whom you claim; invoke his warlike spirit,
And your great-uncle's, Edward the Black Prince,
Who on the French ground play'd a tragedy,   106
Making defeat on the full power of France,
Whiles his most mighty father on a hill
Stood smiling to behold his lion's whelp

Forage in blood of French nobility.   110
O noble English, that could entertain
With half their forces the full pride of France
And let another half stand laughing by,
All out of work and cold for action!
  Ely. Awake remembrance of these valiant dead,
And with your puissant arm renew their feats. 116
You are their heir; you sit upon their throne;
The blood and courage that renowned them
Runs in your veins; and my thrice-puissant liege
Is in the very May-morn of his youth,   120
Ripe for exploits and mighty enterprises.
  Exe. Your brother kings and monarchs of the
    earth
Do all expect that you should rouse yourself,
As did the former lions of your blood.
  West. They know your Grace hath cause and
    means and might;   125
So hath your Highness. Never King of England
Had nobles richer and more loyal subjects,
Whose hearts have left their bodies here in England
And lie pavilion'd in the fields of France.   129
  Cant. O, let their bodies follow, my dear liege,
With blood and sword and fire to win your right;
In aid whereof we of the spiritualty
Will raise your Highness such a mighty sum
As never did the clergy at one time
Bring in to any of your ancestors.   135
  K. Hen. We must not only arm t' invade the
    French,
But lay down our proportions to defend
Against the Scot, who will make road upon us
With all advantages.
  Cant. They of those marches, gracious sovereign,
Shall be a wall sufficient to defend   141
Our inland from the pilfering borderers.
  K. Hen. We do not mean the coursing snatchers
    only,
But fear the main intendment of the Scot,
Who hath been still a giddy neighbour to us;   145
For you shall read that my great-grandfather
Never went with his forces into France
But that the Scot on his unfurnish'd kingdom
Came pouring, like the tide into a breach,
With ample and brim fullness of his force,   150
Galling the gleaned land with hot assays,
Girding with grievous siege castles and towns;
That England, being empty of defence,
Hath shook and trembled at th' ill neighbourhood.
  Cant. She hath been then more fear'd than
    harm'd, my liege;   155
For hear her but exampl'd by herself:

---

72. **find:** provide.   74. **Convey'd:** passed off.   75. **Charlemain:** really, Charles the Bald.   77. **Lewis the Tenth** should be Louis IX.   82. **lineal of:** descended from.   94. **amply to imbar:** frankly to rule out.   106–114. Battle of Crecy, 1346. 114. **for:** for lack of.   137. **proportions:** division of forces.   138. **road:** inroad.   139. **With … advantages:** whenever he sees a good chance.   143. **coursing snatchers:** raiders.   144. **intendment:** intention.   145. **still a giddy:** always a restless. 148. **unfurnish'd:** deprived of defenders.   151. **assays:** assaults.   155. **fear'd:** frightened.

When all her chivalry hath been in France,
And she a mourning widow of her nobles,
She hath herself not only well defended
But taken and impounded as a stray   160
The King of Scots; whom she did send to France
To fill King Edward's fame with prisoner kings,
And make her chronicle as rich with praise
As is the ooze and bottom of the sea
With sunken wrack and sumless treasuries.   165
    [*West.*] But there's a saying very old and true,
      "If that you will France win,
        Then with Scotland first begin."
For once the eagle England being in prey,
To her unguarded nest the weasel Scot   170
Comes sneaking and so sucks her princely eggs,
Playing the mouse in absence of the cat,
To [spoil] and havoc more than she can eat.
    Exe. It follows then the cat must stay at home;
Yet that is but a crush'd necessity,   175
Since we have locks to safeguard necessaries,
And pretty traps to catch the petty thieves.
While that the armed hand doth fight abroad,
Th' advised head defends itself at home;
For government, though high and low and lower,
Put into parts, doth keep in one consent,   181
Congreeing in a full and natural close,
Like music.
    Cant.   Therefore doth heaven divide
The state of man in divers functions,
Setting endeavour in continual motion,   185
To which is fixed, as an aim or butt,
Obedience; for so work the honey-bees,
Creatures that by a rule in nature teach
The act of order to a peopled kingdom.
They have a king and officers of sorts,   190
Where some, like magistrates, correct at home,
Others, like merchants, venture trade abroad,
Others, like soldiers, armed in their stings,
Make boot upon the summer's velvet buds,
Which pillage they with merry march bring
    home
To the tent-royal of their emperor;   196
Who, busied in his majesty, surveys
The singing masons building roofs of gold,
The civil citizens kneading up the honey,
The poor mechanic porters crowding in   200
Their heavy burdens at his narrow gate,
The sad-eyed justice, with his surly hum,
Delivering o'er to executors pale
The lazy yawning drone. I this infer,
That many things, having full reference   205
To one consent, may work contrariously.
As many arrows, loosed several ways,

Come to one mark; as many ways meet in one
    town;
As many fresh streams meet in one salt sea;
As many lines close in the dial's centre;   210
So may a thousand actions, once afoot,
End in one purpose, and be all well borne
Without defeat.   Therefore to France, my liege!
Divide your happy England into four,
Whereof take you one quarter into France,   215
And you withal shall make all Gallia shake.
If we, with thrice such powers left at home,
Cannot defend our own doors from the dog,
Let us be worried and our nation lose
The name of hardiness and policy.   220
    K. Hen. Call in the messengers sent from the
    Dauphin.   [*Exeunt some Attendants.*]
Now are we well resolv'd; and by God's help
And yours, the noble sinews of our power,
France being ours, we'll bend it to our awe,
Or break it all to pieces.   Or there we'll sit, 225
Ruling in large and ample empery
O'er France and all her almost kingly dukedoms,
Or lay these bones in an unworthy urn,
Tombless, with no remembrance over them.
Either our history shall with full mouth   230
Speak freely of our acts, or else our grave,
Like Turkish mute, shall have a tongueless mouth,
Not worshipp'd with a waxen epitaph.

    Enter AMBASSADORS *of France.*

Now are we well prepar'd to know the pleasure
Of our fair cousin Dauphin; for we hear   235
Your greeting is from him, not from the King.
    1. Amb. May 't please your Majesty to give us
    leave
Freely to render what we have in charge,
Or shall we sparingly show you far off
The Dauphin's meaning and our embassy?   240
    K. Hen. We are no tyrant, but a Christian king,
Unto whose grace our passion is as subject
As is our wretches fett'red in our prisons;
Therefore with frank and with uncurbed plainness
Tell us the Dauphin's mind.
    1. Amb.   Thus, then, in few.
Your Highness, lately sending into France,   246
Did claim some certain dukedoms, in the right
Of your great predecessor, King Edward the Third.
In answer of which claim, the prince our master
Says that you savour too much of your youth,   250
And bids you be advis'd there's nought in France
That can be with a nimble galliard won.
You cannot revel into dukedoms there.
He therefore sends you, meeter for your spirit,

---

161. **King of Scots**: David Bruce, 1346. 166. [*West.*] (Capell after Holinshed). *Bish. Ely* F. 169. **in prey**: in search of prey. 173. [spoil] Q. *tame* F. *tear* Rowe. 175. **crush'd**: strained. 179. **advised**: judicious. 181. **consent**: harmony. 182. **Congreeing**: agreeing. **close**: cadence. 190. **sorts**: different kinds. 194. **boot**: booty. 226. **empery**: imperial power. 233. **with ... epitaph**: even with an epitaph written on wax. For *waxen* Q reads *paper*. 252. **galliard**: a dance.

This tun of treasure; and, in lieu of this,   255
Desires you let the dukedoms that you claim
Hear no more of you.   This the Dauphin speaks.
   K. Hen. What treasure, uncle?
   Exe.   Tennis-balls, my liege.
   K. Hen. We are glad the Dauphin is so pleasant
    with us.
His present and your pains we thank you for. 260
When we have match'd our rackets to these balls,
We will, in France, by God's grace, play a set
Shall strike his father's crown into the hazard.
Tell him he hath made a match with such a wrangler
That all the courts of France will be disturb'd 265
With chaces.   And we understand him well,
How he comes o'er us with our wilder days,
Not measuring what use we made of them.
We never valu'd this poor seat of England;
And therefore, living hence, did give ourself   270
To barbarous license; as 'tis ever common
That men are merriest when they are from home.
But tell the Dauphin I will keep my state,
Be like a king, and show my sail of greatness
When I do rouse me in my throne of France. 275
For that I have laid by my majesty
And plodded like a man for working-days,
But I will rise there with so full a glory
That I will dazzle all the eyes of France,
Yea, strike the Dauphin blind to look on us. 280
And tell the pleasant prince this mock of his
Hath turn'd his balls to gun-stones, and his soul
Shall stand sore charged for the wasteful vengeance
That shall fly with them; for many a thousand
   widows
Shall this his mock mock out of their dear hus-
   bands,   285
Mock mothers from their sons, mock castles down;
And some are yet ungotten and unborn
That shall have cause to curse the Dauphin's scorn.
But this lies all within the will of God,
To whom I do appeal; and in whose name   290
Tell you the Dauphin I am coming on
To venge me as I may, and to put forth
My rightful hand in a well-hallow'd cause.
So get you hence in peace; and tell the Dauphin
His jest will savour but of shallow wit,   295
When thousands weep more than did laugh at it. —
Convey them with safe conduct. — Fare you well.
                              [*Exeunt Ambassadors.*
   Exe. This was a merry message.
   K. Hen. We hope to make the sender blush at it.
Therefore, my lords, omit no happy hour   300
That may give furtherance to our expedition;
For we have now no thought in us but France,
Save those to God, that run before our business.
Therefore, let our proportions for these wars

Be soon collected, and all things thought upon 305
That may with reasonable swiftness add
More feathers to our wings; for, God before,
We'll chide this Dauphin at his father's door.
Therefore let every man now task his thought,
That this fair action may on foot be brought. 310
                                [*Exeunt.*

[ACT II]

[PROLOGUE.]

Flourish.   Enter CHORUS.

   [*Chor.*] Now all the youth of England are on fire,
And silken dalliance in the wardrobe lies.
Now thrive the armourers, and honour's thought
Reigns solely in the breast of every man.
They sell the pasture now to buy the horse,   5
Following the mirror of all Christian kings
With winged heels, as English Mercuries.
For now sits Expectation in the air,
And hides a sword from hilts unto the point
With crowns imperial, crowns, and coronets   10
Promis'd to Harry and his followers.
The French, advis'd by good intelligence
Of this most dreadful preparation,
Shake in their fear, and with pale policy
Seek to divert the English purposes.   15
O England! model to thy inward greatness,
Like little body with a mighty heart,
What mightst thou do, that honour would thee do,
Were all thy children kind and natural!
But see thy fault!   France hath in thee found out
A nest of hollow bosoms, which he fills   21
With treacherous crowns; and three corrupted men,
One, Richard Earl of Cambridge, and the second,
Henry Lord Scroop of Masham, and the third,
Sir Thomas Grey, knight, of Northumberland,
Have, for the gilt of France, — O guilt indeed! — 26
Confirm'd conspiracy with fearful France;
And by their hands this grace of kings must die,
If hell and treason hold their promises,
Ere he take ship for France, and in Southampton.
Linger your patience on, and we'll digest   31
The abuse of distance, force a play.
The sum is paid; the traitors are agreed;
The King is set from London; and the scene
Is now transported, gentles, to Southampton.   35
There is the playhouse now, there must you sit;
And thence to France shall we convey you safe,
And bring you back, charming the narrow seas
To give you gentle pass; for, if we may,
We'll not offend one stomach with our play.   40
But, till the King come forth, and not till then,
Unto Southampton do we shift our scene. [*Exit.*

263–266. **hazard, wrangler, courts, chaces:** terms of court tennis used punningly.   267. **comes o'er:** taunts.
Act II, Prol., 18. **would:** would have.   31–32. **digest ... distance:** take care of the violation of the unity of place.

[SCENE I. *London.   A street.*]

Enter CORPORAL NYM *and* LIEUTENANT BARDOLPH.

Bard.   Well met, Corporal Nym.

Nym.   Good morrow, Lieutenant Bardolph.

Bard.   What, are Ancient Pistol and you friends
yet?   4

Nym.   For my part, I care not.   I say little;
but when time shall serve, there shall be smiles;
but that shall be as it may.   I dare not fight,
but I will wink and hold out mine iron.   It is a
simple one, but what though?   It will toast cheese,
and it will endure cold as another man's sword
will; and there's an end.   11

Bard.   I will bestow a breakfast to make you
friends; and we'll be all three sworn brothers to
France.   Let it be so, good Corporal Nym.   14

Nym.   Faith, I will live so long as I may, that's
the certain of it; and when I cannot live any
longer, I will do as I may.   That is my rest, that is
the rendezvous of it.

Bard.   It is certain, corporal, that he is married
to Nell Quickly; and certainly she did you wrong,
for you were troth-plight to her.   21

Nym.   I cannot tell.   Things must be as they
may.   Men may sleep, and they may have their
throats about them at that time; and some say
knives have edges.   It must be as it may.   Though
patience be a tired mare, yet she will plod.   There
must be conclusions.   Well, I cannot tell.   27

Enter PISTOL *and* HOSTESS.

Bard.   Here come Ancient Pistol and his wife.
Good corporal, be patient here.   How now, mine
host Pistol!   30

Pist.   Base tike, call'st thou me host?
Now, by this hand, I swear, I scorn the term;
Nor shall my Nell keep lodgers.   33

Host.   No, by my troth, not long; for we cannot
lodge and board a dozen or fourteen gentlewomen
that live honestly by the prick of their needles
but it will be thought we keep a bawdy house
straight.   [*Nym and Pistol draw.*]   O well a day,
Lady, if he be not [drawn] now!   We shall see
wilful adultery and murder committed.   40

Bard.   Good lieutenant! good corporal! offer
nothing here.

Nym.   Pish!

Pist.   Pish for thee, Iceland dog! thou prick-
ear'd cur of Iceland!

Host.   Good Corporal Nym, show thy valour, and
put up your sword.   46

Nym.   Will you shog off?   I would have you
solus.

Pist.   "Solus," egregious dog!   O viper vile!
The "solus" in thy most mervailous face;   50
The "solus" in thy teeth, and in thy throat,
And in thy hateful lungs, yea, in thy maw, perdy,
And, which is worse, within thy nasty mouth!
I do retort the "solus" in thy bowels;
For I can take, and Pistol's cock is up,
And flashing fire will follow.   56

Nym.   I am not Barbason; you cannot conjure
me.   I have an humour to knock you indifferently
well.   If you grow foul with me, Pistol, I will
scour you with my rapier, as I may, in fair terms.
If you would walk off, I would prick your guts a
little, in good terms, as I may; and that's the
humour of it.   63

Pist.   O braggart vile and damned furious wight!
The grave doth gape, and doting death is near,
Therefore exhale.

Bard.   Hear me, hear me what I say.   He that
strikes the first stroke, I'll run him up to the hilts,
as I am a soldier.   [*Draws.*]

Pist.   An oath of mickle might; and fury shall
abate.   70
Give me thy fist, thy fore-foot to me give.
Thy spirits are most tall.

Nym.   I will cut thy throat, one time or other,
in fair terms: that is the humour of it.

Pist.   "Couple a gorge!"   75
That is the word.   I thee defy again.
O hound of Crete, think'st thou my spouse to get?
No! to the spital go,
And from the powdering-tub of infamy
Fetch forth the lazar kite of Cressid's kind,   80
Doll Tearsheet she by name, and her espouse.
I have, and I will hold, the quondam Quickly
For the only she; and — *pauca*, there's enough.
Go to.   84

Enter the BOY.

Boy.   Mine host Pistol, you must come to my
master, and you, hostess.   He is very sick, and
would to bed.   Good Bardolph, put thy face
between his sheets, and do the office of a warming-
pan.   Faith, he's very ill.

Bard.   Away, you rogue!   90

Host.   By my troth, he'll yield the crow a pudding one of these days.   The King has kill'd his
heart.   Good husband, come home presently.
     [*Exeunt* [*Hostess and Boy*].

Bard.   Come, shall I make you two friends?   We

Sc. i, 3. **Ancient:** ensign.   8. **wink:** shut my eyes.   17. **rest:** what I put my stakes on.   18. **rendezvous.**   It is useless to try
to explain all Nym's and Pistol's assaults on the language.   30. In Q it is Nym who calls Pistol "host."   31. **tike:** cur.
39. **[drawn]** (Hanmer).   *hewne* F.   47. **shog:** jog.   52. **perdy:** *par Dieu.*   57. **Barbason:** a fiend.   66. **exhale:** draw out
(your sword).   75. *Couple a gorge: couper la gorge,* cut the throat.   78. **spital:** hospital.   79. **powdering-tub:** salting tub,
slang for the hot bath used in treating venereal disease.   80. **lazar ... kind.**   A reference to Henryson's sequel to Chaucer's
Troilus, in which Cressida is smitten with leprosy.   83. *pauca:* few (words).   93. **presently:** at once.

must to France together; why the devil should we
keep knives to cut one another's throats?   96
   Pist. Let floods o'erswell, and fiends for food
howl on!
   Nym. You'll pay me the eight shillings I won
of you at betting?
   Pist. Base is the slave that pays.   100
   Nym. That now I will have: that's the humour
of it.
   Pist. As manhood shall compound. Push home.
                   [*They draw.*
   Bard. By this sword, he that makes the first
thrust, I'll kill him; by this sword, I will.   105
   Pist. Sword is an oath, and oaths must have their
course.
   Bard. Corporal Nym, an thou wilt be friends,
be friends; an thou wilt not, why, then, be enemies
with me too. Prithee, put up.
   [*Nym.* I shall have my eight shillings I won from
you at betting?]   111
   Pist. A noble shalt thou have, and present pay;
And liquor likewise will I give to thee,
And friendship shall combine, and brotherhood.
I'll live by Nym, and Nym shall live by me.   115
Is not this just? For I shall sutler be
Unto the camp, and profits will accrue.
Give me thy hand.
   Nym. I shall have my noble?
   Pist. In cash most justly paid.   120
   Nym. Well, then, that's the humour of 't.

           Re-enter HOSTESS.

   Host. As ever you come of women, come in
quickly to Sir John. Ah, poor heart! he is so
shak'd of a burning quotidian tertian, that it is
most lamentable to behold. Sweet men, come to
him.   126
   Nym. The King hath run bad humours on the
knight; that's the even of it.
   Pist. Nym, thou hast spoke the right.
His heart is fracted and corroborate.   130
   Nym. The king is a good King; but it must be
as it may; he passes some humours and careers.
   Pist. Let us condole the knight; for, lambkins,
we will live.   [*Exeunt.*]

[SCENE II. *Southampton. A council-chamber.*]

Enter EXETER, BEDFORD, *and* WESTMORELAND.

   Bed. 'Fore God, his Grace is bold, to trust these
traitors.
   Exe. They shall be apprehended by and by.

   West. How smooth and even they do bear them-
selves!
As if allegiance in their bosoms sat
Crowned with faith and constant loyalty.   5
   Bed. The King hath note of all that they intend,
By interception which they dream not of.
   Exe. Nay, but the man that was his bedfellow,
Whom he hath dull'd and cloy'd with gracious
favours,
That he should, for a foreign purse, so sell   10
His sovereign's life to death and treachery.

   Trumpets sound. Enter KING HENRY, SCROOP,
         CAMBRIDGE, *and* GREY.

   K. Hen. Now sits the wind fair, and we will
aboard.
My Lord of Cambridge, and my kind Lord of
Masham,
And you, my gentle knight, give me your thoughts.
Think you not that the powers we bear with us   15
Will cut their passage through the force of France,
Doing the execution and the act
For which we have in head assembled them?
   Scroop. No doubt, my liege, if each man do his
best.
   K. Hen. I doubt not that, since we are well
persuaded   20
We carry not a heart with us from hence
That grows not in a fair consent with ours,
Nor leave not one behind that doth not wish
Success and conquest to attend on us.
   Cam. Never was monarch better fear'd and
lov'd   25
Than is your Majesty. There's not, I think, a
subject
That sits in heart-grief and uneasiness
Under the sweet shade of your government.
   Grey. True; those that were your father's
enemies
Have steep'd their galls in honey, and do serve you
With hearts create of duty and of zeal.   31
   K. Hen. We therefore have great cause of
thankfulness,
And shall forget the office of our hand
Sooner than quittance of desert and merit
According to the weight and worthiness.   35
   Scroop. So service shall with steeled sinews toil,
And labour shall refresh itself with hope,
To do your Grace incessant services.
   K. Hen. We judge no less. Uncle of Exeter,
Enlarge the man committed yesterday,   40
That rail'd against our person. We consider
It was excess of wine that set him on,

---

103. **compound:** decide. 110–111. [*Nym . . . betting*] Q. Om. F. 112. **noble:** 6*s*.8*d.* 116. **sutler:** seller of provisions.
124. **quotidian tertian:** confusion of medical terms for two kinds of fever. 130. **fracted:** broken. **corroborate:** lit., strengthened. 132. **passes:** lets pass. **careers:** a term of horsemanship.
   Sc. ii, 2. **by and by:** soon. 18. **head:** force. 34. **quittance:** reward. 40. **Enlarge:** set free.

And on his more advice we pardon him.
   Scroop. That's mercy, but too much security.
Let him be punish'd, sovereign, lest example   45
Breed, by his sufferance, more of such a kind.
   K. Hen. O, let us yet be merciful.
   Cam. So may your Highness, and yet punish too.
   Grey. Sir,
You show great mercy if you give him life   50
After the taste of much correction.
   K. Hen. Alas, your too much love and care of me
Are heavy orisons 'gainst this poor wretch!
If little faults, proceeding on distemper,
Shall not be wink'd at, how shall we stretch our eye
When capital crimes, chew'd, swallow'd and di-
    gested,   56
Appear before us? We'll yet enlarge that man,
Though Cambridge, Scroop, and Grey, in their dear
    care
And tender preservation of our person,
Would have him punish'd. And now to our French
    causes.   60
Who are the late commissioners?
   Cam. I one, my lord.
Your Highness bade me ask for it to-day.
   Scroop. So did you me, my liege.
   Grey. And I, my royal sovereign.   65
   K. Hen. Then, Richard Earl of Cambridge, there
    is yours;
There yours, Lord Scroop of Masham; and, sir
    knight,
Grey of Northumberland, this same is yours.
Read them, and know I know your worthiness.
My Lord of Westmoreland, and uncle Exeter,   70
We will aboard to-night. — Why, how now, gentle-
    men?
What see you in those papers that you lose
So much complexion? — Look ye, how they change!
Their cheeks are paper. — Why, what read you
    there
That have so cowarded and chas'd your blood   75
Out of appearance?
   Cam.   I do confess my fault,
And do submit me to your Highness' mercy.
   Grey. }
   Scroop. } To which we all appeal.
   K. Hen. The mercy that was quick in us but late,
By your own counsel is suppress'd and kill'd.   80
You must not dare, for shame, to talk of mercy,
For your own reasons turn into your bosoms,
As dogs upon their masters, worrying you.
See you, my princes and my noble peers,

These English monsters! My Lord of Cambridge
    here,   85
You know how apt our love was to accord
To furnish him with all appertinents
Belonging to his honour; and this man
Hath, for a few light crowns, lightly conspir'd
And sworn unto the practices of France   90
To kill us here in Hampton; to the which
This knight, no less for bounty bound to us
Than Cambridge is, hath likewise sworn. But, O
What shall I say to thee, Lord Scroop? thou cruel,
Ingrateful, savage, and inhuman creature!   95
Thou that didst bear the key of all my counsels,
That knew'st the very bottom of my soul,
That almost mightst have coin'd me into gold,
Wouldst thou have practis'd on me for thy use, —
May it be possible that foreign hire   100
Could out of thee extract one spark of evil
That might annoy my finger? 'Tis so strange,
That, though the truth of it stands off as gross
As black and white, my eye will scarcely see it.
Treason and murder ever kept together,   105
As two yoke-devils sworn to either's purpose,
Working so grossly in a natural cause
That admiration did not whoop at them;
But thou, 'gainst all proportion, didst bring in
Wonder to wait on treason and on murder;   110
And whatsoever cunning fiend it was
That wrought upon thee so preposterously
Hath got the voice in hell for excellence;
And other devils that suggest by treasons
Do botch and bungle up damnation   115
With patches, colours, and with forms being fetch'd
From glist'ring semblances of piety.
But he that temper'd thee, bade thee stand up,
Gave thee no instance why thou shouldst do treason,
Unless to dub thee with the name of traitor.   120
If that same demon that hath gull'd thee thus
Should with his lion gait walk the whole world,
He might return to vasty Tartar back,
And tell the legions, "I can never win
A soul so easy as that Englishman's."   125
O, how hast thou with jealousy infected
The sweetness of affiance! Show men dutiful?
Why, so didst thou. Seem they grave and learned?
Why, so didst thou. Come they of noble family?
Why, so didst thou. Seem they religious?   130
Why, so didst thou. Or are they spare in diet,
Free from gross passion or of mirth or anger,
Constant in spirit, not swerving with the blood,
Garnish'd and deck'd in modest complement,

---

43. **more advice:** thinking better of it. 44. **security:** lack of caution. 46. **his sufferance:** pardoning him. 53. **orisons:** prayers. 54. **on distemper:** from intoxication. 61. **late:** recently appointed. 63. **it:** my commission. 79. **quick:** alive. 86. **accord:** consent. 90. **practices:** plots. 103. **gross:** obvious. 108. **admiration . . . them:** they did not evoke wonder. 113. **voice:** vote. 114. **suggest:** seduce. 116. **colours:** pretexts. 118. **temper'd:** worked on your disposition. **bade . . . up.** The subject of *bade* is probably *that.* *Stand up* like *dub* (l. 120) is part of the formula used in knighting. 121. **gull'd:** fooled. 123. **Tartar:** Tartarus, Hell. 126. **jealousy:** suspicion. 127. **affiance:** trust. **show:** appear. 134. **complement:** demeanor.

Not working with the eye without the ear, 135
And but in purged judgement trusting neither?
Such and so finely bolted didst thou seem.
And thus thy fall hath left a kind of blot
To [mark the] full-fraught man and best indued
With some suspicion. I will weep for thee; 140
For this revolt of thine, methinks, is like
Another fall of man. Their faults are open.
Arrest them to the answer of the law;
And God acquit them of their practices!
  Exe. I arrest thee of high treason, by the name
of Richard Earl of Cambridge. 146
  I arrest thee of high treason, by the name of
[Henry] Lord Scroop of Masham.
  I arrest thee of high treason, by the name of
Thomas Grey, knight, of Northumberland. 150
  Scroop. Our purposes God justly hath discover'd,
And I repent my fault more than my death,
Which I beseech your Highness to forgive,
Although my body pay the price of it.
  Cam. For me, the gold of France did not se-
    duce, 155
Although I did admit it as a motive
The sooner to effect what I intended.
But God be thanked for prevention,
Which I in sufferance heartily will rejoice,
Beseeching God and you to pardon me. 160
  Grey. Never did faithful subject more rejoice
At the discovery of most dangerous treason
Than I do at this hour joy o'er myself,
Prevented from a damned enterprise.
My fault, but not my body, pardon, sovereign. 165
  K. Hen. God quit you in his mercy! Hear your
    sentence.
You have conspir'd against our royal person,
Join'd with an enemy proclaim'd, and from his
    coffers
Receiv'd the golden earnest of our death;
Wherein you would have sold your king to slaugh-
    ter, 170
His princes and his peers to servitude,
His subjects to oppression and contempt,
And his whole kingdom into desolation.
Touching our person seek we no revenge;
But we our kingdom's safety must so tender, 175
Whose ruin you [have] sought, that to her laws
We do deliver you. Get you therefore hence,
Poor miserable wretches, to your death,
The taste whereof God of his mercy give
You patience to endure, and true repentance 180
Of all your dear offences! Bear them hence.

  [*Exeunt* [*Cambridge, Scroop, and Grey*
    guarded].
Now, lords, for France; the enterprise whereof
Shall be to you, as us, like glorious.
We doubt not of a fair and lucky war,
Since God so graciously hath brought to light 185
This dangerous treason lurking in our way
To hinder our beginnings. We doubt not now
But every rub is smoothed on our way.
Then forth, dear countrymen! Let us deliver
Our puissance into the hand of God, 190
Putting it straight in expedition.
Cheerly to sea! The signs of war advance!
No king of England, if not king of France!
             [*Flourish.*

  [SCENE III. *London. Before a tavern.*]

  Enter PISTOL, NYM, BARDOLPH, BOY, *and*
    HOSTESS.

  Host. Prithee honey, sweet husband, let me
bring thee to Staines.
  Pist. No; for my manly heart doth ern.
Bardolph, be blithe; Nym, rouse thy vaunting
    veins;
Boy, bristle thy courage up; for Falstaff he is dead,
And we must ern therefore. 6
  Bard. Would I were with him, wheresome'er he
is, either in heaven or in hell!
  Host. Nay, sure, he's not in hell. He's in Arthur's bosom, if ever man went to Arthur's 10
bosom. 'A made a finer end and went away an it
had been any christom child. 'A parted even just
between twelve and one, even at the turning o' th'
tide: for after I saw him fumble with the sheets,
and play with flowers, and smile upon his fin- 15
gers' ends, I knew there was but one way; for his
nose was as sharp as a pen, and ['a babbled] of
green fields. "How now, Sir John!" quoth I;
"what, man! be o' good cheer." So 'a cried out,
"God, God, God!" three or four times. Now I, 20
to comfort him, bid him 'a should not think of
God; I hop'd there was no need to trouble himself
with any such thoughts yet. So 'a bade me lay
more clothes on his feet. I put my hand into the
bed and felt them, and they were as cold as 25
any stone; then I felt to his knees, [and they were
as cold as any stone;] and so upward and upward,
and all was as cold as any stone.
  Nym. They say he cried out of sack.
  Host. Ay, that 'a did. 30

  135. Not judging a man by looks without talking with him. 137. **bolted:** sifted. 139. [**mark the**] (Theobald). *make thee* F. **full-fraught:** loaded with good qualities. 148. [**Henry**] Q. *Thomas* F. 151. **discover'd:** revealed. 159. **in suffer-ance:** though suffering punishment. 166. **quit:** absolve. 169. **earnest:** payment to bind a bargain. 175. **tender:** regard. 176. [**have**] Q. Om. F₁, three F₂. 181. **dear:** grievous. 188. **rub:** obstacle. 192. **signs of war:** banners.
    Sc. iii, 2. **Staines:** on the way to Southampton. 3. **ern:** grieve; the older form and meaning of *yearn.* 12. **christom:** chrisom, newly christened. 17. [**'a babbled**] (Theobald). *a Table* F. See Introduction. 26–27. [**and ... stone**] Q. Om. F.
  29. **sack:** a Spanish wine.

Bard. And of women.

Host. Nay, that 'a did not.

Boy. Yes, that 'a did; and said they were devils incarnate.

Host. 'A could never abide carnation; 'twas a colour he never lik'd.   36

Boy. 'A said once, the devil would have him about women.

Host. 'A did in some sort, indeed, handle women; but then he was rheumatic, and talk'd of the whore of Babylon.   41

Boy. Do you not remember, 'a saw a flea stick upon Bardolph's nose, and 'a said it was a black soul burning in [hell-fire]?   44

Bard. Well, the fuel is gone that maintain'd that fire. That's all the riches I got in his service.

Nym. Shall we shog? The King will be gone from Southampton.

Pist. Come, let's away. My love, give me thy lips.
Look to my chattels and my movables.   50
Let senses rule; the word is "Pitch and Pay."
Trust none;
For oaths are straws, men's faiths are wafer-
    cakes,
And hold-fast is the only dog, my duck;
Therefore, *Caveto* be thy counsellor.   55
Go, clear thy crystals. Yoke-fellows in arms,
Let us to France; like horse-leeches, my boys,
To suck, to suck, the very blood to suck!

Boy. And that's but unwholesome food, they say.   60

Pist. Touch her soft mouth, and march.

Bard. Farewell, hostess.   [*Kissing her.*]

Nym. I cannot kiss; that is the humour of it; but, adieu.

Pist. Let housewifery appear. **Keep** close, I
    thee command.   65

Host. Farewell; adieu.   [*Exeunt.*]

[Scene IV. *France. The King's palace.*]

Flourish. Enter the French King, *the* Dauphin,
    the Dukes of Berri *and* Bretagne [*the*
    Constable, *and others*].

Fr. King. Thus comes the English with full
        power upon us,
And more than carefully it us concerns
To answer royally in our defences.
Therefore the Dukes of Berri and of Bretagne,
Of Brabant and of Orleans, shall make forth,   5
And you, Prince Dauphin, with all swift dispatch,
To line and new repair our towns of war

With men of courage and with means defendant;
For England his approaches makes as fierce
As waters to the sucking of a gulf.   10
It fits us then to be as provident
As fears may teach us out of late examples
Left by the fatal and neglected English
Upon our fields.

Dau.   My most redoubted father,
It is most meet we arm us 'gainst the foe;   15
For peace itself should not so dull a kingdom
(Though war nor no known quarrel were in ques-
    tion)
But that defences, musters, preparations,
Should be maintain'd, assembled, and collected,
As were a war in expectation.   20
Therefore, I say, 'tis meet we all go forth
To view the sick and feeble parts of France.
And let us do it with no show of fear;
No, with no more than if we heard that England
Were busied with a Whitsun morris-dance;   25
For, my good liege, she is so idly king'd,
Her sceptre so fantastically borne
By a vain, giddy, shallow, humorous youth,
That fear attends her not.

Con.   O peace, Prince Dauphin!
You are too much mistaken in this king.   30
Question your Grace the late ambassadors
With what great state he heard their embassy,
How well supplied with noble counsellors,
How modest in exception, and withal
How terrible in constant resolution,   35
And you shall find his vanities forespent
Were but the outside of the Roman Brutus,
Covering discretion with a coat of folly,
As gardeners do with ordure hide those roots
That shall first spring and be most delicate. 40

Dau. Well, 'tis not so, my Lord High Constable;
But though we think it so, it is no matter.
In cases of defense 'tis best to weigh
The enemy more mighty than he seems,
So the proportions of defence are fill'd;   45
Which, of a weak and niggardly projection,
Doth, like a miser, spoil his coat with scanting
A little cloth.

Fr. King. Think we King Harry strong;
And, Princes, look you strongly arm to meet him.
The kindred of him hath been flesh'd upon us; 50
And he is bred out of that bloody strain
That haunted us in our familiar paths.
Witness our too much memorable shame
When Cressy battle fatally was struck,
And all our princes captiv'd by the hand   55
Of that black name, Edward, Black Prince of Wales;

---

39. **handle:** talk of. 40. **rheumatic.** She probably means *lunatic.* 44. **[hell-fire]** Q. *Hell* F. 55. ***Caveto:*** be cautious.
Sc. iv, 7. **line:** garrison. 10. **gulf:** whirlpool. 13. **fatal and:** fatally. 28. **humorous:** capricious. 34. **exception:** raising objections. 36. **forespent:** former. 37. Brutus pretended madness to conceal conspiracy against Tarquin. 46. **projection:** scale. 50. **flesh'd upon us:** fed on our flesh.

Whiles that his mountain sire, on mountain stand-
ing,
Up in the air, crown'd with the golden sun,
Saw his heroical seed, and smil'd to see him,
Mangle the work of nature and deface 60
The patterns that by God and by French fathers
Had twenty years been made. This is a stem
Of that victorious stock; and let us fear
The native mightiness and fate of him.

Enter a MESSENGER.

Mess. Ambassadors from Harry King of England
Do crave admittance to your Majesty. 66
Fr. King. We'll give them present audience.
Go, and bring them.
[*Exeunt Messenger and certain Lords.*]
You see this chase is hotly follow'd, friends.
Dau. Turn head, and stop pursuit; for coward
dogs
Most spend their mouths when what they seem to
threaten 70
Runs far before them. Good my sovereign,
Take up the English short, and let them know
Of what a monarchy you are the head.
Self-love, my liege, is not so vile a sin
As self-neglecting.

Enter EXETER.

Fr. King. From our brother of England?
Exe. From him; and thus he greets your Majesty:
He wills you, in the name of God Almighty, 77
That you divest yourself, and lay apart
The borrowed glories that by gift of heaven,
By law of nature and of nations, 'longs 80
To him and to his heirs; namely, the crown
And all wide-stretched honours that pertain
By custom and the ordinance of times
Unto the crown of France. That you may know
'Tis no sinister nor no awkward claim 85
Pick'd from the worm-holes of long-vanish'd days,
Nor from the dust of old oblivion rak'd,
He sends you this most memorable line,
In every branch truly demonstrative;
Willing you overlook this pedigree; 90
And when you find him evenly deriv'd
From his most fam'd of famous ancestors,
Edward the Third, he bids you then resign
Your crown and kingdom, indirectly held
From him, the native and true challenger. 95
Fr. King. Or else what follows?
Exe. Bloody constraint; for if you hide the crown
Even in your hearts, there will he rake for it.
Therefore in fierce tempest is he coming,

In thunder and in earthquake, like a Jove, 100
That, if requiring fail, he will compel;
And bids you, in the bowels of the Lord,
Deliver up the crown, and to take mercy
On the poor souls for whom this hungry war
Opens his vasty jaws; and on your head 105
Turning the widows' tears, the orphans' cries,
The dead men's blood, the [pining] maidens' groans,
For husbands, fathers, and betrothed lovers,
That shall be swallowed in this controversy.
This is his claim, his threat'ning, and my message;
Unless the Dauphin be in presence here, 111
To whom expressly I bring greeting too.
Fr. King. For us, we will consider of this
further.
To-morrow shall you bear our full intent 114
Back to our brother of England.
Dau. For the Dauphin,
I stand here for him. What to him from Eng-
land?
Exe. Scorn and defiance. Slight regard, con-
tempt,
And anything that may not misbecome
The mighty sender, doth he prize you at.
Thus says my king: an if your father's Highness 120
Do not, in grant of all demands at large,
Sweeten the bitter mock you sent his Majesty,
He'll call you to so hot an answer of it
That caves and womby vaultages of France
Shall chide your trespass and return your mock 125
In second accent of his ordinance.
Dau. Say, if my father render fair return,
It is against my will; for I desire
Nothing but odds with England. To that end,
As matching to his youth and vanity, 130
I did present him with the Paris balls.
Exe. He'll make your Paris Louvre shake for it,
Were it the mistress-court of mighty Europe;
And, be assur'd, you'll find a difference,
As we his subjects have in wonder found, 135
Between the promise of his greener days
And these he masters now. Now he weighs time
Even to the utmost grain. That you shall read
In your own losses, if he stay in France.
Fr. King. To-morrow shall you know our mind
at full. [*Flourish.* 140
Exe. Dispatch us with all speed, lest that our
king
Come here himself to question our delay;
For he is footed in this land already.
Fr. King. You shall be soon dispatch'd with fair
conditions.
A night is but small breath and little pause 145
To answer matters of this consequence. [*Exeunt.*

57. **mountain**: imposing. 64. **fate of him**: what his destiny holds. 85. **sinister**: illegitimate. 88. **line**: genealogical table. 94. **indirectly**: unjustly. 107. **[pining]** Q. *privy* F. 124. **womby vaultages**: hollow caverns. 126. **second...**: **ordinance**: echo of his ordnance, or artillery.

ACT [III]

[PROLOGUE]

Flourish. Enter CHORUS.

[*Chor.*] Thus with imagin'd wing our swift scene
    flies
In motion of no less celerity
Than that of thought. Suppose that you have seen
The well-appointed king at [Hampton] pier
Embark his royalty, and his brave fleet   5
With silken streamers the young Phœbus fanning.
Play with your fancies, and in them behold
Upon the hempen tackle ship-boys climbing;
Hear the shrill whistle which doth order give
To sounds confus'd; behold the threaden sails, 10
Borne with th' invisible and creeping wind,
Draw the huge bottoms through the furrowed sea,
Breasting the lofty surge. O, do but think
You stand upon the rivage and behold
A city on th' inconstant billows dancing;   15
For so appears this fleet majestical,
Holding due course to Harfleur. Follow, follow!
Grapple your minds to sternage of this navy,
And leave your England, as dead midnight still,
Guarded with grandsires, babies, and old women,
Either past or not arriv'd to pith and puissance. 21
For who is he, whose chin is but enrich'd
With one appearing hair, that will not follow
These cull'd and choice-drawn cavaliers to France?
Work, work your thoughts, and therein see a siege;
Behold the ordnance on their carriages,   26
With fatal mouths gaping on girded Harfleur.
Suppose th' ambassador from the French comes
    back,
Tells Harry that the King doth offer him
Katharine his daughter, and with her, to dowry, 30
Some petty and unprofitable dukedoms.
The offer likes not; and the nimble gunner
With linstock now the devilish cannon touches,
        [*Alarum, and chambers go off.*
And down goes all before them. Still be kind,
And eke out our performance with your mind. 35
        [*Exit.*

[SCENE I. *France. Before*] *Harfleur.*

Alarum. Enter KING HENRY, EXETER, BEDFORD,
  GLOUCESTER, [*and* Soldiers, *with*] *scaling-ladders.*

K. Hen. Once more unto the breach, dear friends,
    once more,
Or close the wall up with our English dead.
In peace there's nothing so becomes a man

As modest stillness and humility;
But when the blast of war blows in our ears,   5
Then imitate the action of the tiger;
Stiffen the sinews, summon up the blood,
Disguise fair nature with hard-favour'd rage;
Then lend the eye a terrible aspect;
Let it pry through the portage of the head   10
Like the brass cannon; let the brow o'erwhelm it
As fearfully as doth a galled rock
O'erhang and jutty his confounded base,
Swill'd with the wild and wasteful ocean.
Now set the teeth and stretch the nostril wide, 15
Hold hard the breath, and bend up every spirit
To his full height. On, on, you [noblest] English,
Whose blood is fet from fathers of war-proof!
Fathers that, like so many Alexanders,
Have in these parts from morn till even fought, 20
And sheath'd their swords for lack of argument.
Dishonour not your mothers; now attest
That those whom you call'd fathers did beget you.
Be copy now to men of grosser blood,
And teach them how to war. And you, good yeo-
    men,   25
Whose limbs were made in England, show us here
The mettle of your pasture; let us swear
That you are worth your breeding, which I doubt
    not;
For there is none of you so mean and base
That hath not noble lustre in your eyes.   30
I see you stand like greyhounds in the slips,
[Straining] upon the start. The game's afoot!
Follow your spirit, and upon this charge
Cry, "God for Harry! England and Saint George!"
    [*Exeunt.*] *Alarum, and chambers go off.*

[SCENE II. *The same.*]

Enter NYM, BARDOLPH, PISTOL, *and* BOY.

Bard. On, on, on, on, on! To the breach, to
the breach!

Nym. Pray thee, corporal, stay. The knocks
are too hot; and, for mine own part, I have not a
case of lives. The humour of it is too hot; that is
the very plain-song of it.   6

Pist. The plain-song is most just, for humours
    do abound.

"Knocks go and come; God's vassals drop and die;
    And sword and shield,
        In bloody field,   10
Doth win immortal fame."

Boy. Would I were in an alehouse in London!

Act III, Prol., 1. **imagin'd wing**: wing of imagination. 4. **[Hampton]** (Theobald). *Dover* F. 14. **rivage**: shore. 18. **sternage**: the sterns. 32. **likes**: pleases. 33. **linstock**: stick holding the match. S.D. **chambers**: small cannon.

Sc. i, 10. **portage**: port-holes. 11. **o'erwhelm**: overhang. 12. **galled**: worn away. 13. **jutty**: project over. **confounded**: wasted away. 14. **Swill'd**: washed. 17. **[noblest]** F2. *noblish* F1. 18. **fet**: fetched. 21. **argument**: cause of quarrel. 31. **slips**: leash. 32. **[Straining]** (Rowe). *Straying* F.

Sc. ii, 5. **case**: set. 6. **plain-song**: simple melody.

I would give all my fame for a pot of ale and safety.

Pist. And I.   15

> "If wishes would prevail with me,
> My purpose should not fail with me,
> But thither would I hie."

Boy. "As duly, but not as truly,
> As bird doth sing on bough."   20

Enter FLUELLEN.

Flu. Up to the breach, you dogs! Avaunt, you cullions!   [*Driving them forward.*]

Pist. Be merciful, great Duke, to men of mould. Abate thy rage, abate thy manly rage, Abate thy rage, great Duke!   25 Good bawcock, bate thy rage; use lenity, sweet chuck!

Nym. These be good humours! Your honour wins bad humours.   [*Exeunt [all but Boy*].

Boy. As young as I am, I have observ'd these three swashers. I am boy to them all three; but 30 all they three, though they would serve me, could not be man to me; for indeed three such antics do not amount to a man. For Bardolph, he is white-liver'd and red-fac'd; by the means whereof 'a faces it out, but fights not. For Pistol, he hath a 35 killing tongue and a quiet sword; by the means whereof 'a breaks words, and keeps whole weapons. For Nym, he hath heard that men of few words are the best men; and therefore he scorns to say his prayers, lest 'a should be thought a coward. But 40 his few bad words are match'd with as few good deeds; for 'a never broke any man's head but his own, and that was against a post when he was drunk. They will steal anything, and call it purchase. Bardolph stole a lute-case, bore it twelve 45 leagues, and sold it for three half-pence. Nym and Bardolph are sworn brothers in filching, and in Calais they stole a fire-shovel. I knew by that piece of service the men would carry coals. They would have me as familiar with men's pockets 50 as their gloves or their handkerchers; which makes much against my manhood, if I should take from another's pocket to put into mine; for it is plain pocketing up of wrongs. I must leave them, and seek some better service. Their villainy goes 55 against my weak stomach, and therefore I must cast it up.   [*Exit.*

Enter GOWER [*and* FLUELLEN].

Gow. Captain Fluellen, you must come presently to the mines. The Duke of Gloucester would speak with you.   60

Flu. To the mines! Tell you the Duke, it is not so good to come to the mines; for, look you, the mines is not according to the disciplines of the war. The concavities of it is not sufficient; for, look you, the athversary, you may discuss unto the Duke, look you, is digt himself four yard under [with] countermines. By Cheshu, I think 'a will plow up all, if there is not better directions.   68

Gow. The Duke of Gloucester, to whom the order of the siege is given, is altogether directed by an Irishman, a very valiant gentleman, i' faith.

Flu. It is Captain Macmorris, is it not?

Gow. I think it be.   73

Flu. By Cheshu, he is an ass, as in the world. I will verify as much in his beard. He has no more directions in the true disciplines of the wars, look you, of the Roman disciplines, than is a puppy-dog.

Enter MACMORRIS *and* CAPTAIN JAMY.

Gow. Here 'a comes; and the Scots captain, Captain Jamy with him.   80

Flu. Captain Jamy is a marvellous falorous gentleman, that is certain; and of great expedition and knowledge in th' aunchient wars, upon my particular knowledge of his directions. By Cheshu, he will maintain his argument as well as any military man in the world, in the disciplines of the pristine wars of the Romans.   87

Jamy. I say gud-day, Captain Fluellen.

Flu. God-den to your worship, good Captain James.

Gow. How now, Captain Macmorris! have you quit the mines? Have the pioners given o'er? 92

Mac. By Chrish, la! 'tish ill done. The work ish give over, the trompet sound the retreat. By my hand I swear, and my father's soul, the work ish ill done; it ish give over. I would have blowed up the town, so Chrish save me, la! in an hour. O, 'tish ill done, 'tish ill done; by my hand, 'tish ill done! 99

Flu. Captain Macmorris, I beseech you now, will you voutsafe me, look you, a few disputations with you, as partly touching or concerning the disciplines of the war, the Roman wars, in the way of argument, look you, and friendly communication; partly to satisfy my opinion, and partly for the 105 satisfaction, look you, of my mind, as touching the direction of the military discipline; that is the point.

Jamy. It sall be very gud, gud feith, gud captains bath: and I sall quit you with gud leve, as I may pick occasion; that sall I, marry.   111

Mac. It is no time to discourse, so Chrish save me. The day is hot, and the weather, and the wars, and the King, and the Dukes. It is no time to discourse. The town is beseech'd, and the trumpet 115

---

22. **cullions:** scoundrels.   26. **bawcock:** Fr. *beau coq*, fine fellow.   32. **antics:** clowns.   49. **carry coals:** put up with an affront.   65. **discuss:** tell.   66. **[with]** (Vaughan).   *the* F.   82. **expedition:** a blunder between *experience* and *erudition* (Evans).   92. **pioners:** trench and mine diggers.   110. **quit:** requite.

call us to the breach, and we talk, and, be Chrish, do
nothing. 'Tis shame for us all. So God sa' me, 'tis
shame to stand still; it is shame, by my hand; and
there is throats to be cut, and works to be done; and
there ish nothing done, so Chrish sa' me, la!   121

Jamy. By the mess, ere theise eyes of mine take
themselves to slomber, I'll de gud service, or I'll
lig i' the grund for it; ay, or go to death; and I'll
pay't as valourously as I may, that sall I suerly
do, that is the breff and the long. Marry, I wad
full fain heard some question 'tween you tway.   128

Flu. Captain Macmorris, I think, look you,
under your correction, there is not many of your
nation —   131

Mac. Of my nation! What ish my nation? Ish
a villain, and a bastard, and a knave, and a rascal?
What ish my nation? Who talks of my nation?   135

Flu. Look you, if you take the matter otherwise
than is meant, Captain Macmorris, peradventure
I shall think you do not use me with that affability
as in discretion you ought to use me, look you, being
as good a man as yourself, both in the disciplines of
war, and in the derivation of my birth, and in other
particularities.   142

Mac. I do not know you so good a man as myself. So Chrish save me, I will cut off your head.

Gow. Gentlemen both, you will mistake each
other.

Jamy. Ah! that's a foul fault.

[*A parley* [*sounded*].

Gow. The town sounds a parley.   149

Flu. Captain Macmorris, when there is more better opportunity to be required, look you, I will be
so bold as to tell you I know the disciplines of war;
and there is an end.   [*Exeunt.* 153

[SCENE III. *The same.*] *Before the gates.*

[*The* GOVERNOR *and some* Citizens *on the walls; the*
English forces below.] *Enter* KING HENRY *and his*
train.

K. Hen. How yet resolves the governor of the
town?
This is the latest parle we will admit;
Therefore to our best mercy give yourselves,
Or like to men proud of destruction
Defy us to our worst; for, as I am a soldier,   5
A name that in my thoughts becomes me best,
If I begin the batt'ry once again,
I will not leave the half-achieved Harfleur
Till in her ashes she lies buried.
The gates of mercy shall be all shut up,   10
And the flesh'd soldier, rough and hard of heart,
In liberty of bloody hand shall range

With conscience wide as hell, mowing like grass
Your fresh fair virgins and your flow'ring infants.
What is it then to me, if impious War,   15
Array'd in flames like to the prince of fiends,
Do with his smirch'd complexion all fell feats
Enlink'd to waste and desolation?
What is't to me, when you yourselves are cause,
If your pure maidens fall into the hand   20
Of hot and forcing violation?
What rein can hold licentious wickedness
When down the hill he holds his fierce career?
We may as bootless spend our vain command
Upon th' enraged soldiers in their spoil   25
As send precepts to the leviathan
To come ashore. Therefore, you men of Harfleur,
Take pity of your town and of your people,
Whiles yet my soldiers are in my command,
Whiles yet the cool and temperate wind of grace   30
O'erblows the filthy and contagious clouds
Of heady murder, spoil, and villainy.
If not, why, in a moment look to see
The blind and bloody soldier with foul hand
[Defile] the locks of your shrill-shrieking daughters;
Your fathers taken by the silver beards,   36
And their most reverend heads dash'd to the walls;
Your naked infants spitted upon pikes,
Whiles the mad mothers with their howls confus'd
Do break the clouds, as did the wives of Jewry   40
At Herod's bloody-hunting slaughtermen.
What say you? Will you yield and this avoid,
Or, guilty in defence, be thus destroy'd?

Gov. Our expectation hath this day an end.
The Dauphin, whom of succours we entreated,   45
Returns us that his powers are yet not ready
To raise so great a siege. Therefore, great King,
We yield our town and lives to thy soft mercy.
Enter our gates; dispose of us and ours;
For we no longer are defensible.   50

K. Hen. Open your gates. Come, uncle Exeter,
Go you and enter Harfleur; there remain,
And fortify it strongly 'gainst the French.
Use mercy to them all. For us, dear uncle,
The winter coming on, and sickness growing   55
Upon our soldiers, we will retire to Calais.
To-night in Harfleur will we be your guest;
To-morrow for the march are we addrest.

[*Flourish.* [*The King and his train*] *enter*
the town.

[SCENE IV. *The French King's palace.*]

Enter KATHARINE *and* [ALICE] *an old Gentlewoman.*

Kath. Alice, tu as été en Angleterre, et tu parles
bien le langage.

124. lig: lie.
Sc. iii, 32. heady: headstrong. 35. [Defile] (Rowe). *Desire* F. 41. Herod's. See *Matthew* II.16-18.
Sc. iv. The French of this scene has been corrected by successive editors. In F it is about as accurate as the Welsh, Irish,
and Scottish dialect in Sc. ii.

Alice. Un peu, madame.

Kath. Je te prie, m'enseignez; il faut que j'apprenne à parler. Comment appelez-vous la main en Anglois? 6

Alice. La main? Elle est appelée de hand.

Kath. De hand. Et les doigts?

Alice. Les doigts? Ma foi, j'oublie les doigts; mais je me souviendrai. Les doigts? Je pense qu'ils sont appelés de fingres; oui, de fingres. 11

Kath. La main, de hand; les doigts, de fingres. Je pense que je suis le bon écolier; j'ai gagné deux mots d'Anglois vîtement. Comment appelez-vous les ongles? 15

Alice. Les ongles? Nous les appelons de nails.

Kath. De nails. Écoutez; dites-moi, si je parle bien: de hand, de fingres, et de nails.

Alice. C'est bien dit, madame; il est fort bon Anglois. 20

Kath. Dites-moi l'Anglois pour le bras.

Alice. De arm, madame.

Kath. Et le coude?

Alice. D'elbow. 24

Kath. D'elbow. Je m'en fais la répétition de tous les mots que vous m'avez appris dès à présent.

Alice. Il est trop difficile, madame, comme je pense.

Kath. Excusez-moi, Alice; écoutez: D'hand, de fingres, de nails, d'arma, de bilbow. 31

Alice. D'elbow, madame.

Kath. O Seigneur Dieu, je m'en oublie! D'elbow. Comment appelez-vous le col?

Alice. De nick, madame. 35

Kath. De nick. Et le menton?

Alice. De chin.

Kath. De sin. Le col, de nick; le menton, de sin.

Alice. Oui. Sauf votre honneur, en vérité, 40 vous prononcez les mots aussi droit que les natifs d'Angleterre.

Kath. Je ne doute point d'apprendre, par la grace de Dieu, et en peu de temps. 44

Alice. N'avez vous pas déjà oublié ce que je vous ai enseigné?

Kath. Non, je reciterai à vous promptement: d' hand, de fingres, de mails, —

Alice. De nails, madame.

Kath. De nails, de arm, de ilbow. 50

Alice. Sauf votre honneur, de elbow.

Kath. Ainsi dis-je; d'elbow, de nick, et de sin. Comment appelez-vous le pied et la robe?

Alice. De foot, madame; et de coun. 54

Kath. De foot et de coun! O Seigneur Dieu! ce sont mots de son mauvais, corruptible, gros, et impudique, et non pour les dames d'honneur d'user. Je ne voudrais prononcer ces mots devant les seigneurs de France pour tout le monde. Foh! le foot et le coun! Néanmoins, je réciterai une autre 60 fois ma leçon ensemble: d'hand, de fingres, de nails, d'arm, d'elbow, de nick, de sin, de foot, de coun.

Alice. Excellent, madame!

Kath. C'est assez pour une fois: allons-nous à dîner. [*Exeunt.* 66

[SCENE V. *The same.*]

Enter the KING OF FRANCE, *the* DAUPHIN, [*the* DUKE OF BOURBON,] *the* CONSTABLE OF FRANCE, *and others.*

Fr. King. 'Tis certain he hath pass'd the river Somme.

Con. An if he be not fought withal, my lord, Let us not live in France; let us quit all And give our vineyards to a barbarous people.

Dau. O Dieu vivant! shall a few sprays of us, 5 The emptying of our fathers' luxury, Our scions put in wild and savage stock, Spirt up so suddenly into the clouds And overlook their grafters?

Bour. Normans, but bastard Normans, Norman bastards! 10 *Mort de ma vie!* if they march along Unfought withal, but I will sell my dukedom, To buy a slobbery and a dirty farm In that nook-shotten isle of Albion.

Con. Dieu de batailles! where have they this mettle? 15 Is not their climate foggy, raw, and dull, On whom, as in despite, the sun looks pale, Killing their fruit with frowns? Can sodden water, A drench for sur-rein'd jades, their barley-broth, Decoct their cold blood to such valiant heat? 20 And shall our quick blood, spirited with wine, Seem frosty? O, for honour of our land, Let us not hang like roping icicles Upon our houses' thatch, whiles a more frosty people Sweat drops of gallant youth in our rich fields! 25 Poor we [may] call them in their native lords.

Dau. By faith and honour, Our madams mock at us, and plainly say Our mettle is bred out, and they will give Their bodies to the lust of English youth 30 To new-store France with bastard warriors.

Bour. They bid us to the English dancing-schools, And teach lavoltas high and swift corantos, Saying our grace is only in our heels, And that we are most lofty runaways. 35

Fr. King. Where is Montjoy the herald? Speed him hence.

Sc. v, 6. **luxury:** lust. 7. **put in:** grafted upon. 14. **nook-shotten:** running out into corners. 18. **sodden:** boiled. 19. **drench...jades:** drink for over-worked horses. 20. **Decoct:** warm. 26. **[may]** F₂. Om. F₁. 33. **lavoltas, corantos:** dances.

Let him greet England with our sharp defiance.
Up, princes! and, with spirit of honour edg'd
More sharper than your swords, hie to the field!
Charles Delabreth, High Constable of France;   40
You Dukes of Orleans, Bourbon, and of Berri,
Alençon, Brabant, Bar, and Burgundy;
Jacques Chatillon, Rambures, Vaudemont,
Beaumont, Grandpré, Roussi, and Fauconberg,
Foix, Lestrale, Bouciqualt, and Charolois;   45
High dukes, great princes, barons, lords, and
        [knights],
For your great seats now quit you of great shames.
Bar Harry England, that sweeps through our land
With pennons painted in the blood of Harfleur.
Rush on his host, as doth the melted snow   50
Upon the valleys, whose low vassal seat
The Alps doth spit and void his rheum upon.
Go down upon him, you have power enough,
And in a captive chariot into Rouen
Bring him our prisoner.
    Con.   This becomes the great.
Sorry am I his numbers are so few,   56
His soldiers sick and famish'd in their march;
For I am sure, when he shall see our army,
He'll drop his heart into the sink of fear
And for achievement offer us his ransom.   60
    Fr. King. Therefore, Lord Constable, haste on
        Montjoy,
And let him say to England that we send
To know what willing ransom he will give.
Prince Dauphin, you shall stay with us in Rouen.
    Dau. Not so, I do beseech your Majesty.   65
    Fr. King. Be patient, for you shall remain with
        us.
Now forth, Lord Constable and princes all,
And quickly bring us word of England's fall.
                                        [*Exeunt.*

[SCENE VI. *The English camp in Picardy.*]

Enter GOWER *and* FLUELLEN [*meeting*].

    Gow. How now, Captain Fluellen! come you from
the bridge?
    Flu. I assure you, there is very excellent services
committed at the bridge.
    Gow. Is the Duke of Exeter safe?   5
    Flu. The Duke of Exeter is as magnanimous as
Agamemnon; and a man that I love and honour
with my soul, and my heart, and my duty, and my
live, and my living, and my uttermost power. He
is not — God be praised and blessed! — any   10
hurt in the world; but keeps the bridge most val-

iantly, with excellent discipline.   There is an
aunchient lieutenant there at the pridge, I think
in my very conscience he is as valiant a man as
Mark Antony; and he is a man of no estimation   15
in the world, but I did see him do as gallant service.
    Gow. What do you call him?
    Flu. He is called Aunchient Pistol.
    Gow. I know him not.   20

Enter PISTOL.

    Flu. Here is the man.
    Pist. Captain, I thee beseech to do me favours.
The Duke of Exeter doth love thee well.
    Flu. Ay, I praise God; and I have merited some
love at his hands.   25
    Pist. Bardolph, a soldier, firm and sound of heart,
And of buxom valour, hath, by cruel fate,
And giddy Fortune's furious fickle wheel,
That goddess blind,
That stands upon the rolling restless stone —   30
    Flu. By your patience, Aunchient Pistol.   For-
tune is painted blind, with a muffler afore his eyes,
to signify to you that Fortune is blind; and she is
painted also with a wheel, to signify to you, which
is the moral of it, that she is turning, and incon-   35
stant, and mutability, and variation; and her foot,
look you, is fixed upon a spherical stone, which
rolls, and rolls, and rolls.   In good truth, the poet
makes a most excellent description of it.   Fortune
is an excellent moral.   40
    Pist. Fortune is Bardolph's foe, and frowns on
        him;
For he hath stolen a pax, and hanged must 'a be, —
A damned death!
Let gallows gape for dog; let man go free,
And let not hemp his windpipe suffocate.   45
But Exeter hath given the doom of death
For pax of little price.
Therefore, go speak; the Duke will hear thy voice;
And let not Bardolph's vital thread be cut
With edge of penny cord and vile reproach.   50
Speak, captain, for his life, and I will thee requite.
    Flu. Aunchient Pistol, I do partly understand
your meaning.
    Pist. Why then, rejoice therefore.   54
    Flu. Certainly, aunchient, it is not a thing to
rejoice at; for if, look you, he were my brother, I
would desire the Duke to use his good pleasure, and
put him to execution; for discipline ought to be
used.
    Pist. Die and be damn'd! and *figo* for thy friend-
ship!   60

---

46. [knights] (Pope).   *Kings* F.   47. quit: clear.   52. rheum: used of any watery discharge.   60. for achievement: in place of victory.
Sc. vi, 27. buxom: lively.   42. pax: a piece of metal with the figure of Christ stamped on it.   It is probably a mistake for Holinshed's *pyx*, the box containing the sacramental wafer.   60. *figo*: fig, a contemptuous gesture made by thrusting the thumb between the next two fingers, or between the teeth.

Flu. It is well.

Pist. The fig of Spain.   [*Exit.*

Flu. Very good.

Gow. Why, this is an arrant counterfeit rascal. I remember him now; a bawd, a cutpurse.   65

Flu. I'll assure you, 'a utt'red as prave words at the pridge as you shall see in a summer's day. But it is very well; what he has spoke to me, that is well, I warrant you, when time is serve.   69

Gow. Why, 'tis a gull, a fool, a rogue, that now and then goes to the wars, to grace himself at his return into London under the form of a soldier. And such fellows are perfect in the great commanders' names; and they will learn you by rote where services were done; at such and such a   75 sconce, at such a breach, at such a convoy; who came off bravely, who was shot, who disgrac'd, what terms the enemy stood on; and this they con perfectly in the phrase of war, which they trick up with new-tuned oaths: and what a beard of the   80 general's cut and a horrid suit of the camp will do among foaming bottles and ale-wash'd wits, is wonderful to be thought on. But you must learn to know such slanders of the age, or else you may be marvellously mistook.   85

Flu. I tell you what, Captain Gower; I do perceive he is not the man that he would gladly make show to the world he is. If I find a hole in his coat, I will tell him my mind. [*Drum heard.*] Hark you, the King is coming, and I must speak with him from the pridge.   91

Drum and colours. Enter KING HENRY, [GLOUCESTER,] *and his poor* Soldiers.

God bless your Majesty!

K. Hen. How now, Fluellen! cam'st thou from the bridge?

Flu. Ay, so please your Majesty. The Duke of Exeter has very gallantly maintain'd the pridge.   95 The French is gone off, look you; and there is gallant and most prave passages. Marry, th' athversary was have possession of the pridge; but he is enforced to retire, and the Duke of Exeter is master of the pridge. I can tell your Majesty, the Duke is a prave man.   101

K. Hen. What men have you lost, Fluellen?

Flu. The perdition of th' athversary hath been very great, reasonable great. Marry, for my part, I think the Duke hath lost never a man, but one   105 that is like to be executed for robbing a church, one Bardolph, if your Majesty know the man. His face is all bubukles, and whelks, and knobs, and flames o' fire; and his lips blows at his nose, and it is like a

coal of fire, sometimes plue and sometimes red; but his nose is executed, and his fire's out.   112

K. Hen. We would have all such offenders so cut off; and we give express charge, that in our marches through the country, there be nothing   115 compell'd from the villages, nothing taken but paid for, none of the French upbraided or abused in disdainful language; for when lenity and cruelty play for a kingdom, the gentler gamester is the soonest winner.   120

Tucket. Enter MONTJOY.

Mont. You know me by my habit.

K. Hen. Well then I know thee. What shall I know of thee?

Mont. My master's mind.

K. Hen. Unfold it.   124

Mont. Thus says my King: Say thou to Harry of England: Though we seem'd dead, we did but sleep; advantage is a better soldier than rashness. Tell him we could have rebuk'd him at Harfleur, but that we thought not good to bruise an injury till it were full ripe. Now we speak upon our cue,   130 and our voice is imperial. England shall repent his folly, see his weakness, and admire our sufferance. Bid him therefore consider of his ransom; which must proportion the losses we have borne, the subjects we have lost, the disgrace we have   135 digested; which in weight to re-answer, his pettiness would bow under. For our losses, his exchequer is too poor; for th' effusion of our blood, the muster of his kingdom too faint a number; and for our disgrace, his own person, kneeling at our feet, but   140 a weak and worthless satisfaction. To this add defiance; and tell him, for conclusion, he hath betrayed his followers, whose condemnation is pronounc'd. So far my King and master; so much my office.   145

K. Hen. What is thy name? I know thy quality.

Mont. Montjoy.

K. Hen. Thou dost thy office fairly. Turn thee back

And tell thy King I do not seek him now,

But could be willing to march on to Calais   150

Without impeachment; for, to say the sooth,

Though 'tis no wisdom to confess so much

Unto an enemy of craft and vantage,

My people are with sickness much enfeebled,

My numbers lessen'd, and those few I have   155

Almost no better than so many French;

Who when they were in health, I tell thee, herald,

I thought upon one pair of English legs

Did march three Frenchmen. Yet, forgive me,
        God,

---

70. **gull:** simpleton.   76. **sconce:** part of a fortification.   108. **bubukles:** carbuncles.   **whelks:** pimples.   119. **game-ster:** player.   S.D. *Tucket:* trumpet call.   MONTJOY: title of the chief herald of France.   121. **habit:** herald's costume.   129. **injury:** boil.   136. **digested:** put up with.   146. **quality:** profession.   151. **impeachment:** hindrance.

That I do brag thus! This your air of France 160
Hath blown that vice in me. I must repent.
Go therefore, tell thy master here I am;
My ransom is this frail and worthless trunk,
My army but a weak and sickly guard;
Yet, God before, tell him we will come on, 165
Though France himself and such another neighbour
Stand in our way. There's for thy labour, Montjoy.
Go, bid thy master well advise himself.
If we may pass, we will; if we be hind'red, 169
We shall your tawny ground with your red blood
Discolour; and so, Montjoy, fare you well.
The sum of all our answer is but this:
We would not seek a battle, as we are;
Nor, as we are, we say we will not shun it.
So tell your master. 175

Mont. I shall deliver so. Thanks to your Highness. [*Exit.*]

Glou. I hope they will not come upon us now.

K. Hen. We are in God's hands, brother, not in
 theirs.
March to the bridge; it now draws toward night.
Beyond the river we'll encamp ourselves, 180
And on to-morrow bid them march away.
           [*Exeunt.*

[SCENE VII. *The French camp, near Agincourt.*]

Enter the CONSTABLE OF FRANCE, *the* LORD
RAMBURES, ORLEANS, DAUPHIN, *with others.*

Con. Tut! I have the best armour of the world.
Would it were day!

Orl. You have an excellent armour; but let my
horse have his due.

Con. It is the best horse of Europe. 5

Orl. Will it never be morning?

Dau. My Lord of Orleans, and my Lord High
Constable, you talk of horse and armour?

Orl. You are as well provided of both as any
prince in the world. 10

Dau. What a long night is this! I will not change
my horse with any that treads but on four [pas-
terns]. Ça, ha! he bounds from the earth, as if his
entrails were hairs; *le cheval volant*, the Pegasus,
[*avec*] *les narines de feu!* When I bestride him, I 15
soar, I am a hawk; he trots the air; the earth sings
when he touches it; the basest horn of his hoof is
more musical than the pipe of Hermes.

Orl. He's of the colour of the nutmeg. 20

Dau. And of the heat of the ginger. It is a beast
for Perseus. He is pure air and fire; and the dull
elements of earth and water never appear in him,

but only in patient stillness while his rider mounts
him. He is indeed a horse, and all other jades you
may call beasts. 26

Con. Indeed, my lord, it is a most absolute and
excellent horse.

Dau. It is the prince of palfreys; his neigh is like
the bidding of a monarch, and his countenance
enforces homage. 31

Orl. No more, cousin.

Dau. Nay, the man hath no wit that cannot,
from the rising of the lark to the lodging of the
lamb, vary deserved praise on my palfrey. It is 35
a theme as fluent as the sea; turn the sands into eloquent tongues, and my horse is argument for them
all. 'Tis a subject for a sovereign to reason on, and
for a sovereign's sovereign to ride on; and for the
world, familiar to us and unknown, to lay apart 40
their particular functions and wonder at him. I
once writ a sonnet in his praise and began thus:
"Wonder of nature," —

Orl. I have heard a sonnet begin so to one's
mistress. 45

Dau. Then did they imitate that which I compos'd to my courser, for my horse is my mistress.

Orl. Your mistress bears well.

Dau. Me well; which is the prescript praise and
perfection of a good and particular mistress. 50

Con. Nay, for methought yesterday your mistress shrewdly shook your back.

Dau. So perhaps did yours.

Con. Mine was not bridled. 54

Dau. O then belike she was old and gentle; and
you rode, like a kern of Ireland, your French hose
off, and in your strait strossers.

Con. You have good judgement in horsemanship.

Dau. Be warn'd by me, then; they that ride 60
so and ride not warily, fall into foul bogs. I had
rather have my horse to my mistress.

Con. I had as lief have my mistress a jade.

Dau. I tell thee, Constable, my mistress wears
his own hair. 65

Con. I could make as true a boast as that, if I had
a sow to my mistress.

Dau. "*Le chien est retourné à son propre vomisse-
ment, et la truie lavée au bourbier.*" Thou mak'st
use of anything. 70

Con. Yet do I not use my horse for my mistress,
or any such proverb so little kin to the purpose.

Ram. My Lord Constable, the armour that I saw
in your tent to-night, are those stars or suns upon
it? 75

Con. Stars, my lord.

161. **blown**: fanned.
Sc. vii, 13. [pasterns] F₂. *postures* F₁. 14. **hairs**: like the stuffing of a tennis ball. **Pegasus**: the winged horse ridden by Perseus (l. 22). 15. [*avec*] (Nicholson conj.) *chez* F. 34. **lodging**: lying down. 49. **prescript**: prescribed, proper. 50. **particular**: belonging to me alone. 56. **kern**: soldier. **French hose**: wide breeches. 57. **strait strossers**: tight trousers. Theobald says the Irish kerns, like the Scotch Highlanders, wore no breeches. 68–69. "*Le chien*, etc." See II *Peter*, ii.22.

Dau. Some of them will fall to-morrow, I hope.

Con. And yet my sky shall not want.

Dau. That may be, for you bear a many super-fluously, and 'twere more honour some were away.   81

Con. Even as your horse bears your praises; who would trot as well, were some of your brags dis-mounted.

Dau. Would I were able to load him with his desert! Will it never be day? I will trot to-morrow a mile, and my way shall be paved with English faces.   88

Con. I will not say so, for fear I should be fac'd out of my way. But I would it were morning; for I would fain be about the ears of the English.   92

Ram. Who will go to hazard with me for twenty prisoners?

Con. You must first go yourself to hazard, ere you have them.   96

Dau. 'Tis midnight; I'll go arm myself. [*Exit.*

Orl. The Dauphin longs for morning.

Ram. He longs to eat the English.

Con. I think he will eat all he kills.   100

Orl. By the white hand of my lady, he's a gallant prince.

Con. Swear by her foot that she may tread out the oath.

Orl. He is simply the most active gentleman of France.   106

Con. Doing is activity; and he will still be doing.

Orl. He never did harm, that I heard of.

Con. Nor will do none to-morrow. He will keep that good name still.   111

Orl. I know him to be valiant.

Con. I was told that by one that knows him bet-ter than you.

Orl. What's he?   115

Con. Marry, he told me so himself; and he said he car'd not who knew it.

Orl. He needs not; it is no hidden virtue in him.   119

Con. By my faith, sir, but it is; never anybody saw it but his lackey. 'Tis a hooded valour; and when it appears, it will bate.

Orl. "Ill will never said well."

Con. I will cap that proverb with "There is flattery in friendship."   125

Orl. And I will take up that with "Give the devil his due."

Con. Well plac'd. There stands your friend for the devil; have at the very eye of that proverb with "A pox of the devil."   130

Orl. You are the better at proverbs, by how

much "A fool's bolt is soon shot."

Con. You have shot over.

Orl. 'Tis not the first time you were overshot.

Enter a MESSENGER.

Mess. My Lord High Constable, the English lie within fifteen hundred paces of your tents.   136

Con. Who hath measur'd the ground?

Mess. The Lord Grandpré.

Con. A valiant and most expert gentleman. Would it were day! Alas, poor Harry of England, he longs not for the dawning as we do.   141

Orl. What a wretched and peevish fellow is this King of England, to mope with his fat-brain'd fol-lowers so far out of his knowledge!

Con. If the English had any apprehension, they would run away.   146

Orl. That they lack; for if their heads had any intellectual armour, they could never wear such heavy head-pieces.

Ram. That island of England breeds very valiant creatures. Their mastiffs are of unmatchable courage.   152

Orl. Foolish curs, that run winking into the mouth of a Russian bear and have their heads crush'd like rotten apples! You may as well say, that's a valiant flea that dare eat his breakfast on the lip of a lion.   157

Con. Just, just; and the men do sympathize with the mastiffs in robustious and rough coming on, leaving their wits with their wives; and then, give them great meals of beef and iron and steel, they will eat like wolves and fight like devils.   162

Orl. Ay, but these English are shrewdly out of beef.

Con. Then shall we find to-morrow they have only stomachs to eat and none to fight. Now is the time to arm. Come, shall we about it?   167

Orl. It is now two o'clock; but, let me see, by ten We shall have each a hundred Englishmen.

[*Exeunt.*

ACT [IV]

[PROLOGUE]

[*Enter* CHORUS.]

Chor. Now entertain conjecture of a time
When creeping murmur and the poring dark
Fills the wide vessel of the universe.
From camp to camp through the foul womb of night
The hum of either army stilly sounds,   5
That the fix'd sentinels almost receive

121–122. **hooded ... bate.** A hawk was hooded till the game was in sight. **bate:** (1) to flap the wings, (2) to be downcast. 142. **peevish:** silly. 143. **mope:** wander in a daze. 158. **sympathize with:** resemble.

Act IV, Prol., 1. conjecture: supposition. 2. **poring dark:** the dark in which people strain to see.

The secret whispers of each other's watch;
Fire answers fire, and through their paly flames
Each battle sees the other's umber'd face;
Steed threatens steed, in high and boastful neighs   10
Piercing the night's dull ear; and from the tents
The armourers, accomplishing the knights,
With busy hammers closing rivets up,
Give dreadful note of preparation.
The country cocks do crow, the clocks do toll,   15
And the third hour of drowsy morning [name].
Proud of their numbers and secure in soul,
The confident and over-lusty French
Do the low-rated English play at dice;
And chide the cripple tardy-gaited Night   20
Who, like a foul and ugly witch, doth limp
So tediously away.   The poor condemned English,
Like sacrifices, by their watchful fires
Sit patiently and inly ruminate
The morning's danger; and their gesture sad,   25
Investing lank-lean cheeks and war-worn coats,
Presented them unto the gazing moon
So many horrid ghosts.   O now, who will behold
The royal captain of this ruin'd band
Walking from watch to watch, from tent to tent,   30
Let him cry, "Praise and glory on his head!"
For forth he goes and visits all his host,
Bids them good morrow with a modest smile,
And calls them brothers, friends, and countrymen.
Upon his royal face there is no note   35
How dread an army hath enrounded him;
Nor doth he dedicate one jot of colour
Unto the weary and all-watched night,
But freshly looks, and over-bears attaint
With cheerful semblance and sweet majesty;   40
That every wretch, pining and pale before,
Beholding him, plucks comfort from his looks.
A largess universal like the sun
His liberal eye doth give to every one,
Thawing cold fear, that mean and gentle all   45
Behold, as may unworthiness define,
A little touch of Harry in the night.
And so our scene must to the battle fly,
Where — O for pity! — we shall much disgrace
With four or five most vile and ragged foils,   50
Right ill-dispos'd in brawl ridiculous,
The name of Agincourt.   Yet sit and see,
Minding true things by what their mockeries be.
                                            [Exit.

[SCENE I. *The English camp at Agincourt.*]

Enter KING HENRY, BEDFORD, *and* GLOUCESTER.

   K. Hen. Gloucester, 'tis true that we are in great
danger;

The greater therefore should our courage be.
Good morrow, brother Bedford.   God Almighty!
There is some soul of goodness in things evil,
Would men observingly distil it out;   5
For our bad neighbour makes us early stirrers,
Which is both healthful and good husbandry.
Besides, they are our outward consciences
And preachers to us all, admonishing
That we should dress us fairly for our end.   10
Thus may we gather honey from the weed,
And make a moral of the devil himself.

Enter ERPINGHAM.

Good morrow, old Sir Thomas Erpingham.
A good soft pillow for that good white head
Were better than a churlish turf of France.   15
   Erp. Not so, my liege; this lodging likes me
      better,
Since I may say, "Now lie I like a king."
   K. Hen. 'Tis good for men to love their present
      pains
Upon example; so the spirit is eas'd;
And when the mind is quick'ned, out of doubt,   20
The organs, though defunct and dead before,
Break up their drowsy grave and newly move,
With casted slough and fresh legerity.
Lend me thy cloak, Sir Thomas.   Brothers both,
Commend me to the princes in our camp;   25
Do my good morrow to them, and anon
Desire them all to my pavilion.
   Glou. We shall, my liege.
   Erp. Shall I attend your Grace?
   K. Hen.   No, my good knight;
Go with my brothers to my lords of England.   30
I and my bosom must debate a while,
And then I would no other company.
   Erp. The Lord in heaven bless thee, noble Harry!
                        [*Exeunt* [*all but King*].
   K. Hen. God-a-mercy, old heart! thou speak'st
      cheerfully.

Enter PISTOL.

   Pist. Qui va là?   35
   K. Hen. A friend.
   Pist. Discuss unto me; art thou officer?
Or art thou base, common, and popular?
   K. Hen. I am a gentleman of a company.
   Pist. Trail'st thou the puissant pike?   40
   K. Hen. Even so.   What are you?
   Pist. As good a gentleman as the Emperor.
   K. Hen. Then you are a better than the King.
   Pist. The King's a bawcock, and a heart of gold,
A lad of life, an imp of fame;   45
Of parents good, of fist most valiant.

9. **umber'd:** dusky.   12. **accomplishing:** equipping.   16. **[name]** (Tyrwhitt).   *nam'd* F.   19. **play:** play for.   25. **gesture:** bearing.   39. **over-bears attaint:** resists stain.   46. **as ... define:** as well as their limitations permit.   53. **Minding:** conceiving. Sc. i, 19. **Upon example:** by comparison.   23. **legerity:** nimbleness.   37. **Discuss:** tell.   38. **popular:** of the people.

I kiss his dirty shoe, and from heart-string
I love the lovely bully.   What is thy name?
   K. Hen. Harry le Roy.
   Pist. Le Roy! a Cornish name.   Art thou of
     Cornish crew?   50
   K. Hen. No, I am a Welshman.
   Pist. Know'st thou Fluellen?
   K. Hen. Yes.
   Pist. Tell him, I'll knock his leek about his pate
Upon Saint Davy's day.   55
   K. Hen. Do not you wear your dagger in your
cap that day, lest he knock that about yours.
   Pist. Art thou his friend?
   K. Hen. And his kinsman too.
   Pist. The *figo* for thee, then!   60
   K. Hen. I thank you.   God be with you!
   Pist. My name is Pistol call'd.   [*Exit.*
   K. Hen. It sorts well with your fierceness.

      Enter FLUELLEN *and* GOWER.

   Gow. Captain Fluellen!   64
   Flu. So! in the name of Jesu Christ, speak fewer.
It is the greatest admiration in the universal world,
when the true and aunchient prerogatifes and laws
of the wars is not kept.   If you would take the
pains but to examine the wars of Pompey the Great,
you shall find, I warrant you, that there is no   70
tiddle taddle nor pibble babble in Pompey's camp.
I warrant you, you shall find the ceremonies of the
wars, and the cares of it, and the forms of it, and
the sobriety of it, and the modesty of it, to be
otherwise.   75
   Gow. Why, the enemy is loud; you hear him all
night.
   Flu. If the enemy is an ass and a fool and a prating coxcomb, is it meet, think you, that we should
also, look you, be an ass and a fool and a prating
coxcomb?   In your own conscience, now?   81
   Gow. I will speak lower.
   Flu. I pray you and beseech you that you will.
           [*Exeunt [Gower and Fluellen].*
   K. Hen. Though it appear a little out of fash-
ion,   85
There is much care and valour in this Welshman.

  Enter three soldiers, JOHN BATES, ALEXANDER
    COURT, *and* MICHAEL WILLIAMS.

   Court. Brother John Bates, is not that the morning which breaks yonder?
   Bates. I think it be; but we have no great cause
to desire the approach of day.   90
   Will. We see yonder the beginning of the day,
but I think we shall never see the end of it.   Who
goes there?

   K. Hen. A friend.
   Will. Under what captain serve you?   95
   K. Hen. Under Sir [Thomas] Erpingham.
   Will. A good old commander and a most kind
gentleman.   I pray you, what thinks he of our
estate?
   K. Hen. Even as men wreck'd upon a sand,
that look to be wash'd off the next tide.   101
   Bates. He hath not told his thought to the King?
   K. Hen. No; nor it is not meet he should.   For,
though I speak it to you, I think the King is but a 105
man, as I am.   The violet smells to him as it does
to me; the element shows to him as it doth to me;
all his senses have but human conditions.   His
ceremonies laid by, in his nakedness he appears but
a man; and though his affections are higher   110
mounted than ours, yet, when they stoop, they
stoop with the like wing.   Therefore, when he sees
reason of fears as we do, his fears, out of doubt, be
of the same relish as ours are; yet, in reason, no
man should possess him with any appearance of
fear, lest he, by showing it, should dishearten his
army.   117
   Bates. He may show what outward courage he
will; but I believe, as cold a night as 'tis, he could
wish himself in Thames up to the neck; and so I
would he were, and I by him, at all adventures, so
we were quit here.   122
   K. Hen. By my troth, I will speak my conscience
of the King: I think he would not wish himself
anywhere but where he is.
   Bates. Then I would he were here alone; so
should he be sure to be ransomed, and a many poor
men's lives saved.   128
   K. Hen. I dare say you love him not so ill to
wish him here alone, howsoever you speak this to
feel other men's minds.   Methinks I could not die
anywhere so contented as in the King's company,
his cause being just and his quarrel honourable.   134
   Will. That's more than we know.
   Bates. Ay, or more than we should seek after;
for we know enough if we know we are the King's
subjects.   If his cause be wrong, our obedience to
the King wipes the crime of it out of us.   139
   Will. But if the cause be not good, the King himself hath a heavy reckoning to make, when all those
legs and arms and heads, chopp'd off in a battle,
shall join together at the latter day and cry all,
"We died at such a place"; some swearing, some
crying for a surgeon, some upon their wives   145
left poor behind them, some upon the debts they
owe, some upon their children rawly left.   I am
afeard there are few die well that die in a battle;
for how can they charitably dispose of anything,

┌ 54–55. **leek … day.** The Welsh wore leeks in their caps to commemorate a victory over the Saxons, as ordered by their patron
saint, David.   96. **[Thomas]** (Pope).   *John* F.   107. **element:** sky.   109. **ceremonies:** ceremonial garments.   114. **relish:**
kind, quality.   123. **conscience:** genuine opinion.   147. **rawly:** unprovided for.

when blood is their argument?   Now, if these men
do not die well, it will be a black matter for the
King that led them to it; who to disobey were
against all proportion of subjection.   153

  K. Hen. So, if a son that is by his father sent
about merchandise do sinfully miscarry upon the
sea, the imputation of his wickedness, by your rule,
should be imposed upon his father that sent him;
or if a servant, under his master's command trans-
porting a sum of money, be assailed by robbers and
die in many irreconcil'd iniquities, you may   160
call the business of the master the author of the
servant's damnation. But this is not so. The King
is not bound to answer the particular endings of
his soldiers, the father of his son, nor the master of
his servant; for they purpose not their death   165
when they purpose their services.   Besides, there
is no king, be his cause never so spotless, if it come
to the arbitrement of swords, can try it out with all
unspotted soldiers.   Some peradventure have on
them the guilt of premeditated and contrived   170
murder; some, of beguiling virgins with the broken
seals of perjury; some, making the wars their bulwark, that have before gored the gentle bosom of
Peace with pillage and robbery.   Now, if these men
have defeated the law and outrun native pun-   175
ishment, though they can outstrip men, they have
no wings to fly from God.   War is his beadle, war is
his vengeance; so that here men are punish'd for
before-breach of the King's laws in now the King's
quarrel.   Where they feared the death, they   180
have borne life away; and where they would be
safe, they perish.   Then if they die unprovided,
no more is the King guilty of their damnation than
he was before guilty of those impieties for the which
they are now visited.   Every subject's duty is   185
the King's; but every subject's soul is his own.
Therefore should every soldier in the wars do as
every sick man in his bed, wash every mote out
of his conscience; and dying so, death is to him
advantage; or not dying, the time was blessedly   190
lost wherein such preparation was gained; and in
him that escapes, it were not sin to think that,
making God so free an offer, He let him outlive
that day to see His greatness and to teach others
how they should prepare.   196

  Will. 'Tis certain, every man that dies ill, the
ill upon his own head, the King is not to answer it.

  Bates. I do not desire he should answer for me;
and yet I determine to fight lustily for him.   201

  K. Hen. I myself heard the King say he would
not be ransom'd.

  Will. Ay, he said so, to make us fight cheerfully;

but when our throats are cut, he may be ransom'd,
and we ne'er the wiser.

  K. Hen. If I live to see it, I will never trust his
word after.   208

  Will. You pay him then.   That's a perilous
shot out of an elder-gun, that a poor and a private
displeasure can do against a monarch!   You may
as well go about to turn the sun to ice with fanning
in his face with a peacock's feather.   You'll
never trust his word after!   Come, 'tis a foolish
saying.   215

  K. Hen. Your reproof is something too round.
I should be angry with you, if the time were convenient.

  Will. Let it be a quarrel between us, if you live.

  K. Hen. I embrace it.   221

  Will. How shall I know thee again?

  K. Hen. Give me any gage of thine, and I will
wear it in my bonnet; then, if ever thou dar'st
acknowledge it, I will make it my quarrel.   225

  Will. Here's my glove; give me another of thine.

  K. Hen. There.

  Wil. This will I also wear in my cap.   If ever
thou come to me and say, after to-morrow, "This
is my glove," by this hand, I will take thee a box
on the ear.   232

  K. Hen. If ever I live to see it, I will challenge it.

  Will. Thou dar'st as well be hang'd.

  K. Hen. Well, I will do it, though I take thee in
the King's company.   237

  Will. Keep thy word; fare thee well.

  Bates. Be friends, you English fools, be friends.
We have French quarrels enow, if you could tell
how to reckon.   241

  K. Hen. Indeed, the French may lay twenty
French crowns to one they will beat us, for they
bear them on their shoulders; but it is no English
treason to cut French crowns, and to-morrow the
King himself will be a clipper. [*Exeunt soldiers.* 246
Upon the King! let us our lives, our souls,
Our debts, our careful wives,
Our children, and our sins lay on the King!
We must bear all.   O hard condition,   250
Twin-born with greatness, subject to the breath
Of every fool whose sense no more can feel
But his own wringing!   What infinite heart's-ease
Must kings neglect, that private men enjoy!
And what have kings, that privates have not too,
Save ceremony, save general ceremony?   256
And what art thou, thou idol Ceremony?
What kind of god art thou, that suffer'st more
Of mortal griefs than do thy worshippers?
What are thy rents?   What are thy comings in?

---

153. **proportion of subjection:** proper relation of subject to sovereign.   155. **sinfully miscarry:** die in his sins.   175. **native:** at home.   197. **ill:** in sin.   210. **elder-gun:** pop-gun, made by removing the pith from a piece of elder.   216. **round:**
harsh.   223. **gage:** pledge.   243, 245. **crowns:** (1) heads, (2) coins.   246. **clipper:** a pun on *clip* (1) to cut off, (2) to trim the
edges of coins for the gold or silver.   248. **careful:** burdened by care.   253. **wringing:** writhing.

O Ceremony, show me but thy worth!   261
What is thy soul of adoration?
Art thou aught else but place, degree, and form,
Creating awe and fear in other men?
Wherein thou art less happy being fear'd   265
Than they in fearing.
What drink'st thou oft, instead of homage sweet,
But poison'd flattery? O, be sick, great greatness,
And bid thy Ceremony give thee cure!
Think'st thou the fiery fever will go out   270
With titles blown from adulation?
Will it give place to flexure and low bending?
Canst thou, when thou command'st the beggar's
          knee,
Command the health of it? No, thou proud dream,
That play'st so subtly with a king's repose;   275
I am a king that find thee, and I know
'Tis not the balm, the sceptre, and the ball,
The sword, the mace, the crown imperial,
The intertissued robe of gold and pearl,
The farced title running 'fore the King,   280
The throne he sits on, nor the tide of pomp
That beats upon the high shore of this world, —
No, not all these, thrice-gorgeous Ceremony,
Not all these, laid in bed majestical,
Can sleep so soundly as the wretched slave,   285
Who with a body fill'd and vacant mind
Gets him to rest, cramm'd with distressful bread,
Never sees horrid night, the child of hell,
But like a lackey from the rise to set
Sweats in the eye of Phœbus, and all night   290
Sleeps in Elysium; next day after dawn,
Doth rise and help Hyperion to his horse,
And follows so the ever-running year
With profitable labour to his grave:
And, but for ceremony, such a wretch,   295
Winding up days with toil and nights with sleep,
Had the fore-hand and vantage of a king.
The slave, a member of the country's peace,
Enjoys it, but in gross brain little wots
What watch the King keeps to maintain the peace,
Whose hours the peasant best advantages.   301

Enter ERPINGHAM.

Erp. My lord, your nobles, jealous of your
          absence,
Seek through your camp to find you.
K. Hen.   Good old knight,
Collect them all together at my tent.
I'll be before thee.
Erp.   I shall do't, my lord.   305
                                        [*Exit.*

K. Hen. O God of battles! steel my soldiers'
          hearts.
Possess them not with fear.   Take from them now
The sense of reckoning, [if] th' opposed numbers
Pluck their hearts from them.   Not to-day, O
          Lord,
O, not to-day, think not upon the fault   310
My father made in compassing the crown!
I Richard's body have interred new,
And on it have bestow'd more contrite tears,
Than from it issu'd forced drops of blood.
Five hundred poor I have in yearly pay,   315
Who twice a day their wither'd hands hold up
Toward heaven, to pardon blood; and I have built
Two chantries, where the sad and solemn priests
Sing still for Richard's soul.   More will I do;
Though all that I can do is nothing worth,   320
Since that my penitence comes after all,
Imploring pardon.

Enter GLOUCESTER.

Glou. My liege!
K. Hen. My brother Gloucester's voice?   Ay;
I know thy errand, I will go with thee.   325
The day, my friends, and all things stay for me.
                                        [*Exeunt.*

[SCENE II. *The French camp.*]

Enter the DAUPHIN, ORLEANS, RAMBURES,
          and others.

Orl. The sun doth gild our armour; up, my lords!
Dau.   Montez à cheval!   My horse, varlet!
          lackey! ha!
Orl. O brave spirit!
Dau. Via! les eaux et la terre.
Orl. Rien puis? L'air et le feu.   5
Dau. Ciel, cousin Orleans.

Enter CONSTABLE.

Now, my Lord Constable!
Con. Hark, how our steeds for present service
          neigh!
Dau. Mount them, and make incision in their
          hides,
That their hot blood may spin in English eyes,   10
And dout them with superfluous courage, ha!
Ram. What, will you have them weep our horses'
          blood?
How shall we, then, behold their natural tears?

---

262. **thy ... adoration:** the secret of the adoration paid thee.   271. **from adulation:** by flatterers.   272. **flexure:** bowing.
277. **balm:** coronation oil.   **ball:** symbol of sovereignty.   280. **farced:** stuffed, pompous.   287. **distressful:** hard earned.
298. **member:** sharer.   301. **best advantages:** employs most profitably, or profits (the peasant).   302. **jealous of:** nervous
about.   308. **[if]** (Tyrwhitt).   *of* F.   *lest* Theobald.   311. **compassing:** getting possession of.
     Sc. ii, 11. **dout:** put out.

Enter MESSENGER.

Mess. The English are embattl'd, you French
    peers.

Con. To horse, you gallant princes! straight to
    horse!   15
Do but behold yond poor and starved band,
And your fair show shall suck away their souls,
Leaving them but the shales and husks of men.
There is not work enough for all our hands;
Scarce blood enough in all their sickly veins   20
To give each naked curtle-axe a stain,
That our French gallants shall to-day draw out
And sheathe for lack of sport. Let us but blow on
    them,
The vapour of our valour will o'erturn them.
'Tis positive 'gainst all exceptions, lords,   25
That our superfluous lackeys and our peasants,
Who in unnecessary action swarm
About our squares of battle, were enow
To purge this field of such a hilding foe,
Though we upon this mountain's basis by   30
Took stand for idle speculation,
But that our honours must not. What's to say?
A very little little let us do,
And all is done. Then let the trumpets sound
The tucket sonance and the note to mount;   35
For our approach shall so much dare the field
That England shall crouch down in fear and yield.

Enter GRANDPRÉ.

Grand. Why do you stay so long, my lords of
    France?
Yond island carrions, desperate of their bones,
Ill-favouredly become the morning field.   40
Their ragged curtains poorly are let loose,
And our air shakes them passing scornfully.
Big Mars seems bankrupt in their beggar'd host
And faintly through a rusty beaver peeps;
The horsemen sit like fixed candlesticks   45
With torch-staves in their hand; and their poor
    jades
Lob down their heads, dropping the hides and hips,
The gum down-roping from their pale-dead eyes,
And in their pale dull mouths the gimmal'd bit
Lies foul with chew'd grass, still and motionless;   50
And their executors, the knavish crows,
Fly o'er them, all impatient for their hour.
Description cannot suit itself in words
To demonstrate the life of such a battle,
In life so lifeless as it shows itself.   55
Con. They have said their prayers, and they stay
    for death.

Dau. Shall we go send them dinners and fresh
    suits
And give their fasting horses provender,
And after fight with them?
Con. I stay but for my guard; on to the field! 60
I will the banner from a trumpet take,
And use it for my haste. Come, come, away!
The sun is high, and we outwear the day. [*Exeunt.*

[SCENE III. *The English camp.*]

Enter GLOUCESTER, BEDFORD, EXETER, ERPING-
HAM, *with all his host:* SALISBURY *and* WEST-
MORELAND.

Glou. Where is the King?
Bed. The King himself is rode to view their battle.
West. Of fighting men they have full threescore
    thousand.
Exe. There's five to one; besides, they all are
    fresh.
Sal. God's arm strike with us! 'tis a fearful odds.
God be wi' you, princes all; I'll to my charge. 6
If we no more meet till we meet in heaven,
Then, joyfully, my noble Lord of Bedford,
My dear Lord Gloucester, and my good Lord
    Exeter,
And my kind kinsman, warriors all, adieu!   10
Bed. Farewell, good Salisbury, and good luck go
    with thee!
Exe. Farewell, kind lord; fight valiantly to-day!
And yet I do thee wrong to mind thee of it,
For thou art fram'd of the firm truth of valour.
                  [*Exit Salisbury.*]
Bed. He is as full of valour as of kindness,   15
Princely in both.

Enter the KING.

West.   O that we now had here
But one ten thousand of those men in England
That do no work to-day!
K. Hen.   What's he that wishes so?
My cousin Westmoreland? No, my fair cousin.
If we are mark'd to die, we are enow   20
To do our country loss; and if to live,
The fewer men, the greater share of honour.
God's will! I pray thee, wish not one man more.
By Jove, I am not covetous for gold,
Nor care I who doth feed upon my cost;   25
It yearns me not if men my garments wear;
Such outward things dwell not in my desires;
But if it be a sin to covet honour
I am the most offending soul alive.   29
No, 'faith, my coz, wish not a man from England.

---

18. **shales:** shells. 21. **curtle-axe:** cutlass. 29. **hilding:** worthless. 31. **speculation:** on-looking. 35. **tucket sonance:** trumpet notes. 36. **dare the field:** daze the enemy (a figure from lark catching). 41. **curtains:** flags. 44. **beaver:** face part of a helmet. 47. **Lob:** hang. 49. **gimmal'd:** jointed.
Sc. iii, 13, 14. **And . . . valour.** In F these lines follow l. 11. 26. **yearns:** grieves.

God's peace! I would not lose so great an honour
As one man more, methinks, would share from me
For the best hope I have. O, do not wish one more!
Rather proclaim it, Westmoreland, through my
　　host,
That he which hath no stomach to this fight,　35
Let him depart. His passport shall be made,
And crowns for convoy put into his purse.
We would not die in that man's company
That fears his fellowship to die with us.
This day is call'd the feast of Crispian.　40
He that outlives this day and comes safe home
Will stand a tip-toe when this day is named,
And rouse him at the name of Crispian.
He that shall [live] this day, and [see] old age,
Will yearly on the vigil feast his neighbours,　45
And say, "To-morrow is Saint Crispian."
Then will he strip his sleeve and show his scars,
[And say, "These wounds I had on Crispin's day."]
Old men forget; yet all shall be forgot,
But he'll remember with advantages　50
What feats he did that day. Then shall our names,
Familiar in his mouth as household words,
Harry the King, Bedford, and Exeter,
Warwick and Talbot, Salisbury and Gloucester,
Be in their flowing cups freshly rememb'red.　55
This story shall the good man teach his son;
And Crispin Crispian shall ne'er go by,
From this day to the ending of the world,
But we in it shall be remembered,
We few, we happy few, we band of brothers.　60
For he to-day that sheds his blood with me
Shall be my brother; be he ne'er so vile,
This day shall gentle his condition;
And gentlemen in England now a-bed　64
Shall think themselves accurs'd they were not here,
And hold their manhoods cheap whiles any speaks
That fought with us upon Saint Crispin's day.

Re-enter SALISBURY.

Sal. My sovereign lord, bestow yourself with
　　speed.
The French are bravely in their battles set,
And will with all expedience charge on us.　70
K. Hen. All things are ready, if our minds be so.
West. Perish the man whose mind is backward
　　now!
K. Hen. Thou dost not wish more help from
　　England, coz?
West. God's will! my liege, would you and I alone,
Without more help, could fight this royal battle!　75
K. Hen. Why, now thou hast unwish'd five
　　thousand men,

Which likes me better than to wish us one.
You know your places. God be with you all!

Tucket. Enter MONTJOY.

Mont. Once more I come to know of thee, King
　　Harry,
If for thy ransom thou wilt now compound,　80
Before thy most assured overthrow;
For certainly thou art so near the gulf,
Thou needs must be englutted. Besides, in mercy,
The Constable desires thee thou wilt mind
Thy followers of repentance; that their souls　85
May make a peaceful and a sweet retire
From off these fields, where, wretches, their poor
　　bodies
Must lie and fester.
K. Hen.　　　　Who hath sent thee now?
Mont. The Constable of France.
K. Hen. I pray thee, bear my former answer
　　back:　90
Bid them achieve me and then sell my bones.
Good God! why should they mock poor fellows thus?
The man that once did sell the lion's skin
While the beast liv'd, was kill'd with hunting him.
A many of our bodies shall no doubt　95
Find native graves, upon the which, I trust,
Shall witness live in brass of this day's work;
And those that leave their valiant bones in France,
Dying like men, though buried in your dunghills,
They shall be fam'd; for there the sun shall greet
　　them,　100
And draw their honours reeking up to heaven;
Leaving their earthly parts to choke your clime,
The smell whereof shall breed a plague in France.
Mark then abounding valour in our English,
That being dead, like to the bullet's grazing,　105
Break out into a second course of mischief,
Killing in relapse of mortality.
Let me speak proudly: tell the Constable
We are but warriors for the working-day.
Our gayness and our gilt are all besmirch'd　110
With rainy marching in the painful field;
There's not a piece of feather in our host —
Good argument, I hope, we will not fly —
And time hath worn us into slovenry;
But, by the mass, our hearts are in the trim;　115
And my poor soldiers tell me, yet ere night
They'll be in fresher robes, or they will pluck
The gay new coats o'er the French soldiers' heads
And turn them out of service. If they do this —
As, if God please, they shall, — my ransom then　120
Will soon be levied. Herald, save thou thy labour.
Come thou no more for ransom, gentle herald.

40, 48. Crispinus and Crispianus were the patron saints of shoemakers, celebrated Oct. 25. 44. [live] ... [see] (Pope). *see ... live* F. 48. [And ... day] Q. Om. F. 62. vile: low born. 63. gentle his condition: make him a gentleman. 68. bestow yourself: take your position. 70. expedience: speed. 80. compound: make terms. 82. gulf: whirlpool. 83. englutted: swallowed. 91. achieve: capture, or kill. 105. grazing: glancing off. 107. relapse of mortality: mortal rebound.

They shall have none, I swear, but these my joints;
Which if they have as I will leave 'em them,
Shall yield them little, tell the Constable.   125
    Mont. I shall, King Harry. And so fare thee
    well;
Thou never shalt hear herald any more.   [*Exit.*
    K. Hen. I fear thou will once more come again
for ransom.

            Enter YORK.
    York. My lord, most humbly on my knee I beg
The leading of the vaward,   130
    K. Hen. Take it, brave York. Now, soldiers,
    march away;
And how thou pleasest, God, dispose the day!
                      [*Exeunt.*

      [SCENE IV. *The field of battle.*]

   Alarum. Excursions. Enter PISTOL, FRENCH
        SOLDIER, *and* BOY.

    Pist. Yield, cur!
    *Fr. Sol. Je pense que vous êtes le gentilhomme de
bonne qualité.*
    Pist. Qualtitie calmie custure me! Art thou a
gentleman? What is thy name? Discuss.   5
    Fr. Sol. O Seigneur Dieu!
    Pist. O, Signieur Dew should be a gentleman.
Perpend my words, O Signieur Dew, and mark:
O Signieur Dew, thou diest on point of fox,
Except, O signieur, thou do give to me   10
Egregious ransom.
    Fr. Sol. O, prenez miséricorde! ayez pitié de moi!
    Pist. Moy shall not serve; I will have forty moys,
Or I will fetch thy rim out at thy throat   15
In drops of crimson blood.
    *Fr. Sol. Est-il impossible d'échapper la force de
ton bras?*
    Pist. Brass, cur!
Thou damned and luxurious mountain goat,   20
Offer'st me brass?
    Fr. Sol. O pardonnez moi!
    Pist. Say'st thou me so? Is that a ton of moys?
Come hither, boy; ask me this slave in French
What is his name.   25
    Boy. Écoutez: comment êtes-vous appelé?
    Fr. Sol. Monsieur le Fer.
    Boy. He says his name is Master Fer.
    Pist. Master Fer! I'll fer him, and firk him, and
ferret him. Discuss the same in French unto him.
    Boy. I do not know the French for fer, and   32
ferret, and firk.
    Pist. Bid him prepare; for I will cut his throat.
    Fr. Sol. Que dit-il, monsieur?   35
    Boy. Il me commande à vous dire que vous faites

*vous prêt; car ce soldat ici est disposé tout à cette
heure de couper votre gorge.*
    Pist. Owy, cuppele gorge, permafoy,
Peasant, unless thou give me crowns, brave crowns;
Or mangled shalt thou be by this my sword.   41
    *Fr. Sol. O, je vous supplie, pour l'amour le Dieu,
me pardonner! Je suis le gentilhomme de bonne
maison; gardez ma vie, et je vous donnerai deux cents
écus.*   45
    Pist. What are his words?
    Boy. He prays you to save his life. He is a
gentleman of a good house; and for his ransom he
will give you two hundred crowns.
    Pist. Tell him my fury shall abate, and I   50
The crowns will take.
    Fr. Sol. Petit monsieur, que dit-il?
    *Boy. Encore qu'il est contre son jurement de par-
donner aucun prisonnier; néanmoins, pour les écus
que vous l'avez promis, il est content de vous donner la
liberté, le franchisement.*   56
    *Fr. Sol. Sur mes genoux je vous donne mille
remercîmens; et je m'estime heureux que je suis tombé
entre les mains d'un chevalier, je pense, le plus brave,
vaillant, et très distingué seigneur d'Angleterre.*   61
    Pist. Expound unto me, boy.
    Boy. He gives you upon his knees, a thousand
thanks; and he esteems himself happy that he hath
fallen into the hands of one (as he thinks) the most
brave, valorous, and thrice-worthy seigneur of
England.
    Pist. As I suck blood, I will some mercy show.
Follow me!   69
    Boy. Suivez-vous le grand capitaine. [*Exeunt
Pistol, and French Soldier.*] I did never know so
full a voice issue from so empty a heart; but the
saying is true, "The empty vessel makes the greatest sound." Bardolph and Nym had ten times
more valour than this roaring devil i' th' old   75
play, that every one may pare his nails with a
wooden dagger; and they are both hang'd; and so
would this be, if he durst steal anything adven-
turously. I must stay with the lackeys with the
luggage of our camp. The French might have a
good prey of us, if he knew of it; for there is none to
guard it but boys.   [*Exit.* 82

    [SCENE V. *Another part of the field.*]
  Enter CONSTABLE, ORLEANS, BOURBON,
       DAUPHIN, *and* RAMBURES.
    Con. O diable!
    Orl. O seigneur! le jour est perdu, tout est perdu!
    Dau. Mort de ma vie! all is confounded, all!
Reproach and everlasting shame

Sc. iv, 4. *Qualtitie ... me:* probably mere nonsense. 9. **fox:** sword. 14. **Moy:** Pistol takes *moi* (l. 13) for the name of a coin. Cf. l. 23 and *brass* (l. 19). 15. **rim:** diaphragm. 20. **luxurious:** lustful. 29. **firk:** beat. 30. **ferret:** worry.

Sits mocking in our plumes.   *O méchante for-*
    tune!   5
Do not run away.   [*A short alarum.*
  Con.   Why, all our ranks are broke.
  Dau. O perdurable shame! let's stab ourselves.
Be these the wretches that we play'd at dice for?
  Orl. Is this the king we sent to for his ransom?
  Bour. Shame and eternal shame, nothing but
    shame!   10
Let's die in [honour]! Once more back again!
And he that will not follow Bourbon now,
Let him go hence, and with his cap in hand
Like a base pandar hold the chamber door
Whilst [by a] slave, no gentler than my dog,   15
His fairest daughter is contaminated.
  Con. Disorder, that hath spoil'd us, friend us
    now!
Let us on heaps go offer up our lives.
  Orl. We are enow yet living in the field
To smother up the English in our throngs   20
If any order might be thought upon.
  Bour. The devil take order now! I'll to the
    throng.
Let life be short, else shame will be too long.
                              [*Exeunt.*

[SCENE VI. *Another part of the field.*]

Alarum. Enter KING HENRY *and his train,*
with prisoners.

  K. Hen. Well have we done, thrice valiant
    countrymen.
But all's not done; yet keep the French the field.
  Exe. The Duke of York commends him to your
    Majesty.
  K. Hen. Lives he, good uncle? Thrice within
    this hour
I saw him down; thrice up again, and fighting.   5
From helmet to the spur all blood he was.
  Exe. In which array, brave soldier, doth he lie,
Larding the plain; and by his bloody side,
Yoke-fellow to his honour-owing wounds,
The noble Earl of Suffolk also lies.   10
Suffolk first died; and York, all haggled over,
Comes to him where in gore he lay insteeped,
And takes him by the beard; kisses the gashes
That bloodily did yawn upon his face.
He cries aloud, "Tarry, my cousin Suffolk!   15
My soul shall thine keep company to heaven;
Tarry, sweet soul, for mine, then fly abreast,
As in this glorious and well-foughten field
We kept together in our chivalry!"
Upon these words I came and cheer'd him up.   20
He smil'd me in the face, raught me his hand,
And, with a feeble gripe, says, "Dear my lord,

Commend my service to my sovereign."
So did he turn and over Suffolk's neck
He threw his wounded arm and kiss'd his lips;   25
And so espous'd to death, with blood he seal'd
A testament of noble-ending love.
The pretty and sweet manner of it forc'd
Those waters from me which I would have stopp'd;
But I had not so much of man in me,   30
And all my mother came into mine eyes
And gave me up to tears.
  K. Hen.   I blame you not;
For, hearing this, I must perforce compound
With mistful eyes, or they will issue too.
                              [*Alarum.*
But, hark! what new alarum is this same?   35
The French have reinforc'd their scatter'd men.
Then every soldier kill his prisoners;
Give the word through.   [*Exeunt.*

[SCENE VII. *Another part of the field.*]

Enter FLUELLEN *and* GOWER.

  Flu. Kill the poys and the luggage! 'Tis expressly against the law of arms. 'Tis as arrant a
piece of knavery, mark you now, as can be offer't;
in your conscience, now, is it not?   4
  Gow. 'Tis certain there's not a boy left alive;
and the cowardly rascals that ran from the battle
ha' done this slaughter. Besides, they have
burned and carried away all that was in the King's
tent; wherefore the King, most worthily, hath
caus'd every soldier to cut his prisoner's throat.
O, 'tis a gallant king!   11
  Flu. Ay, he was porn at Monmouth, Captain
Gower. What call you the town's name where
Alexander the Pig was born!
  Gow. Alexander the Great.   15
  Flu. Why, I pray you, is not pig great? The
pig, or the great, or the mighty, or the huge, or the
magnanimous, are all one reckonings, save the
phrase is a little variations.   19
  Gow. I think Alexander the Great was born in
Macedon. His father was called Philip of Macedon, as I take it.
  Flu. I think it is in Macedon where Alexander
is porn. I tell you, captain, if you look in the
maps of the 'orld, I warrant you sall find, in the   25
comparisons between Macedon and Monmouth,
that the situations, look you, is both alike. There
is a river in Macedon; and there is also moreover a
river at Monmouth. It is call'd Wye at Monmouth; but it is out of my prains what is the name   30
of the other river; but 'tis all one, 'tis alike as
my fingers is to my fingers, and there is salmons in
both. If you mark Alexander's life well, Harry of

Monmouth's life is come after it indifferent well;
for there is figures in all things. Alexander, 35
God knows, and you know, in his rages, and his
furies, and his wraths, and his cholers, and his
moods, and his displeasures, and his indignations,
and also being a little intoxicates in his prains, did,
in his ales and his angers, look you, kill his best
friend, Cleitus. 41

Gow. Our King is not like him in that. He
never kill'd any of his friends.

Flu. It is not well done, mark you now, to take
the tales out of my mouth, ere it is made and 45
finished. I speak but in the figures and comparisons of it. As Alexander kill'd his friend Cleitus,
being in his ales and his cups; so also Harry Monmouth, being in his right wits and his good judgements, turn'd away the fat knight with the 50
great belly doublet. He was full of jests, and gipes,
and knaveries, and mocks; I have forgot his name.

Gow. Sir John Falstaff.

Flu. That is he. I'll tell you there is good men
porn at Monmouth. 56

Gow. Here comes his Majesty.

Alarum. Enter KING HENRY *and [forces;* WARWICK,
GLOUCESTER, EXETER,] *with prisoners. Flourish.*

K. Hen. I was not angry since I came to France
Until this instant. Take a trumpet, herald;
Ride thou unto the horsemen on yond hill. 60
If they will fight with us, bid them come down,
Or void the field; they do offend our sight.
If they'll do neither, we will come to them
And make them skirr away, as swift as stones
Enforced from the old Assyrian slings. 65
Besides, we'll cut the throats of those we have,
And not a man of them that we shall take
Shall taste our mercy. Go and tell them so.

Enter MONTJOY.

Exe. Here comes the herald of the French, my
liege.

Glou. His eyes are humbler than they us'd to
be. 70

K. Hen. How now! what means this, herald?
Know'st thou not
That I have fin'd these bones of mine for ransom?
Com'st thou again for ransom?

Mont.   No, great King;
I come to thee for charitable license,
That we may wander o'er this bloody field 75
To book our dead, and then to bury them;
To sort our nobles from our common men.
For many of our princes — woe the while! —
Lie drown'd and soak'd in mercenary blood;
So do our vulgar drench their peasant limbs 80

In blood of princes; and their wounded steeds
Fret fetlock deep in gore, and with wild rage
Yerk out their armed heels at their dead masters,
Killing them twice. O, give us leave, great King,
To view the field in safety, and dispose 85
Of their dead bodies!

K. Hen.   I tell thee truly, herald,
I know not if the day be ours or no;
For yet a many of your horsemen peer
And gallop o'er the field.

Mont.   The day is yours.

K. Hen. Praised be God, and not our strength,
for it! 90
What is this castle call'd that stands hard by?

Mont. They call it Agincourt.

K. Hen. Then call we this the field of Agincourt,
Fought on the day of Crispin Crispianus. 94

Flu. Your grandfather of famous memory,
an't please your Majesty, and your great-uncle
Edward the Plack Prince of Wales, as I have read
in the chronicles, fought a most prave pattle here
in France.

K. Hen. They did, Fluellen. 100

Flu. Your Majesty says very true. If your
Majesties is rememb'red of it, the Welshmen did
good service in a garden where leeks did grow, wearing leeks in their Monmouth caps; which, your
Majesty know, to this hour is an honourable badge
of the service; and I do believe your Majesty takes
no scorn to wear the leek upon Saint Tavy's
day. 108

K. Hen. I wear it for a memorable honour;
For I am Welsh, you know, good countryman.

Flu. All the water in Wye cannot wash your
Majesty's Welsh plood out of your pody, I can tell
you that. God pless it and preserve it, as long as
it pleases His grace, and His majesty too!

K. Hen. Thanks, good my countryman. 115

Flu. By Jeshu, I am your Majesty's countryman, I care not who know it. I will confess it to
all the 'orld. I need not to be ashamed of your
Majesty, praised be God, so long as your Majesty is
an honest man. 120

K. Hen. God keep me so!

Enter WILLIAMS.

                          Our heralds go with him;
Bring me just notice of the numbers dead
On both our parts. Call yonder fellow hither.

[*Exeunt Heralds with Montjoy.*]

Exe. Soldier, you must come to the King. 124

K. Hen. Soldier, why wear'st thou that glove in
thy cap?

Will. An't please your Majesty, 'tis the gage of
one that I should fight withal, if he be alive.

Sc. vii, 35. **figures:** similes.   64. **skirr:** scurry.   72. **fin'd:** pledged.   76. **book:** list.   88. **peer:** appear.   122. **just notice:** exact record.

K. Hen. An Englishman?   129

Will. An't please your Majesty, a rascal that swagger'd with me last night; who, if alive and ever dare to challenge this glove, I have sworn to take him a box o' th' ear; or if I can see my glove in his cap, which he swore, as he was a soldier, he would wear if alive, I will strike it out soundly.   136

K. Hen. What think you, Captain Fluellen? Is it fit this soldier keep his oath?

Flu. He is a craven and a villain else, an't please your Majesty, in my conscience.   140

K. Hen. It may be his enemy is a gentleman of great sort, quite from the answer of his degree.   143

Flu. Though he be as good a gentleman as the devil is, as Lucifer and Belzebub himself, it is necessary, look your Grace, that he keep his vow and his oath. If he be perjur'd, see you now, his reputation is as arrant a villain and a Jack-sauce, as ever his black shoe trod upon God's ground and His earth, in my conscience, la!   150

K. Hen. Then keep thy vow, sirrah, when thou meet'st the fellow.

Will. So I will, my liege, as I live.

K. Hen. Who serv'st thou under?

Will. Under Captain Gower, my liege.   155

Flu. Gower is a good captain, and is good knowledge and literatured in the wars.

K. Hen. Call him hither to me, soldier.

Will. I will, my liege.   [*Exit.* 159

K. Hen. Here, Fluellen; wear thou this favour for me and stick it in thy cap. When Alençon and myself were down together, I pluck'd this glove from his helm. If any man challenge this, he is a friend to Alençon, and an enemy to our person. If thou encounter any such, apprehend him, an thou dost me love.   166

Flu. Your Grace doo's me as great honours as can be desir'd in the hearts of his subjects. I would fain see the man, that has but two legs, that shall find himself aggrief'd at this glove; that is all. But I would fain see it once, an please God of His grace that I might see.   172

K. Hen. Know'st thou Gower?

Flu. He is my dear friend, an please you.

K. Hen. Pray thee, go seek him, and bring him to my tent.   176

Flu. I will fetch him.   [*Exit.*

K. Hen. My Lord of Warwick, and my brother Gloucester,
Follow Fluellen closely at the heels.
The glove which I have given him for a favour
May haply purchase him a box o' th' ear.   181
It is the soldier's; I by bargain should
Wear it myself. Follow, good cousin Warwick.
If that the soldier strike him, as I judge

By his blunt bearing he will keep his word,   185
Some sudden mischief may arise of it;
For I do know Fluellen valiant
And, touch'd with choler, hot as gunpowder,
And quickly will return an injury.   189
Follow, and see there be no harm between them.
Go you with me, uncle of Exeter.   [*Exeunt.*

[SCENE VIII. *Before King Henry's pavilion.*]

Enter GOWER *and* WILLIAMS.

Will. I warrant it is to knight you, captain.

Enter FLUELLEN.

Flu. God's will and his pleasure, captain, I beseech you now, come apace to the King. There is more good toward you peradventure than is in your knowledge to dream of.   5

Will. Sir, know you this glove?

Flu. Know the glove! I know the glove is a glove.

Will. I know this; and thus I challenge it.
        [*Strikes him.*

Flu. 'Sblood! an arrant traitor as any is in the universal world, or in France, or in England!   11

Gow. How now, sir! you villain!

Will. Do you think I'll be forsworn?

Flu. Stand away, Captain Gower. I will give treason his payment into plows, I warrant you.   15

Will. I am no traitor.

Flu. That's a lie in thy throat. I charge you in his Majesty's name, apprehend him; he's a friend of the Duke Alençon's.   19

Enter WARWICK *and* GLOUCESTER.

War. How now, how now! what's the matter?

Flu. My Lord of Warwick, here is — praised be God for it! — a most contagious treason come to light, look you, as you shall desire in a summer's day. Here is his Majesty.

Enter KING HENRY *and* EXETER.

K. Hen. How now! what's the matter?   25

Flu. My liege, here is a villain and a traitor, that, look your Grace, has struck the glove which your Majesty is take out of the helmet of Alençon.   28

Will. My liege, this was my glove; here is the fellow of it; and he that I gave it to in change promis'd to wear it in his cap. I promis'd to strike him, if he did. I met this man with my glove in his cap, and I have been as good as my word.   34

Flu. Your Majesty hear now, saving your Majesty's manhood, what an arrant, rascally, beggarly, lousy knave it is. I hope your Majesty is pear me testimony and witness, and will

143. **sort:** rank. **quite ... degree:** far above answering the challenge of Williams's rank. 148. **Jack-sauce:** impudent fellow.
Sc. viii, 38. **is pear:** will bear.

avouchment, that this is the glove of Alençon that
your Majesty is give me; in your conscience, now?

K. Hen. Give me thy glove, soldier. Look,
here is the fellow of it.   42
'Twas I, indeed, thou promisedst to strike;
And thou hast given me most bitter terms.

Flu. An it please your Majesty, let his neck
answer for it, if there is any martial law in the
world.   47

K. Hen. How canst thou make me satisfaction?

Will. All offences, my lord, come from the heart.
Never came any from mine that might offend your
Majesty.   51

K. Hen. It was ourself thou didst abuse.

Will. Your Majesty came not like yourself. You
appear'd to me but as a common man; witness the
night, your garments, your lowliness; and what   55
your Highness suffer'd under that shape, I beseech
you take it for your own fault and not mine; for
had you been as I took you for, I made no offence;
therefore, I beseech your Highness, pardon me.   60

K. Hen. Here, uncle Exeter, fill this glove with
       crowns,
And give it to this fellow. Keep it, fellow;
And wear it for an honour in thy cap
Till I do challenge it. Give him his crowns;   65
And, captain, you must needs be friends with him.

Flu. By this day and this light, the fellow has
mettle enough in his belly. Hold, there is twelve
pence for you; and I pray you to serve God, and
keep you out of prawls, and prabbles, and quarrels,
and dissensions, and, I warrant you, it is the better
for you.   71

Will. I will none of your money.

Flu. It is with a good will; I can tell you, it will
serve you to mend your shoes. Come, wherefore
should you be so pashful? Your shoes is not so
good. 'Tis a good silling, I warrant you, or I
will change it.   77

Enter [an English] HERALD.

K. Hen. Now, herald, are the dead numb'red?

Her. Here is the number of the slaught'red French.

K. Hen. What prisoners of good sort are taken,
       uncle?   80

Exe. Charles Duke of Orleans, nephew to the King;
John Duke of Bourbon, and Lord Bouciqualt:
Of other lords and barons, knights and squires,
Full fifteen hundred, besides common men.

K. Hen. This note doth tell me of ten thousand
       French   85
That in the field lie slain; of princes, in this number,
And nobles bearing banners, there lie dead
One hundred twenty-six; added to these,
Of knights, esquires, and gallant gentlemen,
Eight thousand and four hundred; of the which,   90

Five hundred were but yesterday dubb'd knights;
So that, in these ten thousand they have lost,
There are but sixteen hundred mercenaries;
The rest are princes, barons, lords, knights, squires,
And gentlemen of blood and quality.   95
The names of those their nobles that lie dead:
Charles Delabreth, High Constable of France;
Jacques of Chatillon, Admiral of France;
The master of the cross-bows, Lord Rambures;
Great Master of France, the brave Sir Guichard
       Dauphin,   100
John Duke of Alençon, Anthony Duke of Brabant,
The brother to the Duke of Burgundy,
And Edward Duke of Bar; of lusty earls,
Grandpré and Roussi, Fauconberg and Foix,
Beaumont and Marle, Vaudemont and Lestrale.   105
Here was a royal fellowship of death!
Where is the number of our English dead?

       [*Herald shows him another paper.*]
Edward the Duke of York, the Earl of Suffolk,
Sir Richard Ketly, Davy Gam, esquire;
None else of name; and of all other men   110
But five and twenty. — O God, thy arm was here;
And not to us, but to thy arm alone,
Ascribe we all! When, without stratagem,
But in plain shock and even play of battle,
Was ever known so great and little loss   115
On one part and on the other? Take it, God,
For it is none but thine!

Exe.   'Tis wonderful!

K. Hen. Come, go we in procession to the village;
And be it death proclaimed through our host
To boast of this or take that praise from God   120
Which is His only.

Flu. Is it not lawful, an please your Majesty,
to tell how many is kill'd?

K. Hen. Yes, captain, but with this acknow-
       ledgement,
That God fought for us.   125

Flu. Yes, my conscience, He did us great good.

K. Hen. Do we all holy rites.
Let there be sung *Non nobis* and *Te Deum.*
The dead with charity enclos'd in clay,
And then to Calais; and to England then,   130
Where ne'er from France arriv'd more happy
       men.   [*Exeunt.*

ACT V

[PROLOGUE]

Enter CHORUS.

[*Chor.*] Vouchsafe to those that have not read
       the story,
That I may prompt them; and of such as have,
I humbly pray them to admit th' excuse

---

39. **avouchment:** testify.

Of time, of numbers, and due course of things,
Which cannot in their huge and proper life   5
Be here presented. Now we bear the King
Toward Calais; grant him there; there seen,
Heave him away upon your winged thoughts
Athwart the sea. Behold, the English beach
Pales in the flood with men, [with] wives and
    boys,   10
Whose shouts and claps out-voice the deep-mouth'd
    sea,
Which like a mighty whiffler 'fore the King
Seems to prepare his way. So let him land,
And solemnly see him set on to London.
So swift a pace hath thought that even now   15
You may imagine him upon Blackheath,
Where that his lords desire him to have borne
His bruised helmet and his bended sword
Before him through the city. He forbids it,
Being free from vainness and self-glorious pride; 20
Giving full trophy, signal, and ostent
Quite from himself to God. But now behold,
In the quick forge and working-house of thought,
How London doth pour out her citizens!
The mayor and all his brethren in best sort, 25
Like to the senators of th' antique Rome,
With the plebeians swarming at their heels,
Go forth and fetch their conqu'ring Cæsar in;
As, by a lower but loving likelihood,
Were now the general of our gracious empress, 30
As in good time he may, from Ireland coming,
Bringing rebellion broached on his sword,
How many would the peaceful city quit,
To welcome him! Much more, and much more cause,
Did they this Harry. Now in London place
    him;   35
As yet the lamentation of the French
Invites the King of England's stay at home, —
The Emperor 's coming in behalf of France,
To order peace between them; — and omit
All the occurrences, whatever chanc'd, 40
Till Harry's back-return again to France.
There must we bring him; and myself have play'd
The interim, by rememb'ring you 'tis past.
Then brook abridgement, and your eyes advance
After your thoughts, straight back again to France.
                                      [*Exit.* 45

[SCENE I. *France. The English camp.*]

Enter FLUELLEN *and* GOWER.

Gow. Nay, that's right; but why wear you your
leek to-day? Saint Davy's day is past.

Flu. There is occasions and causes why and
wherefore in all things. I will tell you asse my
friend, Captain Gower. The rascally, scald, 5
beggarly, lousy, pragging knave, Pistol, which you
and yourself and all the world know to be no petter
than a fellow, look you now, of no merits, he is
come to me and prings me pread and salt yesterday,
look you, and bid me eat my leek. It was in 10
a place where I could not breed no contention with
him; but I will be so bold as to wear it in my cap
till I see him once again, and then I will tell him a
little piece of my desires.

Enter PISTOL.

Gow. Why, here he comes, swelling like a turkey-
cock.   16
Flu. 'Tis no matter for his swellings nor his
turkey-cocks. God pless you, Aunchient Pistol!
you scurfy, lousy knave, God pless you!
Pist. Ha! art thou bedlam? Dost thou thirst,
    base Troyan, 20
To have me fold up Parca's fatal web?
Hence! I am qualmish at the smell of leek.
Flu. I peseech you heartily, scurfy, lousy knave,
at my desires, and my requests, and my petitions,
to eat, look you, this leek. Because, look you, 25
you do not love it, nor your affections and your
appetites and your disgestions doo's not agree with
it, I would desire you to eat it.
Pist. Not for Cadwallader and all his goats.
Flu. There is one goat for you. (*Strikes him.*)
Will you be so good, scald knave, as eat it? 31
Pist. Base Troyan, thou shalt die.
Flu. You say very true, scald knave, when
God's will is. I will desire you to live in the mean
time, and eat your victuals. Come, there is 35
sauce for it. [*Strikes him.*] You call'd me yesterday mountain-squire; but I will make you to-day
a squire of low degree. I pray you, fall to; if you
can mock a leek, you can eat a leek.
Gow. Enough, captain; you have astonish'd
him.   41
Flu. I say, I will make him eat some part of my
leek, or I will peat his pate four days. Bite, I pray
you; it is good for your green wound and your
ploody coxcomb. 45
Pist. Must I bite?
Flu. Yes, certainly, and out of doubt and out
of question too, and ambiguities.
Pist. By this leek, I will most horribly revenge.
I eat and eat, I swear — 50
Flu. Eat, I pray you. Will you have some more

Act V, Prol., 10. **Pales:** fences. [**with**] F₂. Om. F₁. 12. **whiffler:** one who clears the way for a procession. 21. **signal, and ostent:** signs and shows of victory. 29. **loving** (Seymour). *by loving* F. 30. **general.** The Earl of Essex, who went to Ireland March 27, 1599, to put down Tyrone's rebellion, returning unsuccessful on Sept. 28 of same year. 32. **broached:** spitted. 38. **Emperor:** Sigismund.
Sc. i, 5. **scald:** scabby. 20. **bedlam:** crazy. 21. **Parca's:** Fate's. 29. **Cadwallader:** the last of the Welsh kings. 40. **astonish'd:** stunned.

sauce to your leek? There is not enough leek to
swear by.

Pist. Quiet thy cudgel; thou dost see I eat. 54

Flu. Much good do you, scald knave, heartily.
Nay, pray you, throw none away; the skin is good
for your broken coxcomb. When you take occasions
to see leeks hereafter, I pray you, mock at 'em;
that is all.

Pist. Good. 60

Flu. Ay, leeks is good. **Hold you, there is a**
groat to heal your pate.

Pist. Me a groat!

Flu. Yes, verily and in truth you shall take it;
or I have another leek in my pocket, which you
shall eat. 66

Pist. I take thy groat in earnest of revenge.

Flu. If I owe you anything, I will pay you in
cudgels. You shall be a woodmonger, and buy
nothing of me but cudgels. God be wi' you, and
keep you, and heal your pate. [*Exit.* 71

Pist. All hell shall stir for this.

Gow. Go, go; you are a counterfeit cowardly
knave. Will you mock at an ancient tradition,
begun upon an honourable respect, and worn as
a memorable trophy of predeceased valour, and 75
dare not avouch in your deeds any of your words?
I have seen you gleeking and galling at this gentleman twice or thrice. You thought, because he
could not speak English in the native garb, he 80
could not therefore handle an English cudgel. You
find it otherwise; and henceforth let a Welsh correction teach you a good English condition. Fare
ye well. [*Exit.*

Pist. Doth Fortune play the huswife with me
now? 85
News have I, that my [Nell] is dead i' th' spital
Of malady of France;
And there my rendezvous is quite cut off.
Old I do wax; and from my weary limbs
Honour is cudgell'd. Well, bawd I'll turn. 90
And something lean to cutpurse of quick hand.
To England will I steal, and there I'll steal;
And patches will I get unto these cudgell'd scars,
And swear I got them in the Gallia wars. [*Exit.*

[SCENE II. *France. A royal palace.*]

Enter, at one door, KING HENRY, EXETER, BED-
FORD, [GLOUCESTER,] WARWICK, [WESTMORE-
LAND,] *and other* Lords; *at another, the* FRENCH
KING, QUEEN ISABEL, [*the* PRINCESS KATHARINE,
ALICE, *and other* Ladies;] *the* DUKE OF BUR-
GUNDY, *and other French.*

K. Hen. Peace to this meeting, wherefore we
are met!
Unto our brother France, and to our sister,
Health and fair time of day; joy and good wishes
To our most fair and princely cousin Katharine;
And, as a branch and member of this royalty, 5
By whom this great assembly is contriv'd,
We do salute you, Duke of Burgundy;
And, princes French, and peers, health to you all!

Fr. King. Right joyous are we to behold your
face,
Most worthy brother England; fairly met! 10
So are you, princes English, every one.

Q. Isa. So happy be the issue, brother [England],
Of this good day and of this gracious meeting,
As we are now glad to behold your eyes;
Your eyes, which hitherto have borne in them 15
Against the French that met them in their bent
The fatal balls of murdering basilisks.
The venom of such looks, we fairly hope,
Have lost their quality, and that this day
Shall change all griefs and quarrels into love. 20

K. Hen. To cry amen to that, thus we appear.

Q. Isa. You English princes all, I do salute you.

Bur. My duty to you both, on equal love,
Great Kings of France and England! That I have
labour'd
With all my wits, my pains, and strong endeavours
To bring your most imperial Majesties 26
Unto this bar and royal interview,
Your mightiness on both parts best can witness.
Since then my office hath so far prevail'd
That, face to face and royal eye to eye, 30
You have congreeted, let it not disgrace me,
If I demand, before this royal view,
What rub or what impediment there is,
Why that the naked, poor, and mangled Peace,
Dear nurse of arts, plenties, and joyful births, 35
Should not in this best garden of the world,
Our fertile France, put up her lovely visage?
Alas, she hath from France too long been chas'd,
And all her husbandry doth lie on heaps,
Corrupting in it own fertility. 40
Her vine, the merry cheerer of the heart,
Unpruned dies; her hedges even-pleach'd,
Like prisoners wildly overgrown with hair,
Put forth disorder'd twigs; her fallow leas
The darnel, hemlock, and rank fumitory 45
Doth root upon, while that the coulter rusts
That should deracinate such savagery;
The even mead, that erst brought sweetly forth
The freckled cowslip, burnet, and green clover,
Wanting the scythe, [all] uncorrected, rank, 50

---

62. **groat:** fourpence. 77. **gleeking and galling:** sneering and scoffing. 85. **huswife:** hussy. 86. **[Nell]** (Johnson). *Doll* F.
Sc. ii, 12. **[England]** F$_2$. *Ireland* F$_1$. 17. **basilisks:** (1) fabulous creatures which killed by a glance, (2) large cannon.
27. **bar:** court. 33. **rub:** obstacle. 40. **it:** its. 42. **even-pleach'd:** smoothly interwoven. 47. **deracinate:** uproot. 50.
[all] (Rowe). *withall* F.

Conceives by idleness, and nothing teems
But hateful docks, rough thistles, kexes, burs,
Losing both beauty and utility;
And all our vineyards, fallows, meads, and hedges,
Defective in their natures, grow to wildness.   55
Even so our houses and ourselves and children
Have lost, or do not learn for want of time,
The sciences that should become our country,
But grow like savages, — as soldiers will
That nothing do but meditate on blood, —   60
To swearing and stern looks, diffus'd attire,
And everything that seems unnatural.
Which to reduce into our former favour
You are assembled; and my speech entreats
That I may know the let why gentle Peace   65
Should not expel these inconveniences
And bless us with her former qualities.
    K. Hen. If, Duke of Burgundy, you would the
      peace,
Whose want gives growth to th' imperfections
Which you have cited, you must buy that peace   70
With full accord to all our just demands;
Whose tenours and particular effects
You have enschedul'd briefly in your hands.
    Bur. The King hath heard them; to the which as
      yet   74
There is no answer made.
    K. Hen.   Well, then, the peace,
Which you before so urg'd, lies in his answer.
    Fr. King. I have but with a cursorary eye
O'erglanc'd the articles. Pleaseth your Grace
To appoint some of your council presently
To sit with us once more, with better heed   80
To re-survey them, we will suddenly
Pass our accept and peremptory answer.
    K. Hen. Brother, we shall. Go, uncle Exeter,
And brother Clarence, and you, brother Gloucester,
Warwick, and Huntingdon, go with the King;   85
And take with you free power to ratify,
Augment, or alter, as your wisdoms best
Shall see advantageable for our dignity,
Anything in or out of our demands,
And we'll consign thereto. Will you, fair sister,   90
Go with the princes, or stay here with us?
    Q. Isa. Our gracious brother, I will go with them.
Haply a woman's voice may do some good,
When articles too nicely urg'd be stood on.
    K. Hen. Yet leave our cousin Katharine here
      with us: 95
She is our capital demand, compris'd
Within the fore-rank of our articles.
    Q. Isa. She hath good leave.
          [*Exeunt all except Henry, Katharine* [*and
          Alice*].

    K. Hen.   Fair Katharine, and most fair,
Will you vouchsafe to teach a soldier terms
Such as will enter at a lady's ear   100
And plead his love-suit to her gentle heart?
    Kath. Your Majesty shall mock at me; I cannot
speak your England.
    K. Hen. O fair Katharine, if you will love me
soundly with your French heart, I will be glad to
hear you confess it brokenly with your English
tongue. Do you like me, Kate?   107
    Kath. Pardonnez-moi, I cannot tell wat is "like
me."
    K. Hen. An angel is like you, Kate, and you are
like an angel.   111
    *Kath. Que dit-il? Que je suis semblable à les
anges?*
    Alice. Oui, vraiment, sauf votre grace, ainsi dit-il.
    K. Hen. I said so, dear Katharine; and I must
not blush to affirm it.   117
    *Kath. O bon Dieu! les langues des hommes sont
pleines de tromperies.*
    K. Hen. What says she, fair one? That the
tongues of men are full of deceits?
    Alice. Oui, dat de tongues of de mans is be full
of deceits: dat is de Princess.   123
    K. Hen. The Princess is the better English-
woman. I' faith, Kate, my wooing is fit for thy
understanding. I am glad thou canst speak no
better English; for, if thou couldst, thou wouldst
find me such a plain king that thou wouldst think
I had sold my farm to buy my crown. I know no
ways to mince it in love, but directly to say,   130
"I love you"; then if you urge me farther than to
say, "Do you in faith?" I wear out my suit.
Give me your answer; i' faith, do; and so clap hands
and a bargain. How say you, lady?
    Kath. Sauf votre honneur, me understand
well.   136
    K. Hen. Marry, if you would put me to verses,
or to dance for your sake, Kate, why you undid me;
for the one, I have neither words nor measure, and
for the other I have no strength in measure,   140
yet a reasonable measure in strength. If I could
win a lady at leap-frog, or by vaulting into my
saddle with my armour on my back, under the
correction of bragging be it spoken, I should quickly
leap into a wife. Or if I might buffet for   145
my love, or bound my horse for her favours, I
could lay on like a butcher and sit like a jack-
an-apes, never off. But, before God, Kate, I
cannot look greenly, nor gasp out my eloquence,
nor I have no cunning in protestation; only   150
downright oaths, which I never use till urg'd, nor
never break for urging. If thou canst love a fellow

---

52. **kexes:** dry stalks. 61. **diffus'd:** ragged. 63. **favour:** looks. 65. **let:** hindrance. 77. **cursorary:** cursory. F spells
curselarie. 81. **suddenly:** quickly. 82. **Pass . . . answer:** return our adopted and decisive reply. 90. **consign:** agree. 94.
nicely: punctiliously. 96. **capital:** chief. 139, 140, 141. **measure:** (1) meter, (2) dancing, (3) amount.

of this temper, Kate, whose face is not worth sun-
burning, that never looks in his glass for love of
anything he sees there, let thine eye be thy 155
cook.   I speak to thee plain soldier.   If thou
canst love me for this, take me; if not, to say to
thee that I shall die, is true; but for thy love, by
the Lord, no; yet I love thee too.   And while
thou liv'st, dear Kate, take a fellow of plain 160
and uncoined constancy; for he perforce must do
thee right, because he hath not the gift to woo
in other places; for these fellows of infinite tongue,
that can rhyme themselves into ladies' favours,
they do always reason themselves out again. 165
What! a speaker is but a prater; a rhyme is but a
ballad.   A good leg will fall; a straight back will
stoop; a black beard will turn white; a curl'd pate
will grow bald; a fair face will wither; a full eye
will wax hollow; but a good heart, Kate, is 170
the sun and the moon; or rather the sun and not
the moon; for it shines bright and never changes,
but keeps his course truly.   If thou would have
such a one, take me; and take me, take a soldier;
take a soldier, take a king.   And what say'st 175
thou then to my love?   Speak, my fair, and fairly,
I pray thee.
    Kath. Is it possible dat I should love de enemy
of France?   179
    K. Hen. No; it is not possible you should love
the enemy of France, Kate; but, in loving me, you
should love the friend of France; for I love France
so well that I will not part with a village of it,
I will have it all mine; and, Kate, when France is
mine and I am yours, then yours is France and
you are mine.   186
    Kath. I cannot tell wat is dat.
    K. Hen. No, Kate?   I will tell thee in French;
which I am sure will hang upon my tongue like a
new-married wife about her husband's neck, 190
hardly to be shook off.   *Je quand sur le possession
de France, et quand vous avez le possession de moi, —*
let me see, what then?   Saint Denis be my speed! —
donc votre est France et vous êtes mienne.   It is as
easy for me, Kate, to conquer the kingdom as 195
to speak so much more French.   I shall never
move thee in French, unless it be to laugh at
me.
    Kath. *Sauf votre honneur, le François que vous
parlez, il est meilleur que l'Anglois lequel je parle.* 201
    K. Hen. No, faith, is't not, Kate; but thy
speaking of my tongue, and I thine, most truly-
falsely, must needs be granted to be much at one.
But, Kate, dost thou understand thus much
English: canst thou love me?   206
    Kath. I cannot tell.
    K. Hen. Can any of your neighbours tell, Kate?

I'll ask them.   Come, I know thou lovest me;
and at night, when you come into your closet, 210
you'll question this gentlewoman about me; and
I know, Kate, you will to her dispraise those parts
in me that you love with your heart.   But, good
Kate, mock me mercifully; the rather, gentle
princess, because I love thee cruelly.   If ever 215
thou beest mine, Kate, as I have a saving faith
within me tells me thou shalt, I get thee with
scambling, and thou must therefore needs prove
a good soldier-breeder.   Shalt not thou and I,
between Saint Denis and Saint George, com- 220
pound a boy, half French, half English, that shall
go to Constantinople and take the Turk by the
beard?   Shall we not?   What say'st thou, my fair
flower-de-luce?
    Kath. I do not know dat.   225
    K. Hen. No; 'tis hereafter to know, but now to
promise.   Do but now promise, Kate, you will
endeavour for your French part of such a boy;
and for my English moiety, take the word of a
king and a bachelor.   How answer you, *la plus
belle Katharine du monde, mon très cher et devin
déesse?*   232
    Kath. Your Majestee ave fausse French enough
to deceive de most sage demoiselle dat is en
France.   235
    K. Hen. Now, fie upon my false French!   By
mine honour, in true English, I love thee, Kate;
by which honour I dare not swear thou lovest me;
yet my blood begins to flatter me that thou dost,
notwithstanding the poor and untempering 240
effect of my visage.   Now, beshrew my father's
ambition! he was thinking of civil wars when he
got me; therefore was I created with a stubborn
outside, with an aspect of iron, that, when I come
to woo ladies, I fright them.   But, in faith, 245
Kate, the elder I wax, the better I shall appear.
My comfort is, that old age, that ill layer up of
beauty, can do no more spoil upon my face.   Thou
hast me, if thou hast me, at the worst; and thou
shalt wear me, if thou wear me, better and 250
better; and therefore tell me, most fair Katharine,
will you have me?   Put off your maiden blushes;
avouch the thoughts of your heart with the looks
of an empress; take me by the hand, and say,
Harry of England, I am thine; which word 255
thou shalt no sooner bless mine ear withal, but I
will tell thee aloud, England is thine, Ireland is
thine, France is thine, and Henry Plantagenet is
thine; who, though I speak it before his face, if
he be not fellow with the best king, thou shalt 260
find the best king of good fellows.   Come, your
answer in broken music; for thy voice is music
and thy English broken; therefore, queen of all,

---

155. **be thy cook:** add the garnishing. 161. **uncoined:** of metal not coined so that it can pass from one hand to another.
167. **fall:** lose shape. 210. **closet:** chamber. 218. **scambling:** fighting. 240. **untempering:** uningratiating. 262. **broken
music:** part-music.

Katharine, break thy mind to me in broken English.
Wilt thou have me?   266
  Kath. Dat is as it shall please de *roi mon père.*
  K. Hen. Nay, it will please him well, Kate;
it shall please him, Kate.
  Kath. Den it sall also content me.   270
  K. Hen. Upon that I kiss your hand, and call
you my queen.
  *Kath. Laissez, mon seigneur, laissez, laissez!
Ma foi, je ne veux point que vous abaissez votre
grandeur en baisant la main d'une [de votre seigneurie
indigne] serviteur. Excusez-moi, je vous supplie,
mon très-puissant seigneur.*   277
  K. Hen. Then I will kiss your lips, Kate.
  *Kath. Les dames et demoiselles pour être baisées
devant leur noces, il n'est pas la coutume de   281
France.*
  K. Hen. Madam my interpreter, what says she?
  Alice. Dat it is not be de fashion pour les ladies
of France, — I cannot tell wat is *baiser* en Anglish.
  K. Hen. To kiss.   287
  Alice. Your Majesty *entendre* bettre *que moi.*
  K. Hen. It is not the fashion for the maids in
France to kiss before they are married, would she
say?   291
  Alice. Oui, vraiment.
  K. Hen. O Kate, nice customs curtsy to great
kings. Dear Kate, you and I cannot be confined
within the weak list of a country's fashion.   295
We are the makers of manners, Kate; and the
liberty that follows our places stops the mouth
of all find-faults, as I will do yours, for upholding
the nice fashion of your country in denying me
a kiss; therefore, patiently and yielding.   300
[*Kissing her.*] You have witchcraft in your lips,
Kate; there is more eloquence in a sugar touch
of them than in the tongues of the French council;
and they should sooner persuade Harry of England
than a general petition of monarchs. Here comes
your father.   306

  Re-enter the FRENCH POWER *and the* ENGLISH
LORDS.

  Bur. God save your Majesty! My royal cousin,
teach you our princess English?
  K. Hen. I would have her learn, my fair cousin,
how perfectly I love her; and that is good English.
  Bur. Is she not apt?   312
  K. Hen. Our tongue is rough, coz, and my
condition is not smooth; so that, having neither
the voice nor the heart of flattery about me, I
cannot so conjure up the spirit of love in her,
that he will appear in his true likeness.   317
  Bur. Pardon the frankness of my mirth, if I

answer you for that. If you would conjure in
her, you must make a circle; if conjure up Love
in her in his true likeness, he must appear naked
and blind. Can you blame her then, being a
maid yet ros'd over with the virgin crimson of
modesty, if she deny the appearance of a naked
blind boy in her naked seeing self? It were, my
lord, a hard condition for a maid to consign to. 326
  K. Hen. Yet they do wink and yield, as love is
blind and enforces.
  Bur. They are then excus'd, my lord, when they
see not what they do.
  K. Hen. Then, good my lord, teach your cousin
to consent winking.   332
  Bur. I will wink on her to consent, my lord, if
you will teach her to know my meaning; for maids,
well summer'd and warm kept, are like flies at
Bartholomew-tide, blind, though they have their
eyes; and then they will endure handling, which
before would not abide looking on.   338
  K. Hen. This moral ties me over to time and a
hot summer; and so I shall catch the fly, your
cousin, in the latter end, and she must be blind too.
  Bur. As love is, my lord, before it loves.   342
  K. Hen. It is so; and you may, some of you,
thank love for my blindness, who cannot see many
a fair French city for one fair French maid that
stands in my way.   346
  Fr. King. Yes, my lord, you see them perspectively, the cities turn'd into a maid; for they are
all girdled with maiden walls that war hath [never]
ent'red.   350
  K. Hen. Shall Kate be my wife?
  Fr. King. So please you.
  K. Hen. I am content, so the maiden cities you
talk of may wait on her; so the maid that stood in
the way for my wish shall show me the way to
my will.   356
  Fr. King. We have consented to all terms of
reason.
  K. Hen. Is't so, my lords of England?
  West. The King hath granted every article;
His daughter first, and then in sequel all,
According to their firm proposed natures.   362
  Exe. Only he hath not yet subscribed this:
where your Majesty demands, that the King of
France, having any occasion to write for matter
of grant, shall name your Highness in this form
and with this addition, in French, *Notre très-cher
fils Henri, Roi d'Angleterre, Héritier de France;* and
thus in Latin *Præcarissimus filius noster Henricus,
Rex Angliæ, et Hæres Franciæ.*   370
  Fr. King. Nor this I have not, brother, so denied
But your request shall make me let it pass.

265. **break:** open. 275. [*de ... indigne*] (Camb. edd.) *nostre Seigneur indignie* F. 295. **list:** boundary. 314. **condition:**
disposition. 327. **wink:** close the eyes. 336. **Bartholomew-tide:** Aug. 24. 347. **perspectively:** as through an optical glass
which produces illusions. 349. **[never]** (Rowe). Om. F. 367. **addition:** title.

K. Hen. I pray you then, in love and dear
    alliance,
Let that one article rank with the rest;
And thereupon give me your daughter.   375
    Fr. King. Take her, fair son, and from her blood
    raise up
Issue to me; that the contending kingdoms
Of France and England, whose very shores look pale
With envy of each other's happiness,
May cease their hatred, and this dear conjunction
Plant neighbourhood and Christian-like accord   381
In their sweet bosoms, that never war advance
His bleeding sword 'twixt England and fair France.
    Lords. Amen!
    K. Hen. Now, welcome, Kate; and bear me
    witness all,   385
That here I kiss her as my sovereign queen.
                   [*Flourish.*
    Q. Isa. God, the best maker of all marriages,
Combine your hearts in one, your realms in one!
As man and wife, being two, are one in love,
So be there 'twixt your kingdoms such a spousal,
That never may ill office, or fell jealousy,   391
Which troubles oft the bed of blessed marriage,
Thrust in between the paction of these kingdoms,
To make divorce of their incorporate league;
That English may as French, French Englishmen,
Receive each other.   God speak this Amen!   396
    All. Amen!

---

393. **paction:** agreement.
   Epi., 2. **bending:** i.e., under the weight of his theme.   4. **starts:** fragments.   7. **garden:** i.e., France.   14. **let...take:**
let this play find acceptance.

K. Hen. Prepare we for our marriage; on which
    day,
My Lord of Burgundy, we'll take your oath,
And all the peers', for surety of our leagues.   400
Then shall I swear to Kate, and you to me;
And may our oaths well kept and prosperous be!
              [*Sennet. Exeunt.*

[EPILOGUE]

Enter CHORUS.

[*Chor.*] Thus far, with rough and all-unable pen,
    Our bending author hath pursu'd the story,
In little room confining mighty men,
    Mangling by starts the full course of their glory.
Small time, but in that small most greatly liv'd   5
    This star of England.   Fortune made his sword,
By which the world's best garden he achiev'd,
    And of it left his son imperial lord.
Henry the Sixth, in infant bands crown'd King
    Of France and England, did this king succeed;   10
Whose state so many had the managing,
    That they lost France and made his England
    bleed;
Which oft our stage hath shown; and, for their
    sake,
In your fair minds let this acceptance take.
                      [*Exit.*]

Much Ado About Nothing

MUCH ADO ABOUT NOTHING was entered in the Stationers' Register on August 4, 1600, as one of four plays "to be staied," but, for whatever reason, the prohibition was presently withdrawn and the normal pre-publication entry was made on August 24, a Quarto following before the end of the year. That the manuscript from which the Quarto was set up was the theatrical prompt-copy is established by the appearance in IV.ii. of the names of Kempe and Cowley, actors in Shakespeare's company, in certain speech-prefixes for Dogberry and Verges respectively. That the text in the Folio was printed from a copy of this Quarto which had eventually served in the playhouse is clear from certain changes in stage directions, in particular the insertion at II.iii.39 of the name of Jack Wilson, the actor playing Balthasar. The present text is based on the Quarto, which is the more accurately printed text.

The date of *Much Ado* can be established with gratifying accuracy. Its absence from the list of Meres (for it cannot be *Love's Labour's Won*) argues that it had not been performed at least until the very end of 1598, for so good an acting play could hardly have failed to win Meres's approbation. The title page of the Quarto, however, states that it had been "sundrie times publikely acted" by Shakespeare's company, and this fact, along with the apparent withdrawal of Kempe from the company early in 1599, fixes the date beyond reasonable doubt as some time in the winter of 1598–1599.

The story of Hero and Claudio is mainly derived from the twenty-second tale in a collection of Italian *Novelle* by Matteo Bandello (1554). No English translation of this has been found, but one in French by Belleforest appeared in 1582. As there is nothing in Shakespeare's rendering which could not have come equally well from either the French version or the Italian original, it is impossible to determine which one was actually used. In Bandello the scene is laid as in Shakespeare in Messina at the close of a successful war; Don Pedro of Arragon appears as King Piero d'Aragona, and

Leonato as Lionato de' Lionati; and the thread of the story is the same as in Shakespeare with these main exceptions: the villain is a disappointed lover of Hero's (Fenicia's); there is no Margaret, the deceiving of the bridegroom, Timbreo, being accomplished merely by his being led to see a man enter a window in the heroine's home; the scene in the church, where Claudio casts off Hero, is lacking, the Italian lover sending a friend to announce the breaking off of the match; Timbreo repents of his own accord of his hasty inference; and the dénouement is brought about by the remorse of the villain. Thus it may be seen that in Shakespeare's main plot the character and motive of Don John are quite different, the deceiving of Claudio is made more plausible, and the humors of Dogberry and Verges are introduced to undo the tangle. The rôle of Margaret in this action and the scene at Hero's window appear to have been suggested to Shakespeare by the story of Ariodante and Ginevra in Book V of Ariosto's *Orlando Furioso* (translated into English by John Harrington in 1591), where Ariodante is persuaded that his lady is false after seeing her maid, dressed in the lady's clothes, receive another man at her window. A condensed and altered version appears in Spenser's *Faerie Queene*, II.iv.17.

A number of irregularities and discrepancies in the play have convinced some critics that the received text is Shakespeare's recasting of an earlier play now lost, but the evidence is not conclusive. Confused or redundant stage directions may be owing to no more than Shakespeare's carelessness. For example, at I.i.1 and II.i.1 Innogen, the mother of Hero, is introduced, though she utters not a word and nobody speaks to her in the whole play. This is undeniably odd, but Shakespeare perhaps intended originally to give Innogen a part, discovered, however, as he worked that he did not need her, and then neglected to revise his stage-directions; or Innogen may have been allowed to appear as a mute, as in fact Balthasar does, after an entrance at I.i.96. A kindred peculiarity occurs in the stage direction at II.i.218, where Don John, Borachio, and Conrade are given entrances, though they do not speak in that scene. Likewise Margaret is on the stage in V.iv., but does not speak. There are notable inconsistencies in speech headings; for the outstanding instances see the note on IV.ii.1. If such inconsistencies occurred in this play alone or only rarely in Shakespeare, it might be reasonable to take them as signs of revision, but they crop up in so many plays that one can regard them only as characteristic of Shakespeare's way in composition.

The sub-plot of Benedick and Beatrice and the parts of Dogberry and Verges are original with Shakespeare, and the skill with which he has fused these subordinate elements with his main plot deserves all the praise it has received. The characters of the main plot unite in a plan to make Benedick and Beatrice fall in love with each other, which ruse is carried out effectively in two parallel scenes, but it is the gross wrong to Hero, slandered by Claudio at the very altar, which precipitates the real understanding between them. Alone among the intimates of Hero, Benedick and Beatrice trust in her innocence, and it is Benedick who scents the villainy in Don John. To set the seal upon their affection, Beatrice demands that Benedick kill Claudio, but happily the injunction need go no further than a challenge, for at long last Dogberry and his comrades expose the crime and solve the problem. They were created, of course, to do just that; nevertheless, before they fulfill their office they provide not only diversion from the seriousness of the main plot, but, by their galling stupidities and delays, a fair degree of suspense and dramatic irony.

The villain of the piece is Don John, a "plain-dealing villain" so lacking in subtlety as to seem, in the study at least, almost funny; which is as much as to say, perhaps, that he is the proper kind of villain for a comedy. One cannot, even at the outset, believe that his evil designs are destined to prosper. The title of the play is never quite out of mind. Nevertheless, Shakespeare has given him a plausible human motive for his malignity. After some sort of sedition he has lately been reconciled to his brother (Don Pedro), but Claudio, who distinguished himself in the recent warfare, has been honored at his expense: "That young start-up hath all the glory of my overthrow." Thus Don John

has much the same reason for hating Claudio that Iago has for hating Cassio, whom Othello promoted over his head. But Iago is a villain of quite another order.

Despite the excellence in the structure of the play as a whole, the character and rôle of Margaret seem imperfectly realized. She is made the apparently innocent accomplice in Borachio's machination, though how she could have been so imposed upon, not being unintelligent, is hard to understand. Four important contexts are involved in the problem (II.ii.41–51; III.iii.153–175; IV.i.187–94; V.i. 236–51). Upon the cumulative evidence of these passages it is clear that the guileless Margaret had been induced to dress up in Hero's garments and to be called by Hero's name in a bit of play-acting, the implications of which she cannot have perceived. She should not have been so simple, but the fact remains that she was. There is a crux in Borachio's original outline of the villainy when he tells Don John that Claudio and Don Pedro will "hear me call Margaret Hero, hear Margaret term me Claudio" (II.ii.43–44). Some editors have substituted *Borachio* for *Claudio* in that line, but the change has not been generally adopted. It is idle to wonder why Margaret was not present to witness the repudiation of Hero in the church, or why, hearing of it later, as she could not avoid doing, she did not then explain everything. For Shakespeare had invented the watch to unravel the mystery, and that was that! Margaret is later exonerated in Borachio's confession, and although obviously "at some fault in this," suffers no loss of reputation. Though as a character she is less well developed than Emilia, she is no more consciously guilty in her error than is Iago's wife when she temporarily steals Othello's handkerchief to take a copy of it for her capricious husband.

Hero and Claudio, though the protagonists of the play, are relatively pale and ineffectual characters, by no means so interesting as Benedick and Beatrice, who completely capture one's imagination and affection. Scoffers at love, yet magnetized to each other, sparring at every turn, Benedick and Beatrice are the readiest victims for the Nemesis of Comedy. They are Biron and Rosaline of *Love's Labour's Lost* freed and perfected on a higher plane. Beatrice, though less warm and radiant than some of Shakespeare's women, is one of the most real and lovable of them all.

MUCH ADO ABOUT NOTHING

ACT I

SCENE I. [*Before Leonato's house.*]

Enter LEONATO, HERO, *and* BEATRICE, *with a* MESSENGER.

Leon. I learn in this letter that Don Pedro of Arragon comes this night to Messina.

Mess. He is very near by this. He was not three leagues off when I left him.

Leon. How many gentlemen have you lost in 5 this action?

Mess. But few of any sort, and none of name.

Leon. A victory is twice itself when the achiever brings home full numbers. I find here that Don Pedro hath bestowed much honour on a young 10 Florentine called Claudio.

Mess. Much deserv'd on his part and equally remem'bred by Don Pedro. He hath borne himself beyond the promise of his age, doing, in the figure of a lamb, the feats of a lion. He hath indeed better bett'red expectation than you must expect of me to tell you how. 17

Leon. He hath an uncle here in Messina will be very much glad of it. 19

Mess. I have already delivered him letters, and there appears much joy in him; even so much that joy could not show itself modest enough without a badge of bitterness.

Leon. Did he break out into tears?

Mess. In great measure. 25

Leon. A kind overflow of kindness. There are no faces truer than those that are so wash'd. How much better is it to weep at joy than to joy at weeping!

Beat. I pray you, is Signior Mountanto return'd from the wars or no? 31

Mess. I know none of that name, lady. There was none such in the army of any sort.

Leon. What is he that you ask for, niece?

Hero. My cousin means Signior Benedick of 35 Padua.

Mess. O, he's return'd; and as pleasant as ever he was.

Beat. He set up his bills here in Messina and challeng'd Cupid at the flight; and my uncle's 40

Act I, sc. i. S.D. *Enter* LEONATO. *Enter Leonato . . . Innogen his wife. . . .* Q Ff. 1. **Don Pedro.** *Don Peter* Q. 7. **sort:** rank. **name:** reputation. 26. **kind:** natural. 30. **Mountanto:** an upward cut in fencing. 37. **pleasant:** facetious. 39. **bills:** placards. 40. **flight:** long-range shooting.

fool, reading the challenge, subscrib'd for Cupid, and challeng'd him at the bird-bolt. I pray you, how many hath he kill'd and eaten in these wars? But how many hath he kill'd? for indeed I promised to eat all of his killing.   45

Leon. Faith, niece, you tax Signior Benedick too much; but he'll be meet with you, I doubt it not.

Mess. He hath done good service, lady, in these wars.

Beat. You had musty victual, and he hath   50 holp to eat it. He is a very valiant trencherman; he hath an excellent stomach.

Mess. And a good soldier too, lady.

Beat. And a good soldier to a lady. But what is he to a lord?   55

Mess. A lord to a lord, a man to a man; stuff'd with all honourable virtues.

Beat. It is so, indeed; he is no less than a stuff'd man. But for the stuffing,— well, we are all mortal.   60

Leon. You must not, sir, mistake my niece. There is a kind of merry war betwixt Signior Benedick and her. They never meet but there's a skirmish of wit between them.   64

Beat. Alas! he gets nothing by that. In our last conflict four of his five wits went halting off, and now is the whole man govern'd with one; so that if he have wit enough to keep himself warm, let him bear it for a difference between himself and his horse; for it is all the wealth that he hath left to   70 be known a reasonable creature. Who is his companion now? He hath every month a new sworn brother.

Mess. Is't possible?   74

Beat. Very easily possible. He wears his faith but as the fashion of his hat; it ever changes with the next block.

Mess. I see, lady, the gentleman is not in your books.

Beat. No; an he were, I would burn my study.   80 But, I pray you, who is his companion? Is there no young squarer now that will make a voyage with him to the devil?

Mess. He is most in the company of the right noble Claudio.   85

Beat. O Lord, he will hang upon him like a disease. He is sooner caught than the pestilence, and the taker runs presently mad. God help the noble Claudio! If he have caught the Benedick, it will cost him a thousand pounds ere 'a be cur'd.   90

Mess. I will hold friends with you, lady.

Beat. Do, good friend.

Leon. You will never run mad, niece.

Beat. No, not till a hot January.

Mess. Don Pedro is approach'd.   95

Enter DON PEDRO, CLAUDIO, BENEDICK, BALTHASAR, *and* JOHN *the Bastard.*

D. Pedro. Good Signior Leonato, are you come to meet your trouble? The fashion of the world is to avoid cost, and you encounter it.

Leon. Never came trouble to my house in the likeness of your Grace, for trouble being gone,   100 comfort should remain; but when you depart from me, sorrow abides and happiness takes his leave.

D. Pedro. You embrace your charge too willingly. I think this is your daughter.   104

Leon. Her mother hath many times told me so.

Bene. Were you in doubt, sir, that you ask'd her?

Leon. Signior Benedick, no; for then were you a child.   109

D. Pedro. You have it full, Benedick. We may guess by this what you are, being a man. Truly, the lady fathers herself. Be happy, lady; for you are like an honourable father.

Bene. If Signior Leonato be her father, she would not have his head on her shoulders for all Messina, as like him as she is.   116

Beat. I wonder that you will still be talking, Signior Benedick. Nobody marks you.

Bene. What, my dear Lady Disdain! are you yet living?   120

Beat. Is it possible disdain should die while she hath such meet food to feed it as Signior Benedick? Courtesy itself must convert to disdain, if you come in her presence.   124

Bene. Then is courtesy a turncoat. But it is certain I am loved of all ladies, only you excepted; and I would I could find in my heart that I had not a hard heart, for, truly, I love none.

Beat. A dear happiness to women; they would else have been troubled with a pernicious suitor. I thank God and my cold blood, I am of your   131 humour for that. I had rather hear my dog bark at a crow than a man swear he loves me.

Bene. God keep your ladyship still in that mind! So some gentleman or other shall scape a predestinate scratch'd face.   136

Beat. Scratching could not make it worse, an 'twere such a face as yours were.

Bene. Well, you are a rare parrot-teacher.

Beat. A bird of my tongue is better than a beast of yours.   141

Bene. I would my horse had the speed of your tongue, and so good a continuer. But keep your way, i' God's name; I have done.

Beat. You always end with a jade's trick; I know you of old.   146

42. **bird-bolt:** blunt arrow.   47. **meet:** even, quits.   58. **stuff'd man:** dummy.   69. **difference:** a distinguishing symbol in heraldry.   77. **block:** design (hat-mould).   82. **squarer:** quarreler.   103. **charge:** burden.   129. **dear happiness:** great good luck.   145. **jade's trick,** such as slipping its head out of the halter. Evasion.

D. Pedro. That is the sum of all, Leonato. Signior Claudio and Signior Benedick, my dear friend Leonato hath invited you all. I tell him we shall stay here at the least a month; and he heartily prays some occasion may detain us longer. I 151 dare swear he is no hypocrite, but prays from his heart.

Leon. If you swear, my lord, you shall not be forsworn. [*To Don John.*] Let me bid you wel- 155 come, my lord. Being reconciled to the Prince your brother, I owe you all duty.

D. John. I thank you. I am not of many words, but I thank you.

Leon. Please it your Grace lead on? 160

D. Pedro. Your hand, Leonato; we will go together. [*Exeunt all except Benedick and Claudio.*

Claud. Benedick, didst thou note the daughter of Signior Leonato?

Bene. I noted her not; but I look'd on her. 165

Claud. Is she not a modest young lady?

Bene. Do you question me, as an honest man should do, for my simple true judgement; or would you have me speak after my custom, as being a professed tyrant to their sex? 170

Claud. No; I pray thee speak in sober judgement.

Bene. Why, i' faith, methinks she's too low for a high praise, too brown for a fair praise and too little for a great praise; only this commendation I can 175 afford her, that were she other than she is, she were unhandsome; and being no other but as she is, I do not like her.

Claud. Thou thinkest I am in sport. I pray thee tell me truly how thou lik'st her. 180

Bene. Would you buy her, that you inquire after her?

Claud. Can the world buy such a jewel?

Bene. Yea, and a case to put it into. But speak you this with a sad brow, or do you play the 185 flouting Jack, to tell us Cupid is a good hare-finder and Vulcan a rare carpenter? Come, in what key shall a man take you, to go in the song.

Claud. In mine eye she is the sweetest lady that ever I look'd on. 190

Bene. I can see yet without spectacles and I see no such matter. There's her cousin, an she were not possess'd with a fury, exceeds her as much in beauty as the first of May doth the last of December. But I hope you have no intent to turn husband, have you? 196

Claud. I would scarce trust myself, though I had sworn the contrary, if Hero would be my wife.

Bene. Is't come to this? In faith, hath not the

world one man but he will wear his cap with 200 suspicion? Shall I never see a bachelor of threescore again? Go to, i' faith, an thou wilt needs thrust thy neck into a yoke, wear the print of it, and sigh away Sundays. Look! Don Pedro is returned to seek you. 205

Re-enter DON PEDRO.

D. Pedro. What secret hath held you here, that you followed not to Leonato's?

Bene. I would your Grace would constrain me to tell.

D. Pedro. I charge thee on thy allegiance. 210

Bene. You hear, Count Claudio. I can be secret as a dumb man; I would have you think so; but, on my allegiance, mark you this, on my allegiance. He is in love. With who? Now that is your Grace's part. Mark how short his answer is: — With Hero, Leonato's short daughter. 216

Claud. If this were so, so were it utt'red.

Bene. Like the old tale, my lord: "It is not so, nor 'twas not so, but, indeed, God forbid it should be so." 220

Claud. If my passion change not shortly, God forbid it should be otherwise.

D. Pedro. Amen, if you love her; for the lady is very well worthy.

Claud. You speak this to fetch me in, my lord.

D. Pedro. By my troth, I [speak] my thought. 226

Claud. And, in faith, my lord, I spoke mine.

Bene. And, by my two faiths and troths, my lord, I spoke mine.

Claud. That I love her, I feel. 230

D. Pedro. That she is worthy, I know.

Bene. That I neither feel how she should be loved nor know how she should be worthy, is the opinion that fire cannot melt out of me. I will die in it at the stake. 235

D. Pedro. Thou wast ever an obstinate heretic in the despite of beauty.

Claud. And never could maintain his part but in the force of his will. 239

Bene. That a woman conceived me, I thank her; that she brought me up, I likewise give her most humble thanks; but that I will have a recheat winded in my forehead, or hang my bugle in an invisible baldrick, all women shall pardon me. Because I will not do them the wrong to mistrust 245 any, I will do myself the right to trust none; and the fine is, for the which I may go the finer, I will live a bachelor.

D. Pedro. I shall see thee, ere I die, look pale with love. 250

---

156. **Being:** i.e., since you are. 185. **sad:** serious. 186. **flouting Jack:** mocker. 186-87. '**Cupid . . . carpenter.** Nonsense; for Cupid was blind and Vulcan was a blacksmith. 200. **wear . . . suspicion:** i.e., be suspected of wearing his cap to hide his cuckold's horns. 204. **Sundays,** which one spends with one's wife. 206. s.d. *Re-enter* DON PEDRO. *Enter Don Pedro, John the bastard.* Q Ff. 226. [speak] F. *spoke* Q. 237. **despite:** contempt. 242. **recheat:** a call "winded" on a horn to recall the hounds. 244. **baldrick:** belt carrying the horn. The passage is another joke upon the imaginary horns of the cuckold. 247. **fine:** end. **go the finer:** wear finer clothes.

Bene. With anger, with sickness, or with hunger, my lord, not with love.   Prove that ever I lose more blood with love than I will get again with drinking, pick out mine eyes with a ballad-maker's pen and hang me up at the door of a brothel-house for the sign of blind Cupid.   256

D. Pedro. Well, if ever thou dost fall from this faith, thou wilt prove a notable argument.

Bene. If I do, hang me in a bottle like a cat and shoot at me; and he that hits me, let him be clapp'd on the shoulder, and called Adam.   261

D. Pedro. Well, as time shall try. "In time the savage bull doth bear the yoke."

Bene. The savage bull may; but if ever the sensible Benedick bear it, pluck off the bull's horns 265 and set them in my forehead; and let me be vilely painted, and in such great letters as they write "Here is good horse to hire," let them signify under my sign, "Here you may see Benedick the married man."   270

Claud. If this should ever happen, thou wouldst be horn-mad.

D. Pedro. Nay, if Cupid have not spent all his quiver in Venice, thou wilt quake for this shortly.

Bene. I look for an earthquake too, then. 275

D. Pedro. Well, you will temporize with the hours.   In the meantime, good Signior Benedick, repair to Leonato's; commend me to him, and tell him I will not fail him at supper; for indeed he hath made great preparation.   280

Bene. I have almost matter enough in me for such an embassage; and so I commit you —

Claud. To the tuition of God.   From my house, if I had it, —

D. Pedro. The sixth of July.   Your loving friend, Benedick.   286

Bene. Nay, mock not, mock not.   The body of your discourse is sometime guarded with fragments, and the guards are but slightly basted on neither. Ere you flout old ends any further, examine your conscience; and so I leave you.   [*Exit.* 291

Claud. My liege, your Highness now may do me good.

D. Pedro. My love is thine to teach; teach it but how,
And thou shalt see how apt it is to learn
Any hard lesson that may do thee good.   295

Claud. Hath Leonato any son, my lord?

D. Pedro. No child but Hero; she's his only heir.
Dost thou affect her, Claudio?

Claud.   O, my lord,

When you went onward on this ended action,
I look'd upon her with a soldier's eye,   300
That lik'd, but had a rougher task in hand
Than to drive liking to the name of love.
But now I am return'd and that war-thoughts
Have left their places vacant, in their rooms
Come thronging soft and delicate desires,   305
All prompting me how fair young Hero is,
Saying, I lik'd her ere I went to wars.

D. Pedro. Thou wilt be like a lover presently
And tire the hearer with a book of words.
If thou dost love fair Hero, cherish it,   310
And I will break with her and with her father
And thou shalt have her.   Was 't not to this end
That thou began'st to twist so fine a story?

Claud. How sweetly you do minister to love,
That know love's grief by his complexion!   315
But lest my liking might too sudden seem,
I would have salv'd it with a longer treatise.

D. Pedro. What need the bridge much broader
    than the flood?
The fairest grant is the necessity.
Look, what will serve is fit: 'tis once, thou lovest,
And I will fit thee with the remedy.   321
I know we shall have revelling to-night.
I will assume thy part in some disguise
And tell fair Hero I am Claudio.
And in her bosom I'll unclasp my heart   325
And take her hearing prisoner with the force
And strong encounter of my amorous tale;
Then after to her father will I break;
And the conclusion is, she shall be thine.
In practice let us put it presently.   [*Exeunt.* 330

[Scene II. *A room in Leonato's house.*]

Enter LEONATO *and* ANTONIO, *meeting.*

Leon. How now, brother!   Where is my cousin, your son?   Hath he provided this music?

Ant. He is very busy about it.   But, brother, I can tell you strange news that you yet dreamt not of.   5

Leon. Are they good?

Ant. As the event stamps them; but they have a good cover, they show well outward.   The Prince and Count Claudio, walking in a thick-pleached alley in mine orchard, were thus much over- 10 heard by a man of mine.   The Prince discovered to Claudio that he loved my niece your daughter and meant to acknowledge it this night in a dance; and if he found her accordant, he meant to take the

252–54. I...drinking. It was believed that every sigh cost the heart a drop of blood and that wine generated blood. 259. bottle: wicker basket.   261. Adam: Adam Bell, an archer celebrated in ballads.   263. "In...yoke." Quoted inaccurately from Kyd's *Spanish Tragedy* (II.i.3).   274. Venice.   Then notorious for licentiousness.   276. temporize... hours: surrender eventually.   281. matter: sense.   283. tuition: protection.   288. guarded: trimmed.   298. affect: love. 311. break: open the subject.   319. The...necessity. The best gift is the one which is required.   320. 'tis once: briefly.
Sc. ii. s.d. *Enter Leonato and an old man brother to Leonato* Q.   Q heads Antonio's speeches *Old.*   1. cousin.   Used loosely for *relative.*   7. event: outcome.   9. pleached: with intertwined boughs.   14. accordant: agreeing.

present time by the top and instantly break with you of it.   16

Leon. Hath the fellow any wit that told you this?

Ant. A good sharp fellow. I will send for him; and question him yourself.   20

Leon. No, no; we will hold it as a dream till it appear itself; but I will acquaint my daughter withal, that she may be the better prepared for an answer, if peradventure this be true. Go you and tell her of it. [*Several persons cross the stage.*] Cousin, you know what you have to do. O, I cry 26 you mercy, friend; go you with me, and I will use your skill. Good cousin, have a care this busy time.
                                                [*Exeunt.*]

[SCENE III. *The same.*]

Enter JOHN *the Bastard and* CONRADE.

Con. What the good-year, my lord! Why are you thus out of measure sad?

D. John. There is no measure in the occasion that breeds; therefore the sadness is without limit.

Con. You should hear reason.   6

D. John. And when I have heard it, what blessing brings it?

Con. If not a present remedy, at least a patient sufferance.   10

D. John. I wonder that thou, being, as thou say'st thou art, born under Saturn, goest about to apply a moral medicine to a mortifying mischief. I cannot hide what I am. I must be sad when I have cause, and smile at no man's jests; eat 15 when I have stomach, and wait for no man's leisure; sleep when I am drowsy, and tend on no man's business; laugh when I am merry, and claw no man in his humour.   19

Con. Yea, but you must not make the full show of this till you may do it without controlment. You have of late stood out against your brother, and he hath ta'en you newly into his grace; where it is impossible you should take true root but by the fair weather that you make yourself. It is 25 needful that you frame the season for your own harvest.

D. John. I had rather be a canker in a hedge than a rose in his grace, and it better fits my blood to be disdain'd of all than to fashion a carriage 30 to rob love from any. In this, though I cannot be said to be a flattering honest man, it must not be denied but I am a plain-dealing villain. I am trusted with a muzzle and enfranchis'd with a clog; therefore I have decreed not to sing in my cage. 35

If I had my mouth, I would bite; if I had my liberty, I would do my liking. In the meantime let me be that I am and seek not to alter me.

Con. Can you make no use of your discontent?

D. John. I make all use of it, for I use it only. 41 Who comes here?

Enter BORACHIO.

What news, Borachio?

Bora. I came yonder from a great supper. The Prince your brother is royally entertained by Leonato; and I can give you intelligence of an intended marriage.   47

D. John. Will it serve for any model to build mischief on? What is he for a fool that betroths himself to unquietness?   50

Bora. Marry, it is your brother's right hand.

D. John. Who? The most exquisite Claudio?

Bora. Even he.

D. John. A proper squire! And who, and who? Which way looks he?   55

Bora. Marry, one Hero, the daughter and heir of Leonato.

D. John. A very forward March-chick! How came you to this?   59

Bora. Being entertain'd for a perfumer, as I was smoking a musty room, comes me the Prince and Claudio, hand in hand, in sad conference. I whipt me behind the arras, and there heard it agreed upon that the Prince should woo Hero for himself, and having obtain'd her, give her to Count 65 Claudio.

D. John. Come, come, let us thither; this may prove food to my displeasure. That young startup hath all the glory of my overthrow. If I can cross him any way, I bless myself every way. You are both sure, and will assist me?   71

Con. To the death, my lord.

D. John. Let us to the great supper; their cheer is the greater that I am subdued. Would the cook were o' my mind! Shall we go prove what's to be done?   76

Bora. We'll wait upon your lordship. [*Exeunt.*]

ACT II

[SCENE I. *A hall in Leonato's house.*]

Enter LEONATO, ANTONIO, HERO, BEATRICE, *and a kinsman.*

Leon. Was not Count John here at supper?

Ant. I saw him not.

15. **top:** forelock.   26. **cry you mercy:** beg pardon.
Sc. iii, 1. **What the good-year.** An expletive.   12. **Saturn.** Nativity under the domination of the planet Saturn was supposed to give one a morose disposition.   13. **mortifying mischief:** deadly disease.   18. **claw:** flatter.   28. **canker:** dogrose.   30. **carriage:** behavior.   54. **proper:** fine.   58. **March-chick:** chicken prematurely hatched.   60. **entertain'd for:** employed as.   61. **smoking:** fumigating.   70. **cross:** thwart (with quibbling reference to making the sign of the cross). 71. **sure:** trustworthy.

Act II, sc. i. s.d. Q and F read *Enter Leonato, his brother, his wife, Hero his daughter, and Beatrice his neece, and a kinsman.*

Beat. How tartly that gentleman looks! I never
can see him but I am heart-burn'd an hour after. 5

Hero. He is of a very melancholy disposition.

Beat. He were an excellent man that were made
just in the midway between him and Benedick.
The one is too like an image and says nothing, and
the other too like my lady's eldest son, evermore
tattling. 11

Leon. Then half Signior Benedick's tongue in
Count John's mouth and half Count John's melancholy in Signior Benedick's face, — 14

Beat. With a good leg and a good foot, uncle,
and money enough in his purse, such a man would
win any woman in the world, if 'a could get her
good-will.

Leon. By my troth, niece, thou wilt never get
thee a husband, if thou be so shrewd of thy tongue.

Ant. In faith, she's too curst. 22

Beat. Too curst is more than curst. I shall
lessen God's sending that way; for it is said, "God
sends a curst cow short horns;" but to a cow too
curst he sends none. 26

Leon. So, by being too curst, God will send you
no horns.

Beat. Just, if he send me no husband; for the
which blessing I am at him upon my knees every
morning and evening. Lord, I could not en- 30
dure a husband with a beard on his face! I had
rather lie in the woollen.

Leon. You may light on a husband that hath no
beard. 35

Beat. What should I do with him? Dress him
in my apparel and make him my waiting-gentlewoman? He that hath a beard is more than a
youth, and he that hath no beard is less than a man;
and he that is more than a youth is not for me, 40
and he that is less than a man, I am not for him;
therefore I will even take sixpence in earnest of the
bear-'ard, and lead his apes into hell.

Leon. Well, then, go you into hell? 44

Beat. No, but to the gate; and there will the
devil meet me, like an old cuckold, with horns on
his head, and say, "Get you to heaven, Beatrice,
get you to heaven; here's no place for you maids:"
so deliver I up my apes, and away to Saint Peter
for the heavens. He shows me where the bachelors
sit, and there live we as merry as the day is long. 52

Ant. [*To Hero.*] Well, niece, I trust you will be
rul'd by your father. 54

Beat. Yes, faith; it is my cousin's duty to make
curtsy and say, "[Father], as it please you." But

yet for all that, cousin, let him be a handsome fellow,
or else make another curtsy and say, "Father, as it
please me." 59

Leon. Well, niece, I hope to see you one day fitted
with a husband.

Beat. Not till God make men of some other
metal than earth. Would it not grieve a woman
to be overmaster'd with a piece of valiant dust? to
make an account of her life to a clod of way- 65
ward marl? No, uncle, I'll none. Adam's sons are
my brethren; and, truly, I hold it a sin to match in
my kindred.

Leon. Daughter, remember what I told you. If
the Prince do solicit you in that kind, you know
your answer. 71

Beat. The fault will be in the music, cousin, if
you be not woo'd in good time. If the Prince be too
important, tell him there is measure in every thing
and so dance out the answer. For, hear me, 75
Hero: wooing, wedding, and repenting, is as a
Scotch jig, a measure, and a cinque pace; the first
suit is hot and hasty, like a Scotch jig, and full as
fantastical; the wedding, mannerly-modest, as a
measure, full of state and anciently; and then 80
comes repentance and, with his bad legs, falls into
the cinque pace faster and faster, till he sink into
his grave.

Leon. Cousin, you apprehend passing shrewdly.

Beat. I have a good eye, uncle; I can see a church
by daylight. 86

Leon. The revellers are ent'ring, brother; make
good room. [*Antonio masks.*]

Enter DON PEDRO, CLAUDIO, BENEDICK, *and* BAL-
THASAR, [BORACHIO, MARGARET, URSULA, *and
others*], DON JOHN *masked; with a drum.*

D. Pedro. Lady, will you walk about with your
friend? 90

Hero. So you walk softly and look sweetly and
say nothing, I am yours for the walk; and especially
when I walk away.

D. Pedro. With me in your company?

Hero. I may say so when I please. 95

D. Pedro. And when please you to say so?

Hero. When I like your favour; for God defend
the lute should be like the case!

D. Pedro. My visor is Philemon's roof; within
the house is Jove. 100

Hero. Why, then, your visor should be thatch'd.

D. Pedro. Speak low, if you speak love.

 [*Drawing her aside.*]

10. **eldest son:** a spoiled child. 21. **shrewd:** shrewish, sharp. 22. **curst:** ill-tempered. 32. **lie ... woollen:** sleep between
blankets. 42. **earnest:** advance payment. 43. **lead ... hell.** The punishment for dying an old maid. 51. **bachelors:**
the unmarried of both sexes. 56. **[Father]** (Theobald). Om. QF. 66. **marl:** clay. 74. **important:** importunate. 77.
measure: slow dance. **cinque pace:** lively dance. 80. **ancientry:** antique style. 88. s.d. Q and F read *Enter Prince,
Pedro, Claudio, and Benedicke, and Balthasar, or dumbe John;* F adds *Maskers with a drum.* 89. **about.** Some modern
editors read *a bout.* 90. **friend:** lover. 97. **favour:** face. 99. **visor:** mask. **Philemon's roof.** Jupiter was once entertained *incognito* by the peasants, Baucis and Philemon.

[Balth.] Well, I would you did like me.

Marg. So would not I, for your own sake; 105
for I have many ill qualities.

[Balth.] Which is one?

Marg. I say my prayers aloud.

[Balth.] I love you the better; the hearers may
cry, Amen. 110

Marg. God match me with a good dancer!

[Balth.] Amen.

Marg. And God keep him out of my sight when
the dance is done! Answer, clerk.

Balth. No more words; the clerk is answered. 115

Urs. I know you well enough; you are Signior
Antonio.

Ant. At a word I am not.

Urs. I know you by the waggling of your head.

Ant. To tell you true, I counterfeit him. 121

Urs. You could never do him so ill-well, unless
you were the very man. Here's his dry hand up
and down. You are he, you are he.

Ant. At a word, I am not. 125

Urs. Come, come, do you think I do not know
you by your excellent wit? Can virtue hide itself? Go to, mum, you are he. Graces will appear,
and there's an end.

Beat. Will you not tell me who told you so? 130

Bene. No, you shall pardon me.

Beat. Nor will you not tell me who you are?

Bene. Not now.

Beat. That I was disdainful, and that I had my
good wit out of the "Hundred Merry Tales": —
well, this was Signior Benedick that said so. 136

Bene. What's he?

Beat. I am sure you know him well enough.

Bene. Not I, believe me.

Beat. Did he never make you laugh? 140

Bene. I pray you, what is he?

Beat. Why, he is the Prince's jester, a very dull
fool; only his gift is in devising impossible slanders.
None but libertines delight in him, and the commendation is not in his wit but in his villainy; 145
for he both pleases men and angers them, and then
they laugh at him and beat him. I am sure he is in
the fleet; I would he had boarded me.

Bene. When I know the gentleman, I'll tell him
what you say. 151

Beat. Do, do: he'll but break a comparison or
two on me; which, peradventure not mark'd or not
laugh'd at, strikes him into melancholy; and then
there's a partridge wing saved, for the fool will 155
eat no supper that night. [*Music.*] We must follow
the leaders.

Bene. In every good thing.

Beat. Nay, if they lead to any ill, I will leave
them at the next turning. 160

[*Dance. [Then] exeunt [all except Don John,
Borachio, and Claudio].*

D. John. Sure my brother is amorous on Hero
and hath withdrawn her father to break with him
about it. The ladies follow her and but one visor
remains.

Bora. And that is Claudio. I know him by his
bearing. 166

D. John. Are not you Signior Benedick?

Claud. You know me well; I am he.

D. John. Signior, you are very near my brother
in his love. He is enamour'd on Hero. I pray you,
dissuade him from her; she is no equal for his 171
birth. You may do the part of an honest man in it.

Claud. How know you he loves her?

D. John. I heard him swear his affection. 175

Bora. So did I too; and he swore he would marry
her to-night.

D. John. Come, let us to the banquet.

[*Exeunt Don John and Borachio.*

Claud. Thus answer I in name of Benedick,
But hear these ill news with the ears of Claudio. 180
'Tis certain so; the Prince wooes for himself.
Friendship is constant in all other things
Save in the office and affairs of love;
Therefore all hearts in love use their own tongues.
Let every eye negotiate for itself 185
And trust no agent; for beauty is a witch
Against whose charms faith melteth into blood.
This is an accident of hourly proof.
Which I mistrusted not. Farewell, therefore, Hero!

Re-enter BENEDICK.

Bene. Count Claudio? 190

Claud. Yea, the same.

Bene. Come, will you go with me?

Claud. Whither?

Bene. Even to the next willow, about your own
business, county. What fashion will you wear 195
the garland of? About your neck like an usurer's
chain, or under your arm like a lieutenant's scarf?
You must wear it one way, for the Prince hath got
your Hero.

Claud. I wish him joy of her. 200

Bene. Why, that's spoken like an honest drovier;
so they sell bullocks. But did you think the Prince
would have served you thus?

Claud. I pray you, leave me. 204

Bene. Ho! now you strike like the blind man.

104, 107, 109, 112. **[Balth.]** (Theobald). *Bene.* QFf. 114. **clerk.** The parish clerk read the responses in church. (Cf.
"Amen," ll. 110 and 112.) 122. **do . . . ill-well:** imitate his defects so well. 123. **dry hand.** A sign of age. 135.
"Hundred Merry Tales": a popular collection of coarse stories. 143. **only his gift:** his only talent. 148. **fleet:** i.e.,
company. **boarded:** accosted. 178. **banquet:** dessert. 187. **blood:** passion. 188. **accident:** happening. 194. **willow.**
Emblem of unrequited love.

'Twas the boy that stole your meat, and you'll beat the post.

Claud. If it will not be, I'll leave you.   [*Exit.*

Bene. Alas, poor hurt fowl! now will he creep into sedges. But that my Lady Beatrice should know me, and not know me! The Prince's 210 fool! Ha? It may be I go under that title because I am merry. Yea, but so I am apt to do myself wrong. I am not so reputed. It is the base (though bitter) disposition of Beatrice that puts the 215 world into her person, and so gives me out. Well, I'll be revenged as I may.

Re-enter DON PEDRO.

D. Pedro. Now, signior, where's the count? Did you see him?   219

Bene. Troth, my lord, I have played the part of Lady Fame. I found him here as melancholy as a lodge in a warren. I told him, and I think I told him true, that your Grace had got the good will of this young lady; and I off'red him my company to a willow-tree, either to make him a garland, as 225 being forsaken, or to bind him up a rod, as being worthy to be whipp'd.

D. Pedro. To be whipp'd! What's his fault?

Bene. The flat transgression of a school-boy, who, being overjoyed with finding a birds' nest, shows it his companion, and he steals it.   231

D. Pedro. Wilt thou make a trust a transgression? The transgression is in the stealer.

Bene. Yet it had not been amiss the rod had been made, and the garland too; for the garland he might have worn himself, and the rod he 236 might have bestowed on you, who, as I take it, have stol'n his birds' nest.

D. Pedro. I will but teach them to sing, and restore them to the owner.   240

Bene. If their singing answer your saying, by my faith, you say honestly.

D. Pedro. The Lady Beatrice hath a quarrel to you. The gentleman that danc'd with her told her she is much wrong'd by you.   245

Bene. O, she misus'd me past the endurance of a block! An oak but with one green leaf on it would have answered her. My very visor began to assume life and scold with her. She told me, not thinking I had been myself, that I was the 250 Prince's jester, that I was duller than a great thaw; huddling jest upon jest with such impossible conveyance upon me that I stood like a man at a mark, with a whole army shooting at me. She speaks poniards, and every word stabs. If her breath 255 were as terrible as her terminations, there were no living near her; she would infect to the north star. I would not marry her, though she were endowed with all that Adam had left him before he transgress'd. She would have made Hercules have 260 turn'd spit, yea, and have cleft his club to make the fire too. Come, talk not of her; you shall find her the infernal Ate in good apparel. I would to God some scholar would conjure her; for certainly while she is here, a man may live as quiet in hell as in 265 a sanctuary, and people sin upon purpose, because they would go thither; so, indeed, all disquiet, horror, and perturbation follows her.

Enter CLAUDIO, BEATRICE, HERO, *and* LEONATO.

D. Pedro. Look, here she comes.   270

Bene. Will your Grace command me any service to the world's end? I will go on the slightest errand now to the Antipodes that you can devise to send me on; I will fetch you a toothpicker now from the furthest inch of Asia, bring you the length of 275 Prester John's foot, fetch you a hair off the great Cham's beard, do you any embassage to the Pigmies, rather than hold three words' conference with this harpy. You have no employment for me? 280

D. Pedro. None, but to desire your good company.

Bene. O God, sir, here's a dish I love not. I cannot endure my Lady Tongue.   [*Exit.*

D. Pedro. Come, lady, come; you have lost the heart of Signior Benedick.   286

Beat. Indeed, my lord, he lent it me awhile; and I gave him use for it, a double heart for his single one. Marry, once before he won it of me with false dice, therefore your Grace may well say I have lost it.   291

D. Pedro. You have put him down, lady, you have put him down.

Beat. So I would not he should do me, my lord, lest I should prove the mother of fools. I have brought Count Claudio, whom you sent me to seek.   297

D. Pedro. Why, how now, count! wherefore are you sad?

Claud. Not sad, my lord.   300

D. Pedro. How then? Sick?

Claud. Neither, my lord.

Beat. The count is neither sad, nor sick, nor merry, nor well; but civil count, civil as an orange, and something of that jealous complexion.   306

D. Pedro. I' faith, lady, I think your blazon to be true; though, I'll be sworn, if he be so, his conceit

209. **sedges:** rushes.   213. **though.** Not satisfactorily explained.   221. **Fame:** Rumor.   222. **lodge in a warren:** keeper's house in a game preserve, presumably a solitary place.   252. **impossible conveyance:** incredible adroitness.   253. **mark:** target.   256. **terminations:** terms, words.   263. **Ate:** goddess of discord.   264. **conjure her:** i.e., conjure the evil spirit out of her.   276. **Prester John:** a mythical eastern king.   **the great Cham:** the Mongolian Khan.   288. **use:** interest.   304. **civil:** serious, with a pun on *Seville.*   306. **jealous complexion:** i.e., yellow, a conventional token of jealousy.   307. **blazon:** description.   308. **conceit:** idea.

is false. Here, Claudio, I have wooed in thy name, and fair Hero is won. I have broke with her father, and his good will obtained. Name the day of marriage, and God give thee joy!   312

Leon. Count, take of me my daughter, and with her fortunes. His Grace hath made the match, and all grace say Amen to it.   315

Beat. Speak, Count, 'tis your cue.

Claud. Silence is the perfectest herald of joy; I were but little happy, if I could say how much. Lady, as you are mine, I am yours. I give away myself for you and dote upon the exchange.   320

Beat. Speak, cousin; or, if you cannot, stop his mouth with a kiss, and let not him speak neither.

D. Pedro. In faith, lady, you have a merry heart.   325

Beat. Yea, my lord; I thank it, poor fool, it keeps on the windy side of care. My cousin tells him in his ear that he is in her heart.

Claud. And so she doth, cousin.   329

Beat. Good Lord, for alliance! Thus goes every one to the world but I, and I am sunburnt. I may sit in a corner and cry "Heigh-ho for a husband!"

D. Pedro. Lady Beatrice, I will get you one.

Beat. I would rather have one of your father's getting. Hath your Grace ne'er a brother like   335 you? Your father got excellent husbands, if a maid could come by them.

D. Pedro. Will you have me, lady?

Beat. No, my lord, unless I might have an-   340 other for working-days. Your Grace is too costly to wear every day. But, I beseech your Grace, pardon me; I was born to speak all mirth and no matter.   344

D. Pedro. Your silence most offends me, and to be merry best becomes you; for, out o' question, you were born in a merry hour.

Beat. No, sure, my lord, my mother cried; but then there was a star danc'd, and under that was I born. Cousins, God give you joy!   350

Leon. Niece, will you look to those things I told you of?

Beat. I cry you mercy, uncle. By your Grace's pardon.   [*Exit.*

D. Pedro. By my troth, a pleasant-spirited lady.   356

Leon. There's little of the melancholy element in her, my lord. She is never sad but when she sleeps, and not ever sad then; for I have heard my daughter say, she hath often dreamt of unhappiness and wak'd herself with laughing.   361

D. Pedro. She cannot endure to hear tell of a husband.

Leon. O, by no means; she mocks all her wooers out of suit.   365

D. Pedro. She were an excellent wife for Benedick.

Leon. O Lord, my lord, if they were but a week married, they would talk themselves mad.

D. Pedro. County Claudio, when mean you to go to church?   371

Claud. To-morrow, my lord. Time goes on crutches till love have all his rites.

Leon. Not till Monday, my dear son, which is hence a just seven-night; and a time too brief, too, to have all things answer my mind.   376

D. Pedro. Come, you shake the head at so long a breathing; but, I warrant thee, Claudio, the time shall not go dully by us. I will in the interim under-take one of Hercules' labours; which is, to   380 bring Signior Benedick and the Lady Beatrice into a mountain of affection the one with the other. I would fain have it a match, and I doubt not but to fashion it, if you three will but minister such assist-ance as I shall give you direction.   386

Leon. My lord, I am for you, though it cost me ten nights' watchings.

Claud. And I, my lord.

D. Pedro. And you too, gentle Hero?

Hero. I will do any modest office, my lord, to help my cousin to a good husband.   391

D. Pedro. And Benedick is not the unhopefullest husband that I know. Thus far can I praise him: he is of a noble strain, of approved valour, and confirm'd honesty. I will teach you how to   395 humour your cousin, that she shall fall in love with Benedick; and I, with your two helps, will so practise on Benedick that, in despite of his quick wit and his queasy stomach, he shall fall in love with Beatrice. If we can do this, Cupid is no   400 longer an archer. His glory shall be ours, for we are the only love-gods. Go in with me, and I will tell you my drift.   [*Exeunt.*

[SCENE II. *The same.*]

Enter [DON] JOHN *and* BORACHIO.

D. John. It is so; the Count Claudio shall marry the daughter of Leonato.

Bora. Yea, my lord; but I can cross it.

D. John. Any bar, any cross, any impediment will be med'cinable to me. I am sick in displeas-   5 ure to him, and whatsoever comes athwart his af-

---

327. **windy:** windward (i.e., safe). 330–31. **goes … world:** i.e., gets married. 331. **sunburnt:** i.e., unattractive. 332–33. **"Heigh-ho … husband."** The title of a ballad. 359. **ever:** always. It has been suggested to emend to *even*. 378. **breath-ing:** waiting. 388. **watchings:** i.e., lying awake. 394. **strain:** lineage. **approved:** tested. 399. **queasy stomach:** squeam-ishness. 403. **drift:** scheme.

fection ranges evenly with mine. How canst thou cross this marriage?

Bora. Not honestly, my lord; but so covertly that no dishonesty shall appear in me.   10

D. John. Show me briefly how.

Bora. I think I told your lordship a year since, how much I am in the favour of Margaret, the waiting gentlewoman to Hero.

D. John. I remember.   15

Bora. I can, at any unseasonable instant of the night, appoint her to look out at her lady's chamber-window.

D. John. What life is in that, to be the death of this marriage?   20

Bora. The poison of that lies in you to temper. Go you to the Prince your brother; spare not to tell him that he hath wronged his honour in marrying the renowned Claudio — whose estimation do you mightily hold up — to a contaminated stale, such a one as Hero.   26

D. John. What proof shall I make of that?

Bora. Proof enough to misuse the Prince, to vex Claudio, to undo Hero, and kill Leonato. Look you for any other issue?   30

D. John. Only to despite them, I will endeavour anything.

Bora. Go, then; find me a meet hour to draw Don Pedro and the Count Claudio alone; tell them that you know that Hero loves me; intend a   35 kind of zeal both to the Prince and Claudio, as, — in love of your brother's honour, who hath made this match, and his friend's reputation, who is thus like to be cozen'd with the semblance of a maid, — that you have discover'd thus. They will   40 scarcely believe this without trial. Offer them instances; which shall bear no less likelihood than to see me at her chamber-window, hear me call Margaret Hero, hear Margaret term me Claudio; and bring them to see this the very night before   45 the intended wedding, — for in the meantime I will so fashion the matter that Hero shall be absent, — and there shall appear such seeming truth of Hero's disloyalty, that jealousy shall be call'd assurance and all the preparation overthrown.   51

D. John. Grow this to what adverse issue it can, I will put it in practice. Be cunning in the working this, and thy fee is a thousand ducats.

Bora. Be you constant in the accusation, and my cunning shall not shame me.   56

D. John. I will presently go learn their day of marriage.

[*Exeunt.*

[SCENE III. *Leonato's orchard.*]

Enter BENEDICK *alone.*

Bene. Boy!

[*Enter* BOY.]

Boy. Signior?

Bene. In my chamber-window lies a book; bring it hither to me in the orchard.

Boy. I am here already, sir.   [*Exit.*   5

Bene. I know that; but I would have thee hence, and here again. I do much wonder that one man, seeing how much another man is a fool when he dedicates his behaviours to love, will, after he hath laugh'd at such shallow follies in others, become   10 the argument of his own scorn by falling in love; and such a man is Claudio. I have known when there was no music with him but the drum and the fife; and now had he rather hear the tabor and the pipe. I have known when he would have   15 walk'd ten mile a-foot to see a good armour; and now will he lie ten nights awake, carving the fashion of a new doublet. He was wont to speak plain and to the purpose, like an honest man and a soldier; and now is he turn'd orthography; his   20 words are a very fantastical banquet, just so many strange dishes. May I be so converted and see with these eyes? I cannot tell; I think not. I will not be sworn but love may transform me to an oyster; but I'll take my oath on it, till he have   26 made an oyster of me, he shall never make me such a fool. One woman is fair, yet I am well; another is wise, yet I am well; another virtuous, yet I am well; but till all graces be in one woman, one   30 woman shall not come in my grace. Rich she shall be, that's certain; wise, or I'll none; virtuous, or I'll never cheapen her; fair, or I'll never look on her; mild, or come not near me; noble, or not I for an angel; of good discourse, an excellent mu-   35 sician, and her hair shall be of what colour it please God. Ha! the Prince and Monsieur Love! I will hide me in the arbour.   [*Withdraws.*

Enter DON PEDRO, CLAUDIO, *and* LEONATO. *Music* [*within*].

D. Pedro. Come, shall we hear this music?

Claud. Yea, my good lord. How still the evening is,   40 As hush'd on purpose to grace harmony!

D. Pedro. See you where Benedick hath hid himself?

Claud. O, very well, my lord. The music ended, We'll fit the kid-fox with a pennyworth.

Sc. ii, 21. **temper:** mix. 25. **stale:** harlot. 35. **intend:** pretend. 39. **cozen'd:** cheated. 41. **instances:** proofs. 44. **hear … Claudio.** See Introduction. Some edd. read *Borachio* for *Claudio.* 50. **jealousy:** suspicion.

Sc. iii, 14. **tabor:** small drum. 17. **carving:** planning. 20. **turn'd orthography:** i.e., become a faddist in language. 33. **cheapen:** ask the price of. 34–5. **noble … angel.** Both words, names of coins (worth 6s.8d. and 10s. respectively), are used punningly. 39. s.d. *Music* [*within*]. *Musicke* Q; *and Iacke Wilson* Ff. See Introduction.

Enter BALTHASAR *with music.*

D. Pedro. Come, Balthasar, we'll hear that song
again.   45
Balth. O, good my lord, tax not so bad a voice
To slander music any more than once.
D. Pedro. It is the witness still of excellency
To put a strange face on his own perfection.
I pray thee, sing, and let me woo no more.   50
Balth. Because you talk of wooing, I will sing;
Since many a wooer doth commence his suit
To her he thinks not worthy, yet he wooes,
Yet will he swear he loves.
D. Pedro.   Now, pray thee, come;
Or, if thou wilt hold longer argument,   55
Do it in notes.
Balth.   Note this before my notes;
There's not a note of mine that's worth the noting.
D. Pedro. Why, these are very crotchets that he
speaks;
Note, notes, forsooth, and nothing.   [*Air.*]
Bene. Now, divine air! now is his soul rav-   60
ish'd! Is it not strange that sheeps' guts should
hale souls out of men's bodies? Well, a horn for
my money, when all's done.

THE SONG

[*Balth.*] Sigh no more, ladies, sigh no more,
        Men were deceivers ever,   65
    One foot in sea and one on shore,
        To one thing constant never.
    Then sigh not so, but let them go,
        And be you blithe and bonny,
    Converting all your sounds of woe   70
        Into Hey nonny nonny.

    Sing no more ditties, sing no moe,
        Of dumps so dull and heavy;
    The fraud of men was ever so,
        Since summer first was leafy.   75
        Then sigh not so, etc.

D. Pedro. By my troth, a good song.
Balth. And an ill singer, my lord.
D. Pedro. Ha, no, no, faith; thou sing'st well
enough for a shift.   80
Bene. An he had been a dog that should have
howl'd thus, they would have hang'd him; and
I pray God his bad voice bode no mischief. I had
as lief have heard the night-raven, come what
plague could have come after it.   85
D. Pedro. Yea, marry; dost thou hear, Balthasar?
I pray thee, get us some excellent music; for to-
morrow night we would have it at the Lady Hero's
chamber-window.

Balth. The best I can, my lord.   90
                                        [*Exit Balthasar.*
D. Pedro. Do so; farewell. Come hither, Leonato. What was it you told me of to-day, that
your niece Beatrice was in love with Signior Benedick?
Claud. [*Aside.*] O, ay, stalk on, stalk on; the   95
fowl sits. — I did never think that lady would
have loved any man.
Leon. No, nor I neither; but most wonderful
that she should so dote on Signior Benedick, whom
she hath in all outward behaviours seemed ever
to abhor.   101
Bene. Is't possible? Sits the wind in that
corner?
Leon. By my troth, my lord, I cannot tell what
to think of it but that she loves him with an en-   105
raged affection. It is past the infinite of
thought.
D. Pedro. May be she doth but counterfeit.
Claud. Faith, like enough.
Leon. O God, counterfeit! There was never
counterfeit of passion came so near the life of passion as she discovers it.   111
D. Pedro. Why, what effects of passion shows
she?
Claud. [*Aside.*] Bait the hook well; this fish will
bite.
Leon. What effects, my lord? She will sit   115
you, — you heard my daughter tell you how.
Claud. She did, indeed.
D. Pedro. How, how, I pray you? You amaze
me; I would have thought her spirit had been in-
vincible against all assaults of affection.   120
Leon. I would have sworn it had, my lord; es-
pecially against Benedick.
Bene. I should think this a gull, but that the
white-bearded fellow speaks it. Knavery cannot,
sure, hide himself in such reverence.   125
Claud. [*Aside.*] He hath ta'en th' infection.
Hold it up.
D. Pedro. Hath she made her affection known to
Benedick?
Leon. No; and swears she never will. That's
her torment.   130
Claud. 'Tis true, indeed; so your daughter says.
"Shall I," says she, "that have so oft encount'red
him with scorn, write to him that I love him?"
Leon. This says she now when she is begin-   135
ning to write to him; for she'll be up twenty times a
night, and there will she sit in her smock till she
have writ a sheet of paper. My daughter tells us
all.   139
Claud. Now you talk of a sheet of paper, I remember a pretty jest your daughter told [us of].

58. **crotchets:** (1) whims, (2) musical notes. 59. **nothing:** i.e., with a pun on *noting* (l. 57). 80. **shift:** makeshift. 105. **enraged:** violent. 111. **discovers:** shows. 123. **gull:** trick. 127. **Hold:** keep. 141. **[us of]** F. *of us* Q.

Leon. O, when she had writ it and was reading it over, she found Benedick and Beatrice between the sheet?

Claud. That.   145

Leon. O, she tore the letter into a thousand half-pence; railed at herself, that she should be so immodest to write to one that she knew would flout her. "I measure him," says she, "by my own spirit; for I should flout him, if he writ to me; yea, though I love him, I should."   151

Claud. Then down upon her knees she falls, weeps, sobs, beats her heart, tears her hair, prays, curses; "O sweet Benedick! God give me patience!"   155

Leon. She doth indeed, my daughter says so; and the ecstasy hath so much overborne her that my daughter is sometime afeard she will do a desperate outrage to herself. It is very true.

D. Pedro. It were good that Benedick knew of it by some other, if she will not discover it.   161

Claud. To what end? He would make but a sport of it and torment the poor lady worse.

D. Pedro. An he should, it were an alms to hang him. She's an excellent sweet lady; and, out of all suspicion, she is virtuous.   166

Claud. And she is exceeding wise.

D. Pedro. In every thing but in loving Benedick.

Leon. O, my lord, wisdom and blood com- 170 bating in so tender a body, we have ten proofs to one that blood hath the victory. I am sorry for her, as I have just cause, being her uncle and her guardian.   174

D. Pedro. I would she had bestowed this dotage on me; I would have daff'd all other respects and made her half myself. I pray you, tell Benedick of it, and hear what 'a will say.

Leon. Were it good, think you?   179

Claud. Hero thinks surely she will die; for she says she will die, if he love her not, and she will die, ere she make her love known, and she will die, if he woo her, rather than she will bate one breath of her accustomed crossness.   184

D. Pedro. She doth well. If she should make tender of her love, 'tis very possible he'll scorn it; for the man, as you know all, hath a contemptible spirit.

Claud. He is a very proper man.

D. Pedro. He hath indeed a good outward happiness.   191

Claud. Before God! and, in my mind, very wise.

D. Pedro. He doth indeed show some sparks that are like wit.

Claud. And I take him to be valiant.   195

D. Pedro. As Hector, I assure you; and in the managing of quarrels you may say he is wise, for either he avoids them with great discretion, or undertakes them with a most Christian-like fear.   200

Leon. If he do fear God, 'a must necessarily keep peace. If he break the peace, he ought to enter into a quarrel with fear and trembling.

D. Pedro. And so will he do; for the man doth fear God, howsoever it seems not in him by some large jests he will make. Well, I am sorry for 206 your niece. Shall we go seek Benedick, and tell him of her love?

Claud. Never tell him, my lord. Let her wear it out with good counsel.   210

Leon. Nay, that's impossible; she may wear her heart out first.

D. Pedro. Well, we will hear further of it by your daughter. Let it cool the while. I love Benedick well; and I could wish he would modestly 215 examine himself, to see how much he is unworthy so good a lady.

Leon. My lord, will you walk? Dinner is ready.

Claud. [*Aside.*] If he do not dote on her upon this, I will never trust my expectation.   220

D. Pedro. [*Aside.*] Let there be the same net spread for her; and that must your daughter and her gentlewomen carry. The sport will be, when they hold one an opinion of another's dotage, and no such matter; that's the scene that I would 225 see, which will be merely a dumb-show. Let us send her to call him in to dinner.

[*Exeunt* [*Don Pedro, Claudio, and Leonato*].

Bene. [*Coming forward.*] This can be no trick; the conference was sadly borne. They have the truth of this from Hero. They seem to 230 pity the lady; it seems her affections have their full bent. Love me! why, it must be requited. I hear how I am censur'd. They say I will bear myself proudly, if I perceive the love come from her; they say too that she will rather die than give any 235 sign of affection. I did never think to marry. I must not seem proud. Happy are they that hear their detractions and can put them to mending. They say the lady is fair; 'tis a truth, I can bear them witness; and virtuous; 'tis so, I cannot 240 reprove it; and wise, but for loving me; by my troth, it is no addition to her wit, nor no great argument of her folly, for I will be horribly in love with her. I may chance have some odd quirks and remnants of wit broken on me, because 245 I have rail'd so long against marriage; but doth not the appetite alter? A man loves the meat in his youth that he cannot endure in his age. Shall quips and sentences and these paper bullets of the brain awe a man from the career of his humour?

157. **ecstasy:** madness. 164. **an alms:** charity. 165. **out of:** beyond. 176. **daff'd:** waived. 186. **tender:** offer. 187. **contemptible:** contemptuous. 206. **large:** coarse. 225. **no such matter:** there's nothing in it. 229. **sadly borne:** gravely conducted. 241. **reprove:** disprove. 248. **sentences:** maxims. 249. **career...humour:** course of his inclination.

No, the world must be peopled. When I said 250
I would die a bachelor, I did not think I should live
till I were married. Here comes Beatrice. By
this day! she's a fair lady. I do spy some marks of
love in her. 255

Enter BEATRICE.

Beat. Against my will I am sent to bid you come
in to dinner.

Bene. Fair Beatrice, I thank you for your pains.

Beat. I took no more pains for those thanks
than you take pains to thank me. If it had been
painful, I would not have come. 261

Bene. You take pleasure then in the message?

Beat. Yea, just so much as you may take upon
a knife's point and choke a daw withal. You have
no stomach, signior? Fare you well. [*Exit.* 265

Bene. Ha! "Against my will I am sent to bid
you come in to dinner;" there's a double meaning
in that. "I took no more pains for those thanks
than you took pains to thank me;" that's as much
as to say, "Any pains that I take for you is as 270
easy as thanks." If I do not take pity of her, I am
a villain; if I do not love her, I am a Jew. I will
go get her picture. [*Exit.*

ACT III

[SCENE I. *Leonato's garden.*]

Enter HERO *and two Gentlewomen,* MARGARET *and*
URSULA.

Hero. Good Margaret, run thee to the parlour.
There shalt thou find my cousin Beatrice
Proposing with the Prince and Claudio.
Whisper her ear and tell her, I and Ursula
Walk in the orchard and our whole discourse 5
Is all of her. Say that thou overheard'st us,
And bid her steal into the pleached bower,
Where honeysuckles, ripened by the sun,
Forbid the sun to enter, like favourites 9
Made proud by princes, that advance their pride
Against that power that bred it. There will she
hide her,
To listen our propose. This is thy office;
Bear thee well in it and leave us alone.

Marg. I'll make her come, I warrant you, presently. [*Exit.*]

Hero. Now, Ursula, when Beatrice doth come,
As we do trace this alley up and down, 16
Our talk must only be of Benedick.
When I do name him, let it be thy part
To praise him more than ever man did merit.

My talk to thee must be how Benedick 20
Is sick in love with Beatrice. Of this matter
Is little Cupid's crafty arrow made,
That only wounds by hearsay. Now begin;

Enter BEATRICE [*behind*].

For look where Beatrice, like a lapwing, runs
Close by the ground, to hear our conference. 25

Urs. The pleasant'st angling is to see the fish
Cut with her golden oars the silver stream,
And greedily devour the treacherous bait.
So angle we for Beatrice, who even now
Is couched in the woodbine coverture. 30
Fear you not my part of the dialogue.

Hero. Then go we near her, that her ear lose
nothing
Of the false sweet bait that we lay for it.
[*Approaching the bower.*]
No, truly, Ursula, she is too disdainful.
I know her spirits are as coy and wild 35
As haggards of the rock.

Urs.   But are you sure
That Benedick loves Beatrice so entirely?

Hero. So says the Prince and my new-trothed
lord.

Urs. And did they bid you tell her of it, madam?

Hero. They did entreat me to acquaint her of it;
But I persuaded them, if they lov'd Benedick, 41
To wish him wrestle with affection,
And never to let Beatrice know of it.

Urs. Why did you so? Doth not the gentleman
Deserve as full as fortunate a bed
As ever Beatrice shall couch upon? 45

Hero. O god of love! I know he doth deserve
As much as may be yielded to a man;
But Nature never fram'd a woman's heart
Of prouder stuff than that of Beatrice.
Disdain and scorn ride sparkling in her eyes, 50
Misprising what they look on, and her wit
Values itself so highly that to her
All matter else seems weak. She cannot love,
Nor take no shape nor project of affection, 55
She is so self-endeared.

Urs.   Sure, I think so;
And therefore certainly it were not good
She knew his love, lest she'll make sport at it.

Hero. Why, you speak truth. I never yet saw
man, 59
How wise, how noble, young, how rarely featur'd,
But she would spell him backward. If fair-fac'd,
She would swear the gentleman should be her sister;
If black, why, Nature, drawing of an antic,
Made a foul blot; if tall, a lance ill-headed;
If low, an agate very vilely cut; 65

Act III, sc. i, 3. **proposing:** conversing. 36. **haggards:** untamed female hawks. 52. **misprising:** undervaluing. 55. **project:** idea. 61. **spell him backward:** i.e., say the reverse of him. 63. **black:** dark. **antic:** grotesque figure. 65. **agate:** tiny figure (cut in agate-stone).

If speaking, why, a vane blown with all winds;
If silent, why, a block moved with none.
So turns she every man the wrong side out,
And never gives to truth and virtue that
Which simpleness and merit purchaseth.   70
  Urs. Sure, sure, such carping is not commend-
able.
  Hero. No, not to be so odd and from all fashions
As Beatrice is, cannot be commendable.
But who dare tell her so? If I should speak,
She would mock me into air; O, she would laugh me
Out of myself, press me to death with wit.   76
Therefore let Benedick, like cover'd fire,
Consume away in sighs, waste inwardly.
It were a better death than die with mocks,
Which is as bad as die with tickling.   80
  Urs. Yet tell her of it; hear what she will say.
  Hero. No; rather I will go to Benedick
And counsel him to fight against his passion;
And, truly, I'll devise some honest slanders
To stain my cousin with. One doth not know   85
How much an ill word may empoison liking.
  Urs. O, do not do your cousin such a wrong.
She cannot be so much without true judgement —
Having so swift and excellent a wit
As she is priz'd to have — as to refuse   90
So rare a gentleman as Signior Benedick.
  Hero. He is the only man of Italy,
Always excepted my dear Claudio.
  Urs. I pray you, be not angry with me, madam,
Speaking my fancy; Signior Benedick,   95
For shape, for bearing, argument, and valour,
Goes foremost in report through Italy.
  Hero. Indeed, he hath an excellent good name.
  Urs. His excellence did earn it, ere he had it.
When are you married, madam?   100
  Hero. Why, every day, to-morrow. Come, go in;
I'll show thee some attires, and have thy counsel
Which is the best to furnish me to-morrow.
  Urs. [*Aside.*] She's lim'd, I warrant you. We've
caught her, madam.
  Hero. [*Aside.*] If it proves so, then loving goes
by haps.   105
Some Cupid kills with arrows, some with traps.
                    [*Exeunt [Hero and Ursula].*
  Beat. [*Coming forward.*] What fire is in mine ears?
Can this be true?
  Stand I condemn'd for pride and scorn so much?
Contempt, farewell! and maiden pride, adieu!
  No glory lives behind the back of such.   110
And, Benedick, love on; I will requite thee,
  Taming my wild heart to thy loving hand.
If thou dost love, my kindness shall incite thee
  To bind our loves up in a holy band;

For others say thou dost deserve, and I   115
Believe it better than reportingly.   [*Exit.*

[SCENE II. *A room in Leonato's house.*]

Enter DON PEDRO, CLAUDIO, BENEDICK, *and*
LEONATO.

  D. Pedro. I do but stay till your marriage be
consummate, and then go I toward Arragon.
  Claud. I'll bring you thither, my lord, if you'll
vouchsafe me.
  D. Pedro. Nay, that would be as great a soil   5
in the new gloss of your marriage as to show a child
his new coat and forbid him to wear it. I will only
be bold with Benedick for his company; for, from
the crown of his head to the sole of his foot, he is all
mirth. He hath twice or thrice cut Cupid's   10
bowstring, and the little hangman dare not shoot
at him. He hath a heart as sound as a bell and his
tongue is the clapper, for what his heart thinks his
tongue speaks.
  Bene. Gallants, I am not as I have been.   15
  Leon. So say I; methinks you are sadder.
  Claud. I hope he be in love.
  D. Pedro. Hang him, truant! There's no true
drop of blood in him, to be truly touch'd with love.
If he be sad, he wants money.   20
  Bene. I have the toothache.
  D. Pedro. Draw it.
  Bene. Hang it!
  Claud. You must hang it first, and draw it after-
wards.   25
  D. Pedro. What! sigh for the toothache?
  Leon. Where is but a humour or a worm.
  Bene. Well, every one [can] master a grief but
he that has it.
  Claud. Yet say I, he is in love.   30
  D. Pedro. There is no appearance of fancy in
him, unless it be a fancy that he hath to strange
disguises; as, to be a Dutchman to-day, a Frenchman to-morrow, or in the shape of two countries
at once, as, a German from the waist downward,   35
all slops, and a Spaniard from the hip upward,
no doublet. Unless he have a fancy to this foolery,
as it appears he hath, he is no fool for fancy, as you
would have it appear he is.   39
  Claud. If he be not in love with some woman,
there is no believing old signs. 'A brushes his hat
o' mornings; what should that bode?
  D. Pedro. Hath any man seen him at the barber's?
  Claud. No, but the barber's man hath been   45
seen with him, and the old ornament of his cheek
hath already stuffed tennis-balls.

---

84. **honest:** harmless.   96. **argument:** intelligence.   104. **lim'd:** caught (as by bird-lime).   105. **haps:** chance.   110.
No...such: i.e., such persons are not well spoken of when absent.
  Sc. ii, 28. **[can]** (Pope). *cannot* QF.   31. **fancy:** love.   35. **slops:** loose breeches.

Leon. Indeed, he looks younger than he did, by the loss of a beard.

D. Pedro. Nay, 'a rubs himself with civet. Can you smell him out by that?   51

Claud. That's as much as to say, the sweet youth 's in love.

[*D. Pedro.*] The greatest note of it is his melancholy.   55

Claud. And when was he wont to wash his face?

D. Pedro. Yea, or to paint himself? For the which, I hear what they say of him.   59

Claud. Nay, but his jesting spirit; which is now crept into a lute-string and now govern'd by stops.

D. Pedro. Indeed, that tells a heavy tale for him. Conclude, conclude he is in love.

Claud. Nay, but I know who loves him.   65

D. Pedro. That would I know too. I warrant, one that knows him not.

Claud. Yes, and his ill conditions; and, in despite of all, dies for him.

D. Pedro. She shall be buried with her face upwards.   71

Bene. Yet is this no charm for the toothache. Old signior, walk aside with me; I have studied eight or nine wise words to speak to you, which these hobby-horses must not hear.   75

[*Exeunt Benedick and Leonato.*]

D. Pedro. For my life, to break with him about Beatrice.

Claud. 'Tis even so. Hero and Margaret have by this played their parts with Beatrice; and then the two bears will not bite one another when they meet.   81

Enter JOHN *the Bastard.*

D. John. My lord and brother, God save you!

D. Pedro. Good den, brother.

D. John. If your leisure serv'd, I would speak with you.   85

D. Pedro. In private?

D. John. If it please you; yet Count Claudio may hear, for what I would speak of concerns him.

D. Pedro. What's the matter?   90

D. John. [*To Claudio.*] Means your lordship to be married to-morrow?

D. Pedro. You know he does.

D. John. I know not that, when he knows what I know.   95

Claud. If there be any impediment, I pray you discover it.

D. John. You may think I love you not; let that appear hereafter, and aim better at me by that I

now will manifest. For my brother, I think he   100 holds you well, and in dearness of heart hath holp to effect your ensuing marriage; — surely suit ill spent and labour ill bestowed.

D. Pedro. Why, what's the matter?

D. John. I came hither to tell you; and, cir-   105 cumstances short'ned, for she has been too long a talking of, the lady is disloyal.

Claud. Who? Hero?

D. John. Even she; Leonato's Hero, your Hero, every man's Hero.   110

Claud. Disloyal?

D. John. The word is too good to paint out her wickedness. I could say she were worse; think you of a worse title, and I will fit her to it. Wonder not till further warrant. Go but with me to-night;   115 you shall see her chamber-window ent'red, even the night before her wedding-day. If you love her then, to-morrow wed her; but it would better fit your honour to change your mind.

Claud. May this be so?   120

D. Pedro. I will not think it.

D. John. If you dare not trust that you see, confess not that you know. If you will follow me, I will show you enough; and when you have seen more and heard more, proceed accordingly.   125

Claud. If I see anything to-night why I should not marry her to-morrow, in the congregation, where I should wed, there will I shame her.

D. Pedro. And, as I wooed for thee to obtain her, I will join with thee to disgrace her.   130

D. John. I will disparage her no farther till you are my witnesses. Bear it coldly but till midnight, and let the issue show itself.

D. Pedro. O day untowardly turned!

Claud. O mischief strangely thwarting!   135

D. John. O plague right well prevented! So will you say when you have seen the sequel.

[*Exeunt.*

[SCENE III. *A street.*]

Enter DOGBERRY *and his compartner* [VERGES] *with the* WATCH.

Dog. Are you good men and true?

Verg. Yea, or else it were pity but they should suffer salvation, body and soul.

Dog. Nay, that were a punishment too good for them, if they should have any allegiance in them, being chosen for the Prince's watch.   6

Verg. Well, give them their charge, neighbour Dogberry.

---

50. **civet:** perfume (from the civet cat). 54. [*Don Pedro*] F. *Bene.* Q. 61. **stops:** fingerings (of a stringed instrument). 68. **conditions:** qualities. 69–71. **dies . . . upwards.** I.e., Beatrice will die because of Benedick, not by taking her own life. Suicides were often buried face downwards. 75. **hobby-horses:** buffoons. 78. **Margaret.** Mistake for *Ursula*. 90. Some editors plausibly give this line to Claudio. 99. **aim . . . at:** judge better of.

Sc. iii, 3. **salvation:** blunder for *damnation*, the first of Dogberry's many malapropisms.

Dog. First, who think you the most desertless man to be constable?   10

1. Watch. Hugh Oatcake, sir, or George Seacole; for they can write and read.

Dog. Come hither, neighbour Seacole. God hath bless'd you with a good name. To be a well-favoured man is the gift of fortune, but to write and read comes by nature.   16

2. Watch. Both which, master constable, —

Dog. You have: I knew it would be your answer. Well, for your favour, sir, why, give God thanks, and make no boast of it; and for your writing   20 and reading, let that appear when there is no need of such vanity. You are thought here to be the most senseless and fit man for the constable of the watch; therefore bear you the lantern. This is your charge: you shall comprehend all vagrom men; you are   25 to bid any man stand, in the Prince's name.

2. Watch. How if 'a will not stand?

Dog. Why, then, take no note of him, but let him go; and presently call the rest of the watch together, and thank God you are rid of a knave.   31

Verg. If he will not stand when he is bidden, he is none of the Prince's subjects.

Dog. True, and they are to meddle with none but the Prince's subjects. You shall also make   35 no noise in the streets; for for the watch to babble and to talk is most tolerable and not to be endured.

[2.] Watch. We will rather sleep than talk; we know what belongs to a watch.   40

Dog. Why, you speak like an ancient and most quiet watchman, for I cannot see how sleeping should offend; only, have a care that your bills be not stol'n. Well, you are to call at all the alehouses, and bid those that are drunk get them to bed.   46

[2.] Watch. How if they will not?

Dog. Why, then, let them alone till they are sober. If they make you not then the better answer, you may say they are not the men you took them for.   51

[2.] Watch. Well, sir.

Dog. If you meet a thief, you may suspect him, by virtue of your office, to be no true man; and, for such kind of men, the less you meddle or make with them, why, the more is for your honesty.   56

[2.] Watch. If we know him to be a thief, shall we not lay hands on him?

Dog. Truly, by your office, you may; but I think they that touch pitch will be defil'd. The   60 most peaceable way for you, if you do take a thief, is to let him show himself what he is and steal out of your company.

Verg. You have been always called a merciful man, partner.   65

Dog. Truly, I would not hang a dog by my will, much more a man who hath any honesty in him.

Verg. If you hear a child cry in the night, you must call to the nurse and bid her still it.   70

[2.] Watch. How if the nurse be asleep and will not hear us?

Dog. Why, then, depart in peace, and let the child wake her with crying; for the ewe that will not hear her lamb when it baes will never answer a calf when he bleats.   76

Verg. 'Tis very true.

Dog. This is the end of the charge: you, constable, are to present the Prince's own person. If you meet the Prince in the night, you may stay him.   81

Verg. Nay, by'r lady, that I think 'a cannot.

Dog. Five shillings to one on't, with any man that knows the [statues], he may stay him; marry, not without the Prince be willing; for, indeed,   86 the watch ought to offend no man, and it is an offence to stay a man against his will.

Verg. By'r lady, I think it be so.   89

Dog. Ha, ah ha! Well, masters, good night. An there be any matter of weight chances, call up me. Keep your fellows' counsels and your own, and good night. Come, neighbour.

[2.] Watch. Well, masters, we hear our charge. Let us go sit here upon the church-bench till two, and then all to bed.   96

Dog. One word more, honest neighbours. I pray you, watch about Signior Leonato's door; for the wedding being there to-morrow, there is a great coil to-night. Adieu! Be vigitant, I beseech you.

[Exeunt [Dogberry and Verges].

Enter BORACHIO *and* CONRADE.

Bora. What, Conrade!   102

[2.] Watch. [*Aside.*] Peace! stir not.

Bora. Conrade, I say!

Con. Here, man; I am at thy elbow.   105

Bora. Mass, and my elbow itch'd; I thought there would be a scab follow.

Con. I will owe thee an answer for that; and now forward with thy tale.

Bora. Stand thee close, then, under this pent-   110 house, for it drizzles rain; and I will, like a true drunkard, utter all to thee.

[2.] Watch. [*Aside.*] Some treason, masters; yet stand close.

Bora. Therefore know I have earned of Don John a thousand ducats.   116

Con. Is it possible that any villainy should be so dear?

25. **comprehend:** for *apprehend*. **vagrom:** vagrant. 43. **bills:** halberds, i.e., pikes fixed to long poles. 54. **true:** nonest. 84. **[statues]** F. *statutes* Q; but the error is undoubtedly Dogberry's. 100. **coil:** to-do. 107. **scab.** Also used contemptuously for *scurvy fellow.* 110. **pent-house:** projecting roof.

Bora. Thou shouldst rather ask if it were possible any villainy should be so rich; for when rich villains have need of poor ones, poor ones may make what price they will.   122

Con. I wonder at it.

Bora. That shows thou art unconfirm'd. Thou knowest that the fashion of a doublet, or a hat, or a cloak, is nothing to a man.   126

Con. Yes, it is apparel.

Bora. I mean, the fashion.

Con. Yes, the fashion is the fashion.   129

Bora. Tush! I may as well say the fool's the fool. But seest thou not what a deformed thief this fashion is?

[*2.*] *Watch.* [*Aside.*] I know that Deformed; 'a has been a vile thief this seven years. 'A goes up and down like a gentleman. I remember his name.   136

Bora. Didst thou not hear somebody?

Con. No; 'twas the vane on the house.

Bora. Seest thou not, I say, what a deformed thief this fashion is, how giddily 'a turns about all the hot bloods between fourteen and five-and-   141 thirty, sometimes fashioning them like Pharaoh's soldiers in the reechy painting, sometime like god Bel's priests in the old church-window, sometime like the shaven Hercules in the smirch'd worm-   145 eaten tapestry, where his codpiece seems as massy as his club?

Con. All this I see; and I see that the fashion wears out more apparel than the man. But art not thou thyself giddy with the fashion too, that thou hast shifted out of thy tale into telling me of the fashion?   152

Bora. Not so, neither; but know that I have to-night wooed Margaret, the Lady Hero's gentlewoman, by the name of Hero. She leans me   155 out at her mistress' chamber-window, bids me a thousand times good night, — I tell this tale vilely: — I should first tell thee how the Prince, Claudio, and my master, planted and placed and possessed by my master Don John, saw afar off in the orchard this amiable encounter.   161

Con. And thought they Margaret was Hero?

Bora. Two of them did, the Prince and Claudio; but the devil my master knew she was Mar-   165 garet; and partly by his oaths, which first possess'd them, partly by the dark night, which did deceive them, but chiefly by my villainy, which did confirm any slander that Don John had made, away went

Claudio enrag'd; swore he would meet her, as he   170 was appointed, next morning at the temple, and there, before the whole congregation, shame her with what he saw o'er night, and send her home again without a husband.   175

1. Watch. We charge you, in the Prince's name, stand!

2. Watch. Call up the right master constable. We have here recovered the most dangerous piece of lechery that ever was known in the common-wealth.   181

1. Watch. And one Deformed is one of them. I know him; 'a wears a lock.

Con. Masters, masters, —

2. Watch. You'll be made bring Deformed forth, I warrant you.   186

Con. Masters, —

[*1. Watch.*] Never speak. We charge you let us obey you to go with us.

Bora. We are like to prove a goodly commodity, being taken up of these men's bills.   191

Con. A commodity in question, I warrant you. Come, we'll obey you.   [*Exeunt.*

[SCENE IV. *Hero's apartment.*]

Enter HERO, MARGARET, *and* URSULA.

Hero. Good Ursula, wake my cousin Beatrice, and desire her to rise.

Urs. I will, lady.

Hero. And bid her come hither.

Urs. Well.   [*Exit.*   5

Marg. Troth, I think your other rabato were better.

Hero. No, pray thee, good Meg, I'll wear this.

Marg. By my troth, 's not so good; and I warrant your cousin will say so.   10

Hero. My cousin's a fool, and thou art another. I'll wear none but this.

Marg. I like the new tire within excellently, if the hair were a thought browner; and your gown's a most rare fashion, i' faith. I saw the Duchess of Milan's gown that they praise so.   16

Hero. O, that exceeds, they say.

Marg. By my troth, 's but a night-gown in respect of yours: cloth o' gold, and cuts, and lac'd with silver, set with pearls, down sleeves,   20 side sleeves, and skirts, round underborne with a bluish tinsel; but for a fine, quaint, graceful, and excellent fashion, yours is worth ten on't.

124. **unconfirm'd:** inexperienced. 126. **is...man:** i.e., does not make the man. 143. **reechy:** smoky, dirty. **god Bel's priests.** Alluding to Daniel's overthrow of the priests of Bel, as told in the apocryphal book of *Daniel.* 159. **possessed:** directed. 162. **they** Q. *thy* Ff. 183. **lock:** love-lock, a lock of hair hanging down on the left shoulder. 188. [*1. Watch*] (Theobald). QF print as part of Conrade's speech. 190-91. A punning speech. **commodity:** (1) goods, (2) bargain. **taken up:** (1) taken on credit, (2) arrested. **bills:** (1) bonds, (2) halberds. 192. **in question:** subject to legal trial.
Sc. iv, 6. **rabato:** ruff. 13. **tire:** headdress. **within:** i.e., in the inner room. 17. **exceeds:** excels. 18. **night-gown:** dressing-gown. 19. **cuts:** ornamental slashes showing fabric beneath. 20. **down sleeves:** i.e., the real sleeves. 21. **side sleeves:** ornamental sleeves hanging from the shoulder. 21. **round underborne:** lined around.

Hero. God give me joy to wear it! for my heart is exceeding heavy. 25

Marg. 'Twill be heavier soon by the weight of a man.

Hero. Fie upon thee! art not asham'd?

Marg. Of what, lady? Of speaking honourably? Is not marriage honourable in a beggar? Is not 30 your lord honourable without marriage? I think you would have me say, "saving your reverence, a husband." An bad thinking do not wrest true speaking, I'll offend nobody. Is there any harm in "the heavier for a husband"? None, I think, 35 an it be the right husband and the right wife; otherwise 'tis light, and not heavy. Ask my Lady Beatrice else; here she comes.

Enter BEATRICE.

Hero. Good morrow, coz.

Beat. Good morrow, sweet Hero. 40

Hero. Why, how now? Do you speak in the sick tune?

Beat. I am out of all other tune, methinks.

Marg. Clap's into "Light o' love"; that goes without a burden. Do you sing it, and I'll dance it. 46

Beat. Ye light o' love with your heels! Then, if your husband have stables enough, you'll see he shall lack no barns.

Marg. O illegitimate construction! I scorn that with my heels. 51

Beat. 'Tis almost five o'clock, cousin; 'tis time you were ready. By my troth, I am exceeding ill. Heigh-ho!

Marg. For a hawk, a horse, or a husband? 55

Beat. For the letter that begins them all, H.

Marg. Well, an you be not turn'd Turk, there's no more sailing by the star.

Beat. What means the fool, trow?

Marg. Nothing I; but God send every one their heart's desire! 61

Hero. These gloves the count sent me; they are an excellent perfume.

Beat. I am stuff'd, cousin; I cannot smell.

Marg. A maid, and stuff'd! There's goodly catching of cold. 66

Beat. O, God help me! God help me! How long have you profess'd apprehension?

Marg. Ever since you left it. Doth not my wit become me rarely? 70

Beat. It is not seen enough, you should wear it in your cap. By my troth, I am sick.

Marg. Get you some of this distill'd Carduus

Benedictus, and lay it to your heart. It is the only thing for a qualm. 75

Hero. There thou prick'st her with a thistle.

Beat. Benedictus! why Benedictus? You have some moral in this Benedictus.

Marg. Moral! no, by my troth, I have no moral meaning; I meant, plain holy-thistle. You 80 may think perchance that I think you are in love. Nay, by'r lady, I am not such a fool to think what I list, nor I list not to think what I can, nor indeed I cannot think, if I would think my heart out of thinking, that you are in love or that you will be 85 in love or that you can be in love. Yet Benedick was such another, and now is he become a man. He swore he would never marry, and yet now, in despite of his heart, he eats his meat without grudging; and how you may be converted I know 90 not, but methinks you look with your eyes as other women do.

Beat. What pace is this that thy tongue keeps?

Marg. Not a false gallop. 94

Re-enter URSULA.

Urs. Madam, withdraw; the Prince, the count, Signior Benedick, Don John, and all the gallants of the town, are come to fetch you to church.

Hero. Help to dress me, good coz, good Meg, good Ursula. [*Exeunt.*]

[SCENE V. *Another room in Leonato's house.*]

Enter LEONATO, *with the Constable* [DOGBERRY] *and the Headborough* [VERGES].

Leon. What would you with me, honest neighbour?

Dog. Marry, sir, I would have some confidence with you that decerns you nearly.

Leon. Brief, I pray you; for you see it is a busy time with me. 6

Dog. Marry, this it is, sir.

Verg. Yes, in truth it is, sir.

Leon. What is it, my good friends?

Dog. Goodman Verges, sir, speaks a little off the matter; an old man, sir, and his wits are not so blunt as, God help, I would desire they were; but, in faith, honest as the skin between his brows.

Verg. Yes, I thank God I am as honest as 15 any man living that is an old man and no honester than I.

Dog. Comparisons are odorous. Palabras, neighbour Verges.

33. **wrest:** violate.   37. **light:** with pun on *wanton.*   44. **"Light o' love":** A popular song.   45. **burden:** bass part. 49. **barns:** with pun on *bairns,* children.   56. **H.** Punning on *ache,* pronounced "aitch" in 16th cent.   57. **turn'd Turk.** Common expression for "entirely changed"; here "fallen in love."   64. **I am stuff'd:** I have a cold.   68. **apprehension:** wit. 73. **Carduus Benedictus:** the blessed thistle, a medicinal herb.   78. **moral:** hidden meaning.

Sc. v, S.D. *Headborough:* petty constable.   18. **odorous:** for *odious.*   **Palabras:** for *pocas palabras* (Span.), few words.

Leon. Neighbours, you are tedious.   20

Dog. It pleases your worship to say so, but we are the poor Duke's officers; but truly, for mine own part, if I were as tedious as a king, I could find in my heart to bestow it all of your worship.   25

Leon. All thy tediousness on me, ah?

Dog. Yea, an 'twere a thousand pound more than 'tis; for I hear as good exclamation on your worship as of any man in the city; and though I be but a poor man, I am glad to hear it.   30

Verg. And so am I.

Leon. I would fain know what you have to say.

Verg. Marry, sir, our watch to-night, excepting your worship's presence, ha' ta'en a couple of as arrant knaves as any in Messina.   35

Dog. A good old man, sir; he will be talking: as they say, When the age is in, the wit is out. God help us! It is a world to see. Well said, i' faith, neighbour Verges. Well, God's a good man; an two men ride of a horse, one must ride behind.   40 An honest soul, i' faith, sir; by my troth he is, as ever broke bread; but God is to be worshipp'd; all men are not alike; alas, good neighbour!

Leon. Indeed, neighbour, he comes too short of you.   46

Dog. Gifts that God gives.

Leon. I must leave you.

Dog. One word, sir. Our watch, sir, have indeed comprehended two aspicious persons, and we would have them this morning examined before your worship.   52

Leon. Take their examination yourself and bring it me. I am now in great haste, as it may appear unto you.   55

Dog. It shall be suffigance.

Leon. Drink some wine ere you go. Fare you well.

[*Enter a* MESSENGER.]

Mess. My lord, they stay for you to give your daughter to her husband.   60

Leon. I'll wait upon them; I am ready.

[*Exeunt Leonato and Messenger.*]

Dog. Go, good partner, go, get you to Francis Seacole; bid him bring his pen and inkhorn to the gaol. We are now to examination these men.

Verg. And we must do it wisely.   65

Dog. We will spare for no wit, I warrant you. Here's that shall drive some of them to a non-come; only get the learned writer to set down our excommunication, and meet me at the gaol.

[*Exeunt.*

ACT IV

[SCENE I. *A church.*]

Enter DON PEDRO, [JOHN *the*] BASTARD, LEONATO, FRIAR FRANCIS, CLAUDIO, BENEDICK, HERO, BEATRICE [*and attendants*].

Leon. Come, Friar Francis, be brief; only to the plain form of marriage, and you shall recount their particular duties afterwards.

Friar. You come hither, my lord, to marry this lady.   5

Claud. No.

Leon. To be married to her. Friar, you come to marry her.

Friar. Lady, you come hither to be married to this count.   10

Hero. I do.

Friar. If either of you know any inward impediment why you should not be conjoined, I charge you, on your souls, to utter it.

Claud. Know you any, Hero?   15

Hero. None, my lord.

Friar. Know you any, count?

Leon. I dare make his answer, none.

Claud. O, what men dare do! What men may do! What men daily do, not knowing what they do!   21

Bene. How now! interjections? Why, then, some be of laughing, as, ah, ha, he!

Claud. Stand thee by, friar. Father, by your leave Will you with free and unconstrained soul   25 Give me this maid, your daughter?

Leon. As freely, son, as God did give her me.

Claud. And what have I to give you back,
    whose worth
May counterpoise this rich and precious gift?

D. Pedro. Nothing, unless you render her again.

Claud. Sweet Prince, you learn me noble thank-
    fulness.   31
There, Leonato, take her back again.
Give not this rotten orange to your friend;
She's but the sign and semblance of her honour.
Behold how like a maid she blushes here!   35
O, what authority and show of truth
Can cunning sin cover itself withal!
Comes not that blood as modest evidence
To witness simple virtue? Would you not swear,
All you that see her, that she were a maid,   40
By these exterior shows? But she is none.
She knows the heat of a luxurious bed;
Her blush is guiltiness, not modesty.

Leon. What do you mean, my lord?

Claud.   Not to be married;

37. **When ... out.** Corruption of the proverb, "When ale is in, wit is out." 38. **world:** wonder. 67. **non-come:** *non compos mentis.* 68. **excommunication:** for *examination.*
Act IV, sc. i, 22–23. **interjections ... he.** Benedick is quoting from a grammar. 42. **luxurious:** lustful.

Not to knit my soul to an approved wanton.   45
   Leon. Dear my lord, if you, in your own proof,
Have vanquish'd the resistance of her youth,
And made defeat of her virginity,—
   Claud. I know what you would say.   If I have
    known her,
You will say she did embrace me as a husband,   50
And so extenuate the 'forehand sin.
No, Leonato,
I never tempted her with word too large;
But, as a brother to his sister, show'd
Bashful sincerity and comely love.   55
   Hero. And seem'd I ever otherwise to you?
   Claud. Out on thee!   Seeming!   I will write
    against it:
You seem to me as Dian in her orb,
As chaste as is the bud ere it be blown;
But you are more intemperate in your blood   60
Than Venus, or those pamp'red animals
That rage in savage sensuality.
   Hero. Is my lord well, that he doth speak so
    wide?
   Leon. Sweet Prince, why speak not you?
   D. Pedro.   What should I speak?
I stand dishonour'd, that have gone about   65
To link my dear friend to a common stale.
   Leon. Are these things spoken, or do I but
    dream?
   D. John. Sir, they are spoken, and these things
    are true.
   Bene. This looks not like a nuptial.
   Hero.   True!   O God!
   Claud. Leonato, stand I here?   70
Is this the Prince?   Is this the Prince's brother?
Is this face Hero's?   Are our eyes our own?
   Leon. All this is so; but what of this, my lord?
   Claud. Let me but move one question to your
    daughter;
And, by that fatherly and kindly power   75
That you have in her, bid her answer truly.
   Leon. I charge thee do so, as thou art my child.
   Hero. O, God defend me! how am I beset!
What kind of catechising call you this?   79
   Claud. To make you answer truly to your name.
   Hero. Is it not Hero?   Who can blot that name
With any just reproach?
   Claud.   Marry, that can Hero;
Hero itself can blot out Hero's virtue.
What man was he talk'd with you yesternight
Out at your window betwixt twelve and one?   85
Now, if you are a maid, answer to this.
   Hero. I talk'd with no man at that hour, my lord.
   D. Pedro. Why, then are you no maiden.
    Leonato,
I am sorry you must hear.   Upon mine honour,

Myself, my brother, and this grieved count   90
Did see her, hear her, at that hour last night
Talk with a ruffian at her chamber-window;
Who hath indeed, most like a liberal villain,
Confess'd the vile encounters they have had
A thousand times in secret.   95
   D. John. Fie, fie! they are not to be named, my
    lord,
Not to be spoke of;
There is not chastity enough in language
Without offence to utter them.   Thus, pretty lady,
I am sorry for thy much misgovernment.   100
   Claud. O Hero, what a Hero hadst thou been,
If half thy outward graces had been plac'd
About thy thoughts and counsels of thy heart!
But fare the well, most foul, most fair!   Farewell,
Thou pure impiety and impious purity!   105
For thee I'll lock up all the gates of love,
And on my eyelids shall conjecture hang,
To turn all beauty into thoughts of harm,
And never shall it more be gracious.
   Leon. Hath no man's dagger here a point for me?
                         [Hero swoons.]
   Beat. Why, how now, cousin! wherefore sink you
    down?   111
   D. John. Come, let us go.   These things, come
    thus to light,
Smother her spirits up.
       *[Exeunt Don Pedro, Don John, and
          Claudio.]*
   Bene. How doth the lady?
   Beat.   Dead, I think.   Help, uncle!
Hero! why, Hero! Uncle! Signior Benedick! Friar!
   Leon. O Fate! take not away thy heavy hand.
Death is the fairest cover for her shame   117
That may be wish'd for.
   Beat.   How now, cousin Hero!
   Friar. Have comfort, lady.
   Leon. Dost thou look up?   120
   Friar. Yea, wherefore should she not?
   Leon. Wherefore!   Why, doth not every earthly
    thing
Cry shame upon her?   Could she here deny
The story that is printed in her blood?
Do not live, Hero; do not ope thine eyes;   125
For, did I think thou wouldst not quickly die,
Thought I thy spirits were stronger than thy
    shames,
Myself would, on the rearward of reproaches,
Strike at thy life.   Griev'd I, I had but one?
Chid I for that at frugal nature's frame?   130
O, one too much by thee!   Why had I one?
Why ever wast thou lovely in my eyes?
Why had I not with charitable hand
Took up a beggar's issue at my gates,

---

46. **proof:** trial.   58. **Dian . . . orb.** Diana was goddess of chastity and of the moon.   63. **wide:** wide of the mark.   75. **kindly:** natural.   93. **liberal:** gross, licentious.   107. **conjecture:** suspicion.   128. **on the rearward:** after.   130. **frame:** design.

Who smirched thus and mir'd with infamy,   135
I might have said "No part of it is mine.
This shame derives itself from unknown loins"?
But mine, and mine I lov'd, and mine I prais'd,
And mine that I was proud on, mine so much
That I myself was to myself not mine,   140
Valuing of her, — why, she, O, she is fall'n
Into a pit of ink, that the wide sea
Hath drops too few to wash her clean again,
And salt too little which may season give
To her foul-tainted flesh!
    Bene.   Sir, sir, be patient.   145
For my part, I am so attir'd in wonder,
I know not what to say.
    Beat. O, on my soul, my cousin is belied!
    Bene. Lady, were you her bedfellow last night?
    Beat. No, truly not; although, until last night,
I have this twelvemonth been her bedfellow.   151
    Leon. Confirm'd, confirm'd! O, that is stronger
        made
Which was before barr'd up with ribs of iron!
Would the two princes lie, and Claudio lie,
Who lov'd her so, that, speaking of her foulness,
Wash'd it with tears? Hence from her! Let her
    die.   156
    Friar. Hear me a little;
For I have only been silent so long
And given way unto this course of fortune,
By noting of the lady. I have mark'd   160
A thousand blushing apparitions
To start into her face, a thousand innocent shames
In angel whiteness beat away those blushes;
And in her eye there hath appear'd a fire
To burn the errors that these princes hold   165
Against her maiden truth. Call me a fool;
Trust not my reading nor my observations,
Which with experimental seal doth warrant
The tenour of my book; trust not my age,
My reverence, calling, nor divinity,   170
If this sweet lady lie not guiltless here
Under some biting error.
    Leon.   Friar, it cannot be.
Thou seest that all the grace that she hath left
Is that she will not add to her damnation
A sin of perjury; she not denies it.   175
Why seek'st thou then to cover with excuse
That which appears in proper nakedness?
    Friar. Lady, what man is he you are accus'd of?
    Hero. They know that do accuse me; I know
        none.
If I know more of any man alive   180
Than that which maiden modesty doth warrant,
Let all my sins lack mercy! O my father,

Prove you that any man with me convers'd
At hours unmeet, or that I yesternight
Maintain'd the change of words with any creature,
Refuse me, hate me, torture me to death!   186
    Friar. There is some strange misprision in the
        princes.
    Bene. Two of them have the very bent of
        honour;
And if their wisdoms be misled in this,
The practice of it lives in John the Bastard,   190
Whose spirits toil in frame of villainies.
    Leon. I know not. If they speak but truth of
        her,
These hands shall tear her; if they wrong her
        honour,
The proudest of them shall well hear of it.
Time hath not yet so dried this blood of mine,   195
Nor age so eat up my invention,
Nor fortune made such havoc of my means,
Nor my bad life reft me so much of friends,
But they shall find, awak'd in such a kind,
Both strength of limb and policy of mind,   200
Ability in means and choice of friends,
To quit me of them throughly.
    Friar.   Pause awhile,
And let my counsel sway you in this case.
Your daughter here the princes left for dead.
Let her awhile be secretly kept in,   205
And publish it that she is dead indeed.
Maintain a mourning ostentation
And on your family's old monument
Hang mournful epitaphs, and do all rites
That appertain unto a burial.   210
    Leon. What shall become of this? What will
        this do?
    Friar. Marry, this well carried shall on her behalf
Change slander to remorse; that is some good.
But not for that dream I on this strange course,
But on this travail look for greater birth.   215
She dying, as it must be so maintain'd,
Upon the instant that she was accus'd,
Shall be lamented, pitied, and excus'd
Of every hearer; for it so falls out
That what we have we prize not to the worth   220
Whiles we enjoy it, but being lack'd and lost,
Why, then we rack the value; then we find
The virtue that possession would not show us
Whiles it was ours. So will it fare with Claudio.
When he shall hear she died upon his words,   225
Th' idea of her life shall sweetly creep
Into his study of imagination,
And every lovely organ of her life
Shall come apparell'd in more precious habit,

More moving-delicate and full of life,   230
Into the eye and prospect of his soul,
Than when she liv'd indeed.   Then shall he mourn,
If ever love had interest in his liver,
And wish he had not so accused her,
No, though he thought his accusation true.   235
Let this be so, and doubt not but success
Will fashion the event in better shape
Than I can lay it down in likelihood.
But if all aim but this be levell'd false,
The supposition of the lady's death   240
Will quench the wonder of her infamy.
And if it sort not well, you may conceal her,
As best befits her wounded reputation,
In some reclusive and religious life,
Out of all eyes, tongues, minds, and injuries.   245
  Bene. Signior Leonato, let the friar advise you;
And though you know my inwardness and love
Is very much unto the Prince and Claudio,
Yet, by mine honour, I will deal in this
As secretly and justly as your soul   250
Should with your body.
  Leon.   Being that I flow in grief,
The smallest twine may lead me.
  Friar. 'Tis well consented; presently away,
For to strange sores strangely they strain the cure.
Come, lady, die to live.   This wedding-day   255
Perhaps is but prolong'd; have patience and endure.
          [*Exeunt* [*all but Benedick and Beatrice*].
  Bene. Lady Beatrice, have you wept all this
while?
  Beat. Yea, and I will weep a while longer.
  Bene. I will not desire that.
  Beat. You have no reason; I do it freely.   260
  Bene. Surely I do believe your fair cousin is
wrong'd.
  Beat. Ah, how much might the man deserve of
me that would right her!
  Bene. Is there any way to show such friendship?
  Beat. A very even way, but no such friend.   265
  Bene. May a man do it?
  Beat. It is a man's office, but not yours.
  Bene. I do love nothing in the world so well as
you.   Is not that strange?   270
  Beat. As strange as the thing I know not.   It
were as possible for me to say I lov'd nothing so
well as you: but believe me not; and yet I lie not.
I confess nothing, nor I deny nothing.   I am sorry
for my cousin.   275
  Bene. By my sword, Beatrice, thou lov'st me.
  Beat. Do not swear, and eat it.
  Bene. I will swear by it that you love me; and I
will make him eat it that says I love not you.
  Beat. Will you not eat your word?   280

  Bene. With no sauce that can be devised to it.   I
protest I love thee.
  Beat. Why, then, God forgive me!
  Bene. What offence, sweet Beatrice?
  Beat. You have stayed me in a happy hour.   I
was about to protest I loved you.   286
  Bene. And do it with all thy heart.
  Beat. I love you with so much of my heart that
none is left to protest.
  Bene. Come, bid me do any thing for thee.   290
  Beat. Kill Claudio.
  Bene. Ha! not for the wide world.
  Beat. You kill me to deny it.   Farewell.
  Bene. Tarry, sweet Beatrice.
  Beat. I am gone, though I am here.   There is no
love in you.   Nay, I pray you, let me go.   296
  Bene. Beatrice,—
  Beat. In faith, I will go.
  Bene. We'll be friends first.
  Beat. You dare easier be friends with me than
fight with mine enemy.   301
  Bene. Is Claudio thine enemy?
  Beat. Is 'a not approved in the height a villain,
that hath slandered, scorned, dishonoured my
kinswoman?   O that I were a man!   What, bear
her in hand until they come to take hands;   305
and then, with public accusation, uncover'd slander,
unmitigated rancour, — O God, that I were a man!
I would eat his heart in the market-place.
  Bene. Hear me, Beatrice,—   310
  Beat. Talk with a man out at a window!   A
proper saying!
  Bene. Nay, but, Beatrice,—
  Beat. Sweet Hero!   She is wrong'd, she is
sland'red, she is undone.   315
  Bene. Beat —
  Beat. Princes and counties!   Surely, a princely
testimony, a goodly count, Count Comfect; a sweet
gallant, surely!   O that I were a man for his sake!
or that I had any friend would be a man for   320
my sake!   But manhood is melted into courtesies,
valour into compliment, and men are only turned
into tongue, and trim ones too.   He is now as
valiant as Hercules that only tells a lie and swears
it.   I cannot be a man with wishing, therefore I
will die a woman with grieving.   326
  Bene. Tarry, good Beatrice.   By this hand, I
love thee.
  Beat. Use it for my love some other way than
swearing by it.   330
  Bene. Think you in your soul the Count Claudio
hath wrong'd Hero?
  Beat. Yea, as sure as I have a thought or a soul.
  Bene. Enough, I am engag'd; I will challenge   335

233. **liver:** the supposed seat of passion.   239. **be . . . false:** miscarry.   242. **sort:** turn out.   247. **inwardness:** intimacy.   256. **prolong'd:** postponed.   265. **even:** clear.   285. **in . . . hour:** luckily.   295. **gone:** i.e., in spirit.   304. **bear . . . hand:** delude with false hopes.   306. **uncover'd:** open.   318. **Comfect:** candy.

him. 1 will kiss your hand, and so I leave you. By this hand, Claudio shall render me a dear account. As you hear of me, so think of me. Go, comfort your cousin. I must say she is dead; and so, farewell.   [*Exeunt.*] 340

[SCENE II. *A prison.*]

Enter the Constables [DOGBERRY, VERGES, *and* SEXTON] *in gowns* [*and the* WATCH, *with* CONRADE] *and* BORACHIO.

Dog. Is our whole dissembly appear'd?

Verg. O, a stool and a cushion for the sexton.

Sex. Which be the malefactors?

Dog. Marry, that am I and my partner.

Verg. Nay, that's certain; we have the exhibition to examine.   6

Sex. But which are the offenders that are to be examined? Let them come before master constable.

Dog. Yea, marry, let them come before me. What is your name, friend?   11

Bora. Borachio.

Dog. Pray, write down, Borachio. Yours, sirrah?

Con. I am a gentleman, sir, and my name is Conrade.   16

Dog. Write down, master gentleman Conrade. Masters, do you serve God?

Con. } Yea, sir, we hope.
Bora. }

Dog. Write down, that they hope they serve God; and write God first; for God defend but God 21 should go before such villains! Masters, it is proved already that you are little better than false knaves; and it will go near to be thought so shortly. How answer you for yourselves?   25

Con. Marry, sir, we say we are none.

Dog. A marvellous witty fellow, I assure you; but I will go about with him. Come you hither, sirrah; a word in your ear, sir. I say to you, it is thought you are false knaves.   30

Bora. Sir, I say to you we are none.

Dog. Well, stand aside. 'Fore God, they are both in a tale. Have you writ down, that they are none?   34

Sex. Master constable, you go not the way to examine. You must call forth the watch that are their accusers.

Dog. Yea, marry, that's the eftest way. Let the watch come forth. Masters, I charge you, in the Prince's name, accuse these men.   40

1. Watch. This man said, sir, that Don John, the Prince's brother, was a villain.

Dog. Write down Prince John a villain. Why, this is flat perjury, to call a prince's brother villain.

Bora. Master constable,—   45

Dog. Pray thee, fellow, peace. I do not like thy look, I promise thee.

Sex. What heard you him say else?

2. Watch. Marry, that he had received a thousand ducats of Don John for accusing the Lady Hero wrongfully.   51

Dog. Flat burglary as ever was committed.

Verg. Yea, by mass, that it is.

Sex. What else, fellow?

1. Watch. And that Count Claudio did 55 mean, upon his words, to disgrace Hero before the whole assembly, and not marry her.

Dog. O villain! thou wilt be condemn'd into everlasting redemption for this.

Sex. What else?   60

1. Watch. This is all.

Sex. And this is more, masters, than you can deny. Prince John is this morning secretly stol'n away. Hero was in this manner accus'd, in this very manner refus'd, and upon the grief of this 65 suddenly died. Master constable, let these men be bound, and brought to Leonato's. I will go before and show him their examination.   [*Exit.*]

Dog. Come, let them be opinion'd.

Verg. Let them be in the hands —   70

[*Con.*] Off, coxcomb!

Dog. God's my life, where's the sexton? Let him write down the Prince's officer coxcomb. Come, bind them. Thou naughty varlet!

Con. Away! you are an ass, you are an ass.   75

Dog. Dost thou not suspect my place? Dost thou not suspect my years? O that he were here to write me down an ass! But, masters, remember that I am an ass; though it be not written down, yet forget not that I am an ass. No, thou villain, 80 thou art full of piety, as shall be prov'd upon thee by good witness. I am a wise fellow, and, which is more, an officer, and, which is more, a householder, and, which is more, as pretty a piece of flesh as any is in Messina, and one that knows the law, go to; 85 and a rich fellow enough, go to; and a fellow that hath had losses, and one that hath two gowns and every thing handsome about him. Bring him away. O that I had been writ down an ass!   90
          [*Exeunt.*

Sc. ii, 1. **Dog.** The speech-headings throughout this scene are jumbled. In Q Dogberry's speeches are headed *Keeper* (l. 1), *Andrew* (l. 4), and *Kemp*, abbreviated variously (l. 10 up to l. 76, with the exception of l. 69 which is *Const.*). Verges's speeches are headed *Cowley*, except at l. 53 where *Const.* appears. William Kempe and Richard Cowley were actors in Shakespeare's company. *Keeper* (l. 1) may be the compositor's expansion of the abbreviation *Ke.; Andrew* (l. 4) may stand for "Merry Andrew" or "clown," since Kempe regularly played comic parts. See Introduction. 28. **go about with:** get the better of. 33. **are...tale:** tell the same story. 38. **eftest.** Apparently, easiest or quickest. 69. **opinion'd:** for *pinioned.* 71. **[Con.] Off, coxcomb!** (Warburton). *of Coxcombe* Q. 81. **piety:** for *impiety.*

ACT V

[SCENE I. *Before Leonato's house.*]

Enter LEONATO *and* ANTONIO.

Ant. If you go on thus, you will kill yourself;
And 'tis not wisdom thus to second grief
Against yourself.
Leon.   I pray thee, cease thy counsel,
Which falls into mine ears as profitless
As water in a sieve. Give not me counsel;   5
Nor let no comforter delight mine ear
But such a one whose wrongs do suit with mine.
Bring me a father that so lov'd his child,
Whose joy of her is overwhelm'd like mine,
And bid him speak of patience;   10
Measure his woe the length and breadth of mine,
And let it answer every strain for strain,
As thus for thus, and such a grief for such,
In every lineament, branch, shape, and form;
If such a one will smile and stroke his beard,   15
[Bid] sorrow wag, cry "hem!" when he should groan,
Patch grief with proverbs, make misfortune drunk
With candle-wasters, bring him yet to me,
And I of him will gather patience.
But there is no such man; for, brother, men   20
Can counsel and speak comfort to that grief
Which they themselves not feel; but, tasting it,
Their counsel turns to passion, which before
Would give preceptial medicine to rage,
Fetter strong madness in a silken thread,   25
Charm ache with air and agony with words.
No, no; 'tis all men's office to speak patience
To those that wring under the load of sorrow,
But no man's virtue nor sufficiency
To be so moral when he shall endure   30
The like himself. Therefore give me no counsel;
My griefs cry louder than advertisement.
Ant. Therein do men from children nothing differ.
Leon. I pray thee, peace. I will be flesh and blood;
For there was never yet philosopher   35
That could endure the toothache patiently,
However they have writ the style of gods
And made a push at chance and sufferance.
Ant. Yet bend not all the harm upon yourself;
Make those that do offend you suffer too.   40
Leon. There thou speak'st reason. Nay, I will
  do so.
My soul doth tell me Hero is belied;
And that shall Claudio know; so shall the Prince
And all of them that thus dishonour her.   44

Enter DON PEDRO *and* CLAUDIO.

Ant. Here comes the Prince and Claudio hastily.

D. Pedro. Good den, good den.
Claud.   Good day to both of you.
Leon. Hear you, my lords, —
D. Pedro.   We have some haste, Leonato.
Leon. Some haste, my lord! Well, fare you well,
  my lord.
Are you so hasty now? Well, all is one.
D. Pedro. Nay, do not quarrel with us, good old
  man.   50
Ant. If he could right himself with quarrelling,
Some of us would lie low.
Claud.   Who wrongs him?
Leon. Marry, thou dost wrong me; thou dis-
  sembler, thou, —
Nay, never lay thy hand upon thy sword;
I fear thee not.
Claud.   Marry, beshrew my hand.   55
If it should give your age such cause of fear.
In faith, my hand meant nothing to my sword.
Leon. Tush, tush, man; never fleer and jest at me.
I speak not like a dotard nor a fool,
As under privilege of age to brag   60
What I have done being young, or what would do
Were I not old. Know, Claudio, to thy head,
Thou hast so wrong'd mine innocent child and me
That I am forc'd to lay my reverence by
And, with grey hairs and bruise of many days,   65
Do challenge thee to trial of a man.
I say thou hast belied mine innocent child!
Thy slander hath gone through and through her
  heart,
And she lies buried with her ancestors,
O, in a tomb where never scandal slept,   70
Save this of hers, fram'd by thy villainy!
Claud. My villainy?
Leon.   Thine, Claudio; thine, I say.
D. Pedro. You say not right, old man.
Leon.   My lord, my lord,
I'll prove it on his body, if he dare,
Despite his nice fence and his active practice,   75
His May of youth and bloom of lustihood.
Claud. Away! I will not have to do with you.
Leon. Canst thou so daff me? Thou hast kill'd
  my child.
If thou kill'st me, boy, thou shalt kill a man.
Ant. He shall kill two of us, and men indeed.
But that's no matter; let him kill one first.   81
Win me and wear me; let him answer me.
Come, follow me, boy; come, sir boy, come, follow me.
Sir boy, I'll whip you from your foining fence;
Nay, as I am a gentleman, I will.   85
Leon. Brother, —
Ant. Content yourself. God knows I lov'd my
  niece;

Act V, sc. i, 7. **suit:** match. 16. **[Bid]** (Dyce). *And* Q. **wag:** go packing. 18. **candle-wasters:** revellers. **yet:** then.
24. **preceptial:** made up of precepts. 30. **moral:** moralistic. 32. **advertisement:** advice. 37. **writ...gods:** taken a god-
like tone. 38. **made...at:** pooh-poohed. 55. **beshrew:** curse. 58. **fleer:** sneer. 75. **fence:** fencing. 78. **daff:** put off.
84. **foining:** thrusting.

And she is dead, slander'd to death by villains,
That dare as well answer a man indeed
As I dare take a serpent by the tongue.   90
Boys, apes, braggarts, Jacks, milksops!
    Leon.   Brother Antony,—
    Ant. Hold you content. What, man! I know
       them, yea,
And what they weigh, even to the utmost scruple, —
Scambling, out-facing, fashion-monging boys,
That lie and cog and flout, deprave and slander,   95
Go anticly and show outward hideousness,
And speak off half a dozen dang'rous words,
How they might hurt their enemies, if they durst;
And this is all.
    Leon. But, brother Antony, —
    Ant.   Come, 'tis no matter.
Do not you meddle; let me deal in this.   101
    D. Pedro. Gentlemen both, we will not wake your
       patience.
My heart is sorry for your daughter's death;
But, on my honour, she was charg'd with nothing
But what was true and very full of proof.   105
    Leon. My lord, my lord, —
    D. Pedro. I will not hear you.
    Leon. No? Come, brother, away! I will be
       heard.
    Ant. And shall, or some of us will smart for it.
                   [*Exeunt Leonato and Antonio.*

Enter BENEDICK.

    D. Pedro. See, see; here comes the man we went
       to seek.   110
    Claud. Now, signior, what news?
    Bene. Good day, my lord.
    D. Pedro. Welcome, signior. You are almost
come to part almost a fray.   114
    Claud. We had like to have had our two noses
snapp'd off with two old men without teeth.
    D. Pedro. Leonato and his brother. What
think'st thou? Had we fought, I doubt we should
have been too young for them.
    Bene. In a false quarrel there is no true valour.
I came to seek you both.   121
    Claud. We have been up and down to seek thee;
for we are high-proof melancholy and would fain
have it beaten away. Wilt thou use thy wit?
    Bene. It is in my scabbard; shall I draw it? 125
    D. Pedro. Dost thou wear thy wit by thy side?
    Claud. Never any did so, though very many have
been beside their wit. I will bid thee draw, as we
do the minstrels; draw, to pleasure us.
    D. Pedro. As I am an honest man, he looks pale.
Art thou sick, or angry?   131

    Claud. What, courage, man! What though care
kill'd a cat, thou hast mettle enough in thee to kill
care.
    Bene. Sir, I shall meet your wit in the career, an
you charge it against me. I pray you choose another subject.   137
    Claud. Nay, then, give him another staff. This
last was broke across.
    D. Pedro. By this light, he changes more and
more. I think he be angry indeed.   141
    Claud. If he be, he knows how to turn his girdle.
    Bene. Shall I speak a word in your ear?
    Claud. God bless me from a challenge!   144
    Bene. [*Aside to Claudio.*] You are a villain! I
jest not. I will make it good how you dare, with
what you dare, and when you dare. Do me right,
or I will protest your cowardice. You have kill'd
a sweet lady, and her death shall fall heavy on you.
Let me hear from you.   151
    Claud. Well, I will meet you, so I may have good
cheer.
    D. Pedro. What, a feast, a feast?   154
    Claud. I' faith, I thank him. He hath bid me to
a calf's head and a capon; the which if I do not
carve most curiously, say my knife's naught. Shall
I not find a woodcock too?
    Bene. Sir, your wit ambles well; it goes easily. 159
    D. Pedro. I'll tell thee how Beatrice prais'd thy
wit the other day. I said thou hadst a fine wit.
"True," said she, "a fine little one." "No," said I,
"a great wit." "Right," says she, "a great gross
one." "Nay," said I, "a good wit." "Just," said
she, "it hurts nobody." "Nay," said I, "the 165
gentleman is wise." "Certain," said she, "a wise
gentleman." "Nay," said I, "he hath the tongues."
"That I believe," said she, "for he swore a thing to
me on Monday night, which he forswore on Tuesday
morning. There's a double tongue; there's two 170
tongues." Thus did she, an hour together, trans-
shape thy particular virtues; yet at last she concluded with a sigh, thou wast the proper'st man in
Italy.
    Claud. For the which she wept heartily and said
she car'd not.   176
    D. Pedro. Yea, that she did; but yet, for all that,
an if she did not hate him deadly, she would love
him dearly. The old man's daughter told us all. 180
    Claud. All, all; and, moreover, God saw him when
he was hid in the garden.
    D. Pedro. But when shall we set the savage bull's
horns on the sensible Benedick's head?
    Claud. Yea, and text underneath, "Here dwells
Benedick the married man"?   186

---

94. **Scambling:** quarrelsome. **fashion-monging:** dandified. 95. **cog:** cheat. 96. **anticly:** like a buffoon. 102. **wake your patience.** Not satisfactorily explained. It has been proposed to read *rack* for *wake* or *passions* for *patience*. 123. **high-proof:** exceedingly. 135. **career:** onset. 136. **charge:** level. 138. **staff:** lance. 142. **turn his girdle:** i.e., so that he can more quickly reach his dagger (a gesture of challenge). 148. **protest:** proclaim. 156–58. **calf's head, capon, woodcock.** All figures of stupidity. 157. **curiously:** exquisitely. 167. **hath the tongues:** is a linguist. 171. **trans-shape:** distort.

Bene. Fare you well, boy; you know my mind. I will leave you now to your gossip-like humour. You break jests as braggarts do their blades, which, God be thanked, hurt not. My lord, for your many   190 courtesies I thank you. I must discontinue your company. Your brother the bastard is fled from Messina. You have among you kill'd a sweet and innocent lady. For my Lord Lackbeard there, he and I shall meet; and, till then, peace be with him.

[*Exit.*]

D. Pedro. He is in earnest.   197

Claud. In most profound earnest; and, I'll warrant you, for the love of Beatrice.

D. Pedro. And hath challeng'd thee?   200

Claud. Most sincerely.

D. Pedro. What a pretty thing man is when he goes in his doublet and hose and leaves off his wit!

Claud. He is then a giant to an ape; but then is an ape a doctor to such a man.   206

D. Pedro. But, soft you, let me be. Pluck up, my heart, and be sad. Did he not say, my brother was fled?   209

Enter Constables [DOGBERRY, VERGES, *and the* Watch, *with*] CONRADE *and* BORACHIO.

Dog. Come you, sir. If justice cannot tame you, she shall ne'er weigh more reasons in her balance. Nay, an you be a cursing hypocrite once, you must be look'd to.

D. Pedro. How now? Two of my brother's men, bound! Borachio one!   215

Claud. Hearken after their offence, my lord.

D. Pedro. Officers, what offence have these men done?   218

Dog. Marry, sir, they have committed false report; moreover, they have spoken untruths; secondarily, they are slanders; sixth and lastly, they have belied a lady; thirdly, they have verified unjust things; and, to conclude, they are lying knaves.

D. Pedro. First, I ask thee what they have   225 done; thirdly, I ask thee what's their offence; sixth and lastly, why they are committed; and, to conclude, what you lay to their charge.

Claud. Rightly reasoned, and in his own division; and, by my troth, there's one meaning well suited.

D. Pedro. Who have you offended, masters,   232 that you are thus bound to your answer? This learned constable is too cunning to be understood. What's your offence?   235

Bora. Sweet Prince, let me go no farther to mine answer. Do you hear me, and let this count kill me. I have deceived even your very eyes. What your wisdoms could not discover, these shallow fools have brought to light, who in the night   240

overheard me confessing to this man how Don John your brother incensed me to slander the Lady Hero, how you were brought into the orchard and saw me court Margaret in Hero's garments, how you disgrac'd her, when you should marry her. My   245 villainy they have upon record; which I had rather seal with my death than repeat over to my shame. The lady is dead upon mine and my master's false accusation; and, briefly, I desire nothing but the reward of a villain.   251

D. Pedro. Runs not this speech like iron through your blood?

Claud. I have drunk poison whiles he utter'd it.

D. Pedro. But did my brother set thee on to this?

Bora. Yea, and paid me richly for the practice of it.   256

D. Pedro. He is compos'd and fram'd of treachery. And fled he is upon this villainy.

Claud. Sweet Hero! now thy image doth appear In the rare semblance that I lov'd it first.   260

Dog. Come, bring away the plaintiffs. By this time our sexton hath reformed Signior Leonato of the matter; and, masters, do not forget to specify, when time and place shall serve, that I am an ass.

Verg. Here, here comes master Signior Leonato, and the sexton too.   267

Re-enter LEONATO *and* ANTONIO, *with the* Sexton.

Leon. Which is the villain? Let me see his eyes, That, when I note another man like him   270 I may avoid him. Which of these is he?

Bora. If you would know your wronger, look on me.

Leon. Art thou the slave that with thy breath hast kill'd
Mine innocent child?

Bora.   Yea, even I alone.

Leon. No, not so, villain; thou beliest thyself.   275 Here stand a pair of honourable men,
A third is fled, that had a hand in it.
I thank you, princes, for my daughter's death.
Record it with your high and worthy deeds.
'Twas bravely done, if you bethink you of it.   280

Claud. I know not how to pray your patience;
Yet I must speak. Choose your revenge yourself;
Impose me to what penance your invention
Can lay upon my sin; yet sinn'd I not
But in mistaking.

D. Pedro.   By my soul, nor I;   285
And yet, to satisfy this good old man,
I would bend under any heavy weight
That he'll enjoin me to.

Leon. I cannot bid you bid my daughter live, —
That were impossible; but, I pray you both,   290

---

205. **giant:** i.e., in stature. **to:** compared to.   206. **doctor:** scholar.   216. **Hearken after:** inquire into.   231. **one... suited:** one idea dressed up in four different ways.   233. **bound...answer:** arraigned.   242. **incensed:** instigated.   261. **plaintiffs:** for *defendants*.

Possess the people in Messina here
How innocent she died; and if your love
Can labour ought in sad invention,
Hang her an epitaph upon her tomb
And sing it to her bones, sing it to-night.   295
To-morrow morning come you to my house,
And since you could not be my son-in-law,
Be yet my nephew.   My brother hath a daughter,
Almost the copy of my child that's dead,
And she alone is heir to both of us.   300
Give her the right you should have giv'n her cousin,
And so dies my revenge.
Claud.   O noble sir,
Your over-kindness doth wring tears from me!
I do embrace your offer; and dispose
For henceforth of poor Claudio.   305
Leon. To-morrow then I will expect your coming;
To-night I take my leave.   This naughty man
Shall face to face be brought to Margaret,
Who I believe was pack'd in all this wrong,
Hir'd to it by your brother.
Bora.   No, by my soul, she was not,   310
Nor knew not what she did when she spoke to me,
But always hath been just and virtuous
In anything that I do know by her.
Dog. Moreover, sir, which indeed is not under
white and black, this plaintiff here, the offender, 315
did call me ass.   I beseech you, let it be remem-
b'red in his punishment.   And also, the watch heard
them talk of one Deformed.   They say he wears a
key in his ear and a lock hanging by it, and borrows
money in God's name, the which he hath   320
used so long and never paid that now men grow
hard-hearted and will lend nothing for God's sake.
Pray you, examine him upon that point.
Leon. I thank thee for thy care and honest pains.
Dog. Your worship speaks like a most thankful and
[reverend] youth, and I praise God for you.   326
Leon. There's for thy pains.
Dog. God save the foundation!
Leon. Go, I discharge thee of thy prisoner, and I
thank thee.   330
Dog. I leave an arrant knave with your worship;
which I beseech your worship to correct yourself, for
the example of others.   God keep your worship!   I
wish your worship well.   God restore you to health!
I humbly give you leave to depart; and if a merry
meeting may be wish'd, God prohibit it!   Come,   336
neighbour.
          [Exeunt [Dogberry and Verges].
Leon. Until to-morrow morning, lords, farewell.
Ant. Farewell, my lords.   We look for you to-
          morrow.

D. Pedro. We will not fail.
Claud.   To-night I'll mourn with Hero.
Leon. [To the Watch.] Bring you these fellows on.
We'll talk with Margaret,   341
How her acquaintance grew with this lewd fel-
          low.
          [Exeunt [severally].

[SCENE II.   *Leonato's garden.*]

Enter BENEDICK *and* MARGARET *[meeting].*

Bene. Pray thee, sweet Mistress Margaret, deserve well at my hands by helping me to the speech
of Beatrice.
Marg. Will you then write me a sonnet in praise
of my beauty?   5
Bene. In so high a style, Margaret, that no man
living shall come over it; for, in most comely truth,
thou deservest it.
Marg. To have no man come over me!   Why,
shall I always keep below stairs?   10
Bene. Thy wit is as quick as the greyhound's
mouth; it catches.
Marg. And yours as blunt as the fencer's foils,
which hit, but hurt not.   14
Bene. A most manly wit, Margaret; it will not
hurt a woman.   And so, I pray thee, call Beatrice;
I give thee the bucklers.
Marg. Give us the swords; we have bucklers of
our own.   19
Bene. If you use them, Margaret, you must put
in the pikes with a vice; and they are dangerous
weapons for maids.
Marg. Well, I will call Beatrice to you, who I
think hath legs.   *[Exit Margaret.*
Bene. And therefore will come.   25
[Sings.]   The god of love,
          That sits above,
And knows me, and knows me,
          How pitiful I deserve, —   29
I mean in singing; but in loving, Leander the good
swimmer, Troilus the first employer of panders,
and a whole bookful of these quondam carpet-
mongers, whose names yet run smoothly in the
even road of a blank verse, why, they were never
so truly turn'd over and over as my poor self in
love.   Marry, I cannot show it in rhyme.   I   35
have tried.   I can find out no rhyme to "lady"
but "baby," an innocent rhyme; for "scorn,"
"horn," a hard rhyme; for "school," "fool," a
babbling rhyme; very ominous endings.   No, I
was not born under a rhyming planet, nor I cannot
woo in festival terms.   41

---

291. **possess**: inform.   309. **pack'd**: leagued.   313. **by**: of.   326. **[reverend]** F. *reverent* Q.   328. **God . . . foundation.**
The usual formula upon receiving alms.   342. **lewd**: wicked.
     Sc. ii, 6. style: with a pun on *stile*.   17. **I . . . bucklers**: I yield.   21. **pikes**: spikes (in the center of bucklers).   **vice**:
screw.   32–33. **quondam carpet-mongers**: ancient carpet-knights.

Enter BEATRICE.

Sweet Beatrice, wouldst thou come when I call'd thee?

Beat. Yea, signior, and depart when you bid me.

Bene. O, stay but till then!   45

Beat. "Then" is spoken; fare you well now. And yet, ere I go, let me go with that I came for; which is, with knowing what hath pass'd between you and Claudio.

Bene. Only foul words; and thereupon I will kiss thee.   51

Beat. Foul words is but foul wind, and foul wind is but foul breath, and foul breath is noisome; therefore I will depart unkiss'd.   54

Bene. Thou hast frighted the word out of his right sense, so forcible is thy wit. But I must tell thee plainly, Claudio undergoes my challenge; and either I must shortly hear from him, or I will subscribe him a coward. And, I pray thee now, tell me for which of my bad parts didst thou first fall in love with me?   61

Beat. For them all together, which maintained so politic a state of evil that they will not admit any good part to intermingle with them. But for which of my good parts did you first suffer love for me?   66

Bene. Suffer love! a good epithet! I do suffer love indeed, for I love thee against my will.

Beat. In spite of your heart, I think; alas, poor heart! If you spite it for my sake, I will spite it for yours; for I will never love that which my friend hates.   72

Bene. Thou and I are too wise to woo peaceably.

Beat. It appears not in this confession. There's not one wise man among twenty that will praise himself.   77

Bene. An old, an old instance, Beatrice, that liv'd in the time of good neighbours. If a man do not erect in this age his own tomb ere he dies, he shall live no longer in monument than the bell rings and the widow weeps.   82

Beat. And how long is that, think you?

Bene. Question. Why, an hour in clamour and a quarter in rheum; therefore is it most expedient for the wise, if Don Worm, his conscience, find   86 no impediment to the contrary, to be the trumpet of his own virtues, as I am to myself. So much for praising myself, who, I myself will bear witness, is praiseworthy. And now tell me, how doth your cousin?   91

Beat. Very ill.

Bene. And how do you?

Beat. Very ill too.

Bene. Serve God, love me, and mend. There will I leave you too, for here comes one in haste. 96

Enter URSULA.

Urs. Madam, you must come to your uncle. Yonder's old coil at home. It is proved my Lady Hero hath been falsely accus'd, the Prince and Claudio mightily abus'd; and Don John is the author of all, who is fled and gone. Will you come presently?   102

Beat. Will you go hear this news, signior?

Bene. I will live in thy heart, die in thy lap, and be buried in thy eyes; and moreover I will go with thee to thy uncle's.   [*Exeunt.* 106

[SCENE III. *A church.*]

Enter DON PEDRO, CLAUDIO, *and three or four*
with tapers.

Claud. Is this the monument of Leonato?

A Lord. It is, my lord.

Claud. [*Reading out of a scroll.*]

EPITAPH.

"Done to death by slanderous tongues
    Was the Hero that here lies.
Death, in guerdon of her wrongs,   5
    Gives her fame which never dies.
So the life that died with shame
Lives in death with glorious fame."

Hang thou there upon the tomb,
    Praising her when I am [dumb].   10
Now, music, sound, and sing your solemn hymn.

SONG.

"Pardon, goddess of the night,
    Those that slew thy virgin knight;
For the which, with songs of woe,
    Round about her tomb they go.   15
Midnight, assist our moan;
    Help us to sigh and groan,
        Heavily, heavily.
Graves, yawn and yield your dead,
    Till death be uttered,   20
        Heavily, heavily."

[*Claud.*] Now, unto thy bones good night!
    Yearly will I do this rite.

D. Pedro. Good morrow, masters; put your torches out.
The wolves have prey'd; and look, the gentle day,   25
Before the wheels of Phœbus, round about

57. **undergoes:** has received.   79. **time . . . neighbours:** good old times when neighbors were kindly.   85. **rheum:** tears.
98. **old coil:** great stir.
Sc. iii, 10. **[dumb]** F.   *dead* Q.   20. **uttered:** cast out.   22. **[Claud.]** (Rowe).   *Lo.* Q.

Dapples the drowsy east with spots of grey.
Thanks to you all, and leave us.　Fare you well.
　Claud.　Good morrow, masters.　Each his several
　　way.
　D. Pedro.　Come, let us hence, and put on other
　　weeds;　　　　　　　　　　　　　　　　30
And then to Leonato's we will go.
　Claud.　And Hymen now with luckier issue
　　[speed's]
Than this for whom we rend'red up this woe.
　　　　　　　　　　　　　　　　[Exeunt.

[SCENE IV.　*A room in Leonato's house.*]

Enter LEONATO, *old man* [ANTONIO], BENEDICK,
[BEATRICE,] MARGARET, URSULA, FRIAR FRANCIS,
and HERO.

　Friar.　Did I not tell you she was innocent?
　Leon.　So are the Prince and Claudio, who
　　accus'd her
Upon the error that you heard debated.
But Margaret was in some fault for this,
Although against her will, as it appears　　5
In the true course of all the question.
　Ant.　Well, I am glad that all things sort so well.
　Bene.　And so am I, being else by faith enforc'd
To call young Claudio to a reckoning for it.　9
　Leon.　Well, daughter, and you gentlewomen all,
Withdraw into a chamber by yourselves,
And when I send for you, come hither mask'd.
The Prince and Claudio promis'd by this hour
To visit me.　You know your office, brother.
You must be father to your brother's daughter,　15
And give her to young Claudio.　[*Exeunt Ladies.*
　Ant.　Which I will do with confirm'd countenance.
　Bene.　Friar, I must entreat your pains, I think.
　Friar.　To do what, signior?
　Bene.　To bind me, or undo me; one of them.　20
Signior Leonato, truth it is, good signior,
Your niece regards me with an eye of favour.
　Leon.　That eye my daughter lent her; 'tis most
　　true.
　Bene.　And I do with an eye of love requite her.
　Leon.　The sight whereof I think you had from
　　me,　　　　　　　　　　　　　　　25
From Claudio, and the Prince.　But what's your
　　will?
　Bene.　Your answer, sir, is enigmatical;
But, for my will, my will is your good will
May stand with ours, this day to be conjoin'd
In the state of honourable marriage;　　30
In which, good friar, I shall desire your help.
　Leon.　My heart is with your liking.
　Friar.　　　　　　　　　　　And my help.

Here comes the Prince and Claudio.

Enter DON PEDRO *and* CLAUDIO, *and two or*
three other.

　D. Pedro.　Good morrow to this fair assembly.
　Leon.　Good morrow, Prince; good morrow,
　　Claudio;　　　　　　　　　　　35
We here attend you.　Are you yet determin'd
To-day to marry with my brother's daughter?
　Claud.　I'll hold my mind, were she an Ethiope.
　Leon.　Call her forth, brother; here's the friar
　　ready.　　　　　　　　　　*[Exit Antonio.]*
　D. Pedro.　Good morrow, Benedick.　Why, what's
　　the matter,　　　　　　　　　40
That you have such a February face,
So full of frost, of storm and cloudiness?
　Claud.　I think he thinks upon the savage bull.
Tush, fear not, man; we'll tip thy horns with gold
And all Europa shall rejoice at thee,　　45
As once Europa did at lusty Jove,
When he would play the noble beast in love.
　Bene.　Bull Jove, sir, had an amiable low;
And some such strange bull leap'd your father's cow,
And got a calf in that same noble feat　　50
Much like to you, for you have just his bleat.

Re-enter ANTONIO, *with the* LADIES [*masked*].

　Claud.　For this I owe you: here comes other
　　reck'nings.
Which is the lady I must seize upon?
　[*Ant.*]　This same is she, and I do give you her.
　Claud.　Why, then she's mine.　Sweet, let me
　　see your face.　　　　　　　　55
　Leon.　No, that you shall not, till you take her
　　hand
Before this friar and swear to marry her.
　Claud.　Give me your hand.　Before this holy
　　friar
I am your husband, if you like of me.　　59
　Hero.　And when I liv'd, I was your other wife;
　　　　　　　　　　　　　　　[Unmasking.]
And when you lov'd, you were my other husband.
　Claud.　Another Hero!
　Hero.　　　　　　　　Nothing certainer.
One Hero died defil'd, but I do live;
And surely as I live, I am a maid.　　64
　D. Pedro.　The former Hero!　Hero that is dead!
　Leon.　She died, my lord, but whiles her slander
　　liv'd.
　Friar.　All this amazement can I qualify,
When after that the holy rites are ended,
I'll tell you largely of fair Hero's death.
Meantime let wonder seem familiar,　　70
And to the chapel let us presently.

32. [speed's] (Thirlby conj.): favor us. *speeds* QF.
Sc. iv, 6. question: investigation.　7. sort: turn out.　17. confirm'd: steady, grave.　43. Cf. I.i.263 ff. and V.i.183.
46. Europa.　Jove, in the guise of a white bull, abducted the mortal Europa.　54. [*Ant.*] (Theobald).　*Leon.* QF.　67.
qualify: moderate.　69. largely: in detail.

Bene. Soft and fair, friar.   Which is Beatrice?

Beat. [*Unmasking.*] I answer to that name.
What is your will?

Bene. Do not you love me?

Beat.   Why, no; no more than reason.

Bene. Why, then your uncle and the Prince and
Claudio   75
Have been deceived.   They swore you did.

Beat. Do not you love me?

Bene.   Troth, no; no more than reason.

Beat. Why, then my cousin, Margaret, and
Ursula
Are much deceiv'd, for they did swear you did.

Bene. They swore that you were almost sick
for me.   80

Beat. They swore that you were well-nigh dead
for me.

Bene. 'Tis no such matter.   Then you do not
love me?

Beat. No, truly, but in friendly recompense.

Leon. Come, cousin, I am sure you love the
gentleman.

Claud. And I'll be sworn upon't that he loves
her;   85
For here's a paper written in his hand,
A halting sonnet of his own pure brain,
Fashion'd to Beatrice.

Hero.   And here's another
Writ in my cousin's hand, stol'n from her pocket,
Containing her affection unto Benedick.   90

Bene. A miracle! here's our own hands against
our hearts.   Come, I will have thee; but, by this
light, I take thee for pity.

Beat. I would not deny you; but, by this good
day, I yield upon great persuasion; and partly   95
to save your life, for I was told you were in a consumption.

[*Bene.*] Peace!   I will stop your mouth.

[*Kissing her.*]

D. Pedro. How dost thou, Benedick, the married
man?   100

Bene. I'll tell thee what, Prince; a college of
wit-crackers cannot flout me out of my humour.
Dost thou think I care for a satire or an epigram?
No; if a man will be beaten with brains, 'a shall
wear nothing handsome about him.   In brief,   105
since I do purpose to marry, I will think
nothing to any purpose that the world can say
against it; and therefore never flout at me for
what I have said against it, for man is a giddy
thing, and this is my conclusion.   For thy part,
Claudio, I did think to have beaten thee; but   110
in that thou art like to be my kinsman, live unbruis'd and love my cousin.

Claud. I had well hop'd thou wouldst have
denied Beatrice, that I might have cudgell'd thee
out of thy single life, to make thee a double-   116
dealer; which, out of question, thou wilt be, if my
cousin do not look exceeding narrowly to thee.

Bene. Come, come, we are friends.   Let's have
a dance ere we are married, that we may lighten
our own hearts and our wives' heels.   121

Leon. We'll have dancing afterward.

Bene. First, of my word; therefore play, music.
Prince, thou art sad; get thee a wife, get thee a
wife.   There is no staff more reverend than one
tipp'd with horn.   126

Enter a MESSENGER.

Mess. My lord, your brother John is ta'en in flight,
And brought with armed men back to Messina.

Bene. Think not on him till to-morrow.   I'll
devise thee brave punishments for him.   Strike up,
pipers.   [*Dance.* [*Exeunt.*] 131

98. [*Bene.*] (Theobald).   *Leon.* QF.   104. **beaten with brains**: ridiculed, satirized.   **wear...him**: i.e., to avoid
ridicule.   116. **double-dealer**: (1) married man, (2) unfaithful husband.

As You Like It

UNDER THE DATE of August 4, 1600, *As You Like It* appears in the Stationers' Register, along with *Henry V*, *Much Ado*, and Jonson's *Everyman In His Humour*, as a play "to be staied." The entry was undoubtedly made to forestall piracy and in the case of this play was evidently successful, for no text of *As You Like It* appeared earlier than that of the First Folio. The history of the other Shakespearean plays is, however, otherwise. *Henry V* was printed in a sadly corrupt Quarto in 1600 (despite a formal entry eleven days later to Thomas Pavier), and a good Quarto of *Much Ado* appeared before the end of the year after a regular entry on August 23 to Andrew Wise and William Aspley. That *As You Like It* was not printed before 1623 would suggest that it remained sufficiently popular on the stage to afford Shakespeare's company no temptation to release it for the rewards of publication. The present text is that of the First Folio with some modifications taken from the later Folios and the emendations of modern editors.

The date of the play may be determined within close limits. Since it is not mentioned in the valuable list of Meres, it cannot be earlier than the end of 1598. The quotation from *Hero and Leander*, with the gentle reference to Marlowe as the "dead shepherd" (III.v.81–82), is also significant. That poem was first published in 1598, and though Shakespeare could conceivably have read it in manuscript before Marlowe's death on May 30, 1593, one must hold the printed work much more likely to have inspired the allusion in the play. In the light of the foregoing evidence, the preponderance of prose, and the generally high quality of the composition, 1599 or early 1600 may be taken as a safe date.

Certain discrepancies within the play have caused undue concern. The inconsistencies in connection with the relative statures of Rosalind and Celia (I.ii.284; I.iii.117; IV.iii.88–89), the length of the banished Duke's stay in Arden (I.i.120; I.iii.73; II.i.2), and the identities of the two Dukes are plainly the kind of inadvertence which is to be met with in a great many of Shakespeare's plays. In the Folio the speeches of Rosalind's father, the banished Duke, are headed *Duke* Senior; those of the usurping Duke, Celia's father, simply *Duke*. The former is nowhere called by any name, but from I.ii.246 and V.iv.160 it appears that the name of the latter was Frederick. Thus it seems somewhat odd when, in a line clearly addressed to Celia (I.ii.87), Touchstone calls her father, the *younger* Duke, "old Frederick." Such an inconsistency (if indeed it is one, for perhaps Touchstone is only speaking jocosely with a Clown's license) is not of great moment. It would never be noticed on the stage and it is hardly more disconcerting than Shakespeare's duplicating the conspicuous name of Jaques for the second son of Sir Rowland de Boys. The appearance of an appreciable number of blank verse rhythms in certain passages of prose has been held to indicate that those passages were originally in verse, and this factor, along with the other textual peculiarities already cited, has been taken as evidence of an earlier form of the play (1593) which Shakespeare was revising around 1598. But the occurrence of such "verse fossils" in prose no more calls for elaborate theorizing than do the other matters for which simple explanations are at hand. As has frequently been remarked, verse rhythms are by no means rare in English prose, certainly not in Shakespeare's. Indeed, there would be some reason for surprise if they did not occur in the prose of one who was a supreme master of verse, especially in a play which alternates prose and verse.

As You Like It is a straight dramatization of a pastoral tale in exuberant euphuistic prose called *Rosalynde, Euphues' Golden Legacie* (1590). Thomas Lodge, the author, had based his story upon an anonymous Middle English poem, *The Tale of Gamelyn*, which was at one time erroneously attributed to Chaucer because it is included in certain manuscripts of *The Canterbury Tales*. It does not, however, appear that Shakespeare knew this earlier work. From Lodge's tale he took the substance of his play, with omission and additions as he saw fit. The principal derivatives from Lodge are as follows: the themes of usurpation and banishment (in Lodge, Torismond, King of France, has usurped the throne of his brother Gerismond, the rightful king), the quarrel between Orlando and Oliver (Rosader and Saladyne), the wrestling match, the retreat into Arden, the affection of Rosalind and Celia (Rosalynde and Alinda, cousins as in the play), the wooing of the disguised Rosalind by Orlando (the pseudonym Ganymede also comes from Lodge), the eventual marriage of the remorseful Oliver and Celia, and the affair of Phebe and Silvius (Phoebe and Montanus). Shakespeare has compressed the time covered by the action and has eliminated some of the violent incidents which in the novel attend the quarrel between the hero and his persecuting brother. Oliver's reconciliation with Orlando is somewhat differently motivated in the novel. In the play it springs simply from his gratitude for Orlando's magnanimity in rescuing him from the lion; in the novel Saladyne has already repented of his cruelty to Rosader, owing to persecutions visited upon him by Torismond, and is seeking for his brother when this crisis occurs. Similarly, the marriage of Oliver and Celia is rendered more credible in the novel, because there, in an episode which Shakespeare omits, Saladyne rescues Alinda from a band of robbers who have abducted her. In *Rosalynde*, the restoration of the Duke is brought about by the overthrow and death of the usurper in battle, in contrast with the dramatist's milder device of conversion, which, however unplausible, suits better the mood of the play.

Shakespeare has created a number of new characters, of which Audrey, William, Amiens, Touchstone, and Jaques are the most interesting, the last two being, surely, immortal. Audrey and William, good Warwickshire rustics, add a touch of the true earth to the literary pastoralism of Silvius and Phebe inherited from Lodge. The rôle of Touchstone has something of novelty. Touchstone is the first of Shakespeare's court clowns and looks forward to Feste in *Twelfth Night* and the Fool in

Lear. To put down such a fellow in a pastoral setting was an innovation, but Touchstone, however incongruous in Arden, is merry there, and to good purpose. Often wiser than he is aware of, he breaks his wit over this thing and that with bracing and tonic effect. A genial provider of salutary comic remark, he is of the opposition party, but never with offense. He satirizes court life even while praising it; he ridicules the punctilios of professional quarrelling; he produces a fine "false gallop of verses" that puts Orlando's amorous jingle to shame; and by his grosser passion for Audrey he seems to burlesque, though this time doubtless unintentionally, the other love-making in the play. Jaques, like Touchstone, is a self-appointed critic, but his commentary has a different spirit. Where Touchstone is freely merry, Jaques is caustic. He has been disillusioned, because, one infers, he has been too much in the world. He is a malcontent, a Jonsonian humour character, though by the very distinction of his mind made individual, nursing his melancholy and taking his satisfaction in the contemplation and censure of human folly. His temperament has particular interest because it looks forward to Hamlet's. But whereas Hamlet's melancholy has profound tragic implications, that of Jaques remains a philosophic mood. Jaques, it may be noted, remains true to himself. When the other sojourners in Arden return to Court at the end of the play, he stays in the forest, retiring to the cell of the "convertite" Duke. Neither Touchstone nor Jaques is really necessary to the plot, yet they contribute immeasurably through the quality and the contrast of their personalities to the richness and vitality of the play.

Rosalind has ever enjoyed her due meed of praise. She is one of the most popular of Shakespeare's heroines. Her youth, her gaiety, her candor, and her courage have always captivated. She has, perhaps, the wit of Portia and Beatrice softened by the gentleness of Viola; but whatever the components of her charm, that charm is all her own.

AS YOU LIKE IT

[DRAMATIS PERSONÆ

DUKE, *living in banishment.*
FREDERICK, *his brother, and usurper of his dominions.*
AMIENS,
JAQUES, } *lords attending on the banished Duke.*
LE BEAU, *a courtier attending upon Frederick.*
CHARLES, *wrestler to Frederick.*
OLIVER,
JAQUES, } *sons of Sir Roland de Boys.*
ORLANDO,
ADAM,
DENNIS, } *servants to Oliver.*

TOUCHSTONE, *a clown.*
SIR OLIVER MARTEXT, *a vicar.*
CORIN,
SILVIUS, } *shepherds.*
WILLIAM, *a country fellow, in love with Audrey.*
A person representing Hymen.

ROSALIND, *daughter to the banished Duke.*
CELIA, *daughter to Frederick.*
PHEBE, *a shepherdess.*
AUDREY, *a country wench.*

Lords, pages, attendants, etc.

SCENE: *Oliver's house; Duke Frederick's court; and the Forest of Arden.*]

ACT I

SCENE I. [*Orchard of Oliver's house.*]

Enter ORLANDO *and* ADAM.

Orl. As I remember, Adam, it was upon this fashion: bequeathed me by will but poor a thousand crowns, and, as thou sayest, charged my brother, on his blessing, to breed me well; and there begins my sadness. My brother Jaques he keeps at 5 school, and report speaks goldenly of his profit. For my part, he keeps me rustically at home, or, to speak more properly, stays me here at home un-kept; for call you that keeping for a gentleman of my birth, that differs not from the stalling of an 10 ox? His horses are bred better; for, besides that they are fair with their feeding, they are taught their manage, and to that end riders dearly hir'd; but I, his brother, gain nothing under him but growth; for the which his animals on his dung- 15 hills are as much bound to him as I. Besides this nothing that he so plentifully gives me, the some-thing that nature gave me his countenance seems to take from me. He lets me feed with his hinds, bars me the place of a brother, and, as much as 20 in him lies, mines my gentility with my education. This is it, Adam, that grieves me; and the spirit of my father, which I think is within me, begins to mutiny against this servitude. I will no longer endure it, though yet I know no wise remedy 25 how to avoid it.

Enter OLIVER.

Adam. Yonder comes my master, your brother.
Orl. Go apart, Adam, and thou shalt hear how he will shake me up. 30
Oli. Now, sir! what make you here?
Orl. Nothing. I am not taught to make any thing.
Oli. What mar you then, sir? 34
Orl. Marry, sir, I am helping you to mar that which God made, a poor unworthy brother of yours, with idleness.
Oli. Marry, sir, be better employed, and be naught awhile. 39

Act I, sc. i, 4. **on his blessing:** as a condition to his blessing. 6. **school:** university. 12–13. **taught...manage:** given their training. 18. **countenance:** treatment. 19. **hinds:** menials. 21. **mines:** undermines. 39. **be naught awhile:** clear out.

Orl. Shall I keep your hogs and eat husks with them? What prodigal portion have I spent, that I should come to such penury?

Oli. Know you where you are, sir?

Orl. O, sir, very well; here in your orchard.

Oli. Know you before whom, sir?   45

Orl. Ay, better than him I am before knows me. I know you are my eldest brother; and, in the gentle condition of blood, you should so know me. The courtesy of nations allows you my better, in that you are the first-born; but the same tradi- 50 tion takes not away my blood, were there twenty brothers betwixt us. I have as much of my father in me as you; albeit, I confess, your coming before me is nearer to his reverence.

Oli. What, boy!   55

Orl. Come, come, elder brother, you are too young in this.

Oli. Wilt thou lay hands on me, villain?

Orl. I am no villain; I am the youngest son of Sir Roland de Boys. He was my father, and 60 he is thrice a villain that says such a father begot villains. Wert thou not my brother, I would not take this hand from thy throat till this other had pull'd out thy tongue for saying so. Thou hast rail'd on thyself.   65

Adam. Sweet masters, be patient; for your father's remembrance, be at accord.

Oli. Let me go, I say.

Orl. I will not, till I please. You shall hear me. My father charg'd you in his will to give me 70 good education. You have train'd me like a peasant, obscuring and hiding from me all gentleman-like qualities. The spirit of my father grows strong in me, and I will no longer endure it; therefore allow me such exercises as may become a gentle- 75 man, or give me the poor allottery my father left me by testament. With that I will go buy my fortunes.

Oli. And what wilt thou do? Beg, when that is spent? Well, sir, get you in. I will not long 80 be troubled with you; you shall have some part of your will. I pray you, leave me.

Orl. I will no further offend you than becomes me for my good.

Oli. Get you with him, you old dog.   85

Adam. Is "old dog" my reward? Most true, I have lost my teeth in your service. God be with my old master! He would not have spoke such a word.   89

[*Exeunt Orlando and Adam.*

Oli. Is it even so? Begin you to grow upon me? I will physic your rankness, and yet give no thousand crowns neither. Holla, Dennis!

Enter DENNIS.

Den. Calls your worship?

Oli. Was not Charles, the Duke's wrestler, here to speak with me?   95

Den. So please you, he is here at the door and importunes access to you.

Oli. Call him in. [*Exit Dennis.*] 'Twill be a good way; and to-morrow the wrestling is.

Enter CHARLES.

Cha. Good morrow to your worship.   100

Oli. Good Monsieur Charles, what's the new news at the new court?

Cha. There's no news at the court, sir, but the old news: that is, the old Duke is banished by his younger brother the new Duke; and three or 105 four loving lords have put themselves into voluntary exile with him, whose lands and revenues enrich the new Duke; therefore he gives them good leave to wander.

Oli. Can you tell if Rosalind, the Duke's daughter, be banished with her father?   111

Cha. O, no; for the Duke's daughter, her cousin, so loves her, being ever from their cradles bred together, that [she] would have followed her exile, or have died to stay behind her. She is at the 115 court, and no less beloved of her uncle than his own daughter; and never two ladies loved as they do.

Oli. Where will the old Duke live?   119

Cha. They say he is already in the forest of Arden, and a many merry men with him; and there they live like the old Robin Hood of England. They say many young gentlemen flock to him every day, and fleet the time carelessly, as they did in the golden world.   125

Oli. What, you wrestle to-morrow before the new Duke?

Cha. Marry, do I, sir; and I came to acquaint you with a matter. I am given, sir, secretly to understand that your younger brother, Orlando, 130 hath a disposition to come in disguis'd against me to try a fall. To-morrow, sir, I wrestle for my credit; and he that escapes me without some broken limb shall acquit him well. Your brother is but young and tender; and, for your love, I 135 would be loath to foil him, as I must, for my own honour, if he come in; therefore, out of my love to you, I came hither to acquaint you withal, that either you might stay him from his intendment, or brook such disgrace well as he shall run into, 140 in that it is a thing of his own search, and altogether against my will.

Oli. Charles, I thank thee for thy love to me, which thou shalt find I will most kindly requite.

---

49. **courtesy of nations:** i.e., by virtue of the law of primogeniture. 54. **is...reverence:** gives you better title to the respect due to him. 76. **allottery:** legacy. 90. **grow upon:** take liberties with. 91. **rankness:** exuberant growth, insolence. 114. **[she]** F$_3$. *he* F$_1$. 125. **golden world:** the golden age. 134. **shall:** must.

I had myself notice of my brother's purpose 145
herein, and have by underhand means laboured to
dissuade him from it, but he is resolute. I'll tell
thee, Charles, it is the stubbornest young fellow of
France; full of ambition, an envious emulator of
every man's good parts, a secret and villainous 150
contriver against me his natural brother; therefore
use thy discretion. I had as lief thou didst break
his neck as his finger. And thou wert best look
to't; for if thou dost him any slight disgrace, or if
he do not mightily grace himself on thee, he 155
will practise against thee by poison, entrap thee by
some treacherous device, and never leave thee till
he hath ta'en thy life by some indirect means or
other; for, I assure thee, and almost with tears I
speak it, there is not one so young and so vil- 160
lainous this day living. I speak but brotherly of
him; but should I anatomize him to thee as he is, I
must blush and weep, and thou must look pale and
wonder. 164
Cha. I am heartily glad I came hither to you.
If he come to-morrow, I'll give him his payment.
If ever he go alone again, I'll never wrestle for prize
more. And so, God keep your worship! [*Exit.*
Oli. Farewell, good Charles. 169
Now will I stir this gamester. I hope I shall see
an end of him; for my soul — yet I know not why
— hates nothing more than he. Yet he's gentle;
never school'd, and yet learned; full of noble device; of all sorts enchantingly beloved; and indeed
so much in the heart of the world, and espe- 175
cially of my own people, who best know him, that I
am altogether misprised. But it shall not be so
long; this wrestler shall clear all. Nothing remains
but that I kindle the boy thither, which now I'll
go about. [*Exit.* 180

SCENE II. [*Lawn before the Duke's palace.*]

Enter ROSALIND *and* CELIA.

Cel. I pray thee, Rosalind, sweet my coz, be
merry.
Ros. Dear Celia, I show more mirth than I am
mistress of; and would you yet [I] were merrier?
Unless you could teach me to forget a banished 5
father, you must not learn me how to remember
any extraordinary pleasure.
Cel. Herein I see thou lov'st me not with the full
weight that I love thee. If my uncle, thy banished
father, had banished thy uncle, the Duke my 10
father, so thou hadst been still with me, I could
have taught my love to take thy father for mine.

So wouldst thou, if the truth of thy love to me were
so righteously temper'd as mine is to thee. 15
Ros. Well, I will forget the condition of my
estate, to rejoice in yours.
Cel. You know my father hath no child but I,
nor none is like to have; and, truly, when he dies,
thou shalt be his heir; for what he hath taken 20
away from thy father perforce, I will render thee
again in affection. By mine honour, I will; and
when I break that oath, let me turn monster.
Therefore, my sweet Rose, my dear Rose, be
merry. 25
Ros. From henceforth I will, coz, and devise
sports. Let me see; what think you of falling in love?
Cel. Marry, I prithee, do, to make sport withal.
But love no man in good earnest, nor no further 30
in sport neither than with safety of a pure blush
thou mayst in honour come off again.
Ros. What shall be our sport, then?
Cel. Let us sit and mock the good housewife
Fortune from her wheel, that her gifts may henceforth be bestowed equally. 36
Ros. I would we could do so; for her benefits
are mightily misplaced, and the bountiful blind
woman doth most mistake in her gifts to women. 39
Cel. 'Tis true; for those that she makes fair she
scarce makes honest, and those that she makes
honest she makes very ill-favouredly.
Ros. Nay, now thou goest from Fortune's office
to Nature's. Fortune reigns in gifts of the world,
not in the lineaments of Nature. 45

Enter Clown [TOUCHSTONE].

Cel. No? When Nature hath made a fair
creature, may she not by Fortune fall into the fire?
Though Nature hath given us wit to flout at Fortune, hath not Fortune sent in this fool to cut off
the argument? 50
Ros. Indeed, there is Fortune too hard for
Nature, when Fortune makes Nature's natural the
cutter-off of Nature's wit.
Cel. Peradventure this is not Fortune's work
neither, but Nature's; who, [perceiving] our
natural wits too dull to reason of such goddesses, 55
hath sent this natural for our whetstone; for always the dulness of the fool is the whetstone of the
wits. How now, wit! whither wander you?
Touch. Mistress, you must come away to your
father. 61
Cel. Were you made the messenger?
Touch. No, by mine honour, but I was bid to
come for you.

146. **underhand:** indirect. 151. **natural:** very own. 155. **grace ... thee:** win favor at your expense. 156. **practise:** plot. 167. **go alone:** walk without support. 170. **gamester:** would-be athlete. 173. **device:** aspiration. 174. **enchant-ingly:** as if by enchantment. 177. **misprised:** despised. 179. **kindle:** incite.
Sc. ii, 4. [I] (Rowe). Om. F. 11. **so:** so long as, escape. 41. **honest:** chaste. 42. **ill-favouredly:** ugly. 15. **righteously temper'd:** perfectly composed. 32. **come off:** 52. **natural:** idiot. 54. [perceiving] Ff₂₋₄. *perceiveth* F₁.

Ros. Where learned you that oath, fool?   65

Touch. Of a certain knight that swore by his honour they were good pancakes, and swore by his honour the mustard was naught. Now I'll stand to it, the pancakes were naught and the mustard was good, and yet was not the knight forsworn.   71

Cel. How prove you that, in the great heap of your knowledge?

Ros. Ay, marry, now unmuzzle your wisdom.

Touch. Stand you both forth now. Stroke   75 your chins, and swear by your beards that I am a knave.

Cel. By our beards, if we had them, thou art.   79

Touch. By my knavery, if I had it, then I were. But if you swear by that that is not, you are not forsworn. No more was this knight, swearing by his honour, for he never had any; or if he had, he had sworn it away before ever he saw those pancakes or that mustard.   85

Cel. Prithee, who is't that thou meanest?

Touch. One that old Frederick, your father, loves.

[Cel.] My father's love is enough to honour him. Enough! speak no more of him. You'll be whipp'd for taxation one of these days.   91

Touch. The more pity, that fools may not speak wisely what wise men do foolishly.

Cel. By my troth, thou sayest true; for since the little wit that fools have was silenced, the little   95 foolery that wise men have makes a great show. Here comes Monsieur the Beau.

Enter LE BEAU.

Ros. With his mouth full of news.

Cel. Which he will put on us, as pigeons feed their young.   100

Ros. Then shall we be news-cramm'd.

Cel. All the better; we shall be the more marketable. *Bon jour*, Monsieur Le Beau. What's the news?

Le Beau. Fair princess, you have lost much good sport.   106

Cel. Sport! Of what colour?

Le Beau. What colour, madam? How shall I answer you?

Ros. As wit and fortune will.   110

Touch. Or as the Destinies decrees.

Cel. Well said. That was laid on with a trowel.

Touch. Nay, if I keep not my rank, —

Ros. Thou losest thy old smell.

Le Beau. You amaze me, ladies. I would   115 have told you of good wrestling, which you have lost the sight of.

Ros. Yet tell us the manner of the wrestling.

Le Beau. I will tell you the beginning; and, if it please your ladyships, you may see the end.   120 For the best is yet to do; and here, where you are, they are coming to perform it.

Cel. Well, the beginning, that is dead and buried.

Le Beau. There comes an old man and his three sons, —   126

Cel. I could match this beginning with an old tale.

Le Beau. Three proper young men, of excellent growth and presence.   130

Ros. With bills on their necks, "Be it known unto all men by these presents."

Le Beau. The eldest of the three wrestled with Charles, the Duke's wrestler; which Charles in a moment threw him, and broke three of his ribs,   135 that there is little hope of life in him. So he serv'd the second, and so the third. Yonder they lie; the poor old man, their father, making such pitiful dole over them that all the beholders take his part with weeping.   140

Ros. Alas!

Touch. But what is the sport, monsieur, that the ladies have lost?

Le Beau. Why, this that I speak of.

Touch. Thus men may grow wiser every day.   145 It is the first time that ever I heard breaking of ribs was sport for ladies.

Cel. Or I, I promise thee.

Ros. But is there any else longs to see this broken music in his sides? Is there yet another   150 dotes upon rib-breaking? Shall we see this wrestling, cousin?

Le Beau. You must, if you stay here; for here is the place appointed for the wrestling, and they are ready to perform it.   155

Cel. Yonder, sure, they are coming. Let us now stay and see it.

Flourish. Enter DUKE [FREDERICK], Lords, ORLANDO, CHARLES, *and* Attendants.

Duke F. Come on. Since the youth will not be entreated, his own peril on his forwardness.

Ros. Is yonder the man?   160

Le Beau. Even he, madam.

Cel. Alas, he is too young! Yet he looks successfully.

Duke F. How now, daughter and cousin! Are you crept hither to see the wrestling?   165

Ros. Ay, my liege, so please you give us leave.

Duke F. You will take little delight in it, I can tell you, there is such odds in the man. In pity of the challenger's youth I would fain dissuade   170 him, but he will not be entreated. Speak to him, ladies; see if you can move him.

---

68. **naught:** worthless. 89. **[Cel.]** (Theobald). *Ros.* Ff. 91. **taxation:** satire. 107. **colour.** Le Beau had pronounced sport "spot," as it should probably be spelled in this line. 129. **proper:** handsome. 131. **bills:** proclamations. 138. **dole:** lament. 150. **broken music:** "part" music (for different instruments).

Cel. Call him hither, good Monsieur Le Beau.

Duke F. Do so; I'll not be by.   174

Le Beau. Monsieur the challenger, the princess calls for you.

Orl. I attend them with all respect and duty.

Ros. Young man, have you challeng'd Charles the wrestler?

Orl. No, fair princess; he is the general chal-   180
lenger. I come but in, as others do, to try with him the strength of my youth.

Cel. Young gentleman, your spirits are too bold for your years. You have seen cruel proof of this man's strength. If you saw yourself with your   185
eyes, or knew yourself with your judgement, the fear of your adventure would counsel you to a more equal enterprise. We pray you, for your own sake, to embrace your own safety, and give over this attempt.   190

Ros. Do, young sir; your reputation shall not therefore be misprised. We will make it our suit to the Duke that the wrestling might not go forward.   194

Orl. I beseech you, punish me not with your hard thoughts, wherein I confess me much guilty to deny so fair and excellent ladies any thing. But let your fair eyes and gentle wishes go with me to my trial; wherein if I be foil'd, there is but one sham'd that was never gracious; if kill'd, but one dead that   200
is willing to be so. I shall do my friends no wrong, for I have none to lament me; the world no injury, for in it I have nothing. Only in the world I fill up a place, which may be better supplied when I have made it empty.   205

Ros. The little strength that I have, I would it were with you.

Cel. And mine, to eke out hers.

Ros. Fare you well! Pray heaven I be deceiv'd in you!   210

Cel. Your heart's desires be with you!

Cha. Come, where is this young gallant that is so desirous to lie with his mother earth?

Orl. Ready, sir; but his will hath in it a more modest working.   215

Duke F. You shall try but one fall.

Cha. No, I warrant your Grace, you shall not entreat him to a second, that have so mightily per-suaded him from a first.   219

Orl. You mean to mock me after; you should not have mock'd me before. But come your ways.

Ros. Now Hercules be thy speed, young man!

Cel. I would I were invisible, to catch the strong fellow by the leg.   [*They wrestle.*

Ros. O excellent young man!   225

Cel. If I had a thunderbolt in mine eye I can tell

who should down.   [*Shout.* [*Charles is thrown.*]

Duke F. No more, no more.

Orl. Yes, I beseech your Grace. I am not yet well breath'd.   230

Duke F. How dost thou, Charles?

Le Beau. He cannot speak, my lord.

Duke F. Bear him away. What is thy name, young man?

Orl. Orlando, my liege; the youngest son of Sir Roland de Boys.   235

Duke F. I would thou hadst been son to some man else.
The world esteem'd thy father honourable,
But I did find him still mine enemy.
Thou shouldst have better pleas'd me with this deed
Hadst thou descended from another house.   240
But fare thee well; thou art a gallant youth.
I would thou hadst told me of another father.
        [*Exeunt Duke* [*Fred., train, and Le Beau*].

Cel. Were I my father, coz, would I do this?

Orl. I am more proud to be Sir Roland's son,
His youngest son, — and would not change that calling,   245
To be adopted heir to Frederick.

Ros. My father lov'd Sir Roland as his soul,
And all the world was of my father's mind.
Had I before known this young man his son,
I should have given him tears unto entreaties   250
Ere he should thus have ventur'd.

Cel.   Gentle cousin,
Let us go thank him and encourage him.
My father's rough and envious disposition
Sticks me at heart. Sir, you have well deserv'd.
If you do keep your promises in love   255
But justly, as you have exceeded all promise,
Your mistress shall be happy.

Ros.   Gentleman,
        [*Giving him a chain from her neck.*]
Wear this for me, one out of suits with Fortune,
That could give more, but that her hand lacks means.
Shall we go, coz?

Cel.   Ay. Fare you well, fair gentleman.

Orl. Can I not say, I thank you? My better parts   261
Are all thrown down, and that which here stands up
Is but a quintain, a mere lifeless block.

Ros. He calls us back. My pride fell with my fortunes;
I'll ask him what he would. Did you call, sir?   265
Sir, you have wrestled well, and overthrown
More than your enemies.

Cel.   Will you go, coz?

200. **gracious:** favored. 215. **working:** action. 222. **be thy speed:** favor you. 230. **breath'd:** put into good wind. 245. **calling:** name. 254. **sticks:** pierces. 258. **out...Fortune:** deprived of Fortune's livery, i.e., dismissed by her. 263. **quintain:** a wooden dummy for tilting at.

Ros. Have with you. Fare you well.
         [Exeunt [Rosalind and Celia].
Orl. What passion hangs these weights upon my
   tongue?
I cannot speak to her, yet she urg'd conference. 270

Re-enter LE BEAU.

O poor Orlando, thou art overthrown!
Or Charles or something weaker masters thee.
  Le Beau. Good sir, I do in friendship counsel you
To leave this place. Albeit you have deserv'd
High commendation, true applause, and love, 275
Yet such is now the Duke's condition
That he misconstrues all that you have done.
The Duke is humorous: — what he is, indeed,
More suits you to conceive than I to speak of.
  Orl. I thank you, sir; and, pray you, tell me
  this: 280
Which of the two was daughter of the Duke,
That here was at the wrestling?
  Le Beau. Neither his daughter, if we judge by
  manners;
But yet, indeed, the taller is his daughter.
The other is daughter to the banish'd Duke, 285
And here detain'd by her usurping uncle
To keep his daughter company; whose loves
Are dearer than the natural bond of sisters.
But I can tell you that of late this Duke
Hath ta'en displeasure 'gainst his gentle niece, 290
Grounded upon no other argument
But that the people praise her for her virtues,
And pity her for her good father's sake;
And, on my life, his malice 'gainst the lady
Will suddenly break forth. Sir, fare you well. 295
Hereafter, in a better world than this,
I shall desire more love and knowledge of you.
  Orl. I rest much bounden to you; fare you well.
         [Exit Le Beau.]
Thus must I from the smoke into the smother,
From tyrant Duke unto a tyrant brother. 300
But heavenly Rosalind!   •   *[Exit.*

SCENE III. *[A room in the palace.]*

Enter CELIA *and* ROSALIND.

  Cel. Why, cousin! why, Rosalind! Cupid have
mercy! not a word?
  Ros. Not one to throw at a dog.
  Cel. No, thy words are too precious to be cast
away upon curs; throw some of them at me. Come,
lame me with reasons. 6
  Ros. Then there were two cousins laid up, when

the one should be lam'd with reasons and the other
mad without any.
  Cel. But is all this for your father? 10
  Ros. No, some of it is for my child's father. O,
how full of briers is this working-day world!
  Cel. They are but burs, cousin, thrown upon
thee in holiday foolery. If we walk not in the trodden paths, our very petticoats will catch them. 15
  Ros. I could shake them off my coat. These
burs are in my heart.
  Cel. Hem them away.
  Ros. I would try, if I could cry hem and have
him. 20
  Cel. Come, come, wrestle with thy affections.
  Ros. O, they take the part of a better wrestler
than myself!
  Cel. O, a good wish upon you! you will try in
time, in despite of a fall. But, turning these 25
jests out of service, let us talk in good earnest. Is
it possible, on such a sudden you should fall into so
strong a liking with old Sir Roland's youngest son?
  Ros. The Duke my father lov'd his father
dearly. 31
  Cel. Doth it therefore ensue that you should
love his son dearly? By this kind of chase, I should
hate him, for my father hated his father dearly;
yet I hate not Orlando. 35
  Ros. No, faith, hate him not, for my sake.
  Cel. Why should I not? Doth he not deserve
well?

Enter DUKE FREDERICK, *with* Lords.

  Ros. Let me love him for that, and do you love
him because I do. Look, here comes the Duke. 41
  Cel. With his eyes full of anger.
  Duke F. Mistress, dispatch you with your safest
  haste,
And get you from our court.
  Ros.   Me, uncle?
  Duke F.   You, cousin.
Within these ten days if that thou be'st found 45
So near our public court as twenty miles,
Thou diest for it.
  Ros.   I do beseech your Grace,
Let me the knowledge of my fault bear with me.
If with myself I hold intelligence,
Or have acquaintance with mine own desires; 50
If that I do not dream, or be not frantic, —
As I do trust I am not — then, dear uncle,
Never so much as in a thought unborn
Did I offend your Highness.
  Duke F.   Thus do all traitors.
If their purgation did consist in words, 55

---

  276. **condition:** temper.   278. **humorous:** capricious.   284. **taller.** Inconsistent with other passages; e.g., I.iii.117,
IV.iii.88–89.   291. **argument:** reason.   299. **smoke . . . smother:** frying-pan into the fire.
  Sc. iii, 6. reasons: talk.   18. **Hem:** cough.   37. **deserve well:** i.e., to be hated.   43. **safest haste:** i.e.. all the speed your
safety requires.   55. **purgation:** acquittal.

They are as innocent as grace itself.
Let it suffice thee that I trust thee not.

Ros. Yet your mistrust cannot make me a traitor.
Tell me whereon the likelihood depends.

Duke F. Thou art thy father's daughter; there's
enough.   60

Ros. So was I when your Highness took his duke-
dom.
So was I when your Highness banish'd him.
Treason is not inherited, my lord;
Or, if we did derive it from our friends,
What's that to me? My father was no traitor. 65
Then, good my liege, mistake me not so much
To think my poverty is treacherous.

Cel. Dear sovereign, hear me speak.

Duke F. Ay, Celia; we stay'd her for your sake,
Else had she with her father rang'd along.   70

Cel. I did not then entreat to have her stay;
It was your pleasure and your own remorse.
I was too young that time to value her,
But now I know her. If she be a traitor,
Why so am I. We still have slept together,   75
Rose at an instant, learn'd, play'd, eat together;
And wheresoe'er we went, like Juno's swans,
Still we went coupled and inseparable.

Duke F. She is too subtle for thee; and her
smoothness,
Her very silence, and her patience   80
Speak to the people, and they pity her.
Thou art a fool. She robs thee of thy name,
And thou wilt show more bright and seem more
virtuous
When she is gone. Then open not thy lips.
Firm and irrevocable is my doom   85
Which I have pass'd upon her; she is banish'd.

Cel. Pronounce that sentence then on me, my
liege;
I cannot live out of her company.

Duke F. You are a fool. You, niece, provide
yourself.
If you outstay the time, upon mine honour,   90
And in the greatness of my word, you die.
     [*Exeunt Duke Frederick and Lords.*

Cel. O my poor Rosalind, whither wilt thou go?
Wilt thou change fathers? I will give thee mine.
I charge thee, be not thou more griev'd than I am.

Ros. I have more cause.

Cel.   Thou hast not, cousin; 95
Prithee, be cheerful. Know'st thou not, the Duke
Hath banish'd me, his daughter?

Ros.   That he hath not.

Cel. No, hath not? Rosalind lacks then the love
Which teacheth thee that thou and I am one.
Shall we be sund'red? Shall we part, sweet girl? 100
No; let my father seek another heir.

Therefore devise with me how we may fly,
Whither to go and what to bear with us;
And do not seek to take your [charge] upon you,
To bear your griefs yourself, and leave me out; 105
For, by this heaven, now at our sorrows pale,
Say what thou canst, I'll go along with thee.

Ros. Why, whither shall we go?

Cel. To seek my uncle in the forest of Arden.

Ros. Alas, what danger will it be to us,   110
Maids as we are, to travel forth so far!
Beauty provoketh thieves sooner than gold.

Cel. I'll put myself in poor and mean attire,
And with a kind of umber smirch my face.
The like do you. So shall we pass along   115
And never stir assailants.

Ros.   Were it not better,
Because that I am more than common tall,
That I did suit me all points like a man?
A gallant curtle-axe upon my thigh,
A boar-spear in my hand; and — in my heart 120
Lie there what hidden woman's fear there will —
We'll have a swashing and a martial outside,
As many other mannish cowards have
That do outface it with their semblances.

Cel. What shall I call thee when thou art a
man?   125

Ros. I'll have no worse a name than Jove's own
page,
And therefore look you call me Ganymede.
But what will you be call'd?

Cel. Something that hath a reference to my state;
No longer Celia, but Aliena.   130

Ros. But, cousin, what if we assay'd to steal
The clownish fool out of your father's court?
Would he not be a comfort to our travel?

Cel. He'll go along o'er the wide world with me.
Leave me alone to woo him. Let's away.   135
And get our jewels and our wealth together,
Devise the fittest time and safest way
To hide us from pursuit that will be made
After my flight. Now go we in content
To liberty and not to banishment. [*Exeunt.* 140

ACT II

Scene I. [*The Forest of Arden.*]

Enter Duke *senior,* Amiens, *and two or three*
Lords, *like foresters.*

Duke S. Now, my co-mates and brothers in
exile,
Hath not old custom made this life more sweet
Than that of painted pomp? Are not these woods
More free from peril than the envious court?

---

64. **friends:** kin.   72. **remorse:** compassion.   104. **[charge]** F2: burden.   *change* F1.   114. **umber:** brown pigment.
119. **curtle-axe:** cutlass.

Here feel we not the penalty of Adam,   5
The seasons' difference, as the icy fang
And churlish chiding of the winter's wind,
Which, when it bites and blows upon my body
Even till I shrink with cold, I smile and say,
"This is no flattery: these are counsellors   10
That feelingly persuade me what I am."
Sweet are the uses of adversity,
Which, like the toad, ugly and venomous,
Wears yet a precious jewel in his head;
And this our life, exempt from public haunt,   15
Finds tongues in trees, books in the running brooks,
Sermons in stones, and good in every thing.
 Ami. I would not change it.   Happy is your
  Grace,
That can translate the stubbornness of fortune
Into so quiet and so sweet a style.   20
 Duke S. Come, shall we go and kill us venison?
And yet it irks me the poor dappled fools,
Being native burghers of this desert city,
Should in their own confines with forked heads
Have their round haunches gor'd.
 1. Lord.   Indeed, my lord,
The melancholy Jaques grieves at that;   26
And, in that kind, swears you do more usurp
Than doth your brother that hath banish'd you.
To-day my Lord of Amiens and myself
Did steal behind him as he lay along   30
Under an oak whose antique root peeps out
Upon the brook that brawls along this wood;
To the which place a poor sequest'red stag,
That from the hunter's aim had ta'en a hurt,
Did come to languish; and indeed, my lord,   35
The wretched animal heav'd forth such groans
That their discharge did stretch his leathern coat
Almost to bursting, and the big round tears
Cours'd one another down his innocent nose
In piteous chase; and thus the hairy fool,   40
Much marked of the melancholy Jaques,
Stood on th' extremest verge of the swift brook,
Augmenting it with tears.
 Duke S.   But what said Jaques?
Did he not moralize this spectacle?
 1. Lord. O, yes, into a thousand similes.   45
First, for his weeping into the needless stream:
"Poor deer," quoth he, "thou mak'st a testament
As worldlings do, giving thy sum of more
To that which had too [much]."   Then, being there
 alone,
Left and abandoned of his velvet [friends],   50

"'Tis right," quoth he; "thus misery doth part
The flux of company."   Anon a careless herd,
Full of the pasture, jumps along by him
And never stays to greet him.   "Ay," quoth Jaques,
"Sweep on, you fat and greasy citizens.   55
'Tis just the fashion.   Wherefore do you look
Upon that poor and broken bankrupt there?"
Thus most invectively he pierceth through
The body of [the] country, city, court,
Yea, and of this our life; swearing that we   60
Are mere usurpers, tyrants, and what's worse,
To fright the animals and to kill them up
In their assign'd and native dwelling-place.
 Duke S. And did you leave him in this contempla-
  tion?
 2. Lord. We did, my lord, weeping and com-
  menting   65
Upon the sobbing deer.
 Duke S.   Show me the place.
I love to cope him in these sullen fits,
For then he's full of matter.
 1. Lord. I'll bring you to him straight. [*Exeunt.*

SCENE II. [*A room in the palace.*]

Enter DUKE FREDERICK, *with* LORDS.

 Duke F. Can it be possible that no man saw
  them?
It cannot be.   Some villains of my court
Are of consent and sufferance in this.
 1. Lord. I cannot hear of any that did see her.
The ladies, her attendants of her chamber,   5
Saw her a-bed, and in the morning early
They found the bed untreasur'd of their mistress.
 2. Lord. My lord, the roynish clown, at whom
  so oft
Your Grace was wont to laugh, is also missing.
Hisperia, the princess' gentlewoman,   10
Confesses that she secretly o'erheard
Your daughter and her cousin much commend
The parts and graces of the wrestler
That did but lately foil the sinewy Charles;
And she believes, wherever they are gone,   15
That youth is surely in their company.
 Duke F. Send to his brother.   Fetch that gallant
  hither.
If he be absent, bring his brother to me;
I'll make him find him.   Do this suddenly,
And let not search and inquisition quail   20
To bring again these foolish runaways. [*Exeunt.*

<hr>

Act II, sc. i, 5-6. feel we not. Theobald read *but* for *not.* The Folio phrase, however, means "we do not *mind* the seasons' difference, because that is a blessing compared to the artifice of court life." There had been changeless spring in Eden. **13-14.** It was popularly believed that the toad had in its head a stone which was an antidote for poison. **18. I...it.** Ff. Many editors assign this sentence to the Duke. **24. confines:** territory. **forked heads:** arrows. **40. fool.** Often a term of pity. **41. of:** by. **44. moralize:** draw a moral from. **46. needless:** having no need of more water. **49. [much]** Ff₂₋₄. *must* F₁. **50. [friends]** (Rowe). *friend* F₁. **59. of [the]** Ff₂₋₄. *of* F₁. **67. cope:** encounter. **68. matter:** substance.
 Sc. ii, 8. roynish: scurvy, a vague term of contempt. **19. suddenly:** immediately. **20. inquisition:** inquiry. **quail:** slacken.

SCENE III. [*Before Oliver's house.*]

Enter ORLANDO *and* ADAM, *meeting.*

Orl. Who's there?

Adam. What, my young master?   O my gentle
master!
O my sweet master!   O you memory
Of old Sir Roland!   Why, what make you here?
Why are you virtuous?   Why do people love you?   5
And wherefore are you gentle, strong, and valiant?
Why would you be so fond to overcome
The bonny priser of the humorous Duke?
Your praise is come too swiftly home before you.
Know you not, master, to [some] kind of men   10
Their graces serve them but as enemies?
No more do yours.   Your virtues, gentle master,
Are sanctified and holy traitors to you.
O, what a world is this, when what is comely
Envenoms him that bears it!   15

Orl. Why, what's the matter?

Adam.   O unhappy youth!
Come not within these doors!   Within this roof
The enemy of all your graces lives.
Your brother — no, no brother; yet the son —
Yet not the son, I will not call him son,   20
Of him I was about to call his father,—
Hath heard your praises, and this night he means
To burn the lodging where you use to lie
And you within it.   If he fail of that,
He will have other means to cut you off.   25
I overheard him and his practices.
This is no place; this house is but a butchery.
Abhor it, fear it, do not enter it.

Orl. Why, whither, Adam, wouldst thou have me
go?

Adam. No matter whither, so you come not
here.   30

Orl. What, wouldst thou have me go and beg my
food?
Or with a base and boist'rous sword enforce
A thievish living on the common road?
This I must do, or know not what to do;
Yet this I will not do, do how I can.   35
I rather will subject me to the malice
Of a diverted blood and bloody brother.

Adam. But do not so.   I have five hundred
crowns,
The thrifty hire I sav'd under your father,
Which I did store to be my foster-nurse   40
When service should in my old limbs lie lame,
And unregarded age in corners thrown.
Take that, and He that doth the ravens feed,
Yea, providently caters for the sparrow,
Be comfort to my age!   Here is the gold.   45
All this I give you.   Let me be your servant.
Though I look old, yet I am strong and lusty;
For in my youth I never did apply
Hot and rebellious liquors in my blood,
Nor did not with unbashful forehead woo   50
The means of weakness and debility;
Therefore my age is as a lusty winter,
Frosty, but kindly.   Let me go with you;
I'll do the service of a younger man
In all your business and necessities.   55

Orl. O good old man, how well in thee appears
The constant service of the antique world,
When service sweat for duty, not for meed!
Thou art not for the fashion of these times,
Where none will sweat but for promotion,   60
And having that do choke their service up
Even with the having.   It is not so with thee.
But, poor old man, thou prun'st a rotten tree,
That cannot so much as a blossom yield
In lieu of all thy pains and husbandry.   65
But come thy ways; we'll go along together,
And ere we have thy youthful wages spent,
We'll light upon some settled low content.

Adam. Master, go on, and I will follow thee
To the last gasp, with truth and loyalty.   70
From seventeen years till now almost fourscore
Here lived I, but now live here no more.
At seventeen years many their fortunes seek,
But at fourscore it is too late a week;
Yet fortune cannot recompense me better   75
Than to die well and not my master's debtor.
[*Exeunt.*

SCENE IV. [*The Forest of Arden.*]

Enter ROSALIND *for Ganymede,* CELIA *for
Aliena, and Clown, alias* TOUCHSTONE.

Ros. O Jupiter, how [weary] are my spirits!

Touch. I care not for my spirits, if my legs were
not weary.

Ros. I could find in my heart to disgrace my
man's apparel and to cry like a woman; but I   5
must comfort the weaker vessel, as doublet and hose
ought to show itself courageous to petticoat; therefore, courage, good Aliena.

Cel. I pray you, bear with me; I cannot go no
further.   10

Touch. For my part, I had rather bear with you
than bear you.   Yet I should bear no cross if I did
bear you, for I think you have no money in your
purse.

Ros. Well, this is the forest of Arden.   15

Sc. iii, 8. **bonny priser:** fine champion.   10. **[some]** Ff2–4.   *seeme* F1.   26. **practices:** plots.   27. **place:** i.e., for you.
37. **diverted blood:** perverted kinship.   39. **thrifty . . . saved:** wages I thriftily saved.   65. **lieu of:** return for.   68. **low
content:** lowly contentment.   74. **too . . . week:** much too late.
Sc. iv, 1. **[weary]** (Theobald).   *merry* Ff.   12. **cross:** silver coin with figure of a cross (with a pun).

Touch. Ay, now am I in Arden, the more fool I.
When I was at home, I was in a better place; but
travellers must be content.

Enter CORIN *and* SILVIUS.

Ros. Ay, be so, good Touchstone. Look you,
who comes here; a young man and an old in solemn
talk.   21
Cor. That is the way to make her scorn you still.
Sil. O Corin, that thou knew'st how I do love
her!
Cor. I partly guess; for I have lov'd ere now.
Sil. No, Corin, being old, thou canst not guess,
Though in thy youth thou wast as true a lover   26
As ever sigh'd upon a midnight pillow.
But if thy love were ever like to mine, —
As sure I think did never man love so —
How many actions most ridiculous   30
Hast thou been drawn to by thy fantasy?
Cor. Into a thousand that I have forgotten.
Sil. O, thou didst then ne'er love so heartily!
If thou rememb'rest not the slightest folly
That ever love did make thee run into,   35
Thou hast not lov'd;
Or if thou hast not sat as I do now,
Wearing thy hearer in thy mistress' praise,
Thou hast not lov'd;
Or if thou hast not broke from company   40
Abruptly, as my passion now makes me,
Thou hast not lov'd.
O Phebe, Phebe, Phebe!   [*Exit.*
Ros. Alas, poor shepherd! searching of [thy
wound],
I have by hard adventure found mine own.   45
Touch. And I mine. I remember, when I was
in love I broke my sword upon a stone, and bid him
take that for coming a-night to Jane Smile; and I
remember the kissing of her batler and the cow's
dugs that her pretty chopt hands had milk'd;   50
and I remember the wooing of a peascod instead of
her; from whom I took two cods and, giving her
them again, said with weeping tears, "Wear these
for my sake." We that are true lovers run into
strange capers; but as all is mortal in nature,   55
so is all nature in love mortal in folly.
Ros. Thou speak'st wiser than thou art ware of.
Touch. Nay, I shall ne'er be ware of mine own
wit till I break my shins against it.   60
Ros. Jove, Jove! this shepherd's passion
     Is much upon my fashion.
Touch. And mine; but it grows something stale
with me.

Cel. I pray you, one of you question yond man
If he for gold will give us any food.   65
I faint almost to death.
     Touch.   Holla, you clown!
Ros. Peace, fool; he's not thy kinsman.
Cor.   Who calls?
Touch. Your betters, sir.
Cor.   Else are they very wretched.
Ros. Peace, I say. Good even to [you], friend.
Cor. And to you, gentle sir, and to you all.   70
Ros. I prithee, shepherd, if that love or gold
Can in this desert place buy entertainment,
Bring us where we may rest ourselves and feed.
Here's a young maid with travel much oppressed
And faints for succour.
Cor.   Fair sir, I pity her,   75
And wish, for her sake more than for mine own,
My fortunes were more able to relieve her;
But I am shepherd to another man,
And do not shear the fleeces that I graze.
My master is of churlish disposition,   80
And little recks to find the way to heaven
By doing deeds of hospitality.
Besides, his cote, his flocks, and bounds of feed
Are now on sale, and at our sheep-cote now,
By reason of his absence, there is nothing   85
That you will feed on; but what is, come see,
And in my voice most welcome shall you be.
Ros. What is he that shall buy his flock and pas-
ture?
Cor. That young swain that you saw here but
erewhile,
That little cares for buying any thing.   90
Ros. I pray thee, if it stand with honesty,
Buy thou the cottage, pasture, and the flock,
And thou shalt have to pay for it of us.
Cel. And we will mend thy wages. I like this
     place,
And willingly could waste my time in it.   95
Cor. Assuredly the thing is to be sold.
Go with me. If you like upon report
The soil, the profit, and this kind of life,
I will your very faithful feeder be,
And buy it with your gold right suddenly.   100
     [*Exeunt.*

SCENE V. [*The forest.*]

Enter AMIENS, JAQUES, *and others.*

SONG.

[*Ami.*] Under the greenwood tree
     Who loves to lie with me,

---

31. **fantasy:** love.   38. **Wearing.** F$_1$. *wearying* Ff$_{2-4}$. (Meanings identical.)   44. **searching:** probing. **[thy wound]**
(Rowe). *they would* F$_1$; *their wound* Ff$_{2-4}$.   49. **batler:** small club used by washerwomen. Ff$_{2-4}$ read *batlet.*   50. **chopt:**
chapped.   51. **peascod:** pea pod.   56. **mortal:** excessive.   62. **upon:** after.   69. **[you]** Ff$_{2-4}$. *your* F$_1$.   75. **for:** for want of.
80. **churlish:** miserly.   83. **cote:** cottage. **bounds of feed:** pasturage.   87. **in my voice:** as far as I have anything to say.
91. **stand:** is consistent.   99. **feeder:** shepherd.

And turn his merry note
Unto the sweet bird's throat,
Come hither, come hither, come hither!   5
   Here shall he see
     No enemy
But winter and rough weather.

Jaq. More, more, I prithee, more.

Ami. It will make you melancholy, Monsieur
Jaques.   11

Jaq. I thank it. More, I prithee, more. I can
suck melancholy out of a song, as a weasel sucks
eggs. More, I prithee, more.

Ami. My voice is ragged. I know I cannot
please you.   16

Jaq. I do not desire you to please me; I do desire
you to sing. Come, more; another stanzo. Call
you 'em stanzos?

Ami. What you will, Monsieur Jaques.   20

Jaq. Nay, I care not for their names; they owe
me nothing. Will you sing?

Ami. More at your request than to please myself.   24

Jaq. Well then, if ever I thank any man, I'll
thank you; but that they call compliment is like the
encounter of two dog-apes; and when a man thanks
me heartily, methinks I have given him a penny and
he renders me the beggarly thanks. Come, sing;
and you that will not, hold your tongues.   31

Ami. Well, I'll end the song. Sirs, cover the
while; the Duke will drink under this tree. He
hath been all this day to look you.

Jaq. And I have been all this day to avoid   35
him. He is too disputable for my company. I
think of as many matters as he; but I give heaven
thanks, and make no boast of them. Come,
warble, come.

SONG.   [*All together here.*

Who doth ambition shun,   40
And loves to live i' th' sun,
Seeking the food he eats,
And pleased with what he gets,
Come hither, come hither, come hither!
   Here shall he see   45
     No enemy
But winter and rough weather.

Jaq. I'll give you a verse to this note, that I made
yesterday in despite of my invention.

Ami. And I'll sing it.   50

Jaq. Thus it goes: —

If it do come to pass
That any man turn ass,
  Leaving his wealth and ease
  A stubborn will to please,   55
Ducdame, ducdame, ducdame!
   Here shall he see
     Gross fools as he,
An if he will come to me.

Ami. What's that "ducdame"?   60

Jaq. 'Tis a Greek invocation, to call fools into a
circle. I'll go sleep, if I can; if I cannot, I'll rail
against all the first-born of Egypt.

Ami. And I'll go seek the Duke; his banquet is
prepared.   [*Exeunt.* 65

SCENE VI. [*The forest.*]

Enter ORLANDO *and* ADAM.

Adam. Dear master, I can go no further. O, I
die for food! Here lie I down, and measure out my
grave. Farewell, kind master.

Orl. Why, how now, Adam! no greater heart in
thee? Live a little; comfort a little; cheer thy-   5
self a little. If this uncouth forest yield any thing
savage, I will either be food for it or bring it for
food to thee. Thy conceit is nearer death than
thy powers. For my sake be comfortable; hold
death awhile at the arm's end. I will here be   10
with thee presently; and if I bring thee not something to eat, I will give thee leave to die; but if thou
diest before I come, thou art a mocker of my labour.
Well said! thou look'st cheerly, and I'll be with thee
quickly. Yet thou liest in the bleak air. Come,   15
I will bear thee to some shelter; and thou shalt not
die for lack of a dinner if there live any thing in this
desert. Cheerly, good Adam!   [*Exeunt.*

SCENE VII. [*The forest.*]

[*A table set out.*]   *Enter* DUKE senior, [AMIENS]
and LORDS, *like outlaws.*

Duke S. I think he be transform'd into a beast,
For I can no where find him like a man.

1. Lord. My lord, he is but even now gone hence.
Here was he merry, hearing of a song.

Duke S. If he, compact of jars, grow musical,   5
We shall have shortly discord in the spheres.
Go, seek him; tell him I would speak with him.

Enter JAQUES.

1. Lord. He saves my labour by his own approach.

Sc. **v, 3. turn:** attune.   21. **names:** i.e., as in lists of debtors.   27. **dog-apes:** dog-faced apes.   32. **cover the while:** meanwhile set the table.   49. **in ... invention:** though I have little imagination.   56. **Ducdame.** Probably mere jargon.
Sc. **vi, 8. conceit:** imagination.   14. **Well said:** well done.
Sc. **vii, 5. compact of jars:** composed of discords.   6. **spheres.** In the old Ptolemaic astronomy the spheres were thought to make music in their turning.

Duke S. Why, how now, monsieur! what a life is this,
That your poor friends must woo your company?
What, you look merrily! 11
Jaq. A fool, a fool! I met a fool i' th' forest,
A motley fool. A miserable world!
As I do live by food, I met a fool;
Who laid him down and bask'd him in the sun, 15
And rail'd on Lady Fortune in good terms,
In good set terms, and yet a motley fool.
"Good morrow, fool," quoth I. "No, sir," quoth he,
"Call me not fool till heaven hath sent me fortune."
And then he drew a dial from his poke, 20
And, looking on it with lack-lustre eye,
Says very wisely, "It is ten o'clock.
Thus we may see," quoth he, "how the world wags.
'Tis but an hour ago since it was nine;
And after one hour more 'twill be eleven; 25
And so, from hour to hour, we ripe and ripe,
And then, from hour to hour, we rot and rot;
And thereby hangs a tale." When I did hear
The motley fool thus moral on the time,
My lungs began to crow like chanticleer, 30
That fools should be so deep-contemplative;
And I did laugh sans intermission
An hour by his dial. O noble fool!
A worthy fool! Motley's the only wear.
Duke S. What fool is this? 35
Jaq. O worthy fool! One that hath been a courtier,
And says, if ladies be but young and fair,
They have the gift to know it; and in his brain,
Which is as dry as the remainder biscuit
After a voyage, he hath strange places cramm'd
With observation, the which he vents 41
In mangled forms. O that I were a fool!
I am ambitious for a motley coat.
Duke S. Thou shalt have one.
Jaq. It is my only suit; —
Provided that you weed your better judgements
Of all opinion that grows rank in them 46
That I am wise. I must have liberty
Withal, as large a charter as the wind,
To blow on whom I please; for so fools have;
And they that are most galled with my folly, 50
They most must laugh. And why, sir, must they so?
The "why" is plain as way to parish church.
He that a fool doth very wisely hit
Doth very foolishly, although he smart,

[Not to] seem senseless of the bob; if not, 55
The wise man's folly is anatomiz'd
Even by the squand'ring glances of the fool.
Invest me in my motley. Give me leave
To speak my mind, and I will through and through
Cleanse the foul body of th' infected world, 60
If they will patiently receive my medicine.
Duke S. Fie on thee! I can tell what thou wouldst do.
Jaq. What, for a counter, would I do but good?
Duke S. Most mischievous foul sin, in chiding sin.
For thou thyself hast been a libertine, 65
As sensual as the brutish sting itself;
And all th' embossed sores and headed evils
That thou with license of free foot hast caught,
Wouldst thou disgorge into the general world.
Jaq. Why, who cries out on pride 70
That can therein tax any private party?
Doth it not flow as hugely as the sea,
Till that the [wearer's] very means do ebb?
What woman in the city do I name,
When that I say the city-woman bears 75
The cost of princes on unworthy shoulders?
Who can come in and say that I mean her,
When such a one as she such is her neighbour?
Or what is he of basest function,
That says his bravery is not on my cost, 80
Thinking that I mean him, but therein suits
His folly to the mettle of my speech?
There then; how then? what then? Let me see wherein
My tongue hath wrong'd him. If it do him right,
Then he hath wrong'd himself. If he be free, 85
Why then my taxing like a wild-goose flies,
Unclaim'd of any man. But who comes here?

Enter ORLANDO [*with his sword drawn*].

Orl. Forbear, and eat no more.
Jaq. Why, I have eat none yet.
Orl. Nor shalt not, till necessity be serv'd.
Jaq. Of what kind should this cock come of? 90
Duke S. Art thou thus bolden'd, man, by thy distress?
Or else a rude despiser of good manners,
That in civility thou seem'st so empty?
Orl. You touch'd my vein at first. The thorny point
Of bare distress hath ta'en from me the show 95
Of smooth civility; yet am I inland bred
And know some nurture. But forbear, I say.

---

13. **motley:** wearing motley, i.e., a parti-colored costume.   20. **dial:** watch, or portable sun-dial. **poke:** pouch. **39. dry.** According to Elizabethan physiology a "dry" brain was especially retentive. 40. **strange places:** odd corners. 44. **suit:** (1) costume, (2) request. 55. **[not to]** (Theobald). Om. Ff. **bob:** jibe. 57. **squand'ring glances:** random hits. 63. **counter:** valueless disk of metal used in counting. 66. **brutish sting:** carnal passion. 67. **embossed:** swollen. **headed evils:** sores come to a head. 71. **tax:** censure. 73. **[wearer's]** (Singer). *wearie* Ff. No satisfactory emendation has been proposed. 79. **function:** occupation. 80. **bravery:** finery. 84. **If ... right:** if the glove fits. 85. **free:** innocent. 93. **civility:** courtesy. 94. **You ... vein:** your first question explains my mood. 96. **inland bred:** i.e., near the centers of urbanity. (Cf. *outlandish.*) 97. **nurture:** breeding.

He dies that touches any of this fruit
Till I and my affairs are answered.
   Jaq. An you will not be answer'd with reason,
I must die.   101
   Duke S. What would you have? Your gentle-
   ness shall force,
More than your force move us to gentleness.
   Orl. I almost die for food; and let me have it.
   Duke S. Sit down and feed, and welcome to our
   table.   105
   Orl. Speak you so gently? Pardon me, I pray
   you.
I thought that all things had been savage here,
And therefore put I on the countenance
Of stern commandment. But whate'er you are
That in this desert inaccessible   110
Under the shade of melancholy boughs
Lose and neglect the creeping hours of time;
If ever you have look'd on better days,
If ever been where bells have knoll'd to church,
If ever sat at any good man's feast,   115
If ever from your eyelids wip'd a tear
And know what 'tis to pity and be pitied,
Let gentleness my strong enforcement be;
In the which hope I blush, and hide my sword.
   Duke S. True is it that we have seen better
   days,   120
And have with holy bell been knoll'd to church,
And sat at good men's feasts, and wip'd our eyes
Of drops that sacred pity hath engend'red;
And therefore sit you down in gentleness
And take upon command what help we have   125
That to your wanting may be minist'red.
   Orl. Then but forbear your food a little while,
Whiles, like a doe, I go to find my fawn
And give it food. There is an old poor man,
Who after me hath many a weary step   130
Limp'd in pure love. Till he be first suffic'd,
Oppress'd with two weak evils, age and hunger,
I will not touch a bit.
   Duke S.   Go find him out,
And we will nothing waste till you return.
   Orl. I thank ye; and be blest for your good com-
   fort!   [*Exit.*] 135
   Duke S. Thou seest we are not all alone un-
   happy.
This wide and universal theatre
Presents more woeful pageants than the scene
Wherein we play in.
   Jaq.   All the world's a stage,
And all the men and women merely players.   140
They have their exits and their entrances,
And one man in his time plays many parts,
His acts being seven ages. At first the infant,

Mewling and puking in the nurse's arms.
Then the whining school-boy, with his satchel   145
And shining morning face, creeping like snail
Unwillingly to school. And then the lover,
Sighing like furnace, with a woeful ballad
Made to his mistress' eyebrow. Then a soldier,
Full of strange oaths, and bearded like the pard,   150
Jealous in honour, sudden, and quick in quarrel,
Seeking the bubble reputation
Even in the cannon's mouth. And then the justice,
In fair round belly with good capon lin'd,
With eyes severe and beard of formal cut,   155
Full of wise saws and modern instances;
And so he plays his part. The sixth age shifts
Into the lean and slipper'd pantaloon,
With spectacles on nose and pouch on side,   159
His youthful hose, well sav'd, a world too wide
For his shrunk shank; and his big manly voice,
Turning again toward childish treble, pipes
And whistles in his sound. Last scene of all,
That ends this strange eventful history,
Is second childishness and mere oblivion,   165
Sans teeth, sans eyes, sans taste, sans every thing.

Re-enter ORLANDO, *with* ADAM.

   Duke S. Welcome. Set down your venerable
   burden,
And let him feed.
   Orl. I thank you most for him.
   Adam.   So had you need;
I scarce can speak to thank you for myself.   170
   Duke S. Welcome; fall to. I will not trouble you
As yet, to question you about your fortunes.
Give us some music; and, good cousin, sing.

SONG.

[*Ami.*] Blow, blow, thou winter wind,
        Thou art not so unkind   175
           As man's ingratitude;
        Thy tooth is not so keen,
        Because thou art not seen,
           Although thy breath be rude.
Heigh-ho! sing, heigh-ho! unto the green holly.   180
Most friendship is feigning, most loving mere folly.
        Then, heigh-ho, the holly!
        This life is most jolly.

        Freeze, freeze, thou bitter sky,
        That dost not bite so nigh   185
           As benefits forgot;
        Though thou the waters warp,
        Thy sting is not so sharp
           As friend remem'red not.
Heigh-ho! sing, etc.   190

---

99. **answered**: satisfied.   118. **enforcement**: support.   125. **upon command**: at will.   144. **mewling**: whimpering.
150. **pard**: leopard.   154. **capon.** An allusion to the bribing of justices by gifts of poultry.   156. **saws**: maxims. **modern instances**: trite examples.   158. **pantaloon**: dotard.   175. **unkind**: unnatural.

Duke S. If that you were the good Sir Roland's
    son,
As you have whisper'd faithfully you were,
And as mine eye doth his effigies witness
Most truly limn'd and living in your face,
Be truly welcome hither.   I am the Duke   195
That lov'd your father.   The residue of your for-
    tune,
Go to my cave and tell me.   Good old man,
Thou art right welcome as thy master is.
Support him by the arm.   Give me your hand,
And let me all your fortunes understand.   200
                                    [*Exeunt.*

ACT III

Scene I. [*A room in the palace.*]

Enter DUKE [FREDERICK], OLIVER, *and* Lords.

Duke F. Not see him since?   Sir, sir, that cannot
    be.
But were I not the better part made mercy,
I should not seek an absent argument
Of my revenge, thou present.   But look to it.
Find out thy brother, wheresoe'er he is.   5
Seek him with candle!   Bring him dead or living
Within this twelvemonth, or turn thou no more
To seek a living in our territory.
Thy lands and all things that thou dost call thine
Worth seizure do we seize into our hands,   10
Till thou canst quit thee by thy brother's mouth
Of what we think against thee.
Oli. O that your Highness knew my heart in this!
I never lov'd my brother in my life.
Duke F. More villain thou.   Well, push him out
    of doors;   15
And let my officers of such a nature
Make an extent upon his house and lands.
Do this expediently and turn him going.   [*Exeunt.*

Scene II. [*The forest.*]

Enter ORLANDO [*with a paper*].

Orl. Hang there, my verse, in witness of my love;
    And thou, thrice-crowned queen of night, survey
With thy chaste eye, from thy pale sphere above,
    Thy huntress' name that my full life doth sway.
O Rosalind! these trees shall be my books,   5
    And in their barks my thoughts I'll character;
That every eye which in this forest looks
    Shall see thy virtue witness'd every where.

Run, run, Orlando; carve on every tree
The fair, the chaste, and unexpressive she.   10
                                    [*Exit.*

Enter CORIN *and Clown* [TOUCHSTONE].

Cor. And how like you this shepherd's life, Master Touchstone?
Touch. Truly, shepherd, in respect of itself, it is
a good life; but in respect that it is a shepherd's life,
it is naught.   In respect that it is solitary, I like   15
it very well; but in respect that it is private, it is a
very vile life.   Now, in respect it is in the fields, it
pleaseth me well; but in respect it is not in the
court, it is tedious.   As it is a spare life, look you,
it fits my humour well; but as there is no more   20
plenty in it, it goes much against my stomach.
Hath any philosophy in thee, shepherd?
Cor. No more but that I know the more one
sickens the worse at ease he is; and that he that   25
wants money, means, and content is without three
good friends; that the property of rain is to wet and
fire to burn; that good pasture makes fat sheep, and
that a great cause of the night is lack of the sun; that
he that hath learned no wit by nature nor art   30
may complain of good breeding or comes of a very
dull kindred.
Touch. Such a one is a natural philosopher.
Wast ever in court, shepherd?
Cor. No, truly.   35
Touch. Then thou art damn'd.
Cor. Nay, I hope.
Touch. Truly, thou art damn'd, like an ill-
roasted egg all on one side.
Cor. For not being at court?   Your reason.   40
Touch. Why, if thou never wast at court, thou
never saw'st good manners; if thou never saw'st
good manners, then thy manners must be wicked;
and wickedness is sin, and sin is damnation.   Thou
art in a parlous state, shepherd.   45
Cor. Not a whit, Touchstone.   Those that are
good manners at the court are as ridiculous in the
country as the behaviour of the country is most
mockable at the court.   You told me you salute
not at the court but you kiss your hands.   That   50
courtesy would be uncleanly if courtiers were shepherds.
Touch. Instance, briefly; come, instance.
Cor. Why, we are still handling our ewes, and
their fells, you know, are greasy.   55
Touch. Why, do not your courtier's hands sweat?
And is not the grease of a mutton as wholesome as

---

193. **effigies:** likeness.   194. **limn'd:** painted.
   Act III, sc. i, 11. **quit:** acquit.   16. **of . . . nature:** whose business it is.   17. **extent:** seizure (legal term).   18. **expediently:**
expeditiously.
   Sc. ii, 2. **thrice-crowned queen:** Diana.   She was a triple divinity: Cynthia or Luna in heaven; Diana on earth; Proserpine
or Hecate in the underworld.   6. **character:** inscribe.   10. **unexpressive:** inexpressible.   31. **of:** i.e., of lack of.   45. **parlous:**
perilous.   50. **but you kiss:** without kissing.   55. **fells:** fleeces.

the sweat of a man? Shallow, shallow. A better instance, I say; come.

Cor. Besides, our hands are hard.   60

Touch. Your lips will feel them the sooner. Shallow again. A more sounder instance, come.

Cor. And they are often tarr'd over with the surgery of our sheep; and would you have us kiss tar? The courtier's hands are perfum'd with civet.   66

Touch. Most shallow man! thou worm's-meat, in respect of a good piece of flesh indeed! Learn of the wise, and perpend. Civet is of a baser birth than tar, the very uncleanly flux of a cat. Mend the instance, shepherd.   71

Cor. You have too courtly a wit for me. I'll rest.

Touch. Wilt thou rest damn'd? God help thee, shallow man! God make incision in thee! Thou art raw.   76

Cor. Sir, I am a true labourer. I earn that I eat, get that I wear, owe no man hate, envy no man's happiness, glad of other men's good, content with my harm, and the greatest of my pride is to see my ewes graze and my lambs suck.   81

Touch. That is another simple sin in you, to bring the ewes and the rams together, and to offer to get your living by the copulation of cattle; to be bawd to a bell-wether, and to betray a she-   85
lamb of a twelvemonth to a crooked-pated, old, cuckoldly ram, out of all reasonable match. If thou beest not damn'd for this, the devil himself will have no shepherds. I cannot see else how thou shouldst scape.   90

Cor. Here comes young Master Ganymede, my new mistress's brother.

Enter ROSALIND [*with a paper, reading*].

Ros. From the east to western Ind,
        No jewel is like Rosalind.
    Her worth, being mounted on the wind,
        Through all the world bears Rosalind.   96
    All the pictures fairest lin'd
        Are but black to Rosalind.
    Let no face be kept in mind
        But the fair of Rosalind.   100

Touch. I'll rhyme you so eight years together, dinners and suppers and sleeping-hours excepted. It is the right butter-women's rank to market.

Ros. Out, fool!   105

Touch. For a taste: —
    If a hart do lack a hind,
        Let him seek out Rosalind.

    If the cat will after kind,
        So be sure will Rosalind.   110
    Wint'red garments must be lin'd,
        So must slender Rosalind.
    They that reap must sheaf and bind,
        Then to cart with Rosalind.
    Sweetest nut hath sourest rind,   115
        Such a nut is Rosalind.
    He that sweetest rose will find,
        Must find love's prick and Rosalind.
This is the very false gallop of verses. Why do you infect yourself with them?   120

Ros. Peace, you dull fool! I found them on a tree.

Touch. Truly, the tree yields bad fruit.

Ros. I'll graff it with you, and then I shall graff it with a medlar. Then it will be the earliest   125
fruit i' th' country; for you'll be rotten ere you be half ripe, and that's the right virtue of the medlar.

Touch. You have said; but whether wisely or no, let the forest judge.   130

Enter CELIA, *with a writing.*

Ros. Peace!
Here comes my sister, reading; stand aside.

Cel. [*Reads.*] Why should this a desert be?
        For it is unpeopled? No!
    Tongues I'll hang on every tree,   135
        That shall civil sayings show:
    Some, how brief the life of man
        Runs his erring pilgrimage,
    That the stretching of a span
        Buckles in his sum of age;   140
    Some, of violated vows
        'Twixt the souls of friend and friend;
    But upon the fairest boughs,
        Or at every sentence end,
    Will I Rosalinda write,   145
        Teaching all that read to know
    The quintessence of every sprite
        Heaven would in little show.
    Therefore Heaven Nature charg'd
        That one body should be fill'd   150
    With all graces wide-enlarg'd.
        Nature presently distill'd
    Helen's cheek, but not her heart,
        Cleopatra's majesty,
    Atalanta's better part,   155
        Sad Lucretia's modesty.
    Thus Rosalind of many parts
        By heavenly synod was devis'd;
    Of many faces, eyes, and hearts,

68. in respect of: compared with.   69. perpend: consider.   75. make incision: let blood.   76. raw: crude.   79. content ... harm: uncomplaining at misfortune.   97. lin'd: drawn.   100. fair: beauty.   103. It ... market. I.e., the rhymes, all alike, jog like a row of butter-women going to market.   119. false gallop: canter.   124. graff: graft.   125. medlar: (1) meddler, (2) a fruit like an apple, not good to eat until it decays.   136. civil sayings: serious maxims.   140. Buckles in: encompasses.   155. better part: i.e., her swiftness.

To have the touches dearest priz'd 160
Heaven would that she these gifts should
have,
And I to live and die her slave.
Ros. O most gentle [pulpiter]! what tedious
homily of love have you wearied your parishioners
withal, and never cri'd "Have patience, good
people!"   166
Cel. How now! Back, friends! Shepherd, go off
a little. Go with him, sirrah.
Touch. Come, shepherd, let us make an honourable retreat; though not with bag and baggage,
yet with scrip and scrippage.   171
[*Exeunt [Corin and Touchstone].*
Cel. Didst thou hear these verses?
Ros. O, yes, I heard them all, and more, too;
for some of them had in them more feet than the
verses would bear.   175
Cel. That's no matter. The feet might bear the
verses.
Ros. Ay, but the feet were lame and could not
bear themselves without the verse, and therefore
stood lamely in the verse.   180
Cel. But didst thou hear without wondering how
thy name should be hang'd and carved upon these
trees?
Ros. I was seven of the nine days out of the wonder before you came; for look here what I found 185
on a palm tree. I was never so berhym'd since Pythagoras' time, that I was an Irish rat, which I can
hardly remember.
Cel. Trow you who hath done this?
Ros. Is it a man?   190
Cel. And a chain, that you once wore, about his
neck. Change you colour?
Ros. I prithee, who?
Cel. O Lord, Lord! it is a hard matter for friends
to meet; but mountains may be removed with earth-
quakes and so encounter.   196
Ros. Nay, but who is it?
Cel. Is it possible?
Ros. Nay, I prithee now with most petitionary
vehemence, tell me who it is.   200
Cel. O wonderful, wonderful, and most wonderful wonderful! and yet again wonderful, and after
that, out of all whooping!
Ros. Good my complexion! dost thou think,
though I am caparison'd like a man, I have a 205
doubtlet and hose in my disposition? One inch of
delay more is a South-sea of discovery. I prithee,

tell me who is it quickly, and speak apace. I would
thou couldst stammer, that thou might'st pour this
conceal'd man out of thy mouth, as wine comes 210
out of a narrow-mouth'd bottle, either too much at
once, or none at all. I prithee, take the cork out of
thy mouth that I may drink thy tidings.
Cel. So you may put a man in your belly.   215
Ros. Is he of God's making? What manner of
man? Is his head worth a hat or his chin worth a
beard?
Cel. Nay, he hath but a little beard.   219
Ros. Why, God will send more, if the man will
be thankful. Let me stay the growth of his beard,
if thou delay me not the knowledge of his chin.
Cel. It is young Orlando, that tripp'd up the
wrestler's heels and your heart both in an instant.   225
Ros. Nay, but the devil take mocking. Speak
sad brow and true maid.
Cel. I' faith, coz, 'tis he.
Ros. Orlando?
Cel. Orlando.   230
Ros. Alas the day! what shall I do with my
doublet and hose? What did he when thou saw'st
him? What said he? How look'd he? Wherein
went he? What makes he here? Did he ask for
me? Where remains he? How parted he with 235
thee? And when shalt thou see him again? Answer me in one word.
Cel. You must borrow me Gargantua's mouth
first. 'Tis a word too great for any mouth of this
age's size. To say ay and no to these particulars
is more than to answer in a catechism.   241
Ros. But doth he know that I am in this forest
and in man's apparel? Looks he as freshly as he
did the day he wrestled?
Cel. It is as easy to count atomies as to re- 245
solve the propositions of a lover. But take a taste
of my finding him, and relish it with good observance. I found him under a tree, like a dropp'd
acorn.
Ros. It may well be called Jove's tree, when it
drops forth such fruit.   250
Cel. Give me audience, good madam.
Ros. Proceed.
Cel. There lay he, stretch'd along, like a wounded
knight.
Ros. Though it be pity to see such a sight, it well
becomes the ground.   256
Cel. Cry "holla" to [thy] tongue, I prithee; it

---

160. **touches**: traits. 163. **[pulpiter]** (Spedding). *Jupiter* Ff. 167. **Back, friends!** Addressed to Corin and Touchstone.
171. **scrip**: wallet. 186–87. **Pythagoras'...rat.** A double allusion: (1) to the theory of the transmigration of souls, advanced by the Greek philosopher, Pythagoras; (2) to the belief among Irish peasantry that rats could be killed by rhymed
spells. 189. **Trow**: know. 199. **petitionary**: pleading. 204. **Good my complexion**: i.e., O my blushes! 206. **One...dis-
covery.** I.e., the least delay is to me as long as a voyage of exploration. 221. **stay**: await. 226. **Speak...maid.** I.e., speak
seriously and as an honest maid. 233. **Wherein went he**: what did he wear? 237. **Gargantua**: Rabelais' giant who once
swallowed five pilgrims together. 245. **atomies**: motes. **resolve**: solve. 247. **relish**: sauce (vb.). 247. **observance**:
attention. 249. **Jove's tree**: the oak. 256. **ground.** With pun on *background*. 257. **"holla"**: halt. **[thy]** (Rowe). *the* Ff.

curvets unseasonably. He was furnish'd like a hunter.

Ros. O, ominous! he comes to kill my heart. 260

Cel. I would sing my song without a burden. Thou bring'st me out of tune.

Ros. Do you not know I am a woman? When I think, I must speak. Sweet, say on. 264

Enter ORLANDO *and* JAQUES.

Cel. You bring me out. Soft! comes he not here?

Ros. 'Tis he. Slink by, and note him.

Jaq. I thank you for your company; but, good faith, I had as lief have been myself alone. 270

Orl. And so had I; but yet, for fashion sake, I thank you too for your society.

Jaq. God buy you; let's meet as little as we can.

Orl. I do desire we may be better strangers. 275

Jaq. I pray you, mar no more trees with writing love-songs in their barks.

Orl. I pray you, mar no moe of my verses with reading them ill-favouredly.

Jaq. Rosalind is your love's name? 280

Orl. Yes, just.

Jaq. I do not like her name.

Orl. There was no thought of pleasing you when she was christen'd.

Jaq. What stature is she of? 285

Orl. Just as high as my heart.

Jaq. You are full of pretty answers. Have you not been acquainted with goldsmiths' wives, and conn'd them out of rings? 289

Orl. Not so; but I answer you right painted cloth, from whence you have studied your questions.

Jaq. You have a nimble wit. I think 'twas made of Atalanta's heels. Will you sit down with me? and we two will rail against our mistress the world, and all our misery. 296

Orl. I will chide no breather in the world but myself, against whom I know most faults.

Jaq. The worst fault you have is to be in love. 300

Orl. 'Tis a fault I will not change for your best virtue. I am weary of you.

Jaq. By my troth, I was seeking for a fool when I found you.

Orl. He is drown'd in the brook. Look but in, and you shall see him. 306

Jaq. There I shall see mine own figure.

Orl. Which I take to be either a fool or a cipher.

Jaq. I'll tarry no longer with you. Farewell, good Signior Love. 310

Orl. I am glad of your departure. Adieu, good Monsieur Melancholy. [*Exit Jaques.*]

Ros. [*Aside to Celia.*] I will speak to him like a saucy lackey, and under that habit play the knave with him.— Do you hear, forester? 315

Orl. Very well. What would you?

Ros. I pray you, what is't o'clock?

Orl. You should ask me what time o' day. There's no clock in the forest. 319

Ros. Then there is no true lover in the forest; else sighing every minute and groaning every hour would detect the lazy foot of Time as well as a clock.

Orl. And why not the swift foot of Time? Had not that been as proper? 325

Ros. By no means, sir. Time travels in divers paces with divers persons. I'll tell you who Time ambles withal, who Time trots withal, who Time gallops withal, and who he stands still withal.

Orl. I prithee, who doth he trot withal? 330

Ros. Marry, he trots hard with a young maid between the contract of her marriage and the day it is solemniz'd. If the interim be but a se'nnight, Time's pace is so hard that it seems the length of seven year. 335

Orl. Who ambles Time withal?

Ros. With a priest that lacks Latin, and a rich man that hath not the gout; for the one sleeps easily because he cannot study, and the other lives merrily because he feels no pain; the one lacking the 340 burden of lean and wasteful learning, the other knowing no burden of heavy tedious penury. These Time ambles withal.

Orl. Who doth he gallop withal? 344

Ros. With a thief to the gallows; for though he go as softly as foot can fall, he thinks himself too soon there.

Orl. Who stays it still withal?

Ros. With lawyers in the vacation; for they sleep between term and term, and then they perceive not how Time moves. 351

Orl. Where dwell you, pretty youth?

Ros. With this shepherdess, my sister; here in the skirts of the forest, like fringe upon a petticoat. 355

Orl. Are you native of this place?

Ros. As the cony that you see dwell where she is kindled.

Orl. Your accent is something finer than you could purchase in so removed a dwelling. 360

Ros. I have been told so of many; but indeed an old religious uncle of mine taught me to speak, who was in his youth an inland man; one that knew courtship too well, for there he fell in love. I have heard him read many lectures against it, and I 365

---

258. **curvets:** prances. 261. **burden:** bass part. 265. **bring:** put. 273. **buy:** be with. 289. **out of rings:** i.e., from verses carved in rings, which often have mottoes. 290. **painted cloth:** painted canvas wall-hangings. 331. **hard:** i.e., tediously. 357. **cony:** rabbit. 358. **kindled:** littered. 360. **purchase:** acquire. **removed:** remote. 363. **inland.** Cf. II.vii.96 note. 364. **courtship:** (1) courtiership, (2) wooing.

thank God I am not a woman, to be touch'd with so many giddy offences as he hath generally tax'd their whole sex withal.

Orl. Can you remember any of the principal evils that he laid to the charge of women?   370

Ros. There were none principal; they were all like one another as half-pence are, every one fault seeming monstrous till his fellow-fault came to match it.

Orl. I prithee, recount some of them.   375

Ros. No, I will not cast away my physic but on those that are sick.   There is a man haunts the forest, that abuses our young plants with carving Rosalind on their barks; hangs odes upon haw-thorns and elegies on brambles; all, forsooth, 380 deifying the name of Rosalind.   If I could meet that fancy-monger, I would give him some good counsel, for he seems to have the quotidian of love upon him.   384

Orl. I am he that is so love-shak'd.   I pray you, tell me your remedy.

Ros. There is none of my uncle's marks upon you. He taught me how to know a man in love, in which cage of rushes I am sure you are not prisoner. 390

Orl. What were his marks?

Ros. A lean cheek, which you have not; a blue eye and sunken, which you have not; an unquestion-able spirit, which you have not; a beard neglected, which you have not; but I pardon you for that, 395 for simply your having in beard is a younger broth-er's revenue.   Then your hose should be ungarter'd, your bonnet unbanded, your sleeve unbutton'd, your shoe unti'd, and every thing about you dem-onstrating a careless desolation.   But you are 400 no such man; you are rather point-device in your accoutrements, as loving yourself than seeming the lover of any other.

Orl. Fair youth, I would I could make thee be-lieve I love.   405

Ros. Me believe it! you may as soon make her that you love believe it; which, I warrant, she is apter to do than to confess she does.   That is one of the points in the which women still give the lie to their consciences.   But, in good sooth, are 410 you he that hangs the verses on the trees, wherein Rosalind is so admired?

Orl. I swear to thee, youth, by the white hand of Rosalind, I am that he, that unfortunate he.   415

Ros. But are you so much in love as your rhymes speak?

Orl. Neither rhyme nor reason can express how much.   419

Ros. Love is merely a madness, and, I tell you, deserves as well a dark house and a whip as madmen do; and the reason why they are not so punish'd and cured is, that the lunacy is so ordinary that the whippers are in love too.   Yet I profess curing it by counsel.   425

Orl. Did you ever cure any so?

Ros. Yes, one, and in this manner.   He was to imagine me his love, his mistress, and I set him every day to woo me; at which time would I, being but a moonish youth, grieve, be effeminate, 430 changeable, longing and liking, proud, fantastical, apish, shallow, inconstant, full of tears, full of smiles; for every passion something and for no pas-sion truly any thing, as boys and women are for the most part cattle of this colour; would now 435 like him, now loathe him; then entertain him, then forswear him; now weep for him, then spit at him; that I drave my suitor from his mad humour of love to a living humour of madness; which was, to forswear the full stream of the world and to live 440 in a nook, merely monastic.   And thus I cur'd him; and this way will I take upon me to wash your liver as clean as a sound sheep's heart, that there shall not be one spot of love in 't.   445

Orl. I would not be cured, youth.

Ros. I would cure you, if you would but call me Rosalind and come every day to my cote and woo me.

Orl. Now, by the faith of my love, I will.   Tell me where it is.   451

Ros. Go with me to it and I'll show it you; and by the way you shall tell me where in the forest you live.   Will you go?

Orl. With all my heart, good youth.   455

Ros. Nay, you must call me Rosalind.   Come, sister, will you go?   [*Exeunt.*

SCENE III.   [*The forest.*]

Enter Clown [TOUCHSTONE] *and* AUDREY; JAQUES [*behind*].

Touch. Come apace, good Audrey.   I will fetch up your goats, Audrey.   And how, Audrey, am I the man yet?   Doth my simple feature content you?

Aud. Your features! Lord warrant us! what features?   6

Touch. I am here with thee and thy goats, as the most capricious poet, honest Ovid, was among the Goths.

---

382. **fancy-monger:** dealer in love.   383. **quotidian:** daily fever (suggesting *love-shak'd*, l. 385).   392. **blue eye:** dark shadows under the eye.   393. **unquestionable:** averse to talk.   396. **having:** possession.   401. **point-device:** exact, fault-less.   430. **moonish:** changeable.   439. **living:** actual.   441. **merely:** entirely.   442. **liver:** the supposed seat of love.

Sc. iii, 3. **feature:** shape.   8. **capricious.** With a punning sense, *goat-like*, suggested by *caper* (goat), the Latin root of the word.   **Ovid ... Goths.** Ovid was banished by the Emperor Augustus to the land of the Goths (another pun on *goats*).

Jaq. [*Aside.*] O knowledge ill-inhabited, worse than Jove in a thatch'd house!   11

Touch. When a man's verses cannot be understood, nor a man's good wit seconded with the forward child, understanding, it strikes a man more dead than a great reckoning in a little room. Truly, I would the gods had made thee poetical.   16

Aud. I do not know what "poetical" is. Is it honest in deed and word? Is it a true thing?

Touch. No, truly; for the truest poetry is the most feigning; and lovers are given to poetry, 20 and what they swear in poetry may be said as lovers they do feign.

Aud. Do you wish then that the gods had made me poetical?

Touch. I do, truly; for thou swearest to me 25 thou art honest. Now, if thou wert a poet, I might have some hope thou didst feign.

Aud. Would you not have me honest?

Touch. No, truly, unless thou wert hard-favour'd; for honesty coupled to beauty is to have honey a sauce to sugar.   31

Jaq. [*Aside.*] A material fool!

Aud. Well, I am not fair; and therefore I pray the gods make me honest.   34

Touch Truly, and to cast away honesty upon a foul slut were to put good meat into an unclean dish.

Aud. I am not a slut, though I thank the gods I am foul.   39

Touch. Well, praised be the gods for thy foulness! Sluttishness may come hereafter. But be it as it may be, I will marry thee, and to that end I have been with Sir Oliver Martext, the vicar of the next village, who hath promis'd to meet me in this place of the forest and to couple us.   45

Jaq. [*Aside.*] I would fain see this meeting.

Aud. Well, the gods give us joy!

Touch. Amen. A man may, if he were of a fearful heart, stagger in this attempt; for here we have no temple but the wood, no assembly but horn- 50 beasts. But what though? Courage! As horns are odious, they are necessary. It is said, "Many a man knows no end of his goods." Right; many a man has good horns, and knows no end of them. Well, that is the dowry of his wife; 'tis none of 55 his own getting. Horns? — even so. Poor men alone? No, no; the noblest deer hath them as huge as the rascal. Is the single man therefore blessed? No: as a wall'd town is more worthier than a village, so is the forehead of a married 60 man more honourable than the bare brow of a bachelor; and by how much defence is better than no skill, by so much is a horn more precious than to want.

Enter SIR OLIVER MARTEXT.

Here comes Sir Oliver. Sir Oliver Martext, you are well met. Will you dispatch us here 65 under this tree, or shall we go with you to your chapel?

Sir Oli. Is there none here to give the woman?

Touch. I will not take her on gift of any man.

Sir Oli. Truly, she must be given, or the marriage is not lawful.   71

Jaq. Proceed, proceed. I'll give her.

Touch. Good even, good Master What-ye-call't; how do you, sir? You are very well met. God 75 'ild you for your last company. I am very glad to see you. Even a toy in hand here, sir. Nay, pray be cover'd.

Jaq. Will you be married, motley?   79

Touch. As the ox hath his bow, sir, the horse his curb, and the falcon her bells, so man hath his desires; and as pigeons bill, so wedlock would be nibbling.

Jaq. And will you, being a man of your breeding, be married under a bush like a beggar? Get 85 you to church, and have a good priest that can tell you what marriage is. This fellow will but join you together as they join wainscot; then one of you will prove a shrunk panel, and like green timber warp, warp.   90

Touch. [*Aside.*] I am not in the mind but I were better to be married of him than of another; for he is not like to marry me well; and not being well married, it will be a good excuse for me hereafter to leave my wife.   95

Jaq. Go thou with me, and let me counsel thee.

Touch. Come, sweet Audrey;
We must be married, or we must live in bawdry.
Farewell, good Master Oliver: not, —   100
　　　　　O sweet Oliver,
　　　　　O brave Oliver,
　　　　Leave me not behind thee;
but, —

　　　　　　Wind away,   105
　　　　　Begone, I say,
　　I will not to wedding with thee.
[*Exeunt Jaques, Touchstone, and Audrey.*]

Sir Oli. 'Tis no matter. Ne'er a fantastical knave of them all shall flout me out of my calling.   [*Exit.* 109

---

10. **ill-inhabited:** inappropriately lodged. 11. **Jove...house.** Jupiter was entertained *incognito* by the peasants, Baucis and Philemon. 15. **great reckoning:** big bill. 20. **feigning:** (1) imaginative, (2) lying. 32. **material:** full of good sense. 49. **stagger.** falter. 52. **necessary:** inevitable. 54. **horns.** The inescapable quibble about the cuckold. 58. **rascal:** inferior deer. 62. **defence:** the ability to defend oneself. 64. **want:** lack one. 76. **'ild:** yield, reward. 77. **toy:** trifle. 78. **be cover'd:** put on your hat. 80. **bow:** yoke. 91. **I...mind:** I do not know.

SCENE IV. [*The forest.*]

Enter ROSALIND *and* CELIA.

Ros. Never talk to me; I will weep.

Cel. Do, I prithee; but yet have the grace to consider that tears do not become a man.

Ros. But have I not cause to weep?

Cel. As good cause as one would desire; therefore weep. 6

Ros. His very hair is of the dissembling colour.

Cel. Something browner than Judas's. Marry, his kisses are Judas's own children. 10

Ros. I' faith, his hair is of a good colour.

Cel. An excellent colour. Your chestnut was ever the only colour.

Ros. And his kissing is as full of sanctity as the touch of holy bread. 15

Cel. He hath bought a pair of cast lips of Diana. A nun of winter's sisterhood kisses not more religiously. The very ice of chastity is in them.

Ros. But why did he swear he would come this morning, and comes not? 21

Cel. Nay, certainly, there is no truth in him.

Ros. Do you think so?

Cel. Yes; I think he is not a pick-purse nor a horse-stealer; but for his verity in love, I do 25 think him as concave as a covered goblet or a worm-eaten nut.

Ros. Not true in love?

Cel. Yes, when he is in; but I think he is not in. 30

Ros. You have heard him swear downright he was.

Cel. "Was" is not "is." Besides, the oath of a lover is no stronger than the word of a tapster; they are both the confirmer of false reckonings. 35 He attends here in the forest on the Duke your father.

Ros. I met the Duke yesterday and had much question with him. He asked me of what parentage I was. I told him, of as good as he; so he 40 laugh'd and let me go. But what talk we of fathers, when there is such a man as Orlando?

Cel. O, that's a brave man! He writes brave verses, speaks brave words, swears brave oaths and breaks them bravely, quite traverse, athwart 45 the heart of his lover, as a puisny tilter, that spurs his horse but on one side, breaks his staff like a noble goose. But all's brave that youth mounts and folly guides. Who comes here?

Enter CORIN.

Cor. Mistress and master, you have oft inquired

After the shepherd that complain'd of love, 51
Who you saw sitting by me on the turf,
Praising the proud disdainful shepherdess
That was his mistress.

Cel.   Well, and what of him?

Cor. If you will see a pageant truly play'd, 55
Between the pale complexion of true love
And the red glow of scorn and proud disdain,
Go hence a little and I shall conduct you,
If you will mark it.

Ros.   O, come, let us remove;
The sight of lovers feedeth those in love. 60
Bring us to this sight, and you shall say
I'll prove a busy actor in their play. [*Exeunt.*

SCENE V. [*Another part of the forest.*]

Enter SILVIUS *and* PHEBE.

Sil. Sweet Phebe, do not scorn me; do not, Phebe.
Say that you love me not, but say not so
In bitterness. The common executioner,
Whose heart th' accustom'd sight of death makes hard,
Falls not the axe upon the humbled neck 5
But first begs pardon. Will you sterner be
Than he that dies and lives by bloody drops?

Enter ROSALIND, CELIA, *and* CORIN [*behind*].

Phe. I would not be thy executioner.
I fly thee, for I would not injure thee.
Thou tell'st me there is murder in mine eye: 10
'Tis pretty, sure, and very probable,
That eyes, that are the frail'st and softest things,
Who shut their coward gates on atomies,
Should be called tyrants, butchers, murderers!
Now I do frown on thee with all my heart; 15
And if mine eyes can wound, now let them kill thee.
Now counterfeit to swoon; why, now fall down;
Or if thou canst not, O, for shame, for shame,
Lie not, to say mine eyes are murderers!
Now show the wound mine eye hath made in thee.
Scratch thee but with a pin, and there remains 21
Some scar of it; lean but upon a rush,
The cicatrice and capable impressure
Thy palm some moment keeps; but now mine eyes,
Which I have darted at thee, hurt thee not, 25
Nor, I am sure, there is no force in eyes
That can do hurt.

Sil.   O dear Phebe,
If ever — as that ever may be near —
You meet in some fresh cheek the power of fancy,

Sc. iv, 9. **browner... Judas's.** Judas was traditionally represented with red hair. 15. **holy bread:** sacramental wafer. 16. **cast:** cast-off. 45. **traverse:** across. To break one's lance across an adversary's shield instead of by a direct blow was disgraceful. 46. **puisny:** inexperienced.
Sc. v, 5. **Falls:** lets fall. 7. **dies and lives:** makes his living. 23. **cicatrice:** mark (strictly, *scar*). **capable impressure:** perceptible imprint.

Then shall you know the wounds invisible   30
That love's keen arrows make.
   Phe.   But till that time
Come not thou near me; and when that time comes,
Afflict me with thy mocks, pity me not,
As till that time I shall not pity thee.
   Ros. [*Advancing.*] And why, I pray you? Who
     might be your mother,   35
That you insult, exult, and all at once,
Over the wretched? What though you have no
     beauty, —
As, by my faith, I see no more in you
Than without candle may go dark to bed —
Must you be therefore proud and pitiless?   40
Why, what means this? Why do you look on me?
I see no more in you than in the ordinary
Of nature's sale-work. 'Od's my little life,
I think she means to tangle my eyes too!
No, faith, proud mistress, hope not after it.   45
'Tis not your inky brows, your black silk hair,
Your bugle eyeballs, nor your cheek of cream
That can entame my spirits to your worship.
You foolish shepherd, wherefore do you follow her,
Like foggy south, puffing with wind and rain? 50
You are a thousand times a properer man
Than she a woman. 'Tis such fools as you
That makes the world full of ill-favour'd children.
'Tis not her glass, but you, that flatters her;
And out of you she sees herself more proper 55
Than any of her lineaments can show her.
But, mistress, know yourself. Down on your knees,
And thank heaven, fasting, for a good man's love;
For I must tell you friendly in your ear,
Sell when you can; you are not for all markets. 60
Cry the man mercy; love him; take his offer.
Foul is most foul, being foul to be a scoffer.
So take her to thee, shepherd. Fare you well.
   Phe. Sweet youth, I pray you, chide a year to-
     gether.
I had rather hear you chide than this man woo. 65
   Ros. He's fall'n in love with your foulness, and
she'll fall in love with my anger. If it be so, as
fast as she answers thee with frowning looks, I'll
sauce her with bitter words. Why look you so
upon me?   70
   Phe. For no ill will I bear you.
   Ros. I pray you, do not fall in love with me,
For I am falser than vows made in wine.
Besides, I like you not. If you will know my house,
'Tis at the tuft of olives here hard by.   75
Will you go, sister? Shepherd, ply her hard.
Come, sister. Shepherdess, look on him better,
And be not proud. Though all the world could see,

None could be so abus'd in sight as he.
Come, to our flock.   80
        [*Exeunt* [*Rosalind, Celia, and Corin*].
   Phe. Dead shepherd, now I find thy saw of
     might,
"Who ever lov'd that lov'd not at first sight?"
   Sil. Sweet Phebe, —
   Phe.   Ha, what say'st thou, Silvius?
   Sil. Sweet Phebe, pity me.
   Phe. Why, I am sorry for thee, gentle Silvius. 85
   Sil. Wherever sorrow is, relief would be.
If you do sorrow at my grief in love,
By giving love, your sorrow and my grief
Were both extermin'd.
   Phe. Thou hast my love. Is not that neigh-
     bourly?   90
   Sil. I would have you.
   Phe.   Why, that were covetousness.
Silvius, the time was that I hated thee,
And yet it is not that I bear thee love;
But since that thou canst talk of love so well,
Thy company, which erst was irksome to me, 95
I will endure, and I'll employ thee too.
But do not look for further recompense
Than thine own gladness that thou art employ'd.
   Sil. So holy and so perfect is my love,
And I in such a poverty of grace,   100
That I shall think it a most plenteous crop
To glean the broken ears after the man
That the main harvest reaps. Loose now and then
A scatt'red smile, and that I'll live upon.
   Phe. Know'st thou the youth that spoke to me
     erewhile?   105
   Sil. Not very well, but I have met him oft;
And he hath bought the cottage and the bounds
That the old carlot once was master of.
   Phe. Think not I love him, though I ask for him;
'Tis but a peevish boy; yet he talks well.   110
But what care I for words? Yet words do well
When he that speaks them pleases those that hear.
It is a pretty youth; not very pretty;
But, sure, he's proud, and yet his pride becomes
     him.
He'll make a proper man. The best thing in him
Is his complexion; and faster than his tongue 116
Did make offence his eye did heal it up.
He is not very tall; yet for his years he's tall.
His leg is but so so; and yet 'tis well.
There was a pretty redness in his lip,   120
A little riper and more lusty red
Than that mix'd in his cheek; 'twas just the dif-
     ference
Betwixt the constant red and mingled damask.

---

   37. no. Some edd. omit; others read *some*.   **39. without candle:** without anyone's wanting to see you.   **43. sale-work:** ready-made work.   **47. bugle:** black bead of glass.   **79. abus'd:** deceived.   **81–82.** Shakespeare's tribute to Christopher Marlowe, from whose poem *Hero and Leander* (I,176) line 82 is taken.   **107. bounds:** pasture.   **108. carlot:** peasant.   **123. constant:** uniform.   **mingled damask:** the blended red and white (pink) of the damask rose.

There be some women, Silvius, had they mark'd him
In parcels as I did, would have gone near   125
To fall in love with him; but, for my part,
I love him not nor hate him not; and yet
I have more cause to hate him than to love him,
For what had he to do to chide at me?
He said mine eyes were black and my hair black;
And, now I am rememb'red, scorn'd at me.   131
I marvel why I answer'd not again.
But that's all one; omittance is no quittance
I'll write to him a very taunting letter,
And thou shalt bear it; wilt thou, Silvius?   135
    Sil. Phebe, with all my heart.
    Phe.   I'll write it straight;
The matter's in my head and in my heart.
I will be bitter with him and passing short.
Go with me, Silvius.   [*Exeunt.*

ACT IV

Scene I. [*The forest.*]

Enter Rosalind, Celia, *and* Jaques.

Jaq. I prithee, pretty youth, let me [be] better acquainted with thee.
    Ros. They say you are a melancholy fellow.
    Jaq. I am so; I do love it better than laughing.   4
    Ros. Those that are in extremity of either are abominable fellows, and betray themselves to every modern censure worse than drunkards.
    Jaq. Why, 'tis good to be sad and say nothing.
    Ros. Why then, 'tis good to be a post.   9
    Jaq. I have neither the scholar's melancholy, which is emulation; nor the musician's, which is fantastical; nor the courtier's, which is proud; nor the soldier's, which is ambitious; nor the lawyer's, which is politic; nor the lady's, which is nice; nor the lover's, which is all these: but it is a melan-   15
choly of mine own, compounded of many simples, extracted from many objects; and indeed the sundry contemplation of my travels, in which [my] often rumination wraps me in a most humorous sadness —   20
    Ros. A traveller! By my faith, you have great reason to be sad. I fear you have sold your own lands to see other men's; then, to have seen much, and to have nothing, is to have rich eyes and poor hands.   25
    Jaq. Yes, I have gained my experience.

Enter Orlando.

    Ros. And your experience makes you sad. I

had rather have a fool to make me merry than experience to make me sad; and to travel for it too!
    Orl. Good-day and happiness, dear Rosalind!   30
    Jaq. Nay, then, God buy you, an you talk in blank verse.   [*Exit.*
    Ros. Farewell, Monsieur Traveller. Look you lisp and wear strange suits, disable all the benefits of your own country, be out of love with your   35
nativity, and almost chide God for making you that countenance you are, or I will scarce think you have swam in a gondola. Why, how now, Orlando! Where have you been all this while? You a lover! An you serve me such another trick, never come in my sight more.   41
    Orl. My fair Rosalind, I come within an hour of my promise.
    Ros. Break an hour's promise in love! He that will divide a minute into a thousand parts, and   45
break but a part of the thousandth part of a minute in the affairs of love, it may be said of him that Cupid hath clapp'd him o' th' shoulder but I'll warrant him heart-whole.
    Orl. Pardon me, dear Rosalind.   50
    Ros. Nay, an you be so tardy, come no more in my sight. I had as lief be woo'd of a snail.
    Orl. Of a snail?
    Ros. Ay, of a snail; for though he comes slowly, he carries his house on his head; a better join-   55
ture, I think, than you make a woman. Besides, he brings his destiny with him.
    Orl. What's that?
    Ros. Why, horns, which such as you are fain to be beholding to your wives for. But he comes   60
armed in his fortune and prevents the slander of his wife.
    Orl. Virtue is no horn-maker; and my Rosalind is virtuous.
    Ros. And I am your Rosalind.   65
    Cel. It pleases him to call you so; but he hath a Rosalind of a better leer than you.
    Ros. Come, woo me, woo me; for now I am in a holiday humour and like enough to consent. What would you say to me now, an I were your very very Rosalind?   71
    Orl. I would kiss before I spoke.
    Ros. Nay, you were better speak first; and when you were gravell'd for lack of matter, you might take occasion to kiss. Very good orators,   75
when they are out, they will spit; and for lovers lacking — God warn us! — matter, the cleanliest shift is to kiss.
    Orl. How if the kiss be deni'd?

---

125. **In parcels:** piecemeal.
  Act IV, sc. i, 1. **[be].** Om. F.   7. **modern censure:** ordinary judgment.   14. **nice:** fastidious.   16. **simples:** ingredients.
18. **[my]** F₂. *by* F₁.   19. **humorous:** whimsical.   34. **disable:** disparage.   38. **swam ... gondola:** i.e., been in Venice.
48. **clapp'd ... shoulder:** i.e., arrested.   55. **jointure:** marriage-settlement.   61. **prevents:** anticipates.   67. **leer:** face.
74. **gravell'd:** stuck.   76. **out:** at a loss.   77. **warn:** defend.   **cleanliest shift:** neatest trick.

Ros. Then she puts you to entreaty and there begins new matter.   81

Orl. Who could be out, being before his beloved mistress?

Ros. Marry, that should you if I were your mistress, or I should think my honesty ranker than my wit.   86

Orl. What, of my suit?

Ros. Not out of your apparel, and yet out of your suit. Am not I your Rosalind?

Orl. I take some joy to say you are, because I would be talking of her.   91

Ros. Well, in her person, I say I will not have you.

Orl. Then in mine own person I die.

Ros. No, faith, die by attorney. The poor world is almost six thousand years old, and in all this time there was not any man died in his   95 own person, *videlicet*, in a love-cause. Troilus had his brains dash'd out with a Grecian club; yet he did what he could to die before, and he is one of the patterns of love. Leander, he would have   100 liv'd many a fair year though Hero had turn'd nun, if it had not been for a hot mid-summer night; for, good youth, he went but forth to wash him in the Hellespont and being taken with the cramp was drown'd; and the foolish chroniclers of that age   105 found it was — Hero of Sestos. But these are all lies. Men have died from time to time and worms have eaten them, but not for love.

Orl. I would not have my right Rosalind of this mind; for, I protest, her frown might kill me.   110

Ros. By this hand, it will not kill a fly. But come, now I will be your Rosalind in a more coming-on disposition; and ask me what you will, I will grant it.

Orl. Then love me, Rosalind.   115

Ros. Yes, faith, will I, Fridays and Saturdays and all.

Orl. And wilt thou have me?

Ros. Ay, and twenty such.

Orl. What sayest thou?   120

Ros. Are you not good?

Orl. I hope so.

Ros. Why then, can one desire too much of a good thing? Come, sister, you shall be the priest and marry us. Give me your hand, Orlando. What do you say, sister?   126

Orl. Pray thee, marry us.

Cel. I cannot say the words.

Ros. You must begin, "Will you, Orlando," —

Cel. Go to. Will you, Orlando, have to wife this Rosalind?   131

Orl. I will.

Ros. Ay, but when?

Orl. Why now; as fast as she can marry us.

Ros. Then you must say, "I take thee, Rosalind, for wife."   136

Orl. I take thee, Rosalind, for wife.

Ros. I might ask you for your commission; but I do take thee, Orlando, for my husband. There's a girl goes before the priest; and certainly a woman's thought runs before her actions.   141

Orl. So do all thoughts; they are wing'd.

Ros. Now tell me how long you would have her after you have possess'd her.

Orl. For ever and a day.   145

Ros. Say "a day," without the "ever." No, no, Orlando. Men are April when they woo, December when they wed; maids are May when they are maids, but the sky changes when they are wives. I will be more jealous of thee than a   150 Barbary cock-pigeon over his hen, more clamorous than a parrot against rain, more new-fangled than an ape, more giddy in my desires than a monkey. I will weep for nothing, like Diana in the fountain, and I will do that when you are dispos'd to be   155 merry. I will laugh like a hyen, and that when thou art inclin'd to sleep.

Orl. But will my Rosalind do so?

Ros. By my life, she will do as I do.

Orl. O, but she is wise.   160

Ros. Or else she could not have the wit to do this. The wiser, the waywarder. Make the doors upon a woman's wit and it will out at the casement; shut that and 'twill out at the key-hole; stop that, 'twill fly with the smoke out at the chimney.   166

Orl. A man that had a wife with such a wit, he might say, "Wit, whither wilt?"

Ros. Nay, you might keep that check for it, till you met your wife's wit going to your neighbour's bed.   171

Orl. And what wit could wit have to excuse that?

Ros. Marry, to say she came to seek you there. You shall never take her without her answer,   175 unless you take her without her tongue. O, that woman that cannot make her fault her husband's occasion, let her never nurse her child herself, for she will breed it like a fool!

Orl. For these two hours, Rosalind, I will leave thee.   181

Ros. Alas, dear love, I cannot lack thee two hours!

Orl. I must attend the Duke at dinner. By two o'clock I will be with thee again.   185

Ros. Ay, go your ways, go your ways; I knew

---

85. **honesty ranker:** chastity greater. 96 ff. Troilus and Leander were types of faithful lovers, whose heroism Rosalind facetiously disparages. 138. **commission:** authority. 140. **goes before:** anticipates. 152. **new-fangled:** fond of novelty. 162. **Make:** shut. 168. **"Wit, whither wilt?"** An expression to stop a person talking. 177. **make ... occasion:** make out that her husband is to blame for her fault.

what you would prove. My friends told me as much, and I thought no less. That flattering tongue of yours won me. 'Tis but one cast away, and so, come, death! Two o'clock is your hour?   190

Orl. Ay, sweet Rosalind.

Ros. By my troth, and in good earnest, and so God mend me, and by all pretty oaths that are not dangerous, if you break one jot of your promise or come one minute behind your hour, I will think   195
you the most pathetical break-promise, and the most hollow lover, and the most unworthy of her you call Rosalind, that may be chosen out of the gross band of the unfaithful; therefore beware my censure and keep your promise.   200

Orl. With no less religion than if thou wert indeed my Rosalind; so adieu.

Ros. Well, Time is the old justice that examines all such offenders, and let Time try. Adieu.
          [*Exit [Orlando].*

Cel. You have simply misus'd our sex in your   205
love-prate. We must have your doublet and hose pluck'd over your head, and show the world what the bird hath done to her own nest.

Ros. O coz, coz, coz, my pretty little coz, that thou didst know how many fathom deep I am   210
in love! But it cannot be sounded. My affection hath an unknown bottom, like the bay of Portugal.

Cel. Or rather, bottomless; that as fast as you pour affection in, it runs out.   215

Ros. No, that same wicked bastard of Venus that was begot of thought, conceiv'd of spleen, and born of madness, that blind rascally boy that abuses every one's eyes because his own are out, let him be judge how deep I am in love. I'll tell thee,   220
Aliena, I cannot be out of the sight of Orlando. I'll go find a shadow and sigh till he come.

Cel. And I'll sleep.   [*Exeunt.*

SCENE II. [*The forest.*]

Enter JAQUES, LORDS, *and* FORESTERS.

Jaq. Which is he that killed the deer?

A Lord. Sir, it was I.

Jaq. Let's present him to the Duke, like a Roman conqueror; and it would do well to set the deer's horns upon his head, for a branch of vic-   5
tory. Have you no song, forester, for this purpose?

[*I. For.*] Yes, sir.

Jaq. Sing it. 'Tis no matter how it be in tune, so it make noise enough.   10

SONG.   [*Music.*

[*I. For.*] What shall he have that killed the deer?
          His leather skin and horns to wear.
          Then sing him home.
               [*The rest shall bear this burden.*
          Take thou no scorn to wear the horn;
          It was a crest ere thou wast born;   15
               Thy father's father wore it,
               And thy father bore it.
          The horn, the horn, the lusty horn
          Is not a thing to laugh to scorn.
          [*Exeunt.*

SCENE III. [*The forest.*]

Enter ROSALIND *and* CELIA.

Ros. How say you now? Is it not past two o'clock? And here much Orlando!

Cel. I warrant you, with pure love and troubled brain, (*Enter* SILVIUS) he hath ta'en his bow and arrows and is gone forth — to sleep. Look, who comes here.   5

Sil. My errand is to you, fair youth;
My gentle Phebe bid me give you this.
I know not the contents; but, as I guess
By the stern brow and waspish action
Which she did use as she was writing of it,   10
It bears an angry tenour. Pardon me,
I am but as a guiltless messenger.

Ros. Patience herself would startle at this letter
And play the swaggerer. Bear this, bear all.
She says I am not fair, that I lack manners.   15
She calls me proud, and that she could not love me,
Were man as rare as phœnix. 'Od's my will!
Her love is not the hare that I do hunt.
Why writes she so to me? Well, shepherd, well,
This is a letter of your own device.   20

Sil. No, I protest, I know not the contents.
Phebe did write it.

Ros.   Come, come, you are a fool,
And turn'd into th' extremity of love.
I saw her hand; she has a leathern hand,
A freestone-colour'd hand. I verily did think   25
That her old gloves were on, but 'twas her hands;
She has a huswife's hand; but that's no matter.
I say she never did invent this letter.
This is a man's invention and his hand.

Sil. Sure, it is hers.   30

Ros. Why, 'tis a boisterous and a cruel style,
A style for challengers. Why, she defies me,
Like Turk to Christian. Women's gentle brain
Could not drop forth such giant-rude invention,

---

195. **pathetical:** pitiful.   201. **religion:** devotion.   205. **simply misus'd:** utterly abused.   217. **thought:** melancholy.
spleen: impulsive passion.
Sc. ii, 7. [*I. For.*] *Lord* Ff.
Sc. iii, 7. **bid** F₂.   *did bid* F₁.   17. **phœnix.** A fabulous bird, the only one of its kind, consumed by fire every five hundred years, and rising again from its own ashes.   23. **turn'd:** brought.   25. **freestone:** sandstone.

Such Ethiope words, blacker in their effect   35
Than in their countenance.   Will you hear the
    letter?
    Sil. So please you, for I never heard it yet;
Yet heard too much of Phebe's cruelty.
    Ros. She Phebes me.   Mark how the tyrant
    writes.
[*Reads.*]
    "Art thou god to shepherd turn'd,   40
        That a maiden's heart hath burn'd?"
Can a woman rail thus?
    Sil. Call you this railing?
    Ros. [*Reads.*]
    "Why, thy godhead laid apart,
        Warr'st thou with a woman's heart?"   45
Did you ever hear such railing?
    "Whiles the eye of man did woo me,
        That could do no vengeance to me."
Meaning me a beast.
    "If the scorn of your bright eyne   50
        Have power to raise such love in mine,
    Alack, in me what strange effect
        Would they work in mild aspect!
    Whiles you chid me, I did love;
        How then might your prayers move!   55
    He that brings this love to thee
        Little knows this love in me;
    And by him seal up thy mind,
        Whether that thy youth and kind
    Will the faithful offer take   60
        Of me and all that I can make;
    Or else by him my love deny,
        And then I'll study how to die."
    Sil. Call you this chiding?
    Cel. Alas, poor shepherd!   65
    Ros. Do you pity him?   No, he deserves no pity.
Wilt thou love such a woman?   What, to make
thee an instrument and play false strains upon thee!
Not to be endur'd!   Well, go your way to her —
for I see love hath made thee a tame snake —   70
and say this to her: that if she love me, I charge her
to love thee; if she will not, I will never have her
unless thou entreat for her.   If you be a true lover,
hence, and not a word; for here comes more company.   [*Exit Silvius.*   75

Enter OLIVER.

    Oli. Good morrow, fair ones.   Pray you, if you
    know,
Where in the purlieus of this forest stands
A sheep-cote fenc'd about with olive-trees?
    Cel. West of this place, down in the neighbour
    bottom.
The rank of osiers by the murmuring stream   80

Left on your right hand brings you to the place.
But at this hour the house doth keep itself;
There's none within.
    Oli. If that an eye may profit by a tongue,
Then should I know you by description;   85
Such garments and such years.   "The boy is fair,
Of female favour, and bestows himself
Like a ripe sister; the woman low,
And browner than her brother."   Are not you
The owner of the house I did enquire for?   90
    Cel. It is no boast, being ask'd, to say we are.
    Oli. Orlando doth commend him to you both,
And to that youth he calls his Rosalind
He sends this bloody napkin.   Are you he?
    Ros. I am.   What must we understand by
    this?   95
    Oli. Some of my shame, if you will know of me
What man I am, and how, and why, and where
This handkercher was stain'd.
    Cel.   I pray you, tell it.
    Oli. When last the young Orlando parted from
    you
He left a promise to return again   100
Within an hour; and pacing through the forest,
Chewing the food of sweet and bitter fancy,
Lo, what befell!   He threw his eye aside,
And mark what object did present itself.
Under an oak, whose boughs were moss'd with
    age   105
And high top bald with dry antiquity,
A wretched ragged man, o'ergrown with hair,
Lay sleeping on his back.   About his neck
A green and gilded snake had wreath'd itself,
Who with her head nimble in threats approach'd
The opening of his mouth; but suddenly,   111
Seeing Orlando, it unlink'd itself,
And with indented glides did slip away
Into a bush; under which bush's shade
A lioness, with udders all drawn dry,   115
Lay couching, head on ground, with catlike
    watch,
When that the sleeping man should stir; for 'tis
The royal disposition of that beast
To prey on nothing that doth seem as dead.
This seen, Orlando did approach the man   120
And found it was his brother, his elder brother.
    Cel. O, I have heard him speak of that same
    brother;
And he did render him the most unnatural
That liv'd amongst men.
    Oli.   And well he might so do,
For well I know he was unnatural.   125
    Ros. But, to Orlando.   Did he leave him there,
Food to the suck'd and hungry lioness?

---

35. **Ethiope:** i.e., black.   39. **Phebes me:** i.e., tries her scorn on me.   48. **vengeance:** mischief.   59. **youth and kind:**
youthful nature.   68. **instrument:** (1) tool, (2) musical instrument.   77. **purlieus:** borders.   79. **neighbour bottom:**
neighboring dell.   80. **rank of osiers:** row of willows.   87. **bestows:** carries.   88. **ripe:** mature.   105. **oak** (Pope).   *old
oake* Ff.   113. **indented:** zigzag.   123. **render:** describe.

Oli. Twice did he turn his back and purpos'd so;
But kindness, nobler ever than revenge,
And nature, stronger than his just occasion,   130
Made him give battle to the lioness,
Who quickly fell before him; in which hurtling
From miserable slumber I awaked.
   Cel. Are you his brother?
   Ros.   Was't you he rescu'd?
   Cel. Was't you that did so oft contrive to kill
      him?   135
   Oli. 'Twas I; but 'tis not I. I do not shame
To tell you what I was, since my conversion
So sweetly tastes, being the thing I am.
   Ros. But, for the bloody napkin?
   Oli.   By and by.
When from the first to last betwixt us two   140
Tears our recountments had most kindly bath'd,
As how I came into that desert place, —
In brief, he led me to the gentle Duke,
Who gave me fresh array and entertainment,
Committing me unto my brother's love;   145
Who led me instantly into his cave,
There stripp'd himself, and here upon his arm
The lioness had torn some flesh away,
Which all this while had bled; and now he fainted
And cri'd, in fainting, upon Rosalind.   150
Brief, I recover'd him, bound up his wound;
And, after some small space, being strong at heart,
He sent me hither, stranger as I am,
To tell this story, that you might excuse
His broken promise, and to give this napkin,   155
Dy'd in his blood, unto the shepherd youth
That he in sport doth call his Rosalind.
                                   [*Rosalind swoons.*]
   Cel. Why, how now, Ganymede! sweet Gany-
      mede!
   Oli. Many will swoon when they do look on
      blood.
   Cel. There is more in it. Cousin Ganymede!   160
   Oli. Look, he recovers.
   Ros. I would I were at home.
   Cel.   We'll lead you thither.
I pray you, will you take him by the arm?
   Oli. Be of good cheer, youth. You a man!
You lack a man's heart.   165
   Ros. I do so, I confess it. Ah, sirrah, a body
would think this was well counterfeited! I pray
you, tell your brother how well I counterfeited.
Heigh-ho!   169
   Oli. This was not counterfeit. There is too
great testimony in your complexion that it was a
passion of earnest.
   Ros. Counterfeit, I assure you.
   Oli. Well then, take a good heart and counterfeit
to be a man.   175

   Ros. So I do. But, i' faith, I should have been a
woman by right.
   Cel. Come, you look paler and paler. Pray you,
draw homewards. Good sir, go with us.
   Oli. That will I, for I must bear answer back   180
How you excuse my brother, Rosalind.
   Ros. I shall devise something; but, I pray you,
commend my counterfeiting to him. Will you go?
                                   [*Exeunt.*

ACT V

SCENE I. [*The forest.*]

Enter Clown [TOUCHSTONE] *and* AUDREY.

   Touch. We shall find a time, Audrey; patience,
gentle Audrey.
   Aud. Faith, the priest was good enough, for all
the old gentleman's saying.   4
   Touch. A most wicked Sir Oliver, Audrey, a most
vile Martext. But, Audrey, there is a youth here
in the forest lays claim to you.
   Aud. Ay, I know who 'tis; he hath no interest
in me in the world. Here comes the man you
mean.   10

Enter WILLIAM.

   Touch. It is meat and drink to me to see a clown.
By my troth, we that have good wits have much to
answer for; we shall be flouting; we cannot hold.
   Will. Good ev'n, Audrey.   15
   Aud. God ye good ev'n, William.
   Will. And good ev'n to you, sir,
   Touch. Good ev'n, gentle friend. Cover thy
head, cover thy head; nay, prithee, be cover'd.
How old are you, friend?   20
   Will. Five and twenty, sir.
   Touch. A ripe age. Is thy name William?
   Will. William, sir.
   Touch. A fair name. Was't born i' the forest
here?   25
   Will. Ay, sir, I thank God.
   Touch. "Thank God" — a good answer. Art
rich?
   Will. Faith, sir, so so.
   Touch. "So so" is good, very good, very excel-
lent good; and yet it is not; it is but so so. Art
thou wise?   31
   Will. Ay, sir, I have a pretty wit.
   Touch. Why, thou say'st well. I do now re-
member a saying, "The fool doth think he is wise,
but the wise man knows himself to be a fool."   35
The heathen philosopher, when he had a desire to
eat a grape, would open his lips when he put it
into his mouth; meaning thereby that grapes were

---

141. **recountments:** tales. 151. **recover'd:** revived.
   Act V, sc. i, 11. **clown:** country fellow. Touchstone is a court jester. 14. **shall...flouting:** must have our jest.

made to eat and lips to open. You do love this
maid?   40
Will. I do, sir.
Touch. Give me your hand. Art thou learned?
Will. No, sir.
Touch. Then learn this of me: to have, is to have;
for it is a figure in rhetoric that drink, being   45
pour'd out of a cup into a glass, by filling the one
doth empty the other. For all your writers do
consent that *ipse* is he: now, you are not *ipse*, for
I am he.
Will. Which he, sir?   50
Touch. He, sir, that must marry this woman.
Therefore, you clown, abandon — which is in the
vulgar leave — the society — which in the boorish
is company — of this female — which in the common is woman; which together is, abandon the   55
society of this female; or, clown, thou perishest; or,
to thy better understanding, diest; or, to wit, I kill
thee, make thee away, translate thy life into death,
thy liberty into bondage. I will deal in poison with
thee, or in bastinado, or in steel. I will bandy   60
with thee in faction; I will o'er-run thee with
[policy]; I will kill thee a hundred and fifty ways:
therefore tremble, and depart.
Aud. Do, good William.
Will. God rest you merry, sir.   [*Exit.* 65

Enter CORIN.

Cor. Our master and mistress seeks you. Come,
away, away!
Touch. Trip, Audrey! trip, Audrey! I attend,
I attend.   [*Exeunt.*

SCENE II. [*The forest.*]

Enter ORLANDO *and* OLIVER.

Orl. Is't possible that on so little acquaintance
you should like her? That but seeing you should
love her? And loving woo? And, wooing, she
should grant? And will you persever to enjoy
her?   5
Oli. Neither call the giddiness of it in question,
the poverty of her, the small acquaintance, my
sudden wooing, nor [her] sudden consenting; but
say with me, I love Aliena; say with her that she
loves me; consent with both that we may enjoy
each other. It shall be to your good; for my   10
father's house and all the revenue that was old Sir
Roland's will I estate upon you, and here live and
die a shepherd.   14

Enter ROSALIND.

Orl. You have my consent. Let your wedding

be to-morrow; thither will I invite the Duke and
all 's contented followers. Go you and prepare
Aliena; for look you, here comes my Rosalind.
Ros. God save you, brother.   20
Oli. And you, fair sister.   [*Exit.*]
Ros. O, my dear Orlando, how it grieves me to
see thee wear thy heart in a scarf!
Orl. It is my arm.
Ros. I thought thy heart had been wounded with
the claws of a lion.   26
Orl. Wounded it is, but with the eyes of a lady.
Ros. Did your brother tell you how I counter-
feited to swoon when he show'd me your handkercher?   30
Orl. Ay, and greater wonders than that.
Ros. O, I know where you are. Nay, 'tis true.
There was never any thing so sudden but the fight
of two rams, and Cæsar's thrasonical brag of "I
came, saw, and overcame." For your brother   35
and my sister no sooner met but they look'd;
no sooner look'd but they lov'd; no sooner lov'd
but they sigh'd; no sooner sigh'd but they ask'd one
another the reason; no sooner knew the reason but
they sought the remedy; and in these degrees   40
have they made a pair of stairs to marriage which
they will climb incontinent, or else be incontinent
before marriage. They are in the very wrath of
love and they will together. Clubs cannot part
them.   45
Orl. They shall be married to-morrow, and I
will bid the Duke to the nuptial. But, O, how
bitter a thing it is to look into happiness through
another man's eyes! By so much the more shall I
to-morrow be at the height of heart-heaviness,   50
by how much I shall think my brother happy in
having what he wishes for.
Ros. Why then, to-morrow I cannot serve your
turn for Rosalind?
Orl. I can live no longer by thinking.   55
Ros. I will weary you, then, no longer with idle
talking. Know of me, then, for now I speak to
some purpose, that I know you are a gentleman of
good conceit. I speak not this that you should bear
a good opinion of my knowledge, insomuch I   60
say I know you are; neither do I labour for a greater
esteem than may in some little measure draw a belief from you, to do yourself good and not to grace
me. Believe then, if you please, that I can do
strange things. I have, since I was three year   65
old, convers'd with a magician, most profound in
his art and yet not damnable. If you do love Rosalind so near the heart as your gesture cries it out,
when your brother marries Aliena, shall you marry

---

60. **bastinado:** cudgelling. 62. **[policy]** Ff₂₋₄: cunning. *police* F₁.
Sc. ii, 8. [her] (Rowe). Om. Ff. 13. **estate:** settle. 33. **thrasonical:** boastful (like Thraso, the braggart in Terence's comedy, *Eunuchus*). 42. **incontinent...incontinent:** directly ... unchaste. 43. **wrath:** passion. 59. **conceit:** intelligence.
66. **convers'd:** associated. 67. **damnable.** See note on l. 77. 68. **gesture:** behavior.

her. I know into what straits of fortune she is   70
driven; and it is not impossible to me, if it appear
not inconvenient to you, to set her before your
eyes to-morrow, human as she is, and without any
danger.   75

Orl. Speakest thou in sober meanings?

Ros. By my life, I do; which I tender dearly,
though I say I am a magician. Therefore, put you
in your best array; bid your friends; for if you will
be married to-morrow, you shall; and to Rosalind,
if you will.   81

Enter SILVIUS AND PHEBE.

Look, here comes a lover of mine and a lover of
hers.

Phe. Youth, you have done me much ungentle-
    ness,
To show the letter that I writ to you.

Ros. I care not if I have. It is my study   85
To seem despiteful and ungentle to you.
You are there followed by a faithful shepherd;
Look upon him, love him. He worships you.

Phe. Good shepherd, tell this youth what 'tis to
    love.

Sil. It is to be all made of sighs and tears;   90
And so am I for Phebe.

Phe. And I for Ganymede.

Orl. And I for Rosalind.

Ros. And I for no woman.

Sil. It is to be all made of faith and service;   95
And so am I for Phebe.

Phe. And I for Ganymede.

Orl. And I for Rosalind.

Ros. And I for no woman.

Sil. It is to be all made of fantasy.   100
All made of passion, and all made of wishes;
All adoration, duty, and observance,
All humbleness, all patience, and impatience,
All purity, all trial, all [obedience];
And so am I for Phebe.   105

Phe. And so am I for Ganymede.

Orl. And so am I for Rosalind.

Ros. And so am I for no woman.

Phe. If this be so, why blame you me to love
you?   110

Sil. If this be so, why blame you me to love you?

Orl. If this be so, why blame you me to love you?

Ros. Why do you speak too, "Why blame you
me to love you?"   116

Orl. To her that is not here, nor doth not hear.

Ros. Pray you, no more of this; 'tis like the howling of Irish wolves against the moon. [*To Sil.*] I
will help you, if I can. [*To Phe.*] I would love   120
you, if I could. To-morrow meet me all together.

[*To Phe.*] I will marry you, if ever I marry woman,
and I'll be married to-morrow. [*To Orl.*] I will
satisfy you, if ever I satisfi'd man, and you shall be
married to-morrow. [*To Sil.*] I will content   125
you, if what pleases you contents you, and you
shall be married to-morrow. [*To Orl.*] As you love
Rosalind, meet. [*To Sil.*] As you love Phebe,
meet. And as I love no woman, I'll meet. So, fare
you well. I have left you commands.   131

Sil. I'll not fail, if I live.

Phe. Nor I.

Orl. Nor I.   [*Exeunt.*

SCENE III. [*The forest.*]

Enter Clown [TOUCHSTONE] *and* AUDREY.

Touch. To-morrow is the joyful day, Audrey;
to-morrow will we be married.

Aud. I do desire it with all my heart; and I hope
it is no dishonest desire to desire to be a woman
of the world. Here come two of the banish'd
Duke's pages.   6

Enter two PAGES.

1. Page. Well met, honest gentlemen.

Touch. By my troth, well met. Come, sit, sit,
and a song.

2. Page. We are for you. Sit i' th' middle.   10

1. Page. Shall we clap into't roundly, without
hawking or spitting or saying we are hoarse, which
are the only prologues to a bad voice?   14

2. Page. I' faith, i' faith; and both in a tune, like
two gypsies on a horse.

SONG.

It was a lover and his lass,
  With a hey, and a ho, and a hey nonino,
That o'er the green corn-field did pass
  In the spring time, the only pretty ring time,
When birds do sing, hey ding a ding, ding;   21
Sweet lovers love the spring.

Between the acres of the rye,
  With a hey, and a ho, and a hey nonino,
These pretty country folks would lie,   25
  In spring time, &c.

This carol they began that hour,
  With a hey, and a ho, and a hey nonino,
How that a life was but a flower
  In spring time, &c.   30

And therefore take the present time,
  With a hey, and a ho, and a hey nonino;

77–78. **By ... magician.** Black magic was punishable by death. 104. **[obedience]** (Malone conj.) *observance* Ff.
Sc. iii, 4. **dishonest:** immodest. 4–5. **woman of the world:** married woman. 14. **the only:** only the. 15. **a:** one. 31–34.
F prints this as stanza 2. A version in Morley's *First Booke of Ayres* (1600) places it at the end, where it clearly belongs.

For love is crowned with the prime
In spring time, &c.   34

Touch. Truly, young gentlemen, though there
was no great matter in the ditty, yet the note was
very untuneable.

1. Page. You are deceiv'd, sir. We kept time,
we lost not our time.   39

Touch. By my troth, yes; I count it but time lost
to hear such a foolish song. God buy you — and
God mend your voices! Come, Audrey.   [*Exeunt.*

SCENE IV.   [*The forest.*]

Enter DUKE *senior,* AMIENS, JAQUES, OR-
LANDO, OLIVER, *and* CELIA.

Duke S. Dost thou believe, Orlando, that the boy
Can do all this that he hath promised?

Orl. I sometimes do believe, and sometimes do
not;
As those that fear they hope, and know they fear.

Enter ROSALIND, SILVIUS, *and* PHEBE.

Ros. Patience once more, whiles our compact
is urg'd.   5
You say, if I bring in your Rosalind,
You will bestow her on Orlando here?

Duke S. That would I, had I kingdoms to give
with her.

Ros. And you say, you will have her, when I
bring her.

Orl. That would I, were I of all kingdoms king. 10

Ros. You say, you'll marry me, if I be willing?

Phe. That will I, should I die the hour after.

Ros. But if you do refuse to marry me,
You'll give yourself to this most faithful shepherd?

Phe. So is the bargain.   15

Ros. You say, that you'll have Phebe, if she will?

Sil. Though to have her and death were both one
thing.

Ros. I have promis'd to make all this matter even.
Keep you your word, O Duke, to give your daugh-
ter;   20
You, yours, Orlando, to receive his daughter;
Keep your word, Phebe, that you'll marry me,
Or else, refusing me, to wed this shepherd;
Keep your word, Silvius, that you'll marry her,
If she refuse me; and from hence I go,
To make these doubts all even.   25
                          [*Exeunt Rosalind and Celia.*

Duke S. I do remember in this shepherd boy
Some lively touches of my daughter's favour.

Orl. My lord, the first time that I ever saw him
Methought he was a brother to your daughter.
But, my good lord, this boy is forest-born,   30
And hath been tutor'd in the rudiments
Of many desperate studies by his uncle,
Whom he reports to be a great magician,
Obscured in the circle of this forest.   34

Enter Clown [TOUCHSTONE] *and* AUDREY.

Jaq. There is, sure, another flood toward, and
these couples are coming to the ark. Here comes a
pair of very strange beasts, which in all tongues are
called fools.

Touch. Salutation and greeting to you all!   39

Jaq. Good my lord, bid him welcome. This is
the motley-minded gentleman that I have so often
met in the forest. He hath been a courtier, he
swears.

Touch. If any man doubt that, let him put me
to my purgation. I have trod a measure; I have   45
flatt'red a lady; I have been politic with my friend,
smooth with mine enemy; I have undone three
tailors; I have had four quarrels, and like to have
fought one.

Jaq. And how was that ta'en up?   50

Touch. Faith, we met, and found the quarrel was
upon the seventh cause.

Jaq. How seventh cause? Good my lord, like
this fellow.

Duke S. I like him very well.   55

Touch. God 'ild you, sir; I desire you of the
like. I press in here, sir, amongst the rest of the
country copulatives, to swear and to forswear,
according as marriage binds and blood breaks. A
poor virgin, sir, an ill-favour'd thing, sir, but   60
mine own. A poor humour of mine, sir, to take
that that no man else will. Rich honesty dwells
like a miser, sir, in a poor house, as your pearl in
your foul oyster.

Duke S. By my faith, he is very swift and sententious.   66

Touch. According to the fool's bolt, sir, and such
dulcet diseases.

Jaq. But, for the seventh cause, — how did you
find the quarrel on the seventh cause?   70

Touch. Upon a lie seven times removed, — bear
your body more seeming, Audrey, — as thus, sir.
I did dislike the cut of a certain courtier's beard.
He sent me word, if I said his beard was not cut
well, he was in the mind it was: this is call'd the   75
Retort Courteous. If I sent him word again "it
was not well cut," he would send me word, he cut

---

33. **prime:** spring.   36. **note:** music.   37. **untuneable:** discordant.
Sc. iv, 4. **hope:** i.e., only hope.   19. **make . . . even:** clear up.   22. **your** (Rowe).
35. **toward:** coming.   45. **purgation:** proof.   **measure:** stately dance.   50. **ta'en up:** made up.   58. **copulatives:** people
entering marriage.   59. **blood:** passion.   67. **fool's bolt.**   Alluding to the proverb, "A fool's bolt is soon shot."   68. **dulcet**
diseases.   Intentional nonsense.   72. **seeming:** seemly.   73. **dislike:** criticize.

it to please himself: this is call'd the Quip Modest.
If again "it was not well cut," he disabled my
judgement: this is called the Reply Churlish. If   80
again "it was not well cut," he would answer,
I spake not true: this is called the Reproof Valiant.
If again "it was not well cut," he would say, I lie:
this is call'd the Countercheck Quarrelsome: and so
to Lie Circumstantial and the Lie Direct.   86

Jaq. And how oft did you say his beard was not
well cut?

Touch. I durst go no further than the Lie Circumstantial, nor he durst not give me the Lie   90
Direct; and so we measur'd swords and parted.

Jaq. Can you nominate in order now the degrees
of the lie?

Touch. O sir, we quarrel in print, by the book,
as you have books for good manners. I will   95
name you the degrees. The first, the Retort
Courteous; the second, the Quip Modest; the third,
the Reply Churlish; the fourth, the Reproof
Valiant; the fifth, the Countercheck Quarrelsome;
the sixth, the Lie with Circumstance; the   100
seventh, the Lie Direct. All these you may avoid
but the Lie Direct; and you may avoid that too,
with an If. I knew when seven justices could not
take up a quarrel, but when the parties were met
themselves, one of them thought but of an If,   105
as, "If you said so, then I said so"; and they shook
hands and swore brothers. Your If is the only
peace-maker; much virtue in If.

Jaq. Is not this a rare fellow, my lord? He's as
good at any thing, and yet a fool.   110

Duke S. He uses his folly like a stalking-horse
and under the presentation of that he shoots his wit.

Enter HYMEN, ROSALIND, *and* CELIA. [*Still Music.*

Hym. Then is there mirth in heaven,
    When earthly things made even   115
        Atone together.
Good Duke, receive thy daughter.
Hymen from heaven brought her,
    Yea, brought her hither,
That thou mightst join her hand with his   120
Whose heart within his bosom is.

Ros. [*To the Duke.*] To you I give myself, for I
am yours.
[*To Orl.*] To you I give myself, for I am yours.

Duke S. If there be truth in sight, you are my
daughter.

Orl. If there be truth in sight, you are my
Rosalind.   125

Phe. If sight and shape be true,
    Why then, my love adieu!

Ros. I'll have no father, if you be not he;
I'll have no husband, if you be not he;
Nor ne'er wed woman, if you be not she.   130

Hym. Peace, ho! I bar confusion.
    'Tis I must make conclusion
        Of these most strange events.
    Here's eight that must take hands
    To join in Hymen's bands,   135
        If truth holds true contents.
You and you no cross shall part;
You and you are heart in heart;
You to his love must accord,
Or have a woman to your lord;   140
You and you are sure together,
As the winter to foul weather.
Whiles a wedlock-hymn we sing,
Feed yourselves with questioning;
That reason wonder may diminish,   145
How thus we met, and these things finish.

SONG.

Wedding is great Juno's crown
    O blessed bond of board and bed!
'Tis Hymen peoples every town;
    High wedlock then be honoured.   150
Honour, high honour, and renown,
To Hymen, god of every town!

Duke S. O my dear niece, welcome thou art to me!
Even daughter, welcome in no less degree.

Phe. I will not eat my word, now thou art mine;
Thy faith my fancy to thee doth combine.   156

Enter Second Brother [JAQUES DE BOYS].

Jaq. de B. Let me have audience for a word or
two.
I am the second son of old Sir Roland,
That bring these tidings to this fair assembly.
Duke Frederick, hearing how that every day   160
Men of great worth resorted to this forest,
Address'd a mighty power, which were on foot,
In his own conduct, purposely to take
His brother here and put him to the sword;
And to the skirts of this wild wood he came,   165
Where meeting with an old religious man,
After some question with him, was converted
Both from his enterprise and from the world;
His crown bequeathing to his banish'd brother,
And all their lands restor'd to them again   170
That were with him exil'd. This to be true,
I do engage my life.

Duke S.   Welcome, young man;
Thou offer'st fairly to thy brothers' wedding:

---

78. **Quip:** jest.   94. **by the book.** Touchstone is satirizing the treatises on the etiquette of dueling and quarreling.
111. **stalking-horse:** a horse, real or artificial, underneath which a hunter moved closer to his game.   113. S.D. HYMEN:
god of marriage. *Still Music:* soft music.   116. **Atone together:** are reconciled.   156. **combine:** bind.   162. **Address'd:**
prepared.   **power:** armed force.   166. **religious man:** hermit.   173. **offer'st fairly:** contributest handsomely.

To one his lands withheld; and to the other
A land itself at large, a potent dukedom.   175
First, in this forest let us do those ends
That here were well begun and well begot;
And after, every of this happy number,
That have endur'd shrewd days and nights with us,
Shall share the good of our returned fortune,   180
According to the measure of their states.
Meantime, forget this new-fall'n dignity,
And fall into our rustic revelry.
Play, music! And you, brides and bridegrooms all,
With measure heap'd in joy, to th' measures
    fall.   185
   Jaq. Sir, by your patience. If I heard you
    rightly,
The Duke hath put on a religious life
And thrown into neglect the pompous court?
   Jaq. de B. He hath.
   Jaq. To him will I. Out of these convertites   190
There is much matter to be heard and learn'd.
[*To Duke S.*] You to your former honour I be-
    queath;
Your patience and your virtue well deserves it:
[*To Orl.*] You to a love, that your true faith doth
    merit:
[*To Oli.*] You to your land, and love, and great
    allies: 195
[*To Sil.*] You to a long and well-deserved bed:
[*To Touch.*] And you to wrangling; for thy loving
    voyage
Is but for two months victuall'd. So, to your
    pleasures;
I am for other than for dancing measures.

   Duke S. Stay, Jaques, stay.   200
   Jaq. To see no pastime I. What you would have
I'll stay to know at your abandon'd cave.   [*Exit.*
   Duke S. Proceed, proceed. We will begin these
    rites,
As we do trust they'll end, in true delights.
               [*A dance.*] *Exeunt.*

[EPILOGUE]

   Ros. It is not the fashion to see the lady the
epilogue, but it is no more unhandsome than to
see the lord the prologue. If it be true that good
wine needs no bush, 'tis true that a good play needs
no epilogue; yet to good wine they do use good   5
bushes, and good plays prove the better by the help
of good epilogues. What a case am I in then, that
am neither a good epilogue, nor cannot insinuate
with you in the behalf of a good play! I am not
furnish'd like a beggar, therefore to beg will not   10
become me. My way is to conjure you, and I'll
begin with the women. I charge you, O women,
for the love you bear to men, to like as much of
this play as please you; and I charge you, O men,
for the love you bear to women,—as I perceive   15
by your simpering, none of you hates them — that
between you and the women the play may please.
If I were a woman I would kiss as many of you as
had beards that pleas'd me, complexions that lik'd
me, and breaths that I defi'd not; and, I am   20
sure, as many as have good beards or good faces or
sweet breaths will, for my kind offer, when I make
curtsy, bid me farewell.   [*Exit.*

---

179. **shrewd:** harsh.   181. **states:** ranks.
    Epilogue: 4. **good ... bush.** A bunch of evergreens hung over the door was the common sign of vintners; hence this phrase means "good wine needs no advertising."   8. **insinuate:** ingratiate myself.   18. **If ... woman.** Rosalind's part was, of course, played by a boy in woman's dress.   19. **lik'd:** pleased.   20. **defi'd:** disliked.   23. **bid me farewell:** i.e., with applause.

The Tragedy of Julius Cæsar

IN THE ABSENCE of any Quarto, the text of *Julius Cæsar* must be based upon the First Folio (1623), which prints the play with gratifying accuracy, probably from the theatre manuscript. Several pieces of evidence point convincingly to 1599 as the date of composition. The first of these is negative, the omission of the tragedy in Meres's list of Shakespeare's plays in his *Palladis Tamia* (1598), where we should confidently expect its inclusion if it had been on the stage before the fall of that year. On September 21, 1599, Thomas Platter, a German Swiss traveling in England, saw a "Tragedy vom ersten Keyser Julio Caesare," which is generally presumed to have been Shakespeare's. There is an unequivocal allusion to the speeches of Brutus and Antony to the citizens (III.ii.) in *The Mirror of Martyrs* by John Weever which, though published in 1601, was "made fit for the print," the author declares, some two years earlier. In Jonson's *Every Man Out of his Humour* (acted 1599), Clove, a talker of fustian, is made to say (III.iv.33), "reason long since is fled to animals, you know," perhaps echoing Antony's words, "O judgement! thou art fled to brutish beasts" (III.ii.109).

The relative brevity of the present play, and the number of short lines, have led some critics to surmise that the received text is an abridgment, although the soundness and cohesion of its parts point as plausibly to intentional economy. There is, however, a suggestion of incidental revision. Brutus, who himself tells Cassius about the death of Portia, behaves as if he knew nothing of it when, only a few minutes later, Messala brings news (IV.iii.147–57, 181–95). In all probability the first of these passages was entered in the manuscript as substitute for the second, and a mark cancelling the latter was overlooked by the printer.

The history of Julius Cæsar had been treated on the Elizabethan stage before Shakespeare wrote his tragedy, but there is no indication that he used anything by way of source beyond Plutarch's *Lives* — of Cæsar, Brutus, and Antonius — which he read in the translation by Sir Thomas North (1579, 1595).

Shakespeare follows his source so faithfully that in many passages he is merely turning North's prose into blank verse, with a characteristic heightening of imagination and language. With the exception of Lucius, every character comes from Plutarch, who supplies also several of their individualizing traits, such as the leanness of Cassius, the studiousness of Brutus, and Cæsar's "falling sickness." So, too, with the main events and a multitude of particulars. Yet within these confines of indebtedness Shakespeare is still admirably free, selecting, suppressing, and rearranging details for dramatic effect. Thus he juggles chronology, compressing into the compass of five days (though they are not consecutive) action which in fact covered three years, from the triumph of Cæsar in October, 45 B.C. to the battle at Philippi in October, 42 B.C. The murder of Cæsar, actually committed in the Senate House, Shakespeare transfers to the Capitol. Antony's compact with the conspirators and his demagogic speech, which in the play follow directly upon the murder, came two days later, according to Plutarch, in whose account (*The Life of Brutus*) the reading of the will precedes the speech. Finally, there were in actuality two battles at Philippi, about three weeks apart; the death of Cassius following the first, and the suicide of Brutus, the second. These two engagements Shakespeare unites. Shakespeare also added to what his source provided. The characters of Casca and Lepidus are only hinted at in Plutarch; Cassius's description of the swimming match and of Cæsar's fever, the soliloquy of Brutus rationalizing the need for killing Cæsar, the parley of the conspirators in his orchard, the incident of the assassins' bathing their arms in Cæsar's blood, and the speech of Antony over Cæsar's dead body are wholly Shakespeare's; while the orations of Brutus and Antony at Cæsar's funeral, and the quarrel of Brutus and Cassius, are elaborated from slight suggestions.

It has frequently been asserted that the play is misnamed and is weak in structure because the titular hero is taken off in the middle of the action.

This notion has even inspired the thesis that Shake-speare amalgamated two lost plays dealing respec-tively with the death and the avenging of Cæsar. That Shakespeare's title is a misnomer may be, theoretically, true, for the central figure in the action, the individual in whose mind there is conflict and upon whom our interest is mainly fixed, is Marcus Brutus. But the name of republican Brutus neither has today, nor had in Shakespeare's day, the éclat of imperial Cæsar's; and Shakespeare not un-naturally gave to this play the sovereign title, just as he had named his Histories after the Kings in whose reigns the chief events took place, regardless of the dramatic prominence of their rôles. The charge of disunity, however, is insubstantial, for if Brutus is the tragic protagonist, Cæsar and what he stands for constitute his problem. It is Cæsar's ambition that he fears. He tells the conspirators that they "all stand up against the spirit of Cæsar," and wishes that they could "come by Cæsar's spirit" without killing him (II.i.167–70). That being impossible, they do kill him, but "Cæsar's spirit ranging for revenge," as Antony prophesies (III.i.270), pursues Brutus as his Nemesis. Appear-ing to him at Sardis, the ghost of Cæsar proclaims itself his evil spirit (IV.iii.282). And Brutus ac-knowledges its victory before he dies (V.iii.94–96; V.v.50–51). Thus the spirit of Cæsar, dominant and avenged at the close, gives dramatic warrant for the title of Shakespeare's tragedy.

The character of Cæsar is deliberately foreshort-ened in the play for dramatic purposes. Since Cæsar is to be assassinated, Shakespeare must stress those qualities in him which can justify the deed in the eyes of those who commit it and who must, tempo-rarily, have the sympathy of the audience. Conse-quently, Cæsar is presented without reference to the genuine springs of his greatness, emphasis being placed upon his arrogance and megalomania. This autocrat is a potential tyrant; he would be the Great Dictator. So, at least, it seems to Brutus and his friends. Such pride must have its fall, and Cæsar's murder accords with the ancient belief that those who affect godhead will be destroyed.

The danger embodied in Cæsar is most emphati-cally and resentfully expressed by Cassius, who is the dynamic personality among the rebels. His patri-otism cannot be impugned, but it is not disinter-ested. He is mindful that Cæsar bears him hard, and his dislike of Cæsar is tainted with envy. His speech has occasionally a mordant, derisive tone, remotely suggestive of Iago's or Edmund's. Cæsar estimates him shrewdly, noting his supercilious mien, his humorless solemnity, his sharp intelligence.

For Cassius is a realist, tutored by reading and keen observation, "and he looks quite through the deeds of men" (I.ii.190 ff.). He perceives the need for winning Brutus to the cause, and the means by which he may be won. Yet he is mildly scornful of Brutus for being won. The situation, however, is to have its irony, for at crucial moments later on, Cassius yields his sounder judgment to the ill-calcu-lated wishes of his friend. He sees the peril in allow-ing Antony to give the funeral oration, and he pro-tests the error of marching to Philippi instead of waiting for the enemy at Sardis. The deference of Cassius to the nobility he feels in Brutus bespeaks a strain of gentleness in him, but it insures the final catastrophe.

The figure of Brutus, the tragically conscientious patriot, Shakespeare draws with sympathy. His integrity and gentility, to which Antony himself bears witness in an elegiac tribute at the close (V.v.68–75), are recognized by everybody and are expressed in all he says and does. To emphasize his goodness more fully, Shakespeare lets us see him in his private as well as his public relationships, giving us the touching pictures of his wife's solicitude and his expression of affection for her (II.i.233–303), and creating young Lucius to reveal his kindliness to-ward those who serve him. Studious by nature, and an adherent of the Stoic philosophy (IV.iii. 144–47), Brutus is not passion's slave, nor is he lightly to be moved in serious matters. He is above petty considerations and self-interest, but he is not without a dangerous kind of pride. Cassius plays upon this weakness deftly when he praises Brutus and reminds him of his illustrious ancestry (I.ii. 54–161). And when Brutus has cast the die and joined the conspiracy, this pride makes him per-versely self-confident. As has been noted, some of his judgments are fatal, yet he never admits to him-self the error of his ways. He dies in the high Roman fashion, "the noblest Roman of them all," but a little too aware of superior virtue.

Julius Cæsar is distinguished by a simplicity of outline and of language befitting its classical theme. There are no secondary elements in its rather austere design. The abundant eloquence is disciplined. The great speeches, memorable passages of poised and skillful rhetoric, invite declamation almost too readily. The art which here disguises art likewise restricts effects; the play rather thrills us mechani-cally than moves us deeply. Nevertheless, it looks forward directly to Hamlet, and Brutus the Roman, reflective, scrupulous, idealistic, is related to the Dane. But he never touches us so nearly.

THE TRAGEDY OF
JULIUS CÆSAR

JULIUS CÆSAR.

OCTAVIUS CÆSAR,
MARCUS ANTONIUS, } *triumvirs after the death of Julius Cæsar.*
M. ÆMILIUS LEPIDUS,

CICERO,
PUBLIUS, } *senators.*
POPILIUS LENA,

MARCUS BRUTUS,
CASSIUS,
CASCA,
TREBONIUS, } *conspirators against Julius Cæsar.*
CAIUS LIGARIUS,
DECIUS BRUTUS,
METELLUS CIMBER,
CINNA,

FLAVIUS and MARULLUS, *tribunes.*
ARTEMIDORUS of Cnidos, *a teacher of Rhetoric.*
A Soothsayer.

CINNA, *a poet.*
Another Poet.

LUCILIUS,
TITINIUS,
MESSALA, } *friends to Brutus and Cassius.*
Young CATO,
VOLUMNIUS,

VARRO,
CLITUS,
CLAUDIUS, } *servants to Brutus.*
STRATO,
LUCIUS,
DARDANIUS,

PINDARUS, *servant to Cassius.*

CALPURNIA, *wife to Cæsar.*
PORTIA, *wife to Brutus.*

Senators, Citizens, Guards, Attendants, etc.

SCENE: *Rome; the neighbourhood of Sardis; the neighbourhood of Philippi.*]

ACT I

SCENE I. [*Rome. A street.*]

Enter FLAVIUS, MARULLUS, *and certain* COMMONERS *over the stage.*

Flav. Hence! home, you idle creatures, get you home!
Is this a holiday? What! know you not,
Being mechanical, you ought not walk
Upon a labouring day without the sign
Of your profession? Speak, what trade art thou? 5
Car. Why, sir, a carpenter.
Mar. Where is thy leather apron and thy rule?
What dost thou with thy best apparel on?
You, sir, what trade are you?

Cob. Truly, sir, in respect of a fine workman, I am
but, as you would say, a cobbler. 11
Mar. But what trade art thou? Answer me
directly.
Cob. A trade, sir, that I hope I may use with a
safe conscience; which is, indeed, sir, a mender of
bad soles. 15
[*Mar.*] What trade, thou knave? thou naughty
knave, what trade?
Cob. Nay, I beseech you, sir, be not out with me;
yet, if you be out, sir, I can mend you.
Mar. What mean'st thou by that? Mend me,
thou saucy fellow! 21
Cob. Why, sir, cobble you.
Flav. Thou art a cobbler, art thou?
Cob. Truly, sir, all that I live by is with the awl.

Act I, sc. i, 3. **mechanical**: laborers. 10. **in respect of**: compared with. 11. **cobbler**: (1) mender of shoes, (2) botcher. 16. [*Mar.*] (Capell). *Flav.* F. **naughty**: worthless. 18. **out**: angry. 19. **you be out**: i.e., your shoes have holes.

I meddle with no tradesman's matters, nor 25
women's matters, but with all.   I am, indeed, sir,
a surgeon to old shoes; when they are in great
danger, I re-cover them.   As proper men as ever
trod upon neat's leather have gone upon my handiwork.   30
    Flav. But wherefore art not in thy shop to-day?
Why dost thou lead these men about the streets?
    Cob. Truly, sir, to wear out their shoes, to
get myself into more work.   But, indeed, sir, we
make holiday, to see Cæsar and to rejoice in his
triumph.   36
    Mar. Wherefore rejoice?   What conquest brings
        he home?
What tributaries follow him to Rome
To grace in captive bonds his chariot-wheels?
You blocks, you stones, you worse than senseless
        things!   40
O you hard hearts, you cruel men of Rome,
Knew you not Pompey?   Many a time and oft
Have you climb'd up to walls and battlements,
To tow'rs and windows, yea, to chimney-tops,
Your infants in your arms, and there have sat   45
The live-long day, with patient expectation,
To see great Pompey pass the streets of Rome;
And when you saw his chariot but appear
Have you not made an universal shout,
That Tiber trembled underneath her banks   50
To hear the replication of your sounds
Made in her concave shores?
And do you now put on your best attire?
And do you now cull out a holiday?
And do you now strew flowers in his way   55
That comes in triumph over Pompey's blood?
Be gone!
Run to your houses, fall upon your knees,
Pray to the gods to intermit the plague
That needs must light on this ingratitude.   60
    Flav. Go, go, good countrymen, and, for this
        fault,
Assemble all the poor men of your sort;
Draw them to Tiber banks, and weep your tears
Into the channel, till the lowest stream
Do kiss the most exalted shores of all.   65
                    [*Exeunt all the Commoners.*
See, whe'er their basest metal be not mov'd;
They vanish tongue-tied in their guiltiness.
Go, you down that way towards the Capitol;
This way will I.   Disrobe the images
If you do find them deck'd with ceremonies.   70
    Mar. May we do so?
You know it is the feast of Lupercal.

    Flav. It is no matter; let no images
Be hung with Cæsar's trophies.   I'll about
And drive away the vulgar from the streets;   75
So do you too, where you perceive them thick.
These growing feathers pluck'd from Cæsar's wing
Will make him fly an ordinary pitch,
Who else would soar above the view of men
And keep us all in servile fearfulness. [*Exeunt.* 80

[SCENE II.   *A public place.*]

Enter CÆSAR; ANTONY, *for the course;* CALPURNIA,
    Portia, Decius, Cicero, BRUTUS, CASSIUS, *and*
    CASCA; [*a great crowd following, among them*] *a*
    SOOTHSAYER: *after them* Marullus *and* Flavius.

    Cæs. Calpurnia!
    Casca.   Peace, ho! Cæsar speaks.
    Cæs.   Calpurnia!
    Cal. Here, my lord.
    Cæs. Stand you directly in Antonius' way
When he doth run his course.   Antonius!
    Ant. Cæsar, my lord?   5
    Cæs. Forget not, in your speed, Antonius,
To touch Calpurnia; for our elders say,
The barren, touched in this holy chase,
Shake off their sterile curse.
    Ant.   I shall remember:
When Cæsar says, "Do this," it is perform'd.   10
    Cæs. Set on; and leave no ceremony out.
                                        [*Flourish.*
    Sooth. Cæsar!
    Cæs. Ha! who calls?
    Casca. Bid every noise be still; peace yet again!
    Cæs. Who is it in the press that calls on me?   15
I hear a tongue, shriller than all the music,
Cry "Cæsar!"   Speak; Cæsar is turn'd to hear.
    Sooth. Beware the ides of March.
    Cæs.   What man is that?
    Bru. A soothsayer bids you beware the ides of
        March.
    Cæs. Set him before me; let me see his face.   20
    Cas. Fellow, come from the throng; look upon
        Cæsar.
    Cæs. What say'st thou to me now?   Speak once
        again.
    Sooth. Beware the ides of March.
    Cæs. He is a dreamer; let us leave him.   Pass.
                [*Sennet.   Exeunt all but Brutus and Cassius.*
    Cas. Will you go see the order of the course? 25
    Bru. Not I.
    Cas. I pray you, do.
    Bru. I am not gamesome; I do lack some part

---

28. **proper:** handsome.   29. **neat's leather:** cowhide.   36. **triumph:** triumphal procession.   56. **blood:** offspring.   Cæsar
had just defeated Pompey's sons.   59. **intermit:** withhold.   65. **most...all:** highest flood level.   66. **whe'er:** whether.
where F.   70. **ceremonies:** festal ornaments.   72. **feast of Lupercal:** the Lupercalia, a festival honoring Lupercus, god of
farmers.   75. **vulgar:** populace.
    Sc. ii, S.D. *for the course:* ready for the race.   See ll. 7–9.   18. **ides of March:** March 15th.

Of that quick spirit that is in Antony.
Let me not hinder, Cassius, your desires;   30
I'll leave you.
    Cas. Brutus, I do observe you now of late;
I have not from your eyes that gentleness
And show of love as I was wont to have.
You bear too stubborn and too strange a hand   35
Over your friend that loves you.
    Bru.   Cassius,
Be not deceiv'd. If I have veil'd my look,
I turn the trouble of my countenance
Merely upon myself. Vexed I am
Of late with passions of some difference,   40
Conceptions only proper to myself,
Which give some soil perhaps to my behaviours;
But let not therefore my good friends be griev'd —
Among which number, Cassius, be you one —
Nor construe any further my neglect,   45
Than that poor Brutus, with himself at war,
Forgets the shows of love to other men.
    Cas. Then, Brutus, I have much mistook your
      passion;
By means whereof this breast of mine hath buried
Thoughts of great value, worthy cogitations.   50
Tell me, good Brutus, can you see your face?
    Bru. No, Cassius; for the eye sees not itself
But by reflection, by some other things
    Cas. 'Tis just;
And it is very much lamented, Brutus,   55
That you have no such mirrors as will turn
Your hidden worthiness into your eye
That you might see your shadow. I have heard
Where many of the best respect in Rome,
Except immortal Cæsar, speaking of Brutus   60
And groaning underneath this age's yoke,
Have wish'd that noble Brutus had his eyes.
    Bru. Into what dangers would you lead me,
      Cassius,
That you would have me seek into myself
For that which is not in me?   65
    Cas. Therefore, good Brutus, be prepar'd to
      hear;
And since you know you cannot see yourself
So well as by reflection, I, your glass,
Will modestly discover to yourself
That of yourself which you yet know not of.   70
And be not jealous on me, gentle Brutus.
Were I a common laugher, or did use
To stale with ordinary oaths my love
To every new protester; if you know
That I do fawn on men and hug them hard   75
And after scandal them, or if you know

That I profess myself in banqueting
To all the rout, then hold me dangerous.
                    [Flourish and shout.
    Bru. What means this shouting? I do fear, the
      people
Choose Cæsar for their king.
    Cas.   Ay, do you fear it? 80
Then must I think you would not have it so.
    Bru. I would not, Cassius; yet I love him well.
But wherefore do you hold me here so long?
What is it that you would impart to me?
If it be aught toward the general good,   85
Set honour in one eye and death i' th' other,
And I will look on both indifferently;
For let the gods so speed me as I love
The name of honour more than I fear death.
    Cas. I know that virtue to be in you, Brutus,   90
As well as I do know your outward favour.
Well, honour is the subject of my story.
I cannot tell what you and other men
Think of this life; but, for my single self,
I had as lief not be as live to be   95
In awe of such a thing as I myself.
I was born free as Cæsar, so were you;
We both have fed as well, and we can both
Endure the winter's cold as well as he;
For once, upon a raw and gusty day,   100
The troubled Tiber chafing with her shores,
Cæsar said to me, "Dar'st thou, Cassius, now
Leap in with me into this angry flood,
And swim to yonder point?" Upon the word,
Accoutred as I was, I plunged in   105
And bade him follow; so indeed he did.
The torrent roar'd, and we did buffet it
With lusty sinews, throwing it aside
And stemming it with hearts of controversy;
But ere we could arrive the point propos'd,   110
Cæsar cried, "Help me, Cassius, or I sink!"
I, as Æneas, our great ancestor,
Did from the flames of Troy upon his shoulder
The old Anchises bear, so from the waves of Tiber
Did I the tired Cæsar. And this man   115
Is now become a god, and Cassius is
A wretched creature, and must bend his body
If Cæsar carelessly but nod on him.
He had a fever when he was in Spain,
And when the fit was on him, I did mark   120
How he did shake — 'tis true, this god did shake.
His coward lips did from their colour fly,
And that same eye whose bend doth awe the world
Did lose his lustre; I did hear him groan.
Ay, and that tongue of his that bade the Romans

---

35. **stubborn:** rough.   38–39. **turn...myself:** keep the cause of my sad expression entirely to myself.   40. **of...differ-ence:** conflicting.   42. **soil:** stain.   54. **just:** true.   58. **shadow:** image.   59. **respect:** repute.   69. **modestly:** without ex-aggeration.   74. **protester:** person professing friendship.   77. **profess myself:** profess friendship.   78. **rout:** crowd. 87. **indifferently:** impartially.   91. **favour:** appearance.   109. **of controversy:** excited by rivalry.   122. **His...fly.** The inversion makes clearer the pun on *colour* as (1) hue, (2) flag.   123. **bend:** glance.

Mark him and write his speeches in their books, 126
Alas, it cried, "Give me some drink, Titinius,"
As a sick girl. Ye gods, it doth amaze me
A man of such a feeble temper should
So get the start of the majestic world 130
And bear the palm alone.   [Shout. Flourish.
    Bru. Another general shout!
I do believe that these applauses are
For some new honours that are heap'd on Cæsar.
    Cas. Why, man, he doth bestride the narrow world
Like a Colossus, and we petty men 136
Walk under his huge legs, and peep about
To find ourselves dishonourable graves.
Men at some time are masters of their fates;
The fault, dear Brutus, is not in our stars, 140
But in ourselves, that we are underlings.
Brutus and Cæsar: what should be in that "Cæsar"?
Why should that name be sounded more than yours?
Write them together, yours is as fair a name;
Sound them, it doth become the mouth as well; 145
Weigh them, it is as heavy; conjure with 'em,
"Brutus" will start a spirit as soon as "Cæsar."
Now, in the names of all the gods at once,
Upon what meat doth this our Cæsar feed
That he is grown so great? Age, thou art sham'd! 150
Rome, thou hast lost the breed of noble bloods! 151
When went there by an age since the great flood
But it was fam'd with more than with one man?
When could they say, till now, that talk'd of Rome,
That her wide [walls] encompass'd but one man? 155
Now is it Rome indeed and room enough,
When there is in it but one only man.
O, you and I have heard our fathers say
There was a Brutus once that would have brook'd
Th' eternal devil to keep his state in Rome 160
As easily as a king.
    Bru. That you do love me, I am nothing jealous;
What you would work me to, I have some aim.
How I have thought of this and of these times,
I shall recount hereafter; for this present, 165
I would not, so with love I might entreat you,
Be any further mov'd. What you have said
I will consider; what you have to say
I will with patience hear, and find a time
Both meet to hear and answer such high things. 170
Till then, my noble friend, chew upon this:
Brutus had rather be a villager
Than to repute himself a son of Rome
Under these hard conditions as this time
Is like to lay upon us. 175
    Cas. I am glad that my weak words
Have struck but thus much show of fire from
    Brutus.

Re-enter CÆSAR *and his train.*

    Bru. The games are done and Cæsar is returning.
    Cas. As they pass by, pluck Casca by the sleeve;
And he will, after his sour fashion, tell you 180
What hath proceeded worthy note to-day.
    Bru. I will do so. But, look you, Cassius,
The angry spot doth glow on Cæsar's brow,
And all the rest look like a chidden train.
Calpurnia's cheek is pale; and Cicero 185
Looks with such ferret and such fiery eyes
As we have seen him in the Capitol,
Being cross'd in conference by some senators.
    Cas. Casca will tell us what the matter is.
    Cæs. Antonius! 190
    Ant. Cæsar?
    Cæs. Let me have men about me that are fat,
Sleek-headed men and such as sleep o' nights.
Yond Cassius has a lean and hungry look,
He thinks too much; such men are dangerous. 195
    Ant. Fear him not, Cæsar; he's not dangerous;
He is a noble Roman and well given.
    Cæs. Would he were fatter! but I fear him not.
Yet if my name were liable to fear,
I do not know the man I should avoid 200
So soon as that spare Cassius. He reads much,
He is a great observer, and he looks
Quite through the deeds of men. He loves no plays
As thou dost, Antony; he hears no music;
Seldom he smiles, and smiles in such a sort 205
As if he mock'd himself and scorn'd his spirit
That could be mov'd to smile at anything.
Such men as he be never at heart's ease
Whiles they behold a greater than themselves,
And therefore are they very dangerous. 210
I rather tell thee what is to be fear'd
Than what I fear; for always I am Cæsar.
Come on my right hand, for this ear is deaf,
And tell me truly what thou think'st of him.
    [Sennet. Exeunt Cæsar and all his train
        [but Casca].
    Casca. You pull'd me by the cloak; would you
speak with me? 215
    Bru. Ay, Casca; tell us what hath chanc'd to-day
That Cæsar looks so sad.
    Casca. Why, you were with him, were you not?
    Bru. I should not then ask Casca what had
        chanc'd. 219
    Casca. Why, there was a crown offer'd him; and
being offer'd him, he put it by with the back of his
hand, thus; and then the people fell a-shouting.
    Bru. What was the second noise for?
    Casca. Why, for that too. 225

147. **start:** raise. 152. **flood:** the classical flood, of which Deucalion was the Noah. 155. **[walls]** (Rowe). *walkes* F.
156. **Rome…room.** The words were pronounced alike. (Cf. III.i.288–89.) 159. **a Brutus once.** Lucius Junius Brutus,
who drove out the Tarquins. **brook'd:** tolerated. 162. **nothing jealous:** by no means doubtful. 163. **aim:** guess.
186. **ferret:** red, angry (like a ferret's). 197. **given:** disposed. 199. **my name:** i.e., I myself. 217. **sad:** serious.

Cas. They shouted thrice; what was the last cry
  for?

Casca. Why, for that too.

Bru. Was the crown offer'd him thrice?

Casca. Ay, marry, was't, and he put it by thrice,
every time gentler than other; and at every putting-
by mine honest neighbours shouted. 231

Cas. Who offer'd him the crown?

Casca. Why, Antony.

Bru. Tell us the manner of it, gentle Casca. ' 234

Casca. I can as well be hang'd as tell the manner
of it. It was mere foolery; I did not mark it. I
saw Mark Antony offer him a crown — yet 'twas
not a crown neither, 'twas one of these coronets —
and, as I told you, he put it by once; but, for all
that, to my thinking, he would fain have had it. 240
Then he offered it to him again; then he put it by
again, but, to my thinking, he was very loath to
lay his fingers off it. And then he offered it the
third time; he put it the third time by; and still
as he refus'd it, the rabblement hooted and 245
clapp'd their chapp'd hands and threw up their
sweaty night-caps and uttered such a deal of stinking breath because Cæsar refus'd the crown, that
it had almost choked Cæsar, for he swounded and
fell down at it; and for mine own part, I durst not
laugh, for fear of opening my lips and receiving the
bad air. 252

Cas. But, soft, I pray you; what, did Cæsar
  swound?

Casca. He fell down in the market-place, and
foam'd at mouth, and was speechless.

Bru. 'Tis very like; he hath the falling sickness.

Cas. No, Cæsar hath it not; but you and I
And honest Casca, we have the falling sickness. 258

Casca. I know not what you mean by that, but I
am sure Cæsar fell down. If the tag-rag people did
not clap him and hiss him, according as he pleas'd
and displeas'd them, as they use to do the players in
the theatre, I am no true man.

Bru. What said he when he came unto himself? 264

Casca. Marry, before he fell down, when he
perceiv'd the common herd was glad he refus'd
the crown, he pluck'd me ope his doublet and
offer'd them his throat to cut. An I had been a
man of any occupation, if I would not have taken
him at a word, I would I might go to hell among 270
the rogues. And so he fell. When he came to
himself again, he said, if he had done or said anything amiss, he desir'd their worships to think it
was his infirmity. Three or four wenches, where I
stood, cried, "Alas, good soul!" and forgave him
with all their hearts. But there's no heed to be 276

taken of them; if Cæsar had stabb'd their mothers,
they would have done no less.

Bru. And after that, he came, thus sad, away?

Casca. Ay. 280

Cas. Did Cicero say anything?

Casca. Ay, he spoke Greek.

Cas. To what effect? 283

Casca. Nay, an I tell you that, I'll ne'er look you
i' th' face again; but those that understood him
smil'd at one another and shook their heads; but,
for mine own part, it was Greek to me. I could tell
you more news too. Marullus and Flavius, for
pulling scarfs off Cæsar's images, are put to silence.
Fare you well. There was more foolery yet, if I
could remember it. 291

Cas. Will you sup with me to-night, Casca?

Casca. No, I am promis'd forth.

Cas. Will you dine with me to-morrow?

Casca. Ay, if I be alive and your mind hold and
your dinner worth the eating. 296

Cas. Good; I will expect you.

Casca. Do so. Farewell, both.

[*Exit.*

Bru. What a blunt fellow is this grown to be!
He was quick mettle when he went to school. 300

Cas. So is he now in execution
Of any bold or noble enterprise,
However he puts on this tardy form.
This rudeness is a sauce to his good wit,
Which gives men stomach to digest his words 305
With better appetite.

Bru. And so it is. For this time I will leave
  you;
To-morrow, if you please to speak with me,
I will come home to you; or, if you will,
Come home to me, and I will wait for you. 310

Cas. I will do so; till then, think of the world.

[*Exit Brutus.*

Well, Brutus, thou art noble; yet, I see,
Thy honourable metal may be wrought
From that it is dispos'd; therefore it is meet
That noble minds keep ever with their likes; 315
For who so firm that cannot be seduc'd?
Cæsar doth bear me hard, but he loves Brutus.
If I were Brutus now and he were Cassius,
He should not humour me. I will this night,
In several hands, in at his windows throw, 320
As if they came from several citizens,
Writings all tending to the great opinion
That Rome holds of his name; wherein obscurely
Cæsar's ambition shall be glanced at;
And after this let Cæsar seat him sure, 325
For we will shake him, or worse days endure.

[*Exit.*

256. **falling sickness:** epilepsy. 269. **man ... occupation:** working man. 270. **at a word:** at his word. 289. **scarfs:** streamers, wreaths. 300. **quick mettle:** lively and gifted. 303. **tardy form:** sluggish manner. 314. **that ... dispos'd:** its natural temper. 317. **hard:** i.e., ill-will. 320. **hands:** handwritings.

[SCENE III. *The same. A street.*]

Thunder and lightning. Enter [from opposite sides]
CASCA [*with his sword drawn*] *and* CICERO.

Cic. Good even, Casca; brought you Cæsar home?
Why are you breathless, and why stare you so?
  Casca. Are not you mov'd, when all the sway of
    earth
Shakes like a thing unfirm? O Cicero,
I have seen tempests when the scolding winds   5
Have riv'd the knotty oaks, and I have seen
Th' ambitious ocean swell and rage and foam
To be exalted with the threat'ning clouds;
But never till to-night, never till now,
Did I go through a tempest dropping fire.   10
Either there is a civil strife in heaven,
Or else the world, too saucy with the gods,
Incenses them to send destruction.
  Cic. Why, saw you anything more wonderful?
  Casca. A common slave — you know him well
    by sight —   15
Held up his left hand, which did flame and burn
Like twenty torches join'd, and yet his hand,
Not sensible of fire, remain'd unscorch'd.
Besides — I ha' not since put up my sword —
Against the Capitol I met a lion,   20
Who glaz'd upon me, and went surly by
Without annoying me; and there were drawn
Upon a heap a hundred ghastly women,
Transformed with their fear, who swore they saw
Men all in fire walk up and down the streets.   25
And yesterday the bird of night did sit
Even at noon-day upon the market-place,
Hooting and shrieking. When these prodigies
Do so conjointly meet, let not men say,
"These are their reasons; they are natural";   30
For, I believe, they are portentous things
Unto the climate that they point upon.
  Cic. Indeed, it is a strange-disposed time;
But men may construe things after their fashion
Clean from the purpose of the things themselves.   35
Comes Cæsar to the Capitol to-morrow?
  Casca. He doth; for he did bid Antonius
Send word to you he would be there to-morrow.
  Cic. Good-night then, Casca; this disturbed sky
Is not to walk in.
  Casca.   Farewell, Cicero.   40
                                        [*Exit Cicero.*

Enter CASSIUS.

  Cas. Who's there?
  Casca.   A Roman.
  Cas.   Casca, by your voice.

Casca. Your ear is good. Cassius, what night is
    this!
  Cas. A very pleasing night to honest men.
  Casca. Who ever knew the heavens menace so?
  Cas. Those that have known the earth so full of
    faults.   45
For my part, I have walk'd about the streets,
Submitting me unto the perilous night,
And, thus unbraced, Casca, as you see,
Have bar'd my bosom to the thunder-stone;
And when the cross blue lightning seem'd to open
The breast of heaven, I did present myself   51
Even in the aim and very flash of it.
  Casca. But wherefore did you so much tempt the
    heavens?
It is the part of men to fear and tremble
When the most mighty gods by tokens send   55
Such dreadful heralds to astonish us.
  Cas. You are dull, Casca, and those sparks of life
That should be in a Roman you do want,
Or else you use not. You look pale and gaze
And put on fear and cast yourself in wonder   60
To see the strange impatience of the heavens;
But if you would consider the true cause
Why all these fires, why all these gliding ghosts,
Why birds and beasts from quality and kind,
Why old men, fools, and children calculate,   65
Why all these things change from their ordinance
Their natures and preformed faculties
To monstrous quality, why, you shall find
That Heaven hath infus'd them with these spirits,
To make them instruments of fear and warning   70
Unto some monstrous state.
Now could I, Casca, name to thee a man
Most like this dreadful night,
That thunders, lightens, opens graves, and roars
As doth the lion in the Capitol, —   75
A man no mightier than thyself or me
In personal action, yet prodigious grown
And fearful, as these strange eruptions are.
  Casca. 'Tis Cæsar that you mean; is it not, Cas-
    sius?
  Cas. Let it be who it is; for Romans now   80
Have thews and limbs like to their ancestors,
But, woe the while! our fathers' minds are dead,
And we are govern'd with our mothers' spirits;
Our yoke and sufferance show us womanish.
  Casca. Indeed, they say the senators to-morrow
Mean to establish Cæsar as a king;   86
And he shall wear his crown by sea and land,
In every place, save here in Italy.
  Cas. I know where I will wear this dagger then;
Cassius from bondage will deliver Cassius.   90

Sc. iii, 21. **glaz'd:** stared. 22. **annoying:** harming. 26. **bird of night:** owl. 32. **climate:** region. 48. **unbraced:** with doublet unfastened. 50. **cross:** zigzag. 64. **from … kind:** act contrary to their true nature. 65. **calculate:** forecast, prophesy. 66. **ordinance:** established order. 67. **preformed:** original. 81. **thews:** sinews. 82. **woe the while:** woe to the age. 84. **sufferance:** submission.

Therein, ye gods, you make the weak most strong;
Therein, ye gods, you tyrants do defeat;
Nor stony tower, nor walls of beaten brass,
Nor airless dungeon, nor strong links of iron,
Can be retentive to the strength of spirit;   95
But life, being weary of these worldly bars,
Never lacks power to dismiss itself.
If I know this, know all the world besides,
That part of tyranny that I do bear
I can shake off at pleasure.   [*Thunder still.*
    Casca.   So can I;   100
So every bondman in his own hand bears
The power to cancel his captivity.
    Cas. And why should Cæsar be a tyrant then?
Poor man! I know he would not be a wolf,
But that he sees the Romans are but sheep;   105
He were no lion, were not Romans hinds.
Those that with haste will make a mighty fire
Begin it with weak straws: what trash is Rome,
What rubbish and what offal, when it serves
For the base matter to illuminate   110
So vile a thing as Cæsar! But, O grief,
Where hast thou led me? I perhaps speak this
Before a willing bondman; then I know
My answer must be made. But I am arm'd,
And dangers are to me indifferent.   115
    Casca. You speak to Casca, and to such a man
That is no fleering tell-tale. Hold, — my hand.
Be factious for redress of all these griefs,
And I will set this foot of mine as far
As who goes farthest.
    Cas.   There's a bargain made.   120
Now know you, Casca, I have mov'd already
Some certain of the noblest-minded Romans
To undergo with me an enterprise
Of honourable-dangerous consequence;
And I do know, by this they stay for me   125
In Pompey's Porch; for now, this fearful night,
There is no stir or walking in the streets;
And the complexion of the element
In favour's like the work we have in hand,
Most bloody, fiery, and most terrible.   130

Enter CINNA.

    Casca. Stand close a while, for here comes one in haste.
    Cas. 'Tis Cinna, I do know him by his gait;
He is a friend. Cinna, where haste you so?
    Cin. To find out you. Who's that? Metellus Cimber?
    Cas. No, it is Casca; one incorporate   135
To our attempts. Am I not stay'd for, Cinna?

    Cin. I am glad on't. What a fearful night is this!
There's two or three of us have seen strange sights.
    Cas. Am I not stay'd for? tell me.
    Cin.   Yes, you are.
O Cassius, if you could   140
But win the noble Brutus to our party —
    Cas. Be you content. Good Cinna, take this paper,
And look you lay it in the prætor's chair,
Where Brutus may but find it; and throw this
In at his window; set this up with wax   145
Upon old Brutus' statue. All this done,
Repair to Pompey's Porch, where you shall find us.
Is Decius Brutus and Trebonius there?
    Cin. All but Metellus Cimber; and he's gone
To seek you at your house. Well, I will hie   150
And so bestow these papers as you bade me.
    Cas. That done, repair to Pompey's Theatre.
                    [*Exit Cinna.*
Come, Casca, you and I will yet ere day
See Brutus at his house. Three parts of him
Is ours already, and the man entire   155
Upon the next encounter yields him ours.
    Casca. O, he sits high in all the people's hearts;
And that which would appear offence in us,
His countenance, like richest alchemy,
Will change to virtue and to worthiness.   160
    Cas. Him and his worth and our great need of him
You have right well conceited. Let us go,
For it is after midnight; and ere day
We will awake him and be sure of him. [*Exeunt.*

ACT II

[SCENE I. *Rome.*]

Enter BRUTUS *in his orchard.*

    Bru. What, Lucius, ho!
I cannot by the progress of the stars
Give guess how near to-day. Lucius, I say!
I would it were my fault to sleep so soundly.
When, Lucius, when! Awake, I say! What, Lucius!   5

Enter LUCIUS.

    Luc. Call'd you, my lord?
    Bru. Get me a taper in my study, Lucius.
When it is lighted, come and call me here.
    Luc. I will, my lord.   [*Exit.*
    Bru. It must be by his death; and for my part,   10
I know no personal cause to spurn at him
But for the general. He would be crown'd:

---

106. **hinds:** female deer. 117. **fleering:** flattering. 118. **Be factious:** form a party. 126. **Pompey's Porch:** the portico of Pompey's Theatre. 128. **element:** i.e., sky. 131. **close:** concealed. 143. **prætor's:** magistrate's. 162. **conceited:** understood.

Act II, sc. i, 12. **for the general:** for the sake of the public.

How that might change his nature, there's the
    question.
It is the bright day that brings forth the adder,
And that craves wary walking.   Crown him?
    That —   15
And then, I grant, we put a sting in him
That at his will he may do danger with.
Th' abuse of greatness is when it disjoins
Remorse from power; and, to speak truth of Cæsar,
I have not known when his affections sway'd   20
More than his reason.   But 'tis a common proof
That lowliness is young Ambition's ladder,
Whereto the climber-upward turns his face;
But when he once attains the upmost round,
He then unto the ladder turns his back,   25
Looks in the clouds, scorning the base degrees
By which he did ascend.   So Cæsar may;
Then, lest he may, prevent.   And, since the quarrel
Will bear no colour for the thing he is,
Fashion it thus: that what he is, augmented,   30
Would run to these and these extremities;
And therefore think him as a serpent's egg
Which, hatch'd, would, as his kind, grow mischievous,
And kill him in the shell.

              Re-enter Lucius.

  Luc. The taper burneth in your closet, sir.   35
Searching the window for a flint, I found
This paper, thus seal'd up; and I am sure
It did not lie there when I went to bed.
                   [*Gives him the letter.*
  Bru. Get you to bed again; it is not day.
Is not to-morrow, boy, the [ides] of March?   40
  Luc. I know not, sir.
  Bru. Look in the calendar, and bring me word.
  Luc. I will, sir.   [*Exit.*
  Bru. The exhalations whizzing in the air
Gives so much light that I may read by them.   45
            [*Opens the letter and reads.*
"Brutus, thou sleep'st; awake, and see thyself!
Shall Rome, etc.   Speak, strike, redress!"
"Brutus, thou sleep'st; awake!"
Such instigations have been often dropp'd
Where I have took them up.   50
"Shall Rome, etc."   Thus must I piece it out:
Shall Rome stand under one man's awe?   What,
    Rome?
My ancestors did from the streets of Rome
The Tarquin drive when he was call'd a king.
"Speak, strike, redress!"   Am I entreated   55
To speak and strike? O Rome, I make thee promise,
If the redress will follow, thou receivest
Thy full petition at the hand of Brutus!

              Re-enter Lucius.

  Luc. Sir, March is wasted fifteen days.
                   [*Knocking within.*
  Bru. 'Tis good.   Go to the gate; somebody
    knocks.   [*Exit Lucius.*]   60
Since Cassius first did whet me against Cæsar,
I have not slept.
Between the acting of a dreadful thing
And the first motion, all the interim is
Like a phantasma or a hideous dream.   65
The Genius and the mortal instruments
Are then in council; and the state of a man,
Like to a little kingdom, suffers then
The nature of an insurrection.

              Re-enter Lucius.

  Luc. Sir, 'tis your brother Cassius at the door,   70
Who doth desire to see you.
  Bru.   Is he alone?
  Luc. No, sir, there are more with him.
  Bru.   Do you know them?
  Luc. No, sir; their hats are pluck'd about their
    ears
And half their faces buried in their cloaks,
That by no means I may discover them   75
By any mark of favour.
  Bru.   Let 'em enter.
                   [*Exit Lucius.*]
They are the faction.   O Conspiracy,
Sham'st thou to show thy dangerous brow by night,
When evils are most free?   O, then by day
Where wilt thou find a cavern dark enough   80
To mask thy monstrous visage?   Seek none, Con-
    spiracy!
Hide it in smiles and affability;
For if thou path, thy native semblance on,
Not Erebus itself were dim enough
To hide thee from prevention.   85

Enter the conspirators, Cassius, Casca, Decius,
    Cinna, Metellus Cimber, *and* Trebonius.

  Cas. I think we are too bold upon your rest.
Good morrow, Brutus; do we trouble you?
  Bru. I have been up this hour, awake all night.
Know I these men that come along with you?
  Cas. Yes, every man of them; and no man here
But honours you; and every one doth wish   91
You had but that opinion of yourself
Which every noble Roman bears of you.
This is Trebonius.
  Bru.   He is welcome hither.
  Cas. This, Decius Brutus.
  Bru.   He is welcome too.

---

19. **Remorse:** compassion, conscience.   20. **affections:** passions.   21. **proof:** experience.   29. **Will . . . is:** i.e., is not warranted by his conduct so far.   40. **[ides]** (Theobald). *first* F.   44. **exhalations:** meteors.   64. **motion:** proposal.   65. **phantasma:** hectic vision.   66–67. **The . . . council:** i.e., a man's mind deliberates over the deadly means at his disposal.   70. **brother.**
Cassius had married a sister of Brutus.   83. **path:** goest about.   84. **Erebus:** Hades.   85. **prevention:** being forestalled.

Cas. This, Casca; this, Cinna; and this, Metel-
lus Cimber.   96
Bru. They are all welcome.
What watchful cares do interpose themselves
Betwixt your eyes and night?
Cas. Shall I entreat a word? [*They whisper.* 100
Dec. Here lies the east; doth not the day break
here?
Casca. No.
Cin. O, pardon, sir, it doth; and yon grey lines
That fret the clouds are messengers of day.
Casca. You shall confess that you are both
deceiv'd.   105
Here, as I point my sword, the sun arises,
Which is a great way growing on the south,
Weighing the youthful season of the year.
Some two months hence up higher toward the north
He first presents his fire; and the high east   110
Stands, as the Capitol, directly here.
Bru. Give me your hands all over, one by one.
Cas. And let us swear our resolution.
Bru. No, not an oath! If not the face of men,
The sufferance of our souls, the time's abuse, —
If these be motives weak, break off betimes,   116
And every man hence to his idle bed;
So let high-sighted tyranny range on,
Till each man drop by lottery. But if these,
As I am sure they do, bear fire enough   120
To kindle cowards and to steel with valour
The melting spirits of women, then, countrymen,
What need we any spur but our own cause
To prick us to redress? what other bond
Than secret Romans, that have spoke the word 125
And will not palter? and what other oath
Than honesty to honesty engag'd
That this shall be, or we will fall for it?
Swear priests and cowards and men cautelous,
Old feeble carrions and such suffering souls   130
That welcome wrongs; unto bad causes swear
Such creatures as men doubt; but do not stain
The even virtue of our enterprise,
Nor th' insuppressive mettle of our spirits,
To think that or our cause or our performance 135
Did need an oath; when every drop of blood
That every Roman bears, and nobly bears,
Is guilty of a several bastardy,
If he do break the smallest particle
Of any promise that hath pass'd from him.   140
Cas. But what of Cicero? Shall we sound him?
I think he will stand very strong with us.
Casca. Let us not leave him out.
Cin.   No, by no means.
Met. O, let us have him, for his silver hairs

Will purchase us a good opinion   145
And buy men's voices to commend our deeds.
It shall be said his judgement rul'd our hands;
Our youths and wildness shall no whit appear,
But all be buried in his gravity.
Bru. O, name him not; let us not break with him,
For he will never follow anything   151
That other men begin.
Cas.   Then leave him out.
Casca. Indeed he is not fit.
Dec. Shall no man else be touch'd but only Cæsar?
Cas. Decius, well urg'd. I think it is not meet,
Mark Antony, so well belov'd of Cæsar,   156
Should outlive Cæsar. We shall find of him
A shrewd contriver; and, you know, his means,
If he improve them, may well stretch so far
As to annoy us all; which to prevent,   160
Let Antony and Cæsar fall together.
Bru. Our course will seem too bloody, Caius
Cassius,
To cut the head off and then hack the limbs,
Like wrath in death and envy afterwards;
For Antony is but a limb of Cæsar.   165
Let's be sacrificers, but not butchers, Caius.
We all stand up against the spirit of Cæsar,
And in the spirit of men there is no blood;
O, that we then could come by Cæsar's spirit,
And not dismember Cæsar! But, alas,   170
Cæsar must bleed for it! And, gentle friends,
Let's kill him boldly, but not wrathfully;
Let's carve him as a dish fit for the gods,
Not hew him as a carcass fit for hounds;
And let our hearts, as subtle masters do,   175
Stir up their servants to an act of rage,
And after seem to chide 'em. This shall make
Our purpose necessary and not envious;
Which so appearing to the common eyes,
We shall be call'd purgers, not murderers.   180
And for Mark Antony, think not of him;
For he can do no more than Cæsar's arm
When Cæsar's head is off.
Cas.   Yet I fear him;
For in the ingrafted love he bears to Cæsar —
Bru. Alas, good Cassius, do not think of him. 185
If he love Cæsar, all that he can do
Is to himself — take thought and die for Cæsar;
And that were much he should, for he is given
To sports, to wildness, and much company.
Treb. There is no fear in him; let him not die; 190
For he will live, and laugh at this hereafter.
                                    [*Clock strikes.*
Bru. Peace! count the clock.
Cas.   The clock hath stricken three.

---

107. **growing on:** toward. 118. **high-sighted:** arrogant. 127. **honesty:** personal honor. 129. **cautelous:** deceitful.
130. **suffering:** submissive. 134. **insuppressive:** irrepressible. 150. **break with:** broach the matter to him. 157. **of:** in.
160. **annoy:** injure. 164. **envy:** malice (cf. *envious*, l. 178). 176. **their servants:** i.e., our hands. 187. **take thought:** become melancholy. 188. **were ... should:** is a great deal to expect. 190. **no fear:** nothing to fear.

Treb. 'Tis time to part.

Cas.   But it is doubtful yet
Whether Cæsar will come forth to-day or no;
For he is superstitious grown of late,   195
Quite from the main opinion he held once
Of fantasy, of dreams, and ceremonies.
It may be these apparent prodigies,
The unaccustom'd terror of this night,
And the persuasion of his augurers   200
May hold him from the Capitol to-day.

Dec. Never fear that. If he be so resolv'd,
I can o'ersway him; for he loves to hear
That unicorns may be betray'd with trees,
And bears with glasses, elephants with holes,   205
Lions with toils, and men with flatterers;
But when I tell him he hates flatterers
He says he does, being then most flattered.
Let me work;
For I can give his humour the true bent,   210
And I will bring him to the Capitol.

Cas. Nay, we will all of us be there to fetch him.

Bru. By the eighth hour; is that the uttermost?

Cin. Be that the uttermost, and fail not then.

Met. Caius Ligarius doth bear Cæsar hard,   215
Who rated him for speaking well of Pompey.
I wonder none of you have thought of him.

Bru. Now, good Metellus, go along by him.
He loves me well, and I have given him reasons;
Send him but hither, and I'll fashion him.   220

Cas. The morning comes upon 's. We'll leave
          you, Brutus,
And, friends, disperse yourselves; but all remember
What you have said, and show yourselves true
          Romans.

Bru. Good gentlemen, look fresh and merrily.
Let not our looks put on our purposes,   225
But bear it as our Roman actors do,
With untir'd spirits and formal constancy.
And so good morrow to you every one.

                    [*Exeunt all but Brutus.*

Boy! Lucius! Fast asleep? It is no matter;
Enjoy the honey-heavy dew of slumber.   230
Thou hast no figures nor no fantasies
Which busy care draws in the brains of men;
Therefore thou sleep'st so sound.

Enter PORTIA.

Por.   Brutus, my lord!

Bru. Portia, what mean you? Wherefore rise
          you now?
It is not for your health thus to commit   235
Your weak condition to the raw cold morning.

Por. Nor for yours neither. You've ungently,
          Brutus,
Stole from my bed; and yesternight at supper
You suddenly arose and walk'd about,
Musing and sighing, with your arms across;   240
And when I ask'd you what the matter was,
You star'd upon me with ungentle looks.
I urg'd you further; then you scratch'd your head
And too impatiently stamp'd with your foot.
Yet I insisted; yet you answer'd not,   245
But with an angry [wafture] of your hand
Gave sign for me to leave you. So I did,
Fearing to strengthen that impatience
Which seem'd too much enkindled, and withal
Hoping it was but an effect of humour,   250
Which sometime hath his hour with every man.
It will not let you eat, nor talk, nor sleep,
And could it work so much upon your shape
As it hath much prevail'd on your condition,
I should not know you, Brutus. Dear my lord, 255
Make me acquainted with your cause of grief.

Bru. I am not well in health, and that is all.

Por. Brutus is wise, and, were he not in health,
He would embrace the means to come by it.

Bru. Why, so I do. Good Portia, go to bed.   260

Por. Is Brutus sick? and is it physical
To walk unbraced and suck up the humours
Of the dank morning? What, is Brutus sick,
And will he steal out of his wholesome bed
To dare the vile contagion of the night,   265
And tempt the rheumy and unpurged air
To add unto his sickness? No, my Brutus;
You have some sick offence within your mind,
Which, by the right and virtue of my place,
I ought to know of; and upon my knees   270
I charm you, by my once commended beauty,
By all your vows of love, and that great vow
Which did incorporate and make us one,
That you unfold to me, yourself, your half,
Why you are heavy, and what men to-night   275
Have had resort to you; for here have been
Some six or seven, who did hide their faces
Even from darkness.

Bru.   Kneel not, gentle Portia.

Por. I should not need, if you were gentle Brutus.
Within the bond of marriage, tell me, Brutus, 280
Is it excepted I should know no secrets
That appertain to you? Am I yourself
But, as it were, in sort or limitation,
To keep with you at meals, comfort your bed,
And talk to you sometimes? Dwell I but in the
          suburbs   285

---

196. **main:** strong. 197. **ceremonies,** such as those performed by augurs. 198. **apparent:** manifest. 204. **unicorns…
trees.** It was believed that a unicorn could be caught if, when it charged, the hunter jumped behind a tree, making it bury
its horn in the trunk. 205. **glasses:** mirrors. **holes:** pitfalls. 206. **toils:** nets. 218. **by him:** by his house. 225. **put on:**
reveal. 231. **figures:** imaginings. 236. **condition:** constitution. 237. **ungently:** unkindly. 246. **[wafture]** (Rowe): waving. *wafter* F. 261. **physical:** good for the health. 266. **rheumy:** dank. **unpurged:** not yet purified by the sun.
271. **charm:** conjure. 275. **heavy:** depressed. 283. **in … limitation:** in a limited manner only.

Of your good pleasure?   If it be no more,
Portia is Brutus' harlot, not his wife.
  Bru. You are my true and honourable wife,
As dear to me as are the ruddy drops
That visit my sad heart.   290
  Por. If this were true, then should I know this
    secret.
I grant I am a woman; but withal
A woman that Lord Brutus took to wife.
I grant I am a woman; but withal
A woman well-reputed, Cato's daughter.   295
Think you I am no stronger than my sex,
Being so father'd and so husbanded?
Tell me your counsels, I will not disclose 'em.
I have made strong proof of my constancy,
Giving myself a voluntary wound   300
Here, in the thigh; can I bear that with patience,
And not my husband's secrets?
  Bru.   O ye gods!
Render me worthy of this noble wife!
                   [Knocking within.
Hark, hark! one knocks.   Portia, go in a while,
And by and by thy bosom shall partake   305
The secrets of my heart.
All my engagements I will construe to thee,
All the charactery of my sad brows.
Leave me with haste.
                   [Exit Portia.]
Lucius, who's that knocks?

    Re-enter LUCIUS *with* LIGARIUS.

  Luc. Here is a sick man that would speak with
    you.   310
  Bru. Caius Ligarius, that Metellus spake of.
Boy, stand aside.   Caius Ligarius! how?
  Lig. Vouchsafe good morrow from a feeble
    tongue.
  Bru. O, what a time have you chose out, brave
    Caius,
To wear a kerchief!   Would you were not sick!   315
  Lig. I am not sick, if Brutus have in hand
Any exploit worthy the name of honour.
  Bru. Such an exploit have I in hand, Ligarius,
Had you a healthful ear to hear of it.
  Lig. By all the gods that Romans bow before,
I here discard my sickness!   Soul of Rome!   322
Brave son, deriv'd from honourable loins!
Thou, like an exorcist, hast conjur'd up
My mortified spirit.   Now bid me run,
And I will strive with things impossible;   325
Yea, get the better of them.   What's to do?
  Bru. A piece of work that will make sick men
    whole.

  Lig. But are not some whole that we must make
    sick?
  Bru. That must we also.   What it is, my Caius,
I shall unfold to thee as we are going   330
To whom it must be done.
  Lig.   Set on your foot,
And with a heart new-fir'd I follow you,
To do I know not what; but it sufficeth
That Brutus leads me on.   *[Thunder.*
  Bru.   Follow me, then.
                        [Exeunt.

    [SCENE II.   *Cæsar's house.*]

  Thunder and lightning.   Enter CÆSAR, *in his
            night-gown.*

  Cæs. Nor heaven nor earth have been at peace
    to-night.
Thrice hath Calpurnia in her sleep cried out,
"Help! ho! they murder Cæsar!"   Who's within?

       Enter a SERVANT.

  Serv. My lord?
  Cæs. Go bid the priests do present sacrifice   5
And bring me their opinions of success.
  Serv. I will, my lord.   *[Exit.*

       Enter CALPURNIA.

  Cal. What mean you, Cæsar?   Think you to
    walk forth?
You shall not stir out of your house to-day.
  Cæs. Cæsar shall forth.   The things that
    threaten'd me   10
Ne'er look'd but on my back; when they shall see
The face of Cæsar, they are vanished.
  Cal. Cæsar, I never stood on ceremonies,
Yet now they fright me.   There is one within,
Besides the things that we have heard and seen, 15
Recounts most horrid sights seen by the watch.
A lioness hath whelped in the streets,
And graves have yawn'd and yielded up their dead;
Fierce fiery warriors [fought] upon the clouds
In ranks and squadrons and right form of war,   20
Which drizzl'd blood upon the Capitol;
The noise of battle hurtled in the air,
Horses [did] neigh, and dying men did groan,
And ghosts did shriek and squeal about the streets.
O Cæsar! these things are beyond all use,   25
And I do fear them.
  Cæs.   What can be avoided
Whose end is purpos'd by the mighty gods?
Yet Cæsar shall go forth; for these predictions
Are to the world in general as to Cæsar.

---

    298. **counsels:** secrets.   308. **charactery:** meaning (lit., handwriting).   313. **Vouchsafe:** deign to accept.   324. **mor-**
tified: deadened.
    Sc. ii, S.D. **night-gown:** dressing gown.   5. **present:** immediate.   6. **success:** the outcome.   13. **stood on ceremonies:**
heeded omens.   19. **[fought]** (Grant White).   *fight* F.   23. **[did]** F₂.   *do* F₁.   25. **use:** custom.

Cal. When beggars die there are no comets seen.
The heavens themselves blaze forth the death of
        princes,   31
Cæs. Cowards die many times before their
        deaths;
The valiant never taste of death but once.
Of all the wonders that I yet have heard,
It seems to me most strange that men should fear, 35
Seeing that death, a necessary end,
Will come when it will come.

                    Re-enter SERVANT.

                            What say the augurers?
Serv. They would not have you to stir forth to-
        day.
Plucking the entrails of an offering forth,
They could not find a heart within the beast.   40
Cæs. The gods do this in shame of cowardice;
Cæsar should be a beast without a heart,
If he should stay at home to-day for fear.
No, Cæsar shall not; Danger knows full well
That Cæsar is more dangerous than he.   45
We [are] two lions litter'd in one day,
And I the elder and more terrible;
And Cæsar shall go forth.
Cal.   Alas, my lord,
Your wisdom is consum'd in confidence.
Do not go forth to-day; call it my fear   50
That keeps you in the house, and not your own.
We'll send Mark Antony to the Senate House,
And he shall say you are not well to-day.
Let me, upon my knee, prevail in this.
Cæs. Mark Antony shall say I am not well;   55
And, for thy humour, I will stay at home.

                    Enter DECIUS.
Here's Decius Brutus, he shall tell them so.
Dec. Cæsar, all hail! good morrow, worthy
        Cæsar;
I come to fetch you to the Senate House.
Cæs. And you are come in very happy time   60
To bear my greetings to the Senators
And tell them that I will not come to-day.
Cannot, is false, and that I dare not, falser;
I will not come to-day. Tell them so, Decius.
Cal. Say he is sick.
Cæs.   Shall Cæsar send a lie? 65
Have I in conquest stretch'd mine arm so far,
To be afeard to tell greybeards the truth?
Decius, go tell them Cæsar will not come.
Dec. Most mighty Cæsar, let me know some
        cause,
Lest I be laugh'd at when I tell them so.   70
Cæs. The cause is in my will; I will not come;
That is enough to satisfy the Senate.

But for your private satisfaction,
Because I love you, I will let you know:
Calpurnia here, my wife, stays me at home.   75
She dreamt to-night she saw my statuë,
Which, like a fountain with an hundred spouts,
Did run pure blood; and many lusty Romans
Came smiling and did bathe their hands in it;
And these does she apply for warnings and portents
And evils imminent, and on her knee   81
Hath begg'd that I will stay at home to-day.
Dec. This dream is all amiss interpreted;
It was a vision fair and fortunate.
Your statue spouting blood in many pipes,   85
In which so many smiling Romans bath'd,
Signifies that from you great Rome shall suck
Reviving blood, and that great men shall press
For tinctures, stains, relics, and cognizance.
This by Calpurnia's dream is signified.   90
Cæs. And this way have you well expounded it.
Dec. I have, when you have heard what I can say;
And know it now. The Senate have concluded
To give this day a crown to mighty Cæsar.
If you shall send them word you will not come,   95
Their minds may change. Besides, it were a mock
Apt to be render'd, for some one to say,
"Break up the Senate till another time,
When Cæsar's wife shall meet with better dreams."
If Cæsar hide himself, shall they not whisper,   100
"Lo, Cæsar is afraid"?
Pardon me, Cæsar; for my dear dear love
To your proceeding bids me tell you this;
And reason to my love is liable.
Cæs. How foolish do your fears seem now, Cal-
        purnia!   105
I am ashamed I did yield to them.
Give me my robe, for I will go.

Enter PUBLIUS, BRUTUS, LIGARIUS, METELLUS,
        CASCA, TREBONIUS, *and* CINNA.
And look where Publius is come to fetch me.
Pub. Good morrow, Cæsar.
Cæs.   Welcome, Publius.
What, Brutus, are you stirr'd so early too?   110
Good morrow, Casca. Caius Ligarius,
Cæsar was ne'er so much your enemy
As that same ague which hath made you lean.
What is't o'clock?
Bru.   Cæsar, 'tis strucken eight.
Cæs. I thank you for your pains and courtesy.

                    Enter ANTONY.
See! Antony, that revels long o' nights,   116
Is notwithstanding up. Good morrow, Antony.
Ant. So to most noble Cæsar.
Cæs.   Bid them prepare within;

I am to blame to be thus waited for.
Now, Cinna; now, Metellus.   What, Trebonius!
I have an hour's talk in store for you;   121
Remember that you call on me to-day;
Be near me, that I may remember you.

Treb. Cæsar, I will; [*aside*] and so near will I be,
That your best friends shall wish I had been further.

Cæs. Good friends, go in, and taste some wine
with me;   126
And we, like friends, will straightway go together.

Bru. [*Aside.*] That every like is not the same, O
Cæsar,
The heart of Brutus earns to think upon! [*Exeunt.*

[SCENE III.   *A street near the Capitol.*]

Enter ARTEMIDORUS [*reading a paper*].

Art. "Cæsar, beware of Brutus; take heed of
Cassius; come not near Casca; have an eye to Cinna; trust not Trebonius; mark well Metellus Cim-
ber: Decius Brutus loves thee not: thou hast wrong'd
Caius Ligarius.   There is but one mind in all these 5
men, and it is bent against Cæsar.   If thou beest
not immortal, look about you; security gives way to
conspiracy.   The mighty gods defend thee!   Thy
lover,
                                   ARTEMIDORUS." 10
Here will I stand till Cæsar pass along,
And as a suitor will I give him this.
My heart laments that virtue cannot live
Out of the teeth of emulation.
If thou read this, O Cæsar, thou mayst live;   15
If not, the Fates with traitors do contrive. [*Exit.*

[SCENE IV. *Another part of the same street,*
before the house of Brutus.]

Enter PORTIA *and* LUCIUS.

Por. I prithee, boy, run to the Senate House;
Stay not to answer me, but get thee gone.
Why dost thou stay?

Luc.   To know my errand, madam.

Por. I would have had thee there and here again
Ere I can tell thee what thou shouldst do there.   5
O constancy, be strong upon my side,
Set a huge mountain 'tween my heart and tongue!
I have a man's mind, but a woman's might.
How hard it is for women to keep counsel!
Art thou here yet?

Luc.   Madam, what should I do? 10
Run to the Capitol, and nothing else?
And so return to you, and nothing else?

Por. Yes, bring me word, boy, if thy lord look
well,

For he went sickly forth; and take good note
What Cæsar doth, what suitors press to him.   15
Hark, boy! what noise is that?

Luc. I hear none, madam.

Por.   Prithee, listen well;
I heard a bustling rumour, like a fray,
And the wind brings it from the Capitol.

Luc. Sooth, madam, I hear nothing.   20

Enter the SOOTHSAYER.

Por. Come hither, fellow; which way hast thou
been?

Sooth. At mine own house, good lady.

Por. What is't o'clock?

Sooth.   About the ninth hour, lady.

Por. Is Cæsar yet gone to the Capitol?

Sooth. Madam, not yet; I go to take my stand, 25
To see him pass on to the Capitol.

Por. Thou hast some suit to Cæsar, hast thou
not?

Sooth. That I have, lady; if it will please Cæsar
To be so good to Cæsar as to hear me,
I shall beseech him to befriend himself.   30

Por. Why, know'st thou any harm 's intended
towards him?

Sooth. None that I know will be, much that I
fear may chance.
Good morrow to you.   Here the street is narrow;
The throng that follows Cæsar at the heels,
Of senators, of prætors, common suitors,   35
Will crowd a feeble man almost to death.
I'll get me to a place more void, and there
Speak to great Cæsar as he comes along.   [*Exit.*

Por. I must go in.   Ay me, how weak a thing
The heart of woman is!   O Brutus,   40
The heavens speed thee in thine enterprise!
[*To herself.*] Sure, the boy heard me.   [*To Lucius.*]
Brutus hath a suit
That Cæsar will not grant.   O, I grow faint.
Run, Lucius, and commend me to my lord;
Say I am merry.   Come to me again   45
And bring me word what he doth say to thee.
                              [*Exeunt* [*severally*].

ACT III

[SCENE I. *Rome.   Before the Capitol.*]

[*A crowd of people; among them*] ARTEMIDORUS
and the SOOTHSAYER.   *Flourish.   Enter* CÆSAR,
BRUTUS, CASSIUS, CASCA, DECIUS, METELLUS,
TREBONIUS, CINNA, ANTONY, LEPIDUS, PUB-
LIUS [*and* POPILIUS].

Cæs. [*To the Soothsayer.*] The ides of March are
come.

128. **every ... same:** every apparent friend is not one in fact.   129. **earns:** grieves.
Sc. iii, 7. **security:** over-confidence.   14. **emulation:** envy.
Sc. iv, 6. **constancy:** firmness.   45. **merry:** in good spirits.

Sooth. Ay, Cæsar; but not gone.

Art. Hail, Cæsar! read this schedule.

Dec. Trebonius doth desire you to o'er-read,
At your best leisure, this his humble suit. 5

Art. O Cæsar, read mine first; for mine's a suit
That touches Cæsar nearer. Read it, great Cæsar.

Cæs. What touches us ourself shall be last serv'd.

Art. Delay not, Cæsar; read it instantly.

Cæs. What, is the fellow mad?

Pub. Sirrah, give place.

Cas. What, urge you your petitions in the
street? 11
Come to the Capitol.

[*Cæsar goes up to the Senate-House, the
rest following.*]

Pop. I wish your enterprise to-day may thrive.

Cas. What enterprise, Popilius?

Pop. Fare you well.

[*Advances to Cæsar.*]

Bru. What said Popilius Lena? 15

Cas. He wish'd to-day our enterprise might
thrive.
I fear our purpose is discovered.

Bru. Look, how he makes to Cæsar; mark him.

Cas. Casca, be sudden, for we fear prevention.
Brutus, what shall be done? If this be known, 20
Cassius or Cæsar never shall turn back,
For I will slay myself.

Bru. Cassius, be constant;
Popilius Lena speaks not of our purposes,
For, look, he smiles, and Cæsar doth not change.

Cas. Trebonius knows his time; for, look you,
Brutus, 25
He draws Mark Antony out of the way.

[*Exeunt Antony and Trebonius.*]

Dec. Where is Metellus Cimber? Let him go
And presently prefer his suit to Cæsar.

Bru. He is address'd; press near and second him.

Cin. Casca, you are the first that rears your
hand. 30

Cæs. Are we all ready? What is now amiss
That Cæsar and his senate must redress?

Met. Most high, most mighty, and most puissant
Cæsar,
Metellus Cimber throws before thy seat
An humble heart, — [*Kneeling.*]

Cæs. I must prevent thee, Cimber.
These couchings and these lowly courtesies 36
Might fire the blood of ordinary men,
And turn pre-ordinance and first decree
Into the [law] of children. Be not fond
To think that Cæsar bears such rebel blood 40
That will be thaw'd from the true quality

With that which melteth fools; I mean, sweet
words,
Low-crooked curtsies and base spaniel-fawning.
Thy brother by decree is banished;
If thou dost bend and pray and fawn for him, 45
I spurn thee like a cur out of my way.
Know, Cæsar doth not wrong, nor without cause
Will he be satisfied.

Met. Is there no voice more worthy than my
own,
To sound more sweetly in great Cæsar's ear 50
For the repealing of my banish'd brother?

Bru. I kiss thy hand, but not in flattery, Cæsar;
Desiring thee that Publius Cimber may
Have an immediate freedom of repeal.

Cæs. What, Brutus!

Cas. Pardon, Cæsar; Cæsar, pardon! 55
As low as to thy foot doth Cassius fall,
To beg enfranchisement for Publius Cimber.

Cæs. I could well be mov'd, if I were as you;
If I could pray to move, prayers would move
me;
But I am constant as the northern star, 60
Of whose true-fix'd and resting quality
There is no fellow in the firmament.
The skies are painted with unnumb'red sparks,
They are all fire and every one doth shine;
But there's but one in all doth hold his place. 65
So in the world; 'tis furnish'd well with men,
And men are flesh and blood, and apprehensive;
Yet in the number I do know but one
That unassailable holds on his rank,
Unshak'd of motion; and that I am he, 70
Let me a little show it, even in this:
That I was constant Cimber should be banish'd,
And constant do remain to keep him so.

Cin. O Cæsar, —

Cæs. Hence! wilt thou lift up Olympus?

Dec. Great Cæsar, —

Cæs. Doth not Brutus bootless kneel?

Casca. Speak, hands, for me! 76

[*They stab Cæsar.*

Cæs. *Et tu Brute!* Then fall, Cæsar! [*Dies.*

Cin. Liberty! Freedom! Tyranny is dead!
Run hence, proclaim, cry it about the streets.

Cas. Some to the common pulpits, and cry out, 80
"Liberty, freedom, and enfranchisement!"

Bru. People and senators, be not affrighted;
Fly not; stand still; ambition's debt is paid.

Casca. Go to the pulpit, Brutus.

Dec. And Cassius too.

Bru. Where's Publius? 85

Cin. Here, quite confounded with this mutiny.

Act III, sc. i, 3. **schedule:** document. 28. **presently prefer:** at once present. 29. **address'd:** ready. 36. **couchings:** prostrations. 38. **first:** previous. 39. **[law]** (Johnson conj.). *lane* F. 40. **rebel:** i.e., ready to violate law. 51. **repealing:** recall. 54. **freedom of:** permission for. 61. **resting quality:** stability. 67. **apprehensive:** intelligent. 80. **common pulpits:** public platforms. 86. **mutiny:** uproar.

Met. Stand fast together, lest some friend of
    Cæsar's
Should chance —
    Bru. Talk not of standing. Publius, good cheer;
There is no harm intended to your person,   90
Nor to no Roman else. So tell them, Publius.
    Cas. And leave us, Publius; lest that the people,
Rushing on us, should do your age some mischief.
    Bru. Do so: and let no man abide this deed,
But we the doers.

Re-enter TREBONIUS.

    Cas.   Where is Antony?   95
    Treb. Fled to his house amaz'd.
Men, wives, and children stare, cry out, and run,
As it were doomsday.
    Bru.   Fates, we will know your pleasures.
That we shall die, we know; 'tis but the time
And drawing days out, that men stand upon.   100
    Cas. Why, he that cuts off twenty years of life
Cuts off so many years of fearing death.
    Bru. Grant that, and then is death a benefit;
So are we Cæsar's friends, that have abridg'd
His time of fearing death. Stoop, Romans, stoop,
And let us bathe our hands in Cæsar's blood   106
Up to the elbows, and besmear our swords;
Then walk we forth, even to the market-place,
And, waving our red weapons o'er our heads,
Let's all cry, "Peace, freedom, and liberty!"   110
    Cas. Stoop, then, and wash. How many ages
    hence
Shall this our lofty scene be acted over
In states unborn and accents yet unknown!
    Bru. How many times shall Cæsar bleed in sport,
That now on Pompey's basis lies along   115
No worthier than the dust!
    Cas.   So oft as that shall be,
So often shall the knot of us be call'd
The men that gave their country liberty.
    Dec. What, shall we forth?
    Cas.   Ay, every man away.
Brutus shall lead; and we will grace his heels   120
With the most boldest and best hearts of Rome.

Enter a SERVANT.

    Bru. Soft! who comes here? A friend of An-
    tony's.
    Serv. Thus, Brutus, did my master bid me kneel,
Thus did Mark Antony bid me fall down;
And, being prostrate, thus he bade me say: 125
Brutus is noble, wise, valiant, and honest;
Cæsar was mighty, bold, royal, and loving;
Say I love Brutus, and I honour him;

Say I fear'd Cæsar, honour'd him, and lov'd him.
If Brutus will vouchsafe that Antony   130
May safely come to him, and be resolv'd
How Cæsar hath deserv'd to lie in death,
Mark Antony shall not love Cæsar dead
So well as Brutus living; but will follow
The fortunes and affairs of noble Brutus   135
Thorough the hazards of this untrod state
With all true faith. So says my master Antony.
    Bru. Thy master is a wise and valiant Roman;
I never thought him worse.
Tell him, so please him come unto this place,   140
He shall be satisfied; and, by my honour,
Depart untouch'd.
    Serv.   I'll fetch him presently. [*Exit.*
    Bru. I know that we shall have him well to
    friend.
    Cas. I wish we may; but yet have I a mind
That fears him much, and my misgiving still   145
Falls shrewdly to the purpose.

Re-enter ANTONY.

    Bru. But here comes Antony. Welcome, Mark
    Antony!
    Ant. O mighty Cæsar! dost thou lie so low?
Are all thy conquests, glories, triumphs, spoils,
Shrunk to this little measure? Fare thee well!   150
I know not, gentlemen, what you intend,
Who else must be let blood, who else is rank;
If I myself, there is no hour so fit
As Cæsar's death's hour, nor no instrument
Of half that worth as those your swords, made
    rich   155
With the most noble blood of all this world.
I do beseech ye, if you bear me hard,
Now, whilst your purpled hands do reek and smoke,
Fulfil your pleasure. Live a thousand years,
I shall not find myself so apt to die;   160
No place will please me so, no mean of death,
As here by Cæsar, and by you cut off,
The choice and master spirits of this age.
    Bru. O Antony, beg not your death of us.
Though now we must appear bloody and cruel,   165
As by our hands and this our present act
You see we do, yet see you but our hands
And this the bleeding business they have done.
Our hearts you see not; they are pitiful;
And pity to the general wrong of Rome —   170
As fire drives out fire, so pity pity —
Hath done this deed on Cæsar. For your part,
To you our swords have leaden points, Mark An-
    tony;
Our arms, in strength of malice, and our hearts

---

94. **abide:** pay (the penalty) for.   100. **stand upon:** make much of.   115. **basis:** pedestal.   **along:** prostrate.   131.
be resolv'd: have it explained.   146. **Falls...purpose:** proves very nearly right.   152. **rank:** overgrown, ripe to be cut down.
157. **bear me hard:** have a grudge against me.   160. **apt:** ready.   162. **by Cæsar:** beside Cæsar.   174. **in...malice:**
(though) strong in enmity.

Of brothers' temper, do receive you in   175
With all kind love, good thoughts, and reverence.
    Cas. Your voice shall be as strong as any man's
In the disposing of new dignities.
    Bru. Only be patient till we have appeas'd
The multitude, beside themselves with fear,   180
And then we will deliver you the cause
Why I, that did love Cæsar when I struck him,
Have thus proceeded.
    Ant.   I doubt not of your wisdom.
Let each man render me his bloody hand.
First, Marcus Brutus, will I shake with you;   185
Next, Caius Cassius, do I take your hand;
Now, Decius Brutus, yours; now yours, Metellus;
Yours, Cinna; and, my valiant Casca, yours;
Though last, not least in love, yours, good Tre-
    bonius.
Gentlemen all, — alas, what shall I say?   190
My credit now stands on such slippery ground
That one of two bad ways you must conceit me,
Either a coward or a flatterer.
That I did love thee, Cæsar, O, 'tis true;
If then thy spirit look upon us now,   195
Shall it not grieve thee dearer than thy death,
To see thy Antony making his peace,
Shaking the bloody fingers of thy foes,
Most noble! in the presence of thy corse?
Had I as many eyes as thou hast wounds,   200
Weeping as fast as they stream forth thy blood,
It would become me better than to close
In terms of friendship with thine enemies.
Pardon me, Julius! Here wast thou bay'd, brave
    hart;
Here didst thou fall; and here thy hunters stand, 205
Sign'd in thy spoil, and crimson'd in thy lethe.
O world, thou wast the forest to this hart;
And this, indeed, O world, the heart of thee.
How like a deer, strucken by many princes,
Dost thou here lie!   210
    Cas. Mark Antony, —
    Ant.   Pardon me, Caius Cassius!
The enemies of Cæsar shall say this;
Then, in a friend, it is cold modesty.
    Cas. I blame you not for praising Cæsar so;
But what compact mean you to have with us?   215
Will you be prick'd in number of our friends;
Or shall we on, and not depend on you?
    Ant. Therefore I took your hands, but was, in-
    deed,
Sway'd from the point, by looking down on Cæsar.
Friends am I with you all and love you all,   220
Upon this hope, that you shall give me reasons
Why and wherein Cæsar was dangerous.
    Bru. Or else were this a savage spectacle.

Our reasons are so full of good regard
That were you, Antony, the son of Cæsar,   225
You should be satisfied.
    Ant.   That's all I seek;
And am, moreover, suitor that I may
Produce his body to the market-place
And in the pulpit, as becomes a friend,
Speak in the order of his funeral.   230
    Bru. You shall, Mark Antony.
    Cas.   Brutus, a word with you.
[*Aside to Bru.*] You know not what you do. Do
    not consent
That Antony speak in his funeral.
Know you how much the people may be mov'd
By that which he will utter?
    Bru.   By your pardon. 235
I will myself into the pulpit first
And show the reason of our Cæsar's death.
What Antony shall speak, I will protest
He speaks by leave and by permission,
And that we are contented Cæsar shall   240
Have all true rites and lawful ceremonies.
It shall advantage more than do us wrong.
    Cas. I know not what may fall; I like it not.
    Bru. Mark Antony, here, take you Cæsar's body.
You shall not in your funeral speech blame us, 245
But speak all good you can devise of Cæsar,
And say you do't by our permission;
Else shall you not have any hand at all
About his funeral. And you shall speak
In the same pulpit whereto I am going,   250
After my speech is ended.
    Ant.   Be it so;
I do desire no more.
    Bru. Prepare the body then, and follow us.
                                [*Exeunt all but Antony.*
    Ant. O, pardon me, thou bleeding piece of earth.
That I am meek and gentle with these butchers! 255
Thou art the ruins of the noblest man
That ever lived in the tide of times.
Woe to the hand that shed this costly blood!
Over thy wounds now do I prophesy,
Which, like dumb mouths, do ope their ruby lips 260
To beg the voice and utterance of my tongue:
A curse shall light upon the limbs of men;
Domestic fury and fierce civil strife
Shall cumber all the parts of Italy;
Blood and destruction shall be so in use   265
And dreadful objects so familiar
That mothers shall but smile when they behold
Their infants quartered with the hands of war;
All pity chok'd with custom of fell deeds;
And Cæsar's spirit, ranging for revenge,   270
With Ate by his side come hot from hell,

---

192. **conceit**: regard. 196. **dearer**: more keenly. 204. **bay'd**: brought to bay. 206. **Sign'd ... spoil**: marked with the
signs of death. **lethe**: death. 213. **modesty**: moderation. 216. **prick'd**: marked on the list. 224. **full ... regard**: worthy
of approval. 230. **order**: ceremony. 241. **true**: due. 243. **fall**: happen. 269. **fell**: cruel. 271. **Ate**: goddess of discord.

Shall in these confines with a monarch's voice
Cry "Havoc," and let slip the dogs of war,
That this foul deed shall smell above the earth
With carrion men, groaning for burial.   275

Enter Octavius' SERVANT.

You serve Octavius Cæsar, do you not?
    Serv. I do, Mark Antony.
    Ant. Cæsar did write for him to come to Rome.
    Serv. He did receive his letters, and is coming;
And bid me say to you by word of mouth —   280
O Cæsar! —   [*Seeing the body.*]
    Ant. Thy heart is big; get thee apart and weep.
Passion, I see, is catching; [for] mine eyes,
Seeing those beads of sorrow stand in thine,
Began to water.   Is thy master coming?   285
    Serv. He lies to-night within seven leagues of
        Rome.
    Ant. Post back with speed and tell him what hath
        chanc'd.
Here is a mourning Rome, a dangerous Rome,
No Rome of safety for Octavius yet;
Hie hence, and tell him so.   Yet, stay a while;   290
Thou shalt not back till I have borne this corse
Into the market-place.   There shall I try,
In my oration, how the people take
The cruel issue of these bloody men;
According to the which thou shalt discourse   295
To young Octavius of the state of things.
Lend me your hand.   [*Exeunt [with Cæsar's body].*]

[SCENE II.   *The Forum.*]

Enter BRUTUS *and* CASSIUS, *with the* PLEBEIANS.

    Pleb. We will be satisfied!   Let us be satisfied!
    Bru. Then follow me, and give me audience,
        friends.
Cassius, go you into the other street,
And part the numbers.
Those that will hear me speak, let 'em stay here;   5
Those that will follow Cassius, go with him;
And public reasons shall be rendered
Of Cæsar's death.
    1. Pleb.   I will hear Brutus speak.
    2. Pleb. I will hear Cassius; and compare their
        reasons
When severally we hear them rendered.   10
    [*Exit Cassius, with some of the Plebeians.*]
        Brutus goes into the pulpit.
    3. Pleb. The noble Brutus is ascended; silence!
    Bru. Be patient till the last.
    Romans, countrymen and lovers! hear me for
my cause, and be silent, that you may hear; believe

me for mine honour, and have respect to mine   15
honour, that you may believe; censure me in your
wisdom, and awake your senses, that you may the
better judge.   If there be any in this assembly, any
dear friend of Cæsar's, to him I say, that Brutus'
love to Cæsar was no less than his.   If then   20
that friend demand why Brutus rose against Cæsar,
this is my answer: Not that I lov'd Cæsar less, but
that I lov'd Rome more.   Had you rather Cæsar
were living and die all slaves, than that Cæsar
were dead, to live all free men?   As Cæsar lov'd   25
me, I weep for him; as he was fortunate, I rejoice at
it; as he was valiant, I honour him; but, as he was
ambitious, I slew him.   There is tears for his love;
joy for his fortune; honour for his valour; and
death for his ambition.   Who is here so base   30
that would be a bondman?   If any, speak; for
him have I offended.   Who is here so rude that
would not be a Roman?   If any, speak; for him
have I offended.   Who is here so vile that will not
love his country?   If any, speak; for him have I
offended.   I pause for a reply.   37
    All. None, Brutus, none.
    Bru. Then none have I offended.   I have done
no more to Cæsar than you shall do to Brutus.
The question of his death is enroll'd in the Capitol;
his glory not extenuated, wherein he was worthy,
nor his offences enforc'd, for which he suffered
death.   44

Enter ANTONY [*and others*], *with Cæsar's body.*

Here comes his body, mourn'd by Mark Antony;
who, though he had no hand in his death, shall
receive the benefit of his dying, a place in the commonwealth; as which of you shall not?   With this
I depart, that, as I slew my best lover for the good
of Rome, I have the same dagger for myself, when
it shall please my country to need my death.   52
    All. Live, Brutus! live, live!
    1. Pleb. Bring him with triumph home unto his
        house.
    2. Pleb. Give him a statue with his ancestors.   55
    3. Pleb. Let him be Cæsar.
    4. Pleb.   Cæsar's better parts
Shall be crown'd in Brutus.
    1. Pleb.   We'll bring him to his house
With shouts and clamours.
    Bru.   My countrymen, —
    2. Pleb. Peace, silence!   Brutus speaks.
    1. Pleb.   Peace, ho!
    Bru. Good countrymen, let me depart alone,   60
And, for my sake, stay here with Antony.
Do grace to Cæsar's corpse, and grace his speech
Tending to Cæsar's glories, which Mark Antony,

---

272. **confines**: regions.   273. **"Havoc"**: No quarter!   283. **Passion**: grief.   [for] F₂.   *from* F₁.   294. **issue**: deed.
    Sc. ii, 13. **lovers**: dear friends.   16. **censure**: judge.   32. **rude**: barbarous.   41. **question … enroll'd**: justification for his
death is on record.   43. **enforc'd**: exaggerated.   56. **parts**: qualities.

By our permission, is allow'd to make.
I do entreat you, not a man depart   65
Save I alone, till Antony have spoke.   [*Exit.*
1. Pleb. Stay, ho! and let us hear Mark Antony,
3. Pleb. Let him go up into the public chair;
We'll hear him.   Noble Antony, go up.   69
Ant. For Brutus' sake, I am beholding to you.
     [*Goes into the pulpit.*]
4. Pleb. What does he say of Brutus?
3. Pleb.   He says, for Brutus' sake
He finds himself beholding to us all.
4. Pleb. 'Twere best he speak no harm of Brutus
     here.
1. Pleb. This Cæsar was a tyrant.
3. Pleb.   Nay, that's certain:
We are blest that Rome is rid of him.   75
2. Pleb. Peace! let us hear what Antony can say.
Ant. You gentle Romans, —
All.   Peace, ho! let us hear him.
Ant. Friends, Romans, countrymen, lend me
     your ears!
I come to bury Cæsar, not to praise him.
The evil that men do lives after them,   80
The good is oft interred with their bones;
So let it be with Cæsar.   The noble Brutus
Hath told you Cæsar was ambitious;
If it were so, it was a grievous fault,
And grievously hath Cæsar answer'd it.   85
Here, under leave of Brutus and the rest —
For Brutus is an honourable man;
So are they all, all honourable men —
Come I to speak in Cæsar's funeral.
He was my friend, faithful and just to me;   90
But Brutus says he was ambitious,
And Brutus is an honourable man.
He hath brought many captives home to Rome,
Whose ransoms did the general coffers fill;
Did this in Cæsar seem ambitious?   95
When that the poor have cried, Cæsar hath wept;
Ambition should be made of sterner stuff:
Yet Brutus says he was ambitious,
And Brutus is an honourable man.
You all did see that on the Lupercal   100
I thrice presented him a kingly crown,
Which he did thrice refuse.   Was this ambition?
Yet Brutus says he was ambitious,
And, sure, he is an honourable man.
I speak not to disprove what Brutus spoke,   105
But here I am to speak what I do know.
You all did love him once, not without cause;
What cause withholds you then to mourn for
     him?
O judgement! thou art fled to brutish beasts,
And men have lost their reason.   Bear with me;
My heart is in the coffin there with Cæsar,   111
And I must pause till it come back to me.

1. Pleb. Methinks there is much reason in his
     sayings.
2. Pleb. If thou consider rightly of the matter,
Cæsar has had great wrong.
3. Pleb.   Has he, masters?   115
I fear there will a worse come in his place.
4. Pleb. Mark'd ye his words?   He would not
     take the crown;
Therefore 'tis certain he was not ambitious.
1. Pleb. If it be found so, some will dear abide it.
2. Pleb. Poor soul! his eyes are red as fire with
     weeping.   120
3. Pleb. There's not a nobler man in Rome than
     Antony.
4. Pleb. Now mark him, he begins again to speak.
Ant. But yesterday the word of Cæsar might
Have stood against the world; now lies he there,
And none so poor to do him reverence.   125
O masters, if I were dispos'd to stir
Your hearts and minds to mutiny and rage,
I should do Brutus wrong, and Cassius wrong,
Who, you all know, are honourable men.
I will not do them wrong; I rather choose   130
To wrong the dead, to wrong myself and you,
Than I will wrong such honourable men.
But here's a parchment with the seal of Cæsar;
I found it in his closet; 'tis his will.
Let but the commons hear this testament —   135
Which, pardon me, I do not mean to read —
And they would go and kiss dead Cæsar's wounds
And dip their napkins in his sacred blood,
Yea, beg a hair of him for memory,
And, dying, mention it within their wills,   140
Bequeathing it as a rich legacy
Unto their issue.
4. Pleb. We'll hear the will.   Read it, Mark
     Antony.
All. The will, the will! we will hear Cæsar's will.
Ant. Have patience, gentle friends, I must not
     read it;   145
It is not meet you know how Cæsar lov'd you.
You are not wood, you are not stones, but men;
And, being men, hearing the will of Cæsar,
It will inflame you, it will make you mad.
'Tis good you know not that you are his heirs;   150
For, if you should, O, what would come of it!
4. Pleb. Read the will; we'll hear it, Antony.
You shall read us the will, Cæsar's will.
Ant. Will you be patient?   Will you stay a while?
I have o'ershot myself to tell you of it.   155
I fear I wrong the honourable men
Whose daggers have stabb'd Cæsar; I do fear it.
4. Pleb. They were traitors; honourable men!
All. The will! the testament!
2. Pleb. They were villains, murderers.   The
     will!   Read the will!   160

70. **beholding:** indebted.   134. **closet:** chamber.   135. **commons:** common people.   138. **napkins:** handkerchiefs.

Ant. You will compel me, then, to read the will?
Then make a ring about the corpse of Cæsar,
And let me show you him that made the will.
Shall I descend? and will you give me leave?
All. Come down.   165
2. Pleb. Descend.
3. Pleb. You shall have leave.
    [*Antony comes down from the pulpit.*]
4. Pleb. A ring; stand round.
1. Pleb. Stand from the hearse, stand from the
    body.
2. Pleb. Room for Antony, most noble Antony.
Ant. Nay, press not so upon me; stand far off. 171
All. Stand back; room; bear back!
Ant. If you have tears, prepare to shed them now.
You all do know this mantle; I remember
The first time ever Cæsar put it on.   175
'Twas on a summer's evening, in his tent,
That day he overcame the Nervii.
Look, in this place ran Cassius' dagger through;
See what a rent the envious Casca made;
Through this the well-beloved Brutus stabb'd,   180
And as he pluck'd his cursed steel away,
Mark how the blood of Cæsar followed it,
As rushing out of doors to be resolv'd
If Brutus so unkindly knock'd or no;
For Brutus, as you know, was Cæsar's angel.   185
Judge, O you gods, how dearly Cæsar lov'd him!
This was the most unkindest cut of all;
For when the noble Cæsar saw him stab,
Ingratitude, more strong than traitors' arms,
Quite vanquish'd him.   Then burst his mighty
    heart;   190
And, in his mantle muffling up his face,
Even at the base of Pompey's statuë,
Which all the while ran blood, great Cæsar fell.
O, what a fall was there, my countrymen!
Then I, and you, and all of us fell down,   195
Whilst bloody treason flourish'd over us.
O, now you weep, and I perceive you feel
The dint of pity.   These are gracious drops.
Kind souls, what, weep you when you but behold
Our Cæsar's vesture wounded? Look you here: 200
    [*Lifting Cæsar's mantle.*]
Here is himself, marr'd, as you see, with traitors.
1. Pleb. O piteous spectacle!
2. Pleb. O noble Cæsar!
3. Pleb. O woeful day!
4. Pleb. O traitors, villains!   205
1. Pleb. O most bloody sight!
2. Pleb. We will be reveng'd!
[All.]   Revenge! About!
Seek! Burn! Fire! Kill! Slay!
Let not a traitor live!
Ant.   Stay, countrymen.   210

1. Pleb. Peace there! hear the noble Antony.
2. Pleb. We'll hear him, we'll follow him, we'll
die with him.
Ant. Good friends, sweet friends, let me not stir
    you up
To such a sudden flood of mutiny.   215
They that have done this deed are honourable.
What private griefs they have, alas, I know not,
That made them do it; they are wise and honourable
And will, no doubt, with reasons answer you.
I come not, friends, to steal away your hearts.   220
I am no orator, as Brutus is;
But, as you know me all, a plain blunt man
That love my friend; and that they know full well
That gave me public leave to speak of him;
For I have neither [wit], nor words, nor worth,   225
Action, nor utterance, nor the power of speech
To stir men's blood; I only speak right on.
I tell you that which you yourselves do know;
Show you sweet Cæsar's wounds, poor, poor, dumb
    mouths,
And bid them speak for me.   But were I Brutus,   230
And Brutus Antony, there were an Antony
Would ruffle up your spirits, and put a tongue
In every wound of Cæsar, that should move
The stones of Rome to rise and mutiny.
All. We'll mutiny.   235
1. Pleb. We'll burn the house of Brutus.
3. Pleb. Away, then! come, seek the conspirators.
Ant. Yet hear me, countrymen; yet hear me
    speak.
All. Peace, ho! hear Antony, most noble An-
    tony!
Ant. Why, friends, you go to do you know not
    what.   240
Wherein hath Cæsar thus deserv'd your loves?
Alas, you know not; I must tell you, then.
You have forgot the will I told you of.
All. Most true.   The will!   Let's stay and hear
    the will.
Ant. Here is the will, and under Cæsar's seal.   245
To every Roman citizen he gives,
To every several man, seventy-five drachmas.
2. Pleb. Most noble Cæsar! We'll revenge his
    death.
3. Pleb. O Royal Cæsar!
Ant. Hear me with patience.   250
All. Peace, ho!
Ant. Moreover, he hath left you all his walks,
His private arbours and new-planted orchards,
On this side Tiber; he hath left them you
And to your heirs forever, common pleasures,   255
To walk abroad and recreate yourselves.
Here was a Cæsar!   When comes such another?
1. Pleb. Never, never!   Come, away, away!

169. **hearse:** bier.   177. **Nervii:** a Belgian tribe.   208. *[All.]* (Grant White).   2 F.   225. **[wit]** F$_2$: intellectual capacity.
writ F$_1$.   226. **utterance:** eloquence.   232. **ruffle:** rouse.   255. **pleasures:** pleasure grounds.

We'll burn his body in the holy place,
And with the brands fire the traitors' houses.   260
Take up the body.
 2. Pleb. Go fetch fire.
 3. Pleb. Pluck down benches.
 4. Pleb. Pluck down forms, windows, anything.
     [*Exeunt Plebeians* [*with the body*].
 Ant. Now let it work. Mischief, thou art afoot,
Take thou what course thou wilt!   266

    Enter a SERVANT.

       How now, fellow?
 Serv. Sir, Octavius is already come to Rome.
 Ant. Where is he?
 Serv. He and Lepidus are at Cæsar's house.
 Ant. And thither will I straight to visit him; 270
He comes upon a wish. Fortune is merry,
And in this mood will give us anything.
 Serv. I heard him say, Brutus and Cassius
Are rid like madmen through the gates of Rome.
 Ant. Belike they had some notice of the people, 275
How I had mov'd them. Bring me to Octavius.
         [*Exeunt.*

    [SCENE III. *A street.*]

Enter CINNA *the poet, and after him the* PLEBEIANS.
 Cin. I dreamt to-night that I did feast with
  Cæsar,
And things unluckily charge my fantasy.
I have no will to wander forth of doors,
Yet something leads me forth.
 1. Pleb. What is your name?   5
 2. Pleb. Whither are you going?
 3. Pleb. Where do you dwell?
 4. Pleb. Are you a married man or a bachelor?
 2. Pleb. Answer every man directly.   10
 1. Pleb. Ay, and briefly.
 4. Pleb. Ay, and wisely.
 3. Pleb. Ay, and truly, you were best.
 Cin. What is my name? Whither am I going?
Where do I dwell? Am I a married man or a   15
bachelor? Then, to answer every man directly and
briefly, wisely and truly: wisely I say, I am a bachelor.
 2. Pleb. That's as much as to say, they are fools
that marry. You'll bear me a bang for that, I fear.
Proceed; directly.   21
 Cin. Directly, I am going to Cæsar's funeral.
 1. Pleb. As a friend or an enemy?
 Cin. As a friend.
 2. Pleb. That matter is answered directly.   25
 4. Pleb. For your dwelling, — briefly.
 Cin. Briefly, I dwell by the Capitol.
 3. Pleb. Your name, sir, truly.

 Cin. Truly, my name is Cinna.   30
 1. Pleb. Tear him to pieces; he's a conspirator.
 Cin. I am Cinna the poet, I am Cinna the poet.
 4. Pleb. Tear him for his bad verses, tear him for
  his bad verses.   35
 Cin. I am not Cinna the conspirator.
 4. Pleb. It is no matter, his name's Cinna. Pluck
but his name out of his heart, and turn him going. 39
 3. Pleb. Tear him, tear him! Come, brands,
ho! fire-brands! To Brutus', to Cassius'; burn
all! Some to Decius' house, and some to Casca's;
some to Ligarius'. Away, go!   [*Exeunt.*

     ACT IV

   [SCENE I. *A house in Rome.*]

ANTONY, OCTAVIUS, *and* LEPIDUS [*seated at a table*].
 Ant. These many, then, shall die; their names
  are prick'd.
 Oct. Your brother too must die; consent you,
  Lepidus?
 Lep. I do consent, —
 Oct.   Prick him down, Antony.
 Lep. Upon condition Publius shall not live,
Who is your sister's son, Mark Antony.   5
 Ant. He shall not live; look, with a spot I damn
  him.
But, Lepidus, go you to Cæsar's house;
Fetch the will hither, and we shall determine
How to cut off some charge in legacies.
 Lep. What, shall I find you here?   10
 Oct. Or here, or at the Capitol. [*Exit Lepidus.*
 Ant. This is a slight unmeritable man,
Meet to be sent on errands; is it fit,
The threefold world divided, he should stand
One of the three to share it?
 Oct.   So you thought him;
And took his voice who should be prick'd to die, 16
In our black sentence and proscription.
 Ant. Octavius, I have seen more days than you;
And though we lay these honours on this man
To ease ourselves of divers sland'rous loads,   20
He shall but bear them as the ass bears gold,
To groan and sweat under the business,
Either led or driven, as we point the way;
And having brought our treasure where we will,
Then take we down his load, and turn him off, 25
Like to the empty ass, to shake his ears
And graze in commons.
 Oct.   You may do your will;
But he's a tried and valiant soldier.
 Ant. So is my horse, Octavius; and for that
I do appoint him store of provender.   30
It is a creature that I teach to fight,

  Sc. iii, 2. **unluckily**: ominously. 20. **bear ... bang**: get a blow from me.
  Act IV, sc. i, 9. **charge**: cost. 20. **sland'rous loads**: burdens of slander. 26. **empty**: unburdened.

To wind, to stop, to run directly on,
His corporal motion govern'd by my spirit.
And, in some taste, is Lepidus but so;
He must be taught and train'd and bid go forth;   35
A barren-spirited fellow; one that feeds
On abjects, orts, and imitations,
Which, out of use and stal'd by other men,
Begin his fashion. Do not talk of him
But as a property. And now, Octavius,   40
Listen great things. Brutus and Cassius
Are levying powers; we must straight make
    head;
Therefore let our alliance be combin'd,
Our best friends made, our means stretch'd;
And let us presently go sit in council   45
How covert matters may be best disclos'd
And open perils surest answered.
    Oct. Let us do so; for we are at the stake
And bay'd about with many enemies;
And some that smile have in their hearts, I fear,   50
Millions of mischiefs.   *[Exeunt.*

        [SCENE II. *Camp near Sardis. Before
                    Brutus's tent.*]

Drum. Enter BRUTUS, LUCILIUS, [LUCIUS,] *and
    the army. Titinius and* PINDARUS *meet them.*

    Bru. Stand, ho!
    Lucil. Give the word, ho! and stand.
    Bru. What now, Lucilius! is Cassius near?
    Lucil. He is at hand; and Pindarus is come
To do you salutation from his master.   5
    Bru. He greets me well. Your master, Pindarus,
In his own change, or by ill officers,
Hath given me some worthy cause to wish
Things done undone; but, if he be at hand,
I shall be satisfied.
    Pin.   I do not doubt   10
But that my noble master will appear
Such as he is, full of regard and honour.
    Bru. He is not doubted. A word, Lucilius:
How he receiv'd you let me be resolv'd.
    Lucil. With courtesy and with respect enough;
But not with such familiar instances,   16
Nor with such free and friendly conference,
As he hath us'd of old.
    Bru.   Thou hast describ'd
A hot friend cooling. Ever note, Lucilius,
When love begins to sicken and decay   20
It useth an enforced ceremony.
There are no tricks in plain and simple faith;
But hollow men, like horses hot at hand,

Make gallant show and promise of their mettle;
                            [*Low march within.*
But when they should endure the bloody spur   25
They fall their crests, and, like deceitful jades,
Sink in the trial. Comes his army on?
    Lucil. They mean this night in Sardis to be quar-
        ter'd.
The greater part, the horse in general,
Are come with Cassius.

        Enter CASSIUS *and his Powers.*

    Bru.   Hark! he is arriv'd.   30
March gently on to meet him.
    Cas. Stand, ho!
    Bru. Stand, ho! Speak the word along.
    [*1. Sol.*] Stand!
    [*2. Sol.*] Stand!   35
    [*3. Sol.*] Stand!
    Cas. Most noble brother, you have done me wrong.
    Bru. Judge me, you gods! wrong I mine enemies?
And, if not so, how should I wrong a brother?
    Cas. Brutus, this sober form of yours hides
        wrongs;   40
And when you do them —
    Bru.   Cassius, be content;
Speak your griefs softly; I do know you well.
Before the eyes of both our armies here,
Which should perceive nothing but love from us,
Let us not wrangle. Bid them move away;   45
Then in my tent, Cassius, enlarge your griefs,
And I will give you audience.
    Cas.   Pindarus,
Bid our commanders lead their charges off
A little from this ground.   49
    Bru. [Lucius], do you the like; and let no man
Come to our tent till we have done our conference.
[Lucilius] and Titinius, guard our door.   [*Exeunt.*

        [SCENE III. *Brutus's tent.*]

        [*Enter*] BRUTUS *and* CASSIUS.

    Cas. That you have wrong'd me doth appear in
        this:
You have condemn'd and noted Lucius Pella
For taking bribes here of the Sardians;
Wherein my letters, praying on his side,
Because I knew the man was slighted off, —   5
    Bru. You wrong'd yourself to write in such a case.
    Cas. In such a time as this it is not meet
That every nice offence should bear his comment.
    Bru. Let me tell you, Cassius, you yourself
Are much condemn'd to have an itching palm,   10

32. **wind:** turn. 34. **taste:** degree. 40. **property:** tool. 42. **make head:** raise an army. 44. **our…stretch'd.** F₂ reads *and our best means stretch'd out.* 47. **answered:** met.
    Sc. ii, 16. **familiar instances:** tokens of intimacy. 23. **hollow:** insincere. **hot at hand:** fiery when held back. 26. **fall:** droop. 31. **gently:** slowly. 46. **enlarge:** express fully. 50. [Lucius] (Craik). *Lucilius* F. 52. [Lucilius] (Craik). *Let Lucius* F.
    Sc. iii, 2. **noted:** branded with disgrace. 8. **nice:** trivial. **bear his comment:** receive attention. 10. **to have:** for having.

To sell and mart your offices for gold
To undeservers.
   Cas.   I an itching palm!
You know that you are Brutus that speaks this,
Or, by the gods, this speech were else your last.
   Bru. The name of Cassius honours this corrup-
    tion,   15
And Chastisement doth therefore hide his head.
   Cas. Chastisement!
   Bru. Remember March, the ides of March re-
    member:
Did not great Julius bleed for justice' sake?
What villain touch'd his body, that did stab   20
And not for justice? What, shall one of us,
That struck the foremost man of all this world
But for supporting robbers, shall we now
Contaminate our fingers with base bribes,
And sell the mighty space of our large honours 25
For so much trash as may be grasped thus?
I had rather be a dog, and bay the moon,
Than such a Roman.
   Cas.   Brutus, bait not me;
I'll not endure it. You forget yourself
To hedge me in. I am a soldier, I,   30
Older in practice, abler than yourself
To make conditions.
   Bru.   Go to; you are not, Cassius.
   Cas. I am.
   Bru. I say you are not.
   Cas. Urge me no more, I shall forget myself; 35
Have mind upon your health, tempt me no farther.
   Bru. Away, slight man!
   Cas. Is't possible?
   Bru.   Hear me, for I will speak.
Must I give way and room to your rash choler?
Shall I be frighted when a madman stares?   40
   Cas. O ye gods, ye gods! must I endure all this?
   Bru. All this! ay, more. Fret till your proud
    heart break;
Go show your slaves how choleric you are,
And make your bondmen tremble. Must I budge?
Must I observe you? Must I stand and crouch 45
Under your testy humour? By the gods,
You shall digest the venom of your spleen,
Though it do split you; for, from this day forth,
I'll use you for my mirth, yea, for my laughter,
When you are waspish.
   Cas.   Is it come to this? 50
   Bru. You say you are a better soldier:
Let it appear so; make your vaunting true,
And it shall please me well. For mine own part,
I shall be glad to learn of noble men.
   Cas. You wrong me every way; you wrong me,
    Brutus;   55

I said an elder soldier, not a better.
Did I say "better"?
   Bru.   If you did, I care not.
   Cas. When Cæsar liv'd, he durst not thus have
    mov'd me.
   Bru. Peace, peace! you durst not so have
    tempted him.
   Cas. I durst not!   60
   Bru. No.
   Cas. What, durst not tempt him!
   Bru.   For your life you durst not.
   Cas. Do not presume too much upon my love;
I may do that I shall be sorry for.
   Bru. You have done that you should be sorry for.
There is no terror, Cassius, in your threats, 66
For I am arm'd so strong in honesty
That they pass by me as the idle wind,
Which I respect not. I did send to you
For certain sums of gold, which you deni'd me; 70
For I can raise no money by vile means. —
By heaven, I had rather coin my heart
And drop my blood for drachmas than to wring
From the hard hands of peasants their vile trash
By any indirection. — I did send   75
To you for gold to pay my legions,
Which you deni'd me. Was that done like Cassius?
Should I have answer'd Caius Cassius so?
When Marcus Brutus grows so covetous
To lock such rascal counters from his friends, 80
Be ready, gods, with all your thunderbolts;
Dash him to pieces!
   Cas.   I deni'd you not.
   Bru. You did.
   Cas. I did not. He was but a fool that brought
My answer back. Brutus hath riv'd my heart. 85
A friend should bear his friend's infirmities,
But Brutus makes mine greater than they are.
   Bru. I do not, till you practise them on me.
   Cas. You love me not.
   Bru.   I do not like your faults.
   Cas. A friendly eye could never see such faults. 90
   Bru. A flatterer's would not, though they do
    appear
As huge as high Olympus.
   Cas. Come, Antony, and young Octavius, come,
Revenge yourselves alone on Cassius,
For Cassius is aweary of the world; 95
Hated by one he loves; brav'd by his brother;
Check'd like a bondman; all his faults observ'd,
Set in a note-book, learn'd and conn'd by rote
To cast into my teeth. O, I could weep
My spirit from mine eyes! There is my dagger, 100
And here my naked breast; within, a heart
Dearer than [Plutus'] mine, richer than gold.

---

11. **mart:** market. 30. **hedge me in:** curb me. 32. **make conditions:** manage affairs. 35. **Urge:** press. 36. **tempt:** try. 45. **observe:** be obsequious to. 75. **indirection:** crooked means. 80. **rascal counters:** worthless coins. 85. **riv'd:** split, broken. 97. **Check'd:** rebuked. 102. **[Plutus']** (Pope): the god of wealth. *Pluto's* F.

If that thou be'st a Roman, take it forth;
I, that deni'd thee gold, will give my heart.
Strike, as thou didst at Cæsar; for, I know,   105
When thou didst hate him worst, thou lov'dst him
    better
Than ever thou lov'dst Cassius.
   Bru.   Sheathe your dagger.
Be angry when you will, it shall have scope.
Do what you will, dishonour shall be humour.
O Cassius, you are yoked with a lamb   110
That carries anger as the flint bears fire;
Who, much enforced, shows a hasty spark,
And straight is cold again.
   Cas.   Hath Cassius liv'd
To be but mirth and laughter to his Brutus,
When grief and blood ill-temper'd vexeth him?   115
   Bru. When I spoke that, I was ill-temper'd too.
   Cas. Do you confess so much? Give me your
    hand.
   Bru. And my heart too.
   Cas.   O Brutus!
   Bru.   What's the matter?
   Cas. Have not you love enough to bear with me,
When that rash humour which my mother gave me
Makes me forgetful?
   Bru.   Yes, Cassius; and, from henceforth,
When you are over earnest with your Brutus,   122
He'll think your mother chides, and leave you so.
   Poet. [*Within.*] Let me go in to see the generals.
There is some grudge between 'em; 'tis not meet
They be alone.   126
   Lucil. [*Within.*] You shall not come to them.
   Poet. [*Within.*] Nothing but death shall stay me.

   Enter POET [*followed by* LUCILIUS, TITINIUS,*
            and* LUCIUS].

   Cas. How now! what's the matter?
   Poet. For shame, you generals! what do you
    mean?   130
Love, and be friends, as two such men should be;
For I have seen more years, I'm sure, than ye.
   Cas. Ha, ha! how vilely doth this cynic rhyme!
   Bru. Get you hence, sirrah; saucy fellow, hence!
   Cas. Bear with him, Brutus; 'tis his fashion.   135
   Bru. I'll know his humour, when he knows his
    time.
What should the wars do with these jigging fools?
Companion, hence!
   Cas.   Away, away, be gone!
                       [*Exit Poet.*
   Bru. Lucilius and Titinius, bid the commanders
Prepare to lodge their companies to-night.   140

   Cas. And come yourselves, and bring Messala
    with you
Immediately to us.
                [*Exeunt Lucilius and Titinius.*]
   Bru.   Lucius, a bowl of wine!
                          [*Exit Lucius.*]
   Cas. I did not think you could have been so
    angry.
   Bru. O Cassius, I am sick of many griefs.
   Cas. Of your philosophy you make no use   145
If you give place to accidental evils.
   Bru. No man bears sorrow better. Portia is
    dead.
   Cas. Ha! Portia!
   Bru. She is dead.
   Cas. How scap'd I killing when I cross'd you
    so?   150
O insupportable and touching loss!
Upon what sickness?
   Bru.   Impatient of my absence,
And grief that young Octavius with Mark Antony
Have made themselves so strong, — for with her
    death
That tidings came, — with this she fell distract,   155
And, her attendants absent, swallow'd fire.
   Cas. And died so?
   Bru.   Even so.
   Cas.   O ye immortal gods!

   Re-enter Boy [Lucius], *with wine and tapers.*

   Bru. Speak no more of her. Give me a bowl of
    wine.
In this I bury all unkindness, Cassius.   [*Drinks.*
   Cas. My heart is thirsty for that noble pledge.
Fill, Lucius, till the wine o'erswell the cup;   161
I cannot drink too much of Brutus' love. [*Drinks.*]

   Re-enter TITINIUS, *with* MESSALA.

   Bru. Come in, Titinius!   [*Exit Lucius.*]
                  Welcome, good Messala.
Now sit we close about this taper here,
And call in question our necessities.   165
   Cas. Portia, art thou gone?
   Bru.   No more, I pray you.
Messala, I have here received letters
That young Octavius and Mark Antony
Come down upon us with a mighty power,
Bending their expedition toward Philippi.   170
   Mes. Myself have letters of the self-same [tenour].
   Bru. With what addition?
   Mes. That by proscription and bills of outlawry,

---

109. **dishonour...humour:** I shall count your insults merely as caprice.   110. **yoked with:** like.   115. **blood ill-temper'd:** a bad disposition.   123. **leave you so:** stop at that.   133. **cynic:** rude fellow.   136. **I'll...time:** I'll countenance his eccentricity when he chooses the proper time for it.   138. **Companion:** fellow.   146. **give...evils:** yield to accidents.   154. **her death:** news of her death.   156. **fire.** Plutarch says "hot, burning coals."   165. **call in question:** discuss.   171. **[tenour]** (Theobald). *Tenure* F.

Octavius, Antony, and Lepidus
Have put to death an hundred senators.   175
  Bru. Therein our letters do not well agree;
Mine speak of seventy senators that died
By their proscriptions, Cicero being one.
  Cas. Cicero one!
  Mes.   Cicero is dead,
And by that order of proscription.   180
Had you your letters from your wife, my lord?
  Bru. No, Messala.
  Mes. Nor nothing in your letters writ of her?
  Bru. Nothing, Messala.
  Mes.   That, methinks, is strange.
  Bru. Why ask you? Hear you aught of her in
    yours?   185
  Mes. No, my lord.
  Bru. Now, as you are a Roman, tell me true.
  Mes. Then like a Roman bear the truth I tell:
For certain she is dead, and by strange manner.
  Bru. Why, farewell, Portia. We must die,
    Messala.   190
With meditating that she must die once,
I have the patience to endure it now.
  Mes. Even so great men great losses should
    endure.
  Cas. I have as much of this in art as you,
But yet my nature could not bear it so.   195
  Bru. Well, to our work alive. What do you
    think
Of marching to Philippi presently?
  Cas. I do not think it good.
  Bru.   Your reason?
  Cas.   This it is:
'Tis better that the enemy seek us.
So shall he waste his means, weary his soldiers,   200
Doing himself offence; whilst we, lying still,
Are full of rest, defence, and nimbleness.
  Bru. Good reasons must, of force, give place to
    better.
The people 'twixt Philippi and this ground
Do stand but in a forc'd affection,   205
For they have grudg'd us contribution.
The enemy, marching along by them,
By them shall make a fuller number up,
Come on refresh'd, new-added, and encourag'd;
From which advantage shall we cut him off   210
If at Philippi we do face him there,
These people at our back.
  Cas.   Hear me, good brother.
  Bru. Under your pardon. You must note
    beside
That we have tried the utmost of our friends;
Our legions are brim-full, our cause is ripe.   215

The enemy increaseth every day;
We, at the height, are ready to decline.
There is a tide in the affairs of men
Which, taken at the flood, leads on to fortune;
Omitted, all the voyage of their life   220
Is bound in shallows and in miseries.
On such a full sea are we now afloat,
And we must take the current when it serves
Or lose our ventures.
  Cas.   Then, with your will, go on.
We'll along ourselves, and meet them at Philippi.
  Bru. The deep of night is crept upon our talk   226
And nature must obey necessity,
Which we will niggard with a little rest.
There is no more to say?
  Cas.   No more. Good-night.
Early to-morrow will we rise, and hence.   230
  Bru. Lucius! (*Re-enter Lucius.*) My gown.
    [*Exit Lucius.*] Farewell, good Messala;
Good-night, Titinius. Noble, noble Cassius,
Good-night, and good repose.
  Cas.   O my dear brother!
This was an ill beginning of the night.
Never come such division 'tween our souls!   235
Let it not, Brutus.

Re-enter LUCIUS, *with the gown.*
  Bru.   Everything is well.
  Cas. Good-night, my lord.
  Bru.   Good-night, good brother.
  Tit. Mes. Good-night, Lord Brutus.
  Bru.   Farewell, every one.
    [*Exeunt [all but Brutus and Lucius].*
Give me the gown. Where is thy instrument?
  Luc. Here in the tent.
  Bru.   What, thou speak'st drowsily?   240
Poor knave, I blame thee not; thou art o'erwatch'd.
Call [Claudius] and some other of my men;
I'll have them sleep on cushions in my tent.
  Luc. [Varro] and [Claudius]!

Enter VARRO *and* CLAUDIUS.
  Var. Calls my lord?   245
  Bru. I pray you, sirs, lie in my tent and sleep;
It may be I shall raise you by and by
On business to my brother Cassius.
  Var. So please you, we will stand and watch your
    pleasure.
  Bru. I will not have it so: lie down, good sirs;   250
It may be I shall otherwise bethink me.
    [*Varro and Claudius lie down.*
Look, Lucius, here's the book I sought for so;
I put it in the pocket of my gown.

---

184. **Nothing, Messala.** To explain away this lie by Brutus, it has been suggested that ll. 147 ff. are a later addition.
192. **patience:** fortitude. 194. **art:** philosophic theory. 209. **new-added:** reinforced. 224. **with your will:** as you wish.
228. **niggard:** submit to sparingly. 241. **knave:** boy. **o'er-watch'd:** worn out by keeping awake. 242. **[Claudius]** (Rowe).
Claudio F. So in subsequent lines. 244. **[Varro]** (Rowe). *Varrus* F.

Luc. I was sure your lordship did not give it me.
Bru. Bear with me, good boy, I am much for-
    getful.   255
Canst thou hold up thy heavy eyes a while,
And touch thy instrument a strain or two?
  Luc. Ay, my lord, an't please you.
  Bru.   It does, my boy.
I trouble thee too much, but thou art willing.
  Luc. It is my duty, sir.   260
  Bru. I should not urge thy duty past thy might;
I know young bloods look for a time of rest.
  Luc. I have slept, my lord, already.
  Bru. It was well done; and thou shalt sleep
    again;
I will not hold thee long. If I do live,   265
I will be good to thee.   [*Music, and a song.*
This is a sleepy tune. O murd'rous slumber,
Lay'st thou thy leaden mace upon my boy,
That plays thee music? Gentle knave, good-night;
I will not do thee so much wrong to wake thee.   270
If thou dost nod, thou break'st thy instrument.
I'll take it from thee; and, good boy, good-night.
Let me see, let me see; is not the leaf turn'd down
Where I left reading? Here it is, I think.

Enter the GHOST *of Cæsar.*

How ill this taper burns! Ha! who comes here?
I think it is the weakness of mine eyes   276
That shapes this monstrous apparition.
It comes upon me. Art thou anything?
Art thou some god, some angel, or some devil,
That mak'st my blood cold and my hair to stare? 280
Speak to me what thou art.
  Ghost. Thy evil spirit, Brutus.
  Bru.   Why com'st thou?
  Ghost. To tell thee thou shalt see me at Philippi.
  Bru. Well; then I shall see thee again?   285
  Ghost. Ay, at Philippi.
  Bru. Why, I will see thee at Philippi, then.
                       [*Exit Ghost.*]
Now I have taken heart thou vanishest.
Ill spirit, I would hold more talk with thee.
Boy, Lucius! Varro! Claudius! Sirs, awake! 290
Claudius!
  Luc. The strings, my lord, are false.
  Bru. He thinks he still is at his instrument.
Lucius, awake!
  Luc. My lord?   295
  Bru. Didst thou dream, Lucius, that thou so
    criedst out?
  Luc. My lord, I do not know that I did cry.
  Bru. Yes, that thou didst. Didst thou see any-
    thing?
  Luc. Nothing, my lord.

  Bru. Sleep again, Lucius. Sirrah Claudius! 300
Fellow thou, awake!
  Var. My lord?
  Clau. My lord?
  Bru. Why did you so cry out, sirs, in your sleep?
  Var. Clau. Did we, my lord?
  Bru.   Ay. Saw you anything? 305
  Var. No, my lord, I saw nothing.
  Clau.   Nor I, my lord.
  Bru. Go and commend me to my brother Cas-
    sius;
Bid him set on his powers betimes before,
And we will follow.
  Var. Clau.   It shall be done, my lord.
                         [*Exeunt.*

ACT V

[SCENE I. *The plains of Philippi.*]

Enter OCTAVIUS, ANTONY, *and their army.*

Oct. Now, Antony, our hopes are answered.
You said the enemy would not come down,
But keep the hills and upper regions.
It proves not so: their battles are at hand;
They mean to warn us at Philippi here,   5
Answering before we do demand of them.
  Ant. Tut, I am in their bosoms, and I know
Wherefore they do it. They could be content
To visit other places, and come down
With fearful bravery, thinking by this face   10
To fasten in our thoughts that they have courage;
But 'tis not so.

Enter a MESSENGER.

  Mess.   Prepare you, Generals.
The enemy comes on in gallant show;
Their bloody sign of battle is hung out,
And something to be done immediately.   15
  Ant. Octavius, lead your battle softly on,
Upon the left hand of the even field.
  Oct. Upon the right hand I; keep thou the left.
  Ant. Why do you cross me in this exigent?
  Oct. I do not cross you; but I will do so.   20
                         [*March.*

Drum. Enter BRUTUS, CASSIUS, *and their army*
  [LUCILIUS, TITINIUS, MESSALA, *and others*].

  Bru. They stand, and would have parley.
  Cas. Stand fast, Titinius; we must out and talk.
  Oct. Mark Antony, shall we give sign of battle?
  Ant. No, Cæsar, we will answer on their charge.
Make forth; the generals would have some words. 25
  Oct. Stir not until the signal.

---

280. **stare:** stand on end.
  Act V, sc. i, 4. **battles:** battalions. 5. **warn:** challenge. 7. **am ... bosoms:** know their secrets. 10. **With ... bravery:**
with a show of bravery, though afraid. **face:** exhibition. 19. **exigent:** emergency.

Bru. Words before blows; is it so, countrymen?
Oct. Not that we love words better, as you do.
Bru. Good words are better than bad strokes, Octavius.
Ant. In your bad strokes, Brutus, you give good words;   30
Witness the hole you made in Cæsar's heart,
Crying, "Long live! hail, Cæsar!"
Cas.   Antony,
The posture of your blows are yet unknown;
But for your words, they rob the Hybla bees,
And leave them honeyless.
Ant.   Not stingless too?   35
Bru. O, yes, and soundless too;
For you have stolen their buzzing, Antony,
And very wisely threat before you sting.
Ant. Villains, you did not so, when your vile daggers
Hack'd one another in the sides of Cæsar.   40
You show'd your teeth like apes, and fawn'd like hounds,
And bow'd like bondmen, kissing Cæsar's feet;
Whilst damned Casca, like a cur, behind
Struck Cæsar on the neck. O you flatterers!
Cas. Flatterers! Now, Brutus, thank yourself;   45
This tongue had not offended so to-day
If Cassius might have rul'd.
Oct. Come, come, the cause! If arguing make us sweat,
The proof of it will turn to redder drops.
Look!   50
I draw a sword against conspirators;
When think you that the sword goes up again?
Never, till Cæsar's three and thirty wounds
Be well aveng'd; or till another Cæsar
Have added slaughter to the sword of traitors.   55
Bru. Cæsar, thou canst not die by traitors' hands
Unless thou bring'st them with thee.
Oct.   So I hope;
I was not born to die on Brutus' sword.
Bru. O, if thou wert the noblest of thy strain,
Young man, thou couldst not die more honourable.
Cas. A peevish schoolboy, worthless of such honour,   61
Join'd with a masker and a reveller!
Ant. Old Cassius still!
Oct.   Come, Antony, away!
Defiance, traitors, hurl we in your teeth.
If you dare fight to-day, come to the field;   65
If not, when you have stomachs.
                    [*Exeunt Octavius, Antony, and army.*

Cas. Why, now, blow wind, swell billow, and swim bark!
The storm is up, and all is on the hazard.
Bru. Ho, Lucilius! hark, a word with you.
Lucil.   (*Standing forth.*)   My lord?
        [*Brutus and Lucilius converse apart.*]
Cas. Messala!
Mes. (*Standing forth.*) What says my general?   70
Cas. Messala,
This is my birthday; as this very day
Was Cassius born. Give me thy hand, Messala.
Be thou my witness that against my will,
As Pompey was, am I compell'd to set   75
Upon one battle all our liberties.
You know that I held Epicurus strong
And his opinion; now I change my mind,
And partly credit things that do presage.
Coming from Sardis, on our former ensign   80
Two mighty eagles fell, and there they perch'd,
Gorging and feeding from our soldiers' hands,
Who to Philippi here consorted us.
This morning are they fled away and gone;
And in their steads do ravens, crows, and kites   85
Fly o'er our heads and downward look on us,
As we were sickly prey. Their shadows seem
A canopy most fatal, under which
Our army lies, ready to give up the ghost.
Mes. Believe not so.
Cas.   I but believe it partly;   90
For I am fresh of spirit, and resolv'd
To meet all perils very constantly.
Bru. Even so, Lucilius.
Cas.   Now, most noble Brutus,
The gods to-day stand friendly, that we may,
Lovers in peace, lead on our days to age!   95
But since the affairs of men rest still incertain,
Let's reason with the worst that may befall.
If we do lose this battle, then is this
The very last time we shall speak together.
What are you then determined to do?   100
Bru. Even by the rule of that philosophy
By which I did blame Cato for the death
Which he did give himself,— I know not how,
But I do find it cowardly and vile,
For fear of what might fall, so to prevent   105
The time of life:— arming myself with patience
To stay the providence of some high powers
That govern us below.
Cas.   Then, if we lose this battle,
You are contented to be led in triumph
Thorough the streets of Rome?   110
Bru. No, Cassius, no. Think not, thou noble Roman,
That ever Brutus will go bound to Rome;

---

34. **Hybla:** a town in Sicily.   41. **show'd ... teeth:** grinned.   48. **cause:** i.e., to our real business.   52. **goes up:** will be sheathed.   55. **added ... to:** been slain by.   66. **stomachs:** courage.   80. **former:** foremost.   83. **consorted:** accompanied.   97. **reason with:** consider.   105-106. **prevent ... life:** anticipate death.

He bears too great a mind. But this same day
Must end that work the ides of March begun;
And whether we shall meet again I know not, 115
Therefore our everlasting farewell take.
For ever, and for ever, farewell, Cassius!
If we do meet again, why, we shall smile;
If not, why then, this parting was well made.

Cas. For ever, and for ever, farewell, Brutus! 120
If we do meet again, we'll smile indeed;
If not, 'tis true this parting was well made.

Bru. Why, then, lead on. O, that a man might
    know
The end of this day's business ere it come!
But it sufficeth that the day will end, 125
And then the end is known. Come, ho! away!
                        [Exeunt.

[SCENE II. *The same. The field of battle.*]

Alarum. Enter BRUTUS *and* MESSALA.

Bru. Ride, ride, Messala, ride, and give these
    bills
Unto the legions on the other side. *[Loud alarum.*
Let them set on at once; for I perceive
But cold demeanour in Octavius' wing,
And sudden push gives them the overthrow. 5
Ride, ride, Messala: let them all come down.
                        [Exeunt.

[SCENE III. *Another part of the field.*]

Alarums. Enter CASSIUS *and* TITINIUS.

Cas. O, look, Titinius, look, the villains fly!
Myself have to mine own turn'd enemy.
This ensign here of mine was turning back;
I slew the coward, and did take it from him.

Tit. O Cassius, Brutus gave the word too early;
Who, having some advantage on Octavius, 6
Took it too eagerly. His soldiers fell to spoil,
Whilst we by Antony are all enclos'd.

Enter PINDARUS.

Pin. Fly further off, my lord, fly further off;
Mark Antony is in your tents, my lord; 10
Fly, therefore, noble Cassius, fly far off.

Cas. This hill is far enough. Look, look, Titi-
    nius;
Are those my tents where I perceive the fire?

Tit. They are, my lord.

Cas.   Titinius, if thou lovest me
Mount thou my horse, and hide thy spurs in him 15
Till he have brought thee up to yonder troops
And here again; that I may rest assur'd
Whether yond troops are friend or enemy.

Tit. I will be here again, even with a thought.
                        [Exit.

Cas. Go, Pindarus, get higher on that hill; 20
My sight was ever thick; regard Titinius,
And tell me what thou not'st about the field.
              [Pindarus ascends the hill.]
This day I breathed first; time is come round,
And where I did begin, there shall I end;
My life is run his compass. Sirrah, what news? 25

Pin. (*Above.*) O my lord!

Cas. What news?

Pin. Titinius is enclosed round about
With horsemen, that make to him on the spur;
Yet he spurs on. Now they are almost on him. 30
Now, Titinius! Now some light. O, he lights too.
He's ta'en. (*Shout.*) And, hark! they shout for
    joy.

Cas. Come down, behold no more.
O, coward that I am, to live so long
To see my best friend ta'en before my face! 35
              [Pindarus [descends].
Come hither, sirrah.
In Parthia did I take thee prisoner;
And then I swore thee, saving of thy life,
That whatsoever I did bid thee do,
Thou shouldst attempt it. Come now, keep thine
    oath; 40
Now be a freeman; and with this good sword,
That ran through Cæsar's bowels, search this
    bosom.
Stand not to answer; here, take thou the hilts,
And, when my face is cover'd, as 'tis now,
Guide thou the sword. *[Pindarus stabs him.]* Cæsar,
    thou art reveng'd, 45
Even with the sword that kill'd thee. *[Dies.]*

Pin. So, I am free; yet would not so have been,
Durst I have done my will. O Cassius,
Far from this country Pindarus shall run,
Where never Roman shall take note of him. 50
                        [Exit.]

Re-enter TITINIUS *with* MESSALA.

Mes. It is but change, Titinius; for Octavius
Is overthrown by noble Brutus' power,
As Cassius' legions are by Antony.

Tit. These tidings will well comfort Cassius.

Mes. Where did you leave him?

Tit.   All disconsolate,
With Pindarus his bondman, on this hill. 56

Mes. Is not that he that lies upon the ground?

Tit. He lies not like the living. O my heart!

Mes. Is not that he?

Tit.   No, this was he, Messala,
But Cassius is no more. O setting sun, 60

Sc. ii, 1. bills: orders.

Sc. iii, 3. ensign: standard-bearer. 31. light: dismount. 38. swore thee: made thee swear. 51. change: exchange (of gains).

As in thy red rays thou dost sink to-night,
So in his red blood Cassius' day is set;
The sun of Rome is set! Our day is gone;
Clouds, dews, and dangers come; our deeds are
    done!
Mistrust of my success hath done this deed.   65
    Mes. Mistrust of good success hath done this
    deed.
O hateful error, melancholy's child,
Why dost thou show to the apt thoughts of men
The things that are not? O error, soon conceiv'd,
Thou never com'st unto a happy birth,   70
But kill'st the mother that engend'red thee!
    Tit. What, Pindarus! Where art thou, Pin-
    darus?
    Mes. Seek him, Titinius, whilst I go to meet
The noble Brutus, thrusting this report
Into his ears; I may say, "thrusting" it;   75
For piercing steel and darts envenomed
Shall be as welcome to the ears of Brutus
As tidings of this sight.
    Tit.   Hie you, Messala,
And I will seek for Pindarus the while.
                    [*Exit Messala.*]
Why didst thou send me forth, brave Cassius?   80
Did I not meet thy friends? and did not they
Put on my brows this wreath of victory
And bid me give it thee? Didst thou not hear their
    shouts?
Alas, thou hast misconstrued everything!
But, hold thee, take this garland on thy brow;   85
Thy Brutus bid me give it thee, and I
Will do his bidding. Brutus, come apace,
And see how I regarded Caius Cassius.
By your leave, gods! — this is a Roman's part.
Come, Cassius' sword, and find Titinius' heart.   90
                    [*Kills himself.*

Alarum. Re-enter MESSALA, *with* BRUTUS, *young*
    CATO, STRATO, VOLUMNIUS, LUCILIUS [*and
    others*].

    Bru. Where, where, Messala, doth his body lie?
    Mes. Lo, yonder, and Titinius mourning it.
    Bru. Titinius' face is upward.
    Cato.   He is slain.
    Bru. O Julius Cæsar, thou art mighty yet!
Thy spirit walks abroad, and turns our swords   95
In our own proper entrails.   [*Low alarums.*
    Cato.   Brave Titinius!
Look, whe'er he have not crown'd dead Cassius!
    Bru. Are yet two Romans living such as these?
The last of all the Romans, fare thee well!
It is impossible that ever Rome   100
Should breed thy fellow. Friends, I owe moe tears

To this dead man than you shall see me pay.
I shall find time, Cassius, I shall find time.
Come, therefore, and to [Thassos] send his body;
His funerals shall not be in our camp,   105
Lest it discomfort us. Lucilius, come;
And come, young Cato; let us to the field.
Labeo and [Flavius], set our battles on.
'Tis three o'clock; and, Romans, yet ere night
We shall try fortune in a second fight.   110
                    [*Exeunt.*

[SCENE IV. *Another part of the field.*]

Alarum. Enter BRUTUS, Messala, *young* CATO,
    LUCILIUS, *and* Flavius.

    Bru. Yet, countrymen, O, yet hold up your
    heads!
    Cato. What bastard doth not? Who will go with
    me?
I will proclaim my name about the field.
I am the son of Marcus Cato, ho!
A foe to tyrants, and my country's friend;   5
I am the son of Marcus Cato, ho!

Enter SOLDIERS, *and fight.*

    [*Bru.*] And I am Brutus, Marcus Brutus, I;
Brutus, my country's friend; know me for Brutus!
                    [*Exit.*]
    Lucil. O young and noble Cato, art thou down?
Why, now thou diest as bravely as Titinius,   10
And mayst be honour'd, being Cato's son.
    [*1.*] *Sol.* Yield, or thou diest.
    Lucil.   Only I yield to die:
There is so much that thou wilt kill me straight;
                    [*Offering money.*]
Kill Brutus, and be honour'd in his death.
    [*1.*] *Sol.* We must not. A noble prisoner!   15

Enter ANTONY.

    2. Sol. Room, ho! Tell Antony, Brutus is ta'en.
    1. Sol. I'll tell the news. Here comes the gen-
    eral.
Brutus is ta'en, Brutus is ta'en, my lord!
    Ant. Where is he?
    Lucil. Safe, Antony; Brutus is safe enough.   20
I dare assure thee that no enemy
Shall ever take alive the noble Brutus;
The gods defend him from so great a shame!
When you do find him, or alive or dead,
He will be found like Brutus, like himself.   25
    Ant. This is not Brutus, friend; but, I assure you,
A prize no less in worth. Keep this man safe,
Give him all kindness; I had rather have
Such men my friends than enemies. Go on,

65. **Mistrust:** i.e., on Cassius' part. 71. **mother:** person. 104. **[Thassos]** (Theobald). *Tharsus* F. 106. **discomfort:** dis-
courage. 108. **[Flavius]** F₂. *Flavio* F₁.
    Sc. iv, 12. **Only I yield:** I yield only.

And see whe'er Brutus be alive or dead;   30
And bring us word unto Octavius' tent
How everything is chanc'd.   [*Exeunt.*

SCENE V. [*Another part of the field.*]

Enter BRUTUS, DARDANIUS, CLITUS, STRATO,
and VOLUMNIUS.

Bru. Come, poor remains of friends, rest on this
          rock.
Cli. Statilius show'd the torchlight, but, my
          lord,
He came not back. He is or ta'en or slain.
Bru. Sit thee down, Clitus; slaying is the word,
It is a deed in fashion. Hark thee, Clitus.   5
          [*Whispering.*]
Cli. What, I, my lord? No, not for all the world.
Bru. Peace then! no words.
Cli.   I'll rather kill myself.
Bru. Hark thee, Dardanius.   [*Whispering.*]
Dar.   Shall I do such a deed?
Cli. O Dardanius!
Dar. O Clitus!   10
Cli. What ill request did Brutus make to thee?
Dar. To kill him, Clitus. Look, he meditates.
Cli. Now is that noble vessel full of grief,
That it runs over even at his eyes.
Bru. Come hither, good Volumnius; list a word.
Vol. What says my lord?
Bru.   Why, this, Volumnius: 16
The ghost of Cæsar hath appear'd to me
Two several times by night; at Sardis once,
And, this last night, here in Philippi fields.
I know my hour is come.
Vol.   Not so, my lord.   20
Bru. Nay, I am sure it is, Volumnius.
Thou seest the world, Volumnius, how it goes;
Our enemies have beat us to the pit. [*Low alarums.*
It is more worthy to leap in ourselves
Than tarry till they push us. Good Volumnius,   25
Thou know'st that we two went to school together;
Even for that our love of old, I prithee,
Hold thou my sword-hilts, whilst I run on it.
Vol. That's not an office for a friend, my lord.
          [*Alarum still.*
Cli. Fly, fly, my lord; there is no tarrying here.   30
Bru. Farewell to you, and you, and you, Volum-
          nius.
Strato, thou hast been all this while asleep;
Farewell to thee too, Strato. Countrymen,
My heart doth joy that yet in all my life
I found no man but he was true to me.   35
I shall have glory by this losing day
More than Octavius and Mark Antony
By this vile conquest shall attain unto.

So fare you well at once; for Brutus' tongue
Hath almost ended his life's history.   40
Night hangs upon mine eyes; my bones would rest,
That have but labour'd to attain this hour.
          [*Alarum. Cry within,* "Fly, fly, fly!"
Cli. Fly, my lord, fly.
Bru.   Hence! I will follow.
          [*Exeunt Clitus, Dardanius, and Volum-
          nius.*]
I prithee, Strato, stay thou by thy lord.
Thou art a fellow of a good respect;   45
Thy life hath had some smatch of honour in it.
Hold then my sword, and turn away thy face,
While I do run upon it. Wilt thou, Strato?
Stra. Give me your hand first. Fare you well,
          my lord.
Bru. Farewell, good Strato. [*Runs on his
          sword.*] Cæsar, now be still;   50
I kill'd not thee with half so good a will. [*Dies.*

Alarum. Retreat. Enter OCTAVIUS, ANTONY,
          MESSALA, LUCILIUS, *and the army.*

Oct. What man is that?
Mes. My master's man. Strato, where is thy
          master?
Stra. Free from the bondage you are in, Mes-
          sala;
The conquerors can but make a fire of him,   55
For Brutus only overcame himself,
And no man else hath honour by his death.
Lucil. So Brutus should be found. I thank thee,
          Brutus,
That thou hast prov'd Lucilius' saying true.
Oct. All that serv'd Brutus, I will entertain them.
Fellow, wilt thou bestow thy time with me?   61
Stra. Ay, if Messala will prefer me to you.
Oct. Do so, good Messala.
Mes. How died my master, Strato?
Stra. I held the sword, and he did run on it.   65
Mes. Octavius, then take him to follow thee,
That did the latest service to my master.
Ant. This was the noblest Roman of them all.
All the conspirators, save only he,
Did that they did in envy of great Cæsar;   70
He only, in a general honest thought
And common good to all, made one of them.
His life was gentle, and the elements
So mix'd in him that Nature might stand up
And say to all the world, "This was a man!"   75
Oct. According to his virtue let us use him,
With all respect and rites of burial.
Within my tent his bones to-night shall lie,
Most like a soldier, ordered honourably.
So call the field to rest; and let's away   80
To part the glories of this happy day. [*Exeunt omnes.*

Sc. v, 23. **pit:** i.e., of destruction. 46. **smatch:** smack. 60. **entertain:** take into service. 62. **prefer:** recommend. 73.
gentle: noble. 80. **field:** army. 81. **part:** share.

Twelfth Night; or, What You Will

UNDER THE DATE of February 2, 1601/2, John Manningham, a student at the Middle Temple, wrote in his Diary: "At our feast wee had a play called Twelve Night, or What You Will, much like the Commedy of Errores, or Menechmi in Plautus, but most like and neere to that in Italian called *Inganni*." No one has doubted that the play he witnessed was Shakespeare's, and his record fixes a later limit for the date of composition. An earlier limit cannot be precisely established, but a variety of evidence suggests that the play was still fairly new. There is nothing to indicate either that Manningham was witnessing a first performance or that the play was written for production on Twelfth Night, that is Epiphany, the sixth of January just preceding, though the latter notion has a natural plausibility. The play is, however, despite obvious differences, akin to *As You Like It*, and the part of Feste, unquestionably written for Armin, the comic actor who succeeded Kemp in Shakespeare's company early in 1600, has affinity with that of Touchstone. Of the topical references within the play which have been stressed two may be noted, though they are debatable. The reference to "a pension of thousands to be paid from the Sophy" (II.v.197) may glance at Sir Robert Shirley, who in 1599 returned from a visit to the Shah of Persia laden with gifts of which he is said to have been boastful. Shirley's exploit received considerable publicity, and the likelihood of a topical reference here gains support from another allusion to the Sophy in III.iv.306. The "new map with the augmentation of the Indies" (III.ii.84) is almost certainly that published in England about 1599, giving a larger place to the Indies than any of its predecessors had done. It is barely possible that the name of Orsino was inspired by the visit of Orsino, Duke of Bracciano, to the English Court in 1600. All the available evidence confirms 1601, the generally accepted date, as the true one.

The printing of *Twelfth Night* in the Folio of 1623 was the first, and upon this the present text is based.

The problem of the source of the main plot becomes a study in the transmission of a story. Manningham noted the resemblance of the motivating idea of mistaken identity to that in *The Comedy of Errors* and its source in Plautus, and pointed to a nearer relation in an Italian play called *Inganni* (Cheats). Actually there were two Italian plays of that name, one by Nicolo Secchi (first acted in 1547 at Milan and printed at Florence in 1562) and another by Curzio Gonzaga (printed at Venice in 1592). In the latter the disguised sister takes the name of Cesare, which is provokingly like Viola's assumed name, Cesario. Aside from that fact neither of these plays has any importance, since neither contains the central situation of Olivia's love for Cesario. But a third Italian play, *Gl'Ingannati* (The Cheated), produced at Siena in 1531, does contain the substance of the plot of *Twelfth Night*, and may very likely have been the play which Manningham believed he was citing. *Gl'Ingannati* had a germinal influence, being widely translated and adapted. It was prepared for the French stage in 1549 and for the Spanish in 1556, and a version in Latin was acted at Queen's College, Cambridge, in 1590 and 1598. Its story was retold by Matteo Bandello in his *Novelle*, Part II, no. 36 (1554), and after him by Belleforest in *Histoires Tragiques* (1571). An English rendering, either from Bandello or Belleforest, was put forth by Barnabe Riche as the tale of *Apolonius and Silla*, the second "historie" in *Barnabe Riche, his Farewell to Militarie Profession* (1581). Shakespeare's plot is on the whole closer to this than to any of the others, and there is no reason to doubt that Riche's book came into his hands.

In Riche's story the love of the heroine for the Duke has a preliminary history which Shakespeare wisely ignores. Silla (Viola) had fallen in love with Duke Apolonius (Orsino) when he had been a guest at her father's court in Cyprus. She had made every effort to win him there, but he had returned home to Constantinople unimpressed. Still determined, Silla set out to follow him, taking with her a faithful servant Pedro, who posed as her brother. Her venture met with the shipwreck at which point Shakespeare's play opens. The omission of all these preliminaries not only makes the story more compact, but also permits a finer conception of the heroine. In the adventures of Viola after the shipwreck Shakespeare follows Riche's version, where Silla, in disguise and assuming the name of a brother (physically though not chronologically her twin) takes service with Apolonius, who is now, however, in love with a widow Julina. The relations of Julina (Olivia) and Silvio (Sebastian) are more delicately treated in the play than in the story, and the action is again compressed in the final scene. In Riche the brother, arriving at last in Constantinople after a wide search for his sister, is met and wooed by Julina, who mistakes him for Silla. He accepts her, but departs shortly to continue his search, leaving Julina pregnant. Soon after this, Apolonius, hearing gossip about Julina and Silla, has Silla thrown into a dungeon. Julina goes to him to plead for Silla, whom she supposes to be her husband; Silla is sent for, denies any love-compact with Julina, and under threat of death from the outraged Duke if she will not consent to marry Julina, reveals her identity. Julina departs in dismay and Apolonius promptly offers himself to Silla. The report of their marriage brings Silvio back to the city, where he is joyfully welcomed by his sister. Hearing from Apolonius about all that had transpired, Silvio confesses his former visit and hastens to Julina. They are joyfully reunited and in a few days they are married. This scattering conclusion is in strong contrast to the concentration of Shakespeare's dénouement.

The case for Shakespeare's dependence upon Riche's version of this widely popular story as his main source is further strengthened by his apparent indebtedness to another story in Riche's book for the suggestion of Malvolio's pretended lunacy. In the tale *Of Two Brethren and their Wives*, the younger brother, seeking to cure his wife of her shrewishness, shut her up in "a darke house... with a greate chaine about her legge"; whereupon "callying his neibours about her, he would seeme with great sorrowe to lament his wives distresse, telling them that she was sodainly become lunatique." Her husband and the neighbors then prayed for her and sang the Miserere together outside the house, but "this did so spight and vexe her, that she never gave over her railyng and ragyng againste them all." Apart from this hint for the madness of Malvolio, the underplot, with its array of unforgettable characters, seems to be entirely original.

Indeed, Shakespeare's originality extends to the characterization of the main figures in the play, who are entirely recreated. The sentimentalism of the Duke, as well as the appealing union of wistfulness and arch humor which marks the charm of Viola, is altogether his conception. Orsino, in love with love, with a fondness "high fantastical," might easily have appeared only silly in his fancy, but Shakespeare keeps his sentiment from cloying, blending it with a larger grace and urbanity and giving it the complement of Viola's gentleness. Viola is one of Shakespeare's most lovable heroines. With her youthful freshness, her honesty, her innate refinement, her essential femininity, she has captivated all of Shakespeare's critics. Though her page's disguise and her situation in love are common themes in romance, it is to be noted that she has taken up her service with her master from the necessity of circumstance before she falls in love with him, and that all her conduct, both in his presence and on her missions to his flinty-hearted lady, is marked by a single-minded devotion. Her loyalty and purity are never compromised by so much as a hint; after one initial "aside" on the irony of her position (I.iv.40–42) she pleads her master's cause with genuine vigor and sincerity. Nowhere is Viola more clearly individualized than in her first scene with Olivia. Her address to Olivia is an adroit combination of rebuke and flattery, and she answers Maria, who would put her out, in her own saucy metaphor.

Of the minor characters several are distinguished creations. It is impossible not to associate Sir Toby with Falstaff, though his range of wit is narrower and he lacks entirely Falstaff's capacity for pathos. Sir Andrew Aguecheek is the most absolute fool in Shakespeare; he must be very close to the archetype of fatuity. Feste, the Clown, is the most jovial of Shakespeare's jesters. The character of Malvolio has been variously interpreted. The rather severe usage which he undergoes at the hands of those whom he has provoked, his vengeful resentment of it, and his mistress's pronouncement that he has been "most notoriously abus'd" tend to make a modern audience feel that he has suffered unjustly, but it is quite certain that Elizabethans found him deserving of all he got. He is perhaps more sinned against than sinning, but his utter lack of humor and his inordinate conceit qualify him for a pretty drastic taking down. After all, anyone as "sick of self-love" as Malvolio (and it is noteworthy that the accusation is made by Olivia herself well before his humiliation) is, either in Comedy or in real life, riding for a fall. And to make matters worse, Malvolio not only is a prig himself but obnoxiously sets out to be his brothers' keeper. Sir Toby stigmatizes this defect for all time: "Dost think because thou art virtuous, there shall be no more cakes and ale?"

TWELFTH NIGHT

OR

WHAT YOU WILL

[DRAMATIS PERSONÆ

ORSINO, *Duke of Illyria.*
SEBASTIAN, *brother to Viola.*
ANTONIO, *a sea captain, friend to Sebastian.*
A Sea Captain, *friend to Viola.*
VALENTINE, }
CURIO, } *gentlemen attending on the Duke.*
SIR TOBY BELCH, *uncle to Olivia.*
SIR ANDREW AGUECHEEK.

MALVOLIO, *steward to Olivia.*
FABIAN, }
FESTE, *a clown,* } *servants to Olivia.*

OLIVIA, *a rich countess.*
VIOLA.
MARIA, *Olivia's woman.*

Lords, Priests, Sailors, Officers, Musicians, and other Attendants.

SCENE: *A city in Illyria, and the sea-coast near it.*]

ACT I

SCENE I. [*A room in the Duke's palace.*]

Enter ORSINO, *Duke of Illyria,* CURIO, *and other
Lords* [*Musicians attending*].

Duke. If music be the food of love, play on!
Give me excess of it, that, surfeiting,
The appetite may sicken, and so die.
That strain again! It had a dying fall.
O, it came o'er my ear like the sweet sound   5
That breathes upon a bank of violets,
Stealing and giving odour.   Enough! no more!
'Tis not so sweet now as it was before.
O spirit of love, how quick and fresh art thou,
That, notwithstanding thy capacity   10
Receiveth as the sea, nought enters there,
Of what validity and pitch soe'er,
But falls into abatement and low price
Even in a minute!   So full of shapes is fancy
That it alone is high fantastical.   15

Cur. Will you go hunt, my lord?
Duke.   What, Curio?
Cur. The hart.
Duke. Why, so I do, the noblest that I have.
O, when mine eyes did see Olivia first,
Methought she purg'd the air of pestilence!   20
That instant was I turn'd into a hart;
And my desires, like fell and cruel hounds,
E'er since pursue me.

Enter VALENTINE.

                    How now! what news from her?
Val. So please my lord, I might not be admitted,
But from her handmaid do return this answer: 25
The element itself, till seven years' heat,
Shall not behold her face at ample view;
But, like a cloistress, she will veiled walk,
And water once a day her chamber round
With eye-offending brine: all this to season   30
A brother's dead love, which she would keep fresh
And lasting in her sad remembrance.

Act I, sc. i, 5. **sound** Ff. Pope's emendation, *south,* has been followed by many edd.   12. **validity:** value.   **pitch:** height.
14. **fancy:** love.   15. **fantastical:** imaginative.   21–23. **That... pursue me.** Allusion to Actæon, who, seeing Diana naked,
was changed into a hart and killed by his own dogs.   26. **element:** sky.   **years' heat:** summers.

Duke. O, she that hath a heart of that fine frame
To pay this debt of love but to a brother,
How will she love when the rich golden shaft   35
Hath kill'd the flock of all affections else
That live in her; when liver, brain, and heart,
These sovereign thrones, are all suppli'd, and fill'd
Her sweet perfections with one self king!
Away before me to sweet beds of flowers;   40
Love-thoughts lie rich when canopi'd with bowers.
                                                    [*Exeunt.*

SCENE II.   [*The sea-coast.*]

Enter VIOLA, *a* CAPTAIN, *and Sailors.*

Vio. What country, friends, is this?
Cap. This is Illyria, lady.
Vio. And what should I do in Illyria?
My brother he is in Elysium.
Perchance he is not drown'd. What think you,
    sailors?   5
Cap. It is perchance that you yourself were
    saved.
Vio. O my poor brother! and so perchance may
he be.
Cap. True, madam; and, to comfort you with
    chance,
Assure yourself, after our ship did split,
When you and those poor number sav'd with you
Hung on our driving boat, I saw your brother,   11
Most provident in peril, bind himself,
Courage and hope both teaching him the practice,
To a strong mast that liv'd upon the sea;
Where, like [Arion] on the dolphin's back,   15
I saw him hold acquaintance with the waves
So long as I could see.
Vio.   For saying so, there's gold.
Mine own escape unfoldeth to my hope,
Whereto thy speech serves for authority,   20
The like of him.   Know'st thou this country?
Cap. Ay, madam, well; for I was bred and born
Not three hours' travel from this very place.
Vio. Who governs here?
Cap. A noble duke, in nature as in name.   25
Vio. What is his name?
Cap. Orsino.
Vio. Orsino!   I have heard my father name him.
He was a bachelor then.
Cap. And so is now, or was so very late;   30
For but a month ago I went from hence,
And then 'twas fresh in murmur — as, you know,
What great ones do the less will prattle of —
That he did seek the love of fair Olivia.

Vio. What's she?   35
Cap. A virtuous maid, the daughter of a count
That died some twelvemonth since, then leaving her
In the protection of his son, her brother,
Who shortly also died; for whose dear love,
They say, she hath abjur'd the [company   40
And sight] of men.
Vio.   O that I serv'd that lady,
And might not be delivered to the world,
Till I had made mine own occasion mellow,
What my estate is!
Cap.   That were hard to compass,
Because she will admit no kind of suit,   45
No, not the Duke's.
Vio. There is a fair behaviour in thee, captain;
And though that nature with a beauteous wall
Doth oft close in pollution, yet of thee
I will believe thou hast a mind that suits   50
With this thy fair and outward character.
I prithee, and I'll pay thee bounteously,
Conceal me what I am, and be my aid
For such disguise as haply shall become
The form of my intent.   I'll serve this duke.   55
Thou shalt present me as an eunuch to him.
It may be worth thy pains, for I can sing
And speak to him in many sorts of music
That will allow me very worth his service.
What else may hap, to time I will commit,   60
Only shape thou thy silence to my wit.
Cap. Be you his eunuch, and your mute I'll be.
When my tongue blabs, then let mine eyes not see.
Vio. I thank thee.   Lead me on.   [*Exeunt.*

SCENE III.   [*A room in Olivia's house.*]

Enter SIR TOBY BELCH *and* MARIA.

Sir To. What a plague means my niece, to take
the death of her brother thus?   I am sure care's an
enemy to life.
Mar. By my troth, Sir Toby, you must come in
earlier o' nights.   Your cousin, my lady, takes   5
great exceptions to your ill hours.
Sir To. Why, let her except before excepted.
Mar. Ay, but you must confine yourself within
the modest limits of order.   9
Sir To. Confine!   I'll confine myself no finer than
I am.   These clothes are good enough to drink in,
and so be these boots too; an they be not, let them
hang themselves in their own straps.   13
Mar. That quaffing and drinking will undo you.
I heard my lady talk of it yesterday, and of a fool-

35. **shaft:** i.e., Cupid's.   37. **liver ... heart.**   The supposed seats of the passions.   39. **self:** sole.

Sc. ii, 15. **[Arion]** (Pope)   *Orion* F.   Arion was a Greek poet, saved from drowning by dolphins who were so ravished by his lyre that they carried him to land.   40–41. **[company And sight]** (Hanmer).   *sight And company* F.   42–44. **And ... estate is.**   I.e., And might not have my true condition known until a suitable time.   59. **allow:** show, prove.   61. **wit:** design.

Sc. iii, 7. **except before excepted.**   Quibble upon the legal phrase, *exceptis excipiendis,* "with the exceptions before named."

ish knight that you brought in one night here to be her wooer.   17

Sir To. Who? Sir Andrew Aguecheek?

Mar. Ay, he.

Sir To. He's as tall a man as any's in Illyria.   20

Mar. What's that to th' purpose?

Sir To. Why, he has three thousand ducats a year.

Mar. Ay, but he'll have but a year in all these ducats. He's a very fool and a prodigal.   25

Sir To. Fie, that you'll say so! He plays o' the viol-de-gamboys, and speaks three or four languages word for word without book, and hath all the good gifts of nature.   29

Mar. He hath indeed, almost natural; for besides that he's a fool, he's a great quarreller; and but that he hath the gift of a coward to allay the gust he hath in quarrelling, 'tis thought among the prudent he would quickly have the gift of a grave.   35

Sir To. By this hand, they are scoundrels and substractors that say so of him. Who are they?

Mar. They that add, moreover, he's drunk nightly in your company.   39

Sir To. With drinking healths to my niece. I'll drink to her as long as there is a passage in my throat and drink in Illyria. He's a coward and a coystrill that will not drink to my niece till his brains turn o' th' toe like a parish-top. What, wench! *Castiliano vulgo!* for here comes Sir Andrew Agueface.   46

Enter Sir Andrew Aguecheek.

Sir And. Sir Toby Belch! How now, Sir Toby Belch!

Sir To. Sweet Sir Andrew!

Sir And. Bless you, fair shrew.   50

Mar. And you too, sir.

Sir To. Accost, Sir Andrew, accost.

Sir And. What's that?

Sir To. My niece's chambermaid.

Sir And. Good Mistress Accost, I desire better acquaintance.   56

Mar. My name is Mary, sir.

Sir And. Good Mistress Mary Accost, —

Sir To. You mistake, knight. "Accost" is front her, board her, woo her, assail her.   60

Sir And. By my troth, I would not undertake her in this company. Is that the meaning of "accost"?

Mar. Fare you well, gentlemen.

Sir To. An thou let part so, Sir Andrew, would thou mightst never draw sword again.   66

Sir And. An you part so, mistress, I would I might never draw sword again. Fair lady, do you think you have fools in hand?

Mar. Sir, I have not you by th' hand.   70

Sir And. Marry, but you shall have; and here's my hand.

Mar. Now, sir, "thought is free." I pray you, bring your hand to th' butt'ry-bar and let it drink.

Sir And. Wherefore, sweetheart? What's your metaphor?   76

Mar. It's dry, sir.

Sir And. Why, I think so. I am not such an ass but I can keep my hand dry. But what's your jest?   80

Mar. A dry jest, sir.

Sir And. Are you full of them?

Mar. Ay, sir, I have them at my fingers' ends. Marry, now I let go your hand, I am barren. [*Exit.*

Sir To. O knight, thou lack'st a cup of canary. When did I see thee so put down?   86

Sir And. Never in your life, I think, unless you see canary put me down. Methinks sometimes I have no more wit than a Christian or an ordinary man has; but I am a great eater of beef and I believe that does harm to my wit.   91

Sir To. No question.

Sir And. An I thought that, I'd forswear it. I'll ride home to-morrow, Sir Toby.

Sir To. *Pourquoi,* my dear knight?   95

Sir And. What is "*pourquoi*"? Do or not do? I would I had bestowed that time in the tongues that I have in fencing, dancing, and bear-baiting. O, had I but followed the arts!

Sir To. Then hadst thou had an excellent head of hair.   101

Sir And. Why, would that have mended my hair?

Sir To. Past question; for thou seest it will not [curl by] nature.   105

Sir And. But it becomes me well enough, does't not?

Sir To. Excellent; it hangs like flax on a distaff, and I hope to see a housewife take thee between her legs, and spin it off.   110

Sir And. Faith, I'll home to-morrow, Sir Toby. Your niece will not be seen, or if she be, it's four to one she'll none of me. The Count himself here hard by wooes her.   114

Sir To. She'll none o' th' Count. She'll not match above her degree, neither in estate, years, nor wit; I have heard her swear't. Tut, there's life in't, man.

---

20. **tall**: fine.   27. **viol-de-gamboys**: bass viol.   30. **natural**: (1) naturally, (2) like an idiot.   33. **gust**: gusto, zest.   43. **coystrill**: knave.   45. *Castiliano vulgo.* Probably nonsense.   74. **buttery-bar.** Where drinks were served.   77. **It's dry.** Signifying lack of amorousness.   81. **dry jest**: dull jest.   85. **canary**: a sweet wine (from the Canary Islands).   100. **head of hair.** Sir Toby puns on *tongues* (l. 97) and (curling) tongs.   105. **[curl by]** (Theobald).   *coole my* F.   118. **there's life in't**: there's still hope.

Sir And. I'll stay a month longer. I am a fellow o' the strangest mind i' th' world; I delight in masques and revels sometimes altogether.   121

Sir To. Art thou good at these kickshawses, knight?

Sir And. As any man in Illyria, whatsoever he be, under the degree of my betters; and yet I will not compare with an old man.   126

Sir To. What is thy excellence in a galliard, knight?

Sir And. Faith, I can cut a caper.

Sir To. And I can cut the mutton to't.   130

Sir And. And I think I have the back-trick simply as strong as any man in Illyria.

Sir To. Wherefore are these things hid? Wherefore have these gifts a curtain before 'em? Are they like to take dust, like Mistress Mall's picture? Why dost thou not go to church in a galliard and come home in a coranto? My very walk should be a jig. I would not so much as make water but in a sink-a-pace. What dost thou mean? Is it a world to hide virtues in? I did think, by the excellent constitution of thy leg, it was form'd under the star of a galliard.   140

Sir And. Ay, 'tis strong, and it does indifferent well in a damn'd colour'd stock. Shall we [set] about some revels?   145

Sir To. What shall we do else? Were we not born under Taurus?

Sir And. Taurus! That's sides and heart.

Sir To. No, sir, it is legs and thighs. Let me see thee caper. Ha! Higher! Ha, ha! Excellent!   [*Exeunt.* 151

SCENE IV. [*A room in the Duke's palace.*]

Enter VALENTINE, *and* VIOLA *in man's attire.*

Val. If the Duke continue these favours towards you, Cesario, you are like to be much advanc'd. He hath known you but three days, and already you are no stranger.   4

Vio. You either fear his humour or my negligence, that you call in question the continuance of his love. Is he inconstant, sir, in his favours?

Val. No, believe me.

Enter DUKE, CURIO, *and Attendants.*

Vio. I thank you. Here comes the Count.

Duke. Who saw Cesario, ho?   10

Vio. On your attendance, my lord; here.

Duke. Stand you a while aloof. Cesario, Thou know'st no less but all. I have unclasp'd To thee the book even of my secret soul; Therefore, good youth, address thy gait unto her. Be not deni'd access, stand at her doors,   16 And tell them, there thy fixed foot shall grow Till thou have audience.

Vio.   Sure, my noble lord, If she be so abandon'd to her sorrow As it is spoke, she never will admit me.   20

Duke. Be clamorous and leap all civil bounds Rather than make unprofited return.

Vio. Say I do speak with her, my lord, what then?

Duke. O, then unfold the passion of my love, Surprise her with discourse of my dear faith.   25 It shall become thee well to act my woes. She will attend it better in thy youth Than in a nuncio's of more grave aspect.

Vio. I think not so, my lord.

Duke.   Dear lad, believe it; For they shall yet belie thy happy years,   30 That say thou art a man. Diana's lip Is not more smooth and rubious; thy small pipe Is as the maiden's organ, shrill and sound; And all is semblative a woman's part. I know thy constellation is right apt   35 For this affair. Some four or five attend him, — All, if you will; for I myself am best When least in company. Prosper well in this, And thou shalt live as freely as thy lord, To call his fortunes thine.

Vio.   I'll do my best   40 To woo your lady, — [*aside*] yet, a barful strife! Whoe'er I woo, myself would be his wife.   [*Exeunt.*

SCENE V. [*A room in Olivia's house.*]

Enter MARIA *and* CLOWN.

Mar. Nay, either tell me where thou hast been, or I will not open my lips so wide as a bristle may enter, in way of thy excuse. My lady will hang thee for thy absence.

Clo. Let her hang me! He that is well hang'd in this world needs to fear no colours.   6

Mar. Make that good.

Clo. He shall see none to fear.

Mar. A good lenten answer. I can tell thee where that saying was born, of "I fear no colours."

Clo. Where, good Mistress Mary?   11

122. **kickshawses:** trifles. 126. **old:** (possibly) experienced. 127. **galliard:** a lively dance. 130. Sir Toby puns: mutton is often served with *caper* sauce. 131. **back-trick:** i.e., the reverse step (in the galliard). 137. **coranto:** a fast dance. 139. **sink-a-pace:** (cinque pace) a five-step dance. 144. **damn'd colour'd.** Many editors amend to *flame-coloured.* **stock:** stocking. 144. **[set]** (Rowe). *sit* F. 147. **Taurus.** In the old medical astrology the constellation Taurus was held to control the neck and throat; so both Sir A. and Sir T. are wrong.
Sc. iv, 32. **rubious:** ruby-colored. 33. **sound:** clear. 34. **semblative:** like. 35. **constellation:** nature (which the stars determined). 41. **barful strife:** task full of obstacles.
Sc. v, 6. **colours:** flags (i.e., foes), with a pun on *collars* (the hangman's noose). 9. **lenten:** scanty.

Mar. In the wars; and that may you be bold to say in your foolery.

Clo. Well, God give them wisdom that have it; and those that are fools, let them use their talents.   16

Mar. Yet you will be hang'd for being so long absent; or, to be turn'd away, is not that as good as a hanging to you?

Clo. Many a good hanging prevents a bad 20 marriage; and, for turning away, let summer bear it out.

Mar. You are resolute, then?

Clo. Not so, neither; but I am resolv'd on two points.   25

Mar. That if one break, the other will hold; or, if both break, your gaskins fall.

Clo. Apt, in good faith; very apt. Well, go thy way. If Sir Toby would leave drinking, thou wert as witty a piece of Eve's flesh as any in Illyria. 31

Mar. Peace, you rogue, no more o' that. Here comes my lady. Make your excuse wisely, you were best.   [*Exit.*] 34

Enter LADY OLIVIA [*and retinue*] *with* MALVOLIO.

Clo. Wit, an't be thy will, put me into good fooling! Those wits, that think they have thee, do very oft prove fools; and I, that am sure I lack thee, may pass for a wise man; for what says Quinapalus? "Better a witty fool than a foolish wit." — 40 God bless thee, lady!

Oli. Take the fool away.

Clo. Do you not hear, fellows? Take away the lady.

Oli. Go to, you're a dry fool, I'll no more of you; besides, you grow dishonest.   46

Clo. Two faults, madonna, that drink and good counsel will amend; for give the dry fool drink, then is the fool not dry: bid the dishonest man mend himself; if he mend, he is no longer dishonest; 50 if he cannot, let the botcher mend him. Any thing that's mended is but patch'd; virtue that transgresses is but patch'd with sin, and sin that amends is but patch'd with virtue. If that this simple syllogism will serve, so; if it will not, what remedy? 55 As there is no true cuckold but calamity, so beauty's a flower. The lady bade take away the fool; therefore, I say again, take her away.

Oli. Sir, I bade them take away you.   60

Clo. Misprision in the highest degree! Lady, "*cucullus non facit monachum*"; that's as much to say as I wear not motley in my brain. Good madonna, give me leave to prove you a fool.

Oli. Can you do it?   65

Clo. Dexteriously, good madonna.

Oli. Make your proof.

Clo. I must catechise you for it, madonna. Good my mouse of virtue, answer me.

Oli. Well, sir, for want of other idleness, I'll bide your proof.   71

Clo. Good madonna, why mournest thou?

Oli. Good fool, for my brother's death.

Clo. I think his soul is in hell, madonna.

Oli. I know his soul is in heaven, fool.   75

Clo. The more fool, madonna, to mourn for your brother's soul being in heaven. Take away the fool, gentlemen.

Oli. What think you of this fool, Malvolio? Doth he not mend?   80

Mal. Yes, and shall do till the pangs of death shake him. Infirmity, that decays the wise, doth ever make the better fool.

Clo. God send you, sir, a speedy infirmity, for the better increasing your folly! Sir Toby will be sworn that I am no fox, but he will not pass 85 his word for twopence that you are no fool.

Oli. How say you to that, Malvolio?

Mal. I marvel your ladyship takes delight in such a barren rascal. I saw him put down the 90 other day with an ordinary fool that has no more brain than a stone. Look you now, he's out of his guard already. Unless you laugh and minister occasion to him, he is gagg'd. I protest, I take these wise men that crow so at these set kind of fools no better than the fools' zanies.   96

Oli. O, you are sick of self-love, Malvolio, and taste with a distemper'd appetite. To be generous, guiltless, and of free disposition, is to take those things for bird-bolts that you deem cannon- 100 bullets. There is no slander in an allow'd fool, though he do nothing but rail; nor no railing in a known discreet man, though he do nothing but reprove.

Clo. Now Mercury endue thee with leasing, for thou speak'st well of fools!   106

Re-enter MARIA.

Mar. Madam, there is at the gate a young gentleman much desires to speak with you.

Oli. From the Count Orsino, is it?

Mar. I know not, madam. 'Tis a fair young man, and well attended.   111

Oli. Who of my people hold him in delay?

Mar. Sir Toby, madam, your kinsman.

Oli. Fetch him off, I pray you. He speaks

---

25. **points:** (1) counts, (2) laces to hold up the *gaskins* or breeches.   39. **Quinapalus.** Feste's invention.   45. **dry:** dull. 51. **botcher:** mender of old clothes.   61. **Misprision:** mistake, with a possible reference to the literal sense, taking the wrong person.   62. **cucullus ... monachum:** the cowl does not make the monk.   63. **motley:** the parti-colored costume of jesters.   69. **mouse:** term of affection.   **of virtue:** virtuous.   96. **zanies:** imitators.   100. **bird-bolts:** blunt arrows.   101. **allow'd:** licensed.   105. **leasing:** (gift of) lying.   Mercury was the god of thieves and liars.

nothing but madman; fie on him! [*Exit* 115
Maria.] Go you, Malvolio; if it be a suit from the
Count, I am sick, or not at home, — what you
will, to dismiss it. (*Exit Malvolio.*) Now you see,
sir, how your fooling grows old, and people dislike it.

Clo. Thou hast spoke for us, madonna, as if 120
thy eldest son should be a fool; whose skull Jove
cram with brains! for — here he comes —

Enter SIR TOBY.

one of thy kin has a most weak *pia mater.*

Oli. By mine honour, half drunk. What is he
at the gate, cousin? 125

Sir To. A gentleman.

Oli. A gentleman! What gentleman?

Sir To. 'Tis a gentleman here — a plague o'
these pickle-herring! How now, sot!

Clo. Good Sir Toby! 130

Oli. Cousin, cousin, how have you come so early
by this lethargy?

Sir To. Lechery! I defy lechery. There's one
at the gate.

Oli. Ay, marry, what is he? 135

Sir To. Let him be the devil, an he will, I care
not; give me faith, say I. Well, it's all one. [*Exit.*

Oli. What's a drunken man like, fool?

Clo. Like a drown'd man, a fool, and a madman.
One draught above heat makes him a fool, the 140
second mads him, and a third drowns him.

Oli. Go thou and seek the crowner and let him
sit o' my coz, for he's in the third degree of drink,
he's drown'd. Go, look after him.

Clo. He is but mad yet, madonna; and the fool
shall look to the madman. [*Exit.* 146

Re-enter MALVOLIO.

Mal. Madam, yond young fellow swears he will
speak with you. I told him you were sick. He
takes on him to understand so much, and therefore
comes to speak with you. I told him you were 150
asleep. He seems to have a foreknowledge of
that too, and therefore comes to speak with you.
What is to be said to him, lady? He's fortified
against any denial.

Oli. Tell him he shall not speak with me. 155

Mal. Has been told so; and he says, he'll stand
at your door like a sheriff's post, and be the supporter to a bench, but he'll speak with you.

Oli. What kind o' man is he?

Mal. Why, of mankind. 160

Oli. What manner of man?

Mal. Of very ill manner. He'll speak with you,
will you or no.

Oli. Of what personage and years is he? 164

Mal. Not yet old enough for a man, nor young
enough for a boy; as a squash is before 'tis a peascod, or a codling when 'tis almost an apple. 'Tis
with him in standing water, between boy and man.
He is very well-favour'd and he speaks very shrewishly. One would think his mother's milk were
scarce out of him. 171

Oli. Let him approach. Call in my gentlewoman.

Mal. Gentlewoman, my lady calls. [*Exit.*

Re-enter MARIA.

Oli. Give me my veil. Come, throw it o'er my
face. 175
We'll once more hear Orsino's embassy.

Enter [VIOLA *and Attendants*].

Vio. The honourable lady of the house, which is
she?

Oli. Speak to me; I shall answer for her. Your
will? 180

Vio. Most radiant, exquisite, and unmatchable
beauty, — I pray you, tell me if this be the lady of
the house, for I never saw her. I would be loath
to cast away my speech, for besides that it is excellently well penn'd, I have taken great pains 185
to con it. Good beauties, let me sustain no scorn.
I am very comptible, even to the least sinister usage.

Oli. Whence came you, sir? 189

Vio. I can say little more than I have studied,
and that question's out of my part. Good gentle
one, give me modest assurance if you be the lady
of the house, that I may proceed in my speech.

Oli. Are you a comedian? 194

Vio. No, my profound heart; and yet, by the
very fangs of malice I swear, I am not that I play.
Are you the lady of the house?

Oli. If I do not usurp myself, I am.

Vio. Most certain, if you are she, you do usurp
yourself; for what is yours to bestow is not 200
yours to reserve. But this is from my commission.
I will on with my speech in your praise, and then
show you the heart of my message.

Oli. Come to what is important in't. I forgive
you the praise. 205

Vio. Alas, I took great pains to study it, and
'tis poetical.

Oli. It is the more like to be feigned. I pray
you, keep it in. I heard you were saucy at my
gates, and allow'd your approach rather to won- 210
der at you than to hear you. If you be not mad,
be gone. If you have reason, be brief. 'Tis not
that time of moon with me to make one in so skipping a dialogue.

---

123. *pia mater:* brain.   142. **crowner:** coroner.   157. **sheriff's post:** post before a sheriff's house for notices.   166. **squash:**
unripe pea pod.   167. **codling:** unripe apple.   168. **standing water:** at turn of the tide.   169. **shrewishly:** crossly.   177.
S.D. VIOLA. *Violenta* F.   186. **con:** memorize.   187. **comptible:** sensitive.   201. **from:** out of.   213. **skipping:** flighty.

Mar. Will you hoist sail, sir? Here lies your
way.   216
Vio. No, good swabber, I am to hull here a little
longer. Some mollification for your giant, sweet
lady. Tell me your mind. I am a messenger.   220
Oli. Sure, you have some hideous matter to deliver, when the courtesy of it is so fearful. Speak
your office.
Vio. It alone concerns your ear. I bring no
overture of war, no taxation of homage. I hold 225
the olive in my hand. My words are as full of
peace as matter.
Oli. Yet you began rudely. What are you?
What would you?   229
Vio. The rudeness that hath appear'd in me
have I learn'd from my entertainment. What I
am, and what I would, are as secret as maidenhead; to your ears, divinity, to any other's, profanation.   234
Oli. Give us the place alone; we will hear this
divinity. [*Exeunt Maria and Attendants.*] Now,
sir, what is your text?
Vio. Most sweet lady, —
Oli. A comfortable doctrine, and much may be
said of it. Where lies your text?   240
Vio. In Orsino's bosom.
Oli. In his bosom! In what chapter of his
bosom?
Vio. To answer by the method, in the first of his
heart.   245
Oli. O, I have read it; it is heresy. Have you
no more to say?
Vio. Good madam, let me see your face.
Oli. Have you any commission from your lord to
negotiate with my face? You are now out of   250
your text, but we will draw the curtain and show
you the picture. Look you, sir, such a one I was
— this present. Is't not well done? [*Unveiling.*]
Vio. Excellently done, if God did all.
Oli. 'Tis in grain, sir; 'twill endure wind and
weather.   256
Vio. 'Tis beauty truly blent, whose red and
white
Nature's own sweet and cunning hand laid on.
Lady, you are the cruell'st she alive
If you will lead these graces to the grave   260
And leave the world no copy.
Oli. O, sir, I will not be so hard-hearted; I will
give out divers schedules of my beauty. It shall
be inventoried, and every particle and utensil
labell'd to my will: as, item, two lips, indifferent 265
red; item, two grey eyes, with lids to them; item,

one neck, one chin, and so forth. Were you sent
hither to praise me?
Vio. I see you what you are, you are too proud;
But, if you were the devil, you are fair.   270
My lord and master loves you. O, such love
Could be but recompens'd, though you were
crown'd
The nonpareil of beauty!
Oli.   How does he love me?
Vio. With adorations, [with] fertile tears,
With groans that thunder love, with sighs of fire.
Oli. Your lord does know my mind; I cannot
love him.   276
Yet I suppose him virtuous, know him noble;
Of great estate, of fresh and stainless youth,
In voices well divulg'd, free, learn'd, and valiant,
And in dimension and the shape of nature   280
A gracious person. But yet I cannot love him.
He might have took his answer long ago.
Vio. If I did love you in my master's flame,
With such a suff'ring, such a deadly life,
In your denial I would find no sense.   285
I would not understand it.
Oli.   Why, what would you?
Vio. Make me a willow cabin at your gate,
And call upon my soul within the house;
Write loyal cantons of contemned love
And sing them loud even in the dead of night; 290
Halloo your name to the reverberate hills
And make the babbling gossip of the air
Cry out "Olivia!" O, you should not rest
Between the elements of air and earth,
But you should pity me!
Oli.   You might do much.   295
What is your parentage?
Vio. Above my fortunes, yet my state is well.
I am a gentleman.
Oli.   Get you to your lord.
I cannot love him. Let him send no more, —
Unless, perchance, you come to me again   300
To tell me how he takes it. Fare you well!
I thank you for your pains. Spend this for me.
Vio. I am no fee'd post, lady. Keep your purse.
My master, not myself, lacks recompense.
Love make his heart of flint that you shall love; 305
And let your fervour, like my master's, be
Plac'd in contempt! Farewell, fair cruelty. [*Exit.*
Oli. "What is your parentage?"
"Above my fortunes, yet my state is well.
I am a gentleman." I'll be sworn thou art.   310
Thy tongue, thy face, thy limbs, actions, and
spirit

---

217. **swabber:** washer of decks — keeping up the nautical metaphor in "hoist sail." **hull:** float, drift. 218. **giant.** Ironical reference to Maria's small stature. 225. **taxation:** demand. 231. **my entertainment:** the way I have been received here. 253. **this present:** just now. 255. **in grain:** indelible, not painted. 265. **labell'd:** attached (as a codicil). 268. **praise:** appraise. 274. **[with]** (Pope). Om. F. 279. **In . . . divulg'd:** of good repute. 283. **flame:** passion. 284. **deadly:** doomed to die. 289. **cantons:** cantos, songs. 303. **post:** messenger.

Do give thee five-fold blazon. Not too fast! Soft,
    soft!
Unless the master were the man. How now!
Even so quickly may one catch the plague?
Methinks I feel this youth's perfections   315
With an invisible and subtle stealth
To creep in at mine eyes. Well, let it be.
What ho, Malvolio!

Re-enter MALVOLIO.

Mal.   Here, madam, at your service.
Oli. Run after that same peevish messenger,
The County's man. He left this ring behind him,
Would I or not. Tell him I'll none of it.   321
Desire him not to flatter with his lord,
Nor hold him up with hopes. I'm not for him.
If that the youth will come this way to-morrow,
I'll give him reasons for't. Hie thee, Malvolio.
Mal. Madam, I will.   *[Exit.*   326
Oli. I do I know not what, and fear to find
Mine eye too great a flatterer for my mind.
Fate, show thy force; ourselves we do not owe;
What is decreed must be, and be this so.   330
                                [Exit.]

ACT II

SCENE I. [*The sea-coast.*]

Enter ANTONIO *and* SEBASTIAN.

Ant. Will you stay no longer? Nor will you not
that I go with you?
Seb. By your patience, no. My stars shine
darkly over me. The malignancy of my fate might
perhaps distemper yours, therefore I shall crave   5
of you your leave that I may bear my evils alone.
It were a bad recompense for your love, to lay any
of them on you.
Ant. Let me yet know of you whither you are
bound.   10
Seb. No, sooth, sir. My determinate voyage
is mere extravagancy. But I perceive in you so
excellent a touch of modesty, that you will not extort from me what I am willing to keep in; therefore it charges me in manners the rather to ex-   15
press myself. You must know of me then, Antonio,
my name is Sebastian, which I call'd Roderigo.
My father was that Sebastian of Messaline, whom
I know you have heard of. He left behind him
myself and a sister, both born in an hour. If   20
the heavens had been pleas'd, would we had so
ended! But you, sir, alter'd that; for some hour

before you took me from the breach of the sea was
my sister drown'd.
Ant. Alas the day!   25
Seb. A lady, sir, though it was said she much
resembled me, was yet of many accounted beautiful; but, though I could not with such estimable
wonder overfar believe that, yet thus far I will
boldly publish her: she bore a mind that envy   30
could not but call fair. She is drown'd already,
sir, with salt water, though I seem to drown her
remembrance again with more.
Ant. Pardon me, sir, your bad entertainment.
Seb. O good Antonio, forgive me your trouble.   35
Ant. If you will not murder me for my love, let
me be your servant.
Seb. If you will not undo what you have done,
that is, kill him whom you have recover'd, desire it
not. Fare ye well at once. My bosom is full of   40
kindness, and I am yet so near the manners of my
mother, that upon the least occasion more mine
eyes will tell tales of me. I am bound to the Count
Orsino's court. Farewell.   *[Exit.*
Ant. The gentleness of all the gods go with
    thee!   45
I have many enemies in Orsino's court,
Else would I very shortly see thee there.
But, come what may, I do adore thee so
That danger shall seem sport, and I will go.   49
                                [Exit.

SCENE II. [*A street.*]

Enter VIOLA *and* MALVOLIO, *at several doors.*

Mal. Were you not even now with the Countess
Olivia?
Vio. Even now, sir. On a moderate pace I have
since arriv'd but hither.   4
Mal. She returns this ring to you, sir. You
might have saved me my pains, to have taken it
away yourself. She adds, moreover, that you
should put your lord into a desperate assurance
she will none of him; and — one thing more — that
you be never so hardy to come again in his af-   10
fairs, unless it be to report your lord's taking of
this. Receive it so.
Vio. She took the ring of me. I'll none of it.
Mal. Come, sir, you peevishly threw it to her;
and her will is, it should be so return'd. If it be   15
worth stooping for, there it lies in your eye; if not,
be it his that finds it.   *[Exit.*
Vio. I left no ring with her. What means this
    lady?
Fortune forbid my outside have not charm'd her!

312. **blazon:** proof of nobility.   329. **owe:** own.

Act II, sc. i, 5. distemper: disorder.   11–12. **My ... extravagancy:** my destination is mere wandering.   15. **express:**
reveal.   23. **breach:** breakers, surf.   28. **estimable wonder:** admiring esteem.

Sc. ii, 8. desperate: hopeless.

She made good view of me; indeed, so much 20
That [sure] methought her eyes had lost her tongue,
For she did speak in starts distractedly.
She loves me, sure. The cunning of her passion
Invites me in this churlish messenger.
None of my lord's ring! Why, he sent her none. 25
I am the man! If it be so, as 'tis,
Poor lady, she were better love a dream.
Disguise, I see thou art a wickedness
Wherein the pregnant enemy does much.
How easy is it for the proper-false 30
In women's waxen hearts to set their forms!
Alas, [our] frailty is the cause, not we!
For such as we are made [of], such we be.
How will this fadge? My master loves her dearly;
And I, poor monster, fond as much on him; 35
And she, mistaken, seems to dote on me.
What will become of this? As I am man,
My state is desperate for my master's love;
As I am woman, — now alas the day! —
What thriftless sighs shall poor Olivia breathe! 40
O time! thou must untangle this, not I.
It is too hard a knot for me t' untie! [Exit.]

SCENE III. [A room in Olivia's house.]

Enter SIR TOBY and SIR ANDREW.

Sir To. Approach, Sir Andrew. Not to be a-bed
after midnight is to be up betimes; and "deliculo
surgere," thou know'st, —
Sir And. Nay, by my troth, I know not; but I
know, to be up late is to be up late. 5
Sir To. A false conclusion. I hate it as an unfill'd can. To be up after midnight and to go to
bed then, is early; so that to go to bed after midnight is to go to bed betimes. Does not our lives
consist of the four elements? 10
Sir And. Faith, so they say; but I think it
rather consists of eating and drinking.
Sir To. Thou'rt a scholar; let us therefore eat
and drink. Marian, I say! a stoup of wine!

Enter CLOWN.

Sir And. Here comes the fool, i' faith. 15
Clo. How now, my hearts! Did you never see
the picture of "we three"?
Sir To. Welcome, ass. Now let's have a catch.
Sir And. By my troth, the fool has an excellent
breast. I had rather than forty shillings I had 20
such a leg, and so sweet a breath to sing, as the fool
has. In sooth, thou wast in very gracious fooling

last night, when thou spok'st of Pigrogromitus, of
the Vapians passing the equinoctial of Queubus.
'Twas very good, i' faith. I sent thee sixpence for
thy leman. Hadst it? 26
Clo. I did impeticos thy gratillity; for Malvolio's
nose is no whipstock. My lady has a white hand,
and the Mermidons are no bottle-ale houses.
Sir And. Excellent! Why, this is the best
fooling, when all is done. Now, a song. 31
Sir To. Come on; there is sixpence for you.
Let's have a song.
Sir And. There's a testril of me too. If one
knight give a — 35
Clo. Would you have a love-song, or a song of
good life?
Sir To. A love-song, a love-song.
Sir And. Ay, ay. I care not for good life.
Clo. (Sings.)
O mistress mine, where are you roaming? 40
O, stay and hear, your true love's coming,
That can sing both high and low.
Trip no further, pretty sweeting;
Journeys end in lovers meeting,
Every wise man's son doth know. 45

Sir And. Excellent good, i' faith.
Sir To. Good, good.
Clo. [Sings.]
What is love? 'Tis not hereafter.
Present mirth hath present laughter;
What's to come is still unsure. 50
In delay there lies no plenty;
Then come kiss me, sweet and twenty,
Youth's a stuff will not endure.

Sir And. A mellifluous voice, as I am true
knight. 55
Sir To. A contagious breath.
Sir And. Very sweet and contagious, i' faith.
Sir To. To hear by the nose, it is dulcet in con-
tagion. But shall we make the welkin dance in-
deed? Shall we rouse the night-owl in a catch 60
that will draw three souls out of one weaver?
Shall we do that?
Sir And. An you love me, let's do't. I am dog
at a catch.
Clo. By'r lady, sir, and some dogs will catch
well. 65
Sir And. Most certain. Let our catch be,
"Thou knave."
Clo. "Hold thy peace, thou knave," knight?

---

21. [sure] F₂. Om. F₁. lost: i.e., put at a loss. 29. pregnant: resourceful. 30. proper-false: handsome deceivers. 32.
[our] F₂. O F₁. 33. made [of] (Tyrwhitt). made, if F₁. 34. fadge: turn out.
Sc. iii, 3. deliculo surgere (saluberrimum est): to rise early is most healthful. An extract from Lilly's Latin Grammar.
14. stoup: cup. 17. A picture of two asses or fools entitled "we three," the spectator making the third. 18. catch: round.
20. breast: voice. 23–24. Pigrogromitus ... Queubus. Mock learning. 26. leman: sweetheart. 27. impeticos thy
gratillity. Nonsensical mode of saying "pocket thy gratuity." 28. whipstock: whip handle (i.e., Malvolio's nose is keen).
29. Mermidons: followers of Achilles. 34. testril: sixpence. 56. contagious breath: catchy song. 59. welkin: sky.

I shall be constrain'd in't to call thee knave'
knight.   70

Sir And. 'Tis not the first time I have constrained
one to call me knave. Begin, fool. It begins,
"Hold thy peace."

Clo. I shall never begin if I hold my peace.

Sir And. Good, i' faith. Come, begin.   75

[*Catch sung.*

Enter MARIA.

Mar. What a caterwauling do you keep here! If
my lady have not call'd up her steward Malvolio
and bid him turn you out of doors, never trust
me.   79

Sir To. My lady's a Cataian, we are politicians,
Malvolio's a Peg-a-Ramsey, and "Three merry
men be we." Am not I consanguineous? Am I
not of her blood? Tilly-vally. Lady! [*Sings.*]
"There dwelt a man in Babylon, lady, lady!"   84

Clo. Beshrew me, the knight's in admirable
fooling.

Sir And. Ay, he does well enough if he be dispos'd, and so do I too. He does it with a better
grace, but I do it more natural.   89

Sir To. [*Sings.*] "O, the twelfth day of December," —

Mar. For the love o' God, peace!   92

Enter MALVOLIO.

Mal. My masters, are you mad, or what are
you? Have you no wit, manners, nor honesty, but
to gabble like tinkers at this time of night? Do ye
make an alehouse of my lady's house, that ye
squeak out your coziers' catches without any mitigation or remorse of voice? Is there no respect of
place, persons, nor time in you?   99

Sir To. We did keep time, sir, in our catches.
Sneck up!

Mal. Sir Toby, I must be round with you. My
lady bade me tell you that, though she harbours
you as her kinsman, she's nothing alli'd to your disorders. If you can separate yourself and your   105
misdemeanours, you are welcome to the house; if
not, an it would please you to take leave of her, she
is very willing to bid you farewell.

Sir To. "Farewell, dear heart, since I must
needs be gone."   110

Mar. Nay, good Sir Toby.

Clo. "His eyes do show his days are almost
done."

Mal. Is't even so?

Sir To. "But I will never die."   115

Clo. Sir Toby, there you lie.

Mal. This is much credit to you.

Sir To. "Shall I bid him go?"

Clo. "What an if you do?"

Sir To. "Shall I bid him go, and spare not?"

Clo. "O no, no, no, no, you dare not."   121

Sir To. Out o' tune, sir! Ye lie. Art any more
than a steward? Dost thou think, because thou
art virtuous, there shall be no more cakes and
ale?   125

Clo. Yes, by Saint Anne, and ginger shall be hot
i' th' mouth too.

Sir To. Thou'rt i' th' right. Go, sir, rub your
chain with crumbs. A stoup of wine, Maria!

Mal. Mistress Mary, if you priz'd my lady's   130
favour at anything more than contempt, you would
not give means for this uncivil rule. She shall
know of it, by this hand.   [*Exit.*

Mar. Go shake your ears.   134

Sir And. 'Twere as good a deed as to drink when
a man's a-hungry, to challenge him the field, and
then to break promise with him and make a fool of
him.

Sir To. Do't, knight. I'll write thee a challenge, or I'll deliver thy indignation to him by word
of mouth.   141

Mar. Sweet Sir Toby, be patient for to-night.
Since the youth of the Count's was to-day with my
lady, she is much out of quiet. For Monsieur
Malvolio, let me alone with him. If I do not   145
gull him into a nayword, and make him a common recreation, do not think I have wit enough to
lie straight in my bed. I know I can do it.

Sir To. Possess us, possess us. Tell us something
of him.   150

Mar. Marry, sir, sometimes he is a kind of puritan.

Sir And. O, if I thought that, I'd beat him like a
dog!

Sir To. What, for being a puritan? Thy exquisite reason, dear knight?   156

Sir And. I have no exquisite reason for't, but I
have reason good enough.

Mar. The devil a puritan that he is, or anything
constantly, but a time-pleaser; an affection'd   160
ass, that cons state without book and utters it by
great swarths; the best persuaded of himself, so
cramm'd, as he thinks, with excellencies, that it is
his grounds of faith that all that look on him love
him; and on that vice in him will my revenge find
notable cause to work.   166

Sir To. What wilt thou do?

Mar. I will drop in his way some obscure
epistles of love; wherein, by the colour of his beard,

---

80. **Cataian:** Chinese, rascal. 81. **Peg-a-Ramsey:** a character in a ballad. **Three merry men** (etc.). This and subsequent quotations are from popular songs. 97. **coziers':** cobblers'. 101. **Sneck up:** go hang. 128. **chain:** i.e., steward's
badge. 145. **nayword:** byword. 149. **Possess:** inform. 160. **affection'd:** affected. 161. **cons...book:** memorizes
courtly speeches. 162. **swarths:** swaths.

the shape of his leg, the manner of his gait, the   170
expressure of his eye, forehead, and complexion, he
shall find himself most feelingly personated. I can
write very like my lady your niece. On a forgotten
matter we can hardly make distinction of our
hands.   175

Sir To. Excellent! I smell a device.

Sir And. I have't in my nose too.

Sir To. He shall think, by the letters that thou
wilt drop, that they come from my niece, and that
she's in love with him.   180

Mar. My purpose is, indeed, a horse of that
colour.

Sir And. And your horse now would make him
an ass.

Mar. Ass, I doubt not.   185

Sir And. O, 'twill be admirable!

Mar. Sport royal, I warrant you. I know my
physic will work with him. I will plant you two,
and let the fool make a third, where he shall find
the letter. Observe his construction of it. For   190
this night, to bed, and dream on the event. Farewell.   [*Exit.*

Sir To. Good night, Penthesilea.

Sir And. Before me, she's a good wench.

Sir To. She's a beagle, true-bred, and one that
adores me. What o' that?   196

Sir And. I was ador'd once too.

Sir To. Let's to bed, knight. Thou hadst need
send for more money.

Sir And. If I cannot recover your niece, I am a
foul way out.   201

Sir To. Send for money, knight. If thou hast
her not i' the end, call me cut.

Sir And. If I do not, never trust me, take it how
you will.   205

Sir To. Come, come, I'll go burn some sack; 'tis
too late to go to bed now. Come, knight; come,
knight.   [*Exeunt.*

SCENE IV. [*A room in the Duke's palace.*]

Enter DUKE, VIOLA, CURIO, *and others.*

Duke. Give me some music. Now, — good
    morrow, friends, —
Now, good Cesario, but that piece of song,
That old and antique song we heard last night.
Methought it did relieve my passion much,
More than light airs and recollected terms   5
Of these most brisk and giddy-paced times.
Come, but one verse.

Cur. He is not here, so please your lordship, that
should sing it.

Duke. Who was it?   10

Cur. Feste, the jester, my lord; a fool that the
lady Olivia's father took much delight in. He is
about the house.

Duke. Seek him out, and play the tune the
    while.   [*Exit Curio.*] *Music plays.*
Come hither, boy. If ever thou shalt love,   15
In the sweet pangs of it remember me;
For such as I am all true lovers are,
Unstaid and skittish in all motions else,
Save in the constant image of the creature
That is belov'd. How dost thou like this tune?

Vio. It gives a very echo to the seat   21
Where Love is thron'd.

Duke.   Thou dost speak masterly.
My life upon't, young though thou art, thine eye
Hath stay'd upon some favour that it loves.   25
Hath it not, boy?

Vio.   A little, by your favour.

Duke. What kind of woman is't?

Vio.   Of your complexion.

Duke. She is not worth thee, then. What years,
i' faith?

Vio. About your years, my lord.

Duke. Too old, by heaven. Let still the woman
    take   30
An elder than herself; so wears she to him,
So sways she level in her husband's heart.
For, boy, however we do praise ourselves,
Our fancies are more giddy and unfirm,
More longing, wavering, sooner lost and worn,   35
Than women's are.

Vio.   I think it well, my lord.

Duke. Then let thy love be younger than thy-
    self,
Or thy affection cannot hold the bent.
For women are as roses, whose fair flower
Being once display'd, doth fall that very hour.   40

Vio. And so they are; alas, that they are so!
To die, even when they to perfection grow!

Re-enter CURIO *and* CLOWN.

Duke. O, fellow, come, the song we had last
    night.
Mark it, Cesario, it is old and plain.
The spinsters and the knitters in the sun   45
And the free maids that weave their thread with
    bones
Do use to chant it. It is silly sooth,
And dallies with the innocence of love,
Like the old age.

Clo. Are you ready, sir?   50

Duke. Ay; prithee, sing.   [*Music.*

---

193. **Penthesilea:** Queen of the Amazons. 200. **recover:** win. 201. **out:** i.e., of money. 203. **cut:** horse with docked
tail. 206. **burn:** heat and spice. **sack:** a Spanish wine.

  Sc. iv, 5. **recollected terms:** studied phrases. 18. **motions:** emotions. 25. **favour:** face. 38. **the bent:** its intensity.
46. **free:** carefree. **bones:** bobbins (of bone). 47. **silly sooth:** simple truth. 49. **old age:** golden age.

SONG.

[Clo.] Come away, come away, death,
   And in sad cypress let me be laid.
Fly away, fly away, breath;
   I am slain by a fair cruel maid.   55
My shroud of white, stuck all with yew,
      O, prepare it!
My part of death, no one so true
      Did share it.

Not a flower, not a flower sweet,   60
   On my black coffin let there be strown.
Not a friend, not a friend greet
   My poor corpse, where my bones shall be thrown.
A thousand thousand sighs to save,
     Lay me, O, where   65
Sad true lover never find my grave,
     To weep there!

Duke. There's for thy pains.
Clo. No pains, sir; I take pleasure in singing,
sir.   70
Duke. I'll pay thy pleasure then.
Clo. Truly, sir, and pleasure will be paid, one
time or another.
Duke. Give me now leave to leave thee.   74
Clo. Now, the melancholy god protect thee, and
the tailor make thy doublet of changeable taffeta,
for thy mind is a very opal. I would have men of
such constancy put to sea, that their business might
be everything and their intent everywhere; for
that's it that always makes a good voyage of noth-
ing. Farewell.   *[Exit.* 81
Duke. Let all the rest give place.
           [Curio and Attendants retire.]
           Once more, Cesario,
Get thee to yond same sovereign cruelty.
Tell her, my love, more noble than the world,
Prizes not quantity of dirty lands.   85
The parts that fortune hath bestow'd upon her,
Tell her, I hold as giddily as fortune;
But 'tis that miracle and queen of gems
That nature pranks her in attracts my soul.
Vio. But if she cannot love you, sir?   90
Duke. [I] cannot be so answer'd.
Vio.   Sooth, but you must.
Say that some lady, as perhaps there is,
Hath for your love as great a pang of heart
As you have for Olivia. You cannot love her.
You tell her so. Must she not then be answer'd? 95
Duke. There is no woman's sides
Can bide the beating of so strong a passion

As love doth give my heart; no woman's heart
So big, to hold so much. They lack retention.
Alas, their love may be call'd appetite,   100
No motion of the liver, but the palate,
That suffer surfeit, cloyment, and revolt;
But mine is all as hungry as the sea,
And can digest as much. Make no compare
Between that love a woman can bear me   105
And that I owe Olivia.
Vio.   Ay, but I know —
Duke. What dost thou know?
Vio. Too well what love women to men may owe.
In faith, they are as true of heart as we.
My father had a daughter lov'd a man,   110
As it might be, perhaps, were I a woman,
I should your lordship.
Duke.   And what's her history?
Vio. A blank, my lord. She never told her love,
But let concealment, like a worm i' the bud,
Feed on her damask cheek. She pin'd in
    thought,   115
And with a green and yellow melancholy
She sat, like Patience on a monument,
Smiling at grief. Was not this love indeed?
We men may say more, swear more; but indeed
Our shows are more than will, for still we prove 120
Much in our vows, but little in our love.
Duke. But died thy sister of her love, my boy?
Vio. I am all the daughters of my father's house,
And all the brothers too; — and yet I know not.
Sir, shall I to this lady?
Duke.   Ay, that's the theme.
To her in haste. Give her this jewel. Say   126
My love can give no place, bide no denay.
                   [Exeunt.

SCENE V. [*Olivia's garden.*]

Enter SIR TOBY, SIR ANDREW, *and* FABIAN.

Sir To. Come thy ways, Signior Fabian.
Fab. Nay, I'll come. If I lose a scruple of this
sport, let me be boil'd to death with melancholy. 4
Sir To. Wouldst thou not be glad to have the
niggardly rascally sheep-biter come by some notable
shame?
Fab. I would exult, man. You know, he brought
me out o' favour with my lady about a bear-baiting
here.   10
Sir To. To anger him we'll have the bear again,
and we will fool him black and blue. Shall we not,
Sir Andrew?
Sir And. An we do not, it is pity of our lives. 15

---

53. **cypress:** coffin of cypress wood.   58–59. **My ... share it:** i.e., No truer lover ever died than I.   76. **changeable taffeta:** shot silk.   87. **giddily:** carelessly.   89. **pranks:** adorns.   91. **[I]** (Hanmer). *It* F.   99. **retention:** stability.   102. **cloyment:** satiety. **revolt:** revulsion.   115. **thought:** brooding.   116. **green and yellow,** signifying hope and jealousy.   117. **monument:** tomb.
Sc. v, 6. **sheep-biter:** a vicious dog.

Enter MARIA.

Sir To. Here comes the little villain. How now, my metal of India!

Mar. Get ye all three into the box-tree; Malvolio's coming down this walk. He has been yonder i' the sun practising behaviour to his own 20 shadow this half hour. Observe him, for the love of mockery, for I know this letter will make a contemplative idiot of him. Close, in the name of jesting! Lie thou there [*throws down a letter*], for here comes the trout that must be caught with tickling.   [*Exit.* 26

Enter MALVOLIO.

Mal. 'Tis but fortune. All is fortune. Maria once told me she did affect me; and I have heard herself come thus near, that, should she fancy, it should be one of my complexion. Besides, she 30 uses me with a more exalted respect than any one else that follows her. What should I think on't?

Sir To. Here's an overweening rogue!   34

Fab. O, peace! Contemplation makes a rare turkey-cock of him. How he jets under his advanc'd plumes!

Sir And. 'S light, I could so beat the rogue!

Sir To. Peace, I say.

Mal. To be Count Malvolio!   40

Sir To. Ah, rogue!

Sir And. Pistol him, pistol him.

Sir To. Peace, peace!

Mal. There is example for't. The lady of the Strachy married the yeoman of the wardrobe. 45

Sir And. Fie on him, Jezebel!

Fab. O, peace! now he's deeply in. Look how imagination blows him.

Mal. Having been three months married to her, sitting in my state, —   50

Sir To. O, for a stone-bow, to hit him in the eye!

Mal. Calling my officers about me, in my branch'd velvet gown, having come from a day-bed, where I have left Olivia sleeping, —   55

Sir To. Fire and brimstone!

Fab. O, peace, peace!

Mal. And then to have the humour of state; and after a demure travel of regard, telling them I know my place as I would they should do theirs, to ask for my kinsman Toby, —   61

Sir To. Bolts and shackles!

Fab. O peace, peace, peace! Now, now.

Mal. Seven of my people, with an obedient start, make out for him. I frown the while, and per- 65 chance wind up my watch, or play with my — some

rich jewel. Toby approaches, curtsies there to me, —

Sir To. Shall this fellow live?

Fab. Though our silence be drawn from us with cars, yet peace.   71

Mal. I extend my hand to him thus, quenching my familiar smile with an austere regard of control, —

Sir To. And does not Toby take you a blow o' the lips then?   76

Mal. Saying, "Cousin Toby, my fortunes, having cast me on your niece, give me this prerogative of speech," —

Sir To. What, what?   80

Mal. "You must amend your drunkenness."

Sir To. Out, scab!

Fab. Nay, patience, or we break the sinews of our plot.

Mal. "Besides, you waste the treasure of your time with a foolish knight," —   86

Sir And. That's me, I warrant you.

Mal. "One Sir Andrew," —

Sir And. I knew 'twas I; for many do call me fool.   90

Mal. What employment have we here?

       [*Taking up the letter.*]

Fab. Now is the woodcock near the gin.

Sir To. O, peace, and the spirit of humours intimate reading aloud to him!   94

Mal. By my life, this is my lady's hand. These be her very C's, her U's, and her T's; and thus makes she her great P's. It is, in contempt of question, her hand.

Sir And. Her C's, her U's, and her T's: why that?   100

Mal. [*Reads.*] "To the unknown belov'd, this, and my good wishes": — her very phrases! By your leave, wax. Soft! And the impressure her Lucrece, with which she uses to seal. 'Tis my lady. To whom should this be?   105

Fab. This wins him, liver and all.

Mal. [*Reads.*]

      "Jove knows I love;
        But who?
      Lips, do not move;
      No man must know."

"No man must know." What follows? The numbers alter'd! "No man must know!" If this should be thee, Malvolio?

Sir To. Marry, hang thee, brock!

Mal. [*Reads.*]

      "I may command where I adore;   115

---

17. **metal of India**: gold.   22. **contemplative**: staring or self-regarding; cf. "Contemplation" (l. 35).   26. **tickling.** Trout can be caught by being stroked.   36. **jets**: struts.   45. **Strachy.** This lady, unidentified, obviously married below her station.   50. **state**: chair of state.   54. **branch'd**: flowered.   58. **humour of state**: mood of authority.   59. **demure . . . regard**: grave look about (me).   73. **control**: authority.   92. **woodcock**: a bird noted for its stupidity.   **gin**: snare. 97. **in contempt of**: beyond.   103. **By . . . wax.** Spoken as he breaks the seal.   112. **numbers**: metre.   114. **brock**: badger.

But silence, like a Lucrece knife,
With bloodless stroke my heart doth gore.
M, O, A, I, doth sway my life."
Fab. A fustian riddle!
Sir To. Excellent wench, say I.   120
Mal. "M, O, A, I, doth sway my life." Nay,
but first, let me see, let me see, let me see.
Fab. What dish o' poison has she dress'd him!
Sir To. And with what wing the [staniel] checks
at it!   125
Mal. "I may command where I adore." Why,
she may command me. I serve her. She is my
lady. Why, this is evident to any formal capacity,
there is no obstruction in this. And the end, —
what should that alphabetical position portend? 130
If I could make that resemble something in me! —
Softly! M, O, A, I, —   •
Sir To. O, ay, make up that. He is now at a
cold scent.
Fab. Sowter will cry upon't for all this, though
it be as rank as a fox.   136
Mal. M, — Malvolio; M, — why, that begins
my name.
Fab. Did not I say he would work it out? The
cur is excellent at faults.   140
Mal. M, — but then there is no consonancy in
the sequel. That suffers under probation. A
should follow, but O does.
Fab. And O shall end, I hope.
Sir To. Ay, or I'll cudgel him, and make him
cry O!   146
Mal. And then I comes behind.
Fab. Ay, an you had any eye behind you, you
might see more detraction at your heels than fortunes before you.   150
Mal. M, O, A, I; this simulation is not as the
former. And yet, to crush this a little, it would
bow to me, for every one of these letters are in my
name. Soft! here follows prose.   154
[*Reads.*] "If this fall into thy hand, revolve. In
my stars I am above thee, but be not afraid of
greatness. Some are [born] great, some achieve
greatness, and some have greatness thrust upon 'em.
Thy Fates open their hands, let thy blood and spirit
embrace them; and, to inure thyself to what   160
thou art like to be, cast thy humble slough and
appear fresh. Be opposite with a kinsman, surly
with servants; let thy tongue tang arguments of
state; put thyself into the trick of singularity: she
thus advises thee that sighs for thee. Remem- 165
ber who commended thy yellow stockings, and

wish'd to see thee ever cross-garter'd. I say, remember. Go to, thou art made if thou desir'st to
be so; if not, let me see thee a steward still, the fellow of servants, and not worthy to touch For- 170
tune's fingers. Farewell. She that would alter
services with thee,

THE FORTUNATE UNHAPPY."

Daylight and champaign discovers not more.
This is open. I will be proud, I will read politic 175
authors, I will baffle Sir Toby, I will wash off gross
acquaintance, I will be point-device the very man.
I do not now fool myself, to let imagination jade me;
for every reason excites to this, that my lady loves
me. She did commend my yellow stockings of 180
late, she did praise my leg being cross-garter'd; and
in this she manifests herself to my love, and with a
kind of injunction drives me to these habits of her
liking. I thank my stars I am happy. I will be
strange, stout, in yellow stockings, and cross- 185
garter'd, even with the swiftness of putting on.
Jove and my stars be praised! Here is yet a postscript.
[*Reads.*] "Thou canst not choose but know who
I am. If thou entertain'st my love, let it appear 190
in thy smiling. Thy smiles become thee well;
therefore in my presence still smile, dear my sweet,
I prithee."
Jove, I thank thee. I will smile; I will do everything that thou wilt have me.   [*Exit.* 195
Fab. I will not give my part of this sport for a
pension of thousands to be paid from the Sophy.
Sir To. I could marry this wench for this
device —   200
Sir And. So could I too.
Sir To. And ask no other dowry with her but
such another jest.

Re-enter MARIA.

Sir And. Nor I neither.
Fab. Here comes my noble gull-catcher.   205
Sir To. Wilt thou set thy foot o' my neck?
Sir And. Or o' mine either?
Sir To. Shall I play my freedom at tray-trip,
and become thy bond-slave?
Sir And. I' faith, or I either?   210
Sir To. Why, thou hast put him in such a dream,
that when the image of it leaves him he must run
mad.
Mar. Nay, but say true. Does it work upon
him?   215
Sir To. Like aqua-vitæ with a midwife.

---

119. **fustian:** ridiculous.   124. **[staniel]** (Hanmer): untrained falcon.   *stallion* F.   **checks at it:** turns aside (as to
inferior prey). Cf. III.i.71.   128. **formal:** normal.   135-36. **Sowter...fox.** I.e., Even Sowter (a stupid hound) will
catch this scent though, in fact, it is as strong as a fox's.   Cf. *Shrew*, Ind. i.23.   140. **faults:** failure of the scent.   141.
consonancy: agreement.   142. **probation:** testing.   151. **simulation:** suggestion.   152. **crush:** force (the meaning).   155.
revolve: consider.   157. **[born]** (Rowe).   *become* F.   Cf. III.iv.45 and V.i.378.   161. **slough:** skin (of a snake).   162.
opposite: contradictory.   174. **champaign:** open country.   175. **politic:** i.e., who treat state affairs.   177. **point-device:**
precisely.   178. **jade:** trick.   185. **stout:** haughty.   198. **Sophy:** Shah of Persia.   208. **tray-trip:** a game with dice.

Mar. If you will then see the fruits of the sport, mark his first approach before my lady. He will come to her in yellow stockings, and 'tis a colour she abhors, and cross-garter'd, a fashion she de- 220 tests; and he will smile upon her, which will now be so unsuitable to her disposition, being addicted to a melancholy as she is, that it cannot but turn him into a notable contempt. If you will see it, fol- low me. 225

Sir To. To the gates of Tartar, thou most ex- cellent devil of wit!

Sir And. I'll make one too. [*Exeunt.*

ACT III

Scene I. [*Olivia's garden.*]

Enter Viola *and* Clown [*with a tabor*].

Vio. Save thee, friend, and thy music! Dost thou live by thy tabor?

Clo. No, sir, I live by the church.

Vio. Art thou a churchman? 4

Clo. No such matter, sir. I do live by the church; for I do live at my house, and my house doth stand by the church.

Vio. So thou mayst say, the king lies by a beg- gar, if a beggar dwells near him; or, the church stands by thy tabor, if thy tabor stand by the church. 11

Clo. You have said, sir. To see this age! A sentence is but a chev'ril glove to a good wit. How quickly the wrong side may be turn'd outward! 15

Vio. Nay, that's certain. They that dally nicely with words may quickly make them wanton.

Clo. I would, therefore, my sister had had no name, sir. 20

Vio. Why, man?

Clo. Why, sir, her name's a word, and to dally with that word might make my sister wanton. But, indeed, words are very rascals since bonds disgrac'd them. 25

Vio. Thy reason, man?

Clo. Troth, sir, I can yield you none without words; and words are grown so false, I am loath to prove reason with them. 29

Vio. I warrant thou art a merry fellow and car'st for nothing.

Clo. Not so, sir, I do care for something; but in my conscience, sir, I do not care for you. If that be to care for nothing, sir, I would it would make you invisible. 35

Vio. Art not thou the Lady Olivia's fool?

Clo. No, indeed, sir; the Lady Olivia has no folly. She will keep no fool, sir, till she be married; and fools are as like husbands as pilchards are to her- rings, the husband's the bigger. I am indeed not her fool, but her corrupter of words. 41

Vio. I saw thee late at the Count Orsino's.

Clo. Foolery, sir, does walk about the orb like the sun, it shines everywhere. I would be sorry, sir, but the fool should be as oft with your master as with my mistress. I think I saw your wisdom there. 47

Vio. Nay, an thou pass upon me, I'll no more with thee. Hold, there's expenses for thee.

Clo. Now Jove, in his next commodity of hair, send thee a beard! 51

• *Vio.* By my troth, I'll tell thee, I am almost sick for one, — [*aside*] though I would not have it grow on my chin. Is thy lady within?

Clo. Would not a pair of these have bred, sir? 55

Vio. Yes, being kept together and put to use.

Clo. I would play Lord Pandarus of Phrygia, sir, to bring a Cressida to this Troilus.

Vio. I understand you, sir. 'Tis well begg'd. 60

Clo. The matter, I hope, is not great, sir, begging but a beggar. Cressida was a beggar. My lady is within, sir. I will construe to them whence you come. Who you are and what you would are out of my welkin — I might say "element," but the word is overworn. [*Exit.* 66

Vio. This fellow is wise enough to play the fool, And to do that well craves a kind of wit. He must observe their mood on whom he jests, The quality of persons, and the time, 70 And, like the haggard, check at every feather That comes before his eye. This is a practice As full of labour as a wise man's art; For folly that he wisely shows is fit, But wise men, folly-fall'n, quite taint their wit. 75

Enter Sir Toby *and* Sir Andrew.

Sir To. Save you, gentleman.

Vio. And you, sir.

Sir And. Dieu vous garde, monsieur.

Vio. Et vous aussi; votre serviteur.

Sir And. I hope, sir, you are; and I am yours. 81

Sir To. Will you encounter the house? My niece is desirous you should enter, if your trade be to her.

Vio. I am bound to your niece, sir; I mean, she is the list of my voyage. 86

226. **Tartar:** Tartarus (Hell). Act III, sc. i, 2. **tabor:** small drum. 13. **chev'ril:** kid. 18. **wanton:** equivocal (*unchaste*, l. 23). 24. **disgrac'd them:** i.e., became necessary to bind them. 39. **pilchards:** fish like herring. 48. **pass upon:** jest at. 50. **commodity:** consign- ment. 55. **these:** i.e. coins (see l. 49). 56. **use:** interest. 57. **Pandarus:** uncle to Cressida, who brought her and Troilus together. 62. **Cressida . . . beggar.** In Henryson's *Testament of Cresseid*, Cressida became a leper and begged by the road- side. 71. **haggard:** untrained hawk. 75. **folly-fall'n:** acting like fools. 79–80. *Dieu . . . serviteur:* God keep you, sir. And you, too; I am your servant. 86. **list:** goal.

Sir To. Taste your legs, sir; put them to motion.

Vio. My legs do better understand me, sir, than I understand what you mean by bidding me taste my legs. 91

Sir To. I mean, to go, sir, to enter.

Vio. I will answer you with [gait] and entrance. But we are prevented.

Enter OLIVIA *and Gentlewoman.*

Most excellent accomplish'd lady, the heavens rain odours on you! 96

Sir And. That youth's a rare courtier. "Rain odours;" well.

Vio. My matter hath no voice, lady, but to your own most pregnant and vouchsafed ear. 100

Sir And. "Odours," "pregnant," and "vouchsafed"; I'll get 'em all three all ready.

Oli. Let the garden door be shut, and leave me to hearing. [*Exeunt all but Olivia and Viola.*] Give me your hand, sir. 105

Vio. My duty, madam, and most humble service.

Oli. What is your name?

Vio. Cesario is your servant's name, fair princess.

Oli. My servant, sir! 'Twas never merry world Since lowly feigning was call'd compliment. 110 You're servant to the Count Orsino, youth.

Vio. And he is yours, and his must needs be yours. Your servant's servant is your servant, madam.

Oli. For him, I think not on him. For his thoughts, Would they were blanks, rather than fill'd with me! 115

Vio. Madam, I come to whet your gentle thoughts On his behalf.

Oli.   O, by your leave, I pray you, I bade you never speak again of him; But, would you undertake another suit, I had rather hear you to solicit that 120 Than music from the spheres.

Vio.   Dear lady,—

Oli. Give me leave, beseech you. I did send, After the last enchantment you did here, A ring in chase of you; so did I abuse Myself, my servant, and, I fear me, you. 125 Under your hard construction must I sit, To force that on you, in a shameful cunning, Which you knew none of yours. What might you think? Have you not set mine honour at the stake And baited it with all th' unmuzzled thoughts 130

That tyrannous heart can think? To one of your receiving Enough is shown. A cypress, not a bosom, Hides my heart. So, let me hear you speak.

Vio. I pity you.

Oli.   That's a degree to love.

Vio. No, not a grize; for 'tis a vulgar proof, 135 That very oft we pity enemies.

Oli. Why, then, methinks 'tis time to smile again. O world, how apt the poor are to be proud! If one should be a prey, how much the better To fall before the lion than the wolf! 140 [*Clock strikes.* The clock upbraids me with the waste of time. Be not afraid, good youth, I will not have you; And yet, when wit and youth is come to harvest, Your wife is like to reap a proper man. There lies your way, due west. 145

Vio. Then westward-ho! Grace and good disposition Attend your ladyship! You'll nothing, madam, to my lord by me?

Oli. Stay! I prithee, tell me what thou think'st of me. 150

Vio. That you do think you are not what you are.

Oli. If I think so, I think the same of you.

Vio. Then think you right. I am not what I am.

Oli. I would you were as I would have you be!

Vio. Would it be better, madam, than I am? I wish it might, for now I am your fool. 156

Oli. O, what a deal of scorn looks beautiful In the contempt and anger of his lip! A murd'rous guilt shows not itself more soon Than love that would seem hid. Love's night is noon. 160 Cesario, by the roses of the spring, By maidhood, honour, truth, and everything, I love thee so, that, maugre all thy pride, Nor wit nor reason can my passion hide. Do not extort thy reasons from this clause, 165 For that I woo, thou therefore hast no cause; But rather reason thus with reason fetter, Love sought is good, but given unsought is better.

Vio. By innocence I swear, and by my youth, I have one heart, one bosom, and one truth, 170 And that no woman has; nor never none Shall mistress be of it, save I alone. And so adieu, good madam; nevermore Will I my master's tears to you deplore.

Oli. Yet come again; for thou perhaps mayst move 175 That heart, which now abhors, to like his love. [*Exeunt.*

---

93. [gait] (Johnson). *gate* F. A pun on the two words. 94. **prevented:** anticipated. 100. **pregnant:** ready. 127. **to force:** for forcing. 129–30. **Have...thoughts.** The figure of speech comes from bear-baiting. 131. **receiving:** intelligence. 132. **cypress:** thin crepe. 134. **degree:** step. 135. **grize:** step. **vulgar proof:** common experience. 163. **maugre:** in spite of. 166. **no cause:** i.e., to woo.

SCENE II. [*A room in Olivia's house.*]

Enter SIR TOBY, SIR ANDREW, *and* FABIAN.

Sir And. No, faith, I'll not stay a jot longer.

Sir To. Thy reason, dear venom, give thy reason.

Fab. You must needs yield your reason, Sir Andrew. 5

Sir And. Marry, I saw your niece do more favours to the Count's serving-man than ever she bestow'd upon me. I saw't i' th' orchard.

Sir To. Did she see thee the while, old boy? Tell me that. 10

Sir And. As plain as I see you now.

Fab. This was a great argument of love in her toward you.

Sir And. 'Slight, will you make an ass o' me?

Fab. I will prove it legitimate, sir, upon the oaths of judgement and reason. 16

Sir To. And they have been grand-jurymen since before Noah was a sailor.

Fab. She did show favour to the youth in your sight only to exasperate you, to awake your 20 dormouse valour, to put fire in your heart, and brimstone in your liver. You should then have accosted her; and with some excellent jests, fire-new from the mint, you should have bang'd the youth into dumbness. This was look'd for at 25 your hand, and this was balk'd. The double gilt of this opportunity you let time wash off, and you are now sailed into the north of my lady's opinion, where you will hang like an icicle on a Dutchman's beard, unless you do redeem it by some laudable attempt either of valour or policy. 31

Sir And. An't be any way, it must be with valour; for policy I hate. I had as lief be a Brownist as a politician. 34

Sir To. Why, then, build me thy fortunes upon the basis of valour. Challenge me the Count's youth to fight with him; hurt him in eleven places; my niece shall take note of it; and assure thyself, there is no love-broker in the world can more prevail in man's commendation with woman than report of valour. 41

Fab. There is no way but this, Sir Andrew.

Sir And. Will either of you bear me a challenge to him?

Sir To. Go, write it in a martial hand. Be 45 curst and brief. It is no matter how witty, so it be eloquent and full of invention. Taunt him with the license of ink. If thou thou'st him some thrice, it shall not be amiss; and as many lies as will lie in thy sheet of paper, although the sheet were big 50 enough for the bed of Ware in England, set 'em down. Go about it. Let there be gall enough in thy ink. Though thou write with a goose-pen, no matter. About it.

Sir And. Where shall I find you? 55

Sir To. We'll call thee at the cubiculo. Go.

[*Exit Sir Andrew.*]

Fab. This is a dear manikin to you, Sir Toby.

Sir To. I have been dear to him, lad, some two thousand strong, or so.

Fab. We shall have a rare letter from him. But you'll not deliver't? 61

Sir To. Never trust me, then; and by all means stir on the youth to an answer. I think oxen and wainropes cannot hale them together. For Andrew, if he were open'd and you find so much blood in his liver as will clog the foot of a flea, I'll eat the rest of the anatomy. 67

Fab. And his opposite, the youth, bears in his visage no great presage of cruelty.

Enter MARIA.

Sir To. Look, where the youngest wren of mine comes. 71

Mar. If you desire the spleen, and will laugh yourselves into stitches, follow me. Yond gull Malvolio is turned heathen, a very renegado; for there is no Christian that means to be saved by 75 believing rightly can ever believe such impossible passages of grossness. He's in yellow stockings.

Sir To. And cross-garter'd? 79

Mar. Most villanously; like a pedant that keeps a school i' th' church. I have dogg'd him like his murderer. He does obey every point of the letter that I dropp'd to betray him. He does smile his face into more lines than is in the new map with the augmentation of the Indies. You have 85 not seen such a thing as 'tis. I can hardly forbear hurling things at him. I know my lady will strike him. If she do, he'll smile and take't for a great favour.

Sir To. Come, bring us, bring us where he is. 90

[*Exeunt.*]

SCENE III. [*A street.*]

Enter SEBASTIAN *and* ANTONIO.

Seb. I would not by my will have troubled you; But, since you make your pleasure of your pains, I will no further chide you.

Ant. I could not stay behind you. My desire, More sharp than filed steel, did spur me forth, 5

Sc. ii, 14. **'Slight:** by God's light. 31. **policy:** tact (Sir Andrew interprets as *intrigue*). 33. **Brownist:** member of the sect of Independents, founded by Robert Brown. 46. **curst:** surly. 48. **thou'st:** use "thou" as to an inferior. 51. **bed of Ware:** a famous bed (nearly twelve feet square) in an inn at Ware in Hertfordshire. 56. **cubiculo:** i.e., Sir Andrew's apartment. 64. **wainropes:** cart-ropes. 68. **opposite:** opponent. 70. **mine** Ff. *nine* (Theobald). 72. **spleen:** fit of laughter. 77. **impossible ... grossness:** incredible acts of stupidity. 84. **new ... Indies.** Probably a map published about 1599 by Emerie Molyneux, giving more of the East Indies than any earlier one. See Introduction, p. 279.

And not all love to see you, though so much
As might have drawn one to a longer voyage,
But jealousy what might befall your travel,
Being skilless in these parts; which to a stranger,
Unguided and unfriended, often prove   10
Rough and unhospitable. My willing love,
The rather by these arguments of fear,
Set forth in your pursuit.

Seb.   My kind Antonio,
I can no other answer make but thanks,
And thanks, and ever [thanks. Too] oft good
          turns   15
Are shuffl'd off with such uncurrent pay;
But, were my worth as is my conscience firm,
You should find better dealing. What's to do?
Shall we go see the reliques of this town?

Ant. To-morrow, sir. Best first go see your
          lodging.   20

Seb. I am not weary, and 'tis long to night.
I pray you, let us satisfy our eyes
With the memorials and the things of fame
That do renown this city.

Ant.   Would you'd pardon me.
I do not without danger walk these streets.   25
Once, in a sea-fight, 'gainst the Count his galleys
I did some service; of such note indeed,
That were I ta'en here it would scarce be answer'd.

Seb. Belike you slew great number of his people?

Ant. Th' offence is not of such a bloody nature,
Albeit the quality of the time and quarrel   31
Might well have given us bloody argument.
It might have since been answer'd in repaying
What we took from them, which, for traffic's sake,
Most of our city did; only myself stood out,   35
For which, if I be lapsed in this place,
I shall pay dear.

Seb.   Do not then walk too open.

Ant. It doth not fit me. Hold, sir, here's my
          purse.
In the south suburbs, at the Elephant
Is best to lodge. I will bespeak our diet,   40
Whiles you beguile the time and feed your knowl-
          edge
With viewing of the town. There shall you have me.

Seb. Why I your purse?

Ant. Haply your eye shall light upon some toy
You have desire to purchase; and your store,   45
I think, is not for idle markets, sir.

Seb. I'll be your purse-bearer and leave you
For an hour.

Ant.   To th' Elephant.

Seb.   I do remember.
                                          [*Exeunt.*

SCENE IV. [*Olivia's garden.*]

Enter OLIVIA *and* MARIA.

Oli. [*Aside.*] I have sent after him; he says he'll
          come.
How shall I feast him? What bestow of him?
For youth is bought more oft than begg'd or bor-
          row'd.
I speak too loud. —
Where is Malvolio? He is sad and civil,   5
And suits well for a servant with my fortunes.
Where is Malvolio?

Mar. He's coming, madam, but in very strange
manner. He is, sure, possess'd, madam.

Oli. Why, what's the matter? Does he rave?   10

Mar. No, madam, he does nothing but smile.
Your ladyship were best to have some guard about
you, if he come; for, sure, the man is tainted in's
wits.

Oli. Go call him hither.

Enter MALVOLIO.

                          I am as mad as he, 15
If sad and merry madness equal be.
How now, Malvolio!

Mal. Sweet lady, ho, ho.

Oli. Smil'st thou?
I sent for thee upon a sad occasion.   20

Mal. Sad, lady? I could be sad. This does
make some obstruction in the blood, this cross-
gartering; but what of that? If it please the eye
of one, it is with me as the very true sonnet is,
"Please one, and please all."   25
[*Oli.*] Why, how dost thou, man? What is the
matter with thee?

Mal. Not black in my mind, though yellow in
my legs. It did come to his hands, and commands
shall be executed. I think we do know the sweet
Roman hand.   31

Oli. Wilt thou go to bed, Malvolio?

Mal. To bed! Ay, sweet heart, and I'll come to
thee.

Oli. God comfort thee! Why dost thou smile
so and kiss thy hand so oft?   36

Mar. How do you, Malvolio?

Mal. At your request! Yes. Nightingales
answer daws.

Mar. Why appear you with this ridiculous boldness before my lady?   41

Mal. "Be not afraid of greatness:" 'twas well
writ.

Oli. What mean'st thou by that, Malvolio?

Mal. "Some are born great," —   45

Sc. iii, 8. **jealousy**: suspicion. 9. **skilless**: unacquainted. 15. **And thanks ... oft** (Seymour). *And thankes; and ever*
oft F. 16. **uncurrent**: worthless. 17. **worth**: wealth. 28. **answer'd**: atoned for. 31. **quality**: nature. 36. **lapsed**: caught.
46. **idle markets**: frivolous purchases.
Sc. iv, 5. **sad**: grave. 24. **sonnet**: ballad, of which the quotation is the refrain. 26–27. [*Oli.*] F₂. *Mal.* F₁.

Oli. Ha!

Mal. "Some achieve greatness," —

Oli. What say'st thou?

Mal. "And some have greatness thrust upon them." 50

Oli. Heaven restore thee!

Mal. "Remember who commended thy yellow stockings," —

Oli. Thy yellow stockings!

Mal. "And wish'd to see thee cross-garter'd."

Oli. Cross-garter'd! 56

Mal. "Go to, thou art made, if thou desir'st to be so;" —

Oli. Am I made? 59

Mal. "If not, let me see thee a servant still."

Oli. Why, this is very midsummer madness.

Enter SERVANT.

Ser. Madam, the young gentleman of the Count Orsino's is return'd. I could hardly entreat him back. He attends your ladyship's pleasure. 65

Oli. I'll come to him. [*Exit Servant.*] Good Maria, let this fellow be look'd to. Where's my cousin Toby? Let some of my people have a special care of him. I would not have him miscarry for the half of my dowry. 70

[*Exeunt [Olivia and Maria]*.

Mal. O, ho! do you come near me now? No worse man than Sir Toby to look to me! This concurs directly with the letter. She sends him on purpose, that I may appear stubborn to him, for she incites me to that in the letter. "Cast thy 75 humble slough," says she; "be opposite with a kinsman, surly with servants; let thy tongue tang with arguments of state; put thyself into the trick of singularity;" and consequently sets down the manner how; as, a sad face, a reverend carriage, a 80 slow tongue, in the habit of some sir of note, and so forth. I have lim'd her; but it is Jove's doing, and Jove make me thankful! And when she went away now, "Let this fellow be looked to"; "fellow!" not Malvolio, nor after my degree, but "fel- 85 low." Why, everything adheres together, that no dram of a scruple, no scruple of a scruple, no obstacle, no incredulous or unsafe circumstance — What can be said? Nothing that can be can come between me and the full prospect of my hopes. 90 Well, Jove, not I, is the doer of this, and he is to be thanked.

Re-enter MARIA, *with* SIR TOBY *and* FABIAN.

Sir To. Which way is he, in the name of sanctity?

If all the devils of hell be drawn in little, and Legion himself possess'd him, yet I'll speak to him. 96

Fab. Here he is, here he is. How is't with you, sir? How is't with you, man?

Mal. Go off; I discard you. Let me enjoy my private. Go off. 100

Mar. Lo, how hollow the fiend speaks within him! Did not I tell you? Sir Toby, my lady prays you to have a care of him.

Mal. Ah, ha! Does she so? 104

Sir To. Go to, go to; peace, peace. We must deal gently with him. Let me alone. How do you, Malvolio? How is't with you? What, man, defy the devil! Consider, he's an enemy to mankind.

Mal. Do you know what you say? 110

Mar. La you, an you speak ill of the devil, how he takes it at heart! Pray God he be not bewitch'd!

Fab. Carry his water to the wise woman. 114

Mar. Marry, and it shall be done to-morrow morning if I live. My lady would not lose him for more than I'll say.

Mal. How now, mistress!

Mar. O Lord! 119

Sir To. Prithee, hold thy peace; this is not the way. Do you not see you move him? Let me alone with him.

Fab. No way but gentleness; gently, gently. The fiend is rough, and will not be roughly us'd.

Sir To. Why, how now, my bawcock! How dost thou, chuck? 126

Mal. Sir!

Sir To. Ay, "Biddy, come with me." What, man, 'tis not for gravity to play at cherry-pit with Satan. Hang him, foul collier! 130

Mar. Get him to say his prayers, good Sir Toby, get him to pray.

Mal. My prayers, minx!

Mar. No, I warrant you, he will not hear of godliness. 135

Mal. Go, hang yourselves all! You are idle shallow things; I am not of your element. You shall know more hereafter. [*Exit.*

Sir To. Is't possible?

Fab. If this were played upon a stage now, I could condemn it as an improbable fiction. 141

Sir To. His very genius hath taken the infection of the device, man.

Mar. Nay, pursue him now, lest the device take air and taint. 145

Fab. Why, we shall make him mad indeed.

Mar. The house will be the quieter.

69. **miscarry:** suffer harm. 71. **come near:** begin to understand. 79. **consequently:** thereupon. 82. **lim'd:** caught. 84. **fellow:** originally *companion*, and so taken by Malvolio. 88. **incredulous:** incredible. 95. **little:** miniature. **Legion.** See *Mark* v.9. 124. **rough:** violent. 125. **bawcock:** fine fellow. 129. **cherry-pit:** child's game of throwing cherry stones into a hole. 137. **element:** sphere. 144. **take...taint:** become known and spoiled.

Sir To. Come, we'll have him in a dark room and bound. My niece is already in the belief that he's mad. We may carry it thus, for our pleasure 150 and his penance, till our very pastime, tired out of breath, prompt us to have mercy on him; at which time we will bring the device to the bar and crown thee for a finder of madmen. But see, but see. 155

Enter SIR ANDREW.

Fab. More matter for a May morning.

Sir And. Here's the challenge, read it. I warrant there's vinegar and pepper in't.

Fab. Is't so saucy? 159

Sir And. Ay, is't, I warrant him. Do but read.

Sir To. Give me. [*Reads.*] "Youth, whatsoever thou art, thou art but a scurvy fellow."

Fab. Good, and valiant. 164

Sir To. [*Reads.*] "Wonder not, nor admire not in thy mind, why I do call thee so, for I will show thee no reason for't."

Fab. A good note. That keeps you from the blow of the law. 169

Sir To. [*Reads.*] "Thou com'st to the lady Olivia, and in my sight she uses thee kindly. But thou liest in thy throat; that is not the matter I challenge thee for."

Fab. Very brief, and to exceeding good sense — less. 175

Sir To. [*Reads.*] "I will waylay thee going home; where if it be thy chance to kill me," —

Fab. Good.

Sir To. [*Reads.*] "Thou kill'st me like a rogue and a villain." 180

Fab. Still you keep o' th' windy side of the law; good.

Sir To. [*Reads.*] "Fare thee well, and God have mercy upon one of our souls! He may have mercy upon mine; but my hope is better, and so look 185 to thyself. Thy friend, as thou usest him, and thy sworn enemy,

          ANDREW AGUECHEEK."

If this letter move him not, his legs cannot. I'll give't him. 189

Mar. You may have very fit occasion for't. He is now in some commerce with my lady, and will by and by depart.

Sir To. Go, Sir Andrew, scout me for him at the corner of the orchard like a bum-baily. So soon as ever thou seest him, draw; and, as thou 195 draw'st, swear horrible; for it comes to pass oft that a terrible oath, with a swaggering accent sharply twang'd off, gives manhood more approbation than ever proof itself would have earn'd him. Away!

Sir And. Nay, let me alone for swearing. 201
              [*Exit.*

Sir To. Now will not I deliver his letter; for the behaviour of the young gentleman gives him out to be of good capacity and breeding; his employment between his lord and my niece confirms no 205 less; therefore this letter, being so excellently ignorant, will breed no terror in the youth; he will find it comes from a clodpole. But, sir, I will deliver his challenge by word of mouth, set upon Aguecheek a notable report of valour, and drive the gentle- 210 man, as I know his youth will aptly receive it, into a most hideous opinion of his rage, skill, fury, and impetuosity. This will so fright them both that they will kill one another by the look, like cockatrices. 215

Re-enter OLIVIA *with* VIOLA.

Fab. Here he comes with your niece. Give them way till he take leave, and presently after him.

Sir To. I will meditate the while upon some horrid message for a challenge. 220
      [*Exeunt Sir Toby, Fabian, and Maria.*]

Oli. I have said too much unto a heart of stone, And laid mine honour too unchary on't. There's something in me that reproves my fault; But such a headstrong potent fault it is That it but mocks reproof. 225

Vio. With the same 'haviour that your passion bears
Goes on my master's grief.

Oli. Here, wear this jewel for me; 'tis my picture. Refuse it not; it hath no tongue to vex you; And I beseech you come again to-morrow. 230 What shall you ask of me that I'll deny, That honour sav'd may upon asking give?

Vio. Nothing but this, — your true love for my master.

Oli. How with mine honour may I give him that Which I have given to you?

Vio.   I will acquit you. 235

Oli. Well, come again to-morrow. Fare thee well!
A fiend like thee might bear my soul to hell.
              [*Exit.*]

Re-enter SIR TOBY *and* FABIAN.

Sir To. Gentleman, God save thee!

Vio. And you, sir. 239

Sir To. That defence thou hast, betake thee to't. Of what nature the wrongs are thou hast done him, I know not; but thy intercepter, full of despite, bloody as the hunter, attends thee at the orchard-end. Dismount thy tuck, be yare in thy

---

165. **admire:** be amazed. 168. **note:** point. 181. **windy:** safe. 194. **bum-baily:** petty sheriff's officer (who arrested debtors). 198. **approbation:** credit. 199. **proof:** trial. 214. **cockatrices:** basilisks, fabulous creatures supposed to kill by a mere look. 217. **presently:** immediately. 222. **on't** Ff. *out* (Theobald). 244. **Dismount thy tuck:** draw thy sword. **yare:** quick.

preparation, for thy assailant is quick, skilful, and deadly.   246

Vio. You mistake, sir, I am sure. No man hath any quarrel to me. My remembrance is very free and clear from any image of offence done to any man.   250

Sir To. You'll find it otherwise, I assure you; therefore, if you hold your life at any price, betake you to your guard; for your opposite hath in him what youth, strength, skill, and wrath can furnish man withal.   255

Vio. I pray you, sir, what is he?

Sir To. He is knight, dubb'd with unhatch'd rapier and on carpet consideration; but he is a devil in private brawl. Souls and bodies hath he divorc'd three; and his incensement at this mo- 260 ment is so implacable, that satisfaction can be none but by pangs of death and sepulchre. Hob, nob, is his word; give't or take't.

Vio. I will return again into the house and desire some conduct of the lady. I am no fighter. 265 I have heard of some kind of men that put quarrels purposely on others, to taste their valour. Belike this is a man of that quirk.

Sir To. Sir, no; his indignation derives itself out of a very competent injury; therefore, get you 270 on and give him his desire. Back you shall not to the house, unless you undertake that with me which with as much safety you might answer him; therefore, on, or strip your sword stark naked; for meddle you must, that's certain, or forswear to wear iron about you.   276

Vio. This is as uncivil as strange. I beseech you, do me this courteous office, as to know of the knight what my offence to him is. It is something of my negligence, nothing of my purpose.   280

Sir To. I will do so. Signor Fabian, stay you by this gentleman till my return.   [*Exit.*

Vio. Pray you, sir, do you know of this matter?

Fab. I know the knight is incens'd against 285 you, even to a mortal arbitrement, but nothing of the circumstance more.

Vio. I beseech you, what manner of man is he?

Fab. Nothing of that wonderful promise, to 290 read him by his form, as you are like to find him in the proof of his valour. He is, indeed, sir, the most skilful, bloody, and fatal opposite that you could possibly have found in any part of Illyria. Will you walk towards him? I will make your peace with him if I can.   296

Vio. I shall be much bound to you for't. I am one that had rather go with sir priest than sir

knight. I care not who knows so much of my mettle.   [*Exeunt.* 300

Re-enter SIR TOBY, *with* SIR ANDREW.

Sir To. Why, man, he's a very devil; I have not seen such a firago. I had a pass with him, rapier, scabbard, and all, and he gives me the stuck in with such a mortal motion, that it is inevitable; and on the answer, he pays you as surely as your feet 305 hits the ground they step on. They say he has been fencer to the Sophy.

Sir And. Pox on't, I'll not meddle with him.

Sir To. Ay, but he will not now be pacified. Fabian can scarce hold him yonder.   310

Sir And. Plague on't, an I thought he had been valiant and so cunning in fence, I'd have seen him damn'd ere I'd have challeng'd him. Let him let the matter slip, and I'll give him my horse, grey Capilet.   315

Sir To. I'll make the motion. Stand here; make a good show on't. This shall end without the perdition of souls. [*Aside.*] Marry, I'll ride your horse as well as I ride you.   319

Re-enter FABIAN *and* VIOLA.

[*To Fab.*] I have his horse to take up the quarrel. I have persuaded him the youth's a devil.

Fab. He is as horribly conceited of him; and pants and looks pale, as if a bear were at his heels.   324

Sir To. [*To Vio.*] There's no remedy, sir; he will fight with you for's oath sake. Marry, he hath better bethought him of his quarrel, and he finds that now scarce to be worth talking of; therefore draw, for the supportance of his vow. He protests he will not hurt you.   330

Vio. [*Aside.*] Pray God defend me! A little thing would make me tell them how much I lack of a man.

Fab. Give ground, if you see him furious.   334

Sir To. Come, Sir Andrew, there's no remedy; the gentleman will, for his honour's sake, have one bout with you. He cannot by the duello avoid it; but he has promised me, as he is a gentleman and a soldier, he will not hurt you. Come on; to't.   340

Sir And. Pray God, he keep his oath!

Enter ANTONIO.

Vio. I do assure you, 'tis against my will.
                                          [*They draw.*

Ant. Put up your sword. If this young gentleman
Have done offence, I take the fault on me;

257. **unhatch'd:** unhacked.   258. **carpet consideration.** A "carpet knight" was one who had been dubbed not on the battlefield for valor, but on a carpet for money paid to the king.   265. **conduct:** escort.   268. **quirk:** humor.   274. **meddle:** fight.   286. **arbitrement:** trial.   302. **firago:** virago.   303. **stuck in:** thrust.   305. **on the answer:** on the return.   **pays you:** does for you.   320. **take up:** settle.   323. **is ... conceited:** has as horrible a conception.   337. **duello:** code of dueling.

If you offend him, I for him defy you. 345
Sir To. You, sir! Why, what are you?
Ant. One, sir, that for his love dares yet do more
Than you have heard him brag to you he will.
Sir To. Nay, if you be an undertaker, I am for
you. [*They draw.* 350

Enter OFFICERS.

Fab. O good Sir Toby, hold! Here come the
officers.
Sir To. I'll be with you anon.
Vio. Pray, sir, put your sword up, if you please.
Sir And. Marry, will I, sir; and, for that I 356
promis'd you, I'll be as good as my word. He will
bear you easily and reins well.
1. Off. This is the man; do thy office.
2. Off. Antonio, I arrest thee at the suit of Count
Orsino. 361
Ant. You do mistake me, sir.
1. Off. No, sir, no jot. I know your favour well,
Though now you have no sea-cap on your head.
Take him away; he knows I know him well. 365
Ant. I must obey. [*To Vio.*] This comes with
seeking you.
But there's no remedy; I shall answer it.
What will you do, now my necessity
Makes me to ask you for my purse? It grieves me
Much more for what I cannot do for you 370
Than what befalls myself. You stand amaz'd,
But be of comfort.
2. Off. Come, sir, away.
Ant. I must entreat of you some of that money.
Vio. What money, sir? 375
For the fair kindness you have show'd me here,
And, part, being prompted by your present trouble,
Out of my lean and low ability
I'll lend you something. My having is not much.
I'll make division of my present with you. 380
Hold, there's half my coffer.
Ant. Will you deny me now?
Is't possible that my deserts to you
Can lack persuasion? Do not tempt my misery,
Lest that it make me so unsound a man
As to upbraid you with those kindnesses 385
That I have done for you.
Vio. I know of none,
Nor know I you by voice or any feature.
I hate ingratitude more in a man
Than lying, vainness, babbling, drunkenness,
Or any taint of vice whose strong corruption 390
Inhabits our frail blood.
Ant. O heavens themselves!
2. Off. Come, sir, I pray you, go.
Ant. Let me speak a little. This youth that you
see here

I snatch'd one half out of the jaws of death,
Reliev'd him with such sanctity of love, 395
And to his image, which methought did promise
Most venerable worth, did I devotion.
1. Off. What's that to us? The time goes by;
away!
Ant. But, O, how vile an idol proves this god!
Thou hast, Sebastian, done good feature shame.
In nature there's no blemish but the mind; 401
None can be call'd deform'd but the unkind.
Virtue is beauty, but the beauteous evil
Are empty trunks o'erflourish'd by the devil.
1. Off. The man grows mad; away with him!
Come, come, sir. 405
Ant. Lead me on. [*Exit [with Officers].*
Vio. Methinks his words do from such passion
fly
That he believes himself; so do not I.
Prove true, imagination, O, prove true,
That I, dear brother, be now ta'en for you! 410
Sir To. Come hither, knight; come hither, Fa-
bian; we'll whisper o'er a couplet or two of most
sage saws.
Vio. He nam'd Sebastian. I my brother know
Yet living in my glass; even such and so 415
In favour was my brother, and he went
Still in this fashion, colour, ornament,
For him I imitate. O, if it prove,
Tempests are kind and salt waves fresh in love.
[*Exit.*]
Sir To. A very dishonest paltry boy, and 420
more a coward than a hare. His dishonesty ap-
pears in leaving his friend here in necessity and
denying him; and, for his cowardship, ask Fabian.
Fab. A coward, a most devout coward, religious
in it. 425
Sir And. 'Slid, I'll after him again and beat him.
Sir To. Do; cuff him soundly, but never draw
thy sword.
Sir And. An I do not,— 430
Fab. Come, let's see the event.
Sir To. I dare lay any money 'twill be nothing
yet. [*Exeunt.*

ACT IV

SCENE I. [*Before Olivia's house.*]

Enter SEBASTIAN *and* CLOWN.

Clo. Will you make me believe that I am not
sent for you?
Seb. Go to, go to, thou art a foolish fellow; let
me be clear of thee.
Clo. Well held out, i' faith! No, I do not 5
know you; nor I am not sent to you by my lady, to

bid you come speak with her; nor your name is not
Master Cesario; nor this is not my nose neither.
Nothing that is so is so.

Seb. I prithee, vent thy folly somewhere else.
Thou know'st not me.   11

Clo. Vent my folly! He has heard that word of
some great man and now applies it to a fool. Vent
my folly! I am afraid this great lubber, the world,
will prove a cockney. I prithee now, ungird thy
strangeness and tell me what I shall vent to my lady.
Shall I vent to her that thou art coming?   18

Seb. I prithee, foolish Greek, depart from me.
There's money for thee. If you tarry longer,   20
I shall give worse payment.

Clo. By my troth, thou hast an open hand.
These wise men that give fools money get themselves a good report — after fourteen years' purchase.   25

Enter SIR ANDREW, SIR TOBY, *and* FABIAN.

Sir And. Now, sir, have I met you again?
There's for you.

Seb. Why, there's for thee, and there, and there.
Are all the people mad?

Sir To. Hold, sir, or I'll throw your dagger o'er
the house.   31

Clo. This will I tell my lady straight. I would
not be in some of your coats for two pence.
          [*Exit.*]

Sir To. Come on, sir. Hold!   34

Sir And. Nay, let him alone. I'll go another
way to work with him. I'll have an action of battery against him, if there be any law in Illyria.
Though I struck him first, yet it's no matter for
that.

Seb. Let go thy hand.   40

Sir To. Come, sir, I will not let you go. Come,
my young soldier, put up your iron; you are well
flesh'd. Come on.

Seb. I will be free from thee. What wouldst
thou now?   44
If thou dar'st tempt me further, draw thy sword.

Sir To. What, what? Nay, then I must have an
ounce or two of this malapert blood from you.

Enter OLIVIA.

Oli. Hold, Toby! On thy life I charge thee,
hold!

Sir To. Madam —   50

Oli. Will it be ever thus? Ungracious wretch,
Fit for the mountains and the barbarous caves,

Where manners ne'er were preach'd! Out of my
          sight!
Be not offended, dear Cesario.
Rudesby, be gone!
          [*Exeunt Sir Toby, Sir Andrew, and Fabian.*]
          I prithee, gentle friend,
Let thy fair wisdom, not thy passion, sway   56
In this uncivil and unjust extent
Against thy peace. Go with me to my house,
And hear thou there how many fruitless pranks
This ruffian hath botch'd up, that thou thereby   60
Mayst smile at this. Thou shalt not choose but
          go.
Do not deny. Beshrew his soul for me,
He started one poor heart of mine in thee.

Seb. What relish is in this? How runs the
          stream?
Or I am mad, or else this is a dream.   65
Let fancy still my sense in Lethe steep.
If it be thus to dream, still let me sleep!

Oli. Nay, come, I prithee. Would thou'dst be
          rul'd by me!

Seb. Madam, I will.

Oli.   O, say so, and so be!
          [*Exeunt.*

SCENE II. [*Olivia's house.*]

Enter MARIA *and* CLOWN.

Mar. Nay, I prithee, put on this gown and this
beard. Make him believe thou art Sir Topas the
curate. Do it quickly; I'll call Sir Toby the
whilst.   [*Exit.*]   4

Clo. Well, I'll put it on, and I will dissemble
myself in't; and I would I were the first that ever
dissembled in such a gown. I am not tall enough
to become the function well, nor lean enough to be
thought a good student; but to be said an honest
man and a good housekeeper goes as fairly as to   10
say a careful man and a great scholar. The competitors enter.

Enter SIR TOBY [*and* MARIA].

Sir To. Jove bless thee, master Parson.

Clo. *Bonos dies*, Sir Toby: for, as the old hermit
of Prague, that never saw pen and ink, very   16
wittily said to a niece of King Gorboduc, "That
that is is"; so I, being master Parson, am master
Parson; for, what is "that" but "that," and "is"
but "is"?

Sir To. To him, Sir Topas.   20

Clo. What, ho, I say! Peace in this prison!

Act IV, sc. i, 15. cockney: fop. 19. Greek: jester. 24–25. after...purchase: i.e., at a high price. The value of land
was figured in terms of its annual rental. 43. flesh'd: initiated in bloodshed. 47. malapert: saucy. 55. Rudesby: ruffian.
57. extent: attack. 60. botch'd up: crudely contrived. 63. started: roused. heart: with pun on *hart.* 64. relish: meaning. 66. Lethe: river of forgetfulness.
          Sc. ii, 10. housekeeper: host. 11. competitors: confederates. 15. hermit of Prague. Invented by Feste. 17. Gorboduc:
mythical British king.

Sir To. The knave counterfeits well; a good knave.

Mal. (*Within.*) Who calls there?

Clo. Sir Topas the curate, who comes to visit Malvolio the lunatic. 26

Mal. Sir Topas, Sir Topas, good Sir Topas, go to my lady.

Clo. Out, hyperbolical fiend! How vexest thou this man! Talkest thou nothing but of ladies? 30

Sir To. Well said, master Parson.

Mal. Sir Topas, never was man thus wronged. Good Sir Topas, do not think I am mad. They have laid me here in hideous darkness. 34

Clo. Fie, thou dishonest Satan! I call thee by the most modest terms, for I am one of those gentle ones that will use the devil himself with courtesy. Say'st thou that house is dark?

Mal. As hell, Sir Topas. 39

Clo. Why, it hath bay windows transparent as barricadoes, and the clerestories toward the south north are as lustrous as ebony; and yet complainest thou of obstruction?

Mal. I am not mad, Sir Topas. I say to you, this house is dark. 45

Clo. Madman, thou errest. I say, there is no darkness but ignorance, in which thou art more puzzl'd than the Egyptians in their fog.

Mal. I say, this house is dark as ignorance, though ignorance were as dark as hell; and I 50 say, there was never man thus abus'd. I am no more mad than you are. Make the trial of it in any constant question.

Clo. What is the opinion of Pythagoras concerning wild fowl? 55

Mal. That the soul of our grandam might haply inhabit a bird.

Clo. What think'st thou of his opinion?

Mal. I think nobly of the soul, and no way approve his opinion. 60

Clo. Fare thee well. Remain thou still in darkness. Thou shalt hold th' opinion of Pythagoras ere I will allow of thy wits, and fear to kill a woodcock lest thou dispossess the soul of thy grandam. Fare thee well. 65

Mal. Sir Topas, Sir Topas!

Sir To. My most exquisite Sir Topas!

Clo. Nay, I am for all waters.

Mar. Thou mightst have done this without thy beard and gown. He sees thee not. 70

Sir To. To him in thine own voice, and bring me word how thou find'st him. I would we were well rid of this knavery. If he may be conveniently

deliver'd, I would he were, for I am now so far in offence with my niece that I cannot pursue with 75 any safety this sport to the upshot. Come by and by to my chamber. [*Exit* [*with Maria*].

Clo. [*Singing.*] "Hey, Robin, jolly Robin,
          Tell me how thy lady does."

Mal. Fool! 80

Clo. "My lady is unkind, perdy."

Mal. Fool!

Clo. "Alas, why is she so?"

Mal. Fool, I say!

Clo. "She loves another"— Who calls, ha? 85

Mal. Good fool, as ever thou wilt deserve well at my hand, help me to a candle, and pen, ink, and paper. As I am a gentleman, I will live to be thankful to thee for't.

Clo. Master Malvolio? 90

Mal. Ay, good fool.

Clo. Alas, sir, how fell you besides your five wits?

Mal. Fool, there was never man so notoriously abus'd. I am as well in my wits, fool, as thou art. 96

Clo. But as well? Then you are mad indeed, if you be no better in your wits than a fool.

Mal. They have here propertied me, keep me in darkness, send ministers to me, asses, and do all they can to face me out of my wits. 101

Clo. Advise you what you say; the minister is here. Malvolio, Malvolio, thy wits the heavens restore! Endeavour thyself to sleep, and leave thy vain bibble babble. 105

Mal. Sir Topas!

Clo. Maintain no words with him, good fellow. Who, I, sir? Not I, sir. God buy you, good Sir Topas. Marry, amen. I will, sir, I will.

Mal. Fool, fool, fool, I say! 110

Clo. Alas, sir, be patient. What say you, sir? I am shent for speaking to you.

Mal. Good fool, help me to some light and some paper. I tell thee, I am as well in my wits as any man in Illyria. 115

Clo. Well-a-day that you were, sir!

Mal. By this hand, I am. Good fool, some ink, paper, and light; and convey what I will set down to my lady. It shall advantage thee more than ever the bearing of letter did. 120

Clo. I will help you to't. But tell me true, are you not mad indeed, or do you but counterfeit?

Mal. Believe me, I am not. I tell thee true.

Clo. Nay, I'll ne'er believe a madman till I see his brains. I will fetch you light and paper and ink. 127

29. **hyperbolical:** extravagant. 41. **clerestories:** windows high up in the wall. 48. **Egyptians ... fog.** See *Exodus* x.21. 53. **constant:** logical, rational. 68. **I ... waters:** I can assume any rôle. 92. **wits.** Five by analogy with the five senses; they were common wit, imagination, fantasy, estimation, and memory. 99. **propertied:** treated as a tool. 102. **Advise you:** take care. From this point through l. 109 Feste alternates speaking as Sir Topas and in his own voice. 108. **buy:** be with. 112. **shent:** reproved.

Mal. Fool, I'll requite it in the highest degree.
I prithee, be gone.

    Clo. [*Singing.*] I am gone, sir,   130
               And anon, sir,
               I'll be with you again,
               In a trice,
               Like to the old Vice,
               Your need to sustain;   135

               Who, with dagger of lath,
               In his rage and his wrath,
               Cries, ah, ha! to the devil,
               Like a mad lad.
               Pare thy nails, dad.   140
               Adieu, goodman devil.   [*Exit.*

Scene III. [*Olivia's garden.*]

Enter Sebastian.

Seb. This is the air, that is the glorious sun,
This pearl she gave me, I do feel't and see't;
And though 'tis wonder that enwraps me thus,
Yet 'tis not madness. Where's Antonio, then?
I could not find him at the Elephant;   5
Yet there he was, and there I found this credit,
That he did range the town to seek me out.
His counsel now might do me golden service;
For though my soul disputes well with my sense,
That this may be some error, but no madness,   10
Yet doth this accident and flood of fortune
So far exceed all instance, all discourse,
That I am ready to distrust mine eyes
And wrangle with my reason that persuades me
To any other trust but that I am mad   15
Or else the lady's mad; yet, if 'twere so,
She could not sway her house, command her fol-
      lowers,
Take and give back affairs and their dispatch
With such a smooth, discreet, and stable bearing
As I perceive she does. There's something in't   20
That is deceivable. But here the lady comes.

Enter Olivia *and* Priest.

Oli. Blame not this haste of mine. If you mean
    well,
Now go with me and with this holy man
Into the chantry by; there, before him,
And underneath that consecrated roof,   25
Plight me the full assurance of your faith,
That my most jealous and too doubtful soul
May live at peace. He shall conceal it
Whiles you are willing it shall come to note,

What time we will our celebration keep   30
According to my birth. What do you say?
    Seb. I'll follow this good man, and go with you;
And, having sworn truth, ever will be true.
    Oli. Then lead the way, good father; and heavens
    so shine
That they may fairly note this act of mine!   35
                          [*Exeunt.*

ACT V

Scene I. [*Before Olivia's house.*]

Enter Clown *and* Fabian.

Fab. Now, as thou lov'st me, let me see his letter.
Clo. Good Master Fabian, grant me another re-
quest.
Fab. Anything.   5
Clo. Do not desire to see this letter.
Fab. This is to give a dog and in recompense
desire my dog again.

Enter Duke, Viola, Curio, *and* Lords.

Duke. Belong you to the Lady Olivia, friends?
Clo. Ay, sir! we are some of her trappings.   10
Duke. I know thee well; how dost thou, my good
fellow?
Clo. Truly, sir, the better for my foes and the
worse for my friends.
Duke. Just the contrary; the better for thy
friends.   16
Clo. No, sir, the worse.
Duke. How can that be?
Clo. Marry, sir, they praise me and make an ass
of me. Now my foes tell me plainly I am an   20
ass; so that by my foes, sir, I profit in the knowledge
of myself, and by my friends I am abused; so that,
conclusions to be as kisses, if your four negatives
make your two affirmatives, why then, the worse for
my friends and the better for my foes.   26
Duke. Why, this is excellent.
Clo. By my troth, sir, no; though it please you to
be one of my friends.
Duke. Thou shalt not be the worse for me.
There's gold.   31
Clo. But that it would be double-dealing, sir,
I would you could make it another.
Duke. O, you give me ill counsel.
Clo. Put your grace in your pocket, sir, for this
once, and let your flesh and blood obey it.   36
Duke. Well, I will be so much a sinner, to be a
double-dealer. There's another.

---

134. **the old Vice,** the Fool of the Moralities and Interludes, carried a wooden dagger with which he would attempt to
pare the Devil's nails.
    Sc. iii, 6. was: had been. **credit:** belief. 12. **instance:** example, precedent. **discourse:** reason. 15. **trust:** belief.
18. **Take...dispatch:** undertake and discharge affairs. 21. **deceivable:** deceptive. 24. **chantry:** private chapel. 29.
Whiles: until. 30. **What:** at which.
    Act V, sc. i, 1. his: Malvolio's. 22. **abused:** deceived.

Clo. Primo, secundo, tertio, is a good play; and
the old saying is, the third pays for all.   The   40
triplex, sir, is a good tripping measure; or the bells of
Saint Bennet, sir, may put you in mind; one, two,
three.

Duke. You can fool no more money out of me at
this throw.   If you will let your lady know I am   45
here to speak with her, and bring her along with
you, it may awake my bounty further.

Clo. Marry, sir, lullaby to your bounty till I
come again.   I go, sir, but I would not have you to
think that my desire of having is the sin of   50
covetousness; but, as you say, sir, let your bounty
take a nap, I will awake it anon.   [*Exit.*

Enter ANTONIO *and* OFFICERS.

Vio. Here comes the man, sir, that did rescue me.

Duke. That face of his I do remember well,
Yet, when I saw it last, it was besmear'd   55
As black as Vulcan in the smoke of war.
A bawbling vessel was he captain of,
For shallow draught and bulk unprizable,
With which such scatheful grapple did he make
With the most noble bottom of our fleet,   60
That very envy and the tongue of loss
Cri'd fame and honour on him.   What's the matter?

1. Off. Orsino, this is that Antonio
That took the *Phœnix* and her fraught from Candy,
And this is he that did the *Tiger* board,   65
When your young nephew Titus lost his leg.
Here in the streets, desperate of shame and state,
In private brabble did we apprehend him.

Vio. He did me kindness, sir, drew on my side,
But in conclusion put strange speech upon me.   70
I know not what 'twas but distraction.

Duke. Notable pirate!   Thou salt-water thief!
What foolish boldness brought thee to their mercies
Whom thou, in terms so bloody and so dear,
Hast made thine enemies?

Ant.   Orsino, noble sir,   75
Be pleas'd that I shake off these names you give me.
Antonio never yet was thief or pirate,
Though I confess, on base and ground enough,
Orsino's enemy.   A witchcraft drew me hither.
That most ingrateful boy there by your side,   80
From the rude sea's enrag'd and foamy mouth
Did I redeem.   A wreck past hope he was.
His life I gave him, and did thereto add
My love, without retention or restraint,
All his in dedication.   For his sake   85
Did I expose myself, pure for his love,
Into the danger of this adverse town;

Drew to defend him when he was beset;
Where being apprehended, his false cunning,
Not meaning to partake with me in danger,   90
Taught him to face me out of his acquaintance,
And grew a twenty years removed thing
While one would wink; deni'd me mine own purse,
Which I had recommended to his use
Not half an hour before.

Vio.   How can this be?   95

Duke. When came he to this town?

Ant. To-day, my lord; and for three months
before,
No int'rim, not a minute's vacancy,
Both day and night did we keep company.

Enter OLIVIA *and Attendants.*

Duke. Here comes the countess; now heaven
walks on earth.   100
But for thee, fellow; fellow, thy words are madness.
Three months this youth hath tended upon me;
But more of that anon.   Take him aside.

Oli. What would my lord, but that he may not
have,
Wherein Olivia may seem serviceable?   105
Cesario, you do not keep promise with me.

Vio. Madam!

Duke. Gracious Olivia, —

Oli. What do you say, Cesario?   Good my
lord, —   109

Vio. My lord would speak; my duty hushes me.

Oli. If it be aught to the old tune, my lord,
It is as fat and fulsome to mine ear
As howling after music.

Duke.   Still so cruel!

Oli. Still so constant, lord.

Duke. What, to perverseness?   You uncivil lady,
To whose ingrate and unauspicious altars   116
My soul the faithfull'st off'rings have breath'd out
That e'er devotion tender'd!   What shall I do?

Oli. Even what it please my lord, that shall
become him.

Duke. Why should I not, had I the heart to do it,
Like to th' Egyptian thief at point of death,   121
Kill what I love? — a savage jealousy
That sometime savours nobly.   But hear me this:
Since you to non-regardance cast my faith,
And that I partly know the instrument   125
That screws me from my true place in your favour,
Live you the marble-breasted tyrant still;
But this your minion, whom I know you love,
And whom, by heaven I swear, I tender dearly,
Him will I tear out of that cruel eye,   130

---

39. **Primo . . . tertio:** possibly alluding to throws at dice.   41. **triplex:** triple time in music.   42. **Saint Bennet:** the
church of St. Benedict in London.   57. **bawbling:** trifling.   58. **unprizable:** worthless.   59. **scatheful:** damaging.   64.
Candy: Candia, Crete.   68. **brabble:** brawl.   71. **distraction:** madness.   74. **dear:** dangerous.   112. **fat and fulsome:** i.e.,
repulsive.   121. **Egyptian thief.** The *Ethiopica* of Heliodorus tells how a robber tried to kill his mistress rather than let her
fall into the hands of his enemies.   128. **minion:** favorite.

Where he sits crowned in his master's spite.
Come, boy, with me; my thoughts are ripe in
    mischief.
I'll sacrifice the lamb that I do love,
To spite a raven's heart within a dove.
   Vio. And I, most jocund, apt, and willingly, 135
To do you rest, a thousand deaths would die.
   Oli. Where goes Cesario?
   Vio.   After him I love
More than I love these eyes, more than my life,
More, by all mores, than e'er I shall love wife.
If I do feign, you witnesses above 140
Punish my life for tainting of my love!
   Oli. Ay me, detested! How am I beguil'd!
   Vio. Who does beguile you? Who does do you
    wrong?
   Oli. Hast thou forgot thyself? Is it so long?
Call forth the holy father.
   Duke.   Come, away! 145
   Oli. Whither, my lord? Cesario, husband, stay.
   Duke. Husband!
   Oli.   Ay, husband! Can he that deny?
   Duke. Her husband, sirrah!
   Vio.   No, my lord, not I.
   Oli. Alas, it is the baseness of thy fear
That makes thee strangle thy propriety. 150
Fear not, Cesario; take thy fortunes up.
Be that thou know'st thou art, and then thou art
As great as that thou fear'st.

           Enter PRIEST.

                O, welcome, father!
Father, I charge thee by thy reverence
Here to unfold, though lately we intended 155
To keep in darkness what occasion now
Reveals before 'tis ripe, what thou dost know
Hath newly pass'd between this youth and me.
   Priest. A contract of eternal bond of love,
Confirm'd by mutual joinder of your hands, 160
Attested by the holy close of lips,
Strength'ned by interchangement of your rings;
And all the ceremony of this compact
Seal'd in my function, by my testimony;
Since when, my watch hath told me, toward my
    grave 165
I have travell'd but two hours.
   Duke. O thou dissembling cub! What wilt
    thou be
When time hath sow'd a grizzle on thy case?
Or will not else thy craft so quickly grow,
That thine own trip shall be thine overthrow? 170
Farewell, and take her; but direct thy feet
Where thou and I henceforth may never meet.

   Vio. My lord, I do protest —
   Oli.   O, do not swear!
Hold little faith, though thou hast too much fear.

         Enter SIR ANDREW.

   Sir And. For the love of God, a surgeon! 175
Send one presently to Sir Toby.
   Oli. What's the matter?
   Sir And. Has broke my head across and has
given Sir Toby a bloody coxcomb too. For the
love of God, your help! I had rather than forty
pound I were at home. 181
   Oli. Who has done this, Sir Andrew?
   Sir And. The Count's gentleman, one Cesario.
We took him for a coward, but he's the very devil
incarnate. 185
   Duke. My gentleman, Cesario?
   Sir And. 'Od's lifelings, here he is! You broke
my head for nothing; and that that I did, I was set
on to do't by Sir Toby.
   Vio. Why do you speak to me? I never hurt
    you. 190
You drew your sword upon me without cause;
But I bespake you fair, and hurt you not.

   Enter SIR TOBY *and* CLOWN.

   Sir And. If a bloody coxcomb be a hurt, you
have hurt me. I think you set nothing by a bloody
coxcomb. Here comes Sir Toby halting. You 195
shall hear more; but if he had not been in drink, he
would have tickl'd you othergates than he did.
   Duke. How now, gentleman! How is't with
you? 200
   Sir To. That's all one. Has hurt me, and there's
th' end on't. Sot, didst see Dick surgeon, sot?
   Clo. O, he's drunk, Sir Toby, an hour agone.
His eyes were set at eight i' th' morning. 205
   Sir To. Then he's a rogue, and a passy measures
[pavin]. I hate a drunken rogue.
   Oli. Away with him! Who hath made this havoc
with them?
   Sir And. I'll help you, Sir Toby, because we'll
be dress'd together. 211
   Sir To. Will you help? — an ass-head and a cox-
comb and a knave, a thin-fac'd knave, a gull!
   Oli. Get him to bed, and let his hurt be look'd
to. 215
     [*Exeunt Clown, Fabian, Sir Toby, and Sir
        Andrew.*]

         Enter SEBASTIAN.

   Seb. I am sorry, madam, I have hurt your
kinsman;

---

150. **strangle thy propriety:** deny thyself. 164. **function:** official capacity. 168. **grizzle:** gray hair. **case:** skin. 170.
trip: i.e., as in wrestling. 179. **coxcomb:** head. 185. **incardinate:** incarnate. 197. **othergates:** otherwise. 207.
[pavin] (Malone). *panyn* F. "Passy measures pavin" is an English form of the Italian "Passamezzo pavana," a measured
dance with strains of eight bars each. Toby's outburst is inspired by "set at eight" (l. 205).

But, had it been the brother of my blood,
I must have done no less with wit and safety.
You throw a strange regard upon me, and by that
I do perceive it hath offended you.   220
Pardon me, sweet one, even for the vows
We made each other but so late ago.

   Duke. One face, one voice, one habit, and two
    persons,
A natural perspective, that is and is not!

   Seb. Antonio, O my dear Antonio!   225
How have the hours rack'd and tortur'd me,
Since I have lost thee!

   Ant. Sebastian are you?

   Seb.   Fear'st thou that, Antonio?

   Ant. How have you made division of yourself?
An apple, cleft in two, is not more twin   230
Than these two creatures. Which is Sebastian?

   Oli. Most wonderful!

   Seb. Do I stand there? I never had a brother,
Nor can there be that deity in my nature,
Of here and everywhere. I had a sister,   235
Whom the blind waves and surges have devour'd.
Of charity, what kin are you to me?
What countryman? What name? What parent-
    age?

   Vio. Of Messaline; Sebastian was my father;
Such a Sebastian was my brother too;   240
So went he suited to his watery tomb.
If spirits can assume both form and suit
You come to fright us.

   Seb.   A spirit I am indeed;
But am in that dimension grossly clad
Which from the womb I did participate.   245
Were you a woman, as the rest goes even,
I should my tears let fall upon your cheek,
And say, "Thrice welcome, drowned Viola!"

   Vio. My father had a mole upon his brow.

   Seb. And so had mine.   250

   Vio. And died that day when Viola from her
    birth
Had numb'red thirteen years.

   Seb. O, that record is lively in my soul!
He finished indeed his mortal act
That day that made my sister thirteen years.   255

   Vio. If nothing lets to make us happy both
But this my masculine usurp'd attire,
Do not embrace me till each circumstance
Of place, time, fortune, do cohere and jump
That I am Viola; which to confirm,   260
I'll bring you to a captain in this town,
Where lie my maiden weeds; by whose gentle help

I was preserv'd to serve this noble count.
All the occurrence of my fortune since
Hath been between this lady and this lord.   265

   Seb. [*To Olivia.*] So comes it, lady, you have been
    mistook;
But nature to her bias drew in that.
You would have been contracted to a maid;
Nor are you therein, by my life, deceiv'd,
You are betroth'd both to a maid and man.   270

   Duke. Be not amaz'd, right noble is his blood.
If this be so, as yet the glass seems true,
I shall have share in this most happy wreck.
[*To Viola.*] Boy, thou hast said to me a thousand
    times
Thou never shouldst love woman like to me.   275

   Vio. And all those sayings will I over-swear;
And all those swearings keep as true in soul
As doth that orbed continent the fire
That severs day from night.

   Duke.   Give me thy hand,
And let me see thee in thy woman's weeds.   280

   Vio. The captain that did bring me first on shore
Hath my maid's garments. He upon some action
Is now in durance, at Malvolio's suit,
A gentleman, and follower of my lady's.

   Oli. He shall enlarge him; fetch Malvolio hither.
And yet, alas, now I remember me,   286
They say, poor gentleman, he's much distract.

Re-enter CLOWN *with a letter, and* FABIAN.

A most extracting frenzy of mine own
From my remembrance clearly banish'd his.
How does he, sirrah?   290

   Clo. Truly, madam, he holds Belzebub at the
stave's end as well as a man in his case may
do. Has here writ a letter to you. I should have
given 't you to-day morning, but as a madman's
epistles are no gospels, so it skills not much when
they are deliver'd.   296

   Oli. Open 't and read it.

   Clo. Look then to be well edified when the fool
delivers the madman. [*Shouts.*] "By the Lord,
madam," —   300

   Oli. How now, art thou mad?

   Clo. No, madam, I do but read madness. An
your ladyship will have it as it ought to be, you
must allow Vox.

   Oli. Prithee, read i' thy right wits.   305

   Clo. So I do, madonna; but to read his right wits
is to read thus; therefore perpend, my princess, and
give ear.

---

223. **habit:** dress.   224. **natural perspective:** an optical illusion produced by nature.   228. **Fear'st:** doubtest.   234–35. **Nor ... everywhere:** nor can I, God-like, be everywhere.   241. **suited:** clothed.   244. **in ... clad:** clothed in that material form.   245. **Which ... participate:** which I have possessed since birth.   246. **goes even:** agrees.   256. **lets:** prevents.   259. **jump:** agree.   264. **occurrence:** course.   267. **nature ... drew:** i.e., nature followed her own inclination.   272. **glass.** Probably an allusion to the "perspective" of l. 224.   278. **orbed continent:** the sphere of the sun (according to the Ptolemaic cosmology).   283. **in durance:** under arrest.   288. **extracting:** distracting.   292. **at ... end:** at staff's length.   295. **skills:** matters.   304. **Vox:** i.e., the appropriate (loud) voice.   307. **perpend:** consider.

Oli. Read it you, sirrah.   [*To Fabian.*] 309
Fab. (*Reads.*) "By the Lord, madam, you wrong
me, and the world shall know it.   Though you
have put me into darkness and given your drunken
cousin rule over me, yet have I the benefit of my
senses as well as your ladyship   I have your own
letter that induced me to the semblance I put
on; with the which I doubt not but to do my- 315
self much right, or you much shame.   Think of
me as you please.   I leave my duty a little un-
thought of and speak out of my injury.
    THE MADLY-US'D MALVOLIO."
Oli. Did he write this?   320
Clo. Ay, madam.
Duke. This savours not much of distraction.
Oli. See him deliver'd, Fabian; bring him hither.
                    [*Exit Fabian.*]
My lord, so please you, these things further thought
    on,
To think me as well a sister as a wife,   325
One day shall crown th' alliance on't, so please
    you,
Here at my house and at my proper cost.
    Duke. Madam, I am most apt t' embrace your
        offer.
[*To Viola.*] Your master quits you; and for your
        service done him,
So much against the mettle of your sex,   330
So far beneath your soft and tender breeding,
And since you call'd me master for so long,
Here is my hand.   You shall from this time be
Your master's mistress.
    Oli.   A sister!   You are she.

        Enter MALVOLIO [*and* FABIAN].

Duke. Is this the madman?
Oli.   Ay, my lord, this same. 335
How now, Malvolio!
Mal.   Madam, you have done me wrong,
Notorious wrong.
Oli.   Have I, Malvolio?   No.
Mal. Lady, you have.   Pray you, peruse that
    letter;
You must not now deny it is your hand.
Write from it, if you can, in hand or phrase; 340
Or say 'tis not your seal, not your invention.
You can say none of this.   Well, grant it then
And tell me, in the modesty of honour,
Why you have given me such clear lights of favour,
Bade me come smiling and cross-garter'd to you,
To put on yellow stockings and to frown   346
Upon Sir Toby and the lighter people;
And, acting this in an obedient hope,
Why have you suffer'd me to be imprison'd,

Kept in a dark house, visited by the priest,   350
And made the most notorious geck and gull
That e'er invention play'd on?   Tell me why.
    Oli. Alas, Malvolio, this is not my writing,
Though, I confess, much like the character;
But out of question 'tis Maria's hand.   355
And now I do bethink me, it was she
First told me thou wast mad.   Then cam'st in
    smiling,
And in such forms which here were presuppos'd
Upon thee in the letter.   Prithee, be content. 359
This practice hath most shrewdly pass'd upon
    thee;
But when we know the grounds and authors of
    it,
Thou shalt be both the plaintiff and the judge
Of thine own cause.
    Fab.   Good madam, hear me speak,
And let no quarrel nor no brawl to come
Taint the condition of this present hour,   365
Which I have wond'red at.   In hope it shall not
Most freely I confess, myself and Toby
Set this device against Malvolio here,
Upon some stubborn and uncourteous parts
We had conceiv'd against him.   Maria writ 370
The letter at Sir Toby's great importance,
In recompense whereof he hath married her.
How with a sportful malice it was follow'd
May rather pluck on laughter than revenge,
If that the injuries be justly weigh'd   375
That have on both sides pass'd.
    Oli. Alas, poor fool, how have they baffl'd
        thee!
    Clo. Why, "some are born great, some achieve
greatness, and some have greatness thrown upon
them."   I was one, sir, in this interlude; one Sir 380
Topas, sir; but that's all one.   "By the Lord, fool,
I am not mad."   But do you remember?   "Madam,
why laugh you at such a barren rascal?   An you
smile not, he's gagg'd."   And thus the whirligig of
time brings in his revenges.   385
    Mal. I'll be reveng'd on the whole pack of you.
                        [*Exit.*]
    Oli. He hath been most notoriously abus'd.
    Duke. Pursue him, and entreat him to a peace;
He hath not told us of the captain yet.   390
When that is known and golden time convents,
A solemn combination shall be made
Of our dear souls.   Meantime, sweet sister,
We will not part from hence.   Cesario, come;
For so you shall be, while you are a man;   395
But when in other habits you are seen,
Orsino's mistress and his fancy's queen.
                [*Exeunt [all, except Clown*].

327. **proper:** own.   328. **apt:** ready.   329. **quits:** releases.   330. **mettle:** character.   340. **from:** i.e., differently from.
347. **lighter:** lesser.   351. **geck and gull:** fool and dupe.   358. **presuppos'd:** suggested.   360. **practice:** trick.   **pass'd:**
imposed.   369. **parts:** qualities.   371. **importance:** importunity.   374. **pluck on:** excite.   391. **convents:** suits.

Clo. (Sings.)
When that I was and a little tiny boy,
    With hey, ho, the wind and the rain,
A foolish thing was but a toy,   400
    For the rain it raineth every day.

But when I came to man's estate,
    With hey, ho, &c.
'Gainst knaves and thieves men shut their gate,
    For the rain, &c.   405

But when I came, alas! to wive,
    With hey, ho, &c.

By swaggering could I never thrive,
    For the rain, &c.

But when I came unto my beds,   410
    With hey, ho, &c.
With toss-pots still had drunken heads,
    For the rain, &c.

A great while ago the world begun,
    With hey, ho, &c.   415
But that's all one, our play is done,
    And we'll strive to please you every day.
                                                        [*Exit.*]

400. **toy:** trifle.   412. **toss-pots:** drunkards.

The Tragedy of Hamlet, Prince of Denmark

THE FIRST SURVIVING NOTICE of a Shakespearean *Hamlet* is an entry in the Stationers' Register for July 26, 1602: "The Revenge of Hamlett Prince Denmarke as yt was latelie Acted by the Lord Chamberleyne his servantes." In 1603 appeared the First Quarto, a pirated and badly mutilated text only a little more than half the length of that in the Second Quarto (1604). The Second Quarto, printed "according to the true and perfect Coppie," gives the authorized text of the play as currently performed by Shakespeare's company. This text differs significantly from that in the First Folio; it contains about 218 lines absent in the Folio, but lacks some 85 lines which the Folio has. Since the passages in question are all assuredly genuine, the natural conclusion is that both sets of omissions represent cuts made at different periods for acting purposes. It is likely that the Second Quarto was printed from Shakespeare's manuscript, in which the earlier set of cuts had been marked off. The Folio text, which has more numerous and more explicit stage directions, may have been set up from a transcript which had served as a prompt copy. Both the Second Quarto and the Folio have substantial authority, but the Folio appears to present the later, and therefore perhaps the more approved, acting version utilized by Shakespeare's fellows. The present text is consequently based upon the Folio.

The relationship of the First Quarto to the authoritative texts is a controversial problem. It was once generally held that the First Quarto preserves a corrupt reporting of an earlier handling by Shakespeare of the Hamlet story. The best of recent opinion, however, regards it as a debased rendering of an abridgment of the true text, made for a company on tour. Since the First Quarto reproduces the speeches of Marcellus with striking accuracy, in contrast to the bungling of other parts, it seems almost certain that the pirate was an actor who had played Marcellus. Bad though it is, the First Quarto is not negligible, for at a few points it provides a sound reading where the good texts are unsatisfactory.

The date of composition is conjectural. The entry in the Stationers' Register gives one terminus. A note by Gabriel Harvey in his edition of Speght's Chaucer is suggestive. Harvey remarks the pleasure afforded "the wiser sort" by Shakespeare's *Hamlet*, and since he also mentions commendation of *Albion's England* by the Earl of Essex, it is argued that his note was penned prior to the Earl's death (February 25, 1601). Late 1600 or 1601 is a likely date for the play.

The origin of the Hamlet story lies in the obscure regions of Scandinavian legend. It appears that Hamlet (Amlothi) was the hero of a tale as old as the Old English *Beowulf*, but what his story was like in its ancient form can only be vaguely guessed. The earliest literary account of Hamlet occurs in the *Historia Danica* (c. 1200) by Saxo Grammaticus, who drew upon tradition and the lost Scandinavian sagas. Saxo's narrative was adapted by Belleforest as one of his *Histoires Tragiques* (1576). In Belleforest the story lay ready to the hand of a dramatist. The essential features familiar in Shakespeare's play are present: adultery, fratricide, revenge, the hero's feigned madness, prototypes of Ophelia, Horatio, Polonius, Rosencrantz, and Guildenstern (though Shakespeare's characterization utterly transforms these figures), the journey to England, and the exchange of letters. There are, however, signal differences. In Belleforest the murder of the elder Hamlet is public knowledge. His brother successfully defended it, asserting that he had caught the dead king on the point of murdering his queen and that he had killed him in order to save the queen's life. Hamlet is but a youth, entirely at the mercy of his unscrupulous uncle. He pretends madness as his only means of self-protection until he can avenge his father. His uncle suspects him, however, and is resolved to have him killed if he can prove him sane. The devices employed foreshadow episodes in the play. An effort is made to trap the boy through the agency of a girl whom he loves; later a spy is set in the queen's chamber when Hamlet is to come for an interview with his mother. The first attempt is frustrated because Hamlet has been warned by a friend. On the second occasion Hamlet, still feigning madness, enters the chamber crowing like a cock and waving his arms about; in this fashion he beats the hangings, detects the intruder behind them, and kills him. To his repentant mother Hamlet confides his plan for revenge. On his way to England Hamlet not only procures the death of his companions by the exchange of letters, but requests the king of England to give him his daughter in marriage. After about a year in England Hamlet returns to Denmark and, resuming his feigned madness, enters his uncle's palace during a feast celebrating his own supposed death. He gets the courtiers drunk, sets fire to the hall, and kills the king. Then going before the people with a speech explaining everything, he is proclaimed king. The rest of the story is irrelevant to the play.

The indebtedness of Shakespeare, and his originality, would be easy to determine if this were all one had to consider, but between Belleforest's story and Shakespeare's drama stands a lost play. To its existence there are several witnesses. Henslowe records a performance on June 11, 1594; Lodge alludes in his *Wits Miserie* (1596) to "ye ghost which cried so miserably at ye Theator, like an oister wife, *Hamlet, revenge.*" But the play dates from the previous decade, for Nashe, in the Preface to Greene's *Menaphon* (1589), proclaims that "English *Seneca* read by Candle light yeelds many good sentences ... and if you intreate him faire in a frostie morning, hee will affoord you whole *Hamlets*, I should say handfuls of Tragicall speeches." The author of this lost play is unknown, but evidence points to Kyd. It was clearly a play of the Senecan mode, like *The Spanish Tragedy*, though it may have been by an imitator of Kyd. In any event, it is certain that this lost play had already added to the existent source material the Ghost, probably the play within the play, and the fencing match involving Hamlet's death. Shakespeare must have been indebted to the old play, whatever its content; he may have worked from it directly, though that would presuppose that his company owned the "book," for there is no evidence that the old play was ever printed.

In *Hamlet* the character of the protagonist commands interest above everything else. It is significant that when the Prince is first introduced to us his tragedy has already begun. His impassioned soliloquy (I.ii.129–59) reveals the depth of misery and despair into which the death of a loved father and the hasty and "incestuous" marriage of his mother have plunged him. Because of these things life has lost its savor for him, the world seems contaminated, and he wishes he were dead. Hamlet's condition argues a nature of abnormal sensitivity; he has been, evidently, an idealist, and all that one

can learn of what he was like before disillusion transformed him assumes manifest interest and importance. Through the remarks of others and through speeches of Hamlet himself in relaxed or unguarded moments Shakespeare takes pains to inform us. The famous speech of Ophelia (III.i.158 ff.), wrung from her very heart, describes the noble attributes of the real Hamlet. From this testimony we learn that Hamlet was the embodiment of all courtly virtues, the incarnation of gentility as conceived by the Renaissance. The normal Hamlet can be seen also in the rare moments of gaiety or spontaneity when sudden pleasure makes him forget his melancholy; for example, in his joyous reception of Horatio (I.ii.160 ff.), his hearty welcome to Rosencrantz and Guildenstern (II.ii.226 ff.), and his delight at the arrival of the players (II.ii.440 ff.). In his true nature Hamlet is healthy, frank, and generous, and Claudius, laying his treacherous plot with Laertes, honors his integrity (IV.vii.135–37). Through this very integrity, however, Hamlet is vulnerable at the beginning of the play, as at its close; for it is because he is in morals and in honor finely tuned that his mother's new marriage so offends him. He who had worshiped his father (I.ii.139–53, 187–88; III.iv.55–62) sees his mother's act as treason to an ideal. It is to a mind already depressed and brooding that the Ghost's dread message is imparted.

For Hamlet the Ghost's revelation is a double shock, since he learns not only that his father had been foully murdered, but that his mother, who in his estimation has already fallen so low, had been adulterous while his father was still alive. That Hamlet had never suspected the murder is clear from his exclamation (I.v.26). That he was ignorant of the adultery is equally certain, though he says nothing. Horrified and overcome with pity for his wronged father, Hamlet is speechless, and this silence of grief is one of Shakespeare's finest effects. For fifty lines (I.v.41–91) the Ghost speaks without interruption, while Hamlet stands tense with emotion, and not until the Ghost has vanished does Hamlet find words again.

Hamlet accepts the commission of vengeance with an alacrity which the Ghost commends. To "sweep" to his revenge is his filial duty and his express desire, but he does not do so, and his delay has been the subject of voluminous critical discussion. One must recognize that the postponement of vengeance is a dramatic necessity; without Hamlet's delay there would be no play. Shakespeare's problem was to motivate the delay, and though the motivation he has provided may seem to modern critics unsatisfactory or incomplete, it must be accepted with whatever implications it may carry. When Hamlet swears vengeance, his faith in the authenticity of the Ghost is absolute. Nevertheless, there is the possibility, a commonplace in Elizabethan ghost lore, that the apparition may not be the spirit of his father at all, but rather a demon in the likeness of his father seeking to draw him into evil. This possibility, explicit in the warning of Horatio (I.iv.69 ff.), has already occurred to Hamlet (I.ii.244-46; I.iv.40), though in the moving colloquy with the Ghost suspicion is swept away. Doubt returns subsequently, however, finding memorable expression in the soliloquy of Hamlet inspired by the stirring recitation of his player-friend (II.ii.627-33). To hold, as some critics have, that Hamlet suddenly invents this scruple about the honesty of the Ghost as a pretext for deferring a deed that is repugnant to him is unjust to Hamlet and to Shakespeare. We have heard nothing about this scruple, it is true, since Hamlet swore vengeance, yet it is arbitrary to assume that it recurs for the first time on this occasion. Though Shakespeare does not indicate how soon after the conversation with the Ghost Hamlet's doubt began again to assail him, about two months have passed since that event (cf. I.ii.138 and III.ii.133-36), and one may reasonably suppose that alternate moods of conviction and of uncertainty have possessed Hamlet for some time. Moved by the emotion of the player, Hamlet reviews his own cue for passion, scourges himself for his inaction, and hits upon the play within the play as a means for resolving, once for all, the now insistent question of the Ghost's authenticity.

After the success of Hamlet's "mouse trap" his first opportunity to kill the King comes when he discovers him at prayer, but Hamlet refuses this chance, wishing to take Claudius "in some act that has no relish of salvation in it" and so to damn his soul. Some critics, finding this savage reasoning incompatible with the qualities they admire in Hamlet, construe it as another excuse for procrastination. Nevertheless, one must take Hamlet at his word. To us, this cruel wish is inconsistent with Hamlet's native refinement, but it is no more so than Hamlet's accepting the obligation of vengeance in the first place, and the line of reasoning was familiar to Shakespeare's audience. Individuals in the Renaissance may have outgrown the primitive code of vengeance, but everybody in that period was familiar with it, and the popularity of the contemporary revenge plays, in which vindictiveness touched extremes, gave it fresh notoriety. *Hamlet* is a revenge play, and the fact is that although Shakespeare marvelously transcended the genre, and gave to his hero superior dignity and nobility, he did not eradicate all the earlier crudity of the type. Moreover, Hamlet's particular motive for sparing Claudius was entirely comprehensible to Elizabethans.

With fine skill Shakespeare makes the fact of delay itself dramatic. The play within the play is intensely exciting; the audience is identified with Hamlet in seeking corroboration of the Ghost. Hamlet spares Claudius at prayer, but Claudius has been unable to pray, and thus, ironically, Hamlet loses an opportunity on his own expressed terms. Presently, in his mother's chamber, Hamlet kills Polonius, striking swiftly in the belief that it is the King (III.iv.25, 32). With this mistake his cause is lost, and would have remained forever so had not accident favored him on the voyage to England. Accident, however, merely presents the occasion for action; the energy and the sureness with which Hamlet acts show his mettle. After his return to Denmark, Hamlet kills Claudius at his first real opportunity; for of course he would not attack him at Ophelia's grave. It is easy to convert the simple dramatic necessity of Hamlet's delay into an intricate problem of character, especially in view of Hamlet's melancholy and his habit of self-analysis, but one must be careful not to work these factors too hard. On two notable occasions Hamlet denounces himself for inaction (II.ii.576 ff.; IV.iv.32 ff.) and, unpacking his heart with words, renews his resolve. Like any sensitive man, he can castigate himself unduly; at every crucial point, however, there is a plain reason why his task has not been fulfilled. And letting Hamlet renew his resolve at significant moments is good drama, for it increases suspense as to when and how he will carry it out.

There is no question whatsoever about Hamlet's sanity; his madness is only feigned. His decision to put an antic disposition on when and as he shall see fit, is taken suddenly (I.v.168 ff.), and he never gives any reason for it. This is not the case in Belleforest, where the feigned madness is clearly motivated. There Hamlet, a mere youth, pretends madness as a protection against an uncle who would slay him without hesitation if he could be sure of his sanity. How the madness was motivated in the lost play we do not know. But in Shakespeare, where the deed of Claudius is not known, and where Claudius is eager to be on good terms with Hamlet, this device is not necessary. The fact would seem to be that Shakespeare accepted the feigned madness as an integral factor in his inherited material, either without realizing that with his re-creation of the hero it needed a different motivation, or without caring to invent one. Very likely Shakespeare believed that audiences in the playhouse would be content to assume that Hamlet had reasons of his own. Certainly he knew that the feigned madness would afford moments of comic relief, for he uses it most skillfully to that end. Though Hamlet utters "wild and whirling words" on a few occasions when it is clear that his speech is not a display of the antic disposition (e.g., I.v.117 ff.; III.ii. 282 ff.; V.i.297 ff.), his conduct at such times is no more than the recoil from emotional strain, such as any normal person might exhibit. To particularize briefly, if the nonsensical jingle which Hamlet spouts after the success of the "mouse trap" betrays a neurotic state, we should certainly expect Hamlet to be highly excited when instructing the player in the delivery of the lines he has composed for him and in talking with Horatio before the play begins; but then he is conspicuously calm. For his unseemly conduct at Ophelia's grave he manfully repents; the showy grief of Laertes revolted him and made him forget himself.

Dramatically the rôle of Claudius is the equal of Hamlet's. Urbane, diplomatic, intelligent, courageous, and masterful in the face of danger, Claudius is a worthy antagonist for Hamlet. His self-control is consummate. After the dumb show has revealed to him Hamlet's knowledge of his secret and his consequent imminent peril, Claudius elects to sit out the play, and nearly succeeds. It is not so much the argument of the play as the relentless focus of Hamlet's eyes and his menacing irony that breaks him down. His intrepidity when Laertes storms the palace with the mob at his back is crowned by the skill with which he subdues that rash and misguided young man to his designs. Claudius is the villain of the play, but he is no ordinary villain. For all his apparent callousness, his conscience is alive, and it is the irony of his fate that he cannot relish the fruits of his crime, or expiate it by living at peace with the nephew he has injured, as it had been his honest hope to do.

The Ghost of Hamlet's father is a remarkable creation. He is no horrific apparition, but "the beauteous majesty of buried Denmark." He is seen in his natural and wonted dignity, dressed as he had been dressed in life. "So excellent a king"; all that Hamlet has said of him (I.ii.139–44) is confirmed for us by his courteous action, his graceful speaking, and his noble solicitude for his queen. Shakespeare makes us feel pity, admiration, and affection for the Ghost. Indeed, the personality of the dead king, along with the character of the protagonist, contributes notably to the distinctive refinement of this tragedy of revenge, which stands today as Shakespeare's most popular and most frequently acted play.

THE TRAGEDY OF HAMLET, PRINCE OF DENMARK

[DRAMATIS PERSONÆ

CLAUDIUS, *King of Denmark.*
HAMLET, *son to the late, and nephew to the present, King.*
POLONIUS, *Lord Chamberlain.*
HORATIO, *friend to Hamlet.*
LAERTES, *son to Polonius.*
VOLTIMAND,
CORNELIUS,
ROSENCRANTZ, } *courtiers.*
GUILDENSTERN,
OSRIC,
A Gentleman,
MARCELLUS, } *officers.*
BERNARDO,

FRANCISCO, *a soldier.*
REYNALDO, *servant to Polonius.*
A Priest.
Players.
Two Clowns, *grave-diggers.*
FORTINBRAS, *Prince of Norway.*
A Norwegian Captain.
English Ambassadors.

GERTRUDE, *Queen of Denmark, and mother to Hamlet.*
OPHELIA, *daughter to Polonius.*

Ghost of Hamlet's Father.

Lords, Ladies, Officers, Soldiers, Sailors, Messengers, and other Attendants.

SCENE: *Elsinore, Denmark.*]

ACT I

SCENE I. [*Elsinore. A platform before the castle.*]

FRANCISCO [*at his post. Enter to him*] BERNARDO.

Ber. Who's there?
Fran. Nay, answer me. Stand, and unfold yourself.
Ber. Long live the king!
Fran. Bernardo?
Ber. He.   5
Fran. You come most carefully upon your hour.
Ber. 'Tis now struck twelve. Get thee to bed, Francisco.
Fran. For this relief much thanks. 'Tis bitter cold,
And I am sick at heart.
Ber. Have you had quiet guard?
Fran.   Not a mouse stirring. 10
Ber. Well, good-night.

If you do meet Horatio and Marcellus,
The rivals of my watch, bid them make haste.

Enter HORATIO *and* MARCELLUS.

Fran. I think I hear them. Stand! Who's there?
Hor. Friends to this ground.
Mar.   And liegemen to the Dane. 15
Fran. Give you good-night.
Mar.   O, farewell, honest soldier.
Who hath reliev'd you?
Fran.   Bernardo has my place.
Give you good-night.   [*Exit.*
Mar.   Holla! Bernardo!
Ber.   Say,
What, is Horatio there?
Hor.   A piece of him.
Ber. Welcome, Horatio; welcome, good Marcellus. 20
Mar. What, has this thing appear'd again tonight?

Act I, sc. i, 3. **Long ... king.** A password. 13. **rivals:** partners. 21. **Mar.** F Q₁. *Hora* Q₂.

Ber. I have seen nothing.

Mar. Horatio says 'tis but our fantasy,
And will not let belief take hold of him
Touching this dreaded sight, twice seen of us;   25
Therefore I have entreated him along
With us to watch the minutes of this night,
That, if again this apparition come,
He may approve our eyes and speak to it.

Hor. Tush, tush, 'twill not appear.

Ber.   Sit down a while,   30
And let us once again assail your ears,
That are so fortified against our story,
What we two nights have seen.

Hor.   Well, sit we down,
And let us hear Bernardo speak of this.

Ber. Last night of all,   35
When yond same star that's westward from the pole
Had made his course t' illume that part of heaven
Where now it burns, Marcellus and myself,
The bell then beating one, —

Enter the Ghost.

Mar. Peace, break thee off!   Look, where it
        comes again!   40

Ber. In the same figure, like the King that's
        dead.

Mar. Thou art a scholar; speak to it, Horatio.

Ber. Looks it not like the King?   Mark it,
        Horatio.

Hor. Most like; it harrows me with fear and
        wonder.

Ber. It would be spoke to.

Mar.   Question it, Horatio.   45

Hor. What art thou that usurp'st this time of
        night,
Together with that fair and warlike form
In which the majesty of buried Denmark
Did sometimes march?   By heaven I charge thee,
        speak!

Mar. It is offended.

Ber.   See, it stalks away!   50

Hor. Stay!   Speak, speak!   I charge thee,
        speak!   [*Exit Ghost.*

Mar. 'Tis gone, and will not answer.

Ber. How now, Horatio! You tremble and look
        pale.
Is not this something more than fantasy?
What think you on't?   55

Hor. Before my God, I might not this believe
Without the sensible and true avouch
Of mine own eyes.

Mar.   Is it not like the King?

Hor. As thou art to thyself.
Such was the very armour he had on   60
When [he] th' ambitious Norway combated.
So frown'd he once, when, in an angry parle,
He smote the sledded [Polacks] on the ice.
'Tis strange.

Mar. Thus twice before, and [jump] at this
        dead hour,   65
With martial stalk hath he gone by our watch.

Hor. In what particular thought to work I
        know not;
But, in the gross and scope of my opinion,
This bodes some strange eruption to our state.

Mar. Good now, sit down, and tell me, he that
        knows,   70
Why this same strict and most observant watch
So nightly toils the subject of the land,
And why such daily cast of brazen cannon,
And foreign mart for implements of war;
Why such impress of shipwrights, whose sore task
Does not divide the Sunday from the week.   76
What might be toward, that this sweaty haste
Doth make the night joint-labourer with the day,
Who is't that can inform me?

Hor.   That can I;
At least, the whisper goes so.   Our last king,   80
Whose image even but now appear'd to us,
Was, as you know, by Fortinbras of Norway,
Thereto prick'd on by a most emulate pride,
Dar'd to the combat; in which our valiant Ham-
        let —   84
For so this side of our known world esteem'd him —
Did slay this Fortinbras; who, by a seal'd compact
Well ratified by law and heraldry,
Did forfeit, with his life, all those his lands
Which he stood seiz'd on, to the conqueror;
Against the which, a moiety competent   90
Was gaged by our king; which had return'd
To the inheritance of Fortinbras,
Had he been vanquisher; as, by the same covenant
And carriage of the [articled] design
His fell to Hamlet.   Now, sir, young Fortinbras,   95
Of unimproved mettle hot and full,
Hath in the skirts of Norway here and there
Shark'd up a list of landless resolutes,
For food and diet, to some enterprise
That hath a stomach in't; which is no other —   100
[As] it doth well appear unto our state —
But to recover of us, by strong hand
And terms compulsative, those foresaid lands
So by his father lost; and this, I take it,
Is the main motive of our preparations,   105

29. **approve:** confirm.   42. **scholar.**   One had to exorcise spirits in Latin.   57. **sensible:** of the senses.   61. **[he]** Q$_2$. Om. F.   63. **sledded:** using sleds or sledges.   **[Polacks]** (Malone): Poles.   *Pollax* F.   *pollax* Q$_2$.   65. **[jump]** Q$_2$: precisely. *just* F.   68. **gross and scope:** main drift.   72. **toils:** causes to work.   **subject:** people.   75. **impress:** forced service.   83. **emulate:** envious.   89. **seiz'd on:** possessed of.   90. **moiety competent:** equal share.   91. **gaged:** pledged.   94. **[articled] design** (Edd.).   *article designe* F$_1$.   *article design'd* F$_2$.   The line means: the plan conveyed by the articles of the treaty.   96. **un-improved:** untried.   98. **Shark'd up:** collected swiftly.   **landless** F$_1$.   *lawless* Q$_2$.   100. **hath . . . in't:** takes courage.   101. **[As]** Q$_2$.   *And* F.

The source of this our watch, and the chief head
Of this post-haste and romage in the land.
[*Ber.* I think it be no other but e'en so.
Well may it sort that this portentous figure
Comes armed through our watch, so like the King
That was and is the question of these wars. 111
   Hor. A mote it is to trouble the mind's eye.
In the most high and palmy state of Rome,
A little ere the mightiest Julius fell,
The graves stood tenantless and the sheeted dead 115
Did squeak and gibber in the Roman streets.
.   .   .   .
As stars with trains of fire and dews of blood,
Disasters in the sun; and the moist star
Upon whose influence Neptune's empire stands
Was sick almost to doomsday with eclipse. 120
And even the like precurse of fierce events,
As harbingers preceding still the fates
And prologue to the omen coming on,
Have heaven and earth together demonstrated
Unto our climatures and countrymen.] 125

           Re-enter Ghost.

But soft, behold! Lo, where it comes again!
I'll cross it, though it blast me. Stay, illusion!
If thou hast any sound, or use of voice,
Speak to me;
If there be any good thing to be done 130
That may to thee do ease and grace to me,
Speak to me;
If thou art privy to thy country's fate,
Which, happily, foreknowing may avoid,
O speak! 135
Or if thou hast uphoarded in thy life
Extorted treasure in the womb of earth,
For which, they say, you spirits oft walk in death,
Speak of it; stay, and speak! (*Cock crows.*) Stop
   it, Marcellus.
   Mar. Shall I strike at it with my partisan? 140
   Hor. Do, if it will not stand.
   Ber.   'Tis here!
   Hor.   'Tis here!
   Mar. 'Tis gone!   [*Exit Ghost.*
We do it wrong, being so majestical,
To offer it the show of violence;
For it is, as the air, invulnerable, 145
And our vain blows malicious mockery.
   Ber. It was about to speak, when the cock crew.
   Hor. And then it started like a guilty thing
Upon a fearful summons. I have heard
The cock, that is the trumpet to the [morn], 150

Doth with his lofty and shrill-sounding throat
Awake the god of day; and, at his warning,
Whether in sea or fire, in earth or air,
The extravagant and erring spirit hies
To his confine; and of the truth herein 155
This present object made probation.
   Mar. It faded on the crowing of the cock.
Some [say] that ever 'gainst that season comes
Wherein our Saviour's birth is celebrated,
The bird of dawning singeth all night long; 160
And then, they say, no spirit can walk abroad;
The nights are wholesome; then no planets strike,
No fairy [takes], nor witch hath power to charm,
So hallow'd and so gracious is the time.
   Hor. So have I heard and do in part believe it.
But, look, the morn, in russet mantle clad, 166
Walks o'er the dew of yon high eastern hill.
Break we our watch up; and, by my advice,
Let us impart what we have seen to-night
Unto young Hamlet; for, upon my life, 170
This spirit, dumb to us, will speak to him.
Do you consent we shall acquaint him with it,
As needful in our loves, fitting our duty?
   Mar. Let's do't, I pray; and I this morning
     know
Where we shall find him most conveniently. 175
                          [*Exeunt.*

SCENE II. [*A room of state in the castle.*]
Flourish.   *Enter the* KING, QUEEN, HAMLET,
POLONIUS, LAERTES, OPHELIA, *Lords, and At-
tendants.*
   King. Though yet of Hamlet our dear brother's
     death
The memory be green, and that it us befitted
To bear our hearts in grief, and our whole kingdom
To be contracted in one brow of woe,
Yet so far hath discretion fought with nature 5
That we with wisest sorrow think on him
Together with remembrance of ourselves.
Therefore our sometime sister, now our queen,
Th' imperial jointress of this warlike state,
Have we, as 'twere with a defeated joy,— 10
With one auspicious and one dropping eye,
With mirth in funeral and with dirge in marriage,
In equal scale weighing delight and dole,—
Taken to wife; nor have we herein barr'd
Your better wisdoms, which have freely gone 15
With this affair along. For all, our thanks.
Now follows that you know: young Fortinbras,

---

106. **head:** source. 107. **romage:** bustle. 108–25. [*Ber.... countrymen*] Q2. Om. F. 109. **sort:** fit. 115. **tenant-less** Q4. *tennatlesse* Q2. 116. **Did... streets.** Probably a line has dropped out after l. 116. 118. **Disasters:** unfavor-able aspects. **moist star:** moon. 121. **precurse:** precursor. 125. **climatures:** regions. 127. Q2 adds S.D. *It spreads his arms.* 140. **partisan:** long-handled spear. 150. **trumpet:** trumpeter. [**morn**] Q2. *day* F. 154. **extravagant:** vagrant. **erring:** wandering. 156. **probation:** proof. 158. [**say**] Q2. *sayes* F. 161. **can walk** F. *dare sturre* Q2. 163. [**takes**] Q2: charms. *talks* F.
Sc. ii, 9. **jointress:** joint sovereign. 10. **defeated:** impaired.

Holding a weak supposal of our worth,
Or thinking by our late dear brother's death
Our state to be disjoint and out of frame, 20
Colleagued with the dream of his advantage,
He hath not fail'd to pester us with message
Importing the surrender of those lands
Lost by his father, with all bonds of law,
To our most valiant brother. So much for him. 25

Enter VOLTIMAND *and* CORNELIUS.

Now for ourself and for this time of meeting,
Thus much the business is: we have here writ
To Norway, uncle of young Fortinbras, —
Who, impotent and bed-rid, scarcely hears
Of this his nephew's purpose, — to suppress 30
His further gait herein, in that the levies,
The lists, and full proportions are all made
Out of his subject; and we here dispatch
You, good Cornelius, and you, Voltimand,
For bearing of this greeting to old Norway; 35
Giving to you no further personal power
To business with the king, more than the scope
Of these delated articles allow. [*Giving a paper.*]
Farewell, and let your haste commend your duty.
  [*Cor.*] } In that and all things will we show our
  Vol. }   duty. 40
  King. We doubt it nothing; heartily farewell.
    [*Exeunt Voltimand and Cornelius.*
And now, Laertes, what's the news with you?
You told us of some suit; what is't, Laertes?
You cannot speak of reason to the Dane
And lose your voice. What wouldst thou beg, Laertes, 45
That shall not be my offer, not thy asking?
The head is not more native to the heart,
The hand more instrumental to the mouth,
Than is the throne of Denmark to thy father.
What wouldst thou have, Laertes?
  Laer.   Dread my lord, 50
Your leave and favour to return to France;
From whence though willingly I came to Denmark
To show my duty in your coronation,
Yet now, I must confess, that duty done,
My thoughts and wishes bend again towards France 55
And bow them to your gracious leave and pardon.
  King. Have you your father's leave? What says Polonius?
  Pol. He hath, my lord, [wrung from me my slow leave
By laboursome petition, and at last
Upon his will I seal'd my hard consent.] 60
I do beseech you, give him leave to go.

  King. Take thy fair hour, Laertes. Time be thine,
And thy best graces spend it at thy will!
But now, my cousin Hamlet, and my son, —
  Ham. [*Aside.*] A little more than kin, and less than kind. 65
  King. How is it that the clouds still hang on you?
  Ham. Not so, my lord; I am too much i' th' sun.
  Queen. Good Hamlet, cast thy [nighted] colour off,
And let thine eye look like a friend on Denmark.
Do not for ever with thy vailed lids 70
Seek for thy noble father in the dust.
Thou know'st 'tis common; all that lives must die,
Passing through nature to eternity.
  Ham. Ay, madam, it is common.
  Queen.   If it be,
Why seems it so particular with thee? 75
  Ham. Seems, madam! Nay, it is; I know not "seems."
'Tis not alone my inky cloak, good mother,
Nor customary suits of solemn black,
Nor windy suspiration of forc'd breath,
No, nor the fruitful river in the eye, 80
Nor the dejected haviour of the visage,
Together with all forms, moods, shows of grief,
That can denote me truly. These indeed seem,
For they are actions that a man might play;
But I have that within which passeth show, 85
These but the trappings and the suits of woe.
  King. 'Tis sweet and commendable in your nature, Hamlet,
To give these mourning duties to your father.
But, you must know, your father lost a father;
That father lost, lost his; and the survivor bound 90
In filial obligation for some term
To do obsequious sorrow. But to persever
In obstinate condolement is a course
Of impious stubbornness; 'tis unmanly grief;
It shows a will most incorrect to heaven, 95
A heart unfortified, a mind impatient,
An understanding simple and unschool'd;
For what we know must be, and is as common
As any the most vulgar thing to sense,
Why should we in our peevish opposition 100
Take it to heart? Fie! 'tis a fault to heaven,
A fault against the dead, a fault to nature,
To reason most absurd, whose common theme
Is death of fathers, and who still hath cried,
From the first corse till he that died to-day, 105
"This must be so." We pray you, throw to earth
This unprevailing woe, and think of us
As of a father; for, let the world take note,

---

21. **Colleagued:** joined. **advantage:** superiority. 31. **gait:** proceeding. 32. **proportions:** provisions. 38. **delated:** specified. 40. **[Cor.]** Q2. Om. F. 45. **lose:** waste. 47. **more native:** closer related. 58–60. **[wrung . . . consent]** Q2. Om. F. 65. **kind.** Perhaps with a play on the meaning, nature, natural. 68. **[nighted]** Q2. *nightly* F. 70. **vailed:** downcast. 93. **condolement:** grief. 99. **vulgar:** common. 107. **unprevailing:** unavailing.

You are the most immediate to our throne,
And with no less nobility of love 110
Than that which dearest father bears his son
Do I impart towards you. For your intent
In going back to school in Wittenberg,
It is most retrograde to our desire;
And we beseech you, bend you to remain 115
Here in the cheer and comfort of our eye,
Our chiefest courtier, cousin, and our son.
　　Queen. Let not thy mother lose her prayers,
　　　　Hamlet.
I prithee, stay with us; go not to Wittenberg.
　　Ham. I shall in all my best obey you, madam. 120
　　King. Why, 'tis a loving and a fair reply.
Be as ourself in Denmark. Madam, come;
This gentle and unforc'd accord of Hamlet
Sits smiling to my heart; in grace whereof,
No jocund health that Denmark drinks to-day, 125
But the great cannon to the clouds shall tell,
And the King's rouse the heavens shall bruit again,
Re-speaking earthly thunder. Come away.
　　　　[*Flourish. Exeunt all but Hamlet.*
　　Ham. O, that this too too solid flesh would melt,
Thaw, and resolve itself into a dew! 130
Or that the Everlasting had not fix'd
His canon 'gainst self-slaughter! O God! God!
How weary, stale, flat, and unprofitable,
Seems to me all the uses of this world!
Fie on't! oh fie, fie! 'Tis an unweeded garden, 135
That grows to seed; things rank and gross in nature
Possess it merely. That it should come to this!
But two months dead! Nay, not so much, not two.
So excellent a king; that was, to this,
Hyperion to a satyr; so loving to my mother 140
That he might not beteem the winds of heaven
Visit her face too roughly. Heaven and earth!
Must I remember? Why, she would hang on him
As if increase of appetite had grown
By what it fed on; and yet, within a month, — 145
Let me not think on't! — Frailty, thy name is
　　　　woman! —
A little month, or e'er those shoes were old
With which she followed my poor father's body,
Like Niobe, all tears, — why she, even she —
O [God]! a beast, that wants discourse of reason, 150
Would have mourn'd longer — married with mine
　　　　uncle,
My father's brother, but no more like my father
Than I to Hercules; within a month,
Ere yet the salt of most unrighteous tears
Had left the flushing of her galled eyes, 155
She married. O, most wicked speed, to post

With such dexterity to incestuous sheets!
It is not, nor it cannot come to good. —
But break my heart, for I must hold my tongue.

　　Enter HORATIO, MARCELLUS, *and* BERNARDO.

　　Hor. Hail to your lordship!
　　Ham.　　　　I am glad to see you well. 160
Horatio! — or I do forget myself.
　　Hor. The same, my lord, and your poor servant
　　　　ever.
　　Ham. Sir, my good friend; I'll change that
　　　　name with you.
And what make you from Wittenberg, Horatio?
Marcellus? 165
　　Mar. My good lord!
　　Ham. I am very glad to see you. [*To Ber.*]
　　　　Good even, sir. —
But what, in faith, make you from Wittenberg?
　　Hor. A truant disposition, good my lord.
　　Ham. I would not have your enemy say so, 170
Nor shall you do mine ear that violence,
To make it truster of your own report
Against yourself. I know you are no truant.
But what is your affair in Elsinore?
We'll teach you to drink deep ere you depart. 175
　　Hor. My lord, I came to see your father's funeral.
　　Ham. I pray thee, do not mock me, fellow-student
I think it was to see my mother's wedding.
　　Hor. Indeed, my lord, it followed hard upon.
　　Ham. Thrift, thrift, Horatio! The funeral
　　　　bak'd-meats 180
Did coldly furnish forth the marriage tables.
Would I had met my dearest foe in heaven
Ere I had ever seen that day, Horatio!
My father! — methinks I see my father. 184
　　Hor. Oh, where, my lord?
　　Ham.　　　　In my mind's eye, Horatio.
　　Hor. I saw him once; he was a goodly king.
　　Ham. He was a man, take him for all in all, I
shall not look upon his like again.
　　Hor. My lord, I think I saw him yesternight.
　　Ham. Saw? Who? 190
　　Hor. My lord, the King your father.
　　Ham.　　　　The King my father!
　　Hor. Season your admiration for a while
With an attent ear, till I may deliver,
Upon the witness of these gentlemen,
This marvel to you.
　　Ham.　　　　For [God's] love, let me hear. 195
　　Hor. Two nights together had these gentlemen,
Marcellus and Bernardo, on their watch,
In the dead [waste] and middle of the night,

---

112. **impart.** The object understood is perhaps the succession. 127. **rouse:** bumper. **bruit:** loudly declare. 129. **solid** F. *sallied* Q₂. 132. **canon:** law. 134. **uses:** customs. 137. **merely:** utterly. 140. **Hyperion:** Apollo. 141. **beteem:** allow. 149. **even she** F. Om. Q₂. 150. [**God**] Q₂. *Heaven* F. The same change by F occurs in many other passages, owing to the statute against profanity. **discourse:** power. 155. **flushing:** redness. 170. **have** F. *hear* Q₂. 192. **Season:** temper. **admiration:** astonishment. 198. [**waste**] F₂. *wast* Q₂ F.

Been thus encount'red. A figure like your father,
Arm'd at all points exactly, cap-a-pie,   200
Appears before them, and with solemn march
Goes slow and stately by them. Thrice he walk'd
By their oppress'd and fear-surprised eyes,
Within his truncheon's length; whilst they, [dis-
    till'd]
Almost to jelly with the act of fear,   205
Stand dumb and speak not to him. This to me
In dreadful secrecy impart they did,
And I with them the third night kept the watch;
Where, as they had deliver'd, both in time,
Form of the thing, each word made true and
    good,
The apparition comes. I knew your father;   211
These hands are not more like.

Ham.   But where was this?

Mar. My lord, upon the platform where we
    watch'd.

Ham. Did you not speak to it?

Hor.   My lord, I did;
But answer made it none. Yet once methought   215
It lifted up it head and did address
Itself to motion, like as it would speak;
But even then the morning cock crew loud,
And at the sound it shrunk in haste away,
And vanish'd from our sight.

Ham.   'Tis very strange.   220

Hor. As I do live, my honour'd lord, 'tis true,
And we did think it writ down in our duty
To let you know of it.

Ham. Indeed, indeed, sirs. But this troubles me.
Hold you the watch to-night?

Mar. ⎫
Ber. ⎭   We do, my lord.   225

Ham. Arm'd, say you?

Mar. ⎫
Ber. ⎭   Arm'd, my lord.

Ham. From top to toe?

Mar. ⎫
Ber. ⎭   My lord, from head to foot.

Ham. Then saw you not his face?

Hor. O, yes, my lord; he wore his beaver up.   229

Ham. What, look'd he frowningly?

Hor.   A countenance more
In sorrow than in anger.

Ham.   Pale, or red?

Hor. Nay, very pale.

Ham.   And fix'd his eyes upon you?

Hor. Most constantly.

Ham.   I would I had been there.   235

Hor. It would have much amaz'd you.

Ham. Very like, very like. Stay'd it long?

Hor. While one with moderate haste might tell
    a hundred.

Mar. ⎫
Ber. ⎭   Longer, longer.

Hor. Not when I saw 't.

Ham.   His beard was grizzl'd? No?   240

Hor. It was, as I have seen it in his life,
A sable silver'd.

Ham.   I will watch to-night;
Perchance 'twill [walk] again.

Hor.   I warrant you it will.

Ham. If it assume my noble father's person,
I'll speak to it, though hell itself should gape   245
And bid me hold my peace. I pray you all,
If you have hitherto conceal'd this sight,
Let it be [tenable] in your silence still;
And whatsoever else shall hap to-night,
Give it an understanding, but no tongue.   250
I will requite your loves. So, fare ye well.
Upon the platform 'twixt eleven and twelve,
I'll visit you.

All.   Our duty to your honour.

Ham. Your love, as mine to you; farewell.
                  [*Exeunt* [*all but Hamlet*].
My father's spirit in arms! All is not well;   255
I doubt some foul play. Would the night were
    come!
Till then sit still, my soul. Foul deeds will rise,
Though all the earth o'erwhelm them, to men's
    eyes.   [*Exit.*

SCENE III.   [*A room in Polonius's house.*]

Enter LAERTES *and* OPHELIA.

Laer. My necessaries are embark'd, farewell;
And, sister, as the winds give benefit
And convoy is assistant, do not sleep,
But let me hear from you.

Oph.   Do you doubt that?

Laer. For Hamlet and the trifling of his fa-
    vours,
Hold it a fashion and a toy in blood,   5
A violet in the youth of primy nature,
Forward, not permanent, sweet, not lasting,
The [perfume and] suppliance of a minute;
No more.

Oph. No more but so?

Laer.   Think it no more: 10
For nature crescent does not grow alone
In thews and bulk, but, as [this] temple waxes,
The inward service of the mind and soul
Grows wide withal. Perhaps he loves you now,
And now no soil nor cautel doth besmirch   15

200. **cap-a-pie:** from head to foot.   204. **[distill'd]** Q₂.   *bestil'd* F.   211. **knew:** recognized.   229. **beaver:** visor.
238. **tell:** count.   243. **[walk]** Q₂.   *wake* F.   248. **[tenable]** Q₂: held close.   *treble* F.   256. **doubt:** suspect.
   Sc. iii, 6. **toy in blood:** trifle of passion.   7. **primy:** springlike.   9. **[perfume and]** Q₂. Om. F.   **suppliance:** pastime.
11. **crescent:** growing.   12. **[this]** Q₂.   *his* F.   15. **cautel:** deceit.

The virtue of his [will]; but you must fear,
His greatness weigh'd, his will is not his own;
For he himself is subject to his birth.
He may not, as unvalued persons do,
Carve for himself, for on his choice depends   20
The [sanity] and health of the whole state;
And therefore must his choice be circumscrib'd
Unto the voice and yielding of that body
Whereof he is the head.   Then, if he says he loves
          you,
It fits your wisdom so far to believe it   25
As he in his [particular act and place]
May give his saying deed; which is no further
Than the main voice of Denmark goes withal.
Then weigh what loss your honour may sustain
If with too credent ear you list his songs,   30
Or lose your heart, or your chaste treasure open
To his unmast'red importunity.
Fear it, Ophelia, fear it, my dear sister,
And keep within the rear of your affection,
Out of the shot and danger of desire.   35
The chariest maid is prodigal enough,
If she unmask her beauty to the moon.
Virtue itself scapes not calumnious strokes.
The canker galls the infants of the spring
Too oft before the buttons be disclos'd,   40
And in the morn and liquid dew of youth
Contagious blastments are most imminent.
Be wary then; best safety lies in fear;
Youth to itself rebels, though none else near.
  Oph. I shall th' effect of this good lesson keep,   45
As watchman to my heart.   But, good my brother,
Do not, as some ungracious pastors do,
Show me the steep and thorny way to heaven,
Whilst, like a puff'd and reckless libertine,
Himself the primrose path of dalliance treads,   50
And recks not his own rede.
  Laer.   O, fear me not.

Enter POLONIUS.

I stay too long: but here my father comes.
A double blessing is a double grace;
Occasion smiles upon a second leave.
  Pol. Yet here, Laertes? Aboard, aboard, for
          shame!   55
The wind sits in the shoulder of your sail,
And you are stay'd for.   There; my blessing with
          you!
And these few precepts in thy memory
See thou character.   Give thy thoughts no tongue,
Nor any unproportion'd thought his act.   60
Be thou familiar, but by no means vulgar.

The friends thou hast, and their adoption tried,
Grapple them to thy soul with hoops of steel;
But do not dull thy palm with entertainment
Of each [new]-hatch'd, unfledg'd comrade.   Be-
          ware   65
Of entrance to a quarrel; but being in,
Bear 't that the opposed may beware of thee.
Give every man thine ear, but few thy voice.
Take each man's censure, but reserve thy judge-
          ment.
Costly thy habit as thy purse can buy,   70
But not express'd in fancy; rich, not gaudy;
For the apparel oft proclaims the man,
And they in France of the best rank and station
Are most select and generous in that.
Neither a borrower nor a lender be;   75
For loan oft loses both itself and friend,
And borrowing dulls the edge of husbandry.
This above all: to thine own self be true,
And it must follow, as the night the day,
Thou canst not then be false to any man.   80
Farewell; my blessing season this in thee!
  Laer. Most humbly do I take my leave, my
          lord.
  Pol. The time invites you; go, your servants tend.
  Laer. Farewell, Ophelia, and remember well
What I have said to you.
  Oph.   'Tis in my memory lock'd,   85
And you yourself shall keep the key of it.
  Laer. Farewell.   [*Exit.*
  Pol. What is 't, Ophelia, he hath said to you?
  Oph. So please you, something touching the
          Lord Hamlet.
  Pol. Marry, well bethought.   90
'Tis told me, he hath very oft of late
Given private time to you, and you yourself
Have of your audience been most free and bounte-
          ous.
If it be so — as so 'tis put on me,
And that in way of caution — I must tell you   95
You do not understand yourself so clearly
As it behoves my daughter and your honour.
What is between you?   Give me up the truth.
  Oph. He hath, my lord, of late made many ten-
          ders
Of his affection to me.   100
  Pol. Affection! pooh! You speak like a green
          girl,
Unsifted in such perilous circumstance.
Do you believe his tenders, as you call them?
  Oph. I do not know, my lord, what I should
          think.

16. [will] Q₂. *feare* F.   19. unvalued: of low rank.   21. [sanity] (Theobald). *sanctity* F; *safety* Q₂.   26. [particular act and place] Q₂. *peculiar Sect and force* F.   34. within F. *you in* Q₂.   39. canker: canker-worm.   40. buttons: buds.   47. ungracious: graceless.   51. rede: counsel.   59. character: inscribe.   65. [new]-hatch'd Q₂. *unhatch't* F.   69. censure: opinion.   74. Are...in that (Grant White). *Are of a ... cheff in that* F.   The passage is corrupt.   77. husbandry: thrift. 99. tenders: offers.   102. Unsifted: untried.

Pol. Marry, I'll teach you: think yourself a
baby   105
That you have ta'en his tenders for true pay,
Which are not sterling.   Tender yourself more
dearly,
Or — not to crack the wind of the poor phrase,
[Running] it thus — you'll tender me a fool.
Oph. My lord, he hath importun'd me with
love   110
In honourable fashion.
Pol. Ay, fashion you may call it.   Go to, go to.
Oph. And hath given countenance to his speech,
my lord,
With [almost] all the [holy] vows of heaven.
Pol. Ay, springes to catch woodcocks.   I do
know,   115
When the blood burns, how prodigal the soul
Gives the tongue vows.   These blazes, daughter,
Giving more light than heat, extinct in both
Even in their promise, as it is a-making,
You must not take for fire.   [From] this time,
daughter,   120
Be somewhat scanter of your maiden presence.
Set your entreatments at a higher rate
Than a command to parley.   For Lord Hamlet,
Believe so much in him, that he is young,
And with a larger tether may he walk   125
Than may be given you.   In few, Ophelia,
Do not believe his vows; for they are brokers,
Not of [that dye] which their investments show,
But mere implorators of unholy suits,
Breathing like sanctified and pious [bawds],   130
The better to beguile.   This is for all:
I would not, in plain terms, from this time forth,
Have you so slander any moment leisure
As to give words or talk with the Lord Hamlet.
Look to't, I charge you.   Come your ways.   135
Oph. I shall obey, my lord.   [*Exeunt.*

[SCENE IV.   *The platform.*]

Enter HAMLET, HORATIO, *and* MARCELLUS.

Ham. The air bites shrewdly; [it is] very cold.
Hor. It is a nipping and an eager air.
Ham. What hour now?
Hor.   I think it lacks of twelve.
Mar. No, it is struck.
Hor. Indeed?   I heard it not.   Then it draws
near the season   5

Wherein the spirit held his wont to walk.
    [*A flourish of trumpets, and two pieces go
    off* [*within*].
What does this mean, my lord?
Ham. The King doth wake to-night and takes
his rouse,
Keeps wassails, and the swagg'ring up-spring reels;
And, as he drains his draughts of Rhenish down,   10
The kettle-drum and trumpet thus bray out
The triumph of his pledge.
Hor.   Is it a custom?
Ham. Ay, marry, is't,
[But] to my mind, though I am native here
And to the manner born, it is a custom   15
More honour'd in the breach than the observance.
[This heavy-headed revel east and west
Makes us traduc'd and tax'd of other nations.
They clepe us drunkards, and with swinish phrase
Soil our addition; and indeed it takes   20
From our achievements, though perform'd at
height,
The pith and marrow of our attribute.
So, oft it chances in particular men,
That for some vicious mole of nature in them,
As, in their birth — wherein they are not guilty,   25
Since nature cannot choose his origin —
By their o'ergrowth of some complexion,
Oft breaking down the pales and forts of reason,
Or by some habit that too much o'er-leavens
The form of plausive manners, that these men,   30
Carrying, I say, the stamp of one defect,
Being nature's livery, or fortune's star,—
His virtues else — be they as pure as grace,
As infinite as man may undergo —
Shall in the general censure take corruption   35
From that particular fault.   The dram of evil
Doth all the noble substance often dout
To his own scandal.]

Enter GHOST.

Hor.   Look, my lord, it comes!
Ham. Angels and ministers of grace defend us!
Be thou a spirit of health or goblin damn'd,   40
Bring with thee airs from heaven or blasts from hell,
Be thy [intents] wicked or charitable,
Thou com'st in such a questionable shape
That I will speak to thee.   I'll call thee Hamlet,
King, father; royal Dane, O, answer me!   45
Let me not burst in ignorance, but tell

107. **Tender:** hold. 109. **[Running]** (Collier conj.).   *Roaming* F; *Wrong* Q2. 114. **[almost]** Q2.   Om. F.   **[holy]** Q2.
Om. F. 115. **springes:** snares.   **woodcocks:** proverbially stupid birds. 117. **Gives** F.   *Lends* Q2. 120. **[From]** Q2.   *For*
F. 122. **entreatments:** interviews. 127. **brokers:** procurers. 128. **[that dye]** Q2.   *the eye* F.   **investments:** garments.
130. **[bawds]** (Theobald).   *bonds* Q2 F.
    Sc. iv, 1. **[it is]** Q2.   *is it* F. 2. **eager:** sharp. 8. **wake:** hold revels. 9. **up-spring:** a boisterous dance. 14. **[But]** Q2.
And F. 17–38. **[This . . . scandal]** Q2.   Om. F. 18. **tax'd:** blamed. 19. **clepe:** call. 20. **addition:** title, distinction.
22. **attribute:** reputation. 24. **mole:** defect. 27. **their** Q2.   *the* Pope.   **complexion:** disposition. 28. **pales:** fences. 30.
plausive: pleasing. 35. **general:** popular. 36. **evil** (Keightley conj.).   *eale* Q2. 37. **often dout** (Steevens).   *of a doubt* Q2.
dout: drive out, cancel. 42. **[intents]** Q2.   *events* F. 43. **questionable:** inviting talk. 45. **O** Q2.   *Oh, oh* F.

Why thy canoniz'd bones, hearsed in death,
Have burst their cerements; why the sepulchre,
Wherein we saw thee quietly inurn'd,
Hath op'd his ponderous and marble jaws   50
To cast thee up again. What may this mean,
That thou, dead corse, again in complete steel
Revisits thus the glimpses of the moon,
Making night hideous, and we fools of nature
So horridly to shake our disposition   55
With thoughts beyond the reaches of our souls?
Say, why is this? Wherefore? What should we
   do?   [Ghost beckons Hamlet.
  Hor. It beckons you to go away with it,
As if it some impartment did desire
To you alone.
  Mar.   Look, with what courteous action   60
It wafts you to a more removed ground.
But do not go with it.
  Hor.   No, by no means.
  Ham. It will not speak; then will I follow it.
  Hor. Do not, my lord.
  Ham.   Why, what should be the fear?
I do not set my life at a pin's fee,   65
And for my soul, what can it do to that,
Being a thing immortal as itself?
It waves me forth again. I'll follow it.
  Hor. What if it tempt you toward the flood,
   my lord,
Or to the dreadful summit of the cliff   70
That beetles o'er his base into the sea,
And there assume some other, horrible form,
Which might deprive your sovereignty of reason
And draw you into madness? Think of it.
[The very place puts toys of desperation,   75
Without more motive, into every brain
That looks so many fathoms to the sea
And hears it roar beneath.]
  Ham.   It wafts me still.
Go on, I'll follow thee.
  Mar. You shall not go, my lord.
  Ham.   Hold off your hand.   80
  Hor. Be rul'd; you shall not go.
  Ham.   My fate cries out,
And makes each petty artery in this body
As hardy as the Nemean lion's nerve.
Still am I call'd. Unhand me, gentlemen.
By heaven, I'll make a ghost of him that lets me!   85
I say, away! — Go on, I'll follow thee.
              [Exeunt Ghost and Hamlet.
  Hor. He waxes desperate with imagination.
  Mar. Let's follow. 'Tis not fit thus to obey
   him.
  Hor. Have after. To what issue will this come?

  Mar. Something is rotten in the state of Den-
   mark.   90
  Hor. Heaven will direct it.
  Mar.   Nay, let's follow him.
                    [Exeunt.

[SCENE V. *Another part of the platform.*]

Enter GHOST *and* HAMLET.

  Ham. Where wilt thou lead me? Speak, I'll
   go no further.
  Ghost. Mark me.
  Ham.   I will.
  Ghost.   My hour is almost come,
When I to sulphurous and tormenting flames
Must render up myself.
  Ham.   Alas, poor ghost!
  Ghost. Pity me not, but lend thy serious hearing   5
To what I shall unfold.
  Ham.   Speak; I am bound to hear.
  Ghost. So art thou to revenge, when thou shalt
   hear.
  Ham. What?
  Ghost. I am thy father's spirit,
Doom'd for a certain term to walk the night,   10
And for the day confin'd to fast in fires,
Till the foul crimes done in my days of nature
Are burnt and purg'd away. But that I am forbid
To tell the secrets of my prison-house,
I could a tale unfold whose lightest word   15
Would harrow up thy soul, freeze thy young blood,
Make thy two eyes, like stars, start from their
   spheres,
Thy knotty and combined locks to part
And each particular hair to stand on end,
Like quills upon the fretful porpentine.   20
But this eternal blazon must not be
To ears of flesh and blood. List, Hamlet, O, list!
If thou didst ever thy dear father love —
  Ham. O [God]!
  Ghost. Revenge his foul and most unnatural
   murder.   25
  Ham. Murder!
  Ghost. Murder most foul, as in the best it is,
But this most foul, strange, and unnatural.
  Ham. [Haste] me to know't, that [I], with wings
   as swift
As meditation or the thoughts of love,   30
May sweep to my revenge.
  Ghost.   I find thee apt;
And duller shouldst thou be than the fat weed
That rots itself in ease on Lethe wharf,
Wouldst thou not stir in this. Now, Hamlet, hear.

---

47. **canoniz'd**: sainted. 75–78. **[The . . . beneath]** Q₂. Om. F. 75. **toys**: impulses. 83. **Nemean lion**: lion slain by Hercules. **nerve**: sinew. 85. **lets**: hinders.

    Sc. v, 20. porpentine: porcupine. 21. **eternal blazon**: revelation of eternal things. 29. **[Haste]** Q₂. *Hast, hast* F. **[I]** Q₂. Om. F.

It's given out that, sleeping in mine orchard, 35
A serpent stung me; so the whole ear of Denmark
Is by a forged process of my death
Rankly abus'd; but know, thou noble youth,
The serpent that did sting thy father's life
Now wears his crown.

Ham.   O my prophetic soul! 40
Mine uncle?

Ghost. Ay, that incestuous, that adulterate beast,
With witchcraft of his wit, [with] traitorous gifts, —
O wicked wit and gifts, that have the power
So to seduce! — won [to his] shameful lust 45
The will of my most seeming-virtuous queen.
O Hamlet, what a falling-off was there!
From me, whose love was of that dignity
That it went hand in hand even with the vow
I made to her in marriage, and to decline 50
Upon a wretch whose natural gifts were poor
To those of mine!
But virtue, as it never will be mov'd,
Though lewdness court it in a shape of heaven,
So lust, though to a radiant angel link'd, 55
Will sate itself in a celestial bed
And prey on garbage.
But, soft! methinks I scent the morning's air.
Brief let me be. Sleeping within mine orchard,
My custom always in the afternoon, 60
Upon my secure hour thy uncle stole,
With juice of cursed hebenon in a vial,
And in the porches of mine ears did pour
The leperous distilment; whose effect
Holds such an enmity with blood of man 65
That swift as quicksilver it courses through
The natural gates and alleys of the body,
And with a sudden vigour it doth posset
And curd, like eager droppings into milk,
The thin and wholesome blood. So did it mine, 70
And a most instant tetter [bark'd] about,
Most lazar-like, with vile and loathsome crust,
All my smooth body.
Thus was I, sleeping, by a brother's hand
Of life, of crown, and queen, at once dispatch'd; 75
Cut off even in the blossoms of my sin,
Unhousel'd, disappointed, unanel'd,
No reck'ning made, but sent to my account
With all my imperfections on my head.
O, horrible! O, horrible! most horrible! 80
If thou hast nature in thee, bear it not;
Let not the royal bed of Denmark be
A couch for luxury and damned incest.
But, howsoever thou pursuest this act,
Taint not thy mind, nor let thy soul contrive 85

Against thy mother aught. Leave her to heaven,
And to those thorns that in her bosom lodge
To prick and sting her. Fare thee well at once!
The glow-worm shows the matin to be near,
And 'gins to pale his uneffectual fire. 90
Adieu, adieu! Hamlet, remember me. [*Exit.*

Ham. O all you host of heaven! O earth!
    What else?
And shall I couple hell? O, fie! Hold, my heart,
And you, my sinews, grow not instant old,
But bear me stiffly up. Remember thee! 95
Ay, thou poor ghost, while memory holds a seat
In this distracted globe. Remember thee!
Yea, from the table of my memory
I'll wipe away all trivial fond records,
All saws of books, all forms, all pressures past, 100
That youth and observation copied there,
And thy commandment all alone shall live
Within the book and volume of my brain,
Unmix'd with baser matter. Yes, yes, by heaven!
O most pernicious woman! 105
O villain, villain, smiling, damned villain!
My tables, my tables, — meet it is I set it down
That one may smile, and smile, and be a villain!
At least I'm sure it may be so in Denmark.
So, uncle, there you are. Now to my word; 110
It is "Adieu, adieu! remember me."
I have sworn 't.

Mar. }[*Within.*] My lord, my lord!
Hor. }

Mar.   [*Within.*] Lord Hamlet!
Hor.   [*Within.*] Heaven secure him!
[*Ham.*] So be it!
Hor. [*Within.*] Illo, ho, ho, my lord! 115
Ham. Hillo, ho, ho, boy! Come, bird, come.

Enter HORATIO *and* MARCELLUS.

Mar. How is't, my noble lord?
Hor.   What news, my lord?
Ham. O, wonderful!
Hor. Good my lord, tell it.
Ham.   No, you'll reveal it.
Hor. Not I, my lord, by heaven.
Mar.   Nor I, my lord. 120
Ham. How say you, then, would heart of man
  once think it? —
But you'll be secret?
Hor. }
Mar. }   Ay, by heaven, my lord.
Ham. There's ne'er a villain dwelling in all
  Denmark —
But he's an arrant knave.

37. **process:** account. 38. **abus'd:** deceived. 43. [with] Q2. *hath* F. 45. [to his] Q2. *to to this* F. 61. **secure:** care-free. 62. **hebenon:** yew, considered poisonous. 68. **posset:** curdle. 69. **eager:** sour. 71. **tetter:** scab. [bark'd] Q2. *bak'd* F. 72. **lazar-like:** leper-like. 77. **Unhousel'd:** without the Sacrament. **disappointed:** unabsolved. **un-anel'd:** lacking extreme unction. 83. **luxury:** lust. 97. **globe:** head. 98. **table:** tablet. 99. **fond:** foolish. 100. **pres-sures:** impressions. 110. **word:** motto. 114. [*Ham.*] Q2. *Mar.* F. 115. **Illo, ho, ho:** a falconer's call.

Hor. There needs no ghost, my lord, come from
    the grave   125
To tell us this.
    Ham.   Why, right, you are i' the right.
And so, without more circumstance at all,
I hold it fit that we shake hands and part;
You, as your business and desires shall point you,
For every man has business and desire,   130
Such as it is; and for mine own poor part,
Look you, I'll go pray.
    Hor. These are but wild and [whirling] words,
    my lord.
    Ham. I'm sorry they offend you, heartily;
Yes, faith, heartily.
    Hor.   There's no offence, my lord. 135
    Ham. Yes, by Saint Patrick, but there is,
    [Horatio],
And much offence too. Touching this vision here,
It is an honest ghost, that let me tell you.
For your desire to know what is between us,
O'ermaster 't as you may. And now, good friends,
As you are friends, scholars, and soldiers,   141
Give me one poor request.
    Hor. What is 't, my lord? We will.
    Ham. Never make known what you have seen
    to-night.
    Hor. } My lord, we will not.
    Mar. }
    Ham.   Nay, but swear 't.
    Hor.   In faith, 145
My lord, not I.
    Mar.   Nor I, my lord, in faith.
    Ham. Upon my sword.
    Mar.   We have sworn, my lord, already.
    Ham. Indeed, upon my sword, indeed.
    Ghost. Swear!   [*Ghost cries under the stage.*
    Ham. Ah, ha, boy! say'st thou so? Art thou
    there, truepenny?   150
Come on; you hear this fellow in the cellarage.
Consent to swear.
    Hor.   Propose the oath, my lord.
    Ham. Never to speak of this that you have seen.
Swear by my sword.
    Ghost. [*Beneath.*] Swear.   155
    Ham. Hic et ubique? Then we'll shift [our] ground.
Come hither, gentlemen,
And lay your hands again upon my sword.
Never to speak of this that you have heard,
Swear by my sword.   160
    Ghost. [*Beneath.*] Swear.
    Ham. Well said, old mole! Canst work i' th'
    ground so fast?
A worthy pioner! Once more remove, good friends.

Hor. O day and night, but this is wondrous
    strange!
    Ham. And therefore as a stranger give it wel-
    come.   165
There are more things in heaven and earth, Horatio,
Than are dreamt of in our philosophy.
But come;
Here, as before, never, so help you mercy,
How strange or odd soe'er I bear myself, —   170
As I perchance hereafter shall think meet
To put an antic disposition on —
That you, at such time seeing me, never shall,
With arms encumb'red thus, or [this] headshake,
Or by pronouncing of some doubtful phrase, 175
As "Well, we know," or "We could, an if we
    would,"
Or "If we list to speak," or "There be, an if they
    might."
Or such ambiguous giving out, to note
That you know aught of me, — this not to do,
So grace and mercy at your most need help you, 180
Swear.
    Ghost. [*Beneath.*] Swear.
    Ham. Rest, rest, perturbed spirit! [*They swear.*]
    So, gentlemen,
With all my love I do commend me to you;
And what so poor a man as Hamlet is   185
May do, t' express his love and friending to you,
God willing, shall not lack. Let us go in together;
And still your fingers on your lips, I pray.
The time is out of joint; — O cursed spite,
That ever I was born to set it right!   190
Nay, come, let's go together.   [*Exeunt.*

ACT II

[Scene I. *A room in Polonius's house.*]

Enter Polonius *and* Reynaldo.

Pol. Give him his money and these notes, Rey-
    naldo.
Rey. I will, my lord.
Pol. You shall do marvellous wisely, good Rey-
    naldo,
Before you visit him, [to] make inquiry
Of his behaviour.
    Rey.   My lord, I did intend it.   5
    Pol. Marry, well said, very well said. Look
    you, sir,
Inquire me first what Danskers are in Paris,
And how, and who, what means, and where they
    keep,
What company, at what expense; and finding

---

133. **[whirling]** Q₂ (whurling). *hurling* F. 136. **[Horatio]** Q₂. *my Lord* F. 156. *Hic et ubique:* here and everywhere.
[our] Q₂. *for* F. 159–60. **Never . . . sword** F. Q₂ prints the lines in reverse order. 162. **ground** F. *earth* Q₂. 167.
our F. *your* Q₂. 172. **antic:** fantastic. 174. **[this]** Q₂. *thus* F.
Act II, sc. i, 4. **[to]** Q₂. *you* F. 7. **Danskers:** Danes. 8. **keep:** lodge.

By this encompassment and drift of question   10
That they do know my son, come you more nearer
Than your particular demands will touch it.
Take you, as 'twere, some distant knowledge of
him,
[As] thus, "I know his father and his friends,
And in part him." Do you mark this, Reynaldo?
  Rey. Ay, very well, my lord.   16
  Pol. "And in part him; but," you may say,
"not well.
But, if 't be he I mean, he's very wild,
Addicted so and so;" and there put on him
What forgeries you please; marry, none so rank   20
As may dishonour him, — take heed of that;
But, sir, such wanton, wild, and usual slips
As are companions noted and most known
To youth and liberty.
  Rey.   As gaming, my lord?
  Pol. Ay, or drinking, fencing, swearing, quarrel-
ling,   25
Drabbing; you may go so far.
  Rey. My lord, that would dishonour him.
  Pol. Faith, no, as you may season it in the
charge.
You must not put another scandal on him,
That he is open to incontinency.   30
That's not my meaning. But breathe his faults
so quaintly
That they may seem the taints of liberty,
The flash and outbreak of a fiery mind,
A savageness in unreclaimed blood,
Of general assault.
  Rey.   But, my good lord, —   35
  Pol. Wherefore should you do this?
  Rey.   Ay, my lord,
I would know that.
  Pol.   Marry, sir, here's my drift,
And, I believe, it is a fetch of warrant:
You laying these slight sullies on my son,
As 'twere a thing a little soil'd i' th' working,   40
Mark you,
Your party in converse, him you would sound,
Having ever seen in the prenominate crimes
The youth you breathe of guilty, be assur'd
He closes with you in this consequence: 45
"Good sir," or so, or "friend," or "gentleman,"
According to the phrase and the addition
Of man and country —
  Rey.   Very good, my lord.
  Pol. And then, sir, does he this — he does —   50
What was I about to say? [By the mass,] I was
about to say something. Where did I leave?

  Rey. At "closes in the consequence," at "friend
or so," and "gentleman."
  Pol. At "closes in the consequence," ay, marry.
He closes with you thus: "I know the gentleman.   55
I saw him yesterday, or t' other day,
Or then, or then, with such and such; and, as you
say,
There was he gaming; there o'ertook in 's rouse;
There falling out at tennis;" or, perchance,
"I saw him enter such a house of sale,"   60
Videlicet, a brothel, or so forth.
See you now,
Your bait of falsehood takes this [carp] of truth;
And thus do we of wisdom and of reach,
With windlasses and with assays of bias,   65
By indirections find directions out.
So by my former lecture and advice,
Shall you my son. You have me, have you not?
  Rey. My lord, I have.
  Pol.   God buy you; fare you well.
  Rey. Good my lord.   70
  Pol. Observe his inclination in yourself.
  Rey. I shall, my lord.
  Pol. And let him ply his music.
  Rey.   Well, my lord.
  Pol. Farewell!   [*Exit Reynaldo.*

Enter OPHELIA.
        How now, Ophelia! what's the matter?
  Oph. Alas, my lord, I have been so affrighted!   75
  Pol. With what, in the name of [God]?
  Oph. My lord, as I was sewing in my chamber,
Lord Hamlet, with his doublet all unbrac'd,
No hat upon his head, his stockings foul'd,
Ungart'red, and down-gyved to his ankle,   80
Pale as his shirt, his knees knocking each other,
And with a look so piteous in purport
As if he had been loosed out of hell
To speak of horrors, — he comes before me.
  Pol. Mad for thy love?
  Oph.   My lord, I do not know,
But truly, I do fear it.
  Pol.   What said he?   86
  Oph. He took me by the wrist and held me hard;
Then goes he to the length of all his arm,
And, with his other hand thus o'er his brow,
He falls to such perusal of my face   90
As he would draw it. Long stay'd he so.
At last, a little shaking of mine arm,
And thrice his head thus waving up and down,
He rais'd a sigh so piteous and profound
That it did seem to shatter all his bulk   95

14. **[As]** Q₂. *And* F.   30. **incontinency:** notorious lewdness.   31. **quaintly:** ingeniously.   35. **Of . . . assault:** universal (with youth).   38. **fetch of warrant:** guaranteed device.   43. **prenominate:** aforenamed.   45. **closes:** falls in.   **consequence:** conclusion.   51. **[By the mass]** Q₂. Om. F.   61. **Videlicet:** namely.   63. **[carp]** Q₂ (carpe). *cape* F.   64. **reach:** ability.   65. **windlasses:** roundabout ways.   **assays of bias:** indirect attempts.   71. **in:** by.   80. **down-gyved:** hanging down like fetters.

And end his being. That done, he lets me go;
And, with his head over his shoulder turn'd,
He seem'd to find his way without his eyes,
For out o' doors he went without their help,
And to the last bended their light on me.   100
  Pol. [Come,] go with me, I will go seek the King.
This is the very ecstasy of love,
Whose violent property fordoes itself
And leads the will to desperate undertakings
As oft as any passion under heaven   105
That does afflict our natures. I am sorry, —
What, have you given him any hard words of late?
  Oph. No, my good lord, but, as you did command,
I did repel his letters and deni'd
His access to me.
  Pol.   That hath made him mad.   110
I am sorry that with better [heed] and judgement
I had not quoted him. I fear'd he did but trifle
And meant to wreck thee; but beshrew my jealousy!
It seems it is as proper to our age
To cast beyond ourselves in our opinions   115
As it is common for the younger sort
To lack discretion. Come, go we to the King.
This must be known, which, being kept close, might
    move
More grief to hide than hate to utter love.   119
[Come.]   [*Exeunt.*

SCENE II. [*A room in the castle.*]

Flourish. Enter KING, QUEEN, ROSENCRANTZ,
    GUILDENSTERN, *with others.*

  King. Welcome, dear Rosencrantz and Guilden-
    stern!
Moreover that we much did long to see you,
The need we have to use you did provoke
Our hasty sending. Something have you heard
Of Hamlet's transformation; so I call it,   5
Since not th' exterior nor the inward man
Resembles that it was. What it should be,
More than his father's death, that thus hath put
    him
So much from th' understanding of himself,
I cannot [dream] of. I entreat you both   10
That, being of so young days brought up with him,
And since so neighbour'd to his youth and humour,
That you vouchsafe your rest here in our court
Some little time; so by your companies
To draw him on to pleasures, and to gather   15
So much as from occasions you may glean,
[Whether aught, to us unknown, afflicts him thus,]
That, open'd, lies within our remedy.

  Queen. Good gentlemen, he hath much talk'd
    of you;
That they do know my son, come you and nearer   20
And sure I am two men there are not living
To whom he more adheres. If it will please you
To show us so much gentry and good will
As to expend your time with us a while
For the supply and profit of our hope,   25
Your visitation shall receive such thanks
As fits a king's remembrance.
  Ros.   Both your Majesties
Might, by the sovereign power you have of us,
Put your dread pleasures more into command
Than to entreaty.
  Guil.   We both obey,
And here give up ourselves, in the full bent   30
To lay our services freely at your feet,
To be commanded.
  King. Thanks, Rosencrantz and gentle Guild-
    enstern.
  Queen. Thanks, Guildenstern and gentle Rosen-
    crantz;
And I beseech you instantly to visit   35
My too much changed son. Go, some of ye,
And bring the gentlemen where Hamlet is.
  Guil. Heavens make our presence and our
    practices
Pleasant and helpful to him!
  Queen.   Amen!
    [*Exeunt [Rosencrantz, Guildenstern, and
    some Attendants].*

Enter POLONIUS.

  Pol. Th' ambassadors from Norway, my good
    lord,   40
Are joyfully return'd.
  King. Thou still hast been the father of good
    news.
  Pol. Have I, my lord? Assure you, my good
    liege,
I hold my duty as I hold my soul,
Both to my God [and] to my gracious king.   45
And I do think, or else this brain of mine
Hunts not the trail of policy so sure
As [it hath] us'd to do, that I have found
The very cause of Hamlet's lunacy.
  King. O, speak of that; that I do long to hear. 50
  Pol. Give first admittance to th' ambassadors.
My news shall be the [fruit] to that great feast.
  King. Thyself do grace to them, and bring
    them in.   [*Exit Polonius.*]
He tells me, my sweet queen, that he hath found
The head and source of all your son's distemper.   55

---

101. [Come] Q₂. Om. F. 102. ecstasy: madness. 103. property: quality. fordoes: destroys. 111. [heed] Q₂. speed
F. 112. quoted: observed. 115. cast... ourselves: over-calculate. 120. [Come] Q₂. Om. F.
  Sc. ii, 10. [dream] Q₂. *deeme* F. 11. of: from. 17. [Whether...thus] Q₂. Om. F. 22. gentry: courtesy. 30. in...
bent: to our utmost. 42. still: ever. 45. [and] Q₂. *one* F. 48. [it hath] Q₂. *I have* F. 52. [fruit] Q₂; dessert, *Newes* F.

Queen. I doubt it is no other but the main,
His father's death and our o'erhasty marriage.

Re-enter POLONIUS, *with* VOLTIMAND *and* COR-
NELIUS.

King. Well, we shall sift him. — Welcome,
good friends!
Say, Voltimand, what from our brother Norway?
Volt. Most fair return of greetings and desires. 60
Upon our first, he sent out to suppress
His nephew's levies, which to him appear'd
To be a preparation 'gainst the Polack,
But, better look'd into, he truly found
It was against your Highness. Whereat griev'd,
That so his sickness, age, and impotence   66
Was falsely borne in hand, sends out arrests
On Fortinbras; which he, in brief, obeys,
Receives rebuke from Norway, and in fine
Makes vow before his uncle never more   70
To give th' assay of arms against your Majesty.
Whereon old Norway, overcome with joy,
Gives him three thousand crowns in annual fee,
And his commission to employ those soldiers,
So levied as before, against the Polack;   75
With an entreaty, herein further shown,
                              [*Giving a paper.*]
That it might please you to give quiet pass
Through your dominions for his enterprise,
On such regards of safety and allowance
As therein are set down.
King.   It likes us well;   80
And at our more consider'd time we'll read,
Answer, and think upon this business.
Meantime we thank you for your well-took labour.
Go to your rest; at night we'll feast together.
Most welcome home!
                 [*Exeunt Voltimand and Cornelius.*
Pol.   This business is well ended. 85
My liege, and madam, to expostulate
What majesty should be, what duty is,
Why day is day, night night, and time is time,
Were nothing but to waste night, day, and time,
Therefore, since brevity is the soul of wit,   90
And tediousness the limbs and outward flourishes,
I will be brief. Your noble son is mad.
Mad call I it; for, to define true madness,
What is't but to be nothing else but mad?
But let that go.
Queen.   More matter, with less art.   95
Pol. Madam, I swear I use no art at all.
That he is mad, 'tis true; 'tis true 'tis pity,
And pity ['tis 'tis] true. A foolish figure!
But farewell it, for I will use no art.

Mad let us grant him then; and now remains   100
That we find out the cause of this effect,
Or rather say, the cause of this defect,
For this effect defective comes by cause.
Thus it remains, and the remainder thus.
Perpend.   105
I have a daughter — have whilst she is mine —
Who, in her duty and obedience, mark,
Hath given me this. Now gather, and surmise.
                              [*Reads*] *the letter.*
"To the celestial and my soul's idol, the most
beautified Ophelia," —   110
That's an ill phrase, a vile phrase; "beautified"
is a vile phrase. But you shall hear. [Thus]:
"In her excellent white bosom, these."
Queen. Came this from Hamlet to her?
Pol. Good madam, stay a while. I will be
faithful.   [*Reads.*]   115
      "Doubt thou the stars are fire,
        Doubt that the sun doth move,
        Doubt truth to be a liar,
        But never doubt I love.
"O dear Ophelia, I am ill at these numbers. I   119
have not art to reckon my groans; but that I love
thee best, O most best, believe it. Adieu.
        Thine evermore, most dear lady,
          Whilst this machine is to him,
                                    HAMLET."
This in obedience hath my daughter show'd me, 125
And more above, hath his solicitings,
As they fell out by time, by means, and place,
All given to mine ear.
King.   But how hath she
Receiv'd his love?
Pol.   What do you think of me?
King. As of a man faithful and honourable.   130
Pol. I would fain prove so. But what might
you think,
When I had seen this hot love on the wing, —
As I perceiv'd it, I must tell you that,
Before my daughter told me, — what might you,
Or my dear Majesty your queen here, think,   135
If I had play'd the desk or table-book,
Or given my heart a winking, mute and dumb,
Or look'd upon this love with idle sight,
What might you think? No, I went round to work,
And my young mistress thus I did bespeak: 140
"Lord Hamlet is a prince, out of thy star.
This must not be;" and then I precepts gave her,
That she should lock herself from his resort,
Admit no messengers, receive no tokens.
Which done, she took the fruits of my advice; 145
And he, repulsed — a short tale to make —

---

56. **main:** main cause. 67. **borne in hand:** taken advantage of. 80. **likes:** pleases. 81. **more ... time:** greater leisure for thought. 85. **well** Q₂. *very well* F. 86. **expostulate:** expound. 98. **['tis 'tis]** Q₂. *it is* F. 112. **[Thus]** Q₂. *these* F. 124. **machine:** body. 136. **play'd ... table-book:** i.e., noted the matter secretly. 139. **round:** openly. 141. **star:** i.e., sphere.

Fell into a sadness, then into a fast,
Thence to a watch, thence into a weakness,
Thence to a lightness, and, by this declension,
Into the madness whereon now he raves,   150
And all we wail for.
   King.   Do you think 'tis this?
   Queen. It may be, very likely.
   Pol. Hath there been such a time — I'd fain
      know that —
That I have positively said, "'Tis so,"
When it prov'd otherwise?
   King.   Not that I know.   155
   Pol. Take this from this, if this be otherwise.
If circumstances lead me, I will find
Where truth is hid, though it were hid indeed
Within the centre.
   King.   How may we try it further?
   Pol. You know sometimes he walks four hours
      together   160
Here in the lobby.
   Queen.   So he has, indeed.
   Pol. At such a time I'll loose my daughter to him.
Be you and I behind an arras then;
Mark the encounter. If he love her not,
And be not from his reason fall'n thereon,   165
Let me be no assistant for a state
[But] keep a farm and carters.
   King.   We will try it.

       Enter HAMLET, *reading on a book.*

   Queen. But look where sadly the poor wretch
      comes reading.
   Pol. Away, I do beseech you, both away.
I'll board him presently.
       [Exeunt King, Queen [and Attendants].
          O, give me leave,   170
How does my good Lord Hamlet?
   Ham. Well, God-a-mercy.
   Pol. Do you know me, my lord?
   Ham. Excellent well; you are a fishmonger.
   Pol. Not I, my lord.   175
   Ham. Then I would you were so honest a man.
   Pol. Honest, my lord!
   Ham. Ay, sir. To be honest, as this world goes,
is to be one man pick'd out of two thousand.
   Pol. That's very true, my lord.   180
   Ham. For if the sun breed maggots in a dead
dog, being a good kissing carrion, — Have you a
daughter?
   Pol. I have, my lord.   184
   Ham. Let her not walk i' th' sun. Conception
is a blessing, but not as your daughter may con-
ceive. Friend, look to 't.   187

   Pol. [*Aside.*] How say you by that? Still harping
on my daughter. Yet he knew me not at first; he
said I was a fishmonger. He is far gone, far
gone. And truly in my youth I suff'red much extremity for love; very near this. I'll speak to him
again. — What do you read, my lord?   193
   Ham. Words, words, words.
   Pol. What is the matter, my lord?
   Ham. Between who?
   Pol. I mean, the matter you [read] my lord. 197
   Ham. Slanders, sir; for the satirical slave says
here that old men have grey beards, that their faces
are wrinkled, their eyes purging thick amber or
plum-tree gum, and that they have a plentiful lack
of wit, together with weak hams; all which, sir,
though I most powerfully and potently believe, yet
I hold it not honesty to have it thus set down; for
you yourself, sir, should be old as I am, if like a
crab you could go backward.   206
   Pol. [*Aside.*] Though this be madness, yet there
is method in't. — Will you walk out of the air,
my lord?
   Ham. Into my grave?   210
   Pol. Indeed, that is out o' th' air. [*Aside.*]
How pregnant sometimes his replies are! a happiness
that often madness hits on, which reason and sanity
could not so prosperously be deliver'd of. I will
leave him, and suddenly contrive the means of
meeting between him and my daughter. — My
honourable lord, I will most humbly take my leave
of you.   218
   Ham. You cannot, sir, take from me anything
that I will more willingly part withal, — [*Aside*]
except my life, my life.   221
   Pol. Fare you well, my lord.
   Ham. These tedious old fools!

      Enter ROSENCRANTZ *and* GUILDENSTERN.

   Pol. You go to seek my Lord Hamlet? There
      he is.
   Ros. [*To Polonius.*] God save you, sir!   225
               [Exit Polonius.]
   Guil. Mine honour'd lord!
   Ros. My most dear lord!
   Ham. My excellent good friends! How dost
thou, Guildenstern? Oh, Rosencrantz! Good
lads, how do ye both?   230
   Ros. As the indifferent children of the earth.
   Guil. Happy, in that we are not over-happy.
On Fortune's cap we are not the very button.
   Ham. Nor the soles of her shoe?

148. **watch:** wakefulness. 151. **wail** F. *mourn* Q2. 156. **this from this.** Pol. points to his head and shoulders. 159.
centre: i.e., of the earth. 167. **[But]** Q2. *And* F. 170. **board:** accost. 174. **Excellent** Q2. *Excellent, excellent* F. 179.
two F. *tenne* Q2. 182. **good kissing:** good to kiss. Warburton read *God, kissing.* 185. **Conception:** (1) understanding,
(2) pregnancy. 197. **[read]** Q2. *meane* F. 198. **slave** F. *rogue* Q2. 221. **except . . . life** F. *except my life;* three times Q2.

Ros. Neither, my lord.   235

Ham. Then you live about her waist, or in the middle of her favour?

Guil. Faith, her privates we.

Ham. In the secret parts of Fortune? Oh, most true; she is a strumpet. What's the news?   240

Ros. None, my lord, but that the world's grown honest.

Ham. Then is doomsday near. But your news is not true. Let me question more in particular. What have you, my good friends, deserved at the hands of Fortune, that she sends you to prison hither?   247

Guil. Prison, my lord?

Ham. Denmark's a prison.

Ros. Then is the world one.   250

Ham. A goodly one, in which there are many confines, wards, and dungeons, Denmark being one o' th' worst.

Ros. We think not so, my lord.   254

Ham. Why, then, 'tis none to you; for there is nothing either good or bad, but thinking makes it so. To me it is a prison.

Ros. Why, then, your ambition makes it one. 'Tis too narrow for your mind.   259

Ham. O God, I could be bounded in a nutshell and count myself a king of infinite space, were it not that I have bad dreams.

Guil. Which dreams indeed are ambition, for the very substance of the ambitious is merely the shadow of a dream.   265

Ham. A dream itself is but a shadow.

Ros. Truly, and I hold ambition of so airy and light a quality that it is but a shadow's shadow.

Ham. Then are our beggars bodies, and our monarchs and outstretch'd heroes the beggars' shadows. Shall we to the court? for, by my fay, I cannot reason.   272

Ros. } We'll wait upon you.
Guil. }

Ham. No such matter. I will not sort you with the rest of my servants, for, to speak to you like an honest man, I am most dreadfully attended. But in the beaten way of friendship, what make you at Elsinore?   278

Ros. To visit you, my lord; no other occasion.

Ham. Beggar that I am, I am even poor in thanks, but I thank you; and sure, dear friends, my thanks are too dear a halfpenny. Were you not sent for? Is it your own inclining? Is it a free visitation? Come, deal justly with me. Come, come. Nay, speak.   285

Guil. What should we say, my lord?

Ham. Why, anything, but to the purpose. You were sent for; and there is a kind [of] confession in your looks which your modesties have not craft enough to colour. I know the good king and queen have sent for you.

Ros. To what end, my lord?   292

Ham. That you must teach me. But let me conjure you by the rights of our fellowship, by the consonancy of our youth, by the obligation of our ever-preserved love, and by what more dear a better proposer could charge you withal, be even and direct with me, whether you were sent for or no!   299

Ros. [*Aside to Guil.*] What say you?

Ham. [*Aside.*] Nay, then, I have an eye of you. — If you love me, hold not off.

Guil. My lord, we were sent for.   303

Ham. I will tell you why; so shall my anticipation prevent your discovery, [and] your secrecy to the King and Queen moult no feather. I have of late — but wherefore I know not — lost all my mirth, forgone all custom of exercise; and indeed it goes so [heavily] with my disposition that this goodly frame, the earth, seems to me a sterile   310 promontory, this most excellent canopy, the air, look you, this brave o'erhanging [firmament] this majestical roof fretted with golden fire, why, it appears no other thing to me than a foul and pestilent congregation of vapours. What a piece of   315 work is a man! How noble in reason! How infinite in faculty, in form and moving! How express and admirable in action! How like an angel in apprehension! How like a god! The beauty of the world! The paragon of animals! And yet, to me, what is this quintessence of dust?   320 Man delights not me, — no, nor woman neither, though by your smiling you seem to say so.

Ros. My lord, there was no such stuff in my thoughts.   325

Ham. Why did you laugh [then], when I said, "Man delights not me"?

Ros. To think, my lord, if you delight not in man, what lenten entertainment the players shall receive from you. We coted them on the way, and hither are they coming to offer you service.   331

Ham. He that plays the king shall be welcome; his majesty shall have tribute of me; the adventurous knight shall use his foil and target; the lover shall not sigh gratis; the humorous man shall end his part in peace; the clown shall make those laugh whose lungs are tickle o' the sere; and the lady shall

---

244–76. **Let . . . attended** F. Om. Q₂.   288. **[of]** Q₂. Om. F.   289. **modesties:** sense of shame.   305. **discovery:** disclosure.   **[and]** Q₂. *of* F.   309. **[heavily]** Q₂. *heavenly* F.   312. **[firmament]** Q₂. Om. F.   313. **fretted:** ornamented.   316–19. Our punctuation here substantially follows Q₂. F has question marks after *reason, faculty, admirable, action, angel, god.*   317. **express:** exact.   326. **[then]** Q₂. Om. F.   329. **lenten:** meager.   330. **coted:** outstripped.   337. **tickle . . . sere:** hair-triggered.

say her mind freely, or the blank verse shall halt for't. What players are they? 340

Ros. Even those you were wont to take delight in, the tragedians of the city.

Ham. How chances it they travel? Their residence, both in reputation and profit, was better both ways. 345

Ros. I think their inhibition comes by the means of the late innovation.

Ham. Do they hold the same estimation they did when I was in the city? Are they so follow'd? 350

Ros. No, indeed, they are not.

Ham. How comes it? Do they grow rusty?

Ros. Nay, their endeavour keeps in the wonted pace; but there is, sir, an aery of children, little eyases, that cry out on the top of question, 355 and are most tyrannically clapp'd for't. These are now the fashion, and so berattle the common stages — so they call them — that many wearing rapiers are afraid of goose-quills and dare scarce come thither. 360

Ham. What, are they children? Who maintains 'em? How are they escoted? Will they pursue the quality no longer than they can sing? Will they not say afterwards, if they should grow themselves to common players, — as it is [most like], if their means are no better — their writers do them wrong, to make them exclaim against their own succession? 368

Ros. Faith, there has been much to do on both sides, and the nation holds it no sin to tarre them to controversy. There was for a while no money bid for argument unless the poet and the player went to cuffs in the question. 373

Ham. Is't possible?

Guil. O, there has been much throwing about of brains.

Ham. Do the boys carry it away?

Ros. Ay, that they do, my lord; Hercules and his load too. 379

Ham. It is not strange; for mine uncle is King of Denmark, and those that would make mows at him while my father lived, give twenty, forty, an hundred ducats apiece for his picture in little. ['Sblood,] there is something in this more than natural, if philosophy could find it out. 385

[Flourish for the Players.

Guil. There are the players.

Ham. Gentlemen, you are welcome to Elsinore. Your hands, come. The appurtenance of welcome is fashion and ceremony. Let me comply with you in the garb, lest my extent to the players, 390 which, I tell you, must show fairly outward, should more appear like entertainment than yours. You are welcome; but my uncle-father and aunt-mother are deceiv'd.

Guil. In what, my dear lord? 395

Ham. I am but mad north-north-west. When the wind is southerly I know a hawk from a handsaw.

Enter POLONIUS.

Pol. Well be with you, gentlemen!

Ham. [*Aside to them.*] Hark you, Guildenstern, and you too, at each ear a hearer: that great baby you see there is not yet out of his swathing-clouts. 401

Ros. Happily he is the second time come to them, for they say an old man is twice a child.

Ham. I will prophesy he comes to tell me of the players; mark it. [*Aloud.*] You say right, sir; for o' Monday morning 'twas so indeed. 407

Pol. My lord, I have news to tell you.

Ham. My lord, I have news to tell you. When Roscius [was] an actor in Rome, —

Pol. The actors are come hither, my lord.

Ham. Buzz, buzz!

Pol. Upon mine honour, — 413

Ham. "Then [came] each actor on his ass," —

Pol. The best actors in the world, either for tragedy, comedy, history, pastoral, pastoral-comical, historical-pastoral, tragical-historical, tragical-comical-historical-pastoral, scene individable, or poem unlimited; Seneca cannot be too heavy, nor Plautus too light. For the law of writ and the liberty, these are the only men. 421

Ham. O Jephthah, judge of Israel, what a treasure hadst thou!

Pol. What a treasure had he, my lord?

Ham. Why, 425

　　"One fair daughter, and no more,
　　　　The which he loved passing well."

Pol. [*Aside.*] Still on my daughter.

Ham. Am I not i' the right, old Jephthah?

Pol. If you call me Jephthah, my lord, I have a daughter that I love passing well. 431

---

339. **halt:** i.e., if she is forced to omit vulgarities. 346. **inhibition:** hindrance. 347. **innovation:** the rise of the companies of child actors which proved serious rivals to the adult companies in the opening years of the century. 352–79. **How...load too** F. Om. Q₂. 354. **aery:** nest. 355. **eyases:** young hawks. 355. **cry...question:** cry shrilly above others in controversy. 357. **berattle:** satirize. 358. **common stages:** public theaters, which it became unfashionable to visit. 359. **goose-quills:** i.e., the pens of satirical playwrights. 362. **escoted:** supported. 363. **quality:** profession. 366. **[most like]** (Pope). *like most* F. 368. **succession:** future. 370. **tarre:** provoke. 372. **argument:** plot of a play. 378–79. **Hercules...too.** Referring to the Globe Theatre, which had a sign showing Hercules with a globe. 381. **mows:** grimaces. 384. **['Sblood** Q₂: God's blood. Om. F. 390. **extent:** reception. 398. **handsaw.** With a quibble on "hernshaw" (heron). 410. **[was]** Q₂. Om. F. 414. **[came]** Q₂. *can* F. 418. **scene individable.** Probably a reference to the dramatic unities. 420–21. **law...liberty:** strict regulation versus literary freedom, or, standing by the text versus improvising. 422. **O...Israel:** title of a ballad.

Ham. Nay, that follows not.

Pol. What follows, then, my lord?

Ham. Why,

      "As by lot, God wot,"   435

and then, you know,

 "It came to pass, as most like it was," —

The first row of the [pious] chanson will show you
more, for look where my abridgements come.   439

Enter four or five PLAYERS.

You're welcome, masters, welcome all. I am glad
to see thee well. Welcome, good friends. O, my
old friend! Thy face is [valanc'd] since I saw thee
last; com'st thou to beard me in Denmark? What,
my young lady and mistress! By 'r lady, your
ladyship is nearer heaven than when I saw you 445
last, by the altitude of a chopine. Pray God, your
voice, like a piece of uncurrent gold, be not crack'd
within the ring. Masters, you are all welcome.
We'll e'en to't like French falconers — fly at anything we see; we'll have a speech straight. 450
Come, give us a taste of your quality; come, a passionate speech.

1. Play. What speech, my lord?

Ham. I heard thee speak me a speech once,
but it was never acted; or, if it was, not above 455
once. For the play, I remember, pleas'd not the
million; 'twas caviare to the general; but it was —
as I receiv'd it, and others, whose judgement in
such matters cried in the top of mine — an excellent
play, well digested in the scenes, set down with 460
as much modesty as cunning. I remember, one
said there [were] no sallets in the lines to make the
matter savoury, nor no matter in the phrase that
might indict the author of affectation; but call'd it
an honest method, [as wholesome as sweet, and 465
by very much more handsome than fine.] One
speech in it I chiefly lov'd; 'twas Æneas' tale to
Dido, and thereabout of it especially where he
speaks of Priam's slaughter. If it live in your memory, begin at this line: let me see, let me see — 471
"The rugged Pyrrhus, like th' Hyrcanian beast,"
— It is not so. It begins with Pyrrhus: —
"The rugged Pyrrhus, he whose sable arms,
Black as his purpose, did the night resemble 475
When he lay couched in the ominous horse,
Hath now this dread and black complexion smear'd
With heraldry more dismal. Head to foot
Now is he [total] gules, horribly trick'd

With blood of fathers, mothers, daughters, sons, 480
Bak'd and impasted with the parching streets,
That lend a tyrannous and damned light
To their vile murders. Roasted in wrath and fire,
And thus o'er-sized with coagulate gore,
With eyes like carbuncles, the hellish Pyrrhus 485
Old grandsire Priam seeks."
[So, proceed you.]

Pol. 'Fore God, my lord, well spoken, with good
accent and good discretion.

1. Play.   "Anon he finds him
Striking too short at Greeks. His antique sword,
Rebellious to his arm, lies where it falls,   492
Repugnant to command. Unequal match,
Pyrrhus at Priam drives, in rage strikes wide,
But with the whiff and wind of his fell sword 495
Th' unnerved father falls. Then senseless Ilium,
Seeming to feel his blow, with flaming top
Stoops to his base, and with a hideous crash
Takes prisoner Pyrrhus' ear; for, lo! his sword,
Which was declining on the milky head   500
Of reverend Priam, seem'd i' th' air to stick.
So, as a painted tyrant, Pyrrhus stood
And, like a neutral to his will and matter,
Did nothing.
But, as we often see, against some storm,   505
A silence in the heavens, the rack stand still,
The bold winds speechless, and the orb below
As hush as death, anon the dreadful thunder
Doth rend the region; so, after Pyrrhus' pause,
Aroused vengeance sets him new a-work;   510
And never did the Cyclops' hammers fall
On Mars his armour forg'd for proof eterne
With less remorse than Pyrrhus' bleeding sword
Now falls on Priam.
Out, out, thou strumpet Fortune! All you gods,
In general synod take away her power!   516
Break all the spokes and fellies from her wheel,
And bowl the round nave down the hill of heaven
As low as to the fiends!"

Pol. This is too long.   520

Ham. It shall to the barber's, with your beard.
Prithee, say on; he's for a jig or a tale of bawdry, or
he sleeps. Say on; come to Hecuba.

1. Play. "But who, O, who had seen the [mobled]
queen" —   525

Ham. The [mobled] queen"?

Pol. That's good; "[mobled] queen" is good.

1. Play. "Run barefoot up and down, threat-
'ning the flame

438. **row:** stanza. **[pious]** Q₂. *Pons* F. 439. **abridgements:** (1) entertainments, (2) interrupters. 442. **[valanc'd]**
Q₂: fringed, i.e., bearded. *valiant* F. 446. **chopine:** thick-soled shoe. 457. **caviare . . . general:** i.e., too choice for the
multitude. 459. **cried . . . of:** had more authority than. 462. **[were]** Q₂. *was* F. **sallets:** salads, i.e., spicy jokes.
465–66. **[as wholesome . . . fine]** Q₂. Om. F. 467. **speech** Q₂. *cheefe speech* F. 472. **Hyrcanian beast:** tiger of Hyrcania
in the Caucasus. 479. **[total]** Q₂. *to take* F. **gules:** red. **trick'd:** adorned. 481. **impasted:** crusted. 484. **o'er-sized:**
varnished. 487. **[So . . . you]** Q₂. Om. F. 503. **matter:** task. 506. **rack:** cloud. 509. **region:** i.e., air. 512. **proof:** endurance. 517. **fellies:** rims. 525–26. **[mobled]** Q₂ F₂: muffled. *inobled* F₁. 527. **[mobled] . . . good** F₂. *inobled . . . good* F₁.
Om. Q₂.

With bisson rheum, a clout about that head
Where late the diadem stood, and for a robe,   530
About her lank and all o'er-teemed loins,
A blanket, in the alarm of fear caught up; —
Who this had seen, with tongue in venom steep'd
'Gainst Fortune's state would treason have pro-
     nounc'd.
But if the gods themselves did see her then,   535
When she saw Pyrrhus make malicious sport
In mincing with his sword her husband's limbs,
The instant burst of clamour that she made,
Unless things mortal move them not at all,
Would have made milch the burning eyes of heaven,
And passion in the gods."   541

Pol. Look, whe'er he has not turn'd his colour and
has tears in 's eyes. Pray you, no more.

Ham. 'Tis well; I'll have thee speak out the   545
rest soon. Good my lord, will you see the players
well bestow'd? Do ye hear? Let them be well us'd,
for they are the abstracts and brief chronicles of the
time; after your death you were better have a bad
epitaph than their ill report while you lived.   551

Pol. My lord, I will use them according to their
desert.

Ham. God's bodykins, man, better. Use every
man after his desert, and who should scape whipping? Use them after your own honour and dignity.
The less they deserve, the more merit is in your
bounty. Take them in.

Pol. Come, sirs.   *[Exit.*   559

Ham. Follow him, friends; we'll hear a play to-
morrow. *[Exeunt all the Players but the First.]*
Dost thou hear me, old friend? Can you play "The
Murder of Gonzago"?

I. Play. Ay, my lord.   564

Ham. We'll ha' 't to-morrow night. You could,
for a need, study a speech of some dozen or sixteen
lines, which I would set down and insert in't, could
ye not?

I. Play. Ay, my lord.   569

Ham. Very well. Follow that lord, — and look
you mock him not. *[Exit I. Player.]* My good
friends, I'll leave you till night. You are welcome to
Elsinore.

Ros. Good my lord!

         [Exeunt [Rosencrantz and Guildenstern.]

Ham. Ay, so, God buy ye. — Now I am alone.
O, what a rogue and peasant slave am I!   576
Is it not monstrous that this player here,
But in a fiction, in a dream of passion,
Could force his soul so to his [own] conceit
That from her working all his visage [wann'd],   580

Tears in his eyes, distraction in 's aspect,
A broken voice, and his whole function suiting
With forms to his conceit? And all for nothing!
For Hecuba!
What's Hecuba to him, or he to Hecuba,   585
That he should weep for her? What would he do,
Had he the motive and the cue for passion
That I have? He would drown the stage with tears
And cleave the general ear with horrid speech,
Make mad the guilty and appall the free,   590
Confound the ignorant, and amaze indeed
The very faculty of eyes and ears.
Yet I,
A dull and muddy-mettled rascal, peak,
Like John-a-dreams, unpregnant of my cause,   595
And can say nothing; no, not for a king,
Upon whose property and most dear life
A damn'd defeat was made. Am I a coward?
Who calls me villain, breaks my pate across,
Plucks off my beard and blows it in my face,   600
Tweaks me by th' nose, gives me the lie i' th' throat
As deep as to the lungs? Who does me this?
Ha!
['Swounds,] I should take it; for it cannot be
But I am pigeon-liver'd and lack gall   605
To make oppression bitter, or ere this
I should ha' fatted all the region kites
With this slave's offal. Bloody, bawdy villain!
Remorseless, treacherous, lecherous, kindless villain!
O, vengeance!   610
[Why,] what an ass am I! This is most brave,
That I, the son of [a] dear [father] murder'd,
Prompted to my revenge by heaven and hell,
Must, like a whore, unpack my heart with words,
And fall a-cursing, like a very drab,   615
A scullion!
Fie upon't! Foh! About, my brain! I have
     heard
That guilty creatures sitting at a play
Have by the very cunning of the scene
Been struck so to the soul that presently   620
They have proclaim'd their malefactions;
For murder, though it have no tongue, will speak
With most miraculous organ. I'll have these play-
     ers
Play something like the murder of my father
Before mine uncle. I'll observe his looks;   625
I'll tent him to the quick. If he but blench,
I know my course. The spirit that I have seen
May be the devil; and the devil hath power
T' assume a pleasing shape; yea, and perhaps
Out of my weakness and my melancholy,   630

---

529. **bisson rheum:** blinding tears.   531. **o'er-teemed:** worn out by child-bearing.   540. **milch:** moist.   579. **[own]** Q2.
whole F. **conceit:** imagination.   580. **[wann'd]** Q2 (*wand*). *warm'd* F.   590. **free:** innocent.   591. **amaze:** confound.   594.
muddy-mettled: irresolute. **peak:** mope.   595. **John-a-dreams:** a sleepy fellow. **unpregnant of:** unstirred by.   604.
['Swounds] Q2. *Why* F.   609. **kindless:** unnatural.   611. **[Why]** Q2. *Who* F. *This* Q2. *I sure this* F.   612. **[a] dear**
[father] Q4. *the Deere* F, *a deere* Q2.   617. **About:** to work.   626. **tent:** probe.

As he is very potent with such spirits,
Abuses me to damn me.   I'll have grounds
More relative than this.   The play's the thing
Wherein I'll catch the conscience of the King.
                                        [*Exit.*

[ACT III]

[SCENE I.   *A room in the castle.*]

Enter KING, QUEEN, POLONIUS, OPHELIA,
       ROSENCRANTZ, *and* GUILDENSTERN.

King.   And can you, by no drift of circumstance,
Get from him why he puts on this confusion
Grating so harshly all his days of quiet
With turbulent and dangerous lunacy?
Ros.   He does confess he feels himself distracted;
But from what cause he will by no means speak.   6
Guil.   Nor do we find him forward to be sounded,
But with a crafty madness keeps aloof
When we would bring him on to some confession
Of his true state.
Queen.   Did he receive you well?   10
Ros.   Most like a gentleman.
Guil.   But with much forcing of his disposition.
Ros.   Niggard of question; but of our demands
Most free in his reply.
Queen.   Did you assay him
To any pastime?   15
Ros.   Madam, it so fell out, that certain players
We o'er-raught on the way; of these we told him,
And there did seem in him a kind of joy
To hear of it.   They are about the court,
And, as I think, they have already order   20
This night to play before him.
Pol.   'Tis most true.
And he beseech'd me to entreat your Majesties
To hear and see the matter.
King.   With all my heart; and it doth much con-
        tent me
To hear him so inclin'd.   25
Good gentlemen, give him a further edge,
And drive his purpose on to these delights.
Ros.   We shall, my lord.
            [*Exeunt* [*Rosencrantz and Guildenstern.*]
King.   Sweet Gertrude, leave us too,
For we have closely sent for Hamlet hither,
That he, as 'twere by accident, may [here]   30
Affront Ophelia.
Her father and myself, lawful espials,
Will so bestow ourselves that, seeing unseen,
We may of their encounter frankly judge,
And gather by him, as he is behav'd,   35

If 't be th' affliction of his love or no
That thus he suffers for.
Queen.   I shall obey you.
And for your part, Ophelia, I do wish
That your good beauties be the happy cause
Of Hamlet's wildness.   So shall I hope your virtues
Will bring him to his wonted way again,   41
To both your honours.
Oph.   Madam, I wish it may.
                                    [*Exit Queen.*]
Pol.   Ophelia, walk you here.   Gracious, so please
    ye,
We will bestow ourselves.   [*To Ophelia.*]   Read on
    this book, *prayer book*
That show of such an exercise may colour   45
Your loneliness.   We are oft to blame in this, —
'Tis too much prov'd — that with devotion's visage
And pious action we do [sugar] o'er
The devil himself.
King.   O, 'tis true!
[*Aside.*]   How smart a lash that speech doth give my
        conscience!   50
The harlot's cheek, beautied with plast'ring art,
Is not more ugly to the thing that helps it
Than is my deed to my most painted word.
O heavy burden!
Pol.   I hear him coming.   Let's withdraw, my
    lord.   [*Exeunt* [*King and Polonius*]].   55

Enter HAMLET. *meditates on life in general*

Ham.   To be, or not to be: that is the question.
Whether 'tis nobler in the mind to suffer *finds it*
The slings and arrows of outrageous fortune, *wearying*
Or to take arms against a sea of troubles,
And by opposing end them.   To die; to sleep;   60
No more; and by a sleep to say we end
The heart-ache and the thousand natural shocks
That flesh is heir to.   'Tis a consummation
Devoutly to be wish'd.   To die; to sleep; —
To sleep?   Perchance to dream!   Ay, there's the
    rub;   65
For in that sleep of death what dreams may
    come,
When we have shuffl'd off this mortal coil,
Must give us pause.   There's the respect
That makes calamity of so long life. *calamity for*
For who would bear the whips and scorns of time,
The oppressor's wrong, the [proud] man's con-
        tumely,   71
The pangs of dispriz'd love, the law's delay,
The insolence of office, and the spurns
That patient merit of the unworthy takes,
When he himself might his quietus make   75

631. **spirits**: moods.   633. **relative**: definite.
Act III, sc. i, 13. **question**: conversation.   26. **edge**: incitement.   29. **closely**: secretly.   30. **[here]** Q₂.   *there* F.   31.
Affront: meet.   48. **[sugar]** Q₂.   *surge* F.   52. **to**: in comparison with.   67. **coil**: turmoil.   68. **respect**: consideration.
69. **of ... life**: so long-lived.   71. **[proud]** Q₂.   *poore* F.   72. **dispriz'd** F.   *despiz'd* Q₂.   75. **quietus**: discharge (legal term).

With a bare bodkin? Who would fardels bear,
To grunt and sweat under a weary life,
But that the dread of something after death,
The undiscover'd country from whose bourn
No traveller returns, puzzles the will   80
And makes us rather bear those ills we have
Than fly to others that we know not of?
Thus conscience does make cowards of us all;
And thus the native hue of resolution
Is sicklied o'er with the pale cast of thought,   85
And enterprises of great pith and moment
With this regard their currents turn [awry],
And lose the name of action. — Soft you now!
The fair Ophelia! Nymph, in thy orisons
Be all my sins rememb'red.

Oph.   .   Good my lord,   90
How does your honour for this many a day?

Ham. I humbly thank you, well, well, well.

Oph. My lord, I have remembrances of yours
That I have longed long to re-deliver.
I pray you, now receive them.

Ham.   No, no;   95
I never gave you aught.

Oph. My honour'd lord, I know right well you
        did,
And, with them, words of so sweet breath compos'd
As made the things more rich. [Their] perfume
        [lost],
Take these again; for to the noble mind   100
Rich gifts wax poor when givers prove unkind.
There, my lord.

Ham. Ha, ha! are you honest?

Oph. My lord!

Ham. Are you fair?   105

Oph. What means your lordship?

Ham. That if you be honest and fair, your
honesty should admit no discourse to your beauty.

Oph. Could beauty, my lord, have better commerce than [with] honesty?   110

Ham. Ay, truly; for the power of beauty will
sooner transform honesty from what it is to a
bawd than the force of honesty can translate
beauty into his likeness. This was sometime a
paradox, but now the time gives it proof. I did
love you once.   116

Oph. Indeed, my lord, you made me believe so.

Ham. You should not have believ'd me, for
virtue cannot so inoculate our old stock but we
shall relish of it. I loved you not.   120

Oph. I was the more deceived.

Ham. Get thee to a nunnery; why wouldst thou

be a breeder of sinners? I am myself indifferent
honest, but yet I could accuse me of such things
that it were better my mother had not borne me. 125
I am very proud, revengeful, ambitious, with more
offences at my beck than I have thoughts to put
them in, imagination to give them shape, or time to
act them in. What should such fellows as I do
crawling between heaven and earth? We are 130
arrant knaves all; believe none of us. Go thy ways
to a nunnery. Where's your father?

Oph. At home, my lord.

Ham. Let the doors be shut upon him, that he
may play the fool [nowhere] but in 's own house.
Farewell!   137

Oph. O, help him, you sweet heavens!

Ham. If thou dost marry, I'll give thee this
plague for thy dowry: be thou as chaste as ice, 140
as pure as snow, thou shalt not escape calumny.
Get thee to a nunnery, go. Farewell! Or, if thou
wilt needs marry, marry a fool; for wise men know
well enough what monsters you make of them. To
a nunnery, go, and quickly too. Farewell! 146

Oph. O heavenly powers, restore him!

Ham. I have heard of your [paintings] too, well
enough. God has given you one [face], and you
make yourself another. You [jig], you amble, 150
and you lisp and nick-name God's creatures and
make your wantonness your ignorance. Go to, I'll
no more on't; it hath made me mad. I say, we will
have no more marriages. Those that are married
already (all but one) shall live; the rest shall keep as
they are. To a nunnery, go.   [*Exit.* 157

Oph. O, what a noble mind is here o'erthrown!
The courtier's, soldier's, scholar's, eye, tongue,
        sword;
The expectancy and rose of the fair state,   160
The glass of fashion and the mould of form,
The observ'd of all observers, quite, quite down!
[And] I, of ladies most deject and wretched,
That suck'd the honey of his music vows,
Now see that noble and most sovereign reason, 165
Like sweet bells jangled, out of tune and harsh;
That unmatch'd form and feature of blown youth
Blasted with ecstasy. O, woe is me,
T' have seen what I have seen, see what I see! 169

Re-enter KING *and* POLONIUS.

King. Love! his affections do not that way tend;
Nor what he spake, though it lack'd form a little,
Was not like madness. There's something in his soul
O'er which his melancholy sits on brood,

76. **bodkin:** dagger. **fardels** Q₂: burdens. *these Fardles* F. 83. **conscience:** reflection. 85. **thought:** i.e., melancholy thought, brooding. 86. **pith** F. *pitch* Q₂. 87. **[awry]** Q₂. *away* F. 97. **I know** F. *you know* Q₂. 99. **[Their]** Q₂. *then* F. **[lost]** Q₂. *left* F. 103. **honest:** chaste. 110. **[with]** Q₂. *your* F. 119. **inoculate:** engraft. 120. **relish:** have a trace. **it:** i.e., the old stock. 136. **[nowhere]** Q₂. *no way* F. 148. **[paintings]** Q₂. *pratlings* F. 149. **[face]** Q₂. *pace* F. 150. **[jig]** Q₂ (*gig*). *gidge* F. 152. **make…ignorance:** excuse your wantonness as ignorance. 163. **[And]** Q₂. *Have* F. 167. **blown:** blooming. 170. **affections:** emotions.

And I do doubt the hatch and the disclose
Will be some danger; which [for] to prevent, 175
I have in quick determination
Thus set it down: he shall with speed to England
For the demand of our neglected tribute.
Haply the seas and countries different
With variable objects shall expel 180
This something-settled matter in his heart,
Whereon his brains still beating puts him thus
From fashion of himself. What think you on't?

 Pol. It shall do well; but yet do I believe
The origin and commencement of this grief 185
Sprung from neglected love. How now, Ophelia!
You need not tell us what Lord Hamlet said;
We heard it all. My lord, do as you please,
But, if you hold it fit, after the play
Let his queen mother all alone entreat him 190
To show his griefs. Let her be round with him,
And I'll be plac'd, so please you, in the ear
Of all their conference. If she find him not,
To England send him, or confine him where
Your wisdom best shall think.

 King.   It shall be so. 195
Madness in great ones must not unwatch'd go.

             [*Exeunt.*

[SCENE II. *A hall in the castle.*]

 Enter HAMLET *and* PLAYERS.

 Ham. Speak the speech, I pray you, as I pronounc'd it to you, trippingly on the tongue; but if
you mouth it, as many of your players do, I had
as lief the town-crier had spoke my lines. Nor do
not saw the air too much [with] your hand, thus, 5
but use all gently; for in the very torrent, tempest,
and, as I may say, the whirlwind of passion, you
must acquire and beget a temperance that may
give it smoothness. O, it offends me to the soul to
see a robustious periwig-pated fellow tear a pas- 10
sion to tatters, to very rags, to split the ears of the
groundlings, who for the most part are capable of
nothing but inexplicable dumb-shows and noise. I
could have such a fellow whipp'd for o'erdoing Termagant. It out-herods Herod. Pray you, avoid
it. 16
 [*1.*] *Play.* I warrant your honour.
 Ham. Be not too tame neither, but let your own
discretion be your tutor. Suit the action to the
word, the word to the action; with this special 20
observance, that you [o'erstep] not the modesty of
nature. For anything so overdone is from the purpose of playing, whose end, both at the first and

now, was and is, to hold, as 'twere, the mirror up to
nature; to show virtue her own feature, scorn her 25
own image, and the very age and body of the time
his form and pressure. Now this overdone, or come
tardy off, though it make the unskillful laugh, cannot
but make the judicious grieve; the censure of the
which one must, in your allowance, o'erweigh a 30
whole theatre of others. O, there be players that I
have seen play, and heard others praise, and that
highly, not to speak it profanely, that, neither
having the accent of Christians nor the gait of
Christian, pagan, [nor man,] have so strutted and 35
bellowed that I have thought some of Nature's
journeymen had made men and not made them well,
they imitated humanity so abominably.
 1. Play. I hope we have reform'd that indifferently with us, sir. 41
 Ham. O, reform it altogether. And let those that
play your clowns speak no more than is set down
for them; for there be of them that will themselves
laugh to set on some quantity of barren specta- 45
tors to laugh too, though in the mean time some
necessary question of the play be then to be considered. That's villanous, and shows a most pitiful
ambition in the Fool that uses it. Go, make you
ready.   [*Exeunt Players.* 50

 Enter POLONIUS, ROSENCRANTZ, *and* GUILDEN-
STERN.

How now, my lord! Will the King hear this piece
of work?
 Pol. And the Queen too, and that presently.
 Ham. Bid the players make haste.
          [*Exit Polonius.*
Will you two help to hasten them? 55
 Ros. }
 Guil. } We will, my lord.
    [*Exeunt Rosencrantz and Guildenstern.*
 Ham. What ho! Horatio.

 Enter HORATIO.

 Hor. Here, sweet lord, at your service.
 Ham. Horatio, thou art e'en as just a man
As e'er my conversation cop'd withal. 60
 Hor. O, my dear lord, —
 Ham.   Nay, do not think I flatter,
For what advancement may I hope from thee
That no revenue hast but thy good spirits
To feed and clothe thee? Why should the poor be
flatter'd?
No, let the candied tongue [lick] absurd pomp, 65
And crook the pregnant hinges of the knee

---

175. **[for]** Q2. Om. F. 193. **find him:** learn the truth about him.

 Sc. ii, 5. **[with]** Q2. Om. F. 12. **groundlings:** those who stood in the "pit" of the theatre, the cheapest place. 15.
Termagant: a violent character in the Mystery plays, a god of the Saracens. **Herod,** represented in the Mystery plays as
bombastic. 21. **[o'erstep]** Q2. *ore-stop* F. 28. **tardy:** i.e., ineffectually. 35. **[nor man]** Q2. *or Norman* F. 40. **indifferently:** tolerably. 60. **conversation:** intercourse. **cop'd:** met. 65. **candied:** i.e., flattering. **[lick]** Q2. *like* F. 66. **pregnant:** ready, pliant.

Where thrift may follow [fawning]. Dost thou
　　hear?
Since my dear soul was mistress of my choice
And could of men distinguish, her election
Hath seal'd thee for herself; for thou hast been　70
As one, in suffering all, that suffers nothing,
A man that Fortune's buffets and rewards
Hath ta'en with equal thanks; and blest are those
Whose blood and judgement are so well commingled,
That they are not a pipe for Fortune's finger　75
To sound what stop she please. Give me that man
That is not passion's slave, and I will wear him
In my heart's core, ay, in my heart of heart,
As I do thee. — Something too much of this. —
There is a play to-night before the King.　80
One scene of it comes near the circumstance
Which I have told thee of my father's death.
I prithee, when thou seest that act a-foot,
Even with the very comment of [thy] soul
Observe mine uncle. If his occulted guilt　85
Do not itself unkennel in one speech,
It is a damned ghost that we have seen,
And my imaginations are as foul
As Vulcan's stithy. Give him [heedful] note;
For I mine eyes will rivet to his face,　90
And after we will both our judgements join
To censure of his seeming.
　　Hor. Well, my lord.
If he steal aught the whilst this play is playing,
And scape detecting, I will pay the theft.

Danish march. A flourish. Enter KING, QUEEN,
　POLONIUS, OPHELIA, ROSENCRANTZ, GUILDEN-
　STERN, *and other Lords attendant, with the guard
　carrying torches.*

　　Ham. They are coming to the play; I must be
　　idle.　95
Get you a place.
　　King. How fares our cousin Hamlet?
　　Ham. Excellent, i' faith, — of the chameleon's
dish. I eat the air, promise-cramm'd. You cannot
feed capons so.　100
　　King. I have nothing with this answer, Hamlet;
these words are not mine.
　　Ham. No, nor mine now. [*To Polonius.*] My
lord, you play'd once i' th' university, you say?
　　Pol. That I did, my lord, and was accounted a
good actor.　106
　　Ham. And what did you enact?
　　Pol. I did enact Julius Cæsar. I was kill'd i' th'
Capitol; Brutus kill'd me.
　　Ham. It was a brute part of him to kill so capital
a calf there. Be the players ready?　111

　　Ros. Ay, my lord, they stay upon your patience.
　　Queen. Come hither, my good Hamlet, sit　115
by me.
　　Ham. No, good mother, here's metal more at-
tractive.　[*Lying down at Ophelia's feet.*]
　　Pol. [*To the King.*] O, ho! do you mark that?
　　Ham. Lady, shall I lie in your lap?
　　Oph. No, my lord.　120
　　Ham. I mean, my head upon your lap?
　　Oph. Ay, my lord.
　　Ham. Do you think I meant country matters?
　　Oph. I think nothing, my lord.
　　Ham. That's a fair thought to lie between maids'
legs.　126
　　Oph. What is, my lord?
　　Ham. Nothing.
　　Oph. You are merry, my lord.
　　Ham. Who, I?　130
　　Oph. Ay, my lord.
　　Ham. O God, your only jig-maker. What
should a man do but be merry? For, look you, how
cheerfully my mother looks, and my father died
within 's two hours.　135
　　Oph. Nay, 'tis twice two months, my lord.
　　Ham. So long? Nay then, let the devil wear
black, for I'll have a suit of sables. O heavens! die
two months ago, and not forgotten yet? Then
there's hope a great man's memory may outlive　140
his life half a year; but, by 'r lady; he must build
churches then, or else shall he suffer not thinking on,
with the hobby-horse, whose epitaph is, "For, O,
for, O, the hobby-horse is forgot."　145

Hautboys play. The dumb-show enters.

*Enter a King and Queen very lovingly, the Queen
　embracing him. She kneels and makes show of
　protestation unto him. He takes her up and de-
　clines his head upon her neck; lays him down upon
　a bank of flowers. She, seeing him asleep, leaves
　him. Anon comes in a fellow, takes off his crown,
　kisses it, and pours poison in the King's ears, and
　exit. The Queen returns, finds the King dead, and
　makes passionate action. The poisoner, with some
　two or three Mutes, comes in again, seeming to
　lament with her. The dead body is carried away.
　The poisoner woos the Queen with gifts; she seems
　loath and unwilling a while, but in the end accepts
　his love.　[Exeunt.*

　　Oph. What means this, my lord?
　　Ham. Marry, this is miching mallecho; that
means mischief.
　　Oph. Belike this show imports the argument of
the play?　150

---

67. **thrift:** profit. **[fawning]** Q2. *faining* F. 74. **blood:** passions. 84. **[thy]** Q2. *my* F. 85. **occulted:** hidden. 86.
unkennel: bring into the open. 89. **[heedful]** Q2. *needfull* F. 92. **censure:** judgment. 101. **have...with:** do not
understand. 138. **sables:** fine fur — with a quibble on *sable* as mourning black. 144-45. "**For...forgot.**" A line
from an old ballad. 147. **miching mallecho:** sneaking mischief.

Enter PROLOGUE.

Ham. We shall know by [this fellow]. The
players cannot keep counsel; they'll tell all.
Oph. Will they tell us what this show meant?
Ham. Ay, or any show that you'll show him. Be
not you asham'd to show, he'll not shame to tell
you what it means.   156
Oph. You are naught, you are naught. I'll mark
the play.
Pro. For us, and for our tragedy,
Here stooping to your clemency,   160
We beg your hearing patiently.   [*Exit.*]
Ham. Is this a prologue, or the posy of a ring?
Oph. 'Tis brief, my lord.
Ham. As woman's love.

Enter [*two Players,*] KING *and his* QUEEN.

P. King. Full thirty times hath Phœbus' cart
gone round   165
Neptune's salt wash and Tellus' orbed ground,
And thirty dozen moons with borrowed sheen
About the world have times twelve thirties been,
Since love our hearts and Hymen did our hands
Unite commutual in most sacred bands.   170
[*P. Queen.*] So many journeys may the sun and
moon
Make us again count o'er ere love be done!
But, woe is me, you are so sick of late,
So far from cheer and from your former state,
That I distrust you. Yet, though I distrust,   175
Discomfort you, my lord, it nothing must;
For women's fear and love holds quantity,
In neither aught, or in extremity.
Now, what my love is, proof hath made you know;
And as my love is siz'd, my fear is so.   180
[Where love is great, the littlest doubts are fear;
Where little fears grow great, great love grows
there.]
P. King. Faith, I must leave thee, love, and
shortly too.
My operant powers [their] functions leave to do;
And thou shalt live in this fair world behind, 185
Honour'd, belov'd; and haply one as king
For husband shalt thou —
P. Queen.   O, confound the rest!
Such love must needs be treason in my breast!
In second husband let me be accurst!
None wed the second but who kill'd the first.
Ham. [*Aside.*] Wormwood, wormwood!   191
P. Queen. The instances that second marriage
move
Are base respects of thrift, but none of love.

But w—
Purpose i—
Of violent bi—
Which now, like i—
But fall unshaken wi—
Most necessary 'tis that —
To pay ourselves what to ou—
What to ourselves in passion we—
The passion ending, doth the purpos—
The violence of [either] grief or joy
Their own enactures with themselves destroy.
Where joy most revels, grief doth most lament;
Grief joys, joy grieves, on slender accident.
This world is not for aye, nor 'tis not strange   210
That even our loves should with our fortunes
change,
For 'tis a question left us yet to prove,
Whether love lead fortune, or else fortune love.
The great man down, you mark his favourite flies;
The poor advanc'd makes friends of enemies.   215
And hitherto doth love on fortune tend,
For who not needs shall never lack a friend;
And who in want a hollow friend doth try,
Directly seasons him his enemy.
But, orderly to end where I begun,   220
Our wills and fates do so contrary run
That our devices still are overthrown;
Our thoughts are ours, their ends none of our own.
So think thou wilt no second husband wed;
But die thy thoughts when thy first lord is dead.   225
P. Queen. Nor earth to [me give] food, nor heaven
light!
Sport and repose lock from me day and night!
[To desperation turn my trust and hope!
An anchor's cheer in prison be my scope!]
Each opposite that blanks the face of joy   230
Meet what I would have well and it destroy!
Both here and hence pursue me lasting strife,
If, once a widow, ever I be wife!
Ham. If she should break it now!
P. King. 'Tis deeply sworn. Sweet, leave me
here a while.   235
My spirits grow dull, and fain I would beguile
The tedious day with sleep.   [*Sleeps.*
P. Queen.   Sleep rock thy brain,
And never come mischance between us twain! [*Exit.*
Ham. Madam, how like you this play?
Queen. The lady protests too much, methinks.

...word. 241
...he argument? Is there
...A, I do believe you
...they do but jest, poison in jest.
...th' world. 245
...What do you call the play? *Figuratively*
Ham. "The Mouse-trap." Marry, how? Tropically. This play is the image of a murder done in
Vienna. Gonzago is the duke's name; his wife,
Baptista. You shall see anon. 'Tis a knavish 250
piece of work, but what o' that? Your Majesty
and we that have free souls, it touches us not. Let
the gall'd jade wince, our withers are unwrung.
Chafed horse

Enter LUCIANUS.

This is one Lucianus, nephew to the king.
Oph. You are a good chorus, my lord. 255
Ham. I could interpret between you and your
love, if I could see the puppets dallying.
Oph. You are keen, my lord, you are keen.
Ham. It would cost you a groaning to take off my
edge. 260
Oph. Still better, and worse.
Ham. So you mistake husbands. Begin, mur-
derer; pox, leave thy damnable faces and begin.
Come, "the croaking raven doth bellow for re-
venge." 265
Luc. Thoughts black, hands apt, drugs fit, and
time agreeing;
Confederate season, else no creature seeing.
Thou mixture rank, of midnight weeds collected,
With Hecate's ban thrice blasted, thrice infected,
Thy natural magic and dire property 270
On wholesome life usurp immediately.
[*Pours the poison in* [*to the sleeper's*] *ears.*
Ham. He poisons him i' th' garden for 's estate.
His name's Gonzago; the story is extant, and writ
in choice Italian. You shall see anon how the mur-
derer gets the love of Gonzago's wife. 275
Oph. The King rises.
Ham. What, frighted with false fire?
Queen. How fares my lord?
Pol. Give o'er the play.
King. Give me some light. Away! 280
All. Lights, lights, lights!
[*Exeunt all but Hamlet and Horatio.*
Ham. Why, let the strucken deer go weep,
The hart ungalled play;
For some must watch, while some must
sleep, —
So runs the world away. 285
Would not this, sir, and a forest of feathers — if the

rest of my fortunes turn Turk with me — with two
Provincial roses on my raz'd shoes, get me a fellow-
ship in a cry of players, sir?
Hor. Half a share. 290
Ham. A whole one, I.
For thou dost know, O Damon dear,
This realm dismantled was
Of Jove himself; and now reigns here
A very, very — pajock. 295 *Peacock (Claudius)*
Hor. You might have rhym'd.
Ham. O good Horatio, I'll take the ghost's word
for a thousand pound. Didst perceive?
Hor. Very well, my lord.
Ham. Upon the talk of the poisoning? 300
Hor. I did very well note him.

Re-enter ROSENCRANTZ *and* GUILDENSTERN.

Ham. Ah, ha! Come, some music! Come, the
recorders!
For if the king like not the comedy,
Why then, belike, he likes it not, perdy. 305
Come, some music!
Guil. Good my lord, vouchsafe me a word with
you.
Ham. Sir, a whole history.
Guil. The King, sir, — 310
Ham. Ay, sir, what of him?
Guil. Is in his retirement marvellous distemper'd.
Ham. With drink, sir?
Guil. No, my lord, rather with choler. *indigestion* 315
Ham. Your wisdom should show itself more
richer to signify this to his doctor; for, for me to put
him to his purgation would perhaps plunge him into
far more choler. 319
Guil. Good my lord, put your discourse into some
frame, and start not so wildly from my affair.
Ham. I am tame, sir; pronounce.
Guil. The Queen, your mother, in most great
affliction of spirit, hath sent me to you.
Ham. You are welcome. 325
Guil. Nay, good my lord, this courtesy is not of
the right breed. If it shall please you to make me a
wholesome answer I will do your mother's commandment; if not, your pardon and my return shall
be the end of my business. 330
Ham. Sir, I cannot.
Guil. What, my lord?
Ham. Make you a wholesome answer. My wit's
diseas'd. But, sir, such answers as I can make, you
shall command, or, rather, [as] you say, my mother.
Therefore no more, but to the matter. My mother,
you say, — 337

247. **Tropically:** figuratively. 253. **gall'd jade:** chafed horse. 261. **better, and worse:** i.e., more pointed and less chaste. 262. **mistake** F. *mistake your* Q₂. *must take your* (*husband*) Q₁. 286. **feathers.** Tragic actors wore plumes. 287. **turn Turk:** go bad. 288. **Provincial roses:** rosettes like the rose of Provence. **raz'd:** slashed. 289. **cry:** company. 295. **pajock:** peacock. 315. **choler:** anger; but Hamlet (l. 319) plays upon the other meaning, biliousness. 335. **[as]** Q₂. Om. F.

Ros. Then thus she says: your behaviour hath struck her into amazement and admiration.

Ham. O wonderful son, that can so astonish a mother! But is there no sequel at the heels of this mother-admiration? [Impart.]   342

Ros. She desires to speak with you in her closet ere you go to bed.

Ham. We shall obey, were she ten times our mother. Have you any further trade with us?

Ros. My lord, you once did love me.   348

Ham. So I do still, by these pickers and stealers.

Ros. Good my lord, what is your cause of distemper? You do [surely] bar the door of your own liberty if you deny your griefs to your friend.

Ham. Sir, I lack advancement.   354

Ros. How can that be, when you have the voice of the King himself for your succession in Denmark?

Ham. Ay, but "While the grass grows," — the proverb is something musty.   359

Re-enter one with a recorder.

O, the recorder! Let me see. — To withdraw with you: — why do you go about to recover the wind of me, as if you would drive me into a toil?

Guil. O, my lord, if my duty be too bold, my love is too unmannerly.   364

Ham. I do not well understand that. Will you play upon this pipe?

Guil. My lord, I cannot.

Ham. I pray you.

Guil. Believe me, I cannot.

Ham. I do beseech you.   370

Guil. I know no touch of it, my lord.

Ham. 'Tis as easy as lying. Govern these ventages with your finger and thumb, give it breath with your mouth, and it will discourse most excellent music. Look you, these are the stops.   376

Guil. But these cannot I command to any utterance of harmony. I have not the skill.

Ham. Why, look you now, how unworthy a thing you make of me! You would play upon me,   380 you would seem to know my stops, you would pluck out the heart of my mystery, you would sound me from my lowest note to the top of my compass; and there is much music, excellent voice, in this little organ, yet cannot you make it [speak. 'Sblood,]   385 do you think that I am easier to be play'd on than a pipe? Call me what instrument you will, though you can fret me, you cannot play upon me.

Enter POLONIUS.

God bless you, sir.   390

Pol. My lord, the Queen would speak with you, and presently.

Ham. Do you see that cloud that's almost in shape like a camel?

Pol. By the mass, and it's like a camel, indeed.

Ham. Methinks it is like a weasel.   396

Pol. It is back'd like a weasel.

Ham. Or like a whale?

Pol. Very like a whale.   399

Ham. Then will I come to my mother by and by. [*Aside.*] They fool me to the top of my bent. — I will come by and by.

Pol. I will say so.   [*Exit.*

Ham. "By and by" is easily said. Leave me, friends.   [*Exeunt all but Hamlet.*]   405 'Tis now the very witching time of night When churchyards yawn and hell itself breathes out Contagion to this world. Now could I drink hot blood, And do such bitter business as the day Would quake to look on. Soft! now to my mother. O heart, lose not thy nature! Let not ever   411 The soul of Nero enter this firm bosom; Let me be cruel, not unnatural. I will speak daggers to her, but use none. My tongue and soul in this be hypocrites;   415 How in my words soever she be shent To give them seals never, my soul, consent! [*Exit.*

[SCENE III. *A room in the castle.*]

Enter KING, ROSENCRANTZ, *and* GUILDENSTERN.

King. I like him not, nor stands it safe with us To let his madness range. Therefore prepare you. I your commission will forthwith dispatch, And he to England shall along with you. The terms of our estate may not endure   5 Hazard so dangerous as doth hourly grow Out of his lunacies.

Guil.   We will ourselves provide. Most holy and religious fear it is To keep those many many bodies safe That live and feed upon your Majesty.   10

Ros. The single and peculiar life is bound With all the strength and armour of the mind To keep itself from noyance, but much more That spirit upon whose [weal] depends and rests The lives of many. The cease of majesty   15 Dies not alone, but, like a gulf, doth draw

339. **admiration:** wonder. 342. **mother-admiration** F₄. *Mother admiration* F₁. *mother's admiration* Q₂. **[Impart]** Q₂. Om. F. 343. **closet:** chamber. 349. **pickers and stealers:** i.e., hands. 351. **[surely]** Q₂. *freely* F. 359. **proverb:** "While the grass grows, the steed starves." 360. **withdraw:** speak privately. 361-62. **recover the wind:** get to windward. 362. **toil:** snare. 373. **ventages:** stops. 385. **[speak. 'Sblood]** Q₂. *Why* F. 388. **fret:** (1) finger, (2) vex. 401. **They...** **bent:** they let me play the fool to the limit. 411. **nature:** natural affection. 412. **Nero.** He murdered his mother. 416. **shent:** rebuked. 417. **give... seals:** confirm them by deeds.

Sc. iii, 5. **terms:** condition. 11. **peculiar:** private. 14. **[weal]** Q₂. *spirit* F. 15. **cease:** death. 16. **gulf:** whirlpool.

What's near it with it. It is a massy wheel,
Fixed on the summit of the highest mount,
To whose huge spokes ten thousand lesser things
Are mortis'd and adjoin'd; which, when it falls, 20
Each small annexment, petty consequence,
Attends the boisterous ruin. Never alone
Did the King sigh, but with a general groan.
   King. Arm you, I pray you, to this speedy voyage,
For we will fetters put upon this fear, 25
Which now goes too free-footed.
   Ros. }
   Guil. }   We will haste us.

   [Exeunt Rosencrantz and Guildenstern.

Enter POLONIUS.

   Pol. My lord, he's going to his mother's closet.
Behind the arras I'll convey myself
To hear the process. I'll warrant she'll tax him home;
And, as you said, and wisely was it said, 30
'Tis meet that some more audience than a mother,
Since nature makes them partial, should o'erhear
The speech, of vantage. Fare you well, my liege.
I'll call upon you ere you go to bed
And tell you what I know.
   King.   Thanks, dear my lord.

   [Exit Polonius.]

O, my offence is rank, it smells to heaven; 36
It hath the primal eldest curse upon't,
A brother's murder. Pray can I not,
Though inclination be as sharp as will.
My stronger guilt defeats my strong intent, 40
And, like a man to double business bound,
I stand in pause where I shall first begin,
And both neglect. What if this cursed hand
Were thicker than itself with brother's blood,
Is there not rain enough in the sweet heavens 45
To wash it white as snow? Whereto serves mercy
But to confront the visage of offence?
And what's in prayer but this twofold force,
To be forestalled ere we come to fall,
Or pardon'd being down? Then I'll look up; 50
My fault is past. But, O, what form of prayer
Can serve my turn? "Forgive me my foul murder"?
That cannot be; since I am still possess'd
Of those effects for which I did the murder,
My crown, mine own ambition, and my queen. 55
May one be pardon'd and retain th' offence?
In the corrupted currents of this world
Offence's gilded hand may shove by justice,
And oft 'tis seen the wicked prize itself
Buys out the law. But 'tis not so above: 60
There is no shuffling, there the action lies
In his true nature; and we ourselves compell'd,
Even to the teeth and forehead of our faults,
To give in evidence. What then? What rests?
Try what repentance can. What can it not? 65
Yet what can it when one cannot repent?
O wretched state! O bosom black as death!
O limed soul, that, struggling to be free,
Art more engag'd! Help, angels! Make assay!
Bow, stubborn knees, and, heart with strings of steel, 70
Be soft as sinews of the new-born babe!
All may be well.   *[Retires and] kneels.*

Enter HAMLET

   Ham. Now might I do it pat, now he is praying;
And now I'll do't — And so he goes to heaven;
And so am I reveng'd. That would be scann'd.
A villain kills my father, and for that 76
I, his [sole] son, do this same villain send
To heaven.
Oh, this is hire and salary, not revenge.
He took my father grossly, full of bread, 80
With all his crimes broad blown, as [flush] as May;
And how his audit stands who knows save Heaven?
But in our circumstance and course of thought
'Tis heavy with him. And am I then reveng'd,
To take him in the purging of his soul, 85
When he is fit and season'd for his passage?
No!
Up, sword, and know thou a more horrid hent.
When he is drunk asleep, or in his rage,
Or in th' incestuous pleasure of his bed, 90
At gaming, swearing, or about some act
That has no relish of salvation in't, —
Then trip him, that his heels may kick at heaven,
And that his soul may be as damn'd and black
As hell, whereto it goes. My mother stays. 95
This physic but prolongs thy sickly days.   *[Exit.*
   King. [Rising.] My words fly up, my thoughts remain below.
Words without thoughts never to heaven go.

                                   [Exit.

[SCENE IV. *The Queen's closet.*]

Enter QUEEN *and* POLONIUS.

   Pol. He will come straight. Look you lay home to him.
Tell him his pranks have been too broad to bear with,

24. **Arm:** prepare. 29. **tax:** censure. 33. **of vantage:** from a favorable position. 58. **gilded:** ready to bribe. 64. **rests:** remains. 68. **limed:** caught (as in bird lime). 75. **would be scann'd:** demands scrutiny. 77. **[sole]** Q2. *foule* F. 81. **[flush]** Q2: lusty. *fresh* F. 88. **hent:** grip. 96. **physic:** i.e., prayer.
Sc. iv, 2. **broad:** unrestrained.

And that your Grace hath screen'd and stood be-
    tween
Much heat and him.   I'll silence me e'en here.
Pray you, be round with him.   5
   Ham. [*Within.*] Mother, mother, mother!
   Queen. I'll warrant you, fear me not.   With-
draw, I hear him coming.
             [*Polonius hides behind the arras.*]

         Enter HAMLET.

   Ham. Now, mother, what's the matter?
   Queen. Hamlet, thou hast thy father much of-
    fended.
   Ham. Mother, you have my father much of-
    fended.   10
   Queen. Come, come, you answer with an idle
    tongue.
   Ham. Go, go, you question with [a wicked]
    tongue.
   Queen. Why, how now, Hamlet!
   Ham.   What's the matter now?
   Queen. Have you forgot me?
   Ham.   No, by the rood, not so.
You are the Queen, your husband's brother's wife;
But — would you were not so! — you are my
    mother.   16
   Queen. Nay, then, I'll set those to you that can
    speak.
   Ham. Come, come, and sit you down.   You
    shall not budge.
You go not till I set you up a glass
Where you may see the inmost part of you.   20
   Queen. What wilt thou do?   Thou wilt not mur-
    der me?
Help, help, ho!
   Pol. [*Behind.*] What, ho! help, help, help!
   Ham. [*Drawing.*] How now!   A rat?   Dead,
    for a ducat, dead!
         [*Kills Polonius* [*through the arras*].
   Pol. [*Behind.*]   O, I am slain!
   Queen. O me, what hast thou done?
   Ham.   Nay, I know not.
Is it the King?   26
   Queen. O, what a rash and bloody deed is this!
   Ham. A bloody deed!   Almost as bad, good
    mother,
As kill a king, and marry with his brother.   29
   Queen. As kill a king!
   Ham.   Ay, lady, 'twas my word.
     [*Lifts up the arras and discovers Polonius.*]
Thou wretched, rash, intruding fool, farewell!
I took thee for thy better.   Take thy fortune.
Thou find'st to be too busy is some danger.

   — Leave wringing of your hands.   Peace!   Sit you
    down,
And let me wring your heart; for so I shall,   35
If it be made of penetrable stuff,
If damned custom have not braz'd it so
That it is proof and bulwark against sense.
   Queen. What have I done, that thou dar'st wag
    thy tongue
In noise so rude against me?
   Ham.   Such an act   40
That blurs the grace and blush of modesty,
Calls virtue hypocrite, takes off the rose
From the fair forehead of an innocent love
And [sets] a blister there, makes marriage-vows
As false as dicers' oaths; O, such a deed   45
As from the body of contraction plucks
The very soul, and sweet religion makes
A rhapsody of words.   Heaven's face doth glow,
Yea, this solidity and compound mass,
With tristful visage, as against the doom,   50
Is thought-sick at the act.
   Queen.   Ay me, what act,
That roars so loud and thunders in the index?
   Ham. Look here, upon this picture, and on this,
The counterfeit presentment of two brothers.
See, what a grace was seated on his brow: 55
Hyperion's curls, the front of Jove himself,
An eye like Mars, to threaten or command,
A station like the herald Mercury
New-lighted on a heaven-kissing hill,
A combination and a form indeed,   60
Where every god did seem to set his seal
To give the world assurance of a man.
This was your husband.   Look you now what fol-
    lows:
Here is your husband, like a mildew'd ear,
Blasting his wholesome [brother].   Have you
    eyes?
Could you on this fair mountain leave to feed,   66
And batten on this moor?   Ha! have you eyes?
You cannot call it love, for at your age
The hey-day in the blood is tame, it's humble,
And waits upon the judgement; and what judge-
    ment   70
Would step from this to this?   [Sense sure you
    have,
Else could you not have motion; but sure, that
    sense
Is apoplex'd; for madness would not err,
Nor sense to ecstasy was ne'er so thrall'd
But it reserv'd some quantity of choice,   75
To serve in such a difference.]   What devil was't
That thus hath cozen'd you at hoodman-blind?

12. [a wicked] Q₂. *an idle* F.   14. rood: cross.   37. braz'd: hardened (like brass).   38. sense: feeling.   44. [sets] Q₂. *makes* F.   46. contraction: betrothal.   49. this...mass: the earth.   50. tristful: sorrowful.   doom: Judgement Day. 52. index: prologue.   58. station: bearing.   65. [brother] Q₂. *breath* F.   67. batten: gorge.   71–76. [Sense...difference] Q₂. Om. F.   73. apoplex'd: paralyzed.   77. cozen'd: cheated.   hoodman-blind: blind-man's buff.

[Eyes without feeling, feeling without sight,
Ears without hands or eyes, smelling sans all,
Or but a sickly part of one true sense
Could not so mope.]
O shame! where is thy blush? Rebellious hell,
If thou canst mutine in a matron's bones,
To flaming youth let virtue be as wax
And melt in her own fire. Proclaim no shame 85
When the compulsive ardour gives the charge,
Since frost itself as actively doth burn,
[And] reason panders will.
   Queen.   O Hamlet, speak no more!
Thou turn'st mine eyes into my very soul,
And there I see such black and grained spots 90
As will not leave their tinct.
   Ham.   Nay, but to live
In the rank sweat of an enseamed bed,
Stew'd in corruption, honeying and making love
Over the nasty sty, —
   Queen.   O, speak to me no more!
These words like daggers enter in mine ears. 95
No more, sweet Hamlet!
   Ham.   A murderer and a villain!
A slave that is not twentieth part the tithe
Of your precedent lord! A vice of kings!
A cutpurse of the empire and the rule,
That from a shelf the precious diadem stole, 100
And put it in his pocket!
   Queen.   No more!

            Enter GHOST.

   Ham. A king of shreds and patches! —
Save me, and hover o'er me with your wings,
You heavenly guards! What would you, gracious
     figure?
   Queen. Alas, he's mad! 105
   Ham. Do you not come your tardy son to chide,
That, laps'd in time and passion, lets go by
Th' important acting of your dread command?
O, say!
   Ghost. Do not forget! This visitation 110
Is but to whet thy almost blunted purpose.
But, look, amazement on thy mother sits.
O, step between her and her fighting soul.
Conceit in weakest bodies strongest works.
Speak to her, Hamlet.
   Ham.   How is it with you, lady?
   Queen. Alas, how is't with you, 116
That you [do] bend your eye on vacancy
And with [th' incorporal] air do hold discourse?
Forth at your eyes your spirits wildly peep,

And, as the sleeping soldiers in th' alarm, 120
Your bedded hair, like life in excrements,
Start up and stand on end. O gentle son,
Upon the heat and flame of thy distemper
Sprinkle cool patience. Whereon do you look?
   Ham. On him, on him! Look you, how pale he
     glares! 125
His form and cause conjoin'd, preaching to stones,
Would make them capable. — Do not look upon
     me,
Lest with this piteous action you convert
My stern effects; then what I have to do
Will want true colour, tears perchance for blood. 130
   Queen. To [whom] do you speak this?
   Ham.   Do you see nothing there?
   Queen. Nothing at all, yet all that is I see.
   Ham. Nor did you nothing hear?
   Queen.   No, nothing but ourselves.
   Ham. Why, look you there! Look, how it steals
     away!
My father, in his habit as he lived! 135
Look, where he goes, even now, out at the portal!
                  [*Exit Ghost.*
   Queen. This is the very coinage of your brain.
This bodiless creation ecstasy
Is very cunning in.
   Ham.   Ecstasy!
My pulse, as yours, doth temperately keep time. 140
And makes as healthful music. It is not madness
That I have utt'red. Bring me to the test,
And I the matter will re-word, which madness
Would gambol from. Mother, for love of grace,
Lay not [that] flattering unction to your soul, 145
That not your trespass, but my madness speaks.
It will but skin and film the ulcerous place,
Whilst rank corruption, mining all within,
Infects unseen. Confess yourself to Heaven;
Repent what's past, avoid what is to come, 150
And do not spread the compost on the weeds
To make them rank. Forgive me this my virtue,
For in the fatness of [these] pursy times
Virtue itself of vice must pardon beg,
Yea, curb and woo for leave to do him good, 155
   Queen. O Hamlet, thou hast cleft my heart in
     twain.
   Ham. O, throw away the worser part of it,
And live the purer with the other half.
Good-night; but go not to mine uncle's bed.
Assume a virtue, if you have it not. 160
[That monster, custom, who all sense doth eat
Of habits evil, is angel yet in this,

78–81. [Eyes … mope] Q2. Om. F. 81. mope: be dazed. 88. [And] Q2. *As* F. will: lust. 90. grained: ingrained. 92. enseamed: greasy. 98. vice: the Vice, the mischievous buffoon of the Morality plays. 107. laps'd … passion: having let slip time and the desire for revenge. 117. [do] Q2. Om. F. 118. [th' incorporal] Q2. *their corporal* F. 121. bedded: lying flat. excrements: growths, i.e., hair. 129. effects: i.e., accomplishment of purpose. 131. [whom] Q2. *who* F. 135. habit: garb. 138. ecstasy: madness. 145. [that] Q2. *a* F. 151. unction: salve. 151. compost: manure. 153. [these] Q2. *this* F. pursy: short-winded, out of condition. 155. curb: bow. 161–65. [That … on] Q2. Om. F. 162. evil (Thirlby conj.). *devill* Q2.

That to the use of actions fair and good
He likewise gives a frock or livery,
That aptly is put on.] Refrain to-night,   165
And that shall lend a kind of easiness
To the next abstinence; [the next more easy;
For use almost can change the stamp of nature,
And either master the devil or throw him out,
With wondrous potency.] Once more, good-night;
And when you are desirous to be blest,   171
I'll blessing beg of you. For this same lord,
                              [*Pointing to Polonius.*]
I do repent; but Heaven hath pleas'd it so,
To punish me with this and this with me,
That I must be their scourge and minister.   175
I will bestow him, and will answer well
The death I gave him. So, again, good-night.
I must be cruel, only to be kind.
Thus bad begins and worse remains behind.
[One word more, good lady.]
   Queen.   What shall I do?   180
   Ham. Not this, by no means, that I bid you
      do:
Let the [bloat] king tempt you again to bed,
Pinch wanton on your cheek, call you his mouse,
And let him, for a pair of reechy kisses,
Or paddling in your neck with his damn'd fingers,
Make you to ravel all this matter out,   186
That I essentially am not in madness,
But mad in craft. 'Twere good you let him know;
For who, that's but a queen, fair, sober, wise,
Would from a paddock, from a bat, a gib,   190
Such dear concernings hide? Who would do so?
No, in despite of sense and secrecy,
Unpeg the basket on the house's top,
Let the birds fly, and like the famous ape,
To try conclusions, in the basket creep,   195
And break your own neck down.
   Queen. Be thou assur'd, if words be made of
      breath,
And breath of life, I have no life to breathe
What thou hast said to me.
   Ham. I must to England; you know that?
   Queen.   Alack,
I had forgot. 'Tis so concluded on.   201
   Ham. [There's letters sealed, and my two school-
      fellows,
Whom I will trust as I will adders fang'd,
They bear the mandate. They must sweep my way,
And marshal me to knavery. Let it work;   205
For 'tis the sport to have the enginer
Hoist with his own petar; and 't shall go hard
But I will delve one yard below their mines,

And blow them at the moon. O, 'tis most sweet,
When in one line two crafts directly meet.]   210
This man shall set me packing.
I'll lug the guts into the neighbour room.
Mother, good-night. Indeed this counsellor
Is now most still, most secret, and most grave,
Who was in life a foolish prating knave. —   215
Come, sir, to draw toward an end with you. —
Good-night, mother.
         [*Exeunt* [*severally,*] *Hamlet tugging in
            Polonius.*]

[ACT IV]

[SCENE I. *A room in the castle.*]

Enter KING [QUEEN, Rosencrantz, *and* Guild-
      enstern].
   King. There's matter in these sighs; these pro-
      found heaves
You must translate; 'tis fit we understand them.
Where is your son?
   Queen. [Bestow this place on us a little while.]
         [*Exeunt Rosencrantz and Guildenstern.*]
Ah, my good lord, what have I seen to-night!   5
   King. What, Gertrude? How does Hamlet?
   Queen. Mad as the seas and wind, when both
      contend
Which is the mightier. In his lawless fit,
Behind the arras hearing something stir,
He whips his rapier out, and cries, "A rat, a rat!" 10
And, in his brainish apprehension, kills
The unseen good old man.
   King.   O heavy deed!
It had been so with us, had we been there.
His liberty is full of threats to all,
To you yourself, to us, to every one.   15
Alas, how shall this bloody deed be answer'd?
It will be laid to us, whose providence
Should have kept short, restrain'd, and out of
      haunt
This mad young man. But so much was our love,
We would not understand what was most fit,   20
But, like the owner of a foul disease,
To keep it from divulging, let it feed
Even on the pith of life. Where is he gone?
   Queen. To draw apart the body he hath kill'd,
O'er whom his very madness, like some ore   25
Among a mineral of metals base,
Shows itself pure; he weeps for what is done.
   King. O Gertrude, come away!
The sun no sooner shall the mountains touch,

167–70. [the ... potency] Q2. Om. F. 169. master Q4. Om. Q2. 180. [One ... lady] Q2. Om. F. 182. [bloat] (Warburton). blunt F. blowt Q2. 184. reechy: foul. 190. paddock: toad. gib: tom-cat. 194. ape. A reference to a lost
story of an ape which tried to imitate the birds he had set free. 195. try conclusions: experiment. 202–10. [There's ...
meet] Q2. Om. F. 207. petar: bomb. 210. crafts: plots.
   Act IV, sc. i, 4. [Bestow ... while] Q2. Om. F. 11. brainish: mad. 17. providence: foresight. 18. short: in leash.
haunt: society. 25. ore: vein of gold. 26. mineral: mine.

But we will ship him hence, and this vile deed   30
We must, with all our majesty and skill,
Both countenance and excuse. Ho, Guildenstern!

     [Re-]enter Rosencrantz and Guildenstern.
Friends both, go join you with some further aid.
Hamlet in madness hath Polonius slain,
And from his mother's closet hath he dragg'd him.
Go seek him out; speak fair, and bring the body   36
Into the chapel. I pray you, haste in this.
        [Exeunt Rosencrantz and Guildenstern.
Come, Gertrude, we'll call up our wisest friends
To let them know both what we mean to do
And what's untimely done; [so, haply, slander].   40
[Whose whisper o'er the world's diameter,
As level as the cannon to his blank,
Transports his poisoned shot, may miss our name,
And hit the woundless air.] O, come away!
My soul is full of discord and dismay.   45
                       [Exeunt.

     [Scene II. *Another room in the castle.*]

        Enter Hamlet.

Ham. Safely stow'd.
Ros.   } (*Within.*) Hamlet! Lord Hamlet!
Guil. }
Ham. What noise? Who calls on Hamlet? O,
here they come.

    Enter Rosencrantz *and* Guildenstern.

Ros. What have you done, my lord, with the dead
    body?   5
Ham. Compounded it with dust, whereto 'tis kin.
Ros. Tell us where 'tis, that we may take it
    thence
And bear it to the chapel.
Ham. Do not believe it.
Ros. Believe what?
Ham. That I can keep your counsel and not mine   10
own. Besides, to be demanded of a sponge!
What replication should be made by the son of a
king?
Ros. Take you me for a sponge, my lord?   15
Ham. Ay, sir, that soaks up the King's coun-
tenance, his rewards, his authorities. But such
officers do the King best service in the end. He
keeps them, [as an ape doth nuts], in the corner of
his jaw; first mouth'd, to be last swallowed. When
he needs what you have glean'd, it is but squeezing
you, and, sponge, you shall be dry again.   23

Ros. I understand you not, my lord.
Ham. I am glad of it. A knavish speech sleeps
in a foolish ear.
Ros. My lord, you must tell us where the body
is, and go with us to the King.   28
Ham. The body is with the King, but the King
is not with the body. The King is a thing —
Guil. A thing, my lord!
Ham. Of nothing. Bring me to him. Hide fox,
and all after.   [*Exeunt.*   33

     [Scene III. *Another room in the castle.*]

      Enter King [*and two or three*].

King. I have sent to seek him, and to find the
    body.
How dangerous is it that this man goes loose!
Yet must not we put the strong law on him.
He's lov'd of the distracted multitude,
Who like not in their judgement, but their eyes;   5
And where 'tis so, th' offender's scourge is weigh'd,
But never the offence. To bear all smooth and
    even,
This sudden sending him away must seem
Deliberate pause. Diseases desperate grown
By desperate appliance are reliev'd,   10
Or not at all.

      Enter Rosencrantz.

      How now! What hath befall'n?
Ros. Where the dead body is bestow'd, my lord,
We cannot get from him.
King.   But where is he?
Ros. Without, my lord, guarded, to know your
    pleasure.
King. Bring him before us.   15
Ros. Ho, Guildenstern! bring in my lord.

    Enter Hamlet *and* Guildenstern.

King. Now, Hamlet, where's Polonius?
Ham. At supper.
King. At supper! Where?   19
Ham. Not where he eats, but where he is eaten.
A certain convocation of [politic] worms are e'en at
him. Your worm is your only emperor for diet.
We fat all creatures else to fat us, and we fat our-
selves for maggots. Your fat king and your lean
beggar is but variable service, two dishes, but to one
table; that's the end.   26
[*King.* Alas, alas!
Ham. A man may fish with the worm that hath

---

40. [so ... slander] (Capell). Om. Q₂ F. 41-44. [Whose ... air] Q₂. Om. F. 42. blank: target. 44. woundless:
invulnerable.
    Sc. ii, 12. demanded of: questioned by. 19. [as ... nuts] Q₁. *like an ape* F. *like an apple* Q₂. 32. Hide fox: a game like
hide-and-seek.
    Sc. iii, 9. pause: i.e., planning. 21. [politic] Q₂: statesmanlike. Om. F. 25. variable service: i.e., different ways of
serving the same food. 27-30. [King ... worm] Q₂. Om. F.

eat of a king, and eat of the fish that hath fed of
that worm.] 30

King. What dost thou mean by this?

Ham. Nothing but to show you how a king may
go a progress through the guts of a beggar.

King. Where is Polonius? 34

Ham. In heaven; send thither to see. If your
messenger find him not there, seek him i' th' other
place yourself. But indeed, if you find him not
[within] this month, you shall nose him as you go
up the stairs into the lobby.

King. Go seek him there. 40

[To some Attendants.]

Ham. He will stay till ye come.

[Exeunt Attendants.]

King. Hamlet, this deed, for thine especial
safety, —

Which we do tender, as we dearly grieve

For that which thou hast done, — must send thee
hence

With fiery quickness; therefore prepare thyself. 45

The bark is ready, and the wind at help.

Th' associates tend, and everything is bent

For England.

Ham. For England?

King. Ay, Hamlet.

Ham. Good.

King. So is it, if thou knew'st our purposes.

Ham. I see a cherub that sees [them]. But,
come, for England! Farewell, dear mother. 51

King. Thy loving father, Hamlet.

Ham. My mother. Father and mother is man
and wife, man and wife is one flesh, and so, my
mother. Come, for England! *[Exit.* 55

King. Follow him at foot, tempt him with speed
aboard.

Delay it not; I'll have him hence to-night.

Away! for everything is seal'd and done

That else leans on th' affair. Pray you, make
haste. *[Exeunt Rosencrantz and Guildenstern.]*

And, England, if my love thou hold'st at aught, — 60

As my great power thereof may give the sense,

Since yet thy cicatrice looks raw and red

After the Danish sword, and thy free awe

Pays homage to us — thou mayst not coldly set

Our sovereign process, which imports at full, 65

By letters conjuring to that effect,

The present death of Hamlet. Do it, England;

For like the hectic in my blood he rages,

And thou must cure me. Till I know 'tis done,

Howe'er my haps, my joys were ne'er begun. 70

[Exit.

[SCENE IV. *A plain in Denmark.*]

Enter FORTINBRAS, [*a* CAPTAIN,] *and army,*
[*marching*].

For. Go, captain, from me greet the Danish king.

Tell him that, by his license, Fortinbras

Claims the conveyance of a promis'd march

Over his kingdom. You know the rendezvous.

If that his Majesty would aught with us, 5

We shall express our duty in his eye;

And let him know so.

Cap. I will do't, my lord.

For. Go [softly] on.

[Exeunt Fortinbras [and Soldiers]

[*Enter* HAMLET, ROSENCRANTZ, *and others.*

Ham. Good sir, whose powers are these?

Cap. They are of Norway, sir. 10

Ham. How purpos'd, sir, I pray you?

Cap. Against some part of Poland.

Ham. Who commands them, sir?

Cap. The nephew to old Norway, Fortinbras.

Ham. Goes it against the main of Poland, sir, 15

Or for some frontier?

Cap. Truly to speak, and with no addition,

We go to gain a little patch of ground

That hath in it no profit but the name.

To pay five ducats, five, I would not farm it; 20

Nor will it yield to Norway or the Pole

A ranker rate, should it be sold in fee.

Ham. Why, then the Polack never will defend it.

Cap. Yes, it is already garrison'd.

Ham. Two thousand souls and twenty thousand
ducats 25

Will not debate the question of this straw.

This is th' imposthume of much wealth and peace,

That inward breaks, and shows no cause without

Why the man dies. I humbly thank you, sir.

Cap. God buy you, sir. *[Exit.]*

Ros. Will 't please you go, my lord? 30

Ham. I'll be with you straight. Go a little
before. *[Exeunt all except Hamlet.]*

How all occasions do inform against me,

And spur my dull revenge! What is a man,

If his chief good and market of his time

Be but to sleep and feed? A beast, no more. 35

Sure, He that made us with such large discourse,

Looking before and after, gave us not

That capability and god-like reason

To fust in us unus'd. Now, whether it be

Bestial oblivion, or some craven scruple 40

Of thinking too precisely on th' event, —

---

33. **progress:** royal journey. 38. **[within]** Q₂. Om. F. 42. **deed** Q₂. *deed of thine* F. 46. **at help:** favorable. 63–64. **thy . . . Pays:** thy fear makes thee pay voluntarily. 50. **[them]** Q₂. *him* F. 56. **at foot:** close. 62. **cicatrice:** scar. 64. **set:** regard. 65. **process:** command. 68. **hectic:** fever.

Sc. iv, 3. **conveyance of:** escort for. 6. **eye:** presence. 8. **[softly]** Q₂: slowly. *safely* F. 9–66. **[Enter . . . worth]** Q₂. Om. F. 22. **ranker:** higher. **in fee:** outright. 27. **imposthume:** abscess. 36. **discourse:** reasoning power. 40. **oblivion:** forgetfulness. 41. **event:** outcome.

A thought which, quarter'd, hath but one part wis-
    dom
And ever three parts coward, — I do not know
Why yet I live to say, "This thing's to do,"
Sith I have cause and will and strength and means 45
To do 't.   Examples gross as earth exhort me;
Witness this army of such mass and charge
Led by a delicate and tender prince,
Whose spirit with divine ambition puff'd
Makes mouths at the invisible event,   50
Exposing what is mortal and unsure
To all that fortune, death, and danger dare,
Even for an egg-shell.   Rightly to be great
Is not to stir without great argument,
But greatly to find quarrel in a straw   55
When honour's at the stake.   How stand I then,
That have a father kill'd, a mother stain'd,
Excitements of my reason and my blood,
And let all sleep, while to my shame I see
The imminent death of twenty thousand men,   60
That for a fantasy and trick of fame
Go to their graves like beds, fight for a plot
Whereon the numbers cannot try the cause,
Which is not tomb enough and continent
To hide the slain?   O, from this time forth,   65
My thoughts be bloody, or be nothing worth!]
                         [*Exit.*

    [SCENE V.   *Elsinore.   A room in the castle.*]

   Enter QUEEN, HORATIO [*and a* GENTLEMAN].

  Queen. I will not speak with her.
  [*Gent.*] She is importunate, indeed distract.
Her mood will needs be pitied.
  Queen.   What would she have?
  [*Gent.*] She speaks much of her father; says she
    hears
There's tricks i' th' world, and hems, and beats her
    heart,   5
Spurns enviously at straws, speaks things in doubt
That carry but half sense.   Her speech is nothing,
Yet the unshaped use of it doth move
The hearers to collection.   They aim at it
And botch the words up fit to their own thoughts; 10
Which, as her winks and nods and gestures yield
    them,
Indeed would make one think there would be
    thought,
Though nothing sure, yet much unhappily.
  [*Hor.*] 'Twere good she were spoken with, for she
    may strew
Dangerous conjectures in ill-breeding minds.   15

Let her come in.   [*Exit Gentleman.*]
  Queen. [*Aside.*] To my sick soul, as sin's true
    nature is,
Each toy seems prologue to some great amiss;
So full of artless jealousy is guilt,
It spills itself in fearing to be spilt.   20

      Enter OPHELIA, *distracted.*

  Oph. Where is the beauteous majesty of Den-
    mark?
  Queen. How now, Ophelia!
  Oph. [*Sings.*]
  "How should I your true love know
      From another one?
  By his cockle hat and staff,   25
    And his sandal shoon."
  Queen. Alas, sweet lady, what imports this song?
  Oph. Say you? Nay, pray you, mark.
[*Sings.*] "He is dead and gone, lady,
    He is dead and gone;   30
  At his head a grass-green turf
    At his heels a stone."

        Enter KING.

[O, ho!]
  Queen. Nay, but, Ophelia, —
  Oph. Pray you, mark.
[*Sings.*] "White his shroud as the mountain
      snow," —   35
  Queen. Alas, look here, my lord.
  Oph. [*Sings.*]
  "Larded with sweet flowers;
    Which bewept to the grave did not go
      With true-love showers."
  King. How do you, pretty lady?   40
  Oph. Well, God 'ild you! They say the owl
was a baker's daughter. Lord, we know what we
are, but know not what we may be. God be at
your table! Pray.
  King. Conceit upon her father.   45
  Oph. Pray you, let's have no words of this; but
when they ask you what it means, say you this:
[*Sings.*] "To-morrow is Saint Valentine's day,
    All in the morning betime,
  And I a maid at your window,   50
    To be your Valentine.

  "Then up he rose and donn'd his clothes,
    And dupp'd the chamber door;
  Let in the maid, that out a maid
    Never departed more."   55
  King. Pretty Ophelia!

---

54. argument: cause.   64. continent: receptacle.
  Sc. v, 2, 4. [*Gent.*] Q₂. *Hor.* F (which has no *Gent.* in this scene).   6. Spurns enviously: takes offense spitefully.   in doubt: ambiguously.   9. collection: conjecture.   aim: guess.   14. [*Hor.*] Q. *Qu.* F (which gives ll. 14–20 to the Queen).   19. jealousy: suspicion.   20. spills: destroys.   25. cockle … staff: marks of a pilgrim.   33. [O, ho] Q₂. Om. F.   37. Larded: decked.   41. owl.   Legend tells of a baker's daughter whom Jesus turned into an owl when she complied stingily with his request for bread.   45. Conceit: brooding.   54. dupp'd: opened.

Oph. Indeed, la, without an oath I'll make an
end on't.
  "By Gis, and by Saint Charity,
      Alack! and, Fie for shame!   60
  Young men will do't, if they come to't;
      By Cock, they are to blame.

  "Quoth she, 'Before you tumbled me,
      You promis'd me to wed.'
  'So would I ha' done, by yonder sun,   65
      An thou hadst not come to my bed.'"
  King. How long hath she been thus?
  Oph. I hope all will be well. We must be patient;
but I cannot choose but weep, to think they should
lay him i' th' cold ground. My brother shall   70
know of it; and so I thank you for your good counsel.
Come, my coach! Good-night, ladies; good-night,
sweet ladies; good-night, good-night.   [*Exit.*
  King. Follow her close; give her good watch, I
pray you.   [*Exeunt some.*]   75
O, this is the poison of deep grief; it springs
All from her father's death. O Gertrude, Gertrude,
When sorrows come, they come not single spies,
But in battalions. First, her father slain;   79
Next, your son gone; and he most violent author
Of his own just remove; the people muddied,
Thick and unwholesome in their thoughts and whis-
      pers,
For good Polonius' death; and we have done but
      greenly
In hugger-mugger to inter him; poor Ophelia
Divided from herself and her fair judgement,   85
Without the which we are pictures, or mere beasts;
Last, and as much containing as all these,
Her brother is in secret come from France,
[Feeds] on his wonder, keeps himself in clouds,
And wants not buzzers to infect his ear   90
With pestilent speeches of his father's death,
Wherein necessity, of matter beggar'd,
Will nothing stick our persons to arraign
In ear and ear. O my dear Gertrude, this,
Like to a murd'ring-piece, in many places   95
Gives me superfluous death.   [*A noise within.*

Enter a MESSENGER.

  Queen.   Alack, what noise is this?
  King. Where are my Switzers? Let them guard
      the door.
What is the matter?
  Mess.   Save yourself, my lord!
The ocean, overpeering of his list,
Eats not the flats with more impetuous haste   100

Than young Laertes, in a riotous head,
O'erbears your officers. The rabble call him lord;
And, as the world were now but to begin,
Antiquity forgot, custom not known,
(The ratifiers and props of every word,)   105
They cry, "Choose we! Laertes shall be king!"
Caps, hands, and tongues applaud it to the clouds,
"Laertes shall be king, Laertes king!"
  Queen. How cheerfully on the false trail they
      cry!
O, this is counter, you false Danish dogs!   110

Enter LAERTES [*armed;* DANES *following*].

  King. The doors are broke.   [*Noise within.*
  Laer. Where is [this] king? Sirs, stand you all
      without.
  [*Danes.*] No, let's come in.
  Laer.   I pray you, give me leave.
  [*Danes.*] We will, we will.
                          [*They retire without the door.*]
  Laer. I thank you; keep the door. O thou vile
      king,   115
Give me my father!
  Queen.   Calmly, good Laertes.
  Laer. That drop of blood [that's calm] proclaims
      me bastard,
Cries cuckold to my father, brands the harlot
Even here, between the chaste unsmirched brows
Of my true mother.
  King.   What is the cause, Laertes,   120
That thy rebellion looks so giant-like?
Let him go, Gertrude; do not fear our person.
There's such divinity doth hedge a king
That treason can but peep to what it would,
Acts little of his will. Tell me, Laertes,   125
Why thou art thus incens'd. Let him go, Gertrude.
Speak, man.
  Laer. Where's my father?
  King.   Dead.
  Queen.   But not by him.
  King. Let him demand his fill.
  Laer. How came he dead? I'll not be juggl'd
      with.   130
To heel, allegiance! Vows, to the blackest devil!
Conscience and grace, to the profoundest pit!
I dare damnation. To this point I stand,
That both the worlds I give to negligence,
Let come what comes; only I'll be reveng'd   135
Most throughly for my father.
  King.   Who shall stay you?
  Laer. My will, not all the world.
And for my means, I'll husband them so well,

---

59. **Gis:** contraction of Jesus. 62. **Cock:** corruption of God. 81. **muddied:** confused. 83. **greenly:** foolishly. 84.
In **hugger-mugger:** secretly and hastily. 89. **[Feeds]** Q₂. *Keepes* F. 90. **buzzers:** whisperers. 95. **murd'ring-piece:**
cannon which shoots a kind of shrapnel. 97. **Switzers:** Swiss Guards. 99. **list:** boundary, shore. 101. **in...head:** with
a rebellious force. 110. **counter:** off the scent. 112. **[this]** Q₂. *the* F. 113, 114. **[Danes]** (Capell). *All* F. 117. **[that's
calm]** Q₂. *that calmes* F.

They shall go far with little.

King. Good Laertes,
If you desire to know the certainty　　　　　140
Of your dear father's death, [is't] writ in your
　　revenge
That, swoopstake, you will draw both friend and
　　foe,
Winner and loser?

Laer. None but his enemies.

King. Will you know them then?

Laer. To his good friends thus wide I'll ope my
　　arms.　　　　　145
And like the kind life-rend'ring [pelican],
Repast them with my blood.

King. Why, now you speak
Like a good child and a true gentleman.
That I am guiltless of your father's death,
And am most [sensibly] in grief for it,　　　　150
It shall as level to your judgement pierce
As day does to your eye.
　　　　　[*A noise within:* "Let her come in!"]

Re-enter OPHELIA.

Laer. How now! what noise is that?
O heat, dry up my brains! Tears seven times salt
Burn out the sense and virtue of mine eye!　　155
By heaven, thy madness shall be paid by weight
Till our scale turns the beam. O rose of May!
Dear maid, kind sister, sweet Ophelia!
O heavens! is't possible a young maid's wits
Should be as mortal as an old man's life?　　160
Nature is fine in love, and where 'tis fine,
It sends some precious instance of itself
After the thing it loves.

Oph. [*Sings.*]
　　"They bore him barefac'd on the bier;
　　　　Hey non nonny, nonny, hey nonny;　　165
　　And on his grave rains many a tear," —
Fare you well, my dove!

Laer. Hadst thou thy wits and didst persuade
　　revenge,
It could not move thus.

Oph. You must sing, "Down a-down, and　170
you call him a-down-a." O, how the wheel becomes it! It is the false steward, that stole his
master's daughter.

Laer. This nothing's more than matter.　　174

Oph. There's rosemary, that's for remembrance;
pray, love, remember; and there is pansies, that's
for thoughts.

Laer. A document in madness, thoughts and
remembrance fitted.　　　　　179

Oph. There's fennel for you, and columbines;
there's rue for you, and here's some for me; we may
call it herb [of] grace o' Sundays. O, you must
wear your rue with a difference. There's a daisy.
I would give you some violets, but they wither'd
all when my father died. They say he made a
good end, —　　　　　186
[*Sings.*] "For bonny sweet Robin is all my joy."

Laer. Thought and affliction, passion, hell itself,
She turns to favour and to prettiness.

Oph. [*Sings.*]
　　"And will he not come again?　　　　190
　　　And will he not come again?
　　　　No, no, he is dead;
　　　　Go to thy death-bed;
　　He never will come again.

　　"His beard as white as snow,　　　　195
　　　All flaxen was his poll.
　　　　He is gone, he is gone,
　　　　And we cast away moan.
　　[God 'a' mercy] on his soul!"
And of all Christian souls, I pray God. God buy
ye.　　　　　[*Exit.* 200

Laer. Do you see this, you gods?

King. Laertes, I must commune with your grief,
Or you deny me right. Go but apart,
Make choice of whom your wisest friends you will,
And they shall hear and judge 'twixt you and me. 205
If by direct or by collateral hand
They find us touch'd, we will our kingdom give,
Our crown, our life, and all that we call ours,
To you in satisfaction; but if not,
Be you content to lend your patience to us,　　210
And we shall jointly labour with your soul
To give it due content.

Laer. Let this be so.
His means of death, his obscure burial —
No trophy, sword, nor hatchment o'er his bones,
No noble rite nor formal ostentation —　　215
Cry to be heard, as 'twere from heaven to earth,
That I must call ['t] in question.

King. So you shall;
And where the offence is let the great axe fall.
I pray you, go with me.　　　　　[*Exeunt.*

[SCENE VI.　*Another room in the castle.*]

Enter HORATIO *with an* ATTENDANT.

Hor. What are they that would speak with me?

Att. Sailors, sir. They say they have letters for
　　you.

---

141. [is't] Q₂. *if* F. 146. [pelican] Q₂. *politician* F. The female pelican was believed to feed its own blood to its young. 150. [sensibly] Q₂. *sensible* F. 161. fine: delicate. 171. wheel: (1) refrain, (2) the spinning wheel, at which women sang ballads. 178. document: lesson. 182. [of] Q₂. Om. F. 183. difference: heraldic term for a variation in a coat of arms as borne by different members of a family. 188. Thought: melancholy. passion: suffering. 189. favour: beauty. 199. [God 'a' mercy] Q₂. *Gramercy* F. 207. touch'd: guilty. 214. hatchment: heraldic tablet. 217. ['t] Q₂. Om. F.

Hor. Let them come in.   [*Exit Attendant.*]
I do not know from what part of the world
I should be greeted, if not from Lord Hamlet.   5

Enter SAILOR.

Sail. God bless you, sir.
Hor. Let Him bless thee too.
Sail. He shall, sir, an't please Him.   There's
a letter for you, sir — it comes from the ambassador that was bound for England — if your name
be Horatio, as I am let to know it is.   11

[*Hor.*] (*Reads.*) "Horatio, when thou shalt have
overlook'd this, give these fellows some means to
the King; they have letters for him.   Ere we were
two days old at sea, a pirate of very warlike ap-   15
pointment gave us chase.   Finding ourselves too
slow of sail, we put on a compelled valour.   In
the grapple I boarded them.   On the instant they
got clear of our ship, so I alone became their prisoner.   They have dealt with me like thieves of   20
mercy, but they knew what they did: I am to do a
good turn for them.   Let the King have the letters I
have sent, and repair thou to me with as much haste
as thou wouldest fly death.   I have words to speak
in your ear will make thee dumb, yet are they   25
much too light for the bore of the matter.   These
good fellows will bring thee where I am.   Rosencrantz and Guildenstern hold their course for England; of them I have much to tell thee.   Farewell.   30
                            "He that thou knowest thine,
                                         HAMLET."
Come, I will give you way for these your letters;
And do't the speedier, that you may direct me
To him from whom you brought them.   [*Exeunt.*

[SCENE VII.   *Another room in the castle.*]
Enter KING *and* LAERTES.

King. Now must your conscience my acquit-
          tance seal;
And you must put me in your heart for friend,
Sith you have heard, and with a knowing ear,
That he which hath your noble father slain
Pursued my life.
Laer.   It well appears.   But tell me   5
Why you proceeded not against these feats,
So crimeful and so capital in nature,
As by your safety, wisdom, all things else
You mainly were stirr'd up.
King.   O, for two special reasons,
Which may to you, perhaps, seem much un-
          sinew'd,   10

And yet to me they are strong.   The Queen his
          mother
Lives almost by his looks; and for myself —
My virtue or my plague, be it either which —
She's so conjunctive to my life and soul,
That, as the star moves not but in his sphere,   15
I could not but by her.   The other motive
Why to a public count I might not go
Is the great love the general gender bear him;
Who, dipping all his faults in their affection,
Would, like the spring that turneth wood to stone,   20
Convert his gyves to graces; so that my arrows,
Too slightly timb'red for so loud a wind,
Would have reverted to my bow again,
And not where I had aim'd them.
Laer.   And so have I a noble father lost,   25
A sister driven into desperate terms,
[Whose worth], if praises may go back again,
Stood challenger on mount of all the age
For her perfections.   But my revenge will come.
King.   Break not your sleeps for that.   You
          must not think   30
That we are made of stuff so flat and dull
That we can let our beard be shook with danger
And think it pastime.   You shortly shall hear more.
I lov'd your father, and we love ourself,
And that, I hope, will teach you to imagine —   35

Enter a MESSENGER *with letters*

How now!   What news?
Mess.   Letters, my lord, from Hamlet.
This to your Majesty; this to the Queen.
King.   From Hamlet!   Who brought them?
Mess.   Sailors, my lord, they say; I saw them not.
They were given me by Claudio.   He receiv'd
          them   40
[Of him that brought them].
King.   Laertes, you shall hear them.
Leave us.   [*Exit Messenger.*
[*Reads.*] "High and mighty, You shall know I
am set naked on your kingdom.   To-morrow shall
I beg leave to see your kingly eyes, when I shall,
first asking your pardon thereunto, recount the
occasions of my sudden and more strange re-
turn.   48
                                         HAMLET."
What should this mean?   Are all the rest come
          back?
Or is it some abuse, or no such thing?
Laer.   Know you the hand?
King.   'Tis Hamlet's character.   "Naked!"
And in a postscript here, he says, "alone."
Can you advise me?

Sc. vi, 20–21. **thieves of mercy:** merciful thieves.   26. **bore:** size, importance.
Sc. vii, 17. **count:** reckoning.   18. **general gender:** common people.   21. **gyves:** fetters.   27. **[Whose worth]** Q₂.   *Who*
was F.   41. **[Of ... them]** Q₂. Om. F.   43. **naked:** destitute.   50. **abuse:** deceit.   52. **character:** handwriting.

Laer. I'm lost in it, my lord. But let him come.
It warms the very sickness in my heart   56
That I shall live and tell him to his teeth,
"Thus didest thou."
 King. If it be so, Laertes, ——
As how should it be so? How otherwise? ——
Will you be rul'd by me?
 Laer.   [Ay, my lord,] 60
If so you'll not o'errule me to a peace.
 King. To thine own peace. If he be now re-
  turn'd,
As checking at his voyage, and that he means
No more to undertake it, I will work him
To an exploit, now ripe in my device, 65
Under the which he shall not choose but fall;
And for his death no wind of blame shall breathe,
But even his mother shall uncharge the practice
And call it accident.
 [*Laer.*   My lord, I will be rul'd;
The rather, if you could devise it so 70
That I might be the organ.
 King.   It falls right.
You have been talk'd of since your travel much,
And that in Hamlet's hearing, for a quality
Wherein, they say, you shine. Your sum of parts
Did not together pluck such envy from him 75
As did that one, and that, in my regard,
Of the unworthiest siege.
 Laer.   What part is that, my lord?
 King. A very riband in the cap of youth,
Yet needful too; for youth no less becomes
The light and careless livery that it wears 80
Than settled age his sables and his weeds,
Importing health and graveness.] Two months
 [since]
Here was a gentleman of Normandy; ——
I've seen myself, and serv'd against, the French,
And they [can] well on horseback; but this gallant
Had witchcraft in't. He grew into his seat, 86
And to such wondrous doing brought his horse,
As had he been incorps'd and demi-natur'd
With the brave beast. So far he pass'd my thought,
That I, in forgery of shapes and tricks, 90
Come short of what he did.
 Laer.   A Norman, was't?
 King. A Norman.
 Laer. Upon my life, Lamound.
 King.   The very same.
 Laer. I know him well. He is the brooch indeed
And gem of all [the] nation. 95
 King. He made confession of you,
And gave you such a masterly report

For art and exercise in your defence,
And for your rapier most especially
That he cried out 'twould be a sight indeed 100
If one could match you. [The scrimers of their
 nation,
He swore, had neither motion, guard, nor eye,
If you oppos'd them.] Sir, this report of his
Did Hamlet so envenom with his envy
That he could nothing do but wish and beg 105
Your sudden coming o'er to play with him.
Now, out of this ——
 Laer.   [What] out of this, my lord?
 King. Laertes, was your father dear to you?
Or are you like the painting of a sorrow,
A face without a heart?
 Laer.   Why ask you this? 110
 King. Not that I think you did not love your
 father,
But that I know love is begun by time,
And that I see, in passages of proof,
Time qualifies the spark and fire of it.
[There lives within the very flame of love 115
A kind of wick or snuff that will abate it,
And nothing is at a like goodness still;
For goodness, growing to a plurisy,
Dies in his own too much. That we would do,
We should do when we would; for this "would"
 changes, 120
And hath abatements and delays as many
As there are tongues, are hands, are accidents;
And then this "should" is like a spendthrift
 sigh,
That hurts by easing. But, to the quick o' th'
 ulcer: ——]
Hamlet comes back. What would you undertake,
To show yourself your father's son in deed 126
More than in words?
 Laer.   To cut his throat i' th' church.
 King. No place, indeed, should murder sanc-
 tuarize;
Revenge should have no bounds. But, good
 Laertes,
Will you do this, keep close within your chamber?
Hamlet return'd shall know you are come home. 131
We'll put on those shall praise your excellence
And set a double varnish on the fame
The Frenchman gave you, bring you in fine to-
 gether
And wager on your heads. He, being remiss, 135
Most generous and free from all contriving,
Will not peruse the foils, so that, with ease,
Or with a little shuffling, you may choose

---

60. **[Ay, my lord]** Q₂. Om. F. 63. **checking at:** turning from (as a falcon forsakes its prey). 68. **uncharge the practice:** i.e., fail to see a plot. 69–82. **[*Laer.* . . . graveness]** Q₂. Om. F. 77. **siege:** rank. 82. **Two** Q₂. *Some two* F. **[since]** Q₂. hence F. 85. **[can]** Q₂. *ran* F. 88. **incorps'd:** of one body. 90. **forgery:** imagining. 94. **brooch:** ornament. 95. **[the]** Q₂. our F. 96. **confession:** acknowledgment. 101–103. **[The . . . them]** Q₂. Om. F. 107. **scrimers:** fencers. 107. **[What]** Q₂. *Why* F. 115–24. **[There . . . ulcer]** Q₂. Om. F. 118. **plurisy:** excess. 123. **sigh.** A sigh was supposed to draw blood from the heart. 128. **sanctuarize:** offer asylum to. 134. **in fine:** finally.

A sword unbated, and in a pass of practice
Requite him for your father.
   Laer.   **I will do't;**   140
And, for that purpose, I'll anoint my sword.
I bought an unction of a mountebank,
So mortal [that, but dip] a knife in it,
Where it draws blood no cataplasm so rare,
Collected from all simples that have virtue   145
Under the moon, can save the thing from death
That is but scratch'd withal. I'll touch my point
With this contagion, that, if I gall him slightly,
It may be death.
   King.   Let's further think of this,
Weigh what convenience both of time and means
May fit us to our shape. If this should fail,   151
And that our drift look through our bad perform-
    ance,
'Twere better not assay'd; therefore this project
Should have a back or second, that might hold
If this should blast in proof. Soft! let me see.
We'll make a solemn wager on your cunnings —   156
I ha 't!
When in your motion you are hot and dry —
As make your bouts more violent to that end —
And [that] he calls for drink, I'll have prepar'd him
A chalice for the nonce, whereon but sipping,   161
If he by chance escape your venom'd stuck,
Our purpose may hold there.

           Enter QUEEN.

                How, sweet queen!
   Queen. One woe doth tread upon another's heel,
So fast they follow. Your sister's drown'd, Laertes.
   Laer. Drown'd! O, where?   166
   Queen. There is a willow grows aslant a brook,
That shows his hoar leaves in the glassy stream.
There with fantastic garlands did she come
Of crow-flowers, nettles, daisies, and long purples
That liberal shepherds give a grosser name,   171
But our cold maids do dead men's fingers call them;
There, on the pendent boughs her coronet weeds
Clamb'ring to hang, an envious sliver broke,
When down the weedy trophies and herself   175
Fell in the weeping brook. Her clothes spread
    wide,
And, mermaid-like, a while they bore her up;
Which time she chanted snatches of old tunes,
As one incapable of her own distress,
Or like a creature native and indued   180
Unto that element. But long it could not be

Till that her garments, heavy with [their] drink,
Pull'd the poor wretch from her melodious [lay]
To muddy death.
   Laer.   Alas, then, is she drown'd?
   Queen. Drown'd, drown'd.   185
   Laer. Too much of water hast thou, poor
    Ophelia,
And therefore I forbid my tears. But yet
It is our trick. Nature her custom holds,
Let shame say what it will; when these are gone,
The woman will be out. Adieu, my lord;   190
I have a speech of fire that fain would blaze,
But that this folly douts it.   [*Exit.*
   King.   Let's follow, Gertrude.
How much I had to do to calm his rage!
Now fear I this will give it start again,
Therefore let's follow.   [*Exeunt.*   195

[ACT V]

[SCENE I. *A churchyard.*]

Enter two CLOWNS [*with spades and pickaxes*].

   1. Clo. Is she to be buried in Christian burial that
wilfully seeks her own salvation?
   2. Clo. I tell thee she is, and therefore make her
grave straight. The crowner hath sat on her, and
finds it Christian burial.   5
   1. Clo. How can that be, unless she drown'd herself in her own defence?
   2. Clo. Why, 'tis found so.
   1. Clo. It must be "*se offendendo*," it cannot be
else. For here lies the point: if I drown myself   10
wittingly, it argues an act, and an act hath three
branches; it is [to] act, to do, and to perform; argal,
she drown'd herself wittingly.
   2. Clo. Nay, but hear you, goodman delver, —   15
   1. Clo. Give me leave. Here lies the water;
good. Here stands the man; good. If the man
go to this water and drown himself, it is, will he,
nill he, he goes, — mark you that? But if the
water come to him and drown him, he drowns not
himself; argal, he that is not guilty of his own death
shortens not his own life.   22
   2. Clo. But is this law?
   1. Clo. Ay, marry, is't; crowner's quest law.
   2. Clo. Will you ha' the truth on't? If this had
not been a gentlewoman, she should have been
buried out of Christian burial.   28

---

   139. **unbated:** not blunted. **pass of practice:** treacherous thrust. 142. **mountebank:** quack. 143. **[that... dip]** Q₂. *I
but dipt* F. 144. **cataplasm:** poultice. 145. **simples:** medicinal herbs. 155. **blast in proof:** burst in testing. 160. **[that]**
Q₂. *the* F. 161. **nonce:** purpose. 162. **stuck:** thrust. 168. **hoar:** grey-white. 170. **long purples:** orchids. 171. **liberal:**
free-spoken. 182. **[their]** Q₂. *her* F. 183. **[lay]** Q₂. *buy* F. 188. **trick:** trait, way. 190. **woman:** feminine quality.
192. **douts:** puts out.
   Act V, sc. i, 1. *1. Clo.* F consistently designates *1. Clo.* as *Clown* and *2. Clo.* as *Other.* 4. **crowner:** coroner. 9. *se
offendendo:* blunder for *se defendendo,* self-defence. 12. **[to] act** Q₂. *an Acte* F. **argal:** blunder for *ergo* (therefore).
24. **quest:** inquest.

1. Clo. Why, there thou say'st; and the more pity that great folk should have countenance in this world to drown or hang themselves, more than their even Christian. Come, my spade. There is no ancient gentlemen but gardeners, ditchers, and gravemakers; they hold up Adam's profession.   35

2. Clo. Was he a gentleman?

1. Clo. He was the first that ever bore arms.

2. Clo. Why, he had none.   39

1. Clo. What, art a heathen? How dost thou understand the Scripture? The Scripture says Adam digg'd; could he dig without arms? I'll put another question to thee. If thou answerest me not to the purpose, confess thyself —

2. Clo. Go to.   45

1. Clo. What is he that builds stronger than either the mason, the shipwright, or the carpenter?

2. Clo. The gallows-maker; for that frame outlives a thousand tenants.   50

1. Clo. I like thy wit well, in good faith. The gallows does well; but how does it well? It does well to those that do ill. Now, thou dost ill to say the gallows is built stronger than the church; argal, the gallows may do well to thee. To't again, come.   56

2. Clo. "Who builds stronger than a mason, a shipwright, or a carpenter?"

1. Clo. Ay, tell me that, and unyoke.

2. Clo. Marry, now I can tell.   60

1. Clo. To't.

2. Clo. Mass, I cannot tell.

Enter HAMLET *and* HORATIO, *afar off.*

1. Clo. Cudgel thy brains no more about it, for your dull ass will not mend his pace with beating; and, when you are ask'd this question next, say "a grave-maker"; the houses that he makes lasts till doomsday. Go, get thee to Yaughan; fetch me a stoup of liquor.   68

[*Exit 2. Clown.*]

[*He digs, and*] *sings.*
"In youth, when I did love, did love,
   Methought it was very sweet,
To contract, O, the time for, ah, my behove,
   O, methought, there was nothing meet."   72

Ham. Has this fellow no feeling of his business, that he sings at grave-making?

Hor. Custom hath made it in him a property of easiness.

Ham. 'Tis e'en so. The hand of little employment hath the daintier sense.   78

1. Clo. (*Sings.*)
"But age with his stealing steps
   Hath caught me in his clutch,
And hath shipped me intil the land,
   As if I had never been such."   82

[*Throws up a skull.*]

Ham. That skull had a tongue in it, and could sing once. How the knave jowls it to the ground, as if it were Cain's jaw-bone, that did the first murder! It might be the pate of a politician, which this ass [now o'erreaches]; one that [would] circumvent God, might it not?

Hor. It might, my lord.   89

Ham. Or of a courtier, which could say, "Good morrow, sweet lord! How dost thou, good lord?" This might be my Lord Such-a-one, that prais'd my Lord Such-a-one's horse, when he meant to beg it; might it not?

Hor. Ay, my lord.   95

Ham. Why, e'en so; and now my Lady Worm's; chapless, and knock'd about the mazzard with a sexton's spade. Here's fine revolution, if we had the trick to see 't. Did these bones cost no more the breeding, but to play at loggats with 'em? Mine ache to think on't.   101

1. Clo. (*Sings.*)
"A pick-axe and a spade, a spade,
   For and a shrouding sheet;
O, a pit of clay for to be made
   For such a guest is meet."   105

[*Throws up another skull.*]

Ham. There's another. Why might not that be the skull of a lawyer? Where be his quiddits now, his quillets, his cases, his tenures, and his tricks? Why does he suffer this rude knave now to knock him about the sconce with a dirty shovel, and   110 will not tell him of his action of battery? Hum! This fellow might be in's time a great buyer of land, with his statutes, his recognizances, his fines, his double vouchers, his recoveries. Is this the fine of his fines, and the recovery of his recoveries, to   115 have his fine pate full of fine dirt? Will his vouchers vouch him no more of his purchases, and double ones too, than the length and breadth of a pair of indentures? The very conveyances of his lands will hardly lie in this box, and must the inheritor himself have no more, ha?   121

Hor. Not a jot more, my lord.

Ham. Is not parchment made of sheep-skins?

Hor. Ay, my lord, and of calf-skins too.

Ham. They are sheep and calves that seek out assurance in that. I will speak to this fellow.

---

33. **even:** fellow.   59. **unyoke:** i.e., have done.   67. **Yaughan:** an ale-house keeper.   71. **behove:** advantage.   87. [now o'erreaches] Q₂.   *O're offices* F.   [would] Q₂.   *could* F.   97. **chapless:** without the lower jaw.   **mazzard:** head.   100. **loggats:** a game in which blocks were thrown at a stake.   107. **quiddits:** quibbles.   108. **quillets:** subtleties.   110. **sconce:** head.   113–14. *Statutes* and *recognizances* were bonds securing debts by attaching land and property; *fines* and *recoveries* were legal modes for putting an estate into fee simple.   114. **fine:** end.

Whose grave's this, sir?   127
1. Clo. Mine, sir.
[*Sings.*] "O, a pit of clay for to be made
                For such a guest is meet."
Ham. I think it be thine indeed, for thou liest
in't.   132
1. Clo. You lie out on't, sir, and therefore it is
not yours. For my part, I do not lie in't, and yet
it is mine.
Ham. Thou dost lie in't, to be in't and say 'tis
thine. 'Tis for the dead, not for the quick, therefore thou liest.   138
1. Clo. 'Tis a quick lie, sir; 'twill away again,
from me to you.
Ham. What man dost thou dig it for?
1. Clo. For no man, sir.
Ham. What woman, then?
1. Clo. For none, neither.
Ham. Who is to be buried in't?   145
1. Clo. One that was a woman, sir; but, rest her
soul, she's dead.
Ham. How absolute the knave is! We must
speak by the card, or equivocation will undo us.
By the Lord, Horatio, these three years I have   150
taken note of it; the age is grown so picked that the
toe of the peasant comes so near the heels of our
courtier, he galls his kibe. How long hast thou
been a grave-maker?   154
1. Clo. Of all the days i' the year, I came to't
that day that our last king Hamlet o'ercame
Fortinbras.
Ham. How long is that since?   158
1. Clo. Cannot you tell that? Every fool can
tell that. It was the very day that young Hamlet
was born; he that was mad, and sent into Eng-
land?   164
Ham. Ay, marry, why was he sent into England?
1. Clo. Why, because 'a was mad. He shall recover his wits there; or, if he do not, it's no great
matter there.
Ham. Why?
1. Clo. 'Twill not be seen in him [there]; there the
men are as mad as he.   170
Ham. How came he mad?
1. Clo. Very strangely, they say.
Ham. How "strangely"?
1. Clo. Faith, e'en with losing his wits.
Ham. Upon what ground?   175
1. Clo. Why, here in Denmark. I have been
[sexton] here, man and boy, thirty years.
Ham. How long will a man lie i' th' earth ere he
rot?   179
1. Clo. I' faith, if he be not rotten before he die
— as we have many pocky corses now-a-days, that

will scarce hold the laying in — he will last you
some eight year or nine year. A tanner will last
you nine year.
Ham. Why he more than another?   185
1. Clo. Why, sir, his hide is so tann'd with his
trade that he will keep out water a great while, and
your water is a sore decayer of your whoreson dead
body. Here's a skull now; this skull has lain in
the earth three and twenty years.   191
Ham. Whose was it?
1. Clo. A whoreson mad fellow's it was. Whose
do you think it was?
Ham. Nay, I know not.   195
1. Clo. A pestilence on him for a mad rogue!
'A pour'd a flagon of Rhenish on my head once.
This same skull, sir, was Yorick's skull, the King's
jester.
Ham. This?   200
1. Clo. E'en that.
Ham. Let me see. [*Takes the skull.*] Alas, poor
Yorick! I knew him, Horatio; a fellow of infinite
jest, of most excellent fancy. He hath borne me on
his back a thousand times. And [now] how   205
abhorred [in] my imagination [it] is! My gorge
rises at it. Here hung those lips that I have kiss'd
I know not how oft. Where be your gibes now,
your gambols, your songs, your flashes of merriment, that were wont to set the table on a roar?   210
No one now, to mock your own jeering? Quite
chop-fall'n? Now get you to my lady's chamber,
and tell her, let her paint an inch thick, to this
favour she must come. Make her laugh at that.
Prithee, Horatio, tell me one thing.   216
Hor. What's that, my lord?
Ham. Dost thou think Alexander look'd o' this
fashion i' th' earth?
Hor. E'en so.   220
Ham. And smelt so? Puh!
                              [*Puts down the skull.*]
Hor. E'en so, my lord.
Ham. To what base uses we may return, Horatio! Why may not imagination trace the noble
dust of Alexander, till he find it stopping a bung-
hole?   226
Hor. 'Twere to consider too curiously, to consider so.
Ham. No, faith, not a jot; but to follow him
thither with modesty enough and likelihood to   230
lead it; as thus: Alexander died, Alexander was
buried, Alexander returneth into dust, the dust is
earth, of earth we make loam, and why of that loam
whereto he was converted might they not stop a
beer-barrel?   235
Imperial Cæsar, dead and turn'd to clay,

149. **card:** compass, i.e., punctiliously. 151. **picked:** refined. 153. **kibe:** chilblain. 169. **[there]** Q2. Om. F. 177.
[sexton] Q4. *sixteene* F. 198. **This...sir.** F repeats these words. 205. **[now]** Q2. Om. F. 206. **[in]** Q2. Om. F. **[it]** Q2.
Om. F. 211. **jeering** F. *grinning* Q2. 215. **favour:** appearance. 227. **curiously:** minutely. 230. **modesty:** moderation.

Might stop a hole to keep the wind away.
O, that that earth which kept the world in awe
Should patch a wall t' expel the winter's flaw!
But soft! but soft! Aside! Here comes the King,

Enter [PRIESTS, *etc., in procession;*] KING, QUEEN,
LAERTES, *and a Coffin, with Lords attendant.*

The Queen, the courtiers. Who is that they fol-
low? 241
And with such maimed rites? This doth betoken
The corse they follow did with desperate hand
Fordo it own life. 'Twas [of] some estate.
Couch we a while, and mark. 245
[*Retiring with Horatio.*]
Laer. What ceremony else?
Ham. That is Laertes, a very noble youth.
Mark.
Laer. What ceremony else?
Priest. Her obsequies have been as far enlarg'd
As we have warrantise. Her death was doubtful;
And, but that great command o'ersways the order,
She should in ground unsanctified have lodg'd 252
Till the last trumpet; for charitable prayer,
Shards, flints, and pebbles should be thrown on her.
Yet here she is allowed her virgin rites, 255
Her maiden strewments, and the bringing home
Of bell and burial.
Laer. Must there no more be done?
Priest. No more be done.
We should profane the service of the dead
To sing sage requiem and such rest to her 260
As to peace-parted souls.
Laer. Lay her i' th' earth,
And from her fair and unpolluted flesh
May violets spring! I tell thee, churlish priest,
A minist'ring angel shall my sister be,
When thou liest howling.
Ham. What, the fair Ophelia!
Queen. Sweets to the sweet; farewell! 266
[*Scattering flowers.*]
I hop'd thou shouldst have been my Hamlet's wife.
I thought thy bride-bed to have deck'd, sweet maid,
And not t' have strew'd thy grave.
Laer. O, [treble woe]
Fall ten times treble on that cursed head 270
Whose wicked deed thy most ingenious sense
Depriv'd thee of! Hold off the earth a while,
Till I have caught her once more in mine arms.
[*Leaps in the grave.*
Now pile your dust upon the quick and dead,
Till of this flat a mountain you have made 275
To o'ertop old Pelion, or the skyish head
Of blue Olympus.

Ham. [*Advancing.*] What is he whose grief
Bears such an emphasis, whose phrase of sorrow
Conjures the wand'ring stars and makes them stand
Like wonder-wounded hearers? This is I, 280
Hamlet, the Dane! [*Leaps into the grave.*]
Laer. The devil take thy soul!
[*Grappling with him.*]
Ham. Thou pray'st not well.
I prithee, take thy fingers from my throat.
Sir, though I am not splenitive and rash,
Yet have I something in me dangerous, 285
Which let thy wiseness fear. Away thy hand!
King. Pluck them asunder.
Queen. Hamlet, Hamlet!
[*All.* Gentlemen] —
[*Hor.*] Good my lord, be quiet.
[*The Attendants part them, and they come
out of the grave.*]
Ham. Why, I will fight with him upon this theme
Until my eyelids will no longer wag. 290
Queen. O my son, what theme?
Ham. I lov'd Ophelia. Forty thousand brothers
Could not, with all their quantity of love,
Make up my sum. What wilt thou do for her?
King. O, he is mad, Laertes. 295
Queen. For love of God, forbear him.
Ham. ['Swounds,] show me what thou'lt do.
Woo 't weep? Woo 't fight? [Woo 't fast?]
Woo 't tear thyself?
Woo 't drink up eisel? Eat a crocodile?
I'll do't. Dost thou come here to whine? 300
To outface me with leaping in her grave?
Be buried quick with her, and so will I;
And, if thou prate of mountains, let them throw
Millions of acres on us, till our ground,
Singeing his pate against the burning zone, 305
Make Ossa like a wart! Nay, an thou'lt mouth,
I'll rant as well as thou.
[*Queen.*] This is mere madness,
And thus a while the fit will work on him.
Anon, as patient as the female dove,
When that her golden couplets are disclos'd, 310
His silence will sit drooping.
Ham. Hear you, sir,
What is the reason that you use me thus?
I lov'd you ever. But it is no matter.
Let Hercules himself do what he may,
The cat will mew and dog will have his day. 315
[*Exit.*
King. I pray you, good Horatio, wait upon him.
[*Exit Horatio.*]
[*To Laertes.*] Strengthen your patience in our last
night's speech;

239. flaw: gust. 244. [of] Q₂. Om. F. estate: rank. 250. doubtful: suspicious. 253. for: instead of. 260. sage: solemn. 269. [treble woe] Q₂. *terrible woer* F. 284. splenitive: hot-tempered. 288. [*All.* Gentlemen] Q₂. Om. F. 289. [*Hor.*] Q₂. *Gen.* F. 297. ['Swounds] Q₂. *Come* F. 298. [Woo 't fast] Q₂. Om. F. 299. eisel: vinegar. 305. burning zone: sun's sphere. 307. [*Queen*] Q₂. *Kin.* F. 310. couplets: twins.

We'll put the matter to the present push.
Good Gertrude, set some watch over your son.
This grave shall have a living monument.   320
An hour of quiet shortly shall we see;
Till then, in patience our proceeding be.   [*Exeunt.*

[SCENE II.   *A hall in the castle.*]

Enter HAMLET *and* HORATIO.

Ham. So much for this, sir; now let me see the
   other.
You do remember all the circumstance?
   Hor. Remember it, my lord!
   Ham. Sir, in my heart there was a kind of fight-
   ing
That would not let me sleep.   Methought I lay   5
Worse than the mutines in the bilboes.   Rashly, —
And prais'd be rashness for it; let us know
Our indiscretion sometimes serves us well
When our dear plots do pall; and that should teach
   us
There's a divinity that shapes our ends,   10
Rough-hew them how we will, —
   Hor.   That is most certain.
   Ham. Up from my cabin,
My sea-gown scarf'd about me, in the dark
Grop'd I to find out them; had my desire;
Finger'd their packet; and in fine withdrew   15
To mine own room again, making so bold,
My fears forgetting manners, to unseal
Their grand commission; where I found, Horatio, —
O royal knavery! — an exact command,
Larded with many several sorts of reason   20
Importing Denmark's health and England's too,
With, ho! such bugs and goblins in my life,
That, on the supervise, no leisure bated,
No, not to stay the grinding of the axe,
My head should be struck off.
   Hor.   Is't possible?   25
   Ham. Here's the commission; read it at more
   leisure.
But wilt thou hear me how I did proceed?
   Hor. I beseech you.
   Ham. Being thus be-netted round with vil-
   lanies, —
Ere I could make a prologue to my brains,   30
They had begun the play, — I sat me down,
Devis'd a new commission, wrote it fair.
I once did hold it, as our statists do,
A baseness to write fair, and labour'd much
How to forget that learning; but, sir, now   35

It did me yeoman's service.   Wilt thou know
Th' effects of what I wrote?
   Hor.   Ay, good my lord.
   Ham. An earnest conjuration from the King,
As England was his faithful tributary,
As love between them as the palm should flourish,
As Peace should still her wheaten garland wear   41
And stand a comma 'tween their amities,
And many such-like *as*-es of great charge,
That, on the view and know of these contents,
Without debatement further, more or less,   45
He should the bearers put to sudden death,
Not shriving time allow'd.
   Hor.   How was this seal'd?
   Ham. Why, even in that was Heaven [ordinant].
I had my father's signet in my purse,
Which was the model of that Danish seal;   50
Folded the writ up in [the] form of th' other,
Subscrib'd it, gave't th' impression, plac'd it safely,
The changeling never known.   Now, the next
   day
Was our sea-fight; and what to this was [sequent]
Thou know'st already.   55
   Hor. So Guildenstern and Rosencrantz go to't.
   Ham. Why, man, they did make love to this em-
   ployment;
They are not near my conscience.   Their [defeat]
Doth by their own insinuation grow.
'Tis dangerous when the baser nature comes   60
Between the pass and fell incensed points
Of mighty opposites.
   Hor.   Why, what a king is this!
   Ham. Does it not, thinks 't thee, stand me now
   upon —
He that hath kill'd my king and whor'd my mother,
Popp'd in between th' election and my hopes,   65
Thrown out his angle for my proper life,
And with such cozenage — is't not perfect con-
   science,
To quit him with this arm?   And is't not to be
   damn'd,
To let this canker of our nature come
In further evil?   70
   Hor. It must be shortly known to him from
   England
What is the issue of the business there.
   Ham. It will be short; the interim is mine,
And a man's life's no more than to say "One."
But I am very sorry, good Horatio,   75
That to Laertes I forgot myself,
For by the image of my cause I see
The portraiture of his.   I'll [court] his favours.

318. **present push:** immediate act.
Sc. ii, 6. **mutines:** mutineers.   **bilboes:** fetters.   23. **supervise:** reading.   **bated:** allowed (lit., subtracted).   33. **statists:**
statesmen.   42. **comma:** link.   43. **charge:** burden.   47. **shriving:** absolution.   48. [**ordinant**] Q₂.   *ordinate* F.   51. [**the**]
Q₂.   Om. F.   54. [**sequent**] Q₂.   *sement* F.   58. [**defeat**] Q₂.   *debate* F.   59. **insinuation:** meddling.   61. **pass:** thrust.
fell: cruel.   63. **thinks 't:** seems it to.   78. [**court**] (Theobald).   *count* F.

But, sure, the bravery of his grief did put me
Into a tow'ring passion.

   Hor.   Peace! who comes here?   80

Enter young OSRIC.

   Osr. Your lordship is right welcome back to
Denmark.

   Ham. I humbly thank you, sir. — Dost know
this water-fly?

   Hor. No, my good lord.

   Ham. Thy state is the more gracious, for 'tis 85
a vice to know him. He hath much land, and fertile; let a beast be lord of beasts, and his crib shall
stand at the King's mess. 'Tis a chough, but, as I
[say], spacious in the possession of dirt.   90

   Osr. Sweet lord, if your [lordship] were at leisure,
I should impart a thing to you from his Majesty.

   Ham. I will receive it with all diligence of spirit.
Put your bonnet to his right use; 'tis for the head.

   Osr. I thank your lordship, 'tis very hot.   97

   Ham. No, believe me, 'tis very cold; the wind is
northerly.

   Osr. It is indifferent cold, my lord, indeed.   100

   Ham. Methinks it is very sultry and hot for my
complexion.

   Osr. Exceedingly, my lord; it is very sultry, —
as 'twere, — I cannot tell how. But, my lord, his
Majesty bade me signify to you that he has laid a
great wager on your head. Sir, this is the matter, —

   Ham. I beseech you, remember —   108

   [Hamlet moves him to put on his hat.]

   Osr. Nay, in good faith; for mine ease, in good
faith. [Sir, here is newly come to court Laertes 110
believe me, an absolute gentleman, full of most excellent differences, of very soft society and great
showing; indeed, to speak feelingly of him, he is the
card or calendar of gentry, for you shall find in him
the continent of what part a gentleman would
see.   116

   Ham. Sir, his definement suffers no perdition in
you; though, I know, to divide him inventorially
would dizzy the arithmetic of memory, and yet but
yaw neither, in respect of his quick sail. But, 120
in the verity of extolment, I take him to be a soul
of great article; and his infusion of such dearth and
rareness as, to make true diction of him, his semblable is his mirror; and who else would trace him,
his umbrage, nothing more.   125

   Osr. Your lordship speaks most infallibly of him.

   Ham. The concernancy, sir? Why do we wrap

the gentleman in our more rawer breath?

   Osr. Sir?   130

   Hor. Is't not possible to understand in another
tongue? You will do't, sir, really.

   Ham. What imports the nomination of this
gentleman?

   Osr. Of Laertes?   135

   Hor. His purse is empty already. All's golden
words are spent.

   Ham. Of him, sir.

   Osr. I know you are not ignorant —   139

   Ham. I would you did, sir; yet, in faith, if you
did, it would not much approve me. Well, sir?]

   Osr. You are not ignorant of what excellence
Laertes is —   144

   [Ham. I dare not confess that, lest I should compare with him in excellence; but to know a man well
were to know himself.

   Osr. I mean, sir, for his weapon; but in the imputation laid on him by them, in his meed he's
unfellowed.]   150

   Ham. What's his weapon?

   Osr. Rapier and dagger.

   Ham. That's two of his weapons; but well.

   Osr. The King, sir, has wag'd with him six Barbary horses, against the which he impon'd, as I 155
take it, six French rapiers and poniards, with their
assigns, as girdle, hangers, or so. Three of the
carriages, in faith, are very dear to fancy, very responsive to the hilts, most delicate carriages, and
of very liberal conceit.   160

   Ham. What call you the carriages?

   [Hor. I knew you must be edified by the margent ere you had done.]

   Osr. The carriages, sir, are the hangers.   164

   Ham. The phrase would be more germane to the
matter, if we could carry cannon by our sides; I
would it might be hangers till then. But, on: six
Barbary horses against six French swords, their
assigns, and three liberal-conceited carriages; that's
the French [bet] against the Danish. Why is this
"impon'd," as you call it?   171

   Osr. The King, sir, hath laid that in a dozen
passes between you and him, he shall not exceed
you three hits; he hath [laid on twelve for nine];
and that would come to immediate trial, if your
lordship would vouchsafe the answer.

   Ham. How if I answer no?   177

   Osr. I mean, my lord, the opposition of your person in trial.

   Ham. Sir, I will walk here in the hall; if it

89. **chough:** jackdaw. 90. **[say]** Q2. *saw* F. 91. **[lordship]** Q2. *friendship* F. 110–50. **[Sir ... unfellowed]** Q2. Om.
F., which substitutes only ll. 143–44. 115. **continent:** summary. 119. **dizzy** Q4. *dosie* Q2. 120. **yaw:** falter, stagger.
122. **article:** importance. **infusion:** essence. **dearth:** rarity. 123. **semblable:** likeness. 125. **umbrage:** shadow. 131–32.
another tongue: i.e., when someone else speaks your lingo. **do't** Q3. *too't* Q2. 148. **his** Q6. *this* Q2. 149. **meed:**
merit. 155. **impon'd:** staked. 157. **assigns:** appurtenances. **hangers:** straps. 158. **responsive:** harmonious (in design).
160. **liberal conceit:** elegant design. 162–63. **[Hor. ... done]** Q2. Om. F. 163. **margent:** marginal note. 170. **[bet]**
Q2. *but* F. 174. **[laid ... nine]** Q2. *one twelve for mine* F. 176. **answer:** encounter.

please his Majesty, 'tis the breathing time of day
with me.   Let the foils be brought, the gentleman
willing, and the King hold his purpose, I will win
for him if I can; if not, I'll gain nothing but my
shame and the odd hits.   185

Osr. Shall I re-deliver you e'en so?

Ham. To this effect, sir; after what flourish your
nature will.   188

Osr. I commend my duty to your lordship.

Ham. Yours, yours. [*Exit Osric.*] He does well
to commend it himself; there are no tongues else
for 's [turn].

Hor. This lapwing runs away with the shell on
his head.   194

Ham. He did comply with his dug before he
suck'd it.   Thus had he, and [many] more of the
same bevy that I know the drossy age dotes on,
only got the tune of the time and outward habit of
encounter; a kind of yeasty collection, which carries them through and through the most fond   200
and winnowed opinions; and do but blow them to
their trials, the bubbles are out.

[*Enter a* LORD.

Lord. My lord, his Majesty commended him
to you by young Osric, who brings back to him,
that you attend him in the hall.   He sends to know
if your pleasure hold to play with Laertes, or that
you will take longer time.   207

Ham. I am constant to my purposes; they follow
the King's pleasure.   If his fitness speaks, mine is
ready, now or whensoever, provided I be so able as
now.   211

Lord. The King and Queen and all are coming
down.

Ham. In happy time.   214

Lord. The Queen desires you to use some gentle
entertainment to Laertes before you fall to play.

Ham. She well instructs me.]   [*Exit Lord.*]

Hor. You will lose this wager, my lord.   219

Ham. I do not think so; since he went into
France I have been in continual practice.   I shall
win at the odds.   But thou wouldst not think how
[ill all's] here about my heart.   But it is no matter.

Hor. Nay, good my lord, —   224

Ham. It is but foolery; but it is such a kind of
gain-giving, as would perhaps trouble a woman.

Hor. If your mind dislike anything, obey [it].
I will forestall their repair hither, and say you are
not fit.   229

Ham. Not a whit; we defy augury.   There's a
special providence in the fall of a sparrow.   If it

be now, 'tis not to come; if it be not to come, it will
be now; if it be not now, yet it will come; the readiness is all.   Since no man has aught of what he
leaves, what is't to leave betimes?   [Let be.]   235

Enter KING, QUEEN, LAERTES, [OSRIC,] *Lords,
and other Attendants with foils and gauntlets;
a table and flagons of wine on it.*

King. Come, Hamlet, come, and take this hand
from me.
          [*The King puts Laertes's hand into Ham-
          let's.*]

Ham. Give me your pardon, sir.   I've done you
wrong,
But pardon 't, as you are a gentleman.
This presence knows,
And you must needs have heard, how I am pun-
ish'd   240
With sore distraction.   What I have done
That might your nature, honour, and exception
Roughly awake, I here proclaim was madness.
Was't Hamlet wrong'd Laertes?   Never Hamlet!
If Hamlet from himself be ta'en away,   245
And when he's not himself does wrong Laertes,
Then Hamlet does it not, Hamlet denies it.
Who does it, then?   His madness.   If 't be so,
Hamlet is of the faction that is wrong'd;
His madness is poor Hamlet's enemy.   250
Sir, in this audience,
Let my disclaiming from a purpos'd evil
Free me so far in your most generous thoughts,
That I have shot mine arrow o'er the house
And hurt my [brother].

Laer.   I am satisfied in nature,
Whose motive, in this case, should stir me most   256
To my revenge; but in my terms of honour
I stand aloof, and will no reconcilement
Till by some elder masters of known honour
I have a voice and precedent of peace   260
To keep my name [ungor'd].   But till that time
I do receive your offer'd love like love,
And will not wrong it.

Ham.   I do embrace it freely,
And will this brother's wager frankly play.
Give us the foils.   Come on.

Laer.   Come, one for me.

Ham. I'll be your foil, Laertes; in mine igno-
rance   266
Your skill shall, like a star i' th' darkest night,
Stick fiery off indeed.

Laer.   You mock me, sir.

Ham. No, by this hand.

---

181. **breathing time:** time for exercise.   192. **[turn]** Q₂.   *tongue* F.   196. **[many]** Q₂.   *mine* F.   199. **yeasty:** frothy.   202–
18. **[Enter . . . me]** Q₂.   Om. F.   223. **[ill all's]** Q₂.   *all* F.   226. **gain-giving:** misgiving.   227. **[it]** Q₂.   Om. F.   231. **it:**
death.   235. **[Let be]** Q₂.   Om. F.   239. **presence:** assembled court.   242. **exception:** resentment, disapproval.   255.
[brother] Q₂.   *Mother* F.   260. **voice and precedent:** opinion backed by precedent.   261. **[ungor'd]** Q₂.   *ungorg'd* F.
266. **foil:** (1) rapier, (2) something which, by contrast, enhances a jewel.

King. Give them the foils, young Osric.   Cousin
  Hamlet,   270
You know the wager?
Ham.   Very well, my lord.
Your Grace hath laid the odds o' th' weaker side.
King. I do not fear it, I have seen you both;
But since he is better'd, we have therefore odds.
Laer. This is too heavy, let me see another.
Ham. This likes me well.   These foils have all a
  length?   [*They prepare to play.* 276
Osr. Ay, my good lord.
King. Set me the stoups of wine upon that table.
If Hamlet give the first or second hit,
Or quit in answer of the third exchange,   280
Let all the battlements their ordnance fire.
The King shall drink to Hamlet's better breath,
And in the cup an union shall he throw,
Richer than that which four successive kings
In Denmark's crown have worn.   Give me the
  cups,   285
And let the kettle to the trumpets speak,
The trumpet to the cannoneer without,
The cannons to the heavens, the heaven to earth,
"Now the King drinks to Hamlet."   Come,
  begin;
And you, the judges, bear a wary eye.   290
Ham. Come on, sir.
Laer.   Come, [my lord].   [*They play.*
Ham.   One.
Laer.   No.
Ham.   Judgement.
Osr. A hit, a very palpable hit.
Laer.   Well; again.
King. Stay, give me drink.   Hamlet, this pearl
  is thine;
Here's to thy health!   Give him the cup.   294
      [*Trumpets sound, and shot goes off [with-
        in].*
Ham. I'll play this bout first; set [it] by a while.
Come. [*They play.*] Another hit; what say you?
Laer. A touch, a touch, I do confess.
King. Our son shall win.
Queen.   He's fat, and scant of breath.
[Here, Hamlet, take my] napkin, rub thy brows.
The Queen carouses to thy fortune, Hamlet.   300
Ham. Good madam!
King.   Gertrude, do not drink.
Queen. I will, my lord; I pray you, pardon me.
King. [*Aside.*] It is the poison'd cup; it is too
  late.
Ham. I dare not drink yet, madam; by and
  by.
Queen. Come, let me wipe thy face.   305
Laer. My lord, I'll hit him now.
King.   I do not think 't.

Laer. [*Aside.*] And yet 'tis almost 'gainst my
  conscience.
Ham. Come, for the third, Laertes; you but dally.
I pray you, pass with your best violence.
I am afeard you make a wanton of me.   310
Laer. Say you so?   Come on.   [*They play.*
Osr. Nothing, neither way.
Laer. Have at you now!
      [*Laertes wounds Hamlet; then,*] *in scuffling,
        they change rapiers.*
King.   Part them; they are incens'd.
Ham. Nay, come, again.
      [*Hamlet wounds Laertes.   The Queen
        falls.*]
Osr.   Look to the Queen there!   Ho!
Hor. They bleed on both sides.   How is't, my
  lord!   315
Osr. How is't, Laertes?
Laer. Why, as a woodcock to mine [own] springe,
  Osric;
I am justly kill'd with mine own treachery.
Ham. How does the Queen?
King.   She swounds to see them bleed.
Queen. No, no, the drink, the drink, — O my
  dear Hamlet, —   320
The drink, the drink!   I am poison'd.   [*Dies.*]
Ham. O villainy!   Ho! let the door be lock'd:
Treachery!   Seek it out.
Laer. It is here, Hamlet.   Hamlet, thou art slain.
No medicine in the world can do thee good;   325
In thee there is not half an hour of life.
The treacherous instrument is in thy hand,
Unbated and envenom'd.   The foul practice
Hath turn'd itself on me.   Lo, here I lie,
Never to rise again.   Thy mother's poison'd.   330
I can no more: — the King, the King's to blame.
Ham. The point envenom'd too!
Then, venom, to thy work.   [*Hurts the King.*
All. Treason! treason!
King. O, yet defend me, friends; I am but hurt.
Ham. Here, thou incestuous, murderous, damned
  Dane,   336
Drink off this potion!   Is thy union here?
Follow my mother!   [*King dies.*
Laer.   He is justly serv'd;
It is a poison temp'red by himself.
Exchange forgiveness with me, noble Hamlet.   340
Mine and my father's death come not upon thee,
Nor thine on me!   [*Dies.*
Ham. Heaven make thee free of it!   I follow
  thee.
I am dead, Horatio.   Wretched queen, adieu!
You that look pale and tremble at this chance, 345
That are but mutes or audience to this act,
Had I but time — as this fell sergeant, Death,

283. union: pearl.   286. kettle: kettle-drum.   291. [my lord] Q₂.   on sir F.   295. [it] Q₂.   Om. F.   298. fat: out of
training.   299. [Here ... my] Q₂.   *Heere's a* F.   310. wanton: spoiled child.   317. [own] Q₂.   Om. F.

Is strict in his arrest — O, I could tell you —
But let it be.   Horatio, I am dead;
Thou liv'st.   Report me and my [cause aright]   350
To the unsatisfied.
    Hor.   Never believe it.
I am more an antique Roman than a Dane;
Here's yet some liquor left.
    Ham.   As thou'rt a man,
Give me the cup.   Let go!   By heaven, I'll have't!
O good Horatio, what a wounded name,   355
Things standing thus unknown, shall live behind
        me!
If thou didst ever hold me in thy heart,
Absent thee from felicity a while
And in this harsh world draw thy breath in pain
To tell my story.   [*March afar off, and shot within.*
                    What warlike noise is this?   360
    Osr.   Young Fortinbras, with conquest come
        from Poland,
To the ambassadors of England gives
This warlike volley.
    Ham.   O, I die, Horatio;
The potent poison quite o'er-crows my spirit.
I cannot live to hear the news from England   365
But I do prophesy th' election lights
On Fortinbras; he has my dying voice.
So tell him, with the occurrents, more and less,
Which have solicited — The rest is silence.   [*Dies.*
    Hor.   Now cracks a noble heart.   Good-night,
        sweet prince,   370
And flights of angels sing thee to thy rest!
Why does the drum come hither?   [*March within.*]

    Enter FORTINBRAS *and the* English AMBASSA-
    DOR, *with drum, colours, and Attendants.*

    Fort.   Where is this sight?
    Hor.   What is it ye would see?
If aught of woe or wonder, cease your search.
    Fort.   [This] quarry cries on havoc.   O proud
        Death,   375
What feast is toward in thine eternal cell,
That thou so many princes at a shot
So bloodily hast struck?

    Amb.   The sight is dismal,
And our affairs from England come too late.
The ears are senseless that should give us hearing,
To tell him his commandment is fulfill'd,   381
That Rosencrantz and Guildenstern are dead.
Where should we have our thanks?
    Hor.   Not from his mouth,
Had it th' ability of life to thank you.
He never gave commandment for their death.   385
But since, so jump upon this bloody question,
You from the Polack wars, and you from England,
Are here arriv'd, give order that these bodies
High on a stage be placed to the view;   *Romeo or*
And let me speak to th' yet unknowing world   390   *Juliet*
How these things came about.   So shall you hear
Of carnal, bloody, and unnatural acts,
Of accidental judgements, casual slaughters,
Of deaths put on by cunning and forc'd cause,
And, in this upshot, purposes mistook   395
Fall'n on the inventors' heads: all this can I
Truly deliver.
    Fort.   Let us haste to hear it,
And call the noblest to the audience.
For me, with sorrow I embrace my fortune.
I have some rights of memory in this kingdom,   400
Which [now] to claim, my vantage doth invite me.
    Hor.   Of that I shall have [also] cause to speak,
And from his mouth whose voice will draw on more.
But let this same be presently perform'd
Even while men's minds are wild, lest more mis-
        chance,   405
On plots and errors, happen.
    Fort.   Let four captains
Bear Hamlet, like a soldier, to the stage,
For he was likely, had he been put on,
To have prov'd most royally; and, for his passage,
The soldiers' music and the rites of war   410
Speak loudly for him.
Take up the body.   Such a sight as this
Becomes the field, but here shows much amiss.
Go, bid the soldiers shoot.
                    [*Exeunt marching; after which a peal of
                    ordnance are shot off.*

    350. [cause aright] Q₂.   *causes right* F.   **352. Roman.**   Alluding to the Roman custom of suicide.   **367. voice:** approval,
vote.   **369. solicited:** caused them.   **silence.** F adds *O, o, o, o.*   **375.** [This] Q₂.   *His* F.   **quarry...havoc:** heap of dead
proclaims a massacre.   **383. his:** the King's.   **389. stage:** platform.   **400. of memory:** unforgotten.   **401.** [now] Q₂.   *are*
F.   **402.** [also] Q₂.   *alwayes* F.   **408. put on:** tested.   **409. passage:** i.e., death.   **413. field:** battlefield.

Othello, the Moor of Venice

OTHELLO IS NOTABLE among Shakespeare's plays as being the only one published between his death and the appearance of the First Folio. No First Quarto had been issued after 1609 till that of *Othello* was printed in 1622. The title page carried Shakespeare's name and stated that the tragedy had been "diuerse times acted at the Globe, and at the Black Friers, by his Maiesties Seruants." The text in the First Quarto is a good one, though it is shorter by some 160 lines than that in the First Folio. On the other hand, there are minor omissions and numerous variants in the Folio. Both texts appear to have been printed from manuscripts used in the theatre. The omissions in the Quarto presumably represent cuts, though a few may have been accidental; the preponderance in the Quarto of oaths that have been removed or modified in the Folio suggests that the manuscript from which that edition was printed may have antedated the law of 1606 against profanity on the stage. The text of the present edition is based upon the Folio, with deference to the Quarto where a better reading can be supplied.

There was a performance of *Othello* at Court on November 1, 1604, and authorities are in accord that the composition belongs to an earlier part of that year. There is a possible reference to the death of Desdemona in I.i.37 of Part I of *The Honest Whore* by Dekker and Middleton (1604), and metrical tests indicate a position between *Hamlet* and *Lear*.

The plot of the tragedy is drawn from a tale (the seventh of the third decade) in the *Hecatommithi* (1565) of Giraldi Cinthio, but, as usual, Shakespeare's work is a marvelous transmutation of crude ore. In the Italian story, Desdemona alone is given a name (Disdemona), and the outlines of her character, with those of Othello ("the Moor"), Iago ("the Ensign"), and Cassio ("the Captain") are there faintly indicated. Hardly so much can be said of Emilia and Bianca; for the character of Brabantio there is only the hint that Disdemona's parents opposed her marriage; and Roderigo and the official persons in Venice and Cyprus are Shakespeare's creations. The threat of a Turkish attack upon Cyprus, the separate voyages of Othello and Desdemona, the episode of Cassio's drunkenness, Emilia's part in the stealing of the handkerchief and Bianca's connection with it, are all lacking in the novel. There too, certain of the elements crucial in the drama are quite differently handled. Thus the villain is a disappointed lover of Disdemona's, whose failure turns his passion to hate. Only a trace of this is left in Iago, and the character of Roderigo is built up on the suggestion it affords. In the novel, the handkerchief is stolen by the Ensign himself, who removes it from Disdemona's sash when she is fondling his little girl. The Ensign's wife is aware of his criminal scheming. The Captain (Cassio) is married, and the ocular proof of Disdemona's guilt is given by the Ensign's bringing the Moor to see the Captain's wife sitting at a window making a copy of the lost handkerchief. The Captain is on his way to visit a courtezan when he is attacked by the Ensign, and it is apparently from this hint that Shakespeare creates Bianca, omitting the Captain's wife; although there may be a trace of the latter remaining, perhaps through an oversight, in the cryptic reference to Cassio (I.i.21) as "A fellow almost damn'd in a fair wife."

In the Italian, the arrangement of the catastrophe is also very different. There the Ensign, carrying out a plan approved by the Moor, beats Disdemona to death with a stocking filled with sand, and the two men disguise their crime by pulling down the ceiling and making it appear that she was killed by a falling beam. After a time, however, the Moor, brooding on the memory of Disdemona, comes to hate the Ensign and discharges him; then, in revenge, the Ensign tells the Captain that it was the Moor who wounded him and who caused Disdemona's death. The Moor is accused before the Signiory, is tried and tortured, but refuses to confess. He is banished and is subsequently killed by his wife's relatives. The Ensign goes free, but ultimately dies from the effects of torture inflicted in connection with another charge. The contrast between this sordid and dragged-out conclusion and the swiftness and dignity of Shakespeare's terrible close need not be detailed. The tone of the novel may be gathered from a remark made by the heroine: "I fear I shall prove an example to young girls not to marry against the wishes of their parents, and that the Italian ladies may learn from me not to marry a man whom nature, heaven, and manner of life have separated from us."

Out of this sordid and melodramatic tale, Shakespeare has created a tragic drama of terrifying plausibility. The conviction of reality is extraordinary, considering that the action, regarded in the light of reason, is full of improbability. But Shakespeare knew how easily the light of reason is extinguished in men, especially in certain types of men, and he was, in 1604, so sure a master of characterization and of theatrical illusion, that he could make acceptable in his medium what would not be so in another. He further strengthens credibility by building the action upon relentlessly simple lines. There is no more powerful a destroyer of human happiness than sexual jealousy, which has wrecked the lives of all sorts and conditions of men. Because it is precisely this which ruins Othello, whose happiness with Desdemona seemed ideally perfect, and because Othello, recovering his senses when it is too late, pathetically acknowledges the fact, his tragedy, however peculiar the circumstances, becomes a catastrophe by no means unfamiliar. His tragedy, however, is fraught with uncommon pity and terror, both elements being augmented by an extreme concentration of emotional force. No secondary interest or comic relief is permitted to take our attention from the main course of affairs.

The pathos of Othello's situation is especially acute because he is not constitutionally prone to jealousy. In the early scenes Shakespeare is careful to show us that Othello is a man of high integrity, of commanding presence and simple eloquence, and, most important, of complete self-mastery. When Iago recommends that he avoid Desdemona's irate father, he chooses, rather, to confront him honestly, confident that his perfect record and untarnished conscience will "manifest him rightly." When soon embroilment threatens, he suppresses it with a word. His speech before the Senators, recounting with a winning frankness the history of his courtship, reflects the essential nobility of his character. Furthermore, Othello's story reveals the important fact that Brabantio had respected him and had entertained him often at his house (I.i.127–31). To be sure, Brabantio had never dreamed that his daughter would fall in love with Othello, but in the impression of Othello's nature which Shakespeare is

seeking to convey, his relations with others, including Brabantio, and their opinions of him, are most significant.

How comes it, then, that a man of Othello's confirmed steadiness can be so rankly abused and can so completely lose his true self? Under normal circumstances, doubtless, the calamity would be impossible, but the circumstances are not normal. Othello becomes the victim of an incomparably ingenious and unscrupulous villain, whose hatred of him is increased by contempt for the very qualities which distinguish him. Thus Othello's natural goodness, the native honor which makes duplicity as alien to him as cowardice, becomes a weakness for Iago to play upon (I.iii.405–408). Furthermore, the essential simplicity of Othello's nature is complemented by a lack of certain kinds of experience. His career has been military, and his accomplishments belong to the field rather than to the drawing room (I.iii.81 ff.; III.iii.263–66). He is unacquainted with the ways of Venetian society, as Iago once powerfully reminds him (III.iii.199–204). Because the hero's credulity seems monstrous, one must not underestimate the skill of the intriguer. Nor must one suppose that the hero's noble nature is overcome without a struggle; Othello's mind fights the horrid coil that is being thrown around it (III.iii.176–92; 359–73). Once, however, conviction of Desdemona's guilt is planted in Othello's mind, its consequences are swift and deadly. To gnawing jealousy is added the force of shattered idealism. Desdemona, who has seemed to Othello the embodiment of purity, now seems to him corrupted and defiled. Since hers is now an infectious, not a healthful beauty, she must die, "else she'll betray more men." In this belief, even anger is finally consumed, leaving only unfathomable sorrow; so that when Othello enters Desdemona's chamber to kill her, he conceives of himself as the agent not of vengeance but of divine justice (V.ii.16–22).

The credulity of Othello, his confidence in the "honesty" of Iago, and his failure to place at least an equal trust in his newly wedded wife, when one frank talk would have cleared up everything, are, of course, contrary to reason and common sense. Othello's behavior completely belies his "free and noble nature." It must be remembered, however, that psychological inconsistency of this kind is not felt in the theatre. It may even be possible in real life, for idealists are often easily imposed upon by hypocrites. Men may become for a time "insane with jealousy," and it is conceivable that a man of Othello's make-up might be prevented by a sense of shame from speaking of his jealousy to the person who could logically allay it. In any event, Othello's judgment upon himself is utterly plain and simple. "Oh fool! fool! fool!" he cries, when his eyes are opened to the grossness of his deception. That is all that need be said, except, in fairness, that he was "one not easily jealous, but, being wrought, Perplex'd in the extreme." It is fitting that Othello should pass sentence and execute justice upon himself. In his final moments he recovers his essential nobility and that felicity of language which he commands so well, and his suicide is a kind of atonement.

Iago has become a by-word for consummate villainy. The motives for his evil-doing are explicit. The primary one is professional resentment. Othello has promoted Cassio to the lieutenantcy which he craved and for which he thinks he was better fitted (I.i.8 ff.). The sense of injustice rankles, and if what Iago says about Cassio's military experience in comparison with his own is true, he has something on his side. To supplement this grievance, there is some sexual jealousy (I.iii.392–96; II.i.300–11). At the outset, Iago's aim is only to humiliate Othello, to get Cassio's place, and thus to repair his wounded self-esteem. He has no preconceived plan, but shapes his intrigue gradually from what time and chance afford, becoming more and more deeply involved, until a retreat is finally impossible. In working upon Othello, Iago employs a skillful technique of insinuation and evasion, distilling the poison of jealousy drop by drop, hinting obliquely at evil, recoiling from the suggestion in apparent alarm, but returning to the theme again, each time a little more emphatically. Luck befriends him too. Thus, for example, it is propitious for his scheming that Othello proclaims an evening of revelry in Cyprus (II.ii.), for it becomes easy to get Cassio drunk and ripe for indiscretion. Cassio's leaving Desdemona so self-consciously when Othello and Iago approach (III.iii.29–40) gives the latter a perfect cue for beginning his evil suggestions. The supreme accident is, of course, the dropping of the handkerchief, for with it Iago comes into possession of "ocular proof" of Desdemona's guilt. Finally, however, Iago's luck deserts him, for Roderigo fails to kill Cassio, and his own wife turns out to be his Nemesis. Part of Iago's early good fortune is his reputation. How so wicked a man could acquire and maintain a name for honesty it is futile to wonder, but everybody believes in "honest Iago," and his reputation is at once a primary asset and a hideous irony. The word "honest" becomes a kind of motif, introduced repeatedly in its two meanings, "honorable" and "chaste." The play is charged

with irony too pervasive to be detailed. At points it becomes almost intolerable (e.g., III.iii.106–108; 213–20; III.iv.26–31; IV.ii.148–71), and the spell is not broken until Othello tells Iago's horrified wife that her husband knew all about Desdemona's infidelity. "I say thy husband," he cries. "My friend, thy husband, honest, honest Iago " (V.ii. 154).

Desdemona is essentially a passive heroine, created to love and to suffer. That she is not without spirit is proved by her defiance of convention in marrying Othello, but later when her lover is estranged and her happiness is imperiled, she is impractical and unresisting. For the change in Othello she assumes she must be to blame, though she cannot imagine how. Othello, she is certain, cannot be jealous, and women who would deceive their husbands are beyond her comprehension. Her only refuge is bewilderment and grief. Desdemona is sublimely pure and sublimely innocent, and inexperience is her undoing.

Something should be said about Emilia, and it should be in appreciation. Her relation to the heroine is such that, had the play been a comedy, she might have had a merry rôle. As things are, her capacity for banter is exhibited in two notable passages (II.i.96 ff.; IV.iii.60 ff.). But she is cast in a tragedy and plays an unhappy part. Romance has long since been over for her, though she gets along well enough with her husband. Her "stealing" Desdemona's handkerchief is a grave mistake, but she has only innocent intentions. Iago has expressed a desire for it, and she thinks she may gratify his whim. She purposes to keep it only long enough to make a copy of it, and when Iago snatches the original from her, she protests (III.iii.290 ff.). When Desdemona misses her handkerchief, Emilia (as Desdemona herself is presently to do) tells a venial lie. The only thing that it is difficult to forgive is her later negligence, not to say stupidity, in failing to connect Othello's distemper with the handkerchief and to clear matters up before there is serious trouble. It is only after Desdemona is dead and Othello refers to the handkerchief as proof of her guilt that Emilia comprehends. "O God!" she cries then, "O Heavenly God!" (V.ii.217). The horror in her exclamation proves her innocence, if any proof were needed. Her courageous defiance of Iago in solving the mystery, once her own ignorance has been dispelled, makes us take her to our hearts, and her death by his hand redeems her completely.

OTHELLO, THE MOOR OF VENICE

[DRAMATIS PERSONÆ]

DUKE OF VENICE.
BRABANTIO, [a senator,] father to Desdemona.
[Other] Senators.
GRATIANO, [brother to Brabantio,] } two noble
LUDOVICO, [kinsman to Brabantio,] } Venetians.
OTHELLO, the Moor [in the military service of Venice].
CASSIO, an honourable lieutenant.
IAGO, [an ensign,] a villain.

RODERIGO, a gulled gentleman.
MONTANO, governor of Cyprus [before Othello].
CLOWN [servant to Othello].

DESDEMONA, [daughter to Brabantio and] wife to Othello.
EMILIA, wife to Iago.
BIANCA, a courtezan.

Gentlemen of Cyprus, Sailors [Officers, Messenger, Herald, Musicians, and Attendants].

[SCENE: Venice; a sea-port in Cyprus.]

ACT I

SCENE I. [Venice. A street.]

Enter RODERIGO *and* IAGO.

Rod. [Tush]! never tell me! I take it much un-
kindly
That thou, Iago, who hast had my purse
As if the strings were thine, shouldst know of this.
Iago. ['Sblood], but you'll not hear me.
If ever I did dream of such a matter, 5
Abhor me.
  Rod. Thou told'st me thou didst hold him in thy
hate.
  Iago. Despise me if I do not. Three great ones
of the city,
In personal suit to make me his lieutenant,
Off-capp'd to him; and, by the faith of man, 10
I know my price; I am worth no worse a place.
But he, as loving his own pride and purposes,
Evades them with a bombast circumstance
Horribly stuff'd with epithets of war,
[And, in conclusion,] 15

Nonsuits my mediators; for, "Certes," says he,
"I have already chose my officer."
And what was he?
Forsooth, a great arithmetician,
One Michael Cassio, a Florentine, 20
(A fellow almost damn'd in a fair wife)
That never set a squadron in the field,
Nor the division of a battle knows
More than a spinster, unless the bookish theoric,
Wherein the [toged] consuls can propose 25
As masterly as he. Mere prattle without practice
Is all his soldiership. But he, sir, had th' elec-
tion;
And I, of whom his eyes had seen the proof
At Rhodes, at Cyprus, and on other grounds
Christen'd and heathen, must be be-lee'd and
calm'd 30
By debitor and creditor; this counter-caster,
He, in good time, must his lieutenant be,
And I — [God] bless the mark! — his Moorship's
ancient.
  Rod. By heaven, I rather would have been his
hangman.

Act I, sc. i, 1. [Tush] Q. Om. F. 3. this: Desdemona's elopement. 4. ['Sblood] Q. Om. F. Profane exclamations in brackets, such as this and that in I.i.33, were omitted in F on account of the Act of 1605 against swearing. Frequently *Heaven* was substituted for *God*. 13. circumstance: discourse. 15. [And ... conclusion] Q. Om. F. 21. wife. See Introduction. 23. division: array. 25. [toged] Q: wearing a toga. *tongued* F. 31. counter-caster: accountant. 33. [God] Q. Om. F.

Iago. Why, there's no remedy. 'Tis the curse of
     service,   35
Preferment goes by letter and affection,
And not by old gradation, where each second
Stood heir to th' first.   Now, sir, be judge yourself
Whether I in any just term am affin'd
To love the Moor.
    Rod.   I would not follow him then.   40
    Iago. O, sir, content you;
I follow him to serve my turn upon him.
We cannot all be masters, nor all masters
Cannot be truly follow'd.   You shall mark
Many a duteous and knee-crooking knave   45
That, doting on his own obsequious bondage,
Wears out his time, much like his master's ass,
For nought but provender, and when he's old,
    cashier'd.
Whip me such honest knaves.   Others there are
Who, trimm'd in forms and visages of duty,   50
Keep yet their hearts attending on themselves,
And, throwing but shows of service on their lords,
Do well thrive by them and, when they have lin'd
    their coats,
Do themselves homage.   These fellows have some
    soul;
And such a one do I profess myself.   For, sir,   55
It is as sure as you are Roderigo,
Were I the Moor, I would not be Iago.
In following him, I follow but myself;
Heaven is my judge, not I for love and duty,
But seeming so, for my peculiar end;   60
For when my outward action doth demonstrate
The native act and figure of my heart
In compliment extern, 'tis not long after
But I will wear my heart upon my sleeve
For daws to peck at.   I am not what I am.   65
    Rod. What a full fortune does the thick-lips owe,
If he can carry 't thus!
    Iago.   Call up her father,
Rouse him.   Make after him, poison his delight,
Proclaim him in the streets.   Incense her kins-
    men,
And, though he in a fertile climate dwell,   70
Plague him with flies.   Though that his joy be joy,
Yet throw such [changes] of vexation on't,
As it may lose some colour.
    Rod. Here is her father's house; I'll call aloud.
    Iago. Do, with like timorous accent and dire yell
As when, by night and negligence, the fire   76
Is spied in populous cities.
    Rod. What, ho, Brabantio!   Signior Brabantio,
    ho!

    Iago. Awake! what, ho, Brabantio! thieves!
    thieves!
Look to your house, your daughter, and your bags!
Thieves! thieves!   81

      BRABANTIO [*appears*] *above, at a window.*
    Bra. What is the reason of this terrible summons?
What is the matter there?
    Rod. Signior, is all your family within?
    Iago. Are your doors lock'd?
    Bra.   Why, wherefore ask you this?
    Iago. ['Zounds], sir, you're robb'd!   For shame,
    put on your gown.   86
Your heart is burst, you have lost half your soul;
Even now, now, very now, an old black ram
Is tupping your white ewe.   Arise, arise!
Awake the snorting citizens with the bell,   90
Or else the devil will make a grandsire of you.
Arise, I say!
    Bra.   What, have you lost your wits?
    Rod. Most reverend signior, do you know my
    voice?
    Bra. Not I.   What are you?
    Rod. My name is Roderigo.
    Bra.   The worser welcome;
I have charg'd thee not to haunt about my doors.   96
In honest plainness thou hast heard me say
My daughter is not for thee; and now, in madness,
Being full of supper and distemp'ring draughts,
Upon malicious [bravery] dost thou come   100
To start my quiet.
    Rod. Sir, sir, sir, —
    Bra.   But thou must needs be sure
My spirits and my place have in their power
To make this bitter to thee.
    Rod.   Patience, good sir.
    Bra. What tell'st thou me of robbing?   This is
    Venice;   105
My house is not a grange.
    Rod.   Most grave Brabantio,
In simple and pure soul I come to you.
    Iago. ['Zounds], sir, you are one of those that will
not serve God, if the devil bid you.   Because we
come to do you service and you think we are   110
ruffians, you'll have your daughter cover'd with a
Barbary horse; you'll have your nephews neigh to
you; you'll have coursers for cousins, and gennets
for germans.
    Bra. What profane wretch art thou?   115
    Iago. I am one, sir, that comes to tell you your
daughter and the Moor are [now] making the beast
with two backs.

---

36. **letter:** i.e., of recommendation.   37. **old gradation:** seniority.   39. **affin'd:** bound.   48. **cashier'd:** dismissed.   50.
visages: semblances.   60. **peculiar:** private.   63. **compliment extern:** external show.   66. **thick-lips:** i.e., the Moor.   **owe:**
own.   72. **[changes]** Q.   *chances* F.   75. **timorous:** terrifying.   90. **snorting:** snoring.   99. **distemp'ring:** intoxicating.
100. **[bravery]** Q: swaggering.   *knavery* F.   101. **start:** startle.   106. **grange:** isolated farm.   112. **nephews:** grandsons.
113. **gennets:** Spanish horses.   114. **germans:** relatives.   117. **[now]** Q.   Om. F.

Bra. Thou art a villain.
Iago.   You are — a senator.
Bra. This thou shalt answer; I know thee, Rod-
erigo.   120
Rod. Sir, I will answer anything.   But, I beseech
you,
If 't be your pleasure and most wise consent,
As partly I find it is, that your fair daughter,
At this odd-even and dull watch o' th' night,
Transported, with no worse nor better guard   125
But with a knave of common hire, a gondolier,
To the gross clasps of a lascivious Moor, —
If this be known to you and your allowance,
We then have done you bold and saucy wrongs;
But if you know not this, my manners tell me   130
We have your wrong rebuke.   Do not believe
That, from the sense of all civility,
I thus would play and trifle with your reverence.
Your daughter, if you have not given her leave,
I say again, hath made a gross revolt,   135
Tying her duty, beauty, wit, and fortunes
In an extravagant and wheeling stranger
Of here and everywhere.   Straight satisfy your-
self.
If she be in her chamber or your house,
Let loose on me the justice of the state   140
For thus deluding you.
Bra.   Strike on the tinder, ho!
Give me a taper!   Call up all my people!
This accident is not unlike my dream;
Belief of it oppresses me already.   144
Light, I say! light!   [*Exit* [*above*].
Iago.   Farewell; for I must leave you.
It seems not meet, nor wholesome to my place,
To be produc'd — as, if I stay, I shall —
Against the Moor; for, I do know, the state,
However this may gall him with some check,
Cannot with safety cast him, for he's embark'd   150
With such loud reason to the Cyprus wars,
Which even now [stand] in act, that, for their
souls,
Another of his fathom they have none
To lead their business; in which regard,
Though I do hate him as I do hell-pains,   155
Yet, for necessity of present life,
I must show out a flag and sign of love,
Which is indeed but sign.   That you shall surely
find him,
Lead to the Sagittary the raised search;
And there will I be with him.   So, farewell.   160
                                        [*Exit.*

Enter [*below,*] BRABANTIO *in his night-gown, and
Servants with torches.*

Bra. It is too true an evil; gone she is;
And what's to come of my despised time
Is nought but bitterness.   Now, Roderigo,
Where didst thou see her?   O unhappy girl!
With the Moor, say'st thou?   Who would be a
father!   165
How didst thou know 'twas she?   O, she deceives
me
Past thought!   What said she to you?   Get moe
tapers;
Raise all my kindred.   Are they married, think you?
Rod. Truly, I think they are.
Bra. O heaven!   How got she out?   O treason of
the blood!   170
Fathers, from hence trust not your daughters' minds
By what you see them act.   Is there not charms
By which the property of youth and maidhood
May be abus'd?   Have you not read, Roderigo,
Of some such thing?
Rod.   Yes, sir, I have indeed.   175
Bra. Call up my brother. — O, would you had
had her! —
Some one way, some another. — Do you know
Where we may apprehend her and the Moor?
Rod. I think I can discover him, if you please
To get good guard and go along with me.   180
Bra. Pray you, lead on.   At every house I'll call;
I may command at most.   Get weapons, ho!
And raise some special officers of [night].
On, good Roderigo; I'll deserve your pains.   [*Exeunt.*

SCENE II.   [*Another street.*]

Enter OTHELLO, IAGO, *and Attendants with
torches.*

Iago. Though in the trade of war I have slain
men,
Yet do I hold it very stuff o' th' conscience
To do no contriv'd murder.   I lack iniquity
Sometimes to do me service.   Nine or ten times
I'd thought to have yerk'd him here under the ribs.
Oth. 'Tis better as it is.
Iago.   Nay, but he prated,   6
And spoke such scurvy and provoking terms
Against your honour
That, with the little godliness I have,
I did full hard forbear him.   But, I pray you, sir,   10
Are you fast married?   Be assur'd of this,

124. **odd-even**: midnight.   **dull**: dead.   128. **your allowance**: has your approval.   132. **from**: contrary to.   137. **extrava-gant**: vagabond.   **wheeling**: roving.   149. **check**: rebuke.   150. **cast**: dismiss.   152. **[stand]** (Pope).   *stands* QF.   153. **fathom**: capacity.   159. **Sagittary**: an inn (with a Centaur on its sign).   It has also been proposed that the word is a translation of *Frezzaria*, the Street of the Arrow-makers in Venice.   161. S.D. *night-gown*: dressing gown.   173. **property**: nature.   174. **abus'd**: deceived.   183. **[night]** Q.   *might* F.   184. **deserve**: reward.
Sc. ii, 5. **yerk'd**: stabbed.

That the magnifico is much belov'd,
And hath in his effect a voice potential
As double as the Duke's.   He will divorce you,
Or put upon you what restraint or grievance   15
The law, with all his might to enforce it on,
Will give him cable.
    Oth.   Let him do his spite;
My services which I have done the signiory
Shall out-tongue his complaints.   'Tis yet to
    know, —
Which, when I know that boasting is an honour,   20
I shall promulgate — I fetch my life and being
From men of royal siege, and my demerits
May speak unbonneted to as proud a fortune
As this that I have reach'd; for know, Iago,
But that I love the gentle Desdemona,   25
I would not my unhoused free condition
Put into circumscription and confine
For the sea's worth.   But, look! what lights come
    yond?

Enter CASSIO, *with lights,* Officers, *and torches.*

    Iago. Those are the raised father and his friends.
You were best go in.
    Oth.   Not I; I must be found.   30
My parts, my title, and my perfect soul
Shall manifest me rightly.   Is it they?
    Iago. By Janus, I think no.
    Oth. The servants of the Duke, and my lieutenant.
The goodness of the night upon you, friends!   35
What is the news?
    Cas.   The Duke does greet you, general,
And he requires your haste-post-haste appearance,
Even on the instant.
    Oth.   What is the matter, think you?
    Cas. Something from Cyprus, as I may divine;
It is a business of some heat.   The galleys   40
Have sent a dozen sequent messengers
This very night at one another's heels,
And many of the consuls, rais'd and met,
Are at the Duke's already.   You have been hotly
    call'd for;
When, being not at your lodging to be found,   45
The Senate hath sent about three several quests
To search you out.
    Oth.   'Tis well I am found by you.
I will but spend a word here in the house.
And go with you.   [*Exit.*
    Cas.   Ancient, what makes he here?
    Iago. Faith, he to-night hath boarded a land
    carack.   50
If it prove lawful prize, he's made for ever.

    Cas. I do not understand.
    Iago.   He's married.
    Cas.   To who?

[*Re-enter* OTHELLO.]

    Iago. Marry, to — Come, captain, will you go?
    Oth.   Have with you.
    Cas. Here comes another troop to seek for you.

Enter BRABANTIO, RODERIGO, *and* OFFICERS
    with torches and weapons.

    Iago. It is Brabantio.   General, be advis'd;   55
He comes to bad intent.
    Oth.   Holla! stand there!
    Rod. Signior, it is the Moor.
    Bra.   Down with him, thief!
                    [*They draw on both sides.*]
    Iago. You, Roderigo! come, sir, I am for you.
    Oth. Keep up your bright swords, for the dew will
    rust them.
Good signior, you shall more command with years
Than with your weapons.   61
    Bra. O thou foul thief, where hast thou stow'd
    my daughter?
Damn'd as thou art, thou hast enchanted her;
For I'll refer me to all things of sense,
If she in chains of magic were not bound,   65
Whether a maid so tender, fair, and happy,
So opposite to marriage that she shunn'd
The wealthy curled darlings of our nation,
Would ever have, t' incur a general mock,
Run from her guardage to the sooty bosom   70
Of such a thing as thou — to fear, not to delight.
Judge me the world, if 'tis not gross in sense
That thou hast practis'd on her with foul charms,
Abus'd her delicate youth with drugs or minerals
That weakens motion.   I'll have 't disputed on;   75
'Tis probable, and palpable to thinking.
I therefore apprehend and do attach thee
For an abuser of the world, a practiser
Of arts inhibited and out of warrant.
Lay hold upon him; if he do resist,   80
Subdue him at his peril.
    Oth.   Hold your hands,
Both you of my inclining, and the rest.
Were it my cue to fight, I should have known it
Without a prompter.   [Where] will you that I go
To answer this your charge?
    Bra.   To prison, till fit time
Of law and course of direct session   86
Call thee to answer.
    Oth.   What if [I] do obey?

---

14. double: strong.   22. siege: rank.   demerits: deserts.   23. unbonneted: without taking my hat off, on equal terms.
26. unhoused: unconfined.   31. perfect soul: clear conscience.   40. galleys: i.e., officers of the galleys.   50. carack: large
trading ship.   72. gross in sense: perfectly clear.   75. motion: will power.   disputed on: argued legally.   77. attach: arrest.
79. inhibited: prohibited.   out of warrant: unjustifiable.   82. inclining: party.   84. [Where] Q.   *Whether* F.   *Whither* F₂.
86. course ... session: due course of law.   87. [I] Q.   Om. F.

How may the Duke be therewith satisfi'd,
Whose messengers are here about my side
Upon some present business of the state   90
To bring me to him?
  Off.   'Tis true, most worthy signior.
The Duke 's in council; and your noble self,
I am sure, is sent for.
  Bra.   How! the Duke in council!
In this time of the night! Bring him away;
Mine's not an idle cause. The Duke himself,   95
Or any of my brothers of the state,
Cannot but feel this wrong as 'twere their own;
For if such actions may have passage free,
Bond-slaves and pagans shall our statesmen be.
                                           [*Exeunt.*

SCENE III. [*A council-chamber.*]

The DUKE *and* SENATORS *set at a table, with
lights;* OFFICERS *attending.*

  Duke. There is no composition in [these] news
That gives them credit.
  1. Sen.   Indeed, they are disproportion'd;
My letters say a hundred and seven galleys.
  Duke. And mine, a hundred forty.
  2. Sen.   And mine, two hundred!
But though they jump not on a just account, —   5
As in these cases, where the aim reports,
'Tis oft with difference — yet do they all confirm
A Turkish fleet, and bearing up to Cyprus.
  Duke. Nay, it is possible enough to judgement.
I do not so secure me in the error   10
But the main article I do approve
In fearful sense.
  Sailor. (*Within.*) What, ho! what, ho! what, ho!

Enter a SAILOR.

  Off. A messenger from the galleys.
  Duke.   Now, what's the business?
  Sail. The Turkish preparation makes for Rhodes;
So was I bid report here to the state   15
By Signior Angelo.
  Duke. How say you by this change?
  1. Sen.   This cannot be,
By no assay of reason; 'tis a pageant,
To keep us in false gaze. When we consider
Th' importance of Cyprus to the Turk,   20
And let ourselves again but understand
That, as it more concerns the Turk than Rhodes,
So may he with more facile question bear it,
For that it stands not in such warlike brace,
But altogether lacks th' abilities   25
That Rhodes is dress'd in; if we make thought of
     this,

We must not think the Turk is so unskilful
To leave that latest which concerns him first,
Neglecting an attempt of ease and gain
To wake and wage a danger profitless.   30
  Duke. Nay, in all confidence, he's not for Rhodes.
  Off. Here is more news.

Enter a MESSENGER.

  Mess. The Ottomites, reverend and gracious,
Steering with due course towards the isle of Rhodes,
Have there injointed them with an after fleet. 35
  1. Sen. Ay, so I thought. How many, as you
     guess?
  Mess. Of thirty sail; and now they do restem
Their backward course, bearing with frank appear-
     ance
Their purposes toward Cyprus. Signior Montano,
Your trusty and most valiant servitor,   40
With his free duty recommends you thus,
And prays you to believe him.
  Duke. 'Tis certain, then, for Cyprus.
Marcus Luccicos, is not he in town?
  1. Sen. He's now in Florence.   45
  Duke. Write from us to him; post-post-haste dis-
     patch.
  1. Sen. Here comes Brabantio and the valiant
     Moor.

Enter BRABANTIO, OTHELLO, CASSIO, IAGO,
RODERIGO, *and* Officers.

  Duke. Valiant Othello, we must straight employ
     you
Against the general enemy Ottoman.
[*To Brabantio.*] I did not see you; welcome, gentle
     signior;   50
We lack'd your counsel and your help to-night.
  Bra. So did I yours. Good your Grace, pardon
     me;
Neither my place nor aught I heard of business
Hath rais'd me from my bed, nor doth the general
     care
Take hold on me; for my particular grief   55
Is of so flood-gate and o'erbearing nature
That it englutts and swallows other sorrows
And it is still itself.
  Duke.   Why, what's the matter?
  Bra. My daughter! O, my daughter!
  Sen.   Dead?
  Bra.   Ay, to me;   60
She is abus'd, stol'n from me, and corrupted
By spells and medicines bought of mountebanks;
For nature so prepost'rously to err,
Being not deficient, blind, or lame of sense,
Sans witchcraft could not.

Sc. iii, 1. composition: consistency. [these] Q. *this* F. 5. jump: agree. just: exact. 6. the...reports: the reports
are conjectural. 10. so...error: take such assurance from the disagreement. 11. approve: assent to. 18. pageant: pretence. 23. with...it: capture it more easily. 24. brace: defense. 35. after: i.e., sent after. 55. particular: personal.

Duke. Whoe'er he be that in this foul proceeding
Hath thus beguil'd your daughter of herself   66
And you of her, the bloody book of law
You shall yourself read in the bitter letter
After your own sense, yea, though our proper son
Stood in your action.

  Bra.   Humbly I thank your Grace.
Here is the man, — this Moor, whom now, it seems,
Your special mandate for the state affairs   72
Hath hither brought.

  All.   We are very sorry for 't.

  Duke. [*To Othello.*] What, in your own part, can
  you say to this?

  Bra. Nothing, but this is so.   75

  Oth. Most potent, grave, and reverend signiors,
My very noble and approv'd good masters,
That I have ta'en away this old man's daughter,
It is most true; true, I have married her:
The very head and front of my offending   80
Hath this extent, no more.   Rude am I in my
  speech,
And little bless'd with the soft phrase of peace;
For since these arms of mine had seven years' pith
Till now, some nine moons wasted, they have us'd
Their dearest action in the tented field,   85
And little of this great world can I speak
More than pertains to feats of broils and battle,
And therefore little shall I grace my cause
In speaking for myself.   Yet, by your gracious
  patience,
I will a round unvarnish'd tale deliver   90
Of my whole course of love — what **drugs, what**
  charms,
What conjuration, and what mighty **magic,**
(For such proceeding I am charg'd withal,)
I won his daughter.

  Bra.   A maiden never bold;
Of spirit so still and quiet that her motion   95
Blush'd at herself; and she, in spite of **nature,**
Of years, of country, credit, everything,
To fall in love with what she fear'd to look **on!**
It is a judgement maim'd and most imperfect
That will confess perfection so could err   100
Against all rules of nature, and must be driven
To find out practices of cunning hell,
Why this should be.   I therefore vouch again
That with some mixtures powerful o'er the blood,
Or with some dram conjur'd to this effect,   105
He wrought upon her.

  [*Duke.*]   To vouch this is no proof,
Without more wider and more overt test
Than these thin habits and poor likelihoods
Of modern seeming do prefer against him.

[*1.*] *Sen.* But, Othello, speak.   110
Did you by indirect and forced courses
Subdue and poison this young maid's affections?
Or came it by request and such fair question
As soul to soul affordeth?

  Oth.   I do beseech you,
Send for the lady to the Sagittary,   115
And let her speak of me before her father.
If you do find me foul in her report,
The trust, the office I do hold of you,
Not only take away, but let your sentence
Even fall upon my life.

  Duke.   Fetch Desdemona hither.
        [*Exeunt two or three.*

  Oth. Ancient, conduct them; you best know the
  place.   [*Exit Iago.*]   121
And, till she come, as truly as to heaven
I do confess the vices of my blood,
So justly to your grave ears I'll present
How I did thrive in this fair lady's love,   125
And she in mine.

  Duke. Say it, Othello.

  Oth. Her father lov'd me; oft invited me;
Still question'd me the story of my life
From year to year, the battles, sieges, fortunes,   130
That I have pass'd.
I ran it through, even from my boyish days
To the very moment that he bade me tell it;
Wherein I spoke of most disastrous chances,
Of moving accidents by flood and field,   135
Of hair-breadth scapes i' th' imminent deadly
  breach,
Of being taken by the insolent foe
And sold to slavery, of my redemption **thence**
And portance in my travel's history;
Wherein of antres vast and deserts idle,   140
Rough quarries, rocks, [and] hills whose heads touch
  heaven,
It was my hint to speak, — such was my process, —
And of the Cannibals that each other eat,
The Anthropophagi, and men whose heads
[Do grow] beneath their shoulders.   These to hear
Would Desdemona seriously incline;   146
But still the house-affairs would draw her thence,
Which ever as she could with haste dispatch,
She'd come again, and with a greedy ear
Devour up my discourse: which I observing,   150
Took once a pliant hour, and found good means
To draw from her a prayer of earnest heart
That I would all my pilgrimage dilate,
Whereof by parcels she had something heard,
But not [intentively].   I did consent,   155
And often did beguile her of her tears

---

90. **round:** plain.   95. **motion:** impulses.   106. [*Duke*] Q.   Om. F.   108. **thin habits:** slight semblances.   109. **modern:** ordinary, trivial.   139. **portance:** behavior.   140. **antres:** caves.   **idle:** barren.   141. [**and**] Q.   Om. F.   142. **hint:** occasion.   145. [**Do grow**] Q.   *Grew* F.   **These** Q2.   *These things* F.   151. **pliant:** convenient.   155. [**intentively**] Q: attentively. *instinctively* F.

When I did speak of some distressful stroke
That my youth suffer'd.   My story being done,
She gave me for my pains a world of [sighs].
She swore, in faith, 'twas strange, 'twas passing
    strange,   160
'Twas pitiful, 'twas wondrous pitiful.
She wish'd she had not heard it; yet she wish'd
That Heaven had made her such a man.   She
    thank'd me,
And bade me, if I had a friend that lov'd her,
I should but teach him how to tell my story,   165
And that would woo her.   Upon this hint I spake:
She lov'd me for the dangers I had pass'd,
And I lov'd her that she did pity them.
This only is the witchcraft I have us'd.
Here comes the lady; let her witness it.   170

    Enter DESDEMONA, IAGO, *and Attendants.*

    Duke. I think this tale would win my daughter too.
Good Brabantio,
Take up this mangled matter at the best;
Men do their broken weapons rather use
Than their bare hands.
    Bra.   I pray you, hear her speak.
If she confess that she was half the wooer,   176
Destruction on my head if my bad blame
Light on the man!   Come hither, gentle mistress.
Do you perceive in all this noble company
Where most you owe obedience?
    Des.   My noble father,
I do perceive here a divided duty.   181
To you I am bound for life and education;
My life and education both do learn me
How to respect you; you are the lord of duty;
I am hitherto your daughter.   But here's my hus-
    band;   185
And so much duty as my mother show'd
To you, preferring you before her father,
So much I challenge that I may profess
Due to the Moor, my lord.
    Bra.   God be with you!   I have done.
Please it your Grace, on to the state-affairs.   190
I had rather to adopt a child than get it.
Come hither, Moor.
I here do give thee that with all my heart
Which, but thou hast already, with all my heart
I would keep from thee.   For your sake, jewel,   195
I am glad at soul I have no other child;
For thy escape would teach me tyranny,
To hang clogs on them.   I have done, my lord.
    Duke. Let me speak like yourself, and lay a sen-
    tence,

Which, as a grise or step, may help these lovers   200
[Into your favour].
When remedies are past, the griefs are ended
By seeing the worst, which late on hopes depended.
To mourn a mischief that is past and gone
Is the next way to draw new mischief on.   205
What cannot be preserv'd when fortune takes,
Patience her injury a mock'ry makes.
The robb'd that smiles steals something from the
    thief;
He robs himself that spends a bootless grief.
    Bra. So let the Turk of Cyprus us beguile;   210
We lose it not, so long as we can smile.
He bears the sentence well that nothing bears
But the free comfort which from thence he hears,
But he bears both the sentence and the sorrow
That, to pay grief, must of poor patience borrow.
These sentences, to sugar or to gall   216
Being strong on both sides, are equivocal.
But words are words; I never yet did hear
That the bruis'd heart was pierced through the
    ear.
I humbly beseech you, proceed to the affairs of
    state.   220
    Duke. The Turk with a most mighty preparation
makes for Cyprus.   Othello, the fortitude of the
place is best known to you; and though we have
there a substitute of most allowed sufficiency, yet
opinion, a sovereign mistress of effects, throws a
more safer voice on you.   You must therefore be
content to slubber the gloss of your new fortunes
with this more stubborn and boist'rous expedi-
tion.   229
    Oth. The tyrant custom, most grave senators,
Hath made the flinty and steel couch of war
My thrice-driven bed of down.   I do agnize
A natural and prompt alacrity
I find in hardness, and do undertake
These present wars against the Ottomites.   235
Most humbly therefore bending to your state,
I crave fit disposition for my wife,
Due reference of place and exhibition,
With such accommodation and besort
As levels with her breeding.
    Duke.   [If you please,   240
Be 't at her father's.]
    Bra.   I'll not have it so.
    Oth. Nor I.
    Des.   Nor I; [I would not] there reside,
To put my father in impatient thoughts
By being in his eye.   Most gracious Duke,
To my unfolding lend your prosperous ear;   245

---

159. [sighs] Q. *kisses* F.   166. **hint:** opportunity (not consciously given). Cf. l. 142.   199. **like yourself:** as you should.
200. **grise:** degree.   201. [Into...favour] Q. Om. F.   216. **sentences:** maxims.   217. **equivocal:** equal.   222. **fortitude:**
strength, fortification.   224. **allowed:** admitted.   225. **sovereign** Q. *more sovereign* F.   227. **slubber:** sully.   232. **thrice
driven:** thoroughly sifted.   **agnize:** acknowledge.   238. **reference:** assignment.   **exhibition:** provision.   239. **besort:** company.   240. **levels with:** befits.   240-41. [If...father's] Q. *Why at her Fathers?* F.   242. [I...not] Q. *would I* F.
245. **prosperous:** propitious.

And let me find a charter in your voice
T' assist my simpleness.
   Duke. What would you, Desdemona?
   Des. That I [did] love the Moor to live with him,
My downright violence and storm of fortunes   250
May trumpet to the world. My heart's subdu'd
Even to the very quality of my lord.
I saw Othello's visage in his mind,
And to his honours and his valiant parts
Did I my soul and fortunes consecrate.   255
So that, dear lords, if I were left behind,
A moth of peace, and he go to the war,
The rites for [which] I love him are bereft me,
And I a heavy interim shall support
By his dear absence. Let me go with him.   260
   Oth. Let her have your voice.
Vouch with me, Heaven, I therefore beg it not
To please the palate of my appetite,
Nor to comply with heat, the young affects
In my defunct and proper satisfaction,   265
But to be free and bounteous to her mind;
And Heaven defend your good souls, that you think
I will your serious and great business scant
When she is with me. No, when light-wing'd toys
Of feather'd Cupid seel with wanton dullness   270
My speculative and offic'd instruments
That my disports corrupt and taint my business,
Let housewives make a skillet of my helm,
And all indign and base adversities
Make head against my estimation!   275
   Duke. Be it as you shall privately determine,
Either for her stay or going. Th' affair cries haste,
And speed must answer it.
   1. Sen.   You must away to-night.
   [*Des.* To-night, my lord?
   Duke.   This night.]
   Oth.   With all my heart.
   Duke. At nine i' th' morning here we'll meet
again.   280
Othello, leave some officer behind,
And he shall our commission bring to you,
And such things else of quality and respect
As doth import you.
   Oth.   So please your Grace, my ancient;
A man he is of honesty and trust.   285
To his conveyance I assign my wife,
With what else needful your good Grace shall think
To be sent after me.
   Duke.   Let it be so.
Good-night to every one. [*To Bra.*] And, noble
signior,

If virtue no delighted beauty lack,   290
Your son-in-law is far more fair than black.
   1. Sen. Adieu, brave Moor; use Desdemona well.
   Bra. Look to her, Moor, if thou hast eyes to see;
She has deceiv'd her father, and may thee.
             [*Exeunt* [*Duke, Senators, Officers, etc.*].
   Oth. My life upon her faith! Honest Iago,   295
My Desdemona must I leave to thee.
I prithee, let thy wife attend on her;
And bring them after in the best advantage.
Come, Desdemona; I have but an hour
Of love, of worldly matters and direction,   300
To spend with thee. We must obey the time.
            [*Exeunt Othello and Desdemona.*
   Rod. Iago, —
   Iago. What say'st thou, noble heart?
   Rod. What will I do, think'st thou?
   Iago. Why, go to bed and sleep.   305
   Rod. I will incontinently drown myself.
   Iago. If thou dost, I shall never love thee after.
Why, thou silly gentleman!
   Rod. It is silliness to live when to live is torment;
and then have we a prescription to die when Death is
our physician.   311
   Iago. O villanous! I have look'd upon the world
for four times seven years; and since I could distinguish betwixt a benefit and an injury, I never
found man that knew how to love himself. Ere I
would say I would drown myself for the love of a
guinea-hen, I would change my humanity with a
baboon.   318
   Rod. What should I do? I confess it is my
shame to be so fond, but it is not in my virtue to
amend it.   321
   Iago. Virtue! a fig! 'tis in ourselves that we are
thus or thus. Our bodies are our gardens, to the
which our wills are gardeners; so that if we will plant
nettles or sow lettuce, set hyssop and weed up   325
thyme, supply it with one gender of herbs or distract
it with many, either to have it sterile with idleness
or manured with industry, why, the power and corrigible authority of this lies in our wills. If the
[balance] of our lives had not one scale of reason   330
to poise another of sensuality, the blood and baseness of our natures would conduct us to most preposterous conclusions; but we have reason to cool
our raging motions, our carnal stings, our unbitted
lusts, whereof I take this that you call love to be a
sect or scion.   337
   Rod. It cannot be.
   Iago. It is merely a lust of the blood and a per-

---

246. **charter:** privilege. 249. **[did]** Q. Om. F. 250. **My . . . fortunes:** my precipitate assault upon my fortunes. 258. **[which]** Q. *why* F. 265. **defunct.** The modern meaning is here excluded, and no convincing explanation has been found. 267. **defend:** forbid. 270. **seel:** blind (from falconry). 271. **My . . . instruments:** my faculties whose office is to perceive. 274. **indign:** unworthy. 275. **estimation:** reputation. 279. [*Des.* **To-night . . . night**] Q. Om. F. 284. **import:** concern. 290. **delighted:** delightful. 298. **advantage:** opportunity. 306. **incontinently:** straightway. 325. **hyssop:** fragrant herb. 326. **gender:** kind. 329. **corrigible authority:** corrective power. 330. **[balance]** Q. *braine* F. 335. **motions:** appetites. 337. **sect or scion:** cutting or off-shoot.

mission of the will. Come, be a man! Drown thyself? drown cats and blind puppies! I have profess'd me thy friend, and I confess me knit to thy
deserving with cables of perdurable toughness; I
could never better stead thee than now. Put
money in thy purse; follow thou the wars; defeat 345
thy favour with an usurp'd beard. I say, put
money in thy purse. It cannot be long that Desdemona should continue her love to the Moor, — put
money in thy purse, — nor he his to her. It was a
violent commencement in her, and thou shalt 350
see an answerable sequestration. Put but money
in thy purse. These Moors are changeable in their
wills — fill thy purse with money; — the food that
to him now is as luscious as locusts, shall be to him
shortly as bitter as coloquintida. She must 355
change for youth; when she is sated with his body,
she will find the error of her choice; [she must have
change, she must:] therefore put money in thy
purse. If thou wilt needs damn thyself, do it a
more delicate way than drowning. Make all 360
the money thou canst. If sanctimony and a frail
vow betwixt an erring barbarian and a super-subtle
Venetian be not too hard for my wits and all the
tribe of hell, thou shalt enjoy her; therefore make
money. A pox of drowning thyself! it is clean 365
out of the way. Seek thou rather to be hang'd in
compassing thy joy than to be drown'd and go
without her.

Rod. Wilt thou be fast to my hopes, if I depend
on the issue?   370

Iago. Thou art sure of me. Go, make money.
I had told thee often, and I re-tell thee again and
again, I hate the Moor. My cause is hearted; thine
hath no less reason. Let us be conjunctive in our
revenge against him. If thou canst cuckold 375
him, thou dost thyself a pleasure, me a sport. There
are many events in the womb of time which will be
delivered. Traverse! go, provide thy money. We
will have more of this to-morrow. Adieu.   380

Rod. Where shall we meet i' th' morning?

Iago. At my lodging.

Rod. I'll be with thee betimes.

Iago. Go to; farewell. Do you hear, Roderigo?

[*Rod.* What say you?]   386

Iago. No more of drowning, do you hear?

Rod. I am chang'd;] I'll sell all my land.   [*Exit.*

Iago. Thus do I ever make my fool my purse;
For I mine own gain'd knowledge should profane
If I would time expend with such a snipe   391
But for my sport and profit. I hate the Moor;

And it is thought abroad that 'twixt my sheets
He has done my office. I know not if 't be true;
But I, for mere suspicion in that kind,   395
Will do as if for surety. He holds me well;
The better shall my purpose work on him.
Cassio's a proper man: let me see now:
To get his place and to plume up my will
In double knavery — How, how? — Let's see: —
After some time, to abuse Othello's ear   401
That he is too familiar with his wife.
He hath a person and a smooth dispose
To be suspected, fram'd to make women false.
The Moor is of a free and open nature,   405
That thinks men honest that but seem to be so,
And will as tenderly be led by th' nose
As asses are.
I have't. It is engend'red. Hell and night
Must bring this monstrous birth to the world's
     light.   [*Exit.* 410

ACT II

SCENE I. [*A sea-port in Cyprus. An open
place near the quay.*]

Enter MONTANO *and two* GENTLEMEN.

Mon. What from the cape can you discern at sea?

1. Gent. Nothing at all; it is a high-wrought flood.
I cannot, 'twixt the heaven and the main,
Descry a sail.

Mon. Methinks the wind hath spoke aloud at
     land;   5
A fuller blast ne'er shook our battlements.
If it hath ruffian'd so upon the sea,
What ribs of oak, when mountains melt on them,
Can hold the mortise? What shall we hear of this?

2. Gent. A segregation of the Turkish fleet.   10
For do but stand upon the foaming shore,
The chidden billow seems to pelt the clouds;
The wind-shak'd surge, with high and monstrous
     mane,
Seems to cast water on the burning Bear
And quench the guards of th' ever-fixed Pole.   15
I never did like molestation view
On the enchafed flood.

Mon.   If that the Turkish fleet
Be not enshelter'd and embay'd, they are drown'd;
It is impossible to bear it out.

Enter a third GENTLEMAN.

3. Gent. News, lads! our wars are done.   20

---

343. **perdurable:** eternal.   345-46. **defeat thy favour:** disguise thy face.   351. **sequestration:** separation.   354. **locusts:**
the fruit of the carob tree.   355. **coloquintida:** a bitter fruit.   357-58. [she ... she must] Q. Om. F.   369-70. **depend ...
issue:** rely on the outcome.   373. **hearted:** heart-felt.   374. **conjunctive:** united.   379. **Traverse:** forward.   386-88. [*Rod.*
What ... chang'd] Q. Om. F.   391. **snipe:** woodcock, a silly bird.   398. **proper:** handsome.   399-400. **plume ... In:** brace
myself to.   403. **dispose:** disposition.
     Act II, sc. i, 9. hold the mortise: hold their joints together.   10. **segregation:** dispersion.   15. **guards:** stars in the Little
Bear in line with the pole star.

The desperate tempest hath so bang'd the Turks,
That their designment halts.   A noble ship of
Venice
Hath seen a grievous wreck and sufferance
On most part of their fleet.
     Mon. How! is this true?
     3. Gent.   The ship is here put in.
A Veronese, Michael Cassio,   26
Lieutenant to the warlike Moor Othello,
Is come on shore; the Moor himself at sea,
And is in full commission here for Cyprus.
     Mon. I am glad on't; 'tis a worthy governor.   30
     3. Gent. But this same Cassio, though he speak of
comfort
Touching the Turkish loss, yet he looks sadly
And prays the Moor be safe, for they were parted
With foul and violent tempest.
     Mon.   Pray heavens he be;
For I have serv'd him, and the man commands   35
Like a full soldier.   Let's to the seaside, ho!
As well to see the vessel that's come in
As to throw out our eyes for brave Othello,
Even till we make the main and th' aerial blue
An indistinct regard.
     3. Gent.   Come, let's do so;   40
For every minute is expectancy
Of more arrivance.

Enter CASSIO.

     Cas. Thanks, you the valiant of this warlike isle,
That so approve the Moor!   O, let the heavens
Give him defence against the elements,   45
For I have lost him on a dangerous sea.
     Mon. Is he well shipp'd?
     Cas. His bark is stoutly timber'd, and his pilot
Of very expert and approv'd allowance;
Therefore my hopes, not surfeited to death,   50
Stand in bold cure.   [*Within,* "A sail, a sail, a sail!"]

Enter a [*fourth* GENTLEMAN].

     Cas. What noise?
     [*4.*] *Gent.* The town is empty; on the brow o' th'
sea
Stand ranks of people, and they cry, "A sail!"   54
     Cas. My hopes do shape him for the governor.
                                        [*A shot.*
     2. Gent. They do discharge their shot of courtesy.
Our friends at least.
     Cas.   I pray you, sir, go forth,
And give us truth who 'tis that is arriv'd.
     2. Gent. I shall.   [*Exit.*

     Mon. But, good Lieutenant, is your General
wiv'd?   60
     Cas. Most fortunately.   He hath achiev'd a maid
That paragons description and wild fame;
One that excels the quirks of blazoning pens,
And in th' essential vesture of creation
Does tire the [ingener].

Re-enter second GENTLEMAN.

                    How now! who has put in?
     2. Gent. 'Tis one Iago, ancient to the general.   66
     Cas. He has had most favourable and happy
speed.
Tempests themselves, high seas, and howling winds,
The gutter'd rocks and congregated sands,
Traitors ensteep'd to enclog the guiltless keel,   70
As having sense of beauty, do omit
Their mortal natures, letting go safely by
The divine Desdemona.
     Mon.   What is she?
     Cas. She that I spake of, our great captain's cap-
tain,
Left in the conduct of the bold Iago,   75
Whose footing here anticipates our thoughts
A se'nnight's speed.   Great Jove, Othello guard,
And swell his sail with thine own powerful breath,
That he may bless this bay with his tall ship,
Make love's quick pants in Desdemona's arms,   80
Give renew'd fire to our extinct spirits,
[And bring all Cyprus comfort!]

Enter DESDEMONA, EMILIA, IAGO, RODERIGO
[*and Attendants*].

                              O, behold,
The riches of the ship is come on shore!
You men of Cyprus, let her have your knees.
Hail to thee, lady! and the grace of heaven,   85
Before, behind thee, and on every hand,
Enwheel thee round!
     Des.   I thank you, valiant Cassio.
What tidings can you tell [me] of my lord?
     Cas. He is not yet arriv'd; nor know I aught
But that he's well and will be shortly here.   90
     Des. O, but I fear — How lost you company?
     Cas. The great contention of sea and skies
Parted our fellowship. — But, hark! a sail.
          [*Within,* "A sail, a sail!"]   [*Guns heard.*]
     2. Gent. They give [their] greeting to the citadel.
This likewise is a friend.
     Cas.   See for the news.   96
                                   [*Exit Gentleman.*]

23. **sufferance:** disaster.   26. **A Veronese.** In I.i.20 Cassio is called a Florentine.   49. **approv'd allowance:** tested repute.
50–51. **my hopes . . . cure.**   The sense seems to be: "My hopes, though far from being nourished to excess, yet stand a good chance of being fulfilled."   62. **paragons:** excels.   63. **quirks:** flourishes.   **blazoning:** praising.   64. **essential . . . creation:** i.e., just as she is, in her essential quality.   65. [ingener] (Steevens conj.): inventor (of praise).   *Ingeniver* F.   For *tire the* [*ingener*] Q reads *beare an excellency.*   69. **gutter'd:** furrowed, jagged.   70. **ensteep'd:** submerged.   72. **mortal:** deadly. 82. [And . . . comfort] Q.   Om. F.   88. [me] Q.   Om. F.   95. [their] Q.   *this* F.

Good ancient, you are welcome. [*To Emilia.*]
Welcome, mistress.
Let it not gall your patience, good Iago,
That I extend my manners; 'tis my breeding
That gives me this bold show of courtesy.   100
                           [*Kissing her.*]
Iago. Sir, would she give you so much of her lips
As of her tongue she oft bestows on me,
You'd have enough.
   Des.   Alas, she has no speech.
   Iago. In faith, too much;
I find it still, when I have [list] to sleep.   105
Marry, before your ladyship, I grant,
She puts her tongue a little in her heart,
And chides with thinking.
   Emil. You have little cause to say so.
   Iago. Come on, come on; you are pictures out of
     door,   110
Bells in your parlours, wild-cats in your kitchens,
Saints in your injuries, devils being offended,
Players in your housewifery, and housewives in your
     beds.
   Des. O, fie upon thee, slanderer!
   Iago. Nay, it is true, or else I am a Turk.   115
You rise to play and go to bed to work.
   Emil. You shall not write my praise.
   Iago.   No, let me not.
   Des. What wouldst thou write of me, if thou
     shouldst praise me?
   Iago. O gentle lady, do not put me to't;
For I am nothing if not critical.   120
   Des. Come on, assay. — There's one gone to the
     harbour?
   Iago. Ay, madam.
   Des. I am not merry; but I do beguile
The thing I am by seeming otherwise. —
Come, how wouldst thou praise me?   125
   Iago. I am about it; but indeed my invention
Comes from my pate as birdlime does from frieze;
It plucks out brains and all. But my Muse labours,
And thus she is deliver'd:
If she be fair and wise, fairness and wit,   130
The one 's for use, the other useth it.
   Des. Well prais'd! How if she be black and
     witty?
   Iago. If she be black, and thereto have a wit,
She'll find a white that shall her blackness fit.
   Des. Worse and worse.   135
   Emil. How if fair and foolish?
   Iago. She never yet was foolish that was fair;
For even her folly help'd her to an heir.

   Des. These are old fond paradoxes to make fools
laugh i' th' alehouse. What miserable praise hast
thou for her that's foul and foolish?   141
   Iago. There's none so foul and foolish thereunto,
But does foul pranks which fair and wise ones do.
   Des. O heavy ignorance! thou praisest the worst
best. But what praise couldst thou bestow on a
deserving woman indeed, one that, in the authority
of her merit, did justly put on the vouch of very
malice itself?   148
   Iago. She that was ever fair and never proud,
Had tongue at will and yet was never loud,
Never lack'd gold and yet went never gay,
Fled from her wish and yet said, "Now I may;"
She that being ang'red, her revenge being nigh,
Bade her wrong stay and her displeasure fly;
She that in wisdom never was so frail   155
To change the cod's head for the salmon's tail;
She that could think and ne'er disclose her mind,
See suitors following and not look behind,
She was a wight, if ever such wights were, —
   Des. To do what?   160
   Iago. To suckle fools and chronicle small beer.
   Des. O most lame and impotent conclusion! Do
not learn of him, Emilia, though he be thy husband.
How say you, Cassio? Is he not a most profane and
liberal counsellor?   165
   Cas. He speaks home, madam. You may relish
him more in the soldier than in the scholar.
   Iago. [*Aside.*] He takes her by the palm; ay,
well said, whisper. With as little a web as this will
I ensnare as great a fly as Cassio. Ay, smile 170
upon her, do; I will gyve thee in thine own courtship.
— You say true; 'tis so, indeed. — If such tricks as
these strip you out of your lieutenantry, it had been
better you had not kiss'd your three fingers so oft,
which now again you are most apt to play the sir 175
in. Very good; well kiss'd! an excellent curtsy! 'Tis
so, indeed. Yet again your fingers to your lips?
Would they were clyster-pipes for your sake!
(*Trumpet within.*) — The Moor! I know his
trumpet.   180
   Cas. 'Tis truly so.
   Des. Let's meet him and receive him.
   Cas. Lo, where he comes!

       Enter OTHELLO *and Attendants.*

   Oth. O my fair warrior!
   Des.   My dear Othello!
   Oth. It gives me wonder great as my content 185
To see you here before me. O my soul's joy!

---

105. [list] Q: inclination. *leave* F. 108. **with thinking:** i.e., without words. 110–13. **Come ... beds.** So Q. Prose in F.
111. **Bells:** i.e., clanging tongues. 112. **Saints ... injuries:** i.e., you offend sanctimoniously. 113. **Players:** triflers.
housewives: hussies. 126–29. **I am ... deliver'd.** So Q. Prose in F. 132. **black:** brunette. 134. **white:** with a pun on
wight (person). 147–48. **put ... vouch:** compel the testimony. 156. **cod ... tail:** to take the worthless in exchange for the
worthy. 161. **chronicle small beer:** i.e., to keep petty accounts. 165. **liberal:** free-spoken. 169. **well said:** well done.
171. **gyve:** fetter, entangle. **courtship:** courtesy. 175. **sir:** gentleman. 178. **clyster-pipes:** syringes.

If after every tempest come such calms,
May the winds blow till they have waken'd
    death!
And let the labouring bark climb hills of seas
Olympus-high, and duck again as low   190
As hell's from heaven! If it were now to die,
'Twere now to be most happy; for, I fear,
My soul hath her content so absolute
That not another comfort like to this
Succeeds in unknown fate.

Des.   The heavens forbid 195
But that our lovés and comforts should increase,
Even as our days do grow!

Oth.   Amen to that, sweet powers!
I cannot speak enough of this content;
It stops me here; it is too much of joy.
And this, and this, the greatest discords be 200
                  [*Kissing her.*
That e'er our hearts shall make!

Iago. [*Aside.*] O, you are well tun'd now!
But I'll set down the pegs that make this music,
As honest as I am.

Oth.   Come, let us to the castle.
News, friends: our wars are done, the Turks are
    drown'd.
How does my old acquaintance of this isle? 205
Honey, you shall be well desir'd in Cyprus;
I have found great love amongst them. O my sweet,
I prattle out of fashion, and I dote
In mine own comforts. I prithee, good Iago,
Go to the bay and disembark my coffers. 210
Bring thou the master to the citadel;
He is a good one, and his worthiness
Does challenge much respect. Come, Desdemona,
Once more, well met at Cyprus. 214
    [*Exeunt Othello, Desdemona [and Attendants].*

Iago. Do thou meet me presently at the harbour.
— Come [hither]. If thou be'st valiant, — as, they
say, base men being in love have then a nobility in
their natures more than is native to them, — list me.
The lieutenant to-night watches on the court of
guard; — first, I must tell thee this: Desdemona is
directly in love with him. 221

Rod. With him! why, 'tis not possible.

Iago. Lay thy finger thus, and let thy soul be instructed. Mark me with what violence she first
lov'd the Moor, but for bragging and telling her 225
fantastical lies. To love him still for prating, —
let not thy discreet heart think it. Her eye must be
fed; and what delight shall she have to look on the
devil? When the blood is made dull with the act of
sport, there should be, [again] to inflame it and 230
to give satiety a fresh appetite, loveliness in favour,
sympathy in years, manners, and beauties; all

which the Moor is defective in. Now, for want of
these requir'd conveniences, her delicate tenderness
will find itself abus'd, begin to heave the gorge, 235
disrelish and abhor the Moor. Very nature will instruct her in it and compel her to some second
choice. Now, sir, this granted, — as it is a most
pregnant and unforc'd position — who stands so
eminent in the degree of this fortune as Cassio 240
does? a knave very voluble; no further conscionable than in putting on the mere form of civil and
humane seeming, for the better compassing of his
salt and most hidden loose affection? Why, none;
why, none; a slipper and subtle knave, a finder 245
of occasion, that has an eye can stamp and counterfeit advantages, though true advantage never present itself; a devilish knave. Besides, the knave is
handsome, young, and hath all those requisites 250
in him that folly and green minds look after; a pestilent complete knave, and the woman hath found him
already.

Rod. I cannot believe that in her; she's full of
most bless'd condition. 255

Iago. Bless'd fig's-end! The wine she drinks is
made of grapes. If she had been bless'd, she would
never have lov'd the Moor. Bless'd pudding!
Didst thou not see her paddle with the palm of his
hand? Didst not mark that? 260

Rod. Yes, that I did; but that was but courtesy.

Iago. Lechery, by this hand; an index and
obscure prologue to the history of lust and foul
thoughts. They met so near with their lips
that their breaths embrac'd together. Villan- 265
ous thoughts, Roderigo! When these [mutualities]
so marshal the way, hard at hand comes the master
and main exercise, th' incorporate conclusion.
Pish! But, sir, be you rul'd by me; I have 270
brought you from Venice. Watch you to-night; for
the command, I'll lay 't upon you. Cassio knows
you not. I'll not be far from you. Do you find
some occasion to anger Cassio, either by speaking
too loud, or tainting his discipline; or from what 275
other course you please, which the time shall more
favourably minister.

Rod. Well?

Iago. Sir, he's rash and very sudden in choler,
and haply may strike at you. Provoke him,
that he may; for even out of that will I cause 280
these of Cyprus to mutiny, whose qualification shall
come into no true taste again but by the displanting
of Cassio. So shall you have a shorter journey to
your desires by the means I shall then have to 285
prefer them; and the impediment most profitably
removed, without the which there were no expectation of our prosperity.

---

206. **desir'd:** beloved. 211. **master:** ship's master. 216. **[hither]** Q. *thither* F. 230. **[again]** Q. *a game* F. 235.
heave the gorge: be nauseated. 239. **pregnant:** evident. 241. **conscionable:** conscientious. 244. **salt:** lewd. 245. **slipper:**
slippery. 255. **condition:** character. 266. **[mutualities]** Q: exchanges. *mutabilities* F. 281. **qualification:** appeasement.

Rod. I will do this, if you can bring it to any
opportunity.   290

Iago. I warrant thee. Meet me by and by at the
citadel; I must fetch his necessaries ashore. Farewell.

Rod. Adieu.   [*Exit.*

Iago. That Cassio loves her, I do well believe 't;
That she loves him, 'tis apt and of great credit;   296
The Moor, howbeit that I endure him not,
Is of a constant, loving, noble nature,
And I dare think he'll prove to Desdemona
A most dear husband. Now, I do love her too;   300
Not out of absolute lust, though peradventure
I stand accountant for as great a sin,
But partly led to diet my revenge,
For that I do suspect the lusty Moor
Hath leap'd into my seat; the thought whereof   305
Doth, like a poisonous mineral, gnaw my inwards;
And nothing can or shall content my soul
Till I am even'd with him, wife for [wife];
Or failing so, yet that I put the Moor
At least into a jealousy so strong   310
That judgement cannot cure. Which thing to do,
If this poor trash of Venice, whom I [trash]
For his quick hunting, stand the putting on,
I'll have our Michael Cassio on the hip,
Abuse him to the Moor in the [rank] garb —   315
For I fear Cassio with my night-cap too —
Make the Moor thank me, love me, and reward me
For making him egregiously an ass
And practising upon his peace and quiet
Even to madness. 'Tis here, but yet confus'd;   320
Knavery's plain face is never seen till us'd.   [*Exit.*

SCENE II. [*A street.*]

Enter Othello's HERALD, *with a proclamation*
[*People following*].

Her. It is Othello's pleasure, our noble and
valiant general, that, upon certain tidings now
arriv'd importing the mere perdition of the Turkish
fleet, every man put himself into triumph; some
to dance, some to make bonfires, each man to   5
what sport and revels his [addiction] leads him; for,
beside these beneficial news, it is the celebration of
his nuptial. So much was his pleasure should be
proclaimed. All offices are open, and there is full
liberty of feasting from this present hour of five   10
till the bell have told eleven. [Heaven] bless the isle
of Cyprus and our noble general Othello!   [*Exeunt.*

[SCENE III. *A hall in the castle.*]

Enter OTHELLO, DESDEMONA, CASSIO, *and
Attendants.*

Oth. Good Michael, look you to the guard to-
night.
Let's teach ourselves that honourable stop,
Not to outsport discretion.

Cas. Iago hath direction what to do;
But, notwithstanding, with my personal eye   5
Will I look to't.

Oth.   Iago is most honest.
Michael, good-night; to-morrow with your earliest
Let me have speech with you.   [*To Desdemona.*]
      Come, my dear love,
The purchase made, the fruits are to ensue;
That profit's yet to come 'tween me and you.   10
Good-night.

    [*Exeunt* [*Othello, Desdemona, and Attend-
ants*].

Enter IAGO.

Cas. Welcome, Iago; we must to the watch.

Iago. Not this hour, Lieutenant; 'tis not yet ten
o' th' clock. Our general cast us thus early for the
love of his Desdemona; who let us not therefore
blame. He hath not yet made wanton the night
with her; and she is sport for Jove.   17

Cas. She's a most exquisite lady.

Iago. And, I'll warrant her, full of game.

Cas. Indeed, she's a most fresh and delicate
creature.   21

Iago. What an eye she has! Methinks it sounds
a parley to provocation.

Cas. An inviting eye; and yet methinks right
modest.

Iago. And when she speaks, is it not an alarum to
love?   27

Cas. She is indeed perfection.

Iago. Well, happiness to their sheets! Come,
lieutenant, I have a stoup of wine; and here without
are a brace of Cyprus gallants that would fain have
a measure to the health of black Othello.   33

Cas. Not to-night, good Iago. I have very poor
and unhappy brains for drinking; I could well wish
courtesy would invent some other custom of entertainment.

Iago. O, they are our friends. But one cup; I'll
drink for you.   39

Cas. I have drunk but one cup to-night, and that

---

296. **apt:** natural. **of ... credit:** most credible. 308. **[wife]** Q. **wist** F. 312. **trash:** worthless fellow. **[trash]** (Steevens):
check. *trace* F. *crush* Q. 313. **putting on:** inciting. 315. **[rank]** Q: gross. *right* F. **garb:** manner. 319. **practising
upon:** plotting against.

Sc. ii, 3. **mere:** utter. 6. **[addiction]** Q₂: inclination. *addition* F. *minde* Q. 9. **offices:** kitchens, etc. 11. **[Heaven]** Q.
Om. F.

Sc. iii, 14. **cast:** dismissed.

was craftily qualified too, and, behold, what innova-
tion it makes here. I am unfortunate in the infirm-
ity, and dare not task my weakness with any
more. 44
  Iago. What, man! 'tis a night of revels. The
gallants desire it.
  Cas. Where are they?
  Iago. Here at the door; I pray you, call them in.
  Cas. I'll do't; but it dislikes me. [*Exit.*
  Iago. If I can fasten but one cup upon him, 50
With that which he hath drunk to-night already,
He'll be as full of quarrel and offence
As my young mistress' dog. Now, my sick fool
    Roderigo,
Whom love hath turn'd almost the wrong side out,
To Desdemona hath to-night carous'd 55
Potations pottle-deep; and he's to watch.
Three [lads] of Cyprus, noble swelling spirits
That hold their honours in a wary distance,
The very elements of this warlike isle,
Have I to-night fluster'd with flowing cups, 60
And they watch too. Now, 'mongst this flock of
    drunkards
Am I to put our Cassio in some action
That may offend the isle. But here they come.

    Re-enter CASSIO; *with him* MONTANO *and*
    GENTLEMEN [*Servants follow with wine*].

If consequence do but approve my dream,
My boat sails freely, both with wind and stream. 65
  Cas. 'Fore [God], they have given me a rouse
already.
  Mon. Good faith, a little one; not past a pint, as I
am a soldier.
  Iago. Some wine, ho! 70
[*Sings.*] "And let me the canakin clink, clink;
    And let me the canakin clink.
      A soldier's a man;
      O, man's life's but a span;
    Why, then, let a soldier drink." 75
Some wine, boys!
  Cas. 'Fore [God], an excellent song.
  Iago. I learn'd it in England, where, indeed, they
are most potent in potting; your Dane, your Ger-
man, and your swag-belli'd Hollander — Drink, ho!
— are nothing to your English. 81
  Cas. Is your Englishman so exquisite in his
drinking?
  Iago. Why, he drinks you, with facility, your
Dane dead drunk; he sweats not to overthrow your
Almain; he gives your Hollander a vomit ere the
next pottle can be fill'd. 87
  Cas. To the health of our general!

  Mon. I am for it, Lieutenant; and I'll do you
justice. 90
  Iago. O sweet England!
  "King Stephen was and-a worthy peer,
    His breeches cost him but a crown;
  He held them sixpence all too dear,
    With that he call'd the tailor lown. 95

  "He was a wight of high renown,
    And thou art but of low degree.
  'Tis pride that pulls the country down;
    And take thy auld cloak about thee."
Some wine, ho! 100
  Cas. Why, this is a more exquisite song than the
other.
  Iago. Will you hear 't again?
  Cas. No; for I hold him to be unworthy of his
place that does those things. Well, [God's] above
all; and there be souls must be saved, and there be
souls must not be saved. 107
  Iago. It's true, good Lieutenant.
  Cas. For mine own part — no offence to the
general, nor any man of quality — I hope to be
saved. 111
  Iago. And so do I too, Lieutenant.
  Cas. Ay, but, by your leave, not before me; the
lieutenant is to be saved before the ancient. Let's
have no more of this; let's to our affairs. — 115
[God] forgive us our sins! — Gentlemen, let's look to
our business. Do not think, gentlemen, I am drunk.
This is my ancient; this is my right hand, and this
is my left. I am not drunk now; I can stand well
enough, and I speak well enough. 120
  Gent. Excellent well.
  Cas. Why, very well then; you must not think
then that I am drunk. [*Exit.*
  Mon. To the platform, masters; come, let's set
the watch. 125
  Iago. You see this fellow that is gone before:
He is a soldier fit to stand by Cæsar
And give direction; and do but see his vice.
'Tis to his virtue a just equinox,
The one as long as th' other; 'tis pity of him. 130
I fear the trust Othello puts him in,
On some odd time of his infirmity,
Will shake this island.
  Mon.   But is he often thus?
  Iago. 'Tis evermore his prologue to his sleep.
He'll watch the horologe a double set 135
If drink rock not his cradle.
  Mon.   It were well
The general were put in mind of it.
Perhaps he sees it not; or his good nature

---

  41. **craftily qualified:** slyly diluted. 49. **it dislikes me:** I don't want to. 56. **pottle-deep:** to the bottom of the tankard.
57. **[lads]** Q. *else* F. 58. **hold ... distance:** i.e., are quick to quarrel. 59. **very elements:** true representatives. 66.
rouse: bumper. 86. **Almain:** German. 95. **lown:** fellow, rascal. 129. **equinox:** counterpart, equivalent. 135. **horologe ... set:** clock twice around.

Prizes the virtue that appears in Cassio,
And looks not on his evils. Is not this true?   140

Enter RODERIGO.

Iago. [*Aside to him.*]   How now, Roderigo!
I pray you, after the lieutenant; go.
                                        [*Exit Roderigo.*
Mon. And 'tis great pity that the noble Moor
Should hazard such a place as his own second
With one of an ingraft infirmity.   145
It were an honest action to say
So to the Moor.
Iago.   Not I, for this fair island.
I do love Cassio well; and would do much
To cure him of this evil. — But, hark! what noise?
          [*Cry within:* "Help! help!"]

Re-enter CASSIO, *pursuing* RODERIGO.

Cas. 'Zounds, you rogue! you rascal!
Mon.   What's the matter, Lieutenant?   150
Cas. A knave teach me my duty!
I'll beat the knave into a twiggen bottle.
Rod. Beat me!
Cas.   Dost thou prate, rogue?
                              [*Striking Roderigo.*]
Mon.   Nay, good Lieutenant;
                              [*Staying him.*]
I pray you, sir, hold your hand.
Cas.   Let me go, sir,
Or I'll knock you o'er the mazzard.
Mon.   Come, come, you're drunk.   155
Cas. Drunk!   [*They fight.*
Iago. [*Aside to Roderigo.*] Away, I say; go out,
     and cry a mutiny.   [*Exit Roderigo.*
Nay, good Lieutenant, — [God's will], gentle-
     men; —
Help, ho! — Lieutenant, — sir, — Montano, —
     [sir]; —
Help, masters! — Here's a goodly watch indeed!
                                        [*Bell rings.*
Who's that which rings the bell? — Diablo, ho!   160
The town will rise. Fie, fie, Lieutenant, [hold]!
You will be sham'd for ever.

Re-enter OTHELLO *and Attendants.*

Oth.   What is the matter here?
Mon. ['Zounds], I bleed still; I am hurt to the
     death. He dies!
Oth. Hold, for your lives!   165
Iago. Hold, ho! Lieutenant, — sir, — Mon-
     tano, — gentlemen, —
Have you forgot all [sense of place] and duty?
Hold! the general speaks to you; hold, for shame!

Oth. Why, how now, ho! from whence ariseth
     this?
Are we turn'd Turks, and to ourselves do that   170
Which Heaven hath forbid the Ottomites?
For Christian shame, put by this barbarous brawl.
He that stirs next to carve for his own rage
Holds his soul light; he dies upon his motion.
Silence that dreadful bell; it frights the isle   175
From her propriety. What is the matter, masters?
Honest Iago, that looks dead with grieving,
Speak, who began this? On thy love, I charge thee.
Iago. I do not know. Friends all but now, even
     now,
In quarter, and in terms like bride and groom   180
Devesting them for bed; and then, but now —
As if some planet had unwitted men —
Swords out, and tilting one at other's breast,
In opposition bloody. I cannot speak
Any beginning to this peevish odds;   185
And would in action glorious I had lost
Those legs that brought me to a part of it!
Oth. How comes it, Michael, you are thus forgot?
Cas. I pray you, pardon me; I cannot speak.
Oth. Worthy Montano, you were wont to be
     civil;   190
The gravity and stillness of your youth
The world hath noted, and your name is great
In mouths of wisest censure. What's the matter
That you unlace your reputation thus,
And spend your rich opinion for the name   195
Of a night-brawler? Give me answer to it.
Mon. Worthy Othello, I am hurt to danger.
Your officer, Iago, can inform you —
While I spare speech, which something now offends
     me —
Of all that I do know; nor know I aught   200
By me that's said or done amiss this night,
Unless self-charity be sometimes a vice,
And to defend ourselves it be a sin
When violence assails us.
Oth.   Now, by heaven,
My blood begins my safer guides to rule;   205
And passion, having my best judgement collied,
Assays to lead the way. If I once stir
Or do but lift this arm, the best of you
Shall sink in my rebuke. Give me to know
How this foul rout began, who set it on;   210
And he that is approv'd in this offence,
Though he had twinn'd with me, both at a birth,
Shall lose me. What! in a town of war,
Yet wild, the people's hearts brimful of fear,
To manage private and domestic quarrel,   215
In night, and on the court and guard of safety!

152. **twiggen:** wicker-covered. 155. **mazzard:** head. 157. [**God's will**] Q. *Alas* F. 158. [**sir**] Q. Om. F. 161. [**hold**]
Q. Om. F. 167. [**sense of place**] (Hanmer). *place of sense* QF. 173. **carve . . . rage:** act on his own impulse. 180.
quarter: peace. 185. **peevish odds:** stupid quarrel. 193. **censure:** judgment. 195. **opinion:** reputation. 199. **offends:**
pains. 206. **collied:** darkened. 211. **approv'd:** found guilty. 215. **manage:** carry on.

'Tis monstrous. Iago, who began 't?

Mon. If partially affin'd, or leagu'd in office,
Thou dost deliver more or less than truth,
Thou art no soldier.

Iago.   Touch me not so near.   220
I had rather have this tongue cut from my mouth
Than it should do offence to Michael Cassio;
Yet, I persuade myself, to speak the truth
Shall nothing wrong him. [Thus] it is, General:
Montano and myself being in speech,   225
There comes a fellow crying out for help;
And Cassio following him with determin'd sword
To execute upon him. Sir, this gentleman
Steps in to Cassio and entreats his pause;
Myself the crying fellow did pursue,   230
Lest by his clamour — as it so fell out —
The town might fall in fright. He, swift of foot,
Outran my purpose; and I return'd the rather
For that I heard the clink and fall of swords,
And Cassio high in oath; which till to-night   235
I ne'er might say before. When I came back —
For this was brief — I found them close together,
At blow and thrust; even as again they were
When you yourself did part them.
More of this matter cannot I report.   240
But men are men; the best sometimes forget.
Though Cassio did some little wrong to him,
As men in rage strike those that wish them best,
Yet surely Cassio, I believe, receiv'd
From him that fled some strange indignity   245
Which patience could not pass.

Oth.   I know, Iago,
Thy honesty and love doth mince this matter,
Making it light to Cassio. Cassio, I love thee;
But never more be officer of mine.

Re-enter DESDEMONA, *attended.*

Look, if my gentle love be not rais'd up!   250
I'll make thee an example.

Des.   What's the matter, dear?

Oth. All's well [now], sweeting; come away to bed.
Sir, for your hurts, myself will be your surgeon. —
Lead him off.   [*To Montano, who is led off.*]
Iago, look with care about the town,   255
And silence those whom this vile brawl distracted.
Come, Desdemona; 'tis the soldiers' life
To have their balmy slumbers wak'd with strife.
                    [*Exeunt all but Iago and Cassio.*

Iago. What, are you hurt, Lieutenant?

Cas. Ay, past all surgery.   260

Iago. Marry, God forbid!

Cas. Reputation, reputation, reputation! O,
I have lost my reputation! I have lost the im-
mortal part of myself, and what remains is bestial.
My reputation, Iago, my reputation!   265

Iago. As I am an honest man, I thought you had
received some bodily wound; there is more sense in
that than in reputation. Reputation is an idle
and most false imposition; oft got without merit,
and lost without deserving. You have lost no   270
reputation at all, unless you repute yourself such a
loser. What, man! there are more ways to recover
the general again. You are but now cast in his
mood, a punishment more in policy than in malice;
even so as one would beat his offenceless dog to affright an imperious lion. Sue to him again, and he's
yours.   277

Cas. I will rather sue to be despis'd than to deceive so good a commander with so slight, so
drunken, and so indiscreet an officer. Drunk?
and speak parrot? and squabble? swagger? swear?
and discourse fustian with one's own shadow? O
thou invisible spirit of wine, if thou hast no name
to be known by, let us call thee devil!   284

Iago. What was he that you follow'd with your
sword? What had he done to you?

Cas. I know not.

Iago. Is't possible?   288

Cas. I remember a mass of things, but nothing
distinctly; a quarrel, but nothing wherefore. O
[God], that men should put an enemy in their
mouths to steal away their brains! That we should,
with joy, pleasance, revel, and applause, transform
ourselves into beasts!   294

Iago. Why, but you are now well enough. How
came you thus recovered?

Cas. It hath pleas'd the devil drunkenness to give
place to the devil wrath. One unperfectness shows
me another, to make me frankly despise myself.   300

Iago. Come, you are too severe a moraler. As
the time, the place, and the condition of this country stands, I could heartily wish this had not befallen; but since it is as it is, mend it for your own
good.   305

Cas. I will ask him for my place again; he shall
tell me I am a drunkard! Had I as many mouths
as Hydra, such an answer would stop them all.
To be now a sensible man, by and by a fool, and
presently a beast! O strange! Every inordinate
cup is unbless'd and the ingredient is a devil.   312

Iago. Come, come, good wine is a good familiar
creature, if it be well us'd; exclaim no more against
it. And, good Lieutenant, I think you think I love
you.   316

Cas. I have well approved it, sir. I drunk!

Iago. You or any man living may be drunk at a
time, man. [I'll] tell you what you shall do. Our
general's wife is now the general; — I may say   320
so in this respect, for that he hath devoted and
given up himself to the contemplation, mark, and

---

218. **partially affin'd:** biased because of ties. 224. **[Thus]** Q. *This* F. 252. **[now]** Q. Om. F. 266. **thought** Q. *had thought* F. 272. **recover:** regain favor with. 281. **parrot:** nonsense. 282. **fustian:** nonsense. 319. **[I'll]** Q. *I* F.

[denotement] of her parts and graces; — confess yourself freely to her; importune her help to put you in your place again. She is of so free, so kind, so apt, so blessed a disposition, she holds 325 it a vice in her goodness not to do more than she is requested. This broken joint between you and her husband entreat her to splinter; and, my fortunes against any lay worth naming, this crack of your love shall grow stronger than it was before. 331

Cas. You advise me well.

Iago. I protest, in the sincerity of love and honest kindness. 334

Cas. I think it freely; and betimes in the morning I will beseech the virtuous Desdemona to undertake for me. I am desperate of my fortunes if they check me [here].

Iago. You are in the right. Good-night, lieutenant; I must to the watch. 340

Cas. Good-night, honest Iago.   [*Exit.*

Iago. And what's he then that says I play the villain?

When this advice is free I give and honest,
Probal to thinking and indeed the course
To win the Moor again? For 'tis most easy   345
Th' inclining Desdemona to subdue
In any honest suit; she's fram'd as fruitful
As the free elements. And then for her
To win the Moor, [were't] to renounce his baptism,
All seals and symbols of redeemed sin,   350
His soul is so enfetter'd to her love,
That she may make, unmake, do what she list,
Even as her appetite shall play the god
With his weak function. How am I then a villain
To counsel Cassio to this parallel course,   355
Directly to his good? Divinity of hell!
When devils will the blackest sins put on,
They do suggest at first with heavenly shows,
As I do now; for whiles this honest fool
Plies Desdemona to repair his fortune   360
And she for him pleads strongly to the Moor,
I'll pour this pestilence into his ear,
That she repeals him for her body's lust;
And by how much she strives to do him good,
She shall undo her credit with the Moor.   365
So will I turn her virtue into pitch,
And out of her own goodness make the net
That shall enmesh them all.

         Re-enter RODERIGO.

           How now, Roderigo!

Rod. I do follow here in the chase, not like a hound that hunts, but one that fills up the cry. 370
My money is almost spent; I have been to-night

exceedingly well cudgell'd; and I think the issue will be, I shall have so much experience for my pains; and so, with no money at all and a little more wit, return again to Venice.   375

Iago. How poor are they that have not patience!
What wound did ever heal but by degrees?
Thou know'st we work by wit, and not by witch-
    craft;
And wit depends on dilatory time.
Does't not go well? Cassio hath beaten thee, 380
And thou, by that small hurt, hast cashier'd Cassio.
Though other things grow fair against the sun,
Yet fruits that blossom first will first be ripe.
Content thyself a while. In troth, 'tis morning;
Pleasure and action make the hours seem short.
Retire thee; go where thou art billeted.   386
Away, I say; thou shalt know more hereafter.
Nay, get thee gone. [*Exit Roderigo.*] Two things
    are to be done:
My wife must move for Cassio to her mistress;
I'll set her on;   390
Myself a while to draw the Moor apart,
And bring him jump when he may Cassio find
Soliciting his wife. Ay, that's the way;
Dull not device by coldness and delay.   [*Exit.*

ACT III

SCENE I. [*Cyprus before the castle.*]

Enter CASSIO, *with* MUSICIANS.

Cas. Masters, play here; I will content your
    pains;
Something that's brief; and bid "Good morrow,
    general."   [*They play.*

Enter CLOWN.

Clo. Why, masters, have your instruments been in Naples, that they speak i' th' nose thus?

1. Mus. How, sir, how?   5

Clo. Are these, I pray you, wind-instruments?

1. Mus. Ay, marry, are they, sir.

Clo. O, thereby hangs a tail.

1. Mus. Whereby hangs a tale, sir?   9

Clo. Marry, sir, by many a wind-instrument that I know. But, masters, here's money for you; and the General so likes your music, that he desires you, for love's sake, to make no more noise with it.

1. Mus. Well, sir, we will not.   15

Clo. If you have any music that may not be heard, to't again; but, as they say, to hear music the General does not greatly care.

322. [denotement] Q₂. *devotement* QF.   328. splinter: bind with splints.   330. lay: wager.   338. [here] Q. Om. F.   344. Probal: probable.   347. fruitful: generous.   349. [were't] Q. *were* F.   354. function: mental faculties.   357. put on: incite. 370. cry: pack.   392. jump: at the precise moment.
Act III, sc. i, 1. content: requite.

1. Mus. We have none such, sir.

Clo. Then put up your pipes in your bag, for I'll away. Go, vanish into air, away!   21
              .   [*Exeunt Musicians.*

Cas. Dost thou hear mine honest friend?

Clo. No, I hear not your honest friend; I hear you.   24

Cas. Prithee, keep up thy quillets. There's a poor piece of gold for thee. If the gentlewoman that attends the [General's wife] be stirring, tell her there's one Cassio entreats her a little favour of speech. Wilt thou do this?

Clo. She is stirring, sir. If she will stir hither, I shall seem to notify unto her.   31

Cas. [Do, good my friend.]   [*Exit Clown.*

Enter IAGO.

              In happy time, Iago.

Iago. You have not been a-bed, then?

Cas. Why, no; the day had broke
Before we parted. I have made bold, Iago,   35
To send in to your wife. My suit to her
Is that she will to virtuous Desdemona
Procure me some access.

Iago.   I'll send her to you presently;
And I'll devise a mean to draw the Moor
Out of the way, that your converse and business   40
May be more free.

Cas. I humbly thank you for't. [*Exit Iago.*]
             I never knew
A Florentine more kind and honest.

Enter EMILIA.

Emil. Good morrow, good Lieutenant. I am sorry
For your displeasure; but all will sure be well.   45
The General and his wife are talking of it,
And she speaks for you stoutly. The Moor replies
That he you hurt is of great fame in Cyprus
And great affinity, and that in wholesome wisdom
He might not but refuse you; but he protests he loves you,   50
And needs no other suitor but his likings
[To take the safest occasion by the front]
To bring you in again.

Cas.   Yet, I beseech you,
If you think fit, or that it may be done,
Give me advantage of some brief discourse   55
With Desdemon alone.

Emil.   Pray you, come in.
I will bestow you where you shall have time

To speak your bosom freely.

Cas.   I am much bound to you.
                       [*Exeunt.*

SCENE II. [*A room in the castle.*]

Enter OTHELLO, IAGO, *and* GENTLEMEN.

Oth. These letters give, Iago, to the pilot;
And by him do my duties to the Senate.
That done, I will be walking on the works;
Repair there to me.

Iago.   Well, my good lord, I'll do't.

Oth. This fortification, gentlemen, shall we see't?   5

Gent. We'll wait upon your lordship.   [*Exeunt.*

SCENE III. [*The garden of the castle.*]

Enter DESDEMONA, CASSIO, *and* EMILIA.

Des. Be thou assur'd, good Cassio, I will do
All my abilities in thy behalf.

Emil. Good madam, do. I warrant it grieves my husband
As if the cause were his.

Des. O, that's an honest fellow. Do not doubt, Cassio,   5
But I will have my lord and you again
As friendly as you were.

Cas.   Bounteous madam,
Whatever shall become of Michael Cassio,
He's never anything but your true servant.

Des. I know 't; I thank you. You do love my lord;   10
You have known him long; and be you well assur'd
He shall in strangeness stand no farther off
Than in a politic distance.

Cas.   Ay, but, lady,
That policy may either last so long,
Or feed upon such nice and waterish diet,   15
Or breed itself so out of circumstances,
That, I being absent and my place supplied,
My general will forget my love and service.

Des. Do not doubt that; before Emilia here
I give thee warrant of thy place. Assure thee,   20
If I do vow a friendship, I'll perform it
To the last article. My lord shall never rest;
I'll watch him tame, and talk him out of patience;
His bed shall seem a school, his board a shrift;
I'll intermingle everything he does   25
With Cassio's suit. Therefore be merry, Cassio;
For thy solicitor shall rather die
Than give thy cause away.

---

22. **hear** Q. *hear me* F.   25. **quillets:** quibbles.   27. [General's wife] Q. *general* F.   32. [Do ... friend] Q. Om. F.   45. **displeasure:** disgrace.   49. **affinity:** connections.   52. [To ... front] Q. Om. F. **front:** forelock.
   Sc. ii, 3. **works:** fortifications.
   Sc. iii, 12. **strangeness:** aloofness.   19. **doubt:** fear.   23. **watch him tame:** keep him awake till he gives in.   24. **shrift:** confessional.

Enter OTHELLO *and* IAGO.

Emil. Madam, here comes my lord.

Cas. Madam, I'll take my leave.   30

Des. Why, stay, and hear me speak.

Cas. Madam, not now; I am very ill at ease,
Unfit for mine own purposes.

Des. Well, do your discretion.   [*Exit Cassio.*

Iago. Ha! I like not that.

Oth.   What dost thou say?

Iago. Nothing, my lord; or if — I know not
what.   36

Oth. Was not that Cassio parted from my wife?

Iago. Cassio, my lord! No, sure, I cannot
think it,
That he would steal away so guilty-like,
Seeing your coming.

Oth.   I do believe 'twas he.   40

Des. How now, my lord!
I have been talking with a suitor here,
A man that languishes in your displeasure.

Oth. Who is't you mean?

Des. Why, your lieutenant, Cassio. Good my
lord,   45
If I have any grace or power to move you,
His present reconciliation take;
For if he be not one that truly loves you,
That errs in ignorance and not in cunning,
I have no judgement in an honest face.   50
I prithee, call him back.

Oth.   Went he hence now?

Des. Yes, faith; so humbled
That he hath left part of his grief with me
To suffer with him. Good love, call him back.

Oth. Not now, sweet Desdemon; some other
time.   55

Des. But shall't be shortly?

Oth.   The sooner, sweet, for you.

Des. Shall't be to-night at supper?

Oth.   No, not to-night.

Des. To-morrow dinner, then?

Oth.   I shall not dine at home;
I meet the captains at the citadel.

Des. Why, then, to-morrow night; on Tuesday
morn;   60
On Tuesday noon, or night; on Wednesday
morn.
I prithee, name the time, but let it not
Exceed three days. In faith, he's penitent;
And yet his trespass, in our common reason —
Save that, they say, the wars must make example 65
Out of [their] best — is not almost a fault
T' incur a private check. When shall he come?
Tell me, Othello. I wonder in my soul
What you would ask me that I should deny,

Or stand so mamm'ring on. What! Michael
Cassio,   70
That came a-wooing with you, and so many a time,
When I have spoke of you dispraisingly,
Hath ta'en your part, — to have so much to do
To bring him in! Trust me, I could do much, —

Oth. Prithee, no more; let him come when he
will,   75
I will deny thee nothing.

Des.   Why, this is not a boon.
'Tis as I should entreat you wear your gloves,
Or feed on nourishing dishes, or keep you warm,
Or sue to you to do a peculiar profit
To your own person. Nay, when I have a suit 80
Wherein I mean to touch your love indeed,
It shall be full of poise and difficult weight
And fearful to be granted.

Oth.   I will deny thee nothing;
Whereon, I do beseech thee, grant me this,
To leave me but a little to myself.   85

Des. Shall I deny you? No. Farewell, my
lord.

Oth. Farewell, my Desdemona; I'll come to thee
straight.

Des. Emilia, come. — Be as your fancies teach
you;
Whate'er you be, I am obedient.
                    [*Exeunt Desdemona and Emilia.*

Oth. Excellent wretch! Perdition catch my
soul,   90
But I do love thee! and when I love thee not,
Chaos is come again.

Iago. My noble lord, —

Oth.   What dost thou say, Iago?

Iago. Did Michael Cassio, when [you] woo'd my
lady,
Know of your love?   95

Oth. He did, from first to last. Why dost thou
ask?

Iago. But for a satisfaction of my thought;
No further harm.

Oth.   Why of thy thought, Iago?

Iago. I did not think he had been acquainted
with her.

Oth. O, yes; and went between us very oft.   100

Iago. Indeed!

Oth. Indeed! ay, indeed. Discern'st thou
aught in that?
Is he not honest?

Iago.   Honest, my lord?

Oth.   Honest! ay, honest.

Iago. My lord, for aught I know.

Oth. What dost thou think?

Iago.   Think, my lord?

Oth.   Think, my lord!

66. [their] (Rowe). *her* QF. not almost: hardly. 70. mamm'ring: hesitating. 74. bring…in: i.e., into your favor.
82. poise: weight. 94. [you] Q. *he* F.

[By heaven, he echoes] me,   106
As if there were some monster in [his] thought
Too hideous to be shown. — Thou dost mean some-
    thing.
I heard thee say even now, thou lik'st not that,
When Cassio left my wife. What didst not like? 110
And when I told thee he was of my counsel
[In] my whole course of wooing, thou criedst, "In-
    deed!"
And didst contract and purse thy brow together,
As if thou then hadst shut up in thy brain
Some horrible conceit. If thou dost love me, 115
Show me thy thought.
    Iago. My lord, you know I love you.
    Oth.   I think thou dost;
And, for I know thou'rt full of love and honesty,
And weigh'st thy words before thou giv'st them
    breath,
Therefore these stops of thine fright me the more;
For such things in a false disloyal knave 121
Are tricks of custom; but in a man that's just
They're close dilations, working from the heart
That passion cannot rule.
    Iago.   For Michael Cassio,
I dare be sworn I think that he is honest. 125
    Oth. I think so too.
    Iago.   Men should be what they seem;
Or those that be not, would they might seem
    none!
    Oth. Certain, men should be what they seem.
    Iago. Why, then, I think Cassio's an honest man.
    Oth. Nay, yet there's more in this. 130
I prithee, speak to me as to thy thinkings,
As thou dost ruminate, and give thy worst of
    thoughts
The worst of words.
    Iago.   Good my lord, pardon me.
Though I am bound to every act of duty,
I am not bound to that all slaves are free to. 135
Utter my thoughts? Why, say they are vile and
    false;
As where's that palace whereinto foul things
Sometimes intrude not? Who has that breast so
    pure
[But some] uncleanly apprehensions
Keep leets and law-days and in sessions sit 140
With meditations lawful?
    Oth. Thou dost conspire against thy friend, Iago,
If thou but think'st him wrong'd and mak'st his ear
A stranger to thy thoughts.
    Iago.   I do beseech you —
Though I perchance am vicious in my guess, 145
As, I confess, it is my nature's plague
To spy into abuses, and [oft] my jealousy

Shapes faults that are not — that your wisdom yet,
From one that so imperfectly conceits,
Would take no notice, nor build yourself a trouble
Out of his scattering and unsure observance. 151
It were not for your quiet nor your good,
Nor for my manhood, honesty, and wisdom,
To let you know my thoughts.
    Oth.   What dost thou mean?
    Iago. Good name in man and woman, dear my
    lord,   155
Is the immediate jewel of their souls.
Who steals my purse steals trash; 'tis something,
    nothing;
'Twas mine, 'tis his, and has been slave to thou-
    sands;
But he that filches from me my good name
Robs me of that which not enriches him, 160
And makes me poor indeed.
    Oth. [By heaven,] I'll know thy thoughts.
    Iago. You cannot, if my heart were in your hand;
Nor shall not, whilst 'tis in my custody.
    Oth. Ha!
    Iago.   O, beware, my lord, of jealousy! 165
It is the green-ey'd monster which doth mock
The meat it feeds on. That cuckold lives in bliss
Who, certain of his fate, loves not his wronger;
But, O, what damned minutes tells he o'er
Who dotes, yet doubts, suspects, yet soundly loves!
    Oth. O misery!   171
    Iago. Poor and content is rich, and rich enough;
But riches fineless is as poor as winter
To him that ever fears he shall be poor.
Good heaven, the souls of all my tribe defend 175
From jealousy!
    Oth.   Why, why is this?
Think'st thou I'd make a life of jealousy,
To follow still the changes of the moon
With fresh suspicions? No! to be once in doubt
Is [once] to be resolv'd. Exchange me for a goat
When I shall turn the business of my soul 181
To such exsufflicate and [blown] surmises,
Matching thy inference. 'Tis not to make me
    jealous
To say my wife is fair, feeds well, loves company,
Is free of speech, sings, plays, and dances [well]; 185
Where virtue is, these are more virtuous.
Nor from mine own weak merits will I draw
The smallest fear or doubt of her revolt;
For she had eyes, and chose me. No, Iago;
I'll see before I doubt; when I doubt, prove; 190
And on the proof, there is no more but this, —
Away at once with love or jealousy!
    Iago. I am glad of this, for now I shall have rea-
    son

106. [**By . . . echoes**] Q. *Alas, thou eccho'st* F. 107. [**his**] Q. *thy* F. 112. [**In**] Q. *of* F. 123. **close dilations:** secret (i.e., unconscious) expressions. 139. [**But some**] Q. *Wherein* F. 140. **leets:** court-days. 147. [**oft**] Q. *of* F. **jealousy:** suspicion. 151. **scattering:** random. 173. **fineless:** unlimited. 180. [**once**] Q. Om. F. 182. **exsufflicate:** inflated. [**blown**] Q. *blowed* F. 185. [**well**] Q. Om. F.

To show the love and duty that I bear you
With franker spirit; therefore, as I am bound, 195
Receive it from me.   I speak not yet of proof.
Look to your wife; observe her well with Cassio;
Wear your eyes thus, not jealous nor secure.
I would not have your free and noble nature,
Out of self-bounty, be abus'd; look to't.   200
I know our country disposition well;
In Venice they do let Heaven see the pranks
They dare not show their husbands.   Their best
     conscience
Is not to leave 't undone, but keep 't unknown.
    Oth. Dost thou say so?   205
    Iago. She did deceive her father, marrying you;
And when she seem'd to shake and fear your looks,
She lov'd them most.
    Oth.   And so she did.
    Iago.   Why, go to then.
She that, so young, could give out such a seeming,
To seel her father's eyes up close as oak —   210
He thought 'twas witchcraft — but I am much to
     blame.
I humbly do beseech you of your pardon
For too much loving you.
    Oth.   I am bound to thee for ever.
    Iago. I see this hath a little dash'd your spirits.
    Oth. Not a jot, not a jot.
    Iago.   Trust me! I fear it has.
I hope you will consider what is spoke   216
Comes from [my] love.   But I do see you're mov'd.
I am to pray you not to strain my speech
To grosser issues nor to larger reach
Than to suspicion.   220
    Oth. I will not.
    Iago.   Should you do so, my lord,
My speech should fall into such vile success
Which my thoughts aim'd not at.   Cassio's my
     worthy friend, —
My lord, I see you're mov'd.
    Oth.   No, not much mov'd.
I do not think but Desdemona's honest.   225
    Iago. Long live she so! and long live you to think
     so!
    Oth. And yet, how nature erring from itself, —
    Iago. Ay, there's the point; as — to be bold with
     you —
Not to affect many proposed matches
Of her own clime, complexion, and degree,   230
Whereto we see in all things nature tends —
Foh! one may smell in such, a will most rank,
Foul disproportions, thoughts unnatural.
But pardon me; I do not in position

Distinctly speak of her; though I may fear   235
Her will, recoiling to her better judgement,
May fall to match you with her country forms,
And happily repent.
    Oth.   Farewell, farewell!
If more thou dost perceive, let me know more;
Set on thy wife to observe.   Leave me, Iago.   240
    Iago. [*Going.*] My lord, I take my leave.
    Oth. Why did I marry?   This honest creature
     doubtless
Sees and knows more, much more, than he unfolds.
    Iago. [*Returning.*] My lord, I would I might
     entreat your honour
To scan this thing no farther; leave it to time.   245
Although 'tis fit that Cassio have his place,
For, sure, he fills it up with great ability,
Yet, if you please to [hold] him off a while,
You shall by that perceive him and his means.
Note if your lady strain his entertainment   250
With any strong or vehement importunity;
Much will be seen in that.   In the mean time,
Let me be thought too busy in my fears —
As worthy cause I have to fear I am —
And hold her free, I do beseech your honour.   255
    Oth. Fear not my government.
    Iago. I once more take my leave.   [*Exit.*
    Oth. This fellow 's of exceeding honesty,
And knows all [qualities], with a learn'd spirit,
Of human dealings.   If I do prove her haggard, 260
Though that her jesses were my dear heartstrings,
I'd whistle her off and let her down the wind
To prey at fortune.   Haply, for I am black
And have not those soft parts of conversation
That chamberers have, or for I am declin'd   265
Into the vale of tears, — yet that's not much —
She's gone.   I am abus'd; and my relief
Must be to loathe her.   O curse of marriage,
That we can call these delicate creatures ours,
And not their appetites!   I had rather be a toad 270
And live upon the vapour of a dungeon
Than keep a corner in the thing I love
For others' uses.   Yet, 'tis the plague [of] great
     ones;
Prerogativ'd are they less than the base.
'Tis destiny unshunnable, like death.   275
Even then this forked plague is fated to us
When we do quicken.   Look where she comes,

    Re-enter DESDEMONA *and* EMILIA.

If she be false, [O, then heaven mocks] itself!
I'll not believe 't.
    Des.   How now, my dear Othello!

---

198. **secure**: careless.   200. **self-bounty**: inherent generosity.   217. **[my]** Q.   *your* F.   222. **success**: consequence.   225.
honest: chaste.   232, 236. **will**: desire, appetite.   232. **rank**: foul.   234. **position**: i.e., conviction.   248. **[hold]** Q.   Om. F.
250. **strain his entertainment**: press his reappointment.   255. **free**: guiltless.   256. **government**: management.   259.
[qualities] Q.   *quantities* F.   260. **haggard**: wild.   261. **jesses**: strings by which hawks were held.   264. **parts of conversation**: social graces.   265. **chamberers**: gallants.   273. **[of]** Q.   *to* F.   276. **forked plague**: curse of cuckold's horns.   277.
quicken: begin to live.   278. **[O ... mocks]** Q.   *Heaven mock'd* F.

Your dinner, and the generous islanders   280
By you invited, do attend your presence.
   Oth. I am to blame.
   Des.   Why do you speak so faintly?
Are you not well?
   Oth. I have a pain upon my forehead here.
   Des. Why, that's with watching; 'twill away
     again.   285
Let me but bind it hard, within this hour
It will be well.
   Oth.   Your napkin is too little;
     [*He puts the handkerchief from him; and it
     drops.*]
Let it alone. Come, I'll go in with you.
   Des. I am very sorry that you are not well.
           [*Exeunt* [*Othello and Desdemona*].
   Emil. I am glad I have found this napkin;   290
This was her first remembrance from the Moor.
My wayward husband hath a hundred times
Woo'd me to steal it; but she so loves the token,
For he conjur'd her she should ever keep it,
That she reserves it evermore about her   295
To kiss and talk to. I'll have the work ta'en out
And give 't Iago. What he will do with it
Heaven knows, not I;
I nothing but to please his fantasy.

Re-enter IAGO.

   Iago. How now! what do you here alone?   300
   Emil. Do not you chide; I have a thing for you.
   Iago. A thing for me? It is a common thing —
   Emil. Ha!
   Iago. To have a foolish wife.
   Emil. O, is that all? What will you give me
     now   305
For that same handkerchief?
   Iago.   What handkerchief?
   Emil. What handkerchief!
Why, that the Moor first gave to Desdemona;
That which so often you did bid me steal.
   Iago. Hast stol'n it from her?   310
   Emil. No, [faith;] she let it drop by negligence,
And, to th' advantage, I, being here, took 't up.
Look, here it is.
   Iago.   A good wench; give it me.
   Emil. What will you do with 't, that you have
     been so earnest
To have me filch it?
   Iago. [*Snatching it.*] Why, what is that to you?
   Emil. If it be not for some purpose of import, 316
Give 't me again. Poor lady, she'll run mad
When she shall lack it.
   Iago. Be not acknown on't; I have use for it.
Go, leave me.   [*Exit Emilia.* 320

I will in Cassio's lodging lose this napkin,
And let him find it. Trifles light as air
Are to the jealous confirmations strong
As proofs of holy writ; this may do something.
The Moor already changes with my poison.   325
Dangerous conceits are, in their natures poisons,
Which at the first are scarce found to distaste,
But with a little act upon the blood
Burn like the mines of sulphur. I did say so.

Re-enter OTHELLO.

Look, where he comes! Not poppy, nor mandra-
     gora,   330
Nor all the drowsy syrups of the world
Shall ever medicine thee to that sweet sleep
Which thou ow'dst yesterday.
   Oth.   Ha! ha! false to me?
   Iago. Why, how now, General! no more of that.
   Oth. Avaunt! be gone! thou hast set me on the
     rack.   335
I swear 'tis better to be much abus'd
Than but to know 't a little.
   Iago.   How now, my lord!
   Oth. What sense had I [of] her stol'n hours of
     lust?
I saw 't not, thought it not, it harm'd not me.
I slept the next night well, fed well, was free and
     merry;   340
I found not Cassio's kisses on her lips.
He that is robb'd, not wanting what is stolen,
Let him not know 't, and he's not robb'd at all.
   Iago. I am sorry to hear this.
   Oth. I had been happy, if the general camp,   345
Pioners and all, had tasted her sweet body,
So I had nothing known. O, now, for ever
Farewell the tranquil mind! farewell content!
Farewell the plumed troops and the big wars
That make ambition virtue! O, farewell!   350
Farewell the neighing steed and the shrill trump,
The spirit-stirring drum, th' ear-piercing fife,
The royal banner, and all quality,
Pride, pomp, and circumstance of glorious war!
And, O you mortal engines, whose rude throats   355
Th' immortal Jove's dread clamours counterfeit,
Farewell! Othello's occupation 's gone!
   Iago. Is 't possible, my lord?
   Oth. Villain, be sure thou prove my love a whore;
Be sure of it. Give me the ocular proof;   360
Or, by the worth of mine eternal soul,
Thou hadst been better have been born a dog
Than answer my wak'd wrath!
   Iago.   Is 't come to this?
   Oth. Make me to see 't; or, at the least, so prove
     it

---

280. **generous**: noble. 287. **napkin:** handkerchief. 288. **it**: i.e., his forehead. 296. **work ... out**: pattern copied. 311. [faith] Q. *but* F. 312. **to th' advantage**: opportunely. 319. **acknown**: aware. 328. **act**: action. 330. **mandragora**: a soporific. 333. **ow'dst**: hadst. 338. [of] Q. *in* F. 346. **Pioners**: the lowest rank of soldiers.

That the probation bear no hinge nor loop   365
To hang a doubt on; or woe upon thy life!
  Iago. My noble lord, —
  Oth. If thou dost slander her and torture me,
Never pray more; abandon all remorse;
On horror's head horrors accumulate;   370
Do deeds to make heaven weep, all earth amaz'd;
For nothing canst thou to damnation add
Greater than that.
  Iago.   O grace! O Heaven forgive me!
Are you a man? Have you a soul or sense?
God buy you; take mine office. O wretched fool, 375
That lov'st to make thine honesty a vice!
O monstrous world! Take note, take note, O
     world,
To be direct and honest is not safe.
I thank you for this profit; and from hence
I'll love no friend, sith love breeds such offence. 380
  Oth. Nay, stay. Thou shouldst be honest.
  Iago. I should be wise, for honesty 's a fool
And loses that it works for.
  Oth.   By the world,
I think my wife be honest and think she is not;
I think that thou art just and think thou art
not.   385
I'll have some proof. [Her] name, that was as fresh
As Dian's visage, is now begrim'd and black
As mine own face. If there be cords, or knives,
Poison, or fire, or suffocating streams,
I'll not endure it. Would I were satisfied!   390
  Iago. I see, [sir], you are eaten up with passion;
I do repent me that I put it to you.
You would be satisfied?
  Oth.   Would! nay, I will.
  Iago. And may; but, how? How satisfied, my
     lord?
Would you, the [supervisor], grossly gape on — 395
Behold her topp'd?
  Oth.   Death and damnation! O!
  Iago. It were a tedious difficulty, I think,
To bring them to that prospect; [damn] them then,
If ever mortal eyes do see them bolster
More than their own! What then? How then? 400
What shall I say? Where's satisfaction?
It is impossible you should see this,
Were they as prime as goats, as hot as monkeys,
As salt as wolves in pride, and fools as gross
As ignorance made drunk. But yet, I say,   405
If imputation and strong circumstances
Which lead directly to the door of truth
Will give you satisfaction, you might have't.
  Oth. Give me a living reason she's disloyal.

  Iago. I do not like the office;   410
But, sith I am ent'red in this cause so far,
Prick'd to't by foolish honesty and love,
I will go on. I lay with Cassio lately;
And, being troubled with a raging tooth,
I could not sleep.   415
There are a kind of men so loose of soul,
That in their sleeps will mutter their affairs;
One of this kind is Cassio.
In sleep I heard him say, "Sweet Desdemona,
Let us be wary, let us hide our loves;"   420
And then, sir, would he gripe and wring my hand,
Cry, "O sweet creature!" then kiss me hard,
As if he pluck'd up kisses by the roots
That grew upon my lips; then lay his leg
Over my thigh, and sigh, and kiss; and then   425
Cry, "Cursed fate that gave thee to the Moor!"
  Oth. O monstrous! monstrous!
  Iago.   Nay, this was but his dream.
  Oth. But this denoted a foregone conclusion.
'Tis a shrewd doubt, though it be but a dream. 429
  Iago. And this may help to thicken other proofs
That do demonstrate thinly.
  Oth.   I'll tear her all to pieces.
  Iago. Nay, [but] be wise; yet we see nothing done.
She may be honest yet. Tell me but this,
Have you not sometimes seen a handkerchief
Spotted with strawberries in your wife's hand? 435
  Oth. I gave her such a one; 'twas my first gift.
  Iago. I know not that; but such a handkerchief —
I am sure it was your wife's — did I to-day
See Cassio wipe his beard with.
  Oth.   If it be that, —
  Iago. If it be that, or any [that] was hers,   440
It speaks against her with the other proofs.
  Oth. O, that the slave had forty thousand lives!
One is too poor, too weak for my revenge.
Now do I see 'tis true. Look here, Iago;
All my fond love thus do I blow to heaven.   445
'Tis gone.
Arise, black vengeance, from the hollow hell!
Yield up, O love, thy crown and hearted throne
To tyrannous hate! Swell, bosom, with thy
     fraught,
For 'tis of aspics' tongues!
  Iago.   Yet be content. 450
  Oth. O, blood, blood, blood!
  Iago. Patience, I say; your mind [perhaps] may
     change.
  Oth. Never, Iago. Like to the Pontic Sea,
Whose icy current and compulsive course
Ne'er [feels] retiring ebb, but keeps due on   455

---

375. **buy:** be with. 376. **lov'st** F. *livest* Q. 386. **[Her]** Q. *My* F. 391. **[sir]** Q. Om. F. 393. **nay** Q. *Nay, and* F. 395. **[supervisor]** Q. *supervision* F. 398. **[damn]** Q. Om. F. 399. **bolster:** lie on a bolster (together). 403. **prime:** lecherous. 404. **pride:** heat. 428. **foregone conclusion:** earlier act. 429. **shrewd doubt:** strong reason for suspicion. 432. **[but]** Q. *yet* F. 440. **[that]** (Malone). *it* QF. 449. **fraught:** burden. 450. **aspics':** asps'. 452. **[perhaps]** Q. Om. F 453. **Pontic Sea:** Black Sea. 455. **[feels]** Q₂. *keeps* F.

To the Propontic and the Hellespont,
Even so my bloody thoughts, with violent pace,
Shall ne'er look back, ne'er ebb to humble love,
Till that a capable and wide revenge 459
Swallow them up. Now, by yond marble heaven,
In the due reverence of a sacred vow [Kneels.]
I here engage my words.

Iago.   Do not rise yet.
Witness, you ever-burning lights above,
You elements that clip us round about, [Kneels.
Witness that here Iago doth give up 465
The execution of his wit, hands, heart,
To wrong'd Othello's service! Let him command,
And to obey shall be in me remorse,
What bloody business ever. [They rise.]

Oth.   I greet thy love,
Not with vain thanks, but with acceptance bounteous, 470
And will upon the instant put thee to't:
Within these three days let me hear thee say
That Cassio's not alive.

Iago. My friend is dead; 'tis done at your request.
But let her live.

Oth. Damn her, lewd minx! O, damn her!
damn her! 475
Come, go with me apart; I will withdraw
To furnish me with some swift means of death
For the fair devil. Now art thou my lieutenant.

Iago. I am your own for ever. [Exeunt.

SCENE IV. [Before the castle.]

Enter DESDEMONA, EMILIA, *and* CLOWN.

Des. Do you know, sirrah, where Lieutenant
Cassio lies?

Clo. I dare not say he lies anywhere.

Des. Why, man?

Clo. He's a soldier, and for me to say a soldier
lies, 'tis stabbing. 6

Des. Go to! Where lodges he?

Clo. To tell you where he lodges, is to tell you
where I lie.

Des. Can anything be made of this? 10

Clo. I know not where he lodges, and for me to
devise a lodging and say he lies here or he lies there,
were to lie in mine own throat.

Des. Can you inquire him out, and be edified by
report? 15

Clo. I will catechize the world for him; that is,
make questions, and by them answer.

Des. Seek him, bid him come hither. Tell him
I have mov'd my lord on his behalf, and hope all
will be well. 20

Clo. To do this is within the compass of man's
wit; and therefore I will attempt the doing it. [Exit.

Des. Where should I lose the handkerchief,
Emilia?

Emil. I know not, madam.

Des. Believe me, I had rather have lost my
purse 25
Full of crusadoes; and, but my noble Moor
Is true of mind and made of no such baseness
As jealous creatures are, it were enough
To put him to ill thinking.

Emil.   Is he not jealous?

Des. Who, he? I think the sun where he was
born 30
Drew all such humours from him.

Emil.   Look, where he comes.

Enter OTHELLO.

Des. I will not leave him now till Cassio
Be call'd to him. — How is't with you, my lord?

Oth. Well, my good lady. [Aside.] O, hardness
to dissemble! —
How do you, Desdemona?

Des.   Well, my good lord. 35

Oth. Give me your hand. This hand is moist, my
lady.

Des. It [yet] hath felt no age nor known no sorrow.

Oth. This argues fruitfulness and liberal heart;
Hot, hot, and moist. This hand of yours requires
A sequester from liberty, fasting and prayer, 40
Much castigation, exercise devout;
For here's a young and sweating devil here
That commonly rebels. 'Tis a good hand,
A frank one.

Des.   You may, indeed, say so;
For 'twas that hand that gave away my heart. 45

Oth. A liberal hand. The hearts of old gave
hands;
But our new heraldry is hands, not hearts.

Des. I cannot speak of this. Come now, your
promise.

Oth. What promise, chuck?

Des. I have sent to bid Cassio come speak with
you. 50

Oth. I have a salt and sorry rheum offends me;
Lend me thy handkerchief.

Des.   Here, my lord.

Oth. That which I gave you.

Des.   I have it not about me.

Oth. Not?

Des.   No, indeed, my lord.

Oth. That's a fault. That handkerchief 55
Did an Egyptian to my mother give;
She was a charmer, and could almost read

---

459. **capable:** comprehensive. 464. **clip:** embrace. 466. **execution:** action. 468. **remorse:** obligation.
Sc. iv, 2. **lies:** lodges. 26. **crusadoes:** Portuguese coins stamped with a cross. 37. [yet] Q. Om. F. 40. **sequester:** separation.
47. **our new heraldry.** Probably a topical allusion. 51. **sorry:** distressing. 56. **Egyptian:** gypsy. 57. **charmer:** sorcerer.

The thoughts of people.   She told her, while she
       kept it
'Twould make her amiable and subdue my father
Entirely to her love, but if she lost it,   60
Or made a gift of it, my father's eye
Should hold her loathed and his spirits should hunt
After new fancies.   She, dying, gave it me
And bid me, when my fate would have me wiv'd,
To give it her.   I did so; and take heed on't;   65
Make it a darling like your precious eye.
To lose't or give't away were such perdition
As nothing else could match.
    Des.   Is't possible?
    Oth. 'Tis true; there's magic in the web of it.
A sibyl, that had numb'red in the world   70
The sun to course two hundred compasses,
In her prophetic fury sew'd the work;
The worms were hallowed that did breed the
       silk;
And it was dy'd in mummy which the skilful
Conserv'd of maidens' hearts.
    Des.   Indeed! is't true?
    Oth. Most veritable; therefore look to't well.   76
    Des. Then would to [God] that I had never seen
       't!
    Oth. Ha! wherefore?
    Des. Why do you speak so startingly and rash?
    Oth. Is't lost?   Is't gone?   Speak, is't out o' th'
       way?   80
    Des. [Heaven] bless us!
    Oth. Say you?
    Des. It is not lost; but what an if it were?
    Oth. How?
    Des. I say, it is not lost.
    Oth.   Fetch 't, let me see 't.   85
    Des. Why, so I can, [sir,] but I will not now.
This is a trick to put me from my suit.
Pray you, let Cassio be receiv'd again.
    Oth. Fetch me the handkerchief; my mind mis-
       gives.
    Des. Come, come;   90
You'll never meet a more sufficient man.
    Oth. The handkerchief!
    [*Des.*   I pray, talk me of Cassio.
    Oth. The handkerchief!]
    Des.   A man that all his time
Hath founded his good fortunes on your love,
Shar'd dangers with you, —   95
    Oth. The handkerchief!
    Des. In sooth, you are to blame.
    Oth. ['Zounds!]   [*Exit.*
    Emil. Is not this man jealous?
    Des. I ne'er saw this before.   100
Sure, there's some wonder in this handkerchief;

I am most unhappy in the loss of it.
    Emil. 'Tis not a year or two shows us a man.
They are all but stomachs, and we all but food;
They eat us hungerly, and when they are full   105
They belch us.

              Enter CASSIO *and* IAGO.

            Look you, Cassio and my husband!
    Iago. There is no other way, 'tis she must do't;
And, lo, the happiness!   Go, and importune her.
    Des. How now, good Cassio!   What's the news
       with you?
    Cas. Madam, my former suit.   I do beseech
       you   110
That by your virtuous means I may again
Exist, and be a member of his love
Whom I with all the office of my heart
Entirely honour.   I would not be delay'd.
If my offence be of such mortal kind   115
That nor my service past, nor present sorrows,
Nor purpos'd merit in futurity
Can ransom me into his love again,
But to know so must be my benefit;
So shall I clothe me in a forc'd content,   120
And shut myself up in some other course,
To fortune's alms.
    Des.   Alas, thrice-gentle Cassio!
My advocation is not now in tune.
My lord is not my lord; nor should I know him
Were he in favour as in humour alter'd.   125
So help me every spirit sanctified
As I have spoken for you all my best
And stood within the blank of his displeasure
For my free speech!   You must a while be pa-
       tient.
What I can do I will; and more I will   130
Than for myself I dare.   Let that suffice you.
    Iago. Is my lord angry?
    Emil.   He went hence but now,
And certainly in strange unquietness.
    Iago. Can he be angry?   I have seen the cannon
When it hath blown his ranks into the air,   135
And, like the devil, from his very arm
Puff'd his own brother: — and is he angry?
Something of moment then.   I will go meet him.
There's matter in't indeed, if he be angry.
                             [*Exit Iago.*
    Des. I prithee, do so.   Something, sure, of state,
Either from Venice, or some unhatch'd practice   141
Made demonstrable here in Cyprus to him,
Hath puddled his clear spirit; and in such cases
Men's natures wrangle with inferior things,
Though great ones are their object.   'Tis even so;
For let our finger ache, and it indues   146

---

59. **amiable:** lovable.   74. **mummy:** embalming fluid.   75. **Conserv'd:** prepared.   86. [sir] Q.   Om. F.   92–93. [*Des.
I . . . handkerchief*] Q.   Om. F.   98. ['Zounds] Q.   *Away* F.   108. **happiness:** luck.   111. **virtuous:** effective.   125. **favour:**
appearance.   128. **blank:** target; strictly, the white spot in the center.   141. **practice:** plot.

Our other, healthful members even to a sense
Of pain.   Nay, we must think men are not gods,
Nor of them look for such observancy
As fits the bridal.   Beshrew me much, Emilia,   150
I was, unhandsome warrior as I am,
Arraigning his unkindness with my soul;
But now I find I had suborn'd the witness,
And he's indicted falsely.

   Emil. Pray Heaven it be state-matters, as you
      think,   155
And no conception nor no jealous toy
Concerning you.

   Des. Alas the day!   I never gave him cause.

   Emil. But jealous souls will not be answer'd so;
They are not ever jealous for the cause,   160
But jealous for they're jealous.   It is a monster
Begot upon itself, born on itself.

   Des. Heaven keep the monster from Othello's
      mind!

   Emil. Lady, amen.

   Des. I will go seek him.   Cassio, walk here-
      about;   165
If I do find him fit, I'll move your suit
And seek to effect it to my uttermost.

   Cas. I humbly thank your ladyship.

              [Exeunt [Desdemona and Emilia].

           Enter BIANCA.

   Bian. Save you, friend Cassio!

   Cas.   What make you from home?
How is it with you, my most fair Bianca?   170
Indeed, sweet love, I was coming to your house.

   Bian. And I was going to your lodging, Cassio.
What, keep a week away?   seven days and nights?
Eightscore eight hours? and lovers' absent hours,
More tedious than the dial eightscore times?   175
O weary reck'ning!

   Cas.   Pardon me, Bianca.
I have this while with leaden thoughts been press'd;
But I shall, in a more continuate time,
Strike off this score of absence.   Sweet Bianca,
      [Giving her Desdemona's handkerchief.]
Take me this work out.

   Bian.   O Cassio, whence came this?
This is some token from a newer friend;   181
To the felt absence now I feel a cause.
Is't come to this?   Well, well.

   Cas.   Go to, woman!
Throw your vile guesses in the devils' teeth,
From whence you have them.   You are jealous
      now   185
That this is from some mistress, some remembrance.
No, in good troth, Bianca.

   Bian.   Why, whose is it?

   Cas. I know not, [sweet]; I found it in my
      chamber.

I like the work well; ere it be demanded —
As like enough it will — I'd have it copied.   190
Take it, and do't; and leave me for this time.

   Bian. Leave you!   Wherefore?

   Cas. I do attend here on the General;
And think it no addition, nor my wish,   194
To have him see me woman'd.

   Bian.   Why, I pray you?

   Cas. Not that I love you not.

   Bian.   But that you do not love me.
I pray you, bring me on the way a little,
And say if I shall see you soon at night.

   Cas. 'Tis but a little way that I can bring you,
For I attend here; but I'll see you soon.   200

   Bian. 'Tis very good; I must be circumstanc'd.
                        [Exeunt

ACT IV

SCENE I.   *[Cyprus.   Before the castle.]*

Enter OTHELLO *and* IAGO.

   Iago. Will you think so?

   Oth.   Think so, Iago!

   Iago.   What,
To kiss in private?

   Oth.   An unauthoriz'd kiss.

   Iago. Or to be naked with her friend in bed
An hour or more, not meaning any harm?

   Oth. Naked in bed, Iago, and not mean harm!   5
It is hypocrisy against the devil.
They that mean virtuously, and yet do so,
The devil their virtue tempts, and they tempt
      heaven.

   Iago. If they do nothing, 'tis a venial slip;
But if I give my wife a handkerchief, —   10

   Oth. What then?

   Iago. Why, then, 'tis hers, my lord; and, being
      hers,
She may, I think, bestow 't on any man.

   Oth. She is protectress of her honour too;
May she give that?   15

   Iago. Her honour is an essence that's not seen;
They have it very oft that have it not:
But, for the handkerchief, —

   Oth. By heaven, I would most gladly have forgot
      it.
Thou said'st — O, it comes o'er my memory,   20
As doth the raven o'er the infectious house,
Boding to all — he had my handkerchief.

   Iago. Ay, what of that?

   Oth.   That's not so good now.

   Iago.   What
If I had said I had seen him do you wrong?
Or heard him say, — as knaves be such abroad,   25
Who having, by their own importunate suit,

---

178. **continuate:** uninterrupted.   188. **[sweet]** Q.   *neither* F.   194. **addition:** credit.   201. **circumstanc'd:** reconciled.

Or voluntary dotage of some mistress,
Convinced or suppli'd them, cannot choose
But they must blab —
  Oth.   Hath he said anything? 29
  Iago. He hath, my lord; but be you well assur'd,
No more than he'll unswear.
  Oth.   What hath he said?
  Iago. Why, that he did — I know not what he
  did.
  Oth. What? what?
  Iago. Lie —
  Oth.   With her?
  Iago.   With her, on her; what you will.
  Oth. Lie with her! lie on her! We say lie on 35
her, when they belie her. Lie with her! ['Zounds,]
that's fulsome! — Handkerchief — confessions —
handkerchief! — To confess, and be hang'd for his
labour; — first to be hang'd, and then to confess. —
I tremble at it. Nature would not invest herself
in such shadowing passion without some in- 40
struction. It is not words that shakes me thus.
Pish! Noses, ears, and lips. — Is't possible? —
Confess — handkerchief! — O devil!
                      [Falls in a trance.
  Iago. Work on, 45
My medicine, work! Thus credulous fools are
  caught;
And many worthy and chaste dames even thus,
All guiltless, meet reproach. — What, ho! my lord!
My lord, I say! Othello!

              Enter CASSIO.
            How now, Cassio!
  Cas. What's the matter? 50
  Iago. My lord is fall'n into an epilepsy.
This is his second fit; he had one yesterday.
  Cas. Rub him about the temples.
  Iago.   [No, forbear;]
The lethargy must have his quiet course;
If not, he foams at mouth and by and by 55
Breaks out to savage madness. Look, he stirs.
Do you withdraw yourself a little while;
He will recover straight. When he is gone,
I would on great occasion speak with you. 59
                       [Exit Cassio.
How is it, General? Have you not hurt your
  head?
  Oth. Dost thou mock me?
  Iago.   I mock you not, by heaven.
Would you would bear your fortune like a man!
  Oth. A horned man's a monster and a beast.
  Iago. There's many a beast then in a populous
  city,

And many a civil monster. 65
  Oth. Did he confess it?
  Iago.   Good sir, be a man;
Think every bearded fellow that's but yok'd
May draw with you. There's millions now alive
That nightly lie in those unproper beds
Which they dare swear peculiar; your case is
  better. 70
O, 'tis the spite of hell, the fiend's arch-mock,
To lip a wanton in a secure couch,
And to suppose her chaste! No, let me know;
And knowing what I am, I know what she shall
  be.
  Oth. O, thou art wise; 'tis certain.
  Iago.   Stand you a while apart; 75
Confine yourself but in a patient list.
Whilst you were here o'erwhelmed with your
  grief —
A passion most [unsuiting] such a man —
Cassio came hither. I shifted him away,
And laid good 'scuse upon your ecstasy; 80
Bade him anon return and here speak with me,
The which he promis'd. Do but encave yourself,
And mark the fleers, the gibes, and notable scorns
That dwell in every region of his face;
For I will make him tell the tale anew, 85
Where, how, how oft, how long ago, and when
He hath, and is again to cope your wife.
I say, but mark his gesture. Marry, patience;
Or I shall say you're all in all in spleen,
And nothing of a man.
  Oth.   Dost thou hear, Iago? 90
I will be found most cunning in my patience;
But — dost thou hear? — most bloody.
  Iago.   That's not amiss;
But yet keep time in all. Will you withdraw?
                    [Othello retires.]
Now will I question Cassio of Bianca,
A housewife that by selling her desires 95
Buys herself bread and clothes. It is a creature
That dotes on Cassio, as 'tis the strumpet's plague
To beguile many and be beguil'd by one.
He, when he hears of her, cannot [refrain]
From the excess of laughter. Here he comes. 100

          Re-enter CASSIO.
As he shall smile, Othello shall go mad;
And his unbookish jealousy must [conster]
Poor Cassio's smiles, gestures, and light behaviours
Quite in the wrong. How do you, Lieutenant?
  Cas. The worser that you give me the addition
Whose want even kills me. 106
  Iago. Ply Desdemona well, and you are sure on't.

Act IV, sc. i, 40–41. **invest…instruction:** i.e., create such imaginings unless to teach me. 53. **[No, forbear]** Q. Om. F.
55. **by and by:** straightway. 65. **civil:** civilized. 69. **unproper:** not exclusively their own. 70. **peculiar:** their own. 72.
secure: supposed safe from others. 76. **a patient list:** the bounds of patience. 78. **[unsuiting]** Q. *resulting* F. 80. **ecstasy:**
trance. 89. **spleen:** anger, passion. 99. **[refrain]** Q. *restraine* F. 102. **[conster]** Q: construe. *conserve* F.

[*Speaking lower.*] Now, if this suit lay in Bianca's [power].
How quickly should you speed!
   Cas.   Alas, poor caitiff!
   Oth. Look how he laughs already!   110
   Iago. I never knew woman love man so.
   Cas. Alas, poor rogue! I think, indeed, she loves me.
   Oth. Now he denies it faintly, and laughs it out.
   Iago. Do you hear, Cassio?   115
   Oth. Now he importunes him
To tell it o'er. Go to; well said, well said.
   Iago. She gives it out that you shall marry her. Do you intend it?
   Cas. Ha, ha, ha!   120
   Oth. Do ye triumph, Roman? Do you triumph?
   Cas. I marry [her]!! What? a customer! Prithee, bear some charity to my wit; do not think it so unwholesome. Ha, ha, ha!   125
   Oth. So, so so, so; they laugh that win.
   Iago. Why, the cry goes that you [shall] marry her.
   Cas. Prithee, say true.
   Iago. I am a very villain else.
   Oth. Have you scor'd me? Well.   130
   Cas. This is the monkey's own giving out. She is persuaded I will marry her, out of her own love and flattery, not out of my promise.
   Oth. Iago [beckons] me; now he begins the story.   135
   Cas. She was here even now; she haunts me in every place. I was the other day talking on the sea-bank with certain Venetians; and thither comes the bauble, and, falls me thus about my neck —   140
   Oth. Crying, "O dear Cassio!" as it were; his gesture imports it.
   Cas. So hangs, and lolls, and weeps upon me; so shakes and pulls me. Ha, ha, ha!   144
   Oth. Now he tells how she pluck'd him to my chamber. Oh, I see that nose of yours, but not that dog I shall throw it to.
   Cas. Well, I must leave her company.
   Iago. Before me! look, where she comes.   149

Enter BIANCA.

   Cas. 'Tis such another fitchew! Marry, a perfum'd one. — What do you mean by this haunting of me?
   Bian. Let the devil and his dam haunt you! What did you mean by that same handkerchief you gave me even now? I was a fine fool to take it.   155
I must take out the work? — A likely piece of work, that you should find it in your chamber, and know not who left it there! This is some minx's token, and I must take out the work? There; give it

your hobby-horse. Wheresoever you had it, I'll take out no work on't.   161
   Cas. How now, my sweet Bianca! how now! how now!
   Oth. By heaven, that should be my handkerchief!   165
   Bian. If you'll come to supper to-night, you may; if you will not, come when you are next prepar'd for.   [*Exit.*
   Iago. After her, after her.
   Cas. [Faith,] I must; she'll rail in the streets else.
   Iago. Will you sup there?   172
   Cas. Yes, I intend so.
   Iago. Well, I may chance to see you; for I would very fain speak with you.   175
   Cas. Prithee, come; will you?
   Iago. Go to; say no more.   [*Exit Cassio.*
   Oth. [*Advancing.*] How shall I murder him, Iago?
   Iago. Did you perceive how he laugh'd at his vice?   181
   Oth. O Iago!
   Iago. And did you see the handkerchief?
   Oth. Was that mine?
   Iago. Yours, by this hand. And to see how he prizes the foolish woman your wife! She gave it him, and he hath given it his whore.   187
   Oth. I would have him nine years a-killing. A fine woman! a fair woman! a sweet woman!
   Iago. Nay, you must forget that.   190
   Oth. Ay, let her rot, and perish, and be damn'd to-night; for she shall not live. No, my heart is turn'd to stone; I strike it, and it hurts my hand. O, the world hath not a sweeter creature! She might lie by an emperor's side and command him tasks.   196
   Iago. Nay, that's not your way.
   Oth. Hang her! I do but say what she is. So delicate with her needle! an admirable musician! O! she will sing the savageness out of a bear. Of so high and plenteous wit and invention!   201
   Iago. She's the worse for all this.
   Oth. O, a thousand thousand times. And then, of so gentle a condition!
   Iago. Ay, too gentle.   205
   Oth. Nay, that's certain. But yet the pity of it, Iago! O Iago, the pity of it, Iago!
   Iago. If you are so fond over her iniquity, give her patent to offend; for if it touch not you, it comes near nobody.   210
   Oth. I will chop her into messes. Cuckold me!
   Iago. O, 'tis foul in her.
   Oth. With mine officer!
   Iago. That's fouler.   215
   Oth. Get me some poison, Iago; this night. I'll not expostulate with her, lest her body and beauty

108. [power] Q. *dowre* F. 122. [her] Q. Om. F. **customer**: harlot. 127. [shall] Q. Om. F. 130. **scor'd**: branded. 134. [beckons] Q. *becomes* F. 150. **fitchew**: polecat. 211. **messes**: portions of food.

unprovide my mind again. This night, Iago. 219

Iago. Do it not with poison; strangle her in her
bed, even the bed she hath contaminated.

Oth. Good, good; the justice of it pleases; very
good.

Iago. And for Cassio, let me be his undertaker.
You shall hear more by midnight. 225
                                        [*A trumpet.*

Enter LODOVICO, DESDEMONA, *and Attendants.*

Oth. Excellent good. What trumpet is that
same?

Iago. I warrant, something from Venice. 'Tis
Lodovico, this, comes from the Duke. See, your
wife's with him.

Lod. Save you, worthy General!

Oth.   With all my heart, sir.

Lod. The Duke and Senators of Venice greet
you.   [*Gives him a letter.*] 230

Oth. I kiss the instrument of their pleasures.
                        [*Opens the letter, and reads.*]

Des. And what's the news, good cousin Lodovico?

Iago. I am very glad to see you, signior;
Welcome to Cyprus.

Lod. I thank you. How does Lieutenant
Cassio? 235

Iago. Lives, sir.

Des. Cousin, there 's fall'n between him and my
lord
An unkind breach; but you shall make all well.

Oth. Are you sure of that?

Des. My lord?

Oth. [*Reads.*] "This fail you not to do, as you
will." — 240

Lod. He did not call; he's busy in the paper.
Is there division 'twixt my lord and Cassio?

Des. A most unhappy one. I would do much
T' atone them, for the love I bear to Cassio.

Oth. Fire and brimstone!

Des.   My lord?

Oth.   Are you wise? 245

Des. What, is he angry?

Lod.   May be the letter mov'd him;
For, as I think, they do command him home,
Deputing Cassio in his government.

Des. Trust me, I am glad on 't.

Oth.   Indeed!

Des.   My lord?

Oth. I am glad to see you mad.

Des.   Why, sweet Othello, —

Oth. [*Striking her.*] Devil! 251

Des. I have not deserv'd this.

Lod. My lord, this would not be believ'd in
Venice
Though I should swear I saw 't. 'Tis very much.
Make her amends: she weeps.

Oth.   O devil, devil! 255
If that the earth could teem with woman's tears,
Each drop she falls would prove a crocodile.
Out of my sight!

Des.   I will not stay to offend you.
                                        [*Going.*]

Lod. Truly, [an] obedient lady:
I do beseech your lordship, call her back. 260

Oth. Mistress!

Des.   My lord?

Oth.   What would you with her, sir?

Lod. Who, I, my lord?

Oth. Ay; you did wish that I would make her
turn.
Sir, she can turn, and turn, and yet go on,
And turn again; and she can weep, sir, weep; 265
And she's obedient, as you say, obedient,
Very obedient. Proceed you in your tears.
Concerning this, sir, — O well-painted passion! —
I am commanded home. — Get you away;
I'll send for you anon. — Sir, I obey the man-
date, 270
And will return to Venice. — Hence, avaunt! —
                                [*Exit Desdemona.*]
Cassio shall have my place. And, sir, to-night
I do entreat that we may sup together.
You are welcome, sir, to Cyprus. — Goats and
monkeys!   [*Exit.*

Lod. Is this the noble Moor whom our full
Senate 275
Call all in all sufficient? Is this the nature
Whom passion could not shake? whose solid virtue
The shot of accident nor dart of chance
Could neither graze nor pierce?

Iago.   He is much chang'd.

Lod. Are his wits safe? Is he not light of brain?

Iago. He's that he is; I may not breathe my
censure 281
What he might be. If what he might be is not,
I would to heaven he were!

Lod.   What, strike his wife!

Iago. Faith, that was not so well; yet would I
knew
That stroke would prove the worst!

Lod.   Is it his use? 285
Or did the letters work upon his blood
And new-create [this] fault?

Iago.   Alas, alas!
It is not honesty in me to speak
What I have seen and known. You shall observe
him,
And his own courses will denote him so 290
That I may save my speech. Do but go after,
And mark how he continues.

Lod. I am sorry that I am deceiv'd in him.
                                        [*Exeunt.*

224. **undertaker:** dispatcher. 244. **atone:** reconcile. 256. **teem:** breed. 259. **[an]** Q. Om. F. 287. **[this]** Q. *his* F.

SCENE II. [*A room in the castle.*]

Enter OTHELLO *and* EMILIA.

Oth. You have seen nothing then?

Emil. Nor ever heard, nor ever did suspect.

Oth. Yes, you have seen Cassio and she together.

Emil. But then I saw no harm, and then I heard
Each syllable that breath made up between them.

Oth. What, did they never whisper?

Emil. Never, my lord. 6

Oth. Nor send you out o' th' way?

Emil. Never.

Oth. To fetch her fan, her gloves, her mask, nor
nothing?

Emil. Never, my lord. 10

Oth. That's strange.

Emil. I durst, my lord, to wager she is honest,
Lay down my soul at stake. If you think other,
Remove your thought; it doth abuse your bosom.
If any wretch have put this in your head, 15
Let Heaven requite it with the serpent's curse!
For, if she be not honest, chaste, and true,
There's no man happy; the purest of their wives
Is foul as slander.

Oth. Bid her come hither; go.

[*Exit Emilia.*

She says enough; yet she's a simple bawd 20
That cannot say as much. This is a subtle whore,
A closet lock and key of villanous secrets;
And yet she'll kneel and pray; I have seen her do't.

Enter DESDEMONA *with* EMILIA.

Des. My lord, what is your will?

Oth. Pray, chuck, come hither.

Des. What is your pleasure?

Oth. Let me see your eyes; 25
Look in my face.

Des. What horrible fancy's this?

Oth. [*To Emilia.*] Some of your function, mistress;
Leave procreants alone and shut the door;
Cough, or cry "hem," if anybody come.
Your mystery, your mystery; nay, dispatch. 30

[*Exit Emilia.*

Des. Upon my knee, what doth your speech
import?
I understand a fury in your words,
[But not the words.]

Oth. Why, what art thou?

Des. Your wife, my lord; your true
And loyal wife.

Oth. Come, swear it, damn thyself, 35
Lest, being like one of heaven, the devils themselves

Should fear to seize thee; therefore be double
damn'd,
Swear thou art honest.

Des. Heaven doth truly know it.

Oth. Heaven truly knows that thou art false as
hell.

Des. To whom, my lord? With whom? How
am I false? 40

Oth. Ah, Desdemon! Away! away! away!

Des. Alas the heavy day! Why do you weep?
Am I the motive of these tears, my lord?
If haply you my father do suspect
An instrument of this your calling back, 45
Lay not your blame on me. If you have lost him,
[Why,] I have lost him too.

Oth. Had it pleas'd Heaven
To try me with affliction; had they rain'd
All kind of sores and shames on my bare head,
Steep'd me in poverty to the very lips, 50
Given to captivity me and my utmost hopes,
I should have found in some place of my soul
A drop of patience; but, alas, to make me
The fixed figure for the time of scorn
To point his slow and moving finger at! 55
Yet could I bear that too, well, very well;
But there, where I have garner'd up my heart,
Where either I must live or bear no life;
The fountain from the which my current runs
Or else dries up; to be discarded thence! 60
Or keep it as a cistern for foul toads
To knot and gender in! Turn thy complexion
there,
Patience, thou young and rose-lipp'd cherubin,
[Ay, there] look grim as hell!

Des. I hope my noble lord esteems me honest. 65

Oth. O, ay; as summer flies are in the shambles,
That quicken even with blowing. O thou weed,
Who art so lovely fair and smell'st so sweet
That the sense aches at thee, would thou hadst
ne'er been born! 69

Des. Alas, what ignorant sin have I committed?

Oth. Was this fair paper, this most goodly book,
Made to write "whore" upon? What committed!
Committed! O thou public commoner!
I should make very forges of my cheeks,
That would to cinders burn up modesty, 75
Did I but speak thy deeds. What committed!
Heaven stops the nose at it, and the moon winks;
The bawdy wind, that kisses all it meets,
Is hush'd within the hollow mine of earth
And will not hear it. What committed! 80
[Impudent strumpet!]

Des. By heaven, you do me wrong.

Sc. ii, 24. **Pray** Q. *Pray you* F. 30. **mystery:** trade. 33. **[But...words]** Q. Om. F. 47. **[Why]** Q. Om. F. 54. **time of scorn:** scorn of the age. 55. **slow and moving:** slowly moving. Q reads *slow unmoving.* 62. **Turn thy complexion:** change thy color. 64. **[Ay, there]** (Theobald). *I here* Ff Qq. 67. **quicken...blowing:** come to life as soon as impregnated. 73. **commoner:** harlot. 77. **winks:** shuts her eyes. 81. **[Impudent strumpet]** Q. Om. F.

Oth. Are not you a strumpet?
Des.   No, as I am a Christian.
If to preserve this vessel for my lord
From any other foul unlawful touch
Be not to be a strumpet, I am none.   85
Oth. What, not a whore?
Des.   No, as I shall be sav'd.
Oth. Is't possible?
Des. O, Heaven forgive us!
Oth.   I cry you mercy, then.
I took you for that cunning whore of Venice
That married with Othello. [*Raising his voice.*] —
     You, mistress,   90

Re-enter EMILIA.

That have the office opposite to Saint Peter,
And keeps the gate of hell! You, you, ay, you!
We have done our course; there's money for your
     pains.
I pray you, turn the key and keep our counsel.
                                   [*Exit.*
Emil. Alas, what does this gentleman conceive?
How do you, madam? How do you, my good
     lady?   96
Des. Faith, half asleep.
Emil. Good madam, what's the matter with my
     lord?
Des. With who?
Emil. Why, with my lord, madam.   100
Des. Who is thy lord?
Emil.   He that is yours, sweet lady.
Des. I have none. Do not talk to me, Emilia;
I cannot weep, nor answers have I none
But what should go by water. Prithee, tonight
Lay on my bed my wedding sheets, remember;   105
And call thy husband hither.
Emil.   Here's a change indeed!
                                   [*Exit.*
Des. 'Tis meet I should be us'd so, very meet.
How have I been behav'd, that he might stick
The small'st opinion on my least misuse?

Re-enter EMILIA with IAGO

Iago. What is your pleasure, madam? How
is't with you?   110
Des. I cannot tell. Those that do teach young
     babes
Do it with gentle means and easy tasks.
He might have chid me so; for, in good faith,
I am a child to chiding.
Iago.   What's the matter, lady?
Emil. Alas, Iago, my lord hath so bewhor'd her,
Thrown such despite and heavy terms upon her,   116
That true hearts cannot bear it.
Des. Am I that name, Iago?

Iago.   What name, fair lady?
Des. Such as she said my lord did say I was.
Emil. He call'd her whore. A beggar in his
     drink   120
Could not have laid such terms upon his callet.
Iago. Why did he so?
Des. I do not know; I am sure I am none such.
Iago. Do not weep, do not weep. Alas the day!
Emil. Hath she forsook so many noble matches,
Her father and her country and her friends,   126
To be call'd whore? Would it not make one weep?
Des. It is my wretched fortune.
Iago.   Beshrew him for't!
How comes this trick upon him?
Des.   Nay, Heaven doth know.
Emil. I will be hang'd if some eternal villain,
Some busy and insinuating rogue,   131
Some cogging, cozening slave, to get some office,
Have not devis'd this slander. I'll be hang'd else.
Iago. Fie, there is no such man; it is impossible.
Des. If any such there be, Heaven pardon him!
Emil. A halter pardon him! and hell gnaw his
     bones!   136
Why should he call her whore? Who keeps her
     company?
What place? what time? what form? what likeli-
     hood?
The Moor's abus'd by some most villanous knave,
Some base notorious knave, some scurvy fellow.   140
O heavens, that such companions thou'dst unfold,
And put in every honest hand a whip
To lash the rascals naked through the world
Even from the east to th' west!
Iago.   Speak within door.
Emil. O, fie upon them! Some such squire he
     was   145
That turn'd your wit the seamy side without,
And made you to suspect me with the Moor.
Iago. You are a fool; go to.
Des.   Alas, Iago,
What shall I do to win my lord again?
Good friend, go to him; for, by this light of heaven,
I know not how I lost him. Here I kneel: 151
If e'er my will did trespass 'gainst his love,
Either in discourse of thought or actual deed,
Or that mine eyes, mine ears, or any sense
Delighted them [in] any other form;   155
Or that I do not yet, and ever did,
And ever will — though he do shake me off
To beggarly divorcement — love him dearly,
Comfort forswear me! Unkindness may do much;
And his unkindness may defeat my life,   160
But never taint my love. I cannot say "whore."
It does abhor me now I speak the word;
To do the act that might the addition earn

---

104. **go by water:** be rendered by tears. 109. **opinion:** censure. **misuse:** misconduct. 121. **callet:** whore. 132. **cogging:** lying. **cozening:** cheating. 141. **unfold:** expose. 153. **discourse:** course. 155. **[in]** Q₂. *or* F. 160. **defeat:** destroy.

Not the world's mass of vanity could make me.

Iago. I pray you, be content; 'tis but his humour.
The business of the state does him offence,   166
[And he does chide with you.]

    Des. If 'twere no other, —

    Iago.   It is but so, I warrant.

                        [*Trumpets within.*]
Hark, how these instruments summon to supper!
The messengers of Venice stay the meat.   170
Go in, and weep not; all things shall be well.

          [*Exeunt Desdemona and Emilia.*

            Enter RODERIGO.

How now, Roderigo!

    Rod. I do not find that thou deal'st justly with
me.

    Iago. What in the contrary?   175

    Rod. Every day thou daff'st me with some device,
Iago; and rather, as it seems to me now, keep'st
from me all conveniency than suppliest me with
the least advantage of hope. I will indeed no
longer endure it, nor am I yet persuaded to put up
in peace what already I have foolishly suff'red.   182

    Iago. Will you hear me, Roderigo?

    Rod. I have heard too much, and your words and
performances are no kin together.

    Iago. You charge me most unjustly.   186

    Rod. With nought but truth. I have wasted
myself out of my means. The jewels you have had
from me to deliver Desdemona would half have
corrupted a votarist. You have told me she hath
receiv'd them and return'd me expectations and
comforts of sudden respect and acquaintance, but
I find none.   193

    Iago. Well; go to; very well.

    Rod. Very well! go to! I cannot go to, man;
nor 'tis not very well. Nay, I think it is scurvy,
and begin to find myself fopp'd in it.

    Iago. Very well.   198

    Rod. I tell you 'tis not very well. I will make
myself known to Desdemona. If she will return
me my jewels, I will give over my suit and repent
my unlawful solicitation; if not, assure yourself I
will seek satisfaction of you.

    Iago. You have said now.

    Rod. Ay, and said nothing but what I protest
intendment of doing.   206

    Iago. Why, now I see there's mettle in thee, and
even from this instant do build on thee a better
opinion than ever before. Give me thy hand,
Roderigo. Thou hast taken against me a most
just exception; but yet, I protest, I have dealt most
directly in thy affair.

    Rod. It hath not appear'd.

    Iago. I grant indeed it hath not appear'd, and

your suspicion is not without wit and judgement.
But, Roderigo, if thou hast that in thee indeed,   216
which I have greater reason to believe now than
ever, I mean purpose, courage, and valour, this
night show it. If thou the next night following
enjoy not Desdemona, take me from this world
with treachery and devise engines for my life.   222

    Rod. Well, what is it? Is it within reason and
compass?

    Iago. Sir, there is especial commission come
from Venice to depute Cassio in Othello's place.

    Rod. Is that true? Why, then Othello and
Desdemona return again to Venice.   228

    Iago. O, no; he goes into Mauritania and taketh
away with him the fair Desdemona, unless his
abode be ling'red here by some accident; wherein
none can be so determinate as the removing of
Cassio.   233

    Rod. How do you mean, removing him?

    Iago. Why, by making him uncapable of Othello's
place; knocking out his brains.

    Rod. And that you would have me to do?   237

    Iago. Ay, if you dare do yourself a profit and a
right. He sups to-night with a harlotry, and
thither will I go to him; he knows not yet of his   240
honourable fortune. If you will watch his going
thence, which I will fashion to fall out between
twelve and one, you may take him at your pleasure.
I will be near to second your attempt, and he shall
fall between us. Come, stand not amaz'd at it,   245
but go along with me; I will show you such a necessity in his death that you shall think yourself
bound to put it on him. It is now high supper-
time, and the night grows to waste. About it.   250

    Rod. I will hear further reason for this.

    Iago. And you shall be satisfi'd.   [*Exeunt.*

      SCENE III.   [*Another room in the castle.*]

    Enter OTHELLO, LODOVICO, DESDEMONA,
         EMILIA, *and Attendants.*

    Lod. I do beseech you, sir, trouble yourself no
further.

    Oth. O, pardon me; 'twill do me good to walk.

    Lod. Madam, good-night; I humbly thank your
ladyship.

    Des. Your honour is most welcome.

    Oth.   Will you walk, sir?
O, — Desdemona, —   5

    Des. My lord?

    Oth. Get you to bed on th' instant; I will be
return'd forthwith. Dismiss your attendant there.
Look 't be done.

    Des. I will, my lord.   10

      [*Exeunt* [*Othello, Lodovico, and Attendants*].

167. [And...you] Q. Om. F.   170. **stay the meat:** wait to dine.   176. **daff'st me:** puttest me off.   190. **votarist:**
nun.   192. **sudden respect:** speedy notice.   197. **fopp'd:** duped.   222. **engines:** plots.

Emil. How goes it now? He looks gentler than
  he did.
Des. He says he will return incontinent;
And hath commanded me to go to bed,
And bid me to dismiss you.
Emil.   Dismiss me!
Des. It was his bidding; therefore, good Emilia,
Give me my nightly wearing, and adieu.   16
We must not now displease him.
Emil. I would you had never seen him!
Des. So would not I. My love doth so approve
  him,
That even his stubbornness, his checks, his
  frowns, —   20
Prithee, unpin me, — have grace and favour [in
  them].
Emil. I have laid those sheets you bade me on
  the bed.
Des. All's one. Good [faith], how foolish are
  our minds!
If I do die before, prithee, shroud me   24
In one of these same sheets.
Emil.   Come, come, you talk.
Des. My mother had a maid call'd Barbary;
She was in love, and he she lov'd prov'd mad
And did forsake her. She had a song of "Willow";
An old thing 'twas, but it express'd her fortune,
And she died singing it. That song to-night   30
Will not go from my mind; I have much to do
But to go hang my head all at one side
And sing it like poor Barbary. Prithee, dispatch.
Emil. Shall I go fetch your night-gown?
Des.   No, unpin me here.
This Lodovico is a proper man.   35
Emil. A very handsome man.
Des. He speaks well.
Emil. I know a lady in Venice would have
walk'd barefoot to Palestine for a touch of his
nether lip.   40
Des. [*Singing.*]
"The poor soul sat [sighing] by a sycamore tree,
  Sing all a green willow;
Her hand on her bosom, her head on her knee,
  Sing willow, willow, willow.
The fresh streams ran by her, and murmur'd her
  moans;   45
  Sing willow, willow, willow;
Her salt tears fell from her, and soft'ned the stones;
  Sing willow, willow, willow;"
Lay by these; —
[*Singing.*] "Willow, willow;" —
Prithee, hie thee; he'll come anon; —   50
[*Singing.*]
"Sing all a green willow must be my garland.

Let nobody blame him, his scorn I approve," —
Nay, that's not next. — Hark! who is't that
  knocks?
Emil. It's the wind.
Des. [*Singing.*]
"I call'd my love false love; but what said he
  then?   55
Sing willow, willow, willow.
If I court moe women, you'll couch with moe
  men." —
So, get thee gone; good-night. Mine eyes do itch;
Doth that bode weeping?
Emil.   'Tis neither here nor there.
Des. I have heard it said so. O, these men,
  these men!   60
Dost thou in conscience think, — tell me, Emilia, —
That there be women do abuse their husbands
In such gross kind?
Emil.   There be some such, no question.
Des. Wouldst thou do such a deed for all the
  world?   64
Emil. Why, would not you?
Des.   No, by this heavenly light!
Emil. Nor I neither by this heavenly light;
I might do't as well i' th' dark.
Des. Wouldst thou do such a deed for all the
  world?
Emil. The world's a huge thing; it is a great
  price   69
For a small vice.
Des.   In troth, I think thou wouldst not.
Emil. In troth, I think I should; and undo't
when I had done. Marry, I would not do such a
thing for a joint-ring, nor for measures of lawn, nor
for gowns, petticoats, nor caps, nor any petty exhibition; but, for all the whole world, — ['ud's
pity], who would not make her husband a   75
cuckold to make him a monarch? I should venture
purgatory for't.
Des. Beshrew me, if I would do such a wrong
For the whole world.   79
Emil. Why, the wrong is but a wrong i' th'
world; and having the world for your labour, 'tis a
wrong in your own world, and you might quickly
make it right.
Des. I do not think there is any such woman. 84
Emil. Yes, a dozen; and as many to th' vantage
as would store the world they play'd for.
But I do think it is their husbands' faults
If wives do fall. Say that they slack their duties
And pour our treasures into foreign laps,
Or else break out in peevish jealousies,   90
Throwing restraint upon us; or say they strike us,
Or scant our former having in despite;

Sc. iii, 20. **stubbornness:** roughness. 21. **[in them]** Q. Om. F. 23. **[faith]** Q. *Father* F. 41. **[sighing]** Q₂. *singing* F.
73. **joint-ring:** ring made in separable halves. 74. **exhibition:** allowance. 75. **['ud's pity]** Q: God's pity. *Why* F. 85.
to th' vantage: more, to boot. 90. **peevish:** silly. 92. **having:** allowance.

Why, we have galls, and though we have some
grace,
Yet have we some revenge.   Let husbands know
Their wives have sense like them; they see and
smell   95
And have their palates both for sweet and sour
As husbands have.   What is it that they do
When they change us for others?   Is it sport?
I think it is.   And doth affection breed it?
I think it doth.   Is't frailty that thus errs?   100
It is so too.   And have not we affections,
Desires for sport, and frailty, as men have?
Then let them use us well; else let them know,
The ills we do, their ills instruct us so.
   Des.   Good-night, good-night.   Heaven me such
uses send,   105
Not to pick bad from bad, but by bad mend.
                              [Exeunt.

ACT V

SCENE I.   *[Cyprus.   A street.]*

Enter IAGO *and* RODERIGO.

   Iago.   Here, stand behind this [bulk]; straight
will he come.
Wear thy good rapier bare, and put it home.
Quick, quick; fear nothing; I'll be at thy elbow.
It makes us, or it mars us; think on that,
And fix most firm thy resolution.   5
   Rod.   Be near at hand; I may miscarry in't.
   Iago.   Here, at thy hand; be bold, and take thy
stand.   *[Retires.]*
   Rod.   I have no great devotion to the deed,
And yet he hath given me satisfying reasons.
'Tis but a man gone.   Forth, my sword: he dies.   10
   Iago.   I have rubb'd this young quat almost to
the sense,
And he grows angry.   Now, whether he kill Cassio,
Or Cassio him, or each do kill the other,
Every way makes my gain.   Live Roderigo,
He calls me to a restitution large   15
Of gold and jewels that I bobb'd from him
As gifts to Desdemona;
It must not be.   If Cassio do remain,
He hath a daily beauty in his life
That makes me ugly; and, besides, the Moor   20
May unfold me to him; there stand I in much peril.
No, he must die.   But so; I heard him coming.

Enter CASSIO.

   Rod.   I know his gait, 'tis he. — Villain, thou
diest!   *[Makes a pass at Cassio.]*

   Cas.   That thrust had been mine enemy indeed,
But that my coat is better than thou know'st.   25
I will make proof of thine.
             [Draws, and wounds Roderigo.]
   Rod.   O, I am slain.
    *[Iago from behind wounds Cassio in the leg,
and exit.]*
   Cas.   I am maim'd for ever.   Help, ho! murder!
murder!   *[Falls.]*

Enter OTHELLO.

   Oth.   The voice of Cassio!   Iago keeps his word.
   Rod.   O, villain that I am!
   Oth.   It is even so.
   Cas.   O, help, ho! light! a surgeon!   30
   Oth.   'Tis he! — O brave Iago, honest and just,
That hast such noble sense of thy friend's wrong!
Thou teachest me.   Minion, your dear lies dead,
And your unblest fate hies; strumpet, I come.
[Forth] of my heart those charms, thine eyes, are
blotted;   35
Thy bed, lust-stain'd, shall with lust's blood be
spotted.   *[Exit.*

Enter LODOVICO *and* GRATIANO.

   Cas.   What, ho! no watch? no passage?   Murder!
murder!
   Gra.   'Tis some mischance; the voice is very dire-
ful.
   Cas.   O, help!
   Lod.   Hark!   40
   Rod.   O wretched villain!
   Lod.   Two or three groan.   'Tis heavy night,
These may be counterfeits; let's think 't unsafe
To come in to the cry without more help.
   Rod.   Nobody come?   Then shall I bleed to
death.   45

Re-enter IAGO, *with a light.*

   Lod.   Hark!
   Gra.   Here's one comes in his shirt, with light and
weapons.
   Iago.   Who's there?   Whose noise is this that
cries on murder?
   Lod.   We do not know.
   Iago.   Do not you hear a cry?
   Cas.   Here, here! for Heaven's sake, help me!
   Iago.   What's the matter?   50
   Gra.   This is Othello's ancient, as I take it.
   Lod.   The same indeed; a very valiant fellow.
   Iago.   What are you here that cry so grievously?
   Cas.   Iago?   O, I am spoil'd, undone by villains!
Give me some help.   55

93. **galls:** spirits to resent injury.
Act V, sc. i, 1. **[bulk]** Q: jutting part of a building.   *barke* F.   11. **quat:** pimple.   **the sense:** the quick.   16. **bobb'd:** cheated, swindled.   25. **coat:** i.e., of mail (worn under outer clothing).   33. **Minion:** hussy.   35. **[Forth]** Q.   *For* F.   37. **passage:** passers-by.   42. **heavy:** dark.

Iago. O me, Lieutenant! what villains have done
  this?
Cas. I think that one of them is hereabout
And cannot make away.
Iago.   O treacherous villains!
What are you there? — Come in, and give some
  help.   [*To Lodovico and Gratiano.*]
Rod. O, help me there!   60
Cas. That's one of them.
Iago.   O murd'rous slave! O villain!
              [*Thrusts* [*Roderigo*] *in.*]
Rod. O damn'd Iago! O inhuman dog!
Iago. Kill men i' th' dark! — Where be these
  bloody thieves? —
How silent is this town! — Ho! murder! murder! —
What may you be? Are you of good or evil?   65
Lod. As you shall prove us, praise us.
Iago. Signior Lodovico?
Lod. He, sir.
Iago. I cry you mercy. Here's Cassio hurt by
  villains.
Gra. Cassio!   70
Iago. How is't, brother!
Cas. My leg is cut in two.
Iago.   Marry, heaven forbid!
Light, gentlemen! I'll bind it with my shirt.

Enter BIANCA.

Bian. What is the matter, ho? Who is't that
  cried?
Iago. Who is't that cried!   75
Bian. O my dear Cassio! my sweet Cassio!
O Cassio, Cassio, Cassio!
Iago. O notable strumpet! Cassio, may you
  suspect
Who they should be that have thus mangled you?
Cas. No.   80
Gra. I am sorry to find you thus; I have been
  to seek you.
Iago. Lend me a garter. So. O, for a chair,
To bear him easily hence!
Bian. Alas, he faints! O Cassio, Cassio, Cassio!
Iago. Gentlemen all, I do suspect this trash 85
To be a party in this injury.
Patience a while, good Cassio. Come, come;
Lend me a light. Know we this face or no?
Alas, my friend and my dear countryman
Roderigo! No: — yes, sure: — yes, 'tis Roderigo.
Gra. What, of Venice?   91
Iago. Even he, sir; did you know him?
Gra.   Know him! ay.
Iago. Signior Gratiano? I cry your gentle
  pardon;
These bloody accidents must excuse my manners
That so neglected you.
Gra.   I am glad to see you.   95

Iago. How do you, Cassio? O, a chair, a chair!
Gra. Roderigo!
Iago. He, he, 'tis he. [*A chair brought in.*] O,
  that's well said; the chair.
Some good man bear him carefully from hence;
I'll fetch the General's surgeon.   [*To Bianca.*]
  For you, mistress,   100
Save you your labour. He that lies slain here,
  Cassio,
Was my dear friend. What malice was between
  you?
Cas. None in the world; nor do I know the man.
Iago. [*To Bian.*] What, look you pale? O, bear
  him out o' th' air.
        [*Cassio and Roderigo are borne off.*]
Stay you, good gentlemen. Look you pale, mis-
  tress?   105
Do you perceive the gastness of her eye?
Nay, if you stare, we shall hear more anon.
Behold her well; I pray you, look upon her.
Do you see, gentlemen? Nay, guiltiness will speak,
Though tongues were out of use.   110

Enter EMILIA.

Emil. Alas, what's the matter? What's the
  matter, husband?
Iago. Cassio hath here been set on in the dark
By Roderigo and fellows that are scap'd.
He's almost slain, and Roderigo quite dead.
Emil. Alas, good gentleman! alas, good Cassio!
Iago. This is the fruits of whoring. Prithee,
  Emilia,   116
Go know of Cassio where he supp'd to-night.
[*To Bianca.*] What, do you shake at that?
Bian. He supp'd at my house; but I therefore
  shake not.
Iago. O, did he so? I charge you, go with me. 120
Emil. Oh, fie upon thee, strumpet!
Bian. I am no strumpet, but of life as honest
As you that thus abuse me.
Emil.   As I? Fie upon thee!
Iago. Kind gentlemen, let's go see poor Cassio
  dress'd.
Come, mistress, you must tell's another tale. 125
Emilia, run you to the citadel,
And tell my lord and lady what hath happ'd.
Will you go on afore? [*Aside.*] This is the night
That either makes me or fordoes me quite.
                                      [*Exeunt.*

SCENE II. [*A bedchamber in the castle:*] DESDEMONA
            in bed [*asleep*].

Enter OTHELLO *with a light.*

Oth. It is the cause, it is the cause, my soul, —
Let me not name it to you, you chaste stars! —

82. **chair:** sedan chair. 106. **gastness:** ghastliness. 129. **fordoes:** destroys.

It is the cause.   Yet I'll not shed her blood,
Nor scar that whiter skin of hers than snow,
And smooth as monumental alabaster.   5
Yet she must die, else she'll betray more men.
Put out the light, and then put out the light.
If I quench thee, thou flaming minister,
I can again thy former light restore,
Should I repent me; but once put out thy light,   10
Thou cunning'st pattern of excelling nature,
I know not where is that Promethean heat
That can thy light relume.   When I have pluck'd
  the rose
I cannot give it vital growth again,
It needs must wither.   I'll smell [it] on the tree.   15
                                        [Kisses her.
Oh, balmy breath, that dost almost persuade
Justice to break her sword!   One more, one more.
Be thus when thou art dead, and I will kill thee
And love thee after.   One more, and that's the last;
So sweet was ne'er so fatal.   I must weep,   20
But they are cruel tears.   This sorrow's heavenly;
It strikes where it doth love.   She wakes.
  Des. Who's there?   Othello?
  Oth.   Ay, Desdemona.
  Des. Will you come to bed, my lord?
  Oth. Have you pray'd to-night, Desdemon?
  Des.   Ay, my lord.
  Oth. If you bethink yourself of any crime   26
Unreconcil'd as yet to Heaven and grace,
Solicit for it straight.
  Des. Alack, my lord, what may you mean by
    that?
  Oth. Well, do it, and be brief; I will walk by.   30
I would not kill thy unprepared spirit;
No; heavens forfend!   I would not kill thy soul.
  Des. Talk you of killing?
  Oth.   Ay, I do.
  Des.   Then Heaven
Have mercy on me!
  Oth.   Amen, with all my heart!
  Des. If you say [so], I hope you will not kill
    me.   35
  Oth. Hum!
  Des. And yet I fear you; for you're fatal then
When your eyes roll so.   Why I should fear I know
    not,
Since guiltiness I know not; but yet I feel I fear.
  Oth. Think on thy sins.
  Des.   They are loves I bear to you.   40
  Oth. Ay, and for that thou diest.
  Des. That death's unnatural that kills for loving.
Alas, why gnaw you so your nether lip?
Some bloody passion shakes your very frame.
These are portents; but yet I hope, I hope,   45
They do not point on me.

  Oth.   Peace, and be still!
  Des. I will so.   What's the matter?
  Oth. That handkerchief which I so lov'd and
    gave thee
Thou gav'st to Cassio.
  Des.   No, by my life and soul!
Send for the man, and ask him.
  Oth.   Sweet soul, take heed,   50
Take heed of perjury; thou art on thy deathbed.
  Des. Ay, but not yet to die.
  Oth.   [Yes], presently:
Therefore confess thee freely of thy sin;
For to deny each article with oath
Cannot remove nor choke the strong conception   55
That I do groan withal.   Thou art to die.
  Des. O, Heaven, have mercy on me!
  Oth.   I say, amen.
  Des. And have you mercy too!   I never did
Offend you in my life; never lov'd Cassio
But with such general warranty of heaven   60
As I might love; I never gave him token.
  Oth. By heaven, I saw my handkerchief in 's hand.
O perjur'd woman! thou dost stone my heart,
And makes me call what I intend to do
A murder, which I thought a sacrifice.   65
I saw the handkerchief.
  Des.   He found it then;
I never gave it him.   Send for him hither;
Let him confess a truth.
  Oth.   He hath confess'd.
  Des. What, my lord?   69
  Oth. That he hath us'd thee.
  Des.   How?   unlawfully?
  Oth.   Ay.
  Des. He will not say so.
  Oth.   No, his mouth is stopp'd;
Honest Iago hath ta'en order for't.
  Des. O! my fear interprets.   What, is he dead?
  Oth. Had all his hairs been lives, my great
    revenge
Had stomach for them all.   75
  Des. Alas! he is betray'd and I undone.
  Oth. Out, strumpet! weep'st thou for him to
    my face?
  Des. O, banish me, my lord, but kill me not!
  Oth. Down, strumpet!
  Des. Kill me to-morrow; let me live to-night!   80
  Oth. Nay, if you strive, —
  Des. But half an hour!
  Oth.   Being done, there is no pause.
  Des. But while I say one prayer!
  Oth.   It is too late.
                                        [He smothers her.
  Emil. (*At the door.*) My lord, my lord!
    What, ho! my lord, my lord!

Sc. ii, 12. **Promethean heat:** divine fire.   15. **[it]** Q.   *thee* F.   35. **[so]** Q.   Om. F.   52. **[Yes]** Q.   Om. F.   55. **concep-**
tion: purpose.

Oth. What noise is this? Not dead? not yet
  quite dead? 85
I that am cruel am yet merciful;
I would not have thee linger in thy pain.
So, so.
  Emil. (*Within.*) What, ho! my lord, my lord!
  Oth. Who's there?
  Emil. [*Within.*] O, good my lord, I would speak
    a word with you! 90
  Oth. Yes: — 'tis Emilia. — By and by. — She's
dead.
'Tis like she comes to speak of Cassio's death.
The noise was high. Ha! no more moving?
Still as the grave. Shall she come in? Were't
  good? —
I think she stirs again: — no. What's best to
  do? 95
If she come in, she'll sure speak to my wife.
My wife! my wife! what wife? I have no wife.
O, insupportable! O heavy hour!
Methinks it should be now a huge eclipse
Of sun and moon, and that th' affrighted globe 100
Did yawn at alteration.
  Emil. [*Within.*] I do beseech you
That I may speak with you, O, good my lord!
  Oth. I had forgot thee. O, come in, Emilia.
Soft; by and by. — Let me the curtains draw. —
Where art thou? [*Unlocks the door.*]

Enter EMILIA.

        What's the matter with thee now? 105
  Emil. O, my good lord, yonder's foul murders
    done!
  Oth. What, now?
  Emil. But now, my lord.
  Oth. It is the very error of the moon;
She comes more nearer earth than she was wont, 110
And makes men mad.
  Emil. Cassio, my lord, hath kill'd a young
    Venetian
Call'd Roderigo.
  Oth. Roderigo kill'd!
And Cassio kill'd!
  Emil. No, Cassio is not kill'd.
  Oth. Not Cassio kill'd! Then murder's out
    of tune, 115
And sweet revenge grows harsh.
  Des. O, falsely, falsely murder'd!
  Emil. O Lord, what cry is that?
  Oth. That! what?
  Emil. Out, and alas! that was my lady's voice.
Help! help, ho! help! O lady, speak again! 120
Sweet Desdemona! O sweet mistress, speak!
  Des. A guiltless death I die.
  Emil. O, who hath done this deed?
  Des. Nobody; I myself. Farewell!

Commend me to my kind lord. O, farewell! 125
                         [*Dies.*
  Oth. Why, how should she be murd'red?
  Emil. Alas, who knows?
  Oth. You hear her say herself, it was not I.
  Emil. She said so; I must needs report the truth.
  Oth. She's, like a liar, gone to burning hell.
'Twas I that kill'd her.
  Emil. O, the more angel she, 130
And you the blacker devil!
  Oth. She turn'd to folly, and she was a whore.
  Emil. Thou dost belie her, and thou art a devil.
  Oth. She was false as water.
  Emil. Thou art rash as fire to say
That she was false: O, she was heavenly true! 135
  Oth. Cassio did top her; ask thy husband else.
O, I were damn'd beneath all depth in hell
But that I did proceed upon just grounds
To this extremity. Thy husband knew it all.
  Emil. My husband! 140
  Oth. Thy husband.
  Emil. That she was false to wedlock?
  Oth. Ay, with Cassio. Had she been true,
If Heaven would make me such another world
Of one entire and perfect chrysolite, 145
I'd not have sold her for it.
  Emil. My husband!
  Oth. Ay, 'twas he that told me on her first.
An honest man he is, and hates the slime
That sticks on filthy deeds.
  Emil. My husband!
  Oth. What needs this iterance, woman? I say
    thy husband. 150
  Emil. O mistress, villainy hath made mocks
    with love!
My husband say [that] she was false!
  Oth. He, woman;
I say thy husband; dost understand the word?
My friend, thy husband, honest, honest Iago.
  Emil. If he say so, may his pernicious soul 155
Rot half a grain a day! He lies to the heart.
She was too fond of her most filthy bargain.
  Oth. Ha!
  Emil. Do thy worst!
This deed of thine is no more worthy heaven 160
Than thou wast worthy her.
  Oth. Peace, you were best.
  Emil. Thou hast not half that power to do me
    harm
As I have to be hurt. O gull! O dolt!
As ignorant as dirt! Thou hast done a deed —
I care not for thy sword; I'll make thee known 165
Though I lost twenty lives. — Help! help, ho!
    help!
The Moor hath kill'd my mistress! Murder!
    murder!

---

109. **error:** aberration. 145. **chrysolite:** a precious stone. 150. **iterance:** repetition. 152. **[that]** Q₂. Om. F.

Enter MONTANO, GRATIANO, IAGO, *and others.*

Mon. What is the matter? How now, general!
Emil. O, are you come, Iago? You have done
   well,
That men must lay their murders on your neck. 170
Gra. What is the matter?
Emil. Disprove this villain, if thou be'st a man.
He says thou told'st him that his wife was false.
I know thou didst not, thou'rt not such a villain.
Speak, for my heart is full.   175
   Iago. I told him what I thought, and told no
      more
Than what he found himself was apt and true.
   Emil. But did you ever tell him she was false?
Iago. I did.
Emil. You told a lie, an odious, damned lie; 180
Upon my soul, a lie, a wicked lie.
She false with Cassio! — did you say with Cassio?
   Iago. With Cassio, mistress. Go to, charm your
      tongue.
   Emil. I will not charm my tongue; I am bound
      to speak.
My mistress here lies murdered in her bed, — 185
   All. O heavens forfend!
   Emil. And your reports have set the murderer on.
Oth. Nay, stare not, masters; it is true, indeed.
Gra. 'Tis a strange truth.
Mon. O monstrous act!
Emil.   Villany, villany, villany! 190
I think upon't, — I think I smell 't, — O villany!
I thought so then, — I'll kill myself for grief —
O villany, villany!
   Iago. What, are you mad? I charge you, get
      you home.
   Emil. Good gentlemen, let me have leave to
      speak;   195
'Tis proper I obey him, but not now.
Perchance, Iago, I will ne'er go home.
   Oth. O! O! O!   [*He falls on the bed.*
   Emil.   Nay, lay thee down and roar;
For thou hast kill'd the sweetest innocent
That e'er did lift up eye.
   Oth.   [*Rising.*] O, she was foul!   200
I scarce did know you, uncle; there lies your niece,
Whose breath, indeed, these hands have newly
   stopp'd.
I know this act shows horrible and grim.
   Gra. Poor Desdemon! I am glad thy father's
      dead.
Thy match was mortal to him, and pure grief 205
Shore his old thread in twain. Did he live now,
This sight would make him do a desperate turn,
Yea, curse his better angel from his side,
And fall to reprobance.

Oth. 'Tis pitiful; but yet Iago knows   210
That she with Cassio hath the act of shame
A thousand times committed. Cassio confess'd
   it;
And she did gratify his amorous works
With that recognizance and pledge of love
Which I first gave her. I saw it in his hand; 215
It was a handkerchief, an antique token
My father gave my mother.
   Emil. O [God]! O heavenly [God]!
   Iago. ['Zounds,] hold your peace.
   Emil.   'Twill out, 'twill out! I peace!
No, I will speak as liberal as the north.   220
Let Heaven and men and devils, let them all,
All, all, cry shame against me, yet I'll speak.
   Iago. Be wise, and get you home.
   Emil.   I will not.
                        [*Iago offers to stab Emilia.*]
   Gra.   Fie!
Your sword upon a woman?
   Emil. O thou dull Moor! that handkerchief
      thou speak'st of   225
I found by fortune and did give my husband;
For often, with a solemn earnestness,
More than indeed belong'd to such a trifle,
He begg'd of me to steal 't.
   Iago.   Villanous whore!   229
   Emil. She give it Cassio! No, alas! I found it,
And I did give't my husband.
   Iago.   Filth, thou liest!
   Emil. By heaven, I do not, I do not, gentlemen.
O murd'rous coxcomb! what should such a fool
Do with so good a wife?
   Oth.   Are there no stones in heaven
But what serves for the thunder? — Precious
   villain!   235
              [*He runs at Iago: Iago kills Emilia.*
   Gra. The woman falls; sure, he hath kill'd his
      wife.
   Emil. Ay, ay! O, lay me by my mistress' side.
                                        [*Exit Iago.*
   Gra. He's gone, but his wife's kill'd.
   Mon. 'Tis a notorious villain. Take you this
      weapon
Which I have [here] recover'd from the Moor. 240
Come, guard the door without; let him not pass,
But kill him rather. I'll after that same villain,
For 'tis a damned slave.
              [*Exeunt Montano and Gratiano.*
   Oth.   I am not valiant neither,
But every puny whipster gets my sword.
But why should honour outlive honesty?   245
Let it go all.
   Emil.   What did thy song bode, lady?
Hark, canst thou hear me? I will play the swan,

192. I...then. See IV.ii.130–33. 209. reprobance: damnation. 218. [God] ... [God] Q. *Heaven ... Powers* F.
219. ['Zounds] Q. *Come* F. 220. liberal: freely. 234. stones: bolts. 240. [here] Q. Om. F. 244. whipster: term of contempt.

And die in music. [*Singing.*] "Willow, willow,
     willow!" —
Moor, she was chaste; she lov'd thee, cruel Moor;
So come my soul to bliss, as I speak true;   250
So speaking as I think, alas, I die.   [*Dies.*
   Oth. I have another weapon in this chamber;
It was a sword of Spain, the ice-brook's temper, —
O, here it is.   Uncle, I must come forth.
   Gra. (*Within.*) If thou attempt it, it will cost
     thee dear: 255
Thou hast no weapon, and perforce must suffer.
   Oth. Look in upon me then and speak with me,
Or, naked as I am, I will assault thee.

[*Re-enter* GRATIANO.]

   Gra. What is the matter?
   Oth.   Behold, I have a weapon;
A better never did itself sustain   260
Upon a soldier's thigh.   I have seen the day
That, with this little arm and this good sword,
I have made my way through more impediments
Than twenty times your stop.   But, O vain boast!
Who can control his fate? 'tis not so now.   265
Be not afraid though you do see me weapon'd;
Here is my journey's end, here is my butt
And very sea-mark of my utmost sail.
Do you go back dismay'd?   'Tis a lost fear;
Man but a rush against Othello's breast   270
And he retires.   Where should Othello go?
Now, how dost thou look now?   O ill-starr'd wench!
Pale as thy smock! when we shall meet at compt,
This look of thine will hurl my soul from heaven,
And fiends will snatch at it.   Cold, cold, my girl!   275
Even like thy chastity.   O cursed, cursed slave!
Whip me, ye devils,
From the possession of this heavenly sight!
Blow me about in winds! roast me in sulphur!
Wash me in steep-down gulfs of liquid fire!   280
O Desdemon! dead, Desdemon! dead!
Oh! Oh!

Enter LODOVICO, MONTANO, CASSIO *carried in a
     chair, and* Officers, *with* IAGO [*prisoner*].

   Lod. Where is this rash and most unfortunate
     man?
   Oth. That's he that was Othello; here I am.
   Lod. Where is that viper?   Bring the villain
     forth.   285
   Oth. I look down towards his feet; but that's a
     fable.
If that thou be'st a devil, I cannot kill thee.
                 [*Wounds Iago.*
   Lod. Wrench his sword from him.
   Iago.   I bleed, sir; but not kill'd.

   Oth. I am not sorry neither.   I'd have thee live;
For, in my sense, 'tis happiness to die.   290
   Lod. O thou Othello, that [wast] once so good,
Fall'n in the practice of a cursed slave,
What shall be said to thee?
   Oth.   Why, anything.
An honourable murderer, if you will;
For nought I did in hate, but all in honour.   295
   Lod. This wretch hath part confess'd his villainy.
Did you and he consent in Cassio's death?
   Oth. Ay.
   Cas. Dear General, I never gave you cause.
   Oth. I do believe it, and I ask your pardon.   300
Will you, I pray, demand that demi-devil
Why he hath thus ensnar'd my soul and body?
   Iago. Demand me nothing; what you know, you
     know.
From this time forth I never will speak word.
   Lod. What, not to pray?
   Gra.   Torments will ope your lips.   305
   Oth. Well, thou dost best.
   Lod. Sir, you shall understand what hath befall'n,
Which, as I think, you know not.   Here is a letter
Found in the pocket of the slain Roderigo,
And here another.   The one of them imports   310
The death of Cassio to be undertook
By Roderigo.
   Oth. O villain!
   Cas.   Most heathenish and most gross!
   Lod. Now here's another discontented paper,
Found in his pocket too; and this, it seems,   315
Roderigo meant t' have sent this damned villain;
But that, belike, Iago in the interim
Came in and satisfi'd him.
   Oth.   O thou pernicious caitiff! —
How came you, Cassio, by that handkerchief
That was my wife's?
   Cas.   I found it in my chamber,   320
And he himself confess'd but even now
That there he dropp'd it for a special purpose
Which wrought to his desire.
   Oth.   O fool! fool! fool!
   Cas. There is besides in Roderigo's letter,
How he upbraids Iago, that he made him   325
Brave me upon the watch, whereon it came
That I was cast; and even but now he spake,
After long seeming dead, Iago hurt him,
Iago set him on.
   Lod. You must forsake this room and go with
     us.   330
Your power and your command is taken off,
And Cassio rules in Cyprus.   For this slave,
If there be any cunning cruelty
That can torment him much and hold him long,

---

253. **ice-brook's temper:** its steel tempered in icy water.   258. **naked:** unarmed.   264. **stop:** power to stop.   267. **butt:**
goal.   273. **compt:** accounting, i.e., Judgment Day.   286. **I . . . feet:** i.e., to see if they are cloven.   291. **[wast]** *was* F. *wert*
Q.   292. **practice:** plot.   321. **but** Q. *it but* F.

It shall be his.　You shall close prisoner rest,　335
Till that the nature of your fault be known
To the Venetian state.　Come, bring away.

　Oth.　Soft you; a word or two before you go.
I have done the state some service, and they know 't.
No more of that.　I pray you, in your letters,　340
When you shall these unlucky deeds relate,
Speak of me as I am; nothing extenuate,
Nor set down aught in malice.　Then must you
　　speak
Of one that lov'd not wisely but too well;
Of one not easily jealous, but, being wrought,　345
Perplex'd in the extreme; of one whose hand,
Like the base [Indian], threw a pearl away
Richer than all his tribe; of one whose subdu'd
　　eyes,
Albeit unused to the melting mood,
Drops tears as fast as the Arabian trees　350
Their medicinal gum.　Set you down this;
And say besides, that in Aleppo once,
Where a malignant and a turban'd Turk
Beat a Venetian and traduc'd the state,

I took by th' throat the circumcised dog,　355
And smote him — thus.　　　[*Stabs himself.*

　Lod.　O bloody period!

　Gra.　　　　　All that's spoke is marr'd.

　Oth.　I kiss'd thee ere I kill'd thee: no way but
　　this;
Killing myself, to die upon a kiss.

　　　　　　[*Falls on the bed, and*] *dies.*

　Cas.　This did I fear, but thought he had no
　　weapon;　　　　　　　　360
For he was great of heart.

　Lod.　　　[*To Iago.*]　O Spartan dog,
More fell than anguish, hunger, or the sea!
Look on the tragic loading of this bed;
This is thy work.　The object poisons sight;
Let it be hid.　Gratiano, keep the house,　365
And seize upon the fortunes of the Moor,
For they succeed on you.　To you, Lord Governor,
Remains the censure of this hellish villain;
The time, the place, the torture.　O, enforce it!
Myself will straight aboard; and to the state　370
This heavy act with heavy heart relate.　[*Exeunt.*

346. **Perplex'd**: distraught.　347. **[Indian]** Q.　*Iudean* F.　The allusion has not been identified.　356. **period**: end.
361. **Spartan dog**: bloodhound.　366. **seize upon**: take legal possession of.　368. **censure**: sentencing.

Measure for Measure

AN ENTRY in the Account Books of the Revels Office records a performance of *Measure for Measure* at Court on December 26, 1604, and it is reasonable to assign the composition of the play to that year. It was among the first of Shakespeare's plays to be given for James at Whitehall by Shakespeare's company, now the King's Men; and the lines in I.i.68–73 and II.iv.27–30, touching upon the annoyance which well-intentioned public throngs may cause their rulers, seem calculated to please James, whose aversion to crowds was well known. The central stratagem in the plot links the play directly with *All's Well*, and the splendid passages in II.iv.1–7 and III.i.4–41, 118–132 are unmistakably kin to famous speeches in *Hamlet*.

There is no trace of the play's having been printed before 1623, and a modern text is based perforce on the far from perfect version in the First Folio. The critical problems of the received text suggest that it was set up from a transcribed copy with confusions which in turn may point to revision at some time or other.

The most emphatic hints of revision lie in the speeches or silences of certain characters, yet the significance of some of these has been unduly magnified. It may be odd, for example, that the Duke informs Friar Thomas that Angelo believes him gone into Poland (I.iii.14–16) though he has said nothing about his intentions to Angelo when giving him his commission. This discrepancy, if it is one, is of no great moment; Shakespeare seems to be guilty of nothing more than giving his exposition gradually. Other matters, however, are genuinely strange. Mrs. Overdone, who has told Lucio and his companions about Claudio's arrest and its cause, appears curiously ignorant when shortly afterwards Pompey begins to talk about the same thing (I.ii.60–97); and presently Lucio, encountering Claudio in custody, seems to know nothing of what only a moment ago he has been told about. These inconsistencies are hard to explain. The letter-writing and operations of the Friar-Duke in IV.iii–v are not wholly clear. In IV.iv he has a rendezvous with one Varrius, who walks off with him as soon as they meet and who is on hand, according to the stage direction, in V.i; but his function is entirely obscure and he does not speak. There may be some muddling here owing to revision, though it would probably not be very apparent on the stage in the general excitement of the approaching dénouement. The text of *Measure*

for Measure may have undergone some changes during the years of performance, but it is very doubtful if the revision was ever extensive.

Stories containing the central situation of *Measure for Measure*, the perfidy of Angelo, are common in European literature. The direct source, however, of Shakespeare's play is clearly the double drama of *Promos and Cassandra* (1578) by George Whetstone, who later threw the plot into narrative form in his *Heptameron of Civil Discourses* (1582). Whetstone's source was the fifth novel of the tenth day in the *Hecatommithi* (1565) of Giraldi Cinthio, who dramatized the same story in his *Epitia* (1583). It is likely that Cinthio found the idea for the situation in an actual occurrence reported to have taken place in an Italian town near Milan in 1547. Other cases purporting to be historical are on record, and, indeed, no one can deny that the situation at the core of *Measure for Measure* is realistic enough to have been one or more times a matter of fact.

The scene of Whetstone's comedy is Julio in Hungary, governed by Promos (Angelo) as representative of Corvinus, King of Bohemia. The society of this city is described as seething with moral corruption, a picture transferred by Shakespeare to Vienna. But the typical characters chosen to represent this society are all re-created in *Measure for Measure*, Pompey alone bearing some resemblance to a prototype, the Rosko of Whetstone. The function of the King in the older play is practically confined to the redressing of wrongs in the last act, so that the Duke's disguise as a friar, all his activity in the intrigue, and his final offer of marriage to Isabella, are Shakespeare's. The Deputy in Whetstone is honest in his severity before he sees Cassandra (Isabella), but the subtle portrayal of his austerity, so carefully made in the earlier scenes of the present play, is altogether absent. Shakespeare has changed details of the plot in a way to mitigate the cruelty of Angelo. Whetstone's Promos gives a false pledge of marriage to seal his evil bargain, but with the invention of Mariana, Shakespeare could dispense with this element in his treachery. And whereas Promos ordered the head of the heroine's brother, Andrugio (Claudio), sent to her, Shakespeare avoids this sadism by having Angelo command only that the head be despatched to him. Actually the command is in both instances thwarted: in Whetstone a merciful gaoler defeats the intention by substitut-

ing the head of a newly executed felon; in Shake-
speare the Duke persuades the Provost to send to
Angelo the head of Ragozine, the pirate. The
Provost is a development of Whetstone's gaoler,
but Escalus, the sub-deputy, is the invention of
Shakespeare to serve as a foil to Angelo.

The most profound change is in the creation of
the rôle of Mariana. In the older forms of the
story, the heroine yields to the Deputy, who is
forced to marry her at the end. But for such an
Isabella as Shakespeare conceived, this fate was
clearly impossible. So the device of substitution,
which Shakespeare had used in *All's Well*, was
again employed, and a much loftier type of character made possible for the heroine. This elevation
is apparent throughout the play, but since the
characters of both Isabella and Mariana have been
assailed because of their collaboration in this ruse,
the whole matter must be examined more closely.

In the introduction to *All's Well* it was remarked
that some of Shakespeare's plays contain elements
which can be properly interpreted only when they
are looked at against the background of popular
stories, widely current in Shakespeare's day, in
which these elements were accepted unquestion-
ingly as common, traditional, and wholly respect-
able features. So regarded, the trick of the substituted bedfellow was felt to be in no way degrad-
ing to Helena. The same device, adopted by
Isabella for different motives, is in no wise humili-
ating to her or to Mariana. Moreover, what
Mariana does finds a sanction not alone in the con-
ventions of popular narrative, but in current
Elizabethan mores. For Mariana and Angelo had
earlier been betrothed, and their betrothal had,
according to Elizabethan custom, the validity of
marriage. It was a "handfasting," a kind of pre-
contract which bestowed marital rights, though
individuals thus plighted would not necessarily
avail themselves of them before the final marriage
ceremony. (This custom is important also in considering the gravity of the offence of Claudio and
Juliet.) These important matters are clearly in
the mind of the Friar-Duke when he seeks to enlist
the co-operation of Isabella and Mariana in the
deception scheme (III.i.204–81 and IV.i.72–75)
and rule out of court all charges against the purity
or honor of Isabella and Mariana. Their action
is lawful and the ruse signifies only in so far as
it contributes to good and to a happy issue out of
all their afflictions.

The Duke is another character who must not be
misjudged. Trouble begins when one takes him
too seriously, with moral scruples about his inconsistency and dishonesty. The Duke is created
for the sake of the plot; without his shiftiness, his
scheming, and his falsehoods there would be no
story running through five acts. He is responsible
for the ultimate resolution of the complexities, and
for the dispensation of happiness with which the
play must end. His responsibility is dramatic,
rather than moral, though in his own devious ways,
like Providence, he brings good out of evil.

The character of Claudio is so admirably realized
in the unforgettable first scene of the third act,
that one must regret Shakespeare's failure to fill
out his part. He appears but once before this
(I.ii), when he passes across the scene under arrest
and begs his friend Lucio to acquaint his sister
with his situation. On that occasion he speaks
well, but not with the vitality he exhibits when
Isabella visits him in prison. Then his speech is
moving and his conduct profoundly human. It
is hard not to feel that Isabella, in the swift and
crushing rebuke which she deals him, is somewhat
insensible to her brother's misery. It is well to
remember, however, that Isabella has a saintly
horror of unchastity (even Lucio regards her as
"a thing enskied and sainted," and she has already
anticipated a vocation of celibacy), she has come
to her brother with an agonizing message yet
confident of his understanding, and now his plea
that she comply with Angelo tortures her spirit.
The anger in her reply comes not solely from outraged righteousness; it springs partly from her
feeling that she has misjudged her brother and
partly from the wretchedness of her own predicament. Sympathy must not be denied her because
at the moment one feels intensely for Claudio.
Claudio's repentant outcry after he has regained
his poise, "Let me ask my sister pardon. I am so
out of love with life that I will sue to be rid of it,"
would melt a stony heart, and one would feel better,
perhaps, if Isabella made some reply to it. But
she has moved aside, and there is no evidence that
she hears. She and Claudio exchange no further
words, not even at the end of the play when they
are reunited and when speeches of reconciliation
would seem appropriate. Nevertheless, feelings
may be registered in gesture and expression.

Despite the tragic depths which it probes,
Measure for Measure is a comedy and must, therefore, have a happy ending. The transition from
darkness to light is abrupt for modern taste, but it
would disturb Elizabethans not a jot. Yet we may
believe that Shakespeare found a higher reason
than the theatrical convention of a happy ending
for the pardon of Angelo. Angelo had stood out
for inflexible justice against all the pleas of mercy;
Isabella proves her saintliness by begging mercy
for the man who has injured her, and the Duke dispenses mercy all around. In spite of the title,
the moral of the play is that justice should be
tempered with mercy.

MEASURE FOR MEASURE

[DRAMATIS PERSONÆ]

VINCENTIO, *the Duke.*
ANGELO, *the Deputy.*
ESCALUS, *an ancient Lord.*
CLAUDIO, *a young gentleman.*
LUCIO, *a fantastic.*
Two other like gentlemen.
Provost.
THOMAS, } *two friars.*
PETER,
[A Justice.]
[VARRIUS.]

ELBOW, *a simple constable.*
FROTH, *a foolish gentleman.*
[POMPEY,] *clown* [*servant to Mistress Overdone*].
ABHORSON, *an executioner.*
BARNARDINE, *a dissolute prisoner.*

ISABELLA, *sister to Claudio.*
MARIANA, *betrothed to Angelo.*
JULIET, *beloved of Claudio.*
FRANCISCA, *a nun.*
MISTRESS OVERDONE, *a bawd.*

[Lords, Officers, Citizens, Boy, and Attendants.]

SCENE: *Vienna.*

ACT I

SCENE I. [*An apartment in the Duke's palace.*]

Enter DUKE, ESCALUS, Lords [*and Attendants*].

Duke. Escalus.
Escal. My lord.
Duke. Of government the properties to unfold
Would seem in me to affect speech and discourse,
Since I am put to know that your own science 5
Exceeds, in that, the lists of all advice
My strength can give you. Then no more remains,
But that to your sufficiency . . . .
. . . . as your worth is able,
And let them work. The nature of our people, 10
Our city's institutions, and the terms
For common justice, you're as pregnant in
As art and practice hath enriched any
That we remember. There is our commission,
From which we would not have you warp. Call
    hither, 15

I say, bid come before us Angelo.
                  [*Exit an attendant.*]
What figure of us think you he will bear?
For you must know, we have with special soul
Elected him our absence to supply,
Lent him our terror, dress'd him with our love, 20
And given his deputation all the organs
Of our own power. What think you of it?
Escal. If any in Vienna be of worth
To undergo such ample grace and honour,
It is Lord Angelo.

          Enter ANGELO.

Duke.   Look where he comes. 25
Ang. Always obedient to your Grace's will,
I come to know your pleasure.
Duke.   Angelo,
There is a kind of character in thy life,
That to the observer doth thy history
Fully unfold. Thyself and thy belongings 30

Act I, sc. i, 5. put to know: forced to acknowledge.   6. **lists:** bounds.   8–9. **But . . . able.** F prints as one line. Something necessary to the sense apparently has been lost. Since the line in F is a metrical monstrosity, perhaps the missing words stood originally between *sufficiency* and *as*.   12. **pregnant:** well versed.   15. **warp:** swerve.   17. **figure:** likeness. **18. soul:** assurance.   28. **character:** stamp.   30. **belongings:** attributes.

Are not thine own so proper as to waste
Thyself upon thy virtues, they on thee.
Heaven doth with us as we with torches do,
Not light them for themselves; for if our virtues
Did not go forth of us, 'twere all alike   35
As if we had them not.   Spirits are not finely
    touch'd
But to fine issues, nor Nature never lends
The smallest scruple of her excellence
But, like a thrifty goddess, she determines
Herself the glory of a creditor,   40
Both thanks and use.   But I do bend my speech
To one that can my part in him advertise.
Hold therefore, Angelo:
In our remove be thou at full ourself.
Mortality and mercy in Vienna   45
Live in thy tongue and heart.   Old Escalus,
Though first in question, is thy secondary.
Take thy commission.
    Ang.   Now, good my lord,
Let there be some more test made of my metal
Before so noble and so great a figure   50
Be stamp'd upon it.
    Duke.   No more evasion.
We have with a leaven'd and prepared choice
Proceeded to you; therefore take your honours.
Our haste from hence is of so quick condition
That it prefers itself and leaves unquestion'd   55
Matters of needful value.   We shall write to you,
As time and our concernings shall importune,
How it goes with us, and do look to know
What doth befall you here.   So, fare you well.
To the hopeful execution do I leave you   60
Of your commissions.
    Ang.   Yet give leave, my lord,
That we may bring you something on the way.
    Duke. My haste may not admit it;
Nor need you, on mine honour, have to do
With any scruple.   Your scope is as mine own,   65
So to enforce or qualify the laws
As to your soul seems good.   Give me your hand;
I'll privily away.   I love the people,
But do not like to stage me to their eyes.
Though it do well, I do not relish well   70
Their loud applause and Aves vehement;
Nor do I think the man of safe discretion
That does affect it.   Once more, fare you well.
    Ang. The heavens give safety to your purposes!
    Escal. Lead forth and bring you back in happi-
        ness!   75
    Duke. I thank you.   Fare you well.   [*Exit.*

    Escal. I shall desire you, sir, to give me leave
To have free speech with you; and it concerns me
To look into the bottom of my place.
A power I have, but of what strength and nature   80
I am not yet instructed.
    Ang. 'Tis so with me.   Let us withdraw together,
And we may soon our satisfaction have
Touching that point.
    Escal. I'll wait upon your honour.   [*Exeunt.*

SCENE II. [*A street.*]

Enter LUCIO *and two other* GENTLEMEN.

    Lucio. If the Duke with the other dukes come
not to composition with the King of Hungary,
why then all the dukes fall upon the King.
    1. Gent. Heaven grant us its peace, but not the
King of Hungary's!   5
    2. Gent. Amen.
    Lucio. Thou conclud'st like the sanctimonious
pirate, that went to sea with the Ten Command-
ments, but scrap'd one out of the table.
    2. Gent. "Thou shalt not steal"?   10
    Lucio. Ay, that he raz'd.
    1. Gent. Why, 'twas a commandment to com-
mand the captain and all the rest from their functions; they put forth to steal.   There's not a
soldier of us all, that, in the thanksgiving before
meat, do relish the petition well that prays for
peace.   17
    2. Gent. I never heard any soldier dislike it.
    Lucio. I believe thee; for I think thou never wast
where grace was said.   20
    2. Gent. No?   A dozen times at least.
    1. Gent. What, in metre?
    Lucio. In any proportion or in any language.
    1. Gent. I think, or in any religion.   24
    Lucio. Ay, why not?   Grace is grace, despite
of all controversy; as, for example, thou thyself
art a wicked villain, despite of all grace.
    1. Gent. Well, there went but a pair of shears
between us.
    Lucio. I grant; as there may between the lists and
the velvet.   Thou art the list.   31
    1. Gent. And thou the velvet.   Thou art good
velvet; thou'rt a three-pil'd piece, I warrant thee.
I had as lief be a list of an English kersey as be pil'd,
as thou art pil'd, for a French velvet.   Do I speak
feelingly now?   36
    Lucio. I think thou dost; and, indeed, with most
painful feeling of thy speech.   I will, out of thine

---

31. **thine . . . proper:** so entirely your own.   37. **But . . . issues:** except to bring forth fine things.   38. **scruple:** i.e.,
particle (⅓ of a dram).   41. **use:** interest.   42. **can . . . advertise:** can himself teach the rôle which is mine and which I am
assigning to him.   43. **Hold:** stand fast.   47. **question:** consideration (because the elder).   52. **leaven'd:** matured.   55. **unquestion'd:** undiscussed.   62. **bring:** escort.   66. **qualify:** modify.   71. **Aves:** Hails.

Sc. ii, 2. **composition:** terms.   28–29. **there . . . us:** i.e., we were cut from the same cloth.   30. **lists:** the selvages (edges)
of cloth.   33. **three-pil'd:** superlative.   34. **kersey:** coarse woollen.   35. **pil'd:** peeled (i.e., *bald* from the "French disease").
36. **feelingly:** pointedly.   Lucio next implies that his companion speaks feelingly as a victim of the disease.

own confession, learn to begin thy health; but,
whilst I live, forget to drink after thee.   40
  1. Gent. I think I have done myself wrong, have
I not?
  2. Gent. Yes, that thou hast, whether thou art
tainted or free.   44

Enter Bawd [MISTRESS OVERDONE].

  Lucio. Behold, behold, where Madam Mitigation comes! I have purchas'd as many diseases
under her roof as come to —
  2. Gent. To what, I pray?
  Lucio. Judge.   49
  2. Gent. To three thousand dolours a year.
  1. Gent. Ay, and more.
  Lucio. A French crown more.
  1. Gent. Thou art always figuring diseases in me;
but thou art full of error; I am sound.   54
  Lucio. Nay, not as one would say, healthy; but
so sound as things that are hollow. Thy bones
are hollow; impiety has made a feast of thee.
  1. Gent. How now! which of your hips has the
most profound sciatica?   59
  Mrs. Ov. Well, well; there's one yonder arrested
and carried to prison was worth five thousand of
you all.
  2. Gent. Who's that, I pray thee?
  Mrs. Ov. Marry, sir, that's Claudio, Signior
Claudio.   65
  1. Gent. Claudio to prison? 'Tis not so.
  Mrs. Ov. Nay, but I know 'tis so. I saw him
arrested, saw him carried away; and, which is
more, within these three days his head to be chopp'd
off.   70
  Lucio. But, after all this fooling, I would not
have it so. Art thou sure of this?
  Mrs. Ov. I am too sure of it; and it is for getting
Madam Julietta with child.   74
  Lucio. Believe me, this may be. He promis'd
to meet me two hours since, and he was ever precise
in promise-keeping.
  2. Gent. Besides, you know, it draws something
near to the speech we had to such a purpose.   79
  1. Gent. But, most of all, agreeing with the proclamation.
  Lucio. Away! let's go learn the truth of it.
          [*Exeunt* [*Lucio and Gentlemen*].
  Mrs. Ov. Thus, what with the war, what with
the sweat, what with the gallows, and what with
poverty, I am custom-shrunk.   85

Enter Clown [POMPEY].

How now! what's the news with you?
  Pom. Yonder man is carried to prison.
  Mrs. Ov. Well; what has he done?
  Pom. A woman.
  Mrs. Ov. But what's his offence?   90
  Pom. Groping for trouts in a peculiar river.
  Mrs. Ov. What, is there a maid with child by
him?
  Pom. No, but there's a woman with maid by
him. You have not heard of the proclamation,
have you?   96
  Mrs. Ov. What proclamation, man?
  Pom. All houses in the suburbs of Vienna must
be pluck'd down.
  Mrs. Ov. And what shall become of those in the
city?   101
  Pom. They shall stand for seed. They had gone
down too, but that a wise burgher put in for them.
  Mrs. Ov. But shall all our houses of resort in
the suburbs be pull'd down?   105
  Pom. To the ground, mistress.
  Mrs. Ov. Why, here's a change indeed in the
commonwealth! What shall become of me?
  Pom. Come, fear not you; good counsellors lack
no clients. Though you change your place, you   110
need not change your trade. I'll be your tapster
still. Courage! there will be pity taken on you.
You that have worn your eyes almost out in the
service, you will be considered.   115
  Mrs. Ov. What's to do here, Thomas tapster?
Let's withdraw.
  Pom. Here comes Signior Claudio, led by the
provost to prison; and there's Madam Juliet.
          [*Exeunt.*

Enter PROVOST, CLAUDIO, JULIET, *and* Officers.

  Claud. Fellow, why dost thou show me thus to
      th' world?   120
Bear me to prison, where I am committed.
  Prov. I do it not in evil disposition,
But from Lord Angelo by special charge.
  Claud. Thus can the demigod authority
Make us pay down for our offence by weight   125
The words of heaven: on whom it will, it will;
On whom it will not, so; yet still 'tis just.

[*Re-enter* LUCIO *and two* Gentlemen.]

  Lucio. Why, how now, Claudio! whence comes
      this restraint?

40. after thee: i.e., from the same (infected) cup. 50. dolours: (1) griefs, (2) dollars. 52. French crown: (1) gold coin, (2)
bald head (cf. l. 35 n.). 53. figuring: imagining. 84. sweat: sweating sickness, a form of the plague. 98. suburbs, where the
houses of ill-fame were. 103. put in: bid, applied. 119. provost: jailer. 120. S.D. F marks a new scene here, and gives
Lucio and the two Gentlemen an entrance with the others at this point. Since Juliet says nothing in this scene, her appearance
is strange; in fact much of what is said sounds odd if she herself is present (especially ll. 150 and 160). Perhaps she was
meant to retire at l. 127, before which point she had had something to say which has somehow been lost. Furthermore,
Lucio's questioning of Claudio about the cause of his arrest is queer, considering that only a few moments earlier Mrs. Overdone has informed him. The "two Gentlemen" are also mute in this scene. 126–27. The . . . so. Probably corrupt, though
there seems to be an allusion to *Romans* ix.15.

Claud. From too much liberty, my Lucio, liberty.
As surfeit is the father of much fast,   130
So every scope by the immoderate use
Turns to restraint.   Our natures do pursue,
Like rats that ravin down their proper bane,
A thirsty evil; and when we drink we die.   134
Lucio. If I could speak so wisely under an
arrest, I would send for certain of my creditors;
and yet, to say the truth, I had as lief have the
foppery of freedom as the [morality] of imprison-
ment.   What's thy offence, Claudio?
Claud. What but to speak of would offend again.
Lucio. What, is't murder?   141
Claud. No.
Lucio. Lechery?
Claud. Call it so.
Prov. Away, sir! you must go.   145
Claud. One word, good friend.   Lucio, a word
   with you.
Lucio. A hundred, if they'll do you any good.
Is lechery so look'd after?
Claud. Thus stands it with me: upon a true
   contract
I got possession of Julietta's bed.   150
You know the lady; she is fast my wife,
Save that we do the denunciation lack
Of outward order.   This we came not to,
Only for propagation of a dower
Remaining in the coffer of her friends,   155
From whom we thought it meet to hide our love
Till time had made them for us.   But it chances
The stealth of our most mutual entertainment
With character too gross is writ on Juliet.
Lucio. With child, perhaps?
Claud.   Unhappily, even so.
And the new deputy now for the Duke —   161
Whether it be the fault and glimpse of newness,
Or whether that the body public be
A horse whereon the governor doth ride,
Who, newly in the seat, that it may know   165
He can command, lets it straight feel the spur;
Whether the tyranny be in his place,
Or in his eminence that fills it up,
I stagger in: — but this new governor
Awakes me all the enrolled penalties   170
Which have, like unscour'd armour, hung by the
   wall
So long that nineteen zodiacs have gone round
And none of them been worn; and, for a name,
Now puts the drowsy and neglected act
Freshly on me.   'Tis surely for a name.   175

Lucio. I warrant it is; and thy head stands so
tickle on thy shoulders that a milkmaid, if she be
in love, may sigh it off.   Send after the Duke and
appeal to him.
Claud. I have done so, but he's not to be found.
I prithee, Lucio, do me this kind service.   181
This day my sister should the cloister enter
And there receive her approbation.
Acquaint her with the danger of my state;
Implore her, in my voice, that she make friends 185
To the strict deputy; bid herself assay him.
I have great hope in that; for in her youth
There is a prone and speechless dialect,
Such as move men; beside, she hath prosperous art
When she will play with reason and discourse,
And well she can persuade.   191
Lucio. I pray she may; as well for the encour-
agement of the like, which else would stand under
grievous imposition, as for the enjoying of thy life,
who I would be sorry should be thus foolishly lost
at a game of tick-tack.   I'll to her.   196
Claud. I thank you, good friend Lucio.
Lucio. Within two hours.
Claud.   Come, Officer, away!
                                        [*Exeunt.*

SCENE [III. *A monastery.*]

Enter DUKE *and* FRIAR THOMAS.

Duke. No, holy father; throw away that thought.
Believe not that the dribbling dart of love
Can pierce a complete bosom.   Why I desire thee
To give me secret harbour, hath a purpose
More grave and wrinkled than the aims and ends 5
Of burning youth.
Fri. T.   May your Grace speak of it?
Duke. My holy sir, none better knows than you
How I have ever lov'd the life removed,
And held in idle price to haunt assemblies
Where youth, and cost, [and] witless bravery keeps.
I have deliver'd to Lord Angelo,   11
A man of stricture and firm abstinence,
My absolute power and place here in Vienna,
And he supposes me travell'd to Poland;
For so I have strew'd it in the common ear,   15
And so it is receiv'd.   Now, pious sir,
You will demand of me why I do this.
Fri. T. Gladly, my lord.
Duke. We have strict statutes and most biting
   laws,
The needful bits and curbs to headstrong [steeds],

131. scope: liberty. 133. ravin: gulp. proper bane: own poison. 138. foppery: folly. [morality] (Rowe). *mortality* F.
152. denunciation: proclamation. 154. for: i.e., for the sake of. propagation: increase. 157. for: favorable to. 162. fault
and glimpse: harmful glamour. 167. place: office. 169. stagger in: am not sure. 172. nineteen zodiacs: nineteen years.
In I.iii.21, the Duke says fourteen. 177. tickle: insecure. 183. receive her approbation: begin her novitiate. 194. imposition: punishment. 196. tick-tack: a kind of backgammon.
   Sc. iii, 2. dribbling: feeble. 10. [and] F2–4. Om. F1. bravery: finery. 12. stricture: strictness. 20. [steeds] (Theobald). *weeds* F.

Which for this fourteen years we have let slip;   21
Even like an o'ergrown lion in a cave,
That goes not out to prey.   Now, as fond fathers,
Having bound up the threatening twigs of birch,
Only to stick it in their children's sight   25
For terror, not to use, in time the rod
[Becomes] more mock'd than fear'd; so our decrees,
Dead to infliction, to themselves are dead,
And liberty plucks justice by the nose,
The baby beats the nurse, and quite athwart   30
Goes all decorum.
     Fri. T.   It rested in your Grace
To unloose this tied-up justice when you pleas'd:
And it in you more dreadful would have seem'd
Than in Lord Angelo.
     Duke.   I do fear, too dreadful.
Sith 'twas my fault to give the people scope,   35
'Twould be my tyranny to strike and gall them
For what I bid them do; for we bid this be done,
When evil deeds have their permissive pass
And not the punishment.   Therefore indeed, my
          father,
I have on Angelo impos'd the office;   40
Who may, in th' ambush of my name, strike home,
And yet my nature never in the [sight]
To do [it] slander.   And to behold his sway,
I will, as 'twere a brother of your order,
Visit both prince and people; therefore, I prithee,
Supply me with the habit and instruct me   46
How I may formally in person bear [me]
Like a true friar.   Moe reasons for this action
At our more leisure shall I render you;
Only, this one: Lord Angelo is precise,   50
Stands at a guard with envy, scarce confesses
That his blood flows, or that his appetite
Is more to bread than stone; hence shall we see,
If power change purpose, what our seemers be.
                                        [*Exeunt.*

Scene [IV. *A nunnery.*]

Enter Isabella *and* Francisca, *a Nun.*

Isab. And have you nuns no farther privileges?
Fran. Are not these large enough?
Isab. Yes, truly.   I speak not as desiring more,
But rather wishing a more strict restraint
Upon the sisterhood, the votaries of Saint Clare. 5
Lucio. (*Within.*) Ho! Peace be in this place!
Isab.   Who's that which calls?
Fran. It is a man's voice.   Gentle Isabella,
Turn you the key, and know his business of him.

You may, I may not; you are yet unsworn.
When you have vow'd, you must not speak with
          men   10
But in the presence of the prioress;
Then, if you speak, you must not show your face,
Or, if you show your face, you must not speak.
He calls again; I pray you, answer him.   [*Exit.*
     Isab.   Peace and prosperity!   Who is't that
          calls?   15

                 [*Enter* Lucio.]

Lucio.   Hail, virgin, if you be, as those cheek-
          roses
Proclaim you are no less!   Can you so stead me
As bring me to the sight of Isabella,
A novice of this place and the fair sister
To her unhappy brother Claudio?   20
     Isab.   Why her unhappy brother? let me ask,
The rather for I now must make you know
I am that Isabella and his sister.
     Lucio.   Gentle and fair, your brother kindly
          greets you.
Not to be weary with you, he's in prison.   25
     Isab.   Woe me! for what?
     Lucio.   For that which, if myself might be his
          judge,
He should receive his punishment in thanks.
He hath got his friend with child.
     Isab.   Sir, make me not your story.
     Lucio.   [It is] true.
I would not — though 'tis my familiar sin   31
With maids to seem the lapwing and to jest,
Tongue far from heart — play with all virgins so.
I hold you as a thing enskied and sainted,
By your renouncement an immortal spirit,   35
And to be talk'd with in sincerity,
As with a saint.
     Isab.   You do blaspheme the good in mocking me.
     Lucio.   Do not believe it.   Fewness and truth,
          'tis thus:
Your brother and his lover have embrac'd.   40
As those that feed grow full, as blossoming time
That from the seedness the bare fallow brings
To teeming foison, even so her plenteous womb
Expresseth his full tilth and husbandry.
     Isab.   Some one with child by him?   My cousin
          Juliet?   45
     Lucio.   Is she your cousin?
     Isab.   Adoptedly; as school-maids change their
          names
By vain though apt affection.

---

23. **fond:** foolish.   27. **[Becomes]** (Pope). Om. F.   42–43. **[sight] ... [it]** (Hanmer). *fight ... in* F.   Meaning obscure.
Perhaps the idea is, Without injuring my character since I am out of sight.   47. **[me]** (Capell). Om. F.   48. **Moe:** more.   51.
with envy: against malice.
Sc. iv, 17. **stead:** aid.   25. **weary:** tedious.   30. **story:** i.e., jest.   **[It is]** (Steevens).   *'Tis* F.   32. **lapwing.**   The lapwing
tries to lead intruders from its nest by tricks.   39. **Fewness and truth:** briefly and honestly.   42. **seedness:** sowing.   43.
foison: plenty.   48. **vain:** foolish.   **apt:** spontaneous.

Lucio.   She it is.
Isab. O, let him marry her.
Lucio.   This is the point.
The Duke is very strangely gone from hence;   50
Bore many gentlemen, myself being one,
In hand, [in] hope of action; but we do learn
By those that know the very nerves of state,
His [givings-out] were of an infinite distance
From his true-meant design.   Upon his place,   55
And with full line of his authority,
Governs Lord Angelo, a man whose blood
Is very snow-broth, one who never feels
The wanton stings and motions of the sense,
But doth rebate and blunt his natural edge   60
With profits of the mind, study, and fast.
He — to give fear to use and liberty,
Which have for long run by the hideous law,
As mice by lions — hath pick'd out an act,
Under whose heavy sense your brother's life   65
Falls into forfeit; he arrests him on it;
And follows close the rigour of the statute,
To make him an example.   All hope is gone,
Unless you have the grace by your fair prayer
To soften Angelo.   And that's my pith   70
Of business 'twixt you and your poor brother.
     Isab. Doth he so seek his life?
     Lucio.   Has censur'd him
Already; and, as I hear, the Provost hath
A warrant for his execution.
     Isab. Alas! what poor ability's in me   75
To do him good?
     Lucio.   Assay the power you have.
     Isab. My power?   Alas, I doubt —
     Lucio.   Our doubts are traitors,
And makes us lose the good we oft might win
By fearing to attempt.   Go to Lord Angelo,
And let him learn to know, when maidens sue   80
Men give like gods; but when they weep and
          kneel,
All their petitions are as freely theirs
As they themselves would owe them.
     Isab. I'll see what I can do.
     Lucio.   But speedily.
     Isab. I will about it straight,   85
No longer staying but to give the Mother
Notice of my affair.   I humbly thank you.
Commend me to my brother.   Soon at night
I'll send him certain word of my success.
     Lucio. I take my leave of you.
     Isab.   Good sir, adieu.   90
                              [*Exeunt.*

ACT II

SCENE I.   [*A hall in Angelo's house.*]

Enter ANGELO, ESCALUS, *a* JUSTICE, *and Servants.*

     Ang. We must not make a scarecrow of the law,
Setting it up to fear the birds of prey,
And let it keep one shape, till custom make it
Their perch and not their terror.
     Escal.   Ay, but yet
Let us be keen, and rather cut a little,   5
Than fall, and bruise to death.   Alas, this gentle-
          man
Whom I would save had a most noble father!
Let but your honour know,
Whom I believe to be most strait in virtue,
That, in the working of your own affections,   10
Had time coher'd with place or place with wishing,
Or that the resolute acting of [your] blood
Could have attain'd the effect of your own pur-
          pose,
Whether you had not sometime in your life
Err'd in this point which now you censure him,
And pull'd the law upon you.   16
     Ang. 'Tis one thing to be tempted, Escalus,
Another thing to fall.   I not deny,
The jury, passing on the prisoner's life,
May in the sworn twelve have a thief or two   20
Guiltier than him they try.   What's open made to
          justice,
That justice seizes.   What knows the laws
That thieves do pass on thieves?   'Tis very preg-
          nant,
The jewel that we find, we stoop and take't
Because we see it; but what we do not see   25
We tread upon, and never think of it.
You may not so extenuate his offence
For I have had such faults; but rather tell me,
When I, that censure him, do so offend,   29
Let mine own judgement pattern out my death,
And nothing come in partial.   Sir, he must die.

Enter PROVOST.

     Escal. Be it as your wisdom will.
     Ang.   Where is the Provost?
     Prov. Here, if it like your honour.
     Ang.   See that Claudio
Be executed by nine to-morrow morning.
Bring him his confessor, let him be prepar'd;   35
For that's the utmost of his pilgrimage.
                              [*Exit Provost.*]

51-52. Bore ... In hand: deluded.   52. [in] (Keightley).   *and* F.   action: i.e., war.   54. [givings-out] (Rowe).   *givings-out* F.   60. rebate: dull.   72. censur'd: sentenced.   83. As: as if.   would owe: possessed.   89. my success: the outcome.

Act II, sc. i, 6. fall: let fall (i.e., the sword of justice).   12. [your] (Rowe).   *our* F.   21. open: evident.   22-23. What ... thieves: i.e., the law ignores the hidden crimes of jurors.   23. pregnant: obvious.   28. For: because.   36. pilgrimage: i.e., of life.

Escal. [*Aside.*] Well, Heaven forgive him! and
    forgive us all!
Some rise by sin, and some by virtue fall.
Some run from brakes of [vice] and answer
    none;
And some condemned for a fault alone.   40

    Enter ELBOW, FROTH, *Clown* [POMPEY, *and*]
        Officers.

Elb. Come, bring them away. If these be good
people in a commonweal that do nothing but use
their abuses in common houses, I know no law.
Bring them away.   44
   Ang. How now, sir! What's your name? and
what's the matter?
   Elb. If it please your honour, I am the poor
Duke's constable, and my name is Elbow. I do
lean upon justice, sir, and do bring in here before
your honour two notorious benefactors.   50
   Ang. Benefactors? Well, what benefactors are
they? Are they not malefactors?
   Elb. If it please your honour, I know not well
what they are; but precise villains they are, that I
am sure of; and void of all profanation in the world
that good Christians ought to have.   56
   Escal. This comes off well. Here's a wise officer.
   Ang. Go to; what quality are they of? Elbow
is your name? Why dost thou not speak, Elbow?
   Pom. He cannot, sir; he's out at elbow.   61
   Ang. What are you, sir?
   Elb. He, sir! A tapster, sir; parcel-bawd; one
that serves a bad woman, whose house, sir, was,as
they say, pluck'd down in the suburbs; and now she
professes a hot-house, which, I think, is a very ill
house too.   67
   Escal. How know you that?
   Elb. My wife, sir, whom I detest before Heaven
and your honour, —   70
   Escal. How? Thy wife?
   Elb. Ay, sir; whom, I thank Heaven, is an honest
woman, —
   Escal. Dost thou detest her therefore?   74
   Elb. I say, sir, I will detest myself also, as well
as she, that this house, if it be not a bawd's house,
it is pity of her life, for it is a naughty house.   78
   Escal. How dost thou know that, constable?
   Elb. Marry, sir, by my wife; who, if she had been
a woman cardinally given, might have been accus'd
in fornication, adultery, and all uncleanliness there.
   Escal. By the woman's means?   84
   Elb. Ay, sir, by Mistress Overdone's means; but
as she spit in his face, so she defi'd him.
   Pom. Sir, if it please your honour, this is not so.

   Elb. Prove it before these varlets here, thou
honourable man; prove it.
   Escal. Do you hear how he misplaces?   90
   Pom. Sir, she came in great with child, and longing, saving your honour's reverence, for stew'd
prunes. Sir, we had but two in the house, which
at that very distant time stood, as it were, in a
fruit-dish, a dish of some three-pence. Your
honours have seen such dishes; they are not china
dishes, but very good dishes, —   97
   Escal. Go to, go to; no matter for the dish, sir.
   Pom. No, indeed, sir, not of a pin; you are therein
in the right. But to the point. As I say, this Mistress Elbow, being, as I say, with child, and being
great-bellied, and longing, as I said, for prunes; 102
and having but two in the dish, as I said, Master
Froth here, this very man, having eaten the rest, as
I said, and, as I say, paying for them very honestly;
for, as you know, Master Froth, I could not give
you three-pence again.   107
   Froth. No, indeed.
   Pom. Very well; you being then, if you be rememb'red, cracking the stones of the foresaid
prunes, —   111
   Froth. Ay, so I did indeed.
   Pom. Why, very well. I telling you then, if you
be rememb'red, that such a one and such a one
were past cure of the thing you wot of, unless they
kept very good diet, as I told you, —   116
   Froth. All this is true.
   Pom. Why, very well, then, —
   Escal. Come, you are a tedious fool. To the
purpose. What was done to Elbow's wife, that he
hath cause to complain of? Come me to what
was done to her.   122
   Pom. Sir, your honour cannot come to that yet.
   Escal. No, sir, nor I mean it not.
   Pom. Sir, but you shall come to it, by your
honour's leave. And, I beseech you, look into
Master Froth here, sir; a man of fourscore pound
a year; whose father died at Hallowmas. Was't
not at Hallowmas, Master Froth?   129
   Froth. All-hallond eve.
   Pom. Why, very well; I hope here be truths.
He, sir, sitting, as I say, in a lower chair, sir; 'twas
in the Bunch of Grapes, where indeed you have
a delight to sit, have you not?   134
   Froth. I have so; because it is an open room and
good for winter.
   Pom. Why, very well, then; I hope here be truths.
   Ang. This will last out a night in Russia,
When nights are longest there. I'll take my leave,
And leave you to the hearing of the cause,   141

---

39. **brakes:** thickets. **[vice]** (Rowe). *ice* F. **answer none:** are never called to account. 40. **fault alone:** single
fault. 43. **abuses:** evil practices. 54. **precise:** puritanical. 63. **parcel-bawd:** partly bawd. 66. **hot-house:** bathing house.
69. **detest:** for *protest.* 81. **cardinally:** for *carnally.* 92. **saving... reverence:** begging your honour's pardon. 121. **Come:**
bring. 130. **All-hallond eve:** Hallowe'en. 132. **lower:** reclining. 133. **Bunch of Grapes:** name of a room at the inn.

Hoping you'll find good cause to whip them all.

Escal. I think no less. Good morrow to your lordship.

[*Exit Angelo.*

Now, sir, come on. What was done to Elbow's wife, once more? 145

Pom. Once, sir? There was nothing done to her once.

Elb. I beseech you, sir, ask him what this man did to my wife.

Pom. I beseech your honour, ask me. 150

Escal. Well, sir; what did this gentleman to her?

Pom. I beseech you, sir, look in this gentleman's face. Good Master Froth, look upon his honour; 'tis for a good purpose. Doth your honour mark his face? 156

Escal. Ay, sir, very well.

Pom. Nay, I beseech you, mark it well.

Escal. Well, I do so.

Pom. Doth your honour see any harm in his face? 161

Escal. Why, no.

Pom. I'll be suppos'd upon a book, his face is the worst thing about him. Good, then; if his face be the worst thing about him, how could Master Froth do the constable's wife any harm? I would know that of your honour. 167

Escal. He's in the right. Constable, what say you to it?

Elb. First, an it like you, the house is a respected house; next, this is a respected fellow; and his mistress is a respected woman. 172

Pom. By this hand, sir, his wife is a more respected person than any of us all.

Elb. Varlet, thou liest! Thou liest, wicked varlet! The time is yet to come that she was ever respected with man, woman, or child. 177

Pom. Sir, she was respected with him before he married with her.

Escal. Which is the wiser here, Justice or Iniquity? Is this true? 181

Elb. O thou caitiff! O thou varlet! O thou wicked Hannibal! I respected with her before I was married to her! If ever I was respected with her, or she with me, let not your worship think me the poor Duke's officer. Prove this, thou wicked Hannibal, or I'll have mine action of battery on thee. 188

Escal. If he took you a box o' th' ear, you might have your action of slander too.

Elb. Marry, I thank your good worship for it. What is't your worship's pleasure I shall do with this wicked caitiff? 193

Escal. Truly, officer, because he hath some of-fences in him that thou wouldst discover if thou couldst, let him continue in his courses till thou know'st what they are. 197

Elb. Marry, I thank your worship for it. Thou seest, thou wicked varlet, now, what's come upon thee. Thou art to continue now, thou varlet; thou art to continue. 201

Escal. Where were you born, friend?

Froth. Here in Vienna, sir.

Escal. Are you of fourscore pounds a year?

Froth. Yes, an't please you, sir. 205

Escal. So. What trade are you of, sir?

Pom. A tapster; a poor widow's tapster.

Escal. Your mistress' name?

Pom. Mistress Overdone.

Escal. Hath she had any more than one husband? 211

Pom. Nine, sir; Overdone by the last.

Escal. Nine! Come hither to me, Master Froth. Master Froth, I would not have you acquainted with tapsters; they will draw you, Master Froth, and you will hang them. Get you gone, and let me hear no more of you. 217

Froth. I thank your worship. For mine own part, I never come into any room in a tap-house, but I am drawn in. 220

Escal. Well, no more of it, Master Froth. Farewell. [*Exit Froth.*] Come you hither to me, Master tapster. What's your name, Master tapster? 224

Pom. Pompey.

Escal. What else?

Pom. Bum, sir. 227

Escal. Troth, and your bum is the greatest thing about you, so that in the beastliest sense you are Pompey the Great. Pompey, you are partly a bawd, Pompey, howsoever you colour it in being a tapster, are you not? Come, tell me true; it shall be the better for you. 233

Pom. Truly, sir, I am a poor fellow that would live.

Escal. How would you live, Pompey? By being a bawd? What do you think of the trade, Pompey? Is it a lawful trade? 238

Pom. If the law would allow it, sir.

Escal. But the law will not allow it, Pompey; nor it shall not be allowed in Vienna. 241

Pom. Does your worship mean to geld and splay all the youth of the city?

Escal. No, Pompey. 244

Pom. Truly, sir, in my poor opinion, they will to't then. If your worship will take order for the drabs and the knaves, you need not to fear the bawds.

163. **suppos'd:** for *deposed,* i.e., sworn. 170. **respected:** for *suspected,* of ill fame. 180-81. **Justice or Iniquity:** i.e., Elbow or Pompey, who are referred to as if they were characters in a morality play. 183. **Hannibal:** for *cannibal.* 215. **draw you:** (1) draw liquor for you, (2) hang, draw, and quarter you. 242. **splay:** castrate.

Escal. There is pretty orders beginning, I can tell you. It is but heading and hanging. 250

Pom. If you head and hang all that offend that way but for ten year together, you'll be glad to give out a commission for more heads. If this law hold in Vienna ten year, I'll rent the fairest house in it after three-pence a bay. If you live to see this come to pass, say Pompey told you so. 257

Escal. Thank you, good Pompey; and, in requital of your prophecy, hark you: I advise you, let me not find you before me again upon any 260 complaint whatsoever; no, not for dwelling where you do. If I do, Pompey, I shall beat you to your tent, and prove a shrewd Cæsar to you; in plain dealing, Pompey, I shall have you whipt. So, for this time, Pompey, fare you well. 265

Pom. I thank your worship for your good counsel; [*aside*] but I shall follow it as the flesh and fortune shall better determine.
Whip me? No, no; let carman whip his jade;
The valiant heart's not whipt out of his trade. 270
　　　　　　　　　　　　　　　　　　[*Exit.*

Escal. Come hither to me, Master Elbow; come hither, Master constable. How long have you been in this place of constable?

Elb. Seven year and a half, sir. 274

Escal. I thought, by the readiness in the office, you had continued in it some time. You say, seven years together?

Elb. And a half, sir. 278

Escal. Alas, it hath been great pains to you. They do you wrong to put you so oft upon't. Are there not men in your ward sufficient to serve it?

Elb. Faith, sir, few of any wit in such matters. As they are chosen, they are glad to choose me for them. I do it for some piece of money, and go through with all. 285

Escal. Look you bring me in the names of some six or seven, the most sufficient of your parish.

Elb. To your worship's house, sir?

Escal. To my house. Fare you well.
　　　　　　　　　　　　　　　　[*Exit Elbow.*]
What's o'clock, think you? 290

Just. Eleven, sir.

Escal. I pray you home to dinner with me.

Just. I humbly thank you.

Escal. It grieves me for the death of Claudio;
But there's no remedy. 295

Just. Lord Angelo is severe.

Escal.　　　　　　　　　　　It is but needful.
Mercy is not itself, that oft looks so;
Pardon is still the nurse of second woe.
But yet, — poor Claudio! There is no remedy.
Come, sir.　　　　　　　　　　　　[*Exeunt.* 300

SCENE II. [*Another room in the same.*]

Enter PROVOST *and a* SERVANT.

Serv. He's hearing of a cause; he will come straight.
I'll tell him of you.

Prov.　　　　　　　　Pray you, do.
　　　　　　　　　　　　　　　　[*Exit Servant.*]
　　　　　　　　　　　　　　　　　　I'll know
His pleasure; may be he will relent. Alas,
He hath but as offended in a dream!
All sects, all ages smack of this vice; and he 5
To die for't!

Enter ANGELO.

Ang.　　　Now, what's the matter, Provost?

Prov. Is it your will Claudio shall die to-morrow?

Ang. Did not I tell thee yea? Hadst thou not order?
Why dost thou ask again?

Prov.　　　　　　　　Lest I might be too rash.
Under your good correction, I have seen 10
When, after execution, judgement hath
Repented o'er his doom.

Ang.　　　　　　　Go to; let that be mine.
Do you your office, or give up your place,
And you shall well be spar'd.

Prov.　　　　　　I crave your honour's pardon.
What shall be done, sir, with the groaning Juliet?
She's very near her hour.

Ang.　　　　　　　Dispose of her 16
To some more fitter place, and that with speed.

[*Re-enter* SERVANT.]

Serv. Here is the sister of the man condemn'd
Desires access to you.

Ang.　　　　　　Hath he a sister?

Prov. Ay, my good lord; a very virtuous maid,
And to be shortly of a sisterhood, 21
If not already.

Ang.　　　　Well, let her be admitted.
　　　　　　　　　　　　　　　　[*Exit Servant.*]
See you the fornicatress be remov'd.
Let her have needful but not lavish means;
There shall be order for't.

Enter ISABELLA *and* LUCIO.

Prov.　　　　　　[God] save your honour!

Ang. Stay a little while. [*To Isab.*] You're welcome; what's your will? 26

Isab. I am a woeful suitor to your honour,
Please but your honour hear me.

Ang.　　　　　　Well; what's your suit?

Isab. There is a vice that most I do abhor,
And most desire should meet the blow of justice;

---

250. **heading:** beheading. 255. **after:** at. **bay:** a window with the space round it. 269. **jade:** nag.
Sc. ii, 12. **doom:** sentence. 25. [God] save (Walker conj.). 'Save F.

For which I would not plead, but that I must; 31
For which I must not plead, but that I am
At war 'twixt will and will not.

Ang.   Well; the matter?

Isab. I have a brother is condemn'd to die.
I do beseech you, let it be his fault, 35
And not my brother.

Prov. [Aside.] Heaven give thee moving graces!

Ang. Condemn the fault, and not the actor of it?
Why, every fault's condemn'd ere it be done.
Mine were the very cipher of a function,
To fine the faults whose fine stands in record, 40
And let go by the actor.

Isab.   O just but severe law!
I had a brother, then. Heaven keep your honour!

Lucio. [Aside to Isab.] Give't not o'er so. To
him again, entreat him,
Kneel down before him, hang upon his gown.
You are too cold. If you should need a pin, 45
You could not with more tame a tongue desire it.
To him, I say!

Isab. Must he needs die?

Ang.   Maiden, no remedy.

Isab. Yes; I do think that you might pardon him,
And neither heaven nor man grieve at the mercy.

Ang. I will not do't.

Isab.   But can you, if you would? 51

Ang. Look, what I will not, that I cannot do.

Isab. But might you do't, and do the world no
wrong,
If so your heart were touch'd with that remorse
As mine is to him?

Ang.   He's sentenc'd; 'tis too late.

Lucio. [Aside to Isab.] You are too cold. 56

Isab. Too late? Why, no, I, that do speak a
word,
May call it [back] again. Well, believe this,
No ceremony that to great ones longs, 59
Not the king's crown, nor the deputed sword,
The marshal's truncheon, nor the judge's robe,
Become them with one half so good a grace
As mercy does.
If he had been as you and you as he,
You would have slipt like him; but he, like you, 65
Would not have been so stern.

Ang.   Pray you, be gone.

Isab. I would to heaven I had your potency,
And you were Isabel! Should it then be thus?
No; I would tell what 'twere to be a judge,
And what a prisoner.

Lucio. [Aside to Isab.] Ay, touch him; there's
the vein. 70

Ang. Your brother is a forfeit of the law,

And you but waste your words.

Isab.   Alas, alas!
Why, all the souls that were were forfeit once;
And He that might the vantage best have took
Found out the remedy. How would you be 75
If He, which is the top of judgement, should
But judge you as you are? O, think on that;
And mercy then will breathe within your lips,
Like man new made.

Ang.   Be you content, fair maid.
It is the law, not I condemn your brother. 80
Were he my kinsman, brother, or my son,
It should be thus with him. He must die to-
morrow.

Isab. To-morrow! O, that's sudden! Spare
him, spare him!
He's not prepar'd for death. Even for our kitchens
We kill the fowl of season. Shall we serve Heaven
With less respect than we do minister 86
To our gross selves? Good, good my lord, bethink
you:
Who is it that hath died for this offence?
There's many have committed it.

Lucio.   *[Aside to Isab.]* Ay, well said.

Ang. The law hath not been dead, though it
hath slept. 90
Those many had not dar'd to do that evil,
If [but] the first that did th' edict infringe
Had answer'd for his deed. Now 'tis awake,
Takes note of what is done, and, like a prophet,
Looks in a glass that shows what future evils,
Either [new], or by remissness new-conceiv'd, 96
And so in progress to be hatch'd and born,
Are now to have no successive degrees,
But, [ere] they live, to end.

Isab.   Yet show some pity.

Ang. I show it most of all when I show justice,
For then I pity those I do not know, 101
Which a dismiss'd offence would after gall;
And do him right that, answering one foul wrong,
Lives not to act another. Be satisfied.
Your brother dies to-morrow. Be content. 105

Isab. So you must be the first that gives this
sentence,
And he, that suffers. O, it is excellent
To have a giant's strength; but it is tyrannous
To use it like a giant.

Lucio. [Aside to Isab.] That's well said.

Isab. Could great men thunder 110
As Jove himself does, Jove would ne'er be quiet;
For every pelting, petty officer
Would use his heaven for thunder,
Nothing but thunder! Merciful Heaven, 114

35. **let...fault:** i.e., let his fault die. 40. **fine:** punish. **fine:** punishment. 54. **remorse:** pity. 58. **[back]** F₂₋₄. Om. F₁. 59. **longs:** belongs. 70. **vein:** style. 79. **Like...made:** As God breathed life into Adam. See *Gen.* ii.7. 85. **of season:** i.e., fattened. 92. **[but]** (White). Om. F. 95. **glass:** i.e., magic crystal. 96. **[new]** (Dyce). *now* F. 98. **successive degrees:** development. 99. **[ere]** (Hanmer). *here* F. 112. **pelting:** paltry.

Thou rather with thy sharp and sulphurous bolt
Splits the unwedgeable and gnarled oak
Than the soft myrtle; but man, proud man,
Dress'd in a little brief authority,
Most ignorant of what he's most assur'd,
His glassy essence, like an angry ape,   120
Plays such fantastic tricks before high heaven
As makes the angels weep; who, with our spleens,
Would all themselves laugh mortal.
   Lucio. [*Aside to Isab.*] O, to him, to him, wench!
      he will relent.
He's coming; I perceive't.
   Prov. [*Aside.*] Pray Heaven she win him!   125
   Isab. We cannot weigh our brother with ourself.
Great men may jest with saints; 'tis wit in them,
But in the less foul profanation.
   Lucio. [*Aside.*] Thou'rt i' th' right, girl. More
      o' that.
   Isab. That in the captain's but a choleric word,
Which in the soldier is flat blasphemy.   131
   Lucio. [*Aside to Isab.*] Art avis'd o' that? More
      on't.
   Ang. Why do you put these sayings upon me?
   Isab. Because authority, though it err like others,
Hath yet a kind of medicine in itself,   135
That skins the vice o' th' top. Go to your bosom;
Knock there, and ask your heart what it doth know
That's like my brother's fault. If it confess
A natural guiltiness such as is his,
Let it not sound a thought upon your tongue   140
Against my brother's life.
   Ang.   [*Aside.*] She speaks, and 'tis
Such sense, that my sense breeds with it. — Fare
      you well.
   Isab. Gentle my lord, turn back.
   Ang. I will bethink me. Come again to-morrow.
   Isab. Hark how I'll bribe you. Good my lord,
      turn back.   145
   Ang. How! bribe me?
   Isab. Ay, with such gifts that Heaven shall
      share with you.
   Lucio. [*Aside to Isab.*] You had marr'd all else.
   Isab. Not with fond shekels of the tested gold,
Or stones whose [rates] are either rich or poor   150
As fancy values them; but with true prayers
That shall be up at heaven and enter there
Ere sun-rise, prayers from preserved souls,
From fasting maids whose minds are dedicate
To nothing temporal.
   Ang.   Well, come to me to-morrow.
   Lucio. [*Aside to Isab.*] Go to; 'tis well. Away!
   Isab. Heaven keep your honour safe!
   Ang.   [*Aside.*] Amen! 157

For I am that way going to temptation,
Where prayers cross.
   Isab.   At what hour to-morrow
Shall I attend your lordship?
   Ang.   At any time 'fore noon. 160
   Isab. 'Save your honour!
        [*Exeunt Isabella, Lucio, and Provost.*]
   Ang.   From thee, even from thy virtue.
What's this, what's this? Is this her fault or mine?
The tempter or the tempted, who sins most?
Ha!
Not she, nor doth she tempt; but it is I   165
That, lying by the violet in the sun,
Do as the carrion does, not as the flower,
Corrupt with virtuous season. Can it be
That modesty may more betray our sense
Than woman's lightness? Having waste ground
      enough,   170
Shall we desire to raze the sanctuary
And pitch our evils there? O, fie, fie, fie!
What dost thou, or what art thou, Angelo?
Dost thou desire her foully for those things
That make her good? O, let her brother live!
Thieves for their robbery have authority   176
When judges steal themselves. What, do I love
      her,
That I desire to hear her speak again
And feast upon her eyes? What is't I dream on?
O cunning enemy, that, to catch a saint,   180
With saints dost bait thy hook! Most dangerous
Is that temptation that doth goad us on
To sin in loving virtue. Never could the strumpet,
With all her double vigour, art and nature,
Once stir my temper; but this virtuous maid
Subdues me quite. Ever till now,   186
When men were fond, I smil'd and wond'red how.
                   [*Exit.*

SCENE III. [*A room in a prison.*]

Enter [*severally*] DUKE [*disguised as a friar*]
and PROVOST.

   Duke. Hail to you, Provost! so I think you are.
   Prov. I am the Provost. What's your will, good
      friar?
   Duke. Bound by my charity and my blest order,
I come to visit the afflicted spirits
Here in the prison. Do me the common right   5
To let me see them and to make me know
The nature of their crimes, that I may minister
To them accordingly.
   Prov. I would do more than that, if more were
      needful.

---

120. **glassy essence:** frail spirit. 122. **spleens.** The spleen was the supposed seat of laughter. 123. **mortal:** i.e., to death. 126. **weigh...ourself:** i.e., judge others by ourselves. 132. **avis'd:** aware. 142. **breeds:** is enlivened. 150. **[rates]** (Johnson). *rate* F. 153. **preserved:** kept from evil. 159. **cross:** are at cross purposes. 168. **Corrupt...season:** i.e., decay with the (sun of) summer. 169. **betray our sense:** catch our sensual desire.

Enter JULIET.

Look, here comes one; a gentlewoman of mine, 10
Who, falling in the flaws of her own youth,
Hath blister'd her report. She is with child;
And he that got it, sentenc'd; a young man
More fit to do another such offence
Than die for this. 15
    Duke. When must he die?
    Prov.   As I do think, to-morrow.
I have provided for you. Stay awhile,
                           [*To Juliet.*]
And you shall be conducted.
    Duke. Repent you, fair one, of the sin you carry?
    Jul. I do; and bear the shame most patiently. 20
    Duke. I'll teach you how you shall arraign your
       conscience,
And try your penitence, if it be sound
Or hollowly put on.
    Jul.   I'll gladly learn.
    Duke. Love you the man that wrong'd you? 24
    Jul. Yes, as I love the woman that wrong'd him.
    Duke. So then it seems your most offenceful act
Was mutually committed?
    Jul.   Mutually.
    Duke. Then was your sin of heavier kind than
       his.
    Jul. I do confess it, and repent it, father.
    Duke. 'Tis meet so, daughter; but lest you do
       repent 30
As that the sin hath brought you to this shame, —
Which sorrow is always towards ourselves, not
       heaven,
Showing we would not spare heaven as we love it,
But as we stand in fear, —
    Jul. I do repent me, as it is an evil, 35
And take the shame with joy.
    Duke.   There rest.
Your partner, as I hear, must die to-morrow,
And I am going with instruction to him.
Grace go with you, *Benedicite!*   [*Exit.*
    Jul. Must die to-morrow! O injurious [law], 40
That respites me a life whose very comfort
Is still a dying horror!
    Prov.   'Tis pity of him. [*Exeunt.*

SCENE IV. [*A room in Angelo's house.*]

Enter ANGELO.

    Ang. When I would pray and think, I think and
     pray

To several subjects. Heaven hath my empty
     words,
Whilst my invention, hearing not my tongue,
Anchors on Isabel; Heaven in my mouth,
As if I did but only chew his name, 5
And in my heart the strong and swelling evil
Of my conception. The state, whereon I studied,
Is like a good thing, being often read,
Grown [sear'd] and tedious; yea, my gravity,
Wherein — let no man hear me — I take pride, 10
Could I with boot change for an idle plume,
Which the air beats for vain. O place, O form,
How often dost thou with thy case, thy habit,
Wrench awe from fools and tie the wiser souls
To thy false seeming! Blood, thou art blood. 15
Let's write good angel on the devil's horn;
'Tis not the devil's crest.

Enter a SERVANT.

                How now! who's there?
    Serv. One Isabel, a sister, desires access to you.
    Ang. Teach her the way. [*Exit Serv.*] O
     heavens!
Why does my blood thus muster to my heart, 20
Making both it unable for itself,
And dispossessing all my other parts
Of necessary fitness?
So play the foolish throngs with one that swounds;
Come all to help him, and so stop the air 25
By which he should revive; and even so
The general, subject to a well-wish'd king,
Quit their own part, and in obsequious fondness
Crowd to his presence, where their untaught love
Must needs appear offence.

Enter ISABELLA.

                How now, fair maid?
    Isab. I am come to know your pleasure. 31
    Ang. That you might know it, would much better
     please me
Than to demand what 'tis. Your brother cannot
     live.
    Isab. Even so. Heaven keep your honour!
    Ang. Yet may he live a while; and, it may be, 35
As long as you or I. Yet he must die.
    Isab. Under your sentence?
    Ang. Yea.
    Isab. When, I beseech you? that in his reprieve,
Longer or shorter, he may be so fitted 40
That his soul sicken not.

Ang. Ha! fie, these filthy vices! It were as good
To pardon him that hath from nature stol'n
A man already made, as to remit
Their saucy sweetness that do coin Heaven's image
In stamps that are forbid. 'Tis all as easy   46
Falsely to take away a life true made
As to put metal in restrained means
To make a false one.   49
     Isab. 'Tis set down so in heaven, but not in earth.
     Ang. Say you so? Then I shall pose you quickly.
Which had you rather, that the most just law
Now took your brother's life; [or], to redeem him,
Give up your body to such sweet uncleanness
As she that he hath stain'd?
     Isab.   Sir, believe this,
I had rather give my body than my soul.   56
     Ang. I talk not of your soul; our compell'd sins
Stand more for number than for accompt.
     Isab.   How say you?
     Ang. Nay, I'll not warrant that; for I can speak
Against the thing I say. Answer to this: 60
I, now the voice of the recorded law,
Pronounce a sentence on your brother's life.
Might there not be a charity in sin
To save this brother's life?
     Isab.   Please you to do't,
I'll take it as a peril to my soul,   65
It is no sin at all, but charity.
     Ang. Pleas'd you to do't at peril of your soul,
Were equal poise of sin and charity.
     Isab. That I do beg his life, if it be sin,
Heaven let me bear it! You granting of my suit,
If that be sin, I'll make it my morn prayer   71
To have it added to the faults of mine,
And nothing of your answer.
     Ang.   Nay, but hear me;
Your sense pursues not mine. Either you are ig-
          norant,
Or seem so [craftily]; and that's not good.   75
     Isab. Let [me] be ignorant, and in nothing
          good,
But graciously to know I am no better.
     Ang. Thus wisdom wishes to appear most bright
When it doth tax itself; as these black masks
Proclaim an enshield beauty ten times louder   80
Than beauty could, displayed. But mark me:
To be received plain, I'll speak more gross.
Your brother is to die.
     Isab. So.
     Ang. And his offence is so, as it appears,   85
Accountant to the law upon that pain.

     Isab. True.
     Ang. Admit no other way to save his life, —
As I subscribe not that, nor any other,
But in the [loose] of question, — that you, his sister,
Finding yourself desir'd of such a person,   91
Whose credit with the judge, or own great place,
Could fetch your brother from the manacles
Of the [all-binding] law; and that there were
No earthly mean to save him, but that either   95
You must lay down the treasures of your body
To this supposed, or else to let him suffer;
What would you do?
     Isab. As much for my poor brother as myself:
That is, were I under the terms of death,   100
The impression of keen whips I'd wear as rubies,
And strip myself to death, as to a bed
That, longing, have been sick for, ere I'd yield
My body up to shame.
     Ang.   Then must your brother die.
     Isab. And 'twere the cheaper way.   105
Better it were a brother died at once,
Than that a sister, by redeeming him,
Should die for ever.
     Ang. Were not you then as cruel as the sentence
That you have slander'd so?   110
     Isab. Ignomy in ransom and free pardon
Are of two houses. Lawful mercy
Is nothing kin to foul redemption.
     Ang. You seem'd of late to make the law a tyrant;
And rather prov'd the sliding of your brother   115
A merriment than a vice.
     Isab. O, pardon me, my lord. It oft falls out,
To have what we would have, we speak not what
          we mean.
I something do excuse the thing I hate,
For his advantage that I dearly love.   120
     Ang. We are all frail.
     Isab.   Else let my brother die,
If not a fedary, but only he
Owe and succeed [this] weakness.
     Ang. Nay, women are frail too.
     Isab. Ay, as the glasses where they view them-
          selves;   125
Which are as easy broke as they make forms.
Women! Help, Heaven! men their creation mar
In profiting by them. Nay, call us ten times frail;
For we are soft as our complexions are,   129
And credulous to false prints.
     Ang.   I think it well;
And from this testimony of your own sex, —
Since I suppose we are made to be no stronger

     44. remit: forgive.   **46. 'Tis ... easy:** i.e., it is morally the same.   **48. restrained:** prohibited.   **51. pose you:**
put a puzzling question to you.   **53. [or]** (Rowe).   *and* F.   **58. Stand ... accompt:** are enumerated rather than scored
against us.   **68. poise:** weight.   **73. nothing ... answer:** you not accountable.   **75. [craftily]** (Rowe).   *crafty* F.   **76. [me]** F₂.
Om. F₁.   **79. tax:** accuse.   **80. enshield:** hidden.   **86. pain:** penalty.   **90. [loose]** (Singer conj.): freedom.   *loss* F.   **ques-**
tion: talk.   **94. [all-binding]** (Theobald).   *all-building* F.   **103. have:** I have.   **115. sliding:** backsliding.   **122-23. If ...**
weakness: if he has no fellow in this weakness but he alone inherits (succeed) and possesses (owe) it.   **[this]** (Malone conj.).
thy F.   **127. creation:** nature.   **128. profiting by:** taking advantage of.   **130. credulous:** susceptible.   **prints:** impressions.

Than faults may shake our frames, — let me be
  bold.
I do arrest your words. Be that you are,
That is, a woman; if you be more, you're none; 135
If you be one, as you are well express'd
By all external warrants, show it now,
By putting on the destin'd livery.

Isab. I have no tongue but one; gentle my lord,
Let me entreat you speak the former language. 140

Ang. Plainly conceive, I love you.

Isab. My brother did love Juliet,
And you tell me that he shall die for it.

Ang. He shall not, Isabel, if you give me love.

Isab. I know your virtue hath a license in't. 145
Which seems a little fouler than it is,
To pluck on others.

Ang.   Believe me, on mine honour,
My words express my purpose.

Isab. Ha! little honour to be much believ'd,
And most pernicious purpose! Seeming, seeming!
I will proclaim thee, Angelo. Look for 't! 151
Sign me a present pardon for my brother,
Or with an outstretch'd throat I'll tell the world
  aloud
What man thou art.

Ang.   Who will believe thee, Isabel?
My unsoil'd name, th' austereness of my life, 155
My vouch against you, and my place i' th' state,
Will so your accusation overweigh,
That you shall stifle in your own report
And smell of calumny. I have begun,
And now I give my sensual race the rein. 160
Fit thy consent to my sharp appetite;
Lay by all nicety and prolixious blushes
That banish what they sue for; redeem thy brother
By yielding up thy body to my will;
Or else he must not only die the death, 165
But thy unkindness shall his death draw out
To ling'ring sufferance. Answer me to-morrow,
Or, by the affection that now guides me most,
I'll prove a tyrant to him. As for you, 169
Say what you can, my false o'erweighs your true.
                             [Exit.

Isab. To whom should I complain? Did I tell
  this,
Who would believe me? O perilous mouths,
That bear in them one and the self-same tongue,
Either of condemnation or approof,
Bidding the law make curtsy to their will, 175
Hooking both right and wrong to th' appetite,
To follow as it draws! I'll to my brother.
Though he hath fall'n by prompture of the blood,

Yet hath he in him such a mind of honour
That, had he twenty heads to tender down 180
On twenty bloody blocks, he'd yield them up,
Before his sister should her body stoop
To such abhorr'd pollution.
Then, Isabel, live chaste, and, brother, die;
More than our brother is our chastity. 185
I'll tell him yet of Angelo's request,
And fit his mind to death, for his soul's rest.
                             [Exit.

ACT III

SCENE I. [*A room in the prison.*]

Enter DUKE [*disguised as before,*] CLAUDIO, *and*
PROVOST.

Duke. So then you hope of pardon from Lord
  Angelo?

Claud. The miserable have no other medicine
But only hope.
I've hope to live, and am prepar'd to die.

Duke. Be absolute for death; either death or
  life 5
Shall thereby be the sweeter. Reason thus with
  life:
If I do lose thee, I do lose a thing
That none but fools would keep. A breath thou
  art,
Servile to all the skyey influences,
That dost this habitation where thou keep'st 10
Hourly afflict. Merely, thou art Death's fool;
For him thou labour'st by thy flight to shun
And yet runn'st toward him still. Thou art not
  noble;
For all the accommodations that thou bear'st
Are nurs'd by baseness. Thou'rt by no means
  valiant; 15
For thou dost fear the soft and tender fork
Of a poor worm. Thy best of rest is sleep,
And that thou oft provok'st; yet grossly fear'st
Thy death, which is no more. Thou art not thy-
  self;
For thou exist'st on many a thousand grains 20
That issue out of dust. Happy thou art not;
For what thou hast not, still thou striv'st to get,
And what thou hast, forget'st. Thou art not cer-
  tain,
For thy complexion shifts to strange effects 24
After the moon. If thou art rich, thou'rt poor;
For, like an ass whose back with ingots bows,
Thou bear'st thy heavy riches but a journey,

---

134. **arrest:** seize upon. 138. **livery:** i.e., frailty. 140. **the former language:** i.e., as you did before these lascivious advances.
150. **Seeming:** hypocrisy. 156. **vouch:** assertion. 162. **prolixious:** superfluous. 178. **prompture:** prompting, incitement.
    Act III, sc. i, 5. **absolute:** resolved. 9. **skyey:** i.e., astrological. 10. **keep'st:** livest. 11. **Merely:** absolutely. 14. **ac-
commodations:** qualities. 15. **nurs'd by baseness:** have rotten foundations. 16. **fork:** forked tongue. 17. **worm:** snake.
18. **provok'st:** invitest. 24. **complexion:** disposition.

And Death unloads thee.   Friend hast thou none;
For thine own bowels, which do call thee sire,
The mere effusion of thy proper loins,   30
Do curse the gout, [serpigo], and the rheum,
For ending thee no sooner.   Thou hast nor youth
    nor age,
But, as it were, an after-dinner's sleep,
Dreaming on both; for all thy blessed youth
Becomes as aged, and doth beg the alms   35
Of palsied Eld; and when thou art old and rich,
Thou hast neither heat, affection, limb, nor beauty,
To make thy riches pleasant.   What's yet in this
That bears the name of life?   Yet in this life
Lie hid moe thousand deaths; yet death we fear 40
That makes these odds all even.
    Claud.   I humbly thank you.
To sue to live, I find I seek to die;
And, seeking death, find life.   Let it come on.
    Isab. [*Within.*] What, ho!   Peace here; grace
        and good company!
    Prov. Who's there?   Come in; the wish deserves
        a welcome.   45
    Duke. Dear sir, ere long I'll visit you again.
    Claud. Most holy sir, I thank you.

Enter ISABELLA.

    Isab. My business is a word or two with Claudio.
    Prov. And very welcome.   Look, signior, here's
        your sister.
    Duke. Provost, a word with you.   50
    Prov. As many as you please.
    Duke. Bring [me] to hear [them] speak, where I
may be conceal'd.   [*Exeunt Duke and Provost.*]
    Claud. Now, sister, what's the comfort?
    Isab.   Why,
As all comforts are; most good, most good indeed.
Lord Angelo, having affairs to heaven,   57
Intends you for his swift ambassador,
Where you shall be an everlasting leiger;
Therefore your best appointment make with speed,
To-morrow you set on.
    Claud.   Is there no remedy?   61
    Isab. None but such remedy as, to save a head,
To cleave a heart in twain.
    Claud.   But is there any?
    Isab. Yes, brother, you may live.
There is a devilish mercy in the judge,   65
If you'll implore it, that will free your life,
But fetter you till death.
    Claud.   Perpetual durance?

    Isab. Ay, just; perpetual durance, a restraint,
[Though] all the world's vastidity you had,
To a determin'd scope.
    Claud.   But in what nature? 70
    Isab. In such a one as, you consenting to't,
Would bark your honour from that trunk you bear,
And leave you naked.
    Claud.   Let me know the point.
    Isab. O, I do fear thee, Claudio; and I quake,
Lest thou a feverous life shouldst entertain,   75
And six or seven winters more respect
Than a perpetual honour.   Dar'st thou die?
The sense of death is most in apprehension;
And the poor beetle, that we tread upon,
In corporal sufferance finds a pang as great   80
As when a giant dies.
    Claud.   Why give you me this shame?
Think you I can a resolution fetch
From flow'ry tenderness?   If I must die,
I will encounter darkness as a bride,
And hug it in mine arms.   85
    Isab. There spake my brother; there my father's
        grave
Did utter forth a voice.   Yes, thou must die.
Thou art too noble to conserve a life
In base appliances.   This outward-sainted deputy,
Whose settled visage and deliberate word   90
Nips youth i' th' head and follies doth [enew]
As falcon doth the fowl, is yet a devil;
His filth within being cast, he would appear
A pond as deep as hell.
    Claud.   The prenzie Angelo!
    Isab. O, 'tis the cunning livery of hell,   95
The damned'st body to invest and cover
In prenzie guards!   Dost thou think, Claudio?
If I would yield him my virginity,
Thou mightst be freed.
    Claud.   O heavens! it cannot be.
    Isab. Yes, he would give't thee, from this rank
        offence,   100
So to offend him still.   This night's the time
That I should do what I abhor to name,
Or else thou diest to-morrow.
    Claud.   Thou shalt not do't.
    Isab. O, were it but my life,
I'd throw it down for your deliverance   105
As frankly as a pin.
    Claud.   Thanks, dear Isabel.
    Isab. Be ready, Claudio, for your death to-
        morrow.

---

29. **bowels:** i.e., offspring.   31. **[serpigo]** (Rowe): a skin disease.   *Sapego* F.   35–36. **Becomes...Eld:** grows old and begs the charity that old age must beg.   The passage is very likely corrupt.   37. **limb:** i.e., strength.   40. **moe:** i.e., more than I have spoken of.   52. **[me]...[them]** (Steevens conj.).   *them...me* F.   59. **leiger:** ambassador.   60. **appointment:** preparation.   68. **just:** exactly.   69. **[Though]** (Rowe).   *Through* F.   **vastidity:** vastness.   70. **determin'd scope:** fixed limit.   75. **entertain:** favor.   89. **In...appliances:** by base means.   90. **settled:** composed, grave.   91. **[enew]** (New Camb. Edd.): pursue.   *emmew* F.   The literal meaning is to drive a fowl into the water.   93. **cast:** reckoned.   94, 97. **prenzie:** (apparently) smooth, slick.   F2–4 read *princely*.   97. **guards:** trimmings.   100–01. **give't...still:** grant you freedom, in exchange for my sin, to go on sinning.   106. **frankly:** freely.

Claud. Yes. Has he affections in him,
That thus can make him bite the law by the
    nose,
When he would force it? Sure, it is no sin;   110
Or of the deadly seven it is the least.
   Isab. Which is the least?
   Claud. If it were damnable, he being so wise,
Why would he for the momentary trick
Be perdurably fin'd? O Isabel!   115
   Isab. What says my brother?
   Claud.   Death is a fearful thing.
   Isab. And shamed life a hateful.
   Claud. Ay, but to die, and go we know not where;
To lie in cold obstruction and to rot;
This sensible warm motion to become   120
A kneaded clod, and the delighted spirit
To bathe in fiery floods, or to reside
In thrilling region of thick-ribbed ice;
To be imprison'd in the viewless winds,
And blown with restless violence round about   125
The pendent world; or to be — worse than worst —
Of those that lawless and incertain thought
Imagine howling, — 'tis too horrible!
The weariest and most loathed worldly life
That age, ache, [penury], and imprisonment   130
Can lay on nature is a paradise
To what we fear of death.
   Isab. Alas, alas!
   Claud.   Sweet sister, let me live.
What sin you do to save a brother's life,
Nature dispenses with the deed so far   135
That it becomes a virtue.
   Isab.   O you beast!
O faithless coward! O dishonest wretch!
Wilt thou be made a man out of my vice?
Is't not a kind of incest, to take life
From thine own sister's shame? What should I
    think?   140
Heaven shield my mother play'd my father fair!
For such a warped slip of wilderness
Ne'er issu'd from his blood. Take my defiance!
Die, perish! Might but my bending down
Reprieve thee from thy fate, it should proceed.
I'll pray a thousand prayers for thy death,   146
No word to save thee.
   Claud. Nay, hear me, Isabel.
   Isab.   O, fie, fie, fie!
Thy sin's not accidental, but a trade.
Mercy to thee would prove itself a bawd;   150
'Tis best that thou diest quickly.
   Claud.   O hear me, Isabella!

          [*Re-enter* DUKE.]
   Duke. Vouchsafe a word, young sister, but one
word.
   Isab. What is your will?   153
   Duke. Might you dispense with your leisure, I
would by and by have some speech with you. The
satisfaction I would require is likewise your own
benefit.
   Isab. I have no superfluous leisure; my stay must
be stolen out of other affairs; but I will attend you a
while.   [*Walks apart.*]   160
   Duke. Son, I have overheard what hath pass'd
between you and your sister. Angelo had never
the purpose to corrupt her; only he hath made an
assay of her virtue to practise his judgement with
the disposition of natures. She, having the   165
truth of honour in her, hath made him that gracious
denial which he is most glad to receive. I am confessor to Angelo, and I know this to be true; therefore prepare yourself to death. Do not satisfy your
resolution with hopes that are fallible; to-morrow
you must die. Go to your knees and make ready.
   Claud. Let me ask my sister pardon. I am   173
so out of love with life that I will sue to be rid of it.
   Duke. Hold you there! Farewell. [*Exit
Claudio.*] Provost, a word with you!

          [*Re-enter* PROVOST.]
   Prov. What's your will, father?   178
   Duke. That now you are come, you will be gone.
Leave me a while with the maid. My mind promises with my habit no loss shall touch her by my
company.
   Prov. In good time.   183
         [*Exit* [*Provost. Isabella comes forward*].
   Duke. The hand that hath made you fair hath
made you good; the goodness that is cheap in
beauty makes beauty brief in goodness; but grace,
being the soul of your complexion, shall keep the
body of it ever fair. The assault that Angelo   188
hath made to you, fortune hath convey'd to my understanding; and, but that frailty hath examples
for his falling, I should wonder at Angelo. How
will you do to content this substitute, and to save
your brother?   193
   Isab. I am now going to resolve him. I had
rather my brother die by the law than my son
should be unlawfully born. But, O, how much is
the good Duke deceiv'd in Angelo! If ever he return and I can speak to him, I will open my lips in
vain, or discover his government.   199

---

110. force: enforce. 115. **perdurably fin'd:** eternally punished. 119. obstruction: stagnation (of the blood). 120. **sensible:** sensitive. **motion:** i.e., body. 121. **delighted:** capable of delight. 123. **thrilling:** piercing (with cold). 127. **Of:** among. 130. [penury] F2. *periury* F1. 135. **dispenses with:** condones. 141. **shield:** forbid. 142. **wilderness:** wild growth. 145. **it:** i.e., your fate. 155. **by and by:** directly. 164. **with:** respecting. 169. **satisfy:** feed, nourish. 175. **there:** to that. 183. **In good time:** very well. 187. **complexion:** disposition. 192. **substitute:** deputy. 199. **discover his government:** expose his conduct.

Duke. That shall not be much amiss; yet, as the matter now stands, he will avoid your accusation: he made trial of you only. Therefore fasten your ear on my advisings. To the love I have in doing good a remedy presents itself. I do make myself 205 believe that you may most uprighteously do a poor wronged lady a merited benefit, redeem your brother from the angry law, do no stain to your own gracious person, and much please the absent Duke, if peradventure he shall ever return to have hearing of this business. 211

Isab. Let me hear you speak farther. I have spirit to do anything that appears not foul in the truth of my spirit. 214

Duke. Virtue is bold, and goodness never fearful. Have you not heard speak of Mariana, the sister of Frederick, the great soldier who miscarried at sea?

Isab. I have heard of the lady, and good words went with her name. 220

Duke. She should this Angelo have married; was affianced to her [by] oath, and the nuptial appointed; between which time of the contract and limit of the solemnity, her brother Frederick was wreck'd at sea, having in that perished vessel 225 the dowry of his sister. But mark how heavily this befell to the poor gentlewoman. There she lost a noble and renowned brother, in his love toward her ever most kind and natural; with him, the portion and sinew of her fortune, her marriage-dowry; with both, her combinate husband, this well-seeming Angelo. 232

Isab. Can this be so? Did Angelo so leave her?

Duke. Left her in her tears, and dried not one of them with his comfort; swallowed his vows whole, pretending in her discoveries of dishonour; in few, bestow'd her on her own lamentation, which she yet wears for his sake; and he, a marble to her tears, is washed with them, but relents not. 239

Isab. What a merit were it in death to take this poor maid from the world! What corruption in this life, that it will let this man live! But how out of this can she avail? 243

Duke. It is a rupture that you may easily heal; and the cure of it not only saves your brother, but keeps you from dishonour in doing it.

Isab. Show me how, good father. 247

Duke. This forenamed maid hath yet in her the continuance of her first affection; his unjust unkindness, that in all reason should have quenched 250 her love, hath, like an impediment in the current, made it more violent and unruly. Go you to An-

gelo; answer his requiring with a plausible obedience; agree with his demands to the point; only refer yourself to this advantage, first, that 255 your stay with him may not be long; that the time may have all shadow and silence in it; and the place answer to convenience. This being granted in course, — and now follows all, — we shall advise this wronged maid to stead up your ap- 260 pointment, go in your place. If the encounter acknowledge itself hereafter, it may compel him to her recompense; and here, by this is your brother saved, your honour untainted, the poor Mariana advantaged, and the corrupt deputy scaled. The 265 maid will I frame and make fit for his attempt. If you think well to carry this as you may, the doubleness of the benefit defends the deceit from reproof. What think you of it? 269

Isab. The image of it gives me content already; and I trust it will grow to a most prosperous perfection. 272

Duke. It lies much in your holding up. Haste you speedily to Angelo. If for this night he entreat you to his bed, give him promise of satisfaction. I will presently to Saint Luke's; there, at the moated grange, resides this dejected Mariana. At that place call upon me; and dispatch with Angelo, that it may be quickly. 279

Isab. I thank you for this comfort. Fare you well, good father. [*Exeunt [Isabella and Duke*].

[SCENE II. *The street before the prison.*]

Enter [on one side, DUKE, *disguised as before; on the other,*] ELBOW, *and* Officers *with Clown [*POMPEY].

Elb. Nay, if there be no remedy for it but that you will needs buy and sell men and women like beasts, we shall have all the world drink brown and white bastard.

Duke. O heavens! what stuff is here? 5

Pom. 'Twas never merry world since, of two usuries, the merriest was put down, and the worser allow'd by order of law a furr'd gown to keep him warm; and furr'd with fox and lambskins too, to signify that craft, being richer than innocency, stands for the facing. 11

Elb. Come your way, sir. 'Bless you, good father friar.

Duke. And you, good brother father. What offence hath this man made you, sir? 15

Elb. Marry, sir, he hath offended the law; and, sir, we take him to be a thief too, sir, for we have

201–02. avoid ... he: answer your charge by saying he (etc.). 218. miscarried: perished. 222. [by] F₂. Om. F₁. 224. limit ... solemnity: date of the ceremony. 231. combinate: affianced. 255. refer ... to: i.e., demand for yourself. 264. scaled: weighed. 265. frame: instruct. 276. moated grange: country house with a moat.
Sc. ii, 4. bastard: a sweet Spanish wine (used punningly). 6. two usuries: i.e., prostitution and money-lending. 11. facing: trimming. Pompey means to say that the fox and lambskin facings of the usurer's gown signify that craft is stronger than innocence.

found upon him, sir, a strange picklock, which we
have sent to the deputy.

Duke. Fie, sirrah! a bawd, a wicked bawd!   20
The evil that thou causest to be done,
That is thy means to live.   Do thou but think
What 'tis to cram a maw or clothe a back
From such a filthy vice; say to thyself,
From their abominable and beastly touches   25
I drink, I eat, [array] myself, and live.
Canst thou believe thy living is a life,
So stinkingly depending?   Go mend, go mend.

Pom. Indeed, it does stink in some sort, sir; but
yet, sir, I would prove —   30

Duke. Nay, if the devil have given thee proofs
for sin,
Thou wilt prove his.   Take him to prison, officer.
Correction and instruction must both work
Ere this rude beast will profit.   34

Elb. He must before the deputy, sir; he has given
him warning.   The deputy cannot abide a whoremaster.   If he be a whoremonger, and comes before
him, he were as good go a mile on his errand.

Duke. That we were all, as some would seem to
be,   40
[Free] from our faults, as [from faults] seeming free!

Enter LUCIO.

Elb. His neck will come to your waist, — a cord,
sir.

Pom. I spy comfort; I cry bail.   Here's a gentleman and a friend of mine.   44

Lucio. How now, noble Pompey!   What, at the
wheels of Cæsar?   Art thou led in triumph?   What,
is there none of Pygmalion's images, newly made
woman, to be had now, for putting the hand in the
pocket and extracting [it] clutch'd?   What reply,
ha?   What say'st thou to this tune, matter, and   50
method?   Is't not drown'd i' the last rain, ha?
What say'st thou, Trot?   Is the world as it was,
man?   Which is the way?   Is it sad, and few
words? or how?   The trick of it?   54

Duke. Still thus, and thus; still worse!

Lucio. How doth my dear morsel, thy mistress?
Procures she still, ha?

Pom. Troth, sir, she hath eaten up all her beef,
and she is herself in the tub.   59

Lucio. Why, 'tis good; it is the right of it; it must
be so.   Ever your fresh whore and your powder'd
bawd; an unshunn'd consequence; it must be so.
Art going to prison, Pompey?

Pom. Yes, faith, sir.   64

Lucio. Why, 'tis not amiss, Pompey.   Farewell.

Go, say I sent thee thither.   For debt, Pompey? or
how?

Elb. For being a bawd, for being a bawd.   68

Lucio. Well, then, imprison him.   If imprisonment be the due of a bawd, why, 'tis his right.
Bawd is he doubtless, and of antiquity too; bawd-
born.   Farewell, good Pompey.   Commend me to
the prison, Pompey.   You will turn good husband
now, Pompey; you will keep the house.   74

Pom. I hope, sir, your good worship will be my
bail.

Lucio. No, indeed, will I not, Pompey; it is not
the wear.   I will pray, Pompey, to increase your
bondage.   If you take it not patiently, why, your
mettle is the more.   Adieu, trusty Pompey.   'Bless
you, friar.   81

Duke. And you.

Lucio. Does Bridget paint still, Pompey, ha?

Elb. Come your ways, sir; come.

Pom. You will not bail me, then, sir?   85

Lucio. Then, Pompey, nor now.   What news
abroad, friar? what news?

Elb. Come your ways, sir; come.

Lucio. Go to kennel, Pompey; go.   [*Exeunt Elbow, Pompey, and Officers.*]   What news, friar, of
the Duke?   91

Duke. I know none.   Can you tell me of any?

Lucio. Some say he is with the Emperor of
Russia; other some, he is in Rome; but where is he,
think you?   95

Duke. I know not where; but wheresoever, I wish
him well.

Lucio. It was a mad fantastical trick of him to
steal from the state, and usurp the beggary he was
never born to.   Lord Angelo dukes it well in his
absence; he puts transgression to't.   101

Duke. He does well in't.

Lucio. A little more lenity to lechery would do
no harm in him.   Something too crabbed that way,
friar.

Duke. It is too general a vice, and severity must
cure it.   107

Lucio. Yes, in good sooth, the vice is of a great
kindred, it is well allied; but it is impossible to extirp it quite, friar, till eating and drinking be put
down.   They say this Angelo was not made by man
and woman after this downright way of creation.
Is it true, think you?   113

Duke. How should he be made, then?

Lucio. Some report a sea-maid spawn'd him;
some, that he was begot between two stock-fishes.
But it is certain that when he makes water his urine

---

26. **[array]** (Theobald).   *away* F.   28. **depending:** supported.   38. **he … errand:** he has no chance.   41. **[Free]**
F₂.   Om. F₁.   **[from faults]** (Hanmer).   *faults from* F.   42. **cord:** friar's girdle.   He will be hanged.   49. **[it]**
(Rowe).   Om. F.   **clutch'd:** clenched (holding money).   52. **Trot:** old woman (contemptuously).   59. **tub:** (1) for salting meat, (2) for sweating treatment in venereal disease.   61. **powder'd:** pickled.   62. **unshunn'd:** inevitable.   73. **husband:**
housekeeper.   78. **wear:** fashion.   80. **mettle:** i.e., shackles (with a pun).   110. **extirp:** eradicate.   116. **stock-fishes:**
codfish.

is congeal'd ice; that I know to be true: and he is a
motion generative; that's infallible.   119

Duke. You are pleasant, sir, and speak apace.

Lucio. Why, what a ruthless thing is this in him,
for the rebellion of a codpiece to take away the life
of a man! Would the Duke that is absent have
done this? Ere he would have hang'd a man for the
getting a hundred bastards, he would have paid   125
for the nursing a thousand. He had some feeling
of the sport; he knew the service, and that instructed him to mercy.

Duke. I never heard the absent Duke much
detected for women. He was not inclin'd that way.

Lucio. O, sir, you are deceived.   131

Duke. 'Tis not possible.

Lucio. Who? Not the Duke? Yes, your beggar of fifty; and his use was to put a ducat in her
clack-dish. The Duke had crotchets in him. He
would be drunk too; that let me inform you.   136

Duke. You do him wrong, surely.

Lucio. Sir, I was an inward of his. A shy fellow
was the Duke; and I believe I know the cause of
his withdrawing.   140

Duke. What, I prithee, might be the cause?

Lucio. No, pardon; 'tis a secret must be lock'd
within the teeth and the lips. But this I can let
you understand, the greater file of the subject held
the Duke to be wise.   145

Duke. Wise! Why, no question but he was.

Lucio. A very superficial, ignorant, unweighing
fellow.

Duke. Either this is envy in you, folly, or mistaking. The very stream of his life and the business he hath helmed must, upon a warranted   151
need, give him a better proclamation. Let him be
but testimonied in his own bringings-forth, and he
shall appear to the envious a scholar, a statesman,
and a soldier. Therefore you speak unskilfully; or
if your knowledge be more it is much dark'ned in
your malice.   157

Lucio. Sir, I know him, and I love him.

Duke. Love talks with better knowledge, and
knowledge with [dearer] love.

Lucio. Come, sir, I know what I know.   161

Duke. I can hardly believe that, since you know
not what you speak. But if ever the Duke return,
as our prayers are he may, let me desire you to
make your answer before him. If it be honest you
have spoke, you have courage to maintain it. I am
bound to call upon you; and, I pray you, your
name?   168

Lucio. Sir, my name is Lucio; well known to the
Duke.

Duke. He shall know you better, sir, if I may
live to report you.

Lucio. I fear you not.   173

Duke. O, you hope the Duke will return no more;
or you imagine me too unhurtful an opposite. But
indeed I can do you little harm; you'll forswear this
again.   177

Lucio. I'll be hang'd first; thou art deceiv'd in
me, friar. But no more of this. Canst thou tell if
Claudio die to-morrow or no?   180

Duke. Why should he die, sir?

Lucio. Why? For filling a bottle with a tun-dish.
I would the Duke we talk of were return'd again.
This ungenitur'd agent will unpeople the province
with continency. Sparrows must not build in   185
his house-eaves, because they are lecherous. The
Duke yet would have dark deeds darkly answered;
he would never bring them to light. Would he were
return'd! Marry, this Claudio is condemned for
untrussing. Farewell, good friar; I prithee,   190
pray for me. The Duke, I say to thee again, would
eat mutton on Fridays. He's now past it; yet (and
I say to thee) he would mouth with a beggar, though
she smelt brown bread and garlic. Say that I said
so. Farewell.   [*Exit.* 195

Duke. No might nor greatness in mortality
Can censure scape; back-wounding calumny
The whitest virtue strikes. What king so strong
Can tie the gall up in the slanderous tongue?
But who comes here?   200

Enter ESCALUS, PROVOST, *and* [Officers, *with*]
Bawd [MISTRESS OVERDONE].

Escal. Go; away with her to prison!

Mrs. Ov. Good my lord, be good to me; your
honour is accounted a merciful man. Good my
lord!   204

Escal. Double and treble admonition, and still
forfeit in the same kind! This would make mercy
swear and play the tyrant.

Prov. A bawd of eleven years' continuance, may
it please your honour.   209

Mrs. Ov. My lord, this is one Lucio's information
against me. Mistress Kate Keepdown was with
child by him in the Duke's time. He promis'd her
marriage. His child is a year and a quarter old,
come Philip and Jacob. I have kept it myself, and
see how he goes about to abuse me!   215

Escal. That fellow is a fellow of much license; let

---

119. **motion generative:** a male puppet.   130. **detected for:** accused of.   135. **clack-dish:** covered wooden dish, carried by
beggars for alms; they rattled the cover to get attention.   **crotchets:** caprices.   138. **inward:** intimate.   144. **greater...
subject:** majority of subjects.   147. **unweighing:** thoughtless.   149. **envy:** malice.   151. **helmed:** steered.   **upon...
need:** were assurance needed.   155. **unskilfully:** uncritically.   160. **[dearer]** (Hanmer).   *deare* F.   175. **opposite:** opponent.
182. **tun-dish:** funnel.   184. **ungenitur'd:** impotent.   190. **untrussing:** undressing.   192. **mutton.** Also meant *loose woman.*
196. **mortality:** human life.   206. **forfeit:** guilty.   214. **Philip and Jacob:** the day of St. Philip and St. James (May 1st).

him be call'd before us. Away with her to prison! Go to; no more words. [*Exeunt Officers with Mistress Ov.*] Provost, my brother Angelo will not be alter'd; Claudio must die to-morrow. Let him   220 be furnish'd with divines, and have all charitable preparation. If my brother wrought by my pity, it should not be so with him.

Prov. So please you, this friar hath been with him, and advis'd him for the entertainment of death.   226

Escal. Good even, good father.

Duke. Bliss and goodness on you!

Escal. Of whence are you?

Duke. Not of this country, though my chance is now   230
To use it for my time. I am a brother
Of gracious order, late come from the [See]
In special business from his Holiness.

Escal. What news abroad i' th' world?   234

Duke. None, but that there is so great a fever on goodness, that the dissolution of it must cure it. Novelty is only in request; and it is as dangerous to be aged in any kind of course, as it is virtuous to be constant in any undertaking. There is scarce truth enough alive to make societies secure;   240 but security enough to make fellowships accurst. Much upon this riddle runs the wisdom of the world. This news is old enough, yet it is every day's news. I pray you, sir, of what disposition was the Duke?   245

Escal. One that, above all other strifes, contended especially to know himself.

Duke. What pleasure was he given to?   248

Escal. Rather rejoicing to see another merry, than merry at anything which profess'd to make him rejoice; a gentleman of all temperance. But leave we him to his events, with a prayer they may prove prosperous; and let me desire to know how you find Claudio prepar'd. I am made to understand that you have lent him visitation.   255

Duke. He professes to have received no sinister measure from his judge, but most willingly humbles himself to the determination of justice; yet had he framed to himself, by the instruction of his frailty, many deceiving promises of life, which I by my good leisure have discredited to him, and now is he resolv'd to die.   262

Escal. You have paid the heavens your function, and the prisoner the very debt of your calling. I have labour'd for the poor gentleman to the extremest shore of my modesty; but my brother

justice have I found so severe, that he hath forc'd me to tell him he is indeed Justice.   268

Duke. If his own life answer the straitness of his proceeding, it shall become him well; wherein if he chance to fail, he hath sentenc'd himself.

Escal. I am going to visit the prisoner. Fare you well.   273

Duke. Peace be with you!

[*Exeunt Escalus and Provost.*]
    He who the sword of heaven will bear
    Should be as holy as severe;
    Pattern in himself to know,
    Grace to stand, and virtue go;
    More nor less to others paying
    Than by self-offences weighing.   280
    Shame to him whose cruel striking
    Kills for faults of his own liking!
    Twice treble shame on Angelo,
    To weed my vice and let his grow!
    O, what may man within him hide,   285
    Though angel on the outward side!
    How may likeness made in crimes,
    Making practice on the times,
    To draw with idle spiders' strings
    Most ponderous and substantial things!   290
    Craft against vice I must apply.
    With Angelo to-night shall lie
    His old betrothed but despised;
    So disguise shall, by th' disguised,
    Pay with falsehood false exacting,   295
    And perform an old contracting.   [*Exit.*

ACT IV

SCENE I. [*The moated grange at St. Luke's.*]

Enter MARIANA, *and* BOY *singing.*

SONG

Take, O, take those lips away,
    That so sweetly were forsworn;
And those eyes, the break of day,
    Lights that do mislead the morn;
But my kisses bring again, bring again;   5
Seals of love, but seal'd in vain, seal'd in vain.

Enter DUKE [*disguised as before*].

Mari. Break off thy song, and haste thee quick away.
Here comes a man of comfort, whose advice
Hath often still'd my brawling discontent.
                                          [*Exit Boy.*]

232. [See] (Theobald): i.e., of Rome. *Sea* F.   236. dissolution: death.   237. it is as F₃,₄. *as it is as* F₁,₂. 241. security: (demands for) surety. fellowships: friendships.   252. events: affairs.   256. sinister: unfair.   259. instruction: prompting. 266. shore: limit. 275-96. These octosyllabic lines have been widely proclaimed as un-Shakespearean. They are as feeble as they are unnecessary. 278. go: to go ahead. 284. my: i.e., other people's. 287-90. Probably corrupt and certainly unintelligible. 295. exacting: exaction.
    Act IV, sc. i, 9. brawling: clamorous.

I cry you mercy, sir; and well could wish   10
You had not found me here so musical.
Let me excuse me, and believe me so,
My mirth it much displeas'd, but pleas'd my woe.
    Duke. 'Tis good; though music oft hath such a
      charm
To make bad good, and good provoke to harm. 15
I pray you, tell me, hath anybody inquir'd for me
here to-day?   Much upon this time have I promis'd
here to meet.
    Mari. You have not been inquir'd after.   I have
sat here all day.   20

Enter ISABELLA.

    Duke. I do constantly believe you.   The time
is come even now.   I shall crave your forbearance a
little.   May be I will call upon you anon, for some
advantage to yourself.
    Mari. I am always bound to you.   [*Exit.* 25
    Duke. Very well met, and well come.
What is the news from this good deputy?
    Isab. He hath a garden circummur'd with brick,
Whose western side is with a vineyard back'd,
And to that vineyard is a planched gate   30
That makes his opening with this bigger key.
This other doth command a little door
Which from the vineyard to the garden leads;
There have I made my promise
Upon the heavy middle of the night   35
To call upon him.
    Duke. But shall you on your knowledge find this
      way?
    Isab. I have ta'en a due and wary note upon't.
With whispering and most guilty diligence,
In action all of precept, he did show me   40
The way twice o'er.
    Duke.   Are there no other tokens
Between you 'greed concerning her observance?
    Isab. No, none, but only a repair i' th' dark;
And that I have possess'd him my most stay
Can be but brief; for I have made him know   45
I have a servant comes with me along,
That stays upon me, whose persuasion is
I come about my brother.
    Duke.   'Tis well borne up.
I have not yet made known to Mariana
A word of this.   What ho, within! come forth! 50

Re-enter MARIANA.

I pray you, be acquainted with this maid;
She comes to do you good.

    Isab.   I do desire the like.
    Duke. Do you persuade yourself that I respect
      you?
    Mari. Good friar, I know you do, and have found
      it.
    Duke. Take, then, this your companion by the
      hand,   55
Who hath a story ready for your ear.
I shall attend your leisure; but make haste;
The vaporous night approaches.
    Mari. Will't please you walk aside?
           [*Exeunt [Mariana and Isabella].*
    Duke. O place and greatness! millions of false
      eyes   60
Are stuck upon thee.   Volumes of report
Run with these false and most contrarious [quests]
Upon thy doings; thousand escapes of wit
Make thee the father of their idle dream
And rack thee in their fancies.

Re-enter MARIANA *and* ISABELLA.

           Welcome, how agreed?
    Isab. She'll take the enterprise upon her,
      father,   66
If you advise it.
    Duke.   It is not my consent,
But my entreaty too.
    Isab.   Little have you to say
When you depart from him, but, soft and low,
"Remember now my brother."
    Mari.   Fear me not.   70
    Duke. Nor, gentle daughter, fear you not at all.
He is your husband on a pre-contract:
To bring you thus together, 'tis no sin,
Sith that the justice of your title to him
Doth flourish the deceit.   Come, let us go.   75
Our corn's to reap, for yet our [tilth]'s to sow.
           [*Exeunt.*

SCENE II.   [*A room in the prison.*]

Enter PROVOST *and Clown* [POMPEY].

    Prov. Come hither, sirrah.   Can you cut off a
man's head?
    Pom. If the man be a bachelor, sir, I can; but if
he be a married man, he's his wife's head, and I can
never cut off a woman's head.   5
    Prov. Come, sir, leave me your snatches, and
yield me a direct answer.   To-morrow morning
are to die Claudio and Barnardine.   Here is in our
prison a common executioner, who in his office lacks

---

10. **cry you mercy:** beg your pardon.   21. **constantly:** certainly.   28. **circummur'd:** walled about.   30. **planched:** made
of planks.   35. **heavy:** sleepy.   40. **In ... precept:** with demonstrative gestures.   42. **her:** i.e., Mariana's.   43. **repair:**
tryst.   44. **possess'd:** informed.   47. **persuasion:** understanding.   48. **borne up:** devised.   60. **false:** deceitful.   62.
[**quests**] F$_2$: the cries of the hounds upon the scent.   *quest* F$_1$.   63. **escapes:** sallies.   65. **rack:** distort.   75. **flourish:**
grace, justify.   76. [**tilth**]'s (Warburton): fallow land is.   *tithes* F.
    Sc. ii, 6. **snatches:** quips.   9. **common:** public.

a helper. If you will take it on you to assist him, 10
it shall redeem you from your gyves; if not, you
shall have your full time of imprisonment, and your
deliverance with an unpitied whipping, for you have
been a notorious bawd. 15

Pom. Sir, I have been an unlawful bawd time
out of mind; but yet I will be content to be a lawful
hangman. I would be glad to receive some instruction from my fellow partner.

Prov. What, ho! Abhorson! Where's Abhorson, there? 21

Enter ABHORSON.

Abhor. Do you call, sir?

Prov. Sirrah, here's a fellow will help you to-
morrow in your execution. If you think it meet,
compound with him by the year, and let him 25
abide here with you; if not, use him for the present
and dismiss him. He cannot plead his estimation
with you; he hath been a bawd.

Abhor. A bawd, sir? Fie upon him! he will discredit our mystery. 30

Prov. Go to, sir; you weigh equally. A feather
will turn the scale. [*Exit.*

Pom. Pray, sir, by your good favour, — for
surely, sir, a good favour you have, but that you
have a hanging look, — do you call, sir, your occupation a mystery? 36

Abhor. Ay, sir; a mystery.

Pom. Painting, sir, I have heard say, is a mystery; and your whores, sir, being members of my
occupation, using painting, do prove my occupation
a mystery; but what mystery there should be in
hanging, if I should be hang'd, I cannot imagine. 43

Abhor. Sir, it is a mystery.

Pom. Proof?

Abhor. Every true man's apparel fits your thief.
If it be too little for your thief, your true man thinks
it big enough; if it be too big for your thief, your
thief thinks it little enough; so every true man's
apparel fits your thief. 50

Re-enter PROVOST.

Prov. Are you agreed?

Pom. Sir, I will serve him, for I do find your
hangman is a more penitent trade than your bawd;
he doth oftener ask forgiveness. 54

Prov. You, sirrah, provide your block and your
axe to-morrow four o'clock.

Abhor. Come on, bawd, I will instruct thee in
my trade. Follow. 58

Pom. I do desire to learn, sir; and I hope, if you
have occasion to use me for your own turn, you

shall find me yare; for truly, sir, for your kindness I
owe you a good turn. [*Exit.*

Prov. Call hither Barnardine and Claudio.

[*Exit Abhorson.*]

The one has my pity; not a jot the other,
Being a murderer, though he were my brother. 65

Enter CLAUDIO.

Look, here's the warrant, Claudio, for thy death.
'Tis now dead midnight, and by eight to-morrow
Thou must be made immortal. Where's Bar-
nardine?

Claud. As fast lock'd up in sleep as guiltless
labour
When it lies starkly in the traveller's bones. 70
He will not wake.

Prov. Who can do good on him?
Well, go, prepare yourself. [*Knocking within.*]
But, hark, what noise?
Heaven give your spirits comfort! [*Exit Clau-
dio.*] By and by.
I hope it is some pardon or reprieve
For the most gentle Claudio.

Enter DUKE [*disguised as before*].
Welcome, father.

Duke. The best and wholesom'st spirits of the
night 76
Envelop you, good Provost! Who call'd here of
late?

Prov. None, since the curfew rung.

Duke. Not Isabel?

Prov. No.

Duke. They will, then, ere't be long.

Prov. What comfort is for Claudio? 80

Duke. There's some in hope.

Prov. It is a bitter deputy.

Duke. Not so, not so; his life is parallel'd
Even with the stroke and line of his great justice.
He doth with holy abstinence subdue
That in himself which he spurs on his power 85
To qualify in others. Were he meal'd with that
Which he corrects, then were he tyrannous;
But this being so, he's just. [*Knocking within.*]
Now are they come.
[*Exit Provost.*]
This is a gentle Provost: seldom when
The steeled gaoler is the friend of men. 90
[*Knocking within.*]
How now! what noise? That spirit's possess'd with
haste
That wounds the unsisting postern with these
strokes.

---

11. **gyves**: fetters. 14. **unpitied**: pitiless. 25. **compound**: make contract. 30. **mystery**: profession, trade. 33. **favour**: (1) grace, (2) face. 47–50. **If ... thief.** F gives these lines to the Clown. The correction is Capell's. 61. **yare**: ready. 83. **stroke and line**: line marked out (possibly with allusion to the *stroke* of the executioner's axe and the hangman's *line*, i.e., rope). 86. **qualify**: moderate. **meal'd**: tainted. 92. **unsisting**: unresisting (?). Meaning doubtful.

[Re-enter PROVOST.]

Prov. There he must stay until the officer Arise to let him in. He is call'd up.

Duke. Have you no countermand for Claudio yet 95
But he must die to-morrow?

Prov.   None, sir, none.

Duke. As near the dawning, Provost, as it is, You shall hear more ere morning.

Prov.   Happily
You something know, yet I believe there comes
No countermand; no such example have we. 100
Besides, upon the very siege of justice
Lord Angelo hath to the public ear
Profess'd the contrary.

Enter a MESSENGER.

                      This is his [lordship's] man.
[*Duke.*] And here comes Claudio's pardon.

Mes. [*Giving a paper.*] My lord hath sent 105
you this note; and by me this further charge, that
you swerve not from the smallest article of it,
neither in time, matter, or other circumstance.
Good morrow; for, as I take it, it is almost day.

Prov. I shall obey him. [*Exit Messenger.*] 110

Duke. [*Aside.*] This is his pardon, purchas'd by such sin
For which the pardoner himself is in.
Hence hath offence his quick celerity,
When it is borne in high authority.
When vice makes mercy, mercy's so extended, 115
That for the fault's love is the offender friended.
Now, sir, what news?

Prov. I told you. Lord Angelo, belike thinking
me remiss in mine office, awakens me with this unwonted putting-on; methinks strangely, for he hath
not us'd it before. 121

Duke. Pray you, let's hear.

[*Prov. Reads*] *the letter.*

"Whatsoever you may hear to the contrary, let
Claudio be executed by four of the clock; and in the
afternoon Barnardine. For my better satisfac- 125
tion, let me have Claudio's head sent me by five.
Let this be duly performed, with a thought that
more depends on it than we must yet deliver. Thus
fail not to do your office, as you will answer it at
your peril." 130
What say you to this, sir?

Duke. What is that Barnardine who is to be
executed in the afternoon?

Prov. A Bohemian born, but here nurs'd up and
bred; one that is a prisoner nine years old. 135

Duke. How came it that the absent Duke had
not either deliver'd him to his liberty or executed
him? I have heard it was ever his manner to do
so. 139

Prov. His friends still wrought reprieves for him;
and, indeed, his fact, till now in the government of
Lord Angelo, came not to an undoubtful proof.

Duke. It is now apparent? 144

Prov. Most manifest, and not denied by himself.

Duke. Hath he borne himself penitently in
prison? How seems he to be touch'd? 148

Prov. A man that apprehends death no more
dreadfully but as a drunken sleep; careless, reckless, and fearless of what's past, present, or to come;
insensible of mortality, and desperately mortal.

Duke. He wants advice. 154

Prov. He will hear none. He hath evermore
had the liberty of the prison; give him leave to
escape hence, he would not; drunk many times a
day, if not many days entirely drunk. We have
very oft awak'd him, as if to carry him to execution,
and show'd him a seeming warrant for it; it hath
not moved him at all. 161

Duke. More of him anon. There is written in
your brow, Provost, honesty and constancy. If I
read it not truly, my ancient skill beguiles me; but,
in the boldness of my cunning, I will lay myself 165
in hazard. Claudio, whom here you have warrant
to execute, is no greater forfeit to the law than
Angelo who hath sentenc'd him. To make you
understand this in a manifested effect, I crave but
four days' respite; for the which you are to do me
both a present and a dangerous courtesy. 172

Prov. Pray, sir, in what?

Duke. In the delaying death.

Prov. Alack, how may I do it, having the hour
limited, and an express command, under penalty,
to deliver his head in the view of Angelo? I may
make my case as Claudio's, to cross this in the
smallest. 179

Duke. By the vow of mine order I warrant you,
if my instructions may be your guide. Let this
Barnardine be this morning executed, and his head
borne to Angelo.

Prov. Angelo hath seen them both, and will discover the favour. 185

Duke. O, death's a great disguiser, and you may
add to it. Shave the head, and tie the beard; and
say it was the desire of the penitent to be so bar'd
before his death. You know the course is common.
If anything fall to you upon this, more than thanks

---

98. **Happily:** haply, perhaps.   101. **siege:** seat.   103. **This . . . man.** So Tyrwhitt. F gives this to the Duke, and the next line to the Provost. [**lordship's**] (Pope).   *lords* F.   120. **putting-on:** insistence.   141. **fact:** crime.   153. **mortality:** death. **desperately mortal:** in a desperate spiritual state, unlikely to be saved.   165. **cunning:** knowledge.   **lay . . . hazard:** i.e., stake my very self.   169–70. **in . . . effect:** by direct evidence.   176. **limited:** prescribed.   180. **warrant you:** give you surety.   185. **discover the favour:** recognize the face.

and good fortune, by the saint whom I profess, I will
plead against it with my life.   193

Prov. Pardon me, good father; it is against my
oath.

Duke. Were you sworn to the Duke, or to the
deputy?   197

Prov. To him, and to his substitutes.

Duke. You will think you have made no offence,
if the Duke avouch the justice of your dealing?

Prov. But what likelihood is in that?   202

Duke. Not a resemblance, but a certainty. Yet
since I see you fearful, that neither my coat, integrity, nor persuasion can with ease attempt   205
you, I will go further than I meant, to pluck all
fears out of you. Look you, sir, here is the hand
and seal of the Duke. You know the character, I
doubt not; and the signet is not strange to you.

Prov. I know them both.   210

Duke. The contents of this is the return of the
Duke. You shall anon over-read it at your pleasure; where you shall find, within these two days he
will be here. This is a thing that Angelo knows not;
for he this very day receives letters of strange 215
tenour, perchance of the Duke's death, perchance entering into some monastery, but, by
chance, nothing of what is here writ. Look, the
unfolding star calls up the shepherd. Put not yourself into amazement how these things should be. 220
All difficulties are but easy when they are known.
Call your executioner, and off with Barnardine's
head. I will give him a present shrift and advise
him for a better place. Yet you are amaz'd, but
this shall absolutely resolve you. Come away; it is
almost clear dawn.   [*Exeunt.* 226

SCENE III. [*Another room in the same.*]

Enter Clown [POMPEY].

Pom. I am as well acquainted here as I was in
our house of profession. One would think it were
Mistress Overdone's own house, for here be many
of her old customers. First, here's young Master
Rash. He's in for a commodity of brown paper 5
and old ginger, nine-score and seventeen pounds;
of which he made five marks, ready money. Marry,
then ginger was not much in request, for the old
women were all dead. Then is there here one Master Caper, at the suit of Master Three-pile the 10
mercer, for some four suits of peach-colour'd satin,
which now peaches him a beggar. Then have we
here young Dizzy, and young Master Deep-vow,
and Master Copper-spur, and Master Starve-
lackey the rapier and dagger man, and young 15
Drop-heir that killed lusty Pudding, and Master

Forthlight the tilter, and brave Master Shooty the
great traveller, and wild Half-can that stabb'd Pots,
and, I think, forty more; all great doers in our trade,
and are now "for the Lord's sake."   21

Enter ABHORSON.

Abhor. Sirrah, bring Barnardine hither.

Pom. Master Barnardine! You must rise and
be hang'd, Master Barnardine!

Abhor. What, ho, Barnardine!   25

Bar. (*Within.*) A pox o' your throats! Who
makes that noise there? What are you?

Pom. Your friends, sir; the hangman. You must
be so good, sir, to rise and be put to death.

Bar. [*Within.*] Away, you rogue, away! I am
sleepy.   31

Abhor. Tell him he must awake, and that quickly
too.

Pom. Pray, Master Barnardine, awake till you
are executed, and sleep afterwards.   35

Abhor. Go in to him, and fetch him out.

Pom. He is coming, sir, he is coming. I hear his
straw rustle.

Enter BARNARDINE.

Abhor. Is the axe upon the block, sirrah?

Pom. Very ready, sir.

Bar. How now, Abhorson? What's the news
with you?

Abhor. Truly, sir, I would desire you to clap into
your prayers; for, look you, the warrant's come. 45

Bar. You rogue, I have been drinking all night; I
am not fitted for 't.

Pom. O, the better, sir; for he that drinks all
night, and is hanged betimes in the morning, may
sleep the sounder all the next day.   50

Enter DUKE [*disguised as before*].

Abhor. Look you, sir; here comes your ghostly
father. Do we jest now, think you?

Duke. Sir, induced by my charity, and hearing
how hastily you are to depart, I am come to advise
you, comfort you, and pray with you.   55

Bar. Friar, not I. I have been drinking hard all
night, and I will have more time to prepare me, or
they shall beat out my brains with billets. I will
not consent to die this day, that's certain.

Duke. O, sir, you must; and therefore I beseech
you   60
Look forward on the journey you shall go.

Bar. I swear I will not die to-day for any man's
persuasion.

Duke. But hear you.   64

Bar. Not a word. If you have anything to say

---

203. **resemblance:** probability.   218. **unfolding star:** morning star, at whose rising shepherds lead their flocks from the fold.
  Sc. iii, 5. **commodity:** quantity.   12. **peaches:** impeaches, denounces.   21. **for ... sake.** The cry of prisoners begging alms.   58. **billets:** logs of wood, cudgels.

to me, come to my ward; for thence will not I to-
day.   [*Exit.*

Re-enter PROVOST.

Duke. Unfit to live or die, O gravel heart!
After him, fellows; bring him to the block.
                    [*Exeunt Abhorson and Pompey.*]
Prov. Now sir, how do you find the prisoner?   70
Duke. A creature unprepar'd, unmeet for death;
And to transport him in the mind he is
Were damnable.
Prov.   Here in the prison, father,
There died this morning of a cruel fever
One Ragozine, a most notorious pirate,   75
A man of Claudio's years; his beard and head
Just of his colour. What if we do omit
This reprobate till he were well inclin'd,
And satisfy the deputy with the visage
Of Ragozine, more like to Claudio?   80
Duke. O, 'tis an accident that Heaven provides!
Dispatch it presently. The hour draws on
Prefix'd by Angelo. See this be done,
And sent according to command, whiles I
Persuade this rude wretch willingly to die.   85
Prov. This shall be done, good father, presently.
But Barnardine must die this afternoon;
And how shall we continue Claudio,
To save me from the danger that might come
If he were known alive?
Duke.   Let this be done.   90
Put them in secret holds, both Barnardine
And Claudio.
Ere twice the sun hath made his journal greeting
To [th' under] generation, you shall find
Your safety manifested.
Prov. I am your free dependant.   95
Duke. Quick, dispatch, and send the head to
    Angelo.   [*Exit Provost.*
Now will I write letters to Angelo, —
The Provost, he shall bear them, — whose contents
Shall witness to him I am near at home,
And that, by great injunctions, I am bound   100
To enter publicly. Him I'll desire
To meet me at the consecrated fount
A league below the city; and from thence,
By cold gradation and [well-balanc'd] form,
We shall proceed with Angelo.   105

Re-enter PROVOST.

Prov. Here is the head; I'll carry it myself.
Duke. Convenient is it. Make a swift return;

For I would commune with you of such things
That want no ear but yours.
Prov.   I'll make all speed.
                                       [*Exit.*
Isab. (*Within.*) Peace, ho, be here!   110
Duke. The tongue of Isabel. She's come to
    know
If yet her brother's pardon be come hither.
But I will keep her ignorant of her good,
To make her heavenly comforts of despair,
When it is least expected.

Enter ISABELLA.

Isab.   Ho, by your leave!
Duke. Good morning to you, fair and gracious
    daughter.   116
Isab. The better, given me by so holy a man.
Hath yet the deputy sent my brother's pardon?
Duke. He hath releas'd him, Isabel, from the
    world.
His head is off and sent to Angelo.   120
Isab. Nay, but it is not so.
Duke. It is no other. Show your wisdom,
    daughter,
In your close patience.
Isab. O, I will to him and pluck out his eyes!
Duke. You shall not be admitted to his sight. 125
Isab. Unhappy Claudio! Wretched Isabel!
Injurious world! Most damned Angelo!
Duke. This nor hurts him nor profits you a jot.
Forbear it therefore; give your cause to heaven.
Mark what I say, which you shall find   130
By every syllable a faithful verity.
The Duke comes home to-morrow; — nay, dry
    your eyes; —
One of our covent, and his confessor,
Gives me this instance. Already he hath carried
Notice to Escalus and Angelo,   135
Who do prepare to meet him at the gates,
There to give up their power. If you can, pace
    your wisdom
In that good path that I would wish it go,
And you shall have your bosom on this wretch,
Grace of the Duke, revenges to your heart,   140
And general honour.
Isab.   I am directed by you.
Duke. This letter, then, to Friar Peter give;
'Tis that he sent me of the Duke's return.
Say, by this token, I desire his company
At Mariana's house to-night. Her cause and yours
I'll perfect him withal, and he shall bring you 146

---

77. **omit:** pass by. 88. **continue:** preserve. 93. **journal:** daily. 94. **[th' under]** generation: people underneath, i.e.,
antipodes; or, possibly, the people of this earth. **[th'under]** (Hanmer). *yond* F. 95. **your ... dependant:** entirely your
servant. 97. **to Angelo.** From ll. 134–36 below and IV.iv.6 it appears that Angelo had been instructed to meet the Duke
at the gates. At IV.v.11, however, it is Varrius who meets the Duke, obviously by appointment; perhaps, therefore, *Varrius* should be read for *Angelo* in this line. Nevertheless, note IV.v.1. 104. **cold gradation:** deliberate steps. **[well-
balanc'd]** (Rowe). *weal-balanc'd* F. 123. **close:** silent. 133. **covent:** convent. 134. **instance:** news. 139. **bosom:**
heart's desire. 146. **perfect:** inform (fully).

Before the Duke, and to the head of Angelo
Accuse him home and home. For my poor self,
I am combined by a sacred vow
And shall be absent. Wend you with this letter.
Command these fretting waters from your eyes 151
With a light heart. Trust not my holy order
If I pervert your course. Who's here?

Enter LUCIO.

Lucio. Good even. Friar, where's the Provost?
Duke. Not within, sir. 156
Lucio. O pretty Isabella, I am pale at mine
heart to see thine eyes so red. Thou must be patient. I am fain to dine and sup with water and
bran; I dare not for my head fill my belly; one 160
fruitful meal would set me to't. But they say the
Duke will be here to-morrow. By my troth, Isabel,
I lov'd thy brother. If the old fantastical Duke
of dark corners had been at home, he had lived. 165
[*Exit Isabella.*]
Duke. Sir, the Duke is marvellous little beholding
to your reports; but the best is, he lives not in them.
Lucio. Friar, thou knowest not the Duke so well
as I do. He's a better woodman than thou tak'st
him for. 171
Duke. Well, you'll answer this one day. Fare ye
well.
Lucio. Nay, tarry; I'll go along with thee. I can
tell thee pretty tales of the Duke. 175
Duke. You have told me too many of him already, sir, if they be true; if not true, none were
enough.
Lucio. I was once before him for getting a wench
with child.— 180
Duke. Did you such a thing?
Lucio. Yes, marry, did I; but I was fain to forswear it. They would else have married me to the
rotten medlar. 184
Duke. Sir, your company is fairer than honest.
Rest you well.
Lucio. By my troth, I'll go with thee to the
lane's end. If bawdy talk offend you, we'll have
very little of it. Nay, friar, I am a kind of burr; I
shall stick. [*Exeunt.* 190

SCENE IV. [*A room in Angelo's house.*]
Enter ANGELO *and* ESCALUS.

Escal. Every letter he hath writ hath disvouch'd
other.
Ang. In most uneven and distracted manner.

His actions show much like to madness; pray
Heaven his wisdom be not tainted! And why meet
him at the gates, and [redeliver] our authorities
there? 7
Escal. I guess not.
Ang. And why should we proclaim it in an hour
before his entering, that if any crave redress of injustice, they should exhibit their petitions in the
street? 12
Escal. He shows his reason for that: to have a
dispatch of complaints, and to deliver us from de-
vices hereafter, which shall then have no power to
stand against us. 16
Ang. Well, I beseech you, let it be proclaim'd
betimes i' th' morn. I'll call you at your house.
Give notice to such men of sort and suit as are to
meet him. 20
Escal. I shall, sir. Fare you well.
[*Exit Escalus.*
Ang. Good night.
This deed unshapes me quite, makes me unpreg-
nant
And dull to all proceedings. A deflow'red maid!
And by an eminent body that enforc'd 25
The law against it! But that her tender shame
Will not proclaim against her maiden loss,
How might she tongue me! Yet reason dares her
no;
For my authority bears a credent bulk,
That no particular scandal once can touch 30
But it confounds the breather. He should have
liv'd,
Save that his riotous youth, with dangerous sense,
Might in the times to come have ta'en revenge,
By so receiving a dishonour'd life
With ransom of such shame. Would yet he had
liv'd! 35
Alack, when once our grace we have forgot,
Nothing goes right; we would, and we would not.
[*Exit.*

SCENE V. [*Fields without the town.*]
Enter DUKE [*in his own habit,*] *and* FRIAR PETER.
Duke. These letters at fit time deliver me.
[*Giving letters.*]
The Provost knows our purpose and our plot.
The matter being afoot, keep your instruction,
And hold you ever to our special drift, 4
Though sometimes you do blench from this to that,
As cause doth minister. Go call at Flavius' house,

147. **head:** face. 149. **combined:** bound. 159. **fain:** obliged. 165. **dark corners:** i.e., for meeting women in. 167. **lives ... them:** is not like them. 170. **woodman:** hunter (of women). 184. **medlar:** a kind of apple, edible only at the point of decay. 185. **fairer:** friendlier.
Sc. iv, 1. **disvouch'd:** contradicted. 6. [redeliver] (Capell). *re-liver* F1; *deliver* F2–4. 15. **devices:** plots. 19. **sort:** rank. **suit:** i.e., petitioners. 23. **unpregnant:** unready, inept. 28. **dares her no:** forbids her to dare. 29. **bears a** (Theobald). *bears of a* F. **credent bulk:** weight of credit.
Sc. v, 1. **me:** for me. 5. **blench:** swerve.

And tell him where I stay.   Give the like notice
To [Valentinus], Rowland, and to Crassus,
And bid them bring the trumpets to the gate.
But send me Flavius first.
    Fri. P.   It shall be speeded well.
                                [Exit.]

          Enter VARRIUS.

    Duke. I thank thee, Varrius; thou hast made
      good haste: 11
Come, we will walk.   There's other of our friends
Will greet us here anon, my gentle Varrius.
                            [Exeunt.

    SCENE VI.   [*Street near the city gate.*]
     Enter ISABELLA *and* MARIANA.

    Isab. To speak so indirectly I am loath.
I would say the truth; but to accuse him so,
That is your part.   Yet I am advis'd to do it;
He says, to veil full purpose.
    Mari.   Be rul'd by him.
    Isab. Besides, he tells me that, if peradventure 5
He speak against me on the adverse side,
I should not think it strange; for 'tis a physic
That's bitter to sweet end.

          Enter FRIAR PETER.

    Mari. I would Friar Peter——
    Isab.   O, peace! the friar is come.
    Fri. P. Come, I have found you out a stand most
      fit,   10
Where you may have such vantage on the Duke,
He shall not pass you.   Twice have the trumpets
      sounded,
The generous and gravest citizens
Have hent the gates, and very near upon   14
The Duke is ent'ring; therefore, hence, away!
                            [Exeunt.

              ACT V

      SCENE I.   [*The city gate.*]
Enter DUKE, VARRIUS, Lords, ANGELO, ESCALUS,
  LUCIO, [Provost, Officers, *and*] Citizens, *at
  several doors.*

    Duke. My very worthy cousin, fairly met!
Our old and faithful friend, we are glad to see you.
    Ang. }
    Escal. } Happy return be to your royal Grace!
    Duke. Many and hearty thankings to you both.

We have made inquiry of you, and we hear   5
Such goodness of your justice, that our soul
Cannot but yield you forth to public thanks,
Forerunning more requital.
    Ang.   You make my bonds still greater.
    Duke. O, your desert speaks loud; and I should
      wrong it
To lock it in the wards of covert bosom   10
When it deserves, with characters of brass,
A forted residence 'gainst the tooth of time
And razure of oblivion.   Give [me] your hand,
And let the subject see, to make them know
That outward courtesies would fain proclaim 15
Favours that keep within.   Come, Escalus,
You must walk by us on our other hand;
And good supporters are you.

     Enter FRIAR PETER *and* ISABELLA.

    Fri. P. Now is your time.   Speak loud and kneel
      before him.   19
    Isab. Justice, O royal Duke!   Vail your regard
Upon a wrong'd — I would fain have said a maid!
O worthy Prince, dishonour not your eye
By throwing it on any other object
Till you have heard me in my true complaint
And given me justice, justice, justice, justice! 25
    Duke. Relate your wrongs.   In what?   By
    whom?   Be brief.
Here is Lord Angelo shall give you justice:
Reveal yourself to him.
    Isab.   O worthy Duke,
You bid me seek redemption of the devil.
Hear me yourself; for that which I must speak
Must either punish me, not being believ'd, 31
Or wring redress from you.   Hear me, O hear me,
    [hear]!
    Ang. My lord, her wits, I fear me, are not firm.
She hath been a suitor to me for her brother,
Cut off by course of justice, —
    Isab.   By course of justice!
    Ang. And she will speak most bitterly and
      strange.   36
    Isab. Most strange, but yet most truly, will I
      speak.
That Angelo's forsworn, is it not strange?
That Angelo's a murderer, is't not strange?
That Angelo is an adulterous thief,   40
An hypocrite, a virgin-violator,
Is it not strange and strange?
    Duke.   Nay, it is ten times strange.
    Isab. It is not truer he is Angelo
Than this is all as true as it is strange.

---

8. **[Valentinus]** (Capell).   *Valencius* F.   9. **trumpets:** trumpeters.
Sc. vi, 10. stand: position.   13. **generous:** of noble birth.   14. **hent:** reached.   **near upon:** soon.
Act V, sc. i, 1. cousin. A title used by men of high rank to one another.   8. **bonds:** indebtedness.   10. **wards:** prison
cells.   **covert:** secret.   11. **characters:** letters.   13. **razure:** erasure.   **[me]** F3.   *we* F1.   20. **Vail:** lower.   32. **[hear]**
(Keightley).   *heere* F.

Nay, it is ten times true; for truth is truth   45
To th' end of reckoning.
    Duke.   Away with her! Poor soul,
She speaks this in th' infirmity of sense.
    Isab. O Prince, I conjure thee, as thou believ'st
There is another comfort than this world,
That thou neglect me not, with that opinion   50
That I am touch'd with madness! Make not impossible
    possible
That which but seems unlike. 'Tis not impossible
But one, the wicked'st caitiff on the ground,
May seem as shy, as grave, as just, as absolute
As Angelo. Even so may Angelo,   55
In all his dressings, characts, titles, forms,
Be an arch-villain. Believe it, royal Prince!
If he be less, he's nothing; but he's more,
Had I more name for badness.
    Duke.   By mine honesty,
If she be mad, — as I believe no other, —   60
Her madness hath the oddest frame of sense,
Such a dependency of thing on thing,
As e'er I heard in madness.
    Isab.   O gracious Duke,
Harp not on that, nor do not banish reason
For inequality; but let your reason serve   65
To make the truth appear where it seems hid,
And hide the false seems true.
    Duke.   Many that are not mad
Have, sure, more lack of reason. What would you
    say?
    Isab. I am the sister of one Claudio,
Condemn'd upon the act of fornication   70
To lose his head; condemn'd by Angelo.
I, in probation of a sisterhood,
Was sent to by my brother; one Lucio
As then the messenger, —
    Lucio.   That's I, an't like your Grace.
I came to her from Claudio, and desir'd her   75
To try her gracious fortune with Lord Angelo
For her poor brother's pardon.
    Isab.   That's he indeed.
    Duke. You were not bid to speak.
    Lucio.   No, my good lord;
Nor wish'd to hold my peace.
    Duke.   I wish you now, then.
Pray you, take note of it; and when you have   80
A business for yourself, pray Heaven you then
Be perfect.
    Lucio. I warrant your honour.
    Duke. The warrant's for yourself; take heed to 't.
    Isab. This gentleman told somewhat of my
    tale, —
    Lucio. Right.   85

    Duke. It may be right, but you are i' the wrong
To speak before your time. Proceed.
    Isab.   I went
To this pernicious caitiff deputy, —
    Duke. That's somewhat madly spoken.
    Isab.   Pardon it;
The phrase is to the matter.   90
    Duke. Mended again. The matter; proceed.
    Isab. In brief, to set the needless process by,
How I persuaded, how I pray'd, and kneel'd,
How he refell'd me, and how I repli'd, —
For this was of much length, — the vile conclusion
I now begin with grief and shame to utter.   96
He would not, but by gift of my chaste body
To his concupiscible intemperate lust,
Release my brother; and, after much debatement,
My sisterly remorse confutes mine honour,   100
And I did yield to him; but the next morn betimes,
His purpose surfeiting, he sends a warrant
For my poor brother's head.
    Duke.   This is most likely!
    Isab. O, that it were as like as it is true!
    Duke. By heaven, fond wretch, thou know'st not
    what thou speak'st,   105
Or else thou art suborn'd against his honour
In hateful practice. First, his integrity
Stands without blemish. Next, it imports no
    reason
That with such vehemency he should pursue
Faults proper to himself. If he had so offended,
He would have weigh'd thy brother by himself,   111
And not have cut him off. Some one hath set you
    on.
Confess the truth, and say by whose advice
Thou cam'st here to complain.
    Isab.   And is this all?
Then, O you blessed ministers above,   115
Keep me in patience, and with rip'ned time
Unfold the evil which is here wrapt up
In countenance! Heaven shield your Grace from
    woe,
As I, thus wrong'd, hence unbelieved go!
    Duke. I know you'd fain be gone. An officer!
To prison with her! Shall we thus permit   121
A blasting and a scandalous breath to fall
On him so near us? This needs must be a practice.
Who knew of your intent and coming hither?
    Isab. One that I would were here, Friar Lodo-
    wick.   125
    Duke. A ghostly father, belike. Who knows
    that Lodowick?
    Lucio. My lord, I know him; 'tis a meddling
    friar.

---

52. **unlike:** unlikely. 54. **absolute:** perfect. 56. **characts:** characteristics, marks. 65. **inequality:** injustice. 67. **seems:** which seems. 90. **matter:** point, question. 94. **refell'd:** refuted. 98. **concupiscible:** sensual. 100. **remorse:** pity. 106. **suborn'd:** bribed as false witness. 107. **practice:** plotting. 108. **imports:** carries. 110. **proper to:** owned by. 118. **countenance:** support of authority.

I do not like the man. Had he been lay, my lord,
For certain words he spake against your Grace
In your retirement, I had swing'd him soundly.   130
    Duke. Words against me! That's a good friar,
belike!
And to set on this wretched woman here
Against our substitute! Let this friar be found.
    Lucio. But yesternight, my lord, she and that
    friar,
I saw them at the prison. A saucy friar,   135
A very scurvy fellow.
    Fri. P. Blessed be your royal Grace!
I have stood by, my lord, and I have heard
Your royal ear abus'd. First, hath this woman
Most wrongfully accus'd your substitute,   140
Who is as free from touch or soil with her
As she from one ungot.
    Duke.   We did believe no less.
Know you that Friar Lodowick that she speaks of?
    Fri. P. I know him for a man divine and holy;
Not scurvy, nor a temporary meddler,   145
As he's reported by this gentleman;
And, on my trust, a man that never yet
Did, as he vouches, misreport your Grace.
    Lucio. My lord, most villanously; believe it.
    Fri. P. Well, he in time may come to clear him-
    self;   150
But at this instant he is sick, my lord,
Of a strange fever. Upon his mere request,
Being come to knowledge that there was complaint
Intended 'gainst Lord Angelo, came I hither,
To speak, as from his mouth, what he doth know
Is true and false; and what he with his oath   156
And all probation will make up full clear,
Whensoever he's convented. First, for this
    woman,
To justify this worthy nobleman,
So vulgarly and personally accus'd,   160
Her shall you hear disproved to her eyes,
Till she herself confess it.
    Duke.   Good friar, let's hear it.
    [*Isabella is carried off guarded.*]
Do you not smile at this, Lord Angelo?
O heaven, the vanity of wretched fools!
Give us some seats. Come, cousin Angelo;   165
In this I'll be impartial. Be you judge
Of your own cause. Is this the witness, friar?

        Enter MARIANA [*veiled*].
First, let her show [her] face, and after speak.
    Mari. Pardon, my lord; I will not show my face
Until my husband bid me.   170
    Duke. What, are you married?

    Mari. No, my lord.
    Duke. Are you a maid?
    Mari. No, my lord.
    Duke. A widow, then?   175
    Mari. Neither, my lord.
    Duke. Why, you are nothing then: neither maid,
widow, nor wife?
    Lucio. My lord, she may be a punk; for many of
them are neither maid, widow, nor wife.   180
    Duke. Silence that fellow. I would he had some
    cause
To prattle for himself.
    Lucio. Well, my lord.
    Mari. My lord, I do confess I ne'er was married;
And I confess besides I am no maid.   185
I have known my husband; yet my husband
Knows not that ever he knew me.
    Lucio. He was drunk then, my lord; it can be
    no better.
    Duke. For the benefit of silence, would thou
wert so too!   191
    Lucio. Well, my lord.
    Duke. This is no witness for Lord Angelo.
    Mari. Now I come to't, my lord.
She that accuses him of fornication,   195
In self-same manner doth accuse my husband,
And charges him, my lord, with such a time
When I'll depose I had him in mine arms
With all the effect of love.
    Ang. Charges she moe than me?
    Mari.   Not that I know.
    Duke. No? You say your husband.   201
    Mari. Why, just, my lord, and that is Angelo,
Who thinks he knows that he ne'er knew my body,
But knows he thinks that he knows Isabel's.
    Ang. This is a strange abuse. Let's see thy face.
    Mari. My husband bids me; now I will unmask.
    [*Unveiling.*]   206
This is that face, thou cruel Angelo,
Which once thou swor'st was worth the looking on;
This is the hand which, with a vow'd contract,
Was fast belock'd in thine; this is the body
That took away the match from Isabel,   211
And did supply thee at thy garden-house
In her imagin'd person.
    Duke.   Know you this woman?
    Lucio. Carnally, she says.
    Duke.   Sirrah, no more!
    Lucio. Enough, my lord.   215
    Ang. My lord, I must confess I know this woman;
And five years since there was some speech of mar-
    riage
Betwixt myself and her; which was broke off,

---

128. **lay:** a layman.　130. **swing'd:** beaten.　142. **ungot:** unbegotten, unborn.　145. **temporary:** in temporal affairs.
157. **probation:** proof.　158. **convented:** summoned.　160. **vulgarly:** publicly.　166. **be impartial:** take no part.　168. **[her]**
F₂.　*your* F₁.　179. **punk:** strumpet.　198. **depose:** swear.　200. **moe:** more.　205. **abuse:** deception.　211.
match: appointment.

Partly for that her promised proportions
Came short of composition, but in chief   220
For that her reputation was disvalued
In levity: since which time of five years
I never spake with her, saw her, nor heard from her,
Upon my faith and honour.
    Mari.   Noble Prince,
As there comes light from heaven and words from
       breath,   225
As there is sense in truth and truth in virtue,
I am affianc'd this man's wife as strongly
As words could make up vows; and, my good lord,
But Tuesday night last gone in's garden-house
He knew me as a wife. As this is true,   230
Let me in safety raise me from my knees,
Or else for ever be confixed here,
A marble monument!
    Ang.   I did but smile till now.
Now, good my lord, give me the scope of justice.
My patience here is touch'd. I do perceive   235
These poor informal women are no more
But instruments of some more mightier member
That sets them on. Let me have way, my lord,
To find this practice out.
    Duke.   Ay, with my heart;
And punish them unto your height of pleasure.   240
Thou foolish friar, and thou pernicious woman,
Compact with her that's gone, think'st thou thy
       oaths,
Though they would swear down each particular saint,
Were testimonies against his worth and credit
That's seal'd in approbation? You, Lord Escalus,
Sit with my cousin. Lend him your kind pains   246
To find out this abuse, whence 'tis deriv'd.
There is another friar that set them on;
Let him be sent for.
    Fri. P.   Would he were here, my lord, for he in-
       deed   250
Hath set the women on to this complaint.
Your provost knows the place where he abides,
And he may fetch him.
    Duke.   Go, do it instantly. [*Exit Provost.*]
And you, my noble and well-warranted cousin,
Whom it concerns to hear this matter forth,   255
Do with your injuries as seems you best,
In any chastisement. I for a while will leave you;
But stir not you till you have well determin'd
Upon these slanderers.
    Escal. My lord, we'll do it throughly.   260
                          [*Exit Duke.*
Signior Lucio, did not you say you knew that
Friar Lodowick to be a dishonest person?
    Lucio. Cucullus non facit monachum: honest in

nothing but in his clothes; and one that hath spoke
most villanous speeches of the Duke.   265
    Escal. We shall entreat you to abide here till he
come and enforce them against him. We shall find
this friar a notable fellow.
    Lucio. As any in Vienna, on my word.   269
    Escal. Call that same Isabel here once again; I
would speak with her. [*Exit an attendant.*] Pray
you, my lord, give me leave to question; you shall
see how I'll handle her.
    Lucio. Not better than he, by her own report.
    Escal. Say you?   275
    Lucio. Marry, sir, I think, if you handled her
privately, she would sooner confess. Perchance,
publicly, she'll be asham'd.

Re-enter [Officers *with*] ISABELLA; *and* Provost *with*
    the DUKE [*in his friar's habit*].

    Escal. I will go darkly to work with her.
    Lucio. That's the way, for women are light at
midnight.   281
    Escal. Come on, mistress. Here's a gentlewoman
denies all that you have said.
    Lucio. My lord, here comes the rascal I spoke
of; here with the Provost.   285
    Escal. In very good time. Speak not you to
him till we call upon you.
    Lucio. Mum.
    Escal. Come, sir, did you set these women on to
slander Lord Angelo? They have confess'd you
did.   291
    Duke. 'Tis false.
    Escal. How! know you where you are?
    Duke. Respect to your great place! and let the
       devil
Be sometime honour'd for his burning throne!   295
Where is the Duke? 'Tis he should hear me speak.
    Escal. The Duke's in us; and we will hear you
       speak.
Look you speak justly.
    Duke. Boldly, at least. But, O, poor souls,
Come you to seek the lamb here of the fox?   300
Good night to your redress! Is the Duke gone?
Then is your cause gone too. The Duke's unjust
Thus to retort your manifest appeal,
And put your trial in the villain's mouth
Which here you come to accuse.   305
    Lucio. This is the rascal; this is he I spoke of.
    Escal. Why, thou unreverend and unhallowed
       friar,
Is't not enough thou hast suborn'd these women
To accuse this worthy man, but, in foul mouth
And in the witness of his proper ear,   310

---

219. **proportions:** dowry.   220. **composition:** agreement.   221–22. **disvalued in levity:** depreciated by lightness of conduct.   236. **informal:** crazy, deranged.   242. **Compact:** confederate, leagued.   259. **determin'd:** judged.   263. **Cucullus ... monachum:** a cowl does not make a monk.   279. **darkly:** indirectly.   280. **light:** with pun on sense of *wanton.*   303. **retort:** refer back (to Angelo).   310. **proper:** own.

To call him villain, and then to glance from him
To the Duke himself, to tax him with injustice?
Take him hence; to the rack with him! We'll touse
    you
Joint by joint, but we will know his purpose.
What, "unjust"!
    Duke.   Be not so hot. The Duke   315
Dare no more stretch this finger of mine than he
Dare rack his own. His subject am I not,
Nor here provincial. My business in this state
Made me a looker on here in Vienna,
Where I have seen corruption boil and bubble
Till it o'er-run the stew; laws for all faults,   321
But faults so countenanc'd, that the strong statutes
Stand like the forfeits in a barber's shop,
As much in mock as mark.
    Escal. Slander to the state! Away with him to
    prison!   325
    Ang. What can you vouch against him, Signior
Lucio?
Is this the man that you did tell us of?
    Lucio. 'Tis he, my lord. Come hither, good-
man bald-pate. Do you know me?   329
    Duke. I remember you, sir, by the sound of your
voice. I met you at the prison, in the absence of
the Duke.
    Lucio. O, did you so? And do you remember
what you said of the Duke?
    Duke. Most notedly, sir.   335
    Lucio. Do you so, sir? And was the Duke a
fleshmonger, a fool, and a coward, as you then reported him to be?
    Duke. You must, sir, change persons with me,
ere you make that my report. You, indeed, spoke
so of him, and much more, much worse.   341
    Lucio. O thou damnable fellow! Did not I
pluck thee by the nose for thy speeches?
    Duke. I protest I love the Duke as I love myself.
    Ang. Hark, how the villain would close now, after
his treasonable abuses!   347
    Escal. Such a fellow is not to be talk'd withal.
Away with him to prison! Where is the Provost?
Away with him to prison! Lay bolts enough upon
him. Let him speak no more. Away with those
giglots too, and with the other confederate companion! [*The Provost lays hands on the Duke.*]   353
    Duke. Stay, sir; stay awhile.
    Ang. What, resists he? Help him, Lucio.
    Lucio. Come, sir; come, sir; come, sir; foh, sir!
Why, you bald-pated, lying rascal, you must be
hooded, must you? Show your knave's visage,
with a pox to you! Show your sheep-biting face,

and be hang'd an hour! Will't not off?   360
                  [*Pulls off the friar's hood.*]
    Duke. Thou art the first knave that e'er mad'st
    a duke.
First Provost, let me bail these gentle three.
[*To Lucio.*] Sneak not away, sir; for the friar and
    you
Must have a word anon. Lay hold on him.
    Lucio. This may prove worse than hanging.
    Duke. [*To Escalus.*] What you have spoke I
    pardon. Sit you down;   366
We'll borrow place of him. Sir, [*taking Angelo's
    seat*] by your leave.
Hast thou or word, or wit, or impudence,
That yet can do thee office? If thou hast,
Rely upon it till my tale be heard,   370
And hold no longer out.
    Ang.   O my dread lord,
I should be guiltier than my guiltiness,
To think I can be undiscernible,
When I perceive your Grace, like power divine,
Hath look'd upon my passes. Then, good Prince,
No longer session hold upon my shame,   376
But let my trial be mine own confession;
Immediate sentence, then, and sequent death
Is all the grace I beg.
    Duke.   Come hither, Mariana.
Say, wast thou e'er contracted to this woman?
    Ang. I was, my lord.   381
    Duke. Go take her hence, and marry her in-
stantly.
Do you the office, friar; which consummate,
Return him here again. Go with him, Provost.
          [*Exeunt* [*Angelo, Mariana, Friar Peter, and
             Provost*].
    Escal. My lord, I am more amaz'd at his dis-
honour   385
Than at the strangeness of it.
    Duke.   Come hither, Isabel.
Your friar is now your prince. As I was then
Advertising and holy to your business,
Not changing heart with habit, I am still
Attorney'd at your service.
    Isab.   O, give me pardon,   390
That I, your vassal, have employ'd and pain'd
Your unknown sovereignty!
    Duke.   You are pardon'd, Isabel;
And now, dear maid, be you as free to us.
Your brother's death, I know, sits at your heart;
And you may marvel why I obscur'd myself,   395
Labouring to save his life, and would not rather
Make rash remonstrance of my hidden power

---

313. **touse:** tear. 318. **here provincial:** within this ecclesiastical province. 321. **stew:** (1) kettle, (2) brothel. 323.
forfeits. Apparently alluding to the teeth extracted by barbers, the dentists of the time, and hung up in their shops. 324.
As ... mark: as much spurned as heeded. 335. **notedly:** precisely. 346. **close:** make terms. 352. **giglots:** lewd women.
other: i.e., Friar Peter. 359. **sheep-biting:** thievish. 371. **hold ... out:** bluff no longer. 375. **passes:** acts. 388.
Advertising: attentive. **holy:** dedicated. 393. **free:** generous. 397. **rash remonstrance:** swift show.

Than let him so be lost.   O most kind maid,
It was the swift celerity of his death,
Which I did think with slower foot came on,   400
That brain'd my purpose.   But, peace be with him!
That life is better life, past fearing death,
Than that which lives to fear.   Make it your comfort
So happy is your brother.

Re-enter ANGELO, MARIANA, FRIAR PETER, *and*
PROVOST.

Isab.   I do, my lord.
Duke. For this new-married man approaching
        here,   405
Whose salt imagination yet hath wrong'd
Your well defended honour, you must pardon
For Mariana's sake; but as he adjudg'd your
brother, —
Being criminal, in double violation
Of sacred chastity and of promise-breach   410
Thereon dependent, for your brother's life, —
The very mercy of the law cries out
Most audible, even from his proper tongue,
"An Angelo for Claudio, death for death!"   414
Haste still pays haste, and leisure answers leisure;
Like doth quit like, and *Measure* still *for Measure.*
Then, Angelo, thy fault's thus manifested;
Which, though thou wouldst deny, denies thee
        vantage.
We do condemn thee to the very block
Where Claudio stoop'd to death, and with like
        haste.   420
Away with him!
Mari.   O my most gracious lord,
I hope you will not mock me with a husband.
Duke. It is your husband mock'd you with a
husband.
Consenting to the safeguard of your honour,
I thought your marriage fit; else imputation,   425
For that he knew you, might reproach your life
And choke your good to come.   For his possessions,
Although by [confiscation] they are ours,
We do instate and widow you withal,
To buy you a better husband.
Mari.   O my dear lord,
I crave no other, nor no better man.   431
Duke. Never crave him; we are definitive.
Mari. Gentle my liege, —   [*Kneeling.*]
Duke.   You do but lose your labour.
Away with him to death!   [*To Lucio.*]   Now, sir,
        to you.
Mari. O my good lord!   Sweet Isabel, take my
        part!   435
Lend me your knees, and all my life to come

I'll lend you all my life to do you service.
Duke. Against all sense you do importune her.
Should she kneel down in mercy of this fact,
Her brother's ghost his paved bed would break,
And take her hence in horror.
Mari.   Isabel,   441
Sweet Isabel, do yet but kneel by me.
Hold up your hands, say nothing; I'll speak all.
They say best men are moulded out of faults,
And, for the most, become much more the better
For being a little bad; so may my husband.   446
O Isabel, will you not lend a knee?
Duke. He dies for Claudio's death.
Isab.   [*Kneeling.*]   Most bounteous sir,
Look, if it please you, on this man condemn'd
As if my brother liv'd.   I partly think   450
A due sincerity govern'd his deeds,
Till he did look on me.   Since it is so,
Let him not die.   My brother had but justice,
In that he did the thing for which he died;
For Angelo,   455
His act did not o'ertake his bad intent,
And must be buried but as an intent
That perish'd by the way.   Thoughts are no sub-
        jects;
Intents, but merely thoughts.
Mari.   Merely, my lord.
Duke. Your suit's unprofitable; stand up, I say.
I have bethought me of another fault.   461
Provost, how came it Claudio was beheaded
At an unusual hour?
Prov.   It was commanded so.
Duke. Had you a special warrant for the deed?
Prov. No, my good lord; it was by private mes-
        sage.   465
Duke. For which I do discharge you of your office:
Give up your keys.
Prov.   Pardon me, noble lord.
I thought it was a fault, but knew it not;
Yet did repent me, after more advice.
For testimony whereof, one in the prison,   470
That should by private order else have died,
I have reserv'd alive.
Duke.   What's he?
Prov.   His name is Barnardine.
Duke. I would thou hadst done so by Claudio.
Go fetch him hither; let me look upon him.
                                        [*Exit Provost.*]
Escal. I am sorry, one so learned and so wise   475
As you, Lord Angelo, have still appear'd,
Should slip so grossly, both in the heat of blood,
And lack of temper'd judgement afterward.
Ang. I am sorry that such sorrow I procure;

---

401. **brain'd:** killed, defeated.   406. **salt:** lustful.   418. **vantage:** advantage, i.e., escape.   425. **imputation:** censure.
427. **For:** as for.   428. **[confiscation]** F₂.   *confutation* F₁.   429. **instate ... withal:** confer upon you as a widow's estate.
432. **definitive:** resolved.   458. **subjects:** i.e., to the law.   468. **fault:** mistake.   469. **advice:** thought, consideration.
479. **procure:** cause.

And so deep sticks it in my penitent heart   480
That I crave death more willingly than mercy.
'Tis my deserving, and I do entreat it.

Re-enter PROVOST, *with* BARNARDINE, CLAUDIO
[*muffled*], *and* JULIET.

Duke. Which is that Barnardine?
Prov.   This, my lord.
Duke. There was a friar told me of this man.
Sirrah, thou art said to have a stubborn soul   485
That apprehends no further than this world,
And squar'st thy life according. Thou'rt con-
     demn'd;
But, for those earthly faults, I quit them all;
And pray thee take this mercy to provide
For better times to come. Friar, advise him;   490
I leave him to your hand. What muffl'd fellow's
     that?
Prov. This is another prisoner that I sav'd,
Who should have died when Claudio lost his head;
As like almost to Claudio as himself.
                         [*Unmuffles Claudio.*]
Duke. [*To Isabella.*] If he be like your brother, for
     his sake   495
Is he pardon'd; and, for your lovely sake —
Give me your hand and say you will be mine —
He is my brother too. But fitter time for that.
By this Lord Angelo perceives he's safe;
Methinks I see a quick'ning in his eye.   500
Well, Angelo, your evil quits you well.
Look that you love your wife; her worth worth
     yours.
I find an apt remission in myself;
And yet here's one in place I cannot pardon.
     [*To Lucio.*] You, sirrah, that knew me for a fool,
     a coward,   505
One all of luxury, an ass, a madman,
Wherein have I [deserved so] of you,
That you extol me thus?   508

Lucio. Faith, my lord, I spoke it but according
to the trick. If you will hang me for it, you may;
but I had rather it would please you I might be
whipp'd.   512
Duke. Whipp'd first, sir, and hang'd after.
Proclaim it, Provost, round about the city,
[Is] any woman wrong'd by this lewd fellow,   515
As I have heard him swear himself there's one
Whom he begot with child, let her appear,
And he shall marry her. The nuptial finish'd,
Let him be whipp'd and hang'd.   519
Lucio. I beseech your Highness do not marry me
to a whore. Your Highness said even now, I made
you a duke; good my lord, do not recompense me
in making me a cuckold.
Duke. Upon mine honour, thou shalt marry her.
Thy slanders I forgive; and therewithal   525
Remit thy other forfeits. Take him to prison;
And see our pleasure herein executed.
Lucio. Marrying a punk, my lord, is pressing to
death, whipping, and hanging.
Duke. Slandering a prince deserves it.   530
                    [*Exeunt Officers with Lucio.*]
She, Claudio, that you wrong'd, look you restore.
Joy to you, Mariana! Love her, Angelo!
I have confess'd her and I know her virtue.
Thanks, good friend Escalus, for thy much goodness;
There's more behind that is more gratulate.   535
Thanks, Provost, for thy care and secrecy;
We shall employ thee in a worthier place.
Forgive him, Angelo, that brought you home
The head of Ragozine for Claudio's;
The offence pardons itself. Dear Isabel,   540
I have a motion much imports your good;
Whereto if you'll a willing ear incline,
What's mine is yours and what is yours is mine.
So, bring us to our palace, where we'll show
What's yet behind, that['s] meet you all should
     know.   [*Exeunt.*] 545

488. quit: forgive. 501. quits: requites. 503. apt remission: readiness to pardon. 504. in place: present. 506. luxury:
lust. 507. [deserved so] (Pope). *so deserv'd* F. 515. [Is] (Hart). *If* F. 526. forfeits: penalties. 535. behind: i.e., to
come. gratulate: gratifying. 545. that['s] F₂. *that* F₁.

The Tragedy of King Lear

ON NOVEMBER 26, 1607, "Master William Shakespeare his historye of Kinge Lear" was entered in the Stationers' Register "as yt was played before the Kinges maiestie at Whitehall vppon Sainct Stephens night at Christmas Last." The First Quarto, appearing in 1608, repeats upon its title page Shakespeare's name and the notice of the command performance. This Quarto, known as the "Pied Bull" Quarto because it was printed for Nathaniel Butter and "sold at his shop in Pauls Church-yard at the signe of the Pide Bull," exists in a variety of states, owing to the fact that corrections were made while the work was being printed, corrected and uncorrected sheets being bound up together in several different combinations. A Second Quarto, reprinting the First, has been shown to belong to the year 1619, though the date upon its title page is 1608. The text in the First Quarto is very poorly printed, but it contains some 300 lines absent from the Folio. The Folio text, much more accurate, has, in turn, over one hundred lines lacking in the Quarto. Except for the Fool's prophecy (III.ii.79-95), which the Folio supplies and which is commonly regarded as spurious, all of the passages are held to be authentic, and it is reasonable to suppose that both texts derive from a single original, and that their respective omissions are, at least for the most part, cuts made for acting purposes. Certain features of the Quarto, especially the confounding of prose as verse and verse as prose, may point to a short-hand report as the source of the copy. The present text is based upon the Folio as the more accurately printed version, although the Quarto supplies not only its unique passages but numerous good readings.

For the date of *King Lear* the later limit is fixed by the record of the performance on Saint Stephen's night (December 26) in 1606. An earlier limit is provided by Harsnett's *Declaration of Egregious Popish Impostures* (Stationers' Register, March 16, 1603), from which Shakespeare took the names of the devils in the pretended ravings of Edgar. If, as seems most likely, "these late eclipses" (I.ii.112) were inspired by the eclipses of the sun and moon on October 2 and September 27, 1605 respectively, then the close of 1605 or early 1606 would seem to be a sound conjecture for the date of composition. The chronological relation of *King Lear* to *Macbeth* (1606) cannot be ascertained, but in the light of the available evidence the priority of the former seems more probable.

In its remote origins the story of Lear appears to be a variant of the Cinderella tale, widespread in folklore. Attached to the name of Lear, the legend appears in a fully developed form in the pseudo-historical chronicle, *Historia Regum Britanniae*, by Geoffrey of Monmouth (c. 1135). Thereafter it became an oft-told tale, especially in Tudor days, the most conspicuous versions being those in Holinshed's *Chronicle*, in *The First parte of the Mirrour for Magistrates* by John Higgins, and in Spenser's *Faerie Queene* (II.x.27-32). The story had already been dramatized in an anonymous play, *The True Chronicle History of King Leir* (1605). This play, however, was an old one, having been registered on May 14, 1594 and having been acted, according to Henslowe's records, during the month preceding. It was registered again on May 8, 1605, before its publication in that year as "diuers and sundry times lately acted." It has been urged that the old play was belatedly published to take advantage of the success of Shakespeare's play, but it is easier to believe that the printing, or the revival, of the former moved Shakespeare to handle the time-honored story.

Shakespeare owes little to earlier accounts beyond the broad outlines of the traditional story. From Spenser he may have taken the present form of Cordelia's name, which earlier had been Cordeilla or Cordella. From the old play come minor verbal echoes and perhaps the suggestion for the characters of Kent and Oswald. Comparison of Shakespeare's version with its predecessors, however, reveals mainly his distinctive originality.

Shakespeare transforms the story by substituting a tragic catastrophe for the traditional happy ending, according to which the French forces are victorious and Lear is restored to his kingdom, where he dies in peace after reigning two more years. The old play closes with the restoration of the king. The earlier versions, however, carry the "history" beyond the death of Lear to a calamitous ending involving Cordelia. According to their story, Cordelia and her husband succeed to the throne, but after about five years the sons of Goneril and Regan make war upon Cordelia and cast her into prison, where she kills herself in grief and despair. This appendage to the main story presumably gave Shakespeare the idea for a tragic conclusion to the fortunes of Lear. Having resolved upon this fundamental change, Shakespeare directs all his resources to making the catastrophe terrible. He doubles the pity of it by making not only Lear's death but Cordelia's follow the failure of their cause; he adds immeasurable tragic force through the invention of Lear's madness; he augments pathos and irony through the banishment of the loyal Kent and the creation of the faithful Fool. Finally, he enlarges the dimensions of the tragedy and deepens its intensity by introducing the story of Gloucester and his sons.

This skillfully interwoven underplot is developed from the incident of the King of Paphlagonia in Sidney's *Arcadia* (II.x). The romance tells of a king turned against his legitimate son by the slanders of his bastard, the usurpation of his kingdom and his blinding by the bastard, his rescue by the good son whom he has sought to murder, and the foiling of his attempt at suicide by leaping from a rock. But the pretended madness of Edgar is entirely owing to Shakespeare, as is, of course, the deftness by which this minor plot is engrafted on the story of Lear through the activities of Edgar as Poor Tom and the love of Lear's wicked daughters for Edmund.

By this minor plot Shakespeare not only increases the tragic impact of his drama and deepens the conflict of love and hate in its world, but he both complicates and clarifies the structure through the symmetry of dominant elements. Both Lear and Gloucester suffer from the ingratitude of the children whom they have trusted and are succored by the ones they have cast off. Both meet their injured offspring without recognizing them. Both learn wisdom through adversity — too late. Then there is the remarkable instrumentation upon the theme of madness in the delirium of Lear, in the feigned insanity of Edgar, and in the cracked intelligence of the Fool. *King Lear* is a splendid achievement in dramatic counterpoint.

The much discussed opening affords a perfect illustration of Shakespeare's power to throw the illusion of reality over the improbable and to develop a world of human significance from a core of fable.

The initial situation in the traditional story, the division of Lear's kingdom among his daughters according to their expressions of love for him, involves a double improbability; first that a man of intelligence would do what Lear does, secondly that Cordelia, who loves her father so much, would so risk offending him. This implausibility Shakespeare was bound by as a postulate in his inherited material. As such we too must accept it; but at the same time we should appreciate his skill in disguising it, so that in the clean speed and poise of the opening action it is but faintly perceived. Certain details modify the situation and our impressions of it. For one thing, it is apparent that Lear has fixed his intentions in the division of the Kingdom before the occasion set for the announcement of them (I.i.1-7, 37-39, 84-88, 196-204, 245-47). He has envisaged the proclamation as an official act, duly witnessed, and as an opportunity for a public display of gratitude pleasing to his pride. It is apparent, too, that the portion reserved for Cordelia, his favorite daughter, is richer ("more opulent"), not more extensive, than the territories allotted to her sisters (ll. 81-88), and that Lear's preference for Cordelia, injudiciously stressed, has dictated this "largest bounty" and his expectations of a surpassing avowal of affection from her. When, therefore, Cordelia fails him, he is taken completely by surprise. His pride, both regal and paternal, is sharply wounded, he feels defied and publicly humiliated, and he breaks into a paroxysm of anger. His behavior is unpardonably extreme; on the other hand, he is a king accustomed to obedience, and Cordelia seems blunt in excess of what is needful. She might have indulged him. Our feelings toward her, however, are tempered by her "asides" which express to us the feelings she will not utter (ll. 63, 78-80); we suspect already and are soon to know the hypocrisy in her sisters which sickens her (ll. 271-84); and her defense by Kent and France (ll. 153-56, 185-88, 238-40) makes us understand her. The upshot of all this is that at the end of this first scene of swift and sturdy dialogue we are conscious not of inherent improbability but of grievous misunderstanding, and we sense the threat of worse things to come.

The self-will of Lear which blinds him to the true values about him and drives him to such acts of rashness as the disinheriting of Cordelia and the banishment of Kent, is deeply ingrained and has been fostered by years of autocratic rule. Its grip upon him is shown by his aggressive behavior at the home of Goneril before Goneril herself has begun to show her hand, and by his imprecations upon her after she has done so; and the folly into which it has now betrayed him is irreparable because it has delivered him, in the autumn of his life, into the power of ruthless people. From the wrongs unloosed by his monstrous daughters there is no rescue, but there is redemption for Lear's nature. Through his purgatory of suffering he attains to humble self-knowledge, and when he dies he is transfigured.

The change in Lear is gradual, but there are several points at which its progress is registered. Even at the house of Goneril, though he is still his domineering self and his pride is as yet unyielding, there is an intimation that his mind has begun to glimpse its folly (I.iv.288–94). At Gloucester's castle, where the antipathy of his daughters is becoming clearer every minute, Lear tries to master his rising passion (II.iv.56–58, 122), and this effort at patience and self-control, doubtless unaccustomed, is symptomatic of the transformation that adversity is preparing. Here, though he can still curse Goneril, he kneels to Regan, and when she too shows a heart of stone, Lear knows that he is forsaken. Out in the storm Lear defies the elements with all the vehemence of the passion surging in his heart, resolved to endure what to him is easier to bear than the malice of his daughters. Here his suffering is the beginning of wisdom. An outcast now himself, exposed and wretched, Lear feels bound to all the poor and afflicted for whom he has never before taken thought (III.iv.28–36); and presently, delirium having set in, he would make a philosopher of Poor Tom, who seems to him one of those stricken many whom he has just apostrophized and from whom, therefore, he can tardily learn. This is the new Lear, in whom pride and arrogance are extinguished, a Lear who feels his kinship with common mortals. It is in his reunion with Cordelia, however, that the seal is set upon his transformation. Shakespeare has written nothing more moving than the scene of recognition in which Lear acknowledges his fault and begs his daughter's forgiveness (IV.vii. 45 ff.). The lines, remarkable for their absolute simplicity, are carried "alive into the heart." All Lear cares for now is a refuge in Cordelia's love (V.iii.8–19). After this, the cruelty which parts them is almost too much to bear.

It has been truly noted that Lear's madness is an acute case of delirium brought on by physical exposure and nervous strain. This is clearly understood by the doctor who successfully prescribes for him. There is no hint of earlier mental weakness; Lear's despotic ways are royal prerogatives, not insanity. It is interesting, however, that Shakespeare artistically foreshadows what is to happen, in Lear's repeated dread lest his suffering unhinge his mind (I.V.50–51; II.iv.221, 286–89; III.ii.67; III.iv.21–22).

Shakespeare acknowledges no principle demanding poetic justice at the end of a play in which the powers of injustice have cruelly prevailed. Even Cordelia, whose taking off has seemed to many gratuitously wanton, must be sacrificed, for the wickedness upon which Shakespeare meditates is a perverse and a heartless scourge. Nevertheless, Shakespeare did not conceive this tragedy in a spirit of total negation. The picture of disaster upon which we are made to look is not a denial of good. The wickedness of Goneril and Regan and Edmund is matched by the virtue of Cordelia and Kent and Edgar, and there is a world of difference between the sordid ends of the evil characters and the passing of Lear and Cordelia, purged and reunited. The miserable words of Gloucester (IV.i.38–39),

> As flies to wanton boys, are we to th' gods,
> They kill us for their sport,

have often been quoted as if they abstracted the spirit of the play, in forgetfulness that Gloucester himself learned to think otherwise and, reconciled to affliction, later cried (IV.vi.221–23),

> You ever-gentle gods, take my breath from me;
> Let not my worser spirit tempt me again
> To die before you please!

The meaning of this play is not to be plucked from isolated passages. Indeed, it is difficult to say specifically what the meaning of the play is, unless it be that when reason is abandoned, when natural ties and duties are violated, havoc and suffering are certain to follow. And perhaps one may also discern the implication that suffering may be a way to salvation. For the Lear who expires with Cordelia dead in his arms is a man whom sorrow has ennobled.

THE TRAGEDY OF KING LEAR

[DRAMATIS PERSONÆ

LEAR, *King of Britain.*	Doctor.
KING OF FRANCE.	Fool.
DUKE OF BURGUNDY.	OSWALD, *steward to Goneril.*
DUKE OF CORNWALL.	A Captain employed by Edmund.
DUKE OF ALBANY.	Gentleman attendant on Cordelia.
EARL OF KENT.	A Herald.
EARL OF GLOUCESTER	Servants to Cornwall.
EDGAR, *son to Gloucester.*	
EDMUND, *bastard son to Gloucester.*	GONERIL,
CURAN, *a courtier.*	REGAN, } *daughters to Lear.*
Old Man, *tenant to Gloucester.*	CORDELIA,

Knights of Lear's train, Captains, Messengers, Soldiers, and Attendants.

SCENE: *Britain.*]

ACT I

SCENE I. [*King Lear's palace.*]

Enter KENT, GLOUCESTER, *and* EDMUND.

Kent. I thought the King had more affected the Duke of Albany than Cornwall.

Glou. It did always seem so to us; but now, in the division of the kingdom, it appears not which of the Dukes he values most; for qualities are so weigh'd, that curiosity in neither can make choice of either's moiety.   7

Kent. Is not this your son, my lord?

Glou. His breeding, sir, hath been at my charge. I have so often blush'd to acknowledge him, that now I am braz'd to't.   11

Kent. I cannot conceive you.

Glou. Sir, this young fellow's mother could; whereupon she grew round-womb'd, and had, indeed, sir, a son for her cradle ere she had a husband for her bed. Do you smell a fault?

Kent. I cannot wish the fault undone, the issue of it being so proper.   18

Glou. But I have a son, sir, by order of law, some year elder than this, who yet is no dearer in my account. Though this knave came something saucily to the world before he was sent for, yet was his mother fair; there was good sport at his making, and the whoreson must be acknowledged. Do you know this noble gentleman, Edmund?   25

Edm. No, my lord.

Glou. My Lord of Kent. Remember him hereafter as my honourable friend.

Edm. My services to your lordship.

Kent. I must love you, and sue to know you better.   31

Edm. Sir, I shall study deserving.

Glou. He hath been out nine years, and away he shall again. The King is coming.

Sennet. *Enter one bearing a coronet, then* KING LEAR, *then the* DUKES OF ALBANY *and* CORNWALL, *next* GONERIL, REGAN, CORDELIA, *with followers.*

Lear. Attend the lords of France and Burgundy, Gloucester.   35

Act I, sc. i, 1. **affected:** liked.   5. **qualities** F.   *equalities* Q.   6. **weigh'd:** balanced.   **curiosity:** careful scrutiny.   7. **moiety:** share.   11. **braz'd:** brazened, hardened.   21. **account:** esteem.   33. **out:** in military service.   34. S.D. *Sennet:* set of notes on a trumpet.

Glou. I shall, my lord.

    [Exeunt [Gloucester and Edmund].

  Lear. Meantime we shall express our darker
purpose.
Give me the map there. Know that we have di-
vided
In three our kingdom; and 'tis our fast intent
To shake all cares and business from our age, 40
Conferring them on younger strengths, while we
Unburden'd crawl toward death. Our son of Corn-
wall,
And you, our no less loving son of Albany,
We have this hour a constant will to publish
Our daughters' several dowers, that future strife 45
May be prevented now. The Princes, France and
Burgundy,
Great rivals in our youngest daughter's love,
Long in our court have made their amorous so-
journ,
And here are to be answer'd. Tell me, my daugh-
ters, —
Since now we will divest us both of rule, 50
Interest of territory, cares of state, —
Which of you shall we say doth love us most,
That we our largest bounty may extend
Where nature doth with merit challenge? Goneril,
Our eldest-born, speak first. 55

  Gon. Sir, I love you more than word can wield
the matter;
Dearer than eye-sight, space, and liberty;
Beyond what can be valued, rich or rare;
No less than life, with grace, health, beauty,
honour;
As much as child e'er lov'd, or father found; 60
A love that makes breath poor, and speech unable:
Beyond all manner of so much I love you.

  Cor. *[Aside.]* What shall Cordelia speak? Love
and be silent.

  Lear. Of all these bounds, even from this line to
this,
With shadowy forests and with champains rich'd, 65
With plenteous rivers and wide-skirted meads,
We make thee lady. To thine and Albany's issues
Be this perpetual. What says our second daughter,
Our dearest Regan, wife of Cornwall? [Speak.]

  Reg. I am made of that self metal as my sister, 71
And prize me at her worth. In my true heart
I find she names my very deed of love;
Only she comes too short, that I profess
Myself an enemy to all other joys 75
Which the most precious square of sense [possesses],

And find I am alone felicitate
In your dear Highness' love.

  Cor.   *[Aside.]* Then poor Cordelia!
And yet not so; since, I am sure, my love's
More ponderous than my tongue. 80

  Lear. To thee and thine hereditary ever
Remain this ample third of our fair kingdom;
No less in space, validity, and pleasure,
Than that conferr'd on Goneril. Now, our joy,
Although our last and least, to whose young love 85
The vines of France and milk of Burgundy
Strive to be interess'd, what can you say to draw
A third more opulent than your sisters? Speak.

  Cor. Nothing, my lord.

  Lear. Nothing! 90

  Cor. Nothing.

  Lear. Nothing will come of nothing. Speak
again.

  Cor. Unhappy that I am, I cannot heave
My heart into my mouth. I love your Majesty
According to my bond; no more nor less. 95

  Lear. How, how, Cordelia! Mend your speech
a little,
Lest you may mar your fortunes.

  Cor.   Good my lord,
You have begot me, bred me, lov'd me: I
Return those duties back as are right fit,
Obey you, love you, and most honour you. 100
Why have my sisters husbands, if they say
They love you all? Haply, when I shall wed,
That lord whose hand must take my plight shall
carry
Half my love with him, half my care and duty.
Sure, I shall never marry like my sisters 105
[To love my father all].

  Lear. But goes thy heart with this?

  Cor.   Ay, my good lord.

  Lear. So young, and so untender?

  Cor. So young, my lord, and true.

  Lear. Let it be so; thy truth, then, be thy dower!
For, by the sacred radiance of the sun, 111
The [mysteries] of Hecate and the night;
By all the operation of the orbs
From whom we do exist and cease to be;
Here I disclaim all my paternal care, 115
Propinquity and property of blood,
And as a stranger to my heart and me
Hold thee from this for ever. The barbarous
Scythian,
Or he that makes his generation messes
To gorge his appetite, shall to my bosom 120

51. **Interest:** possession. 54. **Where...challenge:** to the one whose nature and deserts make the best claim. 65. **champains:** plains. 70. **[Speak]** Q. Om. F. 72. **prize...worth:** estimate myself as her equal (in affection). 76. **most...sense:** most exquisite region of my senses. **[possesses]** Q. *professes* F. 77. **felicitate:** made happy. 83. **validity:** value. 85. **our...least** F. *the last not least* Q. 87. **be interess'd:** establish a claim. 95. **bond:** duty. 103. **plight:** troth-plight. 106. **[To...all]** Q. Om. F. 112. **[mysteries]** F₂. *miseries* F₁ *mistresse* Q. **Hecate:** goddess of the infernal regions. 113. **operation:** influence. 119. **generation:** children. But Herodotus says the Scythians ate the aged.

Be as well neighbour'd, piti'd, and reliev'd,
As thou my sometime daughter.
    Kent.   Good my liege, —
    Lear. Peace, Kent!
Come not between the dragon and his wrath.
I lov'd her most, and thought to set my rest   125
On her kind nursery. [*To Cor.*] Hence, and avoid
    my sight! —
So be my grave my peace, as here I give
Her father's heart from her! Call France. — Who
    stirs?
Call Burgundy. Cornwall and Albany,
With my two daughters' dowers digest the third;
Let pride, which she calls plainness, marry her.   131
I do invest you jointly with my power,
Pre-eminence, and all the large effects
That troop with majesty. Ourself, by monthly
    course,
With reservation of an hundred knights   135
By you to be sustain'd, shall our abode
Make with you by due turn. Only we shall
    retain
The name, and all th' addition to a king;
The sway, revenue, execution of the rest,
Beloved sons, be yours; which to confirm,   140
This coronet part between you.
    Kent.   Royal Lear,
Whom I have ever honour'd as my king,
Lov'd as my father, as my master follow'd,
As my great patron thought on in my prayers, —
    Lear. The bow is bent and drawn; make from
    the shaft.   145
    Kent. Let it fall rather, though the fork invade
The region of my heart: be Kent unmannerly
When Lear is mad. What wouldst thou do, old
    man?
Thinkest thou that duty shall have dread to speak
When power to flattery bows? To plainness hon-
    our's bound   150
When majesty falls to folly. Reserve thy state;
And in thy best consideration check
This hideous rashness. Answer my life my judge-
    ment,
Thy youngest daughter does not love thee least;
Nor are those empty-hearted whose low sounds
Reverb no hollowness.
    Lear.   Kent, on thy life, no more.   156
    Kent. My life I never held but as a pawn
To wage against thine enemies, [nor] fear to lose it,
Thy safety being motive.
    Lear.   Out of my sight!
    Kent. See better, Lear; and let me still remain
The true blank of thine eye.   160
    Lear. Now, by Apollo, —

    Kent.   Now, by Apollo, king,
Thou swear'st thy gods in vain.
    Lear.   O, vassal! miscreant!
                 [*Laying his hand on his sword.*]
Alb. }
Corn. } Dear sir, forbear.   164
    Kent. Kill thy physician, and thy fee bestow
Upon the foul disease. Revoke thy gift,
Or, whilst I can vent clamour from my throat,
I'll tell thee thou dost evil.
    Lear.   Hear me, recreant!
On thine allegiance, hear me!   170
That thou hast sought to make us break our vows,
Which we durst never yet, and with strain'd pride
To come betwixt our sentence and our power,
Which nor our nature nor our place can bear,
Our potency made good, take thy reward.   175
Five days we do allot thee, for provision
To shield thee from disasters of the world;
And on the sixth to turn thy hated back
Upon our kingdom. If, on the tenth day follow-
    ing,   179
Thy banish'd trunk be found in our dominions,
The moment is thy death. Away! By Jupiter,
This shall not be revok'd.
    Kent. Fare thee well, king! Sith thus thou wilt
    appear,
Freedom lives hence, and banishment is here.
[*To Cordelia.*] The gods to their dear shelter take
    thee, maid,   185
That justly think'st and hast most rightly said!
[*To Regan and Goneril.*] And your large speeches
    may your deeds approve,
That good effects may spring from words of love.
Thus Kent, O princes, bids you all adieu;
He'll shape his old course in a country new.   190
                     [*Exit.*

Flourish. Re-enter GLOUCESTER, *with* FRANCE,
    BURGUNDY, *and Attendants.*

    Glou. Here's France and Burgundy, my noble
    lord.
    Lear. My Lord of Burgundy,
We first address toward you, who with this king
Hath rivall'd for our daughter. What, in the least,
Will you require in present dower with her,   195
Or cease your quest of love?
    Bur.   Most royal Majesty,
I crave no more than what your Highness offer'd,
Nor will you tender less.
    Lear.   Right noble Burgundy,
When she was dear to us, we did hold her so;
But now her price is fall'n. Sir, there she stands:
If aught within that little-seeming substance,   201

---

125. **set my rest:** stake my all. 126. **nursery:** cherishing. 130. **digest:** absorb. 138. **addition:** title. 146. **fork:** barb. 158. **[nor]** Q. *nere* F. 161. **blank:** center of the target. 172. **strain'd:** exaggerated. 175. **Our...good:** to prove my power. 183. **Sith:** since. 187. **approve:** justify. 198. **tender:** offer.

Or all of it, with our displeasure piec'd,
And nothing more, may fitly like your Grace,
She's there, and she is yours.

Bur.   I know no answer.

Lear. Will you, with those infirmities she owes,
Unfriended, new-adopted to our hate,   206
Dower'd with our curse, and stranger'd with our
        oath,
Take her, or leave her?

Bur.   Pardon me, royal sir;
Election makes not up in such conditions.

Lear. Then leave her, sir; for, by the power that
        made me,   210
I tell you all her wealth. [*To France.*] For you,
        great king,
I would not from your love make such a stray
To match you where I hate; therefore beseech you
T' avert your liking a more worthier way
Than on a wretch whom Nature is asham'd   215
Almost t' acknowledge hers.

France.   This is most strange,
That she, whom even but now was your [best]
        object,
The argument of your praise, balm of your age,
The best, the dearest, should in this trice of time
Commit a thing so monstrous, to dismantle   220
So many folds of favour.   Sure her offence
Must be of such unnatural degree
That monsters it, or your fore-vouch'd affection
Fallen into taint; which to believe of her,
Must be a faith that reason without miracle'   225
Should never plant in me.

Cor.   I yet beseech your Majesty, —
If for I want that glib and oily art
To speak and purpose not, since what I [well] in-
        tend,
I'll do't before I speak, — that you make known
It is no vicious blot, murder, or foulness,   230
No unchaste action, or dishonoured step,
That hath depriv'd me of your grace and favour;
But even for want of that for which I am richer,
A still-soliciting eye, and such a tongue
That I am glad I have not, though not to have it   235
Hath lost me in your liking.

Lear.   Better thou
Hadst not been born than not t' have pleas'd me
        better.

France. Is it but this, — a tardiness in nature
Which often leaves the history unspoke   239
That it intends to do?   My Lord of Burgundy,
What say you to the lady?   Love 's not love

When it is mingled with regards that stands
Aloof from th' entire point.   Will you have her?
She is herself a dowry.

Bur.   Royal king,
Give but that portion which yourself propos'd,
And here I take Cordelia by the hand,   246
Duchess of Burgundy.

Lear. Nothing.   I have sworn; I am firm.

Bur. I am sorry, then, you have so lost a father
That you must lose a husband.

Cor.   Peace be with Burgundy!
Since that respect and fortunes are his love,   251
I shall not be his wife.

France. Fairest Cordelia, that art most rich
        being poor,
Most choice forsaken, and most lov'd despis'd!
Thee and thy virtues here I seize upon,   255
Be it lawful I take up what 's cast away.
Gods, gods! 'tis strange that from their cold'st
        neglect
My love should kindle to inflam'd respect.
Thy dowerless daughter, king, thrown to my chance,
Is queen of us, of ours, and our fair France.   260
Not all the dukes of waterish Burgundy
Can buy this unpriz'd precious maid of me.
Bid them farewell, Cordelia, though unkind;
Thou losest here, a better where to find.

Lear. Thou hast her, France.   Let her be thine;
        for we   265
Have no such daughter, nor shall ever see
That face of hers again. — [*To Cor.*]   Therefore be
        gone
Without our grace, our love, our benison. —
Come, noble Burgundy.

        [*Flourish.   Exeunt [all but France, Goneril,
                Regan, and Cordelia*].

France. Bid farewell to your sisters.   270

Cor. The jewels of our father, with wash'd eyes
Cordelia leaves you.   I know you what you are;
And like a sister am most loath to call
Your faults as they are nam'd.   Love well our
        father.
To your professed bosoms I commit him;   275
But yet, alas, stood I within his grace,
I would prefer him to a better place.
So, farewell to you both.

Reg. Prescribe not us our duty.

Gon.   Let your study   279
Be to content your lord, who hath receiv'd you
At fortune's alms.   You have obedience scanted,
And well are worth the want that you have wanted.

---

203. **like:** please.   205. **owes:** owns.   209. **Election ... conditions:** one cannot make a choice on these terms.   212. **stray:** departure.   217. **[best]** Q. Om. F.   218. **argument:** theme.   223. **monsters:** makes monstrous.   224. **Fallen into taint:** must have decayed.   228. **[well]** Q. *will* F.   242. **regards:** considerations.   251. **respect and:** consideration of.   259. **thrown ... chance:** fallen to my lot.   261. **waterish :** (1) well-watered, (2) poor.   264. **where:** place.   271. **wash'd:** tear-washed.   275. **professed:** making professions (of love).   281. **scanted:** come short in.   282. And have well deserved the loss of that affection in which you were lacking.

Cor. Time shall unfold what plighted cunning
   hides;
Who covers faults, at last shame [them] derides.
Well may you prosper!
   France.   Come, my fair Cordelia. 285
                [Exeunt [France and Cordelia].
   Gon. Sister, it is not little I have to say of what
most nearly appertains to us both. I think our
father will hence to-night.
   Reg. That's most certain, and with you; next
month with us.   290
   Gon. You see how full of changes his age is; the
observation we have made of it hath [not] been
little. He always lov'd our sister most; and with
what poor judgement he hath now cast her off appears too grossly.
   Reg. 'Tis the infirmity of his age; yet he hath ever
but slenderly known himself.   297
   Gon. The best and soundest of his time hath been
but rash; then must we look from his age to receive
not alone the imperfections of long-engraffed condition, but therewithal the unruly waywardness that
infirm and choleric years bring with them.   303
   Reg. Such unconstant starts are we like to have
from him as this of Kent's banishment.
   Gon. There is further compliment of leave-taking
between France and him. Pray you, let['s hit] together; if our father carry authority with such disposition as he bears, this last surrender of his will
but offend us.   310
   Reg. We shall further think of it.
   Gon. We must do something, and i' th' heat.
                              [Exeunt.

SCENE II. *[The Earl of Gloucester's castle.]*

Enter Bastard [EDMUND *with a letter*].

   Edm. Thou, Nature, art my goddess; to thy law
My services are bound. Wherefore should I
Stand in the plague of custom, and permit
The curiosity of nations to deprive me,
For that I am some twelve or fourteen moonshines 5
Lag of a brother? Why bastard? Wherefore base?
When my dimensions are as well compact,
My mind as generous, and my shape as true,
As honest madam's issue? Why brand they us
With base? with baseness? bastardy? base, base? 10
Who, in the lusty stealth of nature, take
More composition and fierce quality
Than doth, within a dull, stale, tired bed,
Go to the creating a whole tribe of fops,

Got 'tween asleep and wake? Well, then,   15
Legitimate Edgar, I must have your land.
Our father's love is to the bastard Edmund
As to th' legitimate. Fine word, "legitimate!"
Well, my legitimate, if this letter speed
And my invention thrive, Edmund the base   20
Shall [top] th' legitimate. I grow; I prosper.
Now, gods, stand up for bastards!

           Enter GLOUCESTER.

   Glou. Kent banish'd thus! and France in choler
   parted!
And the King gone tonight! [subscrib'd] his power!
Confin'd to exhibition! All this done   25
Upon the gad! Edmund, how now! what news?
   Edm. So please your lordship, none.
                    [Putting up the letter.]
   Glou. Why so earnestly seek you to put up that
letter?
   Edm. I know no news, my lord.
   Glou. What paper were you reading?   30
   Edm. Nothing, my lord.
   Glou. No? What needed, then, that terrible
dispatch of it into your pocket? The quality of
nothing hath not such need to hide itself. Let's
see. Come, if it be nothing, I shall not need spec-
tacles.   36
   Edm. I beseech you, sir, pardon me. It is a
letter from my brother that I have not all o'er-
read; and for so much as I have perus'd, I find it
not fit for your o'er-looking.   40
   Glou. Give me the letter, sir.
   Edm. I shall offend either to detain or give it.
The contents, as in part I understand them, are to
blame.
   Glou. Let's see, let's see.   45
   Edm. I hope, for my brother's justification, he
wrote this but as an essay or taste of my virtue.
   Glou. (*Reads.*) "This policy and reverence of
age makes the world bitter to the best of our times;
keeps our fortunes from us till our oldness can- 50
not relish them. I begin to find an idle and fond
bondage in the oppression of aged tyranny; who
sways, not as it hath power, but as it is suffer'd.
Come to me, that of this I may speak more. If
our father would sleep till I wak'd him, you 55
should enjoy half his revenue for ever, and live the
beloved of your brother,   EDGAR."
Hum — conspiracy! — "Sleep till I wake him, you
should enjoy half his revenue!" — My son Edgar!
Had he a hand to write this? a heart and brain to

---

283. **plighted:** folded, complicated.   284. **shame [them]** Q.   *with shame* F.   292. **[not]** Q. Om. F.   295. **grossly:**
obviously.   304. **starts:** impulsive actions.   308. **let['s hit]** Q: let us agree. *let us sit* F.   312. **i' th' heat:** while the iron
is hot.
   Sc. ii, 3. **plague:** vexation.   4. **curiosity of nations:** i.e., the absurd law favoring the first-born.   6. **Lag of:** younger than.
19. **speed:** succeed.   21. **[top]** (Edwards conj.). *to'* F.   24. **[subscrib'd]** Q: surrendered. *prescrib'd* F.   25. **exhibition:** an
allowance.   26. **gad:** spur of the moment.   47. **essay or taste:** trial or test.   48. **policy and reverence:** policy of revering.
49. **times:** lives.   51. **fond:** foolish.

breed it in? — When came this to you? Who brought it? 62

Edm. It was not brought me, my lord; there's the cunning of it. I found it thrown in at the casement of my closet.

Glou. You know the character to be your brother's? 67

Edm. If the matter were good, my lord, I durst swear it were his; but, in respect of that, I would fain think it were not.

Glou. It is his.

Edm. It is his hand, my lord; but I hope his heart is not in the contents. 73

Glou. Has he never before sounded you in this business?

Edm. Never, my lord; but I have heard him oft maintain it to be fit that, sons at perfect age and fathers declin'd, the father should be as ward to the son, and the son manage his revenue. 79

Glou. O villain, villain! His very opinion in the letter! Abhorred villain! Unnatural, detested, brutish villain! worse than brutish! Go, sirrah, seek him; I'll apprehend him. Abominable villain! Where is he? 84

Edm. I do not well know, my lord. If it shall please you to suspend your indignation against my brother till you can derive from him better testimony of his intent, you should run a certain course; where, if you violently proceed against him, mistaking his purpose, it would make a great gap 90 in your own honour and shake in pieces the heart of his obedience. I dare pawn down my life for him that he hath writ this to feel my affection to your honour, and to no other pretence of danger. 95

Glou. Think you so?

Edm. If your honour judge it meet, I will place you where you shall hear us confer of this, and by an auricular assurance have your satisfaction; and that without any further delay than this very evening. 101

Glou. He cannot be such a monster —

[*Edm.* Nor is not, sure.

Glou. To his father, that so tenderly and entirely loves him. Heaven and earth!] Ed- 105 mund, seek him out; wind me into him, I pray you. Frame the business after your own wisdom. I would unstate myself to be in a due resolution.

Edm. I will seek him, sir, presently; convey the business as I shall find means, and acquaint you withal. 111

Glou. These late eclipses in the sun and moon portend no good to us. Though the wisdom of

nature can reason it thus and thus, yet nature finds itself scourg'd by the sequent effects. 115 Love cools, friendship falls off, brothers divide: in cities, mutinies; in countries, discord; in palaces, treason; and the bond crack'd 'twixt son and father. This villain of mine comes under the prediction; there's son against father: the King falls from 120 bias of nature; there's father against child. We have seen the best of our time; machinations, hollowness, treachery, and all ruinous disorders, follow us disquietly to our graves. Find out this villain, Edmund; it shall lose thee nothing; do it care- 125 fully. And the noble and true-hearted Kent banish'd! his offence, honesty! 'Tis strange.

[*Exit.*

Edm. This is the excellent foppery of the world, that, when we are sick in fortune, — often the surfeits of our own behaviour, — we make guilty 130 of our disasters the sun, the moon, and stars, as if we were villains on necessity, fools by heavenly compulsion, knaves, thieves, and treachers by spherical predominance, drunkards, liars, and adulterers by an enforc'd obedience of planetary 135 influence, and all that we are evil in, by a divine thrusting on. An admirable evasion of whoremaster man, to lay his goatish disposition on the charge of a star! My father compounded with my mother under the dragon's tail, and my nativity 140 was under *Ursa major;* so that it follows, I am rough and lecherous. Fut, I should have been that I am, had the maidenliest star in the firmament twinkled on my bastardizing. [Edgar —] 145

Enter EDGAR.

pat he comes like the catastrophe of the old comedy. My cue is villanous melancholy, with a sigh like Tom o' Bedlam. — O, these eclipses do portend these divisions! *fa, sol, la, mi.*

Edg. How now, brother Edmund! what serious contemplation are you in? 151

Edm. I am thinking, brother, of a prediction I read this other day, what should follow these eclipses.

Edg. Do you busy yourself with that? 155

Edm. I promise you, the effects he writes of succeed unhappily; [as of unnaturalness between the child and the parent; death, dearth, dissolutions of ancient amities; divisions in state, menaces and maledictions against king and nobles; needless diffidences, banishment of friends, dissipation of cohorts, nuptial breaches, and I know not what. 163

---

66. **character:** handwriting. 78. **declin'd:** failed. 89. **where:** whereas. 94. **feel:** sound. 95. **pretence of danger:** dangerous intent. 103–105. Q. Om. F. 106. **wind . . . him:** gain his confidence. 108. **unstate . . . resolution:** forfeit my position to be properly assured. 109. **presently:** at once. **convey:** carry on. 120–21. **falls . . . nature:** acts against his natural disposition. 128. **foppery:** foolishness. 133. **treachers:** traitors. 134. **spherical predominance:** influence of the planets. 145. [Edgar —] Q. Om. F. 148. **Tom o' Bedlam:** a lunatic beggar. 157–166. Q. Om. F. 161. **diffidences:** suspicions.

Edg. How long have you been a sectary astronomical?

Edm. Come, come;] when saw you my father last?

Edg. The night gone by.   168

Edm. Spake you with him?

Edg. Ay, two hours together.

Edm. Parted you in good terms? Found you no displeasure in him by word nor countenance?

Edg. None at all.   173

Edm. Bethink yourself wherein you may have offended him; and at my entreaty forbear his presence until some little time hath qualified the heat of his displeasure, which at this instant so rageth in him, that with the mischief of your person it would scarcely allay.

Edg. Some villain hath done me wrong.   180

Edm. That's my fear. I pray you, have a continent forbearance till the speed of his rage goes slower; and, as I say, retire with me to my lodging, from whence I will fitly bring you to hear my lord speak. Pray ye, go; there's my key. If you do stir abroad, go arm'd.   186

Edg. Arm'd, brother!

Edm. Brother, I advise you to the best; I am no honest man if there be any good meaning toward you. I have told you what I have seen and heard; but faintly, nothing like the image and horror of it. Pray you, away.   192

Edg. Shall I hear from you anon?

Edm. I do serve you in this business.

[*Exit Edgar.*

A credulous father and a brother noble,   195
Whose nature is so far from doing harms
That he suspects none; on whose foolish honesty
My practices ride easy. I see the business.
Let me, if not by birth, have lands by wit:
All with me 's meet that I can fashion fit.   200

[*Exit.*

SCENE III. [*The Duke of Albany's palace.*]

Enter GONERIL, *and* [OSWALD, *her*] *Steward.*

Gon. Did my father strike my gentleman for chiding of his Fool?

Osw. Ay, madam.

Gon. By day and night he wrongs me; every hour
He flashes into one gross crime or other
That sets us all at odds. I'll not endure it.   5
His knights grow riotous, and himself upbraids us
On every trifle. When he returns from hunting
I will not speak with him; say I am sick.
If you come slack of former services,

You shall do well; the fault of it I'll answer.   10

Osw. He's coming, madam; I hear him.

[*Horns within.*]

Gon. Put on what weary negligence you please,
You and your fellows; I'd have it come to question.
If he distaste it, let him to my sister,
Whose mind and mine, I know, in that are one,   15
[Not to be over-rul'd. Idle old man,
That still would manage those authorities
That he hath given away! Now, by my life,
Old fools are babes again, and must be us'd
With checks as flatteries, when they are seen abus'd.]
Remember what I have said.

Osw.   Well, madam.   21

Gon. And let his knights have colder looks
among you;
What grows of it, no matter. Advise your fellows
so.
[I would breed from hence occasions, and I shall,
That I may speak.] I'll write straight to my sister
To hold my [very] course. Prepare for dinner.   26

[*Exeunt.*

SCENE IV. [*A hall in the same.*]

Enter KENT [*disguised*].

Kent. If but as well I other accents borrow,
That can my speech defuse, my good intent
May carry through itself to that full issue
For which I raz'd my likeness. Now, banish'd
Kent,
If thou canst serve where thou dost stand condemn'd,   5
So may it come, thy master, whom thou lov'st,
Shall find thee full of labours.

Horns within. Enter LEAR, [KNIGHTS] *and
Attendants.*

Lear. Let me not stay a jot for dinner; go get it
ready. [*Exit an attendant.*] How now! what art
thou?   10

Kent. A man, sir.

Lear. What dost thou profess? What wouldst
thou with us?   13

Kent. I do profess to be no less than I seem; to
serve him truly that will put me in trust; to love
him that is honest; to converse with him that is wise
and says little; to fear judgement; to fight when I
cannot choose; and to eat no fish.   18

Lear. What art thou?

Kent. A very honest-hearted fellow, and as poor
as the King.

Lear. If thou be'st as poor for a subject as he's

---

164. **sectary astronomical**: student of astrology. 176. **qualified**: moderated. 178. **mischief**: injury. 198. **practices: plots.**

Sc. iii, 13. **question**: discussion. 16–20. [**Not ... abus'd**] Q. Om. F. 20. **as**: as well as. **abus'd**: misled. 24–25. [**I ... speak**] Q. Om. F. 26. [**very**] Q: identical. Om. F.

Sc. iv, 2. **defuse**: disguise. 4. **raz'd my likeness**: changed my appearance. 18. **eat no fish**: be a Protestant.

for a king, thou art poor enough. What wouldst
thou?   24
   Kent. Service.
   Lear. Who wouldst thou serve?
   Kent. You.
   Lear. Dost thou know me, fellow?
   Kent. No, sir; but you have that in your coun-
tenance which I would fain call master.   30
   Lear. What's that?
   Kent. Authority.
   Lear. What services canst thou do?   33
   Kent. I can keep honest counsel, ride, run, mar a
curious tale in telling it, and deliver a plain message
bluntly. That which ordinary men are fit for, I
am qualified in; and the best of me is diligence. 38
   Lear. How old art thou?
   Kent. Not so young, sir, to love a woman for
singing, nor so old to dote on her for anything. I
have years on my back forty-eight.   42
   Lear. Follow me; thou shalt serve me. If I like
thee no worse after dinner, I will not part from thee
yet. Dinner, ho, dinner! Where's my knave? my
Fool? Go you, and call my Fool hither.   47
                              [*Exit an attendant.*

       Enter Steward [OSWALD].
You, you, sirrah, where's my daughter?
   Osw. So please you, —   [*Exit.*
   Lear. What says the fellow there? Call the
clotpoll back. [*Exit a knight.*] Where's my Fool,
ho? I think the world's asleep.   52

       [*Re-enter* KNIGHT.]
How now! where's that mongrel?
   Knight. He says, my lord, your daughter is not
well.   55
   Lear. Why came not the slave back to me when
I call'd him?
   Knight. Sir, he answered me in the roundest
manner, he would not.
   Lear. He would not!   60
   Knight. My lord, I know not what the matter is;
but, to my judgement, your Highness is not en-
tertain'd with that ceremonious affection as you
were wont. There's a great abatement of kindness
appears as well in the general dependants as in the
Duke himself also and your daughter.   67
   Lear. Ha! say'st thou so?
   Knight. I beseech you, pardon me, my lord, if I
be mistaken; for my duty cannot be silent when I
think your Highness wrong'd.   71
   Lear. Thou but rememb'rest me of mine own
conception. I have perceived a most faint neglect
of late, which I have rather blamed as mine own
jealous curiosity than as a very pretence and pur-

pose of unkindness. I will look further into't.
But where's my Fool? I have not seen him this
two days.   78
   Knight. Since my young lady's going into France,
sir, the Fool hath much pined away.
   Lear. No more of that; I have noted it well.
Go you, and tell my daughter I would speak with
her. [*Exit an attendant.*] Go you, call hither my
Fool. [*Exit an attendant.*]   84

     Re-enter Steward [OSWALD].
O, you sir, you, come you hither, sir. Who am I,
sir?
   Osw. My lady's father.
   Lear. "My lady's father"! My lord's knave!
You whoreson dog! you slave! you cur!   89
   Osw. I am none of these, my lord; I beseech your
pardon.
   Lear. Do you bandy looks with me, you rascal?
                              [*Striking him.*]
   Osw. I'll not be strucken, my lord.   94
   Kent. Nor tripp'd neither, you base foot-ball
player.   [*Tripping up his heels.*]
   Lear. I thank thee, fellow. Thou serv'st me,
and I'll love thee.   98
   Kent. Come, sir, arise, away! I'll teach you
differences. Away, away! If you will measure
your lubber's length again, tarry; but away! go to.
Have you wisdom? So.   [*Pushes Oswald out.*]
   Lear. Now, my friendly knave, I thank thee.
There's earnest of thy service.   104
                           [*Giving Kent money.*]

       Enter FOOL.
   Fool. Let me hire him too; here's my coxcomb.
                  [*Offering Kent his cap.*]
   Lear. How now, my pretty knave! how dost
thou?
   Fool. Sirrah, you were best take my coxcomb.
[*Kent.* Why, Fool?]   110
   Fool. Why? For taking one's part that's out
of favour. Nay, an thou canst not smile as the
wind sits, thou'lt catch cold shortly. There, take
my coxcomb. Why, this fellow has banish'd two
on 's daughters, and did the third a blessing against
his will; if thou follow him, thou must needs wear
my coxcomb. — How now, nuncle! Would I had
two coxcombs and two daughters!   118
   Lear. Why, my boy?
   Fool. If I gave them all my living, I'd keep my
coxcombs myself. There's mine; beg another of
thy daughters.
   Lear. Take heed, sirrah; the whip.   123
   Fool. Truth's a dog must to kennel; he must be

---

51. **clotpoll:** blockhead. 75. **jealous curiosity:** suspicious fussiness. **very pretence:** real intention. 104. **earnest:** advance payment. 110. [**Kent ... Fool**] Q. *Lear. Why my Boy?* F.

whipp'd out, when [Lady the] brach may stand by
the fire and stink.

Lear. A pestilent gall to me!

Fool. Sirrah, I'll teach thee a speech.

Lear. Do.

Fool. Mark it, nuncle: 130

"Have more than thou showest,
  Speak less than thou knowest,
  Lend less than thou owest,
  Ride more than thou goest,
  Learn more than thou trowest, 135
  Set less than thou throwest;
  Leave thy drink and thy whore,
  And keep in-a-door,
  And thou shalt have more
  Than two tens to a score." 140

Kent. This is nothing, Fool.

Fool. Then 'tis like the breath of an unfee'd
lawyer; you gave me nothing for't. Can you make
no use of nothing, nuncle?

Lear. Why, no, boy; nothing can be made out
of nothing.   146

Fool. [*To Kent.*] Prithee, tell him so much the
rent of his land comes to. He will not believe a
Fool.

Lear. A bitter fool!   150

Fool. Dost thou know the difference, my boy,
between a bitter fool and a sweet one?

Lear. No, lad; teach me.

[*Fool.* "That lord that counsell'd thee
    To give away thy land, 155
  Come place him here by me,
  Do thou for him stand:
  The sweet and bitter fool
  Will presently appear;
  The one in motley here, 160
  The other found out there."

Lear. Dost thou call me fool, boy?

Fool. All thy other titles thou hast given away;
that thou wast born with.

Kent. This is not altogether fool, my lord. 165

Fool. No, faith, lords and great men will not let
me; if I had a monopoly out, they would have part
on't. And ladies, too, they will not let me have all
the fool to myself; they'll be snatching.] Nuncle,
give me an egg, and I'll give thee two crowns.

Lear. What two crowns shall they be? 172

Fool. Why, after I have cut the egg i' th' middle
and eat up the meat, the two crowns of the egg.
When thou clovest thy crown i' th' middle and
gav'st away both parts, thou bor'st thine ass on thy
back o'er the dirt. Thou hadst little wit in thy
bald crown when thou gav'st thy golden one away.

If I speak like myself in this, let him be whipp'd
that first finds it so. 180

"Fools had ne'er less grace in a year;
  For wise men are grown foppish,
And know not how their wits to wear,
  Their manners are so apish."

Lear. When were you wont to be so full of songs,
sirrah? 186

Fool. I have used it, nuncle, e'er since thou
mad'st thy daughters thy mothers; for when thou
gav'st them the rod, and puttest down thine own
breeches, 190

"Then they for sudden joy did weep,
  And I for sorrow sung,
That such a king should play bo-peep,
  And go the fools among." 194

Prithee, nuncle, keep a schoolmaster that can teach
thy Fool to lie. I would fain learn to lie.

Lear. And you lie, sirrah, we'll have you
whipp'd. 198

Fool. I marvel what kin thou and thy daughters
are. They'll have me whipp'd for speaking true,
thou'lt have me whipp'd for lying; and sometimes
I am whipp'd for holding my peace. I had rather
be any kind o' thing than a Fool; and yet I would
not be thee, nuncle; thou hast pared thy wit o' both
sides, and left nothing i' th' middle. Here comes
one o' the parings. 206

Enter GONERIL.

Lear. How now, daughter! what makes that
frontlet on? [Methinks] you are too much of late
i' th' frown. 209

Fool. Thou wast a pretty fellow when thou hadst
no need to care for her frowning; now thou art an O
without a figure. I am better than thou art now;
I am a Fool, thou art nothing. [*To Gon.*] Yes, forsooth, I will hold my tongue; so your face bids me,
though you say nothing. Mum, mum, 216

"He that keeps nor crust nor crumb,
  Weary of all, shall want some."

[*Pointing to Lear.*] That's a sheal'd peascod.

Gon. Not only, sir, this your all-licens'd Fool,
But other of your insolent retinue 221
Do hourly carp and quarrel, breaking forth
In rank and not-to-be-endured riots. Sir,
I had thought, by making this well known unto
  you,
To have found a safe redress; but now grow fearful,
By what yourself, too, late have spoke and done, 226
That you protect this course and put it on
By your allowance; which if you should, the fault
Would not scape censure, nor the redresses sleep,

---

125. [Lady the] (Malone). *The Lady* F. brach: bitch. 133. owest: ownest. 134. goest: walkest. 136. Set: stake.
throwest: win at a throw of the dice. 154–170. [*Fool . . . snatching*] Q. Om. F. 208. frontlet: frown (lit., a forehead
band). [Methinks] Q. Om. F. 219. sheal'd: empty. 227. put it on: encourage it. 228. allowance: approval.

Which, in the tender of a wholesome weal, 230
Might in their working do you that offence,
Which else were shame, that then necessity
Will call discreet proceeding.
    Fool. For, you know, nuncle,
    "The hedge-sparrow fed the cuckoo so long, 235
    That it had it head bit off by it young."
So, out went the candle, and we were left dark-
    ling.
    Lear. Are you our daughter?
    Gon. [Come, sir,]
I would you would make use of your good wis-
    dom, 240
Whereof I know you are fraught, and put away
These dispositions which of late transport you
From what you rightly are.
    Fool. May not an ass know when the cart draws
the horse? "Whoop, Jug! I love thee."
    Lear. Doth any here know me? This is not
    Lear. 246
Doth Lear walk thus? speak thus? Where are his
    eyes?
Either his notion weakens, his discernings
Are lethargied — Ha! waking? 'Tis not so.
Who is it that can tell me who I am? 250
    Fool. Lear's shadow.
    [*Lear.* I would learn that; for, by the marks of
sovereignty, knowledge, and reason, I should be
false persuaded I had daughters.
    Fool. Which they will make an obedient father.]
    Lear. Your name, fair gentlewoman? 257
    Gon. This admiration, sir, is much o' the savour
Of other your new pranks. I do beseech you
To understand my purposes aright. 260
As you are old and reverend, should be wise.
Here do you keep a hundred knights and squires,
Men so disorder'd, so debosh'd and bold,
That this our court, infected with their manners,
Shows like a riotous inn. Epicurism and lust 265
Makes it more like a tavern or a brothel
Than a grac'd palace. The shame itself doth speak
For instant remedy. Be then desir'd
By her, that else will take the thing she begs,
A little to disquantity your train; 270
And the remainders that shall still depend
To be such men as may besort your age,
Which know themselves and you.
    Lear.   Darkness and devils!
Saddle my horses; call my train together!
Degenerate bastard! I'll not trouble thee; 275
Yet have I left a daughter.

    Gon. You strike my people; and your disorder'd
    rabble
Make servants of their betters.

    Enter ALBANY.

    Lear. Woe, that too late repents! — [O, sir, are
    you come?]
Is it your will? Speak, sir. — Prepare my horses. —
Ingratitude, thou marble-hearted fiend, 281
More hideous when thou show'st thee in a child
Than the sea-monster!
    Alb.   Pray, sir, be patient.
    Lear. [*To Gon.*] Detested kite! thou liest.
My train are men of choice and rarest parts, 285
That all particulars of duty know,
And in the most exact regard support
The worships of their name. O most small fault,
How ugly didst thou in Cordelia show! 289
Which, like an engine, wrench'd my frame of nature
From the fix'd place; drew from my heart all love
And added to the gall. O Lear, Lear, Lear!
Beat at this gate, that let thy folly in
                [*Striking his head.*]
And thy dear judgement out! Go, go, my people.
    Alb. My lord, I am guiltless as I am ignorant 295
Of what hath moved you.
    Lear.   It may be so, my lord.
Hear, Nature! hear, dear goddess, hear!
Suspend thy purpose, if thou didst intend
To make this creature fruitful!
Into her womb convey sterility! 300
Dry up in her the organs of increase,
And from her derogate body never spring
A babe to honour her! If she must teem,
Create her child of spleen, that it may live
And be a thwart disnatur'd torment to her! 305
Let it stamp wrinkles in her brow of youth,
With cadent tears fret channels in her cheeks,
Turn all her mother's pains and benefits
To laughter and contempt, that she may feel
How sharper than a serpent's tooth it is 310
To have a thankless child! — Away, away! [*Exit.*
    Alb. Now, gods that we adore, whereof comes
    this?
    Gon. Never afflict yourself to know more of it,
But let his disposition have that scope
As dotage gives it. 315

    Re-enter LEAR.

    Lear. What, fifty of my followers at a clap!
Within a fortnight!

---

230. **tender of:** care for. **weal:** commonweal. 236. **it:** its. 237. **darkling:** in the dark. 239. **[Come, sir]** Q. Om. F.
241. **fraught:** furnished with. 248. **notion:** mental power. 252–256. [*Lear*...*father*] Q. Om. F. 252. **by**...**of:** tested by.
258. **admiration:** (pretended) surprise. 263. **debosh'd:** debauched. 265. **Epicurism:** gluttony. 270. **disquantity:** reduce.
271. **depend:** be your dependants. 272. **besort:** suit. 279. [O...**come**] Q. Om. F. 288. **worships**...**name:** their honorable reputation. 290. **engine:** rack. 302. **derogate:** debased. 305. **thwart:** distorted, perverse. **disnatur'd:** unnatural.
307. **cadent:** falling. 313. **more of it:** F. *the cause* Q.

Alb.   What's the matter, sir?
Lear. I'll tell thee. [*To Gon.*] Life and death!
  I am asham'd
That thou hast power to shake my manhood thus;
That these hot tears, which break from me per-
  force,   320
Should make thee worth them.   Blasts and fogs
  upon thee!
Th' untented woundings of a father's curse
Pierce every sense about thee!   Old fond eyes,
Beweep this cause again, I'll pluck ye out,
And cast you, with the waters that you loose,   325
To temper clay.   Ha! [is it come to this?]
Let it be so: I have another daughter,
Who, I am sure, is kind and comfortable.
When she shall hear this of thee, with her nails
She'll flay thy wolvish visage.   Thou shalt find   330
That I'll resume the shape which thou dost think
I have cast off for ever.   [Thou shalt, I warrant
  thee.]   [*Exeunt* [*Lear, Kent, and attendants*].
Gon. Do you mark that?
Alb. I cannot be so partial, Goneril,
To the great love I bear you, —   335
Gon. Pray you, content. — What, Oswald, ho!
[*To the Fool.*] You, sir, more knave than fool, after
  your master.
Fool. Nuncle Lear, nuncle Lear, tarry!   Take
the Fool with thee.
      A fox, when one has caught her,   340
      And such a daughter,
      Should sure to the slaughter,
      If my cap would buy a halter.
      So the Fool follows after.   [*Exit.*
Gon. This man hath had good counsel, — a
  hundred knights!   345
'Tis politic and safe to let him keep
At point a hundred knights; yes, that, on every
  dream,
Each buzz, each fancy, each complaint, dislike,
He may enguard his dotage with their powers,
And hold our lives in mercy.   Oswald, I say!   350
Alb. Well, you may fear too far.
Gon.   Safer than trust too far.
Let me still take away the harms I fear,
Not fear still to be taken.   I know his heart.
What he hath utter'd I have writ my sister.
If she sustain him and his hundred knights,   355
When I have show'd th' unfitness, —

          Re-enter Steward [OSWALD].
                          How now, Oswald!
What, have you writ that letter to my sister?

Osw. Ay, madam.
Gon. Take you some company, and away to horse.
Inform her full of my particular fear;   360
And thereto add such reasons of your own
As may compact it more.   Get you gone;
And hasten your return. [*Exit Oswald.*]   No, no,
  my lord,
This milky gentleness and course of yours
Though I condemn not, yet, under pardon,   365
You are much more at task for want of wisdom
Than prais'd for harmful mildness.
Alb. How far your eyes may pierce I cannot tell.
Striving to better, oft we mar what's well.
Gon. Nay, then —   370
Alb. Well, well; th' event.   [*Exeunt.*

Scene V. [*Court before the same.*]
      Enter LEAR, KENT, *and* FOOL.

Lear. Go you before to Gloucester with these
letters.   Acquaint my daughter no further with
anything you know than comes from her demand
out of the letter.   If your diligence be not speedy,
I shall be there afore you.   5
Kent. I will not sleep, my lord, till I have de-
livered your letter.   [*Exit.*
Fool. If a man's brains were in 's heels, were't
not in danger of kibes?
Lear. Ay, boy.   10
Fool. Then, I prithee, be merry; thy wit shall not
go slip-shod.
Lear. Ha, ha, ha!
Fool. Shalt see thy other daughter will use thee
kindly; for though she's as like this as a crab's like
an apple, yet I can tell what I can tell.   16
Lear. What canst tell, boy?
Fool. She will taste as like this as a crab does to a
crab.   Thou canst tell why one's nose stands i' th'
middle on 's face?   20
Lear. No.
Fool. Why, to keep one's eyes of either side 's
nose, that what a man cannot smell out, he may
spy into.
Lear. I did her wrong —   25
Fool. Canst tell how an oyster makes his shell?
Lear. No.
Fool. Nor I neither; but I can tell why a snail
has a house.   30
Lear. Why?
Fool. Why, to put 's head in; not to give it away
to his daughters and leave his horns without a
case.   34

322. **untented:** not to be probed.   326. **[is it come to this?]** Q.   Om. F.   328. **comfortable:** comforting.   332. **[Thou ...
thee]** Q.   Om. F.   347. **At point:** armed.   350. **in mercy:** at his mercy.   362. **compact:** confirm.   366. **at task:** to be
blamed.   371. **th' event:** (we'll see) the outcome.
   Sc. v, 1. **Gloucester:** the city.   9. **kibes:** chilblains.   11. **thy ... slip-shod:** i.e., because there is no sense in your proposed
journey.   15. **kindly:** (1) in friendly fashion, (2) according to her nature.

Lear. I will forget my nature. So kind a father!
Be my horses ready?

Fool. Thy asses are gone about 'em. The reason
why the seven stars are no moe than seven is a
pretty reason.

Lear. Because they are not eight?   40

Fool. Yes, indeed. Thou wouldst make a good
Fool.

Lear. To take 't again perforce! Monster ingratitude!

Fool. If thou wert my Fool, nuncle, I'd have
thee beaten for being old before thy time.   46

Lear. How's that?

Fool. Thou shouldst not have been old till thou
hadst been wise.

Lear. O, let me not be mad, not mad, sweet
heaven!   50
Keep me in temper; I would not be mad!

[*Enter* GENTLEMAN.]

How now! are the horses ready?

Gent. Ready, my lord.

Lear. Come, boy.

Fool. She that's a maid now, and laughs at my
departure,   55
Shall not be a maid long, unless things be cut
shorter.   [*Exeunt.*

ACT II

SCENE I. [*The Earl of Gloucester's castle.*]

Enter Bastard [EDMUND] *and* CURAN, *severally.*

Edm. Save thee, Curan.

Cur. And you, sir. I have been with your father,
and given him notice that the Duke of Cornwall and
Regan his duchess will be here with him this night.

Edm. How comes that?   6

Cur. Nay, I know not. You have heard of the
news abroad; I mean the whisper'd ones, for they
are yet but ear-kissing arguments?

Edm. Not I. Pray you, what are they?   10

Cur. Have you heard of no likely wars toward,
'twixt the Dukes of Cornwall and Albany?

Edm. Not a word.

Cur. You may do, then, in time. Fare you well,
sir.   [*Exit.* 15

Edm. The Duke be here to-night? The better!
best!
This weaves itself perforce into my business.
My father hath set guard to take my brother;
And I have one thing, of a queasy question,
Which I must act. Briefness and fortune, work! 20

Enter EDGAR.

Brother, a word; descend. Brother, I say!
My father watches; O sir, fly this place;
Intelligence is given where you are hid;
You have now the good advantage of the night.
Have you not spoken 'gainst the Duke of Corn-
wall?   25
He's coming hither, now, i' th' night, i' th' haste,
And Regan with him. Have you nothing said
Upon his party 'gainst the Duke of Albany?
Advise yourself.

Edg.   I am sure on't, not a word.

Edm. I hear my father coming. Pardon me, 30
In cunning I must draw my sword upon you.
Draw; seem to defend yourself; now quit you well.
Yield! Come before my father. Light, ho, here! —
Fly, brother. — Torches, torches! — So, farewell.
     [*Exit Edgar.*
Some blood drawn on me would beget opinion 35
     [*Wounds his arm.*
Of my more fierce endeavour. I have seen drunk-
ards
Do more than this in sport. — Father, father! —
Stop, stop! — No help?

Enter GLOUCESTER, *and* Servants *with torches.*

Glou. Now, Edmund, where's the villain?

Edm. Here stood he in the dark, his sharp sword
out,   40
Mumbling of wicked charms, conjuring the moon
To stand ['s] auspicious mistress, —

Glou.   But where is he?

Edm. Look, sir, I bleed.

Glou.   Where is the villain, Edmund?

Edm. Fled this way, sir. When by no means he
could —

Glou. Pursue him, ho! Go after. [*Exeunt some
Servants.*] By no means what?   45

Edm. Persuade me to the murder of your lord-
ship;
But that I told him, the revenging gods
'Gainst parricides did all the thunder bend;
Spoke, with how manifold and strong a bond
The child was bound to th' father; sir, in fine, 50
Seeing how loathly opposite I stood
To his unnatural purpose, in fell motion,
With his prepared sword he charges home
My unprovided body, latch'd mine arm;
And when he saw my best alarum'd spirits, 55
Bold in the quarrel's right, rous'd to th' encounter,
Or whether gasted by the noise I made,
Full suddenly he fled.

Glou.   Let him fly far.

Act II, sc. i, 9. **ear-kissing arguments:** whispered topics. 11. **toward:** imminent. 19. **of...question:** requiring delicate
handling. 20. **Advise yourself:** consider. 42. ['s] Q: his. Om. F. **stand...mistress:** to shed favorable influence on him.
52. **in fell motion:** with a fierce stab. 54. **latch'd:** caught. 57. **gasted:** scared.

Not in this land shall he remain uncaught;
And found, — dispatch.   The noble Duke my
 master,   60
My worthy arch and patron, comes to-night.
By his authority I will proclaim it,
That he which finds him shall deserve our thanks,
Bringing the murderous coward to the stake;
He that conceals him, death.   65
 Edm. When I dissuaded him from his intent,
And found him pight to do it, with curst speech
I threaten'd to discover him; he replied,
"Thou unpossessing bastard! dost thou think,
If I would stand against thee, would the reposal 70
Of any trust, virtue, or worth in thee
Make thy words faith'd?   No! what [I should]
 deny, —
As this I would; [ay,] though thou didst produce
My very character, — I'd turn it all
To thy suggestion, plot, and damned practice; 75
And thou must make a dullard of the world
If they not thought the profits of my death
Were very pregnant and potential [spurs]
To make thee seek it."
 Glou.   • O strange and fast'ned villain!
Would he deny his letter?   [I never got him.] 80
            [Tucket within.
Hark, the Duke's trumpets!   I know not [why] he
 comes.
All ports I'll bar, the villain shall not scape;
The Duke must grant me that.   Besides, his
 picture
I will send far and near, that all the kingdom
May have due note of him; and of my land, 85
Loyal and natural boy, I'll work the means
To make thee capable.

  Enter CORNWALL, REGAN, *and Attendants.*

 Corn. How now, my noble friend! since I came
 hither,
Which I can call but now, I have heard [strange
 news].
 Reg. If it be true, all vengeance comes too
 short   90
Which can pursue th' offender.   How dost, my lord?
 Glou. O, madam, my old heart is crack'd, it's
 crack'd!
 Reg. What, did my father's godson seek your
 life?
He whom my father nam'd? your Edgar?
 Glou. O, lady, lady, shame would have it hid! 95
 Reg. Was he not companion with the riotous
 knights

That tended upon my father?
 Glou. I know not, madam.   'Tis too bad, too bad.
 Edm. Yes, madam, he was of that consort.
 Reg. No marvel, then, though he were ill af-
 fected: 100
'Tis they have put him on the old man's death,
To have th' expense and waste of his revenues.
I have this present evening from my sister
Been well inform'd of them; and with such cautions,
That if they come to sojourn at my house, 105
I'll not be there.
 Corn.   Nor I, assure thee, Regan.
Edmund, I hear that you have shown your father
A child-like office.
 Edm.   'Twas my duty, sir.
 Glou. He did bewray his practice; and receiv'd
This hurt you see, striving to apprehend him. 110
 Corn. Is he pursued?
 Glou.   Ay, my good lord.
 Corn. If he be taken he shall never more
Be fear'd of doing harm. • Make your own purpose,
How in my strength you please.   For you, Edmund,
Whose virtue and obedience doth this instant 115
So much commend itself, you shall be ours.
Natures of such deep trust we shall much need;
You we first seize on.
 Edm.   I shall serve you, sir,
Truly, however else.
 Glou.   For him I thank your Grace.
 Corn. You know not why we came to visit you, —
 Reg. Thus out of season, threading dark-ey'd
 night?   121
Occasions, noble Gloucester, of some [poise],
Wherein we must have use of your advice.
Our father he hath writ, so hath our sister,
Of differences, which I best thought it fit 125
To answer from our home; the several messengers
From hence attend dispatch.   Our good old friend,
Lay comforts to your bosom; and bestow
Your needful counsel to our businesses,
Which craves the instant use.
 Glou.   I serve you, madam.
Your Graces are right welcome.   131
            [Exeunt.   Flourish.

   SCENE II.   [*Before Gloucester's castle.*]

 Enter KENT *and Steward* [OSWALD], *severally.*

 Osw. Good dawning to thee, friend.   Art of this
house?
 Kent. Ay.
 Osw. Where may we set our horses?

---

 61. **arch:** chief.   66. **dissuaded:** tried to dissuade.   67. **pight:** pitched, determined.   68. **discover:** reveal.   72. **faith'd:**
trusted.   [I should] Q.   *should I* F.   73. [ay] *I* Q.   Om. F.   75. **practice:** conspiracy.   78. [spurs] Q.   *spirits* F.   79.
fast'ned: hardened.   80. [I . . . him] Q.   *said he?* F.   s.d. *Tucket:* flourish on a trumpet.   81. [why] Q.   *wher* F.   87. **capa-**
ble: able to inherit.   89. [strange news] Q.   *strangeness* F.   102. **expense and waste:** power of spending and wasting.   108.
child-like: filial.   109. **bewray:** reveal.   114. **strength:** authority.   122. [poise] Q: weight.   *prize* F.   126. **from:** away from.

Kent. I' th' mire.   5
Osw. Prithee, if thou lov'st me, tell me.
Kent. I love thee not.
Osw. Why, then, I care not for thee.
Kent. If I had thee in Lipsbury pinfold, I would make thee care for me.   10
Osw. Why dost thou use me thus? I know thee not.
Kent. Fellow, I know thee.
Osw. What dost thou know me for?   14
Kent. A knave; a rascal; an eater of broken meats; a base, proud, shallow, beggarly, three-suited, hundred-pound, filthy, worsted-stocking knave; a lily-livered, action-taking, whoreson, glass-gazing, superserviceable, finical rogue; one-trunk-inheriting slave; one that wouldst be a 20
bawd in way of good service, and art nothing but the composition of a knave, beggar, coward, pandar, and the son and heir of a mongrel bitch; one whom I will beat into clamorous whining, if thou deni'st the least syllable of thy addition.   26
Osw. Why, what a monstrous fellow art thou, thus to rail on one that is neither known of thee nor knows thee!   29
Kent. What a brazen-fac'd varlet art thou, to deny thou knowest me! Is it two days since I tripp'd up thy heels, and beat thee before the King? Draw, you rogue; for, though it be night, yet the moon shines. I'll make a sop o' th' moonshine of you, you whoreson cullionly barber-monger! Draw!   [*Drawing his sword.*] 36
Osw. Away! I have nothing to do with thee.
Kent. Draw, you rascal! You come with letters against the King; and take Vanity the puppet's part against the royalty of her father. Draw, you rogue, or I'll so carbonado your shanks, — draw, you rascal! Come your ways.   42
Osw. Help, ho! murder! help!
Kent. Strike, you slave! Stand, rogue, stand! You neat slave, strike.   [*Beating him.*]
Osw. Help, ho! murder! murder!   46

Enter Bastard [EDMUND] *with his rapier drawn,*
CORNWALL, REGAN, GLOUCESTER, *and* Servants.

Edm. How now! What's the matter? Part.
Kent. With you, goodman boy, if you please. Come, I'll flesh ye; come on, young master.
Glou. Weapons! arms! What's the matter here?
Corn. Keep peace, upon your lives!   52
He dies that strikes again. What is the matter?

Reg. The messengers from our sister and the King.   55
Corn. What is your difference? Speak.
Osw. I am scarce in breath, my lord.
Kent. No marvel, you have so bestirr'd your valour. You cowardly rascal, Nature disclaims in thee. A tailor made thee.   60
Corn. Thou art a strange fellow. A tailor make a man?
Kent. A tailor, sir. A stone-cutter or a painter could not have made him so ill, though they had been but two years o' th' trade.   65
Corn. Speak yet, how grew your quarrel?
Osw. This ancient ruffian, sir, whose life I have spar'd at suit of his grey beard, —   68
Kent. Thou whoreson zed! thou unnecessary letter! My lord, if you will give me leave, I will tread this unbolted villain into mortar, and daub the wall of a jakes with him. Spare my grey beard, you wagtail?
Corn. Peace, sirrah!
You beastly knave, know you no reverence?   75
Kent. Yes, sir; but anger hath a privilege.
Corn. Why art thou angry?
Kent. That such a slave as this should wear a sword,
Who wears no honesty. Such smiling rogues as these,
Like rats, oft bite the holy cords a-twain   80
Which are too intrinse t' unloose; smooth every passion
That in the natures of their lords rebel;
[Bring] oil to fire, snow to their colder moods;
[Renege,] affirm, and turn their halcyon beaks
With every gale and vary of their masters,   85
Knowing nought, like dogs, but following.
A plague upon your epileptic visage!
Smile you my speeches, as I were a fool?
Goose, if I had you upon Sarum Plain,
I'd drive ye cackling home to Camelot.   90
Corn. What, art thou mad, old fellow?
Glou. How fell you out? Say that.
Kent. No contraries hold more antipathy
Than I and such a knave.
Corn. Why dost thou call him knave? What is his fault?   95
Kent. His countenance likes me not.
Corn. No more, perchance, does mine, nor his, nor hers.
Kent. Sir, 'tis my occupation to be plain;

Sc. ii, 9. Lipsbury pinfold: my teeth (?). **18. lily-livered:** cowardly. **action-taking:** preferring going to law to fighting. **19. glass-gazing:** vain. **superserviceable:** officious. **22. composition:** combination. **26. thy addition:** the titles I have given you. **35. cullionly:** rascally. **barber-monger:** frequenter of barber-shops. **41. carbonado:** slash. **45. neat:** foppish. **59. disclaims in:** renounces. **69. zed:** Z, often omitted in old dictionaries. **71. unbolted:** coarse. **72. jakes:** privy. **80. holy cords:** i.e., of natural affection. **81. intrinse:** intricate. **smooth:** humor. **83. [Bring]** Q. *Being* F. **84. [Renege]** F₂: deny. *Revenge* F₁. **halcyon:** kingfisher, which, if hung up, was believed always to turn with its bill to the wind. **89. Sarum:** Salisbury. **90. Camelot:** Winchester. **96. likes:** pleases.

I have seen better faces in my time
Than stands on any shoulder that I see   100
Before me at this instant.
   Corn.   This is some fellow
Who, having been prais'd for bluntness, doth affect
A saucy roughness, and constrains the garb
Quite from his nature. He cannot flatter, he;
An honest mind and plain, he must speak truth!
An they will take it, so; if not, he's plain.   106
These kind of knaves I know, which in this plain-
    ness
Harbour more craft and more corrupter ends
Than twenty silly ducking observants
That stretch their duties nicely.   110
   Kent. Sir, in good sooth, in sincere verity,
Under the allowance of your great aspect,
Whose influence, like the wreath of radiant fire
On [flickering] Phœbus' front, —
   Corn.   What mean'st by this?   114
   Kent. To go out of my dialect, which you dis-
commend so much. I know, sir, I am no flatterer.
He that beguil'd you in a plain accent was a plain
knave; which for my part I will not be, though I
should win your displeasure to entreat me to't.   120
   Corn. What was th' offence you gave him?
   Osw. I never gave him any.
It pleas'd the King his master very late
To strike at me, upon his misconstruction;
When he, compact, and flattering his displeasure,
Tripp'd me behind; being down, insulted, rail'd,   126
And put upon him such a deal of man
[That 't] worthied him, got praises of the King
For him attempting who was self-subdued;
And, in the fleshment of this [dread] exploit,   130
Drew on me here again.
   Kent.   None of these rogues and cowards
But Ajax is their fool.
   Corn.   Fetch forth the stocks!
You stubborn ancient knave, you reverend brag-
    gart,
We'll teach you —
   Kent.   Sir, I am too old to learn.
Call not your stocks for me; I serve the King,   135
On whose employment I was sent to you.
You shall do small respects, show too bold malice
Against the grace and person of my master,
Stocking his messenger.
   Corn. Fetch forth the stocks! As I have life and
    honour,   140
There shall he sit till noon.

   Reg. Till noon! Till night, my lord; and all night
    too.
   Kent. Why, madam, if I were your father's dog,
You should not use me so.
   Reg.   Sir, being his knave, I will.
                       [*Stocks brought out.*
   Corn. This is a fellow of the self-same colour   145
Our sister speaks of. Come, bring away the stocks!
   Glou. Let me beseech your Grace not to do so.
[His fault is much, and the good King his master
Will check him for't. Your purpos'd low correc-
    tion
Is such as basest and contemned'st wretches   150
For pilferings and most common trespasses
Are punish'd with.] The King must take it ill
That he, so slightly valued in his messenger,
Should have him thus restrain'd.
   Corn.   I'll answer that.
   Reg. My sister may receive it much more worse
To have her gentleman abus'd, assaulted,   156
[For following her affairs. Put in his legs.]
              [*Kent is put in the stocks.*
[Come, my good] lord, away.
         [*Exeunt [all but Gloucester and Kent].*
   Glou. I am sorry for thee, friend; 'tis the Duke's
    pleasure,
Whose disposition, all the world well knows,   160
Will not be rubb'd nor stopp'd. I'll entreat for
    thee.
   Kent. Pray, do not, sir. I have watch'd and
    travell'd hard;
Some time I shall sleep out, the rest I'll whistle.
A good man's fortune may grow out at heels.
Give you good morrow!   165
   Glou. The Duke's to blame in this; 'twill be ill
    taken.   [*Exit.*
   Kent. Good King, that must approve the com-
    mon saw,
Thou out of heaven's benediction com'st
To the warm sun!
Approach, thou beacon to this under globe,   170
That by thy comfortable beams I may
Peruse this letter! Nothing almost sees miracles
But misery. I know 'tis from Cordelia,
Who hath most fortunately been inform'd
Of my obscured course; [*reads*] " — and shall find
    time   175
From this enormous state — seeking to give
Losses their remedies." — All weary and o'er-
    watch'd,

---

103. **constrains the garb:** forces the manner. 109. **observants:** obsequious attendants. 110. **nicely:** punctiliously. 114. [flickering] Q. *flicking* F. 125. **compact:** taking his side. 127. **put...man:** took such a heroic attitude. 128. [That 't] (Anon.) *That* F. *That* Q. 129. **attempting:** attacking. 130. **fleshment:** excitement from first success. [dread] Q. *dead* F. 132. **But...fool:** but pick on a plain blunt fellow like Ajax (?). 148-152. [His...with] Q. Om. F. 150. **contemned'st** (Capell). *temnest* or *contened* Q. 152. **King** Q. *King his master needs* F. 157. [For...legs] Q. Om. F. 158. [Come, my good] Q. *Corn. Come my* F. 162. **watch'd:** been awake long. Cf. l. 177. 167. **approve...saw:** prove the proverb true. 168-169. **out...sun:** from better to worse.

Take vantage, heavy eyes, not to behold
This shameful lodging.
Fortune, good-night!   Smile once more; turn thy
    wheel!   [*Sleeps.*] 180

[SCENE III.   *The same.*]

Enter EDGAR.

  Edg. I heard myself proclaim'd;
And by the happy hollow of a tree
Escap'd the hunt.   No port is free; no place
That guard and most unusual vigilance
Does not attend my taking.   Whiles I may scape 5
I will preserve myself, and am bethought
To take the basest and most poorest shape
That ever penury, in contempt of man,
Brought near to beast.   My face I'll grime with
    filth,
Blanket my loins, elf all my hairs in knots, 10
And with presented nakedness out-face
The winds and persecutions of thy sky.
The country gives me proof and precedent
Of Bedlam beggars, who, with roaring voices,
Strike in their numb'd and mortified arms 15
Pins, wooden pricks, nails, sprigs of rosemary;
And with this horrible object, from low farms,
Poor pelting villages, sheep-cotes, and mills,
Sometimes with lunatic bans, sometimes with
    prayers, 19
Enforce their charity.   Poor Turlygod! poor Tom!
That's something yet.   Edgar I nothing am.
                      [*Exit.*

[SCENE IV.   *The same.*]

Enter LEAR, FOOL, *and* GENTLEMAN.   [KENT
in the stocks.]

  Lear. 'Tis strange that they should so depart
    from home,
And not send back my messengers.
  Gent.   As I learn'd,
The night before there was no purpose in them
Of this remove.
  Kent.   Hail to thee, noble master!
  Lear. Ha!   5
Mak'st thou this shame thy pastime?
  Kent.   No, my lord.
  Fool. Ha, ha! he wears cruel garters.   Horses are
tied by the heads, dogs and bears by th' neck, mon-
keys by th' loins, and men by th' legs.   When a
man's over-lusty at legs, then he wears wooden
nether-stocks.   11

  Lear. What's he that hath so much thy place
    mistook
To set thee here?
  Kent.   It is both he and she;
Your son and daughter.
  Lear. No.   15
  Kent. Yes.
  Lear. No, I say.
  Kent. I say, yea.
  [*Lear.* No, no, they would not.
  Kent. Yes, they have.]   20
  Lear. By Jupiter, I swear, no.
  Kent. By Juno, I swear, ay.
  Lear.   They durst not do't;
They could not, would not do't.   'Tis worse than
    murder
To do upon respect such violent outrage.
Resolve me with all modest haste which way 25
Thou mightst deserve, or they impose, this usage,
Coming from us.
  Kent.   My lord, when at their home
I did commend your Highness' letters to them,
Ere I was risen from the place that show'd
My duty kneeling, came there a reeking post, 30
Stew'd in his haste, half breathless, panting forth
From Goneril his mistress salutations;
Deliver'd letters, spite of intermission,
Which presently they read.   On those contents,
They summon'd up their meiny, straight took
    horse;
Commanded me to follow, and attend   36
The leisure of their answer; gave me cold looks:
And meeting here the other messenger,
Whose welcome, I perceiv'd, had poison'd mine, —
Being the very fellow which of late   40
Display'd so saucily against your Highness, —
Having more man than wit about me, drew.
He rais'd the house with loud and coward cries.
Your son and daughter found this trespass worth
The shame which here it suffers.   45
  Fool. Winter's not gone yet, if the wild geese fly
that way.
      "Fathers that wear rags
        Do make their children blind;
      But fathers that bear bags   50
        Shall see their children kind.
      Fortune, that arrant whore,
        Ne'er turns the key to th' poor."
But, for all this, thou shalt have as many dolours
for thy daughters as thou canst tell in a year. 55
  Lear. O, how this mother swells up toward my
    heart!

---

180. **Smile ... wheel.** Q attaches *once more* to *turn* rather than *smile.*
  Sc. iii, 5. **attend my taking:** wait to capture me. 10. **elf:** tangle as in elf-locks. 11. **presented:** exposed. 17. **object:** aspect. 18. **pelting:** petty. 19. **bans:** curses. 21. **Edgar ... am:** of Edgar nothing will remain.
  Sc. iv, 11. **nether-stocks:** stockings. 19–20. [*Lear ... have*] Q. Om. F. 24. **upon respect:** deliberately. 25. **Resolve:** inform. 33. **spite of intermission:** careless of interrupting. 35. **meiny:** retinue. 41. **Display'd:** showed himself. 54. **dolours:** with a pun on *dollars.* 55. **tell:** count. 56. **mother:** hysteria.

Hysterica passio, down, thou climbing sorrow,
Thy element's below! — Where is this daughter?
  Kent. With the Earl, sir, here within.
  Lear.   Follow me not;
Stay here.   [*Exit.* 60
  Gent. Made you no more offence but what you
speak of?
  Kent. None.
How chance the King comes with so small a number?
  Fool. An thou hadst been set i' th' stocks for that
question, thou'dst well deserv'd it.   66
  Kent. Why, Fool?
  Fool. We'll set thee to school to an ant, to teach
thee there's no labouring i' th' winter. All that
follow their noses are led by their eyes but 70
blind men; and there's not a nose among twenty
but can smell him that's stinking. Let go thy hold
when a great wheel runs down a hill, lest it break
thy neck with following; but the great one that
goes upward, let him draw thee after. When a 75
wise man gives thee better counsel, give me mine
again; I would have none but knaves follow it,
since a fool gives it.
    "That sir which serves and seeks for gain,
      And follows but for form,   80
    Will pack when it begins to rain,
      And leave thee in the storm.
    But I will tarry; the Fool will stay,
      And let the wise man fly.
    The knave turns fool that runs away; 85
      The Fool no knave, perdy."

      Re-enter LEAR *and* GLOUCESTER.

  Kent. Where learn'd you this, Fool?
  Fool. Not i' th' stocks, fool.
  Lear. Deny to speak with me? They are sick?
    They are weary?
They have travell'd all the night? Mere fetches; 90
The images of revolt and flying off.
Fetch me a better answer.
  Glou.   My dear lord,
You know the fiery quality of the Duke;
How unremovable and fix'd he is
In his own course.   95
  Lear. Vengeance! plague! death! confusion!
"Fiery"? What "quality"? Why, Gloucester,
Gloucester,
I'd speak with the Duke of Cornwall and his
  wife.
  Glou. Well, my good lord, I have inform'd them
so.
  Lear. "Inform'd" them! Dost thou under-
  stand me, man?   100
  Glou. Ay, my good lord.

  Lear. The King would speak with Cornwall; the
  dear father
Would with his daughter speak, commands [her]
  service.
Are they "inform'd" of this? My breath and
  blood!
"Fiery"? The fiery duke? Tell the hot duke
  that —   105
No, but not yet; may be he is not well.
Infirmity doth still neglect all office
Whereto our health is bound; we are not ourselves
When nature, being oppress'd, commands the mind
To suffer with the body. I'll forbear;   110
And am fallen out with my more headier will,
To take the indispos'd and sickly fit
For the sound man. — Death on my state! where-
  fore   [*Looking on Kent.*]
Should he sit here? This act persuades me
That this remotion of the Duke and her   115
Is practice only. Give me my servant forth.
Go tell the Duke and 's wife I'd speak with them,
Now, presently. Bid them come forth and hear me,
Or at their chamber-door I'll beat the drum
Till it cry sleep to death.   120
  Glou. I would have all well betwixt you. [*Exit.*
  Lear. O me, my heart, my rising heart! But,
  down!
  Fool. Cry to it, nuncle, as the cockney did to the
eels when she put 'em i' th' paste alive; she knapp'd
'em o' th' coxcombs with a stick, and cried, "Down,
wantons, down!" 'Twas her brother that, in pure
kindness to his horse, buttered his hay.   128

    Enter CORNWALL, REGAN, GLOUCESTER, *and*
           Servants.

  Lear. Good morrow to you both.
  Corn.   Hail to your Grace!
                  [*Kent is set at liberty.*
  Reg. I am glad to see your Highness.
  Lear. Regan, I think you are; I know what rea-
  son
I have to think so. If thou shouldst not be glad, 132
I would divorce me from thy mother's tomb,
Sepulchring an adulteress. [*To Kent.*] O, are you
  free?
Some other time for that. Beloved Regan,
Thy sister's naught. O Regan, she hath tied
Sharp-tooth'd unkindness, like a vulture, here.
                [*Points to his heart.*]
I can scarce speak to thee; thou'lt not believe
With how deprav'd a quality — O Regan!   139
  Reg. I pray you, sir, take patience. I have hope
You less know how to value her desert
Than she to scant her duty.

90. **fetches:** tricks. 91. **images:** signs. **flying off:** deserting. 103. [her] Q. *tends* F. 107. **office:** duty. 111. **headier:** impetuous. 115. **remotion:** removal. 116. **practice:** trickery. 120. **cry...to death:** murder. 136. **naught:** wicked. 139. **quality:** manner.

Lear.   Say, how is that?

Reg. I cannot think my sister in the least
Would fail her obligation. If, sir, perchance
She have restrain'd the riots of your followers, 145
'Tis on such ground and to such wholesome end
As clears her from all blame.

Lear. My curses on her!

Reg.   O, sir, you are old;
Nature in you stands on the very verge
Of her confine. You should be rul'd and led 150
By some discretion that discerns your state
Better than you yourself. Therefore, I pray you,
That to our sister you do make return;
Say you have wrong'd her, sir.

Lear.   Ask her forgiveness?
Do you but mark how this becomes the house: 155
"Dear daughter, I confess that I am old;

[*Kneeling.*]

Age is unnecessary. On my knees I beg
That you'll vouchsafe me raiment, bed, and food."

Reg. Good sir, no more; these are unsightly tricks.
Return you to my sister.

Lear. [*Rising.*] Never, Regan: 160
She hath abated me of half my train;
Look'd black upon me; struck me with her tongue,
Most serpent-like, upon the very heart.
All the stor'd vengeances of heaven fall
On her ingrateful top! Strike her young bones, 165
You taking airs, with lameness!

Corn.   Fie, sir, fie!

Lear. You nimble lightnings, dart your blinding
           flames
Into her scornful eyes! Infect her beauty,
You fen-suck'd fogs, drawn by the powerful sun,
To fall and [blast her pride!]   170

Reg. O the blest gods! so will you wish on me,
When the rash mood is on.

Lear. No, Regan, thou shalt never have my
           curse.
Thy tender-hefted nature shall not give
Thee o'er to harshness. Her eyes are fierce; but
           thine   175
Do comfort and not burn. 'Tis not in thee
To grudge my pleasures, to cut off my train,
To bandy hasty words, to scant my sizes,
And in conclusion to oppose the bolt
Against my coming in. Thou better know'st 180
The offices of nature, bond of childhood,
Effects of courtesy, dues of gratitude.
Thy half o' th' kingdom hast thou not forgot,
Wherein I thee endow'd.

Reg.   Good sir, to th' purpose.

[*Tucket within.*]

Lear. Who put my man i' th' stocks?

Enter Steward [OSWALD].

Corn.   What trumpet 's that?

Reg. I know 't; my sister's. This approves her
           letter,   186
That she would soon be here. [*To Oswald.*] Is
           your lady come?

Lear. This is a slave whose easy-borrowed pride
Dwells in the [fickle] grace of her he follows.
Out, varlet, from my sight!

Corn.   What means your Grace? 190

Enter GONERIL.

Lear. Who stock'd my servant? Regan, I have
           good hope
Thou didst not know on't. — Who comes here?
           O heavens,
If you do love old men, if your sweet sway
Allow obedience, if you yourselves are old,
Make it your cause; send down, and take my
           part!   195
[*To Gon.*] Art not asham'd to look upon this beard?
O Regan, will you take her by the hand?

Gon. Why not by th' hand, sir? How have I
           offended?
All's not offence that indiscretion finds   199
And dotage terms so.

Lear.   O sides, you are too tough;
Will you yet hold? How came my man i' th' stocks?

Corn. I set him there, sir; but his own disorders
Deserv'd much less advancement.

Lear.   You! did you?

Reg. I pray you, father, being weak, seem so.
If, till the expiration of your month,   205
You will return and sojourn with my sister,
Dismissing half your train, come then to me.
I am now from home, and out of that provision
Which shall be needful for your entertainment.

Lear. Return to her, and fifty men dismiss'd! 210
No, rather I abjure all roofs, and choose
To wage against the enmity o' th' air;
To be a comrade with the wolf and owl, —
Necessity's sharp pinch. Return with her?
Why, the hot-blooded France, that dowerless took
Our youngest born, I could as well be brought 216
To knee his throne, and, squire-like, pension beg
To keep base life afoot. Return with her?
Persuade me rather to be slave and sumpter
To this detested groom. [*Pointing at Oswald.*]

Gon.   At your choice, sir.   220

Lear. I prithee, daughter, do not make me mad;
I will not trouble thee, my child; farewell!

---

155. **house:** royal family. 157. **Age is unnecessary:** old people are useless. 165. **top:** head. **young bones:** bones of her unborn child. 166. **taking:** infectious. 170. **fall:** humble. [**blast her pride**] Q. *blister* F. 174. **tender-hefted:** gentle. 178. **sizes:** allowances. 182. **Effects:** manifestations. 188. **easy-borrowed:** not justified by his own qualities, but on the reflection of his mistress's position. 189. [**fickle**] Q. *sickly* F. 194. **Allow:** approve. 212. **wage:** contend. 219. **sumpter:** pack-horse.

We'll no more meet, no more see one another.
But yet thou art my flesh, my blood, my daughter;
Or rather a disease that's in my flesh,   225
Which I must needs call mine; thou art a boil,
A plague-sore, an embossed carbuncle,
In my corrupted blood. But I'll not chide thee;
Let shame come when it will, I do not call it.
I do not bid the thunder-bearer shoot,   230
Nor tell tales of thee to high-judging Jove.
Mend when thou canst; be better at thy leisure.
I can be patient; I can stay with Regan,
I and my hundred knights.
    Reg.   Not altogether so;
I look'd not for you yet, nor am provided   235
For your fit welcome. Give ear, sir, to my sister;
For those that mingle reason with your passion
Must be content to think you old, and so —
But she knows what she does.
    Lear.   Is this well spoken?
    Reg. I dare avouch it, sir. What, fifty follow-
ers!   240
Is it not well? What should you need of more?
Yea, or so many, sith that both charge and danger
Speak 'gainst so great a number? How, in one house,
Should many people under two commands
Hold amity? 'Tis hard; almost impossible.   245
    Gon. Why might not you, my lord, receive at-
tendance
From those that she calls servants or from mine?
    Reg. Why not, my lord? If then they chanc'd to
slack ye,
We could control them. If you will come to me, —
For now I spy a danger — I entreat you   250
To bring but five and twenty; to no more
Will I give place or notice.
    Lear. I gave you all.
    Reg.   ＊ And in good time you gave it.
    Lear. Made you my guardians, my depositaries,
But kept a reservation to be followed   255
With such a number. What, must I come to you
With five and twenty, Regan? Said you so?
    Reg. And speak 't again, my lord; no more with
me.
    Lear. Those wicked creatures yet do look well-
favour'd
When others are more wicked; not being the worst
Stands in some rank of praise. [*To Gon.*] I'll go
with thee.   261
Thy fifty yet doth double five and twenty,
And thou art twice her love.
    Gon.   Hear me, my lord:
What need you five and twenty, ten, or five,
To follow in a house where twice so many   265
Have a command to tend you?

    Reg.   What need one?
    Lear. O, reason not the need! Our basest beggars
Are in the poorest thing superfluous.
Allow not nature more than nature needs,
Man's life is cheap as beast's. Thou art a lady;   270
If only to go warm were gorgeous,
Why, nature needs not what thou gorgeous wear'st,
Which scarcely keeps thee warm. But, for true
need, —
You heavens, give me that patience, patience I
need!
You see me here, you gods, a poor old man,   275
As full of grief as age; wretched in both!
If it be you that stirs these daughters' hearts
Against their father, fool me not so much
To bear it tamely; touch me with noble anger,
And let not women's weapons, water-drops,   280
Stain my man's cheeks! No, you unnatural hags,
I will have such revenges on you both
That all the world shall — I will do such things,
What they are, yet I know not; but they shall be
The terrors of the earth. You think I'll weep: 285
No, I'll not weep.
I have full cause of weeping; but this heart
                    (*Storm and tempest.*)
Shall break into a hundred thousand flaws,
Or ere I'll weep. O, Fool! I shall go mad!
        [*Exeunt Lear, Gloucester, Kent, and Fool.*
    Corn. Let us withdraw; 'twill be a storm.   290
    Reg. This house is little; the old man and 's peo-
ple
Cannot be well bestow'd.
    Gon. 'Tis his own blame; hath put himself from
rest,
And must needs taste his folly.
    Reg. For his particular, I'll receive him gladly,
But not one follower.
    Gon.   So am I purpos'd.   296
Where is my Lord of Gloucester?

            Re-enter GLOUCESTER.

    Corn. Follow'd the old man forth. He is re-
turn'd.
    Glou. The King is in high rage.
    Corn.   Whither is he going?
    Glou. He calls to horse; but will I know not
whither.   300
    Corn. 'Tis best to give him way; he leads him-
self.
    Gon. My lord, entreat him by no means to stay.
    Glou. Alack, the night comes on, and the high
winds
Do sorely ruffle; for many miles about
There 's scarce a bush.

227. **embossed:** swollen. 242. **charge:** expense. 248. **slack:** be lacking in their services. 268. **Are...superfluous:** have at the worst more than bare necessities. 288. **flaws:** fragments. 295. **For his particular:** as far as he himself is concerned. 304. **ruffle:** bluster.

Reg.   O, sir, to wilful men,   305
The injuries that they themselves procure
Must be their schoolmasters.   Shut up your doors.
He is attended with a desperate train,
And what they may incense him to, being apt
To have his ear abus'd, wisdom bids fear.   310
   Corn. Shut up your doors, my lord; 'tis a wild
      night:
My Regan counsels well.   Come out o' th' storm.
                                          [*Exeunt.*

ACT III

Scene I. [*The open country near Gloucester's
              castle.*]

Storm still.   Enter Kent *and a* Gentleman,
                  severally.

Kent. Who's there, besides foul weather?
Gent. One minded like the weather, most un-
      quietly.
Kent. I know you.   Where's the King?
Gent. Contending with the fretful elements;
Bids the wind blow the earth into the sea,   5
Or swell the curled waters 'bove the main,
That things might change or cease; [tears his white
      hair,
Which the impetuous blasts with eyeless rage
Catch in their fury, and make nothing of;
Strives in his little world of man to out-scorn   10
The to-and-fro-conflicting wind and rain.
This night, wherein the cub-drawn bear would couch,
The lion and the belly-pinched wolf
Keep their fur dry, unbonneted he runs,
And bids what will take all.]
   Kent.   But who is with him?
Gent. None but the Fool, who labours to out-
      jest   16
His heart-struck injuries.
   Kent.   Sir, I do know you,
And dare upon the warrant of my note
Commend a dear thing to you.   There is division,
Although as yet the face of it is cover'd   20
With mutual cunning, 'twixt Albany and Cornwall;
Who have — as who have not, that their great stars
Thron'd and set high? — servants, who seem no
      less,
Which are to France the spies and speculations
Intelligent of our state.   What hath been seen,   25
Either in snuffs and packings of the Dukes,

Or the hard rein which both of them have borne
Against the old kind king, or something deeper,
Whereof perchance these are but furnishings —
[But, true it is, from France there comes a power   30
Into this scattered kingdom; who already,
Wise in our negligence, have secret feet
In some of our best ports, and are at point
To show their open banner.   Now to you:
If on my credit you dare build so far   35
To make your speed to Dover, you shall find
Some that will thank you, making just report
Of how unnatural and bemadding sorrow
The King hath cause to plain.
I am a gentleman of blood and breeding;   40
And, from some knowledge and assurance, offer
This office to you.]
   Gent. I will talk further with you.
   Kent.   No, do not.
For confirmation that I am much more
Than my out-wall, open this purse and take   45
What it contains.   If you shall see Cordelia, —
As fear not but you shall, — show her this ring,
And she will tell you who that fellow is
That yet you do not know.   Fie on this storm!
I will go seek the King.   50
   Gent. Give me your hand.   Have you no more
      to say?
   Kent. Few words, but, to effect, more than all
      yet;
That, when we have found the King, — in which
      your pain
That way, I'll this, — he that first lights on him
Holla the other.   [*Exeunt* [*severally*].   55

Scene II. [*The same.*]   *Storm still.*

Enter Lear *and* Fool.

   Lear. Blow, winds, and crack your cheeks! Rage!
      Blow!
You cataracts and hurricanoes, spout
Till you have drench'd our steeples, drown'd the
      cocks!
You sulph'rous and thought-executing fires,
Vaunt-couriers of oak-cleaving thunderbolts,   5
Singe my white head!   And thou, all-shaking thun-
      der,
Strike flat the thick rotundity o' th' world!
Crack nature's moulds, all germens spill at once
That makes ingrateful man!   9
   Fool. O nuncle, court holy-water in a dry house

310. **abus'd:** misled.
   Act III, sc. i, 6. main: mainland. 7-15. [**tears . . . all**] Q. Om. F. 12. **cub-drawn:** sucked dry. 18. **note:** knowledge
(of you). 19. **dear:** important. 24. **speculations:** observers. 25. **Intelligent:** giving information. 26. **snuffs:** resent-
ments. **packings:** plots. 30-42. [**But . . . you**] Q. Om. F. 30. **power:** armed force. 31. **scattered:** divided. 33. **at
point:** ready. 39. **plain:** complain. 45. **out-wall:** exterior. 52. **to effect:** in effect, in importance.
   Sc. ii, 3. cocks: weathercocks. 5. **Vaunt-couriers:** forerunners. 8. **germens:** germs, seeds. 10. **court holy-water:**
flattery.

is better than this rain water out o' door. Good
nuncle, in; ask thy daughters' blessing. Here's a
night pities neither wise men nor fools.

Lear. Rumble thy bellyful! Spit, fire! Spout,
  rain!
Nor rain, wind, thunder, fire are my daughters. 15
I tax not you, you elements, with unkindness;
I never gave you kingdom, call'd you children;
You owe me no subscription. Then let fall
Your horrible pleasure. Here I stand your slave,
A poor, infirm, weak, and despis'd old man;   20
But yet I call you servile ministers,
That will with two pernicious daughters join
Your high-engender'd battles 'gainst a head
So old and white as this. Oh! Oh! 'tis foul!

Fool. He that has a house to put 's head in has a
good head-piece.   26
  "The cod-piece that will house
      Before the head has any,
    The head and he shall louse;
      So beggars marry many.   30
    The man that makes his toe
      What he his heart should make
    Shall of a corn cry woe,
      And turn his sleep to wake."
For there was never yet fair woman but she made
mouths in a glass.   36

Enter KENT.

Lear. No, I will be the pattern of all patience; I
will say nothing.
Kent. Who's there?
Fool. Marry, here's grace and a cod-piece; that's
a wise man and a fool.   41
Kent. Alas, sir, are you here? Things that love
  night
Love not such nights as these; the wrathful skies
Gallow the very wanderers of the dark,
And make them keep their caves. Since I was
  man,   45
Such sheets of fire, such bursts of horrid thunder,
Such groans of roaring wind and rain, I never
Remember to have heard. Man's nature cannot
  carry
Th' affliction nor the fear.
Lear.   Let the great gods,
That keep this dreadful pudder o'er our heads,   50
Find out their enemies now. Tremble, thou
  wretch
That hast within thee undivulged crimes,
Unwhipp'd of justice! Hide thee, thou bloody hand;
Thou perjur'd, and thou simular of virtue
That art incestuous! Caitiff, to pieces shake, 55

That under covert and convenient seeming
Has practis'd on man's life! Close pent-up guilts,
Rive your concealing continents, and cry
These dreadful summoners grace. I am a man
More sinn'd against than sinning.
Kent.   Alack, bare-headed!
Gracious my lord, hard by here is a hovel;   61
Some friendship will it lend you 'gainst the tempest.
Repose you there, while I to this hard house —
More harder than the stones whereof 'tis rais'd,
Which even but now, demanding after you,   65
Deni'd me to come in — return, and force
Their scanted courtesy.
Lear.   My wits begin to turn.
Come on, my boy. How dost, my boy? Art cold?
I am cold myself. Where is this straw, my fellow?
The art of our necessities is strange   70
And can make vile things precious. Come, your
  hovel.
Poor Fool and knave, I have one part in my heart
That's sorry yet for thee.
Fool. [*Singing.*]
"He that has and a little tiny wit, —
    With heigh-ho, the wind and the rain, —   75
  Must make content with his fortunes fit,
    For the rain it raineth every day."
Lear. True, boy. Come, bring us to this hovel.
                              [*Exeunt* [*Lear and Kent*].
Fool. This is a brave night to cool a courtezan.
I'll speak a prophecy ere I go: 80
  When priests are more in word than matter;
  When brewers mar their malt with water;
  When nobles are their tailors' tutors;
  No heretics burn'd, but wenches' suitors;
  When every case in law is right;   85
  No squire in debt, nor no poor knight;
  When slanders do not live in tongues;
  Nor cutpurses come not to throngs;
  When usurers tell their gold i' th' field;
  And bawds and whores do churches build;   90
  Then shall the realm of Albion
  Come to great confusion.
  Then comes the time, who lives to see 't,
  That going shall be us'd with feet.
This prophecy Merlin shall make; for I live before
  his time.   [*Exit.* 95

SCENE III. [*Gloucester's castle.*]

Enter GLOUCESTER and EDMUND.

Glou. Alack, alack, Edmund, I like not this unnatural dealing. When I desired their leave that
I might pity him, they took from me the use of

---

18. **subscription:** allegiance. 23. **high-engender'd:** produced in the heavens. 44. **Gallow:** frighten. 50. **pudder:** turmoil. 54. **simular of:** pretender to. 58. **continents:** disguises. 58–59. **cry ... grace:** ask mercy. 66. **Deni'd ... in:** refused
to admit me. 70. **art of:** skill created by. 80–95. This prophecy is influenced by a so-called "Chaucer's Prophecy," and
is probably not by Shakespeare.

mine own house; charg'd me on pain of perpetual
displeasure neither to speak of him, entreat for him,
or any way sustain him.   6

Edm. Most savage and unnatural!

Glou. Go to; say you nothing. There is division
between the Dukes, and a worse matter than that.
I have received a letter this night; 'tis danger- 10
ous to be spoken; I have lock'd the letter in my
closet. These injuries the King now bears will be
revenged home; there is part of a power already
footed. We must incline to the King. I will look
him and privily relieve him. Go you and main- 15
tain talk with the Duke that my charity be not of
him perceived. If he ask for me, I am ill and gone
to bed. If I die for it, as no less is threat'ned me,
the King my old master must be relieved. There
is strange things toward, Edmund; pray you, be
careful.   [*Exit.* 21

Edm. This courtesy, forbid thee, shall the Duke
Instantly know; and of that letter too.
This seems a fair deserving, and must draw me
That which my father loses; no less than all. 25
The younger rises when the old doth fall. [*Exit.*

SCENE IV. [*The open country. Before a hovel.*]

Enter LEAR, KENT, *and* FOOL.

Kent. Here is the place, my lord; good my lord,
    enter.
The tyranny of the open night 's too rough
For nature to endure.   [*Storm still.*

Lear.   Let me alone.

Kent. Good my lord, enter here.

Lear.   Wilt break my heart?

Kent. I had rather break mine own. Good
my lord, enter.   5

Lear. Thou think'st 'tis much that this conten-
    tious storm
Invades us to the skin; so 'tis to thee;
But where the greater malady is fix'd,
The lesser is scarce felt. Thou'dst shun a bear;
But if thy flight lay toward the roaring sea, 10
Thou'dst meet the bear i' th' mouth. When the
    mind 's free,
The body 's delicate; the tempest in my mind
Doth from my senses take all feeling else
Save what beats there. Filial ingratitude!
Is it not as this mouth should tear this hand 15
For lifting food to't? But I will punish home.
No, I will weep no more. In such a night
To shut me out! Pour on! I will endure.
In such a night as this! O Regan, Goneril!
Your old kind father, whose frank heart gave all, —

O, that way madness lies; let me shun that; 21
No more of that.

Kent.   Good my lord, enter here.

Lear. Prithee, go in thyself; seek thine own ease.
This tempest will not give me leave to ponder
On things would hurt me more. But I'll go in. 25
[*To the Fool.*] In, boy; go first. You houseless
    poverty, —
Nay, get thee in. I'll pray, and then I'll sleep.
              [*Exit [Fool*].
Poor naked wretches, wheresoe'er you are,
That bide the pelting of this pitiless storm,
How shall your houseless heads and unfed sides, 30
Your loop'd and window'd raggedness, defend you
From seasons such as these? O, I have ta'en
Too little care of this! Take physic, pomp;
Expose thyself to feel what wretches feel,
That thou mayst shake the superflux to them, 35
And show the heavens more just.

Edg. [*Within.*] Fathom and half, fathom and
    half! Poor Tom!
           [*The Fool runs out from the hovel.*]

Fool. Come not in here, nuncle, here's a spirit.
Help me, help me!   40

Kent. Give me thy hand. Who's there?

Fool. A spirit, a spirit! He says his name 's poor
Tom.

Kent. What art thou that dost grumble there i'
th' straw? Come forth.   45

[*Enter* EDGAR, *disguised as a madman.*]

Edg. Away! the foul fiend follows me!
"Through the sharp hawthorn blow the winds."
Hum! go to thy bed, and warm thee.

Lear. Did'st thou give all to thy daughters, and
art thou come to this?   50

Edg. Who gives anything to poor Tom? whom
the foul fiend hath led through fire and through
flame, and through [ford] and whirlpool, o'er bog
and quagmire; that hath laid knives under his pillow, and halters in his pew; set ratsbane by his 55
porridge; made him proud of heart, to ride on a bay
trotting-horse over four-inch'd bridges, to course
his own shadow for a traitor. Bless thy five wits!
Tom's a-cold, — O, do de, do de, do de. Bless thee
from whirlwinds, star-blasting, and taking! 60
Do poor Tom some charity, whom the foul fiend
vexes. There could I have him now, — and there,
— and there again, and there.   [*Storm still.*

Lear. Has his daughters brought him to this
    pass?   65
Couldst thou save nothing? Wouldst thou give
    'em all?

Sc. iii, 14. **footed**: landed. 22. **forbid thee**: which you are forbidden to render. 24. **deserving**: action by which I shall
acquire merit.

Sc. iv, 12. **delicate**: sensitive. 31. **loop'd and window'd**: full of holes. 53. **[ford]** *foord* Q. *Sword* F. 57. **course**: chase.
60. **taking**: infection.

Fool. Nay, he reserv'd a blanket, else we had been all sham'd.

Lear. Now, all the plagues that in the pendulous air Hang fated o'er men's faults light on thy daughters!   70

Kent. He hath no daughters, sir.

Lear. Death, traitor! nothing could have subdu'd nature
To such a lowness but his unkind daughters.
Is it the fashion, that discarded fathers
Should have thus little mercy on their flesh?   75
Judicious punishment! 'Twas this flesh begot
Those pelican daughters.

Edg. "Pillicock sat on Pillicock-hill."
Alow, alow, loo, loo!

Fool. This cold night will turn us all to fools and madmen.   81

Edg. Take heed o' th' foul fiend. Obey thy parents; keep thy [word justly]; swear not; commit not with man's sworn spouse; set not thy sweet heart on proud array. Tom 's a-cold.

Lear. What hast thou been?   86

Edg. A serving-man, proud in heart and mind; that curl'd my hair; wore gloves in my cap; serv'd the lust of my mistress' heart and did the act of darkness with her; swore as many oaths as I   90
spake words, and broke them in the sweet face of heaven: one that slept in the contriving of lust, and wak'd to do it. Wine lov'd I dearly, dice dearly; and in woman out-paramour'd the Turk: false of heart, light of ear, bloody of hand; hog in   95
sloth, fox in stealth, wolf in greediness, dog in madness, lion in prey. Let not the creaking of shoes nor the rustling of silks betray thy poor heart to woman. Keep thy foot out of brothels, thy hand out of plackets, thy pen from lenders' books, and defy the foul fiend.   101
"Still through the hawthorn blows the cold wind."
Says suum, mun, nonny. Dolphin my boy, boy, sessa! let him trot by.   [*Storm still.*

Lear. Thou wert better in a grave than to   105
answer with thy uncover'd body this extremity of the skies. Is man no more than this? Consider him well. Thou ow'st the worm no silk, the beast no hide, the sheep no wool, the cat no perfume. Ha! here 's three on 's are sophisticated! Thou   110
art the thing itself; unaccommodated man is no more but such a poor, bare, forked animal as thou art. Off, off, you lendings! come, unbutton here.   114
[*Tearing off his clothes.*]

Enter GLOUCESTER, *with a torch.*

Fool. Prithee, nuncle, be contented; 'tis a naughty night to swim in. Now a little fire in a wild field were like an old lecher's heart; a small spark, all the rest on 's body cold. Look, here comes a walking fire.   119

Edg. This is the foul [fiend] Flibbertigibbet; he begins at curfew, and walks [till the] first cock; he gives the web and the pin, squints the eye, and makes the hare-lip; mildews the white wheat, and hurts the poor creature of earth.
"St. Withold footed thrice the 'old;   125
    He met the night-mare and her ninefold;
        Bid her alight,
        And her troth plight,
    And, aroint thee, witch, aroint thee!"

Kent. How fares your Grace?   130

Lear. What's he?

Kent. Who's there? What is't you seek?

Glou. What are you there? Your names?

Edg. Poor Tom, that eats the swimming frog, the toad, the tadpole, the wall-newt, and the   135
water; that in the fury of his heart, when the foul fiend rages, eats cow-dung for salads; swallows the old rat and the ditch-dog; drinks the green mantle of the standing pool; who is whipp'd from tithing to tithing, and stock'd, punish'd, and im-   140
prison'd; who hath three suits to his back, six shirts to his body.
    Horse to ride, and weapon to wear;
    But mice and rats, and such small deer,
    Have been Tom's food for seven long year.
Beware my follower. Peace, Smulkin; peace, thou fiend!   146

Glou. What, hath your Grace no better company?

Edg. The prince of darkness is a gentleman.
Modo he's call'd, and Mahu.

Glou. Our flesh and blood, my lord, is grown so vile   150
That it doth hate what gets it.

Edg. Poor Tom 's a-cold.

Glou. Go in with me; my duty cannot suffer
To obey in all your daughters' hard commands.
Though their injunction be to bar my doors   155
And let this tyrannous night take hold upon you,
Yet have I ventur'd to come seek you out,
And bring you where both fire and food is ready.

Lear. First let me talk with this philosopher.

---

69. **pendulous:** suspended. 77. **pelican.** Young pelicans were believed to feed on their mother's blood. 83. [**word justly**] (Pope). *words justice* F; *words justly* Q. 88. **gloves,** as his mistress's favors. 94. **Turk:** Sultan. 95. **light of ear:** credulous. 100. **placket:** opening in a petticoat. 109. **cat:** civet cat. 111. **unaccommodated:** naked. 114. **lendings:** things not really belonging to one, clothes. 120. [**fiend**] Q. Om. F. **Flibbertigibbet.** See Introduction. 121. [**till the**] Q. *at* F. 122. **web...pin:** cataract. 125. **St. Withold** (Theobald) is supposed to be St. Vitalis. *Swithold* F. **'old:** wold. 126. **ninefold:** nine foals (?), imps (?). 129. **aroint thee:** begone. 136. **water:** water-newt, a lizard. 140. **tithing:** district. 151. **gets:** begets.

What is the cause of thunder?   160

  Kent. Good my lord, take his offer; go into th' house.

  Lear. I'll talk a word with this same learned Theban.

What is your study?

  Edg. How to prevent the fiend, and to kill vermin.

  Lear. Let me ask you one word in private.   165

  Kent. Importune him once more to go, my lord;

His wits begin t' unsettle.

  Glou.   Canst thou blame him?

                         [*Storm still.*

His daughters seek his death. Ah, that good Kent!

He said it would be thus, poor banish'd man!

Thou say'st the King grows mad; I'll tell thee, friend,   170

I am almost mad myself. I had a son,

Now outlaw'd from my blood; he sought my life,

But lately, very late. I lov'd him, friend.

No father his son dearer; true to tell thee,

The grief hath craz'd my wits. What a night 's this!   175

I do beseech your Grace, —

  Lear.   O, cry you mercy, sir.

Noble philosopher, your company.

  Edg. Tom 's a-cold.

  Glou. In, fellow, there, into th' hovel; keep thee warm.

  Lear. Come, let 's in all.

  Kent.   This way, my lord.

  Lear.   With him;

I will keep still with my philosopher.   181

  Kent. Good my lord, soothe him; let him take the fellow.

  Glou. Take him you on.

  Kent. Sirrah, come on; go along with us.

  Lear. Come, good Athenian.   185

  Glou. No words, no words: hush.

  Edg. "Child Rowland to the dark tower came;

His word was still, 'Fie, foh, and fum,

I smell the blood of a British man.'"

                         [*Exeunt.*

Scene V. [*Gloucester's castle.*]

Enter Cornwall *and* Edmund.

  Corn. I will have my revenge ere I depart his house.

  Edm. How, my lord, I may be censured that nature thus gives way to loyalty, something fears me to think of.   5

  Corn. I now perceive, it was not altogether your brother's evil disposition made him seek his death; but a provoking merit, set a-work by a reproveable badness in himself.   9

  Edm. How malicious is my fortune, that I must repent to be just! This is the letter which he spoke of, which approves him an intelligent party to the advantages of France. O heavens! that this treason were not, or not I the detector!   14

  Corn. Go with me to the Duchess.

  Edm. If the matter of this paper be certain, you have mighty business in hand.

  Corn. True or false, it hath made thee Earl of Gloucester. Seek out where thy father is, that he may be ready for our apprehension.   20

  Edm. [*Aside.*] If I find him comforting the King, it will stuff his suspicion more fully. — I will persevere in my course of loyalty, though the conflict be sore between that and my blood.   24

  Corn. I will lay trust upon thee; and thou shalt find a [dearer] father in my love.   [*Exeunt.*

Scene VI. [*A building attached to Gloucester's castle.*]

Enter Kent *and* Gloucester.

  Glou. Here is better than the open air; take it thankfully. I will piece out the comfort with what addition I can. I will not be long from you. [*Exit.*

  Kent. All the power of his wits have given way to his impatience. The gods reward your kindness!   6

Enter Lear, Edgar, *and* Fool.

  Edg. Frateretto calls me; and tells me Nero is an angler in the lake of darkness. Pray, innocent, and beware of the foul fiend.

  Fool. Prithee, nuncle, tell me whether a madman be a gentleman or a yeoman?   11

  Lear. A king, a king!

  Fool. No, he's a yeoman that has a gentleman to his son; for he's a mad yeoman that sees his son a gentleman before him.   15

  Lear. To have a thousand with red burning spits Come hissing in upon 'em, —

  [*Edg.* The foul fiend bites my back.

  Fool. He's mad that trusts in the tameness of a wolf, a horse's health, a boy's love, or a whore's oath.   21

  Lear. It shall be done; I will arraign them straight.

[*To Edgar.*] Come, sit thou here, most learned justicer;

[*To the Fool.*] Thou, sapient sir, sit here. Now, you she foxes!

  Edg. Look, where he stands and glares!   25

---

164. **prevent:** anticipate.

Sc. v, 3. **censured:** judged.   7. **his:** Gloucester's.   8. **provoking merit:** a good quality that incited him.   12. **intelligent:** informed.   22. **stuff:** strengthen.   26. **[dearer]** Q. *deere* F.

Sc. vi, 18–59. **[Edg. ... scape?]** Q. Om. F.   23. **justicer:** Theobald's correction of *Justice* Q.

I effort to destroy evil - good is destroyed too - that is the tragedy.

Wantest thou eyes at trial, madam?
  "Come o'er the bourn, Bessy, to me," —
Fool. "Her boat hath a leak,
    And she must not speak
    Why she dares not come over to thee."   30
  Edg. The foul fiend haunts poor Tom in the
voice of a nightingale. Hopdance cries in Tom's
belly for two white herring. Croak not, black
angel; I have no food for thee.
  Kent. How do you, sir? Stand you not so
    amaz'd: *bewildered*   35
Will you lie down and rest upon the cushions?
  Lear. I'll see their trial first. Bring in their
    evidence.
[*To Edgar.*] Thou robed man of justice, take thy
    place;
[*To the Fool.*] And thou, his yoke-fellow of equity,
Bench by his side. [*To Kent.*] You are o' th' com-
    mission,   40
Sit you too.
  Edg. Let us deal justly.
  "Sleepest or wakest thou, jolly shepherd?
    Thy sheep be in the corn;
    And for one blast of thy minikin mouth,   45
    Thy sheep shall take no harm."
Purr! the cat is grey.
  Lear. Arraign her first; 'tis Goneril. I here take
my oath before this honourable assembly, she kick'd
the poor king her father.   50
  Fool. Come hither, mistress. Is your name
Goneril?
  Lear. She cannot deny it.
  Fool. Cry you mercy, I took you for a joint-
stool.   55
  Lear. And here's another, whose warp'd looks
    proclaim
What store her heart is made on. Stop her there!
Arms, arms, sword, fire! Corruption in the place!
False justicer, why hast thou let her scape?]
  Edg. Bless thy five wits!   60
  Kent. O pity! Sir, where is the patience now
That you so oft have boasted to retain?
  Edg. [*Aside.*] My tears begin to take his part so
    much,
They mar my counterfeiting.
  Lear. The little dogs and all, *even dogs against* 65
Tray, Blanch, and Sweetheart, see, they bark at me.
  Edg. Tom will throw his head at them. Avaunt,
you curs!
    Be thy mouth or black or white,
    Tooth that poisons if it bite;   70
    Mastiff, greyhound, mongrel grim,
    Hound or spaniel, brach or [lym],

    Or bobtail [tike] or trundle-tail,
    Tom will make him weep and wail;
    For, with throwing thus my head,   75
    Dogs leapt the hatch, and all are fled.
Do de, de, de. Sessa! Come, march to wakes
and fairs and market-towns. Poor Tom, thy horn
is dry.   79
  Lear. Then let them anatomize Regan; see
what breeds about her heart. Is there any cause
in nature that make these hard hearts? [*To Edg.*]
You, sir, I entertain for one of my hundred;
only I do not like the fashion of your garments.
You will say they are Persian, but let them be
chang'd.   86

Re-enter GLOUCESTER.

  Kent. Now, good my lord, lie here and rest a
while.
  Lear. Make no noise, make no noise; draw the
curtains; so, so, so. We'll go to supper i' th' morn-
ing.   91
  Fool. And I'll go to bed at noon. *last words of Fool.*
  Glou. Come hither, friend; where is the King my
    master?
  Kent. Here, sir; but trouble him not, his wits are
    gone.
  Glou. Good friend, I prithee, take him in thy
    arms;   95
I have o'erheard a plot of death upon him.
There is a litter ready; lay him in't,
And drive toward Dover, friend, where thou shalt
    meet
Both welcome and protection. Take up thy mas-
    ter.
If thou shouldst dally half an hour, his life,   100
With thine and all that offer to defend him
Stand in assured loss. Take up, take up;
And follow me, that will to some provision
Give thee quick conduct.
  Kent.   [Oppressed nature sleeps.
This rest might yet have balm'd thy broken sinews,
Which, if convenience will not allow,   106
Stand in hard cure. (*To the Fool.*) Come, help to
    bear thy master;
Thou must not stay behind.]
  Glou.   Come, come, away.
    [*Exeunt* [*all but Edgar*].
  [*Edg.* When we our betters see bearing our woes,
We scarcely think our miseries our foes.   110
Who alone suffers, suffers most i' th' mind,
Leaving free things and happy shows behind;
But then the mind much sufferance doth o'erskip,
When grief hath mates, and bearing fellowship.

fool taking less part - Edgar taking his place

---

27. **bourn:** burn, brook. 45. **minikin:** dainty. 57. **store:** material. 72. **[lym]** (Hanmer): bloodhound. *Hym* F. 73.
[tike] Q: cur. *tight* F. **trundle-tail:** curled tail. 76. **hatch:** lower half of a divided door. 83. **entertain:** engage. 104–
108. **[Oppressed...behind]** Q. Om. F. 105. **sinews:** nerves. 109–122. **[Edg....lurk]** Q. Om. F. 114. **bearing:**
suffering.

doesn't seem pure Shakespearian - but fits into play.

Edgar developing into a wiser man.

Regan always add to any evil anyone suggests.

How light and portable my pain seems now, 115
When that which makes me bend makes the King
 bow,
He childed as I fathered! Tom, away!
Mark the high noises; and thyself bewray
When false opinion, whose wrong thoughts defile thee,
In thy just proof repeals and reconciles thee. 120
What will hap more to-night, safe scape the King!
Lurk, lurk.]   [*Exit.*]

SCENE VII. [*Gloucester's castle.*]

Enter CORNWALL, REGAN, GONERIL, *Bastard*
  [EDMUND], *and* SERVANTS.

Corn. [*To Gon.*] Post speedily to my lord your
husband; show him this letter. The army of France
is landed. — Seek out the traitor Gloucester.
      [*Exeunt some of the Servants.*]
Reg. Hang him instantly.
Gon. Pluck out his eyes.   5
Corn. Leave him to my displeasure. — Edmund,
keep you our sister company; the revenges we are
bound to take upon your traitorous father are not
fit for your beholding. Advise the Duke, where
you are going, to a most festinate preparation; we
are bound to the like. Our posts shall be swift
and intelligent betwixt us. Farewell, dear sister;
farewell, my Lord of Gloucester. (*Edmund*) 13

    Enter Steward [OSWALD].

How now! where's the King?
Osw. My Lord of Gloucester hath convey'd him
 hence.   15
Some five or six and thirty of his knights,
Hot questrists after him, met him at gate,
Who, with some other of the lord's dependants,
Are gone with him toward Dover, where they boast
To have well-armed friends.
Corn.   Get horses for your mistress.
Gon. Farewell, sweet lord, and sister. 21
Corn. Edmund, farewell.
   [*Exeunt* [*Goneril, Edmund, and Oswald*].
    Go seek the traitor Gloucester,
Pinion him like a thief, bring him before us.
       [*Exeunt other Servants.*]
Though well we may not pass upon his life
Without the form of justice, yet our power 25
Shall do a court'sy to our wrath, which men
May blame, but not control.

   Enter GLOUCESTER *and* SERVANTS.

    Who's there? The traitor?
Reg. Ingrateful fox! 'tis he.

Cornwall cant tell Glou. knows't right —

Corn. Bind fast his corky arms.
Glou. What means your Graces? Good my
 friends, consider   30
You are my guests. Do me no foul play, friends.
Corn. Bind him, I say. [*Servants bind him.*]
Reg.   Hard, hard. O filthy traitor!
Glou. Unmerciful lady as you are, I'm none.
Corn. To this chair bind him. Villain, thou
 shalt find — [*Regan plucks his beard.*]
Glou. By the kind gods, 'tis most ignobly done
To pluck me by the beard.   36
Reg. So white, and such a traitor! *a strong expression in those days*
Glou.   Naughty lady,
These hairs, which thou dost ravish from my chin,
Will quicken, and accuse thee. I am your host:
With robber's hands my hospitable favours 40
You should not ruffle thus. What will you do?
Corn. Come, sir, what letters had you late from
 France?
Reg. Be simple-answer'd, for we know the truth.
Corn. And what confederacy have you with the
 traitors
Late footed in the kingdom?   45
Reg. To whose hands you have sent the lunatic
 king,
Speak.
Glou. I have a letter guessingly set down,
Which came from one that's of a neutral heart,
And not from one oppos'd.
Corn.   Cunning.
Reg.   And false.
Corn. Where hast thou sent the King? 50
Glou. To Dover.
Reg. Wherefore to Dover? Wast thou not
 charg'd at peril —
Corn. Wherefore to Dover? Let him answer
 that. *Cornwall is master over Reg.*
Glou. I am tied to th' stake, and I must stand the
 course.
Reg. Wherefore to Dover?   55
Glou. Because I would not see thy cruel nails *irony*
Pluck out his poor old eyes; nor thy fierce sister
In his anointed flesh stick boarish fangs.
The sea, with such a storm as his bare head
In hell-black night endur'd, would have buoy'd
 up   60
And quench'd the stelled fires;
Yet, poor old heart, he holp the heavens to rain.
If wolves had at thy gate howl'd that stern time,
Thou shouldst have said, "Good porter, turn the
 key."
All cruels else subscribe; but I shall see 65
The winged vengeance overtake such children.

---

115. **portable:** bearable. 118. **bewray:** disclose. 120. **repeals:** recalls. 121. **What:** whatever.
 Sc. vii, 10. **festinate:** speedy. 17. **questrists:** searchers. 29. **corky:** withered. 39. **quicken:** become alive. 40. **favours:** features. 41. **ruffle:** outrage. 54. **course:** attack of the dogs (bear-baiting). 61. **stelled fires:** stars. 65. **All...subscribe.** Not satisfactorily explained. All other cruelties yield to this (?).

Corn. See 't shalt thou never. Fellows, hold the
chair.
Upon these eyes of thine I'll set my foot.
Glou. He that will think to live till he be old,
Give me some help! — O cruel! O you gods! 70
Reg. One side will mock another; th' other
too.
Corn. If you see vengeance, —
[*r.*] *Serv.* Hold your hand, my lord!
I have serv'd you ever since I was a child;
But better service have I never done you
Than now to bid you hold.
Reg. How now, you dog!
[*r.*] *Serv.* If you did wear a beard upon your
chin, 76
I'd shake it on this quarrel. What do you mean?
Corn. My villain! [*They draw and fight.*]
[*r.*] *Serv.* Nay, then, come on, and take the
chance of anger.
Reg. Give me thy sword. A peasant stand up
thus? 80
[*Takes a sword, and runs at him behind.*]
[*r.*] *Serv.* Oh, I am slain! My lord, you have
one eye left
To see some mischief on him. Oh! [*Dies.*]
Corn. Lest it see more, prevent it. Out, vile
jelly!
Where is thy lustre now?
Glou. All dark and comfortless. Where's my son
Edmund? 85
Edmund, enkindle all the sparks of nature,
To quit this horrid act.
Reg. Out, treacherous villain!
Thou call'st on him that hates thee. It was he
That made the overture of thy treasons to us,
Who is too good to pity thee. 90
Glou. O my follies! then Edgar was abus'd.
Kind gods, forgive me that, and prosper him!
Reg. Go thrust him out at gates, and let him
smell
His way to Dover. (*Exit [one] with Gloucester.*)
How is't, my lord? How look you?
Corn. I have received a hurt; follow me, lady. 95
Turn out that eyeless villain; throw this slave
Upon the dunghill. Regan, I bleed apace;
Untimely comes this hurt. Give me your arm.
[*Exit Cornwall, led by Regan.*]
[*2. Serv.* I'll never care what wickedness I do,
If this man come to good.
3. Serv. If she live long, 100
And in the end meet the old course of death,
Women will all turn monsters.

2. Serv. Let's follow the old earl, and get the Bedlam
To lead him where he would: his roguish madness
Allows itself to anything. 105
3. Serv. Go thou: I'll fetch some flax and whites
of eggs
To apply to his bleeding face. Now, Heaven help
him!] [*Exeunt [severally].*

ACT IV

SCENE I. [*The open country near Gloucester's
castle.*]

Enter EDGAR.

Edg. Yet better thus, and known to be con-
temn'd,
Than, still contemn'd and flatter'd, to be worst.
The lowest and most dejected thing of fortune
Stands still in esperance, lives not in fear.
The lamentable change is from the best; 5
The worst returns to laughter. Welcome, then,
Thou unsubstantial air that I embrace!
The wretch that thou hast blown unto the worst
Owes nothing to thy blasts.

Enter GLOUCESTER, *led by an* OLD MAN.

But who comes here?
My father, poorly led? World, world, O world! 10
But that thy strange mutations make us hate thee,
Life would not yield to age.
Old Man. O, my good lord, I have been your
tenant, and your father's tenant, these fourscore
years. 15
Glou. Away, get thee away! Good friend, be
gone;
Thy comforts can do me no good at all;
Thee they may hurt.
Old Man. You cannot see your way.
Glou. I have no way, and therefore want no
eyes;
I stumbled when I saw. Full oft 'tis seen, 21
Our means secure us, and our mere defects
Prove our commodities. O dear son Edgar,
The food of thy abused father's wrath!
Might I but live to see thee in my touch, 25
I'd say I had eyes again!
Old Man. How now! Who's there?
Edg. [*Aside.*] O gods! Who is't can say, "I am
at the worst"?
I am worse than e'er I was.
Old Man. 'Tis poor mad Tom.

---

77. **What ... mean?** Probably this should be given to Cornwall or Regan. 89. **made the overture:** disclosed. 91.
abus'd: wronged. 99-107. [**2. Serv....him**] Q. Om. F. 101. **old:** usual.
Act IV, sc. i, 1. **contemn'd:** despised. 4. **esperance:** hope. 6. **The worst...laughter:** any change from the worst must
be for the better. 9. **Owes nothing:** cannot be called on to pay anything more. 12. **Life...age:** we should never live to
be old. 22. **secure:** make careless. 23. **commodities:** advantages. 24. **food:** object. **abused:** deceived.

Edg. [*Aside.*] And worse I may be yet; the worst
  is not
So long as we can say, "This is the worst."   30
  Old Man. Fellow, where goest?
  Glou.   Is it a beggar-man?
  Old Man. Madman and beggar too.
  Glou. He has some reason, else he could not beg.
I' th' last night's storm I such a fellow saw,
Which made me think a man a worm. My son
Came then into my mind, and yet my mind   36
Was then scarce friends with him. I have heard
  more since.
As flies to wanton boys, are we to th' gods,
They kill us for their sport.
  Edg.   [*Aside.*] How should this be?
Bad is the trade that must play fool to sorrow,   40
Ang'ring itself and others. — Bless thee, master!
  Glou. Is that the naked fellow?
  Old Man.   Ay, my lord.
  Glou. [Then, prithee,] get thee away. If, for
  my sake,
Thou wilt o'ertake us hence a mile or twain
I' th' way toward Dover, do it for ancient love;   45
And bring some covering for this naked soul,
Which I'll entreat to lead me.
  Old Man.   Alack, sir, he is mad.
  Glou. 'Tis the time's plague, when madmen lead
  the blind.
Do as I bid thee, or rather do thy pleasure;
Above the rest, be gone.   50
  Old Man. I'll bring him the best 'parel that I
  have,
Come on't what will.   [*Exit.*
  Glou. Sirrah, naked fellow, —
  Edg. Poor Tom 's a-cold. [*Aside.*] I cannot daub
  it further.
  Glou. Come hither, fellow.   55
  Edg. [*Aside.*] And yet I must. — Bless thy sweet
  eyes, they bleed.
  Glou. Know'st thou the way to Dover?
  Edg. Both stile and gate, horse-way and foot-
path. Poor Tom hath been scar'd out of his good
wits. Bless thee, good man's son, from the foul   60
fiend! [Five fiends have been in poor Tom at once;
of lust, as Obidicut; Hobbididence, prince of dumbness; Mahu, of stealing; Modo, of murder; Flibbertigibbet, of mopping and mowing, who since possesses chambermaids and waiting-women. So, bless
thee, master!]   66
  Glou. Here, take this purse, thou whom the
  heavens' plagues
Have humbled to all strokes. That I am wretched

Makes thee the happier; heavens, deal so still!
Let the superfluous and lust-dieted man,   70
That slaves your ordinance, that will not see
Because he does not feel, feel your power quickly;
So distribution should undo excess,
And each man have enough. Dost thou know
  Dover?
  Edg. Ay, master.   75
  Glou. There is a cliff, whose high and bending
  head
Looks fearfully in the confined deep.
Bring me but to the very brim of it,
And I'll repair the misery thou dost bear
With something rich about me. From that place   80
I shall no leading need.
  Edg.   Give me thy arm;
Poor Tom shall lead thee.   [*Exeunt.*

SCENE II. [*Before the Duke of Albany's
  palace.*]

Enter GONERIL, *Bastard* [EDMUND], *and Steward* [OSWALD].

  Gon. Welcome, my lord! I marvel our <u>mild</u> hus-
band
Not met us on the way. — Now, where's your mas-
  ter?
  Osw. Madam, within; but never man so chang'd.
I told him of the army that was landed;
He smil'd at it. I told him you were coming;   5
His answer was, "The worse." Of Gloucester's
  treachery,
And of the loyal service of his son,
When I inform'd him, then he call'd me sot,
And told me I had turn'd the wrong side out.
What most he should dislike seems pleasant to him;
What like, offensive.   10
  Gon. [*To Edm.*] Then shall you go no further.
It is the cowish terror of his spirit,
That dares not undertake; he'll not feel wrongs
Which tie him to an answer. Our wishes on the
  way
May prove effects. Back, Edmund, to my brother;
Hasten his musters and conduct his powers.   16
I must change [arms] at home, and give the distaff
Into my husband's hands. This trusty servant
Shall pass between us. Ere long you are like to
  hear,
If you dare venture in your own behalf,   20
A mistress's command. Wear this; spare speech;
Decline your head. This kiss, if it durst speak,
Would stretch thy spirits up into the air.

---

43. [**Then, prithee**] Q. Om. F.   54. **daub**: dissemble.   61–66. [**Five ... master!**] Q. Om. F.   64. **mopping and mowing**: making faces.   70. **superfluous**: having too much.   71. **slaves your ordinance**: makes your laws subordinate to his
desires.   76. **bending**: overhanging.
  Sc. ii, 8. **sot**: fool.   12. **cowish**: cowardly.   15. **prove effects**: be realized.   17. [**arms**] Q. *names* F. Goneril will take the
sword.

Conceive, and fare thee well.
  Edm. Yours in the ranks of death.   [*Exit.*
  Gon.   My most dear Gloucester!
O, the difference of man and man!   26
To thee a woman's services are due;
My Fool usurps my body.
  Osw.   Madam, here comes my lord.
                         [*Exit.*

Enter the DUKE OF ALBANY.

  Gon. I have been worth the whistle.
  Alb.   O Goneril!
You are not worth the dust which the rude wind 30
Blows in your face. [I fear your disposition.
That nature which contemns its origin
Cannot be bordered certain in itself.
She that herself will sliver and disbranch
From her material sap, perforce must wither 35
And come to deadly use.
  Gon. No more; the text is foolish.
  Alb. Wisdom and goodness to the vile seem vile;
Filths savour but themselves. What have you done?
Tigers, not daughters, what have you perform'd? 40
A father, and a gracious aged man,
Whose reverence even the head-lugg'd bear would
    lick,
Most barbarous, most degenerate! have you madded.
Could my good brother suffer you to do it?
A man, a prince, by him so benefited!   45
If that the heavens do not their visible spirits
Send quickly down to tame these vile offences,
It will come,
Humanity must perforce prey on itself,
Like monsters of the deep.]
  Gon.   Milk-liver'd man! 50
That bear'st a cheek for blows, a head for wrongs,
Who hast not in thy brows an eye discerning
Thine honour from thy suffering, [that not know'st
Fools do those villains pity who are punish'd
Ere they have done their mischief, where's thy
    drum?   55
France spreads his banners in our noiseless land,
With plumed helm thy state begins to threat;
Whiles thou, a moral fool, sits still, and criest,
"Alack, why does he so?"]
  Alb.   See thyself, devil!
Proper deformity seems not in the fiend 60
So horrid as in woman.
  Gon.   O vain fool!
  [*Alb.* Thou changed and self-cover'd thing, for
    shame!
Be-monster not thy feature. Were't my fitness
To let these hands obey my blood,

They are apt enough to dislocate and tear 65
Thy flesh and bones. Howe'er thou art a fiend,
A woman's shape doth shield thee.
  Gon. Marry, your manhood — Mew!

Enter a MESSENGER.

  Alb. What news?]
  Mess. O, my good lord, the Duke of Cornwall 's
    dead;   70
Slain by his servant, going to put out
The other eye of Gloucester.
  Alb.   Gloucester's eyes!
  Mess. A servant that he bred, thrill'd with re-
    morse,
Oppos'd against the act, bending his sword
To his great master; who, thereat enrag'd, 75
Flew on him, and amongst them fell'd him dead;
But not without that harmful stroke which since
Hath pluck'd him after.
  Alb.   This shows you are above,
You [justicers,] that these our nether crimes
So speedily can venge! But, O poor Gloucester!
Lost he his other eye?
  Mess.   Both, both, my lord. 81
This letter, madam, craves a speedy answer.
'Tis from your sister.
  Gon. [*Aside.*] One way I like this well;
But being widow, and my Gloucester with her, 85
May all the building in my fancy pluck
Upon my hateful life. Another way,
The news is not so tart. — I'll read, and answer.
                      [*Exit.*
  Alb. Where was his son when they did take his
    eyes?
  Mess. Come with my lady hither.
  Alb.   He is not here.
  Mess. No, my good lord; I met him back again. 91
  Alb. Knows he the wickedness?
  Mess. Ay, my good lord; 'twas he inform'd against
    him;
And quit the house on purpose that their punish-
    ment
Might have the freer course.
  Alb.   Gloucester, I live 95
To thank thee for the love thou show'dst the King,
And to revenge thine eyes. Come hither, friend;
Tell me what more thou know'st.   [*Exeunt.*

[SCENE III. *The French camp near Dover.*

Enter KENT and a GENTLEMAN.

  Kent. Why the King of France is so suddenly
gone back, know you no reason?

31–50. [I fear ... deep] Q. Om. F. 33. bordered certain: kept within bounds. 35. material: essential to life. 53–59. [that ... so?] Q. Om. F. 56. noiseless: peaceful. 60. Proper: that belongs to him. 62–69. [Alb.... news?] Q. Om. F. 62. self-cover'd: whose real self is hidden. 63. Were't my fitness: were it suitable for me. 64. blood: impulse. 73. remorse: pity. 79. [justicers] Q. justices F. nether: committed here below. 86. pluck: pull down.

Gent. Something he left imperfect in the state,
which since his coming forth is thought of; which
imports to the kingdom so much fear and danger
that his personal return was most required and
necessary.   7

Kent. Who hath he left behind him General?

Gent. The Marshal of France, Monsieur La Far.

Kent. Did your letters pierce the Queen to any
demonstration of grief?   12

Gent. [Ay, sir]; she took them, read them in my
    presence;
And now and then an ample tear trill'd down
Her delicate cheek. It seem'd she was a queen   15
Over her passion, who, most rebel-like,
Sought to be king o'er her.

Kent.   O, then it mov'd her.

Gent. Not to a rage; patience and sorrow [strove]
Who should express her goodliest. You have seen
Sunshine and rain at once: her smiles and tears   20
Were like a better way; those happy smilets
That play'd on her ripe lip seem'd not to know
What guests were in her eyes, which, parted thence,
As pearls from diamonds dropp'd. In brief,
Sorrow would be a rarity most beloved,   25
If all could so become it.

Kent.   Made she no verbal question?

Gent. Faith, once or twice she heav'd the name
    of "father"
Pantingly forth, as if it press'd her heart;
Cried, "Sisters! sisters! Shame of ladies! sisters!
Kent! father! sisters! What, i' th' storm? i' th'
    night?   30
Let pity not be believ'd!" There she shook
The holy water from her heavenly eyes;
And clamour moistened; then away she started
To deal with grief alone.

Kent.   It is the stars,
The stars above us, govern our conditions;   35
Else one self mate and make could not beget
Such different issues. You spoke not with her
    since?

Gent. No.

Kent. Was this before the King return'd?

Gent.   No, since.

Kent. Well, sir, the poor distressed Lear 's i' th'
    town;   40
Who sometime, in his better tune, remembers
What we are come about, and by no means
Will yield to see his daughter.

Gent.   Why, good sir?

Kent. A sovereign shame so elbows him. His
    own unkindness,
That stripp'd her from his benediction, turn'd her   45
To foreign casualties, gave her dear rights
To his dog-hearted daughters, — these things sting
His mind so venomously, that burning shame
Detains him from Cordelia.

Gent.   Alack, poor gentleman!

Kent. Of Albany's and Cornwall's powers you
    heard not?   50

Gent. 'Tis so, they are afoot.

Kent. Well, sir, I'll bring you to our master Lear,
And leave you to attend him. Some dear cause
Will in concealment wrap me up a while;
When I am known aright, you shall not grieve   55
Lending me this acquaintance. I pray you, go
Along with me.]   [*Exeunt.*

SCENE [IV. *The same. A tent.*]

Enter, with drum and colours, CORDELIA, [DOC-
TOR], *and* Soldiers.

Cor. Alack, 'tis he! Why, he was met even now
As mad as the vex'd sea, singing aloud,
Crown'd with rank fumiter and furrow-weeds,
With hardocks, hemlock, nettles, cuckoo-flowers,
Darnel, and all the idle weeds that grow   5
In our sustaining corn. A [sentry] send forth;
Search every acre in the high-grown field,
And bring him to our eye. [*Exit an Officer.*] What
    can man's wisdom
In the restoring his bereaved sense?
He that helps him take all my outward worth.   10

[*Doct.*] There is means, madam.
Our foster-nurse of nature is repose,
The which he lacks; that to provoke in him,
Are many simples operative, whose power
Will close the eye of anguish.

Cor.   All blest secrets,   15
All you unpublish'd virtues of the earth,
Spring with my tears! be aidant and remediate
In the good man's [distress]! Seek, seek for him,
Lest his ungovern'd rage dissolve the life
That wants the means to lead it.

Enter a MESSENGER.

Mess.   News, madam!
The British powers are marching hitherward.   21

Cor. 'Tis known before; our preparation stands
In expectation of them. O dear father,

Sc. iii, Q. F omits scene. **13. [Ay, sir]** (Johnson). *I say* Q. **18. [strove]** (Pope). *streme* Q. **21. like a better way:** more beautiful than "sunshine and rain at once." **25. rarity:** something precious. **33. clamour moistened.** Q adds *her.* The passage is probably corrupt. Tears followed her outcry (?). **36. self mate and make:** same husband and wife. **43. yield:** consent. **44. sovereign:** over-mastering. **elbows:** holds him aloof (?). **46. casualties:** risks. **53. dear:** important. **Sc. iv,** S.D. [DOCTOR] Q. *Gentlemen* F. **3. fumiter:** fumitory. **4. hardocks:** perhaps for *burdocks* or *harlock,* wild mustard. **5. Darnel:** a general term for weed; sometimes specifically rye-grass. **6. [sentry]** (Johnson). *Centery* F. *centurie* Q. **11. [Doct.]** Q. *Gent.* F. **14. simples:** medicinal herbs. **17. aidant:** helpful. **remediate:** healing. **18. [distress]** Q. *desires* F.

Oswald loyal to Goneril

It is thy business that I go about;
Therefore great France   25
My mourning and importun'd tears hath pitied.
No blown ambition doth our arms incite,
But love, dear love, and our ag'd father's right.
Soon may I hear and see him!   [*Exeunt.*

SCENE [V. *Gloucester's castle.*]

Enter REGAN *and* Steward [OSWALD].

Reg. But are my brother's powers set forth?
Osw.   Ay, madam.
Reg. Himself in person there?
Osw.   Madam, with much ado.
Your sister is the better soldier.
Reg. Lord Edmund spake not with your lord at
    home?
Osw. No, madam.   5
Reg. What might import my sister's letter to
    him?
Osw. I know not, lady.
Reg. Faith, he is posted hence on serious matter.
It was great ignorance, Gloucester's eyes being out,
To let him live; where he arrives he moves   10
All hearts against us. Edmund, I think, is gone,
In pity of his misery, to dispatch
His nighted life; moreover, to descry
The strength o' th' enemy.
Osw. I must needs after him, madam, with my
    letter.   15
Reg. Our troops set forth to-morrow, stay with
    us;
The ways are dangerous.
Osw.   I may not, madam;
My lady charg'd my duty in this business.
Reg. Why should she write to Edmund? Might
    not you
Transport her purposes by word? Belike   20
Some things — I know not what. I'll love thee
    much —
Let me unseal the letter.
Osw.   Madam, I had rather —
Reg. I know your lady does not love her husband;
I am sure of that; and at her late being here   24
She gave strange œillades and most speaking looks
To noble Edmund. I know you are of her bosom.
Osw. I, madam?
Reg. I speak in understanding; y' are, I know 't.
Therefore I do advise you, take this note:
My lord is dead; Edmund and I have talk'd;   30
And more convenient is he for my hand
Than for your lady's. You may gather more.
If you do find him, pray you, give him this;

And when your mistress hears thus much from you,
I pray, desire her call her wisdom to her.   35
So, fare you well.
If you do chance to hear of that blind traitor,
Preferment falls on him that cuts him off.
Osw. Would I could meet him, madam! I should
    show
What party I do follow.
Reg.   Fare thee well.   40
                     [*Exeunt.*

SCENE [VI. *Fields near Dover.*]

Enter GLOUCESTER *and* EDGAR [*dressed like a
peasant*].

Glou. When shall I come to th' top of that same
    hill?
Edg. You do climb up it now; look, how we la-
    bour.
Glou. Methinks the ground is even.
Edg.   Horrible steep.
Hark, do you hear the sea?
Glou.   No, truly.
Edg. Why, then, your other senses grow im-
    perfect   5
By your eyes' anguish.
Glou.   So may it be, indeed.
Methinks thy voice is alter'd, and thou speak'st
In better phrase and matter than thou didst.
Edg. You're much deceiv'd. In nothing am I
    chang'd
But in my garments.
Glou.   Methinks you're better spoken.
Edg. Come on, sir, here's the place; stand still.
    How fearful   11
And dizzy 'tis, to cast one's eyes so low!
The crows and choughs that wing the midway air
Show scarce so gross as beetles. Half way down
Hangs one that gathers samphire, dreadful trade!   15
Methinks he seems no bigger than his head.
The fishermen, that walk upon the beach,
Appear like mice; and yond tall anchoring bark,
Diminish'd to her cock; her cock, a buoy
Almost too small for sight. The murmuring surge,
That on th' unnumb'red idle pebbles chafes,   21
Cannot be heard so high. I'll look no more,
Lest my brain turn, and the deficient sight
Topple down headlong.
Glou.   Set me where you stand.
Edg. Give me your hand; you are now within a
    foot   25
Of th' extreme verge. For all beneath the moon
Would I not leap upright.

---

26. **importun'd:** importunate, urgent. *important* Q. 27. **blown:** puffed up.
Sc. v, 2. **with much ado:** persuaded with difficulty. 13. **nighted:** blinded. 25. **œillades:** amorous glances. 26. **of her bosom:** in her confidence. 29. **take this note:** note this.
Sc. vi, 13. **choughs:** jackdaws. 14. **gross:** big. 15. **samphire:** sea-fennel, used for pickling. 19. **cock:** cock-boat.

Glou.   Let go my hand.
Here, friend, 's another purse; in it a jewel
Well worth a poor man's taking. Fairies and gods
Prosper it with thee! Go thou further off;   30
Bid me farewell, and let me hear thee going.
   Edg. Now fare ye well, good sir.
   Glou.   With all my heart.
   Edg. Why I do trifle thus with his despair
Is done to cure it.   *[Glou.* [*Kneeling.*] O you mighty gods!
This world I do renounce, and in your sights   35
Shake patiently my great affliction off.
If I could bear it longer, and not fall
To quarrel with your great opposeless wills,
My snuff and loathed part of nature should
Burn itself out. If Edgar live, O bless him!   40
Now, fellow, fare thee well.   [*He falls.*
   Edg.   Gone, sir; farewell!
— And yet I know not how conceit may rob
The treasury of life, when life itself
Yields to the theft. Had he been where he thought,
By this had thought been past. Alive or dead? —
Ho, you sir! friend! Hear you, sir! speak! —   46
Thus might he pass indeed; yet he revives. —
What are you, sir?
   Glou.   Away, and let me die.
   Edg. Hadst thou been aught but gossamer, feathers, air,
So many fathom down precipitating,   50
Thou 'dst shiver'd like an egg: but thou dost breathe;
Hast heavy substance; bleed'st not; speak'st; art sound.
Ten masts at each make not the altitude
Which thou hast perpendicularly fell.
Thy life's a miracle. Speak yet again.   55
   Glou. But have I fall'n, or no?
   Edg. From the dread summit of this chalky bourn.
Look up a-height; the shrill-gorg'd lark so far
Cannot be seen or heard. Do but look up.
   Glou. Alack, I have no eyes.   60
Is wretchedness depriv'd that benefit,
To end itself by death? 'Twas yet some comfort,
When misery could beguile the tyrant's rage,
And frustrate his proud will.
   Edg.   Give me your arm.
Up: so. How is't? Feel you your legs? You stand.   65
   Glou. Too well, too well.
   Edg.   This is above all strangeness.
Upon the crown o' th' cliff, what thing was that

Which parted from you?
   Glou.   A poor unfortunate beggar.
   Edg. As I stood here below, methought his eyes
Were two full moons; he had a thousand noses,   70
Horns whelk'd and waved like the [enridged] sea.
It was some fiend; therefore, thou happy father,
Think that the clearest gods, who make them honours
Of men's impossibilities, have preserv'd thee.
   Glou. I do remember now. Henceforth I'll bear
Affliction till it do cry out itself   76
"Enough, enough," and die. That thing you speak of,
I took it for a man; often 't would say,
"The fiend, the fiend!" He led me to that place.
   Edg. Bear free and patient thoughts.

     Enter LEAR [*fantastically dressed with wild flowers*].

          But who comes here?
The safer sense will ne'er accommodate   81
His master thus.
   Lear. No, they cannot touch me for [coining];
I am the King himself.
   Edg. O thou side-piercing sight!   85
   Lear. Nature's above art in that respect. There's
your press-money. That fellow handles his bow
like a crow-keeper; draw me a clothier's yard.
Look, look, a mouse! Peace, peace; this piece of
toasted cheese will do't. There's my gauntlet; I'll
prove it on a giant. Bring up the brown bills. O,
well flown, bird! I' th' clout, i' th' clout! Hewgh!
Give the word.   93
   Edg. Sweet marjoram.
   Lear. Pass.
   Glou. I know that voice.   96
   Lear. Ha! Goneril, with a white beard! They
flatter'd me like a dog, and told me I had the white
hairs in my beard ere the black ones were there.
To say "ay" and "no" to everything that I said!
"Ay" and "no" too was no good divinity.   101
When the rain came to wet me once, and the wind
to make me chatter; when the thunder would not
peace at my bidding; there I found 'em, there I
smelt 'em out. Go to, they are not men o' their
words: they told me I was everything; 'tis a lie, I
am not ague-proof.   107
   Glou. The trick of that voice I do well remember.
Is't not the King?
   Lear.   Ay, every inch a king!
When I do stare, see how the subject quakes.   110
I pardon that man's life. What was thy cause?

39. **snuff:** burnt wick, useless remnant. 42. **conceit:** imagination. 47. **pass:** die. 53. **at each:** end to end. 57. **bourn:** boundary. 58. **a-height:** on high. 71. **whelk'd:** twisted. [**enridged**] Q. *enraged* F. 73. **clearest:** most pure. 80. **free:** fearless. 81. **The safer sense:** a sane mind. **accommodate:** dress up. 83. [**coining**] Q. *crying* F. 87. **press-money:** money given to a conscript. 88. **clothier's yard:** an arrow a cloth-yard long. 91. **brown bills:** men carrying pikes stained brown. 92. **clout:** center of the target. 111. **cause:** accusation.

Adultery?
Thou shalt not die.   Die for adultery!   No:
The wren goes to't, and the small gilded fly
Does lecher in my sight.   115
Let copulation thrive; for Gloucester's bastard son
Was kinder to his father than my daughters
Got 'tween the lawful sheets.
To't, luxury, pell-mell! for I lack soldiers.
Behold yond simp'ring dame,   120
Whose face between her forks presages snow,
That minces virtue, and does shake the head
To hear of pleasure's name, —
The fitchew nor the soiled horse goes to't
With a more riotous appetite.   125
Down from the waist they are Centaurs,
Though women all above;
But to the girdle do the gods inherit,
Beneath is all the fiends';
There's hell, there's darkness, there's the sulphurous
      pit,   130
Burning, scalding, stench, consumption; fie, fie, fie!
pah, pah!   Give me an ounce of civet; good apothe-
cary, sweeten my imagination.   There's money
for thee.
    Glou. O, let me kiss that hand!   135
    Lear. Let me wipe it first; it smells of mortality.
    Glou. O ruin'd piece of nature!   This great world
Shall so wear out to nought.   Dost thou know me?
    Lear. I remember thine eyes well enough.   Dost
thou squiny at me?   No, do thy worst, blind
Cupid; I'll not love.   Read thou this challenge; mark
but the penning of it.   142
    Glou. Were all thy letters suns, I could not see.
    Edg. [Aside.] I would not take this from report.
      It is;
And my heart breaks at it.   145
    Lear. Read.
    Glou. What, with the case of eyes?
    Lear. O, ho, are you there with me?   No eyes
in your head, nor no money in your purse?   Your
eyes are in a heavy case, your purse in a light; yet
you see how this world goes.
    Glou. I see it feelingly.   152
    Lear. What, art mad?   A man may see how this
world goes with no eyes.   Look with thine ears; see
how yond justice rails upon yond simple thief.
Hark, in thine ear: change places, and, handy-
dandy, which is the justice, which is the thief?
Thou hast seen a farmer's dog bark at a beggar? 159
    Glou. Ay, sir.
    Lear. And the creature run from the cur?   There
thou mightst behold the great image of authority:
a dog's obey'd in office.

Thou rascal beadle, hold thy bloody hand!
Why dost thou lash that whore?   Strip thy own
      back;   165
Thou hotly lusts to use her in that kind
For which thou whip'st her.   The usurer hangs the
      cozener.
Through tatter'd clothes great vices do appear;
Robes and furr'd gowns hide all.   [Plate] sins with
      gold,
And the strong lance of justice hurtless breaks;   170
Arm it in rags, a pigmy's straw does pierce it.
None does offend, none, I say, none; I'll able 'em.
Take that of me, my friend, who have the power
To seal th' accuser's lips.   Get thee glass eyes,
And, like a scurvy politician, seem   175
To see the things thou dost not.   Now, now, now,
      now.
Pull off my boots; harder, harder: so.
    Edg. O, matter and impertinency mix'd!
Reason in madness!
    Lear. If thou wilt weep my fortunes, take my
      eyes.   180
I know thee well enough; thy name is Gloucester.
Thou must be patient; we came crying hither.
Thou know'st, the first time that we smell the
      air,
We wawl and cry.   I will preach to thee; mark.
    Glou. Alack, alack the day!   185
    Lear. When we are born, we cry that we are come
To this great stage of fools. — This' a good block.
It were a delicate stratagem, to shoe
A troop of horse with felt.   I'll put 't in proof;
And when I have stol'n upon these son-in-laws,   190
Then, kill, kill, kill, kill, kill, kill!

    Enter a GENTLEMAN [with Attendants].

    Gent. O, here he is!   Lay hand upon him.   Sir,
Your most dear daughter —
    Lear. No rescue?   What, a prisoner?   I am even
The natural fool of fortune.   Use me well;   195
You shall have ransom.   Let me have surgeons;
I am cut to th' brains.
    Gent.   You shall have anything.
    Lear. No seconds?   All myself?
Why, this would make a man a man of salt,
To use his eyes for garden water-pots,   200
[Ay, and laying autumn's dust.
    Gent.   Good sir, —]
    Lear. I will die bravely, like a smug bridegroom.
      What!
I will be jovial.   Come, come; I am a king,
My masters, know you that?
    Gent. You are a royal one, and we obey you.   205

119. luxury: lust.   121. forks: part of the head-dress.   snow: coldness, chastity.   122. minces: affects coyly.   124.
fitchew: pole-cat.   soiled: richly fed.   128. inherit: possess.   140. squiny: squint.   147. case: sockets.   167. cozener: petty
cheat.   169. [Plate] (Theobald).   Place F.   The reference is to plate armor.   172. able: warrant.   178. impertinency:
irrelevance.   187. block: hat.   198. seconds: supporters.   199. salt: tears.   201. [Ay ... sir] Q.   Om. F.

Lear. Then there's life in't. Come, an you get it, you shall get it by running. Sa, sa, sa, sa.
      [*Exit [running; attendants follow]*].

Gent. A sight most pitiful in the meanest wretch,
Past speaking of in a king! Thou hast [one] daughter
Who redeems Nature from the general curse   210
Which twain have brought her to.

Edg. Hail, gentle sir.

Gent.   Sir, speed you: what's your will?

Edg. Do you hear aught, sir, of a battle toward?

Gent. Most sure and vulgar; every one hears that,
Which can distinguish sound.

Edg.   But, by your favour,   215
How near's the other army?

Gent. Near and on speedy foot; the main descry
Stands on the hourly thought.

Edg.   I thank you, sir; that's all.

Gent. Though that the Queen on special cause is here,
Her army is mov'd on.   [*Exit*.

Edg.   I thank you, sir.   220

Glou. You ever-gentle gods, take my breath from me;
Let not my worser spirit tempt me again
To die before you please!

Edg.   Well pray you, father.

Glou. Now, good sir, what are you?

Edg. A most poor man, made tame to fortune's blows;   225
Who, by the art of known and feeling sorrows,
Am pregnant to good pity. Give me your hand,
I'll lead you to some biding.

Glou.   Hearty thanks;
The bounty and the benison of Heaven
To boot, and boot!

Enter Steward [OSWALD].

Osw. A proclaim'd prize! Most happy!   230
That eyeless head of thine was first fram'd flesh
To raise my fortunes. Thou old unhappy traitor,
Briefly thyself remember; the sword is out
That must destroy thee.

Glou.   Now let thy friendly hand
Put strength enough to't.   [*Edgar interposes.*]

Osw.   Wherefore, bold peasant,   235
Dar'st thou support a publish'd traitor? Hence;
Lest that the infection of his fortune take
Like hold on thee. Let go his arm.

Edg. 'Chill not let go, zir, without vurther 'casion.

Osw. Let go, slave, or thou diest!   241

Edg. Good gentleman, go your gait, and let poor volk pass. An 'chud ha' bin zwagger'd out of my life, 'twould not ha' bin zo long as 'tis by a vortnight. Nay, come not near th' old man; keep out, 'che vor ye, or Ise try whether your costard or my ballow be the harder. 'Chill be plain with you.   248

Osw. Out, dunghill!

Edg. 'Chill pick your teeth, zir. Come, no matter vor your foins.   251
      [*They fight, and Edgar knocks him down.*]

Osw. Slave, thou hast slain me. Villain, take my purse.
If ever thou wilt thrive, bury my body;
And give the letters which thou find'st about me   254
To Edmund Earl of Gloucester; seek him out
Upon the English party. O, untimely death!
Death!   [*Dies.*

Edg. I know thee well; a serviceable villain,
As duteous to the vices of thy mistress
As badness would desire.

Glou.   What, is he dead?

Edg. Sit you down, father; rest you.   260
Let's see these pockets; the letters that he speaks of
May be my friends. He's dead; I am only sorry
He had no other death's-man. Let us see.
Leave, gentle wax; and, manners, blame us not.
To know our enemies' minds, we rip their hearts;
Their papers, is more lawful.   266

(*Reads the letter.*) "Let our reciprocal vows be rememb'red. You have many opportunities to cut him off; if your will want not, time and place will be fruitfully offer'd. There is nothing done, if he return the conqueror; then am I the prisoner, and his bed my gaol; from the loathed warmth whereof deliver me, and supply the place for your labour.   274
      "Your — wife, so I would say —
            "Affectionate servant,
                  "GONERIL."

O indistinguish'd space of woman's will!
A plot upon her virtuous husband's life;
And the exchange my brother! Here, in the sands,   280
Thee I'll rake up, the post unsanctified
Of murderous lechers; and in the mature time
With this ungracious paper strike the sight
Of the death-practis'd duke. For him 'tis well
That of thy death and business I can tell.   285

Glou. The King is mad; how stiff is my vile sense
That I stand up and have ingenious feeling
Of my huge sorrows! Better I were distract;

---

209. [one] Q. *a* F. 213. **toward:** imminent. 214. **vulgar:** of common knowledge. 217-218. **the main ... thought:** every hour we expect to catch sight of the main body. 226. **art:** experience. 227. **pregnant:** ready. 228. **biding:** dwelling. 233. **thyself remember:** think on your soul's welfare. 239. **'Chill:** I will. Edgar takes the part of a peasant and uses Southern dialect. 243. **An 'chud:** if I could. 246. **'che vor:** I warn. **Ise:** I shall. **costard:** head. 248. **ballow:** cudgel. 251. **foins:** thrusts. 264. **Leave:** by your leave. 276. **servant:** lover. 278. **indistinguish'd space:** unlimited range. **will:** lust. 281. **rake:** cover. 284. **death-practis'd:** whose death is plotted. 287. **ingenious:** conscious.

[handwritten: Gloucester tries to run away from suffering. Edgar gains strength & dominates latter part of play.]

So should my thoughts be sever'd from my griefs,
                        [Drum afar off.
And woes by wrong imaginations lose   290
The knowledge of themselves.
    Edg.   Give me your hand.
Far off, methinks, I hear the beaten drum.
Come, father, I'll bestow you with a friend.
                        [Exeunt.

SCENE VII. *[A tent in the French camp.]*

Enter CORDELIA, KENT, *and* [DOCTOR].

    Cor. O thou good Kent, how shall I live and work
To match thy goodness? My life will be too short,
And every measure fail me.
    Kent. To be acknowledg'd, madam, is o'erpaid.
All my reports go with the modest truth;   5
Nor more nor clipp'd, but so.
    Cor.   Be better suited;
These weeds are memories of those worser hours.
I prithee, put them off.
    Kent.   Pardon, dear madam;
Yet to be known shortens my made intent.
My boon I make it, that you know me not   10
Till time and I think meet.
    Cor. Then be't so, my good lord. *[To the Doctor.]*
      How does the King?
    [*Doct.*] Madam, sleeps still.
    Cor. O you kind gods,
Cure this great breach in his abused nature!   15
Th' untun'd and jarring senses, O, wind up
Of this child-changed father!
    [*Doct.*]   So please your Majesty
That we may wake the King? He hath slept long.
    Cor. Be govern'd by your knowledge, and proceed
I' th' sway of your own will.

Enter LEAR *in a chair carried by* Servants.
    [GENTLEMAN *in attendance.*]
                  Is he array'd?   20
    Gent. Ay, madam; in the heaviness of sleep
We put fresh garments on him.
    [*Doct.*] Be by, good madam, when we do awake
      him;
I doubt [not] of his temperance.
    [*Cor.*]   Very well.
    Doct. Please you, draw near. — Louder the
      music there!]   25
    Cor. O my dear father! Restoration hang
Thy medicine on my lips; and let this kiss

Repair those violent harms that my two sisters
Have in thy reverence made!
    Kent.   Kind and dear princess!
    Cor. Had you not been their father, these white
      flakes   30
Did challenge pity of them. Was this a face
To be oppos'd against the [warring] winds?
[To stand against the deep dread-bolted thunder?
In the most terrible and nimble stroke
Of quick, cross lightning? to watch — poor perdu! —
With this thin helm?] Mine enemy's dog,   36
Though he had bit me, should have stood that night
Against my fire; and wast thou fain, poor father,
To hovel thee with swine and rogues forlorn
In short and musty straw? Alack, alack!   40
'Tis wonder that thy life and wits at once
Had not concluded all. He wakes; speak to him.
    Doct. Madam, do you; 'tis fittest.
    Cor. How does my royal lord? How fares your
      Majesty?
    Lear. You do me wrong to take me out o' th'
      grave.   45
Thou art a soul in bliss; but I am bound
Upon a wheel of fire, that mine own tears
Do scald like molten lead.
    Cor.   Sir, do you know me?
    Lear. You are a spirit, I know; where did you die?
    Cor. Still, still, far wide!   50
    Doct. He's scarce awake; let him alone a while.
    Lear. Where have I been? Where am I? Fair
      daylight?
I am mightily abus'd. I should ev'n die with pity,
To see another thus. I know not what to say.
I will not swear these are my hands. Let's see; 55
I feel this pin prick. Would I were assur'd
Of my condition!
    Cor.   O, look upon me, sir,
And hold your hand in benediction o'er me.
[No, sir,] you must not kneel.
    Lear.   Pray, do not mock me.
I am a very foolish fond old man,   60
Fourscore and upward, not an hour more nor less;
And, to deal plainly,
I fear I am not in my perfect mind.
Methinks I should know you, and know this man;
Yet I am doubtful; for I am mainly ignorant 65
What place this is, and all the skill I have
Remembers not these garments; nor I know not
Where I did lodge last night. Do not laugh at me;
For, as I am a man, I think this lady
To be my child Cordelia.

---

293. bestow: lodge.
Sc. vii, s.d. [DOCTOR] Q. *Gentlemen* F. 9. shortens: interferes with. made: prearranged. 13, 17, 23. [*Doct.*] Q. *Gent.* F. 16. wind up. The figure is of a stringed instrument. 17. child-changed: changed by his children's conduct. 24. [not] Q. Om. F. temperance: sanity. 24–25. [*Cor.*...there] Q. Om. F. 32. [warring] Q. *iarring* F. 33–36. [To... helm?] Q. Om. F. 35. cross: zigzag. perdu: a sentinel placed in a dangerous station. 36. helm: covering (of hair). 42. all: altogether. 50. wide: astray. 59. [No, sir] Q. Om. F. 65. mainly: completely.

Cordelia cannot speak
when in deep emotion
few words show
the emotion

Cor.   And so I am, I am.   70
Lear. Be your tears wet? Yes, faith. I pray,
     weep not.
If you have poison for me, I will drink it.
I know you do not love me; for your sisters
Have, as I do remember, done me wrong: 74
You have some cause, they have not.
Cor.   No cause, no cause.
Lear. Am I in France?
Kent.   In your own kingdom, sir.
Lear. Do not abuse me.
Doct. Be comforted, good madam; the great rage,
You see, is kill'd in him: [and yet it is danger
To make him even o'er the time he has lost.]   80
Desire him to go in; trouble him no more
Till further settling.
Cor. Will't please your Highness walk?
Lear.   You must bear with me.
Pray you now, forget and forgive; I am old and
     foolish.
               [*Exeunt* [*all but Kent and Gentleman*].
[*Gent.* Holds it true, sir, that the Duke of Corn-
wall was so slain?   86
Kent. Most certain, sir.
Gent. Who is conductor of his people?
Kent. As 'tis said, the bastard son of Gloucester.
Gent. They say Edgar, his banish'd son, is with
the Earl of Kent in Germany.   91
Kent. Report is changeable. 'Tis time to look
about; the powers of the kingdom approach apace.
Gent. The arbitrement is like to be bloody.
Fare you well, sir.   [*Exit.*] 96
Kent. My point and period will be throughly
     wrought,
Or well or ill, as this day's battle's fought.] [*Exit.*

ACT V

SCENE I. [*The British camp, near Dover.*]

Enter, with drum and colours, EDMUND, REGAN,
Gentlemen, *and* Soldiers.

Edm. Know of the Duke if his last purpose hold,
Or whether since he is advis'd by aught
To change the course. He's full of alteration
And self-reproving; bring his constant pleasure.
               [*To a Gentleman, who goes out.*]
Reg. Our sister's man is certainly miscarried. 5
Edm. 'Tis to be doubted, madam.
Reg.   Now, sweet lord,
You know the goodness I intend upon you.

Tell me — but truly — but then speak the truth,
Do you not love my sister?
Edm.   In honour'd love.
Reg. But have you never found my brother's
     way   10
To the forfended place?
[*Edm.*   That thought abuses you.
Reg. I am doubtful that you have been conjunct
And bosom'd with her, — as far as we call hers.]
Edm. No, by mine honour, madam.
Reg. I never shall endure her. Dear my lord,
Be not familiar with her.
Edm.   Fear me not.   16
She and the Duke her husband!

Enter, with drum and colours, ALBANY, GONERIL,
and Soldiers.

[*Gon.* [*Aside.*] I had rather lose the battle than
     that sister
Should loosen him and me.]
Alb. Our very loving sister, well be-met.   20
Sir, this I heard: the King is come to his daughter,
With others whom the rigour of our state
Forc'd to cry out. [Where I could not be honest,
I never yet was valiant. For this business,
It toucheth us, as France invades our land,   25
Not bolds the King, with others, whom, I fear,
Most just and heavy causes make oppose.
Edm. Sir, you speak nobly.] *Sarcastic*
Reg.   Why is this reason'd?
Gon. Combine together 'gainst the enemy;
For these domestic and particular broils   30
Are not the question here.
Alb.   Let's then determine
With the ancient of war on our proceeding.
[*Edm.* I shall attend you presently at your tent.]
Reg. Sister, you'll go with us?
Gon. No.   35
Reg. 'Tis most convenient; pray you, go with us.
Gon. [*Aside.*] O, ho, I know the riddle. — I will
     go.   [*Exeunt both the armies.*

[*As they are going out,*] *enter* EDGAR [*disguised.*
Albany remains*].

Edg. If e'er your Grace had speech with man so
     poor,
Hear me one word.
Alb.   I'll overtake you. — Speak.
Edg. Before you fight the battle, ope this letter.
If you have victory, let the trumpet sound   41
For him that brought it. Wretched though I seem,
challenge to be resolv'd

79–80. **[and … lost]** Q. Om. F. 85–98. **[Gent. … fought]** Q. Om. F. 97. **My … period:** the question of my end.
Act V, sc. i, 4. constant pleasure: fixed decision. 5. **is … miscarried:** has met disaster. 6. **doubted:** feared. Cf. l. 12,
doubtful. 11. **forfended:** forbidden. **abuses:** deceives. 11–13. **[Edm. … hers]** Q. Om. F. 13. **bosom'd:** intimate. **as
… hers:** to the utmost limit. 18–19. **[Gon. … me]** Q. Om. F. 23–28. **[Where … nobly]** Q. Om. F. 26. **Not bolds:**
not as it encourages. 28. **reason'd:** discussed. 32. **ancient:** veterans. 33. **[Edm. … tent]** Q. Om. F. 36. **convenient:**
suitable.

Edgar ready to accept everything life bring

ACT V, SCENE III   KING LEAR   611

I can produce a champion that will prove
What is avouched there. If you miscarry,
Your business of the world hath so an end,   45
And machination ceases. Fortune love you!
 Alb. Stay till I have read the letter.
 Edg.   I was forbid it.
When time shall serve, let but the herald cry,
And I'll appear again.   [*Exit.*
 Alb. Why, fare thee well; I will o'erlook thy
  paper.   50

    Re-enter EDMUND.

 Edm. The enemy's in view; draw up your powers.
Here is the guess of their true strength and forces
By diligent discovery; but your haste
Is now urg'd on you.
 Alb.   We will greet the time.
          [*Exit.*
 Edm. To both these sisters have I sworn my
  love;   55
Each jealous of the other as the stung
Are of the adder. Which of them shall I take?
Both? one? or neither? Neither can be enjoy'd,
If both remain alive. To take the widow
Exasperates, makes mad her sister Goneril;   60
And hardly shall I carry out my side,
Her husband being alive. Now then we'll use
His countenance for the battle; which being done,
Let her who would be rid of him devise
His speedy taking off. As for the mercy   65
Which he intends to Lear and to Cordelia,
The battle done, and they within our power,
Shall never see his pardon; for my state
Stands on me to defend, not to debate. [*Exit.*

  Shortest battle in Shakespeare.

 SCENE II. [*A field between the two camps.*]

*Alarum within. Enter, with drum and colours,
Lear, Cordelia, and Soldiers, over the stage; and
exeunt.*

  Enter EDGAR *and* GLOUCESTER.

 Edg. Here, father, take the shadow of this tree
For your good host; pray that the right may thrive.
If ever I return to you again,
I'll bring you comfort.
 Glou.   Grace go with you, sir!
        [*Exit* [*Edgar.*]

Alarum and retreat within. Re-enter EDGAR.

 Edg. Away, old man; give me thy hand; away!   5
King Lear hath lost, he and his daughter ta'en.

Give me thy hand; come on.
 Glou. No further, sir; a man may rot even here.
 Edg. What, in ill thoughts again? Men must
  endure
Their going hence even as their coming hither;   10
Ripeness is all. Come on.
 Glou.   And that's true too.
         [*Exeunt.*

 SCENE III. [*The British camp near Dover.*]

Enter, in conquest, with drum and colours, EDMUND;
 LEAR *and* CORDELIA *as prisoners:* CAPTAIN,
 Soldiers, *etc.*

 Edm. Some officers take them away. Good
  guard,
Until their greater pleasures first be known
That are to censure them.
 Cor.   We are not the first
Who with best meaning have incurr'd the worst.
For thee, oppressed king, I am cast down;   5
Myself could else out-frown false Fortune's frown.
Shall we not see these daughters and these sis-
  ters?
 Lear. No, no, no, no! Come, let's away to
  prison;
We two alone will sing like birds i' th' cage.
When thou dost ask me blessing, I'll kneel down   10
And ask of thee forgiveness. So we'll live,
And pray, and sing, and tell old tales, and laugh
At gilded butterflies, and hear poor rogues
Talk of court news; and we'll talk with them too,
Who loses and who wins; who's in, who's out;   15
And take upon 's the mystery of things
As if we were God's spies; and we'll wear out,
In a wall'd prison, packs and sects of great ones,
That ebb and flow by th' moon.
 Edm.   Take them away.
 Lear. Upon such sacrifices, my Cordelia,   20
The gods themselves throw incense. Have I
  caught thee?
He that parts us shall bring a brand from heaven,
And fire us hence like foxes. Wipe thine eyes;
The good-years shall devour them, flesh and fell,
Ere they shall make us weep. We'll see 'em
  starv'd first.   25
Come. [*Exeunt* [*Lear and Cordelia, guarded*].
 Edm. Come hither, captain; hark.
Take thou this note [*giving a paper*]; go follow them
  to prison.
One step I have advanc'd thee; if thou dost
As this instructs thee, thou dost make thy way
To noble fortunes. Know thou this, that men   30

---

53. **discovery:** scouting. 54. **greet the time:** meet the occasion. 69. **Stands on:** requires.
Sc. ii, 2. host: shelterer.
 Sc. iii, 2. their greater pleasures: the desires of those greater persons. 3. **censure:** judge. 17. **God's spies:** spies on God's ways. 23. **foxes.** Foxes were driven from their holes by fire and smoke. 24. **good-years:** an expression for some vague evil influence. **fell:** skin.

Are as the time is; to be tender-minded
Does not become a sword. Thy great employment
Will not bear question; either say thou'lt do't,
Or thrive by other means.
    Capt.   I'll do't, my lord.
    Edm. About it; and write happy when thou'st
      done.   35
Mark, I say instantly; and carry it so
As I have set it down.
    [*Capt.* I cannot draw a cart, nor eat dried oats;
If it be man's work, I'll do't.]   [*Exit.*

    Flourish. Enter ALBANY, GONERIL, REGAN,
      [*another* CAPTAIN] *and* Soldiers.

    Alb. Sir, you have show'd to-day your valiant
      strain,   40
And fortune led you well. You have the captives
Who were the opposites of this day's strife;
I do require them of you, so to use them
As we shall find their merits and our safety
May equally determine.
    Edm.   Sir, I thought it fit   45
To send the old and miserable king
To some retention [and appointed guard];
Whose age had charms in it, whose title more,
To pluck the common bosom on his side,
And turn our impress'd lances in our eyes   50
Which do command them. With him I sent the
    Queen,
My reason all the same; and they are ready
To-morrow, or at further space, t' appear
Where you shall hold your session. [At this time
We sweat and bleed: the friend hath lost his friend;
And the best quarrels, in the heat, are curs'd   56
By those that feel their sharpness:
The question of Cordelia and her father
Requires a fitter place.]
    Alb.   Sir, by your patience,
I hold you but a subject of this war,   60
Not as a brother.
    Reg.   That's as we list to grace him.
Methinks our pleasure might have been demanded,
Ere you had spoke so far. He led our powers,
Bore the commission of my place and person;
The which immediacy may well stand up,   65
And call itself your brother.
    Gon.   Not so hot.
In his own grace he doth exalt himself,
More than in your addition.
    Reg.   In my rights,
By me invested, he compeers the best.

    Alb. That were the most, if he should husband
      you.   70
    Reg. Jesters do oft prove prophets.
    Gon.   Holla, holla!
That eye that told you so look'd but a-squint.
    Reg. Lady, I am not well; else I should answer
From a full-flowing stomach. General,
Take thou my soldiers, prisoners, patrimony;   75
Dispose of them, of me; the walls are thine.
Witness the world, that I create thee here
My lord and master.
    Gon.   Mean you to enjoy him?
    Alb. The let-alone lies not in your good will.
    Edm. Nor in thine, lord.
    Alb.   Half-blooded fellow, yes.   80
    Reg. [*To Edmund.*] Let the drum strike, and
      prove my title thine.
    Alb. Stay yet; hear reason. Edmund, I arrest thee
On capital treason; and, in thy arrest,
This gilded serpent. [*Pointing to Gon.*] For your
    claim, fair sister,
I bar it in the interest of my wife.   85
'Tis she is sub-contracted to this lord,
And I, her husband, contradict your bans.
If you will marry, make your loves to me,
My lady is bespoke.
    Gon.   An interlude!
    Alb. Thou art arm'd, Gloucester; let the trumpet
      sound.   90
If none appear to prove upon thy person
Thy heinous, manifest, and many treasons,
There is my pledge [*throwing down a glove*]. I'll
    [prove] it on thy heart,
Ere I taste bread, thou art in nothing less
Than I have here proclaim'd thee.
    Reg.   Sick, O, sick! 95
    Gon. [*Aside.*] If not, I'll ne'er trust medicine.
    Edm. There's my exchange [*throwing down a
      glove*]. What in the world he is
That names me traitor, villain-like he lies.
Call by the trumpet; — he that dares approach,
On him, on you, who not? I will maintain   100
My truth and honour firmly.
    Alb. A herald, ho!
    [*Edm.*   A herald, ho, a herald!]
    Alb. Trust to thy single virtue; for thy soldiers,
All levied in my name, have in my name   104
Took their discharge.
    Reg.   My sickness grows upon me.
    Alb. She is not well; convey her to my tent.
            [*Exit Regan, led.*]

32. sword: soldier. 35. write happy: call yourself lucky. 38-39. [*Capt*....do't] Q. Om. F. 47. [and...guard] Q. Om. F. 49. common bosom: affection of the multitude. 50. impress'd lances: weapons of our soldiers who have been pressed into our army. 54-59. [At...place] Q. Om. F. 65. immediacy: close connection. 68. your addition: what you call him. 69. compeers: equals. 74. stomach: anger. 76. the walls. Theobald proposed to read they all. 79. let-alone: power of preventing it. 89. interlude: comedy. 93. [prove] Q. make F. 102. [*Edm*....herald] Q. Om. F. 103. virtue: strength.

duel- theatrical scene
— combat between 2 brothers.

Enter a HERALD.

Come hither, herald, — Let the trumpet sound —
And read out this.
   [*Capt.* Sound, trumpet!]   109
                      [*A trumpet sounds.*
   Her. (*Reads.*) "If any man of quality or degree
within the lists of the army will maintain upon
Edmund, supposed Earl of Goucester, that he is a
manifold traitor, let him appear by the third sound
of the trumpet. He is bold in his defence."   114
   [*Edm.* Sound!]   [*First trumpet.*
   Her. Again!   [*Second trumpet.*
   Her. Again!   [*Third trumpet.*
              [*Trumpet answers within.*

Enter EDGAR, *at the third sound, armed, with
a trumpet before him.*

   Alb. Ask him his purposes, why he appears
Upon this call o' th' trumpet.
   Her.   What are you?
Your name, your quality? and why you answer   120
This present summons?
   Edg.   Know, my name is lost,
By treason's tooth bare-gnawn and canker-bit,
Yet am I noble as the adversary
I come to cope.
   Alb.   Which is that adversary?
   Edg. What's he that speaks for Edmund Earl of
     Gloucester?   125
   Edm. Himself; what say'st thou to him?
   Edg.   Draw thy sword.
That, if my speech offend a noble heart,
Thy arm may do thee justice; here is mine.
Behold, it is the privilege of mine honours,
My oath, and my profession. I protest,   130
Maugre thy strength, place, youth, and eminence,
Despite thy victor-sword and fire-new fortune,
Thy valour, and thy heart, thou art a traitor;
False to thy gods, thy brother, and thy father;
Conspirant 'gainst this high illustrious prince;   135
And, from th' extremest upward of thy head
To the descent and dust below thy foot,
A most toad-spotted traitor. Say thou "No,"
This sword, this arm, and my best spirits are bent
To prove upon thy heart, whereto I speak,   140
Thou liest.
   Edm.   In wisdom I should ask thy name;
But, since thy outside looks so fair and warlike,
And that thy tongue some 'say of breeding breathes,
What safe and nicely I might well delay
By rule of knighthood, I disdain and spurn.   145
Back do I toss these treasons to thy head;

With the hell-hated lie o'erwhelm thy heart;
Which, for they yet glance by and scarcely bruise,
This sword of mine shall give them instant way
Where they shall rest for ever. Trumpets, speak!
     [*Alarums. They fight.* [*Edmund falls.*]
   Alb. Save him, save him!   151
   Gon.   This is [mere] practice, Gloucester.
By th' law of war thou wast not bound to answer
An unknown opposite. Thou art not vanquish'd,
But cozen'd and beguil'd.
   Alb.   Shut your mouth, dame,
Or with this paper shall I stop it. Hold, sir. —   155
Thou worse than any name, read thine own evil.
No tearing, lady; I perceive you know it.
   Gon. Say, if I do, the laws are mine, not thine.
Who can arraign me for't?   [*Exit.*]
   Alb.   Most monstrous! oh! —
Know'st thou this paper?
   Edm.   Ask me not what I know.   160
   Alb. Go after her; she's desperate; govern her.
   Edm. What you have charg'd me with, that have
    I done;
And more, much more; the time will bring it out.
'Tis past, and so am I. But what art thou
That hast this fortune on me? If thou'rt noble,   165
I do forgive thee.
   Edg.   Let's exchange charity.
I am no less in blood than thou art, Edmund;
If more, the more thou'st wrong'd me.
My name is Edgar, and thy father's son.
The gods are just, and of our pleasant vices,   170
Make instruments to plague us.
The dark and vicious place where thee he got
Cost him his eyes.
   Edm.   Thou'st spoken right, 'tis true.
The wheel is come full circle; I am here.
   Alb. Methought thy very gait did prophesy   175
A royal nobleness. I must embrace thee.
Let sorrow split my heart, if ever I
Did hate thee or thy father!
   Edg.   Worthy prince, I know't.
   Alb. Where have you hid yourself?
How have you known the miseries of your father?
   Edg. By nursing them, my lord. List a brief
    tale;   181
And when 'tis told, oh, that my heart would burst!
The bloody proclamation to escape,
That follow'd me so near, — oh, our lives' sweetness!
That we the pain of death would hourly die   185
Rather than die at once! — taught me to shift
Into a madman's rags, t' assume a semblance
That very dogs disdain'd; and in this habit
Met I my father with his bleeding rings,   189

109. [*Capt.* ... trumpet!] Q. Om. F. 112. supposed: pretended. 115. [*Edm.* Sound!] Q. Om. F. 122. canker-bit: worm-eaten. 129. the privilege (Pope). *my privilege, The* F. honours: rank. 131. Maugre: in spite of. 132. fire-new: brand-new. 137. descent: lowest part. 143. 'say: trace. 144. safe and nicely: safely and with technical correctness. 151. [mere] Q. Om. F. 161. govern: restrain.

noble didn't have to fight anyone of lower rank
*— Edmund willing to take chance - didn't know it
was Edgar.*

Their precious stones new lost; became his guide,
Led him, begg'd for him, sav'd him from despair;
Never, — O fault! — reveal'd myself unto him,
Until some half-hour past, when I was arm'd.
Not sure, though hoping, of this good success,   195
I ask'd his blessing, and from first to last
Told him our pilgrimage; but his flaw'd heart,
Alack, too weak the conflict to support!
'Twixt two extremes of passion, joy and grief,
Burst smilingly.
   Edm.   This speech of yours hath mov'd me,
And shall perchance do good. But speak you on;
You look as you had something more to say.   201
   Alb. If there be more, more woeful, hold it in;
For I am almost ready to dissolve,
Hearing of this.
   [*Edg.*   This would have seem'd a period
To such as love not sorrow; but another,   205
To amplify too much, would make much more,
And top extremity.
Whilst I was big in clamour came there in a man,
Who, having seen me in my worst estate,
Shunn'd my abhorr'd society; but then, finding   210
Who 'twas that so endur'd, with his strong arms
He fastened on my neck, and bellowed out
As he'd burst heaven; threw him on my father;
Told the most piteous tale of Lear and him
That ever ear receiv'd; which in recounting,   215
His grief grew puissant, and the strings of life
Began to crack. Twice then the trumpets sounded,
And there I left him tranc'd.
   Alb.   But who was this?
   Edg. Kent, sir, the banish'd Kent; who in disguise
Follow'd his enemy king, and did him service   220
Improper for a slave.]

     Enter a GENTLEMAN *with a bloody knife.*

   Gent. Help, help, O, help!
   Edg.   What kind of help?
   Alb.   Speak, man.
   Edg. What means this bloody knife?
   Gent.   'Tis hot, it smokes;
It came even from the heart of — O, she's dead!
   Alb. Who dead? Speak, man.   225
   Gent. Your lady, sir, your lady; and her sister
By her is poison'd; she confesses it.
   Edm. I was contracted to them both. All three
Now marry in an instant.
   Edg.   Here comes Kent.

     Enter KENT.

   Alb. Produce the bodies, be they alive or dead.
This judgement of the heavens, that makes us
     tremble,   231

Touches us not with pity.   [*Exit Gentleman.*]
     — O, is this he?
The time will not allow the compliment
Which very manners urges.
   Kent.   I am come
To bid my king and master aye good-night.   235
Is he not here?
   Alb.   Great thing of us forgot!
Speak, Edmund, where's the King? and where's
     Cordelia?
     [*The bodies of* Goneril *and* Regan *are
       brought in.*
See'st thou this object, Kent?
   Kent. Alack, why thus?
   Edm.   Yet Edmund was belov'd!
The one the other poison'd for my sake,   240
And after slew herself.
   Alb. Even so. Cover their faces.
   Edm. I pant for life. Some good I mean to do,
Despite of mine own nature. Quickly send,
Be brief in it, to th' castle; for my writ   245
Is on the life of Lear and on Cordelia.
Nay, send in time.
   Alb.   Run, run, O, run!
   Edg. To who, my lord? Who has the office?
     Send
Thy token of reprieve.
   Edm. Well thought on. Take my sword,   250
Give it the captain.
   Edg.   Haste thee, for thy life.
     [*Exit Gentleman.*]
   Edm. He hath commission from thy wife and me
To hang Cordelia in the prison, and
To lay the blame upon her own despair,
That she fordid herself.   255
   Alb. The gods defend her! Bear him hence a
     while.   [*Edmund is borne off.*]

     Re-enter LEAR *with Cordelia in his arms*
       [GENTLEMAN *following*].

   Lear. Howl, howl, howl! O, you are men of
     stones!
Had I your tongues and eyes, I'd use them so
That heaven's vault should crack. She's gone
     for ever!
I know when one is dead, and when one lives;   260
She's dead as earth. Lend me a looking-glass;
If that her breath will mist or stain the stone,
Why, then she lives.
   Kent.   Is this the promis'd end?
   Edg. Or image of that horror?
   Alb.   Fall, and cease!
   Lear. This feather stirs; she lives! If it be so,
It is a chance which does redeem all sorrows   266

---

196. **flaw'd:** cracked. 204–221. [*Edg.... slave*] Q. Om. F. 205–207. **but ... extremity:** one more such circumstance, amplifying what is already too much, would increase it and pass all limits. 208. **big in clamour:** loud in grief. 213. **him** (Theobald). *me* Q. 218. **tranc'd:** unconscious. 255. **fordid:** destroyed. 262. **stone:** polished crystal, mirror. 263. **promis'd end:** Last Judgment.

[handwritten: Lear never consistent recognizes preoccupied with cordelia]

That ever I have felt.

Kent. [*Kneeling.*] O my good master!

Lear. Prithee, away.

Edg.   'Tis noble Kent, your friend.

Lear. A plague upon you, murderers, traitors all!
I might have sav'd her; now she's gone for ever!   270
Cordelia, Cordelia! stay a little. Ha!
What is't thou say'st? Her voice was ever soft,
Gentle, and low; an excellent thing in woman. ✓
I kill'd the slave that was a-hanging thee.

Gent. 'Tis true, my lords, he did.

Lear.   Did I not, fellow?   275
I have seen the day, with my good biting falchion
I would have made him skip. I am old now,
And these same crosses spoil me. Who are you?
Mine eyes are not o' th' best. I'll tell you straight.

Kent. If Fortune brag of two she lov'd and
    hated,   280
One of them we behold.

Lear. This is a dull sight. Are you not Kent?

Kent.   The same,
Your servant Kent. Where is your servant Caius?

Lear. He's a good fellow, I can tell you that;
He'll strike, and quickly too. He's dead and rotten.

Kent. No, my good lord; I am the very man, —

Lear. I'll see that straight.   287

Kent. — That, from your first of difference and
    decay,
Have follow'd your sad steps —

Lear.   You are welcome hither.

Kent. Nor no man else; All's cheerless, dark,
    and deadly.   290
Your eldest daughters have fordone themselves,
And desperately are dead.

Lear.   Ay, so I think.

Alb. He knows not what he says; and vain is it
That we present us to him. *[handwritten: whole mind on Cordelia]*

Enter a MESSENGER.

Edg.   Very bootless.

Mess. Edmund is dead, my lord.

Alb.   That's but a trifle here. —   295 *[handwritten: little out & under her but]*
You lords and noble friends, know our intent. *[handwritten: necessary]*
What comfort to this great decay may come *[handwritten: for rounding]*
Shall be appli'd. For us, we will resign,
During the life of this old majesty, *[handwritten: albany's intentions]*
To him our absolute power; [*to Edgar and Kent*]
    you, to your rights,   300
With boot, and such addition as your honours
Have more than merited. All friends shall taste
The wages of their virtue, and all foes
The cup of their deservings. O, see, see!

Lear. And my poor fool is hang'd! No, no, no *[handwritten: Cordelia]*
    life!   305
Why should a dog, a horse, a rat, have life,
And thou no breath at all? Thou'lt come no more,
Never, never, never, never, never! *[handwritten: force — decisive line]*
Pray you, undo this button. Thank you, sir.
Do you see this? Look on her, look, her lips,   310 *[handwritten: have to bring things back to earth]*
Look there, look there! *[handwritten: heart breaks]* . [*Dies.*]

Edg.   He faints! My lord, my lord!

Kent. Break, heart; I prithee, break!

Edg.   Look up, my lord.

Kent. Vex not his ghost; O, let him pass! He *[handwritten: yet can't bother]*
    hates him
That would upon the rack of this tough world
Stretch him out longer.

Edg.   He is gone, indeed.   315

Kent. The wonder is he hath endur'd so long;
He but usurp'd his life.

Alb. Bear them from hence. Our present
    business
Is general woe. [*To Kent and Edgar.*] Friends of
    my soul, you twain
Rule in this realm, and the gor'd state sustain.   320

Kent. I have a journey, sir, shortly to go.
My master calls me; I must not say no.

Edg. The weight of this sad time we must obey;
Speak what we feel, not what we ought to say.
The oldest hath borne most; we that are young   325
Shall never see so much, nor live so long.
       [*Exeunt, with a dead march.*

278. **crosses:** sufferings.   288. **first...decay:** beginning of the change and decay of your fortunes.   305. **poor fool:** *[handwritten: pet name]* Cordelia.   320. **gor'd:** wounded.   323. *Edg.* F. *Duke* Q.

[handwritten: Fool, Kent, Cordelia, Gloucester — Lear's greatest friends all gone.]

The Tragedy of Macbeth

MACBETH, NEXT TO *The Comedy of Errors*, Shakespeare's shortest play, was first published in the Folio of 1623, which consequently becomes the basis for all modern texts. The nature of the stage directions suggests that a theatrical manuscript, probably a transcript of the original with revisions, served as copy. The play's exceptional brevity, along with an abnormal number of broken lines, occasionally abrupt transitions, considerable misline-ation, and mangling of metre, points to abridgment. On the other hand, such hints of cutting are offset by evidence of additions, and it is unlikely that the play was ever significantly longer than the surviving version. In particular, III.v. and IV.i.39–43, introducing the superfluous character of Hecate, whose speeches differ from the rest of the play in tone and metre, are manifest intrusions. Stage directions at III.v.34 and IV.i.43 call for songs which are to be found in full in *The Witch* by Thomas Middleton (c. 1614), and these, together with the appearance of Hecate as a conspicuous character in that play, strongly suggest Middleton as the interpolator. The genuineness of other portions has also been doubted (e.g., I.ii., I.iii.1–37, II.iii.1–23, III.vi., IV. iii.140–59, V.vi., and V.viii). These passages cannot all be discussed, but the authenticity of most of them can be reasonably vindicated. For example, the second scene of the play, though perhaps not memorable, provides imperative exposition quite adequately. The soliloquy of the Porter (II.iii), with its rare blend of low humor and high irony, ought never to have failed of appreciation. Act III, scene vi, presents another expository colloquy not unworthy of Shakespeare; the irony of Lennox should not be missed, and the fact that his interlocutor is an anonymous Lord need disturb nobody.

Several matters bear upon the date of the play, though none is conclusive. When King James visited Oxford on August 27, 1605, his advent was celebrated by a little drama enacted at the gates. Three students, dressed as Sibyls, recited Latin verses (by Dr. Matthew Gwinne) based upon the prophesies of the weird sisters to Banquo, the fabled head of James's royal line, and hailed the King in sequence as ruler of Scotland, England, and Ireland, and again as sovereign of Great Britain, Ireland, and France (cf. IV.i.121–22). It is entirely plausible that Shakespeare was moved by a report of this episode, which greatly pleased the King, to turn again to his favorite Holinshed, where he knew the story of Banquo was to be found, and that, doing so, he became inspired to write a play, not around Banquo, concerning whom dramatic material was insufficient, but around his more vivid associate, Macbeth. Though Banquo could not serve for protagonist, Shakespeare (was he not one of the King's men?) found other ways of gratifying James. Naturally he stresses the integrity of Banquo in contrast to the criminality of Macbeth (which involves, incidentally, a diplomatic departure from his source, for Holinshed represents Banquo as Macbeth's accomplice) and emphasizes the prophecy respecting Banquo's descendants. He alludes deferentially to the healing of scrofula by royal touch (IV.iii.146 ff.), a practice in which James had been ceremoniously indulging since the winter of 1604. If, as is conceivable, the Porter's treasonable equivocator (II.iii. 9–12) glances at the Jesuit Superior, Henry Garnet, who in his trial (1606) for complicity in the Gunpowder Plot defended the doctrine of equivocation, James must have been duly appreciative. All in all, it seems likely that *Macbeth* was composed near the middle or end of 1606, and a recollection of Banquo's Ghost in *The Knight of the Burning Pestle* (Beaumont and Fletcher, 1607) confirms the probability. It has been conjectured that Shakespeare prepared *Macbeth* with special reference to a performance at Court and that when his company gave three plays (unnamed in the Revels Account) for the entertainment of "his Maiestie and the kinge of Denmarke" in the summer of 1606, *Macbeth* was offered as new.

As already noted, the source for *Macbeth* is the *Chronicles* of Holinshed. Most of the substance is taken from the account of the reigns of Duncan and Macbeth (A.D. 1034–1057), but Shakespeare has made the rebellion of Macdonwald and the invasion by the Norwegian Sueno, though originally independent activities, sequential episodes of the same campaign, and has enriched dramatic effect by details drawn from other parts of the *Chronicles*. Thus, whereas the *Chronicles* record the assassination of Duncan in the single statement that Macbeth slew him at Inverness, Shakespeare appropriates the drugging of the grooms and the portents described in II.iv from the account of the murder of Duncan's ancestor Duffe (A.D. 972); and the voice that cried "Sleep no more!" to the troubled conscience of Duffe's brother Kenneth (who had poisoned a nephew) is assigned to harry the mind of Macbeth.

Of the witches Holinshed writes: " ... the common opinion was, that these women were either the weird sisters, that is (as ye would say) the goddesses of destinie, or else some nymphs or feiries, indued with knowledge of prophesie by their necromanticall science, bicause everie thing came to passe as they had spoken." It may be that from this somewhat non-committal statement Shakespeare's imagination apprehended these creatures unequivocally as powers of destiny, the Norns of Scandinavian mythology, but it cannot be proved that he knew about the Norns. Furthermore, as Shakespeare pursued the story in Holinshed, he found the influence of these figures upon Macbeth superseded by that of others. It was "certeine wizzards, in whose words he put great confidence," who told him "how that he ought to take heed of Makduffe," and the prediction that "he should never be slaine with man borne of anie woman, nor vanquished till the wood of Bernane came to the castell of Dunsinane" was made by "a certeine witch, whome hee had in great trust" (cf. IV.i.71–72, 92–94). The several oracular agents in Holinshed were fused by Shakespeare into the prophetic "instruments of darkness" of his play. Though the text consistently names them "weird sisters" (or an equivalent), in the stage directions they are called simply "witches"; and the figures they cut upon the stage and the language they speak are in accord with this conception. Shakespeare's audiences must have viewed these "secret, black, and midnight hags" in the light of current witch lore, but they may also have felt that they were no common witches, since Shakespeare has raised them to a fresh level of imagination, giving them an unearthly air and a spiritual significance in relation to the character of Macbeth.

To Shakespeare's Macbeth crime is at the outset neither natural nor congenial. Unlike the Macbeth of Holinshed, who is described as "somewhat cruel of nature," he is, when the play opens, a man of unblemished record. He is a gentleman of honor and a superlative soldier, and the "golden opinions" lately won "from all sorts of people" through his heroic achievements in the field bear no shadow of reservation. To these testimonies is added the private judgment of his wife, who stresses his probity and his humanity, in what is unquestionably a candid and true evaluation of him (I.v.17–26). Macbeth is "not without ambition," but ambition is proper to a man of his station, and Macbeth, she says, would not "play false" in the pursuit of it. Left to himself, Macbeth would not have fallen to crime, but a unique combination of temptation and circumstance coerce his will. Macbeth has no justification for killing Duncan, and every reason for not, as he knows only too well, and when he says (I.vii. 25–27) that he has no incitement but ambition he is honest with himself. The native ambition to which his wife has referred becomes perverted; one must therefore inquire what that ambition may earlier have amounted to.

On that point evidence is reasonably clear, but it must be interpreted carefully. Macbeth's excitement, perceptible to Banquo, upon the witches' prophetic salutation (I.iii.48–50) and the readiness with which he imagines murder as, after the immediate confirmation respecting Cawdor, he ponders the "supernatural solicitings," suggest that the witches have quickened a thought that is not new in Macbeth's mind. One may legitimately suppose that Macbeth had wished for the kingship, the monarchy in Scotland being elective (cf. I.iv.37–50; II.iv.29–32); but that he had heretofore seriously entertained criminal means of getting it is not a necessary consequence. The image of murder that rises in his mind (I.iii.130 ff.) betrays no contemplated purpose or antecedent temptation; rather it is the way in which his abnormally sensitive imagination develops the inevitable thought that unless he should murder Duncan, the prophecy of his future kingship must be long in fulfillment. The horror inspired by the notion argues that he has not made it familiar, and the natural conclusion for the moment comes in his words, "If chance will have me King, why, chance may crown me without my stir." The utterances of the witches, nevertheless, are calculated to rouse an ambitious man, and the thought of murder as the nearest way of realizing the "greatest" of them, repellent though he finds it, will not out of Macbeth's mind; so that when he reaches home, his wife reads in his face what he has been thinking (I.v.63 ff.). She too has been thinking about murder, and with her, thoughts are purposes. Though neither of them utters the word, Macbeth understands that she has resolved upon murder as the course to take, and he ends their talk with a determination to "speak further." It is during this further conversation, which we must think of as taking place between this action and the beginning of scene vii, that Macbeth makes up his mind, for when we hear him then in soliloquy, he has fixed his intent. At least, so he believes. When shortly Lady Macbeth taunts him in an effort to screw his failing courage to the sticking point, she refers to matters in their off-stage talk (I.vii.35 ff.). And it is her slurs upon his courage that finally rivet his resolve. Thus swiftly does evil suggestion corrupt honest ambition, making harmless desire appear as manifest destiny. To the fateful promptings of supernatural agency are added exceptional opportunity and irresistible urging. Events may move more rapidly than in actual life, but Shakespeare has obtained illusion of reality complete for dramatic purposes. He makes it clear that in murdering Duncan Macbeth murders his better nature. His heart is not in the deed; he repents it as soon as it is done, and a Nemesis of fear dogs him afterwards and drives him to more hideous crime and ultimate destruction.

The most memorable passages in this tragedy have, therefore, distinctive psychological interest. Macbeth is endowed with an imagination of appalling, indeed pathological, intensity. Though he is essentially an extrovert, his mind renders palpable and alive its plainest ideas and impressions. Thus the idea that he might murder the King becomes instantly the terrifying picture of himself doing it; thus, when in fact he is about to do it, his heated brain conjures a dagger, the handle toward his hand, pointing the way that he is going; thus, when the deed is done, he thinks he hears a voice cry "Sleep no more," and pictures his bloody hands coloring the oceans red. As time goes on, imagination tortures him less in this precise fashion, but harries him nonetheless with insecurity and fear. We hear of the terrible dreams which shake him nightly, and of his envy of Duncan, who after life's fitful fever sleeps well, while his murderer's mind is "full of scorpions." So Macbeth wades forward in blood, to make assurance double sure and take a bond of the fate that he but brings closer with every step.

Banquo's Ghost has for Macbeth a peculiar horror and presents a special problem. By many critics the Ghost is regarded as merely an hallucination, because Macbeth's mind has already conjured other figments, because it is seen by nobody but Macbeth, because it does not speak, because Lady Macbeth scouts it, and because, when the fit is passed, Macbeth refers it to his "strange and self-abuse." None of these facts, however, militates against its objectivity. In Elizabethan ghost lore it was understood that spectres could be visible to as many or as few in a company as they should choose, and unless their mission required it, as is not the case with Banquo's Ghost, they did not necessarily speak. Lady Macbeth, who sees nothing, naturally ridicules the apparition, and Macbeth, once it has vanished and he is himself again, quite as naturally begins to doubt

what he has seen. Under the circumstances his doubt is merely human. For the Elizabethans, on the other hand, familiar with ghosts in drama, the reality of this one would be clinched by its actual appearance on the stage, and that Shakespeare intended its introduction is attested by the stage direction (III.iv.37) describing its entrance and its usurping of Macbeth's place at the banquet. The effectiveness of this highly dramatic business is enhanced by its implications. For Macbeth, ironically, has bidden Banquo not to fail his feast, and the Ghost, with finer irony, keeps the date.

Lady Macbeth is Shakespeare's own remarkable creation. Holinshed merely mentions her as "verie ambitious, burning in unquenchable desire to beare the name of a queene." This yearning Shakespeare redirects. In the play Lady Macbeth wishes greatness only for her husband; otherwise, though she speaks of herself and of their "great business," she appears self-abnegating. In Macbeth's interests she is passionate and unswerving. She is a woman of supreme will and nerve, supplying both where he wavers. In these respects (and these dominate) she is masculine; but she is also distinctly feminine. She plays the hostess consummately. Apparently Shakespeare conceived her as physically slight (III.ii.45; V.i.57), as women of nervous intensity generally are. There are limits to this reserve of energy and control, however, as her need of a stimulant (II.ii.1–2), her swoon (II.iii.124), and her ultimate mental collapse show. In her single-mindedness, in her courage, and especially in the steadiness she exhibits during her husband's crisis in the banquet scene she is superb. And as if meeting that crisis had taxed her resources to the breaking point, we hear no more of her until we come to witness her tragic change. Her breakdown has its own peculiar irony. For it is not the susceptible, haunted mind of Macbeth that snaps, but hers, which, in contrast, had shown itself ever literal, practical, prosaic, and had spurned the visionary tendencies of his. In the sleep-walking scene (V.i) Lady Macbeth relives salient moments of the dreadful past, and the recapitulation, in chronological disorder, is pitiful. After the murder of Duncan, when Macbeth had stared in agony at the blood upon his hands, she had confidently proclaimed, "A little water clears us of this deed"; now she strives perpetually to wash the imagined blood from her own hands, which "all the perfumes of Arabia will not sweeten." Before the murder of Banquo, seeking to quell her husband's gloomy fears, she had scornfully asserted, "What's done is done"; now she cries in desperation, "What's done cannot be undone." It is somehow meet, though inglorious, that she who had been so masterful should take her own life.

When the news that his lady is dead is brought

to Macbeth, he accepts it without emotion, expressing in words of mournfullest cadence not personal grief, but the vanity and emptiness of life (V.v.17 ff.). Not that he has not loved her; she lived for him, and he knows it. They shared together fully, but they staked their happiness on evil and lost it. For each the end is bitter disillusionment. But the disillusionment of Macbeth is the greater, for he had once foreseen, though he had willfully ignored, that the assassination might not trammel up the consequence and that their bloody instructions might return to plague them. Now that even-handed justice has taken off his wife and is closing in on him, Macbeth is careless. Life to him now is but "a walking shadow," a "tale told by an idiot." The speech embracing that thought is Macbeth's elegy for his wife and a confession of their common failure. In spirit it expresses the negation of all that he was and might have been, the blasting of those golden opinions which he had deliberately sacrificed and upon the loss of which he reflects in unforgettable lines (V.iii.22–28). Though Macbeth rouses himself to meet his enemies and to die fighting with his old valor, he knows where he stands. He acknowledges the moral isolation he has brought upon himself, and the words, "I have lived long enough," revealing his weariness not alone with life but with himself, inform us that the death which he defies will be welcome to him. Macbeth proved a desperately wicked man, but as we observe him at the end we are reassured that he was more than the butcher the avenging Malcolm not unnaturally calls him.

THE TRAGEDY OF MACBETH

[DRAMATIS PERSONÆ

DUNCAN, *King of Scotland.*

MALCOLM, } *his sons.*
DONALBAIN,

MACBETH, } *generals of the King's army.*
BANQUO,

MACDUFF,
LENNOX,
ROSS,
MENTEITH, } *noblemen of Scotland.*
ANGUS,
CAITHNESS,

FLEANCE, *son to Banquo.*

SIWARD, *earl of Northumberland, commanding the English forces.*

Young SIWARD, *his son.*

SEYTON, *an officer attending on Macbeth.*

Boy, *son to Macduff.*

An English Doctor.
A Scotch Doctor.
A Captain.
A Porter.
An Old Man.

LADY MACBETH.
LADY MACDUFF.
Gentlewoman attending on Lady Macbeth.

HECATE.
Three Witches.
Apparitions.

Lords, Gentlemen, Officers, Soldiers, Murderers, Attendants, and Messengers.

SCENE: *Scotland; England.*]

ACT I

SCENE I. [*A heath.*]

Thunder and lightning. Enter three WITCHES.

1. Witch. When shall we three meet again
In thunder, lightning, or in rain?
2. Witch. When the hurlyburly's done,
When the battle's lost and won.
3. Witch. That will be ere the set of sun.   5
1. Witch. Where the place?
2. Witch.   Upon the heath.
3. Witch. There to meet with Macbeth.
1. Witch. I come, Graymalkin!
[*2. Witch.*] Paddock calls: — [*3. Witch.*] Anon! 10
All. Fair is foul, and fool is fair;
Hover through the fog and filthy air.   [*Exeunt.*

SCENE II. [*A camp near Forres.*]

Alarum within. Enter DUNCAN, MALCOLM, Donalbain, LENNOX, *with* Attendants, *meeting a bleeding* CAPTAIN.

Dun. What bloody man is that? He can report,
As seemeth by his plight, of the revolt
The newest state.
Mal.   This is the sergeant
Who like a good and hardy soldier fought
'Gainst my captivity. Hail, brave friend!   5
Say to the King the knowledge of the broil
As thou didst leave it.
Cap.   Doubtful it stood,
As two spent swimmers that do cling together
And choke their art. The merciless Macdonwald —
Worthy to be a rebel, for to that   10

Act I, sc. i, 9–10. Graymalkin (little gray cat) and **Paddock** (toad) are the names of the spirits serving the Witches. The third Witch answers without calling her spirit by name, but at IV.i.3 the name appears to be *Harpier* (derived, apparently, from "Harpy"). 10–12. The distribution of speeches follows a suggestion of Hunter's adopted by Singer. F assigns to *All.*
Sc. ii, 1. The speeches of Duncan are all headed *King* in F. 3. **sergeant.** Called "Captain" in the s.d. by F, which heads his speeches *Cap.* Some editors alter one title or the other to obtain consistency. 6. **broil:** battle. 10. **that:** i.e., that end.

The multiplying villanies of nature
Do swarm upon him — from the Western Isles
Of kerns and gallowglasses is suppli'd;
And Fortune, on his damned [quarrel] smiling,
Show'd like a rebel's whore. But all's too weak;   15
For brave Macbeth — well he deserves that
     name —
Disdaining Fortune, with his brandish'd steel,
Which smok'd with bloody execution,
Like Valour's minion carv'd out his passage
Till he fac'd the slave;   20
Which ne'er shook hands, nor bade farewell to him,
Till he unseam'd him from the nave to th' chaps,
And fix'd his head upon our battlements.
     Dun. O valiant cousin! worthy gentleman!
     Cap. As whence the sun gins his reflection   25
Shipwrecking storms and direful thunders [break],
So from that spring whence comfort seem'd to come
Discomfort swells. Mark, King of Scotland, mark!
No sooner justice had, with valour arm'd,
Compell'd these skipping kerns to trust their heels,
But the Norweyan lord, surveying vantage,   31
With furbish'd arms and new supplies of men
Began a fresh assault.
     Dun.   Dismay'd not this
Our captains, Macbeth and Banquo?
     Cap.   Yes;
As sparrows eagles, or the hare the lion.   35
If I say sooth, I must report they were
As cannons overcharg'd with double cracks; so they
Doubly redoubled strokes upon the foe.
Except they meant to bathe in reeking wounds,
Or memorize another Golgotha,   40
I cannot tell.
But I am faint, my gashes cry for help.
     Dun. So well thy words become thee as thy
     wounds;
They smack of honour both. Go get him surgeons.
                    [*Exit Captain, attended.*]

                Enter Ross *and* Angus.
Who comes here?
     Mal.   The worthy thane of Ross.   45
     Len. What a haste looks through his eyes! So
     should he look
That seems to speak things strange.
     Ross.   God save the King!
     Dun. Whence cam'st thou, worthy thane?

     Ross.   From Fife, great king;
Where the Norweyan banners flout the sky
And fan our people cold. Norway himself,   50
With terrible numbers,
Assisted by that most disloyal traitor,
The thane of Cawdor, began a dismal conflict;
Till that Bellona's bridegroom, lapp'd in proof,
Confronted him with self-comparisons,   55
Point against point, rebellious arm 'gainst arm,
Curbing his lavish spirit; and, to conclude,
The victory fell on us; —
     Dun.   Great happiness!
     Ross.   That now
Sweno, the Norways' king, craves composition;
Nor would we deign him burial of his men   60
Till he disbursed at Saint Colme's inch
Ten thousand dollars to our general use.
     Dun. No more that thane of Cawdor shall de-
     ceive
Our bosom interest. Go pronounce his present
     death,
And with his former title greet Macbeth.   65
     Ross. I'll see it done.
     Dun. What he hath lost, noble Macbeth hath
     won.   [*Exeunt.*

          SCENE III. [*A heath near Forres.*]

          Thunder.   Enter the three WITCHES.

     1. Witch. Where hast thou been, sister?
     2. Witch. Killing swine.
     3. Witch. Sister, where thou?
     1. Witch. A sailor's wife had chestnuts in her lap,
And munch'd, and munch'd, and munch'd. "Give
     me!" quoth I.   5
"Aroint thee, witch!" the rump-fed ronyon cries.
Her husband's to Aleppo gone, master o' th' Tiger;
But in a sieve I'll thither sail,
And, like a rat without a tail,
I'll do, I'll do, and I'll do.   10
     2. Witch. I'll give thee a wind.
     1. Witch. Thou'rt kind.
     3. Witch. And I another.
     1. Witch. I myself have all the other,
And the very ports they blow,   15
All the quarters that they know
I' th' shipman's card.
I'll drain him dry as hay.

---

13. Of: with. **kerns and gallowglasses:** Irish foot soldiers. 14. [quarrel] (Hanmer). *quarry* F. 19. **minion:** darling.
22. **nave:** navel. **chaps:** jaws. 26. [break] (Pope). Om. F. 31. **surveying vantage:** seeing opportunity. 37.
cracks: charges. 39. **Except:** unless. 40. **memorize ... Golgotha:** make the field memorable as another Golgotha, i.e.,
Calvary, "the place of skulls." 47. **to:** about to. 49. **flout:** mock. 54. **Bellona's bridegroom:** i.e., Macbeth. Bellona was
the goddess of war. **lapp'd in proof:** clad in armor. 55. **self-comparisons:** deeds the equal of his own. 57. **lavish:** uncon-
trolled. 59. **composition:** terms of peace. 61. **Saint ... inch:** St. Columba's island, Inchcolm. 64. **bosom interest:** close
affection.
     Sc. iii, 6. **Aroint:** be gone. **rump-fed:** fed on refuse, or, perhaps, pampered. **ronyon:** scabby person. 9. **like:** in the shape
of. 15. **blow:** blow toward. 17. **card:** compass.

Sleep shall neither night nor day
Hang upon his pent-house lid;   20
He shall live a man forbid.
Weary sev'nights nine times nine
Shall he dwindle, peak, and pine.
Though his bark cannot be lost,
Yet it shall be tempest-tost.   25
Look what I have.
   2. Witch. Show me, show me.
   1. Witch. Here I have a pilot's thumb,
Wreck'd as homeward he did come. [*Drum within.*
   3. Witch. A drum, a drum!   30
Macbeth doth come.
   All. The [weird] sisters, hand in hand,
Posters of the sea and land,
Thus do go about, about;
Thrice to thine, and thrice to mine,   35
And thrice again, to make up nine.
Peace! the charm's wound up.

     Enter MACBETH *and* BANQUO.

   Macb. So foul and fair a day I have not seen.
   Ban. How far is't call'd to [Forres]?   What are
    these
So wither'd and so wild in their attire,   40
That look not like th' inhabitants o' th' earth,
And yet are on't?   Live you? or are you aught
That man may question?   You seem to understand
    me,
By each at once her choppy finger laying
Upon her skinny lips.   You should be women,   45
And yet your beards forbid me to interpret
That you are so.
   Macb. Speak, if you can.   What are you?
   1. Witch. All hail, Macbeth! hail to thee, thane
    of Glamis!
   2. Witch. All hail, Macbeth! hail to thee, thane
    of Cawdor!
   3. Witch. All hail, Macbeth, that shalt be King
    hereafter!   50
   Ban. Good sir, why do you start, and seem to
    fear
Things that do sound so fair?   [*To the Witches.*]   I'
    th' name of truth,
Are ye fantastical, or that indeed
Which outwardly ye show?   My noble partner
You greet with present grace and great prediction
Of noble having and of royal hope,   56
That he seems rapt withal; to me you speak not.
If you can look into the seeds of time,
And say which grain will grow and which will not,

Speak then to me, who neither beg nor fear   60
Your favours nor your hate.
   1. Witch. Hail!
   2. Witch. Hail!
   3. Witch. Hail!
   1. Witch. Lesser than Macbeth, and greater.   65
   2. Witch. Not so happy, yet much happier.
   3. Witch. Thou shalt get kings, though thou be
    none;
So all hail, Macbeth and Banquo!
   1. Witch. Banquo and Macbeth, all hail!
   Macb. Stay, you imperfect speakers, tell me
    more.   70
By Sinel's death I know I am thane of Glamis;
But how of Cawdor?   The thane of Cawdor lives,
A prosperous gentleman; and to be king
Stands not within the prospect of belief
No more than to be Cawdor.   Say from whence   75
You owe this strange intelligence, or why
Upon this blasted heath you stop our way
With such prophetic greeting.   Speak, I charge you.
                  [*Witches vanish.*
   Ban. The earth hath bubbles, as the water has,
And these are of them.   Whither are they van-
    ish'd?   80
   Macb. Into the air; and what seem'd corporal
    melted
As breath into the wind.   Would they had stay'd!
   Ban. Were such things here as we do speak about,
Or have we eaten on the insane root
That takes the reason prisoner?   85
   Macb. Your children shall be kings.
   Ban.   You shall be King.
   Macb. And thane of Cawdor too; went it not so?
   Ban. To the self-same tune and words.   Who's
    here?

     Enter ROSS *and* ANGUS.

   Ross. The King hath happily receiv'd, Macbeth,
The news of thy success; and when he reads   90
Thy personal venture in the rebels' fight,
His wonders and his praises do contend
Which should be thine or his.   Silenc'd with that,
In viewing o'er the rest o' th' self-same day,
He finds thee in the stout Norweyan ranks,   95
Nothing afeard of what thyself didst make,
Strange images of death.   As thick as [hail]
[Came] post with post; and every one did bear
Thy praises in his kingdom's great defence,
And pour'd them down before him.
   Ang.   We are sent

---

20. **pent-house:** sloping like the roof of a lean-to.   21. **forbid:** accursed.   32. **[weird]** (Theobald).   *weyward* F. (and elsewhere, sometimes as *weyard*).   For the weird sisters, see Introduction.   33. **Posters of:** swift travellers over.   39. **[Forres]** (Pope).   *Soris* F.   43. **question:** talk to.   44. **choppy:** chapped.   53. **fantastical:** imaginary.   56. **having:** possessions.   57. **rapt:** carried out of himself.   67. **get:** beget.   71. **Sinel's:** Macbeth's father.   76. **owe:** have.   84. **insane:** causing insanity.   97. **[hail]** (Rowe).   *tale* F.   98. **[Came]** (Rowe).   *Can* F.   **post with post:** one messenger after another.

To give thee from our royal master thanks;   101
Only to herald thee into his sight,
Not pay thee.
    Ross. And for an earnest of a greater honour,
He bade me, from him, call thee thane of Cawdor;
In which addition, hail, most worthy thane!   106
For it is thine.
    Ban. [*Aside.*] What, can the devil speak true?
    Macb. The thane of Cawdor lives; why do you
        dress me
In borrowed robes?
    Ang.   Who was the thane lives yet;
But under heavy judgement bears that life   110
Which he deserves to lose.   Whether he was com-
        bin'd
With those of Norway, or did line the rebel
With hidden help and vantage, or that with both
He labour'd in his country's wreck, I know not;
But treasons capital, confess'd and prov'd,   115
Have overthrown him.
    Macb. [*Aside.*] Glamis, and thane of Cawdor!
The greatest is behind.   [*To Ross and Angus.*]
        Thanks for your pains.
[*To Ban.*] Do you not hope your children shall be
        kings,
When those that gave the thane of Cawdor to me
Promis'd no less to them?
    Ban. [*Aside to Macbeth.*] That, trusted home,
Might yet enkindle you unto the crown,   121
Besides the thane of Cawdor.   But 'tis strange;
And oftentimes, to win us to our harm,
The instruments of darkness tell us truths,
Win us with honest trifles, to betray 's   125
In deepest consequence.
Cousins, a word, I pray you.
    Macb.   [*Aside.*] Two truths are told,
As happy prologues to the swelling act
Of the imperial theme. — I thank you, gentlemen.
[*Aside.*] This supernatural soliciting   130
Cannot be ill, cannot be good.   If ill,
Why hath it given me earnest of success,
Commencing in a truth?   I'm thane of Cawdor.
If good, why do I yield to that suggestion
Whose horrid image doth unfix my hair   135
And make my seated heart knock at my ribs,
Against the use of nature?   Present fears
Are less than horrible imaginings.
My thought, whose murder yet is but fantastical,
Shakes so my single state of man that function
Is smother'd in surmise, and nothing is   141
But what is not.

    Ban.   Look, how our partner's rapt.
    Macb. [*Aside.*] If chance will have me King,
        why, chance may crown me
Without my stir.
    Ban.   New honours come upon him,
Like our strange garments, cleave not to their
        mould   145
But with the aid of use.
    Macb.   [*Aside.*] Come what come may,
Time and the hour runs through the roughest day.
    Ban. Worthy Macbeth, we stay upon your lei-
        sure.
    Macb. Give me your favour; my dull brain was
        wrought
With things forgotten.   Kind gentlemen, your
        pains   150
Are regist'red where every day I turn
The leaf to read them.   Let us toward the King.
[*To Ban.*] Think upon what hath chanc'd, and,
        at more time,
The interim having weigh'd it, let us speak   154
Our free hearts each to other.
    Ban.   Very gladly.
    Macb. Till then, enough.   Come, friends.
                                        [*Exeunt.*

SCENE IV. [*Forres.   The palace.*]

Flourish.   Enter [DUNCAN], MALCOLM, Donal-
        bain, Lennox, *and* Attendants.

    Dun. Is execution done on Cawdor?   [Are] not
Those in commission yet return'd?
    Mal.   My liege,
They are not yet come back.   But I have spoke
With one that saw him die; who did report
That very frankly he confess'd his treasons,   5
Implor'd your Highness' pardon, and set forth
A deep repentance.   Nothing in his life
Became him like the leaving it.   He died
As one that had been studied in his death
To throw away the dearest thing he ow'd,   10
As 'twere a careless trifle.
    Dun.   There's no art
To find the mind's construction in the face.
He was a gentleman on whom I built
An absolute trust.

Enter MACBETH, BANQUO, ROSS, *and* ANGUS.
                            O worthiest cousin!
The sin of my ingratitude even now   15
Was heavy on me.   Thou art so far before

---

106. **addition:** title.   112. **line:** support.   120. **home:** fully.   122. **thane:** thanedom.   126. **deepest consequence:** very
important matters.   130. **soliciting:** incitement.   139. **whose:** in which.   140. **single:** weak.   140–42. **function . . .
not:** my faculties are overwhelmed by imagination and nothing exists for me but the unrealized future.   144. **stir:** making an effort.   145. **strange:** new.   **their mould:** i.e., our shape.   155. **free hearts:** hearts freely.

Sc. iv, 1. [Are] F$_2$. *Or* F$_1$.   2. **in commission:** delegated to the task.   10. **dearest . . . ow'd:** i.e., his life.   11. **careless:**
worthless.   12. **construction:** interpretation.

That swiftest wing of recompense is slow
To overtake thee. Would thou hadst less deserv'd,
That the proportion both of thanks and payment
Might have been mine! Only I have left to say, 20
More is thy due than more than all can pay.

  Macb. The service and the loyalty I owe,
In doing it, pays itself. Your Highness' part
Is to receive our duties; and our duties
Are to your throne and state children and servants,
Which do but what they should, by doing every-
    thing   26
Safe toward your love and honour.

  Dun.   Welcome hither!
I have begun to plant thee, and will labour
To make thee full of growing. Noble Banquo,
That hast no less deserv'd, nor must be known 30
No less to have done so, let me infold thee
And hold thee to my heart.

  Ban.   There if I grow,
The harvest is your own.

  Dun.   My plenteous joys,
Wanton in fulness, seek to hide themselves
In drops of sorrow. Sons, kinsmen, thanes, 35
And you whose places are the nearest, know
We will establish our estate upon
Our eldest, Malcolm, whom we name hereafter
The Prince of Cumberland; which honour must
Not unaccompanied invest him only,   40
But signs of nobleness, like stars, shall shine
On all deservers. From hence to Inverness,
And bind us further to you.

  Macb. The rest is labour, which is not us'd for you.
I'll be myself the [harbinger] and make joyful 45
The hearing of my wife with your approach;
So humbly take my leave.

  Dun.   My worthy Cawdor!
  Macb. [*Aside.*] The Prince of Cumberland!
    That is a step
On which I must fall down, or else o'erleap,
For in my way it lies. Stars, hide your fires; 50
Let not light see my black and deep desires;
The eye wink at the hand; yet let that be
Which the eye fears, when it is done, to see. [*Exit.*

  Dun. True, worthy Banquo; he is full so valiant,
And in his commendations I am fed;   55
It is a banquet to me. Let's after him,
Whose care is gone before to bid us welcome.
It is a peerless kinsman.   [*Flourish. Exeunt.*

SCENE V. [*Inverness. Macbeth's castle.*]

Enter MACBETH'S WIFE, *alone, with a letter.*

  Lady M. [*Reads.*] "They met me in the day of

success; and I have learn'd by the perfect'st report, they have more in them than mortal knowledge. When I burn'd in desire to question them
further, they made themselves air, into which they
vanish'd. Whiles I stood rapt in the wonder of it, 5
came missives from the King, who all-hail'd me
'Thane of Cawdor'; by which title, before, these
weird sisters saluted me, and referr'd me to the coming on of time with 'Hail, King that shalt be!' 10
This have I thought good to deliver thee, my dearest
partner of greatness, that thou mightst not lose the
dues of rejoicing by being ignorant of what greatness
is promis'd thee. Lay it to thy heart, and farewell."
Glamis thou art, and Cawdor; and shalt be   16
What thou art promis'd. Yet do I fear thy nature;
It is too full o' th' milk of human kindness
To catch the nearest way. Thou wouldst be great,
Art not without ambition, but without   20
The illness should attend it. What thou wouldst
    highly,
That wouldst thou holily; wouldst not play false,
And yet wouldst wrongly win. Thou'dst have,
    great Glamis,
That which cries, "Thus thou must do, if thou
    have it";
And that which rather thou dost fear to do   25
Than wishest should be undone. Hie thee hither
That I may pour my spirits in thine ear,
And chastise with the valour of my tongue
All that impedes thee from the golden round
Which fate and metaphysical aid doth seem   30
To have thee crown'd withal.

        Enter a MESSENGER.

                        What is your tidings?
  Mess. The King comes here to-night.
  Lady M.   Thou'rt mad to say it!
Is not thy master with him? who, were 't so,
Would have inform'd for preparation.
  Mess. So please you, it is true; our thane is com-
    ing.   35
One of my fellows had the speed of him,
Who, almost dead for breath, had scarcely more
Than would make up his message.
  Lady M.   Give him tending;
He brings great news.   [*Exit Messenger.*
                  The raven himself is hoarse
That croaks the fatal entrance of Duncan   40
Under my battlements. Come, you spirits
That tend on mortal thoughts, unsex me here,
And fill me from the crown to the toe top-full
Of direst cruelty! Make thick my blood;
Stop up th' access and passage to remorse,   45

19–20. **the proportion...mine:** I might thank and pay you in proportion to your deserts.   27. **Safe toward:** to secure.   34. **Wanton:** profuse.   39. **Prince of Cumberland:** the title of the heir apparent.   45. **[harbinger]** (Rowe): officer sent ahead to provide lodging. *Herbenger* F.   52. **wink at:** fail to see.
  Sc. v, 1. Lady M. Here and throughout the play F heads the speeches of Lady Macbeth simply *Lady.*   6. **missives:** messengers.   21. **illness:** evil (cruelty).   29. **round:** crown.   30. **metaphysical:** supernatural.   42. **mortal:** murderous.

That no compunctious visitings of nature
Shake my fell purpose, nor keep peace between
Th' effect and [it]! Come to my woman's breasts
And take my milk for gall, you murd'ring ministers,
Wherever in your sightless substances   50
You wait on nature's mischief! Come, thick night,
And pall thee in the dunnest smoke of hell,
That my keen knife see not the wound it makes,
Nor heaven peep through the blanket of the dark
To cry, "Hold, hold!"

Enter MACBETH.

           Great Glamis! worthy Cawdor!
Greater than both, by the all-hail hereafter!   56
Thy letters have transported me beyond
This ignorant present, and I feel now
The future in the instant.
     Macb.   My dearest love,   59
Duncan comes here to-night.
     Lady M.   And when goes hence?
     Macb. To-morrow, as he purposes.
     Lady M.   O, never
Shall sun that morrow see!
Your face, my thane, is as a book where men
May read strange matters. To beguile the time,
Look like the time; bear welcome in your eye,   65
Your hand, your tongue; look like the innocent
     flower,
But be the serpent under 't. He that's coming
Must be provided for; and you shall put
This night's great business into my dispatch,
Which shall to all our nights and days to come   70
Give solely sovereign sway and masterdom.
     Macb. We will speak further.
     Lady M.   Only look up clear;
To alter favour ever is to fear.
Leave all the rest to me.   [*Exeunt.*

SCENE VI. [*Before Macbeth's castle.*]

Hautboys and torches. Enter [DUNCAN], Malcolm,
     Donalbain, BANQUO, Lennox, Macduff, Ross,
     Angus, *and* Attendants.

     Dun. This castle hath a pleasant seat; the air
Nimbly and sweetly recommends itself
Unto our gentle senses.
     Ban.   This guest of summer,
The temple-haunting [martlet] does approve,

By his loved [mansionry], that the heaven's breath   5
Smells wooingly here; no jutty, frieze,
Buttress, nor coign of vantage, but this bird
Hath made his pendent bed and procreant cradle.
Where they [most] breed and haunt, I have observ'd
The air is delicate.

Enter LADY [MACBETH].

     Dun.   See, see, our honour'd hostess!
The love that follows us sometime is our trouble,   11
Which still we thank as love. Herein I teach you
How you shall bid God 'ield us for your pains,
And thank us for your trouble.
     Lady M.   All our service
In every point twice done and then done double   15
Were poor and single business to contend
Against those honours deep and broad wherewith
Your Majesty loads our house. For those of old,
And the late dignities heap'd up to them,   19
We rest your hermits.
     Dun.   Where's the thane of Cawdor?
We cours'd him at the heels, and had a purpose
To be his purveyor; but he rides well,
And his great love, sharp as his spur, hath holp him
To his home before us. Fair and noble hostess,
We are your guest to-night.
     Lady M.   Your servants ever
Have theirs, themselves, and what is theirs, in
     compt,   26
To make their audit at your Highness' pleasure,
Still to return your own.
     Dun.   Give me your hand;
Conduct me to mine host. We love him highly,
And shall continue our graces towards him.   30
By your leave, hostess.   [*Exeunt.*

SCENE VII. [*Within Macbeth's castle.*]

Hautboys and torches. Enter a Sewer, *and divers*
     Servants *with dishes and service, over the stage.*
     Then enter MACBETH.

     Macb. If it were done when 'tis done, then 'twere
     well
It were done quickly. If the assassination
Could trammel up the consequence, and catch
With his surcease success; that but this blow
Might be the be-all and the end-all here,   5
But here, upon this bank and [shoal] of time,

We'd jump the life to come.   But in these cases
We still have judgement here, that we but teach
Bloody instructions, which, being taught, return
To plague th' inventor.   This even-handed justice
Commends th' ingredients of our poison'd chalice   11
To our own lips.   He's here in double trust:
First, as I am his kinsman and his subject,
Strong both against the deed; then, as his host,
Who should against his murderer shut the door,
Not bear the knife myself.   Besides, this Duncan   16
Hath borne his faculties so meek, hath been
So clear in his great office, that his virtues
Will plead like angels, trumpet-tongu'd, against
The deep damnation of his taking-off;   20
And pity, like a naked new-born babe
Striding the blast, or heaven's cherubin hors'd
Upon the sightless couriers of the air,
Shall blow the horrid deed in every eye,
That tears shall drown the wind.   I have no spur   25
To prick the sides of my intent, but only
Vaulting ambition, which o'erleaps itself
And falls on th' other —

Enter LADY MACBETH

How now! what news?
Lady M. He has almost supp'd.   Why have you
left the chamber?
Macb. Hath he ask'd for me?
Lady M.   Know you not he has?
Macb. We will proceed no further in this business.
He hath honour'd me of late; and I have bought
Golden opinions from all sorts of people,
Which would be worn now in their newest gloss,
Not cast aside so soon.
Lady M.   Was the hope drunk   35
Wherein you dress'd yourself?   Hath it slept since?
And wakes it now, to look so green and pale
At what it did so freely?   From this time
Such I account thy love.   Art thou afeard
To be the same in thine own act and valour   40
As thou art in desire?   Wouldst thou have that
Which thou esteem'st the ornament of life,
And live a coward in thine own esteem,
Letting "I dare not" wait upon "I would,"
Like the poor cat i' th' adage?
Macb.   Prithee, peace!   45
I dare do all that may become a man;
Who dares [do] more is none.
Lady M.   What beast was 't, then,
That made you break this enterprise to me?
When you durst do it, then you were a man;
And, to be more than what you were, you would   50
Be so much more the man.   Nor time nor place

Did then adhere, and yet you would make both.
They have made themselves, and that their fitness
now
Does unmake you.   I have given suck, and know
How tender 'tis to love the babe that milks me;   55
I would, while it was smiling in my face,
Have pluck'd my nipple from his boneless gums
And dash'd the brains out, had I so sworn as you
Have done to this.
Macb.   If we should fail?
Lady M.   We fail?
But screw your courage to the sticking-place,   60
And we'll not fail.   When Duncan is asleep —
Whereto the rather shall his day's hard journey
Soundly invite him — his two chamberlains
Will I with wine and wassail so convince
That memory, the warder of the brain,   65
Shall be a fume, and the receipt of reason
A limbeck only.   When in swinish sleep
Their drenched natures lie as in a death,
What cannot you and I perform upon
Th' unguarded Duncan? what not put upon   70
His spongy officers, who shall bear the guilt
Of our great quell?
Macb.   Bring forth men-children only;
For thy undaunted mettle should compose
Nothing but males.   Will it not be receiv'd,
When we have mark'd with blood those sleepy two
Of his own chamber and us'd their very daggers,   76
That they have done 't?
Lady M.   Who dares receive it other,
As we shall make our griefs and clamour roar
Upon his death?
Macb.   I am settled, and bend up
Each corporal agent to this terrible feat.   80
Away, and mock the time with fairest show;
False face must hide what the false heart doth know.
[*Exeunt.*

ACT II

SCENE I.   [*Within Macbeth's castle.*]

Enter BANQUO, *and* FLEANCE *with a torch before him.*

Ban. How goest the night, boy?
Fle. The moon is down; I have not heard the
clock.
Ban. And she goes down at twelve.
Fle.   I take 't, 'tis later, sir.
Ban. Hold, take my sword.   There's husbandry
in heaven;
Their candles are all out.   Take thee that too.   5
A heavy summons lies like lead upon me,

---

7. **jump:** risk.   17. **faculties:** powers.   18. **clear:** blameless.   37. **green:** sickly.   45. **th' adage.** "The cat would eat fish, and would not wet her feet."   47. **[do]** (Rowe).   *no* F.   48. **break:** disclose.   52. **adhere:** agree.   60. **But:** only. 64. **wassail:** carousal.   **convince:** overpower.   67. **limbeck:** retort, still.   71. **spongy:** drunken.   72. **quell:** killing.
Act II, sc. i, 4. **husbandry:** economy.   5. **that:** his dagger.

And yet I would not sleep.   Merciful powers,
Restrain in me the cursed thoughts that nature
Gives way to in repose!

    Enter MACBETH, *and a* Servant *with a torch.*
               Give me my sword.
Who's there?   10
  Macb. A friend.
  Ban. What, sir, not yet at rest?   The King's
a-bed.
He hath been in unusual pleasure, and
Sent forth great largess to your offices.
This diamond he greets your wife withal,   15
By the name of most kind hostess; and shut up
In measureless content.
  Macb.   Being unprepar'd,
Our will became the servant to defect;
Which else should free have wrought.
  Ban.   All's well.
I dreamt last night of the three weird sisters: 20
To you they have show'd some truth.
  Macb.   I think not of them;
Yet when we can entreat an hour to serve,
We would spend it in some words upon that busi-
    ness,
If you would grant the time.
  Ban.   At your kind'st leisure.
  Macb. If you shall cleave to my consent, when
    'tis,   25
It shall make honour for you.
  Ban.   So I lose none
In seeking to augment it, but still keep
My bosom franchis'd and allegiance clear,
I shall be counsell'd.
  Macb.   Good repose the while!
  Ban. Thanks, sir; the like to you!   30
             [*Exeunt Banquo* [*and Fleance*].
  Macb. Go bid thy mistress, when my drink is
    ready,
She strike upon the bell.   Get thee to bed.
                  [*Exit* [*Servant*].
Is this a dagger which I see before me,
The handle toward my hand?   Come, let me clutch
    thee.
I have thee not, and yet I see thee still.   35
Art thou not, fatal vision, sensible
To feeling as to sight? or art thou but
A dagger of the mind, a false creation,
Proceeding from the heat-oppressed brain?
I see thee yet, in form as palpable   40
As this which now I draw.

Thou marshall'st me the way that I was going,
And such an instrument I was to use.
Mine eyes are made the fools o' th' other senses,
Or else worth all the rest.   I see thee still,   45
And on thy blade and dudgeon gouts of blood,
Which was not so before.   There's no such thing.
It is the bloody business which informs
Thus to mine eyes.   Now o'er the one half-world
Nature seems dead, and wicked dreams abuse   50
The curtain'd sleep.   Witchcraft celebrates
Pale Hecate's offerings, and wither'd Murder,
Alarum'd by his sentinel, the wolf,
Whose howl's his watch, thus with his stealthy pace,
With Tarquin's ravishing [strides], towards his de-
    sign   55
Moves like a ghost.   Thou [sure] and firm set earth,
Hear not my steps, which [way they] walk, for fear
The very stones prate of my whereabout
And take the present horror from the time,   59
Which now suits with it.   Whiles I threat, he lives:
Words to the heat of deeds too cold breath gives.
                        [*A bell rings.*
I go, and it is done; the bell invites me.
Hear it not, Duncan; for it is a knell
That summons thee to heaven or to hell.   [*Exit.*

         SCENE II.   [*The same.*]

        Enter LADY [MACBETH].
  Lady M. That which hath made them drunk hath
    made me bold;
What hath quench'd them hath given me fire.
    Hark!   Peace!
It was the owl that shriek'd the fatal bellman
Which gives the stern'st good-night.   He is about it.
The doors are open, and the surfeited grooms   5
Do mock their charge with snores.   I have drugg'd
    their possets,
That death and nature do contend about them
Whether they live or die.

          Enter MACBETH.
  Macb. Who's there?   What, ho!
  Lady M. Alack, I am afraid they have awak'd, 10
And 'tis not done.   Th' attempt and not the deed
Confounds us.   Hark!   I laid their daggers ready;
He could not miss 'em.   Had he not resembled
My father as he slept, I had done 't. — My husband!
  Macb. I have done the deed.   Didst thou not hear
    a noise?   15

---

   14. **largess:** gifts.   **offices:** servants' quarters.   16. **shut up:** concluded.   18. **defect:** deficiency.   19. **free:** bountifully.
25. **consent:** party, interests.   **when 'tis:** when the time comes.   28. **franchis'd:** free from guilt.   36. **sensible:** perceptible.   46. **dudgeon:** handle.   **gouts:** drops.   48. **informs:** speaks.   50. **abuse:** deceive.   52. **Hecate:** goddess of night
and of witchcraft.   55. [strides] (Pope).   *sides* F.   56. [sure] (Pope conj.).   *sowre* F.   57. [way they] (Rowe).   *they may* F.
   Sc. ii, 3. **bellman.**   The night watchman customarily visited prisoners the night before their execution.   5. **grooms:**
king's body servants.   6. **possets:** drink made of wine, hot milk, etc.

Lady M. I heard the owl scream and the crickets
    cry.
Did not you speak?
    Macb.   When?
    Lady M.   Now.
    Macb.   As I descended?
    Lady M. Ay.
    Macb. Hark!
Who lies i' th' second chamber?
    Lady M.   Donalbain.   20
    Macb. This is a sorry sight.
                 [*Looking on his hands.*]
    Lady M. A foolish thought, to say a sorry sight.
    Macb. There's one did laugh in 's sleep, and one
    cried, "Murder!"
That they did wake each other. I stood and heard
    them;
But they did say their prayers, and address'd them
Again to sleep.
    Lady M.   There are two lodg'd together. 26
    Macb. One cried, "God bless us!" and "Amen"
    the other,
As they had seen me with these hangman's hands.
List'ning their fear. I could not say "Amen"
When they did say "God bless us!"
    Lady M.   Consider it not so deeply.
    Macb. But wherefore could not I pronounce
    "Amen"?   31
I had most need of blessing, and "Amen"
Stuck in my throat.
    Lady M. These deeds must not be thought
After these ways; so, it will make us mad.
    Macb. Methought I heard a voice cry, "Sleep
    no more!   35
Macbeth does murder sleep." — the innocent sleep,
Sleep that knits up the ravell'd sleave of care,
The death of each day's life, sore labour's bath,
Balm of hurt minds, great nature's second course,
Chief nourisher in life's feast.
    Lady M.   What do you mean?
    Macb. Still it cried, "Sleep no more!" to all the
    house;   41
"Glamis hath murder'd sleep, and therefore Cawdor
Shall sleep no more; Macbeth shall sleep no more."
    Lady M. Who was it that thus cried? Why,
    worthy thane,
You do unbend your noble strength, to think   45
So brainsickly of things. Go get some water,
And wash this filthy witness from your hand.
Why did you bring these daggers from the place?
They must lie there. Go carry them; and smear
The sleepy grooms with blood.
    Macb.   I'll go no more.   50

I am afraid to think what I have done;
Look on't again I dare not.
    Lady M.   Infirm of purpose!
Give me the daggers. The sleeping and the dead
Are but as pictures; 'tis the eye of childhood
That fears a painted devil. If he do bleed,   55
I'll gild the faces of the grooms withal;
For it must seem their guilt.
              [*Exit. Knocking within.*
    Macb.   Whence is that knocking?
How is't with me, when every noise appalls me?
What hands are here? Ha! they pluck out mine
    eyes.
Will all great Neptune's ocean wash this blood 60
Clean from my hand? No, this my hand will rather
The multitudinous seas incarnadine,
Making the green one red.

        Re-enter LADY [MACBETH]

    Lady M. My hands are of your colour; but I
    shame
To wear a heart so white. (*Knocking.*) I hear a
    knocking   65
At the south entry. Retire we to our chamber.
A little water clears us of this deed;
How easy is it, then! Your constancy
Hath left you unattended. (*Knocking.*) Hark!
    more knocking.
Get on your nightgown, lest occasion call us 70
And show us to be watchers. Be not lost
So poorly in your thoughts.
    Macb. To know my deed, 'twere best not know
    myself.   [*Knocking.*
Wake Duncan with thy knocking! I would thou
    couldst!   [*Exeunt.*

        SCENE III. [*The same.*]

    Enter a PORTER. *Knocking within.*

Porter. Here's a knocking indeed! If a man were
porter of hell-gate, he should have old turning
the key. (*Knocking.*) Knock, knock, knock!
Who's there, i' th' name of Beelzebub? Here's a
farmer, that hang'd himself on th' expectation 5
of plenty. Come in time; have napkins enow about
you; here you'll sweat for't. (*Knocking.*) Knock,
knock! Who's there, in th' other devil's name?
Faith, here's an equivocator, that could swear in
both the scales against either scale; who com- 10
mitted treason enough for God's sake, yet could not
equivocate to heaven. O, come in, equivocator.
(*Knocking.*) Knock, knock, knock! Who's there?
Faith, here's an English tailor come hither for steal-

---

    37. ravell'd: tangled. **sleave:** skein.   **62. incarnadine:** turn blood-red.   **68–69. constancy . . . unattended:** firmness
has quit you.   **70. nightgown:** dressing-gown.
    Sc. iii, 2. old: a grand old time.   **5–6. farmer . . . plenty.** The farmer, having hoarded grain to sell at high prices, foresaw
his ruin when crops proved plentiful.   **6. napkins:** handkerchiefs.   **9–10. swear . . . scale:** swear to an ambiguity.

ing out of a French hose. Come in, tailor; here 15
you may roast your goose. (*Knocking*.) Knock,
knock; never at quiet! What are you? But this
place is too cold for hell. I'll devil-porter it no
further. I had thought to have let in some of 20
all professions that go the primrose way to th' everlasting bonfire. (*Knocking*.) Anon, anon. I pray
you, remember the porter.   [*Opens the gate*.]

Enter MACDUFF *and* LENNOX.

Macd. Was it so late, friend, ere you went to bed,
That you do lie so late?   25
Port. Faith, sir, we were carousing till the second
cock; and drink, sir, is a great provoker of three
things.
Macd. What three things does drink especially
provoke?   30
Port. Marry, sir, nose-painting, sleep, and urine.
Lechery, sir, it provokes, and unprovokes; it provokes the desire, but it takes away the performance;
therefore, much drink may be said to be an equivocator with lechery: it makes him, and it mars 35
him; it sets him on, and it takes him off; it persuades
him, and disheartens him; makes him stand to, and
not stand to; in conclusion, equivocates him in a
sleep, and, giving him the lie, leaves him.   40
Macd. I believe drink gave thee the lie last night.
Port. That it did, sir, i' the very throat on me.
But I requited him for his lie; and, I think, being too
strong for him, though he took up my legs sometime,
yet I made a shift to cast him.   46

Enter MACBETH.

Macd. Is thy master stirring?
Our knocking has awak'd him; here he comes.
Len. Good morrow, noble sir.
Macb.   Good morrow, both.
Macd. Is the King stirring, worthy thane?
Macb.   Not yet.
Macd. He did command me to call timely on
    him.   51
I have almost slipp'd the hour.
Macb.   I'll bring you to him.
Macd. I know this is a joyful trouble to you;
But yet 'tis one.
Macb. The labour we delight in physics pain.
This is the door.
Macd.   I'll make so bold to call,   56
For 'tis my limited service.   [*Exit*.
Len. Goes the King hence to-day?
Macb.   He does; — he did appoint so.
Len. The night has been unruly. Where we lay,
Our chimneys were blown down; and, as they say,

Lamentings heard i' th' air; strange screams of
    death,   61
And prophesying with accents terrible
Of dire combustion and confus'd events
New hatch'd to th' woeful time. The obscure bird
Clamour'd the livelong night; some say, the earth 65
Was feverous and did shake.
Macb.   'Twas a rough night.
Len. My young remembrance cannot parallel
A fellow to it.

Re-enter MACDUFF.

Macd. O horror, horror, horror! Tongue nor
    heart
Cannot conceive nor name thee!
Macb.⎱
Len.⎰   What's the matter?
Macd. Confusion now hath made his master-
    piece!   71
Most sacrilegious murder hath broke ope
The Lord's anointed temple, and stole thence
The life o' th' building!
Macb.   What is't you say? The life?
Len. Mean you his Majesty?   75
Macd. Approach the chamber, and destroy your
    sight
With a new Gorgon. Do not bid me speak;
See, and then speak yourselves.
                    [*Exeunt Macbeth and Lennox*.
                                Awake, awake!
Ring the alarum-bell. Murder and treason!
Banquo and Donalbain! Malcolm! awake!   80
Shake off this downy sleep, death's counterfeit,
And look on death itself! Up, up, and see
The great doom's image! Malcolm! Banquo!
As from your graves rise up, and walk like sprites,
To countenance this horror! Ring the bell.   85
                                [*Bell rings*.

Enter LADY MACBETH.

Lady M. What's the business,
That such a hideous trumpet calls to parley
The sleepers of the house? Speak, speak!
Macd.   O gentle lady,
'Tis not for you to hear what I can speak;
The repetition in a woman's ear   90
Would murder as it fell.

Enter BANQUO.

                        O Banquo, Banquo,
Our royal master's murder'd!
Lady M.   Woe, alas!
What, in our house?

15–16. **French hose.** A tight-fitting kind, in the making of which it would be hard for tailors to steal any cloth. 16.
goose: pressing iron. 26–27. **the second cock:** 3 A.M. 41. **gave thee the lie:** (1) floored thee, (2) lied to thee. 46. **cast:** (1)
throw, (2) vomit. 51. **timely:** early. 55. **physics:** cures. 57. **limited:** appointed. 63. **combustion:** tumult. 64. **obscure bird:** owl. 71. **Confusion:** destruction. 77. **Gorgon.** The Gorgon Medusa turned to stone anyone who looked in
her face. 83. **doom's image:** image of Doomsday. 85. **countenance:** be in keeping with.

Ban.   Too cruel anywhere.
Dear Duff, I prithee, contradict thyself,
And say it is not so.   95

Re-enter MACBETH *and* LENNOX, *with* ROSS.

Macb. Had I but died an hour before this chance,
I had liv'd a blessed time; for, from this instant,
There's nothing serious in mortality.
All is but toys; renown and grace is dead;
The wine of life is drawn, and the mere lees   100
Is left this vault to brag of.

Enter MALCOLM *and* DONALBAIN.

Don. What is amiss?
Macb.   You are, and do not know 't.
The spring, the head, the fountain of your blood
Is stopp'd; the very source of it is stopp'd.
Macd. Your royal father's murder'd.
Mal.   O, by whom?
Len. Those of his chamber, as it seem'd, had
    done 't.   106
Their hands and faces were all badg'd with blood;
So were their daggers, which unwip'd we found
Upon their pillows.
They star'd, and were distracted; no man's life   110
Was to be trusted with them.
Macb. O, yet I do repent me of my fury,
That I did kill them.
Macd.   Wherefore did you so?
Macb. Who can be wise, amaz'd, temp'rate and
    furious,
Loyal and neutral, in a moment?   No man.   115
The expedition of my violent love
Outrun the pauser, reason.   Here lay Duncan,
His silver skin lac'd with his golden blood,   118
And his gash'd stabs look'd like a breach in nature
For ruin's wasteful entrance; there, the murderers,
Steep'd in the colours of their trade, their daggers
Unmannerly breech'd with gore.   Who could refrain,
That had a heart to love, and in that heart
Courage to make 's love known?
Lady M.   Help me hence, ho!
Macd. Look to the lady.
Mal. [*Aside to Don.*]   Why do we hold our
    tongues,   125
That most may claim this argument for ours?
Don. [*Aside to Mal.*]   What should be spoken
    here, where our fate,
Hid in an auger-hole, may rush and seize us?
Let's away;
Our tears are not yet brew'd.

Mal. [*Aside to Don.*]   Nor our strong sorrow
Upon the foot of motion.
Ban.   Look to the lady;   131
    [*Lady Macbeth is carried out.*]
And when we have our naked frailties hid,
That suffer in exposure, let us meet
And question this most bloody piece of work,
To know it further.   Fears and scruples shake us.
In the great hand of God I stand, and thence   136
Against the undivulg'd pretence I fight
Of treasonous malice.
Macd.   And so do I.
All.   So all.
Macb. Let's briefly put on manly readiness,
And meet i' th' hall together.
All.   Well contented.   140
    [*Exeunt* [*all but Malcolm and Donalbain*].
Mal. What will you do?   Let's not consort with
    them;
To show an unfelt sorrow is an office
Which the false man does easy.   I'll to England.
Don. To Ireland, I; our separated fortune
Shall keep us both the safer.   Where we are,   145
There's daggers in men's smiles; the near in blood,
The nearer bloody.
Mal.   This murderous shaft that's shot
Hath not yet lighted, and our safest way
Is to avoid the aim.   Therefore, to horse;
And let us not be dainty of leave-taking,   150
But shift away.   There's warrant in that theft
Which steals itself, when there's no mercy left.
    [*Exeunt.*

SCENE IV.   [*Outside Macbeth's castle.*]

Enter ROSS *and an* OLD MAN.

Old M. Threescore and ten I can remember well;
Within the volume of which time I have seen
Hours dreadful and things strange; but this sore
    night
Hath trifled former knowings.
Ross.   Ah, good father,
Thou seest the heavens, as troubled with man's act,
Threatens his bloody stage.   By th' clock 'tis day, 6
And yet dark night strangles the travelling lamp.
Is't night's predominance or the day's shame
That darkness does the face of earth entomb,
When living light should kiss it?
Old M.   'Tis unnatural,   10
Even like the deed that's done.   On Tuesday last,
A falcon, tow'ring in her pride of place,

---

98. **mortality:** human life.   99. **toys:** trifles.   103. **head:** source.   107. **badg'd:** marked.   114. **amaz'd:** confused.
116. **expedition:** haste.   122. **breech'd:** covered.   126. **argument:** subject.   128. **auger-hole:** obscure spot.   131.
Upon...motion: ready to act.   132. **our...hid:** clothed ourselves.   135. **scruples:** suspicions.   139. **briefly:** quickly.
readiness: dress.   146-47. **the near...bloody:** i.e., the closer the blood ties, the greater the danger (**near:** nearer).   150.
dainty of: particular about.
Sc. iv, 3. **sore:** dreadful.   4. **trifled:** made trivial.   12. **tow'ring...place:** mounting proudly to the summit of her flight.

Was by a mousing owl hawk'd at and kill'd.

Ross.   And Duncan's horses — a thing most
    strange and certain —
Beauteous and swift, the minions of their race, 15
Turn'd wild in nature, broke their stalls, flung out,
Contending 'gainst obedience, as they would make
War with mankind.

Old M.   'Tis said they eat each other.

Ross.   They did so, to th' amazement of mine eyes
That look'd upon't.

Enter MACDUFF.

          Here comes the good Macduff. 20
How goes the world, sir, now?

Macd.   Why, see you not?

Ross.   Is't known who did this more than bloody
    deed?

Macd.   Those that Macbeth hath slain.

Ross.   Alas, the day!
What good could they pretend?

Macd.   They were suborn'd.
Malcolm and Donalbain, the King's two sons, 25
Are stol'n away and fled; which puts upon them
Suspicion of the deed.

Ross.   'Gainst nature still!
Thriftless ambition, that will ravin up
Thine own life's means!   Then 'tis most like
The sovereignty will fall upon Macbeth. 30

Macd.   He is already nam'd, and gone to Scone
To be invested.

Ross.   Where is Duncan's body?

Macd.   Carried to Colmekill,
The sacred storehouse of his predecessors 34
And guardian of their bones.

Ross.   Will you to Scone?

Macd.   No, cousin, I'll to Fife.

Ross.   Well, I will thither.

Macd.   Well, may you see things well done there,
    — adieu! —
Lest our old robes sit easier than our new!

Ross.   Farewell, father.

Old M.   God's benison go with you; and with
    those   40
That would make good of bad, and friends of foes!
                               [Exeunt.

ACT III

Scene I.   [*Forres.   The palace.*]

Enter BANQUO.

Ban.   Thou hast it now: King, Cawdor, Glamis,
    all,
As the weird women promis'd, and, I fear,

Thou play'dst most foully for't; yet it was said
It should not stand in thy posterity,
But that myself should be the root and father   5
Of many kings.   If there come truth from them —
As upon thee, Macbeth, their speeches shine —
Why, by the verities on thee made good,
May they not be my oracles as well,
And set me up in hope?   But hush! no more.   10

Sennet sounded.   Enter MACBETH, *as King*, LADY
    [MACBETH, *as Queen*], Lennox, Ross, Lords,
    [Ladies,] *and* SERVANTS.

Macb.   Here's our chief guest.

Lady M.   If he had been forgotten,
It had been as a gap in our great feast,
And all-thing unbecoming.

Macb.   To-night we hold a solemn supper, sir,
And I'll request your presence.

Ban.   Let your Highness
Command upon me; to the which my duties   16
Are with a most indissoluble tie
For ever knit.

Macb.   Ride you this afternoon?

Ban.   Ay, my good lord.   20

Macb.   We should have else desir'd your good ad-
    vice,
Which still hath been both grave and prosperous,
In this day's council; but we'll take to-morrow.
Is't far you ride?

Ban.   As far, my lord, as will fill up the time   25
'Twixt this and supper.   Go not my horse the
    better,
I must become a borrower of the night
For a dark hour or twain.

Macb.   Fail not our feast.

Ban.   My lord, I will not.   29

Macb.   We hear our bloody cousins are bestow'd
In England and in Ireland, not confessing
Their cruel parricide, filling their hearers
With strange invention.   But of that to-morrow,
When therewithal we shall have cause of state
Craving us jointly.   Hie you to horse; adieu,   35
Till you return at night.   Goes Fleance with you?

Ban.   Ay, my good lord.   Our time does call
    upon 's.

Macb.   I wish your horses swift and sure of foot;
And so I do commend you to their backs.
Farewell.   *[Exit Banquo.* 40
Let every man be master of his time
Till seven at night.   To make society
The sweeter welcome, we will keep ourself
Till supper-time alone; while then, God be with you!
          [Exeunt [all but Macbeth, and a Servant].

---

24. **pretend:** intend. **suborn'd:** criminally incited.   28. **ravin:** devour ravenously.   31. **Scone.** Where Scottish kings were always crowned.   33. **Colmekill:** Iona (Columba's cell), then the burial place of Scottish royalty.   40. **benison:** blessing.
    Act III, sc. i, 7. **shine:** i.e., in fulfillment.   10. s.d. *Sennet:* trumpet call.   14. **solemn:** formal.   22. **still:** ever.   30. **are bestow'd:** have taken refuge.   35. **Craving us jointly:** requiring our joint attention.   44. **while:** until.

Sirrah, a word with you.   Attend those men   45
Our pleasure?
  Serv. They are, my lord, without the palace gate.
  Macb. Bring them before us.   [*Exit Servant.*
                          To be thus is nothing,
But to be safely thus.   Our fears in Banquo
Stick deep; and in his royalty of nature   50
Reigns that which would be fear'd.   'Tis much he
          dares;
And, to that dauntless temper of his mind,
He hath a wisdom that doth guide his valour
To act in safety.   There is none but he
Whose being I do fear; and, under him,   55
My Genius is rebuk'd, as, it is said,
Mark Antony's was by Cæsar.   He chid the sisters
When first they put the name of king upon me,
And bade them speak to him; then prophet-like
They hail'd him father to a line of kings.   60
Upon my head they plac'd a fruitless crown,
And put a barren sceptre in my gripe,
Thence to be wrench'd with an unlineal hand,
No son of mine succeeding.   If 't be so,
For Banquo's issue have I fil'd my mind;   65
For them the gracious Duncan have I murder'd;
Put rancours in the vessel of my peace
Only for them; and mine eternal jewel
Given to the common enemy of man,
To make them kings, the [seed] of Banquo kings!   70
Rather than so, come fate into the list,
And champion me to th' utterance!   Who's there?

          Re-enter Servant, *with two* MURDERERS.

Now go to the door, and stay there till we call.
                          [*Exit Servant.*
Was it not yesterday we spoke together?
  [*1.*] *Mur.* It was, so please your Highness.
  Macb.   Well then, now
Have you consider'd of my speeches?   Know   76
That it was he in the times past which held you
So under fortune, which you thought had been
Our innocent self.   This I made good to you
In our last conference, pass'd in probation with you
How you were borne in hand, how cross'd, the in-
          struments,   81
Who wrought with them, and all things else that
          might
To half a soul and to a notion craz'd
Say, "Thus did Banquo."
  1. Mur.   You made it known to us.
  Macb. I did so, and went further, which is now   85
Our point of second meeting.   Do you find

Your patience so predominant in your nature
That you can let this go?   Are you so gospell'd
To pray for this good man and for his issue,   89
Whose heavy hand hath bow'd you to the grave
And beggar'd yours for ever?
  1. Mur.   We are men, my liege.
  Macb. Ay, in the catalogue ye go for men,
As hounds and greyhounds, mongrels, spaniels,
          curs,
Shoughs, water-rugs, and demi-wolves are clept
All by the name of dogs; the valued file   95
Distinguishes the swift, the slow, the subtle,
The housekeeper, the hunter, every one,
According to the gift which bounteous nature
Hath in him clos'd; whereby he does receive
Particular addition, from the bill   100
That writes them all alike; and so of men.
Now, if you have a station in the file,
Not i' th' worst rank of manhood, say 't;
And I will put that business in your bosoms,
Whose execution takes your enemy off,   105
Grapples you to the heart and love of us,
Who wear our health but sickly in his life,
Which in his death were perfect.
  2. Mur.   I am one, my liege,
Whom the vile blows and buffets of the world
Hath so incens'd that I am reckless what   110
I do to spite the world.
  1. Mur.   And I another
So weary with disasters, tugg'd with fortune,
That I would set my life on any chance,
To mend it or be rid on't.
  Macb.   Both of you
Know Banquo was your enemy.
  [*Both*] *Mur.*   True, my lord.   115
  Macb. So is he mine; and in such bloody distance,
That every minute of his being thrusts
Against my near'st of life; and though I could
With barefac'd power sweep him from my sight
And bid my will avouch it, yet I must not,   120
For certain friends that are both his and mine,
Whose loves I may not drop, but wail his fall
Who I myself struck down; and thence it is,
That I to your assistance do make love,
Masking the business from the common eye   125
For sundry weighty reasons.
  2. Mur.   We shall, my lord,
Perform what you command us.
  1. Mur.   Though our lives—
  Macb. Your spirits shine through you.   Within
          this hour at most

---

48. **thus:** i.e., king.   51. **would:** must.   52. **to:** added to.   57. **Cæsar:** Octavius Cæsar.   62. **gripe:** grasp.   65. **fil'd:**
defiled.   68–69. **mine…man:** given my soul to the devil.   70. **[seed]** (Pope).   *Seedes* F.   71. **list:** arena of combat.
72. **th' utterance:** the death.   77. **he:** Banquo.   80. **pass'd in probation:** reviewed and proved.   81. **borne in hand:**
deceived.   **cross'd:** thwarted.   83. **notion:** mind.   88. **gospell'd:** filled with the gospel.   92. **go:** pass.   94. **Shoughs:**
shaggy dogs.   **water-rugs:** water-dogs.   **clept:** called.   95. **valued file:** list which specifies values.   97. **housekeeper:**
watchdog.   100. **addition:** title.   101. **writes…alike:** enters them indiscriminately.   112. **tugg'd with:** pulled about
by.   116. **distance:** enmity.   118. **near'st of life:** most vital spot.   120. **avouch:** justify.

I will advise you where to plant yourselves,   129
Acquaint you with the perfect spy o' th' time,
The moment on't; for't must be done to-night,
And something from the palace; always thought
That I require a clearness: and with him —
To leave no rubs nor botches in the work —
Fleance his son, that keeps him company,   135
Whose absence is no less material to me
Than is his father's, must embrace the fate
Of that dark hour.   Resolve yourselves apart;
I'll come to you anon.
     [*Both*] *Mur.*   We are resolv'd, my lord.
     Macb. I'll call upon you straight; abide within.
                       [*Exeunt Murderers.*]
It is concluded.   Banquo, thy soul's flight,   141
If it find heaven, must find it out to-night.   [*Exit.*

SCENE II.   [*The same.*]

Enter LADY MACBETH *and a* SERVANT.

     Lady M. Is Banquo gone from court?
     Serv. Ay, madam, but returns again to-night.
     Lady M. Say to the King, I would attend his
leisure
For a few words.
     Serv.   Madam, I will.   [*Exit.*
     Lady M.   Nought's had, all's spent,
Where our desire is got without content.   5
'Tis safer to be that which we destroy
Than by destruction dwell in doubtful joy.

Enter MACBETH.

How now, my lord! why do you keep alone,
Of sorriest fancies your companions making,
Using those thoughts which should indeed have
died   10
With them they think on?   Things without all
remedy
Should be without regard; what's done is done.
     Macb. We have [scotch'd] the snake, not kill'd it;
She'll close and be herself, whilst our poor malice
Remains in danger of her former tooth.   15
But let the frame of things disjoint, both the worlds
suffer,
Ere we will eat our meal in fear and sleep
In the affliction of these terrible dreams
That shake us nightly.   Better be with the dead
Whom we, to gain our peace, have sent to peace,   20
Than on the torture of the mind to lie
In restless ecstasy.   Duncan is in his grave;

After life's fitful fever he sleeps well.
Treason has done his worst; nor steel, nor poison,
Malice domestic, foreign levy, nothing,   25
Can touch him further.
     Lady M.   Come on,
Gentle my lord, sleek o'er your rugged looks;
Be bright and jovial among your guests to-night.
     Macb. So shall I, love; and so, I pray, be you.
Let your remembrance apply to Banquo;   30
Present him eminence both with eye and tongue.
Unsafe the while that we
Must lave our honours in these flattering streams,
And make our faces vizards to our hearts,
Disguising what they are.
     Lady M.   You must leave this.   35
     Macb. O, full of scorpions is my mind, dear wife!
Thou know'st that Banquo and his Fleance lives.
     Lady M. But in them nature's copy's not eterne.
     Macb. There's comfort yet; they are assailable.
Then be thou jocund; ere the bat hath flown   40
His cloister'd flight, ere to black Hecate's summons
The shard-borne beetle with his drowsy hums
Hath rung night's yawning peal, there shall be done
A deed of dreadful note.
     Lady M.   What's to be done?
     Macb. Be innocent of the knowledge, dearest
chuck,   45
Till thou applaud the deed.   Come, seeling night,
Scarf up the tender eye of pitiful day,
And with thy bloody and invisible hand
Cancel and tear to pieces that great bond
Which keeps me pale!   Light thickens, and the
crow   50
Makes wing to th' rooky wood;
Good things of day begin to droop and drowse,
Whiles night's black agents to their preys do rouse.
Thou marvell'st at my words, but hold thee still;
Things bad begun make strong themselves by ill.
So, prithee, go with me.   [*Exeunt.*   56

SCENE III.   [*A park near the palace.*]

Enter three MURDERERS.

     1. Mur. But who did bid thee join with us?
     3. Mur.   Macbeth.
     2. Mur. He needs not our mistrust, since he de-
livers
Our offices and what we have to do
To the direction just.
     1. Mur.   Then stand with us;

---

     130. **perfect...time:** exact time.   132. **something:** some distance.   133. **I...clearness:** I must not be suspected.
134. **rubs:** slips.   138. **Resolve yourselves:** make up your minds.
     Sc. ii, 5. **content:** contentment.   10. **Using:** keeping company with.   13. **[scotch'd]** (Theobald): gashed. *scorch'd* F.
14. **close:** reunite.   22. **ecstasy:** frenzy.   27. **sleek:** smooth.   31. **eminence:** special favor.   34. **vizards:** masks.   38. **in
...eterne:** their lease (copy) of life is not eternal.   42. **shard-borne:** borne on hard wings.   46. **seeling:** blinding.   The
eyes of falcons were sewed up (seeled) in order to tame them.   49. **bond:** Banquo's life.   51. **rooky:** haunted by rooks.
     Sc. iii, 1. The speeches of the murderers are headed by numbers alone in F.   3. **offices:** duties.   4. **To...just:** precisely
according to his directions.

The west yet glimmers with some streaks of day. 5
Now spurs the lated traveller apace
To gain the timely inn; and near approaches
The subject of our watch.
 3. Mur.   Hark! I hear horses.
 Ban. (Within.) Give us a light there, ho!
 2. Mur.   Then 'tis he; the rest
That are within the note of expectation 10
Already are i' th' court.
 1. Mur.   His horses go about.
 3. Mur. Almost a mile; but he does usually,
So all men do, from hence to th' palace gate
Make it their walk.

   Enter BANQUO, *and* FLEANCE *with a torch.*

 2. Mur.   A light, a light!
 3. Mur.   'Tis he.
 1. Mur. Stand to't. 15
 Ban. It will be rain to-night.
 1. Mur.   Let it come down.
       [*They set upon Banquo.*]
 Ban. O, treachery! Fly, good Fleance, fly, fly, fly!
Thou mayst revenge. O slave!
     [*Dies. Fleance escapes.*]
 3. Mur. Who did strike out the light?
 1. Mur.   Was 't not the way?
 3. Mur. There's but one down; the son is fled.
 2. Mur.   We have lost 20
Best half of our affair.
 1. Mur. Well, let's away, and say how much is
  done.   [*Exeunt.*

   SCENE IV. [*Hall in the palace.*]

A banquet prepared. Enter MACBETH, LADY
[MACBETH], ROSS, LENNOX, Lords, *and* Attendants.

 Macb. You know your own degrees; sit down.
  At first
And last, the hearty welcome.
 Lords.   Thanks to your Majesty.
 Macb. Ourself will mingle with society
And play the humble host.
Our hostess keeps her state, but in best time 5
We will require her welcome.
 Lady M. Pronounce it for me, sir, to all our
  friends,
For my heart speaks they are welcome.

   First MURDERER [*appears at the door*].

 Macb. See, they encounter thee with their hearts'
  thanks. 9
Both sides are even; here I'll sit i' th' midst.

Be large in mirth; anon we'll drink a measure
The table round. [*Approaching the door.*]—There's
  blood upon thy face.
 Mur. 'Tis Banquo's then.
 Macb. 'Tis better thee without than he within.
Is he dispatch'd? 15
 Mur. My lord, his throat is cut; that I did for
  him.
 Macb. Thou art the best o' th' cut-throats; yet
  he's good
That did the like for Fleance. If thou didst it,
Thou art the nonpareil.
 Mur.   Most royal sir,
Fleance is scap'd. 20
 Macb. Then comes my fit again. I had else been
  perfect,
Whole as the marble, founded as the rock,
As broad and general as the casing air;
But now I am cabin'd, cribb'd, confin'd, bound in
To saucy doubts and fears. But Banquo's safe?
 Mur. Ay, my good lord; safe in a ditch he bides,
With twenty trenched gashes on his head, 27
The least a death to nature.
 Macb.   Thanks for that;
There the grown serpent lies. The worm that's
  fled
Hath nature that in time will venom breed, 30
No teeth for th' present. Get thee gone; to-morrow
We'll hear ourselves again. [*Exit Murderer.*
 Lady M.   My royal lord,
You do not give the cheer. The feast is sold
That is not often vouch'd, while 'tis a-making,
'Tis given with welcome. To feed were best at
  home; 35
From thence, the sauce to meat is ceremony;
Meeting were bare without it.

   Enter the Ghost of Banquo, *and sits in*
    Macbeth's place.

 Macb.   Sweet remembrancer!
Now, good digestion wait on appetite,
And health on both!
 Len. May 't please your Highness sit.
 Macb. Here had we now our country's honour
  roof'd, 40
Were the grac'd person of our Banquo present,
Who may I rather challenge for unkindness
Than pity for mischance.
 Ross.   His absence, sir,
Lays blame upon his promise. Please 't your High-
  ness
To grace us with your royal company? 45
 Macb. The table's full.

Len.   Here is a place reserv'd, sir.
Macb. Where?
Len. Here, my good lord. What is't that
    moves your Highness?
Macb. Which of you have done this?
Lords.   What, my good lord?
Macb. Thou canst not say I did it; never shake 50
Thy gory locks at me.
Ross. Gentlemen, rise: his Highness is not well.
Lady M. Sit, worthy friends; my lord is often
    thus,
And hath been from his youth. Pray you, keep
    seat;
The fit is momentary; upon a thought   55
He will again be well. If much you note him,
You shall offend him and extend his passion.
Feed, and regard him not. Are you a man?
Macb. Ay, and a bold one, that dare look on that
Which might appall the devil.
Lady M.   O proper stuff!   60
This is the very painting of your fear;
This is the air-drawn dagger which, you said,
Led you to Duncan. O, these flaws and starts,
Impostors to true fear, would well become
A woman's story at a winter's fire,   65
Authoriz'd by her grandam. Shame itself!
Why do you make such faces? When all's done,
You look but on a stool.
Macb. Prithee, see there! behold! look! lo! how
    say you?
Why, what care I? If thou canst nod, speak too. 70
If charnel-houses and our graves must send
Those that we bury back, our monuments
Shall be the maws of kites.   *[Ghost vanishes.]*
Lady M.   What, quite unmann'd in folly?
Macb. If I stand here, I saw him.
Lady M.   Fie, for shame!
Macb. Blood hath been shed ere now, i' th'
    olden time,   75
Ere humane statute purg'd the gentle weal;
Ay, and since too, murders have been perform'd
Too terrible for the ear. The [time] has been,
That, when the brains were out, the man would die,
And there an end; but now they rise again.   80
With twenty mortal murders on their crowns,
And push us from our stools. This is more strange
Than such a murder is.
Lady M.   My worthy lord,
Your noble friends do lack you.
Macb.   I do forget.
Do not muse at me, my most worthy friends;   85

I have a strange infirmity, which is nothing
To those that know me. Come, love and health
    to all;
Then I'll sit down. Give me some wine; fill full.

        Re-enter Ghost.

I drink to th' general joy o' th' whole table,
And to our dear friend Banquo, whom we miss;
Would he were here! to all and him we thirst,   91
And all to all.
Lords.   Our duties, and the pledge.
Macb. Avaunt! and quit my sight! let the earth
    hide thee!
Thy bones are marrowless, thy blood is cold;
Thou hast no speculation in those eyes   95
Which thou dost glare with!
Lady M.   Think of this, good peers,
But as a thing of custom; 'tis no other.
Only it spoils the pleasure of the time.
Macb. What man dare, I dare.
Approach thou like the rugged Russian bear,   100
The arm'd rhinoceros, or th' Hyrcan tiger;
Take any shape but that, and my firm nerves
Shall never tremble. Or be alive again,
And dare me to the desert with thy sword;
If trembling I inhabit then, protest me   105
The baby of a girl. Hence, horrible shadow!
Unreal mock'ry, hence!   *[Ghost vanishes.]*
                  Why, so; being gone,
I am a man again. Pray you, sit still.
Lady M. You have displac'd the mirth, broke
    the good meeting,
With most admir'd disorder.
Macb.   Can such things be,
And overcome us like a summer's cloud,   111
Without our special wonder? You make me
    strange
Even to the disposition that I owe,
When now I think you can behold such sights,
And keep the natural ruby of your cheeks,   115
When mine is blanch'd with fear.
Ross.   What sights, my lord?
Lady M. I pray you, speak not; he grows worse
    and worse;
Question enrages him. At once, good-night.
Stand not upon the order of your going,   119
But go at once.
Len.   Good-night; and better health
Attend his Majesty!
Lady M.   A kind good-night to all!
                      [Exeunt Lords.

---

55. **upon a thought:** in a moment. 57. **offend:** make worse. **extend his passion:** prolong his attack. 60. **proper stuff:** fine business! 63. **flaws:** outbursts. 64. **Impostors to:** (mere) frauds compared with. 66. **Authoriz'd:** vouched for. 73. **Shall ... kites:** had better be the stomachs of hawks (i.e., we should leave our dead unburied to be devoured). 76. **purg'd ... weal:** cleansed the state of violence, making it gentle. 78. **[time] has** (Grant White). *times has* F. *times have* F₂. 81. **mortal murders:** deadly wounds. 84. **lack:** miss. 85. **muse:** wonder. 91. **thirst:** i.e., eagerly drink. 95. **speculation:** comprehending sight. 101. **Hyrcan:** of Hyrcania, near the Caspian Sea. 105. **inhabit:** i.e., continue. Perhaps corrupt. 106. **baby:** doll. 110. **admir'd:** amazing. 111. **like ... cloud:** i.e., suddenly. 112-13. **make ... owe:** make me wonder if I have the courage I supposed.

Macb. It will have blood, they say; blood will
    have blood.
Stones have been known to move and trees to
    speak;
Augures and understood relations have
By maggot-pies and choughs and rooks brought
    forth   125
The secret'st man of blood. What is the night?
    Lady M. Almost at odds with morning, which is
    which.
    Macb. How say'st thou that Macduff denies his
    person
At our great bidding?
    Lady M.   Did you send to him, sir?
    Macb. I hear it by the way; but I will send. 130
There's not a one of them but in his house
I keep a servant fee'd. I will to-morrow,
And betimes I will, to the weird sisters.
More shall they speak; for now I am bent to know,
By the worst means, the worst. For mine own
    good   135
All causes shall give way. I am in blood
Stepp'd in so far that, should I wade no more,
Returning were as tedious as go o'er.
Strange things I have in head, that will to hand,
Which must be acted ere they may be scann'd. 140
    Lady M. You lack the season of all natures, sleep.
    Macb. Come, we'll to sleep. My strange and
    self-abuse
Is the initiate fear that wants hard use;
We are yet but young in deed.   [*Exeunt.*

SCENE V. [*A heath.*]

Thunder. Enter the three WITCHES, *meeting*
    HECATE.

    1. Witch. Why, how now, Hecate! you look an-
    gerly.
    Hec. Have I not reason, beldams as you are,
Saucy and overbold? How did you dare
To trade and traffic with Macbeth
In riddles and affairs of death;   5
And I, the mistress of your charms,
The close contriver of all harms,
Was never call'd to bear my part,
Or show the glory of our art?
And, which is worse, all you have done   10
Hath been but for a wayward son,
Spiteful and wrathful, who, as others do,
Loves for his own ends, not for you.
But make amends now; get you gone,

And at the pit of Acheron   15
Meet me i' th' morning; thither he
Will come to know his destiny.
Your vessels and your spells provide,
Your charms and everything beside.
I am for th' air; this night I'll spend   20
Unto a dismal and a fatal end;
Great business must be wrought ere noon.
Upon the corner of the moon
There hangs a vap'rous drop profound;
I'll catch it ere it come to ground;   25
And that, distill'd by magic sleights,
Shall raise such artificial sprites
As by the strength of their illusion
Shall draw him on to his confusion.
He shall spurn fate, scorn death, and bear   30
His hopes 'bove wisdom, grace, and fear;
And, you all know, security
Is mortals' chiefest enemy.   [*Music, and a song.*
Hark! I am call'd; my little spirit, see,
Sits in a foggy cloud, and stays for me.   [*Exit.*]
    [*Sing within:* "Come away, come away,"
    etc.
    1. Witch. Come, let's make haste; she'll soon be
    back again.   [*Exeunt.* 36

SCENE VI. [*Forres. The palace.*]

Enter LENNOX *and another* LORD.

    Len. My former speeches have but hit your
    thoughts,
Which can interpret farther; only, I say,
Things have been strangely borne. The gracious
    Duncan
Was pitied of Macbeth; marry, he was dead.
And the right-valiant Banquo walk'd too late;   5
Whom, you may say, if 't please you, Fleance
    kill'd,
For Fleance fled; men must not walk too late.
Who cannot want the thought how monstrous
It was for Malcolm and for Donalbain
To kill their gracious father? Damned fact!   10
How it did grieve Macbeth! Did he not straight
In pious rage the two delinquents tear,
That were the slaves of drink and thralls of
    sleep?
Was not that nobly done? Ay, and wisely too;
For 'twould have anger'd any heart alive   15
To hear the men deny 't. So that, I say,
He has borne all things well; and I do think
That, had he Duncan's sons under his key —

124. **Augures...relations:** omens and significances rightly comprehended. 125. **By:** by means of. **maggot-pies:** magpies. **choughs:** jackdaws. 136. **causes:** considerations. 141. **season:** preservative. 142. **strange and self-abuse:** strange self-delusion. 143. **initiate...use:** fear felt by the novice unhardened (in crime).

Sc. v, 2. **beldams:** hags. 7. **close:** secret. 24. **profound:** having deep potency. 29. **confusion:** ruin. 32. **security:** over-confidence.

Sc. vi, 3. **borne:** managed. 10. **fact:** crime.

As, an't please Heaven, he shall not — they should
find
What 'twere to kill a father; so should Fleance. 20
But, peace! for from broad words, and, 'cause he
fail'd
His presence at the tyrant's feast, I hear
Macduff lives in disgrace.   Sir, can you tell
Where he bestows himself?
    Lord.   The son of Duncan,
From whom this tyrant holds the due of birth, 25
Lives in the English court, and is receiv'd
Of the most pious Edward with such grace
That the malevolence of Fortune nothing
Takes from his high respect.   Thither Macduff
Is gone to pray the holy king, upon his aid   30
To wake Northumberland and warlike Siward;
That by the help of these — with Him above
To ratify the work — we may again
Give to our tables meat, sleep to our nights,
Free from our feasts and banquets bloody knives, 35
Do faithful homage and receive free honours;
All which we pine for now: and this report
Hath so exasperate [the] King that he
Prepares for some attempt of war.
    Len.   Sent he to Macduff?
    Lord. He did; and with an absolute "Sir, not
I,"   40
The cloudy messenger turns me his back,
And hums, as who should say, "You'll rue the time
That clogs me with this answer."
    Len.   And that well might
Advise him to a caution, t' hold what distance
His wisdom can provide.   Some holy angel   45
Fly to the court of England and unfold
His message ere he come, that a swift blessing
May soon return to this our suffering country
Under a hand accurs'd!
    Lord.   I'll send my prayers with him.
                                           [Exeunt.

ACT IV

SCENE I. [*A cavern. In the middle, a boiling
cauldron.*]

Thunder. Enter the three WITCHES.

  1. Witch. Thrice the brinded cat hath mew'd.
  2. Witch. Thrice, and once the hedge-pig whin'd.
  3. Witch. Harpier cries; 'tis time, 'tis time.
  1. Witch. Round about the cauldron go;
In the poison'd entrails throw.   5
Toad, that under cold stone
Days and nights has thirty-one

Swelt'red venom sleeping got,
Boil thou first i' th' charmed pot.
  All. Double, double, toil and trouble;   10
Fire burn and cauldron bubble.
  2. Witch. Fillet of a fenny snake,
In the cauldron boil and bake;
Eye of newt and toe of frog,
Wool of bat and tongue of dog,   15
Adder's fork and blind-worm's sting,
Lizard's leg and howlet's wing,
For a charm of pow'rful trouble,
Like a hell-broth boil and bubble.
  All. Double, double, toil and trouble;   20
Fire burn and cauldron bubble.
  3. Witch. Scale of dragon, tooth of wolf,
Witches' mummy, maw and gulf
Of the ravin'd salt-sea shark,
Root of hemlock digg'd i' th' dark,   25
Liver of blaspheming Jew,
Gall of goat, and slips of yew
Sliver'd in the moon's eclipse,
Nose of Turk and Tartar's lips,
Finger of birth-strangled babe   30
Ditch-deliver'd by a drab,
Make the gruel thick and slab.
Add thereto a tiger's chaudron,
For th' ingredients of our cauldron.
  All. Double, double, toil and trouble;   35
Fire burn and cauldron bubble.
  2. Witch. Cool it with a baboon's blood,
Then the charm is firm and good.

Enter HECATE *to the other three Witches.*

  Hec. O, well done! I commend your pains;
And every one shall share i' th' gains.   40
And now about the cauldron sing,
Like elves and fairies in a ring,
Enchanting all that you put in.
         [*Music and a song:* "Black spirits," *etc.*
                                [*Hecate retires.*]
  2. [*Witch*]. By the pricking of my thumbs,
Something wicked this way comes.   45
      Open, locks,
      Whoever knocks!

Enter MACBETH.

  Macb. How now, you secret, black, and midnight
hags!
What is't you do?
  All.   A deed without a name.
  Macb. I conjure you by that which you profess, 50
Howe'er you come to know it, answer me!
Though you untie the winds and let them fight

25. **holds:** withholds. 27. **Edward:** Edward the Confessor. 30. **upon:** for. 38. **[the]** (Hanmer). *their* F. 41. **cloudy:** sullen.
    Act IV, sc. i, 8. **Swelt'red:** in sweaty drops. 12. **Fillet:** slice. **fenny:** swamp-dwelling. 16. **fork:** forked tongue. 17.
howlet's: owl's. 23. **mummy:** medicinal substance made from a mummy. **gulf:** gullet. 32. **slab:** sticky. 33. **chaudron:**
entrails.

Against the churches; though the yesty waves
Confound and swallow navigation up;
Though bladed corn be lodg'd and trees blown
    down;   55
Though castles topple on their warders' heads;
Though palaces and pyramids do slope
Their heads to their foundations; though the treas-
    ure
Of nature's [germens] tumble all together,
Even till destruction sicken; answer me   60
To what I ask you.
    1. Witch.   Speak.
    2. Witch.   Demand.
    3. Witch.   We'll answer.
    1. Witch. Say, if th' hadst rather hear it from our
    mouths,
Or from our masters'?
    Macb.   Call 'em; let me see 'em.
    1. Witch. Pour in sow's blood, that hath eaten
Her nine farrow; grease that's sweaten   65
From the murderer's gibbet throw
Into the flame.
    All.   Come, high or low;
Thyself and office deftly show!

    Thunder. First APPARITION, *an armed Head.*
    Macb. Tell me, thou unknown power, —
    1. Witch.   He knows thy thought.
Hear his speech, but say thou nought.   70
    1. App. Macbeth! Macbeth! Macbeth! beware
    Macduff;
Beware the thane of Fife. Dismiss me. Enough.
                   [*Descends.*
    Macb. Whate'er thou art, for thy good caution,
    thanks;
Thou hast harp'd my fear aright. But one word
    more, —
    1. Witch. He will not be commanded. Here's
    another,   75
More potent than the first.

    Thunder. Second APPARITION, *a bloody Child.*
    2. App. Macbeth! Macbeth! Macbeth!
    Macb. Had I three ears, I'd hear thee.
    2. App. Be bloody, bold, and resolute; laugh to
    scorn
The pow'r of man; for none of woman born   80
Shall harm Macbeth.   [*Descends.*
    Macb. Then live, Macduff: what need I fear of
    thee?
But yet I'll make assurance double sure

And take a bond of fate. Thou shalt not live;
That I may tell pale-hearted fear it lies,   85
And sleep in spite of thunder.

    Thunder. Third APPARITION, *a Child crowned,*
    with a tree in his hand.
                   What is this
That rises like the issue of a king,
And wears upon his baby-brow the round
And top of sovereignty?
    All.   Listen, but speak not to't.
    3. App. Be lion-mettled, proud, and take no
    care   90
Who chafes, who frets, or where conspirers are.
Macbeth shall never vanquish'd be until
Great Birnam wood to high Dunsinane hill
Shall come against him.   [*Descends.*
    Macb.   That will never be.
Who can impress the forest, bid the tree   95
Unfix his earth-bound root? Sweet bodements!
    good!
[Rebellion's head], rise never till the wood
Of Birnam rise, and our high-plac'd Macbeth
Shall live the lease of nature, pay his breath
To time and mortal custom. Yet my heart   100
Throbs to know one thing: tell me, if your art
Can tell so much, shall Banquo's issue ever
Reign in this kingdom?
    All.   Seek to know no more.
    Macb. I will be satisfied! Deny me this,
And an eternal curse fall on you! Let me know. 105
Why sinks that cauldron? And what noise is this?
                   [*Hautboys.*
    1. Witch. Show!
    2. Witch. Show!
    3. Witch. Show!
    All. Show his eyes, and grieve his heart;   110
Come like shadows, so depart!

    A show of Eight Kings, [*the last*] *with a glass in his*
    hand; [*Banquo's Ghost following*].
    Macb. Thou art too like the spirit of Banquo;
    down!
Thy crown does sear mine eye-balls. And thy hair,
Thou other gold-bound brow, is like the first.
A third is like the former. Filthy hags!   115
Why do you show me this? A fourth! Start, eyes!
What, will the line stretch out to th' crack of doom?
Another yet! A seventh! I'll see no more.
And yet the eighth appears, who bears a glass
Which shows me many more; and some I see   120

53. **yesty:** foamy. 55. **lodg'd:** beaten down. 59. **[germens]** (Camb. edd.): seeds. *Germaine* F. 65. **farrow:** litter. 69. s.d. ***armed Head.*** Perhaps signifying Macduff's rebellion. 77. s.d. ***a bloody Child.*** Signifying Macduff (see V.viii.15–16). 86. s.d. ***a Child crowned.*** Signifying Malcolm. ***tree.*** Foreshadowing the action of the soldiers of Malcolm in V.iv.4 ff. 89. **top:** crown. 95. **impress:** force into service. 96. **bodements:** prophecies. 97. **[Rebellion's head]** (Theobald conj.). *Rebellious dead* F. 112. s.d. F reads "A shew of eight Kings, and Banquo last, with a glasse in his hand." ***glass:*** mirror.

That twofold balls and treble sceptres carry.
Horrible sight! Now, I see, 'tis true;
For the blood-bolter'd Banquo smiles upon me,
And points at them for his. [*Apparitions vanish.*]
  What, is this so?
  1. [*Witch*]. Ay, sir, all this is so; but why 125
Stands Macbeth thus amazedly?
Come, sisters, cheer we up his sprites,
And show the best of our delights.
I'll charm the air to give a sound,
While you perform your antic round;   130
That this great king may kindly say
Our duties did his welcome pay.
          [*Music. The Witches dance, and vanish*
          [*with Hecate*].
  Macb. Where are they? Gone? **Let this per-**
nicious hour
Stand aye accursed in the calendar!   134
Come in, without there!

Enter LENNOX.

  Len.   What's your Grace's will?
  Macb. Saw you the weird sisters?
  Len.   No, my lord.
  Macb. Came they not by you?
  Len.   No, indeed, my lord.
  Macb. Infected be the air whereon they ride,
And damn'd all those that trust them! I did
    hear
The galloping of horse; who was 't came by? 140
  Len. 'Tis two or three, my lord, that bring you
    word
Macduff is fled to England.
  Macb.   Fled to England!
  Len. Ay, my good lord.
  Macb. [*Aside.*] Time, thou anticipat'st my dread
    exploits:
The flighty purpose never is o'ertook   145
Unless the deed go with it. From this moment
The very firstlings of my heart shall be
The firstlings of my hand. And even now,
To crown my thoughts with acts, be it thought and
    done.
The castle of Macduff I will surprise;   150
Seize upon Fife; give to the edge o' th' sword
His wife, his babes, and all unfortunate souls
That trace him in his line. No boasting like a fool;
This deed I'll do before this purpose cool.
But no more sights! — Where are these gentlemen?
Come, bring me where they are. [*Exeunt.* 156

SCENE II. [*Fife, Macduff's castle.*]

  Enter LADY [MACDUFF], *her* SON, *and* ROSS.

  L. Macd. What had he done, to make him fly
    the land?
  Ross. You must have patience, madam.
  L. Macd.   He had none;
His flight was madness. When our actions do not,
Our fears do make us traitors.
  Ross.   You know not
Whether it was his wisdom or his fear.   5
  L. Macd. Wisdom! to leave his wife, to leave his
    babes,
His mansion and his titles, in a place
From whence himself does fly? He loves us not,
He wants the natural touch; for the poor wren,
The most diminutive of birds, will fight,   10
Her young ones in her nest, against the owl.
All is the fear and nothing is the love;
As little is the wisdom, where the flight
So runs against all reason.
  Ross.   My dearest coz,
I pray you school yourself; but for your husband,
He is noble, wise, judicious, and best knows   16
The fits o' th' season. I dare not speak much fur-
    ther;
But cruel are the times when we are traitors
And do not know ourselves; when we hold rumour
From what we fear, yet know not what we fear, 20
But float upon a wild and violent sea
Each way and move. I take my leave of you;
Shall not be long but I'll be here again.
Things at the worst will cease, or else climb up-
    ward
To what they were before. My pretty cousin, 25
Blessing upon you!
  L. Macd. Father'd he is, and yet he's fatherless.
  Ross. I am so much a fool, should I stay longer,
It would be my disgrace and your discomfort.
I take my leave at once.   [*Exit.*
  L. Macd.   Sirrah, your father's dead;
And what will you do now? How will you live? 31
  Son. As birds do, mother.
  L. Macd.   What, with worms and flies?
  Son. With what I get, I mean; and so do they.
  L. Macd. Poor bird! thou'dst never fear the net
    nor lime,
The pitfall nor the gin.   35
  Son. Why should I, mother? Poor birds they
    are not set for.
My father is not dead, for all your saying.

---

121. twofold ... sceptres. Referring respectively to England and Scotland, and to King James's taking the title "King of Great Britain, France and Ireland." Banquo was the mythical ancestor of James. **123. blood-bolter'd:** with hair matted with blood. **126. amazedly:** as in a trance. **130. antic round:** fantastic circular dance. **145. flighty:** fleeting. **147. firstlings:** first-born. **153. trace:** follow.
Sc. ii, 1. L. Macd. The speeches of Lady Macduff are headed *Wife* in F. **7. titles:** title deeds, hence estates. **17. fits ... season:** emergencies of the time. **19. hold:** judge. **20. From:** because of. **22. move.** Perhaps corrupt. Camb. edd. read *none*. **29. It ... discomfort:** i.e., I should weep. **35. gin:** snare.

L. Macd. Yes, he is dead. How wilt thou do for
  a father?
Son. Nay, how will you do for a husband?
L. Macd. Why, I can buy me twenty at any mar-
  ket.   40
Son. Then you'll buy 'em to sell again.
L. Macd. Thou speak'st with all thy wit; and yet,
  i' faith,
With wit enough for thee.
  Son. Was my father a traitor, mother?
L. Macd. Ay, that he was.   45
Son. What is a traitor?
L. Macd. Why, one that swears and lies.
Son. And be all traitors that do so?
L. Macd. Every one that does so is a traitor, and
must be hang'd.   50
Son. And must they all be hang'd that swear and
lie?
L. Macd. Every one.
Son. Who must hang them?
L. Macd. Why, the honest men.   55
Son. Then the liars and swearers are fools; for
there are liars and swearers enow to beat the honest
men and hang up them.
L. Macd. Now, God help thee, poor monkey!
But how wilt thou do for a father!   60
Son. If he were dead, you'd weep for him; if you
would not, it were a good sign that I should quickly
have a new father.
L. Macd. Poor prattler, how thou talk'st!

Enter a MESSENGER.

Mess. Bless you, fair dame! I am not to you
  known.   65
Though in your state of honour I am perfect.
I doubt some danger does approach you nearly.
If you will take a homely man's advice,
Be not found here; hence, with your little
  ones.
To fright you thus, methinks, I am too savage;   70
To do worse to you were fell cruelty,
Which is too nigh your person. Heaven preserve
  you!
I dare abide no longer.   [*Exit.*
L. Macd.   Whither should I fly?
I have done no harm. But I remember now
I am in this earthly world, where to do harm   75
Is often laudable, to do good sometime
Accounted dangerous folly. Why then, alas,
Do I put up that womanly defence,
To say I have done no harm?

Enter MURDERERS.

                What are these faces?
[1.] *Mur.* Where is your husband?   80
L. Macd. I hope, in no place so unsanctified
Where such as thou mayst find him.
[1.] *Mur.*   He's a traitor.
Son. Thou liest, thou shag-ear'd villain!
[1.] *Mur.*   What, you egg!
                         [*Stabbing him.*]
Young fry of treachery!
Son.   He has kill'd me, mother:
Run away, I pray you!   [*Dies.*] 85
  [*Exit* [*Lady Macduff*] *crying* "Murder!"
  [*Exeunt Murderers, following her.*]

SCENE III. [*England. Before the King's
                     palace.*]

Enter MALCOLM *and* MACDUFF.

Mal. Let us seek out some desolate shade, and
  there
Weep our sad bosoms empty.
  Macd.   Let us rather
Hold fast the mortal sword, and like good men
Bestride our down-fall'n birthdom. Each new
  morn
New widows howl, new orphans cry, new sorrows   5
Strike heaven on the face, that it resounds
As if it felt with Scotland, and yell'd out
Like syllable of dolour.
  Mal.   What I believe I'll wail,
What know believe, and what I can redress,
As I shall find the time to friend, I will.   10
What you have spoke, it may be so perchance.
This tyrant, whose sole name blisters our tongues,
Was once thought honest; you have lov'd him well.
He hath not touch'd you yet. I am young; but
  something
You may [deserve] of him through me, and wis-
  dom   15
To offer up a weak poor innocent lamb
T' appease an angry god.
  Macd. I am not treacherous.
  Mal.   But Macbeth is.
A good and virtuous nature may recoil
In an imperial charge. But I shall crave your par-
  don;   20
That which you are my thoughts cannot transpose.
Angels are bright still, though the brightest fell.
Though all things foul would wear the brows of
  grace,
Yet grace must still look so.

---

47. **swears and lies:** takes an oath and breaks it.   66. **in ... perfect:** I know your rank.   67. **doubt:** fear.   68. **homely:** plain.   71. **fell:** fierce.   83. **shag-ear'd:** with ears like a shaggy dog's.

Sc. iii, 8. **Like ... dolour:** similar cry of pain.   10. **to friend:** favorable.   12. **sole:** mere.   15. [**deserve**] (Theobald): win. *discerne* F.   **wisdom:** it were wise.   19-20. **recoil ... charge:** give way under a king's command.   21. **transpose:** change.

Macd.   I have lost my hopes.
Mal. Perchance even there where I did find my
    doubts.   25
Why in that rawness left you wife and child,
Those precious motives, those strong knots of love,
Without leave-taking?   I pray you,
Let not my jealousies be your dishonours,   29
But mine own safeties.   You may be rightly just,
Whatever I shall think.
Macd.   Bleed, bleed, poor country!
Great tyranny! lay thou thy basis sure,
For goodness dare not check thee; wear thou thy
    wrongs;
The title is [affeer'd]!   Fare thee well, lord:
I would not be the villain that thou think'st   35
For the whole space that's in the tyrant's grasp,
And the rich East to boot.
Mal.   Be not offended;
I speak not as in absolute fear of you.
I think our country sinks beneath the yoke;
It weeps, it bleeds; and each new day a gash   40
Is added to her wounds.   I think withal
There would be hands uplifted in my right;
And here from gracious England have I offer
Of goodly thousands.   But, for all this,
When I shall tread upon the tyrant's head,   45
Or wear it on my sword, yet my poor country
Shall have more vices than it had before,
More suffer and more sundry ways than ever,
By him that shall succeed.
Macd.   What should he be?
Mal. It is myself I mean; in whom I know   50
All the particulars of vice so grafted
That, when they shall be open'd, black Macbeth
Will seem as pure as snow, and the poor state
Esteem him as a lamb, being compar'd
With my confineless harms.
Macd.   Not in the legions   55
Of horrid hell can come a devil more damn'd
In evils to top Macbeth.
Mal.   I grant him bloody,
Luxurious, avaricious, false, deceitful,
Sudden, malicious, smacking of every sin
That has a name; but there's no bottom, none,   60
In my voluptuousness.   Your wives, your daughters,
Your matrons, and your maids could not fill up
The cistern of my lust, and my desire
All continent impediments would o'erbear
That did oppose my will.   Better Macbeth   65
Than such an one to reign.
Macd.   Boundless intemperance

In nature is a tyranny; it hath been
Th' untimely emptying of the happy throne
And fall of many kings.   But fear not yet
To take upon you what is yours.   You may   70
Convey your pleasures in a spacious plenty,
And yet seem cold; the time you may so hoodwink.
We have willing dames enough; there cannot be
That vulture in you to devour so many
As will to greatness dedicate themselves,   75
Finding it so inclin'd.
Mal.   With this there grows
In my most ill-compos'd affection such
A stanchless avarice that, were I King,
I should cut off the nobles for their lands,
Desire his jewels and this other's house;   80
And my more-having would be as a sauce
To make me hunger more, that I should forge
Quarrels unjust against the good and loyal,
Destroying them for wealth.
Macd.   This avarice
Sticks deeper, grows with more pernicious root   85
Than summer-seeming lust, and it hath been
The sword of our slain kings.   Yet do not fear;
Scotland hath foisons to fill up your will,
Of your mere own.   All these are portable,
With other graces weigh'd.   90
Mal. But I have none.   The king-becoming
    graces,
As justice, verity, temp'rance, stableness,
Bounty, perseverance, mercy, lowliness,
Devotion, patience, courage, fortitude,
I have no relish of them, but abound   95
In the division of each several crime,
Acting it many ways.   Nay, had I power, I should
Pour the sweet milk of concord into hell,
Uproar the universal peace, confound
All unity on earth.
Macd.   O Scotland, Scotland!   100
Mal. If such an one be fit to govern, speak.
I am as I have spoken.
Macd.   Fit to govern!
No, not to live.   O nation miserable,
With an untitled tyrant bloody-scept'red,
When shalt thou see thy wholesome days again,
Since that the truest issue of thy throne   106
By his own interdiction stands accurs'd
And does blaspheme his breed?   Thy royal father
Was a most sainted king; the queen that bore thee,
Oftener upon her knees than on her feet,   110
Died every day she liv'd.   Fare thee well!
These evils thou repeat'st upon thyself

---

24. **hopes:** i.e., of Malcolm's cooperation. 25. **doubts:** i.e., of Macduff's honor. 26. **rawness:** haste, unpreparedness. 28. **jealousies:** suspicions. 33. **wrongs:** things wrongly gained. 34. **[affeer'd]** (Hanmer): confirmed (legal term). *affear'd* F. 57. **top:** surpass. 58. **Luxurious:** lecherous. 59. **Sudden:** violent. 64. **continent:** restraining. 69. **yet:** nevertheless. 71. **Convey:** manage secretly. 72. **cold:** chaste. 77. **affection:** character. 78. **stanchless:** insatiable. 86. **summer-seeming:** typical only of early age. 88. **foisons:** abundance. 89. **portable:** bearable. 90. **weigh'd:** balanced. 95. **relish:** trace. 99. **Uproar:** make tumultuous. 108. **blaspheme:** slander. 111. **Died:** i.e., to the world.

Hath banish'd me from Scotland. O my breast,
Thy hope ends here!
 Mal.   Macduff, this noble passion,
Child of integrity, hath from my soul 115
Wip'd the black scruples, reconcil'd my thoughts
To thy good truth and honour. Devilish Macbeth
By many of these trains hath sought to win me
Into his power, and modest wisdom plucks me
From over-credulous haste. But God above 120
Deal between thee and me! for even now
I put myself to thy direction, and
Unspeak mine own detraction; here abjure
The taints and blames I laid upon myself,
For strangers to my nature. I am yet 125
Unknown to woman, never was forsworn,
Scarcely have coveted what was mine own,
At no time broke my faith, would not betray
The devil to his fellow, and delight
No less in truth than life; my first false speaking 130
Was this upon myself. What I am truly,
Is thine and my poor country's to command;
Whither indeed, before thy here-approach,
Old Siward, with ten thousand warlike men,
Already at a point, was setting forth. 135
Now we'll together; and the chance of goodness
Be like our warranted quarrel! Why are you
 silent?
 Macd. Such welcome and unwelcome things at
 once
'Tis hard to reconcile.

    Enter a DOCTOR.

 Mal. Well; more anon. — Comes the King forth,
 I pray you? 140
 Doct. Ay, sir; there are a crew of wretched souls
That stay his cure. Their malady convinces
The great assay of art; but at his touch —
Such sanctity hath Heaven given his hand —
They presently amend.
 Mal.   I thank you, doctor. 145
        [*Exit Doctor.*
 Macd. What's the disease he means?
 Mal.   'Tis call'd the evil:
A most miraculous work in this good king;
Which often, since my here-remain in England,
I have seen him do. How he solicits Heaven,
Himself best knows; but strangely-visited people,
All swoll'n and ulcerous, pitiful to the eye, 151
The mere despair of surgery, he cures,
Hanging a golden stamp about their necks,
Put on with holy prayers; and 'tis spoken,
To the succeeding royalty he leaves 155

The healing benediction. With this strange virtue,
He hath a heavenly gift of prophecy,
And sundry blessings hang about his throne
That speak him full of grace.

    Enter ROSS.

 Macd.   See, who comes here?
 Mal. My countryman; but yet I know him not.
 Macd. My ever-gentle cousin, welcome hither. 161
 Mal. I know him now. Good God, betimes re-
 move
The means that makes us strangers!
 Ross.   Sir, amen.
 Macd. Stand Scotland where it did?
 Ross.   Alas, poor country!
Almost afraid to know itself. It cannot 165
Be call'd our mother, but our grave; where nothing,
But who knows nothing, is once seen to smile;
Where sighs and groans and shrieks that rend the
 air
Are made, not mark'd; where violent sorrow seems
A modern ecstasy. The dead man's knell 170
Is there scarce ask'd for who; and good men's lives
Expire before the flowers in their caps,
Dying or ere they sicken.
 Macd.   O, relation
Too nice, and yet too true!
 Mal.   What's the newest grief?
 Ross. That of an hour's age doth hiss the speaker;
Each minute teems a new one.
 Macd.   How does my wife? 176
 Ross. Why, well.
 Macd.   And all my children?
 Ross.   Well too.
 Macd. The tyrant has not batter'd at their
 peace?
 Ross. No; they were well at peace when I did
 leave 'em.
 Macd. Be not a niggard of your speech; how
 goes 't? 180
 Ross. When I came hither to transport the tid-
 ings,
Which I have heavily borne, there ran a rumour
Of many worthy fellows that were out;
Which was to my belief witness'd the rather,
For that I saw the tyrant's power afoot. 185
Now is the time of help; your eye in Scotland
Would create soldiers, make our women fight,
To doff their dire distresses.
 Mal.   Be 't their comfort
We're coming thither. Gracious England hath
Lent us good Siward and ten thousand men; 190

118. **trains**: devices. 135. **at a point**: fully prepared. 136. **goodness**: success. 137. **like...quarrel**: as good as our just cause. 142. **convinces**: defeats. 143. **great...art**: best medical skill. 147. **evil**: scrofula ("the king's evil," supposedly healed by royal touch). 150. **strangely-visited**: strangely afflicted. 152. **mere**: utter. 153. **stamp**: coin. 156. **virtue**: power. 160. **know**: recognize. 170. **modern ecstasy**: commonplace emotion. 174. **nice**: precise. 175. **hiss...speaker**: cause the speaker to be hissed (for telling old stuff). 176. **teems**: brings forth. 182. **heavily**: sorrowfully. 183. **out**: in arms.

An older and a better soldier none
That Christendom gives out.

Ross.   Would I could answer
This comfort with the like! But I have words
That would be howl'd out in the desert air,
Where hearing should not latch them.

Macd.   What concern they?
The general cause? Or is it a fee-grief   196
Due to some single breast?

Ross.   No mind that's honest
But in it shares some woe, though the main part
Pertains to you alone.

Macd.   If it be mine,
Keep it not from me, quickly let me have it.   200

Ross. Let not your ears despise my tongue for
ever,
Which shall possess them with the heaviest sound
That ever yet they heard.

Macd.   Hum! I guess at it.

Ross. Your castle is surpris'd; your wife and
babes
Savagely slaughter'd. To relate the manner,   205
Were, on the quarry of these murder'd deer,
To add the death of you.

Mal.   Merciful heaven!
What, man! ne'er pull your hat upon your brows;
Give sorrow words. The grief that does not
speak
Whispers the o'er-fraught heart and bids it break.

Macd. My children too?

Ross.   Wife, children, servants, all 211
That could be found.

Macd.   And I must be from thence!
My wife kill'd too?

Ross.   I have said.

Mal.   Be comforted.
Let's make us med'cines of our great revenge
To cure this deadly grief.   215

Macd. He has no children. — All my pretty
ones?
Did you say all? O hell-kite! All?
What, all my pretty chickens and their dam
At one fell swoop?

Mal. Dispute it like a man.

Macd.   I shall do so;   220
But I must also feel it as a man.
I cannot but remember such things were,
That were most precious to me. Did heaven look
on,
And would not take their part? Sinful Macduff,
They were all struck for thee! naught that I am, 225
Not for their own demerits, but for mine,

Fell slaughter on their souls. Heaven rest them
now!

Mal. Be this the whetstone of your sword; let
grief
Convert to anger; blunt not the heart, enrage it.

Macd. O, I could play the woman with mine
eyes   230
And braggart with my tongue! But, gentle heav-
ens,
Cut short all intermission. Front to front
Bring thou this fiend of Scotland and myself;
Within my sword's length set him; if he scape,
Heaven forgive him too!

Mal.   This [tune] goes manly. 235
Come, go we to the King; our power is ready;
Our lack is nothing but our leave. Macbeth
Is ripe for shaking, and the powers above
Put on their instruments. Receive what cheer you
may;
The night is long that never finds the day.   240
                                        [*Exeunt.*

ACT V

Scene I. [*Dunsinane. Ante-room in the castle.*]

Enter a Doctor *of Physic and a* Waiting Gentlewoman.

Doct. I have two nights watch'd with you, but
can perceive no truth in your report. When was it
she last walk'd?   3

Gent. Since his Majesty went into the field, I
have seen her rise from her bed, throw her night-
gown upon her, unlock her closet, take forth paper,
fold it, write upon 't, read it, afterwards seal it, and
again return to bed; yet all this while in a most
fast sleep.   9

Doct. A great perturbation in nature, to receive
at once the benefit of sleep and do the effects of
watching! In this slumb'ry agitation, besides her
walking and other actual performances, what, at
any time, have you heard her say?   15

Gent. That, sir, which I will not report after her.

Doct. You may to me: and 'tis most meet you
should.

Gent. Neither to you nor any one; having no
witness to confirm my speech.   21

Enter Lady [Macbeth], *with a taper.*

Lo, you, here she comes! This is her very guise;
and, upon my life, fast asleep. Observe her; stand
close.

---

195. **latch:** catch. 196. **fee-grief:** private woe. 206. **quarry:** slaughtered heap. 210. **o'er-fraught:** over-burdened. 220. **Dispute:** fight. 225. **naught:** wicked. 235. **[tune]** (Rowe). *time* F. 237. **Our...leave:** we need only to take leave (of King Edward). 239. **Put...instruments:** urge on their agents (us).

Act V, sc. i, 11–12. **do...watching:** act as if awake. 12. **agitation:** activity. 22. **her very guise:** exactly what she has been doing. 24. **close:** out of sight.

Doct. How came she by that light? 25

Gent. Why, it stood by her. She has light by her continually: 'tis her command.

Doct. You see her eyes are open.

Gent. Ay, but their sense are shut.

Doct. What is it she does now? Look how she rubs her hands. 31

Gent. It is an accustom'd action with her, to seem thus washing her hands. I have known her continue in this a quarter of an hour.

Lady M. Yet here's a spot. 35

Doct. Hark! she speaks. I will set down what comes from her, to satisfy my remembrance the more strongly. 38

Lady M. Out, damned spot! out, I say! — One: two: why, then 'tis time to do't. — Hell is murky! — Fie, my lord, fie! a soldier, and afeard? What need we fear who knows it, when none can call our pow'r to account? — Yet who would have thought the old man to have had so much blood in him? 45

Doct. Do you mark that?

Lady M. The thane of Fife had a wife; where is she now? — What, will these hands ne'er be clean? — No more o' that, my lord, no more o' that; you mar all with this starting. 50

Doct. Go to, go to; you have known what you should not.

Gent. She has spoke what she should not, I am sure of that; Heaven knows what she has known. 55

Lady M. Here's the smell of the blood still; all the perfumes of Arabia will not sweeten this little hand. Oh, oh, oh!

Doct. What a sigh is there! The heart is sorely charg'd. 60

Gent. I would not have such a heart in my bosom for the dignity of the whole body.

Doct. Well, well, well, —

Gent. Pray God it be, sir. 64

Doct. This disease is beyond my practice; yet I have known those which have walk'd in their sleep who have died holily in their beds.

Lady M. Wash your hands, put on your nightgown; look not so pale. — I tell you yet again, Banquo's buried; he cannot come out on 's grave. 71

Doct. Even so?

Lady M. To bed, to bed! there's knocking at the gate. Come, come, come, come, give me your hand. What's done cannot be undone. — To bed, to bed, to bed! [*Exit.* 76

Doct. Will she go now to bed?

Gent. Directly.

Doct. Foul whisp'rings are abroad; unnatural deeds

Do breed unnatural troubles; infected minds 80
To their deaf pillows will discharge their secrets.
More needs she the divine than the physician.
God, God, forgive us all! Look after her;
Remove from her the means of all annoyance,
And still keep eyes upon her. So, good-night! 85
My mind she has mated, and amaz'd my sight.
I think, but dare not speak.

Gent. Good-night, good doctor.
[*Exeunt.*

SCENE II. [*The country near Dunsinane.*]

Drum and colours. Enter MENTEITH, CAITH-
NESS, ANGUS, LENNOX, *and* Soldiers.

Ment. The English pow'r is near, led on by Malcolm,
His uncle Siward, and the good Macduff.
Revenges burn in them; for their dear causes
Would to the bleeding and the grim alarm
Excite the mortified man.

Ang. Near Birnam wood 5
Shall we well meet them; that way are they coming.

Caith. Who knows if Donalbain be with his brother?

Len. For certain, sir, he is not; I have a file
Of all the gentry. There is Siward's son,
And many unrough youths that even now 10
Protest their first of manhood.

Ment. What does the tyrant?

Caith. Great Dunsinane he strongly fortifies.
Some say he's mad, others that lesser hate him
Do call it valiant fury; but, for certain,
He cannot buckle his distemper'd cause 15
Within the belt of rule.

Ang. Now does he feel
His secret murders sticking on his hands;
Now minutely revolts upbraid his faith-breach;
Those he commands move only in command,
Nothing in love. Now does he feel his title 20
Hang loose about him, like a giant's robe
Upon a dwarfish thief.

Ment. Who then shall blame
His pester'd senses to recoil and start,
When all that is within him does condemn
Itself for being there?

Caith. Well, march we on 25
To give obedience where 'tis truly ow'd.
Meet we the med'cine of the sickly weal,
And with him pour we in our country's purge
Each drop of us.

Len. Or so much as it needs

37. **satisfy**: assure. 60. **charg'd**: burdened. 84. **annoyance**: self-harm. 86. **mated**: bewildered.
Sc. ii, 3. **dear**: deeply felt. 4. **bleeding ... alarm**: grim and bloody battle. 5. **mortified**: weakened, sickly. 6. **well**: probably. 10. **unrough**: beardless. 11. **Protest**: assert. 15–16. **buckle ... rule**: uphold his evil cause by controlled measures. 18. **minutely**: every minute. 27. **med'cine**: i.e., Malcolm. **weal**: state.

To dew the sovereign flower and drown the weeds.
Make we our march towards Birnam.   31

                         [Exeunt, marching.

SCENE III. [*Dunsinane. A room in the castle.*]

Enter MACBETH, DOCTOR, *and* Attendants.

Macb. Bring me no more reports; let them fly all;
Till Birnam wood remove to Dunsinane
I cannot taint with fear. What's the boy Malcolm?
Was he not born of woman? The spirits that know
All mortal consequences have pronounc'd me thus:
"Fear not, Macbeth; no man that's born of wo-
    man   6
Shall e'er have power upon thee." Then fly, false
    thanes,
And mingle with the English epicures!
The mind I sway by and the heart I bear
Shall never sag with doubt nor shake with fear.   10

Enter a SERVANT.

The devil damn thee black, thou cream-fac'd loon!
Where got'st thou that goose look?
    Serv. There is ten thousand —
    Macb.   Geese, villain?
    Serv.   Soldiers, sir.
    Macb. Go prick thy face, and over-red thy fear,
Thou lily-liver'd boy. What soldiers, patch?   15
Death of thy soul! those linen cheeks of thine
Are counsellors to fear. What soldiers, whey-face?
    Serv. The English force, so please you.
    Macb. Take thy face hence.   *Exit Servant.*]
                      Seyton! — I am sick at heart
When I behold — Seyton, I say! — This push   20
Will cheer me ever, or [disseat] me now.
I have liv'd long enough. My way of life
Is fallen into the sear, the yellow leaf;
And that which should accompany old age,
As honour, love, obedience, troops of friends,   25
I must not look to have; but, in their stead,
Curses, not loud but deep, mouth-honour, breath
Which the poor heart would fain deny, and dare not.
Seyton!

Enter SEYTON.

    Sey. What's your gracious pleasure?
    Macb.   What news more?
    Sey. All is confirm'd, my lord, which was re-
    ported.   31
    Macb. I'll fight till from my bones my flesh be
    hack'd.
Give me my armour.

    Sey.   'Tis not needed yet.
    Macb. I'll put it on.
Send out moe horses; skirr the country round;   35
Hang those that talk of fear. Give me mine
    armour.
How does your patient, doctor?
    Doct.   Not so sick, my lord,
As she is troubled with thick-coming fancies
That keep her from her rest.
    Macb.   Cure her of that.
Canst thou not minister to a mind diseas'd,   40
Pluck from the memory a rooted sorrow,
Raze out the written troubles of the brain,
And with some sweet oblivious antidote
Cleanse the stuff'd bosom of that perilous stuff
Which weighs upon the heart?
    Doct.   Therein the patient
Must minister to himself.   46
    Macb. Throw physic to the dogs; I'll none of it.
Come, put mine armour on; give me my staff.
Seyton, send out. Doctor, the thanes fly from me.
Come, sir, dispatch. If thou couldst, doctor, cast
The water of my land, find her disease,   51
And purge it to a sound and pristine health,
I would applaud thee to the very echo,
That should applaud again. — Pull 't off, I say. —
What rhubarb, [senna], or what purgative drug,
Would scour these English hence? Hear'st thou of
    them?   56
    Doct. Ay, my good lord; your royal preparation
Makes us hear something.
    Macb.   Bring it after me.
I will not be afraid of death and bane,
Till Birnam forest come to Dunsinane.   60
    Doct. [*Aside.*] Were I from Dunsinane away and
    clear,
Profit again should hardly draw me here.   [*Exeunt.*

SCENE IV. [*Country near Birnam wood.*]

Drum and colours. Enter MALCOLM, *old* SIWARD
and his Son, MACDUFF, MENTEITH, Caithness,
Angus, [Lennox, Ross,] *and* SOLDIERS, *marching.*

    Mal. Cousins, I hope the days are near at hand
That chambers will be safe.
    Ment.   We doubt it nothing.
    Siw. What wood is this before us?
    Ment.   The wood of Birnam.
    Mal. Let every soldier hew him down a bough
And bear 't before him; thereby shall we shadow   5
The numbers of our host and make discovery
Err in report of us.

    Sc. iii, 3. **taint:** be infected. 5. **mortal consequences:** human fortunes. 9. **sway:** act. 15. **patch:** fool. 17. **Are . . . to:**
inspire. 20. **push:** crisis. 21. **cheer.** Many edd. read *chair.* [**disseat**] (Steevens): dethrone. *dis-eate* F₁. *disease* F₂₋₄.
35. **skirr:** scour. 42. **Raze:** blot. 43. **oblivious:** causing forgetfulness. 48. **staff:** lance. 50. **cast:** analyze. 51. **water:**
urine. 52. **pristine:** perfect (as in former times). 55. [**senna**] F₄. *Cyme* F₁. 58. **it:** the armor.
    Sc. iv, 2. **chambers.** Alluding to Duncan's murder. 6. **discovery:** Macbeth's scouts.

Soldiers.   It shall be done.

Siw. We learn no other but the confident tyrant
Keeps still in Dunsinane, and will endure
Our setting down before 't.

Mal.   'Tis his main hope;   10
For where there is advantage to be given,
Both more and less have given him the revolt,
And none serve with him but constrained things,
Whose hearts are absent too.

Macd.   Let our just censures
Attend the true event, and put we on   15
Industrious soldiership.

Siw.   The time approaches
That will with due decision make us know
What we shall say we have and what we owe.
Thoughts speculative their unsure hopes relate,
But certain issue strokes must arbitrate;   20
Towards which advance the war.

[*Exeunt, marching.*

SCENE V. [*Dunsinane.   Within the castle.*]

Enter MACBETH, SEYTON, *and* Soldiers, *with
drum and colours.*

Macb. Hang out our banners on the outward
    walls;
The cry is still, "They come!" Our castle's
    strength
Will laugh a siege to scorn; here let them lie
Till famine and the ague eat them up.
Were they not forc'd with those that should be
    ours,   5
We might have met them dareful, beard to beard,
And beat them backward home.

[*A cry of women within.*
    What is that noise?

Sey. It is the cry of women, my good lord.

[*Exit.*

Macb. I have almost forgot the taste of fears.
The time has been, my senses would have cool'd
To hear a night-shriek, and my fell of hair   11
Would at a dismal treatise rouse and stir
As life were in 't. I have supp'd full with horrors;
Direness, familiar to my slaughterous thoughts,
Cannot once start me.

[*Re-enter* SEYTON.]
    Wherefore was that cry?

Sey. The Queen, my lord, is dead.   16

Macb. She should have died hereafter;
There would have been a time for such a word.
To-morrow, and to-morrow, and to-morrow
Creeps in this petty pace from day to day   20

To the last syllable of recorded time;
And all our yesterdays have lighted fools
The way to dusty death. Out, out, brief candle!
Life's but a walking shadow, a poor player
That struts and frets his hour upon the stage   25
And then is heard no more. It is a tale
Told by an idiot, full of sound and fury,
Signifying nothing.

Enter a MESSENGER.

Thou com'st to use thy tongue; thy story quickly.

Mess. Gracious my lord,   30
I should report that which I say I saw,
But know not how to do it.

Macb.   Well, say, sir.

Mess. As I did stand my watch upon the hill,
I look'd toward Birnam, and anon, methought,
The wood began to move.

Macb.   Liar and slave!   35

Mess. Let me endure your wrath, if 't be not so.
Within this three mile may you see it coming;
I say, a moving grove.

Macb.   If thou speak'st false,
Upon the next tree shalt thou hang alive,
Till famine cling thee; if thy speech be sooth,   40
I care not if thou dost for me as much.
I pull in resolution, and begin
To doubt th' equivocation of the fiend
That lies like truth. "Fear not, till Birnam wood
Do come to Dunsinane;" and now a wood   45
Comes toward Dunsinane. Arm, arm, and out!
If this which he avouches does appear,
There is nor flying hence nor tarrying here.
I gin to be aweary of the sun,   49
And wish th' estate o' th' world were now undone.
Ring the alarum-bell! Blow, wind! come, wrack!
At least we'll die with harness on our back.

[*Exeunt.*

SCENE VI. [*Dunsinane.   Before the castle.*]

Drum and colours. Enter MALCOLM, *old* SIWARD,
MACDUFF, *and their* Army, *with boughs.*

Mal. Now near enough; your leavy screens throw
    down,
And show like those you are. You, worthy uncle,
Shall, with my cousin, your right noble son,
Lead our first battle. Worthy Macduff and we
Shall take upon 's what else remains to do,   5
According to our order.

Siw.   Fare you well.
Do we but find the tyrant's power to-night,
Let us be beaten if we cannot fight.

10. **setting down:** laying siege.   11. **advantage:** chance.   14. **censures:** judgments.   15. **Attend…event:** await the outcome.
Sc. v, 5. **forc'd:** reinforced.   10. **cool'd:** i.e., with terror.   11. **fell of hair:** head of hair.   12. **treatise:** story.   17. **should …died:** was bound to die.   40. **cling:** shrivel.   42. **pull:** rein, draw.   51. **wrack:** ruin.
Sc. vi, 4. **battle:** battalion.

Macd. Make all our trumpets speak; give them
    all breath,   9
Those clamorous harbingers of blood and death.
            [Exeunt. Alarums continued.

SCENE VII.   [*Another part of the field.*]

Enter MACBETH.

Macb. They have tied me to a stake; I cannot fly,
But, bear-like, I must fight the course.   What's he
That was not born of woman?   Such a one
Am I to fear, or none.

Enter young SIWARD.

Y. Siw. What is thy name?
Macb.   Thou'lt be afraid to hear it.
Y. Siw. No; though thou call'st thyself a hotter
    name   6
Than any is in hell.
Macb.   My name's Macbeth.
Y. Siw. The devil himself could not pronounce
    a title
More hateful to mine ear.
Macb.   No, nor more fearful.
Y. Siw. Thou liest, abhorred tyrant; with my
    sword   10
I'll prove the lie thou speak'st.
        [They fight and young Siward is slain.
Macb.   Thou wast born of woman.
But swords I smile at, weapons laugh to scorn,
Brandish'd by man that's of a woman born. [*Exit.*

Alarums.   Enter MACDUFF.

Macd. That way the noise is.   Tyrant, show thy
    face!
If thou be'st slain and with no stroke of mine,   15
My wife and children's ghosts will haunt me still.
I cannot strike at wretched kerns, whose arms
Are hir'd to bear their staves; either thou, Macbeth,
Or else my sword with an unbattered edge
I sheathe again undeeded.   There thou shouldst
    be;   20
By this great clatter one of greatest note
Seems bruited.   Let me find him, Fortune!
And more I beg not.   [*Exit. Alarums.*

Enter MALCOLM *and old* SIWARD.

Siw. This way, my lord; the castle's gently
    rend'red:
The tyrant's people on both sides do fight;   25
The noble thanes do bravely in the war;

The day almost itself professes yours,
And little is to do.
Mal.   We have met with foes
That strike beside us.
Siw.   Enter, sir, the castle.
               [Exeunt. Alarums.

[SCENE VIII.   *Another part of the field.*]

Enter MACBETH.

Macb. Why should I play the Roman fool, and
    die
On mine own sword?   Whiles I see lives, the gashes
Do better upon them.

Enter MACDUFF.

Macd.   Turn, hell-hound, turn!
Macb. Of all men else I have avoided thee.
But get thee back; my soul is too much charg'd   5
With blood of thine already.
Macd.   I have no words;
My voice is in my sword, thou bloodier villain
Than terms can give thee out!
            [They fight.   Alarum.
Macb.   Thou losest labour.
As easy mayst thou the intrenchant air
With thy keen sword impress as make me bleed.   10
Let fall thy blade on vulnerable crests;
I bear a charmed life, which must not yield
To one of woman born.
Macd.   Despair thy charm;
And let the angel whom thou still hast serv'd
Tell thee, Macduff was from his mother's womb
Untimely ripp'd.   16
Macb. Accursed be that tongue that tells me so,
For it hath cow'd my better part of man!
And be these juggling fiends no more believ'd
That palter with us in a double sense,   20
That keep the word of promise to our ear,
And break it to our hope.   I'll not fight with thee.
Macd. Then yield thee, coward,
And live to be the show and gaze o' th' time!
We'll have thee, as our rarer monsters are,   25
Painted upon a pole, and underwrit,
"Here may you see the tyrant."
Macb.   I will not yield,
To kiss the ground before young Malcolm's feet
And to be baited with the rabble's curse.
Though Birnam wood be come to Dunsinane,   30
And thou oppos'd, being of no woman born,
Yet I will try the last.   Before my body

Sc. vii, 2. **course:** a round of bear-baiting.   18. **staves:** spears.   22. **bruited:** proclaimed.   24. **gently rend'red:** tamely
surrendered.   29. **strike ... us:** only pretend to strike us, or fight on our side.
    Sc. viii.   F begins no new scene at this point.   8. **terms ... out:** words can describe.   9. **intrenchant:** that cannot be cut.
14. **angel:** evil genius.   18. **better ... man:** i.e., courage.   26. **Painted ... pole:** i.e., with your picture carried on a pole.
32. **the last:** i.e., my last hope, viz., to fight.

I throw my warlike shield. Lay on, Macduff,
And damn'd be him that first cries, "Hold,
      enough!"   [*Exeunt, fighting. Alarums.*

Retreat. Flourish. Enter, with drum and colours,
  MALCOLM, *old* SIWARD, ROSS, *the other* Thanes,
  and Soldiers.

  Mal. I would the friends we miss were safe
      arriv'd.   35
  Siw. Some must go off; and yet, by these I see,
So great a day as this is cheaply bought.
  Mal. Macduff is missing, and your noble son.
  Ross. Your son, my lord, has paid a soldier's debt.
He only liv'd but till he was a man;   40
The which no sooner had his prowess confirm'd
In the unshrinking station where he fought,
But like a man he died.
  Siw.   Then he is dead?
  Ross. Ay, and brought off the field.   Your cause
      of sorrow
Must not be measur'd by his worth, for then   45
It hath no end.
  Siw.   Had he his hurts before?
  Ross. Ay, on the front.
  Siw.   Why then, God's soldier be he!
Had I as many sons as I have hairs,
I would not wish them to a fairer death.   49
And so, his knell is knoll'd.
  Mal.   He's worth more sorrow,
And that I'll spend for him.
  Siw.   He's worth no more.

They say he parted well, and paid his score;
And so, God be with him! Here comes newer comfort.

  Re-enter MACDUFF, *with Macbeth's head.*

  Macd. Hail, king! for so thou art.   Behold where
      stands
Th' usurper's cursed head.   The time is free.   55
I see thee compass'd with thy kingdom's pearl,
That speak my salutation in their minds;
Whose voices I desire aloud with mine:
Hail, King of Scotland!
  All.   Hail, King of Scotland!
                                           [*Flourish.*
  Mal. We shall not spend a large expense of time
Before we reckon with your several loves   61
And make us even with you.   My thanes and kins-
      men,
Henceforth be earls, the first that ever Scotland
In such an honour nam'd.   What's more to do,
Which would be planted newly with the time,   65
As calling home our exil'd friends abroad
That fled the snares of watchful tyranny;
Producing forth the cruel ministers
Of this dead butcher and his fiend-like queen,
Who, as 'tis thought, by self and violent hands
Took off her life; this, and what needful else   71
That calls upon us, by the grace of Grace
We will perform in measure, time, and place.
So, thanks to all at once and to each one,
Whom we invite to see us crown'd at Scone.   75
                                  [*Flourish. Exeunt.*

34. S.D. **Alarums.** F adds *Enter Fighting, and Macbeth slaine.*   36. **go off:** die.   50. **knoll'd:** tolled.   55. **time:** i.e.,
country, nation.   56. **compass'd . . . pearl:** surrounded by the finest in your realm.   61. **reckon with:** i.e., reward.

The Tragedy of Antony and Cleopatra

Historical play

ON MAY 20, 1608, Edward Blount entered in the Stationers' Register "a booke Called Anthony and Cleopatra," which does not seem to have been actually issued. Blount was one of the publishers of the First Folio, and in spite of the fact that Shakespeare's drama, first appearing there, was registered in 1623 along with the other plays "not formerly entered to any man," it is generally conceded that the entry of 1608 refers to it. Upon this evidence one may reasonably conjecture 1607 as the date of composition. A time very early in that year, or late in 1606, may be indicated by revisions in Samuel Daniel's *Cleopatra* (originally published in 1594 and newly printed in 1607), which may possibly have been inspired by Shakespeare's play. The First Folio, which, despite numerous misprints and some faulty lining, preserves a sound text, is the basis for all other editions.

Cleopatra had frequently been made the subject of dramatic treatment in the sixteenth century, but none of these earlier plays seems to have influenced Shakespeare. His sole source was Plutarch's *Life of Marcus Antonius*, in the translation from Amyot's French version by Sir Thomas North. This he followed with remarkable fidelity. Not only are practically all the incidents of the plot found in the biography, and in almost the same order, but there are numerous passages in the play — and these among the most brilliant — which follow the very diction of North as closely as verse can follow prose. Yet no play of Shakespeare's is less prosaic in style, and in none is the splendor of his imagination more superbly exhibited in the presentation of human character.

In Plutarch, then, who was an artist in the selection of detail and had an intense appreciation of greatness, Shakespeare found much of his work done for him. Yet between the *Life* and the tragedy there are contrasts of greatest significance. In the treatment of the whole action, which in reality covered ten years (from the death of Fulvia, in 40 B.C., to the deaths of Antony and Cleopatra in 30 B.C.), Shakespeare discarded long series of events,

like Antony's campaigns against the Parthians, which are described at length by Plutarch but which had no bearing on the tragic theme; and he relegated to the background important figures such as Cæsar and Octavia. Thus he makes no reference to the children of Antony and Octavia, he suppresses the fact that Octavia won Antony away from Cleopatra for a number of years, and he reduces Antony's protracted stay in Rome to a short visit. Similarly he compresses into a matter of days the months between the battle of Actium (September, 31 B.C.) and the deaths of Antony and Cleopatra, which, in their turn, were actually several days apart. Shakespeare has added something, too, to the great panorama. The vivid impressions of oriental luxury in the Alexandrian scenes are due in part to Shakespeare's imagination, in part to Plutarch; the orgy on Pompey's galley is developed from Plutarch's simple statement that Pompey gave a banquet there; the portraits of Iras and Charmian are elaborated from meagre sketches; the incident of Cleopatra's chastisement of the messenger is Shakespeare's invention; the character of Enobarbus is his creation.

Antony and Cleopatra is in effect a sequel to *Julius Cæsar*, though separated from it by some eight years. The infatuated protagonist of this play is the man whose oratory doomed the conspirators and who, joined with Octavius, now his rival, defeated Brutus and Cassius at Philippi. The tragedy in *Julius Cæsar* is the spiritual tragedy of Brutus, and the great tragedies intervening are signalized by a struggle within the hero. But here, although the crowning interest is the tragic passion of Antony, which is the cause of his ruin, the structure of the play is determined by the external and political struggle between the forces of Octavius and the forces of Antony. It is Rome against Egypt, and the love affair of Antony which precipitates the contest and determines its conclusion is at first subordinate to the larger issue. It is not until the outcome of the martial conflict is clear and Antony's ruin is imminent that the lovers' tragedy gains primary ascendancy. Then all the resources of a splendid orchestration give it immortal beauty. Then and not before does Shakespeare begin to dwell upon tragic emotion and strife in the mind of the hero. Earlier there is little of this. There is a mild struggle as Antony rouses himself to break his "strong Egyptian fetters"; he is pained and embarrassed taking leave of Cleopatra (I.iii.); but there is no upheaval in the mind now possessed by "Roman thoughts." The agitation is Cleopatra's, and it is not yet of tragic cast. In Rome Antony proceeds with the same assurance to make his peace with Cæsar, and with cool diplomacy to make his marriage of convenience. Yet in all of this we are not deceived, for Enobarbus declares that Antony will again to Egypt, and his prophecy is only hours old when Antony himself confirms it. The readiness with which he resolves to return to Cleopatra pointedly indicates that his heart has never been elsewhere. The words of the Soothsayer (II. iii.10 ff.) serve to rationalize the heart's desire. Though Antony's obedience to his sense of duty in shaking off his "dotage" may have been sincere enough under the impact of Fulvia's death and "the business she hath broached in the state," it could not endure. Of that fact there is sufficient intimation, for in the opening scene we witness the fullness of Antony's surrender to his eastern pleasures, and we soon learn on further testimony the range and potent magnetism of Cleopatra's charms. Indeed, in the scene of parting, Cleopatra, honest, yet "cunning past man's thought," caps her protests with amorous benediction, and Antony proclaims that in separation they are not divided (I.iii.86–105). Shakespeare's reason for minimizing emotional conflict in his hero during the early part of the action now emerges. Cleopatra must appear essentially irresistible; she must have no really credible rival in Antony's mind and heart.

To Plutarch, the love of Antony for Cleopatra was merely a baneful spell which stirred up the evil elements in his character and quenched what was left of good; and Cleopatra herself was a sensual coquette, full of trickery and deceit, whose grief for Antony at the end was genuine enough, but was disfigured by petulance, fear, and vacillation. Shakespeare ignores the more vulgar libertine elements in Antony's character, and presents him as a man with a genius for friendship, a splendid practical capacity, and a highly sensuous temperament, who is subdued by a passion which, however unworthy in some aspects, is redeemed from meanness by its magnificent intensity. The picture of the Egyptian queen is equally skillful and even more subtle. Shakespeare preserves nearly all the characteristics of selfishness

and guile that are found in Plutarch's sketch, and, save that he condenses and omits some ugly physical details, spares us nothing of the weakness and falsehood that are constantly appearing almost to the last. But he alternates these with amazing flashes of a magical fascination that render the creation unique; and he closes with a scene which, without any inconsistency with previous revelations of character, lifts both her and her Herculean Roman into the sphere of loftiest tragedy.

Enobarbus is remarkable among Shakespeare's minor characters. A caustic observer of Antony's gradual downfall, he serves as a kind of Chorus. But he is much more than this. As Antony's truest friend, he magnifies the tragic hero through his affection. Even his desertion, when Antony's fortunes are at lowest ebb, helps to raise the sunken hero in our eyes. For it prompts Antony to an act of splendid magnanimity (IV.v.12–17), and the remorse of Enobarbus, who dies broken-hearted, is a supreme expression of loyalty (IV.vi.30–39, IV.ix. 12–23). Similarly, the loyalty of Scarus and of Eros assist in reviving our esteem for Antony. And of Enobarbus one may remark that it is he who gives the magnificent description of Cleopatra in her barge (II.ii.195 ff.), a rich transmutation of the prose of North, where the account is given by Antony. One would not, perhaps, expect these raptures from the mocking realist, but Shakespeare's letting Enobarbus bear witness to the glory of Cleopatra adds important conviction; for Antony would be a prejudiced reporter.

When early in his career Shakespeare wrote a tragedy of love he gave us Romeo and Juliet, idealizing the pure passion of youth. When at the height of that career he turns to write a tragedy of love he gives us Antony and Cleopatra, celebrating a passion as mature, experienced, and artful as the other was artless and unabashed. Each, one may believe, would have been impossible in the other's place; for at the time of writing the first Shakespeare had not lived long enough to write the second, yet when he wrote the second he had lived too long to write the first. What taught Shakespeare to understand the infatuation of an Antony, the temperament of a Cleopatra, the greatness of a passion that exalts what it destroys, we cannot hope to know. But it could hardly have been insight alone. In the lyric impulse of Romeo and Juliet one acknowledges an affinity with Shakespeare's Sonnets. If the richer music of Antony and Cleopatra does not invite recollection of the Sonnets, the amorous theme does, and it is conceivable that through his enigmatic Dark Lady, Shakespeare was assisted in imagining what Antony's Cleopatra was like.

THE TRAGEDY OF
ANTONY AND CLEOPATRA

[DRAMATIS PERSONÆ

MARK ANTONY,
OCTAVIUS CÆSAR, } triumvirs.
M. ÆMILIUS LEPIDUS,
SEXTUS POMPEIUS.
DOMITIUS ENOBARBUS,
VENTIDIUS,
EROS,
SCARUS, } friends to Antony.
DERCETAS,
DEMETRIUS,
PHILO,
CANIDIUS, lieutenant-general to Antony.
MÆCENAS,
AGRIPPA,
DOLABELLA, } friends to Cæsar.
PROCULEIUS,
THYREUS,
GALLUS,

TAURUS, lieutenant-general to Cæsar.
MENAS,
MENECRATES, } friends to Pompey.
VARRIUS,
SILIUS, an officer in Ventidius's army.
EUPHRONIUS, an ambassador from Antony to
   Cæsar.
ALEXAS,
MARDIAN, a eunuch, } attendants on Cleopatra.
SELEUCUS,
DIOMEDES,
A Soothsayer.
A Clown.

CLEOPATRA, Queen of Egypt.
OCTAVIA, sister to Cæsar and wife to Antony.
CHARMIAN, } attendants on Cleopatra.
IRAS,

Officers, Soldiers, Messengers, and other Attendants.

SCENE: In several parts of the Roman Empire.]

ACT I

SCENE I. [Alexandria. A room in Cleopatra's
palace.]

Enter DEMETRIUS and PHILO.

Phi. Nay, but this dotage of our general's
O'erflows the measure. Those his goodly eyes,
That o'er the files and musters of the war
Have glow'd like plated Mars, now bend, now
   turn
The office and devotion of their view   5
Upon a tawny front; his captain's heart,
Which in the scuffles of great fights hath burst
The buckles on his breast, reneges all temper,
And is become the bellows and the fan   9
To cool a gipsy's lust.

Flourish. Enter ANTONY, CLEOPATRA, *her Ladies,
the train, with Eunuchs fanning her.*

    Look, where they come!
Take but good note, and you shall see in him
The triple pillar of the world transform'd
Into a strumpet's fool. Behold and see.
   Cleo. If it be love indeed, tell me how much.
   Ant. There's beggary in the love that can be
   reckon'd.   15

Act I, sc. i, 4. **plated:** in armor. 5. **office:** service. 8. **reneges:** renounces. **temper:** discipline. 12. **triple pillar.** Antony as one of the triumvirs.

Cleo. I'll set a bourn how far to be belov'd.

Ant. Then must thou needs find out new heaven, new earth.

Enter a MESSENGER.

Mess. News, my good lord, from Rome.

Ant.   Grates me: the sum.

Cleo. Nay, hear them, Antony.

Fulvia perchance is angry; or, who knows   20
If the scarce-bearded Cæsar have not sent
His powerful mandate to you: "Do this, or this;
Take in that kingdom, and enfranchise that;
Perform 't, or else we damn thee."

Ant.   How, my love!

Cleo. Perchance? Nay, and most like.   25
You must not stay here longer; your dismission
Is come from Cæsar; therefore hear it, Antony.
Where's Fulvia's process? — Cæsar's, I would say.
Both?
Call in the messengers. As I am Egypt's queen,
Thou blushest, Antony, and that blood of thine   30
Is Cæsar's homager; else so thy cheek pays shame
When shrill-tongu'd Fulvia scolds. The messengers.

Ant. Let Rome in Tiber melt, and the wide arch
Of the rang'd empire fall! Here is my space.
Kingdoms are clay; our dungy earth alike   35
Feeds beast as man; the nobleness of life
Is to do thus, when such a mutual pair
                    [*Embracing.*]
And such a twain can do 't, in which I bind,
On pain of punishment, the world to weet
We stand up peerless.

Cleo.   Excellent falsehood!   40
Why did he marry Fulvia, and not love her?
                    [*Aside.*]
I'll seem the fool I am not. — Antony
Will be himself.

Ant.   But stirr'd by Cleopatra.
Now, for the love of Love and her soft hours,
Let's not confound the time with conference harsh.   45
There's not a minute of our lives should stretch
Without some pleasure now. What sport to-night?

Cleo. Hear the ambassadors.

Ant.   Fie, wrangling queen!
Whom everything becomes — to chide, to laugh,
To weep; [whose] every passion fully strives   50
To make itself, in thee, fair and admir'd!
No messenger but thine; and all alone

To-night we'll wander through the streets and note
The qualities of people. Come, my queen;   54
Last night you did desire it. — Speak not to us.
          [*Exeunt [Ant. and Cleo.] with their train.*]

Dem. Is Cæsar with Antonius priz'd so slight?

Phi. Sir, sometimes, when he is not Antony,
He comes too short of that great property
Which still should go with Antony.

Dem.   I am full sorry
That he approves the common liar, who   60
Thus speaks of him at Rome; but I will hope
Of better deeds to-morrow. Rest you happy!
                    [*Exeunt.*

[SCENE II. *The same. Another room.*]

Enter ENOBARBUS, Lamprius, *a* SOOTHSAYER, Rannius, Lucilius, CHARMIAN, IRAS, Mardian *the Eunuch, and* ALEXAS.

Char. [Lord] Alexas, sweet Alexas, most anything Alexas, almost most absolute Alexas, where's the soothsayer that you prais'd so to th' Queen? O, that I knew this husband, which, you say, must [charge] his horns with garlands!   5

Alex. Soothsayer!

Sooth. Your will?

Char. Is this the man? Is 't you, sir, that know things?

Sooth. In nature's infinite book of secrecy
A little I can read.

Alex.   Show him your hand.   10

Eno. Bring in the banquet quickly; wine enough
Cleopatra's health to drink.

Char. Good sir, give me good fortune.

Sooth. I make not, but foresee.

Char. Pray, then, foresee me one.   15

Sooth. You shall be yet far fairer than you are.

Char. He means in flesh.

Iras. No, you shall paint when you are old.

Char. Wrinkles forbid!

Alex. Vex not his prescience; be attentive.   20

Char. Hush!

Sooth. You shall be more beloving than beloved.

Char. I had rather heat my liver with drinking.

Alex. Nay, hear him.   24

Char. Good now, some excellent fortune! Let me be married to three kings in a forenoon and widow them all. Let me have a child at fifty, to whom Herod of Jewry may do homage. Find me to marry me with Octavius Cæsar, and companion me with my mistress.   30

Sooth. You shall outlive the lady whom you serve.

16. **bourn**: limit. 18. **Grates**: it vexes. **the sum**: be brief. 28. **process**: summons. 31. **homager**: vassal. 34. **rang'd**: ordered. 39. **weet**: know. 43. **stirr'd**: inspired. 45. **confound**: spoil. 50. [whose] F₂. who F₁. 54. **qualities**: characters. 58. **property**: quality. 60. **approves**: confirms.

Sc. ii, 1. [**Lord**] (Johnson). *L. F.* 5. [**charge**] (Theobald). *change* F. **with garlands**: i.e., like a sacrificial beast. The reference is to the imaginary horns of the cuckold. 23. **drinking**: i.e., as opposed to loving (l. 22).

Char. O excellent! I love long life better than figs.

Sooth. You have seen and proved a fairer former fortune
Than that which is to approach.   34

Char. Then belike my children shall have no names. Prithee, how many boys and wenches must I have?

Sooth. If every of your wishes had a womb,
And [fertile] every wish, a million.

Char. Out, fool! I forgive thee for a witch.   40

Alex. You think none but your sheets are privy to your wishes.

Char. Nay, come, tell Iras hers.

Alex. We'll know all our fortunes.

Eno. Mine, and most of our fortunes to-night, shall be — drunk to bed.   46

Iras. There's a palm presages chastity, if nothing else.

Char. E'en as the o'erflowing Nilus presageth famine.   50

Iras. Go, you wild bedfellow, you cannot sooth-say.

Char. Nay, if an oily palm be not a fruitful prognostication, I cannot scratch mine ear. Prithee, tell her but a worky-day fortune.   55

Sooth. Your fortunes are alike.

Iras. But how, but how? Give me particulars.

Sooth. I have said.

Iras. Am I not an inch of fortune better than she?   60

Char. Well, if you were but an inch of fortune better than I, where would you choose it?

Iras. Not in my husband's nose.

Char. Our worser thoughts heavens mend! Alexas, — come, his fortune, his fortune! O let   65
him marry a woman that cannot go, sweet Isis, I beseech thee! and let her die too, and give him a worse! and let worse follow worse, till the worst of all follow him laughing to his grave, fifty-fold a cuckold! Good Isis, hear me this prayer, though thou deny me a matter of more weight; good Isis, I beseech thee!   72

Iras. Amen. Dear goddess, hear that prayer of the people! for, as it is a heart-breaking to see a handsome man loose-wiv'd, so it is a deadly sorrow to behold a foul knave uncuckolded; therefore, dear Isis, keep decorum, and fortune him accordingly! 78

Char. Amen.

Alex. Lo, now, if it lay in their hands to make me a cuckold, they would make themselves whores but they'd do't!

Enter CLEOPATRA.

Eno. Hush! here comes Antony.

Char.   Not he; the Queen.   83

Cleo. [Saw] you my lord?

Eno.   No, lady.

Cleo.   Was he not here?

Char. No, madam.

Cleo. He was dispos'd to mirth, but on the sudden   86
A Roman thought hath struck him. Enobarbus!

Eno. Madam?

Cleo. Seek him, and bring him hither. Where's Alexas?

Alex. Here, at your service. My lord approaches.   90

Enter ANTONY *with a* MESSENGER [*and* ATTENDANTS].

Cleo. We will not look upon him. Go with us.
                        [*Exeunt* [*Cleo. and train*].

Mess. Fulvia thy wife first came into the field.

Ant. Against my brother Lucius?

Mess. Ay;   94
But soon that war had end, and the time's state
Made friends of them, jointing their force 'gainst Cæsar;
Whose better issue in the war from Italy,
Upon the first encounter, drave them.

Ant.   Well, what worst?

Mess. The nature of bad news infects the teller.

Ant. When it concerns the fool or coward. On:
Things that are past are done with me. 'Tis thus:
Who tells me true, though in his tale lie death, 102
I hear him as he flatter'd.

Mess.   Labienus —
This is stiff news — hath with his Parthian force
Extended Asia from Euphrates,   105
His conquering banner shook from Syria
To Lydia and to Ionia,
Whilst —

Ant.   Antony, thou wouldst say, —

Mess.   O, my lord!

Ant. Speak to me home; mince not the general tongue.
Name Cleopatra as she is call'd in Rome;   110
Rail thou in Fulvia's phrase, and taunt my faults
With such full license as both truth and malice
Have power to utter. O, then we bring forth weeds
When our quick [minds] lie still; and our ills told us
Is as our earing. Fare thee well a while.   115

Mess. At your noble pleasure.   [*Exit.*

Ant. From Sicyon, [ho], the news! Speak there!

---

39. **[fertile]** (Theobald). *foretell* F. 40. **witch:** wizard. 53. **oily.** A moist palm indicated licentiousness. 55. **worky-day:** ordinary. 64. **Alexas** (Theobald). *Alexas.* F (as speech-heading). 66. **go:** walk. 84. **[Saw]** F₂. *Save* F₁. 105. **Extended:** seized. 109. **home:** plainly. **general tongue:** common talk. 114. **quick:** fertile. **[minds]** (Hanmer). *windes* F. 115. **as our earing:** as beneficial to us as plowing (earing) to weedy soil. 117. **[ho]** (Dyce). *how* F.

1. [*Att.*] The man from Sicyon, — is there such
    an one?
2. [*Att.*] He stays upon your will.
  Ant.   Let him appear.
These strong Egyptian fetters I must break,   120
Or lose myself in dotage.

     Enter another MESSENGER *with a letter.*
                    What are you?
[*2.*] *Mess.* Fulvia thy wife is dead.
  Ant.   Where died she?
[*2.*] *Mess.* In Sicyon:
Her length of sickness, with what else more
    serious
Importeth thee to know, this bears.
                    [*Gives a letter.*]
  Ant.   Forbear me.
               [*Exit 2. Messenger.*]
There's a great spirit gone! Thus did I desire it.
What our contempts doth often hurl from us, 127
We wish it ours again; the present pleasure,
By revolution low'ring, does become
The opposite of itself. She's good, being gone;
The hand could pluck her back that shov'd
    her on.
I must from this enchanting queen break off; 132
Ten thousand harms, more than the ills I know,
My idleness doth hatch.

     Re-enter ENOBARBUS.
              How now! Enobarbus!
  Eno. What's your pleasure, sir?   135
  Ant. I must with haste from hence.
  Eno. Why, then, we kill all our women. We see
how mortal an unkindness is to them; if they suffer
our departure, death's the word.
  Ant. I must be gone.   140
  Eno. Under a compelling occasion, let women
die. It were pity to cast them away for nothing;
though, between them and a great cause, they
should be esteemed nothing. Cleopatra, catching
but the least noise of this, dies instantly; I 145
have seen her die twenty times upon far poorer
moment. I do think there is mettle in Death,
which commits some loving act upon her, she hath
such a celerity in dying.
  Ant. She is cunning past man's thought. 150
  Eno. Alack, sir, no; her passions are made of
nothing but the finest part of pure love. We cannot call her winds and waters sighs and tears; they

are greater storms and tempests than almanacs can
report. This cannot be cunning in her; if it be, she
makes a shower of rain as well as Jove.   157
  Ant. Would I had never seen her!
  Eno. O, sir, you had then left unseen a won-
derful piece of work; which not to have been blest
withal would have discredited your travel.
  Ant. Fulvia is dead.   162
  Eno. Sir?
  Ant. Fulvia is dead.
  Eno. Fulvia!
  Ant. Dead.   166
  Eno. Why, sir, give the gods a thankful sacrifice.
When it pleaseth their deities to take the wife of a
man from him, it shows to man the tailors of the
earth; comforting therein, that when old robes 170
are worn out, there are members to make new. If
there were no more women but Fulvia, then had
you indeed a cut, and the case to be lamented.
This grief is crown'd with consolation; your old
smock brings forth a new petticoat; and indeed the
tears live in an onion that should water this sor-
row.   177
  Ant. The business she hath broached in the state
Cannot endure my absence.
  Eno. And the business you have broach'd here
cannot be without you; especially that of Cleo-
patra's, which wholly depends on your abode. 182
  Ant. No more light answers. Let our officers
Have notice what we purpose. I shall break
The cause of our expedience to the Queen,   185
And get her [leave] to part. For not alone
The death of Fulvia, with more urgent touches,
Do strongly speak to us, but the letters too
Of many our contriving friends in Rome
Petition us at home. Sextus Pompeius   190
[Hath] given the dare to Cæsar, and commands
The empire of the sea. Our slippery people,
Whose love is never link'd to the deserver
Till his deserts are past, begin to throw
Pompey the Great and all his dignities   195
Upon his son; who, high in name and power,
Higher than both in blood and life, stands up
For the main soldier; whose quality, going on,
The sides o' th' world may danger. Much is breed-
    ing
Which, like the courser's hair, hath yet but life, 200
And not a serpent's poison. Say, our pleasure,
To such whose [place is] under us, [requires]
Our quick remove from hence.
  Eno. I shall do't.   [*Exeunt.*]

118, 119. [*Att.*] (Capell). *Mes.* F. 122. [*2.*]. *3.* F. 123. [*2.*]. Om. F. 125. **Forbear:** leave. 129. **By . . . low'ring:** growing worse through change. 131. **could:** would gladly. 169. **tailors . . . earth:** i.e., those who can provide a new wife as easily as tailors can make a new garment. 173. **cut:** bad luck. 178. **broached:** set going. 182. **abode:** staying. 185. **expedience:** haste. 186. [**leave**] (Pope). *love* F. 187. **touches:** motives. 191. [**Hath**] F₂. *Have* F₁. 194. **throw:** bestow. 198. **main:** leading. 199. **sides:** frame. 200. **courser's hair.** Allusion to the belief that a horse's hair, put into water, would become a snake. 202. [**place is**] . . . [**requires**] F₂. *places . . . require* F₁.

[SCENE III. *The same. Another room.*]

Enter CLEOPATRA, CHARMIAN, IRAS, *and* ALEXAS.

Cleo. Where is he?
Char.   I did not see him since.
Cleo. See where he is, who's with him, what he
    does.
I did not send you. If you find him sad,
Say I am dancing; if in mirth, report
That I am sudden sick. Quick, and return.   5
                                      [*Exit Alexas.*]
    Char. Madam, methinks, if you did love him
        dearly,
You do not hold the method to enforce
The like from him.
    Cleo.   What should I do, I do not?
    Char. In each thing give him way, cross him in
        nothing.
    Cleo. Thou teachest like a fool: the way to lose
        him.   10
    Char. Tempt him not so too far; I wish, forbear.
In time we hate that which we often fear.

                Enter ANTONY.

But here comes Antony.
    Cleo.   I am sick and sullen.
    Ant. I am sorry to give breathing to my pur-
        pose, —
    Cleo. Help me away, dear Charmian; I shall fall.
It cannot be thus long, the sides of nature   16
Will not sustain it.
    Ant.   Now, my dearest queen, —
    Cleo. Pray you, stand farther from me.
    Ant.   What's the matter?
    Cleo. I know, by that same eye, there's some
        good news.
What says the married woman? You may go.   20
Would she had never given you leave to come!
Let her not say 'tis I that keep you here;
I have no power upon you; hers you are.
    Ant. The gods best know, —
    Cleo.   O, never was there queen
So mightily betray'd! Yet at the first   25
I saw the treasons planted.
    Ant.   Cleopatra, —
    Cleo. Why should I think you can be mine and
        true,
Though you in swearing shake the throned gods,
Who have been false to Fulvia? Riotous madness,
To be entangled with those mouth-made vows,   30
Which break themselves in swearing!
    Ant.   Most sweet queen, —
    Cleo. Nay, pray you, seek no colour for your going,

But bid farewell and go. When you sued staying,
Then was the time for words; no going then;
Eternity was in our lips and eyes,   35
Bliss in our brows' bent; none our parts so poor
But was a race of heaven. They are so still,
Or thou, the greatest soldier of the world,
Art turn'd the greatest liar.
    Ant.   How now, lady!
    Cleo. I would I had thy inches; thou shouldst
        know   40
There were a heart in Egypt.
    Ant.   Hear me, Queen.
The strong necessity of time commands
Our services a while; but my full heart
Remains in use with you. Our Italy
Shines o'er with civil swords; Sextus Pompeius 45
Makes his approaches to the port of Rome;
Equality of two domestic powers
Breed scrupulous faction; the hated, grown to
        strength,
Are newly grown to love; the condemn'd Pompey,
Rich in his father's honour, creeps apace   50
Into the hearts of such as have not thrived
Upon the present state, whose numbers threaten;
And quietness, grown sick of rest, would purge
By any desperate change. My more particular,
And that which most with you should safe my
        going,   55
Is Fulvia's death.
    Cleo. Though age from folly could not give me
        freedom,
It does from childishness. Can Fulvia die?
    Ant. She's dead, my queen.
Look here, and at thy sovereign leisure read   60
The garboils she awak'd: at the last, best;
See when and where she died.
    Cleo.   O most false love!
Where be the sacred vials thou shouldst fill
With sorrowful water? Now I see, I see,
In Fulvia's death, how mine receiv'd shall be. 65
    Ant. Quarrel no more, but be prepar'd to know
The purposes I bear; which are, or cease,
As you shall give the advice. By the fire
That quickens Nilus' slime, I go from hence
Thy soldier, servant; making peace or war   70
As thou [affect'st].
    Cleo.   Cut my lace, Charmian, come!
But let it be; I am quickly ill and well,
So Antony loves.
    Ant.   My precious queen, forbear;
And give true evidence to his love, which stands
An honourable trial.
    Cleo.   So Fulvia told me.   75

Sc. iii, 11. **forbear:** i.e., that you would forbear.   32. **colour:** pretext.   33. **sued staying:** begged to stay.   37. **a . . .
heaven:** of divine origin.   45. **civil:** of civil war.   48. **scrupulous faction:** carping dissension.   53. **purge:** i.e., seek cure.
54. **particular:** personal concern.   55. **safe:** make safe.   61. **garboils:** turmoils.   63. **sacred vials.** The small vials sometimes buried by the Romans with their dead were supposed to be for tears.   71. **[affect'st]** F₂: pleasest.   *affects* F₁.

I prithee, turn aside and weep for her;
Then bid adieu to me, and say the tears
Belong to Egypt. Good now, play one scene
Of excellent dissembling; and let it look
Like perfect honour.
   Ant.   You'll heat my blood. No more.
   Cleo. You can do better yet; but this is meetly. 81
   Ant. Now, by [my] sword, —
   Cleo.   And target. — Still he mends;
But this is not the best. Look, prithee, Charmian,
How this Herculean Roman does become
The carriage of his chafe. 85
   Ant. I'll leave you, lady.
   Cleo.   Courteous lord, one word.
Sir, you and I must part, but that's not it;
Sir, you and I have lov'd, but there's not it;
That you know well. Something it is I would, —
O, my oblivion is a very Antony, 90
And I am all forgotten.
   Ant.   But that your royalty
Holds idleness your subject, I should take you
For idleness itself.
   Cleo.   'Tis sweating labour
To bear such idleness so near the heart
As Cleopatra this. But, sir, forgive me, 95
Since my becomings kill me when they do not
Eye well to you. Your honour calls you hence;
Therefore be deaf to my unpitied folly,
And all the gods go with you! Upon your sword
Sit laurell'd victory, and smooth success 100
Be strew'd before your feet!
   Ant.   Let us go. — Come;
Our separation so abides and flies,
That thou, residing here, [goest] yet with me,
And I, hence fleeting, here remain with thee.
Away!   [*Exeunt.* 105

[SCENE IV. *Rome. Cæsar's house.*]

Enter OCTAVIUS [CÆSAR], *reading a letter,* LEPIDUS, *and their train.*

   Cæs. You may see, Lepidus, and henceforth know,
It is not Cæsar's natural vice to hate
[Our] great competitor. From Alexandria
This is the news: he fishes, drinks, and wastes
The lamps of night in revel; is not more manlike 5
Than Cleopatra, nor the queen of Ptolemy
More womanly than he; hardly gave audience, or

Vouchsaf'd to think he had partners. You shall find there
A man who is the abstract of all faults
That all men follow.
   Lep.   I must not think there are
Evils enow to darken all his goodness. 11
His faults, in him, seem as the spots of heaven,
More fiery by night's blackness; hereditary,
Rather than purchas'd; what he cannot change,
Than what he chooses. 15
   Cæs. You are too indulgent. Let's grant it is not
Amiss to tumble on the bed of Ptolemy;
To give a kingdom for a mirth; to sit
And keep the turn of tippling with a slave;
To reel the streets at noon, and stand the buffet 20
With knaves that smell of sweat: say this becomes him, —
As his composure must be rare indeed
Whom these things cannot blemish, — yet must Antony
No way excuse his foils, when we do bear
So great weight in his lightness. If he fill'd 25
His vacancy with his voluptuousness,
Full surfeits and the dryness of his bones
Call on him for't; but to confound such time
That drums him from his sport and speaks as loud
As his own state and ours, 'tis to be chid 30
As we rate boys who, being mature in knowledge,
Pawn their experience to their present pleasure,
And so rebel to judgement.

Enter a MESSENGER.

   Lep.   Here's more news.
   Mess. Thy biddings have been done, and every hour,
Most noble Cæsar, shalt thou have report 35
How 'tis abroad. Pompey is strong at sea,
And it appears he is belov'd of those
That only have fear'd Cæsar. To the ports
The discontents repair, and men's reports 39
Give him much wrong'd.
   Cæs.   I should have known no less.
It hath been taught us from the primal state,
That he which is was wish'd until he were;
And the ebb'd man, ne'er loved till ne'er worth love,
Comes [dear'd] by being lack'd. This common body,
Like to a vagabond flag upon the stream, 45
Goes to and back, [lackeying] the varying tide,
To rot itself with motion.

81. **meetly:** pretty good. 82. **[my]** F$_2$. Om. F$_1$. **target:** shield. 84–85. **How...chafe:** How well his anger becomes him. 84. **Herculean.** Antony claimed descent from Hercules. 90. **oblivion:** i.e., slippery memory. 92. **idleness:** flippancy. 97. **Eye:** seem. 103. **[goest]** F$_2$. *goes* F$_1$.

Sc. iv, 3. **[Our]** (Johnson conj.). *One* F. **competitor:** partner. 9. **abstract:** epitome. 14. **purchas'd:** acquired. 22. **composure:** constitution. 24. **foils:** disgraces. 25. **in his lightness:** because of his levity. 26. **vacancy:** idleness. 28. **Call on him:** make him pay. **confound:** waste. 31. **rate:** scold. 33. **to judgement:** against their own common sense. 40. **Give:** represent. 42. **is:** is in power. 43. **ebb'd:** declined in fortune. 44. **[dear'd]** (Theobald). *fear'd* F. 45. **flag:** iris. 46. **[lackeying]** (Theobald): following (like a flunkey). *lacking* F.

Mess.   Cæsar, I bring thee word
Menecrates and Menas, famous pirates,
Makes the sea serve them, which they ear and wound
With keels of every kind.   Many hot inroads   50
They make in Italy; the borders maritime
Lack blood to think on't, and flush youth revolt.
No vessel can peep forth but 'tis as soon
Taken as seen; for Pompey's name strikes more
Than could his war resisted.
Cæs.   Antony,   55
Leave thy lascivious [wassails].   When thou once
Was beaten from Modena, where thou slew'st
Hirtius and Pansa, consuls, at thy heel
Did famine follow; whom thou fought'st against,
Though daintily brought up, with patience more
Than savages could suffer.   Thou didst drink   61
The stale of horses and the gilded puddle
Which beasts would cough at; thy palate then did
    deign
The roughest berry on the rudest hedge;
Yea, like the stag, when snow the pasture sheets, 65
The barks of trees thou [browsed'st]; on the Alps
It is reported thou didst eat strange flesh,
Which some did die to look on; and all this —
It wounds thine honour that I speak it now —
Was borne so like a soldier, that thy cheek   70
So much as lank'd not.
Lep.   'Tis pity of him.
Cæs. Let his shames quickly
Drive him to Rome. 'Tis time we twain
Did show ourselves i' th' field, and to that end
Assemble we immediate council. Pompey   75
Thrives in our idleness.
Lep.   To-morrow, Cæsar,
I shall be furnish'd to inform you rightly
Both what by sea and land I can be able
To front this present time.
Cæs.   Till which encounter,
It is my business too. Farewell.   80
Lep. Farewell, my lord. What you shall know
    meantime
Of stirs abroad, I shall beseech you, sir,
To let me be partaker.
Cæs.   Doubt not, sir;
I knew it for my bond.   [*Exeunt.*

[SCENE V. *Alexandria. Cleopatra's palace.*]

Enter CLEOPATRA, CHARMIAN, Iras, *and*
        MARDIAN.

Cleo. Charmian!
Char. Madam?

Cleo. Ha, ha!
Give me to drink mandragora.
Char.   Why, madam?
Cleo. That I might sleep out this great gap of
    time   5
My Antony is away.
Char.   You think of him too much.
Cleo. O, 'tis treason!
Char.   Madam, I trust not so.
Cleo. Thou, eunuch Mardian!
Mar.   What's your Highness' pleasure?
Cleo. Not now to hear thee sing; I take no pleas-
    ure
In aught an eunuch has. 'Tis well for thee,   10
That, being unseminar'd, thy freer thoughts
May not fly forth of Egypt. Hast thou affections?
Mar. Yes, gracious madam.
Cleo. Indeed!
Mar. Not in deed, madam, for I can do nothing
But what indeed is honest to be done;   16
Yet have I fierce affections, and think
What Venus did with Mars.
Cleo.   O Charmian,
Where think'st thou he is now? Stands he, or sits
    he?
Or does he walk? Or is he on his horse?   20
O happy horse, to bear the weight of Antony!
Do bravely, horse! for wot'st thou whom thou
    mov'st?
The demi-Atlas of this earth, the arm
And burgonet of men. He's speaking now,
Or murmuring, "Where's my serpent of old Nile?"
For so he calls me. Now I feed myself   26
With most delicious poison. Think on me,
That am with Phœbus' amorous pinches black,
And wrinkled deep in time? Broad-fronted Cæsar,
When thou wast here above the ground, I was   30
A morsel for a monarch; and great Pompey
Would stand and make his eyes grow in my brow;
There would he anchor his aspect and die
With looking on his life.

              Enter ALEXAS.

Alex.   Sovereign of Egypt, hail!
Cleo. How much unlike art thou Mark Antony!
Yet, coming from him, that great med'cine hath   36
With his tinct gilded thee.
How goes it with my brave Mark Antony?
Alex. Last thing he did, dear queen,
He kiss'd, — the last of many doubled kisses, —   40
This orient pearl. His speech sticks in my heart.
Cleo. Mine ear must pluck it thence.

---

49. **ear:** plow.   52. **Lack blood:** grow pale. **flush:** lusty.   54. **strikes:** accomplishes.   55. **resisted:** if it were resisted.
56. **[wassails]** (Pope). *Vassailes* F. 62. **stale:** urine. **gilded:** covered with yellow slime. 66. **[browsed'st]** F₂. *brows'd*
F₁. 71. **lank'd not:** did not grow thin. 84. **bond:** duty.

Sc. v, 4. **mandragora:** juice of the mandrake (a soporific).   11. **unseminar'd:** castrated.   12. **affections:** sexual passion.
23. **demi-Atlas:** supporter of half the world.   24. **burgonet:** helmet, i.e., defender.   28. **black:** swarthy.   29. **Broad-
fronted:** with broad forehead. **Cæsar:** Julius Cæsar.   33. **aspect:** gaze.   34. s.d. *Enter* ALEXAS. F adds *from Cæsar.*
37. **tinct:** tincture.

Alex.   "Good friend," quoth he,
"Say the firm Roman to great Egypt sends
This treasure of an oyster; at whose foot,
To mend the petty present, I will piece   45
Her opulent throne with kingdoms. All the East,
Say thou, shall call her mistress." So he nodded,
And soberly did mount an arm-gaunt steed,
Who neigh'd so high that what I would have spoke
Was beastly [dumb'd] by him.

     Cleo.   What, was he sad or merry?

     Alex. Like to the time o' th' year between the
          extremes   51
Of hot and cold, he was nor sad nor merry.

     Cleo. O well-divided disposition! Note him,
Note him, good Charmian, 'tis the man; but note him:
He was not sad, for he would shine on those   55
That make their looks by his; he was not merry,
Which seem'd to tell them his remembrance lay
In Egypt with his joy; but between both.
O heavenly mingle! Be'st thou sad or merry,
The violence of either thee becomes,   60
So does it no man else. Met'st thou my posts?

     Alex. Ay, madam, twenty several messengers.
Why do you send so thick?

     Cleo.   Who's born that day
When I forget to send to Antony,
Shall die a beggar. Ink and paper, Charmian.   65
Welcome, my good Alexas. Did I, Charmian,
Ever love Cæsar so?

     Char.   O that brave Cæsar!

     Cleo. Be chok'd with such another emphasis!
Say "the brave Antony."

     Char.   The valiant Cæsar!

     Cleo. By Isis, I will give thee bloody teeth,   70
If thou with Cæsar paragon again
My man of men.

     Char.   By your most gracious pardon,
I sing but after you.

     Cleo.   My salad days,
When I was green in judgement, cold in blood,
To say as I said then! But, come, away;   75
Get me ink and paper.
He shall have every day a several greeting,
Or I'll unpeople Egypt.   [*Exeunt.*

[ACT II]

[SCENE I. *Messina. Pompey's house.*]

Enter POMPEY, MENECRATES, *and* MENAS, *in
warlike manner.*

     Pom. If the great gods be just, they shall assist
The deeds of justest men.

     Mene.   Know, worthy Pompey,
That what they do delay, they not deny.

     Pom. Whiles we are suitors to their throne,
          decays
The thing we sue for.

     Mene.   We, ignorant of ourselves,
Beg often our own harms, which the wise powers   6
Deny us for our good; so find we profit
By losing of our prayers.

     Pom.   I shall do well.
The people love me, and the sea is mine;
My powers are crescent, and my auguring hope   10
Says it will come to th' full. Mark Antony
In Egypt sits at dinner, and will make
No wars without-doors. Cæsar gets money where
He loses hearts. Lepidus flatters both,
Of both is flatter'd; but he neither loves,   15
Nor either cares for him.

     Mene.   Cæsar and Lepidus
Are in the field; a mighty strength they carry.

     Pom. Where have you this? 'Tis false.

     Mene.   From Silvius, sir.

     Pom. He dreams. I know they are in Rome
          together,
Looking for Antony. But all the charms of love, 20
Salt Cleopatra, soften thy [wan'd] lip!
Let witchcraft join with beauty, lust with both!
Tie up the libertine in a field of feasts,
Keep his brain fuming; Epicurean cooks
Sharpen with cloyless sauce his appetite,   25
That sleep and feeding may prorogue his honour
Even till a Lethe'd dulness!

Enter VARRIUS.

          How now, Varrius!

     Var. This is most certain that I shall deliver:
Mark Antony is every hour in Rome
Expected; since he went from Egypt 'tis   30
A space for farther travel.

     Pom.   I could have given less matter
A better ear. Menas, I did not think
This amorous surfeiter would have donn'd his helm
For such a petty war. His soldiership
Is twice the other twain; but let us rear   35
The higher our opinion, that our stirring
Can from the lap of Egypt's widow pluck
The [ne'er] lust-wearied Antony.

     [*Menas.*]   I cannot hope
Cæsar and Antony shall well greet together.
His wife that's dead did trespasses to Cæsar;   40
His brother [warr'd] upon him, although, I think,
Not mov'd by Antony.

---

48. **arm-gaunt:** gaunt with carrying armed warriors.   50. **[dumb'd]** (Theobald): made inaudible. *dumbe* F.   62. **several:** separate.   71. **paragon:** match.   73. **salad days:** days of inexperience.

Act II, sc. i, 10. **crescent:** increasing.   21. **Salt:** wanton. **[wan'd]** (Percy conj.): faded. *wand* F.   26. **prorogue:** suspend (from action).   27. **Lethe'd:** oblivious.   31. **space:** interval long enough.   36. **opinion:** i.e., of ourselves.   37. **widow.** Cleopatra had been married to Ptolemy, her brother.   38. **[ne'er]** (Pope). *neere* F. **[Menas]** (Malone). *Mene.* F.   39. **greet.** Furness suggests *gree*.   41. **[warr'd]** F$_2$. *wan'd* F$_1$.

Pom.   I know not, Menas,
How lesser enmities may give way to greater.
Were't not that we stand up against them all,
'Twere pregnant they should square between them-
    selves,   45
For they have entertained cause enough
To draw their swords; but how the fear of us
May cement their divisions and bind up
The petty difference, we yet not know.
Be't as our gods will have't! It only stands   50
Our lives upon to use our strongest hands.
Come, Menas.   [*Exeunt.*

[SCENE II. *Rome. The house of Lepidus.*]

Enter ENOBARBUS *and* LEPIDUS.

Lep. Good Enobarbus, 'tis a worthy deed,
And shall become you well, to entreat your captain
To soft and gentle speech.
Eno.   I shall entreat him
To answer like himself. If Cæsar move him,
Let Antony look over Cæsar's head   5
And speak as loud as Mars. By Jupiter,
Were I the wearer of Antonius' beard,
I would not shave't to-day.
Lep.   'Tis not a time
For private stomaching.
Eno.   Every time
Serves for the matter that is then [born] in't.   10
Lep. But small to greater matters must give way.
Eno. Not if the small come first.
Lep.   Your speech is passion;
But, pray you, stir no embers up. Here comes
The noble Antony.

Enter ANTONY *and* Ventidius.

Eno.   And yonder, Cæsar.

Enter CÆSAR, MÆCENAS, *and* AGRIPPA.

Ant. If we compose well here, to Parthia!   15
Hark, Ventidius.
Cæs.   I do not know,
Mæcenas; ask Agrippa.
Lep.   Noble friends,
That which combin'd us was most great, and let not
A leaner action rend us. What's amiss,
May it be gently heard; when we debate   20
Our trivial difference loud, we do commit
Murder in healing wounds; then, noble partners,
The rather, for I earnestly beseech,
Touch you the sourest points with sweetest terms,

Nor curstness grow to th' matter.
Ant.   'Tis spoken well.
Were we before our armies, and to fight,   26
I should do thus.   [*Flourish.*
Cæs. Welcome to Rome.
Ant.   Thank you.
Cæs.   Sit.
Ant.   Sit, sir.
Cæs.   Nay, then.
Ant. I learn you take things ill which are not so,
Or being, concern you not.
Cæs.   I must be laugh'd at
If, or for nothing or a little, I   31
Should say myself offended, and with you
Chiefly i' th' world; more laugh'd at that I should
Once name you derogately, when to sound your
    name
It not concern'd me.
Ant.   My being in Egypt, Cæsar,
What was't to you?   36
Cæs. No more than my residing here at Rome
Might be to you in Egypt; yet, if you there
Did practise on my state, your being in Egypt
Might be my question.
Ant.   How intend you, practis'd?   40
Cæs. You may be pleas'd to catch at mine intent
By what did here befall me. Your wife and brother
Made wars upon me, and their contestation
Was theme for you; you were the word of war.
Ant. You do mistake your business; my brother
    never   45
Did urge me in his act. I did inquire it,
And have my learning from some true reports
That drew their swords with you. Did he not
    rather
Discredit my authority with yours,
And make the wars alike, against my stomach,   50
Having alike your cause? Of this my letters
Before did satisfy you. If you'll patch a quarrel,
As matter whole you have [not] to make it with,
It must not be with this.
Cæs.   You praise yourself
By laying defects of judgement to me; but   55
You patch'd up your excuses.
Ant.   Not so, not so.
I know you could not lack, I am certain on't,
Very necessity of this thought, that I,
Your partner in the cause 'gainst which he fought,
Could not with graceful eyes attend those wars   60
Which fronted mine own peace. As for my wife,
I would you had her spirit in such another.

45. **pregnant:** most probable. **square:** fight. 50–51. **It...upon:** it is imperative for us.
Sc. ii, 4. **move:** anger. 8. **shave't:** i.e., to avoid having it plucked as a challenge. 9. **stomaching:** resentment. 10.
[born] F₃. *borne* F₁. 15. **compose:** agree. 25. **Nor...grow:** nor let scolding be added. 34. **derogately:** disparagingly.
39. **practise on:** plot against. 40. **question:** business. 44. **theme for you:** your business. 46. **urge me:** use my name.
50. **stomach:** desire. 51. **Having:** i.e., I having. 52. **patch a quarrel:** make a quarrel from a shred. 53. [not] (Rowe).
Om. F. 60. **graceful:** i.e., approving. 61. **fronted:** opposed.

Octavia lightly regarded.
— everyone speaks well of her
except Cleo

The third o' th' world is yours, which with a snaffle
You may pace easy, but not such a wife.

Eno. Would we had all such wives, that the men
might go to wars with the women!   66

Ant. So much uncurable her garboils, Cæsar,
Made out of her impatience, which not wanted
Shrewdness of policy too, I grieving grant
Did you too much disquiet. For that you must
But say, I could not help it.

Cæs.   I wrote to you   71
When rioting in Alexandria; you
Did pocket up my letters, and with taunts
Did gibe my missive out of audience.

Ant.   Sir,
He fell upon me ere admitted. Then   75
Three kings I had newly feasted, and did want
Of what I was i' th' morning; but next day
I told him of myself, which was as much
As to have ask'd him pardon. Let this fellow
Be nothing of our strife; if we contend,   80
Out of our question wipe him.

Cæs.   You have broken
The article of your oath; which you shall never
Have tongue to charge me with.

Lep.   Soft, Cæsar!

Ant.   No,
Lepidus, let him speak.
The honour is sacred which he talks on now,   85
Supposing that I lack'd it. But, on, Cæsar:
The article of my oath.

Cæs. To lend me arms and aid when I requir'd
them;
The which you both denied.

Ant.   Neglected, rather;
And then when poisoned hours had bound me up   90
From mine own knowledge. As nearly as I may,
I'll play the penitent to you; but mine honesty
Shall not make poor my greatness, nor my power
Work without it. Truth is, that Fulvia,
To have me out of Egypt, made wars here;   95
For which myself, the ignorant motive, do
So far ask pardon as befits mine honour
To stoop in such a case.

Lep.   'Tis noble spoken.

Mæc. If it might please you, to enforce no further
The griefs between ye: to forget them quite   100
Were to remember that the present need
Speaks to atone you.

Lep.   Worthily spoken, Mæcenas.

Eno. Or, if you borrow one another's love for
the instant, you may, when you hear no more
words of Pompey, return it again. You shall
have time to wrangle in when you have nothing
else to do.   107

Ant. Thou art a soldier only; speak no more.

Eno. That truth should be silent I had almost
forgot.

Ant. You wrong this presence; therefore speak
no more.   111

Eno. Go to, then; your considerate stone.

Cæs. I do not much dislike the matter, but
The manner of his speech; for't cannot be
We shall remain in friendship, our conditions   115
So diff'ring in their acts. Yet, if I knew
What hoop should hold us stanch, from edge to edge
O' th' world I would pursue it.

Agr.   Give me leave, Cæsar,—

Cæs. Speak, Agrippa.

Agr. Thou hast a sister by the mother's side,   120
Admir'd Octavia. Great Mark Antony
Is now a widower.

Cæs.   Say not [so] Agrippa.
If Cleopatra heard you, your [reproof]
Were well deserved of rashness.

Ant. I am not married, Cæsar; let me hear
Agrippa further speak.   126

Agr. To hold you in perpetual amity,
To make you brothers, and to knit your hearts
With an unslipping knot, take Antony
Octavia to his wife; whose beauty claims   130
No worse a husband than the best of men;
Whose virtue and whose general graces speak
That which none else can utter. By this marriage,
All little jealousies, which now seem great,   134
And all great fears, which now import their dangers,
Would then be nothing. Truths would be tales,
Where now half-tales be truths. Her love to both
Would each to other and all loves to both
Draw after her. Pardon what I have spoke;
For 'tis a studied, not a present thought,   140
By duty ruminated.

Ant.   Will Cæsar speak?

Cæs. Not till he hears how Antony is touch'd
With what is spoke already.

Ant.   What power is in Agrippa,
If I would say, "Agrippa, be it so,"
To make this good?

Cæs.   The power of Cæsar, and   145
His power unto Octavia.

Ant.   May I never
To this good purpose, that so fairly shows,
Dream of impediment! Let me have thy hand.
Further this act of grace; and from this hour
The heart of brothers govern in our loves   150
And sway our great designs!

Cæs.   There's my hand.
A sister I bequeath you, whom no brother
Did ever love so dearly. Let her live

---

67. **garboils:** broils. 74. **missive:** messenger. 94. **it:** i.e., his greatness (position in the state), or, perhaps, honesty. 102. **atone:** reconcile. 112. **considerate:** reflective. 115. **conditions:** dispositions. 122. **[so]** (Rowe). *say* F. 123. **[reproof]** (Warburton conj.). *proofe* F. 135. **import:** carry with them.

Half effect here is on the poetry

To join our kingdoms and our hearts; and never
Fly off our loves again!

Lep.   Happily, amen!   155

Ant. I did not think to draw my sword 'gainst
    Pompey;
For he hath laid strange courtesies and great
Of late upon me. I must thank him only,
Lest my remembrance suffer ill report;
At heel of that, defy him.

Lep.   Time calls upon 's.   160
Of us must Pompey presently be sought,
Or else he seeks out us.

Ant.   Where lies he?

Cæs. About the mount Misenum.

Ant. What is his strength by land?

Cæs. Great and increasing; but by sea   165
He is an absolute master.

Ant.   So is the fame.
Would we had spoke together! Haste we for it;
Yet, ere we put ourselves in arms, dispatch we
The business we have talk'd of.

Cæs.   With most gladness;
And do invite you to my sister's view,   170
Whither straight I'll lead you.

Ant.   Let us, Lepidus,
Not lack your company.

Lep.   Noble Antony,
Not sickness should detain me.

    [*Flourish. Exeunt Cæsar, Antony, Lepidus,*
       and Ventidius.

Mæc. Welcome from Egypt, sir.   174

Eno. Half the heart of Cæsar, worthy Mæcenas!
My honourable friend, Agrippa!

Agr. Good Enobarbus!

Mæc. We have cause to be glad that matters
are so well digested. You stay'd well by 't in
Egypt.   180

Eno. Ay, sir; we did sleep day out of countenance, and made the night light with drinking.

Mæc. Eight wild boars roasted whole at a
breakfast, and but twelve persons there; is this
true?   185

Eno. This was but as a fly by an eagle. We had
much more monstrous matter of feast, which
worthily deserved noting.

Mæc. She's a most triumphant lady, if report
be square to her.   190

Eno. When she first met Mark Antony, she
purs'd up his heart, upon the river of Cydnus.

Agr. There she appear'd indeed, or my reporter
devis'd well for her.

Eno. I will tell you.   195
The barge she sat in, like a burnish'd throne,
Burn'd on the water. The poop was beaten gold;

Purple the sails, and so perfumed that
The winds were love-sick with them. The oars
    were silver,
Which to the tune of flutes kept stroke, and made
The water which they beat to follow faster,   201
As amorous of their strokes. For her own person,
It beggar'd all description: she did lie
In her pavilion — cloth-of-gold of tissue —
O'er-picturing that Venus where we see   205
The fancy outwork nature. On each side her
Stood pretty dimpled boys, like smiling Cupids,
With divers-colour'd fans, whose wind did seem
To [glow] the delicate cheeks which they did cool,
And what they undid did.

Agr.   O, rare for Antony!

Eno. Her gentlewomen, like the Nereides,   211
So many mermaids, tended her i' th' eyes,
And made their bends adornings. At the helm
A seeming mermaid steers; the silken tackle
Swell with the touches of those flower-soft hands   215
That yarely frame the office. From the barge
A strange invisible perfume hits the sense
Of the adjacent wharfs. The city cast
Her people out upon her; and Antony
Enthron'd i' th' market-place, did sit alone,   220
Whistling to th' air, which, but for vacancy,
Had gone to gaze on Cleopatra too
And made a gap in nature.

Agr.   Rare Egyptian!

Eno. Upon her landing, Antony sent to her,
Invited her to supper. She replied,   225
It should be better he became her guest;
Which she entreated. Our courteous Antony,
Whom ne'er the word of "No" woman heard
    speak,
Being barber'd ten times o'er, goes to the feast,
And for his ordinary pays his heart   230
For what his eyes eat only.

Agr.   Royal wench!
She made great Cæsar lay his sword to bed.
He plough'd her, and she cropp'd.

Eno.   I saw her once
Hop forty paces through the public street;
And having lost her breath, she spoke, and
    panted,
That she did make defect perfection   236
And, breathless, power breathe forth.

Mæc. Now Antony must leave her utterly.

Eno. Never; he will not.
Age cannot wither her, nor custom stale   240
Her infinite variety. Other women cloy
The appetites they feed, but she makes hungry
Where most she satisfies; for vilest things
Become themselves in her, that the holy priests

---

166. **fame:** rumor. 167. **spoke:** i.e., to thank him (ll. 157–58). 204. **cloth...tissue:** cloth woven of gold and silver threads.
209. **[glow]** (Rowe): make glow. *glove* F. 213. **bends:** bows. 216. **yarely frame:** nimbly do. 218. **wharfs:** banks. 221.
vacancy: i.e., causing a vacuum. 230. **ordinary:** meal. 237. **power:** i.e., charm. 244. **Become themselves:** are becoming.

Enobarbus here gives information

Bless her when she is riggish.   245

Mæc. If beauty, wisdom, modesty, can settle
The heart of Antony, Octavia is
A blessed lottery to him.

Agr.   Let us go.
Good Enobarbus, make yourself my guest
Whilst you abide here.

Eno.   Humbly, sir, I thank you.   250
                      [*Exeunt.*

       [SCENE III.   *Rome.   Cæsar's house.*]

Enter ANTONY, CÆSAR, OCTAVIA *between them*
            [*and Attendants*].

Ant. The world and my great office will some-
     times
Divide me from your bosom.

Octa.   All which time
Before the gods my knee shall bow my prayers
To them for you.

Ant.   Good-night, sir.   My Octavia,
Read not my blemishes in the world's report.   5
I have not kept my square; but that to come
Shall all be done by th' rule.   Good-night, dear
     lady.
Good-night, sir.

Cæs. Good-night.   [*Exeunt* [*Cæsar and Octavia*].

          Enter SOOTHSAYER.

Ant. Now, sirrah, you do wish yourself in Egypt?

Sooth. Would I had never come from thence, nor
     you   11
Thither!

Ant. If you can, your reason?

Sooth.   I see it in
My motion, have it not in my tongue; but yet
Hie you to Egypt again.

Ant.   Say to me,   15
Whose fortunes shall rise higher, Cæsar's or mine?

Sooth. Cæsar's.
Therefore, O Antony, stay not by his side.
Thy demon, that thy spirit which keeps thee, is
Noble, courageous, high, unmatchable,   20
Where Cæsar's is not; but, near him, thy angel
Becomes a fear, as being o'erpower'd: therefore
Make space between you.

Ant.   Speak this no more.

Sooth. To none but thee; no more, but when to
     thee.
If thou dost play with him at any game,   25
Thou art sure to lose; and, of that natural luck,
He beats thee 'gainst the odds.   Thy lustre thickens
When he shines by.   I say again, thy spirit

Is all afraid to govern thee near him;
But, he [away], 'tis noble.

Ant.   Get thee gone. —   30
Say to Ventidius I would speak with him;
                  [*Exit* [*Soothsayer*].
He shall to Parthia. — Be it art or hap,
He hath spoken true.   The very dice obey him,
And in our sports my better cunning faints
Under his chance.   If we draw lots, he speeds;   35
His cocks do win the battle still of mine,
When it is all to nought; and his quails ever
Beat mine, inhoop'd, at odds.   I will to Egypt;
And though I make this marriage for my peace,
I' th' East my pleasure lies.

           Enter VENTIDIUS.

               O, come, Ventidius,
You must to Parthia.   Your commission 's ready;
Follow me and receive 't.   [*Exeunt.*

       [SCENE IV.   *Rome.   A street.*]

    Enter LEPIDUS, MÆCENAS, *and* AGRIPPA.

Lep. Trouble yourselves no further; pray you,
     hasten
Your generals after.

Agr.   Sir, Mark Antony
Will e'en but kiss Octavia, and we'll follow.

Lep. Till I shall see you in your soldier's dress,
Which will become you both, farewell.

Mæc.   We shall,
As I conceive the journey, be at [th'] Mount   6
Before you, Lepidus.

Lep.   Your way is shorter;
My purposes do draw me much about.
You'll win two days upon me.

Both.   Sir, good success!

Lep. Farewell.   [*Exeunt.*   10

    [SCENE V.   *Alexandria.   Cleopatra's palace.*]

     Enter CLEOPATRA, CHARMIAN, IRAS, *and*
                Alexas.

Cleo. Give me some music; music, moody food
Of us that trade in love.

All.   The music, ho!

       Enter MARDIAN *the Eunuch*.

Cleo. Let it alone; let's to billiards.   Come,
     Charmian.

Char. My arm is sore; best play with Mardian.

Cleo. As well a woman with an eunuch play'd   5
As with a woman.   Come, you'll play with me, sir?

Mar. As well as I can, madam.

---

245. **riggish:** wanton.   248. **lottery:** prize.
Sc. iii, 6. **kept my square:** done as I ought.   14. **motion:** intuition.   26. **of:** by.   27. **thickens:** grows dim.   30. **[away]**
(Pope).   *alway* F.   35. **chance:** luck.   38. **inhoop'd:** fighting in an enclosure.
Sc. iv, 6. **[th']** F₂.   Om. F₁.   **Mount:** Mount Misenum.

Cleo. And when good will is showed, though 't
   come too short,
The actor may plead pardon. I'll none now.
Give me mine angle, we'll to th' river; there,   10
My music playing far off, I will betray
[Tawny-finn'd] fishes; my bended hook shall pierce
Their slimy jaws; and, as I draw them up,
I'll think them every one an Antony,
And say, "Ah, ha! you're caught."
Char.   'Twas merry when
You wager'd on your angling; when your diver   16
Did hang a salt-fish on his hook, which he
With fervency drew up.
Cleo.   That time, — O times! —
I laugh'd him out of patience; and that night
I laugh'd him into patience; and next morn,   20
Ere the ninth hour, I drunk him to his bed;
Then put my tires and mantles on him, whilst
I wore his sword Philippan.

        Enter a MESSENGER.
                 O, from Italy!
Ram thou thy fruitful tidings in mine ears,
That long time have been barren.
Mess.   Madam, madam, —
Cleo. Antonio's dead! — If thou say so, villain, 26
Thou kill'st thy mistress; but well and free,
If thou so yield him, there is gold, and here
My bluest veins to kiss; a hand that kings
Have lipp'd, and trembled kissing.   30
Mess. First, madam, he is well.
Cleo.   Why, there's more gold.
But, sirrah, mark, we use
To say the dead are well. Bring it to that,
The gold I give thee will I melt and pour
Down thy ill-uttering throat.   35
Mess. Good madam, hear me.
Cleo.   Well, go to, I will.
But there's no goodness in thy face; if Antony
Be free and healthful, [why] so tart a favour
To trumpet such good tidings? If not well,
Thou shouldst come like a Fury crown'd with
   snakes,   40
Not like a formal man.
Mess.   Will 't please you hear me?
Cleo. I have a mind to strike thee ere thou
   speak'st;
Yet, if thou say Antony lives, [is] well,
Or friends with Cæsar, or not captive to him,
I'll set thee in a shower of gold, and hail   45
Rich pearls upon thee.
Mess.   Madam, he's well.
Cleo.   Well said.
Mess. And friends with Cæsar.

Cleo.   Thou'rt an honest man.
Mess. Cæsar and he are greater friends than ever.
Cleo. Make thee a fortune from me.
Mess.   But yet, madam, —
Cleo. I do not like "But yet," it does allay   50
The good precedence; fie upon "But yet"!
"But yet" is as a gaoler to bring forth
Some monstrous malefactor. Prithee, friend,
Pour out the pack of matter to mine ear,
The good and bad together. He's friends with
   Cæsar;   55
In state of health thou say'st; and thou say'st free.
Mess. Free, madam? No; I made no such report.
He's bound unto Octavia.
Cleo.   For what good turn?
Mess. For the best turn i' th' bed.
Cleo.   I am pale, Charmian.
Mess. Madam, he's married to Octavia.   60
Cleo. The most infectious pestilence upon thee!
                [*Strikes him down.*
Mess. Good madam, patience.
Cleo.   What say you? Hence,
                [*Strikes him again.*
Horrible villain! or I'll spurn thine eyes
Like balls before me; I'll unhair thy head.
           [*She hales him up and down.*
Thou shalt be whipp'd with wire, and stew'd in
   brine,   65
Smarting in ling'ring pickle.
Mess.   Gracious madam,
I that do bring the news made not the match.
Cleo. Say 'tis not so, a province I will give thee,
And make thy fortunes proud; the blow thou
   hadst
Shall make thy peace for moving me to rage;   70
And I will boot thee with what gift beside
Thy modesty can beg.
Mess.   He's married, madam.
Cleo. Rogue, thou hast liv'd too long.
                [*Draws a knife.*
Mess.   Nay, then I'll run.
What mean you, madam? I have made no fault.
                [*Exit.*
Char. Good madam, keep yourself within your-
   self: 75
The man is innocent.
Cleo. Some innocents scape not the thunderbolt.
Melt Egypt into Nile! and kindly creatures
Turn all to serpents! Call the slave again.
Though I am mad, I will not bite him; call.   80
Char. He is afeard to come.
Cleo.   I will not hurt him.
              [*Exit Charmian.*
These hands do lack nobility that they strike

Sc. v, 10. **angle:** rod and line.   12. **[Tawny-finn'd]** (Theobald).   *Tawny fine* F.   22. **tires:** head-dresses.   38. **[why]**
(Rowe). Om. F.   **tart a favour:** sour a face.   41. **formal:** ordinary.   43. **[is]** (Tyrwhitt conj.).   *'tis* F.   50. **allay:** qualify.
51. **precedence:** news which preceded (it).   63. **spurn:** kick.   71. **boot thee with:** give thee also.

A meaner than myself, since I myself
Have given myself the cause.

Re-enter [CHARMIAN *and*] MESSENGER.

Come hither, sir.
Though it be honest, it is never good 85
To bring bad news. Give to a gracious message
An host of tongues, but let ill tidings tell
Themselves when they be felt.
Mess.   I have done my duty.
Cleo. Is he married?
I cannot hate thee worser than I do, 90
If thou again say yes.
Mess.   He's married, madam.
Cleo. The gods confound thee! Dost thou hold
   there still?
Mess. Should I lie, madam?
Cleo.   O, I would thou didst,
So half my Egypt were submerg'd and made
A cistern for scal'd snakes! Go, get thee hence! 95
Hadst thou Narcissus in thy face, to me
Thou wouldst appear most ugly. He is married?
Mess. I crave your Highness' pardon.
Cleo.   He is married?
Mess. Take no offence that I would not offend
you.
To punish me for what you make me do 100
Seems much unequal. He's married to Octavia.
Cleo. O, that his fault should make a knave of
   thee,
That art not what thou'rt sure of. Get thee hence;
The merchandise which thou hast brought from
   Rome 104
Are all too dear for me. Lie they upon thy hand,
And be undone by 'em!   [*Exit Messenger.*]
Char.   Good your Highness, patience.
Cleo. In praising Antony I have disprais'd Cæsar.
Char. Many times, madam.
Cleo.   I am paid for't now.
Lead me from hence;
I faint, O Iras, Charmian! 'Tis no matter. 110
Go to the fellow, good Alexas; bid him
Report the feature of Octavia, her years,
Her inclination; let him not leave out
The colour of her hair. Bring me word quickly.
     [*Exit Alexas.*]
Let him for ever go; — let him not — Charmian,
Though he be painted one way like a Gorgon, 116
The other [way 's] a Mars. Bid you Alexas
     [*To Mardian.*
Bring me word how tall she is. Pity me, Charmian,

But do not speak to me. Lead me to my chamber.
     [*Exeunt.*

[SCENE VI. *Near Misenum.*]

Flourish. Enter POMPEY *and* MENAS *at one door,
with drum and trumpet: at another,* CÆSAR, AN-
TONY, LEPIDUS, ENOBARBUS, Mæcenas, Agrippa,
with Soldiers *marching.*

Pom. Your hostages I have, so have you mine;
And we shall talk before we fight.
Cæs.   Most meet
That first we come to words, and therefore have we
Our written purposes before us sent;
Which, if thou hast considered, let us know 5
If 'twill tie up thy discontented sword,
And carry back to Sicily much tall youth
That else must perish here.
Pom.   To you all three,
The senators alone of this great world,
Chief factors for the gods, I do not know 10
Wherefore my father should revengers want,
Having a son and friends; since Julius Cæsar,
Who at Philippi the good Brutus ghosted,
There saw you labouring for him. What was't
That mov'd pale Cassius to conspire; and what 15
Made [the] all-honour'd, honest Roman, Brutus,
With the arm'd rest, courtiers of beauteous freedom,
To drench the Capitol, but that they would
Have one man but a man? And that is it
Hath made me rig my navy, at whose burden 20
The anger'd ocean foams; with which I meant
To scourge th' ingratitude that despiteful Rome
Cast on my noble father.
Cæs.   Take your time.
Ant. Thou canst not fear us, Pompey, with thy
   sails; 24
We'll speak with thee at sea. At land, thou know'st
How much we do o'er-count thee.
Pom.   At land, indeed,
Thou dost o'er-count me of my father's house;
But since the cuckoo builds not for himself,
Remain in't as thou mayst.
Lep.   Be pleas'd to tell us —
For this is from the present — how you take 30
The offers we have sent you.
Cæs.   There's the point.
Ant. Which do not be entreated to, but weigh
What it is worth embrac'd.
Cæs.   And what may follow,
To try a larger fortune.
Pom.   You have made me offer

---

94. **So:** even if. 96. **Narcissus:** a mythical figure famous for his beauty. 103. **what... of:** i.e., the hateful news.
112. **feature:** shape, appearance. 113. **inclination:** disposition. 117. **[way 's]** F₄: way he is. *wayes* F₁. The reference is
to "perspectives," pictures which showed different objects, according to the angle of view.
 Sc. vi, 7. **tall:** valiant. 13. **ghosted:** haunted. 16. **[the]** F₂. Om. F₁. 24. **fear:** frighten. 26. **o'er-count:** outnumber.
27. **o'er-count:** cheat. Plutarch writes that Antony, having bought the elder Pompey's house, refused to pay for it. 30.
present: i.e., present business.

Of Sicily, Sardinia; and I must   35
Rid all the sea of pirates; then, to send
Measures of wheat to Rome. This 'greed upon,
To part with unhack'd edges and bear back
Our targes undinted.
   All. That's our offer.
   Pom.   Know, then,
I came before you here a man prepar'd   41
To take this offer; but Mark Antony
Put me to some impatience. — Though I lose
The praise of it by telling, you must know,
When Cæsar and your brother were at blows,   45
Your mother came to Sicily and did find
Her welcome friendly.
   Ant.   I have heard it, Pompey,
And am well studied for a liberal thanks
Which I do owe you.
   Pom.   Let me have your hand.
I did not think, sir, to have met you here.   50
   Ant. The beds i' th' East are soft; and thanks to
    you,
That call'd me timelier than my purpose hither
For I have gain'd by 't.
   Cæs.   Since I saw you last,
There is a change upon you.
   Pom.   Well, I know not
What counts harsh Fortune casts upon my face;   55
But in my bosom shall she never come,
To make my heart her vassal.
   Lep.   Well met here.
   Pom. I hope so, Lepidus. Thus we are agreed.
I crave our composition may be written,
And seal'd between us.
   Cæs.   That's the next to do.
   Pom. We'll feast each other ere we part; and
    let's   61
Draw lots who shall begin.
   Ant.   That will I, Pompey.
   Pom. No, Antony, take the lot; but, first
Or last, your fine Egyptian cookery
Shall have the fame. I have heard that Julius
    Cæsar   65
Grew fat with feasting there.
   Ant.   You have heard much.
   Pom. I have fair [meanings], sir.
   Ant.   And fair words to them.
   Pom. Then so much have I heard;
And I have heard, Apollodorus carried —
   Eno. No more [of] that; he did so.
   Pom.   What, I pray you?
   Eno. A certain queen to Cæsar in a mattress.   71
   Pom. I know thee now. How far'st thou, sol-
    dier?
   Eno Well;
And well am like to do, for, I perceive,

Four feasts are toward.
   Pom.   Let me shake thy hand;   75
I never hated thee. I have seen thee fight,
When I have envied thy behaviour.
   Eno.   Sir,
I never lov'd you much; but I ha' prais'd ye
When you have well deserv'd ten times as much
As I have said you did.
   Pom.   Enjoy thy plainness;   80
It nothing ill becomes thee.
Aboard my galley I invite you all:
Will you lead, lords?
   All.   Show [us] the way, sir.
   Pom.   Come.
         [*Exeunt all but Menas and Enobarbus.*
   Men. [*Aside.*] Thy father, Pompey, would ne'er
have made this treaty. — You and I have known,
sir.   86
   Eno. At sea, I think.
   Men. We have, sir.
   Eno. You have done well by water.
   Men. And you by land.   90
   Eno. I will praise any man that will praise me;
though it cannot be denied what I have done by
land.
   Men. Nor what I have done by water.   94
   Eno. Yes, something you can deny for your own
safety. You have been a great thief by sea.
   Men. And you by land.
   Eno. There I deny my land service. But give me
your hand, Menas. If our eyes had authority, here
they might take two thieves kissing.   101
   Men. All men's faces are true, whatsome'er their
hands are.
   Eno. But there is never a fair woman has a true
face.   105
   Men. No slander; they steal hearts.
   Eno. We came hither to fight with you.
   Men. For my part, I am sorry it is turn'd to a
drinking. Pompey doth this day laugh away his
fortune.   110
   Eno. If he do, sure, he cannot weep 't back
again.
   Men. You've said, sir. We look'd not for Mark
Antony here. Pray you, is he married to Cleo-
patra?   115
   Eno. Cæsar's sister is called Octavia.
   Men. True, sir; she was the wife of Caius
Marcellus.
   Eno. But she is now the wife of Marcus Antonius.
   Men. Pray ye, sir?   120
   Eno. 'Tis true.
   Men. Then is Cæsar and he for ever knit together.
   Eno. If I were bound to divine of this unity, I
would not prophesy so.   125

---

38. edges: swords.   **55. counts:** accounts.   **59. composition:** agreement.   **67. [meanings]** (Heath conj.). *meaning* F.
70. [of] F₃. Om. F₁.   **75. toward:** being prepared.   **85. known:** been acquainted.

Men. I think the policy of that purpose made more in the marriage than the love of the parties.

Eno. I think so too. But you shall find the band that seems to tie their friendship together will be the very strangler of their amity. Octavia is of a holy, cold, and still conversation.   131

Men. Who would not have his wife so?

Eno. Not he that himself is not so; which is Mark Antony. He will to his Egyptian dish again. Then shall the sighs of Octavia blow the fire up in   135 Cæsar; and, as I said before, that which is the strength of their amity shall prove the immediate author of their variance. Antony will use his affection where it is; he married but his occasion here.   140

Men. And thus it may be. Come, sir, will you aboard? I have a health for you.

Eno. I shall take it, sir; we have us'd our throats in Egypt.

Men. Come, let's away.   [*Exeunt.*   145

[SCENE VII. *On board Pompey's galley, off Misenum.*]

Music plays. Enter two or three SERVANTS *with a banquet.*

1. [*Serv.*] Here they'll be, man. Some o' their plants are ill-rooted already; the least wind i' th' world will blow them down.

2. Serv. Lepidus is [high-colour'd].

1. Serv. They have made him drink alms-drink.   6

2. Serv. As they pinch one another by the disposition, he cries out, "No more"; reconciles them to his entreaty, and himself to th' drink.

1. Serv. But it raises the greater war between him and his discretion.   11

2. Serv. Why, this it is to have a name in great men's fellowship. I had as lief have a reed that will do me no service as a partisan I could not heave.   15

1. Serv. To be called into a huge sphere, and not to be seen to move in't, are the holes where eyes should be, which pitifully disaster the cheeks.

A sennet sounded. Enter CÆSAR, ANTONY, LEPIDUS, POMPEY, *Agrippa,* Mæcenas, ENOBARBUS, MENAS, *with other captains.*

Ant. [*To Cæsar.*] Thus do they, sir: they take the flow o' th' Nile   20
By certain scales i' th' pyramid; they know,
By th' height, the lowness, or the mean, if dearth
Or foison follow. The higher Nilus swells,
The more it promises; as it ebbs, the seedsman
Upon the slime and ooze scatters his grain,   25
And shortly comes to harvest.

Lep. You've strange serpents there?

Ant. Ay, Lepidus.

Lep. Your serpent of Egypt is bred now of your mud by the operation of your sun. So is your crocodile.   31

Ant. They are so.

Pom. Sit, — and some wine! A health to Lepidus!

Lep. I am not so well as I should be, but I'll ne'er out.   36

Eno. Not till you have slept; I fear me you'll be in till then.

Lep. Nay, certainly, I have heard the Ptolemies' pyramises are very goodly things; without contradiction, I have heard that.   41

Men. [*Aside to Pom.*] Pompey, a word.

Pom. [*Aside to Men.*] Say in mine ear: what is't?

Men. [*Aside to Pom.*] Forsake thy seat, I do beseech thee, captain,
And hear me speak a word.

Pom. (*Whispers in's ear.*) Forbear me till anon.—
This wine for Lepidus!   45

Lep. What manner o' thing is your crocodile?

Ant. It is shap'd, sir, like itself; and it is as broad as it hath breadth. It is just so high as it is, and moves with it own organs. It lives by that which nourisheth it; and the elements once out of it, it transmigrates.   51

Lep. What colour is it of?

Ant. Of it own colour too.

Lep. 'Tis a strange serpent.

Ant. 'Tis so. And the tears of it are wet.   55

Cæs. Will this description satisfy him?

Ant. With the health that Pompey gives him, else he is a very epicure.

Pom. [*Aside to Men.*] Go hang, sir, hang! Tell me of that? Away!
Do as I bid you. — Where's this cup I call'd for?   60

Men. [*Aside to Pom.*] If for the sake of merit thou wilt hear me,
Rise from thy stool.

Pom. [*Aside to Men.*] I think thou'rt mad. The matter?   [*Rises, and walks aside.*]

Men. I have ever held my cap off to thy fortunes.

Pom. Thou hast serv'd me with much faith. What's else to say? —
Be jolly, lords.

Ant.   These quick-sands, Lepidus,   65
Keep off them, for you sink.

Men. Wilt thou be lord of all the world?

Pom.   What say'st thou?

Men. Wilt thou be lord of the whole world? That's twice.

---

131. **conversation:** deportment.   140. **occasion:** expediency.

Sc. vii, 1, etc. [*Serv.*] (Rowe). F designates the servants *1* and *2*.   2. **plants:** soles (of the feet).   4. [**high-colour'd**] F₂: intoxicated. *high Conlord* F₁.   5. **alms-drink:** i.e., in addition to his own share.   6–7. **pinch ... disposition:** fall to quarreling. 14. **partisan:** long-handled spear with double blade.   18. **disaster:** disfigure.   23. **foison:** plenty.   36. **out:** fail to drink my share.   38. **in:** in drink.   63. **held ... off:** been respectful.

ironic picture of 3 rulers
of world - feasting, drinking.

Pom. How should that be?

Men.   But entertain it,
And, though thou think me poor, I am the man   70
Will give thee all the world.

Pom.   Hast thou drunk well?

Men. No, Pompey, I have kept me from the cup.
Thou art, if thou dar'st be, the earthly Jove.
Whate'er the ocean pales, or sky inclips,
Is thine, if thou wilt ha't.

Pom.   Show me which way.

Men. These three world-sharers, these competi-
          tors,   76
Are in thy vessel: let me cut the cable;
And, when we are put off, fall to their throats.
All there is thine.

Pom.   Ah, this thou shouldst have done,
And not have spoke on't! In me 'tis villany;   80
In thee 't had been good service. Thou must know,
'Tis not my profit that does lead mine honour;
Mine honour, it. Repent that e'er thy tongue
Hath so betray'd thine act. Being done unknown,
I should have found it afterwards well done   85
But must condemn it now. Desist, and drink.

Men. [*Aside.*] For this,
I'll never follow thy pall'd fortunes more.
Who seeks, and will not take when once 'tis offer'd,
Shall never find it more.

Pom.   This health to Lepidus!

Ant. Bear him ashore. I'll pledge it for him,
          Pompey,   91

Eno. Here's to thee, Menas!

Men.   Enobarbus, welcome!

Pom. Fill till the cup be hid.

Eno. There's a strong fellow, Menas.
          [*Pointing to the Attendant who carries off
          Lepidus.*]

Men. Why?   95

Eno. 'A bears the third part of the world, man;
see'st not?

Men. The third part, then, is drunk. Would it
          were all,
That it might go on wheels!

Eno. Drink thou; increase the reels.   100

Men. Come.

Pom. This is not yet an Alexandrian feast.

Ant. It ripens towards it. Strike the vessels, ho!
Here's to Cæsar!

Cæs.   I could well forbear 't.
It's monstrous labour when I wash my brain   105
And it [grows] fouler.

Ant.   Be a child o' th' time.

Cæs. Possess it, I'll make answer.

But I had rather fast from all, four days,
Than drink so much in one.   109

Eno. Ha, my brave emperor!   [*To Antony.*
Shall we dance now the Egyptian Bacchanals
And celebrate our drink?

Pom.   Let's ha't, good soldier.

Ant. Come, let's all take hands
Till that the conquering wine hath steep'd our sense
In soft and delicate Lethe.

Eno.   All take hands.
Make battery to our ears with the loud music; 116
The while I'll place you; then the boy shall sing.
The holding every man shall [bear] as loud
As his strong sides can volley.
          [*Music plays. Enobarbus places them hand
          in hand.*

THE SONG.

Come, thou monarch of the vine,   120
Plumpy Bacchus with pink eyne!
In thy fats our cares be drown'd,
With thy grapes our hairs be crown'd!
Cup us till the world go round,
Cup us till the world go round!   125

Cæs. What would you more? Pompey, good-
          night. Good brother,
Let me request you [off]; our graver business
Frowns at this levity. Gentle lords, let's part;
You see we have burnt our cheeks. Strong Enobarb
Is weaker than the wine, and mine own tongue   130
Splits what it speaks; the wild disguise hath almost
Antick'd us all. What needs more words? Good-
          night.
Good Antony, your hand.

Pom.   I'll try you on the shore.

Ant. And shall, sir; give 's your hand.

Pom.   O Antony,
You have my father's house, — But, what? we are
          friends.   135
Come, down into the boat.

Eno.   Take heed you fall not.
          [*Exeunt all but Enobarbus and Menas.*
Menas, I'll not on shore.

[Men.]   No, to my cabin.
These drums! these trumpets, flutes! what!
Let Neptune hear we bid a loud farewell
To these great fellows. Sound and be hang'd,
          sound out!   [*Sound a flourish, with drums.*

Eno. Ho! says 'a. There's my cap.   141

Men. Ho! Noble captain, come.
                              [*Exeunt.*

74. **pales:** fences in. **inclips:** embraces. 88. **pall'd:** waned. 99. **go on wheels:** run smoothly (proverbial). 103. **Strike the vessels:** clink the cups. 106. [grows] F₂. *grow* F₁. 107. **Possess it:** have your way, go ahead. 118. **holding:** refrain. [bear] (Theobald). *beate* F. 121. **pink:** small. 122. **fats:** vats. 127. [off] (Rowe and Hanmer): i.e., to excuse me. *of* F. 131. **disguise:** drunkenness. 132. **Antick'd:** made buffoons of. 133. **try you:** test your drinking powers. 138. [Men.] (Capell). Om. F.

[ACT III]

[Scene I. *A plain in Syria.*]

Enter Ventidius *as it were in triumph* [*with* Silius, *and other* Romans, Officers, *and* Soldiers;] *the dead body of Pacorus borne before him.*

Ven. Now, darting Parthia, art thou struck; and now
Pleas'd Fortune does of Marcus Crassus' death
Make me revenger. Bear the King's son's body
Before our army. Thy Pacorus, Orodes,   4
Pays this for Marcus Crassus.
  [*Sil.*]   Noble Ventidius,
Whilst yet with Parthian blood thy sword is warm,
The fugitive Parthians follow.   Spur through Media,
Mesopotamia, and the shelters whither
The routed fly; so thy grand captain, Antony,
Shall set thee on triumphant chariots and   10
Put garlands on thy head.
  Ven.   O Silius, Silius,
I have done enough; a lower place, note well,
May make too great an act.   For learn this, Silius:
Better to leave undone, than by our deed   14
Acquire too high a fame when him we serve 's away.
Cæsar and Antony have ever won
More in their officer than person.   Sossius,
One of my place in Syria, his lieutenant,
For quick accumulation of renown,   19
Which he achiev'd by th' minute, lost his favour.
Who does i' th' wars more than his captain can
Becomes his captain's captain; and ambition,
The soldier's virtue, rather makes choice of loss,
Than gain which darkens him.
I could do more to do Antonius good,   25
But 'twould offend him; and in his offence
Should my performance perish.
  [*Sil.*]   Thou hast, Ventidius, that
Without the which a soldier and his sword
Grants scarce distinction.   Thou wilt write to Antony?
  Ven. I'll humbly signify what in his name,   30
That magical word of war, we have effected;
How, with his banners and his well-paid ranks,
The ne'er-yet-beaten horse of Parthia
We have jaded out o' th' field.
  [*Sil.*]   Where is he now?
  Ven. He purposeth to Athens; whither, with what haste   35
The weight we must convey with 's will permit,

We shall appear before him. On, there; pass along!
                [*Exeunt.*

[Scene II. *Rome. An Ante-chamber in Cæsar's house.*]

Enter Agrippa *at one door*, Enobarbus *at another.*

  Agr. What, are the brothers parted?
  Eno. They have dispatch'd with Pompey, he is gone;
The other three are sealing. Octavia weeps
To part from Rome; Cæsar is sad; and Lepidus,
Since Pompey's feast, as Menas says, is troubled   5
With the green sickness.
  Agr.   'Tis a noble Lepidus.
  Eno. A very fine one. O, how he loves Cæsar!
  Agr. Nay, but how dearly he adores Mark Antony!
  Eno. Cæsar? Why, he's the Jupiter of men.
  Agr. What's Antony? The god of Jupiter.   10
  Eno. Spake you of Cæsar? How! the nonpareil!
  Agr. O Antony! O thou Arabian bird!
  Eno. Would you praise Cæsar, say "Cæsar"; go no further.
  Agr. Indeed, he plied them both with excellent praises.
  Eno. But he loves Cæsar best; yet he loves Antony.   15
Ho! hearts, tongues, figures, scribes, bards, poets, cannot
Think, speak, cast, write, sing, number, ho!
His love to Antony. But as for Cæsar,
Kneel down, kneel down, and wonder.
  Agr.   Both he loves.
  Eno. They are his shards, and he their beetle.
      [*Trumpets within.*] So;   20
This is to horse. Adieu, noble Agrippa.
  Agr. Good fortune, worthy soldier; and farewell.

Enter Cæsar, Antony, Lepidus, *and* Octavia.

  Ant. No further, sir.
  Cæs. You take from me a great part of myself;
Use me well in't. Sister, prove such a wife   25
As my thoughts make thee, and as my farthest band
Shall pass on thy approof. Most noble Antony,
Let not the piece of virtue which is set
Betwixt us as the cement of our love,
To keep it builded, be the ram to batter   30

Act III, sc. i, 1. **darting.** The Parthians were famous for their skill in throwing darts, especially to cover retreats. 5, 27, 34. [*Sil.*] (Theobald). *Romaine* or *Rom.* F. 12. **lower place:** subordinate. 29. **Grants…distinction:** are hardly distinguishable. 34. **jaded:** driven.
  Sc. ii, 3. **sealing:** i.e., their agreement. 6. **green sickness:** usually anemia; here, effects of his debauch. 12. **Arabian bird:** Phoenix, a fabulous bird, only one of which was said to exist at a time. 20. **shards:** wing cases. 26. **band:** pledge. 27. **pass…approof:** certify thou shalt prove to be.

The fortress of it; for better might we
Have lov'd without this mean, if on both parts
This be not cherish'd.

Ant.   Make me not offended
In your distrust.

Cæs.   I have said.

Ant.   You shall not find,
Though you be therein curious, the least cause   35
For what you seem to fear. So, the gods keep
    you,
And make the hearts of Romans serve your ends!
We will here part.

Cæs. Farewell, my dearest sister, fare thee well!
The elements be kind to thee, and make   40
Thy spirits all of comfort! Fare thee well!

Oct. My noble brother!

Ant. The April's in her eyes; it is love's spring,
And these the showers to bring it on. Be cheerful.

Oct. Sir, look well to my husband's house; and —

Cæs.   What,   45
Octavia?

Oct. I'll tell you in your ear.

Ant. Her tongue will not obey her heart, nor can
Her heart inform her tongue, — the swan's down-
    feather,
That stands upon the swell at full of th' tide
And neither way inclines.

Eno. [*Aside to Agr.*] Will Cæsar weep?   50

Agr. [*Aside to Eno.*] He has a cloud in 's face.

Eno. [*Aside to Agr.*] He were the worse for that,
    were he a horse;
So is he, being a man.

Agr. [*Aside to Eno.*] Why, Enobarbus,
When Antony found Julius Cæsar dead,
He cried almost to roaring; and he wept   55
When at Philippi he found Brutus slain.

Eno. [*Aside to Agr.*] That year, indeed, he was
    troubled with a rheum;
What willingly he did confound he wail'd,
Believe 't, till I [wept] too.

Cæs.   No, sweet Octavia,
You shall hear from me still; the time shall not   60
Out-go my thinking on you.

Ant.   Come, sir, come;
I'll wrestle with you in my strength of love.
Look, here I have you; thus I let you go,
And give you to the gods.

Cæs.   Adieu; be happy!   64

Lep. Let all the number of the stars give light
To thy fair way!

Cæs.   Farewell, farewell!
                        [*Kisses Octavia.*

Ant.   Farewell!
               [*Trumpets sound. Exeunt.*

[SCENE III. *Alexandria. Cleopatra's palace.*]

Enter CLEOPATRA, CHARMIAN, IRAS, *and* ALEXAS.

Cleo. Where is the fellow?

Alex.   Half afeard to come.

Cleo. Go to, go to. Come hither, sir.

Enter the MESSENGER *as before.*

Alex.   Good Majesty,
Herod of Jewry dare not look upon you
But when you are well pleas'd.

Cleo.   That Herod's head
I'll have; but how, when Antony is gone,   5
Through whom I might command it? Come thou
    near.

Mess. Most gracious Majesty, —

Cleo. Didst thou behold Octavia?

Mess. Ay, dread queen.

Cleo. Where?   10

Mess. Madam, in Rome;
I look'd her in the face, and saw her led
Between her brother and Mark Antony.

Cleo. Is she as tall as me?

Mess.   She is not, madam.

Cleo. Didst hear her speak? Is she shrill-tongu'd
    or low?   15

Mess. Madam, I heard her speak; she is low-
    voic'd.

Cleo. That's not so good. He cannot like her long?

Char. Like her! O Isis! 'tis impossible.

Cleo. I think so, Charmian. Dull of tongue,
    and dwarfish!
What majesty is in her gait? Remember,   20
If e'er thou [look'dst] on majesty.

Mess.   She creeps;
Her motion and her station are as one;
She shows a body rather than a life,
A statue than a breather.

Cleo.   Is this certain?   24

Mess. Or I have no observance.

Char.   Three in Egypt
Cannot make better note.

Cleo.   He's very knowing;
I do perceive 't. There's nothing in her yet.
The fellow has good judgement.

Char.   Excellent.

Cleo. Guess at her years, I prithee.

Mess.   Madam,
She was a widow, —

Cleo.   Widow! Charmian, hark.

Mess. And I do think she's thirty.   31

Cleo. Bear'st thou her face in mind? Is't long
    or round?

Mess. Round even to faultiness.

---

35. **curious:** meticulous. 40. **elements:** weather. 51. **cloud:** dark spot. 57. **rheum:** cold, causing watery eyes. 58. **confound:** destroy. **wail'd:** bewailed. 59. [**wept**] (Theobald). *weepe* F.
    Sc. iii, 21. [**look'dst**] (Pope). *look'st* F. 22. **station:** standing.

Cleo. For the most part, too, they are foolish
     that are so.
Her hair, what colour?   35
     Mess. Brown, madam; and her forehead
As low as she would wish it.
     Cleo.   There's gold for thee.
Thou must not take my former sharpness ill.
I will employ thee back again; I find thee
Most fit for business.   Go make thee ready;   40
Our letters are prepar'd.   [*Exit Messenger.*]
     Char.   A proper man.
     Cleo. Indeed, he is so; I repent me much
That so I harried him.   Why, methinks, by him,
This creature's no such thing.
     Char.   Nothing, madam.
     Cleo. The man hath seen some majesty, and
     should know.   45
     Char. Hath he seen majesty?   Isis else defend,
And serving you so long!
     Cleo. I have one thing more to ask him yet,
     good Charmian:
But 'tis no matter; thou shalt bring him to me
Where I will write.   All may be well enough.   50
     Char. I warrant you, madam.   [*Exeunt.*

[SCENE IV.   *Athens.*   *A room in Antony's house.*]

Enter ANTONY *and* OCTAVIA.

     Ant. Nay, nay, Octavia, not only that, —
That were excusable, that, and thousands more
Of semblable import, — but he hath wag'd
New wars 'gainst Pompey; made his will, and read it
To public ear;   5
Spoke scantly of me; when perforce he could not
But pay me terms of honour, cold and sickly
He vented them; most narrow measure lent me,
When the best hint was given him, he not [took 't],
Or did it from his teeth.
     Oct.   O my good lord,   10
Believe not all; or, if you must believe,
Stomach not all.   A more unhappy lady,
If this division chance, ne'er stood between,
Praying for both parts.
The good gods will mock me presently,   15
When I shall pray "O, bless my lord and husband!"
Undo that prayer, by crying out as loud,
"O, bless my brother!"   Husband win, win brother,
Prays, and destroys the prayer; no midway
'Twixt these extremes at all.
     Ant.   Gentle Octavia,   20
Let your best love draw to that point which seeks

Best to preserve it.   If I lose mine honour,
I lose myself, better I were not yours
Than yours so branchless.   But, as you requested,
Yourself shall go between 's.   The meantime, lady,
I'll raise the preparation of a war   26
Shall stain your brother.   Make your soonest haste;
So your desires are yours.
     Oct.   Thanks to my lord.
The Jove of power make me most weak, most weak,
Your reconciler!   Wars 'twixt you twain would be
As if the world should cleave, and that slain men   31
Should solder up the rift.
     Ant. When it appears to you where this begins,
Turn your displeasure that way, for our faults
Can never be so equal that your love   35
Can equally move with them.   Provide your going;
Choose your own company, and command what cost
Your heart has mind to.   [*Exeunt.*

[SCENE V.   *The same.*   *Another room.*]

Enter ENOBARBUS *and* EROS [*meeting*].

     Eno. How now, friend Eros!
     Eros. There's strange news come, sir.
     Eno. What, man?
     Eros. Cæsar and Lepidus have made wars upon
Pompey.
     Eno. This is old; what is the success?   6
     Eros. Cæsar, having made use of him in the
wars 'gainst Pompey, presently denied him rivality,
would not let him partake in the glory of the
action; and not resting here, accuses him of letters
he had formerly wrote to Pompey; upon his own
appeal, seizes him.   So the poor third is up, till
death enlarge his confine.   13
     Eno. Then, [world], thou [hast] a pair of chaps,
     no more;
And throw between them all the food thou hast,
They'll grind [the one] the other.   Where's Antony?
     Eros. He's walking in the garden — thus; and
     spurns
The rush that lies before him; cries, "Fool Lepidus!"
And threats the throat of that his officer   19
That murd'red Pompey.
     Eno.   Our great navy's rigg'd.
     Eros. For Italy and Cæsar.   More, Domitius;
My lord desires you presently; my news
I might have told hereafter.
     Eno.   'Twill be nought:
But let it be.   Bring me to Antony.
     Eros. Come, sir.   [*Exeunt.* 25

---

37. **she . . . it:** i.e., as could be.   41. **proper:** fine.   44. **such:** great.
   Sc. iv, 3. **semblable:** like.   6. **scantly:** grudgingly.   9. **hint:** opportunity.   **[took 't]** (Thirlby conj.).   *look't* F.   10. **from his teeth:** i.e., not from his heart.   12. **Stomach:** resent.   27. **stain:** eclipse.
   Sc. **v,** 6. **success:** outcome.   .8. **rivality:** equal rights as partner.   11–12. **his own appeal:** Cæsar's own accusation.
14. **[world] . . . [hast]** (Hanmer).   *would . . . hadst* F.   **chaps:** jaws.   16. **[the one]** (Johnson conj.).   Om. F.   22. **presently:** at once.

[handwritten annotations in top margin: "affront to Romans - as giving the empire - such part to the public - being not done in Rome!" and "redeeming feature / Octavian's character is his affection for his sister"]

[SCENE VI. *Rome. Cæsar's house.*]

Enter CÆSAR, AGRIPPA, *and* MÆCENAS.

Cæs. Contemning Rome, he has done all this
  and more
In Alexandria. Here's the manner of 't:
I' th' market-place, on a tribunal silver'd,
Cleopatra and himself in chairs of gold
Were publicly enthron'd. At the feet sat   5
Cæsarion, whom they call my father's son,
And all the unlawful issue that their lust
Since then hath made between them. Unto her
He gave the stablishment of Egypt; made her
Of lower Syria, Cyprus, Lydia,   10
Absolute queen.
  Mæc.   This in the public eye?
  Cæs. I' th' common show-place, where they
  exercise.
His sons [he there] proclaim'd the kings of kings:
Great Media, Parthia, and Armenia
He gave to Alexander; to Ptolemy he assign'd   15
Syria, Cilicia, and Phœnicia. She
In th' habiliments of the goddess Isis
That day appear'd; and oft before gave audience,
As 'tis reported, so.
  Mæc.   Let Rome be thus
Inform'd.
  Agr.   Who, queasy with his insolence   20
Already, will their good thoughts call from him.
  Cæs. The people knows it; and have now receiv'd
His accusations.
  Agr.   Who does he accuse?
  Cæs. Cæsar; and that, having in Sicily
Sextus Pompeius spoil'd, we had not rated him   25
His part o' th' isle. Then does he say he lent me
Some shipping unrestor'd. Lastly, he frets
That Lepidus of the triumvirate
Should be depos'd; and, being, that we detain
All his revenue.
  Agr.   Sir, this should be answer'd.   30
  Cæs. 'Tis done already, and the messenger gone.
I have told him Lepidus was grown too cruel;
That he his high authority abus'd,
And did deserve his change. For what I have con-
  quer'd,
I grant him part; but then, in his Armenia   35
And other of his conquer'd kingdoms, I
Demand the like.
  Mæc.   He'll never yield to that.
  Cæs. Nor must not then be yielded to in this.

Enter OCTAVIA *with her train.*

  Oct. Hail, Cæsar, and my lord! Hail, most dear
  Cæsar!
  Cæs. That ever I should call thee castaway!   40

  Oct. You have not call'd me so, nor have you
  cause.
  Cæs. Why have you stolen upon us thus? You
  come not
Like Cæsar's sister. The wife of Antony
Should have an army for an usher, and
The neighs of horse to tell of her approach   45
Long ere she did appear; the trees by th' way
Should have borne men, and expectation fainted,
Longing for what it had not; nay, the dust
Should have ascended to the roof of heaven,   49
Rais'd by your populous troops. But you are come
A market-maid to Rome, and have prevented
The ostentation of our love, which, left unshown,
Is often left unlov'd. We should have met you
By sea and land, supplying every stage
With an augmented greeting.
  Oct.   Good my lord,   55
To come thus was I not constrain'd, but did
On my free will. My lord, Mark Antony,
Hearing that you prepar'd for war, acquainted
My grieved ear withal; whereon, I begg'd
His pardon for return.
  Cæs.   Which soon he granted,
Being an [obstruct] 'tween his lust and him.   61
  Oct. Do not say so, my lord.
  Cæs.   I have eyes upon him,
And his affairs come to me on the wind.
Where is he now?
  Oct.   My lord, in Athens.
  Cæs. No, my most wronged sister; Cleopatra   65
Hath nodded him to her. He hath given his empire
Up to a whore; who now are levying
The kings o' th' earth for war. He hath assembled
Bocchus, the King of Libya; Archelaus,
Of Cappadocia; Philadelphos, King   70
Of Paphlagonia; the Thracian king, Adallas;
King Malchus of Arabia; King of Pont;
Herod of Jewry; Mithridates, King
Of Comagene; Polemon and Amyntas,
The Kings of Mede and Lycaonia,   75
With a more larger list of sceptres.
  Oct.   Ay me, most wretched,
That have my heart parted betwixt two friends
That do afflict each other!
  Cæs.   Welcome hither!
Your letters did withhold our breaking forth,
Till we perceiv'd both how you were wrong led   80
And we in negligent danger. Cheer your heart.
Be you not troubled with the time, which drives
O'er your content these strong necessities;
But let determin'd things to destiny
Hold unbewail'd their way. Welcome to Rome;   85
Nothing more dear to me. You are abus'd
Beyond the mark of thought; and the high gods,

Sc. vi, 3. **tribunal:** platform. 13. [**he there**] (Johnson). *hither* F. 20. **queasy:** disgusted. 25. **spoil'd:** plundered.
rated: allotted. 61. [**obstruct**] (Theobald): obstruction. *abstract* F. 81. **negligent:** unheeded.

[handwritten annotation at bottom: "moon Goddess - appropriate for changeable Cleo."]

To do you justice, [make them] ministers
Of us and those that love you.   Best of comfort,
And ever welcome to us.
   Agr.   Welcome, lady.   90
   Mæc. Welcome, dear madam.
Each heart in Rome does love and pity you;
Only th' adulterous Antony, most large
In his abominations, turns you off,
And gives his potent regiment to a trull.   95
That noises it against us.
   Oct.   Is it so, sir?
   Cæs. Most certain.   Sister, welcome.   Pray you,
Be ever known to patience.   My dear'st sister!
                            [*Exeunt.*

   [SCENE VII.   *Near Actium.   Antony's camp.*]

     Enter CLEOPATRA *and* ENOBARBUS.

   Cleo. I will be even with thee, doubt it not.
   Eno. But why, why, why?
   Cleo. Thou hast forspoke my being in these wars,
And say'st it is not fit.
   Eno.   Well, is it, is it?
   Cleo. [Is't] not denounc'd against us?   Why
    should not we   5
Be there in person?
   Eno.   Well, I could reply:
If we should serve with horse and mares together,
The horse were merely lost; the mares would bear
A soldier and his horse.
   Cleo.   What is 't you say?   10
   Eno. Your presence needs must puzzle Antony;
Take from his heart, take from his brain, from 's
    time,
What should not then be spar'd.   He is already
Traduc'd for levity; and 'tis said in Rome
That Photinus an eunuch and your maids   15
Manage this war.
   Cleo.   Sink Rome, and their tongues rot
That speak against us!   A charge we bear i' th' war,
And, as the president of my kingdom, will
Appear there for a man.   Speak not against it;
I will not stay behind.

     Enter ANTONY *and* CANIDIUS.

   Eno.   Nay, I have done.   20
Here comes the Emperor.
   Ant.   Is it not strange, Canidius,
That from Tarentum and Brundusium
He could so quickly cut the Ionian Sea,
And take in Toryne?   You have heard on't, sweet?
   Cleo. Celerity is never more admir'd   25
Than by the negligent.

   Ant.   A good rebuke,
Which might have well becom'd the best of men,
To taunt at slackness.   Canidius, we
Will fight with him by sea.
   Cleo.   By sea! what else?   29
   Can. Why will my lord do so?
   Ant.   For that he dares us to't.
   Eno. So hath my lord dar'd him to single fight.
   Can. Ay, and to wage this battle at Pharsalia,
Where Cæsar fought with Pompey; but these offers,
Which serve not for his vantage, he shakes off;
And so should you.
   Eno.   Your ships are not well mann'd;
Your mariners are [muleters], reapers, people   36
Ingross'd by swift impress.   In Cæsar's fleet
Are those that often have 'gainst Pompey fought.
Their ships are yare; yours, heavy.   No disgrace
Shall fall you for refusing him at sea,   40
Being prepar'd for land.
   Ant.   By sea, by sea.
   Eno. Most worthy sir, you therein throw away
The absolute soldiership you have by land;
Distract your army, which doth most consist
Of war-mark'd footmen; leave unexecuted   45
Your own renowned knowledge; quite forgo
The way which promises assurance; and
Give up yourself merely to chance and hazard,
From firm security.
   Ant.   I'll fight at sea.
   Cleo. I have sixty sails, Cæsar none better.   50
   Ant. Our overplus of shipping will we burn;
And, with the rest full-mann'd, from th' head of
    Actium
Beat the approaching Cæsar.   But if we fail,
We then can do't at land.

     Enter a MESSENGER.

                 Thy business?
   Mess. The news is true, my lord; he is descried;
Cæsar has taken Toryne.   56
   Ant. Can he be there in person?   'Tis impossible;
Strange that his power should be.   Canidius,
Our nineteen legions thou shalt hold by land,
And our twelve thousand horse.   We'll to our ship;
Away, my Thetis!

     Enter a SOLDIER.

             How now, worthy soldier!   61
   Sold. O noble emperor, do not fight by sea;
Trust not to rotten planks!   Do you misdoubt
This sword and these my wounds?   Let the Egyp-
    tians
And the Phœnicians go a-ducking; we   65

   88. [make them] (Capell).   *makes his* F.   95. regiment: government.   96. noises it: is clamorous.
   Sc. vii, 3. forspoke: spoken against.   5. [Is't] (Tyrwhitt conj.).   *If* F.   denounc'd: declared.   9. merely: utterly.   11.
puzzle: confuse.   36. [muleters] F₂ (Muliters).   *Militers* F₁.   37. Ingross'd: enrolled.   impress: forced levy.   39. yare:
easily managed.   61. Thetis: a sea goddess.

Have us'd to conquer, standing on the earth,
And fighting foot to foot.

Ant.   Well, well: away!

    [*Exeunt Antony, Cleopatra, and Enobarbus.*

Sold. By Hercules, I think I am i' th' right.

Can. Soldier, thou art; but his whole action grows
Not in the power on't. So our [leader's led],   70
And we are women's men.

Sold.   You keep by land
The legions and the horse whole, do you not?

[*Can.*] Marcus Octavius, Marcus Justeius,
Publicola, and Cælius, are for sea;   74
But we keep whole by land. This speed of Cæsar's
Carries beyond belief.

Sold.   While he was yet in Rome,
His power went out in such distractions as
Beguil'd all spies.

Can.   Who's his lieutenant, hear you?

Sold. They say, one Taurus.

Can.   Well I know the man.

         Enter a MESSENGER.

Mess. The Emperor calls Canidius.   80

Can. With news the time's with labour, and
    throes forth
Each minute some.   [*Exeunt.*

    [SCENE VIII. *A plain near Actium.*]

    Enter CÆSAR [*and* TAURUS], *with his army,*
          marching.

Cæs. Taurus!

Taur. My lord?

Cæs. Strike not by land; keep whole; provoke
    not battle
Till we have done at sea. Do not exceed
The prescript of this scroll. Our fortune lies   5
Upon this jump.   [*Exeunt.*

    [SCENE IX. *Another part of the plain.*]

      Enter ANTONY *and* Enobarbus.

Ant. Set we our squadrons on yond side o' th'
    hill,
In eye of Cæsar's battle; from which place
We may the number of the ships behold,
And so proceed accordingly.   [*Exeunt.*

    [SCENE X. *Another part of the plain.*]

*Canidius marcheth with his land army one way over
the stage; and Taurus, the lieutenant of Cæsar, the
other way. After their going in, is heard the noise
of a sea-fight.*

     Alarum. Enter ENOBARBUS.

Eno. Nought, nought, all nought! I can behold
    no longer.
Th' Antoniad, the Egyptian admiral,
With all their sixty, fly and turn the rudder.
To see 't mine eyes are blasted.

        Enter SCARUS.

Scar.   Gods and goddesses,
All the whole synod of them!

Eno.   What's thy passion?   5

Scar. The greater cantle of the world is lost
With very ignorance; we have kiss'd away
Kingdoms and provinces.

Eno.   How appears the fight.

Scar. On our side like the token'd pestilence,
Where death is sure. Yon ribaldried nag of
    Egypt, —   10
Whom leprosy o'ertake! — i' th' midst o' th' fight,
When vantage like a pair of twins appear'd,
Both as the same, or rather ours the elder,
The breese upon her, like a cow in June,
Hoists sails and flies.   15

Eno. That I beheld.
Mine eyes did sicken at the sight and could not
Endure a further view.

Scar.   She once being loof'd,
The noble ruin of her magic, Antony,
Claps on his sea-wing, and, like a doting mallard, 20
Leaving the fight in height, flies after her.
I never saw an action of such shame;
Experience, manhood, honour, ne'er before
Did violate so itself.

Eno   Alack, alack!   24

       Enter CANIDIUS.

Can. Our fortune on the sea is out of breath
And sinks most lamentably. Had our general
Been what he knew himself, it had gone well.
O, [he] has given example for our flight,
Most grossly, by his own!

Eno.   Ay, are you thereabouts?

69–70. **his ... on't:** his (purposed) conduct is not based on his true source of power.   70. **[leader's led]** (Theobald).
Leaders leade F.   73. **[Can.]** (Pope). *Ven.* F.   77. **distractions:** (small) detachments.   81. **throes:** brings painfully
(forth).

   Sc. viii, 5. **prescript:** direction.   6. **jump:** hazard.

   Sc. ix, 2. **battle:** army.

   Sc. x, 2. **Antoniad:** the flag-ship.   5. **synod:** assembly.   6. **cantle:** corner, i.e., part.   9. **token'd:** spotted.   10. **Yon
ribaldried:** yon lewd. *Yon rebaudred* F₁₋₃. *Your ribauldred* F₄.   12–13. **When ... same:** when chances were evenly balanced.   14. **breese:** gadfly.   18. **being loof'd:** having sailed away.   20. **mallard:** drake.   28. **[he]** F₂. *His* F₁.   29. **thereabouts:** of that mind.

Why, then, good-night indeed.   30
  Can. Toward Peloponnesus are they fled.
  Scar. 'Tis easy to't; and there I will attend
What further comes.
  Can.   To Cæsar will I render
My legions and my horse. Six kings already
Show me the way of yielding.
  Eno.   I'll yet follow   35
The wounded chance of Antony, though my reason
Sits in the wind against me.   [*Exeunt.*]

[SCENE XI. *Alexandria. Cleopatra's palace.*]

Enter ANTONY *with* ATTENDANTS.

  Ant. Hark! the land bids me tread no more upon
    't;
It is asham'd to bear me! Friends, come hither.
I am so lated in the world, that I
Have lost my way for ever. I have a ship
Laden with gold; take that, divide it; fly,   5
And make your peace with Cæsar.
  All.   Fly! not we.
  Ant. I have fled myself, and have instructed
    cowards
To run and show their shoulders. Friends, be gone;
I have myself resolv'd upon a course
Which has no need of you; be gone.   10
My treasure's in the harbour; take it. O,
I follow'd that I blush to look upon.
My very hairs do mutiny; for the white
Reprove the brown for rashness, and they them
For fear and doting. Friends, be gone; you shall
Have letters from me to some friends that will   16
Sweep your way for you. Pray you, look not sad,
Nor make replies of loathness. Take the hint
Which my despair proclaims; let [that] be left
Which leaves itself. To the sea-side straightway;
I will possess you of that ship and treasure.   21
Leave me, I pray, a little; pray you now.
Nay, do so; for, indeed, I have lost command,
Therefore I pray you. I'll see you by and by.
[*Sits down.*

Enter CLEOPATRA, *led by* CHARMIAN *and* [IRAS;]
EROS [*following*].

  Eros. Nay, gentle madam, to him; comfort him.
  Iras. Do, most dear queen.   26
  Char. Do! Why, what else?
  Cleo. Let me sit down. O Juno!
  Ant. No, no, no, no, no.
  Eros. See you here, sir?   30
  Ant. O fie, fie, fie!

  Char. Madam!
  Iras. Madam, O good empress!
  Eros. Sir, sir, —
  Ant. Yes, my lord, yes; he at Philippi kept   35
His sword e'en like a dancer, while I struck
The lean and wrinkled Cassius; and 'twas I
That the mad Brutus ended. He alone
Dealt on lieutenantry and no practice had
In the brave squares of war; yet now — No matter.
  Cleo. Ah, stand by.   41
  Eros. The Queen, my lord, the Queen.
  Iras. Go to him, madam, speak to him;
He is unqualitied with very shame.
  Cleo. Well then, sustain me. Oh!   45
  Eros. Most noble sir, arise; the Queen ap-
    proaches.
Her head's declin'd, and death will [seize] her, but
Your comfort makes the rescue.
  Ant. I have offended reputation,
A most unnoble swerving.
  Eros.   Sir, the Queen.   50
  Ant. O, whither hast thou led me, Egypt? See
How I convey my shame out of thine eyes
By looking back what I have left behind
'Stroy'd in dishonour.
  Cleo.   O my lord, my lord,
Forgive my fearful sails! I little thought   55
You would have followed.
  Ant.   Egypt, thou knew'st too well
My heart was to thy rudder tied by th' strings,
And thou shouldst [tow] me after. O'er my spirit
[Thy] full supremacy thou knew'st, and that
Thy beck might from the bidding of the gods   60
Command me
  Cleo.   O, my pardon!
  Ant.   Now I must
To the young man send humble treaties, dodge
And palter in the shifts of lowness, who
With half the bulk o' th' world play'd as I pleas'd,
Making and marring fortunes. You did know   65
How much you were my conqueror, and that
My sword, made weak by my affection, would
Obey it on all cause.
  Cleo.   Pardon, pardon!
  Ant. Fall not a tear, I say; one of them rates
All that is won and lost. Give me a kiss.   70
Even this repays me. We sent our schoolmaster;
Is 'a come back? Love, I am full of lead.
Some wine, within there, and our viands! Fortune
    knows
We scorn her most when most she offers blows.
[*Exeunt.*

---

37. **Sits...against:** opposes.
  Sc. xi, 3. **lated:** benighted. 19. **[that]** (Capell). *them* F. 35. **kept:** i.e., in its sheath. 39. **Dealt on lieutenantry:** fought through subordinates. 40. **squares:** squadrons. 44. **unqualitied:** without his natural qualities. 47. **[seize]** F₂. *cease* F₁. 53. **what:** upon what. 58. **[tow]** (Rowe). *stowe* F. 59. **[Thy]** (Theobald). *the* F. 62. **treaties:** proposals. 63. **palter...lowness:** haggle by mean trickery. 69. **rates:** is worth.

[SCENE XII. *Egypt. Cæsar's camp.*]

Enter CÆSAR, Agrippa, DOLABELLA, [THYREUS,]
with others.

Cæs. Let him appear that's come from Antony.
Know you him?
Dol.   Cæsar, 'tis his schoolmaster;
An argument that he is pluck'd, when hither
He sends so poor a pinion of his wing,
Which had superfluous kings for messengers   5
Not many moons gone by.

Enter [EUPHRONIUS,] *ambassador from Antony.*

Cæs.   Approach and speak.
[*Euph.*] Such as I am, I come from Antony.
I was of late as petty to his ends
As is the morn-dew on the myrtle-leaf
To his grand sea.
Cæs.   Be't so: declare thine office.   10
[*Euph.*] Lord of his fortunes he salutes thee, and
Requires to live in Egypt; which not granted,
He [lessens] his requests and to thee sues
To let him breathe between the heavens and earth,
A private man in Athens. This for him.   15
Next, Cleopatra does confess thy greatness,
Submits her to thy might; and of thee craves
The circle of the Ptolemies for her heirs,
Now hazarded to thy grace.
Cæs.   For Antony,
I have no ears to his request. The Queen   20
Of audience nor desire shall fail, so she
From Egypt drive her all-disgraced friend,
Or take his life there. This if she perform,
She shall not sue unheard. So to them both.
[*Euph.*] Fortune pursue thee!
Cæs.   Bring him through the bands.
                              [*Exit Euphronius.*]
[*To Thyreus.*] To try thy eloquence, now 'tis time;
    dispatch.   26
From Antony win Cleopatra; promise,
And in our name, what she requires; add more,
From thine invention, offers. Women are not
In their best fortunes strong, but want will perjure
The ne'er-touch'd vestal. Try thy cunning,
    [Thyreus];   31
Make thine own edict for thy pains, which we
Will answer as a law.
Thyr.   Cæsar, I go.
Cæs. Observe how Antony becomes his flaw,
And what thou think'st his very action speaks 35

In every power that moves.
Thyr.   Cæsar, I shall.
                              [*Exeunt.*

[SCENE XIII. *Alexandria. Cleopatra's palace.*]

Enter CLEOPATRA, ENOBARBUS, Charmian, *and*
                    Iras.

Cleo. What shall we do, Enobarbus?
Eno.   Think, and die.
Cleo. Is Antony or we in fault for this?
Eno. Antony only, that would make his will
Lord of his reason. What though you fled
From that great face of war, whose several ranges 5
Frighted each other? Why should he follow?
The itch of his affection should not then
Have nick'd his captainship, at such a point,
When half to half the world oppos'd, he being
The mered question. 'Twas a shame no less   10
Than was his loss, to course your flying flags,
And leave his navy gazing.
Cleo.   Prithee, peace.

Enter ANTONY *with* [EUPHRONIUS,] *the Am-
                    bassador.*

Ant. Is that his answer?
[*Euph.*] Ay, my lord.
Ant. The Queen shall then have courtesy, so she
Will yield us up.
[*Euph.*]   He says so.
Ant.   Let her know't.   16
To the boy Cæsar send this grizzled head,
And he will fill thy wishes to the brim
With principalities.
Cleo.   That head, my lord?
Ant. To him again. Tell him he wears the rose
Of youth upon him, from which the world should
    note   21
Something particular. His coin, ships, legions,
May be a coward's; whose ministers would prevail
Under the service of a child as soon
As i' th' command of Cæsar. I dare him therefore
To lay his gay comparisons apart   26
And answer me declin'd, sword against sword,
Ourselves alone. I'll write it. Follow me.
                  [*Exeunt Antony and Euphronius.*
Eno. [*Aside.*]   Yes, like enough high-battl'd
    Cæsar will
Unstate his happiness and be stag'd to th' show 30
Against a sworder! I see men's judgements are

Sc. xii, 7. [*Euph.*] (Capell). *Amb.* F. (throughout). 8. to: compared to. 12. Requires: requests. 13. [lessens] F₂. Lessons F₁. 18. circle: crown. 31. [Thyreus] (Theobald). *Thidias* F (throughout; *Thid.* in speech-headings). 32. Make ... edict: name ... reward. 34. becomes his flaw: bears his disaster. 35. speaks: signifies. 36. power that moves: i.e., gesture.
Sc. xiii, 1. Think: take thought. 3. will: desire. 8. nick'd: impaired. 10. mered question: sole point at issue. 11. course: chase. 26. comparisons: superior advantages. 27. declin'd: i.e., in fortunes and in years. 30. Unstate: strip of dignity. stag'd ... show: exhibited publicly. 31. sworder: gladiator.

A parcel of their fortunes, and things outward,
Do draw the inward quality after them,
To suffer all alike.   That he should dream,
Knowing all measures, the full Cæsar will   35
Answer his emptiness!   Cæsar, thou hast subdu'd
His judgement too.

Enter a SERVANT.

Serv.   A messenger from Cæsar.
Cleo. What, no more ceremony?   See, my wo-
    men!
Against the blown rose may they stop their nose
That kneel'd unto the buds.   Admit him, sir.   40
                                [Exit Servant.]
Eno. [Aside.]   Mine honesty and I begin to
    square.
The loyalty well held to fools does make
Our faith mere folly; yet he that can endure
To follow with allegiance a fall'n lord
Does conquer him that did his master conquer,   45
And earns a place i' th' story.

Enter [THYREUS].

Cleo.   Cæsar's will?
[Thyr.] Hear it apart.
Cleo.   None but friends: say boldly.
[Thyr.] So, haply, are they friends to Antony.
Eno. He needs as many, sir, as Cæsar has,
Or needs not us.   If Cæsar please, our master   50
Will leap to be his friend; for us, you know
Whose he is we are, and that is Cæsar's.
[Thyr.]   So.
Thus then, thou most renown'd: Cæsar entreats
Not to consider in what case thou stand'st
Further than he is [Cæsar].
Cleo.   Go on: right royal.   55
[Thyr.] He knows that you embrace not Antony
As you did love, but as you fear'd him.
Cleo.   Oh!
[Thyr.] The scars upon your honour, therefore,
    he
Does pity, as constrained blemishes,
Not as deserv'd.
Cleo.   He is a god and knows   60
What is most right.   Mine honour was not yielded,
But conquer'd merely.
Eno. [Aside.]   To be sure of that,
I will ask Antony.   Sir, sir, thou art so leaky
That we must leave thee to thy sinking, for
Thy dearest quit thee.   [Exit.
[Thyr.]   Shall I say to Cæsar   65
What you require of him? for he partly begs
To be desir'd to give.   It much would please him
That of his fortunes you should make a staff

To lean upon; but it would warm his spirits
To hear from me you had left Antony   70
And put yourself under his shroud,
The universal landlord.
Cleo.   What's your name?
[Thyr.] My name is [Thyreus].
Cleo.   Most kind messenger,
Say to great Cæsar this: in [deputation]   74
I kiss his conqu'ring hand.   Tell him, I am prompt
To lay my crown at 's feet, and there to kneel;
Tell him, from his all-obeying breath I hear
The doom of Egypt.
[Thyr.]   'Tis your noblest course.
Wisdom and fortune combating together,
If that the former dare but what it can,   80
No chance may shake it.   Give me grace to lay
My duty on your hand.
Cleo.   Your Cæsar's father oft,
When he hath mus'd of taking kingdoms in,
Bestow'd his lips on that unworthy place,   84
As it rain'd kisses.

Re-enter ANTONY and ENOBARBUS.

Ant.   Favours, by Jove that thunders!
What art thou, fellow?
[Thyr.]   One that but performs
The bidding of the fullest man, and worthiest
To have command obey'd.
Eno.   [Aside.] You will be whipp'd.
Ant. Approach there!   Ah, you kite!   Now, gods
    and devils!
Authority melts from me.   Of late, when I cried
    "Ho!"   90
Like boys unto a muss, kings would start forth
And cry, "Your will?"   Have you no ears?   I am
Antony yet.

Enter a SERVANT.

                Take hence this Jack and whip him.
Eno. [Aside.]   'Tis better playing with a lion's
    whelp
Than with an old one dying.
Ant.   Moon and stars!   95
Whip him!   Were 't twenty of the greatest tribu-
    taries
That do acknowledge Cæsar, should I find them
So saucy with the hand of she here, — what's her
    name,
Since she was Cleopatra?   Whip him, fellows,
Till, like a boy, you see him cringe his face   100
And whine aloud for mercy.   Take him hence.
[Thyr.] Mark Antony, —
Ant.   Tug him away.   Being whipp'd,
Bring him again; [this] Jack of Cæsar's shall

    32. A parcel of: of a piece with.   41. honesty: honor.   square: quarrel.   55. [Cæsar] F₂: i.e., himself, a magnanimous
victor.   Cæsars F₁.   71. shroud: i.e., protection.   74. in [deputation] (Theobald): by deputy.   in disputation F.   77. all-
obeying: obeyed by all.   89. kite: harlot.   91. muss: scramble.   103. [this] (Pope).   the F.

Bear us an errand to him. —

[*Exit Servant with* [*Thyreus*].

You were half blasted ere I knew you; ha!   105
Have I my pillow left unpress'd in Rome,
Forborne the getting of a lawful race,
And by a gem of women, to be abus'd
By one that looks on feeders?

Cleo.   Good my lord, —

Ant. You have been a boggler ever: 110
And when we in our viciousness grow hard —
O misery on 't! — the wise gods seel our eyes;
In our own filth drop our clear judgements; make us
Adore our errors; laugh at 's while we strut
To our confusion.

Cleo.   O, is 't come to this?   115

Ant. I found you as a morsel cold upon
Dead Cæsar's trencher; nay, you were a fragment
Of Cneius Pompey's; besides what hotter hours,
Unregist'red in vulgar fame, you have
Luxuriously pick'd out; for, I am sure,   120
Though you can guess what temperance should be,
You know not what it is.

Cleo.   Wherefore is this?

Ant. To let a fellow that will take rewards
And say "God quit you!" be familiar with
My playfellow, your hand, this kingly seal   125
And plighter of high hearts! O, that I were
Upon the hill of Basan, to outroar
The horned herd! For I have savage cause;
And to proclaim it civilly were like
A halter'd neck which does the hangman thank
For being yare about him.

Re-enter SERVANT *with* [*Thyreus.*]

          Is he whipp'd?   131

Serv. Soundly, my lord.

Ant.   Cried he? and begg'd a pardon?

Serv. He did ask favour.

Ant. If that thy father live, let him repent
Thou wast not made his daughter; and be thou
          sorry   135
To follow Cæsar in his triumph, since
Thou hast been whipp'd for following him. Hence-
          forth
The white hand of a lady fever thee;
Shake thou to look on 't. Get thee back to Cæsar;
Tell him thy entertainment. Look thou say   140
He makes me angry with him; for he seems
Proud and disdainful, harping on what I am,
Not what he knew I was. He makes me angry;
And at this time most easy 'tis to do 't,
When my good stars, that were my former guides,

Have empty left their orbs and shot their fires   146
Into th' abysm of hell. If he mislike
My speech and what is done, tell him he has
Hipparchus, my enfranched bondman, whom
He may at pleasure whip, or hang, or torture,   150
As he shall like, to quit me. Urge it thou.
Hence with thy stripes, begone! [*Exit* [*Thyreus*].

Cleo. Have you done yet?

Ant.   Alack, our terrene moon
Is now eclips'd, and it portends alone
The fall of Antony!

Cleo.   I must stay his time.   155

Ant. To flatter Cæsar, would you mingle eyes
With one that ties his points?

Cleo.   Not know me yet?

Ant. Cold-hearted toward me?

Cleo.   Ah, dear, if I be so,
From my cold heart let heaven engender hail
And poison it in the source, and the first stone
Drop in my neck; as it determines, so   161
Dissolve my life! The next Cæsarion [smite]!
Till by degrees the memory of my womb,
Together with my brave Egyptians all,
By the [discandying] of this pelleted storm,   165
Lie graveless, till the flies and gnats of Nile
Have buried them for prey!

Ant.   I am satisfied.
Cæsar [sits] down in Alexandria, where
I will oppose his fate. Our force by land
Hath nobly held; our sever'd navy too   170
Have knit again, and fleet, threat'ning most sealike.
Where hast thou been, my heart? Dost thou hear,
          lady?
If from the field I shall return once more
To kiss these lips, I will appear in blood;
I and my sword will earn our chronicle.   175
There's hope in 't yet.

Cleo. That's my brave lord!

Ant. I will be treble-sinew'd, hearted, breath'd,
And fight maliciously; for when mine hours
Were nice and lucky, men did ransom lives   180
Of me for jests; but now I'll set my teeth
And send to darkness all that stop me. Come,
Let's have one other gaudy night. Call to me
All my sad captains; fill our bowls once more;
Let's mock the midnight bell.

Cleo.   It is my birthday.
I had thought t' have held it poor; but, since my
          lord   186
Is Antony again, I will be Cleopatra.

Ant. We will yet do well.

Cleo. Call all his noble captains to my lord.

---

109. **feeders:** servants.   110. **boggler:** shifty one.   112. **seel:** sew up.   120. **luxuriously:** lustfully.   124. **quit:** requite.
127. **Basan.** See *Psalms*, 22.12 and 68.15.   128. **horned herd:** (1) bulls, (2) cuckolds.   131. **yare:** quick.   146. **orbs:** spheres.
149. **enfranched:** freed.   Hipparchus had deserted Antony.   153. **terrene:** earthly.   157. **points:** laces (of clothing).   161.
determines: melts.   162. [**smite**] (Rowe).   *smile* F.   163. **memory:** memorials.   165. [**discandying**] (Thirlby conj.): thawing.   *discandering* F.   168. [**sits**] (Johnson).   *sets* F.   171. **fleet:** float.   180. **nice:** favorable.

Ant. Do so, we'll speak to them; and tonight I'll
 force 190
The wine peep through their scars. Come on, my
 queen;
There's sap in't yet. The next time I do fight,
I'll make Death love me; for I will contend
Even with his pestilent scythe.
     [*Exeunt [all but Enobarbus].*

Eno. Now he'll outstare the lightning. To be
 furious, 195
Is to be frighted out of fear; and in that mood
The dove will peck the estridge; and I see still
A diminution in our captain's brain
Restores his heart. When valour [preys on] reason,
It eats the sword it fights with. I will seek 200
Some way to leave him.   [*Exit.*

[ACT IV]

[SCENE I. *Before Alexandria. Cæsar's camp.*]

Enter CÆSAR, Agrippa, *and* MÆCENAS, *with his
Army; Cæsar reading a letter.*

Cæs. He calls me boy, and chides as he had power
To beat me out of Egypt. My messenger
He hath whipp'd with rods; dares me to personal
 combat,
Cæsar to Antony. Let the old ruffian know
I have many other ways to die; meantime 5
Laugh at his challenge.

Mæc.   Cæsar must think,
When one so great begins to rage, he's hunted
Even to falling. Give him no breath, but now
Make boot of his distraction. Never anger
Made good guard for itself.

Cæs.   Let our best heads 10
Know that to-morrow the last of many battles
We mean to fight. Within our files there are,
Of those that serv'd Mark Antony but late,
Enough to fetch him in. See it done,
And feast the army; we have store to do't, 15
And they have earn'd the waste. Poor Antony!
          [*Exeunt.*

[SCENE II. *Alexandria. Cleopatra's palace.*]

Enter ANTONY, CLEOPATRA, ENOBARBUS,
Charmian, Iras, Alexas, *with others.*

Ant. He will not fight with me, Domitius.

Eno.   No?

Ant. Why should he not?

Eno. He thinks, being twenty times of better
 fortune,
He is twenty men to one.

Ant.   To-morrow, soldier, 5
By sea and land I'll fight; or I will live,
Or bathe my dying honour in the blood
Shall make it live again. Woo't thou fight well?

Eno. I'll strike, and cry, "Take all!"

Ant.   Well said; come on.
Call forth my household servants; let's tonight
Be bounteous at our meal.

Enter three or four SERVITORS.

       Give me thy hand, 10
Thou hast been rightly honest; — so hast thou; —
Thou, — and thou, — and thou. You have serv'd
 me well,
And kings have been your fellows.

Cleo.   [*Aside to Eno.*] What means this?

Eno. [*Aside to Cleo.*] 'Tis one of those odd tricks
 which sorrow shoots
Out of the mind.

Ant.   And thou art honest too. 15
I wish I could be made so many men,
And all of you clapp'd up together in
An Antony, that I might do you service
So good as you have done.

All.   The gods forbid!

Ant. Well, my good fellows, wait on me tonight.
Scant not my cups; and make as much of me 21
As when mine empire was your fellow too,
And suffer'd my command.

Cleo. [*Aside to Eno.*] What does he mean?

Eno. [*Aside to Cleo.*] To make his followers weep.

Ant.   Tend me tonight;
May be it is the period of your duty: 25
Haply you shall not see me more; or if,
A mangled shadow. Perchance to-morrow
You'll serve another master. I look on you
As one that takes his leave. Mine honest friends,
I turn you not away; but, like a master 30
Married to your good service, stay till death.
Tend me to-night two hours, I ask no more,
And the gods yield you for't!

Eno.   What mean you, sir,
To give them this discomfort? Look, they weep;
And I, an ass, am onion-ey'd. For shame, 35
Transform us not to women.

Ant.   Ho, ho, ho!
Now the witch take me, if I meant it thus!
Grace grow where those drops fall! My hearty
 friends,
You take me in too dolorous a sense; 39
For I spake to you for your comfort, did desire you
To burn this night with torches. Know, my hearts,
I hope well of to-morrow, and will lead you
Where rather I'll expect victorious life

---

193. **contend:** compete. 197. **estridge:** falcon. 199. **[preys on]** (Rowe). *prayes* in F.
Act IV, sc. i, 9. boot: profit. 14. **fetch him in:** capture him. 16. **waste:** cost.
Sc. ii, 8. "Take all!": i.e., winner take everything. 33. **yield:** reward.

[handwritten annotation at top: believe god Hercules is leaving a, love for god Hercules — a deified with Hercules & Cleo with Isis - gives them greatness in spite of human weakness.]

Than death and honour. Let's to supper, come,
And drown consideration.   [*Exeunt.* 45

[SCENE III. *The same. Before the palace.*]

Enter a Company of SOLDIERS.

1. Sold. Brother, good-night; to-morrow is the
    day.
2. Sold. It will determine one way; fare you
    well.
Heard you of nothing strange about the streets?
1. Sold. Nothing. What news?
2. Sold. Belike 'tis but a rumour. Good-night
    to you.   5
1. Sold. Well, sir, good-night.

They meet other SOLDIERS.

2. Sold. Soldiers, have careful watch.
[3.] Sold. And you. Good-night, good-night.
        [*They place themselves in every corner of
        the stage.*
[4.] Sold. Here we. And if to-morrow
Our navy thrive, I have an absolute hope   10
Our landmen will stand up.
[3.] Sold.   'Tis a brave army,
And full of purpose.
        [*Music of the hautboys is under the stage.*
2. Sold.   Peace! what noise?
1. Sold.   List, list!
2. Sold. Hark!
1. Sold.   Music i' th' air.
3. Sold.   Under the earth.
4. Sold. It signs well, does it not?
3. Sold.   No.
1. Sold.   Peace, I say.
What should this mean?   15
2. Sold. 'Tis the god Hercules, whom Antony
    lov'd,
Now leaves him.
1. Sold. Walk; let's see if other watchmen
Do hear what we do.
        [*They advance to another post.*
2. Sold.   How now, masters!
        [*Speak together.*
All.   How now!
How now! do you hear this?
1. Sold.   Ay; is't not strange?
3. Sold. Do you hear, masters? Do you hear? 21
1. Sold. Follow the noise so far as we have quarter;
Let's see how it will give off.
All.   Content. 'Tis strange.
        [*Exeunt.*

[SCENE IV. *The same. A room in the palace.*]

Enter ANTONY *and* CLEOPATRA, [CHARMIAN,]
and others [*attending*].

Ant. Eros! mine armour, Eros!
Cleo.   Sleep a little.
Ant. No, my chuck. Eros, come; mine armour,
    Eros!

Enter EROS [*with armour*].

Come, good fellow, put [mine] iron on.
If Fortune be not ours to-day, it is   4
Because we brave her. Come.
Cleo.   Nay, I'll help too.
What's this for?
[Ant.]   Ah, let be, let be! thou art
The armourer of my heart. False, false; this, this.
Cleo. Sooth, la, I'll help. Thus it must be.
Ant.   Well, well;
We shall thrive now. Seest thou, my good fellow?
Go put on thy defences.
Eros.   Briefly, sir.   10
Cleo. Is not this buckled well?
Ant.   Rarely, rarely:
He that unbuckles this, till we do please
To daff 't for our repose, shall hear a storm.
Thou fumblest, Eros, and my queen's a squire   14
More tight at this than thou. Dispatch. O love,
That thou couldst see my wars to-day, and knew'st
The royal occupation! Thou shouldst see
A workman in't.

Enter an armed SOLDIER.

                Good-morrow to thee; welcome.
Thou look'st like him that knows a warlike charge.
To business that we love we rise betime   20
And go to't with delight.
Sold.   A thousand, sir,
Early though 't be, have on their riveted trim,
And at the port expect you.
        [*Shout. Trumpets flourish.*

Enter CAPTAINS *and* SOLDIERS.

[Capt.] The morn is fair. Good-morrow, general.
All. Good-morrow, general.
Ant.   'Tis well blown, lads.
This morning, like the spirit of a youth   26
That means to be of note, begins betimes.
So, so; come, give me that. This way; well said.
Fare thee well, dame, whate'er becomes of me.
This is a soldier's kiss; rebukeable   30
And worthy shameful check it were, to stand

[handwritten right margin: G. ready for battle. Puts on harness like a soldier]

Sc. iii, 8, 9, 12. [*3.*], [*4.*], [*3.*] (Capell). F assigns to *1, 2,* and *1* respectively. 14. **signs well:** is a good omen. 22. **quarter:**
beat. 23. **give off:** end.
Sc. iv, 3. [mine] (Hanmer). *thine* F. 5. **brave:** defy. 6. [*Ant.*] (Malone). F continues to *Cleo.* 7. **False:** wrong.
10. **Briefly:** quickly. 15. **tight:** deft. 23. **port:** gate. 24. [*Capt.*] (Rowe). *Alex.* F. 25. **blown.** See s.d. l. 24. 28.
said: done. 31. **check:** rebuke.

On more mechanic compliment. I'll leave thee
Now, like a man of steel. You that will fight,
Follow me close; I'll bring you to't. Adieu. 34
    [*Exeunt* [*Antony, Eros, Captains, and Soldiers*].
  Char. Please you, retire to your chamber.
  Cleo.   Lead me.
He goes forth gallantly. That he and Cæsar might
Determine this great war in single fight!
Then, Antony, — but now — Well, on.   [*Exeunt.*

[SCENE V. *Alexandria. Antony's camp.*]

Trumpets sound. Enter ANTONY *and* EROS.
    [*A* SOLDIER *meets them.*]

  [*Sold.*] The gods make this a happy day to
Antony!
  Ant. Would thou and those thy scars had once
prevail'd
To make me fight at land!
  [*Sold.*]   Hadst thou done so,
The kings that have revolted, and the soldier
That has this morning left thee, would have still 5
Followed thy heels.
  Ant.   Who's gone this morning?
  [*Sold.*]   Who!
One ever near thee. Call for Enobarbus,
He shall not hear thee, or from Cæsar's camp
Say "I am none of thine."
  Ant.   What sayest thou?
  Sold.   Sir,
He is with Cæsar.
  Eros.   Sir, his chests and treasure 10
He has not with him.
  Ant.   Is he gone?
  Sold.   Most certain.
  Ant. Go, Eros, send his treasure after; do it;
Detain no jot, I charge thee. Write to him —
I will subscribe — gentle adieus and greetings;
Say that I wish he never find more cause 15
To change a master. O, my fortunes have
Corrupted honest men! Dispatch, — Enobarbus!
                              [*Exeunt.*

[SCENE VI. *Alexandria. Cæsar's camp.*]

Flourish. Enter CÆSAR, AGRIPPA, *with* ENOBARBUS,
and Dolabella.

  Cæs. Go forth, Agrippa, and begin the fight.
Our will is Antony be took alive;
Make it so known.
  Agr. Cæsar, I shall.   [*Exit.*

  Cæs. The time of universal peace is near. 5
Prove this a prosperous day, the three-nook'd world
Shall bear the olive freely.

Enter a MESSENGER.

  Mess.   Antony
Is come into the field.
  Cæs.   Go charge Agrippa
Plant those that have revolted in the van,
That Antony may seem to spend his fury 10
Upon himself.   [*Exeunt* [*all but Enobarbus*].
  Eno. Alexas did revolt and went to Jewry on
Affairs of Antony; there did [persuade]
Great Herod to incline himself to Cæsar
And leave his master Antony; for this pains 15
Cæsar hath hang'd him. Canidius and the rest
That fell away have entertainment, but
No honourable trust. I have done ill;
Of which I do accuse myself so sorely
That I will joy no more.

Enter a SOLDIER *of Cæsar's.*

  Sold.   Enobarbus, Antony 20
Hath after thee sent all thy treasure, with
His bounty overplus. The messenger
Came on my guard, and at thy tent is now
Unloading of his mules.
  Eno.   I give it you.
  Sold. Mock not, Enobarbus; 25
I tell you true. Best you saf'd the bringer
Out of the host; I must attend mine office,
Or would have done 't myself. Your emperor
Continues still a Jove.   [*Exit.*
  Eno. I am alone the villain of the earth, 30
And feel I am so most. O Antony,
Thou mine of bounty, how wouldst thou have paid
My better service, when my turpitude
Thou dost so crown with gold! This blows my heart.
If swift thought break it not, a swifter means 35
Shall outstrike thought; but thought will do't, I
    feel.
I fight against thee! No! I will go seek
Some ditch wherein to die; the foul'st best fits
My latter part of life.   [*Exit.*

[SCENE VII. *Field of battle between the camps.*]

Alarum. Drums and trumpets. Enter AGRIPPA
[*and others*].

  Agr. Retire, we have engag'd ourselves too far.
Cæsar himself has work, and our oppression
Exceeds what we expected.   [*Exeunt.*

Sc. v, 1. [*Sold.*] (Thirlby conj.). *Eros.* F. 3, 7. [*Sold.*] (Capell). *Eros.* F. 14. subscribe: sign.
Sc. vi, 6. three-nook'd: three-cornered. 13. [persuade] (Rowe). *disswade* F. 17. entertainment: employment. 26.
saf'd: convoyed. 34. blows: swells.
Sc. vii, 2. oppression: opposition.

Alarums. Enter ANTONY, *and* SCARUS *wounded.*

Scar. O my brave emperor, this is fought indeed!
Had we done so at first, we had droven them home 5
With clouts about their heads.

Ant.   Thou bleed'st apace,

Scar. I had a wound here that was like a T,
But now 'tis made an H.

Ant.   They do retire.

Scar. We'll beat 'em into bench-holes. I have yet
Room for six scotches more.   10

Enter EROS.

Eros. They are beaten, sir; and our advantage serves
For a fair victory.

Scar.   Let us score their backs,
And snatch 'em up, as we take hares, behind.
'Tis sport to maul a runner.

Ant.   I will reward thee
Once for thy sprightly comfort, and tenfold 15
For thy good valour. Come thee on.

Scar.   I'll halt after.
                                    [*Exeunt.*

[SCENE VIII. *Under the walls of Alexandria.*]

Alarum. Enter ANTONY, *in a march;* Scarus,
with others.

Ant. We have beat him to his camp. Run one before,
And let the Queen know of our [gests]. To-morrow,
Before the sun shall see 's, we'll spill the blood
That has to-day escap'd. I thank you all;
For doughty-handed are you, and have fought 5
Not as you serv'd the cause, but as 't had been
Each man's like mine; you have shown all Hectors.
Enter the city, clip your wives, your friends,
Tell them your feats; whilst they with joyful tears
Wash the congealment from your wounds, and kiss
The honour'd gashes whole.

Enter CLEOPATRA [*attended*].

[*To Scarus.*]   Give me thy hand; 11
To this great fairy I'll commend thy acts,
Make her thanks bless thee. [*To Cleo.*] O thou
day o' th' world,
Chain mine arm'd neck; leap thou, attire and all,
Through proof of harness to my heart, and there 15
Ride on the pants triumphing!

Cleo.   Lord of lords!
O infinite virtue, com'st thou smiling from

The world's great snare uncaught?

Ant.   My nightingale,
We have beat them to their beds. What, girl!
though grey
Do something mingle with our younger brown, yet
ha' we   20
A brain that nourishes our nerves, and can
Get goal for goal of youth. Behold this man;
Commend unto his lips thy [favouring] hand.
Kiss it, my warrior; he hath fought to-day
As if a god, in hate of mankind, had   25
Destroyed in such a shape.

Cleo.   I'll give thee, friend,
An armour all of gold; it was a king's.

Ant. He has deserv'd it, were it carbuncled
Like holy Phœbus' car. Give me thy hand.
Through Alexandria make a jolly march;   30
Bear our hack'd targets like the men that owe them.
Had our great palace the capacity
To camp this host, we all would sup together
And drink carouses to the next day's fate,
Which promises royal peril. Trumpeters,   35
With brazen din blast you the city's ear;
Make mingle with our rattling tabourines,
That heaven and earth may strike their sounds
together,
Applauding our approach.   [*Exeunt.*

[SCENE IX. *Cæsar's camp.*]

Enter a SENTRY, *and his* COMPANY. ENOBARBUS
follows.

Sent. If we be not reliev'd within this hour,
We must return to th' court of guard. The night
Is shiny, and they say we shall embattle
By the second hour i' th' morn.

1. [*Sold.*]   This last day was
A shrewd one to 's.

Eno.   O, bear me witness, night,— 5

2. Sold. What man is this?

1. Sold.   Stand close, and list him.

Eno. Be witness to me, O thou blessed moon,
When men revolted shall upon record
Bear hateful memory, poor Enobarbus did
Before thy face repent!

Sent.   Enobarbus!

2. Sold.   Peace! 10
Hark further.

Eno. O sovereign mistress of true melancholy,
The poisonous damp of night disponge upon me,
That life, a very rebel to my will,
May hang no longer on me. Throw my heart 15

---

6. **clouts:** bandages. 10. **scotches:** cuts.
    Sc. viii, 2. **[gests]** (Theobald): deeds. *guests* F. 8. **clip:** embrace. 15. **proof of harness:** tested armor. 17. **virtue:** valor. 23. **[favouring]** (Theobald). *savouring* F. 31. **owe:** own. 37. **tabourines:** drums.
    Sc. ix, 4. **[Sold.]** (Malone). *Watch* F. Elsewhere in this scene the speeches of the soldiers are designated *1* or *2* by F.
    5. **shrewd:** ill. 13. **disponge:** drop as from a squeezed sponge.

Against the flint and hardness of my fault;
Which, being dried with grief, will break to powder,
And finish all foul thoughts.   O Antony,
Nobler than my revolt is infamous,
Forgive me in thine own particular; *for yourself*   20
But let the world rank me in register
A master-leaver and a fugitive.
O Antony!   O Antony!   [*Dies.*]
    1. Sold.   Let's speak
To him.
    Sent. Let's hear him, for the things he speaks 25
May concern Cæsar.
    2. Sold.   Let's do so.   But he sleeps.
    Sent. Swoons rather; for so bad a prayer as his
Was never yet for sleep.
    1. Sold.   Go we to him.
    2. Sold. Awake, sir, awake; speak to us.
    1. Sold.   Hear you, sir?
    Sent. The hand of death hath raught him.
        (*Drums afar off.*)   Hark! the drums   30
Demurely wake the sleepers.   Let us bear him
To th' court of guard; he is of note.   Our hour
Is fully out.
    2. Sold.   Come on, then;
He may recover yet.   [*Exeunt* [*with the body*].

[SCENE X.   *Between the two camps.*]

Enter ANTONY *and* SCARUS, *with their Army.*

    Ant. Their preparation is to-day by sea;
We please them not by land.
    Scar.   For both, my lord.
    Ant. I would they'd fight i' th' fire or i' th' air;
We'd fight there too.   But this it is: our foot
Upon the hills adjoining to the city   5
Shall stay with us.   Order for sea is given;
They have put forth the haven.   [Go we up]
Where their appointment we may best discover
And look on their endeavour.   [*Exeunt.*

[SCENE XI.   *Another part of the same.*]

Enter CÆSAR, *and his Army.*

    Cæs. But being charg'd, we will be still by land,
Which, as I take 't, we shall; for his best force
Is forth to man his galleys.   To the vales,
And hold our best advantage.   [*Exeunt.*

[SCENE XII.   *Another part of the same.*]

Enter ANTONY *and* SCARUS.

    Ant. Yet they are not join'd.   Where yond pine
does stand

I shall discover all; I'll bring thee word
Straight how 'tis like to go.   [*Exit.*
    Scar.   Swallows have built
In Cleopatra's sails their nests.   The [augurers]
Say they know not, they cannot tell; look grimly, 5
And dare not speak their knowledge.   Antony
Is valiant, and dejected; and, by starts,
His fretted fortunes give him hope and fear,
Of what he has and has not.
     [*Alarum afar off, as at a sea-fight.*

Re-enter ANTONY.

    Ant.   All is lost!   10
This foul Egyptian hath betrayed me.
My fleet hath yielded to the foe, and yonder
They cast their caps up and carouse together
Like friends long lost.   Triple-turn'd whore! 'tis
    thou
Hast sold me to this novice, and my heart
Makes only wars on thee.   Bid them all fly;   15
For when I am reveng'd upon my charm,
I have done all.   Bid them all fly; begone.
                   [*Exit Scarus.*]
O sun, thy uprise shall I see no more:
Fortune and Antony part here; even here
Do we shake hands.   All come to this?   The hearts
That [spaniel'd] me at heels, to whom I gave   21
Their wishes, do discandy, melt their sweets
On blossoming Cæsar; and this pine is bark'd,
That overtopp'd them all.   Betray'd I am.
O this false soul of Egypt! this grave charm, —   25
Whose eye beck'd forth my wars and call'd them
    home,
Whose bosom was my crownet, my chief end, —
Like a right gipsy, hath at fast and loose
Beguil'd me to the very heart of loss.
What, Eros, Eros!

Enter CLEOPATRA.

        Ah, thou spell!   Avaunt!   30
    Cleo. Why is my lord enrag'd against his love?
    Ant. Vanish, or I shall give thee thy deserving
And blemish Cæsar's triumph.   Let him take thee
And hoist thee up to the shouting plebeians!
Follow his chariot, like the greatest spot   35
Of all thy sex; most monster-like, be shown
For poor'st diminutives, for dolts; and let
Patient Octavia plough thy visage up
With her prepared nails.   [*Exit Cleopatra.*
'T is well thou'rt gone,

20. in ... particular: for yourself. 29. raught: reached. 31. Demurely: quietly.
Sc. x, 7. [Go we up] (Grant White). Om. F.
Sc. xi, 1. But being: unless we are.
Sc. xii, 4. sails: ships. [augurers] (Capell). *Auguries* F. 9. s.d. *Alarum* etc. Between sc. xi and xii in F. 13. Triple-
turn'd: thrice faithless. 16. charm: charmer. 21. [spaniel'd] (Hanmer). *pannelled* F. 27. crownet: coronet. 28. fast
and loose: a cheating game. 37. diminutives ... dolts: contemptuous terms for the crowd. Many edd. read *doits* and explain both as small coins charged for admission.

If it be well to live; but better 'twere   40
Thou fell'st into my fury, for one death
Might have prevented many.   Eros, ho!
The shirt of Nessus is upon me.   Teach me,
Alcides, thou mine ancestor, thy rage.
Let me lodge Lichas on the horns o' th' moon;   45
And with those hands, that grasp'd the heaviest
     club,
Subdue my worthiest self.   The witch shall die.
To the young Roman boy she hath sold me, and I
     fall
Under this plot.   She dies for't.   Eros, ho!   [*Exit.*

[SCENE XIII.   *Alexandria.   Cleopatra's*
palace.]

Enter CLEOPATRA, CHARMIAN, IRAS, *and* MARDIAN.

   Cleo.   Help me, my women!   O, he is more mad
Than Telamon for his shield; the boar of Thessaly
Was never so emboss'd.
   Char.   To th' monument!
There lock yourself, and send him word you are
     dead.
The soul and body rive not more in parting   5
Than greatness going off.
   Cleo.   To th' monument!
Mardian, go tell him I have slain myself;
Say that the last I spoke was "Antony,"
And word it, prithee, piteously.   Hence, Mardian,
And bring me how he takes my death.   To th'
     monument!   [*Exeunt.*   10

[SCENE XIV.   *The same.   Another room.*]

Enter ANTONY *and* EROS.

   Ant.   Eros, thou yet behold'st me?
   Eros.   Ay, noble lord.
   Ant.   Sometime we see a cloud that's dragonish;
A vapour sometime like a bear or lion,
A tower'd citadel, a pendent rock,
A forked mountain, or blue promontory   5
With trees upon 't that nod unto the world
And mock our eyes with air.   Thou hast seen these
     signs;
They are black vesper's pageants.
   Eros.   Ay, my lord.
   Ant.   That which is now a horse, even with a
     thought
The rack [dislimns], and makes it indistinct   10
As water is in water.
   Eros.   It does, my lord.

   Ant.   My good knave Eros, now thy captain is
Even such a body.   Here I am Antony;
Yet cannot hold this visible shape, my knave.
I made these wars for Egypt; and the Queen, —   15
Whose heart I thought I had, for she had mine,
Which whilst it was mine had annex'd unto 't
A million moe, now lost, — she, Eros, has
Pack'd cards with Cæsar, and false-play'd my glory
Unto an enemy's triumph.   20
Nay, weep not, gentle Eros; there is left us
Ourselves to end ourselves.

Enter MARDIAN.

                    O, thy vile lady!
She has robb'd me of my sword.
   Mar.   No, Antony;
My mistress lov'd thee, and her fortunes mingled
With thine entirely.
   Ant.   Hence, saucy eunuch; peace!
She hath betray'd me and shall die the death.   26
   Mar.   Death of one person can be paid but once,
And that she has discharg'd.   What thou wouldst
     do
Is done unto thy hand; the last she spake
Was "Antony! most noble Antony!"   30
Then in the midst a tearing groan did break
The name of Antony; it was divided
Between her heart and lips.   She rend'red life,
Thy name so buried in her.
   Ant.   Dead, then?
   Mar.   Dead.
   Ant.   Unarm, Eros; the long day's task is done,   35
And we must sleep.   [*To* Mar.]   That thou de-
     part'st hence safe
Does pay thy labour richly; go.   [*Exit* Mardian.
                    Off, pluck off!
The seven-fold shield of Ajax cannot keep
The battery from my heart.   O, cleave, my sides!
Heart, once be stronger than thy continent,   40
Crack thy frail case!   Apace, Eros, apace.
No more a soldier.   Bruised pieces, go;
You have been nobly borne. — From me a while.
                    [*Exit* Eros.
I will o'ertake thee, Cleopatra, and
Weep for my pardon.   So it must be, for now   45
All length is torture; since the torch is out,
Lie down, and stray no farther.   Now all labour
Mars what it does; yea, very force entangles
Itself with strength.   Seal then, and all is done.
Eros! — I come, my queen! — Eros! — Stay for
     me!   50

43–45. **shirt . . . Lichas.** Deianeira, wife of Hercules (Alcides), innocently sent him, as a love charm, a shirt which had been dipped in the poisoned blood of the Centaur Nessus. In his pain Hercules hurled Lichas, who had brought it to him, into the sea. **Sc. xiii, 2. Telamon.** Ajax Telamon went mad and killed himself when, after the Trojan war, the armor of Achilles was given to Ulysses instead of to him. **boar of Thessaly,** sent by Diana to ravage Calydon. 3. **emboss'd:** foaming. **Sc. xiv, 10. rack:** cloud. [**dislimns**] (Theobald): effaces. *dislimes* F. 12. **knave:** boy. 19. **Pack'd:** stacked. 40. **thy continent:** what contains thee. 49. **Seal:** conclude (the business).

Where souls do couch on flowers, we'll hand in hand,
And with our sprightly port make the ghosts gaze.
Dido and her Æneas shall want troops,
And all the haunt be ours. Come, Eros, Eros!

Re-enter EROS.

Eros. What would my lord?

Ant. Since Cleopatra died
I have liv'd in such dishonour that the gods   56
Detest my baseness. I, that with my sword
Quarter'd the world, and o'er green Neptune's back
With ships made cities, condemn myself to lack
The courage of a woman; less noble mind   60
Than she which by her death our Cæsar tells,
"I am conqueror of myself." Thou art sworn, Eros,
That, when the exigent should come, which now
Is come indeed, when I should see behind me
The inevitable prosecution of   65
Disgrace and horror, that, on my command,
Thou then wouldst kill me. Do't; the time is come.
Thou strik'st not me, 'tis Cæsar thou defeat'st.
Put colour in thy cheek.

Eros.   The gods withhold me!
Shall I do that which all the Parthian darts,   70
Though enemy, lost aim and could not?

Ant.   Eros,
Wouldst thou be window'd in great Rome and
    see
Thy master thus with pleach'd arms, bending down
His corrigible neck, his face subdu'd
To penetrative shame, whilst the wheel'd seat   75
Of fortunate Cæsar, drawn before him, branded
His baseness that ensued?

Eros.   I would not see 't.

Ant. Come, then; for with a wound I must be
    cur'd.
Draw that thy honest sword, which thou hast worn
Most useful for thy country.

Eros.   O, sir, pardon me!

Ant. When I did make thee free, swor'st thou not
    then   81
To do this when I bade thee? Do it at once;
Or thy precedent services are all
But accidents unpurpos'd. Draw, and come.

Eros. Turn from me, then, that noble coun-
    tenance,   85
Wherein the worship of the whole world lies.

Ant. Lo thee!   [*Turning from him.*]

Eros. My sword is drawn.

Ant.   Then let it do at once
The thing why thou hast drawn it.

Eros.   My dear master,
My captain, and my emperor, let me say,   90
Before I strike this bloody stroke, farewell.

Ant. 'Tis said, man; and farewell.

Eros. Farewell, great chief. Shall I strike now?

Ant.   Now, Eros.

Eros. Why, there then. (*Kills himself.*) Thus
    I do escape the sorrow
Of Antony's death.

Ant.   Thrice-nobler than myself!   95
Thou teachest me, O valiant Eros, what
I should, and thou couldst not. My queen and Eros
Have by their brave instruction got upon me
A nobleness in record; but I will be
A bridegroom in my death, and run into 't   100
As to a lover's bed. Come, then; and, Eros,
Thy master dies thy scholar: to do thus
    [*Falling on his sword.*
I learn'd of thee. How! not dead? not dead?
The guard, ho! O, dispatch me!

Enter [DERCETAS *and*] GUARD.

1. Guard.   What's the noise?

Ant. I have done my work ill, friends. O, make
    an end   105
Of what I have begun.

2. Guard.   The star is fall'n.

1. Guard. And time is at his period.

All.   Alas, and woe!

Ant. Let him that loves me strike me dead.

1. Guard.   Not I.

2. Guard. Nor I.

3. Guard. Nor any one.   [*Exeunt Guard.*   110

Der. Thy death and fortunes bid thy followers
    fly.
This sword but shown to Cæsar, with this tidings,
Shall enter me with him.

Enter DIOMEDES.

Dio. Where's Antony?

Der.   There, Diomed, there.

Dio.   Lives he?
Wilt thou not answer, man?   [*Exit Dercetas.*   115

Ant. Art thou there, Diomed? Draw thy sword,
    and give me
Sufficing strokes for death.

Dio.   Most absolute lord,
My mistress Cleopatra sent me to thee.

Ant. When did she send thee?

Dio.   Now, my lord.

Ant.   Where is she?

Dio. Lock'd in her monument. She had a pro-
    phesying fear   120
Of what hath come to pass; for when she saw —
Which never shall be found — you did suspect
She had dispos'd with Cæsar, and that your rage

---

52. **port:** bearing. 54. **haunt:** society, company. 63. **exigent:** emergency. 73. **pleach'd:** folded. 74. **corrigible:** submissive. 77. **ensued:** followed. 98. **got upon me:** gained over me. 113. **enter me:** bring me to favor. 120. **monument:** the tomb she had prepared for herself. 123. **dispos'd:** made terms.

Would not be purg'd, she sent you word she was
　　dead;
But, fearing since how it might work, hath sent
Me to proclaim the truth; and I am come,　　126
I dread, too late.

Ant. Too late, good Diomed.　Call my guard, I
　　prithee.

Dio. What, ho, the Emperor's guard!　The
　　guard, what, ho!
Come, your lord calls!　　130

Enter four or five of the GUARD *of Antony.*

Ant. Bear me, good friends, where Cleopatra
　　bides;
'Tis the last service that I shall command you.

1. Guard. Woe, woe are we, sir, you may not live
　　to wear
All your true followers out.

All.　　　　　　　　　　Most heavy day!

Ant. Nay, good my fellows, do not please sharp
　　fate　　135
To grace it with your sorrows; bid that welcome
Which comes to punish us, and we punish it
Seeming to bear it lightly.　Take me up.
I have led you oft; carry me now, good friends,
And have my thanks for all.　　140
　　　　　　　　　　[*Exeunt, bearing Antony.*

[SCENE XV.　*The same.　A monument.*]

Enter CLEOPATRA, *and her maids aloft, with*
CHARMIAN *and* IRAS.

Cleo. O Charmian, I will never go from hence.

Char. Be comforted, dear madam.

Cleo.　　　　　　　　　　No, I will not.
All strange and terrible events are welcome,
But comforts we despise; our size of sorrow,
Proportion'd to our cause, must be as great　　5
As that which makes it.

Enter [*below*] DIOMEDES.

　　　　　　　　How now! is he dead?

Dio. His death's upon him, but not dead.
Look out o' th' other side your monument;
His guard have brought him thither.

Enter [*below*] ANTONY, *borne by the* Guard.

Cleo.　　　　　　　　　　O sun,
Burn the great sphere thou mov'st in!　Darkling
　　stand　　10
The varying shore o' th' world.　O Antony,
Antony, Antony!　Help, Charmian, help, Iras, help;
Help, friends below; let's draw him hither.

Ant.　　　　　　　　　　Peace!

Not Cæsar's valour hath o'erthrown Antony,
But Antony's hath triumph'd on itself.　　15

Cleo. So it should be, that none but Antony
Should conquer Antony; but woe 'tis so!

Ant. I am dying, Egypt, dying; only
I here importune death a while, until
Of many thousand kisses the poor last　　20
I lay upon thy lips.

Cleo.　　　　　　I dare not, dear, —
Dear my lord, pardon, — I dare not,
Lest I be taken.　Not th' imperious show
Of the full-fortun'd Cæsar ever shall
Be brooch'd with me; if knife, drugs, serpents,
　　have
Edge, sting, or operation, I am safe.　　26
Your wife Octavia, with her modest eyes
And still conclusion, shall acquire no honour
Demuring upon me.　But come, come, Antony, —
Help me, my women, — we must draw thee up.
Assist, good friends.

Ant.　　　　　　O, quick, or I am gone.　　31

Cleo. Here's sport indeed!　How heavy weighs
　　my lord!
Our strength is all gone into heaviness,
That makes the weight.　Had I great Juno's power,
The strong-wing'd Mercury should fetch thee up　35
And set thee by Jove's side.　Yet come a little, —
Wishers were ever fools, — O, come, come, come;
　　　　　[*They heave Antony aloft to Cleopatra.*
And welcome, welcome!　Die [where] thou hast
　　liv'd;
Quicken with kissing.　Had my lips that power,
Thus would I wear them out.

All.　　　　　　　　　　A heavy sight!　　40

Ant. I am dying, Egypt, dying.
Give me some wine, and let me speak a little.

Cleo. No, let me speak; and let me rail so high,
That the false housewife Fortune break her wheel,
Provok'd by my offence.

Ant.　　　　　　One word, sweet queen:
Of Cæsar seek your honour, with your safety.　O!　46

Cleo. They do not go together.

Ant.　　　　　　　　　　Gentle, hear me:
None about Cæsar trust but Proculeius.

Cleo. My resolution and my hands I'll trust;
None about Cæsar.　　50

Ant. The miserable change now at my end
Lament nor sorrow at; but please your thoughts
In feeding them with those my former fortunes
Wherein I liv'd, the greatest prince o' th' world,
The noblest; and do now not basely die,　　55
Not cowardly put off my helmet to
My countryman, — a Roman by a Roman
Valiantly vanquish'd.　Now my spirit is going;
I can no more.

Sc. xv, 10. **Darkling:** in darkness.　21. **dare not:** i.e., come down from the monument.　25. **brooch'd:** adorned.　28. **still conclusion:** silent judgment.　33. **heaviness:** (1) grief, (2) weight.　38. [**where**] (Pope).　*when* F.　39. **Quicken:** revive.

Cleo. Noblest of men, woo 't die?
Hast thou no care of me? Shall I abide 60
In this dull world, which in thy absence is
No better than a sty? O, see, my women.
         [Antony dies.]
The crown o' th' earth doth melt. My lord!
O, wither'd is the garland of the war,
The soldier's pole is fall'n! Young boys and girls
Are level now with men; the odds is gone, 66
And there is nothing left remarkable
Beneath the visiting moon.   *[Faints.]*
 Char.   O, quietness, lady!
 Iras. She is dead too, our sovereign.
 Char.   Lady!
 Iras.   Madam!
 Char. O madam, madam, madam!
 Iras.   Royal Egypt,
Empress!   71
 Char. Peace, peace, Iras!
 Cleo. No more but [e'en] a woman, and commanded
By such poor passion as the maid that milks
And does the meanest chares. It were for me 75
To throw my sceptre at the injurious gods,
To tell them that this world did equal theirs
Till they had stol'n our jewel. All's but nought;
Patience is sottish, and impatience does
Become a dog that's mad: then is it sin 80
To rush into the secret house of death
Ere death dare come to us? How do you, women?
What, what! good cheer! Why, how now, Charmian!
My noble girls! Ah, women, women, look,
Our lamp is spent, it's out! Good sirs, take heart.
We'll bury him; and then, what's brave, what's
  noble,   86
Let's do it after the high Roman fashion,
And make Death proud to take us. Come, away;
This case of that huge spirit now is cold.
Ah, women, women! come; we have no friend 90
But resolution and the briefest end.
   *[Exeunt; [those above] bearing off Antony's
   body.*

[ACT V]

[SCENE I. *Alexandria. Cæsar's camp.*]

Enter CÆSAR, AGRIPPA, DOLABELLA, [MÆCENAS,
 GALLUS, PROCULEIUS, *and others,*] *his council of
 war.*

 Cæs. Go to him, Dolabella, bid him yield;
Being so frustrate, tell him he mocks
The pauses that he makes.
 Dol.   Cæsar, I shall. *[Exit.]*

Enter DERCETAS *with the sword of Antony.*

 Cæs. Wherefore is that? and what art thou that
  dar'st
Appear thus to us?
 Der.   I am call'd Dercetas; 5
Mark Antony I serv'd, who best was worthy
Best to be serv'd. Whilst he stood up and spoke,
He was my master; and I wore my life
To spend upon his haters. If thou please
To take me to thee, as I was to him 10
I'll be to Cæsar; if thou pleasest not,
I yield thee up my life.
 Cæs.   What is't thou say'st?
 Der. I say, O Cæsar, Antony is dead.
 Cæs. The breaking of so great a thing should make
A greater crack. The round world 15
Should have shook lions into civil streets,
And citizens to their dens. The death of Antony
Is not a single doom; in the name lay
A moiety of the world.
 Der.   He is dead, Cæsar;
Not by a public minister of justice, 20
Nor by a hired knife; but that self hand
Which writ his honour in the acts it did
Hath, with the courage which the heart did lend it,
Splitted the heart. This is his sword;
I robb'd his wound of it; behold it stain'd 25
With his most noble blood.
 Cæs.   Look you sad, friends?
The gods rebuke me, but it is tidings
To wash the eyes of kings.
 [Agr.]   And strange it is
That nature must compel us to lament
Our most persisted deeds.
 Mæc.   His taints and honours
Wag'd equal with him.
 [Agr.]   A rarer spirit never 31
Did steer humanity; but you gods will give us
Some faults to make us men. Cæsar is touch'd.
 Mæc. When such a spacious mirror 's set before
  him,
He needs must see himself.
 Cæs.   O Antony! 35
I have followed thee to this; but we do lance
Diseases in our bodies. I must perforce
Have shown to thee such a declining day,
Or look on thine; we could not stall together
In the whole world: but yet let me lament, 40
With tears as sovereign as the blood of hearts,
That thou, my brother, my competitor
In top of all design, my mate in empire,
Friend and companion in the front of war,
The arm of mine own body, and the heart 45
Where mine his thoughts did kindle,—that our stars,

---

65. **pole:** standard. 73. **[e'en]** (Johnson). *in* F. 75. **chares:** chores. **were:** i.e., would be proper.
 Act V, sc. i, 2–3. **he...makes:** his delays are ridiculous. 19. **moiety:** half. 28, 31. **[Agr.]** (Theobald). **Dol.** F. 39.
stall: dwell.

Unreconciliable, should divide
Our equalness to this.   Hear me, good friends, —
But I will tell you at some meeter season.

Enter an EGYPTIAN.

The business of this man looks out of him;   50
We'll hear him what he says, — Whence are you?

Egyp. A poor Egyptian yet.   The Queen my
          mistress,
Confin'd in all she has, her monument,
Of thy intents desires instruction,
That she preparedly may frame herself   55
To th' way she's forc'd to.

Cæs.   Bid her have good heart.
She soon shall know of us, by some of ours,
How honourable and how kindly we
Determine for her; for Cæsar cannot [live]
To be ungentle.

Egyp.   So the gods preserve thee!   60
                                   [*Exit.*

Cæs. Come hither, Proculeius.   Go and say
We purpose her no shame.   Give her what com-
          forts
The quality of her passion shall require,
Lest, in her greatness, by some mortal stroke
She do defeat us; for her life in Rome   65
Would be eternal in our triumph.   Go,
And with your speediest bring us what she says,
And how you find of her.

Pro.   Cæsar, I shall.   [*Exit.*
Cæs. Gallus, go you along.   [*Exit Gallus.*]
          Where's Dolabella,
To second Proculeius?

All.   Dolabella!   70
Cæs. Let him alone, for I remember now
How he's employ'd; he shall in time be ready.
Go with me to my tent, where you shall see
How hardly I was drawn into this war,
How calm and gentle I proceeded still   75
In all my writings.   Go with me, and see
What I can show in this.   [*Exeunt.*

[SCENE II.   *Alexandria.   A room in the monument.*]

Enter CLEOPATRA, CHARMIAN, IRAS, *and* Mardian.

Cleo. My desolation does begin to make
A better life.   'Tis paltry to be Cæsar;
Not being Fortune, he's but Fortune's knave,
A minister of her will: and it is great
To do that thing that ends all other deeds;   5
Which shackles accidents and bolts up change;
Which sleeps, and never palates more the dung,
The beggar's nurse and Cæsar's.

Enter [*to the gates of the monument*] PROCULEIUS
          [GALLUS *and* Soldiers].

Pro. Cæsar sends greeting to the Queen of Egypt,
And bids thee study on what fair demands   10
Thou mean'st to have him grant thee.

Cleo.   What's thy name?
Pro. My name is Proculeius.

Cleo.   Antony
Did tell me of you, bade me trust you; but
I do not greatly care to be deceiv'd,
That have no use for trusting.   If your master   15
Would have a queen his beggar, you must tell him
That majesty, to keep decorum, must
No less beg than a kingdom.   If he please
To give me conquer'd Egypt for my son,
He gives me so much of mine own as I   20
Will kneel to him with thanks.

Pro.   Be of good cheer.
You're fallen into a princely hand; fear nothing.
Make your full reference freely to my lord,
Who is so full of grace that it flows over
On all that need.   Let me report to him   25
Your sweet dependency, and you shall find
A conqueror that will pray in aid for kindness
Where he for grace is kneel'd to.

Cleo.   Pray you, tell him
I am his fortune's vassal, and I send him
The greatness he has got.   I hourly learn   30
A doctrine of obedience, and would gladly
Look him i' th' face.

Pro.   This I'll report, dear lady.
Have comfort, for I know your plight is pitied
Of him that caus'd it.

          [*Gall.*] You see how easily she may be surpris'd.   35
          [*Here Proculeius and two of the Guard enter
                    the monument by a ladder to a window and
                    come down behind Cleopatra.*]
Guard her till Cæsar come.   [*Exit.*]

Iras. Royal queen!
Char. O Cleopatra! thou art taken, Queen.
Cleo. Quick, quick, good hands.
                    [*Drawing a dagger.*]
Pro.   Hold, worthy lady, hold!
                    [*Seizes and disarms her.*]
Do not yourself such wrong, who are in this   40
Reliev'd, but not betray'd.

Cleo.   What, of death too,
That rids our dogs of languish?

Pro.   Cleopatra,
Do not abuse my master's bounty by
Th' undoing of yourself.   Let the world see
His nobleness well acted, which your death   45
Will never let come forth.

Cleo.   Where art thou, Death?

---

59. **[live]** (Rowe).   *leave* F.   66. **eternal:** eternally glorious.
Sc. ii, 3. **knave:** servant.   7. **never...dung:** no longer tastes (the) base food.   8. **nurse:** nourisher.   14. **to be:** i.e., if I
am.   23. **reference:** appeal.   27. **pray in aid:** summon assistance (legal term).   29. **send him:** i.e., acknowledge in him.
35. The introduction of Gallus (l. 8) and the S.D. here are based on Plutarch.   42. **languish:** lingering disease.

Come hither, come!　Come, come, and take a queen
Worth many babes and beggars!
　Pro.　　　　　　　　　　O, temperance, lady!
　Cleo.　Sir, I will eat no meat; I'll not drink, sir;
If idle talk will once be necessary,　　　　　50
I'll not sleep neither; this mortal house I'll ruin,
Do Cæsar what he can.　Know, sir, that I
Will not wait pinion'd at your master's court;
Nor once be chastis'd with the sober eye
Of dull Octavia.　Shall they hoist me up　　55
And show me to the shouting varletry
Of censuring Rome?　Rather a ditch in Egypt
Be gentle grave unto me!　Rather on Nilus' mud
Lay me stark nak'd, and let the water-flies
Blow me into abhorring!　Rather make　　60
My country's high pyramides my gibbet,
And hang me up in chains!
　Pro.　　　　　　　　　　You do extend
These thoughts of horror further than you shall
Find cause in Cæsar.

　　　　　Enter DOLABELLA.

　Dol.　　　　　　　　Proculeius,
What thou hast done thy master Cæsar knows,
And he hath sent for thee.　For the Queen,　66
I'll take her to my guard.
　Pro.　　　　　　So, Dolabella,
It shall content me best.　Be gentle to her.
[*To Cleo.*] To Cæsar I will speak what you shall
　please,
If you'll employ me to him.
　Cleo.　　　　　　　Say, I would die.　70
　　　　　　[*Exeunt Proculeius* [*and Soldiers*].
　Dol.　Most noble empress, you have heard of me?
　Cleo.　I cannot tell.
　Dol.　　　　　　　Assuredly you know me.
　Cleo.　No matter, sir, what I have heard or known.
You laugh when boys or women tell their dreams;
Is't not your trick?
　Dol.　　　　I understand not, madam.　75
　Cleo.　I dream'd there was an Emperor Antony.
O, such another sleep, that I might see
But such another man?
　Dol.　　　　　　If it might please ye, —
　Cleo.　His face was as the heavens; and therein
　stuck　　　　　　　　　　　79
A sun and moon, which kept their course and lighted
The little O, the earth.
　Dol.　　　　　　Most sovereign creature, —
　Cleo.　His legs bestrid the ocean; his rear'd arm
Crested the world; his voice was propertied
As all the tuned spheres, and that to friends;
But when he meant to quail and shake the orb,
He was as rattling thunder.　For his bounty,　86

There was no winter in't; [an autumn 'twas]
That grew the more by reaping.　His delights
Were dolphin-like: they show'd his back above
The element they liv'd in.　In his livery　90
Walk'd crowns and crownets; realms and islands
　were
As plates dropp'd from his pocket.
　Dol.　　　　　　　　Cleopatra!
　Cleo.　Think you there was or might be such a man
As this I dream'd of?
　Dol.　　　　　　Gentle madam, no.
　Cleo.　You lie, up to the hearing of the gods!　95
But, if there be [or] ever were one such,
It's past the size of dreaming.　Nature wants stuff
To vie strange forms with fancy; yet, t' imagine
An Antony were nature's piece 'gainst fancy,
Condemning shadows quite.
　Dol.　　　　　　Hear me, good madam.　100
Your loss is as yourself, great; and you bear it
As answering to the weight.　Would I might never
O'ertake pursu'd success, but I do feel,
By the rebound of yours, a grief that [smites]
My very heart at root.
　Cleo.　　　　　　I thank you, sir.　105
Know you what Cæsar means to do with me?
　Dol.　I am loath to tell you what I would you
　knew.
　Cleo.　Nay, pray you, sir, —
　Dol.　　　　　　Though he be honourable, —
　Cleo.　He'll lead me, then, in triumph?
　Dol.　Madam, he will; I know 't.　　110
　　　　　　　　　　　　[*Flourish.*

　Enter CÆSAR, Gallus, PROCULEIUS, Mæcenas,
　　[SELEUCUS,] *and others of his train.*

　All.　Make way there!　Cæsar!
　Cæs.　Which is the Queen of Egypt?
　Dol.　It is the Emperor, madam.
　　　　　　　　　　　[*Cleopatra kneels.*
　Cæs.　Arise, you shall not kneel.
I pray you, rise; rise, Egypt.
　Cleo.　　　　　　Sir, the gods　　115
Will have it thus; my master and my lord
I must obey.
　Cæs.　　　Take to you no hard thoughts.
The record of what injuries you did us,
Though written in our flesh, we shall remember
As things but done by chance.
　Cleo.　　　　　　Sole sir o' th' world,
I cannot project mine own cause so well　　121
To make it clear; but do confess I have
Been laden with like frailties which before
Have often sham'd our sex.
　Cæs.　　　　　　Cleopatra, know

---

50. **If...necessary:** i.e., to keep awake.　56. **varletry:** rabble.　83–84. **was...spheres:** had the music of the spheres in it.
87. **[an autumn 'twas]** (Thirlby conj.).　*Anthony it was* F.　92. **plates:** coins.　96. **[or]** F₃.　*nor* F₁.　97. **size:** capacity.　98.
vie: compete in.　99. **piece 'gainst:** masterpiece in the competition with.　103. **but:** unless.　104. **[smites]** (Capell).　*suites* F.

We will extenuate rather than enforce.   125
If you apply yourself to our intents,
Which towards you are most gentle, you shall find
A benefit in this change; but if you seek
To lay on me a cruelty, by taking
Antony's course, you shall bereave yourself   130
Of my good purposes, and put your children
To that destruction which I'll guard them from
If thereon you rely.   I'll take my leave.

    Cleo. And may, through all the world; 't is yours;
     and we,
Your scutcheons and your signs of conquest, shall
Hang in what place you please.   Here, my good
     lord.   136

    Cæs. You shall advise me in all for Cleopatra.

    Cleo. This is the brief of money, plate, and jewels
I am possess'd of.   'Tis exactly valued,
Not petty things admitted.   Where's Seleucus?

    Sel. Here, madam.   141

    Cleo. This is my treasurer; let him speak, my lord,
Upon his peril, that I have reserv'd
To myself nothing.   Speak the truth, Seleucus.

    Sel. Madam,   145
I had rather seal my lips than to my peril
Speak that which is not.

    Cleo.   What have I kept back?

    Sel. Enough to purchase what you have made
     known.

    Cæs. Nay, blush not, Cleopatra; I approve   149
Your wisdom in the deed.

    Cleo.   See, Cæsar! O, behold,
How pomp is followed!   Mine will now be yours;
And, should we shift estates, yours would be mine.
Th' ingratitude of this Seleucus does
Even make me wild.   O slave, of no more trust
Than love that's hir'd!   What, goest thou back?
     Thou shalt   155
Go back, I warrant thee; but I'll catch thine eyes,
Though they had wings.   Slave, soulless villain, dog!
O rarely base!

    Cæs.   Good queen, let us entreat you.

    Cleo. O Cæsar, what a wounding shame is this,
That thou, vouchsafing here to visit me,   160
Doing the honour of thy lordliness
To one so meek, that mine own servant should
Parcel the sum of my disgraces by
Addition of his envy!   Say, good Cæsar,
That I some lady trifles have reserv'd,   165
Immoment toys, things of such dignity
As we greet modern friends withal: and say,
Some nobler token I have kept apart
For Livia and Octavia, to induce
Their mediation; must I be unfolded   170

With one that I have bred?   The gods! it smites me
Beneath the fall I have.   [*To Seleucus.*]   Prithee,
     go hence;
Or I shall show the cinders of my spirits
Through th' ashes of my chance.   Wert thou a man,
Thou wouldst have mercy on me.

    Cæs.   Forbear, Seleucus.
           [*Exit Seleucus.*]

    Cleo. Be it known that we, the greatest, are mis-
     thought   176
For things that others do; and, when we fall,
We answer others' merits in our name,
Are therefore to be pitied.

    Cæs.   Cleopatra,
Not what you have reserv'd, nor what acknowl-
     edg'd,   180
Put we i' th' roll of conquest.   Still be 't yours,
Bestow it at your pleasure; and believe,
Cæsar 's no merchant, to make prize with you
Of things that merchants sold.   Therefore be cheer'd;
Make not your thoughts your prisons; no, dear
     queen;   185
For we intend so to dispose you as
Yourself shall give us counsel.   Feed, and sleep.
Our care and pity is so much upon you,
That we remain your friend; and so, adieu.   189

    Cleo. My master, and my lord!

    Cæs.   Not so.   Adieu.
     [*Flourish.   Exeunt Cæsar and his train.*

    Cleo. He words me, girls, he words me, that I
     should not
Be noble to myself; but, hark thee, Charmian.
           [*Whispers Charmian.*]

    Iras. Finish, good lady; the bright day is done,
And we are for the dark.

    Cleo.   Hie thee again.
I have spoke already, and it is provided;   195
Go put it to the haste.

    Char.   Madam, I will.

Re-enter DOLABELLA.

    Dol. Where is the Queen?

    Char.   Behold, sir.   [*Exit.*]

    Cleo.   Dolabella!

    Dol. Madam, as thereto sworn by your command,
Which my love makes religion to obey,
I tell you this: Cæsar through Syria   200
Intends his journey, and within three days
You with your children will he send before.
Make your best use of this.   I have perform'd
Your pleasure and my promise.

    Cleo.   Dolabella,
I shall remain your debtor.

---

125. **enforce:** stress.   163. **Parcel:** increase.   164. **envy:** malice.   166. **Immoment toys:** insignificant trifles.   167. **modern:** ordinary.   169. **Livia:** Cæsar's wife.   170–71. **unfolded With:** exposed by.   173. **spirits:** i.e., anger.   174. **chance:** misfortune.   175. **Forbear:** withdraw.   176. **misthought:** misjudged.   178. **merits:** demerits.   185. **Make . . . prisons:** do not regard yourself a prisoner.   193. **Finish:** die.   195. **it:** i.e., the asp.

Dol.   I your servant.   205
Adieu, good queen; I must attend on Cæsar.
                               [*Exit.*

   Cleo. Farewell, and thanks! Now, Iras, what
     think'st thou?
Thou, an Egyptian puppet, shall be shown
In Rome as well as I. Mechanic slaves
With greasy aprons, rules, and hammers, shall   210
Uplift us to the view; in their thick breaths,
Rank of gross diet, shall we be encloud'd,
And forc'd to drink their vapour.

   Iras.   The gods forbid!

   Cleo. Nay, 'tis most certain, Iras. Saucy lictors
Will catch at us like strumpets, and scald rhymers
Ballad us out o' tune. The quick comedians   216
Extemporally will stage us, and present
Our Alexandrian revels; Antony
Shall be brought drunken forth, and I shall see
Some squeaking Cleopatra boy my greatness   220
I' th' posture of a whore.

   Iras.   O the good gods!

   Cleo. Nay, that's certain.

   Iras. I'll never see 't; for, I am sure, [my] nails
Are stronger than mine eyes.

   Cleo.   Why, that's the way
To fool their preparation, and to conquer   225
Their most absurd intents.

Re-enter CHARMIAN.

                Now, Charmian!
Show me, my women, like a queen. Go fetch
My best attires; I am again for Cydnus
To meet Mark Antony. Sirrah Iras, go.
Now, noble Charmian, we'll dispatch indeed;   230
And, when thou hast done this chare, I'll give thee
     leave
To play till doomsday. Bring our crown and all.
Wherefore's this noise?
           [*Exit Iras.*]   *A noise within.*

Enter a GUARDSMAN.

   Guard.   Here is a rural fellow
That will not be deni'd your Highness' presence.
He brings you figs.   235

   Cleo. Let him come in.   [*Exit Guardsman.*
                What poor an instrument
May do a noble deed! He brings me liberty.
My resolution 's plac'd, and I have nothing
Of woman in me; now from head to foot
I am marble-constant; now the fleeting moon   240
No planet is of mine.

Re-enter GUARDSMAN, *with* CLOWN [*bringing in a
basket*].

   Guard.   This is the man.

   Cleo. Avoid, and leave him.   [*Exit Guardsman.*
Hast thou the pretty worm of Nilus there,
That kills and pains not?   244

   Clown. Truly, I have him; but I would not be
the party that should desire you to touch him, for
his biting is immortal; those that do die of it do
seldom or never recover.

   Cleo. Remember'st thou any that have died
on't?   249

   Clown. Very many, men and women too. I
heard of one of them no longer than yesterday; a
very honest woman, but something given to lie, as
a woman should not do but in the way of honesty;
how she died of the biting of it, what pain she felt;
truly, she makes a very good report o' th' worm.   255
But he that will believe all that they say, shall never
be saved by half that they do. But this is most
falliable, the worm 's an odd worm.

   Cleo. Get thee hence; farewell.   260

   Clown. I wish you all joy of the worm.
                      [*Setting down his basket.*]

   Cleo. Farewell.

   Clown. You must think this, look you, that the
worm will do his kind.

   Cleo. Ay, ay; farewell.   265

   Clown. Look you, the worm is not to be trusted
but in the keeping of wise people; for, indeed, there
is no goodness in the worm.

   Cleo. Take thou no care; it shall be heeded.

   Clown. Very good. Give it nothing, I pray you,
for it is not worth the feeding.   271

   Cleo. Will it eat me?

   Clown. You must not think I am so simple but
I know the devil himself will not eat a woman. I
know that a woman is a dish for the gods, if the   275
devil dress her not. But, truly, these same whereson
devils do the gods great harm in their women; for
in every ten that they make, the devils mar five.

   Cleo. Well, get thee gone; farewell.   280

   Clown. Yes, forsooth; I wish you joy o' th' worm.
                                 [*Exit.*

[*Re-enter* IRAS *with a robe, crown, etc.*]

   Cleo. Give me my robe, put on my crown; I have
Immortal longings in me. Now no more
The juice of Egypt's grape shall moist this lip.   285
Yare, yare, good Iras; quick. Methinks I hear
Antony call; I see him rouse himself
To praise my noble act; I hear him mock
The luck of Cæsar, which the gods give men
To excuse their after wrath. Husband, I come!
Now to that name my courage prove my title!   291
I am fire and air; my other elements
I give to baser life. So; have you done?
Come then, and take the last warmth of my lips.

   215. **scald:** scurvy. 216. **quick:** lively. 220. **boy.** Referring to the playing of female rôles by boys on the Elizabethan
stage. 223. [my] *mine* F. 231. **chare:** task. 240. **fleeting:** changeable. 242. **Avoid:** depart. 243. **worm:** serpent.
264. **his kind:** what his nature dictates. 292. **other elements:** earth and water.

Farewell, kind Charmian; Iras, long farewell.   295
          [*Kisses them. Iras falls and dies.*]
Have I the aspic in my lips? Dost fall?
If thou and nature can so gently part,
The stroke of death is as a lover's pinch,
Which hurts, and is desir'd. Dost thou lie still?
If thus thou vanishest, thou tell'st the world   300
It is not worth leave-taking.
   Char. Dissolve, thick cloud, and rain; that I may say
The gods themselves do weep!
   Cleo.   This proves me base.
If she first meet the curled Antony,
He'll make demand of her, and spend that kiss   305
Which is my heaven to have. Come, thou mortal wretch,
          [*To an asp, which she applies to her breast.*]
With thy sharp teeth this knot intrinsicate
Of life at once untie. Poor venomous fool,
Be angry, and dispatch. O, couldst thou speak,
That I might hear thee call great Cæsar ass   310
Unpolicied!
   Char.   O eastern star!
   Cleo.   Peace, peace!
Dost thou not see my baby at my breast,
That sucks the nurse asleep?
   Char.   O, break! O, break!
   Cleo. As sweet as balm, as soft as air, as gentle, —
O Antony! — Nay, I will take thee too: 315
          [*Applying another asp to her arm.*]
What should I stay —   [*Dies.*
   Char. In this vile world? So, fare thee well!
Now boast thee, death, in thy possession lies
A lass unparallel'd. Downy windows, close;
And golden Phœbus never be beheld   320
Of eyes again so royal! Your crown 's [awry];
I'll mend it, and then play —

          Enter the GUARD, *rushing in.*

   1. Guard. Where's the Queen?
   Char.   Speak softly, wake her not.
   1. Guard. Cæsar hath sent —
   Char.   Too slow a messenger.
          [*Applies an asp.*]
O, come apace, dispatch! I partly feel thee.   325
   1. Guard. Approach, ho! All 's not well; Cæsar 's beguil'd.
   2. Guard. There 's Dolabella sent from Cæsar; call him.
   1. Guard. What work is here! Charmian, is this well done?
   Char. It is well done, and fitting for a princess
Descended of so many royal kings.   330
Ah, soldier!   [*Dies.*

          Re-enter DOLABELLA.
   Dol. How goes it here?
   2. Guard.   All dead.
   Dol.   Cæsar, thy thoughts
Touch their effects in this; thyself art coming
To see perform'd the dreaded act which thou
So sought'st to hinder.   335

          Re-enter CÆSAR *and all his train, marching.*
   All. A way there, a way for Cæsar!
   Dol. O sir, you are too sure an augurer;
That you did fear is done.
   Cæs.   Bravest at the last,
She levell'd at our purposes, and, being royal,
Took her own way. The manner of their deaths?
I do not see them bleed.   340
   Dol.   Who was last with them?
   1. Guard. A simple countryman, that brought her figs.
This was his basket.
   Cæs.   Poison'd, then.
   1. Guard.   O Cæsar,
This Charmian liv'd but now; she stood and spake.
I found her trimming up the diadem   345
On her dead mistress. Tremblingly she stood
And on the sudden dropp'd.
   Cæs.   O noble weakness!
If they had swallow'd poison, 'twould appear
By external swelling; but she looks like sleep,
As she would catch another Antony   350
In her strong toil of grace.
   Dol.   Here, on her breast,
There is a vent of blood and something blown.
The like is on her arm.
   1. Guard. This is an aspic's trail; and these fig-leaves
Have slime upon them, such as the aspic leaves   355
Upon the caves of Nile.
   Cæs.   Most probable
That so she died; for her physician tells me
She hath pursu'd conclusions infinite
Of easy ways to die. Take up her bed;
And bear her women from the monument.   360
She shall be buried by her Antony;
No grave upon the earth shall clip in it
A pair so famous. High events as these
Strike those that make them; and their story is
No less in pity than his glory which   365
Brought them to be lamented. Our army shall
In solemn show attend this funeral;
And then to Rome. Come, Dolabella, see
High order in this great solemnity.
          [*Exeunt omnes.*

296. **aspic**: asp. 305. **make . . . her**: ask her about me. 307. **intrinsicate**: intricate. 321. **[awry]** (Rowe). away F. 333. **Touch . . . effects**: are realized. 339. **levell'd at**: guessed. 352. **blown**: swollen. 358. **conclusions**: experiments. 362. **clip**: enclose.

The Tragedy of Coriolanus

FOR THE TEXT of *Coriolanus* the First Folio (1623) is the sole authority. This is marred by considerable misprinting and mislineation, but unusually full stage-directions establish the authenticity of the copy and suggest Shakespeare's hand.

Evidence for the date is quite inconclusive. It is conceivable but unlikely that the simile of the "coal of fire upon the ice" (I.i.177) was reminiscent of the ice upon the Thames, which in January of 1608 froze over the first time since 1565; Shakespeare might have seen fires upon frozen streams more than once. A line in Ben Jonson's *Epicoene* (1609), "You have lurch'd your friends of the better halfe of the garland" (V.iv.227), which bears so close a likeness to "He lurch'd all swords of the garland" in II.ii.105, may be one of those gibing allusions of which Jonson was fond; but the expression was perhaps a current one. Another possible reference appears in the Preface to Robert Armin's poem *The Italian Tailor and His Boy* (1609), where the striking image of throwing up one's cap at the horns of the moon may have been plucked from I.i.216-17 of the present play. Armin was one of "the Principall Actors" of Shakespeare's company at the time his poem was printed. The foregoing evidence, for what it is worth, combines with that from style and metre to indicate a time late in 1608 or early in 1609 as the period of composition.

The source of the plot is Plutarch's *Life of Coriolanus*, which Shakespeare knew in the translation of Sir Thomas North. As in the case of *Julius Cæsar* and *Antony and Cleopatra*, which are also based on Plutarch, he followed his authority closely. Whole passages of some of the most notable speeches, such as the fable related by Menenius (I.i.99 ff.), the speech of Coriolanus presenting himself to Aufidius (IV.v.71 ff.), and the appeal of Volumnia to her son on behalf of Rome (V.iii.94 ff.), are couched almost in the words of the biography. The main lines of the characters are also followed faithfully, though many of the more subtle points are introduced by Shakespeare. For example, the episode in which Coriolanus begs of Cominius freedom for his Vol-

scian host is in Plutarch, but the finely characteristic touch by which he is represented as having forgotten the man's name is Shakespeare's (I.ix.79-90). The demagogic tribunes, Brutus and Sicinius, are virtually Shakespeare's creations, for in Plutarch their personalities are barely suggested. The portrait of Menenius is greatly elaborated in the play. Plutarch assigns to him merely the part of a dignified patrician who makes a single attempt to pacify the rebellious plebeians; Shakespeare conceives him as a genial and self-important old gentleman, who takes a touching pride in his intimacy with the hero, who is appreciated, even by the people, for his civic virtue, and who, with his command of salty, homely language and his skill in repartee, is responsible for most of the humor which helps to relieve the prevailing somberness of the tragedy. The dialogues of the citizens and such scenes as those with the servants of Aufidius are wholly invented; while as a basis for the actual language in which Coriolanus expresses his haughty and contemptuous nature, Shakespeare had merely Plutarch's statement that he was rough and insolent in conversation and undisciplined in temper. Although what is most attractive in Volumnia is provided by Plutarch, the harshness in her character is the addition of Shakespeare. In the biography, it is Valeria who induces the wife and mother of Coriolanus to go to plead with him, and her share in the action is treated with considerable fullness. This is represented in the play merely by her presence in the deputation; but Shakespeare supplies from his own imagination the admirable scene (I.iii) where she calls on Volumnia and Virgilia and finds them sewing. Virgilia is little more than a name in the source, and the skill with which in the play she is drawn in some half dozen lines is all Shakespeare's.

The facts of the political situation in which the action takes place Shakespeare has deliberately altered. The dignified secession of the *plebs*, which in Plutarch is a measure of passive resistance to severe economic oppression, he represents as the rioting of a hungry mob shouting for cheap corn; and the picture of the common crowd in this play, as elsewhere, is unflattering. It is wrong, however, to suppose that Shakespeare conceived this play primarily as a political document. One cannot recall too often that Shakespeare was a dramatist, not an essayist, and that therefore dramatic considerations always govern. In the present play class conflict is a postulate inherited from the source, and in making the narrative dramatic Shakespeare underlines the elements of opposition. Like most of his articulate contemporaries, Shakespeare viewed the established social order as part or counterpart of the rational order of the universe, in which all classes had their place and function. Therefore, although no champion of the masses, Shakespeare was, on the other hand, not their enemy. In *Coriolanus*, one should observe, the true source of danger is not in the nature of the people but in the pride of the leading aristocrat. Had Coriolanus had a modicum of charity or humility, even, one might say, of common sense, disaster might have been avoided. But he is a patrician bigot, identifying his own class with the State, ready in his fanatical scorn to take from the people even their traditional privileges. With such an attitude Shakespeare, of course, had no sympathy. It is useful to note, furthermore, that although the citizens are muddle-headed, fickle, and stupidly pliable, they have good instincts and honest intentions. When they cry, "That we did, we did for the best," they speak the truth (IV.vi.143). Until he has spurned their good will irretrievably, Coriolanus never lacks advocates among them. In the first scene when the crowd is out to kill him, a voice is raised recalling his services and warning against holding "what he cannot help in his nature" as a vice in him (I.i.42). When at the election Coriolanus demands of a citizen the price of the consulship, he is told that "the price is to ask it kindly" (II.iii.81). He does not ask it kindly, yet these citizens elect him just the same. Coriolanus could have their devotion if he would show them a decent respect.

The vocation of Coriolanus is war, and in that he is great. From his youth he has been dedicated to fighting, and he won distinction early (I.iii.1 ff.; II.ii.91 ff.). Success has not turned his head, and although he is haughty to excess with those whom he disdains, he is not vainglorious because of his victories. He is embarrassed by praise, and it is interesting to note that his indifference to it is a touch invented by Shakespeare. Not that he does not covet distinction; he does, and his deprecation of his exploits and his exaggerated impatience with eulogy look like a negative expression of his pride. His honesty, though too often tactless, is essentially to his credit. "What his breast forges, that his tongue must vent" (III.i.258). He knows the necessity for strategy in war, but of pacific diplomacy he is totally incapable. His pride wears no mask, and the people know what he thinks of them. He has done much for Rome which only he could do, and the idea most hideous to his imagination is that of traitor. When Sicinius calls him one he is enraged (III.i.162–72; III.iii.63–74), and it is a mighty irony that with this abhorrence of the crime, he should ever stoop to treason.

The capitulation of Coriolanus to the entreaties of his mother is highly revealing with respect to both his character and hers. This stalwart woman, one of Shakespeare's truly remarkable creations, is in a real sense responsible for the destiny of her son. He is bone of her bone and flesh of her flesh; she has directed his spirit and shaped his ideals, and she cherishes him as a projection of herself. "Thou art my warrior; I holp to frame thee," are the first words she speaks after he has raised her from her knees in Corioli (V.iii.62). His wounds incurred for Rome have ever been glorious in her eyes. In the victory which makes him "Coriolanus," her dreams for him — "my very wishes and the buildings of my fancy" — are realized, except for the consulship, which she is confident Rome will now bestow upon him (II.i.214–218). Though she despises the populace as much as he, she would have him dissimulate, and it is her rebuke of that pride which she has done so much to foster in him that moves him to his ill-fated effort (III.ii.128–30). But more than family and more than class, she loves her country, and when her son has shamed them all, she can abase her spirit in a last effort to save Rome. In her pleading with her son it is to his honor, not his pity, that she appeals; her personal feelings are consumed in her country's peril. It is not for Rome's sake, however, or for honor, that Coriolanus yields; it is because his family kneels and his mother begs. He had sworn that he would never be "such a gosling" as to obey instinct, and that he would deny his kin (V.iii.34 ff.). But that is the one thing he cannot do. Nature sways where no arguments avail, and when he tells his mother what she must but too well have divined, that his submission may prove most mortal to him, her feelings are too deep for words.

THE TRAGEDY OF CORIOLANUS

CAIUS MARCIUS, *afterwards* CAIUS MARCIUS CORIOLANUS.

TITUS LARTIUS, } *generals against the Volscians.*
COMINIUS,

MENENIUS AGRIPPA, *friend to Coriolanus.*

SICINIUS VELUTUS, } *tribunes of the people.*
JUNIUS BRUTUS,

Young MARCIUS, *son to Coriolanus.*

A Roman Herald.

TULLUS AUFIDIUS, *general of the Volscians.*

Lieutenant to Aufidius.
Conspirators with Aufidius.
A Citizen of Antium.
Two Volscian Guards.

VOLUMNIA, *mother to Coriolanus.*
VIRGILIA, *wife to Coriolanus.*
VALERIA, *friend to Virgilia.*
Gentlewoman, *attending on Virgilia.*

Roman and Volscian Senators, Patricians, Ædiles, Lictors, Soldiers, Citizens, Messengers, Servants to Aufidius, and other Attendants.

SCENE: *Rome and the neighbourhood; Corioli and the neighbourhood; Antium.*]

ACT I

SCENE I. [*Rome. A street.*]

Enter a company of mutinous CITIZENS, *with staves, clubs, and other weapons.*

1. Cit. Before we proceed any further, hear me speak.

All. Speak, speak.

1. Cit. You are all resolv'd rather to die than to famish?   5

All. Resolv'd, resolv'd.

1. Cit. First, you know Caius Marcius is chief enemy to the people.

All. We know 't, we know 't.   9

1. Cit. Let us kill him, and we'll have corn at our own price. Is 't a verdict?

All. No more talking on 't; let it be done. Away, away!

2. Cit. One word, good citizens.   15

1. Cit. We are accounted poor citizens, the patricians good. What authority surfeits on would relieve us; if they would yield us but the superfluity while it were wholesome, we might guess they relieved us humanely; but they think we are too dear. The leanness that afflicts us, the 20 object of our misery, is as an inventory to particularize their abundance; our sufferance is a gain to them. Let us revenge this with our pikes ere we become rakes; for the gods know I speak this in hunger for bread, not in thirst for revenge.   25

2. Cit. Would you proceed especially against Caius Marcius?

All. Against him first; he's a very dog to the commonalty.   29

2. Cit. Consider you what services he has done for his country?

1. Cit. Very well; and could be content to give him good report for 't, but that he pays himself with being proud.

[*2. Cit.*] Nay, but speak not maliciously.   35

1. Cit. I say unto you, what he hath done famously, he did it to that end. Though soft-conscienc'd men can be content to say it was for his country, he did it to please his mother, and to be partly proud; which he is, even to the altitude of his virtue.   41

2. Cit. What he cannot help in his nature, you

Act I, sc. i, 21. **object:** sight.   22. **sufferance:** suffering.   24. **rakes:** i.e., thin.   35. [*2. Cit.*] (Malone).   *All* F.

account a vice in him. You must in no way say he
is covetous.   44

  1. Cit. If I must not, I need not be barren of accusations; he hath faults, with surplus, to tire in
repetition. (*Shouts within.*) What shouts are
these? The other side o' th' city is risen; why stay
we prating here? To th' Capitol!

  All. Come, come.   50

  1. Cit. Soft! who comes here?

Enter MENENIUS AGRIPPA.

  2. Cit. Worthy Menenius Agrippa, one that hath
always lov'd the people.

  1. Cit. He's one honest enough; would all the rest
were so!   55

  Men. What work 's, my countrymen, in hand?
       Where go you
With bats and clubs? The matter? Speak, I pray
you.

  2. Cit. Our business is not unknown to th' Senate.
They have had inkling this fortnight what we intend
to do, which now we'll show 'em in deeds. They
say poor suitors have strong breaths; they shall
know we have strong arms too.   62

  Men. Why, masters, my good friends, mine
       honest neighbours,
Will you undo yourselves?

  2. Cit. We cannot, sir, we are undone already.

  Men. I tell you, friends, most charitable care
Have the patricians of you. For your wants,
Your suffering in this dearth, you may as well
Strike at the heaven with your staves as lift them   70
Against the Roman state, whose course will on
The way it takes, cracking ten thousand curbs
Of more strong link asunder than can ever
Appear in your impediment. For the dearth,
The gods, not the patricians, make it, and   75
Your knees to them, not arms, must help. Alack,
You are transported by calamity
Thither where more attends you, and you slander
The helms o' th' state, who care for you like fathers
When you curse them as enemies.   80

  2. Cit. Care for us! True, indeed! They ne'er
car'd for us yet: suffer us to famish, and their store-
houses cramm'd with grain; make edicts for usury,
to support usurers; repeal daily any wholesome act
established against the rich, and provide more   85
piercing statutes daily, to chain up and restrain the
poor. If the wars eat us not up, they will; and
there's all the love they bear us.

  Men. Either you must   90
Confess yourselves wondrous malicious,

Or be accus'd of folly. I shall tell you
A pretty tale. It may be you have heard it;
But, since it serves my purpose, I will venture
To [stale 't] a little more.   95

  2. Cit. Well, I'll hear it, sir; yet you must not
think to fob off our disgrace with a tale. But, an't
please you, deliver.

  Men. There was a time when all the body's
       members
Rebell'd against the belly, thus accus'd it: 100
That only like a gulf it did remain
I' th' midst o' th' body, idle and unactive,
Still cupboarding the viand, never bearing
Like labour with the rest, where th' other instru-
       ments
Did see and hear, devise, instruct, walk, feel   105
And, mutually participate, did minister
Unto the appetite and affection common
Of the whole body. The belly answer'd —

  2. Cit. Well, sir, what answer made the belly? 110

  Men. Sir, I shall tell you. With a kind of smile,
Which ne'er came from the lungs, but even thus —
For, look you, I may make the belly smile
As well as speak — it [tauntingly] replied
To th' discontented members, the mutinous parts
That envied his receipt; even so most fitly   116
As you malign our senators for that
They are not such as you.

  2. Cit.   Your belly's answer? What?
The kingly-crowned head, the vigilant eye,
The counsellor heart, the arm our soldier,   120
Our steed the leg, the tongue our trumpeter,
With other muniments and petty helps
In this our fabric, if that they —

  Men.   What then?
'Fore me, this fellow speaks! What then? what
       then?

  2. Cit. Should by the cormorant belly be re-
       strain'd.   125
Who is the sink o' th' body, —

  Men.   Well, what then?

  2. Cit. The former agents, if they did complain,
What could the belly answer?

  Men.   I will tell you.
If you'll bestow a small — of what you have little —
Patience a while, you'st hear the belly's answer. 130

  2. Cit. Ye're long about it.

  Men.   Note me this, good friend;
Your most grave belly was deliberate,
Not rash like his accusers, and thus answered:
"True is it, my incorporate friends," quoth he,
"That I receive the general food at first   135

---

  58. *2. Cit.* Many edd. change to *1. Cit.* here and throughout the rest of the scene.   79. **helms:** pilots.   95. [**stale 't**]
(Theobald). *scale 't* F.   97. **fob ... disgrace:** cajole us from our feeling of injury.   101. **gulf:** whirlpool.   106. **participate:**
cooperating.   107. **affection:** desire.   112. **ne'er ... lungs:** i.e., was not a laugh.   113. [**tauntingly**] F4. *taintingly* F1.
116. **receipt:** what he received.   122. **muniments:** furnishings.   130. **you'st:** you shall.   134. **incorporate:** united in
one body.

Which you do live upon; and fit it is,
Because I am the store-house and the shop
Of the whole body.   But, if you do remember,
I send it through the rivers of your blood,
Even to the court, the heart, to th' seat o' th' brain;
And, through the cranks and offices of man,   141
The strongest nerves and small inferior veins
From me receive that natural competency
Whereby they live.   And though that all at once,
You, my good friends," — this says the belly, mark
    me, —   145
    2. Cit.   Ay, sir; well, well.
    Men.   "Though all at once cannot
See what I do deliver out to each,
Yet I can make my audit up, that all
From me do back receive the flour of all,   149
And leave me but the bran."   What say you to't?
    2. Cit.   It was an answer.   How apply you this?
    Men.   The senators of Rome are this good belly,
And you the mutinous members; for examine
Their counsels and their cares, digest things rightly
Touching the weal o' th' common, you shall find
No public benefit which you receive   156
But it proceeds or comes from them to you
And no way from yourselves.   What do you think,
You, the great toe of this assembly?
    2. Cit.   I the great toe!   Why the great toe?   160
    Men.   For that, being one o' th' lowest, basest,
        poorest,
Of this most wise rebellion, thou goest foremost;
Thou rascal, that art worst in blood to run,
Lead'st first to win some vantage.
But make you ready your stiff bats and clubs;   165
Rome and her rats are at the point of battle,
The one side must have bale.

Enter CAIUS MARCIUS.

                                   Hail, noble Marcius!
    Mar.   Thanks.   What's the matter, you dissen-
        tious rogues,
That, rubbing the poor itch of your opinion,   169
Make yourselves scabs?
    2. Cit.   We have ever your good word.
    Mar.   He that will give good words to thee will
        flatter
Beneath abhorring.   What would you have, you
        curs,
That like nor peace nor war?   The one affrights you,
The other makes you proud.   He that trusts to you,
Where he should find you lions, finds you hares;   175
Where foxes, geese.   You are no surer, no,
Than is the coal of fire upon the ice,

Or hailstone in the sun.   Your virtue is
To make him worthy whose offence subdues him,
And curse that justice did it.   Who deserves great-
        ness   180
Deserves your hate; and your affections are
A sick man's appetite, who desires most that
Which would increase his evil.   He that depends
Upon your favours swims with fins of lead
And hews down oaks with rushes.   Hang ye!   Trust
        ye?   185
With every minute you do change a mind,
And call him noble that was now your hate,
Him vile that was your garland.   What's the mat-
        ter,
That in these several places of the city
You cry against the noble Senate, who,   190
Under the gods, keep you in awe, which else
Would feed on one another?   What's their seeking?
    Men.   For corn at their own rates; whereof, they
        say,
The city is well stor'd.
    Mar.   Hang 'em!   They say!
They'll sit by th' fire, and presume to know   195
What's done i' th' Capitol; who's like to rise,
Who thrives, and who declines; side factions, and
        give out
Conjectural marriages; making parties strong,
And feebling such as stand not in their liking
Below their cobbled shoes.   They say there's grain
        enough!   200
Would the nobility lay aside their ruth
And let me use my sword, I'd make a quarry
With thousands of these quarter'd slaves as high
As I could pick my lance.
    Men.   Nay, these are almost thoroughly per-
        suaded;   205
For though abundantly they lack discretion,
Yet are they passing cowardly.   But, I beseech you,
What says the other troop?
    Mar.   They are dissolv'd, hang 'em!
They said they were an-hungry; sigh'd forth prov-
        erbs,
That hunger broke stone walls, that dogs must eat,
That meat was made for mouths, that the gods sent
        not   211
Corn for the rich men only.   With these shreds
They vented their complainings; which being
        answer'd,
And a petition granted them, — a strange one
To break the heart of generosity,   215
And make bold power look pale, — they threw their
        caps
As they would hang them on the horns o' th' moon,

---

141. **cranks:** winding passages.   **offices:** service rooms.   163. **rascal:** lean deer (therefore not worth hunting).   **blood:** condition.   167. **bale:** disaster.   170. **scabs:** (1) sores, (2) scurvy rascals.   179. **whose...him:** whose own fault has ruined him.   180. **that...it:** the justice that punished him.   197. **side:** take sides with.   198. **marriages:** i.e., political alliances.   **strong:** i.e., in report.   202. **quarry:** heap of dead.   203. **quarter'd:** slaughtered.   204. **pick:** pitch.   215. **generosity:** the gentry.

Shouting their emulation.

Men.   What is granted them?

Mar. Five tribunes to defend their vulgar wisdoms,

Of their own choice. One's Junius Brutus,   220

Sicinius Velutus, and I know not — 'Sdeath!

The rabble should have first unroof'd the city

Ere so prevail'd with me. It will in time

Win upon power and throw forth greater themes

For insurrection's arguing.

Men.   This is strange.   225

Mar. Go, get you home, you fragments!

Enter a MESSENGER, *hastily.*

Mess. Where's Caius Marcius?

Mar.   Here. What's the matter?

Mess. The news is, sir, the Volsces are in arms.

Mar. I am glad on't. Then we shall ha' means to vent

Our musty superfluity. See, our best elders.   230

Enter COMINIUS, TITUS LARTIUS, *and other* SENATORS; JUNIUS BRUTUS *and* SICINIUS VELUTUS.

1. Sen. Marcius, 'tis true that you have lately told us;

The Volsces are in arms.

Mar.   They have a leader,

Tullus Aufidius, that will put you to't.

I sin in envying his nobility,

And were I anything but what I am,   235

I would wish me only he.

Com.   You have fought together?

Mar. Were half to half the world by th' ears and he

Upon my party, I'd revolt, to make

Only my wars with him. He is a lion

That I am proud to hunt.

1. Sen.   Then, worthy Marcius,

Attend upon Cominius to these wars.   241

Com. It is your former promise.

Mar.   Sir, it is;

And I am constant. Titus [Lartius], thou

Shalt see me once more strike at Tullus' face.

What, art thou stiff? Stand'st out?

Lart.   No, Caius Marcius;

I'll lean upon one crutch and fight with t'other   246

Ere stay behind this business.

Men.   O, true-bred!

[1.] Sen. Your company to th' Capitol; where, I know,

Our greatest friends attend us.

Lart.   [*To Com.*] Lead you on.

[*To Mar.*] Follow Cominius; we must follow you;

Right worthy you priority.

Com.   Noble Marcius!   251

[1.] Sen. [*To the Citizens.*] Hence to your homes; begone!

Mar.   Nay, let them follow.

The Volsces have much corn; take these rats thither

To gnaw their garners. Worshipful mutiners,

Your valour puts well forth; pray, follow.   255

     [*Citizens steal away. Exeunt all but Sicinius and Brutus.*

Sic. Was ever man so proud as is this Marcius?

Bru. He has no equal.

Sic. When we were chosen tribunes for the people, —

Bru. Mark'd you his lip and eyes?

Sic.   Nay, but his taunts.

Bru. Being mov'd, he will not spare to gird the gods.   260

Sic. Be-mock the modest moon.

Bru. The present wars devour him! He is grown

Too proud to be so valiant.

Sic.   Such a nature,

Tickled with good success, disdains the shadow

Which he treads on at noon. But I do wonder   265

His insolence can brook to be commanded

Under Cominius.

Bru.   Fame, at the which he aims,

In whom already he's well grac'd, cannot

Better be held nor more attain'd than by

A place below the first; for what miscarries   270

Shall be the general's fault, though he perform

To th' utmost of a man, and giddy censure

Will then cry out of Marcius, "O, if he

Had borne the business!"

Sic.   Besides, if things go well,

Opinion that so sticks on Marcius shall   275

Of his demerits rob Cominius.

Bru.   Come.

Half all Cominius' honours are to Marcius,

Though Marcius earn'd them not, and all his faults

To Marcius shall be honours, though indeed

In aught he merit not.

Sic.   Let's hence, and hear   280

How the dispatch is made, and in what fashion,

More than his singularity, he goes

Upon this present action.

Bru.   Let's along.   [*Exeunt.*

[SCENE II. *Corioli. The Senate-house.*]

Enter TULLUS AUFIDIUS *with* SENATORS *of Corioli.*

1. Sen. So, your opinion is, Aufidius,

That they of Rome are ent'red in our counsels

---

218. **emulation**: factiousness.   229. **vent**: get rid of.   233. **put you to't**: keep you busy.   243. [**Lartius**] (Rowe). *Lucius* F (as elsewhere).   248, 252. [**1.**] (Rowe). Om. F.   255. **puts well forth**: shows up well.   260. **gird**: scoff at.   276. **demerits**: deserts.   282. **More … singularity**: apart from his individual peculiarities.

And know how we proceed.

Auf.   Is it not yours?
What ever have been thought on in this state,
That could be brought to bodily act ere Rome   5
Had circumvention? 'Tis not four days gone
Since I heard thence; these are the words: — I think
I have the letter here; yes, here it is: —
[*Reads.*] "They have press'd a power, but it is not
     known
Whether for east or west. The dearth is great;   10
The people mutinous; and it is rumour'd,
Cominius, Marcius your old enemy,
Who is of Rome worse hated than of you,
And Titus Lartius, a most valiant Roman,
These three lead on this preparation   15
Whither 'tis bent. Most likely 'tis for you;
Consider of it."

1. Sen.   Our army's in the field.
We never yet made doubt but Rome was ready
To answer us.

Auf.   Nor did you think it folly
To keep your great pretences veil'd till when   20
They needs must show themselves; which in the
     hatching,
It seem'd, appear'd to Rome. By the discovery
We shall be short'ned in our aim, which was
To take in many towns ere almost Rome
Should know we were afoot.

2. Sen.   Noble Aufidius,   25
Take your commission; hie you to your bands;
Let us alone to guard Corioli.
If they set down before 's, for the remove
Bring up your army; but, I think, you'll find
They've not prepar'd for us.

Auf.   O, doubt not that;   30
I speak from certainties. Nay, more;
Some parcels of their power are forth already,
And only hitherward. I leave your honours.
If we and Caius Marcius chance to meet,
'Tis sworn between us we shall ever strike   35
Till one can do no more.

All.   The gods assist you!

Auf. And keep your honours safe!

1. Sen.   Farewell.

2. Sen.   Farewell.

All. Farewell.   [*Exeunt.*

[SCENE III. *Rome. A room in Marcius' house.*]

Enter VOLUMNIA *and* VIRGILIA: *they set them
down on two low stools, and sew.*

Vol. I pray you, daughter, sing; or express yourself in a more comfortable sort. If my son were my
husband, I should freelier rejoice in that absence
wherein he won honour than in the embracements
of his bed where he would show most love. When   5
yet he was but tender-bodied and the only son of my
womb, when youth with comeliness pluck'd all gaze
his way, when for a day of kings' entreaties a mother
should not sell him an hour from her beholding, I,
considering how honour would become such a   10
person, that it was no better than picture-like to
hang by th' wall, if renown made it not stir, was
pleas'd to let him seek danger where he was like to
find fame. To a cruel war I sent him; from whence
he return'd, his brows bound with oak. I tell   15
thee, daughter, I sprang not more in joy at first
hearing he was a man-child than now in first seeing
he had proved himself a man.   19

Vir. But had he died in the business, madam,
how then?

Vol. Then his good report should have been my
son; I therein would have found issue. Hear me
profess sincerely: had I a dozen sons, each in my love
alike and none less dear than thine and my good   25
Marcius, I had rather had eleven die nobly for their
country than one voluptuously surfeit out of action.

Enter a GENTLEWOMAN.

Gent. Madam, the Lady Valeria is come to visit
     you.

Vir. Beseech you, give me leave to retire myself.

Vol. Indeed, you shall not.   31
Methinks I hear hither your husband's drum;
See him pluck Aufidius down by the hair;
As children from a bear, the Volsces shunning him.
Methinks I see him stamp thus, and call thus: 35
"Come on, you cowards! you were got in fear,
Though you were born in Rome." His bloody brow
With his mail'd hand then wiping, forth he goes,
Like to a harvest-man that's task'd to mow
Or all or lose his hire.   40

Vir. His bloody brow! O Jupiter, no blood!

Vol. Away, you fool! it more becomes a man
Than gilt his trophy. The breasts of Hecuba,
When she did suckle Hector, look'd not lovelier
Than Hector's forehead when it spit forth blood   45
At Grecian sword, [*contemning.* Tell] Valeria,
We are fit to bid her welcome.   [*Exit Gent.*

Vir. Heavens bless my lord from fell Aufidius!

Vol. He'll beat Aufidius' head below his knee
And tread upon his neck.   50

Enter VALERIA, *with an* Usher *and* Gentlewoman.

Val. My ladies both, good day to you.

Vol. Sweet madam.

Sc. ii, 6. **circumvention:** means to circumvent.   9. **press'd a power:** conscripted troops.   20. **pretences:** designs.   28. **for the remove:** to raise the siege.

Sc. iii, 11. **person:** comely figure.   39. **task'd:** committed.   43. **trophy:** monument.   46. **[contemning. Tell]** (Collier conj.). *Contenning tell* F.

Vir. I am glad to see your ladyship.

Val. How do you both?   You are manifest house-keepers.   What are you sewing here?   A fine spot, in good faith.   How does your little son?   57

Vir. I thank your ladyship; well, good madam.

Vol. He had rather see the swords and hear a drum than look upon his schoolmaster.   61

Val. O' my word, the father's son.   I'll swear, 'tis a very pretty boy.   O' my troth, I look'd upon him o' Wednesday half an hour together; has such a confirm'd countenance.   I saw him run after a   65 gilded butterfly; and when he caught it, he let it go again; and after it again; and over and over he comes, and up again; catch'd it again; or whether his fall enrag'd him, or how 'twas, he did so set his teeth and tear it.   O, I warrant, how he mammock'd it!   71

Vol. One on 's father's moods.

Val. Indeed, la, 'tis a noble child.

Vir. A crack, madam.   74

Val. Come, lay aside your stitchery; I must have you play the idle housewife with me this afternoon.

Vir. No, good madam; I will not out of doors.

Val. Not out of doors!

Vol. She shall, she shall.   80

Vir. Indeed, no, by your patience; I'll not over the threshold till my lord return from the wars.

Val. Fie, you confine yourself most unreasonably.   Come, you must go visit the good lady that lies in.   86

Vir. I will wish her speedy strength, and visit her with my prayers; but I cannot go thither.

Vol. Why, I pray you?

Vir. 'Tis not to save labour, nor that I want love.   91

Val. You would be another Penelope: yet, they say, all the yarn she spun in Ulysses' absence did but fill Ithaca full of moths.   Come; I would your cambric were sensible as your finger, that you might leave pricking it for pity.   Come, you shall go with us.   97

Vir. No, good madam, pardon me; indeed, I will not forth.

Val. In truth, la, go with me; and I'll tell you excellent news of your husband.   101

Vir. O, good madam, there can be none yet.

Val. Verily, I do not jest with you; there came news from him last night.

Vir. Indeed, madam?   105

Val. In earnest, it's true; I heard a senator speak it.   Thus it is: the Volsces have an army forth; against whom Cominius the general is gone, with one part of our Roman power.   Your lord and Titus Lartius are set down before their city Corioli;   110

they nothing doubt prevailing and to make it brief wars.   This is true, on mine honour; and so, I pray, go with us.

Vir. Give me excuse, good madam; I will obey you in everything hereafter.   115

Vol. Let her alone, lady.   As she is now, she will but disease our better mirth.

Val. In troth, I think she would.   Fare you well, then.   Come, good sweet lady.   Prithee, Virgilia, turn thy solemness out o' door, and go along with us.   121

Vir. No, at a word, madam; indeed, I must not. I wish you much mirth.

Val. Well, then, farewell.   [*Exeunt.*

[SCENE IV.]   *Before Corioli.*

Enter, with drum and colours, MARCIUS, TITUS LARTIUS, Captains *and* Soldiers.   *To them a* MESSENGER.

Mar. Yonder comes news.   A wager they have met.

Lart. My horse to yours, no.

Mar.   'Tis done.

Lart.   Agreed.

Mar. Say, has our general met the enemy?

Mess. They lie in view; but have not spoke as yet.

Lart. So, the good horse is mine.

Mar.   I'll buy him of you.

Lart. No, I'll nor sell nor give him; lend you him I will   6

For half a hundred years.   Summon the town.

Mar. How far off lie these armies?

Mess.   Within this mile and half.

Mar. Then shall we hear their 'larum, and they ours.

Now, Mars, I prithee, make us quick in work,   10

That we with smoking swords may march from hence

To help our fielded friends!   Come, blow thy blast.

They sound a parley.   Enter two SENATORS *with others on the walls.*

Tullus Aufidius, is he within your walls?

1. Sen. No, nor a man that fears you less than he,

That's lesser than a little.   [*Drum afar off.*]   Hark! our drums   15

Are bringing forth our youth.   We'll break our walls,

Rather than they shall pound us up.   Our gates,

Which yet seem shut, we have but pinn'd with rushes;

They'll open of themselves.   [*Alarum afar off.*] Hark you, far off!

56. **spot:** pattern.   65. **confirm'd:** resolute.   71. **mammock'd:** tore to pieces.   72. **on's:** of his.   74. **crack:** rascal. 95. **sensible:** sensitive.   117. **disease:** disturb.   122. **at a word:** absolutely.

Sc. iv, 4. **spoke:** engaged in fight.   14. **less.** Apparently a slip for *more.*   17. **pound:** impound, shut.

There is Aufidius; list, what work he makes   20
Amongst your cloven army.
Mar.   O, they are at it!
Lart. Their noise be our instruction. Ladders, ho!

Enter the army of the Volsces.

Mar. They fear us not, but issue forth their city.
Now put your shields before your hearts, and fight
With hearts more proof than shields.   Advance,
        brave Titus!   25
They do disdain us much beyond our thoughts,
Which makes me sweat with wrath.   Come on, my
        fellows!
He that retires, I'll take him for a Volsce,
And he shall feel mine edge.   [*Exit.*]

Alarum.   The Romans are beat back to their trenches.
        Re-enter MARCIUS, *cursing.*

Mar. All the contagion of the south light on you,
You shames of Rome! you herd of — Boils and
        plagues   31
Plaster you o'er, that you may be abhorr'd
Further than seen, and one infect another
Against the wind a mile!   You souls of geese,
That bear the shapes of men, how have you run   35
From slaves that apes would beat!   Pluto and hell!
All hurt behind!   Backs red, and faces pale
With flight and agued fear!   Mend and charge
        home,
Or, by the fires of heaven, I'll leave the foe   39
And make my wars on you.   Look to't; come on!
If you'll stand fast, we'll beat them to their wives,
As they us to our trenches followed.

    Another alarum.   [The Volsces fly,] and MAR-
            CIUS *follows them to the gates*

So, now the gates are ope; now prove good seconds.
'Tis for the followers fortune widens them,
Not for the fliers.   Mark me, and do the like.   45
                            [*Enters the gates.*
1. Sol. Fool-hardiness; not I.
2. Sol.   Nor I.
                            [*Marcius is shut in.*
1. Sol. See, they have shut him in.
                            [*Alarum continues.*
All.   To th' pot, I warrant him.

    Re-enter TITUS LARTIUS.

Lart. What is become of Marcius?
All.   Slain, sir, doubtless.
1. Sol. Following the fliers at the very heels,
With them he enters; who, upon the sudden,   50
Clapp'd to their gates.   He is himself alone,
To answer all the city.

Lart.   O noble fellow!
Who sensibly outdares his senseless sword
And, when it bows, stand'st up.   Thou art left,
        Marcius;
A carbuncle entire, as big as thou art,   55
Were not so rich a jewel.   Thou wast a soldier
Even to [Cato's] wish, not fierce and terrible
Only in strokes; but, with thy grim looks and
The thunder-like percussion of thy sounds,
Thou mad'st thine enemies shake, as if the world 60
Were feverous and did tremble.

Re-enter MARCIUS, *bleeding, assaulted by the enemy.*

1. Sol.   Look, sir.
Lart.   O, 'tis Marcius!
Let's fetch him off, or make remain alike.
                [*They fight, and all enter the city.*

        [SCENE V.   *Corioli.   A street.*]

    Enter certain ROMANS, *with spoils.*

1. Rom. This will I carry to Rome.
2. Rom. And I this.
3. Rom. A murrain on't!   I took this for silver.
            [*Exeunt.   Alarum continues still afar off.*

    Enter MARCIUS *and* TITUS [LARTIUS] *with a*
            Trumpet.

Mar. See here these movers that do prize their
        hours   5
At a crack'd drachma!   Cushions, leaden spoons,
Irons of a doit, doublets that hangmen would
Bury with those that wore them, these base slaves,
Ere yet the fight be done, pack up.   Down with
        them!
And hark, what noise the general makes!   To him!
There is the man of my soul's hate, Aufidius,   11
Piercing our Romans; then, valiant Titus, take
Convenient numbers to make good the city;
Whilst I, with those that have the spirit, will haste
To help Cominius.
Lart.   Worthy sir, thou bleed'st.   15
Thy exercise hath been too violent for
A second course of fight.
Mar.   Sir, praise me not,
My work hath yet not warm'd me; fare you well.
The blood I drop is rather physical
Than dangerous to me.   To Aufidius thus   20
I will appear, and fight.
Lart.   Now the fair goddess, Fortune,
Fall deep in love with thee; and her great charms
Misguide thy opposers' swords!   Bold gentleman,
Prosperity be thy page!
Mar.   Thy friend no less

25. **proof:** stout.   30. **south:** south wind (pestilential).   38. **Mend:** reform your lines.   43. **seconds:** helpers.   47. **th'**
pot: i.e., destruction.   57. [**Cato's**] (Theobald).   *Calves* F.   62. **make ... alike:** stay to share his fate.
Sc. v, 5. **movers:** looters.   6. **drachma:** Greek coin.   7. **of a doit:** worth a doit (small coin).   19. **physical:** healthful.

Than those she placeth highest! So, farewell. 25
  Lart. Thou worthiest Marcius! [*Exit Marcius.*]
Go sound thy trumpet in the market-place;
Call thither all the officers o' th' town,
Where they shall know our mind. Away! [*Exeunt.*

[SCENE VI. *Near the camp of Cominius.*]

Enter COMINIUS, *as it were in retire, with soldiers.*

  Com. Breathe you, my friends; well fought. We
    are come off
Like Romans, neither foolish in our stands
Nor cowardly in retire. Believe me, sirs,
We shall be charg'd again. Whiles we have struck,
By interims and conveying gusts we have heard 5
The charges of our friends. [Ye] Roman gods!
Lead their successes as we wish our own,
That both our powers, with smiling fronts en-
    count'ring,
May give you thankful sacrifice.

Enter a MESSENGER.

                       Thy news?
  Mess. The citizens of Corioli have issued 10
And given to Lartius and to Marcius battle.
I saw our party to their trenches driven,
And then I came away.
  Com.   Though thou speak'st truth,
Methinks thou speak'st not well. How long is't
    since?
  Mess. Above an hour, my lord. 15
  Com. 'Tis not a mile; briefly we heard their
    drums.
How couldst thou in a mile confound an hour
And bring thy news so late?
  Mess.   Spies of the Volsces
Held me in chase, that I was forc'd to wheel
Three or four miles about, else had I, sir, 20
Half an hour since brought my report.

Enter MARCIUS.

  Com.   Who's yonder,
That does appear as he were flay'd? O gods!
He has the stamp of Marcius; and I have
Before-time seen him thus.
  Mar.   Come I too late?
  Com. The shepherd knows not thunder from a
    tabor 25
More than I know the sound of Marcius' tongue
From every meaner man.
  Mar.   Come I too late?
  Com. Ay, if you come not in the blood of others,
But mantled in your own.
  Mar.   O, let me clip ye

In arms as sound as when I woo'd, in heart 30
As merry as when our nuptial day was done
And tapers burn'd to bedward!
  Com.   Flower of warriors,
How is't with Titus Lartius?
  Mar. As with a man busied about decrees:
Condemning some to death, and some to exile; 35
Ransoming him, or pitying, threat'ning th' other;
Holding Corioli in the name of Rome,
Even like a fawning greyhound in the leash,
To let him slip at will.
  Com.   Where is that slave
Which told me they had beat you to your trenches?
Where is he? Call him hither.
  Mar.   Let him alone; 41
He did inform the truth. But for our gentlemen, —
The common file — a plague! tribunes for them! —
The mouse ne'er shunn'd the cat as they did budge
From rascals worse than they.
  Com.   But how prevail'd you? 45
  Mar. Will the time serve to tell? I do not think.
Where is the enemy? Are you lords o' th' field?
If not, why cease you till you are so?
  Com.   Marcius,
We have at disadvantage fought, and did
Retire to win our purpose. 50
  Mar. How lies their battle? Know you on which
    side
They have plac'd their men of trust?
  Com.   As I guess, Marcius,
Their bands i' th' vaward are the [Antiates],
Of their best trust; o'er them Aufidius,
Their very heart of hope.
  Mar.   I do beseech you, 55
By all the battles wherein we have fought,
By th' blood we have shed together, by the vows
We have made to endure friends, that you directly
Set me against Aufidius and his Antiates;
And that you not delay the present, but, 60
Filling the air with swords advanc'd and darts,
We prove this very hour.
  Com.   Though I could wish
You were conducted to a gentle bath
And balms applied to you, yet dare I never
Deny your asking. Take your choice of those 65
That best can aid your action.
  Mar.   Those are they
That most are willing. If any such be here —
As it were sin to doubt — that love this painting
Wherein you see me smear'd; if any fear
[Lesser] his person than an ill report; 70
If any think brave death outweighs bad life,
And that his country's dearer than himself;
Let him alone, or so many so minded,

  Sc. vi, 5. By . . . gusts: at intervals, by gusts of wind. **6.** [Ye] (Hanmer). *The* F. **16. briefly:** a short time ago. **17.
confound:** waste. **25. tabor:** small drum. **29. clip:** embrace. **53. vaward:** vanguard. **[Antiates]** (Pope). *Antients* F.
60. present: i.e., affair. **62. prove:** try out. **70. [Lesser]** F₃: less. *Lessen* F₁. **person:** personal harm.

Wave thus, to express his disposition
And follow Marcius.   75
       [They all shout and wave their swords,
           take him up in their arms, and cast up
           their caps.
O, me alone, make you a sword of me?
If these shows be not outward, which of you
But is four Volsces? None of you but is
Able to bear against the great Aufidius
A shield as hard as his. A certain number,   80
Though thanks to all, must I select from all; the rest
Shall bear the business in some other fight,
As cause will be obey'd. Please you to march;
And four shall quickly draw out my command,
Which men are best inclin'd.
  Com.   March on, my fellows! 85
Make good this ostentation, and you shall
Divide in all with us.   *[Exeunt.*

[SCENE VII. *The gates of Corioli.*]

TITUS LARTIUS, *having set a guard upon Corioli,*
going with drum and trumpet toward Cominius and
Caius Marcius, enters with a LIEUTENANT, *other*
Soldiers, and a Scout.

  Lart. So, let the ports be guarded; keep your
     duties,
As I have set them down. If I do send, dispatch
Those centuries to our aid; the rest will serve
For a short holding. If we lose the field,
We cannot keep the town.
  Lieu.   Fear not our care, sir.
  Lart. Hence, and shut your gates upon 's.   6
Our guider, come; to th' Roman camp conduct us.
                               [Exeunt.

[SCENE VIII. *A field of battle.*]

Alarum as in battle. Enter MARCIUS *and* AU-
FIDIUS *at several doors.*

  Mar. I'll fight with none but thee, for I do hate
     thee
Worse than a promise-breaker.
  Auf.   We hate alike.
Not Afric owns a serpent I abhor
More than thy fame and envy. Fix thy foot.
  Mar. Let the first budger die the other's slave, 5
And the gods doom him after!
  Auf.   If I fly, Marcius,
Holloa me like a hare.
  Mar.   Within these three hours, Tullus,
Alone I fought in your Corioli walls

And made what work I pleas'd. 'Tis not my blood
Wherein thou seest me mask'd; for thy revenge 10
Wrench up thy power to th' highest.
  Auf.   Wert thou the Hector
That was the whip of your bragg'd progeny,
Thou shouldst not scape me here.
       [Here they fight, and certain Volsces come in
          the aid of Aufidius. Marcius fights till
          they be driven in breathless.
Officious, and not valiant, you have sham'd me
In your condemned seconds.   *[Exeunt.]* 15

[SCENE IX. *The Roman camp.*]

Flourish. Alarum. A retreat is sounded. Enter,
   at one door, COMINIUS *with the* Romans; *at another*
   door, MARCIUS, *with his arm in a scarf.*

  Com. If I should tell thee o'er this thy day's work,
Thou'lt not believe thy deeds; but I'll report it
Where senators shall mingle tears with smiles,
Where great patricians shall attend and shrug,
I' th' end admire, where ladies shall be frighted 5
And, gladly quak'd, hear more; where the dull
    tribunes,
That with the fusty plebeians hate thine honours,
Shall say against their hearts, "We thank the gods
Our Rome hath such a soldier."
Yet cam'st thou to a morsel of this feast,   10
Having fully din'd before.

  Enter TITUS [LARTIUS], *with his power, from the*
             pursuit.

  Lart.   O General,
Here is the steed, we the caparison.
Hadst thou beheld —
  Mar.   Pray now, no more. My mother,
Who has a charter to extol her blood,   14
When she does praise me grieves me. I have
    done
As you have done, that's what I can; induc'd
As you have been, that's for my country.
He that has but effected his good will
Hath overta'en mine act.
  Com.   You shall not be   19
The grave of your deserving; Rome must know
The value of her own. 'Twere a concealment
Worse than a theft, no less than a traducement,
To hide your doings and to silence that
Which, to the spire and top of praises vouch'd,
Would seem but modest; therefore, I beseech you —
In sign of what you are, not to reward   26
What you have done — before our army hear me.

---

83. **cause:** occasion.
  Sc. vii, 1. **ports:** gates. 3. **centuries:** companies.
  Sc. viii, 12. **of ... progeny:** possessed by your boasted ancestry (the Trojans). 15. **seconds:** support.
  Sc. ix, 4. **attend and shrug:** listen incredulously. 5. **admire:** be amazed. 6. **quak'd:** trembling. 7. **fusty:** mouldy.
12. **caparison:** trappings. 22. **traducement:** calumny.

Mar.   I have some wounds upon me, and they
     smart
To hear themselves remem'red.
     Com.   Should they not,
Well might they fester 'gainst ingratitude,   30
And tent themselves with death.   Of all the horses,
Whereof we have ta'en good and good store, of all
The treasure in this field achiev'd and city,
We render you the tenth, to be ta'en forth,
Before the common distribution, at   35
Your only choice.
     Mar.   I thank you, General;
But cannot make my heart consent to take
A bribe to pay my sword.   I do refuse it,
And stand upon my common part with those
That have beheld the doing.   40
     [*A long flourish.   They all cry, "Marcius!*
       Marcius!" cast up their caps and lances.
       Cominius and Lartius stand bare.
May these same instruments, which you profane,
Never sound more!   When drums and trumpets
     shall
I' th' field prove flatterers, let courts and cities be
Made all of false-fac'd soothing!
When steel grows soft as the parasite's silk,   45
Let him be made [a coverture] for th' wars!
No more, I say!   For that I have not wash'd
My nose that bled, or foil'd some debile wretch, —
Which, without note, here's many else have done, —
You [shout] me forth   50
In acclamations hyperbolical,
As if I lov'd my little should be dieted
In praises sauc'd with lies.
     Com.   Too modest are you;
More cruel to your good report than grateful
To us that give you truly.   By your patience,   55
If 'gainst yourself you be incens'd, we'll put you,
Like one that means his proper harm, in manacles,
Then reason safely with you.   Therefore be it
     known,
As to us, to all the world, that Caius Marcius
Wears this war's garland; in token of the which,   60
My noble steed, known to the camp, I give him
With all his trim belonging; and from this time,
For what he did before Corioli, call him,
With all th' applause and clamour of the host,
[CAIUS MARCIUS] CORIOLANUS!   Bear   65
Th' addition nobly ever!
     [*Flourish.   Trumpets sound, and drums.*
     All. [Caius Marcius] Coriolanus!
     Cor.   I will go wash;

And when my face is fair, you shall perceive
Whether I blush or no; howbeit, I thank you.   70
I mean to stride your steed, and at all times
To undercrest your good addition
To th' fairness of my power.
     Com.   So, to our tent;
Where, ere we do repose us, we will write
To Rome of our success.   You, Titus Lartius,   75
Must to Corioli back, send us to Rome
The best, with whom we may articulate
For their own good and ours.
     Lart.   I shall, my lord.
     Cor.   The gods begin to mock me.   I, that now
Refus'd most princely gifts, am bound to beg   80
Of my Lord General.
     Com.   Take't; 'tis yours.   What is't?
     Cor.   I sometime lay here in Corioli
At a poor man's house; he us'd me kindly.
He cried to me, — I saw him prisoner, —
But then Aufidius was within my view,   85
And wrath o'erwhelm'd my pity.   I request you
To give my poor host freedom.
     Com.   O well begg'd!
Were he the butcher of my son, he should
Be free as is the wind.   Deliver him, Titus.
     Lart.   Marcius, his name?
     Cor.   By Jupiter! forgot.
I am weary; yea, my memory is tir'd.   91
Have we no wine here?
     Com.   Go we to our tent.
The blood upon your visage dries; 'tis time
It should be look'd to.   Come.   [*Exeunt.*

[SCENE X.   *The camp of the Volsces.*]

A flourish.   Cornets.   Enter TULLUS AUFIDIUS,
     bloody, with two or three SOLDIERS.

     Auf.   The town is ta'en!
     [*1.*] *Sol.*   'Twill be deliver'd back on good condi-
     tion.
     Auf.   Condition!
I would I were a Roman; for I cannot,
Being a Volsce, be that I am.   Condition!   5
What good condition can a treaty find
I' th' part that is at mercy?   Five times, Marcius,
I have fought with thee; so often hast thou beat me,
And wouldst do so, I think, should we encounter
As often as we eat.   By th' elements,   10
If e'er again I meet him beard to beard,
He's mine, or I am his.   Mine emulation

---

31. **tent**: cure.   32. **good store**: plenty.   44. **soothing**: flattery.   44–51. Some edd. rearrange, beginning the lines with *Made, Soft, A, For, Or, Here's, In.*   46. **him**: perhaps *it*, but the passage is probably corrupt.   [**a coverture**] (Tyrwhitt). *an Overture* F.   48. **foil'd**: defeated.   **debile**: weak.   55. **give**: report.   57. **proper**: own.   65, 67. [CAIUS MARTIUS] (Rowe). *Marcus Caius* F (also II.i.181).   72. **undercrest**: wear as a crest.   **addition**: title.   73. **fairness . . . power**: best of my ability. 77. **articulate**: discuss terms.
     Sc. x, 2, etc.   [*1.*] *Sol.*   (Capell).   *Sol.* F.   **condition**: terms.   7. **part . . . mercy**: conquered side.   12. **emulation**: rivalry.

Hath not that honour in't it had; for where
I thought to crush him in an equal force,
True sword to sword, I'll potch at him some way; 15
Or wrath or craft may get him.

   [*1.*] *Sol.*　　　　　　　　　　He's the devil.

   Auf. Bolder, though not so subtle. My valour's
poison'd
With only suff'ring stain by him; for him
Shall fly out of itself. Nor sleep nor sanctuary,
Being naked, sick, nor fane nor Capitol, 20
The prayers of priests nor times of sacrifice,
Embargements all of fury, shall lift up
Their rotten privilege and custom 'gainst
My hate to Marcius. Where I find him, were
it
At home, upon my brother's guard, even there, 25
Against the hospitable canon, would I
Wash my fierce hand in 's heart. Go you to th'
city;
Learn how 'tis held, and what they are that must
Be hostages for Rome.

   [*1.*] *Sol.*　　　　　　Will not you go?

   Auf. I am attended at the cypress grove. I
pray you — 30
'Tis south the city mills — bring me word thither
How the world goes, that to the pace of it
I may spur on my journey.

   [*1.*] *Sol.*　　　　　　　I shall, sir.

                       [*Exeunt.*]

ACT II

[SCENE I. *Rome. A public place.*]

Enter MENENIUS, *with the two Tribunes of the people,*
SICINIUS *and* BRUTUS.

   Men. The augurer tells me we shall have news
to-night.

   Bru. Good or bad?

   Men. Not according to the prayer of the people,
for they love not Marcius. 5

   Sic. Nature teaches beasts to know their friends.

   Men. Pray you, who does the wolf love?

   Sic. The lamb.

   Men. Ay, to devour him; as the hungry plebeians
would the noble Marcius. 11

   Bru. He's a lamb indeed, that baes like a
bear.

   Men. He's a bear indeed, that lives like a
lamb. You two are old men: tell me one thing that
I shall ask you. 16

   Both. Well, sir.

   Men. In what enormity is Marcius poor in, that
you two have not in abundance?

   Bru. He's poor in no one fault, but stor'd with
all. 21

   Sic. Especially in pride.

   Bru. And topping all others in boasting.

   Men. This is strange now. Do you two know
how you are censured here in the city, I mean of
us o' th' right-hand file? Do you? 26

   Both. Why, how are we censur'd?

   Men. Because you talk of pride now, — will you
not be angry?

   Both. Well, well, sir, well. 30

   Men. Why, 'tis no great matter; for a very little
thief of occasion will rob you of a great deal of
patience. Give your dispositions the reins and be
angry at your pleasures; at the least, if you take it
as a pleasure to you in being so. You blame
Marcius for being proud? 36

   Bru. We do it not alone, sir.

   Men. I know you can do very little alone, for
your helps are many, or else your actions would
grow wondrous single; your abilities are too 40
infant-like for doing much alone. You talk of pride:
O that you could turn your eyes toward the napes
of your necks and make but an interior survey of
your good selves! O that you could!

   Both. What then, sir? 45

   Men. Why, then you should discover a brace of
unmeriting, proud, violent, testy magistrates, alias
fools, as any in Rome.

   Sic. Menenius, you are known well enough
too. 50

   Men. I am known to be a humorous patrician,
and one that loves a cup of hot wine with not a drop
of allaying Tiber in't; said to be something imperfect in favouring the first complaint; hasty and
tinder-like upon too trivial motion; one that con- 55
verses more with the buttock of the night than with
the forehead of the morning. What I think, I utter,
and spend my malice in my breath. Meeting two
such wealsmen as you are — I cannot call you
Lycurguses — if the drink you give me touch 60
my palate adversely, I make a crooked face at it.
I [can't] say your worships have deliver'd the matter
well, when I find the ass in compound with the major
part of your syllables; and though I must be content
to bear with those that say you are reverend 65
grave men, yet they lie deadly that tell you have
good faces. If you see this in the map of my
microcosm, follows it that I am known well enough

---

15. **potch**: stab. 19. **fly out of itself**: change its nature. 20. **fane**: temple. 22. **Embargements**: impediments. 25. **upon**: under. 26. **hospitable canon**: law of hospitality. 30. **attended**: awaited.
   Act II, sc. i, 25. **censured**: estimated. 26. **right-hand file**: upper class. 40. **single**: feeble. 51. **humorous**: whimsical. 53. **allaying Tiber**: i.e., diluting water. 54. **in... complaint**: i.e., without hearing the other side. 55. **tinder-like**: inflammable. 55. **motion**: cause. 59. **wealsmen**: statesmen. 60. **Lycurguses**. Lycurgus was a famous Spartan law-giver. 62. **[can't]** (Theobald). *can* F. 67–68. **map ... microcosm**: my face.

too? What harm can your [bisson] conspectuities
glean out of this character, if I be known well
enough too?   72
  Bru. Come, sir, come, we know you well enough.
  Men. You know neither me, yourselves, nor anything. You are ambitious for poor knaves' caps and
legs. You wear out a good wholesome forenoon in
hearing a cause between an orange-wife and a
faucet-seller and then rejourn the controversy of
three pence to a second day of audience. When 80
you are hearing a matter between party and party,
if you chance to be pinch'd with the colic, you make
faces like mummers, set up the bloody flag against
all patience, and, in roaring for a chamber-pot, dismiss the controversy bleeding, the more entan- 85
gled by your hearing. All the peace you make in
their cause is calling both the parties knaves. You
are a pair of strange ones.   89
  Bru. Come, come, you are well understood to be
a perfecter giber for the table than a necessary
bencher in the Capitol.
  Men. Our very priests must become mockers if
they shall encounter such ridiculous subjects as 94
you are. When you speak best unto the purpose,
it is not worth the wagging of your beards; and
your beards deserve not so honourable a grave as
to stuff a botcher's cushion, or to be entomb'd in
an ass's pack-saddle. Yet you must be saying
Marcius is proud; who, in a cheap estimation, is 100
worth all your predecessors since Deucalion, though
peradventure some of the best of 'em were hereditary hangmen. God-den to your worships. More
of your conversation would infect my brain, being
the herdsmen of the beastly plebeians. I will be
bold to take my leave of you.   105
              [*Brutus and Sicinius go aside.*

Enter VOLUMNIA, VIRGILIA, *and* VALERIA.
How now, my as fair as noble ladies — and the
moon, were she earthly, no nobler — whither do
you follow your eyes so fast?   109
  Vol. Honourable Menenius, my boy Marcius
approaches. For the love of Juno, let's go.
  Men. Ha! Marcius coming home?
  Vol. Ay, worthy Menenius; and with most prosperous approbation.
  Men. Take my cap, Jupiter, [*tosses it up*] and I
thank thee. Hoo! Marcius coming home!   116
  2 Ladies. Nay, 'tis true.
  Vol. Look, here's a letter from him; the state
hath another, his wife another, and, I think, there's
one at home for you.   120

  Men. I will make my very house reel to-night.
A letter for me!
  Vir. Yes, certain, there's a letter for you; I
saw 't.   124
  Men. A letter for me! it gives me an estate of
seven years' health, in which time I will make a lip
at the physician. The most sovereign prescription
in Galen is but empiricutic and, to this preservative,
of no better report than a horse-drench. Is he not
wounded? He was wont to come home wounded.
  Vir. O, no, no, no.   132
  Vol. O, he is wounded; I thank the gods
for't.
  Men. So do I too, if it be not too much. Brings
'a victory in his pocket? The wounds become
him.   136
  Vol. On 's brows. Menenius, he comes the third
time home with the oaken garland.
  Men. Has he disciplin'd Aufidius soundly?
  Vol. Titus Lartius writes they fought together,
but Aufidius got off.   141
  Men. And 'twas time for him too, I'll warrant
him that. An he had stay'd by him, I would not
have been so fidius'd for all the chests in Corioli,
and the gold that's in them. Is the Senate possess'd
of this?   146
  Vol. Good ladies, let's go. — Yes, yes, yes; the
Senate has letters from the General, wherein he
gives my son the whole name of the war. He hath
in this action outdone his former deeds doubly. 151
  Val. In troth, there's wondrous things spoke of
him.
  Men. Wondrous! ay, I warrant you, and not
without his true purchasing.   155
  Vir. The gods grant them true!
  Vol. True! pow, wow.
  Men. True! I'll be sworn they are true. Where
is he wounded? [*To the Tribunes.*] God save your
good worships! Marcius is coming home; he has
more cause to be proud. — Where is he wounded? 162
  Vol. I' th' shoulder and i' th' left arm. There
will be large cicatrices to show the people, when he
shall stand for his place. He received in the repulse
of Tarquin seven hurts i' th' body.   166
  Men. One i' th' neck, and two i' th' thigh, —
there's nine that I know.
  Vol. He had, before this last expedition, twenty-
five wounds upon him.   170
  Men. Now it's twenty-seven; every gash was an
enemy's grave. Hark! the trumpets.
                        [*A shout and flourish.*]
  Vol. These are the ushers of Marcius; before him

70. [bisson] (Theobald): blind. *beesome* F. conspectuities: vision. 75–76. caps and legs: bowings and scrapings. 79.
rejourn: adjourn. 83. mummers: masked players. bloody flag: banner of war. 92. bencher: senator. 98. botcher:
mender of old clothes. 101. Deucalion: the classical Noah. 103. God-den: good evening. 114. most...approbation:
greatest triumph. 126. lip: grimace. 128. Galen: famous Greek physician (2d cent. A.D.). empiricutic: quackish. 144.
fidius'd: in Aufidius's place. 149. name: honor. 164. cicatrices: scars.

he carries noise, and behind him he leaves tears. 176
Death, that dark spirit, in 's nervy arm doth lie,
Which, being advanc'd, declines, and then men die.

A sennet. Trumpets sound. Enter COMINIUS *the
General, and* TITUS LARTIUS; *between them,* CORIO-
LANUS, *crown'd with an oaken garland; with Cap-
tains and Soldiers, and a* HERALD.

Her. Know, Rome, that all alone Marcius did
    fight
Within Corioli gates; where he hath won,   180
With fame, a name to [Caius Marcius]; these
In honour follows Coriolanus.
Welcome to Rome, renowned Coriolanus!
                           [Flourish.
 All. Welcome to Rome, renowned Coriolanus!
 Cor. No more of this; it does offend my heart.
Pray now, no more.
   Com.   Look, sir, your mother!
 Cor.   O, 186
You have, I know, petition'd all the gods
For my prosperity!   *[Kneels.*
 Vol.   Nay, my good soldier, up;
My gentle Marcius, worthy Caius, and
By deed-achieving honour newly nam'd, —   190
What is it? — Coriolanus must I call thee? —
But, O, thy wife!
 Cor.   My gracious silence, hail!
Wouldst thou have laugh'd had I come coffin'd
    home,
That weep'st to see me triumph? Ah, my dear,
Such eyes the widows in Corioli wear,   195
And mothers that lack sons.
   Men.   Now, the gods crown thee!
 [*Cor.*] And live you yet? [*To Valeria.*] O my
    sweet lady, pardon.
 Vol. I know not where to turn. O, welcome
    home;
And welcome, General; and you're welcome all.
 Men. A hundred thousand welcomes! I could
    weep   200
And I could laugh; I am light and heavy. Welcome!
A curse begin at very root on 's heart,
That is not glad to see thee! You are three
That Rome should dote on; yet, by the faith of men,
We have some old crab-trees here at home that will
    not   205
Be grafted to your relish. Yet welcome, warriors;
We call a nettle but a nettle and
The faults of fools but folly.
  Com.   Ever right.

 Cor. Menenius ever, ever.
 Her. Give way there, and go on!
 Cor. [*To Volumnia and Virgilia.*] Your hand,
    and yours.   210
Ere in our own house I do shade my head,
The good patricians must be visited;
From whom I have receiv'd not only greetings,
But with them change of honours.
 Vol.   I have liv'd
To see inherited my very wishes   215
And the buildings of my fancy; only
There's one thing wanting, which I doubt not but
Our Rome will cast upon thee.
  Cor.   Know, good mother,
I had rather be their servant in my way
Than sway with them in theirs.
  Com.   On, to the Capitol!
    [*Flourish. Cornets. Exeunt in state, as
        before. Brutus and Sicinius [come for-
        ward].*
 Bru. All tongues speak of him, and the bleared
    sights   221
Are spectacled to see him. Your prattling nurse
Into a rapture lets her baby cry
While she chats him; the kitchen Malkin pins
Her richest lockram 'bout her reechy neck,   225
Clamb'ring the walls to eye him; stalls, bulks,
    windows,
Are smother'd up, leads fill'd, and ridges hors'd
With variable complexions, all agreeing
In earnestness to see him. Seld-shown flamens
Do press among the popular throngs and puff 230
To win a vulgar station; our veil'd dames
Commit the war of white and damask in
Their nicely-gawded cheeks to th' wanton spoil
Of Phœbus' burning kisses; — such a pother
As if that whatsoever god who leads him   235
Were slily crept into his human powers
And gave him graceful posture.
 Sic.   On the sudden,
I warrant him consul.
 Bru.   Then our office may,
During his power, go sleep.
 Sic. He cannot temp'rately transport his honours
From where he should begin and end, but will 241
Lose those he hath won.
 Bru.   In that there's comfort.
 Sic.   Doubt not
The commoners, for whom we stand, but they
Upon their ancient malice will forget   244
With the least cause these his new honours, which

---

177. **nervy:** sinewy. 178. **advanc'd:** raised. **declines:** descends. 179. S.D. *sennet:* trumpet signal. 197. [*Cor.*] *Com.*
F. 201. **light and heavy:** merry and sad. 214. **change of honours:** fresh honors. 215. **inherited:** realized. 220. **sway:**
rule. 223. **rapture:** fit. 224. **chats:** chats about. **Malkin:** slattern. 225. **lockram:** linen. **reechy:** filthy. 226. **bulks:**
stalls. 227. **leads:** leaded roofs. **hors'd:** bestridden. 228. **variable complexions:** all sorts of people. 229. **flamens:**
priests. 230. **popular:** vulgar. 233. **nicely-gawded:** daintily decorated. 234. **Phœbus'... kisses:** the blazing sun.
245. **which:** which cause.

That he will give them make I as little question
As he is proud to do't.
   Bru.   I heard him swear,
Were he to stand for consul, never would he
Appear i' th' market-place, nor on him put
The napless vesture of humility,   250
Nor, showing, as the manner is, his wounds
To th' people, beg their stinking breaths.
   Sic.   'Tis right.
   Bru. It was his word.   O, he would miss it rather
Than carry it but by the suit of the gentry to him
And the desire of the nobles.
   Sic.   I wish no better 255
Than have him hold that purpose and to put it
In execution.
   Bru.   'Tis most like he will.
   Sic. It shall be to him then as our good wills,
A sure destruction.
   Bru.   So it must fall out
To him or our authorities for an end.   260
We must suggest the people in what hatred
He still hath held them; that to 's power he would
Have made them mules, silenc'd their pleaders, and
Dispropertied their freedoms, holding them,
In human action and capacity,   265
Of no more soul nor fitness for the world
Than camels in [the] war, who have their provand
Only for bearing burdens, and sore blows
For sinking under them.
   Sic.   This, as you say, suggested
At some time when his soaring insolence   270
Shall [touch] the people — which time shall not
     want,
If he be put upon 't; and that's as easy
As to set dogs on sheep — will be his fire
To kindle their dry stubble; and their blaze
Shall darken him for ever.

Enter a MESSENGER.

   Bru.   What's the matter?
   Mess. You are sent for to the Capitol.   'Tis
     thought   276
That Marcius shall be consul.
I have seen the dumb men throng to see him, and
The blind to hear him speak.   Matrons flung gloves,
Ladies and maids their scarfs and handkerchers 280
Upon him as he pass'd; the nobles bended,
As to Jove's statue, and the commons made
A shower and thunder with their caps and shouts.
I never saw the like.
   Bru.   Let's to the Capitol;
And carry with us ears and eyes for th' time,

But hearts for the event.
   Sic.   Have with you. 286
[*Exeunt.*

[SCENE II.   *The same.*]   *The Capitol.*

Enter two OFFICERS, *to lay cushions.*

   1. Off. Come, come, they are almost here.   How
many stand for consulships?
   2. Off. Three, they say; but 'tis thought of every
one Coriolanus will carry it.   4
   1. Off. That's a brave fellow; but he's vengeance
proud, and loves not the common people.
   2. Off. Faith, there hath been many great men
that have flatter'd the people, who ne'er loved
them; and there be many that they have loved, 10
they know not wherefore; so that, if they love they
know not why, they hate upon no better a ground.
Therefore, for Coriolanus neither to care whether
they love or hate him manifests the true knowledge
he has in their disposition, and out of his noble carelessness lets them plainly see 't.   17
   1. Off. If he did not care whether he had their
love or no, he waved indifferently 'twixt doing them
neither good nor harm; but he seeks their hate with
greater devotion than they can render it him, 21
and leaves nothing undone that may fully discover
him their opposite.   Now, to seem to affect the
malice and displeasure of the people is as bad as
that which he dislikes, to flatter them for their love.
   2. Off. He hath deserved wortnily of his country;
and his ascent is not by such easy degrees as those
who, having been supple and courteous to the
people, bonneted, without any further deed to have
them at all into their estimation and report. 31
But he hath so planted his honours in their eyes
and his actions in their hearts that for their tongues
to be silent and not confess so much were a kind
of ingrateful injury; to report otherwise were a 35
malice that, giving itself the lie, would pluck reproof
and rebuke from every ear that heard it.
   1. Off. No more of him; he's a worthy man.
Make way, they are coming.   40

A sennet.   Enter, with Lictors before them, COMINIUS
the consul, MENENIUS, CORIOLANUS, SENATORS,
SICINIUS *and* BRUTUS.   *The Senators take their
places; the Tribunes take their places by themselves.
Coriolanus stands.*

   Men. Having determin'd of the Volsces and
To send for Titus Lartius, it remains,
As the main point of this our after-meeting,

<hr>

250. **napless:** threadbare.   258. **as ... wills:** as we desire.   260. **for an end:** ultimately.   262. **still:** ever.   264. **Dis-**
propertied: robbed them of.   267. [**the**] (Hanmer).   *their* F.   **provand:** provender.   271. [**touch**] (Hanmer).   *teach* F.
want: be lacking.   286. **event:** outcome.

Sc. ii, 5. **vengeance:** desperately.   8. **who:** i.e., the people.   19. **waved:** wavered.   22. **discover:** show.   23. **opposite:**
adversary.   **affect:** desire.   30. **bonneted:** doffed their caps.

To gratify his noble service that
Hath thus stood for his country; therefore, please
    you, 45
Most reverend and grave elders, to desire
The present consul and last general
In our well-found successes, to report
A little of that worthy work perform'd
By [Caius Marcius] Coriolanus, whom 50
We met here both to thank and to remember
With honours like himself.   [*Coriolanus sits.*]
  1. Sen.   Speak, good Cominius:
Leave nothing out for length, and make us think
Rather our state's defective for requital
Than we to stretch it out.   [*To the Tribunes.*]
       Masters o' th' people, 55
We do request your kindest ears, and after,
Your loving motion toward the common body
To yield what passes here.
  Sic.   We are convented
Upon a pleasing treaty, and have hearts
Inclinable to honour and advance 60
The theme of our assembly.
  Bru.   Which the rather
We shall be blest to do, if he remember
A kinder value of the people than
He hath hereto priz'd them at.
  Men.   That's off, that's off;
I would you rather had been silent. Please you 65
To hear Cominius speak?
  Bru.   Most willingly;
But yet my caution was more pertinent
Than the rebuke you give it.
  Men.   He loves your people;
But tie him not to be their bedfellow.
Worthy Cominius, speak. (*Coriolanus rises and*
    offers to go away.) Nay, keep your place. 70
  [*1.*] *Sen.* Sit, Coriolanus; never shame to hear
What you have nobly done.
  Cor.   Your honours' pardon;
I had rather have my wounds to heal again
Than hear say how I got them.
  Bru.   Sir, I hope
My words disbench'd you not.
  Cor.   No, sir; yet oft, 75
When blows have made me stay, I fled from words.
You sooth'd not, therefore hurt not; but your people,
I love them as they weigh.
  Men.   Pray now, sit down.
  Cor. I had rather have one scratch my head i'
    th' sun

When the alarum were struck, than idly sit   80
To hear my nothings monster'd.   [*Exit.*
  Men.   Masters of the people,
Your multiplying spawn how can he flatter —
That's thousand to one good one — when you now
    see
He had rather venture all his limbs for honour
Than [one on 's] ears to hear it? Proceed, Co-
    minius.   85
  Com. I shall lack voice; the deeds of Coriolanus
Should not be utter'd feebly. It is held
That valour is the chiefest virtue and
Most dignifies the haver; if it be,
The man I speak of cannot in the world   90
Be singly counterpois'd. At sixteen years,
When Tarquin made a head for Rome, he fought
Beyond the mark of others. Our then dictator,
Whom with all praise I point at, saw him fight,
When with his Amazonian [chin] he drove   95
The bristled lips before him. He bestrid
An o'er-press'd Roman, and i' th' consul's view
Slew three opposers. Tarquin's self he met,
And struck him on his knee. In that day's feats,
When he might act the woman in the scene,   100
He prov'd best man i' th' field, and for his meed
Was brow-bound with the oak. His pupil age
Man-ent'red thus, he waxed like a sea,
And in the brunt of seventeen battles since
He lurch'd all swords of the garland. For this
    last,   105
Before and in Corioli, let me say,
I cannot speak him home. He stopp'd the fliers,
And by his rare example made the coward
Turn terror into sport; as weeds before
A vessel under sail, so men obey'd   110
And fell below his stem. His sword, death's stamp,
Where it did mark, it took; from face to foot
He was a thing of blood, whose every motion
Was tim'd with dying cries. Alone he ent'red
The mortal gate of th' city, which he painted   115
With shunless destiny; aidless came off,
And with a sudden reinforcement struck
Corioli like a planet; now all's his.
When, by and by, the din of war 'gan pierce
His ready sense, then straight his doubled spirit
Re-quick'ned what in flesh was fatigate,   121
And to the battle came he, where he did
Run reeking o'er the lives of men, as if
'Twere a perpetual spoil; and till we call'd
Both field and city ours, he never stood   125

---

    44. **gratify:** reward.   47. **last:** late.   52. **like himself:** appropriate.   54–55. **Rather . . . out:** our state lacks means to reward him rather than we willingness to stretch those means.   58. **yield:** report.   **convented:** convened.   59. **treaty:** proposal.   62. **blest:** most happy.   64. **off:** amiss.   71. [*1.*] (Rowe). Om. F.   77. **sooth'd:** flattered.   78. **weigh:** are worthy.   85. [**one on 's**] F₂: one of his. *on ones* F₁.   91. **singly counterpois'd:** equalled by any one.   92. **made . . . for:** raised a force to attack.   95. **Amazonian:** i.e., beardless. [**chin**] F₃. *Shinne* F₁.   99. **on:** to.   100. **in the scene:** on the stage; alluding to the playing of female parts by boys.   105. **lurch'd:** robbed.   107. **speak him home:** praise him duly.   116. **shunless destiny:** the blood of the unavoidably doomed.   118. **planet.** A reference to the supposed malign influence of planets.   121. **fatigate:** fatigued.   124. **spoil:** slaughter.

To ease his breast with panting.

Men.   Worthy man!

[*1.*] *Sen.* He cannot but with measure fit the
    honours
Which we devise him.

Com.   Our spoils he kick'd at,
And look'd upon things precious as they were
The common muck of the world. He covets less 130
Than misery itself would give, rewards
His deeds with doing them, and is content
To spend the time to end it.

Men.   He's right noble.
Let him be call'd for.

[*1.*] *Sen.*   Call Coriolanus.

Off. He doth appear.   135

       Re-enter CORIOLANUS.

Men. The Senate, Coriolanus, are well pleas'd
To make thee consul.

Cor.   I do owe them still
My life and services.

Men.   It then remains
That you do speak to the people.

Cor.   I do beseech you,
Let me o'erleap that custom; for I cannot   140
Put on the gown, stand naked and entreat them
For my wounds' sake to give their suffrage. Please
    you
That I may pass this doing.

Sic.   Sir, the people
Must have their voices; neither will they bate
One jot of ceremony.

Men.   Put them not to't.   145
Pray you, go fit you to the custom and
Take to you, as your predecessors have,
Your honour with your form.

Cor.   It is a part
That I shall blush in acting, and might well
Be taken from the people.

Bru.   Mark you that?   150

Cor. To brag unto them, "Thus I did, and thus";
Show them th' unaching scars which I should
    hide,
As if I had receiv'd them for the hire
Of their breath only!

Men.   Do not stand upon 't.   154
We recommend to you, tribunes of the people,
Our purpose to them; and to our noble consul
Wish we all joy and honour.

Senators. To Coriolanus come all joy and honour!

    [*Flourish of cornets. Exeunt all but Sicinius*
        and Brutus.

Bru. You see how he intends to use the people.

Sic. May they perceive 's intent! He will require
    them   160
As if he did contemn what he requested
Should be in them to give.

Bru.   Come, we'll inform them
Of our proceedings here. On th' market-place,
I know, they do attend us.

                      [Exeunt.

[SCENE III.   *The same.   The Forum.*]

    Enter seven or eight CITIZENS.

1. Cit. Once if he do require our voices, we ought
not to deny him.

2. Cit. We may, sir, if we will.

3. Cit. We have power in ourselves to do it, but
it is a power that we have no power to do; for   5
if he show us his wounds and tell us his deeds, we
are to put our tongues into those wounds and speak
for them; so, if he tell us his noble deeds, we must
also tell him our noble acceptance of them. Ingratitude is monstrous, and for the multitude to   10
be ingrateful were to make a monster of the multitude; of the which we being members, should bring
ourselves to be monstrous members.   14

1. Cit. And to make us no better thought of, a
little help will serve; for once we stood up about
the corn, he himself stuck not to call us the many-
headed multitude.   18

3. Cit. We have been called so of many; not that
our heads are some brown, some black, some auburn,
some bald, but that our wits are so diversely colour'd;
and truly I think if all our wits were to issue out
of one skull, they would fly east, west, north, south,
and their consent of one direct way should be at
once to all the points o' th' compass.   26

2. Cit. Think you so? Which way do you judge
my wit would fly?

3. Cit. Nay, your wit will not so soon out as
another man's will, 'tis strongly wedg'd up in a
block-head; but if it were at liberty, 'twould, sure,
southward.   32

2. Cit. Why that way?

3. Cit. To lose itself in a fog, where being three
parts melted away with rotten dews, the fourth
would return for conscience' sake to help to get
thee a wife.

2. Cit. You are never without your tricks; you
may, you may.   39

3. Cit. Are you all resolv'd to give your voices?
But that's no matter, the greater part carries it.
I say, if he would incline to the people, there was
never a worthier man.

127, 134. [*1.*] (Rowe). Om. F.   127. **with measure:** becomingly.   133. **to end it:** to pass the time.   143. **pass:**
omit.   144. **voices:** votes.   148. **your form:** the usual formality.   154. **breath:** i.e., votes. **Do ... upon't:** don't insist.
155. **recommend:** entrust.   160. **require:** solicit.

Sc. iii, 17. **stuck:** hesitated.   25. **consent of:** agreement about.   42. **incline to:** favor.

Enter CORIOLANUS *in a gown of humility, with*
MENENIUS.

Here he comes, and in the gown of humility; mark
his behaviour. We are not to stay all together, 45
but to come by him where he stands, by ones, by
twos, and by threes. He's to make his requests by
particulars, wherein every one of us has a single
honour, in giving him our own voices with our own
tongues; therefore follow me, and I'll direct you how
you shall go by him.   52
All. Content, content.   [*Exeunt citizens.*]
Men. O sir, you are not right. Have you not
     known
The worthiest men have done 't?
Cor.   What must I say?
"I pray, sir," — Plague upon 't! I cannot bring 56
My tongue to such a pace, — "look, sir, my wounds!
I got them in my country's service, when
Some certain of your brethren roar'd and ran
From the noise of our own drums."
Men.   O me, the gods!
You must not speak of that. You must desire them 61
To think upon you.
Cor.   Think upon me! Hang 'em!
I would they would forget me, like the virtues
Which our divines lose by 'em.
Men.   You'll mar all.
I'll leave you. Pray you, speak to 'em, I pray you,
In wholesome manner.   [*Exit.* 66

Re-enter three of the CITIZENS.

Cor.   Bid them wash their faces
And keep their teeth clean. So, here comes a brace. —
You know the cause, sir, of my standing here.
3. Cit. We do, sir; tell us what hath brought you
to 't.   70
Cor. Mine own desert.
2. Cit. Your own desert!
Cor. Ay, [not] mine own desire.
3. Cit. How not your own desire?
Cor. No, sir, 'twas never my desire yet to trouble
the poor with begging.   76
3. Cit. You must think, if we give you anything,
we hope to gain by you.
Cor. Well then, I pray, your price o' th' consul
ship?   80
1. Cit. The price is to ask it kindly.
Cor. Kindly, sir, I pray, let me ha 't. I have
wounds to show you, which shall be yours in private.
Your good voice, sir; what say you?
2. Cit. You shall ha' it, worthy sir.   85
Cor. A match, sir. There's in all two worthy
voices begg'd. I have your alms; adieu.

3. Cit. But this is something odd.
2. Cit. An't were to give again, — but 'tis no
matter.   [*Exeunt [the three Citizens].*   90

Re-enter two other CITIZENS.

Cor. Pray you now, if it may stand with the tune
of your voices that I may be consul, I have here the
customary gown.
[4.] Cit. You have deserved nobly of your country, and you have not deserved nobly.   95
Cor. Your enigma?
[4.] Cit. You have been a scourge to her enemies,
you have been a rod to her friends; you have not
indeed loved the common people.   99
Cor. You should account me the more virtuous
that I have not been common in my love. I will,
sir, flatter my sworn brother, the people, to earn a
dearer estimation of them; 'tis a condition they
account gentle. And since the wisdom of their
choice is rather to have my hat than my heart, 105
I will practise the insinuating nod and be off to
them most counterfeitly; that is, sir, I will counterfeit the bewitchment of some popular man and give
it bountiful to the desirers. Therefore, beseech you,
I may be consul.   110
[5.] Cit. We hope to find you our friend; and
therefore give you our voices heartily.
[4.] Cit. You have received many wounds for
your country.   114
Cor. I will not seal your knowledge with showing
them. I will make much of your voices, and so
trouble you no further.
Both Cit. The gods give you joy, sir, heartily!
                                         [*Exeunt.*]

Cor. Most sweet voices!
Better it is to die, better to starve,   120
Than crave the hire which first we do deserve.
Why in this [woolless toge] should I stand here
To beg of Hob and Dick, that [do] appear,
Their needless vouches? Custom calls me to 't.
What custom wills, in all things should we do 't,
The dust on antique time would lie unswept, 126
And mountainous error be too highly heapt
For truth to o'er-peer. Rather than fool it so,
Let the high office and the honour go
To one that would do thus. — I am half through; 130
The one part suffer'd, th' other will I do.

Re-enter three CITIZENS *more.*

Here come moe voices. —
Your voices! For your voices I have fought;
Watch'd for your voices; for your voices bear

48. **by particulars:** to each in turn.   64. **lose by 'em:** lose their time preaching to them (because they neglect to practise them).   73. [not] F₃.   *but* F₁.   91. **stand:** accord.   94, 97, 113. **[4.]** (Camb. edd.).   *1.* F.   106. **be off:** doff my hat.   107. **counterfeitly:** hypocritically.   111. **[5.]** (Camb. edd.).   *2.* F.   122. [woolless] (Collier). Cf. *napless* II.i.250. *Wool-vish* F. [toge] (Steevens): toga. *tongue* F₁. *gowne* F₂₋₄.   123. [do] F₄. *does* F₁.   128. **fool it:** play the fool.   134. **Watch'd:** kept guard.

Of wounds two dozen odd; battles thrice six   135
I have seen and heard of; for your voices have
Done many things, some less, some more.   Your
     voices.
Indeed, I would be consul.
     [6.] Cit. He has done nobly, and cannot go with-
out any honest man's voice.   140
     [7.] Cit. Therefore let him be consul.   The gods
give him joy, and make him good friend to the
people!
     All Cit. Amen, amen.   God save thee, noble
     consul!   [Exeunt.]
     Cor. Worthy voices!   145

     Re-enter MENENIUS, with BRUTUS and SICINIUS.
     Men. You have stood your limitation, and the
     tribunes
Endue you with the people's voice.   Remains
That, in th' official marks invested, you
Anon do meet the Senate.
     Cor.   Is this done?
     Sic. The custom of request you have discharg'd.
The people do admit you, and are summon'd   151
To meet anon upon your approbation.
     Cor. Where?   At the Senate-house?
     Sic.   There, Coriolanus.
     Cor. May I change these garments?
     Sic.   You may, sir.
     Cor. That I'll straight do, and, knowing myself
     again,   155
Repair to th' Senate-house.
     Men. I'll keep you company.   Will you along?
     Bru. We stay here for the people.
     Sic.   Fare you well.
            [Exeunt Coriolanus and Menenius.
He has it now, and by his looks methinks
'Tis warm at 's heart.   160
     Bru. With a proud heart he wore his humble
     weeds.
Will you dismiss the people?

             Enter the PLEBEIANS.
     Sic. How now, my masters! have you chose this
     man?
     1. Cit. He has our voices, sir.
     Bru. We pray the gods he may deserve your
     loves.   165
     2. Cit. Amen, sir.   To my poor unworthy notice,
He mock'd us when he begg'd our voices.
     3. Cit.   Certainly
He flouted us downright.
     1. Cit. No, 'tis his kind of speech; he did not
     mock us.

     2. Cit. Not one amongst us, save yourself, but
     says   170
He us'd us scornfully.   He should have show'd us
His marks of merit, wounds receiv'd for 's country.
     Sic. Why, so he did, I am sure.
     All.   No, no; no man saw 'em.
     3. Cit. He said he had wounds, which he could
     show in private;
And with his hat, thus waving it in scorn,   175
"I would be consul," says he; "aged custom,
But by your voices, will not so permit me;
Your voices therefore."   When we granted that,
Here was "I thank you for your voices; thank you;
Your most sweet voices.   Now you have left your
     voices,   180
I have no further with you." Was not this mockery?
     Sic. Why either were you ignorant to see 't,
Or, seeing it, of such childish friendliness
To yield your voices?
     Bru.   Could you not have told him
As you were lesson'd: when he had no power,   185
But was a petty servant to the state,
He was your enemy, ever spake against
Your liberties and the charters that you bear
I' th' body of the weal; and now, arriving
A place of potency and sway o' th' state,   190
If he should still malignantly remain
Fast foe to th' plebeii, your voices might
Be curses to yourselves?   You should have said
That as his worthy deeds did claim no less
Than what he stood for, so his gracious nature
Would think upon you for your voices and   196
Translate his malice towards you into love,
Standing your friendly lord.
     Sic.   Thus to have said,
As you were fore-advis'd, had touch'd his spirit
And tried his inclination; from him pluck'd   200
Either his gracious promise, which you might,
As cause had call'd you up, have held him to;
Or else it would have gall'd his surly nature,
Which easily endures not article
Tying him to aught; so putting him to rage,   205
You should have ta'en th' advantage of his choler
And pass'd him unelected.
     Bru.   Did you perceive
He did solicit you in free contempt
When he did need your loves, and do you think
That his contempt shall not be bruising to you   210
When he hath power to crush?   Why, had your
     bodies
No heart among you?   Or had you tongues to cry
Against the rectorship of judgement?
     Sic.   Have you
Ere now deni'd the asker, and now again

139, 141. [6.], [7.] (Camb. edd.).   1, 2 F.   146. limitation: prescribed time.   148. official marks: insignia of office.
152. upon... approbation: to confirm your election.   182. ignorant: too dull.   189. weal: commonwealth.   199. touch'd:
tested.   204. article: stipulation.   212. heart: courage.   213. rectorship: rule.

Of him that did not ask but mock, bestow   215
Your sued-for tongues?
   3. Cit. He's not confirm'd; we may deny him yet.
   2. Cit. And will deny him.
I'll have five hundred voices of that sound.
   1. Cit. I twice five hundred and their friends to
     piece 'em.   220
   Bru. Get you hence instantly, and tell those
     friends
They have chose a consul that will from them take
Their liberties, make them of no more voice
Than dogs, that are as often beat for barking
As therefore kept to do so.
   Sic.   Let them assemble,
And on a safer judgement all revoke   226
Your ignorant election. Enforce his pride
And his old hate unto you; besides, forget not
With what contempt he wore the humble weed,
How in his suit he scorn'd you; but your loves,   230
Thinking upon his services, took from you
The apprehension of his present portance,
Which most gibingly, ungravely, he did fashion
After th' inveterate hate he bears you.
   Bru.   Lay
A fault on us, your tribunes, that we labour'd,   235
No impediment between, but that you must
Cast your election on him.
   Sic.   Say you chose him
More after our commandment than as guided
By your own true affections, and that your minds,
Pre-occupi'd with what you rather must do   240
Than what you should, made you against the grain
To voice him consul. Lay the fault on us.
   Bru. Ay, spare us not. Say we read lectures to
     you,
How youngly he began to serve his country,   244
How long continued, and what stock he springs of,—
The noble house o' th' Marcians, from whence came
That Ancus Marcius, Numa's daughter's son,
Who, after great Hostilius, here was king;
Of the same house Publius and Quintus were,
That our best water brought by conduits hither;
[And Censorinus, nobly named so,   251
Twice being by the people chosen censor,]
Was his great ancestor.
   Sic.   One thus descended,
That hath beside well in his person wrought
To be set high in place, we did commend   255
To your remembrances; but you have found,
Scaling his present bearing with his past,
That he's your fixed enemy, and revoke
Your sudden approbation.
   Bru.   Say, you ne'er had done 't —

Harp on that still — but by our putting on;   260
And presently, when you have drawn your number,
Repair to t' Capitol.
   All.   We will so. Almost all
Repent in their election.   [*Exeunt Citizens.*
   Bru.   Let them go on;
This mutiny were better put in hazard
Than stay, past doubt, for greater.   265
If, as his nature is, he fall in rage
With their refusal, both observe and answer
The vantage of his anger.
   Sic.   To th' Capitol, come.
We will be there before the stream o' th' people;
And this shall seem, as partly 'tis, their own,   270
Which we have goaded onward.   [*Exeunt.*

ACT III

[SCENE I. *Rome. A street.*]

Cornets. Enter CORIOLANUS, MENENIUS, *all the*
  Gentry, COMINIUS, TITUS LARTIUS, *and other*
  SENATORS.

   Cor. Tullus Aufidius then had made new head?
   Lart. He had, my lord; and that it was which
     caus'd
Our swifter composition.
   Cor. So then the Volsces stand but as at first,   4
Ready, when time shall prompt them, to make road
Upon 's again.
   Com.   They are worn, Lord Consul, so
That we shall hardly in our ages see
Their banners wave again.
   Cor.   Saw you Aufidius?
   Lart. On safe-guard he came to me, and did curse
Against the Volsces for they had so vilely   10
Yielded the town. He is retired to Antium.
   Cor. Spoke he of me?
   Lart.   He did, my lord.
   Cor.   How? What?
   Lart. How often he had met you, sword to sword;
That of all things upon the earth he hated
Your person most; that he would pawn his fortunes
To hopeless restitution, so he might   16
Be call'd your vanquisher.
   Cor.   At Antium lives he?
   Lart. At Antium.
   Cor. I wish I had a cause to seek him there,
To oppose his hatred fully. Welcome home.   20

Enter SICINIUS *and* BRUTUS.

Behold, these are the tribunes of the people,
The tongues o' th' common mouth. I do despise them

215. **Of:** on.   220. **piece:** increase.   227. **Enforce:** stress.   232. **portance:** demeanor.   233. **ungravely:** frivolously.
251–52. **[And ... censor]** (Camb. edd.).   *And Nobly nam'd, so twice being Censor* F.   257. **Scaling:** weighing.   260. **putting
on:** urging.   265. **stay:** (to) wait.   267–68. **answer ... vantage:** take advantage of.
  Act III, sc. i, 1. made new head: raised a new force.   3. **composition:** coming to terms.   16. **To ... restitution:** beyond
hope of recovery.

For they do prank them in authority,
Against all noble sufferance.
  Sic.   Pass no further.
  Cor. Ha! what is that?   25
  Bru. It will be dangerous to go on. No further.
  Cor. What makes this change?
  Men. The matter?
  Com. Hath he not pass'd the noble and the
      common?
  Bru. Cominius, no.
  Cor.   Have I had children's voices?
  [*I.*] *Sen.* Tribunes, give way; he shall to the
      market-place.   31
  Bru. The people are incens'd against him.
  Sic.   Stop,
Or all will fall in broil.
  Cor.   Are these your herd?
Must these have voices, that can yield them now
And straight disclaim their tongues? What are
      your offices?   35
You being their mouths, why rule you not their
      teeth?
Have you not set them on?
  Men.   Be calm, be calm.
  Cor. It is a purpos'd thing, and grows by plot,
To curb the will of the nobility.
Suffer 't, and live with such as cannot rule   40
Nor ever will be rul'd.
  Bru.   Call 't not a plot.
The people cry you mock'd them, and of late,
When corn was given them gratis, you repin'd,
Scandal'd the suppliants for the people, call'd them
Time-pleasers, flatterers, foes to nobleness.   45
  Cor. Why, this was known before.
  Bru.   Not to them all.
  Cor. Have you inform'd them sithence?
  Bru.   How! I inform them!
  Com. You are like to do such business.
  Bru.   Not unlike,
Each way, to better yours.
  Cor. Why, then, should I be consul? By yond
      clouds,   50
Let me deserve so ill as you, and make me
Your fellow tribune.
  Sic.   You show too much of that
For which the people stir. If you will pass
To where you are bound, you must inquire your
      way,
Which you are out of, with a gentler spirit,   55
Or never be so noble as a consul,
Nor yoke with him for tribune.
  Men.   Let's be calm.

  Com. The people are abus'd; set on. This
      palt'ring
Becomes not Rome, nor has Coriolanus
Deserv'd this so dishonour'd rub, laid falsely   60
I' th' plain way of his merit.
  Cor.   Tell me of corn!
This was my speech, and I will speak 't again —
  Men. Not now, not now.
  [*I.*] *Sen.*   Not in this heat, sir, now.
  Cor. Now, as I live, I will. My nobler friends,
I crave their pardons;   65
For the mutable, rank-scented [many], let them
Regard me as I do not flatter, and
Therein behold themselves. I say again,
In soothing them we nourish 'gainst our Senate
The cockle of rebellion, insolence, sedition,   70
Which we ourselves have plough'd for, sow'd, and
      scatter'd,
By mingling them with us, the honour'd number,
Who lack not virtue, no, nor power, but that
Which they have giv'n to beggars.
  Men.   Well, no more.
  [*I.*] *Sen.* No more words, we beseech you.
  Cor.   How! no more!
As for my country I have shed my blood,   76
Not fearing outward force, so shall my lungs
Coin words till their decay against those measles,
Which we disdain should tetter us, yet sought
The very way to catch them.
  Bru.   You speak o' th' people
As if you were a god to punish, not   81
A man of their infirmity.
  Sic.   'Twere well
We let the people know 't.
  Men.   What, what? his choler?
  Cor. Choler!
Were I as patient as the midnight sleep,   85
By Jove, 'twould be my mind!
  Sic.   It is a mind
That shall remain a poison where it is,
Not poison any further.
  Cor.   Shall remain!
Hear you this Triton of the minnows? Mark you
His absolute "shall"?
  Com.   'Twas from the canon.
  Cor.   "Shall"!
O [good] but most unwise patricians! why,   91
You grave but [reckless] senators, have you thus
Given Hydra here to choose an officer,
That with his peremptory "shall," being but
The horn and noise o' th' monster's, wants not
      spirit   95

24. **Against...sufferance:** beyond the toleration of the nobility.   30, 63, 75. [*I.*] (Capell). Om. F.   47. **sithence:** since.   58. **abus'd:** deceived.   60. **rub:** impediment.   66. [many] F₄. *Meynie* F₁.   70. **cockle:** weed.   78. **measles:** leprosy.   79. **tetter:** infect.   89. **Triton:** a sea god.   90. **from the canon:** against the law.   91. [good] (Theobald). *God* F.   92. [reckless] (Hanmer). *wreaklesse* F.   93. **Hydra:** many-headed beast, i.e., the multitude.   95. **horn and noise:** noisy horn. *Horn* may refer back to Triton, *noise* to Hydra.

To say he'll turn your current in a ditch,
And make your channel his?   If he have power,
Then [vail] your ignorance; if none, awake
Your dangerous lenity.   If you are learn'd,
Be not as common fools; if you are not,   100
Let them have cushions by you.   You are plebeians,
If they be senators; and they are no less,
When, both your voices blended, the great'st taste
Most palates theirs.   They choose their magistrate,
And such a one as he, who puts his "shall,"   105
His popular "shall," against a graver bench
Than ever frown'd in Greece.   By Jove himself!
It makes the consuls base; and my soul aches
To know, when two authorities are up,
Neither supreme, how soon confusion   110
May enter 'twixt the gap of both and take
The one by th' other.
    Com.   Well, on to th' market-place.
    Cor.   Whoever gave that counsel, to give forth
The corn o' th' storehouse gratis, as 'twas us'd
Sometime in Greece, —
    Men.   Well, well, no more of that.
    Cor.   Though there the people had more absolute
        power,   116
I say, they nourish'd disobedience, fed
The ruin of the state.
    Bru.   Why, shall the people give
One that speaks thus their voice?
    Cor.   I'll give my reasons,
More worthier than their voices.   They know the
        corn   120
Was not our recompense, resting well assur'd
That ne'er did service for't; being press'd to th'
        war,
Even when the navel of the state was touch'd,
They would not thread the gates.   This kind of
        service   124
Did not deserve corn gratis.   Being i' th' war,
Their mutinies and revolts, wherein they show'd
Most valour, spoke not for them.   Th' accusation
Which they have often made against the Senate,
All cause unborn, could never be the [motive]
Of our so frank donation.   Well, what then?   130
How shall this bosom-multiplied digest
The Senate's courtesy?   Let deeds express
What's like to be their words: "We did request it;
We are the greater poll, and in true fear   134
They gave us our demands."   Thus we debase
The nature of our seats and make the rabble
Call our cares fears; which will in time
Break ope the locks o' th' Senate and bring in

The crows to peck the eagles.
    Men.   Come, enough.
    Bru.   Enough, with over-measure.
    Cor.   No, take more!
What may be sworn by, both divine and human,   141
Seal what I end withal!   This double worship,
Where one part does disdain with cause, the other
Insult without all reason; where gentry, title,
        wisdom,
Cannot conclude but by the yea and no   145
Of general ignorance, — it must omit
Real necessities and give way the while
To unstable slightness; purpose so barr'd, it follows
Nothing is done to purpose.   Therefore, beseech
        you, —
You that will be less fearful than discreet,   150
That love the fundamental part of state
More than you doubt the change on't, that prefer
A noble life before a long, and wish
To jump a body with a dangerous physic
That's sure of death without it, at once pluck out
The multitudinous tongue; let them not lick   156
The sweet which is their poison.   Your dishonour
Mangles true judgement and bereaves the state
Of that integrity which should become 't,   159
Not having the power to do the good it would,
For th' ill which doth control 't.
    Bru.   Has said enough.
    Sic.   Has spoken like a traitor, and shall answer
As traitors do.
    Cor.   Thou wretch, despite o'erwhelm thee!
What should the people do with these bald tribunes?
On whom depending, their obedience fails   166
To the greater bench.   In a rebellion,
When what's not meet, but what must be, was law,
Then were they chosen; in a better hour,
Let what is meet be said it must be meet,   170
And throw their power i' th' dust.
    Bru.   Manifest treason!
    Sic.   This a consul?   No!
    Bru.   The ædiles, ho!

Enter an Ædile.
            — Let him be apprehended.
    Sic.   Go, call the people; [*Exit Ædile*] in whose
        name myself
Attach thee as a traitorous innovator,   175
A foe to th' public weal.   Obey, I charge thee,
And follow to thine answer.
    Cor.   Hence, old goat!

98. [vail] your ignorance: submit yourselves in your ignorance.   [vail] F₄.   *vale* F₁.   101. cushions: i.e., seats in the Senate.
103–104. the . . . theirs: the dominant flavor comes from them, i.e., their votes decide.   111. take: overthrow.   121. recompense: payment for service.   124. thread: go through.   129. [motive] (Johnson conj.).   *native* F.   131. bosom-
multiplied: multitudinous bosom (cf. l. 156 below and II.iii.18), the common herd.   Many edd. emend to *bisson* (blind)
multitude.   142. Seal: confirm.   144. Insult: exult.   without: beyond.   145. conclude: make a decision, decree.   152.
doubt: fear.   154. jump: risk.   167. greater bench: senate.   173. ædiles: officers attached to the Tribunes.   175. Attach:
arrest.

[*Senators, etc.*] We'll surety him.

Com.   Ag'd sir, hands off.

Cor. Hence, rotten thing! or I shall shake thy bones
Out of thy garments.

Sic.   Help, ye citizens!   180

Enter a rabble of PLEBEIANS, *with the* ÆDILES.

Men. On both sides more respect.

Sic. Here's he that would take from you all
    your power.

Bru. Seize him, ædiles!

[*Citizens.*] Down with him! down with him!

2. Sen. Weapons, weapons, weapons!   185
        [*They all bustle about Coriolanus* [*crying,*]
Tribunes! Patricians! Citizens! What, ho!
Sicinius! Brutus! Coriolanus! Citizens!

All. Peace, peace, peace! Stay, hold, peace!

Men. What is about to be? I am out of breath;
Confusion's near; I cannot speak. You, tribunes
To the people! Coriolanus, patience!   191
Speak, good Sicinius.

Sic.   Hear me, people; peace!

[*Citizens.*] Let's hear our tribune; peace! Speak,
    speak, speak!

Sic. You are at point to lose your liberties.
Marcius would have all from you; Marcius,   195
Whom late you have nam'd for consul.

Men.   Fie, fie, fie!
This is the way to kindle, not to quench.

[*1.*] *Sen.* To unbuild the city and to lay all flat.

Sic. What is the city but the people?

[*Citizens.*]   True,
The people are the city.   200

Bru. By the consent of all, we were establish'd
The people's magistrates.

[*Citizens.*]   You so remain.

Men. And so are like to do.

Com. That is the way to lay the city flat,
To bring the roof to the foundation   205
And bury all, which yet distinctly ranges,
In heaps and piles of ruin.

Sic.   This deserves death.

Bru. Or let us stand to our authority,
Or let us lose it. We do here pronounce,
Upon the part o' th' people, in whose power   210
We were elected theirs, Marcius is worthy
Of present death.

Sic.   Therefore lay hold of him;
Bear him to th' rock Tarpeian, and from thence
Into destruction cast him.

Bru.   Ædiles, seize him!

[*Citizens.*] Yield, Marcius, yield!

Men.   Hear me one word;
Beseech you, tribunes, hear me but a word.   216

Æd. Peace, peace!

Men. [*To Brutus.*] Be that you seem, truly your
    country's friend,
And temp'rately proceed to what you would
Thus violently redress.

Bru.   Sir, those cold ways   220
That seem like prudent helps are very poisonous
Where the disease is violent. — Lay hands upon
    him
And bear him to the rock.

Cor.   No, I'll die here.
                                [*Drawing his sword.*
There's some among you have beheld me fighting;
Come, try upon yourselves what you have seen me.

Men. Down with that sword! Tribunes, with-
    draw a while.   226

Bru. Lay hands upon him.

Com.   Help Marcius, help;
You that be noble, help him, young and old!

[*Citizens.*] Down with him, down with him!
        [*In this mutiny, the Tribunes, the Ædiles,
            and the People, are beat in.*

Men. [*to Cor.*] Go, get you to [your] house;
    begone, away!   230
All will be naught else.

2. Sen.   Get you gone.

Com.   Stand fast;
We have as many friends as enemies.

Men. Shall it be put to that?

[*1.*] *Sen.*   The gods forbid!
I prithee, noble friend, home to thy house;
Leave us to cure this cause.

Men.   For 'tis a sore upon us   235
You cannot tent yourself. Begone, beseech you.

[*Com.*] Come, sir, along with us.

[*Cor.*] I would they were barbarians — as they
    are,
Though in Rome litter'd — not Romans — as they
    are not,
Though calv'd i' th' porch o' th' Capitol!

[*Men.*]   Begone!
Put not your worthy rage into your tongue;   241
One time will owe another.

Cor.   On fair ground
I could beat forty of them.

Men.   I could myself
Take up a brace o' th' best of them; yea, the two
    tribunes.

Com. But now 'tis odds beyond arithmetic;   245
And manhood is call'd foolery when it stands
Against a falling fabric. Will you hence

178. [*Senators, etc.*] *All* F.   184, etc. [*Citizens*] (Capell). *All* F. (and elsewhere).   186. S.D. [*crying*] (Camb. edd.).
Om. F.   206. **distinctly ranges:** has an independent setting.   213. **rock Tarpeian:** from which criminals were hurled.   230.
[**your**] (Rowe).   *our* F.   237. [**Com.**] F₂.   *Corio.* F₁.   238. [**Cor.**] (Tyrwhitt conj.).   *Mene.* F.   240. [**Men.**] Om. F.
242. **One . . . another:** i.e., a good time will come.   247. **fabric:** structure.

Before the tag return, whose rage doth rend
Like interrupted waters, and o'erbear
What they are us'd to bear?
Men.   Pray you, begone.
I'll try whether my old wit be in request   251
With those that have but little.   This must be
    patch'd
With cloth of any colour.
    Com.   Nay, come away.
    [*Exeunt Coriolanus, Cominius [and others].*
    A Patrician.   This man has marr'd his fortune.
    Men.   His nature is too noble for the world;   255
He would not flatter Neptune for his trident,
Or Jove for 's power to thunder.   His heart's his
    mouth;
What his breast forges, that his tongue must vent;
And, being angry, does forget that ever   259
He heard the name of death.   [*A noise within.*
Here's goodly work!
    A Patrician.   I would they were a-bed!
    Men.   I would they were in Tiber!   What the
    vengeance!
Could he not speak 'em fair?

    Re-enter BRUTUS *and* SICINIUS, *with the rabble.*
    Sic.   Where is this viper
That would depopulate the city and   264
Be every man himself?
    Men.   You worthy tribunes, —
    Sic.   He shall be thrown down the Tarpeian rock
With rigorous hands.   He hath resisted law,
And therefore law shall scorn him further trial
Than the severity of the public power
Which he so sets at nought.
    1. Cit.   He shall well know
The noble tribunes are the people's mouths,   271
And we their hands.
    [*Citizens.*]   He shall, sure on't.
    Men.   Sir, sir, —
    Sic.   Peace!
    Men.   Do not cry havoc where you should but
    hunt   275
With modest warrant.
    Sic.   Sir, how comes 't that you
Have help to make this rescue?
    Men.   Hear me speak.
As I do know the consul's worthiness,
So can I name his faults, —
    Sic.   Consul! what consul?
    Men.   The consul Coriolanus.
    Bru.   He consul!   280
    [*Citizens.*]   No, no, no, no, no.
    Men.   If, by the tribunes' leave, and yours, good
    people,

I may be heard, I would crave a word or two;
The which shall turn you to no further harm
Than so much loss of time.
    Sic.   Speak briefly then;
For we are peremptory to dispatch   286
This viperous traitor.   To eject him hence
Were but one danger, and to keep him here
[Our] certain death; therefore it is decreed
He dies to-night.
    Men.   Now the good gods forbid   290
That our renowned Rome, whose gratitude
Towards her deserved children is enroll'd
In Jove's own book, like an unnatural dam
Should now eat up her own!
    Sic.   He's a disease that must be cut away.   295
    Men.   O, he's a limb that has but a disease;
Mortal, to cut it off; to cure it, easy.
What has he done to Rome that's worthy death?
Killing our enemies, the blood he hath lost —
Which I dare vouch, is more than that he hath,   300
By many an ounce — he dropp'd it for his country;
And what is left, to lose it by his country
Were to us all that do't and suffer it
A brand to th' end o' th' world.
    Sic.   This is clean kam.
    Bru.   Merely awry.   When he did love his
    country,   305
It honour'd him.
    Men.   The service of the foot
Being once gangren'd, is not then respected
For what before it was, —
    Bru.   We'll hear no more.
Pursue him to his house and pluck him thence,
Lest his infection, being of catching nature,   310
Spread further.
    Men.   One word more, one word.
This tiger-footed rage, when it shall find
The harm of unscann'd swiftness, will too late
Tie leaden pounds to 's heels.   Proceed by process,
Lest parties, as he is belov'd, break out   315
And sack great Rome with Romans.
    Bru.   If it were so, —
    Sic.   What do ye talk?
Have we not had a taste of his obedience?
Our ædiles smote? ourselves resisted?   Come.
    Men.   Consider this: he has been bred i' th' wars
Since 'a could draw a sword, and is ill school'd   321
In bolted language; meal and bran together
He throws without distinction.   Give me leave;
I'll go to him, and undertake to bring him
Where he shall answer, by a lawful form,   325
In peace, to his utmost peril.
    1. Sen.   Noble tribunes,
It is the humane way.   The other course

---

248. **tag:** rabble.   275. **cry havoc:** give the signal for general slaughter.   289. **[Our]** (Theobald).   *One* F.   292. **de-**
served: deserving.   304. **clean kam:** all wrong.   305. **Merely:** entirely.   313. **unscann'd:** inconsiderate.   314. **process:**
legal means.   315. **parties:** factions.   322. **bolted:** refined.   324. **bring him** (Pope).   *bring him in peace* F.

Will prove too bloody, and the end of it
Unknown to the beginning.

   Sic.   Noble Menenius,
Be you then as the people's officer.   330
Masters, lay down your weapons.

   Bru.   Go not home.

   Sic. Meet on the market-place. We'll attend
    you there;
Where, if you bring not Marcius, we'll proceed
In our first way.

   Men.   I'll bring him to you.
[*To the Senators.*] Let me desire your company. He
    must come,   335
Or what is worst will follow.

   [*1.*] *Sen.*   Pray you, let's to him.
                             [*Exeunt.*

[SCENE II. *A room in Coriolanus's house.*]

Enter CORIOLANUS, *with* NOBLES.

   Cor. Let them pull all about mine ears, present
    me
Death on the wheel or at wild horses' heels,
Or pile ten hills on the Tarpeian rock,
That the precipitation might down stretch
Below the beam of sight, yet will I still   5
Be thus to them.

Enter VOLUMNIA.

   Noble.   You do the nobler.

   Cor. I muse my mother
Does not approve me further, who was wont
To call them woollen vassals, things created   9
To buy and sell with groats, to show bare heads
In congregations, to yawn, be still and wonder
When one but of my ordinance stood up
To speak of peace or war. — I talk of you.
                            [*To Vol.*]
Why did you wish me milder? Would you have me
False to my nature? Rather say I play   15
The man I am.

   Vol.   O, sir, sir, sir,
I would have had you put your power well on,
Before you had worn it out.

   Cor.   Let go.

   Vol. You might have been enough the man you
    are,
With striving less to be so. Lesser had been   20
The [thwartings] of your dispositions, if
You had not show'd them how ye were dispos'd,
Ere they lack'd power to cross you.

   Cor.   Let them hang!

   Vol. [*Aside.*] Ay, and burn too.

Enter MENENIUS *with the* SENATORS.

   Men. Come, come, you have been too rough,
    something too rough;   25
You must return and mend it.

   [*1.*] *Sen.*   There's no remedy;
Unless, by not so doing, our good city
Cleave in the midst and perish.

   Vol.   Pray, be counsell'd.
I have a heart as little apt as yours.
But yet a brain that leads my use of anger   30
To better vantage.

   Men.   Well said, noble woman!
Before he should thus stoop to the [herd], but that
The violent fit o' th' time craves it as physic
For the whole state, I would put mine armour on, 34
Which I can scarcely bear.

   Cor.   What must I do?

   Men. Return to th' tribunes.

   Cor.   Well, what then? what then?

   Men. Repent what you have spoke.

   Cor. For them! I cannot do it to the gods;
Must I then do't to them?

   Vol.   You are too absolute;
Though therein you can never be too noble,   40
But when extremities speak. I have heard you say
Honour and policy, like unsever'd friends,
I' th' war do grow together. Grant that, and tell
    me
In peace what each of them by th' other lose
That they combine not there.

   Cor.   Tush, tush!

   Men.   A good demand.

   Vol. If it be honour in your wars to seem   46
The same you are not, which, for your best ends,
You adopt your policy, how is it less or worse
That it shall hold companionship in peace
With honour, as in war, since that to both   50
It stands in like request?

   Cor.   Why force you this?

   Vol. Because that now it lies you on to speak
To th' people; not by your own instruction,
Nor by the matter which your heart prompts you,
But with such words that are but roted in   55
Your tongue, though but bastards and syllables
Of no allowance to your bosom's truth.
Now, this no more dishonours you at all
Than to take in a town with gentle words,
Which else would put you to your fortune and 60
The hazard of much blood.
I would dissemble with my nature where
My fortunes and my friends at stake requir'd
I should do so in honour. I am in this
Your wife, your son, these senators, the nobles;

Sc. ii, 4. **precipitation:** steepness. 5. **beam:** i.e., reach. 7. **muse:** marvel. 10. **groats:** fourpenny coins. 12. **ordinance:** rank. 18. **Let go:** enough. 21. **[thwartings]** (Theobald). *things* F. 29. **apt:** docile. 32. **[herd]** (Warburton). *heart* F. 48. **adopt:** adopt as. 51. **It...request:** it is equally necessary. **force:** urge. 55. **roted:** learned by rote, memorized. 57. **Of...to:** unacknowledged by. 59. **take in:** capture. 64. **I am:** I am speaking for.

And you will rather show our general louts   66
How you can frown, than spend a fawn upon 'em
For the inheritance of their loves and safeguard
Of what that want might ruin.

Men.   Noble lady!
Come, go with us; speak fair. You may salve so,
Not what is dangerous present, but the loss   71
Of what is past.

Vol.   I prithee now, my son,
Go to them, with this bonnet in thy hand;
And thus far having stretch'd it — here be with
  them —   74
Thy knee bussing the stones — for in such business
Action is eloquence, and the eyes of th' ignorant
More learned than the ears — waving thy head,
Which often, thus, correcting thy stout heart,
Now humble as the ripest mulberry
That will not hold the handling — or say to them,
Thou art their soldier, and, being bred in broils,   81
Hast not the soft way which, thou dost confess,
Were fit for thee to use as they to claim,
In asking their good loves; but thou wilt frame
Thyself, forsooth, hereafter theirs, so far   85
As thou hast power and person.

Men.   This but done,
Even as she speaks, why, their hearts were yours;
For they have pardons, being ask'd, as free
As words to little purpose.

Vol.   Prithee now,
Go, and be rul'd; although I know thou hadst rather
Follow thine enemy in a fiery gulf   91
Than flatter him in a bower.

Enter COMINIUS.

                          Here is Cominius.
Com. I have been i' th' market-place; and, sir,
  'tis fit
You make strong party, or defend yourself
By calmness or by absence. All's in anger.   95
Men. Only fair speech.
Com.   I think 'twill serve, if he
Can thereto frame his spirit.
Vol.   He must, and will.
Prithee now, say you will, and go about it.
Cor. Must I go show them my unbarb'd sconce?
  Must I
With my base tongue give to my noble heart   100
A lie that it must bear? Well, I will do't;
Yet, were there but this single plot to lose,
This mould of Marcius, they to dust should grind it
And throw 't against the wind. To th' market-
  place!   104
You have put me now to such a part which never
I shall discharge to th' life.

Com.   Come, come, we'll prompt you.
Vol. I prithee now, sweet son, as thou hast said
My praises made thee first a soldier, so,
To have my praise for this, perform a part
Thou hast not done before.
Cor.   Well, I must do't.   110
Away, my disposition, and possess me
Some harlot's spirit! My throat of war be turn'd,
Which choir'd with my drum, into a pipe
Small as an eunuch's, or the virgin voice
That babies lull asleep! The smiles of knaves   115
Tent in my cheeks, and schoolboys' tears take up
The glasses of my sight! A beggar's tongue
Make motion through my lips, and my arm'd knees,
Who bow'd but in my stirrup, bend like his
That hath receiv'd an alms! — I will not do't,   120
Lest I surcease to honour mine own truth
And by my body's action teach my mind
A most inherent baseness.
Vol.   At thy choice, then.
To beg of thee, it is my more dishonour
Than thou of them. Come all to ruin! Let   125
Thy mother rather feel thy pride than fear
Thy dangerous stoutness; for I mock at death
With as big heart as thou. Do as thou list.
Thy valiantness was mine, thou suck'st it from me,
But owe thy pride thyself.
Cor.   Pray, be content.   130
Mother, I am going to the market-place;
Chide me no more. I'll mountebank their loves,
Cog their hearts from them, and come home belov'd
Of all the trades in Rome. Look, I am going;
Commend me to my wife. I'll return consul,   135
Or never trust to what my tongue can do
I' th' way of flattery further.
Vol.   Do your will. [*Exit.*
Com. Away! the tribunes do attend you. Arm
  yourself
To answer mildly; for they are prepar'd
With accusations, as I hear, more strong   140
Than are upon you yet.
Cor. The word is "mildly." Pray you, let us go.
Let them accuse me by invention, I
Will answer in mine honour.
Men.   Ay, but mildly.
Cor. Well, mildly be it then. Mildly!   145
                                        [*Exeunt.*

[SCENE III.   *The same.   The Forum.*]

Enter SICINIUS *and* BRUTUS.

Bru. In this point charge him home, that he
  affects
Tyrannical power. If he evade us there,

---

69. **want:** lack of their loves.   70. **salve:** remedy.   71. **Not:** not only.   74. **here...them:** i.e., this is the way to win
them.   75. **bussing:** kissing.   77. **waving:** bowing.   80. **hold:** bear.   83. **they:** for them.   99. **unbarb'd sconce:** bare head.
102. **this...plot:** only this body.   103. **mould:** form.   121. **surcease:** cease.   130. **owe:** own.   132. **mountebank:** win
by quackery.   133. **Cog:** cheat.   138. **Arm:** prepare.   143. **invention:** fraud.
  Sc. iii, 1. **affects:** wants.

Enforce him with his envy to the people,
And that the spoil got on the Antiates
Was ne'er distributed.

Enter an ÆDILE.

                  What, will he come?   5
Æd. He's coming.
Bru.   How accompanied?
Æd. With old Menenius and those senators
That always favour'd him.
Sic.   Have you a catalogue
Of all the voices that we have procur'd
Set down by th' poll?
Æd.   I have; 'tis ready. 10
Sic. Have you collected them by tribes?
Æd.   I have.
Sic. Assemble presently the people hither;
And when they hear me say, "It shall be so
I' th' right and strength o' th' commons," be it
    either
For death, for fine, or banishment, then let them, 15
If I say fine, cry "Fine!" if death, cry "Death!"
Insisting on the old prerogative
And power i' th' truth o' th' cause.
Æd.   I shall inform them.
Bru. And when such time they have begun to
    cry,
Let them not cease, but with a din confus'd 20
Enforce the present execution
Of what we chance to sentence.
Æd.   Very well.
Sic. Make them be strong and ready for this hint
When we shall hap to give 't them.
Bru.   Go about it.
                [Exit Ædile.]
Put him to choler straight. He hath been us'd
Ever to conquer, and to have his worth 26
Of contradiction. Being once chaf'd, he cannot
Be rein'd again to temperance; then he speaks
What's in his heart, and that is there which looks
With us to break his neck.

Enter CORIOLANUS, MENENIUS, *and* COMINIUS,
  with others [SENATORS *and* Patricians].

Sic.   Well, here he comes.
Men. Calmly, I do beseech you. 31
Cor. Ay, as an ostler, that [for the] poorest piece
Will bear the knave by th' volume. Th' honour'd
    gods
Keep Rome in safety, and the chairs of justice
Supplied with worthy men! plant love among 's! 35
[Throng] our large temples with the shows of peace,

And not our streets with war!
1. Sen.   Amen, amen.
Men. A noble wish.

Re-enter ÆDILE, with CITIZENS.

Sic. Draw near, ye people.
Æd. List to your tribunes. Audience! peace, I
    say! 40
Cor. First, hear me speak.
Both Tri.   Well, say. Peace, ho!
Cor. Shall I be charg'd no further than this
    present?
Must all determine here?
Sic.   I do demand
If you submit you to the people's voices,
Allow their officers, and are content 45
To suffer lawful censure for such faults
As shall be prov'd upon you?
Cor.   I am content.
Men. Lo, citizens, he says he is content.
The warlike service he has done, consider; think
Upon the wounds his body bears, which show 50
Like graves i' th' holy churchyard.
Cor.   Scratches with briers,
Scars to move laughter only.
Men.   Consider further,
That when he speaks not like a citizen,
You find him like a soldier. Do not take
His rougher [accents] for malicious sounds, 55
But, as I say, such as become a soldier
Rather than envy you.
Com.   Well, well, no more.
Cor. What is the matter
That being pass'd for consul with full voice,
I am so dishonour'd that the very hour 60
You take it off again?
Sic.   Answer to us.
Cor. Say, then; 'tis true, I ought so.
Sic. We charge you, that you have contriv'd to
    take
From Rome all season'd office and to wind
Yourself into a power tyrannical; 65
For which you are a traitor to the people.
Cor. How! traitor!
Men.   Nay, temperately; your promise.
Cor. The fires i' th' lowest hell fold in the people!
Call me their traitor! Thou injurious tribune!
Within thine eyes sat twenty thousand deaths, 70
In thy hands clutch'd as many millions, in
Thy lying tongue both numbers, I would say
"Thou liest" unto thee with a voice as free
As I do pray the gods.
Sic.   Mark you this, people?

3. **envy:** malice. 12. **presently:** straightway. 21. **present:** immediate. 26. **worth:** fill. 29. **looks:** promises. 32.
[for the] F₃. *fourth* F₁. **piece:** coin. 33. **Will...volume:** will swallow quantities of insults. 36. [Throng] (Theobald).
Through F. 45. **Allow:** acknowledge. 55. [accents] (Theobald). *Actions* F. 57. **envy you:** as malice toward you. 63.
contriv'd: plotted. 64. **season'd:** established. 69. **injurious:** insulting.

[*Citizens.*] To th' rock, to th' rock with him!

Sic.   Peace!

We need not put new matter to his charge.   76

What you have seen him do and heard him speak,

Beating your officers, cursing yourselves,

Opposing laws with strokes and here defying

Those whose great power must try him; even this

So criminal and in such capital kind,   81

Deserves th' extremest death.

Bru.   But since he hath

Serv'd well for Rome, —

Cor.   What do you prate of service?

Bru. I talk of that, that know it.

Cor. You?   85

Men. Is this the promise that you made your mother?

Com. Know, I pray you, —

Cor.   I'll know no further.

Let them pronounce the steep Tarpeian death,

Vagabond exile, flaying, pent to linger

But with a grain a day, I would not buy   90

Their mercy at the price of one fair word;

Nor check my courage for what they can give,

To have 't with saying "Good morrow."

Sic.   For that he has,

As much as in him lies, from time to time

Envi'd against the people, seeking means   95

To pluck away their power, as now at last

Given hostile strokes, and that not in the presence

Of dreaded justice, but on the ministers

That [do] distribute it; in the name o' th' people

And in the power of us the tribunes, we,   100

Even from this instant, banish him our city,

In peril of precipitation

From off the rock Tarpeian never more

To enter our Rome gates. I' th' people's name,

I say it shall be so.   105

[*Citizens.*] It shall be so, it shall be so. Let him away!

He's banish'd, and it shall be so.

Com. Hear me, my masters, and my common friends, —

Sic. He's sentenc'd; no more hearing.

Com.   Let me speak.

I have been consul, and can show [for] Rome   110

Her enemies' marks upon me. I do love

My country's good with a respect more tender,

More holy and profound, than mine own life,

My dear wife's estimate, her womb's increase

And treasure of my loins; then if I would   115

Speak that, —

Sic.   We know your drift; speak what?

Bru. There's no more to be said, but he is banish'd

As enemy to the people and his country.

It shall be so.

[*Citizens.*]   It shall be so, it shall be so.

Cor. You common cry of curs! whose breath I hate   120

As reek o' th' rotten fens, whose loves I prize

As the dead carcasses of unburied men

That do corrupt my air, I banish you!

And here remain with your uncertainty!

Let every feeble rumour shake your hearts!   125

Your enemies, with nodding of their plumes,

Fan you into despair! Have the power still

To banish your defenders, till at length

Your ignorance, which finds not till it feels,

Making [not] reservation of yourselves,   130

Still your own foes, deliver you as most

Abated captives to some nation

That won you without blows! Despising,

For you, the city, thus I turn my back;

There is a world elsewhere.   135

  [*Exeunt Coriolanus, Cominius* [*Menenius,*
  Senators, and Patricians]. *They all
  shout, and throw up their caps.*

Æd. The people's enemy is gone, is gone!

[*Citizens.*] Our enemy is banish'd! he is gone! Hoo! hoo!

Sic. Go, see him out at gates, and follow him,

As he hath follow'd you, with all despite;

Give him deserv'd vexation. Let a guard   140

Attend us through the city.

[*Citizens.*] Come, come; let's see him out at gates; come.

The gods preserve our noble tribunes! Come.

  [*Exeunt.*

ACT IV

[SCENE I. *Rome. Before a gate of the city.*]

Enter CORIOLANUS, VOLUMNIA, VIRGILIA, MENE-
NIUS, COMINIUS, *with the young Nobility of Rome.*

Cor. Come, leave your tears: a brief farewell. The beast

With many heads butts me away. Nay, mother,

Where is your ancient courage? You were us'd

To say extremity was the trier of spirits;

That common chances common men could bear;

That when the sea was calm all boats alike   6

Show'd mastership in floating; fortune's blows,

When most struck home, being gentle, wounded, craves

89. **pent:** imprisoned.   97. **not:** not merely.   99. [do] F$_3$. *doth* F$_1$.   110. [for] (Theobald). *from* F.   114. **estimate:** reputation.   120. **cry:** pack.   124. **uncertainty:** fickleness.   129. **finds:** learns.   **feels:** suffers.   130. **Making...of:** sparing not even. [not] (Capell). *but* F.   132. **Abated:** humiliated.

Act IV, sc. i, 7–9. **fortune's...cunning:** when Fortune's blows are heaviest, to behave like a gentleman, if wounded, takes a noble mind.

A noble cunning.   You were us'd to load me
With precepts that would make invincible   10
The heart that conn'd them.
  Vir. O heavens! O heavens!
  Cor.   Nay, I prithee, woman, —
  Vol. Now the red pestilence strike all trades in
    Rome,
And occupations perish!
  Cor.   What, what, what!
I shall be lov'd when I am lack'd.   Nay, mother,
Resume that spirit when you were wont to say,   16
If you had been the wife of Hercules,
Six of his labours you'd have done, and sav'd
Your husband so much sweat.   Cominius,   19
Droop not; adieu.   Farewell, my wife, my mother;
I'll do well yet.   Thou old and true Menenius,
Thy tears are salter than a younger man's,
And venomous to thine eyes.   My sometime
    General,
I have seen thee stern, and thou hast oft beheld
Heart-hard'ning spectacles; tell these sad women 25
'Tis fond to wail inevitable strokes,
As 'tis to laugh at 'em.   My mother, you wot well
My hazards still have been your solace; and
Believe 't not lightly — though I go alone,
Like to a lonely dragon, that his fen   30
Makes fear'd and talk'd of more than seen — your
    son
Will or exceed the common or be caught
With cautelous baits and practice.
  Vol.   My first son,
[Whither wilt] thou go?   Take good Cominius
With thee a while; determine on some course,   35
More than a wild exposture to each chance
That starts i' th' way before thee.
  Cor.   O the gods!
  Com. I'll follow thee a month, devise with thee
Where thou shalt rest, that thou mayst hear of us
And we of thee; so if the time thrust forth   40
A cause for thy repeal, we shall not send
O'er the vast world to seek a single man
And lose advantage, which doth ever cool
I' th' absence of the needer.
  Cor.   Fare ye well!
Thou hast years upon thee, and thou art too full
Of the wars' surfeits to go rove with one   46
That's yet unbruis'd.   Bring me but out at gate.
Come, my sweet wife, my dearest mother, and
My friends of noble touch; when I am forth,
Bid me farewell, and smile.   I pray you, come.
While I remain above the ground, you shall   51
Hear from me still, and never of me aught
But what is like me formerly.
  Men.   That's worthily

As any ear can hear.   Come, let's not weep.
If I could shake off but one seven years   55
From these old arms and legs, by the good gods,
I'd with thee every foot.
  Cor.   Give me thy hand:
Come.   [*Exeunt.*

[SCENE II. *The same. A street near the gate.*]

  Enter SICINIUS, BRUTUS, *and an* Ædile.

  Sic. Bid them all home; he's gone, and we'll no
    further.
The nobility are vexed, whom we see have sided
In his behalf.
  Bru.   Now we have shown our power,
Let us seem humbler after it is done
Than when it was a-doing.
  Sic.   Bid them home.   5
Say their great enemy is gone, and they
Stand in their ancient strength.
  Bru.   Dismiss them home.
                       [*Exit Ædile.*]
Here comes his mother.

  Enter VOLUMNIA, VIRGILIA, *and* MENENIUS.

  Sic.   Let's not meet her.
  Bru.   Why?
  Sic. They say she's mad.
  Bru. They have ta'en note of us; keep on your
    way.   10
  Vol. O, you're well met.   The hoarded plague o'
    th' gods
Requite your love!
  Men.   Peace, peace; be not so loud.
  Vol. If that I could for weeping, you should
    hear, —
Nay, and you shall hear some.   [*To Brutus.*]   Will
    you be gone?
  Vir. [*To Sicinius.*]   You shall stay too.   I would
    I had the power   15
To say so to my husband.
  Sic.   Are you mankind?
  Vol. Ay, fool; is that a shame?   Note but this,
    fool.
Was not a man my father?   Hadst thou foxship
To banish him that struck more blows for Rome 19
Than thou hast spoken words?
  Sic.   O blessed heavens!
  Vol. Moe noble blows than ever thou wise words,
And for Rome's good.   I'll tell thee what: — yet
    go.
Nay, but thou shalt stay too: — I would my son
Were in Arabia and thy tribe before him,
His good sword in his hand.

---

26. fond: foolish. 27. wot: know. 33. cautelous: crafty. practice: treachery. 34. [Whither wilt] (Capell). *Whether will* F. 36. exposture: exposure. 49. noble touch: proved nobleness.
  Sc. ii, 16. mankind: human. 18. foxship: craft.

Sic. What then?
Vir. What then!
He'd make an end of thy posterity. 26
  Vol. Bastards and all!
Good man, the wounds that he does bear for Rome!
  Men. Come, come, peace.
  Sic. I would he had continued to his country 30
As he began, and not unknit himself
The noble knot he made.
  Bru. I would he had.
  Vol. "I would he had"! 'Twas you incens'd the
    rabble;
Cats, that can judge as fitly of his worth
As I can of those mysteries which heaven 35
Will not have earth to know.
  Bru. Pray, let's go.
  Vol. Now, pray, sir, get you gone;
You have done a brave deed. Ere you go, hear
    this:
As far as doth the Capitol exceed
The meanest house in Rome, so far my son — 40
This lady's husband here, this, do you see? —
Whom you have banish'd, does exceed you all.
  Bru. Well, well, we'll leave you.
  Sic. Why stay we to be baited
With one that wants her wits?
      [*Exeunt Tribunes.*
  Vol. Take my prayers with you.
I would the gods had nothing else to do 45
But to confirm my curses! Could I meet 'em
But once a-day, it would unclog my heart
Of what lies heavy to't.
  Men. You have told them home;
And, by my troth, you have cause. You'll sup
    with me?
  Vol. Anger's my meat; I sup upon myself, 50
And so shall starve with feeding. Come, let's go.
[*To Virgilia.*] Leave this faint puling, and lament
    as I do,
In anger, Juno-like. Come, come, come. [*Exeunt.*
  Men. Fie, fie, fie! [*Exit.*

[SCENE III. *A highway between Rome and Antium.*]

Enter a ROMAN *and a* VOLSCE [*meeting*].

  Rom. I know you well, sir, and you know me.
Your name, I think, is Adrian.
  Vols. It is so, sir. Truly, I have forgot you.
  Rom. I am a Roman; and my services are, as
you are, against 'em. Know you me yet? 5
  Vols. Nicanor? No?
  Rom. The same, sir.
  Vols. You had more beard when I last saw you;
but your favour is well appear'd by your tongue.
What's the news in Rome? I have a note from

the Volscian state, to find you out there. You
have well saved me a day's journey. 12
  Rom. There hath been in Rome strange insur-
rections; the people against the senators, patricians,
and nobles.
  Vols. Hath been! Is it ended, then? Our
state thinks not so. They are in a most warlike
preparation and hope to come upon them in the
heat of their division. 19
  Rom. The main blaze of it is past, but a small
thing would make it flame again; for the nobles
receive so to heart the banishment of that worthy
Coriolanus, that they are in a ripe aptness to
take all power from the people and to pluck from
them their tribunes for ever. This lies glowing,
I can tell you, and is almost mature for the violent
breaking out. 27
  Vols. Coriolanus banish'd!
  Rom. Banish'd, sir.
  Vols. You will be welcome with this intelligence,
Nicanor. 31
  Rom. The day serves well for them now. I have
heard it said, the fittest time to corrupt a man's wife
is when she's fallen out with her husband. Your
noble Tullus Aufidius will appear well in these wars,
his great opposer, Coriolanus, being now in no request of his country. 38
  Vols. He cannot choose. I am most fortunate
thus accidentally to encounter you. You have
ended my business, and I will merrily accompany
you home. 42
  Rom. I shall, between this and supper, tell you
most strange things from Rome; all tending to the
good of their adversaries. Have you an army ready,
say you? 46
  Vols. A most royal one; the centurions and their
charges, distinctly billeted, already in th' entertainment, and to be on foot at an hour's warning. 50
  Rom. I am joyful to hear of their readiness, and
am the man, I think, that shall set them in present
action. So, sir, heartily well met, and most glad of
your company. 54
  Vols. You take my part from me, sir; I have the
most cause to be glad of yours.
  Rom. Well, let us go together. [*Exeunt.*

[SCENE IV. *Antium. Before Aufidius's house.*]

Enter CORIOLANUS, *in mean apparel, disguis'd
and muffled.*

  Cor. A goodly city is this Antium. City,
'Tis I that made thy widows; many an heir
Of these fair edifices 'fore my wars
Have I heard groan and drop. Then know me
    not,

Sc. iii, 9. **favour:** face. **appear'd:** manifested. 48. **distinctly:** separately. **in th' entertainment:** enlisted.
Sc. iv, 3. **wars:** attacks.

Lest that thy wives with spits and boys with stones
In puny battle slay me.

Enter a CITIZEN.

Save you, sir.   6

Cit. And you.

Cor.   Direct me, if it be your will,
Where great Aufidius lies. Is he in Antium?

Cit. He is, and feasts the nobles of the state
At his house this night.

Cor.   Which is his house, beseech you?   10

Cit. This, here before you.

Cor.   Thank you, sir: farewell.
                              [*Exit Citizen.*

O world, thy slippery turns! Friends now fast
          sworn,
Whose double bosoms seem to wear one heart,
Whose hours, whose bed, whose meal and exercise
Are still together, who twin, as 'twere, in love   15
Unseparable, shall within this hour,
On a dissension of a doit, break out
To bitterest enmity; so, fellest foes,
Whose passions and whose plots have broke their
          sleep
To take the one the other, by some chance,   20
Some trick not worth an egg, shall grow dear friends
And interjoin their issues. So with me;
My birthplace [hate] I, and my love's upon
This enemy town. I'll enter. If he slay me,
He does fair justice; if he give me way,   25
I'll do his country service.   [*Exit.*

[SCENE V. *The same. A hall in Aufidius's house.*]

Music within. Enter a SERVINGMAN.

1. Serv. Wine, wine, wine! What service is here!
I think our fellows are asleep.   [*Exit.*

Enter a second SERVINGMAN.

2. Serv. Where's Cotus? my [master] calls for him.
Cotus!   [*Exit.*

Enter CORIOLANUS.

Cor. A goodly house! The feast smells well but I
Appear not like a guest.   6

Re-enter the first SERVINGMAN.

1. Serv. What would you have, friend? Whence
are you? Here's no place for you; pray, go to the
door.   [*Exit.*

Cor. I have deserv'd no better entertainment   10
In being Coriolanus.

Re-enter second SERVINGMAN.

2. Serv. Whence are you, sir? Has the porter his

eyes in his head, that he gives entrance to such companions? Pray, get you out.

Cor. Away!   15

2. Serv. Away! get you away.

Cor. Now thou'rt troublesome.

2. Serv. Are you so brave? I'll have you talk'd
with anon.

Enter a third SERVINGMAN. *The first meets him.*

3. Serv. What fellow's this?   20

1. Serv. A strange one as ever I look'd on; I
cannot get him out o' th' house. Prithee, call my
master to him.   [*Retires.*]

3. Serv. What have you to do here, fellow? Pray
you, avoid the house.   25

Cor. Let me but stand; I will not hurt your hearth.

3. Serv. What are you?

Cor. A gentleman.

3. Serv. A marv'llous poor one.   30

Cor. True, so I am.

3. Serv. Pray you, poor gentleman, take up some
other station; here's no place for you. Pray you,
avoid. Come.   34

Cor. Follow your function, go and batten on cold
bits.   [*Pushes him away from him.*

3. Serv. What, you will not? Prithee, tell my
master what a strange guest he has here.

2. Serv. And I shall.   [*Exit.*

3. Serv. Where dwell'st thou?   40

Cor. Under the canopy.

3. Serv. Under the canopy?

Cor. Ay.

3. Serv. Where's that?

Cor. I' th' city of kites and crows.   45

3. Serv. I' th' city of kites and crows! What an
ass it is! Then thou dwell'st with daws too?

Cor. No, I serve not thy master.

3. Serv. How, sir! do you meddle with my
master?   51

Cor. Ay; 'tis an honester service than to meddle
with thy mistress.
Thou prat'st and prat'st; serve with thy trencher,
          hence!
          [*Beats him away.* [*Exit third Servingman.*]

Enter AUFIDIUS *with the* [*second*] SERVINGMAN.

Auf. Where is this fellow?   55

2. Serv. Here, sir. I'd have beaten him like a dog,
but for disturbing the lords within. [*Retires.*]

Auf. Whence com'st thou? What wouldst thou?
          Thy name?
Why speak'st not? Speak, man: what's thy name?

Cor. If, Tullus [*unmuffling*], not yet thou   60
know'st me, and, seeing me, dost not think me for

17. doit: small coin. 22. interjoin...issues: intermarry their children. 23. [hate] (Capell). *have* F.
Sc. v, 3. [master] F₄. *M.* F₁. 14. companions: scurvy fellows. 18. brave: saucy. 25. avoid: quit. 35. Follow...
function: attend to your job. batten: fatten. 41. canopy: sky. 47. daws: jackdaws (foolish birds).

the man I am, necessity commands me name myself.

Auf. What is thy name?

Cor. A name unmusical to the Volscians' ears,
And harsh in sound to thine.

Auf.   Say, what's thy name?
Thou hast a grim appearance, and thy face   66
Bears a command in't; though thy tackle's torn,
Thou show'st a noble vessel. What's thy name?

Cor. Prepare thy brow to frown. Know'st thou
   me yet?

Auf. I know thee not. Thy name?   70

Cor. My name is Caius Marcius, who hath done
To thee particularly and to all the Volsces
Great hurt and mischief; thereto witness may
My surname, Coriolanus. The painful service,
The extreme dangers, and the drops of blood   75
Shed for my thankless country are requited
But with that surname; a good memory
And witness of the malice and displeasure
Which thou shouldst bear me. Only that name re-
   mains.
The cruelty and envy of the people,   80
Permitted by our dastard nobles, who
Have all forsook me, hath devour'd the rest
And suffer'd me by th' voice of slaves to be
Whoop'd out of Rome. Now this extremity
Hath brought me to thy hearth; not out of hope —
Mistake me not — to save my life, for if   86
I had fear'd death, of all the men i' th' world
I would have 'voided thee, but in mere spite,
To be full quit of those my banishers,
Stand I before thee here. Then if thou hast   90
A heart of wreak in thee, that wilt revenge
Thine own particular wrongs and stop those maims
Of shame seen through thy country, speed thee
   straight
And make my misery serve thy turn. So use it
That my revengeful services may prove   95
As benefits to thee, for I will fight
Against my cank'red country with the spleen
Of all the under fiends. But if so be
Thou dar'st not this, and that to prove more for-
   tunes
Thou'rt tired, then, in a word, I also am   100
Longer to live most weary, and present
My throat to thee and to thy ancient malice;
Which not to cut would show thee but a fool,
Since I have ever followed thee with hate,
Drawn tuns of blood out of thy country's breast,   105
And cannot live but to thy shame, unless
It be to do thee service.

Auf.   O Marcius, Marcius!
Each word thou hast spoke hath weeded from my
   heart

A root of ancient envy. If Jupiter
Should from yond cloud speak divine things,   110
And say "'Tis true," I'd not believe them more
Than thee, all noble Marcius. Let me twine
Mine arms about that body, whereagainst
My grained ash an hundred times hath broke
And scarr'd the moon with splinters. Here I clip
The anvil of my sword, and do contest   116
As hotly and as nobly with thy love
As ever in ambitious strength I did
Contend against thy valour. Know thou first,
I lov'd the maid I married; never man   120
Sigh'd truer breath; but that I see thee here,
Thou noble thing, more dances my rapt heart
Than when I first my wedded mistress saw
Bestride my threshold. Why, thou Mars, I tell
   thee,
We have a power on foot; and I had purpose   125
Once more to hew thy target from thy brawn,
Or lose mine arm for't. Thou hast beat me out
Twelve several times, and I have nightly since
Dreamt of encounters 'twixt thyself and me;
We have been down together in my sleep,   130
Unbuckling helms, fisting each other's throat,
And wak'd half dead with nothing. Worthy Mar-
   cius,
Had we no quarrel else to Rome but that
Thou art thence banish'd, we would muster all
From twelve to seventy, and pouring war   135
Into the bowels of ungrateful Rome,
Like a bold flood o'er-beat. O, come, go in,
And take our friendly senators by th' hands;
Who now are here, taking their leaves of me,
Who am prepar'd against your territories,   140
Though not for Rome itself.

Cor.   You bless me, gods!

Auf. Therefore, most absolute sir, if thou wilt
   have
The leading of thine own revenges, take
Th' one half of my commission; and set down —
As best thou art experienc'd, since thou know'st   145
Thy country's strength and weakness, — thine own
   ways;
Whether to knock against the gates of Rome,
Or rudely visit them in parts remote,
To fright them ere destroy. But come in;
Let me commend thee first to those that shall   150
Say yea to thy desires. A thousand welcomes!
And more a friend than e'er an enemy;
Yet, Marcius, that was much. Your hand; most
   welcome!
     [*Exeunt Coriolanus and Aufidius. The two
      Servingmen* [*come forward*].

1. Serv. Here's a strange alteration!   154

---

77. memory: reminder. **91. wreak:** vengeance. **92–93. maims Of shame:** shameful injuries. **99. prove:** try. **114. grained ash:** spear. **116. anvil:** i.e., Coriolanus. **133. quarrel** F3. *other quarrel* F1. **137. o'er-beat:** beat (all) down. **142. absolute:** perfect.

2. Serv. By my hand, I had thought to have strucken him with a cudgel; and yet my mind gave me his clothes made a false report of him.

1. Serv. What an arm he has! He turn'd me about with his finger and his thumb as one would set up a top.   161

2. Serv. Nay, I knew by his face that there was something in him. He had, sir, a kind of face, me-thought, — I cannot tell how to term it.

1. Serv. He had so; looking as it were — would I were hang'd, but I thought there was more in him than I could think.   167

2. Serv. So did I, I'll be sworn. He is simply the rarest man i' th' world.

1. Serv. I think he is; but a greater soldier than he you wot one.   171

2. Serv. Who? My master?

1. Serv. Nay, it's no matter for that.

2. Serv. Worth six on him.

1. Serv. Nay, not so neither; but I take him to be the greater soldier.   176

2. Serv. Faith, look you, one cannot tell how to say that. For the defence of a town, our general is excellent.

1. Serv. Ay, and for an assault too.   180

Re-enter third SERVINGMAN.

3. Serv. O slaves, I can tell you news, — news, you rascals!

1. and 2. Serv. What, what, what? Let's partake.

3. Serv. I would not be a Roman, of all nations; I had as lieve be a condemn'd man.   186

1. and 2. Serv. Wherefore? wherefore?

3. Serv. Why, here's he that was wont to thwack our general, Caius Marcius.

1. Serv. Why do you say, "thwack our general"?   191

3. Serv. I do not say, "thwack our general"; but he was always good enough for him.

2. Serv. Come, we are fellows and friends; he was ever too hard for him; I have heard him say so himself.   196

1. Serv. He was too hard for him directly, to say the troth on't. Before Corioli he scotch'd him and notch'd him like a carbonado.

2. Serv. An he had been cannibally given, he might have boil'd and eaten him too.   201

1. Serv. But more of thy news.

3. Serv. Why, he is so made on here within as if he were son and heir to Mars; set at upper end o' th' table; no question ask'd him by any of the 205 senators but they stand bald before him. Our general himself makes a mistress of him; sanctifies

himself with 's hand and turns up the white o' th' eye to his discourse. But the bottom of the news is, our general is cut i' th' middle and but one 210 half of what he was yesterday; for the other has half by the entreaty and grant of the whole table. He'll go, he says, and sowl the porter of Rome gates by th' ears. He will mow all down before him, and leave his passage poll'd.   215

2. Serv. And he's as like to do't as any man I can imagine.

3. Serv. Do't! he will do't; for, look you, sir, he has as many friends as enemies; which friends, sir, as it were, durst not, look you, sir, show themselves, as we term it, his friends whilst he's in directi-tude.   222

1. Serv. Directitude! What's that?

3. Serv. But when they shall see, sir, his crest up again and the man in blood, they will out of their burrows like conies after rain, and revel all with him.   227

1. Serv. But when goes this forward?

3. Serv. To-morrow; to-day; presently; you shall have the drum struck up this afternoon. 'Tis, as it were, a parcel of their feast, and to be executed ere they wipe their lips.   232

2. Serv. Why, then we shall have a stirring world again. This peace is nothing but to rust iron, in-crease tailors, and breed ballad-makers.   235

1. Serv. Let me have war, say I; it exceeds peace as far as day does night; it's spritely, [waking], audible, and full of vent. Peace is a very apoplexy, lethargy; mull'd, deaf, sleepy, insensible; a getter of more bastard children than war's a destroyer of men.   241

2. Serv. 'Tis so; and as wars, in some sort, may be said to be a ravisher, so it cannot be denied but peace is a great maker of cuckolds.

1. Serv. Ay, and it makes men hate one an-other.   246

3. Serv. Reason; because they then less need one another. The wars for my money! I hope to see Romans as cheap as Volscians. — They are rising, they are rising.   250

1. and 2. Serv. In, in, in, in!   [*Exeunt.*

[SCENE VI. *Rome. A public place.*]

Enter SICINIUS *and* BRUTUS.

Sic. We hear not of him, neither need we fear him;
His remedies are tame. The present peace
And quietness of the people, which before
Were in wild hurry here, do make his friends

---

157. **gave**: told.   161. **set up**: spin.   197. **directly**: plainly.   198. **scotch'd**: slashed.   199. **carbonado**: meat cut for broiling.   213. **sowl**: drag.   215. **poll'd**: cleared.   222. **directitude**: blunder for *discredit*.   226. **conies**: rabbits.   237. [**waking**] (Pope): wide awake. *walking* F.   238. **audible**: sharp-eared. **vent**: activity (lit. outlet).   239. **mull'd**: drowsy. Sc. vi, 2. **remedies**: powers of redress.   4. **do** (Hanmer). *do we* F.

Blush that the world goes well, who rather had, 5
Though they themselves did suffer by 't, behold
Dissentious numbers pest'ring streets than see
Our tradesmen singing in their shops and going
About their functions friendly.

Enter MENENIUS.

Bru. We stood to't in good time. Is this
Menenius?   10
Sic. 'Tis he, 'tis he. O, he is grown most kind of
    late.
Hail, sir!
Men.   Hail to you both!
Sic.   Your Coriolanus
Is not much miss'd but with his friends.
The commonwealth doth stand, and so would
    do,
Were he more angry at it.   15
Men.   All's well; and might have been much
    better, if
He could have temporiz'd.
Sic.   Where is he, hear you?
Men.   Nay, I hear nothing; his mother and his
    wife
Hear nothing from him.

Enter three or four CITIZENS.

[*Citizens.*] The gods preserve you both!
Sic.   God-den, our neighbours, 20
Bru. God-den to you all, god-den to you all.
1. Cit. Ourselves, our wives, and children, on our
    knees,
Are bound to pray for you both.
Sic.   Live, and thrive!
Bru. Farewell, kind neighbours! We wish'd
    Coriolanus   24
Had lov'd you as we did.
[*Citizens.*]   Now the gods keep you!
Both Tri. Farewell, farewell. [*Exeunt Citizens.*
Sic. This is a happier and more comely time
Than when these fellows ran about the streets,
Crying confusion.
Bru.   Caius Marcius was
A worthy officer i' th' war, but insolent,   30
O'ercome with pride, ambitious past all thinking,
Self-loving, —
Sic.   And affecting one sole throne,
Without assistance.
Men.   I think not so.
Sic. We should by this, to all our lamentation,
If he had gone forth consul, found it so.   35
Bru. The gods have well prevented it, and
    Rome
Sits safe and still without him.

Enter an ÆDILE.

Æd.   Worthy tribunes,
There is a slave, whom we have put in prison,
Reports the Volsces with two several powers
Are ent'red in the Roman territories,   40
And with the deepest malice of the war
Destroy what lies before 'em.
Men.   'Tis Aufidius,
Who, hearing of our Marcius' banishment,
Thrusts forth his horns again into the world,
Which were inshell'd when Marcius stood for
    Rome,   45
And durst not once peep out.
Sic.   Come, what talk you
Of Marcius?
Bru. Go see this rumourer whipp'd. It cannot
    be
The Volsces dare break with us.
Men.   Cannot be!
We have record that very well it can;
And three examples of the like hath been   50
Within my age. But reason with the fellow,
Before you punish him, where he heard this,
Lest you shall chance to whip your information
And beat the messenger who bids beware
Of what is to be dreaded.
Sic.   Tell not me!   55
I know this cannot be.
Bru.   Not possible.

Enter a MESSENGER.

Mess. The nobles in great earnestness are
    going
All to the Senate-house; some news is [come]
That turns their countenances.
Sic.   'Tis this slave, —
Go whip him 'fore the people's eyes, — his raising;
Nothing but his report.
Mess.   Yes, worthy sir,   61
The slave's report is seconded; and more,
More fearful, is deliver'd.
Sic.   What more fearful?
Mess. It is spoke freely out of many mouths —
How probable I do not know — that Marcius,   65
Join'd with Aufidius, leads a power 'gainst Rome,
And vows revenge as spacious as between
The young'st and oldest thing.
Sic.   This is most likely!
Bru. Rais'd only that the weaker sort may wish
Good Marcius home again.
Sic.   The very trick on 't.   70
Men. This is unlikely.
He and Aufidius can no more atone
Than violent'st contrariety.

7. **pest'ring:** blocking. 19, etc. [*Citizens*] (Capell). *All* F. 51. **reason:** talk. 58. **[come]** (Rowe). *comming* F. 67.
between: i.e., to embrace. 69. **Rais'd:** made up. 72. **atone:** be reconciled.

Enter [a second] MESSENGER.

[2.] *Mess.* You are sent for to the Senate.
A fearful army, led by Caius Marcius   75
Associated with Aufidius, rages
Upon our territories; and have already
O'erborne their way, consum'd with fire, and took
What lay before them.

Enter COMINIUS.

Com. O, you have made good work!
Men.   What news? what news?
Com. You have holp to ravish your own daughters
    and   81
To melt the city leads upon your pates,
To see your wives dishonour'd to your noses, —
Men. What's the news? what's the news?
Com. Your temples burned in their cement, and
Your franchises, whereon you stood, confin'd 86
Into an auger's bore.
Men.   Pray now, your news? —
You have made fair work, I fear me. — Pray, your
    news?
If Marcius should be join'd with Volscians, —
Com.   If!
He is their god.   He leads them like a thing 90
Made by some other deity than Nature,
That shapes man better; and they follow him
Against us brats with no less confidence
Than boys pursuing summer butterflies,   94
Or butchers killing flies.
Men.   You have made good work,
You and your apron-men; you that stood so much
Upon the voice of occupation and
The breath of garlic-eaters!
Com.   He will shake
Your Rome about your ears.
Men.   As Hercules
Did shake down mellow fruit.   You have made fair
    work!   100
Bru. But is this true, sir?
Com.   Ay; and you'll look pale
Before you find it other.   All the regions
Do smilingly revolt; and who resists
Are mock'd for valiant ignorance
And perish constant fools.   Who is't can blame
    him?   105
Your enemies and his find something in him.
Men. We are all undone, unless
The noble man have mercy.
Com.   Who shall ask it?
The tribunes cannot do't for shame; the people
Deserve such pity of him as the wolf   110
Does of the shepherds.   For his best friends, if they

Should say, "Be good to Rome," they charg'd him
    even
As those should do that had deserv'd his hate,
And therein show'd like enemies.
Men.   'Tis true.
If he were putting to my house the brand   115
That should consume it, I have not the face
To say, "Beseech you, cease."   You have made
    fair hands,
You and your crafts!   You have crafted fair!
Com.   You have brought
A trembling upon Rome, such as was never
S' incapable of help.
[*Both*] *Tri.*   Say not we brought it. 120
Men. How!   Was 't we?   We lov'd him; but,
    like beasts,
[The] cowardly nobles gave way unto your clusters,
Who did hoot him out o' th' city.
Com.   But I fear
They'll roar him in again.   Tullus Aufidius,
The second name of men, obeys his points   125
As if he were his officer.   Desperation
Is all the policy, strength, and defence
That Rome can make against them.

Enter a troop of CITIZENS.

Men.   Here come the clusters.
And is Aufidius with him?   You are they
That made the air unwholesome, when you cast 130
Your stinking greasy caps in hooting at
Coriolanus' exile.   Now he's coming;
And not a hair upon a soldier's head
Which will not prove a whip.   As many coxcombs
As you threw caps up will he tumble down,   135
And pay you for your voices.   'Tis no matter;
If he could burn us all into one coal,
We have deserv'd it.
[*Citizens.*] Faith, we hear fearful news.
I. Cit.   For mine own part,
When I said banish him, I said 'twas pity.   140
2. Cit. And so did I.
3. Cit. And so did I; and, to say the truth, so did
very many of us.   That we did, we did for the best;
and though we willingly consented to his banish-
ment, yet it was against our will.   146
Com. You're goodly things, you voices!
Men.   You have made
Good work, you and your cry!   Shall 's to the Capi-
    tol?
Com. O, ay, what else?
                        [*Exeunt Cominius and Menenius.*
Sic. Go, masters, get you home; be not dismay'd.
These are a side that would be glad to have   151

74. [2.] (Hanmer).   Om. F.   78. O'erborne: surged over.   86. stood: insisted.   confin'd: shrunk.   96. apron-men:
artisans.   97. occupation: workingmen.   105. constant: steadfast.   112. charg'd: would be beseeching.   114. show'd:
would look.   117. made...hands: done fine work.   120. [Both] (Dyce).   Om. F.   122. [The] (Gould conj.).   And F.
clusters: mobs.   125. points: directions.   134. coxcombs: fool's heads.

This true which they so seem to fear.   Go home,
And show no sign of fear.

1. Cit. The gods be good to us!   Come, masters,
let's home.   I ever said we were i' th' wrong when
we banish'd him.   156

2. Cit. So did we all.   But, come, let's home.
                                        [*Exeunt Citizens.*

Bru. I do not like this news.

Sic. Nor I.   159

Bru. Let's to the Capitol.   Would half my wealth
Would buy this for a lie!

Sic.   Pray, let's go.   [*Exeunt.*

[SCENE VII.   *A camp, at a small distance from
Rome.*]

Enter AUFIDIUS *with his* LIEUTENANT.

Auf. Do they still fly to th' Roman?

Lieu. I do not know what witchcraft's in him, but
Your soldiers use him as the grace 'fore meat,
Their talk at table, and their thanks at end;
And you are dark'ned in this action, sir,   5
Even by your own.

Auf.   I cannot help it now,
Unless, by using means, I lame the foot
Of our design.   He bears himself more proudlier,
Even to my person, than I thought he would
When first I did embrace him; yet his nature   10
In that's no changeling, and I must excuse
What cannot be amended.

Lieu.   Yet I wish, sir, —
I mean for your particular, — you had not
Join'd in commission with him; but either
[Had] borne the action of yourself, or else   15
To him had left it solely.

Auf. I understand thee well; and be thou sure,
When he shall come to his account, he knows not
What I can urge against him.   Although it seems,
And so he thinks, and is no less apparent   20
To th' vulgar eye, that he bears all things fairly,
And shows good husbandry for the Volscian state,
Fights dragon-like, and does achieve as soon
As draw his sword; yet he hath left undone
That which shall break his neck or hazard mine   25
Whene'er we come to our account.

Lieu. Sir, I beseech you, think you he'll carry
Rome?

Auf. All places yield to him ere he sits down,
And the nobility of Rome are his.
The senators and patricians love him too;   30
The tribunes are no soldiers, and their people

Will be as rash in the repeal as hasty
To expel him thence.   I think he'll be to Rome
As is the osprey to the fish, who takes it
By sovereignty of nature.   First he was   35
A noble servant to them, but he could not
Carry his honours even.   Whether 'twas pride,
Which out of daily fortune ever taints
The happy man; whether [defect] of judgement,
To fail in the disposing of those chances   40
Which he was lord of; or whether nature,
Not to be other than one thing, not moving
From th' casque to th' cushion, but commanding
    peace
Even with the same austerity and garb
As he controll'd the war; but one of these, —   45
As he hath spices of them all — not all, —
For I dare so far free him, — made him fear'd;
So, hated; and so, banish'd; but he has a merit
To choke it in the utt'rance.   So our virtues
Lie in th' interpretation of the time;   50
And power, unto itself most commendable,
Hath not a tomb so evident as a chair
T' extol what it hath done.
One fire drives out one fire; one nail, one nail;
Rights by rights [falter], strengths by strengths do
    fail.   55
Come, let's away.   When, Caius, Rome is thine,
Thou art poor'st of all; then shortly art thou mine.
                                        [*Exeunt.*

ACT V

[SCENE I.   *Rome.   A public place.*]

Enter MENENIUS, COMINIUS, SICINIUS, BRUTUS,
    with others.

Men. No, I'll not go.   You hear what he hath
    said
Which was sometime his general who lov'd him
In a most dear particular.   He call'd me father;
But what o' that?   Go, you that banish'd him;
A mile before his tent fall down, and knee   5
The way into his mercy.   Nay, if he coy'd
To hear Cominius speak, I'll keep at home.

Com. He would not seem to know me.

Men.   Do you hear?

Com. Yet one time he did call me by my name.
I urg'd our old acquaintance, and the drops   10
That we have bled together.   Coriolanus
He would not answer to; forbade all names;
He was a kind of nothing, titleless,

Sc. vii, 13. **particular**: personal good.   14. **commission**: command.   15. **[Had]** (Pope).   *Have* F.   **of**: by.   22. **husbandry**: economy.   28. **sits down**: lays siege.   34. **osprey**: fish hawk.   39. **happy**: lucky.   **[defect]** F₂.   *detect* F₁.   41. **nature**: i.e., it was his nature.   42. **moving**: i.e., changing his behavior when moving.   43. **casque**: helmet, i.e., battlefield.   **cushion**: i.e., senate-house.   49. **it**: i.e., the enmity.   52–53. **Hath ... done**: is never so near its end as when it proclaims its own deserts.   55. **[falter]** (Dyce).   *fouler* F.   Other emendations are *founder, suffer.*

Act V, sc. i, 3. **particular**: personal way.   6. **coy'd**: was reluctant.

Till he had forg'd himself a name o' th' fire
Of burning Rome.

Men. Why, so; you have made good work! 15
A pair of tribunes that have wrack'd [fair] Rome
To make coals cheap! A noble memory!

Com. I minded him how royal 'twas to pardon
When it was less expected; he replied,
It was a bare petition of a state 20
To one whom they had punish'd.

Men.   **Very well;**
Could he say less?

Com. I offered to awaken his regard
For 's private friends; his answer to me was,
He could not stay to pick them in a pile 25
Of noisome musty chaff. He said 'twas folly,
For one poor grain or two, to leave unburnt
And still to nose th' offence.

Men.   For one poor grain or two!
I am one of those; his mother, wife, his child,
And this brave fellow too, we are the grains. 30
You are the musty chaff, and you are smelt
Above the moon; we must be burnt for you.

Sic. Nay, pray, be patient. If you refuse your
    aid
In this so never-needed help, yet do not
Upbraid 's with our distress. But, sure, if you 35
Would be your country's pleader, your good tongue,
More than the instant army we can make,
Might stop our countryman.

Men.   No, I'll not meddle.

Sic. Pray you, go to him.

Men.   What should I do?

Bru. Only make trial what your love can do 40
For Rome, towards Marcius.

Men.   Well, and say that Marcius
Return me, as Cominius is return'd,
Unheard; what then?
But as a discontented friend, grief-shot
With his unkindness? Say 't be so?

Sic.   Yet your good will
Must have that thanks from Rome, after the
    measure 46
As you intended well.

Men.   I'll undertake 't.
I think he'll hear me. Yet, to bite his lip
And hum at good Cominius much unhearts me.
He was not taken well; he had not din'd. 50
The veins unfill'd, our blood is cold, and then
We pout upon the morning, are unapt
To give or to forgive; but when we have stuff'd
These pipes and these conveyances of our blood
With wine and feeding, we have suppler souls 55
Than in our priest-like fasts: therefore I'll watch
    him

Till he be dieted to my request,
And then I'll set upon him.

Bru. You know the very road into his kindness,
And cannot lose your way.

Men.   Good faith, I'll prove him,
Speed how it will. I shall ere long have know-
    ledge 61
Of my success.   [*Exit.*

Com.   He'll never hear him.

Sic.   Not?

Com. I tell you, he does sit in gold, his eye
Red as 'twould burn Rome; and his injury
The gaoler to his pity. I kneel'd before him; 65
'Twas very faintly he said, "Rise"; dismiss'd me
Thus, with his speechless hand. What he would
    do
He sent in writing after me; what he would not,
Bound with an oath to yield to his conditions;
So that all hope is vain, 70
Unless [in 's] noble mother and his wife,
Who, as I hear, mean to solicit him
For mercy to his country. Therefore, let's hence,
And with our fair entreaties haste them on.
                      [*Exeunt.*

[SCENE II. *Entrance of the Volscian camp before
    Rome.*] *The* WATCH *on guard.*

Enter to them, MENENIUS.

1. Watch. Stay! Whence are you?

2. Watch.   Stand, and go back.

Men. You guard like men; 'tis well; but, by your
    leave,
I am an officer of state, and come
To speak with Coriolanus.

1. Watch.   From whence?

Men.   From Rome.

1. Watch. You may not pass, you must return;
    our general 5
Will no more hear from thence.

2. Watch. You'll see your Rome embrac'd with
    fire before
You'll speak with Coriolanus.

Men.   Good my friends,
If you have heard your general talk of Rome
And of his friends there, it is lots to blanks 10
My name hath touch'd your ears; it is Menenius.

1. Watch. Be it so; go back. The virtue of your
    name
Is not here passable.

Men.   I tell thee, fellow,
Thy general is my lover. I have been
The book of his good acts, whence men have read 15
His fame unparallel'd haply amplified;

16. [fair] (Hanmer). *for* F.   20. bare: mere.   23. offered: tried.   37. instant: improvised.   50. taken well: approached at a good time.   63. in gold: on a throne of gold.   69. Bound: i.e., binding us.   71. [in 's] *his* F.
    Sc. ii, 10. lots to blanks: certain (terms from lottery).   13. passable: current.

For I have ever verified my friends,
Of whom he's chief, with all the size that verity
Would without lapsing suffer; nay, sometimes,
Like to a bowl upon a subtle ground,   20
I have tumbled past the throw; and in his praise
Have almost stamp'd the leasing. Therefore, fellow,
I must have leave to pass.

1. Watch. Faith, sir, if you had told as many lies
in his behalf as you have uttered words in your
own, you should not pass here; no, though it were
as virtuous to lie as to live chastely. Therefore, go
back.   28

Men. Prithee, fellow, remember my name is
Menenius, always factionary on the party of your
general.   31

2. Watch. Howsoever you have been his liar, as
you say you have, I am one that, telling true under
him, must say you cannot pass. Therefore, go
back.   35

Men. Has he din'd, canst thou tell? for I would
not speak with him till after dinner.

1. Watch. You are a Roman, are you?

Men. I am, as thy general is.   39

1. Watch. Then you should hate Rome, as he
does. Can you, when you have push'd out your
gates the very defender of them, and, in a violent
popular ignorance, given your enemy your shield,
think to front his revenges with the easy groans of
old women, the virginal palms of your daughters,   45
or with the palsied intercession of such a decay'd
dotant as you seem to be? Can you think to blow
out the intended fire your city is ready to flame in,
with such weak breath as this? No, you are de-   50
ceiv'd; therefore, back to Rome, and prepare for
your execution. You are condemn'd; our general
has sworn you out of reprieve and pardon.   54

Men. Sirrah, if thy captain knew I were here,
he would use me with estimation.

1. Watch. Come, my captain knows you not.

Men. I mean, thy general.   58

1. Watch. My general cares not for you. Back,
I say, go; lest I let forth your half-pint of blood.
Back, that's the utmost of your having; back!

Men. Nay, but, fellow, fellow, —

Enter CORIOLANUS *with* AUFIDIUS.

Cor. What's the matter?   64

Men. Now, you companion, I'll say an errand
for you. You shall know now that I am in estimation; you shall perceive that a Jack guardant cannot
office me from my son Coriolanus. Guess but [by]

my entertainment with him if thou stand'st not i'
th' state of hanging, or of some death more long   70
in spectatorship and crueller in suffering; behold
now presently, and swoon for what's to come upon
thee. [*To Cor.*] The glorious gods sit in hourly
synod about thy particular prosperity, and love thee
no worse than thy old father Menenius does! O   75
my son, my son! thou art preparing fire for us; look
thee, here's water to quench it. I was hardly moved
to come to thee; but being assured none but myself
could move thee, I have been blown out of our   80
gates with sighs, and conjure thee to pardon Rome
and thy petitionary countrymen. The good gods
assuage thy wrath, and turn the dregs of it upon
this varlet here, — this, who, like a block, hath
denied my access to thee.   85

Cor. Away!

Men. How! away!

Cor. Wife, mother, child I know not. My
affairs
Are servanted to others; though I owe
My revenge properly, my remission lies   90
In Volscian breasts. That we have been familiar,
Ingrate forgetfulness shall poison rather
Than pity note how much. Therefore, begone
Mine ears against your suits are stronger than
Your gates against my force. Yet, for I loved
thee,   95
Take this along. I writ it for thy sake,
                   [*Gives a letter.*]
And would have sent it. Another word, Menenius,
I will not hear thee speak. This man, Aufidius,
Was my belov'd in Rome; yet thou behold'st!

Auf. You keep a constant temper.   100
         [*Exeunt* [*Coriolanus and Aufidius*].

1. Watch. Now, sir, is your name Menenius?

2. Watch. 'Tis a spell, you see, of much power.
You know the way home again.

1. Watch. Do you hear how we are shent for keeping your greatness back?   105

2. Watch. What cause do you think I have to
swoon?

Men. I neither care for th' world nor your general; for such things as you, I can scarce think
there's any, you're so slight. He that hath a   110
will to die by himself fears it not from another.
Let your general do his worst. For you, be that
you are, long; and your misery increase with your
age! I say to you, as I was said to, "Away!" [*Exit.*

1. Watch. A noble fellow, I warrant him.   115

2. Watch. The worthy fellow is our general. He's
the rock, the oak not to be wind-shaken. [*Exeunt.*

---

17. **verified:** credited. Many emendations have been proposed, as *magnified, glorified, amplified.*   20. **subtle:** deceptive.
21. **throw:** mark.   22. **stamp'd the leasing:** certified a falsehood.   30. **factionary on:** adhering to.   47. **dotant:** dotard.
65. **say an errand:** deliver a message.   67. **Jack guardant:** ill-mannered guard.   68. **[by]** (Malone).   *my* F.   77.
hardly: with difficulty.   84. **block:** blockhead.   89. **servanted:** subjected.   90. **properly:** to myself.   **remission:** mercy.
104. **shent:** scolded.   111. **himself:** his own hand.

[SCENE III.   *The tent of Coriolanus.*]

Enter CORIOLANUS, AUFIDIUS [*and others*].

Cor. We will before the walls of Rome to-morrow
Set down our host.   My partner in this action,
You must report to th' Volscian lords, how plainly
I have borne this business.

Auf.   Only their ends
You have respected; stopp'd your ears against   5
The general suit of Rome; never admitted
A private whisper, no, not with such friends
That thought them sure of you.

Cor.   This last old man,
Whom with a crack'd heart I have sent to Rome,
Lov'd me above the measure of a father;   10
Nay, godded me, indeed.   Their latest refuge
Was to send him; for whose old love I have,
Though I show'd sourly to him, once more offer'd
The first conditions, which they did refuse
And cannot now accept.   To grace him only   15
That thought he could do more, a very little
I have yielded to.   Fresh embassies and suits,
Nor from the state nor private friends, hereafter
Will I lend ear to.   Ha! what shout is this?

                     [*Shout within.*

Shall I be tempted to infringe my vow   20
In the same time 'tis made?   I will not.

Enter [*in mourning habits*] VIRGILIA, VOLUMNIA
[*leading*] *young* MARCIUS, Valeria, *with Attendants.*

My wife comes foremost; then the honour'd mould
Wherein this trunk was fram'd, and in her hand
The grandchild to her blood.   But out, affection!
All bond and privilege of nature, break!   25
Let it be virtuous to be obstinate.
What is that curtsy worth? or those doves' eyes,
Which can make gods forsworn?   I melt, and am
    not
Of stronger earth than others.   My mother bows,
As if Olympus to a molehill should   30
In supplication nod; and my young boy
Hath an aspect of intercession which
Great nature cries, "Deny not."   Let the Volsces
Plough Rome and harrow Italy, I'll never
Be such a gosling to obey instinct, but stand   35
As if a man were author of himself
And knew no other kin.

Vir.   My lord and husband!

Cor. These eyes are not the same I wore in Rome.

Vir. The sorrow that delivers us thus chang'd
Makes you think so.

Cor.   Like a dull actor now   40
I have forgot my part, and I am out,

Even to a full disgrace.   Best of my flesh,
Forgive my tyranny; but do not say
For that, "Forgive our Romans."   O, a kiss
Long as my exile, sweet as my revenge!   45
Now, by the jealous queen of heaven, that kiss
I carried from thee, dear; and my true lip
Hath virgin'd it e'er since.   You gods! I [prate],
And the most noble mother of the world
Leave unsaluted.   Sink, my knee, i' th' earth;

                     [*Kneels.*

Of thy deep duty more impression show   51
Than that of common sons.

Vol.   O, stand up bless'd!
Whilst, with no softer cushion than the flint,
I kneel before thee, and unproperly
Show duty, as mistaken all this while   55
Between the child and parent.   [*Kneels.*]

Cor. [*Instantly raising her.*] What's this?
Your knees to me? to your corrected son?
Then let the pebbles on the hungry beach
Fillip the stars; then let the mutinous winds
Strike the proud cedars 'gainst the fiery sun,   60
Murd'ring impossibility, to make
What cannot be, slight work.

Vol.   Thou art my warrior;
I holp to frame thee.   Do you know this lady?

Cor. The noble sister of Publicola,
The moon of Rome, chaste as the icicle   65
That's curded by the frost from purest snow
And hangs on Dian's temple.   Dear Valeria!

Vol. This is a poor epitome of yours,
Which by th' interpretation of full time
May show like all yourself.

Cor.   The god of soldiers,
With the consent of supreme Jove, inform   71
Thy thoughts with nobleness; that thou mayst prove
To shame unvulnerable, and stick i' th' wars
Like a great sea-mark, standing every flaw
And saving those that eye thee!

Vol.   Your knee, sirrah.

Cor. That's my brave boy!   76

Vol. Even he, your wife, this lady, and myself,
Are suitors to you.

Cor.   I beseech you, peace;
Or, if you'd ask, remember this before:
The thing I have forsworn to grant may never
Be held by you denials.   Do not bid me   81
Dismiss my soldiers, or capitulate
Again with Rome's mechanics; tell me not
Wherein I seem unnatural; desire not
To allay my rages and revenges with   85
Your colder reasons.

Vol.   O, no more, no more!

You have said you will not grant us anything,
For we have nothing else to ask but that
Which you deny already. Yet we will ask,
That, if you fail in our request, the blame   90
May hang upon your hardness; therefore hear us.
  Cor. Aufidius, and you Volsces, mark; for we'll
Hear nought from Rome in private. Your request?
  Vol. Should we be silent and not speak, our
    raiment
And state of bodies would bewray what life   95
We have led since thy exile. Think with thyself
How more unfortunate than all living women
Are we come hither; since that thy sight, which
    should
Make our eyes flow with joy, hearts dance with
    comforts,
Constrains them weep and shake with fear and
    sorrow;   100
Making the mother, wife, and child to see
The son, the husband, and the father tearing
His country's bowels out. And to poor we
Thine enmity's most capital. Thou barr'st us
Our prayers to the gods, which is a comfort   105
That all but we enjoy; for how can we,
Alas, how can we for our country pray,
Whereto we are bound, together with thy victory,
Whereto we are bound? Alack, or we must lose
The country, our dear nurse, or else thy person, 110
Our comfort in the country. We must find
An evident calamity, though we had
Our wish, which side should win; for either thou
Must, as a foreign recreant, be led
With manacles through our streets, or else   115
Triumphantly tread on thy country's ruin
And bear the palm for having bravely shed
Thy wife and children's blood. For myself, son,
I purpose not to wait on fortune till
These wars determine. If I cannot persuade thee
Rather to show a noble grace to both parts   121
Than seek the end of one, thou shalt no sooner
March to assault thy country than to tread —
Trust to't, thou shalt not — on thy mother's womb
That brought thee to this world.
  Vir.   Ay, and on mine,
That brought you forth this boy, to keep your
    name   126
Living to time.
  Young Mar. 'A shall not tread on me.
I'll run away till I am bigger, but then I'll fight.
  Cor. Not of a woman's tenderness to be,
Requires nor child nor woman's face to see.   130
I have sat too long.   [*Rising.*]
  Vol.   Nay, go not from us thus.

If it were so that our request did tend
To save the Romans, thereby to destroy
The Volsces whom you serve, you might condemn
    us,
As poisonous of your honour. No; our suit   135
Is that you reconcile them: while the Volsces
May say, "This mercy we have show'd"; the
    Romans,
"This we receiv'd"; and each in either side
Give the all-hail to thee and cry, "Be blest
For making up this peace!" Thou know'st, great
    son,   140
The end of war's uncertain, but this certain,
That, if thou conquer Rome, the benefit
Which thou shalt thereby reap is such a name
Whose repetition will be dogg'd with curses,
Whose chronicle thus writ: "The man was noble,
But with his last attempt he wip'd it out,   146
Destroy'd his country, and his name remains
To th' ensuing age abhorr'd." Speak to me, son.
Thou hast affected the [fine] strains of honour,
To imitate the graces of the gods;   150
To tear with thunder the wide cheeks o' th' air,
And yet to [charge] thy sulphur with a bolt
That should but rive an oak. Why dost not speak?
Think'st thou it honourable for a noble man
Still to remember wrongs? Daughter, speak you;
He cares not for your weeping. Speak thou, boy; 156
Perhaps thy childishness will move him more
Than can our reasons. There's no man in the world
More bound to 's mother; yet here he lets me prate
Like one i' th' stocks. — Thou hast never in thy
    life   160
Show'd thy dear mother any courtesy,
When she, poor hen, fond of no second brood,
Has cluck'd thee to the wars and safely home,
Loaden with honour. Say my request 's unjust,
And spurn me back; but if it be not so,   165
Thou art not honest; and the gods will plague thee
That thou restrain'st from me the duty which
To a mother's part belongs. — He turns away.
Down, ladies; let us shame him with our knees.
To his surname Coriolanus longs more pride   170
Than pity to our prayers. Down! an end;
This is the last. So we will home to Rome,
And die among our neighbours. — Nay, behold 's!
This boy, that cannot tell what he would have,
But kneels and holds up hands for fellowship,   175
Does reason our petition with more strength
Than thou hast to deny 't. — Come, let us go.
This fellow had a Volscian to his mother;
His wife is in Corioli, and his child
Like him by chance. — Yet give us our dispatch. 180

---

   90. **fail in:** refuse.   95. **bewray:** reveal.   114. **recreant:** traitor.   120. **determine:** end.   124. **Trust...not.** In sense, this parenthesis follows "sooner," l. 122.   146. **attempt:** enterprise.   149. **[fine]** (Johnson). *five* F.   152. **[charge]** (Warburton). | *change* F.   **sulphur:** the supposed source of lightning.   153. **rive an oak:** i.e., do little real harm.   167. **restrain'st:** withholdest.   170. **longs:** belongs.   176. **reason:** argue.   180. **dispatch:** dismissal.

I am hush'd until our city be a-fire,
And then I'll speak a little.

              [He holds her by the hand, silent.

Cor.   O mother, mother!
What have you done? Behold, the heavens do ope,
The gods look down, and this unnatural scene
They laugh at. O my mother, mother! O!   185
You have won a happy victory to Rome;
But, for your son, — believe it, O believe it —,
Most dangerously you have with him prevail'd,
If not most mortal to him. But, let it come.
Aufidius, though I cannot make true wars,   190
I'll frame convenient peace. Now, good Aufidius,
Were you in my [stead], would you have heard
A mother less, or granted less, Aufidius?

Auf.   I was mov'd withal.

Cor.   I dare be sworn you were;
And, sir, it is no little thing to make   195
Mine eyes to sweat compassion. But, good sir,
What peace you'll make, advise me. For my part,
I'll not to Rome, I'll back with you; and pray you,
Stand to me in this cause. — O mother! wife!

               [Speaks apart with them.]

Auf. [*Aside.*] I am glad thou hast set thy mercy
    and thy honour   200
At difference in thee. Out of that I'll work
Myself a former fortune.

Cor. [*To Volumnia, Virgilia, etc.*] Ay, by and by;
But we will drink together; and you shall bear
A better witness back than words, which we,
On like conditions, will have counter-seal'd.   205
Come, enter with us. Ladies, you deserve
To have a temple built you. All the swords
In Italy, and her confederate arms,
Could not have made this peace.   *[Exeunt.*

[SCENE IV. *Rome. A public place.*]

Enter MENENIUS *and* SICINIUS.

Men. See you yond coign o' th' Capitol, yond
corner-stone?

Sic. Why, what of that?

Men. If it be possible for you to displace it with
your little finger, there is some hope the ladies of   5
Rome, especially his mother, may prevail with him.
But I say there is no hope in 't; our throats are
sentenc'd and stay upon execution.

Sic. Is't possible that so short a time can alter
the condition of a man?   10

Men. There is difference between a grub and a
butterfly; yet your butterfly was a grub. This
Marcius is grown from man to dragon; he has wings;
he's more than a creeping thing.

Sic. He lov'd his mother dearly.   15

Men. So did he me; and he no more remembers
his mother now than an eight-year-old horse.
The tartness of his face sours ripe grapes; when he
walks, he moves like an engine, and the ground
shrinks before his treading. He is able to pierce   20
a corslet with his eye; talks like a knell, and his
hum is a battery. He sits in his state, as a thing
made for Alexander. What he bids be done is
finish'd with his bidding. He wants nothing of a
god but eternity and a heaven to throne in.   26

Sic. Yes, mercy, if you report him truly.

Men. I paint him in the character. Mark what
mercy his mother shall bring from him. There is
no more mercy in him than there is milk in a male
tiger; that shall our poor city find: and all this is
long of you.   32

Sic. The gods be good unto us!

Men. No, in such a case the gods will not be good
unto us. When we banish'd him, we respected not
them; and, he returning to break our necks, they
respect not us.   37

Enter a MESSENGER.

Mess. Sir, if you'd save your life, fly to your
    house.
The plebeians have got your fellow-tribune
And hale him up and down, all swearing, if   40
The Roman ladies bring not comfort home,
They'll give him death by inches.

Enter a second MESSENGER.

Sic.   What's the news?

[2.] *Mess.* Good news, good news! The ladies
    have prevail'd,
The Volscians are dislodg'd, and Marcius gone.
A merrier day did never yet greet Rome,   45
No, not th' expulsion of the Tarquins.

Sic.   Friend,
Art thou certain this is true? Is't most certain?

[2.] *Mess.* As certain as I know the sun is fire.
Where have you lurk'd, that you make doubt of it?
Ne'er through an arch so hurried the blown tide,   50
As the recomforted through th' gates. Why, hark
    you!

        [Trumpets; hautboys; drums beat; all to-
        gether.

The trumpets, sackbuts, psalteries, and fifes,
Tabors and cymbals and the shouting Romans,
Make the sun dance. Hark you!

               [A shout within.

Men.   This is good news;
I will go meet the ladies. This Volumnia   55

---

192. [stead] F₄. steed F₁. 199. **Stand to**: support. 201–202. **work . . . fortune**: retrieve my former fortune.

Sc. iv, 1. **coign**: corner. 8. **stay upon**: await. 10. **condition**: nature. 19. **engine**: instrument of war. 22. **state**: chair of state. 32. **long**: because. 35. **respected**: considered. 44. **dislodg'd**: decamped. 52. s.d. *hautboys*: oboes. **sackbuts**: trombones. **psalteries**: stringed instruments.

Is worth of consuls, senators, patricians,
A city full; of tribunes, such as you,
A sea and land full. You have pray'd well to-day.
This morning for ten thousand of your throats
I'd not have given a doit. Hark, how they joy!
      [*Sound still, with the shouts.*
  Sic. First, the gods bless you for your tidings;
      next,   61
Accept my thankfulness.
  [2.] *Mess.*   Sir, we have all
Great cause to give great thanks.
  Sic.   They are near the city?
  [2.] *Mess.* Almost at point to enter.
  Sic.   We will meet them,
And help the joy.   [*Exeunt.* 65

[SCENE V. *The same. A street near the gate.*]

Enter two SENATORS *with Ladies* [Volumnia, Virgilia,
      Valeria, etc.], *passing over the stage, with other
      Lords.*

  [*1.*] *Sen.* Behold our patroness, the life of Rome!
Call all your tribes together, praise the gods,
And make triumphant fires!   Strew flowers before
      them!
Unshout the noise that banish'd Marcius!
Repeal him with the welcome of his mother;   5
Cry, "Welcome, ladies, welcome!"
  All.   Welcome, ladies,
Welcome!   [*A flourish with drums and trumpets.*
                                          [*Exeunt.*]

[SCENE VI. *Corioli. A public place.*]

Enter TULLUS AUFIDIUS, *with Attendants.*

  Auf. Go tell the lords o' th' city I am here;
Deliver them this paper.   Having read it,
Bid them repair to th' market-place, where I,
Even in theirs and in the commons' ears,
Will vouch the truth of it.   Him I accuse   5
The city ports by this hath enter'd, and
Intends to appear before the people, hoping
To purge himself with words.   Dispatch.
                                  [*Exeunt Attendants.*]

Enter three or four CONSPIRATORS *of Aufidius'
      faction.*

Most welcome!
  1. Con. How is it with our general?
  Auf.   Even so   10
As with a man by his own alms empoison'd,
And with his charity slain.
  2. Con.   Most noble sir,
If you do hold the same intent wherein
You wish'd us parties, we'll deliver you

Of your great danger.
  Auf.   Sir, I cannot tell.   15
We must proceed as we do find the people.
  3. Con. The people will remain uncertain whilst
'Twixt you there's difference; but the fall of either
Makes the survivor heir of all.
  Auf.   I know it;
And my pretext to strike at him admits   20
A good construction.   I rais'd him, and I pawn'd
Mine honour for his truth; who being so heighten'd,
He watered his new plants with dews of flattery,
Seducing so my friends; and, to this end,
He bow'd his nature, never known before   25
But to be rough, unswayable, and free.
  3. Con. Sir, his stoutness
When he did stand for consul, which he lost
By lack of stooping, —
  Auf.   That I would have spoke of.   29
Being banish'd for't, he came unto my hearth,
Presented to my knife his throat.   I took him;
Made him joint-servant with me; gave him way
In all his own desires; nay, let him choose
Out of my files, his projects to accomplish,
My best and freshest men; serv'd his designments
In mine own person; holp to reap the fame   36
Which he did end all his, and took some pride
To do myself this wrong; till, at the last,
I seem'd his follower, not partner, and
He wag'd me with his countenance as if   40
I had been mercenary.
  1. Con.   So he did, my lord.
The army marvell'd at it, and, in the last,
When he had carried Rome and that we look'd
For no less spoil than glory, —
  Auf.   There was it,
For which my sinews shall be stretch'd upon him.
At a few drops of women's rheum, which are   46
As cheap as lies, he sold the blood and labour
Of our great action.   Therefore shall he die,
And I'll renew me in his fall.   But, hark!
      [*Drums and trumpets sound, with great
            shouts of the People.*
  1. Con. Your native town you enter'd like a post,
And had no welcomes home; but he returns,   51
Splitting the air with noise.
  2. Con.   And patient fools,
Whose children he hath slain, their base throats tear
With giving him glory.
  3. Con.   Therefore, at your vantage,
Ere he express himself or move the people   55
With what he would say, let him feel your sword,
Which we will second.   When he lies along,
After your way his tale pronounc'd shall bury
His reasons with his body.
  Auf.   Say no more.
Here come the lords.   60

Sc. vi, 40. **wag'd . . . countenance:** paid me with his favor, patronized me.   45. **upon:** against.   46. **rheum:** tears.   50.
post: messenger.   57. **along:** prostrate, dead.   58. **After . . . pronounc'd:** your version of the story.

Enter the LORDS *of the city.*

All the Lords. You are most welcome home.

Auf.   I have not deserv'd it.
But, worthy lords, have you with heed perused
What I have written to you?

Lords.   We have.

1. Lord.   And grieve to hear 't.
What faults he made before the last, I think
Might have found easy fines; but there to end   65
Where he was to begin, and give away
The benefit of our levies, answering us
With our own charge, making a treaty where
There was a yielding, — this admits no excuse.

Auf. He approaches; you shall hear him.   70

Enter CORIOLANUS, *marching with drum and
      colours;* Commoners *being with him.*

Cor. Hail, lords! I am return'd your soldier,
No more infected with my country's love
Than when I parted hence, but still subsisting
Under your great command. You are to know
That prosperously I have attempted and   75
With bloody passage led your wars even to
The gates of Rome. Our spoils we have brought home
Doth more than counterpoise a full third part
The charges of the action. We have made peace
With no less honour to the Antiates   80
Than shame to th' Romans; and we here deliver,
Subscrib'd by th' consuls and patricians,
Together with the seal o' th' Senate, what
We have compounded on.

Auf.   Read it not, noble lords;
But tell the traitor, in the highest degree   85
He hath abus'd your powers.

Cor. "Traitor!" How now!

Auf.   Ay, traitor, Marcius!

Cor.   "Marcius!"

Auf. Ay, Marcius, Caius Marcius! Dost thou
    think
I'll grace thee with that robbery, thy stol'n name,
Coriolanus, in Corioli?   90
You lords and heads o' th' state, perfidiously
He has betray'd your business, and given up,
For certain drops of salt, your city Rome,
I say "your city," to his wife and mother;
Breaking his oath and resolution like   95
A twist of rotten silk; never admitting
Counsel o' th' war; but at his nurse's tears
He whin'd and roar'd away your victory,
That pages blush'd at him and men of heart
Look'd wond'ring each at others.

Cor.   Hear'st thou, Mars?   100

Auf. Name not the god, thou boy of tears!

Cor.   Ha!

Auf. No more.

Cor. Measureless liar, thou hast made my heart
Too great for what contains it. "Boy!" O slave!
Pardon me, lords, 'tis the first time that ever   105
I was forc'd to scold. Your judgements, my grave
    lords,
Must give this cur the lie; and his own notion —
Who wears my stripes impress'd upon him, that
Must bear my beating to his grave — shall join
To thrust the lie unto him.   110

1. Lord. Peace, both, and hear me speak.

Cor. Cut me to pieces, Volsces; men and lads,
Stain all your edges on me. "Boy!" False hound!
If you have writ your annals true, 'tis there
That, like an eagle in a dove-cote, I   115
[Flutter'd] your Volscians in Corioli;
Alone I did it. "Boy!"

Auf.   Why, noble lords,
Will you be put in mind of his blind fortune,
Which was your shame, by this unholy braggart,
'Fore your own eyes and ears?

All Consp.   Let him die for't.   120

All the people. Tear him to pieces! Do it
presently! —He kill'd my son! — My daughter! —
He kill'd my cousin Marcus! — He kill'd my father!

2. Lord. Peace, ho! no outrage: peace!   125
The man is noble and his fame folds in
This orb o' th' earth. His last offences to us
Shall have judicious hearing. Stand, Aufidius,
And trouble not the peace.

Cor.   O that I had him,
With six Aufidiuses, or more, his tribe,   130
To use my lawful sword!

Auf.   Insolent villain!

All Consp. Kill, kill, kill, kill, kill him!

> [*Both the Conspirators draw, and kill
> Coriolanus, who falls: Aufidius stands
> on him.*

Lords.   Hold, hold, hold, hold!

Auf. My noble masters, hear me speak.

1. Lord.   O Tullus!

2. Lord. Thou hast done a deed whereat valour
    will weep.

3. Lord. Tread not upon him. Masters all, be
    quiet;   135
Put up your swords.

Auf. My lords, when you shall know — as in
    this rage,
Provok'd by him, you cannot — the great danger
Which this man's life did owe you, you'll rejoice
That he is thus cut off. Please it your Honours
To call me to your Senate, I'll deliver   141
Myself your loyal servant, or endure
Your heaviest censure.

1. Lord.   Bear from hence his body;

---

65. **easy fines:** light penalties. 67–68. **answering ... charge:** only repaying us the cost of our war (cf. ll. 77–79). 84. **compounded:** agreed. 107. **notion:** sense. 116. **[Flutter'd]** F$_3$. *Flatter'd* F$_1$. 139. **did owe:** had in store for. 141. **deliver:** prove.

And mourn you for him. Let him be regarded
As the most noble corse that ever herald 145
Did follow to his urn.
  2. Lord.   His own impatience
Takes from Aufidius a great part of blame.
Let's make the best of it.
  Auf.   My rage is gone,
And I am struck with sorrow. Take him up.
Help, three o' th' chiefest soldiers; I'll be one. 150

Beat thou the drum, that it speak mournfully.
Trail your steel pikes. Though in this city he
Hath widow'd and unchilded many a one,
Which to this hour bewail the injury,
Yet he shall have a noble memory. 155
Assist.

   [Exeunt, bearing the body of Coriolanus.
    A dead march sounded.

Cymbeline

CYMBELINE FIRST APPEARED in print in the Folio of 1623, and there is no evidence of any previous attempt at publication. The text must therefore be based upon this original.

For the date of production the later limit is fixed by the death, on September 12, 1611, of Simon Forman, astrologer and quack physician, whose *Booke of Plaies* records a performance of *Cymbeline* which he had seen. The entry, undated, appears to have been made between notes on performances of *Macbeth* and *Richard II* (not Shakespeare's play) dated respectively Saturday, April 20, 1610, and Tuesday, April 30, 1611. But April 20th fell on a Saturday in 1611, not in 1610, and inasmuch as the entries of the other plays witnessed by Forman are headed 1611, it is likely that Forman made an error in the case of *Macbeth*, and that he saw both that play and *Cymbeline* in 1611. If this is true, it seems reasonable to suppose that, unless the play was very new, *Cymbeline* was composed some time in 1610, and features of style and metre support this date.

Cymbeline conforms in its general theatrical nature to the tragi-comic romances with which Beaumont and Fletcher were winning at about this time remarkable success, and to their *Philaster* (c. 1610) in particular, with which it exhibits some striking resemblances. The question of influence and indebtedness may never, perhaps, be unequivocally resolved, because the date of *Philaster* cannot be fixed with precision. In 1608 Beaumont and Fletcher had produced *The Faithful Shepherdess*, which, though a pastoral and written in couplets, may be regarded as anticipating the new kind of tragi-comedy to which both *Cymbeline* and *Philaster* belong. It may be conjectured that after writing *Cymbeline*, Shakespeare was encouraged to continue working the same vein in *The Winter's Tale* and *The Tempest*, not only because of his presumable satisfaction with *Cymbeline* but also because of the success of Beaumont and Fletcher. In such cases influence may be reciprocal. Furthermore, it may be recalled that *Pericles* (1608) has many of the features of the tragi-comic romance.

Doubt has been cast upon the authorship of the vision of Posthumus in V.iv. The device itself is paralleled by the spectacular elements in *The Winter's Tale* and *The Tempest*, but the vastly inferior quality of the verses has led most authorities to believe that many, at least, must be by another hand than Shakespeare's. Critics differ, however, in the amount they would assign to him. To consider V.iv.30–113 as un-Shakespearean is a conservative judgment, but that is all that one can relieve him of with any confidence, and lines 93–113 may be genuine. Moreover, one must see a collaborator here rather than an interpolator, for the extended reference to the vision in V.v.425–59 shows that Shakespeare was cognizant of what had gone before.

For the intricate plot of *Cymbeline* Shakespeare chose to place a familiar romantic tale in a semi-historical setting. Though the story of a man who makes a wager upon the chastity of his wife is widespread in Western Europe, the version in the ninth novel of the second day in Boccaccio's *Decameron* is assuredly the one which served Shakespeare. In the essential features of the story up to the point where the heroine sets out to seek her fortunes in disguise, Shakespeare closely follows his source, but the rest of her history bears no relation to Boccaccio's narrative. Moreover, Shakespeare has made two notable changes in the material he derived from Boccaccio. Whereas the prototype of Posthumus (Bernabo) is a merchant, Shakespeare makes Posthumus a noble; and Imogen, whose original (Ginevra) is, like her husband, bourgeois, Shakespeare makes the daughter of a king. In Boccaccio the wager is proposed by the husband himself; in the play the suggestion comes from the villain Iachimo. These alterations significantly affect characterization.

His romantic plot Shakespeare has skillfully woven into a background derived from Holinshed's *Chronicle*. This background is chiefly legendary; of authentic history there is little beyond the fact of the existence, about the beginning of the Christian era, of a British king, Cunobelinus. The *Chronicle* represents him as brought up at Rome and knighted by Augustus Caesar, who showed him great favor, and as the father of two sons, Guiderius and Arviragus. Conflicting stories are reported about the payment of tribute to Rome, but Holinshed stresses the friendship between Cymbeline and the Emperor, and makes the refusal of tribute come from Guiderius after his father's death. The references to previous conflicts between Rome and Britain are derived from the *Chronicle*. The account of the battle in the fifth act, and of the saving of the day by Belarius and the two princes, is based upon Holinshed's story of a fight between the Danes and the Scots, in which the fleeing Scots were rallied in a lane by a husbandman and his two sons. The names given to the Britons in the play, even the pseudonyms of the princes Shakespeare picked up in a variety of places in Holinshed.

In the matter of the stolen princes, their education according to nature by the banished Belarius, and their loving hospitality to their disguised sister, Shakespeare seems to have been largely original. Yet some hints he probably found in an old anonymous play, *The Rare Triumphs of Love and Fortune* (printed 1589), which presents one Hermione (whose name Shakespeare appropriated for the queen in *The Winter's Tale*) as a king's ward, who is banished for marrying the princess Fidelia against her father's wishes. Fidelia, seeking her lover, is succored at the cave of a hermit, a courtier who had been banished (like Belarius) on false charges. Fidelia, whose name seems to have inspired "Fidele" for the disguised Imogen, has a cowardly Brother (Armenio) who may have suggested to Shakespeare the character of Cloten. The relation of the Queen to her son and Imogen recalls the familiar stepmother motive of Germanic folk-lore. But whatever sources may have assisted Shakespeare in these various matters, the skillful interweaving and the atmosphere are all his own, and all the wealth of poetry and characterization which gives the drama its charm.

In the brand of tragi-comedy of which *Cymbeline* is typical the widest gamut of emotion, sensation, and surprise was enjoined, anything being permissible and welcome, provided only that ultimately tragic consequences should be avoided and the protagonists brought finally to complete happiness. The audience could surrender to the manifold adventure, sentiment, and pathos, safe in the assurance of a happy ending. To judge plays of this kind by realistic criteria is entirely wrong, yet this need not preclude observing where Shakespeare has evidently sought to make the extraordinary appear more natural.

Several of the characters in *Cymbeline* are more memorable than the dexterously contrived plot. The weak king and his wicked queen, indeed, are rather flat, but Cloten, a crass bully and coward is individualized. Vulgar, boastful, and stupid though he is, he is a patriot and speaks to the Roman Lucius in so honest and telling a fashion that one is almost persuaded he is more like his betters than he is known to be. One would be tempted to accuse Shakespeare of inconsistent characterization, if life did not amply confirm that vain and arrogant men often sincerely love their country.

The other villain, Iachimo, is of the subtle, crafty type. As a clever strategist and opportunist who takes an artist's satisfaction in the execution of his villainy, he may be called the Iago of Shakespearean comedy.

Posthumus plays a rôle so uncongenial to modern minds that he has been widely misjudged. He has been condemned for his compact with Iachimo, for his crediting Iachimo's story, and for his revenge upon Imogen. No Elizabethan, however, would have censured him. He is no simpleton and no criminal. Shakespeare takes pains to stress his fine traits through the conversation of the "first Gentleman" at court and the good report of Iachimo to his friends in Rome. Clearly his confidence in his wife's honor was construed as a virtue, and as a gentleman he was bound to go to any extreme in its defense. That the circumstantial detail supporting Iachimo's story is simply overwhelming, does not, of course, justify Posthumus in planning his wife's murder, but in the literature on which the Elizabethans fed, guilty women were not spared.

The lady whom he so trusts and wrongs is in truth a "heavenly angel," almost too bright and good for human nature's daily food. And yet she is completely human, a flesh and blood creature, at least most of the time. In her seem to be compacted the several excellences of Shakespeare's earlier romantic heroines: the dignity of Portia, the energy of Beatrice, the radiant high spirits of Rosalind, the sweetness of Viola. And she has courage beyond them all, as circumstances demand. It would be difficult to conceive words more compelling than those which spontaneously burst from her after she has read the false letter telling her to meet her lord at Milford Haven (III.ii.49–84), or those she utters when she is reunited with him at the last (V.v.261–263). The indignation with which she rejects the accusation of infidelity shows her fine mettle (III.iv.42–66); the mingled reserve and sharpness in her repulse of Cloten show her high breeding (II.iii.91–160). Only in the woodland scenes does Imogen's natural sweetness (cf. I.i.109–114 and I.iii.14–37) come perilously near to cloying, and her clear, strong voice sound thin — an impression accentuated by the artificiality of the situation and the sentimentality of the spotless youths, her brothers. In this respect the grafting of the Belarius branch upon the main plot proved unfortunate for the heroine. But while one may regret this, and her subordination in the finale where everything is made to serve the technical triumph of unravelling all the strands of the intricate web, one will hardly stint his devotion to Imogen, whom many have thought to stand supreme among the women of Shakespeare's comedies.

CYMBELINE

[DRAMATIS PERSONÆ

CYMBELINE, *king of Britain.*
CLOTEN, *son to the Queen by a former husband.*
POSTHUMUS LEONATUS, *a gentleman, husband to Imogen.*
BELARIUS, *a banished lord disguised under the name of Morgan.*
GUIDERIUS,
ARVIRAGUS, } *sons to Cymbeline, disguised under the names of Polydore and Cadwal, supposed sons to Morgan.*
PHILARIO, *friend to Posthumus,* }
IACHIMO, *friend to Philario,* } *Italians.*
CAIUS LUCIUS, *general of the Roman forces.*

PISANIO, *servant to Posthumus.*
CORNELIUS, *a physician.*
A Roman Captain.
Two British Captains.
A Frenchman, friend to Philario.
Two Lords of Cymbeline's court.
Two Gentlemen of the same.
Two Gaolers.

QUEEN, *wife to Cymbeline.*
IMOGEN, *daughter to Cymbeline by a former Queen.*
HELEN, *a lady attending on Imogen.*

Lords, Ladies, Roman Senators, Tribunes, a Soothsayer, a Dutchman, a Spaniard, Musicians, Officers, Captains, Soldiers, Messengers, and other Attendants.

Apparitions.

SCENE: *Britain; Rome.*]

ACT I

SCENE I. [*Britain. The garden of Cymbeline's palace.*]

Enter two GENTLEMEN.

1. Gent. You do not meet a man but frowns. Our bloods
No more obey the heavens than our courtiers
Still seem as does the [King].
  2. Gent.   But what's the matter?
  1. Gent. His daughter, and the heir of 's kingdom, whom
He purpos'd to his wife's sole son — a widow 5
That late he married — hath referr'd herself
Unto a poor but worthy gentleman. She's wedded,
Her husband banish'd, she imprison'd; all

Is outward sorrow, though I think the King
Be touch'd at very heart.
  2. Gent.   None but the King?
  1. Gent. He that hath lost her too; so is the Queen,
That most desir'd the match; but not a courtier,
Although they wear their faces to the bent
Of the King's looks, hath a heart that is not
Glad at the thing they scowl at.
  2. Gent.   And why so?
  1. Gent. He that hath miss'd the Princess is a thing 16
Too bad for bad report; and he that hath her —
I mean, that married her, alack, good man!
And therefore banish'd — is a creature such
As, to seek through the regions of the earth 20
For one his like, there would be something failing

Act I, sc. i, 1. **bloods:** moods. 3. **[King]** (Tyrwhitt conj.). *kings* F. 4. **1. Gent.** From this point to l. 68 F designates *1. Gent.* and *2. Gent.* as *1.* and *2.* This holds generally throughout the play. 6. **referr'd:** given. 13. **bent:** inclination.

In him that should compare. I do not think
So fair an outward and such stuff within
Endows a man but he.

    2. Gent.   You speak him far.

    1. Gent. I do extend him, sir, within himself,   25
Crush him together rather than unfold
His measure duly.

    2. Gent.   What's his name and birth?

    1. Gent. I cannot delve him to the root. His
        father
Was call'd Sicilius, who did gain his honour
Against the Romans with Cassibelan,   30
But had his titles by Tenantius whom
He serv'd with glory and admir'd success,
So gain'd the sur-addition Leonatus;
And had, besides this gentleman in question,
Two other sons, who in the wars o' th' time   35
Died with their swords in hand; for which their
        father,
Then old and fond of issue, took such sorrow
That he quit being, and his gentle lady,
Big of this gentleman our theme, deceas'd
As he was born. The King he takes the babe   40
To his protection, calls him Posthumus Leonatus,
Breeds him and makes him of his bed-chamber,
Puts to him all the learnings that his time
Could make him the receiver of; which he took,
As we do air, fast as 'twas minist'red,   45
And in 's spring became a harvest; liv'd in court —
Which rare it is to do — most prais'd, most lov'd,
A sample to the youngest, to the more mature
A glass that feated them, and to the graver
A child that guided dotards; to his mistress,   50
For whom he now is banish'd, — her own price
Proclaims how she esteem'd him and his virtue;
By her election may be truly read
What kind of man he is.

    2. Gent.   I honour him
Even out of your report. But, pray you, tell me,   55
Is she sole child to the King?

    1. Gent.   His only child.
He had two sons, — if this be worth your hearing,
Mark it — the eldest of them at three years old,
I' th' swathing-clothes the other, from their nursery
Were stol'n, and to this hour no guess in knowl-
        edge   60
Which way they went.

    2. Gent.   How long is this ago?

    1. Gent. Some twenty years.

    2. Gent. That a king's children should be so
        convey'd,
So slackly guarded, and the search so slow,
That could not trace them!

    1. Gent.   Howsoe'er 'tis strange,   65

Or that the negligence may well be laugh'd at,
Yet is it true, sir.

    2. Gent.   I do well believe you.

    1. Gent. We must forbear; here comes the gentle-
    man,
The Queen, and Princess.   *[Exeunt.*

    Enter the QUEEN, POSTHUMUS, *and* IMOGEN.

    Queen. No, be assur'd you shall not find me,
        daughter,   70
After the slander of most stepmothers,
Evil-ey'd unto you. You're my prisoner, but
Your gaoler shall deliver you the keys
That lock up your restraint. For you, Posthumus,
So soon as I can win th' offended King,   75
I will be known your advocate. Marry, yet
The fire of rage is in him, and 'twere good
You lean'd unto his sentence with what patience
Your wisdom may inform you.

    Post.   Please your Highness,
I will from hence to-day.

    Queen.   You know the peril.
I'll fetch a turn about the garden, pitying   81
The pangs of barr'd affections, though the King
Hath charg'd you should not speak together.
                                [Exit.

    Imo.   O
Dissembling courtesy! How fine this tyrant
Can tickle where she wounds! My dearest hus-
    band,   85
I something fear my father's wrath, but nothing —
Always reserv'd my holy duty — what
His rage can do on me. You must be gone;
And I shall here abide the hourly shot
Of angry eyes, not comforted to live,   90
But that there is this jewel in the world
That I may see again.

    Post.   My queen! my mistress!
O lady, weep no more, lest I give cause
To be suspected of more tenderness
Than doth become a man. I will remain   95
The loyal'st husband that did e'er plight troth.
My residence in Rome at one [Philario's],
Who to my father was a friend, to me
Known but by letter; thither write, my queen,
And with mine eyes I'll drink the words you
    send,   100
Though ink be made of gall.

    Re-enter QUEEN.

    Queen.   Be brief, I pray you.
If the King come, I shall incur I know not
How much of his displeasure. *[Aside.]* Yet I'll
    move him

---

24. **speak ... far**: praise him very highly. F₂ reads *fair*.   33. **sur-addition**: added title.   37. **fond of issue**: desirous of offspring.   43. **time**: years.   49. **feated them**: gave them a flattering reflection.   51. **price**: valuation.   70. s.d. F begins Sc. ii here.   78. **lean'd**: submitted.   97. **[Philario's]** (Rowe). *Filorio's* F.

To walk this way.   I never do him wrong
But he does buy my injuries, to be friends;   105
Pays dear for my offences.   [*Exit.*]
    Post.   Should we be taking leave
As long a term as yet we have to live,
The loathness to depart would grow.   Adieu!
    Imo. Nay, stay a little;
Were you but riding forth to air yourself,   110
Such parting were too petty.   Look here, love;
This diamond was my mother's.   Take it, heart;
But keep it till you woo another wife,
When Imogen is dead.
    Post.   How, how! another?
You gentle gods, give me but this I have,   115
And cere up my embracements from a next
With bonds of death!   [*Putting on the ring.*]
        Remain, remain thou here
While sense can keep it on.   And, sweetest, fairest,
As I my poor self did exchange for you,
To your so infinite loss, so in our trifles   120
I still win of you; for my sake wear this.
It is a manacle of love; I'll place it
Upon this fairest prisoner.
            [*Putting a bracelet upon her arm.*]
    Imo.   O the gods!
When shall we see again?

        Enter CYMBELINE *and* Lords.

    Post.   Alack, the King!
    Cym. Thou basest thing, avoid!   Hence, from
        my sight!   125
If after this command thou fraught the court
With thy unworthiness, thou diest.   Away!
Thou'rt poison to my blood.
    Post.   The gods protect you!
And bless the good remainders of the court!
I am gone.   [*Exit.*
    Imo.   There cannot be a pinch in death   130
More sharp than this is.
    Cym.   O disloyal thing,
That shouldst repair my youth, thou heap'st
A year's age on me.
    Imo.   I beseech you, sir,
Harm not yourself with your vexation.
I am senseless of your wrath; a touch more rare   135
Subdues all pangs, all fears.
    Cym.   Past grace? obedience?
    Imo. Past hope, and in despair; that way, past
        grace.
    Cym. That mightst have had the sole son of my
        queen!
    Imo. O blest, that I might not! I chose an eagle,
And did avoid a puttock.   140

    Cym. Thou took'st a beggar; wouldst have made
        my throne
A seat for baseness.
    Imo.   No; I rather added
A lustre to it.
    Cym.   O thou vile one!
    Imo.   Sir,
It is your fault that I have lov'd Posthumus.
You bred him as my playfellow, and he is   145
A man worth any woman; overbuys me
Almost the sum he pays.
    Cym.   What, art thou mad?
    Imo. Almost, sir; heaven restore me!   Would
        I were
A neat-herd's daughter, and my Leonatus
Our neighbour shepherd's son!

        Re-enter QUEEN.

    Cym.   Thou foolish thing!
— They were again together; you have done   151
Not after our command.   Away with her,
And pen her up.
    Queen.   Beseech your patience.   Peace,
Dear lady daughter, peace!   Sweet sovereign,
Leave us to ourselves; and make yourself some
        comfort   155
Out of your best advice.
    Cym.   Nay, let her languish
A drop of blood a day; and, being aged,
Die of this folly!   [*Exeunt* [*Cymbeline and Lords*].

        Enter PISANIO.

    Queen.   Fie! you must give way.
Here is your servant.   How now, sir!   What
        news?   159
    Pis. My lord your son drew on my master.
    Queen.   Ha!
No harm, I trust, is done?
    Pis.   There might have been,
But that my master rather play'd than fought
And had no help of anger.   They were parted
By gentlemen at hand.
    Queen.   I am very glad on't.
    Imo. Your son's my father's friend; he takes
        his part   165
To draw upon an exile.   O brave sir!
I would they were in Afric both together;
Myself by with a needle, that I might prick
The goer-back.   Why came you from your master?
    Pis. On his command.   He would not suffer
        me   170
To bring him to the haven; left these notes
Of what commands I should be subject to,

105. **buy:** reward.   116. **cere up:** shroud.   Cerecloths were waxed shrouds.   125. **avoid:** get out.   126. **fraught:** burden.   129. **remainders of:** those who remain in.   132. **repair:** renew.   135. **senseless:** insensible.   **touch more rare:** feeling more keen.   140. **puttock:** kite.   146–47. **overbuys...pays:** i.e., his superiority to me is almost equal to his whole worth.   149. **neat-herd's:** cowherd's.   156. **advice:** self-counsel.

When't pleas'd you to employ me.
Queen.   This hath been
Your faithful servant. I dare lay mine honour
He will remain so.
Pis.   I humbly thank your Highness. 175
Queen. Pray, walk a while.
Imo. [to Pis.] About some half-hour hence,
[I] pray you, speak with me; you shall at least
Go see my lord aboard. For this time leave
me.   [Exeunt.

SCENE [II. The same. A public place.]

Enter CLOTEN and two LORDS.

1. Lord. Sir, I would advise you to shift a shirt;
the violence of action hath made you reek as a
sacrifice. Where air comes out, air comes in;
there's none abroad so wholesome as that you vent. 5
Clo. If my shirt were bloody, then to shift it.
Have I hurt him?
2. Lord. [Aside.] No, faith; not so much as his
patience.   9
1. Lord. Hurt him! His body's a passable
carcass, if he be not hurt; it is a throughfare for
steel, if it be not hurt.
2. Lord. [Aside.] His steel was in debt; it went
o' th' backside the town.
Clo. The villain would not stand me.   15
2. Lord. [Aside.] No; but he fled forward still,
toward your face.
1. Lord. Stand you! You have land enough of
your own, but he added to your having, gave you
some ground.   20
2. Lord. [Aside.] As many inches as you have
oceans. Puppies!
Clo. I would they had not come between us.
2. Lord. [Aside.] So would I, till you had measur'd how long a fool you were upon the ground. 26
Clo. And that she should love this fellow and
refuse me!
2. Lord. [Aside.] If it be a sin to make a true
election, she is damn'd.   30
1. Lord. Sir, as I told you always, her beauty
and her brain go not together. She's a good sign,
but I have seen small reflection of her wit.
2. Lord. [Aside.] She shines not upon fools,
lest the reflection should hurt her.   35
Clo. Come, I'll to my chamber. Would there
had been some hurt done!
2. Lord. [Aside.] I wish not so; unless it had been
the fall of an ass, which is no great hurt.

Clo. You'll go with us?   40
1. Lord. I'll attend your lordship.
Clo. Nay, come, let's go together.
2. Lord. Well, my lord.   [Exeunt.

SCENE [III. A room in Cymbeline's palace.]

Enter IMOGEN and PISANIO.

Imo. I would thou grew'st unto the shores o'
th' haven,
And question'dst every sail. If he should write
And I not have it, 'twere a paper lost
As offer'd mercy is. What was the last   4
That he spake to thee?
Pis.   It was his queen, his queen!
Imo. Then wav'd his handkerchief?
Pis.   And kiss'd it, madam.
Imo. Senseless linen! happier therein than I!
And that was all?
Pis.   No, madam; for so long
As he could make me with [this] eye or ear
Distinguish him from others, he did keep   10
The deck, with glove or hat or handkerchief
Still waving, as the fits and stirs of 's mind
Could best express how slow his soul sail'd on,
How swift his ship.
Imo.   Thou shouldst have made him
As little as a crow, or less, ere left   15
To after-eye him.
Pis.   Madam, so I did.
Imo. I would have broke mine eye-strings,
crack'd them, but
To look upon him, till the diminution
Of space had pointed him sharp as my needle;
Nay, follow'd him till he had melted from   20
The smallness of a gnat to air, and then
Have turn'd mine eye and wept. But, good
Pisanio,
When shall we hear from him?
Pis.   Be assur'd, madam,
With his next vantage.   24
Imo. I did not take my leave of him, but had
Most pretty things to say. Ere I could tell him
How I would think on him at certain hours
Such thoughts and such, or I could make him swear
The shes of Italy should not betray
Mine interest and his honour, or have charg'd
him,   30
At the sixth hour of morn, at noon, at midnight,
T' encounter me with orisons, for then
I am in heaven for him; or ere I could

176. walk: withdraw. 177. [I] (Capell). Om. F.
Sc. ii, 1. 1. Lord. In this scene speeches of the Lords are designated in F merely 1. and 2. 5. abroad: outside you. 10.
passable: easy (for a rapier) to pass through. 13. in debt: i.e., paid no scores (blows). 13-14. went... town: was afraid
to go through the town; i.e., it missed. 32. sign: appearance.
Sc. iii, 4. offer'd mercy: pardon not received. 9. [this] (Theobald). his F. 24. vantage: opportunity. 32. orisons:
prayers.

Give him that parting kiss which I had set
Betwixt two charming words, comes in my father 35
And like the tyrannous breathing of the north
Shakes all our buds from growing.

Enter a LADY.

Lady.   The Queen, madam,
Desires your Highness' company.
Imo. Those things I bid you do, get them dis-
patch'd.
I will attend the Queen.
Pis.   Madam, I shall.   40
                                        [*Exeunt.*

SCENE [IV.   *Rome.   Philario's house.*]

Enter PHILARIO, IACHIMO, *a* FRENCHMAN, *a* Dutchman, *and a* Spaniard.

Iach. Believe it, sir, I have seen him in Britain.
He was then of a crescent note, expected to prove
so worthy as since he hath been allowed the name
of; but I could then have look'd on him without the
help of admiration, though the catalogue of his
endowments had been tabled by his side and I to
peruse him by items.   7
Phi. You speak of him when he was less furnish'd
than now he is with that which makes him both
without and within.
French. I have seen him in France. We had
very many there could behold the sun with as firm
eyes as he.   13
Iach. This matter of marrying his king's daughter, wherein he must be weighed rather by her
value than his own, words him, I doubt not, a great
deal from the matter.
French. And then his banishment.   18
Iach. Ay, and the approbation of those that
weep this lamentable divorce under her colours
are wonderfully to extend him, be it but to fortify
her judgement, which else an easy battery might
lay flat for taking a beggar without less quality.
But how comes it he is to sojourn with you? How
creeps acquaintance?   25
Phi. His father and I were soldiers together;
to whom I have been often bound for no less
than my life.

Enter POSTHUMUS.

Here comes the Briton. Let him be so entertained
amongst you as suits with gentlemen of your know-

ing to a stranger of his quality. — I beseech you 30
all, be better known to this gentleman, whom I
commend to you as a noble friend of mine. How
worthy he is I will leave to appear hereafter,
rather than story him in his own hearing.   35
French. Sir, we have known together in Orleans.
Post. Since when I have been debtor to you for
courtesies, which I will be ever to pay and yet
pay still.   40
French. Sir, you o'er-rate my poor kindness.
I was glad I did atone my countryman and you.
It had been pity you should have been put together with so mortal a purpose as then each bore,
upon importance of so slight and trivial a nature. 45
Post. By your pardon, sir, I was then a young
traveller; rather shunn'd to go even with what I
heard than in my every action to be guided by
others' experiences: but upon my mended judgement — if I offend [not] to say it is mended — my
quarrel was not altogether slight.   51
French. Faith, yes, to be put to the arbitrement
of swords, and by such two that would by all likelihood have confounded one the other, or have
fallen both.   55
Iach. Can we, with manners, ask what was the
difference?
French. Safely, I think; 'twas a contention in
public, which may, without contradiction, suffer
the report. It was much like an argument that 60
fell out last night, where each of us fell in praise of
our country-mistresses; this gentleman at that
time vouching — and upon warrant of bloody af-
firmation — his to be more fair, virtuous, wise,
chaste, constant, qualified, and less attemptable
than any the rarest of our ladies in France.   66
Iach. That lady is not now living, or this gentleman's opinion by this worn out.
Post. She holds her virtue still, and I my mind.
Iach. You must not so far prefer her 'fore ours
of Italy.   71
Post. Being so far provok'd as I was in France,
I would abate her nothing, though I profess myself
her adorer, not her friend.   74
Iach. As fair and as good — a kind of hand-in-
hand comparison — had been something too fair
and too good for any lady in Britain. If she went
before others I have seen, as that diamond of yours
outlustres many I have beheld, I could not [but]
believe she excelled many. But I have not seen
the most precious diamond that is, nor you the
lady.   82

---

35. **charming:** having a charm or spell.
Sc. iv, 2. **crescent note:** growing distinction. 5. **admiration:** astonishment. 6. **tabled:** listed. 12-13. **many...he:**
many there as good as he. 16-17. **words...matter:** represents him as very different from what he really is. 20. **colours:**
banners; i.e., those on her side. 21. **extend:** magnify. 23. **without.** A mistake for *with*. 24. **quality:** rank. 36. **known**
together: been acquainted. 42. **atone:** reconcile. 43. **put together:** opposed (in a duel). 47. **go even:** agree. 50. **[not]**
(Rowe). Om. F. 54. **confounded:** destroyed. 65. **qualified:** endowed. **attemptable:** i.e., in virtue. 73. **abate:**
depreciate. 74. **friend:** lover. 75. **hand-in-hand comparison:** comparison of equals. 79. **[but]** (Malone). Om. F.

Post. I prais'd her as I rated her; so do I my stone.

Iach. What do you esteem it at?

Post. More than the world enjoys.

Iach. Either your unparagon'd mistress is dead, or she's outpriz'd by a trifle.   88

Post. You are mistaken. The one may be sold or given, or if there were wealth enough for the purchase, or merit for the gift; the other is not a thing for sale, and only the gift of the gods.

Iach. Which the gods have given you?

Post. Which, by their graces, I will keep.   95

Iach. You may wear her in title yours; but, you know, strange fowl light upon neighbouring ponds. Your ring may be stol'n too; so your brace of un-prizable estimations, the one is but frail and the other casual. A cunning thief, or a that-way-accomplish'd courtier, would hazard the winning both of first and last.   102

Post. Your Italy contains none so accomplish'd a courtier to convince the honour of my mistress, if, in the holding or loss of that, you term her frail. I do nothing doubt you have store of thieves; notwithstanding, I fear not my ring.   108

Phi. Let us leave here, gentlemen.

Post. Sir, with all my heart. This worthy signior, I thank him, makes no stranger of me; we are familiar at first.   112

Iach. With five times so much conversation, I should get ground of your fair mistress, make her go back, even to the yielding, had I admittance, and opportunity to friend.

Post. No, no.   117

Iach. I dare thereupon pawn the moiety of my estate to your ring; which, in my opinion, o'ervalues it something. But I make my wager rather against your confidence than her reputation; and, to bar your offence herein too, I durst attempt it against any lady in the world.   123

Post. You are a great deal abus'd in too bold a persuasion, and I doubt not you sustain what you're worthy of by your attempt.

Iach. What's that?

Post. A repulse; though your attempt, as you call it, deserve more, — a punishment too.   129

Phi. Gentlemen, enough of this; it came in too suddenly. Let it die as it was born, and, I pray you, be better acquainted.

Iach. Would I had put my estate and my neigh-bour's on th' approbation of what I have spoke!

Post. What lady would you choose to assail?   136

Iach. Yours, whom in constancy you think stands so safe. I will lay you ten thousand ducats to your ring that, commend me to the court where

your lady is, with no more advantage than the opportunity of a second conference, and I will bring from thence that honour of hers which you imagine so reserv'd.   143

Post. I will wage against your gold, gold to it. My ring I hold dear as my finger; 'tis part of it.

Iach. You are [afraid], and therein the wiser. If you buy ladies' flesh at a million a dram, you cannot preserve it from tainting. But I see you have some religion in you, that you fear.   149

Post. This is but a custom in your tongue; you bear a graver purpose, I hope.

Iach. I am the master of my speeches, and would undergo what's spoken, I swear.   153

Post. Will you? I shall but lend my diamond till your return. Let there be covenants drawn between 's. My mistress exceeds in goodness the hugeness of your unworthy thinking. I dare you to this match; here's my ring.

Phi. I will have it no lay.   159

Iach. By the gods, it is one. If I bring you no sufficient testimony that I have enjoy'd the dearest bodily part of your mistress, my ten thousand ducats are yours; so is your diamond too. If I come off and leave her in such honour as you have trust in, she your jewel, this your jewel, and my gold are yours; provided I have your commendation for my more free entertainment.   167

Post. I embrace these conditions; let us have articles betwixt us. Only, thus far you shall answer: if you make your voyage upon her and give me directly to understand you have prevail'd, I am no further your enemy; she is not worth our debate. If she remain unseduc'd, you not making it appear otherwise, for your ill opinion and the assault you have made to her chastity you shall answer me with your sword.   176

Iach. Your hand; a covenant. We will have these things set down by lawful counsel, and straight away for Britain, lest the bargain should catch cold and starve. I will fetch my gold and have our two wagers recorded.   181

Post. Agreed. [*Exeunt Posthumus and Iachimo.*]

French. Will this hold, think you?

Phi. Signior Iachimo will not from it. Pray, let us follow 'em.   [*Exeunt.*

SCENE [V. *Britain. A room in Cymbeline's palace.*]

Enter QUEEN, LADIES, *and* CORNELIUS.

Queen. Whiles yet the dew's on ground, gather those flowers;

99. **unprizable estimations:** priceless values.   100. **casual:** subject to accident.   104. **convince:** overcome.   108. **fear:** fear for.   109. **leave:** desist.   116. **to friend:** as aid.   118. **moiety:** half.   124. **abus'd:** deceived.   125. **persuasion:** opinion.   134. **approbation:** proof.   146. **[afraid]** (Theobald).   *a Friend* F.   149. **that:** because.   153. **undergo:** undertake.   159. **lay:** wager.   180. **starve:** die.

Make haste. Who has the note of them?
[*1.*] *Lady.*   I, madam.
Queen. Dispatch.   [*Exeunt Ladies.*
Now, master doctor, have you brought those drugs?
  Cor. Pleaseth your Highness, ay. Here they
    are, madam.   [*Presenting a small box.*] 5
But I beseech your Grace, without offence, —
My conscience bids me ask — wherefore you have
Commanded of me these most poisonous com-
    pounds,
Which are the movers of a languishing death,
But though slow, deadly.
  Queen.   I wonder, doctor, 10
Thou ask'st me such a question. Have I not been
Thy pupil long? Hast thou not learn'd me how
To make perfumes? distil? preserve? yea, so
That our great king himself doth woo me oft
For my confections?   Having thus far pro-
    ceeded, — 15
Unless thou think'st me devilish — is't not meet
That I did amplify my judgement in
Other conclusions? I will try the forces
Of these thy compounds on such creatures as
We count not worth the hanging, — but none
    human — 20
To try the vigour of them and apply
Allayments to their act, and by them gather
Their several virtues and effects.
  Cor.   Your Highness
Shall from this practice but make hard your heart.
Besides, the seeing these effects will be 25
Both noisome and infectious.
  Queen.   O, content thee.

Enter PISANIO.

[*Aside.*] Here comes a flattering rascal; upon him
Will I first work. He's for his master,
And enemy to my son. How now, Pisanio!
Doctor, your service for this time is ended; 30
Take your own way.
  Cor.   [*Aside.*] I do suspect you, madam;
But you shall do no harm.
  Queen.   [*To Pisanio.*] Hark thee, a word.
  Cor. [*Aside.*] I do not like her. She doth think
she has
Strange ling'ring poisons. I do know her spirit,
And will not trust one of her malice with 35
A drug of such damn'd nature. Those she has
Will stupefy and dull the sense a while,
Which first, perchance, she'll prove on cats and
    dogs,
Then afterward up higher; but there is
No danger in what show of death it makes, 40

More than the locking-up the spirits a time,
To be more fresh, reviving. She is fool'd
With a most false effect; and I the truer,
So to be false with her.
  Queen.   No further service, doctor,
Until I send for thee.
  Cor.   I humbly take my leave. 45
                                        [*Exit.*
  Queen. Weeps she still, say'st thou? Dost
    thou think in time
She will not quench and let instructions enter
Where folly now possesses? Do thou work.
When thou shalt bring me word she loves my son,
I'll tell thee on the instant thou art then 50
As great as is thy master, — greater, for
His fortunes all lie speechless and his name
Is at last gasp. Return he cannot, nor
Continue where he is. To shift his being
Is to exchange one misery with another, 55
And every day that comes comes to decay
A day's work in him. What shalt thou expect
To be depender on a thing that leans,
Who cannot be new built, nor has no friends
So much as but to prop him? [*The Queen drops
    the box: Pisanio takes it up.*]
                             Thou tak'st up
Thou know'st not what; but take it for thy labour.
It is a thing I made, which hath the King 62
Five times redeem'd from death. I do not know
What is more cordial. Nay, I prithee, take it;
It is an earnest of a further good 65
That I mean to thee. Tell thy mistress how
The case stands with her; do't as from thyself.
Think what a chance thou changest on, but think
Thou hast thy mistress still; to boot, my son,
Who shall take notice of thee. I'll move the
    King 70
To any shape of thy preferment such
As thou'lt desire; and then myself, I chiefly,
That set thee on to this desert, am bound
To load thy merit richly. Call my women.
Think on my words.   [*Exit Pisanio.*
              A sly and constant knave,
Not to be shak'd; the agent for his master 76
And the remembrancer of her to hold
The hand-fast to her lord. I have given him that
Which, if he take, shall quite unpeople her
Of liegers for her sweet, and which she after, 80
Except she bend her humour, shall be assur'd
To taste of too.

Re-enter PISANIO *and* Ladies.
            So, so; well done, well done.

The violets, cowslips, and the primroses,
Bear to my closet.   Fare thee well, Pisanio;
Think on my words.   [*Exeunt Queen and Ladies.*
  Pis.   And shall do;   85
But when to my good lord I prove untrue,
I'll choke myself.   There's all I'll do for you.
                                          [*Exit.*

SCENE [VI.   *The same.   Another room in the
                    palace.*]

                Enter IMOGEN *alone.*

  Imo. A father cruel, and a step-dame false;
A foolish suitor to a wedded lady
That hath her husband banish'd; — O, that
        husband!
My supreme crown of grief! and those repeated
Vexations of it!   Had I been thief-stolen,   5
As my two brothers, happy! but most miserable
Is the desire that's glorious.   Blessed be those,
How mean soe'er, that have their honest wills,
Which seasons comfort.   Who may this be?   Fie!

                Enter PISANIO *and* IACHIMO.

  Pis. Madam, a noble gentleman of Rome,   10
Comes from my lord with letters.
  Iach.   Change you, madam?
The worthy Leonatus is in safety
And greets your Highness dearly.
                                [*Presents a letter.*]
  Imo.   Thanks, good sir;
You're kindly welcome.
  Iach. [*Aside.*] All of her that is out of door
        most rich!   15
If she be furnish'd with a mind so rare,
She is alone, th' Arabian bird, and I
Have lost the wager.   Boldness be my friend!
Arm me, audacity, from head to foot!
Or, like the Parthian, I shall flying fight;   20
Rather, directly fly.
  Imo. (*Reads.*) " — He is one of the noblest note,
to whose kindnesses I am most infinitely tied.
Reflect upon him accordingly, as you value your
trust —   LEONATUS."   25
So far I read aloud —
But even the very middle of my heart
Is warm'd by th' rest — and take it thankfully.
You are as welcome, worthy sir, as I
Have words to bid you, and shall find it so   30
In all that I can do.
  Iach.   Thanks, fairest lady.
What, are men mad?   Hath nature given them eyes

To see this vaulted arch and the rich crop
Of sea and land, which can distinguish 'twixt
The fiery orbs above and the twinn'd stones   35
Upon [th' unnumber'd] beach, and can we not
Partition make with spectacles so precious
'Twixt fair and foul?
  Imo.   What makes your admiration?
  Iach. It cannot be i' th' eye, for apes and
        monkeys
'Twixt two such shes would chatter this way
        and   40
Contemn with mows the other; nor i' th' judge-
        ment,
For idiots in this case of favour would
Be wisely definite; nor i' th' appetite;
Sluttery to such neat excellence oppos'd
Should make desire vomit emptiness,   45
Not so allur'd to feed.
  Imo. What is the matter, trow?
  Iach.   The cloyed will, —
That satiate yet unsatisfi'd desire, that tub
Both fill'd and running, — ravening first the lamb,
Longs after for the garbage.
  Imo.   What, dear sir,   50
Thus raps you?   Are you well?
  Iach. Thanks, madam; well.   [*To Pisanio.*]
Beseech you, sir, desire
My man's abode where I did leave him.   He
Is strange and peevish.
  Pis.   I was going, sir,
To give him welcome.   [*Exit.*   55
  Imo. Continues well my lord?   His health,
        beseech you?
  Iach. Well, madam.
  Imo. Is he dispos'd to mirth?   I hope he is.
  Iach. Exceeding pleasant; none a stranger there
So merry and so gamesome.   He is call'd   60
The Briton reveller.
  Imo.   When he was here,
He did incline to sadness, and oft-times
Not knowing why.
  Iach.   I never saw him sad.
There is a Frenchman his companion, one
An eminent monsieur that, it seems, much loves 65
A Gallian girl at home.   He furnaces
The thick sighs from him, whiles the jolly Briton —
Your lord, I mean — laughs from 's free lungs,
        cries "O,
Can my sides hold, to think that man, who knows
By history, report, or his own proof,   70
What woman is, yea, what she cannot choose
But must be, will his free hours languish for

Sc. vi, 4. **repeated**: which I have enumerated.   7. **that's glorious**: for glory.   8. **wills**: desires.   9. **seasons**: gives zest to.
11. **Change**: i.e., change color.   17. **alone**: unique.   **Arabian bird**: the phoenix, a fabulous bird, one only existing at a time.
24. **Reflect upon**: regard.   35. **twinn'd**: identical.   36. **[th' unnumber'd]** (Theobald).   *the number'd* F.   37. **spectacles**:
eyes.   38. **admiration**: wonder.   41. **mows**: grimaces.   42. **case of favour**: question of beauty.   49. **ravening**: devouring.
51. **raps**: transports.   52–53. **desire ... abode**: ask my servant to remain.   54. **strange**: a stranger.   66. **Gallian**: Gallic.

Assured bondage?"
  Imo.   Will my lord say so?
  Iach. Ay, madam, with his eyes in flood with
    laughter.
It is a recreation to be by   75
And hear him mock the Frenchman. But, heavens
    know,
Some men are much to blame.
  Imo.   Not he, I hope.
  Iach. Not he; but yet heaven's bounty towards
    him might
Be us'd more thankfully. In himself, 'tis much;
In you — which I account his — beyond all
    talents.   80
Whilst I am bound to wonder, I am bound
To pity too.
  Imo.   What do you pity, sir?
  Iach. Two creatures heartily.
  Imo.   Am I one, sir?
You look on me; what wreck discern you in me
Deserves your pity?
  Iach.   Lamentable! What, 85
To hide me from the radiant sun, and solace
I' th' dungeon by a snuff!
  Imo.   I pray you, sir,
Deliver with more openness your answers
To my demands. Why do you pity me?
  Iach. That others do,   90
I was about to say, enjoy your — But
It is an office of the gods to venge it,
Not mine to speak on't.
  Imo.   You do seem to know
Something of me, or what concerns me: pray you, —
Since doubting things go ill often hurts more 95
Than to be sure they do; for certainties
Either are past remedies, or, timely knowing,
The remedy then born — discover to me
What both you spur and stop.
  Iach.   Had I this cheek
To bathe my lips upon; this hand, whose touch, 100
Whose every touch, would force the feeler's soul
To the oath of loyalty; this object, which
Takes prisoner the wild motion of mine eye,
[Fixing] it only here; should I, damn'd then,
Slaver with lips as common as the stairs 105
That mount the Capitol; join gripes with hands
Made hard with hourly falsehood — falsehood, as
With labour; then [lie] peeping in an eye
Base and [illustrous] as the smoky light
That's fed with stinking tallow: it were fit 110
That all the plagues of hell should at one time

Encounter such revolt.
  Imo.   My lord, I fear,
Has forgot Britain.
  Iach.   And himself. Not I,
Inclin'd to this intelligence, pronounce
The beggary of his change; but 'tis your graces 115
That from my mutest conscience to my tongue
Charms this report out.
  Imo.   Let me hear no more.
  Iach. O dearest soul! your cause doth strike
    my heart
With pity that doth make me sick. A lady
So fair, and fasten'd to an empery 120
Would make the great'st king double, — to be
    partner'd
With tomboys hir'd with that self-exhibition
Which your own coffers yield! with diseas'd ven-
    tures
That play with all infirmities for gold
Which rottenness can lend nature! such boil'd
    stuff 125
As well might poison poison! Be reveng'd;
Or she that bore you was no queen, and you
Recoil from your great stock.
  Imo.   Reveng'd!
How should I be reveng'd? If this be true, —
As I have such a heart that both mine ears 130
Must not in haste abuse — if it be true,
How should I be reveng'd?
  Iach.   Should he make me
Live, like Diana's priest, betwixt cold sheets,
Whiles he is vaulting variable ramps,
In your despite, upon your purse? Revenge it. 135
I dedicate myself to your sweet pleasure,
More noble than that runagate to your bed,
And will continue fast to your affection,
Still close as sure.
  Imo.   What, ho, Pisanio!
  Iach. Let me my service tender on your lips. 140
  Imo. Away! I do condemn mine ears that have
So long attended thee. If thou wert honourable,
Thou wouldst have told this tale for virtue, not
For such an end thou seek'st, — as base as strange.
Thou wrong'st a gentleman, who is as far 145
From thy report as thou from honour, and
[Solicit'st] here a lady that disdains
Thee and the devil alike. What ho, Pisanio!
The King my father shall be made acquainted
Of thy assault. If he shall think it fit 150
A saucy stranger in his court to mart
As in a Romish stew, and to expound

80. **talents**: riches. 87. **snuff**: candle wick. 99. **spur and stop**: impel (to speak) and check. 104. [**Fixing**] F₂. *Fiering* F₁. 108. [**lie**] (Johnson conj.). *by* F. 109. [**illustrous**] (Collier); lack-lustre. *illustrious* F. 112. **Encounter**: befall. **revolt**: infidelity. 113–14. **Not...intelligence**: I, reluctant to give this news. 120. **empery**: empire. 122. **tomboys**: strumpets. 122–23. **with...yield**: with money from you. 123. **ventures**: adventuresses. 125. **Which**: referring to *infirmities*. **boil'd**: sweated, referring to the treatment for certain diseases. 128. **Recoil**: degenerate. 134. **ramps**: prostitutes. 137. **runagate**: renegade. 139. **close**: secret. 147. [**Solicit'st**]. *Solicites* F. 151. **mart**: bargain. 152. **stew**: brothel.

His beastly mind to us, he hath a court
He little cares for and a daughter who
He not respects at all. What, ho, Pisanio!   155
  Iach. O happy Leonatus! I may say.
The credit that thy lady hath of thee
Deserves thy trust, and thy most perfect goodness
Her assur'd credit. Blessed live you long
A lady to the worthiest sir that ever   160
Country call'd his! and you his mistress, only
For the most worthiest fit! Give me your pardon.
I have spoke this to know if your affiance
Were deeply rooted, and shall make your lord,
That which he is, new o'er; and he is one   165
The truest manner'd, such a holy witch
That he enchants societies into him;
Half all men's hearts are his.
  Imo.   You make amends.
  Iach. He sits 'mongst men like a [descended] god:
He hath a kind of honour sets him off,   170
More than a mortal seeming. Be not angry,
Most mighty princess, that I have adventur'd
To try your taking of a false report; which hath
Honour'd with confirmation your great judgement
In the election of a sir so rare,   175
Which you know cannot err. The love I bear him
Made me to fan you thus; but the gods made you,
Unlike all others, chaffless. Pray, your pardon.
  Imo. All's well, sir. Take my power i' th'
    court for yours.
  Iach. My humble thanks. I had almost forgot
To entreat your Grace but in a small request, 181
And yet of moment too, for it concerns
Your lord; myself, and other noble friends,
Are partners in the business.
  Imo.   Pray, what is't?
  Iach. Some dozen Romans of us and your
    lord —   185
The best feather of our wing — have mingled sums
To buy a present for the Emperor;
Which I, the factor for the rest, have done
In France. 'Tis plate of rare device, and jewels
Of rich and exquisite form, their values great; 190
And I am something curious, being strange,
To have them in safe stowage. May it please you
To take them in protection?
  Imo.   Willingly;
And pawn mine honour for their safety. Since
My lord hath interest in them, I will keep them 195
In my bedchamber.
  Iach.   They are in a trunk,
Attended by my men. I will make bold
To send them to you, only for this night;

I must aboard to-morrow.
  Imo.   O, no, no.   200
  Iach. Yes, I beseech; or I shall short my word
By length'ning my return. From Gallia
I cross'd the seas on purpose and on promise
To see your Grace.
  Imo.   I thank you for your pains:
But not away to-morrow!
  Iach.   O, I must, madam;
Therefore I shall beseech you, if you please 205
To greet your lord with writing, do't to-night.
I have outstood my time; which is material
To the tender of our present.
  Imo.   I will write.
Send your trunk to me; it shall safe be kept,
And truly yielded you. You're very welcome. 210
                   [*Exeunt.*

ACT II

Scene I. [*Britain. Before Cymbeline's palace.*]

Enter Cloten *and the two* Lords.

  Clo. Was there ever man had such luck! When I kiss'd the jack, upon an up-cast to be hit away! I had a hundred pound on't; and then a whoreson jackanapes must take me up for swearing, as if I borrowed mine oaths of him and might not spend them at my pleasure.   6
  1. Lord. What got he by that? You have broke his pate with your bowl.
  2. Lord. [*Aside.*] If his wit had been like him that broke it, it would have run all out.   10
  Clo. When a gentleman is dispos'd to swear, it is not for any standers-by to curtail his oaths, ha?
  2. Lord. No, my lord; [*aside*] nor crop the ears of them.   15
  Clo. Whoreson dog! I gave him satisfaction! Would he had been one of my rank!
  2. Lord. [*Aside.*] To have smelt like a fool.   18
  Clo. I am not vex'd more at anything in th' earth; a pox on't! I had rather not be so noble as I am. They dare not fight with me because of the Queen my mother. Every Jack-slave hath his bellyful of fighting, and I must go up and down like a cock that nobody can match.   24
  2. Lord. [*Aside.*] You are cock and capon too; and you crow, cock, with your comb on.
  Clo. Sayest thou?
  2. Lord. It is not fit your lordship should undertake every companion that you give offence to.   30
  Clo. No, I know that; but it is fit I should commit offence to my inferiors.

157. **credit:** trust. 166. **witch:** wizard, charmer. 169. **[descended]** F₂. *defended* F₁. 177. **fan:** winnow, i.e., test. 188. **factor:** agent. 191. **curious...strange:** anxious, being a stranger. 200. **short:** fall short of. 208. **tender:** bestowing.
Act II, sc. i, 2. **kiss'd the jack:** touched the target bowl. **up-cast:** final shot. 4. **take me up:** rebuke me. 22. **Jack-slave:** base fellow. 26. **comb:** coxcomb, fool's cap. 30. **companion:** fellow.

2. Lord. Ay, it is fit for your lordship only.

Clo. Why, so I say.

1. Lord. Did you hear of a stranger that's come to court [to-night]?   36

Clo. A stranger, and I not know on't!

2. Lord. [*Aside.*] He's a strange fellow himself, and knows it not.

1. Lord. There's an Italian come; and, 'tis thought, one of Leonatus' friends.   41

Clo. Leonatus! a banish'd rascal; and he's another, whatsoever he be. Who told you of this stranger?

1. Lord. One of your lordship's pages.   45

Clo. Is it fit I went to look upon him? Is there no derogation in't?

2. Lord. You cannot derogate, my lord.

Clo. Not easily, I think.   49

2. Lord. [*Aside.*] You are a fool granted; therefore your issues, being foolish, do not derogate.

Clo. Come, I'll go see this Italian. What I have lost to-day at bowls I'll win to-night of him. Come, go.   55

2. Lord. I'll attend your lordship.

[*Exeunt* [*Cloten and First Lord*].

That such a crafty devil as is his mother
Should yield the world this ass! A woman that
Bears all down with her brain; and this her son
Cannot take two from twenty, for his heart,   60
And leave eighteen. Alas, poor princess,
Thou divine Imogen, what thou endur'st,
Betwixt a father by thy step-dame govern'd,
A mother hourly coining plots, a wooer
More hateful than the foul expulsion is   65
Of thy dear husband, [than] that horrid act
Of the divorce he'd make! The heavens hold firm
The walls of thy dear honour, keep unshak'd
That temple, thy fair mind, that thou mayst stand,
T' enjoy thy banish'd lord and this great land!   70

[*Exit.*

SCENE II. [*Imogen's bedchamber in Cymbeline's palace: a trunk in one corner of it.*]

IMOGEN *in her bed* [*reading*]; *and a* LADY [*attending*].

Imo. Who's there? My woman Helen?

Lady.   Please you, madam.

Imo. What hour is it?

Lady.   Almost midnight, madam.

Imo. I have read three hours then. Mine eyes are weak.
Fold down the leaf where I have left. To bed.
Take not away the taper, leave it burning;   5
And if thou canst awake by four o' th' clock,

I prithee, call me. Sleep hath seiz'd me wholly.

[*Exit Lady.*]

To your protection I commend me, gods.
From fairies and the tempters of the night
Guard me, beseech ye.   10

[*Sleeps. Iachimo* [*comes*] *from the trunk.*

Iach. The crickets sing, and man's o'er-labour'd sense
Repairs itself by rest. Our Tarquin thus
Did softly press the rushes ere he waken'd
The chastity he wounded. Cytherea!
How bravely thou becom'st thy bed, fresh lily,   15
And whiter than the sheets! That I might touch!
But kiss one kiss! Rubies unparagon'd,
How dearly they do't! 'Tis her breathing that
Perfumes the chamber thus. The flame o' th' taper
Bows toward her, and would under-peep her lids   20
To see th' enclosed lights, now canopied
Under these windows white and azure, lac'd
With blue of heaven's own tinct. But my design,
To note the chamber. I will write all down:
Such and such pictures; there the window; such   25
Th' adornment of her bed; the arras, figures,
Why, such and such, and the contents o' th' story.
Ah, but some natural notes about her body,
Above ten thousand meaner moveables
Would testify, t' enrich mine inventory.   30
O sleep, thou ape of death, lie dull upon her!
And be her sense but as a monument,
Thus in a chapel lying! Come off, come off!

[*Taking off her bracelet.*]

As slippery as the Gordian knot was hard!
'Tis mine; and this will witness outwardly,   35
As strongly as the conscience does within,
To th' madding of her lord. On her left breast
A mole cinque-spotted, like the crimson drops
I' th' bottom of a cowslip. Here's a voucher,
Stronger than ever law could make; this secret   40
Will force him think I have pick'd the lock and ta'en
The treasure of her honour. No more. To what end?
Why should I write this down, that's riveted,
Screw'd to my memory? She hath been reading late
The tale of Tereus; here the leaf's turn'd down   45
Where Philomel gave up. I have enough.
To th' trunk again, and shut the spring of it.
Swift, swift, you dragons of the night, that dawning
May bare the raven's eye! I lodge in fear;
Though this a heavenly angel, hell is here.   50

[*Clock strikes.*

One, two, three; time, time! [*Goes into the trunk.*]

---

36. **[to-night]** F₂. *night* F₁.   47. **derogation:** loss of dignity.   66. **husband, [than]** F₄. *husband. Then* F₁.

Sc. ii, 13. **rushes.** Floors of Elizabethan houses were covered with rushes (an anachronism).   14. **Cytherea:** Venus.   18. **they do't:** her lips kiss each other.   27. **story:** the picture on the arras.   29. **moveables:** pieces of furniture.   38. **cinque-spotted:** with five spots.   45. **Tereus:** a Thracian king who defiled his sister-in-law Philomela.

SCENE III. [*An ante-chamber adjoining Imogen's apartments.*]

Enter CLOTEN *and* LORDS.

1. Lord. Your lordship is the most patient man in loss, the most coldest that ever turn'd up ace.

Clo. It would make any man cold to lose.   4

1. Lord. But not every man patient after the noble temper of your lordship. You are most hot and furious when you win.

Clo. Winning will put any man into courage. If I could get this foolish Imogen, I should have gold enough. It's almost morning, is't not?   10

1. Lord. Day, my lord.

Clo. I would this music would come. I am advised to give her music o' mornings; they say it will penetrate.   14

Enter Musicians.

Come on; tune. If you can penetrate her with your fingering, so; we'll try with tongue too. If none will do, let her remain; but I'll never give o'er. First, a very excellent good-conceited thing; after, a wonderful sweet air, with admirable rich words to it; and then let her consider.   20

SONG.

Hark, hark! the lark at heaven's gate sings,
     And Phœbus gins arise
His steeds to water at those springs
     On chalic'd flowers that lies;
And winking Mary-buds begin   25
     To ope their golden eyes;
With every thing that pretty is,
     My lady sweet, arise,
         Arise, arise.   30

[*Clo.*] So, get you gone. If this penetrate, I will consider your music the better; if it do not, it is a [vice] in her ears, which horsehairs and calves' guts, nor the voice of unpaved eunuch to boot, can never amend.   [*Exeunt Musicians.*] 35

Enter CYMBELINE *and* QUEEN.

2. Lord. Here comes the King.

Clo. I am glad I was up so late, for that's the reason I was up so early. He cannot choose but take this service I have done fatherly. — Good morrow to your Majesty and to my gracious mother!   41

Cym. Attend you here the door of our stern
     daughter?
Will she not forth?

Clo. I have assail'd her with musics, but she vouchsafes no notice.   45

Cym. The exile of her minion is too new;
She hath not yet forgot him. Some more time
Must wear the print of his remembrance on't,
And then she's yours.

Queen.   You are most bound to th' King,
Who lets go by no vantages that may   50
Prefer you to his daughter. Frame yourself
To orderly [soliciting], and be friended
With aptness of the season; make denials
Increase your services; so seem as if
You were inspir'd to do those duties which   55
You tender to her, that you in all obey her,
Save when command to your dismission tends,
And therein you are senseless.

Clo.   Senseless! not so.

[*Enter a* MESSENGER.]

Mess. So like you, sir, ambassadors from Rome;
The one is Caius Lucius.

Cym.   A worthy fellow,   60
Albeit he comes on angry purpose now;
But that's no fault of his. We must receive him
According to the honour of his sender;
And towards himself, his goodness forespent on us,
We must extend our notice. Our dear son,   65
When you have given good morning to your mistress,
Attend the Queen and us; we shall have need
T' employ you towards this Roman. Come, our
     queen.   [*Exeunt [all but Cloten].*]

Clo. If she be up, I'll speak with her; if not,
Let her lie still and dream. [*Knocks.*] By your
     leave, ho!   70
I know her women are about her; what
If I do line one of their hands? 'Tis gold
Which buys admittance; oft it doth; yea, and makes
Diana's rangers false themselves, yield up   74
Their deer to th' stand o' th' stealer; and 'tis gold
Which makes the true man kill'd and saves the thief,
Nay, sometime hangs both thief and true man. What
Can it not do and undo? I will make
One of her women lawyer to me, for
I yet not understand the case myself.   80
By your leave.   [*Knocks.*

Enter a LADY.

Lady. Who's there that knocks?

Clo.   A gentleman.

Lady.   No more?

Clo. Yes, and a gentlewoman's son.

Lady.   That's more

Sc. iii, 2. **ace:** lowest throw of the dice.   18. **good-conceited:** fanciful.   25. **winking Mary-buds:** closed marigold buds. 32. **consider:** requite.   33. **[vice]** (Rowe). *voyce* F.   **horsehairs:** bow strings.   33. **calves' guts:** violin strings.   **unpaved:** castrated.   39. **fatherly.** Modifies *take*.   46. **minion:** darling.   48. **on't** F₁. *ou't* F₂. *out* Rowe.   51. **Prefer:** commend. 52. **[soliciting]** (Collier). *solicity* F.   58. **are senseless:** must fail to understand.   64. **forespent:** formerly bestowed. 74. **rangers:** gamekeepers; here, her nymphs.   75. **stand...stealer:** the stalking hunter.

Than some, whose tailors are as dear as yours,
Can justly boast of.   What's your lordship's pleas-
          ure?   85
   Clo. Your lady's person.   Is she ready?
   Lady.   Ay,
To keep her chamber.
   Clo.   There is gold for you;
Sell me your good report.
   Lady. How! my good name?   Or to report of you
What I shall think is good? — The Princess!   90

           Enter IMOGEN.

   Clo. Good morrow, fairest sister; your sweet
          hand.   [*Exit Lady.*]
   Imo. Good morrow, sir.   You lay out too much
          pains
For purchasing but trouble.   The thanks I give
Is telling you that I am poor of thanks
And scarce can spare them.
   Clo.   Still, I swear I love you.
   Imo. If you but said so, 'twere as deep with me.
If you swear still, your recompense is still   97
That I regard it not.
   Clo.   This is no answer.
   Imo. But that you shall not say I yield being
          silent,
I would not speak.   I pray you, spare me.   Faith,
I shall unfold equal discourtesy   101
To your best kindness.   One of your great knowing
Should learn, being taught, forbearance.
   Clo. To leave you in your madness, 'twere my sin.
I will not.   105
   Imo. Fools are not mad folks.
   Clo.   Do you call me fool?
   Imo. As I am mad, I do.
If you'll be patient, I'll no more be mad;
That cures us both.   I am much sorry, sir,
You put me to forget a lady's manners,   110
By being so verbal; and learn now, for all,
That I, which know my heart, do here pronounce,
By th' very truth of it, I care not for you,
And am so near the lack of charity
To accuse myself I hate you; which I had rather   115
You felt than make 't my boast.
   Clo.   You sin against
Obedience, which you owe your father.   For
The contract you pretend with that base wretch,
One bred of alms and foster'd with cold dishes,
With scraps o' th' court — it is no contract, none;
And though it be allow'd in meaner parties —   121
Yet who than he more mean? — to knit their
          souls —

On whom there is no more dependency
But brats and beggary, — in self-figur'd knot,
Yet you are curb'd from that enlargement by   125
The consequence o' th' crown, and must not foil
The precious note of it with a base slave,
A hilding for a livery, a squire's cloth,
A pantler, not so eminent.
   Imo.   Profane fellow!
Wert thou the son of Jupiter and no more   130
But what thou art besides, thou wert too base
To be his groom.   Thou wert dignified enough,
Even to the point of envy, if 'twere made
Comparative for your virtues, to be styl'd   134
The under-hangman of his kingdom, and hated
For being preferr'd so well.
   Clo.   The south-fog rot him!
   Imo. He never can meet more mischance than
          come
To be but nam'd of thee.   His meanest **garment**
That ever hath but clipp'd his body, is dearer
In my respect than all the hairs above thee,   140
Were they all made such men.   How now? [*Miss-*
          ing the bracelet.]   Pisanio!

           Enter PISANIO.

   Clo. "His garment!"   Now the devil —
   Imo. To Dorothy my woman hie thee pre-
          sently —
   Clo. "His garment!"
   Imo.   I am sprited with a fool,
Frighted, and ang'red worse.   Go bid my woman
Search for a jewel that too casually   146
Hath left mine arm.   It was thy master's.   Shrew me
If I would lose it for a revenue
Of any king's in Europe.   I do think
I saw 't this morning; confident I am   150
Last night 'twas on mine arm; I kiss'd it.
I hope it be not gone to tell my lord
That I kiss aught but he.
   Pis.   'Twill not be lost.
   Imo. I hope so; go and search.   [*Exit Pisanio.*]
   Clo.   You have abus'd me.
"His meanest garment!"
   Imo.   Ay, I said so, sir.   155
If you will make 't an action, call witness to 't.
   Clo. I will inform your father.
   Imo.   Your mother too.
She's my good lady, and will conceive, I hope,
But the worst of me.   So, I leave you, sir,
To the worst of discontent.   [*Exit.*
   Clo.   I'll be reveng'd.
"His meanest garment!"   Well.   [*Exit.* 161

---

86. **ready:** dressed.   111. **verbal:** profuse, plain-spoken.   123–24. **there ... beggary:** no more people are dependent
than brats and beggars.   124. **self-figur'd:** self-made.   125. **enlargement:** freedom.   126. **consequence:** succession.   **foil:**
foul, mar.   127. **note:** distinction.   128. **hilding ... livery:** worthless fellow fit for a livery.   129. **pantler:** pantry servant.
134. **Comparative for:** a comparison befitting.   139. **clipp'd:** embraced.   140. **respect:** regard.   144. **sprited:** haunted.
156. **action:** i.e., at law.

SCENE IV. [*Rome.   Philario's house.*]

Enter POSTHUMUS *and* PHILARIO.

Post. Fear it not, sir.   I would I were so sure
To win the King as I am bold her honour
Will remain hers.

Phi.   What means do you make to him?

Post. Not any, but abide the change of time,
Quake in the present winter's state, and wish
That warmer days would come.   In these fear'd
     hopes   6
I barely gratify your love; they failing,
I must die much your debtor.

Phi. Your very goodness and your company
O'erpays all I can do.   By this, your king   10
Hath heard of great Augustus.   Caius Lucius
Will do 's commission throughly; and I think
He'll grant the tribute, send th' arrearages,
Or look upon our Romans, whose remembrance
Is yet fresh in their grief.

Post.   I do believe,   15
Statist though I am none, nor like to be,
That this will prove a war; and you shall hear
The legion now in Gallia sooner landed
In our not-fearing Britain than have tidings
Of any penny tribute paid.   Our countrymen   20
Are men more order'd than when Julius Cæsar
Smil'd at their lack of skill, but found their courage
Worthy his frowning at.   Their discipline,
Now [mingled] with their courages, will make
     known
To their approvers they are people such   25
That mend upon the world.

Enter IACHIMO.

Phi.   See! Iachimo!

Post. The swiftest harts have posted you by land,
And winds of all the corners kiss'd your sails,
To make your vessel nimble.

Phi.   Welcome, sir.

Post. I hope the briefness of your answer made
The speediness of your return.

Iach.   Your lady   31
Is one of the fairest that I have look'd upon.

Post. And therewithal the best; or let her beauty
Look through a casement to allure false hearts
And be false with them.

Iach.   Here are letters for you.   35

Post. Their tenour good, I trust.

Iach.   'Tis very like.

[*Phi.*] Was Caius Lucius in the Britain court
When you were there?

Iach.   He was expected then,
But not approach'd.

Post.   All is well yet.

Sparkles this stone as it was wont, or is't not   40
Too dull for your good wearing?

Iach.   If I have lost it,
I should have lost the worth of it in gold.
I'll make a journey twice as far, to enjoy
A second night of such sweet shortness which
Was mine in Britain; for the ring is won.   45

Post. The stone's too hard to come by.

Iach.   Not a whit,
Your lady being so easy.

Post.   Make not, sir,
Your loss your sport.   I hope you know that we
Must not continue friends.

Iach.   Good sir, we must,
If you keep covenant.   Had I not brought   50
The knowledge of your mistress home, I grant
We were to question farther; but I now
Profess myself the winner of her honour,
Together with your ring; and not the wronger
Of her or you, having proceeded but   55
By both your wills.

Post.   If you can make't apparent
That you have tasted her in bed, my hand
And ring is yours; if not, the foul opinion
You had of her pure honour gains or loses
Your sword or mine, or masterless leaves both   60
To who shall find them.

Iach.   Sir, my circumstances,
Being so near the truth as I will make them,
Must first induce you to believe; whose strength
I will confirm with oath, which, I doubt not,
You'll give me leave to spare when you shall find   65
You need it not.

Post.   Proceed.

Iach.   First, her bedchamber, —
Where, I confess, I slept not, but profess
Had that was well worth watching — it was hang'd
With tapestry of silk and silver; the story
Proud Cleopatra, when she met her Roman,   70
And Cydnus swell'd above the banks, or for
The press of boats or pride; a piece of work
So bravely done, so rich, that it did strive
In workmanship and value; which I wonder'd
Could be so rarely and exactly wrought,   75
Since the true life on't was —

Post.   This is true;
And this you might have heard of here, by me,
Or by some other.

Iach.   More particulars
Must justify my knowledge.

Post.   So they must,
Or do your honour injury.

Iach.   The chimney   80
Is south the chamber, and the chimney-piece

Sc. iv, 6. **fear'd**: mistrustful.   7. **gratify**: requite.   14. **Or**: before.   16. **Statist**: statesman.   21. **order'd**: disciplined.
24. **[mingled]** F₂.   *wing-led* F₁.   25. **approvers**: those who try them out.   37. **[Phi.]** (Capell).   *Post.* F.   52. **question**:
dispute (in a duel).   61. **circumstances**: particulars.   68. **watching**: keeping awake for.   73. **bravely**: splendidly.

Chaste Dian bathing. Never saw I figures
So likely to report themselves. The cutter
Was as another Nature, dumb; outwent her,
Motion and breath left out.

Post.   This is a thing   85
Which you might from relation likewise reap,
Being, as it is, much spoke of.

Iach.   The roof o' th' chamber
With golden cherubins is fretted. Her andirons —
I had forgot them — were two winking Cupids
Of silver, each on one foot standing, nicely   90
Depending on their brands.

Post.   This is her honour!
Let it be granted you have seen all this — and
     praise
Be given to your remembrance — the description
Of what is in her chamber nothing saves
The wager you have laid.

Iach.   Then, if you can,   95
     [Showing the bracelet.]
Be pale. I beg but leave to air this jewel; see!
And now 'tis up again. It must be married
To that your diamond; I'll keep them.

Post.   Jove!
Once more let me behold it. Is it that
Which I left with her?

Iach.   Sir — I thank her — that.
She stripp'd it from her arm. I see her yet.   101
Her pretty action did outsell her gift,
And yet enrich'd it too. She gave it me, and said
She priz'd it once.

Post.   May be she pluck'd it off
To send it me.

Iach.   She writes so to you, doth she? 105

Post. O, no, no, no! 'tis true. Here, take this too;
     [Gives the ring.]
It is a basilisk unto mine eye,
Kills me to look on't. Let there be no honour
Where there is beauty; truth, where semblance;
     love,
Where there's another man. The vows of women
Of no more bondage be to where they are made   111
Than they are to their virtues, which is nothing.
O, above measure false!

Phi.   Have patience, sir,
And take your ring again; 'tis not yet won.
It may be probable she lost it; or   115
Who knows if one [of] her women, being corrupted,
Hath stol'n it from her?

Post.   Very true;
And so, I hope, he came by't. Back my ring!
Render to me some corporal sign about her,
More evident than this; for this was stol'n.   120

Iach. By Jupiter, I had it from her arm.

Post. Hark you, he swears; by Jupiter he swears.
'Tis true, — nay, keep the ring — 'tis true. I am
     sure
She would not lose it. Her attendants are
All sworn and honourable. They induc'd to steal
     it?   125
And by a stranger? No, he hath enjoy'd her.
The cognizance of her incontinency
Is this. She hath bought the name of whore thus
     dearly.
There, take thy hire; and all the fiends of hell
Divide themselves between you!

Phi.   Sir, be patient.
This is not strong enough to be believ'd   131
Of one persuaded well of —

Post.   Never talk on't;
She hath been colted by him.

Iach.   If you seek
For further satisfying, under her breast —
Worthy [the] pressing — lies a mole, right proud
Of that most delicate lodging. By my life,   136
I kiss'd it; and it gave me present hunger
To feed again, though full. You do remember
This stain upon her?

Post.   Ay, and it doth confirm
Another stain, as big as hell can hold,   140
Were there no more but it.

Iach.   Will you hear more?

Post. Spare your arithmetic; never count the
     turns;
Once, and a million!

Iach.   I'll be sworn —

Post.   No swearing.
If you will swear you have not done't, you lie;
And I will kill thee if thou dost deny   145
Thou'st made me cuckold.

Iach.   I'll deny nothing.

Post. O, that I had her here, to tear her limb-
     meal!
I will go there and do't, i' th' court, before
Her father. I'll do something —   *[Exit.*

Phi.   Quite besides
The government of patience! You have won.   150
Let's follow him and pervert the present wrath
He hath against himself.

Iach.   With all my heart.
     [Exeunt.

[SCENE V. *Another room in Philario's house.*]

Enter POSTHUMUS.

Post. Is there no way for men to be, but women

---

83. **So . . . themselves:** such speaking likenesses. 84. **dumb:** but could not give speech. 88. **fretted:** carved. 89. **wink-ing:** blind. 91. **Depending:** leaning. **brands:** torches. 97. **up:** put away. 107. **basilisk:** a fabulous serpent, believed to kill by its glance. 111. **Of . . . made:** i.e., no more bind them to their men. 116. **[of]** F₂. Om. F₁. 127. **cognizance:** token. 135. **[the]** (Rowe). *her* F. 147. **limbmeal:** limb from limb. 151. **pervert:** divert.

Must be half-workers? We are all bastards;
And that most venerable man which I
Did call my father, was I know not where
When I was stamp'd. Some coiner with his tools   5
Made me a counterfeit; yet my mother seem'd
The Dian of that time. So doth my wife
The nonpareil of this. O, vengeance, vengeance!
Me of my lawful pleasure she restrain'd
And pray'd me oft forbearance; did it with   10
A pudency so rosy the sweet view on't
Might well have warm'd old Saturn; that I thought
     her
As chaste as unsunn'd snow. O, all the devils!
This yellow Iachimo, in an hour, — was't not? —
Or less, — at first? — perchance he spoke not, but,
Like a full-acorn'd boar, a [German one],   16
Cried "O!" and mounted; found no opposition
But what he look'd for should oppose and she
Should from encounter guard. Could I find out
The woman's part in me! For there's no motion
That tends to vice in man, but I affirm   21
It is the woman's part: be it lying, note it,
The woman's flattering, hers; deceiving, hers;
Lust and rank thoughts, hers, hers; revenges, hers;
Ambitions, covetings, change of prides, disdain,   25
Nice longing, slanders, mutability,
All faults that [may be nam'd], nay, that hell knows,
Why, hers, in part or all; but rather, all.
For even to vice
They are not constant, but are changing still   30
One vice but of a minute old, for one
Not half so old as that. I'll write against them,
Detest them, curse them; yet 'tis greater skill
In a true hate, to pray they have their will;
The very devils cannot plague them better.   35
                             [*Exit.*

ACT III

SCENE I. [*Britain. A hall in Cymbeline's
palace.*]

Enter in state, CYMBELINE, QUEEN, CLOTEN, *and*
Lords *at one door, and at another,* CAIUS LUCIUS
and Attendants.

     Cym. Now say, what would Augustus Cæsar
       with us?
     Luc. When Julius Cæsar, whose remembrance
       yet
Lives in men's eyes and will to ears and tongues
Be theme and hearing ever, was in this Britain
And conquer'd it, Cassibelan, thine uncle, —   5

Famous in Cæsar's praises, no whit less
Than in his feats deserving it — for him
And his succession granted Rome a tribute,
Yearly three thousand pounds, which by thee lately
Is left untender'd.
     Queen.   And, to kill the marvel,   10
Shall be so ever.
     Clo.   There be many Cæsars,
Ere such another Julius. Britain is
A world by itself, and we will nothing pay
For wearing our own noses.
     Queen.   That opportunity
Which then they had to take from 's, to resume   15
We have again. Remember, sir, my liege,
The kings your ancestors, together with
The natural bravery of your isle, which stands
As Neptune's park, ribbed and paled in
With [rocks] unscaleable and roaring waters,   20
With sands that will not bear your enemies' boats
But suck them up to th' topmast. A kind of con-
     quest
Cæsar made here, but made not here his brag
Of "Came and saw and overcame." With shame —
The first that ever touch'd him — he was carried   25
From off our coast, twice beaten; and his shipping —
Poor ignorant baubles! — on our terrible seas,
Like egg-shells mov'd upon their surges, crack'd
As easily 'gainst our rocks; for joy whereof
The fam'd Cassibelan, who was once at point —   30
O giglot fortune! — to master Cæsar's sword,
Made Lud's town with rejoicing fires bright
And Britons strut with courage.   33
     Clo. Come, there's no more tribute to be paid.
Our kingdom is stronger than it was at that time;
and, as I said, there is no moe such Cæsars. Other
of them may have crook'd noses, but to owe such
straight arms, none.
     Cym. Son, let your mother end.   39
     Clo. We have yet many among us can gripe as
hard as Cassibelan. I do not say I am one, but I
have a hand. Why tribute? Why should we pay
tribute? If Cæsar can hide the sun from us with a
blanket, or put the moon in his pocket, we will pay
him tribute for light; else, sir, no more tribute, pray
you now.   46
     Cym. You must know,
Till the injurious Romans did extort
This tribute from us, we were free. Cæsar's am-
     bition,
Which swell'd so much that it did almost stretch   50
The sides o' th' world, against all colour here
Did put the yoke upon 's; which to shake off

Sc. v, 2. half-workers: i.e., in procreation.   **11. pudency:** modesty.   **16. full-acorn'd:** full of acorns.   **[German one]**
(Rowe).   *Iarmen on* F.   No convincing emendation has been proposed.   **25. prides:** vanities.   **26. Nice:** fastidious.   **27.**
[may be nam'd] F₂.   *name* F₁.
     Act III, sc. i, 20. [rocks] (Seward conj.).   *Oakes* F.   **27. ignorant:** silly.   **31. giglot:** wanton woman.   **32. Lud's town:**
London.   Lud was a mythical king of Britain.   **37. owe:** own.   **48. injurious:** insulting.   **51. colour:** excuse.

Becomes a warlike people, whom we reckon
Ourselves to be.   We do say then to Cæsar,
Our ancestor was that Mulmutius which   55
Ordain'd our laws, whose use the sword of Cæsar
Hath too much mangled, whose repair and franchise
Shall, by the power we hold, be our good deed,
Though Rome be therefore angry.   Mulmutius
     made our laws,
Who was the first of Britain which did put   60
His brows within a golden crown and call'd
Himself a king.

Luc.   I am sorry, Cymbeline,
That I am to pronounce Augustus Cæsar —
Cæsar, that hath moe kings his servants than
Thyself domestic officers — thine enemy.   65
Receive it from me, then: War and confusion
In Cæsar's name pronounce I 'gainst thee; look
For fury not to be resisted.   Thus defi'd,
I thank thee for myself.

Cym.   Thou art welcome, Caius.
Thy Cæsar knighted me; my youth I spent   70
Much under him; of him I gather'd honour,
Which he to seek of me again, perforce,
Behoves me keep at utterance.   I am perfect
That the Pannonians and Dalmatians for
Their liberties are now in arms, a precedent
Which not to read would show the Britons cold.   76
So Cæsar shall not find them.

Luc.   Let proof speak.
Clo. His Majesty bids you welcome.   Make
pastime with us a day or two, or longer.   If you
seek us afterwards in other terms, you shall find us
in our salt-water girdle; if you beat us out of it, it is
yours; if you fall in the adventure, our crows shall
fare the better for you; and there's an end.   84
Luc. So, sir.
Cym. I know your master's pleasure and he mine:
All the remain is "Welcome!"   [*Exeunt.*

SCENE II.   [*Another room in the palace.*]

Enter PISANIO, *reading a letter.*

Pis. How? of adultery?   Wherefore write you
     not
What [monster's her accuser]?   Leonatus!
O master! what a strange infection
Is fall'n into thy ear!   What false Italian,
As poisonous-tongu'd as handed, hath prevail'd   5
On thy too ready hearing?   Disloyal?   No!
She's punish'd for her truth, and undergoes,
More goddess-like than wife-like, such assaults
As would take in some virtue.   O my master!

Thy mind to her is now as low as were   10
Thy fortunes.   How? that I should murder her?
Upon the love and truth and vows which I
Have made to thy command?   I, her?   Her blood?
If it be so to do good service, never
Let me be counted serviceable.   How look I   15
That I should seem to lack humanity
So much as this fact comes to?   [*Reading.*] "Do't;
     the letter
That I have sent her, by her own command
Shall give thee opportunity."   O damn'd paper,
Black as the ink that's on thee!   Senseless bauble,
Art thou a fedary for this act, and look'st   21
So virgin-like without?   Lo, here she comes.

Enter IMOGEN.

I am ignorant in what I am commanded.
Imo. How now, Pisanio!
Pis. Madam, here is a letter from my lord.
Imo. Who?   Thy lord?   That is my lord
     Leonatus!   26
O, learn'd indeed were that astronomer
That knew the stars as I his characters;
He'd lay the future open.   You good gods,
Let what is here contain'd relish of love,   30
Of my lord's health, of his content, — yet not
That we two are asunder; let that grieve him:
Some griefs are med'cinable; that is one of them,
For it doth physic love — of his content,
All but in that!   Good wax, thy leave.   Blest be
You bees that make these locks of counsel! Lovers
And men in dangerous bonds pray not alike;   37
Though forfeiters you cast in prison, yet
You clasp young Cupid's tables.   Good news,
     gods!   39
[*Reads.*] "Justice, and your father's wrath should
he take me in his dominion, could not be so cruel to
me as you, O the dearest of creatures, would even
renew me with your eyes.   Take notice that I am
in Cambria, at Milford-Haven; what your own love
will out of this advise you, follow.   So he wishes
you all happiness, that remains loyal to his vow,
and your increasing in love
         LEONATUS POSTHUMUS."   49
O, for a horse with wings!   Hear'st thou, Pisanio?
He is at Milford-Haven.   Read, and tell me
How far 'tis thither.   If one of mean affairs
May plod it in a week, why may not I
Glide thither in a day?   Then, true Pisanio, —
Who long'st like me to see thy lord; who long'st, —
O, let me bate, — but not like me — yet long'st,   56
But in a fainter kind; — O, not like me,

<hr/>

57. **franchise:** free use.   72. **he to seek:** his seeking.   73. **at utterance:** to the last extremity.   **perfect:** well informed.
Sc. ii 2. **[monster's her accuser]** (Capell).   *Monsters her accuse* F.   9. **take in:** subdue.   10. **to:** compared to.   17. **fact:** crime.   21. **fedary:** confederate.   23. **I . . . in:** I will act as if I knew not.   28. **characters:** handwriting.   30. **relish:** taste.   35. **Good . . . leave.**   She breaks the seal.   36. **counsel:** secrets.   37. **pray not alike.**   Lovers pray for blessings on the bees, forfeiters for curses.   38. **forfeiters:** i.e., of bonds sealed with your wax.   39. **You . . . tables:** you seal love-letters.   42. **as:** but that.   44. **Cambria:** Wales.   52. **mean affairs:** small business.   56. **bate:** abate, qualify.

For mine's beyond beyond — say, and speak
    thick, —
Love's counsellor should fill the bores of hearing, 59
To th' smothering of the sense — how far it is
To this same blessed Milford; and by th' way
Tell me how Wales was made so happy as
T' inherit such a haven; but first of all,
How we may steal from hence, and for the gap
That we shall make in time, from our hence-going
And our return, to excuse. But first, how get
    hence? 66
Why should excuse be born or ere begot?
We'll talk of that hereafter. Prithee, speak,
How many [score] of miles may we well ride
'Twixt hour and hour?
    Pis.   One score 'twixt sun and sun,
Madam, 's enough for you, and too much too. 71
    Imo. Why, one that rode to's execution, man,
Could never go so slow. I have heard of riding
    wagers,
Where horses have been nimbler than the sands
That run i' th' clock's behalf. But this is foolery.
Go bid my woman feign a sickness, say 76
She'll home to her father; and provide me presently
A riding-suit, no costlier than would fit
A franklin's housewife.
    Pis.   Madam, you're best consider.
    Imo. I see before me, man; nor here, [nor] here,
Nor what ensues, but have a fog in them 81
That I cannot look through. Away, I prithee;
Do as I bid thee. There's no more to say.
Accessible is none but Milford way.   [*Exeunt.*

SCENE III. [*Wales: a mountainous country with
    a cave.*]

Enter [from the cave] BELARIUS; GUIDERIUS
    and ARVIRAGUS [*following*].

    Bel. A goodly day not to keep house with such
Whose roof's as low as ours! [Stoop], boys; this
    gate
Instructs you how t' adore the heavens and bows
    you
To a morning's holy office. The gates of monarchs
Are arch'd so high that giants may jet through
And keep their impious turbans on without 6
Good morrow to the sun. Hail, thou fair heaven!
We house i' th' rock, yet use thee not so hardly
As prouder livers do.
    Gui.   Hail, heaven!
    Arv.   Hail, heaven!

    Bel. Now for our mountain sport. Up to yond
    hill! 10
Your legs are young; I'll tread these flats. Con-
    sider,
When you above perceive me like a crow,
That it is place which lessens and sets off;
And you may then revolve what tales I have told
    you
Of courts of princes, of the tricks in war; 15
This service is not service, so being done,
But being so allow'd. To apprehend thus
Draws us a profit from all things we see;
And often, to our comfort, shall we find
The sharded beetle in a safer hold 20
Than is the full-wing'd eagle. O, this life
Is nobler than attending for a check,
Richer than doing nothing for a [bribe],
Prouder than rustling in unpaid-for silk.
Such gains the cap of him that makes him fine, 25
Yet keeps his book uncross'd. No life to ours.
    Gui. Out of your proof you speak; we, poor un-
    fledg'd,
Have never wing'd from view o' th' nest, nor know
    not
What air's from home. Haply this life is best,
If quiet life be best; sweeter to you 30
That have a sharper known; well corresponding
With your stiff age; but unto us it is
A cell of ignorance, travelling a-bed,
A prison [of] a debtor that not dares
To stride a limit.
    Arv.   What should we speak of 35
When we are old as you? When we shall hear
The rain and wind beat dark December, how,
In this our pinching cave, shall we discourse
The freezing hours away? We have seen nothing.
We are beastly; subtle as the fox for prey, 40
Like warlike as the wolf for what we eat.
Our valour is to chase what flies. Our cage
We make a choir, as doth the prison'd bird,
And sing our bondage freely.
    Bel.   How you speak!
Did you but know the city's usuries, 45
And felt them knowingly; the art o' th' court,
As hard to leave as keep, whose top to climb
Is certain falling, or so slipp'ry that
The fear 's as bad as falling; the toil o' th' war,
A pain that only seems to seek out danger 50
I' th' name of fame and honour which dies i' th'
    search,
And hath as oft a slanderous epitaph

---

58. **thick:** quickly. 63. **inherit:** possess. 67. **or ere begot:** before the thing has happened. 69. **[score]** F₂. *store* F₁.
79. **franklin's:** small landowner's. 80. **[nor]** F₂. *not* F₁. 80–82. **I . . . through:** i.e., I see only Milford; all else lies in a fog.
    Sc. iii, 1. **keep house:** stay inside. 2. **[Stoop]** (Hanmer). *Sleepe* F. 5. **jet:** strut. 13. **sets off:** enhances. 17. **allow'd:**
acknowledged. 20. **sharded:** with scaly wing covers. 22. **attending . . . check:** doing service only to get a rebuke. 23.
[bribe] (Hanmer). *Babe* F. 25. **the cap . . . fine:** the salute of his tailor. 26. **book uncross'd:** account unpaid. 27. **proof:**
experience. 29. **Haply:** perhaps. 34. **[of]** (Vaughan). *or* F. 35. **stride a limit:** over-step a boundary. 40. **beastly:**
like beasts.

As record of fair act; nay, many times,
Doth ill deserve by doing well; what's worse,
Must curtsy at the censure; — O boys, this story 55
The world may read in me. My body's mark'd
With Roman swords, and my report was once
First with the best of note. Cymbeline lov'd me,
And when a soldier was the theme, my name
Was not far off. Then was I as a tree   60
Whose boughs did bend with fruit; but in one night,
A storm or robbery, call it what you will,
Shook down my mellow hangings, nay, my leaves,
And left me bare to weather.
    Gui.   Uncertain favour!
    Bel. My fault being nothing — as I have told you
oft —   65
But that two villains, whose false oaths prevail'd
Before my perfect honour, swore to Cymbeline
I was confederate with the Romans; so
Follow'd my banishment, and this twenty years
This rock and these demesnes have been my
        world,   70
Where I have liv'd at honest freedom, paid
More pious debts to heaven than in all
The fore-end of my time. But up to th' moun-
        tains!
This is not hunters' language. He that strikes
The venison first shall be the lord o' th' feast;
To him the other two shall minister;   76
And we will fear no poison, which attends
In place of greater state. I'll meet you in the
        valleys. [*Exeunt* [*Guiderius and Arviragus*].
How hard it is to hide the sparks of nature!
These boys know little they are sons to th' King, 80
Nor Cymbeline dreams that they are alive.
They think they're mine; and, though train'd up
        thus meanly
I' th' cave [wherein they bow], their thoughts do hit
The roofs of palaces, and nature prompts them
In simple and low things to prince it much   85
Beyond the trick of others. This Polydore,
The heir of Cymbeline and Britain, who
The King his father call'd Guiderius, — Jove!
When on my three-foot stool I sit and tell
The warlike feats I have done, his spirits fly out 90
Into my story; say, "Thus mine enemy fell,
And thus I set my foot on's neck;" even then
The princely blood flows in his cheek, he sweats,
Strains his young nerves, and puts himself in posture
That acts my words. The younger brother, Cad-
        wal,   95
Once Arviragus, in as like a figure,
Strikes life into my speech and shows much more
His own conceiving. — Hark, the game is rous'd! —
O Cymbeline! heaven and my conscience knows

Thou didst unjustly banish me; whereon,   100
At three and two years old, I stole these babes,
Thinking to bar thee of succession, as
Thou reft'st me of my lands. Euriphile,
Thou wast their nurse; they took thee for their
        mother,
And every day do honour to her grave.   105
Myself, Belarius, that am Morgan call'd,
They take for natural father. — The game is up.
                                               [*Exit.*

SCENE IV. [*Wales Country near Milford-Haven.*]

        Enter Pisanio *and* Imogen.

    Imo. Thou told'st me, when we came from horse,
        the place
Was near at hand. Ne'er long'd my mother so
To see me first, as I have now. Pisanio! man!
Where is Posthumus? What is in thy mind
That makes thee stare thus? Wherefore breaks
        that sigh   5
From th' inward of thee? One but painted thus
Would be interpreted a thing perplex'd
Beyond self-explication. Put thyself
Into a haviour of less fear, ere wildness
Vanquish my staider senses. What's the matter?
Why tender'st thou that paper to me with   11
A look untender? If 't be summer news,
Smile to't before; if winterly, thou need'st
But keep that countenance still. My husband's
        hand!
That drug-damn'd Italy hath out-crafted him,
And he's at some hard point. Speak, man! Thy
        tongue   16
May take off some extremity, which to read
Would be even mortal to me.
    Pis.   Please you, read;
And you shall find me, wretched man, a thing
The most disdain'd of fortune.   20
    Imo. (*Reads.*)   "Thy mistress, Pisanio, hath
played the strumpet in my bed, the testimonies
whereof lie bleeding in me. I speak not out of
weak surmises, but from proof as strong as my grief
and as certain as I expect my revenge. That part
thou, Pisanio, must act for me, if thy faith be 25
not tainted with the breach of hers. Let thine own
hands take away her life. I shall give thee opportunity at Milford-Haven. She hath my letter for
the purpose; where, if thou fear to strike and to
make me certain it is done, thou art the pander to
her dishonour and equally to me disloyal."   33
    Pis. What shall I need to draw my sword? The
        paper
Hath cut her throat already. No, 'tis slander,

---

54. **deserve:** earn. 83. [**wherein they bow**] (Warburton). *whereon the Bowe* F. 94. **nerves:** sinews. 98. **conceiving:** imagination.
Sc. iv, 9. **of . . . fear:** less fearsome. **wildness:** madness. 16. **hard point:** crisis. 32. **pander:** go-between.

Whose edge is sharper than the sword, whose
    tongue   36
Outvenoms all the worms of Nile, whose breath
Rides on the posting winds and doth belie
All corners of the world.   Kings, queens, and states,
Maids, matrons, nay, the secrets of the grave   40
This viperous slander enters.   What cheer, madam?
  Imo.   False to his bed!   What is it to be false?
To lie in watch there and to think on him?
To weep 'twixt clock and clock? if sleep charge
    nature,
To break it with a fearful dream of him   45
And cry myself awake?   That's false to 's bed, is it?
  Pis.   Alas, good lady!
  Imo.   I false!   Thy conscience witness! —
    Iachimo,
Thou didst accuse him of incontinency;
Thou then look'dst like a villain; now methinks 50
Thy favour's good enough.   Some jay of Italy,
Whose mother was her painting, hath betray'd him!
Poor I am stale, a garment out of fashion;
And, for I am richer than to hang by th' walls,
I must be ripp'd. — To pieces with me! — O,   55
Men's vows are women's traitors!   All good seeming,
By thy revolt, O husband, shall be thought
Put on for villainy; not born where't grows,
But worn a bait for ladies.
  Pis.   Good madam, hear me.
  Imo.   True honest men, being heard like false
    Æneas,   60
Were in his time thought false, and Sinon's weeping
Did scandal many a holy tear, took pity
From most true wretchedness; so thou, Posthumus,
Wilt lay the leaven on all proper men;
Goodly and gallant shall be false and perjur'd   65
From thy great fail. — Come, fellow, be thou hon-
    est!
Do thou thy master's bidding.   When thou see'st
    him,
A little witness my obedience.   Look!
I draw the sword myself.   Take it, and hit
The innocent mansion of my love, my heart.   70
Fear not; 'tis empty of all things but grief.
Thy master is not there, who was indeed
The riches of it.   Do his bidding; strike.
Thou mayst be valiant in a better cause,   74
But now thou seem'st a coward.
  Pis.   Hence, vile instrument!
Thou shalt not damn my hand.
  Imo.   Why, I must die;
And if I do not by thy hand, thou art

No servant of thy master's.   Against self-slaughter
There is a prohibition so divine
That cravens my weak hand.   Come, here's my
    heart,   80
(Something's [afore't], — soft, soft! we'll no de-
    fence,)
Obedient as the scabbard.   What is here?
The scriptures of the loyal Leonatus,
All turn'd to heresy?   Away, away,
Corrupters of my faith! you shall no more   85
Be stomachers to my heart.   [*Drawing his letters
    from her bodice.*]   Thus may poor fools
Believe false teachers.   Though those that are
    betray'd
Do feel the treason sharply, yet the traitor
Stands in worse case of woe.
And thou, Posthumus, [thou] that didst set up
My disobedience 'gainst the King my father,   90
And make me put into contempt the suits
Of princely fellows, shalt hereafter find
It is no act of common passage, but
A strain of rareness; and I grieve myself   95
To think, when thou shalt be disedg'd by her
That now thou tirest on, how thy memory
Will then be pang'd by me.   Prithee, dispatch!
The lamb entreats the butcher.   Where's thy knife?
Thou art too slow to do thy master's bidding,   100
When I desire it too.
  Pis.   O gracious lady,
Since I receiv'd command to do this business
I have not slept one wink.
  Imo.   Do't, and to bed then.
  Pis.   I'll wake mine eye-balls [out] first.
  Imo.   Wherefore then
Didst undertake it?   Why hast thou abus'd   105
So many miles with a pretence?   This place?
Mine action and thine own?   Our horses' labour?
The time inviting thee?   The perturb'd court
For my being absent?   whereunto I never
Purpose return.   Why hast thou gone so far,   110
To be unbent when thou hast ta'en thy stand,
Th' elected deer before thee?
  Pis.   But to win time
To lose so bad employment; in the which
I have consider'd of a course.   Good lady,   114
Hear me with patience.
  Imo.   Talk thy tongue weary; speak.
I have heard I am a strumpet, and mine ear,
Therein false struck, can take no greater wound,
Nor tent to bottom that.   But speak.
  Pis.   Then, madam,

37. **worms:** serpents.   38. **posting:** speeding.   **belie:** calumniate.   39. **states:** statesmen.   51. **favour's:** countenance is.
jay: strumpet.   52. **Whose...painting:** i.e., born of the paint pot.   54. **richer than:** too rich.   60. **Æneas.** Æneas deserted Dido.   61. **Sinon's weeping.**   By false pretenses Sinon caused the downfall of Troy.   62. **scandal:** make disreputable.   64. **lay...on:** discredit.   80. **cravens:** makes cowardly.   81. [**afore't**] (Rowe).   *a-foot* F.   89. [**thou**] (Capell).
Om. F.   **set up:** inspire, incite.   94. **It:** i.e., my choice.   **passage:** occurrence.   96. **disedg'd:** satiated.   97. **tirest on:** de-
vourest.   104. [**out**] (Johnson conj.).   Om. F.   111. **unbent:** i.e., with bow unbent.   118. **tent...that:** probe to reach the
bottom of that wound.

I thought you would not back again.

Imo.　　　　　　　　　　　　Most like;
Bringing me here to kill me.

Pis.　　　　　　　　　　　Not so, neither;
But if I were as wise as honest, then　　121
My purpose would prove well.　It cannot be
But that my master is abus'd.
Some villain, ay, and singular in his art,
Hath done you both this cursed injury.　125

Imo. Some Roman courtezan.

Pis.　　　　　　　　　　No, on my life.
I'll give but notice you are dead, and send him
Some bloody sign of it; for 'tis commanded
I should do so.　You shall be miss'd at court,
And that will well confirm it.

Imo.　　　　　　　　　Why, good fellow,
What shall I do the while?　Where bide?　How
live?　　　　　　　　　　　　　　　131
Or in my life what comfort, when I am
Dead to my husband?

Pis.　　　　　　　If you'll back to th' court —

Imo. No court, no father; nor no more ado　134
With that harsh, [nothing] noble, simple nothing,
That Cloten, whose love-suit hath been to me
As fearful as a siege.

Pis.　　　　　　　　If not at court,
Then not in Britain must you bide.

Imo.　　　　　　　　　　　Where then?
Hath Britain all the sun that shines?　Day, night,
Are they not but in Britain?　I' th' world's volume
Our Britain seems as of it, but not in't;　141
In a great pool a swan's nest.　Prithee, think
There's livers out of Britain.

Pis.　　　　　　　　I am most glad
You think of other place.　Th' ambassador,
Lucius the Roman, comes to Milford-Haven　145
To-morrow.　Now, if you could wear a mind
Dark as your fortune is, and but disguise
That which, to appear itself, must not yet be
But by self-danger, you should tread a course
Pretty and full of view; yea, haply, near　150
The residence of Posthumus; so nigh at least
That though his actions were not visible, yet
Report should render him hourly to your ear
As truly as he moves.

Imo.　　　　　　　O, for such means,
Though peril to my modesty, not death on't,　155
I would adventure.

Pis.　　　　　Well, then, here's the point.
You must forget to be a woman; change
Command into obedience; fear and niceness —
The handmaids of all women, or, more truly,
Woman it pretty self — into a waggish courage;　160

Ready in gibes, quick-answer'd, saucy, and
As quarrelous as the weasel; nay, you must
Forget that rarest treasure of your cheek,
Exposing it — but, O, the harder heart!
Alack, no remedy! — to the greedy touch　165
Of common-kissing Titan, and forget
Your laboursome and dainty trims, wherein
You made great Juno angry.

Imo.　　　　　　　　　Nay, be brief.
I see into thy end and am almost
A man already.

Pis.　　　　First, make yourself but like one.
Fore-thinking this, I have already fit —　171
'Tis in my cloak-bag — doublet, hat, hose, all
That answer to them.　Would you in their serving,
And with what imitation you can borrow
From youth of such a season, 'fore noble Lucius　175
Present yourself, desire his service, tell him
Wherein you're happy, — which will make him
know
If that his head have ear in music, — doubtless
With joy he will embrace you, for he's honourable,
And doubling that, most holy.　Your means
abroad —　　　　　　　　　　　　　180
You have me, rich; and I will never fail
Beginning nor supplyment.

Imo.　　　　　　　Thou art all the comfort
The gods will diet me with.　Prithee, away.
There's more to be consider'd; but we'll even
All that good time will give us.　This attempt　185
I am soldier to, and will abide it with
A prince's courage.　Away, I prithee.

Pis. Well, madam, we must take a short farewell,
Lest, being miss'd, I be suspected of
Your carriage from the court.　My noble mis-
tress,　　　　　　　　　　　　　　　190
Here is a box — I had it from the Queen —
What's in't is precious.　If you are sick at sea,
Or stomach-qualm'd at land, a dram of this
Will drive away distemper.　To some shade,
And fit you to your manhood.　May the gods　195
Direct you to the best!

Imo. Amen!　I thank thee.

　　　　　　　　　　　　[Exeunt [severally].

SCENE V.　[*Britain.　A room in Cymbeline's
palace.*]

Enter CYMBELINE, QUEEN, CLOTEN, LUCIUS,
Lords [*and* ATTENDANTS].

Cym. Thus far; and so farewell.

Luc.　　　　　　　　Thanks, royal sir.
My emperor hath wrote I must from hence,

123. **abus'd:** deceived.　124. **singular:** unique.　135. **[nothing]** (Dowden conj.).　Om. F.　147. **Dark:** lowly.　148. **That which:** i.e., her sex.　150. **view:** opportunity.　160. **it:** its.　164. **harder heart:** i.e., the too hard heart (that could demand this).　166. **Titan:** the sun.　167. **laboursome:** elaborate.　173. **in ... serving:** with their help.　175. **season:** age.　177. **happy:** accomplished.　184. **even:** avail ourselves fully of.

And am right sorry that I must report ye
My master's enemy.

Cym.   Our subjects, sir,
Will not endure his yoke; and for ourself   5
To show less sovereignty than they, must needs
Appear unkinglike.

Luc.   So, sir. I desire of you
A conduct over-land to Milford-Haven.
Madam, all joy befall your Grace, and you!

Cym. My lords, you are appointed for that
    office;   10
The due of honour in no point omit.
So farewell, noble Lucius.

Luc.   Your hand, my lord.

Clo. Receive it friendly; but from this time forth
I wear it as your enemy.

Luc.   Sir, the event
Is yet to name the winner. Fare you well.   15

Cym. Leave not the worthy Lucius, good my
    lords,
Till he have cross'd the Severn. Happiness!

       [*Exeunt Lucius and Lords.*

Queen. He goes hence frowning; but it honours us
That we have given him cause.

Clo.   'Tis all the better;
Your valiant Britons have their wishes in it.   20

Cym. Lucius hath wrote already to the Emperor
How it goes here. It fits us therefore ripely
Our chariots and our horsemen be in readiness.
The powers that he already hath in Gallia
Will soon be drawn to head, from whence he moves
His war for Britain.   26

Queen.   'Tis not sleepy business,
But must be look'd to speedily and strongly.

Cym. Our expectation that it would be thus
Hath made us forward. But, my gentle queen,
Where is our daughter? She hath not appear'd   30
Before the Roman, nor to us hath tender'd
The duty of the day. She looks us like
A thing more made of malice than of duty;
We have noted it. Call her before us, for
We have been too slight in sufferance.

       [*Exit an attendant.*

Queen.   Royal sir,
Since the exile of Posthumus, most retir'd   36
Hath her life been; the cure whereof, my lord,
'Tis time must do. Beseech your Majesty,
Forbear sharp speeches to her; she's a lady
So tender of rebukes that words are strokes   40
And strokes death to her.

      Re-enter ATTENDANT.

Cym.   Where is she, sir? How
Can her contempt be answer'd?

Atten.   Please you, sir,

Her chambers are all lock'd; and there's no answer
That will be given to the [loudest] noises we make.

Queen. My lord, when last I went to visit her,
She pray'd me to excuse her keeping close;   46
Whereto constrain'd by her infirmity,
She should that duty leave unpaid to you,
Which daily she was bound to proffer. This
She wish'd me to make known; but our great
    court   50
Made me to blame in memory.

Cym.   Her doors lock'd?
Not seen of late? Grant, heavens, that which I fear
Prove false!   [*Exit.*

Queen.   Son, I say, follow the King.

Clo. That man of hers, Pisanio, her old servant,
I have not seen these two days.   [*Exit.*

Queen [*to attendant*].   Go, look after
Pisanio, thou, that stands so for Posthumus.   56

       [*Exit attendant.*

He hath a drug of mine; I pray his absence
Proceed by swallowing that, for he believes
It is a thing most precious. But for her,
Where is she gone? Haply, despair hath seiz'd
    her,   60
Or, wing'd with fervour of her love, she's flown
To her desir'd Posthumus. Gone she is
To death or to dishonour; and my end
Can make good use of either. She being down,
I have the placing of the British crown.   65

      Re-enter CLOTEN.

How now, my son!

Clo.   'Tis certain she is fled.
Go in and cheer the King. He rages; none
Dare come about him.

Queen.   [*Aside.*] All the better. May
This night forestall him of the coming day!

       [*Exit.*

Clo. I love and hate her; for she's fair and royal,
And that she hath all courtly parts more exqui-
    site   71
Than lady, ladies, woman; from every one
The best she hath, and she, of all compounded,
Outsells them all. I love her therefore; but
Disdaining me and throwing favours on   75
The low Posthumus slanders so her judgement
That what's else rare is chok'd; and in that point
I will conclude to hate her, nay, indeed,
To be reveng'd upon her. For when fools
Shall —

      Enter PISANIO.

Who is here? What, are you packing, sirrah?
Come hither. Ah, you precious pandar! Vil-
    lain,   81

Sc. v, 14. **event:** outcome. 22. **ripely:** urgently. 35. **slight in sufferance:** slack in allowing this. 44. **[loudest]** (Rowe). *lowd of* F. 50. **great court:** i.e., the reception to Lucius. 69. **forestall:** deprive. 80. **packing:** plotting.

Where is thy lady?   In a word; or else
Thou art straightway with the fiends.
    Pis.   O, good my lord!
    Clo. Where is thy lady? or, by Jupiter,
I will not ask again.   Close villain,   85
I'll have this secret from thy heart, or rip
Thy heart to find it.   Is she with Posthumus,
From whose so many weights of baseness cannot
A dram of worth be drawn?
    Pis.   Alas, my lord,   89
How can she be with him?   When was she miss'd?
He is in Rome.
    Clo.   Where is she, sir?   Come nearer.
No further halting.   Satisfy me home
What is become of her.
    Pis. O, my all-worthy lord!
    Clo.   All-worthy villain!
Discover where thy mistress is at once,   95
At the next word.   No more of "worthy lord!"
Speak, or thy silence on the instant is
Thy condemnation and thy death.
    Pis.   Then, sir,
This paper is the history of my knowledge
Touching her flight.   [*Presenting a letter.*]
    Clo.   Let's see't.   I will pursue her   100
Even to Augustus' throne.
    Pis.   [*Aside.*] Or this, or perish.
She's far enough; and what he learns by this
May prove his travel, not her danger.
    Clo.   Hum!
    Pis. [*Aside.*] I'll write to my lord she's dead.   O
         Imogen,   104
Safe mayst thou wander, safe return again!
    Clo. Sirrah, is this letter true?
    Pis. Sir, as I think.   107
    Clo. It is Posthumus' hand; I know't.   Sirrah,
if thou wouldst not be a villain, but do me true service, undergo those employments wherein I should
have cause to use thee with a serious industry, that
is, what villainy soe'er I bid thee do, to perform it
directly and truly, I would think thee an honest
man.   Thou shouldst neither want my means for
thy relief nor my voice for thy preferment.   116
    Pis. Well, my good lord.
    Clo. Wilt thou serve me?   For since patiently
and constantly thou hast stuck to the bare fortune
of that beggar Posthumus, thou canst not, in the
course of gratitude, but be a diligent follower of
mine.   Wilt thou serve me?   122
    Pis. Sir, I will.
    Clo. Give me thy hand; here's my purse.   Hast
any of thy late master's garments in thy possession?   126
    Pis. I have, my lord, at my lodging, the same

suit he wore when he took leave of my lady and mistress.
    Clo. The first service thou dost me, fetch that
suit hither.   Let it be thy first service; go.   131
    Pis. I shall, my lord.   [*Exit.*
    Clo. Meet thee at Milford-Haven! — I forgot
to ask him one thing; I'll remember't anon; —
even there, thou villain Posthumus, will I kill   135
thee.   I would these garments were come.   She
said upon a time — the bitterness of it I now belch
from my heart — that she held the very garment
of Posthumus in more respect than my noble and
natural person, together with the adornment of   140
my qualities.   With that suit upon my back will I
ravish her, — first kill him, and in her eyes; there
shall she see my valour, which will then be a torment to her contempt, — he on the ground, my
speech of insultment ended on his dead body;   145
and when my lust hath dined, — which, as I say, to
vex her I will execute in the clothes that she so
prais'd, — to the court I'll knock her back, foot
her home again.   She hath despis'd me rejoicingly,
and I'll be merry in my revenge.   150

     Re-enter PISANIO [*with the clothes*].

Be those the garments?
    Pis. Ay, my noble lord.
    Clo. How long is't since she went to Milford-
Haven?
    Pis. She can scarce be there yet.   155
    Clo. Bring this apparel to my chamber; that is
the second thing that I have commanded thee; the
third is, that thou wilt be a voluntary mute to my
design.   Be but duteous, and true preferment shall
tender itself to thee.   My revenge is now at Milford;
would I had wings to follow it!   Come, and be
true.   [*Exit.* 162
    Pis. Thou bidd'st me to my loss; for true to thee
Were to prove false, which I will never be,
To him that is most true.   To Milford go,
And find not her whom thou pursuest.   Flow, flow,
You heavenly blessings, on her!   This fool's speed
Be cross'd with slowness; labour be his meed!   168
                              [*Exit.*

SCENE VI. [*Wales.   Before the cave of Belarius.*]

    Enter IMOGEN, *alone* [*in boy's clothes*].

    Imo. I see a man's life is a tedious one.
I have tir'd myself, and for two nights together
Have made the ground my bed.   I should be sick,
But that my resolution helps me.   Milford,
When from the mountain-top Pisanio show'd thee,
Thou wast within a ken.   O Jove!   I think   6

---

   85. **Close:** secretive.   91. **Come nearer:** answer more to the point.   92. **home:** completely.   148. **foot:** kick.   168.
cross'd: thwarted.
   Sc. vi, 6. **a ken:** view.

Foundations fly the wretched; such, I mean,
Where they should be reliev'd. Two beggars told
me
I could not miss my way: will poor folks lie,
That have afflictions on them, knowing 'tis   10
A punishment or trial? Yes; no wonder,
When rich ones scarce tell true. To lapse in fulness
Is sorer than to lie for need; and falsehood
Is worse in kings than beggars. My dear lord!
Thou art one o' th' false ones. Now I think on
thee,   15
My hunger's gone; but even before, I was
At point to sink for food. But what is this?
Here is a path to 't. 'Tis some savage hold.
I were best not call; I dare not call; yet famine,
Ere clean it o'erthrow nature, makes it valiant.   20
Plenty and peace breeds cowards; hardness ever
Of hardiness is mother. Ho! who's here?
If anything that's civil, speak; if savage,
Take or lend. Ho! No answer? Then I'll enter.
Best draw my sword; and if mine enemy   25
But fear the sword like me, he'll scarcely look on 't.
Such a foe, good heavens!   [*Exit* [*to the cave*].

Enter BELARIUS, GUIDERIUS, *and* ARVIRAGUS.

Bel. You, Polydore, have prov'd best woodman
and
Are master of the feast. Cadwal and I
Will play the cook and servant; 'tis our match.   30
The sweat of industry would dry and die,
But for the end it works to. Come; our stomachs
Will make what's homely savoury; weariness
Can snore upon the flint, when resty sloth   34
Finds the down pillow hard. Now peace be here,
Poor house, that keep'st thyself!
Gui.   I am throughly weary.
Arv. I am weak with toil, yet strong in appetite.
Gui. There is cold meat i' th' cave; we'll browse
on that,
Whilst what we have kill'd be cook'd.
Bel. [*Looking into the cave.*] Stay; come not in.
But that it eats our victuals, I should think   41
Here were a fairy.
Gui.   What's the matter, sir?
Bel. By Jupiter, an angel! or, if not,
An earthly paragon! Behold divineness
No elder than a boy!   45

Re-enter IMOGEN.

Imo. Good masters, harm me not.
Before I enter'd here I call'd, and thought
To have begg'd or bought what I have took. Good
troth,

I have stol'n nought, nor would not, though I had
found
Gold strew'd i' th' floor. Here's money for my
meat.   50
I would have left it on the board so soon
As I had made my meal, and parted with
Prayers for the provider.
Gui.   Money, youth?
Arv. All gold and silver rather turn to dirt!
As 'tis no better reckon'd, but of those   55
Who worship dirty gods.
Imo.   I see you're angry.
Know, if you kill me for my fault, I should
Have died had I not made it.
Bel.   Whither bound?
Imo. To Milford-Haven.
Bel. What's your name?   60
Imo. Fidele, sir. I have a kinsman who
Is bound for Italy; he embark'd at Milford;
To whom being going, almost spent with hunger,
I am fall'n in this offence.
Bel.   Prithee, fair youth,
Think us no churls, nor measure our good minds
By this rude place we live in. Well encounter'd!   66
'Tis almost night: you shall have better cheer
Ere you depart; and thanks to stay and eat it.
Boys, bid him welcome.
Gui.   Were you a woman, youth,
I should woo hard but be your groom. In hon-
esty,   70
I bid for you as [I'd] buy.
Arv.   I'll make 't my comfort
He is a man; I'll love him as my brother;
And such a welcome as I'd give to him
After long absence, such is yours. Most welcome!
Be sprightly, for you fall 'mongst friends.
Imo.   'Mongst friends,
If brothers. [*Aside.*] Would it had been so, that
they   76
Had been my father's sons! Then had my prize
Been less, and so more equal ballasting
To thee, Posthumus.
Bel.   He wrings at some distress.
Gui. Would I could free 't!
Arv.   Or I, whate'er it be,   80
What pain it cost, what danger. Gods!
Bel.   Hark, boys.
                           [*Whispering.*]
Imo. [*Aside.*] Great men,
That had a court no bigger than this cave,
That did attend themselves and had the virtue
Which their own conscience seal'd them, laying by
That nothing-gift of differing multitudes,   86

---

7. **Foundations:** houses of charity.   11. **trial:** i.e., of their virtue.   21. **hardness:** hardship.   24. **Take or lend:** i.e., perhaps, blows. Obscure.   30. **match:** agreement.   34. **resty:** idle.   38. **browse:** nibble.   70. **but to be:** but to be.   71. **[I'd]** (Tyrwhitt conj.).   *I do* F.   **buy:** pay.   77. **prize:** value.   With her brothers alive, Imogen would not be heir.   79. **wrings:** writhes.   85. **seal'd:** assured.   86. **nothing...multitudes:** worthless gift of being attended by mobs of suitors.

Could not out-peer these twain. Pardon me, gods!
I'd change my sex to be companion with them,
Since Leonatus false.

Bel.   It shall be so.
Boys, we'll go dress our hunt. Fair youth, come
   in.   90
Discourse is heavy, fasting; when we have supp'd,
We'll mannerly demand thee of thy story,
So far as thou wilt speak it.

Gui.   Pray, draw near.
Arv. The night to th' owl and morn to th' lark
   less welcome.

Imo. Thanks, sir.   95
Arv. I pray, draw near.   [*Exeunt.*

SCENE VII. [*Rome. A public place.*]

Enter two Roman SENATORS *and* TRIBUNES.

1. Sen. This is the tenour of the Emperor's writ:
That since the common men are now in action
'Gainst the Pannonians and Dalmatians,
And that the legions now in Gallia are
Full weak to undertake our wars against   5
The fall'n-off Britons, that we do incite
The gentry to this business. He creates
Lucius proconsul; and to you the tribunes,
For this immediate levy, he commands
His absolute commission. Long live Cæsar!   10

1. Tri. Is Lucius general of the forces?
2. Sen.   Ay.
1. Tri. Remaining now in Gallia?
1. Sen.   With those legions
Which I have spoke of, whereunto your levy
Must be supplyant. The words of your commission
Will tie you to the numbers and the time   15
Of their dispatch.

1. Tri.   We will discharge our duty.
                               [*Exeunt.*

ACT IV

SCENE I. [*Wales. Near the cave of Belarius.*]

Enter CLOTEN *alone.*

Clo. I am near to th' place where they should
meet, if Pisanio have mapp'd it truly. How fit
his garments serve me! Why should his mistress,
who was made by him that made the tailor, not be
fit too? the rather — saving reverence of the   5
word — for 'tis said a woman's fitness comes by
fits. Therein I must play the workman. I dare

speak it to myself — for it is not vain-glory for a
man and his glass to confer in his own chamber —
I mean, the lines of my body are as well drawn as
his; no less young, more strong, not beneath   10
him in fortunes, beyond him in the advantage of the
time, above him in birth, alike conversant in general services, and more remarkable in single oppositions; yet this imperceiverant thing loves him in   15
my despite. What mortality is! Posthumus, thy
head, which now is growing upon thy shoulders,
shall within this hour be off; thy mistress enforced;
thy garments cut to pieces before [her] face: and
all this done, spurn her home to her father; who   20
may haply be a little angry for my so rough usage;
but my mother, having power of his testiness, shall
turn all into my commendations. My horse is
tied up safe. Out, sword, and to a sore purpose!
Fortune, put them into my hand! This is the   25
very description of their meeting-place; and the
fellow dares not deceive me.   [*Exit.*

SCENE II. [*Before the cave of Belarius.*]

Enter BELARIUS, GUIDERIUS, ARVIRAGUS, *and*
IMOGEN, *from the cave.*

Bel. [*To Imogen.*] You are not well. Remain
   here in the cave;
We'll come to you after hunting.

Arv.   [*To Imogen.*] Brother, stay here.
Are we not brothers?

Imo.   So man and man should be;
But clay and clay differs in dignity,
Whose dust is both alike. I am very sick.   5

Gui. Go you to hunting; I'll abide with him.
Imo. So sick I am not, yet I am not well;
But not so citizen a wanton as
To seem to die ere sick. So please you, leave me;
Stick to your journal course. The breach of cus-
   tom   10
Is breach of all. I am ill, but your being by me
Cannot amend me; society is no comfort
To one not sociable. I am not very sick,
Since I can reason of it. Pray you, trust me here.
I'll rob none but myself; and let me die,   15
Stealing so poorly.

Gui.   I love thee; I have spoke it;
How much the quantity, the weight as much,
As I do love my father.

Bel.   What! how! how!
Arv. If it be sin to say so, sir, I yoke me
In my good brother's fault. I know not why   20
I love this youth; and I have heard you say,
Love's reason's without reason. The bier at door,

---

87. **out-peer:** surpass.
Sc. vii, 6. **fall'n-off:** rebelling. 9. **commands:** commends. 14. **supplyant:** supplementary. 15. **tie you to:** inform you of.
Act IV, sc. i, 14. **oppositions:** combats. **imperceiverant:** undiscerning. 19. **[her]** (Hanmer). *thy* F.
Sc. ii, 8. **citizen a wanton:** delicate a spoiled child. 10. **journal:** daily.

And a demand who is't shall die, I'd say
My father, not this youth.
Bel. [*Aside.*] O noble strain!
O worthiness of nature! breed of greatness!　25
Cowards father cowards and base things sire base:
Nature hath meal and bran, contempt and grace.
I'm not their father; yet who this should be
Doth miracle itself, lov'd before me. —
'Tis the ninth hour o' th' morn.
Arv.　　　　　　　　Brother, farewell.　30
Imo. I wish ye sport.
Arv.　　　　　You health. — So please you, sir.
Imo. [*Aside.*] These are kind creatures. Gods,
　　what lies I have heard!
Our courtiers say all's savage but at court.
Experience, O, thou disprov'st report!
The imperious seas breed monsters; for the dish　35
Poor tributary rivers as sweet fish.
I am sick still, heart-sick. Pisanio,
I'll now taste of thy drug.　　[*Swallows some.*]
Gui.　　　　　I could not stir him.
He said he was gentle, but unfortunate;
Dishonestly afflicted, but yet honest.　40
Arv. Thus did he answer me; yet said, hereafter
I might know more.
Bel.　　　　To th' field, to th' field!
We'll leave you for this time. Go in and rest.
Arv. We'll not be long away.
Bel.　　　　　Pray, be not sick,
For you must be our housewife.
Imo.　　　　　Well or ill,　45
I am bound to you.　　[*Exit* [*to the cave*].
Bel.　　　　And shalt be ever.
This youth, howe'er distress'd, appears he hath had
Good ancestors.
Arv.　　　How angel-like he sings!
Gui. But his neat cookery! He cut our roots
In characters,
And sauc'd our broths, as Juno had been sick　50
And he her dieter.
Arv.　　　　Nobly he yokes
A smiling with a sigh, as if the sigh
Was that it was for not being such a smile;
The smile mocking the sigh, that it would fly
From so divine a temple to commix　55
With winds that sailors rail at.
Gui.　　　　　I do note
That grief and patience, rooted in [him] both,
Mingle their spurs together.
Arv.　　　　Grow, [patience]!
And let the stinking elder, grief, untwine
His perishing root with th' increasing vine!　60
Bel. It is great morning. Come, away! —
　　Who's there?

Enter CLOTEN.
Clo. I cannot find those runagates; that villain
Hath mock'd me. I am faint.
Bel.　　　　　Those runagates!
Means he not us? I partly know him. 'Tis
Cloten, the son o' th' Queen. I fear some ambush.
I saw him not these many years, and yet　66
I know 'tis he. We are held as outlaws; hence!
Gui. He is but one. You and my brother search
What companies are near. Pray you, away;
Let me alone with him.
　　　　　[*Exeunt Belarius and Arviragus.*]
Clo.　　　　Soft! What are you　70
That fly me thus? Some villain mountaineers?
I have heard of such. What slave art thou?
Gui.　　　　　　A thing
More slavish did I ne'er than answering
A "slave" without a knock.
Clo.　　　　Thou art a robber,
A law-breaker, a villain. Yield thee, thief.　75
Gui. To who? To thee? What art thou?
　　Have not I
An arm as big as thine? a heart as big?
Thy words, I grant, are bigger; for I wear not
My dagger in my mouth. Say what thou art,
Why I should yield to thee.
Clo.　　　　Thou villain base,　80
Know'st me not by my clothes?
Gui.　　　　No, nor thy tailor, rascal,
Who is thy grandfather. He made those clothes,
Which, as it seems, make thee.
Clo.　　　　Thou precious varlet,
My tailor made them not.
Gui.　　　　Hence, then, and thank
The man that gave them thee. Thou art some
　　fool;　85
I am loath to beat thee.
Clo.　　　　Thou injurious thief,
Hear but my name, and tremble.
Gui.　　　　　What's thy name?
Clo. Cloten, thou villain.
Gui. Cloten, thou double villain, be thy name,
I cannot tremble at it. Were it Toad, or Adder,
　　Spider,　90
'Twould move me sooner.
Clo.　　　　To thy further fear,
Nay, to thy mere confusion, thou shalt know
I am son to th' Queen.
Gui.　　　I am sorry for't; not seeming
So worthy as thy birth.
Clo.　　　　Art not afeard?
Gui. Those that I reverence, those I fear, the
　　wise.　95
At fools I laugh, not fear them.
Clo.　　　　Die the death!

---

29. **Doth miracle itself:** is miraculous.　39. **gentle:** nobly born.　49. **characters:** letters, emblems.　57. **[him]** (Pope).
them F.　58. **spurs:** roots. **[patience]** (Theobald). *patient* F.　92. **mere:** utter.

When I have slain thee with my proper hand,
I'll follow those that even now fled hence,
And on the gates of Lud's town set your heads.
Yield, rustic mountaineer.   [*Fight and exeunt.*   100

Re-enter BELARIUS *and* ARVIRAGUS.

Bel. No company's abroad?
Arv. None in the world.   You did mistake him,
     sure.
Bel. I cannot tell, — long is it since I saw him.
But time hath nothing blurr'd those lines of favour
Which then he wore.   The snatches in his voice,   105
And burst of speaking, were as his.   I am absolute
'Twas very Cloten.
Arv.   In this place we left them.
I wish my brother make good time with him,
You say he is so fell.
Bel.   Being scarce made up,
I mean, to man, he had not apprehension   110
Of roaring terrors; for the defect of judgement
Is oft the [cease] of fear.

Re-enter GUIDERIUS [*with Cloten's head*].
         But, see, thy brother.
Gui. This Cloten was a fool, an empty purse;
There was no money in't.   Not Hercules
Could have knock'd out his brains, for he had none.
Yet I not doing this, the fool had borne   116
My head as I do his.
Bel.   What hast thou done?
Gui. I am perfect what: cut off one Cloten's head,
Son to the Queen, after his own report;
Who call'd me traitor, mountaineer, and swore
With his own single hand he'd take us in,   121
Displace our heads where — thank the gods! —
     they grow.
And set them on Lud's town.
Bel.   We are all undone.
Gui. Why, worthy father, what have we to lose,
But that he swore to take, our lives?   The law   125
Protects not us; then why should we be tender
To let an arrogant piece of flesh threat us,
Play judge and executioner all himself,
For we do fear the law?   What company
Discover you abroad?
Bel.   No single soul   130
Can we set eye on; but in all safe reason
He must have some attendants.   Though his [hu-
     mour]
Was nothing but mutation, ay, and that
From one bad thing to worse, not frenzy, not
Absolute madness could so far have rav'd   135
To bring him here alone; although perhaps
It may be heard at court that such as we

Cave here, hunt here, are outlaws, and in time
May make some stronger head; the which he hear-
     ing —
As it is like him — might break out and swear   140
He'd fetch us in; yet is't not probable
To come alone, either he so undertaking,
Or they so suffering.   Then on good ground we fear,
If we do fear this body hath a tail
More perilous than the head.
Arv.   Let ordinance   145
Come as the gods foresay it; howsoe'er,
My brother hath done well.
Bel.   I had no mind
To hunt this day; the boy Fidele's sickness
Did make my way long forth.
Gui.   With his own sword,
Which he did wave against my throat, I have ta'en
His head from him.   I'll throw't into the creek   151
Behind our rock; and let it to the sea,
And tell the fishes he's the Queen's son, Cloten.
That's all I reck.   [*Exit.*
Bel.   I fear 'twill be reveng'd.
Would, Polydore, thou hadst not done't! though
     valour   155
Becomes thee well enough.
Arv.   Would I had done't,
So the revenge alone pursu'd me!   Polydore,
I love thee brotherly, but envy much
Thou hast robb'd me of this deed.   I would re-
     venges,
That possible strength might meet, would seek us
     through   160
And put us to our answer.
Bel.   Well, 'tis done.
We'll hunt no more to-day, nor seek for danger
Where there's no profit.   I prithee, to our rock;
You and Fidele play the cooks.   I'll stay
Till hasty Polydore return, and bring him   165
To dinner presently.
Arv.   Poor sick Fidele!
I'll willingly to him.   To gain his colour
I'd let a parish of such Clotens blood,
And praise myself for charity.   [*Exit.*
Bel.   O thou goddess,
Thou divine Nature, [how] thyself thou blazon'st
In these two princely boys!   They are as gentle
As zephyrs blowing below the violet,   172
Not wagging his sweet head; and yet as rough,
Their royal blood enchaf'd, as the rud'st wind
That by the top doth take the mountain pine   175
And make him stoop to th' vale.   'Tis wonder
That an invisible instinct should frame them
To royalty unlearn'd, honour untaught,
Civility not seen from other, valour

---

104. **favour:** appearance.   105. **snatches:** catches, breaks.   112. **[cease]** Herr.   *cause* F.   129. **For:** because.   132.
[humour] (Theobald).   *honor* F.   139. **head:** armed force.   143. **suffering:** permitting.   145. **ordinance:** what is ordained.   167. **gain his colour:** restore color to his cheeks.   170. **[how]** (Pope).   *thou* F.   174. **enchaf'd:** heated.

That wildly grows in them but yields a crop   180
As if it had been sow'd.   Yet still it's strange
What Cloten's being here to us portends,
Or what his death will bring us.

Re-enter GUIDERIUS.

Gui.   Where's my brother?
I have sent Cloten's clotpoll down the stream
In embassy to his mother.   His body's hostage   185
For his return.   [*Solemn music.*
Bel.   My ingenious instrument!
Hark, Polydore, it sounds!   But what occasion
Hath Cadwal now to give it motion?   Hark!
Gui. Is he at home?
Bel.   He went hence even now.
Gui. What does he mean?   Since death of my
    dear'st mother   190
It did not speak before.   All solemn things
Should answer solemn accidents.   The matter?
Triumphs for nothing and lamenting toys
Is jollity for apes and grief for boys.
Is Cadwal mad?

Re-enter ARVIRAGUS, *with* IMOGEN [*as*] *dead,*
bearing her in his arms.

Bel.   Look, here he comes,   195
And brings the dire occasion in his arms
Of what we blame him for.
Arv.   The bird is dead
That we have made so much on.   I had rather
Have skipp'd from sixteen years of age to sixty,
To have turn'd my leaping-time into a crutch,   200
Than have seen this.
Gui.   O sweetest, fairest lily!
My brother wears thee not the one half so well
As when thou grew'st thyself.
Bel.   O melancholy!
Who ever yet could sound thy bottom? find
The ooze, to show what coast thy sluggish [crare]
[Might] easiliest harbour in?   Thou blessed thing!
Jove knows what man thou mightst have made;
    but I,   207
Thou diedst, a most rare boy, of melancholy.
How found you him?
Arv.   Stark, as you see;
Thus smiling, as some fly had tickled slumber, 210
Not as death's dart, being laugh'd at; his right
    cheek
Reposing on a cushion.
Gui.   Where?
Arv.   O' th' floor,
His arms thus leagu'd.   I thought he slept, and put
My clouted brogues from off my feet, whose rude-
    ness

Answer'd my steps too loud.
Gui.   Why, he but sleeps!
If he be gone, he'll make his grave a bed.   216
With female fairies will his tomb be haunted,
And worms will not come to thee.
Arv.   With fairest flowers
Whilst summer lasts and I live here, Fidele,
I'll sweeten thy sad grave.   Thou shalt not lack 220
The flower that's like thy face, pale primrose, nor
The azur'd harebell, like thy veins, no, nor
The leaf of eglantine, whom not to slander,
Out-sweet'ned not thy breath.   The ruddock
    would,
With charitable bill, — O bill, sore shaming   225
Those rich-left heirs that let their fathers lie
Without a monument! — bring thee all this;
Yea, and furr'd moss besides, when flowers are none,
To winter-ground thy corse.
Gui.   Prithee, have done;
And do not play in wench-like words with that
Which is so serious.   Let us bury him,   231
And not protract with admiration what
Is now due debt.   To th' grave!
Arv.   Say, where shall's lay him?
Gui. By good Euriphile, our mother.
Arv.   Be't so;
And let us, Polydore, though now our voices   235
Have got the mannish crack, sing him to th' ground,
As once our mother; use like note and words,
Save that Euriphile must be Fidele.
Gui. Cadwal,
I cannot sing.   I'll weep, and word it with thee; 240
For notes of sorrow out of tune are worse
Than priests and fanes that lie.
Arv.   We'll speak it, then.
Bel. Great griefs, I see, med'cine the less; for
    Cloten
Is quite forgot.   He was a queen's son, boys;
And though he came our enemy, remember   245
He was paid for that.   Though mean and mighty,
    rotting
Together, have one dust, yet reverence,
That angel of the world, doth make distinction
Of place 'tween high and low.   Our foe was princely;
And though you took his life, as being our foe,   250
Yet bury him as a prince.
Gui.   Pray you, fetch him hither.
Thersites' body is as good as Ajax',
When neither are alive.
Arv.   If you'll go fetch him,
We'll say our song the whilst.   Brother, begin.
                    [*Exit Belarius.*]
Gui. Nay, Cadwal, we must lay his head to the
    east;   255

184. clotpoll: blockhead.   192. **accidents:** events.   193. **toys:** trifles.   205. [crare] (Sympson conj.): small trading vessel. *care* F.   206. [Might] F₂. *Might'st* F₁.   207. **but I:** but I know that. But perhaps *I* should read *ay* or *ah.*   223. **eglantine:** sweet briar.   224. **ruddock:** robin.   229. **winter-ground:** protect in winter.   237. **our** (Pope). *to our* F.

My father hath a reason for't.
Arv.   'Tis true.
Gui. Come on then, and remove him.
Arv.   So. Begin.

SONG.

Gui. Fear no more the heat o' th' sun,
    Nor the furious winter's rages;
    Thou thy worldly task hast done,   260
    Home art gone, and ta'en thy wages.
    Golden lads and girls all must,
    As chimney-sweepers, come to dust.

Arv. Fear no more the frown o' th' great;
    Thou art past the tyrant's stroke.   265
    Care no more to clothe and eat;
    To thee the reed is as the oak.
    The sceptre, learning, physic, must
    All follow this, and come to dust.

Gui. Fear no more the lightning-flash,   270
Arv. Nor the all-dreaded thunder-stone;
Gui. Fear not slander, censure rash;
Arv. Thou hast finish'd joy and moan.
Both. All lovers young, all lovers must
    Consign to thee, and come to dust.   275

Gui. No exorciser harm thee!
Arv. Nor no witchcraft charm thee!
Gui. Ghost unlaid forbear thee!
Arv. Nothing ill come near thee!
Both. Quiet consummation have,   280
    And renowned be thy grave!

Re-enter BELARIUS, *with the body of Cloten.*

Gui. We have done our obsequies. Come, lay
    him down.
Bel. Here's a few flowers; but 'bout midnight,
    more.
The herbs that have on them cold dew o' th' night
Are strewings fitt'st for graves. Upon their faces.
You were as flowers, now wither'd; even so   286
These herblets shall, which we upon you strew.
Come on, away; apart upon our knees.
The ground that gave them first has them again.
Their pleasures here are past, so [is] their pain. 290
    [*Exeunt* [Belarius, Guiderius, and Arvira-
    gus].
Imo. [*Awaking.*] Yes, sir, to Milford-Haven;
    which is the way? —
I thank you. — By yond bush? — Pray, how far
    thither?
'Ods pittikins! can it be six mile yet?
I have gone all night. Faith, I'll lie down and sleep.

But, soft! no bedfellow! — O gods and god-
    desses!   [*Seeing the body of Cloten.*] 295
These flowers are like the pleasures of the world;
This bloody man, the care on't. I hope I dream;
For so I thought I was a cave-keeper
And cook to honest creatures. But 'tis not so.
'Twas but a bolt of nothing, shot at nothing, 300
Which the brain makes of fumes. Our very eyes
Are sometimes like our judgements, blind. Good
    faith,
I tremble still with fear; but if there be
Yet left in heaven as small a drop of pity
As a wren's eye, fear'd gods, a part of it!   305
The dream's here still, even when I wake. It is
Without me, as within me; not imagin'd, felt.
A headless man! The garments of Posthumus!
I know the shape of 's leg; this is his hand,
His foot Mercurial, his Martial thigh,   310
The brawns of Hercules; but his Jovial face —
Murder in heaven? — How! — 'Tis gone. Pisanio,
All curses madded Hecuba gave the Greeks,
And mine to boot, be darted on thee! Thou,
Conspir'd with that irregulous devil, Cloten, 315
Hath here cut off my lord. To write and read
Be henceforth treacherous! Damn'd Pisanio
Hath with his forged letters, — damn'd Pisanio —
From this most bravest vessel of the world
Struck the main-top! O Posthumus! alas,   320
Where is thy head? Where's that? Ay me!
    where's that?
Pisanio might have kill'd thee at the heart
And left this head on. How should this be? Pi-
    sanio?
'Tis he and Cloten. Malice and lucre in them
Have laid this woe here. O, 'tis pregnant, preg-
    nant!   325
The drug he gave me, which he said was precious
And cordial to me, have I not found it
Murd'rous to the senses? That confirms it home.
This is Pisanio's deed, and Cloten's. O!
Give colour to my pale cheek with thy blood,   330
That we the horrider may seem to those
Which chance to find us. O, my lord, my lord!
    [*Falls on the body.*]

Enter LUCIUS, CAPTAINS, *and a* SOOTHSAYER.

1. Cap. To him the legions garrison'd in Gallia,
After your will, have cross'd the sea, attending
You here at Milford-Haven with your ships.   335
They're here in readiness.
Luc.   But what from Rome?
1. Cap. The senate hath stirr'd up the confiners
And gentlemen of Italy, most willing spirits
That promise noble service; and they come

276. **exorciser:** conjuror. 287. **shall:** shall become. 290. **[is]** (Pope). **are** F. 293. **'Ods pittikins:** God's (little) pity. 310. **Mercurial:** like Mercury. **Martial:** like Mars. 311. **Jovial:** like Jove. 315. **irregulous:** lawless. 325. **pregnant:** evident. 337. **confiners:** borderers.

Under the conduct of bold Iachimo, 340
Sienna's brother.
Luc. When expect you them?
I. Cap. With the next benefit o' th' wind.
Luc. This forwardness
Makes our hopes fair. Command our present
numbers
Be muster'd; bid the captains look to 't. Now, sir,
What have you dream'd of late of this war's pur-
pose? 345
Sooth. Last night the very gods show'd me a
vision —
I fast and pray'd for their intelligence — thus:
I saw Jove's bird, the Roman eagle, wing'd
From the spongy south to this part of the west,
There vanish'd in the sunbeams; which portends —
Unless my sins abuse my divination — 351
Success to the Roman host.
Luc. Dream often so,
And never false. Soft, ho! what trunk is here
Without his top? The ruin speaks that sometime
It was a worthy building. How! a page! 355
Or dead, or sleeping on him? But dead rather;
For nature doth abhor to make his bed
With the defunct, or sleep upon the dead.
Let's see the boy's face.
I. Cap. He's alive, my lord.
Luc. He'll then instruct us of this body. Young
one, 360
Inform us of thy fortunes, for it seems
They crave to be demanded. Who is this
Thou mak'st thy bloody pillow? Or who was he
That, otherwise than noble nature did,
Hath alter'd that good picture? What's thy in-
terest 365
In this sad wreck? How came it? Who is it?
What art thou?
Imo. I am nothing: or if not,
Nothing to be were better. This was my master,
A very valiant Briton and a good,
That here by mountaineers lies slain. Alas! 370
There is no more such masters. I may wander
From east to occident, cry out for service,
Try many, all good, serve truly, never
Find such another master.
Luc. 'Lack, good youth!
Thou mov'st no less with thy complaining than 375
Thy master in bleeding. Say his name, good friend.
Imo. Richard du Champ. [*Aside.*] If I do lie
and do
No harm by it, though the gods hear, I hope
They'll pardon it. — Say you, sir?
Luc. Thy name?
Imo. Fidele, sir.
Luc. Thou dost approve thyself the very same;

Thy name well fits thy faith, thy faith thy name.
Wilt take thy chance with me? I will not say 382
Thou shalt be so well master'd, but, be sure,
No less belov'd. The Roman Emperor's letters,
Sent by a consul to me, should not sooner 385
Than thine own worth prefer thee. Go with me.
Imo. I'll follow, sir. But first, an't please the
gods,
I'll hide my master from the flies, as deep
As these poor pickaxes can dig; and when
With wild-wood leaves and weeds I ha' strew'd his
grave, 390
And on it said a century of prayers,
Such as I can, twice o'er, I'll weep and sigh;
And leaving so his service, follow you,
So please you entertain me.
Luc. Ay, good youth;
And rather father thee than master thee. 395
My friends,
The boy hath taught us manly duties. Let us
Find out the prettiest daisied plot we can,
And make him with our pikes and partisans
A grave. Come, arm him. Boy, he is preferr'd 400
By thee to us, and he shall be interr'd
As soldiers can. Be cheerful; wipe thine eyes.
Some falls are means the happier to arise.
[*Exeunt.*

SCENE III. [*Britain. A room in Cymbeline's
palace.*]

Enter CYMBELINE, LORDS, PISANIO [*and Attendants*].

Cym. Again; and bring me word how 'tis with
her. [*Exit an attendant.*]
A fever with the absence of her son,
A madness, of which her life's in danger. Heavens,
How deeply you at once do touch me! Imogen,
The great part of my comfort, gone; my queen 5
Upon a desperate bed, and in a time
When fearful wars point at me; her son gone,
So needful for this present: it strikes me, past
The hope of comfort. But for thee, fellow,
Who needs must know of her departure and 10
Dost seem so ignorant, we'll enforce it from thee
By a sharp torture.
Pis. Sir, my life is yours;
I humbly set it at your will; but, for my mistress,
I nothing know where she remains, why gone,
Nor when she purposes return. Beseech your High-
ness, 15
Hold me your loyal servant.
I. Lord. Good my liege,
The day that she was missing he was here.
I dare be bound he's true and shall perform

---

341. **Sienna's:** i.e., the lord of Sienna's. 389. **pickaxes:** i.e., her fingers. 394. **entertain:** employ. 399. **partisans:** long-handled weapons with a blade. 400. **arm him:** pick him up. **preferr'd:** advanced.

All parts of his subjection loyally. For Cloten,
There wants no diligence in seeking him,   20
And will, no doubt, be found.
    Cym.   The time is troublesome.
[*To Pisanio.*] We'll slip you for a season; but our
    jealousy
Does yet depend.
    1. Lord.   So please your Majesty,
The Roman legions, all from Gallia drawn,
Are landed on your coast, with a supply   25
Of Roman gentlemen, by the senate sent.
    Cym. Now for the counsel of my son and queen!
I am amaz'd with matter.
    1. Lord.   Good my liege,
Your preparation can affront no less
Than what you hear of. Come more, for more
    you're ready;   30
The want is but to put those powers in motion
That long to move.
    Cym.   I thank you. Let's withdraw,
And meet the time as it seeks us. We fear not
What can from Italy annoy us; but
We grieve at chances here. Away!   35
             [*Exeunt [all but Pisanio].*
    Pis. I heard no letter from my master since
I wrote him Imogen was slain. 'Tis strange.
Nor hear I from my mistress, who did promise
To yield me often tidings; neither know I
What is betid to Cloten; but remain   40
Perplex'd in all. The heavens still must work.
Wherein I am false I am honest; not true, to be true.
These present wars shall find I love my country,
Even to the note o' th' King, or I'll fall in them.
All other doubts, by time let them be clear'd;   45
Fortune brings in some boats that are not steer'd.
             [*Exit.*

SCENE IV. [*Wales. Before the cave of Belarius.*]

Enter BELARIUS, GUIDERIUS, *and* ARVIRAGUS.

    Gui. The noise is round about us.
    Bel.   Let us from it.
    Arv. What pleasure, sir, [find we] in life, to lock it
From action and adventure?
    Gui.   Nay, what hope
Have we in hiding us? This way, the Romans
Must or for Britons slay us, or receive us   5
For barbarous and unnatural revolts
During their use, and slay us after.
    Bel.   Sons,
We'll higher to the mountains; there secure us.
To the King's party there's no going. Newness

Of Cloten's death — we being not known, not mus-
    ter'd   10
Among the bands — may drive us to a render
Where we have liv'd, and so extort from 's that
Which we have done, whose answer would be death
Drawn on with torture.
    Gui.   This is, sir, a doubt
In such a time nothing becoming you,   15
Nor satisfying us.
    Arv.   It is not likely
That when they hear [the] Roman horses neigh,
Behold their quarter'd fires, have both their eyes
And ears so cloy'd importantly as now,
That they will waste their time upon our note,   20
To know from whence we are.
    Bel.   O, I am known
Of many in the army. Many years,
Though Cloten then but young, you see, not wore
    him
From my remembrance. And besides, the King
Hath not deserv'd my service nor your loves,   25
Who find in my exile the want of breeding,
The certainty of this hard life; aye hopeless
To have the courtesy your cradle promis'd,
But to be still hot Summer's tanlings and
The shrinking slaves of Winter.
    Gui.   Than be so   30
Better to cease to be. Pray, sir, to th' army.
I and my brother are not known; yourself
So out of thought, and thereto so o'ergrown,
Cannot be question'd.
    Arv.   By this sun that shines,
I'll thither. What thing is it that I never   35
Did see man die! scarce ever look'd on blood,
But that of coward hares, hot goats, and venison!
Never bestrid a horse, save one that had
A rider like myself, who ne'er wore rowel
Nor iron on his heel! I am asham'd   40
To look upon the holy sun, to have
The benefit of his blest beams, remaining
So long a poor unknown.
    Gui.   By heavens, I'll go.
If you will bless me, sir, and give me leave,
I'll take the better care; but if you will not,   45
The hazard therefore due fall on me by
The hands of Romans!
    Arv.   So say I; amen.
    Bel. No reason I, since of your lives you set
So slight a valuation, should reserve
My crack'd one to more care. Have with you,
    boys!   50
If in your country wars you chance to die,

    Sc. iii, 22. **slip:** release. **jealousy:** suspicion. 23. **depend:** hang in suspense. 28. **amaz'd ... matter:** confused with the
rush of affairs. 29. **affront:** encounter. 44. **note:** notice.
    Sc. iv, 2. **[find we]** F₂. *we finde* F₁. 4. **This way:** i.e., if we hide. 6. **revolts:** rebels. 7. **During ... use:** while they use
us. 11. **render:** confession. 17. **[the]** (Rowe). *their* F. 18. **their ... fires:** camp fires. 19. **cloy'd importantly:** filled
with urgent matters. 20. **upon our note:** noticing us. 29. **tanlings:** those tanned by. 33. **o'ergrown:** heavily bearded.

That is my bed too, lads, and there I'll lie.
Lead, lead! [*Aside.*] The time seems long; their
    blood thinks scorn
Till it fly out and show them princes born.
                         [*Exeunt.*

ACT V

Scene I. [*Britain. The Roman camp.*]

Enter POSTHUMUS [*with a bloody handkerchief*].

Post. Yea, bloody cloth, I'll keep thee, for I
    wish'd
Thou shouldst be colour'd thus.   You married ones,
If each of you should take this course, how many
Must murder wives much better than themselves
For wrying but a little!   O Pisanio!   5
Every good servant does not all commands;
No bond but to do just ones.   Gods! if you
Should have ta'en vengeance on my faults, I never
Had liv'd to put on this; so had you sav'd
The noble Imogen to repent, and struck   10
Me, wretch, more worth your vengeance.   But,
    alack,
You snatch some hence for little faults; that's love,
To have them fall no more: you some permit
To second ills with ills, each elder worse,
And make them dread it, to the doers' thrift.
But Imogen is your own; do your best wills,   16
And make me blest to obey!   I am brought hither
Among th' Italian gentry, and to fight
Against my lady's kingdom.   'Tis enough
That, Britain, I have kill'd thy mistress; peace! 20
I'll give no wound to thee.   Therefore, good
    heavens,
Hear patiently my purpose: I'll disrobe me
Of these Italian weeds and suit myself
As does a Briton peasant; so I'll fight
Against the part I come with; so I'll die   25
For thee, O Imogen, even for whom my life
Is every breath a death; and thus, unknown,
Pitied nor hated, to the face of peril
Myself I'll dedicate.   Let me make men know
More valour in me than my habits show.   30
Gods, put the strength o' th' Leonati in me!
To shame the guise o' th' world, I will begin
The fashion: less without and more within. [*Exit.*

Scene II. [*Field between the British and Roman
camps.*]

Enter LUCIUS, IACHIMO, *and the* Roman Army *at
one door; and the* Briton Army *at another;* LEONA-
TUS POSTHUMUS *following, like a poor soldier.*

*They march over and go out.   Then enter again, in
skirmish,* IACHIMO *and* POSTHUMUS: *he vanquisheth
and disarmeth* IACHIMO, *and then leaves him.*

Iach. The heaviness and guilt within my bosom
Takes off my manhood.   I have belied a lady,
The Princess of this country, and the air on't
Revengingly enfeebles me; or could this carl,
A very drudge of Nature's, have subdu'd me   5
In my profession?   Knighthoods and honours,
    borne
As I wear mine, are titles but of scorn.
If that thy gentry, Britain, go before
This lout as he exceeds our lords, the odds
Is that we scarce are men and you are gods.   10
                         [*Exit.*

The battle continues; the Britons *fly;* CYMBELINE
is taken: then enter, to his rescue, BELARIUS,
GUIDERIUS, *and* ARVIRAGUS.

Bel. Stand, stand!   We have th' advantage of
    the ground;
The lane is guarded.   Nothing routs us but
The villainy of our fears.
Gui. ⎫
Arv. ⎬   Stand, stand, and fight!

Re-enter POSTHUMUS, *and seconds the* Britons.
They rescue CYMBELINE, *and exeunt.   Then re-
enter* LUCIUS, IACHIMO, *and* IMOGEN.

Luc. Away, boy, from the troops, and save thy-
    self;
For friends kill friends, and the disorder's such   15
As war were hoodwink'd.
Iach.   'Tis their fresh supplies.
Luc. It is a day turn'd strangely.   Or betimes
Let's reinforce, or fly.   [*Exeunt.*

Scene III. [*Another part of the field.*]

Enter POSTHUMUS *and a* Briton LORD.

Lord. Cam'st thou from where they made the
    stand?
Post.   I did;
Though you, it seems, come from the fliers.
Lord.   I did.
Post. No blame be to you, sir, for all was lost
But that the heavens fought; the King himself
Of his wings destitute, the army broken,   5
And but the backs of Britons seen, all flying
Through a strait lane; the enemy full-hearted,
Lolling the tongue with slaught'ring, having work
More plentiful than tools to do 't, struck down
Some mortally, some slightly touch'd, some falling

Act V, sc. i, 1. **wish'd** (Pope).   *am wisht* F.   5. **wrying:** swerving.   9. **put on:** instigate.   14. **elder.**   One should expect
later.   15. **thrift:** profit; i.e., because the "doer" has learned to repent.   30. **habits:** clothes.   32. **guise:** custom.
Sc. ii 4. **carl:** churl, peasant.   16. **hoodwink'd:** blindfolded.

Merely through fear; that the strait pass was
    damm'd   11
With dead men hurt behind, and cowards living
To die with length'ned shame.
    Lord.   Where was this lane?
    Post. Close by the battle, ditch'd, and wall'd with
    turf;
Which gave advantage to an ancient soldier,   15
(An honest one, I warrant) who deserv'd
So long a breeding as his white beard came to,
In doing this for 's country. Athwart the lane,
He, with two striplings — lads more like to run
The country base than to commit such slaughter, 20
With faces fit for masks, or rather fairer
Than those for preservation cas'd, or shame, —
Made good the passage; cried to those that fled,
"Our Britain's harts die flying, not our men.
To darkness fleet souls that fly backwards. Stand,
Or we are Romans and will give you that   26
Like beasts which you shun beastly, and may save
But to look back in frown. Stand, stand!" These
    three,
Three thousand confident, in act as many —
For three performers are the file when all   30
The rest do nothing — with this word "Stand,
    stand!"
Accommodated by the place, more charming
With their own nobleness, which could have turn'd
A distaff to a lance, gilded pale looks.
Part shame, part spirit renew'd; that some, turn'd
    coward   35
But by example — O, a sin in war,
Damn'd in the first beginners! — gan to look
The way that they did, and to grin like lions
Upon the pikes o' th' hunters. Then began
A stop i' th' chaser, a retire, anon   40
A rout, confusion thick. Forthwith they fly
Chickens, the way which they [stoop'd] eagles;
    slaves,
The strides [they] victors made: and now our cow-
    ards,
Like fragments in hard voyages, became
The life o' th' need. Having found the backdoor
    open   45
Of th' unguarded hearts, heavens, how they wound!
Some slain before; some dying; some their friends
O'er-borne i' th' former wave; then, chas'd by one,
Are now each one the slaughter-man of twenty.
Those that would die or ere resist are grown   50
The mortal bugs o' th' field.
    Lord.   This was strange chance.

A narrow lane, an old man, and two boys!
    Post. Nay, do not wonder at it; you are made
Rather to wonder at the things you hear
Than to work any. Will you rhyme upon 't,   55
And vent it for a mockery? Here is one:
"Two boys, an old man twice a boy, a lane,
Preserv'd the Britons, was the Romans' bane."
    Lord. Nay, be not angry, sir.
    Post.   'Lack, to what end?
Who dares not stand his foe, I'll be his friend;   60
For if he'll do as he is made to do,
I know he'll quickly fly my friendship too.
You have put me into rhyme.
    Lord.   Farewell; you're angry.
                                    [*Exit.*
    Post. **Still** going? This is a lord! O noble
    misery,
To be i' th' field, and ask "what news?" of me! 65
To-day how many would have given their honours
To have sav'd their carcases! took heel to do 't,
And yet died too! I, in mine own woe charm'd,
Could not find Death where I did hear him groan,
Nor feel him where he struck. Being an ugly mon-
    ster,   70
'Tis strange he hides him in fresh cups, soft beds,
Sweet words; or hath moe ministers than we
That draw his knives i' th' war. Well, I will find
    him;
For being now a favourer to the Briton,
No more a Briton, I have resum'd again   75
The part I came in. Fight I will no more,
But yield me to the veriest hind that shall
Once touch my shoulder. Great the slaughter is
Here made by th' Roman; great the answer be
Britons must take. For me, my ransom's death.
On either side I come to spend my breath;   81
Which neither here I'll keep nor bear again,
But end it by some means for Imogen.

    Enter two [British] CAPTAINS *and* Soldiers.

    1. [*Cap.*] Great Jupiter be prais'd! Lucius is
    taken.   84
'Tis thought the old man and his sons were angels.
    2. [*Cap.*] There was a fourth man, in a silly
    habit,
That gave the affront with them.
    1. [*Cap.*]   So 'tis reported;
But none of 'em can be found. Stand! who's there?
    Post. A Roman,
Who had not now been drooping here, if seconds 90
Had answer'd him.

Sc. iii, 19–20. **run . . . base:** play prisoner's base. 22. **cas'd:** masked. **shame:** modesty. 27–28. **save . . . frown:** avert
if you will only look back defiantly. Cf. ll. 36–38, below. 30. **file:** rank. 32. **charming:** bewitching. 35. **Part . . . part:**
some . . . others. 38. **they:** i.e., the three. 42. **[stoop'd]** (Rowe): swooped. *stopt* F. 43. **[they]** (Theobald). *the* F.
42–43. **slaves . . . made:** retrace like slaves the ground they strode like victors. 44. **fragments:** i.e., of food. 45. **life . . .
need:** i.e., food for life in (dire) need. 51. **mortal bugs:** deadly terrors. 64. **noble misery:** titled wretchedness. 68.
charm'd: made invulnerable. 86. **silly:** simple. 90. **seconds:** supporters.

2. [Cap.]   Lay hands on him; a dog!
A leg of Rome shall not return to tell
What crows have peck'd them here.   He brags
    his service
As if he were of note.   Bring him to th' King.

Enter Cymbeline, Belarius, Guiderius, Arviragus,
Pisanio [Soldiers, Attendants] *and* Roman
Captives. *The* Captains *present* Posthumus *to*
Cymbeline, *who delivers him over to a* Gaoler.
[*Then exeunt omnes.*]

SCENE IV.   [*A British prison.*]

Enter POSTHUMUS *and* [*two*] GAOLER[S].

[*1.*] *Gaol.* You shall not now be stol'n, you have
    locks upon you;
So graze as you find pasture.

2. Gaol.   Ay, or a stomach.
                     [*Exeunt Gaolers.*]

Post. Most welcome, bondage! for thou art a
    way,
I think, to liberty; yet am I better
Than one that's sick o' th' gout, since he had
    rather   5
Groan so in perpetuity than be cur'd
By th' sure physician, Death, who is the key
T' unbar these locks.   My conscience, thou art
    fetter'd
More than my shanks and wrists.   You good gods,
    give me
The penitent instrument to pick that bolt;   10
Then, free for ever!   Is't enough I am sorry?
So children temporal fathers do appease;
Gods are more full of mercy.   Must I repent,
I cannot do it better than in gyves,
Desir'd more than constrain'd; to satisfy,   15
If of my freedom 'tis the main part, take
No stricter render of me than my all.
I know you are more clement than vile men,
Who of their broken debtors take a third,
A sixth, a tenth, letting them thrive again   20
On their abatement.   That's not my desire.
For Imogen's dear life take mine; and though
'Tis not so dear, yet 'tis a life; you coin'd it.
'Tween man and man they weigh not every stamp;
Though light, take pieces for the figure's sake;   25
You rather mine, being yours; and so, great powers,
If you will take this audit, take this life,
And cancel these cold bonds.   O Imogen!
I'll speak to thee in silence.   [*Sleeps.*]

Solemn music.   Enter, as in an apparition, SICILIUS
    LEONATUS, *father to Posthumus, an old man,*

*attired like a warrior; leading in his hand an
ancient matron, his wife and mother to Posthumus,
with music before them.   Then, after other music,
follow the two young* LEONATI, *brothers to Posthumus, with wounds as they died in the wars.   They
circle Posthumus round, as he lies sleeping.*

Sici. No more, thou Thunder-master, show   30
    Thy spite on mortal flies:
With Mars fall out, with Juno chide,
    That thy adulteries
      Rates and revenges.
Hath my poor boy done aught but well,   35
    Whose face I never saw?
I died whilst in the womb he stay'd
    Attending Nature's law;
Whose father then, as men report
    Thou orphans' father art,   40
Thou shouldst have been, and shielded him
    From this earth-vexing smart.

Moth. Lucina lent not me her aid,
    But took me in my throes;
That from me was Posthumus ript,   45
    Came crying 'mongst his foes,
      A thing of pity!

Sici. Great Nature, like his ancestry,
    Moulded the stuff so fair,
That he deserv'd the praise o' th' world,   50
    As great Sicilius' heir.

1. Bro. When once he was mature for man,
    In Britain where was he
That could stand up his parallel,
    Or fruitful object be   55
In eye of Imogen, that best
    Could deem his dignity?

Moth. With marriage wherefore was he mock'd,
    To be exil'd, and thrown
From Leonati seat, and cast   60
    From her his dearest one,
      Sweet Imogen?

Sici. Why did you suffer Iachimo,
    Slight thing of Italy,
To taint his nobler heart and brain   65
    With needless jealousy;
And to become the geck and scorn
    O' th' other's villainy?

2. Bro. For this from stiller seats we came,
    Our parents and us twain,   70

Sc. iv, 14. gyves: fetters.   **16–17. If…me:** If it is essential for my freedom of conscience, take from me no greater
payment.   **24. stamp:** coin.   **25. figure's:** i.e., the image (or the amount) stamped on the coin.   **26. You…yours:** You
(gods) should sooner take the light coin of my life, since you made it.   **34. rates:** scolds.   **38. Attending:** awaiting.   **43.
Lucina:** goddess of childbirth.   **67. geck:** dupe.

That striking in our country's cause
Fell bravely and were slain,
Our fealty and Tenantius' right
With honour to maintain.

1. Bro.   Like hardiment Posthumus hath   75
Too Cymbeline perform'd.
Then, Jupiter, thou king of gods,
Why hast thou thus adjourn'd
The graces for his merits due,
Being all to dolours turn'd?   80

Sici.   Thy crystal window ope; look out;
No longer exercise
Upon a valiant race thy harsh
And potent injuries.

Moth.   Since, Jupiter, our son is good,   85
Take off his miseries.

Sici.   Peep through thy marble mansion; help;
Or we poor ghosts will cry
To th' shining synod of the rest
Against thy deity.   90

Both Bro.   Help, Jupiter; or we appeal,
And from thy justice fly.

JUPITER *descends in thunder and lightning, sitting
upon an eagle: he throws a thunderbolt. The
Ghosts fall on their knees.*

Jup.   No more, you petty spirits of region low,
Offend our hearing; hush! How dare you ghosts
Accuse the Thunderer, whose bolt, you know,   95
Sky-planted batters all rebelling coasts?
Poor shadows of Elysium, hence, and rest
Upon your never-with'ring banks of flowers.
Be not with mortal accidents opprest;
No care of yours it is; you know 'tis ours.   100
Whom best I love I cross; to make my gift,
The more delay'd, delighted. Be content;
Your low-laid son our godhead will uplift.
His comforts thrive, his trials well are spent.
Our jovial star reign'd at his birth, and in   105
Our temple was he married. Rise, and fade.
He shall be lord of Lady Imogen,
And happier much by his affliction made.
This tablet lay upon his breast, wherein
Our pleasure his full fortune doth confine.   110
And so, away! No farther with your din
Express impatience, lest you stir up mine.
Mount, eagle, to my palace crystalline.
                      [*Ascends.*
Sici. He came in thunder; his celestial breath
Was sulphurous to smell. The holy eagle   115

Stoop'd, as to foot us. His ascension is
More sweet than our blest fields. His royal bird
Prunes the immortal wing and cloys his beak,
As when his god is pleas'd.
All.   Thanks, Jupiter!
Sici. The marble pavement closes, he is enter'd
His radiant roof. Away! and, to be blest,   121
Let us with care perform his great behest.
                  [*The Ghosts*] *vanish.*
Post. [*Waking.*] Sleep, thou hast been a grandsire
    and begot
A father to me, and thou hast created
A mother and two brothers; but, O scorn!   125
Gone! they went hence so soon as they were born.
And so I am awake. Poor wretches that depend
On greatness' favour dream as I have done,
Wake and find nothing. But, alas, I swerve.
Many dream not to find, neither deserve,   130
And yet are steep'd in favours; so am I,
That have this golden chance and know not why.
What fairies haunt this ground? A book? O
    rare one!
Be not, as is our fangled world, a garment
Nobler than that it covers! Let thy effects   135
So follow, to be most unlike our courtiers,
As good as promise!
   (*Reads.*) "Whenas a lion's whelp shall, to him-
self unknown, without seeking find, and be em-
brac'd by a piece of tender air; and when from a
stately cedar shall be lopp'd branches, which,   140
being dead many years, shall after revive, be
jointed to the old stock and freshly grow; then
shall Posthumus end his miseries, Britain be for-
tunate and flourish in peace and plenty."   145
'Tis still a dream, or else such stuff as madmen
Tongue and brain not; either both or nothing;
Or senseless speaking, or a speaking such
As sense cannot untie. Be what it is,
The action of my life is like it, which   150
I'll keep, if but for sympathy.

            Re-enter GAOLER.

Gaol. Come, sir, are you ready for death?
Post. Over-roasted rather; ready long ago.
Gaol. Hanging is the word, sir. If you be ready
for that, you are well cook'd.   156
Post. So, if I prove a good repast to the spectators, the dish pays the shot.
Gaol. A heavy reckoning for you, sir. But the
comfort is, you shall be called to no more pay-   160
ments, fear no more tavern-bills, which are often
the sadness of parting, as the procuring of mirth.
You come in faint for want of meat, depart reeling
with too much drink; sorry that you have paid too

---

102. **delighted:** delightful.   116. **foot:** grasp with his talons.   **ascension:** i.e., his breath when ascending.   118. **Prunes:** preens.   **cloys:** claws.   125. **scorn:** mockery.   129. **swerve:** digress.   134. **fangled:** showy.   146. **brain:** understand. 151. **for sympathy:** because of the resemblance.   158. **shot:** reckoning.

much, and sorry that you are paid too much;   165
purse and brain both empty; the brain the heavier
for being too light, the purse too light, being drawn
of heaviness.   O, of this contradiction you shall
now be quit.   O, the charity of a penny cord!   It
sums up thousands in a trice.   You have no   170
true debitor and creditor but it; of what's past, is,
and to come, the discharge.   Your neck, sir, is pen,
book, and counters; so the acquittance follows.

Post. I am merrier to die than thou art to live. 176

Gaol. Indeed, sir, he that sleeps feels not the
toothache; but a man that were to sleep your sleep,
and a hangman to help him to bed, I think he
would change places with his officer; for, look you,
sir, you know not which way you shall go.

Post. Yes indeed do I, fellow.   183

Gaol. Your Death has eyes in's head then; I have
not seen him so pictur'd.   You must either be
directed by some that take upon them to know,
or to take upon yourself that which I am sure you
do not know, or jump the after-inquiry on your own
peril; and how you shall speed in your journey's
end, I think you'll never return to tell one.   191

Post. I tell thee, fellow, there are none want eyes
to direct them the way I am going, but such as
wink and will not use them.   194

Gaol. What an infinite mock is this, that a man
should have the best use of eyes to see the way of
blindness!   I am sure hanging's the way of winking.

Enter a MESSENGER.

Mess. Knock off his manacles; bring your
prisoner to the King.   200

Post. Thou bring'st good news; I am call'd to
be made free.

Gaol. I'll be hang'd then.

Post. Thou shalt be then freer than a gaoler;
no bolts for the dead.   205

[*Exeunt all but the Gaoler.*]

Gaol. Unless a man would marry a gallows and
beget young gibbets, I never saw one so prone.
Yet, on my conscience, there are verier knaves
desire to live, for all he be a Roman; and there be
some of them too that die against their wills.   210
So should I, if I were one.   I would we were all
of one mind, and one mind good.   O, there were
desolation of gaolers and gallowses!   I speak against
my present profit, but my wish hath a preferment
in't.   [*Exit.* 215

SCENE V.   [*Cymbeline's tent.*]

Enter CYMBELINE, BELARIUS, GUIDERIUS, ARVI-
RAGUS, PISANIO, Lords [Officers, *and* Attendants].

Cym. Stand by my side, you whom the gods have
made
Preservers of my throne.   Woe is my heart
That the poor soldier that so richly fought,
Whose rags sham'd gilded arms, whose naked breast
Stepp'd before targes of proof, cannot be found.   5
He shall be happy that can find him, if
Our grace can make him so.

Bel.   I never saw
Such noble fury in so poor a thing;
Such precious deeds in one that promis'd nought
But beggary and poor looks.

Cym.   No tidings of him?

Pis. He hath been search'd among the dead and
living,   11
But no trace of him.

Cym.   To my grief, I am
The heir of his reward; [*to Belarius, Guiderius, and
Arviragus*] which I will add
To you, the liver, heart and brain of Britain,
By whom I grant she lives.   'Tis now the time
To ask of whence you are.   Report it.

Bel.   Sir,   16
In Cambria are we born, and gentlemen.
Further to boast were neither true nor modest,
Unless I add we are honest.

Cym.   Bow your knees.
Arise my knights o' th' battle.   I create you   20
Companions to our person and will fit you
With dignities becoming your estates.

Enter CORNELIUS *and* LADIES.

There's business in these faces.   Why so sadly
Greet you our victory?   You look like Romans,
And not o' th' court of Britain.

Cor.   Hail, great King!
To sour your happiness, I must report   26
The Queen is dead.

Cym.   Who worse than a physician
Would this report become?   But I consider,
By med'cine life may be prolong'd, yet death
Will seize the doctor too.   How ended she?   30

Cor. With horror, madly dying, like her life,
Which, being cruel to the world, concluded
Most cruel to herself.   What she confess'd
I will report, so please you.   These her women
Can trip me, if I err; who with wet cheeks   35
Were present when she finish'd.

Cym.   Prithee, say.

Cor. First, she confess'd she never lov'd you; only
Affected greatness got by you, not you;
Married your royalty, was wife to your place,
Abhorr'd your person.

Cym.   She alone knew this;   40

167. **drawn:** emptied.   171. **debitor and creditor:** accountant.   173. **counters:** metal discs used in counting.   188.
jump: risk.   194. **wink:** close.   207. **prone:** eager (to die).   214. **preferment:** promotion.
Sc. v, 5. **targes of proof:** shields proved impenetrable.   35. **trip:** refute.   38. **Affected:** loved.

And, but she spoke it dying, I would not
Believe her lips in opening it.   Proceed.
   Cor. Your daughter, whom she bore in hand to
    love
With such integrity, she did confess
Was as a scorpion to her sight; whose life,   45
But that her flight prevented it, she had
Ta'en off by poison.
   Cym.   O most delicate fiend!
Who is't can read a woman?   Is there more?
   Cor. More, sir, and worse.   She did confess she
    had
For you a mortal mineral, which, being took,   50
Should by the minute feed on life, and ling'ring,
By inches waste you; in which time she purpos'd,
By watching, weeping, tendance, kissing, to
O'ercome you with her show, and, in time,
When she had fitted you with her craft, to work   55
Her son into th' adoption of the crown;
But, failing of her end by his strange absence,
Grew shameless-desperate; open'd, in despite
Of heaven and men, her purposes; repented
The evils she hatch'd were not effected; so   60
Despairing died.
   Cym.   Heard you all this, her women?
   Lad. We did, so please your Highness.
   Cym.   Mine eyes
Were not in fault, for she was beautiful;
Mine ears, that [heard] her flattery; nor my heart,
That thought her like her seeming.   It had been
    vicious   65
To have mistrusted her; yet — O my daughter! —
That it was folly in me, thou mayst say,
And prove it in thy feeling.   Heaven mend all!

Enter Lucius, Iachimo, [*the* Soothsayer] *and other*
   Roman Prisoners [*guarded*]; Posthumus *behind,*
   and Imogen.

Thou com'st not, Caius, now for tribute; that
The Britons have raz'd out, though with the loss   70
Of many a bold one, whose kinsmen have made suit
That their good souls may be appeas'd with
    slaughter
Of you their captives, which ourself have granted.
So think of your estate.
   Luc. Consider, sir, the chance of war.   The day
Was yours by accident.   Had it gone with us,   76
We should not, when the blood was cool, have
    threaten'd
Our prisoners with the sword.   But since the gods
Will have it thus, that nothing but our lives
May be call'd ransom, let it come.   Sufficeth   80
A Roman with a Roman's heart can suffer.
Augustus lives to think on't; and so much
For my peculiar care.   This one thing only

I will entreat: my boy, a Briton born,
Let him be ransom'd.   Never master had   85
A page so kind, so duteous, diligent,
So tender over his occasions, true,
So feat, so nurse-like.   Let his virtue join
With my request, which I'll make bold your High-
    ness
Cannot deny.   He hath done no Briton harm,   90
Though he have serv'd a Roman.   Save him, sir,
And spare no blood beside.
   Cym.   I have surely seen him;
His favour is familiar to me.   Boy,
Thou hast look'd thyself into my grace
And art mine own.   I know not why, wherefore,   95
To say "Live, boy."   Ne'er thank thy master; live,
And ask of Cymbeline what boon thou wilt,
Fitting my bounty and thy state, I'll give it,
Yea, though thou do demand a prisoner,   99
The noblest ta'en.
   Imo.   I humbly thank your Highness.
   Luc. I do not bid thee beg my life, good lad;
And yet I know thou wilt.
   Imo.   No, no, alack;
There's other work in hand.   I see a thing
Bitter to me as death; your life, good master,
Must shuffle for itself.
   Luc.   The boy disdains me;   105
He leaves me, scorns me.   Briefly die their joys
That place them on the truth of girls and boys.
Why stands he so perplex'd?
   Cym.   What wouldst thou, boy?
I love thee more and more; think more and more
What's best to ask.   Know'st him thou look'st on?
    Speak,   110
Wilt have him live?   Is he thy kin? thy friend?
   Imo. He is a Roman, no more kin to me
Than I to your Highness; who, being born your
    vassal,
Am something nearer.
   Cym.   Wherefore ey'st him so?
   Imo. I'll tell you, sir, in private, if you please 115
To give me hearing.
   Cym.   Ay, with all my heart,
And lend my best attention.   What's thy name?
   Imo. Fidele, sir.
   Cym.   Thou'rt my good youth, my page;
I'll be thy master.   Walk with me; speak freely.
            [*Cymbeline and Imogen talk apart.*]
   Bel. Is not this boy, reviv'd from death, —
   Arv.   One sand another
Not more resembles, — that sweet rosy lad   121
Who died, and was Fidele?   What think you?
   Gui. The same dead thing alive.
   Bel. Peace, peace! see further.   He eyes us not;
    forbear;

---

42. **opening:** revealing. 43. **bore in hand:** pretended. 47. **delicate:** artful. 55. **fitted:** prepared. 64. **[heard]** F₃. *heare*
F₁. 83. **peculiar:** personal. 87. **occasions:** needs. 88. **feat:** adroit.

Creatures may be alike. Were 't he, I am sure 125
He would have spoke to us.
  Gui.   But we [saw] him dead.
  Bel. Be silent; let's see further.
  Pis.   *[Aside.]* It is my mistress.
Since she is living, let the time run on
To good or bad.
      [Cymbeline and Imogen come forward.]
  Cym.   Come, stand thou by our side;
Make thy demand aloud. *[To Iachimo.]* Sir, step
    you forth;   130
Give answer to this boy, and do it freely;
Or, by our greatness and the grace of it,
Which is our honour, bitter torture shall
Winnow the truth from falsehood. On, speak to
    him.
  Imo. My boon is, that this gentleman may
    render   135
Of whom he had this ring.
  Post.   *[Aside.]* What's that to him?
  Cym. That diamond upon your finger, say
How came it yours?
  Iach. Thou'lt torture me to leave unspoken that
Which, to be spoke, would torture thee.
  Cym.   How! me?
  Iach. I am glad to be constrain'd to utter that
Which torments me to conceal. By villainy 142
I got this ring. 'Twas Leonatus' jewel,
Whom thou didst banish; and — which more may
    grieve thee,
As it doth me — a nobler sir ne'er liv'd 145
'Twixt sky and ground. Wilt thou hear more,
    my lord?
  Cym. All that belongs to this.
  Iach.   That paragon, thy daughter, —
For whom my heart drops blood, and my false
    spirits
Quail to remember, — Give me leave; I faint.
  Cym. My daughter! what of her? Renew thy
    strength.   150
I had rather thou shouldst live while Nature will
Than die ere I hear more. Strive, man, and speak.
  Iach. Upon a time, — unhappy was the clock
That struck the hour! — it was in Rome, — ac-
    curs'd
The mansion where! — 'twas at a feast, — O,
    would   155
Our viands had been poison'd, or at least
Those which I heav'd to head! — the good Post-
    humus —
What should I say? He was too good to be
Where ill men were, and was the best of all
Amongst the rar'st of good ones, — sitting sadly,
Hearing us praise our loves of Italy 161

For beauty that made barren the swell'd boast
Of him that best could speak; for feature, lam-
    ing
The shrine of Venus or straight-pight Minerva,
Postures beyond brief nature; for condition, 165
A shop of all the qualities that man
Loves woman for, besides that hook of wiving,
Fairness which strikes the eye —
  Cym.   I stand on fire:
Come to the matter.
  Iach.   All too soon I shall,
Unless thou wouldst grieve quickly. This Post-
    humus,   170
Most like a noble lord in love and one
That had a royal lover, took his hint;
And, not dispraising whom we prais'd, — therein
He was as calm as virtue, — he began
His mistress' picture; which by his tongue being
    made,   175
And then a mind put in't, either our brags
Were crack'd of kitchen-trulls, or his description
Prov'd us unspeaking sots.
  Cym.   Nay, nay, to th' purpose.
  Iach. Your daughter's chastity — there it begins.
He spake of her, as Dian had hot dreams, 180
And she alone were cold; whereat I, wretch,
Made scruple of his praise, and wager'd with him
Pieces of gold 'gainst this which then he wore
Upon his honour'd finger, to attain
In suit the place of 's bed and win this ring 185
By hers and mine adultery. He, true knight,
No lesser of her honour confident
Than I did truly find her, stakes this ring;
And would so, had it been a carbuncle
Of Phœbus' wheel, and might so safely, had it 190
Been all the worth of 's car. Away to Britain
Post I in this design. Well may you, sir,
Remember me at court, where I was taught
Of your chaste daughter the wide difference
'Twixt amorous and villainous. Being thus
    quench'd   195
Of hope, not longing, mine Italian brain
Gan in your duller Britain operate
Most vilely; for my vantage, excellent;
And, to be brief, my practice so prevail'd,
That I return'd with simular proof enough 200
To make the noble Leonatus mad,
By wounding his belief in her renown
With tokens thus, and thus; averring notes
Of chamber-hanging, pictures, this her bracelet, —
O cunning, how I got [it]! — nay, some marks
Of secret on her person, that he could not 206
But think her bond of chastity quite crack'd,
I having ta'en the forfeit. Whereupon —

Methinks, I see him now —
  Post.   [*Advancing.*] Ay, so thou dost,
Italian fiend! Ay me, most credulous fool,   210
Egregious murderer, thief, anything
That's due to all the villains past, in being,
To come! O, give me cord, or knife, or poison,
Some upright justicer! Thou, King, send out
For torturers ingenious; it is I   215
That all th' abhorred things o' th' earth amend
By being worse than they. I am Posthumus,
That kill'd thy daughter: — villain-like, I lie —
That caused a lesser villain than myself,
A sacrilegious thief, to do't. The temple   220
Of Virtue was she; yea, and she herself.
Spit, and throw stones, cast mire upon me, set
The dogs o' th' street to bay me; every villain
Be call'd Posthumus Leonatus, and
Be villainy less than 'twas! O Imogen!   225
My queen, my life, my wife! O Imogen,
Imogen, Imogen!
  Imo.   Peace, my lord; hear, hear —
  Post. Shall 's have a play of this? Thou scornful
    page,
There lie thy part.   [*Striking her; she falls.*]
  Pis.   O, gentlemen, help
Mine and your mistress! O, my Lord Posthumus!
You ne'er kill'd Imogen till now. Help, help!   231
Mine honour'd lady!
  Cym.   Does the world go round?
  Post. How comes these staggers on me?
  Pis.   Wake, my mistress!
  Cym. If this be so, the gods do mean to strike me
To death with mortal joy.
  Pis.   How fares my mistress?
  Imo. O, get thee from my sight;   236
Thou gav'st me poison. Dangerous fellow, hence!
Breathe not where princes are.
  Cym.   The tune of Imogen!
  Pis. Lady,
The gods throw stones of sulphur on me, if   240
That box I gave you was not thought by me
A precious thing. I had it from the Queen.
  Cym. New matter still?
  Imo.   It poison'd me.
  Cor.   O gods!
I left out one thing which the Queen confess'd,
Which must approve thee honest. "If Pisanio
Have," said she, "given his mistress that confection
Which I gave him for cordial, she is serv'd   247
As I would serve a rat."
  Cym.   What's this, Cornelius?
  Cor. The Queen, sir, very oft importun'd me
To temper poisons for her, still pretending   250
The satisfaction of her knowledge only
In killing creatures vile, as cats and dogs,

Of no esteem. I, dreading that her purpose
Was of more danger, did compound for her
A certain stuff, which, being ta'en, would cease   255
The present power of life, but in short time
All offices of nature should again
Do their due functions. Have you ta'en of it?
  Imo. Most like I did, for I was dead.
  Bel.   My boys,
There was our error.
  Gui.   This is, sure, Fidele.   260
  Imo. Why did you throw your wedded lady from
    you?
Think that you are upon a [lock], and now
Throw me again.   [*Embracing him.*
  Post.   Hang there like fruit, my soul,
Till the tree die!
  Cym.   How now, my flesh, my child!
What, mak'st thou me a dullard in this act?
Wilt thou not speak to me?
  Imo.   [*Kneeling.*] Your blessing, sir.   266
  Bel. [*To Guiderius and Arviragus.*] Though you
    did love this youth, I blame ye not;
You had a motive for't.
  Cym.   My tears that fall
Prove holy water on thee! Imogen,
Thy mother's dead.
  Imo.   I am sorry for't, my lord.
  Cym. O, she was naught; and long of her it was
That we meet here so strangely; but her son   272
Is gone, we know not how nor where.
  Pis.   My lord,
Now fear is from me, I'll speak troth. Lord Cloten,
Upon my lady's missing, came to me   275
With his sword drawn; foam'd at the mouth and
    swore,
If I discover'd not which way she was gone,
It was my instant death. By accident
I had a feigned letter of my master's
Then in my pocket, which directed him   280
To seek her on the mountains near to Milford;
Where, in a frenzy, in my master's garments,
Which he enforc'd from me, away he posts
With unchaste purpose and with oath to violate
My lady's honour. What became of him   285
I further know not.
  Gui.   Let me end the story:
I slew him there.
  Cym.   Marry, the gods forfend!
I would not thy good deeds should from my lips
Pluck a hard sentence. Prithee, valiant youth,
Deny 't again.
  Gui.   I have spoke it, and I did it.   290
  Cym. He was a prince.
  Gui. A most incivil one. The wrongs he did me
Were nothing prince-like; for he did provoke me

With language that would make me spurn the sea
If it could so roar to me.   I cut off 's head;   295
And am right glad he is not standing here
To tell this tale of mine.

Cym.   I am [sorry] for thee.
By thine own tongue thou art condemn'd, and must
Endure our law.   Thou'rt dead.

   Imo.   That headless man
I thought had been my lord.

   Cym.   Bind the offender   300
And take him from our presence.

   Bel.   Stay, sir King;
This man is better than the man he slew,
As well descended as thyself; and hath
More of thee merited than a band of Clotens
Had ever scar for.   [*To the Guard.*] Let his arms
   alone;   305
They were not born for bondage.

   Cym.   Why, old soldier,
Wilt thou undo the worth thou art unpaid for,
By tasting of our wrath?   How of descent
As good as we?

   Arv.   In that he spake too far.

   Cym. And thou shalt die for't.

   Bel.   We will die all three
But I will prove that two on 's are as good   311
As I have given out him.   My sons, I must
For mine own part unfold a dangerous speech,
Though, haply, well for you.

   Arv.   Your danger's ours.

   Gui. And our good his.

   Bel.   Have at it then, by leave.
Thou hadst, great King, a subject who   316
Was call'd Belarius.

   Cym.   What of him?   He is
A banish'd traitor.

   Bel.   He it is that hath
Assum'd this age, indeed a banish'd man;
I know not how a traitor.

   Cym.   Take him hence.   320
The whole world shall not save him.

   Bel.   Not too hot.
First pay me for the nursing of thy sons;
And let it be confiscate all so soon
As I've receiv'd it.

   Cym.   Nursing of my sons!

   Bel. I am too blunt and saucy; here's my knee.
Ere I arise, I will prefer my sons;   326
Then spare not the old father.   Mighty sir,
These two young gentlemen, that call me father
And think they are my sons, are none of mine;
They are the issue of your loins, my liege,   330
And blood of your begetting.

   Cym.   How! my issue!

   Bel. So sure as you your father's.   I, old Morgan,

Am that Belarius whom you sometime banish'd.
Your pleasure was my mere offence, my punishment
Itself, and all my treason; that I suffer'd   335
Was all the harm I did.   These gentle princes —
For such and so they are — these twenty years
Have I train'd up.   Those arts they have as I
Could put into them; my breeding was, sir, as
Your Highness knows.   Their nurse, Euriphile,   340
Whom for the theft I wedded, stole these children
Upon my banishment I mov'd her to't,
Having receiv'd the punishment before,
For that which I did then.   Beaten for loyalty
Excited me to treason.   Their dear loss,   345
The more of you 'twas felt, the more it shap'd
Unto my end of stealing them.   But, gracious sir,
Here are your sons again; and I must lose
Two of the sweet'st companions in the world.
The benediction of these covering heavens   350
Fall on their heads like dew! for they are worthy
To inlay heaven with stars.

   Cym.   Thou weep'st, and speak'st.
The service that you three have done is more
Unlike than this thou tell'st.   I lost my children;
If these be they, I know not how to wish   355
A pair of worthier sons.

   Bel.   Be pleas'd awhile.
This gentleman, whom I call Polydore,
Most worthy prince, as yours, is true Guiderius;
This gentleman, my Cadwal, Arviragus,
Your younger princely son.   He, sir, was lapp'd   360
In a most curious mantle, wrought by the hand
Of his queen mother, which for more probation
I can with ease produce.

   Cym.   Guiderius had
Upon his neck a mole, a sanguine star;
It was a mark of wonder.

   Bel.   This is he,   365
Who hath upon him still that natural stamp.
It was wise Nature's end in the donation,
To be his evidence now.

   Cym.   O, what, am I
A mother to the birth of three?   Ne'er mother
Rejoic'd deliverance more.   Blest pray you be,   370
That, after this strange starting from your orbs,
You may reign in them now!   O Imogen,
Thou hast lost by this a kingdom.

   Imo.   No, my lord;
I have got two worlds by't.   O my gentle brothers,
Have we thus met?   O, never say hereafter   375
But I am truest speaker.   You call'd me brother,
When I was but your sister; I you brothers,
When [ye] were so indeed.

   Cym.   Did you e'er meet?

   Arv. Ay, my good lord.

   Gui.   And at first meeting lov'd;

297. **[sorry]** F₂. *sorrow* F₁. 319. **Assum'd**: reached. 334. **pleasure**: caprice. **mere**: entire. 346. **shap'd**: suited.
354. **Unlike**: improbable. 362. **probation**: proof. 364. **sanguine**: red. 378. **[ye]** (Rowe). *we* F.

Continu'd so, until we thought he died.   380
   Cor. By the Queen's dram she swallow'd.
   Cym.   O rare instinct!
When shall I hear all through? This fierce abridgement
Hath to it circumstantial branches, which
Distinction should be rich in. Where, how liv'd
    you?   384
And when came you to serve our Roman captive?
How parted with your brothers? How first met
    them?
Why fled you from the court? and whither? These
And your three motives to the battle, with
I know not how much more, should be demanded,
And all the other by-dependencies,   390
From chance to chance; but nor the time nor place
Will serve our long inter'gatories. See
Posthumus anchors upon Imogen,
And she, like harmless lightning, throws her eye
On him, her brothers, me, her master, hitting   395
Each object with a joy; the counterchange
Is severally in all. Let's quit this ground,
And smoke the temple with our sacrifices.
[*To Belarius.*] Thou art my brother; so we'll hold
    thee ever.
   Imo. You are my father too, and did relieve me
To see this gracious season.
   Cym.   All o'erjoy'd,   401
Save these in bonds. Let them be joyful too,
For they shall taste our comfort.
   Imo.   My good master,
I will yet do you service.
   Luc.   Happy be you!   404
   Cym. The forlorn soldier, that so nobly fought,
He would have well becom'd this place, and grac'd
The thankings of a king.
   Post.   I am, sir,
The soldier that did company these three
In poor beseeming; 'twas a fitment for
The purpose I then follow'd. That I was he,   410
Speak, Iachimo. I had you down and might
Have made you finish.
   Iach.   [*Kneeling.*] I am down again;
But now my heavy conscience sinks my knee,
As then your force did. Take that life, beseech
    you,
Which I so often owe; but your ring first,   415
And here the bracelet of the truest princess
That ever swore her faith.
   Post.   Kneel not to me.
The power that I have on you is to spare you,
The malice towards you to forgive you. Live,

And deal with others better.
   Cym.   Nobly doom'd!   420
We'll learn our freeness of a son-in-law;
Pardon's the word to all.
   Arv.   You holp us, sir,
As you did mean indeed to be our brother;
Joy'd are we that you are.
   Post. Your servant, Princes. Good my lord of
    Rome,   425
Call forth your soothsayer. As I slept, methought
Great Jupiter, upon his eagle back'd,
Appear'd to me, with other spritely shows
Of mine own kindred. When I wak'd, I found
This label on my bosom, whose containing   430
Is so from sense in hardness, that I can
Make no collection of it. Let him show
His skill in the construction.
   Luc.   Philarmonus!
   Sooth. Here, my good lord.
   Luc.   Read, and declare the meaning.   434
   [*Sooth.*] (*Reads.*) "Whenas a lion's whelp shall,
to himself unknown, without seeking find, and be
embrac'd by a piece of tender air; and when from a
stately cedar shall be lopp'd branches, which, being
dead many years, shall after revive, be jointed to
the old stock, and freshly grow; then shall Posthu-
mus end his miseries, Britain be fortunate and
flourish in peace and plenty."   442
Thou, Leonatus, art the lion's whelp;
The fit and apt construction of thy name,
Being *leo-natus,* doth import so much.   445
[*To Cymbeline.*] The piece of tender air, thy virtu-
    ous daughter,
Which we call *mollis aer;* and *mollis aer*
We term it *mulier;* which *mulier* I divine
Is this most constant wife, who, even now,
Answering the letter of the oracle,   450
Unknown to you, unsought, were clipp'd about
With this most tender air.
   Cym.   This hath some seeming.
   Sooth. The lofty cedar, royal Cymbeline,
Personates thee; and thy lopp'd branches point
Thy two sons forth; who, by Belarius stol'n,   455
For many years thought dead, are now reviv'd,
To the majestic cedar join'd, whose issue
Promises Britain peace and plenty.
   Cym.   Well;
My peace we will begin. And, Caius Lucius,
Although the victor, we submit to Cæsar,   460
And to the Roman empire, promising
To pay our wonted tribute, from the which
We were dissuaded by our wicked queen;

---

382. **fierce abridgement:** extravagant entertainment. 383–84. **which … in:** which should be rich in interest. 388. **your three motives:** what incited you three. 391. **chance:** happening. 397. **severally in all:** in each according to his relationship. 400. **relieve:** rescue. 405. **forlorn:** lost. 409. **fitment:** outfit. 428. **spritely:** ghostly. 430. **label:** parchment. 432. **collection:** interpretation. 445. *leo-natus:* lion-born. 447. *mollis aer:* tender air, an imagined etymology of *mulier,* woman. 451. **clipp'd:** embraced. 452. **seeming:** likelihood.

Whom heavens, in justice, both on her and hers,
Have laid most heavy hand.   465
    Sooth.   The fingers of the powers above do tune
The harmony of this peace.   The vision
Which I made known to Lucius, ere the stroke
Of [this yet] scarce-cold battle, at this instant
Is full accomplish'd; for the Roman eagle,   470
From south to west on wing soaring aloft,
Lessen'd herself, and in the beams o' th' sun
So vanish'd; which foreshow'd our princely eagle,
Th' imperial Cæsar, should again unite
His favour with the radiant Cymbeline,   475

Which shines here in the west.
    Cym.   Laud we the gods;
And let our crooked smokes climb to their nostrils
From our bless'd altars.   Publish we this peace
To all our subjects.   Set we forward.   Let
A Roman and a British ensign wave   480
Friendly together.   So through Lud's town march;
And in the temple of great Jupiter
Our peace we'll ratify; seal it with feasts.
Set on there!   Never was a war did cease,   484
Ere bloody hands were wash'd, with such a peace.
                        [*Exeunt.*

469. [this yet] F₃.   *yet this* F₁.

The Winter's Tale

NO QUARTO of *The Winter's Tale* was published, nor is the title found in the Stationers' Register before 1623. The earliest edition is that in the First Folio, in which it is the last of the Comedies. On this, which is unusually accurate, the present text is based. The bibliographical features which render the Folio text of *The Two Gentlemen of Verona* peculiar, prevail here, though to a less extent; and the same reasons for opposing the theory of an "assembled" text may be advanced in this instance also.

Simon Forman saw *The Winter's Tale* on May 15, 1611. It is highly probable that the dance of twelve satyrs (IV.iv.331–52), three of whom had "danced before the king," was suggested by the anti-masque in Jonson's *Masque of Oberon*, performed at court on January 1, 1611. There is, therefore, good reason for believing that the play was written within the early months of 1611, and all the metrical evidence, as well as the atmosphere and method of treatment, is in harmony with this late date.

The source of the plot is Robert Greene's euphuistic romance, *Pandosto. The Triumph of Time* (1588). Some of the changes wrought by Shakespeare in his material are interesting to note. For no discernible reason Bohemia and Sicily are interchanged, Greene's Pandosto (Leontes) being king of Bohemia, and Egistus (Polixenes), king of Sicily. Fawnia (Perdita) is put to sea in a rudderless boat, instead of being exposed on a desert shore. The proposal to consult the oracle comes from the queen (Bellaria) in the novel, from Leontes in the play; yet Pandosto accepts the answer of the oracle at once, while Leontes denies its truth until brought to his senses by the death of his son and the apparent death of Hermione. This latter change is significant because it touches upon the much-discussed problem of Leontes's jealousy, of which more must presently be said. In the novel the instant remorse of Pandosto upon hearing the oracle is succeeded by the announcement that his son Garinter (Mamillius) has suddenly died, at which news Bellaria (Hermione) falls dead. The old shepherd comes from Greene, but the Clown is substituted by Shakespeare for the shepherd's wife. The wooing of Fawnia is related at great length in the novel, and the situation is complicated by Egistus's wish to marry his son to a princess of Denmark. In his flight from his father's court Dorastus (Florizel) has the assistance of a servant, Capnio, whom Shakespeare discards, but whose functions in the plot are divided between Camillo (Franion) and Autolycus. When the prince arrives at the court of Pandosto he conceals his identity, and is thrown into prison while the king makes love to Fawnia. This unpleasant incident of the courtship of the unrecognized daughter by her father Shakespeare omits, keeping Leontes faithful to the memory of Hermione. The omission makes possible the happy ending for all and does away with the depression and suicide of Pandosto with which Greene closes his narrative. The most important change made by Shakespeare is in saving the life of Hermione, thus opening the way for the situation which, though more defiant of likelihood than any of the improbabilities in the source, gives to the play its undeniably effective conclusion. The characters of Antigonus, Paulina, Emilia, Mopsa, Dorcas, the Clown, and Autolycus are all of Shakespeare's invention. And through the delightful rustic figures, particularly in the beautiful scene of the sheep-shearing feast, Shakespeare converts the artificial pastoralism of his source into something authentically of his own England.

Certain subsidiary indebtednesses may be mentioned. It seems clear that Shakespeare found the trick by which Autolycus picks the pocket of the shepherd's son (IV.iii.53–81) substantially described in Greene's *Second Part of Conny-Catching* (1592). The device of bringing an apparent statue to life could have been suggested by Lyly's *Woman in the Moon* (1597) or Marston's *Pygmalion's Image* (1598), but Shakespeare must have known the story of Pygmalion for years in Ovid's *Metamorphoses*. The names of Leontes, Antigonus, Cleomenes, Archidamus, and Mopsa are derived from Sidney's *Arcadia*; that of Florizel, probably, from *Amadis de Gaule*; and Autolycus from the *Odyssey* (XIX, 394) or from Ovid.

Ever since Ben Jonson remarked to Drummond

of Hawthornden that "Sheakspear in a play brought in a number of men saying they had suffered Ship-wrack in Bohemia, wher ther is no Sea neer by some 100 Miles," critics have been amused or vexed by the fact. To worry about such a matter is to be a "snapper-up of unconsidered trifles" with a vengeance. Shakespeare's (and Greene's) error needs neither censure nor vindication in a play where Apollo's Delphic oracle, Whitsun pastorals, Puritans singing hymns to hornpipes, a queen who is the daughter of a Russian emperor, and "that rare Italian master, Julio Romano" are all charmingly contemporary.

Criticism has been concerned to better purpose with the jealousy of Leontes, a problem which merits consideration. As it is presented, the jealousy of Leontes is obviously a case of temporary insanity; when the requisite shock is administered, the termination of the seizure is as abrupt as the on-slaught has been. The amazement of those intimate with Leontes indicates that nothing remotely like it has ever been seen in him before. In the novel, the jealousy of Pandosto appears, upon comparison, to be better motivated. Pandosto, having observed the familiarity of his wife and Egistus, becomes suspicious, but he ponders his fears before giving rein to them. His "doubtfull thoughtes a long time smoothering in his stomache, beganne at last to kindle in his minde a secret mistrust, which increased by suspition, grewe at last to be a flaming Iealousie, that so tormented him as he could take no rest." The necessity inherent in the source that the jealousy of Leontes must set the entire plot in motion presented a real problem in verisimilitude, which was made no easier by the fact that the delusions of Leontes are self-engendered. Leontes's sole enemy is his own imagination; the problem for the dramatist is simpler, and the attaining of plausibility easier, when the deceived character is, like Othello and Posthumus, the victim of another's machinations. Though Shakespeare must have been aware of the difficulties confronting him, it is doubtful if he let them trouble him. He must have felt confident that his audience, accustomed to accepting improbabilities in the very premises of romantic story and drama, would accept whatever was to be postulated in this one. And the jealousy of Leontes, demanded almost at the beginning of the play, is in the nature of a postulate. Psychiatrists might even argue today that the case of Leontes is credible. But to subject the matter to rigorous scrutiny is doubtless mistaken effort, for this kind of tragi-comedy asks by its very nature exemption from too close questioning. Indeed, it would seem that in the title of his play Shakespeare has sought to remind us of this fact. For a "winter's tale" is proverbially one "to drive away the time," a good story, that is, which is to be taken with just as much or as little seriousness as one will.

One must accept with a willing suspension of disbelief the incredible seclusion of Hermione for sixteen years. That is a thing which it is absurd to rationalize; it is there for the sake of the plot, for the sake of the striking climax which Shakespeare was reserving, the dramatic descent of Hermione from her pedestal, which, *coup de théâtre* though it is, is profoundly moving. For the sake of this scene, furthermore, Shakespeare sacrifices another which would have been almost as effective, namely, the revelation of Perdita's identity and her restoration to her father. He has been censured for describing these things through conversations (V.ii) instead of representing them dramatically, but surely, had he chosen the latter course, he would have rendered the scene with Hermione a conspicuous anti-climax. He paid the price of seeming ineptitude in order to keep the greater scene unrivalled.

The Winter's Tale is a play which takes a firmer hold upon one's affections with every reading. This is owing equally to certain of its characters and to the beauty of its poetry. With respect to characterization in general it may be said that, whatever the improbabilities in situation, the behavior of the characters is completely credible, once the situation is granted. Hermione is throughout nobly conceived. Her serene dignity, which almost raises her above pity, never deserts her, either in her hour of trial or in her exalted hour of reconcilement. In the final scene, Shakespeare exhibits a fine dramatic sense in according but one speech to Hermione. To her husband she says no word, expressing the fullness of her heart in her embrace; her words are reserved for the daughter whom she has never known. And the rich simplicity of her address to Perdita must stir the heart of the most stolid spectator or reader. Of Perdita it is hard to speak controlledly. She is exquisite, one with the beauty of the flowers she knows and loves so well, joining somehow an other-worldliness with the earthiness of the English countryside. Her gay rustic friends and, of course, Autolycus, one of the most engaging rogues in Shakespeare, contribute much to the realism of the pastoral scenes. Perdita is the queen of curds and cream, but there can be no doubt of the blood that runs in her veins. In her speech to Florizel after her dream has been shattered by the cruel words of Polixenes, are mingled courage and dignity inherited from her mother, and the simplicity derived from her environment (IV.iv.451–59). Nothing she says "but smacks of something greater than herself," and no strain is put upon the imagination picturing her moving with the same ease and charm in the new life to which the happy turn of fortune finally brings her.

THE WINTER'S TALE

[DRAMATIS PERSONÆ]

LEONTES, *king of Sicilia.*
MAMILLIUS, *young prince of Sicilia.*
CAMILLO,
ANTIGONUS,
CLEOMENES, } *lords of Sicilia.*
DION,
POLIXENES, *king of Bohemia.*
FLORIZEL, *prince of Bohemia.*
ARCHIDAMUS, *a lord of Bohemia.*
Old Shepherd, reputed father of Perdita.
Clown, his son.
AUTOLYCUS, *a rogue.*

[A Mariner.]
[A Gaoler.]

HERMIONE, *Queen to Leontes.*
PERDITA, *daughter to Leontes and Hermione.*
PAULINA, *wife to Antigonus.*
EMILIA, *a lady* [*attending on Hermione*].
MOPSA,
DORCAS, } *shepherdesses.*]

[TIME, *as Chorus.*]

Other Lords and Gentlemen [Ladies, Officers] and Servants, Shepherds, and Shepherdesses.

[SCENE: *Sicilia and Bohemia.*]

ACT I

SCENE I. [*Sicilia. Ante-chamber in the palace of Leontes.*]

Enter CAMILLO *and* ARCHIDAMUS.

Arch. If you shall chance, Camillo, to visit Bohemia on the like occasion whereon my services are now on foot, you shall see, as I have said, great difference betwixt our Bohemia and your Sicilia. 5
Cam. I think, this coming summer, the King of Sicilia means to pay Bohemia the visitation which he justly owes him.
Arch. Wherein our entertainment shall shame us we will be justified in our loves; for indeed —
Cam. Beseech you, — 11
Arch. Verily, I speak it in the freedom of my knowledge. We cannot with such magnificence — in so rare — I know not what to say. We will give you sleepy drinks, that your senses, unintelligent of our insufficience, may, though they cannot praise us, as little accuse us. 17

Cam. You pay a great deal too dear for what's given freely.
Arch. Believe me, I speak as my understanding instructs me and as mine honesty puts it to utterance. 22
Cam. Sicilia cannot show himself over-kind to Bohemia. They were train'd together in their childhoods; and there rooted betwixt them then such an affection, which cannot choose but branch now. Since their more mature dignities and royal necessities made separation of their society, 28 their encounters, though not personal, hath been royally attorneyed with interchange of gifts, letters, loving embassies; that they have seem'd to be together, though absent; shook hands, as over a vast; and embrac'd, as it were, from the ends of opposed winds. The heavens continue their loves! 35
Arch. I think there is not in the world either malice or matter to alter it. You have an unspeakable comfort of your young prince Mamillius. It is a gentleman of the greatest promise that ever came into my note. 40

Act I, sc. i, 10. **be justified**: make amends. 30. **attorneyed**: performed by proxy. 32. **vast**: wide expanse. 40. **note**: observation (cf. Sc.ii.2).

Cam. I very well agree with you in the hopes of him. It is a gallant child; one that indeed physics the subject, makes old hearts fresh. They that went on crutches ere he was born desire yet their life to see him a man.   45

Arch. Would they else be content to die?

Cam. Yes; if there were no other excuse why they should desire to live.

Arch. If the King had no son, they would desire to live on crutches till he had one.   50

[*Exeunt.*

SCENE II. [*A room of state in the same.*]

Enter LEONTES, HERMIONE, MAMILLIUS, PO-
LIXENES, CAMILLO [*and* Attendants].

Pol. Nine changes of the wat'ry star hath been
The shepherd's note since we have left our throne
Without a burden; time as long again
Would be fill'd up, my brother, with our thanks,
And yet we should, for perpetuity,   5
Go hence in debt; and therefore, like a cipher,
Yet standing in rich place, I multiply
With one "We thank you" many thousands moe
That go before it.

Leon.   Stay your thanks a while,
And pay them when you part.

Pol.   Sir, that's to-morrow.
I am question'd by my fears of what may chance
Or breed upon our absence; that may blow   12
No sneaping winds at home, to make us say,
"This is put forth too truly." Besides, I have
      stay'd
To tire your Royalty.

Leon.   We are tougher, brother,
Than you can put us to't.

Pol.   No longer stay.   16

Leon. One sev'n-night longer.

Pol.   Very sooth, to-morrow.

Leon. We'll part the time between's then; and in
      that
I'll no gainsaying.

Pol.   Press me not, beseech you, so.
There is no tongue that moves, none, none i' th'
      world,   20
So soon as yours could win me. So it should now,
Were there necessity in your request, although
'Twere needful I deni'd it. My affairs
Do even drag me homeward; which to hinder
Were, in your love, a whip to me; my stay   25
To you a charge and trouble. To save both,

Farewell, our brother.

Leon.   Tongue-tied our Queen? Speak you.

Her. I had thought, sir, to have held my peace
      until
You had drawn oaths from him not to stay. You,
      sir,
Charge him too coldly. Tell him you are sure   30
All in Bohemia's well; this satisfaction
The by-gone day proclaim'd. Say this to him,
He's beat from his best ward.

Leon.   Well said, Hermione.

Her. To tell he longs to see his son were strong;
But let him say so then, and let him go;   35
But let him swear so, and he shall not stay;
We'll thwack him hence with distaffs.
Yet of your royal presence I'll adventure
The borrow of a week. When at Bohemia
You take my lord, I'll give him my commission 40
To let him there a month behind the gest
Prefix'd for 's parting; yet, good deed, Leontes,
I love thee not a jar o' th' clock behind
What lady she her lord. You'll stay?

Pol.   No, madam.

Her. Nay, but you will?

Pol.   I may not, verily.   45

Her. Verily!
You put me off with limber vows; but I,
Though you would seek to unsphere the stars with
      oaths,
Should yet say, "Sir, no going." Verily,
You shall not go; a lady's "Verily" 's   50
As potent as a lord's. Will you go yet?
Force me to keep you as a prisoner,
Not like a guest? So you shall pay your fees
When you depart, and save your thanks. How say
      you?
My prisoner or my guest? By your dread "Verily,"
One of them you shall be.

Pol.   Your guest, then, madam. 56
To be your prisoner should import offending,
Which is for me less easy to commit
Than you to punish.

Her.   Not your gaoler, then,
But your kind hostess. Come, I'll question you 60
Of my lord's tricks and yours when you were boys.
You were pretty lordings then?

Pol.   We were, fair Queen,
Two lads that thought there was no more behind
But such a day to-morrow as to-day,
And to be boy eternal.

Her.   Was not my lord   65

42. **physics the subject:** does the people good.
Sc. ii, 1. wat'ry star: the moon (that governs the tides). 6. **like a cipher.** A cipher, though worthless itself, may, when added to a small number, increase it. 11. **question'd:** i.e., motivated. 12. **that may blow:** may there blow. 13. **sneaping:** nipping. 14. **"This...truly":** our present fears are only too true. 16. **Than...to't:** i.e., than anything you can lay upon us. 19. **I'll no gainsaying:** I'll take no denial. 25. **in your love:** i.e., though inspired by your love. **whip:** punishment. 32. **The...day:** yesterday. 33. **ward:** position of defense. 40. **take:** charm (as in several passages in this play). 41. **let:** allow. **gest:** time. 53. **fees.** Prisoners leaving jail had to pay for their keep.

The verier wag o' th' two?

Pol. We were as twinn'd lambs that did frisk i'
   th' sun,
And bleat the one at th' other.   What we chang'd
Was innocence for innocence; we knew not
The doctrine of ill-doing, [no], nor dream'd   70
That any did.   Had we pursu'd that life,
And our weak spirits ne'er been higher rear'd
With stronger blood, we should have answer'd
   Heaven
Boldly, "Not guilty"; the imposition clear'd
Hereditary ours.

Her.   By this we gather   75
You have tripp'd since.

Pol.   O my most sacred lady,
Temptations have since then been born to 's; for
In those unfledg'd days was my wife a girl;
Your precious self had then not cross'd the eyes
Of my young play-fellow.

Her.   Grace to boot!   80
Of this make no conclusion, lest you say
Your Queen and I are devils.   Yet go on;
Th' offences we have made you do we'll answer,
If you first sinn'd with us, and that with us
You did continue fault, and that you slipp'd not   85
With any but with us.

Leon.   Is he won yet?

Her. He'll stay, my lord.

Leon.   At my request he would not.
Hermione, my dearest, thou never spok'st
To better purpose.

Her.   Never?

Leon.   Never, but once.

Her. What! have I twice said well?   When was 't
   before?   90
I prithee tell me; cram 's with praise, and make 's
As fat as tame things.   One good deed dying
   tongueless
Slaughters a thousand waiting upon that.
Our praises are our wages; you may ride 's
With one soft kiss a thousand furlongs ere   95
With spur we heat an acre.   But to th' goal:
My last good deed was to entreat his stay;
What was my first?   It has an elder sister,
Or I mistake you.   O, would her name were
   Grace!
But once before I spoke to th' purpose; when?   100
Nay, let me have 't; I long.

Leon.   Why, that was when

Three crabbed months had sour'd themselves to
   death,
Ere I could make thee open thy white hand
And clap thyself my love; then didst thou utter,
"I am yours for ever."

Her.   'Tis grace indeed.   105
Why, lo you now, I have spoke to th' purpose
   twice:
The one for ever earn'd a royal husband;
Th' other for some while a friend.

                  [*Gives her hand to Polixenes.*]

Leon.   [*Aside.*]   Too hot, too hot!
To mingle friendship far is mingling bloods.
I have *tremor cordis* on me; my heart dances,   110
But not for joy; not joy.   This entertainment
May a free face put on, derive a liberty
From heartiness, from bounty, fertile bosom,
And well become the agent; 't may, I grant;
But to be paddling palms and pinching fingers,   115
As now they are, and making practis'd smiles,
As in a looking-glass; and then to sigh, as 'twere
The mort o' th' deer; — O, that is entertainment
My bosom likes not, nor my brows!   Mamillius,
Art thou my boy?

Mam.   Ay, my good lord.

Leon.   I' fecks!
Why, that's my bawcock.   What, hast smutch'd
   thy nose?   121
They say it is a copy out of mine.   Come, captain,
We must be neat; not neat, but cleanly, captain:
And yet the steer, the heifer, and the calf
Are all call'd neat. — Still virginalling   125
Upon his palm! — How now, you wanton calf!
Art thou my calf?

Mam.   Yes, if you will, my lord.

Leon. Thou want'st a rough pash and the shoots
   that I have,
To be full like me; yet they say we are
Almost as like as eggs; women say so,   130
That will say anything.   But were they false
As o'er-dy'd blacks, as wind, as waters, false
As dice are to be wish'd by one that fixes
No bourn 'twixt his and mine, yet were it true
To say this boy were like me.   Come, sir page,   135
Look on me with your welkin eye.   Sweet villain!
Most dear'st! my collop!   Can thy dam? — may 't
   be? —
Affection! thy intention stabs the centre.
Thou dost make possible things not so held,

70. [no] F₂. Om. F₁.   74–75. the ... ours: absolved even from our inherited guilt (i.e., original sin).   80. Grace to
boot: heavenly grace help me.   96. heat: speed over.   104. clap: pledge (by handclasp).   110. tremor cordis: fluttering
of the heart.   112. free: innocent.   113. fertile: generous.   118. mort: blast of a hunting horn, announcing the death of
the deer.   119. brows.   Referring to the horns of the cuckold (cf. ll. 146 and 186).   120. I' fecks: in faith.   121. bawcock:
fine fellow.   123. not neat.   *Neat*, cattle, suggests "horns" to Leontes.   125. virginalling: fingering (as upon the virginals,
an early kind of piano).   128. rough pash: shaggy head.   shoots: horns.   132. o'er-dy'd blacks: black garments spoiled by
too much dyeing.   136. welkin: sky-blue.   137. my collop: piece of my flesh.   138–43. Affection ... something.   The
general sense is: that since Desire can fix upon imagined objects so powerfully, it is all the more credible that it should
pursue real ones.   138. Affection: sexual desire.   centre: soul.

Communicat'st with dreams; — how can this
   be? —   140
With what's unreal thou co-active art,
And fellow'st nothing. Then 'tis very credent
Thou mayst co-join with something; and thou
   dost,
And that beyond commission, and I find it,
And that to the infection of my brains   145
And hardening of my brows.

Pol.   What means Sicilia?

Her. He something seems unsettled.

Pol.   How, my lord!
What cheer? How is 't with you, best brother?

Her.   You look
As if you held a brow of much distraction.
Are you mov'd, my lord?

Leon.   No, in good earnest.
How sometimes nature will betray its folly,   151
Its tenderness, and make itself a pastime
To harder bosoms! Looking on the lines
Of my boy's face, methoughts I did [recoil]
Twenty-three years, and saw myself unbreech'd
In my green velvet coat, my dagger muzzl'd   156
Lest it should bite its master, and so prove,
As ornaments oft do, too dangerous.
How like, methought, I then was to this kernel,
This squash, this gentleman. Mine honest friend,
Will you take eggs for money?   161

Mam. No, my lord, I'll fight.

Leon. You will! Why, happy man be 's dole!
   My brother,
Are you so fond of your young prince as we
Do seem to be of ours?

Pol.   If at home, sir,   165
He's all my exercise, my mirth, my matter,
Now my sworn friend and then mine enemy,
My parasite, my soldier, statesman, all.
He makes a July's day short as December,
And with his varying childness cures in me   170
Thoughts that would thick my blood.

Leon.   So stands this squire
Offic'd with me. We two will walk, my lord,
And leave you to your graver steps. Hermione,
How thou lov'st us, show in our brother's welcome;
Let what is dear in Sicily be cheap.   175
Next to thyself and my young rover, he's
Apparent to my heart.

Her.   If you would seek us,
We are yours i' th' garden. Shall 's attend you
   there?

Leon. To your own bents dispose you; you'll be
   found,

Be you beneath the sky. [*Aside.*] I am angling
   now,   180
Though you perceive me not how I give line.
Go to, go to!
How she holds up the neb, the bill to him!
And arms her with the boldness of a wife
To her allowing husband!

   [*Exeunt Polixenes, Hermione, and attendants.*]

                 Gone already!   185
Inch-thick, knee-deep, o'er head and ears a fork'd
   one!
Go, play, boy, play. Thy mother plays, and I
Play too, but so disgrac'd a part, whose issue
Will hiss me to my grave; contempt and clamour
Will be my knell. Go, play, boy, play. There have
   been,   190
Or I am much deceiv'd, cuckolds ere now;
And many a man there is, even at this present,
Now while I speak this, holds his wife by th' arm,
That little thinks she has been sluic'd in 's absence
And his pond fish'd by his next neighbour, by   195
Sir Smile, his neighbour. Nay, there's comfort in 't
Whiles other men have gates, and those gates
   open'd,
As mine, against their will. Should all despair
That have revolted wives, the tenth of mankind
Would hang themselves. Physic for 't there is
   none.   200
It is a bawdy planet, that will strike
Where 'tis predominant; and 'tis powerful, think it,
From east, west, north, and south. Be it concluded,
No barricado for a belly; know 't;
It will let in and out the enemy   205
With bag and baggage. Many thousand on 's
Have the disease, and feel 't not. How now, boy!

Mam. I am like you, [they] say.

Leon.   Why, that's some comfort.
What, Camillo there?

Cam. Ay, my good lord.   210

Leon. Go play, Mamillius; thou 'rt an honest
   man.   [*Exeunt Mamillius.*]
Camillo, this great sir will yet stay longer.

Cam. You had much ado to make his anchor
   hold.
When you cast out, it still came home.

Leon.   Didst note it?

Cam. He would not stay at your petitions; made
His business more material.

Leon.   Didst perceive it?   216

[*Aside.*] They're here with me already, whispering,
   rounding,

142. **fellow'st nothing:** art companion to what does not exist. 144. **commission:** what is lawful. 148. **What ... brother** (Rann). F gives this line to Leontes. 153–55. **Looking ... years.** These lines indicate that Leontes must be about thirty. 154. **[recoil]** F₃. *requoyle* F₁. 160. **squash:** unripe pea-pod. 161. **take ... money:** i.e., let yourself be cheated. 163. **happy ... dole:** may his lot be happy. 170. **childness:** childish ways. 171–72. **So ... me:** such is the part this boy plays in my life. 177. **Apparent:** heir apparent. 185. **allowing:** approving. 186. **fork'd:** horned. 201. **strike:** spread ruin. 202. **predominant:** in the ascendant. 208. **[they]** F₂. Om. F₁. 214. **still ... home:** always failed to hold. 216. **material:** urgent. 217. **here ... me:** i.e., mocking me. **rounding:** whispering.

"Sicilia is a so-forth." 'Tis far gone,
When I shall gust it last. — How came 't, Camillo,
That he did stay?
    Cam.   At the good Queen's entreaty.
    Leon. At the Queen's be 't; "good" should be
      pertinent;   221
But, so it is, it is not. Was this taken
By any understanding pate but thine?
For thy conceit is soaking, — will draw in
More than the common blocks. Not noted, is 't,
But of the finer natures? By some severals 226
Of head-piece extraordinary? Lower messes
Perchance are to this business purblind? Say.
    Cam. Business, my lord! I think most under-
      stand
Bohemia stays here longer.
    Leon.   Ha!
    Cam.   Stays here longer.
    Leon. Ay, but why?   231
    Cam. To satisfy your Highness and the entreaties
Of our most gracious mistress.
    Leon.   Satisfy!
Th' entreaties of your mistress! Satisfy!
Let that suffice. I have trusted thee, Camillo, 235
With all the nearest things to my heart, as well
My chamber-counsels, wherein, priest-like, thou
Hast cleans'd my bosom, ay, from thee departed
Thy penitent reform'd; but we have been
Deceiv'd in thy integrity, deceiv'd 240
In that which seems so.
    Cam.   Be it forbid, my lord!
    Leon. To bide upon 't, thou art not honest, or,
If thou inclin'st that way, thou art a coward,
Which hoxes honesty behind, restraining
From course requir'd; or else thou must be counted
A servant grafted in my serious trust 246
And therein negligent; or else a fool
That seest a game play'd home, the rich stake
    drawn,
And tak'st it all for jest.
    Cam.   My gracious lord,
I may be negligent, foolish, and fearful; 250
In every one of these no man is free
But that his negligence, his folly, fear,
Among the infinite doings of the world,
Sometime puts forth. In your affairs, my lord,
If ever I were wilful-negligent, 255
It was my folly; if industriously
I play'd the fool, it was my negligence,
Not weighing well the end; if ever fearful
To do a thing, where I the issue doubted,
Whereof the execution did cry out 260

Against the non-performance, 'twas a fear
Which oft infects the wisest: these, my lord,
Are such allow'd infirmities that honesty
Is never free of. But, beseech your Grace,
Be plainer with me; let me know my trespass 265
By its own visage. If I then deny it,
'Tis none of mine.
    Leon.   Ha' not you seen, Camillo, —
But that's past doubt; you have, or your eye-glass
Is thicker than a cuckold's horn, — or heard, —
For to a vision so apparent rumour 270
Cannot be mute, — or thought, — for cogitation
Resides not in that man that does not think, —
My wife is slippery? If thou wilt confess,
Or else be impudently negative,
To have nor eyes nor ears nor thought, then say
My wife 's a hobby-horse, — deserves a name 276
As rank as any flax-wench that puts to
Before her troth-plight: say 't and justify 't.
    Cam. I would not be a stander-by to hear
My sovereign mistress clouded so, without 280
My present vengeance taken. Shrew my heart,
You never spoke what did become you less
Than this; which to reiterate were sin
As deep as that, though true.
    Leon.   Is whispering nothing?
Is leaning cheek to cheek? Is meeting noses?
Kissing with inside lip? stopping the career 286
Of laughter with a sigh? — a note infallible
Of breaking honesty; — horsing foot on foot?
Skulking in corners? wishing clocks more swift?
Hours, minutes? noon, midnight? and all eyes 290
Blind with the pin-and-web but theirs, theirs only,
That would unseen be wicked? Is this nothing?
Why, then the world and all that's in 't is nothing;
The covering sky is nothing; Bohemia nothing;
My wife is nothing; nor nothing have these no-
    things, 295
If this be nothing.
    Cam.   Good my lord, be cur'd
Of this diseas'd opinion, and betimes;
For 'tis most dangerous.
    Leon.   Say it be, 'tis true.
    Cam. No, no, my lord.
    Leon.   It is; you lie, you lie!
I say thou liest, Camillo, and I hate thee, 300
Pronounce thee a gross lout, a mindless slave,
Or else a hovering temporizer, that
Canst with thine eyes at once see good and evil,
Inclining to them both. Were my wife's liver
Infected as her life, she would not live 305
The running of one glass.

---

219. **gust:** taste, perceive. 222. **so it is:** as things are. 224. **conceit:** understanding. **soaking:** absorbent. 225. **blocks:** blockheads. 226. **severals:** individuals. 227. **Lower messes:** those occupying inferior seats at meals. 237. **chamber-counsels:** private concerns. 242. **bide:** insist. 244. **hoxes:** hamstrings. 254. **puts forth:** appears. 256. **industriously:** purposely. 268. **eye-glass:** lens of the eye. 270. **vision so apparent:** sight so obvious. 277. **flax-wench:** a coarse woman. 284. **that ... true:** that offense, if it were true. 286. **career:** swift course (equestrian figure). 288. **honesty:** chastity. **horsing:** setting. 291. **pin-and-web:** cataract. 302. **hovering:** wavering. 306. **glass:** hour-glass.

Cam.   Who does infect her?
Leon. Why, he that wears her like her medal
    hanging
About his neck, Bohemia; who, if I
Had servants true about me, that bare eyes
To see alike mine honour as their profits,   310
Their own particular thrifts, they would do that
Which should undo more doing; ay, and thou,
His cup-bearer, — whom I from meaner form
Have bench'd and rear'd to worship, who mayst see
Plainly as heaven sees earth and earth sees heaven,
How I am gall'd, — mightst bespice a cup,   316
To give mine enemy a lasting wink;
Which draught to me were cordial.
Cam.   Sir, my lord,
I could do this, and that with no rash potion,
But with a ling'ring dram that should not work 320
Maliciously like poison; but I cannot
Believe this crack to be in my dread mistress,
So sovereignly being honourable.
I have lov'd thee, —
Leon.   Make that thy question, and go rot!
Dost think I am so muddy, so unsettled,   325
To appoint myself in this vexation, sully
The purity and whiteness of my sheets,
Which to preserve is sleep, which being spotted
Is goads, thorns, nettles, tails of wasps,
Give scandal to the blood o' th' Prince my son,
Who I do think is mine and love as mine,   331
Without ripe moving to 't? Would I do this?
Could man so blench?
Cam.   I must believe you, sir;
I do; and will fetch off Bohemia for 't;
Provided that, when he's removed, your Highness
Will take again your queen as yours at first, 336
Even for your son's sake; and thereby forsealing
The injury of tongues in courts and kingdoms
Known and allied to yours.
Leon.   Thou dost advise me
Even so as I mine own course have set down.
I'll give no blemish to her honour, none.   341
Cam. My lord,
Go then; and with a countenance as clear
As friendship wears at feasts, keep with Bohemia
And with your queen. I am his cupbearer: 345
If from me he have wholesome beverage,
Account me not your servant.
Leon.   This is all.
Do 't and thou hast the one half of my heart;
Do 't not, thou split'st thine own.
Cam.   I'll do 't, my lord.

Leon. I will seem friendly, as thou hast advis'd
    me.   *[Exit.* 350
Cam. O miserable lady! But, for me,
What case stand I in? I must be the poisoner
Of good Polixenes; and my ground to do 't
Is the obedience to a master, one
Who, in rebellion with himself, will have   355
All that are his so too. To do this deed,
Promotion follows. If I could find example
Of thousands that had struck anointed kings
And flourish'd after, I'd not do 't; but since
Nor brass nor stone nor parchment bears not one,
Let villainy itself forswear 't. I must   361
Forsake the court. To do 't, or no, is certain
To me a break-neck. Happy star reign now!
Here comes Bohemia.

Re-enter POLIXENES.

Pol.   This is strange; methinks
My favour here begins to warp. Not speak! 365
Good day, Camillo.
Cam.   Hail, most royal sir!
Pol. What is the news i' th' court?
Cam.   None rare, my lord.
Pol. The King hath on him such a countenance
As he had lost some province and a region
Lov'd as he loves himself. Even now I met him
With customary compliment; when he,   371
Wafting his eyes to th' contrary and falling
A lip of much contempt, speeds from me, and
So leaves me to consider what is breeding
That changeth thus his manners.   375
Cam. I dare not know, my lord.
Pol. How! dare not? Do not! Do you know,
    and dare not?
Be intelligent to me: 'tis thereabouts;
For, to yourself, what you do know, you must,
And cannot say you dare not. Good Camillo, 380
Your chang'd complexions are to me a mirror
Which shows me mine chang'd too; for I must be
A party in this alteration, finding
Myself thus alter'd with 't.
Cam.   There is a sickness
Which puts some of us in distemper, but   385
I cannot name the disease; and it is caught
Of you that yet are well.
Pol.   How! caught of me!
Make me not sighted like the basilisk.
I have look'd on thousands, who have sped the
    better
By my regard, but kill'd none so. Camillo, —

---

311. **particular thrifts:** personal gains. 313. **meaner form:** lower seat. 314. **bench'd:** raised to an official seat. **worship:** dignity. 317. **wink:** sleep. 322. **dread:** revered. 324. **question:** topic. 326. **appoint...in:** bring myself into. 332. **ripe moving:** good reason. 333. **blench:** swerve (from sense). 334. **fetch off:** kill. 337. **forsealing:** sealing up tight. 372. **falling:** letting droop. 378. **Be intelligent:** make yourself clear. **thereabouts:** something like that. 379-80. **For... not:** i.e., for, as to yourself, what you know must be clear to yourself, and you cannot say you dare not. 388. **basilisk:** fabulous snake, supposed to kill by its glance.

As you are certainly a gentleman, thereto   391
Clerk-like experienc'd, which no less adorns
Our gentry than our parents' noble names,
In whose success we are gentle, — I beseech you,
If you know aught which does behove my knowl-
         edge   395
Thereof to be inform'd, imprison 't not
In ignorant concealment.
    Cam.   I may not answer.
    Pol. A sickness caught of me, and yet I well!
I must be answer'd. Dost thou hear, Camillo?
I conjure thee, by all the parts of man   400
Which honour does acknowledge, whereof the least
Is not this suit of mine, that thou declare
What incidency thou dost guess of harm
Is creeping toward me; how far off, how near;
Which way to be prevented, if to be;   405
If not, how best to bear it.
    Cam.   Sir, I will tell you,
Since I am charg'd in honour and by him
That I think honourable; therefore mark my
         counsel,
Which must be even as swiftly follow'd as
I mean to utter it, or both yourself and me   410
Cry lost, and so good night!
    Pol.   On, good Camillo.
    Cam. I am appointed him to murder you.
    Pol. By whom, Camillo?
    Cam.   By the King.
    Pol.   For what?
    Cam. He thinks, nay, with all confidence he
         swears,
As he had seen 't or been an instrument   415
To vice you to 't, that you have touch'd his queen
Forbiddenly.
    Pol.   O, then my best blood turn
To an infected jelly, and my name
Be yok'd with his that did betray the Best!
Turn then my freshest reputation to   420
A savour that may strike the dullest nostril
Where I arrive, and my approach be shunn'd,
Nay, hated too, worse than the great'st infection
That e'er was heard or read!
    Cam.   Swear his thought over
By each particular star in heaven and   425
By all their influences, you may as well
Forbid the sea for to obey the moon
As or by oath remove or counsel shake
The fabric of his folly, whose foundation
Is pil'd upon his faith and will continue   430
The standing of his body.
    Pol.   How should this grow?

    Cam. I know not; but I am sure 'tis safer to
Avoid what's grown than question how 'tis born.
If therefore you dare trust my honesty,
That lies enclosed in this trunk which you   435
Shall bear along impawn'd, away to-night!
Your followers I will whisper to the business,
And will by twos and threes at several posterns
Clear them o' th' city. For myself, I'll put
My fortunes to your service, which are here   440
By this discovery lost. Be not uncertain;
For, by the honour of my parents, I
Have utt'red truth, which if you seek to prove,
I dare not stand by; nor shall you be safer
Than one condemn'd by th' King's own mouth,
         thereon   445
His execution sworn.
    Pol.   I do believe thee;
I saw his heart in 's face. Give me thy hand.
Be pilot to me, and thy places shall
Still neighbour mine. My ships are ready and
My people did expect my hence departure   450
Two days ago. This jealousy
Is for a precious creature. As she 's rare,
Must it be great; and as his person 's mighty,
Must it be violent; and as he does conceive
He is dishonour'd by a man which ever   455
Profess'd to him, why, his revenges must
In that be made more bitter. Fear o'ershades me.
Good expedition be my friend, and comfort
The gracious queen, — part of his theme, but
         nothing
Of his ill-ta'en suspicion! Come, Camillo;   460
I will respect thee as a father if
Thou bear'st my life off hence. Let us avoid.
    Cam. It is in mine authority to command
The keys of all the posterns. Please your Highness
To take the urgent hour. Come, sir, away.   465
                                        [*Exeunt.*

ACT II

SCENE I. [*Sicilia. A room in the palace.*]

Enter HERMIONE, MAMILLIUS, *and* LADIES.

Her. Take the boy to you; he so troubles me,
'Tis past enduring.
    [*I.*] *Lady.*   Come, my gracious lord,
Shall I be your playfellow?
    Mam.   No, I'll none of you.
    [*I.*] *Lady.* Why, my sweet lord?
    Mam. You'll kiss me hard and speak to me
         as if   5

392. **Clerk-like:** like a scholar.   394. **In ... gentle:** from whom we inherit our noble rank.   400. **parts:** duties.   403.
incidency: happening.   412. **him:** the one.   416. **vice:** force.   419. **his ... Best:** i.e., the name of Judas.   424.
Swear ... over: though you seek to annul his thought by swearing.   431. **The ... body:** whilst he lives.   435. **trunk:**
body.   436. **impawn'd:** as a pledge of my honesty.   441. **discovery:** disclosure.   448–49. **thy ... mine:** i.e., I shall keep
you in offices ever close to me.   456. **Profess'd:** professed friendship.

I were a baby still. — I love you better.
  2. Lady. And why so, my lord?
  Mam.   Not for because
Your brows are blacker; yet black brows, they say,
Become some women best, so that there be not
Too much hair there, but in a semicircle,   10
Or a half-moon made with a pen.
  2. Lady.   Who taught ' this?
  Mam. I learn'd it out of women's faces. Pray now
What colour are your eyebrows?
  [*1.*] *Lady.*   Blue, my lord.
  Mam. Nay, that's a mock. I have seen a lady's
    nose
That has been blue, but not her eyebrows.
  [*1.*] *Lady.*   Hark ye;
The Queen your mother rounds apace. We shall   16
Present our services to a fine new prince
One of these days; and then you'd wanton with us,
If we would have you.
  2. Lady.   She is spread of late   20
Into a goodly bulk. Good time encounter her!
  Her. What wisdom stirs amongst you? Come,
  — sir, now
I am for you again. Pray you, sit by us,
And tell 's a tale.
  Mam.   Merry or sad shall't be?
  Her. As merry as you will.
  Mam. A sad tale's best for winter. I have one   25
Of sprites and goblins.
  Her.   Let's have that, good sir.
Come on, sit down; come on, and do your best
To fright me with your sprites; you're powerful at it.
  Mam. There was a man —
  Her.   Nay, come, sit down; then on.
  Mam. Dwelt by a churchyard. I will tell it
    softly;   30
Yond crickets shall not hear it.
  Her.   Come on, then,
And give 't me in mine ear.

[*Enter* LEONTES, *with* ANTIGONUS, LORDS, *and
    others.*]

  Leon. Was he met there? his train? Camillo
    with him?
  [*1.*] *Lord.* Behind the tuft of pines I met them;
    never
Saw I men scour so on their way. I ey'd   35
Them even to their ships.
  Leon.   How blest am I
In my just censure, in my true opinion!
Alack, for lesser knowledge! How accurs'd
In being so blest! There may be in the cup
A spider steep'd, and one may drink, depart,   40

And yet partake no venom, for his knowledge
Is not infected; but if one present
Th' abhorr'd ingredient to his eye, make known
How he hath drunk, he cracks his gorge, his sides,
With violent hefts. I have drunk, and seen the
    spider.   45
Camillo was his help in this, his pander.
There is a plot against my life, my crown.
All's true that is mistrusted. That false villain
Whom I employ'd was pre-employ'd by him.
He has discover'd my design, and I   50
Remain a pinch'd thing; yea, a very trick
For them to play at will. How came the posterns
So easily open?
  [*1.*] *Lord.*   By his great authority;
Which often hath no less prevail'd than so
On your command.
  Leon.   I know 't too well.   55
Give me the boy. I am glad you did not nurse him.
Though he does bear some signs of me, yet you
Have too much blood in him.
  Her.   What is this? Sport?
  Leon. Bear the boy hence; he shall not come
    about her.
Away with him! and let her sport herself   60
With that she's big with; for 'tis Polixenes
Has made thee swell thus.
  Her.   But I'd say he had not,
And I'll be sworn you would believe my saying,
Howe'er you lean to th' nayward.
  Leon.   You, my lords,
Look on her, mark her well; be but about   65
To say she is a goodly lady, and
The justice of your hearts will thereto add
'Tis pity she's not honest, honourable.
Praise her but for this her without-door form,
Which on my faith deserves high speech, and
    straight   70
The shrug, the hum or ha, these petty brands
That calumny doth use — O, I am out —
That mercy does, for calumny will sear
Virtue itself; these shrugs, these hums and has,
When you have said she's goodly, come between   75
Ere you can say she's honest: but be't known,
From him that has most cause to grieve it should be,
She's an adultress.
  Her.   Should a villain say so,
The most replenish'd villain in the world,
He were as much more villain: you, my lord,   80
Do but mistake.
  Leon.   You have mistook, my lady,
Polixenes for Leontes. O thou thing!
Which I'll not call a creature of thy place,

Act II, sc. i. 18. **wanton:** play. 31. **crickets:** chattering women. 37. **censure:** judgment. 38. **for ... knowledge:** would that I knew less. 45. **hefts:** heavings, retchings. 48. **mistrusted:** suspected. 51. **pinch'd:** made ridiculous. 64. **to th' nayward:** in the opposite direction. 68. **honest:** chaste. 69. **without-door:** outward. 72. **out:** wrong. 79. **replenish'd:** complete. 83. **Which ... place:** a term I'll not apply to one of your rank.

Lest barbarism, making me the precedent,
Should a like language use to all degrees,   85
And mannerly distinguishment leave out
Betwixt the prince and beggar. I have said
She's an adultress; I have said with whom;
More, she's a traitor, and Camillo is
A [fedary] with her, and one that knows   90
What she should shame to know herself
But with her most vile principal, that she's
A bed-swerver, even as bad as those
That vulgars give bold'st titles; ay, and privy
To this their late escape.
  Her.   No, by my life,   95
Privy to none of this. How will this grieve you,
When you shall come to clearer knowledge, that
You thus have publish'd me! Gentle, my lord,
You scarce can right me throughly then to say
You did mistake.
  Leon.   No; if I mistake   100
In those foundations which I build upon,
The centre is not big enough to bear
A school-boy's top. Away with her, to prison!
He who shall speak for her is afar off guilty
But that he speaks.
  Her.   There's some ill planet reigns;
I must be patient till the heavens look   106
With an aspect more favourable. Good my lords,
I am not prone to weeping, as our sex
Commonly are, the want of which vain dew
Perchance shall dry your pities; but I have   110
That honourable grief lodg'd here which burns
Worse than tears drown. Beseech you all, my
        lords,
With thoughts so qualified as your charities
Shall best instruct you, measure me; and so
The King's will be perform'd!
  Leon.   Shall I be heard?
  Her. Who is 't that goes with me? Beseech your
        Highness,   116
My women may be with me; for you see
My plight requires it. Do not weep, good fools;
There is no cause. When you shall know your
        mistress
Has deserv'd prison, then abound in tears   120
As I come out; this action I now go on
Is for my better grace. Adieu, my lord.
I never wish'd to see you sorry; now
I trust I shall. My women, come; you have leave.
  Leon. Go, do our bidding; hence!   125
           [Exit Queen guarded, with Ladies.]
  [*1.*] *Lord.* Beseech your Highness, call the Queen
        again.

  Ant. Be certain what you do, sir, lest your jus-
        tice
Prove violence; in the which three great ones suffer,
Yourself, your queen, your son.
  [*1.*] *Lord.*   For her, my lord,
I dare my life lay down, and will do 't, sir,   130
Please you to accept it, that the Queen is spotless
I' th' eyes of Heaven and to you; I mean,
In this which you accuse her.
  Ant.   If it prove
She's otherwise, I'll keep my stables where
I lodge my wife; I'll go in couples with her;   135
Than when I feel and see her no farther trust her;
For every inch of woman in the world,
Ay, every dram of woman's flesh is false,
If she be.
  Leon. Hold your peaces.
  [*1.*] *Lord.*   Good my lord, —
  Ant. It is for you we speak, not for ourselves. 140
You are abus'd, and by some putter-on
That will be damn'd for 't; would I knew the villain,
I would land-damn him. Be she honour-flaw'd,
I have three daughters; the eldest is eleven;
The second and the third, nine, and some five;
If this prove true, they'll pay for 't. By mine
        honour,   146
I'll geld 'em all; fourteen they shall not see
To bring false generations. They are co-heirs;
And I had rather glib myself than they
Should not produce fair issue.
  Leon.   Cease; no more.
You smell this business with a sense as cold   151
As is a dead man's nose; but I do see 't and feel 't,
As you feel doing thus; and see withal
The instruments that feel.
  Ant.   If it be so,
We need no grave to bury honesty.   155
There's not a grain of it the face to sweeten
Of the whole dungy earth.
  Leon.   What! lack I credit?
  [*1.*] *Lord.* I had rather you did lack than I, my
        lord,
Upon this ground; and more it would content me
To have her honour true than your suspicion,   160
Be blam'd for 't how you might.
  Leon.   Why, what need we
Commune with you of this, but rather follow
Our forceful instigation? Our prerogative
Calls not your counsels, but our natural goodness
Imparts this; which if you, or stupefied   165
Or seeming so in skill, cannot or will not
Relish a truth like us, inform yourselves

---

90. **[fedary]** (Dyce): confederate. *Federarie* F.   102. **centre:** earth.   104–105. **afar ... speaks:** indirectly guilty merely through speaking.   113. **so qualified:** of such a nature.   115. **heard:** obeyed.   134–35. **I'll ... wife:** i.e., I'll lock up my wife like my mares.   141. **abus'd:** deceived. **putter-on:** plotter.   143. **land-damn.** Probably corrupt.   149. **glib:** geld.   153–54. **As ... feel.** The usual stage business here is pulling Antigonus's nose.   159. **ground:** matter.   163. **instigation:** impulse.   164. **Calls not:** has no call for.   166. **skill:** craft.

We need no more of your advice. The matter,
The loss, the gain, the ord'ring on't, is all
Properly ours.
    Ant.   And I wish, my liege,   170
You had only in your silent judgement tried it,
Without more overture.
    Leon.   How could that be?
Either thou art most ignorant by age,
Or thou wert born a fool. Camillo's flight,
Added to their familiarity, —   175
Which was as gross as ever touch'd conjecture,
That lack'd sight only, nought for approbation
But only seeing, all other circumstances
Made up to th' deed, — doth push on this proceed-
    ing.
Yet, for a greater confirmation,   180
For in an act of this importance 'twere
Most piteous to be wild, I have dispatch'd in post
To sacred Delphos, to Apollo's temple,
Cleomenes and Dion, whom you know
Of stuff'd sufficiency. Now from the oracle   185
They will bring all; whose spiritual counsel had,
I shall stop or spur me. Have I done well?
    [*1.*] *Lord.* Well done, my lord.
    Leon. Though I am satisfi'd and need no more
Than what I know, yet shall the oracle   190
Give rest to th' minds of others, such as he
Whose ignorant credulity will not
Come up to th' truth. So have we thought it
    good
From our free person she should be confin'd,
Lest that the treachery of the two fled hence   195
Be left her to perform. Come, follow us;
We are to speak in public, for this business
Will raise us all.
    Ant. [*Aside.*] To laughter, as I take it,
If the good truth were known.   [*Exeunt.* 200

      SCENE II. [*Outer ward of a prison.*]

Enter PAULINA, *a* Gentleman, [*and* Attendants].

    Paul. The keeper of the prison, call to him;
Let him have knowledge who I am.   [*Exit Gent.*]
                    Good lady,
No court in Europe is too good for thee;
What dost thou then in prison?

    [*Re-enter* Gentleman, *with the* GAOLER.]
                  Now, good sir,
You know me, do you not?
    Gaol.   For a worthy lady,   5
And one who much I honour.
    Paul.   Pray you then,

Conduct me to the Queen.
    Gaol.   I may not, madam.
To the contrary I have express commandment.
    Paul. Here's ado,
To lock up honesty and honour from   10
Th' access of gentle visitors! Is't lawful, pray
    you,
To see her women? Any of them? Emilia?
    Gaol. So please you, madam,
To put apart these your attendants, I
Shall bring Emilia forth.
    Paul.   I pray now, call her.
Withdraw yourselves.
            [*Exeunt Gentleman and attendants.*]
    Gaol.   And, madam,   16
I must be present at your conference.
    Paul. Well, be't so, prithee.   [*Exit Gaoler.*]
Here's such ado to make no stain a stain
As passes colouring.

    [*Re-enter* GAOLER, *with* EMILIA.]
                Dear gentlewoman,   20
How fares our gracious lady?
    Emil. As well as one so great and so forlorn
May hold together. On her frights and griefs,
Which never tender lady hath borne greater,
She is something before her time deliver'd.   25
    Paul. A boy?
    Emil.   A daughter, and a goodly babe,
Lusty and like to live. The Queen receives
Much comfort in't; says, "My poor prisoner,
I am innocent as you."
    Paul.   I dare be sworn.
These dangerous unsafe lunes i' th' King, beshrew
    them!   30
He must be told on't, and he shall. The office
Becomes a woman best; I'll take't upon me.
If I prove honey-mouth'd, let my tongue blister
And never to my red-look'd anger be
The trumpet any more. Pray you, Emilia,   35
Commend my best obedience to the Queen.
If she dares trust me with her little babe,
I'll show't the King and undertake to be
Her advocate to th' loud'st. We do not know
How he may soften at the sight o' th' child.   40
The silence often of pure innocence
Persuades when speaking fails.
    Emil.   Most worthy madam,
Your honour and your goodness is so evident
That your free undertaking cannot miss
A thriving issue. There is no lady living   45
So meet for this great errand. Please your lady-
    ship
To visit the next room, I'll presently

---

172. **overture:** publicity. 176. **touch'd conjecture:** i.e., conjecture reached to. 177. **approbation:** proof. 182. **wild:** rash.
185. **stuff'd sufficiency:** complete competence. 194. **free:** accessible. 198. **raise:** rouse.
    Sc. ii, 20. **colouring:** (1) dyeing, (2) excusing. 30. **lunes:** fits of lunacy. 47. **presently:** immediately.

Acquaint the Queen of your most noble offer;
Who but to-day hammer'd of this design,
But durst not tempt a minister of honour,   50
Lest she should be deni'd.
  Paul.   Tell her, Emilia,
I'll use that tongue I have. If wit flow from 't
As boldness from my bosom, let 't not be doubted
I shall do good.
  Emil.   Now be you blest for it!
I'll to the Queen. Please you, come something
        nearer.   55
  Gaol. Madam, if 't please the Queen to send the
        babe,
I know not what I shall incur to pass it,
Having no warrant.
  Paul.   You need not fear it, sir.
This child was prisoner to the womb and is
By law and process of great Nature thence   60
Freed and enfranchis'd, not a party to
The anger of the King nor guilty of,
If any be, the trespass of the Queen.
  Gaol. I do believe it.
  Paul. Do not you fear. Upon mine honour, I
Will stand betwixt you and danger. [*Exeunt.* 66

SCENE III. [*A room in Leontes' palace.*]

Enter LEONTES, ANTIGONUS, LORDS, *and* SERVANTS.

  Leon. Nor night nor day no rest. It is but weak-
        ness
To bear the matter thus; mere weakness. If
The cause were not in being, — part o' th' cause,
She the adultress; for the harlot king
Is quite beyond mine arm, out of the blank   5
And level of my brain, plot-proof; but she
I can hook to me: say that she were gone,
Given to the fire, a moiety of my rest
Might come to me again. Who's there?
  [*1.*] *Serv.*   My lord?
  Leon. How does the boy?
  [*1.*] *Serv.*   He took good rest to-night;
'Tis hop'd his sickness is discharg'd.   11
  Leon. To see his nobleness!
Conceiving the dishonour of his mother,
He straight declin'd, droop'd, took it deeply,
Fasten'd and fix'd the shame on 't in himself,
Threw off his spirit, his appetite, his sleep,   16
And downright languish'd. Leave me solely; go,
See how he fares. [*Exit Serv.*] Fie, fie! no thought
        of him;
The very thought of my revenges that way
Recoil upon me: in himself too mighty,   20
And in his parties, his alliance. Let him be
Until a time may serve; for present vengeance,

Take it on her. Camillo and Polixenes
Laugh at me, make their pastime at my sorrow.
They should not laugh if I could reach them,
        nor   25
Shall she within my power.

Enter PAULINA [*with a babe*].

  [*1.*] *Lord.*   You must not enter.
  Paul. Nay, rather, good my lords, be second to
        me.
Fear you his tyrannous passion more, alas,
Than the Queen's life? A gracious innocent soul,
More free than he is jealous.
  Ant.   That's enough.
  [*2.*] *Serv.* Madam, he hath not slept to-night;
        commanded   31
None should come at him.
  Paul.   Not so hot, good sir;
I come to bring him sleep. 'Tis such as you,
That creep like shadows by him and do sigh
At each his needless heavings, such as you   35
Nourish the case of his awaking. I
Do come with words as med'cinal as true,
Honest as either, to purge him of that humour
That presses him from sleep.
  Leon.   [What] noise there, ho?
  Paul. No noise, my lord; but needful conference
About some gossips for your Highness.
  Leon.   How!   41
Away with that audacious lady! Antigonus,
I charg'd thee that she should not come about me:
I knew she would.
  Ant.   I told her so, my lord,
On your displeasure's peril and on mine,   45
She should not visit you.
  Leon.   What, canst not rule her?
  Paul. From all dishonesty he can. In this,
Unless he take the course that you have done,
Commit me for committing honour, trust it,
He shall not rule me.
  Ant.   La you now, you hear.
When she will take the rein I let her run;   51
But she'll not stumble.
  Paul.   Good my liege, I come;
And, I beseech you, hear me, who professes
Myself your loyal servant, your physician,
Your most obedient counsellor, yet that dares   55
Less appear so in comforting your evils,
Than such as most seem yours. I say, I come
From your good queen.
  Leon.   Good queen!
  Paul.   Good queen, my lord,
Good queen; I say good queen;
And would by combat make her good, so were I   60

49. **hammer'd of**: deliberated. 52. **wit**: wisdom.
  Sc. iii, 5. **blank**: white spot in the centre of a target. 6. **level: aim**. 18. **him**: Polixenes. 39. **[What]** F₂. *Who* F₁.
41. **gossips**: sponsors in baptism. 49. **Commit**: imprison. 57. **yours**: your loyal servants.

A man, the worst about you.

Leon.   Force her hence.

Paul. Let him that makes but trifles of his eyes
First hand me.   On mine own accord I'll off,
But first I'll do my errand.   The good queen,
For she is good, hath brought you forth a daughter;
Here 'tis; commends it to your blessing.

                              [*Laying down the child.*]

Leon.   Out!   66
A mankind witch!   Hence with her, out o' door!
A most intelligencing bawd!

Paul.   Not so.
I am as ignorant in that as you
In so entitling me, and no less honest   70
Than you are mad; which is enough, I'll warrant,
As this world goes, to pass for honest.

Leon.   Traitors!
Will you not push her out?   Give her the bastard,
Thou dotard! thou art woman-tir'd, unroosted
By thy dame Partlet here.   Take up the bastard;
Take 't up, I say; give 't to thy crone.

Paul.   For ever
Unvenerable be thy hands, if thou   77
Tak'st up the Princess by that forced baseness
Which he has put upon 't!

Leon.   He dreads his wife.

Paul. So I would you did; then 'twere past all
        doubt   80
You'd call your children yours.

Leon.   A nest of traitors!

Ant. I am none, by this good light.

Paul.   Nor I, nor any
But one that's here, and that's himself; for he
The sacred honour of himself, his queen's,
His hopeful son's, his babe's, betrays to slander,   85
Whose sting is sharper than the sword's, and will
        not —
For, as the case now stands, it is a curse
He cannot be compell'd to 't — once remove
The root of his opinion, which is rotten
As ever oak or stone was sound.

Leon.   A callat   90
Of boundless tongue, who late hath beat her hus-
        band
And now baits me!   This brat is none of mine;
It is the issue of Polixenes.
Hence with it, and together with the dam
Commit them to the fire!

Paul.   It is yours;   95
And, might we lay th' old proverb to your charge,
So like you, 'tis the worse.   Behold, my lords,
Although the print be little, the whole matter
And copy of the father, — eye, nose, lip,
The trick of 's frown, his forehead, nay, the valley,

The pretty dimples of his chin and cheek,   101
His smiles,
The very mould and frame of hand, nail, finger;
And thou, good goddess Nature, which hast made it
So like to him that got it, if thou hast   105
The ordering of the mind too, 'mongst all colours
No yellow in 't, lest she suspect, as he does,
Her children not her husband's!

Leon.   A gross hag!
And, lozel, thou art worthy to be hang'd,   109
That wilt not stay her tongue.

Ant.   Hang all the husbands
That cannot do that feat, you'll leave yourself
Hardly one subject.

Leon.   Once more, take her hence.

Paul. A most unworthy and unnatural lord
Can do no more.

Leon.   I'll ha' thee burnt.

Paul.   I care not;
It is an heretic that makes the fire,   115
Not she which burns in 't.   I'll not call you tyrant;
But this most cruel usage of your queen,
Not able to produce more accusation
Than your own weak-hing'd fancy, something
        savours
Of tyranny, and will ignoble make you,   120
Yea, scandalous to the world.

Leon.   On your allegiance,
Out of the chamber with her!   Were I a tyrant,
Where were her life?   She durst not call me so,
If she did know me one.   Away with her!

Paul. I pray you, do not push me; I'll be gone.
Look to your babe, my lord; 'tis yours.   Jove send
        her   126
A better guiding spirit!   What needs these hands?
You, that are thus so tender o'er his follies,
Will never do him good, not one of you.
So, so; farewell; we are gone.   [*Exit.*   130

Leon. Thou, traitor, hast set on thy wife to this.
My child?   Away with 't!   Even thou, that hast
A heart so tender o'er it, take it hence
And see it instantly consum'd with fire;
Even thou and none but thou.   Take it up straight.
Within this hour bring me word 'tis done,   136
And by good testimony, or I'll seize thy life,
With what thou else call'st thine.   If thou refuse
And wilt encounter with my wrath, say so;
The bastard brains with these my proper hands
Shall I dash out.   Go, take it to the fire;   141
For thou set'st on thy wife.

Ant.   I did not, sir.
These lords, my noble fellows, if they please,
Can clear me in 't.

Lords.   We can.   My royal liege,

---

67. **mankind:** ferocious.   74. **woman-tir'd:** henpecked.   **unroosted:** driven off the perch.   75. **Partlet:** the hen in the fable of the cock and the fox.   78. **by...baseness:** i.e., under that false name of bastard.   90. **callat:** scold.   107. **yellow:** the color of jealousy.   109. **lozel:** scoundrel.   127. **What...hands:** i.e., you don't have to push me out.

He is not guilty of her coming hither.   145
  Leon. You're liars all.
  [*1.*] *Lord.* Beseech your Highness, give us better
    credit.
We have always truly serv'd you, and beseech
So to esteem of us; and on our knees we beg,
As recompense of our dear services   150
Past and to come, that you do change this pur-
    pose,
Which being so horrible, so bloody, must
Lead on to some foul issue. We all kneel.
  Leon. I am a feather for each wind that blows.
Shall I live on to see this bastard kneel   155
And call me father? Better burn it now
Than curse it then. But be it; let it live.
It shall not neither. You, sir, come you hither;
You that have been so tenderly officious
With Lady Margery, your midwife there,   160
To save this bastard's life, — for 'tis a bastard,
So sure as this beard's gray, — what will you ad-
    venture
To save this brat's life?
  Ant.   Anything, my lord,
That my ability may undergo
And nobleness impose; at least thus much: 165
I'll pawn the little blood which I have left
To save the innocent. Anything possible.
  Leon. It shall be possible. Swear by this sword
Thou wilt perform my bidding.
  Ant.   I will, my lord.
  Leon. Mark and perform it; see'st thou? for the
    fail   170
Of any point in 't shall not only be
Death to thyself but to thy lewd-tongu'd wife,
Whom for this time we pardon. We enjoin thee,
As thou art liege-man to us, that thou carry
This female bastard hence, and that thou bear it
To some remote and desert place quite out   176
Of our dominions, and that there thou leave it,
Without more mercy, to it own protection
And favour of the climate. As by strange fortune
It came to us, I do in justice charge thee,   180
On thy soul's peril and thy body's torture,
That thou commend it strangely to some place
Where chance may nurse or end it. Take it up.
  Ant. I swear to do this, though a present death
Had been more merciful. Come on, poor babe.   185
Some powerful spirit instruct the kites and ravens
To be thy nurses! Wolves and bears, they say,
Casting their savageness aside, have done
Like offices of pity. Sir, be prosperous
In more than this deed does require! And blessing
Against this cruelty fight on thy side,   191

Poor thing, condemn'd to loss!
                   [*Exit* [*with the babe*].
  Leon.   No, I'll not rear
Another's issue.

           Enter a SERVANT.

  Serv.   Please your Highness, posts
From those you sent to th' oracle are come
An hour since. Cleomenes and Dion,   195
Being well arriv'd from Delphos, are both landed,
Hasting to the court.
  [*1.*] *Lord.*   So please you, sir, their speed
Hath been beyond accompt.
  Leon.   Twenty-three days
They have been absent; 'tis good speed; foretells
The great Apollo suddenly will have   200
The truth of this appear. Prepare you, lords;
Summon a session, that we may arraign
Our most disloyal lady, for, as she hath
Been publicly accus'd, so shall she have
A just and open trial. While she lives   205
My heart will be a burden to me. Leave me,
And think upon my bidding.   [*Exeunt.*

ACT III

SCENE I. [*A street in a Sicilian town.*]

Enter CLEOMENES *and* DION.

  Cleo. The climate's delicate, the air most sweet,
Fertile the isle, the temple much surpassing
The common praise it bears.
  Dion.   I shall report,
For most it caught me, the celestial habits
(Methinks I so should term them), and the rev-
    erence   5
Of the grave wearers. O, the sacrifice!
How ceremonious, solemn, and unearthly
It was i' th' off'ring!
  Cleo.   But of all, the burst
And the ear-deaf'ning voice o' th' oracle,
Kin to Jove's thunder, so surpris'd my sense,   10
That I was nothing.
  Dion.   If th' event o' th' journey
Prove as successful to the Queen, — O be 't so! —
As it hath been to us rare, pleasant, speedy,
The time is worth the use on't.
  Cleo.   Great Apollo
Turn all to th' best! These proclamations,   15
So forcing faults upon Hermione,
I little like.
  Dion.   The violent carriage of it
Will clear or end the business. When the oracle,

---

162. **So … gray.** Leontes perhaps plucks the beard of Antigonus. Cf. I.ii.153–55 and note. 182. **strangely:** as an alien. 190. **does require:** deserves. 192. **loss:** destruction. 198. **accompt:** precedent. 200. **suddenly:** at once.

Act III, sc. i, 2. isle. Shakespeare repeats an error in his source, confusing Delos, the island sacred as Apollo's birthplace, with Delphi, the seat of his oracle. 4. **habits:** garments. 14. **worth … on't:** well spent.

Thus by Apollo's great divine seal'd up,
Shall the contents discover, something rare   20
Even then will rush to knowledge.   Go; fresh
    horses!
And gracious be the issue!   [*Exeunt.*

SCENE II.   [*Sicilia.   A place of justice.*]

Enter LEONTES, LORDS, *and* OFFICERS.

Leon. This sessions (to our great grief we pro-
    nounce)
Even pushes 'gainst our heart, — the party tried
The daughter of a king, our wife, and one
Of us too much belov'd.   Let us be clear'd
Of being tyrannous, since we so openly   5
Proceed in justice, which shall have due course
Even to the guilt or the purgation.
Produce the prisoner.

Off. It is his Highness' pleasure that the Queen
Appear in person here in court.   Silence!   10

[*Enter* HERMIONE (*as to her trial*); PAULINA *and*
LADIES *attending.*]

Leon. Read the indictment.

Off. [*Reads.*] "Hermione, Queen to the worthy
Leontes, King of Sicilia, thou art here accused and
arraigned of high treason, in committing adultery
with Polixenes, King of Bohemia, and conspiring   15
with Camillo to take away the life of our sovereign
lord the King, thy royal husband: the pretence
whereof being by circumstances partly laid open,
thou, Hermione, contrary to the faith and allegiance
of a true subject, didst counsel and aid them, for
their better safety, to fly away by night."   22

Her. Since what I am to say must be but that
Which contradicts my accusation, and
The testimony on my part no other   25
But what comes from myself, it shall scarce boot me
To say "Not guilty."   Mine integrity
Being counted falsehood, shall, as I express it,
Be so receiv'd.   But thus: — If powers divine
Behold our human actions, as they do,   30
I doubt not then but innocence shall make
False accusation blush, and tyranny
Tremble at patience.   You, my lord, best know,
[Who] least will seem to do so, my past life
Hath been as continent, as chaste, as true,   35
As I am now unhappy; which is more
Than history can pattern, though devis'd
And play'd to take spectators.   For behold me,
A fellow of the royal bed, which owe
A moiety of the throne, a great king's daughter,

The mother to a hopeful prince, here standing   41
To prate and talk for life and honour 'fore
Who please to come and hear.   For life, I prize it
As I weigh grief, which I would spare; for honour,
'Tis a derivative from me to mine,   45
And only that I stand for.   I appeal
To your own conscience, sir, before Polixenes
Came to your court, how I was in your grace,
How merited to be so; since he came,
With what encounter so uncurrent I   50
Have strain'd t' appear thus; if one jot beyond
The bound of honour, or in act or will
That way inclining, hard'ned be the hearts
Of all that hear me, and my near'st of kin
Cry fie upon my grave!

Leon.   I ne'er heard yet   55
That any of these bolder vices wanted
Less impudence to gainsay what they did
Than to perform it first.

Her.   That's true enough;
Though 'tis a saying, sir, not due to me.

Leon. You will not own it.

Her.   More than mistress of
Which comes to me in name of fault, I must not
At all acknowledge.   For Polixenes,   62
With whom I am accus'd, I do confess
I lov'd him as in honour he requir'd,
With such a kind of love as might become   65
A lady like me, with a love even such,
So and no other, as yourself commanded;
Which not t' have done I think had been in me
Both disobedience and ingratitude
To you and toward your friend, whose love had
    spoke,   70
Even since it could speak, from an infant, freely
That it was yours.   Now, for conspiracy,
I know not how it tastes, though it be dish'd
For me to try how.   All I know of it
Is that Camillo was an honest man;   75
And why he left your court, the gods themselves,
Wotting no more than I, are ignorant.

Leon. You knew of his departure, as you know
What you have underta'en to do in 's absence.

Her. Sir,   80
You speak a language that I understand not.
My life stands in the level of your dreams,
Which I'll lay down.

Leon.   Your actions are my dreams;
You had a bastard by Polixenes,
And I but dream'd it.   As you were past all
    shame, —   85
Those of your fact are so, — so past all truth,

19. **great divine:** high priest.
Sc. ii, 7. **purgation:** acquittal.   17. **pretence:** design.   34.
38. **take:** charm.   39. **owe:** own.   40. **moiety:** half.   43–44. **For . . . spare:** as for life, I esteem it as I do grief — a thing
I would do without.   50. **encounter:** behavior.   **uncurrent:** improper.   51. **strain'd . . . thus:** strained propriety, so that
I should be so brought to trial.   59. **due:** applicable.   60–61. **More . . . fault:** i.e., more than I am guilty of.   77. **Wotting:**
if they know.   82. **in . . . of:** within the range of, i.e., at the mercy of.   86. **fact:** crime.
[Who] (Rowe).   *Whom* F.   36. **which:** which unhappiness.

Which to deny concerns more than avails; for as
Thy brat hath been cast out, like to itself,
No father owning it, — which is, indeed,
More criminal in thee than it, — so thou   90
Shalt feel our justice, in whose easiest passage
Look for no less than death.
  Her.   Sir, spare your threats.
The bug which you would fright me with I seek;
To me can life be no commodity.
The crown and comfort of my life, your favour,   95
I do give lost; for I do feel it gone,
But know not how it went.   My second joy
And first-fruits of my body, from his presence
I am barr'd, like one infectious.   My third comfort,
Starr'd most unluckily, is from my breast,   100
The innocent milk in it most innocent mouth,
Hal'd out to murder; myself on every post
Proclaim'd a strumpet; with immodest hatred
The child-bed privilege deni'd, which longs
To women of all fashion; lastly, hurried   105
Here to this place, i' th' open air, before
I have got strength of limit.   Now, my liege,
Tell me what blessings I have here alive,
That I should fear to die?   Therefore proceed.
But yet hear this: mistake me not; no life,   110
I prize it not a straw; but for mine honour,
Which I would free, — if I shall be condemn'd
Upon surmises, all proofs sleeping else
But what your jealousies awake, I tell you
'Tis rigour and not law.   Your honours all,   115
I do refer me to the oracle:
Apollo be my judge!
  [*i.*] *Lord.*   This your request
Is altogether just; therefore bring forth,
And in Apollo's name, his oracle.
                      [*Exeunt certain Officers.*]
  Her. The Emperor of Russia was my father:
O that he were alive, and here beholding   121
His daughter's trial! that he did but see
The flatness of my misery, yet with eyes
Of pity, not revenge!

[*Re-enter* OFFICERS, *with* CLEOMENES *and* DION.]

  Off. You here shall swear upon this sword of
      justice,   125
That you, Cleomenes and Dion, have
Been both at Delphos, and from thence have
      brought
This seal'd-up oracle, by the hand deliver'd
Of great Apollo's priest, and that since then
You have not dar'd to break the holy seal   130
Nor read the secrets in't.

  Cleo. Dion.   All this we swear.
  Leon. Break up the seals and read.
  Off. [*Reads.*]   "Hermione is chaste; Polixenes
blameless; Camillo a true subject; Leontes a jealous
tyrant; his innocent babe truly begotten; and the
King shall live without an heir, if that which is lost
be not found."   137
  Lords. Now blessed be the great Apollo!
  Her.   Praised!
  Leon. Hast thou read truth?
  Off.   Ay, my lord; even so
As it is here set down.   140
  Leon. There is no truth at all i' th' oracle.
The sessions shall proceed; this is mere falsehood.

[*Enter a* SERVANT.]

  Serv. My lord the King, the King!
  Leon.   What is the business?
  Serv. O sir, I shall be hated to report it!
The Prince your son, with mere conceit and fear 145
Of the Queen's speed, is gone.
  Leon.   How! gone?
  Serv.   Is dead.
  Leon. Apollo's angry; and the heavens them-
      selves
Do strike at my injustice.   [*Hermione swoons.*]
      How now there!
  Paul. This news is mortal to the Queen.   Look
      down   149
And see what Death is doing.
  Leon.   Take her hence;
Her heart is but o'ercharg'd; she will recover.
I have too much believ'd mine own suspicion.
Beseech you, tenderly apply to her
Some remedies for life.
            [*Exeunt Paulina and Ladies, with Her-
              mione.*]
                      Apollo, pardon
My great profaneness 'gainst thine oracle!   155
I'll reconcile me to Polixenes,
New woo my queen, recall the good Camillo,
Whom I proclaim a man of truth, of mercy;
For, being transported by my jealousies
To bloody thoughts and to revenge, I chose   160
Camillo for the minister to poison
My friend Polixenes; which had been done,
But that the good mind of Camillo tardied
My swift command, though I with death and with
Reward did threaten and encourage him,   165
Not doing't and being done.   He, most humane
And fill'd with honour, to my kingly guest
Unclasp'd my practice, quit his fortunes here,

---

87. **concerns . . . avails:** is more important to you than effective with me.   88. **like to itself:** i.e., as a bastard should be.
93. **bug:** bogey.   94. **commodity:** profit.   100. **Starr'd . . . unluckily:** born under a most unlucky star.   103. **immodest:**
immoderate.   104. **longs:** belongs.   105. **fashion:** sorts.   107. **of limit:** from the due time of rest after childbirth.   110.
no life: i.e., I do not ask for life.   115. **rigour:** tyranny.   123. **flatness:** completeness.   145. **conceit:** idea.   146. **speed:**
fortune.   168. **Unclasp'd my practice:** disclosed my plot.

Which you knew great, and to the [certain] hazard
Of all incertainties himself commended,   170
No richer than his honour.   How he glisters
Through my [dark] rust!   And how his piety
Does my deeds make the blacker!

[*Re-enter* PAULINA.]

Paul.   Woe the while!
O, cut my lace, lest my heart, cracking it,
Break too!

[1.] *Lord.* What fit is this, good lady?   175

Paul. What studied torments, tyrant, hast for
me?
What wheels? racks? fires?   What flaying? boiling
In leads or oils?   What old or newer torture
Must I receive, whose every word deserves
To taste of thy most worst?   Thy tyranny   180
Together working with thy jealousies,
Fancies too weak for boys, too green and idle
For girls of nine, — O, think what they have done,
And then run mad indeed, stark mad! for all
Thy by-gone fooleries were but spices of it.   185
That thou betray'dst Polixenes, 'twas nothing;
That did but show thee of a fool, inconstant
And damnable ingrateful; nor was 't much
Thou wouldst have poison'd good Camillo's honour,
To have him kill a king; poor trespasses,   190
More monstrous standing by; whereof I reckon
The casting forth to crows thy baby-daughter
To be or none or little, though a devil
Would have shed water out of fire ere done't;
Nor is't directly laid to thee, the death   195
Of the young Prince, whose honourable thoughts,
Thoughts high for one so tender, cleft the heart
That could conceive a gross and foolish sire
Blemish'd his gracious dam; this is not, no,
Laid to thy answer: but the last, — O lords,   200
When I have said, cry "Woe!" — the Queen, the
Queen,
The sweet'st, dear'st creature's dead, and vengeance
for't
Not dropp'd down yet.

[1.] *Lord.*   The higher pow'rs forbid!

Paul. I say she's dead; I'll swear't.   If word nor
oath
Prevail not, go and see.   If you can bring   205
Tincture or lustre in her lip, her eye,
Heat outwardly or breath within, I'll serve you
As I would do the gods.   But, O thou tyrant!
Do not repent these things, for they are heavier
Than all thy woes can stir; therefore betake thee   210
To nothing but despair.   A thousand knees
Ten thousand years together, naked, fasting,

Upon a barren mountain, and still winter
In storm perpetual, could not move the gods
To look that way thou wert.

Leon.   Go on, go on;   215
Thou canst not speak too much.   I have deserv'd
All tongues to talk their bitt'rest.

[1.] *Lord.*   Say no more.
Howe'er the business goes, you have made fault
I' th' boldness of your speech.

Paul.   I am sorry for't.
All faults I make, when I shall come to know them,
I do repent.   Alas!   I have show'd too much
The rashness of a woman; he is touch'd   222
To th' noble heart.   What's gone and what's past
help
Should be past grief.   Do not receive affliction
At my petition; I beseech you, rather   225
Let me be punish'd, that have minded you
Of what you should forget.   Now, good my liege,
Sir, royal sir, forgive a foolish woman.
The love I bore your queen — lo, fool again! —
I'll speak of her no more, nor of your children;   230
I'll not remember you of my own lord,
Who is lost too.   Take your patience to you,
And I'll say nothing.

Leon.   Thou didst speak but well
When most the truth; which I receive much better
Than to be pitied of thee.   Prithee, bring me   235
To the dead bodies of my queen and son.
One grave shall be for both; upon them shall
The causes of their death appear, unto
Our shame perpetual.   Once a day I'll visit
The chapel where they lie, and tears shed there   240
Shall be my recreation.   So long as nature
Will bear up with this exercise, so long
I daily vow to use it.   Come and lead me
To these sorrows.   [*Exeunt.*

SCENE III. [*Bohemia.   A desert country near
the sea.*]

Enter ANTIGONUS, *with the* Babe, *and a* MARINER.

Ant. Thou art perfect then, our ship hath touch'd
upon
The deserts of Bohemia?

Mar.   Ay, my lord; and fear
We have landed in ill time: the skies look grimly
And threaten present blusters.   In my conscience,
The heavens with that we have in hand are angry   5
And frown upon 's.

Ant. Their sacred wills be done!   Go, get aboard;
Look to thy bark.   I'll not be long before
I call upon thee.

Mar. Make your best haste, and go not 10
Too far i' th' land; 'tis like to be loud weather.
Besides, this place is famous for the creatures
Of prey that keep upon 't.

Ant.   Go thou away;
I'll follow instantly.

Mar.   I am glad at heart
To be so rid o' th' business.   [*Exit.*

Ant.   Come, poor babe.
I have heard, but not believ'd, the spirits o' th'
  dead 16
May walk again. If such thing be, thy mother
Appear'd to me last night, for ne'er was dream
So like a waking. To me comes a creature,
Sometimes her head on one side, some another;
I never saw a vessel of like sorrow, 21
So fill'd and so becoming. In pure white robes,
Like very sanctity, she did approach
My cabin where I lay; thrice bow'd before me,
And, gasping to begin some speech, her eyes 25
Became two spouts; the fury spent, anon
Did this break from her: "Good Antigonus,
Since fate, against thy better disposition,
Hath made thy person for the thrower-out
Of my poor babe, according to thine oath, 30
Places remote enough are in Bohemia,
There weep and leave it crying; and, for the babe
Is counted lost for ever, Perdita,
I prithee, call 't. For this ungentle business,
Put on thee by my lord, thou ne'er shalt see 35
Thy wife Paulina more." And so, with shrieks,
She melted into air. Affrighted much,
I did in time collect myself and thought
This was so, and no slumber. Dreams are toys;
Yet for this once, yea, superstitiously, 40
I will be squar'd by this. I do believe
Hermione hath suffer'd death, and that
Apollo would, this being indeed the issue
Of King Polixenes, it should here be laid,
Either for life or death, upon the earth 45
Of its right father. Blossom, speed thee well!
There lie, and there thy character; there these,
Which may, if Fortune please, both breed thee,
  pretty,
  [*Laying down the babe, with a paper and a
  bundle.*]
And still rest thine. The storm begins. Poor wretch,
That for thy mother's fault art thus expos'd 50
To loss and what may follow! Weep I cannot,
But my heart bleeds; and most accurs'd am I
To be by oath enjoin'd to this. Farewell!
The day frowns more and more; thou 'rt like to have

A lullaby too rough. I never saw 55
The heavens so dim by day. — A savage clamour!
Well may I get aboard! This is the chase;
I am gone for ever. [*Exit, pursued by a bear.*

[*Enter a* SHEPHERD.]

Shep. I would there were no age between ten and
three-and-twenty, or that youth would sleep 60
out the rest; for there is nothing in the between but
getting wenches with child, wronging the ancientry,
stealing, fighting — [*Horns.*] Hark you now!
Would any but these boil'd brains of nineteen and
two-and-twenty hunt this weather? They have 65
scar'd away two of my best sheep, which I fear the
wolf will sooner find than the master. If anywhere
I have them, 'tis by the seaside, browsing of ivy.
Good luck, an 't be thy will! what have we here?
Mercy on 's, a barne; a very pretty barne! A 70
boy or a child, I wonder? A pretty one; a very
pretty one: sure, some scape. Though I am not
bookish, yet I can read waiting-gentlewoman in the
scape. This has been some stair-work, some trunk-
work, some behind-door-work; they were warmer 75
that got this than the poor thing is here. I'll take
it up for pity: yet I'll tarry till my son come; he
halloo'd but even now. Whoa, ho, hoa!

Enter CLOWN.

Clo. Hilloa, loa! 80

Shep. What, art so near? If thou'lt see a thing
to talk on when thou art dead and rotten, come
hither. What ail'st thou, man? 83

Clo. I have seen two such sights, by sea and by
land! But I am not to say it is a sea, for it is now
the sky; betwixt the firmament and it you cannot
thrust a bodkin's point.

Shep. Why, boy, how is it? 88

Clo. I would you did but see how it chafes, how
it rages, how it takes up the shore! But that 's
not to the point. O, the most piteous cry of the
poor souls! Sometimes to see 'em, and not to see
'em; now the ship boring the moon with her main-
mast, and anon swallowed with yeast and froth, as
you'd thrust a cork into a hogshead. And then 95
for the land-service, to see how the bear tore out his
shoulder-bone; how he cried to me for help and said
his name was Antigonus, a nobleman. But to make
an end of the ship, to see how the sea flap-dragon'd
it; but, first, how the poor souls roared, and the 100
sea mock'd them; and how the poor gentleman
roared and the bear mock'd him, both roaring
louder than the sea or weather. 104

22. **So ... becoming:** so complete (in sorrow) and yet so beautiful. 39. **toys:** trifles. 41. **squar'd:** ruled. 47. **character:** evidence of identity. **these:** the gold and jewels. 48–49. **both ... thine:** both pay for thy upbringing and still leave something for thine own. 57. **chase:** hunted animal. 58. s.d. It is quite likely that Shakespeare's company introduced a tame bear upon the stage. 62. **ancientry:** old people. 64. **boil'd:** hot. 70. **barne:** child. 71. **child:** girl. 74. **scape:** escapade. 99. **flap-dragon'd:** swallowed, as a flap-dragon (a raisin floating on burning brandy).

Shep. Name of mercy, when was this, boy?

Clo. Now, now; I have not wink'd since I saw these sights. The men are not yet cold under water, nor the bear half din'd on the gentleman. He's at it now. 109

Shep. Would I had been by, to have help'd the old man!

Clo. I would you had been by the ship side, to have help'd her; there your charity would have lack'd footing. 114

Shep. Heavy matters! heavy matters! But look thee here, boy. Now bless thyself; thou met'st with things dying, I with things new-born. Here's a sight for thee; look thee, a bearing-cloth for a squire's child! Look thee here; take up, take up, boy; open't. So, let's see. It was told me I should be rich by the fairies. This is some changeling; open't. What's within, boy? 123

Clo. You're a made old man; if the sins of your youth are forgiven you, you're well to live. Gold! all gold! 126

Shep. This is fairy gold, boy, and 'twill prove so. Up with't, keep it close. Home, home, the next way. We are lucky, boy; and to be so still requires nothing but secrecy. Let my sheep go. Come, good boy, the next way home. 131

Clo. Go you the next way with your findings. I'll go see if the bear be gone from the gentleman and how much he hath eaten. They are never curst but when they are hungry. If there be any of him left, I'll bury it. 136

Shep. That's a good deed. If thou mayest discern by that which is left of him what he is, fetch me to the sight of him.

Clo. Marry, will I; and you shall help to put him i' th' ground. 141

Shep. 'Tis a lucky day, boy, and we'll do good deeds on't. [*Exeunt.*

ACT IV

Scene I.

Enter TIME, *the* Chorus.

Time. I, that please some, try all, both joy and terror
Of good and bad, that makes and unfolds error,
Now take upon me, in the name of Time,
To use my wings. Impute it not a crime
To me or my swift passage, that I slide 5
O'er sixteen years and leave the growth untri'd
Of that wide gap, since it is in my power
To o'erthrow law and in one self-born hour

To plant and o'erwhelm custom. Let me pass
The same I am, ere ancient'st order was 10
Or what is now receiv'd. I witness to
The times that brought them in; so shall I do
To th' freshest things now reigning, and make stale
The glistering of this present, as my tale
Now seems to it. Your patience this allowing, 15
I turn my glass and give my scene such growing
As you had slept between. Leontes leaving,
Th' effects of his fond jealousies so grieving
That he shuts up himself, imagine me,
Gentle spectators, that I now may be 20
In fair Bohemia; and remember well,
I mention'd a son o' th' King's, which Florizel
I now name to you; and with speed so pace
To speak of Perdita, now grown in grace
Equal with wond'ring. What of her ensues 25
I list not prophesy; but let Time's news
Be known when 'tis brought forth. A shepherd's
　　daughter,
And what to her adheres, which follows after,
Is th' argument of Time. Of this allow,
If ever you have spent time worse ere now; 30
If never, yet that Time himself doth say
He wishes earnestly you never may. [*Exit.*

Scene II. [*Bohemia. The palace of Polixenes.*]

Enter POLIXENES *and* CAMILLO.

Pol. I pray thee, good Camillo, be no more importunate. 'Tis a sickness denying thee anything; a death to grant this. 3

Cam. It is fifteen years since I saw my country; though I have for the most part been aired abroad, I desire to lay my bones there. Besides, the penitent king, my master, hath sent for me; to whose feeling sorrows I might be some allay, or I o'erween to think so, which is another spur to my departure. 10

Pol. As thou lov'st me, Camillo, wipe not out the rest of thy services by leaving me now. The need I have of thee thine own goodness hath made. Better not to have had thee than thus to want thee. Thou, having made me businesses which none 15 without thee can sufficiently manage, must either stay to execute them thyself or take away with thee the very services thou hast done; which if I have not enough considered (as too much I cannot), to be more thankful to thee shall be my study, and 20 my profit therein the heaping friendships. Of that fatal country, Sicilia, prithee speak no more; whose very naming punishes me with the remembrance of that penitent, as thou call'st him, and reconciled 25

118. **bearing-cloth:** christening-robe. 128. **close:** secret. **next:** nearest. 135. **curst:** fierce.
Act IV, sc. i, 6. **untri'd:** unexamined. 8. **self-born:** self-same. 15. **seems:** seems stale. 25. **with wond'ring:** to the amazement it creates.
Sc. ii, 4. **fifteen.** Cf. IV.i.6. 21. **heaping friendships:** piling up of favors.

king, my brother; whose loss of his most precious
queen and children are even now to be afresh lamented.   Say to me, when saw'st thou the Prince
Florizel, my son?   Kings are no less unhappy, their
issue not being gracious, than they are in losing
them when they have approved their virtues.   32

Cam.   Sir, it is three days since I saw the Prince.
What his happier affairs may be, are to me unknown:
but I have missingly noted, he is of late much retired
from court and is less frequent to his princely exercises than formerly he hath appeared.   38

Pol.   I have considered so much, Camillo, and
with some care; so far that I have eyes under my
service which look upon his removedness; from
whom I have this intelligence, that he is seldom
from the house of a most homely shepherd, a man,
they say, that from very nothing, and beyond the
imagination of his neighbours, is grown into an unspeakable estate.   46

Cam.   I have heard, sir, of such a man, who hath
a daughter of most rare note.   The report of her is
extended more than can be thought to begin from
such a cottage.   50

Pol.   That's likewise part of my intelligence; but,
I fear, the angle that plucks our son thither.   Thou
shalt accompany us to the place; where we will, not
appearing what we are, have some question with the
shepherd; from whose simplicity I think it not   55
uneasy to get the cause of my son's resort thither.
Prithee, be my present partner in this business, and
lay aside the thoughts of Sicilia.

Cam.   I willingly obey your command.   60

Pol.   My best Camillo!   We must disguise ourselves.   [*Exeunt.*

SCENE III.   [*A road near the Shepherd's cottage.*]

Enter AUTOLYCUS [*very ragged*], *singing.*

"When daffodils begin to peer,
    With heigh! the doxy over the dale,
Why, then comes in the sweet o' the year;
    For the red blood reigns in the winter's pale.

"The white sheet bleaching on the hedge,   5
    With heigh! the sweet birds, O, how they sing!
Doth set my pugging tooth on edge;
    For a quart of ale is a dish for a king.

"The lark, that tirra-lyra chants,
    With heigh! [with heigh!] the thrush and the
        jay,   10
Are summer songs for me and my aunts,
    While we lie tumbling in the hay."

I have serv'd Prince Florizel, and in my time wore
three-pile; but now I am out of service.

"But shall I go mourn for that, my dear?   15
    The pale moon shines by night;
And when I wander here and there,
    I then do most go right.

"If tinkers may have leave to live,
    And bear the sow-skin budget,   20
Then my account I well may give,
    And in the stocks avouch it."

My traffic is sheets; when the kite builds, look to
lesser linen.   My father nam'd me Autolycus, who
being, as I am, litter'd under Mercury, was like-   25
wise a snapper-up of unconsidered trifles.   With die
and drab I purchas'd this caparison, and my revenue is the silly cheat.   Gallows and knock are too
powerful on the highway; beating and hanging are
terrors to me; for the life to come, I sleep out the
thought of it.   A prize! a prize!   32

Enter CLOWN.

Clo.   Let me see: every 'leven wether tods; every
tod yields pound and odd shilling; fifteen hundred
shorn, what comes the wool to?

Aut.   [*Aside.*] If the springe hold, the cock's
mine.   37

Clo.   I cannot do 't without compters.   Let me
see: what am I to buy for our sheep-shearing feast?
Three pound of sugar, five pound of currants, rice,
— what will this sister of mine do with rice?   40
But my father hath made her mistress of the feast,
and she lays it on.   She hath made me four-and-
twenty nosegays for the shearers, three-man song-
men all, and very good ones; but they are most of
them means and bases; but one Puritan amongst   45
them, and he sings psalms to hornpipes.   I must
have saffron to colour the warden pies; mace; dates
— none, that's out of my note; nutmegs, seven;
a race or two of ginger, but that I may beg;
four pounds of prunes, and as many of raisins
o' th' sun.   52

---

32. **approved:** proved.   35. **missingly:** with a sense of loss.   40–41. **eyes … removedness:** spies keeping watch upon his
absences.   52. **angle:** baited hook.

Sc. iii, 2. **doxy:** beggar's wench.   4. **in … pale:** in place of the winter's pale blood.   7. **pugging:** thievish.   10. **[with
heigh]** F₂.   Om. F₁.   11. **aunts:** wenches.   14. **three-pile:** costly velvet.   20. **budget:** wallet.   23–24. **My … linen:** i.e.,
watch your sheets when I'm around, as you guard your smaller pieces from the kite, who likes to steal them.   25. **under
Mercury.** The mythical Autolycus was the son of Mercury, god of thieves; Shakespeare's Autolycus was born when the
planet Mercury was rising.   26–27. **With … caparison:** through dice and women have I come into this outfit (i.e., rags).
28. **the … cheat:** from petty thieving.   33. **every … tods:** every eleven sheep yield a tod (28 lbs.) of wool.   36. **springe:**
snare.   **cock:** woodcock (a proverbially silly bird).   38. **compters:** counters, metal discs used for counting.   43. **three …
men:** singers of catches.   45. **means:** tenors.   46. **hornpipes:** dance tunes.   47. **saffron:** orange-red coloring.   **warden:**
made of winter pears.   49. **race:** root.   52. **o' th' sun:** sun-dried.

Aut. O that ever I was born!

[*Grovelling on the ground.*]

Clo. I' th' name of me —

Aut. O, help me, help me! Pluck but off these
rags, and then, death, death!   56

Clo. Alack, poor soul! thou hast need of more
rags to lay on thee, rather than have these off.

Aut. O sir, the loathsomeness of them offend me
more than the stripes I have received, which are
mighty ones and millions.   61

Clo. Alas, poor man! a million of beating may
come to a great matter.

Aut. I am robb'd, sir, and beaten; my money
and apparel ta'en from me, and these detestable
things put upon me.   66

Clo. What, by a horseman or a footman?

Aut. A footman, sweet sir, a footman.

Clo. Indeed, he should be a footman by the garments he has left with thee. If this be a horseman's
coat, it hath seen very hot service. Lend me thy
hand, I'll help thee. Come, lend me thy hand.   73

Aut. O, good sir, tenderly, O!

Clo. Alas, poor soul!

Aut. O, good sir, softly, good sir! I fear, sir, my
shoulder-blade is out.   77

Clo. How now! canst stand?

Aut. Softly, dear sir; [*picking his pocket*] good sir,
softly. You ha' done me a charitable office.

Clo. Dost lack any money? I have a little
money for thee.   83

Aut. No, good sweet sir; no, I beseech you, sir.
I have a kinsman not past three quarters of a mile
hence, unto whom I was going. I shall there have
money, or anything I want. Offer me no money, I
pray you; that kills my heart.

Clo. What manner of fellow was he that robb'd
you?   90

Aut. A fellow, sir, that I have known to go about
with troll-my-dames. I knew him once a servant
of the Prince. I cannot tell, good sir, for which of
his virtues it was, but he was certainly whipp'd out
of the court.   95

Clo. His vices, you would say; there's no virtue
whipp'd out of the court. They cherish it to make
it stay there; and yet it will no more but abide.   99

Aut. Vices, I would say, sir. I know this man
well. He hath been since an ape-bearer; then a
process-server, a bailiff; then he compass'd a motion of the Prodigal Son, and married a tinker's wife
within a mile where my land and living lies;
and, having flown over many knavish profes-   105

sions, he settled only in rogue. Some call him
Autolycus.

Clo. Out upon him! prig, for my life, prig. He
haunts wakes, fairs, and bear-baitings.

Aut. Very true, sir; he, sir, he. That's the rogue
that put me into this apparel.   111

Clo. Not a more cowardly rogue in all Bohemia.
If you had but look'd big and spit at him, he'd have
run.

Aut. I must confess to you, sir, I am no fighter.
I am false of heart that way; and that he knew, I
warrant him.   117

Clo. How do you now?

Aut. Sweet sir, much better than I was; I can
stand and walk. I will even take my leave of you,
and pace softly towards my kinsman's.   121

Clo. Shall I bring thee on the way?

Aut. No, good-fac'd sir; no, sweet sir.

Clo. Then fare thee well. I must go buy spices
for our sheep-shearing.   [*Exit.*   125

Aut. Prosper you, sweet sir! — Your purse is not
hot enough to purchase your spice. I'll be with
you at your sheep-shearing too. If I make not this
cheat bring out another and the shearers prove
sheep, let me be unroll'd and my name put in the
book of virtue!   131

(*Sings.*) "Jog on, jog on, the foot-path way,
          And merrily hent the stile-a;
     A merry heart goes all the day
          Your sad tires in a mile-a."   [*Exit.*   135

SCENE IV. [*Bohemia.   The Shepherd's cottage.*]

Enter FLORIZEL *and* PERDITA.

Flo. These your unusual weeds to each part of
          you
[Do] give a life; no shepherdess, but Flora,
Peering in April's front. This your sheep-shearing
Is as a meeting of the petty gods,
And you the queen on't.

Per.   Sir, my gracious lord,
To chide at your extremes it not becomes me.   6
O, pardon, that I name them! Your high self,
The gracious mark o' th' land, you have obscur'd
With a swain's wearing, and me, poor lowly maid,
Most goddess-like prank'd up. But that our feasts
In every mess have folly, and the feeders   11
Digest [it] with a custom, I should blush
To see you so attir'd; sworn, I think,
To show myself a glass.

Flo.   I bless the time

92. **troll-my-dames:** a game, something like bagatelle.   99. **abide:** stay briefly.   101. **ape-bearer:** man with a trained
monkey.   102. **compass'd a motion:** obtained a puppet show.   108. **prig:** thief.   130. **unroll'd:** struck from the roll of
thieves.   133. **hent:** take, leap over.

Sc. iv, 1. **weeds:** garments.   2. **[Do]** (Theobald).   *Do's* F.   3. **Peering...front:** peeping in early April.   8. **mark:**
pattern.   11. **mess:** group.   12. **Digest...custom:** accept from habit.   **[it]** F2.   Om. F1.   13–14. **sworn...glass:** bound
to see myself as in a mirror.   Many edd. follow Theobald in reading *swoon.*

When my good falcon made her flight across   15
Thy father's ground.
    Per.   Now Jove afford you cause!
To me the difference forges dread; your greatness
Hath not been us'd to fear.   Even now I tremble
To think your father, by some accident,
Should pass this way as you did. O, the Fates!   20
How would he look to see his work, so noble,
Vilely bound up? What would he say? Or how
Should I, in these my borrowed flaunts, behold
The sternness of his presence?
    Flo.   Apprehend
Nothing but jollity. The gods themselves,   25
Humbling their deities to love, have taken
The shapes of beasts upon them. Jupiter
Became a bull and bellow'd; the green Neptune
A ram and bleated; and the fire-rob'd god,
Golden Apollo, a poor humble swain,   30
As I seem now. Their transformations
Were never for a piece of beauty rarer,
Nor in a way so chaste, since my desires
Run not before mine honour, nor my lusts
Burn hotter than my faith.
    Per.   O, but, sir,   35
Your resolution cannot hold when 'tis
Oppos'd, as it must be, by th' power of the King.
One of these two must be necessities,
Which then will speak that you must change this
       purpose,
Or I my life.
    Flo.   Thou dearest Perdita,   40
With these forc'd thoughts, I prithee, darken not
The mirth o' th' feast. Or I'll be thine, my fair,
Or not my father's; for I cannot be
Mine own, nor anything to any, if
I be not thine. To this I am most constant,   45
Though destiny say no. Be merry, gentle!
Strangle such thoughts as these with anything
That you behold the while. Your guests are com-
       ing.
Lift up your countenance, as it were the day
Of celebration of that nuptial which   50
We two have sworn shall come.
    Per.   O lady Fortune,
Stand you auspicious!
    Flo.   See, your guests approach.
Address yourself to entertain them sprightly,
And let's be red with mirth.

[*Enter* SHEPHERD, CLOWN, MOPSA, DORCAS, *and
    others, with* POLIXENES *and* CAMILLO *disguised.*]
    Shep. Fie, daughter! when my old wife liv'd,
       upon   55

This day she was both pantler, butler, cook,
Both dame and servant; welcom'd all, serv'd all;
Would sing her song and dance her turn; now here,
At upper end o' th' table, now i' th' middle;
On his shoulder, and his; her face o' fire   60
With labour; and the thing she took to quench it,
She would to each one sip. You are retir'd,
As if you were a feasted one and not
The hostess of the meeting. Pray you, bid   64
These unknown friends to 's welcome, for it is
A way to make us better friends, more known.
Come, quench your blushes, and present yourself
That which you are, mistress o' th' feast. Come on,
And bid us welcome to your sheep-shearing,
As your good flock shall prosper.
    Per.   [*To Pol.*] Sir, welcome.
It is my father's will I should take on me   71
The hostess-ship o' th' day. [*To Cam*] You're
       welcome, sir.
Give me those flowers there, Dorcas. Reverend sirs,
For you there's rosemary and rue; these keep
Seeming and savour all the winter long.   75
Grace and remembrance be to you both,
And, welcome to our shearing!
    Pol.   Shepherdess, —
A fair one are you — well you fit our ages
With flowers of winter.
    Per.   Sir, the year growing ancient,
Not yet on summer's death, nor on the birth   80
Of trembling winter, the fairest flowers o' th' season
Are our carnations and streak'd [gillyflowers],
Which some call Nature's bastards. Of that kind
Our rustic garden 's barren; and I care not   84
To get slips of them.
    Pol.   Wherefore, gentle maiden,
Do you neglect them?
    Per.   For I have heard it said
There is an art which in their piedness shares
With great creating Nature.
    Pol.   Say there be;
Yet Nature is made better by no mean
But Nature makes that mean; so, over that art   90
Which you say adds to Nature, is an art
That Nature makes. You see, sweet maid, we
       marry
A gentler scion to the wildest stock,
And make conceive a bark of baser kind
By bud of nobler race. This is an art   95
Which does mend Nature, change it rather, but
The art itself is Nature.
    Per.   So it is.
    Pol. Then make [your] garden rich in gilly-
       flowers,

---

17. **difference**: i.e., between our ranks. 23. **flaunts**: finery. 33. **Nor ... chaste.** The reference is to "transformations," not to "piece." 41. **forc'd**: far-fetched. 56. **pantler**: pantry servant. 82. **[gillyflowers]** (Rowe); clove-scented pinks. The name was also applied to wallflowers and stocks. *Gilly-vors* F. 83. **Nature's bastards.** Because grown artificially. 98. **[your]** F₂. *you* F₁.

And do not call them bastards.
    Per.   I'll not put
The dibble in earth to set one slip of them;   100
No more than were I painted I would wish
This youth should say 'twere well, and only there-
    fore
Desire to breed by me.   Here's flowers for you;
Hot lavender, mints, savory, marjoram;
The marigold, that goes to bed wi' th' sun   105
And with him rises weeping.   These are flowers
Of middle summer, and I think they are given
To men of middle age.   You're very welcome.
    Cam.   I should leave grazing, were I of your flock,
And only live by gazing.
    Per.   Out, alas!   110
You'd be so lean, that blasts of January
Would blow you through and through.   Now, my
    fair'st friend,
I would I had some flowers o' th' spring that might
Become your time of day; and yours, and yours,
That wear upon your virgin branches yet   115
Your maidenheads growing.   O Proserpina,
For the flowers now, that frighted thou let'st fall
From Dis's waggon! daffodils,
That come before the swallow dares, and take
The winds of March with beauty; violets dim,
But sweeter than the lids of Juno's eyes   121
Or Cytherea's breath; pale primroses,
That die unmarried, ere they can behold
Bright Phœbus in his strength — a malady
Most incident to maids; bold oxlips and   125
The crown imperial; lilies of all kinds,
The flower-de-luce being one!   O, these I lack,
To make you garlands of, and my sweet friend,
To strew him o'er and o'er!
    Flo.   What, like a corse?
    Per.   No, like a bank for love to lie and play on;
Not like a corse; or if, not to be buried,   131
But quick and in mine arms.   Come, take your
    flowers.
Methinks I play as I have seen them do
In Whitsun pastorals.   Sure this robe of mine
Does change my disposition.
    Flo.   What you do   135
Still betters what is done.   When you speak, sweet,
I'd have you do it ever; when you sing,
I'd have you buy and sell so, so give alms,
Pray so; and for the ord'ring your affairs,
To sing them too.   When you do dance, I wish you
A wave o' th' sea, that you might ever do   141
Nothing but that; move still, still so,
And own no other function.   Each your doing,
So singular in each particular,

Crowns what you are doing in the present deeds,   145
That all your acts are queens.
    Per.   O Doricles,
Your praises are too large.   But that your youth,
And the true blood which peeps [so] fairly through't,
Do plainly give you out an unstain'd shepherd,
With wisdom I might fear, my Doricles,   150
You woo'd me the false way.
    Flo.   I think you have
As little skill to fear as I have purpose
To put you to 't.   But come; our dance, I pray.
Your hand, my Perdita.   So turtles pair,
That never mean to part.
    Per.   I'll swear for 'em.   155
    Pol.   This is the prettiest low-born lass that ever
Ran on the green-sward.   Nothing she does or
    seems
But smacks of something greater than herself,
Too noble for this place.
    Cam.   He tells her something
That makes her blood look out.   Good sooth, she is
The queen of curds and cream.
    Clo.   Come on, strike up!   161
    Dor.   Mopsa must be your mistress; marry, garlic,
To mend her kissing with!
    Mop.   Now, in good time!
    Clo.   Not a word, a word; we stand upon our
    manners.
Come, strike up!   165
    [*Music.*] *Here a dance of Shepherds and*
        Shepherdesses.
    Pol.   Pray, good shepherd, what fair swain is this
Which dances with your daughter?
    Shep.   They call him Doricles; and boasts himself
To have a worthy feeding; but I have it
Upon his own report, and I believe it.   170
He looks like sooth.   He says he loves my daughter.
I think so too; for never gaz'd the moon
Upon the water as he'll stand and read,
As 'twere, my daughter's eyes; and, to be plain,
I think there is not half a kiss to choose   175
Who loves another best.
    Pol.   She dances featly.
    Shep.   So she does anything, though I report it,
That should be silent.   If young Doricles
Do light upon her, she shall bring him that
Which he not dreams of.   180

           Enter a SERVANT.

    Serv.   O master, if you did but hear the pedlar at
the door, you would never dance again after a tabor
and pipe; no, the bagpipe could not move you.   He
sings several tunes faster than you'll tell money.

---

100. **dibble:** tool for making holes.   104. **Hot:** fragrant.   126. **crown imperial:** fritillary.   127. **flower-de-luce:** iris.
132. **quick:** alive.   134. **Whitsun pastorals:** morris dances at Whitsuntide.   144. **singular:** distinctly yours.   148. **[so]**
(Capell). Om. F.   152. **skill:** reason.   154. **turtles:** turtle-doves.   163. **in…time.** An expression of indignation.   169.
feeding: pasture land.   171. **like sooth:** honest.   176. **featly:** gracefully.   182. **tabor:** small drum.   184. **tell:** count.

He utters them as he had eaten ballads and all men's ears grew to his tunes. 186

Clo. He could never come better; he shall come in. I love a ballad but even too well, if it be doleful matter merrily set down, or a very pleasant thing indeed and sung lamentably. 190

Serv. He hath songs for man or woman, of all sizes; no milliner can so fit his customers with gloves. He has the prettiest love-songs for maids; so without bawdry, which is strange; with such delicate burdens of dildos and fadings, "jump 195 her and thump her;" and where some stretch-mouth'd rascal would, as it were, mean mischief and break a foul gap into the matter, he makes the maid to answer, "Whoop, do me no harm, good man;" puts him off, slights him, with "Whoop, do me no harm, good man." 201

Pol. This is a brave fellow.

Clo. Believe me, thou talkest of an admirable conceited fellow. Has he any unbraided wares? 204

Serv. He hath ribbons of all the colours i' th' rainbow; points more than all the lawyers in Bohemia can learnedly handle, though they come to him by th' gross; inkles, caddises, cambrics, lawns. Why, he sings 'em over as they were gods or goddesses; you would think a smock were a she-angel, he so chants to the sleeve-hand and the work about the square on't. 212

Clo. Prithee bring him in; and let him approach singing.

Per. Forewarn him that he use no scurrilous words in 's tunes. [*Exit Servant.*] 216

Clo. You have of these pedlars, that have more in them than you'd think, sister.

Per. Ay, good brother, or go about to think.

Enter AUTOLYCUS, *singing.*

"Lawn as white as driven snow; 220
Cypress black as e'er was crow;
Gloves as sweet as damask roses;
Masks for faces and for noses;
Bugle bracelet, necklace amber,
Perfume for a lady's chamber; 225
Golden quoifs and stomachers
For my lads to give their dears;
Pins and poking-sticks of steel;
What maids lack from head to heel.
Come buy of me, come; come buy, come buy; 230
Buy, lads, or else your lasses cry.
Come buy."

Clo. If I were not in love with Mopsa, thou shouldst take no money of me; but being enthrall'd as I am, it will also be the bondage of certain ribbons and gloves. 236

Mop. I was promis'd them against the feast; but they come not too late now.

Dor. He hath promis'd you more than that, or there be liars. 240

Mop. He hath paid you all he promis'd you. May be he has paid you more, which will shame you to give him again. 243

Clo. Is there no manners left among maids? Will they wear their plackets where they should bear their faces? Is there not milking-time, when you are going to bed, or kiln-hole, to whistle off these secrets, but you must be tittle-tattling before all our guests? 'Tis well they are whisp'ring. Clamour your tongues, and not a word more. 251

Mop. I have done. Come, you promis'd me a tawdry-lace and a pair of sweet gloves.

Clo. Have I not told thee how I was cozen'd by the way and lost all my money? 255

Aut. And indeed, sir, there are cozeners abroad; therefore it behoves men to be wary.

Clo. Fear not thou, man, thou shalt lose nothing here. 259

Aut. I hope so, sir; for I have about me many parcels of charge.

Clo. What hast here? Ballads?

Mop. Pray now, buy some. I love a ballad in print, o' life, for then we are sure they are true. 264

Aut. Here's one to a very doleful tune, how a usurer's wife was brought to bed of twenty money-bags at a burden, and how she long'd to eat adders' heads and toads carbonado'd.

Mop. Is it true, think you?

Aut. Very true, and but a month old. 270

Dor. Bless me from marrying a usurer!

Aut. Here's the midwife's name to't, one Mistress Tale-porter, and five or six honest wives that were present. Why should I carry lies abroad? 275

Mop. Pray you now, buy it.

Clo. Come on, lay it by, and let's first see moe ballads. We'll buy the other things anon. 278

Aut. Here's another ballad, of a fish that appeared upon the coast on Wednesday the fourscore of April, forty thousand fathom above water, and sung this ballad against the hard hearts of maids. It was thought she was a woman and was turned into a cold fish for she would not exchange

---

195. **dildos and fadings:** words familiar in ballad refrains. 196. **stretch-mouth'd:** foul-mouthed. 198. **break... matter:** thrust in a lewd phrase. 204. **conceited:** clever. **unbraided:** fresh. 206. **points:** (1) metal-tagged laces, (2) arguments. 208. **inkles:** linen tapes. **caddises:** worsted tapes for garters. 211. **sleeve-hand:** wrist-band. 212. **square:** yoke. 217. **You have:** there are some. 219. **go about:** intend. 221. **Cypress:** crepe. 224. **Bugle:** black-beaded. 226. **quoifs:** caps. 228. **poking-sticks:** metal rods for adjusting the plaits of ruffs. 237. **against:** for. 245. **plackets:** petticoats. 247. **kiln-hole:** furnace-room of a kiln. 251. **Clamour:** silence. 253. **tawdry-lace:** a silk neckerchief (named for St. Audrey). 261. **charge:** value. 268. **carbonado'd:** cut up for broiling.

flesh with one that lov'd her. The ballad is very pitiful and as true. 286

Dor. Is it true too, think you?

Aut. Five justices' hands at it, and witnesses more than my pack will hold.

Clo. Lay it by too. Another.

Aut. This is a merry ballad, but a very pretty one. 292

Mop. Let's have some merry ones.

Aut. Why, this is a passing merry one and goes to the tune of "Two maids wooing a man." There's scarce a maid westward but she sings it. 'Tis in request, I can tell you. 297

Mop. We can both sing it. If thou'lt bear a part, thou shalt hear. 'Tis in three parts.

Dor. We had the tune on't a month ago. 300

Aut. I can bear my part; you must know 'tis my occupation. Have at it with you.

SONG.

A. Get you hence, for I must go
    Where it fits not you to know.
D. Whither? *M.* O, whither? *D.* Whither?
M. It becomes thy oath full well, 306
    Thou to me thy secrets tell.
D. Me too, let me go thither.
M. Or thou goest to th' grange or mill.
D. If to either, thou dost ill. 310
A. Neither. *D.* What, neither? *A.* Neither.
D. Thou hast sworn my love to be.
M. Thou hast sworn it more to me.
Then whither goest? Say, whither? 314

Clo. We'll have this song out anon by ourselves. My father and the gentlemen are in sad talk, and we'll not trouble them. Come, bring away thy pack after me. Wenches, I'll buy for you both. Pedlar, let's have the first choice. Follow me, girls. 320
[*Exit with Dorcas and Mopsa.*]

Aut. And you shall pay well for 'em.

"Will you buy any tape,
    Or lace for your cape,
My dainty duck, my dear-a?
    Any silk, any thread,
    Any toys for your head, 325
Of the new'st and fin'st, fin'st wear-a?
    Come to the pedlar;
    Money's a meddler
That doth utter all men's ware-a." [*Exit.* 330

[*Re-enter* SERVANT.]

Serv. Master, there is three carters, three shepherds, three neat-herds, three swine-herds, that

have made themselves all men of hair. They call themselves Saltiers; and they have a dance which the wenches say is a gallimaufry of gambols, 335 because they are not in't; but they themselves are o' th' mind, if it be not too rough for some that know little but bowling, it will please plentifully. 339

Shep. Away! we'll none on't. Here has been too much homely foolery already. I know, sir, we weary you.

Pol. You weary those that refresh us. Pray, let's see these four threes of herdsmen. 344

Serv. One three of them, by their own report, sir, hath danc'd before the King; and not the worst of the three but jumps twelve foot and a half by the squire.

Shep. Leave your prating. Since these good men are pleas'd, let them come in; but quickly now. 351

Serv. Why, they stay at door, sir. [*Exit.*]

Here a dance of twelve Satyrs.

Pol. O, father, you'll know more of that hereafter.

[*To Cam.*] Is it not too far gone? 'Tis time to part them.

He's simple and tells much. [*To Flor.*] How now, fair shepherd! 355
Your heart is full of something that does take
Your mind from feasting. Sooth, when I was young
And handed love as you do, I was wont
To load my she with knacks. I would have ransack'd
The pedlar's silken treasury and have pour'd it 360
To her acceptance; you have let him go
And nothing marted with him. If your lass
Interpretation should abuse and call this
Your lack of love or bounty, you were straited
For a reply; at least if you make a care 365
Of happy holding her.

Flo.   Old sir, I know
She prizes not such trifles as these are.
The gifts she looks from me are pack'd and lock'd
Up in my heart; which I have given already,
But not deliver'd. O, hear me breathe my life 370
Before this ancient sir, [who], it should seem,
Hath sometime lov'd! I take thy hand, this hand,
As soft as dove's down and as white as it,
Or Ethiopian's tooth, or the fann'd snow that's
    bolted 374
By the northern blasts twice o'er.

Pol.   What follows this?
How prettily the young swain seems to wash
The hand was fair before! I have put you out.
But to your protestation; let me hear
What you profess.

Flo.   Do, and be witness to 't.
Pol. And this my neighbour too?
Flo.   And he, and more
Than he, and men, the earth, the heavens, and
    all;   381
That, were I crown'd the most imperial monarch,
Thereof most worthy, were I the fairest youth
That ever made eye swerve, had force and knowl-
        edge
More than was ever man's, I would not prize them
Without her love; for her employ them all;   386
Commend them and condemn them to her service
Or to their own perdition.
Pol.   Fairly offer'd.
Cam. This shows a sound affection.
Shep.   But, my daughter,
Say you the like to him?
Per.   I cannot speak   390
So well, nothing so well; no, nor mean better.
By th' pattern of mine own thoughts I cut out
The purity of his.
Shep.   Take hands, a bargain!
And, friends unknown, you shall bear witness to 't:
I give my daughter to him, and will make   395
Her portion equal his.
Flo.   O, that must be
I' th' virtue of your daughter. One being dead,
I shall have more than you can dream of yet.
Enough then for your wonder. But, come on,
Contract us 'fore these witnesses.
Shep.   Come, your hand;   400
And, daughter, yours.
Pol.   Soft, swain, a while, beseech you.
Have you a father?
Flo.   I have; but what of him?
Pol. Knows he of this?
Flo.   He neither does nor shall.
Pol. Methinks a father
Is at the nuptial of his son a guest   405
That best becomes the table. Pray you once more,
Is not your father grown incapable
Of reasonable affairs? Is he not stupid
With age and alt'ring rheums? Can he speak?
    hear?
Know man from man? dispute his own estate?   410
Lies he not bed-rid? and again does nothing
But what he did being childish?
Flo.   No, good sir;
He has his health, and ampler strength indeed
Than most have of his age.
Pol.   By my white beard,
You offer him, if this be so, a wrong   415
Something unfilial. Reason my son

Should choose himself a wife, but as good reason
The father, all whose joy is nothing else
But fair posterity, should hold some counsel
In such a business.
Flo.   I yield all this;   420
But for some other reasons, my grave sir,
Which 'tis not fit you know, I not acquaint
My father of this business.
Pol.   Let him know 't.
Flo. He shall not.
Pol.   Prithee, let him.
Flo.   No, he must not.
Shep. Let him, my son. He shall not need to
    grieve   425
At knowing of thy choice.
Flo.   Come, come, he must not.
Mark our contract.
Pol.   Mark your divorce, young sir,
                               [*Discovering himself.*]
Whom son I dare not call. Thou art too base
To be acknowledg'd. Thou, a sceptre's heir,
That thus affects a sheep-hook! Thou old traitor,
I am sorry that by hanging thee I can   431
But shorten thy life one week. And thou, fresh
    piece
Of excellent witchcraft, [who] of force must know
The royal fool thou cop'st with, —
Shep.   O, my heart!
Pol. I'll have thy beauty scratch'd with briers
    and made   435
More homely than thy state. For thee, fond boy,
If I may ever know thou dost but sigh
That thou no more shalt see this knack, as never
I mean thou shalt, we'll bar thee from succession,
Not hold thee of our blood, no, not our kin,   440
Far than Deucalion off. Mark thou my words.
Follow us to the court. Thou, churl, for this time,
Though full of our displeasure, yet we free thee
From the dead blow of it. And you, enchant-
    ment, —
Worthy enough a herdsman, yea, him too,   445
That makes himself, but for our honour therein,
Unworthy thee, — if ever henceforth thou
These rural latches to his entrance open,
Or hoop his body more with thy embraces,
I will devise a death as cruel for thee   450
As thou art tender to 't.   [*Exit.*
Per.   Even here undone!
I was not much afeard; for once or twice
I was about to speak, and tell him plainly
The self-same sun that shines upon his court
Hides not his visage from our cottage, but   455
Looks on alike. Will 't please you, sir, be gone?

384. **made eye swerve**: attracted notice. 409. **alt'ring rheums**: weakening colds. 410. **dispute**: discuss. 416. **Reason**: it is reasonable. 433. **[who]** *whom* F₁. 434. **cop'st**: dealest. 436. **fond**: foolish. 438. **That**: because. **shalt** (Rowe). *shalt ne'er* F. **knack**: toy. 441. **Far**: farther (*Farre* F). **Deucalion**: the Noah of Greek mythology.
445-47. **him ... thee**: i.e., worthy also of him, who (the question of our royalty aside) makes himself unworthy of thee.

I told you what would come of this.   Beseech you,
Of your own state take care.   This dream of mine,—
Being now awake, I'll queen it no inch farther,
But milk my ewes and weep.

Cam.   Why, how now, father! 460
Speak ere thou diest.

Shep.   I cannot speak, nor think,
Nor dare to know that which I know.   O sir!
You have undone a man of fourscore three,
That thought to fill his grave in quiet, yea,
To die upon the bed my father died,   465
To lie close by his honest bones; but now
Some hangman must put on my shroud and lay me
Where no priest shovels in dust. — O cursed
    wretch,
That knew'st this was the Prince, and wouldst
    adventure
To mingle faith with him!   Undone! undone!
If I might die within this hour, I have liv'd   471
To die when I desire.   [*Exit.*

Flo.   Why look you so upon me?
I am but sorry, not afeard; delay'd,
But nothing alt'red.   What I was, I am;
More straining on for plucking back, not following
My leash unwillingly.

Cam.   Gracious my lord,   476
You know your father's temper.   At this time
He will allow no speech, which I do guess
You do not purpose to him; and as hardly
Will he endure your sight as yet, I fear.   480
Then, till the fury of his Highness settle,
Come not before him.

Flo.   I not purpose it.
I think, Camillo?

Cam.   Even he, my lord.

Per. How often have I told you 'twould be thus!
How often said, my dignity would last   485
But till 'twere known!

Flo.   It cannot fail but by
The violation of my faith; and then
Let Nature crush the sides o' th' earth together
And mar the seeds within!   Lift up thy looks.
From my succession wipe me, father; I   490
Am heir to my affection.

Cam.   Be advis'd.

Flo. I am, and by my fancy.   If my reason
Will thereto be obedient, I have reason;
If not, my senses, better pleas'd with madness,
Do bid it welcome.

Cam.   This is desperate, sir.   495

Flo. So call it, but it does fulfil my vow;
I needs must think it honesty.   Camillo,
Not for Bohemia, nor the pomp that may
Be thereat gleaned, for all the sun sees or
The close earth wombs or the profound seas hides

In unknown fathoms, will I break my oath   501
To this my fair belov'd; therefore, I pray you,
As you have ever been my father's honour'd friend,
When he shall miss me, — as, in faith, I mean not
To see him any more, — cast your good counsels
Upon his passion; let myself and Fortune   506
Tug for the time to come.   This you may know
And so deliver: I am put to sea
With her who here I cannot hold on shore;
And most opportune to [our] need I have   510
A vessel rides fast by, but not prepar'd
For this design.   What course I mean to hold
Shall nothing benefit your knowledge, nor
Concern me the reporting.

Cam.   O my lord!
I would your spirit were easier for advice,   515
Or stronger for your need.

Flo.   Hark, Perdita!
                          [*Drawing her aside.*]
I'll hear you [*to Cam.*] by and by.

Cam.   He's irremoveable,
Resolv'd for flight.   Now were I happy, if
His going I could frame to serve my turn,
Save him from danger, do him love and honour, 520
Purchase the sight again of dear Sicilia
And that unhappy king, my master, whom
I so much thirst to see.

Flo.   Now, good Camillo;
I am so fraught with curious business that
I leave out ceremony.

Cam.   Sir, I think   525
You have heard of my poor services i' th' love
That I have borne your father?

Flo.   Very nobly
Have you deserv'd.   It is my father's music
To speak your deeds, not little of his care
To have them recompens'd as thought on.

Cam.   Well, my lord,
If you may please to think I love the King   531
And through him what's nearest to him, which is
Your gracious self, embrace but my direction.
If your more ponderous and settled project
May suffer alteration, on mine honour,   535
I'll point you where you shall have such receiv-
    ing
As shall become your Highness; where you may
Enjoy your mistress, from the whom, I see,
There's no disjunction to be made, but by —
As heavens forefend! — your ruin; marry her,   540
And, with my best endeavours in your absence,
Your discontenting father strive to qualify
And bring him up to liking.

Flo.   How, Camillo,
May this, almost a miracle, be done?
That I may call thee something more than man 545

---

492. **fancy**: love.   507. **Tug...come**: combat for the future.   510. **[our]** (Theobald).   *her* F.   524. **curious**: anxious.
542. **qualify**: appease.   543. **liking**: i.e., approving your choice.

And after that trust to thee.
    Cam.   Have you thought on
A place whereto you'll go?
    Flo.   Not any yet:
But as th' unthought-on accident is guilty
To what we wildly do, so we profess
Ourselves to be the slaves of chance, and flies   550
Of every wind that blows.
    Cam.   Then list to me.
This follows: if you will not change your purpose
But undergo this flight, make for Sicilia,
And there present yourself and your fair princess,
For so I see she must be, 'fore Leontes.   555
She shall be habited as it becomes
The partner of your bed. Methinks I see
Leontes opening his free arms and weeping
His welcomes forth; asks thee, the son, forgiveness,
As 'twere i' th' father's person; kisses the hands 560
Of your fresh princess; o'er and o'er divides him
'Twixt his unkindness and his kindness; the one
He chides to hell and bids the other grow
Faster than thought or time.
    Flo.   Worthy Camillo,
What colour for my visitation shall I   565
Hold up before him?
    Cam.   Sent by the King your father
To greet him and to give him comforts. Sir,
The manner of your bearing towards him, with
What you as from your father shall deliver,   569
Things known betwixt us three, I'll write you down;
The which shall point you forth at every sitting
What you must say; that he shall not perceive
But that you have your father's bosom there
And speak his very heart.
    Flo.   I am bound to you.
There is some sap in this.
    Cam.   A course more promising
Than a wild dedication of yourselves   576
To unpath'd waters, undream'd shores, most certain
To miseries enough; no hope to help you,
But as you shake off one to take another;
Nothing so certain as your anchors, who   580
Do their best office, if they can but stay you
Where you'll be loath to be. Besides, you know,
Prosperity's the very bond of love,
Whose fresh complexion and whose heart together
Affliction alters.
    Per.   One of these is true.   585
I think affliction may subdue the cheek,
But not take in the mind.
    Cam.   Yea, say you so?
There shall not at your father's house these seven
years

Be born another such.
    Flo.   My good Camillo,
She is as forward of her breeding as   590
She is i' th' rear o' our birth.
    Cam.   I cannot say 'tis pity
She lacks instructions, for she seems a mistress
To most that teach.
    Per.   Your pardon, sir; for this
I'll blush you thanks.
    Flo.   My prettiest Perdita!
But O, the thorns we stand upon! Camillo,   595
Preserver of my father, now of me,
The medicine of our house, how shall we do?
We are not furnish'd like Bohemia's son,
Nor shall appear in Sicilia.
    Cam.   My lord,
Fear none of this. I think you know my fortunes
Do all lie there. It shall be so my care   601
To have you royally appointed as if
The scene you play were mine. For instance, sir,
That you may know you shall not want, one
    word.   *[They talk aside.]* 604

Re-enter AUTOLYCUS.

    Aut. Ha, ha! what a fool Honesty is! and Trust,
his sworn brother, a very simple gentleman! I
have sold all my trumpery; not a counterfeit stone,
not a ribbon, glass, pomander, brooch, table-book,
ballad, knife, tape, glove, shoe-tie, bracelet, horn-
ring, to keep my pack from fasting. They 610
throng who should buy first, as if my trinkets had
been hallowed and brought a benediction to the
buyer; by which means I saw whose purse was
best in picture, and what I saw, to my good use
I remem b'red. My clown, who wants but 615
something to be a reasonable man, grew so in
love with the wenches' song, that he would not
stir his pettitoes till he had both tune and words;
which so drew the rest of the herd to me that all
their other senses stuck in ears. You might 620
have pinched a placket, it was senseless; 'twas
nothing to geld a codpiece of a purse; I would
have fil'd keys off that hung in chains. No hearing, no feeling, but my sir's song, and admiring
the nothing of it. So that in this time of 625
lethargy I pick'd and cut most of their festival
purses; and had not the old man come in with a
whoo-bub against his daughter and the King's son
and scar'd my choughs from the chaff, I had not
left a purse alive in the whole army. 630
    [Camillo, Florizel, and Perdita come for-
        ward.]

---

558. **free:** gracious.   561. **him:** i.e., his speech.   565. **colour:** excuse.   571. **point you forth:** show you.   **sitting:** conference.   586. **subdue:** i.e., with tears.   587. **take in:** overcome.   599. **appear:** i.e., appear as such.   608. **pomander:**
scent-ball.   **table-book:** notebook.   614. **picture:** looks.   618. **pettitoes:** pig's feet.   622. **geld ... codpiece:** rob a trouser
pocket.   624. **my sir's:** i.e., the clown's.   629. **choughs:** jackdaws.

Cam. Nay, but my letters, by this means being
  there
So soon as you arrive, shall clear that doubt.
  Flo. And those that you'll procure from King
  Leontes?
  Cam. Shall satisfy your father.
  Per.   Happy be you!
All that you speak shows fair.
  Cam.   Who have we here?
                        [*Seeing Autolycus.*]
We'll make an instrument of this, omit   636
Nothing may give us aid.
  Aut. [*Aside.*] If they have overheard me now,
why, hanging.   639
  Cam. How now, good fellow! why shak'st thou
so?   Fear not, man; here's no harm intended to
thee.
  Aut. I am a poor fellow, sir.   643
  Cam. Why, be so still; here's nobody will steal
that from thee.   Yet for the outside of thy poverty
we must make an exchange; therefore discase thee
instantly, — thou must think there's a necessity
in't, — and change garments with this gentleman.
Though the pennyworth on his side be the worst,
yet hold thee, there's some boot.   650
  Aut. I am a poor fellow, sir.   [*Aside.*] I know ye
well enough.
  Cam. Nay, prithee, dispatch.   The gentleman
is half [flay'd] already.
  Aut. Are you in earnest, sir?   [*Aside.*] I smell
the trick on't.   656
  Flo. Dispatch, I prithee.
  Aut. Indeed, I have had earnest; but I cannot
with conscience take it.
  Cam. Unbuckle, unbuckle.   660
  [*Florizel and Autolycus exchange garments.*]
Fortunate mistress, — let my prophecy
Come home to ye! — you must retire yourself
Into some covert.   Take your sweetheart's hat
And pluck it o'er your brows, muffle your face,
Dismantle you, and, as you can, disliken   665
The truth of your own seeming; that you may —
For I do fear eyes over — to shipboard
Get undescri'd.
  Per.   I see the play so lies
That I must bear a part.
  Cam.   No remedy.   669
Have you done there?
  Flo.   Should I now meet my father,
He would not call me son.
  Cam.   Nay, you shall have no hat.
                        [*Giving it to Perdita.*]
Come, lady, come.   Farewell, my friend.
  Aut.   Adieu, sir.

  Flo. O Perdita, what have we twain forgot!
Pray you, a word.
  Cam. [*Aside.*] What I do next shall be to tell
  the King   675
Of this escape and whither they are bound;
Wherein my hope is I shall so prevail
To force him after; in whose company
I shall re-view Sicilia, for whose sight
I have a woman's longing.
  Flo.   Fortune speed us!
Thus we set on, Camillo, to th' sea-side.   681
  Cam. The swifter speed the better.
            [*Exeunt [Florizel, Perdita, and Camillo].*]
  Aut. I understand the business, I hear it.   To
have an open ear, a quick eye, and a nimble hand,
is necessary for a cut-purse; a good nose is   685
requisite also, to smell out work for th' other senses.
I see this is the time that the unjust man doth
thrive.   What an exchange had this been without
boot!   What a boot is here with this exchange!
Sure the gods do this year connive at us, and   690
we may do anything extempore.   The Prince himself is about a piece of iniquity, stealing away from
his father with his clog at his heels.   If I thought
it were a piece of honesty to acquaint the King
withal, I would not do 't.   I hold it the more   695
knavery to conceal it; and therein am I constant
to my profession.

  Re-enter CLOWN *and* SHEPHERD
Aside, aside; here is more matter for a hot brain.
Every lane's end, every shop, church, session,
hanging, yields a careful man work.   701
  Clo. See, see; what a man you are now!   There
is no other way but to tell the King she's a change-
ling and none of your flesh and blood.   705
  Shep. Nay, but hear me.
  Clo. Nay, but hear me.
  Shep. Go to, then.
  Clo. She being none of your flesh and blood,
your flesh and blood has not offended the King;   710
and so your flesh and blood is not to be punish'd
by him.   Show those things you found about her,
those secret things, all but what she has with her.
This being done, let the law go whistle.   I warrant
you.   715
  Shep. I will tell the King all, every word, yea,
and his son's pranks too; who, I may say, is no
honest man, neither to his father nor to me, to go
about to make me the King's brother-in-law.   720
  Clo. Indeed, brother-in-law was the farthest off
you could have been to him, and then your blood
had been the dearer by I know how much an ounce.
  Aut. [*Aside.*] Very wisely, puppies!   725

646. discase: undress.   649. the pennyworth: his side of the bargain.   650. some boot: something in addition.   654.
[flay'd] (Rowe): undressed.   *fled* F.   658. earnest: down-payment (to bind a bargain).   661. prophecy: i.e., as implied
in "Fortunate mistress."   665. disliken: disguise.   667. eyes over: spying eyes.   723. know F.   *know not* Hanmer.

Shep. Well, let us to the King. There is that in this fardel will make him scratch his beard.

Aut. [*Aside.*] I know not what impediment this complaint may be to the flight of my master.

Clo. Pray heartily he be at palace. 730

Aut. [*Aside.*] Though I am not naturally honest, I am so sometimes by chance. Let me pocket up my pedlar's excrement. [*Takes off his false beard.*] How now, rustics! whither are you bound? 735

Shep. To th' palace, an it like your worship.

Aut. Your affairs there? What, with whom, the condition of that fardel, the place of your dwelling, your names, your ages, of what having, breeding, and anything that is fitting to be known, discover? 741

Clo. We are but plain fellows, sir.

Aut. A lie; you are rough and hairy. Let me have no lying. It becomes none but tradesmen, and they often give us soldiers the lie; but we pay them for it with stamped coin, not stabbing steel; therefore they do not give us the lie. 748

Clo. Your worship had like to have given us one, if you had not taken yourself with the manner.

Shep. Are you a courtier, an't like you, sir? 752

Aut. Whether it like me or no, I am a courtier. Seest thou not the air of the court in these enfoldings? Hath not my gait in it the measure of the court? Receives not thy nose court-odour from me? Reflect I not on thy baseness court-contempt? Think'st thou, for that I insinuate, [or] touse from thee thy business, I am therefore no courtier? I am courtier cap-a-pie, and one that will either 760 push on or pluck back thy business there; whereupon I command thee to open thy affair.

Shep. My business, sir, is to the King.

Aut. What advocate hast thou to him? 765

Shep. I know not, an't like you.

Clo. Advocate's the court-word for a pheasant. Say you have none.

Shep. None, sir; I have no pheasant, cock nor hen. 770

Aut. How bless'd are we that are not simple men!
Yet Nature might have made me as these are,
Therefore I will not disdain.

Clo. This cannot be but a great courtier.

Shep. His garments are rich, but he wears them not handsomely. 776

Clo. He seems to be the more noble in being fantastical. A great man, I'll warrant; I know by the picking on 's teeth.

Aut. The fardel there? What's i' th' fardel?

Wherefore that box? 781

Shep. Sir, there lies such secrets in this fardel and box, which none must know but the King; and which he shall know within this hour, if I may come to th' speech of him. 785

Aut. Age, thou hast lost thy labour.

Shep. Why, sir?

Aut. The King is not at the palace. He is gone aboard a new ship to purge melancholy and air himself; for, if thou be'st capable of things serious, thou must know the King is full of grief. 791

Shep. So 'tis said, sir; about his son, that should have married a shepherd's daughter.

Aut. If that shepherd be not in hand-fast, let him fly. The curses he shall have, the tortures he shall feel, will break the back of man, the heart of monster.

Clo. Think you so, sir? 798

Aut. Not he alone shall suffer what wit can make heavy and vengeance bitter, but those that are germane to him, though remov'd fifty times, shall all come under the hangman; which though it be great pity, yet it is necessary. An old 803 sheep-whistling rogue, a ram-tender, to offer to have his daughter come into grace! Some say he shall be ston'd; but that death is too soft for him, say I. Draw our throne into a sheep-cote! All deaths are too few, the sharpest too easy.

Clo. Has the old man e'er a son, sir, do you hear, an't like you, sir? 810

Aut. He has a son, who shall be flay'd alive; then 'nointed over with honey, set on the head of a wasp's nest; then stand till he be three quarters and a dram dead; then recover'd again with aqua-vitæ or some other hot infusion; then, raw as 815 he is, and in the hottest day prognostication proclaims, shall he be set against a brick-wall, the sun looking with a southward eye upon him, where he is to behold him with flies blown to death. But what talk we of these traitorly rascals, 820 whose miseries are to be smil'd at, their offences being so capital? Tell me, for you seem to be honest plain men, what you have to the King. Being something gently consider'd, I'll bring you where he is aboard, tender your persons to his presence, whisper him in your behalfs; and if it be in man besides the King to effect your suits, here is man shall do it. 828

Clo. He seems to be of great authority. Close with him, give him gold; and though authority be a stubborn bear, yet he is oft led by the nose with gold. Show the inside of your purse to the

---

727. **fardel**: bundle. 733. **excrement**: beard. 739. **having**: property. 751. **with the manner**: in the act. 754. **enfoldings**: garments. 758. **insinuate**: wheedle. [or] F₂. *at* F₁. **touse**: tear (*toaze* F₁). 760. **cap-a-pie**: from head to foot. 769. **pheasant**. Judges were sometimes bribed by gifts such as game. 779. **picking...teeth**: the way he picks his teeth. 794. **hand-fast**: custody. 814. **aqua-vitæ**: brandy. 816. **prognostication**: the almanac. 824. **Being...consider'd**: if nobly recompensed.

outside of his hand, and no more ado. Remember
"ston'd," and "flay'd alive."   834
Shep. An't please you, sir, to undertake the
business for us, here is that gold I have. I'll make
it as much more, and leave this young man in
pawn till I bring it you.
Aut. After I have done what I promised?
Shep. Ay, sir.   840
Aut. Well, give me the moiety. Are you a
party in this business?
Clo. In some sort, sir; but though my case be a
pitiful one, I hope I shall not be flay'd out of it.
Aut. O, that's the case of the shepherd's son.
Hang him, he'll be made an example.   846
Clo. Comfort, good comfort! We must to the
King and show our strange sights. He must
know 'tis none of your daughter nor my sister;
we are gone else. Sir, I will give you as much as
this old man does when the business is performed,
and remain, as he says, your pawn till it be brought
you.   853
Aut. I will trust you. Walk before toward the
sea-side; go on the right hand. I will but look upon
the hedge and follow you.
Clo. We are blest in this man, as I may say,
even blest.
Shep. Let's before as he bids us. He was provided to do us good.   860
[*Exeunt Shepherd and Clown.*]
Aut. If I had a mind to be honest, I see Fortune
would not suffer me; she drops booties in my
mouth. I am courted now with a double occasion,
gold and a means to do the Prince my master good;
which who knows how that may turn back to   865
my advancement? I will bring these two moles,
these blind ones, aboard him. If he think it fit to
shore them again, and that the complaint they
have to the King concerns him nothing, let him
call me rogue for being so far officious; for   870
I am proof against that title and what shame else
belongs to't. To him will I present them. There
may be matter in it.   [*Exit.* 873

ACT V

Scene I. [*Sicilia. A room in Leontes' palace.*]

Enter Leontes, Cleomenes, Dion, Paulina,
and Servants.

Cleo. Sir, you have done enough, and have
    perform'd
A saint-like sorrow. No fault could you make
Which you have not redeem'd; indeed, paid down
More penitence than done trespass. At the last

Do as the heavens have done, forget your evil;   5
With them forgive yourself.
Leon.   Whilst I remember
Her and her virtues, I cannot forget
My blemishes in them, and so still think of
The wrong I did myself; which was so much
That heirless it hath made my kingdom, and   10
Destroy'd the sweet'st companion that e'er man
Bred his hopes out of.
Paul.   True, too true, my lord.
If, one by one, you wedded all the world,
Or, from the all that are, took something good
To make a perfect woman, she you kill'd   15
Would be unparallel'd.
Leon.   I think so. Kill'd!
She I kill'd! I did so; but thou strik'st me
Sorely, to say I did. It is as bitter
Upon thy tongue as in my thought. Now, good
    now,
Say so but seldom.
Cleo.   Not at all, good lady.   20
You might have spoken a thousand things that
    would
Have done the time more benefit and grac'd
Your kindness better.
Paul.   You are one of those
Would have him wed again.
Dion.   If you would not so,
You pity not the state, nor the remembrance   25
Of his most sovereign name; consider little
What dangers, by his Highness' fail of issue,
May drop upon his kingdom and devour
Incertain lookers on. What were more holy
Than to rejoice the former queen is well?   30
What holier than, for royalty's repair,
For present comfort and for future good,
To bless the bed of majesty again
With a sweet fellow to't?
Paul.   There is none worthy,
Respecting her that's gone. Besides, the gods   35
Will have fulfill'd their secret purposes;
For has not the divine Apollo said,
Is't not the tenour of his oracle,
That King Leontes shall not have an heir
Till his lost child be found? which that it shall,   40
Is all as monstrous to our human reason
As my Antigonus to break his grave
And come again to me; who, on my life,
Did perish with the infant. 'Tis your counsel
My lord should to the heavens be contrary,   45
Oppose against their wills. [*To Leontes.*] Care
    not for issue;
The crown will find an heir. Great Alexander
Left his to th' worthiest; so his successor

---

843. **case:** (1) plight, (2) skin.
Act V, sc. i, 12. **True, too true.** Theobald. F continues the first *true* to Leontes. 29. **Incertain:** wavering. 35. **Respect-**
ing: compared with.

Was like to be the best.

Leon.   Good Paulina,
Who hast the memory of Hermione,
I know, in honour, O, that ever I   50
Had squar'd me to thy counsel! then, even now,
I might have look'd upon my queen's full eyes,
Have taken treasure from her lips —

Paul.   And left them
More rich for what they yielded.

Leon.   Thou speak'st truth.
No more such wives; therefore, no wife. One
     worse,   56
And better us'd, would make her sainted spirit
Again possess her corpse, and on this stage,
(Where we offenders now appear) soul-vex'd,
Begin, "[And] why to me — ?"

Paul.   Had she such power,   60
She had just cause.

Leon.   She had; and would incense me
To murder her I married.

Paul.   I should so.
Were I the ghost that walk'd, I'd bid you mark
Her eye, and tell me for what dull part in't
You chose her; then I'd shriek, that even your
     ears   65
Should rift to hear me; and the words that follow'd
Should be "Remember mine."

Leon.   Stars, stars,
And all eyes else dead coals! Fear thou no wife;
I'll have no wife, Paulina.

Paul.   Will you swear
Never to marry but by my free leave?   70

Leon. Never, Paulina; so be blest my spirit!

Paul. Then, good my lords, bear witness to his
     oath.

Cleo. You tempt him over-much.

Paul.   Unless another,
As like Hermione as is her picture,   74
Affront his eye.

Cleo.   Good madam, —

Paul.   I have done.
Yet, if my lord will marry, — if you will, sir,
No remedy, but you will, — give me the office
To choose you a queen. She shall not be so
     young
As was your former; but she shall be such
As, walk'd your first queen's ghost, it should take
     joy   80
To see her in your arms.

Leon.   My true Paulina,
We shall not marry till thou bid'st us.

Paul.   That
Shall be when your first queen's again in breath;
Never till then.

Enter a SERVANT.

Serv. One that gives out himself Prince Florizel,
Son of Polixenes, with his princess, she   86
The fairest I have yet beheld, desires access
To your high presence.

Leon.   What with him? He comes not
Like to his father's greatness. His approach,
So out of circumstance and sudden, tells us   90
'Tis not a visitation fram'd, but forc'd
By need and accident. What train?

Serv.   But few,
And those but mean.

Leon.   His princess, say you, with him?

Serv. Ay, the most peerless piece of earth, I
     think,
That e'er the sun shone bright on.

Paul.   O Hermione,
As every present time doth boast itself   96
Above a better gone, so must thy grave
Give way to what's seen now! Sir, you yourself
Have said and writ so, but your writing now   99
Is colder than that theme, "She had not been,
Nor was not to be equall'd;" — thus your verse
Flow'd with her beauty once. 'Tis shrewdly ebb'd,
To say you have seen a better.

Serv.   Pardon, madam:
The one I have almost forgot, — your pardon, —
The other, when she has obtain'd your eye,   105
Will have your tongue too. This is a creature,
Would she begin a sect, might quench the zeal
Of all professors else, make proselytes
Of who she but bid follow.

Paul.   How? Not women!

Serv. Women will love her, that she is a woman
More worth than any man; men, that she is   111
The rarest of all women.

Leon.   Go, Cleomenes;
Yourself, assisted with your honour'd friends,
Bring them to our embracement. Still, 'tis strange
                    [*Exeunt [Cleomenes and others*].
He thus should steal upon us.

Paul.   Had our prince,   115
Jewel of children, seen this hour, he had pair'd
Well with this lord. There was not full a month
Between their births.

Leon. Prithee, no more; cease. Thou know'st
He dies to me again when talk'd of. Sure,   120
When I shall see this gentleman, thy speeches
Will bring me to consider that which may
Unfurnish me of reason. They are come.

Re-enter CLEOMENES *and others, with* FLORIZEL
          and PERDITA.

Your mother was most true to wedlock, Prince,

---

52. **squar'd**: adjusted. 60. Begin, **[And]** (Capell). *And begin* F. **why to me**: i.e., why the insult you put upon me?
66. **rift**: split. 75. **Affront**: confront. **I have done.** Capell. F continues to Cleomenes. 91. **fram'd**: planned. 102.
shrewdly: grievously. 108. **professors else**: adherents of other sects.

For she did print your royal father off,   125
Conceiving you. Were I but twenty-one,
Your father's image is so hit in you,
His very air, that I should call you brother,   128
As I did him, and speak of something wildly
By us perform'd before. Most dearly welcome!
And your fair princess, — goddess! — O, alas!
I lost a couple, that 'twixt heaven and earth
Might thus have stood begetting wonder as
You, gracious couple, do; and then I lost —
All mine own folly — the society,   135
Amity too, of your brave father, whom,
Though bearing misery, I desire my life
Once more to look on him.
    Flo.   By his command
Have I here touch'd Sicilia, and from him
Give you all greetings that a king, at friend,
Can send his brother; and, but infirmity   141
Which waits upon worn times hath something seiz'd
His wish'd ability, he had himself
The lands and waters 'twixt your throne and his   144
Measur'd to look upon you; whom he loves —
He bade me say so — more than all the sceptres
And those that bear them living.
    Leon.   O my brother,
Good gentleman! the wrongs I have done thee stir
Afresh within me, and these thy offices,
So rarely kind, are as interpreters   150
Of my behind-hand slackness. Welcome hither,
As is the spring to th' earth. And hath he too
Expos'd this paragon to the fearful usage,
(At least ungentle,) of the dreadful Neptune,
To greet a man not worth her pains, much less   155
Th' adventure of her person?
    Flo.   Good my lord,
She came from Libya.
    Leon.   Where the warlike Smalus,
That noble honour'd lord, is fear'd and lov'd?
    Flo. Most royal sir, from thence; from him, whose
        daughter   159
His tears proclaim'd his, parting with her; thence,
A prosperous south-wind friendly, we have cross'd,
To execute the charge my father gave me
For visiting your Highness. My best train
I have from your Sicilian shores dismiss'd;
Who for Bohemia bend, to signify   165
Not only my success in Libya, sir,
But my arrival and my wife's in safety
Here where we are.
    Leon.   The blessed gods
Purge all infection from our air whilst you
Do climate here! You have a holy father,   170
A graceful gentleman, against whose person,
So sacred as it is, I have done sin;

For which the heavens, taking angry note,
Have left me issueless; and your father's blest,
As he from heaven merits it, with you   175
Worthy his goodness. What might I have been,
Might I a son and daughter now have look'd on,
Such goodly things as you?

           Enter a LORD.

    Lord.   Most noble sir,
That which I shall report will bear no credit,
Were not the proof so nigh. Please you, great sir,
Bohemia greets you from himself by me;   181
Desires you to attach his son, who has —
His dignity and duty both cast off —
Fled from his father, from his hopes, and with   184
A shepherd's daughter.
    Leon.   Where's Bohemia? Speak.
    Lord. Here in your city; I now came from him.
I speak amazedly, and it becomes
My marvel and my message. To your court
Whiles he was hast'ning, in the chase, it seems,
Of this fair couple, meets he on the way   190
The father of this seeming lady and
Her brother, having both their country quitted
With this young prince.
    Flo.   Camillo has betray'd me;
Whose honour and whose honesty till now   194
Endur'd all weathers.
    Lord.   Lay 't so to his charge:
He's with the King your father.
    Leon.   Who? Camillo?
    Lord. Camillo, sir; I spake with him; who now
Has these poor men in question. Never saw I
Wretches so quake. They kneel, they kiss the
    earth,
Forswear themselves as often as they speak.   200
Bohemia stops his ears, and threatens them
With divers deaths in death.
    Per.   O my poor father!
The heaven sets spies upon us, will not have
Our contract celebrated.
    Leon.   You are married?
    Flo. We are not, sir, nor are we like to be.   205
The stars, I see, will kiss the valleys first;
The odds for high and low 's alike.
    Leon.   My lord,
Is this the daughter of a king?
    Flo.   She is,
When once she is my wife.
    Leon. That "once," I see by your good father's
        speed,   210
Will come on very slowly. I am sorry,
Most sorry, you have broken from his liking
Where you were tied in duty, and as sorry

---

129. **wildly:** boisterously.   140. **at friend:** in friendship.   142. **worn times:** old age.   149. **offices:** kindnesses.   170. **climate:** stay (in this climate).   182. **attach:** arrest.   187. **amazedly:** confusedly.   188. **marvel:** wonder.   202. **deaths in death:** i.e., tortures.   207. **The . . . alike:** i.e., Fortune cheats high and low alike.

Your choice is not so rich in worth as beauty,
That you might well enjoy her.
Flo.   Dear, look up.
Though Fortune, visible an enemy,   216
Should chase us with my father, pow'r no jot
Hath she to change our loves. Beseech you, sir,
Remember since you ow'd no more to time
Than I do now. With thought of such affections,
Step forth mine advocate. At your request   221
My father will grant precious things as trifles.
Leon. Would he do so, I'd beg your precious mis-
          tress,
Which he counts but a trifle.
Paul.   Sir, my liege,
Your eye hath too much youth in't. Not a month
'Fore your queen died, she was more worth such
          gazes   226
Than what you look on now.
Leon.   I thought of her,
Even in these looks I made. [*To Florizel.*] But
          your petition
Is yet unanswer'd. I will to your father.
Your honour not o'erthrown by your desires,   230
I am friend to them and you; upon which errand
I now go toward him; therefore follow me
And mark what way I make. Come, good my lord.
                                        [*Exeunt.*

SCENE II. [*Before Leontes' palace.*]

Enter AUTOLYCUS *and a* GENTLEMAN.

Aut. Beseech you, sir, were you present at this
relation?
1. Gent. I was by at the opening of the fardel,
heard the old shepherd deliver the manner how he
found it; whereupon, after a little amazedness, we
were all commanded out of the chamber; only this
methought I heard the shepherd say, he found the
child.   8
Aut. I would most gladly know the issue of it.
1. Gent. I make a broken delivery of the business;
but the changes I perceived in the King and Camillo
were very notes of admiration. They seem'd almost, with staring on one another, to tear the cases
of their eyes. There was speech in their dumbness,
language in their very gesture; they look'd as   15
they had heard of a world ransom'd, or one destroyed. A notable passion of wonder appeared in
them; but the wisest beholder, that knew no more
but seeing, could not say if th' importance were joy
or sorrow; but in the extremity of the one, it must
needs be.   21

Enter another GENTLEMAN.

Here comes a gentleman that haply knows more.
The news, Rogero?
2. Gent. Nothing but bonfires. The oracle is
fulfill'd; the King's daughter is found; such a deal
of wonder is broken out within this hour that ballad-
makers cannot be able to express it.   27

Enter a third GENTLEMAN.

Here comes the Lady Paulina's steward: he can   28
deliver you more. How goes it now, sir? This
news which is call'd true is so like an old tale, that
the verity of it is in strong suspicion. Has the
King found his heir?   32
3. Gent. Most true, if ever truth were pregnant
by circumstance. That which you hear you'll
swear you see, there is such unity in the proofs.
The mantle of Queen Hermione's, her jewel about
the neck of it, the letters of Antigonus found with
it, which they know to be his character, the majesty
of the creature in resemblance of the mother, the
affection of nobleness which nature shows above   40
her breeding, and many other evidences proclaim
her with all certainty to be the King's daughter.
Did you see the meeting of the two kings?
2. Gent. No.   45
3. Gent. Then have you lost a sight which was to
be seen, cannot be spoken of. There might you
have beheld one joy crown another, so and in such
manner that it seem'd sorrow wept to take leave of
them, for their joy waded in tears. There was   50
casting up of eyes, holding up of hands, with countenance of such distraction that they were to be
known by garment, not by favour. Our king, being ready to leap out of himself for joy of his found
daughter, as if that joy were now become a loss,   55
cries, "O, thy mother, thy mother!" then asks
Bohemia forgiveness; then embraces his son-in-law;
then again worries he his daughter with clipping
her; now he thanks the old shepherd, which stands
by like a weather-bitten conduit of many kings'   60
reigns. I never heard of such another encounter,
which lames report to follow it and undoes description to do it.
2. Gent. What, pray you, became of Antigonus,
that carried hence the child?   65
3. Gent. Like an old tale still, which will have
matter to rehearse, though credit be asleep and not
an ear open. He was torn to pieces with a bear;
this avouches the shepherd's son, who has not only
his innocence, which seems much, to justify him,

214. **worth:** rank.   219–20. **since . . . now:** when you were as young as I am.
Sc. ii, 10. **broken delivery:** incoherent story.   12. **notes of admiration:** exclamation points.   13. **cases:** sockets.   19.
importance: import.   33. **pregnant by circumstance:** clear from evidence.   38. **character:** handwriting.   40. **affection of:**
inclination to.   51. **countenance:** appearance.   53. **favour:** face.   58. **clipping:** embracing.   60. **weather-bitten conduit:**
weather-beaten fountain (in the form of a statue).   63. **do:** report.   70. **innocence:** simplicity.

but a handkerchief and rings of his that Paulina knows.   72

1. Gent. What became of his bark and his followers?

3. Gent. Wreck'd the same instant of their 75 master's death and in the view of the shepherd; so that all the instruments which aided to expose the child were even then lost when it was found. But O, the noble combat that 'twixt joy and sorrow was fought in Paulina! She had one eye declin'd 80 for the loss of her husband, another elevated that the oracle was fulfill'd. She lifted the Princess from the earth, and so locks her in embracing, as if she would pin her to her heart that she might no more be in danger of losing.   85

1. Gent. The dignity of this act was worth the audience of kings and princes; for by such was it acted.

3. Gent. One of the prettiest touches of all, and that which angl'd for mine eyes, caught the 90 water though not the fish, was when, at the relation of the Queen's death, with the manner how she came to't bravely confess'd and lamented by the King, how attentively wounded his daughter; till, from one sign of dolour to another, she did with an 95 "Alas," I would fain say, bleed tears, for I am sure my heart wept blood. Who was most marble there changed colour; some swooned, all sorrowed. If all the world could have seen 't, the woe had been universal.   100

1. Gent. Are they returned to the court?

3. Gent. No. The Princess hearing of her mother's statue, which is in the keeping of Paulina, — a piece many years in doing and now newly perform'd by that rare Italian master, Julio Ro- 105 mano, who, had he himself eternity and could put breath into his work, would beguile Nature of her custom, so perfectly he is her ape. He so near to Hermione hath done Hermione that they say one would speak to her and stand in hope of answer. Thither with all greediness of affection are they gone, and there they intend to sup.   112

2. Gent. I thought she had some great matter there in hand; for she hath privately twice or thrice a day, ever since the death of Hermione, visited that removed house. Shall we thither and with our company piece the rejoicing?   117

1. Gent. Who would be thence that has the benefit of access? Every wink of an eye some new grace will be born. Our absence makes us unthrifty to our knowledge. Let's along.   121

              [Exeunt [Gentlemen].

Aut. Now, had I not the dash of my former life in me, would preferment drop on my head. I

brought the old man and his son aboard the Prince, told him I heard them talk of a fardel and I 125 know not what; but he at that time, overfond of the shepherd's daughter, so he then took her to be, who began to be much sea-sick, and himself little better, extremity of weather continuing, this mystery remained undiscover'd. But 'tis all one to me; for had I been the finder out of this secret, it would not have relish'd among my other discredits.   133

Enter SHEPHERD *and* CLOWN.

Here come those I have done good to against my will, and already appearing in the blossoms of their fortune.

Shep. Come, boy; I am past moe children, but thy sons and daughters will be all gentlemen born.   138

Clo. You are well met, sir. You deni'd to fight with me this other day, because I was no gentleman born. See you these clothes? Say you see them not and think me still no gentleman born. You were best say these robes are not gentlemen born. Give me the lie, do, and try whether I am not now a gentleman born.   145

Aut. I know you are now, sir, a gentleman born.

Clo. Ay, and have been so any time these four hours.

Shep. And so have I, boy.   149

Clo. So you have; but I was a gentleman born before my father. For the King's son took me by the hand, and call'd me brother; and then the two kings call'd my father brother; and then the Prince my brother and the Princess my sister call'd my father father; and so we wept, and there was the first gentleman-like tears that ever we shed. 156

Shep. We may live, son, to shed many more.

Clo. Ay; or else 'twere hard luck, being in so preposterous estate as we are.   159

Aut. I humbly beseech you, sir, to pardon me all the faults I have committed to your worship, and to give me your good report to the Prince my master.

Shep. Prithee, son, do; for we must be gentle, now we are gentlemen.   165

Clo. Thou wilt amend thy life?

Aut. Ay, an it like your good worship.

Clo. Give me thy hand: I will swear to the Prince thou art as honest a true fellow as any is in Bohemia.   170

Shep. You may say it, but not swear it.

Clo. Not swear it, now I am a gentleman? Let boors and franklins say it, I'll swear it.

Shep. How if it be false, son?   175

Clo. If it be ne'er so false, a true gentleman may swear it in the behalf of his friend; and I'll swear to

94. **attentiveness:** listening. 104. **perform'd:** completed. 105. **Julio Romano:** Italian artist (d. 1546). 107. **beguile:** rob. 108. **custom:** trade. 117. **piece:** increase. 133. **relish'd:** been acceptable. 174. **boors:** peasants. **franklins:** small landowners.

the Prince thou art a tall fellow of thy hands and
that thou wilt not be drunk; but I know thou art no
tall fellow of thy hands and that thou wilt be drunk;
but I'll swear it, and I would thou wouldst be a tall
fellow of thy hands. 182

Aut. I will prove so, sir, to my power.

Clo. Ay, by any means prove a tall fellow. If I
do not wonder how thou dar'st venture to be drunk,
not being a tall fellow, trust me not. Hark! the
kings and the princes, our kindred, are going to see
the Queen's picture. Come, follow us; we'll be thy
good masters. 189

[*Exeunt.*

SCENE III. [*A chapel in Paulina's house.*]

Enter LEONTES, POLIXENES, FLORIZEL, PER-
DITA, CAMILLO, PAULINA, Lords, *etc.*

Leon. O grave and good Paulina, the great comfort
That I have had of thee!

Paul.   What, sovereign sir,
I did not well I meant well. All my services
You have paid home; but that you have vouchsaf'd,
With your crown'd brother and these your con-
tracted 5
Heirs of your kingdoms, my poor house to visit,
It is a surplus of your grace, which never
My life may last to answer.

Leon.   O Paulina,
We honour you with trouble. But we came
To see the statue of our queen. Your gallery 10
Have we pass'd through, not without much content
In many singularities; but we saw not
That which my daughter came to look upon,
The statue of her mother.

Paul.   As she liv'd peerless,
So her dead likeness, I do well believe, 15
Excels whatever yet you look'd upon
Or hand of man hath done; therefore I keep it
Lonely, apart. But here it is. Prepare
To see the life as lively mock'd as ever 19
Still sleep mock'd death. Behold, and say 'tis well.

[*Paulina draws a curtain, and discovers
Hermione standing like a statue.*]

I like your silence; it the more shows off
Your wonder; but yet speak. First, you, my liege;
Comes it not something near?

Leon.   Her natural posture!
Chide me, dear stone, that I may say indeed
Thou art Hermione; or rather, thou art she 25
In thy not chiding, for she was as tender
As infancy and grace. But yet, Paulina,
Hermione was not so much wrinkled, nothing

So aged as this seems.

Pol.   O, not by much. 29

Paul. So much the more our carver's excellence,
Which lets go by some sixteen years and makes her
As she liv'd now.

Leon.   As now she might have done,
So much to my good comfort as it is
Now piercing to my soul. O, thus she stood,
Even with such life of majesty, warm life, 35
As now it coldly stands, when first I woo'd her!
I am asham'd; does not the stone rebuke me
For being more stone than it? O royal piece
There's magic in thy majesty, which has
My evils conjur'd to remembrance, and 40
From thy admiring daughter took the spirits,
Standing like stone with thee.

Per.   And give me leave,
And do not say 'tis superstition, that
I kneel and then implore her blessing. Lady,
Dear queen, that ended when I but began, 45
Give me that hand of yours to kiss.

Paul.   O, patience!
The statue is but newly fix'd, the colour's
Not dry.

Cam. My lord, your sorrow was too sore laid on,
Which sixteen winters cannot blow away, 50
So many summers dry. Scarce any joy
Did ever so long live; no sorrow
But kill'd itself much sooner.

Pol.   Dear my brother,
Let him that was the cause of this have power
To take off so much grief from you as he 55
Will piece up in himself.

Paul.   Indeed, my lord,
If I had thought the sight of my poor image
Would thus have wrought you, — for the stone is
mine —
I'd not have show'd it.

Leon.   Do not draw the curtain.

Paul. No longer shall you gaze on't, lest your
fancy 60
May think anon it moves.

Leon.   Let be, let be.
Would I were dead but that, methinks, already —
What was he that did make it? See, my lord,
Would you not deem it breath'd, and that those
veins
Did verily bear blood?

Pol.   Masterly done! 65
The very life seems warm upon her lip.

Leon. The fixure of her eye has motion in't,
As we are mock'd with art.

Paul.   I'll draw the curtain.
My lord 's almost so far transported that

---

178. **tall ... hands:** brave fellow in action.

Sc. iii, 4. **home:** fully.   12. **singularities:** rarities.   58. **wrought:** moved.   62. **Would ... already:** i.e., may I die if it is
not beginning to move.   67. **fixure:** fixedness.   68. **As:** as if.

He'll think anon it lives.

Leon.   O sweet Paulina,   70
Make me to think so twenty years together!
No settled senses of the world can match
The pleasure of that madness. Let 't alone.

Paul. I am sorry, sir, I have thus far stirr'd you;
    but
I could afflict you farther.

Leon.   Do, Paulina;   75
For this affliction has a taste as sweet
As any cordial comfort. Still, methinks,
There is an air comes from her. What fine chisel
Could ever yet cut breath? Let no man mock me,
For I will kiss her.

Paul.   Good my lord, forbear.   80
The ruddiness upon her lip is wet;
You'll mar it if you kiss it, stain your own
With oily painting. Shall I draw the curtain?

Leon. No, not these twenty years.

Per.   So long could I
Stand by, a looker on.

Paul.   Either forbear,   85
Quit presently the chapel, or resolve you
For more amazement. If you can behold it,
I'll make the statue move indeed, descend
And take you by the hand; but then you'll think —
Which I protest against — I am assisted   90
By wicked powers.

Leon.   What you can make her do,
I am content to look on; what to speak,
I am content to hear; for 'tis as easy
To make her speak as move.

Paul.   It is requir'd
You do awake your faith. Then all stand still;
[Or], those that think it is unlawful business   96
I am about, let them depart.

Leon.   Proceed;
No foot shall stir.

Paul.   Music, awake her; strike!
                                 [*Music.*]
'Tis time; descend; be stone no more; approach.   99
Strike all that look upon with marvel. Come,
I'll fill your grave up. Stir, nay, come away,
Bequeath to death your numbness; for from him
Dear life redeems you. You perceive she stirs.
             [*Hermione comes down.*]
Start not; her actions shall be holy as
You hear my spell is lawful. Do not shun her
Until you see her die again, for then   106
You kill her double. Nay, present your hand.
When she was young you woo'd her; now in age
Is she become the suitor?

Leon.   O, she's warm!
If this be magic, let it be an art   110
Lawful as eating.

Pol.   She embraces him.

Cam. She hangs about his neck.
If she pertain to life let her speak too.

Pol. Ay, and make 't manifest where she has
    liv'd,
Or how stolen from the dead.

Paul.   That she is living,
Were it but told you, should be hooted at   116
Like an old tale; but it appears she lives,
Though yet she speak not. Mark a little while.
Please you to interpose, fair madam; kneel
And pray your mother's blessing. Turn, good
    lady;   120
Our Perdita is found.

Her.   You gods, look down
And from your sacred vials pour your graces
Upon my daughter's head! Tell me, mine own,
Where hast thou been preserv'd? where liv'd? how
    found
Thy father's court? for thou shalt hear that I,
Knowing by Paulina that th' oracle   126
Gave hope thou wast in being, have preserv'd
Myself to see the issue.

Paul.   There's time enough for that;
Lest they desire upon this push to trouble
Your joys with like relation. Go together,   130
You precious winners all; your exultation
Partake to every one. I, an old turtle,
Will wing me to some wither'd bough and there
My mate, that's never to be found again,
Lament till I am lost.

Leon.   O, peace, Paulina!   135
Thou shouldst a husband take by my consent,
As I by thine a wife; this is a match,
And made between 's by vows. Thou hast found
    mine;
But how, is to be question'd; for I saw her,   139
As I thought, dead, and have in vain said many
A prayer upon her grave. I'll not seek far —
For him, I partly know his mind — to find thee
An honourable husband. Come, Camillo,
And take her by the hand, whose worth and hon-
    esty
Is richly noted and here justified   145
By us, a pair of kings. Let's from this place.
What! look upon my brother. Both your pardons,
That e'er I put between your holy looks
My ill suspicion. This your son-in-law   149
And son unto the King, whom heavens directing,
Is troth-plight to your daughter. Good Paulina,
Lead us from hence, where we may leisurely
Each one demand and answer to his part
Perform'd in this wide gap of time since first
We were dissever'd. Hastily lead away.   155
                                   [*Exeunt.*

---

96. **[Or]** (Hanmer). *On* F.   129. **upon … push:** under the pressure of these events.   130. **relation:** narrative.   132. **Partake:** impart.   145. **justified:** confirmed.   149. **This:** i.e., this is.

The Tempest

THE TEMPEST FIRST APPEARED in print as the opening play in the First Folio. It is generally held to be Shakespeare's last independent contribution to the stage, and the suggestion has been made that this distinction, coupled with the established success of the play, led to its eminence in the Folio. It was one of numerous plays performed at Court by Shakespeare's company during the winter of 1612–1613 as part of the wedding festivities of King James's daughter Elizabeth, who was betrothed to Frederick, the Elector Palatine, on December 27, and married on February 14. The play was written, however, somewhat earlier. An entry in the Revels Accounts, relieved by recent scholarship of a long-standing charge of forgery, records a performance of *The Tempest* before the King at Whitehall on Hallowmas Night (November 1) in 1611. Details in the play inspired by accounts of the wreck of Sir George Somers in the Bermudas (1609), about which more will be said, point to a date early in 1611, for no news of Somers's experiences reached England before September, 1610.

It is a reasonable assumption that the received text, a thoroughly good one, presents the drama as it was given on the occasion connected with the royal marriage, and the suggestion that its unusually full stage directions were prepared by Shakespeare himself with special care in anticipation of that performance has welcome plausibility.

For the main thread of the plot no source has been discovered. Resemblances to *Die Schöne Sidea* of Jacob Ayrer of Nuremberg, who died in 1605, are more interesting than significant. In both plays we have a dispossessed prince devoted to magic and driven into exile with a daughter who ultimately marries the son of his enemy; an attendant spirit; and, especially striking, the imposition of log-carrying upon the captive prince, and the fixing of his sword in its scabbard. But there is absolutely no similarity in character, and Ayrer's devil has nothing in common with Ariel, save his function as a supernatural servant. The fixing of the sword is a commonplace of magic, and even the carrying or splitting of logs is found as a task imposed by a magician on a captive prince in folktales having no connection with the present plays. Since English comedians were in Nuremberg in 1604, it is barely possible that Shakespeare learned the plot of Ayrer's play from some actor, but the more credible view is that both dramas may go back to a common origin, which, in all likelihood, was remote.

The origin of certain details can be pointed out with more assurance. Gonzalo's ideal commonwealth (II.i.147 ff.) was inspired by passages in Montaigne's essay "Of the Cannibales," which Shakespeare could have read in Florio's translation (1603). Prospero's abjuration speech (V.i.33–57) shows the influence of Ovid's *Metamorphoses* (VII.192 ff.), which Shakespeare could have known either through Golding's translation (1567), or in the original. The name of Setebos is taken from Richard Eden's *History of Travayle in the West and East Indies* (1577), where it occurs as that of the devil-god of the Patagonian giants, and in the same source are also to be found the names of Alonso, Sebastian, Antonio, Ferdinand, and Gonzalo. The names Prospero and Stephano were given to characters in the first edition of *Every Man in his Humour* (in which Shakespeare himself is reputed to have played a rôle) before Jonson substituted English for Italian ones; and Prospero is to be found also in William Thomas's *Historie of Italye* (1549). Ariel appears in *Isaiah*, and is the name of a prince of spirits in cabalistic literature. Caliban seems to be an anagram for "cannibal." Miranda is evidently a significant coinage, like Marina and Perdita. Finally, Shakespeare's interest in certain events which had but recently excited considerable public attention, is noteworthy.

On June 2, 1609, an expedition of nine ships set sail from Plymouth for the colony at Jamestown, Virginia, founded two years before. On July 25 a terrific storm dispersed the fleet. All the vessels reached Jamestown safely, however, with the exception of the *Sea Adventure*, which, with about one hundred and fifty aboard, including Sir George Somers (the Admiral), Sir Thomas Gates (the new Governor), and Sir Christopher Newport (one of the first founders), was believed lost. When, therefore, some months later (May 23, 1610), they all sailed into Jamestown, the others could hardly believe their eyes. The *Sea Adventure* had been driven south from her course until finally wrecked on the reefs of Bermuda. Not a life had been lost, and after considerable time, during which they made out a fair subsistence on the islands, the party built two small pinnaces in which they effected their own rescue. On June 10, 1610, Gates and Newport sailed back to England and, arriving in September, astonished London with the first news of their preservation.

The lively public interest in these events could be capitalized, and certain members of the *Sea Adventure's* party lent their aid. In October of 1610, Silvester Jourdan, one of the crew, published a pamphlet entitled *A Discovery of the Bermudas, otherwise called the Isle of Divels*. Soon afterwards there followed *A True Declaration of the Colonie in Virginia*, to which William Strachey, another member of the group, may have contributed data. Strachey was the writer of a letter, dated July 15, 1610, which was published only in 1625 in *Purchas his Pilgrimes* under the title, "A true reportory of the wracke, and redemption of Sir Thomas Gates, Knight." There can be no doubt, however, that it had circulated freely in manuscript and that somehow its contents reached Shakespeare. Numerous parallels and echoes in *The Tempest*, especially with reference to the storm, the climate, and the means of livelihood on Prospero's island, make it clear that Shakespeare had read the aforementioned narratives with keen attention, and may, indeed, have supplemented them with details gathered from some of the survivors. Nevertheless, it does not follow that Shakespeare intended to identify Prospero's island with Bermuda.

The Tempest is, with the exception of *The Comedy of Errors*, the shortest play Shakespeare wrote, and it is unique in the canon for its observance of the unity of time. The total action comprises little more than three hours. This compression suited Shakespeare's purpose, but he may still have taken a sly joy in proving to his classical friend, Ben Jonson, what he could do with a rule when he wished. He gave the freest possible rein to imagination, however, and Jonson, as if in retort, jovially slapped both *The Tempest* and *The Winter's Tale* in the Induction to his *Bartholomew Fair* (acted at Court, November 1, 1614): "If there bee never a *Seruant-monster* i' the Fayre; who can helpe it? he [Jonson] sayes; nor a nest of *Antiques*? Hee is loth to make Nature afraid in his *Playes*, like those that beget *Tales, Tempests*, and such like *Drolleries*."

The Tempest presents a comprehensive kind of entertainment: idyllic romance in the love of Ferdinand and Miranda, set against the background of Prospero's wrongs, of which, through his "rarer action" preferring virtue to vengeance, it is the benign outcome; realistic intrigue in the designs of Sebastian and Antonio upon Alonso, to which the conspiracy of Caliban and his confederates against Prospero is a kind of comic counterpart; excellent fooling in the trio of Caliban, Stephano, and Trinculo; overseeing wisdom and charity in Prospero, the master of the revels. For Prospero is master. It is clear from the beginning that the destinies of all, including his own, are in his hands, and we never doubt his providential guidance.

The harmony in which the heterogeneous elements of the play are blended, and the delicate poise maintained throughout between the illusions of fancy and reality, are miraculous. We surrender to the play as to a fairy tale of perennial charm, yet we do not entirely forget the world we live in.

Ariel, blithely serving out his time to win again his elemental freedom, enthralls the imagination, like the fairies of *A Midsummer Night's Dream*, to whom aesthetically he is kin. He has their vitality and their poetry, but while they make their own sport with foolish mortals, he performs the will of a human master.

If Ariel charms the imagination, Caliban, his gross opposite, teases it. The offspring of the Devil and a witch Sycorax, Caliban is a native of Prospero's island. His physique, kept by Shakespeare purposely indeterminate, it is impossible to visualize. Though he is "not honoured with a human shape," appears, in fact, to be "a strange fish," he is "legged like a man, and his fins [are] like arms" (II.ii.35); he has long nails and he can carry wood. That is about all that one can say. Prospero once calls him "tortoise" (I.ii.316), but this alludes to his sloth. Prospero has made him a slave, and he feels a peculiar hatred for this master, who has dispossessed him. There is a touch of pathos in Caliban's protesting claim to his island (I.ii.331–44). But his baser instincts have been his real enemy, for Prospero was fond of him at first and attempted to educate him (I.ii.353–65) with disappointing results. It would be interesting to know how much of Shakespeare's considered thought on the subject of the savage is reflected here. Indeed, when one recalls the fresh English interest in colonization and the reflections in *The Tempest* of the Virginia enterprise, it is tempting to see manifold problems adumbrated in the play: the relations of colonists with native populations, the question of government, the question of slavery, the missionary question, and so on. But all such speculation is perilous and can be indulged only with reserve and with a sense of humor to fall back upon. In a last word about Caliban it may be remarked that in his repudiation of his folly he is almost heroic (V.i.295–97).

Take it how one will, *The Tempest* remains an infinitely suggestive play, and not the least of its intimations concern the dramatist himself. Without resort to allegorical interpretation, of which there has been much, one may yet assert that Shakespeare's ripest thoughts upon life inform certain of the speeches of Prospero. The best known lines of the play (IV.i.148–58) constitute one of the most beautiful expressions in the language of the evanescence of earthly things. The words in which Prospero commends reason and virtue (V.i.25–30) express the goal of human wisdom. And when one reads Prospero's eloquent speech of abdication of his art (V.i.32–57), the notion that in penning it Shakespeare must have felt the analogy with the closing of his own career is too potent to be denied.

THE TEMPEST

ALONSO, *king of Naples.*
SEBASTIAN, *his brother.*
PROSPERO, *the right duke of Milan.*
ANTONIO, *his brother, the usurping duke of Milan.*
FERDINAND, *son to the king of Naples.*
GONZALO, *an honest old Counsellor.*
ADRIAN,
FRANCISCO, } *Lords.*
CALIBAN, *a savage and deformed Slave.*
TRINCULO, *a Jester.*

STEPHANO, *a drunken Butler.*
Master of a Ship.
Boatswain.
Mariners.
MIRANDA, *daughter to Prospero.*
ARIEL, *an airy Spirit.*
IRIS,
CERES,
JUNO, } *Spirits.*
Nymphs,
Reapers,

[Other Spirits attending on Prospero.]

SCENE: [*A ship at sea;*] *an uninhabited island.*

ACT I

SCENE I. [*On a ship at sea:*] *a tempestuous noise of thunder and lightning heard.*

Enter a SHIP-MASTER *and a* BOATSWAIN.

Mast. Boatswain!

Boats. Here, master; what cheer?

Mast. Good; speak to th' mariners. Fall to't, yarely, or we run ourselves aground. Bestir, bestir. [*Exit.* 5

Enter MARINERS.

Boats. Heigh, my hearts! cheerly, cheerly, my hearts! yare, yare! Take in the topsail. Tend to the master's whistle. — Blow till thou burst thy wind, if room enough!

Enter ALONSO, SEBASTIAN, ANTONIO, FERDINAND, GONZALO, *and others.*

Alon. Good boatswain, have care. Where's the master? Play the men. 11

Boats. I pray now, keep below.

Ant. Where is the master, bos'n?

Boats. Do you not hear him? You mar our labour. Keep your cabins; you do assist the storm.

Gon. Nay, good, be patient. 16

Boats. When the sea is. Hence! What cares these roarers for the name of king? To cabin! silence! trouble us not.

Gon. Good, yet remember whom thou hast aboard. 21

Boats. None that I more love than myself. You are a counsellor; if you can command these elements to silence, and work the peace of the present, we will not hand a rope more; use your authority. If you cannot, give thanks you have liv'd so long, and make yourself ready in your cabin for the mischance of the hour, if it so hap. — Cheerly, good hearts! — Out of our way, I say. [*Exit.* 29

Gon. I have great comfort from this fellow. Methinks he hath no drowning mark upon him; his complexion is perfect gallows. Stand fast, good Fate, to his hanging; make the rope of his destiny our cable, for our own doth little advantage. If he be not born to be hang'd, our case is miserable. [*Exeunt.* 36

Act I, sc. i, 4. **yarely:** nimbly. 16. **good:** i.e., good friend. 32. **his ... gallows:** his look shows he was born for hanging. 34. **advantage:** help (us).

Re-enter BOATSWAIN.

Boats. Down with the topmast! yare! lower, lower! Bring her to try wi' th' main-course. A plague   (*A cry within.*)

Re-enter SEBASTIAN, ANTONIO, *and* GONZALO.

upon this howling! They are louder than the weather or our office. — Yet again! What do   40
you here? Shall we give o'er and drown? Have you a mind to sink?

Seb. A pox o' your throat, you bawling, blasphemous, incharitable dog!

Boats. Work you, then.   45

Ant. Hang, cur! hang, you whoreson, insolent noisemaker! We are less afraid to be drown'd than thou art.

Gon. I'll warrant him for drowning though the ship were no stronger than a nut-shell and as leaky as an unstanched wench.   51

Boats. Lay her a-hold, a-hold! Set her two courses off to sea again! Lay her off.

Enter MARINERS *wet.*

Mariners. All lost! To prayers, to prayers! All lost!   55

Boats. What, must our mouths be cold?

Gon. The King and Prince at prayers! Let's assist them,
For our case is as theirs.

Seb.   I'm out of patience.

Ant. We are merely cheated of our lives by drunkards.
This wide-chopp'd rascal — would thou mightst lie drowning   60
The washing of ten tides!

Gon.   He'll be hang'd yet,
Though every drop of water swear against it
And gape at wid'st to glut him.

            [*A confused noise within.*
            Mercy on us!
We split, we split! Farewell, my wife and children!   65
Farewell, brother! We split, we split, we split!

Ant. Let's all sink wi' th' King.

Seb. Let's take leave of him.

            [*Exit.*
Gon. Now would I give a thousand furlongs of sea for an acre of barren ground, long heath, brown [furze], anything. The wills above be done! but I would fain die a dry death.   72
            [*Exeunt.*

SCENE II. [*The island. Before Prospero's cell.*]

Enter PROSPERO *and* MIRANDA.

Mir. If by your art, my dearest father, you have Put the wild waters in this roar, allay them.
The sky, it seems, would pour down stinking pitch, But that the sea, mounting to th' welkin's cheek, Dashes the fire out. O, I have suffer'd   5
With those that I saw suffer! A brave vessel, Who had, no doubt, some noble creature in her, Dash'd all to pieces! O, the cry did knock Against my very heart. Poor souls, they perish'd. Had I been any god of power, I would   10
Have sunk the sea within the earth or ere It should the good ship so have swallow'd and The fraughting souls within her.

Pros.   Be collected;
No more amazement. Tell your piteous heart There's no harm done.

Mir.   O, woe the day!

Pros.   No harm.
I have done nothing but in care of thee,   16
Of thee, my dear one, thee, my daughter, who Art ignorant of what thou art, nought knowing Of whence I am, nor that I am more better Than Prospero, master of a full poor cell,   20
And thy no greater father.

Mir.   More to know
Did never meddle with my thoughts.

Pros.   'Tis time
I should inform thee farther. Lend thy hand, And pluck my magic garment from me. So,
            [*Lays down his mantle.*
Lie there, my art. Wipe thou thine eyes; have comfort.   25
The direful spectacle of the wreck, which touch'd The very virtue of compassion in thee,
I have with such provision in mine art
So safely ordered that there is no soul —
No, not so much perdition as an hair   30
Betid to any creature in the vessel
Which thou heard'st cry, which thou saw'st sink.
            Sit down;
For thou must now know farther.

Mir.   You have often
Begun to tell me what I am, but stopp'd
And left me to a bootless inquisition,   35
Concluding, "Stay, not yet."

Pros.   The hour's now come;
The very minute bids thee ope thine ear.
Obey and be attentive. Canst thou remember
A time before we came unto this cell?

38. **Bring...try:** sail her near to the wind. **main-course:** mainsail. 49. **for:** against. 52. **a-hold:** close to the wind. 53. **courses:** points of the compass. **off:** i.e., away from shore. 59. **merely:** absolutely. 60. **wide-chopp'd:** wide-jawed. 63. **glut:** swallow. 71. **[furze]** (Hanmer). *firrs* F.

Sc. ii, 4. **welkin's:** sky's. 6. **brave:** fine, gallant. 13. **fraughting:** making the cargo. 14. **amazement:** terror. **piteous:** pitying. 22. **meddle:** mingle. 28. **provision:** foresight. 35. **bootless inquisition:** useless inquiry.

I do not think thou canst, for then thou wast not 40
Out three years old.

Mir.   Certainly, sir, I can.

Pros. By what? By any other house or person?
Of anything the image tell me, that
Hath kept with thy remembrance.

Mir.   'Tis far off
And rather like a dream than an assurance   45
That my remembrance warrants. Had I not
Four or five women once that tended me?

Pros. Thou hadst, and more, Miranda. But
    how is it
That this lives in thy mind? What seest thou else
In the dark backward and abysm of time?   50
If thou rememb'rest aught ere thou cam'st here,
How thou cam'st here thou may'st.

Mir.   But that I do not.

Pros. Twelve year since, Miranda, twelve year
    since,
Thy father was the Duke of Milan and   54
A prince of power.

Mir.   Sir, are not you my father?

Pros. Thy mother was a piece of virtue, and
She said thou wast my daughter; and thy father
Was Duke of Milan, and his only heir
And princess no worse issued.

Mir.   O the heavens!
What foul play had we, that we came from thence?
Or blessed was 't we did?

Pros.   Both, both, my girl. 61
By foul play, as thou say'st, were we heav'd thence,
But blessedly holp hither.

Mir.   O, my heart bleeds
To think o' th' teen that I have turn'd you to,
Which is from my remembrance! Please you, far-
    ther.   65

Pros. My brother and thy uncle, call'd Antonio —
I pray thee, mark me — that a brother should
Be so perfidious! — he whom next thyself
Of all the world I lov'd, and to him put
The manage of my state; as at that time   70
Through all the signories it was the first,
And Prospero the prime duke, being so reputed
In dignity, and for the liberal arts
Without a parallel; those being all my study,
The government I cast upon my brother   75
And to my state grew stranger, being transported
And rapt in secret studies. Thy false uncle —
Dost thou attend me?

Mir.   Sir, most heedfully.

Pros. Being once perfected how to grant suits,
How to deny them, who t' advance and who   80

To trash for overtopping, new created
The creatures that were mine, I say, or chang'd 'em,
Or else new form'd 'em; having both the key
Of officer and office, set all hearts i' th' state
To what tune pleas'd his ear; that now he was   85
The ivy which had hid my princely trunk,
And suck'd my verdure out on 't. Thou attend'st
    not.

Mir. O, good sir, I do.

Pros.   I pray thee, mark me.
I, thus neglecting worldly ends, all dedicated
To closeness and the bettering of my mind   90
With that which, but by being so retir'd,
O'er-priz'd all popular rate, in my false brother
Awak'd an evil nature; and my trust,
Like a good parent, did beget of him
A falsehood, in its contrary as great   95
As my trust was; which had indeed no limit,
A confidence sans bound. He being thus lorded,
Not only with what my revenue yielded,
But what my power might else exact, — like one
Who having into truth, by telling of it,   100
Made such a sinner of his memory
To credit his own lie, — he did believe
He was indeed the Duke. Out o' th' substitution,
And executing the outward face of royalty,   104
With all prerogative, hence his ambition growing —
Dost thou hear?

Mir.   Your tale, sir, would cure deafness.

Pros. To have no screen between this part he
    play'd
And him he play'd it for, he needs will be
Absolute Milan. Me, poor man! — my library
Was dukedom large enough — of temporal royal-
    ties   110
He thinks me now incapable; confederates —
So dry he was for sway — wi' th' King of Naples
To give him annual tribute, do him homage,
Subject his coronet to his crown, and bend
The dukedom yet unbow'd — alas, poor Milan! —
To most ignoble stooping.

Mir.   O the heavens!   116

Pros. Mark his condition and th' event, then tell
    me
If this might be a brother.

Mir.   I should sin
To think but nobly of my grandmother.
Good wombs have borne bad sons.

Pros.   Now the condition.
This King of Naples, being an enemy   121
To me inveterate, hearkens my brother's suit;
Which was, that he, in lieu o' th' premises,

---

41. **Out:** fully.   56. **piece:** masterpiece.   59. **issued:** born.   64. **teen:** trouble, grief.   79. **perfected:** expert.
81. **trash ... overtopping:** check for going too far ahead (hunting term).   83. **key:** (1) key to office, (2) tuning key.
90. **closeness:** seclusion.   92. **rate:** estimation.   97. **sans:** without.   100–102. **Who ... lie:** who, having told a lie so often,
came to believe it true.   107. **screen:** distinction.   108. **him ... for:** i.e., himself.   109. **Absolute Milan:** the actual Duke.
112. **dry:** thirsty.   117. **condition:** compact. **event:** outcome.   123. **lieu ... premises:** return for the stipulations.

Of homage, and I know not how much tribute,
Should presently extirpate me and mine   125
Out of the dukedom, and confer fair Milan
With all the honours on my brother; whereon,
A treacherous army levied, one midnight
Fated to th' purpose did Antonio open   129
The gates of Milan; and, i' th' dead of darkness,
The ministers for th' purpose hurried thence
Me and thy crying self.
　　Mir.　　　　　　　　Alack, for pity!
I, not rememb'ring how I cried out then,
Will cry it o'er again.　It is a hint   134
That wrings mine eyes to't.
　　Pros.　　　　　　　　Hear a little further,
And then I'll bring thee to the present business
Which now's upon 's, without the which this story
Were most impertinent.
　　Mir.　　　　　　Wherefore did they not
That hour destroy us?
　　Pros.　　　　　Well demanded, wench;
My tale provokes that question.　Dear, they durst
　　not   140
(So dear the love my people bore me) set
A mark so bloody on the business; but
With colours fairer painted their foul ends.
In few, they hurried us aboard a bark,
Bore us some leagues to sea; where they prepared
A rotten carcass of a butt, not rigg'd,   146
Nor tackle, sail, nor mast; the very rats
Instinctively have quit it.　There they hoist us,
To cry to th' sea that roar'd to us, to sigh
To th' winds whose pity, sighing back again,   150
Did us but loving wrong.
　　Mir.　　　　　　Alack, what trouble
Was I then to you!
　　Pros.　　　　　O, a cherubin
Thou wast that did preserve me.　Thou didst smile,
Infused with a fortitude from heaven,   154
When I have deck'd the sea with drops full salt,
Under my burden groan'd; which rais'd in me
An undergoing stomach, to bear up
Against what should ensue.
　　Mir.　　　　　　How came we ashore?
　　Pros.　By Providence divine.
Some food we had and some fresh water that   160
A noble Neapolitan, Gonzalo,
Out of his charity, who being then appointed
Master of this design, did give us, with
Rich garments, linens, stuffs, and necessaries,
Which since have steaded much; so, of his gentle-
　　ness,   165
Knowing I lov'd my books, he furnish'd me
From mine own library with volumes that

I prize above my dukedom.
　　Mir.　　　　　　Would I might
But ever see that man!
　　Pros.　　　　　Now I arise.
　　　　　　　　　　　[*Puts on his robe.*]
Sit still, and hear the last of our sea-sorrow.   170
Here in this island we arriv'd; and here
Have I, thy schoolmaster, made thee more profit
Than other princess can that have more time
For vainer hours and tutors not so careful.
　　Mir.　Heavens thank you for't!　And now, I
　　pray you, sir,   175
For still 'tis beating in my mind, your reason
For raising this sea-storm?
　　Pros.　　　　　Know thus far forth.
By accident most strange, bountiful Fortune,
Now my dear lady, hath mine enemies
Brought to this shore; and by my prescience   180
I find my zenith doth depend upon
A most auspicious star, whose influence
If now I court not but omit, my fortunes
Will ever after droop.　Here cease more questions.
Thou art inclin'd to sleep; 'tis a good dulness, 185
And give it way.　I know thou canst not choose.
　　　　　　　　　　　[*Miranda sleeps.*]
Come away, servant, come; I am ready now.
Approach, my Ariel; come.

　　　　　　　Enter ARIEL.

　　Ari.　All hail, great master! grave sir, hail! I come
To answer thy best pleasure, be't to fly,   190
To swim, to dive into the fire, to ride
On the curl'd clouds.　To thy strong bidding task
Ariel and all his quality.
　　Pros.　　　　　Hast thou, spirit,
Perform'd to point the tempest that I bade thee?
　　Ari.　To every article.   195
I boarded the king's ship; now on the beak,
Now in the waist, the deck, in every cabin,
I flam'd amazement.　Sometime I'd divide,
And burn in many places.　On the topmast,
The yards and bowsprit, would I flame distinctly,
Then meet and join.　Jove's lightnings, the pre-
　　cursors   201
O' th' dreadful thunder-claps, more momentary
And sight-outrunning were not; the fire and cracks
Of sulphurous roaring the most mighty Neptune
Seem to besiege, and make his bold waves tremble,
Yea, his dread trident shake.
　　Pros.　　　　　My brave spirit!
Who was so firm, so constant, that this coil   207
Would not infect his reason?
　　Ari.　　　　　Not a soul

---

134. **hint:** occasion.　141. **set** (Wright conj.).　*nor set* F.　144. **few:** short.　146. **butt:** tub.　155. **deck'd:** sprinkled.　157. **undergoing stomach:** courage to undergo.　165. **steaded:** helped.　173. **princess:** i.e., princesses.　Rowe reads *princes*.　181. **zenith:** height of fortune.　183. **omit:** ignore.　193. **quality:** (1) skill, (2) profession (i.e., fellow spirits).　194. **to point:** in every detail.　207. **coil:** turmoil.

But felt a fever of the mad, and play'd
Some tricks of desperation. All but mariners 210
Plung'd in the foaming brine and quit the vessel,
Then all afire with me. The King's son, Fer-
dinand,
With hair up-staring, — then like reeds, not hair, —
Was the first man that leap'd; cried, "Hell is
    empty,   214
And all the devils are here."
    Pros.   Why, that's my spirit!
But was not this nigh shore?
    Ari.   Close by, my master.
    Pros. But are they, Ariel, safe?
    Ari.   Not a hair perish'd;
On their sustaining garments not a blemish,
But fresher than before; and, as thou bad'st me,
In troops I have dispers'd them 'bout the isle. 220
The King's son have I landed by himself,
Whom I left cooling of the air with sighs
In an odd angle of the isle, and sitting,
His arms in this sad knot.
    Pros.   Of the King's ship
The mariners say how thou hast dispos'd,   225
And all the rest o' th' fleet.
    Ari.   Safely in harbour
Is the King's ship; in the deep nook, where once
Thou call'dst me up at midnight to fetch dew
From the still-vex'd Bermoothes, there she's hid;
The mariners all under hatches stow'd,   230
Who, with a charm join'd to their suff'red labour,
I have left asleep; and for the rest o' th' fleet,
Which I dispers'd, they all have met again,
And are upon the Mediterranean float
Bound sadly home for Naples,   235
Supposing that they saw the King's ship wreck'd
And his great person perish.
    Pros.   Ariel, thy charge
Exactly is perform'd; but there's more work.
What is the time o' th' day?
    Ari.   Past the mid season.
    Pros. At least two glasses. The time 'twixt six
    and now   240
Must by us both be spent most preciously.
    Ari. Is there more toil? Since thou dost give me
    pains,
Let me remember thee what thou hast promis'd,
Which is not yet perform'd me.
    Pros.   How now? moody?
What is't thou canst demand?
    Ari.   My liberty.   245
    Pros. Before the time be out? No more!
    Ari.   I prithee,
Remember I have done thee worthy service,
Told thee no lies, made thee no mistakings, serv'd

Without or grudge or grumblings. Thou did
    promise
To bate me a full year.
    Pros.   Dost thou forget   250
From what a torment I did free thee?
    Ari.   No.
    Pros. Thou dost, and think'st it much to tread
    the ooze
Of the salt deep,
To run upon the sharp wind of the north,
To do me business in the veins o' th' earth   255
When it is bak'd with frost.
    Ari.   I do not, sir.
    Pros. Thou liest, malignant thing! Hast thou
    forgot
The foul witch Sycorax, who with age and envy
Was grown into a hoop? Hast thou forgot her?
    Ari. No, sir.
    Pros.   Thou hast. Where was she born?
    Speak; tell me.   260
    Ari. Sir, in Argier.
    Pros.   O, was she so? I must
Once in a month recount what thou hast been,
Which thou forget'st. This damn'd witch Sycorax,
For mischiefs manifold and sorceries terrible
To enter human hearing, from Argier,   265
Thou know'st, was banish'd; for one thing she did
They would not take her life. Is not this true?
    Ari. Ay, sir.
    Pros. This blue-ey'd hag was hither brought with
    child,
And here was left by th' sailors. Thou, my slave,
As thou report'st thyself, was then her servant; 271
And, for thou wast a spirit too delicate
To act her earthly and abhorr'd commands,
Refusing her grand hests, she did confine thee,
By help of her more potent ministers   275
And in her most unmitigable rage,
Into a cloven pine; within which rift
Imprison'd thou didst painfully remain
A dozen years; within which space she died
And left thee there, where thou didst vent thy
    groans   280
As fast as mill-wheels strike. Then was this
    island —
Save for the son that [she] did litter here,
A freckl'd whelp, hag-born, — not honour'd with
A human shape.
    Ari.   Yes, Caliban her son.
    Pros. Dull thing, I say so; he, that Caliban 285
Whom now I keep in service. Thou best know'st
What torment I did find thee in; thy groans
Did make wolves howl, and penetrate the breasts
Of ever-angry bears. It was a torment

218. **sustaining:** supporting. 229. **still-vex'd Bermoothes:** ever-stormy Bermudas. 234. **float:** sea. 240. **glasses:** hour-glasses. 242. **pains:** labor. 250. **bate:** remit. 258. **envy:** malice. 261. **Argier:** Algiers. 269. **blue-ey'd:** with dark circles round the eyes; frequently emended to *blear-eyed.* 274. **hests:** commands. 282. **[she]** (Dryden). *he* F.

Caliban – earth
Ariel – air

elves could only work certain parts of night

To lay upon the damn'd, which Sycorax   290
Could not again undo. It was mine art,
When I arriv'd and heard thee, that made gape
The pine, and let thee out.
    Ari.   I thank thee, master.
    Pros. If thou more murmur'st, I will rend an oak
And peg thee in his knotty entrails till   295
Thou hast howl'd away twelve winters.
    Ari.   Pardon, master;
I will be correspondent to command
And do my spriting gently.
    Pros.   Do so, and after two days
I will discharge thee.
    Ari.   That's my noble master!
What shall I do? say what. What shall I do?   300
    Pros. Go make thyself like a nymph o' th' sea;
    be subject
To no sight but thine and mine, invisible
To every eyeball else. Go take this shape
And hither come in't. Go, hence with diligence!
                      [*Exit Ariel.*
Awake, dear heart, awake! Thou hast slept well;
Awake!   306
    Mir. The strangeness of your story put
Heaviness in me.
    Pros.   Shake it off. Come on;
We'll visit Caliban my slave, who never
Yields us kind answer.
    Mir.   'Tis a villain, sir,
I do not love to look on.
    Pros.   But, as 'tis,   310
We cannot miss him. He does make our fire,
Fetch in our wood, and serves in offices
That profit us. What, ho! slave! Caliban!
Thou earth, thou! speak.
    Cal. (*Within.*) There's wood enough within.

Caliban

    Pros. Come forth, I say! there's other business
    for thee.   315
Come, thou tortoise! when?

         Re-enter ARIEL *like a water-nymph.*

Fine apparition! My quaint Ariel,
Hark in thine ear.
    Ari.   My lord, it shall be done.
                          [*Exit.*
    Pros. Thou poisonous slave, got by the devil
    himself
Upon thy wicked dam, come forth!   320

            Enter CALIBAN.

    Cal. As wicked dew as e'er my mother brush'd
With raven's feather from unwholesome fen
Drop on you both! A south-west blow on ye
And blister you all o'er!   *wind which brings diseases*

    Pros. For this, be sure, to-night thou shalt have
    cramps,   325
Side-stitches that shall pen thy breath up; urchins
Shall, for that vast of night that they may work,
All exercise on thee; thou shalt be pinch'd
As thick as honeycomb, each pinch more stinging
Than bees that made 'em.
    Cal.   I must eat my dinner.
This island's mine, by Sycorax my mother,   331
Which thou tak'st from me. When thou cam'st first,
Thou [strok'dst] me and made much of me, wouldst
    give me
Water with berries in't, and teach me how
To name the bigger light, and how the less,   335
That burn by day and night; and then I lov'd thee
And show'd thee all the qualities o' th' isle,
The fresh springs, brine-pits, barren place and
    fertile.
Curs'd be I that did so! All the charms
Of Sycorax, toads, beetles, bats, light on you!
For I am all the subjects that you have,   341
Which first was mine own king; and here you *sty*
    me
In this hard rock, whiles you do keep from me
The rest o' th' island.
    Pros.   Thou most lying slave,
Whom stripes may move, not kindness! I have
    us'd thee,   345
Filth as thou art, with human care, and lodg'd thee
In mine own cell, till thou didst seek to violate
The honour of my child.
    Cal. O ho, O ho! would 't had been done!
Thou didst prevent me; I had peopl'd else   350
This isle with Calibans.
    [*Pros.*]   Abhorred slave,
Which any print of goodness wilt not take,
Being capable of all ill! I pitied thee,
Took pains to make thee speak, taught thee each
    hour   354
One thing or other. When thou didst not, savage,
Know thine own meaning, but wouldst gabble like
A thing most brutish, I endow'd thy purposes
With words that made them known. But thy vile
    race, *inherited nature*
Though thou didst learn, had that in't which good
    natures
Could not abide to be with; therefore wast thou
Deservedly confin'd into this rock,   361
Who hadst deserv'd more than a prison.
    Cal. You taught me language; and my profit
    on't *allegory?*
Is, I know how to curse. The red plague rid you
For learning me your language!
    Pros.   Hag-seed, hence!

---

297. **correspondent:** obedient.   311. **miss:** do without.   317. **quaint:** dainty.   326. **urchins:** goblins (lit., hedgehogs).
327. **vast:** dark void.   333. **[strok'dst]** (Rowe).   *stroakst* F.   351. **[Pros.]** (Dryden).   *Mira.* F.   358. **race:** inherited nature.
364. **rid:** destroy.

Prospero, Miranda watching [handwritten]

Fetch us in fuel; and be quick, thou 'rt best, 366
To answer other business. Shrug'st thou, malice?
If thou neglect'st or dost unwillingly
What I command, I'll rack thee with old cramps,
Fill all thy bones with achës, make thee roar 370
That beasts shall tremble at thy din.
    Cal.   No, pray thee.
[*Aside.*] I must obey. His art is of such power
It would control my dam's god, Setebos, *Caliban's god* [handwritten]
And make a vassal of him.
    Pros.   So, slave; hence! 375
                            [*Exit Caliban.*

Re-enter ARIEL, *invisible, playing and singing;*
    FERDINAND [*following*].

        ARIEL'S SONG.

    Come unto these yellow sands,   *Song* [handwritten]
        And then take hands.
    Curtsied when you have, and kiss'd   *about a dance* [handwritten]
        The wild waves whist,   *silent* [handwritten]
    Foot it featly here and there,   380
    And, sweet sprites, the burden bear.
Burden (*dispersedly*). Hark, hark!
                    Bow-wow.   *fantastic* [handwritten]
    The watch-dogs bark!   *song they heard, spread out on feet* [handwritten]
                    Bow-wow.
Ari. Hark, hark! I hear
    The strain of strutting chanticleer   385
    Cry, "Cock-a-diddle-dow."

Fer. Where should this music be? I' th' air or
        th' earth?
It sounds no more; and, sure, it waits upon
Some god o' th' island. Sitting on a bank,
Weeping again the King my father's wreck, 390
This music crept by me upon the waters,
Allaying both their fury and my passion
With its sweet air; thence I have follow'd it,
Or it hath drawn me rather. But 'tis gone.
No, it begins again.   395

        ARIEL'S SONG.

    Full fathom five thy father lies;   *this* [handwritten]
        Of his bones are coral made;
    Those are pearls that were his eyes: *isn't true* [handwritten]
        Nothing of him that doth fade
    But doth suffer a sea-change   400
    Into something rich and strange.
    Sea-nymphs hourly ring his knell:
Burden.   Ding-dong.
Ari. Hark! now I hear them, — ding-dong, bell.
Fer. The ditty does remember my drown'd
        father.   405

This is no mortal business, nor no sound
That the earth owes. I hear it now above me.
    Pros. The fringed curtains of thine eye advance
And say what thou seest yond.
    Mir.   What is 't? A spirit?
Lord, how it looks about! Believe me, sir, 410
It carries a brave form. But 'tis a spirit.
    Pros. No, wench; it eats and sleeps and hath such
        senses
As we have, such. This gallant which thou seest
Was in the wreck; and, but he's something stain'd
With grief, that's beauty's canker, thou mightst   *tear stained* [handwritten]
        call him   415
A goodly person. He hath lost his fellows
And strays about to find 'em.
    Mir.   I might call him
A thing divine; for nothing natural
I ever saw so noble.
    Pros. [*Aside.*] It goes on, I see,
As my soul prompts it. Spirit, fine spirit! I'll free
        thee   420
Within two days for this.
    Fer.   Most sure, the goddess   *Miranda* [handwritten]
On whom these airs attend! Vouchsafe my prayer
May know if you remain upon this island,
And that you will some good instruction give
How I may bear me here. My prime request, 425
Which I do last pronounce, is, O you wonder!
If you be maid or no?
    Mir.   No wonder, sir,
But certainly a maid.
    Fer.   My language! heavens!
I am the best of them that speak this speech, 429
Were I but where 'tis spoken.
    Pros.   How? the best?
What wert thou, if the King of Naples heard thee?
    Fer. A single thing, as I am now, that wonders
To hear thee speak of Naples. He does hear me;
And that he does I weep. Myself am Naples,
Who with mine eyes, never since at ebb, beheld 435
The King my father wreck'd.
    Mir.   Alack, for mercy!   *Miranda pity* [handwritten]
    Fer. Yes, faith, and all his lords; the Duke of
        Milan
And his brave son being twain.
    Pros.   [*Aside.*] The Duke of Milan
And his more braver daughter could control thee,
If now 'twere fit to do 't. At the first sight 440
They have chang'd eyes. Delicate Ariel,
I'll set thee free for this. [*To Fer.*] A word, good
        sir;
I fear you have done yourself some wrong; a word.
    Mir. Why speaks my father so ungently? This

---

370. **achës.** Pronounced "aitches." 379. **whist:** (being) silent. 380. **featly:** nimbly. 381. **the burden bear** Q 1674.
beare the burthen F. 382. s.d. **Burden:** refrain. **dispersedly:** from several directions. 405. **remember:** commemorate.
407. **owes:** owns. 408. **advance:** raise. 415. **canker:** canker-worm. 432. **single:** solitary, helpless. 439. **control:** confute.
441. **chang'd eyes:** exchanged loving glances.

Is the third man that e'er I saw, the first   445
That e'er I sigh'd for.   Pity move my father
To be inclin'd my way!
   Fer.   O, if a virgin,
And your affection not gone forth, I'll make you
The Queen of Naples.
   Pros.   Soft, sir! one word more.
[*Aside.*] They are both in either's powers; but this
    swift business   450
I must uneasy make, lest too light winning
Make the prize light.   [*To Fer.*] One word more; I
    charge thee
That thou attend me.   Thou dost here usurp
The name thou ow'st not; and hast put thyself
Upon this island as a spy, to win it   455
From me, the lord on't.
   Fer.   No, as I am a man.
   Mir.   There's nothing ill can dwell in such a
    temple.
If the ill spirit have so fair a house,
Good things will strive to dwell with 't.
   Pros.   Follow me.
Speak not you for him; he's a traitor.   Come,   460
I'll manacle thy neck and feet together.
Sea-water shalt thou drink; thy food shall be
The fresh-brook mussels, wither'd roots and husks
Wherein the acorn cradled.   Follow.
   Fer.   No;
I will resist such entertainment till   465
Mine enemy has more power.
     [*He draws, and is charmed from moving.*
   Mir.   O dear father,
Make not too rash a trial of him, for
He's gentle and not fearful.
   Pros.   What! I say;
My foot my tutor?   Put thy sword up, traitor,
Who mak'st but a show but dar'st not strike, thy con-
    science   470
Is so possess'd with guilt.   Come from thy ward,
For I can here disarm thee with this stick
And make thy weapon drop.
   Mir.   Beseech you, father.
   Pros.   Hence! hang not on my garments.
   Mir.   Sir, have pity;
I'll be his surety.
   Pros.   Silence! one word more   475
Shall make me chide thee if not hate thee.   What!
An advocate for an impostor! hush!
Thou think'st there is no more such shapes as he,
Having seen but him and Caliban.   Foolish wench!
To th' most of men this is a Caliban,   480
And they to him are angels.
   Mir.   My affections
Are then most humble; I have no ambition

To see a goodlier man.
   Pros.   Come on; obey.
Thy nerves are in their infancy again
And have no vigour in them.
   Fer.   So they are.   485
My spirits, as in a dream, are all bound up.
My father's loss, the weakness which I feel,
The wreck of all my friends, nor this man's threats
To whom I am subdu'd, are but light to me,
Might I but through my prison once a day   490
Behold this maid.   All corners else o' th' earth
Let liberty make use of; space enough
Have I in such a prison.
   Pros. [*Aside.*] It works.   [*To Fer.*]   Come on.
— Thou hast done well, fine Ariel!   [*To Fer.*] Fol-
    low me.
[*To Ari.*]   Hark what thou else shalt do me.
   Mir.   Be of comfort;
My father's of a better nature, sir,   496
Than he appears by speech.   This is unwonted
Which now came from him.
   Pros.   [*To Ari.*] Thou shalt be as free
As mountain winds; but then exactly do
All points of my command.
   Ari.   To th' syllable.   500
   Pros. [*To Mir. and Fer.*]   Come, follow.   Speak
    not for him.   [*Exeunt.*

ACT II

SCENE I.   [*Another part of the island.*]

Enter ALONSO, SEBASTIAN, ANTONIO, GONZALO,
   ADRIAN, FRANCISCO, *and others.*

   Gon.   Beseech you, sir, be merry; you have cause,
So have we all, of joy; for our escape
Is much beyond our loss.   Our hint of woe
Is common; every day some sailor's wife,
The masters of some merchant, and the merchant   5
Have just our theme of woe; but for the miracle,
I mean our preservation, few in millions
Can speak like us.   Then wisely, good sir, weigh
Our sorrow with our comfort.
   Alon.   Prithee, peace.
   Seb.   He receives comfort like cold porridge.   10
   Ant.   The visitor will not give him o'er so.
   Seb.   Look, he's winding up the watch of his wit;
by and by it will strike.
   Gon.   Sir, —
   Seb.   One.   Tell.   15
   Gon.   When every grief is entertain'd that's
    offer'd,
Comes to th' entertainer —
   Seb.   A dollar.

---

468. **fearful:** dangerous.   469. **foot:** subordinate, i.e., Miranda.   471. **Come . . . ward:** drop your posture of defense.
484. **nerves:** sinews.   486. **spirits:** vital powers.
   Act II, sc. i, 5. **merchant:** merchant vessel.   11. **visitor:** spiritual guide.   15. **Tell:** count.

Gon. Dolour comes to him, indeed; you have spoken truer than you purpos'd.   20

Seb. You have taken it wiselier than I meant you should.

Gon. Therefore, my lord, —

Ant. Fie, what a spendthrift is he of his tongue!

Alon. I prithee, spare.   25

Gon. Well, I have done. But yet, —

Seb. He will be talking.

Ant. Which, of he or Adrian, for a good wager, first begins to crow?

Seb. The old cock.   *Gonzalo*   30

Ant. The cock'rel.   *Adrian*

Seb. Done. The wager?

Ant. A laughter. *— pun (setting of eggs).*

Seb. A match!   34

Adr. Though this island seem to be desert, —

Seb. Ha, ha, ha! [Antonio]! So you're paid.

Adr. Uninhabitable and almost inaccessible, —

Seb. Yet, —

Adr. Yet, —

Ant. He could not miss't.   40

Adr. It must needs be of subtle, tender, and delicate temperance.

Ant. Temperance was a delicate wench.

Seb. Ay, and a subtle; as he most learnedly deliver'd.   45

Adr. The air breathes upon us here most sweetly.

Seb. As if it had lungs and rotten ones.

Ant. Or as 'twere perfum'd by a fen.

Gon. Here is everything advantageous to life.

Ant. True; save means to live.   50

Seb. Of that there's none, or little.

Gon. How lush and lusty the grass looks! How green!

Ant. The ground indeed is tawny.   *Gonzalo*

Seb. With an eye of green in't.   *easily deceived*   55

Ant. He misses not much.

Seb. No; he doth but mistake the truth totally.

Gon. But the rarity of it is, — which is indeed almost beyond credit, —

Seb. As many vouch'd rarities are.   60

Gon. That our garments, being, as they were, drench'd in the sea, hold notwithstanding their freshness and glosses, being rather new-dy'd than stain'd with salt water.

Ant. If but one of his pockets could speak, would it not say he lies?   66

Seb. Ay, or very falsely pocket up his report.

Gon. Methinks our garments are now as fresh as when we put them on first in Afric, at the marriage of the King's fair daughter Claribel to the King of Tunis.   71

Seb. 'Twas a sweet marriage, and we prosper well in our return.

Adr. Tunis was never grac'd before with such a paragon to their queen.   75

Gon. Not since widow Dido's time.

Ant. Widow! a pox o' that! How came that widow in? Widow Dido!

Seb. What if he had said "widower Æneas" too? Good Lord, how you take it!   80

Adr. "Widow Dido" said you? You make me study of that. She was of Carthage, not of Tunis.

Gon. This Tunis, sir, was Carthage.

Adr. Carthage?

Gon. I assure you, Carthage.   85

Ant. His word is more than the miraculous harp.

Seb. He hath rais'd the wall and houses too.

Ant. What impossible matter will he make easy next?

Seb. I think he will carry this island home in his pocket and give it his son for an apple.   91

Ant. And, sowing the kernels of it in the sea, bring forth more islands.

Gon. Ay.

Ant. Why, in good time.   95

Gon. Sir, we were talking that our garments seem now as fresh as when we were at Tunis at the marriage of your daughter, who is now Queen.

Ant. And the rarest that e'er came there.

Seb. Bate, I beseech you, widow Dido.   100

Ant. O, widow Dido! ay, widow Dido.

Gon. Is not, sir, my doublet as fresh as the first day I wore it? I mean, in a sort.

Ant. That "sort" was well fish'd for.

Gon. When I wore it at your daughter's marriage?   105

Alon. You cram these words into mine ears against
The stomach of my sense. Would I had never
Married my daughter there! for, coming thence,
My son is lost and, in my rate, she too,
Who is so far from Italy removed   110
I ne'er again shall see her. O thou mine heir
Of Naples and of Milan, what strange fish
Hath made his meal on thee?

Fran.   Sir, he may live.
I saw him beat the surges under him
And ride upon their backs. He trod the water,   115
Whose enmity he flung aside, and breasted
The surge most swoln that met him. His bold head
'Bove the contentious waves he kept, and oar'd
Himself with his good arms in lusty stroke
To th' shore, that o'er his wave-worn basis bowed,
As stooping to relieve him. I not doubt   121

---

33. **laughter:** (1) a laugh, (2) sitting of eggs.   34. **match:** bargain.   36. **Ha . . . paid.** Since Adrian speaks first, Sebastian loses the bet and pays Antonio his laugh. **[Antonio]** (Liddell). *Ant.* F (as speech-tag).   40. **miss't:** miss saying "yet," or, do without the island.   42. **temperance:** temperature.   55. **eye:** spot.   86. **harp:** the harp of Amphion, whose music raised the walls of Thebes.   100. **Bate:** except.   107. **stomach:** inclination.   109. **rate:** judgment.

He came alive to land.

Alon.   No, no, he's gone.

Seb. Sir, you may thank yourself for this great
     loss,
That would not bless our Europe with your daughter,
But rather loose her to an African;   125
Where she at least is banish'd from your eye,
Who hath cause to wet the grief on't.

Alon.   Prithee, peace.

Seb. You were kneel'd to and importun'd other-
     wise
By all of us, and the fair soul herself
Weigh'd between loathness and obedience, at
Which end o' th' beam should bow. We have lost
     your son,   131
I fear, for ever. Milan and Naples have
Moe widows in them of this business' making
Than we bring men to comfort them.
The fault's your own.

Alon.   So is the dear'st o' th' loss.

Gon. My lord Sebastian,   136
The truth you speak doth lack some gentleness
And time to speak it in. You rub the sore,
When you should bring the plaster.

Seb.   Very well.

Ant. And most chirurgeonly.   140

Gon. It is foul weather in us all, good sir,
When you are cloudy.

Seb.   Foul weather?

Ant.   Very foul.

Gon. Had I plantation of this isle, my lord, —

Ant. He'd sow't with nettle-seed.

Seb.   Or docks, or mallows.

Gon. And were the king on't, what would I do?

Seb. Scape being drunk for want of wine.   146

Gon. I' th' commonwealth I would by contraries
Execute all things; for no kind of traffic
Would I admit; no name of magistrate;
Letters should not be known; riches, poverty, 150
And use of service, none; contract, succession,
Bourn, bound of land, tilth, vineyard, none;
No use of metal, corn, or wine, or oil;
No occupation; all men idle, all;
And women too, but innocent and pure;   155
No sovereignty; —

Seb.   Yet he would be king on't.

Ant. The latter end of his commonwealth forgets
the beginning.

Gon. All things in common nature should pro-
     duce   159
Without sweat or endeavour: treason, felony,

Sword, pike, knife, gun, or need of any engine,
Would I not have; but nature should bring forth,
Of it own kind, all foison, all abundance,
To feed my innocent people.

Seb. No marrying 'mong his subjects?   165

Ant. None, man; all idle; whores and knaves.

Gon. I would with such perfection govern, sir,
T' excel the golden age.

Seb.   Save his Majesty!

Ant. Long live Gonzalo!

Gon.   And, — do you mark me, sir?

Alon. Prithee, no more; thou dost talk nothing to
me.   171

Gon. I do well believe your Highness; and did it
to minister occasion to these gentlemen, who are of
such sensible and nimble lungs that they always use
to laugh at nothing.   175

Ant. 'Twas you we laugh'd at.

Gon. Who in this kind of merry fooling am nothing to you. So you may continue and laugh at nothing still.

Ant. What a blow was there given!   180

Seb. An it had not fallen flatlong.

Gon. You are gentlemen of brave mettle; you
would lift the moon out of her sphere, if she would
continue in it five weeks without changing.

Enter ARIEL [*invisible*], *playing solemn music.*

Seb. We would so, and then go a bat-fowling.

Ant. Nay, good my lord, be not angry.   186

Gon. No, I warrant you; I will not adventure my
discretion so weakly. Will you laugh me asleep,
for I am very heavy?

Ant. Go sleep, and hear us.   190

     [*All sleep except Alon., Seb., and Ant.*]

Alon. What, all so soon asleep! I wish mine eyes
Would, with themselves, shut up my thoughts. I
     find
They are inclin'd to do so.

Seb.   Please you, sir,
Do not omit the heavy offer of it.
It seldom visits sorrow; when it doth,   195
It is a comforter.

Ant.   We two, my lord,
Will guard your person while you take your rest,
And watch your safety.

Alon.   Thank you. Wondrous heavy.

     [*Alonso sleeps. Exit Ariel.*]

Seb. What a strange drowsiness possesses them!

Ant. It is the quality o' th' climate.

Seb.   Why   200

---

125. **loose her:** turn her loose. 127. **Who:** which (eye). 130. **Weigh'd:** poised. **loathness:** unwillingness. 135. **dear'st:**
most keenly felt. 140. **chirurgeonly:** like a surgeon. 143. **plantation:** colonizing. 147. **by contraries:** contrary to custom.
150. **Letters:** learning. 151. **service:** servants. **succession:** inheritance. 152. **Bourn:** boundary. **tilth:** tilling of soil.
161. **engine:** instrument of war. 163. **it:** its. **foison:** plenty. 174. **sensible:** sensitive. 181. **flatlong:** with the flat of
the sword. 185. **bat-fowling:** hunting birds by night. *Bat* is a stick for knocking them down. 187. **adventure:** risk.
194. **omit:** neglect.

Handwritten note at top: by time Claribel hears her father dead + gets there with an army — Ant will be well established by then

Doth it not then our eyelids sink? I find not
Myself dispos'd to sleep.
Ant.   Nor I; my spirits are nimble.
They fell together all, as by consent;
They dropp'd, as by a thunder-stroke. What
    might,
Worthy Sebastian, O, what might —? No more: —
And yet methinks I see it in thy face,   206
What thou shouldst be. Th' occasion speaks thee,
    and
My strong imagination sees a crown
Dropping upon thy head.
    Seb.   What, art thou waking?
    Ant. Do you not hear me speak?
    Seb.   I do; and surely
It is a sleepy language, and thou speak'st   211
Out of thy sleep. What is it thou didst say?
This is a strange repose, to be asleep
With eyes wide open; standing, speaking, moving,
And yet so fast asleep.
    Ant.   Noble Sebastian,   215
Thou let'st thy fortune sleep — die, rather;
    wink'st
Whiles thou art waking.
    Seb.   Thou dost snore distinctly;
There's meaning in thy snores.
    Ant. I am more serious than my custom; you
Must be so too, if heed me; which to do   220
Trebles thee o'er.
    Seb.   Well, I am standing water.
    Ant. I'll teach you how to flow.
    Seb.   Do so. To ebb
Hereditary sloth instructs me.
    Ant.   O,
If you but knew how you the purpose cherish
Whiles thus you mock it! how, in stripping it, 225
You more invest it! Ebbing men, indeed,
Most often do so near the bottom run
By their own fear or sloth.
    Seb.   Prithee, say on.
The setting of thine eye and cheek proclaim
A matter from thee, and a birth indeed   230
Which throes thee much to yield.
    Ant.   Thus, sir:
Although this lord of weak remembrance, this
Who shall be of as little memory
When he is earth'd, hath here almost persuaded —
For he's a spirit of persuasion, only   235
Professes to persuade — the King his son's alive,
'Tis as impossible that he's undrown'd

As he that sleeps here swims.
    Seb.   I have no hope
That he's undrown'd.
    Ant.   O, out of that no hope
What great hope have you! No hope that way is
Another way so high a hope that even   241
Ambition cannot pierce a wink beyond,
But doubt discovery there. Will you grant with
    me
That Ferdinand is drown'd?
    Seb.   He's gone.
    Ant.   Then, tell me,
Who's the next heir of Naples?
    Seb.   Claribel.   245
    Ant. She that is Queen of Tunis; she that dwells
Ten leagues beyond man's life; she that from
    Naples
Can have no note, unless the sun were post —
The Man i' th' Moon's too slow — till newborn
    chins   249
Be rough and razorable; she that — from whom
We all were sea-swallow'd, though some cast again,
And by that destiny to perform an act
Whereof what's past is prologue, what to come
In yours and my discharge.
    Seb.   What stuff is this! How say you?
'Tis true, my brother's daughter 's Queen of
    Tunis;
So is she heir of Naples; 'twixt which regions   256
There is some space.
    Ant.   A space whose every cubit
Seems to cry out, "How shall that Claribel
Measure us back to Naples? Keep in Tunis,
And let Sebastian wake." Say this were death   260
That now hath seiz'd them; why, they were no
    worse
Than now they are. There be that can rule Naples
As well as he that sleeps; lords that can prate
As amply and unnecessarily
As this Gonzalo; I myself could make   265
A chough of as deep chat. O, that you bore
The mind that I do! what a sleep were this
For your advancement! Do you understand me?
    Seb. Methinks I do.
    Ant.   And how does your content
Tender your own good fortune?
    Seb.   I remember   270
You did supplant your brother Prospero.
    Ant.   True.
And look how well my garments sit upon me;

203. **consent:** agreement. 207. **speaks:** proclaims. 216. **wink'st:** closest thine eyes. 221. **Trebles...o'er:** triples thy greatness. **standing water:** between ebb and flow, i.e., undecided. 225–26. **in...it:** in making little of it, you give it more meaning. 231. **throes:** pains. 232. **this lord:** probably Francisco. See ll. 113 ff. 234. **earth'd:** buried. 242–43. **cannot...there:** cannot imagine anything higher beyond, but can only find it difficult to believe what it sees there. 247. **man's life:** a lifetime journey. 248. **note:** news. 250. **from:** coming from. 251. **cast:** (1) cast up, (2) cast as actors. 254. **discharge:** performance. 259. **Measure us:** travel over us (the cubits). **Keep:** i.e., let her stay. 260. **wake:** i.e., awake to fortune. 266. **chough...chat:** jackdaw chatter as wisely. 269. **content:** desire. 270. **Tender:** regard.

Much feater than before. My brother's servants
Were then my fellows; now they are my men.
   Seb. But, for your conscience?   275
   Ant. Ay, sir, where lies that? If 'twere a kibe,
'Twould put me to my slipper; but I feel not
This deity in my bosom. Twenty consciences,
That stand 'twixt me and Milan, candied be they
And melt ere they molest! Here lies your brother,
No better than the earth he lies upon   281
If he were that which now he's like, that's dead;
Whom I, with this obedient steel, three inches of it,
Can lay to bed for ever; whiles you, doing thus,
To the perpetual wink for aye might put   285
This ancient morsel, this Sir Prudence, who
Should not upbraid our course. For all the rest,
They'll take suggestion as a cat laps milk;
They'll tell the clock to any business that   289
We say befits the hour.
   Seb.   Thy case, dear friend,
Shall be my precedent; as thou got'st Milan,
I'll come by Naples. Draw thy sword. One stroke
Shall free thee from the tribute which thou payest,
And I the King shall love thee.
   Ant.   Draw together;
And when I rear my hand, do you the like,   295
To fall it on Gonzalo.
   Seb.   O, but one word.
                    [They talk apart.]

Re-enter ARIEL *[invisible], with music and song.*

   Ari. My master through his art foresees the danger
That you, his friend, are in; and sends me forth —
For else his project dies — to keep them living.
                [Sings in Gonzalo's ear.
     While you here do snoring lie,   300
     Open-ey'd Conspiracy
       His time doth take.
     If of life you keep a care,
     Shake off slumber, and beware;
       Awake, awake!   305
   Ant. Then let us both be sudden.
   Gon. [Waking.]   Now, good angels
Preserve the King!   *[Wakes Alon.]*
   Alon. Why, how now? — Ho, awake! — Why
are you drawn?   308
Wherefore this ghastly looking?
   Gon.   What's the matter?
   Seb. Whiles we stood here securing your repose,
Even now, we heard a hollow burst of bellowing
Like bulls, or rather lions. Did 't not wake you?
It struck mine ear most terribly.
   Alon.   I heard nothing.
   Ant. O, 'twas a din to fright a monster's ear,
To make an earthquake! Sure, it was the roar   315

Of a whole herd of lions.
   Alon.   Heard you this, Gonzalo?
   Gon. Upon mine honour, sir, I heard a humming,
And that a strange one too, which did awake me.
I shak'd you, sir, and cried. As mine eyes open'd,
I saw their weapons drawn. There was a noise,
That's verily. 'Tis best we stand upon our guard,
Or that we quit this place. Let's draw our weapons.   322
   Alon. Lead off this ground; and let's make further search
For my poor son.
   Gon. Heavens keep him from these beasts!
For he is, sure, i' th' island.
   Alon.   Lead away.   325
   Ari. Prospero my lord shall know what I have done.
So, King, go safely on to seek thy son.   *[Exeunt.*

SCENE II. *[Another part of the island.]*

Enter CALIBAN *with a burden of wood. A noise
of thunder heard.*

   Cal. All the infections that the sun sucks up
From bogs, fens, flats, on Prosper fall and make him
By inch-meal a disease! His spirits hear me
And yet I needs must curse. But they'll nor pinch,
Fright me with urchin-shows, pitch me i' th' mire,
Nor lead me, like a firebrand, in the dark   6
Out of my way, unless he bid 'em; but
For every trifle are they set upon me,
Sometime like apes that mow and chatter at me
And after bite me, then like hedgehogs which   10
Lie tumbling in my barefoot way and mount
Their pricks at my footfall; sometime am I
All wound with adders who with cloven tongues
Do hiss me into madness.

Enter TRINCULO.
                Lo, now, lo!
Here comes a spirit of his, and to torment me   15
For bringing wood in slowly. I'll fall flat;
Perchance he will not mind me.
   Trin. Here's neither bush nor shrub to bear off
any weather at all, and another storm brewing; I
hear it sing i' th' wind. Yond same black cloud,   20
yond huge one, looks like a foul bombard that
would shed his liquor. If it should thunder as it
did before, I know not where to hide my head; yond
same cloud cannot choose but fall by pailfuls.
What have we here? A man or a fish? Dead   25
or alive? A fish; he smells like a fish; a very ancient and fish-like smell; a kind of not-of-the-newest
Poor-John. A strange fish! Were I in England

273. **feater:** more becomingly. 276. **kibe:** chilblain. 279. **candied:** frozen. 308. **Ho, awake!** To the other sleepers.
Sc. ii, 3. **By inch-meal:** inch by inch. 6. **like:** in the shape of. 21. **bombard:** leather bottle. 28. **Poor-John:** salted hake.

[handwritten annotations in top margin: "ambiguity Elizabethan love of a code ... ?"]

now, as once I was, and had but this fish painted,
not a holiday fool there but would give a piece of   30
silver.   There would this monster make a man; any
strange beast there makes a man.   When they will
not give a doit to relieve a lame beggar, they will
lay out ten to see a dead Indian.   Legg'd like a
man! and his fins like arms!   Warm o' my troth!   35
I do now let loose my opinion, hold it no longer: this
is no fish, but an islander, that hath lately suffered
by a thunderbolt.   [*Thunder.*]   Alas, the storm is
come again!   My best way is to creep under his
gaberdine; there is no other shelter hereabout.   40
Misery acquaints a man with strange bedfellows.
I will here shroud till the dregs of the storm be past.

Enter STEPHANO, *singing* [: *a bottle in his hand*].

   Ste. "I shall no more to sea, to sea,
       Here shall I die ashore —"   45
This is a very scurvy tune to sing at a man's funeral.   Well, here's my comfort.   [*Drinks.*

(*Sings.*) "The master, the swabber, the boatswain,
    and I,
       The gunner and his mate *[a sailor's song]*
Lov'd Moll, Meg, and Marian, and Margery,   50
    But none of us car'd for Kate;
    For she had a tongue with a tang,
    Would cry to a sailor, 'Go hang!'
She lov'd not the savour of tar nor of pitch,   54
Yet a tailor might scratch her where'er she did itch;
    Then to sea, boys, and let her go hang!"

This is a scurvy tune too; but here's my comfort.
                    [*Drinks.*
Cal. Do not torment me!   Oh!   58
Ste. What's the matter?   Have we devils here?
Do you put tricks upon 's with savages and men of
Ind, ha?   I have not scap'd drowning to be afeard
now of your four legs; for it hath been said, "As
proper a man as ever went on four legs cannot make
him give ground"; and it shall be said so again
while Stephano breathes at nostrils.   65
Cal. The spirit torments me!   Oh!
Ste. This is some monster of the isle with four
legs, who hath got, as I take it, an ague.   Where the
devil should he learn our language?   I will give him
some relief, if it be but for that.   If I can re-   70
cover him and keep him tame and get to Naples
with him, he's a present for any emperor that ever
trod on neat's-leather.
Cal. Do not torment me, prithee; I'll bring my
wood home faster.   75

Ste. He's in his fit now and does not talk after
the wisest.   He shall taste of my bottle; if he have
never drunk wine afore, it will go near to remove his
fit.   If I can recover him and keep him tame, I will
not take too much for him; he shall pay for him that
hath him, and that soundly.   81
Cal. Thou dost me yet but little hurt; thou wilt
anon, I know it by thy trembling.   Now Prosper
works upon thee.   84
Ste. Come on your ways.   Open your mouth;
here is that which will give language to you, cat.
Open your mouth; this will shake your shaking, I
can tell you, and that soundly.   You cannot tell
who's your friend.   Open your chaps again.   89
Trin. I should know that voice; it should be —
but he is drown'd; and these are devils.   O defend
me!   92
Ste. Four legs and two voices; a most delicate
monster!   His forward voice now is to speak well
of his friend; his backward voice is to utter foul
speeches and to detract.   If all the wine in my bottle will recover him, I will help his ague.   Come.
Amen!   I will pour some in thy other mouth.   99
Trin. Stephano!
Ste. Doth thy other mouth call me?   Mercy,
mercy!   This is a devil, and no monster.   I will
leave him; I have no long spoon.   103
Trin. Stephano!   If thou beest Stephano, touch
me and speak to me; for I am Trinculo, — be not
afeard — thy good friend Trinculo.   106
Ste. If thou beest Trinculo, come forth.   I'll pull
thee by the lesser legs.   If any be Trinculo's legs,
these are they.   Thou art very Trinculo indeed!
How cam'st thou to be the siege of this moon-calf?
Can he vent Trinculos?   111
Trin. I took him to be kill'd with a thunder-
stroke.   But art thou not drown'd, Stephano?   I
hope now thou art not drown'd.   Is the storm over-
blown?   I hid me under the dead mooncalf's gaberdine for fear of the storm.   And art thou living, Stephano?   O Stephano, two Neapolitans
scap'd!   117
Ste. Prithee, do not turn me about; my stomach
is not constant.
Cal. [*Aside.*]   These be fine things, an if they be
    not sprites.
That's a brave god and bears celestial liquor.
I will kneel to him.   122
Ste. How didst thou scape?   How cam'st thou
hither?   Swear by this bottle how thou cam'st
hither, — I escap'd upon a butt of sack which the
sailors heaved o'erboard — by this bottle, which I

---

31. **man:** i.e., man's fortune.   33. **doit:** Dutch coin worth less than a farthing.   40. **gaberdine:** cloak.   63. **proper:** handsome.   71. **recover:** restore.   73. **neat's-leather:** cowhide.   83. **trembling.**   Caliban takes this as a sign he is possessed of
a devil.   86. **cat.**   Allusion to the proverb, "Good liquor will make a cat speak."   93. **delicate:** charming.   103. **long
spoon.**   Allusion to the proverb, "It takes a long spoon to sup with the devil."   110. **siege:** stool, excrement.   **moon-calf:**
monstrosity (caused by the influence of the moon).   125. **sack:** sherry-like wine.

[handwritten annotations at bottom: "Caliban fears Stephano / Stephano fears Caliban / Caliban has no regard for Trinculo"]

made of the bark of a tree with mine own hands
since I was cast ashore.   128
  Cal. I'll swear upon that bottle to be thy true
subject, for the liquor is not earthly.
  Ste. Here; swear then how thou escap'dst.
  Trin. Swam ashore, man, like a duck. I can
swim like a duck, I'll be sworn.   133
  Ste. Here, kiss the book. [*Passing the bottle.*]
Though thou canst swim like a duck, thou art made
like a goose.
  Trin. O Stephano, hast any more of this?
  Ste. The whole butt, man. My cellar is in a rock
by th' seaside where my wine is hid. How now,
moon-calf! how does thine ague?   139
  Cal. Hast thou not dropp'd from heaven?
  Ste. Out o' th' moon, I do assure thee. I was the
Man i' the Moon when time was.
  Cal. I have seen thee in her and I do adore thee.
My mistress show'd me thee and thy dog and thy
  bush.   144
  Ste. Come, swear to that; kiss the book. I will
furnish it anon with new contents. Swear.
  Trin. By this good light, this is a very shallow
monster! I afeard of him! A very weak monster!
The Man i' th' Moon! A most poor credulous
monster! Well drawn, monster, in good sooth! 150
  Cal. I'll show thee every fertile inch o' th' island;
And I will kiss thy foot. I prithee, be my god.
  Trin. By this light, a most perfidious and
drunken monster! When 's god 's asleep, he'll rob
his bottle.   155
  Cal. I'll kiss thy foot. I'll swear myself thy sub-
ject.
  Ste. Come on then; down, and swear.
  Trin. I shall laugh myself to death at this puppy-
headed monster. A most scurvy monster! I could
find in my heart to beat him —   160
  Ste. Come, kiss.
  Trin. But that the poor monster's in drink. An
abominable monster!
  Cal. I'll show thee the best springs; I'll pluck
  thee berries;
I'll fish for thee and get thee wood enough.   165
A plague upon the tyrant that I serve!
I'll bear him no more sticks, but follow thee,
Thou wondrous man.
  Trin. A most ridiculous monster, to make a won-
der of a poor drunkard!   170
  Cal. I prithee, let me bring thee where crabs
  grow;
And I with my long nails will dig thee pig-nuts,
Show thee a jay's nest, and instruct thee how

To snare the nimble marmoset. I'll bring thee
To clust'ring filberts and sometimes I'll get thee
Young scamels from the rock. Wilt thou go with
  me?   176
  Ste. I prithee now, lead the way without any
more talking. Trinculo, the King and all our com-
pany else being drown'd, we will inherit here.
Here! bear my bottle. Fellow Trinculo, we'll fill
him by and by again.   181
  Cal. (*Sings drunkenly.*)
    Farewell, master; farewell, farewell!
  Trin. A howling monster; a drunken monster!
  Cal. No more dams I'll make for fish;
    Nor fetch in firing   185
      At requiring;
    Nor scrape trenchering, nor wash dish.
      'Ban, 'Ban, Ca-Caliban
      Has a new master, get a new man.
Freedom, high-day! high-day, freedom! freedom,
high-day, freedom!   191
  Ste. O brave monster! Lead the way.
                                            [*Exeunt.*

ACT III

SCENE I. [*Before Prospero's cell.*]

Enter FERDINAND, *bearing a log.*

Fer. There be some sports are painful, and their
  labour
Delight in them [sets] off; some kinds of baseness
Are nobly undergone, and most poor matters
Point to rich ends. This my mean task
Would be as heavy to me as odious, but   5
The mistress which I serve quickens what's dead
And makes my labours pleasures. O, she is
Ten times more gentle than her father's crabbed,
And he's compos'd of harshness. I must remove
Some thousands of these logs and pile them up,
Upon a sore injunction. My sweet mistress   11
Weeps when she sees me work, and says such base-
  ness
Had never like executor. I forget;
But these sweet thoughts do even refresh my la-
  bours,   14
Most busy least when I do it.

Enter MIRANDA; *and* PROSPERO [*at a distance,
  unseen*].

Mir.   Alas, now, pray you,
Work not so hard. I would the lightning had
Burnt up those logs that you are enjoin'd to pile!

---

142. **when…was:** once upon a time.   150. **drawn:** drunk.   171. **crabs:** crab-apples.   174. **marmoset:** monkey.   176.
scamels. Unexplained. *Seamells* (seagulls) is a common emendation.   187. **trenchering:** wooden plates.
Act III, sc. i, 2. [sets] off: cancels. [sets] (Theobald). set F. 11. sore injunction: orders with a severe penalty for dis-
obeying. 15. **Most…it.** The passage may be corrupt, but the general sense seems to be: I feel the burden of my labors
least when occupied with these thoughts. Holt reads *busiest* for F *busy lest.*

Pray, set it down and rest you. When this burns,
'Twill weep for having wearied you. My father
Is hard at study; pray now, rest yourself;   20
He's safe for these three hours.

Fer.   O most dear mistress,
The sun will set before I shall discharge
What I must strive to do.

Mir.   If you'll sit down,
I'll bear your logs the while. Pray, give me that;
I'll carry it to the pile.

Fer.   No, precious creature;   25
I had rather crack my sinews, break my back,
Than you should such dishonour undergo,
While I sit lazy by.

Mir.   It would become me
As well as it does you; and I should do it
With much more ease, for my good will is to it,   30
And yours it is against.

Pros.   Poor worm, thou art infected!
This visitation shows it.

Mir.   You look wearily.

Fer. No, noble mistress; 'tis fresh morning with
    me
When you are by at night. I do beseech you —
Chiefly that I might set it in my prayers —   35
What is your name?

Mir.   Miranda. — O my father,
I have broke your hest to say so!

Fer.   Admir'd Miranda!
Indeed the top of admiration! worth
What's dearest to the world! Full many a lady
I have ey'd with best regard, and many a time   40
Th' harmony of their tongues hath into bondage
Brought my too diligent ear; for several virtues
Have I lik'd several women, never any
With so full soul but some defect in her
Did quarrel with the noblest grace she ow'd   45
And put it to the foil; but you, O you,
So perfect and so peerless, are created
Of every creature's best!

Mir.   I do not know
One of my sex; no woman's face remember,
Save, from my glass, mine own; nor have I seen   50
More that I may call men than you, good friend,
And my dear father. How features are abroad,
I am skilless of; but, by my modesty,
The jewel in my dower, I would not wish
Any companion in the world but you,   55
Nor can imagination form a shape,
Besides yourself, to like of. But I prattle
Something too wildly, and my father's precepts
I therein do forget.

Fer.   I am in my condition
A prince, Miranda; I do think, a king;   60

I would, not so! — and would no more endure
This wooden slavery than to suffer
The flesh-fly blow my mouth. Hear my soul speak.
The very instant that I saw you, did
My heart fly to your service; there resides,   65
To make me slave to it; and for your sake
Am I this patient log-man.

Mir.   Do you love me?

Fer. O heaven, O earth, bear witness to this
    sound,
And crown what I profess with kind event
If I speak true! if hollowly, invert   70
What best is boded me to mischief! I,
Beyond all limit of what else i' th' world,
Do love, prize, honour you.

Mir.   I am a fool
To weep at what I am glad of.

Pros.   Fair encounter   74
Of two most rare affections! Heavens rain grace
On that which breeds between 'em!

Fer.   Wherefore weep you?

Mir. At mine unworthiness, that dare not offer
What I desire to give, and much less take
What I shall die to want. But this is trifling;
And all the more it seeks to hide itself,   80
The bigger bulk it shows. Hence, bashful cunning!
And prompt me, plain and holy innocence!
I am your wife, if you will marry me;
If not, I'll die your maid. To be your fellow
You may deny me; but I'll be your servant,   85
Whether you will or no.

Fer.   My mistress, dearest;
And I thus humble ever.

Mir.   My husband, then?

Fer. Ay, with a heart as willing
As bondage e'er of freedom. Here's my hand.

Mir. And mine, with my heart in't. And now
    farewell   90
Till half an hour hence.

Fer.   A thousand thousand!
           [*Exeunt* [*Fer. and Mir. severally*].

Pros. So glad of this as they I cannot be,
Who are surpris'd withal; but my rejoicing
At nothing can be more. I'll to my book,
For yet ere supper-time must I perform   95
Much business appertaining.   [*Exit.*

SCENE II. [*Another part of the island.*]

Enter CALIBAN, STEPHANO, *and* TRINCULO.

Ste. Tell not me. When the butt is out, we will
drink water; not a drop before; therefore bear up
and board 'em. Servant-monster, drink to me.   4

---

42. **several:** particular.   45. **ow'd:** owned.   46. **put . . . foil:** defeated it.   52. **abroad:** in the world.   53. **skilless:** ignorant.   59. **condition:** status, rank.   69. **event:** outcome.   70. **invert:** convert.   71. **boded:** destined.   79. **to want:** if I lack.   84. **maid:** handmaiden.   **fellow:** mate.

Trin. Servant-monster! the folly of this island!
They say there's but five upon this isle: we are
three of them; if the other two be brain'd like us,
the state totters.

Ste. Drink, servant-monster, when I bid thee.
Thy eyes are almost set in thy head.   10

Trin. Where should they be set else? He were
a brave monster indeed, if they were set in his
tail.   13

Ste. My man-monster hath drown'd his tongue
in sack. For my part, the sea cannot drown me; I
swam, ere I could recover the shore, five and thirty
leagues off and on. By this light, thou shalt be my
lieutenant, monster, or my standard.

Trin. Your lieutenant, if you list; he's no standard.   20

Ste. We'll not run, Monsieur Monster.

Trin. Nor go neither; but you'll lie like dogs and
yet say nothing neither.

Ste. Moon-calf, speak once in thy life, if thou
beest a good moon-calf.   25

Cal. How does thy honour? Let me lick thy
shoe.
I'll not serve him; he's not valiant.   27

Trin. Thou liest, most ignorant monster! I am
in case to justle a constable. Why, thou debosh'd
fish, thou, was there ever man a coward that hath
drunk so much sack as I to-day? Wilt thou tell a
monstrous lie, being but half a fish and half a monster?   33

Cal. Lo, how he mocks me! Wilt thou let him,
my lord?

Trin. "Lord" quoth he! That a monster should
be such a natural!   37

Cal. Lo, lo, again! Bite him to death, I prithee.

Ste. Trinculo, keep a good tongue in your head.
If you prove a mutineer, — the next tree! The
poor monster's my subject and he shall not suffer
indignity.

Cal. I thank my noble lord. Wilt thou be pleas'd
to hearken once again to the suit I made to thee? 45

Ste. Marry, will I; kneel and repeat it. I will
stand, and so shall Trinculo.

Enter ARIEL, *invisible.*

Cal. As I told thee before, I am subject to a
tyrant, a sorcerer, that by his cunning hath cheated
me of the island.   50

Ari. Thou liest.

Cal. Thou liest, thou jesting monkey, thou. I
would my valiant master would destroy thee! I do
not lie.   54

Ste. Trinculo, if you trouble him any more in's

tale, by this hand, I will supplant some of your
teeth.

Trin. Why, I said nothing.

Ste. Mum, then, and no more. Proceed.

Cal. I say by sorcery he got this isle;   60
From me he got it. If thy greatness will
Revenge it on him, — for I know thou dar'st,
But this thing dare not, —

Ste. That's most certain.   64

Cal. Thou shalt be lord of it and I'll serve thee.

Ste. How now shall this be compass'd? Canst
thou bring me to the party?

Cal. Yea, yea, my lord. I'll yield him thee
asleep,
Where thou mayst knock a nail into his head.

Ari. Thou liest; thou canst not.   70

Cal. What a pied ninny's this! Thou scurvy
patch!
I do beseech thy greatness, give him blows
And take his bottle from him. When that's gone
He shall drink nought but brine; for I'll not show
him
Where the quick freshes are.   75

Ste. Trinculo, run into no further danger. Interrupt the monster one word further, and, by this
hand, I'll turn my mercy out o' doors and make a
stock-fish of thee.

Trin. Why, what did I? I did nothing. I'll go
farther off.   81

Ste. Didst thou not say he lied?

Ari. Thou liest.

Ste. Do I so? Take thou that. [*Beats Trin.*]
As you like this, give me the lie another time.   85

Trin. I did not give the lie. Out o' your wits
and hearing too? A pox o' your bottle! this can
sack and drinking do. A murrain on your monster,
and the devil take your fingers!

Cal. Ha, ha, ha!   90

Ste. Now, forward with your tale. Prithee,
stand farther off.

Cal. Beat him enough. After a little time I'll
beat him too.

Ste.   Stand farther. Come, proceed. 94

Cal. Why, as I told thee, 'tis a custom with him,
I' th' afternoon to sleep. There thou mayst brain
him,
Having first seiz'd his books, or with a log
Batter his skull, or paunch him with a stake,
Or cut his wezand with thy knife. Remember
First to possess his books; for without them   100
He's but a sot, as I am, nor hath not
One spirit to command. They all do hate him
As rootedly as I. Burn but his books.

Sc. ii, 10. **set:** fixed by drink. 18. **standard:** standard-bearer (with a pun in l. 20). 22. **go:** walk. 29. **case:** condition.
29. **debosh'd:** debauched. 37. **natural:** idiot. 71. **pied ninny:** jester in many-colored costume. **patch:** fool. 75. **quick
freshes:** springs of fresh water. 79. **stock-fish:** dried cod, which was beaten before cooking. 88. **murrain:** plague. 98.
paunch him: stab him in the belly. 99. **wezand:** windpipe.

Sympathy for Caliban here — human element here (handwritten)

He has brave utensils, — for so he calls them, —
Which, when he has a house, he'll deck withal.   105
And that most deeply to consider is
The beauty of his daughter.   He himself
Calls her a nonpareil.   I never saw a woman
But only Sycorax my dam and she;
But she as far surpasseth Sycorax   110
As greatest does least.
      Ste.   Is it so brave a lass?
      Cal. Ay, lord; she will become thy bed, I war-
            rant,
And bring thee forth brave brood.
      Ste. Monster, I will kill this man.   His daughter
and I will be king and queen, — save our Graces! —
and Trinculo and thyself shall be viceroys.   Dost
thou like the plot, Trinculo?   117
      Trin. Excellent.
      Ste. Give me thy hand.   I am sorry I beat thee;
but, while thou liv'st, keep a good tongue in thy
head.   121
      Cal. Within this half hour will he be asleep.
Wilt thou destroy him then?
      Ste.   Ay, on mine honour.
      Ari. This will I tell my master.
      Cal. Thou mak'st me merry; I am full of pleas-
ure.   125
Let us be jocund.   Will you troll the catch
You taught me but while-ere?
      Ste. At thy request, monster, I will do reason,
any reason.   Come on, Trinculo, let us sing.
                              [*Sings.*
            Flout 'em and [scout] 'em   130
            And scout 'em and flout 'em;
                  Thought is free.
      Cal. That's not the tune.
            [*Ariel plays the tune on a tabor and pipe.*
      Ste. What is this same?
      Trin. This is the tune of our catch, played by the
picture of Nobody.   136
      Ste. If thou beest a man, show thyself in thy
likeness.   If thou be'st a devil, take't as thou list.
      Trin. O, forgive me my sins!
      Ste. He that dies pays all debts.   I defy thee.
Mercy upon us!   141
      Cal. Art thou afeard?
      Ste. No, monster, not I.
      Cal. Be not afeard.   The isle is full of noises,
Sounds and sweet airs, that give delight and hurt
            not.   145
Sometimes a thousand twangling instruments
Will hum about mine ears, and sometime voices
That, if I then had wak'd after long sleep,
Will make me sleep again; and then, in dreaming,
The clouds methought would open and show riches

Ready to drop upon me, that, when I wak'd,   151
I cried to dream again.
      Ste. This will prove a brave kingdom to me,
where I shall have my music for nothing.
      Cal. When Prospero is destroy'd.   155
      Ste. That shall be by and by.   I remember the
story.
      Trin. The sound is going away.   Let's follow it,
and after do our work.
      Ste. Lead, monster; we'll follow.   I would I
could see this taborer; he lays it on.   161
      Trin. Wilt come?   I'll follow Stephano.
                              [*Exeunt.*

SCENE III.   [*Another part of the island.*]

Enter ALONSO, SEBASTIAN, ANTONIO, GONZALO,
            ADRIAN, FRANCISCO, *etc.*

      Gon. By'r lakin, I can go no further, sir;
My old bones ache.   Here's a maze trod indeed
Through forth-rights and meanders!   By your pa-
            tience,
I needs must rest me.
      Alon.   Old lord, I cannot blame thee,
Who am myself attach'd with weariness   5
To th' dulling of my spirits.   Sit down, and rest.
Even here I will put off my hope and keep it
No longer for my flatterer.   He is drown'd
Whom thus we stray to find, and the sea mocks
Our frustrate search on land.   Well, let him go.   10
      Ant. [*Aside to Seb.*]   I am right glad that he's so
            out of hope.
Do not, for one repulse, forgo the purpose
That you resolv'd t' effect.
      Seb. [*Aside to Ant.*]   The next advantage
Will we take throughly.
      Ant. [*Aside to Seb.*]   Let it be to-night;
For, now they are oppress'd with travel, they   15
Will not, nor cannot, use such vigilance
As when they are fresh.

Solemn and strange music; and PROSPERO *on the top
      invisible.   Enter several strange shapes, bringing in
      a banquet; and dance about it with gentle actions of
      salutation; and, inviting the King, etc., to eat, they
      depart.*

      Seb. [*Aside to Ant.*]   I say, to-night.   No more.
      Alon. What harmony is this?   My good friends,
            hark!
      Gon. Marvellous sweet music!
      Alon. Give us kind keepers, heavens!   What
            were these?   20
      Seb. A living drollery.   Now I will believe
That there are unicorns, that in Arabia

126. **troll the catch:** sing the part-song.   130. **[scout]** (Rowe).   *cout* F.   133. S.D. **tabor:** a small drum.
      Sc. iii, 1. **By'r lakin:** by our Lady (the Virgin Mary).   3. **forth-rights:** straight paths.   **meanders:** winding paths.   5.
attach'd: seized.   17. S.D. **top:** the upper stage.   21. **drollery:** puppet show.

There is one tree, the phœnix' throne, one phœnix
At this hour reigning there.
   Ant.   I'll believe both;
And what does else want credit, come to me,   25
And I'll be sworn 'tis true. Travellers ne'er did lie,
Though fools at home condemn 'em.
   Gon.   If in Naples
I should report this now, would they believe me?
If I should say, I saw such [islanders] —
For, certes, these are people of the island —   30
Who, though they are of monstrous shape, yet, note,
Their manners are more gentle, kind, than of
Our human generation you shall find
Many, nay, almost any.
   Pros.   [*Aside.*] Honest lord,   34
Thou hast said well; for some of you there present
Are worse than devils.
   Alon.   I cannot too much muse
Such shapes, such gesture, and such sound, express-
    ing,
Although they want the use of tongue, a kind
Of excellent dumb discourse.
   Pros.   [*Aside.*] Praise in departing.
   Fran. They vanish'd strangely.
   Seb.   No matter, since
They have left their viands behind, for we have
    stomachs.   41
Will't please you taste of what is here?
   Alon.   Not I.
   Gon. Faith, sir, you need not fear. When we
    were boys,
Who would believe that there were mountaineers
Dew-lapp'd like bulls, whose throats had hanging
    at 'em   45
Wallets of flesh? or that there were such men
Whose heads stood in their breasts? which now we
    find
Each putter-out of five for one will bring us
Good warrant of.
   Alon.   I will stand to and feed.
Although my last. No matter, since I feel   50
The best is past. Brother, my lord the Duke,
Stand to and do as we.

Thunder and lightning. Enter ARIEL, *like a harpy;
   claps his wings upon the table; and, with a quaint
   device, the banquet vanishes.*

   Ari. You are three men of sin, whom Destiny,
That hath to instrument this lower world
And what is in't, the never-surfeited sea   55
Hath caus'd to belch up you; and on this island

Where man doth not inhabit; you 'mongst men
Being most unfit to live. I have made you mad;
And even with such-like valour men hang and
    drown
Their proper selves.
       [*Alon., Seb., etc., draw their swords.*]
             You fools! I and my fellows
Are ministers of Fate. The elements,   61
Of whom your swords are temper'd, may as well
Wound the loud winds, or with bemock'd-at stabs
Kill the still-closing waters, as diminish
One dowle that's in my plume. My fellow-minis-
    ters   65
Are like invulnerable. If you could hurt,
Your swords are now too massy for your strengths
And will not be uplifted. But remember —
For that's my business to you — that you three
From Milan did supplant good Prospero;   70
Expos'd unto the sea, which hath requit it,
Him and his innocent child; for which foul deed
The powers, delaying, not forgetting, have
Incens'd the seas and shores, yea, all the creatures,
Against your peace. Thee of thy son, Alonso,   75
They have bereft; and do pronounce by me
Ling'ring perdition, worse than any death
Can be at once, shall step by step attend
You and your ways; whose wraths to guard you
    from —
Which here, in this most desolate isle, else falls   80
Upon your heads — is nothing but heart's sorrow
And a clear life ensuing.

*He vanishes in thunder; then, to soft music, enter the
   shapes again, and dance, with mocks and mows,
   and carrying out the table.*

   Pros. Bravely the figure of this harpy hast thou
Perform'd, my Ariel; a grace it had, devouring.
Of my instruction hast thou nothing bated   85
In what thou hadst to say; so, with good life
And observation strange, my meaner ministers
Their several kinds have done. My high charms
    work,
And these mine enemies are all knit up
In their distractions. They now are in my power;
And in these fits I leave them, while I visit   91
Young Ferdinand, whom they suppose is drown'd,
And his and mine lov'd darling.   [*Exit above.*]
   Gon. I' th' name of something holy, sir, why
    stand you   94
In this strange stare?
   Alon.   O, it is monstrous, monstrous!
Methought the billows spoke and told me of it;

---

29. **[islanders]** F₂. *Islands* F₁. 36. **muse:** marvel at. 39. **Praise in departing:** keep your praise until your entertainment is over (Proverbial). 45. **Dew-lapp'd:** with a fold of loose skin hanging from the throat (a reference to goitre). 48.
Each . . . one. Travelers took out a kind of insurance, depositing money with an agent, who was bound to pay a specified
number of times as much if they returned safely. 52. s.d. *harpy:* fabulous monster with woman's head and vulture's body.
quaint device: ingenious mechanism. 54. **to:** for. 60. **proper:** own. 65. **dowle:** tiny feather. 67. **massy:** heavy. 71.
requit: requited, avenged. 82. **clear:** blameless. 84. **devouring:** i.e., as you whisked it away. 86. **life:** likeness to life.
88. **kinds:** parts, rôles.

Loose style of speech—more powerful form of verse.—Lachs knchner pr. 9

The winds did sing it to me, and the thunder,
That deep and dreadful organ-pipe, pronounc'd
The name of Prosper; it did bass my trespass.
Therefore my son i' th' ooze is bedded, and   100
I'll seek him deeper than e'er pummet sounded
And with him there lie mudded.   [*Exit.*]
   Seb.   But one fiend at a time,
I'll fight their legions o'er.
   Ant.   I'll be thy second.
                 [*Exeunt* [*Seb. and Ant.*].
   Gon. All three of them are desperate: their great
     guilt,
Like poison given to work a great time after,   105
Now gins to bite the spirits. I do beseech you
That are of suppler joints, follow them swiftly
And hinder them from what this ecstasy
May now provoke them to.
   Adr.   Follow, I pray you.
                              [*Exeunt.*

ACT IV

SCENE I. [*Before Prospero's cell.*]

Enter PROSPERO, FERDINAND, *and* MIRANDA.

   Pros. If I have too austerely punish'd you,
Your compensation makes amends, for I
Have given you here a third of mine own life,
Or that for which I live; who once again
I tender to thy hand. All thy vexations   5
Were but my trials of thy love, and thou
Hast strangely stood the test. Here, afore Heaven,
I ratify this my rich gift. O Ferdinand,
Do not smile at me that I boast her off,
For thou shalt find she will outstrip all praise 10
And make it halt behind her.
   Fer.   I do believe it
Against an oracle.
   Pros. Then, as my [gift] and thine own acquisi-
     tion
Worthily purchas'd, take my daughter. But
If thou dost break her virgin-knot before   15
All sanctimonious ceremonies may
With full and holy rite be minist'red,
No sweet aspersion shall the heavens let fall
To make this contract grow; but barren Hate,
Sour-eyed Disdain, and Discord shall bestrew   20
The union of your bed with weeds so loathly
That you shall hate it both. Therefore take heed,
As Hymen's lamps shall light you.
   Fer.   As I hope

For quiet days, fair issue, and long life,
With such love as 'tis now, the murkiest den,   25
The most opportune place, the strong'st suggestion
Our worser genius can, shall never melt
Mine honour into lust, to take away
The edge of that day's celebration   29
When I shall think or Phœbus' steeds are founder'd
Or Night kept chain'd below.
   Pros.   Fairly spoke.
Sit then and talk with her; she is thine own.
What, Ariel! my industrious servant, Ariel!

Enter ARIEL.

   Ari. What would my potent master? Here I am.
   Pros. Thou and thy meaner fellows your last
     service   35
Did worthily perform; and I must use you
In such another trick. Go bring the rabble,
O'er whom I give thee power, here to this place.
Incite them to quick motion; for I must
Bestow upon the eyes of this young couple   40
Some vanity of mine art. It is my promise,
And they expect it from me.
   Ari.   Presently?
   Pros. Ay, with a twink.
   Ari. Before you can say "come" and "go,"
     And breathe twice and cry "so, so,"   45
     Each one, tripping on his toe,
     Will be here with mop and mow.
     Do you love me, master? No?
   Pros. Dearly, my delicate Ariel. Do not ap-
     proach
Till thou dost hear me call.
   Ari.   Well, I conceive.   50
                                [*Exit.*
   Pros. Look thou be true; do not give dalliance
Too much the rein. The strongest oaths are straw
To th' fire i' th' blood. Be more abstemious,
Or else good night your vow!
   Fer.   I warrant you, sir;
The white cold virgin snow upon my heart   55
Abates the ardour of my liver.
   Pros.   Well.
Now come, my Ariel! bring a corollary,
Rather than want a spirit. Appear, and pertly!
No tongue! all eyes! Be silent. [*Soft music.* *Masque*

Enter IRIS.

   Iris. Ceres, most bounteous lady, thy rich leas
Of wheat, rye, barley, vetches, oats, and pease; 61
Thy turfy mountains, where live nibbling sheep,

99. **bass:** proclaim in deep tones. 108. **ecstasy:** frenzy.
   Act IV, sc. i, 3. **third.** Variously explained. Perhaps the "thirds" are Prospero, his dukedom, and his daughter; or, better, past, present, and future. 7. **strangely:** unusually well. 13. [**gift**] (Rowe). *guest* F. 18. **aspersion:** sprinkling (of dew). 26. **suggestion:** temptation. 27. **can:** i.e., can offer. 41. **vanity:** trifling illusion. 42. **Presently:** instantly. 47. **mop and mow.** Both words mean grimace. 50. **conceive:** understand. 56. **liver:** the supposed seat of love. 57. **corollary:** surplus, extra. 58. **pertly:** briskly.

And flat meads thatch'd with stover, them to keep;
Thy banks with pioned and twilled brims,
Which spongy April at thy hest betrims   65
To make cold nymphs chaste crowns; and thy
      broom groves,
Whose shadow the dismissed bachelor loves,
Being lass-lorn; thy pole-clipp'd vineyard;
And thy sea-marge, sterile and rocky-hard,
Where thou thyself dost air; — the queen o' th' sky,
Whose wat'ry arch and messenger am I,   71
Bids thee leave these, and with her sovereign grace,
                            [Juno descends.
Here on this grass-plot, in this very place,
To come and sport; here peacocks fly amain.
Approach, rich Ceres, her to entertain.   75

            Enter CERES.

  Cer. Hail, many-coloured messenger, that ne'er
Dost disobey the wife of Jupiter;
Who with thy saffron wings upon my flowers
Diffusest honey-drops, refreshing showers,
And with each end of thy blue bow dost crown   80
My bosky acres and my unshrubb'd down,
Rich scarf to my proud earth; why hath thy queen
Summon'd me hither, to this short-grass'd green?
  Iris. A contract of true love to celebrate;
And some donation freely to estate   85
On the blest lovers.
  Cer.   Tell me, heavenly bow,
If Venus or her son, as thou dost know,
Do now attend the Queen? Since they did plot
The means that dusky Dis my daughter got,
Her and her blind boy's scandal'd company   90
I have forsworn.
  Iris.   Of her society
Be not afraid. I met her deity
Cutting the clouds towards Paphos, and her son
Dove-drawn with her. Here thought they to have
      done
Some wanton charm upon this man and maid,   95
Whose vows are, that no bed-right shall be paid
Till Hymen's torch be lighted; but in vain.
Mars's hot minion is return'd again;
Her waspish-headed son has broke his arrows,
Swears he will shoot no more, but play with spar-
      rows   100
And be a boy right out.   [Juno alights.]
  Cer.   Highest queen of state,
Great Juno, comes; I know her by her gait.
  Juno. How does my bounteous sister? Go with
      me

To bless this twain, that they may prosperous be
And honour'd in their issue.   [They sing. 105
  Juno. Honour, riches, marriage-blessing,
      Long continuance, and increasing,
      Hourly joys be still upon you!
      Juno sings her blessings on you.

  [Cer.] Earth's increase, foison plenty,   110
      Barns and garners never empty,
      Vines with clust'ring bunches growing,
      Plants with goodly burden bowing.
      Spring come to you at the farthest
      In the very end of harvest!   115
      Scarcity and want shall shun you;
      Ceres' blessing so is on you.
  Fer. This is a most majestic vision, and
Harmonious charmingly. May I be bold
To think these spirits?
  Pros.   Spirits, which by mine art
I have from their confines call'd to enact   121
My present fancies.
  Fer.   Let me live here ever;
So rare a wond'red father and a wise
Makes this place Paradise.
  Pros.   Sweet, now, silence!
Juno and Ceres whisper seriously.   125
There's something else to do; hush and be mute,
Or else our spell is marr'd.
            [Juno and Ceres whisper, and send Iris on
                  employment.
  Iris. You nymphs, call'd Naiads, of the wind'ring
      brooks,
With your sedg'd crowns and ever-harmless looks,
Leave your crisp channels, and on this green land
Answer your summons; Juno does command.   131
Come, temperate nymphs, and help to celebrate
A contract of true love; be not too late.

            Enter certain Nymphs.

You sunburnt sicklemen, of August weary,
Come hither from the furrow and be merry.   135
Make holiday; your rye-straw hats put on
And these fresh nymphs encounter every one
In country footing.

Enter certain Reapers, properly habited: they join
      with the Nymphs in a graceful dance; towards the
      end whereof Prospero starts suddenly, and speaks;
      after which, to a strange, hollow, and confused noise,
      they heavily vanish.

63. stover: hay.   64. pioned and twilled. Meaning uncertain, the most satisfactory interpretation being "furrowed
and ridged." 66. broom groves. So F. brown groves Hanmer. 68. pole-clipp'd: surrounded by poles. 71. wat'ry arch:
rainbow. 72. S.D. As Juno does not seem to be present before l. 101, this F direction is the cue for operating the
machinery for her descent. 81. bosky: wooded. 85. estate: bestow. 89. Dis: Pluto, who abducted Proserpine to be
his queen in Hades. 90. scandal'd: scandalous. 98. hot minion: lustful darling (Venus). 99. waspish-headed: irritable.
110. [Cer.] (Theobald). Om. F. 123. wond'red: wonder-doing. wise. Some copies of F read wife. 128. wind'ring:
wandering or winding or both. winding (Rowe); wand'ring (Steevens). 138. S.D. heavily: reluctantly.

Pros. [*Aside.*] I had forgot that foul conspiracy
Of the beast Caliban and his confederates   140
Against my life. The minute of their plot
Is almost come. [*To the Spirits.*] Well done!
          avoid. No more!
Fer. This is strange. Your father's in some pas-
          sion
That works him strongly.
Mir.   Never till this day   144
Saw I him touch'd with anger, so distemper'd.
Pros. You do look, my son, in a mov'd sort,
As if you were dismay'd. Be cheerful, sir,
Our revels now are ended. These our actors,
As I foretold you, were all spirits, and
Are melted into air, into thin air;   150
And, like the baseless fabric of this vision,
The cloud-capp'd towers, the gorgeous palaces,
The solemn temples, the great globe itself,
Yea, all which it inherit, shall dissolve
And, like this insubstantial pageant faded,   155
Leave not a rack behind. We are such stuff
As dreams are made on, and our little life
Is rounded with a sleep. Sir, I am vex'd, —
Bear with my weakness — my old brain is troubled.
Be not disturb'd with my infirmity.   160
If you be pleas'd, retire into my cell
And there repose. A turn or two I'll walk,
To still my beating mind.
Fer. Mir.   We wish your peace.
                              [*Exeunt.*
Pros. Come with a thought. I thank thee,
          Ariel; come.

                  Enter ARIEL.

Ari. Thy thoughts I cleave to. What's thy
          pleasure?
Pros.   Spirit,   165
We must prepare to meet with Caliban.
Ari. Ay, my commander. When I presented
          Ceres,
I thought to have told thee of it, but I fear'd
Lest I might anger thee.
Pros. Say again, where didst thou leave these
          varlets?   170
Ari. I told you, sir, they were red-hot with
          drinking;
So full of valour that they smote the air
For breathing in their faces; beat the ground
For kissing of their feet; yet always bending
Towards their project. Then I beat my tabor;
At which, like unback'd colts, they prick'd their
          ears,   176
Advanc'd their eyelids, lifted up their noses

As they smelt music. So I charm'd their ears
That calf-like they my lowing follow'd through
Tooth'd briers, sharp furzes, pricking [gorse] and
          thorns,   180
Which ent'red their frail shins. At last I left them
I' th' filthy-mantled pool beyond your cell,
There dancing up to the chins, that the foul lake
O'erstunk their feet.
Pros.   This was well done, my bird.
Thy shape invisible retain thou still.   185
The trumpery in my house, go bring it hither,
For stale to catch these thieves.
Ari.   I go, I go.
                              [*Exit.*
Pros. A devil, a born devil, on whose nature
Nurture can never stick; on whom my pains,
Humanely taken, all, all lost, quite lost;   190
And as with age his body uglier grows,
So his mind cankers. I will plague them all,
Even to roaring.

Re-enter ARIEL, *loaden with glittering apparel,*
          etc.

          Come, hang [them on] this line.

[*Prospero and Ariel remain, invisible.*] *Enter*
CALIBAN, STEPHANO, *and* TRINCULO, *all wet.*
Cal. Pray you, tread softly, that the blind mole
          may not
Hear a foot fall; we now are near his cell.   195
Ste. Monster, your fairy, which you say is a
harmless fairy, has done little better than play'd
the Jack with us.
Trin. Monster, I do smell all horse-piss, at which
my nose is in great indignation.   200
Ste. So is mine. Do you hear, monster? If I
should take a displeasure against you, look you, —
Trin. Thou wert but a lost monster.
Cal. Good my lord, give me thy favour still.
Be patient, for the prize I'll bring thee to   205
Shall hoodwink this mischance; therefore speak
          softly.
All's hush'd as midnight yet.
Trin. Ay, but to lose our bottles in the pool, —
Ste. There is not only disgrace and dishonour in
that, monster, but an infinite loss.   210
Trin. That's more to me than my wetting; yet
this is your harmless fairy, monster!
Ste. I will fetch off my bottle, though I be o'er
ears for my labour,
Cal. Prithee, my king, be quiet. See'st thou
          here,   215
This is the mouth o' th' cell. No noise, and enter,

---

142. **avoid:** begone. 156. **rack:** cloud. 176. **unback'd:** unbroken. 180. **[gorse]** (Collier). *goss* F. 182. **filthy-mantled:**
slime covered. 186. **trumpery:** stuff, the "glittering apparel" of s.d. (l.193). 187. **stale:** decoy. 193. **[them on]** (Rowe).
on them F. **line:** lime-tree. 198. **Jack:** knave. 206. **hoodwink:** cover up, make you blind to.

Do that good mischief which may make this island
Thine own for ever, and I, thy Caliban,
For aye thy foot-licker.

Ste. Give me thy hand. I do begin to have
bloody thoughts. 221

Trin. O King Stephano! O peer! O worthy
Stephano! look what a wardrobe here is for thee!

Cal. Let it alone, thou fool; it is but trash.

Trin. O, ho, monster! we know what belongs to
a frippery. O King Stephano! 226

Ste. Put off that gown, Trinculo; by this hand,
I'll have that gown.

Trin. Thy Grace shall have it.

Cal. The dropsy drown this fool! what do you
mean 230
To dote thus on such luggage? [Let 't] alone
And do the murder first. If he awake,
From toe to crown he'll fill our skins with pinches,
Make us strange stuff. 234

Ste. Be you quiet, monster. Mistress line, is not
this my jerkin? Now is the jerkin under the line.
Now, jerkin, you are like to lose your hair and
prove a bald jerkin.

Trin. Do, do; we steal by line and level, an't like
your Grace. 240

Ste. I thank thee for that jest; here's a garment
for't. Wit shall not go unrewarded while I am
king of this country. "Steal by line and level" is
an excellent pass of pate; there's another garment
for't. 245

Trin. Monster, come, put some lime upon your
fingers, and away with the rest.

Cal. I will have none on't. We shall lose our
time,
And all be turn'd to barnacles, or to apes
With foreheads villainous low. 250

Ste. Monster, lay-to your fingers. Help to bear
this away where my hogshead of wine is, or I'll turn
you out of my kingdom. Go to, carry this.

Trin. And this.

Ste. Ay, and this. 255

*A noise of hunters heard. Enter divers Spirits, in
shape of dogs and hounds, hunting them about,
Prospero and Ariel setting them on.*

Pros. Hey, Mountain, hey!

Ari. Silver! there it goes, Silver!

Pros. Fury, Fury! there, Tyrant, there! hark!
hark!

[*Cal., Ste., and Trin. are driven out.*]
Go charge my goblins that they grind their joints

With dry convulsions, shorten up their sinews 260
With aged cramps, and more pinch-spotted make
them
Than pard or cat o' mountain.

Ari. Hark, they roar!

Pros. Let them be hunted soundly. At this hour
Lies at my mercy all mine enemies.
Shortly shall all my labours end, and thou 265
Shalt have the air at freedom. For a little
Follow, and do me service. [*Exeunt.*]

ACT V

SCENE I. [*Before Prospero's cell.*]

Enter PROSPERO *in his magic robes, and* ARIEL.

Pros. Now does my project gather to a head.
My charms crack not; my spirits obey; and Time
Goes upright with his carriage. How's the day?

Ari. On the sixth hour; at which time, my lord,
You said our work should cease.

Pros.   I did say so, 5
When first I rais'd the tempest. Say, my spirit,
How fares the King and 's followers?

Ari.   Confin'd together
In the same fashion as you gave in charge,
Just as you left them; all prisoners, sir,
In the line-grove which weather-fends your cell; 10
They cannot budge till your release. The King,
His brother, and yours, abide all three distracted,
And the remainder mourning over them,
Brimful of sorrow and dismay; but chiefly
Him that you term'd, sir, "the good old lord, Gon-
zalo," 15
His tears run down his beard like winter's drops
From eaves of reeds. Your charm so strongly
works 'em
That if you now beheld them, your affections
Would become tender.

Pros.   Dost thou think so, spirit?

Ari. Mine would, sir, were I human.

Pros.   And mine shall.
Hast thou, which art but air, a touch, a feeling 21
Of their afflictions, and shall not myself,
One of their kind, that relish all as sharply
Passion as they, be kindlier mov'd than thou art?
Though with their high wrongs I am struck to th'
quick, 25
Yet with my nobler reason 'gainst my fury
Do I take part. The rarer action is
In virtue than in vengeance. They being penitent,

---

222. **King...peer.** Allusion to an old song beginning, "King Stephen was a worthy peer." 226. **frippery:** old clothes
shop. 231. **[Let 't]** (Rowe). *let's* F. 236. **line:** (1) lime-tree, (2) equator. Stephano has taken the jerkin down from
the lime-tree. The jerkin will "lose its hair" (fur trimming?), as men lose hair through tropical fevers. 239. **Do, do:** i.e.,
bravo! **by...level:** by plumb line and carpenter's level, i.e., systematically. 244. **pass of pate:** stroke of wit. 246. **lime:**
bird lime. 249. **barnacles:** wild geese, thought to be hatched from the shell fish. 262. **pard:** leopard.

Act V, sc. i, 3. carriage: burden. 11. **your release:** you release them. 23. **relish:** am susceptible to.

The sole drift of my purpose doth extend
Not a frown further. Go release them, Ariel.   30
My charms I'll break, their senses I'll restore,
And they shall be themselves.
    Ari.   I'll fetch them, sir.
                                      [*Exit.*
    Pros. Ye elves of hills, brooks, standing lakes,
        and groves,
And ye that on the sands with printless foot
Do chase the ebbing Neptune, and do fly him   35
When he comes back; you demi-puppets that
By moonshine do the green sour ringlets make,
Whereof the ewe not bites; and you whose pastime
Is to make midnight mushrooms, that rejoice
To hear the solemn curfew; by whose aid,   40
Weak masters though ye be, I have bedimm'd
The noontide sun, call'd forth the mutinous winds,
And 'twixt the green sea and the azur'd vault
Set roaring war; to the dread rattling thunder
Have I given fire, and rifted Jove's stout oak   45
With his own bolt; the strong-bas'd promontory
Have I made shake, and by the spurs pluck'd up
The pine and cedar; graves at my command
Have wak'd their sleepers, op'd, and let 'em forth
By my so potent art. But this rough magic   50
I here abjure, and, when I have requir'd
Some heavenly music, which even now I do,
To work mine end upon their senses that
This airy charm is for, I'll break my staff,
Bury it certain fathoms in the earth,   55
And deeper than did ever plummet sound
I'll drown my book.   [*Solemn music.*

Here enters ARIEL *before: then* ALONSO, *with a frantic
    gesture, attended by* GONZALO; SEBASTIAN *and
    *Antonio *in like manner, attended by* Adrian *and*
    Francisco. *They all enter the circle which Pros-
    pero had made, and there stand charmed; which
    Prospero observing, speaks.*

A solemn air and the best comforter
To an unsettled fancy cure thy brains,
Now useless, boil'd within thy skull! There stand,
For you are spell-stopp'd.   61
Holy Gonzalo, honourable man,
Mine eyes, ev'n sociable to the shew of thine,
Fall fellowly drops. The charm dissolves apace,
And as the morning steals upon the night,   65
Melting the darkness, so their rising senses
Begin to chase the ignorant fumes that mantle
Their clearer reason. O good Gonzalo,
My true preserver, and a loyal sir
To him thou follow'st! I will pay thy graces   70
Home both in word and deed.   Most cruelly

Did thou, Alonso, use me and my daughter.
Thy brother was a furtherer in the act.
Thou art pinch'd for't now, Sebastian. Flesh and
    blood,
You, brother mine, that entertain'd ambition,   75
Expell'd remorse and nature, [who], with Sebastian,
Whose inward pinches therefore are most strong,
Would here have kill'd your king, I do forgive thee,
Unnatural though thou art. — Their understanding
Begins to swell, and the approaching tide   80
Will shortly fill the reasonable shore
That now [lies] foul and muddy. Not one of them
That yet looks on me, or would know me! Ariel,
Fetch me the hat and rapier in my cell;
I will discase me, and myself present   85
As I was sometime Milan. Quickly, spirit;
Thou shalt ere long be free.   [*Exit Ariel.*]

    *Ariel [returning] sings and helps to attire
    him.*
    Ari. "Where the bee sucks, there suck I.
        In a cowslip's bell I lie;
          There I couch when owls do cry.   90
          On the bat's back I do fly
          After summer merrily.
      Merrily, merrily shall I live now
      Under the blossom that hangs on the bough."

    Pros. Why, that's my dainty Ariel! I shall miss
    thee;   95
But yet thou shalt have freedom. So, so, so.
To the King's ship, invisible as thou art;
There shalt thou find the mariners asleep
Under the hatches. The master and the boatswain
Being awake, enforce them to this place,   100
And presently, I prithee.
    Ari. I drink the air before me, and return
Or ere your pulse twice beat.   [*Exit.*
    Gon. All torment, trouble, wonder, and amaze-
    ment
Inhabits here. Some heavenly power guide us   105
Out of this fearful country!
    Pros.   Behold, sir King,
The wronged Duke of Milan, Prospero.
For more assurance that a living prince
Does now speak to thee, I embrace thy body;
And to thee and thy company I bid   110
A hearty welcome.
    Alon.   Whe'er thou be'st he or no,
Or some enchanted trifle to abuse me,
As late I have been, I not know. Thy pulse
Beats as of flesh and blood; and, since I saw thee,
Th' affliction of my mind amends, with which,   115

---

37. **green sour ringlets:** small circles of dark grass called fairy-rings.   40. **curfew.**   After curfew spirits were free to
wander.   45. **given fire:** added lightning.   51. **requir'd:** requested.   63. **sociable:** sympathetic.   70–71. **pay...Home:**
requite the favors thoroughly.   76. **[who]** (Rowe).   *whom* F.   81. **reasonable shore:** shore of reason.   82. **[lies]** F₃-₄.   *ly*
F₁-₂.   85. **discase me:** take off these clothes.   112. **trifle:** magic trick. **abuse:** deceive.

I fear, a madness held me. This must crave,
An if this be at all, a most strange story.
Thy dukedom I resign and do entreat
Thou pardon me my wrongs. But how should Prospero
Be living and be here?
    Pros.   First, noble friend,   120
Let me embrace thine age, whose honour cannot
Be measur'd or confin'd.
    Gon.   Whether this be
Or be not, I'll not swear.
    Pros.   You do yet taste
Some subtleties o' th' isle, that will not let you
Believe things certain. Welcome, my friends all!
[*Aside to Seb. and Ant.*] But you, my brace of lords,
    were I so minded,   126
I here could pluck his Highness' frown upon you
And justify you traitors. At this time
I will tell no tales.
    Seb.   [*Aside.*] The devil speaks in him.
    Pros.   No.
For you, most wicked sir, whom to call brother   130
Would even infect my mouth, I do forgive
Thy rankest fault, — all of them; and require
My dukedom of thee, which perforce, I know,
Thou must restore.
    Alon.   If thou be'st Prospero,
Give us particulars of thy preservation,
How thou hast met us here, [who] three hours since   135
Were wreck'd upon this shore, where I have lost —
How sharp the point of this remembrance is! —
My dear son Ferdinand.
    Pros.   I am woe for't, sir.
    Alon. Irreparable is the loss, and Patience   140
Says it is past her cure.
    Pros.   I rather think
You have not sought her help, of whose soft grace
For the like loss I have her sovereign aid
And rest myself content.
    Alon.   You the like loss!   144
    Pros. As great to me as late; and, supportable
To make the dear loss, have I means much weaker
Than you may call to comfort you, for I
Have lost my daughter.
    Alon.   A daughter?
O heavens, that they were living both in Naples,
The King and Queen there! That they were, I wish   150
Myself were mudded in that oozy bed
Where my son lies. When did you lose your daughter?
    Pros. In this last tempest. I perceive, these lords
At this encounter do so much admire
That they devour their reason and scarce think   155

Their eyes do offices of truth, their words
Are natural breath; but, howsoe'er you have
Been jostled from your senses, know for certain
That I am Prospero and that very duke
Which was thrust forth of Milan, who most strangely   160
Upon this shore, where you were wreck'd, was landed,
To be the lord on't. No more yet of this;
For 'tis a chronicle of day by day,
Not a relation for a breakfast nor
Befitting this first meeting. Welcome, sir;   165
This cell's my court. Here have I few attendants,
And subjects none abroad. Pray you, look in.
My dukedom since you have given me again,
I will requite you with as good a thing;
At least bring forth a wonder, to content ye   170
As much as me my dukedom.

Here Prospero discovers FERDINAND *and* MIRANDA
playing at chess.

    Mir. Sweet lord, you play me false.
    Fer.   No, my dearest love,
I would not for the world.
    Mir. Yes, for a score of kingdoms you should wrangle,
And I would call it fair play.
    Alon.   If this prove   175
A vision of the island, one dear son
Shall I twice lose.
    Seb.   A most high miracle!
    Fer. Though the seas threaten, they are merciful;
I have curs'd them without cause.
                            [*Kneels.*]
    Alon.   Now all the blessings
Of a glad father compass thee about!   180
Arise, and say how thou cam'st here.
    Mir.   O, wonder!
How many goodly creatures are there here!
How beauteous mankind is! O brave new world,
That has such people in't!
    Pros.   'Tis new to thee.
    Alon. What is this maid with whom thou wast at
    play?   185
Your eld'st acquaintance cannot be three hours.
Is she the goddess that hath sever'd us,
And brought us thus together?
    Fer.   Sir, she is mortal,
But by immortal Providence she's mine.
I chose her when I could not ask my father   190
For his advice, nor thought I had one. She
Is daughter to this famous Duke of Milan,
Of whom so often I have heard renown,
But never saw before; of whom I have
Receiv'd a second life; and second father   195

---

124. **subtleties:** illusions. 128. **justify:** prove. 136. **[who]** F$_{2-4}$. *whom* F$_1$. 145. **late:** recent. 154. **admire:** wonder.
171. s.d. *discovers:* discloses. 186. **eld'st:** longest possible.

This lady makes him to me.
Alon.   I am hers.
But, O, how oddly will it sound that I
Must ask my child forgiveness!
Pros.   There, sir, stop.
Let us not burden our remembrances with
A heaviness that's gone.
Gon.   I have inly wept,   200
Or should have spoke ere this.   Look down, you
          gods,
And on this couple drop a blessed crown!
For it is you that have chalk'd forth the way
Which brought us hither.
Alon.   I say, Amen, Gonzalo!
Gon. Was Milan thrust from Milan, that his
          issue   205
Should become Kings of Naples?   O, rejoice
Beyond a common joy, and set it down
With gold on lasting pillars: in one voyage
Did Claribel her husband find at Tunis,
And Ferdinand, her brother, found a wife   210
Where he himself was lost, Prospero his dukedom
In a poor isle, and all of us ourselves
When no man was his own.
Alon. [*To Fer. and Mir.*]   Give me your hands.
Let grief and sorrow still embrace his heart
That doth not wish you joy!
Gon.   Be it so!   Amen!

Re-enter ARIEL, *with the* Master *and* BOATSWAIN
          amazedly following.

O, look, sir, look, sir! here is more of us.   216
I prophesi'd, if a gallows were on land,
This fellow could not drown.   Now, blasphemy,
That swear'st grace o'erboard, not an oath on
          shore?
Hast thou no mouth by land?   What is the news?
Boats. The best news is, that we have safely
          found   221
Our king and company; the next, our ship —
Which, but three glasses since, we gave out split —
Is tight and yare and bravely rigg'd as when
We first put out to sea.
Ari. [*Aside to Pros.*]   Sir, all this service   225
Have I done since I went.
Pros.   [*Aside to Ari.*]   My tricksy spirit!
Alon. These are not natural events; they
          strengthen
From strange to stranger.   Say, how came you
          hither?
Boats. If I did think, sir, I were well awake,
I'd strive to tell you.   We were dead of sleep,
And — how we know not — all clapp'd under
          hatches;   231

Where but even now with strange and several noises
Of roaring, shrieking, howling, jingling chains,
And moe diversity of sounds, all horrible,
We were awak'd; straightway, at liberty;   235
Where we, in all [her] trim, freshly beheld
Our royal, good, and gallant ship, our master
Cap'ring to eye her.   On a trice, so please you,
Even in a dream, were we divided from them
And were brought moping hither.
Ari.   [*Aside to Pros.*] Was't well done?   240
Pros. [*Aside to Ari.*]   Bravely, my diligence.
          Thou shalt be free.
Alon. This is as strange a maze as e'er men trod;
And there is in this business more than nature
Was ever conduct of.   Some oracle
Must rectify our knowledge.
Pros.   Sir, my liege,   245
Do not infest your mind with beating on
The strangeness of this business.   At pick'd leisure,
Which shall be shortly, single I'll resolve you,
Which to you shall seem probable, of every
These happen'd accidents; till when, be cheerful
And think of each thing well. [*Aside to Ari.*]   Come
          hither, spirit.   251
Set Caliban and his companions free;
Untie the spell.   [*Exit Ariel.*]   How fares my gra-
          cious sir?
There are yet missing of your company
Some few odd lads that you remember not.   255

Re-enter ARIEL, *driving in* CALIBAN, STEPHANO *and*
          TRINCULO, *in their stolen apparel.*

Ste. Every man shift for all the rest, and let no
man take care for himself; for all is but fortune.
Coragio, bully-monster, coragio!
Trin. If these be true spies which I wear in my
head, here's a goodly sight.   260
Cal. O Setebos, these be brave spirits indeed!
How fine my master is!   I am afraid
He will chastise me.
Seb.   Ha, ha!
What things are these, my lord Antonio?
Will money buy 'em?
Ant.   Very like; one of them   265
Is a plain fish, and, no doubt, marketable.
Pros. Mark but the badges of these men, my
          lords,
Then say if they be true.   This mis-shapen knave,
His mother was a witch, and one so strong
That could control the moon, make flows and ebbs,
And deal in her command without her power.   271
These three have robb'd me; and this demi-devil —
For he's a bastard one — had plotted with them
To take my life.   Two of these fellows you

214. **still**: ever.   224. **yare**: ready.   236. **[her]** (Thirlby conj.).   *our* F.   240. **moping**: dazed.   244. **conduct**: director.
245. **rectify**: verify, confirm.   246. **infest**: harass.   248. **single**: in private, or, one by one.   258. **Coragio**: courage.
267. **badges**: liveries; here, the stolen garments.   271. **deal . . . power**: act in the moon's domain independently.

Must know and own; this thing of darkness I 275
Acknowledge mine.

Cal. I shall be pinch'd to death.

Alon. Is not this Stephano, my drunken butler?

Seb. He is drunk now. Where had he wine?

Alon. And Trinculo is reeling ripe. Where
should they
Find this grand liquor that hath gilded 'em? 280
How cam'st thou in this pickle?

Trin. I have been in such a pickle since I saw you
last that, I fear me, will never out of my bones. I
shall not fear fly-blowing.

Seb. Why, how now, Stephano! 285

Ste. O, touch me not; I am not Stephano, but a
cramp.

Pros. You'd be king o' the isle, sirrah?

Ste. I should have been a sore one then,

Alon. This is a strange thing as e'er I look'd on.
[*Pointing to Caliban.*

Pros. He is as disproportion'd in his manners
As in his shape. Go, sirrah, to my cell; 291
Take with you your companions. As you look
To have my pardon, trim it handsomely.

Cal. Ay, that I will; and I'll be wise hereafter
And seek for grace. What a thrice-double ass 295
Was I, to take this drunkard for a god
And worship this dull food!

Pros. Go to; away!

Alon. Hence, and bestow your luggage where you
found it.

Seb. Or stole it, rather. 299
[*Exeunt Cal., Ste., and Trin.*]

Pros. Sir, I invite your Highness and your train
To my poor cell, where you shall take your rest
For this one night; which, part of it, I'll waste
With such discourse as, I not doubt, shall make it
Go quick away, — the story of my life
And the particular accidents gone by 305
Since I came to this isle. And in the morn
I'll bring you to your ship and so to Naples,

Where I have hope to see the nuptial
Of these our dear-belov'd solemnized;
And thence retire me to my Milan, where 310
Every third thought shall be my grave.

Alon. I long
To hear the story of your life, which must
Take the ear strangely.

Pros. I'll deliver all;
And promise you calm seas, auspicious gales,
And sail so expeditious that shall catch 315
Your royal fleet far off. [*Aside to Ari.*] My Ariel,
chick,
That is thy charge. Then to the elements
Be free, and fare thou well! Please you, draw near.
[*Exeunt omnes.*

EPILOGUE

SPOKEN BY PROSPERO.

Now my charms are all o'erthrown,
And what strength I have's mine own,
Which is most faint. Now, 'tis true,
I must be here confin'd by you,
Or sent to Naples. Let me not, 5
Since I have my dukedom got
And pardon'd the deceiver, dwell
In this bare island by your spell;
But release me from my bands
With the help of your good hands. 10
Gentle breath of yours my sails
Must fill, or else my project fails,
Which was to please. Now I want
Spirits to enforce, art to enchant,
And my ending is despair, 15
Unless I be reliev'd by prayer,
Which pierces so that it assaults
Mercy itself and frees all faults.
As you from crimes would pardon'd be.
Let your indulgence set me free. [*Exit.* 20

280. **gilded:** intoxicated. 288. **sore:** (1) pained, (2) severe. 313. **deliver:** relate.
Epilogue, 10. **hands:** applause.

INDEX TO THE CHARACTERS IN SHAKESPEARE'S PLAYS

This Index records the act and scene in which each character first speaks, not necessarily the same as that in which he first appears. Only persons who speak are included, except a few marked with asterisk.

Abbess, Lady.   CofE. V. i.
Abhorson.   Meas. IV. ii.
Abraham.   R&J. I. i.
Adam.   AYLI. I. i.
Adrian.   Tmp. II. i.
Adriana.   CofE. II. i.
Ædile, an.   Cor. III. i.
Ægeon.   CofE. I. i.
Æmilia.   CofE. V. i.
Agrippa.   A&C. II. ii.
Aguecheek, Sir Andrew.   TwN. I. iii.
Albany, Duke of.   Lear I. i.
Alexas.   A&C. I. ii.
Alice.   H5. III. iv.
Alonso.   Tmp. I. i.
Ambassadors.   Hml. V. ii; H5. I. ii.
Amiens.   AYLI. II. i. v.
Angelo.   CofE. III. i.
Angelo.   Meas. I. i.
Angus.   Mcb. I. ii.
Anne, Lady.   R3. I. ii.
Antigonus.   WT. II. i.
Antipholus of Ephesus.   CofE. III. i.
Antipholus of Syracuse.   CofE. I. ii.
Antonio.   Merch. I. i.
Antonio.   MAdo. I. ii.
Antonio.   Tmp. I. i.
Antonio.   TwN. II. i.
Antony.   JC. I. ii; A&C. I. i.
Apothecary.   R&J. V. i.
Apparitions.   Mcb. IV. i.
Archbishop.   *See* York, Canterbury.
Archidamus.   WT. I. i.
Ariel.   Tmp. I. ii.
Arragon, Prince of.   Merch. II. ix.
Artemidorus.   JC. II. iii.
Arviragus.   Cym. III. iii.
Attendants.   A&C. I. ii; Hml. IV. vi.   *See* Servants.

Audrey.   AYLI. III. iii.
Aufidius, Tullus.   Cor. I. ii.
Aumerle, Duke of.   R2. I. iii.
Autolycus.   WT. IV. iii.

Bagot.   R2. II. ii.
Balthasar.   MAdo. II. iii.
Balthazar.   CofE. III. i.
Balthazar.   Merch. III. iv.
Balthazar.   R&J. I. i.
Banquo.   Mcb. I. iii.
Bardolph.   1H4. II. ii; 2H4. II. i; H5. II. i.
Bardolph, Lord.   2H4. I. i.
Barnardine.   Meas. IV. iii.
Bassanio.   Merch. I. i.
Bastard.   *See* Edmund.
Bates.   H5. IV. i.
Bawd.   *See* Overdone.
Beadles.   2H4. V. iv.
Beatrice.   MAdo. I. i.
Beaufort, Thomas, Duke of Exeter.   H5. I. ii.
Bedford, Duke of.   H5. II. ii.
Belarius.   Cym. III. iii.
Belch, Sir Toby.   TwN. I. iii.
Benedick.   MAdo. I. i.
Benvolio.   R&J. I. i.
Berkeley.   R3. I. iii.*
Berkeley, Lord.   R2. II. iii.
Bernardo.   Hml. I. i.
Bianca.   Oth. III. iv.
Blunt, Sir James.   R3. V. ii.
Blunt, Sir Walter.   1H4. I. iii.
Boatswain.   Tmp. I. i.
Bolingbroke, afterwards King Henry IV.   R2. I. i.
Borachio.   MAdo. I. iii.
Bottom.   MND. I. ii.
Bourbon, Duke of.   H5. III. v.
Bourchier, Cardinal.   R3. III. i.

Boys. H5. II. i; Mcb. IV. ii; Meas. IV. i; MAdo. II. iii; R3. II. ii. *See* Pages.
Brabantio. Oth. I. i.
Brakenbury, Sir Robert. R3. I. i.
Brothers, to Posthumus, ghosts. Cym. V. iv.
Brutus, Decius. JC. II. i.
Brutus, Junius. Cor. I. i.
Brutus, Marcus. JC. I. ii.
Buckingham, Duke of. R3. I. iii.
Bullcalf. 2H4. III. ii.
Burgundy, Duke of. H5. V. ii.
Burgundy, Duke of. Lear I. i.
Bushy. R2. I. iv.

Cæsar. *See* Julius *and* Octavius.
Caithness. Mcb. V. ii.
Caius Ligarius. JC. II. i.
Caius Lucius. Cym. III. i.
Caius Marcius (Coriolanus). Cor. I. i.
Caliban. Tmp. I. ii.
Calpurnia. JC. I. ii.
Cambridge, Earl of. H5. II. ii.
Camillo. WT. I. i.
Canidius. A&C. III. x.
Canterbury, Archbishop of. H5. I. i. *See* Bourchier.
Captains. A&C. IV. iv; Cym. IV. ii, V. iii; Hml. IV. iv; Lear V. iii; Mcb. I. ii; R2. II. iv. *See* Sea Captain.
Capulet. R&J. I. i.
Capulet, Lady. R&J. I. i.
Capulet, second. R&J. I. v.
Carlisle, Bishop of. R2. III. ii.
Carpenter. JC. I. i.
Carriers. 1H4. II. i.
Casca. JC. I. ii.
Cassio. Oth. I. ii.
Cassius. JC. I. ii.
Cato, young. JC. V. iii.
Catesby, Sir William. R3. I. iii.
Celia. AYLI. I. ii.
Ceres. Tmp. IV. i.
Chamberlain. 1H4. II. i.
Charles, a wrestler. AYLI. I. i.
Charles VI, King of France. H5. II. iv.
Charmian. A&C. I. ii.
Chief Justice. 2H4. I. ii.
Chorus. H5; R&J. W.T.
Cicero. JC. I. iii.
Cimber, Metellus. JC. II. i.
Cinna, a conspirator. JC. I. iii.
Cinna, a poet. JC. III. iii.
Citizens. Cor. I. i; R3. II. iii; R&J. III. i.
Clarence, George, Duke of. R3. I. i.
Clarence, Thomas, Duke of. 2H4. IV. iv.
Clarence, son and daughter of. R3. II. ii.
Claudio. Meas. I. ii.

Claudio. MAdo. I. i.
Claudius, King of Denmark. Hml. I. ii.
Claudius. JC. IV. iii.
Cleomenes. WT. III. i.
Cleopatra. A&C. I. i.
Clitus. JC. V. v.
Cloten. Cym. I. ii.
Clowns. A&C. V. ii; Hml. V. ii; Oth. III. i; WT. IV. iii. *See* Feste, Peter, Pompey, etc.
Cobbler. JC. I. i.
Cobweb. MND. III. i.
Colville, Sir John. 2H4. IV. iii.
Cominius. Cor. I. i.
Conrade. MAdo. I. iii.
Conspirators. Cor. V. vi.
Constable of France. H5. II. iv.
Cordelia. Lear I. i.
Corin. AYLI. II. iv.
Coriolanus. Cor. I. i.
Cornelius, a physician. Cym. I. v.
Cornelius. Hml. I. ii.
Cornwall, Duke of. Lear I. i.
Court. H5. IV. i.
Courtesan. CofE. IV. iii.
Curan. Lear II. i.
Curio. TwN. I. i.
Cymbeline, King. Cym. I. i.

Dancer, A. 2H4. Epi.
Dardanius. JC. V. v.
Dauphin. H5. II. iv.
Davy. 2H4. V. i.
Demetrius. A&C. I. i.
Demetrius. MND. I. i.
Dennis. AYLI. I. i.
Derby, Earl of. R3. I. iii.
Dercetas. A&C. IV. xiv.
Desdemona. Oth. I. iii.
Diomedes. A&C. IV. xiv.
Dion. WT. III. i.
Doctor. Lear IV. iv.
Doctor, English. Mcb. IV. iii.
Doctor, Scotch. Mcb. V. i.
Dogberry. MAdo. III. iii.
Dolabella. A&C. III. xii.
Doll Tearsheet. 2H4. II. iv.
Donalbain. Mcb. II. iii.
Don John. MAdo. I. i.
Don Pedro. MAdo. I. i.
Dorcas. WT. IV. iv.
Dorset, Marquis of. R3. I. iii.
Douglas, Archibald, Earl of. 1H4. IV. i.
Drawers. 2H4. II. iv.
Dromio of Ephesus. CofE. I. ii.
Dromio of Syracuse. CofE. I. ii.
Duke, in banishment. AYLI. II. i.
Duke Frederick. AYLI. I. ii.

Herbert, Sir Walter. R3. V. ii.
Hereford, Duke of. *See* Henry IV. R2. I. i.
Herminia. MND. I. i.
Hermione. WT. I. ii.
Hero. MAdo. I. i.
Hippolyta. MND. I. i.
Horatio. Hml. I. i.
Hostess. H5. II. i. *See* Quickly.
Hotspur. 1H4. I. iii. *See* Percy.
Humphrey of Gloucester. 2H4. IV, iv; H5. III. vii.
Hymen. AYLI. V. iv.

Iachimo. Cym. I. iv.
Iago. Oth. I. i.
Imogen. Cym. I. i.
Iras. A&C. I. ii.
Iris. Tmp. IV. i.
Isabel, Queen of France. H5. V. ii.
Isabella. Meas. I. iv.

Jamy. H5. III. ii.
Jaques. AYLI. II. v.
Jaques, son of Sir Roland de Boys. AYLI.*
Jessica. Merch. II. iii.
John of Lancaster. 1H4. V. iv; 2H4. IV. ii.
Juliet. Meas. I. ii.
Juliet. R&J. I. iii.
Julius Cæsar. JC. I. ii.
Juno. Tmp. IV. i.
Jupiter. Cym. V. iv.

Katherine, Princess of France. H5. III. iv.
Keepers. R2. V. v; R3. I. iv. *See* Gaolers.
Kent, Earl of. Lear I. i.
Knights. Lear I. iv.

Ladies. Cor. II. i; Cym. I. v; R2. III. iv; WT. II. i.
Laertes. Hml. I. ii.
Lamprius. A&C. I. ii.
Launcelot Gobbo. Merch. II. ii.
Lear, King. Lear I. i.
Le Beau. AYLI. I. ii.
Lennox. Mcb. I. ii.
Leonardo. Merch. II. ii.
Leonato. MAdo. I. i.
Leonatus, Posthumus. Cym. I. i.
Leontes. WT. I. ii.
Lepidus. JC. IV. i; A&C. I. iv.
Lewis, the Dauphin. H5. II. iv.
Lieutenant. Cor. IV. vii.
Ligarius. JC. II. i.
Lion. MND. V. i.
Lords. AYLI. II. i; Cor. V. vi; Cym. I. ii; Hml. V. ii; Mcb. III. iv; R3. V. iii; WT. II. ii.
Lorenzo. Merch. I. i.
Lovel, Lord. R3. III. iv.

Luce. CofE. III. i.
Luciana. CofE. II. i.
Lucianus. Hml. III. ii.
Lucilius. JC. IV. ii.
Lucio. Meas. I. ii.
Lucius, Caius. Cym. III. i.
Lucius. JC. II. i.
Ludovico. Oth. IV. i.
Lysander. MND. I. i.

Macbeth. Mcb. I. iii.
Macbeth, Lady. Mcb. I. v.
Macduff. Mcb. II. iii.
Macduff, Lady. Mcb. IV. ii.
Macduff's son. Mcb. IV. ii.
Macmorris. H5. III. ii.
Mæcenas. A&C. II. ii.
Malcolm. Mcb. I. ii.
Malvolio. TwN. I. v.
Mamillius. WT. I. ii.
Marcellus. Hml. I. i.
Marcus Antonius (Antony). JC. I. ii; A&C. I. i.
Mardian. A&C. I. v.
Margaret. MAdo. II. i.
Margaret, Queen. R3. I. iii.
Margaret Plantagenet, daughter of Clarence. R3. II. ii.
Maria. TwN. I. iii.
Mariana. Meas. IV. i.
Mariner. WT. III. iii; Tmp. I. i.
Marshal, Lord. R2. I. iii.
Martext, Sir Oliver. AYLI. III. iii.
Marullus. JC. I. i.
Master, of a ship. Tmp. I. i.
Mayor of London. R3. III. i.
Menas. A&C. II. i.
Menecrates. A&C. II. i.
Menenius Agrippa. Cor. I. i.
Menteith. Mcb. V. ii.
Merchants. CofE. I. ii.
Mercutio. R&J. I. iv.
Messala. JC. IV. iii.
Messengers. A&C. I. i, iii; CofE. V. i; Cor. I. i; Cym. V. iv; Hml. IV. v; 1H4. IV. i; 2H4. IV. i; H5. II. v; JC. IV. iii; Lear IV. ii; Mcb. I. v; Meas. IV. ii; Merch. II. ix; MAdo. I. i; Oth. I. iii; R3. III. ii.
Metellus Cimber. JC. II. i.
Michael, Sir. 1H4. IV. iv.
Miranda. Tmp. I. ii.
Montague. R&J. I. i.
Montague, Lady. R&J. I. i.
Montano. Oth. II. i.
Montjoy. H5. III. vi.
Moonshine. MND. V. i.
Mopsa. WT. IV. iv.
Morocco, Prince of. Merch. II. i.
Mortimer, Edmund, Earl of March. 1H4. III. i.

Mortimer, Lady. 1H4. III. i.
Morton. 2H4. I. i.
Morton, John, Bishop of Ely. R3. III. iv.
Moth. MND. III. i.
Mother to Posthumus, a ghost. Cym. V. iv.
Mouldy. 2H4. III. ii.
Mowbray, Lord. 2H4. I. iii.
Mowbray, Thomas, Duke of Norfolk. R2. I. i.
Murderers. Mcb. III. i; R3. I. iii.
Musicians. Merch. V. i; Oth. III. i; R&J. IV. v.
Mustardseed. MND. III. i.

Nerissa. Merch. I. ii.
Noble, a. Cor. III. ii.
Norfolk, Duke of. R3. V. iii.
Norfolk, Duke of, Thomas Mowbray. R2. I. i.
Northumberland. *See* Percy.
Northumberland, Lady. 2H4. II. iii.
Nurse. R&J. I. 3.
Nym. H5. II. i.

Oberon. MND. II. i.
Octavia. A&C. III. ii.
Octavius Cæsar (Augustus). JC. IV. i; A&C. I. iv.
Officers. CofE. IV. i; Cor. II. ii; Oth. I. iii; R&J.
   I. i; TwN. III. iv; WT. III. ii.
Old Man. Lear IV. i; Mcb. II. iv.
Oliver. AYLI. I. i.
Oliver Martext, Sir. AYLI. III. iii.
Olivia. TwN. I. v.
Ophelia. Hml. I. iii.
Orlando. AYLI. I. i.
Orleans, Duke of. H5. III. vii.
Orsino, Duke of Illyria. TwN. I. i.
Osric. Hml. V. ii.
Ostler. 1H4. II. i.
Oswald. Lear I. iii.
Othello. Oth. I. ii.
Overdone, Mrs. Meas. I. ii.
Oxford, Earl of. R3. V. ii.

Pages. AYLI. V. iii; 2H4. I. ii; R3. IV. ii; R&J.
   V. ii. *See* Boys.
Paris. R&J. I. ii.
Patrician. Cor. III. i.
Paulina. WT. II. ii.
Peaseblossom. MND. III. i.
Pedro, Don. MAdo. I. i.
Percy, Henry, Earl of Northumberland. 1H4. I.
   iii; 2H4. I. i; R2. III. i.
Percy, Henry (Hotspur). 1H4. I. iii; R2. II. iii.
Percy, Lady (wife of Hotspur). 1H4. II. iii; 2H4.
   II. iii.
Percy, Thomas, Earl of Worcester. 1H4. I. iii.
Perdita. WT. IV. iv.
Peter. R&J. II. iv.
Peto. 1H4. II. ii; 2H4. II. iv.

Phebe. AYLI. III. v.
Philario. Cym. I. iv.
Philo. A&C. I. i.
Philostrate. MND. V. i.
Physicians. Cym. I. v; Lear IV. iv; Mcb. IV. iii.
Pierce, Sir, of Exton. R2. V. iv.
Pinch. CofE. IV. iv.
Pindarus. JC. IV. ii.
Pisanio. Cym. I. i.
Pistol. 2H4. II. iv; H5. II. i.
Player King. Hml. III. ii.
Player Queen. Hml. III. ii.
Players. Hml. II. ii.
Plebeians. JC. III. ii. *See* Citizens.
Poet. JC. IV. iii.
Poins. 1H4. I. ii; 2H4. II. ii.
Polixenes. WT. I. ii.
Polonius. Hml. I. ii.
Pompeius, Sextus. A&C. II. i.
Pompey. Meas. I. ii.
Popilius. JC. III. i.
Porters. 2H4. I. i; Mcb. II. iii.
Portia. JC. II. i.
Portia. Merch. I. ii.
Posthumus Leonatus. Cym. I. i.
Priests. Hml. V. i; R3. III. ii; TwN. v. i.
Proculeius. A&C. V. i.
Prologue. R&J; H5; MND; Hml. III. ii.
Prospero. Tmp. I. ii.
Provost. Meas. I. ii.
Publius. JC. II. ii.
Puck, Robin Goodfellow. MND. II. i.
Pursuivant. R3. III. ii.
Pyramus. MND. V. i.

Queen, wife of Cymbeline. Cym. I. i.
Queen, wife of Richard II. R2. II. i.
Quickly, Mrs. 1H4. II. iv; 2H4. II. i; H5. II. i.
Quince. MND. I. ii.

Rambures. H5. III. vii.
Ratcliff, Sir Richard. R3. III. iii.
Regan. Lear I. i.
Reynaldo. Hml. II. i.
Richard II, King. R2. I. i.
Richard II, Queen to. R2. II. i.
Richard III, King (at first Gloucester). R3. I. i.
Richard, Duke of York, son of Edward IV. R3.
   II. iv.
Richmond, Earl of, later Henry VII. R3. V. iii.
Rivers, Lord. R3. I. iii.
Robin Goodfellow. MND. II. i.
Roderigo. Oth. I. i.
Roman, a. Cor. IV. iii. *See* Citizens.
Romeo. R&J. I. i.
Rosalind. AYLI. i. ii.
Rosencrantz. Hml. II. ii.

Ross. Mcb. I. ii.
Ross, Lord. R2. II. i.
Rotherham, Thomas. Archbishop of York. R3. II. iv.
Rumour. 2H4. Ind.

Sailors. Hml. IV. vi; Oth. I. iii.
Salanio. Merch. I. i.
Salarino. Merch. I. i.
Salerio. Merch. III. ii.
Salisbury, Earl of. H5. IV. iii.
Salisbury, Earl of. R2. II. iv.
Sampson. R&J. I. i.
Scarus. A&C. III. x.
Scrivener. R3. III. vi.
Scroop, Lord. H5. II. ii.
Scroop, Richard, Archbishop of York. 1H4. IV. iv; 2H4. I. iii.
Scroop, Sir Stephen. R2. III. ii.
Sea-Captain (Lieut.). TwN. I. ii.
Sebastian. Tmp. I. i.
Sebastian. TwN. II. i.
Seleucus. A&C. V. ii.
Senators, Roman. Cor. I. i; Cym. III. vii; Venetian. Oth. I. iii; Coriolanian. Cor. I. ii.
Sentry. A&C. IV. ix.
Servants. A&C. II. vii; Hml. IV. vi; 1H4. II. iii; 2H4. I. ii; JC. II. ii; Lear III. vii; Mcb. III. i; Meas. II. ii; Merch. III. i; R2. II. ii; TwN. III. iv; WT. II. iii.
Servingmen. Cor. IV. v; Merch. I. ii.
Seyton. Mcb. V. iii.
Sexton. MAdo. I. i.
Sextus Pompeius. A&C. II. i.
Shadow. 2H4. III. ii.
Shallow, Justice. 2H4. III. ii.
Shepherd, Old. WT. III. iii.
Sheriff. 1H4. II. iv; R3. V. i.
Shylock. Merch. I. iii.
Sicilius Leonatus, a ghost. Cym. V. iv.
Sicinius Velutus. Cor. I. i.
Silence. 2H4. III. ii.
Silius. A&C. III. i.
Silvius. AYLI. II. iv.
Siward. Mcb. V. iv.
Siward, young. Mcb. V. vii.
Snare. 2H4. II. i.
Snout. MND. I. ii.
Snug. MND. I. ii.
Soldiers. A&C. III. vii; Cor. I. iv; H5. IV. iv; JC. IV. ii; Mcb. V. iv.
Solinus, Duke of Ephesus. CofE. I. i.
Soothsayers. A&C. I. ii; Cym. IV. ii; JC. I. ii.
Stanley, Lord, Earl of Derby. R3. I. iii.
Starveling. MND. I. ii.
Stephano. Merch.*
Stephano. Tmp. II. ii.

Strato. JC. V. v.
Surrey, Earl of. 2H4.*
Surrey, Earl of. R2. IV. i.
Surrey, Earl of. R3. V. iii.

Taurus. A&C. III. viii.
Theseus. MND. I. i.
Thieves. 1H4. II. ii.
Thisbe. MND. V. i.
Thomas, Friar. Meas. I. iii.
Thyreus (Thidias). A&C. III. xii.
Time (chorus). WT. IV. i.
Titania. MND. II. i.
Titinius. JC. IV. iii.
Titus Lartius. Cor. I. i.
Touchstone. AYLI. I. ii.
Travellers. 1H4. II. ii.
Travers. 2H4. I. i.
Trebonius. JC. II. i.
Tressel. R3. I. iii.*
Tribunes, Roman. Cym. III. vii.
Trinculo. Tmp. II. ii.
Tubal. Merch. III. i.
Tullus Aufidius. Cor. I. ii.
Tybalt. R&J. I. i.
Tyrrel, Sir James. R3. IV. ii.

Ursula. MAdo. II. i.
Urswick, Christopher. R3. IV. v.

Valentine. TwN. I. iv.
Valeria. Cor. I. iii.
Varrius. A&C. II. i.
Varro. JC. IV. iii.
Vaughan, Sir Thomas. R3. III. iii.
Venice, Duke of. Merch. IV. i.
Venice, Duke of. Oth. I. iii.
Ventidius. A&C. III. i.
Verges. MAdo. III. iii.
Vernon, Sir Richard. 1H4. IV. i.
Vincentio, Duke. Meas. I. i.
Vintner. 1H4. II. iv.
Viola. TwN. I. ii.
Virgilia. Cor. I. iii.
Volsce, a. Cor. IV. iii.
Voltimand. Hml. I. ii.
Volumnia. Cor. I. iii.
Volumnius. JC. V. v.

Wall. MND. V. i.
Wart. 2H4. III. ii.
Warwick (Beauchamp), Earl of. 2H4. III. i; H5. IV. viii.
Watchmen: Cor. V. ii; MAdo. III. iii; R&J. V. iii.
Westminster, Abbot of. R2. IV. i.

Mrs. Elsie Bean
c/o Dr Belden
20 Buckingham St
    London WC 2

Box 222 - Johnson Hall
411 West 116 St.
n. y 27 - n. y.